STREET ATLAS
London

www.philips-maps.co.uk

First published in 2000 by

Philip's, a division of
Octopus Publishing Group Ltd
www.octopusbooks.co.uk
Endeavour House
189 Shaftesbury Avenue
London WC2H 8JG
An Hachette UK Company
www.hachette.co.uk

Fourth edition 2010
First impression 2010
LONDA

ISBN 978-1-84907-058-4 (standard spiral-bound)
ISBN 978-1-84907-059-1 (standard paperback)

© Philip's 2010

o|s Ordnance Survey®

This product includes mapping data licensed from
Ordnance Survey® with the permission of the
Controller of Her Majesty's Stationery Office.
© Crown copyright 2010. All rights reserved.
Licence number 100011710.

Data for the speed cameras supplied by
PocketGPSWorld.com Ltd

Post Office is a trade mark of Post Office Ltd in the
UK and other countries.

Printed and bound in China

Contents

II **Key to map pages**

IV Administrative and Postcode boundaries

VI **Route planning**

XXIV **Key to map symbols**

1 **Street maps**

228 **Keys to enlarged map pages and symbols**

229 **Enlarged street maps**

271 **Index**

429 **List of numbered locations**

450 West End theatres and cinemas

452 Central London buses

454 Local rail and London Underground

Digital Data

The exceptionally high-quality mapping fo[...]
easily convertible to other bitmapped (rast[...]

The index is also available in digital form a[...]
printed index together with the National Gr[...]

For further information and to discuss your [...]
philips@mapsinternational.co.uk

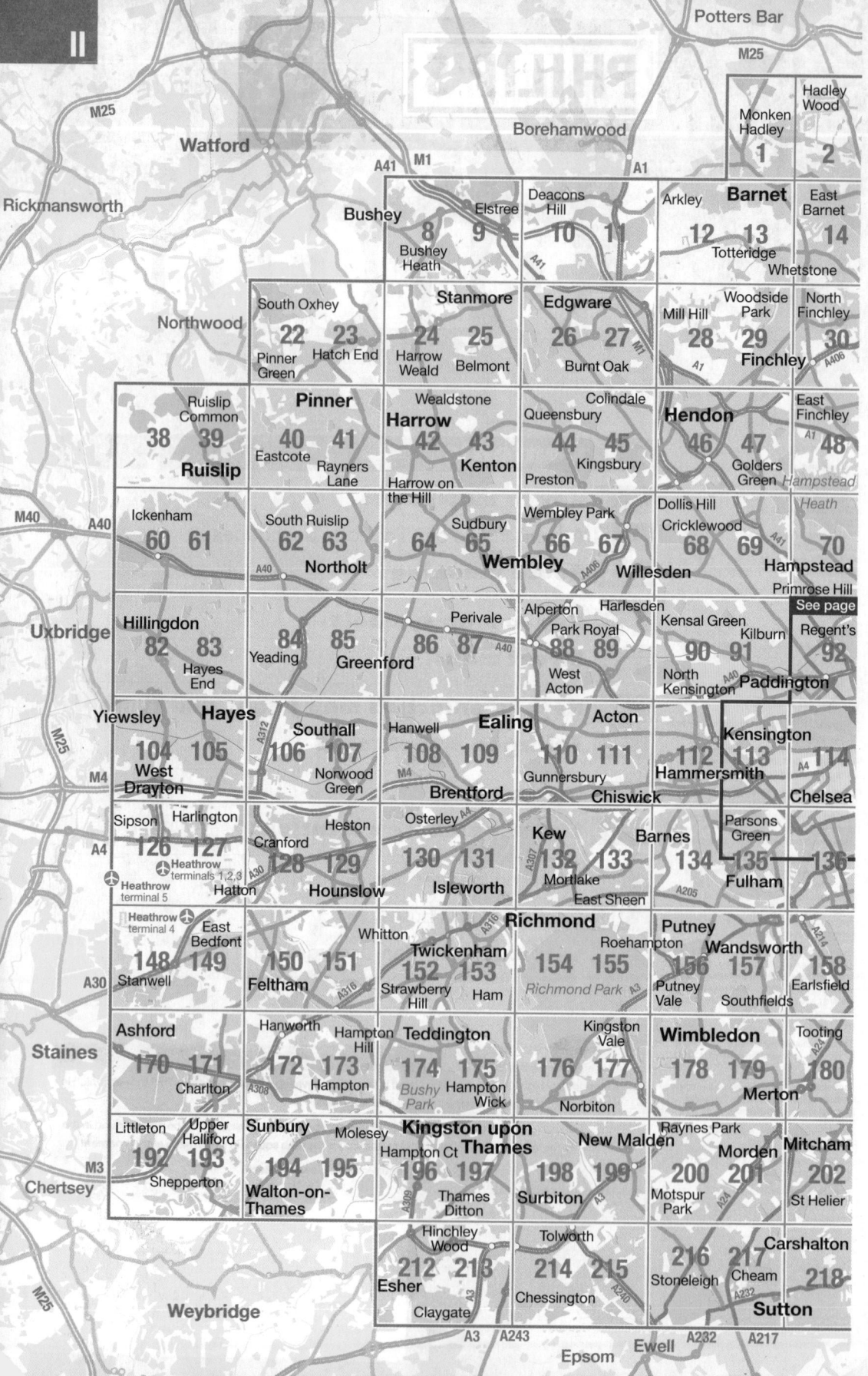

Potters Bar

M25

M25

Watford

Rickmansworth

Borehamwood

Monken Hadley **1**   Hadley Wood **2**

A41   M1   A1

Bushey   Elstree **9**   Deacons Hill **10**   **11**   Arkley **12**   **Barnet** **13**   East Barnet **14**

8   Bushey Heath

A41

Northwood   South Oxhey **22** **23**   Pinner Green   Hatch End   Stanmore **24** **25**   Harrow Weald   Belmont   Edgware **26** **27**   Burnt Oak   Mill Hill **28**   Woodside Park **29**   North Finchley **30**   **Finchley**   A406

Ruislip Common **38** **39**   **Ruislip**   **Pinner** **40** **41**   Eastcote   Rayners Lane   **Harrow** **42** **43**   **Kenton**   Harrow on the Hill   Wealdstone   Queensbury   Colindale **44** **45**   Preston   Kingsbury   **Hendon** **46** **47**   Golders Green **48**   East Finchley   A1   Hampstead

M40   A40   Ickenham **60** **61**   A40   South Ruislip **62** **63**   **Northolt**   Sudbury **64** **65**   **Wembley**   Wembley Park **66** **67**   Willesden   Dollis Hill   Cricklewood **68** **69**   **Hampstead** **70**   Primrose Hill   Heath

Uxbridge   Hillingdon **82** **83**   Hayes End   Yeading **84** **85**   **Greenford**   Perivale **86** **87**   A40   Alperton   Park Royal **88** **89**   West Acton   Harlesden   Kensal Green **90** **91**   Kilburn   North Kensington   **Paddington**   A40   See page   Regent's **92**

M4   **Hayes**   Yiewsley   **104** **105**   West Drayton   **Southall** **106** **107**   Norwood Green   Hanwell **108** **109**   **Ealing**   Brentford   **110** **111**   Gunnersbury   Chiswick   Acton   **Hammersmith** **112** **113**   **Kensington**   A4 **114**   **Chelsea**

A4   Sipson   Harlington **126** **127**   Cranford **128** **129**   Heston   Hatton   Hounslow   Osterley   A4 **130** **131**   **Isleworth**   **Kew** **132** **133**   Mortlake   East Sheen   **Barnes** **134**   Parsons Green **135**   **136**   **Fulham**   A205

Heathrow terminals 1,2,3   Heathrow terminal 5

Heathrow terminal 4   East Bedfont **148** **149**   Stanwell   **150** **151**   **Feltham**   Whitton   A316   **Twickenham** **152** **153**   Strawberry Hill   Ham   **Richmond**   **154** **155**   Richmond Park   A3   Roehampton   **Putney** **156** **157**   Putney Vale   Southfields   **Wandsworth**   A214 **158**   Earlsfield

A30   Ashford **170** **171**   Charlton   Hanworth **172** **173**   A308   Hampton   Hampton Hill   **Teddington** **174** **175**   Bushy Park   Hampton Wick   Kingston Vale **176** **177**   Norbiton   **Wimbledon** **178** **179**   **Merton**   A24   Tooting **180**

Staines   Littleton **192** **193**   Shepperton   Upper Halliford   **Sunbury** **194** **195**   **Walton-on-Thames**   Molesey   Hampton Ct **196** **197**   Thames Ditton   **Kingston upon Thames**   A309   **Surbiton** **198** **199**   A3   **New Malden**   Raynes Park **200** **201**   Motspur Park   **Morden**   A24   **Mitcham** **202**   St Helier

Chertsey   M3

Weybridge   Esher   Hinchley Wood **212** **213**   Claygate   A3   **214** **215**   Chessington   A240   Tolworth   **216** **217**   Stoneleigh   Cheam   A232   **Sutton** **218**   **Carshalton**

A3   A243   A232   A217   Ewell

Epsom

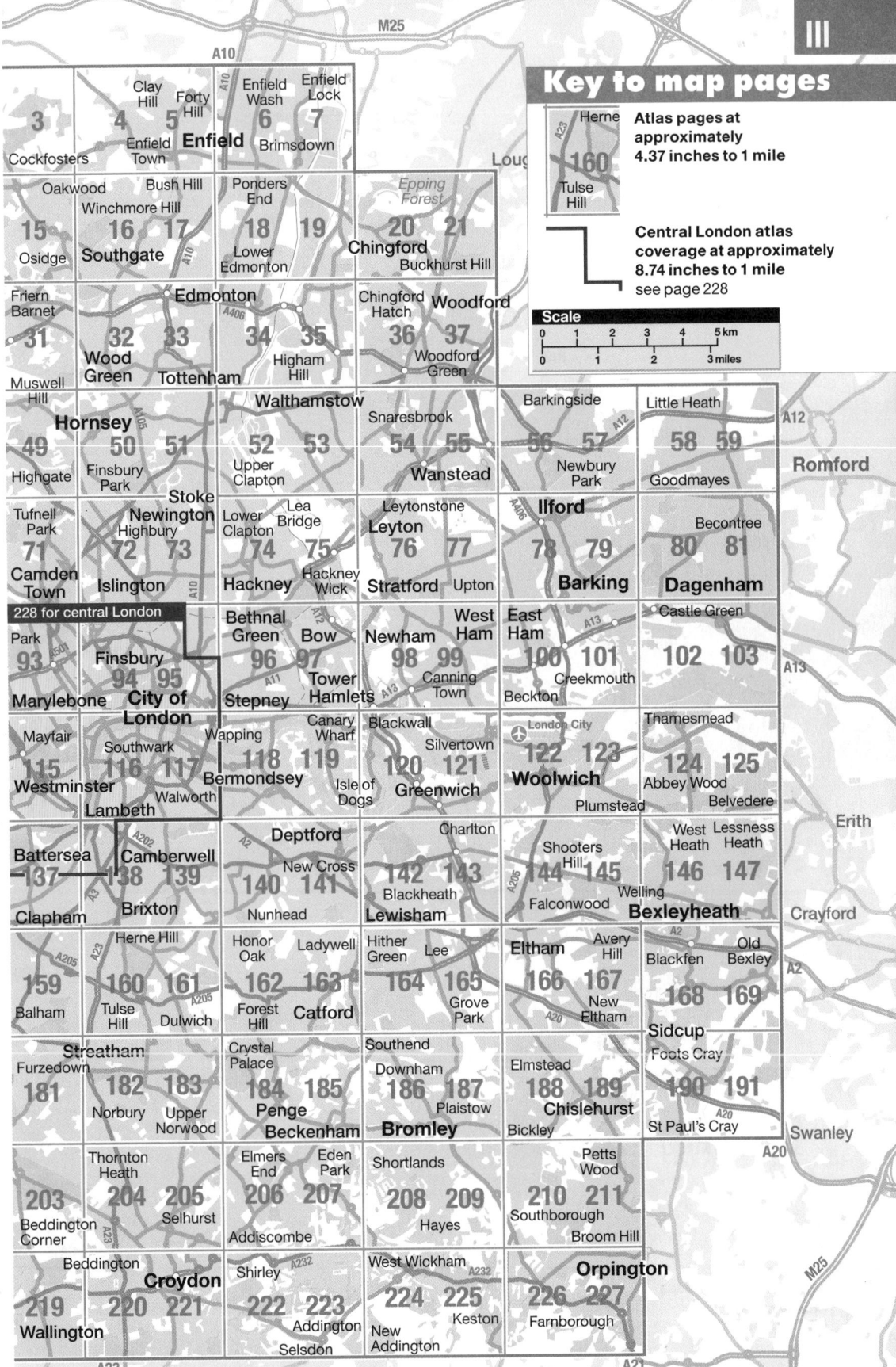

Key to map pages

Herne
160
Tulse
Hill

Atlas pages at
approximately
4.37 inches to 1 mile

Central London atlas
coverage at approximately
8.74 inches to 1 mile
see page 228

Scale

0   1   2   3   4   5 km
0   1   2   3 miles

Cockfosters **3**
Clay Hill **4**
Forty Hill **5**
Enfield Town
Enfield
Enfield Wash **6**
Enfield Lock **7**
Brimsdown

Oakwood
Winchmore Hill
Bush Hill
Osidge **15**
16 **17**
Southgate
Ponders End
Lower Edmonton
18 **19**
20 **21**
Chingford
Buckhurst Hill
Epping Forest

Friern Barnet
Muswell Hill
31
32 **33**
Wood Green
Tottenham
34 **35**
Higham Hill
Chingford Hatch
36 **37**
Woodford
Woodford Green

Highgate
Hornsey
49
50 **51**
Finsbury Park
Walthamstow
52 **53**
Upper Clapton
Snaresbrook
54 **55**
Wanstead
Barkingside
56 **57**
Newbury Park
Little Heath
58 **59**
Goodmayes
Romford

Tufnell Park
71
Camden Town
72 **73**
Islington
Stoke Newington
Highbury
Lower Clapton
74 **75**
Hackney
Lea Bridge
Hackney Wick
Leytonstone
Leyton
76 **77**
Stratford Upton
Ilford
78 **79**
Barking
Becontree
80 **81**
Dagenham

Park
93
Marylebone
Finsbury
94 **95**
City of London
Bethnal Green
96 **97**
Stepney
Bow
Tower Hamlets
Newham
98 **99**
West **Ham**
East **Ham**
100 **101**
Creekmouth
Beckton
Canning Town
Castle Green
102 **103**

Mayfair
115
Westminster
Southwark
116 **117**
Bermondsey
Walworth
Lambeth
Wapping
118 **119**
Canary Wharf
Isle of Dogs
Blackwall
120 **121**
Greenwich
Silvertown
London City
122 **123**
Woolwich
Plumstead
Thamesmead
124 **125**
Abbey Wood
Belvedere
Erith

228 for central London

Battersea
137
Clapham
Camberwell
138 **139**
Brixton
Deptford
140 **141**
New Cross
Nunhead
Charlton
142 **143**
Blackheath
Lewisham
Shooters Hill
144 **145**
Falconwood Welling
West Heath
Lessness Heath
146 **147**
Bexleyheath
Crayford

Furzedown
159
Balham
Herne Hill
160 **161**
Tulse Hill Dulwich
Honor Oak
162 **163**
Forest Hill
Ladywell
Catford
Hither Green
164 **165**
Lee
Grove Park
Eltham
166 **167**
New Eltham
Avery Hill
Blackfen
168 **169**
Old Bexley
Sidcup
Foots Cray
190 **191**
St Paul's Cray
Swanley

Streatham
181
182 **183**
Norbury Upper Norwood
Crystal Palace
184 **185**
Penge
Beckenham
Southend
Downham
186 **187**
Plaistow
Bromley
Elmstead
188 **189**
Chislehurst
Bickley
Petts Wood
210 **211**
Southborough
Broom Hill

Thornton Heath
203
Beddington Corner
204 **205**
Selhurst
Elmers End
206 **207**
Addiscombe
Eden Park
Shortlands
208 **209**
Hayes

Beddington
219
Wallington
220 **221**
Croydon
Shirley
222 **223**
Addington
Selsdon
West Wickham
224 **225**
New Addington
Keston
226 **227**
Farnborough
Orpington

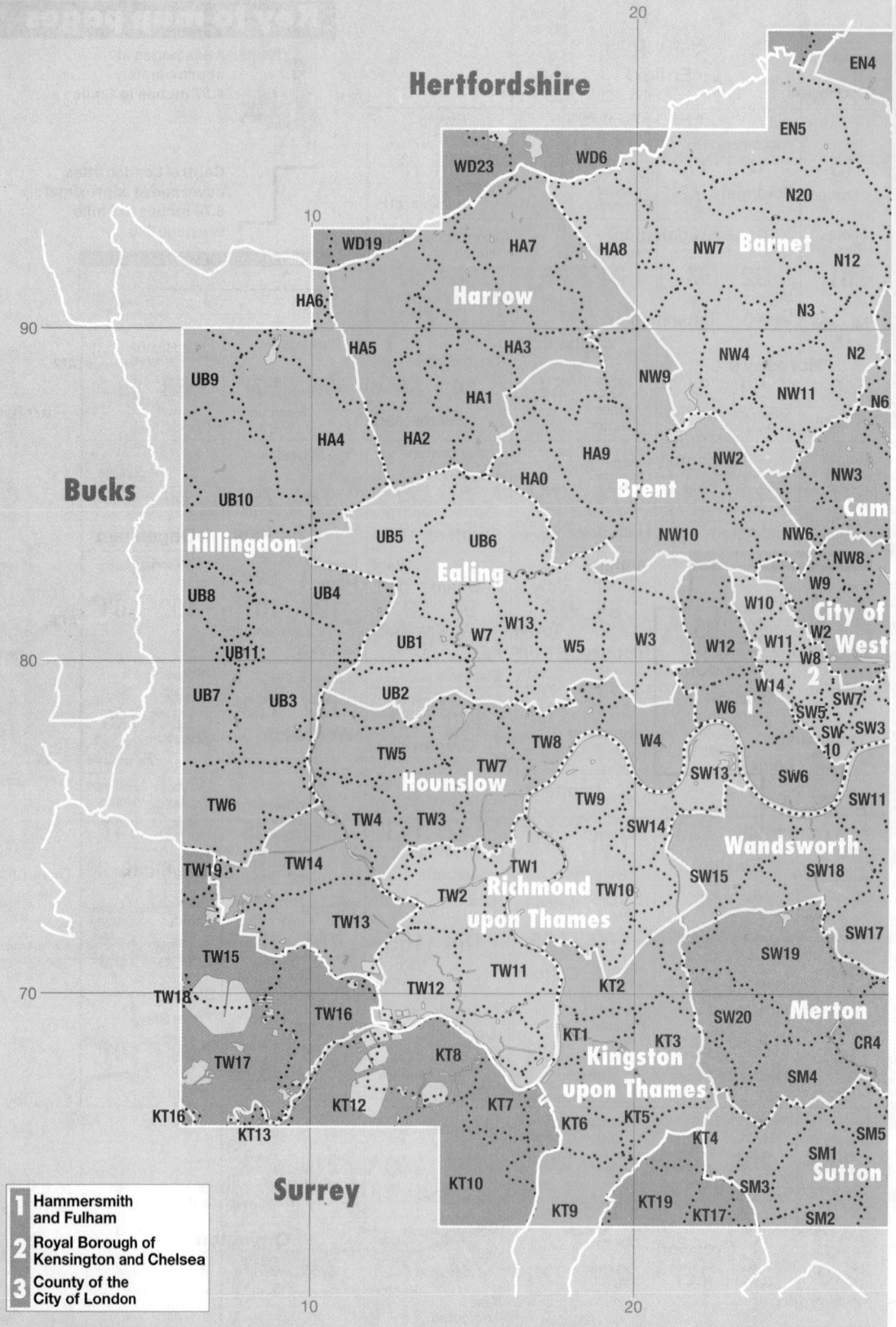

Hertfordshire

WD23

WD6

EN4

EN5

N20

WD19

HA7

HA8

NW7

Barnet

N12

HA6

N3

HA5

HA3

NW4

N2

Harrow

UB9

HA1

NW9

NW11

N6

HA4

HA2

HA9

NW2

NW3

Bucks

UB10

HA0

Brent

Cam

Hillingdon

UB5

UB6

NW10

NW6

NW8

UB8

UB4

Ealing

W9

W10

City of

UB11

UB1

W7

W13

W5

W3

W12

W11

W2

West

UB7

UB3

UB2

W8

W14

SW7

2

UB2

W6

1

SW5

SW3

TW5

TW8

W4

SW10

Hounslow

TW7

TW9

SW13

SW6

SW11

TW6

TW9

SW14

TW4

TW3

Wandsworth

TW19

TW14

SW15

SW18

TW1

SW17

TW13

TW2

Richmond

TW10

TW15

upon Thames

SW19

TW11

TW18

TW12

KT2

Merton

TW16

SW20

CR4

TW17

KT1

KT3

SM4

KT8

Kingston

KT16

KT12

KT7

upon Thames

SM1

SM5

KT13

KT6

KT5

KT4

SM3

Sutton

Surrey

KT10

KT19

KT17

SM2

KT9

1 Hammersmith and Fulham

2 Royal Borough of Kensington and Chelsea

3 County of the City of London

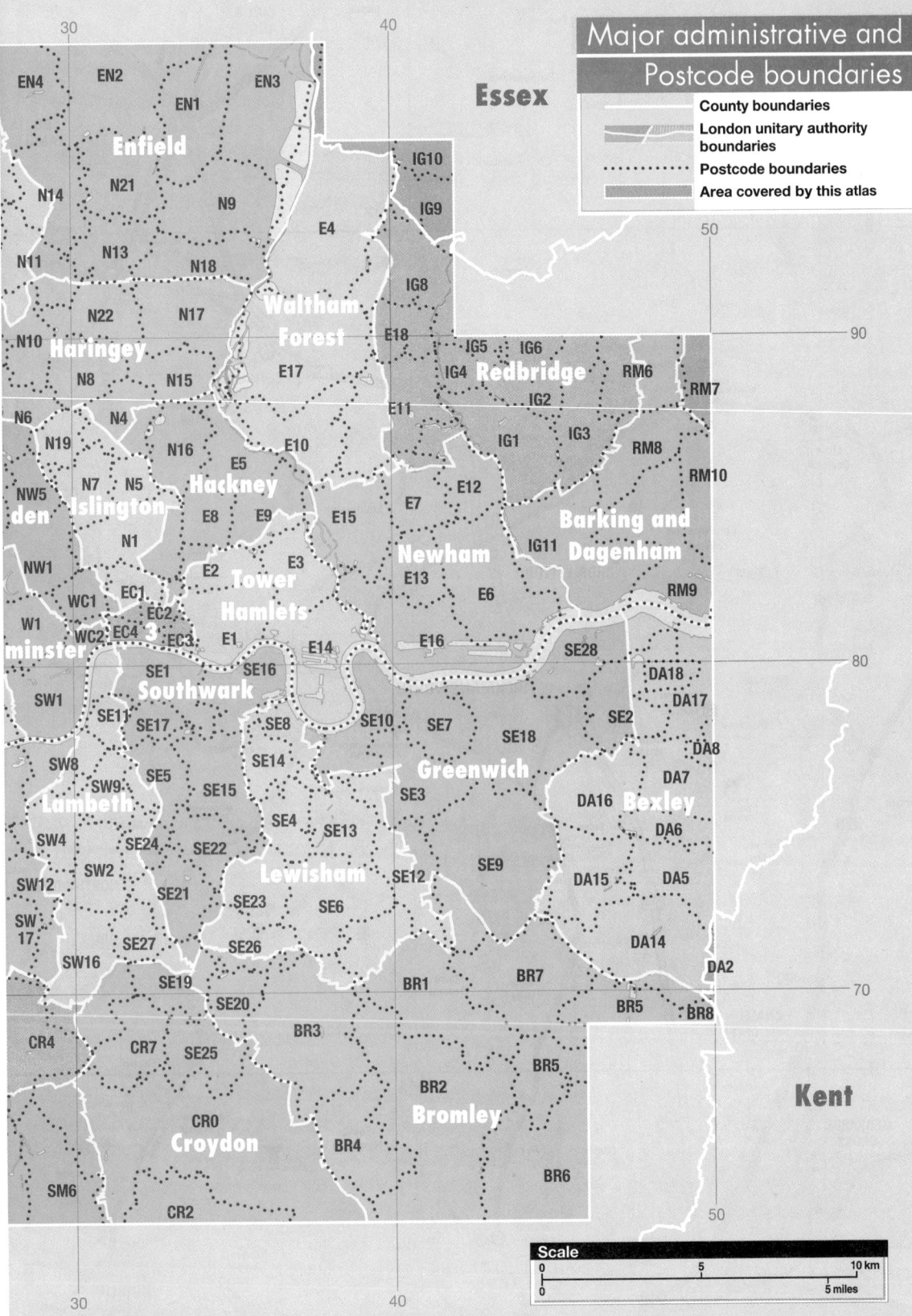

V

Major administrative and Postcode boundaries

County boundaries
London unitary authority boundaries
.... Postcode boundaries
Area covered by this atlas

Essex

Kent

EN4 EN2 EN1 EN3
IG10
Enfield
N14 N21 N9 IG9
E4
N11 N13 N18 IG8
N22 N17 Waltham E18 IG5 IG6 RM6
N10 N8 N15 Forest IG4 Redbridge RM7
Haringey E17 IG2 RM8
N6 N4 E11 IG1 IG3 RM10
N19 N16 E10 E12
N7 N5 Hackney E5 E7 Barking and RM9
NW5 N1 E8 E9 E15 IG11 Dagenham
den Islington E2 E3 Newham
NW1 WC1 EC1 Tower E13 E6 RM9
W1 EC2 Hamlets E1 E14 E16 SE28 DA18
minster WC2 EC4 3 EC3 E1 E14 E16 SE28 DA17
SE1 SE16 SE10 SE7 SE2
SW1 Southwark SE8 SE18 DA8
SE11 SE17 SE14 Greenwich DA7
SW8 SE5 SE15 SE3 DA16 Bexley DA6
Lambeth SE4 SE13 DA5
SW4 SE24 SE22 Lewisham SE12 SE9 DA15
SW2 SE21 SE23 SE6 DA14
SW12 SE27 SE26 DA2
SW17 SE19 BR1 BR7 BR5 BR8
SW16 SE20
CR4 CR7 SE25 BR3
SE25 BR5
CR0 BR2
Croydon BR4 Bromley
SM6 CR2 BR6

Scale
0   5   10 km
0   5 miles

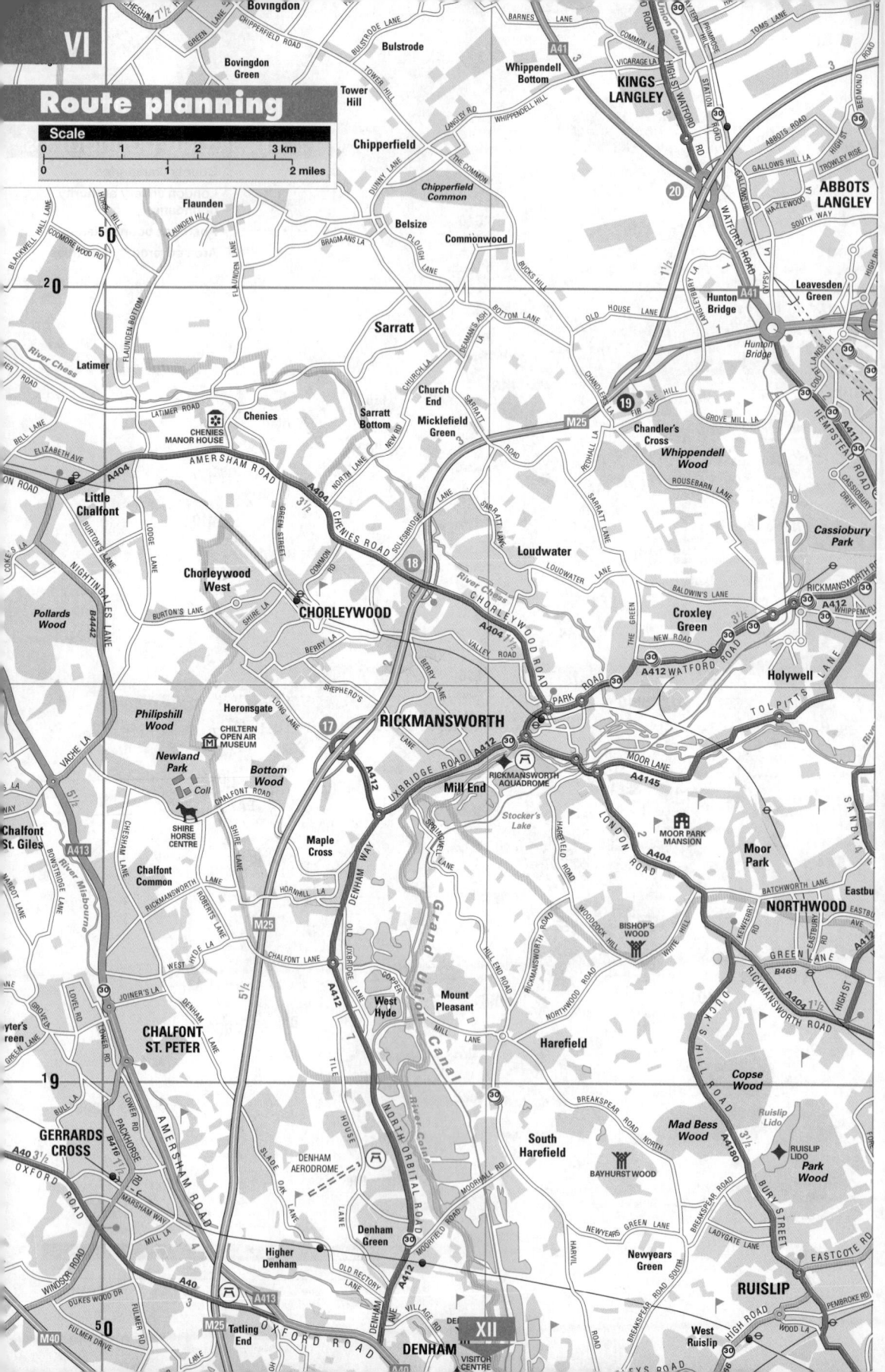

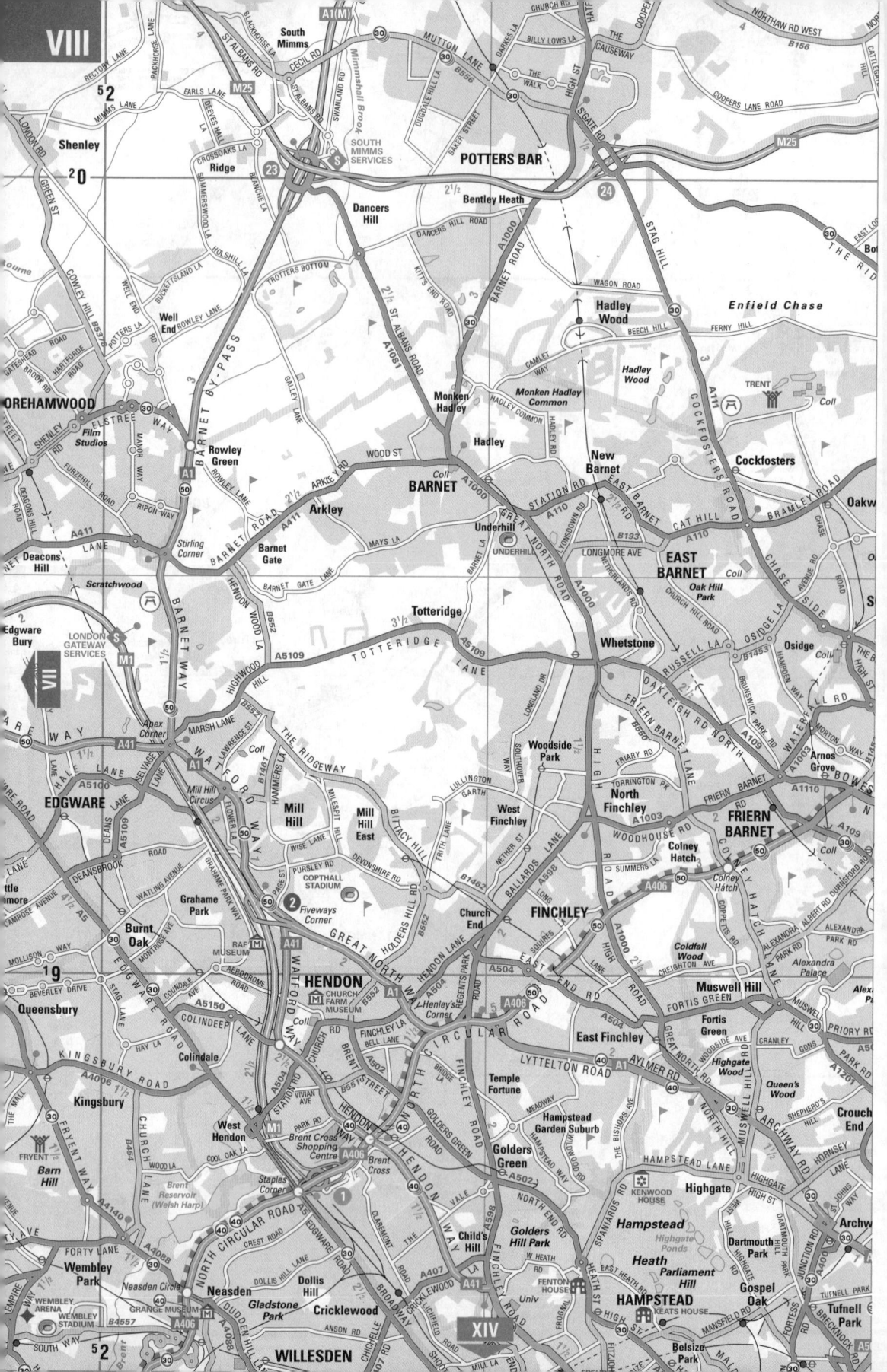

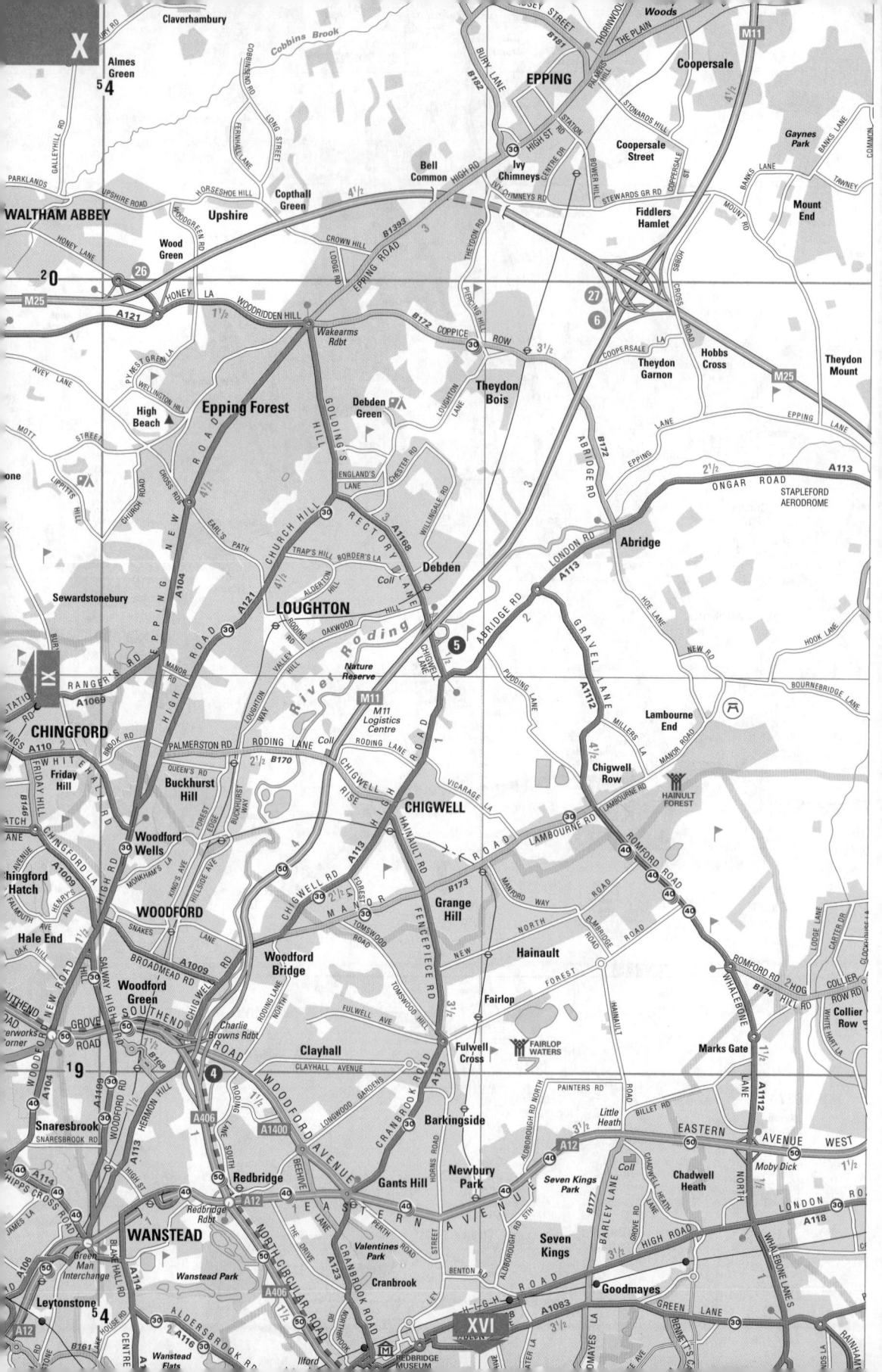

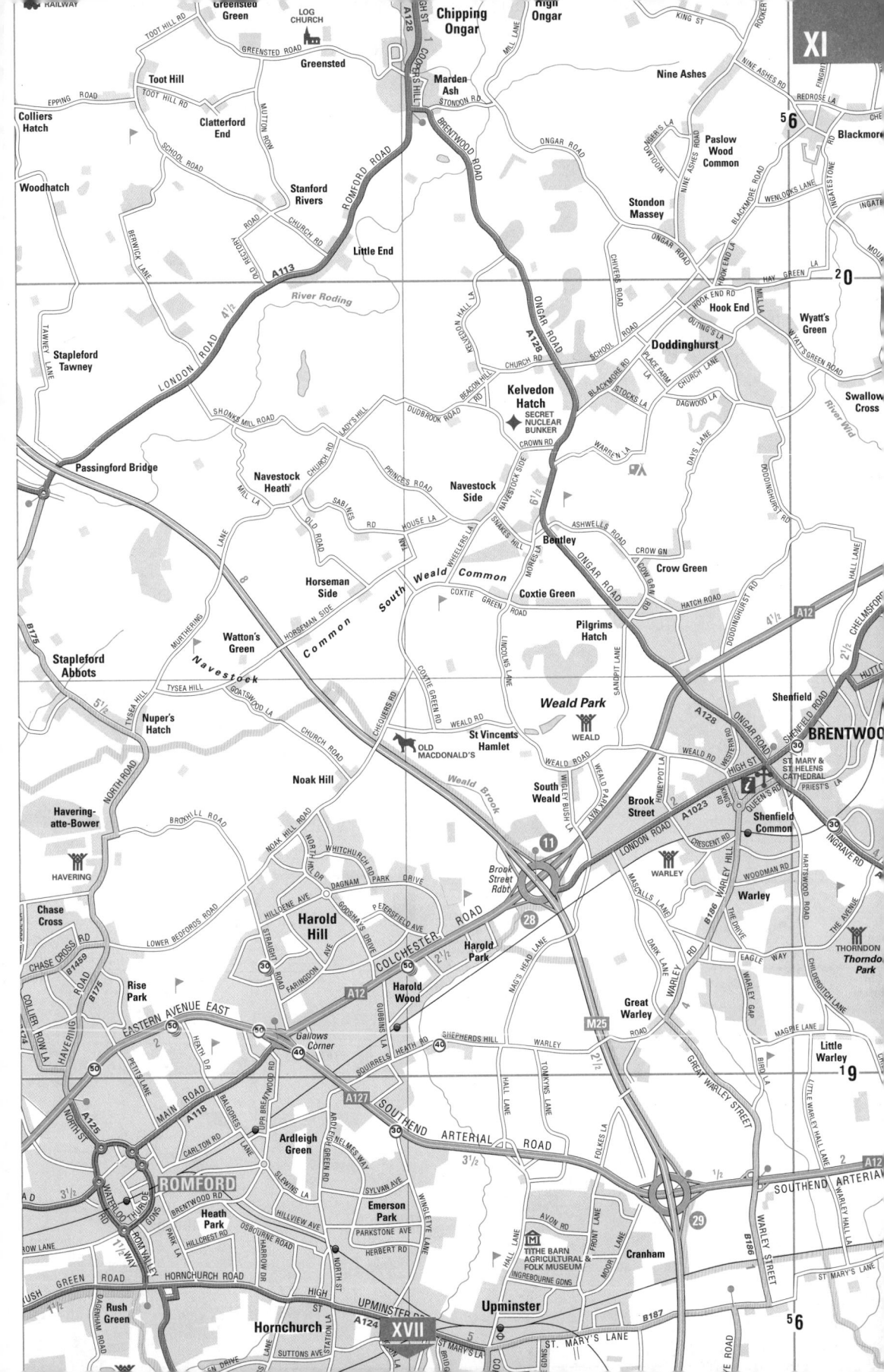

RAILWAY

Greensted Green

LOG CHURCH

Chipping Ongar

High Ongar

Nine Ashes

Blackmore

Greensted

Greensted Road

Marden Ash

5 6

Toot Hill

Stondon Rd.

Paslow Wood Common

Toot Hill Rd.

Clatterford End

Brentwood Road

Ongar Road

Stanford Rivers

Stondon Massey

Colliers Hatch

Mutton Row

School Road

Epping Road

Romford Road

Redrose La.

Woodhatch

Church Rd

Little End

A113

Ongar Road

Hook End

2 0

River Roding

Old Rectory

Ongar Road

Wyatt's Green

Stapleford Tawney

Ongar Road

Church Rd.

Doddinghurst

Swallow Cross

London Road

Kelvedon Hatch SECRET NUCLEAR BUNKER

Blackmore Rd.

Stocks La.

Dagwood La.

River Wid

Passingford Bridge

Shonks Mill Road

Dudbrook Road

Lady's Hill

Crown Rd.

Warren La.

Day's Lane

Navestock Heath

Princes Road

Navestock Side

Ashwells Road

Bentley

Crow Green

Horseman Side

Old Road

Mouse La.

South Weald Common

Coxtie Green

Crow Gn.

Hatch Road

A12

Watton's Green

Navestock

Coxtie Green

Pilgrims Hatch

Shenfield

Nuper's Hatch

Tysea Hill

Church Road

Weald Rd.

Weald Park WEALD

St Vincents Hamlet

Sandpit Lane

A128

BRENTWOOD

Stapleford Abbots

Goatswood La.

Chequers Rd.

Coxtie Green Rd.

ST. MARY & ST. HELENS CATHEDRAL

Havering-atte-Bower

Broxhill Road

OLD MACDONALD'S

Weald Brook

South Weald

Wigley Bush La.

Brook Street

Shenfield Common

HAVERING

North Road

Noak Hill

11

Brook Street Rdbt

London Road

A1023

Warley

Ingrave Rd.

Chase Cross

Hilldene Ave

Dagnam Park Drive

P etersfield Ave

28

Harold Hill

Harold Park

Woodman Rd.

Thorndon Park

Rise Park

Harold Wood

Great Warley

Warley

Eastern Avenue East

Gallows Corner

Shepherds Hill

M25

Little Warley

1 9

ROMFORD

Ardleigh Green

A127

SOUTHEND ARTERIAL ROAD

A12

Emerson Park

29

Cranham

A12

Southend Arteria

Rush Green

Hornchurch

A124

XVII

Upminster

TITHE BARN AGRICULTURAL & FOLK MUSEUM

B187

5 6

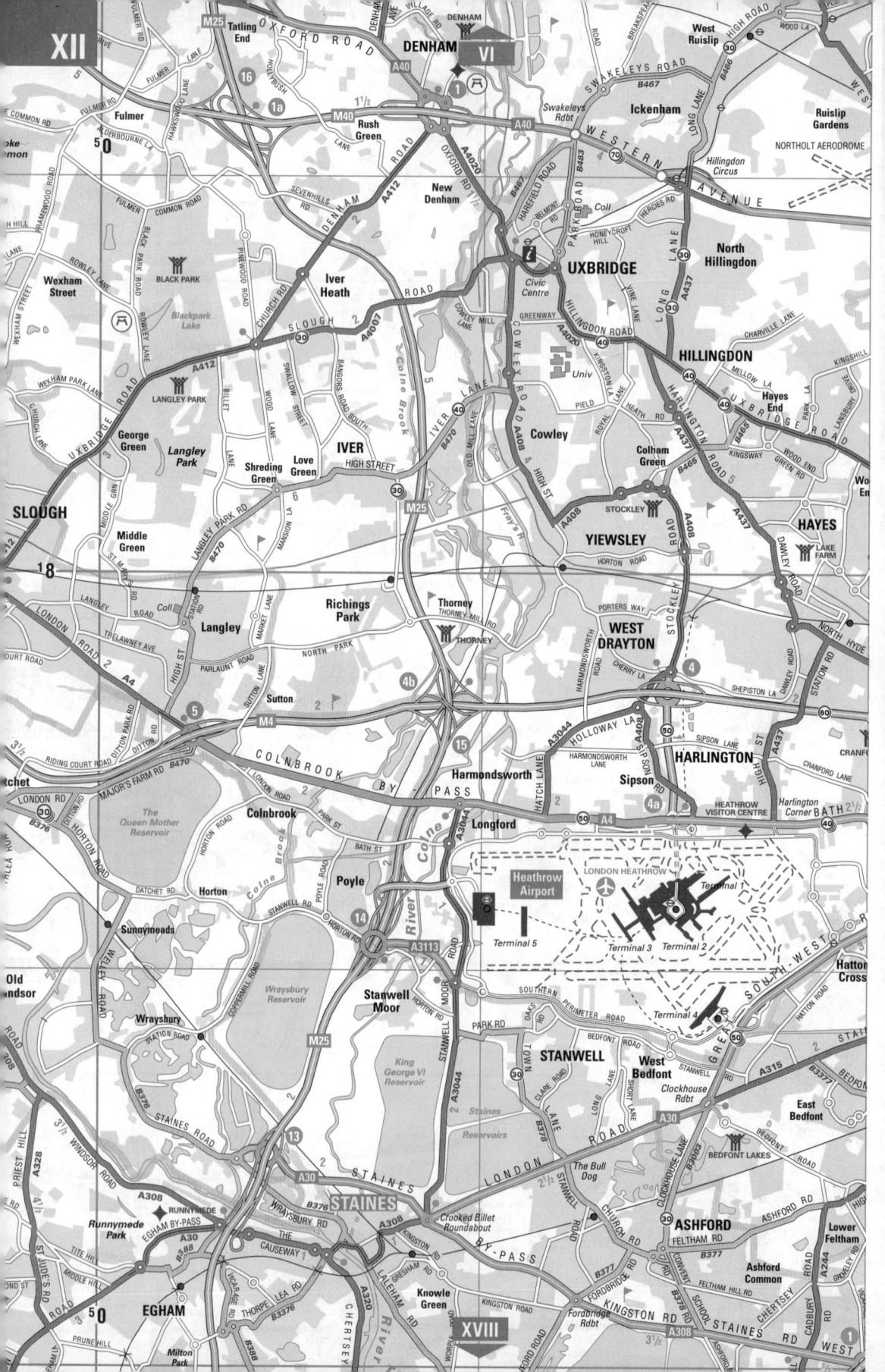

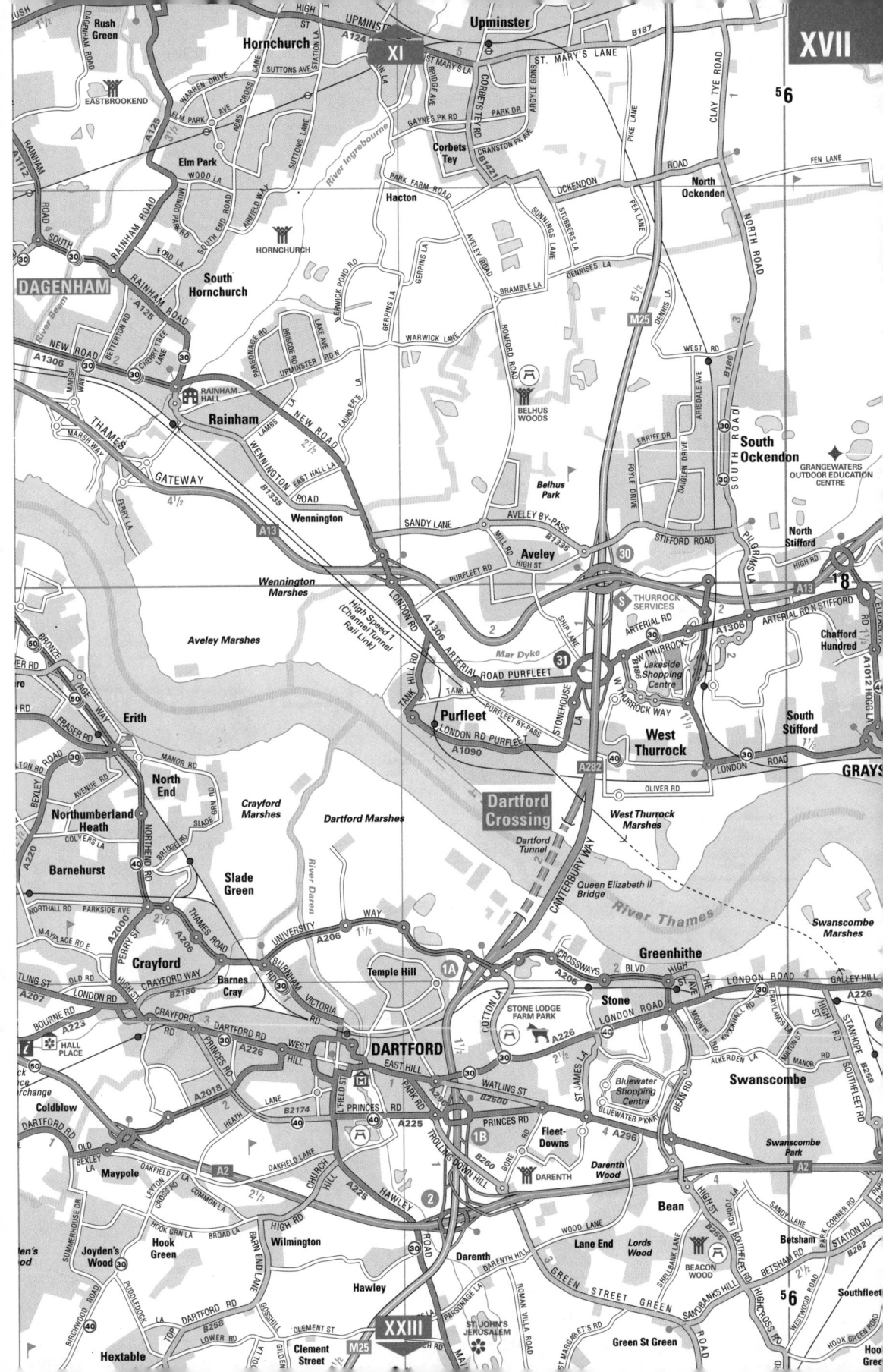

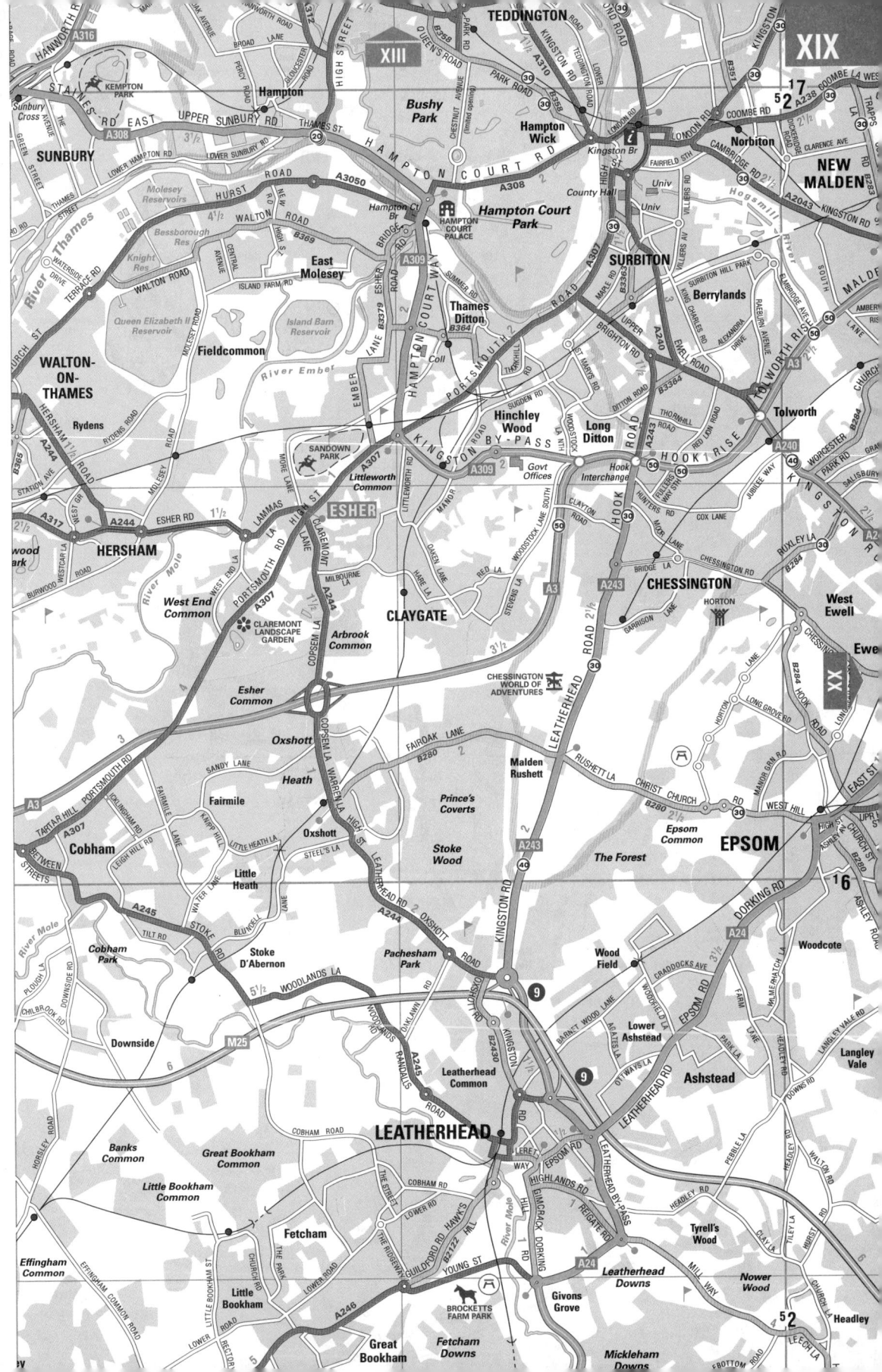

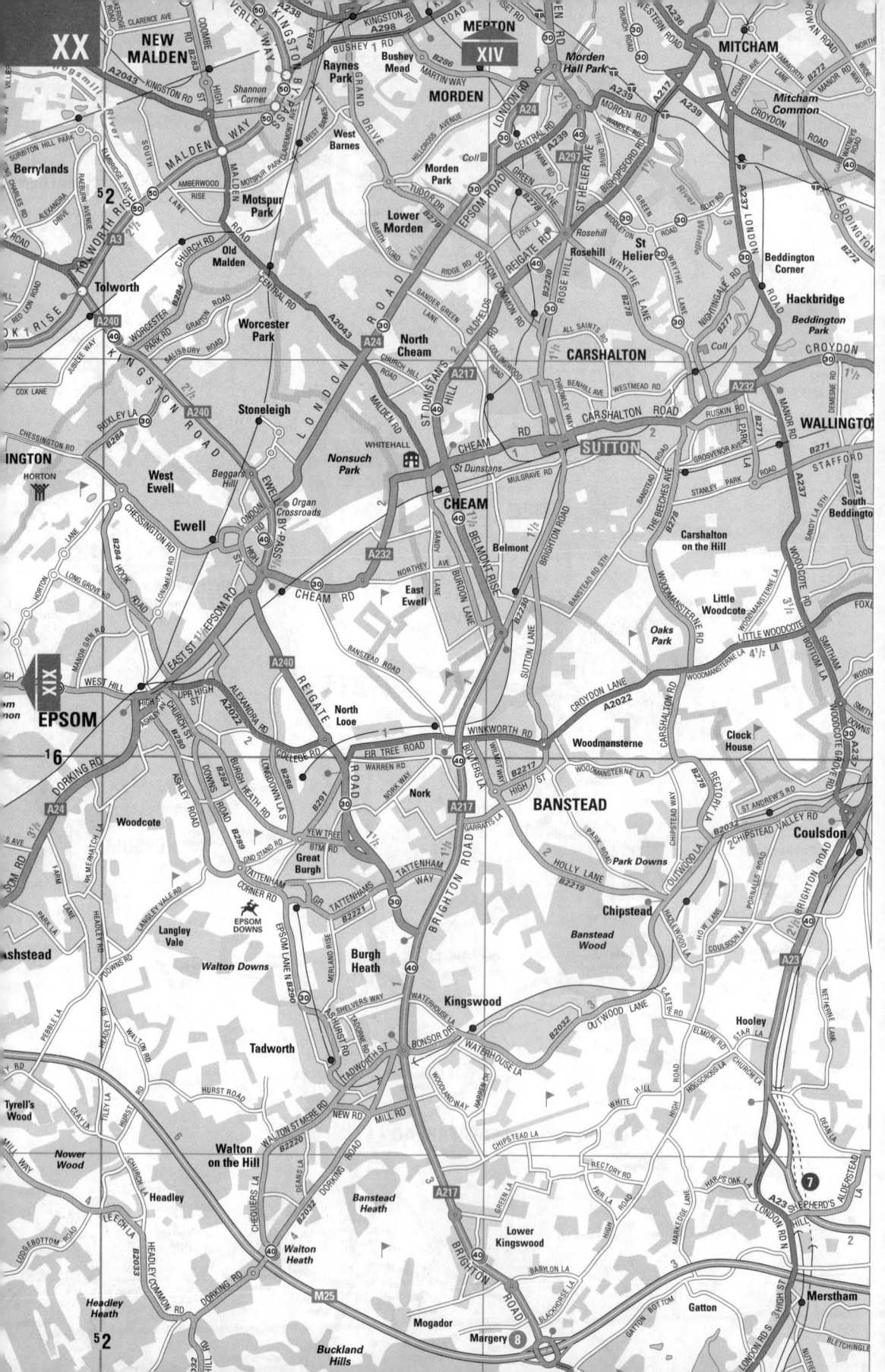

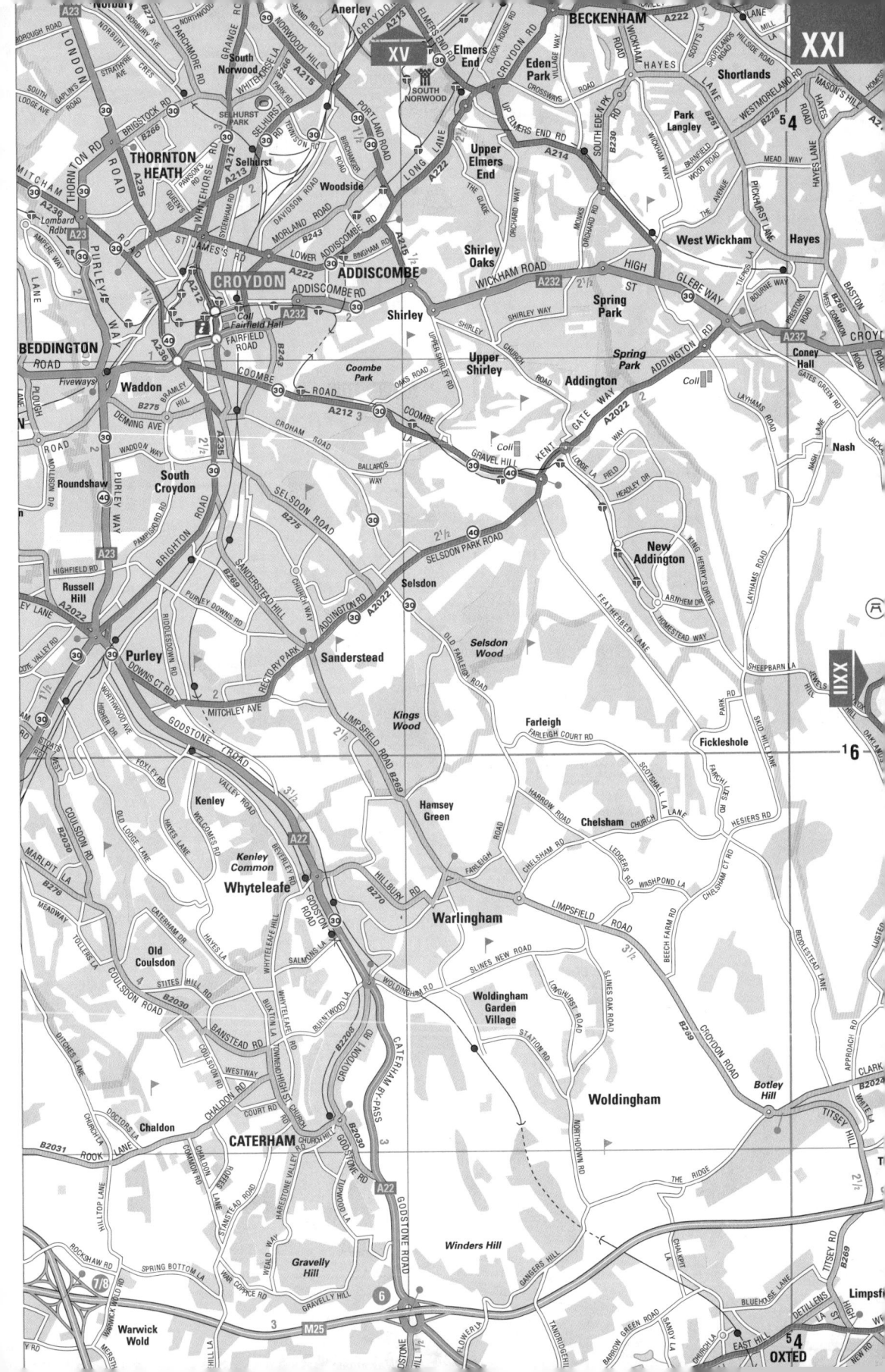

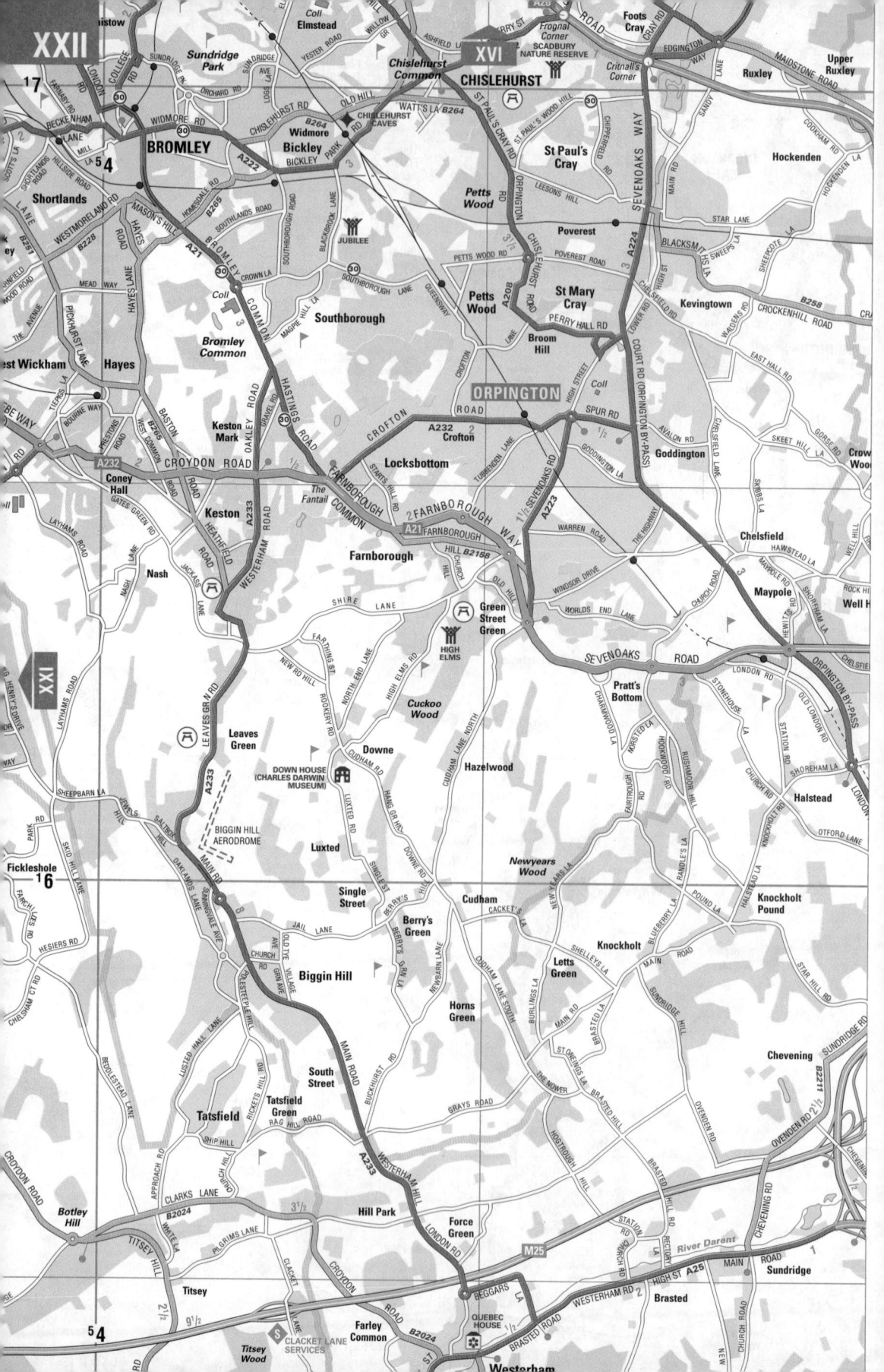

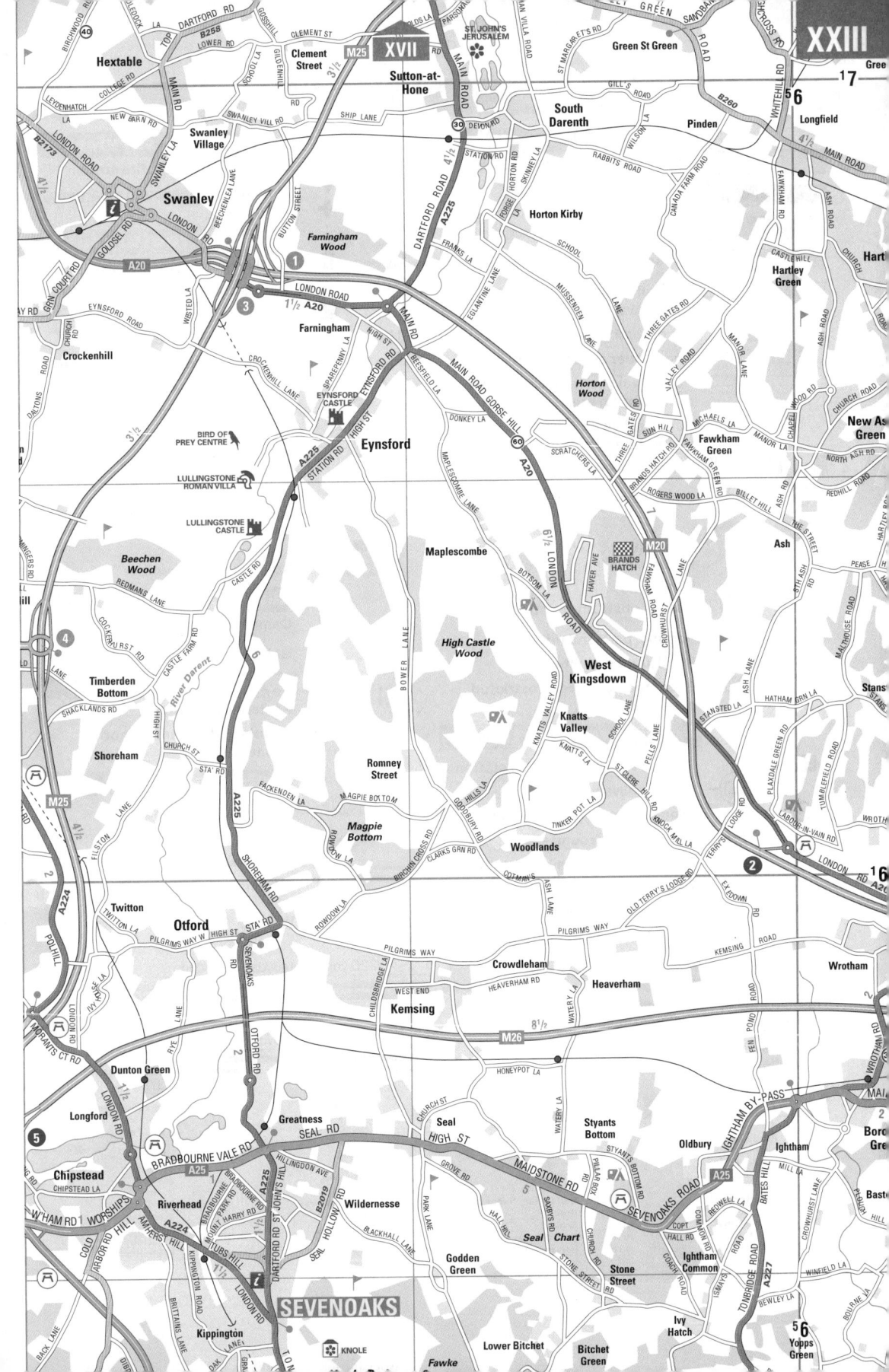

Key to map symbols

Roads

Motorway with junction number

Primary route – single, dual carriageway

A road – single, dual carriageway

B road – single, dual carriageway

Through-route – single, dual carriageway

Minor road – single, dual carriageway

Road under construction

Rural track, private road or narrow road in urban area

Path, bridleway, byway open to all traffic, restricted byway

Tunnel, covered road

Speed camera – single, multiple

Congestion Charge Zone boundary
Roads within the zone are outlined in green

Gate or obstruction, car pound

Parking, park and ride

Road junction name

Pedestrianised area, restricted access area

Public transport

Railway with National Rail station

Private railway station

London Underground station

London Overground station

Docklands Light Railway station

Tramway or miniature railway

Riverbus or ferry pier

Bus or coach station, tram stop

Emergency services

Ambulance, police, fire station

Hospital, accident and emergency entrance

General features

Market, public amenity site

Sports stadium, shopping centre

Information centre, post office

Roman, non-Roman antiquity

House number, spot height – metres

Christian place of worship

Mosque, synagogue

Other place of worship

Houses, important buildings

Woods, parkland/common

Adjoining page number

VILLA   House
100   .304

Leisure facilities

Camp site, caravan site

Golf course, picnic site, view point

Boundaries

Postcode boundaries

County and unitary authority boundaries

NW6

Westminster

Water features

Tidal water, water name

River or canal – minor, major

Stream

Water

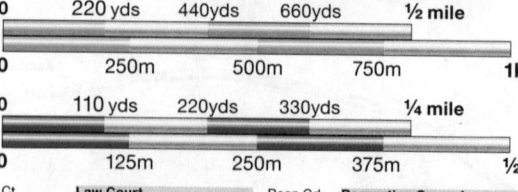

Barking Creek

Scales

The map scale on the pages numbered in blue is
4.37 inches to 1 mile • 6.9cm to 1 km • 1 : 14 492

The map scale on the pages numbered in red is
8.74 inches to 1 mile, see page 228

0   220 yds   440yds   660yds   ½ mile
0   250m   500m   750m   1km

0   110 yds   220yds   330yds   ¼ mile
0   125m   250m   375m   ½km

Abbreviations

Acad	Academy	Crem	Crematorium	Ct	Law Court
Allot Gdns	Allotments	Crkt	Cricket	L Ctr	Leisure Centre
Bndstd	Bandstand	Ent	Enterprise	LC	Level Crossing
Btcl	Botanical	Ex H	Exhibition Hall	Liby	Library
Bwg Gn	Bowling	Fball	Football	Mkt	Market
Cemy	Cemetery	Gdns	Gardens	Meml	Memorial
Ctr	Centre	Glf C	Golf Course	Mon	Monument
C Ctr	Civic Centre	Glf Crs	Golf Course	Mus	Museum
CH	Club House	Drv Rng	Golf Driving Range	Nat Res	Nature Reserve
Ctry Pk	Country Park	Gn	Green	Obsy	Observatory
Coll	College	Gd	Ground	Pav	Pavilion
Ct	Court	Hort	Horticultural	Pk	Park
		Ind Est	Industrial Estate	Pl Fld	Playing Field
		Inst	Institute	Pal	Royal Palace
		Int	Interchange	PH	Public House

Recn Gd	Recreation Ground
Resr	Reservoir
Ret Pk	Retail Park
Sch	School
Sh Ctr	Shopping Centre
Sp	Sports
Stad	Stadium
Sw Pool	Swimming Pool
Tenn Cts	Tennis
TH	Town Hall
Trad Est	Trading Estate
Univ	University
YH	Youth Hostel

Crooked Billet

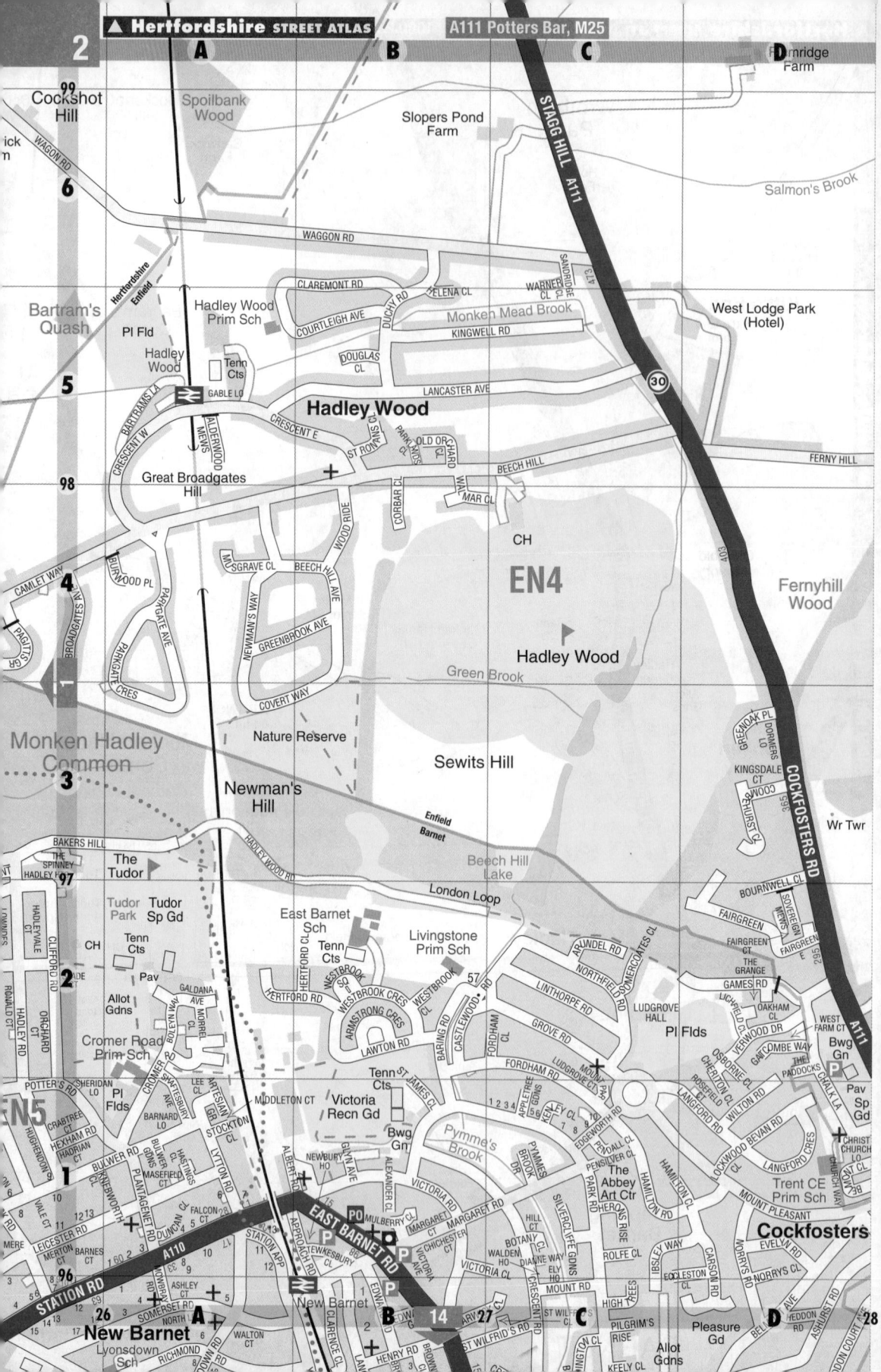

Fernridge Farm

99 Cockshot Hill

6 WAGON RD

ick n

Spoilbank Wood

Slopers Pond Farm

STAGG HILL A111

Salmon's Brook

WAGGON RD

Hertfordshire Enfield

CLAREMONT RD

DUCHY RD

HELENA CL

WARNER CL

SANDRIDGE CL

A111

West Lodge Park (Hotel)

Bartram's Quash

Pl Fld

Hadley Wood Prim Sch

COURTLEIGH AVE

Monken Mead Brook

KINGWELL RD

5 Hadley Wood

Tenn Cts

DOUGLAS CL

LANCASTER AVE

30

BARTRAMS LA

GABLE LO

CRESCENT E

ALDERWOOD MEWS

Hadley Wood

ST RONANS CL

PARK RD

OLD ORCHARD

BEECH HILL

FERNY HILL

CRESCENT W

98 Great Broadgates Hill

CORBAR CL

WALMAR CL

BROADGATES AVE

BURWOOD PL

WOOD RIDE

MUSGRAVE CL

BEECH HILL AVE

CH

EN4

Fernyhill Wood

CAMLET WAY

4 PARKGATE AVE

NEWMAN'S WAY

GREENBROOK AVE

Hadley Wood

GREENDAK PL

DORMERS LO

COCKFOSTERS RD

PAGITS GR

PARKGATE CRES

COVERT WAY

Green Brook

KINGSDALE CT

KWOOD

SHURST CL

Wr Twr

1

Monken Hadley Common

Nature Reserve

Sewits Hill

BOURNWELL CL

3 Newman's Hill

HADLEY WOOD RD

Enfield Barnet

Beech Hill Lake

FAIRGREEN

SOVEREIGN MEWS

FAIRGREEN CT

BAKERS HILL

THE SPINNEY

97 Hadley Ho

The Tudor

London Loop

FAIRGREEN

THE GRANGE

GAMES RD

LICHFIELD CL

HADLEYVALE CT

CLIFFORD RD

Tudor Park

Tudor Sp Gd

CH

Tenn Cts

East Barnet Sch

Tenn Cts

Livingstone Prim Sch

ARUNDEL RD

NORTHFIELD RD

SOMERCOATES CL

OAKHAM CT

THE PADDOCKS

OSBORNE CL

VERWOOD DR

COMBE WAY

WEST FARM CT

Bwg Gn

Pav Sp Gd

A111

2 Pav

Allot Gdns

GALDANA AVE

BOLEYN WAY

MORELL

WESTBROOK SQ

HERTFORD CL

Tenn Cts

WESTBROOK CRES

57

Ludgrove Hall

LINTHORPE RD

GROVE RD

Pl Flds

CHERLTON CL

PENSILVER CL

WILTON RD

LANGFORD RD

LANGFORD CRES

CHRIST CHURCH LO

CHURCH WAY

Cromer Road Prim Sch

HADLEY RD

ORCHARD RD

RONALD CT

HERTFORD RD

ARMSTRONG CRES

LAWTON RD

CASTLEWOOD RD

BARING RD

FORDHAM CL

FORDHAM RD

LUDGROVE CL

MOUNT

The Abbey Art Ctr

HAMILTON CL

LOCKWOOD BEVAN RD

GALT COMBE WAY

Trent CE Prim Sch

Cockfosters

N5

POTTER'S RD

SHERIDAN LO

Pl Flds

CROMER RD

SHAFTESBURY

LEE LA

ARTESIAN GR

MIDDLETON CT

ST JAMES' CL

Tenn Cts

Victoria Recn Gd

Bwg Gn

Pymme's Brook

APPLETREE GDNS

PYMMES GDNS

KELLY CL

EDGEWORTH RD

TYNDALL CL

SILVERCLIFFE GDNS

HAMILTON RD

HEROES RISE

MOUNT PLEASANT

IBSLEY WAY

EVELYN CL

MORRYS RD

Pleasure Gd

CRABTREE CT

HEXHAM RD

HADRIAN CT

RUGHENDON

NORTH

BARNARD LO

HASTINGS

STOCKTON CL

LYTTON RD

ALBERT RD

NEWBURY HO

GLYN AVE

ALEXANDER CL

VICTORIA RD

MARGARET RD

MARGARET

CHICHESTER CL

BOTANY WALDEN HO

DIANNE WAY

ELY HO

PARK RD

ROLFE CL

MOUNT RD

CARSON RD

NORRYS CL

NORRYS RD

BELL AVE

CHRIST CHURCH

COURT

EN5

96 STATION RD

A110

VALE CT

LEICESTER CT

MERTON CT

BARNES CT

BULWER RD

KNEBWORTH

PLANTAGENET GDNS

MASEFIELD

DUNCAN CT

FALCON

STATION APP

APPROACH RD

EAST BARNET RD

MULBERRY CL

TEWKESBURY CL

EDWARD RD

BROWN

ST WILFRID'S RD

PILGRIM'S RISE

HIGH CRES

Allot Gdns

LONDON COURT

HEDDON RD

ASHURST CL

26 New Barnet

Lyonsdown Sch

SOMERSET RD

WALTON CT

RICHMOND RD

HENRY RD

New Barnet

Victoria Cl

ST WILFRID'S RD

KINGSTON RD

14

27

Cockfosters

28

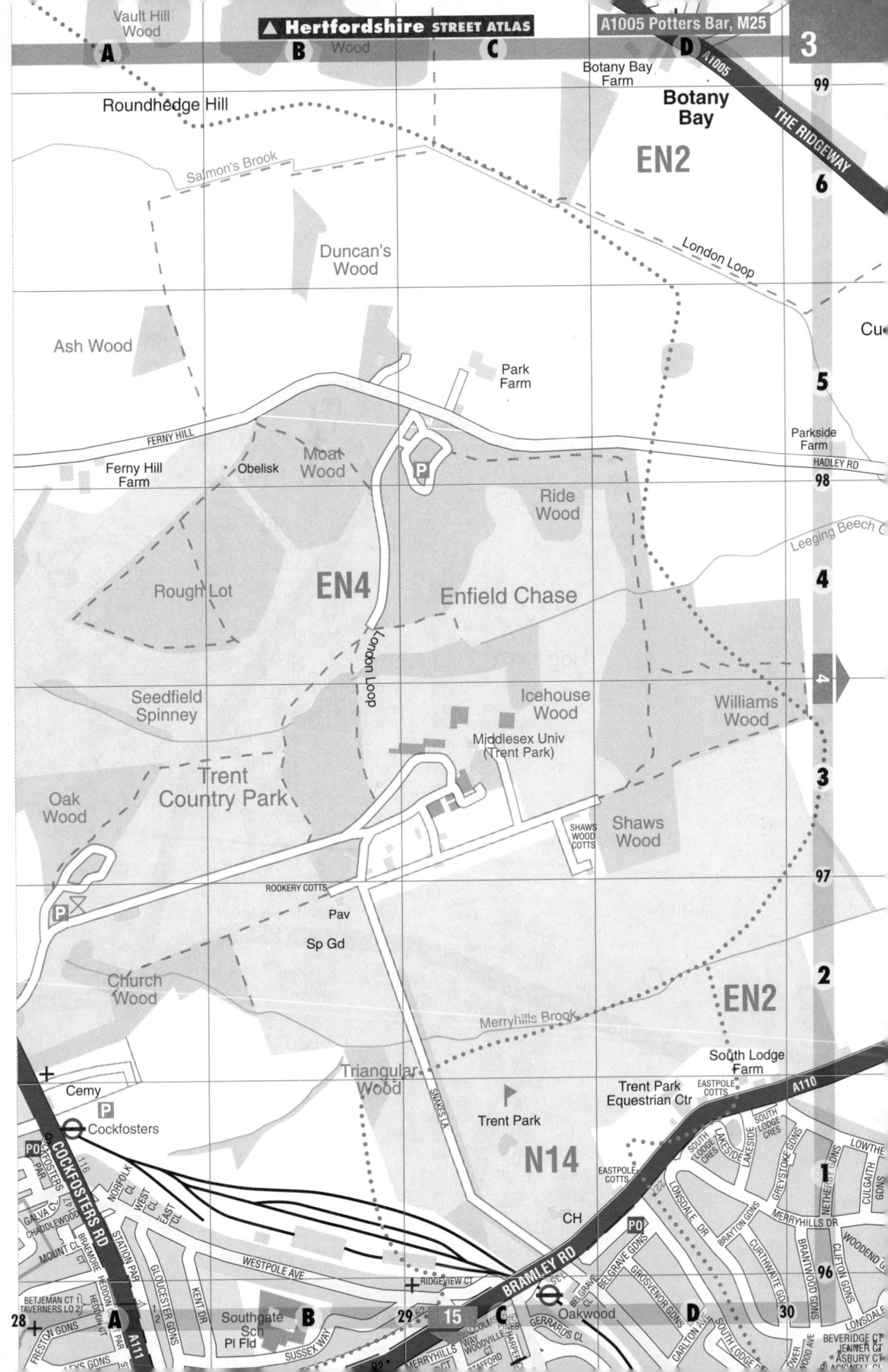

A1005 Potters Bar, M25

3

A   B   Wood   C   D

99

Vault Hill Wood

Roundhedge Hill

Botany Bay Farm

Botany Bay

EN2

Salmon's Brook

London Loop

Duncan's Wood

6

Ash Wood

Park Farm

5

THE RIDGEWAY

A1005

Cu

Parkside Farm

FERNY HILL

Ferny Hill Farm

Obelisk

Moat Wood

P

HADLEY RD

98

Ride Wood

Leeging Beech C

EN4

Rough Lot

Enfield Chase

London Loop

4

Williams Wood

4

Seedfield Spinney

Icehouse Wood

3

Middlesex Univ (Trent Park)

Trent Country Park

Oak Wood

SHAWS WOOD COTTS

Shaws Wood

97

ROOKERY COTTS

Pav

Sp Gd

Church Wood

P

Merryhills Brook

EN2

2

South Lodge Farm

EASTPOLE COTTS

A110

Triangular Wood

SNAKES LA

Trent Park Equestrian Ctr

Trent Park Cotts

Cemy

P

Cockfosters

Trent Park

N14

SOUTH LODGE CRES

LAKESIDE

SOUTH LODGE CRES

LAKESIDE

GREYSTOKE GDNS

CULGAITH

LOWTHE

EASTPOLE COTTS

1

COCKFOSTERS RD

NORFOLK CL

WEST CL

EAST CL

CH

PO

LONSDALE DR

BRAYTON GDNS

CURTHWAITE GDNS

MERRYHILLS DR

BRANTWOOD GDNS

CLIFTON GDNS

WOODEND GD

LONSDALE

96

CHADDLEWOOD

MOUNT CL

STATION PAR

GLOUCESTER GDNS

KENT DR

WESTPOLE AVE

BRAMLEY RD

BELGRAVE CL

BELGRAVE GDNS

GROSVENOR GDNS

CARLTON AVE

SOUTH LODGE

TOWER

LONSDALE

BEVERIDGE CT

JENNER CT

ASBURY CT

BLACKWELL CL

28

BETJEMAN CT

TAVERNERS

FRESTON GDNS

A111

BRAEMORE CT

HEDDON CT

A   B   Southgate Sch Pl Fld   29   15   C   Oakwood   D   30

SUSSEX WAY

RIDGEVIEW CT

MERRYHILLS

WAY WOODVILLE CL

STAFFORD

GERRARDS CL

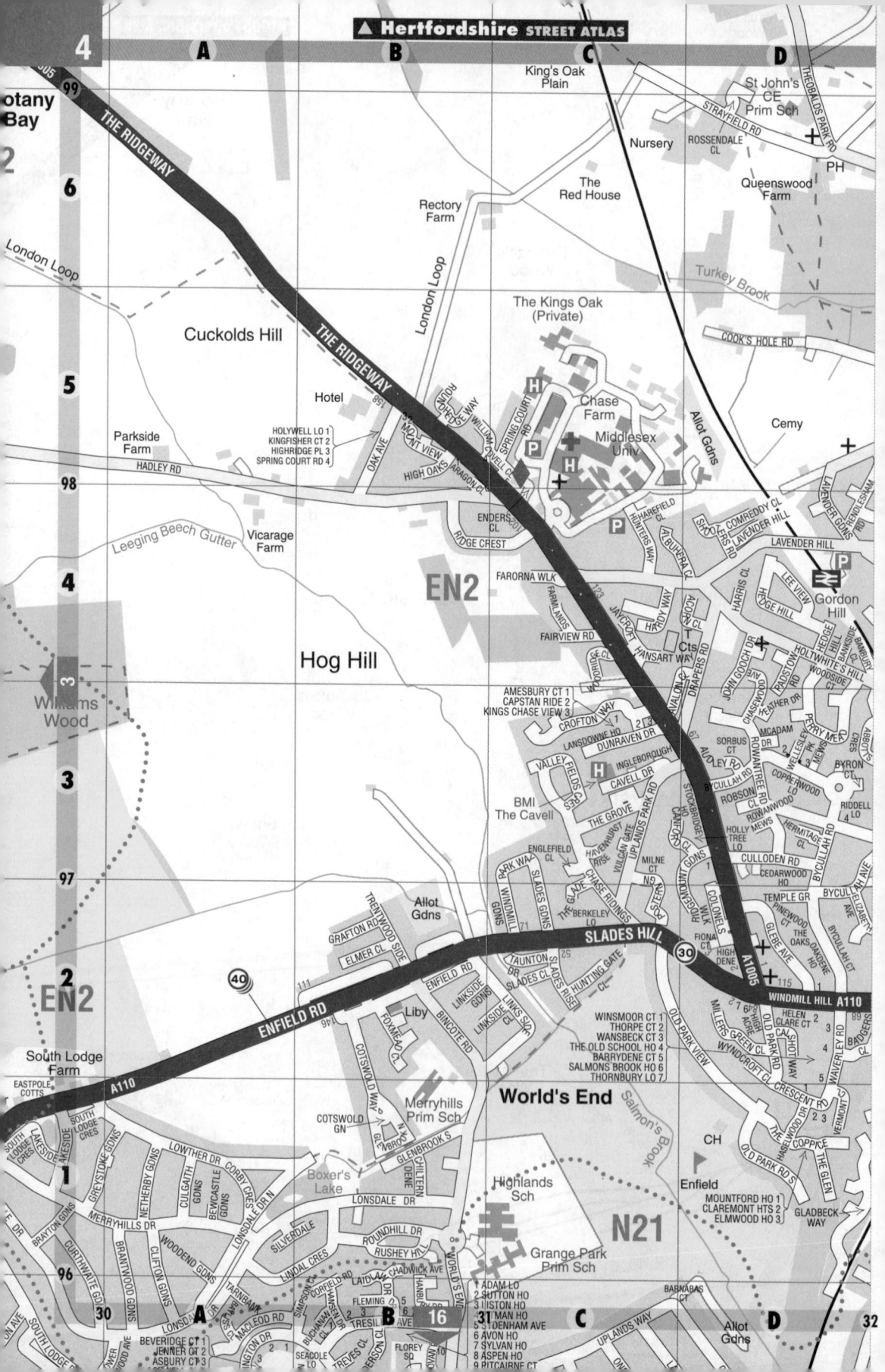

4

A | B | C | D

99

otany
Bay

2

THE RIDGEWAY

6

London Loop

Cuckolds Hill

THE RIDGEWAY

5

Hotel

Parkside
Farm

HADLEY RD

98

Leeging Beech Gutter

Vicarage
Farm

4

Williams
Wood

3

Hog Hill

3

97

EN2

2

EN2

40

ENFIELD RD

South Lodge
Farm

A110

EASTPOLE
COTTS

1

96

30

A

King's Oak
Plain

Nursery

The
Red House

Rectory
Farm

London Loop

The Kings Oak
(Private)

HOLYWELL LO 1
KINGFISHER CT 2
HIGHRIDGE PL 3
SPRING COURT RD 4

H

P

Chase
Farm

Middlesex
Univ

H

OAK AVE

HIGH OAKS

MONT VIEW

ARAGON CL

WILLIAM WAY

SPRING COURT RD

FELTON CL

ENDERS
CL

RIDGE CREST

FARORNA WLK

FARMLANDS

FAIRVIEW RD

P

HAREFIELD
CL

HUNTERS WAY

ALBUFERA CL

AMESBURY CT 1
CAPSTAN RIDE 2
KINGS CHASE VIEW 3

CROFTON WAY

LANSDOWNE RD

VALLEY FIELDS

DUNRAVEN DR

Ingleborough

H

CAVELL DR

BMI
The Cavell

THE GROVE

PARK WAY

WINDMILL GDNS

SLADES GDNS

SLADES RISE

SLADES CL

HUNTING GATE
CL

ENGLEFIELD
CL

HAVENHURST
RISE

VULCAN GATE

MILNE
CT

BERKELEY
LO

CHASE RIDINGS

UPLANDS PARK RD

CANFORD

SLADES HILL

30

A1005

TAUNTON
DR

Allot
Gdns

GRAFTON CL

ELMER CL

TRENWOOD SIDE

111

146

ENFIELD RD

LINKSIDE

LINKSIDE
GDNS

COTSWOLD WAY

FOXMEAD CT

BINCOTE CT

LINKSIDE

COTSWOLD
GN

Liby

Merryhills
Prim Sch

GLENBROOK S

CHILTERN
DENE

GLENBROOK N

Boxer's
Lake

LONSDALE DR

Highlands
Sch

WINSMOOR CT 1
THORPE CT 2
WANSBECK CT 3
THE OLD SCHOOL HO 4
BARRYDENE CT 5
SALMONS BROOK HO 6
THORNBURY LO 7

World's End

OLD PARK VIEW

Salmon's Brook

MILLERS GREEN CL

WYNDCROFT CL

CRESCENT RD

OLD PARK RD

CH

Enfield

MOUNTFORD HO 1
CLAREMONT HTS 2
ELMWOOD HO 3

OLD PARK RD S

GLADBECK
WAY

N21

Grange Park
Prim Sch

SOUTH
LODGE CRES

LAKESIDE

SOUTH LODGE
CRES

GREYSTOKE GDNS

NETHERBY GDNS

LOWTHER DR

CULGAITH
GDNS

CORBY CRES

BEWCASTLE
GDNS

LONSDALE DR N

WOODEND GDNS

CLIFTON GDNS

BRAYTON GDNS

BRANTWOOD GDNS

CURTHWAITE GDNS

MERRYHILLS DR

SILVERDALE

LINDAL CRES

LONSDALE DR

ROUNDHILL DR

RUSHEY HL

CHADWICK AVE

WORLD'S END

HANBURY

SOUTH LODGE

96

30

A

B

1 ADAM LO
2 SUTTON HO
3 USTON HO
4 MAN HO
5 DENHAM AVE
6 AVON HO
7 SYLVAN HO
8 ASPEN HO
9 PITCAIRNE C

16

31

C

St John's
CE
Prim Sch

STRAYFIELD RD

THEOBALDS PARK RD

ROSSENDALE
CL

PH

Queenswood
Farm

COOK'S HOLE RD

Turkey Brook

Cemy

LAVENDER GDNS

COMREDDY CL

LAVENDER HILL

LAVENDER HILL

P

Gordon
Hill

HOLTWHITE'S HILL

LEE VIEW

HOGE HILL

HARRIS CL

JOHN GOOCH DR

CHASEWOOD

HEATHER DR

PERRY MEAD

WELLESLEY RD

MCADAM

ROWANTREE RD

SORBUS
CT

ROWANWOOD

COPPERWOOD

HERMITAGE
CL

CEDARWOOD
HO

CULLODEN RD

TEMPLE GR

PINEWOOD

THE OAKS

GLEBE AVE

WINDMILL HILL

A110

HELEN
CT

CALSHOT WAY

WAVERLEY RD

VERMONT CL

THE GLEN

COPPICE

MASLEWOOD DR

OLD PARK RD

BADGERS

BARNABAS
CT

Allot
Gdns

UPLANDS WAY

D

32

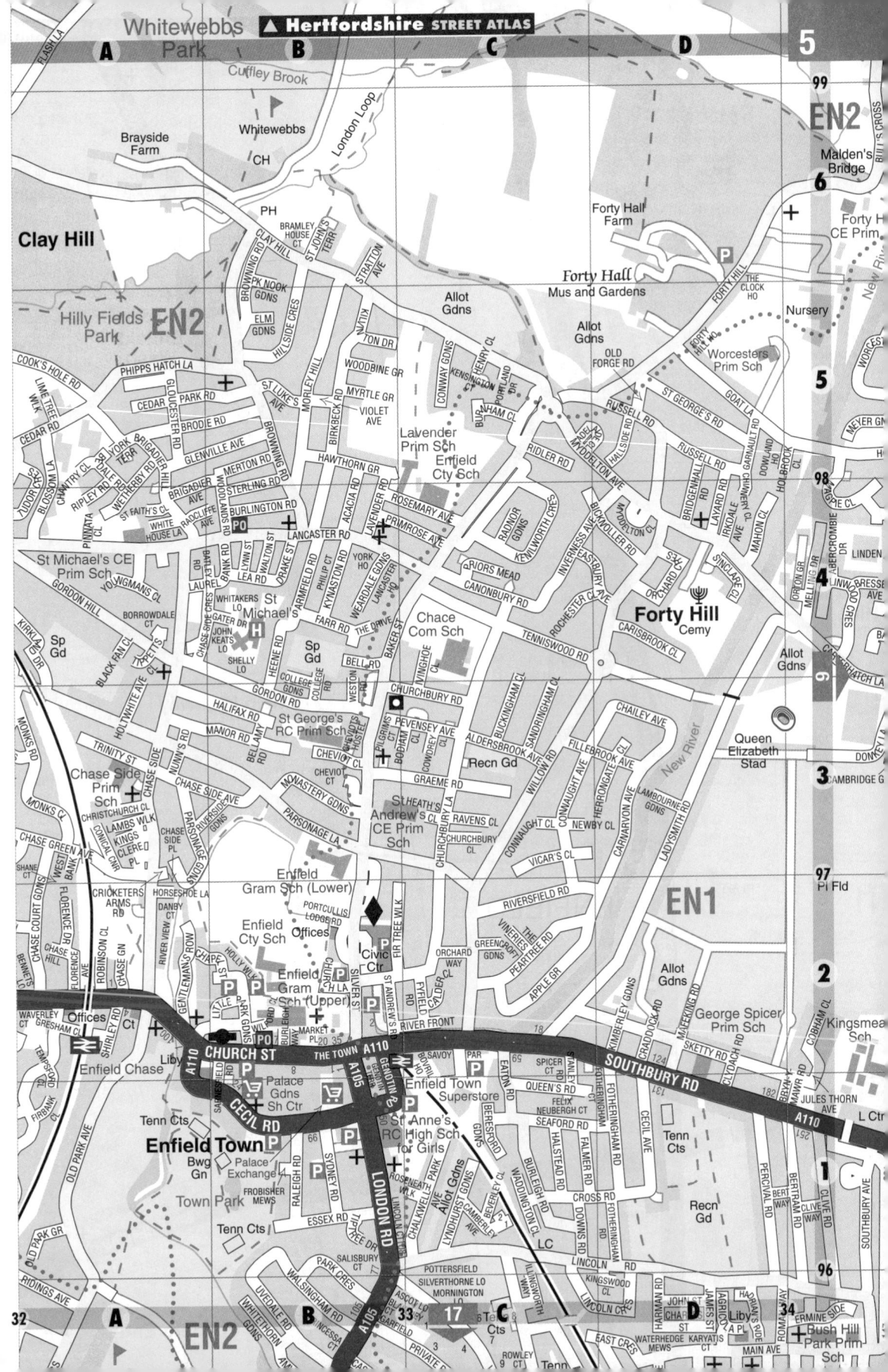

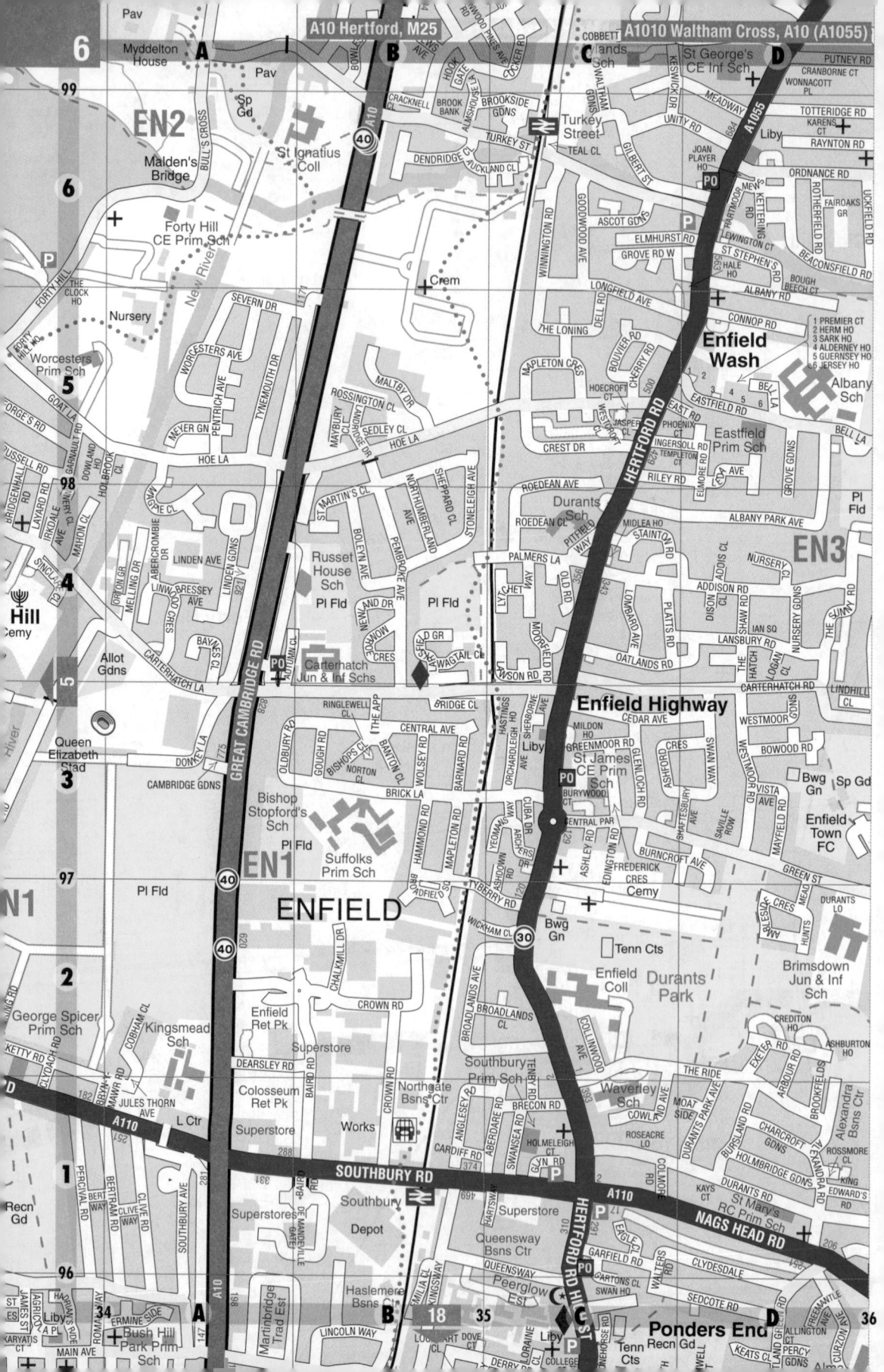

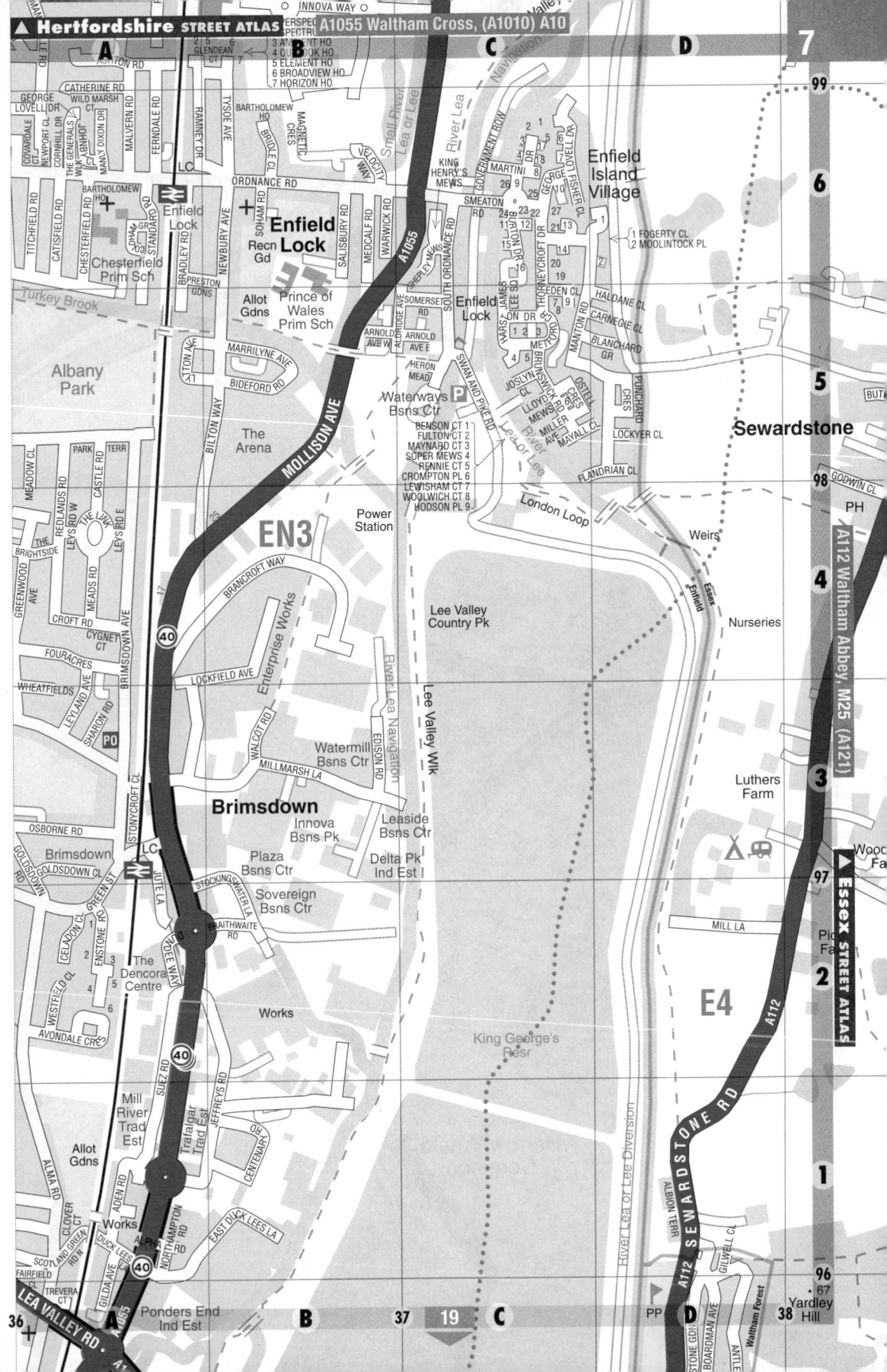

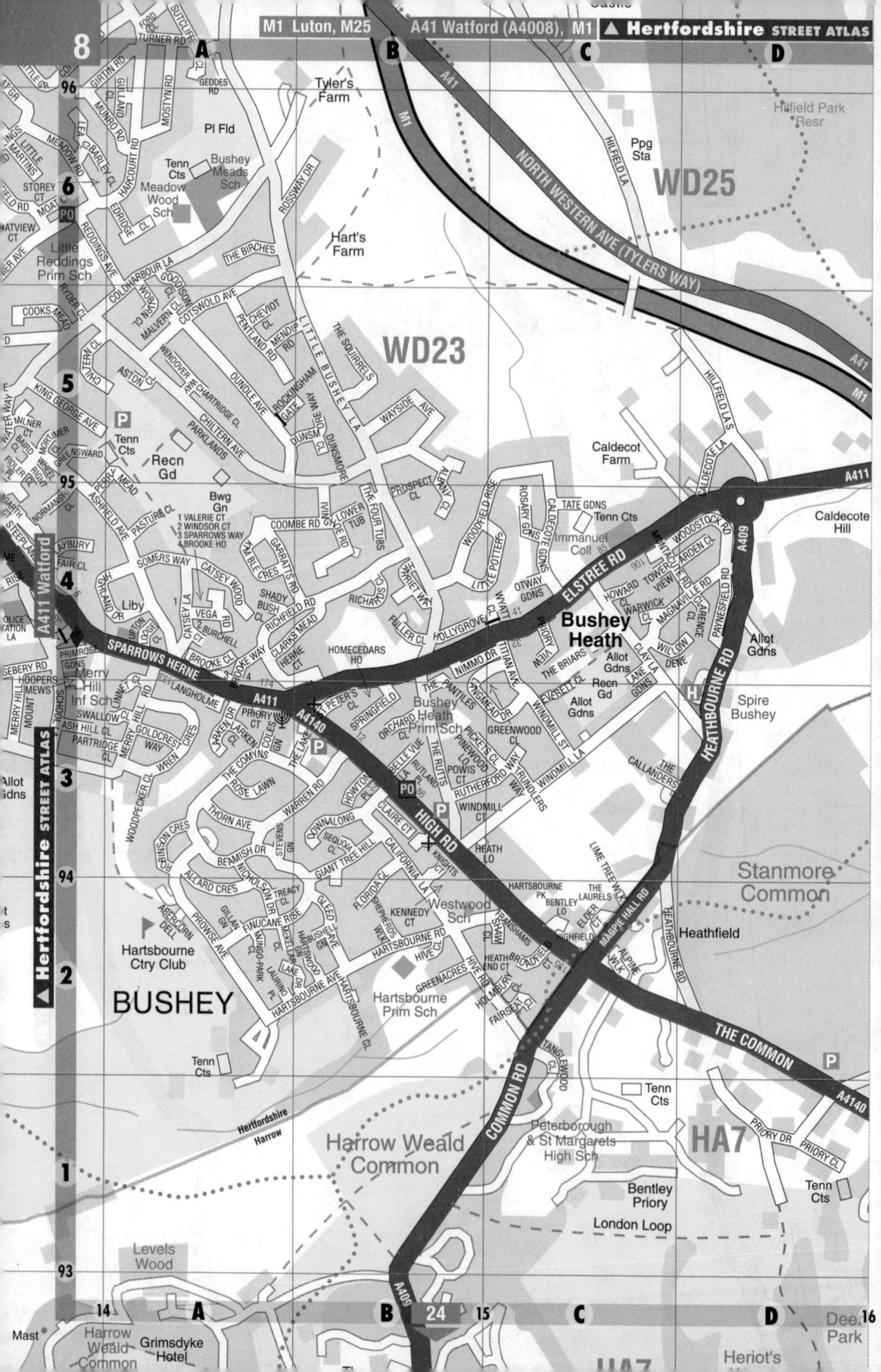

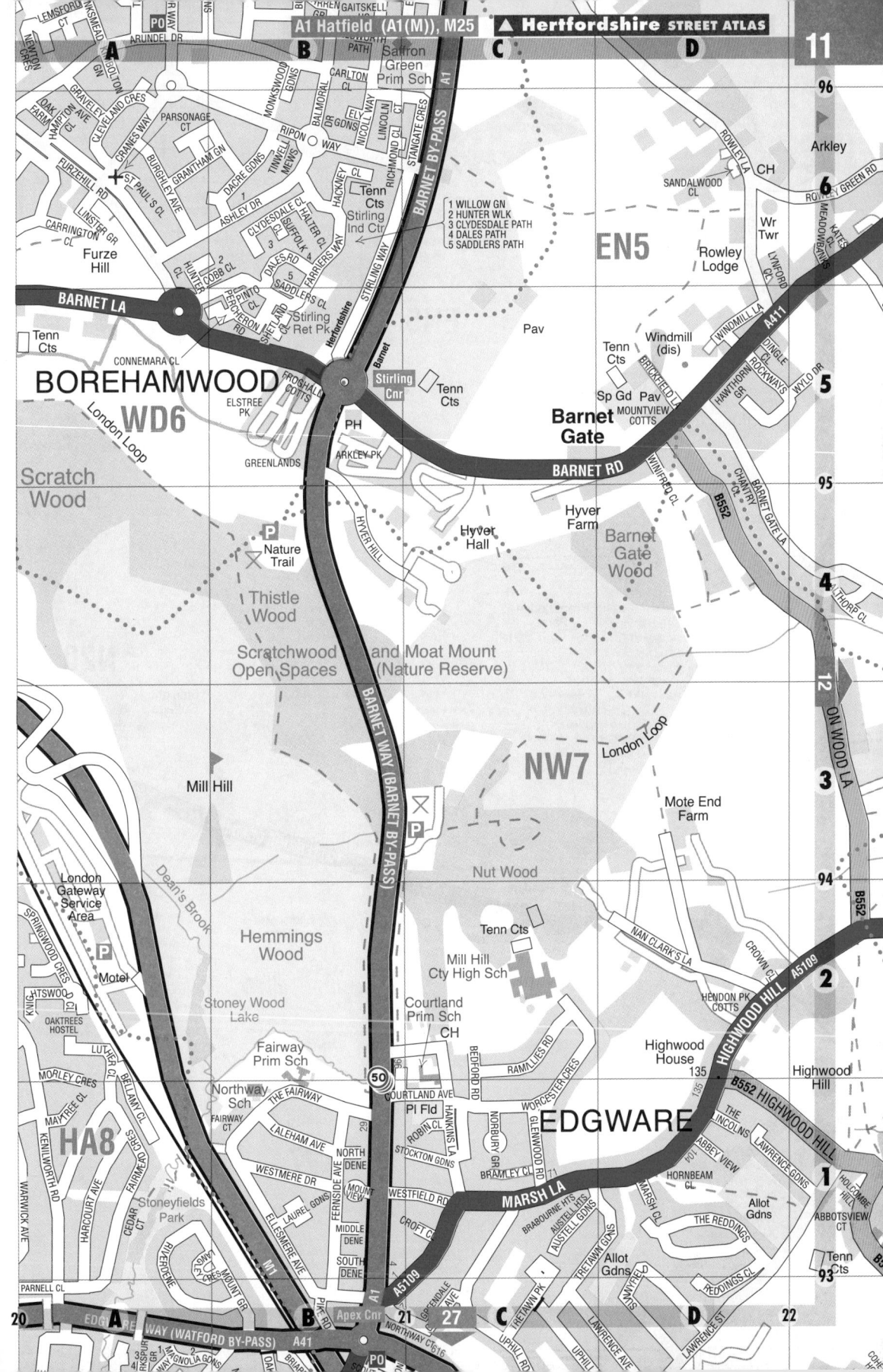

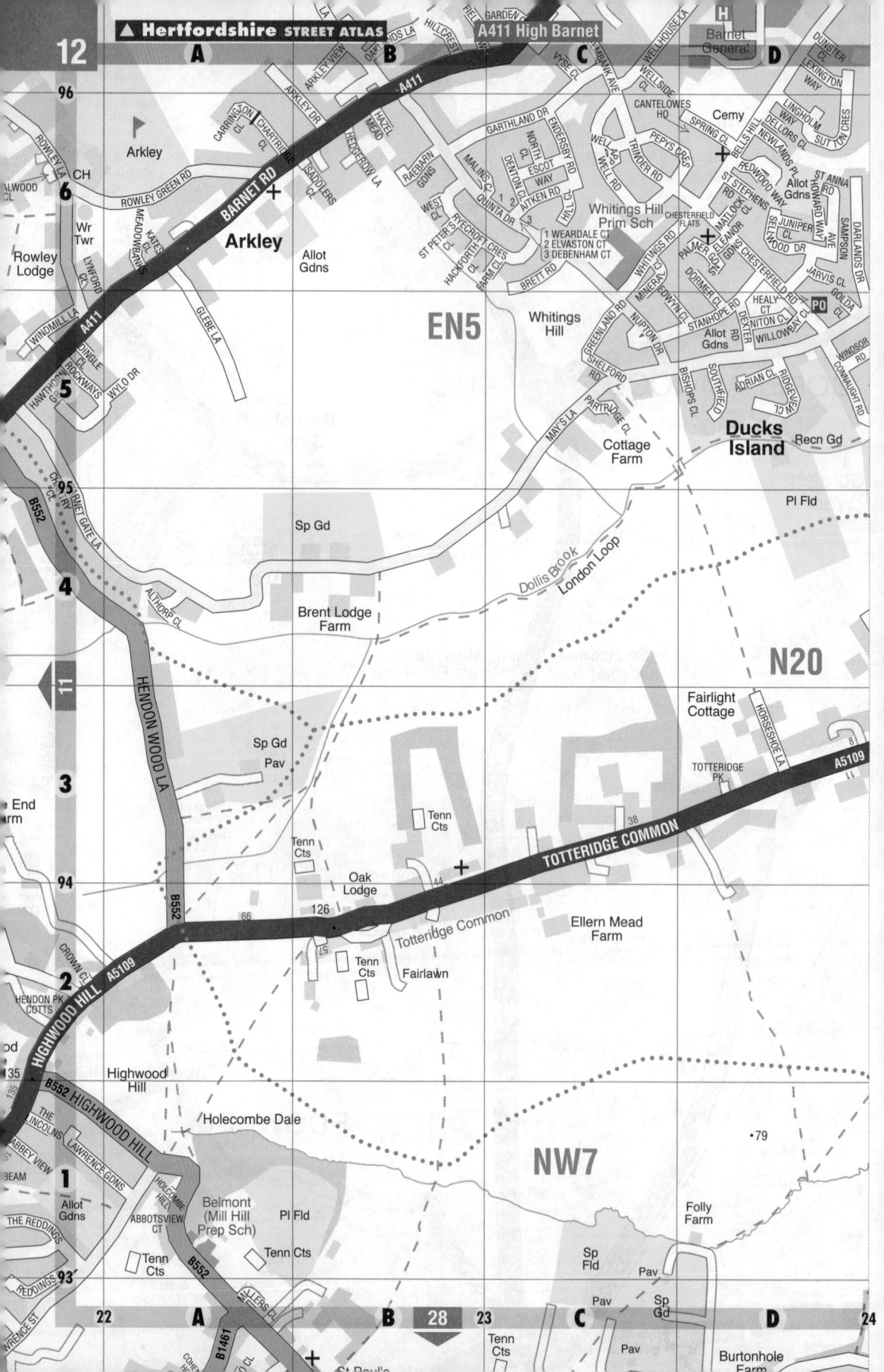

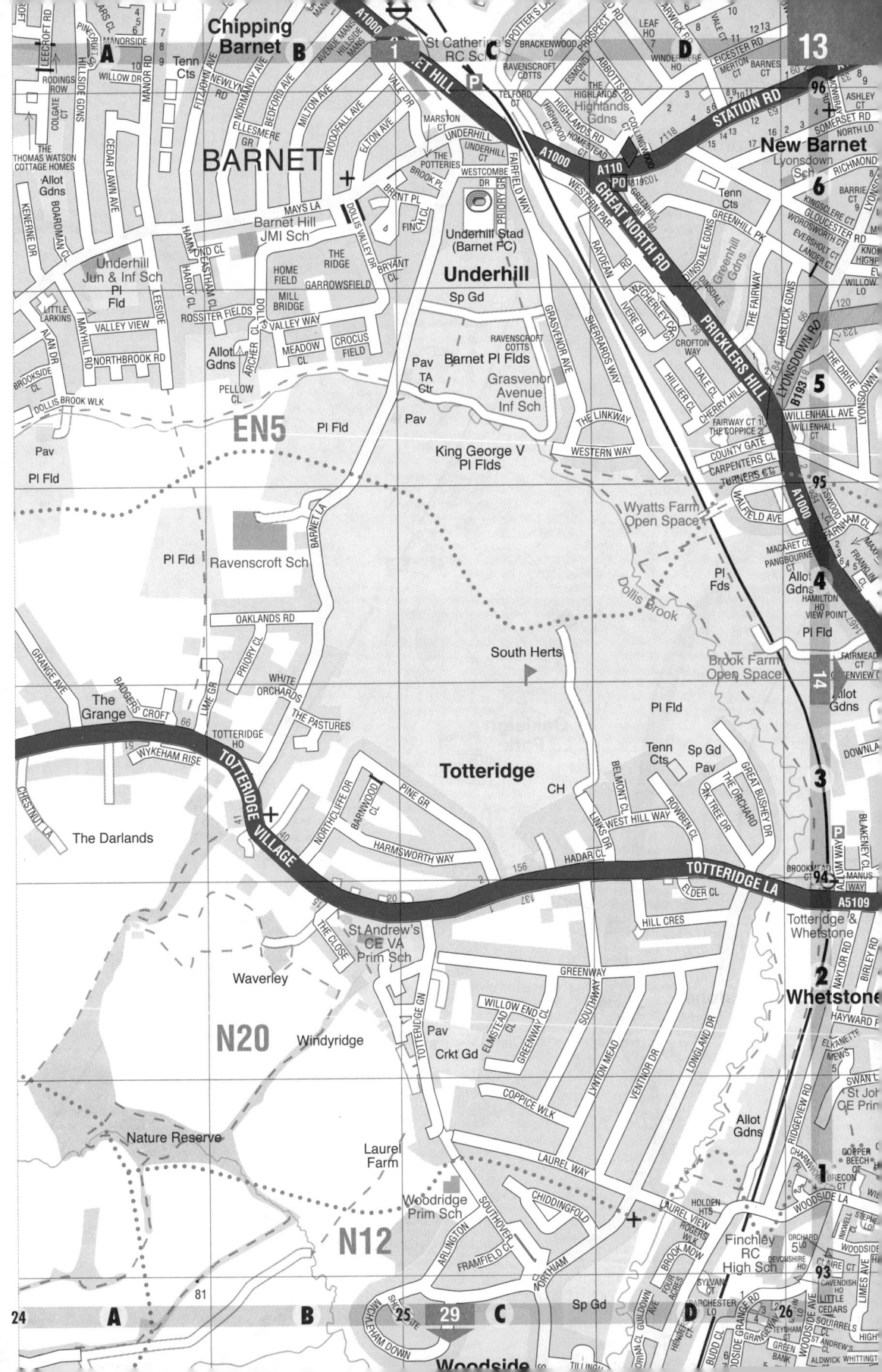

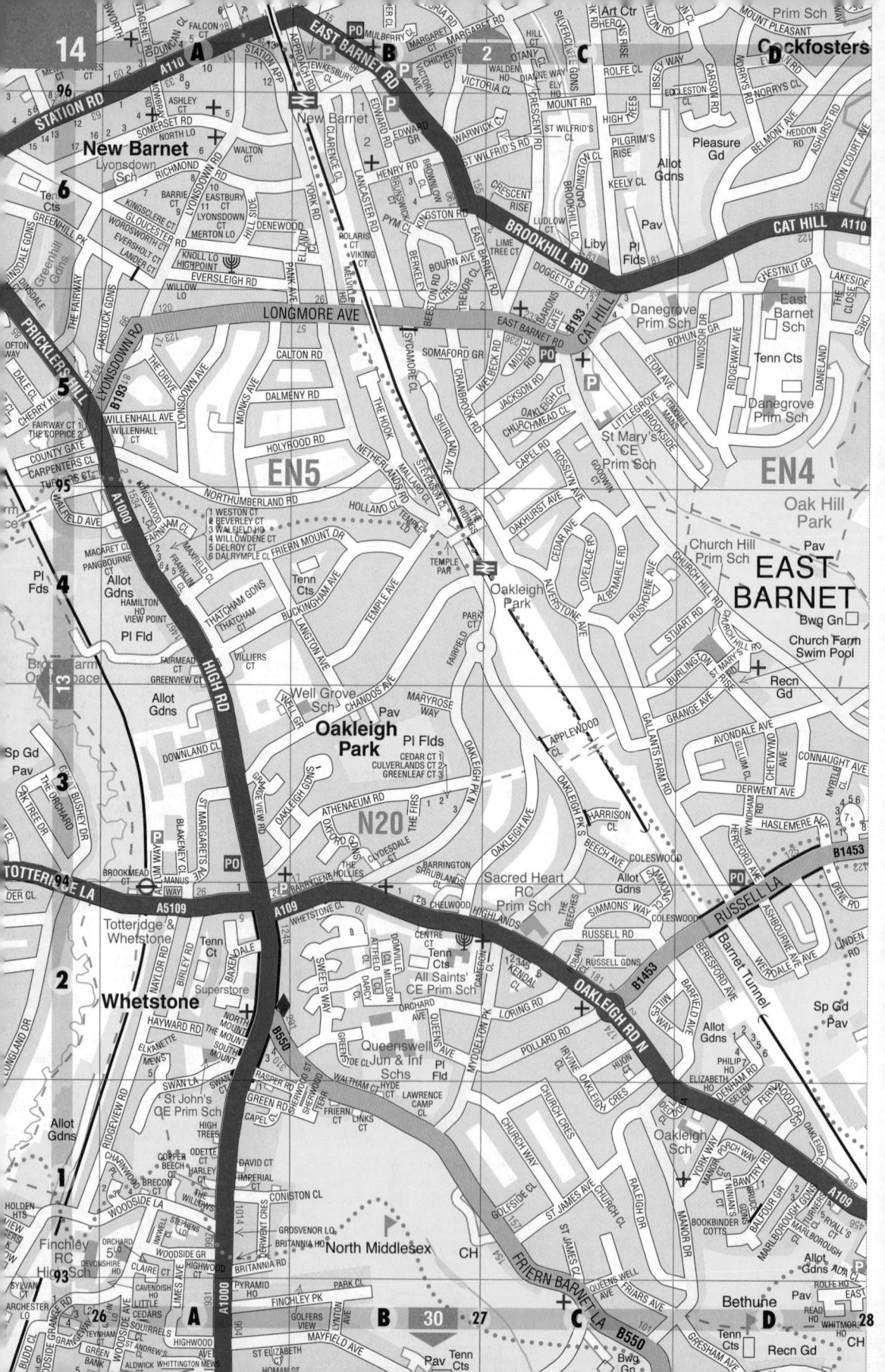

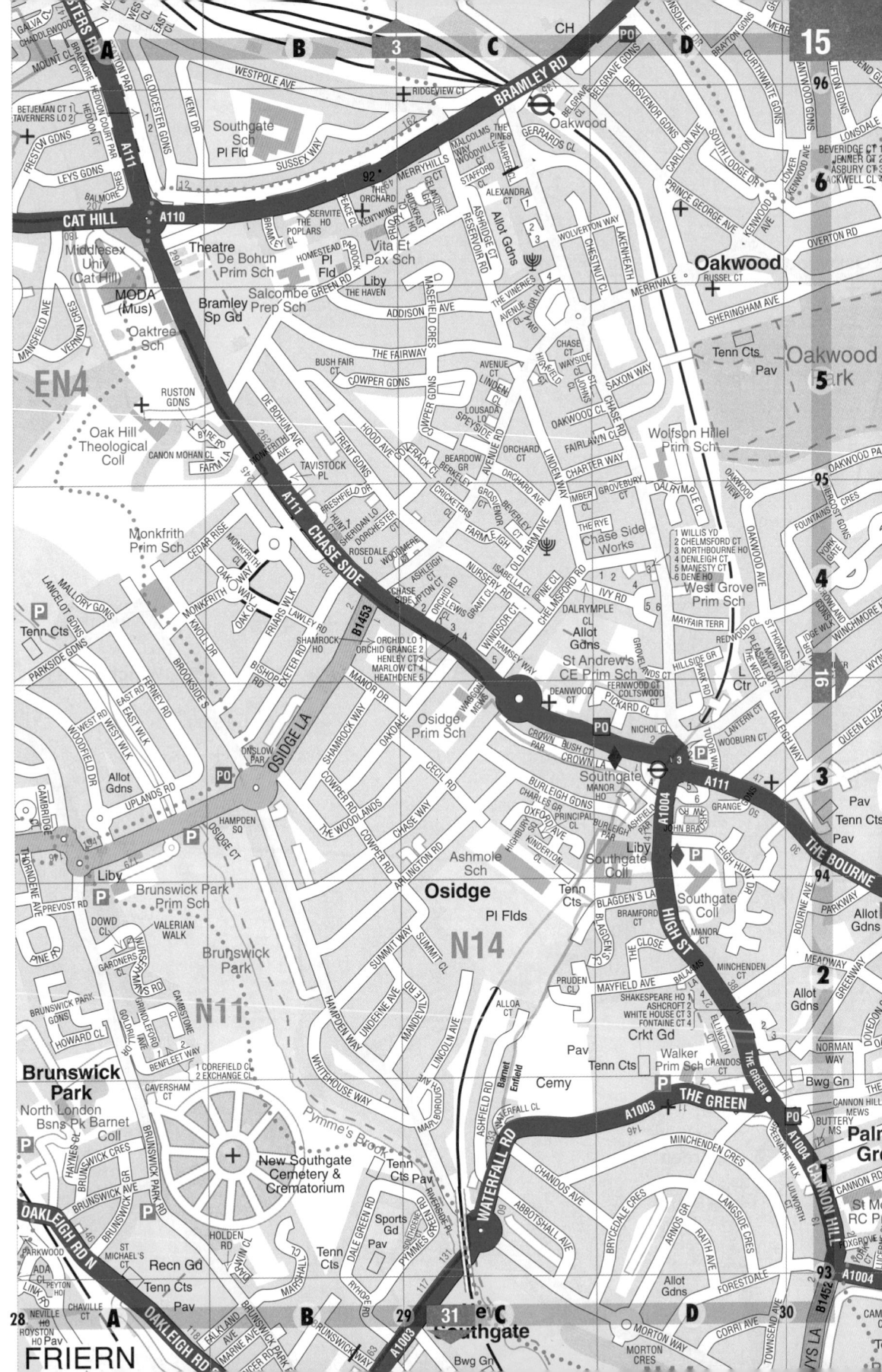

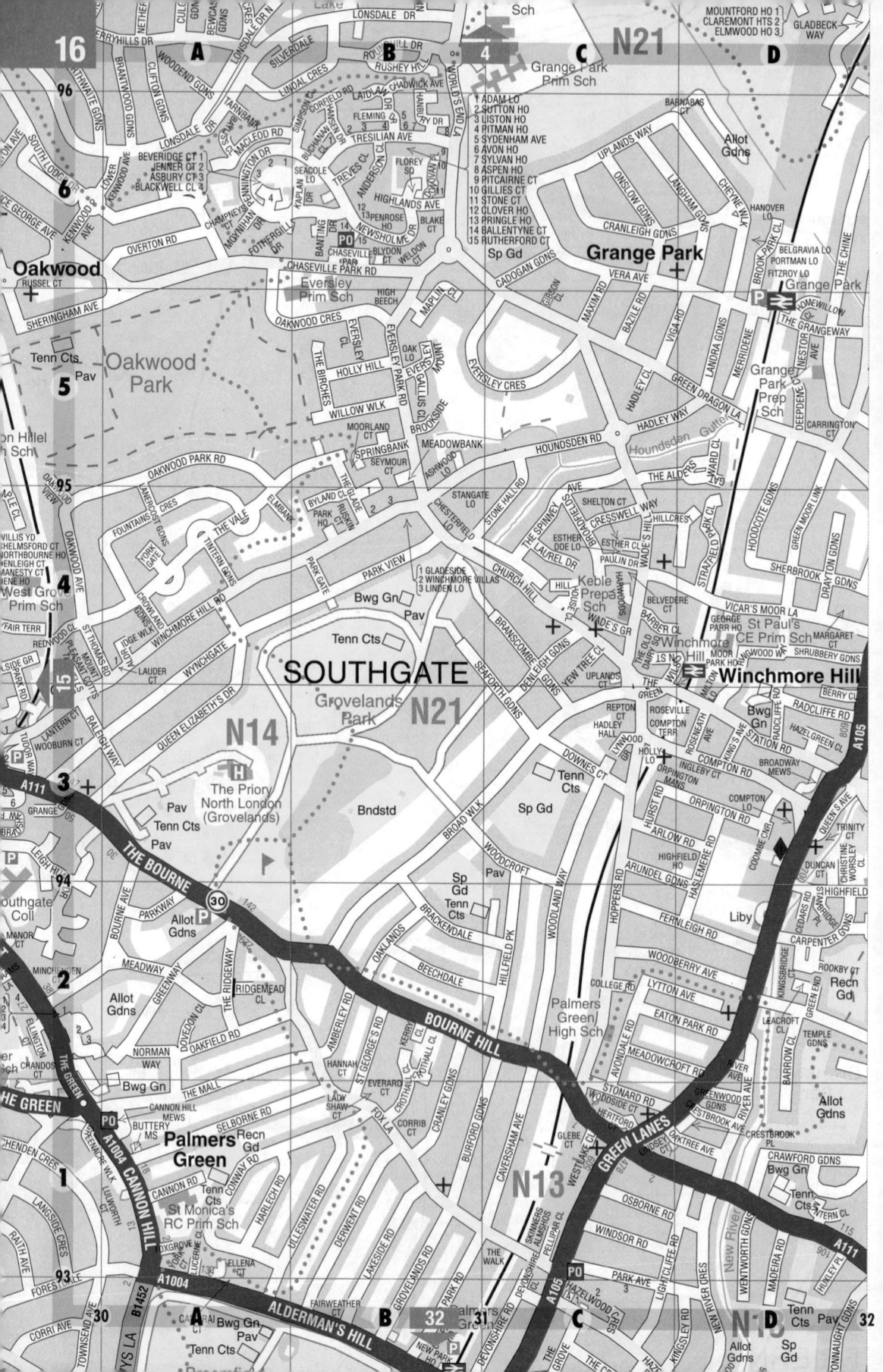

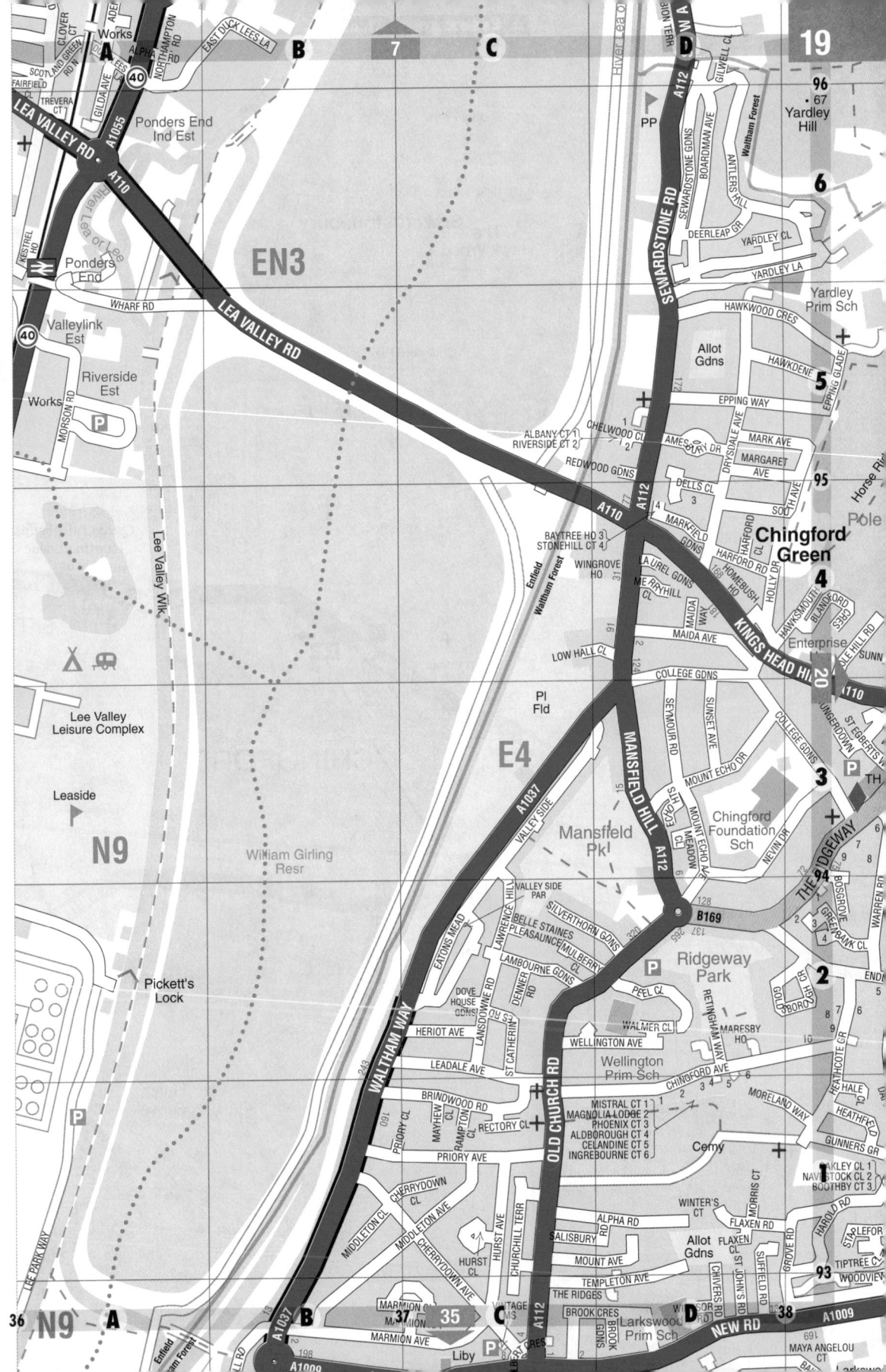

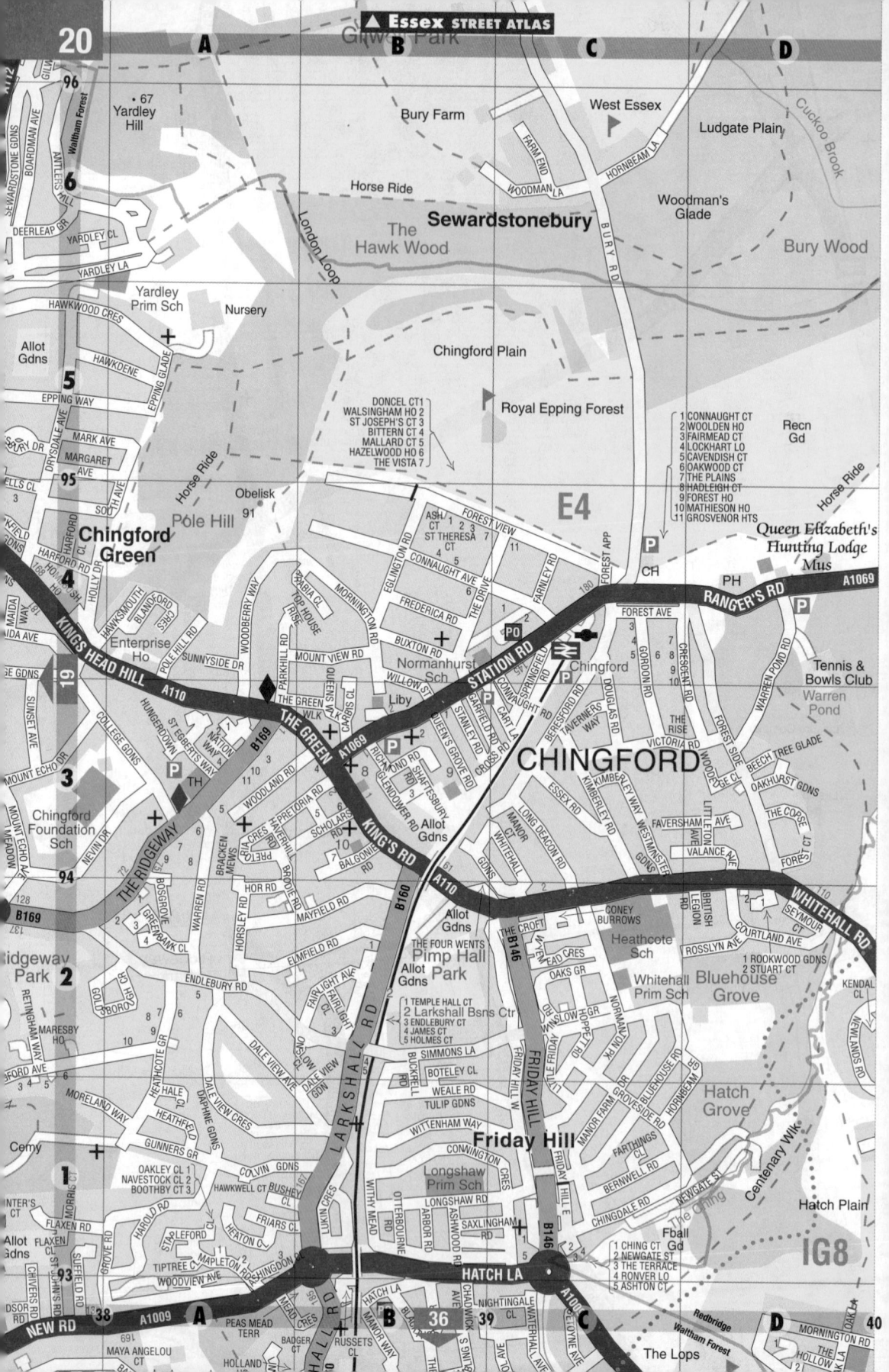

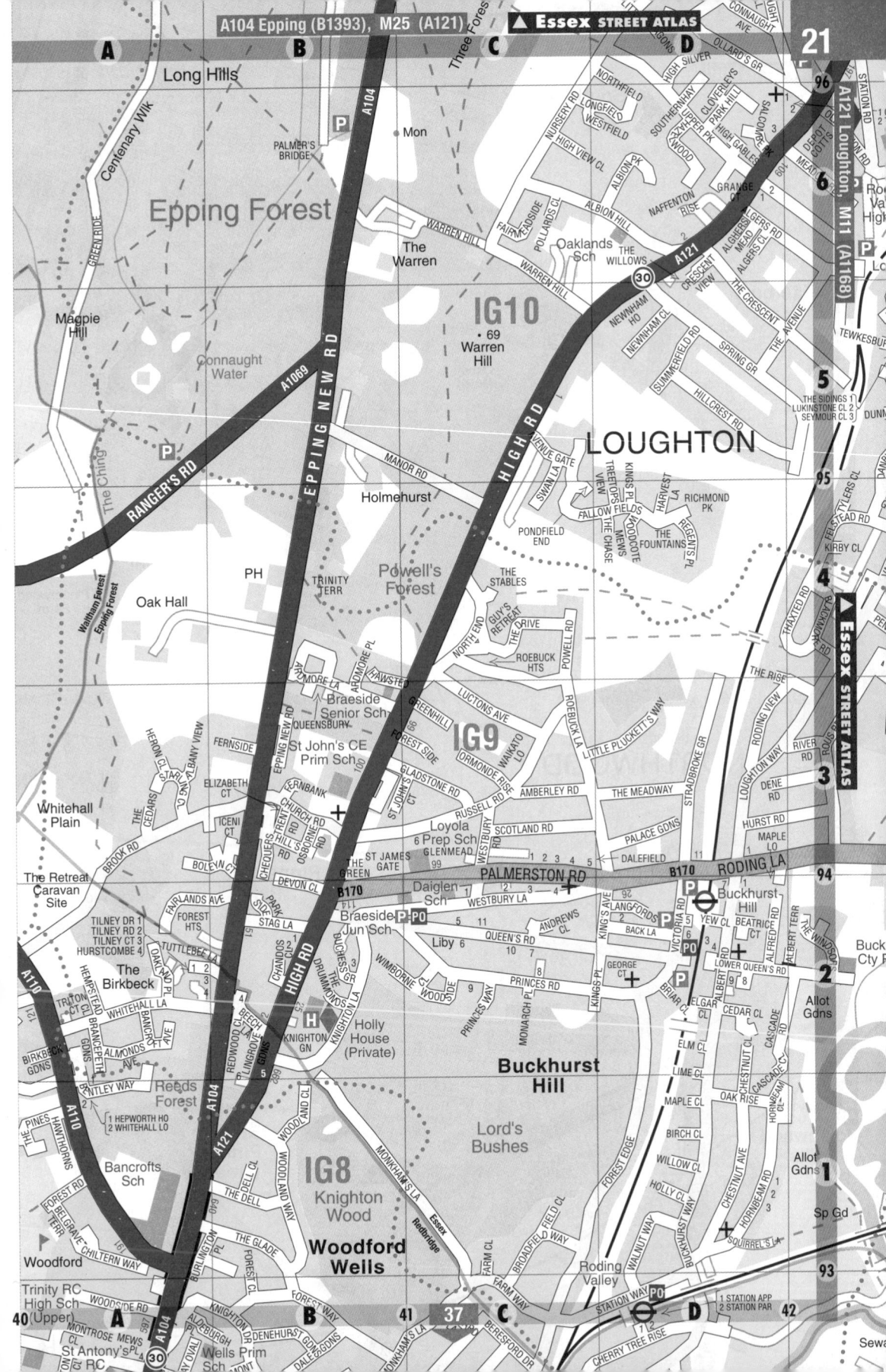

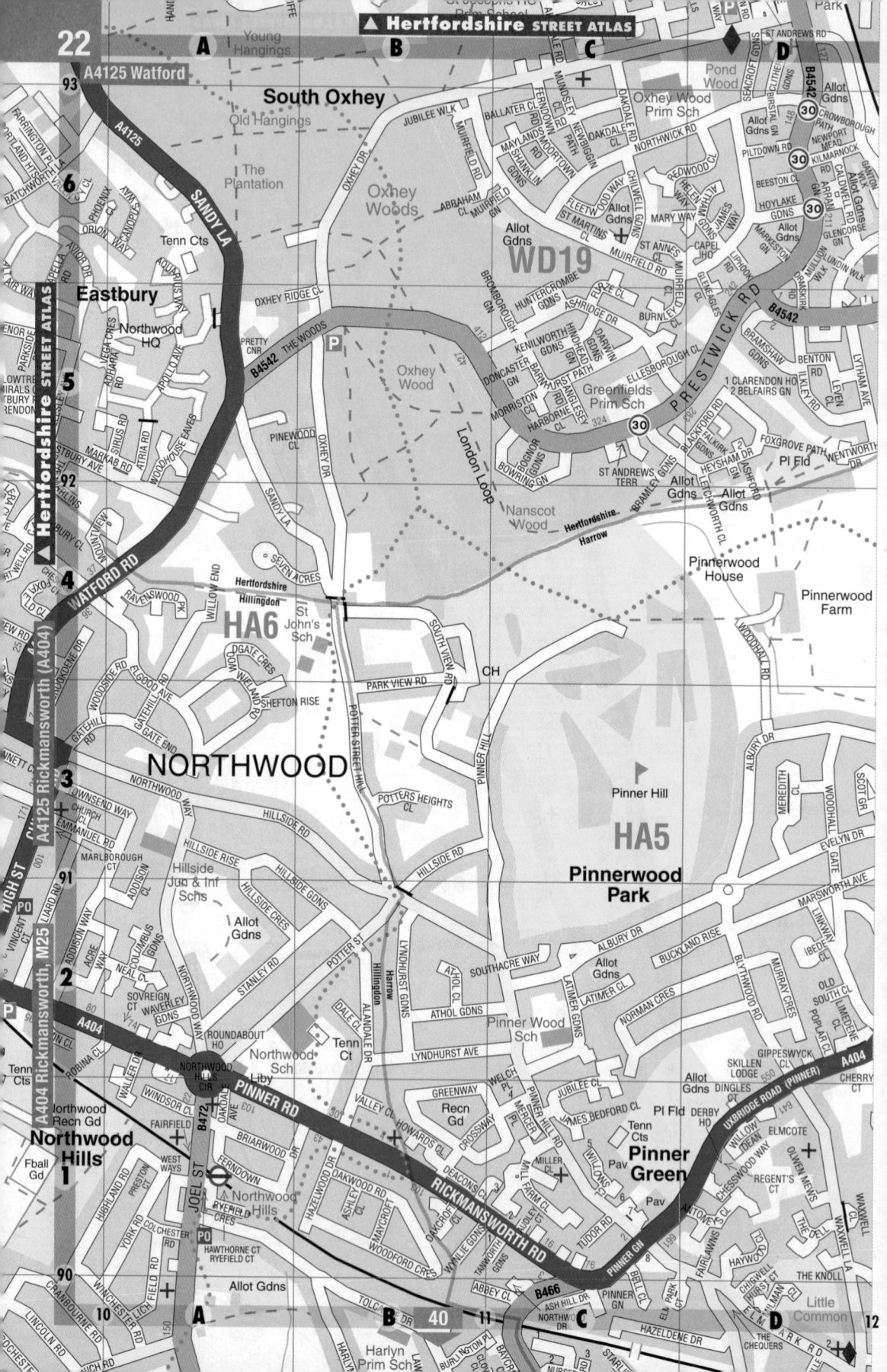

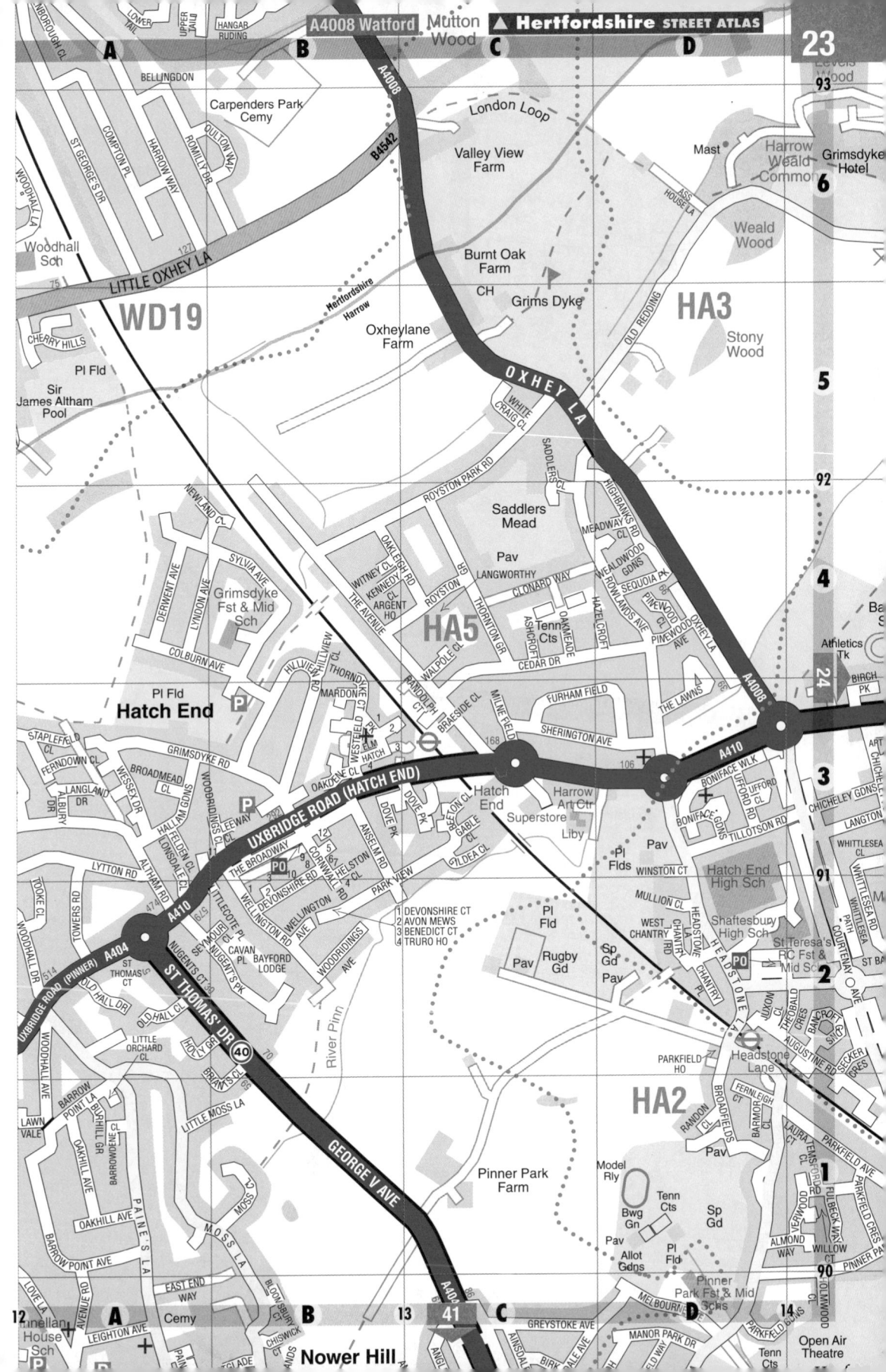

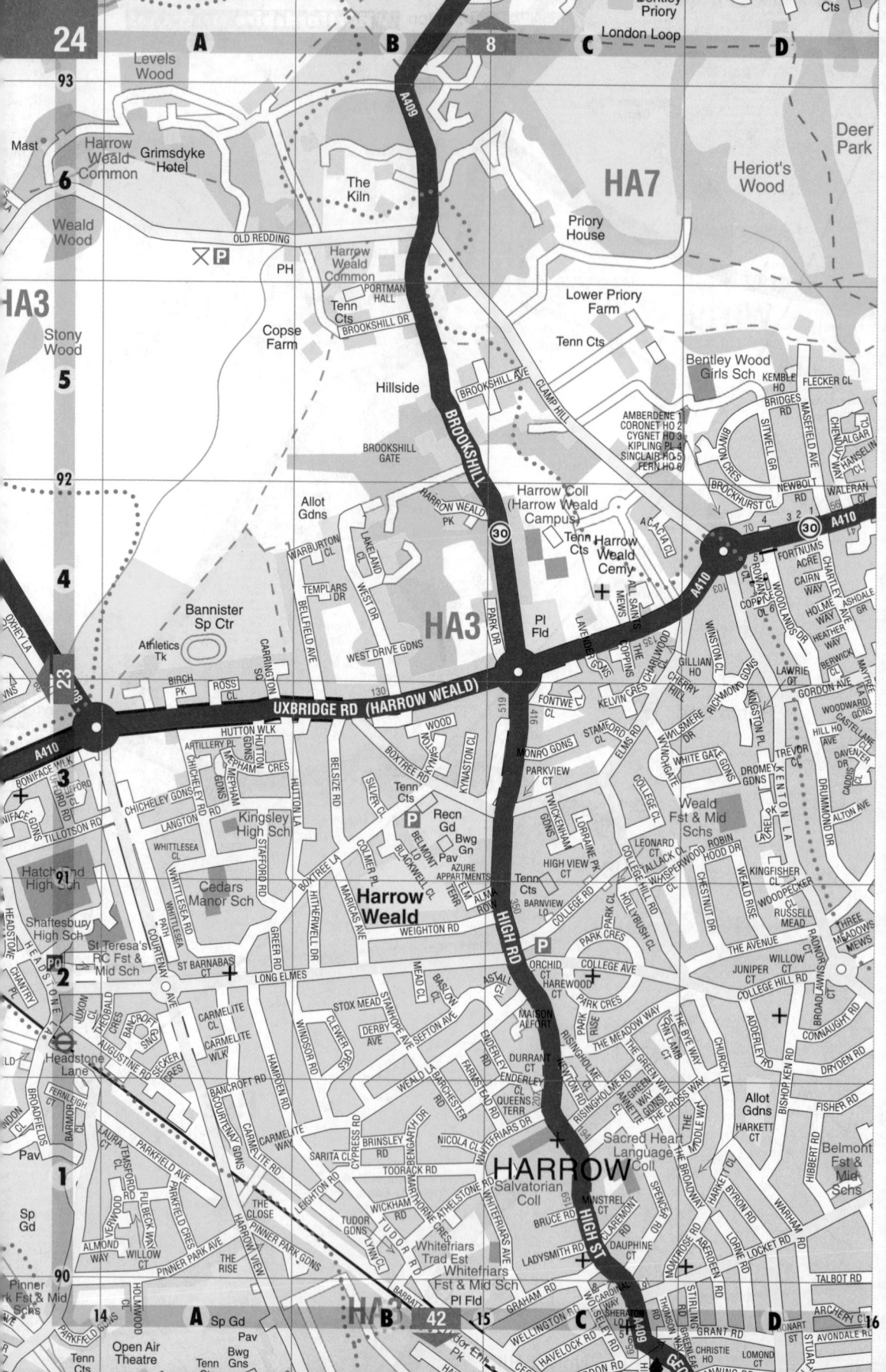

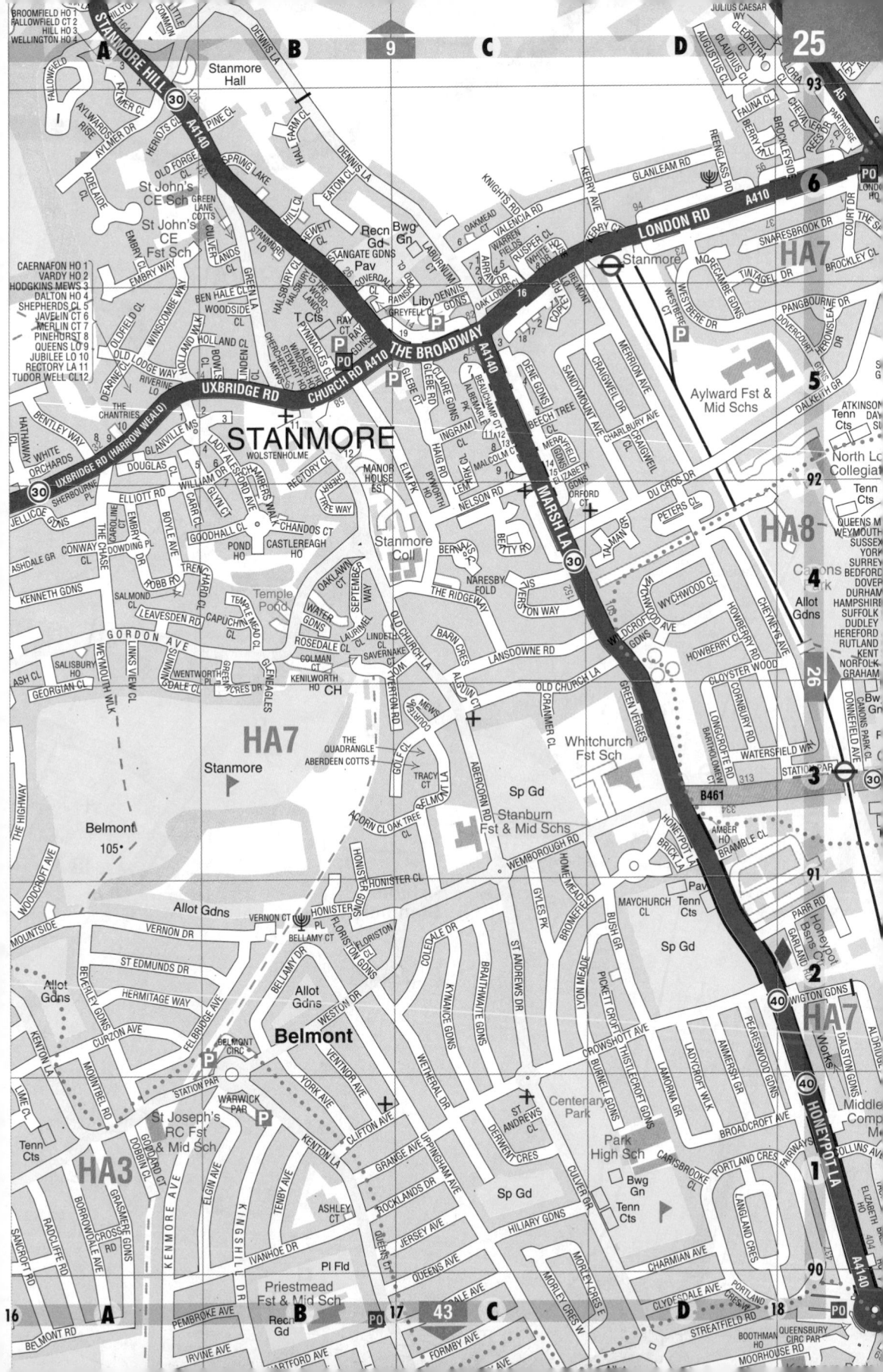

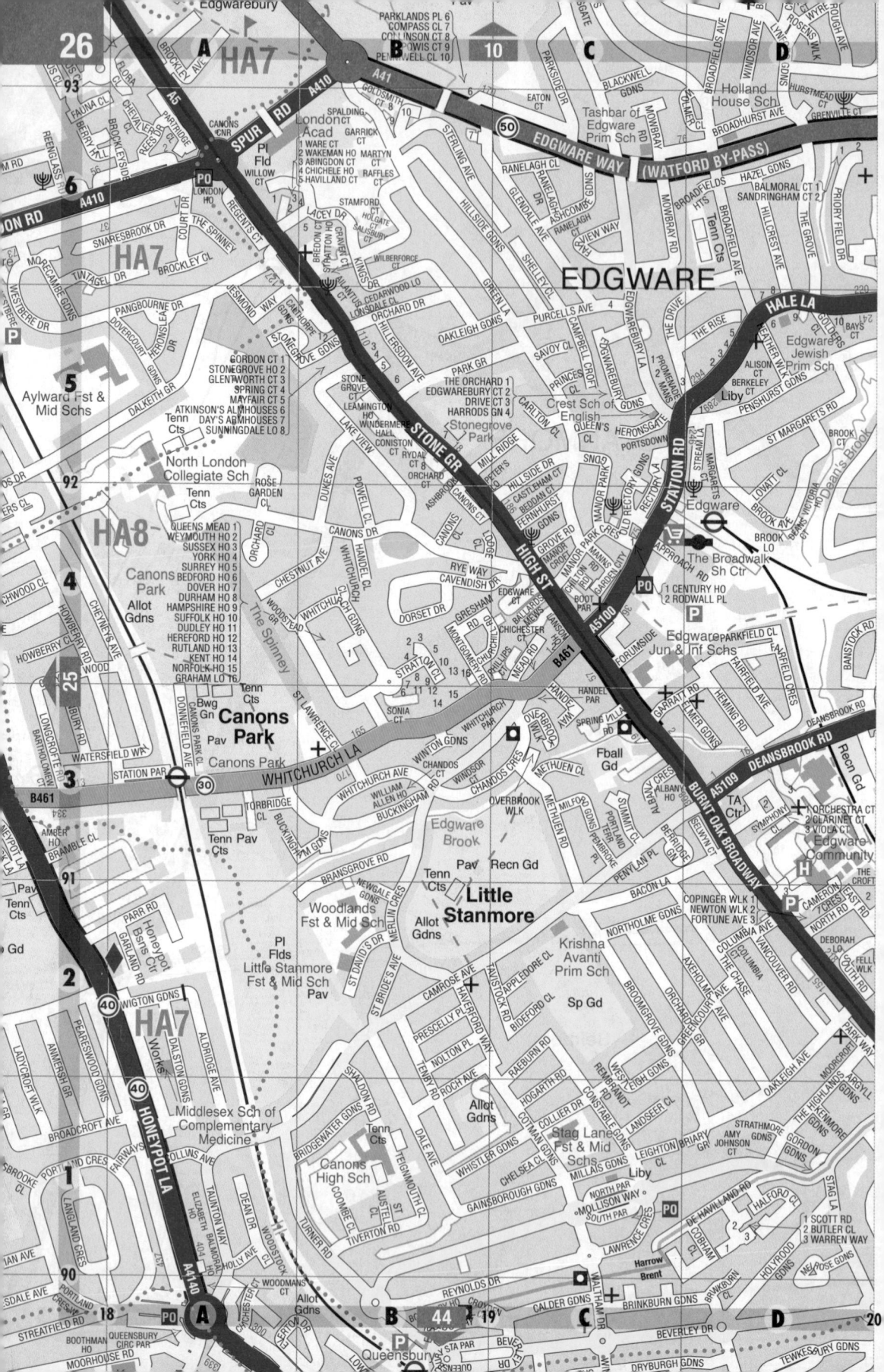

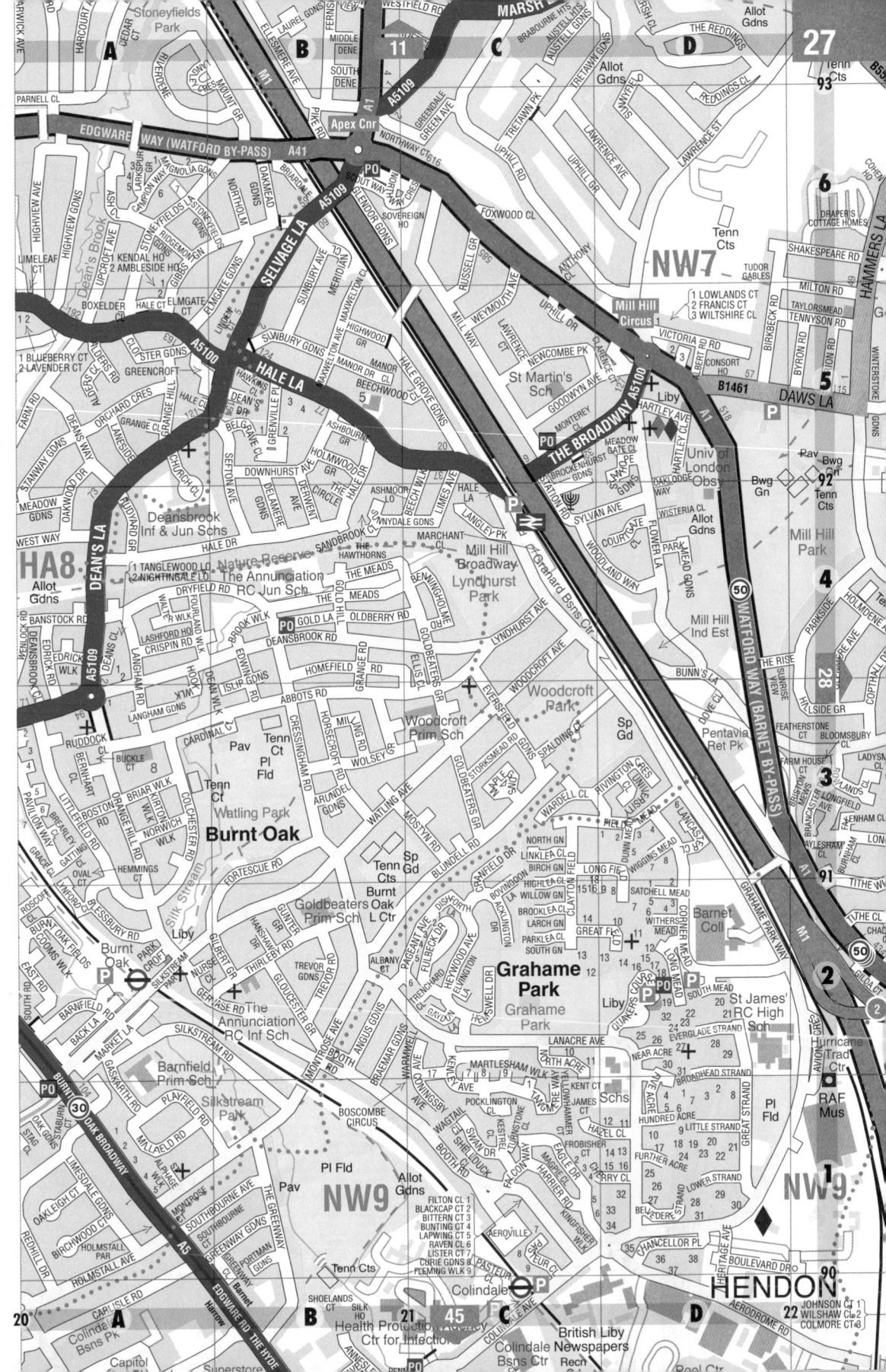

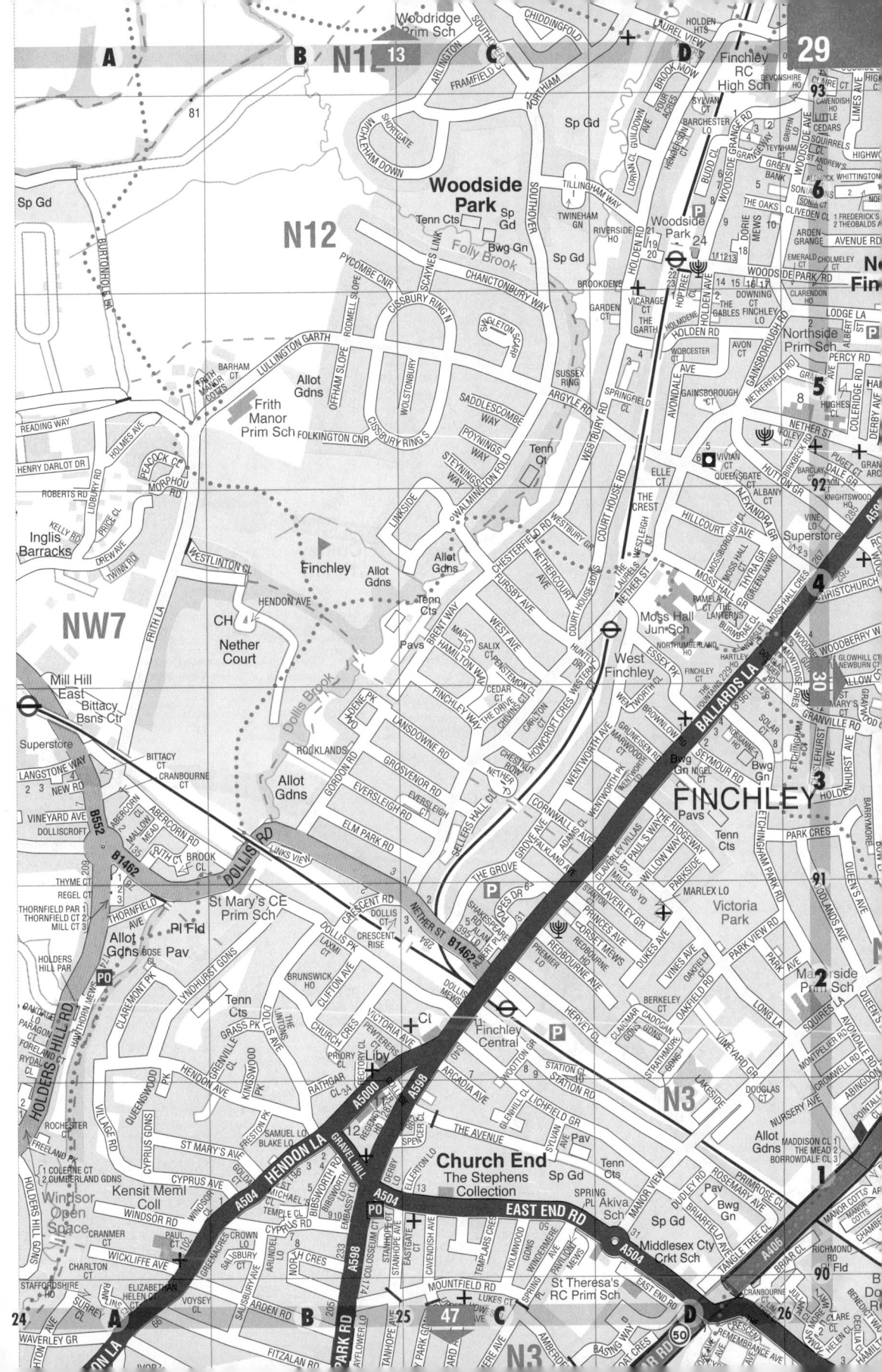

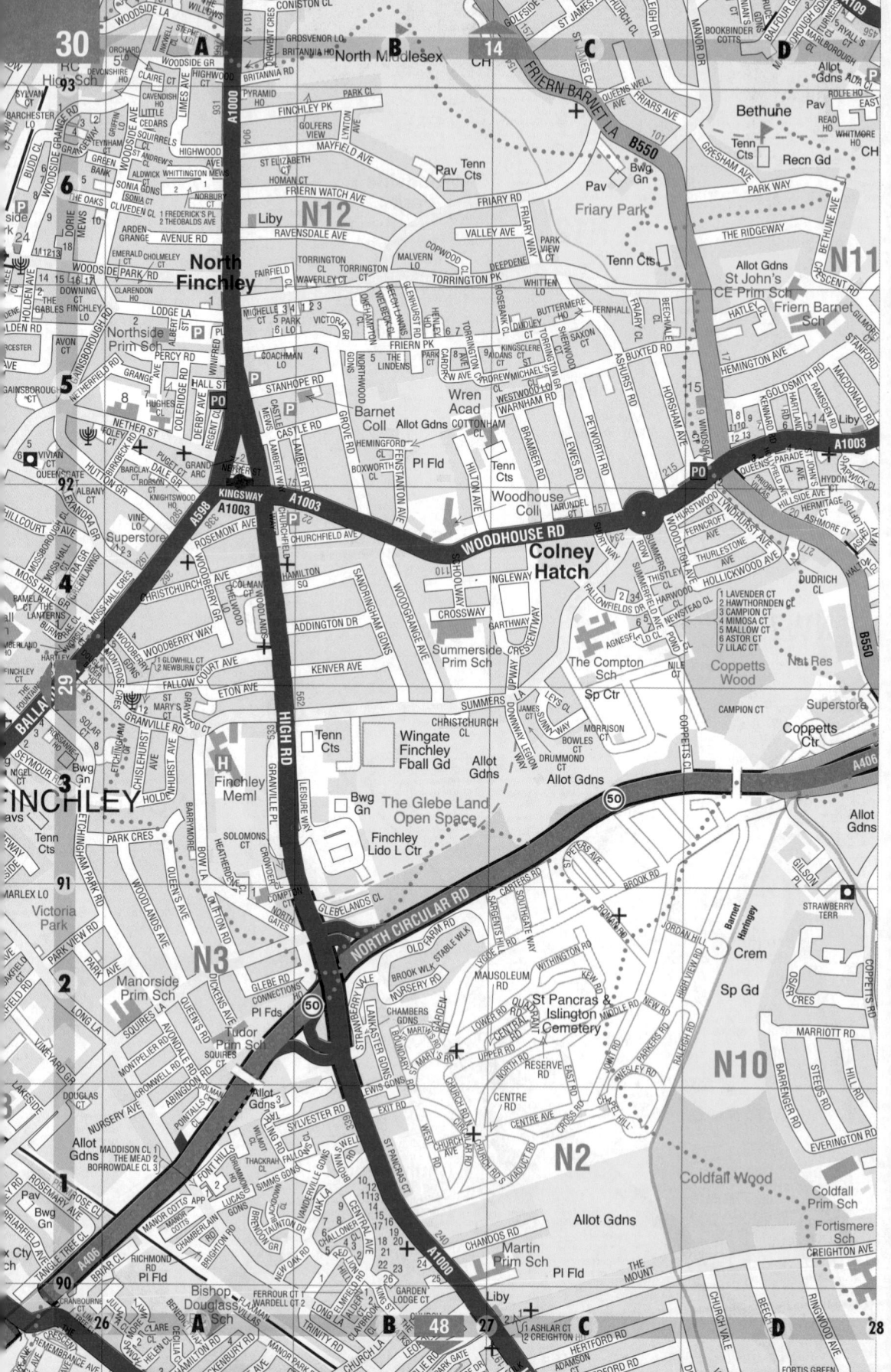

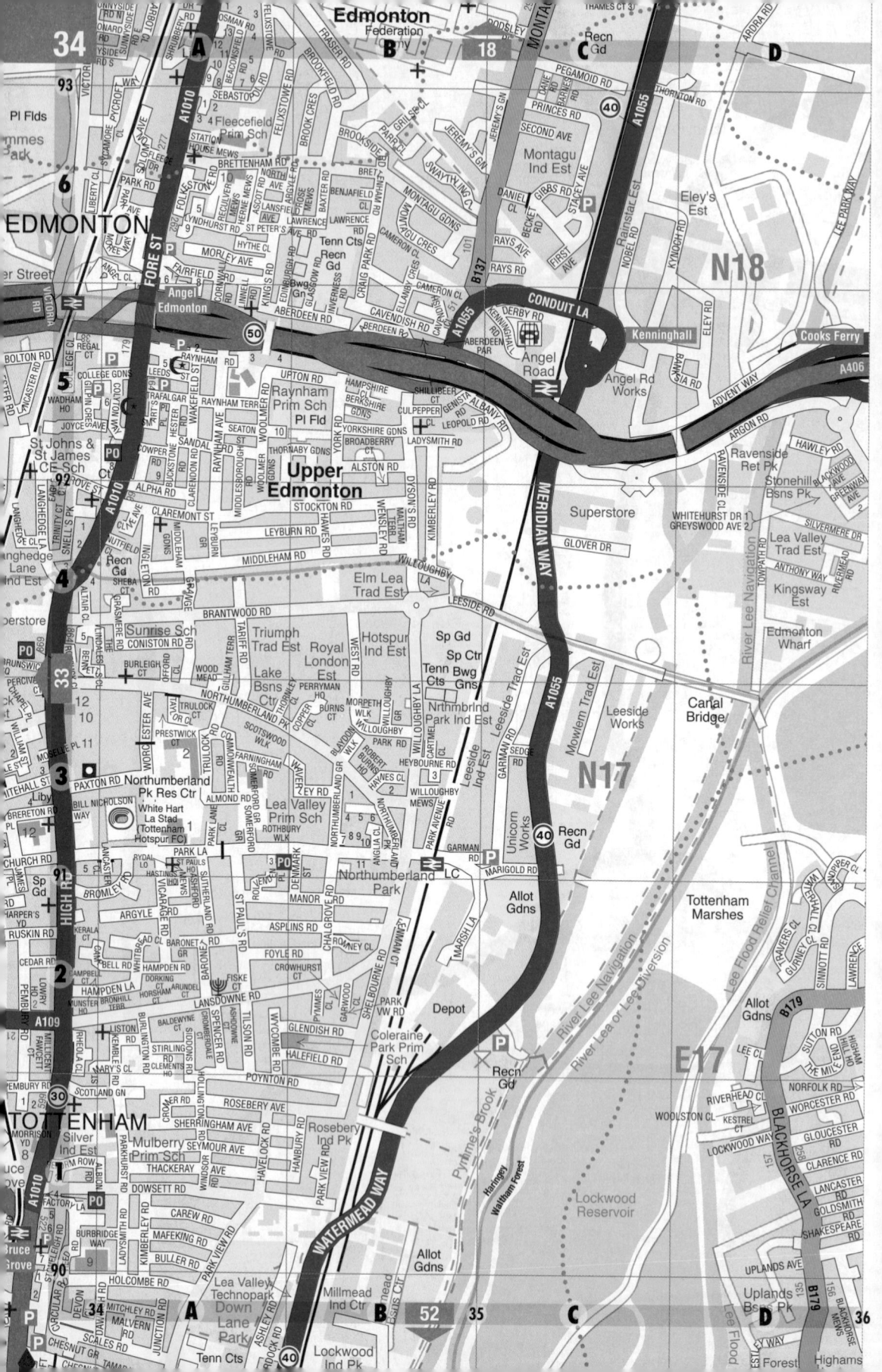

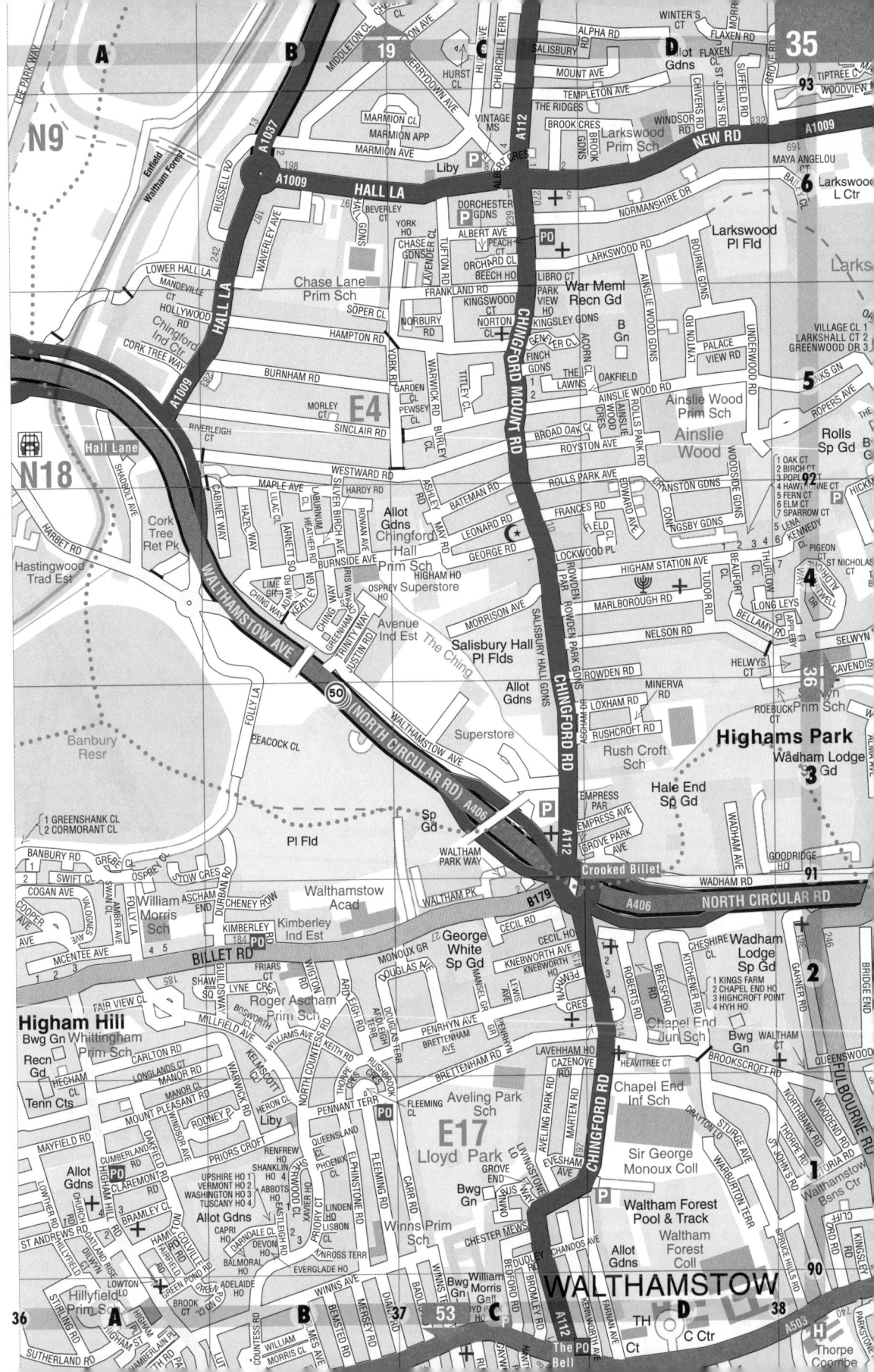

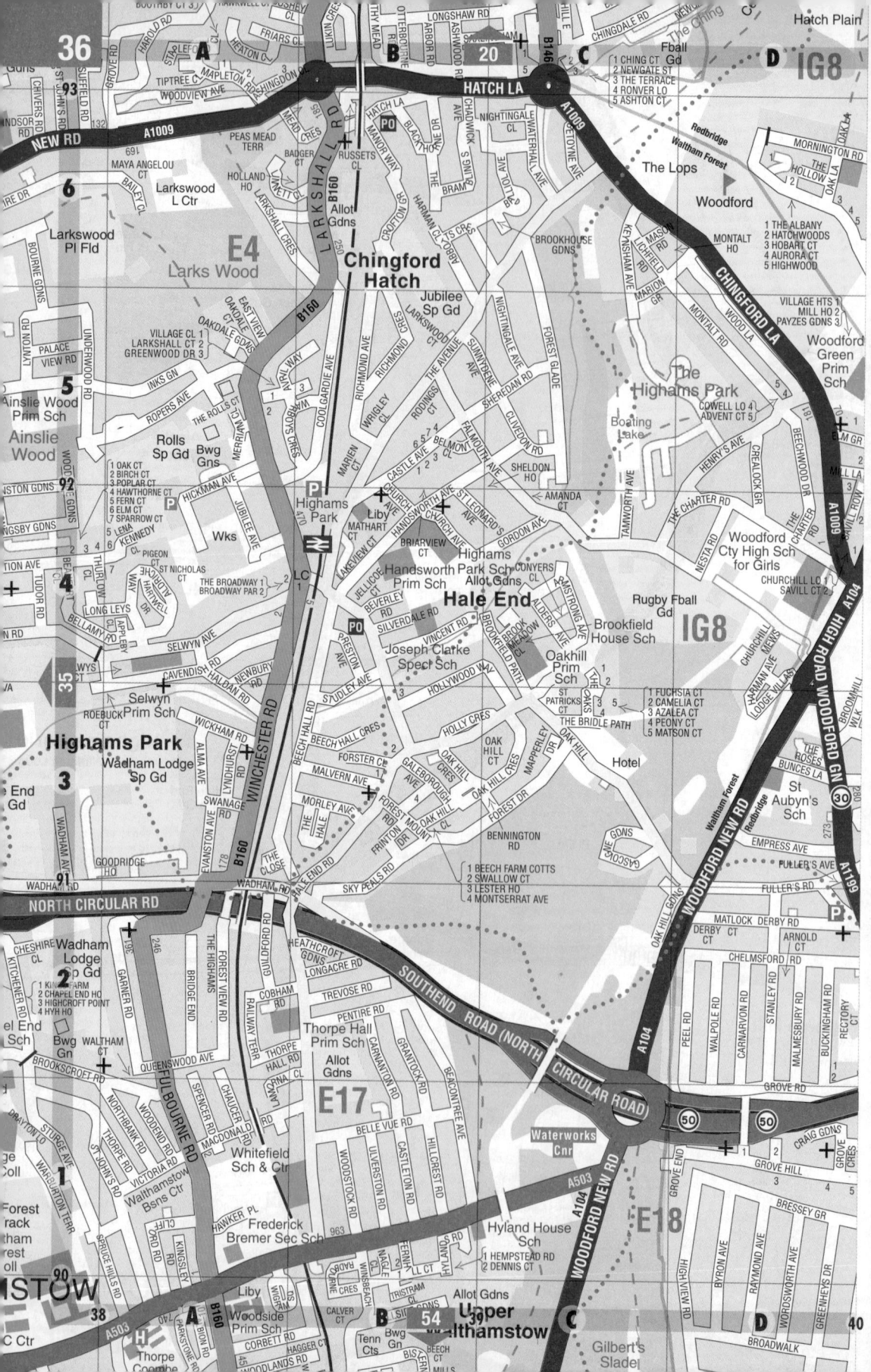

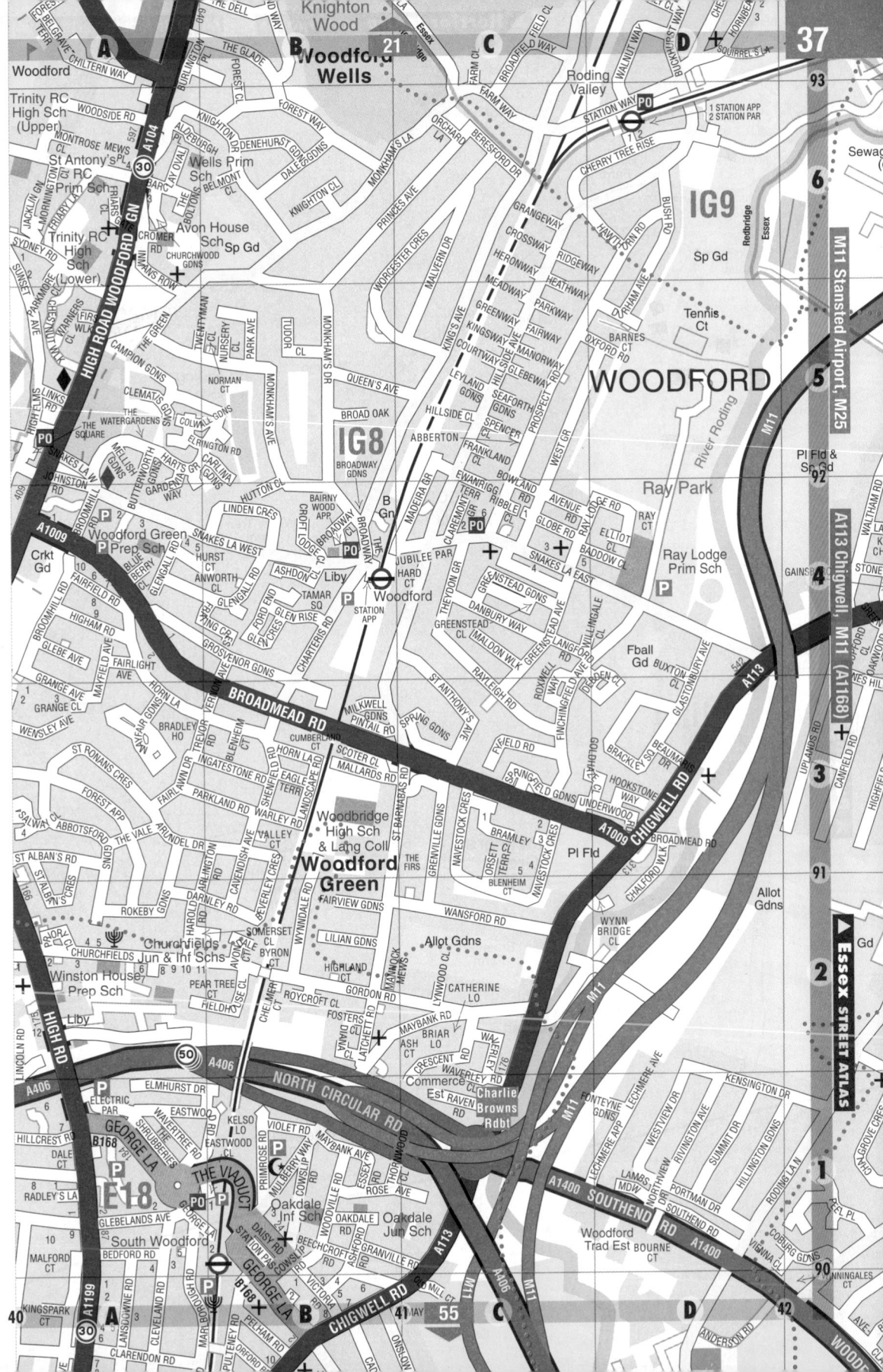

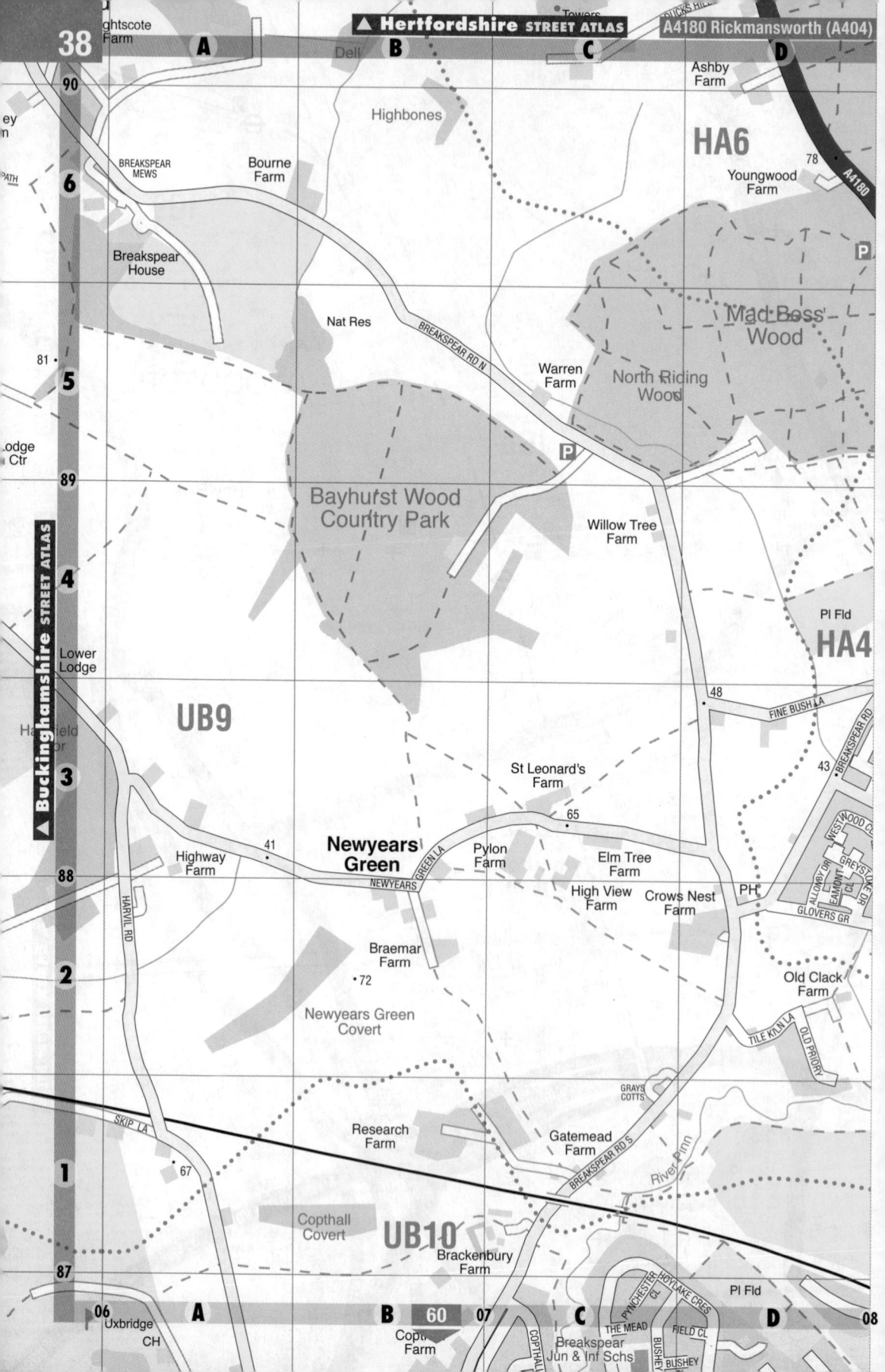

A

B

C

D

ghtscote
Farm

Dell

Towers

BUCKS HILL

Ashby
Farm

90

Highbones

HA6

Youngwood
Farm

78

A4180

BREAKSPEAR
MEWS

Bourne
Farm

6

Breakspear
House

PATH

P

81

Nat Res

BREAKSPEAR RD N

Warren
Farm

North Riding
Wood

Mad Bess
Wood

P

5

89

Bayhurst Wood
Country Park

P

Willow Tree
Farm

Pl Fld

HA4

4

Lower
Lodge

odge
Ctr

48

FINE BUSH LA

BREAKSPEAR RD

△ **Buckinghamshire** STREET ATLAS

UB9

Harvilfield
or

3

St Leonard's
Farm

43

WESTWOOD CT

GREYSTONE DR

65

Highway
Farm

41

**Newyears
Green**

GREEN LA

Pylon
Farm

Elm Tree
Farm

ALLONBY DR

EAMONT CL

88

NEWYEARS

High View
Farm

Crows Nest
Farm

PH

GLOVERS GR

HARVIL RD

2

Braemar
Farm

72

Old Clack
Farm

Newyears Green
Covert

TILE KILN LA

OLD PRIORY

GRAYS
COTTS

SKIP LA

Research
Farm

Gatemead
Farm

BREAKSPEAR RD S

River Pinn

1

67

Copthall
Covert

UB10

Brackenbury
Farm

Pl Fld

87

06

A

B

60

07

C

D

08

Uxbridge
CH

Copt
Farm

PYNCHESTER CL

THE MEAD

Breakspear
Jun & Inf Schs

HOYLAKE CRES

FIELD CL

BUSHEY

BUSHEY

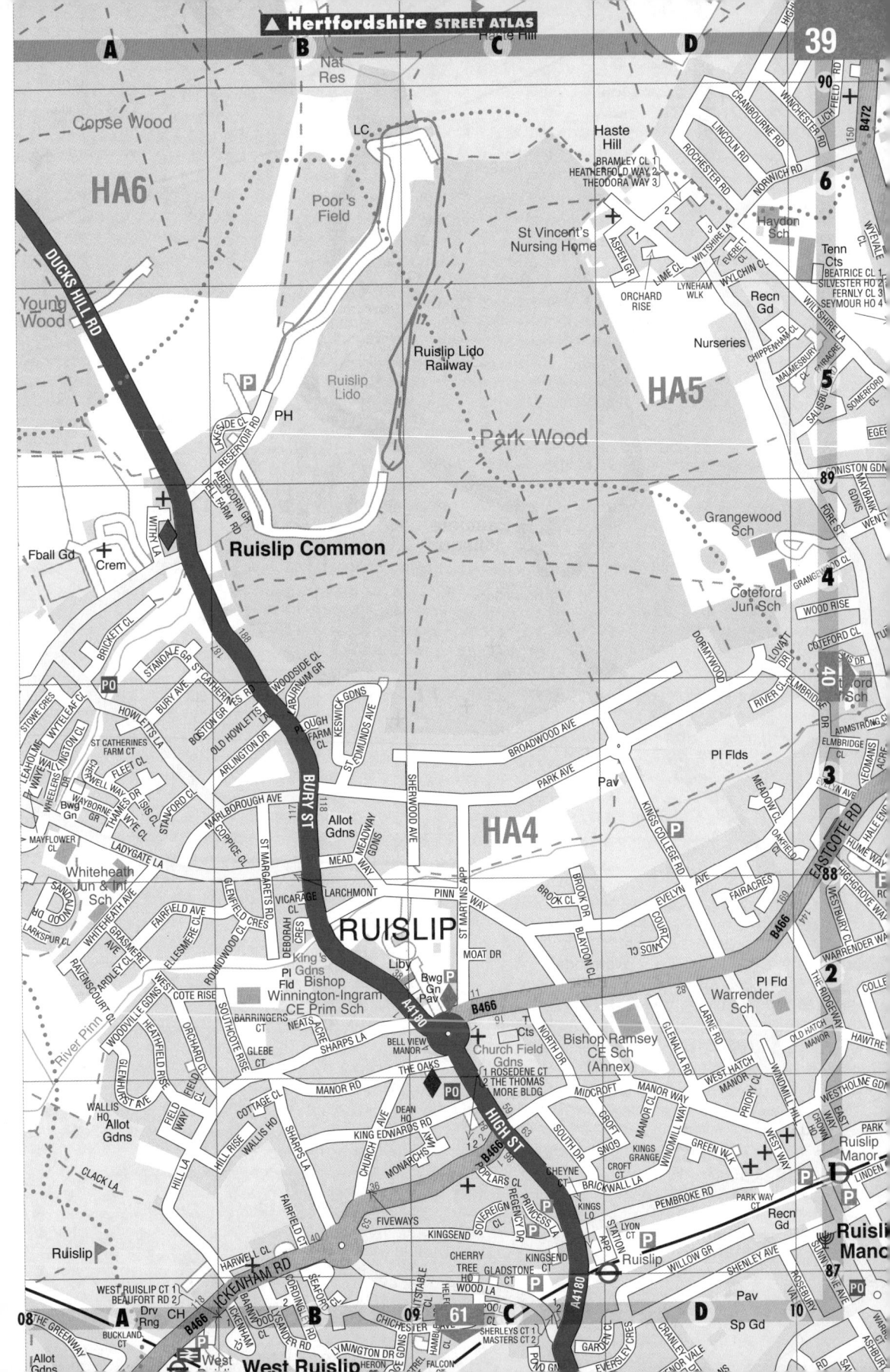

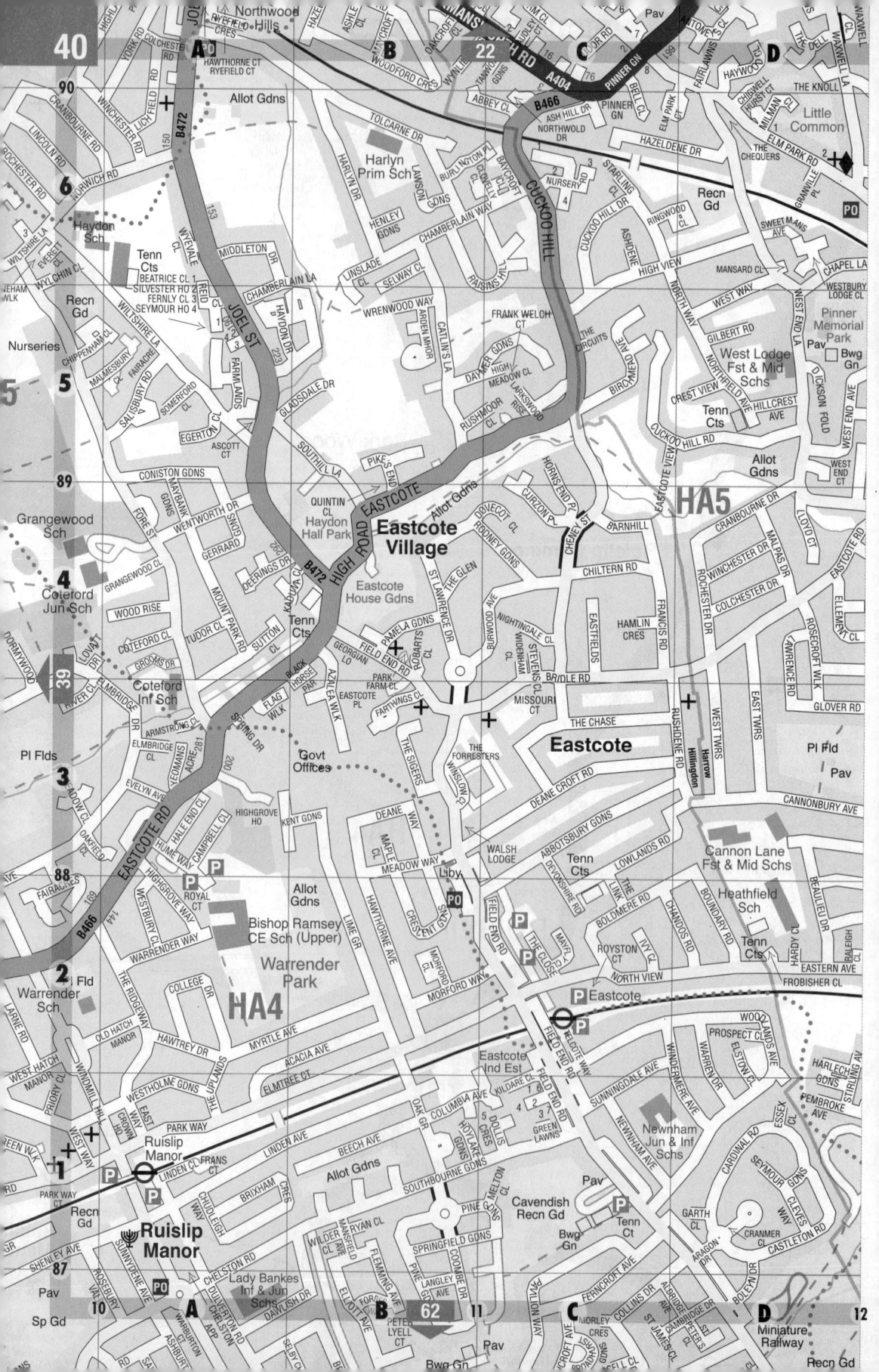

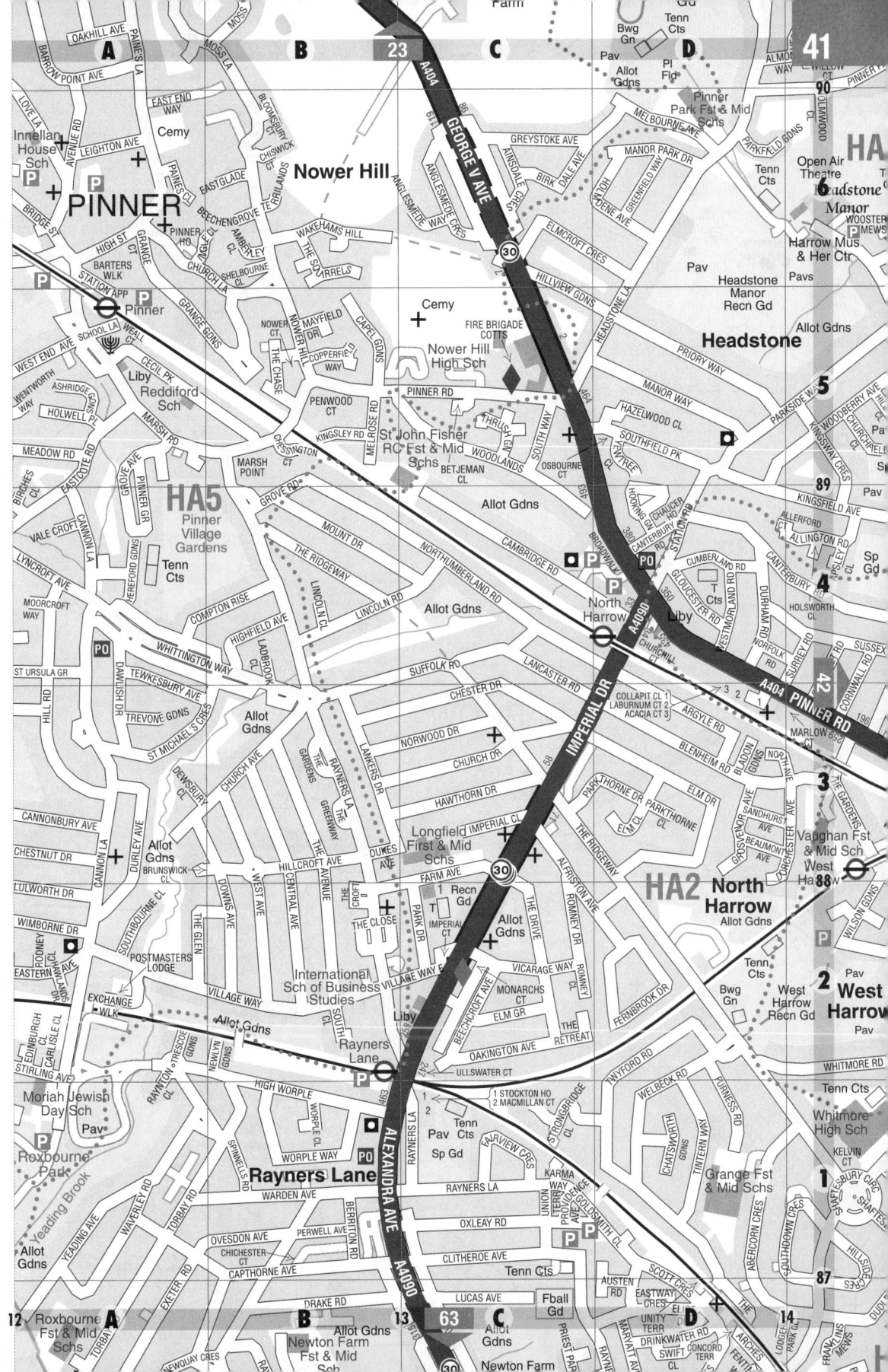

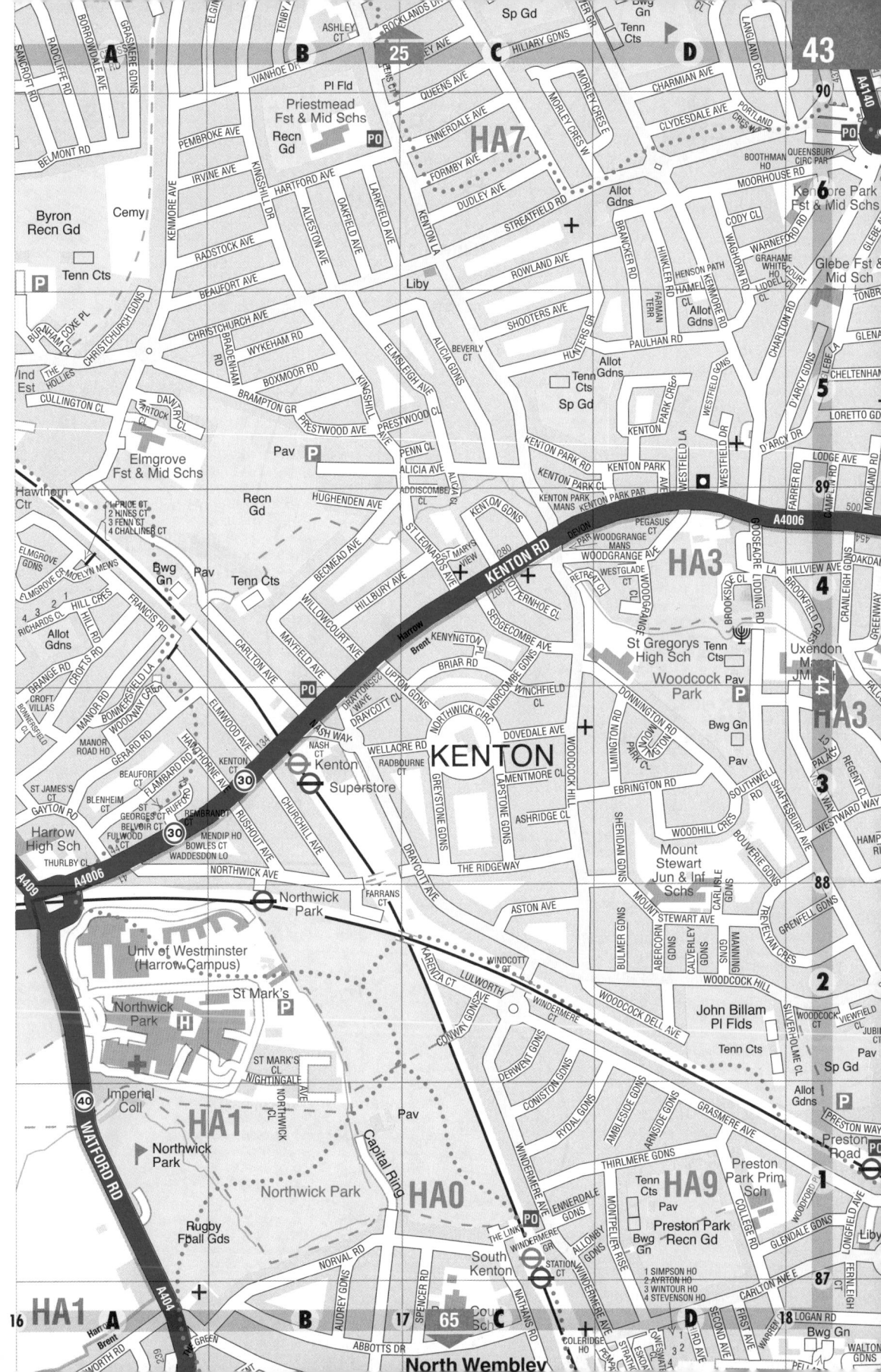

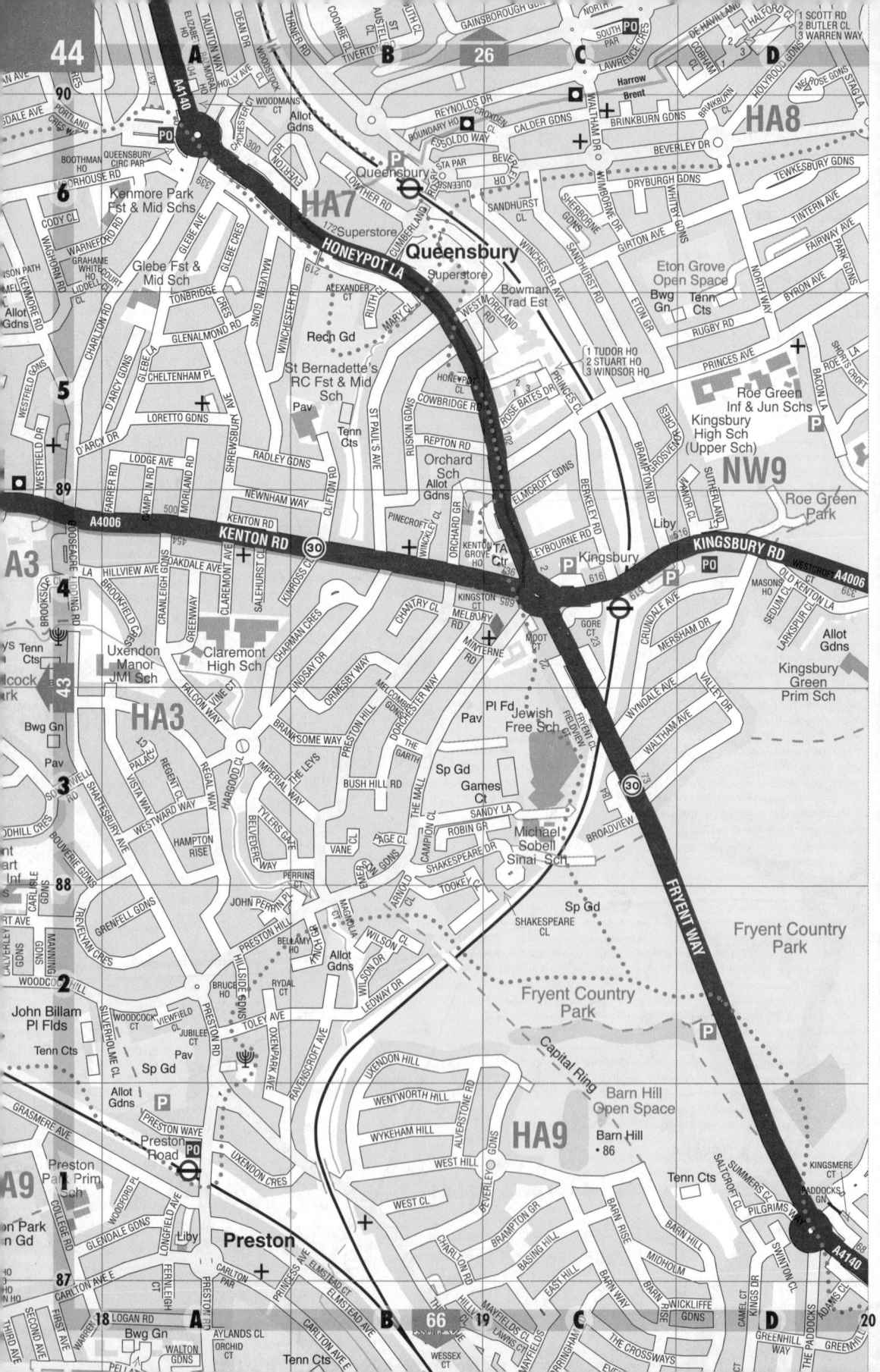

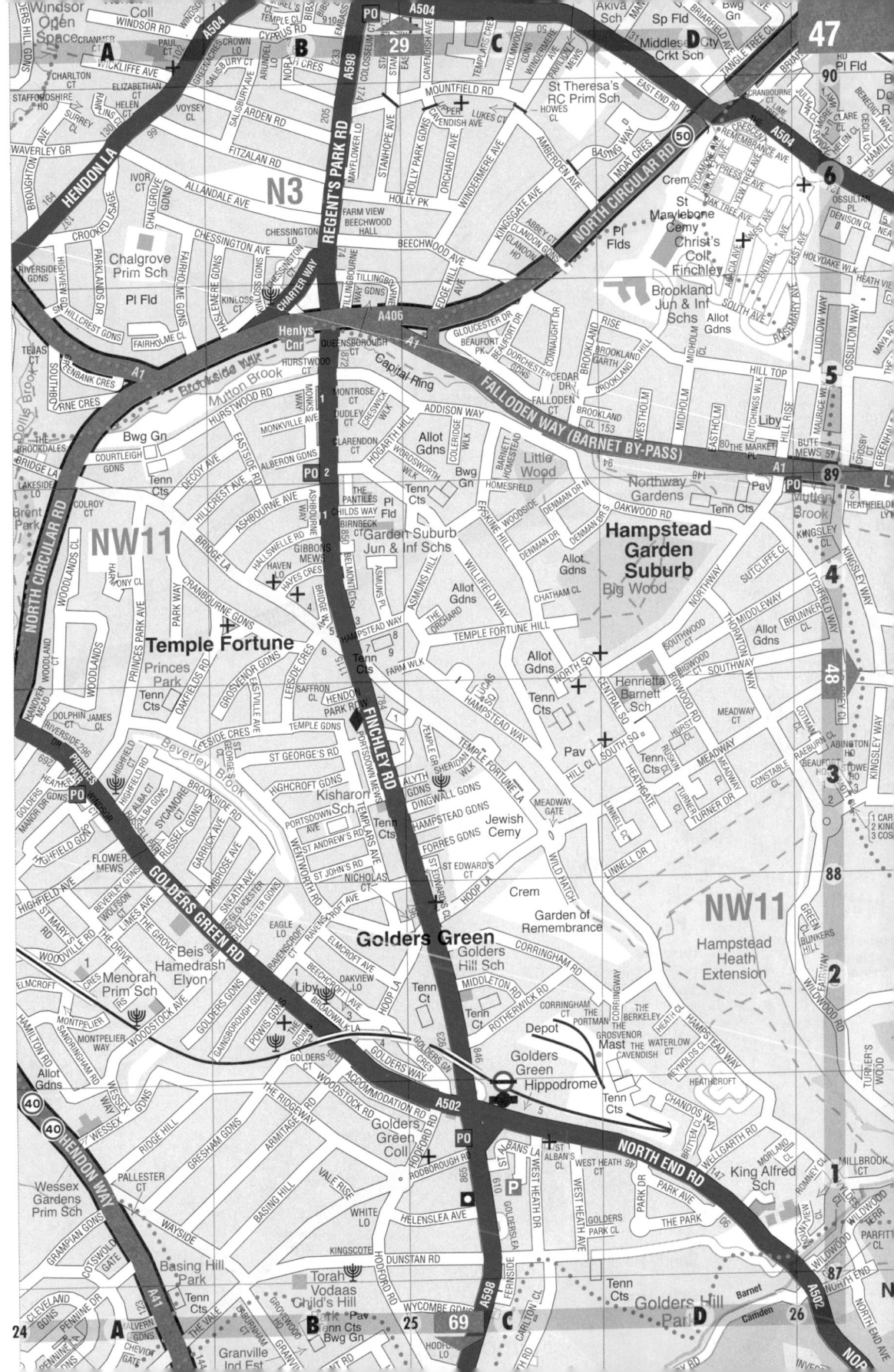

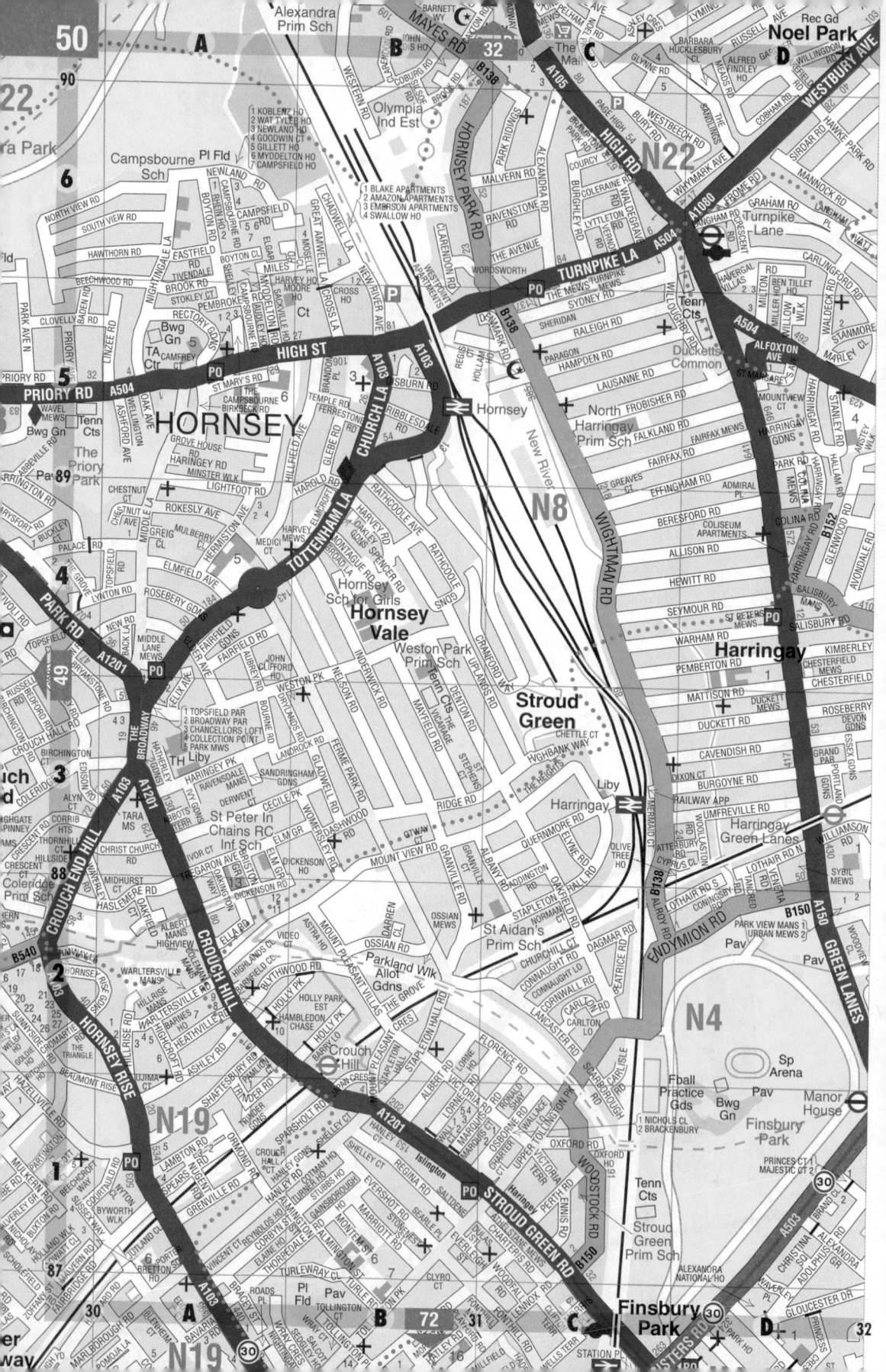

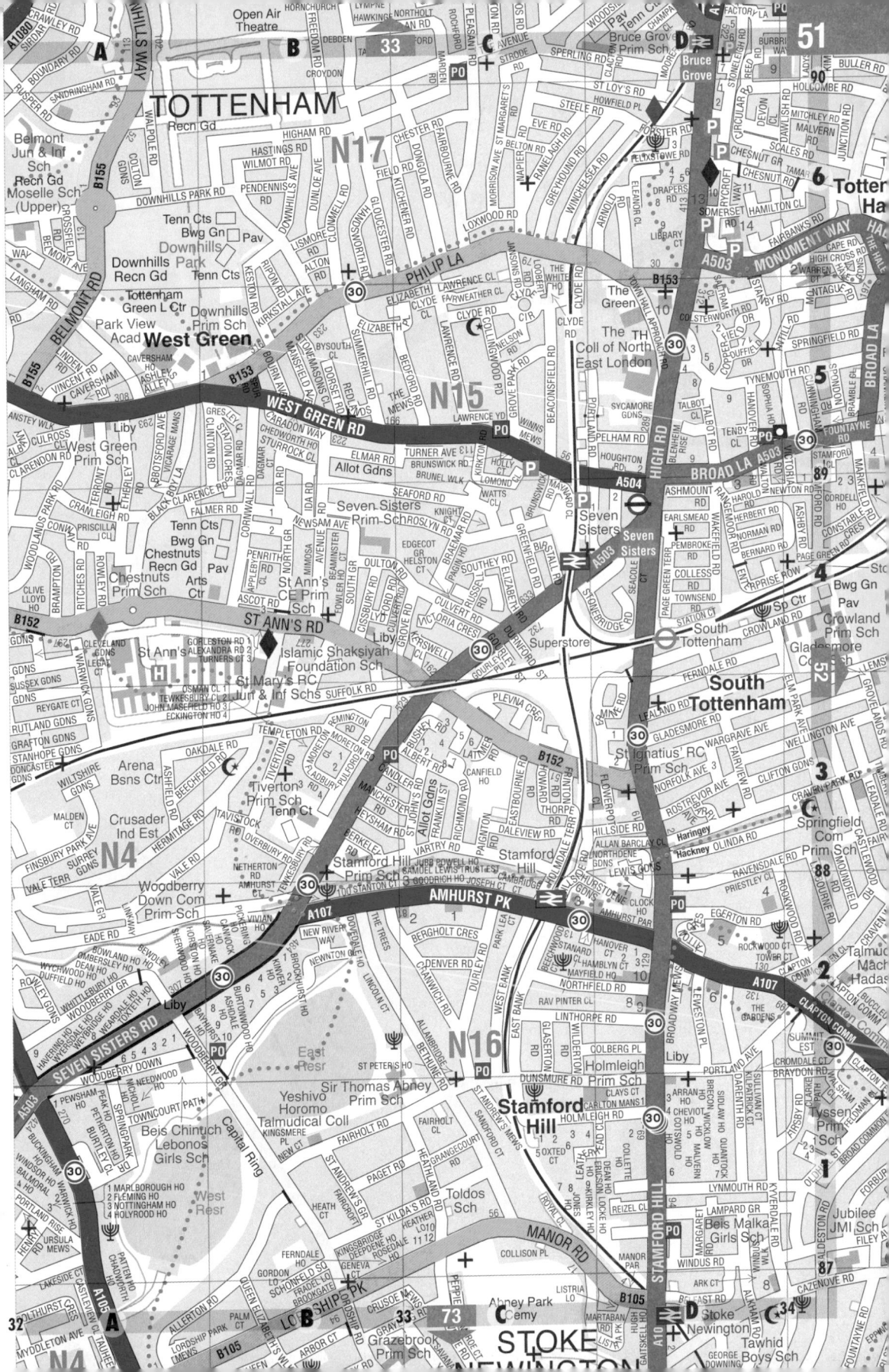

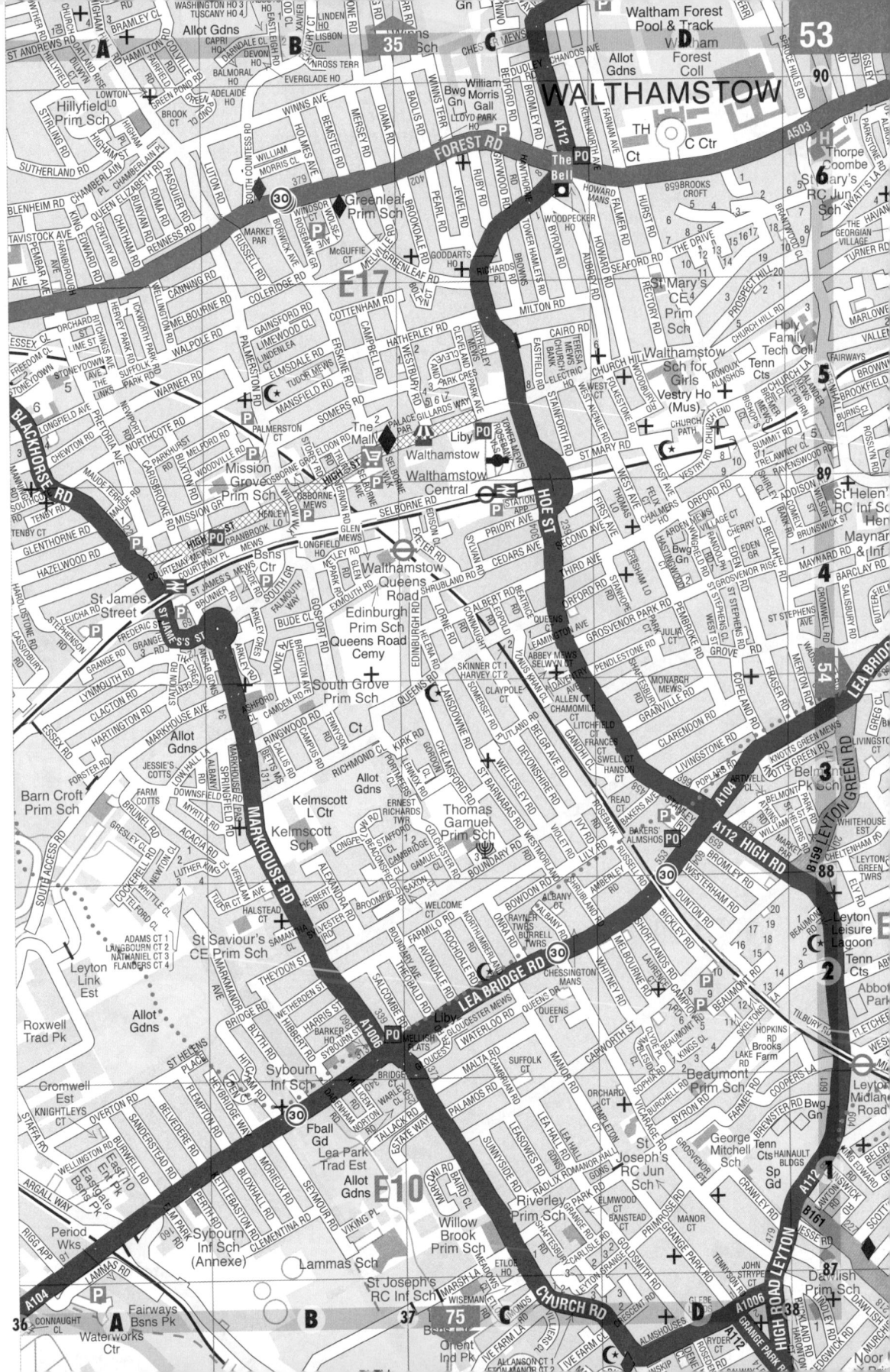

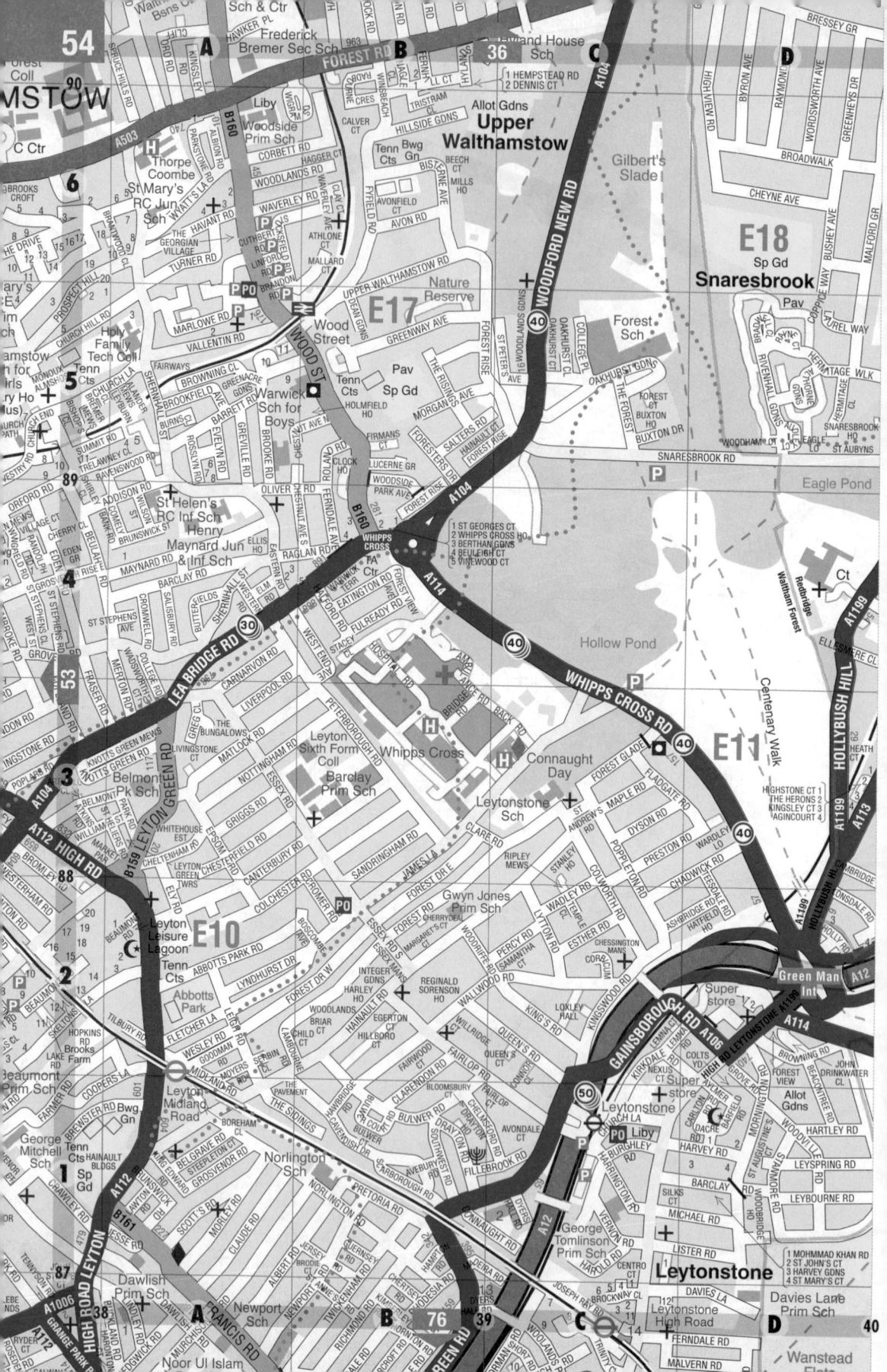

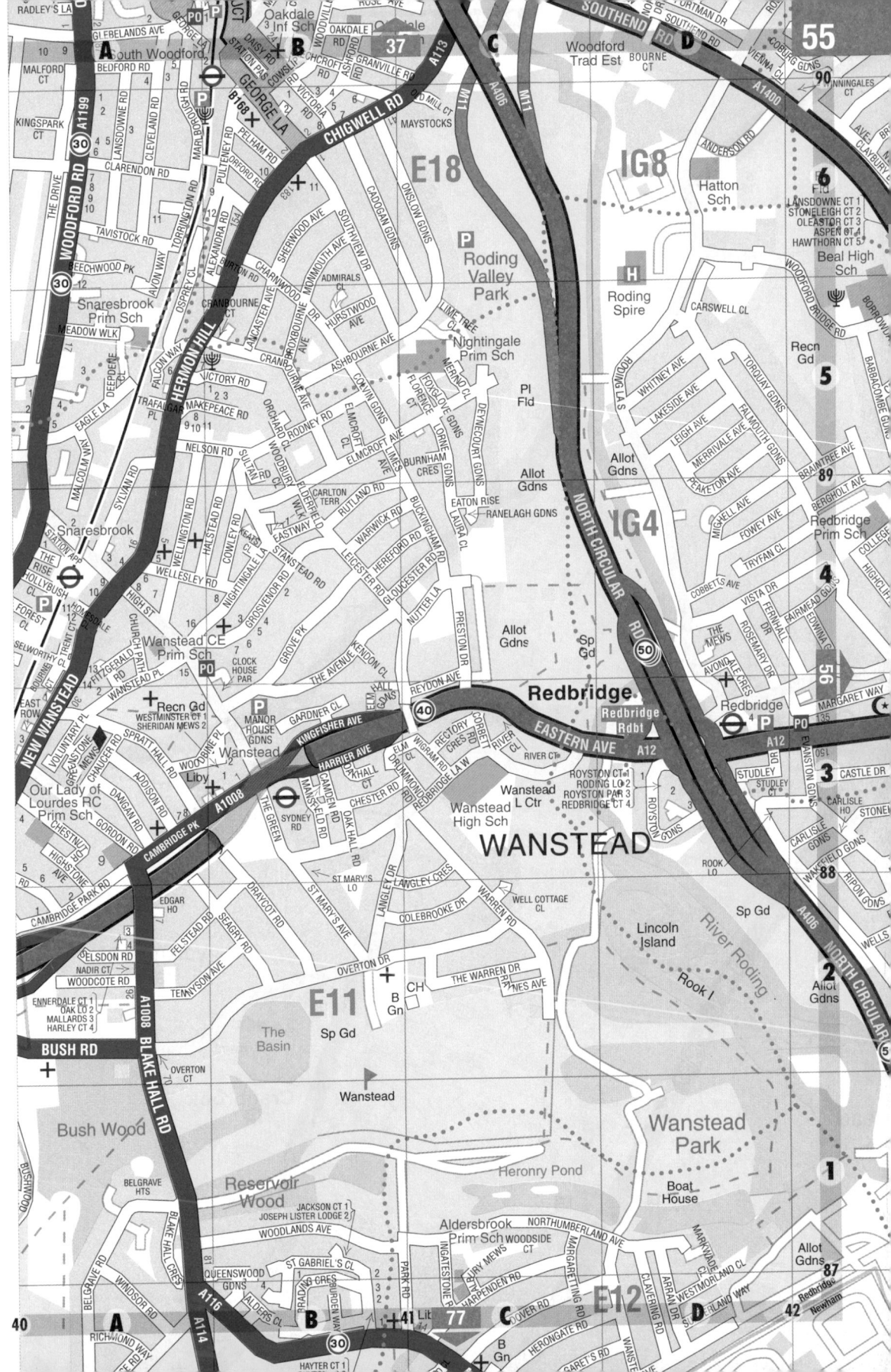

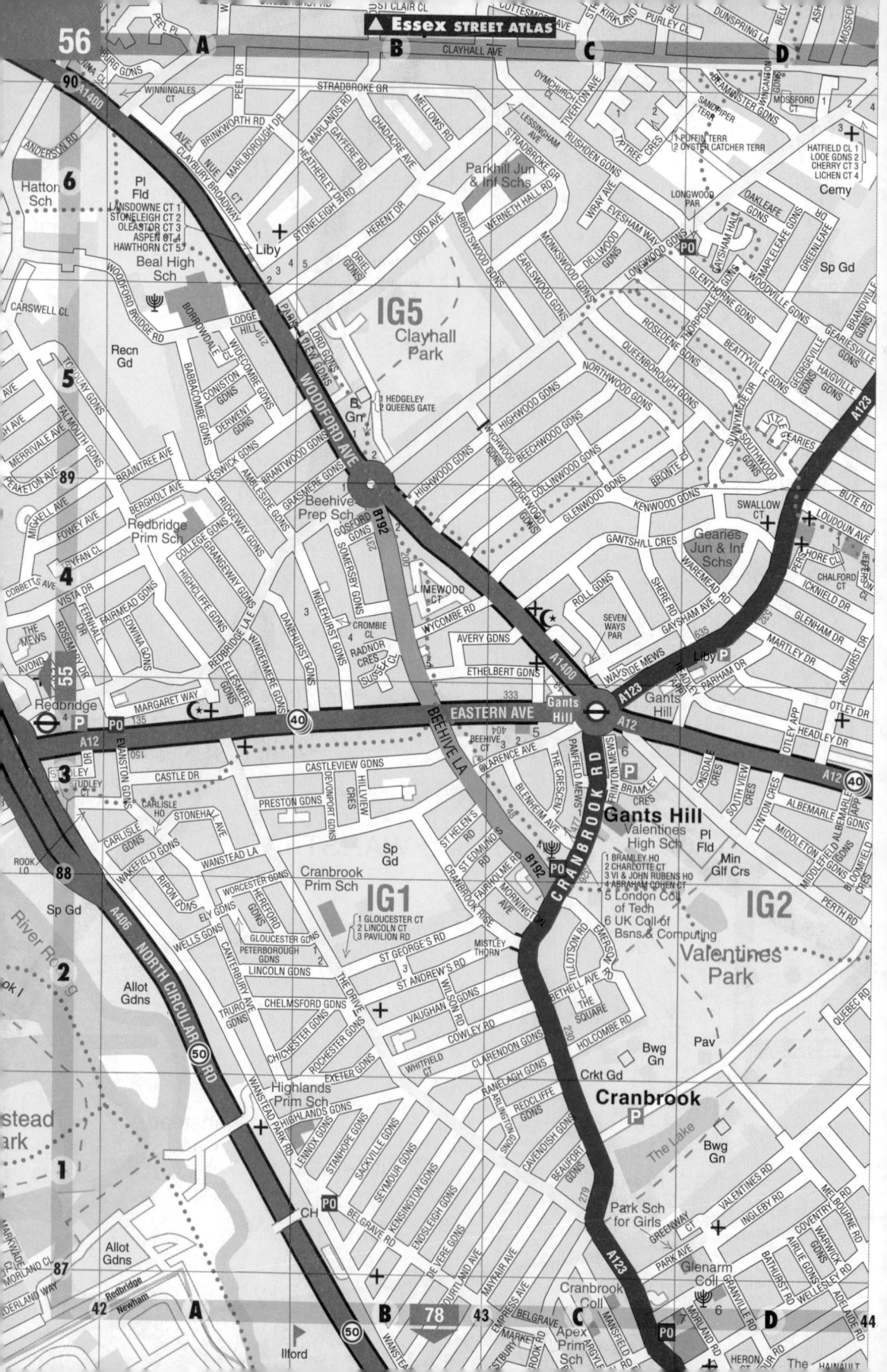

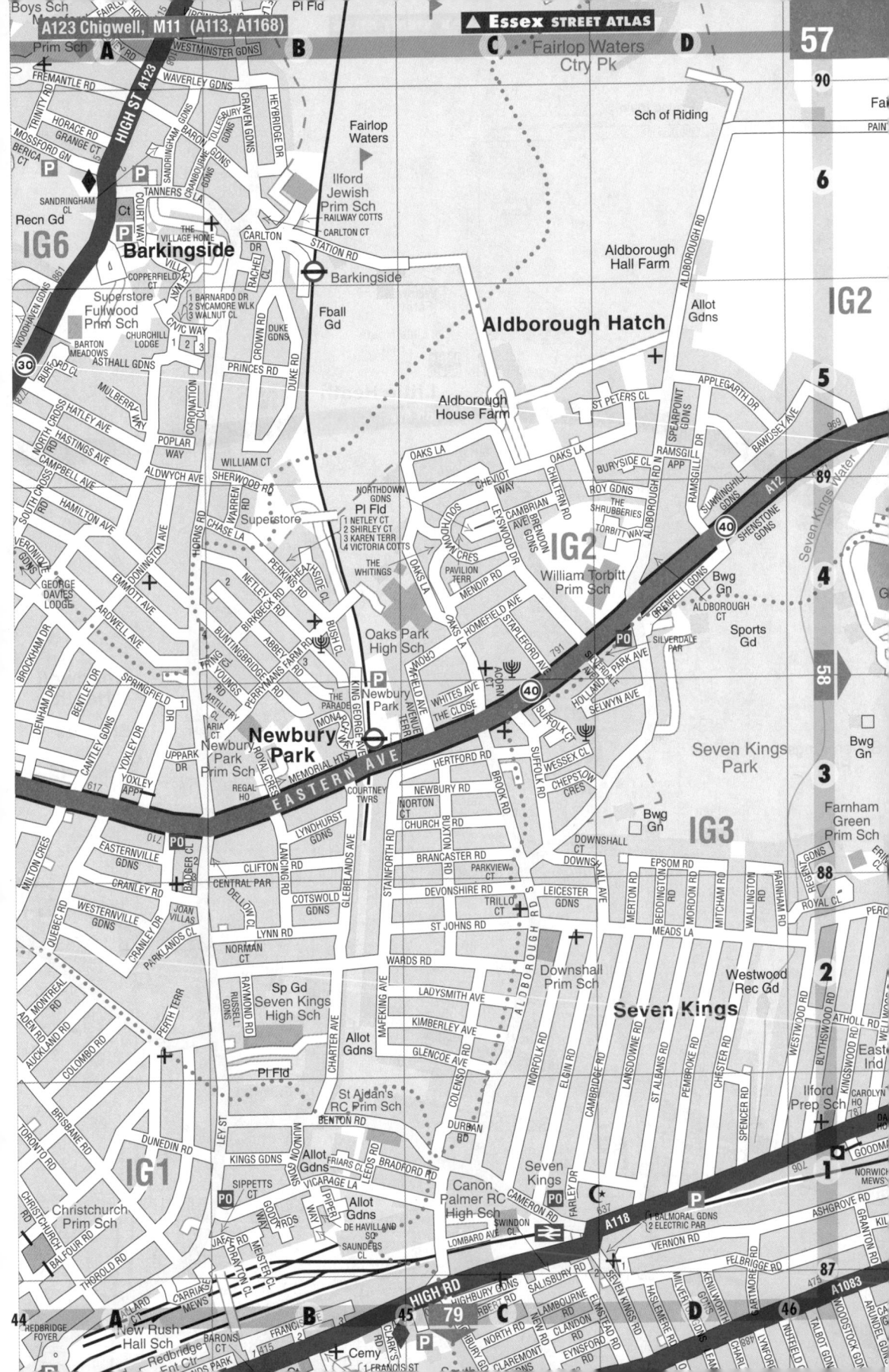

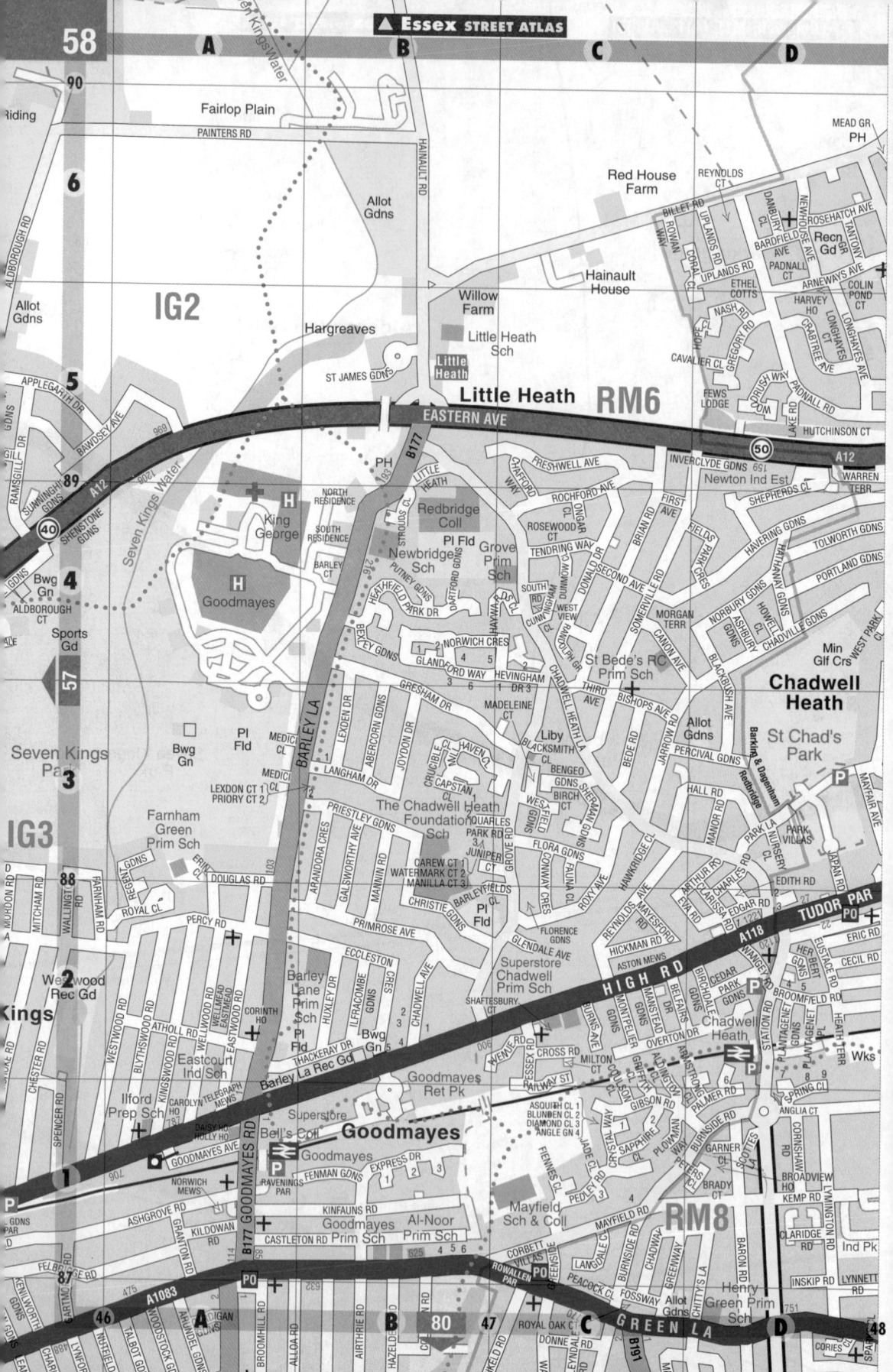

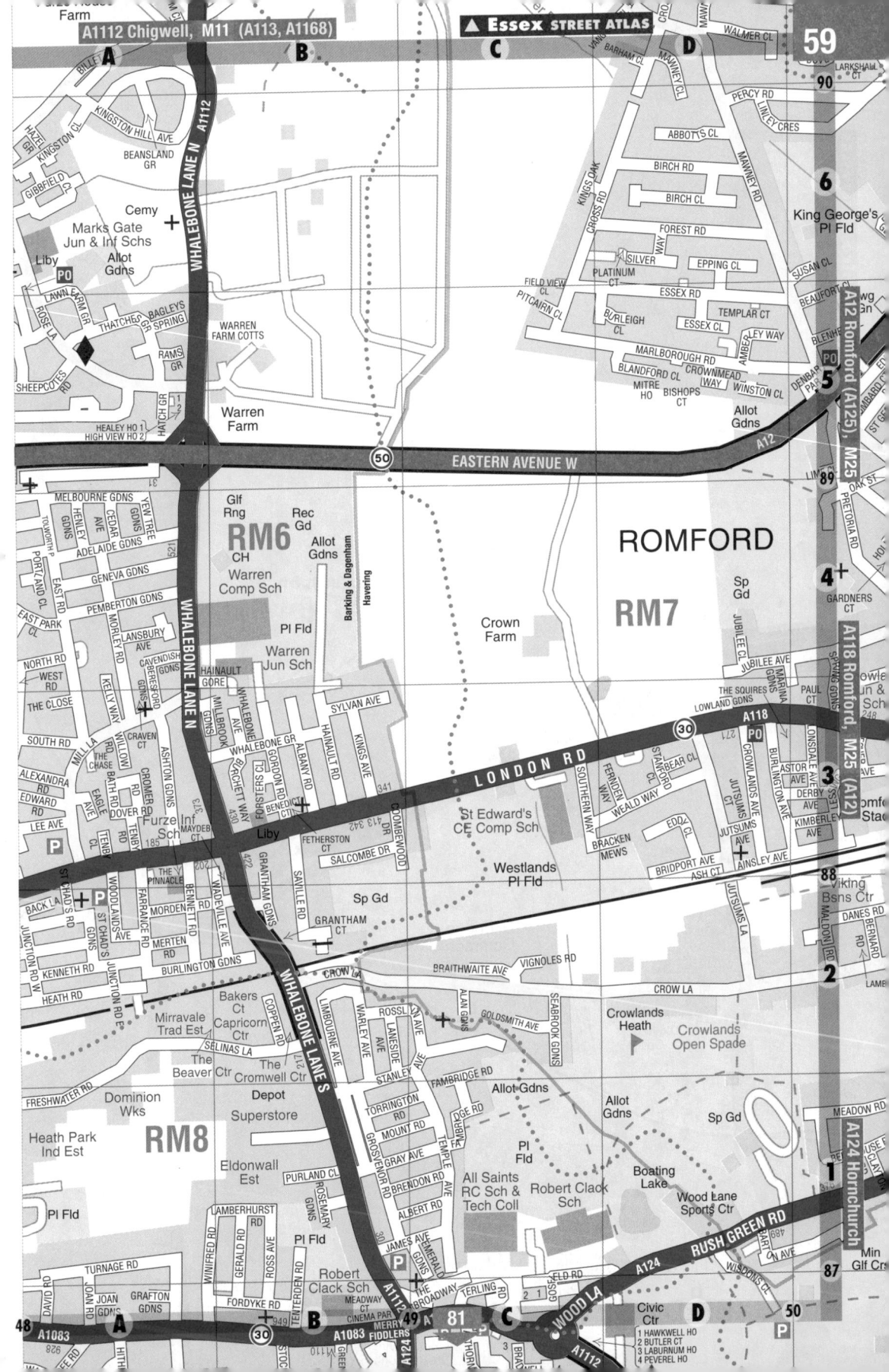

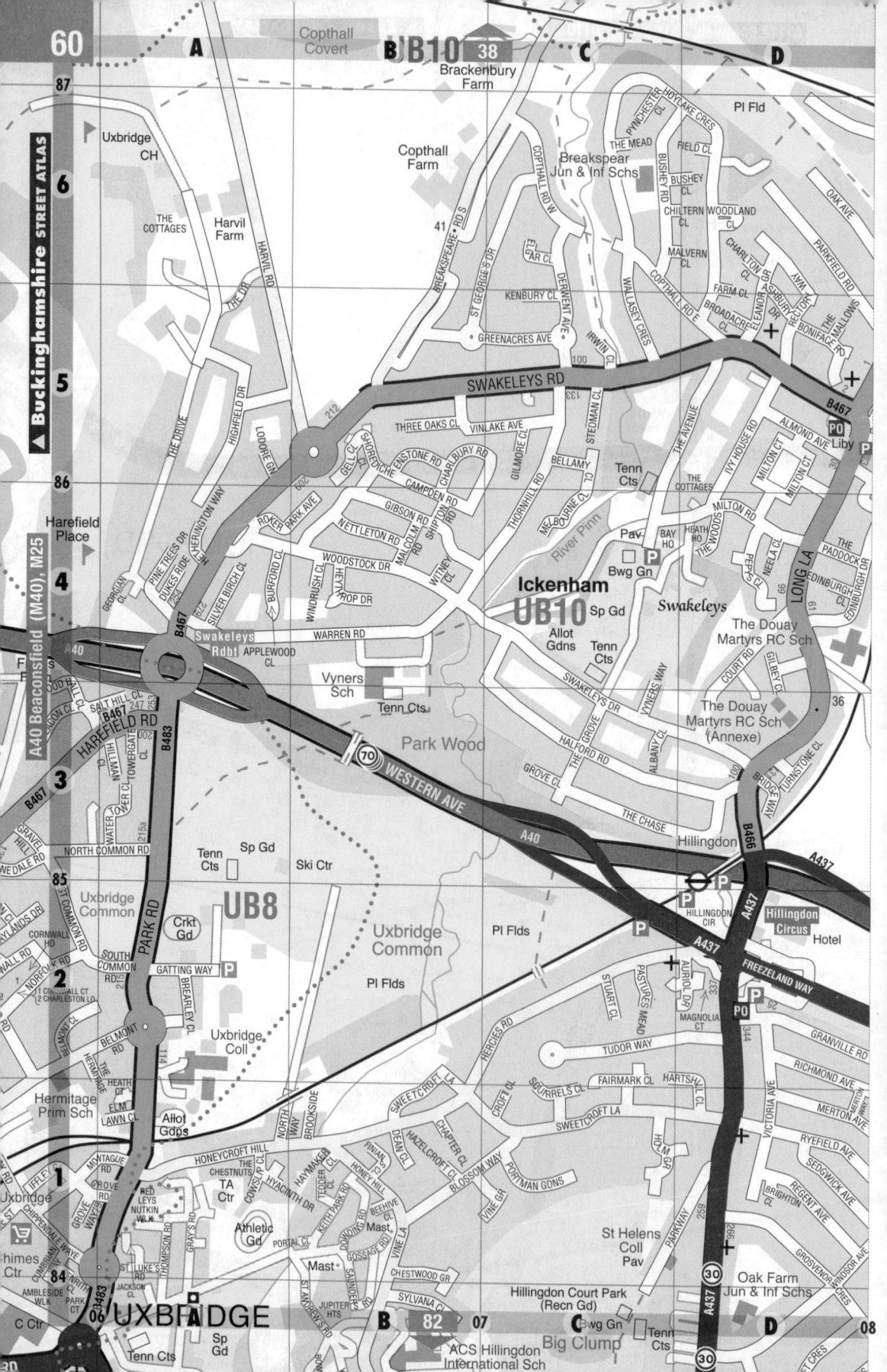

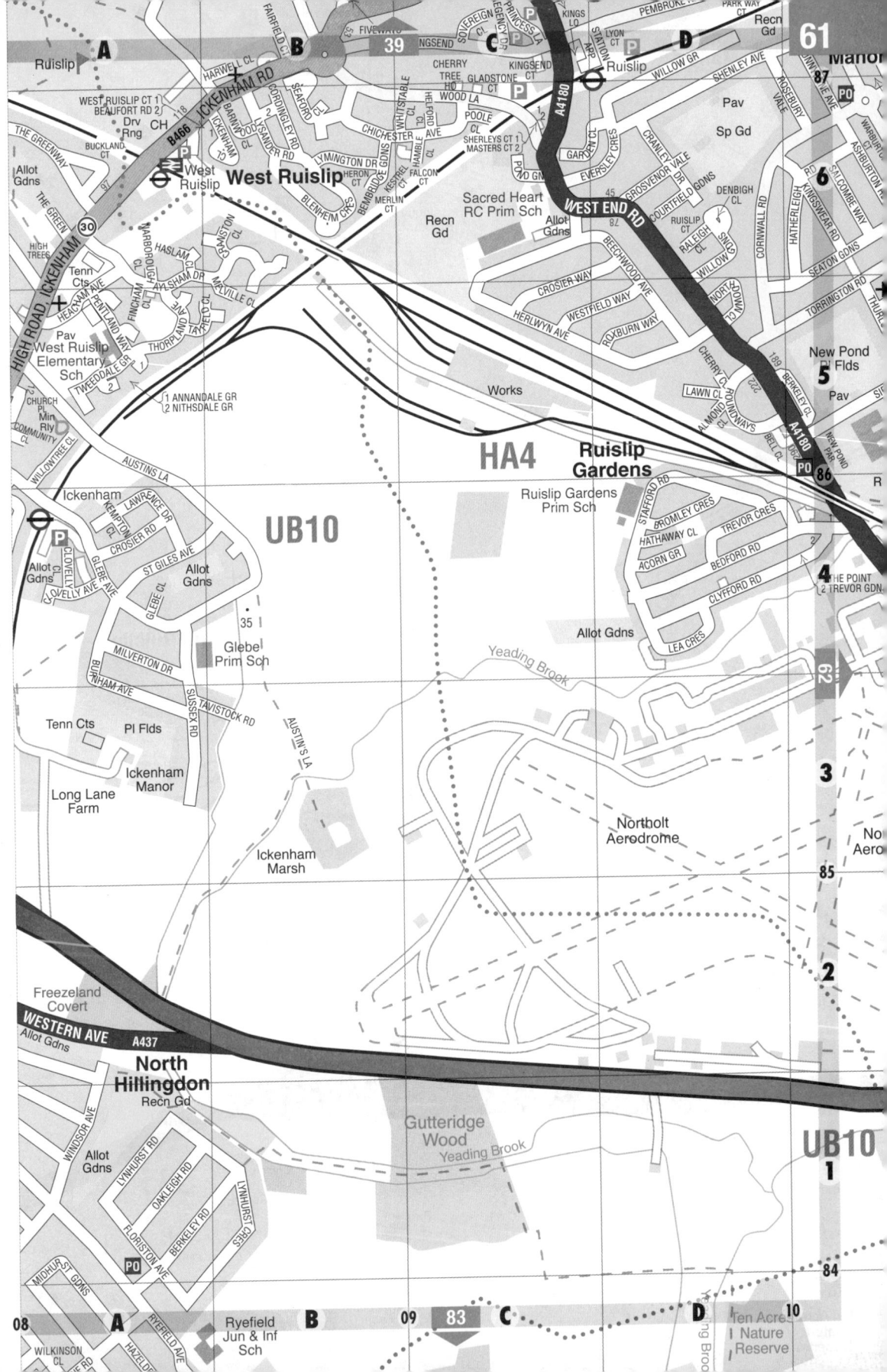

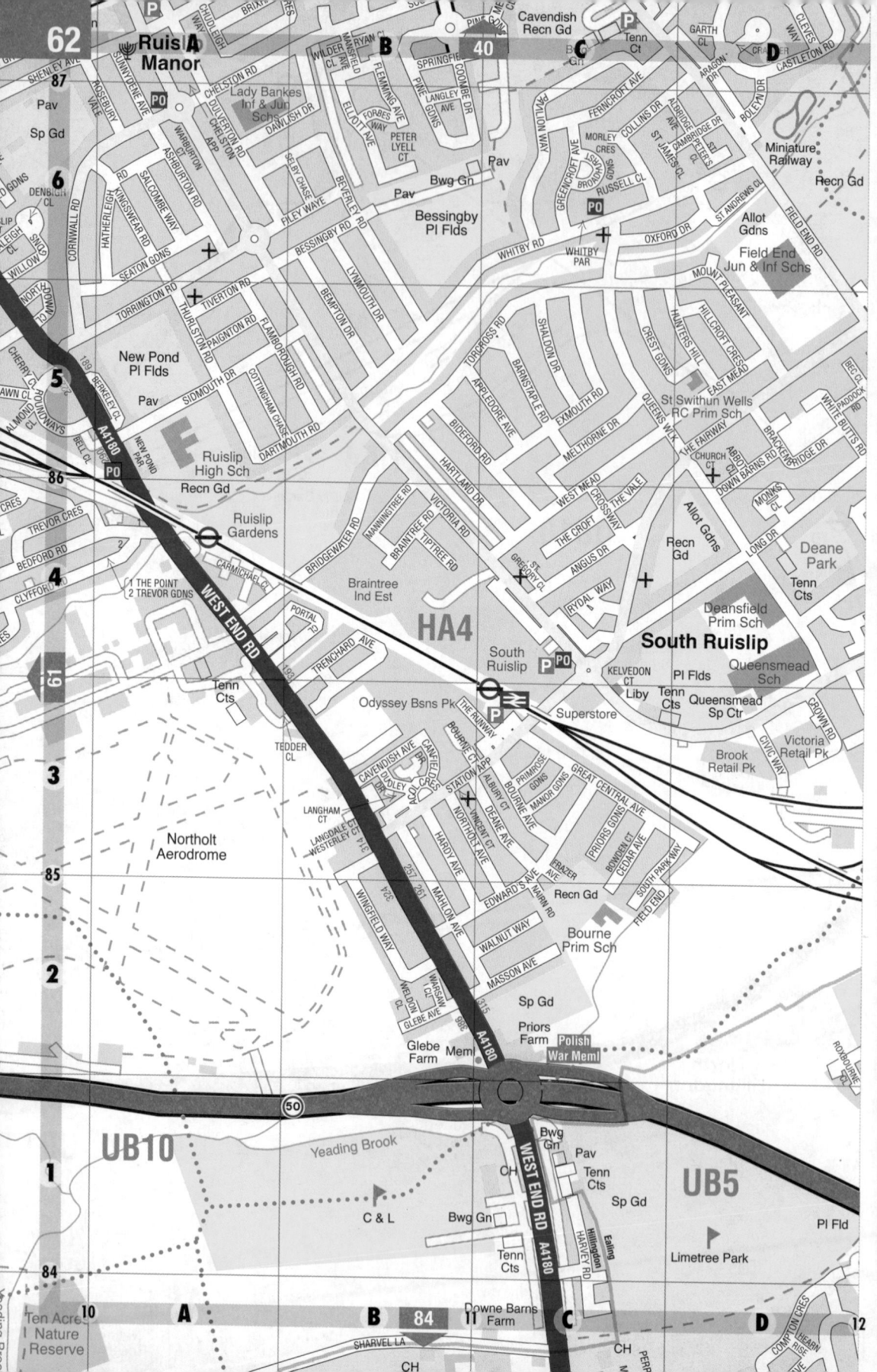

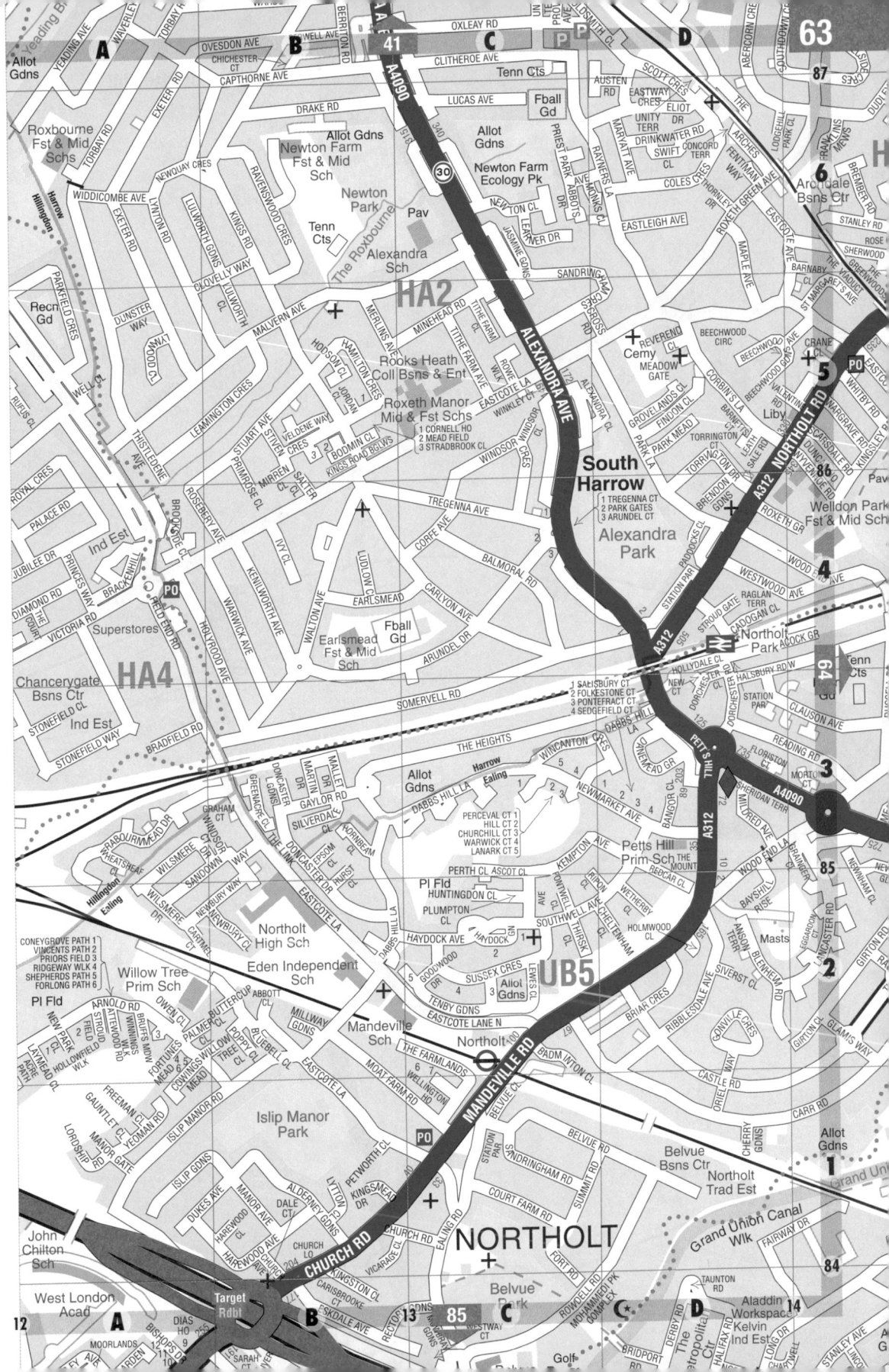

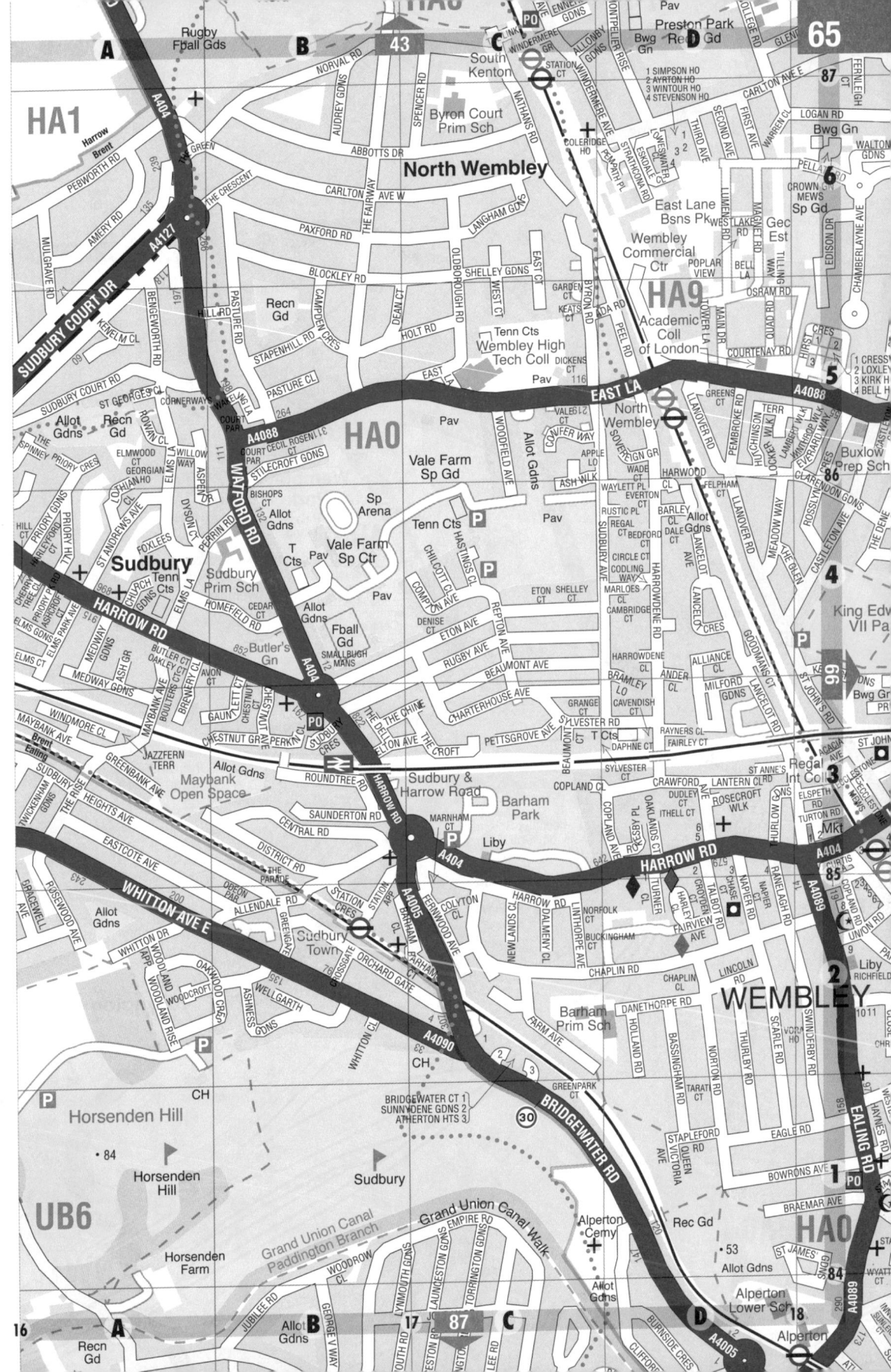

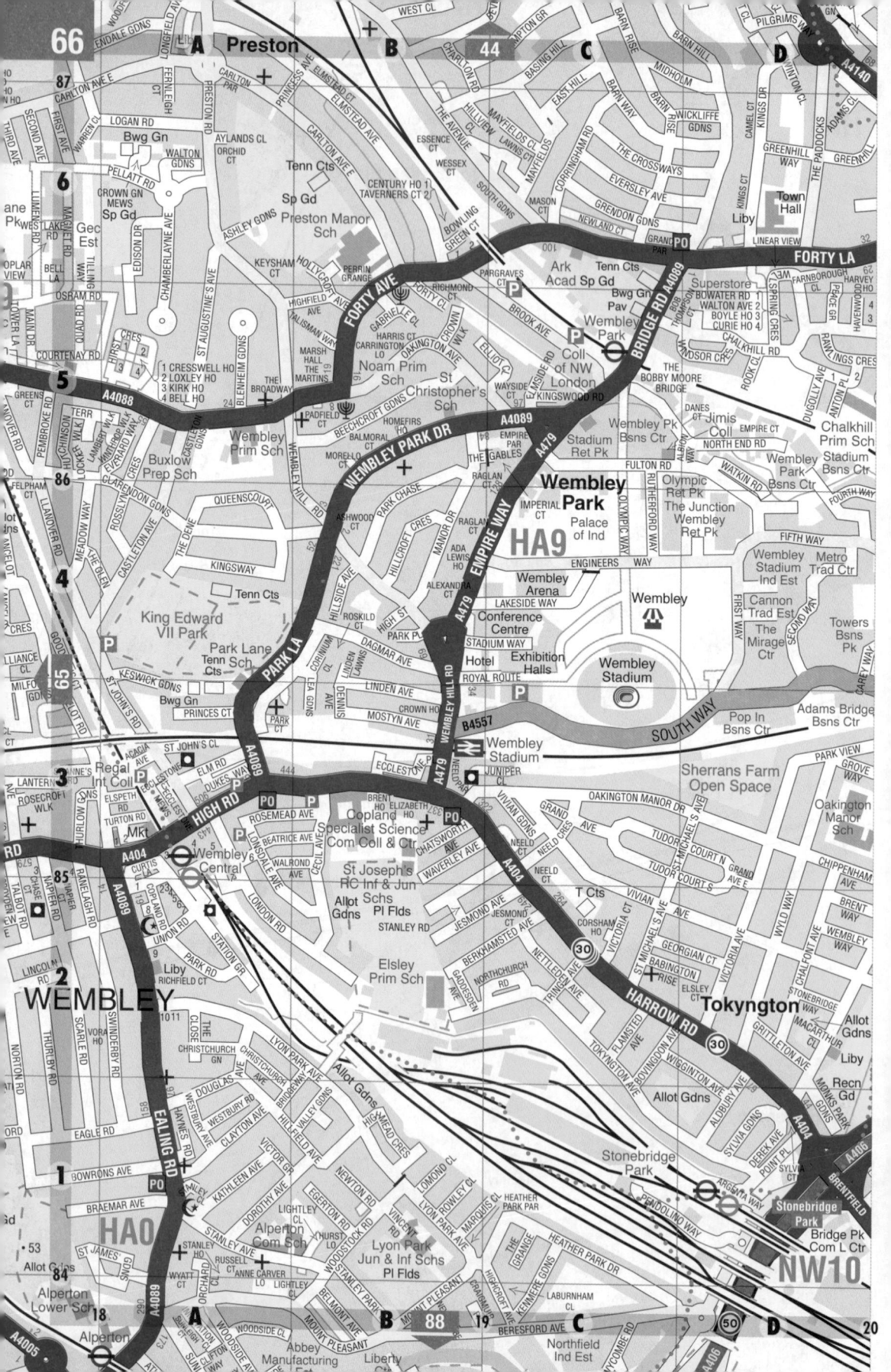

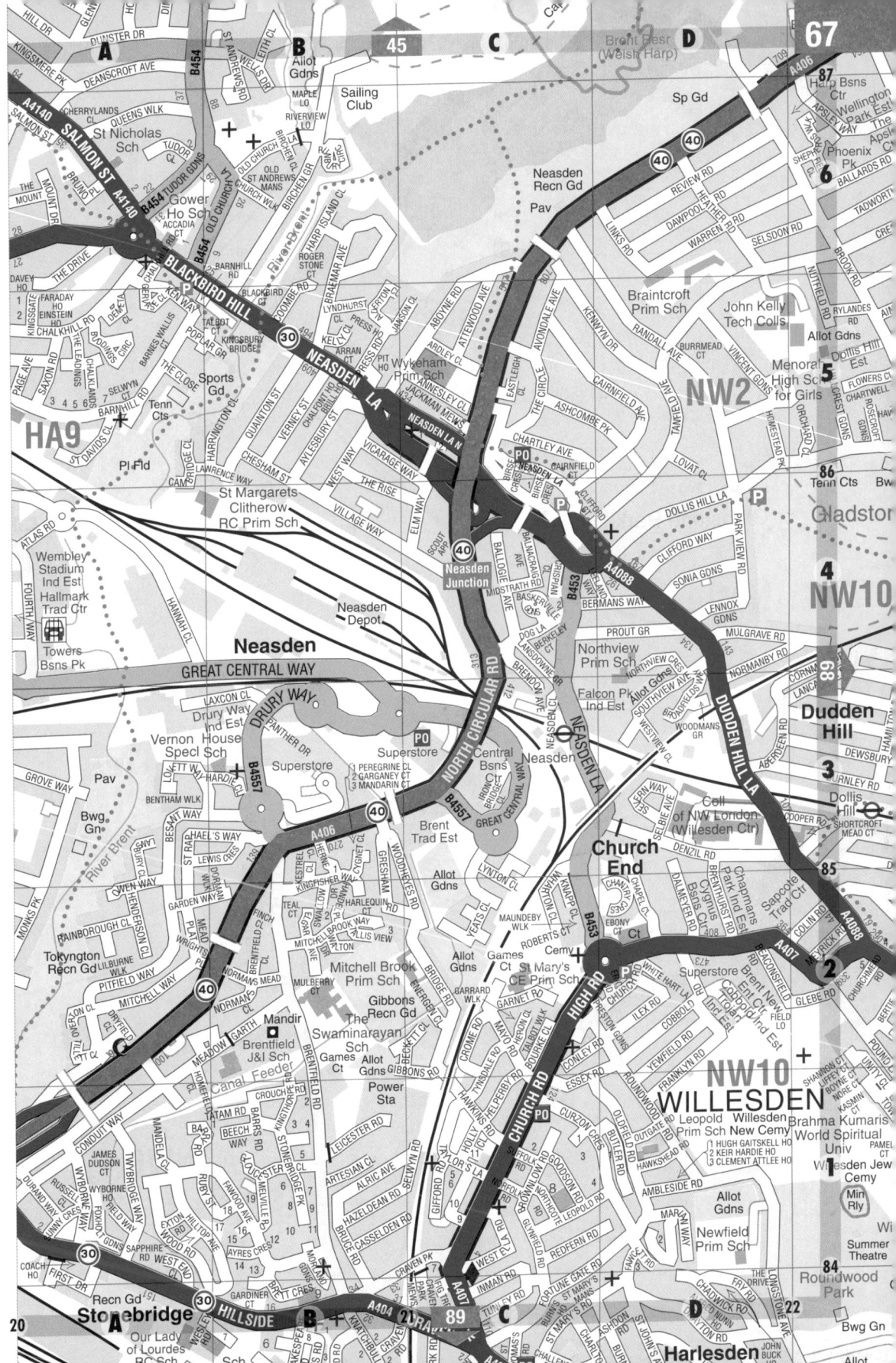

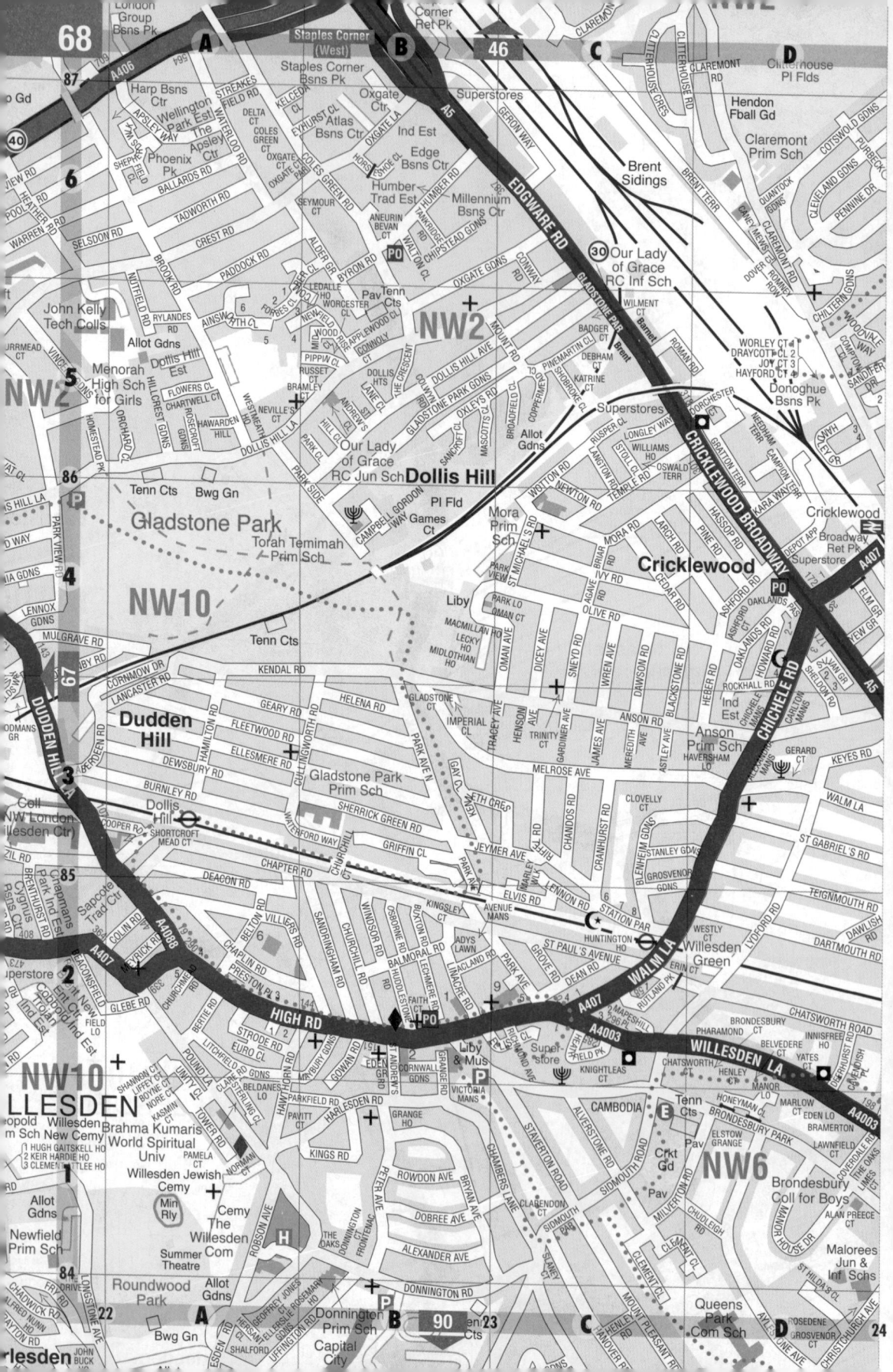

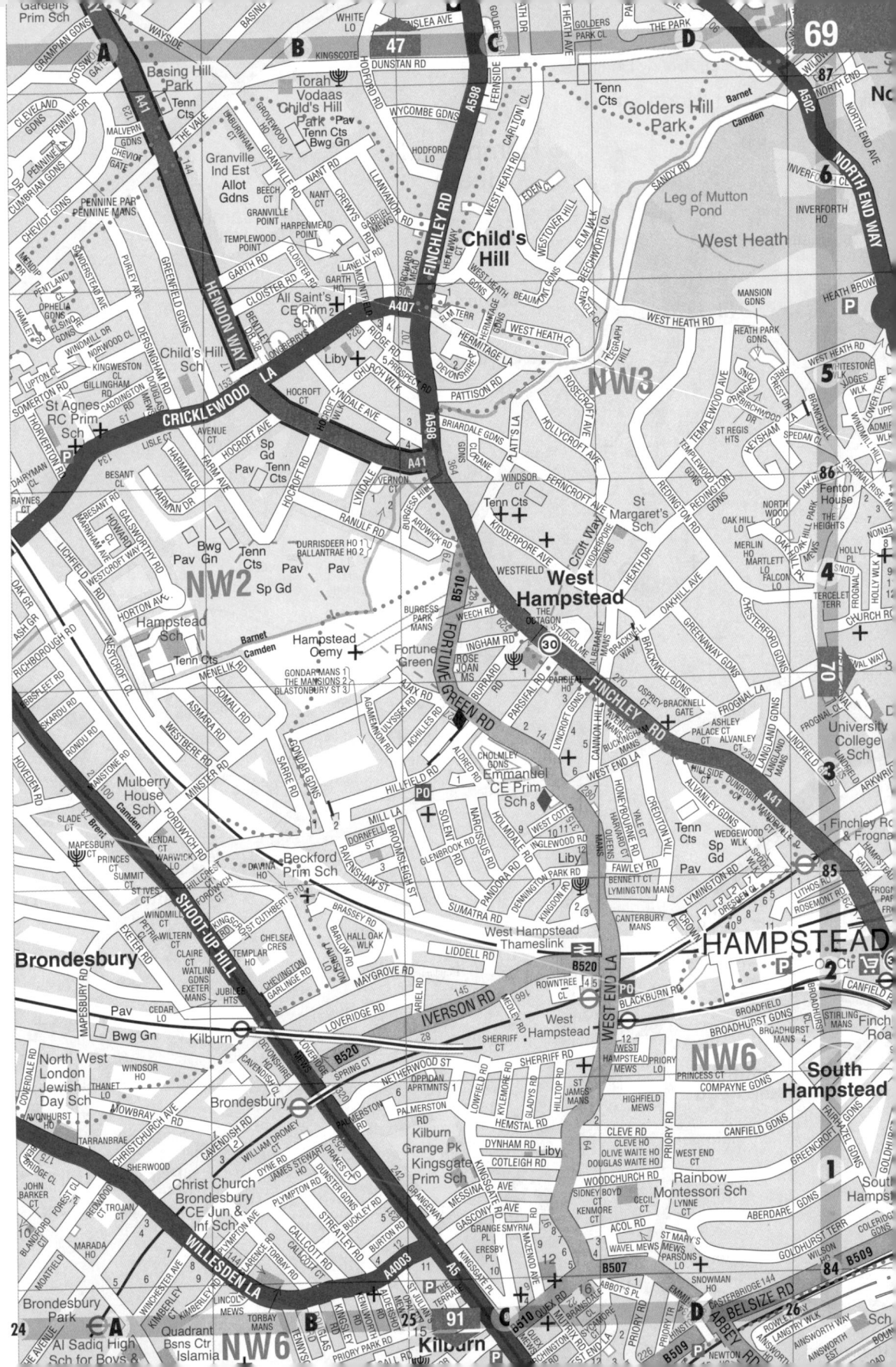

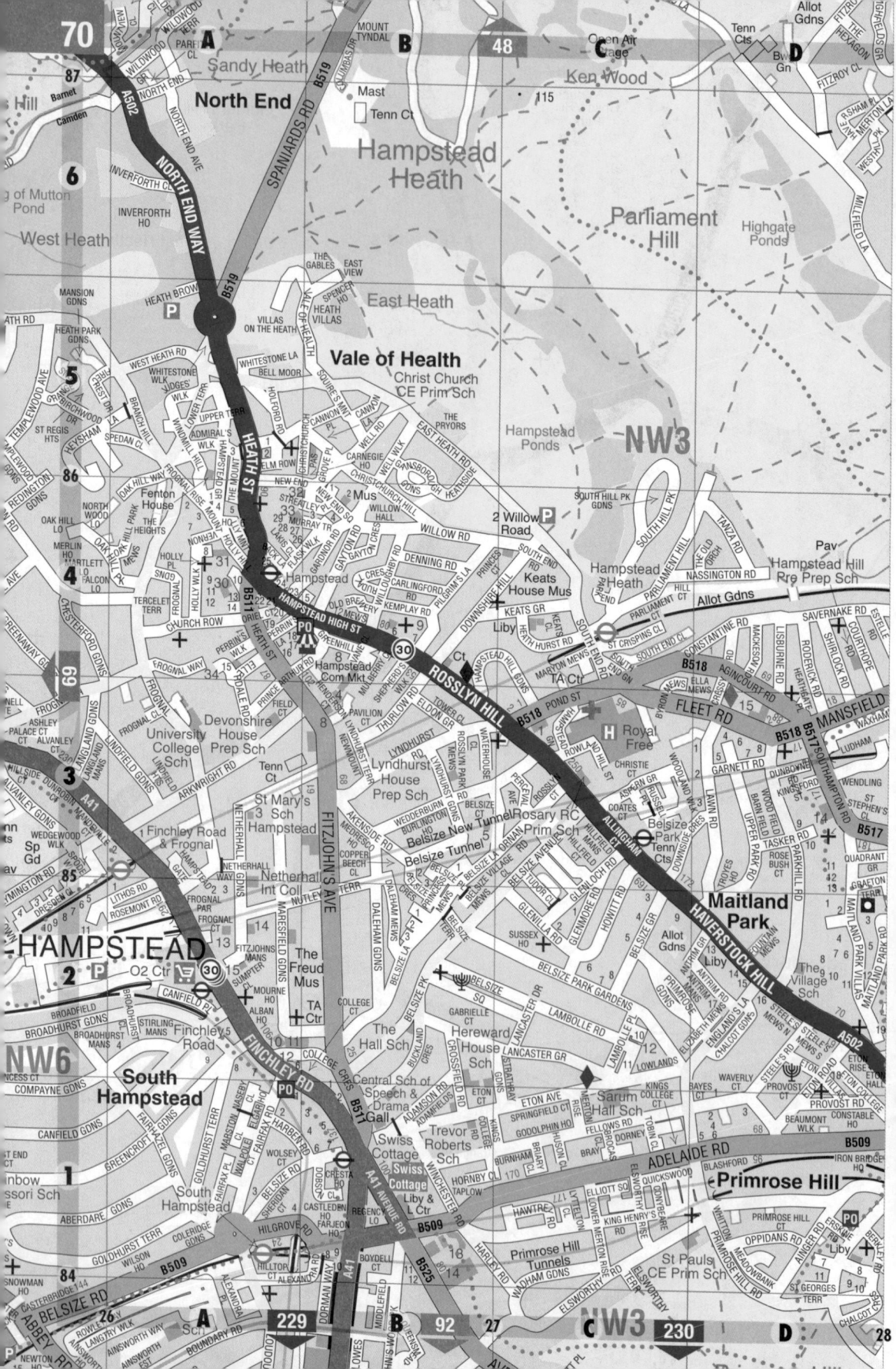

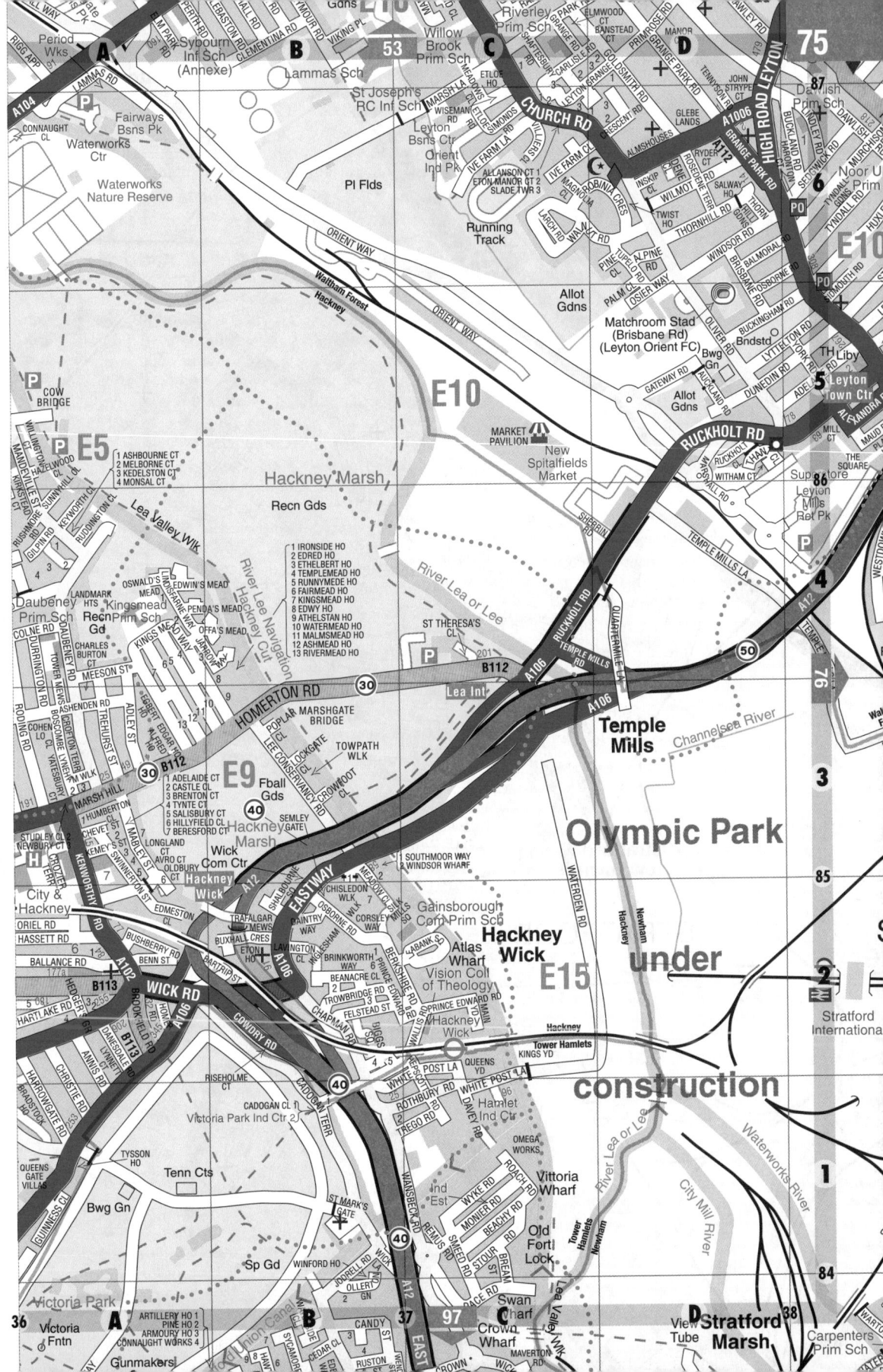

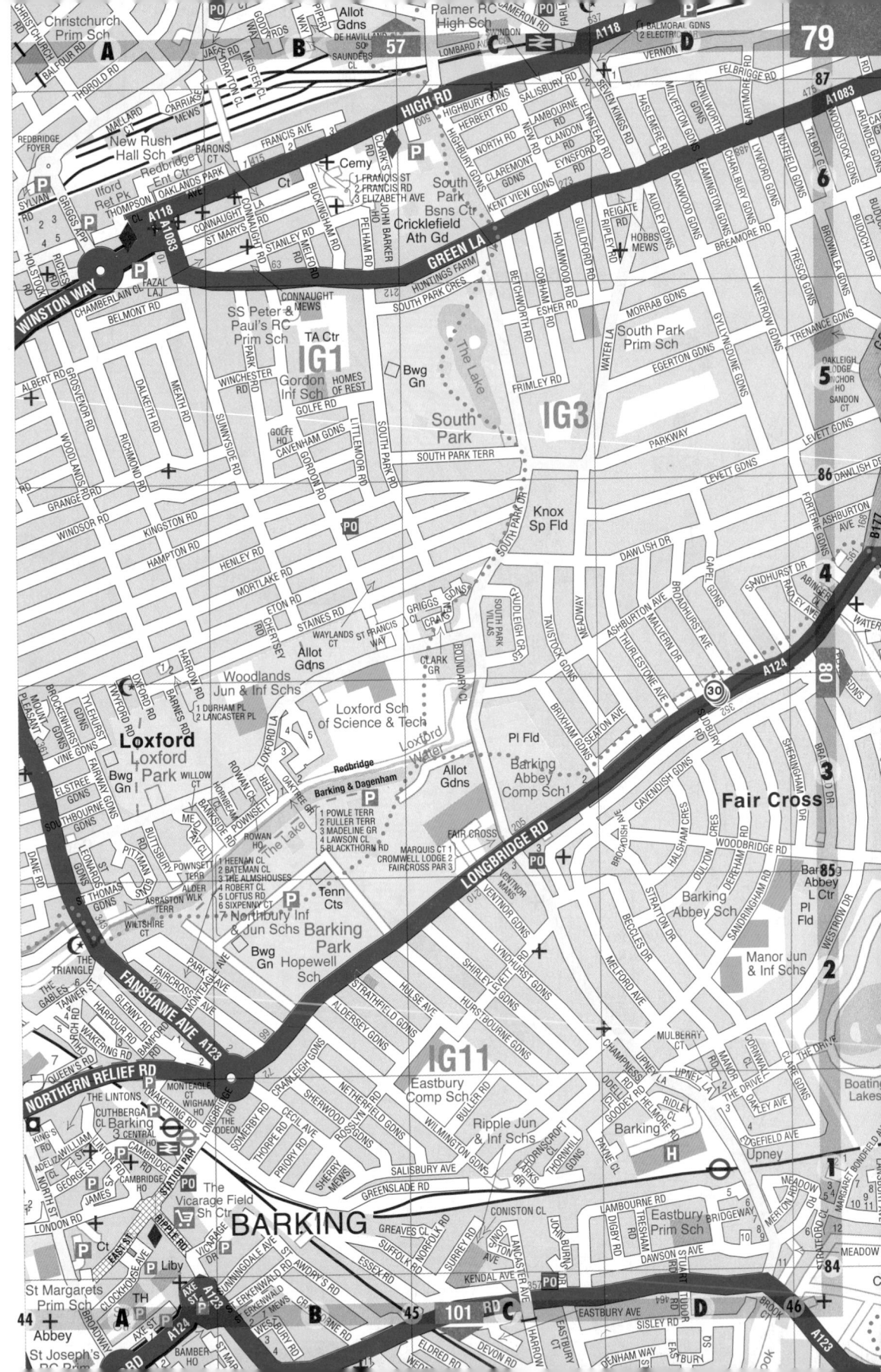

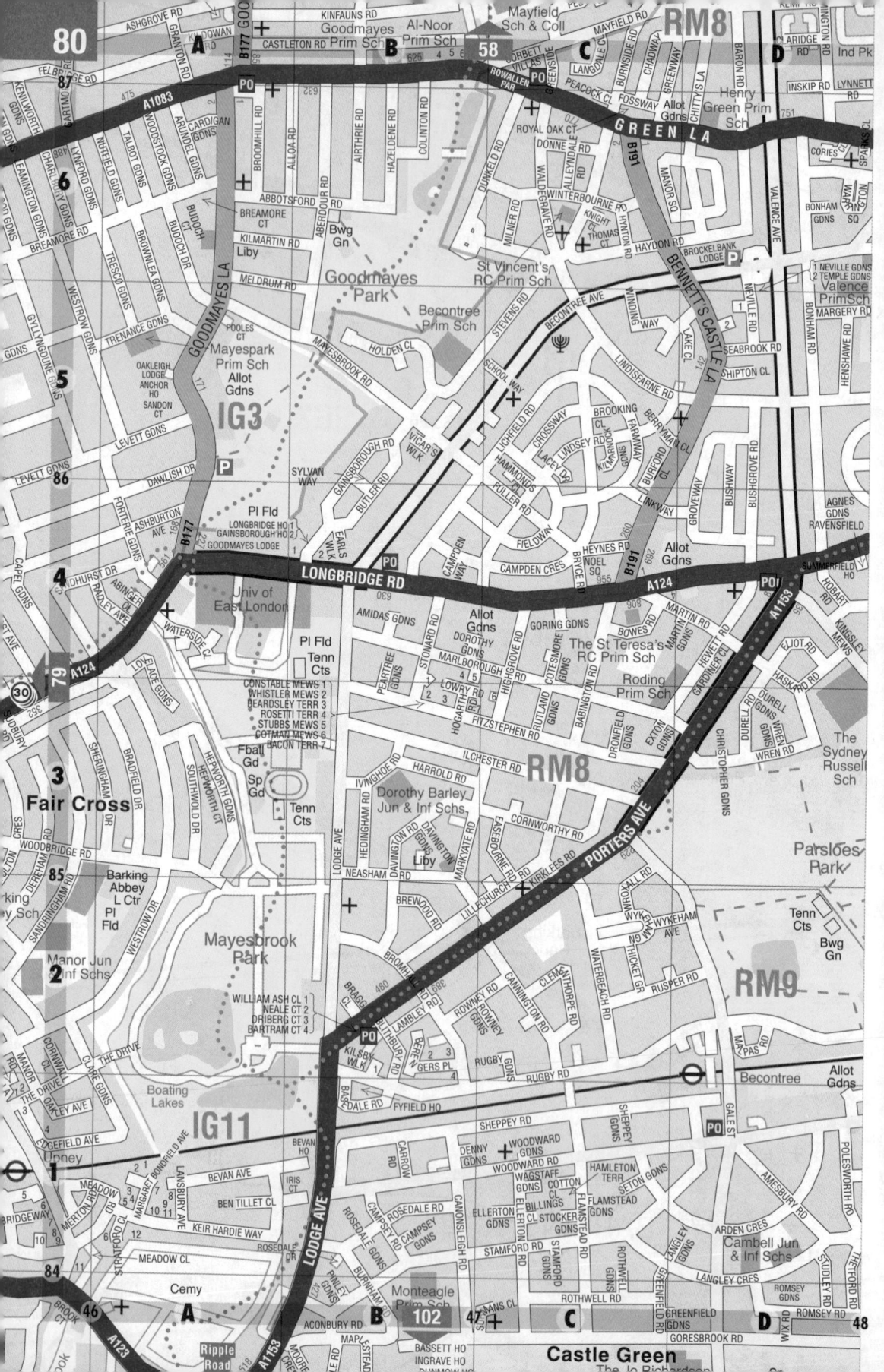

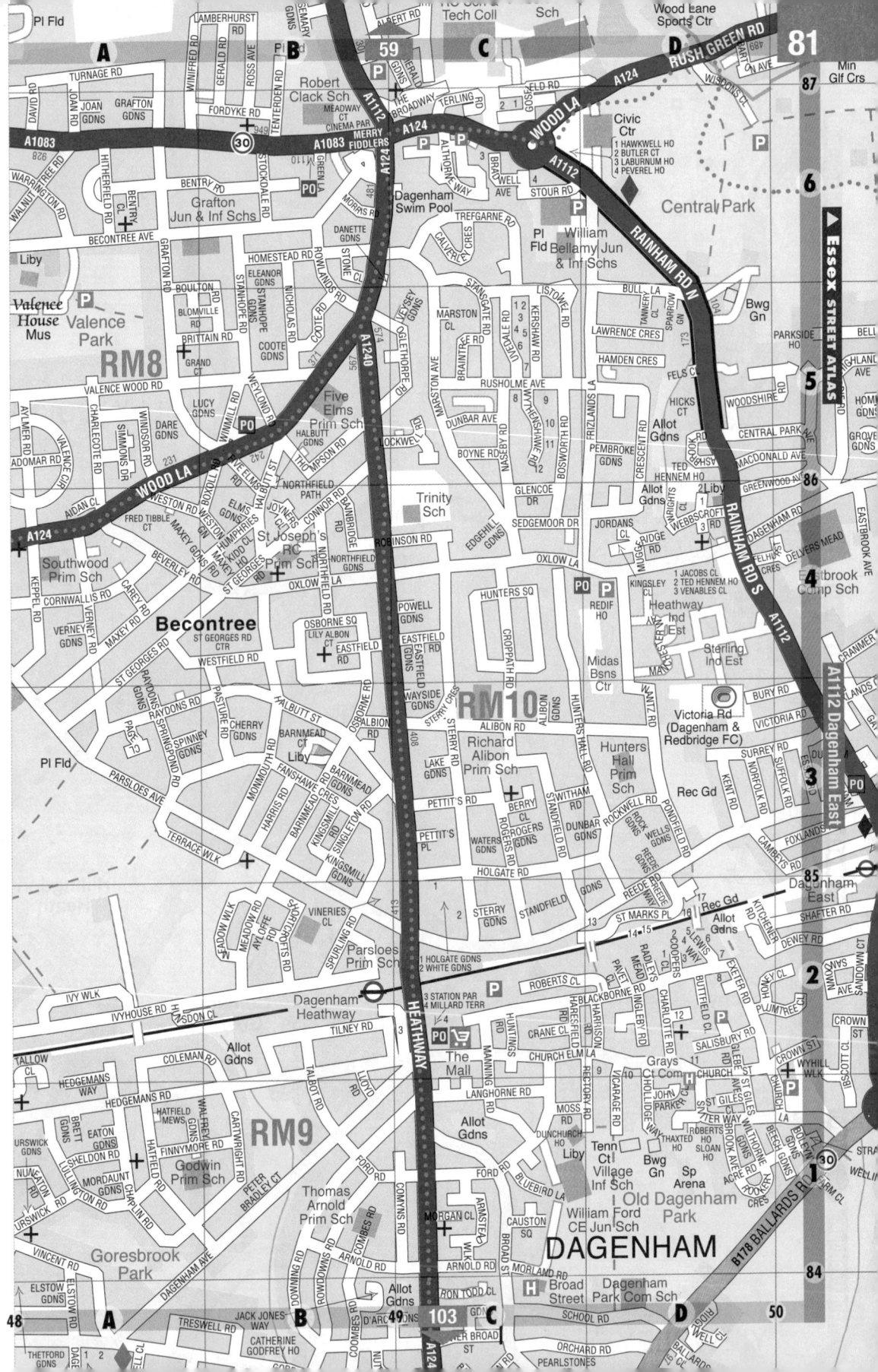

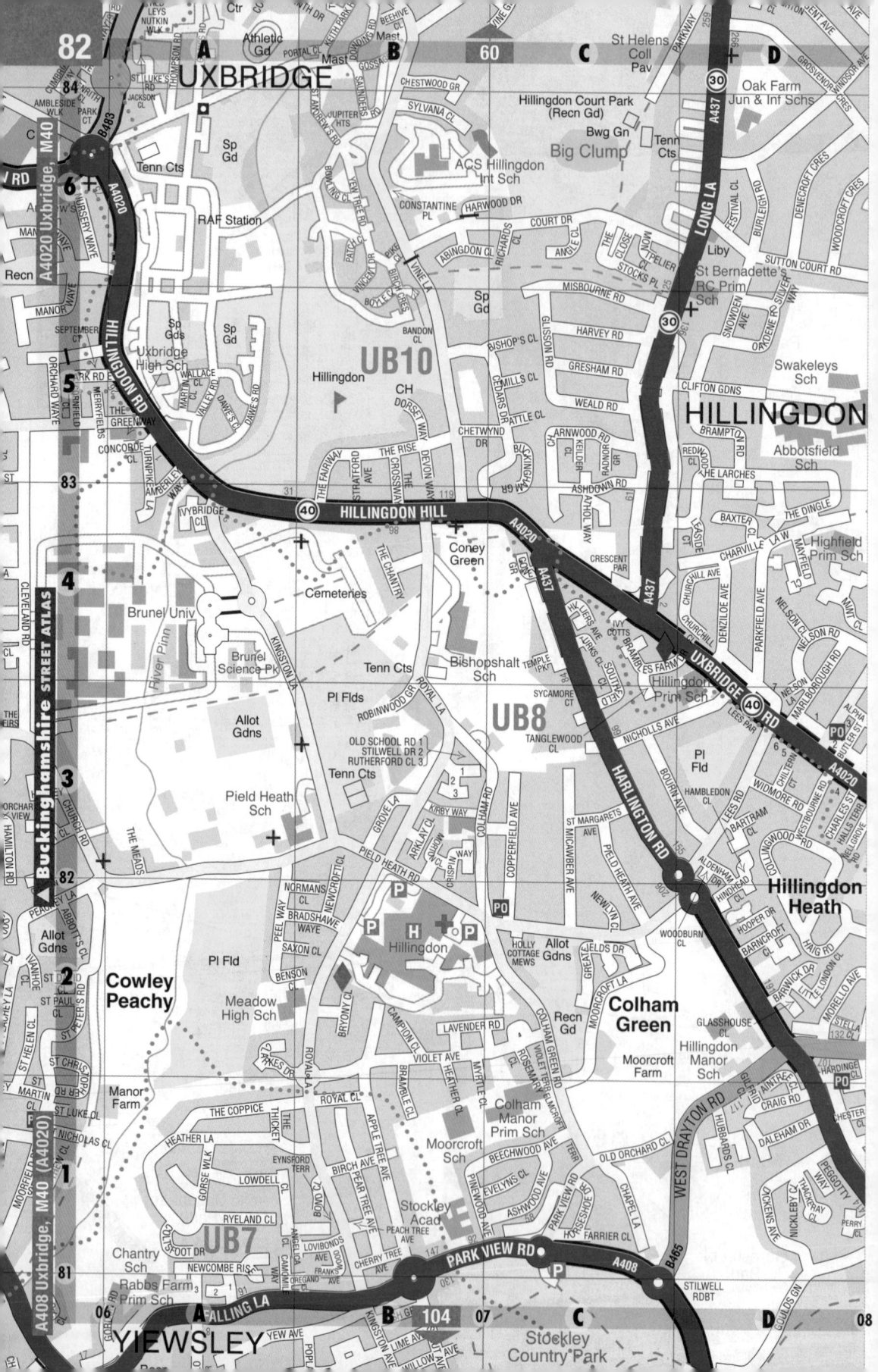

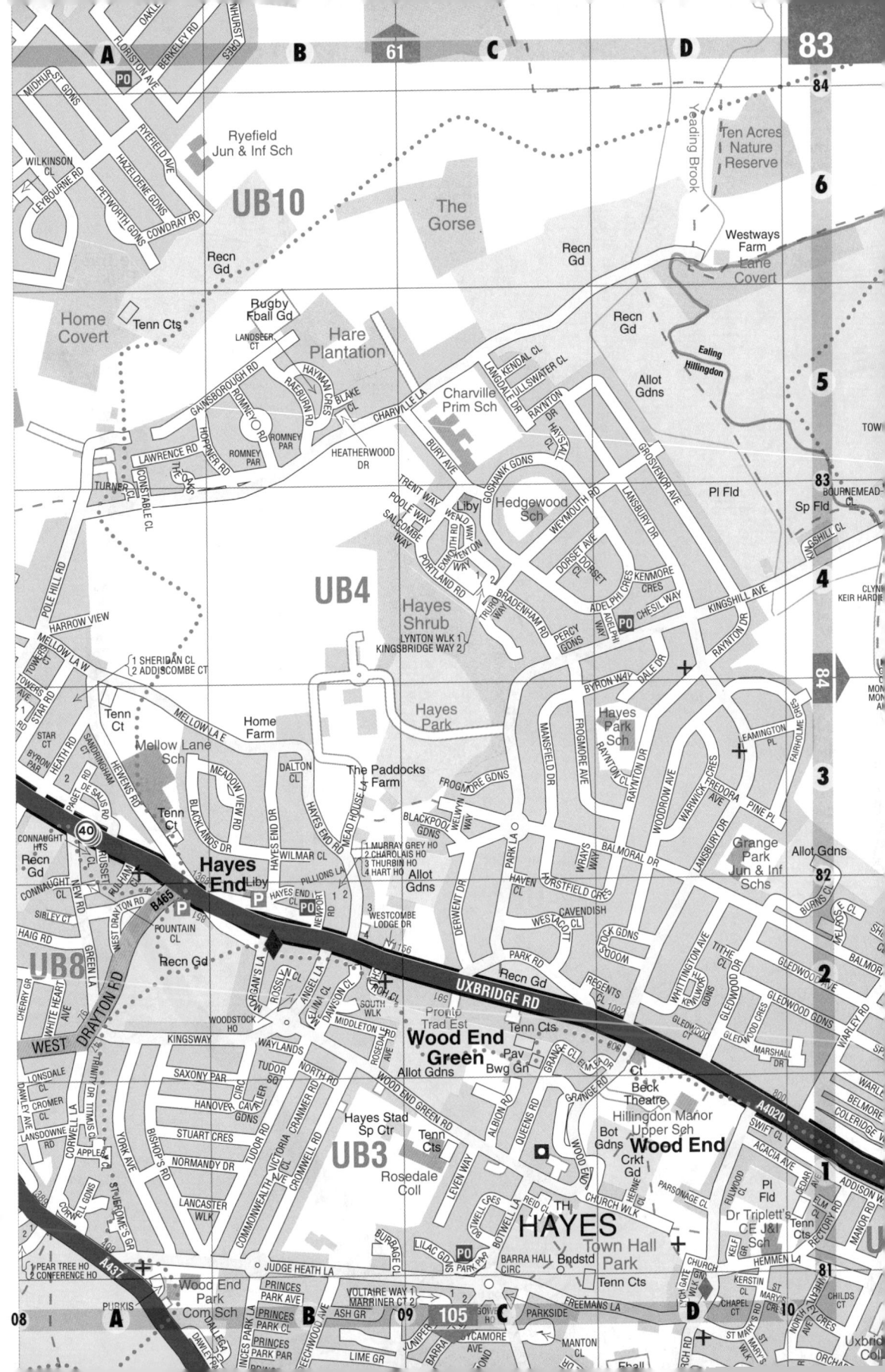

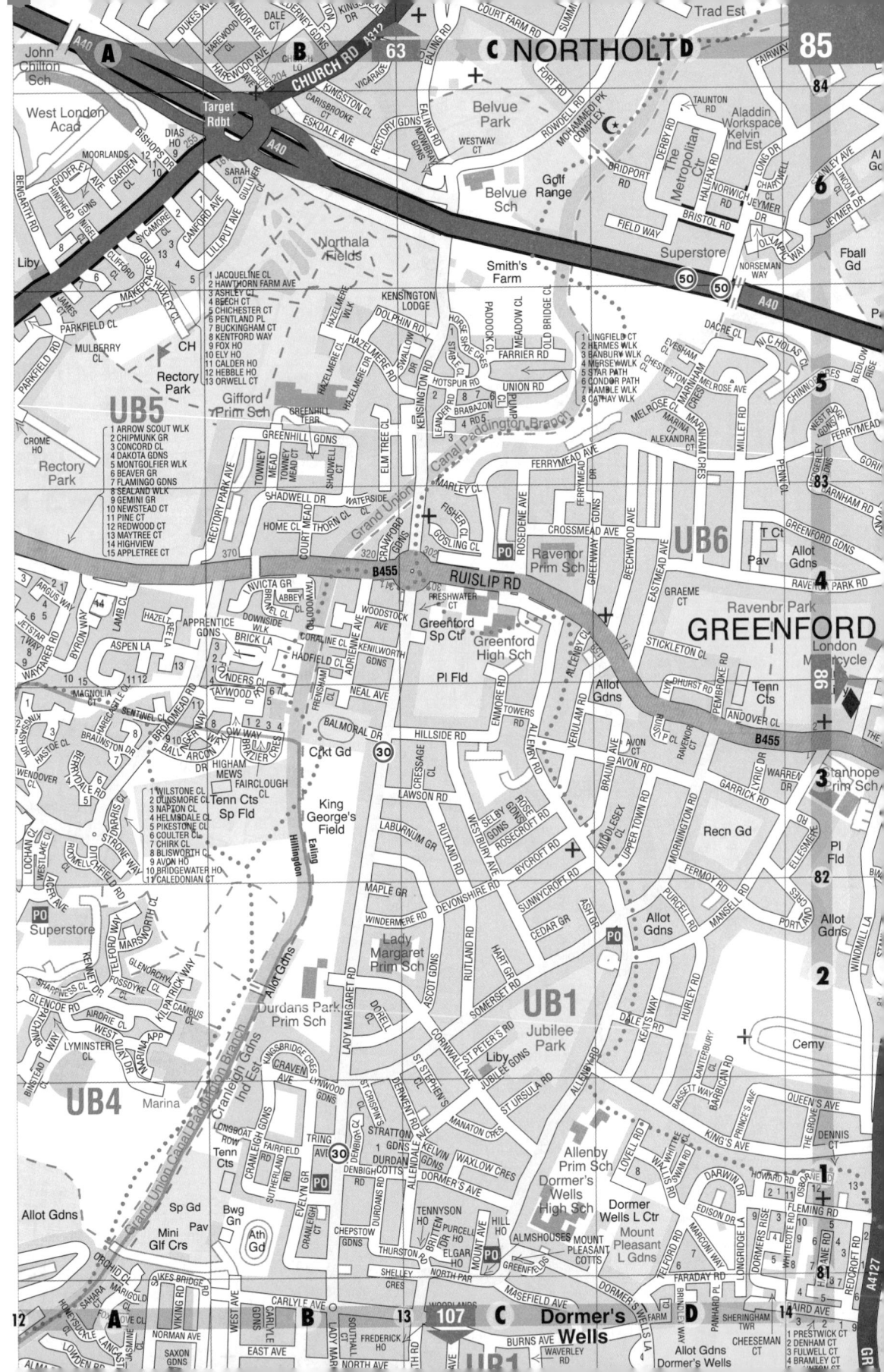

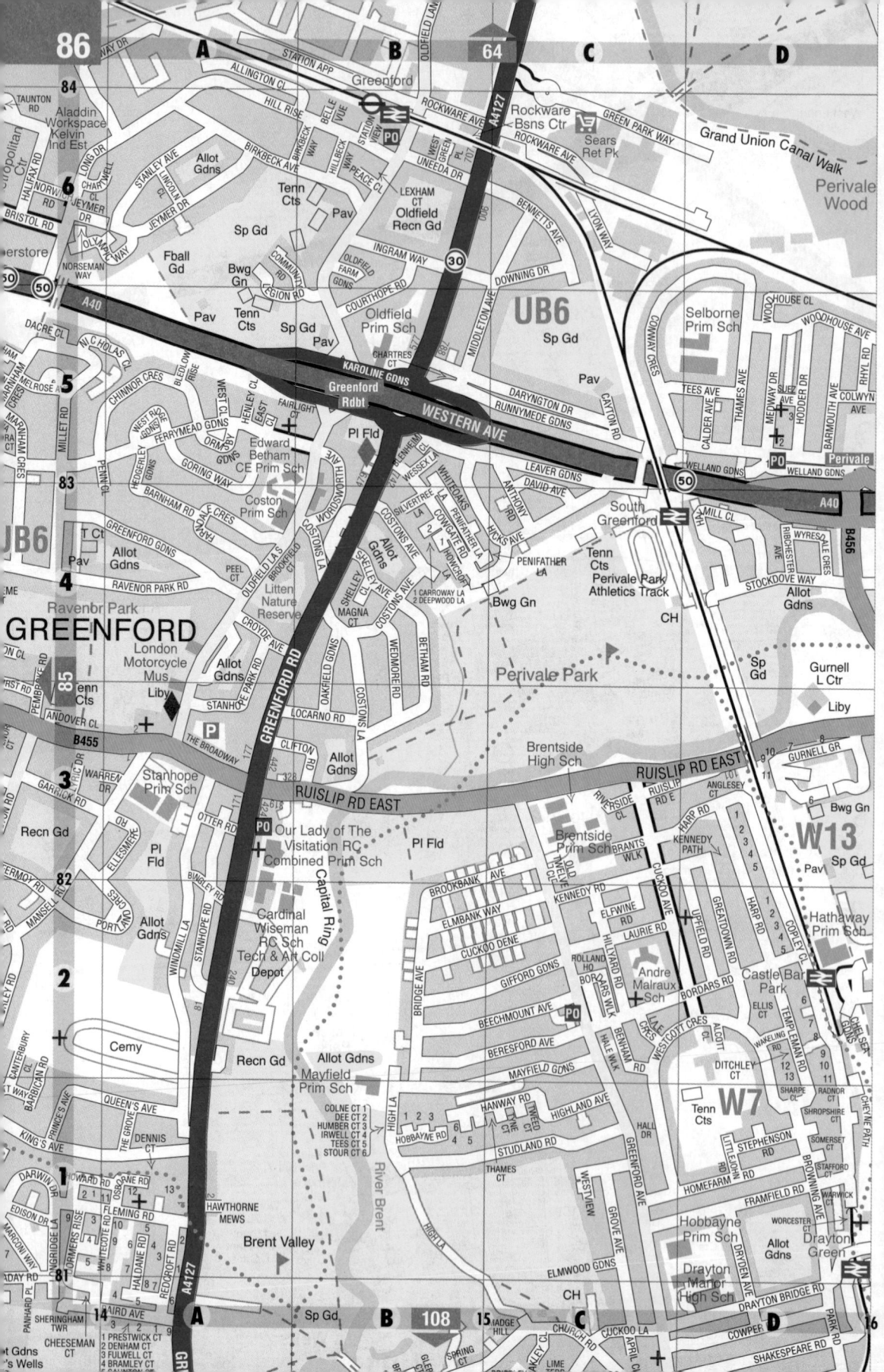

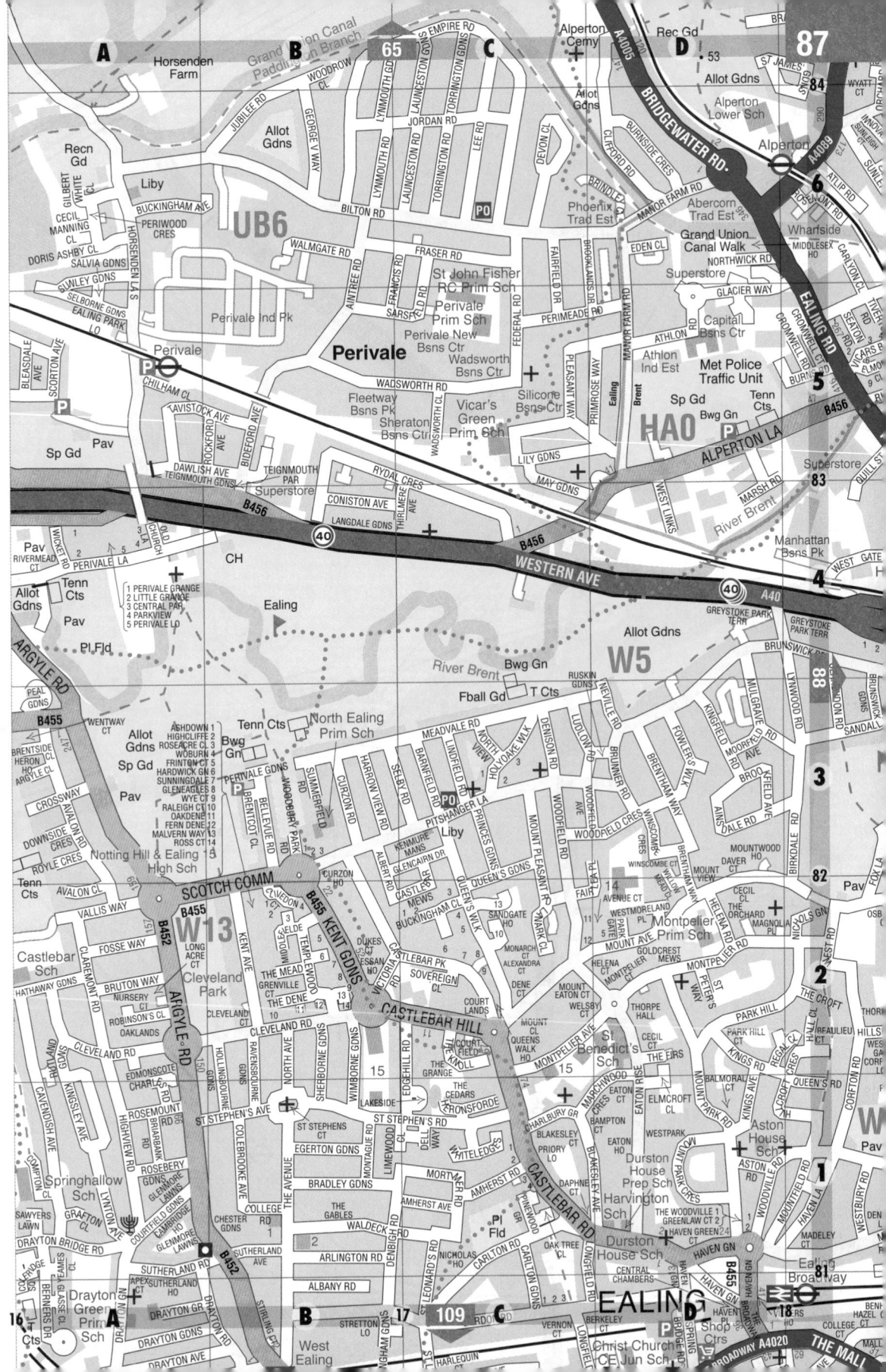

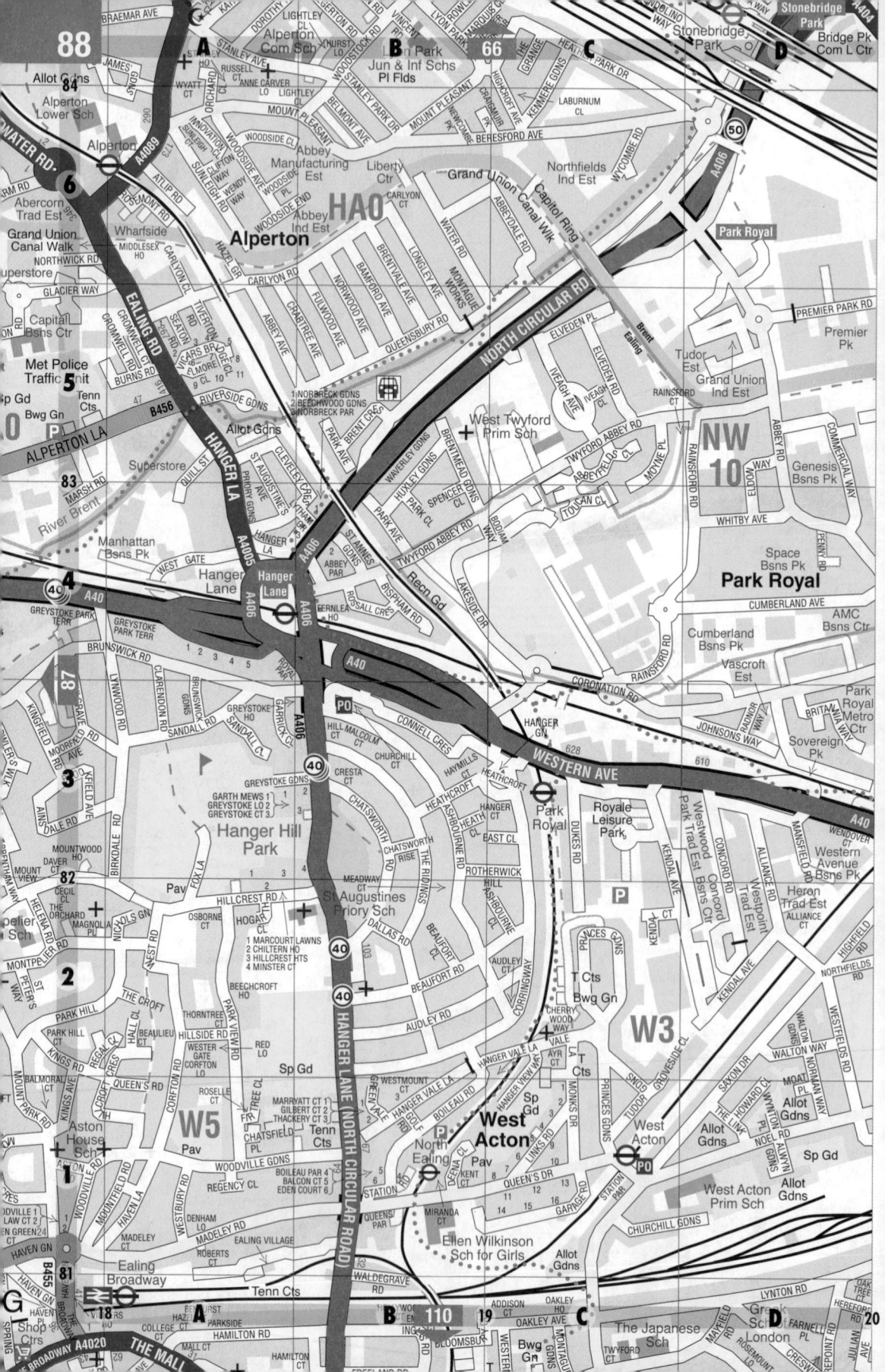

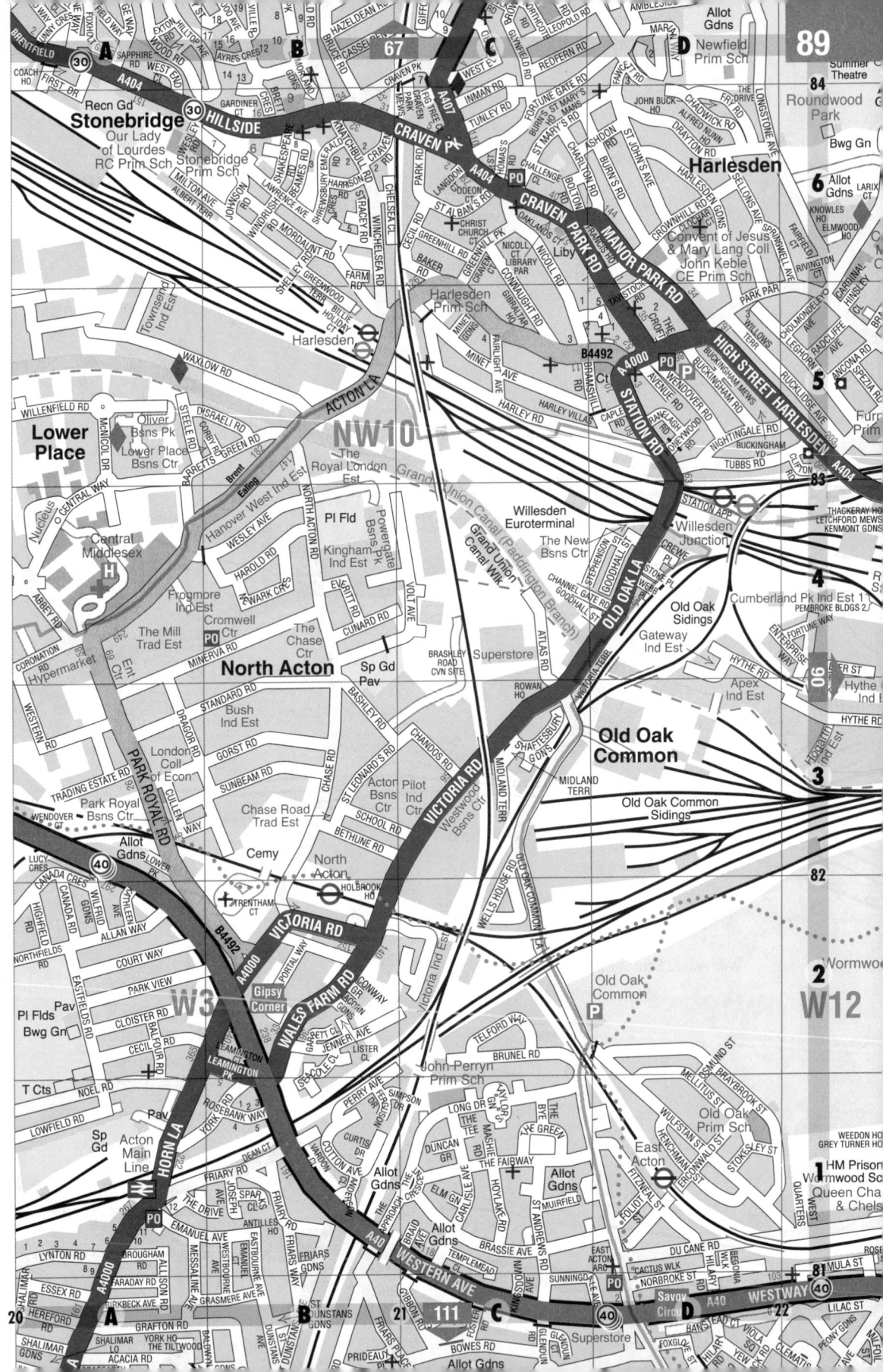

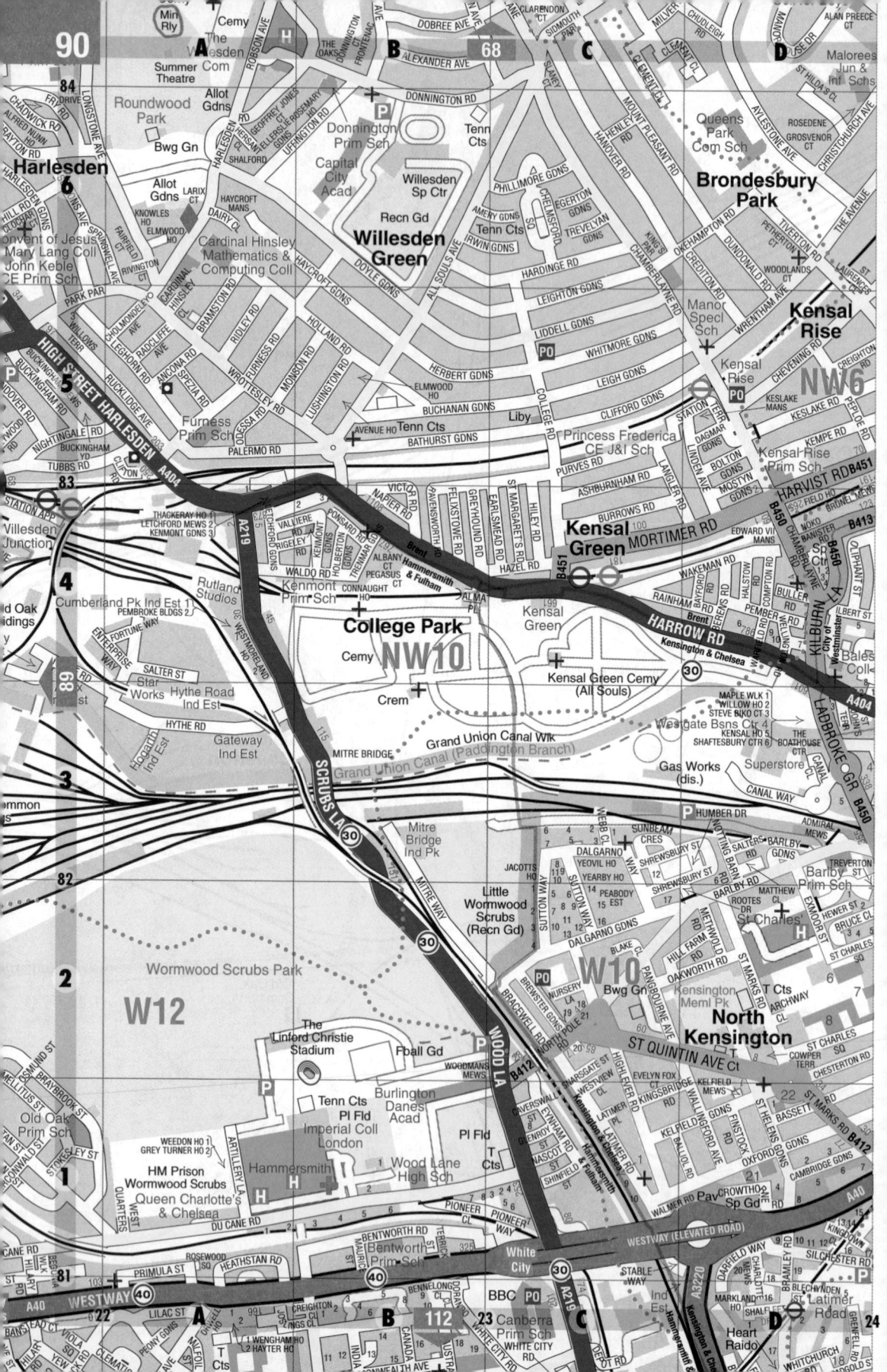

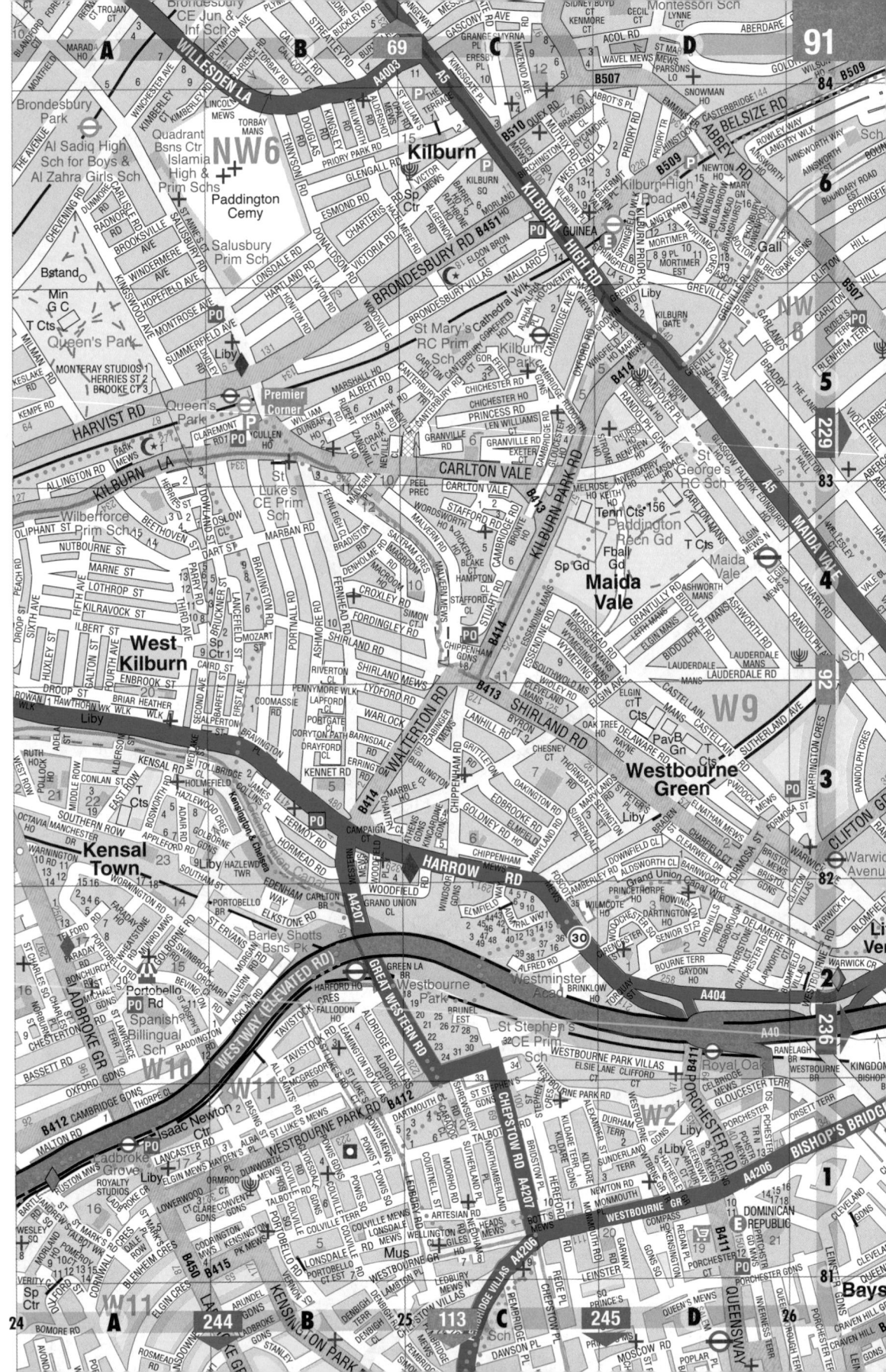

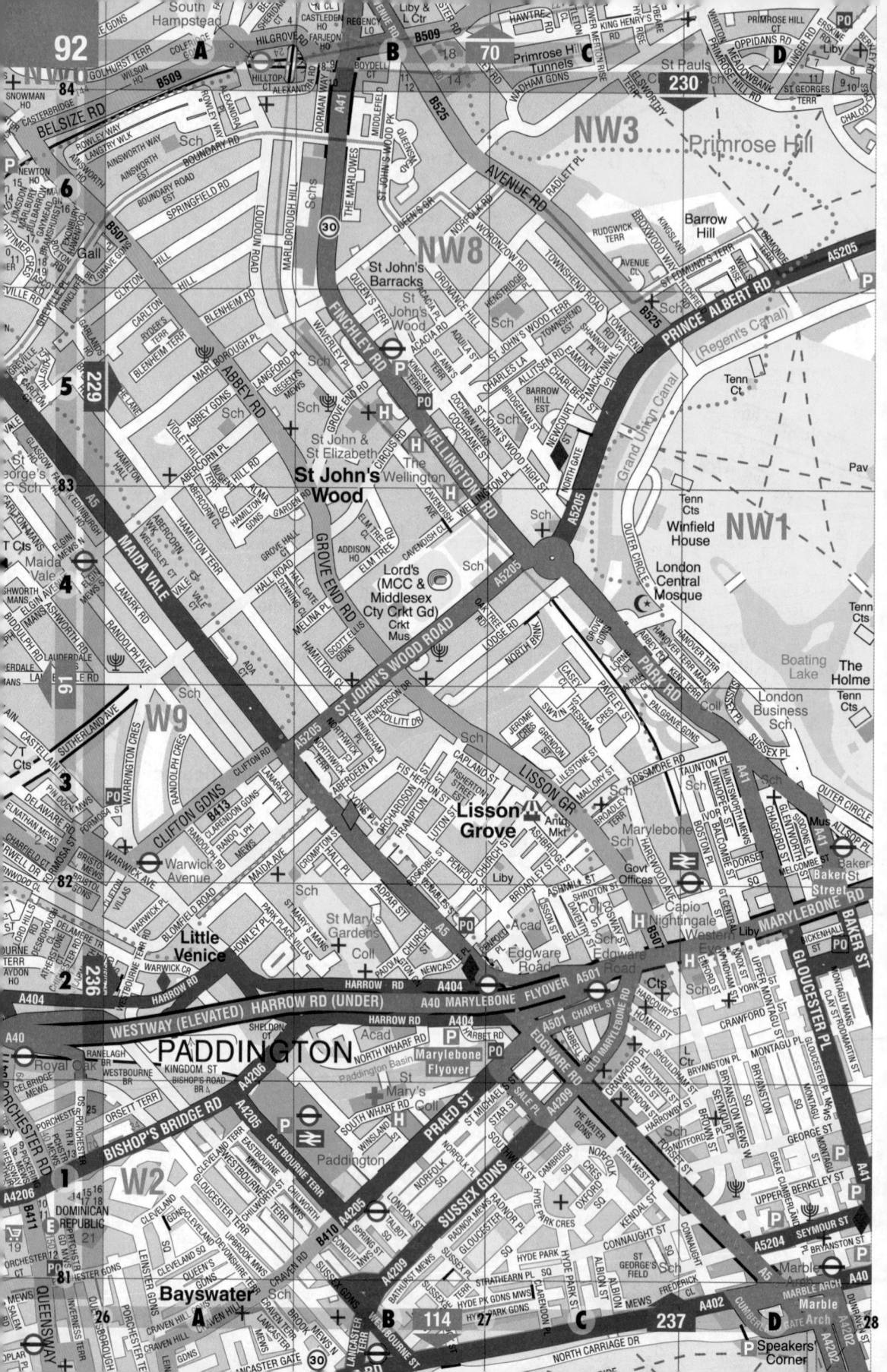

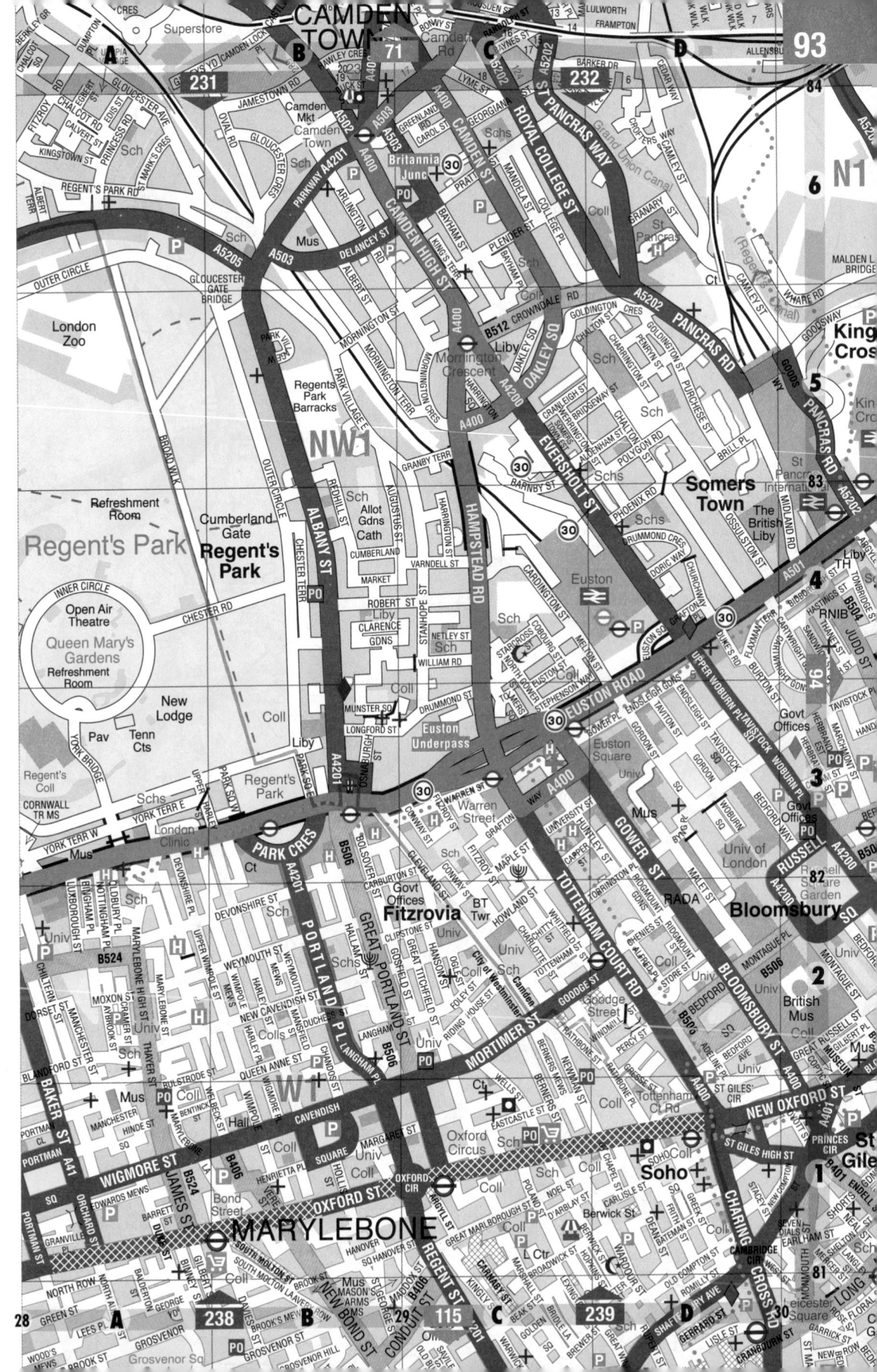

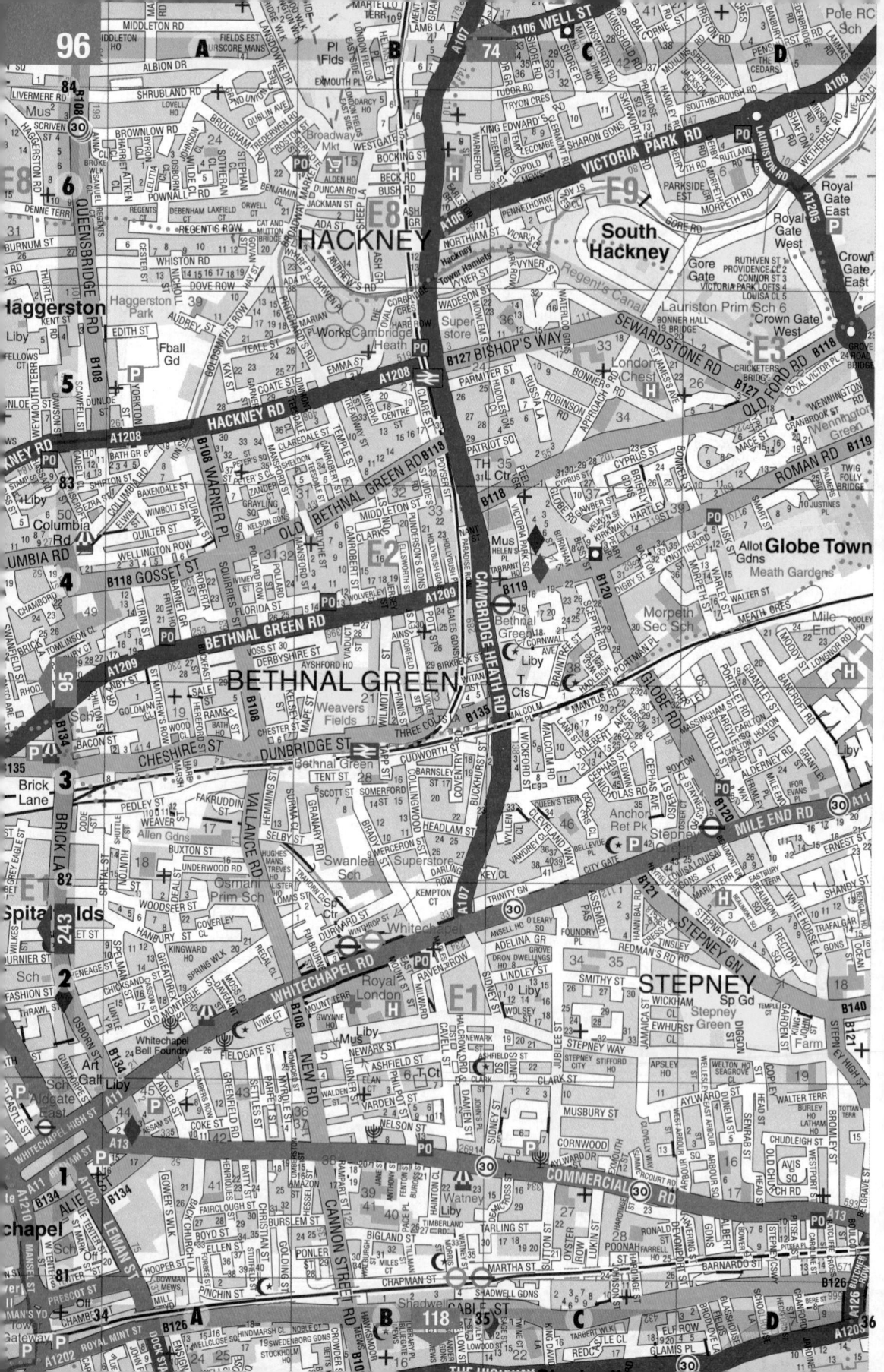

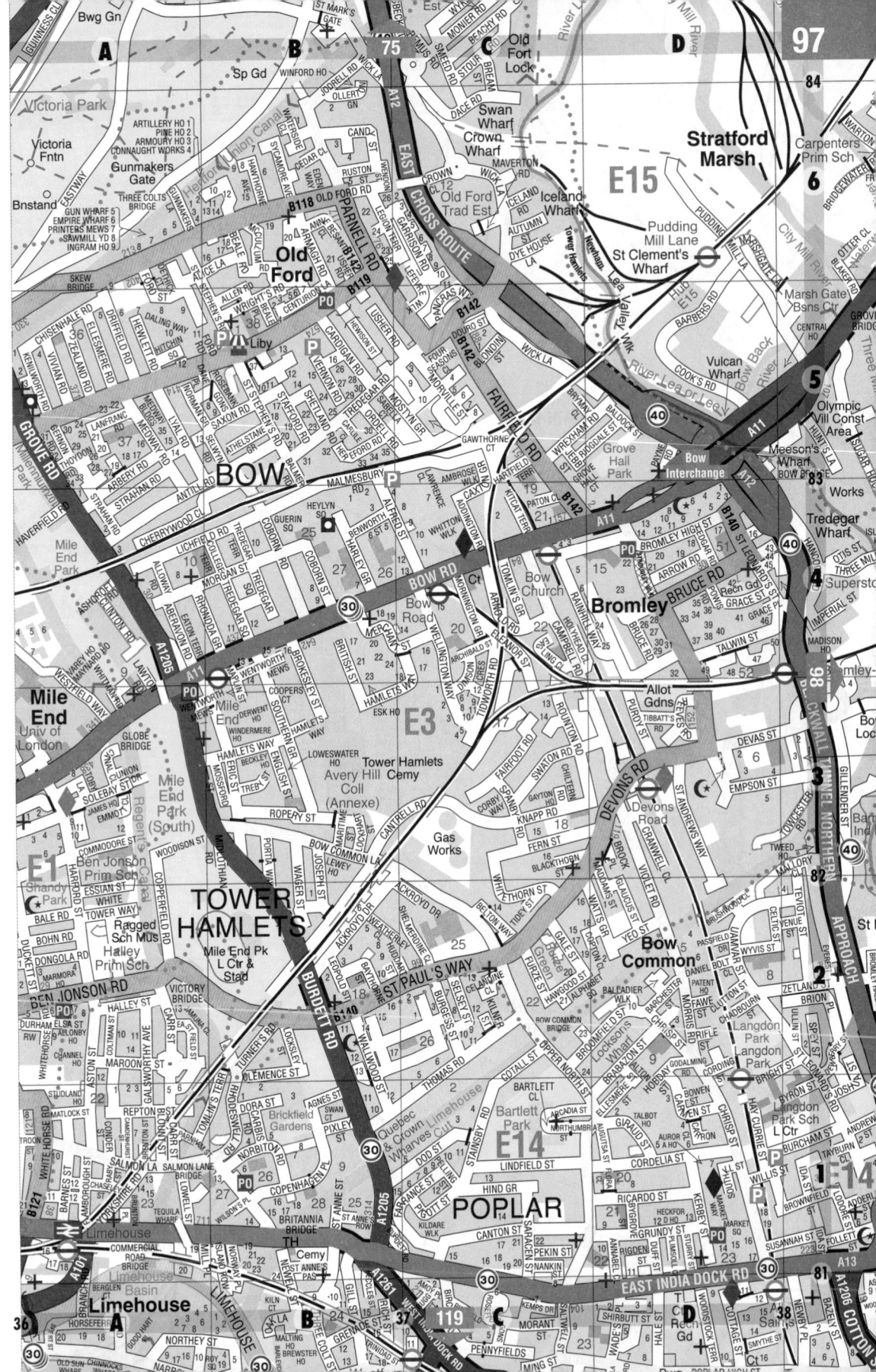

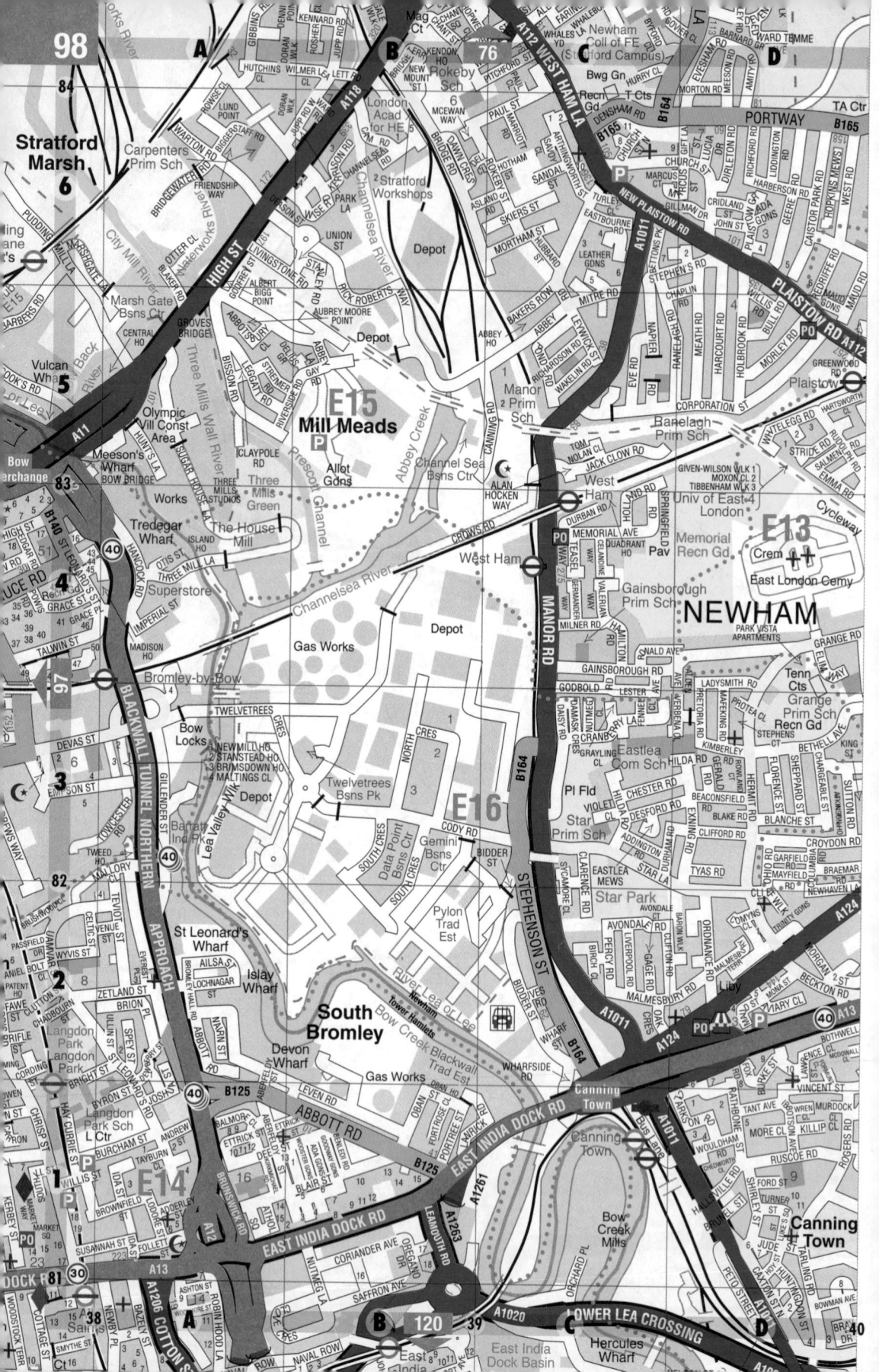

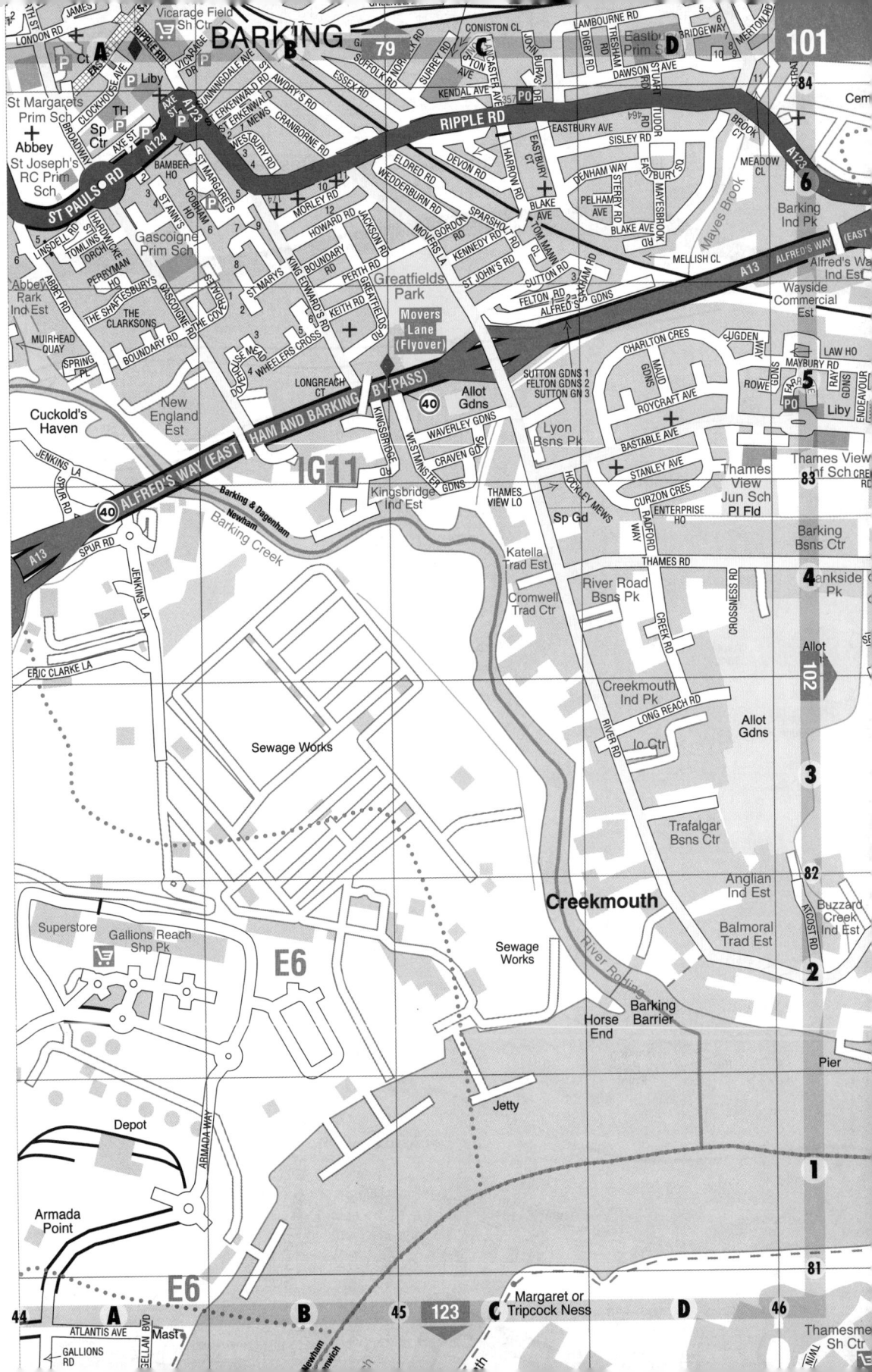

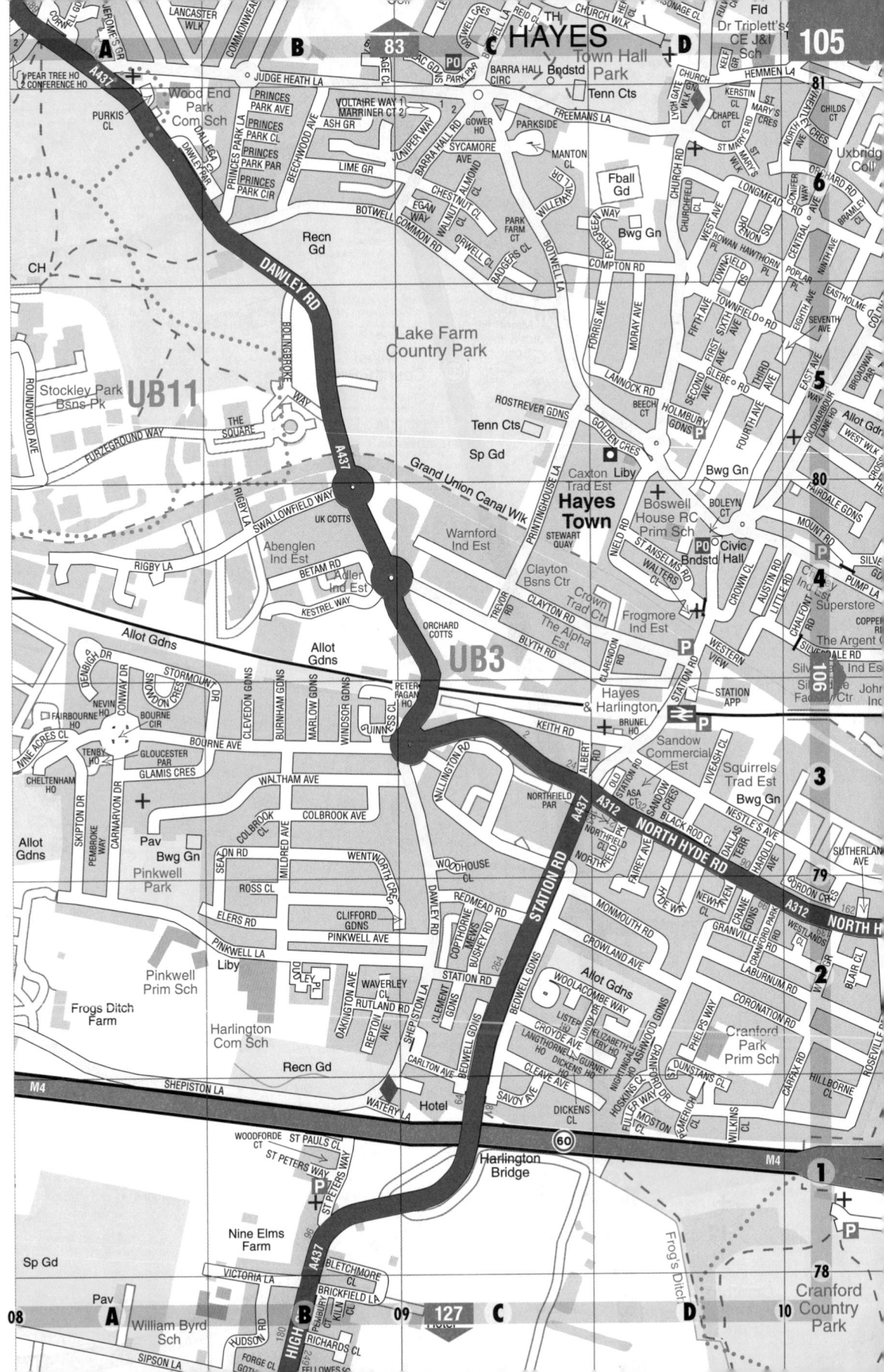

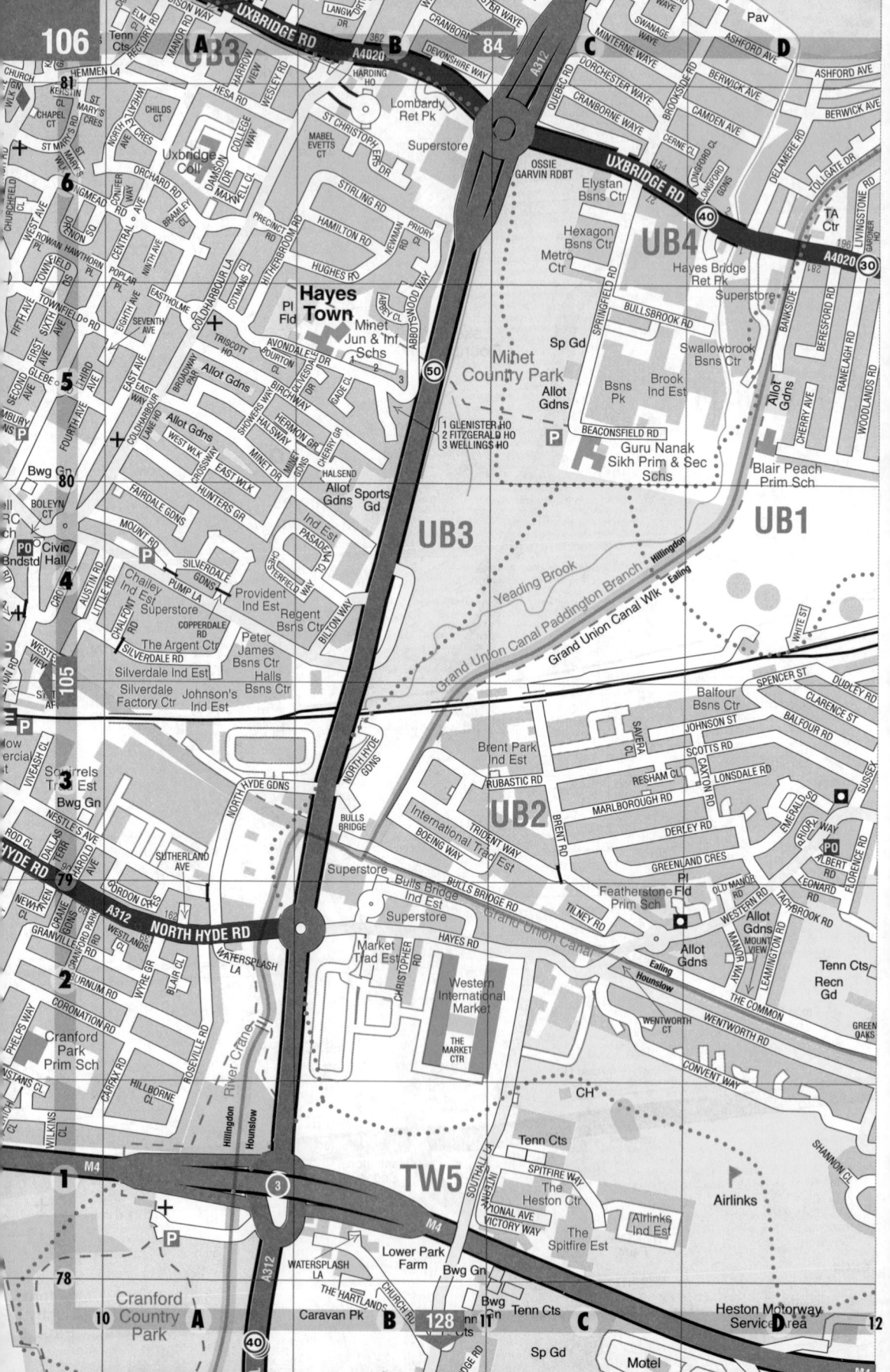

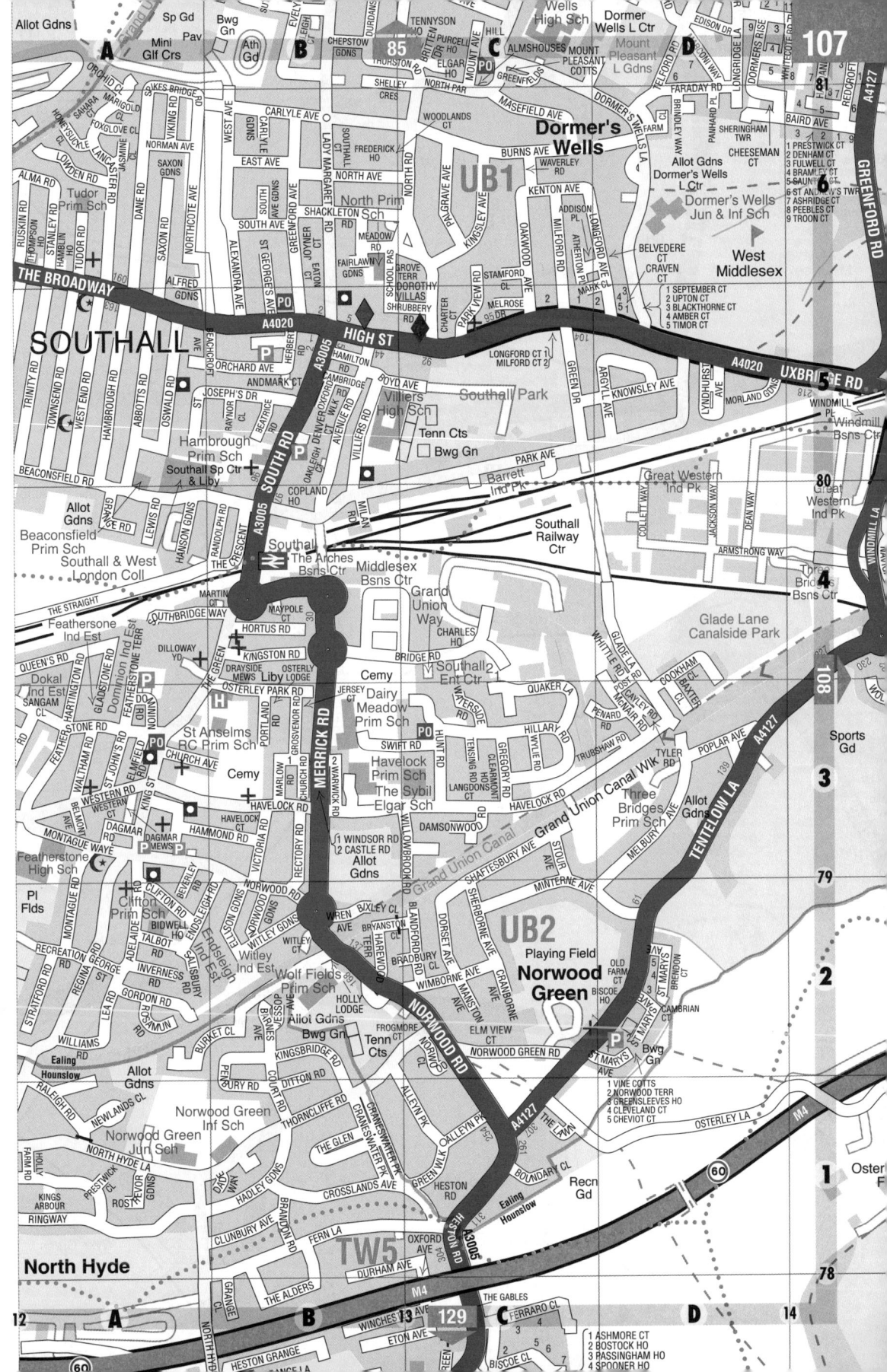

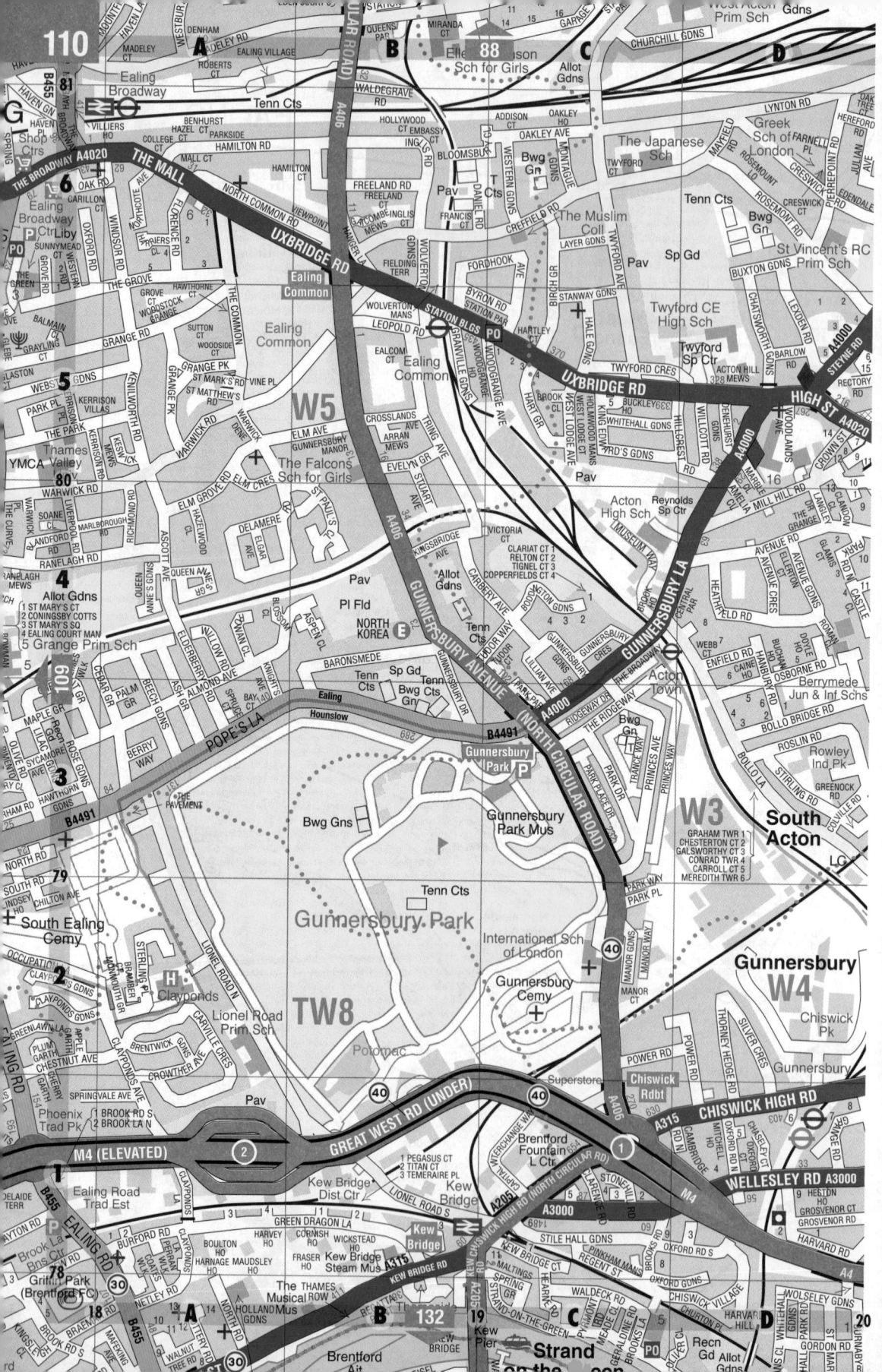

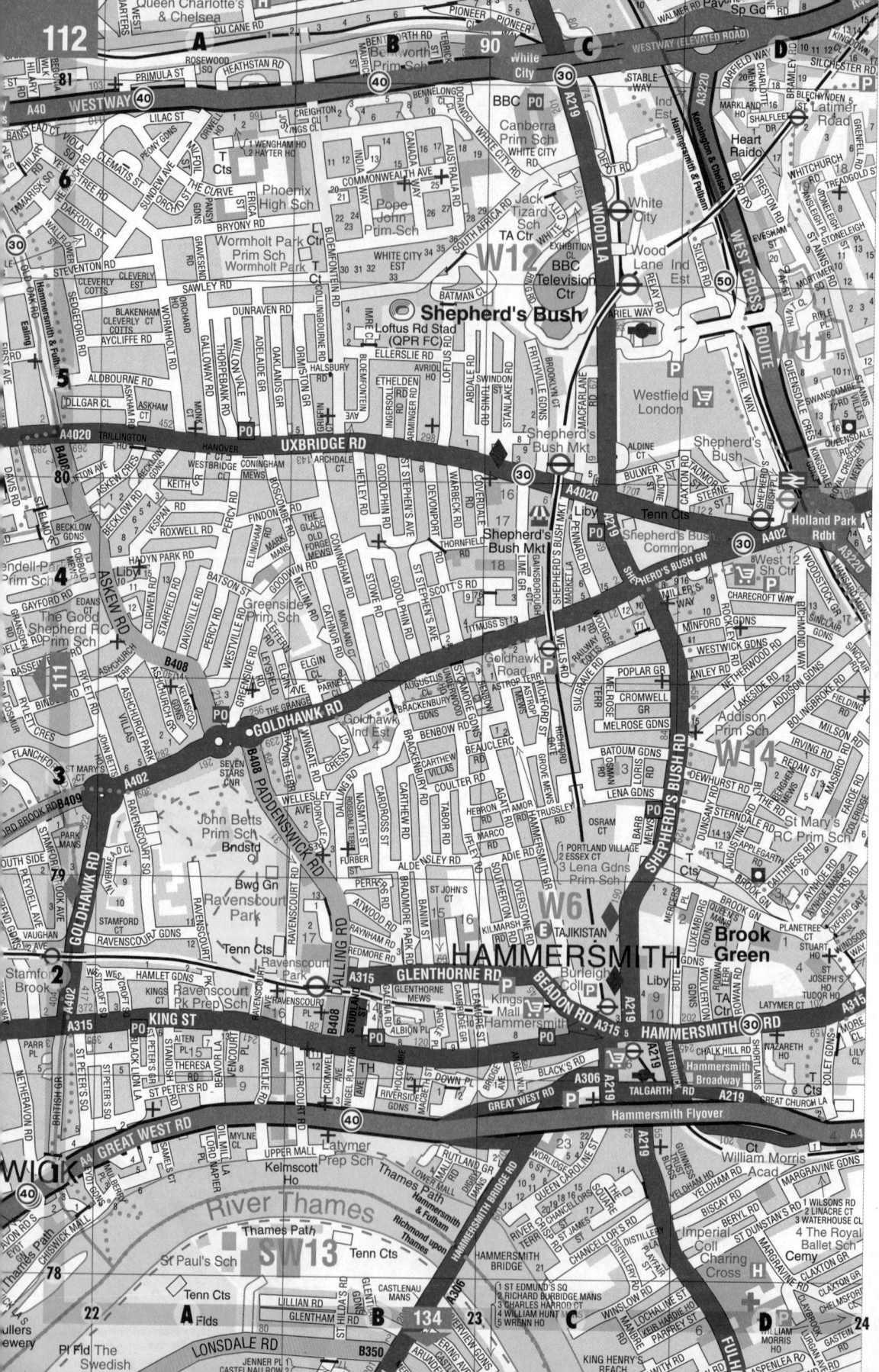

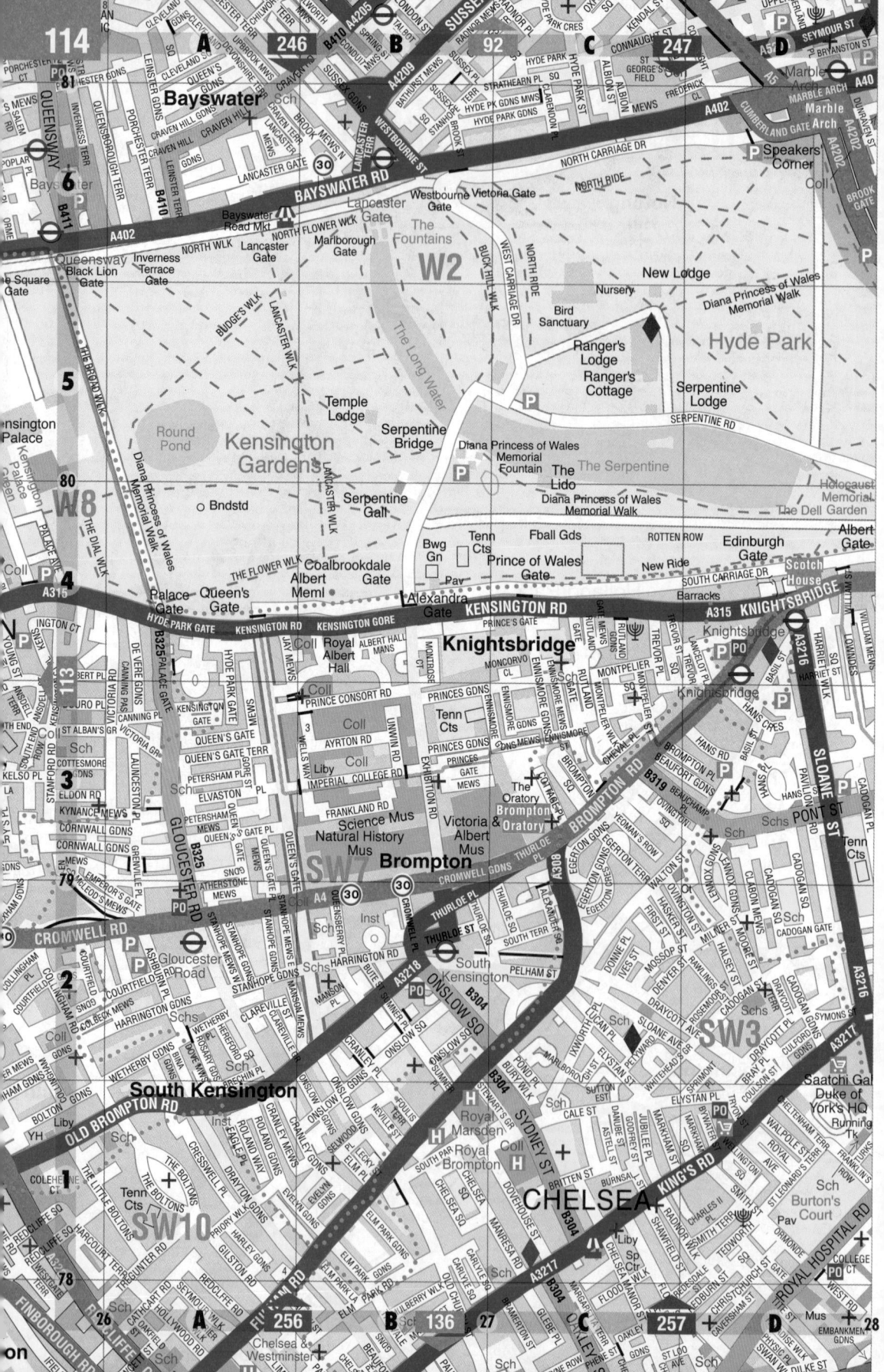

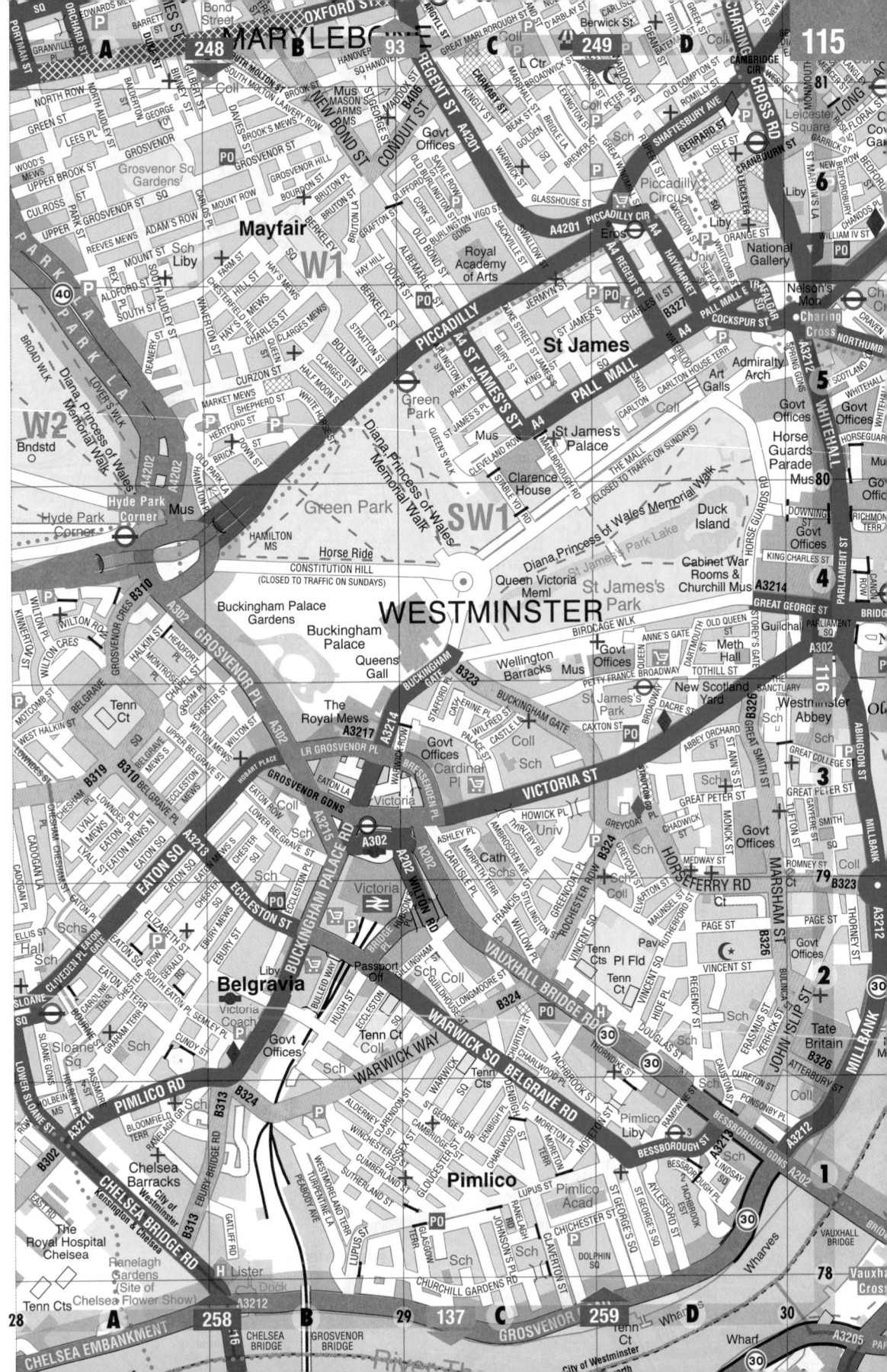

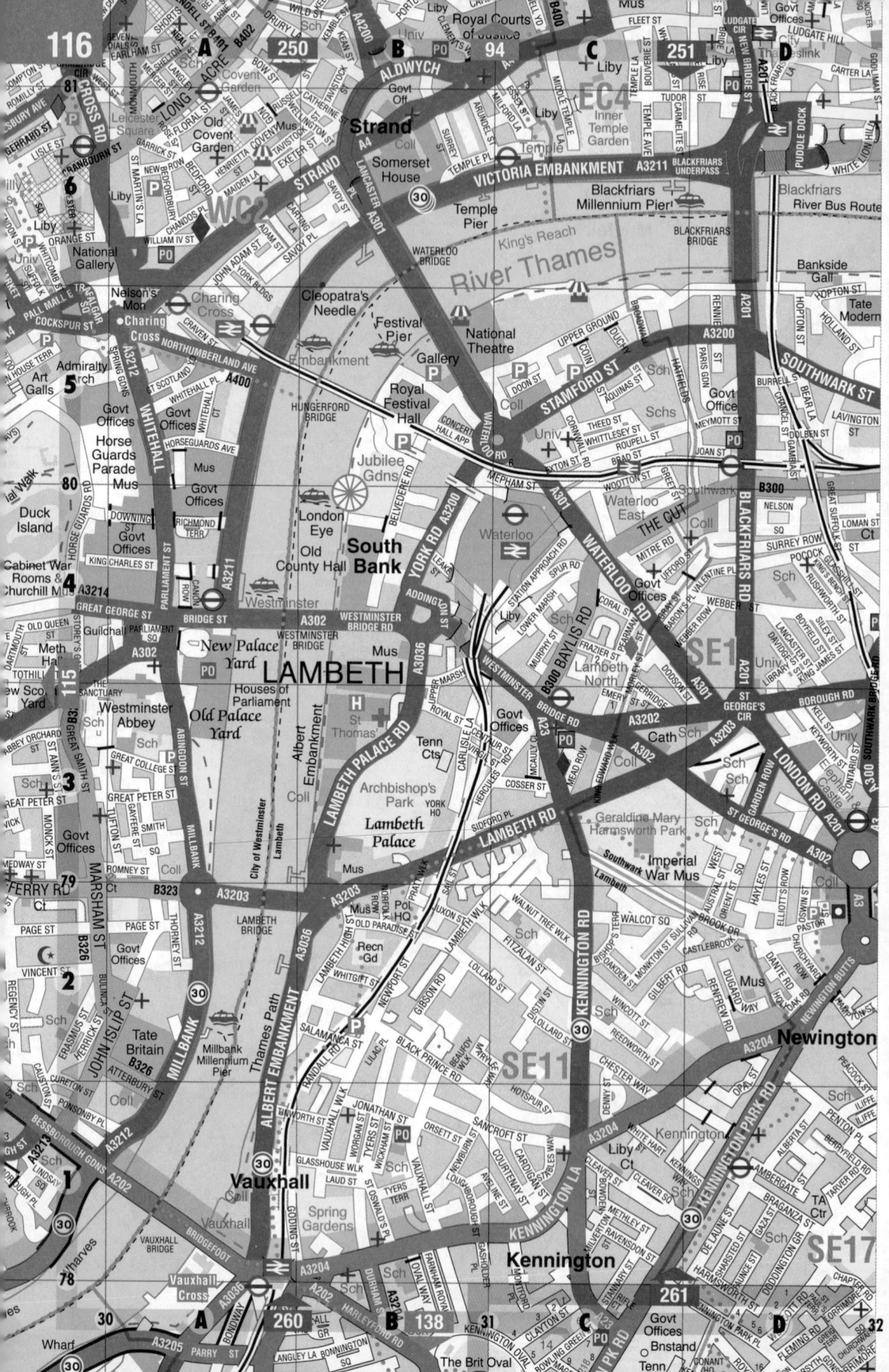

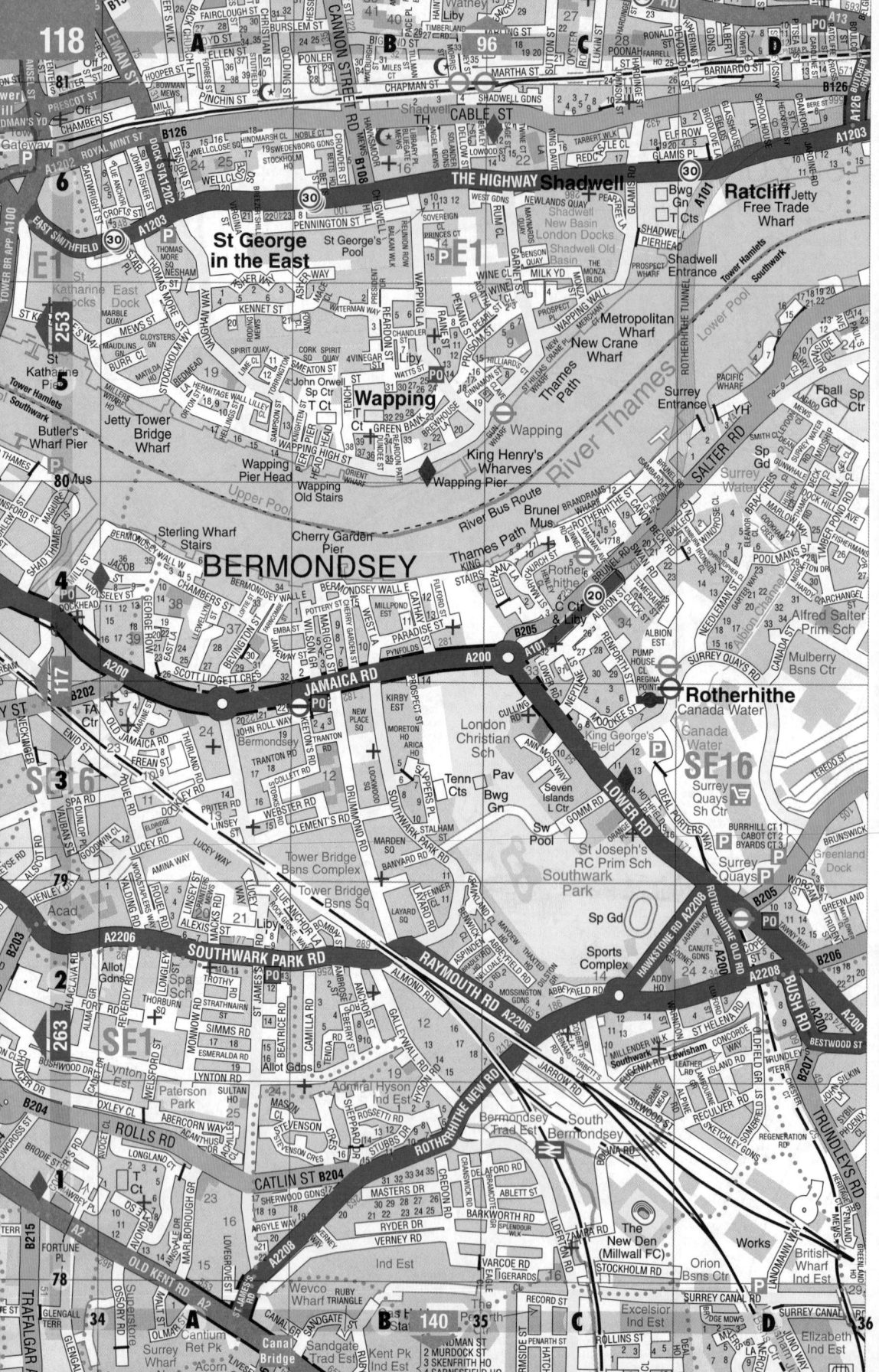

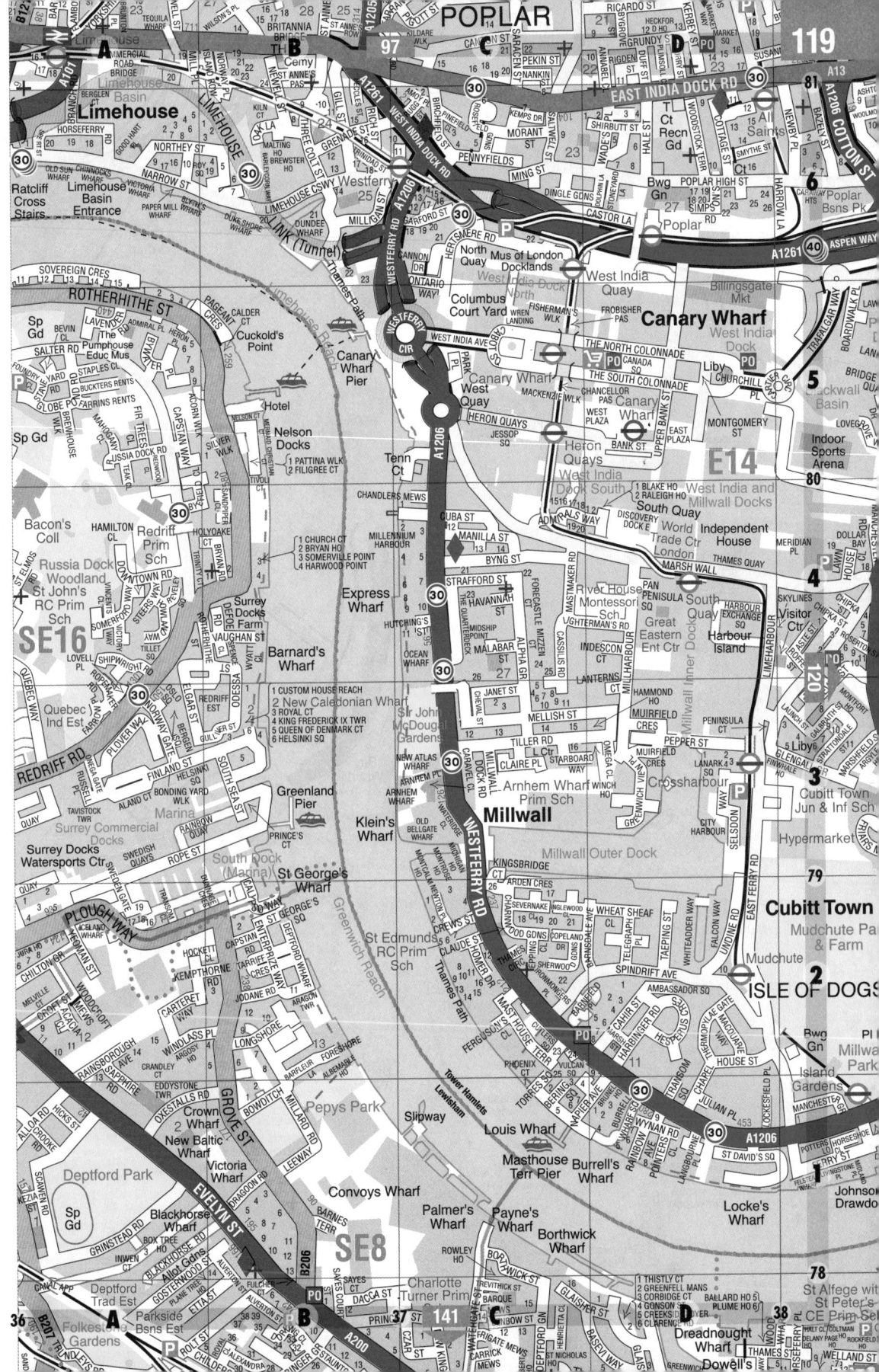

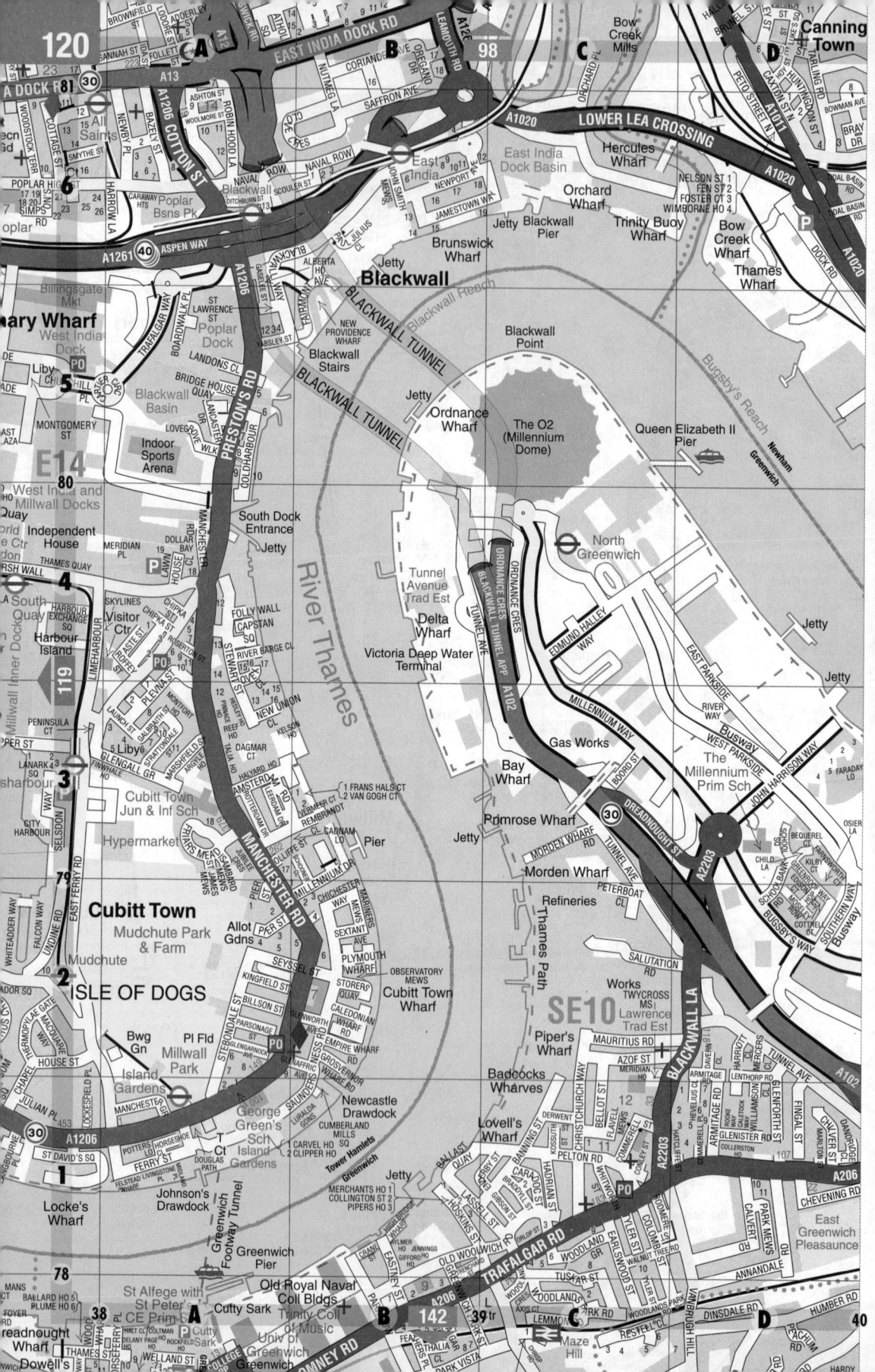

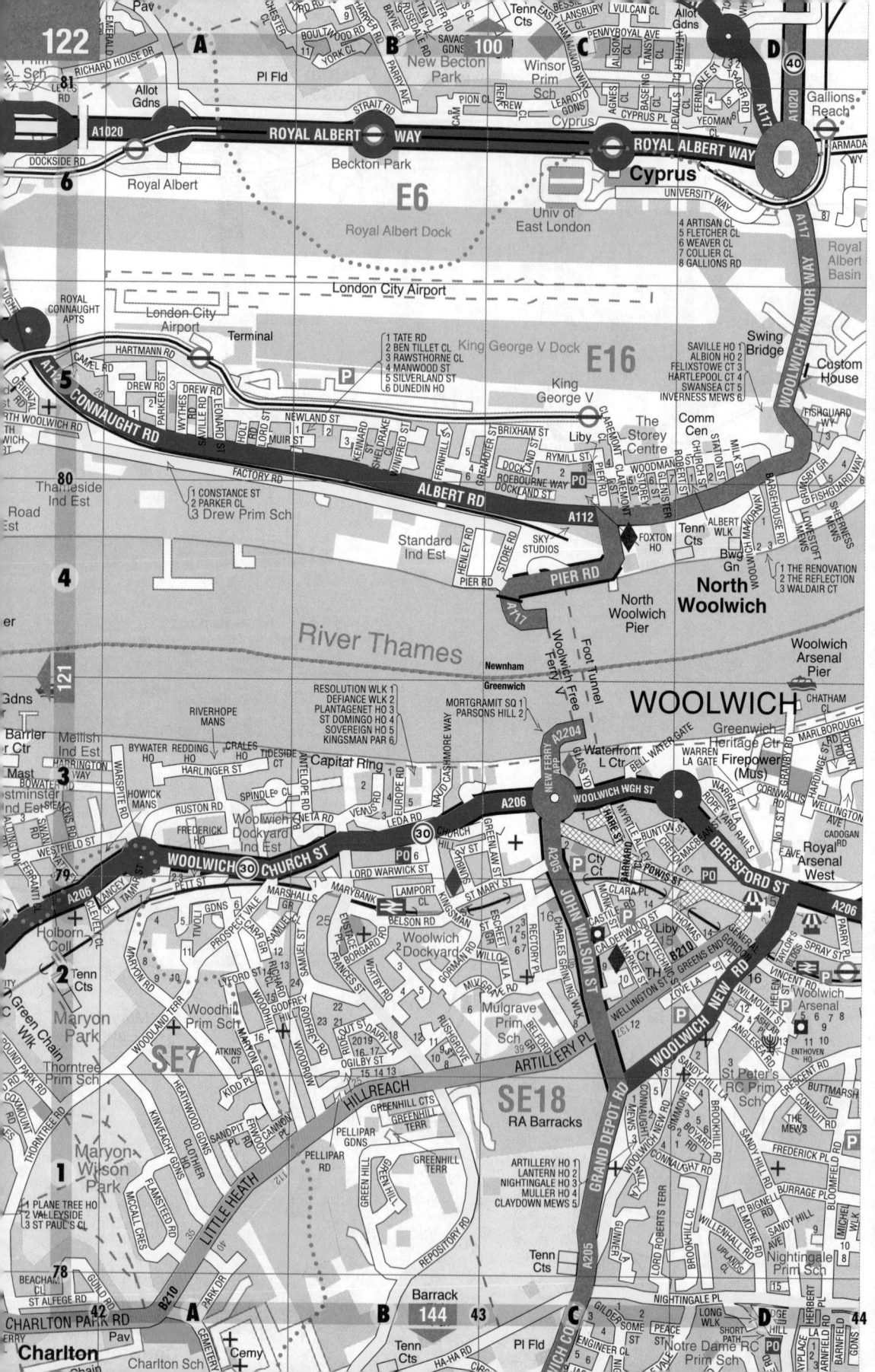

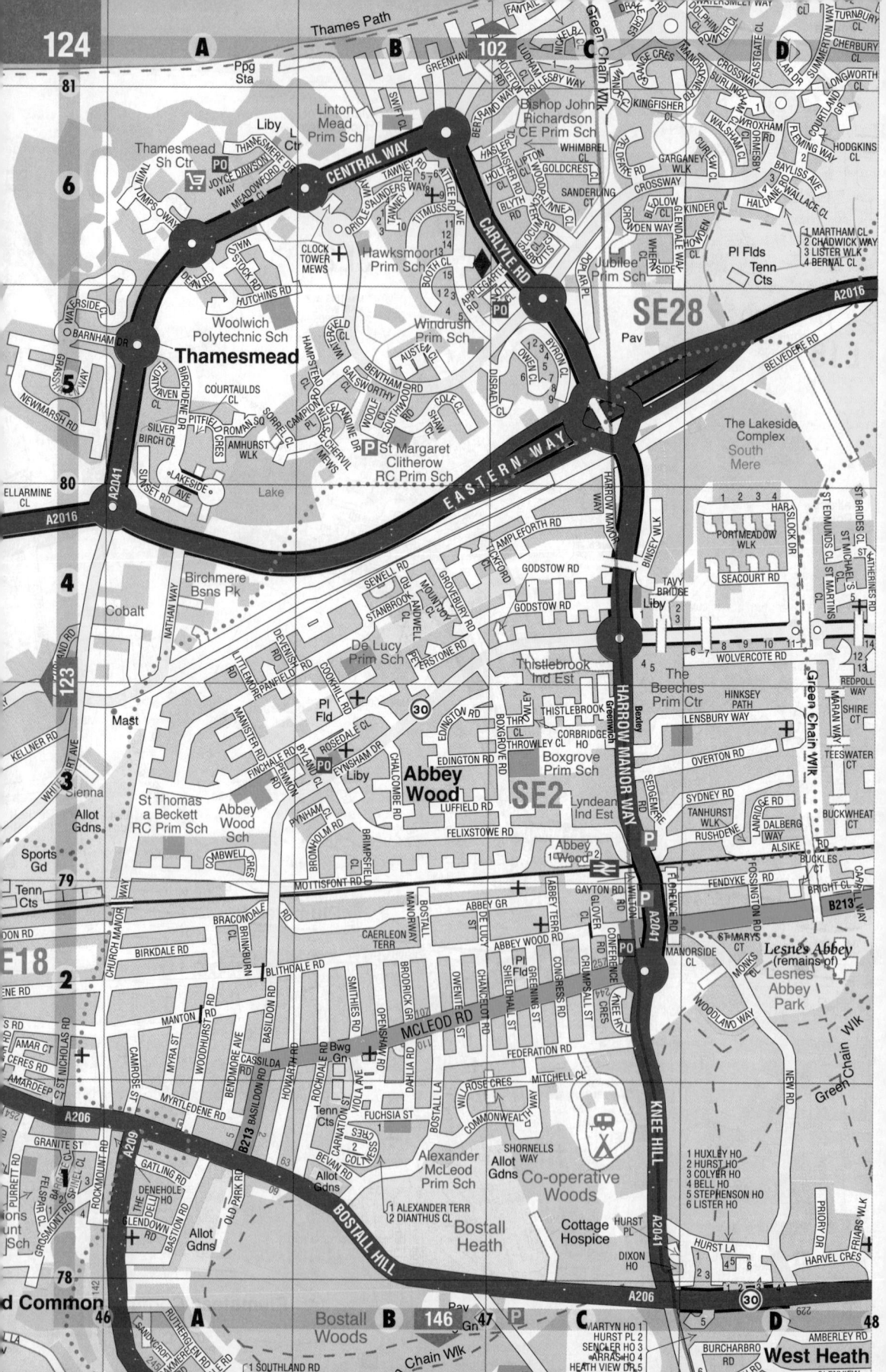

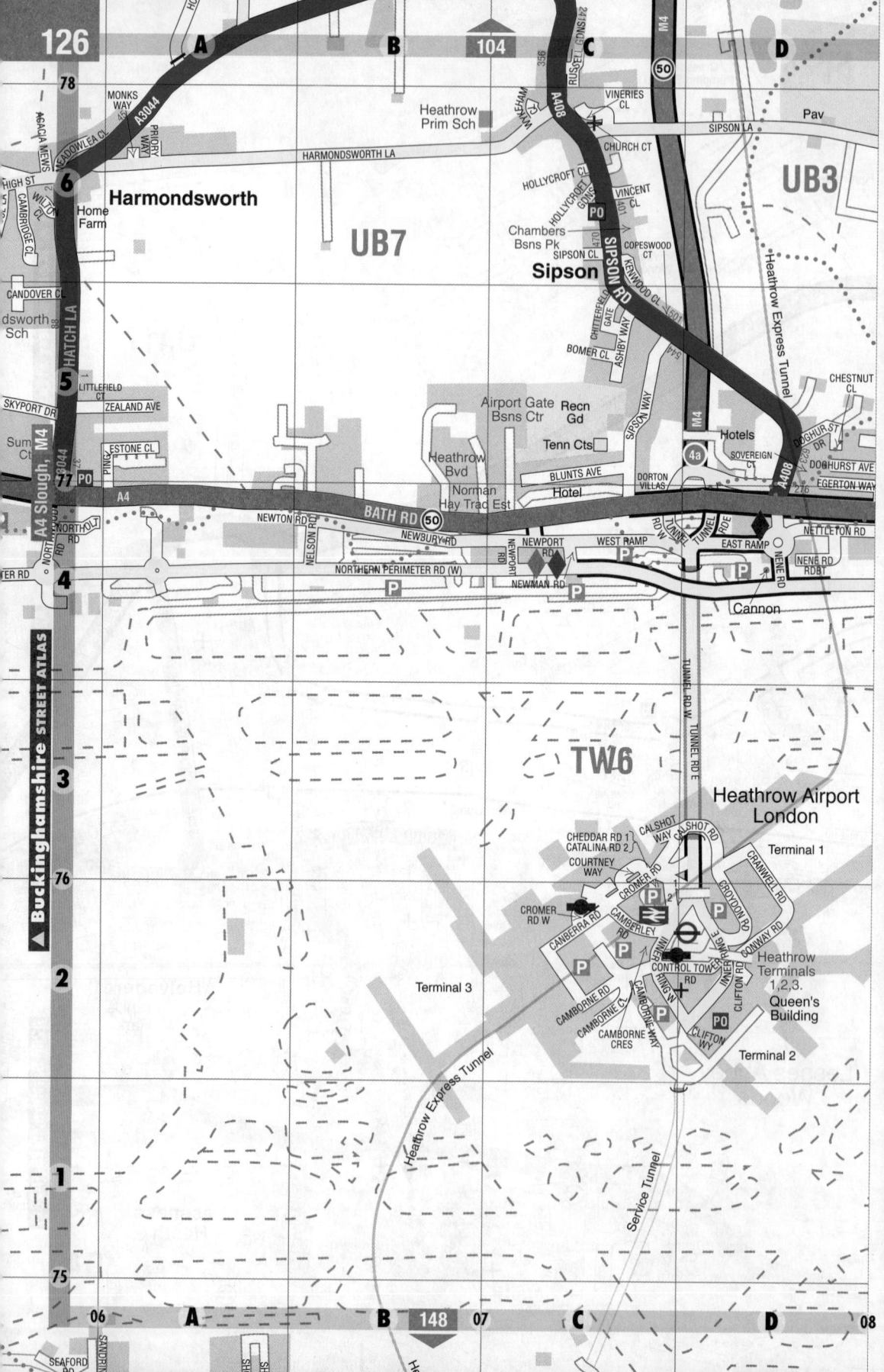

78

MONKS WAY
A3044

MEADOWLEA CL

PRIORY WAY

High St

ACACIA MEWS

WILTON

CAMBRIDGE CL

6

Home Farm

Harmondsworth

CANDOVER CL

dsworth Sch

88

HATCH LA

5

LITTLEFIELD CT

SKYPORT DR

ZEALAND AVE

Sum Ct

North A4 Slough, M4

A3044

77 PO

PING

ESTONE CL

A4

4

NORTHOLT RD

ER RD

UB7

HARMONDSWORTH LA

Heathrow Prim Sch

WINEHAM

A408

104

A3044

336

RUSSELL GDNS

C

50

VINERIES CL

SIPSON LA

Pav

CHURCH CT

HOLLYCROFT CL

HOLLYCROFT GDNS

PO

VINCENT CL

A401

Sipson

Chambers Bsns Pk

SIPSON CL

SIPSON RD

KENWOOD CL

CHITTERFIELD GATE

BOMER CL

ASHBY WAY

COPESWOOD CT

M4

UB3

Heathrow Express Tunnel

CHESTNUT CL

DOGHUR ST DR

A408

D

Airport Gate Bsns Ctr

Recn Gd

SIPSON WAY

Tenn Cts

Heathrow Bvd

Norman Hay Trad Est

BLUNTS AVE

Hotel

DORTON VILLAS

4a

Hotels

SOVEREIGN CT

DOGHURST AVE

EGERTON WAY

276

NEWTON RD

NELSON RD

BATH RD 50

NEWBURY RD

NEWPORT RD

WEST RAMP

P

NENE RD

EAST RAMP

P

NETTLETON RD

NENE RD RDBT

NORTHERN PERIMETER RD (W)

NEWMAN RD

P

P

TUNNEL RD W

TUNNEL RD E

Cannon

P

TW6

Heathrow Airport London

CALSHOT WAY

CALSHOT RD

Terminal 1

CHEDDAR RD 1
CATALINA RD 2

COURTNEY WAY

CROMER RD

CRANWELL RD

CROMER RD W

CANBERRA RD

CAMBERLEY RD

P

CROYDON RD

P

INNER RING E

CONWAY RD

Terminal 3

CAMBORNE RD

CAMBORNE CL

CLIFTON RD

CONTROL TOW RD

INNER RING W

Heathrow Terminals 1,2,3. Queen's Building

CAMBORNE WAY

CLIFTON WY

PO

CAMBORNE CRES

Terminal 2

Heathrow Express Tunnel

Service Tunnel

3

76

2

1

75

06

A

B

148

07

C

D

08

SEAFORD RD

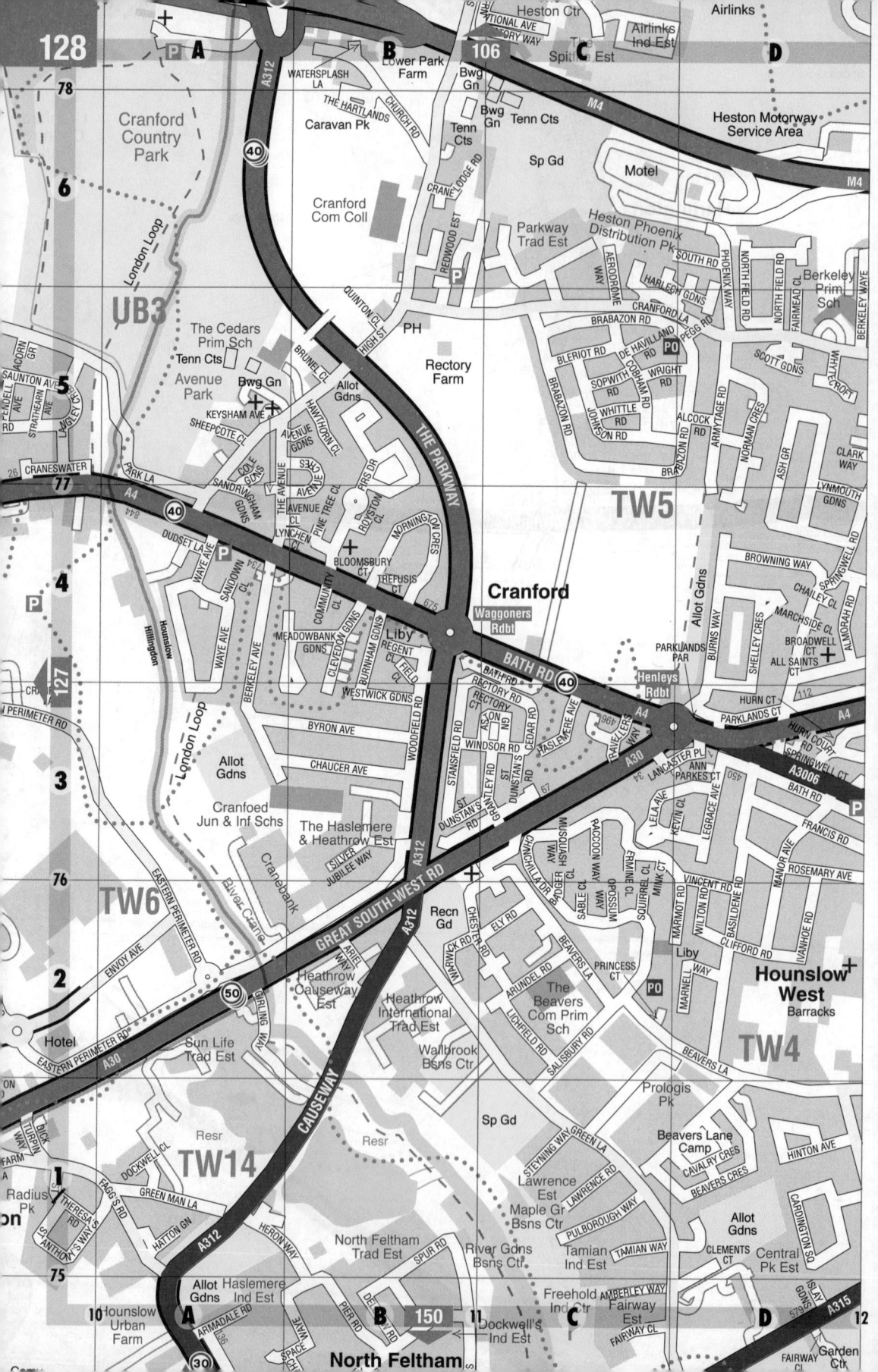

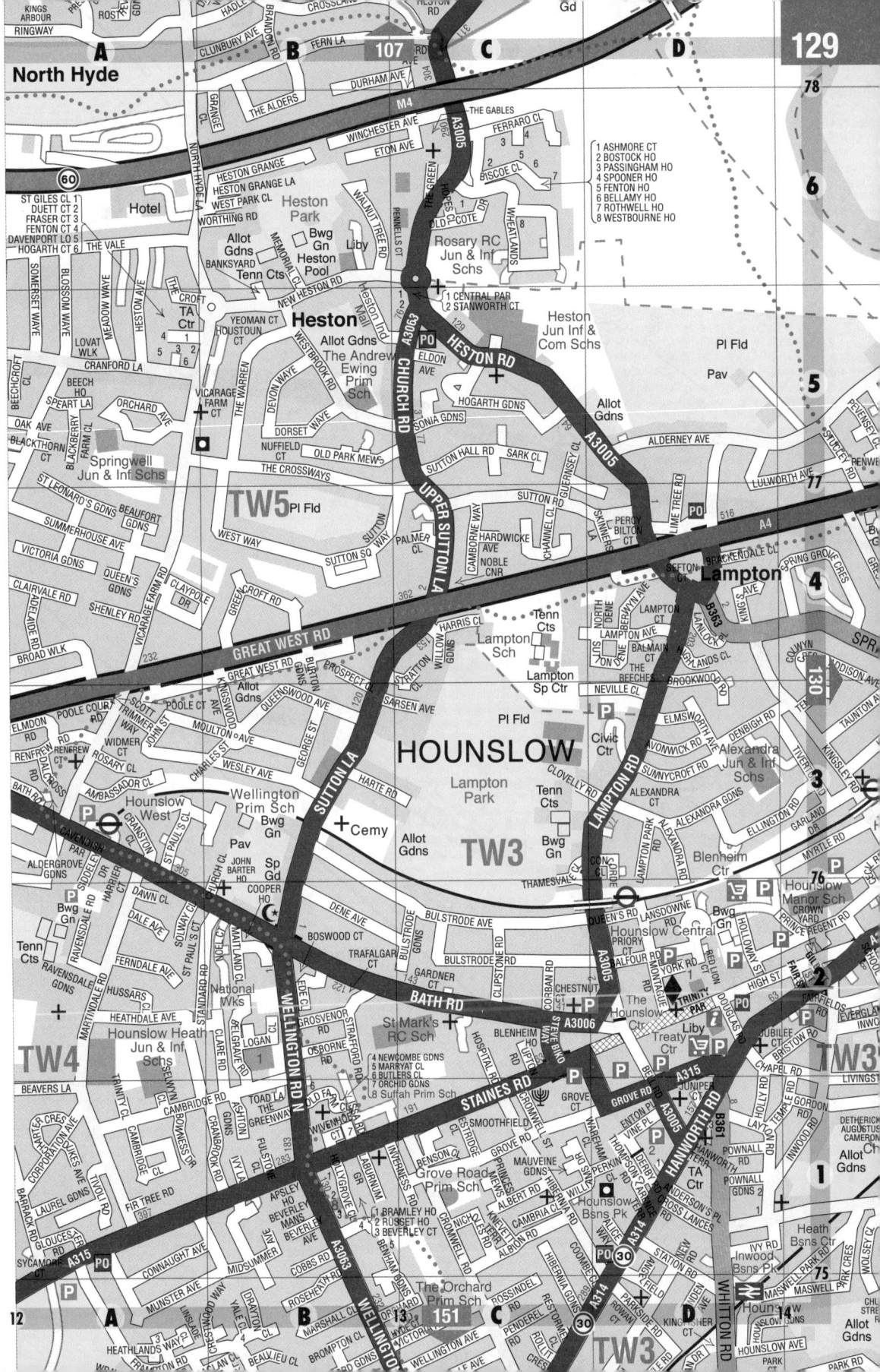

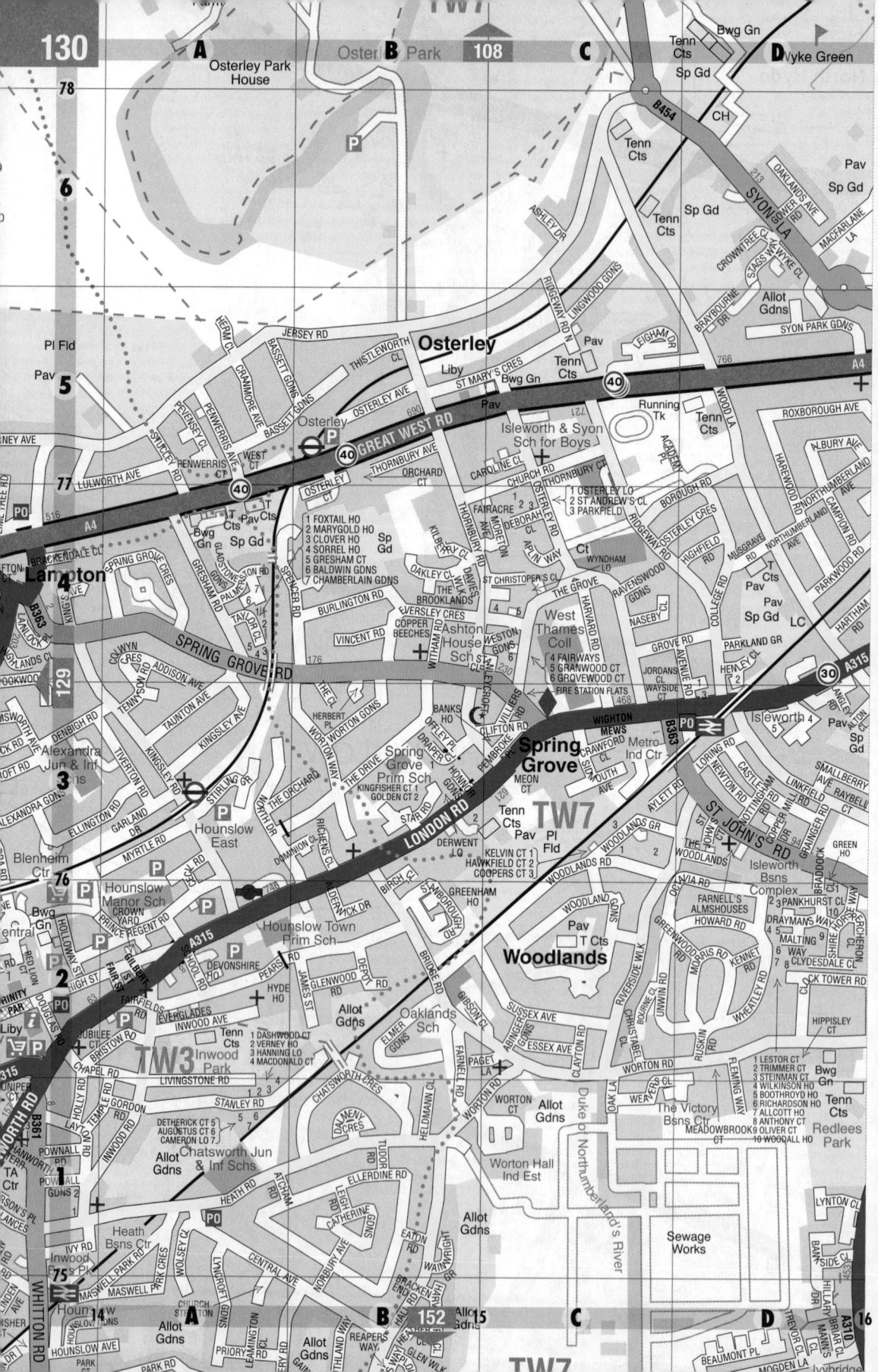

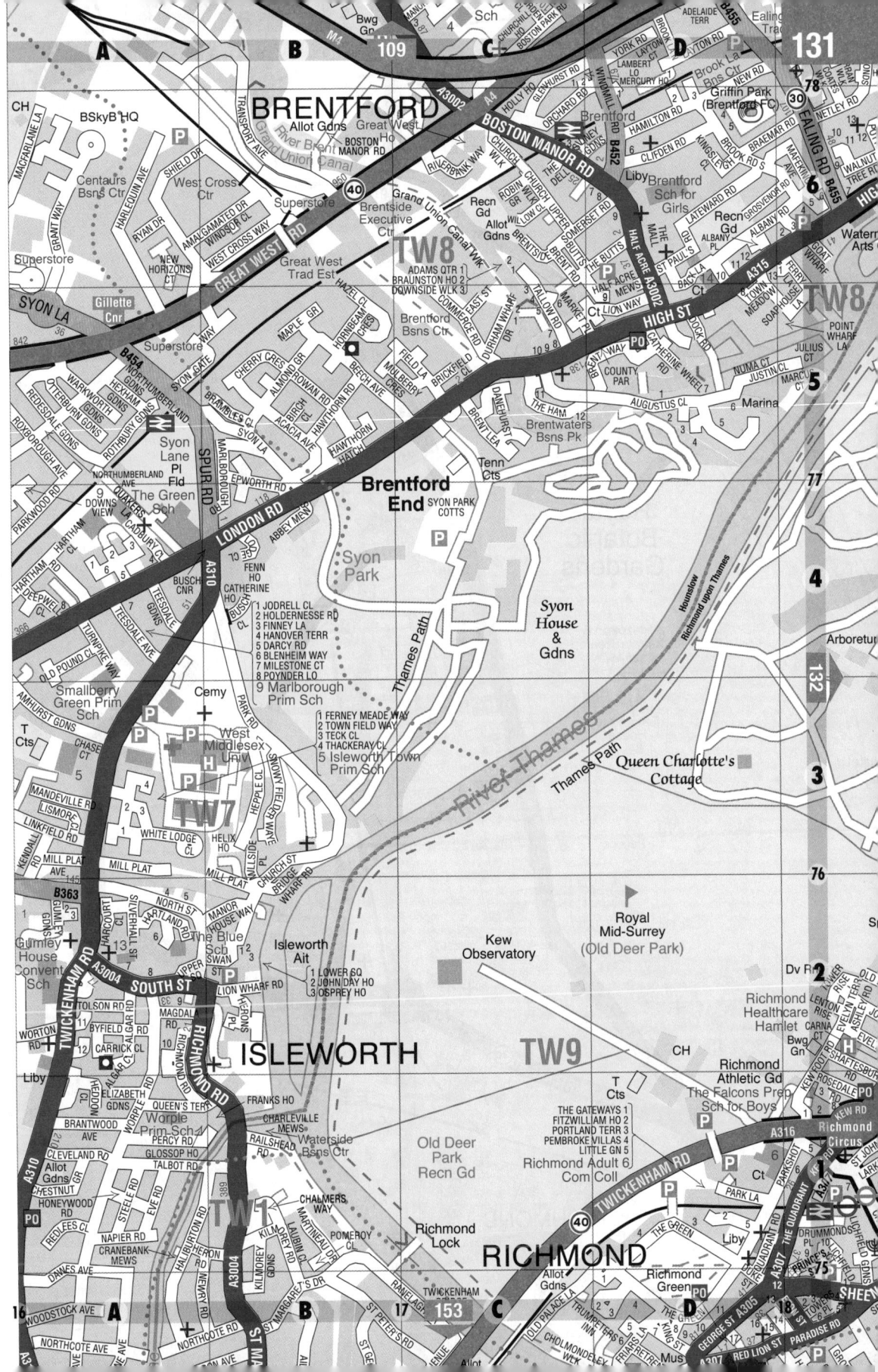

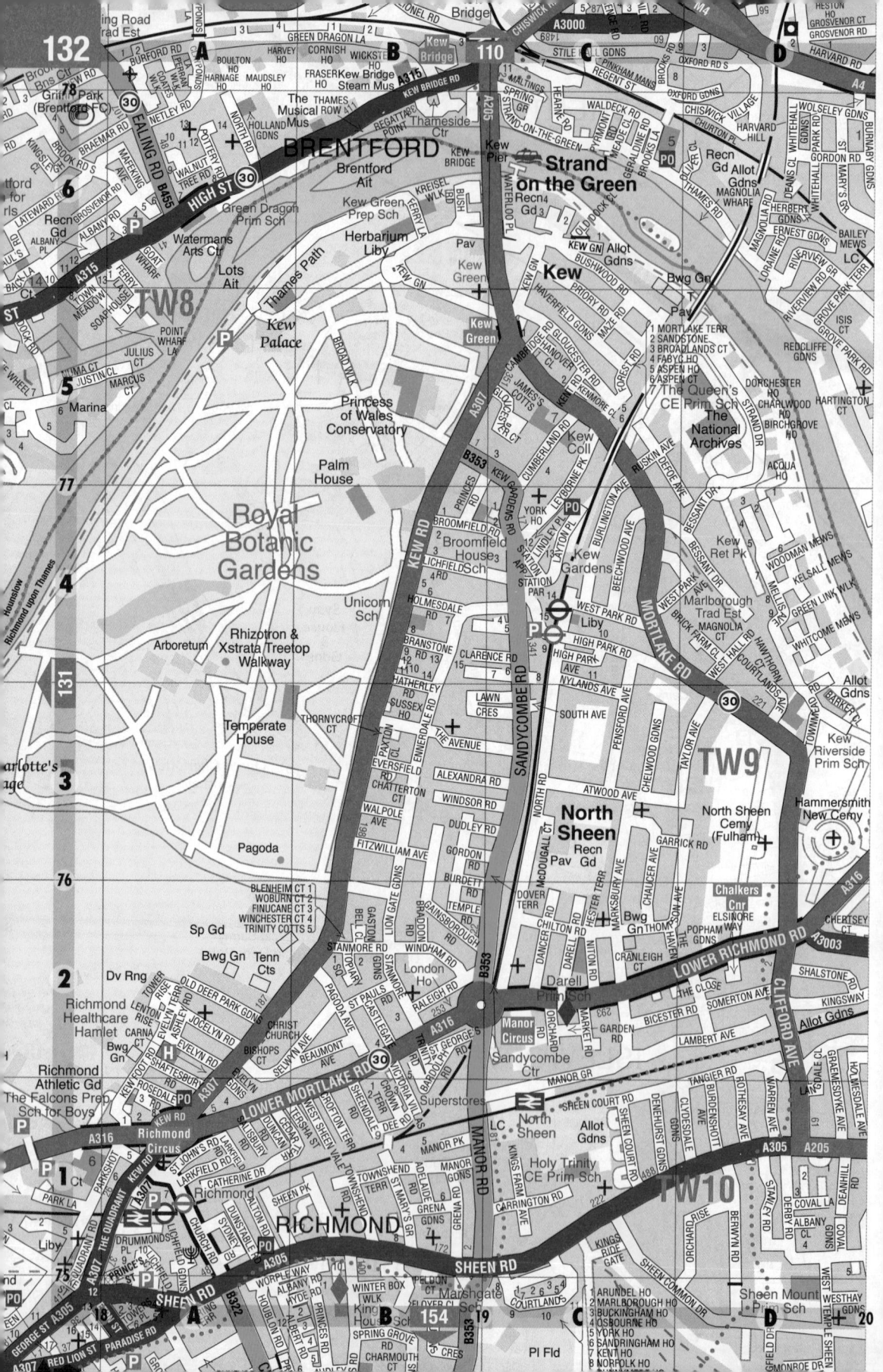

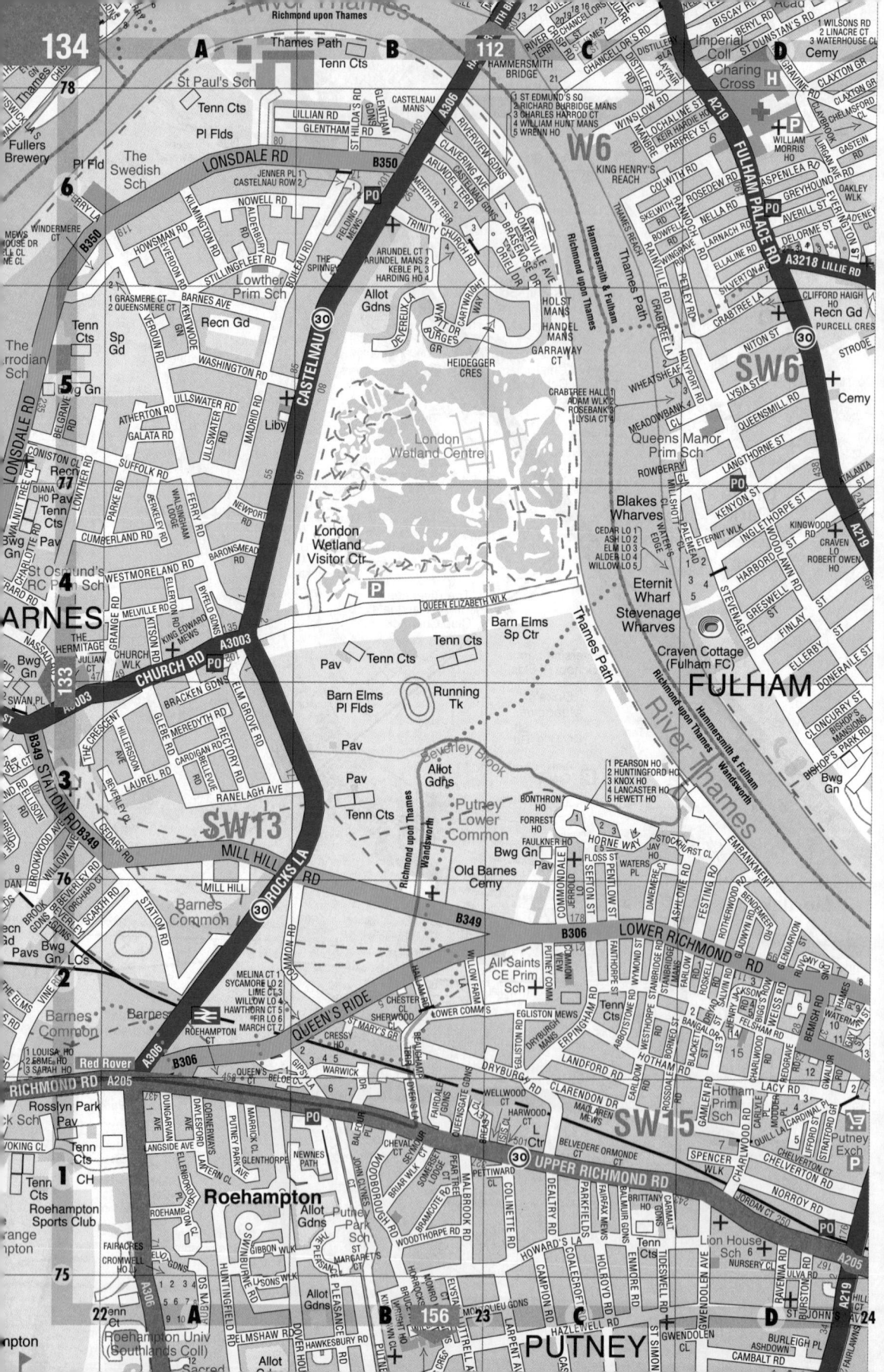

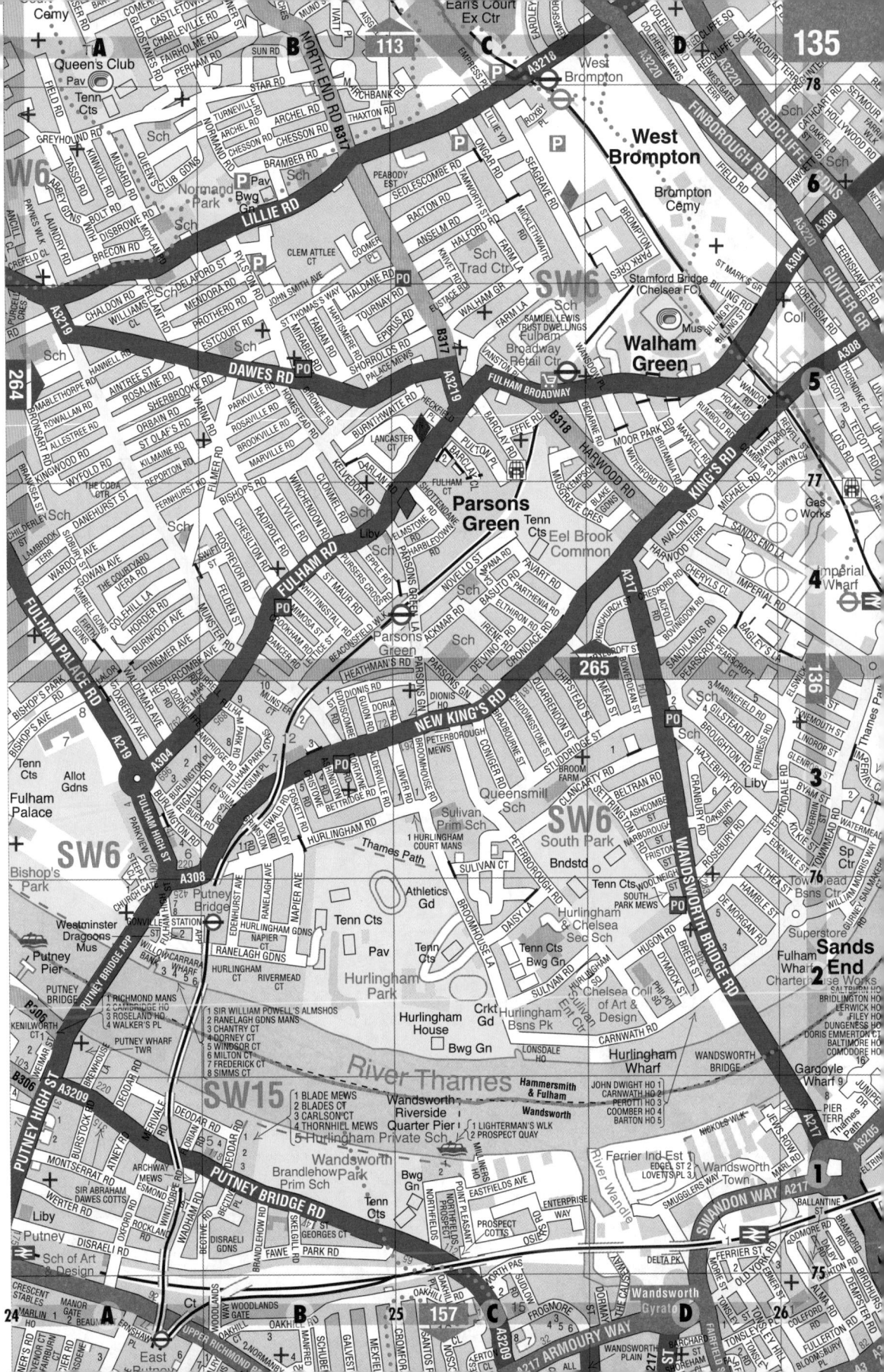

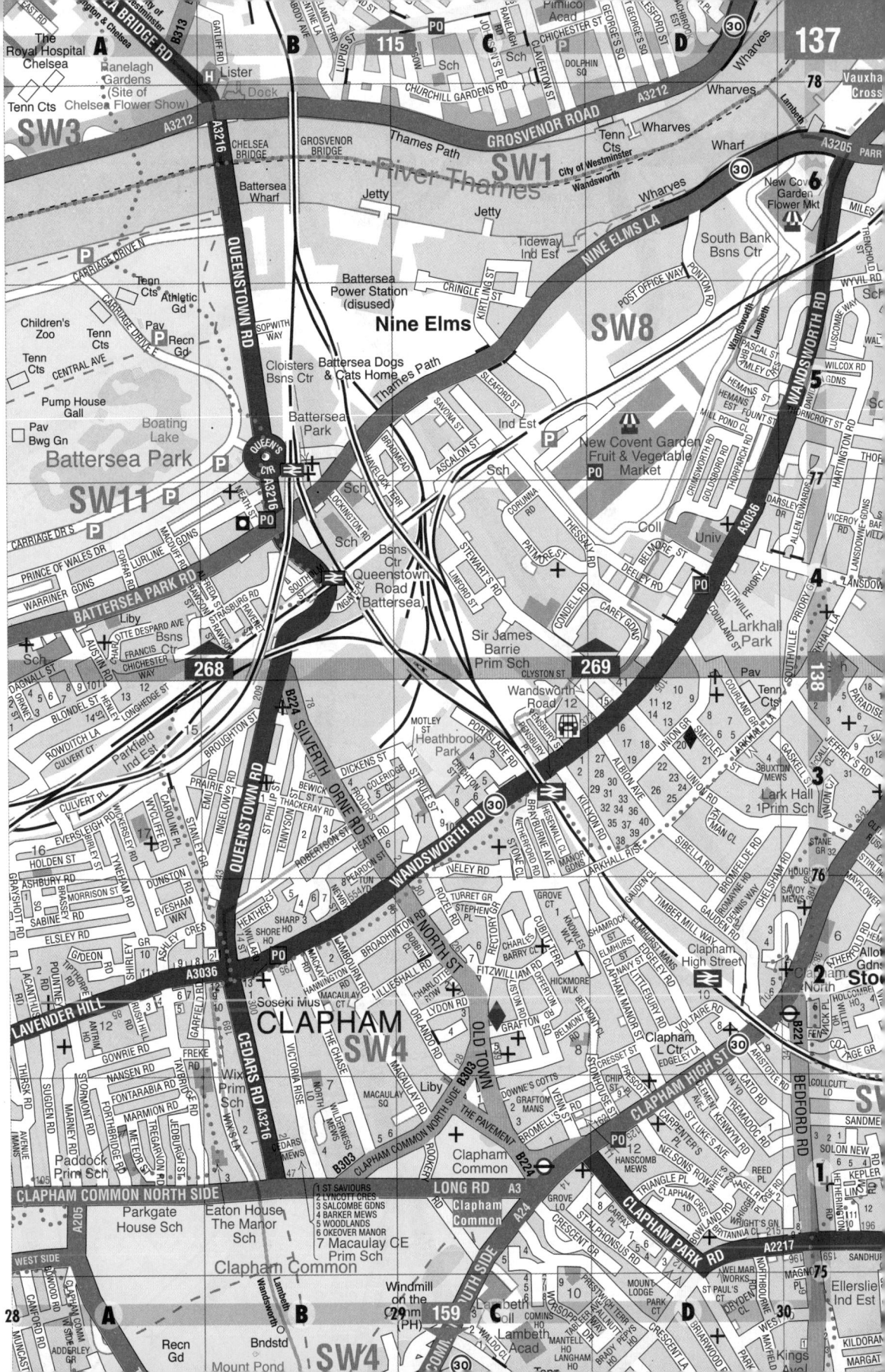

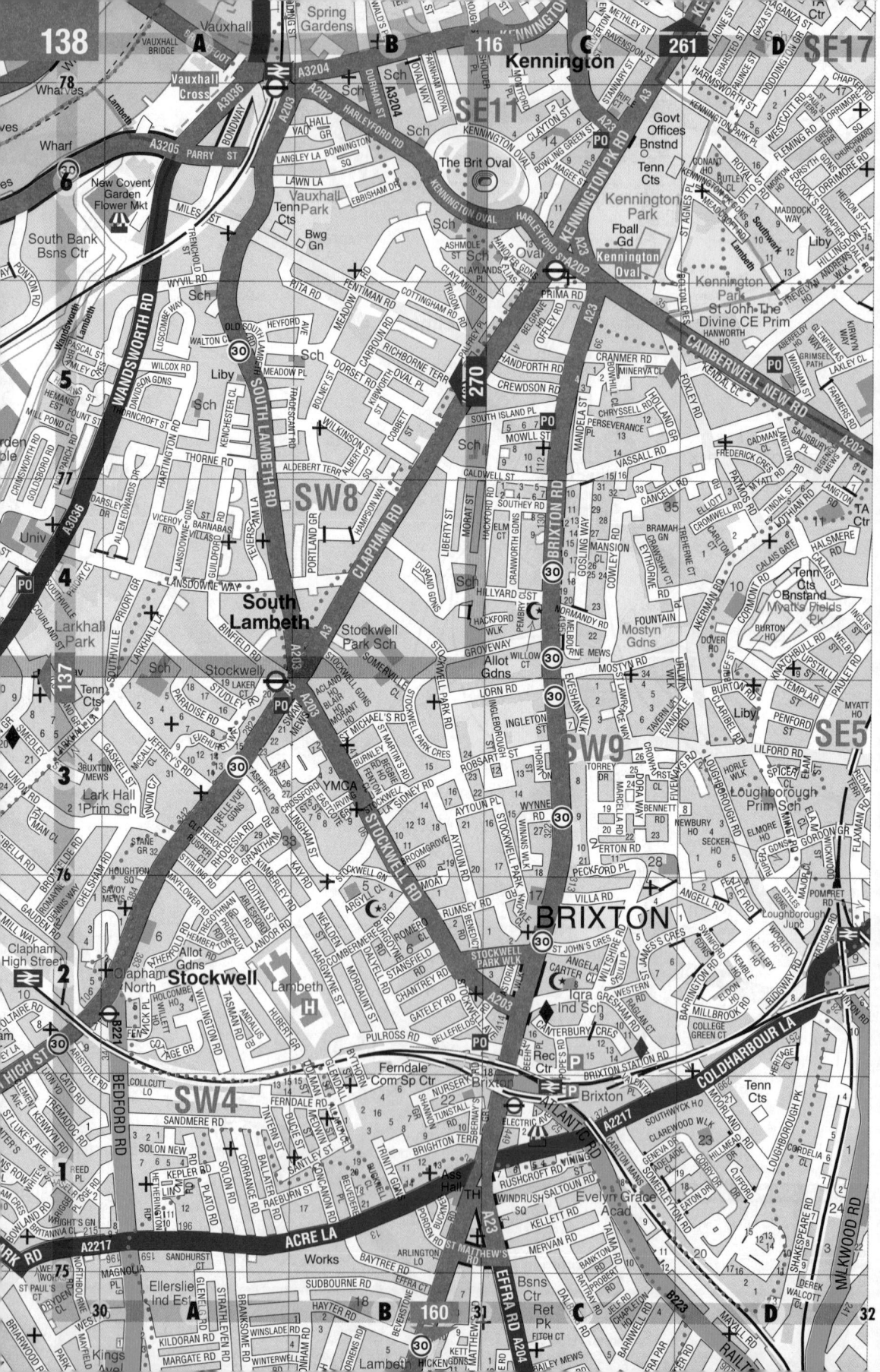

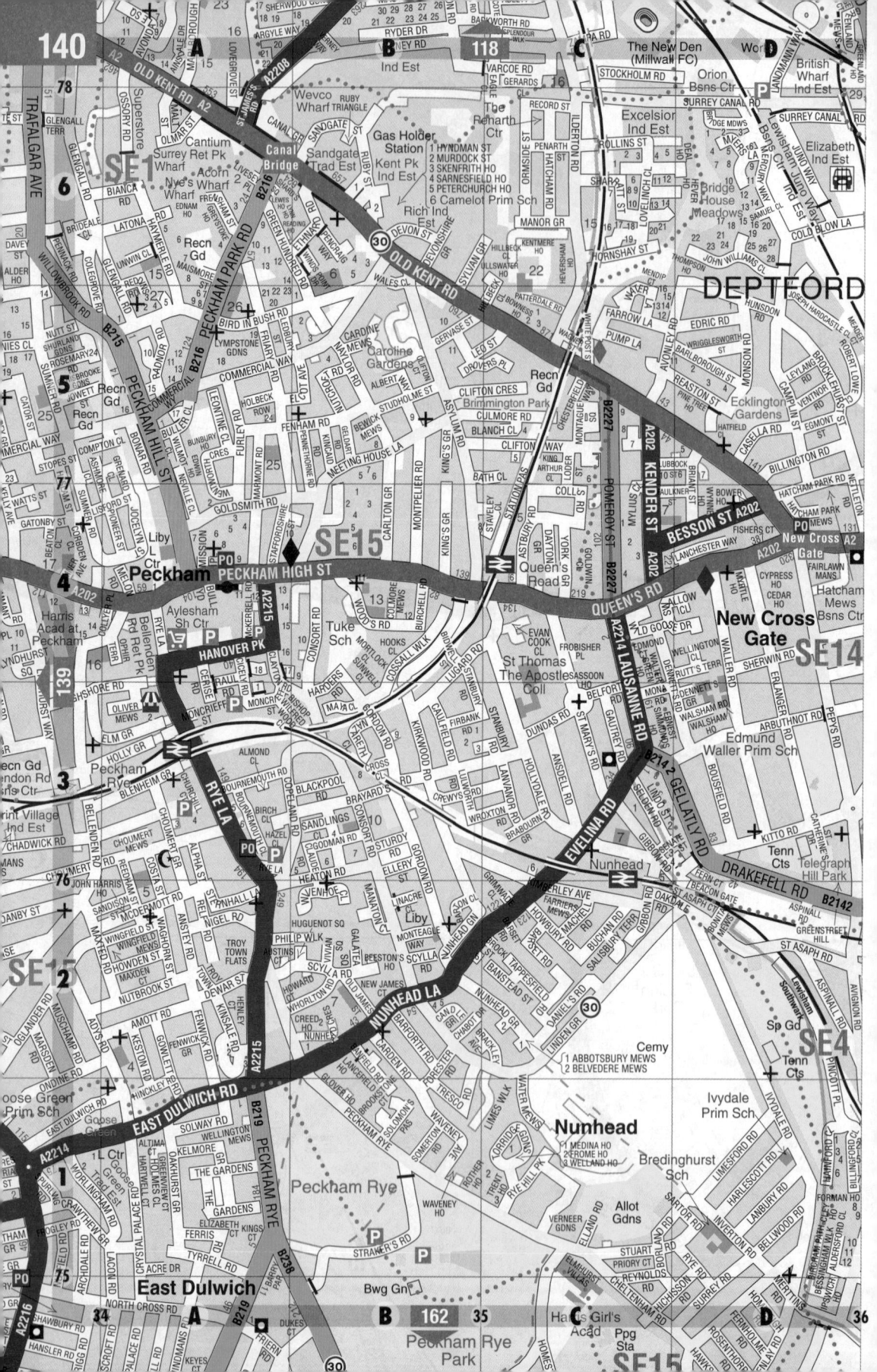

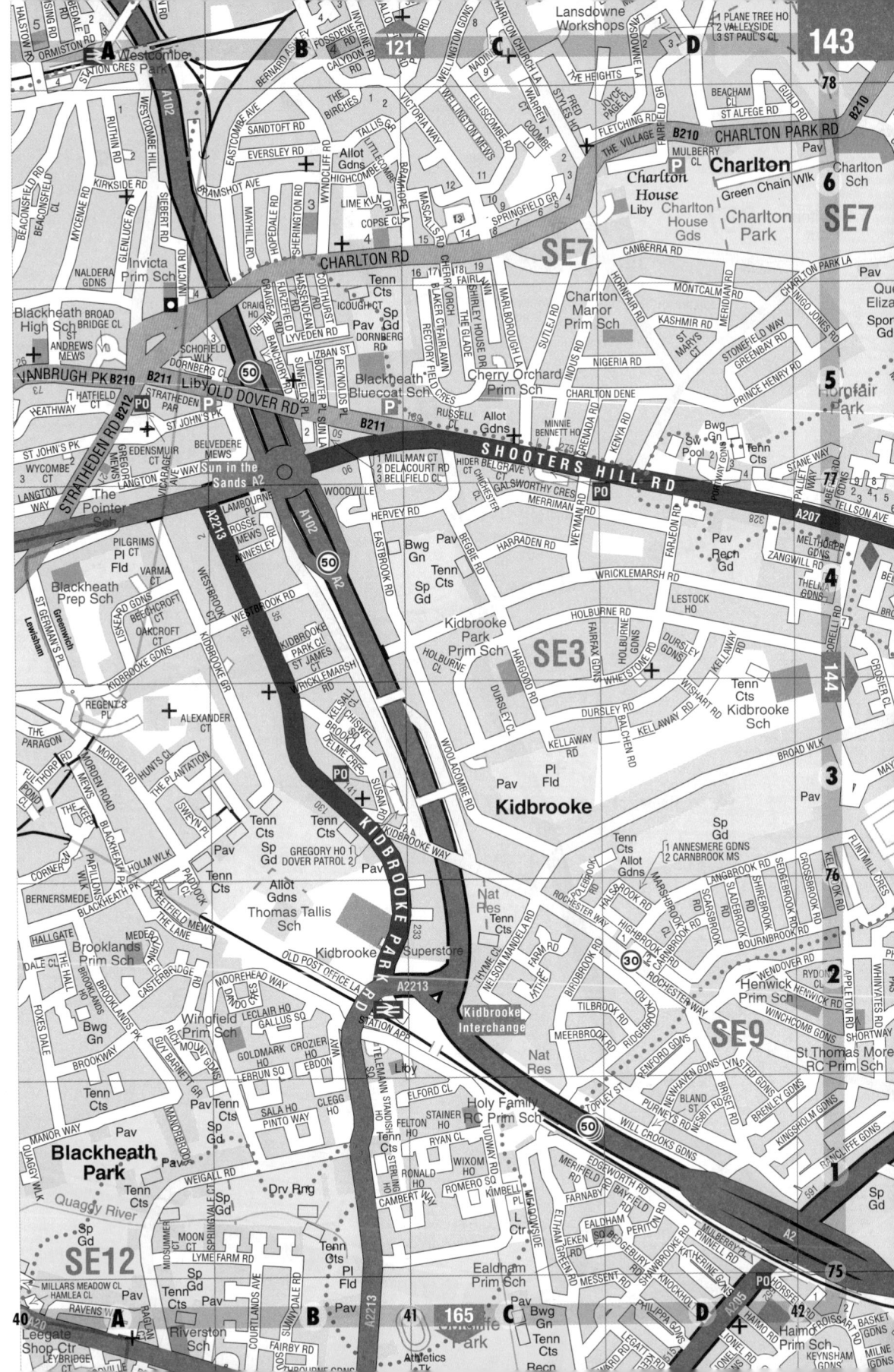

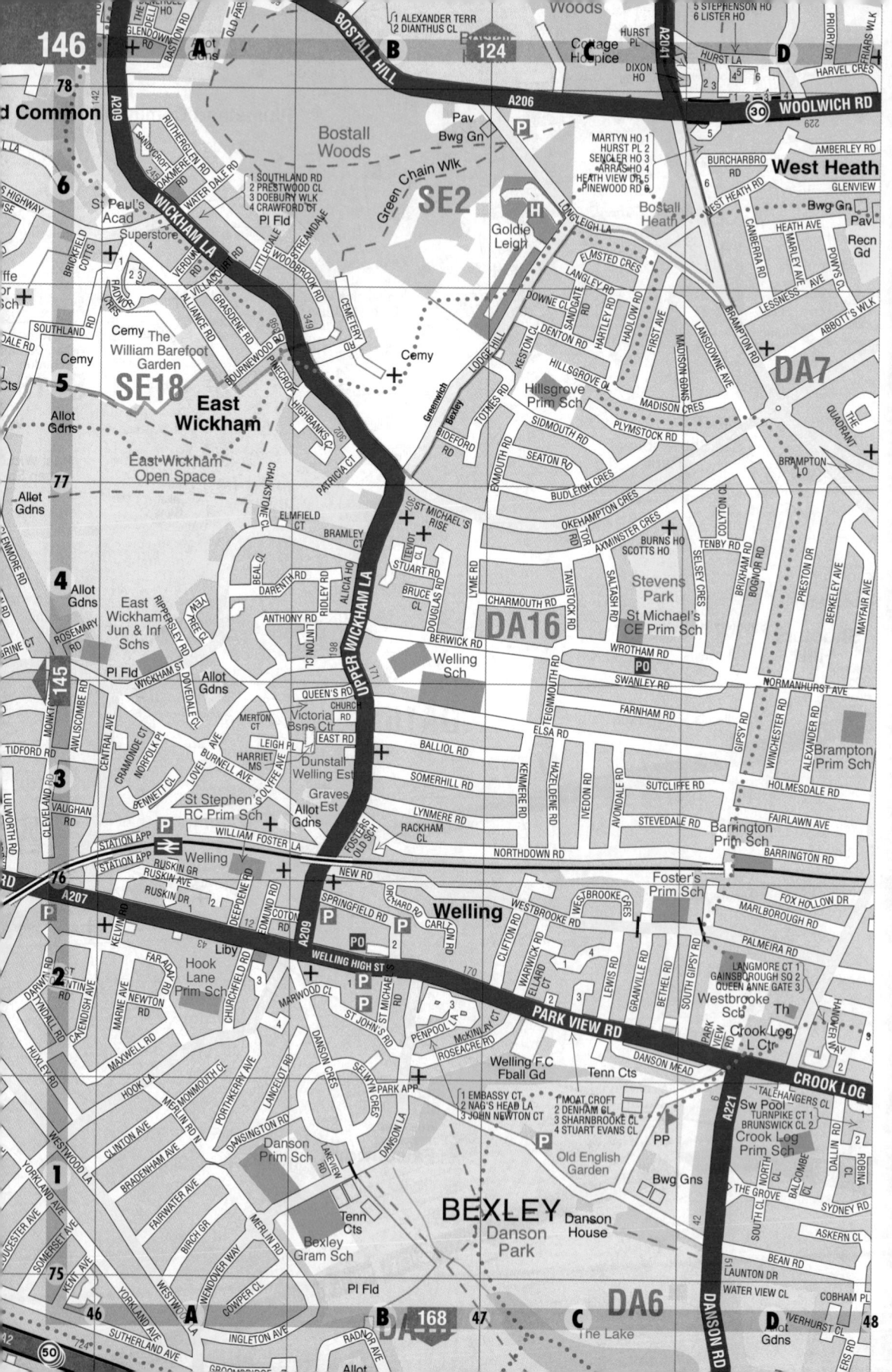

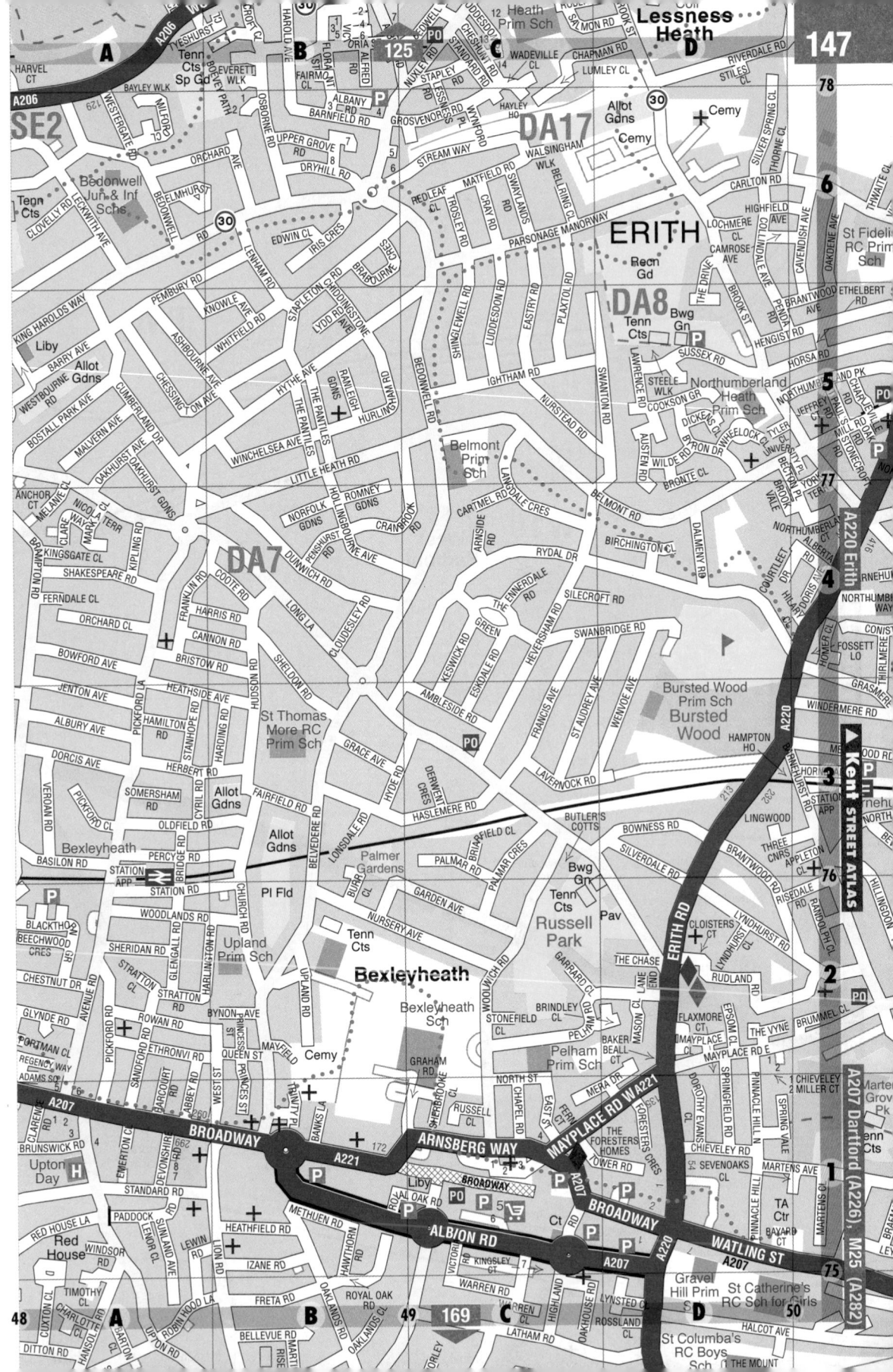

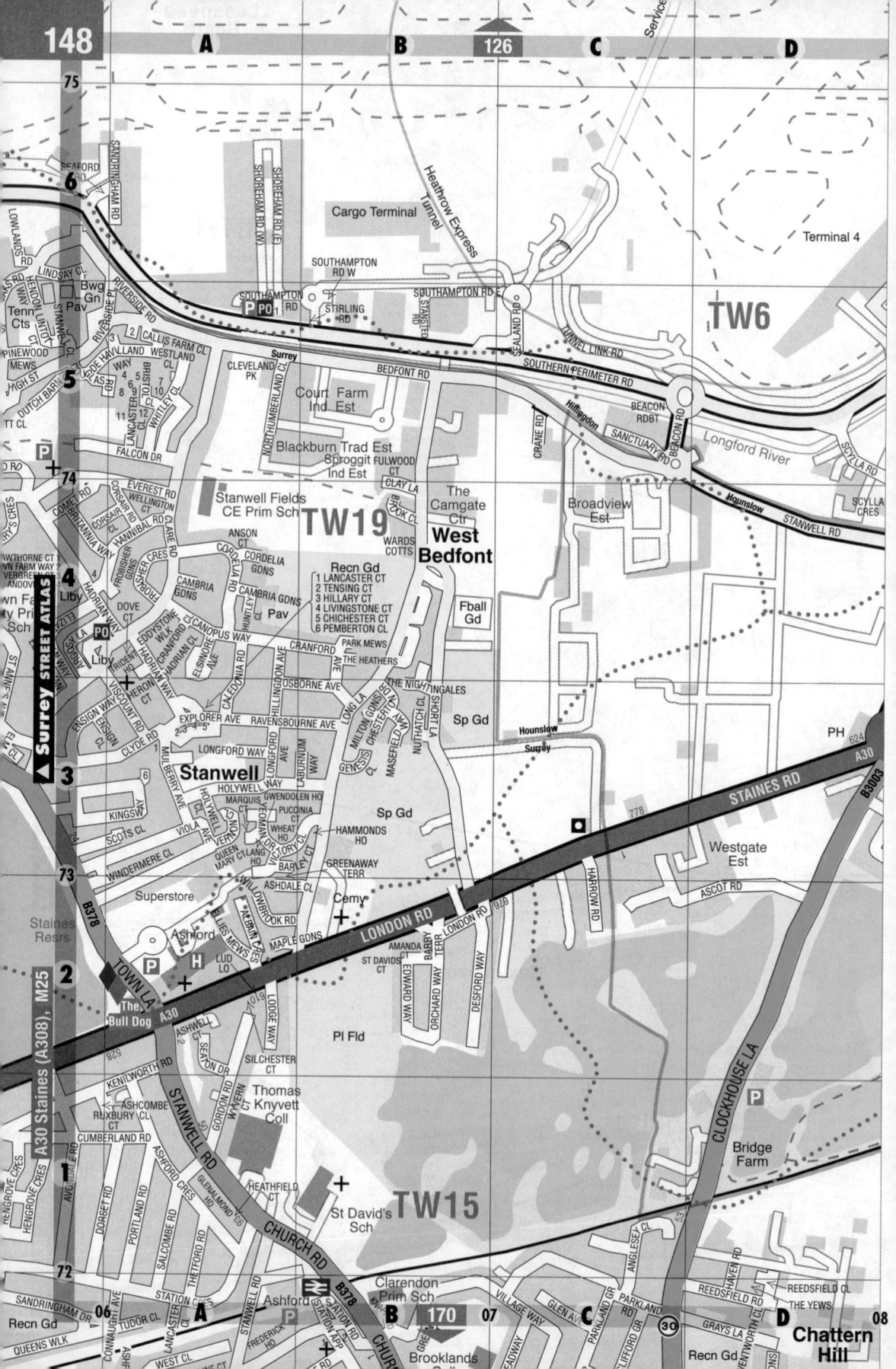

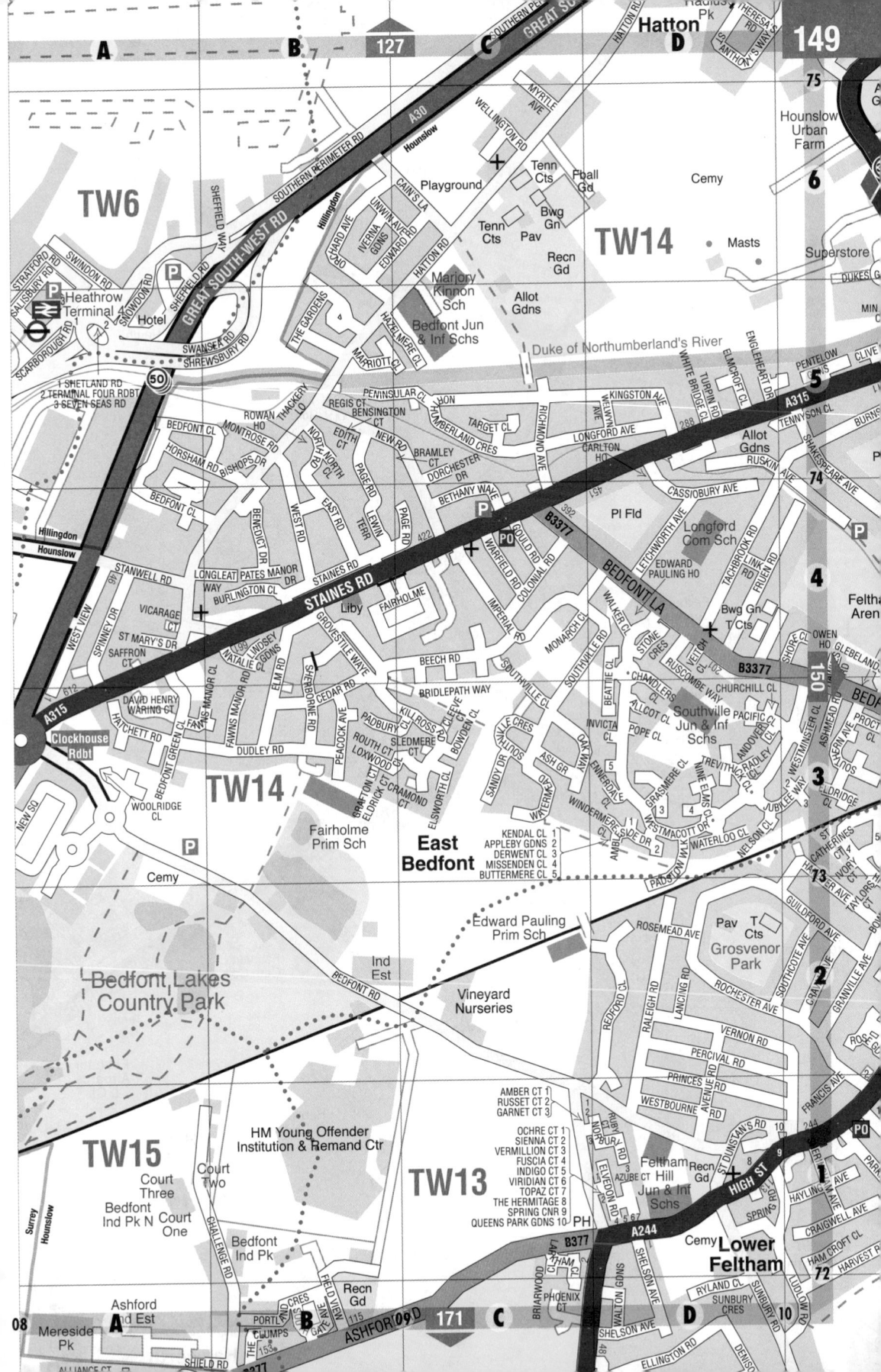

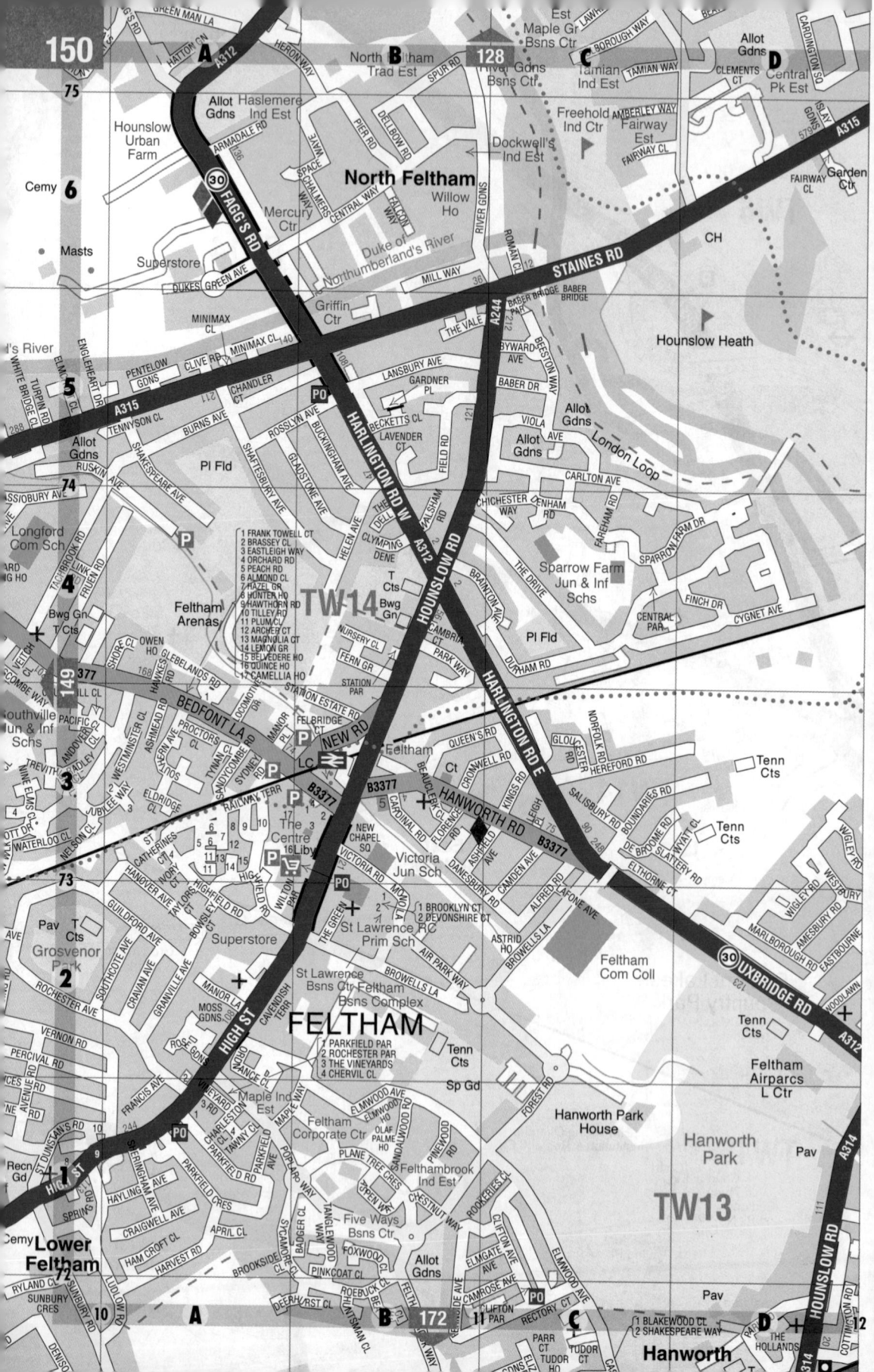

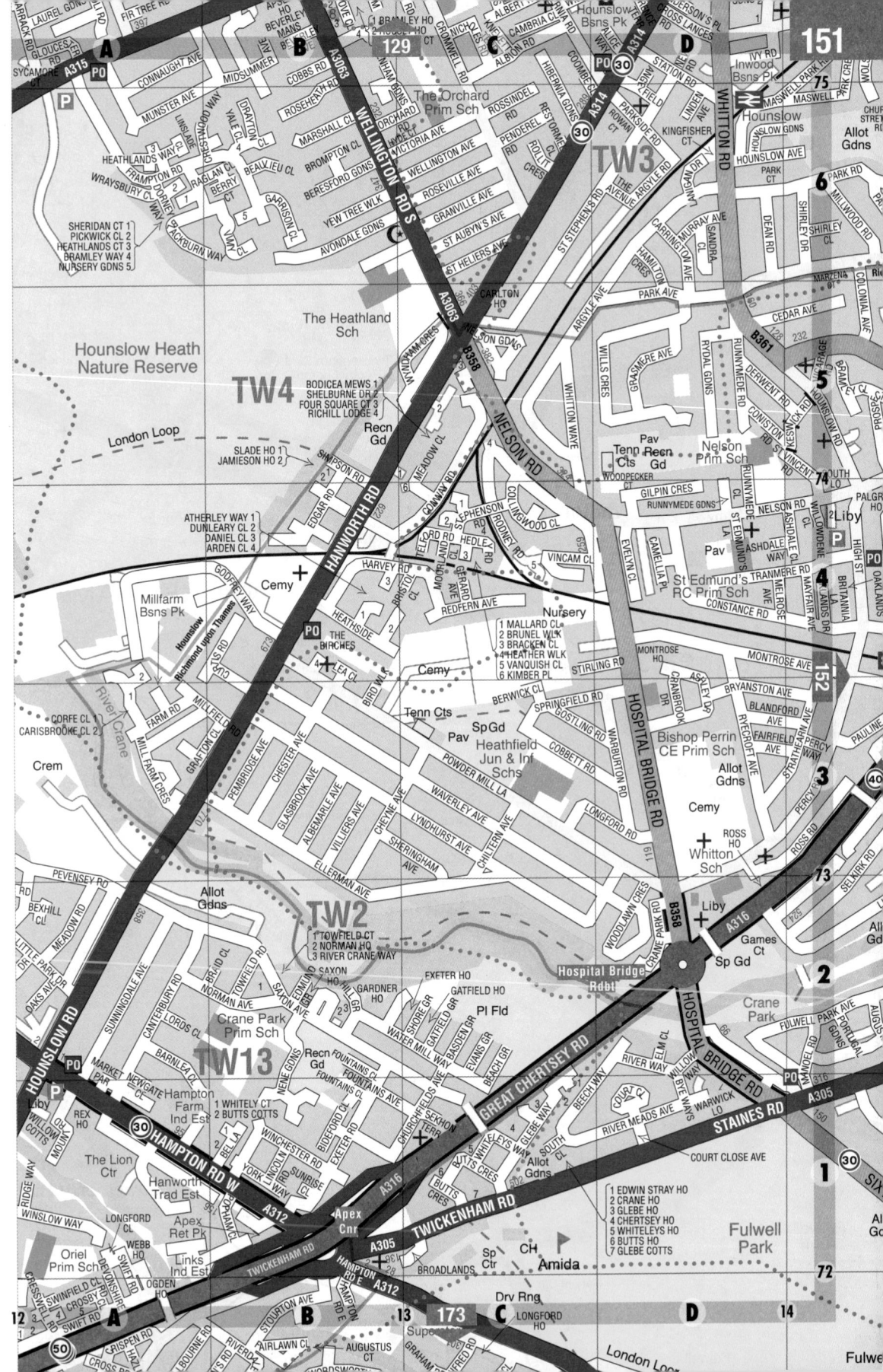

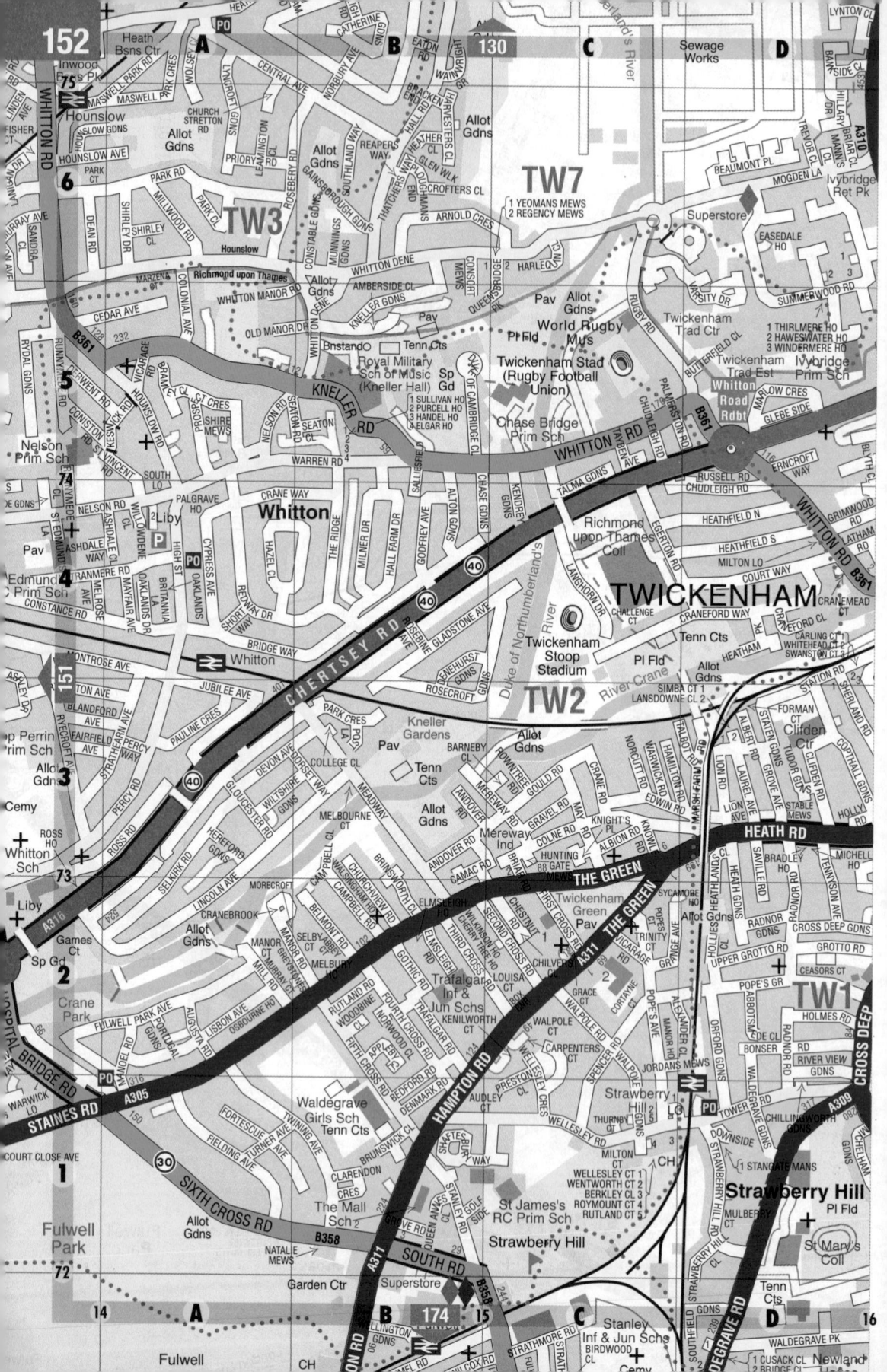

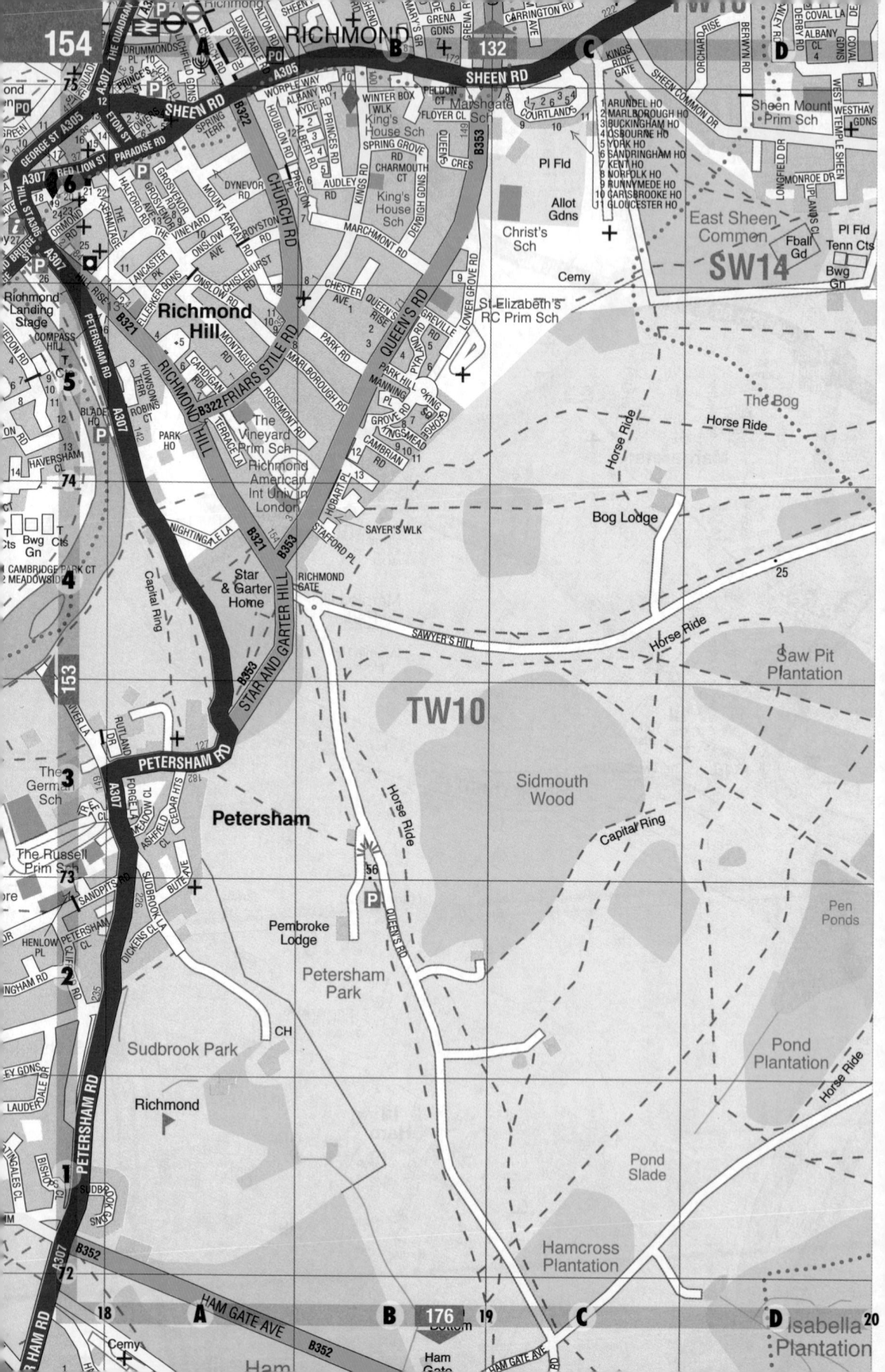

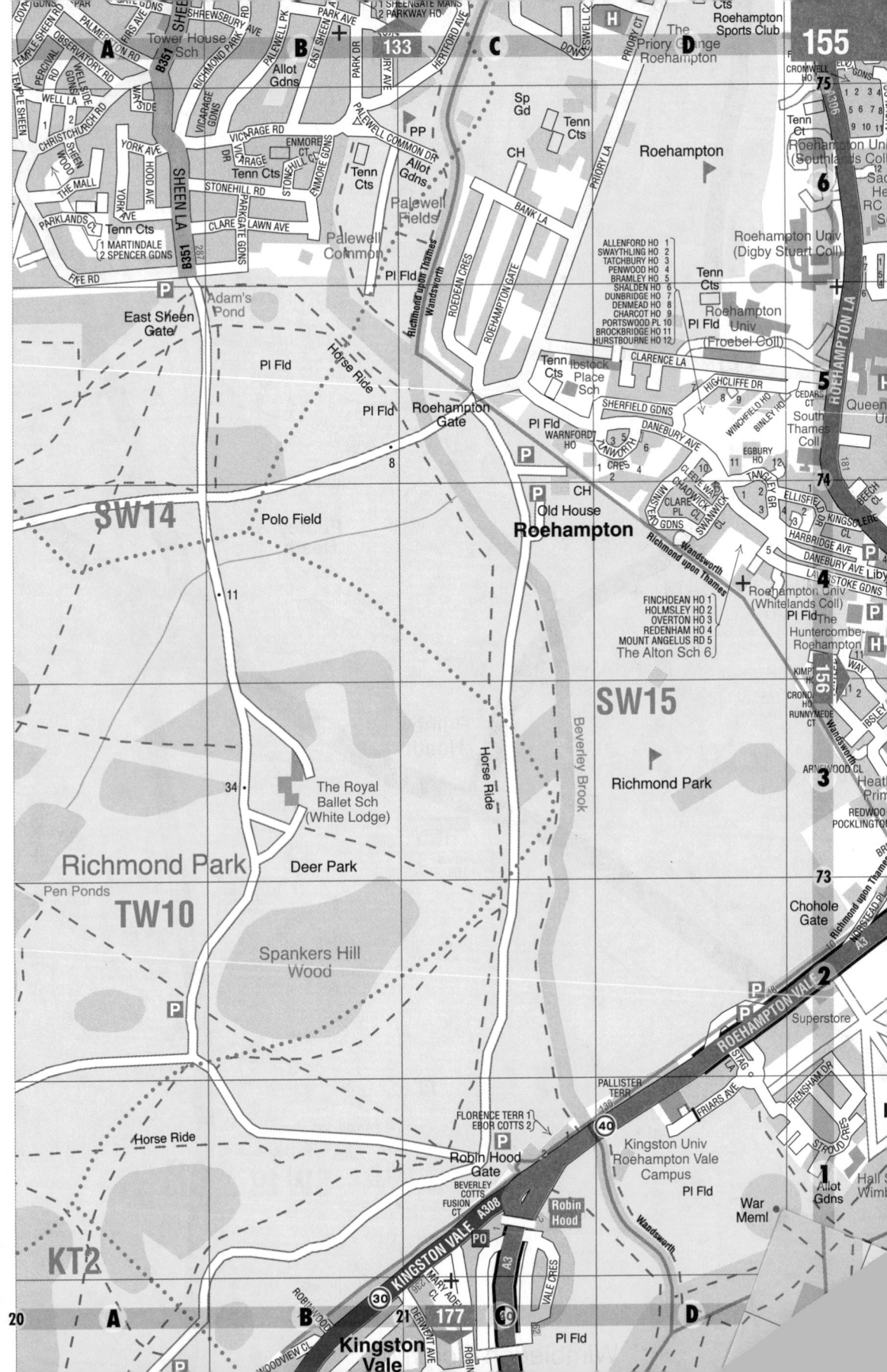

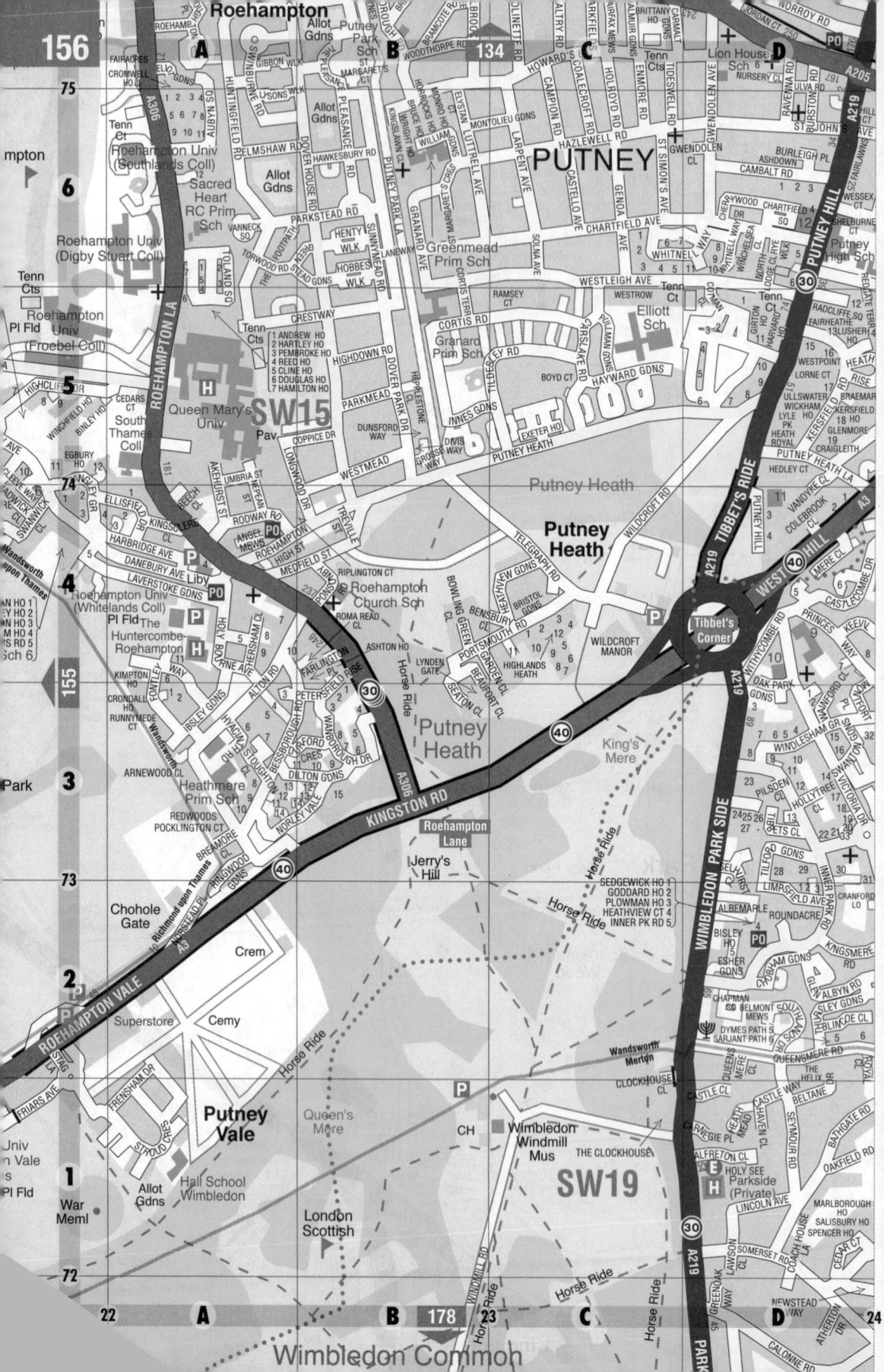

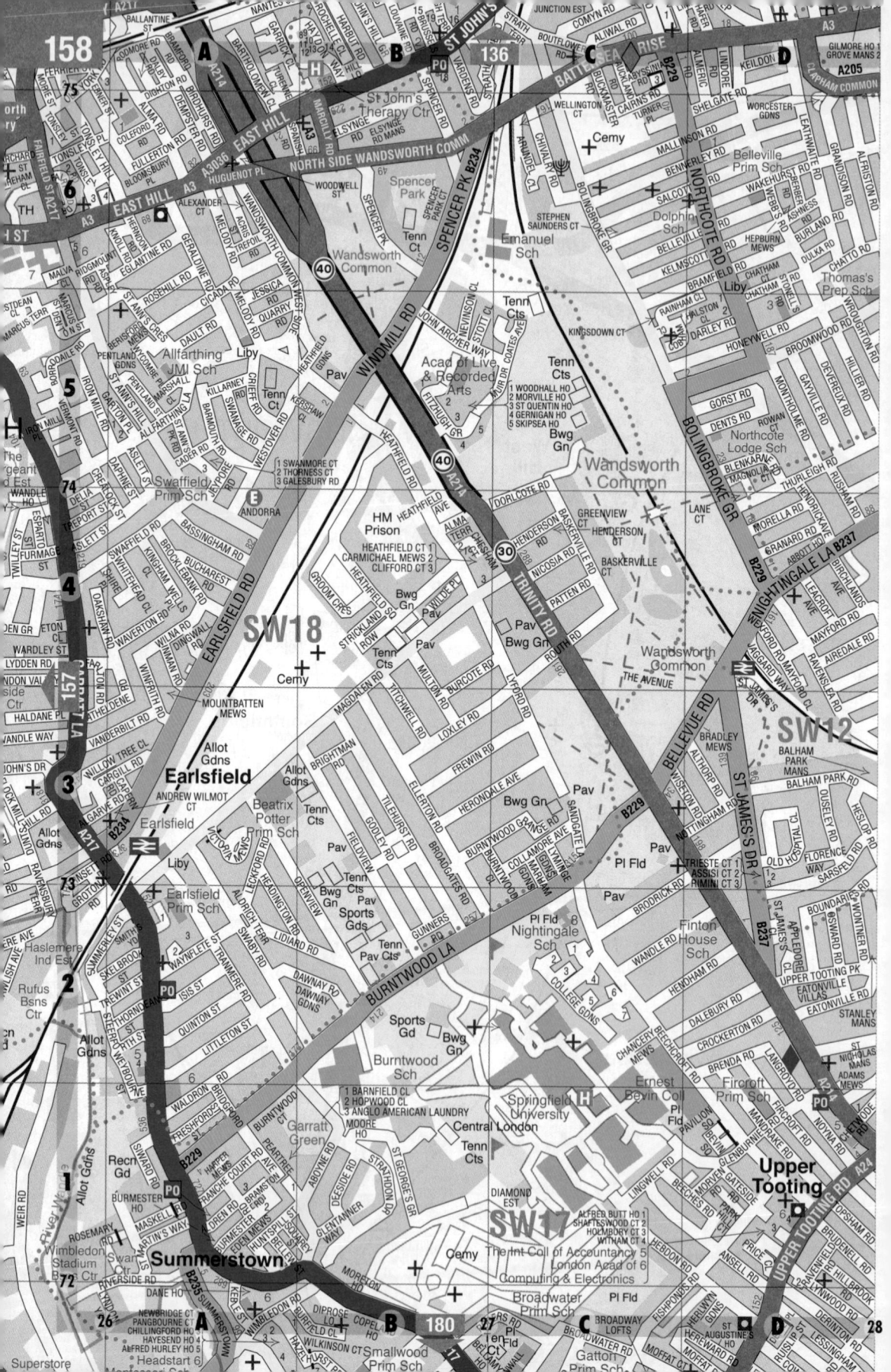

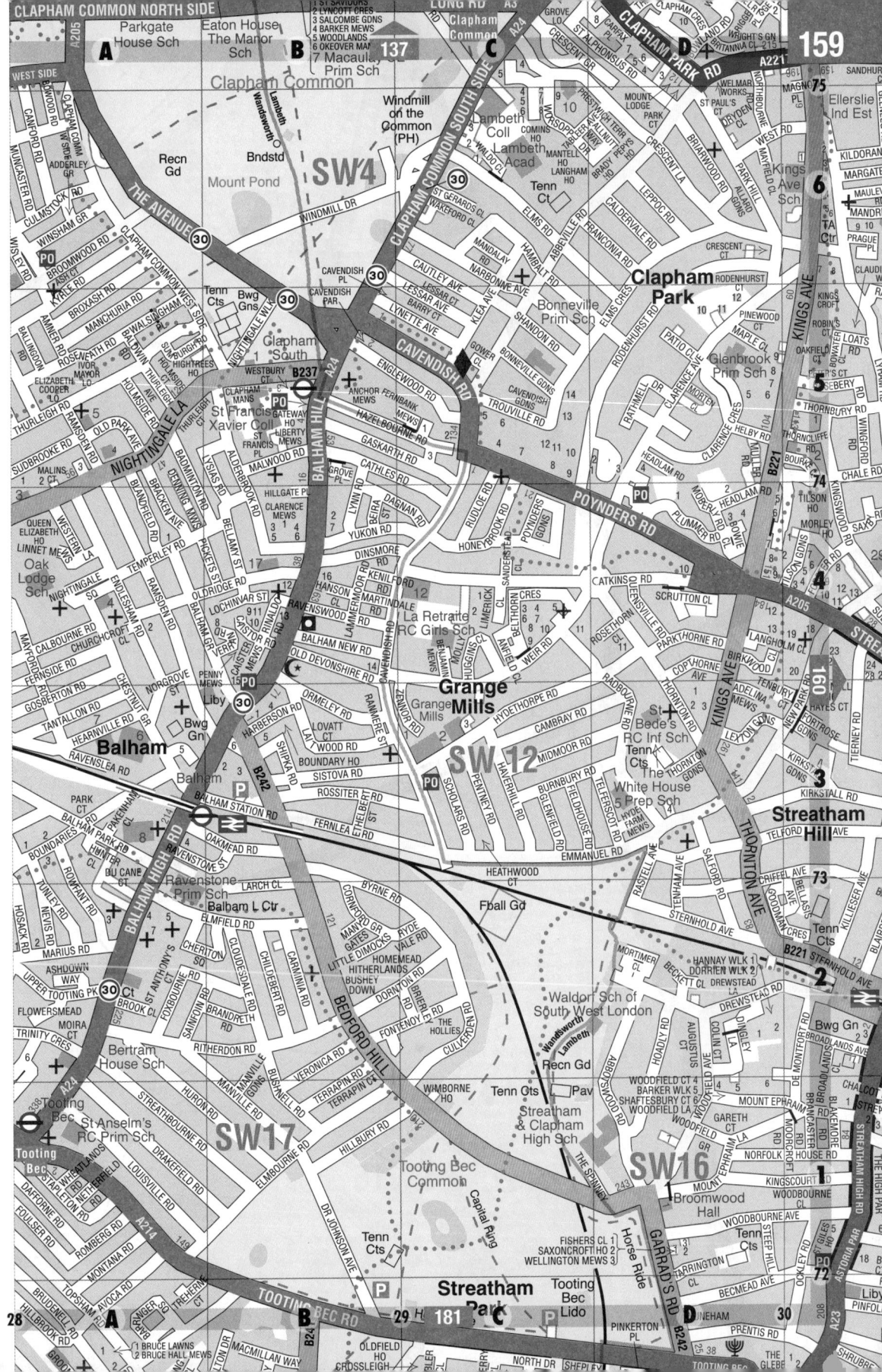

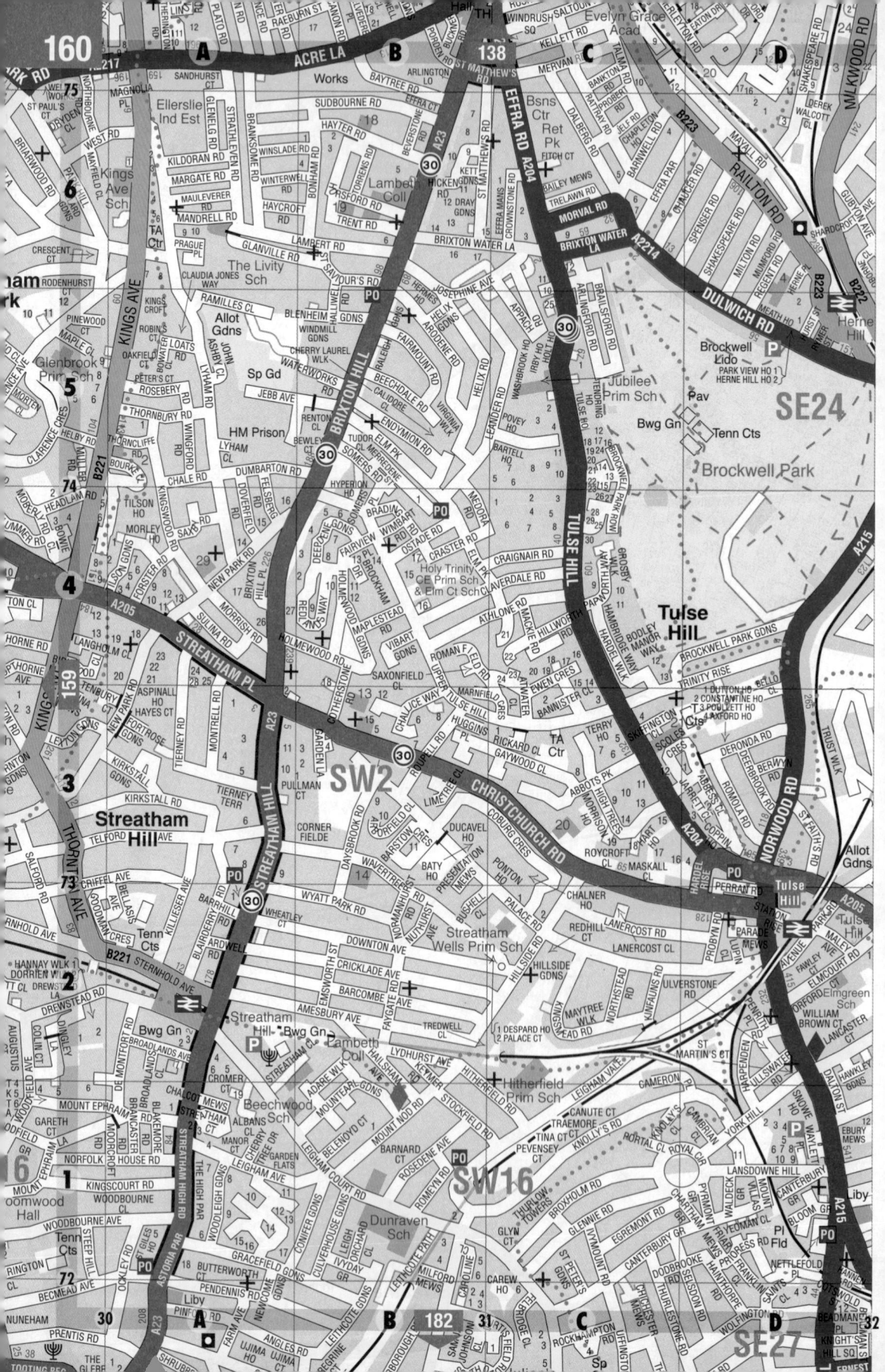

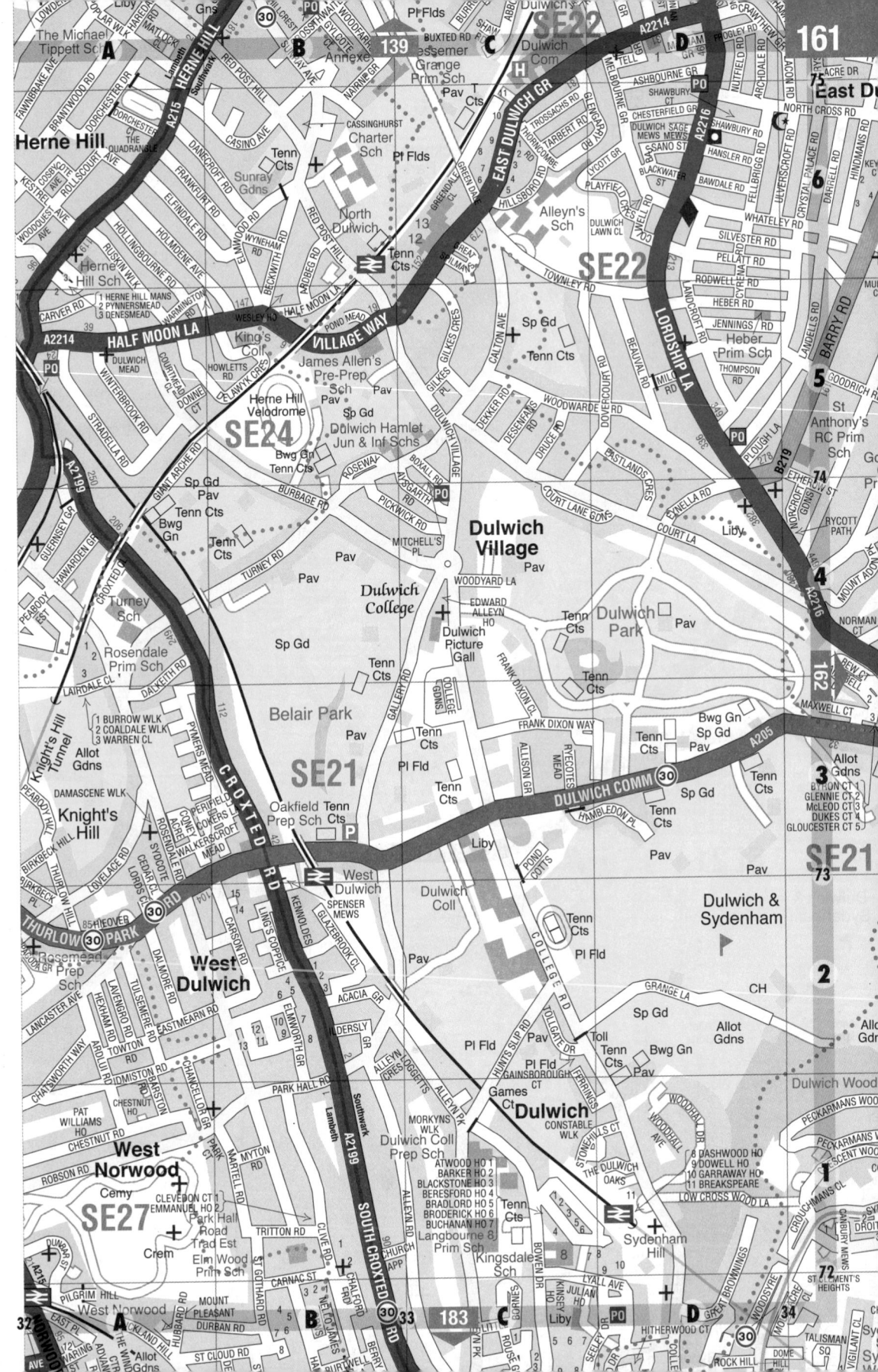

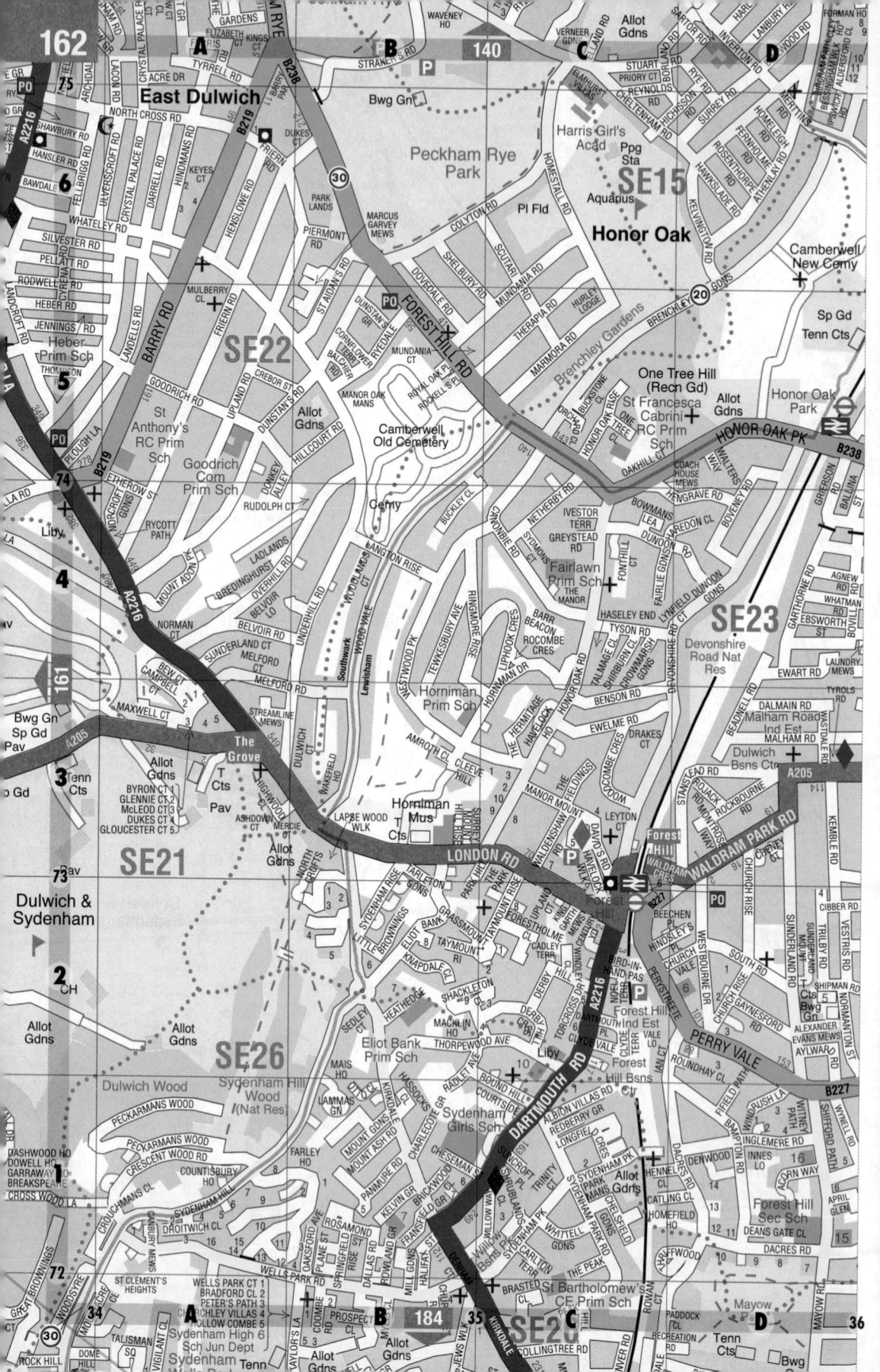

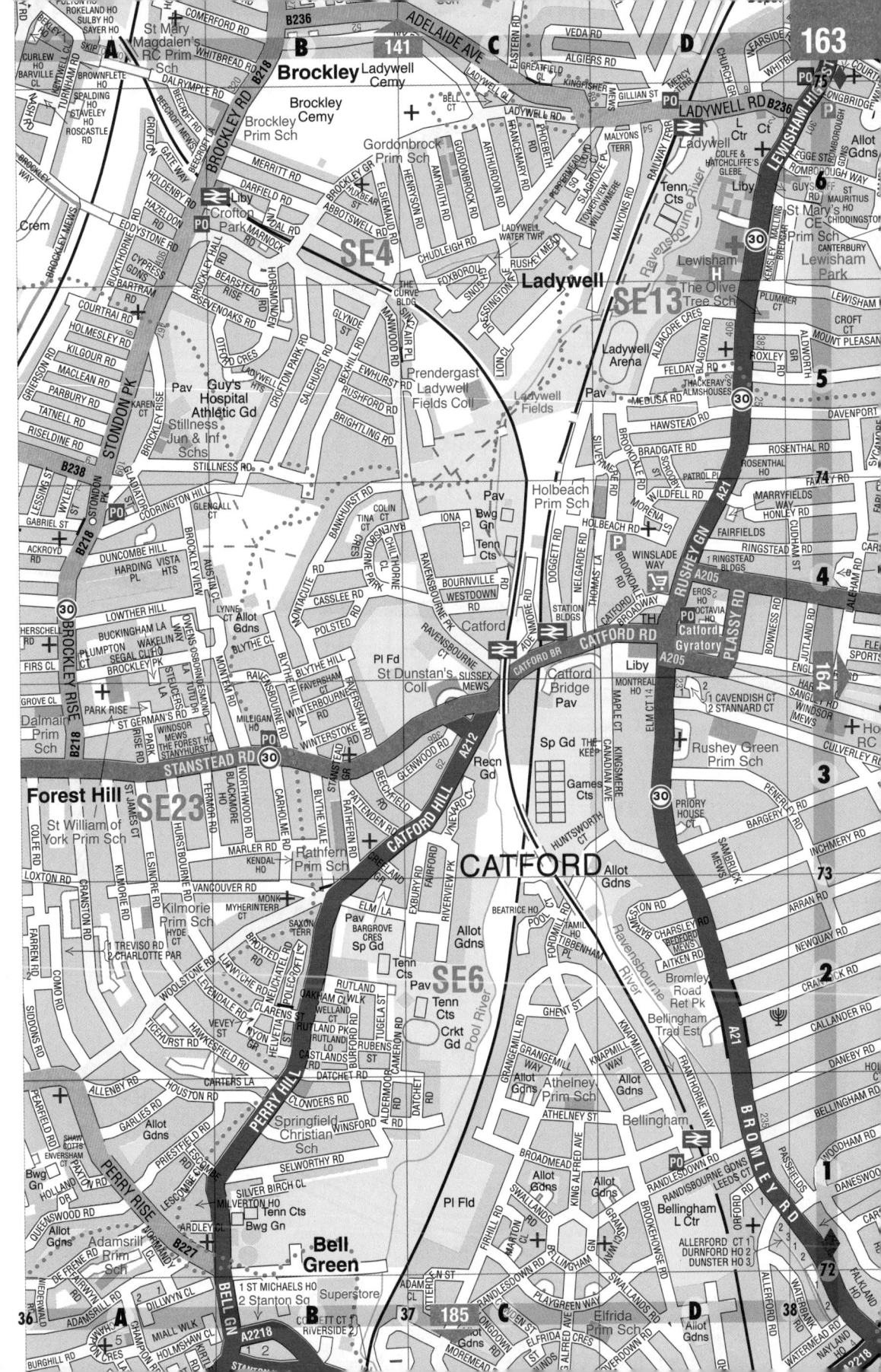

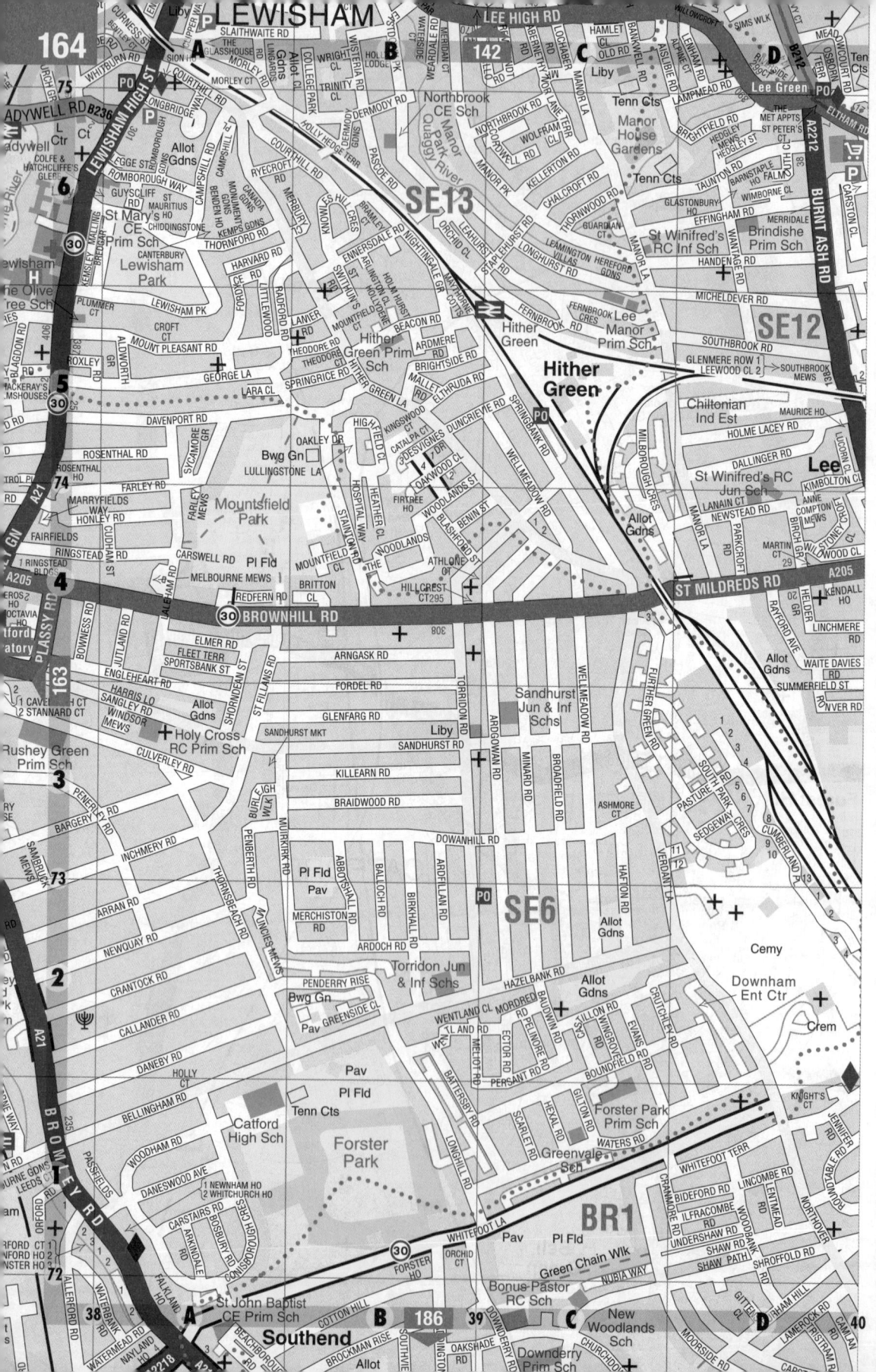

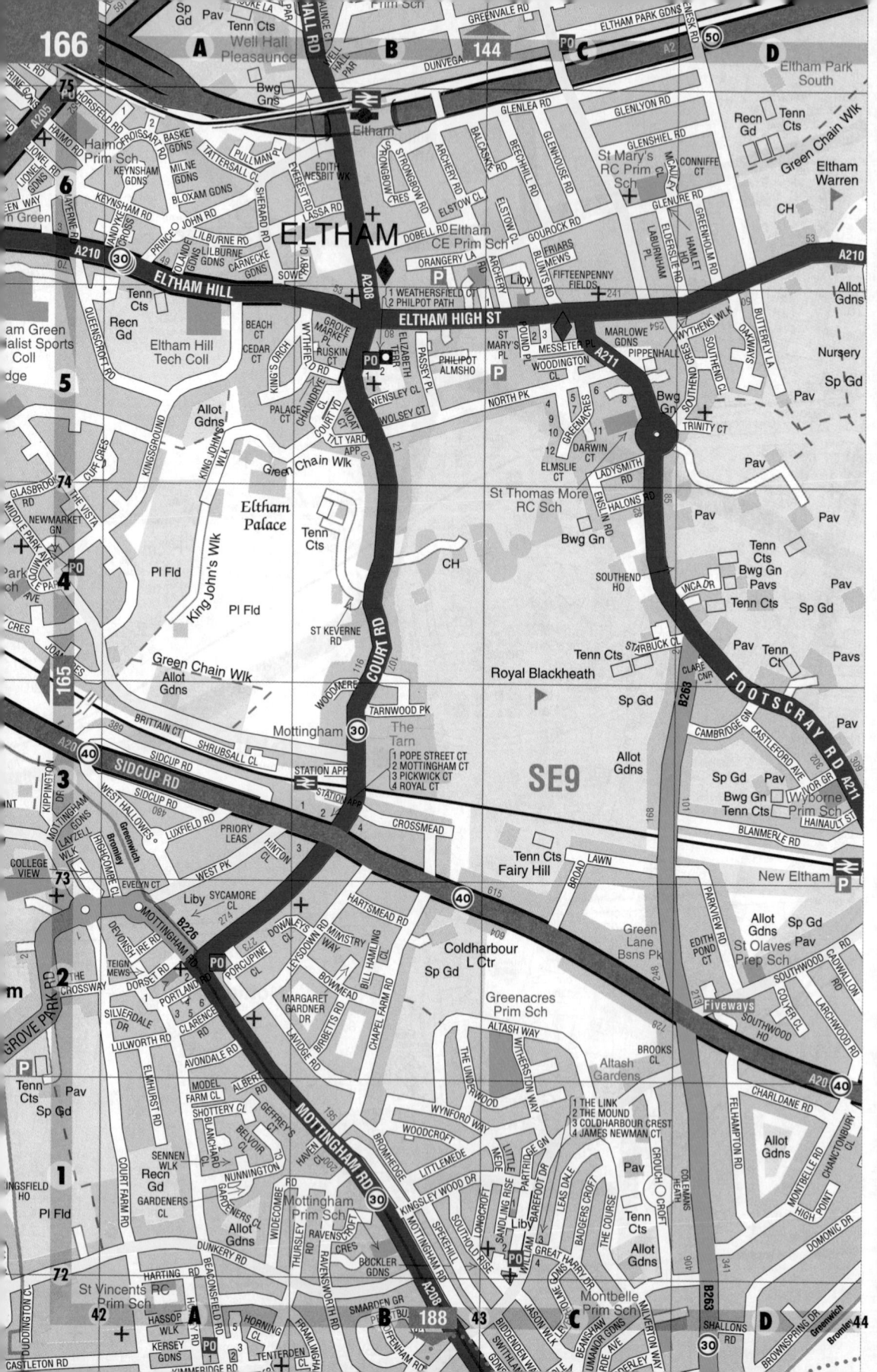

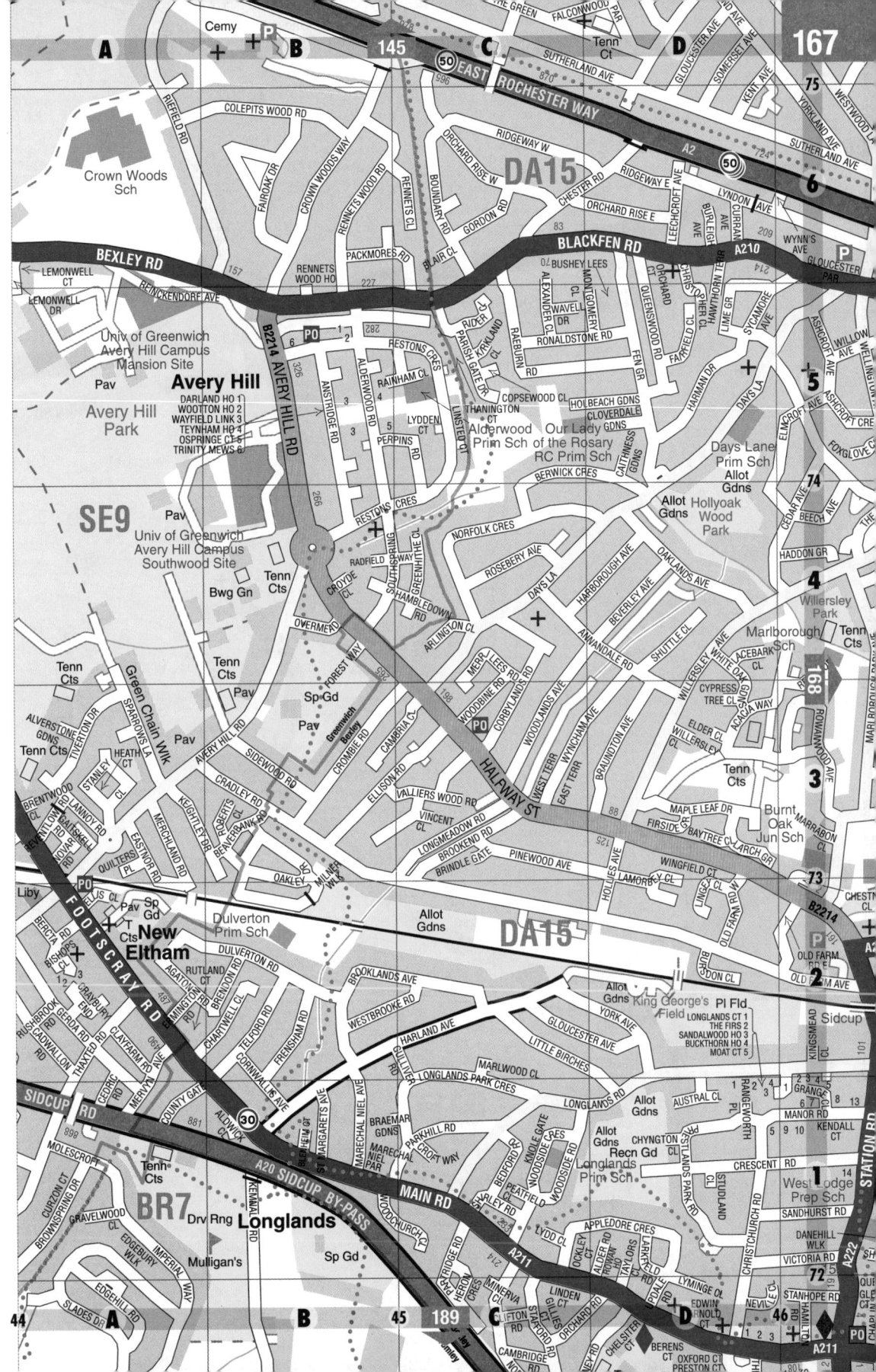

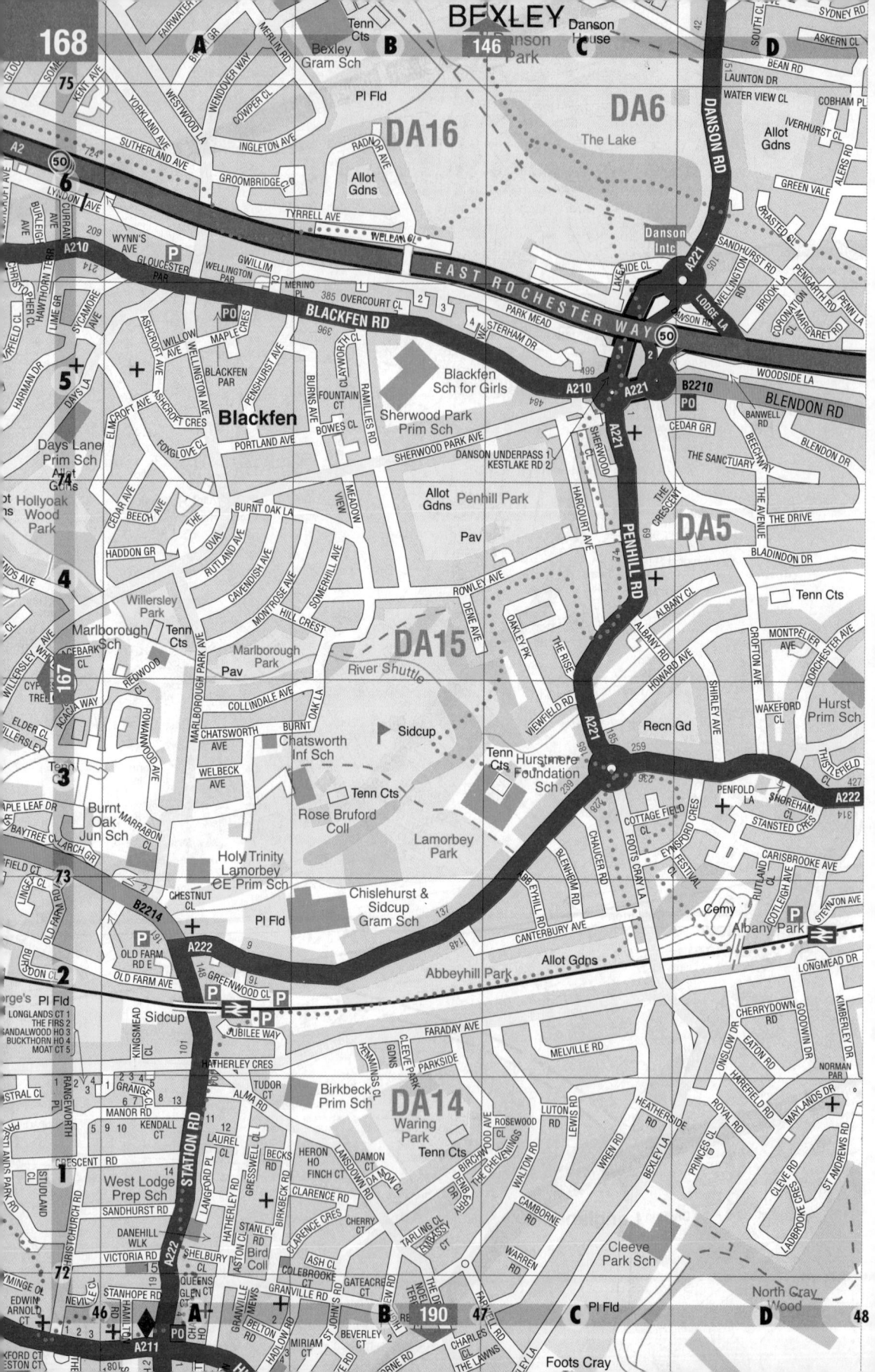

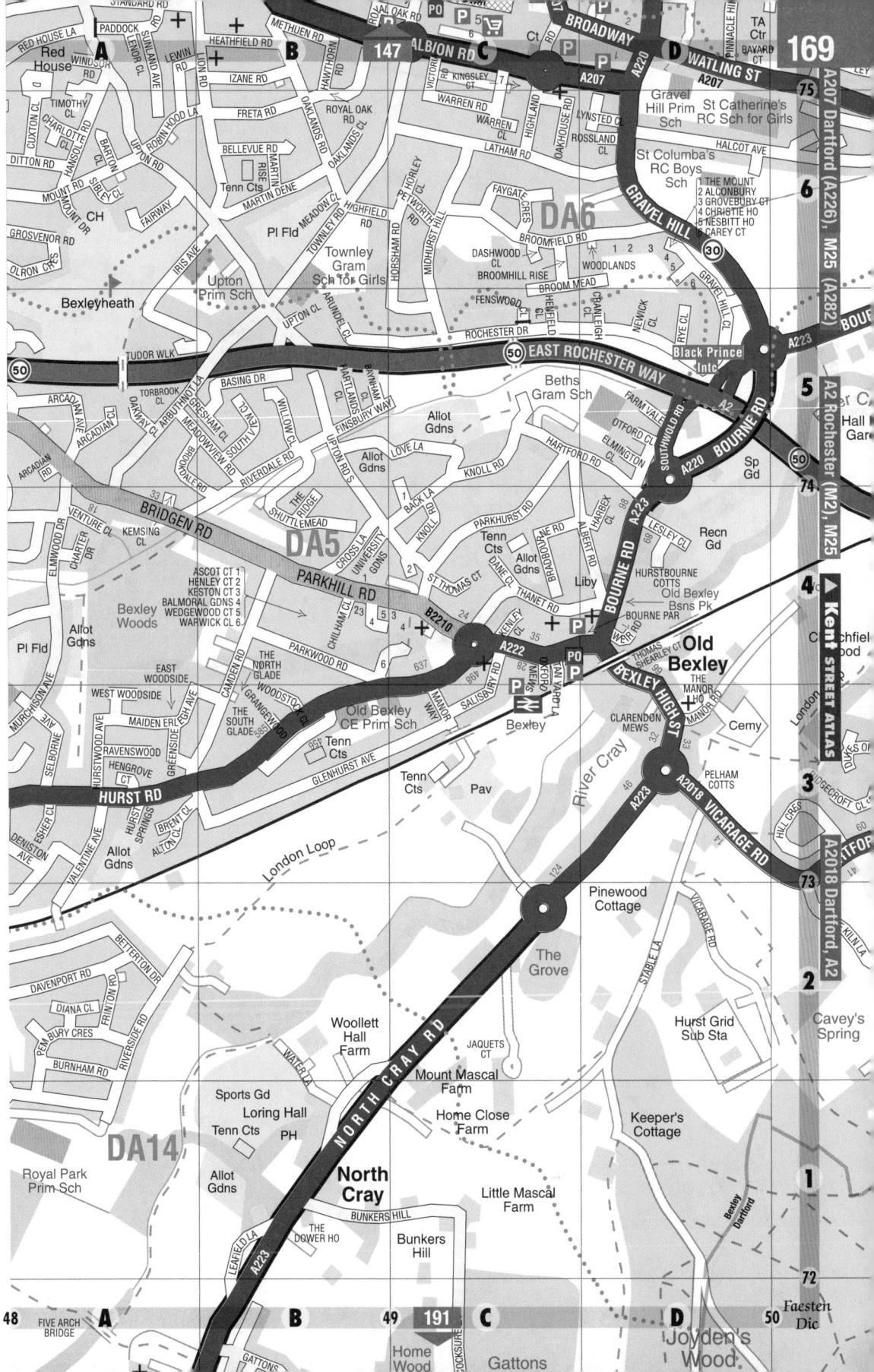

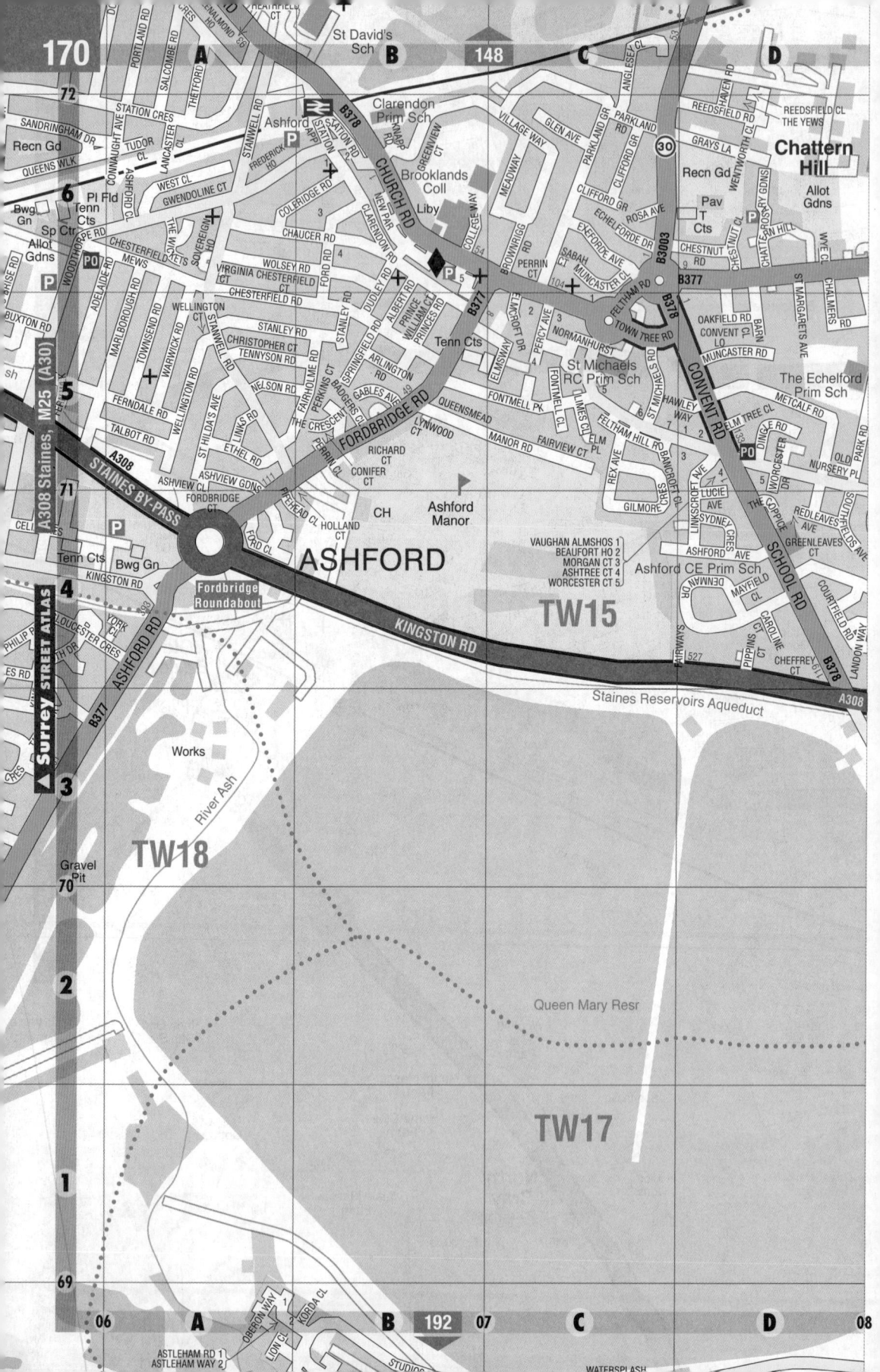

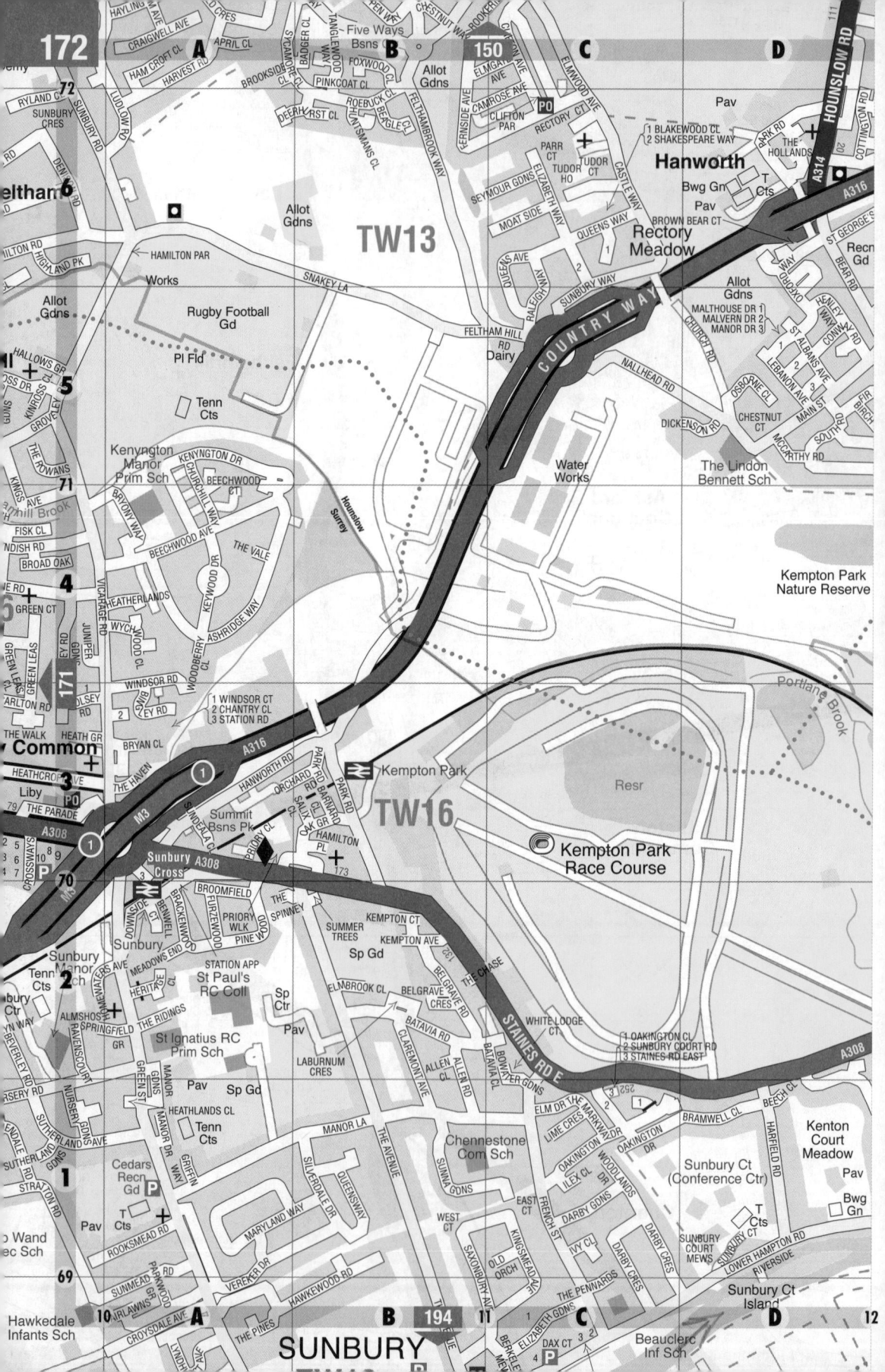

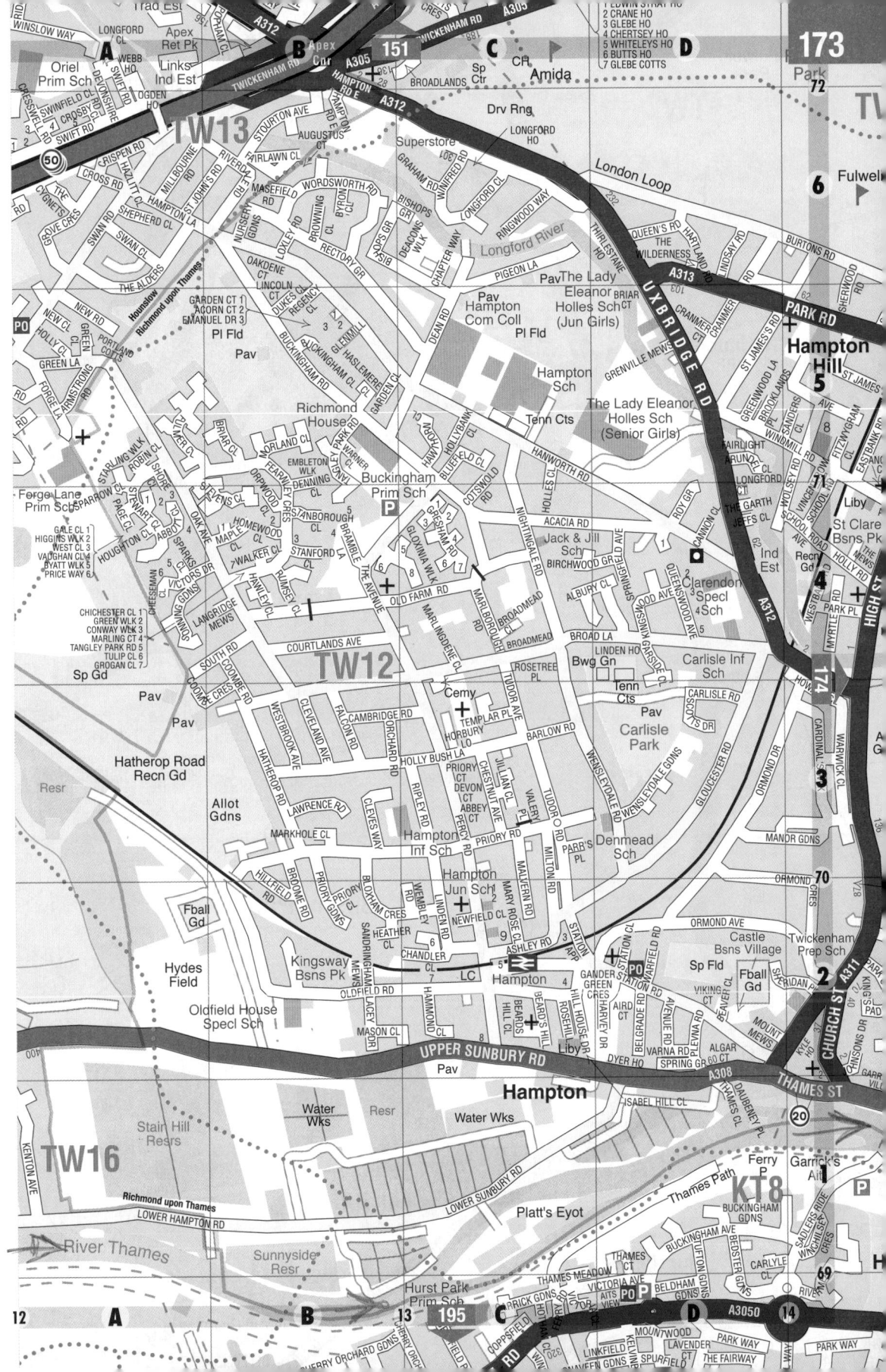

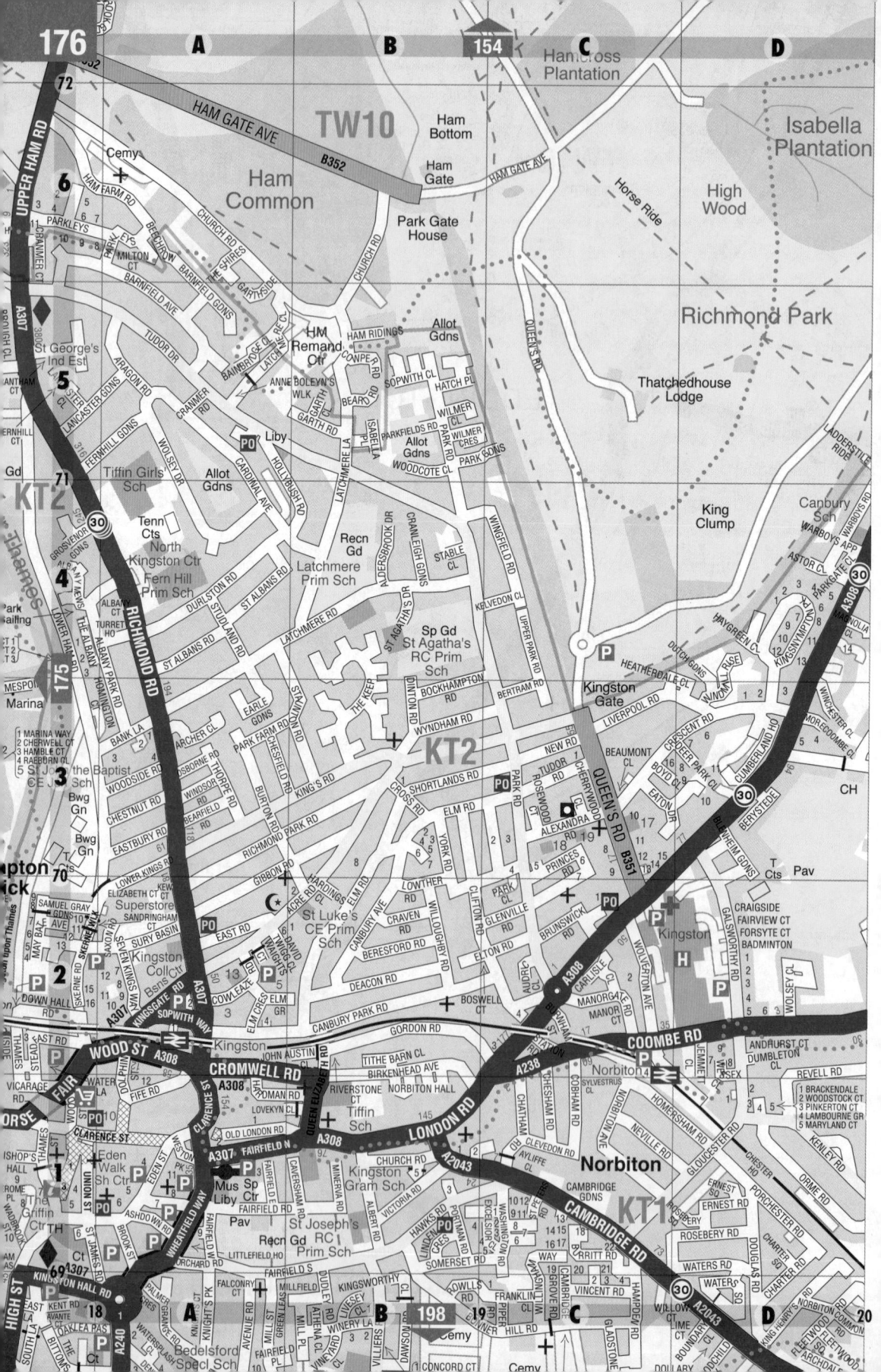

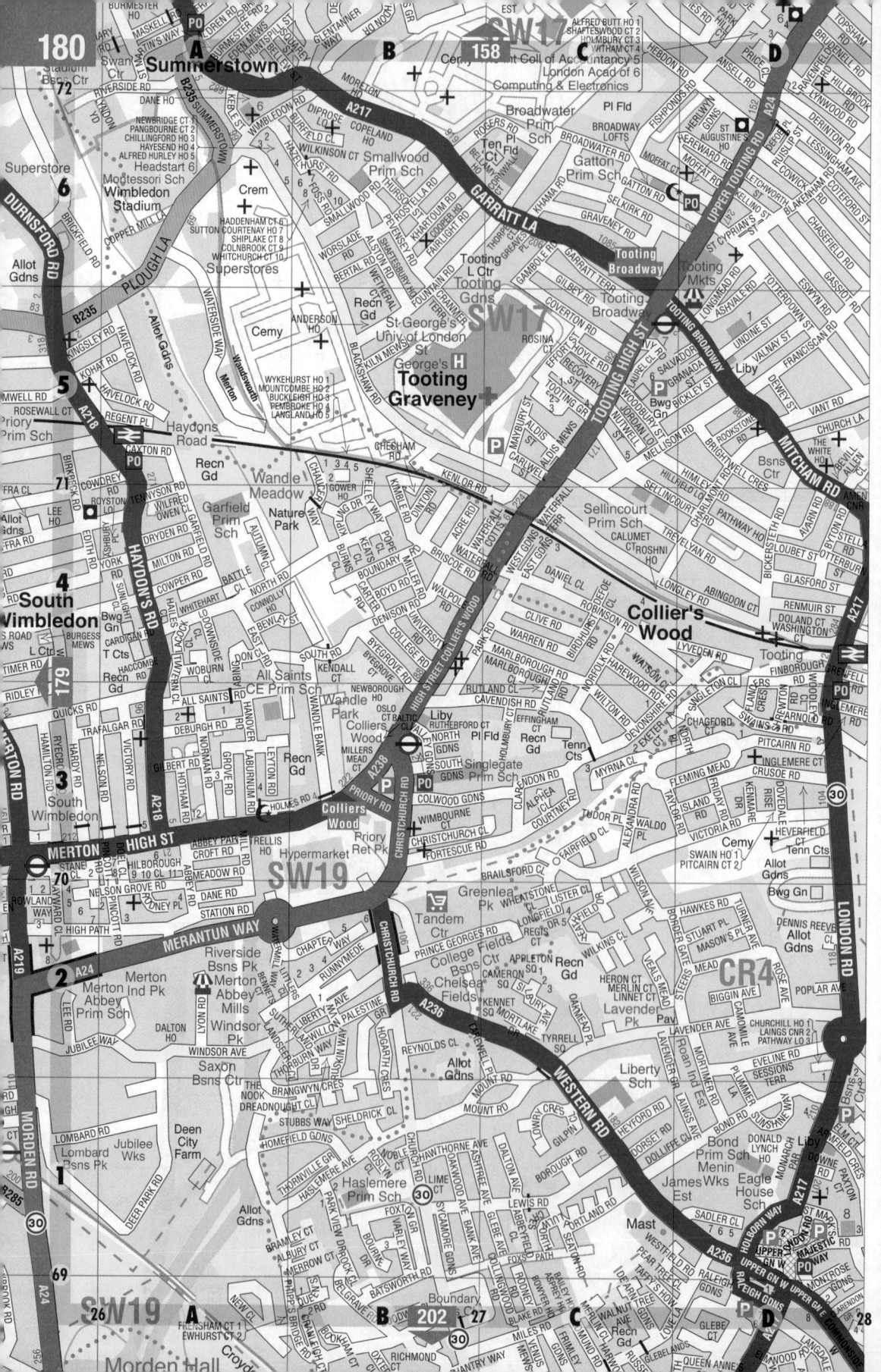

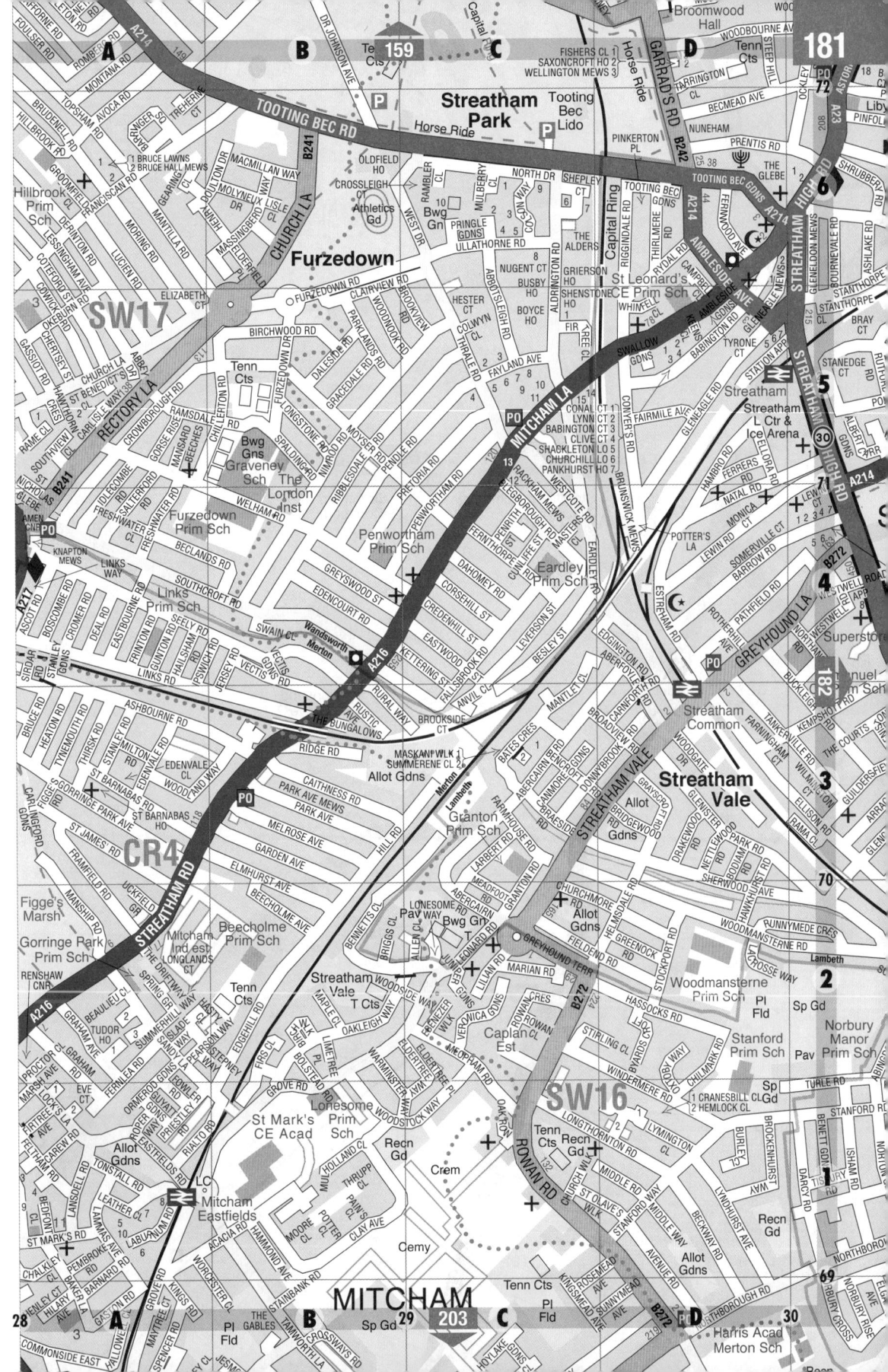

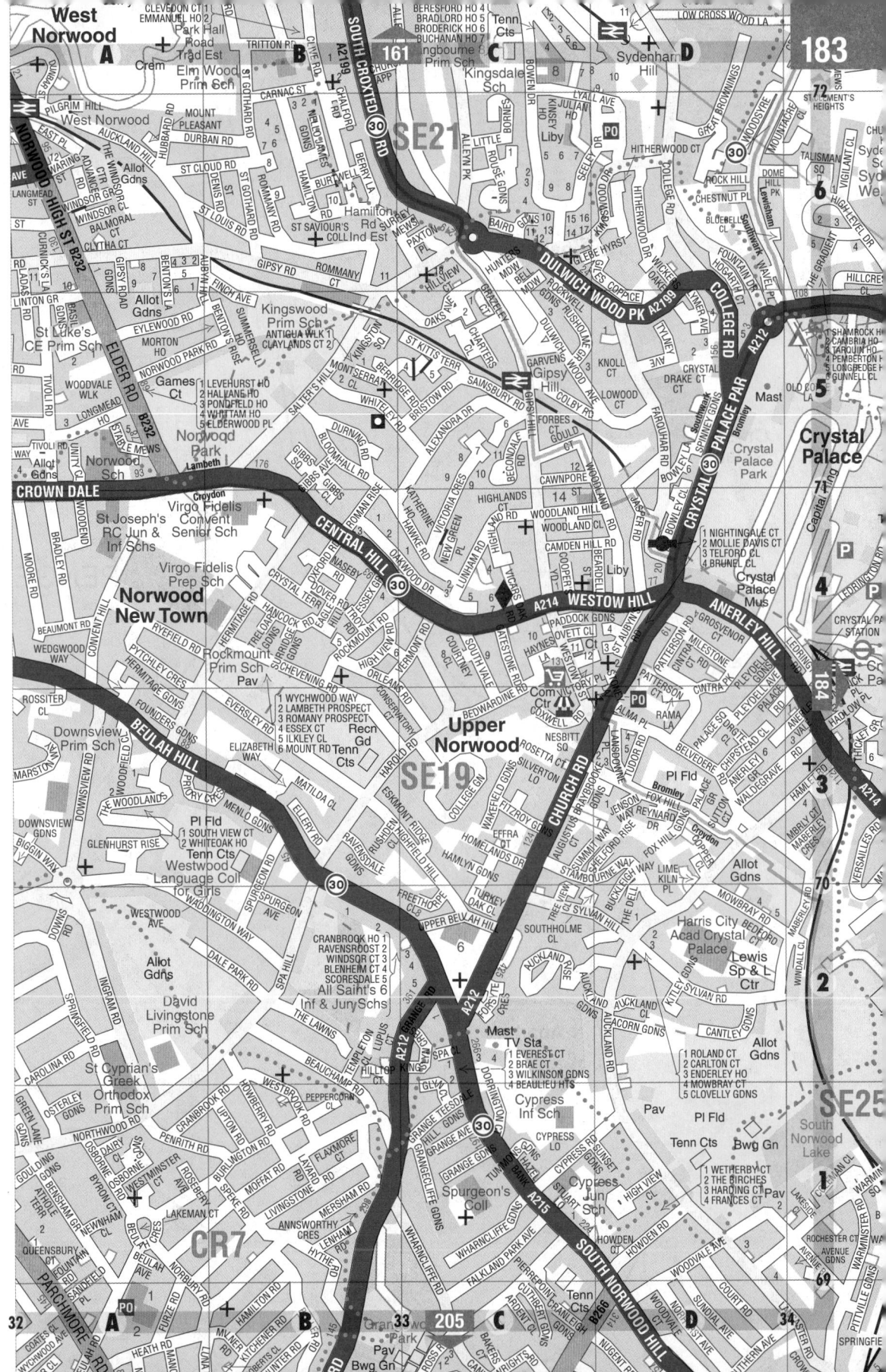

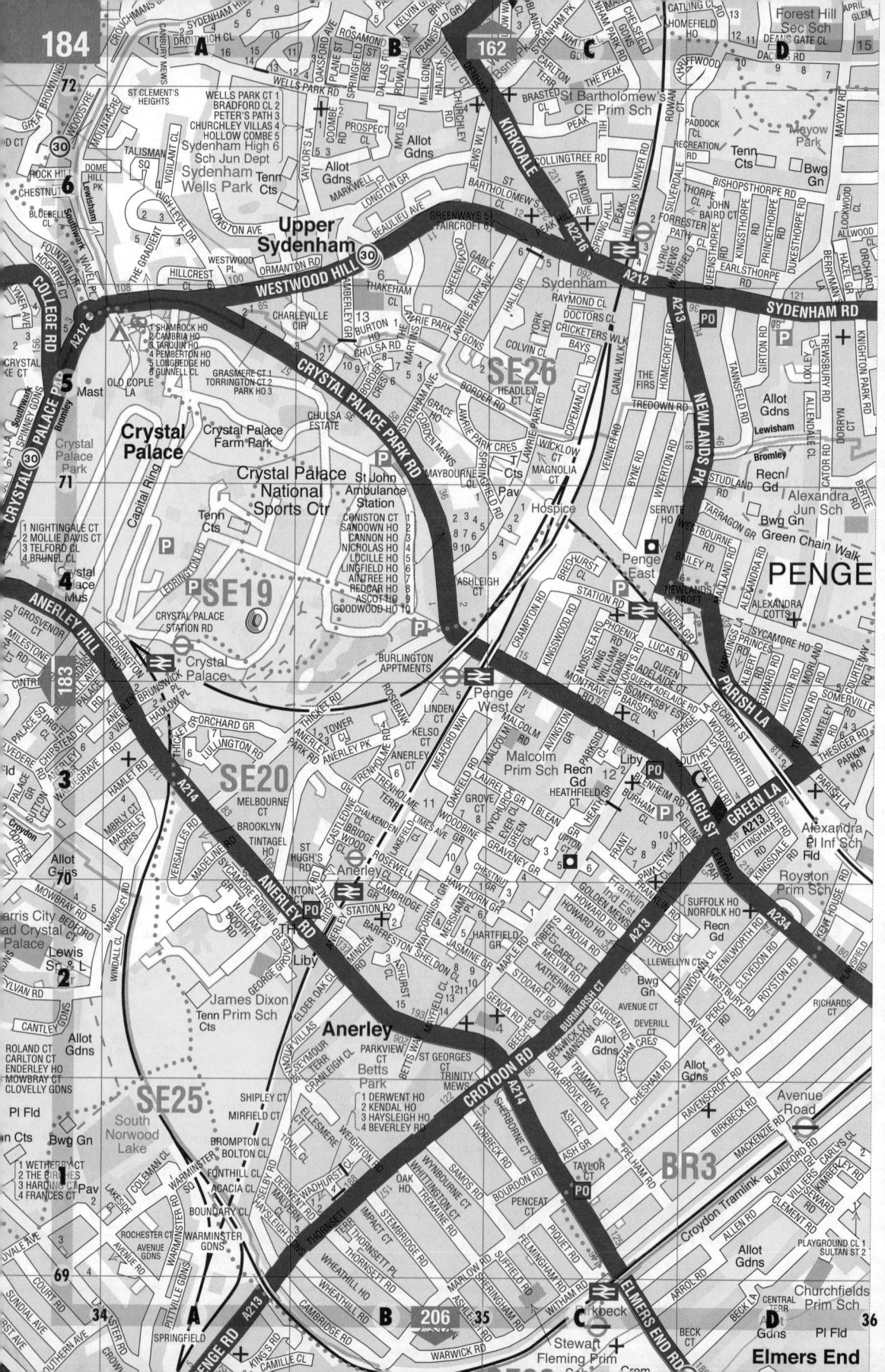

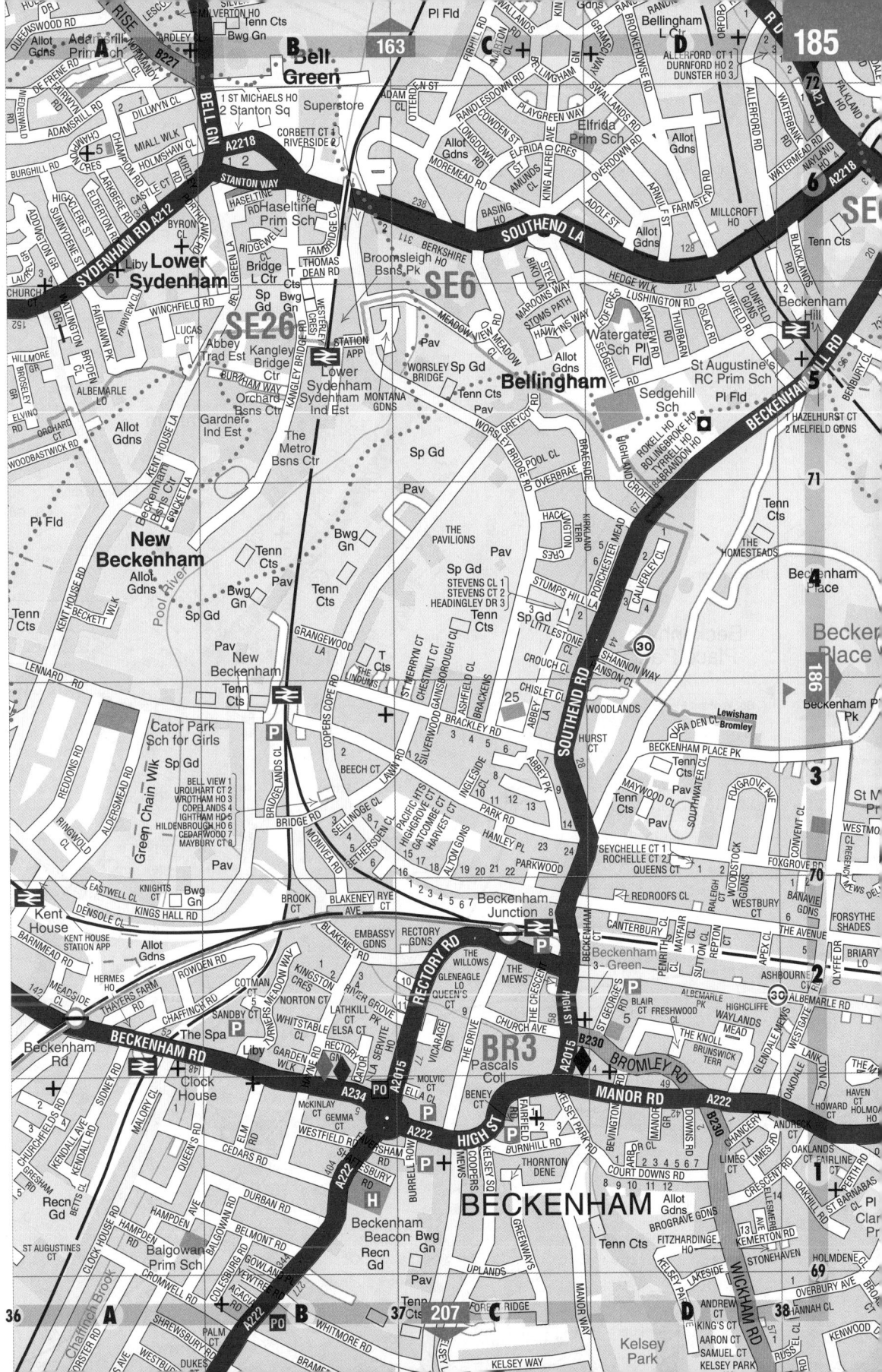

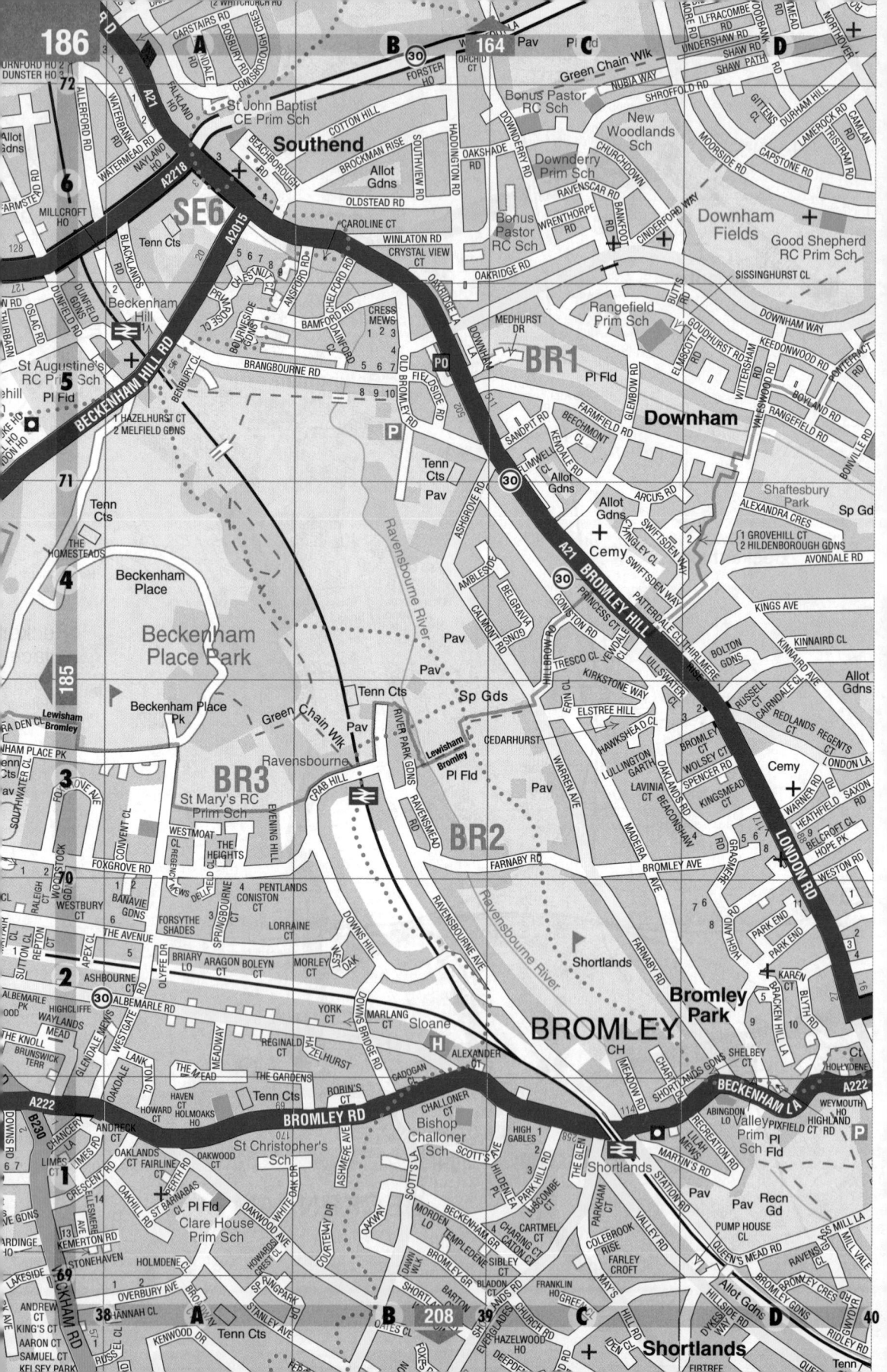

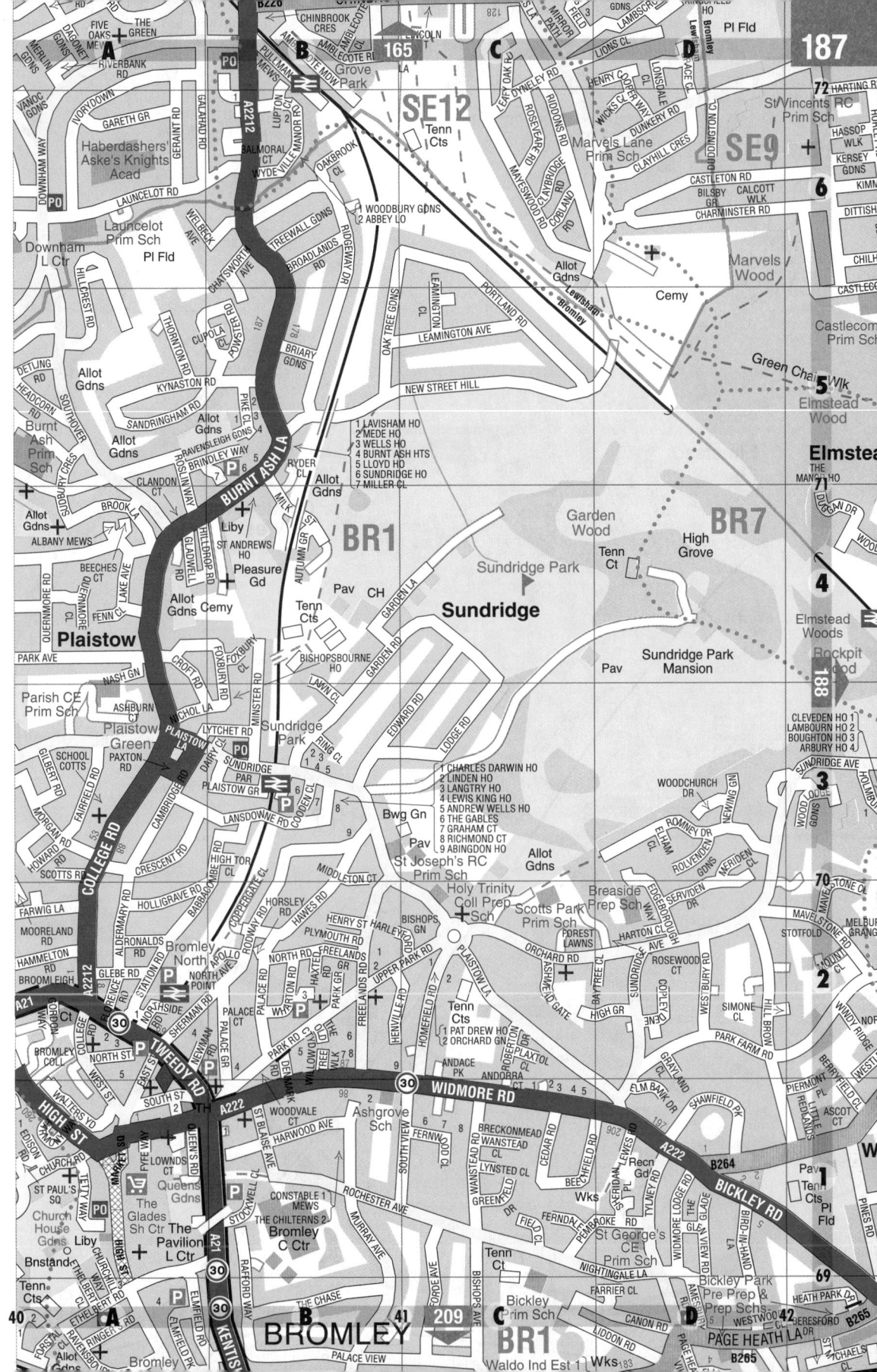

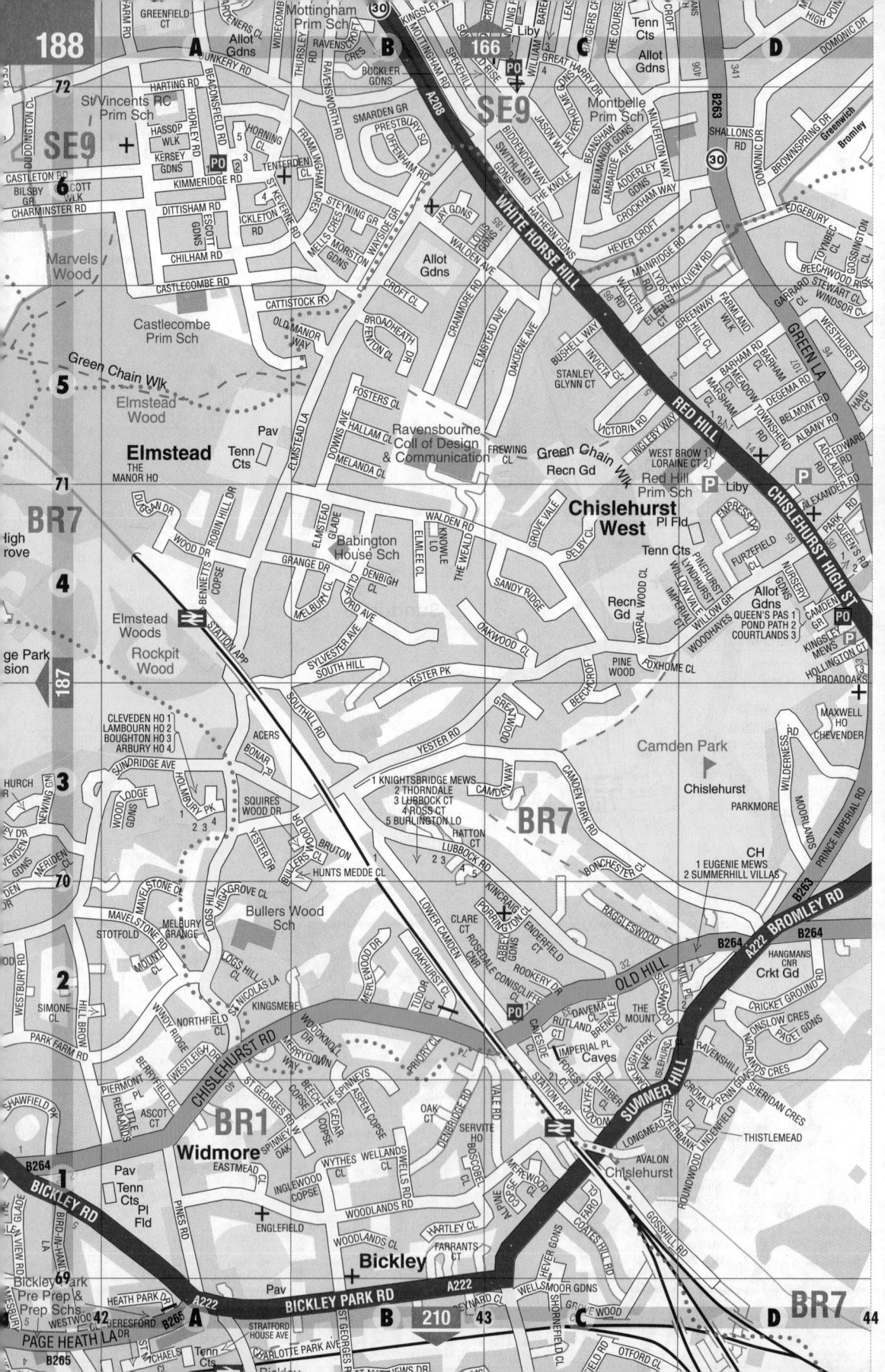

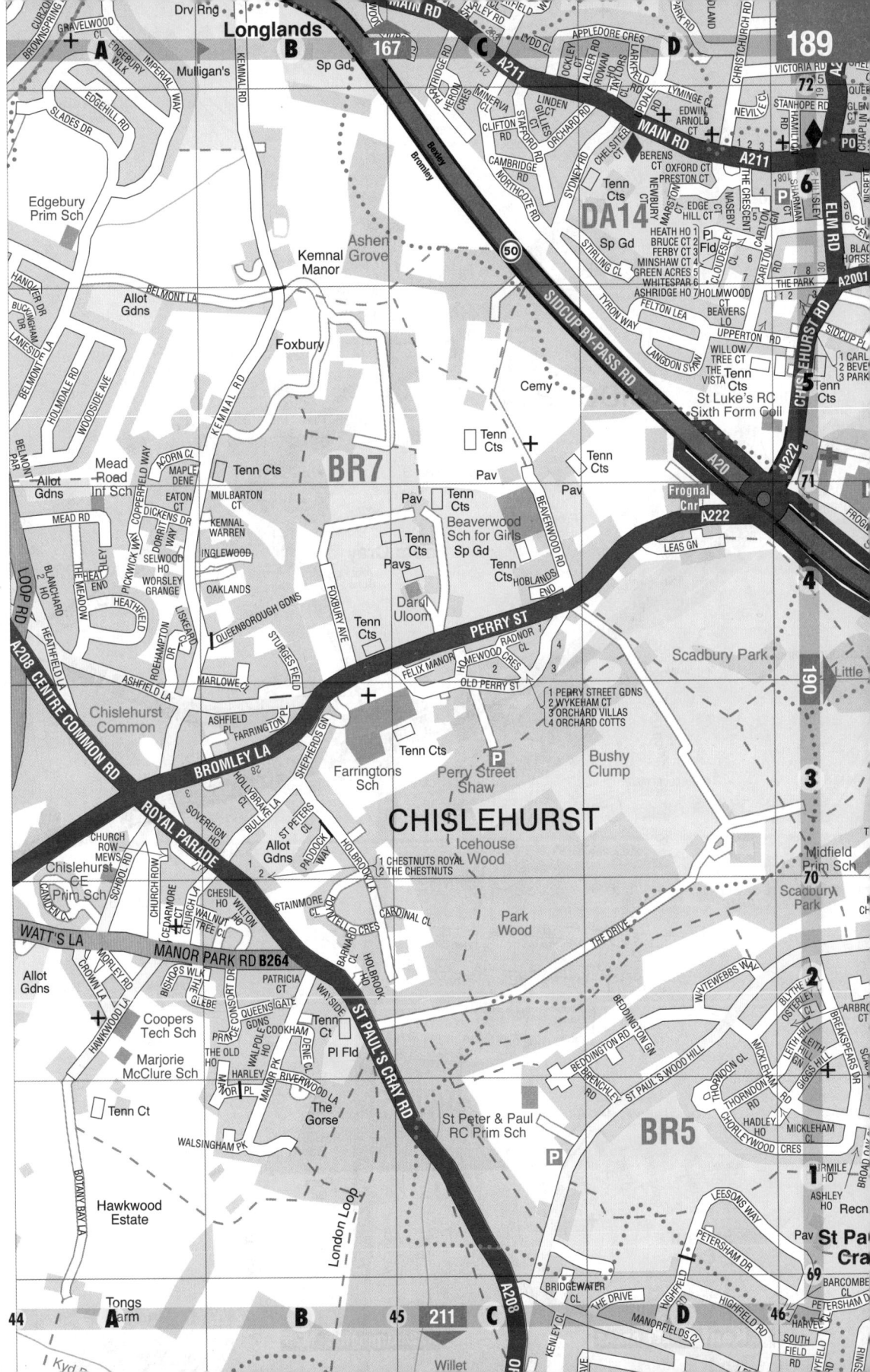

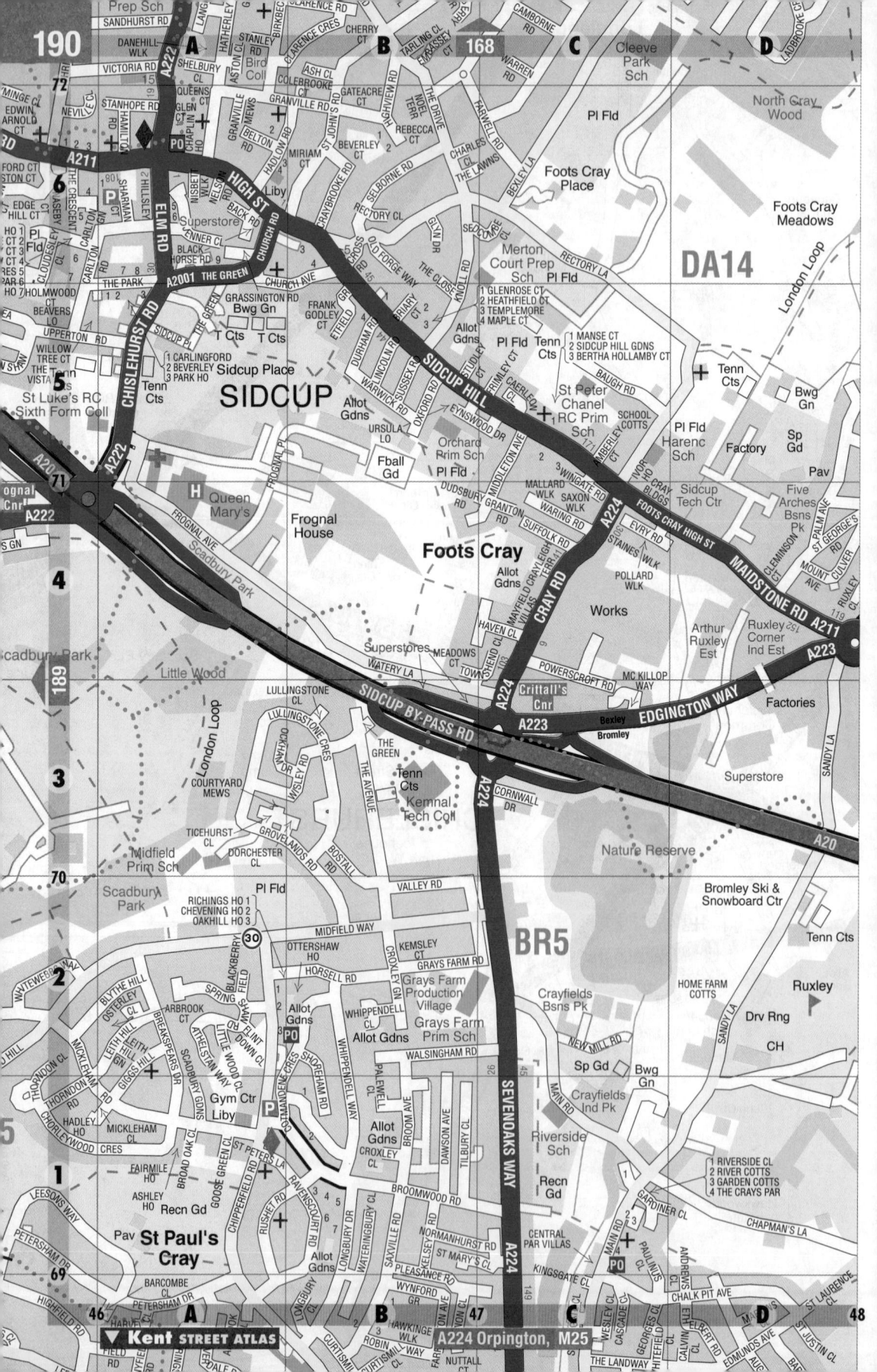

SIDCUP

Foots Cray

DA14

BR5

A224 Orpington, M25

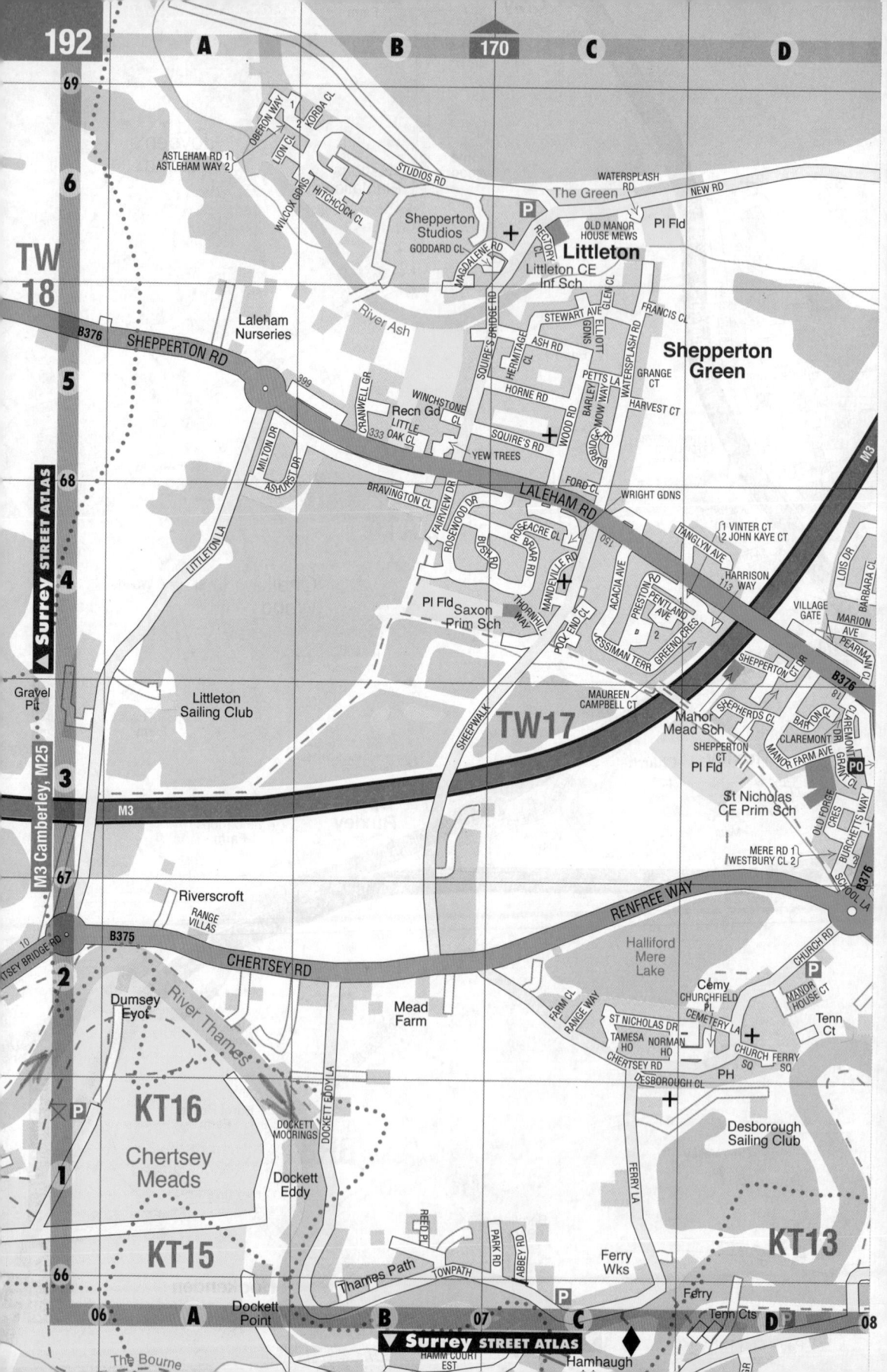

A   B   170   C   D

69

6

TW
18

B376   SHEPPERTON RD

5

68

4

3

67

2

1

66

06   A   07   B   C   08   D

ASTLEHAM RD 1
ASTLEHAM WAY 2

OBERON WAY
KORDA CL
LION CL
WILCOX GDNS
HITCHCOCK CL

STUDIOS RD

Shepperton Studios

GODDARD CL

MAGDALENE RD

RECTORY RD

WATERSPLASH RD
The Green

NEW RD

Pl Fld

OLD MANOR HOUSE MEWS

Littleton
Littleton CE Inf Sch

Laleham Nurseries

River Ash

STEWART AVE

FRANCIS CL

GLEN CL

Shepperton Green

HERMITAGE CL
ASH RD
ELLIOTT GDNS

GRANGE CT

WINCHSTONE CL

HORNE RD

BARLEY MOW WAY
PETTS LA
WATERSPLASH RD

HARVEST CT

CRANWELL GR

LITTLE OAK CL

SQUIRE'S RD

YEW TREES

WOOD RD

BLUEBRIDGE RD

Recn Gd
333

399

MILTON DR

ASHURST DR

LITTLETON LA

BRAVINGTON CL

FAIRVIEW DR
ROSEWOOD DR
BUSH RD

ROSEACRE CL
BAAR RD

MANDEVILLE RD

FORD CL

LALEHAM RD

WRIGHT GDNS

150

TANGLYN AVE

1 VINTER CT
2 JOHN KAYE CT

HARRISON WAY
113

LOIS DR

BARBARA CL

VILLAGE GATE

MARION AVE
PEARMAN CL

B376

THORNHILL WAY

POOL END CL

ACACIA AVE

PRESTON RD
PENTLAND AVE

GREENO CRES

SESSIMAN TERR

Pl Fld
Saxon Prim Sch

SHEEPWALK

TW17

MAUREEN CAMPBELL CT

SHEPPERTON CT

Manor Mead Sch

SHEPHERDS CL

BARTON CL

CLAREMONT CL

SHEPPERTON CT

Pl Fld

MANOR FARM AVE

GRANT CL

CLAREMONT DR

OLD FORGE CRES

BURCHETTS WAY

PO

SCHOOL LA

B376

St Nicholas CE Prim Sch

MERE RD 1
WESTBURY CL 2

Gravel Pit

Littleton Sailing Club

M3

M3 Camberley, M25

Riverscroft

RANGE VILLAS

ITSEY BRIDGE RD

B375

CHERTSEY RD

Dumsey Eyot

River Thames

Mead Farm

RENFREE WAY

FARM CL

RANGE WAY

Halliford Mere Lake

Cemy
CHURCHFIELD PL
CEMETERY LA

MANOR HOUSE CT

CHURCH RD

Tenn Ct

P

ST NICHOLAS DR

TAMESA HO

NORMAN HO

CHERTSEY RD

DESBOROUGH CL

FERRY LA

CHURCH FERRY SQ

CHURCH FERRY SQ

PH

KT16

Chertsey Meads

DOCKETT MOORINGS

DOCKETT EDDY LA

Dockett Eddy

RED PL

PARK RD

ABBEY RD

Desborough Sailing Club

Ferry Wks

KT15

KT13

Dockett Point

Thames Path

TOWPATH

Ferry

Tenn Cts

P

Surrey STREET ATLAS

Hamhaugh

HAMM COURT EST

The Bourne

Surrey STREET ATLAS

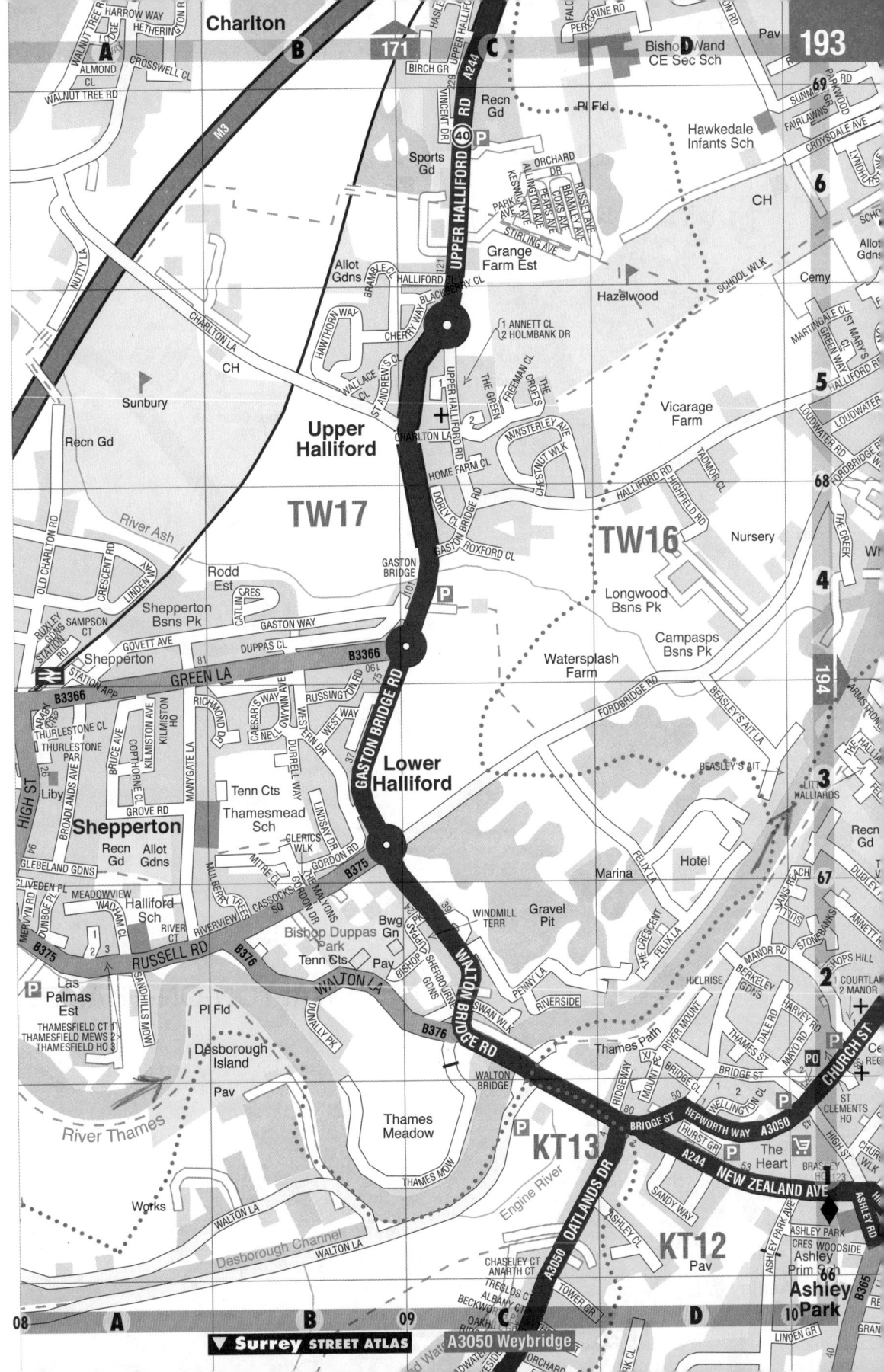

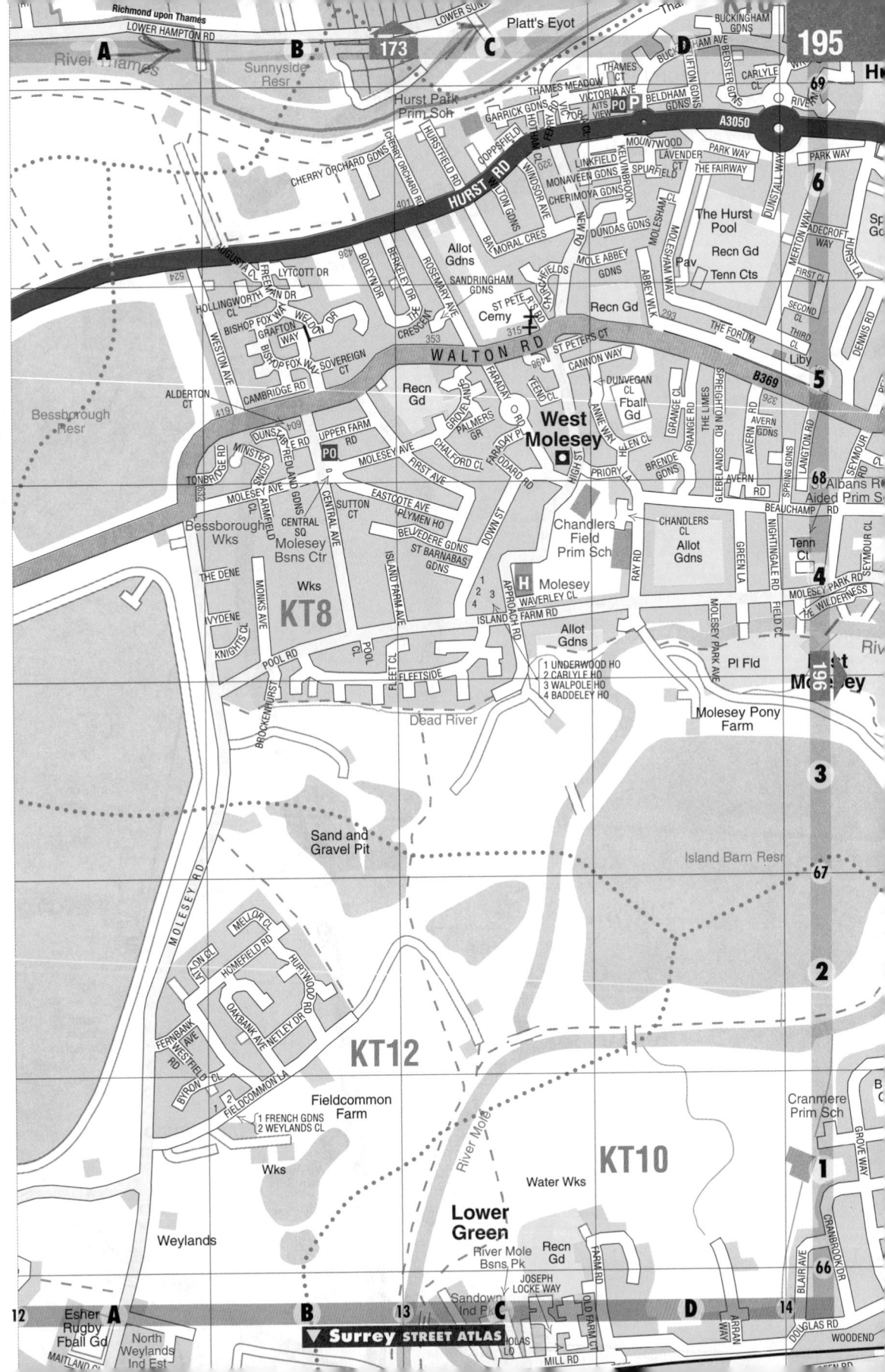

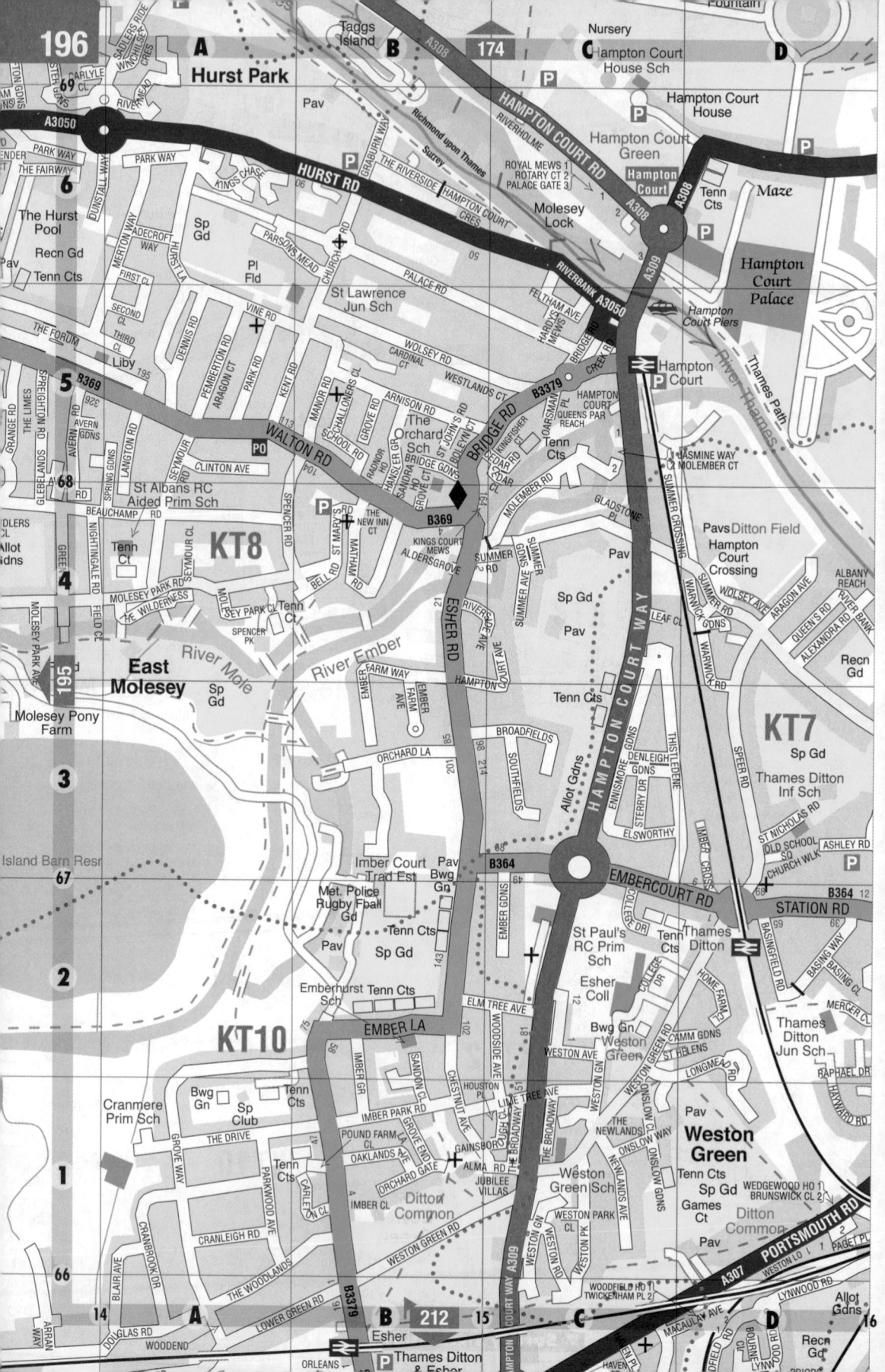

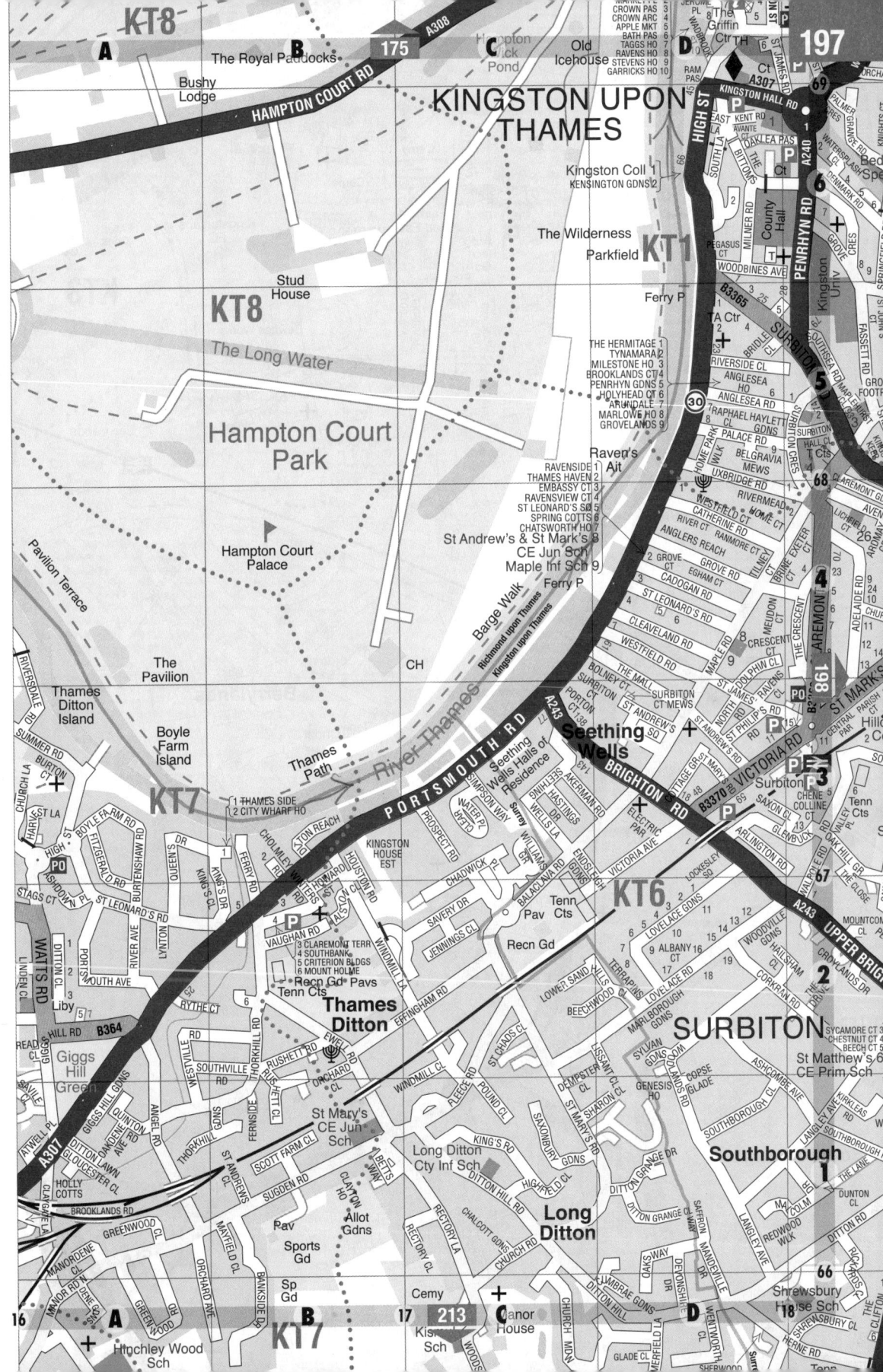

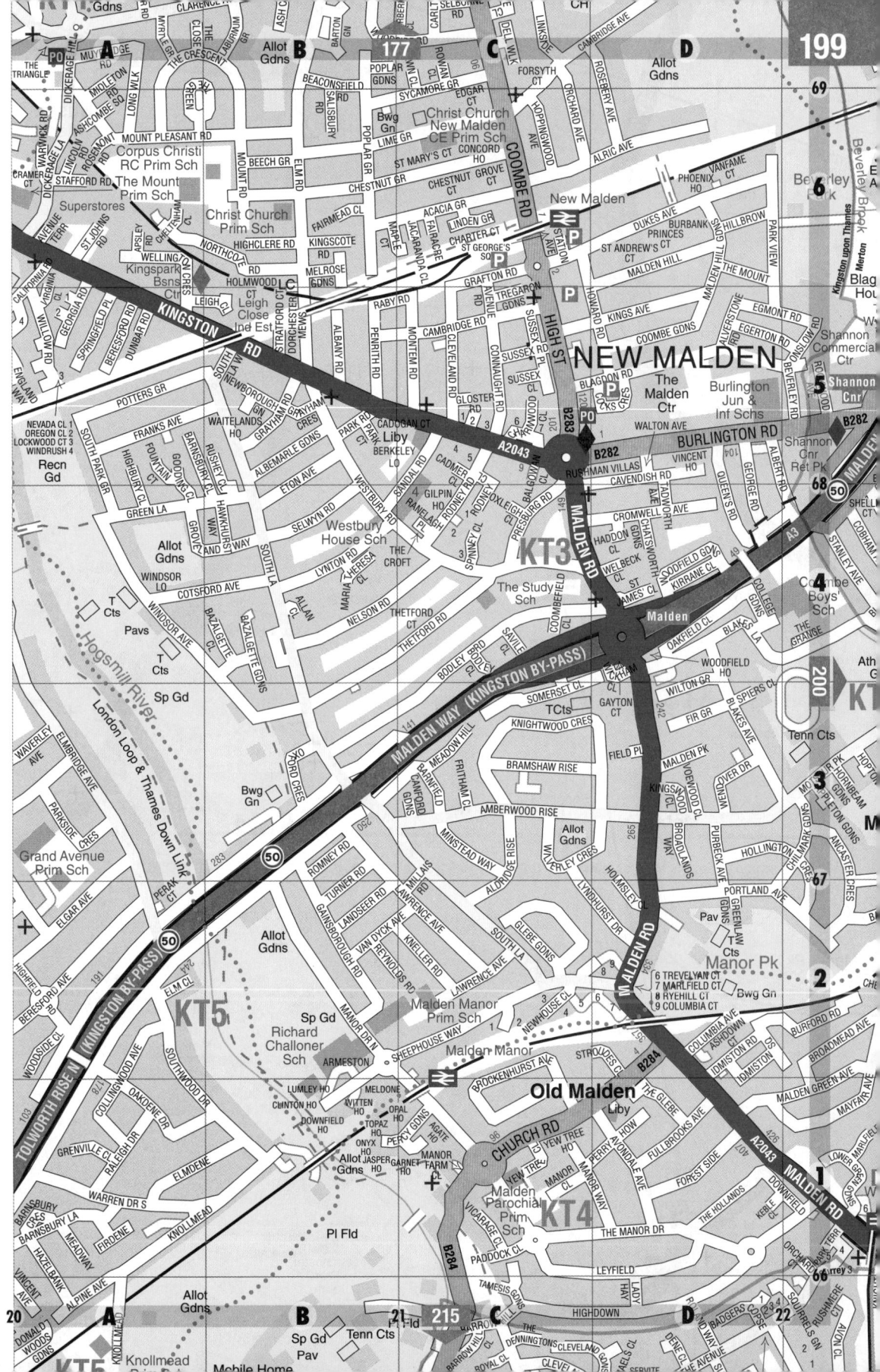

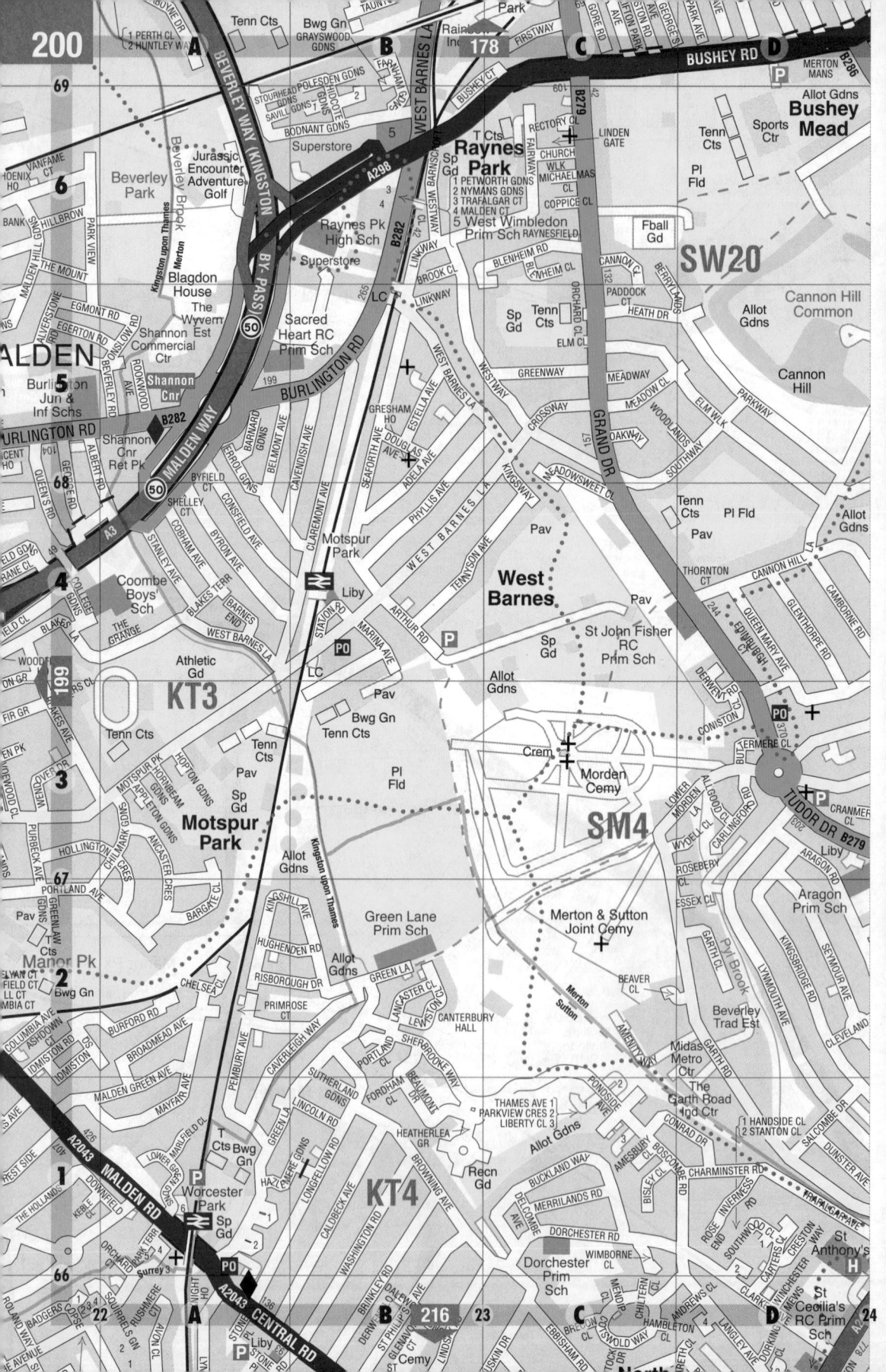

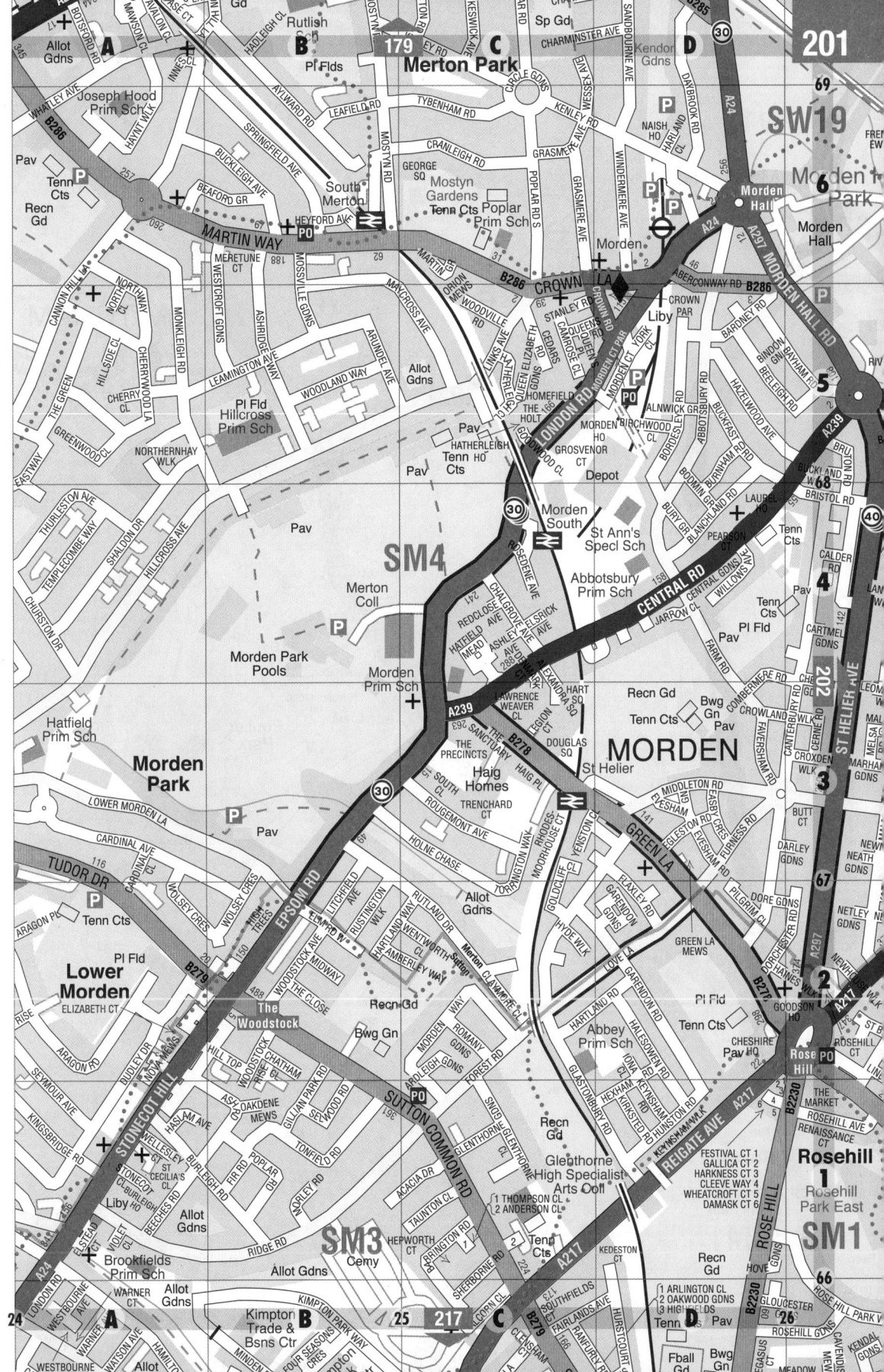

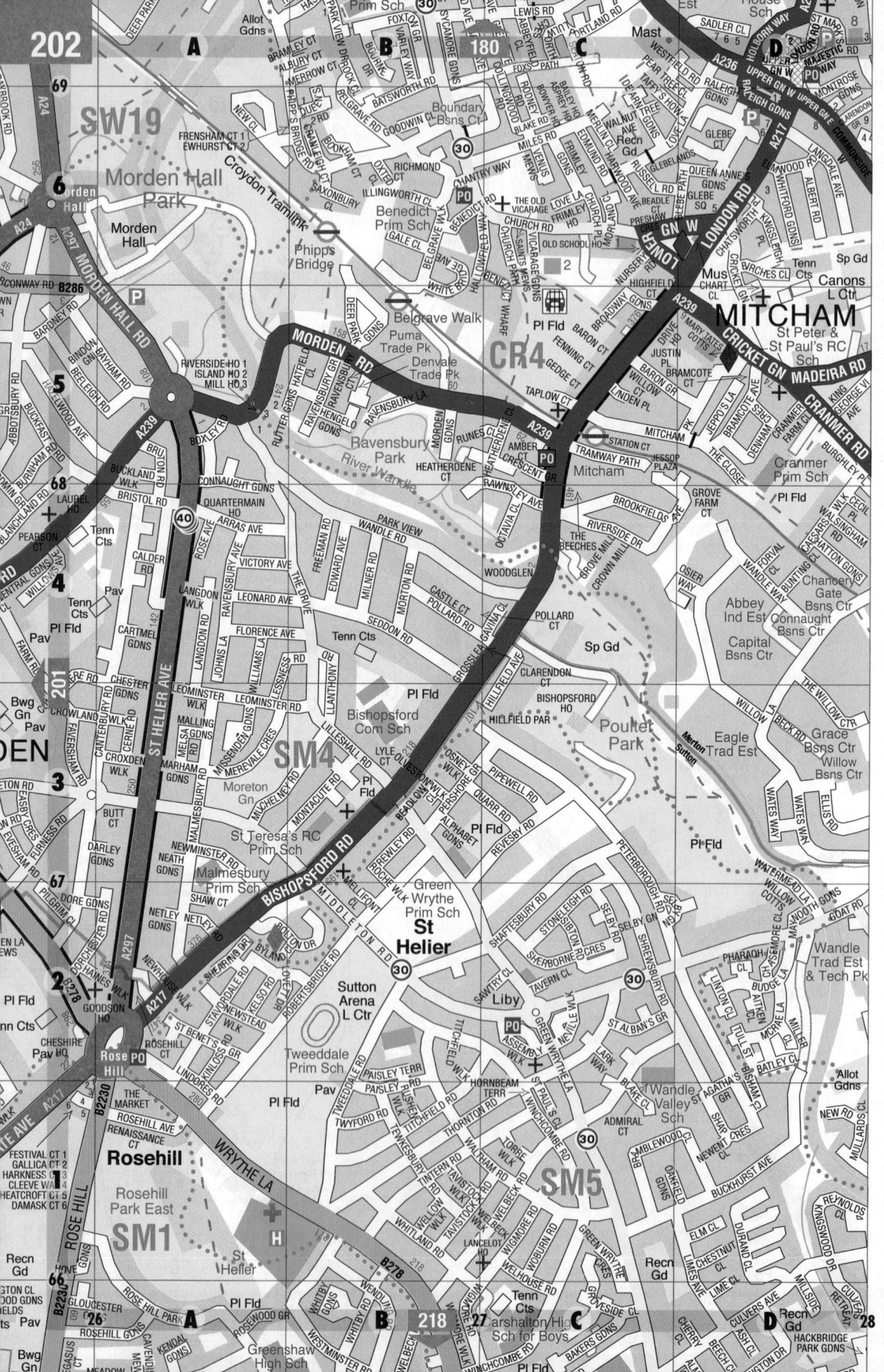

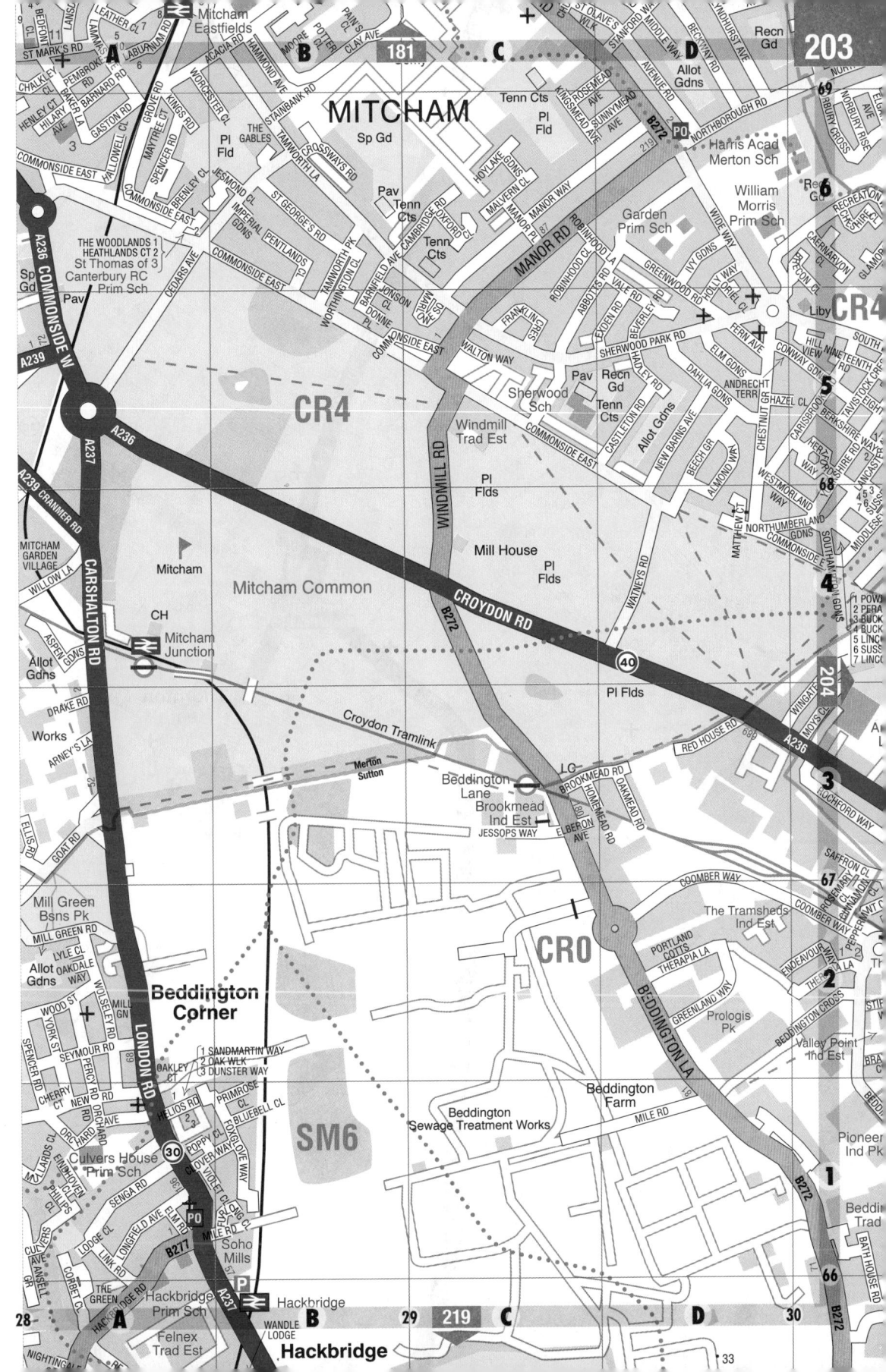

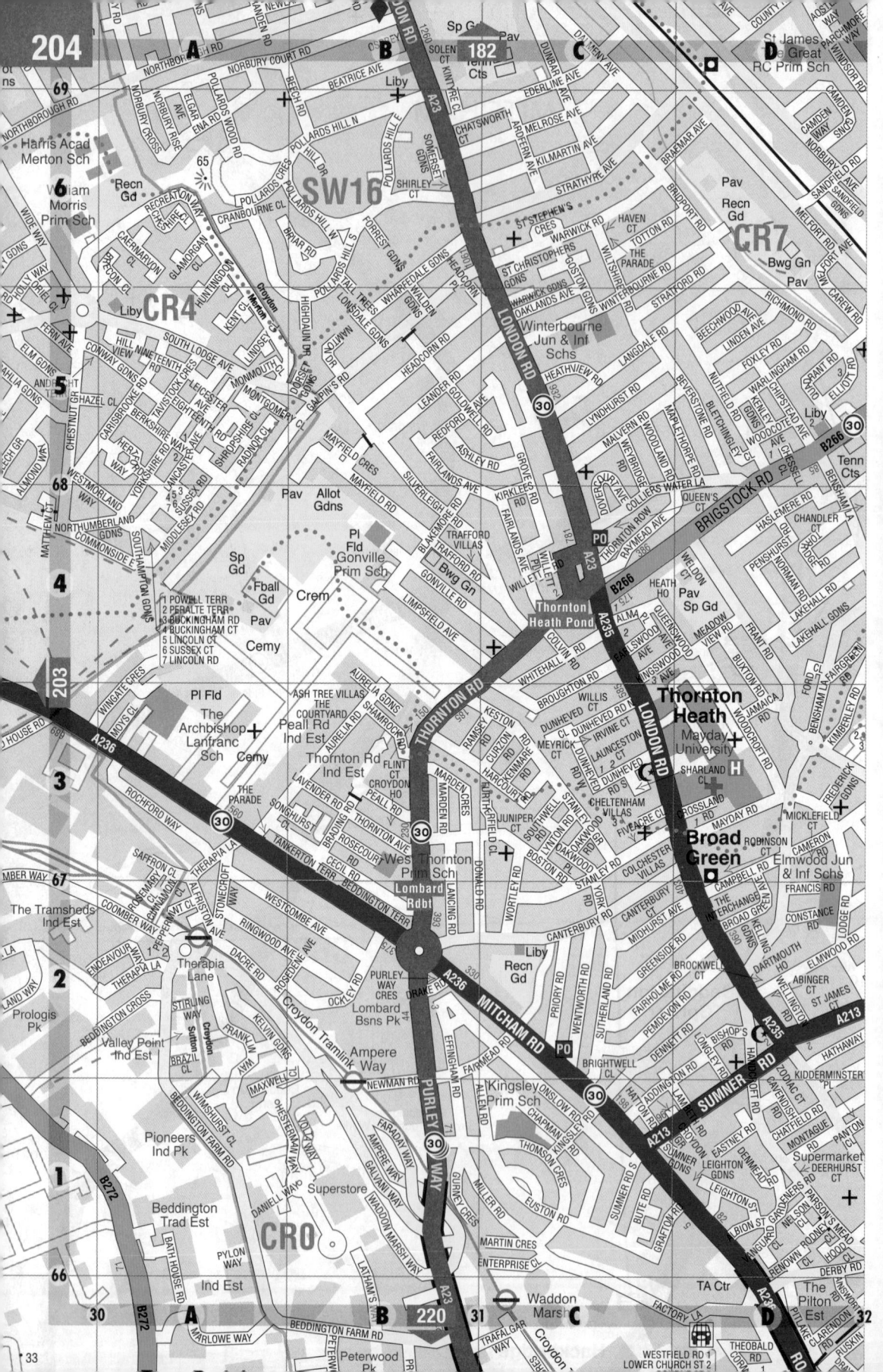

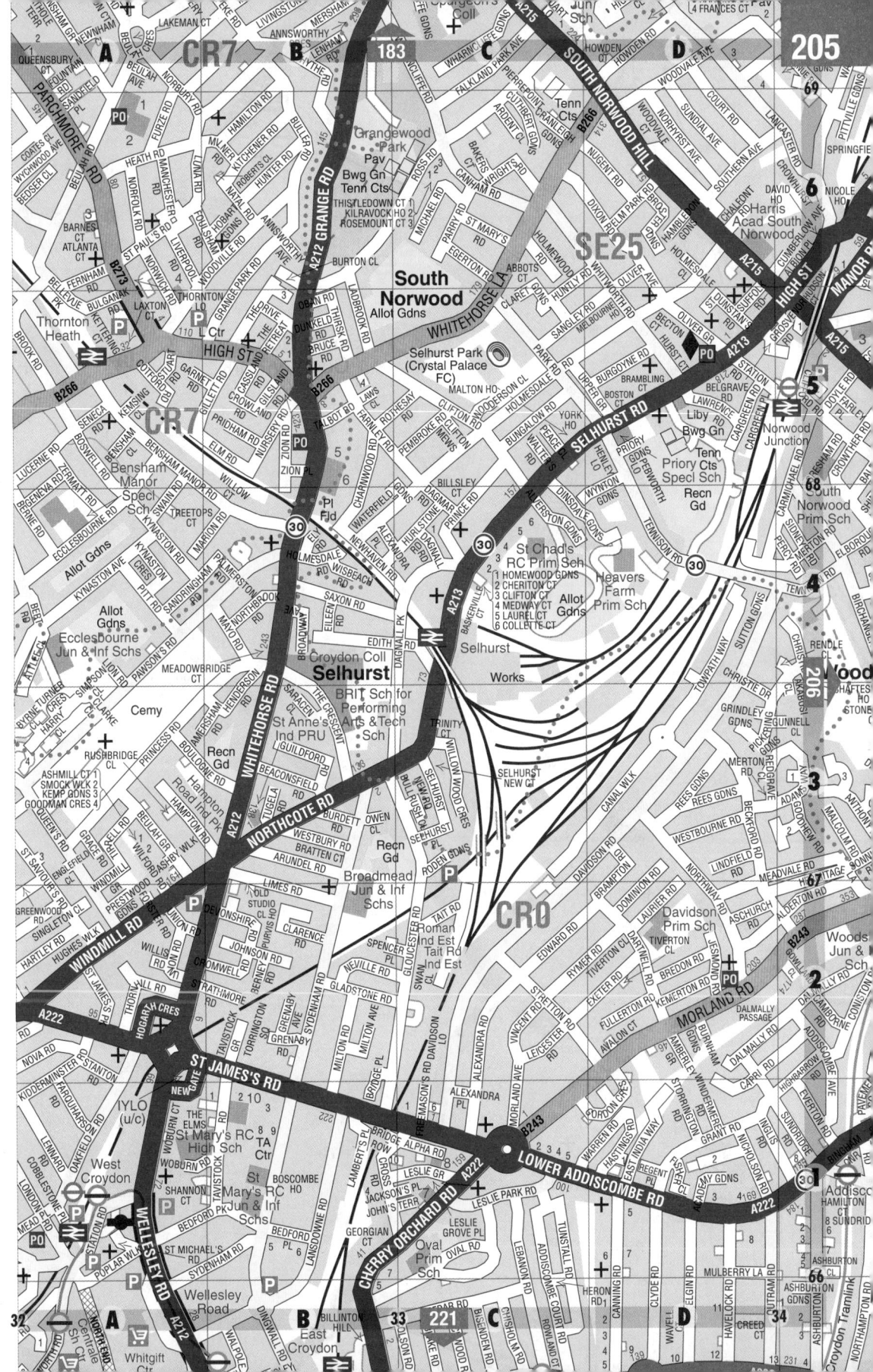

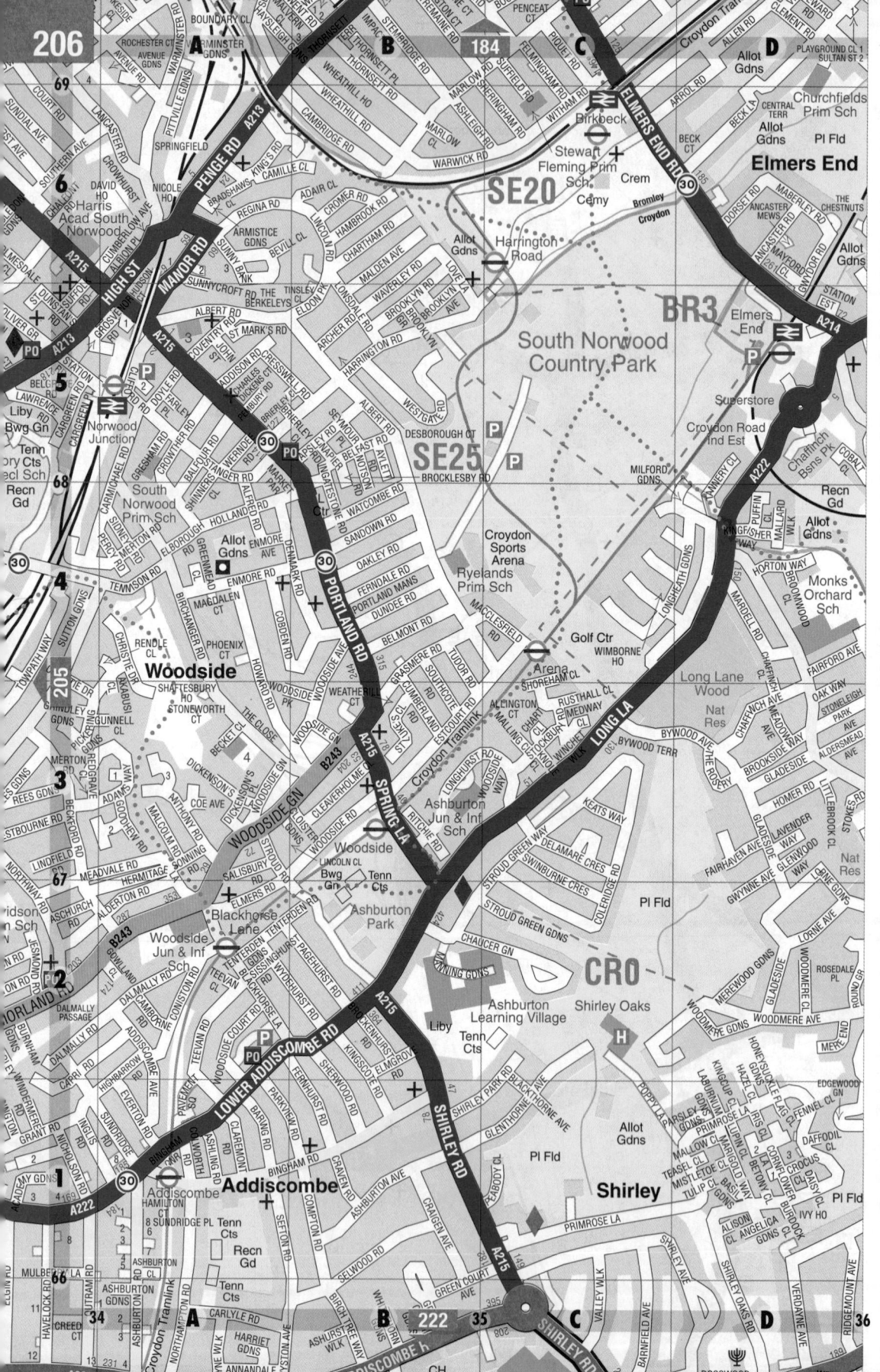

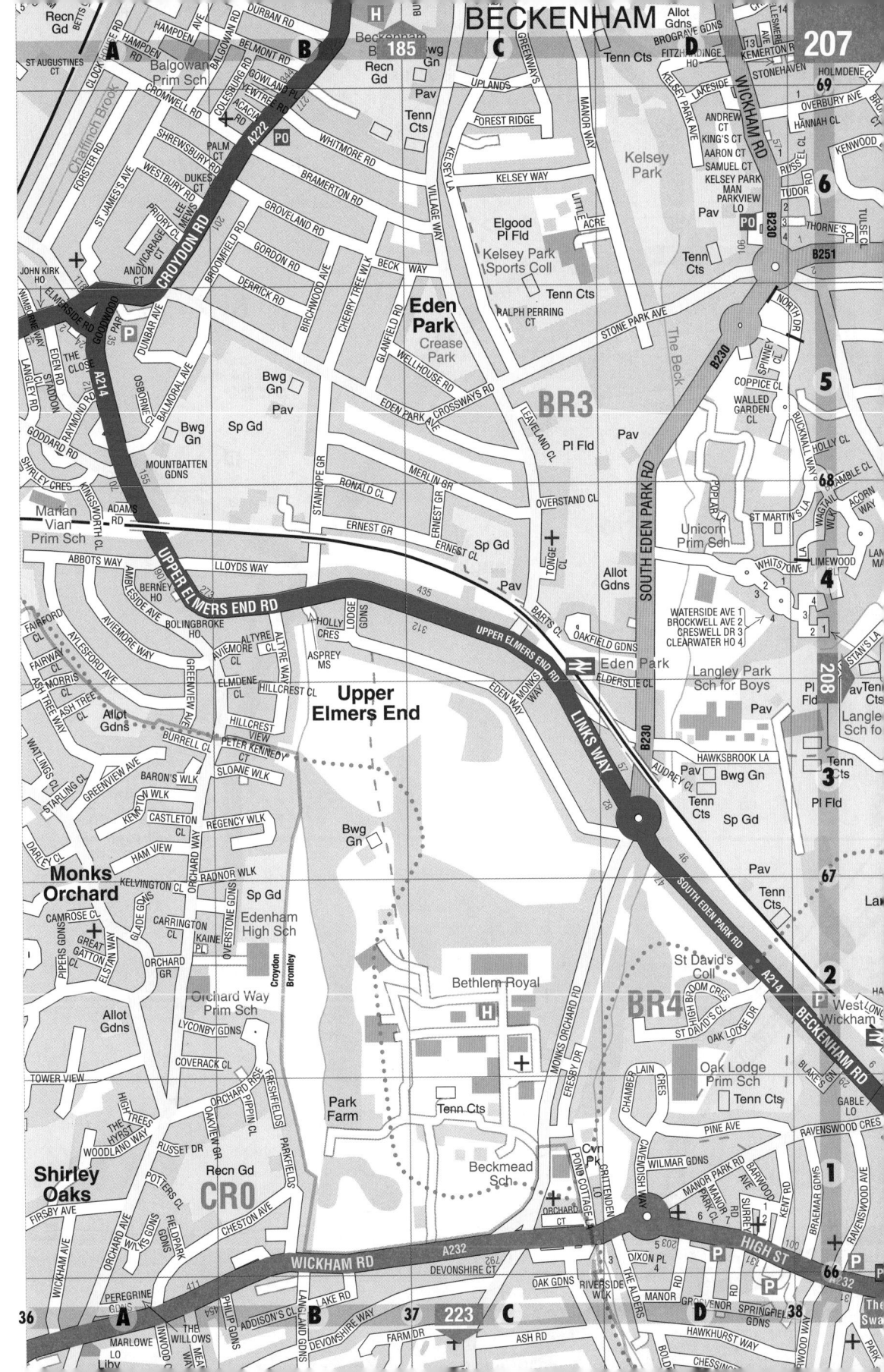

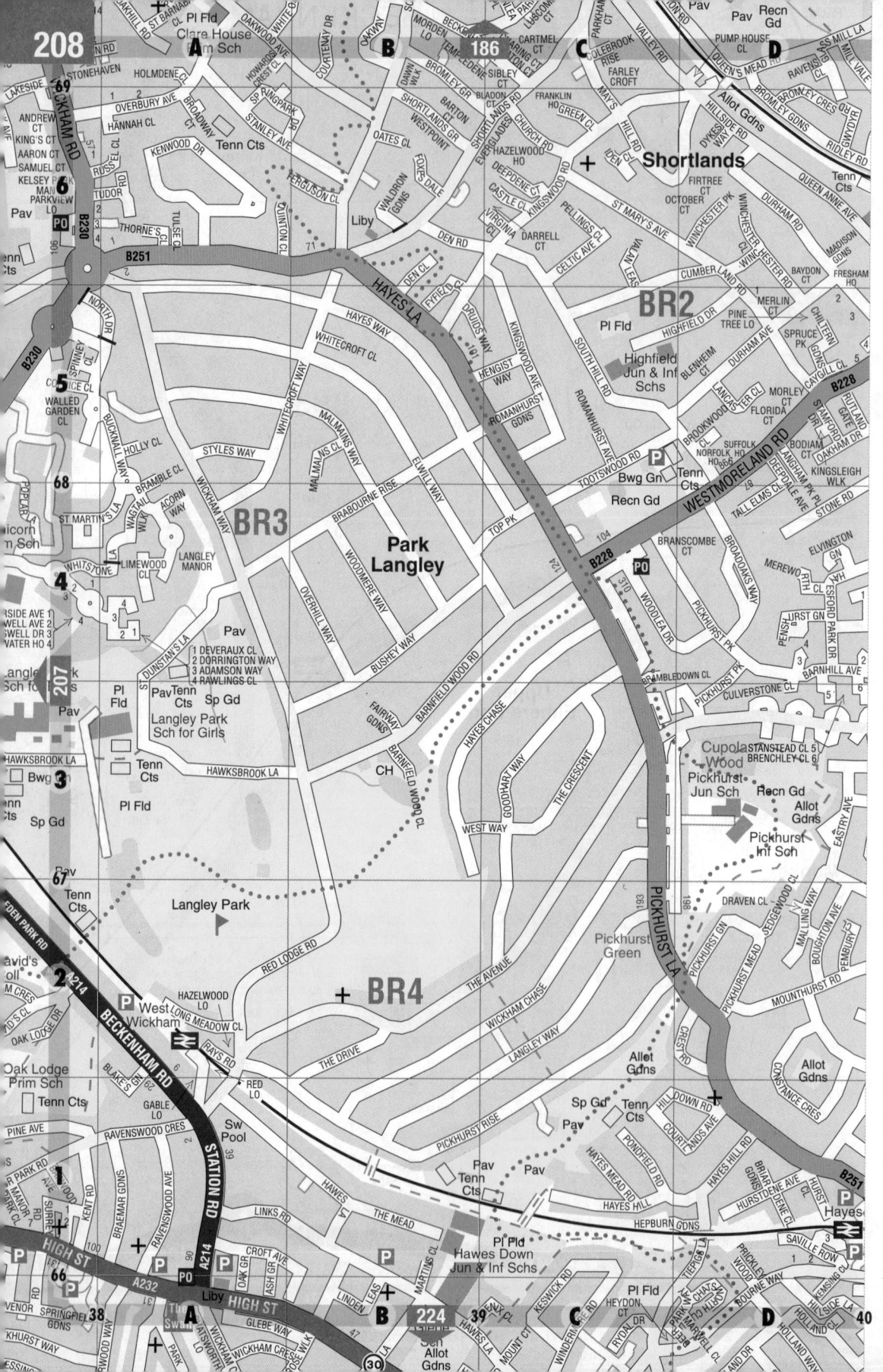

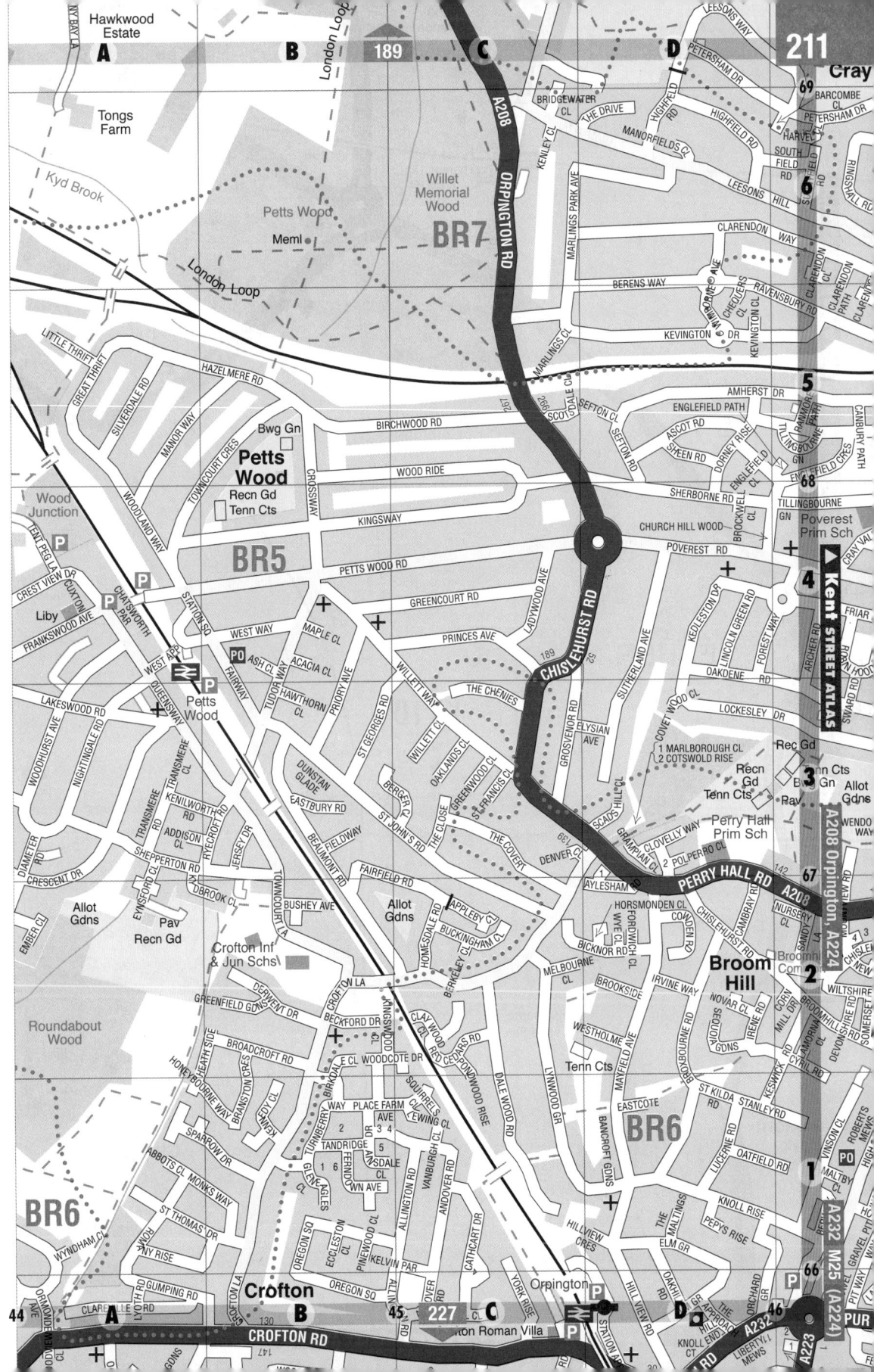

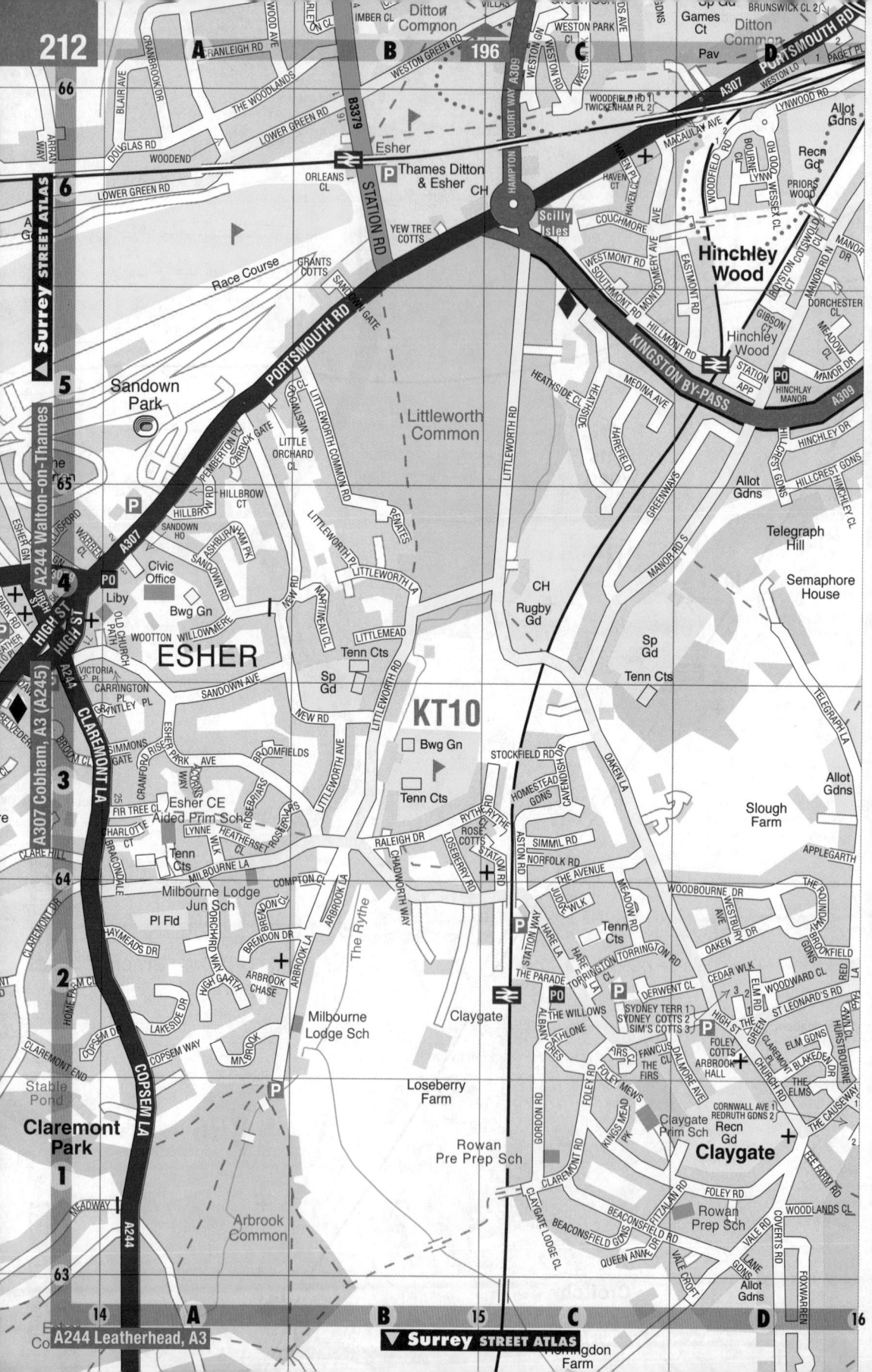

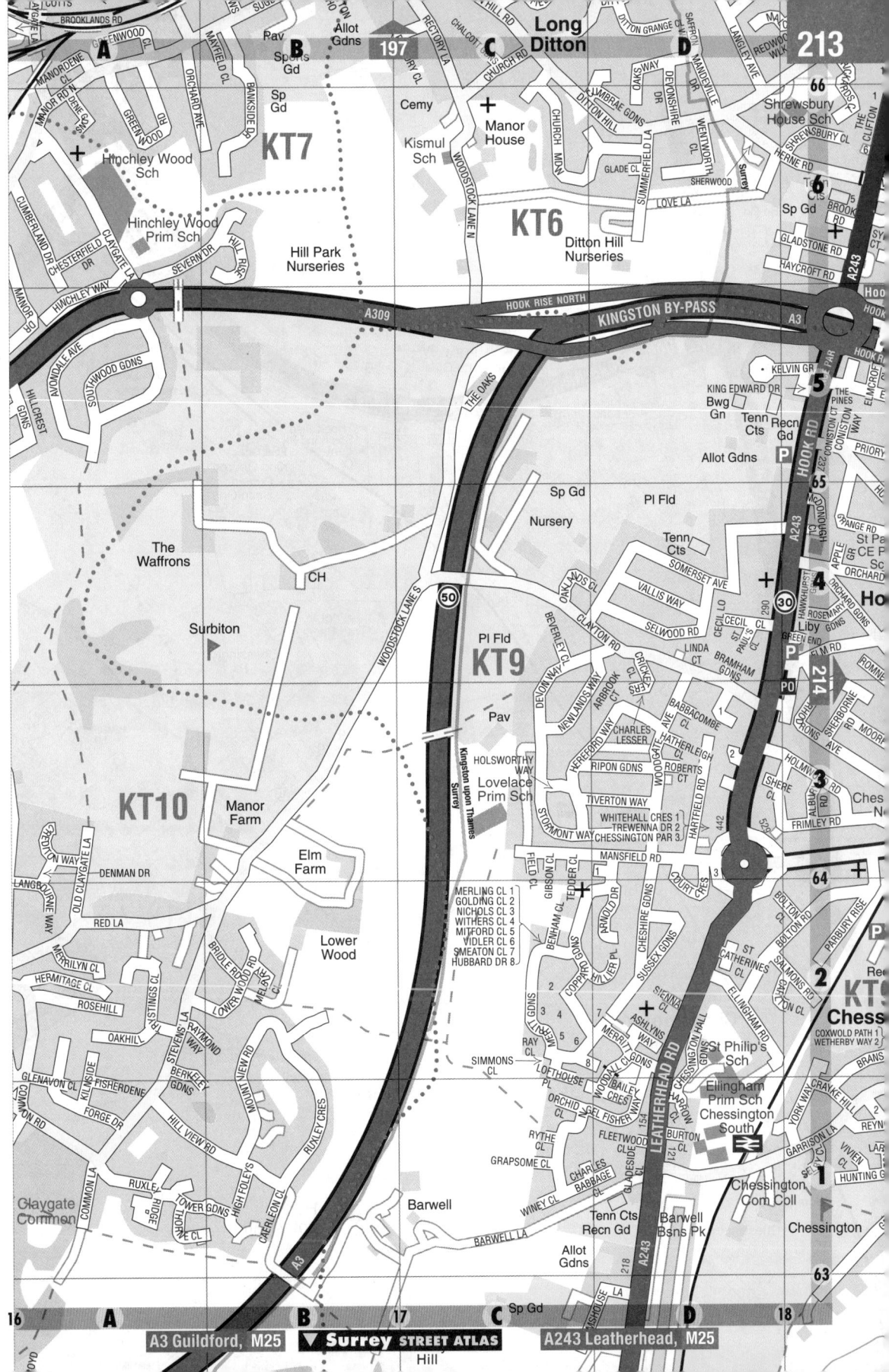

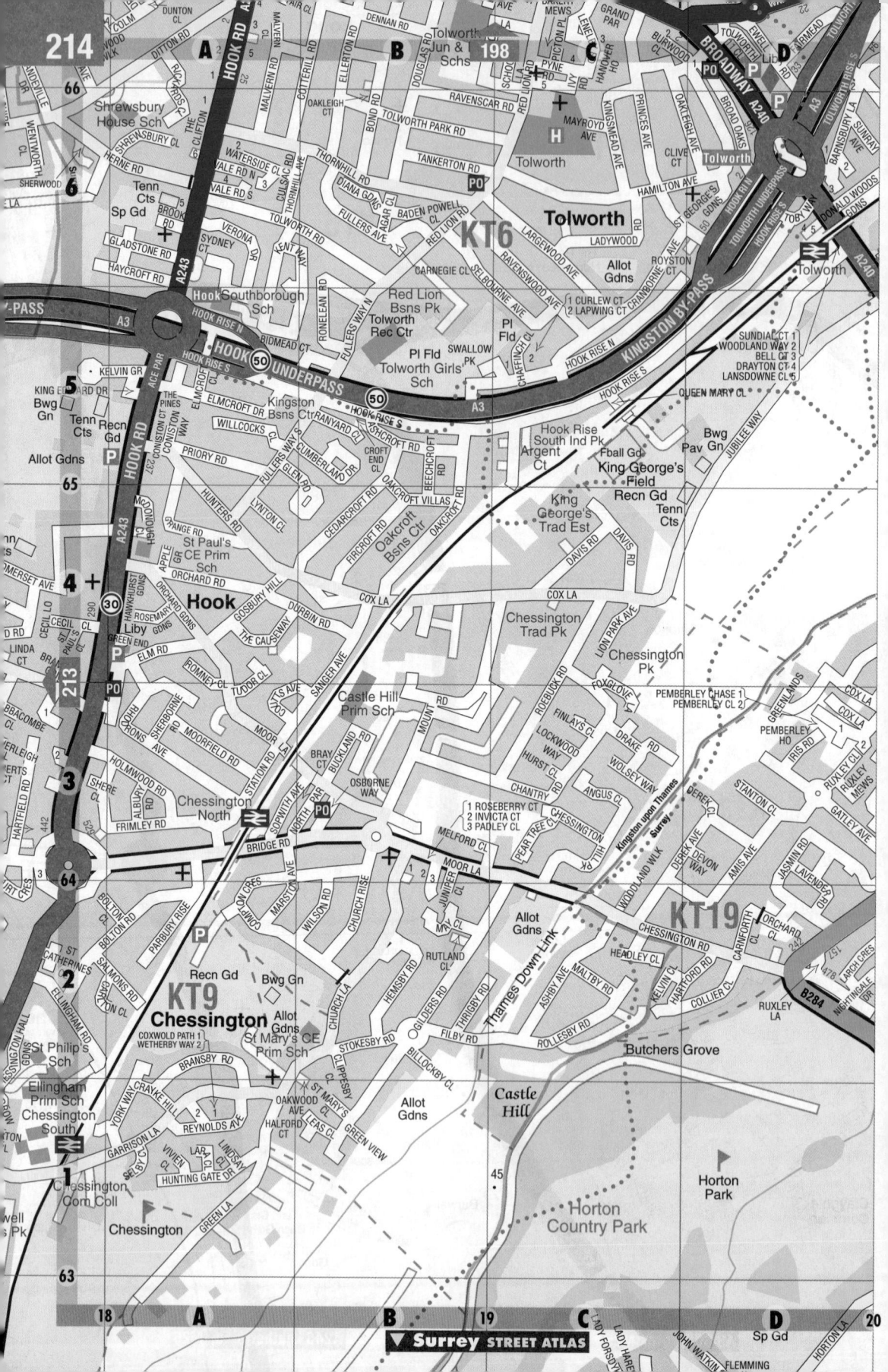

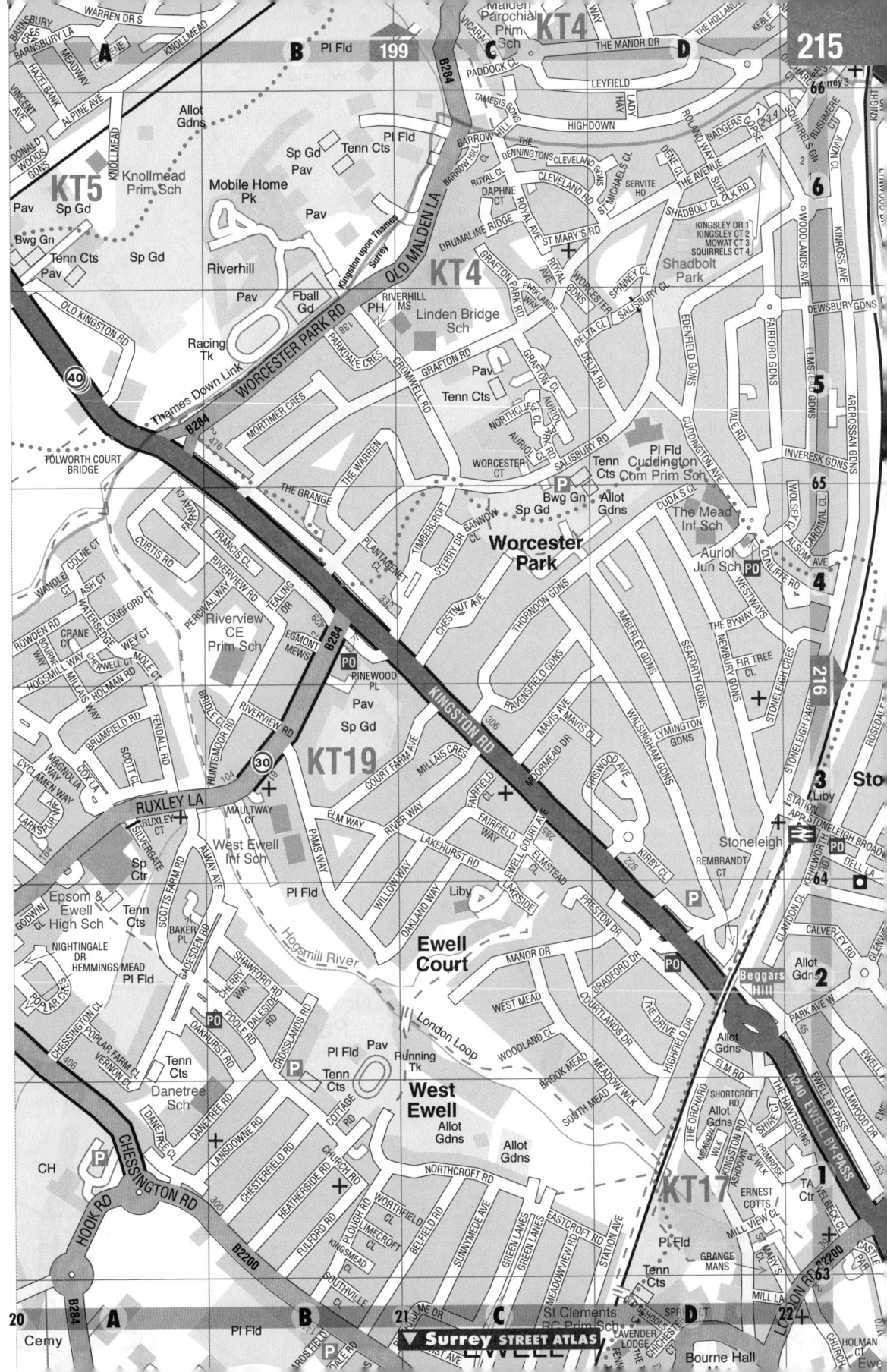

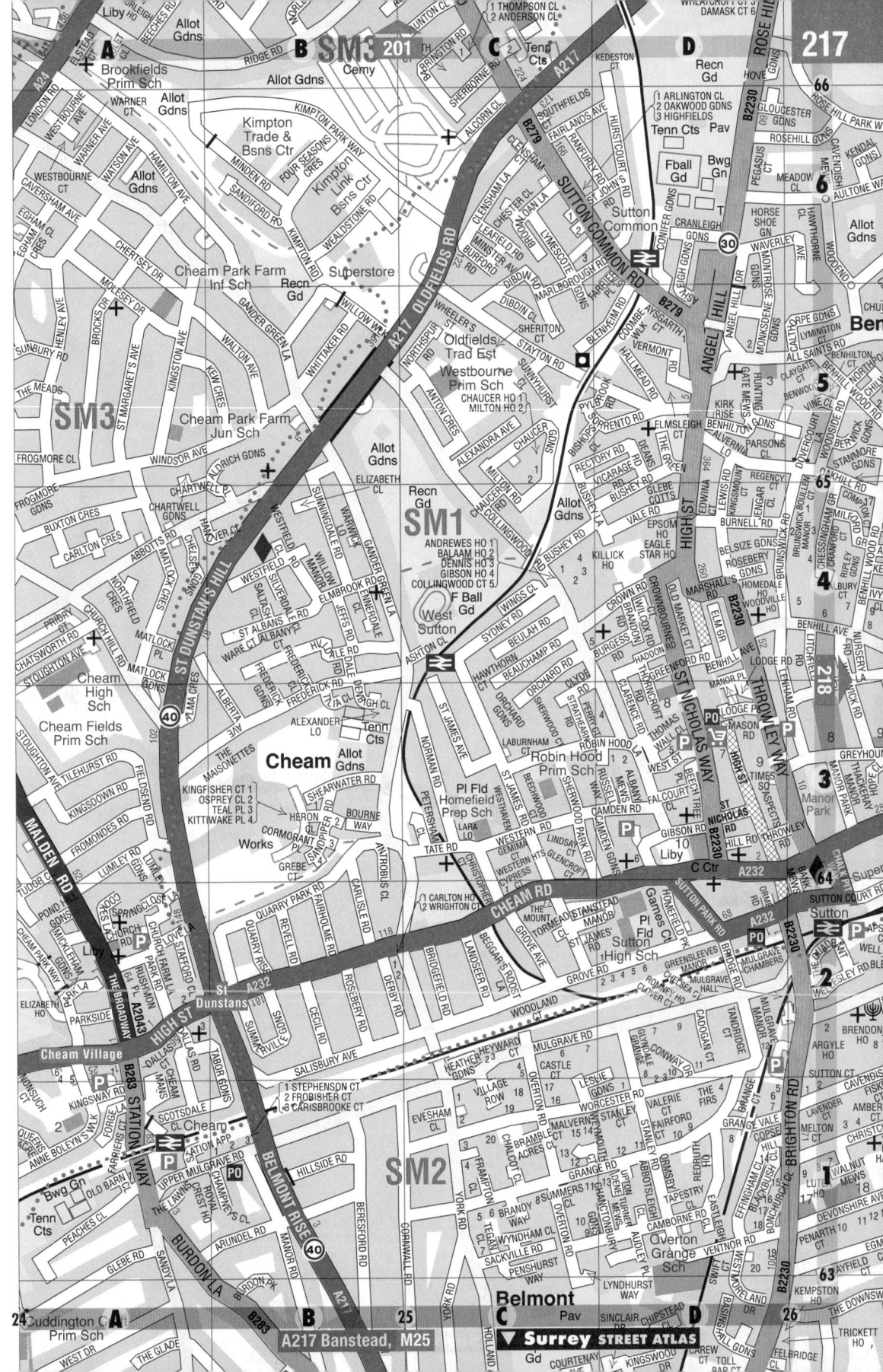

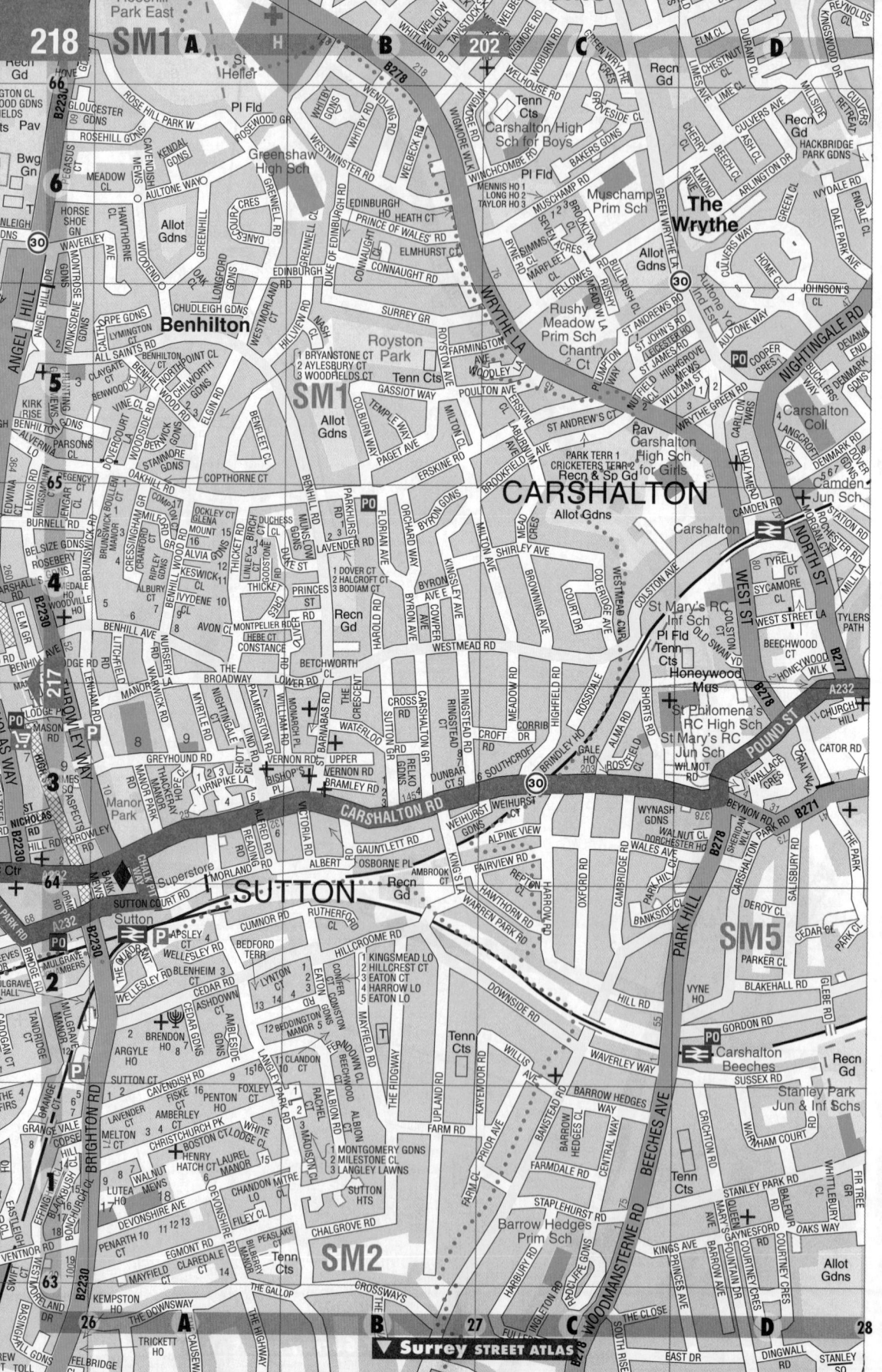

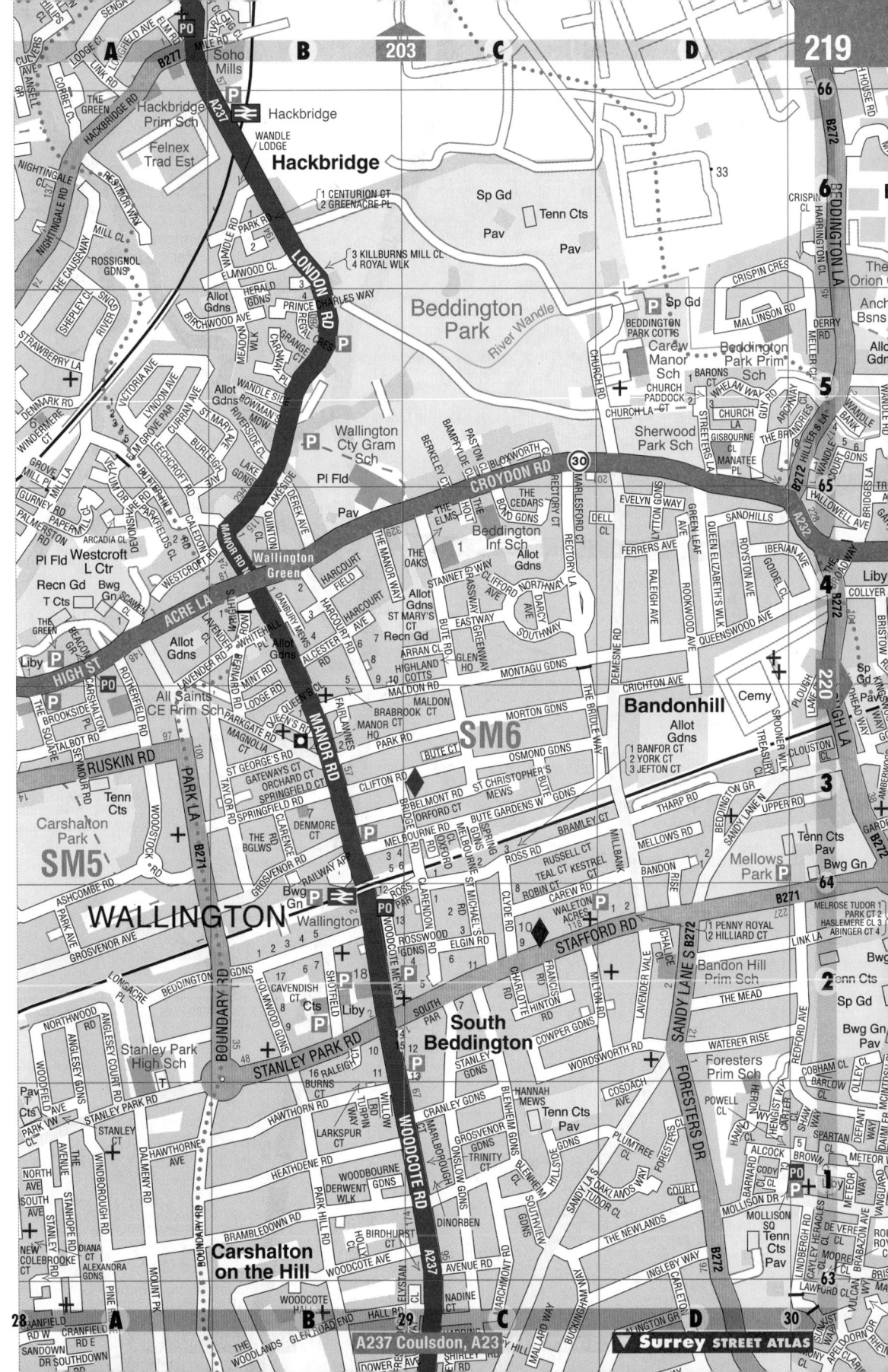

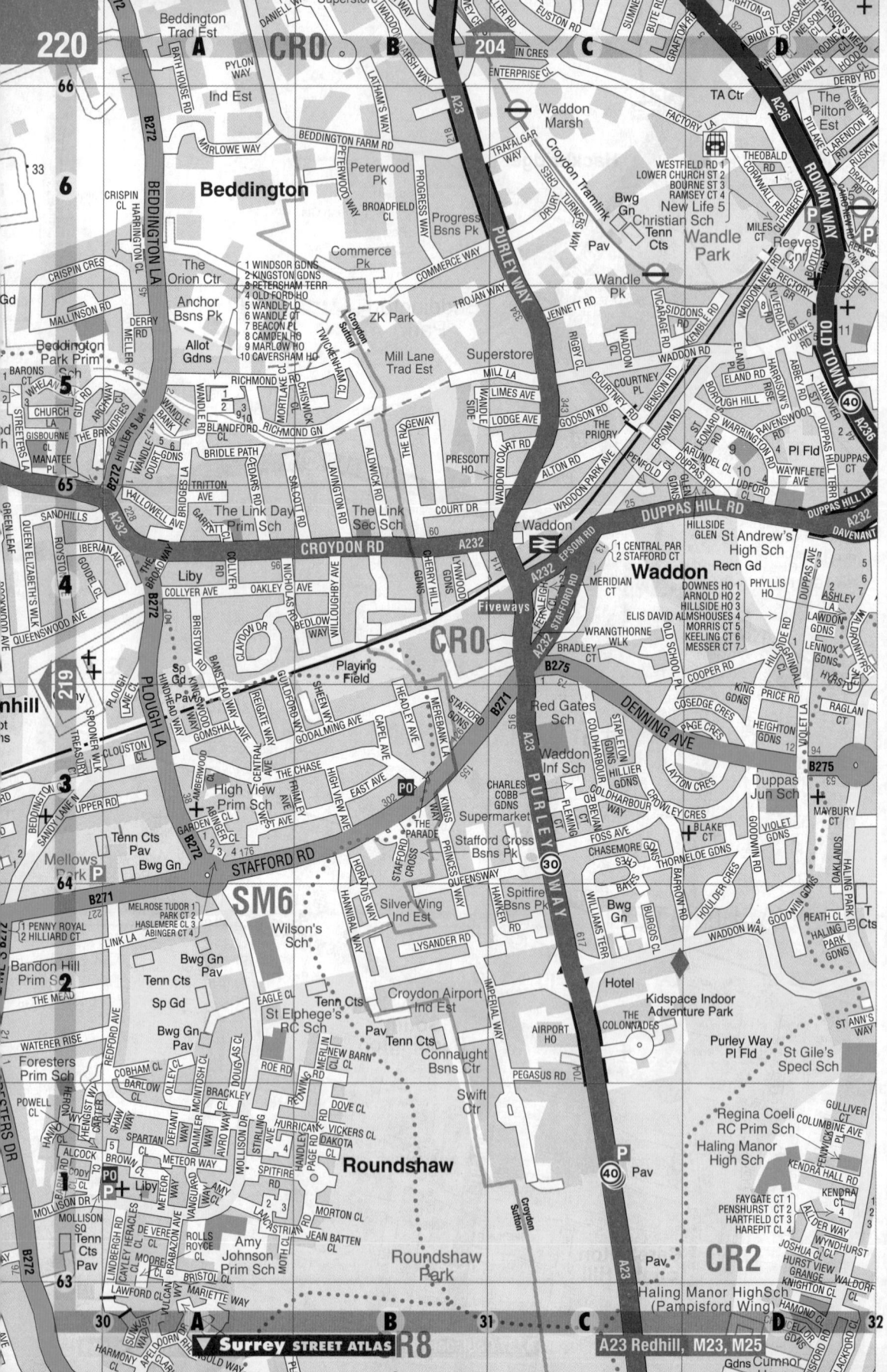

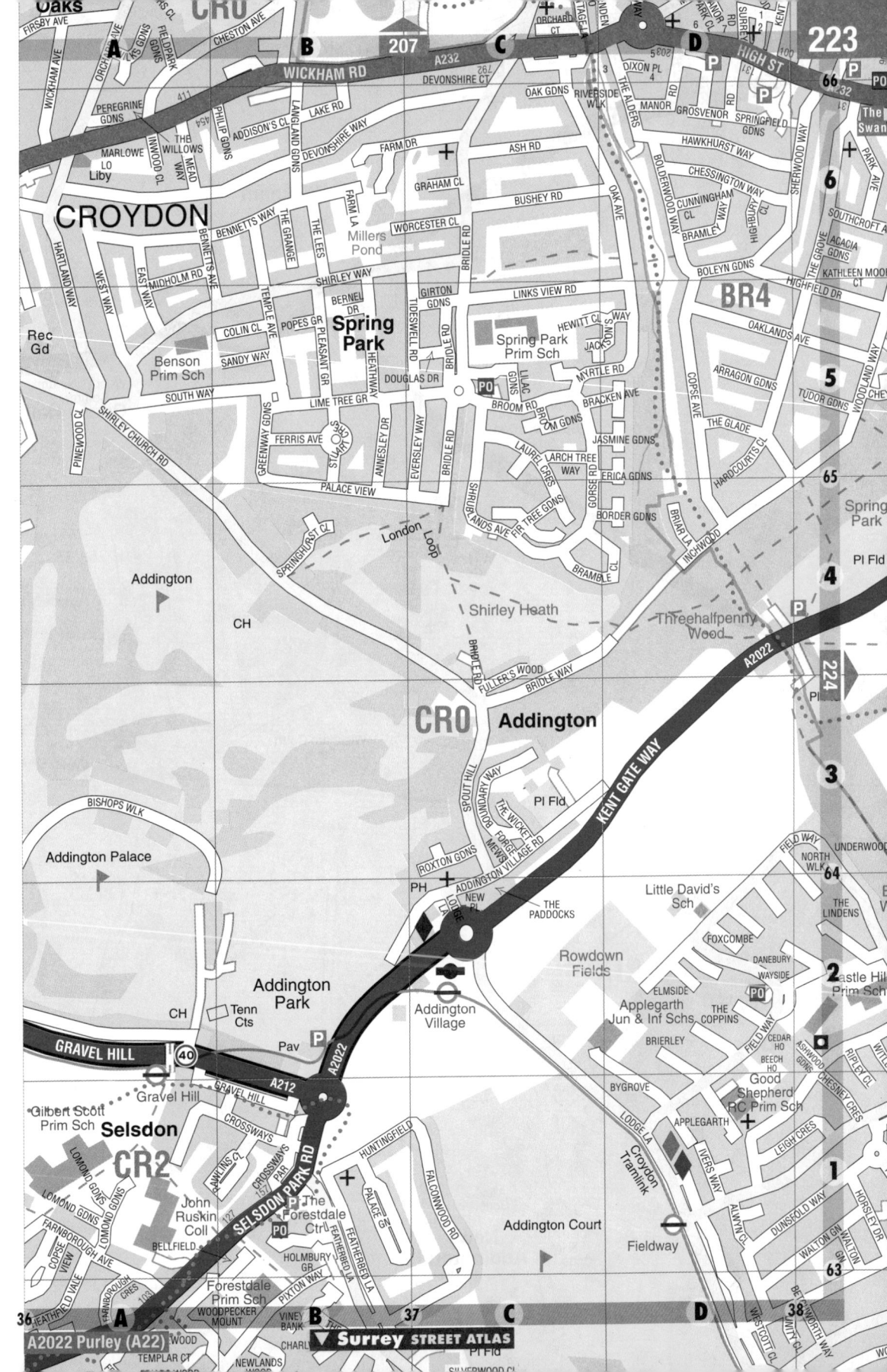

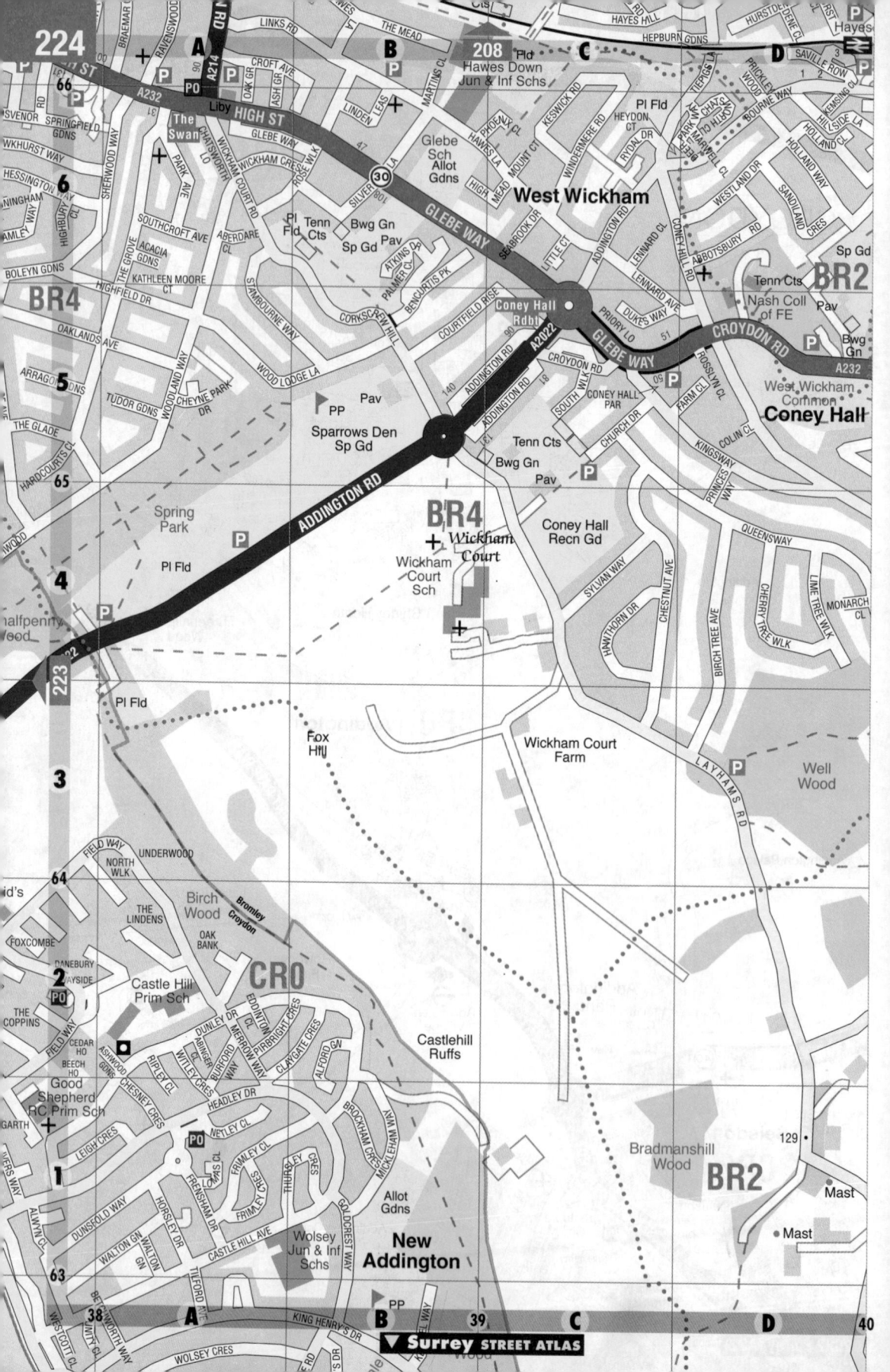

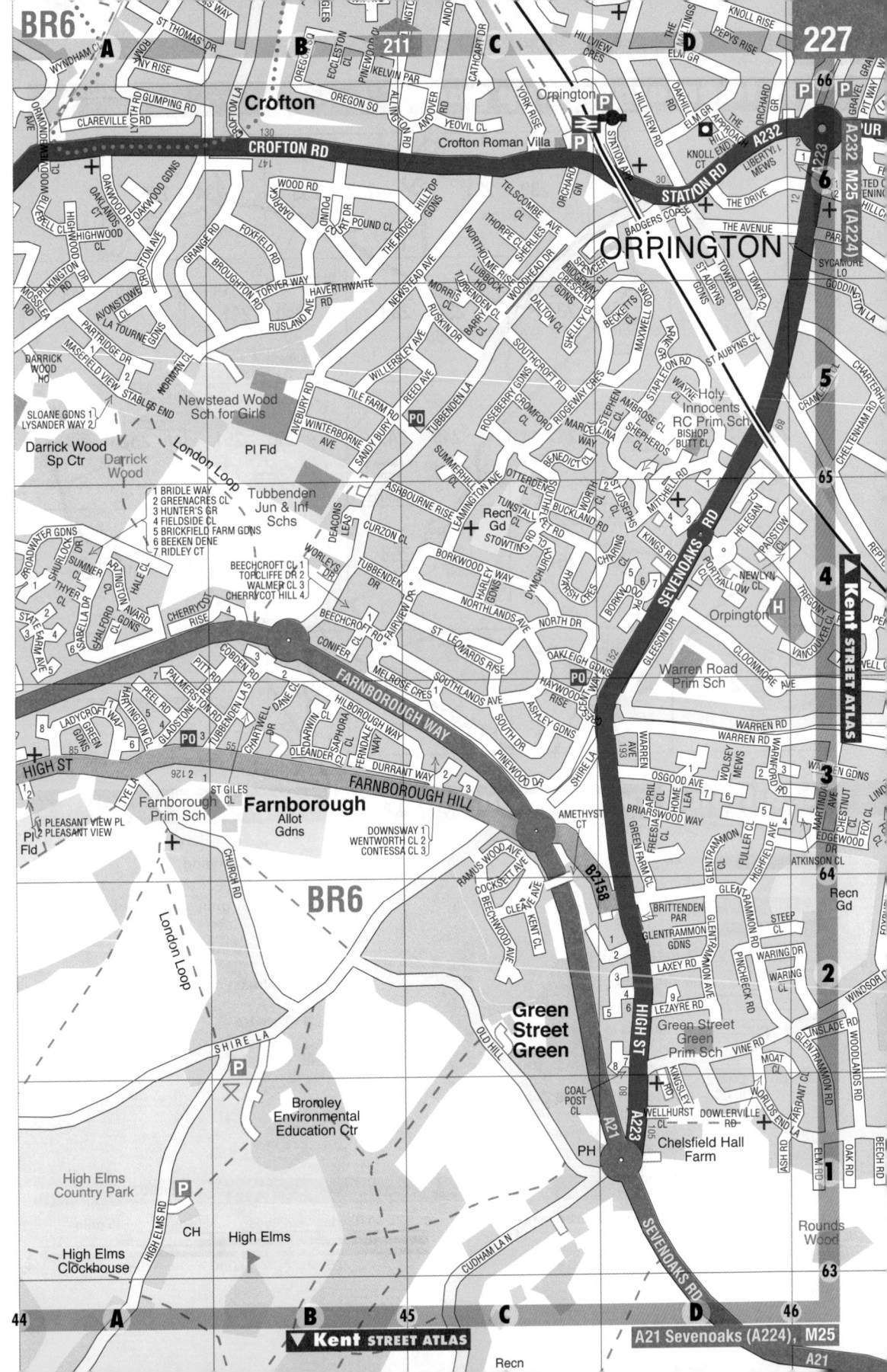

Key to enlarged map pages

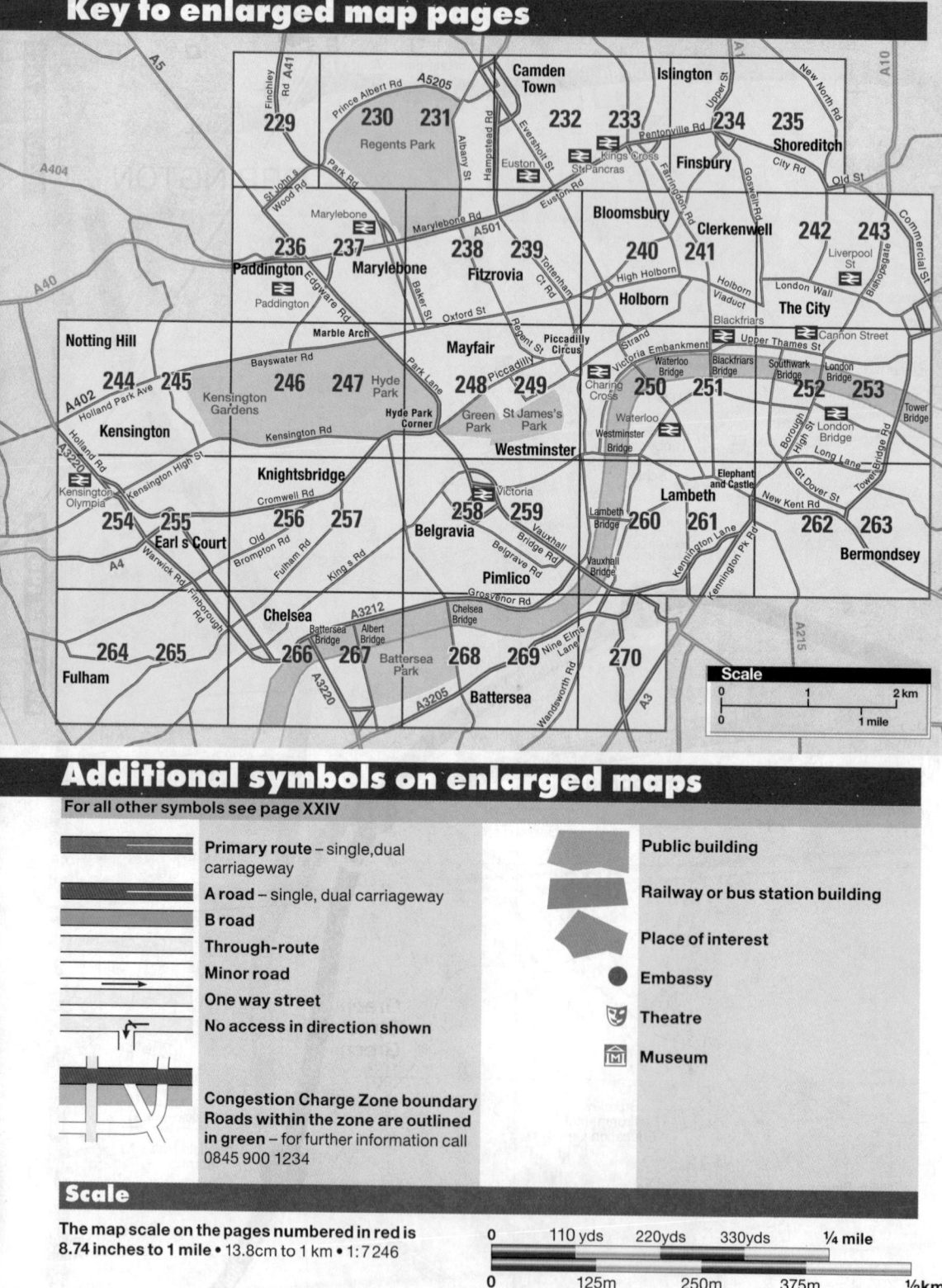

229 230 231 Camden Town 232 233 234 235 Shoreditch
Finchley Rd A41 Prince Albert Rd A5205 Islington Upper St New North Rd A10
A5 Regents Park Hampstead Rd Eversholt St Pentonville Rd Shoreditch
A404 St John's Wood Rd Albany St Euston Euston St Pancras Kings Cross Finsbury City Rd Old St
Marylebone 236 237 238 239 240 241 Clerkenwell 242 243
Paddington Marylebone Rd A501 Bloomsbury Liverpool St
A40 Edgware Rd Fitzrovia Tottenham Ct Rd Holborn Holborn Viaduct London Wall Bishopsgate Commercial St
Paddington Baker St Oxford St High Holborn Holborn Blackfriars The City

Notting Hill 244 245 Bayswater Rd 246 247 Hyde Park 248 249 250 251 252 253
A402 Holland Park Ave Kensington Gardens Park Lane Mayfair Piccadilly Circus Strand Victoria Embankment Upper Thames St Cannon Street
Kensington Kensington Rd Hyde Park Corner Piccadilly Charing Cross Waterloo Bridge Blackfriars Bridge Southwark Bridge London Bridge Tower Bridge
Green Park St James's Park Waterloo Westminster Borough High St London Bridge Long Lane
Kensington High St 254 255 Knightsbridge 256 257 258 259 Westminster 260 261 Lambeth 262 263
Kensington Olympia Cromwell Rd Victoria Elephant and Castle Gt Dover St Tower Bridge Rd Bermondsey
Earl's Court Old Brompton Rd Fulham Rd King's Rd Belgravia Vauxhall Bridge Rd Belgrave Rd Lambeth Bridge Vauxhall Bridge Kennington Lane Kennington Pk Rd New Kent Rd
Chelsea Pimlico Grosvenor Rd A2
264 265 266 267 268 269 270
Fulham Battersea Bridge Albert Bridge Battersea Park Chelsea Bridge Nine Elms Lane Wandsworth Rd A215
A3220 A3205 Battersea A3

Scale

| 0 | 1 | 2 km |
| 0 | | 1 mile |

Additional symbols on enlarged maps

For all other symbols see page XXIV

Primary route – single, dual carriageway

A road – single, dual carriageway

B road

Through-route

Minor road

One way street

No access in direction shown

Congestion Charge Zone boundary Roads within the zone are outlined in green – for further information call 0845 900 1234

Public building

Railway or bus station building

Place of interest

● **Embassy**

Theatre

Museum

Scale

The map scale on the pages numbered in red is **8.74 inches to 1 mile** • **13.8cm to 1 km** • **1:7 246**

| 0 | 110 yds | 220yds | 330yds | ¼ mile |
| 0 | 125m | 250m | 375m | ½km |

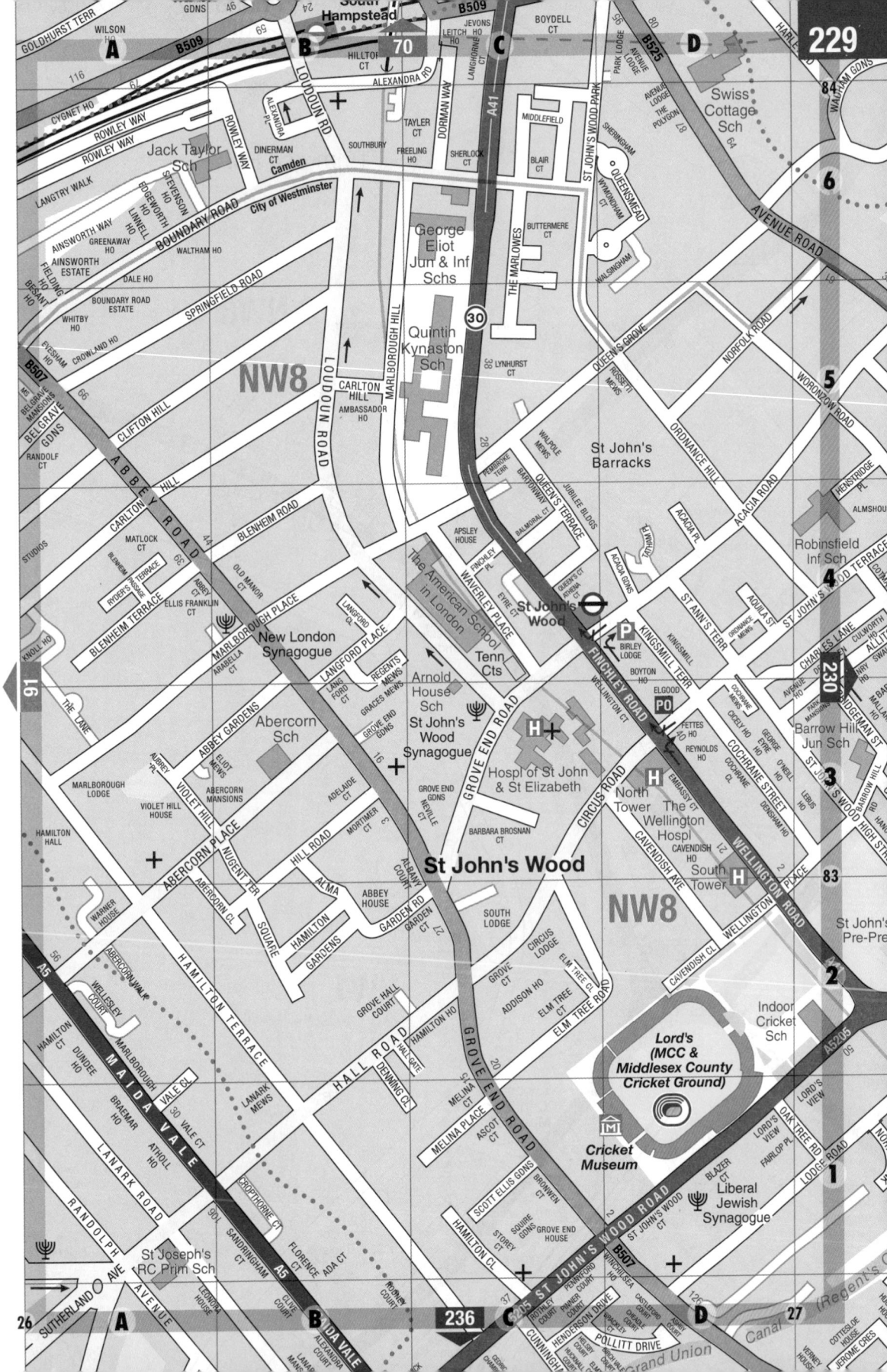

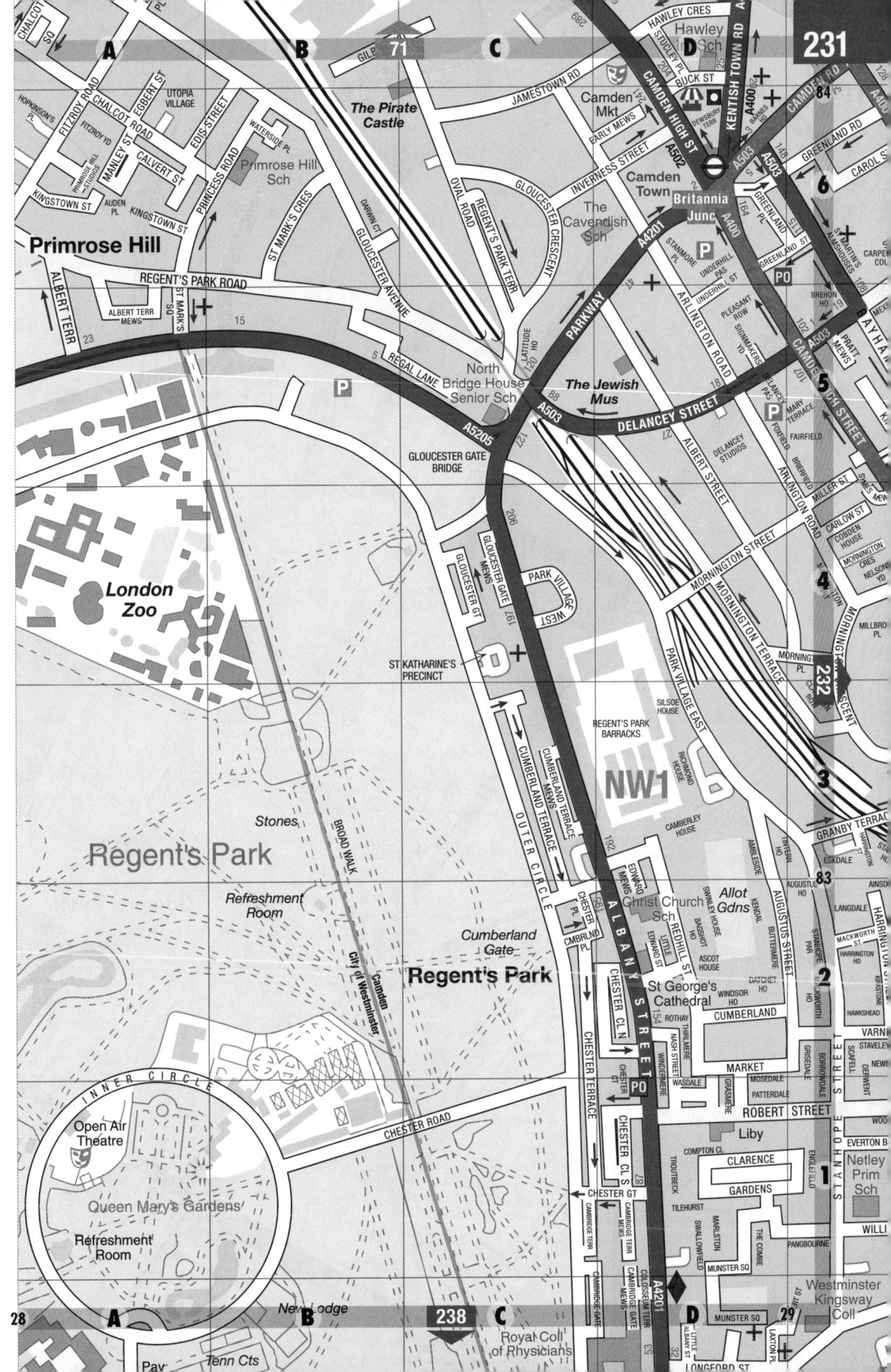

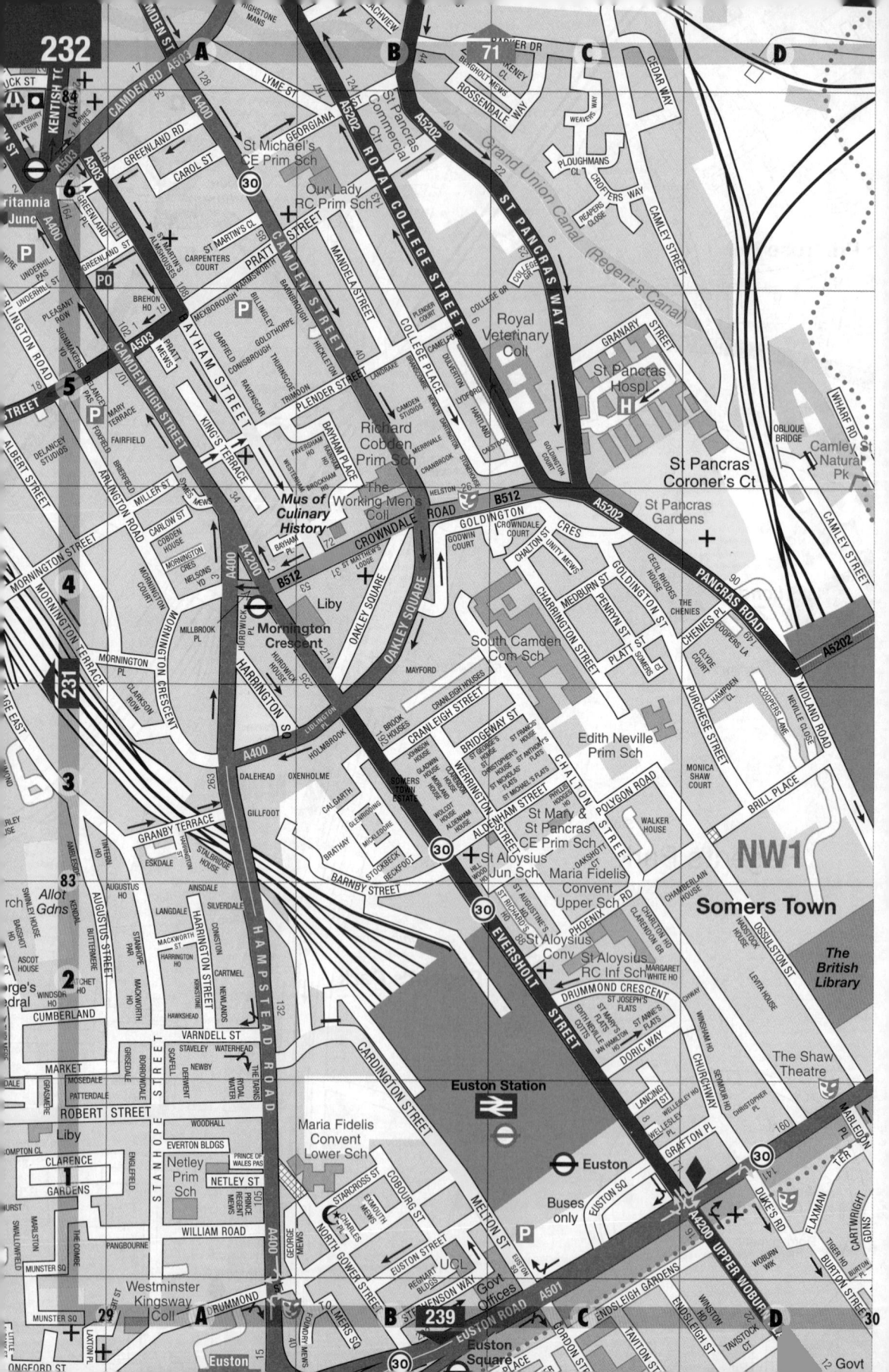

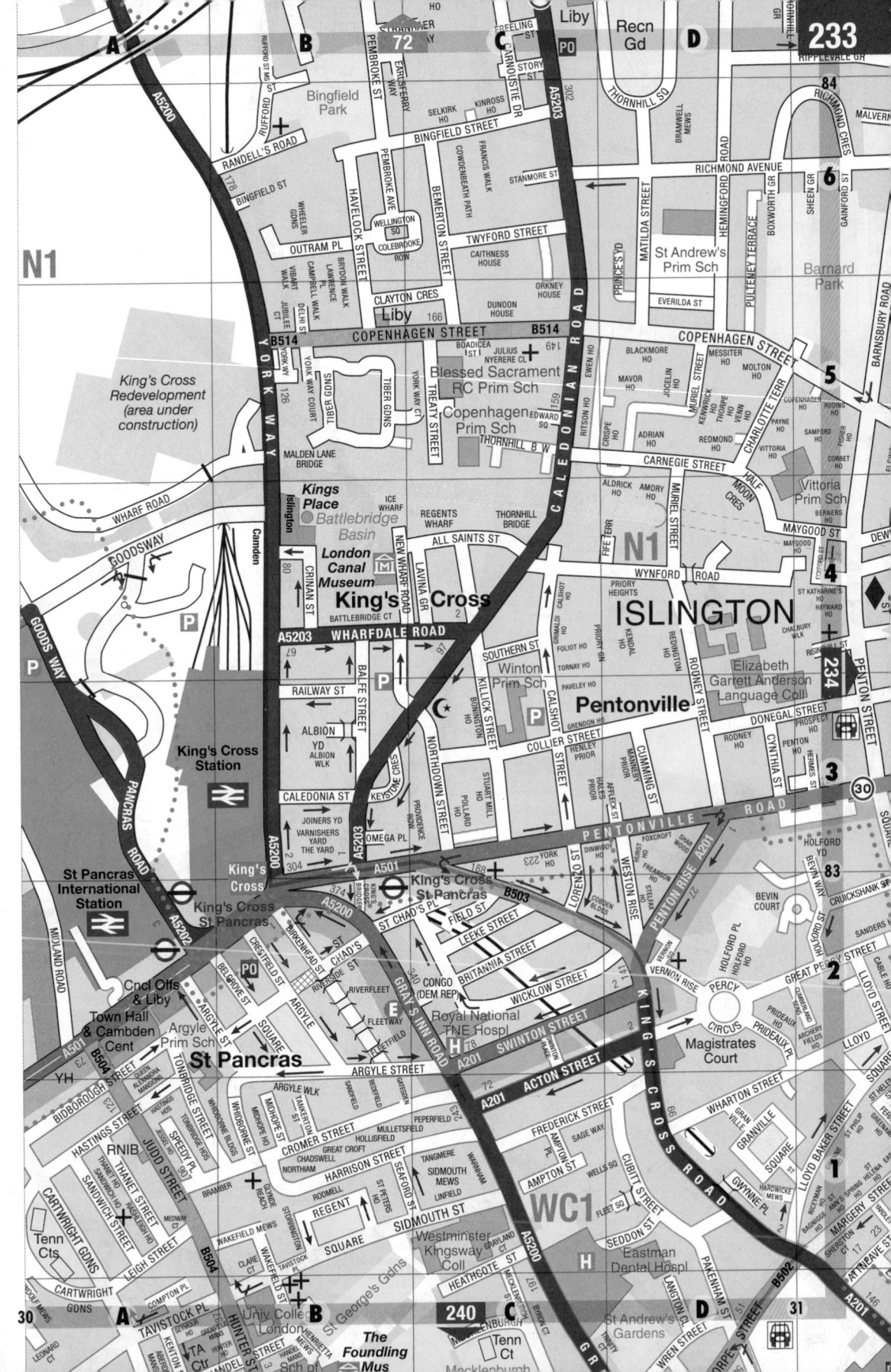

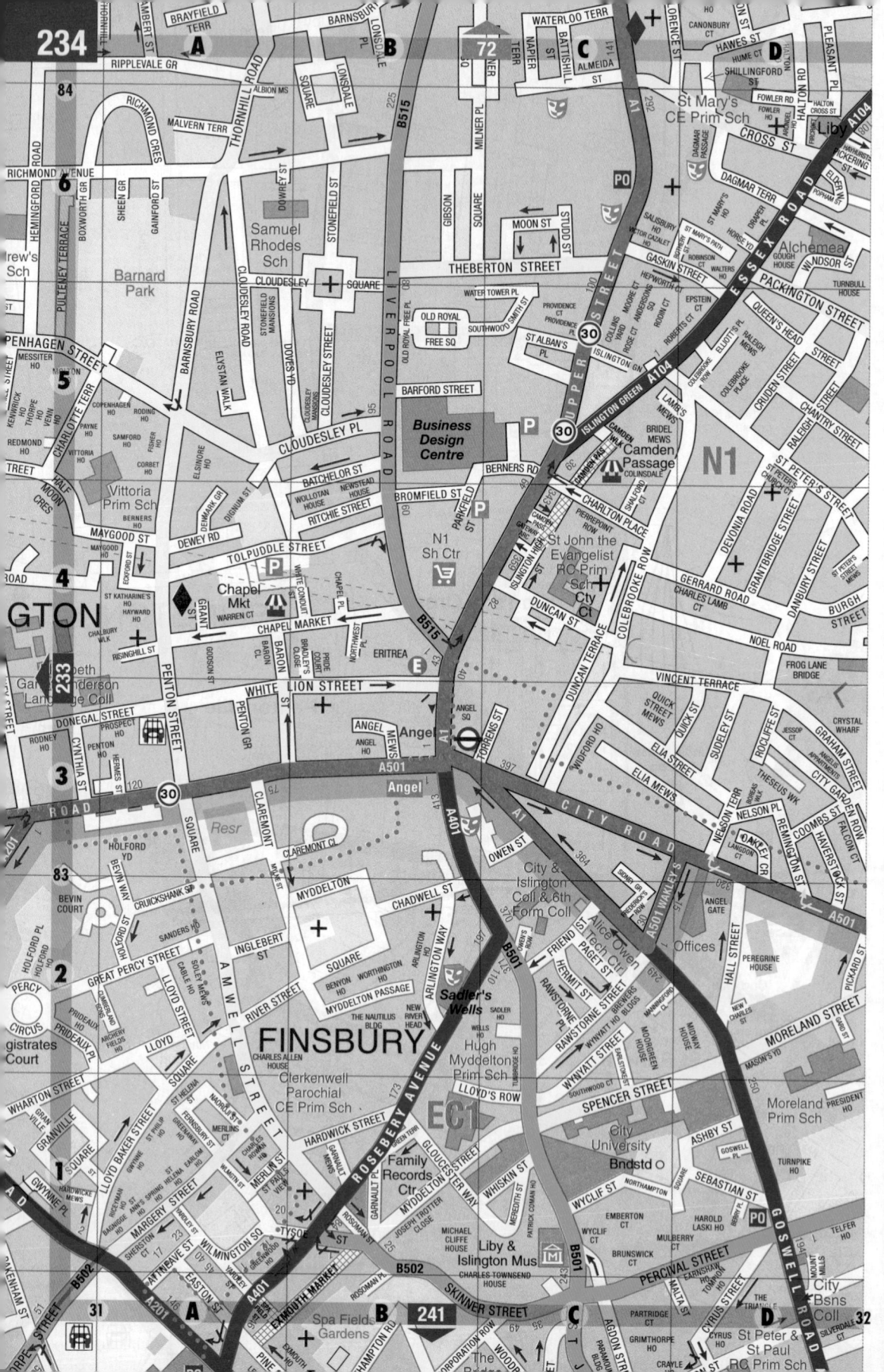

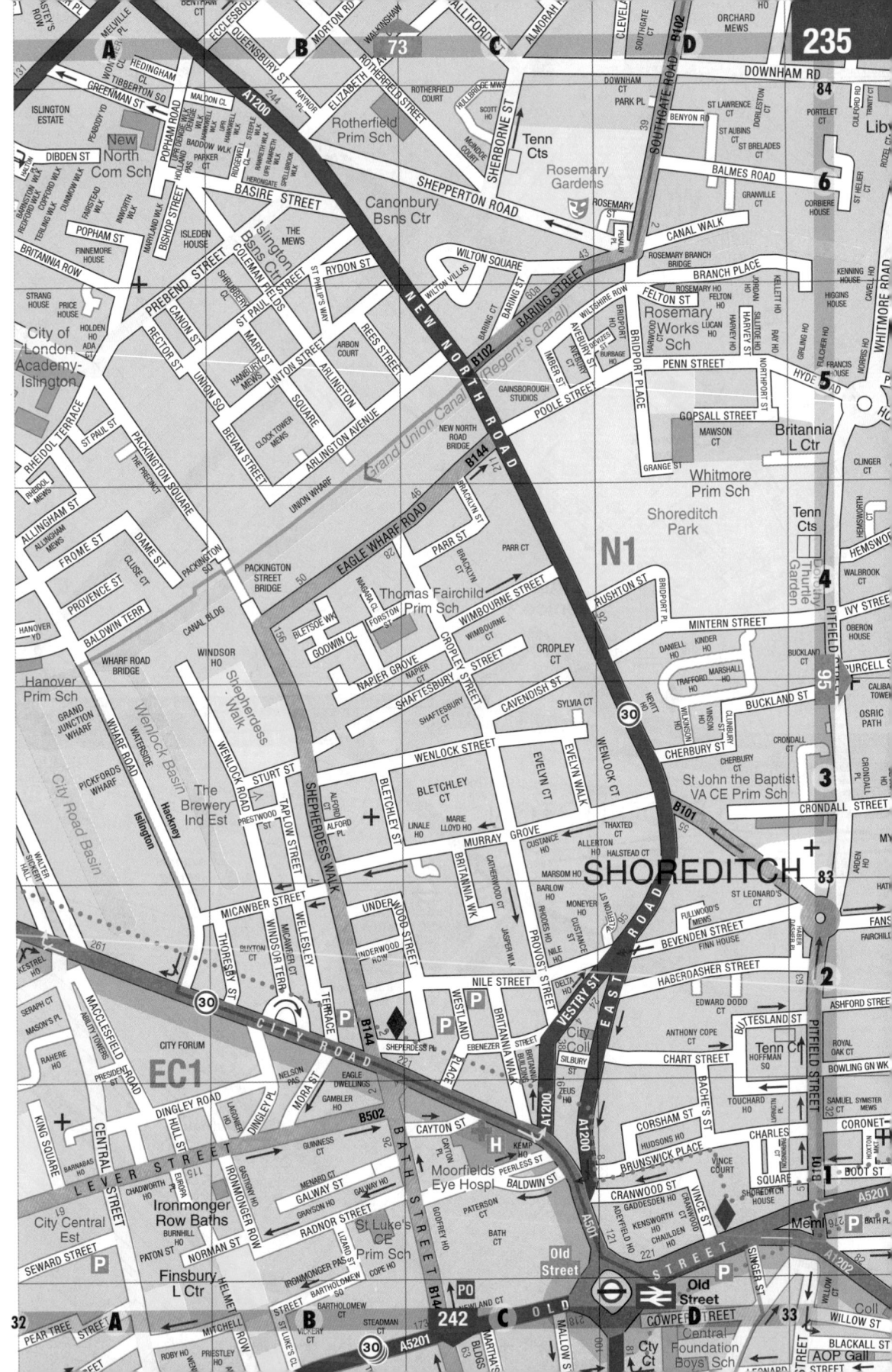

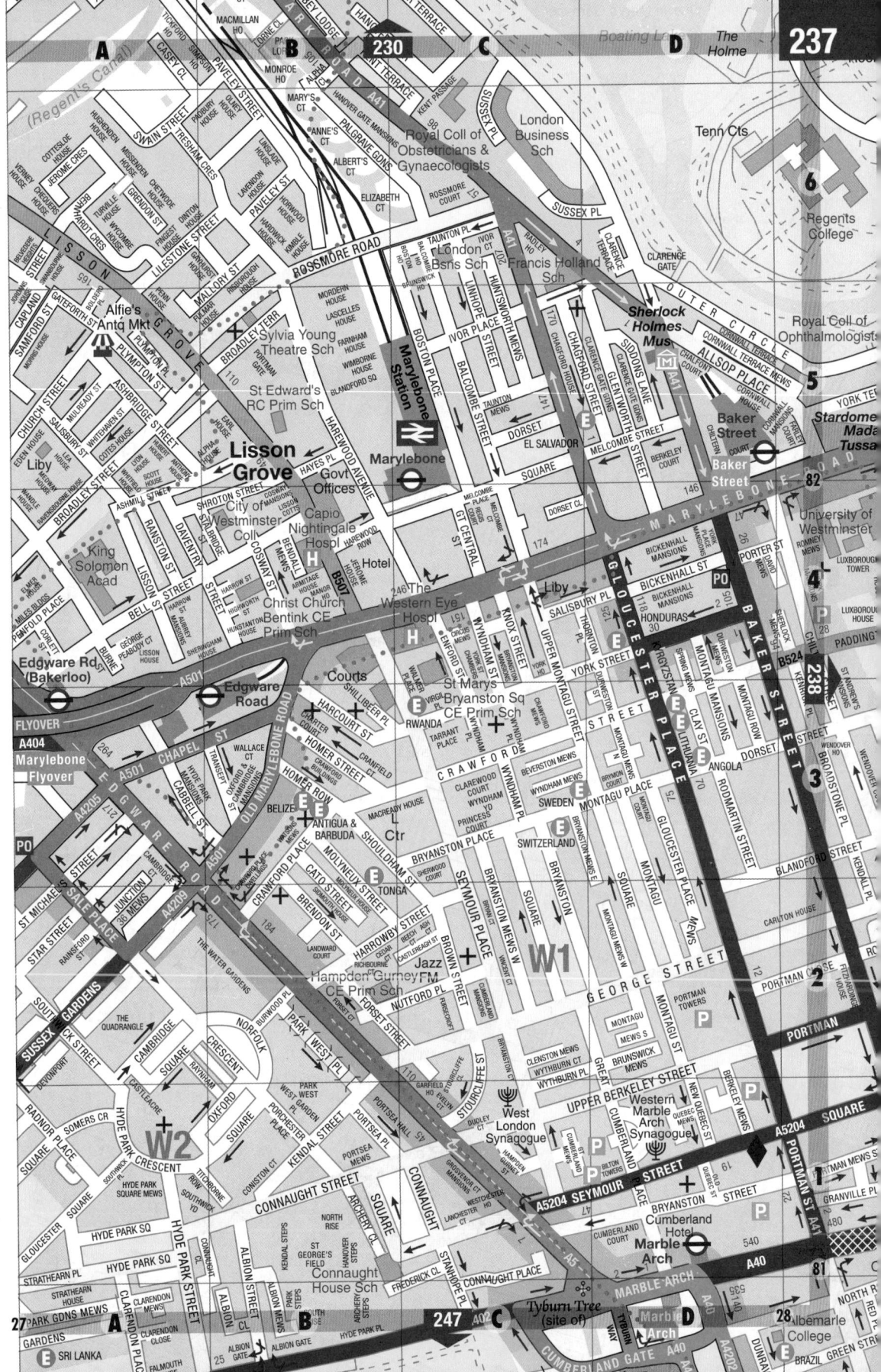

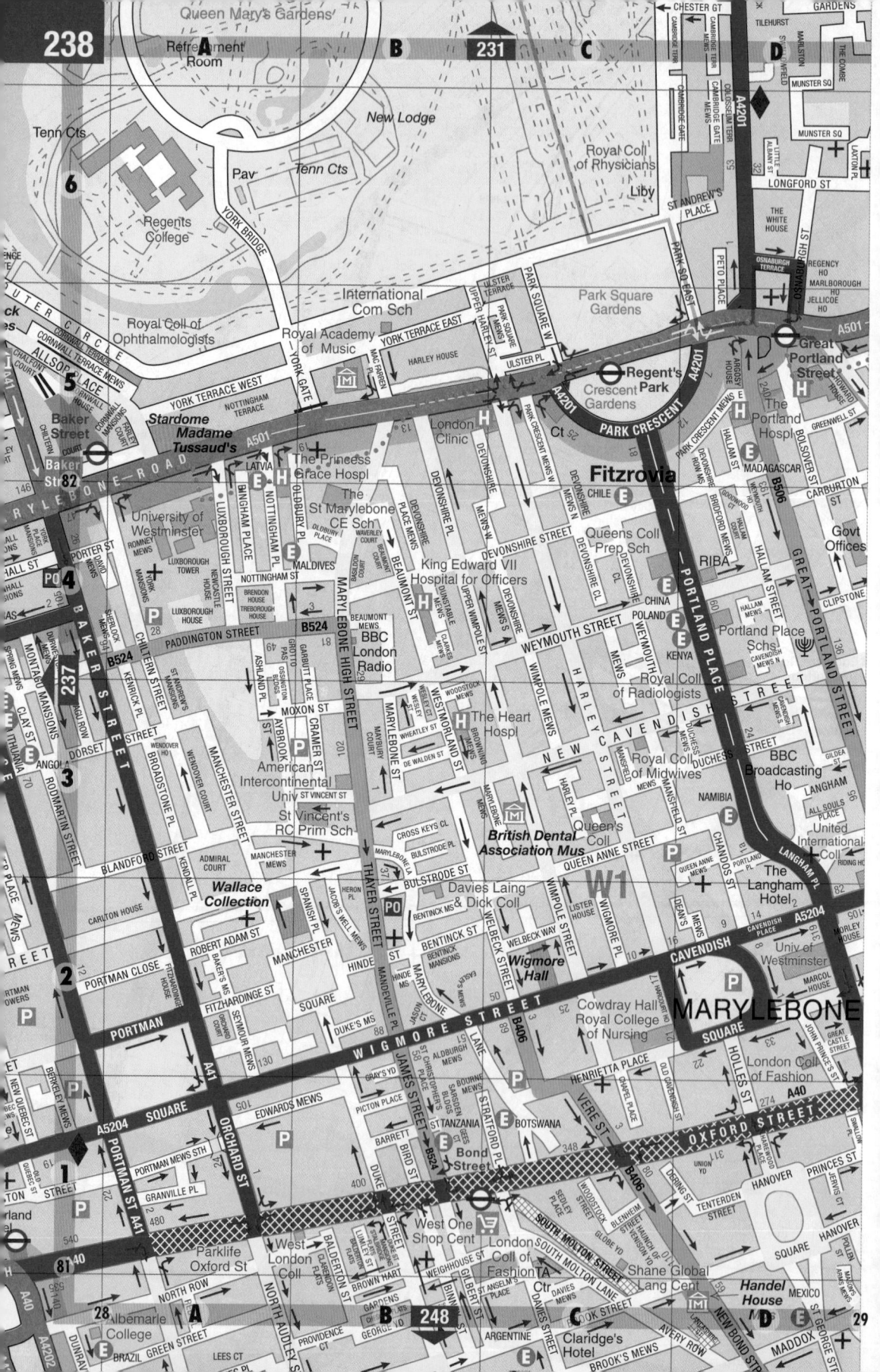

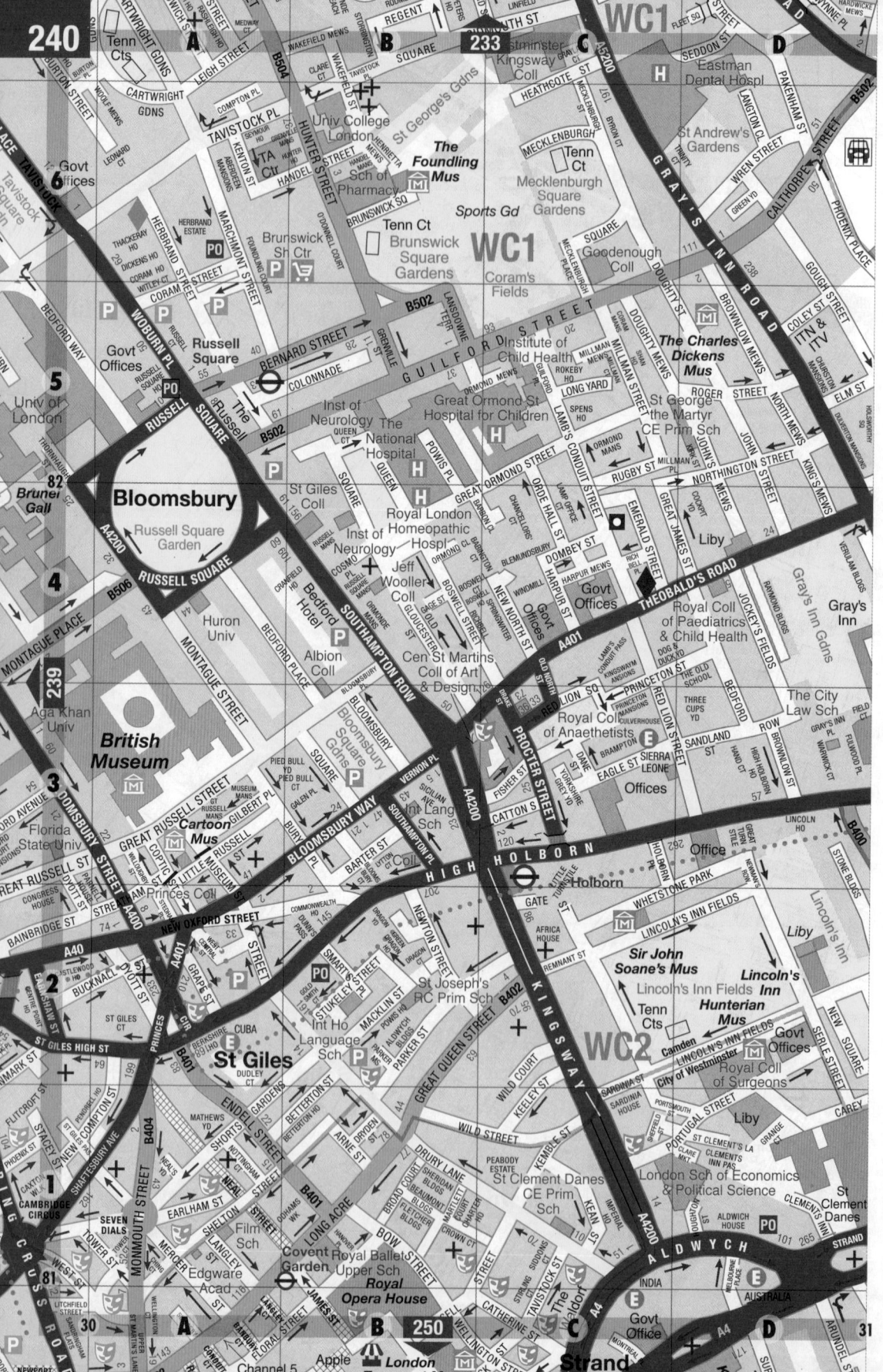

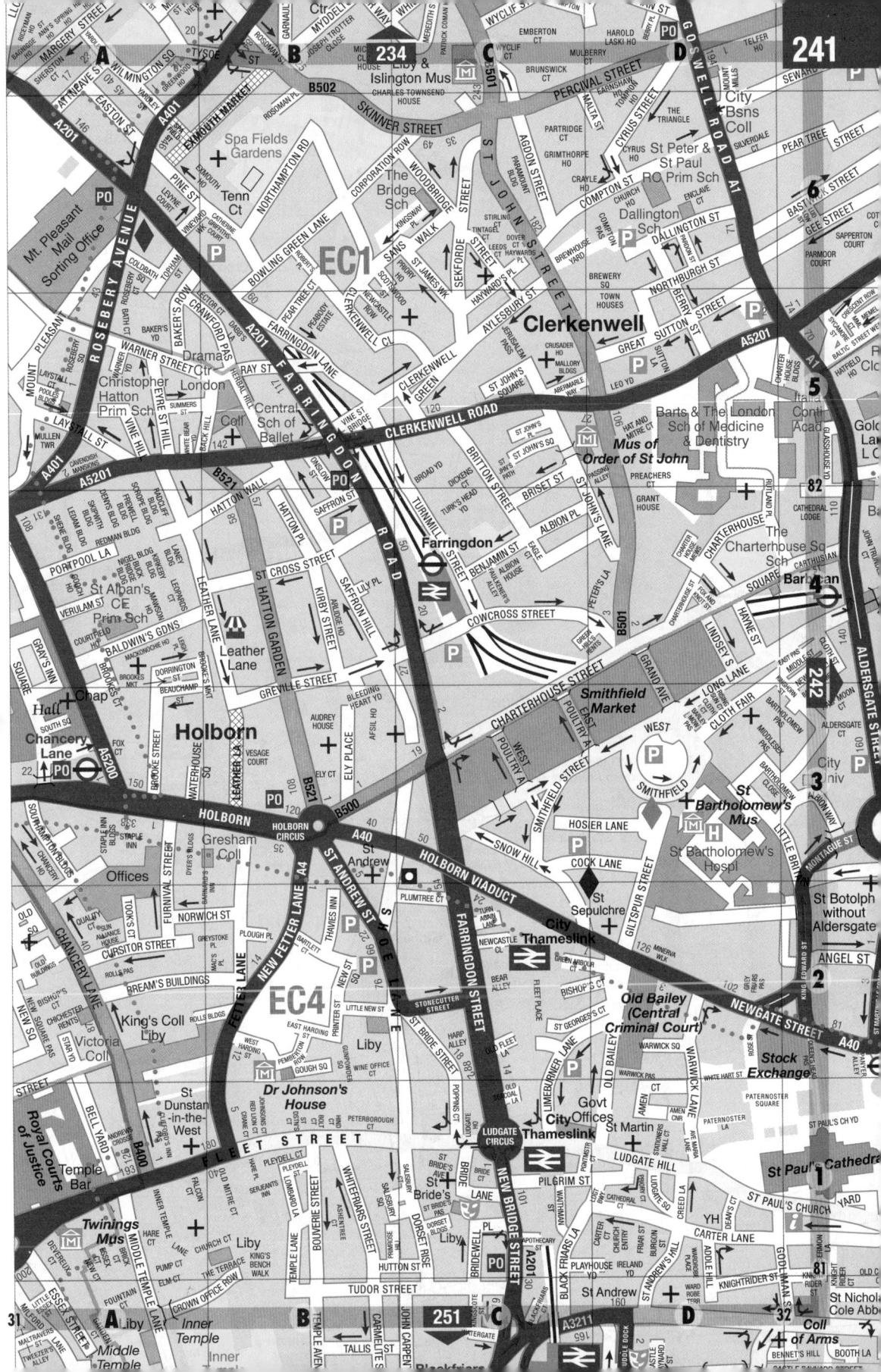

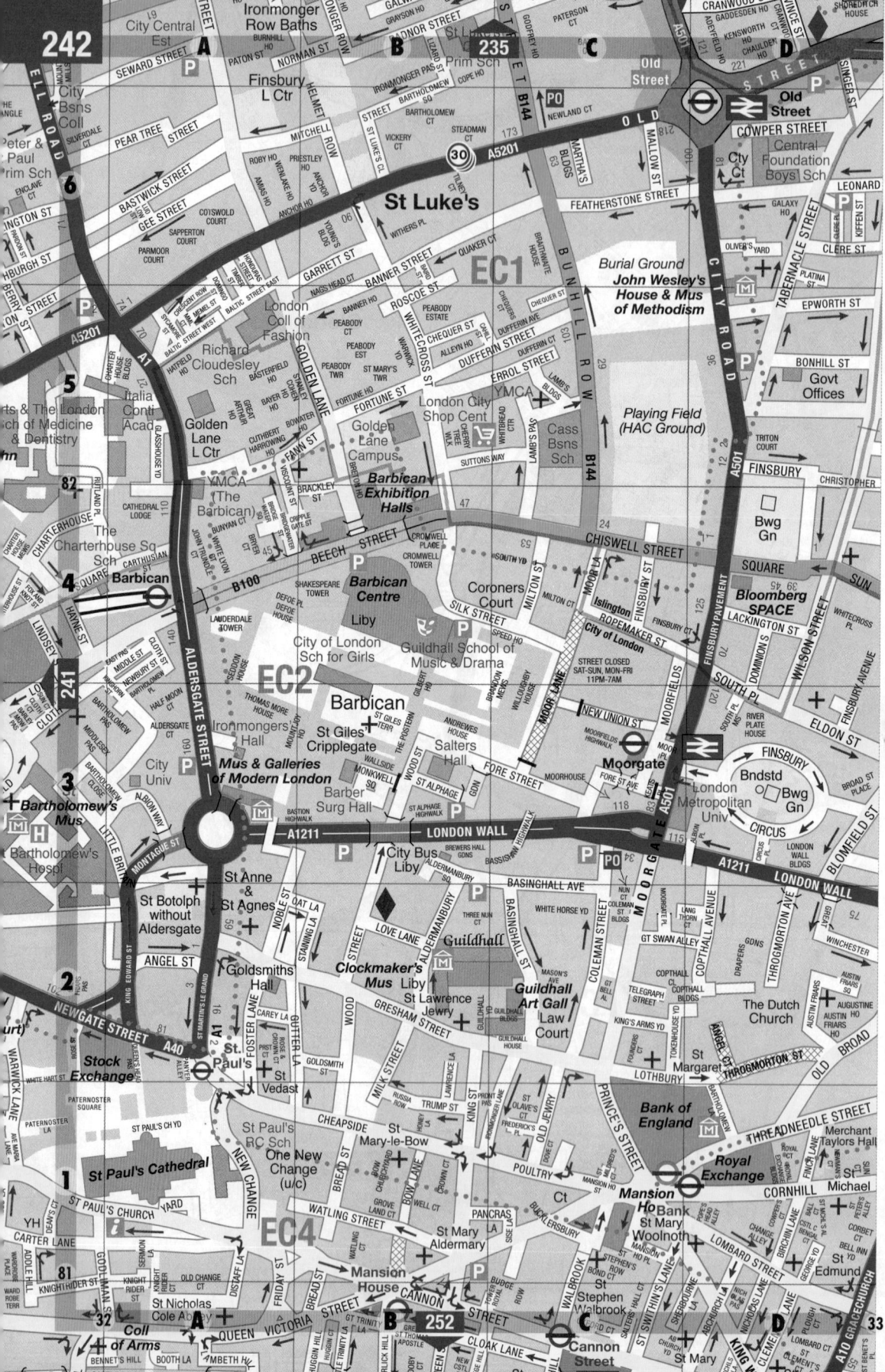

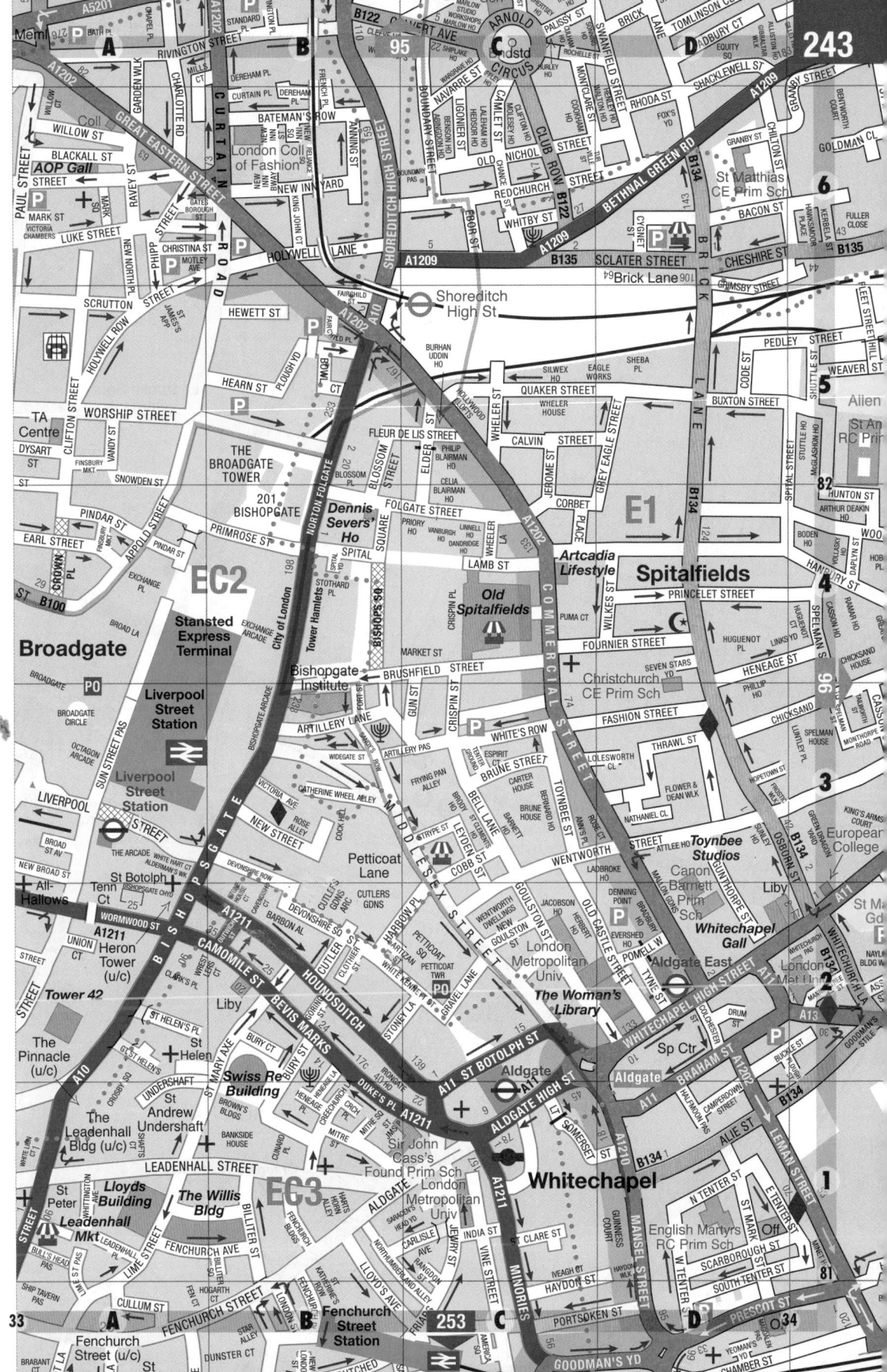

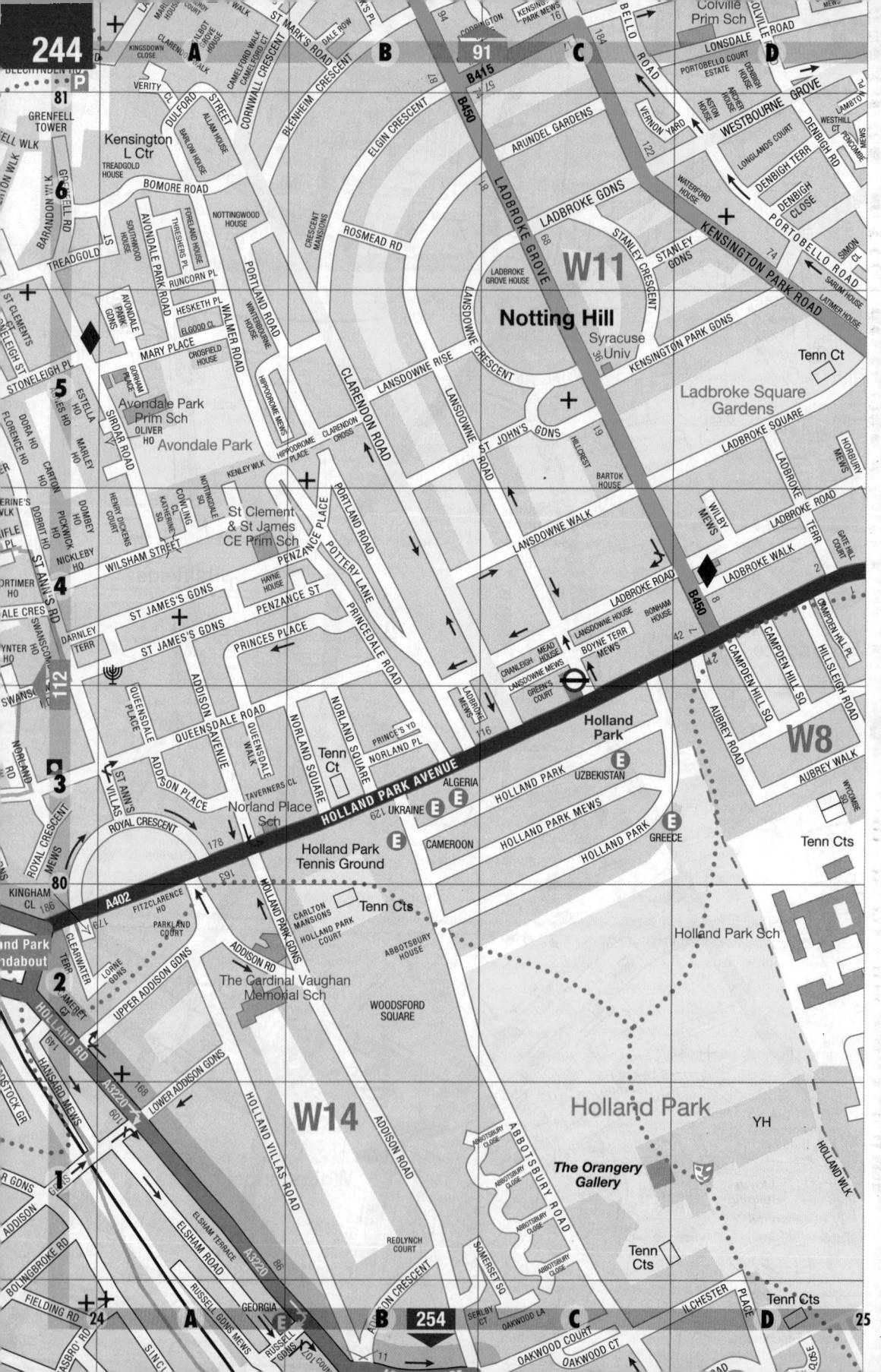

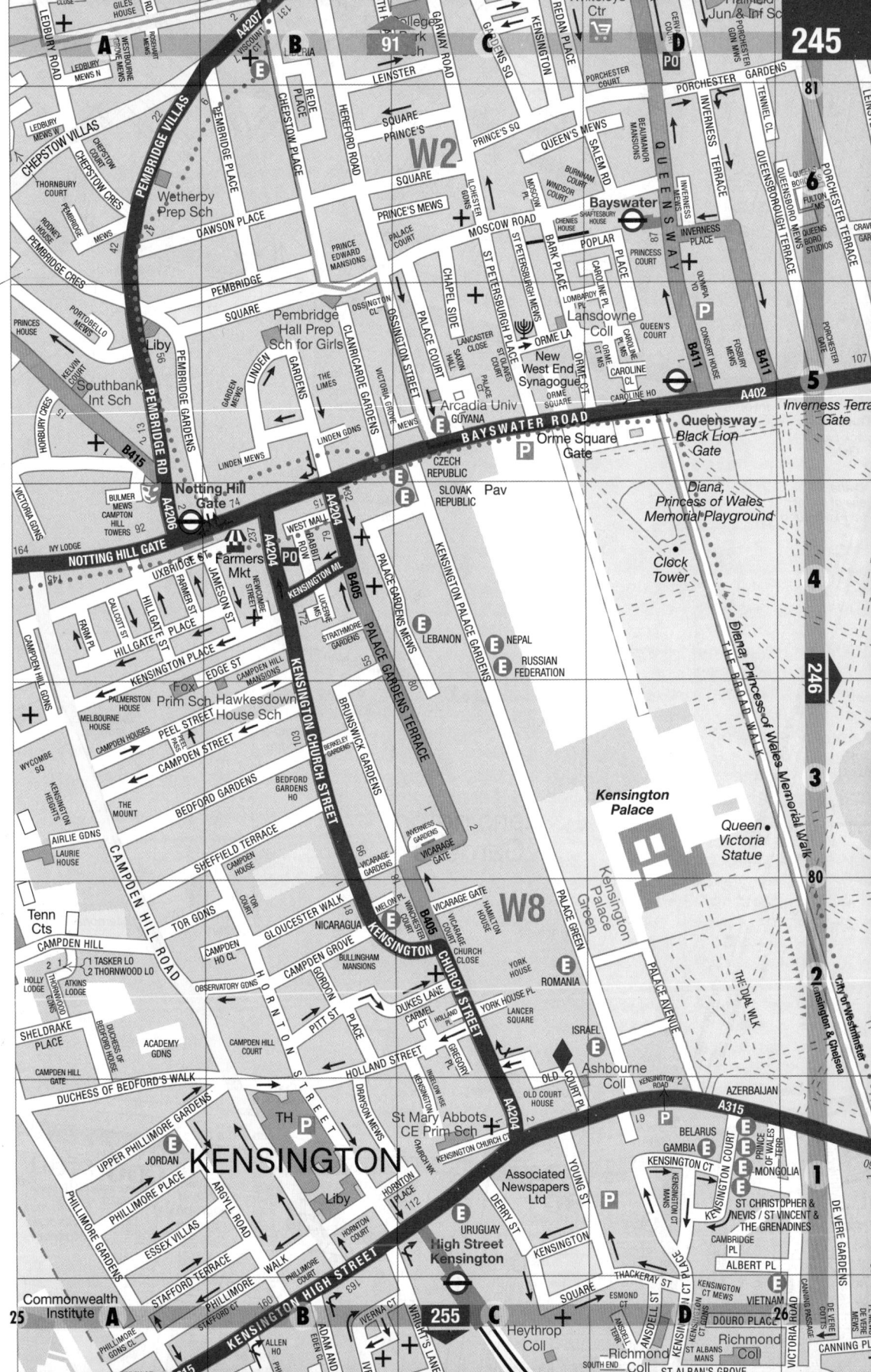

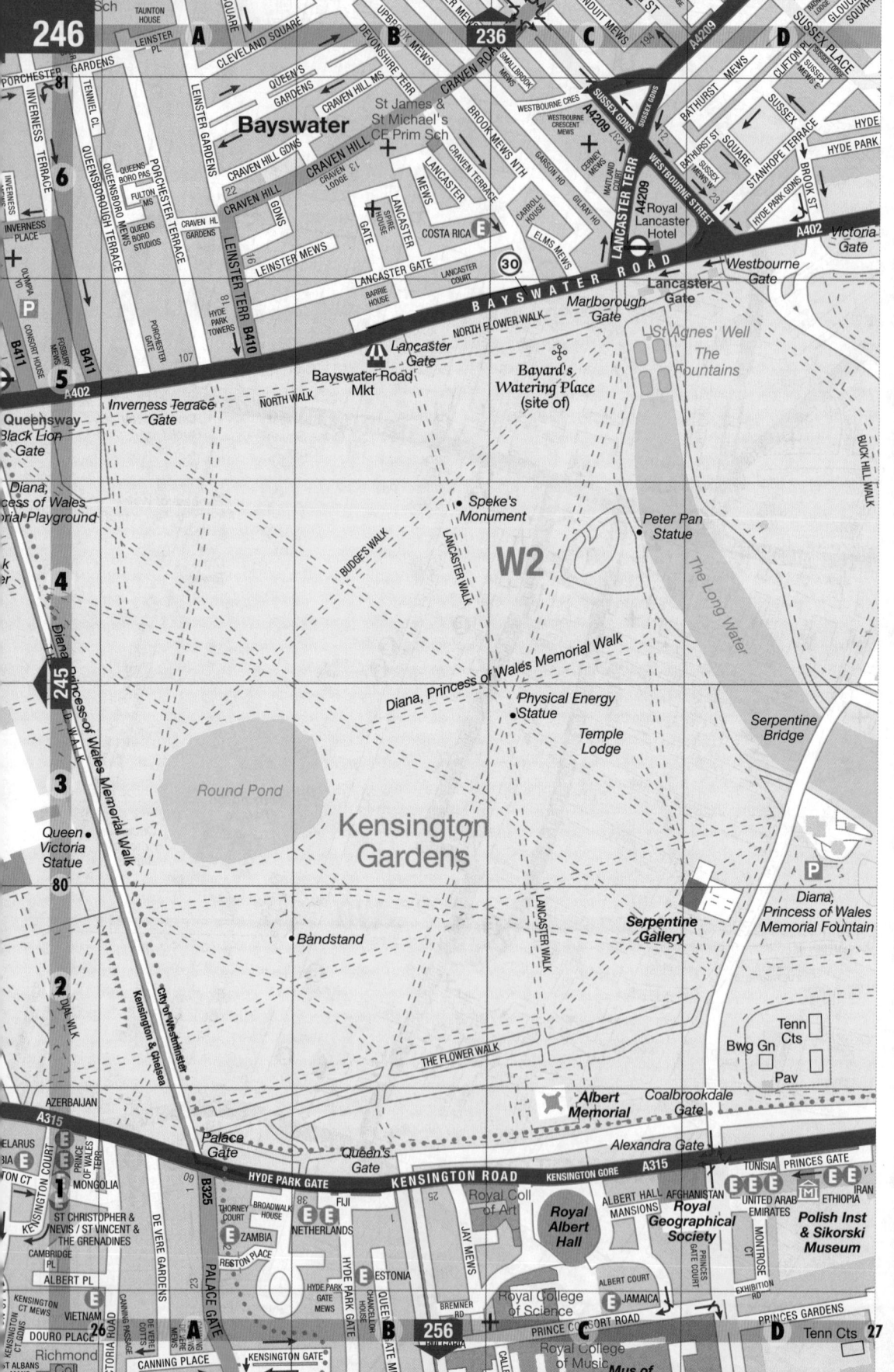

236

C

D

SUSSEX PLACE

GLOUCES

SQUARE

CONDUIT MEWS

LONG ST

A4209

CLIFTON PL

SUSSEX

BATHURST

MEWS

SQUARE

STANHOPE TERRACE

HYDE

HYDE PARK

Victoria
Gate

A402

A

B

SQUARE

TAUNTON
HOUSE

LEINSTER
PL

CLEVELAND SQUARE

QUEEN'S
GARDENS

UPBROOK MEWS

DEVONSHIRE TERR

CRAVEN ROAD

SMALLBROOK

BROOK MEWS NTH

CRAVEN HILL MS

St James &
St Michael's
CF Prim Sch

Bayswater

CRAVEN HILL

LANCASTER
MEWS

CRAVEN TERRACE

WESTBOURNE CRES

WESTBOURNE
CRESCENT
MEWS

CARSON HO

GARSON HO

GILRAY HO

MAITLAND
COURT

Royal
Lancaster
Hotel

WESTBOURNE STREET

CRAVEN HILL GDNS

CRAVEN HILL

13

CRAVEN HL GARDENS

22

CRAVEN HILL

16

LANCASTER
COURT

SPIRE
HOUSE

CARROLL
HOUSE

ELMS MEWS

Costa Rica

LANCASTER
COURT

BARRIE
HOUSE

Lancaster
Gate

E

30

Marlborough
Gate

Westbourne
Gate

Lancaster
Gate

BAYSWATER ROAD

NORTH FLOWER WALK

Bayswater Road
Mkt

North Walk

Inverness Terrace Gate

NORTH WALK

Bayard's
Watering Place
(site of)

Queensway
Black Lion
Gate

St Agnes' Well
The
Fountains

Diana,
cess of Wales
rial Playground

Speke's
Monument

Peter Pan
Statue

BUDGE'S WALK

LANCASTER WALK

W2

The Long Water

BUCK HILL WALK

245

Princess of Wales Memorial Walk

Diana, Princess of Wales Memorial Walk

Physical Energy
Statue

Temple
Lodge

Serpentine
Bridge

Round Pond

Kensington
Gardens

Serpentine
Gallery

Diana,
Princess of Wales
Memorial Fountain

Queen
Victoria
Statue

80

Bandstand

LANCASTER WALK

Tenn
Cts

Bwg Gn

Pav

THE FLOWER WALK

AZERBAIJAN

A315

Albert
Memorial

Coalbrookdale
Gate

Palace
Gate

Queen's
Gate

Alexandra Gate

BELARUS

PRINCE OF WALES TERR

MONGOLIA

HYDE PARK GATE

KENSINGTON ROAD

KENSINGTON GORE

A315

TUNISIA

PRINCES GATE

AFGHANISTAN

UNITED ARAB
EMIRATES

IRAN

ETHIOPIA

ST CHRISTOPHER &
NEVIS / ST VINCENT &
THE GRENADINES

ZAMBIA

NETHERLANDS

FIJI

Royal Coll
of Art

Royal
Albert
Hall

ALBERT HALL
MANSIONS

Royal
Geographical
Society

Polish Inst
& Sikorski
Museum

CAMBRIDGE
PL

ALBERT PL

VIETNAM

ESTONIA

JAY MEWS

ALBERT COURT

JAMAICA

MONTROSE
CT

PRINCES GATE COURT

EXHIBITION
RD

PRINCES GARDENS

Richmond
Coll

26

A

256

B

Royal College
of Science

PRINCE CONSORT ROAD

D

27

Royal College
of Music

Mus of
Instruments

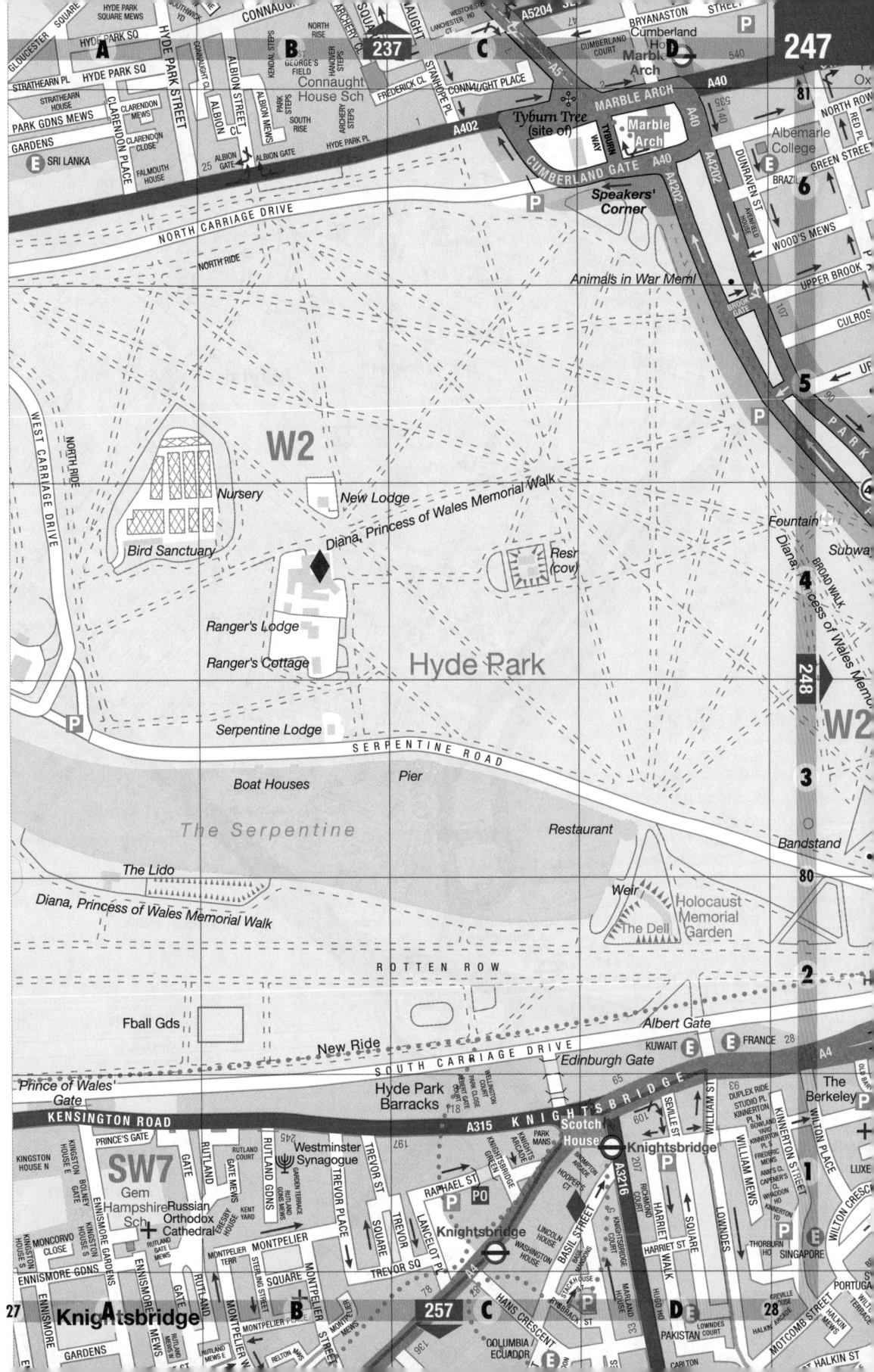

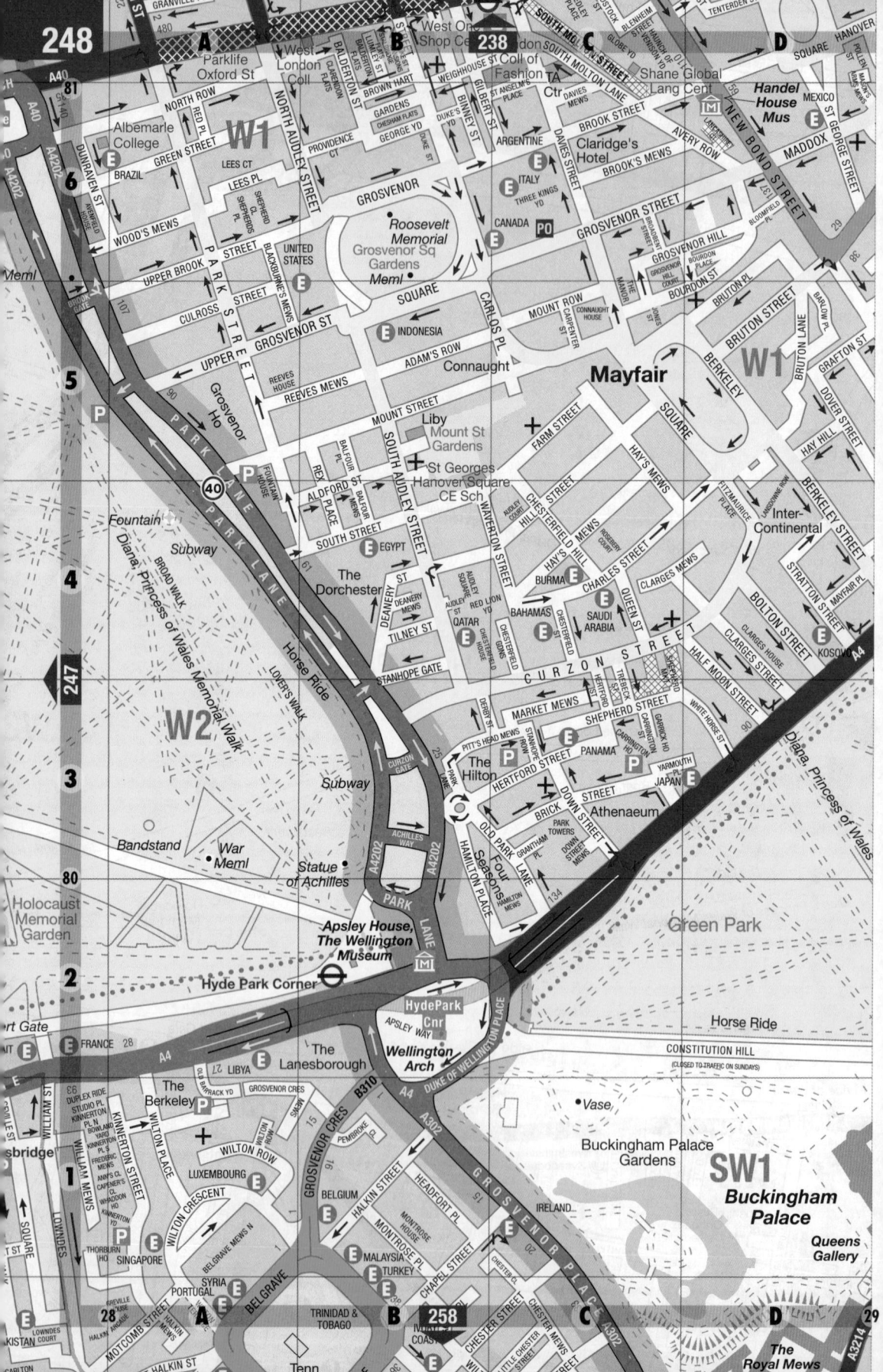

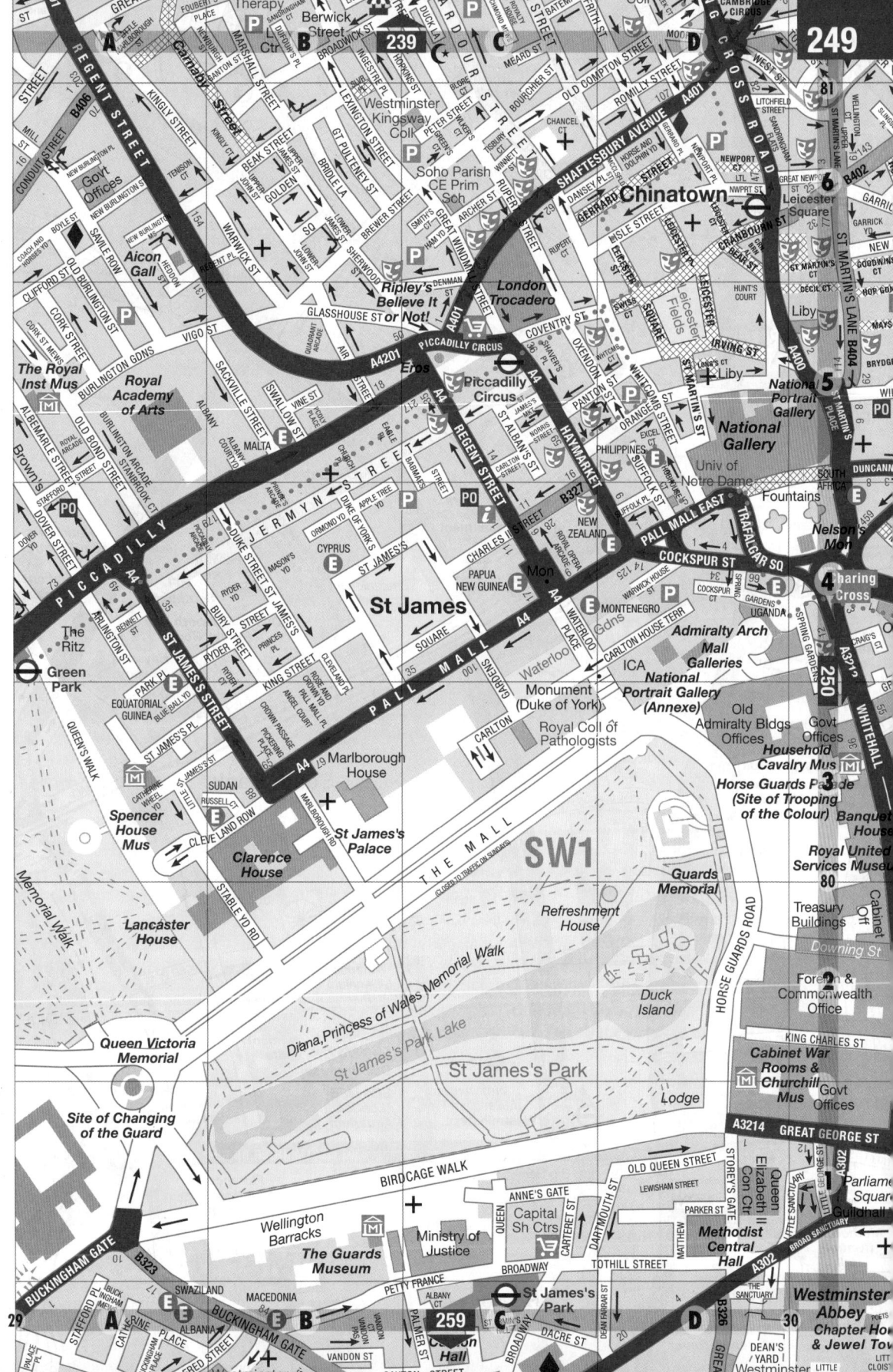

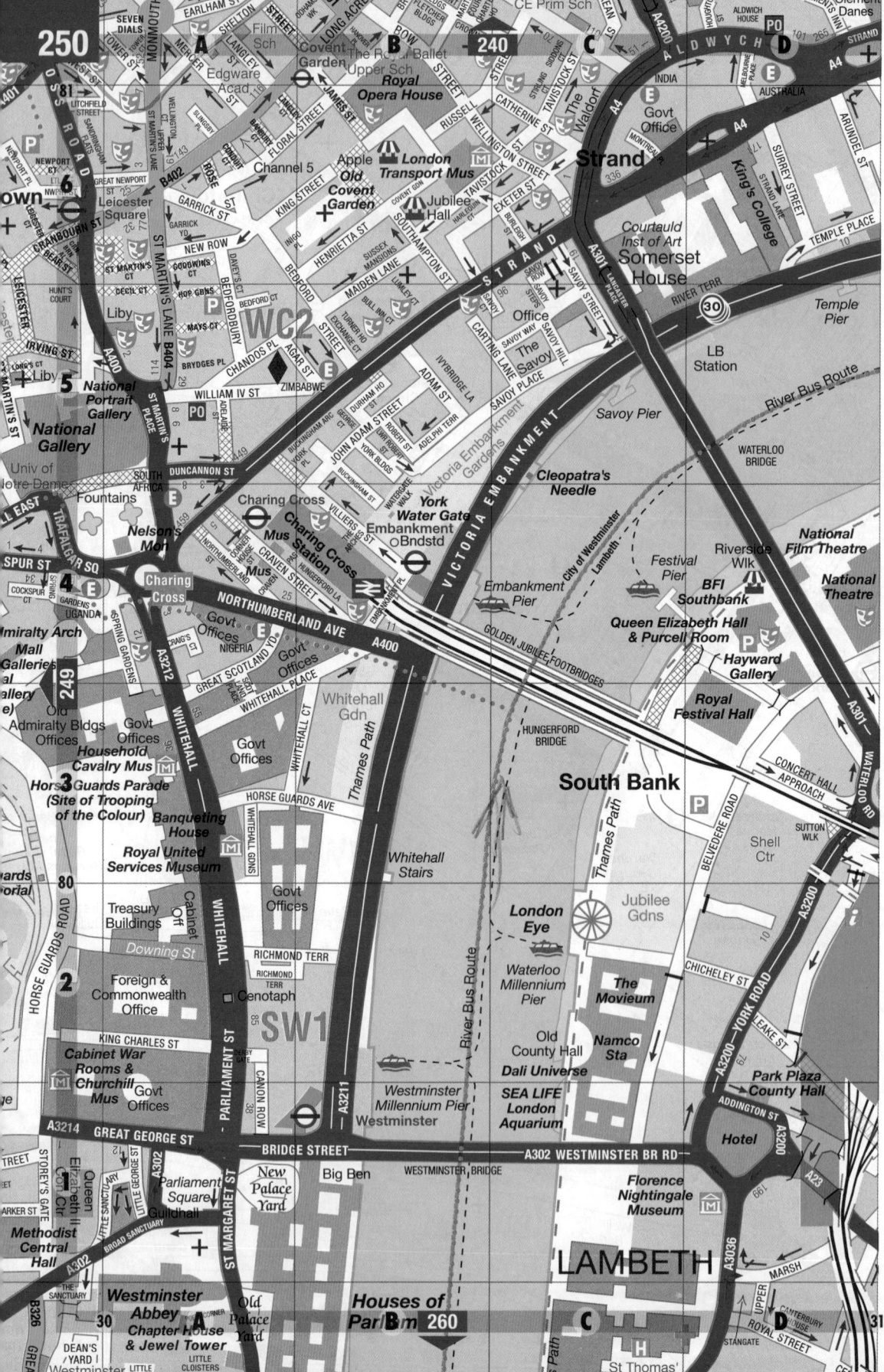

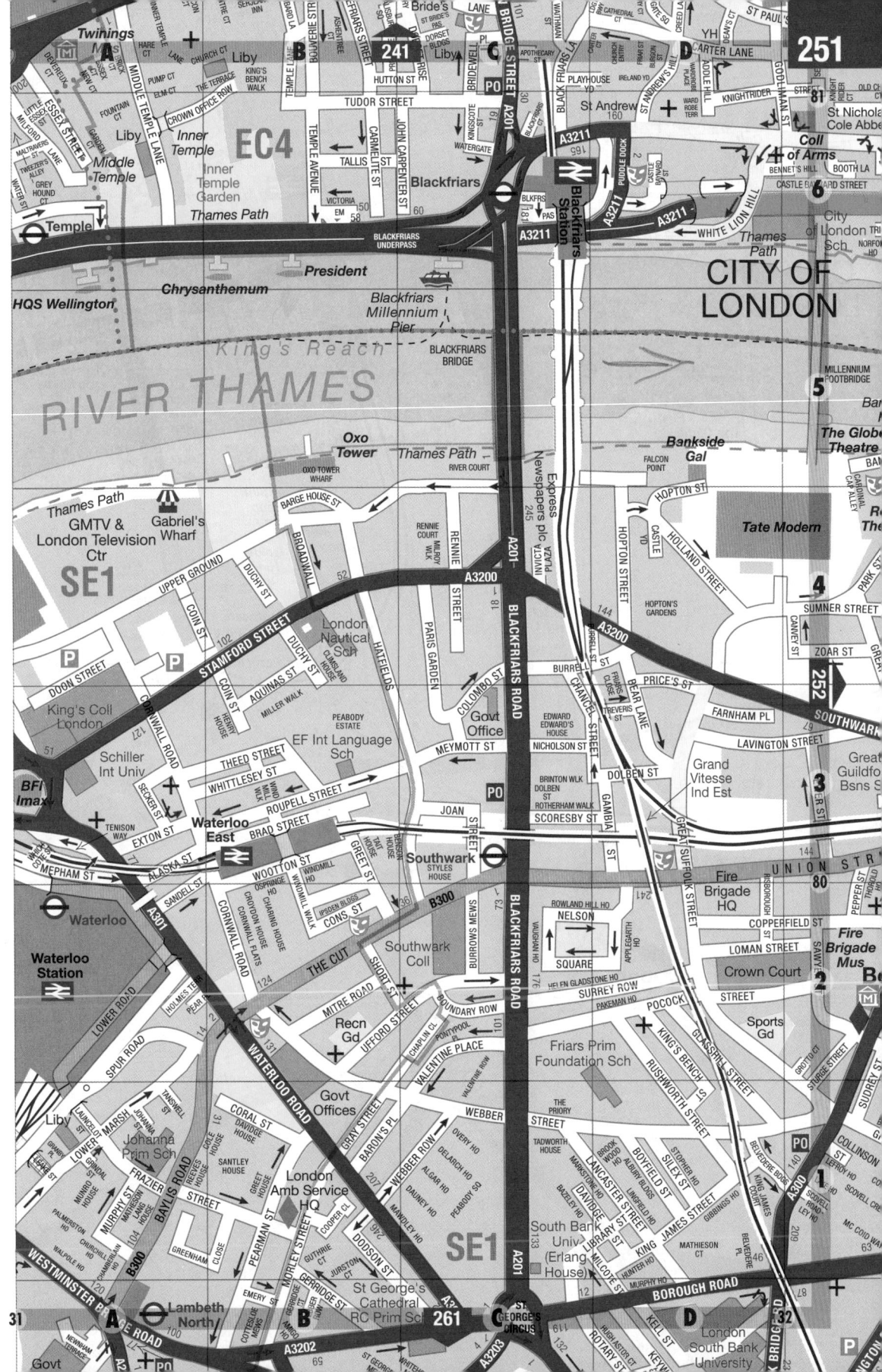

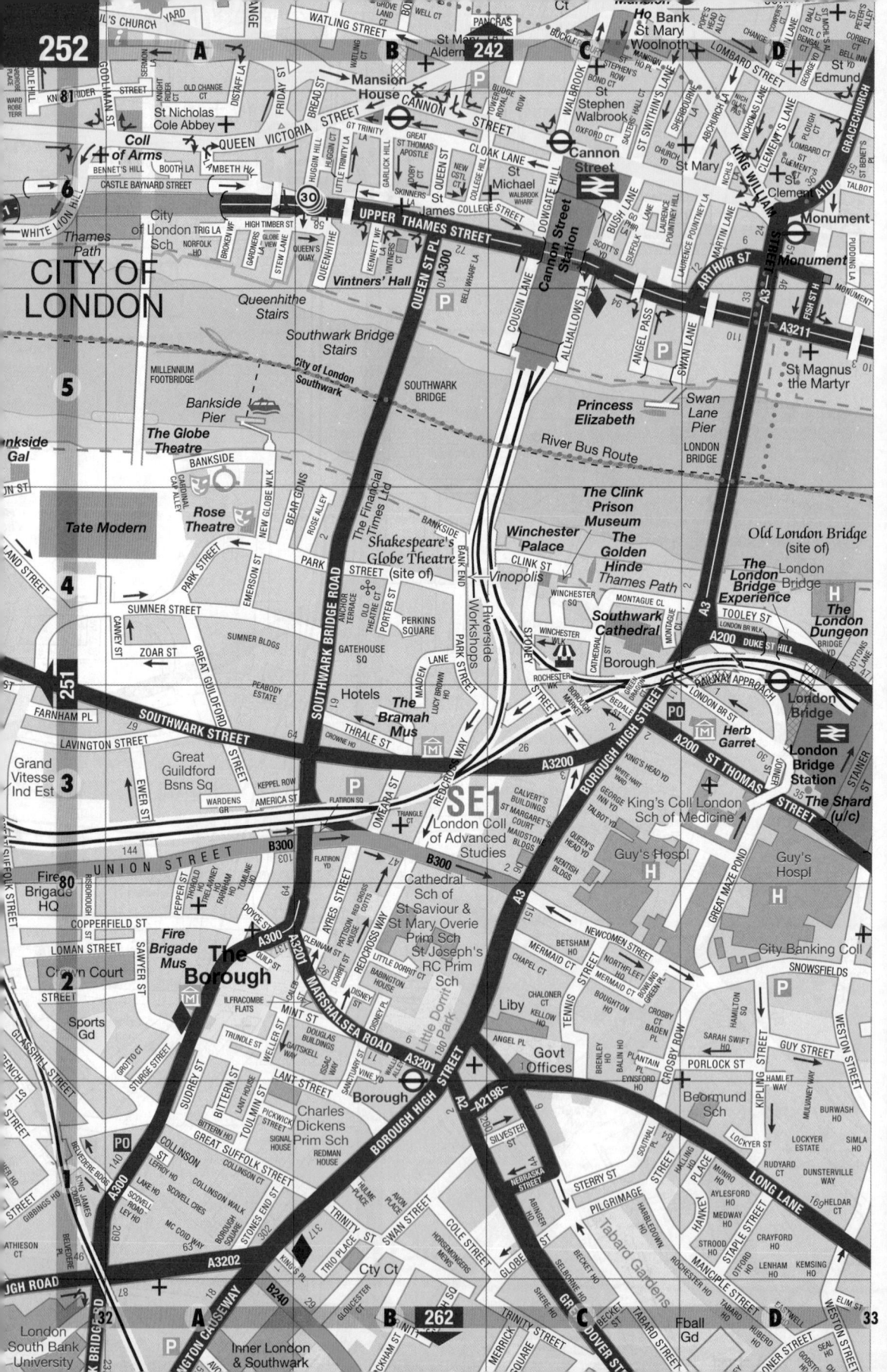

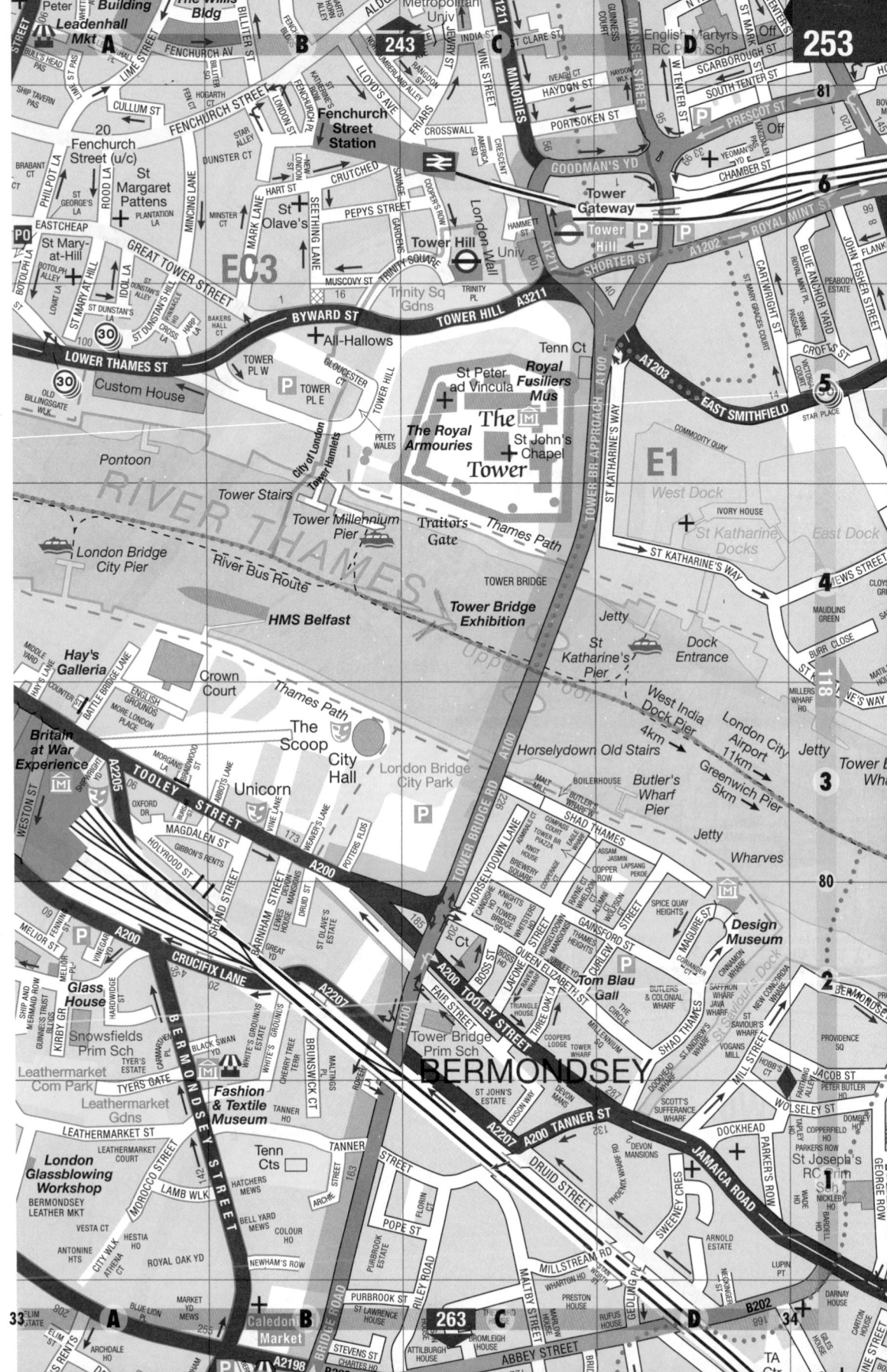

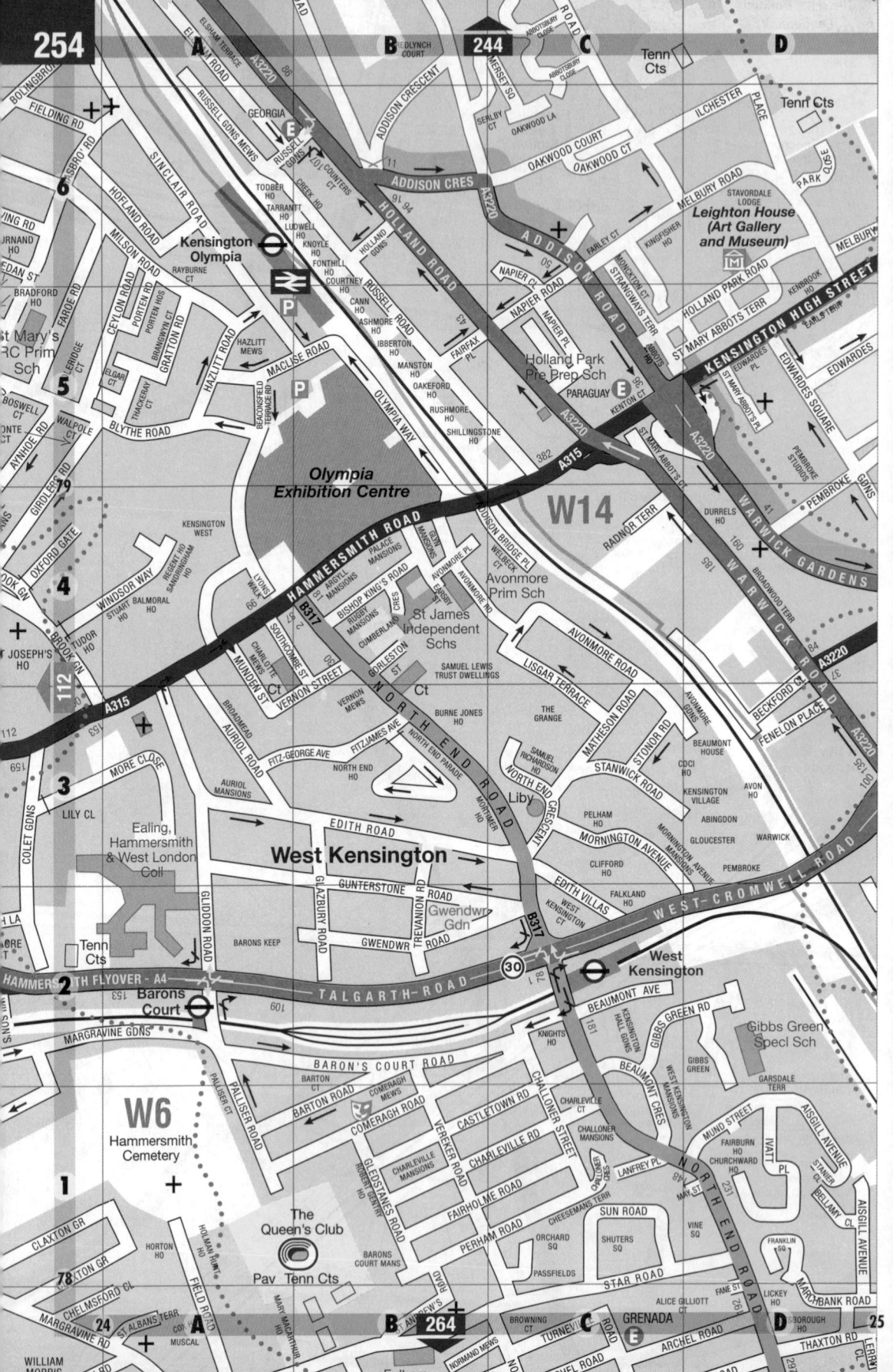

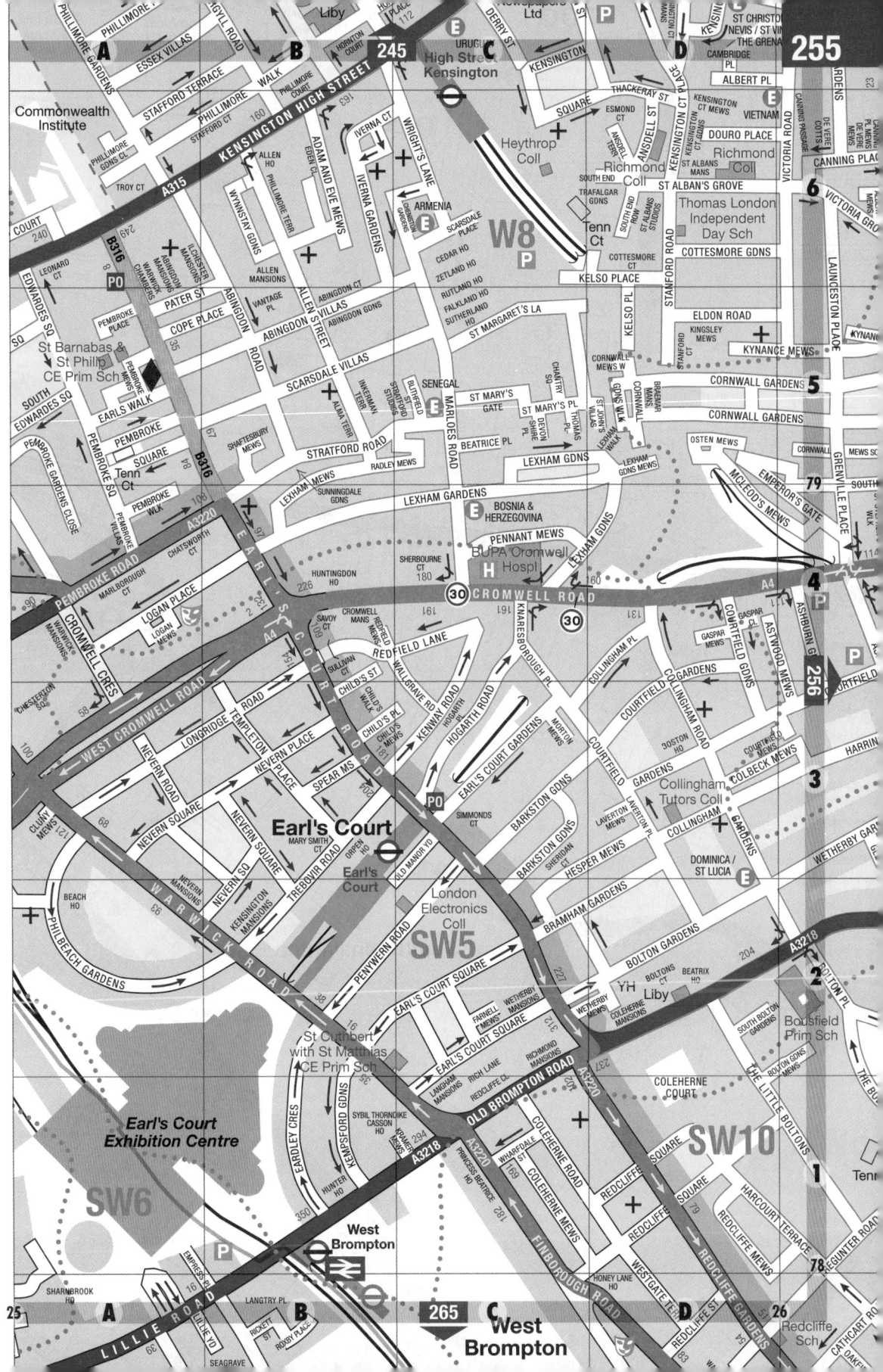

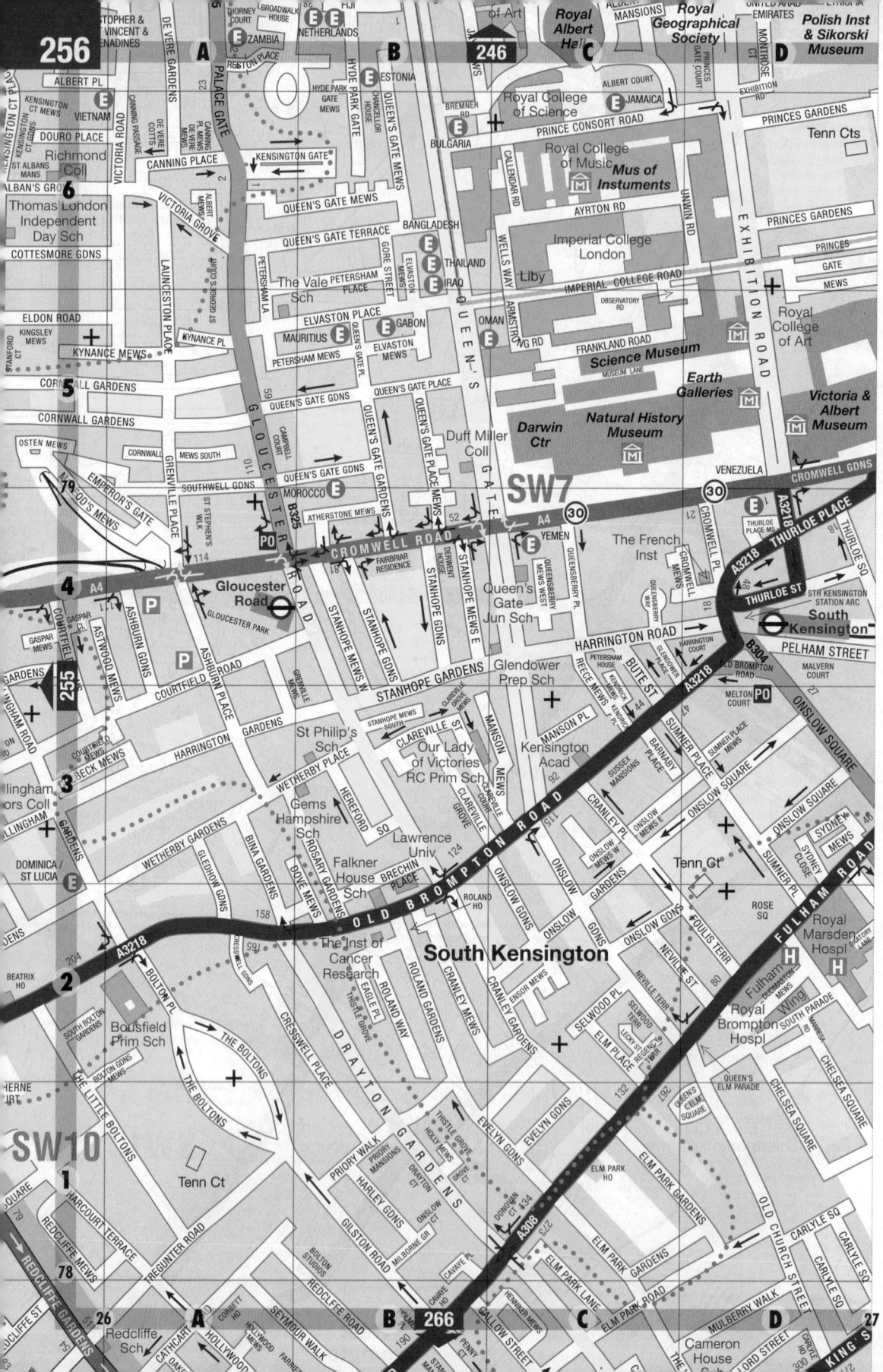

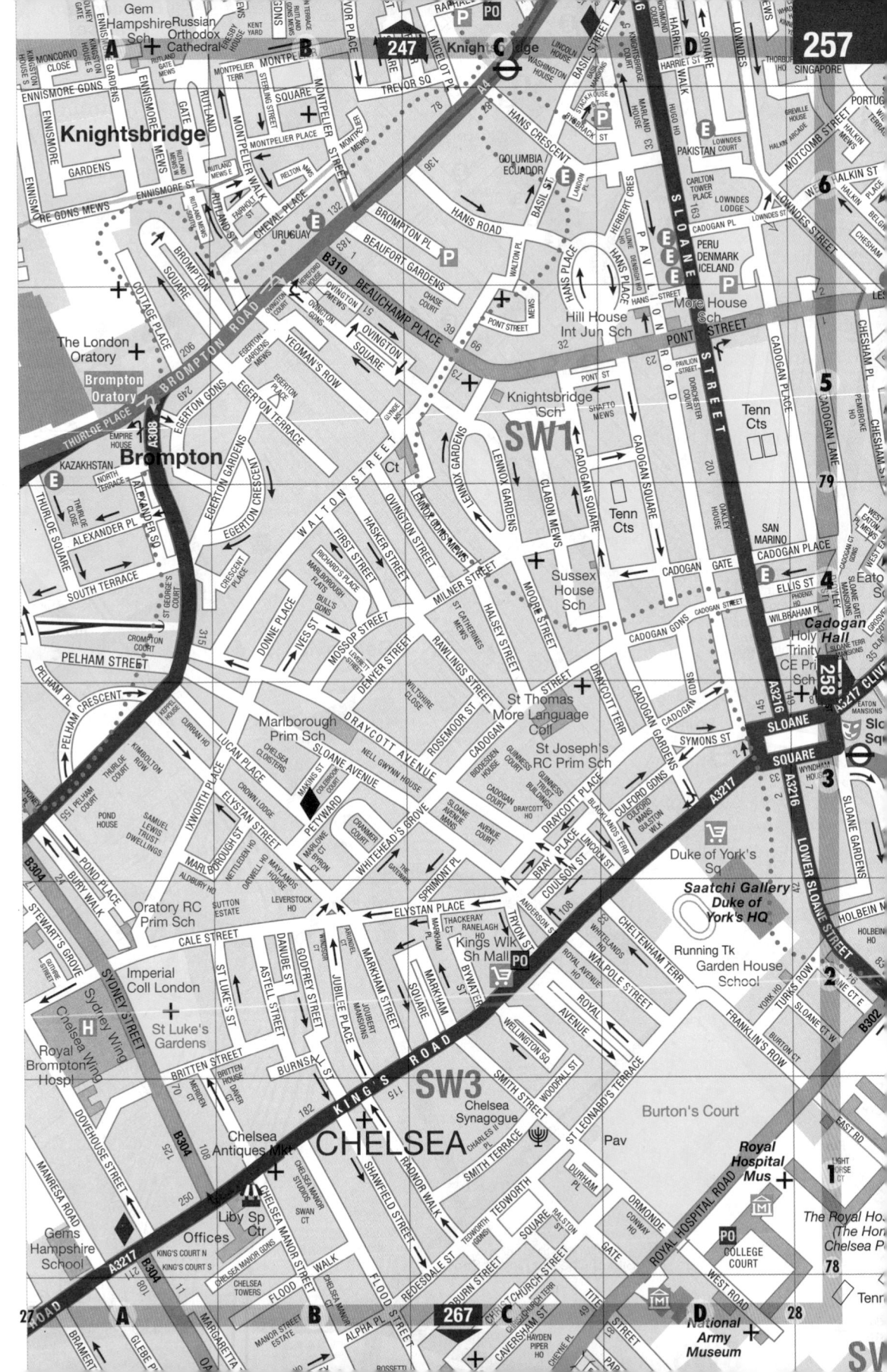

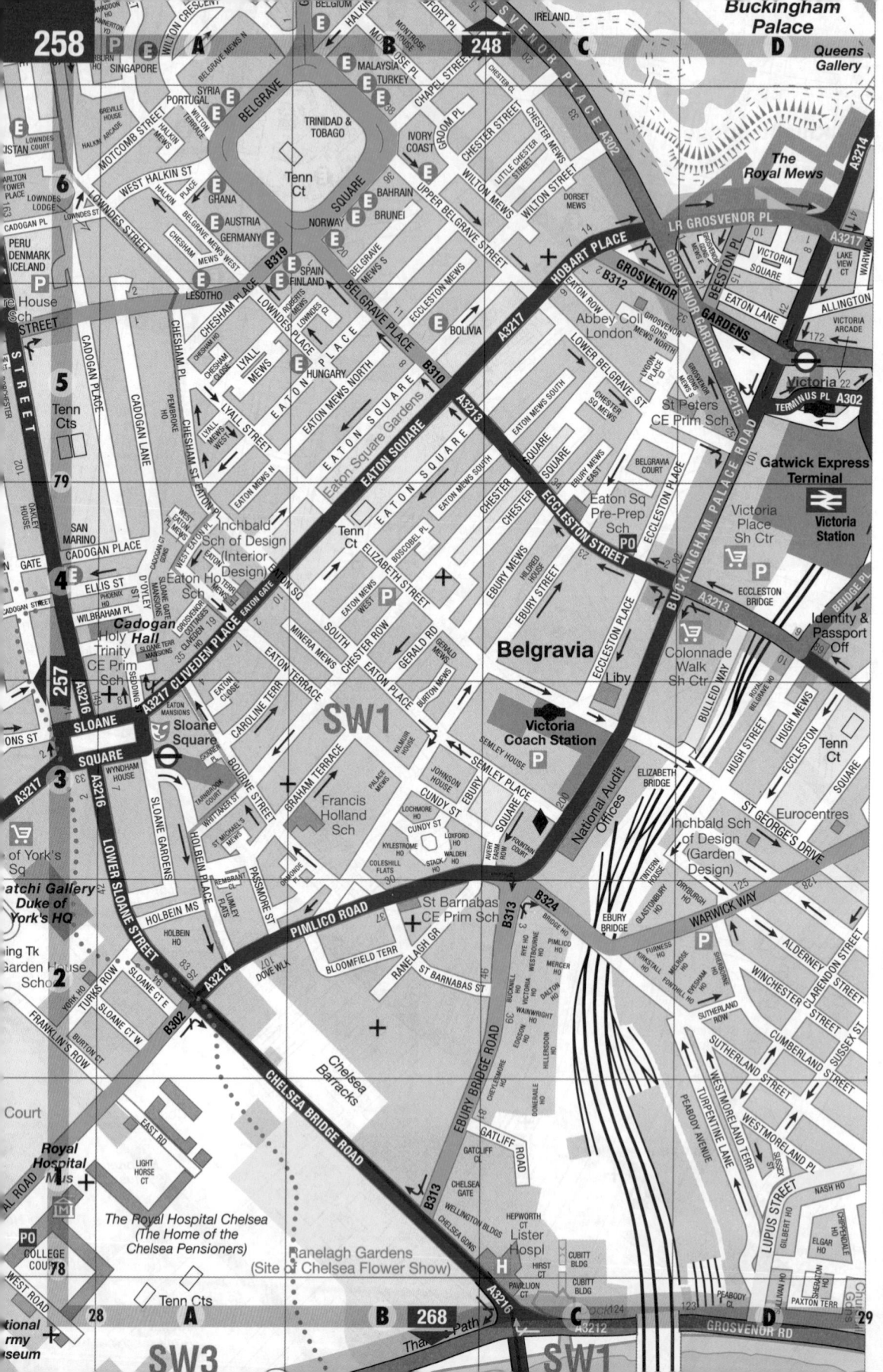

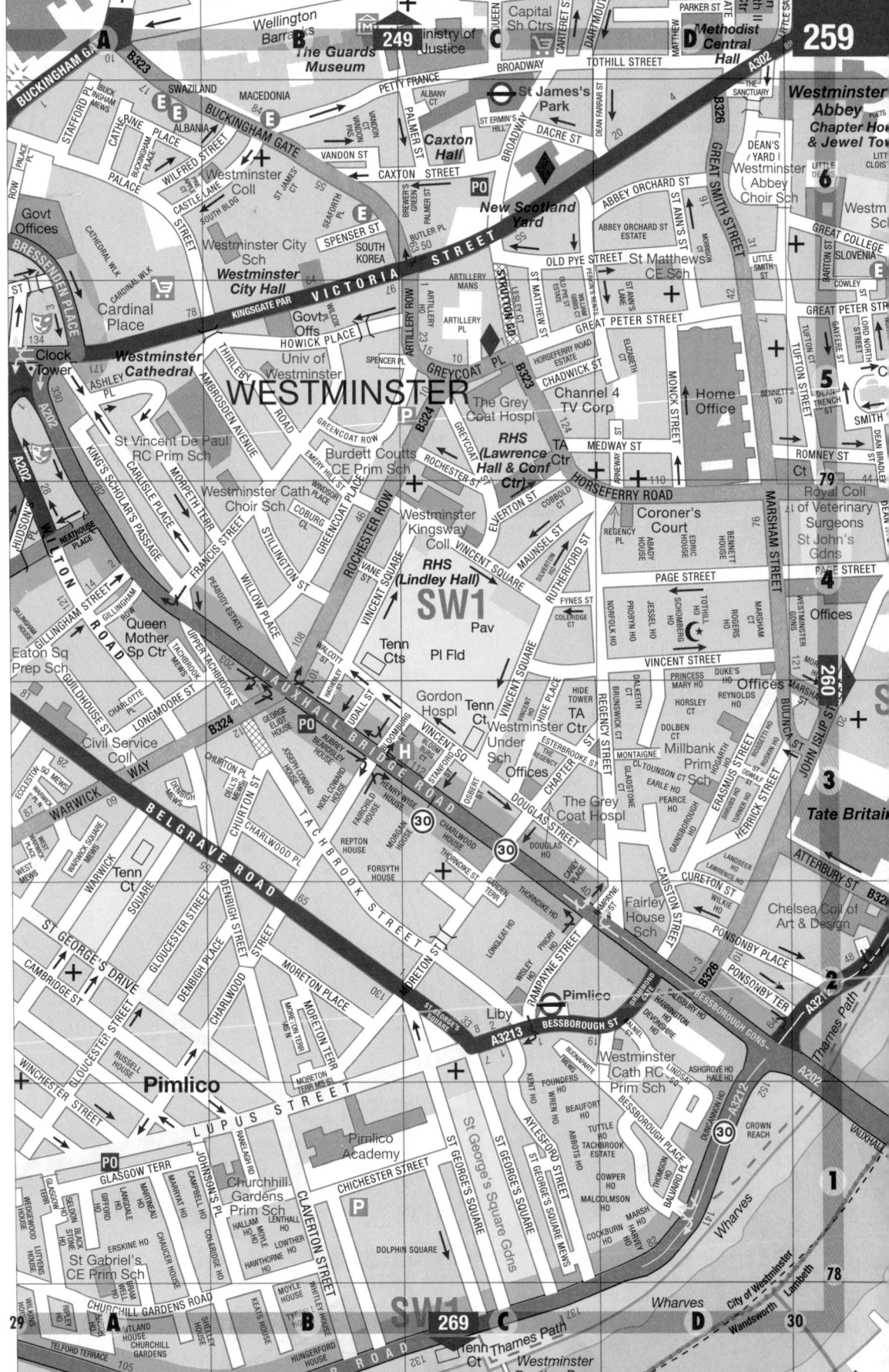

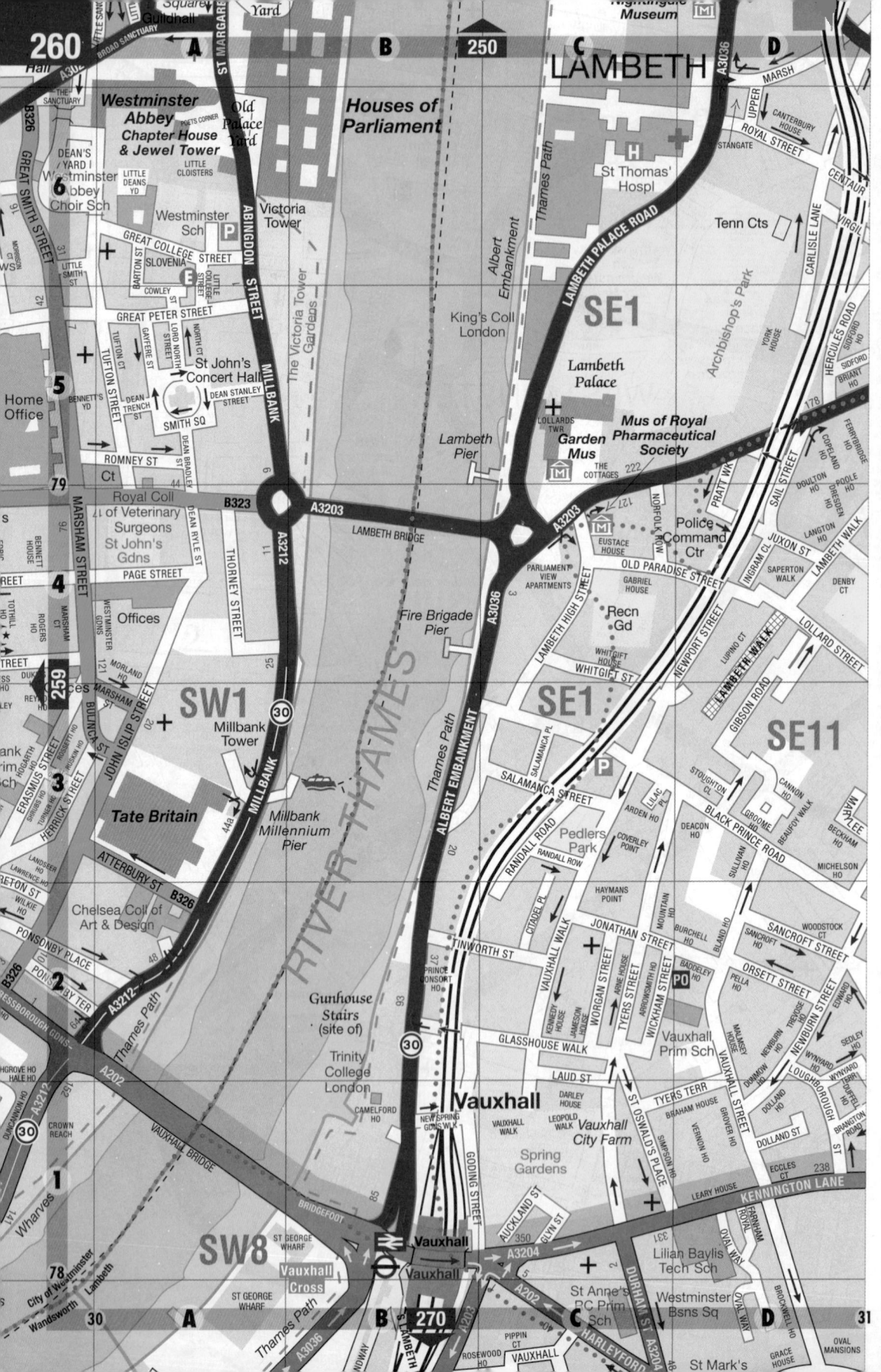

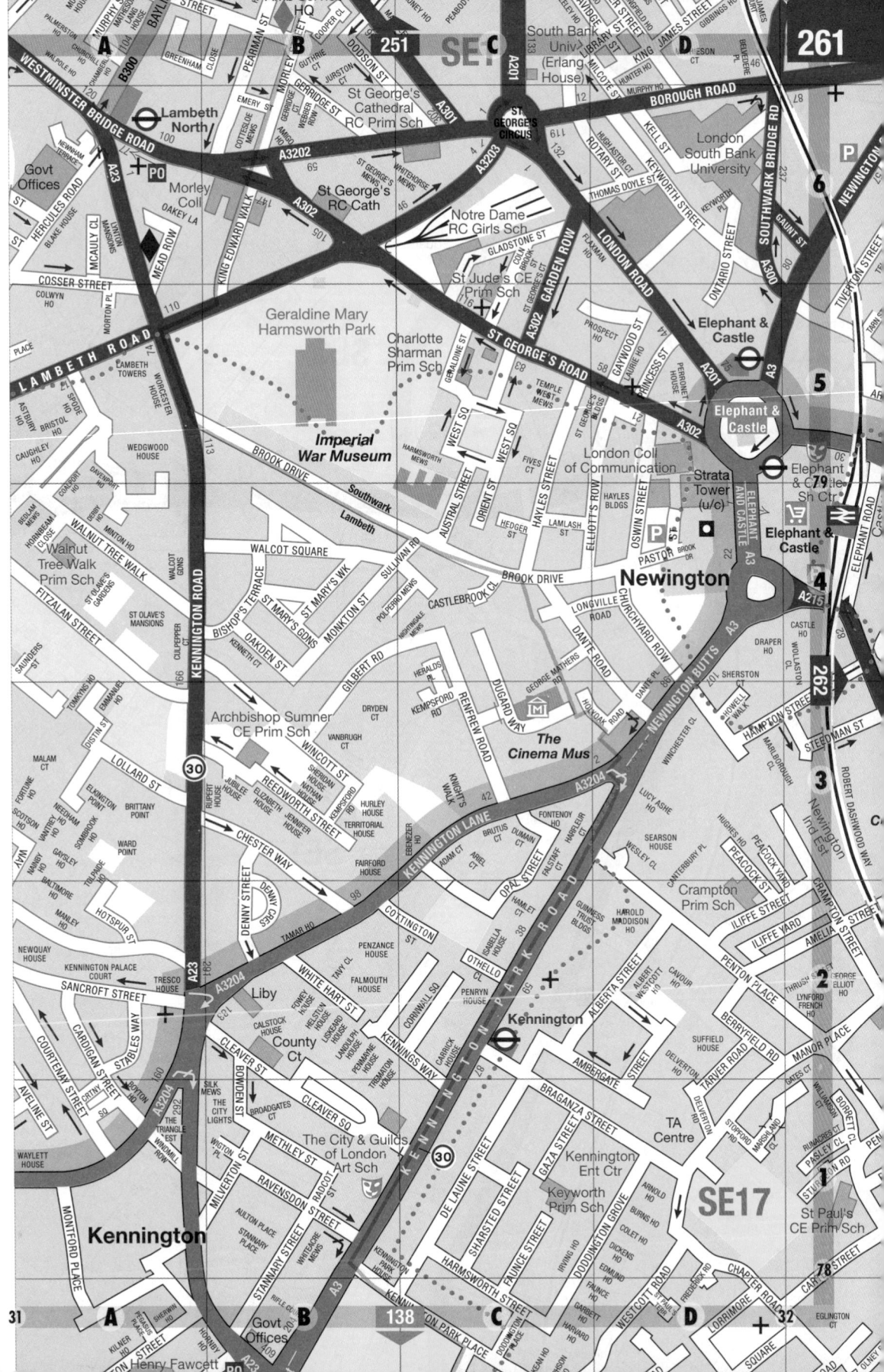

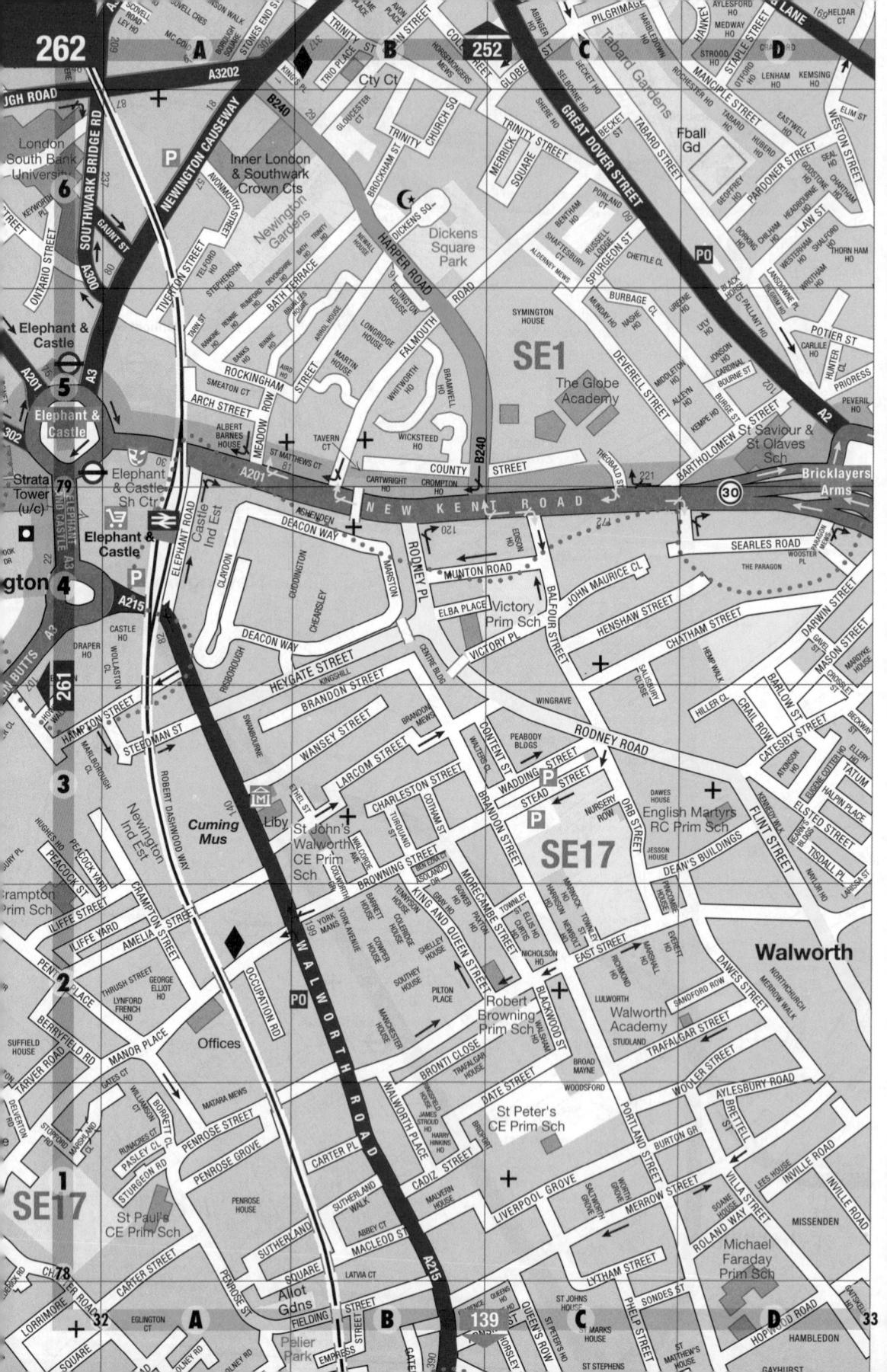

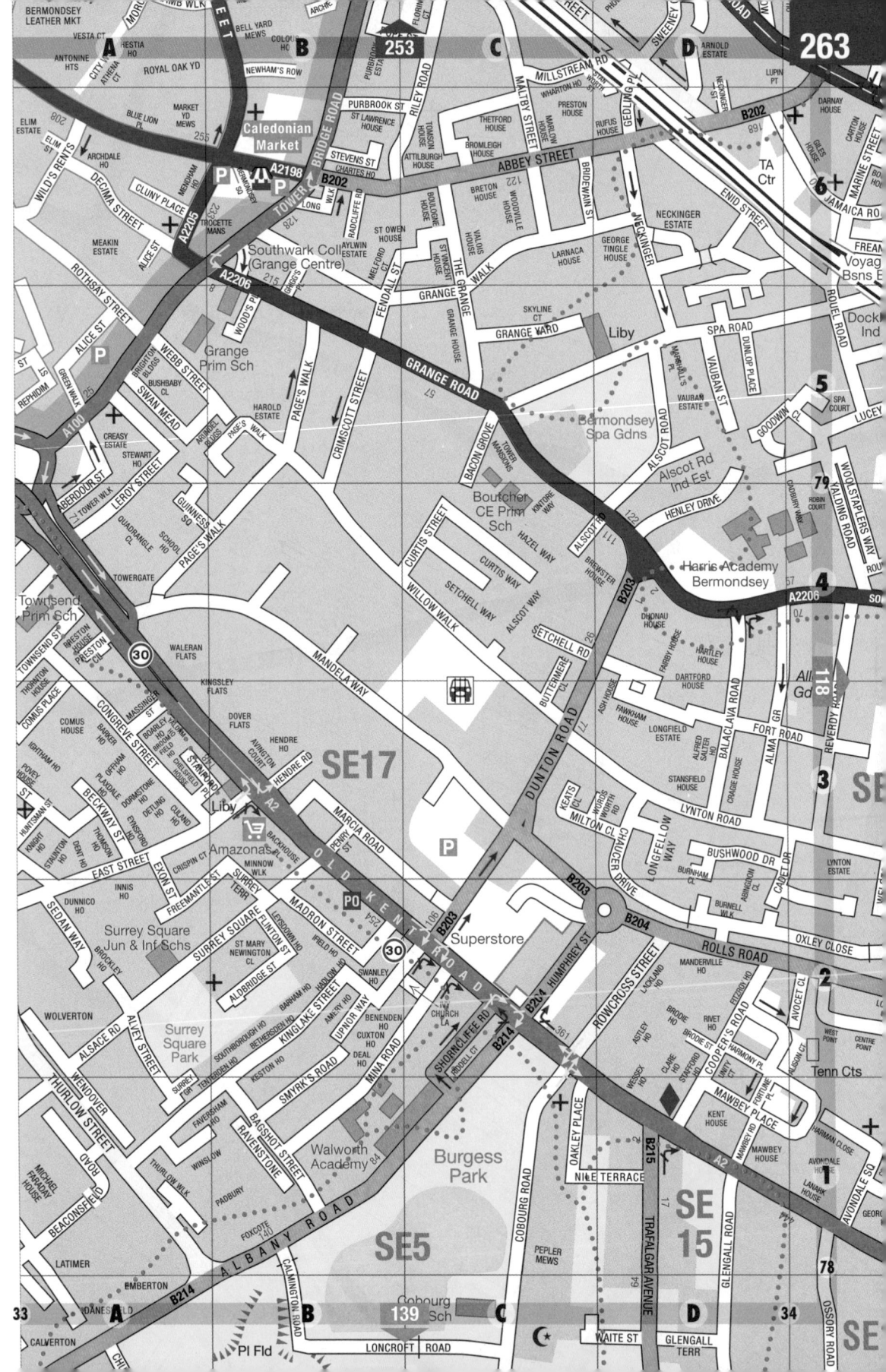

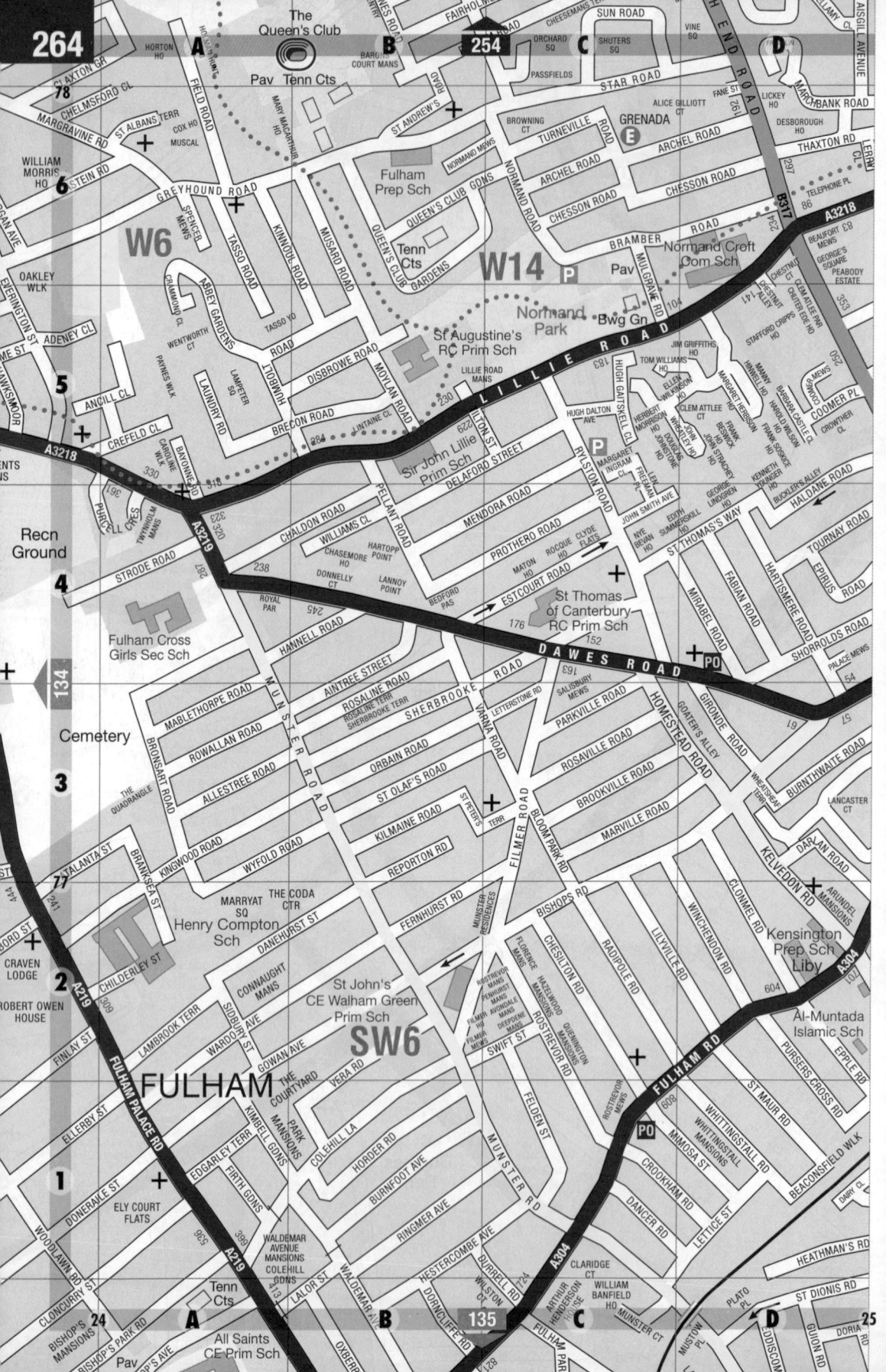

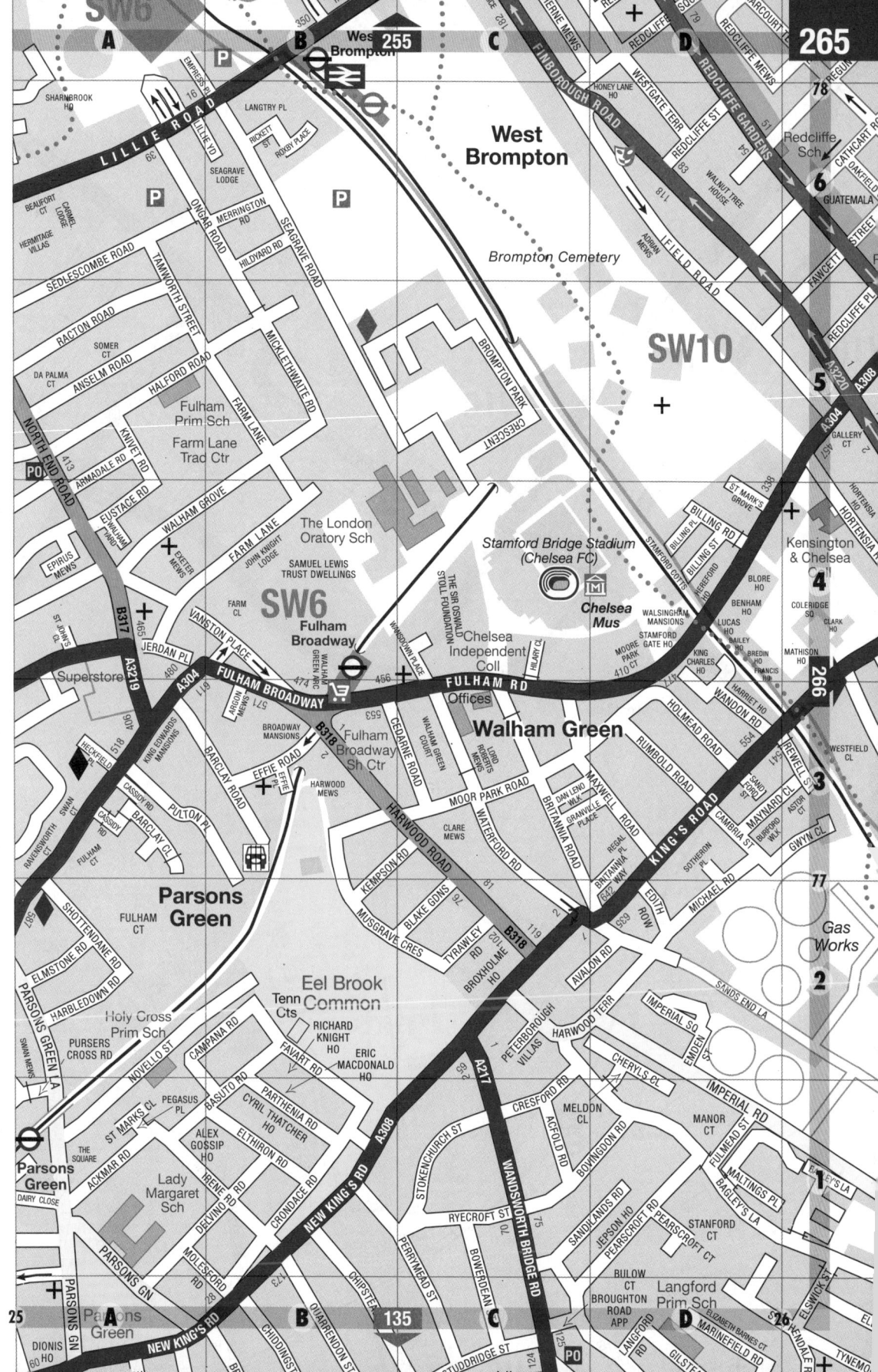

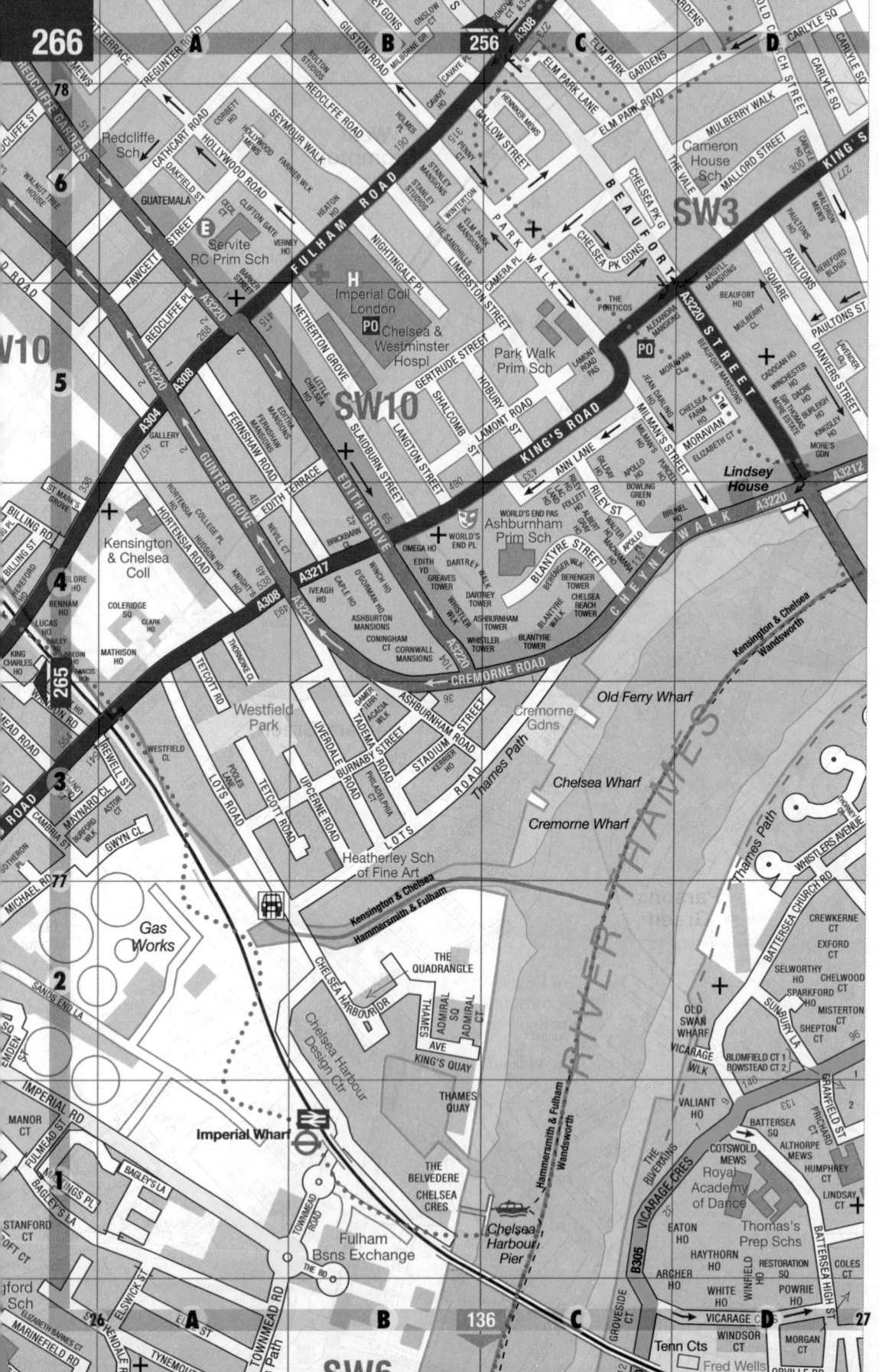

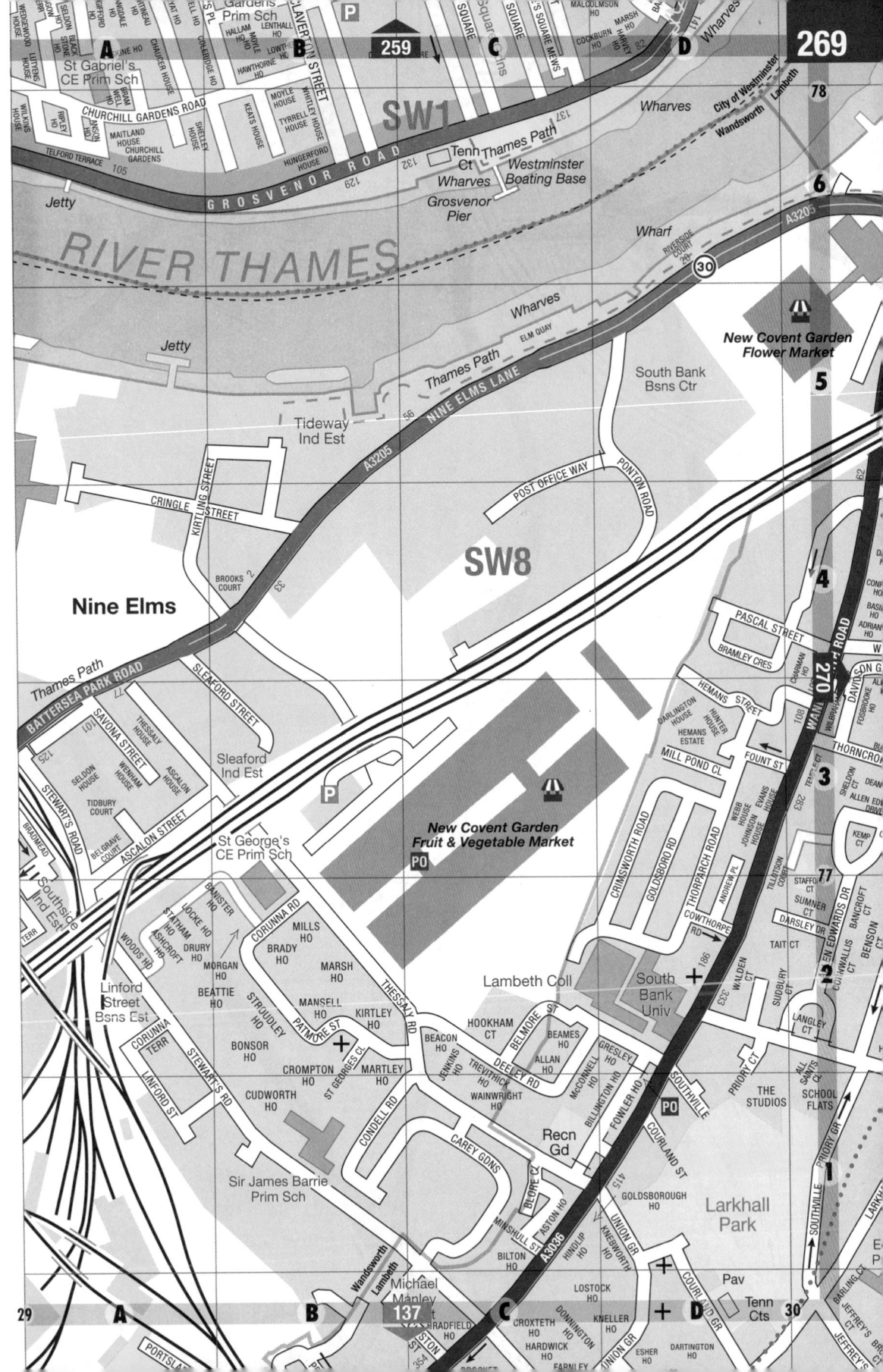

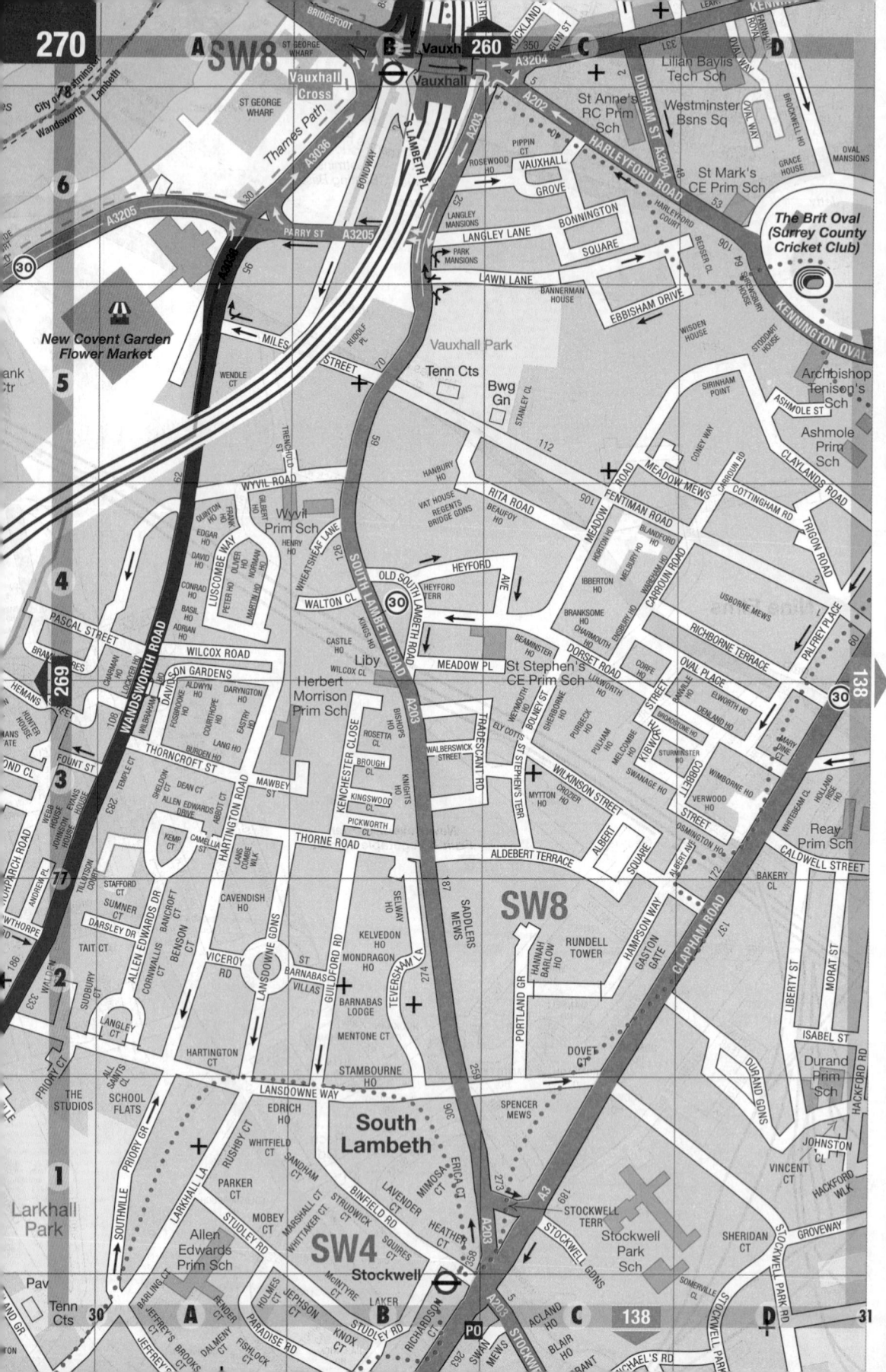

Index

Place name May be abbreviated on the map

Location number Present when a number indicates the place's position in a crowded area of mapping

Locality, town or village Shown when more than one place has the same name

Postcode district District for the indexed place

Map page number and grid square References to the large-scale maps on pages 229–270 are underlined in red

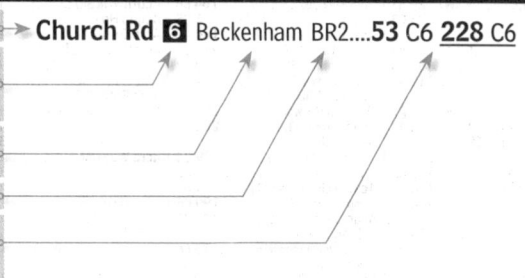

Church Rd **6** Beckenham BR2....**53** C6 **228** C6

Cities, towns and villages are listed in CAPITAL LETTERS. **Public and commercial buildings** are highlighted in magenta. **Places of interest** are highlighted in blue with a star ★

Abbreviations used in the index

Acad	**Academy**	Ct	**Court**	Hts	**Heights**	Pl	**Place**
App	**Approach**	Ctr	**Centre**	Ind	**Industrial**	Prec	**Precinct**
Arc	**Arcade**	Ctry	**Country**	Inst	**Institute**	Prom	**Promenade**
Ave	**Avenue**	Cty	**County**	Int	**International**	Rd	**Road**
Bglw	**Bungalow**	Dr	**Drive**	Intc	**Interchange**	Recn	**Recreation**
Bldg	**Building**	Dro	**Drove**	Junc	**Junction**	Ret	**Retail**
Bsns, Bus	**Business**	Ed	**Education**	L	**Leisure**	Sh	**Shopping**
Bvd	**Boulevard**	Emb	**Embankment**	La	**Lane**	Sq	**Square**
Cath	**Cathedral**	Est	**Estate**	Liby	**Library**	St	**Street**
Cir	**Circus**	Ex	**Exhibition**	Mdw	**Meadow**	Sta	**Station**
Cl	**Close**	Gd	**Ground**	Meml	**Memorial**	Terr	**Terrace**
Cnr	**Corner**	Gdn	**Garden**	Mkt	**Market**	TH	**Town Hall**
Coll	**College**	Gn	**Green**	Mus	**Museum**	Univ	**University**
Com	**Community**	Gr	**Grove**	Orch	**Orchard**	Wk, Wlk	**Walk**
Comm	**Common**	H	**Hall**	Pal	**Palace**	Wr	**Water**
Cott	**Cottage**	Ho	**House**	Par	**Parade**	Yd	**Yard**
Cres	**Crescent**	Hospl	**Hospital**	Pas	**Passage**		
Cswy	**Causeway**	HQ	**Headquarters**	Pk	**Park**		

Index of towns, villages, streets, hospitals, industrial estates, railway stations, schools, shopping centres, universities and places of interest

176 Gall★ NW5..........71 A2
201 Bishopgate EC2 .... **243** B4

A

Aaron Ct BR3 .... 207 D6
Aaron Hill Rd E6.........100 C2
Abady Ho SW1.........**259** D4
Abberley Mews **9** SW8 .**137** B2
Abberton IG8............37 C5
Abbess Cl **11** Newham E6 ..100 A2
Abbeville Mews **3** SW4 . 137 D1
Abbeville Rd
　Clapham Pk SW4 ......159 C6
　Hornsey N8..............49 D5
Abbey Ave HA0 ....88 A5
Abbey Bsns Ctr
　SW8 ....137 B4 **268** D2
Abbey Cl Hayes UB3 ....106 B5
　Northolt UB5 ....85 B4
　Pinner HA5.............40 C6
Abbey Coll London
　SW1...........115 B3 **258** C5
Abbey Cres DA17 ......125 C2
Abbey Ct
　6 Bedford Pk W12 ....111 C3
　Camberwell SE17......**262** B1
　Church End N3..........47 C6
　5 Edgware HA8 ....26 D5
　Hampton TW12.........173 C3
　St John's Wood NW8 ...**229** A4
　Twickenham TW2 ....152 B2
Abbeydale Rd HA0 ....88 C6
Abbey Dr SW17 ....181 A5
Abbeyfield Cl CR4......180 C1
Abbeyfield Rd SE16 ....118 C2
Abbeyfields Cl NW10 ....88 C5

Abbey Gdns
　10 Bermondsey SE16.....118 A2
　Chislehurst BR7 ....188 C2
　St John's Wood
　　NW8..........92 A5 **229** B3
　West Kensington
　　W6 ....135 A6 **264** A5
Abbey Gr SE2............**124** B2
Abbeyhill Rd DA15 ......168 C2
Abbey Ho Newham E15 ....98 C5
　St John's Wood NW8 ...**229** B2
Abbey Ind Est Ealing HA0...88 B6
　Mitcham CR4 ....202 D4
Abbey La Beckenham BR3 .185 C3
　Mill Meads E15...........98 B5
Abbey Lane Commercial Est
　1 E15...................98 C5
Abbey Lo Bromley SE12....187 B6
　1 Ealing W5 ....109 C6
　Lisson Gr NW8 ....**230** B1
Abbey Manufacturing Est
　HA0....................88 B6
Abbey Mews
　Brentford TW7 ....131 A4
　Walthamstow E17 ....53 C4
Abbey Mount DA17 ......125 B1
Abbey Orchard St
　SW1..........115 D3 **259** D6
Abbey Orchard Street Est
　SW1..................**259** D6
Abbey Par Ealing NW10 ....88 B4
　Merton SW19 ....180 A3
Abbey Park Ind Est
　IG11....................101 A6
Abbey Pk BR3 ....185 C3
Abbey Prim Sch SM4.....201 C2
Abbey Rd Barking IG11....100 D6
　Bexley DA7 ....147 A1
　Croydon CR0...........220 D5

Abbey Rd continued
　Enfield EN1...............17 C6
　Erith DA17 ....125 A3
　Ilford IG2..................57 B4
　Lower Halliford TW17.....192 C1
　Merton SW19 ....180 A2
　Newham E15 ....98 C5
　St John's Wood
　　NW8........92 A5 **229** A4
　Wembley NW10 ....88 D5
Abbey Sports Ctr IG11 ...101 A6
Abbey St
　Bermondsey SE1 . 117 D3 **263** C6
　Newham E13 ....99 A3
　Walthamstow E17 ....35 B1
Abbey Terr SE2 ....124 C2
Abbey Trad Est SE26.....185 B5
Abbey View NW7 ....11 D1
Abbey Wlk KT8 ....195 D5
ABBEY WOOD 124 B3
Abbey Wood Rd SE2 ....124 C2
Abbey Wood Sch SE2 ....124 A3
Abbey Wood Sta SE2....124 C3
Abbot Cl HA4 ....62 D5
Abbot Ct SW8 ....**270** A3
Abbot Ho **14** E14 ....119 D6
Abbotsbury Cl
　Kensington W14....113 B4 **244** C5
　Mill Meads E15..........98 A5
Abbotsbury Gdns HA5....40 C3
Abbotsbury Ho W14......**244** B2
Abbotsbury Mews SE15 ..140 C2
Abbotsbury Prim Sch
　SM4...................201 D4
Abbotsbury Rd
　Coney Hall BR2, BR4....224 D6
　Kensington W14....113 B4 **244** C1
　Morden SM4............201 D5
Abbots Cl BR5 ....211 A1
Abbots Ct SE25 ....205 C6

Abbots Dr HA2...........63 C6
Abbotsfield Sch UB10....82 D5
Abbotsford Ave N15.....51 A5
Abbotsford Rd IG3......80 B6
Abbots Gdns N2..........48 B5
Abbots Gn CR0, CR2 ....222 D2
Abbots Green CR2 ......222 D2
Abbotshade Rd **13** SE16 .118 D5
Abbotshall Ave N14......15 C1
Abbotshall Rd SE6......164 B2
Abbots Ho
　Kensington W14.........**254** C5
　Pimlico SW1..............**259** C1
Abbots La SE1 ....117 C5 **253** B3
Abbotsleigh Cl SM2......217 D1
Abbotsleigh Rd SW16....181 C5
Abbotsmede Cl TW1 ....152 D2
Abbots Pk SW2 ....160 C3
Abbot's Pl NW6..........91 D6
Abbots Rd Burnt Oak HA8...27 B3
　Newham E6 ....99 D6
Abbot St E8 ....73 D2
Abbots Terr N8 ....50 A3
Abbotstone Ho **4** E5 .....74 A6
Abbotstone Rd SW15....134 C2
Abbotsview Ct NW7......12 A1
Abbots Way BR3 ....207 A4
Abbotswell Rd SE4......163 B6
Abbotswood Cl **7** DA17 ..27 B3
Abbotswood Gdns IG5....56 B6
Abbotswood Rd
　London SE22............139 C1
　Streatham SW16 ......159 D1
Abbotswood Way UB3....106 B5
Abbott Ave SW20 ......178 D2
Abbott Cl Hampton TW12 .173 A4
　Northolt UB5 ....63 B2

| | 176–Abe |

Abbott Ho SW12 .... 158 D4
Abbott Rd E14 ....98 B1
　Romford RM7 ....59 D6
　Woolwich SE28.........124 C6
Abbotts Cres Chingford E4 . 36 B6
　Enfield EN2..............4 D3
Abbotts Ct HA2..........64 B6
Abbotts Dr HA0..........65 B6
Abbotts Park Rd E10 ....54 A2
Abbotts Rd Barnet EN5....1 D1
　Cheam SM3 ....217 A4
　Mitcham CR4 ....203 C5
　Southall UB1............107 A5
Abbotts Wharf **4** E14...97 C1
Abbott's Wlk DA7......146 D5
Abchurch La EC2,
　EC4........117 B6 **252** D6
Abchurch Yd EC4 ....**252** C6
Abdale Rd W12 ....112 B5
Abel Ho
　7 Kennington SE11....138 C6
　1 Woolwich SE18 .....123 A2
Abenglen Ind Est UB3....105 B4
Aberavon Rd E3...........97 A4
Abercairn Rd SW16......181 C3
Aberconway Rd SM4....201 D5
Abercorn Cl Finchley NW7 ..29 A3
　St John's Wood
　　NW8........92 A4 **229** A2
Abercorn Cres HA2.......41 D1
Abercorn Dell WD23 .....8 A2
Abercorn Gdns
　Harrow HA3 ....43 D2
　Ilford RM6 ....58 B3
Abercorn Gr HA4 ....39 D5

Abercorn Mans NW8.... **229** B3
Abercorn Mews **10**
  TW10....................**132** B1
Abercorn Pl NW8 . . **92** A5 **229** A3
Abercorn Rd Finchley NW7 . **29** A3
  Stanmore HA7 ....**25** C3
Abercorn Sch
  NW8............**92** A5 **229** B3
Abercorn Trad Est HA0 ...**87** D6
Abercorn Way SE1.........**118** A1
Abercorn Wlk
  NW8............**92** A4 **229** A4
Abercrombie Dr EN1......**6** A4
Abercrombie Ho **1**
  W12....................**112** B6
Abercrombie St SW11....**136** C3
Aberdale Ct **22** SE16.....**118** D4
Aberdare Cl BR4...........**224** A6
Aberdare Gdns
  Finchley NW7..........**28** D3
  South Hampstead NW6.....**69** D1
Aberdare Rd EN3.........**6** C1
Aberdeen Cotts HA7......**25** C3
Aberdeen Ct
  Canonbury N5............**73** A3
  Paddington W2.........**236** C5
Aberdeen Ctr N5 ....**73** A3
Aberdeen La N5 ....**73** A3
Aberdeen Mans NW1.....**240** A6
Aberdeen Par N18.........**34** B5
Aberdeen Pk N5...........**73** A3
Aberdeen Pl NW8..**92** B3 **236** C6
Aberdeen Rd
  Canonbury N5............**73** A4
  Croydon CR0.............**221** B4
  Dudden Hill NW10........**67** D3
  Edmonton N18...........**34** B5
  Harrow HA3..............**24** D1
Aberdeen Terr SE3.........**142** B3
Aberdour Rd IG3...........**80** B6
Aberdour St SE1..**117** C2 **263** A4
Aberfeldy Ho SE18.........**138** D5
Aberfeldy St E14..........**98** A1
Aberford Gdns SE18......**144** A4
Aberfoyle Rd SW16........**181** D4
Abergeldie Rd SE12......**165** B5
Abernethy Rd SE13........**142** C1
Abery St SE18............**123** C2
Ability Plaza **8** E8........**73** D1
Ability Twrs EC1.........**235** A2
Abingdon W14............**254** D3
Abingdon Cl Fulham SE1 . **254** D3
  Hillingdon UB10.........**82** B6
  Kentish Town NW1.......**71** D2
  North Cheam KT4.......**216** B5
  Wimbledon SW19........**180** A4
Abingdon Ct Earl's Ct W8 . **255** B5
  Edgware HA8 ....**26** A6
  Upper Tooting SW17......**180** D4
Abingdon Gdns W8 ......**255** B5
Abingdon Ho
  Bromley BR1.............**187** B3
  Spitalfields E2...........**243** C6
Abingdon Lo **2** Barnet EN5. . **1** A1
  Bromley BR2.............**186** D1
Abingdon Mans W8......**255** A6
Abingdon Rd Finchley N3...**30** A1
  Kensington W8......**113** C3 **255** B5
  Thornton Heath SW16....**182** A4
Abingdon St
  SW1..........**116** A3 **260** A6
  W8..........**113** C3 **255** B6
Abinger Cl Barking IG11....**80** A4
  Bickley BR1.............**210** A6
  New Addington CR0......**224** A2
  Wallington SM6.........**220** A3
Abinger Ct **3** Ealing W5...**109** C6
  Thornton Heath CR0......**204** D2
  Wallington SM6.........**220** A3
Abinger Gdns SW7.......**130** C2
Abinger Gr SE8............**141** B6
Abinger Ho
  Borough The SE1.......**252** C1
  2 Kingston u T KT2 ....**176** D3
Abinger Mews W9.........**91** C3
Abinger Rd W4............**111** C3
Abington Ho NW11......**48** A3
Ablett St SE16............**118** C1
Abney Gdns **5** N16 ....**73** D6
Abney Park Cemetery★
  N16....................**73** C6
Abney Park Ct N16.........**73** D6
Aborfield **5** NW5........**71** C3
Aboyne Dr SW20..........**178** A1
Aboyne Rd Neasden NW10...**67** C5
  Wandsworth SW17.......**158** B1
Abraham Cl WD19.........**22** B6
Abraham Cohen Ct IG1 . . **56** C3
Abraham Fisher Ho **2**
  E12....................**78** C3
Abridge Way IG11.........**102** B5
Abyssinia Cl SW11........**136** C1
Abyssinia Rd SW11........**136** C1
Acacia Ave
  Brentford TW8............**131** B5

Acacia Ave continued
  East Finchley N2...........**47** D6
  Hayes UB3 ....**83** D1
  Littleton TW17..........**192** C4
  Ruislip HA4 ....**40** B2
  Tottenham N17...........**33** B3
  Wembley HA9............**66** A3
  Yiewsley UB7 ....**104** B6
Acacia Bsns Ctr **1** E11....**76** C5
  Petts Wood BR5..........**211** B4
  Rotherhithe SE8..........**119** A2
  Stanmore HA7...........**24** C4
Acacia Ct Harrow HA1.....**41** D3
  5 West Norwood SW16 ..**182** C5
Acacia Dr SM3............**201** C1
Acacia Gdns
  St John's Wood NW8......**229** D4
  West Wickham BR4 ......**224** A6
Acacia Gr Dulwich SE21....**161** B2
  Kingston u T KT3.........**199** C6
Acacia Ho Brockley SE4...**141** B1
  1 New Malden KT3......**199** C5
  Stoke Newington N16......**73** B6
  Wood Green N22.........**32** C2
Acacia Lo **6** N3..........**29** B1
Acacia Pl NW8......**92** B5 **229** D4
Acacia Rd Acton W3.......**111** A6
  Beckenham BR3.........**207** B6
  Enfield EN2..............**5** B4
  Hampton TW12...........**173** C4
  Leyton E11 ....**76** C6
  Mitcham CR4............**181** B1
  St John's Wood
    NW8............**92** B5 **229** D4
  Thornton Heath SW16....**182** A2
  Walthamstow E17 ....**53** A3
  Wood Green N22.........**32** C2
Acacias Lo EN4 ....**14** B6
Acacias The EN4...........**14** B6
Acacia Way DA15.........**167** D3
Acacia Wlk SW10.........**266** B3
Academia Way N17......**33** C4
Academic Coll of London
  HA0....................**65** D5
Academy Ct **13** E2........**96** C4
Academy Gdns
  Croydon CR0............**205** D1
  Kensington W8..........**245** A2
  Northolt UB5.............**84** D5
Academy Pl
  Hounslow TW7 ....**130** C5
  Woolwich SE18..........**144** C4
Academy Rd SE18.........**144** B5
Academy Sch The **9**
  NW3...................**70** B4
Academy The **2** N19....**49** C1
Acad of Live & Recorded Arts
  SW18..................**158** B5
Acanthus Dr SE1..........**118** A1
Acanthus Rd SW11........**137** A2
Accadia Ct NW9...........**67** A6
Accommodation Rd
  NW11...................**47** B1
Ace Par KT9..............**214** A5
Acer Ave UB4.............**85** A2
Acer Ct
  2 Cricklewood NW2......**68** D4
  3 Enfield EN3 ....**7** A2
Acer Rd E8...............**73** D1
Acers BR7................**188** A3
Acfold Rd SW6............**265** C1
Achilles Cl SE1...........**118** A1
Achilles Ho **16** E2........**96** B5
Achilles Rd NW6..........**69** C3
Achilles St SE14..........**141** A5
Achilles Way W1..........**248** B3
Acklam Rd W10...........**91** B2
Acklington Dr NW9.......**27** C2
Ackmar Rd SW6 ..**135** C4 **265** A1
Ackroyd Dr E3............**97** C2
Ackroyd Rd SE23.........**163** A4
Acland Burghley Sch
  NW5...................**71** B4
Acland Cl SE18...........**145** B5
Acland Cres SE5..........**139** B2
Acland Ho SW9...........**138** B3
Acland Rd NW2...........**68** B2
Acock Gr UB5.............**64** A4
Acol Cres HA4............**62** B3
Acol Ct **3** NW6..........**69** C1
Acol Rd NW6.............**69** D1
Aconbury Rd RM9.........**102** B6
Acorn Cl Chingford E4.....**35** D5
  Enfield EN2..............**4** D4
  1 Hampton TW12......**173** D4
  Stanmore HA7 ....**25** B3
Acorn Ct **5** Bow E3........**97** C5
  Hampton TW12..........**173** B5
  Ilford IG2...............**57** C4
  Upton Pk E6 ....**78** A1
  Wood Green N11..........**31** D4
Acorn Gdns
  North Acton W3..........**89** B2
  South Norwood SE19......**183** D2
Acorn Gr Harlington UB3.. **127** D5
  Ruislip HA4.............**61** D4
Acorn Par **7** SE15.......**140** B5
Acorn Production Ctr N7.. **72** A1

Acorns The **21** SW19 ....**156** D3
Acorns Way KT10........**212** A3
Acorn Way
  Beckenham BR3.........**208** A4
  Forest Hill SE23.........**162** D1
  Orpington BR6..........**226** D4
Acorn Wharf SE15........**140** A6
Acorn Wlk SE16..........**119** A5
Acqua Ho TW9............**132** D5
Acre Dr SE22.............**140** A1
Acrefield Ho **4** NW4.....**46** D5
Acre La Brixton SW2......**138** B1
  Wallington SM5.........**219** A4
Acre Path SM5............**63** A2
Acre Rd Dagenham RM10 .. **81** D1
  Kingston u T KT2.........**176** B2
  Mitcham SW19.........**180** B4
Acre Way HA6............**22** A2
Acris St SW18............**158** A6
ACS Hillingdon International
  Sch UB10 ....**82** B6
Action Ct TW15..........**171** A2
ACTON................**111** B5
Acton Bsns Ctr NW10......**89** B3
Acton Central Ind Est **4**
  W3....................**110** D5
Acton Central Sta W3......**111** B5
Acton Cl N9..............**18** A2
ACTON GREEN.........**111** A2
Acton High Sch W3........**110** C4
Acton Hill Mews W3......**110** D5
Acton Ho **5** Acton W3....**89** A1
  16 Haggerston E8.......**95** D6
Acton La Acton Green W4 ..**111** A2
  Acton W3..............**111** A4
  Harlesden NW10..........**89** B5
Acton Main Line Sta W3....**89** A1
Acton Mews E8............**95** D6
Acton Park Ind Est W3....**111** B4
Acton St WC1.....**94** B4 **233** C1
Acton Vale Ind Pk W3....**111** D5
Acton & West London Coll **10**
  W3....................**110** D5
Acuba Ho SW18...........**157** D3
Acuba Rd SW18...........**157** D2
Acworth Cl N9............**18** C4
Acworth Ho **11** SE18.....**144** D6
Ada Ct Islington N1........**235** A5
  St John's Wood W9 . . **92** A4 **229** B1
Ada Gdns Plaistow E15......**98** D6
  South Bromley E14.......**98** B1
Ada Ho **23** E2...........**96** A6
Adair Cl SE25.............**206** B6
Adair Ho SW3............**267** B6
Adair Rd W10............**91** A3
Adair Twr **7** W10........**91** A3
Ada Kennedy Ct **6**
  SE10...................**142** A5
Ada Lewis Ho HA9.........**66** B4
Adam Cl SE6.............**185** C6
Adam Ct Newington SE11 . **261** C3
  15 Sutton SM1..........**218** A4
Adam & Eve Ct W1........**239** B2
Adam & Eve Mews
  W8..............**113** C3 **255** B6
Adamfields NW3...........**70** B1
Adam La N21.............**16** B6
Adam Rd E4..............**35** B4
Adams Bridge Bsns Ctr
  HA9...................**66** D3
Adams Cl Finchley N3 .....**29** C3
  Surbiton KT5............**198** B3
  Wembley Pk NW9.........**66** D6
Adams Ct E17.............**53** A3
Adams Gardens Est **5**
  SE16...................**118** C4
Adams Ho
  3 South Bromley E14....**98** B1
  3 Streatham SW16......**181** C5
Adams Mews
  Upper Tooting SW17......**158** D2
  Wood Green N22 ....**32** B3
Adamson Ct N2...........**48** C6
Adamson Rd
  Hampstead NW3........**70** B1
  Newham E16 ....**99** A1
Adamson Way BR3........**208** A4
Adams Pl N7.............**72** B3
Adams Qtr TW8..........**131** C6
Adams Rd
  Beckenham BR3.........**207** A4
  Tottenham N17...........**33** B1
Adamsrill Cl EN1..........**17** B5
Adamsrill Prim Sch
  SE26...................**163** A1
Adamsrill Rd SE26........**185** A6
Adam's Row W1 ...**115** A4 **248** B5
Adams Sq DA6............**147** A2
Adam St WC2......**116** A4 **250** B5
Adams Way CR0..........**206** A3
Adams Wlk **11** KT1.......**176** A1
Adam Wlk SW6...........**134** C5
Ada Pl E2................**96** A6
Ada Rd Camberwell SE5...**139** C5
  Wembley HA0, HA9 ......**65** D5
Adare Wlk SW16, SW2....**160** B2
Ada St E8................**96** B6
Adcot Wlk **6** BR6.........**227** D4
Adderley Gdns SE9........**188** C6

Adderley Gr SW11........**159** A6
Adderley Rd HA3.........**24** D2
Adderley St E14..........**98** A1
Addey Ho SE8............**141** B5
Addey & Stanhope Sch **11**
  SE14...................**141** C4
ADDINGTON...........**223** C3
Addington Ct **7** SW14...**133** B2
Addington Dr N12.........**30** B4
Addington Gr SE26......**185** A6
Addington Ho **13** SW9...**138** B3
Addington Rd Bow E3......**97** C4
  Newham E16 ....**98** C3
  Stroud Green N4.........**50** C3
  Thornton Heath CR0......**204** C1
  West Wickham BR4 ......**224** C6
  West Wickham BR4, CR0..**224** B4
Addington Sq SE5.........**139** B5
Addington St
  SE1..........**116** B4 **250** D1
Addington Village Rd
  CR0...................**223** C3
Addington Village Sta
  CR0...................**223** C2
Addis Cl EN3.............**6** D4
ADDISCOMBE.........**206** A1
Addiscombe Ave CR0.....**206** A2
Addiscombe Cl HA3.......**43** C4
Addiscombe Court Rd
  CR0...................**221** C6
Addiscombe Ct UB10.....**83** A3
Addiscombe Rd CR0......**222** B6
Addiscombe Sta CR0......**206** A1
Addis Ho **13** E1..........**96** C2
Addison Ave
  Hounslow TW3..........**130** A4
  Notting Hill W11.....**113** A5 **244** A3
  Southgate N14...........**15** C5
Addison Bridge Pl
  W14.............**113** B2 **254** C4
Addison Cl Northwood HA6 . **22** A2
  Orpington BR5..........**211** A3
Addison Cres
  W14.............**113** A3 **254** B6
Addison Ct
  3 Belmont SM2........**217** D1
  Ealing W5..............**110** C6
  Twickenham TW1 ....**153** A3
Addison Dr SE12.........**165** B6
Addison Gdns
  Hammersmith W14 ......**112** D3
  Kingston u T KT5........**198** B5
Addison Gr W4...........**111** C3
Addison Ho **2** NW8 . . **92** A4 **229** C2
Addison Park Mans **12**
  W14...................**112** D4
Addison Pl
  Notting Hill W11 ....**113** A5 **244** A3
  Southall UB1............**107** C6
Addison Prim Sch W14....**112** D3
Addison Rd Bromley BR2 . **209** D4
  Croydon SE25...........**206** A5
  Enfield EN3..............**6** D4
  Kensington W14.....**113** B3 **254** C6
  Teddington TW11........**175** B4
  Walthamstow E17 ....**54** A4
  Wanstead E11 ....**55** A3
Addison's Cl CR0..........**223** B6
Addison Way
  Hampstead Garden Suburb
    NW11..................**47** C5
  Hayes UB3 ....**84** A1
  Northwood HA6 ....**22** A2
Addle Hill EC4...........**241** D1
Addlestone Ho **4** W10...**90** C2
Addy Ho SE16............**118** C2
Adecroft Way KT8.........**196** A6
Adela Ave KT3...........**200** B5
Adela Ho **9** W6..........**112** C1
Adelaide Ave SE4.........**141** C1
Adelaide Cl Brixton SW9...**138** C1
  Enfield EN1.............**5** C5
  Stanmore HA7 ....**25** A6
Adelaide Ct
  15 Beckenham BR3......**185** C3
  Hackney E5.............**75** A3
  Hanwell W7 ....**108** D4
  St John's Wood NW8 .....**229** B3
Adelaide Gdns RM6.......**59** A4
Adelaide Gr W12.........**112** A5
Adelaide Ho E17..........**53** B6
Adelaide Rd
  Ashford TW15...........**170** A6
  Chislehurst BR7.........**188** D5
  Ealing W13.............**109** A4
  Heston TW5.............**129** A4
  Ilford IG1...............**78** D6
  Kingston u T KT6........**198** A4
  Leyton E10 ....**76** A5
  Primrose Hill NW3........**70** C1
  Richmond TW9..........**132** B1
  Southall UB2............**107** A2
  Teddington TW11........**174** D4
  2 Wandsworth SW18....**157** C6
Adelaide St WC2.........**250** A5
Adelaide Terr TW8........**109** D1
Adela St W10.............**91** A3
Adelina Gr E1............**96** C2
Adelina Mews SW12......**159** D3
Adeline Pl WC1.....**93** D2 **239** D3

Adelphi Cres UB4.........**83** D4
Adelphi Ct **19** Finchley N2. . **30** B1
  20 Rotherhithe SE16.....**118** D4
Adelphi Terr WC2........**250** B5
Adelphi Way UB4.........**83** D4
Adeney Cl W6............**134** D6
Aden Gr N16.............**73** B4
Aden Ho **15** E1..........**96** D2
Aden Lo N16.............**73** B4
Adenmore Rd SE6........**163** C4
Aden Rd Enfield EN3.......**7** A1
  Ilford IG1...............**57** A2
Adeyfield Ho EC1........**235** D1
Adhara Rd HA6...........**22** A5
Adie Rd W6..............**112** C3
Adine Rd E13............**99** B3
Adisham Ho **4** E5.......**74** B3
Adler Ind Est UB3.........**105** B4
Adler St E1..............**96** A1
Adley St E5..............**75** A3
Adlington Cl N18.........**33** C5
Admaston Rd SE18........**145** A6
Admiral Ct Barking IG11...**102** C5
  Carshalton SM5.........**202** C1
  Chelsea SW10 ....**136** A4 **266** B2
  Hendon NW4 ....**46** A4
  Marylebone W1.........**238** A3
Admiral Ho TW11.........**175** A6
Admiral Hyson Ind Est
  SE16...................**118** B1
Admiral Mews W10.......**90** D3
Admiral Pl Harringay N8....**50** D5
  Rotherhithe SE16.........**119** A5
Admirals Cl E18...........**55** B5
Admirals Ct
  Bermondsey SE1........**253** C3
  3 Newham E6...........**100** D1
  32 Putney SW19.........**156** B1
Admiral Seymour Rd
  SE9....................**144** B1
Admirals Gate SE10.......**141** D4
Admiral Sq SW10 .**136** A4 **266** B2
Admiral St SE8...........**141** C4
Admirals Way E14.........**119** C4
Admiral's Wlk NW3.......**70** A5
Admiralty Arch★ SW1 . . **249** D4
Admiralty Cl
  1 London SE8..........**141** C4
  West Drayton UB7.......**104** B4
Admiralty Rd TW11.......**174** D4
Admiral Wlk W9..........**91** C2
Adolf St SE6.............**185** D6
Adolphus Rd N4..........**50** D1
Adolphus St SE8..........**141** B5
Adomar Rd RM8..........**81** A5
Adpar St W2......**92** B2 **236** C4
Adrian Ave NW2.........**46** B1
Adrian Bolt Ho **2** E2.....**96** B4
Adrian Cl EN5............**12** D5
Adrian Ho Islington N1....**233** D5
  South Lambeth SW8......**270** A4
  Stratford E15............**76** B1
Adrian Mews SW10.......**265** D6
Adriatic Bldg **18** E14....**119** A6
Adriatic Ho **18** E1.......**96** C3
Adrienne Ave UB1........**85** B4
Adron Ho **13** SE16.......**118** C2
Adstock Ho **5** N1........**72** D1
Advance Rd SE27.........**183** A6
Advent Ct **17** E14........**120** B6
Advent Way N18..........**34** D5
Adyar Ct **3** SW19........**179** A3
Adys Lawn NW2..........**68** B2
Adys Rd SE15............**139** D2
Aegean Apts **7** E16......**121** A4
Aegon Ho **3** E14........**119** C3
Aerodrome Rd NW4, NW9. . **45** D6
Aerodrome Way TW5......**128** C6
Aeroville NW9............**27** C1
Affleck St N1............**233** D3
Afghan Rd SW11..........**136** C3
Africa Ho WC2...........**240** C2
Afsil Ho EC1.............**241** B3
Aga Khan Univ WC1......**239** D3
Agamemnon Rd NW6.....**69** B3
Agar Cl KT6..............**214** B6
Agar Gr NW1.............**71** D1
Agar Ho **6** KT1..........**198** A6
Agar Pl NW1.............**71** C1
Agar St WC2............**250** B5
Agate Cl E16.............**99** D1
Agate Ho
  New Malden KT4 ....**199** C1
  12 Penge SE26..........**184** B5
Agate Rd W6.............**112** C3
Agatha Cl E1.............**118** C5
Agaton Rd SE9...........**167** A2
Agave Rd NW2...........**68** C4
Agdon St EC1......**94** C3 **241** C6
Agincourt E11............**54** D3
Agincourt Rd NW3........**70** D4
Agnes Ave IG1............**78** B4
Agnes Cl E6.............**122** C6
Agnes Ct **11** SW18.......**136** B1
Agnesfield Cl N12.........**30** C4
Agnes Gdns RM8..........**80** D4
Agnes Ho **13** W11.......**112** D6
Agnes Rd W3.............**111** D4

Agnes St E14 . . . . .97 B1
Agnew Rd SE23 . . . . .162 D4
Agricola Pl EN1 . . . . .17 D6
Aicon Gall★ SW1 . . . . . . .249 A6
Aidan Cl RM8 . . . . .81 A4
Aidans Ct N12 . . . . .30 C5
Aigburth Mans [5] SW9 . .138 C5
Ailanthe Cl HA8 . . . . .26 B5
Aileen Wlk E15 . . . . .76 D1
Ailsa Ave TW1 . . . . .153 B6
Ailsa Rd TW1 . . . . .153 B6
Ailsa St E14 . . . . .98 A2
Ainger Rd NW3 . . . . .70 D1
Ainsdale NW1 . . . . .232 A2
Ainsdale Cl BR6 . . . . .211 B1
Ainsdale Cres HA5 . . . . . . .41 C6
Ainsdale Dr SE1 . . . . .118 A1
Ainsdale Rd W5 . . . . .87 D3
Ainsley Ave RM7 . . . . .59 D3
Ainsley Cl N2 . . . . .17 C3
Ainsley St E2 . . . . .96 B4
Ainslie Ct [2] HA0 . . . . .88 A5
Ainslie Ho [1] E4 . . . . .35 C5
Ainslie Wlk [8] SW12 . . . .159 B4
Ainslie Wood Cres E4 . . . .35 D5
Ainslie Wood Gdns E4 . . . .35 D5
Ainslie Wood Prim Sch
E4 .35 D5
Ainslie Wood Rd E4 . . . . . .35 D5
Ainsty St [20] SE16 . . . . . .118 C4
Ainsworth Cl
Camberwell SE5 . . . . . . .139 C3
Dollis Hill NW2 . . . . .68 A5
Ainsworth Est
NW8 . . . . .92 A6 229 A6
Ainsworth Ho NW8 . . . . . .91 D6
Ainsworth Rd
Croydon CR0 . . . . .220 D6
Hackney E9 . . . . .74 C1
Ainsworth Way
NW8 . . . . .92 A6 229 A6
Aintree Ave E6 . . . . .100 A6
Aintree Cl UB8 . . . . .82 D2
Aintree Ho SE26 . . . . .184 B4
Aintree Rd UB6 . . . . .87 B5
Aintree St SW6 . . . .135 A5 264 B4
Airborne Ho [10] SM6 . . . . .219 B4
Airco Cl NW9 . . . . .45 B6
Aird Ct TW12 . . . . .173 D2
Aird Ho SE1 . . . . .262 A5
Airdrie Cl Barnsbury N1 . . .72 B1
Hayes UB4 . . . . .85 A2
Airedale Ave W4 . . . . . . .111 D1
Airedale Ave S W4 . . . . . .111 D1
Airedale Rd
Balham SW12 . . . . .158 D4
Ealing W5 . . . . .109 D3
Airlie Gdns Ilford IG1 . . . . .56 D1
Kensington W8 . . . . 113 C5 245 A3
Airlinks Ind Est TW5 . . . .106 C1
Air Park Way TW13 . . . . .150 B2
Airport Gate Bsns Ctr
UB7 . . . . .126 C5
Airport Ho CR0 . . . . .220 C2
Airport Rdbt E16 . . . . . . .121 D5
Air St W1 . . . . .249 B5
Airthrie Rd IG3 . . . . .80 B6
Aisgill Ave SW5 . . . .113 B1 254 D1
Aisher Rd SE28 . . . . .124 C6
Aislabie Ho N21 . . . . .17 B5
Aislibie Rd SE12 . . . . . . .142 C1
Aiten Pl W6 . . . . .112 A2
Aithan Ho [19] E14 . . . . .97 B1
Aitken Cl Carshalton CR4 . .202 D2
Hackney E8 . . . . .96 A6
Aitken Rd Barnet EN5 . . . . .12 C6
Catford SE6 . . . . .163 D2
Aits View KT8 . . . . .195 D6
Ajax Ave NW9 . . . . .45 C6
Ajax Ct NW9 . . . . .45 C6
Ajax Ho [15] E2 . . . . .96 B5
Ajax Rd NW6 . . . . .69 C3
Akabusi Cl SE25 . . . . .206 A3
Akbar Ho [7] E14 . . . . .119 D2
Akehurst St SW15 . . . . . .156 A4
Akenside Ct [3] NW3 . . . . . .70 B3
Akenside Rd NW3 . . . . .70 B3
Akerman Rd Brixton SW9 . .138 D4
Kingston u T KT6 . . . . . . .197 C3
Akintaro Ho [7] SE8 . . . . . .141 B6
Akiva Sch N3 . . . . .29 D1
Alabama St SE18 . . . . . . .145 C5
Alacross Rd W5 . . . . .109 D4
Aladdin Workspace UB6 . . .85 D6
Alamaro Lo [5] SE10 . . . . .120 D3
Alandale Dr HA5 . . . . .22 B2
Aland Ct SE16 . . . . .119 A3
Alander Mews E17 . . . . . . .54 A5
Alan Dr EN5 . . . . .13 A5
Alan Gdns RM7 . . . . .59 C2
Alan Hocken Way E15 . . . .98 C5
Alan Lo N3 . . . . .29 C2
Alan Preece Ct NW6 . . . . . .68 D1
Alan Rd SW19 . . . . .179 A5
Alanthus Cl SE12 . . . . . . .165 A5
Alaska Bldg [12] SE13 . . . .141 D4
Alaska St SE1 . . . . .251 A3
Alastor Ho [10] E14 . . . . . .120 A3
Alba Cl UB4 . . . . .84 D3
Albacore Cres SE13 . . . . .163 D5

Alba Gdns NW11 . . . . .47 A3
Albain Cres TW15 . . . . . .148 A2
Alba Mews SW18, SW19 . .157 C2
Alban Ho Hampstead NW3 . .70 A2
New Cross SE14 . . . . .141 B4
Albans Cl SW16 . . . . .160 A1
Albany W1 . . . . .249 A5
Albany Ct Bushey WD23 . . . .8 B5
Ickenham UB10 . . . . .60 C3
Mortlake SW14 . . . . .132 D1
Sidcup DA5 . . . . .168 D4
West Green N15 . . . . .51 A5
Albany Coll NW4 . . . . .46 C4
Albany Coll Hendry Ho
NW4 . . . . .46 B4
Albany Cres
Claygate KT10 . . . . .212 C2
Edgware HA8 . . . . .26 C3
Albany Ct Ashford TW15 . .171 B4
Cheam SM1 . . . . .217 B4
Chingford E4 . . . . .19 D5
College Pk NW10 . . . . .90 B4
Finchley N12 . . . . .29 D4
Grahame Pk HA8 . . . . .27 B2
Kingston u T KT2 . . . . . . .176 A4
NW8 . . . . .229 C3
Richmond TW10 . . . . .153 B1
Surbiton KT6 . . . . .197 D2
Walthamstow E10 . . . . . . .53 C2
Westminster SW1 . . . . . . .259 C6
[8] Whitechapel E1 . . . . . . .96 A1
Albany Ctyd W1 . . . . .249 B5
Albany Ho
[6] Brentford TW8 . . . . . . .132 A6
Edgware HA8 . . . . .26 C3
Upper Clapton E5 . . . . .74 C6
Albany Mans
Camberwell SE5 . . . . .139 A6
Islington N1 . . . . .72 C1
Kingston u T KT2 . . . . . . .175 D4
Plaistow BR1 . . . . .187 A4
Stanmore SM1 . . . . .217 D3
Albany Par [4] TW8 . . . . . .132 A6
Albany Park Ave EN3 . . . . . .6 D4
Albany Park Rd KT2 . . . . .176 A4
Albany Pas [12] TW10 . . . .154 A6
Albany Pk Canoe & Sailing
Ctr KT2 . . . . .175 D4
Albany Pl Brentford TW8 . .131 D6
Camberwell SE5 . . . . .139 C6
Chislehurst BR1 . . . . .188 D5
Dagenham RM6 . . . . .59 B3
Ealing W13 . . . . .109 B6
Enfield EN3 . . . . .6 D5
Erith DA17 . . . . .147 B6
Leyton E10 . . . . .53 C2
Manor Pk E12 . . . . .77 D4
New Malden KT3 . . . . . . .199 B5
Richmond TW10 . . . . .154 A6
Sidcup DA5 . . . . .168 C4
Stroud Green N4 . . . . .50 C3
Upper Edmonton N18 . . . . .34 C5
Walthamstow E17 . . . . . . .53 A3
Wimbledon SW19 . . . . . .179 D5
Albany Reach KT7 . . . . . .196 D4
Albany Sch EN3 . . . . .6 D5
Albany St NW1 . . . .93 B4 231 D2
Albany Terr [6] TW10 . . . .154 B6
Albany The
Kingston u T KT2 . . . . . . .175 D4
Woodford IG8 . . . . .36 D6
Albany View IG9 . . . . .21 A3
Albany Wlk N15 . . . . .50 D5
Alba Pl W11 . . . . .91 B1
Albatross NW9 . . . . .27 D1
Albatross Cl E6 . . . . .100 B3
Albatross St SE18 . . . . . . .145 C5
Albemarle SW19 . . . . .156 D2
Albemarle App IG2 . . . . . . .56 D3
Albemarle Ave TW2 . . . . .151 B3
Albemarle Coll W1 . . . . . .247 D6
Albemarle Gdns
Ilford IG2 . . . . .56 D3
New Malden KT3 . . . . . . .199 B5
Albemarle Ho
[2] Brixton SW9 . . . . .138 C2
Rotherhithe SE16 . . . . . . .119 B2
Albemarle Lo SE26 . . . . . .185 A5
Albemarle Mans NW3 . . . . .69 D4
Albemarle Pk
Beckenham BR3 . . . . .185 D2
Stanmore HA7 . . . . .25 C5
Albemarle Prim Sch
SW19 . . . . .157 A2
Albemarle Rd
Beckenham BR2, BR3 . . . .186 A2
East Barnet EN4 . . . . .1 C4
Albemarle St W1 . .115 C6 249 A5
Alberon Gdns NW11 . . . . . .47 B5
Alberta Ave SM1 . . . . .217 B3
Alberta Ct [1] TW10 . . . . . .154 B6
Alberta Est SE17 . . .116 D1 261 D2
Alberta Ho Blackwall E14 . .120 A5
Hayes UB4 . . . . .84 B4
Alberta Rd EN1 . . . . .18 A5
Alberta St SE17 . . . .116 D1 261 D2
Albert Ave Chingford E4 . . . .35 C6

Albert Ave continued
South Lambeth SW8 . . . . .270 C3
Albert Barnes Ho SE1 . . . .262 A5
Albert Basin Way E16 . . . .123 A6
Albert Bigg Point E15 . . . . .98 A6
Albert Bridge Rd
SW11 . . . . .136 D3 267 C3
Albert Carr Gdns SW16 . .182 A5
Albert Cl [11] Hackney E9 . . .96 B6
Wood Green N22 . . . . .31 D2
Albert Cotts [2] E1 . . . . .96 A2
Albert Cres E4 . . . . .35 C6
Albert Ct
Knightsbridge SW7 . . . . . .246 C1
[9] Putney SW19 . . . . .157 A3
Albert Dr SW19 . . . . .157 A3
Albert Emb SE1 . .116 A2 260 B3
Albert Gate Ct SW1 . . . . .247 C1
Albert Gdns E1 . . . . .96 D1
Albert Gr SW20 . . . . .178 D2
Albert Gray Ho SW10 . . . .266 C4
Albert Hall Mans
SW7 . . . . .114 B4 246 C1
Albert Ho Stanmore HA7 . . .25 B5
[5] Wanstead E18 . . . . .55 B6
[2] Woolwich SE28 . . . . . .123 A4
Albert Mans
Battersea SW11 . . . . .267 C2
Hornsey N8 . . . . .50 A2
Albert Meml★
SW7 . . . . .114 B4 246 C1
Albert Mews W8 . . .114 B4 256 A6
Albert Palace Mans
SW11 . . . . .268 B2
Kensington W8 . . . . .113 D4 245 D1
Albert Pl Finchley N3 . . . . . .29 C2
Kensington W8 . . . . .113 D4 245 D1
Albert Rd Ashford TW15 . .170 B3
Bromley Comm BR2 . . . . .209 D4
Buckhurst Hill IG9 . . . . . . .21 D2
Chislehurst SE9 . . . . .166 A1
Croydon SE25 . . . . .206 A6
Dagenham RM8 . . . . .59 C1
Ealing W5 . . . . .87 B3
East Barnet EN4 . . . . .2 A1
Erith DA17 . . . . .125 B1
Finsbury Pk N4 . . . . .50 B2
Hampton TW12 . . . . .174 A5
Harrow HA2 . . . . .42 A6
Hayes UB3 . . . . .105 C3
Hendon NW4 . . . . .46 D5
Hounslow TW3 . . . . .129 C1
Ilford IG1 . . . . .79 A5
Kilburn NW6 . . . . .91 B5
Kingston u T KT1 . . . . . . .176 B1
Leyton E10 . . . . .54 A1
Mill Hill NW7 . . . . .27 D5
Mitcham CR4 . . . . .202 D6
New Barnet EN4 . . . . .2 B4
New Malden KT3 . . . . . . .199 D5
Penge SE20 . . . . .184 D4
Richmond TW10 . . . . .154 A6
Sidcup DA5 . . . . .169 D4
South Tottenham N15 . . . . .51 C3
Sutton SM1 . . . . .218 B3
Teddington TW11 . . . . . . .174 D4
Twickenham TW1 . . . . . . .152 D3
Walthamstow E17 . . . . . . .53 C4
[4] Wanstead E18 . . . . .55 B6
Wood Green N22 . . . . .31 D2
Yiewsley UB7 . . . . .104 A5
Albert's Ct NW1 . . . . .237 B6
Albert Sleet Ct N9 . . . . .18 B1
Albert Sq Leyton E15 . . . . .76 C3
South Lambeth
SW8 . . . . .138 B5 270 C3
Albert St
Camden Town
NW1 . . . . .93 B6 231 D5
North Finchley N12 . . . . . . .30 A5
Albert Starr Ho [7] SE8 . . . .118 D2
Albert Studios SW11 . . . .267 C4
Albert Terr
Buckhurst Hill IG9 . . . . . . .21 D2
Camden Town NW1 . .93 A6 231 D5
Stonebridge NW10 . . . . . . .89 A6
Albert Terr Mews NW1 . . .231 A5
Albert Victoria Ho N22 . . . .32 C2
Albert Way SE15 . . . . .140 B5
Albert Westcott Ho SE17 . .261 D2
Albert Whicher Ho [3]
E17 . . . . .54 A5
Albert Wlk E16 . . . . .144 D4
Albion Ave Clapham SW8 . .137 D3
Muswell Hill N10 . . . . .31 A2
Albion Cl W2 . . . . .247 B6
Albion Coll WC1 . . .94 A2 240 B3
Albion Ct
[7] Hammersmith W6 . . . .112 B2
Sutton SM2 . . . . .218 B1
[2] Woolwich SE18 . . . . . .122 A4
Albion Dr E8 . . . . .74 A1
Albion Est SE16 . . . . .118 C4
Albion Gate W2 . . . . .247 B6
Albion Gdns [1] W6 . . . . . .112 B2
Albion Gr N16 . . . . .73 C4
Albion Hill IG10 . . . . .21 D6
Albion Ho
[17] Deptford SE8 . . . . . . .141 C5
EC1 . . . . .241 C4

Albion Ho continued
Newham E16 . . . . .122 D5
Albion Mews
Bayswater W2 . . . . .114 C6 247 B6
[6] Hammersmith W6 . . . .112 B2
Islington N1 . . . . .234 A6
Albion Pk IG10 . . . . .21 D6
Albion Pl Broadgate EC2 . .242 D3
Clerkenwell EC1 . . . . .241 C4
Hammersmith W6 . . . . . . .112 B2
South Norwood SE25 . . . .206 A6
Albion Prim Sch [34]
SE16 . . . . .118 C4
Albion Rd Bexley DA6 . . . .147 C1
Dagenham RM10 . . . . .81 B3
Hayes UB3 . . . . .83 C1
Hounslow TW3 . . . . .129 C1
Kingston u T KT2 . . . . . . .177 A2
Stoke Newington N16 . . . . .73 B4
Sutton SM2 . . . . .218 B1
Tottenham N17 . . . . .34 A1
Twickenham TW2 . . . . . . .152 C3
Walthamstow E17 . . . . . . .54 A6
Albion Riverside SW11 . . .267 A4
Albion Sq E8 . . . . .73 D1
Albion St
Bayswater W2 . . . . .114 C6 247 B6
Rotherhithe SE16 . . . . . . .118 C4
Thornton Heath CR0 . . . . .204 D1
Albion Terr Hackney E8 . . . .73 D1
Sewardstone E4 . . . . .7 D1
Albion Villas Rd SE23,
SE26 . . . . .162 C1
Albion Way Barbican EC1 . .242 A3
Lewisham SE13 . . . . .142 A1
Wembley HA9 . . . . .66 C5
Albion Wlk N1 . . . . .233 B3
E8 . . . . .74 A3
Albion Works Studios [14]
E8 . . . . .74 A3
Albion Yd N1 . . . . .233 B3
Albon Ho SW18 . . . . .157 D5
Albrighton Rd SE5, SE22 . .139 C2
Albuhera Cl EN2 . . . . .4 C4
Albury Ave
Bexleyheath DA7 . . . . . . .147 A3
Hounslow TW7 . . . . .130 D5
Albury Bldgs SE1 . . . . . . .251 D1
Albury Cl TW12 . . . . .173 D4
Albury Ct
Deptford SE8 . . . . .141 C6
Mitcham CR4 . . . . .180 B1
[4] Croydon CR0 . . . . .221 A4
[6] Northolt UB5 . . . . .84 C4
Ruislip HA4 . . . . .62 C3
Sutton SM1 . . . . .218 A4
Albury Dr HA5 . . . . .22 D3
Albury Lo [7] SW2 . . . . . . .160 B4
Albury Mews E12 . . . . .77 C6
Albury Rd KT9 . . . . .214 A3
Albury St SE8 . . . . .141 C6
Albyfield BR1 . . . . .210 B6
Albyn Rd SE8 . . . . .141 C4
Alcester Cres E5 . . . . .74 B6
Alcester Ct [4] SM6 . . . . . .219 B4
Alcester Rd SM6 . . . . .219 B4
Alchemea Coll of Audio
Engineering N1 . .94 D6 234 D6
Alcock Cl SM6 . . . . .219 D1
Alcock Rd TW5 . . . . .128 D5
Alconbury DA6 . . . . .169 D6
Alconbury Rd E5 . . . . .74 A6
Alcorn Cl SM3 . . . . .217 C6
Alcott Cl W7 . . . . .86 D2
Aldborough Ct
Chingford E4 . . . . .19 D1
Ilford IG2 . . . . .57 D4
ALDBOROUGH HATCH 57 C5
Aldborough Rd IG2 . . . . . . .57 D6
Aldborough Rd N IG2 . . . . .57 D4
Aldborough Rd S IG3 . . . . .57 C2
Aldbourne Rd W12 . . . . . .112 A5
Aldbridge St
SE17 . . . . .117 C1 263 B2
Aldburgh Mews W1 . . . . .238 B2
Aldbury Ave HA9 . . . . .66 D1
Aldbury Ho SW3 . . . . .257 A3
Aldbury Mews N9 . . . . .17 C6
Aldebert Terr
SW8 . . . . .138 B5 270 C3
Aldeburgh Cl [16] E5 . . . . . .74 B6
Aldeburgh Pl
Greenwich SE10 . . . . .121 A2
Woodford IG8 . . . . .37 A6
Aldeburgh St SE10 . . . . . .121 A1
Alden Ave E15 . . . . .98 D4
Alden Ct
South Croydon CR0 . . . . .221 C5
Wimbledon SW19 . . . . . .179 C4
Aldenham Ctry Pk WD6 . . . .9 B6
Aldenham Dr UB8 . . . . .82 D3
Aldenham Ho NW1 . . . . . .232 B3
Aldenham Rd WD6 . . . . .9 B6
Aldenham St NW1 . .93 D5 232 C3
Aldensley Rd W6 . . . . .112 B3
Alderbrook Prim Sch [17]
SW12 . . . . .159 B4
Alderbrook Rd SW12 . . . .159 B5
Alderbury Rd SW13 . . . . .134 A6
Alder Ct East Finchley N2 . . .48 B6

Alder Ct continued
[3] West Norwood SW16 . .182 C5
Alder Gr NW2 . . . . .68 B6
Aldergrove Gdns TW4 . . . .129 A3
Aldergrove Ho [3] E5 . . . . . .74 A6
Alder Ho
Camberwell SE15 . . . . . . .139 D6
[1] Maitland Pk NW3 . . . . . .70 D2
St Johns SE4 . . . . .141 C2
Alderley Ho [36] SW8 . . . . .137 D3
Alder Lo SW6 . . . . .134 D4
Alder Lodge N9 . . . . .17 C3
Alderman Ave IG11 . . . . . .102 A4
Aldermanbury
EC2 . . . . .95 A1 242 B2
Aldermanbury Sq 2 . . . . .242 B3
Alderman Ct [13] N11 . . . . . .30 D5
Alderman Judge Mall [6]
KT1 . . . . .176 A1
Alderman's Hill N13 . . . . . .32 B6
Alderman's Wlk EC2 . . . . .243 C1
Aldermary Rd BR1 . . . . . .187 A2
Aldermead [2] TW3 . . . . . .129 C1
Alder Mews [12] N19 . . . . . .71 C6
Aldermoor Rd SE6 . . . . . .163 B1
Alderney Ave TW5 . . . . . .129 D5
Alderney Gdns UB5 . . . . . .63 B1
Alderney Ho
[20] Canonbury N1 . . . . . . .73 A2
Enfield EN3 . . . . .6 D5
Alderney Mews SE1 . . . . .262 C6
Alderney Rd E1 . . . . .96 D3
Alderney St SW1 . . .115 B3 258 D2
Alder Rd Mortlake SW14 . .133 B2
Sidcup DA14 . . . . .167 D1
Alders Ave IG8 . . . . .36 C4
ALDERSBROOK 77 C6
Aldersbrook Ave EN1 . . . . . .5 C3
Aldersbrook Dr KT2 . . . . .176 B4
Aldersbrook La E12 . . . . . .78 B5
Aldersbrook Prim Sch
E12 . . . . .77 C6
Aldersbrook Rd E11, E12 . .77 C6
Alders Cl Ealing W5 . . . . . .109 D3
Edgware HA8 . . . . .27 A5
Wanstead E11 . . . . .77 B6
Alders Ct N17 . . . . .52 B5
Aldersey Gdns IG11 . . . . . .79 B2
Aldersford Cl SE4 . . . . . . .140 C1
Aldersgate Ct EC1 . . . . . .242 A3
Aldersgate St EC1 . .95 A2 242 A3
Aldersgrove KT8 . . . . .196 B4
Aldersgrove Ave SE9,
SE12 . . . . .165 D1
Aldershot Rd NW6 . . . . . . .91 B6
Aldersmead Ave CR0 . . . .206 D3
Aldersmead Rd BR3 . . . . .185 A3
Alderson Pl UB2 . . . . .108 A5
Alderson St W10 . . . . .91 A3
Alders Rd HA8 . . . . .27 A5
Alders The
Feltham TW13 . . . . .173 A6
Heston TW5 . . . . .129 B6
Southgate N21 . . . . .16 C5
Streatham SW16 . . . . .181 C6
West Wickham BR4 . . . . . .223 D6
Alderton [9] KT2 . . . . .176 D2
Alderton Cl NW10 . . . . .67 B5
Alderton Cres NW4 . . . . . . .46 B4
Alderton Rd KT8 . . . . .195 B5
Croydon CR0 . . . . .206 A2
Alderton Way NW4 . . . . . . .46 B4
Alderville Rd SW6 . . . . . . .135 B3
Alderwick Ct N7 . . . . .72 B2
Alderwick Dr TW3 . . . . . .130 B2
Alder Wlk IG11 . . . . .79 A2
Alderwood Mews EN4 . . . . .2 A5
Alderwood Prim Sch
SE9 . . . . .167 C5
Alderwood Rd SE9 . . . . . .167 B5
Aldford St W1 . . . . .115 A5 248 B4
Aldgate EC3 . . . . . . .95 C1 243 C1
Aldgate East Sta
E1 . . . . .95 D1 243 D1
Aldgate High St
EC3 . . . . .95 D1 243 C1
Aldgate Sta EC3 . . .95 D1 243 C1
Aldham Hall [1] E11 . . . . . .55 A3
Aldham Ho SE4 . . . . .141 B4
Aldine Ct W12 . . . . .112 C5
Aldine St W12 . . . . .112 C5
Aldington Cl RM8 . . . . .58 C1
Aldington Ct [1] E8 . . . . .74 A1
Aldington Rd SE18 . . . . . .121 D3
Aldis Mews
[3] Holbrook EN3 . . . . .7 C6
Upper Tooting SW17 . . . . .180 C5
Aldis St SW17 . . . . .180 C5
Aldred Rd NW6 . . . . .69 C3
Aldren Rd SW17 . . . . .158 A1
Aldrich Way E4 . . . . .36 A4
Aldrich Gdns SM3 . . . . . .217 B5
Aldrich Terr SW18 . . . . . .158 A2
Aldrick Ho N1 . . . . .233 D4
Aldridge Ave
Edgware HA8 . . . . .10 D1

Aldridge Ave *continued*
Holdbrook EN3 7 C5
Ruislip HA4 62 D6
Stanmore HA7 26 A2
Aldridge Ct W11 91 B2
Aldridge Rd Villas W11 91 B2
Aldridge Rise KT3 199 C3
Aldridge Wlk N14 16 A4
Aldrington Rd SW16 181 C6
Aldsworth Cl W9 91 D3
Aldwich Ho WC2 240 D1
Aldwick Cl SE9 167 B1
Aldwick Ct N12 30 A6
Aldwick Rd CR0 220 B4
Aldworth Gr SE13 164 A5
Aldworth Rd E15 76 C1
Aldwych WC2 94 B1 240 D1
Aldwych Ave IG6 57 A5
Aldwych Bldgs WC2 240 B2
Aldwyn Ho SW8 270 A3
Alers Rd DA6 168 D6
Alesia Cl N22 32 A3
Alestan Beck Rd E16 99 D1
Alexa Ct 4 SM2 217 C2
Alexander Ave NW10 68 B1
Alexander Cl Barnet EN4 2 B1
Hayes BR2 209 A1
Sidcup DA15 167 C5
Southall UB2 108 A5
Twickenham TW2 152 D2
Alexander Ct
Beckenham BR3 186 B2
Greenwich SE3 143 B3
Stanmore HA7 44 B6
14 Surbiton KT6 197 D2
Wandsworth SW18 158 A6
Alexander Evans Mews
SE23 162 D2
Alexander Fleming Laboratory Mus* W2 236 D2
Alexander Ho
8 Kingston u T KT2 176 A2
15 Millwall E14 119 C3
16 Sutton SM2 218 A2
Alexander Lo SM1 217 B3
Alexander McLeod Prim Sch
SE2 124 B1
Alexander Mews 2 W2 91 D1
Alexander Pl SW7 257 A4
Alexander Rd
Bexley DA7 146 D3
Chislehurst BR7 188 D5
Upper Holloway N19 72 A6
Alexander Sq
SW3 114 C2 257 A4
Alexander St W2 91 C1
Alexander Terr SE2 124 B1
Alexandra Ave
Battersea SW11 268 A1
Harrow HA2 63 C5
Southall UB1 107 B6
Sutton SM1 217 C5
Wood Green N22 31 D2
Alexandra Bsns Ctr EN3 6 D1
Alexandra Cl
Ashford TW15 171 B3
Deptford SE8 141 B6
Harrow HA2 63 D5
Alexandra Cotts
New Cross SE14 141 B4
Penge SE20 184 D4
Alexandra Cres BR1 186 D4
Alexandra Ct
Ashford TW15 171 B4
Ealing W5 87 C2
Greenford UB6 85 D5
Hounslow TW3 129 D3
Paddington W9 236 B6
4 Shacklewell N16 73 D4
5 Shepherd's Bush W12 112 A4
Southgate N14 15 C6
Wembley HA9 66 B4
Alexandra Dr
Surbiton KT5 198 C2
West Norwood SE19 183 C5
Alexandra Gdns
Chiswick W4 133 C5
Cranley Gdns N10 49 B5
Hounslow TW3 129 D3
Wallington SM5 219 A1
Alexandra Gr Finchley N12 29 D4
Finsbury Pk N4 50 D1
Alexandra Ho 13 W6 112 C1
Alexandra Inf Sch
19 Kingston u T KT2 176 C3
Penge BR3 184 D3
Alexandra Jun & Inf Schs
TW3 129 D3
Alexandra Jun Sch
SE26 184 D4
Alexandra Mans
Chelsea SW3 266 C5
Cricklewood NW2 68 D3
6 Hampstead NW6 69 C3
9 Shepherd's Bush W12 112 C5
Alexandra Mews N2 48 D6
Alexandra National Ho
N4 72 D6
Alexandra Pal* N22 31 D1
Alexandra Palace Sta
N22 32 A1
Alexandra Palace Way
N10 49 C6
Alexandra Park Rd N10, N22 31 D2
Alexandra Park Sch N11 31 C2
Alexandra Pl
Croydon CR0 205 C1
South Norwood SE25 205 B4
St John's Wood NW8 92 A6 229 B6
Alexandra Prim Sch N22 32 B1
Alexandra Rd Acton W4 111 B4
Ashford TW15 171 C4
10 Brentford TW8 131 D6
Croydon CR0 205 C2
Dagenham RM6 59 A3
Edmonton N9 18 B4
Enfield EN3 6 D1
Hampstead NW8 70 B1
Hendon NW4 46 D5
Hornsey N8, N22 50 C6
Hounslow TW3 129 D3
Kingston u T KT2 176 C3
Leyton E10 76 A5
Mitcham SW19 180 C3
Mortlake SW14 133 B2
Muswell Hill N10 31 B3
Penge SE26 184 D4
Richmond TW9 132 B3
Thames Ditton KT7 196 D4
Tottenham N15 51 B4
Twickenham TW1 153 C5
Wallend E6 100 C4
Walthamstow E17 53 B2
Wanstead E18 55 B6
Wimbledon SW19 179 C5
Alexandra Sch HA2 63 C6
Alexandra Sq SM4 201 C4
Alexandra St
5 Deptford SE14 141 A5
Newham E16 99 A2
Alexandra Wlk 8 SE19 183 C5
Alexandria Rd W13 109 B6
Alex Gossip Ho SW6 265 A1
Alexis St SE16 118 A2
Al Falah Sch 7 E5 74 B5
Alfearn Rd E5 74 C4
Alfie's Antique Mkt*
NW8 92 C3 237 A5
Alford Ct
18 Belmont SM2 217 D1
Shoreditch N1 235 B3
Alford Gn CR0 224 B2
Alford Ho Crouch End N6 49 C3
6 Woolwich SE18 144 D6
Alford Pl N1 235 B3
Alfoxton Ave N8, N15 50 D5
Alfreda Ct SW11 268 C1
Alfreda St SW11 137 B4 268 C1
Alfred Butt Ho SW17 158 D1
Alfred Cl W4 111 B2
Alfred Findley Ho N22 32 D1
Alfred Gdns UB1 107 A6
Alfred Ho E9 75 A3
Alfred Hurley Ho SW17 180 A6
Alfred Mews W1, WC1 239 C4
Alfred Nunn Ho NW10 89 D6
Alfred Pl WC1 93 D2 239 C4
Alfred Prior Ho 7 E12 78 C4
Alfred Rd Acton W3 111 A5
Buckhurst Hill IG9 21 D2
Croydon SE25 206 A4
Erith DA17 125 B1
Feltham TW13 150 C2
Kingston u T KT1 198 B6
Leyton E15 76 D3
Paddington W2 91 C2
Sutton SM1 218 A3
Alfred Salter Ho SE1 263 D3
Alfred Salter Prim Sch
SE16 118 D4
Alfred's Gdns IG11 101 C5
Alfred St E3 97 B4
Alfred's Way (East Ham & Barking By-Pass) IG11 101 B5
Alfred's Way Ind Est
IG11 102 A6
Alfred Villas 9 E17 54 A5
Alfreton Cl SW19 156 D1
Alfriston KT5 198 B3
Alfriston Ave Harrow HA2 41 C2
Thornton Heath CR0 204 A2
Alfriston Cl 5 KT5 198 B3
Alfriston Rd SW11 158 D6
Algar Cl Isleworth TW7 131 A2
Stanmore HA7 24 D5
Algar Ct TW12 173 D2
Algar Ho SE1 251 C1
Algar Rd TW7 131 A2
Algarve Rd SW18 157 D3
Algernon Rd Hendon NW4 46 A3
Kilburn NW6 91 C6
Lewisham SE13 141 D1
Algers Cl IG10 21 D6
Algers Rd IG10 21 D6
Alghers Mead IG10 21 D6
Algiers Rd SE13 141 C1
Alguin Ct HA7 25 C3
Alibon Gdns RM10 81 C3
Alibon Rd RM10 81 C3
Alice Cl 13 EN5 2 A1
Alice Ct 10 N3 29 C2
Alice Gilliott Ct W14 264 D6
Alice La E3 97 B6
Alice Mews 3 TW11 174 D5
Alice Owen Tech Ctr
EC1 234 C2
Alice Shepherd Ho 12
E14 120 A4
Alice St SE1 117 C3 263 A5
Alice Thompson Cl
SE12 165 C2
Alice Walker Cl 8 SE24 138 D1
Alice Way TW3 129 D1
Alicia Ave HA3 43 C5
Alicia Cl HA3 43 C5
Alicia Gdns HA3 43 C5
Alicia Ho DA16 146 B4
Alie St E1 95 D1 243 D1
Alington Cres NW9 45 A1
Alison Cl Croydon CR0 206 D1
Newham E6 100 C1
Alison Ct HA8 26 D5
Aliwal Rd SW11 136 C1
Alkerden Rd W4 111 C1
Al Khair Prim & Sec Sch 7
CR0 205 C1
Alkham Rd N16 73 D6
Allam Ho W11 244 A6
Allan Barclay Cl N15 51 D3
Allanbridge N16 51 C2
Allan Cl KT3 199 B4
Allandale Ave N3 47 B6
Allan Ho SW8 269 C2
Allanson Ct E10 75 C6
Allan Way W3 89 A2
Allard Cres WD23 8 A2
Allard Gdns SW4 159 D6
Allardyce St SW4, SW9 138 B1
Allbrook Cl TW11 174 C5
Allbrook Ho 4 SW15 156 A4
Allcot Cl TW14 149 D3
Allcott Ho TW7 130 D2
Allcroft Rd NW5 71 A2
Allder Way CR2 220 D1
Allenby Cl UB6 85 C4
Allenby Prim Sch UB1 85 C1
Allenby Rd
Forest Hill SE23 163 A1
Southall UB1 85 C3
Woolwich SE28 123 A3
Allen Cl Streatham CR4 181 C2
Sunbury TW16 172 B2
Allen Ct Greenford UB6 64 D3
Walthamstow E17 53 C3
Allendale Ave UB1 85 C1
Allendale Cl
Camberwell SE5 139 B4
Forest Hill SE26 184 D5
Allendale Rd UB6 65 B2
Allen Edwards Dr
SW8 138 A4 270 A2
Allen Edwards Prim Sch
SW4 138 A4 270 A1
Allenford Ho SW15 155 D5
All England Lawn Tennis & Croquet Club The
SW19 157 A1
Allen Ho W8 255 B6
Allen Mans W8 255 B6
Allen Rd Old Ford E3 97 B5
Penge BR3 184 D1
Stoke Newington N16 73 C4
Sunbury TW16 172 B1
Thornton Heath CR0 204 C1
Allensbury Pl
7 Camden Town NW1 71 D1
Camden Town NW1 72 A1
Allens Rd EN3 18 C6
Allen St W8 113 C3 255 B5
Allenswood 12 SW19 157 A3
Allenswood Rd SE9 144 B3
Allerdale Ho 7 N4 51 B2
Allerford Ct Catford SE6 163 D1
Harrow HA2 42 A4
Allerford Rd SE6 185 D6
Allerton Ct
5 Hendon NW4 28 D1
North Cheam SM3 216 D6
Allerton Ho
4 Merton SW19 180 A3
Shoreditch N1 235 D3
Allerton Rd N16 73 A6
Allerton St N1 235 D2
Allerton Wlk 11 N7 72 B6
Allestree Rd
SW6 135 A5 264 A3
Alleyn Cres SE21 161 B2
Alleyndale Rd RM8 80 C6
Alleyn Ho
Bermondsey SE1 262 C5
St Luke's EC1 242 B5
Alleyn Pk Dulwich SE21 161 C1
Southall UB2 107 C1
Alleyn Rd SE21 161 C1
Alleyn's Sch SE22 161 C6
Allfarthing JMI Sch
SW18 158 A5
Allfarthing La SW18 158 A5
Allgood Cl SM4 200 D3
Allgood St 10 E2 95 D5
Allhallows La EC4 252 C5
Allhallows Rd E6 100 A1
All Hallows Rd N17 33 C2
Alliance Cl HA0 65 D4
Alliance Ct Acton W3 88 D2
Ashford TW15 171 A6
Alliance Rd Acton W3 88 D3
East Wickham SE18 146 A5
1 Newham E16 99 C2
Allied Ind Est W3 111 C5
Allied Way W3 111 C4
Allingham Cl W7 108 D6
Allingham Ct NW3 70 C3
Allingham Mews N1 235 A4
Allingham St N1 95 A5 235 A4
Allington Ave
Tottenham N17 33 C4
Upper Halliford TW17 193 C6
Allington Cl
Greenford UB6 64 A1
3 Wimbledon SW19 178 D5
Allington Ct
6 Clapham SW8 137 C3
Croydon CR0 206 C3
Enfield EN3 18 D6
Allington Rd Harrow HA2 42 A4
Hendon NW4 46 B3
Kensal Rise W10 91 A5
Orpington BR6 211 C1
Allington St SW1 258 D5
Allison Cl SE10 142 A4
Allison Gr SE21 161 C3
Allison Rd Acton W3 111 A6
Harringay N8 50 D4
Alliston Ho 27 E2 95 D4
Allitsen Rd NW8 92 C5 230 A4
All Nations Ho 10 E8 74 B1
Allnutt Way SW4 159 D6
Alloa Ct N14 15 C2
Alloa Rd IG3 80 A6
Allom Ct 11 SW4 138 A3
Allonby Dr HA4 38 D2
Allonby Gdns HA9 43 C1
Allonby Ho E14 97 A2
Alloway Rd E3 97 A4
Allport Ho SE5 139 B2
Allport Mews 44 E1 96 C3
All Saints' Benhilton CE Prim Sch 3 SM1 217 D5
All Saints CE Prim Sch
8 Fulham SW6 135 A3
Merton SW19 180 A3
Putney SW15 134 C2
All Saints' CE Prim Sch
Blackheath Vale SE3 142 C3
Child's Hill NW2 69 B5
East Barnet N20 14 B2
Wallington SM5 219 A3
All Saints Church 9 N19 71 D5
All Saints' Cl N9 18 A2
All Saints Ct Heston TW5 128 D4
Lower Clapton E5 74 C4
10 Shadwell E1 118 C6
All Saints Dr SE3 142 D3
All Saints Ho 2 W11 91 B2
All Saint's Inf & Jun Schs
SE19 183 C2
All Saints Mews HA3 24 C4
All Saints Pas SW18 157 C6
All Saints RC Sch & Tech Coll
RM8 59 C1
All Saints Rd
Merton SW19 180 A3
Notting Hill W11 91 B1
Sutton SM1 218 A5
All Saints' Rd W3 111 A3
All Saints St N1 94 B5 233 C4
All Saints Sta E14 119 D6
All Saints Twr 19 E10 53 D2
Allsop Pl NW1 92 D3 237 D5
All Souls Ave NW10 90 B6
All Souls CE Prim Sch
W1 93 C2 239 A4
All Souls Pl W1 238 D3
Allum La WD6 10 A6
Allum Way N20 14 A3
Allwood Cl SE26 184 D6
Alma Ave E4 36 A3
Alma Birk Ho 1 NW6 69 B1
Almack Rd E5 74 C4
Alma Cl N10 31 B2
Alma Cres SM1 217 A3
Alma Gr SE1 117 D2 263 D3
Alma Ho
7 Brentford TW8 132 A6
2 Edmonton N9 34 A6
Alma Pl College Pk NW10 90 B4
Penge SE19 183 D3
Thornton Heath CR7 204 C4
Alma Prim Sch
21 Bermondsey SE16 118 A2
Enfield EN3 18 D6
Alma Rd Carshalton SM5 218 C3
Enfield EN3 7 A1
Alma Rd *continued*
Muswell Hill N10 31 B3
Sidcup DA14 168 A1
Southall UB1 107 A6
Thames Ditton KT10, KT7 196 C1
Wandsworth SW18 158 A6
Alma Row HA3 24 B2
Alma Sq NW8 92 A4 229 B2
Alma St Camden Town NW5 71 B2
Stratford New Town E15 76 B2
Alma Terr Earl's Ct W8 255 B5
Wandsworth SW18 158 B4
Almeida St 10 N1 72 D1
Almeric Rd SW11 136 D1
Almer Rd SW20 178 A3
Almington St N4 50 B1
Almond Ave
Carshalton SM5 218 D6
Ealing W5 110 A3
Uxbridge UB10 60 D5
West Drayton UB7 104 C3
Almond Cl Bromley BR2 210 C2
Charlton TW17 171 A1
Feltham TW14 150 A3
Hayes UB3 105 C6
Peckham SE15 140 A3
Ruislip HA4 61 D5
Almond Gr TW8 131 B5
Almond Ho SE4 141 B3
Almond Rd
Bermondsey SE16 118 B2
Tottenham N17 34 A3
Almonds Ave IG9 21 A2
Almond Way
Bromley BR2 210 C2
Harrow HA2 24 A1
Mitcham CR4 203 D5
Almorah Rd
De Beauvoir Town N1 73 B1
Heston TW5 128 D4
Almshouse La EN1 6 B6
Almshouses Edmonton N9 17 D2
Leyton E10 75 D6
Southall UB1 85 C1
Sunbury TW16 171 D2
Almshouses The IG11 79 A2
Al-Muntada Islamic Sch
SW6 135 B4 264 D2
Alnmouth Ct 10 UB1 86 A1
Al-Noor Prim Sch IG3 58 B1
Alnwick 8 N17 34 B3
Alnwick Gr SM4 201 D5
Alnwick Rd Eltham SE12 165 B4
Newham E16 99 C1
Alonso Ho 4 DA17 125 C1
ALPERTON 88 A6
Alperton Com Sch HA0 66 B1
Alperton La UB6 87 D5
Alperton Lower Sch HA0 87 D6
Alperton St W10 91 B3
Alperton Sta HA0 88 A6
Alphabet Gdns SM5 202 B3
Alphabet Sq E3 97 C2
Alpha Bsns Ctr E17 53 B4
Alpha Cl NW8 92 C4 230 B1
Alpha Ct 6 NW5 71 B2
Alpha Est The UB3 105 C4
Alpha Gr E14 119 C4
Alpha Ho 19 Brixton SW4 138 B1
Kilburn NW6 91 C5
Lisson Gr NW8 237 B5
Alpha Pl
Chelsea SW3 136 C6 267 B6
Kilburn NW6 91 C5
Alpha Prep Sch HA1 42 C4
Alpha Rd Chingford E4 19 D1
Croydon CR0 205 C1
Edmonton N18 34 A4
Enfield EN3 7 A1
Hillingdon UB10 82 D3
New Cross SE14 141 B4
Surbiton KT5 198 B3
Teddington TW12 174 B5
Alpha St SE15 140 A3
Alphea Cl SW19 180 C3
Alpine Ave KT5 215 A6
Alpine Bsns Ctr E6 100 C2
Alpine Cl CR0 221 C5
Alpine Copse BR1 188 C1
Alpine Ct SE12 142 D1
Alpine Gr 37 E9 74 C1
Alpine Rd Deptford SE16 118 D1
Leyton E10 75 D6
Walton-on-T KT12 194 A2
Alpine View SM5 218 C3
Alpine Way E6 100 C2
Alpine Wlk HA7 8 C2
Alric Ave
Kingston u T KT3 199 D6
Willesden NW10 67 B1
Al-risaala Sec Sch 1
SW17 180 D6
Alroy Rd N4 50 C2
Alsace Rd SE17 117 C1 263 A2
Al Sadiq High Sch for Boys & Al Zahra Girls Sch NW6 91 A6
Alscot Rd SE1 117 D3 263 D5
Alscot Road Ind Est SE1 263 D5
Alscot Way SE1 263 C4
Alsike Rd DA18 125 A3

Alsom Ave KT19, KT4 ..... 216 A4
Alston Cl KT7 ..... 197 B2
Alston Ct [2] EN5 ..... 1 A2
Alstone Ct N9 ..... 18 A2
Alston Rd Edmonton N18 ..... 34 B5
High Barnet EN5 ..... 1 A2
Upper Tooting SW17 ..... 180 B6
Altair Cl N17 ..... 33 D4
Altair Ct N1 ..... 73 B2
Altash Way SE9 ..... 166 C2
Altenburg Ave W13 ..... 109 B3
Altenburg Gdns SW11 ..... 136 D1
Alt Gr SW19 ..... 179 B3
Altham Gdns WD19 ..... 22 D6
Altham Rd HA5 ..... 23 A3
Althea St SW6 ..... 135 D2
Althorne Gdns E18 ..... 54 D5
Althorne Way RM10 ..... 81 C6
Althorp Cl EN5 ..... 12 A4
Althorpe Mews SW11 ..... 266 D1
Althorpe Rd HA1 ..... 42 A4
Althorp Rd SW17 ..... 158 D3
Altima Ct SE22 ..... 140 A1
Altior Ct N6 ..... 49 C3
Altmore Ave E6 ..... 100 B6
Altmore Inf Sch E6 ..... 100 B6
Alton Ave HA7 ..... 24 D3
Alton Cl Isleworth TW7 ..... 130 D3
Sidcup DA5 ..... 169 A3
Alton Ct [18] BR3 ..... 185 C3
Alton Gdns
Beckenham BR3 ..... 185 C3
Twickenham TW2 ..... 152 B4
Alton Ho [3] E3 ..... 97 D4
Alton Rd Croydon CR0 ..... 220 C5
Richmond TW10, TW9 ..... 132 A1
Roehampton SW15 ..... 156 A3
Tottenham N17 ..... 51 B6
Alton Sch The SW15 ..... 155 D4
Alton St E14 ..... 97 D2
Altyre Cl BR3 ..... 207 B4
Altyre Rd CR0 ..... 221 B6
Altyre Way BR3 ..... 207 B4
Alum Ct KT5 ..... 198 B3
Alumni Ct SE1 ..... 253 D2
Alvanley Ct NW3 ..... 69 D3
Alvanley Gdns NW6 ..... 69 D3
Alvanley Ho [14] SW9 ..... 138 C4
Alvernia Lo SM1 ..... 217 D5
Alverstone Ave
East Barnet EN4 ..... 14 C4
Wimbledon SW18, SW19 ..... 157 C2
Alverstone Gdns SE9 ..... 167 A3
Alverstone Ho [11] SE11 ..... 138 C6
Alverstone Rd
Little Ilford E12 ..... 78 C4
New Malden KT3 ..... 199 D5
Wembley HA9 ..... 44 B1
Willesden NW2 ..... 68 C1
Alverston Gdns SE25 ..... 205 C4
Alverton St SE8 ..... 141 B6
Alveston Ave HA3 ..... 43 B6
Alveston Sq [5] E18 ..... 37 A1
Alvey St SE17 ..... 263 A2
Alvia Gdns SM1 ..... 218 A4
Alvington Cres E8 ..... 73 D3
Alway Ave KT19 ..... 215 B3
Alwen Cotts CR0 ..... 222 D4
Alwold Cres SE12 ..... 165 C5
Alwyn Ave W4 ..... 111 B1
Alwyn Cl
Borehamwood WD6 ..... 10 B5
New Addington CR0 ..... 223 D1
Alwyne La N1 ..... 72 D1
Alwyne Mans SW19 ..... 179 B4
Alwyne Pl N1 ..... 73 A1
Alwyne Rd Canonbury N1 ..... 73 A1
Ealing W7 ..... 108 C6
Wimbledon SW19 ..... 179 B4
Alwyne Sq N1 ..... 73 A2
Alwyne Villas N1 ..... 72 D1
Alwyn Gdns Acton W3 ..... 88 D1
Hendon NW9 ..... 46 A5
Alyn Ct N8 ..... 49 D3
Alyth Gdns NW11 ..... 47 C3
Alzette Ho [11] E2 ..... 96 D5
Amalgamated Dr TW8 ..... 131 B6
Amanda Ct Ashford TW15 ..... 148 B2
Chingford E4 ..... 36 C4
Aman Dalvi Ho [2] SW18 ..... 157 A4
Amar Ct SE18 ..... 123 D2
Amardeep Ct SE18 ..... 123 D1
Amazon Apartments N8 ..... 50 B6
Amazonas SE1 ..... 117 C2 263 B3
Amazon St E1 ..... 96 B1
Ambassador Cl TW3 ..... 129 A3
Ambassador Ct
[9] Hampstead NW6 ..... 69 C3
Hendon NW4 ..... 46 D4
Ambassador Gdns E6 ..... 100 B2
Ambassador Ho
Harrow HA3 ..... 42 C6
St John's Wood NW8 ..... 229 B5
Ambassador Sq E14 ..... 119 D2
Amber Ave E17 ..... 35 A2
Amber Ct Feltham TW13 ..... 149 C1
Islington N7 ..... 72 C2
Mitcham CR4 ..... 202 C5
Southall UB1 ..... 107 D5
Amberden Ave N3 ..... 47 C6
Amberdene HA7 ..... 24 D4
Ambergate St
SE17 ..... 116 D1 261 D2
Amber Gr NW2 ..... 46 D1
Amber Ho HA7 ..... 25 D3
Amberley Cl
[2] Orpington BR6 ..... 227 D3
Pinner HA5 ..... 41 B6
Amberley Ct
[2] Brixton SW9 ..... 138 D2
Sidcup DA14 ..... 190 C5
Sutton SM2 ..... 218 A1
Amberley Gdns
Enfield EN1 ..... 17 C4
Worcester Pk KT19 ..... 215 D4
Amberley Gr
Croydon CR0 ..... 205 D2
Penge SE26 ..... 184 B5
Amberley Ho
[8] Barnet EN5 ..... 1 D1
[7] Ealing W7 ..... 108 C5
Amberley Rd
Buckhurst Hill IG9 ..... 21 C3
Enfield EN1 ..... 17 D5
Palmers Green N13 ..... 16 B2
Walthamstow E10 ..... 53 D2
Westbourne Green W9 ..... 91 C2
West Heath SE2 ..... 146 D6
Amberley Way
Heston TW4 ..... 150 C6
Morden SM4 ..... 201 B2
Romford RM7 ..... 59 D5
Uxbridge UB10 ..... 82 A5
Amberside Cl TW2 ..... 152 B5
Amber Wharf [29] E2 ..... 95 D6
Amberwood Cl SM6 ..... 220 A3
Amberwood Rise KT3 ..... 199 C3
Amblecote Cl SE12 ..... 165 B1
Amblecote Mdws SE12 ..... 165 B1
Amblecote Rd SE12 ..... 165 B1
Ambler Prim Sch [2] N4 ..... 72 D6
Ambler Rd N4 ..... 72 D5
Ambleside Catford BR1 ..... 186 B4
[13] Putney SW19 ..... 157 A3
Regent's Pk NW1 ..... 231 D3
Ambleside Ave
Beckenham BR3 ..... 207 A4
Streatham SW16 ..... 181 D6
Walton-on-T KT12 ..... 194 C1
Ambleside Cl
Lower Clapton E9 ..... 74 C3
[5] Tottenham N17 ..... 51 D6
Walthamstow E10 ..... 53 D2
Ambleside Cres EN3 ..... 6 D2
Ambleside Dr TW14 ..... 149 D3
Ambleside Gdns
Redbridge IG4 ..... 56 A4
Streatham SW16 ..... 181 D5
Sutton SM2 ..... 218 A2
Wembley HA9 ..... 43 D1
Ambleside Ho HA8 ..... 27 A5
Ambleside Point [1]
SE15 ..... 140 C5
Ambleside Rd
Bexleyheath DA7 ..... 147 C3
Willesden NW10 ..... 67 D1
Ambrook Ct SM1 ..... 218 B3
Ambrook Rd DA17 ..... 125 C3
Ambrosden Ave
SW1 ..... 115 C3 259 B5
Ambrose Ave NW11 ..... 47 B3
Ambrose Cl
[6] Newham E6 ..... 100 B2
Orpington BR6 ..... 227 D5
Ambrose Ho [9] E14 ..... 97 C2
Ambrose Mews [2]
SW11 ..... 136 D3
Ambrose St SE16 ..... 118 B2
Ambrose Wlk E3 ..... 97 C5
Ambulance Rd E11 ..... 54 B4
AMC Bsns Ctr NW10 ..... 88 D4
Amelia Cl W3 ..... 110 D4
Amelia Ho [5] W6 ..... 112 C1
Amelia St SE17 ..... 117 A1 262 A2
Amen Cnr Holborn EC4 ..... 241 D1
Streatham SW17 ..... 181 A4
Amen Ct EC4 ..... 94 D1 241 D1
Amenity Way SM4 ..... 200 C2
American Intercontinental
Univ W1 ..... 93 A2 238 B3
American Sch in London The
NW8 ..... 92 B5 229 C4
American Univ in London
The [3] N7 ..... 72 B5
America Sq EC3 ..... 253 C6
America St SE1 ..... 252 A3
Amerland Rd SW18 ..... 157 B5
Amersham Ave N18 ..... 33 B4
Amersham Gr SE14 ..... 141 B5
Amersham Rd
New Cross SE14 ..... 141 B4
Thornton Heath CR0 ..... 205 B3
Amersham Vale SE14,
SE8 ..... 141 B5
Amery Gdns NW10 ..... 90 B6
Amery Ho SE17 ..... 263 B2
Amery Rd HA1 ..... 65 A6
Amesbury Ave SW2 ..... 160 B2
Amesbury Cl KT4 ..... 200 C1
Amesbury Ct EN2 ..... 4 C3
Amesbury Dr E4 ..... 19 D5
Amesbury Rd
Bromley BR1 ..... 209 D6
Dagenham RM9 ..... 80 D1
Feltham TW13 ..... 150 D2
Amesbury Twr [4] SW8 ..... 137 C3
Ames Cotts [12] E3 ..... 97 A2
Ames Ho [10] E2 ..... 96 D5
Amethyest Ct [1] EN3 ..... 7 A2
Amethyst Cl N11 ..... 31 D3
Amethyst Ct BR6 ..... 227 C3
Amethyst Rd E15 ..... 76 B4
Amherst Ave W13 ..... 87 C1
Amherst Dr BR5 ..... 211 D5
Amherst Gdns [2] W13 ..... 87 C1
Amherst Rd W13 ..... 87 C1
Amhurst Ct N4 ..... 51 B2
Amhurst Gdns TW7 ..... 131 A3
Amhurst Par N16 ..... 51 D2
Amhurst Pk N4, N16 ..... 51 C2
Amhurst Rd E8, N16 ..... 74 A4
Amhurst Terr E8 ..... 74 A4
Amhurst Wlk SE28 ..... 124 A5
Amias Ho EC1 ..... 242 A6
Amidas Gdns RM8 ..... 80 B4
Amiel St [15] E1 ..... 96 C3
Amies St SW11 ..... 136 D2
Amigo Ho SE1 ..... 261 B6
Amina Way SE16 ..... 118 A3
Amis Ave KT19 ..... 214 D3
Amity Gr SW20 ..... 178 C2
Amity Rd E15 ..... 76 D1
Ammanford Gn NW9 ..... 45 C3
Ammonite Ho [3] E15 ..... 76 D1
Amner Rd SW11 ..... 159 A5
Amora [8] HA7 ..... 25 C6
Amor Rd W6 ..... 112 C3
Amory Ho N1 ..... 233 D4
Amott Rd SE15 ..... 140 A2
Amoy Pl E14 ..... 119 C6
Ampere Way Sta CR0 ..... 204 B1
Ampleforth Rd SE2 ..... 124 C4
Ampton Pl WC1 ..... 233 C1
Ampton St WC1 ..... 94 B4 233 C1
Amroth Cl SE23 ..... 162 B3
Amroth Gn NW9 ..... 45 C3
Amstel Ct [12] SE15 ..... 139 D5
Amsterdam Rd E14 ..... 120 A3
Amundsen Ct [7] E14 ..... 119 C1
Amundsen Ho [6] NW10 ..... 67 B1
Amwell Cl EN2 ..... 17 B6
Amwell St EC1 ..... 94 C4 234 A2
Amyand Cotts [12] TW1 ..... 153 B5
Amyand Park Gdns [2]
TW1 ..... 153 B4
Amyand Park Rd TW1 ..... 153 B4
Amy Cl SM6 ..... 220 A1
Amy Johnson Ct HA8 ..... 26 D1
Amy Johnson Prim Sch
SM6 ..... 220 A1
Amyruth Rd SE4 ..... 163 C6
Amy Warne Cl E6 ..... 100 A3
Anarth Ct KT13 ..... 193 C1
Anatola Rd N19 ..... 71 C6
Ancaster Cres KT3 ..... 200 A3
Ancaster Mews CR0 ..... 206 D6
Ancaster Rd BR3 ..... 206 D6
Ancaster St SE18 ..... 145 C5
Anchorage Cl SW19 ..... 179 C5
Anchorage Point [1] E14 ..... 119 C4
Anchorage Point Ind Est
SE7 ..... 121 C3
Anchor Bsns Pk CR0,
SM6 ..... 220 A5
Anchor Cl IG11 ..... 102 B4
Anchor Ct Bexley DA7 ..... 147 A4
[5] Enfield EN1 ..... 17 C6
Anchor Ho Ilford IG3 ..... 80 A5
Newham E16 ..... 99 C1
St Luke's EC1 ..... 242 A6
Anchor & Hope La SE7 ..... 121 C2
Anchor Mews SW12 ..... 159 B5
Anchor Rd E12 ..... 77 D6
Anchor Ret Pk E1 ..... 96 C3
Anchor St SE16 ..... 118 B2
Anchor Terr SE1 ..... 252 B4
Anchor Yd EC1 ..... 242 B6
Ancill Cl W6 ..... 135 A6 264 A5
Ancona Rd
Plumstead SE18 ..... 123 B1
Willesden Green NW10 ..... 90 A5
Andace Pk BR1 ..... 187 C2
Andalus Rd SW9 ..... 138 A2
Andaman Ho [3] E1 ..... 97 A2
Ander Cl HA0 ..... 65 D4
Andersens Wharf [9] E14 ..... 97 B1
Anderson Cl
Morden SM3 ..... 201 C1
North Acton W3 ..... 89 B1
Southgate N21 ..... 16 B6
Anderson Ct NW2 ..... 46 C2
Anderson Dr TW15 ..... 171 A6
Anderson Ho
[1] Barking IG11 ..... 101 B5
[10] Blackwall E14 ..... 120 A6
Upper Tooting SW17 ..... 180 B5
Anderson Rd Homerton E9 ..... 74 D2
Redbridge IG8 ..... 55 D6
Anderson's Pl TW3 ..... 129 D1
Andersons Sq N1 ..... 234 C5
Anderson St SW3 ..... 257 C2
Anderson Way
Erith DA17 ..... 125 D4
Erith DA17 ..... 125 D4
Anderton Cl SE5 ..... 139 B2
Anderton Ct N22 ..... 31 D1
Andhurst Ct KT2 ..... 176 D2
Andmark Ct UB1 ..... 107 B5
Andon Ct BR3 ..... 207 A6
Andorra Ct BR1 ..... 187 C2
Andover Ave E16 ..... 99 D1
Andover Cl
East Bedfont TW14 ..... 149 D3
Greenford UB6 ..... 85 D3
Andover Ho [5] N7 ..... 72 B6
Andover Pl NW6 ..... 91 D5
Andover Rd Finsbury Pk N7 ..... 72 B6
Orpington BR6 ..... 211 C1
Twickenham TW2 ..... 152 B3
Andoversford Ct [2]
SE15 ..... 139 C6
Andrecht Terr CR4 ..... 203 D5
Andreck Ct BR3 ..... 186 A1
Andre Malraux Sch W7 ..... 86 C2
Andre St E8 ..... 74 A3
Andrew Borde St WC2 ..... 239 D2
Andrew Ct
Beckenham BR3 ..... 207 D6
[2] Forest Hill SE23 ..... 162 D2
Andrewes Ct [2] W7 ..... 108 C5
Andrewes Gdns E6 ..... 100 A1
Andrewes Ho
Barbican EC2 ..... 242 B3
Sutton SM1 ..... 217 C4
Andrew Ewing Prim Sch The
TW5 ..... 129 B5
Andrew Ho Enfield EN3 ..... 18 C6
New Cross SE4 ..... 141 B3
Putney SW15 ..... 156 A6
Andrew Logan's
Glasshouse★
SE1 ..... 253 A2
Andrew Marvell Ho [12]
N16 ..... 73 C4
Andrew Pl SW8 ..... 269 D2
Andrew Reed Ho [3]
SW18 ..... 157 A4
Andrews Cl
Buckhurst Hill IG9 ..... 21 C2
Harrow HA1 ..... 42 B2
North Cheam KT4 ..... 216 D6
Sidcup BR5 ..... 190 D1
Andrews Crosse WC2 ..... 241 A1
Andrew's Rd E8 ..... 96 B6
Andrew St E14 ..... 98 A1
Andrews Wharf [14] E8 ..... 96 B6
Andrews Wlk SE17 ..... 138 D6
Andrew Wells Ho BR1 ..... 187 B3
Andrew Wilmot Ct
SW18 ..... 158 A3
Andridge Ct SW19 ..... 179 B2
Andringham Lo [4] BR1 ..... 187 B2
Andrula Ct N22 ..... 32 D2
Andwell Cl SE2 ..... 124 B4
ANERLEY 184 B2
Anerley Ct SE20 ..... 184 B3
Anerley Gr SE19 ..... 183 D3
Anerley Hill SE19 ..... 183 D4
Anerley Park Rd SE20 ..... 184 B3
Anerley Pk SE20 ..... 184 B3
Anerley Rd SE20 ..... 184 B2
Anerley Sta SE20 ..... 184 B2
Anerley Station Rd SE20 ..... 184 B2
Anerley Vale SE19 ..... 184 A3
Aneurin Bevan Ct NW2 ..... 68 B6
Aneurin Bevan Ho N11 ..... 31 D3
Anfield Cl SW12 ..... 159 C4
Angel EC1 ..... 94 D5 234 D3
Angela Carter Cl SW9 ..... 138 C2
Angela Ct [2] SE23 ..... 162 C3
Angela Davis Ind Est [20]
SW9 ..... 138 D1
Angel Cl Edmonton N18 ..... 34 A6
Hampton TW12 ..... 174 A5
Angel Corner Par [6] N18 ..... 34 A6
Angel Ct Broadgate EC2 ..... 242 D2
St James SW1 ..... 249 B3
[5] Willesden NW2 ..... 68 A2
Angel Edmonton N18 ..... 34 A5
Angelfield TW3 ..... 151 D6
Angel Gate EC1 ..... 234 D2
Angel Hill SM1 ..... 217 D5
Angel Hill Dr SM1 ..... 217 D5
Angel Ho N1 ..... 234 B3
Angelica Cl UB7 ..... 82 B1
Angelica Dr E6 ..... 100 C2
Angelica Gdns CR0 ..... 206 D1
Angelina Ho [2] SE15 ..... 140 A4
Angelis Appartments N1 ..... 234 D3
Angel La Hayes UB3 ..... 83 B2
Stratford E15 ..... 76 B2
Angell Park Gdns [4]
SW9 ..... 138 C2
Angell Rd SW9 ..... 138 D2
Angel Mews Finsbury N1 ..... 234 B3
Putney SW15 ..... 156 A4
Stepney E1 ..... 118 B6
Angel Pas EC4 ..... 117 B6 252 C5
Angel Pl Borough The SE1 ..... 252 C2
[1] Edmonton N18 ..... 34 A5
Angel Rd Harrow HA1 ..... 42 C3
Thames Ditton KT7 ..... 197 A1
Angel Rd (North Circular Rd)
N18 ..... 34 B5
Angel Rd Works N18 ..... 34 C5
Angel Road Sta N18 ..... 34 C5
Angel Sq N1 ..... 234 B3
Angel St EC1 ..... 95 A1 242 A2
Angel Sta EC1 ..... 94 C5 234 B3
Angel Wlk W6 ..... 112 C2
Angerstein Bsns Pk
SE10 ..... 121 A2
Angerstein La SE3 ..... 142 D4
Anglebury [5] W2 ..... 91 C1
Angle Cl UB10 ..... 82 C6
Angle Gn RM8 ..... 58 C1
Anglers Cl TW10 ..... 175 C6
Anglers La NW5 ..... 71 B2
Anglers Reach KT6 ..... 197 D4
Anglesea Ave [4] SE18 ..... 122 D2
Anglesea Ho KT1 ..... 197 D5
Anglesea Mews [12] SE18 ..... 122 D2
Anglesea Rd
Kingston u T KT1 ..... 197 D5
Woolwich SE18 ..... 122 D2
Anglesey Cl TW15 ..... 148 C1
Anglesey Court Rd SM5 ..... 219 A2
Anglesey Ct W7 ..... 86 D3
Anglesey Gdns SM5 ..... 219 A2
Anglesey Ho [18] E14 ..... 97 C1
Anglesey Rd Enfield EN3 ..... 6 B1
South Oxhey WD19 ..... 22 C5
Anglesmede Cres HA5 ..... 41 C6
Anglesmede Way HA5 ..... 41 C6
Angles Rd SW16 ..... 182 A6
Anglia Cl N17 ..... 34 B3
Anglia Ct RM8 ..... 58 D1
Anglia Ho [13] E14 ..... 97 A1
Anglian Ind Est IG11 ..... 101 D2
Anglian Rd E11 ..... 76 B5
Anglia Wlk E6 ..... 100 C6
Anglo American Laundry
SW17 ..... 158 A1
Anglo Rd [16] E3 ..... 97 B5
Angrave Ct [4] E8 ..... 95 D6
Angrave Pas [5] E8 ..... 95 D6
Angus Cl KT9 ..... 214 C3
Angus Dr HA4 ..... 62 C4
Angus Gdns NW9 ..... 27 B2
Angus Ho [12] SW12 ..... 159 D4
Angus Rd E13 ..... 99 C4
Angus St SE14 ..... 141 A5
Anhalt Rd SW11 ..... 136 C5 267 B4
Animals in War Meml★
W1 ..... 247 D6
Ankerdine Cres SE18 ..... 144 D4
Anlaby Rd TW11 ..... 174 C5
Anley Rd W14 ..... 112 D4
Anmersh Gr HA7 ..... 25 D2
Annabel Cl E14 ..... 97 D1
Anna Cl E8 ..... 95 D6
Annadale N22 ..... 32 B5
Annandale Gr UB10 ..... 61 A5
Annandale Rd
Chiswick W4 ..... 111 C1
Croydon CR0 ..... 222 A6
Greenwich SE10 ..... 120 D1
Sidcup DA15 ..... 167 D4
Anna Neagle Cl [2] E7 ..... 77 A4
Anne Boleyn's Wlk
Belmont SM3 ..... 217 A1
Kingston u T KT2 ..... 176 A5
Anne Compton Mews
SE12 ..... 164 D4
Anne Goodman Ho [3] E1 ..... 96 C1
Anne Kerr Ct [18] SW15 ..... 156 D5
Anne's Ct NW8 ..... 237 B6
Annesley Ave NW9 ..... 45 B6
Annesley Cl NW10 ..... 67 C5
Annesley Dr CR0 ..... 223 B5
Annesley Ho
[31] Brixton SW9 ..... 138 C4
[15] Kennington SW9 ..... 138 C5
Annesley Rd SE3 ..... 143 B4
Annesley Wlk N19 ..... 71 C6
Annesmere Gdns SE3 ..... 143 D2
Anne St E13 ..... 99 A3
Annett Cl TW17 ..... 193 C5
Annette Cl HA3 ..... 24 C1
Annette Cres [16] N1 ..... 73 A1
Annette Ct N7 ..... 72 B5
Annette Rd N7 ..... 72 B4
Annette White Lo [20] N2 ..... 30 B1
Annett Rd KT12 ..... 194 A2
Anne Way KT8 ..... 195 D5
Annie Besant Cl E3 ..... 97 B6
Annie Taylor Ho [2] E12 ..... 78 C4
Anning St EC2 ..... 243 B6
Annington Rd N2 ..... 48 D6
Annis Rd E9 ..... 75 A2
Ann La SW10 ..... 136 B6 266 C5
Ann Moss Way SE16 ..... 118 C3
Ann Parkes Ct TW5 ..... 128 D3
Ann's Cl SW1 ..... 248 A1
Ann's Pl E1 ..... 243 C3
Ann St SE18 ..... 123 B2
Ann Stroud Ct SE12 ..... 165 A6

Annsworthy Ave CR7 ... 205 B6
Annsworthy Cres CR7 ... 183 B1
Annunciation RC Inf Sch The HA8 ... 27 B2
Annunciation RC Jun Sch The HA8 ... 27 B4
Ansar Gdns E17 ... 53 B4
Ansdell Rd SE15 ... 140 C3
Ansdell St W8 ... 113 D3 255 D6
Ansdell Terr W8 .. 113 D3 255 D6
Ansell Gr SM5 ... 203 A1
Ansell Ho E1 ... 96 C2
Ansell Rd SW17 ... 158 D1
Anselm Cl CR0 ... 221 D5
Anselm Rd Hatch End HA5 .. 23 B3
West Brompton SW6 ... 135 C6 265 A5
Ansford Rd BR1, SE6 ... 186 B6
Ansleigh Pl W11 ... 112 D6
Anson 30 NW9 ... 27 D1
Anson Ct TW19 ... 148 A4
Anson Ho Pimlico SW1 ... 269 A6
6 Tower Hamlets E1 ... 97 A3
Anson Pl SE28 ... 123 B4
Anson Prim Sch NW2 ... 68 D3
Anson Rd
Cricklewood NW2 ... 68 C3
Tufnell Pk N7 ... 71 D4
Anson Terr UB5 ... 63 D2
Anstey Ct 6 W3 ... 110 D4
Anstey Ho 7 E9 ... 96 C6
Anstey Lo EN1 ... 17 C5
Anstey Rd SE15 ... 140 A2
Anstey Wlk N15 ... 51 A5
Anstice Cl W4 ... 133 C5
Anstridge Rd SE9 ... 167 B5
Antelope Rd SE18 ... 122 B3
Antenor Ho 11 E2 ... 96 B5
Anthony Cl NW7 ... 27 C6
Anthony Cope Ct N1 ... 235 D2
Anthony Ct Harrow HA1 ... 42 B2
Isleworth TW7 ... 130 D2
Anthony Ho NW8 ... 237 A5
Anthony Kendal Ho 4 E5 ... 74 B5
Anthony Rd
Croydon SE25 ... 206 A3
East Wickham DA16 ... 146 A4
Greenford UB6 ... 86 C4
Anthony St E1 ... 96 B1
Antigua Wlk SE19 ... 183 B5
Antilles Bay 19 E14 ... 120 A4
Antilles Ho W3 ... 89 B1
Antill Rd Mile End E3 ... 97 A4
Tottenham Hale N15 ... 52 A5
Antill Terr 5 E1 ... 96 D1
Antlers Hill E4 ... 19 D6
Anton Cres SM1 ... 217 C5
Antoneys Cl HA5 ... 22 D1
Antonine Hts SE1 ... 253 A1
Anton Pl HA9 ... 66 D5
Anton St E8 ... 74 A3
Antony Ho
4 Deptford SE14 ... 140 D5
2 Rotherhithe SE16 ... 118 C2
Antrim Gr NW3 ... 70 D2
Antrim Ho SW11 ... 137 A2
Antrim Mans NW3 ... 70 D2
Antrim Rd NW3 ... 70 D2
Antrobus Cl SM1 ... 217 B3
Antrobus Rd W4 ... 111 A3
Anvil Cl SW16 ... 181 C3
Anvil Ho 10 N9 ... 18 A1
Anvil Rd TW16 ... 194 A6
Anworth Cl IG8 ... 37 B4
AOP Gall* EC2 ... 243 A6
Apex Cl BR3 ... 185 D2
Apex Cnr Edgware NW7 ... 27 B6
Twickenham TW13 ... 151 B1
Apex Ct W13 ... 87 A1
Apex Ind Est NW10 ... 89 D3
Apex Lo 10 EN5 ... 14 A6
Apex Prim Sch
3 Barking IG11 ... 79 A1
Ilford IG1 ... 78 C6
Apex Ret Pk TW13 ... 151 B1
Aphrodite Ct 11 E14 ... 119 C2
Aplin Ct 4 SM1 ... 217 D2
Aplin Way TW7 ... 130 C4
Apollo Ave Bromley BR1 ... 187 B2
Loughton HA6 ... 22 A5
Apollo Bldg 2 E14 ... 119 C2
Apollo Ho Chelsea SW10 ... 266 C5
32 Hackney E2 ... 96 B5
Highgate N6 ... 48 D2
Apollo Ind Bsns Ctr 29 SE8 ... 140 D6
Apollo Pl Chelsea SW10 .. 266 C4
6 Leyton E11 ... 76 C5
Apollo Studios 18 NW5 ... 71 D3
Apollo Way 1 SE18 ... 123 B3
Apostle Way CR7 ... 182 D1
Apothecary St EC4 ... 241 C1
Appach Rd SW2 ... 160 C5
Appin Ct HA1 ... 42 C2
Appleby Cl Chingford E4 ... 36 A4
Hayes UB3, UB8 ... 83 A1

Appleby Cl *continued*
Orpington BR5 ... 211 C2
Twickenham TW2 ... 152 B2
West Green N15 ... 51 B4
Appleby Ct W3 ... 111 A4
Appleby Gdns TW14 ... 149 D3
Appleby Rd Hackney E8 ... 74 A1
Newham E16 ... 99 A1
Appleby St E2 ... 95 D5
Appledore Ave HA4 ... 62 C5
Appledore Cl
Bromley BR2 ... 209 A4
Edgware HA8 ... 26 C2
Upper Tooting SW12, SW17 ... 158 D2
Appledore Cres DA14 ... 167 D1
Appledore Way NW7 ... 28 D3
Appleford 8 NW5 ... 71 C3
Appleford Ho 6 W10 ... 91 A3
Appleford Rd W10 ... 91 A3
Applegarth
Claygate KT10 ... 212 D3
New Addington CR0 ... 223 D1
Apple Garth TW8 ... 109 D2
Applegarth Dr IG2 ... 57 D5
Applegarth Ho
Borough The SE1 ... 251 D2
9 Camberwell SE15 ... 140 A5
Applegarth Inf Sch CR0 . 223 D2
Applegarth Jun Sch CR0 ... 223 D2
Applegarth Rd
Hammersmith W14 ... 112 D3
Woolwich SE28 ... 124 C6
Apple Gr Chessington KT9 . 214 A4
Enfield EN1 ... 5 C2
Apple Lo HA0 ... 65 C5
Apple Mkt KT1 ... 175 D1
Apple Mkt* WC2 ... 250 B6
Apple Rd E11 ... 76 C5
Appleshaw Ho 4 SE5 ... 139 C2
Appleton Ct 30 E8 ... 74 B3
Appleton Gdns KT3 ... 200 A3
Appleton Rd SE9 ... 144 A2
Appleton Sq CR4 ... 180 C2
Apple Tree Ave UB7 ... 82 B1
Appletree Cl 5 SE20 ... 184 B2
Appletree Ct
Lewisham SE13 ... 142 B1
Northolt UB5 ... 85 A4
Appletree Gdns EN4 ... 2 C1
Apple Tree Yd SW1 ... 249 B4
Applewood Cl
Dollis Hill NW2 ... 68 B5
Ickenham UB10 ... 60 A4
Oakleigh Pk N20 ... 14 C3
Applewood Dr E13 ... 99 B3
Appold St EC2 ... 95 C2 243 A4
Appollo Ct 7 SW9 ... 138 C4
Apprentice Gdns UB5 ... 85 B4
Apprentice Way 5 E5 ... 74 B4
Approach Cl N16 ... 73 C4
Approach Rd
Ashford TW15 ... 171 A4
Bethnal Green E2 ... 96 C5
East Molesey KT8 ... 195 C4
Edgware HA8 ... 26 C4
Merton SW20 ... 178 C1
New Barnet EN4, EN5 ... 2 B1
Approach The Acton W3 ... 89 B1
Enfield EN1 ... 6 B3
Hendon NW4 ... 46 D4
Orpington BR6 ... 227 D6
Aprey Gdns NW4 ... 46 C5
April Cl Ealing W7 ... 108 C6
Feltham TW13 ... 150 A1
Orpington BR6 ... 227 D3
April Ct 20 E2 ... 96 A5
April Glen SE23 ... 162 D1
April St E8 ... 73 D4
Apsley Cl HA2 ... 42 A4
Apsley Ct SM2 ... 218 A2
Apsley Ctr The NW2 ... 68 A6
Apsley Ho Enfield EN1 ... 17 C5
Hounslow TW4 ... 129 B1
Stepney E1 ... 96 C2
St John's Wood NW8 ... 229 C4
Apsley Ho, The Wellington Mus* SW1 ... 115 A4 248 B2
Apsley Rd Croydon SE25 ... 206 B5
Kingston u T KT3 ... 199 A6
Apsley Way Dollis Hill NW2 . 68 A6
Mayfair W1 ... 248 B2
Aquarius TW1 ... 153 B3
Aquarius Bsns Pk NW2 ... 46 A1
Aquarius Way HA6 ... 22 A6
Aquila St NW8 ... 92 B5 229 D4
Aquinas St SE1 ... 116 C5 251 B3
Arabella Ct NW8 ... 229 B4
Arabella Dr SW15 ... 133 C1
Arabia Cl E4 ... 20 B4
Arabian Ho 8 E1 ... 97 A3
Arabin Rd SE4 ... 141 B1
Aragon Ave KT7 ... 196 D4
Aragon Cl Ashford TW16 ... 171 D3
Bromley BR2 ... 210 B1
Enfield EN2 ... 4 B5
Aragon Ct
Beckenham BR3 ... 186 A2
East Molesey KT8 ... 196 A5

Aragon Dr HA4 ... 40 D1
Aragon Pl SM4 ... 201 A2
Aragon Prim Sch SM4 ... 200 D2
Aragon Rd
Kingston u T KT2 ... 176 A5
West Barnes SM4 ... 201 A2
Aragon Twr SE8 ... 119 B2
Arakan Ho 4 N16 ... 73 B4
Aral Ho 14 E1 ... 96 D3
Arandora Cres RM6 ... 58 B2
Aranya Ct 3 E17 ... 35 A1
Arapiles Ho 6 E14 ... 98 B1
Arbery Rd E3 ... 97 A5
Arbon Ct N1 ... 235 B5
Arbor Cl BR3 ... 185 D1
Arbor Ct N16 ... 73 B6
Arborfield Cl SW2 ... 160 B3
Arborfield Ho 7 E14 ... 119 C6
Arbor Rd E4 ... 20 B1
Arbour Ho 3 E1 ... 96 D1
Arbour Rd EN3 ... 6 D2
Arbour Sq E1 ... 96 D1
Arbroath Rd SE9 ... 144 A2
Arbrook Chase KT10 ... 212 A2
Arbrook Ct
Chessington KT9 ... 213 D3
St Paul's Cray BR5 ... 190 A2
Arbrook Hall KT10 ... 212 D2
Arbrook La KT10 ... 212 B2
Arbury Ho BR1 ... 188 A3
Arbury Terr 3 SE26 ... 162 B1
Arbuthnot La DA5 ... 169 A5
Arbuthnot Rd SE14 ... 140 D3
Arbutus St E8 ... 95 D6
Arcade Ho 7 NW11 ... 47 B4
Arcade The
Broadgate EC2 ... 243 A3
2 Eltham SE9 ... 166 C5
1 Tufnell Pk N7 ... 72 A4
Walthamstow E17 ... 53 C5
Arcadia Ave N3 ... 29 C2
Arcadia Centre The W5 .. 109 D6
Arcadia Cl SM5 ... 219 A4
Arcadian Ave DA5 ... 169 A5
Arcadian Cl DA5 ... 169 A5
Arcadian Gdns N22 ... 32 C3
Arcadian Ho SW6 ... 136 A3
Arcadian Pl SW18 ... 157 B4
Arcadian Rd DA5 ... 169 A5
Arcadia St E14 ... 97 C1
Arcadia Univ W2. 113 D6 245 C5
Archangel St SE16 ... 118 D4
Archbishop Coggan Ho SE13 ... 142 B1
Archbishop Lanfranc Sch The CR0 ... 204 A3
Archbishop's Pl 1 SW2 ... 160 B4
Archbishop Sumner CE Prim Sch SE11 ... 116 C2 261 B3
Archbishop Tenison's CE Sch CR0 ... 221 D5
Archbishop Tenison's Sch SE11 ... 138 B6 270 D5
Archdale Bsns Ctr HA2 ... 64 A6
Archdale Ct W12 ... 112 B5
Archdale Ho SE1 ... 263 A6
Archdale Pl KT3 ... 198 D6
Archdale Rd SE22 ... 139 D1
Archdeacon Cambridge's CE Prim Sch 2 TW2 ... 152 C2
Archel Rd W14 ... 135 B6 264 C6
Archer Cl Barnet EN5 ... 13 B5
Kingston u T KT2 ... 176 A3
Archer Ct TW13 ... 150 A3
Archer Ho
1 Battersea SW11 ... 136 B3
Ealing W13 ... 109 B5
24 Hoxton N1 ... 95 C6
1 New Cross SE14 ... 141 A4
Notting Hill W11 ... 244 D6
Rotherhithe SE8 ... 119 A2
Archer Mews TW12 ... 174 A4
Archer Rd SE25 ... 206 B5
Archers Ct 3 CR2 ... 221 A3
Archers Dr EN3 ... 6 C3
Archers Lo 22 SE16 ... 118 A1
Archer Sq SE14 ... 141 A6
Archer St W1 ... 249 C6
Archer Terr UB7 ... 104 A6
Archery Cl Harrow HA3 ... 42 D6
Paddington W2 ... 237 B1
Archery Fields Ho WC1 ... 234 A2
Archery Rd SE9 ... 166 B6
Archery Stps W2 ... 247 B6
Arches Bsns Ctr The UB2 ... 107 B4
Arches The Harrow HA2 ... 63 D6
Strand WC2 ... 250 B4
Archgate Bsns Ctr 1 N12 ... 30 A5
Archibald Mews W1 ... 248 C5
Archibald Rd N7 ... 71 D4
Archibald St E3 ... 97 C4
Archie Cl UB7 ... 104 C4
Archie St SE1 ... 253 B1
Arch St SE1 ... 117 A3 262 A5
Archway N19 ... 71 C6
Archway Bsns Ctr 5 N19 .. 71 D5
Archway Cl
North Kensington W10 ... 90 D2
2 Upper Holloway N19 ... 71 C6

Archway Cl *continued*
Wallington SM6 ... 220 A5
Wimbledon SW19 ... 179 D6
Archway Hts 5 N19 ... 49 C1
Archway L Ctr N19 ... 71 C6
Archway Mews SW15 ... 135 A1
Archway Rd N6 ... 49 B2
Archway St SW13, SW14 .. 133 C2
Archway Sta N19 ... 71 C6
Arcola St E8 ... 73 D3
Arcon Dr UB5 ... 85 A3
Arctic St NW5 ... 71 B3
Arcus Rd BR1 ... 186 C4
Ardbeg Rd SE24 ... 161 B6
Arden 17 SW19 ... 156 D3
Arden Cl
Bushey Heath WD23 ... 8 D4
Erith SE28 ... 102 D1
Harrow HA1 ... 64 B5
Twickenham TW2 ... 151 B4
Arden Court Gdns N2 ... 48 B3
Arden Cres
Dagenham RM9 ... 80 D1
Millwall E14 ... 119 C2
Arden Gr BR6 ... 226 D4
Arden Grange N12 ... 30 A6
Arden Ho 21 Hoxton N1 ... 95 C5
29 Stockwell SW9 ... 138 A3
Vauxhall SE11 ... 260 C3
Arden Mews E17 ... 53 D4
Arden Mhor HA5 ... 40 B5
Arden Rd Ealing W13 ... 109 C6
Finchley N3 ... 47 B6
Ardent Cl SE25 ... 205 C6
Ardent Ho 30 E3 ... 97 A5
Ardfern Ave SW16 ... 204 C6
Ardfillan Rd SE6 ... 164 B2
Ardgowan Rd SE6 ... 164 C3
Ardilaun Rd N5 ... 73 A4
Ardingly Cl CR0 ... 222 D5
Ardleigh Gdns SM3 ... 201 C2
Ardleigh Ho 4 IG11 ... 101 A6
Ardleigh Rd Kingsland N1 .. 73 C2
Walthamstow E17 ... 35 B2
Ardleigh Terr E17 ... 35 B2
Ardley Cl Forest Hill SE6 .. 163 A1
Neasden NW10 ... 67 C5
Ruislip HA4 ... 39 A2
Ardlui Rd SE27 ... 161 A2
Ardmay Gdns KT6 ... 198 A4
Ardmere Rd SE13 ... 164 B5
Ardmore La IG9 ... 21 B4
Ardmore Pl IG9 ... 21 B4
Ardoch Rd SE6 ... 164 B2
Ardra Rd N9 ... 18 D1
Ardrossan Gdns KT4 ... 216 A5
Ardshiel Cl 6 SW15 ... 134 D2
Ardwell Ave IG6 ... 57 A4
Ardwell Rd SW2 ... 160 A2
Ardwick Rd NW2 ... 69 C4
Arena Bsns Ctr N4 ... 51 A3
Arena Est N4 ... 50 D3
Arena Sta SE25 ... 206 C4
Arena The EN3 ... 7 B5
Ares Ct 16 E14 ... 119 C2
Arethusa Ho 8 E14 ... 119 D2
Argali Ho 3 DA18 ... 125 A3
Argall Ave E10 ... 52 D1
Argall Way E10 ... 53 A1
Argenta Way NW10 ... 66 D1
Argent Ct KT6 ... 214 C5
Argent Ctr The UB3 ... 106 A4
Argent Ho HA5 ... 23 B4
Argo Bsns Ctr 7 NW6 ... 91 C4
Argon Mews SW6 ... 265 B3
Argon Rd N18 ... 34 D5
Argos Ct 5 SW9 ... 138 C4
Argos Ho 8 E2 ... 96 B5
Argosy Ho Fitzrovia W1 ... 238 D5
Rotherhithe SE8 ... 119 A2
Argus Way UB5 ... 85 A4
Argyle Cl W13 ... 87 A3
Argyle Ho
Cubitt Town E14 ... 120 A3
Richmond TW10 ... 153 C2
Sutton SM2 ... 218 A2
Teddington TW11 ... 174 C5
Argyle Mans 4 NW2 ... 68 D4
Argyle Pl W6 ... 112 B2
Argyle Prim Sch WC1 ... 94 A4 233 A2
Argyle Rd Ealing W13 ... 87 A2
Edmonton N18 ... 34 A6
Harrow HA2 ... 41 D3
Hounslow TW3 ... 151 D6
Ilford IG1 ... 78 C6
Leyton E15 ... 76 C4
Newham E16 ... 99 B1
Stepney E1 ... 96 D3
Tottenham N17 ... 34 A2
Woodside Pk N12 ... 29 C5
Argyle Sq WC1 ... 94 A4 233 B2
Argyle St WC1 ... 94 A4 233 B2
Argyle Way SE16 ... 118 A1
Argyle Wlk WC1 ... 233 B1
Argyll Ave UB1 ... 107 D5
Argyll Cl SW9 ... 138 B2
Argyll Ct 15 SW2 ... 160 A4
Argyll Gdns HA8 ... 26 D2
Argyll Mans Chelsea SW3. 266 D6

Argyll Mans *continued*
West Kensington W14 ... 254 B4
Argyll Rd
Kensington W8 ... 113 C4 245 B1
Woolwich SE18 ... 123 A3
Argyll St W1 ... 93 C1 239 A1
Aria Ct IG2 ... 57 A3
Arica Ho SE16 ... 118 B3
Arica Rd SE4 ... 141 A2
Ariel Ct
5 Belvedere DA17 ... 125 C1
5 Hammersmith W12 ... 112 A3
Newington SE11 ... 261 C3
Ariel Rd NW6 ... 69 C2
Ariel Way Hounslow TW4 .. 128 B2
Shepherd's Bush W11, W12 ... 112 D5
Aristotle Rd SW4 ... 137 D2
Arizona Bldg 10 SE13 ... 141 D4
Ark Acad HA9 ... 65 C6
Arkansas Ho 21 N19 ... 49 D2
Ark Ct N16 ... 73 D6
Arkell Gr SW16 ... 182 D3
Arkindale Rd SE6 ... 164 A1
Arklay Cl UB8 ... 82 B3
ARKLEY ... 12 A6
Arkley Cres E17 ... 53 B4
Arkley Dr EN5 ... 12 B6
Arkley Pk EN5 ... 11 B5
Arkley Rd E17 ... 53 B4
Arklow Ho SE17 ... 139 B6
Arklow Mews 4 KT6 ... 214 A6
Arklow Rd SE14 ... 141 B6
Arklow Road Trad Est SE14 ... 141 B6
Arkwright Ho 23 SW2 ... 160 A4
Arkwright Mans 1 NW3 ... 70 A3
Arkwright Rd NW3 ... 70 A3
Arlesey Cl SW15 ... 157 A6
Arlesford Rd SW9 ... 138 A2
Arless Ho 8 HA1 ... 42 D4
Arlidge Ho EC1 ... 241 B4
Arlingford Rd SW2 ... 160 C5
Arlington N12 ... 13 C1
Arlington Ave N1 .. 95 A6 235 B5
Arlington Cl
Lewisham SE13 ... 164 B6
Sidcup DA15 ... 167 C4
Sutton SM1 ... 217 C6
Twickenham TW1 ... 153 C5
Arlington Ct
13 Acton W3 ... 110 D5
Highgate N6 ... 49 A3
4 Twickenham TW1 ... 153 C5
Arlington Dr
Carshalton SM5 ... 218 D6
Ruislip HA4 ... 39 B3
Arlington Gdns
Acton Green W4 ... 111 A1
Ilford IG1 ... 56 C1
Arlington Gn NW7 ... 28 D3
Arlington Ho
3 Deptford SE8 ... 141 B6
Finsbury EC1 ... 234 B2
1 Shepherd's Bush W12 ... 112 B5
Arlington Lo SW2 ... 138 B1
Arlington Park Mans 1 W4 ... 111 A1
Arlington Pl 7 SE10 ... 142 A5
Arlington Rd
Ashford TW15 ... 170 B5
Camden Town NW1 . 93 B6 231 D5
Ealing W13 ... 87 B1
Osidge N14 ... 15 C3
Richmond TW10 ... 153 D2
Surbiton KT6 ... 197 D3
Teddington TW11 ... 174 D6
Twickenham TW1 ... 153 C5
Woodford IG8 ... 37 B3
Arlington Sq N1 ... 95 A6 235 B5
Arlington St SW1 ... 115 C5 249 A4
Arlington Way EC1 ... 94 C4 234 B2
Arliss Way UB5 ... 84 C6
Arlow Rd N21 ... 16 C3
Armada Ct 11 SE8 ... 141 C6
Armadale Cl N17 ... 52 B5
Armadale Rd
Feltham TW14 ... 150 A6
West Brompton SW6 ... 265 A5
Armada St 10 SE8 ... 141 C6
Armada Way Newham E6 .. 101 B1
Newham E16 ... 122 D6
Armagh Rd E3 ... 97 B6
Armeston KT3 ... 199 B2
Armfield Cl KT8 ... 195 B4
Armfield Cotts 3 SW19 . 180 D1
Armfield Cres CR4 ... 180 D1
Armfield Rd EN2 ... 5 B4
Arminger Rd W12 ... 112 B5
Armistice Gdns SE25 ... 206 A6
Armitage Ho NW1 . 92 C2 237 B4
Armitage Rd
Golders Green NW11 ... 47 B1
Greenwich SE10 ... 120 D1
Armour Cl N7 ... 72 B2
Armoury Ho E3 ... 97 A6
Armoury Rd SE8 ... 141 D3
Armoury Way SW18 ... 157 C6

Armsby Ho 17 E1 . . . . .96 C2
Armstead Wlk RM10 . . . .81 C1
Armstrong Ave IG8 . . . . .36 C4
Armstrong Cl
Bickley BR1. . . . . .210 A6
Dagenham RM8 . . . . .58 D2
Newham E6 . . . . .100 B1
Pinner HA5 . . . . .40 A3
Walton-on-T KT12 . . . . . .194 A3
Armstrong Cres EN4 . . . . . .2 B2
Armstrong Ho 8 SW15. . .156 D5
Armstrong Rd
East Acton W3 . . . . .111 D5
Feltham TW13 . . . . .173 A5
Knightsbridge SW7 . . . . .256 C5
10 Willesden NW0 . . . . . . .67 C1
Woolwich SE18. . . . . .123 A3
Armstrong Way UB2 . . . .107 D4
Armytage Rd TW5. . . . . . .128 D5
Arnal Cres SW18 . . . . .157 A4
Arncliffe NW6 . . . . .91 D6
Arncliffe Cl N11 . . . . .31 A4
Arncroft Ct IG11 . . . . .102 B4
Arndale Wlk 6 SW18 . . . .157 D6
Arndell Ho 16 SM1 . . . . . .218 A4
Arne Gr BR6 . . . . .227 D5
Arne Ho SE11. . . . . .260 C2
Arne St WC2 . . . . .94 A1 240 B1
Arnett Sq E4 . . . . .35 B4
Arneways Ave RM6. . . . . . .58 C4
Arneway St SW1 . . . . . . .259 D5
Arne Wlk SE3 . . . . .142 D1
Arnewood Cl SW15 . . . . .156 A3
Arney's La CR4 . . . . .203 A3
Arngask Rd SE6. . . . . .164 B4
Arnhem Pl E14 . . . . .119 C3
Arnhem Way 3 SE22 . . . .161 C6
Arnhem Wharf E14 . . . . . .119 C3
Arnhem Wharf Prim Sch
E14. . . . . .119 C3
Arnison Rd KT8 . . . . .196 B5
Arnold Ave E EN3 . . . . .7 C5
Arnold Ave W EN3 . . . . .7 B5
Arnold Cir E2. . . . . .95 D4
Arnold Cl HA3 . . . . .44 B2
Arnold Cres TW7. . . . . . . .152 B6
Arnold Ct E18 . . . . .36 D2
Arnold Dr KT9 . . . . .213 D2
Arnold Est SE1. . . . . .253 D1
Arnold Gdns N13 . . . . .32 D5
Arnold Ho Croydon CR0. . .220 D4
Newington SE17. . . . . . . .261 D1
9 Stoke Newington N16 . . .73 C5
Arnold House Sch
NW8 . . . . .92 B5 229 C3
Arnold Rd Bow E3 . . . . . . .97 C4
Dagenham RM10 . . . . .81 C1
Mitcham SW17 . . . . .180 D3
Northolt UB5 . . . . .63 A2
Tottenham N15. . . . . .51 D6
Arnos Gr N14 . . . . .15 D1
Arnos Grove Ct 4 N11 . . . .31 C5
Arnos Grove Sta N11 . . . . .31 C6
Arnos Rd N11. . . . . .31 C6
Arnot Ho 27 SE5 . . . . .139 A5
Arnott Cl Acton Green W4 . .111 B2
Thamesmead SE28 . . . . . .124 C5
Arnould Ave SE5 . . . . .139 B1
Arnsberg Way DA6, DA7 . . .147 C1
Arnside Gdns HA9 . . . . . . .43 D1
Arnside Ho 2 SE17 . . . . . .139 B6
Arnside Rd DA7. . . . . .147 C4
Arnside St SE17. . . . . .139 A6
Arnulf St SE6 . . . . .185 D6
Arnull's Rd SW16 . . . . . . .182 D4
Arodene Rd SW2 . . . . .160 B5
Arosa Rd 8 TW1. . . . . . . .153 D5
Arragon Gdns
Streatham SW16 . . . . .182 A3
West Wickham BR4 . . . . . .223 D5
Arragon Rd Newham E6. . . .99 D6
4 Twickenham TW1. . . . . .153 A3
Wandsworth SW18 . . . . . .157 C3
Arran Cl SM6 . . . . .219 C4
Arran Ct Edgware HA8. . . . .10 D2
32 Hendon NW9. . . . . .27 D1
Neasden NW0 . . . . .67 B5
Arrandene Ho 3 BR5 . . . .190 B1
Arran Dr Stanmore HA7. . . .25 C6
Wanstead E12 . . . . .77 D6
Arran Ho
5 Canary Wharf E14 . . . . .120 A5
Stoke Newington N16. . . . .51 D1
Arran Mews W5 . . . . .110 B5
Arran Rd SE6 . . . . .164 A2
Arran Wlk N1. . . . . .73 A1
Arras Ave SM4. . . . . .202 A4
Arras Ho SE2 . . . . .146 D6
Arrol Ho SE1. . . . . .262 B5
Arrol Rd BR3 . . . . .206 D6
Arrowe Ct 6 E5 . . . . .74 B4
Arrow Ho 23 N1. . . . . .95 C6
Arrow Rd E3. . . . . .97 D4
Arrow Scout Wlk UB5 . . . .85 A4
Arrowsmith Ho SE11. . . . .260 C2
Arsenal Rd SE9 . . . . .144 B2
Arsenal Sta N5 . . . . .72 C5
Arsenal Way SE18. . . . . . .123 A3
Arta Ho 26 E1. . . . . .96 C1
Artcadia Lifestyle★ EC2. .243 C4

Artemis Ct 14 E14. . . . . . .119 C2
Artemis Pl SW18. . . . . . . .157 B4
Arterberry Rd SW20,
SW19. . . . . .178 D2
Artesian Cl NW10 . . . . . . .67 B1
Artesian Gr EN5 . . . . .2 A1
Artesian Rd W2 . . . . .91 C1
Artesian Wlk 4 E11. . . . . .76 C5
Arthingworth St E15 . . . . .98 C6
Arthur Ct Battersea SW11 . .268 B1
10 North Kensington W10 . . .90 D1
Paddington W2. . . . . .91 D1
South Croydon CR0. . . . . .221 B5
Arthur Deakin Ho 1 E1 . . .96 A2
Arthurdon Rd SE4 . . . . . . .163 C6
Arthur Gr SE18 . . . . .123 A2
Arthur Henderson Ho
9 Crouch End N19 . . . . .49 D2
9 Fulham SW6 . . . . .135 B3
Arthur Newton Ho 19
SW11. . . . . .136 B2
Arthur Rd Dagenham RM6 . . .58 D3
Edmonton N9 . . . . .17 D2
6 Kingston u T KT2 . . . . .176 C3
Lower Holloway N7 . . . . . .72 B4
Newham E6 . . . . .100 B5
West Barnes KT3 . . . . . . .200 B4
Wimbledon SW19 . . . . . . .179 C6
Arthur Ruxley Est DA14. . .190 D4
Arthur St EC4. . . . .117 B6 252 C6
Arthur Wade Ho 7 E2 . . . . .95 D4
Arthur Walls Ho 3 E12. . . .78 C5
Artichoke Hill 8 E1. . . . . .118 B6
Artichoke Mews 5 SE5 . . .139 B4
Artichoke Pl SE5. . . . . .139 B4
Artillery Cl IG2 . . . . .57 A3
Artillery Ho Bow E3. . . . . . .97 A6
Woolwich SE18. . . . . .122 C1
Artillery La
Broadgate E1 . . . . .95 C2 243 B3
North Kensington W12. . . . .90 A1
Artillery Pas E1. . . . . .243 B3
Artillery Pl
Harrow Weald HA3. . . . . . .24 A3
Westminster SW1 . . . . . . .259 C5
Woolwich SE18. . . . . .122 C2
Artillery Row SW1 . . . . . .259 C5
Artington Cl BR6. . . . . .227 A4
Artisan Cl E16 . . . . .122 D6
Artisan Ct E8 . . . . .74 A2
Artisan Mews 9 NW10. . . .90 D4
Artisan Quarter 10 NW10 . .90 D4
Artizan St E1 . . . . .243 B2
Arton Wilson Ho 12
SW15. . . . . .156 A6
Art Pilgrim★ NW3 . . . . . . .70 B1
Artsdepot★ N12 . . . . .30 A3
Arts Educational Sch The 14
W4 . . . . .111 C2
Artwell Cl E10 . . . . .53 D3
Arundale Cl E13 . . . . .197 D5
Arundel Ave SM4 . . . . .201 B5
Arundel Bldgs SE1 . . . . . .263 B5
Arundel Cl Croydon CR0 . . .220 D5
Hampton TW12. . . . . .173 D5
Leyton E15 . . . . .76 C4
Sidcup DA5. . . . . .169 B5
Wandsworth SW11 . . . . . .158 C6
Arundel Ct Barnes SW13 . .134 B6
8 Beckenham BR2 . . . . . .186 C1
2 Bexley DA6 . . . . .147 A1
Chelsea SW3 . . . . .257 B2
Colney Hatch N12. . . . . . . .30 C4
3 Croydon CR0 . . . . .220 D5
Harrow HA2 . . . . .63 C4
Putney SW15 . . . . .156 D6
Tottenham N17. . . . . .34 A2
Arundel Dr
Borehamwood WD6 . . . . . .11 A6
Harrow HA2 . . . . .63 C4
Woodford IG8. . . . . .37 A3
Arundel Gdns
Burnt Oak HA8 . . . . .27 B3
Ilford IG3 . . . . .80 A6
Notting Hill W11. . . . .113 B6 244 C6
Southgate N21 . . . . .16 C3
Arundel Gr N16. . . . . .73 C3
Arundel Ho Croydon CR0 . .221 B3
Islington N1. . . . . . .94 D4 234 D6
Richmond TW10 . . . . .154 C6
3 South Acton W3. . . . . . .110 D4
Arundel Lo Church End N3 . .29 B1
9 Upper Holloway N19 . . . .72 A4
Arundel Mans
Barnes SW13 . . . . .134 B6
Fulham SW6 . . . . .264 D2
Arundel Pl N1, N7 . . . . .72 C2
Arundel Rd Belmont SM2 . .217 B1
Cockfosters EN4. . . . . .2 C2
Hounslow TW4 . . . . .128 C2
Kingston u T KT1 . . . . . . .177 A1
Thornton Heath CR0. . . . .205 B3
Arundel Sq N7. . . . . .72 C2
Arundel St WC2. . . .116 B6 250 D6
Arundel Terr SW13 . . . . . .134 B6
Arungford Mews 12
SW2. . . . . .160 C6
Arun Ho 5 KT2 . . . . .175 D2
Arvon Rd N5. . . . . .72 C3

Asa Ct UB3 . . . . .105 D3
Asaph Ho SE14 . . . . .141 B4
Asbaston Terr IG11 . . . . . . .79 A2
Asbury Ct N21. . . . . .16 A6
Ascalon Ct 16 SW2 . . . . . .160 B4
Ascalon Ho SW8. . . . . .269 A3
Ascalon St SW8. . . .137 C5 269 A3
Ascham Dr E4 . . . . .35 C3
Ascham End E17 . . . . .35 A2
Ascham St NW5 . . . . .71 C3
Aschurch Rd CR0 . . . . .205 D2
Ascot Cl
Borehamwood WD6 . . . . . .10 C6
Northolt UB5 . . . . .63 C3
Ascot Ct 8 Brixton SW2 . . .138 A1
Bromley BR1. . . . . .188 A1
Old Bexley DA5. . . . . .169 B4
St John's Wood NW8 . . . . .229 C1
Southall UB1. . . . . .85 C2
Ascot Gdns Enfield EN3. . . . .6 C6
Southall UB1. . . . . .85 C2
Ascot Ho
6 Acton Green W4 . . . . . .111 A1
1 Paddington W9 . . . . .91 C2
Penge SE26 . . . . .184 B4
Regent's Pk NW1 . . . . . . .231 D2
Paddington W9 . . . . .91 D5
Ascot Par 9 SW4 . . . . .138 A1
Ascot Pl 12 HA7 . . . . .25 C5
Ascot Rd
East Bedfont TW14. . . . . .148 D2
Edmonton N18 . . . . .34 A6
Newham E6 . . . . .100 B4
Orpington BR5 . . . . .211 D5
Streatham SW17 . . . . .181 A4
Tottenham N15. . . . . .51 B4
Ascott Ave W5 . . . . .110 A4
Ascott Ct HA5. . . . . .40 A5
Ashbourne Ave
East Barnet N20 . . . . .14 D2
Erith DA7. . . . . .147 A5
Harrow HA2 . . . . .64 B6
Temple Fortune NW11 . . . . .47 C2
Wanstead E18 . . . . .55 B5
Ashbourne Cl Ealing W5. . . .88 C2
18 Woodside Pk N12 . . . . .29 C6
Ashbourne Coll
W8 . . . . .113 D4 245 C1
Ashbourne Ct
Beckenham BR3 . . . . .186 A2
Clapton Pk E5 . . . . .75 A4
13 Woodside Pk N12 . . . . .29 D6
Ashbourne Gr
Chiswick W4. . . . . .111 C1
East Dulwich SE22 . . . . . .139 D1
Edgware NW7 . . . . .27 B5
Ashbourne Lo 2 N13 . . . . . .32 C6
Ashbourne Par 2 NW11 . . .47 B4
Ashbourne Rd Ealing W5 . . .88 B3
Mitcham CR4 . . . . .181 A3
Ashbourne Rise BR6 . . . . .227 C4
Ashbourne Terr 1
SW19. . . . . .179 C3
Ashbourne Way NW11 . . . .47 B4
Ashbridge Ct 3 W6. . . . . .112 B3
Ashbridge Rd E11. . . . . .54 D2
Ashbridge St NW8 .92 C3 237 A5
Ashbrook HA8 . . . . .26 B4
Ashbrook Rd
Dagenham RM10 . . . . .81 D5
Upper Holloway N19 . . . . . .71 D6
Ashburn Ct BR1. . . . . .187 A3
Ashburn Gdns SW7 . . . . . .256 A4
Ashburnham Ave HA1 . . . . .42 D3
Ashburnham Cl N2 . . . . . . .48 B5
Ashburnham Gdns HA1 . . . .42 D3
Ashburnham Gr SE10 . . . .141 D5
Ashburnham Pk KT10 . . . .212 A4
Ashburnham Pl SE10 . . . . .141 D5
Ashburnham Prim Sch
SW10 . . . . .266 C4
Ashburnham Rd
Chelsea SW10 . . . . .136 A5 266 B3
Kensal Rise NW10 . . . . . . .90 C5
Richmond TW10 . . . . .153 B1
Ashburnham Retreat 4
SE10 . . . . .141 D5
Ashburnham Twr SW10. . . .266 C4
Ashburn Pl SW7 . . .114 A2 256 A3
Ashburton Ave
Croydon CR0. . . . . .206 B1
Ilford IG3 . . . . .79 D4
Ashburton Cl CR0 . . . . .206 A1
Ashburton Ct 1 HA5. . . . . .40 D6
Ashburton Gdns CR0. . . . .222 A6
Ashburton Ho Enfield EN3 . . .6 D2
2 Wallington SM6 . . . . . . .219 D3
Ashburton Jun & Inf Sch
CR0. . . . . .206 B3
Ashburton Learning Village
CR9. . . . . .206 B2
Ashburton Mans SW10 . . .266 B4
Ashburton Rd
Croydon CR0. . . . . .222 A6
Newham E16. . . . . .99 A1
Ruislip HA4. . . . . .62 A6
Ashburton Terr 2 E13. . . . .99 A5
Ashbury Dr UB10 . . . . .60 D5
Ashbury Gdns RM6. . . . . . .58 D4
Ashbury Pl SW19 . . . . .180 A4

Ashbury Rd SW11 . . . . . . .137 A2
Ashby Ave KT19, KT9. . . . .214 C2
Ashby Ct NW8 . . . . .236 D6
Ashby Gr N1 . . . . .73 A1
Ashby Grange 7 SM6 . . . .219 C2
Ashby Ho 6 Brixton SW9. . .138 D3
17 Islington N1 . . . . .73 A1
3 Northolt UB5 . . . . .85 B3
14 Surbiton KT6. . . . . . . .198 A3
Ashby Mews
10 Clapham Pk SW2. . . . .160 A6
New Cross SE4 . . . . .141 B3
Ashby Rd New Cross SE4. . .141 B3
South Tottenham N15. . . . .52 A4
Ashby St EC1 . . . . .94 D4 234 D1
Ashby Way UB7 . . . . .126 C5
Ashby Wlk CR0 . . . . .205 A3
Ashchurch Ct 2 W12 . . . . .112 A3
Ashchurch Gr W12. . . . . . .112 A3
Ashchurch Park Villas
W12. . . . . .112 A3
Ashchurch Terr W12. . . . . .112 A3
Ash Cl Carshalton SM5. . . .218 D6
Edgware HA8. . . . . .27 A6
Kingston u T KT3 . . . . . . .177 B1
Penge SE20 . . . . .184 C1
Petts Wood BR5 . . . . .211 B4
Sidcup DA14. . . . . .168 B1
Stanmore HA7 . . . . .25 A4
Ashcombe Ave KT6 . . . . . .197 D2
Ashcombe Cl TW15 . . . . . .148 A1
Ashcombe Ct 4 SW15 . . . .157 A6
Ashcombe Gdns HA8. . . . . .26 C6
Ashcombe Ho 8 E3 . . . . . . .97 D4
Ashcombe Pk NW2 . . . . . . .67 C5
Ashcombe Rd
Wallington SM5 . . . . .219 A2
Wimbledon SW19 . . . . . . .179 C5
Ashcombe Sq KT3 . . . . . . .199 A6
Ashcombe St SW6 . . . . . . .135 D3
Ashcroft Hatch End HA5. . . .23 C4
Osidge N14. . . . . .15 D2
Ashcroft Ave DA15 . . . . . . .168 A5
Ashcroft Cres DA15 . . . . . .168 A5
Ashcroft Ct
5 Eltham SE9 . . . . .166 C5
3 Whetstone N20. . . . . . . .14 B2
Ashcroft Ho SW8 . . . . .269 A2
Ashcroft Rd Bow E3 . . . . . .97 A4
Chessington KT9 . . . . . . .213 D5
Ashcroft Sq 8 W6 . . . . . . .112 C2
Ashcroft Tech Acad
SW15. . . . . .157 B6
Ash Ct Chingford E4 . . . . . . .20 B4
Clapham SW11 . . . . .159 A6
Lee SE12. . . . . .165 A4
Marylebone W1 . . . . .237 C2
Romford RM7 . . . . .59 D3
6 Rotherhithe SE16 . . . . . .119 A5
West Ewell KT19. . . . . .215 A4
2 West Norwood SE19. . . .182 C5
9 Wimbledon SW19 . . . . .179 A3
Woodford E18. . . . . .37 C2
Ashdale Cl
Stanwell TW19 . . . . .148 A2
Twickenham TW2 . . . . . . .152 A4
Ashdale Ho N4 . . . . .51 B2
Ashdale Rd SE12 . . . . .165 B3
Ashdale Way TW2 . . . . . . .151 D4
Ashdene
6 Deptford SE15. . . . . .140 B5
Pinner HA5. . . . . .40 C6
Ashdene Cl TW15 . . . . .171 A3
Ashdon Cl IG8. . . . . .37 B4
Ashdon Rd NW10 . . . . .89 D6
Ashdown Ealing W13. . . . . . .87 B2
Putney SW15 . . . . .156 D6
Ashdown Cl 13 BR3 . . . . . .185 D1
Ashdown Cres NW5. . . . . . .71 A3
Ashdown Ct
Dulwich SE22 . . . . .162 A3
Ilford IG1 . . . . .78 D2
New Malden KT4 . . . . .199 D2
Sutton SM2. . . . . .218 A2
Ashdowne Ct N17. . . . . .34 A2
Ashdown Ho 5 E5 . . . . .74 A6
Ashdown Pl Ewell KT17 . . .215 D1
Thames Ditton KT7 . . . . . .197 A2
Ashdown Rd Enfield EN3. . . . .6 C3
Hillingdon UB10 . . . . .82 C5
Kingston u T KT1. . . . . . . .176 A1
Ashdown Way SW17. . . . . .159 A2
Ashdown Wlk 20 E14. . . . . .119 C2
Ashe Ho 9 TW1 . . . . .153 D5
Ashen E6 . . . . .100 C1
Ashenden SE17 . . . . .262 B4
Ashenden Rd E5 . . . . .75 A3
Ashen Gr SW19 . . . . .157 C2
Ashentree Ct EC4. . . . . . . .241 B1
Asher Loftus Way N11. . . . .30 C4
Asher Way E1 . . . . .118 A6
Ashfield Ave Bushey WD23. . .8 A4
Feltham TW13 . . . . .150 B3
Ashfield Cl
Beckenham BR3 . . . . .185 C3
Richmond TW10 . . . . .154 A3

Ashfield Ho 5 N5. . . . . .73 A3
Ashfield La BR7. . . . . .189 A3
Ashfield Par N14. . . . . .15 D3
Ashfield Pl BR7. . . . . .189 B3
Ashfield Rd
East Acton W3 . . . . .111 D5
New Southgate N14. . . . . . .15 C1
Tottenham N4. . . . . .51 A3
Ashfield St E1 . . . . .96 C2
4 Whitechapel E1 . . . . . . .96 B2
Ashfield Yd 21 E1 . . . . .96 C2
ASHFORD 170 B4
Ashford Ave
Ashford TW15. . . . . .170 D4
Hayes UB4 . . . . .84 D1
Hornsey N8. . . . . .50 A5
Ashford Bsns Complex
TW15 . . . . .171 A6
Ashford CE Prim Sch
TW15 . . . . .170 D4
Ashford Cl Ashford TW15. . .170 A6
Walthamstow E17 . . . . . . .53 B3
ASHFORD COMMON 171 B4
Ashford Cres EN3 . . . . .6 C3
Ashford Ct
Cricklewood NW2. . . . . . . .68 D4
Edgware HA8. . . . . .10 D1
Ashford Gn WD19 . . . . .22 D5
Ashford Ho
14 Brixton SW9. . . . . .138 D1
11 Deptford SE8. . . . . . . .141 B6
Ashford Hospl TW15 . . . . . .148 A4
Ashford Ind Est TW15 . . . .171 A6
Ashford Mews N17. . . . . . . .34 A2
Ashford Rd
Cricklewood NW2. . . . . . . .68 D4
Feltham TW13, TW15 . . . .171 B6
Littleton TW15, TW17. . . . .171 A3
Staines TW18 . . . . .170 A4
Wallend E6 . . . . .78 C1
Woodford E18. . . . . .37 B1
Ashford St N1 . . . . .95 C4
Ashford Sta TW15. . . . . . . .170 B6
Ash Gr
Cranley Gardens N10 . . . . .49 B5
Cricklewood NW2. . . . . . . .69 A4
Ealing W5 . . . . .110 A3
East Bedfont TW14. . . . . .149 C3
Edmonton N13 . . . . .17 A1
Enfield EN1. . . . . .17 C4
Hackney E8. . . . . .96 B6
Hayes UB3 . . . . .105 B6
Heston TW5 . . . . .128 D5
Penge SE20 . . . . .184 C1
Southall UB1. . . . . .85 C2
Wembley HA0. . . . . .65 A4
West Wickham BR4 . . . . . .208 A1
Yiewsley UB7 . . . . .104 B6
Ashgrove SE12 . . . . .165 A3
Ashgrove Ct 2 W9. . . . . . . .91 C2
Ashgrove Ho SW1. . . . . . . .259 D2
Ashgrove Rd
Ashford TW15. . . . . .171 B5
Catford BR1 . . . . .186 B4
Ashgrove Sch BR1. . . . . . . .187 B1
Ash Hill Dr HA5. . . . . .40 C6
Ash Ho
3 Canary Wharf E14. . . . .120 A4
Fulham SE1. . . . . .263 D3
Kenton NW9. . . . . .45 A6
Lewisham SE12 . . . . .165 A3
2 Teddington TW11. . . . . .175 C3
Ashingdon Cl E4. . . . . .20 A1
Ashington 1 NW5 . . . . .71 B2
Ashington Ho 16 E1. . . . . . .96 B3
Ashington Rd SW6. . . . . . . .135 B3
Ashlake Rd SW16 . . . . .182 A6
Ashland Pl W1. . . . . .238 A4
Ashlar Ct N12. . . . . .48 C6
Ashlar Pl SE18. . . . . .122 C2
Ashleigh Commercial Est
SE7. . . . . .121 D3
Ashleigh Ct Ealing W5. . . . .109 D2
Osidge N14. . . . . .15 C4
Penge SE26 . . . . .184 B4
Ashleigh Gdns SM1 . . . . . .217 D6
Ashleigh Ho
Mortlake SW14 . . . . .133 C2
1 Streatham SW16. . . . . . .182 B6
Ashleigh Point 8 SE26. . . . .162 D1
Ashleigh Rd
Mortlake SW14 . . . . .133 C2
Penge SE20 . . . . .206 B6
Ashley Ave SM4. . . . . .201 C4
Ashley Cres
Clapham SW11 . . . . .137 A2
Wood Green N22 . . . . .32 C5
Ashley Ct St Hampstead NW3 . .69 D1
Hendon NW4 . . . . .28 C1
19 Kingsland EN5. . . . . . .73 C3
New Barnet EN5. . . . . .14 A6
Northolt UB5 . . . . .85 A6
Stanmore HA7 . . . . .25 B1
Yiewsley UB7 . . . . .104 A5

Ashley Dr
Borehamwood WD6 11 B6
Hounslow TW7 130 C6
Twickenham TW2 151 D3
Ashley Gdns
Edmonton N13 33 A6
Orpington BR6 227 C3
Richmond TW10 153 D2
Wembley HA9 66 A6
Ashley Ho BR5 190 A1
Ashley La Croydon CR0 220 D4
Edgware NW7 28 D3
Hendon NW4 28 C1
Ashley Park Ave KT12 193 D1
Ashley Park Cres KT12 194 A1
Ashley Pl
Walton-on-T KT12 194 A1
Westminster SW1 115 C3 259 A5
Ashley Prim Sch KT12 194 A1
Ashley Rd Chingford E4 35 C4
Enfield EN3 6 C3
Hampton TW12 173 C2
Hornsey N19 50 A2
Richmond TW9 132 A2
Thames Ditton KT7 196 D3
Thornton Heath CR7 204 B5
Tottenham Hale N17 52 A6
Upton E7 77 C1
Walton-on-T KT12 194 A1
Wimbledon SW19 179 D4
Ashleys Alley N15 51 A5
Ashley Wlk NW7 28 D3
Ashling Ho 2 N17 33 D1
Ashling Rd CR0 206 A1
Ashlin Rd E15 76 B4
Ash Lo 2 Ashford TW16 171 D3
Fulham SW6 134 D4
Ashlone Rd SW15 134 D2
Ashlyns Way KT9 213 D2
Ashmead 4 N14 15 C6
Ashmead Bsns Ctr 2 E16 98 B3
Ashmead Gate BR1 187 C2
Ashmead Ho E9 75 A3
Ashmead Mews 1 SE8 141 C3
Ashmead Prim Sch SE8 141 C3
Ashmead Rd
East Bedfont TW14 150 A3
St Johns SE8 141 C3
Ashmere Ave BR3 186 B1
Ashmere Cl SM3 216 D3
Ashmere Gr 11 SW2, SW4 138 A1
Ashmere Ho 10 SW2 138 A1
Ashmill Ct CR0 205 A3
Ashmill St NW8 92 C2 237 A4
Ashmole Prim Sch SW8 138 B6 270 D5
Ashmole Sch N14 15 C3
Ashmole St SW8 138 B6 270 D5
Ashmoor Lo NW7 27 B4
Ashmore NW1 71 D1
Ashmore Cl SE15 139 D5
Ashmore Ct Catford SE6 164 C3
Colney Hatch N11 30 D4
Heston TW5 129 C6
Ashmore Gr DA16 145 C2
Ashmore Ho W14 254 B5
Ashmore Rd W9 91 B4
Ashmount Prim Sch N19 49 C2
Ashmount Rd
Crouch End N19 49 D2
South Tottenham N15 51 D4
Ashmount Terr W5 109 D2
Ashneal Gdns HA1 64 B5
Ashness Gdns UB6 65 B2
Ashness Rd SW11 158 D6
Ashpark Ho 4 E14 97 B1
Ash Rd Cheam SM3 201 B1
Croydon CR0 223 C6
Littleton TW17 192 C5
Orpington BR6 227 D1
Plashet E15 76 D3
Ashridge Cl HA3 43 C3
Ashridge Cres SE18 145 A5
Ashridge Ct Southall UB1 108 A6
Southgate N14 15 C6
Ashridge Dr WD19 22 C5
Ashridge Gdns
Bowes Pk N13 32 A5
Pinner HA5 41 A5
Ashridge Ho DA14 189 D6
Ashridge Way
Ashford TW16 172 A4
Merton SM4 201 B5
Ash Row BR2 210 C3
Ashtead Ct 15 SW19 156 D3
Ashtead Rd E5 52 A2
Ashton Cl SM1 217 C4
Ashton Ct
1 Beckenham BR3 185 B2
Chingford E4 20 C1
Harrow HA1 64 D5
Ashton Gdns
Dagenham RM6 59 A3
Hounslow TW4 129 B1
Ashton Ho
13 Kennington SW9 138 C5
Ashton Ho *continued*
Roehampton SW15 156 B4
Ashton House Sch TW7 130 B4
Ashton Rd E15 76 B3
Ashton St E14 120 A6
Ashtree Ave CR4 180 B1
Ashtree Cl BR6 226 D4
Ash Tree Cl Croydon CR0 207 A3
1 Surbiton KT6 198 A1
Ashtree Ct TW15 170 D5
Ash Tree Dell NW9 45 B4
Ash Tree Villas CR0 204 B3
Ash Tree Way CR0 207 A3
Ashurst Cl SE20 184 B2
Ashurst Dr Ilford IG2, IG6 57 A4
Littleton TW17 192 A4
Ashurst Lo 4 N5 72 D3
Ashurst Rd
Cockfosters EN4 14 D6
Colney Hatch N12 30 C5
Ashurst Wlk CR0 222 B6
Ashvale Rd SW17 180 D5
Ashview Cl TW15 170 A5
Ashview Gdns TW15 170 A5
Ashville Rd E11 76 B6
Ashwater Rd SE12 165 A3
Ashway Ctr 5 KT2 176 A2
Ashwell Cl 8 E6 100 A1
Ashwell Ct TW15 148 A2
Ashwin St E8 73 D2
Ash Wlk HA0 65 C4
Ashwood Ave UB8 82 C1
Ashwood Ct HA9 66 B4
Ashwood Gdns
Hayes UB3 105 D2
New Addington CR0 224 A2
Ashwood Ho 10 NW4 46 C5
Ashwood Lo
9 New Barnet EN5 13 D6
Southgate N21 16 B5
Ashwood Pk 6 SM2 217 C1
Ashwood Rd E4 20 B1
Ashworth Cl SE5 139 B3
Ashworth Mans W9 91 D4
Ashworth Rd W9 91 D4
Aske Ho 2 N1 95 C4
Asker Ho N7 72 A4
Askern Cl DA6 146 D1
Aske St N1 95 C4
Askew Cres W12 112 A4
Askew Mans 14 W12 112 A4
Askew Rd W12 112 A4
Askham Ct W12 112 A5
Askham Lo 5 SE12 165 A4
Askham Rd W12 112 A5
Askill Dr SW15 157 A6
Asland Rd E15 98 B6
Aslett St SW18 158 A4
Asmara Rd NW2 69 A3
Asmuns Hill NW11 47 C4
Asmuns Pl NW11 47 B4
Asolando Dr SE17 262 B3
Aspect Ho 7 E14 120 A4
Aspects SM1 217 D3
Aspen Cl Ealing W5 110 B4
13 Upper Holloway N19 71 C6
Yiewsley UB7 104 B5
Aspen Copse BR1 188 B1
Aspen Ct 10 Acton W3 89 A1
12 Hackney E8 74 A3
Redbridge IG5 56 A6
Richmond TW9 132 C5
Aspen Dr HA0 65 A5
Aspen Gdns
Ashford TW15 171 A5
2 Hammersmith W6 112 B1
Mitcham CR4 203 A4
Aspen Gn DA18 125 B3
Aspen Gr HA5 39 D6
Aspen Ho
8 Deptford SE15 140 C6
4 Maitland Pk NW3 70 D2
Richmond TW9 132 C5
2 Sidcup DA15 168 A1
Southgate N21 16 B6
Aspen La UB5 85 A4
Aspenlea Rd W6 134 D6
Aspen Lo 1 SW19 179 B4
Aspen Way
Canary Wharf E14 120 A6
Feltham TW13 150 B1
Aspern Gr NW3 70 C3
Aspinall Ho SW12 160 A3
Aspinall Rd SE4 140 D2
Aspinden Rd SE16 118 B2
Aspire Bld 10 SW15 157 B6
Aspley Rd SW18 157 D6
Asplins Rd N17 34 B2
Asprey Ho CR4 202 C6
Asprey Mews BR3 207 B4
Asquith Cl RM8 58 C1
Assam SE1 253 D3
Assam St E1 96 A1
Assata Mews N1 72 D2
Assembly Pas E1 96 C2
Assembly Wlk SM5 202 C2
Assheton-Bennett Ho 15 KT6 198 A4
Ass House La HA3 23 D6
Assisi Ct
Upper Tooting SW12 158 D3
Wembley HA0 64 D5
Assunah Sch 8 N17 33 D1
Astall Cl HA3 24 C2
Astbury Bsns Pk 5 SE15 140 C4
Astbury Ho SE11 261 A5
Astbury Rd SE15 140 C4
Astell St SW3 114 C1 257 B2
Aster Ct 3 HA8 27 A6
Aster Ho 3 SE13 142 A3
Aste St E14 120 A4
Astey's Row 1 N1 73 A1
Asthall Gdns IG6 57 A5
Astins Ho 4 E17 53 D5
Astleham Rd TW17 192 A6
Astleham Way TW17 192 A6
Astle St SW11 137 A3
Astley Ave NW2 68 C3
Astley Ho Fulham SE1 263 D2
39 Paddington W2 91 C2
8 West Norwood SE27 183 A6
Aston Ave HA3 43 C2
Aston Cl Bushey WD23 8 A5
Sidcup DA14 168 A1
Aston Ct
Stoke Newington N4 73 A6
3 Wimbledon SW19 178 C3
10 Woodford IG8 37 A4
Aston Gn TW5 128 C3
Aston Ho Notting Hill W11 244 D6
South Lambeth SW8 269 C1
Aston House Sch W5 87 D1
Aston Mews RM6 58 C2
Aston Pl SW16 182 D4
Aston Rd Claygate KT10 212 C3
Ealing W5 87 D1
Merton SW20 178 C1
Aston St E14 97 A2
Astonville St SW18 157 C3
Astor Ave RM7 59 D3
Astor Cl KT2 176 D4
Astor Ct Colney Hatch N12 30 C4
Newham E16 99 C1
Walham Green SW6 266 A3
Astoria Mans 18 SW16 160 A1
Astoria Par SW16 160 A1
Astoria Wlk SW9 138 C2
Astra Ct W13 109 A5
Astra Ho 4 Bow E3 97 B4
Hornsey N4 50 B2
Astrid Ho TW13 150 C2
Astrop Mews W6 112 C3
Astrop Terr W6 112 C4
Astwood Mews SW7 256 A4
Asylum Rd SE15 140 B5
Atalanta St SW6 134 D5 264 A3
Atbara Ct TW11 175 B4
Atbara Rd TW11 175 B4
Atcham Rd TW3 130 A1
Atcost Rd IG11 102 A2
Atheldene Rd SW18 158 A3
Athelney Prim Sch SE6 163 C1
Athelney St SE6 163 C1
Athelstan Ct E6 100 C5
Athelstane Gr E3 97 B5
Athelstane Mews N4 50 C1
Athelstan Gdns 8 NW6 69 A1
Athelstan Ho
Hackney Wick E9 75 B3
Kingston u T KT1 198 B5
Stoke Newington N16 73 C4
Athelstan House Sch 9 TW12 173 C2
Athelstan Rd KT1 198 B5
Athelstan Way BR5 190 A2
Athelstone Rd HA3 24 B1
Athena Cl Harrow HA2 64 C6
Kingston u T KT1 198 B6
Athena Ct
Bermondsey SE1 253 A1
St John's Wood NW8 229 C4
Athenaeum Pl 3 N10 49 B6
Athenaeum Rd N20 14 B3
Athenia Ho 7 E14 98 B1
Athenlay Rd SE15 162 D6
Athenoeum Ct N5 73 A4
Athens Gdns W9 91 C3
Atherden Rd E5 74 C4
Atherfield Ct SW18 157 D5
Atherfold Rd SW9 138 A2
Atherley Way TW4 151 B4
Atherstone Ct W2 91 D2
Atherstone Mews SW7 114 A2 256 B4
Atherton Dr SW19 178 D6
Atherton Ho CR2 221 C2
Atherton Hts HA0 65 C2
Atherton L Ctr E15 76 D2
Atherton Mews E7 77 A2
Atherton Pl Harrow HA2 42 B6
Southall UB1 107 C6
Atherton Rd
Barnes SW13 134 A5
Stratford E7 76 D2
Atherton St SW11 136 C3
Athlone KT10 212 C2
Athlone Cl 24 E5 74 B3
Athlone Ct Lewisham SE6 164 B4
Athlone Ct *continued*
Upper Walthamstow E17 54 B6
Athlone Ho
16 Camden Town NW5 71 A2
9 Stepney E1 96 C1
Athlone Rd SW2 160 C4
Athlone St NW5 71 A2
Athlon Ind Est HA0 87 D5
Athlon Rd HA0 87 D5
Athol Cl HA5 22 B2
Athol Ct 13 N4 72 B6
Athole Gdns EN1 17 C6
Athole Terr CR7 183 A1
Athol Gdns HA5 22 B2
Atholl Ho W9 229 A1
Atholl Rd IG3 58 A2
Athol Sq E14 98 A1
Athol Way UB10 82 C4
Atkins Ct 13 Old Ford E3 97 B6
Woolwich SE7 122 A2
Atkins Dr BR4 224 B6
Atkins Lo W8 245 A2
Atkinson Ct 3 E10 53 D2
Atkinson Ho
11 Battersea SW11 137 A3
Battersea SW11 268 A1
15 Hackney E2 96 A5
Newham E13 98 D3
Walworth SE17 262 D3
Atkinson Rd E16 99 C2
Atkinson's Almhouses HA8 26 B5
Atkins Rd
Streatham SW4, SW12 159 D4
Walthamstow E10 53 D3
Atlanta Bldg 8 SE13 141 D4
Atlanta Ct CR7 205 A6
Atlantic Ct 19 E14 120 B6
Atlantic Ho
5 Putney SW15 157 B6
4 Tower Hamlets E1 97 A2
Atlantic Rd SW2, SW9, SE24 138 C1
Atlantis Ave E16 123 A6
Atlantis Cl IG11 102 B4
Atlas Bsns Ctr NW2 68 B6
Atlas Cres HA8 10 D2
Atlas Gdns SE7 121 C2
Atlas Mews Dalston E8 73 D2
Islington N7 72 B2
Atlas Rd Friern Barnet N11 31 A4
Newham E13 99 A5
North Acton NW10 89 C4
Wembley HA9 67 A4
Atlip Rd HA0 88 A6
Atney Rd SW15 135 A1
Atria Rd HA6 22 A5
Atrium 9 IG9 21 D2
Atterbury Rd N4 50 D3
Atterbury St SW1 116 A2 260 A3
Attewood Ave NW10 67 C5
Attewood Rd UB5 63 A2
Attfield Cl N20 14 B2
Attilburgh Ho SE1 263 C6
Attleborough Ct 4 SE21 162 B2
Attle Cl UB10 82 C5
Attlee Cl Hayes UB4 84 B4
Thornton Heath CR7 205 A4
Attlee Ct UB4 84 B4
Attlee Ho E1 243 D3
Attlee Rd Hayes UB4 84 B4
Thamesmead SE28 124 B6
Attlee Terr 3 E17 53 D5
Attneave St WC1 234 A1
Atwater Cl SW2 160 C3
Atwell Pl KT7 197 A1
Atwell Rd 6 SE15 140 A3
Atwood Ave TW9 132 C3
Atwood Ho SE21 161 C1
Atwood Rd W6 112 B2
Aubert Ct N5 72 D4
Aubert Pk N5 72 D4
Aubert Rd N5 72 D4
Aubrey Beardsley Ho SW1 259 B3
Aubrey Mans NW1 237 A4
Aubrey Moore Point E15 98 A5
Aubrey Pl NW8 229 A3
Aubrey Rd Hornsey N8 50 A4
Kensington W14 113 B5 244 D3
Walthamstow E17 53 D6
Aubrey Wlk W14 113 B5 244 D3
Auburn Cl SE14 141 A5
Aubyn Hill SE27 183 B6
Aubyn Sq SW15 156 A6
Auckland Cl Enfield EN1 6 B6
South Norwood SE19 183 D2
Auckland Ct UB4 84 C3
Auckland Gdns SE19 183 D2
Auckland Hill SE27 183 A6
Auckland Ho 11 W12 112 B6
Auckland Rd
Clapham SW11 136 C1
Ilford IG1 57 A2
Kingston u T KT1 198 B5
Leyton E10 75 D5
South Norwood SE19 183 D2
Auckland Rise SE19 183 C2
Auckland St SE11 260 C1
Audax 29 NW9 27 D1
Auden Dr WD6 10 C6
Auden Pl NW1 231 A6
Audley Cl
8 Clapham SW11 137 A2
Muswell Hill N10 31 B3
Audley Ct Ealing W5 88 C2
Mayfair W1 248 C4
Northolt UB5 84 C4
Pinner Green HA5 22 C1
Snaresbrook E11, E18 54 D5
Surbiton KT5 198 B3
Twickenham TW2 152 B1
Audley Dr 3 E16 121 B5
Audley Gdns IG3 79 D6
Audley Ho N8 50 A5
Audley Pl SM2 217 D1
Audley Rd Ealing W5 88 B2
Enfield EN2 4 D3
Hendon NW4 46 B3
Richmond TW10 154 B6
Audley Sq W1 248 B4
Audley St W1 248 B4
Audrey Cl BR3 207 D3
Audrey Gdns HA0 65 B6
Audrey Ho EC1 241 B3
Audrey Rd IG1 78 D5
Audrey St E2 96 A5
Audric Cl KT2 176 C2
Augurs La 3 E13 99 B4
Augusta Cl KT8 195 B6
Augusta Ct NW4 28 C1
Augusta Rd TW2 152 A2
Augusta St E14 97 D1
Augustine Ho
Broadgate EC2 242 D2
New Cross SE4 141 B4
Augustine Rd
Hammersmith W14 112 D3
Harrow Weald HA3 24 A2
Augustines Ct E9 74 C3
Augustus Cl
Brentford TW8 131 D5
Hammersmith W12 112 B3
Stanmore HA7 9 D1
Augustus Ct
Feltham TW13 173 B6
Isleworth TW3 130 A1
8 Putney SW19 157 A3
South Norwood SE19 183 C3
Streatham SW16 159 D2
Augustus Ho NW1 232 A2
Augustus Rd
33 Putney SW19 156 D3
Putney SW19 157 A3
Augustus St NW1 93 B4 231 D2
Aulay Lawrence Ct N9 18 B1
Aultone Way
Carshalton SM5 218 D5
Sutton SM1 218 A6
Aultone Yd Ind Est SM5 218 D5
Aulton Pl SE11 261 B1
Aura Ho 3 TW9 132 D4
Aurelia Gdns CR0 204 B3
Aurelia Rd CR0 204 B3
Auriga Mews N1 73 B3
Auriol Cl KT4 215 C5
Auriol Dr Greenford UB6 64 B1
Hillingdon UB10 60 D2
Auriol Jun Sch KT19 215 D4
Auriol Mans W14 254 A3
Auriol Park Rd KT4 215 C5
Auriol Rd W14 113 A2 254 A3
Aurora Bldg 4 E14 120 A5
Aurora Ct IG8 36 D6
Aurora Ho E14 97 D1
Austell Gdns NW7 11 C1
Austell Hts NW7 11 C1
Austen Cl SE28 124 B5
Austen Ho 5 NW6 91 C4
Austen Rd Erith DA8 147 D5
Harrow HA2 63 D6
Austin Ave BR1, BR2 210 A4
Austin Cl Forest Hill SE23 163 B4
Twickenham TW1 153 C6
Austin Ct 9 Enfield EN1 17 C6
9 Newham E6 99 C6
Austin Friars EC2 242 D2
Austin Friars Ho EC2 242 D2
Austin Friars Sq EC2 242 D2
Austin Ho
6 Brixton SW2 160 B6
19 Kingston u T KT6 198 A4
1 New Cross SE14 141 B5
Austin Rd
Battersea SW11 137 A4 268 A1
Hayes UB3 105 D4
Austins Ct SE15 140 A2
Austins La UB10 61 A5
Austin St E2 95 D4
Austral Cl DA15 167 D1
Australia Rd W12 112 B6
Austral St SE11 116 D2 261 C4
Austyn Gdns KT5 198 D1
Autumn Cl Enfield EN1 6 A4
Wimbledon SW19 180 A4
Autumn Gr BR1 187 B4
Autumn Lo CR2 221 C4
Autumn Rise 9 W4 111 B1

Autumn St E3 . . . . .97 C6
Avalon BR7 . . . . .188 C1
Avalon Cl Ealing W13 . . . .87 A2
  Enfield EN2 . . . . .4 C3
  Merton SW20 . . . . .179 A1
Avalon Ct CR0 . . . . .205 D2
Avalon Ho Ealing W13 . . . .87 A3
  Parsons Green
  SW6 . . . . .135 D4 265 C2
Avante Ct KT1 . . . . .197 D6
Avard Gdns BR6 . . . . . . .227 A4
Avarn Rd SW17 . . . . . . .180 D4
Avebury Ct N1 . . . . .235 C5
Avebury Rd
  Leytonstone E11 . . . . .54 B1
  Merton SW19 . . . . .179 B2
  Orpington BR6 . . . . .227 B5
Avebury St N1 . . . . .235 C5
Aveley Ct 15 E5 . . . . .74 B6
Aveley Mans 1 IG11 . . . .78 D1
Aveline St SE11 . . . .116 C1 261 A1
Aveling Ho 12 N19 . . . . . .71 C5
Aveling Park Rd E17 . . . . .35 C1
Aveling Park Sch E17 . . . .35 C1
Ave Maria La EC4 . . . . . .241 D1
Avenell Mans N5 . . . . .72 D4
Avenell Rd N5 . . . . .72 D5
Avenfield Ho W1 . . . . . . .247 D6
Avening Rd SW18 . . . . . .157 C4
Avening Terr SW18 . . . . .157 C4
Avenons Rd E13 . . . . .99 A3
Avenue Cl Cranford TW5 . .128 B4
  Primrose Hill NW8 . .92 C6 230 B5
  Southgate N14 . . . . .15 C5
Avenue Cres
  Cranford TW5 . . . . .128 B5
  South Acton W3 . . . . . . .110 D4
Avenue Ct Chelsea SW3 . .257 C3
  Cricklewood NW2 . . . . . . .69 A5
  Ealing W5 . . . . .87 D2
  Penge SE20 . . . . .184 C2
  Redbridge IG5 . . . . .56 A6
  Southgate N14 . . . . .15 C5
Avenue Elmers KT6 . . . . .198 A4
Avenue Gate IG10 . . . . . . .21 C5
Avenue Gdns
  Cranford TW5 . . . . .128 B5
  Mortlake SW14 . . . . . . .133 C2
  South Acton W3 . . . . . . .110 D4
  South Norwood SE25 . . . .184 A1
  Teddington TW11 . . . . . .174 D4
Avenue Hall N6 . . . . .49 D3
Avenue Ho
  St John's Wood NW8 . . . .230 A1
  Upper Clapton N16 . . . . . .74 A6
  Willesden Green NW10 . . . .90 B5
Avenue House Sch 2
  W13 . . . . .87 B1
Avenue Ind Est E4 . . . . . . .35 B4
Avenue Lo 1 NW8 . . . . . . .70 B1
Avenue Mans Barnet EN5 . . .1 A2
  Clapham SW11 . . . . . . .137 A1
  Hampstead NW3 . . . . .69 D3
  Muswell Hill N10 . . . . . . .31 C1
  Willesden NW2 . . . . .68 B2
Avenue Mews N10 . . . . . . .49 B6
Avenue Par Southgate N21 . .17 B4
  Sunbury TW16 . . . . .194 B6
Avenue Park Rd SE21,
  SE27 . . . . .160 D2
Avenue Prim Sch E12 . . . . .78 A3
Avenue Rd
  Bexley DA6, DA7 . . . . . .147 A2
  Brentford TW8 . . . . .109 C1
  Crouch End N6 . . . . .49 D2
  Feltham TW13 . . . . .149 D1
  Forest Gate E7 . . . . .77 B4
  Hampton TW12 . . . . . . .173 D2
  Harlesden NW10 . . . . .89 D5
  Hounslow TW7 . . . . .130 D4
  Ilford RM6 . . . . .58 C2
  Kingston u T KT1 . . . . . .198 A6
  Mitcham SW16 . . . . .181 D1
  New Malden KT3 . . . . . .199 C5
  North Finchley N12 . . . . . .30 A6
  Penge BR3, SE20 . . . . . .184 D2
  Pinner HA5 . . . . .41 A6
  Primrose Hill NW8 . .92 C6 230 A6
  South Acton W3 . . . . . . .110 D4
  Southall UB1 . . . . .107 B5
  Southgate N14 . . . . .15 C5
  South Norwood SE25 . . . .184 A1
  Teddington TW11 . . . . . .175 A4
  Tottenham N15 . . . . .51 B4
  Wallington SM6 . . . . . . .219 C1
  Wimbledon SW6 . . . . . . .178 B1
  Woodford IG8 . . . . .37 C4
Avenue Road Sta BR3 . . . .184 D1
Avenue S KT5 . . . . .198 C2
Avenue Terr Ilford IG2 . . . . .57 C3
  Kingston u T KT3 . . . . . .199 A6
Avenue The Barnet EN5 . . . .1 A1
  Beckenham BR3 . . . . . . .186 A2
  Bedford Pk W4 . . . . .111 C3
  Bromley BR1 . . . . .209 D6
  Brondesbury Pk NW6 . . . . .91 A6
  8 Buckhurst Hill IG9 . . . . .21 C2
  Chingford E4 . . . . .36 B5
  Clapham SW4 . . . . .159 A6
  Claygate KT10 . . . . .212 C3

Avenue The continued
  Cranford TW5 . . . . .128 A4
  3 Ealing W13 . . . . .87 B1
  Finchley N3 . . . . .29 C1
  Friern Barnet N11 . . . . . . .31 B5
  Greenwich SE10 . . . . . . .142 B5
  Hampton TW12 . . . . . . .173 B4
  Harrow HA3 . . . . .24 D2
  Hatch End HA5 . . . . .23 B4
  Hornsey N8 . . . . .50 C6
  Hounslow TW3 . . . . .151 D6
  Isleworth TW1 . . . . .153 B6
  Keston Mark BR2 . . . . . .225 D5
  Loughton IG10 . . . . .21 D5
  Muswell Hill N10 . . . . . . .31 C1
  4 New Malden KT4 . . . . .200 A1
  Orpington BR6 . . . . .227 D6
  Pinner HA5 . . . . .41 B3
  Richmond TW9 . . . . .132 B3
  Sidcup DA5 . . . . .168 D4
  South Croydon CR0 . . . . .221 C5
  Stoneleigh KT17, SM3 . . .216 C1
  St Paul's Cray BR5 . . . . . .190 B3
  Sunbury TW16 . . . . .172 B1
  Surbiton KT5 . . . . .198 B3
  Tottenham N17 . . . . .33 C1
  Uxbridge UB10 . . . . .60 D5
  Wallington SM5 . . . . . . .219 A1
  Wandsworth SW18, SW12 .158 C4
  Wanstead E11 . . . . .55 B4
  Wembley HA9 . . . . .44 B1
  West Wickham BR4 . . . . .208 C2
  Worcester Pk KT4 . . . . . .215 D6
Averil Gr SW16 . . . . .182 D4
Averill St W6 . . . . .134 D6
Avern Gdns KT8 . . . . . . .195 D5
Avern Rd KT8 . . . . .195 D5
Avery Ct 1 SE20 . . . . . . .184 B3
Avery Farm Row SW1 . . . .258 C3
Avery Gdns IG2 . . . . .56 B4
AVERY HILL 167 B5
Avery Hill Coll (Mile End
  Annexe) 8 . . . . .97 B3
Avery Hill Rd SE9 . . . . . .167 B3
Avery Row W1 . . . . .115 B6 248 D6
Aviary Ct E16 . . . . .98 D2
Aviemore Cl BR3 . . . . . . .207 B4
Aviemore Way BR3 . . . . .207 A4
Avignon Rd SE4 . . . . .140 D2
Avingdor Ct 10 W3 . . . . . .111 A5
Avington Ct SE1 . . . . . . .263 B3
Avington Gr SE20 . . . . . .184 C3
Avion Cres NW7, NW9 . . . .28 A2
Avis Sq E1 . . . . .96 D1
Avoca Rd SW17 . . . . .181 A6
Avocet Cl SE1 . . . . .118 A1
Avocet Mews SE28 . . . . .123 B3
Avon Cl Hayes UB4 . . . . . .84 C3
  Sutton SM1 . . . . .218 A4
  Worcester Pk KT4 . . . . . .216 A6
Avon Ct 1 Acton W3 . . . . .89 A1
  11 Chingford E4 . . . . .20 A3
  Greenford UB6 . . . . .85 D3
  North Finchley N12 . . . . . .29 D5
  12 Putney SW15 . . . . . . .157 A6
  Woodford E18 . . . . .37 B2
Avondale N12 . . . . .29 D5
Avondale Ave Barnet EN4 . .14 D3
  Finchley N12 . . . . .29 D5
  Hinchley Wood KT10 . . . .213 A5
  Neasden NW2 . . . . .67 C5
  New Malden KT4 . . . . . . .199 D1
Avondale Cres Enfield EN3 . . .7 A2
  Redbridge IG4 . . . . .55 D4
Avondale Ct
  Canning Town E16 . . . . . . .98 C2
  Leytonstone E11 . . . . .54 C1
  9 Sutton SM2 . . . . .218 A1
  Woodford E18 . . . . .37 B2
Avondale Dr UB3 . . . . . . .106 B5
Avondale Gdns TW4 . . . . .151 B6
Avondale Ho
  11 Bermondsey SE1 . . . . .118 A1
  6 Mortlake SW14 . . . . . .133 B2
Avondale Mans SW6 . . . .264 C2
Avondale Park Gdns
  W11 . . . . .113 A6 244 A5
Avondale Park Prim Sch
  W11 . . . . .113 A6 244 A6
Avondale Park Rd
  W11 . . . . .113 A6 244 A6
Avondale Pavement 7
  SE1 . . . . .118 A1
Avondale Rd
  Bexley DA16 . . . . .146 C3
  Bromley BR1 . . . . .186 D4
  Chislehurst SE9 . . . . . . .166 A2
  Finchley N3 . . . . .30 A2
  Harringay N15 . . . . .50 D4
  Harrow HA3 . . . . .42 D6
  Mortlake SW14 . . . . . . .133 B2
  Newham E16 . . . . .98 C2
  South Croydon CR2 . . . . .221 A4
  Southgate N13 . . . . .16 C2
  Walthamstow E17 . . . . . . .53 C2
  Wimbledon SW19 . . . . . .179 D5
Avondale Rise SE15 . . . . .139 D2
Avondale Sq SE1 . . . . . . .118 A1
Avonfield Ct E17 . . . . .54 B6
Avon Ho 2 Islington N1 . . . .72 C1

Avon Ho continued
  7 Kingston u T KT2 . . . . .175 D2
  Northolt UB5 . . . . .85 A3
  Southgate N21 . . . . .16 B6
  14 Stoke Newington N16 . . .73 B4
  West Kensington W14 . . . .254 D3
Avon House Sch IG8 . . . . . .37 A6
Avonhurst Ho NW6 . . . . . . .69 A1
Avonley Rd SE14 . . . . . . .140 C5
Avon Mews HA5 . . . . .23 B2
Avonmore Gdns W14 . . . .254 D3
Avonmore Pl W14 . . . . . .254 D3
Avonmore Prim Sch
  W14 . . . . .113 A2 254 B4
Avonmore Rd
  W14 . . . . .113 B2 254 C4
Avonmouth St SE1 . . . . . .262 A6
Avon Path CR0 . . . . .221 A1
Avon Pl SE1 . . . . .252 B1
Avon Rd Ashford TW16 . . .171 D3
  Greenford UB6 . . . . .85 D3
  St Johns SE4 . . . . .141 C2
  Upper Walthamstow E17 . . .54 B6
Avonstone Cl BR6 . . . . . .227 A5
Avon Way E18 . . . . .55 A6
Avonwick Rd TW3 . . . . . .129 D3
Avril Way E4 . . . . .36 A5
Avriol Ho W12 . . . . .112 B5
Avro Ct E9 . . . . .75 A3
Avro Way SM6 . . . . .220 A1
Awlfield Ave N17 . . . . . . .33 B2
Awliscombe Rd DA16 . . . .145 D3
Axeholm Ave HA8 . . . . . . .26 D2
Axe St IG11 . . . . .101 A6
Axford Ho SW2 . . . . .160 D3
Axiom Apartments 5
  BR2 . . . . .209 B5
Axis Ct
  7 Bermondsey SE16 . . . . .118 A4
  Greenwich SE10 . . . . . . .142 C6
Axminster Cres DA16 . . . .146 C4
Axminster Rd N7 . . . . .72 B5
Axon Pl 5 IG1 . . . . .79 A6
Aybrook St W1 . . . .93 A2 238 A3
Aycliffe Cl BR1 . . . . .210 B5
Aycliffe Rd W12 . . . . .112 A5
Ayerst Ct 1 E10 . . . . .54 A2
Aylands Cl HA9 . . . . .66 A6
Aylesbury Cl E7 . . . . .76 D2
Aylesbury Ct SM1 . . . . . .218 A5
Aylesbury Ho 19 SE15 . . . .140 A6
Aylesbury Rd
  Bromley BR2 . . . . .209 A6
  Walworth SE17 . . . . 117 B1 262 D1
Aylesbury St
  Clerkenwell EC1 . . . . .94 D3 241 C5
  Neasden NW10 . . . . .67 B5
Ayles Ct UB4 . . . . .84 B4
Aylesford Ave BR3 . . . . . .207 A4
Aylesford Ho SE1 . . . . . . .252 D1
Aylesford St
  SW1 . . . . .115 D1 259 C1
Aylesham Cl NW7 . . . . .28 A3
Aylesham Rd BR6 . . . . . . .211 D2
Aylesham Sh Ctr SE15 . . .140 A4
Ayles Rd UB4 . . . . .84 B4
Aylestone Ave NW6 . . . . . .90 D6
Aylestone Ct 10 HA0 . . . . . .66 A2
Aylett Rd Croydon SE25 . . .206 B5
  Isleworth TW7 . . . . .130 C3
Ayley Croft EN1 . . . . .18 A6
Ayliffe Cl HA7 . . . . .25 A6
Aylmer Cl HA7 . . . . .25 A6
Aylmer Ct N2 . . . . .48 D4
Aylmer Dr HA7 . . . . .25 A6
Aylmer Ho SE10 . . . . . . .120 B1
Aylmer Par N2 . . . . .48 D4
Aylmer Rd Acton W12 . . . .111 D4
  Dagenham RM8 . . . . .81 A5
  East Finchley N2 . . . . .48 C4
  Leytonstone E11 . . . . .54 D1
Aylofe Rd RM9 . . . . .81 B2
Aylsham Dr UB10 . . . . . . .61 A6
Ayliton Est 28 SE16 . . . . .118 C4
Aylward Fst & Mid Schs
  HA7 . . . . .25 D5
Aylward Rd
  Forest Hill SE23 . . . . . . .162 D2
  Merton SW20 . . . . .201 B6
Aylwards Rise HA7 . . . . . . .25 A6
Aylward St E1 . . . . .96 D1
Aylwin Est SE1 . . . . .263 B6
Aynhoe Mans W14 . . . . . .112 D2
Aynhoe Rd W14 . . . . .112 D3
Ayr Ct W3 . . . . .88 C2
Ayres Cl E13 . . . . .99 A4
Ayres Cres NW10 . . . . .67 B1
Ayres St SE1 . . . . .117 A4 252 B2
Ayrsome Rd N16 . . . . .73 C5
Ayrton Gould Ho 9 E2 . . . .96 D4
Ayrton Ho HA9 . . . . .65 D6
Ayrton Rd SW7 . . . . 114 B3 256 C6
Aysgarth Ct SM1 . . . . . . .217 D5
Aysgarth Rd SE21 . . . . . .161 C4
Ayshford Ho E1 . . . . .96 B4
Ayston Ho 19 SE8 . . . . . .118 D2
Aytoun Ct 17 SW9 . . . . . .138 B3
Aytoun Pl SW9 . . . . .138 B3
Aytoun Rd SW9 . . . . .138 B3
Azalea Cl Ealing W7 . . . . .108 D5

Azalea Cl continued
  Ilford IG1 . . . . .78 D3
Azalea Ct Chingford IG8 . . .36 C3
  Ealing W7 . . . . .108 D5
Azalea Ho
  2 Feltham TW13 . . . . . . .150 B3
  New Cross SE14 . . . . . . .141 B5
Azalea Wlk HA5 . . . . .40 B3
Azania Mews NW5 . . . . . .71 B2
Azenby Rd SE15 . . . . . . .139 D3
Azhar Acad E7 . . . . .77 A2
Azof St SE10 . . . . .120 C2
Azov Ho 10 E1 . . . . .97 A3
Aztec Ct 3 N16 . . . . .73 C2
Azure Appartments HA3 . .24 B3
Azure Ct TW13 . . . . .149 D1
Azure Ho 28 E2 . . . . .96 A4

B

Baalbec Rd N5 . . . . .72 D3
Babbacombe Cl IG4 . . . . . .56 A5
Babbacombe Gdns IG4 . . . .56 A5
Babbacombe Rd BR1 . . . .187 A2
Baber Bridge Par TW14 . . .150 C5
Baber Dr TW14 . . . . .150 C5
Babington Ct
  Bloomsbury WC1 . . . . . . .240 B4
  Streatham SW16 . . . . . . .181 D5
Babington Ho SE1 . . . . . .252 B2
Babington House Sch
  BR7 . . . . .188 B4
Babington Rd
  Dagenham RM8 . . . . .80 C4
  Hendon NW4 . . . . .46 B5
  Streatham SW16 . . . . . . .181 D5
Babington Rise HA9 . . . . . .66 C2
Babmaes St SW1 . . . . . . .249 C5
Bacchus Wlk 12 N1 . . . . . .95 C5
Bache's St N1 . . . . .95 B4 235 D1
Back Church La E1 . . . . . . .96 A1
Back Hill EC1 . . . . .241 B5
Backhouse Pl SE1 . . . . . .263 B3
Back La Brentford TW8 . . .131 D6
  Buckhurst Hill IG9 . . . . . .21 D2
  Burnt Oak HA8 . . . . .27 A2
  Dagenham RM6 . . . . .59 A2
  Hampstead NW3 . . . . .70 A4
  Hornsey N8 . . . . .50 A4
  Richmond TW10 . . . . . . .153 C2
  Sidcup DA5 . . . . .169 C4
Backley Gdns SE25 . . . . .206 A3
Back Rd Leytonstone E11 . . .54 C3
  Sidcup DA14 . . . . .190 A6
  Teddington TW11 . . . . . .174 C3
Bacon Gr SE1 . . . . 117 D3 263 C6
Bacon La Edgware HA8 . . . .26 C2
  Queensbury NW9 . . . . .44 D5
  Bacon's Coll SE16 . . . . . .119 A4
Bacon La N6 . . . . .49 A1
Bacon St E2 . . . . . .95 D3 243 D6
Bacon Terr RM8 . . . . .80 B3
Bacton St E2 . . . . .96 C4
Baddeley Cl 11 EN3 . . . . . . .7 C6
Baddeley Ho
  East Molesey KT8 . . . . . .195 C4
  Vauxhall SE11 . . . . .260 D2
Baddow Cl
  Dagenham RM10 . . . . . . .103 C6
  Woodford IG8 . . . . .37 D4
Baddow Wlk N1 . . . . .235 A6
Baden Cl N11 . . . . .31 D3
Baden Pl SE1 . . . . .252 C2
Baden Powell Cl
  Dagenham RM9 . . . . .103 A6
  Surbiton KT6 . . . . .214 B6
Baden Powell Ho 11
  DA17 . . . . .125 A6
Baden Powell Sch 8 E5 . . .74 B5
Baden Rd Hornsey N8 . . . . .49 D5
  Ilford IG1 . . . . .78 D3
Badger Cl Feltham TW13 . .150 B1
  Hounslow TW4 . . . . .128 C2
  Ilford IG2 . . . . .57 A2
Badger Ct Chingford E4 . . . .36 B6
  Dollis Hill NW2 . . . . .68 C5
Badgers Cl Ashford TW15 . .170 B5
  Enfield EN2 . . . . .4 D2
  Harrow HA1 . . . . .42 B3
  Hayes UB3 . . . . .105 C6
Badgers Copse
  Orpington BR6 . . . . .227 D6
  Worcester Pk KT4 . . . . . .215 D6
Badgers Croft Barnet N20 . .13 A3
  Chislehurst SE9 . . . . . . .166 C1
Badgers Hole CR0 . . . . . .222 D4
Badgers Wlk KT3 . . . . . . .177 C1
Badlis Rd E17 . . . . .53 C6
Badma Cl N9 . . . . .18 C1
Badminton Cl 9 N4 . . . . . . .51 A2
  Harrow HA1 . . . . .42 C5
  Northolt UB5 . . . . .63 C2
Badminton Ho SE22 . . . . .139 C1
Badminton Mews 9
  E16 . . . . .121 A5
Badminton Rd SW12 . . . . .159 A5

Badsworth Rd 3 SE5 . . . .139 A4
Bagley Cl UB7 . . . . .104 A4
Bagley's La SW6 . . 135 D4 265 D1
Bagleys Spring RM6 . . . . . .59 A5
Bagnigge Ho WC1 . . . . . . .234 A1
Bagshot Ho NW1 . . . . . . .231 D2
Bagshot Rd EN1 . . . . .17 D5
Bagshot St SE17 . . . 117 C1 263 B1
Baildon 27 E2 . . . . .96 C5
Baildon St SE8 . . . . .141 B5
Bailey Cl Chingford E4 . . . . .36 A6
  Wood Green N11 . . . . .31 D3
  Woolwich SE28 . . . . . . .123 C5
Bailey Cres KT9 . . . . .213 D1
Bailey Ct 4 Chingford E4 . . .36 B5
  9 Shepherd's Bush W12 . .112 A4
Bailey Ho Mitcham CR4 . . .202 C6
  11 Penge SE26 . . . . .184 B5
  Walham Green SW10 . . . .265 D4
Bailey Mews
  Brixton SW2 . . . . .160 C6
  Chiswick W4 . . . . .132 D6
Bailey Pl SE26 . . . . .184 C4
Bainbridge Rd RM9 . . . . . .81 B4
Bainbridge St WC1 . . . . . .239 D2
Baines Cl CR22 . . . . .221 B3
Bain Ho 23 SW9 . . . . . . .138 A3
Baird Ave UB1 . . . . .108 A6
Baird Cl Kingsbury NW9 . . .45 A3
  Walthamstow E10 . . . . . . .53 C1
Baird Gdns SE19 . . . . . . .183 C6
Baird Ho
  12 Belvedere DA17 . . . . .125 C3
  29 Shepherd's Bush W12 . .112 B6
Baird Rd EN1 . . . . .6 B1
Baird St EC1 . . . . .242 B6
Bairny Wood App IG8 . . . . .37 B4
Baizdon Rd SE3 . . . . .142 C3
Baker Beall Ct DA7 . . . . . .147 D2
Baker Ct E11 . . . . .76 B5
Baker Ho 12 Bromley E3 . . . .97 D4
  Ealing W7 . . . . .108 D5
Baker La CR4 . . . . .203 A6
Baker Pl KT19 . . . . .215 A2
Baker Rd Harlesden NW10 . .89 C5
  Kidbrooke SE18 . . . . . . .144 A4
Bakers Ave E17 . . . . .53 D3
Bakers Ct RM8 . . . . .59 B2
Bakers Ct SE25 . . . . .205 C6
Bakers End SW20 . . . . . .179 A1
Bakers Field N7 . . . . .72 A4
Bakers Gdns SM5 . . . . . .218 C6
Bakers Hall Ct EC3 . . . . . .253 B5
Bakers Hill Barnet EN5 . . . . .1 D3
  Upper Clapton E5 . . . . . . .52 C1
Bakers Ho W5 . . . . .109 D5
Baker's La N6 . . . . .48 D3
Bakers Mews 9 BR6 . . . . .227 D2
Baker's Mews W1 . . . . . . .238 A2
Bakers Pas 22 NW3 . . . . . .70 A4
Bakers Rents 13 E2 . . . . . .95 D4
Bakers Row E15 . . . . .98 C5
Baker's Row EC1 . . 94 C3 241 A6
Bakers St Enfield EN1 . . . . . .5 B4
  Marylebone W1 . . . 92 D2 237 D6
Baker Street W1 . . . 92 D2 237 A4
Baker Street Sta
  NW1 . . . . .92 D3 237 D5
Baker's Yd EC1 . . . . .241 A6
Bakery Cl SW9 . . . . .270 D3
Bakery Mews KT6 . . . . . . .198 C1
Bakewell Way KT3 . . . . . .177 C1
Balaam Ho SM1 . . . . .217 C4
Balaams L Ctr E13 . . . . . . .99 A3
Balaams La N14 . . . . .15 D2
Balaam St E13 . . . . .99 B4
Balaclava Rd
  Bermondsey SE1 . . 117 D2 263 D3
  Kingston u T KT6 . . . . . .197 C2
Bala Gn NW9 . . . . .45 C3
Balcaskie Rd SE9 . . . . . . .166 B6
Balchen Rd SE3 . . . . .143 D3
Balchier Rd SE22 . . . . . . .162 B5
Balcombe Cl DA6 . . . . . . .146 D1
Balcombe Ho
  Lisson Gr NW1 . . . . .237 C6
  3 Streatham SW2 . . . . . .160 B3
Balcombe St NW1 . 92 D3 237 C5
Balcon Ct W5 . . . . .88 B1
Balcorne St E9 . . . . .74 C1
Balder Rise SE12 . . . . . . .165 B2
Balderton Flats W1 . . . . . .238 B1
Balderton St W1 . . .93 A1 238 B1
Baldewyne Ct N17 . . . . . . .34 A2
Baldock Ho 31 SE5 . . . . . .139 A3
Baldock St E3 . . . . .97 D5
Baldrey Ho 1 SE10 . . . . . .120 D1
Baldry Gdns SW16 . . . . . .182 A4
Baldwin Cres SE5 . . . . . . .139 A4
Baldwin Gdns TW3 . . . . . .130 A4
Baldwin Ho
  15 Streatham SW2 . . . . .160 C3
  Wallend E12 . . . . .78 C1
Baldwin Rd SW12 . . . . . . .159 A5

Baldwin's Gdns
EC1 . . . . 94 C2 241 A4
Baldwin St EC1 . . . . . 235 C1
Baldwin Terr N1 . . .95 A5 235 A4
Baldwyn Gdns W3 . . . . .111 B6
Balearic Apts 3 E16 . . . .121 A6
Bale Rd E1 . . . . .97 A2
Bales Coll W10 . . . . . .90 D4
Balfern Gr W4 . . . . . . .111 C1
Balfern St SW11 . . . . .136 C3
Balfe St N1 . . . . 94 A5 233 B3
Balfour Ave W7 . . . . . .108 D5
Balfour Bsns Ctr UB2. . .106 D3
Balfour Gr N20 . . . . . . .14 D1
Balfour Ho 4 W10 . . . . .90 D2
Balfour Mews
 Edmonton N9 . . . . . . .18 A1
 Mayfair W1 . . . . 248 B4
 Putney SW15 . . . . . . .134 B1
Balfour Rd
 Bromley Comm BR2 . . .209 D4
 Croydon SE25 . . . . . . .206 A5
 Ealing W13 . . . . .109 B4
 Harrow HA1 . . . . .42 B4
 Highbury N5 . . . . .73 A4
 Hounslow TW3 . . . . . .129 D2
 Ilford IG1 . . . . .57 A1
 Merton SW19 . . . . . . .179 D3
 North Acton W3 . . . . . .89 A2
 Southall UB1 . . . . . . .106 D3
 Wallington SM5 . . . . . .218 D1
Balfour St SE17 . . .117 B2 262 C4
Balfront Twr 4 E14 . . . . .98 A1
Balgonie Rd E4 . . . . . . .20 B3
Balgowan Cl KT3 . . . . . .199 C5
Balgowan Prim Sch
 BR3 . . . . .185 A1
Balgowan Rd BR3 . . . . . .185 B1
Balgowan St SE18 . . . . .123 D2
BALHAM 159 A3
Balham Gr SW12 . . . . . .159 A4
Balham High Rd SW12,
 SW17 . . . . .159 A3
Balham Hill SW12 . . . . . .159 B5
Balham L Ctr SW12 . . . .159 B2
Balham New Rd SW12 . . .159 B4
Balham Park Mans
 SW12 . . . . .158 D3
Balham Park Rd SW12,
 SW17 . . . . .158 D3
Balham Rd N9 . . . . .18 A2
Balham Sta SW12 . . . . . .159 B3
Balham Station Rd
 SW12 . . . . .159 B3
Balin Ho SE1 . . . . .252 C2
Balkan Wlk E1 . . . . . . .118 B6
Balladier Wlk E14 . . . . . .97 D2
Ballamore Rd BR1 . . . . . .165 A1
Ballance Rd E9 . . . . .75 A2
Ballantine St SW18 . . . . .136 A1
Ballantrae Ho NW2 . . . . . .69 B4
Ballantyne Cl 5 SE9 . . . .188 A6
Ballard Cl KT2 . . . . .177 B3
Ballard Ho SE10 . . . . . . .141 D6
Ballards Cl RM10. . . . . . .103 D6
Ballards Farm Rd CR0,
 CR2 . . . . .222 A2
Ballards La N3. . . . . . . .29 D3
Ballards Mews HA8 . . . . .26 C4
Ballards Rd
 Dagenham RM10 . . . . . .103 D6
 Dollis Hill NW2 . . . . . .68 A6
Ballards Rise CR2. . . . . .222 A4
Ballards Way CR0, CR2 . . .222 B2
Ballast Quay SE10. . . . . .120 B1
Ballater Cl WD19. . . . . . .22 C6
Ballater Rd
 Brixton SW2, SW4 . . . . .138 A1
 South Croydon CR2. . . . .221 D3
Ball Ct EC3 . . . . .242 D1
Ballentyne Ct N21 . . . . . .16 B6
Ballina St SE23 . . . . . . .162 D4
Ballin Ct 14 E14. . . . . . .120 A4
Ballingdon Rd SW11 . . . .159 A5
Ballinger Point 18 E3 . . . .97 D4
Ballinger Way UB5. . . . . .85 A3
Balliol Ave E4 . . . . .36 C6
Balliol Ho 11 SW15. . . . .156 D5
Balliol Rd Bexley DA16 . . .146 B3
 North Kensington W10. . .90 D1
 Tottenham N17. . . . . . . .33 C2
Balloch Rd SE6 . . . . . . .164 B2
Ballogie Ave NW10. . . . . .67 C4
Ballow Cl 15 SE5. . . . . . .139 C5
Ball's Pond Pl 3 N1 . . . .73 B2
Ball's Pond Rd N1 . . . . . .73 A2
Balmain Cl W5. . . . . . . .109 D5
Balmain Ct TW3 . . . . . . .129 D4
Balman Ho 3 SE16 . . . . .118 D2
Balmer Rd E3. . . . . .97 B5
Balmes Rd N1 . . .95 B6 235 D6
Balmoral Ave
 Beckenham BR3 . . . . . .207 A5
 Friern Barnet N11 . . . . . .31 B5
Balmoral Cl 1 SW15. . . . .156 D5
Balmoral Cres KT8. . . . . .195 C6

Balmoral Ct
 18 Belmont SM2. . . . . .217 C1
 Ealing W5 . . . . .87 D1
 Edgware HA8 . . . . .26 D6
 Grove Pk SE12 . . . . . . .187 B6
 North Cheam KT4. . . . . .216 B6
 21 Redbridge IG6 . . . . .118 D5
 St John's Wood NW8 . . .229 C4
 Wembley HA9. . . . . . . .66 B5
 West Norwood SE27 . . . .183 A6
Balmoral Dr
 Borehamwood WD6 . . . . .11 B6
 Hayes UB4 . . . . .83 D3
 Southall UB1. . . . . . . .85 B3
Balmoral Gdns
 Ealing W13 . . . . .109 A3
 Ilford IG3 . . . . .57 D1
 Old Bexley DA5. . . . . . .169 B4
Balmoral Gr N7. . . . . . . .72 B2
Balmoral Ho
 2 Isle Of Dogs E14 . . . .119 D3
 Stanmore HA7 . . . . . . .26 A1
 Stoke Newington N4. . . .51 A1
 Walthamstow E17 . . . . . .35 B1
 West Kensington W14 . . .254 A4
Balmoral Lo BR6. . . . . . .226 C4
Balmoral Mews W12. . . . .111 D3
Balmoral Rd
 Forest Gate E7 . . . . . . .77 C3
 Harrow HA2 . . . . .63 C4
 Kingston u T KT1. . . . . .198 B5
 Leyton E10 . . . . .75 D6
 North Cheam KT4. . . . . .216 B6
 Willesden NW2. . . . . . . .68 B2
Balmoral Trad Est IG11. . .101 D2
Balmore Cl E14. . . . . . . .98 A1
Balmore Cres EN4 . . . . . .15 A6
Balmore St N19 . . . . . . .71 B6
Balmuir Gdns SW15. . . . .134 C1
Balnacraig Ave NW10. . . . .67 C4
Balniel Gate SW1 . . . . . .259 D2
Balsam Ho 9 E14. . . . . . .119 D6
Baltic Apts 5 E16. . . . . . .121 A6
Baltic Ho 7 SE5 . . . . . . .139 A3
Baltic St E EC1. . . .95 A3 242 A5
Baltic St W EC1. . . .95 A3 242 A5
Baltimore Ho
 Clapham SW18. . . . . . .136 A1
 Kennington SE11 . . . . . .261 A2
 Merton SW19 . . . . . . .179 D3
Baltimore Pl DA16 . . . . . .145 D3
Balvaird Pl SW1 . . . . . . .259 D1
Balvernie Gr SW18. . . . . .157 C4
Bamber Ho IG11. . . . . . .101 A6
Bamber Rd 5 SE15 . . . . .139 D4
Bamborough Gdns 12
 W12. . . . . .112 C4
Bamburgh 9 N17 . . . . . . .34 B3
Bamford Ave HA0. . . . . . .88 B5
Bamford Rd Barking IG11. . .79 A2
 Catford BR1 . . . . .186 B5
Bampfylde Cl SM6 . . . . . .219 C5
Bampton Ct W5. . . . . . . .87 D1
Bampton Dr NW7 . . . . . . .28 A3
Bampton Rd SE23. . . . . . .162 D1
Banavie Gdns BR3 . . . . . .186 A2
Banbury Ct EN2. . . . . . . .4 D4
Banbury Ct
 11 Belmont SM2. . . . . .217 C1
 Ealing W13 . . . . .109 A3
 Strand WC2 . . . . .250 A6
Banbury Ho 5 E9. . . . . . .74 D1
Banbury Rd
 Higham Hill E17 . . . . . . .35 A3
 Homerton E9 . . . . .74 D1
Banbury St 3 SW11. . . . .136 C3
Banbury Wlk UB5. . . . . . .85 C5
Banchory Rd SE3 . . . . . . .143 B5
Bancroft Ave
 East Finchley N2 . . . . . .48 C4
 Woodford IG9. . . . . . . .21 A2
Bancroft Ct TW15. . . . . . .170 C5
 South Lambeth SW8. . . .270 A2
Bancroft Gdns
 Harrow Weald HA3. . . . .24 A2
 Orpington BR6. . . . . . .211 D1
Bancroft Ho 11 E1 . . . . . .96 C3
Bancroft Rd
 Bethnal Green E1 . . . . . .96 D3
 Harrow Weald HA3. . . . .24 A1
Bancrofts Sch IG8 . . . . . .21 A1
Bandon Cl UB10 . . . . . . .82 B5
BANDONHILL 219 D3
Bandon Hill Prim Sch
 SM6. . . . . .219 D2
Bandon Rise SM6. . . . . . .219 D3
Banff Ho 1 NW3. . . . . . . .70 C2
Banfield Rd SE15 . . . . . . .140 B2
Banfor Ct SM6. . . . . .219 C3
Bangabandhu Prim Sch 38
 E2. . . . . .96 C4
Bangalore St SW15 . . . . .134 D2
Bangor Cl UB5. . . . . . . .63 D3
Banim St W6. . . . . .112 B2
Banister Ho Hackney E9. . .74 D3
 Nine Elms SW8. . . . . . .269 B2
 9 West Kilburn W10. . . . .91 A4
Banister Rd W10. . . . . . . .90 D4

Bank Ave CR4. . . . . . . .180 B1
Bank Bldgs 13 SW16. . . . .181 C5
Bank Ct SW11 . . . . .268 C2
Bank End SE1. . . . . . . .252 B4
Bankfoot Rd BR1 . . . . . .186 C6
Bankhurst Rd SE6. . . . . . .163 B4
Bank La Kingston u T KT2. .176 A3
 Roehampton SW15. . . . .155 C6
Bank Mews SM1 . . . . . . .218 A2
Bank of England★ EC2. . .242 C1
Bank of England Mus★
 EC2. . . . . .95 B1 242 C1
Bank Par N11. . . . . .31 B5
Banks Ho Silvertown TW7. .130 C3
 Newington SE1. . . . . . .262 A5
Banksia Rd N18. . . . . . . .34 D5
Bankside
 Borough The SE1. . .117 A6 252 A5
 Borough The SE1. . . . . .252 B4
 Enfield EN2. . . . . .4 D4
 Southall UB1. . . . . . . .106 D5
 South Croydon CR2. . . . .221 D2
Bankside Ave
 1 Lewisham SE13. . . . . .142 A2
 Northolt UB5 . . . . .84 A5
Bankside Cl
 Carshalton SM5 . . . . . .218 C2
 Isleworth TW7 . . . . . . .130 D1
Bankside Dr KT7. . . . . . .213 B6
Bankside Gall★
 SE1. . . . . .116 D6 251 D5
Bankside Ho EC3 . . . . . . .243 B1
Bankside Pier
 SE1. . . . . .117 A6 252 A5
Bankside Pk IG11. . . . . . .102 A4
Bankside Rd IG1. . . . . . . .79 B3
Bankside Way 6 SE19 . . .183 C4
Banks La DA6. . . . . .147 B1
Bank St E14 . . . . .119 D5
Bank Sta EC3 . . . .95 B1 242 D1
Banks Way E12 . . . . .78 C4
Banksyard TW5. . . . . . . .129 B6
Bank The N6. . . . . .49 B1
Bankton Rd SW2. . . . . . .138 C1
Bankwell Rd SE13. . . . . . .142 C1
Banner Ct 5 SE16 . . . . . .118 C2
Banner Ho EC1 . . . . .242 B5
Bannerman Ho SW8 . . . . .270 C5
Banner St EC1 . . . .95 A3 242 B6
Banning Ho 4 SW19 . . . .156 D3
Banning St SE10 . . . . . . .120 C1
Bannister Cl
 Greenford UB6 . . . . . . .64 B3
 Streatham SW2 . . . . . . .160 C3
Bannister Ho
 28 Deptford SE14. . . . . .140 D6
 Harrow HA3 . . . . .42 C6
Bannister Sports Ctr HA3. .24 A4
Bannockburn Prim Sch
 SE18. . . . . .123 D2
Bannockburn Rd SE18 . . .123 D2
Bannow Cl KT19. . . . . . .215 C4
Banqueting Ho★ SW1. . . .250 A3
Banstead Ct
 East Acton W12 . . . . . . .111 D6
 Stoke Newington N4. . . .51 A1
Banstead Gdns N9. . . . . . .17 C1
Banstead Rd SM5 . . . . . . .218 C1
Banstead St SE15 . . . . . .140 C2
Banstead Way SM6. . . . . .220 A3
Banstock Rd HA8 . . . . . . .26 D4
Banting Dr N21 . . . . .16 B6
Banting Ho 6 NW2 . . . . . .68 A5
Bantock Ct 1 N20 . . . . . . .14 D2
Bantock Ho 8 W10 . . . . . .91 A4
Banton Cl EN1. . . . . .6 B3
Bantry Ho 13 E1 . . . . . . .96 D3
Bantry St SE5. . . . . .139 B5
Banville Ho SW8. . . . . . . .270 D3
Banwell Rd DA5 . . . . . . .168 D5
Banyan Ho 8 NW3. . . . . . .69 D2
Banyard Rd SE16. . . . . . . .118 B3
Baptist Gdns NW5. . . . . . .71 A2
Barandon Wlk 6 W11 . . . .112 D6
Barbanel Ho 26 E1. . . . . . .96 C3
Barbara Brosnan Ct
 NW8 . . . . .229 D3
Barbara Castle Cl SW6. . .264 D5
Barbara Cl TW17. . . . . . .192 D4
Barbara Hucklesbury Cl
 N22. . . . . .32 D1
Barbara Martin Ho 1
 N11. . . . . .31 C5
Barbara Rudolph Ct 5
 N19 . . . . .50 A2
Barbara Ward Ct 3 E11. . .76 C6
Barbauld Rd N16 . . . . . . .73 C5
Barber Beaumont Ho 21
 E1. . . . . .96 D4
Barber Cl N21. . . . . .16 C4
Barberry Ct E15 . . . . .76 C2
Barbers Alley 1 E13. . . . . .99 B4
Barbers Rd E15 . . . . .97 D5
BARBICAN. 95 A2
Barbican★ EC2. . . .95 A2 242 B3
Barbican Ctr★
 EC2. . . . . .95 A2 242 B4
Barbican Rd UB1. . . . . . .85 D1
Barb Mews W6 . . . . .112 C3

Barbon Alley EC3. . . . . . .243 B2
Barbon Cl WC1. . . . . . . .240 C4
Barbot Cl N9 . . . . .18 A1
Barbrook Ho E9 . . . . .74 C2
Barchard St SW18 . . . . . .157 D6
Barchester Cl W7. . . . . . . .108 D5
Barchester Lo N12. . . . . . . .29 D6
Barchester Rd HA3 . . . . . . .24 B1
Barchester St E14 . . . . .97 D2
Barclay Cl SW6 . . .135 C5 265 A3
Barclay Ct N12. . . . . .30 A5
Barclay Ho 21 E9 . . . . .74 C1
Barclay Oval IG8. . . . . .37 A6
Barclay Prim Sch E10 . . . .54 B3
Barclay Rd Edmonton N18 . .33 B4
 Leyton E11 . . . . .54 D1
 Newham E13 . . . . .99 C3
 Parsons Green
 SW6 . . . . .135 C5 265 A3
 South Croydon CR0. . . . .221 B5
 Walthamstow E17 . . . . . .54 A4
Barcombe Ave SW2. . . . . .160 B2
Barcom Trad Est 1
 CR0. . . . . .204 A2
Bardell Ho 17 SE1. . . . . . .118 A4
Barden St SE18. . . . . . . .145 C5
Bardfield Ave RM6 . . . . . . .58 D6
Bardney Rd SM4 . . . . .201 D5
Bardolph Rd
 Richmond TW9. . . . . . .132 B2
 Tufnell Pk N7. . . . . .72 A4
Bard Rd W10 . . . . .112 D6
Bardsey Pl 41 E1. . . . . .96 C3
Bardsey Wlk 5 N1. . . . . . . .73 A2
Bardsley Cl CR0. . . . . .221 D5
Bardsley Ho 5 SE10 . . . . .142 A6
Bardsley La SE10. . . . . . . .142 A6
Barents Ho 10 E1 . . . . .96 D3
Barfett St W10. . . . . .91 B3
Barfield Ave N20. . . . . .14 D2
Barfield Rd
 Bromley BR1, BR7 . . . . .210 C6
 Leytonstone E11. . . . . . . .54 D1
Barfleur La SE8 . . . . .119 B2
Barford Cl NW4. . . . . .28 A2
Barford Ho 23 E3 . . . . .97 B5
Barford St N1. . . . . .94 C6 234 B5
Barforth Rd SE15 . . . . . . .140 B2
Barfreston Way SE20. . . . .184 B2
Bargate Cl
 New Malden KT3. . . . . . .200 A2
 Plumstead Comm SE18 . .123 D1
Bargehouse Rd E16. . . . . .122 D4
Barge House St SE1. . . . . .251 B4
Barge La 10 E3 . . . . .97 B6
Bargery Rd SE6. . . . . .163 D3
Bargrove Cl 8 SE20. . . . . .184 A3
Bargrove Cres SE6. . . . . . .163 B2
Barham Cl
 Chislehurst BR7 . . . . . . .188 D5
 Keston Mark BR2 . . . . . .210 A1
 Wembley HA0. . . . . .65 C2
Barham Ct
 8 Croydon CR2 . . . . . . .221 A4
 Keston Mark BR2 . . . . . .210 A1
 Wembley HA0. . . . . .65 C2
 Woodside Pk N12 . . . . . . .29 B5
Barham Ho SE17 . . . . .263 B2
Barham Prim Sch HA0 . . . .65 C2
Barham Rd
 Chislehurst BR7 . . . . . . .188 D5
 Croydon CR2. . . . . .221 A3
 Wimbledon SW20. . . . . . .178 A3
Baring Cl SE12. . . . . .165 A2
Baring Ct N1 . . . . .235 C5
Baring Ho 5 E14. . . . . .97 C1
Baring Prim Sch SE12. . . .165 A4
Baring Rd Barnet EN4 . . . . .2 B2
 Croydon CR0. . . . . .206 A1
 Grove Pk SE12 . . . . .165 A2
Baring St N1 . . . . .95 B6 235 C5
Barker Cl
 Kingston u T KT3. . . . . . .198 D5
 Richmond TW9. . . . . . . .132 D3
Barker Dr NW1 . . . . .71 D1
Barker Ho Dulwich SE21. . .161 C1
 3 Harringay N15. . . . . . . .50 D5
 Walthamstow E17 . . . . . .53 B2
 Walworth SE17 . . . . .263 A3
Barker Mews SW4 . . . . . .137 B1
Barker St SW10 . . . . .266 A6
Barker Wlk SW16 . . . . . . .159 D1
Barkham Rd N17. . . . . .33 C3
BARKING. 79 B1
Barking Abbey Comp Sch
 (Sports & Humanities Coll))
 IG11. . . . . .79 C3
Barking Abbey L Ctr
 IG11. . . . . .80 A2
Barking Abbey (ruins of)★
 IG11. . . . . .101 A1
Barking Abbey Sch (Sports &
 Humanities Coll) IG11. . .79 D2
Barking Bsns Ctr IG11 . . .102 A4
Barking Flyover IG11. . . . . .78 D1
Barking Hospl IG11. . . . . . .79 D1
Barking Ind Pk IG11. . . . . .102 A6
Barking Rd East Ham E6. . .100 B6
 Plaistow E13. . . . . .99 B4
BARKINGSIDE. 57 A6

Barkingside Sta IG6 . . . . . .57 B6
Barking Sta IG11. . . . . .79 A1
Bark Pl W2. . . . . .113 D6 245 C6
Barkston Gdns
 SW5. . . . . .113 D2 255 C3
Barkway Cl BR6. . . . . .226 C4
Barkway Ct N4 . . . . .73 A6
Barkwith Ho 27 SE14 . . . .140 D6
Barkworth Rd SE16 . . . . . .118 C1
Barlborough St SE14. . . . .140 D5
Barlby Gdns W10 . . . . .90 D3
Barlby Prim Sch W10 . . . . .90 D3
Barlby Rd W10. . . . . .90 D2
Barley Cl Bus WD23. . . . . . .8 A6
 Wembley HA9. . . . . .65 C4
Barleycorn Way E14 . . . . .119 B6
Barley Ct Ilford IG3 . . . . . . .58 B4
Barleyfields Cl RM6. . . . . . .58 C2
Barley La IG3. . . . . .58 B3
Barley Lane Prim Sch
 RM6. . . . . .58 B2
Barley Mow Pas
 Chiswick W4. . . . . .111 B1
 Clerkenwell EC1 . . . . . . .241 D3
Barley Mow Way TW17 . . .192 C5
Barley Shotts Bsns Pk
 W10 . . . . .91 B2
Barling 6 NW1. . . . . .71 B1
Barling Ct 11 SW4 . . . . . .138 A3
Barlings Ho 2 SE4. . . . . . .140 D1
Barloch Ho 14 SW11 . . . .137 A3
Barlow Cl SM6. . . . . .220 A1
Barlow Dr SE18 . . . . .144 A4
Barlow Ho
 14 Bermondsey SE16. . . .118 B2
 Notting Hill W11. . . . . . . .244 A6
 Shoreditch N1. . . . . .235 C2
Barlow Pl W1. . . . . .248 D5
Barlow Rd Acton W3 . . . . .110 D5
 Brondesbury NW6 . . . . . .69 B2
 Hampton TW12. . . . . . . .173 C3
Barlow St SE17 . . .117 B2 262 D3
Barmeston Rd SE6. . . . . . .163 D2
Barmor Cl HA2 . . . . .23 D1
Barmouth Ave UB6. . . . . . .86 D5
Barmouth Ho 6 N7. . . . . . .72 B6
Barmouth Rd
 Croydon CR0. . . . . .222 D6
 Wandsworth SW18 . . . . .158 A5
Barnabas Ct N21. . . . . .16 D6
Barnabas Ho EC1. . . . . . . .235 A1
Barnabas Lo SW8. . . . . . . .270 B2
Barnabas Rd E9 . . . . .74 D3
Barnaby Cl HA2. . . . . .64 A6
Barnaby Ct NW9 . . . . .45 C6
Barnaby Pl SW7 . . . . .256 C3
Barnard Cl
 Chislehurst BR7 . . . . . . .189 B2
 Sunbury TW16 . . . . .172 B3
 Wallington SM6 . . . . . . .219 D1
 Woolwich SE18 . . . . .122 C3
Barnard Ct SW16 . . . . . . .160 B1
Barnard Gdns Hayes UB4. .84 B3
 West Barnes KT3 . . . . . .200 A5
Barnard Gr E15 . . . . .76 D1
Barnard Hill N10. . . . . .31 B2
Barnard Ho 17 E2. . . . . . . .96 B4
Barnard Lo New Barnet EN5. .2 A1
 10 Paddington W9 . . . . . .91 C2
Barnard Mews SW11. . . . .136 C1
Barnardo Dr IG6. . . . . .57 A5
Barnardo Gdns 1 E1 . . . .118 D6
Barnardo St E1. . . . . .96 D6
Barnard Rd
 Clapham SW11. . . . . .136 C1
 Enfield EN1. . . . . .6 B3
 Mitcham CR4 . . . . .181 A1
Barnard's Inn EC4 . . . . . . .241 B2
Barnbrough NW1 . . . . .232 A5
Barnby Sq 1 E15. . . . . .98 C6
Barnby St
 Somers Town
 NW1. . . . . .93 C4 232 B2
 2 West Ham E15. . . . . . . .98 C6
Barn Cl Ashford TW15 . . . .170 D5
 19 Kentish Town NW5 . . . .71 D3
 Northolt UB5. . . . . .84 C5
Barn Cres HA7. . . . . .25 C4
Barncroft Cl UB8. . . . . .82 D2
Barn Croft Prim Sch E17. . .53 A3
Barnehurst Rd DA7 . . . . . .147 D3
Barneby Cl TW2. . . . . .152 C3
Barnes Ave Barnet EN5. . . . .1 C1
 Southall UB2. . . . . .107 B2
Barnes Bridge Sta
 SW13 . . . . .133 C3
Barnes Cl E12 . . . . .77 D4
Barnes Common★
 SW13 . . . . .134 A2
Barnes Ct Barnet EN5 . . . . .1 C1
 Islington N1 . . . . .72 C1
 3 Newham E16. . . . . .99 C2
 South Norwood CR7 . . . .205 A6
 Woodford IG8. . . . . .37 D5
 Wood Green N22 . . . . . . .32 A3
Barnes End KT3. . . . . .200 A4

Barnes High St SW13.... 133 D3
Barnes Ho
 8 Barking IG11.........101 B6
 14 Bethnal Green E2......96 C5
 Camden Town NW1......231 D6
 26 Deptford SE14.......140 D6
 Hornsey N8............50 A2
Barnes Hospl SW14.... 133 C2
Barnes Prim Sch SW13. 133 D2
Barnes Qtr **6** TW8....131 C5
Barnes Rd Edmonton N18.. 34 C6
 Ilford IG1...........79 A3
Barnes St E14..........97 A1
Barnes Sta SW13.......134 A2
Barnes Terr SE8.......119 B1
Barnes Wallis Ct HA9...67 A5
BARNET...............13 B6
Barnet By-Pass WD6....11 C6
Barnet Coll (Grahame Park)
 NW9.................27 A1
Barnet Coll (North London
 Bsns Pk) N11........15 A1
Barnet Coll (Stanhope Rd)
 N12.................30 B5
Barnet Coll (Wood St) EN5.. 1 B1
Barnet Dr BR2.........226 A6
BARNET GATE..........11 C5
Barnet Gate La EN5....11 D4
Barnet Gr E2..........96 A4
Barnet Hill EN5........1 C1
Barnet Hill JMI Sch EN5.. 13 B6
Barnet Ho **35** SE5.....139 A3
Barnet La Barnet EN5, N20.. 13 B4
 Borehamwood WD6......10 B5
 Barnet Mus ***** EN5.....1 A1
Barnet Rd Barnet EN5.....1 B5
 Edgware EN5..........11 C5
Barnett Ho **1** 243 C3
Barnett Homestead
 NW11................47 C5
Barnet Trad Est EN5.....1 B2
Barnetts Ct HA2.......63 D5
Barnet St **18** E1......96 B1
Barnet Way (Barnet By-Pass)
 EN5, NW7, WD6.......11 B3
Barnet Wood Rd BR2....225 C6
Barney Cl SE7.........121 C1
Barnfield KT3.........199 C3
Barn Field NW3........70 D3
Barnfield Ave
 Croydon CR0.........222 C6
 Kingston u T KT2......176 A5
 Mitcham CR4..........203 B6
Barnfield Cl London N4...50 A2
 Wandsworth SW17......158 A1
Barnfield Gdns
 Kingston u T KT2......176 A5
 Shooters Hill SE18.....144 D6
Barnfield Pl E14......119 C2
Barnfield Prim Sch HA8..27 A2
Barnfield Rd
 Burnt Oak HA8........27 A2
 Ealing W5............87 C3
 Erith DA17..........147 B6
 Shooters Hill SE18.....144 D6
Barnfield Wood Cl BR3..208 B3
Barnfield Wood Rd BR3..208 B3
Barnham Dr SE28......123 D5
Barnham Rd UB6.......86 A4
Barnham St SE1.......253 B2
Barnhill HA5..........40 C4
Barn Hill HA9.........44 D1
Barnhill Ave BR2......208 D4
Barnhill Com High Sch
 UB4.................84 C4
Barnhill Ct UB4.......84 B4
Barnhill La UB4.......84 B4
Barnhill Rd Hayes UB4...84 C3
 Wembley HA9.........67 A5
Barnhurst Path WD19...22 C5
Barningham Way NW9...45 B3
Barnlea Cl TW13.......151 A2
Barnmead Rd RM9......81 B3
Barnmead Gdns RM9....81 B3
Barnmead Rd
 Dagenham RM9........81 B3
 Penge BR3...........185 A2
Barn Rise HA9.........66 C6
BARNSBURY............72 A1
Barnsbury Cl KT3......199 A5
Barnsbury Cres KT5....199 A1
Barnsbury Gr N7.......72 B1
Barnsbury Ho **12** SW4..159 D5
Barnsbury La KT5......199 A1
Barnsbury Pk N1.......72 C1
Barnsbury Rd N1..94 C6 234 A5
Barnsbury Sq N1.......72 C1
Barnsbury St N1.......72 C1
Barnsbury Terr N1.....72 B1
Barnscroft SW20......200 B6
Barnsdale Ave E14.....119 C2
Barnsdale Rd W9.......91 B3
Barnsley St E1........96 B3
Barn St N16...........73 C6
Barnstaple Ho SE12....164 D6
Barnstaple La SE13....142 A1
Barnstaple Rd HA4.....62 C5
Barnston Wlk N1......235 A6
Barnview Lo HA3.......24 C2
Barn Way HA9..........66 C6

Barnwell Ho **1** SE5.....139 C4
Barnwell Rd SW2.......160 C6
Barnwood Cl Barnet N20..13 B3
 Ruislip HA4............61 B6
 Westbourne Green W9....91 D3
Baron Cl Friern Barnet N11..31 B5
 Islington N1..........234 A4
Baron Ct Barnet EN5.....1 D1
 Mitcham CR4..........202 C5
Baroness Rd **5** E2.....95 D4
Baronet Gr N17.........34 A2
Baronet Rd N17.........34 A2
Baron Gdns IG6........57 A6
Baron Gr E2...........204 C5
Baron Ho **6** SW19.....180 B2
Baron Rd RM8..........58 D1
Barons **14** BR3.......185 D1
Barons Court Mans W14..254 B1
Baron's Court Rd
 W14.........113 A1 254 B2
Barons Court Sta
 W14.........113 A1 254 A2
Barons Ct Ilford IG1.....79 B6
 Kingsbury NW9.........45 B3
 Wallington SM6........219 D5
Baronsfield Rd TW1....153 B5
Barons Gate
 East Barnet EN4.......14 C5
 13 South Acton W4....111 A3
Barons Keep
 W14.........113 A1 254 A2
Barons Lo **9** E14.....120 A2
Barons Mead HA1.......42 C5
Baronsmead Rd SW13....134 A4
Baronsmede W5.........110 B4
Baronsmere Ct **9** EN5...1 A1
Baronsmere Rd N2......48 C5
Baron's Pl SE1....116 C4 251 B1
Baron St N1....94 C5 234 A4
Barons The TW1........153 B5
Baron's Wlk CR0.......207 A3
Baron Wlk E16.........98 D2
Barque Mews SE8......141 C6
Barrack Rd TW4........129 A1
Barradell Ho **18** W14..112 D3
Barra Hall Cir UB3.....83 C1
Barra Hall Rd UB3.....105 C6
Barrass Cl **7** EN3.....7 C6
Barratt Ave N22........32 B1
Barratt Ho **15** N1.....72 D1
Barratt Ind Pk Poplar E3..98 A3
 Southall UB1..........107 C5
Barratt Way HA3.......42 B6
Barra Beacon SE23.....162 C4
Barrenger Rd N10......30 D1
Barret Ho NW6.........91 C6
Barrett Ct **2** NW10...89 C5
Barrett Rd E17........54 A5
Barrett's Gr N16.......73 C3
Barretts Green Rd NW10..89 B5
Barrett St W1.....93 A1 238 B1
Barrhill Rd SW2.......160 A2
Barrie Ct EN5.........14 A6
Barriedale SE14.......141 A3
Barrie Ho Acton W3.....111 A4
 Bayswater W2.........246 B5
 Edmonton N9..........18 B4
 Primrose Hill NW8.....230 B5
 8 Stoke Newington N16..73 C5
Barrier Gdns Pier SE18..121 D3
Barrier Point Rd E16...121 C4
Barringers Ct HA4.....39 B2
Barrington Sq SW17....181 A6
Barrington N20........14 B3
Barrington Ct **7** NW5..71 A3
Barrington Ct
 9 Acton W3........110 D4
 Kentish Town NW5......71 A3
 4 Muswell Hill N10...31 B1
 31 South Lambeth SW8..138 A3
Barrington Prim Sch
 DA7.................146 D3
Barrington Rd
 Bexley DA7...........146 D3
 Brixton SW9..........138 D2
 Cheam SM3...........201 C1
 Hornsey N8...........49 D4
 Little Ilford E12.......78 C2
Barrington Villas SE18..144 C4
Barrington Wlk **9** SE19..183 C4
Barrow Ave SM5.......218 D1
Barrow Cl N21.........16 D2
Barrow Ct **6** SE6.....164 D3
Barrowdene Cl HA5.....23 A1
Barrowell Gn N21......17 A2
Barrowfield Cl N9......18 C1
Barrowgate Ho W4......111 B1
Barrowgate Rd W4......111 B1
Barrow Hedges Cl SM5..218 C1
Barrow Hedges Prim Sch
 SM5................218 C1
Barrow Hedges Way
 SM5................218 C1
Barrow Hill KT4.......215 C6
Barrow Hill Cl KT4....215 C6
Barrow Hill Est
 NW8.........92 C5 230 A3
Barrow Hill Jun Sch
 NW8.........92 C5 230 A3
Barrow Hill Rd NW8....230 A3

Barrow Point Ave HA5...23 A1
Barrow Point La HA5....23 A1
Barrow Rd Croydon CR0..220 C3
 Streatham SW16.......181 D4
Barrow Wlk **1** TW8....109 C1
Barrs Rd NW10.........67 B1
Barry Ave Erith DA7....147 A5
 South Tottenham N15....51 D3
Barry Cl BR6..........227 C5
Barry Ct SW4..........159 C5
Barrydene N20.........14 B2
Barrydene Ct EN2.......4 D2
Barry Ho **4** SE16.....118 B1
Barry Lo N4...........50 B2
Barrymore N12.........30 A3
Barry Par SE22........162 A6
Barry Rd London SE22...162 A6
 Newham E6...........100 A1
 Willesden NW10........67 A1
Barry Terr TW15.......148 B2
Barset Rd SE15........140 C2
Barsons Cl SE20......184 C3
Barston Rd SE27......161 A1
Barstow Cres SW2.....160 B3
Bartell Ho SW2.......160 C5
Barter St WC1....94 A2 240 B3
Barters Wlk HA5.......41 A6
Barth Mews SE18......123 C2
Bartholomew Cl
 Barbican EC1.........242 A3
 Wandsworth SW18.....136 A1
Bartholomew Ct
 16 Blackwall E14....120 B6
 Edgware HA8..........25 D3
 St Luke's EC1........242 B6
Bartholomew Ho
 22 Camberwell SE5....139 A3
 Enfield EN3..........7 A6
Bartholomew La EC2....242 D1
Bartholomew Pas EC1...241 D3
Bartholomew Pl EC1....242 A3
Bartholomew Rd NW5...71 C2
Bartholomew Sq
 18 Bethnal Green E1...96 B3
 St Luke's EC1........242 B6
Bartholomew St
 SE1.........117 B3 262 D5
Bartholomew Villas NW5..71 C2
Barth Rd SE18........123 C2
Bartle Ave E6.........100 A5
Bartle Rd W11.........91 A1
Bartlett Cl E14.......97 C1
Bartlett Ct EC4.......241 B2
Bartletts Cotts **4** EN5..1 A2
Bartlett St CR2.......221 B3
Bartok Ho W11........244 C5
Barton Ave RM7.......59 D1
Barton Cl Bexley DA6...169 A6
 Hackney E9...........74 C3
 Hendon NW4..........46 A5
 2 Newham E6........100 B1
 Peckham SE15.........140 B2
 Shepperton TW17......192 D3
Barton Ct
 Beckenham BR2........208 B6
 10 South Lambeth SW4..138 A3
 3 Sutton SM1.......217 D2
 West Kensington W14...254 B2
Barton Gn KT3........177 B1
Barton Ho **3** Bromley E3..97 D4
 Islington N1..........72 D1
 Sands End SW6........135 D2
Barton Mdws IG6.......57 A5
Barton Rd Sidcup DA14..191 A4
 West Kensington
 W14.........113 A1 254 B1
Barton St SW1........260 A6
Bartons The WD6......9 D5
Bartonway NW8........229 C4
Bartram Cl UB8........82 D3
Bartram Ct RM9........80 B2
Bartram Rd SE4........163 A5
Bartrams La EN4.......2 A5
Bartrip St E9.........75 B2
Barts Cl BR3.........207 C4
Barts & The London Sch of
 Medicine & Dentistry
 EC1............94 D3 241 D5
Barville Cl SE4.......141 A1
Barwell Bsns Pk KT9...213 D1
Barwell Ho **7** E2.....96 A3
Barwell La KT9........213 C1
Barwick Dr UB8.......82 D2
Barwick Ho **3** W3....111 A4
Barwick Rd E7........77 B4
Barwood Ave BR4......207 D1
Bascome St **13** SW2...160 C5
Basden Gr TW13.......151 C2
Base Apartments **8** N1..73 A1
 Borough The SE1.......262 B6
Basedale Rd RM9......80 B1
Baseing Ct E6........100 A4
Baseline Business Studios **18**
 W11................112 D6
Basevi Way SE8.......141 D6
Bashley Rd NW10......89 B3
Basil Ave E6.........100 A4
Basil Ct **11** EN5......2 A1
Basildene Rd TW4, TW5..128 D2
Basildon Ct W1.......238 B4

Basildon Rd SE2.......124 A1
Basil Gdns Croydon CR0..206 D1
 West Norwood SE27.....183 A5
Basil Ho
 South Lambeth SW8.....270 A4
 22 Whitechapel E1....96 A1
Basil Mans SW1.......247 C1
Basilon Rd DA7.......147 A3
Basil Spence Ho N22....32 B2
Basil St
 Knightsbridge
 SW1.........114 D4 247 C1
 Knightsbridge SW1,
 SW3.........114 D3 257 C6
Basin App **20** E14.....97 A1
Basing Cl KT7........196 D2
Basing Ct **13** SE15....139 D4
Basingdon Way SE5.....139 B1
Basing Dr DA5........169 B5
Basingfield Rd KT7.....196 D2
Basinghall Ave
 EC2............95 B3 242 C2
Basinghall St EC2..95 B1 242 C2
Basing Hill London NW11..47 B1
 Wembley HA9..........44 C1
Basing Ho
 7 Barking IG11.....101 B6
 Catford SE6..........185 C6
Basing House Yd **22** E2..95 C4
Basing Pl E2.........95 C4
Basing St W11........91 B1
Basing Way London N3...47 D6
 Thames Ditton KT7.....196 D2
Basire St N1....95 A6 235 B6
Baskerville Ct
 South Norwood SE25....205 C4
 Wandsworth SW18.....158 C4
Baskerville Gdns NW10...67 A5
Baskerville Rd SW18....158 C4
Basket Gdns SE9......166 A6
Basle Ho **3** E15.......76 C3
Baslow Cl HA3........24 B2
Baslow Wlk E5........74 D4
Basnett Rd **9** SW11...137 A2
Basque Ct **21** SE16...118 D4
Bassano St SE22......161 D6
Bassant Rd SE18......123 C4
Bassein Park Rd W12...111 D4
Bassett Gdns TW7.....130 A5
Bassett Ho RM9.......102 B6
Bassett House Sch **22**
 W10................90 D1
Bassett Rd W10.......90 D1
Bassetts Cl BR6......226 D4
Bassett St NW5.......71 A2
Bassetts Way BR6.....226 D4
Bassett Way UB1......85 D1
Bassingbourn Ho **3** N1..72 D1
Bassingham Rd
 Wandsworth SW18.....158 A4
 Wembley HA0.........65 D2
Bassishaw Highwalk
 EC2................242 C3
Basswood Cl **5** SE15...140 B2
Bastable Ave IG11.....102 A5
Basterfield Ho EC1....242 A5
Bastion Highwalk EC2...242 C3
Bastion Rd SE18, SE2...124 A1
Baston Manor Rd BR2,
 BR4................225 B4
Baston Rd BR2........225 B5
Baston Sch BR2.......225 B6
Bastwick St EC1..95 A3 242 A6
Basuto Rd SW6...135 C4 265 B1
Batavia Cl TW16......172 C2
Batavia Ho **1** SE14....141 A5
Batavia Mews **3** SE14..141 A5
Batavia Rd Deptford SE14..141 A5
 Sunbury TW16........172 B2
Batchelor St N1...94 C6 234 B5
Bateman Ho **8** SE17...138 D6
Bateman Rd E4........35 C4
Bateman's Bldgs W1....239 C1
Bateman's Row
 EC2............95 C3 243 B6
Bateman St W1....93 D1 239 C1
Bates Cres Croydon CR0..220 C3
 Streatham SW16.......181 C3
Bateson St **3** SE18...123 C2
Bate St E10..........119 B6
Bath Cl SE15.........140 B5
Bath Ct Finsbury EC1...235 C1
 3 Forest Hill SE26..162 A1
 Holborn EC1.........241 A5
Bathgate Ho **8** SW9...138 D4
Bathgate Rd SW19.....156 D1
Bath Gr E2...........95 D5
Bath Ho Bethnal Green E2..96 A3
 Borough The SE1......262 B6
Bath House Rd CR0.....204 A1
Bath Pl Barnet EN5......1 B2
 14 Hammersmith W6...112 C1
 11 Shoreditch EC2....95 C4
Bath Rd Acton W4......111 B2
 Cranford TW3, TW4, TW5..128 C4
 Dagenham RM6........59 A3
 Harlington TW6, UB7, TW5..127 B4
 Harmondsworth TW6, UB7..126 B4

Bath Rd continued
 Lower Edmonton N9....18 C2
 Upton E7............77 D2
Baths Rd BR1, BR2.....209 D5
Bath St EC1......95 B4 235 C1
Bath Terr SE1....117 A3 262 A6
Bathurst Ave SW19....179 D2
Bathurst Gdns NW10...90 B5
Bathurst Ho **2** W12...112 B6
Bathurst Mews
 W2..........114 B6 246 D6
Bathurst Rd IG1.......56 D1
Bathurst St W2.......246 D6
Bathway **11** SE18.....122 C2
Batley Cl CR4........202 D2
Batley Pl **3** N16......73 D5
Batley Rd Enfield EN2...5 B4
 Shacklewell N16......73 D5
Batman Cl W12........112 B5
Batoum Gdns W6......112 C3
Batson Ho **29** E1......96 A1
Batson St W12........112 A4
Batsworth Rd CR4.....202 B6
Battenburg Wlk **10** SE19..183 C5
Batten Cl E6.........100 B1
Batten Ho
 1 London SW4.....159 C6
 4 Walthamstow E17..53 D6
 10 West Kilburn W10..91 A4
Batten St SW11.......136 C2
Battersby Rd SE6......164 B1
BATTERSEA...........136 D4
Battersea Bridge Rd
 SW11..........136 C5 267 A3
Battersea Bsns Ctr
 SW11..............137 A2
Battersea Church Rd
 SW11..........136 B4 266 D2
Battersea Dogs & Cats Home
 SW8.........137 B5 268 B3
Battersea High St SW11..136 B3
Battersea Mews SW11...136 D2
Battersea Park *****
 SW11..........137 A5 268 A3
Battersea Park Rd SW11,
 SW8..............267 D1
Battersea Park Sch
 SW11..........136 D4 267 D1
Battersea Park Sta
 SW8.........137 B5 268 C3
Battersea Power Station(dis)
 SW8.........137 B6 268 D6
Battersea Rise SW11....136 C1
Battersea Sq SW11....266 C1
Battery Rd SE28......123 C4
Battishill St **9** N1....72 C1
Battlebridge Ct NW1...233 B4
Battle Bridge La
 SE1.........117 C5 253 A3
Battle Cl SW19.......180 A4
Battledean Rd N5......72 D3
Battle Ho **8** SE15....140 A6
Battle House Mews **7**
 EN5................2 A1
Batty St E1..........96 A1
Baty Ho SW2.........160 B3
Baudwin Rd SE6.......164 C2
Baugh Rd DA14........190 C5
BaulkThe SW18.......157 C4
Bavant Rd SW16......182 B1
Bavaria Rd N19.......72 A6
Bavdene Mews NW4....46 B5
Bavent Rd SE5........139 A3
Bawdale Rd SE22......161 D6
Bawdsey Ave IG2......57 D5
Bawtree Rd SE14......141 A5
Bawtry Rd N20........14 D1
Baxendale N20........14 A2
Baxendale St E2......96 A4
Baxter Cl Bromley BR1..210 D6
 Hillingdon UB10.......82 D4
 Southall UB2.........107 C3
Baxter Ho **11** E3......97 C4
Baxter Rd Edmonton N18..34 B6
 Ilford IG1...........78 D3
 Islington N1.........73 B2
 Newham E16.........99 C1
Bayard Ct DA7........147 D1
Baycliffe Ho **8** E9....74 D2
Baycroft Cl HA5......40 C6
Bay Ct Ealing W5......110 A3
 7 Stepney E1.......96 D3
Baydon Ct BR2........208 D6
Bayer Ho EC1........242 A5
Bayes Ct NW3........70 D1
Bayeux Ho **10** SE7...143 C6
Bayfield Ho **3** SE4....140 D1
Bayfield Rd SE9......143 D1
Bayford Lodge HA5....23 B2
Bayford Rd NW10......90 D4
Bayford St Ind Ctr **4** E8..74 D1
Bayford St **5** E8......74 D1
Baygrove Mews KT1....175 C2
Bayham Pl NW1...93 C6 232 B5
Bayham Rd Acton W3...111 B3
 Ealing W13..........109 B5
 Morden SM4.........202 A5

Bayham St NW1 . . .93 C6 232 A5
Bay Ho UB10. . . . . .60 C4
Bayhurst Ho N4. . . . . .51 A2
Bayhurst Wood Country Park
UB9. . . . . .38 B4
Bayleaf Cl TW12 . . . . .174 B5
Bayley St WC1 . . . . .239 C3
Bayley Wlk SE2 . . . . .125 A1
Baylis Mews TW1 . . . . .153 A4
Baylis Rd SE1. . . . .116 C4 251 A1
Bayliss Ave SE28 . . . . .124 D6
Bayliss Cl 4 Southall UB1. . .85 D1
Southgate N21 . . . . .16 A6
Bayne Cl E6 . . . . .100 B1
Baynes Cl EN1 . . . . .6 A4
Baynes Mews 2 NW3 . . . . . .70 B2
Baynes St NW1 . . . . .71 C1
Baynham Ct DA5. . . . . .169 B5
Bayon Ho 27 N19 . . . . .49 D2
Bayonne Rd W6 . . . . .264 A5
Bays Cl SE26. . . . . .184 C5
Bays Ct HA8 . . . . .26 D5
Bayshill Rise UB5 . . . . .63 D2
Bayston Rd N16. . . . . .73 D5
BAYSWATER. 114 A6
Bayswater Rd
W2. . . . . .114 B6 246 C5
Bayswater Rd Mkt*
W2. . . . . .114 A6 246 B5
Bayswater Sta
W2 . . . . .113 D6 245 D6
Bayton Ct 2 E8. . . . . .74 A1
Baytree Cl Bromley BR1 . . .187 D2
Sidcup DA15. . . . . .167 D3
Baytree Ho E4 . . . . .19 D4
Baytree Rd SW2 . . . . .138 B1
Bazalgette Cl KT3. . . . . . . .199 B4
Bazalgette Gdns KT3. . . . . .199 B4
Bazalgette Ho NW8 . . . . . .236 D6
Bazeley Ho SE1. . . . . .251 C1
Bazely St E14. . . . . .120 A6
Bazile Rd N21 . . . . .16 C5
BBC Television Ctr W12 . . .112 C5
Beacham Cl SE7 . . . . .143 D6
Beachborough Rd BR1. . . . .186 A6
Beachcroft Ave UB1. . . . . . .107 B5
Beachcroft Rd E11. . . . . . . .76 C5
Beach Ct SE9 . . . . .166 A5
Beach Gr TW13 . . . . .151 C2
Beach Ho SW5. . . . . .255 A2
Beachy Rd E3 . . . . .75 C1
Beaconfield Terrace Rd
W14. . . . . .254 A5
Beacon Gate SE14 . . . . . . .140 D2
Beacon Gr SM5. . . . . .219 A4
Beacon Hill N7 . . . . .72 A3
Beacon Ho
11 Camberwell SE5 . . . . .139 C5
7 Isle of Dogs E14. . . . .119 D1
10 Penge SE26. . . . . . . .184 B5
South Lambeth SW8. . . . .269 C2
Beacon Pl CR0. . . . . .220 A6
Beacon Rd
Harlington TW19, TW6. . . .148 C5
Hither Green SE13. . . . . .164 B5
Beacon Rdbt TW6. . . . . . . .148 C5
Beacons Cl 10 E6 . . . . .100 A2
Beaconsfield Cl
Acton Green W4 . . . . . . .111 A1
Friern Barnet N11 . . . . . .31 A5
Greenwich SE3. . . . . . . .143 A6
Beaconsfield Ct N11. . . . . . .31 A5
Beaconsfield Gdns KT10 .212 C1
Beaconsfield Par 1
SE9 . . . . .188 A6
Beaconsfield Prim Sch
UB2. . . . . .107 A5
Beaconsfield Rd
Acton W4 . . . . .111 B3
Bromley BR1. . . . . .209 D6
Claygate KT10 . . . . .212 C1
Ealing W5 . . . . .109 D4
Edmonton N9 . . . . .18 A1
Elmstead SE9 . . . . .188 A6
Enfield EN3 . . . . .6 D6
Friern Barnet N11 . . . . . .31 A6
Greenwich SE3 . . . . .143 A5
Hayes UB4 . . . . .106 C5
Kingston u T KT3 . . . . . .177 B1
Leyton E10 . . . . .76 A5
Newham E16 . . . . .98 D3
Southall UB1. . . . . .107 A5
South Tottenham N15. . . .51 C5
Surbiton KT5. . . . . .198 B2
Thornton Heath CR0. . . . .205 B3
Twickenham TW1. . . . . . .153 B5
Walthamstow E17 . . . . . .53 B3
Walworth SE17. . . .117 C1 263 A1
Willesden NW10. . . . . . . .67 C2
Beaconsfield Wlk
SW6. . . . . .135 B4 264 D1
Beaconshaw BR1. . . . . .186 C3
Beacontree Ave E17 . . . . . . .36 B1
Beacontree Rd E11 . . . . . . .54 D2
Beadle Ct CR4 . . . . .202 C6
Beadlow Cl SM4 . . . . .202 B3
Beadman Pl SE27 . . . . .182 D6

Beadman St SE27 . . . . .182 D6
Beadnell Rd SE23 . . . . .162 D3
Beadon Rd Bromley BR2. .209 A4
Hammersmith W6 . . . . . .112 C2
Beaford Gr SW20 . . . . .201 B6
Beagle Cl TW13 . . . . .172 B6
Beak St W1. . . . . . . .115 C6 249 B6
Beal Cl DA16. . . . . .146 A4
Beale Ho 7 SW9 . . . . .138 B3
Beale Pl E3. . . . . .97 B5
Beale Rd E3 . . . . .97 B6
Beal High Sch IG5. . . . . . . .56 A5
Beal Rd IG1 . . . . .78 C6
Beam Ave RM10 . . . . .103 D6
Beames Ho SW8 . . . . .269 C2
Beames Rd NW10. . . . . .89 B6
Beaminster Ct N15. . . . . . . .51 B4
Beaminster Gdns IG6 . . . . . .56 D6
Beaminster Ho SW8 . . . . . .270 C4
Beamish Dr WD23. . . . . .8 A3
Beamish Ho 7 SE16 . . . . . .118 C2
Beamish Rd N9. . . . . .18 A3
Beanacre Cl E9. . . . . .75 B2
Bean Rd DA6 . . . . .146 D1
Beanshaw SE9. . . . . .188 C6
Beansland Gr RM6. . . . . . . .59 A6
Bear Alley EC4. . . . . .241 C2
Bear Cl RM7 . . . . .59 D3
Bear Croft Ho 6 SW6 . . . . .135 B3
Beardow Gr N14. . . . . .15 C5
Beard Rd KT2. . . . . .176 B5
Beardsfield E13 . . . . .99 A5
Beard's Hill TW12. . . . . . . .173 A5
Beards Hill Cl TW12. . . . . .173 C2
Beardsley Terr RM8. . . . . . . .80 B3
Beardsley Way W3 . . . . . . .111 B4
Beard's Rd TW15, TW16. . . .171 C4
Bearfield Rd KT2. . . . . .176 A3
Bear Gdns SE1. . . .117 A5 252 A4
Bear La SE1 . . . . .116 D5 251 D3
Bear Rd TW13 . . . . .172 D6
Bear St WC2 . . . . .249 D6
Bearstead Rise SE4 . . . . . .163 B6
Bearsted Terr 7 BR3. . . . . .185 C2
Beasley's Ait TW17. . . . . . .193 D3
Beasley's Ait La TW16,
TW17. . . . . .193 D3
Beaton Cl SE15 . . . . .139 D4
Beatrice Ave
Thornton Heath SW16. . . .182 B1
Wembley HA9. . . . . .66 A3
Beatrice Cl Newham E13 . . .99 A3
Pinner HA5. . . . . .40 A5
Beatrice Ct
Buckhurst Hill IG9 . . . . . .21 D2
Hendon NW4 . . . . .46 C4
Beatrice Ho
1 Brixton SW2 . . . . .160 B6
Forest Hill SE6 . . . . .163 C2
4 Hammersmith W6. . . .112 C1
2 Stepney E1 . . . . .96 D2
Beatrice Lo 3 N12. . . . . . . .30 A4
Beatrice Pl W8 . . . . .255 C5
Beatrice Rd
Bermondsey SE1 . . . . . . .118 A2
Edmonton N9 . . . . .18 C4
Finsbury Pk N4 . . . . .50 C2
2 Richmond TW10 . . . . .154 B6
Southall UB1. . . . . .107 B5
Walthamstow E17 . . . . . .53 C4
Beatrice Tate Sch 33 E2 . . .96 B4
Beatrice Webb Ho 4 E3. . .97 A5
Beatrix Ho SW5. . . . . .255 D2
Beatrix Potter Prim Sch
SW18. . . . . .158 A3
Beatson Wlk 22 SE16. . . . . .118 D5
Beattie Cl TW14. . . . . .149 D3
Beattie Ho SW8. . . . . .269 B2
Beattock Rise N10. . . . . . . .49 B5
Beatty Ho 16 E14. . . . . .119 C4
Beatty Rd Stanmore HA7. . .25 C4
Stoke Newington N16. . . .73 C4
Beattyville Gdns IG6. . . . . . .56 D5
Beauchamp Cl 17 W4 . . . . .111 A3
Beauchamp Ct HA7 . . . . . . .25 C5
Beauchamp Pl
SW3. . . . . .114 C3 257 B6
Beauchamp Rd
Clapham SW11. . . . . . . .136 D1
East Molesey KT8. . . . . . .196 A4
South Norwood SE19 . . . .183 B2
Sutton SM1. . . . . .217 C4
Twickenham TW1. . . . . . .153 A4
Upton E7. . . . . .77 B1
Beauchamp St EC1. . . . . . .241 A3
Beauchamp Terr SW15. . . .134 B2
Beauclerc Inf Sch TW16. . . .194 C6
Beauclerc Rd W6 . . . . .112 B3
Beauclerk Ho 1 SM2 . . . . .218 A1
Beauclerk Cl 1 TW13. . . . .150 B3
Beauclerk Ho 10 SW16. . . .160 A1
Beaudesert Mews UB7. . . . .104 A4
Beaufort Ct
Beaufort Ave HA3. . . . . . .43 B6
Beaufort Cl Chingford E4 . . .35 B4
Ealing W5 . . . . .88 B2
Putney SW19 . . . . .156 B4

Beaufort Ct
Friern Barnet N11 . . . . . .31 B5
Harrow HA3. . . . . .43 A3
3 New Barnet EN5 . . . . .14 A6
Richmond TW10 . . . . . . .175 C6
West Brompton SW6 . . . .265 A6
Beaufort Dr NW11 . . . . .47 C5
Beaufort Gdns
Hendon NW4 . . . . .46 C3
Heston TW5 . . . . .129 A4
Ilford IG1 . . . . .56 C1
Knightsbridge
SW3. . . . . .114 C3 257 B6
South Norwood SW16 . . . .182 B3
Beaufort Ho
Ashford TW15. . . . . .170 D5
Battersea SW11 . . . . . . .136 C3
Chelsea SW3 . . . . .266 D5
Hampstead Garden Suburb
NW11. . . . . .48 A3
20 Millwall E14. . . . . . . .119 C4
Pimlico SW1. . . . . .259 C1
8 South Tottenham N15 . .51 D5
1 Wimbledon SW20 . . . .178 D2
Beaufort Mans SW3. . . . . .266 D5
Beaufort Mews SW6 . . . . . .264 D6
Beaufort Pk NW11 . . . . .47 C5
Beaufort Rd Ealing W5 . . . . .88 B2
Kingston u T KT1, KT5,
KT6. . . . . .198 A5
Richmond TW10 . . . . . . .175 C6
Ruislip HA4. . . . . .61 B6
Twickenham TW1. . . . . . .153 C4
Beaufort St SW3 . .136 B6 266 C6
Beaufort Way KT17 . . . . . . .216 A1
Beaufoy Ho
South Lambeth SW8. . . . .270 A4
3 West Norwood SE27 . . .160 D1
Beaufoy Rd
11 London SW8 . . . . . . .137 B2
Tottenham N17. . . . . .33 C3
Beaufoy Wlk
SE11. . . . . .116 B2 260 D3
Beaulieu Ave
Forest Hill SE26 . . . . . . .184 B6
1 Newham E16 . . . . . . .121 B5
Beaulieu Cl
Camberwell SE5 . . . . . . .139 B2
Colindale NW9. . . . . .45 C5
Hounslow TW4 . . . . .151 B6
Mitcham CR4 . . . . .181 A4
14 Twickenham TW1. . . .153 D5
Beaulieu Ct W5. . . . . .88 A2
Beaulieu Dr HA5. . . . . .40 D2
Beaulieu Gdns N21 . . . . . . .17 A4
Beaulieu Ho 6 NW4 . . . . . .28 D1
Beaulieu Hts CR7 . . . . .183 C2
Beaulieu Pl W4 . . . . .111 A3
Beaumanor Gdns SE9. . . . .188 C6
Beaumanor Mans W2 . . . . .245 D6
Beaumaris 5 N11. . . . . .32 A4
Beaumaris Dr IG8 . . . . .37 D3
Beaumaris Gn NW9 . . . . . . .45 C3
Beaumaris Twr 2 W3 . . . . .110 D4
Beaumont SW15. . . . . .157 A6
Beaumont Ave
Harrow HA2. . . . . .41 D3
Richmond TW9 . . . . .132 B2
Wembley HA0. . . . . .65 C4
West Kensington
W14. . . . . .113 B1 254 C2
Beaumont Bldgs WC2. . . .240 B1
Beaumont Cl
East Finchley N2. . . . . . . .48 C5
Kingston u T KT2. . . . . . .176 C3
Beaumont Cres
W14. . . . . .113 B1 254 C1
Beaumont Ct
10 Acton Green W4 . . . .111 A1
16 Hendon NW9. . . . . . .27 D1
Lower Clapton E5 . . . . . . .74 B5
Marylebone W1 . . . . .238 B4
7 Mile End E1 . . . . .97 A4
6 Mitcham CR4. . . . . . . .181 A1
Wembley HA0. . . . . .65 C3
17 Wimbledon SW19 . . .178 D3
Beaumont Dr
Ashford TW15. . . . . .171 B5
New Malden KT4 . . . . . . .200 B2
Beaumont Gdns NW3 . . . . .69 C5
Beaumont Gr E1. . . . . .96 D3
Beaumont Ho
12 Leyton E10. . . . . .53 D2
1 Streatham SW2. . . . . .160 A3
West Kensington W14 . . .254 D3
Wimbledon SW19 . . . . . .157 C1
Beaumont Lo E8. . . . . .74 A2
Beaumont Pl Barnet EN5 . . .1 B4
Fitzrovia NW1, WC1,
W1. . . . . .93 C3 239 B6
Isleworth TW7 . . . . .152 B6
Beaumont Prim Sch E10 . . .53 D1
Beaumont Rd Leyton E10. . .53 D2
Newham E13 . . . . .99 B4
Orpington BR5. . . . . .211 B3
Putney SW15, SW19. . . . .157 A4
South Acton W4 . . . . . . .111 A3
South Norwood SE19 . . . .183 A4
Beaumont Rise N19. . . . . . .49 D1
Beaumont Sq E1. . . . . .96 D2

Beaumont St W1 . . . . .238 B4
Beaumont Terr 1 SE13. .164 C4
Beaumont Wlk NW3 . . . . . . .70 D1
Beauvais Terr UB5 . . . . .84 D4
Beauvale 6 NW1 . . . . .71 A1
Beaver Cl Hampton TW12 . .173 D2
8 Penge SE20. . . . . . . .184 A3
West Barnes SM4. . . . . . .200 C2
Beaver Ctr The RM8. . . . . . .59 A2
Beaver Gr UB5. . . . . .85 A4
Beaverbank Rd SE9. . . . . . .167 B3
Beavers Com Prim Sch The
TW4 . . . . .128 C2
Beavers Cres TW4 . . . . .128 D1
Beavers La TW4. . . . . .128 C2
Beavers Lo DA14. . . . . .189 D5
Beaverwood Rd BR7. . . . . . .189 C4
Beaverwood Sch for Girls
BR7. . . . . .189 C4
Beavis Ho N16. . . . . .73 C5
Beavor La W6 . . . . .112 A1
Bebbington Rd SE18 . . . . . .123 C2
Beblets Cl 4 BR6. . . . . .227 D3
Bec Cl HA4 . . . . .62 D5
Beccles Dr IG11 . . . . .79 D2
Beccles St E14. . . . . .119 B6
Bechervaise Ct 2 E10 . . . . .53 D1
Beck Cl SE13 . . . . .141 D4
Beck Ct BR3. . . . . .206 D6
BECKENHAM. 185 C1
Beckenham Beacon Hospl
BR3. . . . . .185 B3
Beckenham Bsns Ctr
BR3. . . . . .185 A4
Beckenham Ct BR3. . . . . . .185 C2
Beckenham Gdns N9. . . . . . .17 C1
Beckenham Gr BR2. . . . . . .186 B1
Beckenham Hill Rd BR3,
SE6. . . . . .186 A5
Beckenham Hill Sta SE6. . .186 A5
Beckenham Junction Sta
BR3. . . . . .185 C2
Beckenham La BR1, BR2. . .186 D1
Beckenham Place Pk
BR3 . . . . .185 D3
Beckenham Rd
Penge BR3. . . . . .185 D1
West Wickham BR3, BR4 . .208 A2
Beckers The N16. . . . . .74 A4
Becket Ave E6 . . . . .100 C4
Becket Cl Croydon SE25 . . .206 A3
2 Merton SW19 . . . . . . .179 D2
Becket Fold 10 HA1 . . . . . . .42 D4
Becket Ho SE1. . . . . .252 C1
Becket Rd N18. . . . . .34 C6
Becket St SE1 . . . . .262 C6
Beckett Cl
Abbey Wood DA17. . . . . .125 B3
Streatham SW16 . . . . . . .159 D2
Willesden NW10. . . . . . . .67 C2
Beckett Ho
28 London SW9 . . . . . . .138 A3
15 Stepney E1 . . . . .96 C2
Becketts Cl
Feltham TW14 . . . . .150 B5
Orpington BR6. . . . . .227 D5
Becketts Pl KT1. . . . . .175 D2
Beckett Wlk BR3. . . . . .185 A4
Beckfoot NW1. . . . . .232 B3
Beckford Cl W14. . . . . .254 D3
Beckford Dr BR5. . . . . .211 B2
Beckford Ho 16 N16. . . . . . .73 C3
Beckford Prim Sch NW6 . . .69 B3
Beckford Rd CR0. . . . . .205 D3
Beckham Ho SE11. . . . . . . .260 D3
Beck Ho 4 Edmonton N18. .34 A5
Stoke Newington N16. . . .73 C5
Beckington 18 NW5 . . . . . . .71 A2
Beck La BR3. . . . . .206 D6
Beckley Ho E3. . . . . .97 B3
Becklow Gdns
Chiswick W12. . . . . .111 D4
1 Shepherd's Bush W12. .112 A4
Becklow Mews 9 W12. . . . .112 A4
Becklow Rd W12. . . . . .112 A4
Beckmead Sch BR3. . . . . . .207 C1
Beck Rd E8. . . . . .96 B6
Mitcham CR4 . . . . .202 D3
Beck River Pk 10 BR3. . . . .185 C2
Becks Rd DA14. . . . . .168 A1
BECKTON. 100 D2
Beckton Alps E6. . . . . .100 D3
Beckton Alps Ski Ctr E6. . .100 C3
Beckton Park Sta E6. . . . . .122 B6
Beckton Rd E16. . . . . .98 D2
Beckton Ret Pk E6. . . . . . . .100 C2
Beckton Sta E6. . . . . .100 C2
Beckton Triangle Ret Pk
E6. . . . . .100 D3
Beck Way BR3. . . . . .207 B6
Beckway Rd SW16. . . . . . . .181 D1
Beckway St SE17 .117 C2 263 A3
Beckwith Ho 22 E2. . . . . . . .96 B5
Beckwith Rd SE24 . . . . . . .161 B6
Beclands Rd SW17. . . . . . . .181 A4
Becmead Ave Harrow HA3. .43 B6
Streatham SW16 . . . . . . .181 D6
Becondale Rd SE19 . . . . . .183 C5

BECONTREE. 81 A4
Becontree Ave RM8. . . . . . .80 C5
Becontree Prim Sch RM8 . .80 B5
Becontree Sta RM9 . . . . . . .80 D2
Bective Pl SW15 . . . . .135 B1
Bective Rd E7 Forest Gate E7 . .77 A4
Putney SW15. . . . . .135 B1
Becton Pl DA8 . . . . .147 D5
Bedale Rd EN2. . . . . .5 A5
Bedale St SE1 . . . . .252 C3
Beddan Ct HA8 . . . . .26 C4
BEDDINGTON. 220 A6
BEDDINGTON CORNER. . . .203 A2
Beddington Cross CR0 . . . .204 A2
Beddington Farm Rd
CR0. . . . . .204 A1
Beddington Gdns SM5,
SM6. . . . . .219 A2
Beddington Gn BR5. . . . . . .189 D2
Beddington Gr SM6. . . . . . .219 D3
Beddington Inf Sch
SM6 . . . . .219 C4
Beddington La
Wallington CR0. . . . . . . .203 D2
Wallington CR0. . . . . . . .220 A6
Beddington Lane Sta
CR0. . . . . .203 C3
Beddington Manor SM2. .218 B2
Beddington Park Cotts
SM6. . . . . .219 D5
Beddington Park Prim Sch
CR0. . . . . .219 D5
Beddington Rd Ilford IG3 . .57 D2
St Paul's Cray BR5. . . . . .189 D2
Beddington Terr CR0. . . . . .204 B2
Beddington Trad Est
CR0. . . . . .204 A1
Bede Cl HA5. . . . . .22 D2
Bedefield WC1. . . . . .233 B1
Bede Ho London SE14. . . . .141 B4
5 Putney SW15. . . . . . . .156 D5
Bedelsford Specl Sch
KT1. . . . . .198 A6
Bedens Rd DA14. . . . . .191 A5
Bede Rd RM6. . . . . .58 C3
Bedevere Rd N9 . . . . .18 A1
Bedfont Cl
East Bedfont TW14. . . . . .149 A5
Mitcham CR4 . . . . .181 A1
Bedfont Green Cl TW14. . . .149 A3
Bedfont Ind Pk TW15. . . . .149 D6
Bedfont Ind Pk NTW15. . . .149 A1
Bedfont Jun & Inf Schs
TW14 . . . . .149 C5
Bedfont La TW14, TW13. . . .149 D4
Bedfont Lakes Ctry Pk
TW14 . . . . .149 A2
Bedfont Rd
East Bedfont TW13,
TW14 . . . . .149 B2
Stanwell TW19 . . . . .148 B5
Bedford Ave Barnet EN5. . . .13 B6
Bloomsbury WC1 . . .93 D2 239 D3
Hayes UB4 . . . . .84 B1
Bedfordbury
WC2. . . . . .116 A6 250 A5
Bedford Cl Chiswick W4 . . .133 D6
Muswell Hill N10 . . . . . . .31 A3
Bedford Cnr 3 W4. . . . . . . .111 C2
Bedford Court Mans
WC1. . . . . .239 D3
Bedford Ct
6 Richmond TW9 . . . . . .132 B1
South Norwood SE19 . . . .183 D2
St James WC2 . . . . .250 A5
Wembley HA0. . . . . .65 D4
Bedford Gardens Ho W8 . .245 B3
Bedford Gdns
W8. . . . . .113 C5 245 B3
Bedford Hill SW12 . . . . . . .159 B2
Bedford Ho 2 Acton W4 . . .111 C2
Edgware HA8. . . . . .26 B3
7 Stockwell SW4 . . . . . .138 A1
Bedford Mews SE6. . . . . . .163 D2
BEDFORD PARK. 111 C3
Bedford Park Cnr 5
W4. . . . . .111 C2
Bedford Park Mans 4
W4. . . . . .111 B2
Bedford Pas SW6 . . . . .264 B4
Bedford Pk CR0. . . . . .205 A1
Bedford Pl
Bloomsbury WC1 . . .94 A2 240 A4
Croydon CR0. . . . . .205 B1
Bedford Rd Acton W4 . . . . .111 C3
Barking IG11 . . . . .100 C6
Crouch End N8. . . . . .49 C6
Ealing W13 . . . . .109 B6
East Finchley N2. . . . . . . .48 C6
Edgware HA7. . . . . .11 C1
Edmonton N9 . . . . .18 B4
Harrow HA1 . . . . .42 A3
Ilford IG1 . . . . .78 D5
North Cheam KT4. . . . . . .216 C6
Ruislip HA4. . . . . .61 D4
Sidcup DA15. . . . . .167 C1
South Tottenham N15. . . .51 C5
Stockwell SW2, SW4 . . . .138 A1
Twickenham TW2 . . . . . . .152 B1
Walthamstow E17 . . . . . .53 C6

Bedford Rd continued
Woodford E18. . . . .**37** A1
Wood Green N22 . . . .**32** A1
Bedford Row WC1 . .**94** B2 **240** D3
Bedford Sq WC1 . . .**93** D2 **239** D3
Bedford St WC2. . . . .**116** A6 **250** B5
Bedford Terr SM2. . . . .**218** A2
Bedford Villas **3** SM5 . . . .**218** D5
Bedford Way WC1. . .**93** D3 **239** D3
Bedgebury Gdns SW19. . . . .**157** A2
Bedgebury Rd SE9 . . . .**143** D1
Bedivere Rd BR1. . . . .**165** A1
Bedlam Mews SE11. . . . . . .**261** A4
Bedlow Cl NW8. . . . .**236** D5
Bedlow Way CR0. . . . .**220** B4
Bedonwell Inf Sch DA17. . .**147** A6
Bedonwell Jun Sch
DA17. . . . .**147** A6
Bedonwell Rd
Bexley DA17. . . . .**147** A6
Erith DA7. . . . .**147** C5
Bedser Cl
Kennington SE11. . . . .**270** D6
South Norwood CR7. . . . . .**205** A6
Bedser Ct **7** SW4. . . . .**138** A3
Bedser Dr UB6. . . . .**64** B3
Bedster Gdns KT8. . . . .**195** D6
Bedwardine Rd SE19. . . . . .**183** C3
Bedwell Ct **4** RM6. . . . . . .**58** D2
Bedwell Gdns UB3. . . . . . .**105** C2
Bedwell Ho **18** SW9. . . . . .**138** C3
Bedwell Rd
Belvedere DA17. . . . .**125** C1
Tottenham N17. . . . .**33** C2
Beeby Rd E16. . . . .**99** B2
Beech Ave Acton W3 . . . . . .**111** C5
Brentford TW8. . . . .**131** B5
4 Chigwell IG9 . . . .**21** B2
East Barnet N20 . . . .**14** C3
Ruislip HA4. . . . .**40** B1
Sidcup DA15. . . . .**168** A4
Beech Cl Ashford TW15. . . .**171** B5
Carshalton SM5 . . . .**218** D6
Deptford SE8 . . . .**141** B6
Enfield N9. . . . .**18** B5
Putney SW15 . . . .**156** A4
Sunbury TW16 . . . .**172** D1
West Drayton UB7 . . . .**104** C3
Wimbledon SW19. . . . .**178** C4
Beech Copse Bickley BR1. .**188** B1
South Croydon CR2. . . . . .**221** C3
Beechcroft
Chislehurst BR7 . . . .**188** C3
3 Kingston u T KT2 . . . . .**176** D2
Beechcroft Ave
Golders Green NW11 . . . . . .**47** B2
Harrow HA2. . . . .**41** C2
Kingston u T KT1, KT3 . . . .**177** A1
Beechcroft Cl
Heston TW5 . . . .**129** A5
Orpington BR6. . . . .**227** B4
Streatham SW16 . . . .**182** B5
Beechcroft Ct
3 Golders Green NW11 . . . .**47** B2
Greenwich SE3 . . . .**143** A4
8 Woodside Pk N12. . . . . .**29** D6
Beech Croft Ct N5 . . . .**72** D4
Beechcroft Gdns HA9 . . . . .**66** B5
Beechcroft Ho W5. . . . .**88** A2
Beechcroft Lo **6** SM2. . . . .**218** A1
Beechcroft Mans SW16 . . .**182** B5
Beechcroft Rd
Chessington KT9 . . . .**214** B5
Mortlake SW14 . . . .**133** A2
Orpington BR6. . . . .**227** B4
Upper Tooting SW17. . . . . .**158** C2
Woodford E18. . . . .**37** B1
Beechcroft Way N19 . . . . . .**49** D1
Beech Ct Beckenham BR3. .**185** B3
3 Buckhurst Hill IG9. . . . .**21** D2
Child's Hill NW2. . . . .**69** B6
Hayes UB3 . . . .**105** D5
6 Ilford E12 . . . .**78** C5
Marylebone W1. . . . .**237** C2
Northolt UB5. . . . .**85** A6
43 Notting Hill W2 . . . . . .**91** C2
7 Rotherhithe SE16 . . . . .**119** A5
Surbiton KT6. . . . .**198** A2
Teddington TW11 . . . .**175** C4
Walthamstow E17 . . . .**54** B6
4 West Norwood SW16 . . .**182** C5
Beechdale N21. . . . .**16** B2
Beechdale Rd SW2. . . . . . .**160** B5
Beech Dell BR2, BR6. . . . . .**226** B4
Beechdene **4** SE15. . . . . .**140** B4
Beech Dr N2 . . . .**48** D6
Beechen Cliff Way **2**
TW7. . . . .**130** D3
Beechengrove HA5. . . . .**41** B6
Beechen Pl SE23. . . . .**162** C2
Beeches Ave SM5. . . . .**218** C1
Beeches Cl SE20 . . . .**184** C2
Beeches Ct BR1. . . . .**187** A4
Beeches Prim Ctr The
SE2. . . . .**124** C3
Beeches Rd Cheam SM3. . .**201** A1
Upper Tooting SW17. . . . . .**158** D1
Beeches The Ealing W7. . . .**108** D4
East Barnet N20. . . . .**14** C2
East Ham E12. . . . .**78** B1

Beeches The continued
Hounslow TW3. . . . .**129** D4
Mitcham CR4 . . . .**202** C4
1 Upper Holloway N19. . . .**50** A1
Beechey Ho **30** E1 . . . .**118** B5
Beech Farm Cotts IG8 . . . . .**36** B3
Beechfield Cotts BR1. . . . .**187** C1
Beechfield Ct **7** CR2. . . . .**221** B4
Beechfield Rd
Bromley BR1. . . . .**187** C1
Forest Hill SE6. . . . .**163** B3
Harringay N4 . . . .**51** A3
Beech Gdns
Dagenham RM10 . . . .**81** D1
Ealing W5. . . . .**110** A3
Beech Gr
Kingston u T KT3 . . . .**199** B6
Mitcham CR4 . . . .**203** D5
Beech Hall Cres E4. . . . .**36** B3
Beech Hall Rd E4 . . . .**36** B3
Beech Hill EN4 . . . .**2** C5
Beech Hill Ave EN4. . . . .**2** B4
Beech Ho Chingford E4 . . . . .**35** C6
Hayes UB4 . . . .**84** D2
Heston TW5 . . . .**129** A5
6 Maitland Pk NW3 . . . . . .**70** D2
New Addington CR0 . . . . . .**223** D2
22 Rotherhithe SE16 . . . . .**118** C4
7 Sidcup DA15 . . . .**168** A1
5 Stoke Newington N16. . . .**73** B6
12 Wallington SM6. . . . . . .**219** C2
Beech La IG9. . . . .**21** B2
Beech Lawns N12. . . . .**30** B5
Beechmont Cl BR1. . . . . . .**186** C5
Beechmore Gdns SM3 . . . .**216** D6
Beechmore Rd
SW11. . . . .**136** D4 **267** D1
Beechmount Ave W7. . . . . . .**86** C2
Beecholme **15** N12. . . . .**29** D6
Beecholme Ave CR4 . . . . . .**181** B2
Beecholme Est E5 . . . .**74** B5
Beecholme Prim Sch
CR4. . . . .**181** B2
Beech Rd Bowes Pk N11 . . . .**32** A4
East Bedfont TW14. . . . . . .**149** C4
Thornton Heath SW16 . . . .**204** B6
Beechrow KT2. . . . .**176** A6
Beech St EC2. . . . . .**95** A2 **242** B4
Beech Tree Cl
Islington N1. . . . .**72** C1
Stanmore HA7 . . . .**25** C5
Beech Tree Glade E4 . . . . . .**20** D3
Beech Tree Pl SM1 . . . .**217** D3
Beechvale Cl N12. . . . .**30** C5
Beechway DA5 . . . .**168** D5
Beech Way
Twickenham TW2 . . . .**151** C1
Willesden NW10. . . . .**67** B1
Beech Wlk NW7 . . . .**27** C4
Beechwood Ave
Ashford TW16. . . . .**172** A4
East Finchley N3. . . . .**47** C6
Greenford UB6. . . . .**85** D4
Harrow HA2 . . . .**63** D5
Hayes UB3 . . . .**105** B6
Hillingdon UB8. . . . .**82** C1
Orpington BR6 . . . .**227** C2
Richmond TW9 . . . .**132** C4
Ruislip HA4. . . . .**61** D6
Thornton Heath CR7. . . . . .**204** D5
Beechwood Circ HA2. . . . . .**63** D5
Beechwood Cl
Edgware NW7 . . . .**27** C5
Fortis Green N2 . . . .**48** D5
Surbiton KT6. . . . .**197** D2
Beechwood Cres DA7 . . . . .**147** A2
Beechwood Ct
Ashford TW16. . . . .**172** A5
Carshalton SM5 . . . .**218** D4
Cheam SM1 . . . .**217** C3
Chiswick W4. . . . .**133** B6
Stamford Hill N16. . . . .**51** C2
Sutton SM2. . . . .**218** B2
Beechwood Dr
Keston BR2. . . . .**225** D4
Woodford IG8. . . . .**36** D5
Beechwood Gdns
Ealing NW10. . . . .**88** B4
Harrow HA2 . . . .**63** D5
Ilford IG5. . . . .**56** C5
Beechwood Gr W3. . . . .**111** C6
Beechwood Hall N3. . . . . . .**47** B6
Beechwood Ho **23** E2 . . . . .**96** B5
Beechwood Mews **2** N9. .**18** A2
Beechwood Pk E18. . . . .**55** A6
Beechwood Rd Dalston E8 . .**73** C2
London N8 . . . .**50** A5
South Croydon CR2. . . . . .**221** C1
Beechwood Rise BR7 . . . . .**188** D6
Beechwoods Ct **5** SE19. .**183** D5
Beechworth Cl NW3 . . . .**69** C6
Beecroft La SE4. . . . .**163** A6
Beecroft Mews SE4. . . . . . .**163** A6
Beecroft Rd SE4. . . . .**163** A6
Beehive Cl Dalston E8. . . . . .**73** D1
Elstree WD6. . . . .**9** D5
Hillingdon UB10 . . . .**60** B1

Beehive Ct IG1. . . . .**56** B3
Beehive La IG1. . . . .**56** B3
Beehive Pl SW9. . . . .**138** C2
Beehive Prep Sch IG4. . . . . .**56** B4
Beeken Dene BR6. . . . .**227** A4
Beeleigh Rd SM4 . . . .**201** D5
Beeston Cl **5** Dalston E8 . . .**74** A3
South Oxhey WD19. . . . . . .**22** D6
Beeston Pl SW1 . . . .**258** D6
Beeston Rd EN4 . . . .**14** B5
Beeston's Ho SE15. . . . . . .**140** B2
Beeston Way TW14. . . . . . .**150** C5
Beethoven Rd WD6 . . . .**9** D5
Beethoven St W10. . . . .**91** A4
Beeton Cl HA5. . . . .**23** C3
Begbie Ho SW9. . . . .**138** B3
Begbie Rd SE3. . . . .**143** C4
Beggars Hill KT17. . . . .**215** D2
Beggar's Roost La SM1. . . .**217** C2
Begonia Cl E6. . . . .**100** B3
Begonia Pl **1** TW12. . . . . .**173** C4
Begonia Wlk W12. . . . .**89** D1
Beira St SW12. . . . .**159** B4
Beis Chinuch Lebonos Girls
Sch N4. . . . .**51** A2
Beis Hamedrash Elyon
NW11. . . . .**47** A2
Beis Malka Girls Sch N16. .**51** D1
Beis Rochel d'Satmar Girls
Sch **1** N16. . . . .**51** C2
Beis Soroh Schneirer (Sch)
4 NW4. . . . .**46** A3
Beis Yaakov Prim Sch
NW9. . . . .**45** B6
Bekesbourne St **17** E14. . . .**97** A1
Belcroft Cl BR1. . . . .**186** D3
Beldanes Lo NW10. . . . .**68** A1
Beldham Gdns KT8 . . . .**195** D6
Belenoyd Ct SW16. . . . . . .**160** B1
Belfairs Dr RM6. . . . .**58** C2
Belfairs Gn WD19. . . . .**22** D5
Belfast Rd Croydon SE25. .**206** B5
Stoke Newington N16. . . . . .**73** D6
Belfield Rd KT19. . . . .**215** C1
Belford Gr SE18. . . . .**122** C2
Belford Ho **7** E8. . . . .**95** D6
Belfort Rd SE15. . . . .**140** C3
Belfry Cl **33** SE16. . . . . . .**118** B1
Belfry Rd E12. . . . .**77** D6
Belgrade Ho N16. . . . .**73** C4
Belgrade Rd
Hampton TW12. . . . .**173** D2
Stoke Newington N16. . . . . .**73** C4
Belgrave Cl **1** Acton W3 .**111** A4
Burnt Oak NW7. . . . .**27** B5
Southgate N14 . . . .**15** C6
Belgrave Cres TW16. . . . . .**172** B2
Belgrave Ct
8 Acton Green W4 . . . . . .**111** A1
Charlton SE3. . . . .**143** C5
22 Limehouse E14 . . . . . .**119** B6
Newham E13 . . . .**99** C3
Nine Elms SW8. . . . .**269** A3
Belgrave Gdns
Kilburn NW8. . . . .**91** D6
Southgate N14 . . . .**3** D1
1 Stanmore HA7. . . . .**25** C5
St John's Wood NW8 . . . . .**229** A5
Belgrave Ho SW9 . . . .**138** C5
Belgrave Hts **11** **55** A1
Belgrave Mans NW8 . . . . . .**229** A5
Belgrave Market IG1. . . . . . .**78** C6
Belgrave Mews N SW1 . . . .**248** A1
Belgrave Mews S
SW1. . . . .**115** A3 **258** B6
Belgrave Mews W SW1. . . .**258** A6
Belgrave Pl SW1. . . .**115** A3 **258** B5
Belgrave Rd
Barnes SW13 . . . .**133** D5
Hounslow TW4. . . . .**129** B2
Leyton E10 . . . .**54** A1
Mitcham CR4 . . . .**202** B6
Newham E13 . . . .**99** C3
Redbridge IG1. . . . .**56** B1
South Norwood SE25. . . . .**205** D5
Sunbury TW16 . . . .**172** B2
Walthamstow E17 . . . .**53** C3
Wanstead E11 . . . .**55** A1
Westminster SW1 .**115** C2 **259** A3
Belgrave Sq
SW1. . . . .**115** A3 **258** A6
Belgrave St E1. . . . .**96** D1
Belgrave Terr IG8. . . . .**21** A1
Belgrave Wlk CR4. . . . .**202** B6
Belgrave Wlk Sta CR4. . . . .**202** B5
Belgrave Yd SW1 . . . .**258** C5
BELGRAVIA. **115** B2
Belgravia Cl EN5. . . . .**1** B2
Belgravia Ct SW1. . . . .**258** C5
Belgravia Gdns BR1. . . . . .**186** C4
Belgravia Ho
11 London SW4 . . . .**159** D5
1 Teddington TW11. . . . . .**175** C3
Belgravia Lo N21. . . . .**16** D6
Belgravia Mews KT1 . . . . . .**197** D5
Belgrove St WC1. . . . .**233** B2
Belham Wlk **13** SE5. . . . . .**139** B4
Belinda Rd **8** SW9. . . . . . .**138** D2
Belitha Villas N1. . . . .**72** C1

Bel La TW13. . . . .**151** B1
Bellamy Cl Edgware HA8 . . .**11** A1
13 Millwall E14. . . . .**119** C4
Uxbridge UB10 . . . .**60** C5
West Kensington SW5 . . . .**254** D1
Bellamy Ct HA7. . . . .**25** B2
Bellamy Dr HA7. . . . .**25** B2
Bellamy Ho Harrow HA3. . . .**44** A2
Heston TW5 . . . .**129** C6
Upper Tooting SW17. . . . . .**180** B6
Bellamy Rd Chingford E4 . . .**35** D4
Enfield EN3. . . . .**6** D5
Bellamy's Ct **16** SE16. . . . .**118** D5
Bellamy St SW12. . . . .**159** B4
Bellarmine Cl SE28 . . . . . .**123** D4
Bellasis Ave SW2. . . . .**160** A2
Bell Ave UB7. . . . .**104** B3
Bell Cl Pinner HA5 . . . .**40** C6
Ruislip HA4. . . . .**61** D5
Bellclose Rd UB7. . . . .**104** A4
Bell Ct Hendon NW4. . . . . . .**46** C5
Ladywell SE13 . . . .**163** C6
Tolworth KT5 . . . .**214** D6
Bell Dr SW18. . . . .**157** A4
Bellefields Rd SW9 . . . . . .**138** B2
Bellegrove Cl DA16 . . . . . .**145** D3
Bellegrove Par DA16. . . . . .**145** D2
Bellegrove Rd DA16. . . . . .**145** D3
Bellenden Prim Sch **5**
SE15. . . . .**140** A2
Bellenden Rd SE15. . . . . . .**139** D3
Bellenden Rd Ret Pk
SE15. . . . .**140** A4
Bellenden Road Bsns Ctr
SE15. . . . .**139** D3
Bellerbys Coll SE8 . . . .**141** C6
Belle Staines Pleasaunce
E4 . . . .**19** C2
Belleville Prim Sch
SW11. . . . .**158** D6
Belleville Rd SW11. . . . . . .**158** D6
Belle Vue UB6. . . . .**86** B6
Belle Vue La WD23 . . . .**8** B3
Belle Vue Gdns SW9. . . . . .**138** A3
Bellevue Mews N11. . . . . . .**31** A5
Bellevue Pk CR7. . . . .**205** A5
Bellevue Pl E1. . . . .**96** C3
Bellevue Rd
Barnes SW13 . . . .**134** A3
Bexley DA6. . . . .**169** B6
Ealing W13 . . . .**87** B3
Friern Barnet N11. . . . .**31** A5
Kingston u T KT1. . . . .**198** A6
Upper Tooting SW17. . . . . .**158** D3
Belle Vue Rd
Chingford E4. . . . .**36** B1
8 Hendon NW4. . . . .**46** C5
Bellew St SW17. . . . .**158** A1
Bellfield CR0. . . . .**223** B1
Bellfield Ave HA3 . . . .**24** B4
Bellfield Cl SE3. . . . .**143** B5
Bell Flats **4** NW2. . . . .**68** A2
Bellflower Cl **2** E6. . . . . .**100** A2
Bellflower Ct SE13. . . . . . .**141** D1
Bellgate Mews NW5 . . . . . .**71** B5
Bell Gn SE26. . . . .**185** B6
Bellgrave Lo **9** W4. . . . . . .**110** D1
Bell Green La SE26. . . . . . .**185** B6
Bell Ho
6 Dagenham RM10. . . . . .**81** D2
Greenwich SE10. . . . .**142** A6
15 Streatham SW2. . . . . .**160** C4
Wembley HA9. . . . .**66** A5
West Heath SE2. . . . .**124** D1
Bellina Mews NW5. . . . .**71** C4
Bell Ind Est **2** W4 . . . .**111** A4
Bellingham Rd SE6. . . . . . .**164** A1
Bellingham Sta SE6. . . . . . .**163** D1
Bellingham Trad Est
SE6. . . . .**163** D2
Bell Inn Yd EC3 . . . .**242** D1
Bell La Enfield EN3 . . . .**6** D5
Hendon NW4 . . . .**46** D5
Newham E16 . . . .**121** A5
Spitalfields E1. . . . . .**95** D2 **243** D3
Twickenham TW1 . . . .**153** A3
Wembley HA9 . . . .**65** D6
Bell Lane Prim Sch **7**
NW4. . . . .**46** D5
Bell Language Sch
W1. . . . .**93** C3 **239** A5
Bellmaker Ct **13** E3 . . . .**97** C2
Bell Mdw SE19. . . . .**183** C6
Bell Moor NW3 . . . .**70** B4
Bellmore Ct **5** CR0. . . . . .**205** D1
Bello Cl SE24, SW2 . . . . . .**160** D3
Bellot Gdns **1** SE10. . . . . .**120** C1
Bellot St SE10 . . . .**120** C1
Bell Rd East Molesey KT8. .**196** B4
Enfield EN1. . . . .**5** B4
Hounslow TW3. . . . .**129** D1
Bellring Cl DA17. . . . .**147** C6
Bell's Coll IG3. . . . .**58** A1
Bells Hill EN5. . . . .**12** D6

Bell St Kidbrooke SE18. . . . .**144** A4
Paddington NW1 . . . .**92** C2 **237** A4
Bell The E17. . . . .**53** C6
Bell View BR3. . . . .**185** B3
Bell View Manor HA4. . . . . .**39** C2
Bell Water Gate SE18. . . . .**122** C3
Bell Wharf La EC4. . . . .**252** B6
Bell Yard Mews SE1. . . . . .**140** D1
Bell Yd WC2 . . . .**94** C2 **241** A1
BELMONT. **25** B2
Belmont Ave
Bowes Pk N13. . . . .**32** B5
Cockfosters EN4. . . . .**14** C6
Edmonton N9 . . . .**18** A3
Falconwood DA16. . . . .**145** C2
Southall UB2. . . . .**107** A3
Tottenham N17. . . . .**51** A6
Wembley HA0. . . . .**88** B6
West Barnes KT3. . . . .**200** A5
Belmont Circ HA3. . . . .**25** B2
Belmont Cl **1** Chingford E4. .**36** B5
Clapham SW4 . . . .**137** C2
Cockfosters EN4. . . . .**2** D1
Totteridge N20 . . . .**13** D3
Uxbridge UB8 . . . .**60** A2
Woodford IG8. . . . .**37** B6
Belmont Ct Highbury N5. . . .**73** A4
6 Stamford Hill N16. . . . . .**51** C1
Temple Fortune NW11 . . . . .**47** B4
1 Whetstone N20 . . . .**14** A1
Wood Green N13 . . . .**31** D3
Belmont Fst & Mid Schs
HA3 . . . .**24** D1
Belmont Gr Chiswick W4 . .**111** B2
Lewisham SE13 . . . .**142** B2
Belmont Hall Ct SE13. . . . .**142** B2
Belmont Hill SE13. . . . .**142** B2
Belmont Jun & Inf Sch
N22. . . . .**51** A6
Belmont La
Chislehurst BR7 . . . .**189** A5
Stanmore HA7 . . . .**25** C3
Belmont Lo Harrow HA3. . . .**24** B3
Stanmore HA7 . . . .**25** C6
Belmont Mews SW19 . . . . .**156** D2
Belmont (Mill Hill Prep Sch)
NW7. . . . .**12** A1
Belmont Par
Chislehurst BR7 . . . .**189** A5
2 Temple Fortune NW11. . .**47** B4
Belmont Park Cl SE13. . . . .**142** C1
Belmont Park Rd E10. . . . . .**53** D3
Belmont Pk SE13. . . . .**142** C1
Belmont Pk Sch E10. . . . . . .**54** A3
Belmont Prim Sch
10 Chiswick W4. . . . .**111** B2
Erith DA8. . . . .**147** C5
Belmont Rd
Beckenham BR3. . . . .**185** B1
Chislehurst BR7 . . . .**188** D5
Clapham SW4 . . . .**137** C2
Croydon SE25. . . . .**206** B4
Erith DA8. . . . .**147** B4
Harrow HA3 . . . .**43** A6
Ilford IG1. . . . .**79** A5
London N4 . . . .**111** B2
Twickenham TW2 . . . .**152** B2
Uxbridge UB8 . . . .**60** A2
Wallington SM6. . . . .**219** C3
West Green N15, N17. . . . . .**51** A6
Belmont Rise SM1, SM2. . .**217** B1
Belmont St NW1 . . . .**71** A1
Belmont Terr W4. . . . .**111** B2
Belmor WD6. . . . .**10** C5
Belmore Ave UB4 . . . .**84** A1
Belmore Ho N7. . . . .**71** D3
Belmore La N7 . . . .**71** D3
Belmore Prim Sch UB4. . . . .**84** B4
Belmore St SW8 . .**137** D4 **269** C2
Beloe Cl SW15. . . . .**134** A1
Belper Ct **11** E5. . . . .**74** D4
Belsham St E9 . . . .**74** C1
Belsize Ave Bowes Pk N13 . .**32** B4
Ealing W13 . . . .**109** B3
Maitland Pk NW3 . . . .**70** C3
Belsize Court Garages **1**
NW3 . . . .**70** B3
Belsize Cres NW3 . . . .**70** B3
Belsize Ct NW3 . . . .**70** B3
Belsize Gdns SM1. . . . .**217** D4
Belsize Gn NW3 . . . .**70** B3
Belsize La NW3. . . . .**70** B3
Belsize Mews NW3. . . . .**70** B3
Belsize Park Gdns NW3 . . . .**70** C2
Belsize Park Mews **1**
NW3 . . . .**70** B3
Belsize Park Sta NW3 . . . . . .**70** C3
Belsize Pk NW3 . . . .**70** C3
Belsize Rd Harrow HA3. . . . .**24** B3
Kilburn NW6. . . . .**91** D6
Belsize Sq NW3. . . . .**70** B2
Belsize Terr NW3. . . . .**70** B2
Belson Rd SE18. . . . .**122** B2
Beltane Dr SW19. . . . .**156** D1

Belthorn Cres SW12 . . . . . .159 C4
Belton Rd Leyton E11 . . . .76 C4
Sidcup DA14. . . . . .190 A6
Tottenham N17 . . . . .51 C6
Upton E7. . . . . .77 B1
Willesden NW2. . . . . .68 A2
Belton Way E3. . . . . .97 C2
Beltran Rd SW6. . . . . . .135 D3
BELVEDERE 125 D2
Belvedere Ave SW19 . . . .179 A5
Belvedere Bldgs SE1. . . .251 D1
Belvedere Cl TW11. . . . . .174 C5
Belvedere Ct
Abbey Wood DA17. . . . . .125 B3
Brondesbury NW2 . . . . . . .68 D2
  7 Clapham Pk SW4. . . .159 D5
East Finchley N2. . . . . . . .48 B4
  8 Kingston u T KT2 . . . .176 C3
Putney SW15 . . . . .134 C1
  33 Shoreditch N1 . . . . . . .95 C6
Southall UB1. . . . . .107 D6
Southgate N21 . . . . .16 C4
Belvedere Dr SW19 . . . . .179 A5
Belvedere Gdns KT8 . . . .195 C4
Belvedere Gr SW19 . . . . .179 A5
Belvedere Ho TW14 . . . . .150 A3
Belvedere Htss NW8 . . . .237 A6
Belvedere Jun & Inf Sch
  DA17. . . . . .125 D3
Belvedere Mews
  Greenwich SE3. . . . . . .143 B5
  Nunhead SE15 . . . . . . .140 C2
Belvedere Pl
  Brixton SW2. . . . . .138 B1
  Lambeth SE1. . . . . .251 D1
Belvedere Rd
  Bexleyheath DA7. . . . . .147 B3
  Erith SE2, SE28. . . . . . .124 D5
  Hanwell W7 . . . . .108 D3
  Lambeth SE1. . . .116 B5 250 D3
  Penge SE19 . . . . .183 D3
  Walthamstow E10 . . . . . .53 A1
Belvedere Sq SW19 . . . . .179 A5
Belvedere Sta DA17. . . . .125 D3
Belvedere Strand NW9. . . .27 D1
Belvedere The SW10 . . . .266 B1
Belvedere Way HA3. . . . . .44 A3
Belvoir Cl SE9 . . . . .166 A1
Belvoir Ct HA3. . . . . .43 A3
Belvoir Lo SE22. . . . . . . .162 A4
Belvoir Rd SE22 . . . . . . .162 A4
Belvue Bsns Ctr UB5 . . . .63 D1
Belvue Cl UB5 . . . . .63 C1
Belvue Rd UB5. . . . . .63 C1
Belvue Sch UB5. . . . . . . .85 C6
Bembridge Cl NW6 . . . . . .69 A1
Bembridge Gdns HA4 . . . .61 B6
Bembridge Ho
  9 Deptford SE8. . . . . . .119 B2
  Wandsworth SW18 . . . . .157 D5
Bemersyde Point **6** E13 . .99 B4
Bemerton St N1 . . . .94 B6 233 C6
Bemish Rd SW15. . . . . . .134 D2
Bempton Dr HA4. . . . . . . .62 B5
Bemsted Rd E17. . . . . . . .53 B6
Benabo Ct **6** E8. . . . . . . .74 A3
Benares Rd SE18, SE2. . .123 D2
Benbow Ct W6. . . . . .112 B3
Benbow Ho **12** SE8. . . . . .141 C6
Benbow Rd W6. . . . . . . .112 B3
Benbow St SE8 . . . . .141 C6
Benbury Cl BR1. . . . . . . .186 A5
Bence Ho **13** SE8. . . . . . . .119 A2
Bench Field CR2. . . . . . .221 D3
Bencroft Rd SW16 . . . . . .181 C3
Bencurtis Pk BR4. . . . . . .224 B6
Bendall Mews NW1 . . . . .237 B4
Bendemeer Rd SW15 . . . .134 D2
Benden Ho SE13. . . . . . .164 A6
Bendish Point SE28. . . . .123 A4
Bendish Rd E6. . . . . .78 A1
Bendmore Ave SE2 . . . . .124 A2
Bendon Valley SW18 . . . .157 D4
Benedict Cl
  9 Erith DA17. . . . . . . .125 A3
  Orpington BR6 . . . . .227 C5
Benedict Ct
  Dagenham RM9 . . . . .59 B3
  Pinner HA5. . . . . .23 B2
Benedict Dr TW14. . . . . . .149 B4
Benedict House Sch **15**
  DA15. . . . . .168 A1
Benedict Prim Sch CR4 . .202 B6
Benedict Rd London SW9. .138 D2
  Mitcham CR4 . . . . .202 B6
Benedict Way N2. . . . . . . .48 A6
Benedict Wharf CR4. . . . .202 C6
Benenden Gn BR2. . . . . .209 A4
Benenden Ho SE17. . . . .263 B2
Benett Gdns SW16. . . . . .182 A1
Beney Ct BR3. . . . . .185 C1
Ben Ezra Ct SE17. . . . . .262 B3
Benfleet Cl SM1. . . . . . . .218 A5
Benfleet Ct **6** E8. . . . . . . .95 D6
Benfleet Way N11. . . . . . .15 A2
Bengal Ct EC3. . . . . .242 D1
Bengal Ho E1. . . . . .96 D2

Bengal Rd IG1. . . . . .78 D5
Bengarth Dr HA3 . . . . . . .24 B1
Bengarth Rd UB5 . . . . . . .85 A6
Bengeo Gdns RM6 . . . . . .58 C3
Bengeworth Rd
  Camberwell SE5. . . . . . .139 A2
  Harrow HA1. . . . . .65 A5
Ben Hale Cl HA7 . . . . .25 B5
Benham Cl KT9 . . . . .213 C2
Benham Gdns TW3, TW4 . .151 B6
Benham Ho SW10. . . . . .265 D4
Benham Rd W7. . . . . .86 C2
Benham's Pl **11** NW3. . . . . .70 A4
Benhill Ave SM1. . . . . . . .218 A4
Benhill Rd London SE5 . . .139 B4
  Sutton SM1. . . . . .218 B4
Benhill Wood Rd SM1. . . .218 A4
BENHILTON. 218 A5
Benhilton Ct SM1. . . . . . .218 A5
Benhilton Gdns SM1 . . . .217 D5
Benhurst Ct Ealing W5. . . .110 A6
  West Norwood SW16. . . .182 C5
Benhurst La SW16. . . . . .182 C5
Benington Ct N4. . . . . . . .73 A6
Benin St SE13. . . . . .164 B4
Benjafield Cl N18. . . . . . . .34 B6
Benjamin Cl E8. . . . . .96 A6
Benjamin Ct
  4 Ealing W7. . . . . . . .108 C5
  4 Erith DA17. . . . . . . .147 B6
  Littleton TW15 . . . . .171 A3
Benjamin Franklin House *
  SW1 . . . . .250 A4
Benjamin Ho **12** W3. . . . . .110 D5
Benjamin Mews SW12 . . .159 C4
Benjamin St EC1. . . . . . .241 C4
Ben Jonson Ct **30** N1. . . . . .95 C5
Ben Jonson Rd E1 . . . . . .97 A2
Ben Jonson Prim Sch E1. .97 A3
Benledi Rd E14. . . . . .98 B1
Bennelong Cl W12. . . . . . .90 B1
Bennerley Rd SW11. . . . .158 D6
Bennet Cl KT1. . . . . .175 C2
Bennets St SW19 . . . . . .180 A2
Bennetsfield Rd UB11. . . .104 D5
Bennet's Hill EC4 . . . . . .251 D6
Bennets Lo EN2. . . . . .5 A2
Bennett Cl
  Twickenham TW4 . . . . . .151 A6
  Welling DA16. . . . . .146 A3
Bennett Ct
  Hampstead NW6 . . . . . . .69 D2
  Lower Holloway N7 . . . . . .72 B5
  7 South Acton W3. . . . .110 D4
Bennett Gr SE13 . . . . . . .141 D4
Bennett Ho
  2 Streatham SW4. . . . .159 D4
  Westminster SW1 . . . . . .259 D4
Bennett Pk SE3 . . . . .142 D2
Bennett Rd Brixton SW9. . .138 C3
  Dagenham RM6 . . . . . . .59 A2
  Newham E13 . . . . .99 C3
Bennetts Ave
  Croydon CR0. . . . . .223 A6
  Greenford UB6. . . . . .86 C6
Bennett's Castle La RM8 . .80 D5
Bennetts Cl
  Mitcham CR4, SW16. . . .181 B2
  Tottenham N17. . . . . . . .33 D4
Bennetts Copse BR7 . . . .188 A4
Bennett St Chiswick W4 . .111 C1
  St James SW1 . . . . .249 A4
Bennetts Way CR0 . . . . . .223 B6
Bennett's Yd SW1 . . . . . .259 D5
  7 Bethnal Green E2 . . . .96 A4
Benningholme Rd HA8. . . .27 C4
Bennington Rd
  Chingford IG8. . . . . .36 C3
  Tottenham N17. . . . . .33 C2
Benn St E9 . . . . .75 A2
Benns Wlk **8** TW9. . . . . . .132 A1
Bensbury Cl SW15 . . . . .156 C4
Bensham Cl CR7. . . . . . .205 A5
Bensham Gr CR7. . . . . . .183 A1
Bensham La CR0, CR7. . .204 D3
Bensham Manor Rd
  CR7. . . . . .205 A4
Bensham Manor Specl Sch
  CR7. . . . . .205 A4
Bensington Ct TW14 . . . .149 B5
Bensley Cl **7** N11. . . . . . .30 D5
Ben Smith Way **21** SE16 . .118 A3
Benson Ave E13, E6. . . . . .99 D5
Benson Cl Hillingdon UB8. .82 A2
  Hounslow TW3. . . . . . . .129 C1
Benson Ct Holbrook EN3. . .7 C5
  South Lambeth SW8. . . . .270 A2
  1 Tufnell Pk N19 . . . . . .71 C4
Benson Ho Lambeth SE1. .251 B3
  1 Richmond TW10 . . . .153 C1
  Shoreditch E2. . . . . .243 C6
Benson Prim sch CR0 . . . .223 A5
Benson Quay E1 . . . . . . .118 C6
Benson Rd Croydon CR0. .220 C5
  Forest Hill SE23 . . . . . . .162 C3
Bentall Sh Ctr The **10**
  KT1. . . . . .176 A1
Bentfield Gdns SE9 . . . . .165 D1

Benthal Ct N16. . . . . .74 A5
Benthal Prim Sch N16 . . . .74 A5
Benthal Rd N16. . . . . .74 A5
Bentham Ct **11** N1. . . . . . .73 A1
Bentham Ho SE1. . . . . . .262 C6
Bentham Rd Homerton E9. .74 D2
  Woolwich SE28. . . . . . . .124 B5
Bentham Wlk NW10. . . . . .67 A3
Ben Tillet Cl E16. . . . . . . .122 B5
Ben Tillet Ho N15. . . . . . . .50 D6
Bentinck Cl NW8. . . . . . .230 B3
Bentinck Ho
  4 Richmond TW10 . . . .153 C1
  4 Shepherd's Bush W12. .112 B6
Bentinck Mans W1. . . . . .238 B2
Bentinck Mews W1 . . . . .238 B2
Bentinck Rd UB7. . . . . . .104 A5
Bentinck St W1 . . . .93 A1 238 B2
Bentley Cl SW19 . . . . . . .157 C1
Bentley Dr SE13. . . . . . . .142 A1
Bentley Dr Child's Hill NW2. .69 B5
  Ilford IG2. . . . . .57 A3
Bentley Ho **6** Bow E3. . . . .97 C3
  4 Camberwell SE5 . . . .139 C4
Bentley Lo WD23. . . . . . . .8 C2
Bentley Mews EN1. . . . . . .17 B5
Bentley Rd N1 . . . . .73 C2
Bentley Way
  Stanmore HA7 . . . . .25 A5
  Woodford IG8. . . . . .21 A1
Bentley Wood Girls Sch
  HA7. . . . . .24 D5
Benton Rd Ilford IG1, IG2. . .57 B1
  South Oxhey WD19. . . . . .22 D5
Benton's La SE27. . . . . . .183 A6
Benton's Rise SE27 . . . . .183 B5
Bentry Cl RM8 . . . . .81 A6
Bentry Rd RM8. . . . . .81 B6
Bentworth Ct **1** E2. . . . . . .96 A3
Bentworth Prim Sch W12 . .90 B1
Bentworth Rd W12. . . . . . .90 B1
Ben Uri Gall * NW8 . . . . . .91 D6
Benwell Ct TW16. . . . . . .172 A2
Benwell Rd N7 . . . . .72 C3
Benwick Cl SE16. . . . . . .118 B2
Benwick Ct SE20. . . . . . .184 C2
Benwood Ct SM1 . . . . . . .218 A5
Benworth St E3. . . . . .97 B4
Benyon Ho EC1. . . . . . . .234 B2
Benyon Rd N1 . . . .95 B6 235 D6
Benyon Wharf **81** E8 . . . . . .95 C6
Beormund Sch
  SE1. . . . . .117 B4 252 D1
Bequerel Ct SE10 . . . . . .120 D3
Berberis Ct IG1. . . . . .78 D2
Berberis Ho **17** E3 . . . . . . .97 C2
Berberis Wlk UB7. . . . . . .104 A2
Berber Par **8** SE18. . . . . .144 A4
Berber Rd SW11. . . . . . . .158 D6
Berber Rd SW11. . . . . . . .158 D6
Berberry Cl **5** HA8. . . . . . .27 A6
Bercta Rd SE9 . . . . .167 A2
Berebinder Ho **21** E3. . . . . .97 B5
Berengers Pl RM9 . . . . . .80 B2
Berenger Twr SW10. . . . .266 C4
Berenger Wlk SW10. . . . .266 C4
Berens Ct DA14. . . . . . . .189 D6
Berens Rd NW10. . . . . . . .90 D4
Berens Way BR5, BR7. . . .211 D6
Beresford Ave Ealing W7. . .86 C2
  Friern Barnet N20 . . . . . .14 D2
  Tolworth KT5. . . . . .199 A2
  Twickenham TW1 . . . . . .153 C5
  Wembley HA0. . . . . .88 C6
Beresford Ct Homerton E9. .75 A3
  11 Twickenham TW1. . . .153 C5
Beresford Dr Bickley BR1. .210 A6
  Woodford IG8. . . . . .37 C6
Beresford Gdns
  Dagenham RM6 . . . . . . .59 A4
  Enfield EN1. . . . . .5 C1
  Hounslow TW4 . . . . .151 B6
Beresford Ho
  Dulwich SE21. . . . . .161 C1
  15 Stockwell SW4 . . . . .138 A1
Beresford Lo N4. . . . . .73 B3
Beresford Rd
  Belmont SM2. . . . . .217 B1
  Canonbury N5. . . . . .73 B3
  Chingford E4. . . . . .20 C3
  East Finchley N2. . . . . . . .48 C6
  Harringay N8 . . . . .50 D4
  Harrow HA1. . . . . .42 B4
  Kingston u T KT2. . . . . . .176 B2
  New Malden KT3 . . . . . .199 A5
  Southall UB1. . . . . .106 D5
  Walthamstow E17 . . . . . .35 D2
Beresford Sq **1** SE18 . . . .122 D2
Beresford Square Mkt
  SE18. . . . . .122 D2
Beresford Terr **3** N5. . . . . .73 A3
Bere St E1. . . . . .118 D6
Berestede Rd **4** W6 . . . . .111 D1
Bergen Ho **6** SE5. . . . . . .139 A3
Bergenia Ho **11** TW13. . . .150 B3
Bergen Sq SE16. . . . . . . .119 A3
Berger Cl BR5. . . . . .211 C3
Berger Prim Sch **30** E9. . .74 D2
Berger Rd E9. . . . . .74 D2
Berghem Mews W14. . . . .112 D3

Bergholt Ave IG4. . . . . . . .56 A4
Bergholt Cres N16. . . . . . .51 C2
Bergholt Mews **4** NW1 . . .71 D1
Berglen Ct E14. . . . . .119 A6
Berica Ct IG6. . . . . .57 A6
Bering Sq E14. . . . . .119 C1
Bering Wlk E16. . . . . .99 D1
Berisford Mews SW18. . . .158 A5
Berkeley Ave
  Cranford TW4. . . . . .128 A3
  Erith DA16. . . . . .146 D4
  Northolt UB6 . . . . .64 C2
Berkeley Cl
  Borehamwood WD6 . . . . .10 C6
  Broom Hill BR5. . . . . . . .211 C2
  2 Kingston u T KT2 . . . .176 A3
  Ruislip HA4. . . . . .62 A5
Berkeley Cres EN4 . . . . . .14 B6
Berkeley Ct Ealing W5. . . .109 C6
  Edgware HA8. . . . . .26 D5
  Finchley N3. . . . . .29 D2
  1 Golders Green NW11 . .47 B2
  Marylebone NW1 . . . . . .237 D5
  Southgate N14 . . . . .15 C5
  Wallington SM6 . . . . . . .219 C4
  Willesden NW10. . . . . . . .67 C4
Berkeley Dr KT8 . . . . . . .195 C6
Berkeley Gdns
  Claygate KT10 . . . . .213 A2
  Kensington W8 . . . . .245 B3
  Southgate N21 . . . . .17 B4
  Walton-on-T KT12 . . . . . .193 D2
Berkeley Ho **17** Bow E3. . . .97 C4
  11 Brentford TW8 . . . . .131 D6
  8 Deptford SE8. . . . . . .119 B1
Berkeley Lo Enfield EN2 . . .4 C2
  New Malden KT3 . . . . . .199 C5
Berkeley Mews
  Marylebone W1 . . . . . . .237 D1
  Sunbury TW16 . . . . .194 C6
Berkeley Pl SW19 . . . . . .178 D4
Berkeley Prim Sch TW5 . .128 C5
Berkeley Rd
  Barnes SW13. . . . . .134 A4
  Crouch End N8 . . . . .49 D3
  Hillingdon UB10 . . . . .61 A1
  Manor Pk E12. . . . . .78 A3
  Queensbury NW9. . . . . . .44 C4
  Stamford Hill N15. . . . . . .51 B3
Berkeley Sq W1. . .115 B6 248 D5
Berkeley St W1 . . .115 B5 248 D4
Berkeleys The SE25 . . . . .206 A5
Berkeley The NW11 . . . . . .47 D2
Berkeley Waye TW5. . . . .128 D5
Berkeley Wlk **1** N7. . . . . . .72 B6
Berkhampstead Rd
  DA17. . . . . .125 C1
Berkhamsted Ave HA9. . . .66 C2
Berkley Ct TW2 . . . . .152 C1
Berkley Ct **8** TW1. . . . . . .153 A4
Berkley Gr NW1. . . . . .71 A1
Berkley Rd NW1 . . . . .70 D1
Berkshire Ct **1** W7. . . . . . .86 D3
Berkshire Gdns
  Bowes Pk N13. . . . . .32 C4
  Upper Edmonton N18. . . .34 B5
Berkshire Ho
  Catford SE6 . . . . .185 C6
  St Giles WC2. . . . . .240 A2
Berkshire Rd E9 . . . . .75 B2
Berkshire Way CR4 . . . . .204 A5
Bermans Way NW10 . . . . .67 D4
BERMONDSEY. 118 A4
Bermondsey Leather Mkt
  SE1. . . . . .253 A1
Bermondsey Sq SE1 . . . .263 B6
Bermondsey St
  SE1. . . . . .117 C4 253 A1
Bermondsey Sta SE16. . . .118 B3
Bermondsey Trad Est
  SE16. . . . . .118 C1
Bermondsey Wall E
  SE16. . . . . .118 B4
Bermondsey Wall W SE1,
  SE16. . . . . .118 B4
Bermuda Ho HA1. . . . . . . .64 B5
Bernal Cl SE28. . . . . .124 D6
Bernard Angell Ho **4**
  SE10 . . . . .142 B6
Bernard Ashley Dr SE7. . .121 B1
Bernard Ave W13 . . . . . .109 B3
Bernard Cassidy St **2**
  E16. . . . . .98 D2
Bernard Gdns SW19. . . . .179 B5
Bernard Ho E1. . . . . .243 C3
Bernard Rd
  South Tottenham N15. . . .51 D4
  Wallington SM5, SM6. . . .219 B4
Bernard Shaw Cl **5** NW1. .71 C1
Bernard Shaw Ho **2**
  NW10 . . . . .89 B6
Bernard St WC1. . .94 A3 240 B5
Bernays Cl HA7. . . . . .25 C4
Bernay's Gr SW9. . . . . . .138 B1
Bernel Dr CR0 . . . . .223 B5
Berne Rd CR7. . . . . .205 A4
Berners Dr W13 . . . . .109 A6
Berners Ho N1 . . . . .234 A4
Bernersmede SE3 . . . . . .143 A2
Berners Mews W1 . .93 C2 239 B3

Berners Pl W1. . . . . .239 B2
Berners Rd Islington N1. . .234 C5
  Wood Green N22 . . . . . . .32 C1
Berners St W1. . . .93 C1 239 B2
Berner Terr **27** E1. . . . . . . .96 A1
Berney Ho BR3. . . . . .207 A4
Berney Rd CR0. . . . . .205 B2
Bernhard Baron Ho **23**
  E1. . . . . .96 A1
Bernhardt Cres NW8. . . . .237 A6
Bernhart Cl HA8 . . . . .27 A3
Bernie Grant Ho **40** E9 . . .74 C1
Bernwell Rd E4. . . . . .20 C1
Bernwood Ho **6** N4 . . . . . .51 B2
Berridge Gn HA8. . . . . . . .26 C3
Berridge Mews NW6. . . . . .69 C3
Berridge Rd SE19. . . . . . .183 C5
Berriman Rd N7 . . . . .72 B5
Berrite Works UB7. . . . . .104 C4
Berriton Rd HA2. . . . . .41 B1
Berrybank Cl **4** E4 . . . . . . .20 A2
Berry Cl Dagenham RM10 . .81 C3
  Southgate N21 . . . . .16 D3
Berry Cotts **2** E14 . . . . . . .97 A1
Berry Ct TW4. . . . . .151 B6
Berrydale Rd UB4. . . . . . . .85 A3
Berryfield Cl **8** E17. . . . . .188 A1
Berry Field Cl **8** E17. . . . . .53 D5
Berryfield Rd
  SE17. . . . . .116 D1 261 D2
Berryhill SE9. . . . . .144 D1
Berry Hill HA7 . . . . .25 D6
Berryhill Gdns SE9. . . . . .144 D1
Berry Ho
  10 Battersea SW11 . . . .136 D3
  25 Bethnal Green E1 . . . .96 B3
Berry La SE21. . . . . .183 B6
BERRYLANDS. 198 C3
Berrylands Surbiton KT5. . .198 C3
  West Barnes SW20 . . . . .200 C5
Berrylands Ct **16** SM2 . . . .217 D1
Berrylands Rd KT5. . . . . .198 B3
Berrylands Sta KT5 . . . . .198 C3
Berryman Rd RM8. . . . . . .80 C5
Berryman's La SE26. . . . .184 D6
Berrymead Gdns W3. . . . .111 A4
Berrymede Inf Sch W3 . . .110 D4
Berrymede Jun Sch W3 . .110 D4
Berrymede Rd W4. . . . . . .111 B3
Berry Pl EC1. . . . . .234 D1
Berry St EC1. . . . . .241 D5
Berry Way W5 . . . . .110 A3
Bertal Rd SW17 . . . . .180 B6
Bertha Hollamby Ct
  DA14. . . . . .190 C5
Bertha James Ct BR2 . . . .209 B5
Bertha Neuberg Ho **1**
  SE5 . . . . .139 A4
Berthan Gdns E17 . . . . . . .54 B4
Berthon St SE8. . . . . . . .141 C6
Bertie Rd Penge SE26. . . .184 D4
  Willesden NW10. . . . . . . .68 A2
Bertram Cotts SW19 . . . .179 C3
Bertram Rd Enfield EN1 . . .6 A1
  Hendon NW4. . . . . .46 A3
  Kingston u T KT2. . . . . . .176 C3
Bertram St N19 . . . . .71 B6
Bertrand Ho **11** SW16 . . . .160 A1
Bertrand St SE13 . . . . . . .141 D2
Bertrand Way SE28 . . . . .124 C6
Bert Rd CR7 . . . . .205 A3
Bert Reilly Ho **1** SE18. . . .123 B1
Bertram House Sch
  SW17 . . . . .159 A2
Bert Way EN1. . . . . .5 D1
Berwick Ave UB4 . . . . . . .106 D6
Berwick Cl Harrow HA7 . . .24 D4
  Twickenham TW2 . . . . . .151 C3
Berwick Cres DA15. . . . . .167 C5
Berwick Ct **8** BR3. . . . . . .185 C2
Berwick Gdns SM1. . . . . .218 A5
Berwick Ho **10** N2. . . . . . . .30 B1
Berwick Rd Newham E16. . .99 C1
  Tottenham N22. . . . . .32 D2
  Welling DA16 . . . . .146 A4
Berwick St W1. . . .93 C1 239 B1
Berwick Street Mkt *
  W1. . . . . .93 C1 239 B1
Berwyn Ave **3** TW3. . . . . .129 D4
Berwyn Ho **3** N16. . . . . . .51 D1
Berwyn Rd
  Mortlake SW14, TW10 . . .132 D1
  Streatham SE24. . . . . . . .160 D3
Beryl Ave E6. . . . . .100 A2
Beryl Harding Ho **3**
  SW19. . . . . .178 D3
Beryl Ho SE18 . . . . .123 D1
Beryl Rd W6. . . . . .112 D1
Berystede KT2. . . . . .176 D3
Besant Ct NW2. . . . . .69 B6
Besant Ho Canonbury N1 . .73 B3
  15 Thamesmead SE28 . . .124 B6
Besant Rd NW8. . . . . . . .229 A5
Besant Pl SE22 . . . . .139 D1
Besant Rd NW2. . . . . .69 A4
Besant Way NW10 . . . . . . .67 A3
Besant Wlk N7. . . . . .72 B6
Besford Ho **28** E2. . . . . . . .96 A5
Besley St SW16. . . . . . . .181 C4
Bessant Dr TW9. . . . . . . .132 D4

Bessborough Gdns SW1 . . . 115 D1 259 D2
Bessborough Pl SW1 . . . 115 D1 259 D2
Bessborough Rd
Harrow HA1 . . . 42 B1
Roehampton SW15 . . . 156 A3
Bessborough St SW1 . . . 115 D1 259 C2
Bessborough Wks KT8 . . . 195 B4
Bessemer Ct 7 NW1 . . . 71 C1
Bessemer Grange Prim Sch SE5 . . . 139 C1
Bessemer Park Ind Est 3 SE24 . . . 138 D1
Bessemer Rd SE5 . . . 139 A3
Bessie Lansbury Cl E6 . . . 100 C1
Bessingby Rd HA4 . . . 62 B6
Bessingham Wlk SE4 . . . 162 D6
Besson St SE14 . . . 140 D4
Bessy St E2 . . . 96 C4
Bestwood St SE8 . . . 118 D2
Beswick Mews 1 NW6 . . . 69 D2
Betam Rd UB3 . . . 105 B4
Beta Pl 20 SW4 . . . 138 B1
Betchworth Cl SM1 . . . 218 B3
Betchworth Ho 8 N7 . . . 71 D3
Betchworth Rd IG3 . . . 79 C5
Betham Rd UB6 . . . 86 B4
Bethany Ct 8 DA6 . . . 147 A1
Bethany Waye TW14 . . . 149 C4
Bethecar Rd HA1 . . . 42 C4
Bethel Cl NW4 . . . 46 D4
Bethell Ave Ilford IG1 . . . 56 C2
Newham E13, E16 . . . 98 D3
Bethel Lo N11 . . . 31 C5
Bethel Rd DA16 . . . 146 C2
Bethersden Cl BR3 . . . 185 B3
Bethersden Ho SE17 . . . 263 B2
Bethesda Ct 5 SE20 . . . 184 C3
Beth Jacob Gram Sch 6 NW4 . . . 46 D5
Bethlehem Ho 13 E14 . . . 119 B6
Bethlem Royal Hospl BR3 . . . 207 C2
BETHNAL GREEN . . . 96 B4
Bethnal Green Rd
Bethnal Green E2 . . . 96 A4
Shoreditch E1, E2 . . . 95 D3 243 D6
Bethnal Green Sta
Bethnal Green E1 . . . 96 B3
Bethnal Green E2 . . . 96 C4
Bethnal Green Tech Coll 49 E2 . . . 95 D4
Beths Gram Sch DA5 . . . 169 D5
Bethune Ave N11 . . . 30 D6
Bethune Rd
North Acton NW10 . . . 89 B3
Stamford Hill N16 . . . 51 C2
Bethwin Rd SE5 . . . 139 A5
Betjeman Cl HA5 . . . 41 C5
Betjeman Ct EN4 . . . 15 A6
Betony Cl CR0 . . . 206 D1
Betoyne Ave E4 . . . 36 C6
Betsham Ho SE1 . . . 252 C2
Betspath Ho 6 N11 . . . 31 C5
Betstyle Circus N11 . . . 31 B6
Betstyle Ho 2 N10 . . . 31 A3
Betstyle Rd N11 . . . 31 B6
Betterton Dr DA14 . . . 169 A2
Betterton Ho WC2 . . . 240 B1
Betterton St WC2 . . 94 A1 240 B1
Bettons Pk E15 . . . 98 C6
Bettridge Rd SW6 . . . 135 B3
Betts Cl BR3 . . . 185 A1
Betts Ho E1 . . . 118 B6
Betts Mews E17 . . . 53 B3
Betts Rd E16 . . . 121 B6
Betts St E1 . . . 118 B6
Betts Way
Long Ditton KT6 . . . 197 B1
Penge SE20 . . . 184 B2
Bettswood Ct 15 SE20 . . . 184 B2
Betty Brooks Ho E11 . . . 76 B5
Betty Layward Prim Sch 1 N16 . . . 73 B5
Betty May Gray Ho 2 E14 . . . 120 A2
Beulah Ave CR7 . . . 183 A1
Beulah Cl HA8 . . . 10 D1
Beulah Cres CR7 . . . 183 A1
Beulah Gr CR0 . . . 205 A3
Beulah Hill SE19 . . . 183 A3
Beulah Inf Sch 2 CR7 . . . 205 A6
Beulah Jun Sch 1 CR7 . . . 205 A6
Beulah Rd Merton SW19 . . . 179 B3
South Norwood CR7 . . . 205 A6
Sutton SM1 . . . 217 C4
Walthamstow E17 . . . 53 D4
Beuleigh Ct E17 . . . 54 B4
Bevan Ave IG11 . . . 80 A1
Bevan Ct Croydon CR0 . . . 220 C3
10 Twickenham TW1 . . . 153 D5
Bevan Ho IG11 . . . 80 B1
Bevan Rd Cockfosters EN4 . . . 2 D1
Plumstead Comm SE2 . . . 124 B1
Bevan St N1 . . . 95 A6 235 B5
Bev Callender Cl 4 SW8 . . . 137 B2
Bevenden St N1 . . . 95 B4 235 D2
Bevercote Wlk 1 DA17 . . . 147 B6
Beveridge Ct
Southgate N21 . . . 16 A6
1 Thamesmead SE28 . . . 124 B6
Beveridge Rd 1 NW10 . . . 67 C1
Beverley DA14 . . . 190 A5
Beverley Ave
Hounslow TW4 . . . 129 B1
Sidcup DA15 . . . 167 D4
Wimbledon SW20 . . . 177 D2
Beverley Cl Barnes SW13 . . 134 A3
Chessington KT9 . . . 213 C4
Edmonton N21 . . . 17 A3
Enfield EN1 . . . 5 C1
6 Wandsworth SW11 . . . 136 B1
Beverley Cotts SW15 . . . 155 C1
Beverley Cres IG8 . . . 37 B2
Beverley Ct
9 Acton Green W4 . . . 111 A1
5 Acton W12 . . . 111 C4
Brockley SE4 . . . 141 B2
6 Cheam SM2 . . . 217 C2
Chingford Hatch E4 . . . 35 B6
Fortis Green N2 . . . 48 D5
Harrow HA2 . . . 42 B6
Hounslow TW4 . . . 129 B1
Islington N5 . . . 72 D2
Northolt UB5 . . . 84 C5
Oakleigh Pk N20 . . . 14 A4
Oakwood N14 . . . 15 C4
Sidcup DA14 . . . 190 B6
Wimbledon SW20 . . . 177 D2
Beverley Dr HA8 . . . 44 C6
Beverley Gdns
Barnes SW13 . . . 133 D2
Hendon NW11 . . . 47 A2
2 New Malden KT4 . . . 200 A1
Stanmore HA7 . . . 25 A2
Wembley HA9 . . . 44 C1
Beverley Ho 5 BR1 . . . 186 B5
Beverley Hyrst 10 CR0 . . . 221 D6
Beverley La KT2 . . . 177 C3
Beverley Lo 6 TW10 . . . 154 A6
Beverley Mans TW4 . . . 129 B1
Beverley Path 9 SW13 . . . 133 D3
Beverley Rd
Barnes SW13 . . . 133 D2
Chingford E4 . . . 36 B4
Chiswick W4 . . . 111 D1
Dagenham RM9 . . . 81 A4
Keston Mark BR2 . . . 226 A6
Mitcham CR4 . . . 203 D5
Newham E6 . . . 99 D4
North Cheam KT4 . . . 216 C6
Penge SE20 . . . 184 B1
Ruislip HA4 . . . 62 B6
Southall UB2 . . . 107 A3
Sunbury TW16 . . . 171 D2
Teddington KT1 . . . 175 C2
West Barnes KT3 . . . 200 A5
Beverley Trad Est SM4 . . . 200 D2
Beverley Way KT3, SW20, KT2 . . . 177 D2
Beverley Way (Kingston By-Pass) KT3, SW20 . . . 200 A6
Beverly Ct HA3 . . . 43 C5
Beversbrook Rd N19 . . . 71 D5
Beverstone Rd
London SW2 . . . 160 B6
Thornton Heath CR7 . . . 204 D5
Beverston Mews NW1 . . . 237 C3
Bevill Allen Cl SW17 . . . 180 D5
Bevill Cl SE25 . . . 206 A6
Bevin Cl SE16 . . . 119 A5
Bevin Ct WC1 . . . 233 D2
Bevington Prim Sch 15 W10 . . . 91 A2
Bevington Rd
Beckenham BR3 . . . 185 D1
Kensal Town W10 . . . 91 A2
Bevington St SE16 . . . 118 A4
Bevin Ho
35 Bethnal Green E2 . . . 96 C4
8 Bow E3 . . . 97 C4
Bevin Rd UB4 . . . 84 B4
Bevin Sq SW17 . . . 158 D1
Bevin Way WC1 . . . 234 A2
Bevis Marks EC3 . . . 95 C1 243 B2
Bewcastle Gdns EN2 . . . 4 A1
Bew Ct SE21 . . . 162 A4
Bewdley Ho N4 . . . 51 A2
Bewdley St N1 . . . 72 C1
Bewick Mews SE15 . . . 140 B5
Bewick St SW8 . . . 137 B3
Bewley Ct SW2 . . . 160 B5
Bewley Ho 7 E1 . . . 118 B6
Bewley St Stepney E1 . . . 118 B6
Wimbledon SW19 . . . 180 A4
Bewlys Rd SE27 . . . 182 D5
Bexhill Cl TW13 . . . 151 A2
Bexhill Rd Catford SE4 . . . 163 B5
Mortlake SW14 . . . 133 A2
Wood Green N11 . . . 31 D5
Bexhill Wlk 6 E15 . . . 98 C6
BEXLEY . . . 146 B1
Bexley Coll (Erith Rd Campus) DA17 . . . 125 D1
Bexley Gdns Edmonton N9 . . 17 B1
Ilford RM6 . . . 58 B4
Bexley Gram Sch DA16 . . . 146 B1
BEXLEYHEATH . . . 147 B2
Bexleyheath Sch DA6 . . . 147 C2
Bexleyheath Sta DA7 . . . 147 A3
Bexley High St DA5 . . . 169 D3
Bexley Ho SE4 . . . 141 A1
Bexley La DA14 . . . 168 C1
Bexley Rd SE9 . . . 167 A6
Bexley Sta DA5 . . . 169 C3
Beynon Rd SM5 . . . 218 D3
BFI Imax (Cinema) SE1 . . . 116 C5 251 A3
BFI Southbank* SE1 . . . 250 D4
Bglws The SM6 . . . 219 B3
Bianca Rd SE1, SE15 . . . 140 A6
Bibsworth Lo N3 . . . 29 B1
Bibsworth Rd N3 . . . 29 B1
Bicester Rd TW9 . . . 132 D2
Bickenhall Mans W1 . . . 237 D4
Bickenhall St W1 . . 92 D2 237 D4
Bickersteth Rd SW17 . . . 180 D4
Bickerton Rd N19 . . . 71 C6
BICKLEY . . . 188 B1
Bickley Cres BR1 . . . 210 A5
Bickley Ct
10 Merton SW19 . . . 179 C3
1 Stanmore HA7 . . . 25 C6
Bickley Park Rd BR1, BR7 . . . 210 B6
Bickley Pk Pre Prep Sch BR1 . . . 209 D6
Bickley Pk Prep Sch BR1 . . . 209 D6
Bickley Prim Sch BR1 . . . 209 C6
Bickley Rd Bromley BR1 . . . 187 D1
Leyton E10 . . . 53 D2
Bickley St SW17 . . . 180 D5
Bickley Sta BR1 . . . 210 A6
Bicknell Ho 34 E1 . . . 96 A1
Bicknell Rd SE5 . . . 139 A2
Bicknoller Rd EN1 . . . 5 D4
Bicknor Ho 2 E5 . . . 74 B3
Bicknor Rd BR6 . . . 211 D2
Bidborough Cl 3 BR2 . . . 208 D4
Bidborough St N1, WC1 . . . 94 A4 233 A1
Biddenden Way SE9 . . . 188 C6
Biddenham Ho 18 SE16 . . . 118 D2
Bidder St E16 . . . 98 C2
Biddesden Ho SW3 . . . 257 C3
Biddestone Rd N7 . . . 72 B4
Biddulph Ho 22 SE18 . . . 122 B2
Biddulph Mans W9 . . . 91 D4
Biddulph Rd W9 . . . 91 D4
Bideford Ave UB6 . . . 87 B5
Bideford Cl Edgware HA8 . . . 26 C2
Twickenham TW13 . . . 151 B1
Bideford Gdns EN1 . . . 17 C4
Bideford Rd Catford BR1 . . 164 D1
East Wickham DA16 . . . 146 B5
Enfield EN3 . . . 7 B5
Ruislip HA4 . . . 62 B5
Bidmead Ct KT6 . . . 214 A5
Bidwell Gdns N11 . . . 31 C3
Bidwell Ho Southall UB2 . . . 107 A2
3 Willesden NW2 . . . 68 A5
Bidwell St SE15 . . . 140 B4
Big Ben* SW1 . . . 250 B1
Bigbury Cl N17 . . . 33 C3
Biggerstaff Rd E15 . . . 98 A6
Biggerstaff St N4 . . . 72 C6
Biggin Ave CR4 . . . 180 D2
Biggin Hill SE19 . . . 182 D3
Biggin Hill Cl KT2 . . . 175 C5
Biggin Way SE19 . . . 183 A3
Bigginwood Rd SW16 . . . 182 D2
Bigg's Row SW15 . . . 134 D2
Biggs Sq E9 . . . 75 B2
Big Hill E5 . . . 52 B1
Bigland Green Prim Sch 41 E1 . . . 96 B1
Bigland St E1 . . . 96 B1
Bignell Rd SE18 . . . 122 D1
Bignold Rd E7 . . . 77 A4
Bigwood Ct NW11 . . . 47 D4
Bigwood Rd NW11 . . . 47 D3
Biko Ho 1 NW10 . . . 67 B1
Bilberry Ho 18 E3 . . . 97 C2
Bilberry Manor SM2 . . . 218 A1
Billet Rd Ilford RM6 . . . 58 C6
Walthamstow E17 . . . 35 B2
Billetts Hart Cl W7 . . . 108 C4
Bill Hamling Cl SE9 . . . 166 B2
Billie Holiday Ct NW10 . . . 89 B5
Billingford Cl SE4 . . . 140 D1
Billing Ho 7 E1 . . . 96 D1
Billingley NW1 . . . 232 A5
Billing Pl SW10 . . 135 D5 265 D4
Billing Rd SW10 . . 135 D5 265 D4
Billings Cl RM9 . . . 80 C1
Billingsgate Mkt E14 . . . 119 D5
Billing St SW10 . . 135 D5 265 D4
Billington Ho SW8 . . . 269 D1
Billington Rd SE14 . . . 140 D5
Billinton Hill CR0 . . . 221 B6
Billiter Sq EC3 . . . 243 B1
Billiter St EC3 . . . 95 C1 243 B1
Bill Nicholson Way N17 . . . 33 D3
Billockby Cl KT9 . . . 214 B2
Billsley Ct SE25 . . . 205 C5
Billson St E14 . . . 120 A2
Bilsby Gr SE9 . . . 187 D6
Bilton Ho SW8 . . . 269 C1
Bilton Rd UB6 . . . 87 B6
Bilton Twrs W1 . . . 237 D1
Bilton Way Enfield EN3 . . . 7 B5
Hayes UB3 . . . 106 B4
Bina Gdns SW5 . . . 114 A2 256 A3
Binbrook Ho 13 W10 . . . 90 C2
Bincote Rd EN2 . . . 4 B2
Binden Rd W12 . . . 111 D3
Bindon Gn SM4 . . . 201 D5
Binfield Ct SE5 . . . 139 A3
Binfield Rd
London SW4 . . . 138 A4 270 B1
South Croydon CR2 . . . 221 D3
Bingfield St N1 . . . 94 B6 233 C6
Bingham Cnr CR0 . . . 206 A1
Bingham Ct 1 N1 . . . 72 D1
Bingham Pl W1 . . . 93 A2 238 A4
Bingham Point 11 SE18 . . . 122 D2
Bingham Rd CR0 . . . 206 B1
Bingham St N1 . . . 73 B2
Bingley Rd Ashford TW16 . . . 172 A3
Newham E16 . . . 99 C1
Southall UB6 . . . 86 A2
Binley Ho SW15 . . . 155 D5
Binney St W1 . . . 93 A1 238 B1
Binnie Ct SE10 . . . 141 D5
Binnie Ho SE1 . . . 262 A5
Binns Rd W4 . . . 111 C1
Binns Terr 3 W4 . . . 111 C1
Binsey Wlk 1 SE2 . . . 124 C4
Binstead Cl UB4 . . . 85 A2
Binstead Ho SW18 . . . 157 D5
Binyon Cres HA7 . . . 24 D5
Binyon Ho 8 N16 . . . 73 C4
Birbeck Ho 4 N19 . . . 49 D1
Birbetts Rd SE9 . . . 166 B2
Bircham Path SE4 . . . 140 D1
Birchanger Rd SE25 . . . 206 A4
Birch Ave Edmonton N13 . . . 17 A1
Hillingdon UB7 . . . 82 B1
Birch Cl Brentford TW8 . . . 131 B5
Buckhurst Hill IG9 . . . 21 D1
Hounslow TW3 . . . 130 B3
Newham E16 . . . 98 C2
Peckham SE15 . . . 140 A3
Romford RM7 . . . 59 D6
Teddington TW11 . . . 175 A5
Upper Holloway N19 . . . 71 C6
Birch Cres UB10 . . . 82 B6
Birch Ct Chingford E4 . . . 35 D4
Forest Gate E7 . . . 76 D4
Ilford RM6 . . . 58 C3
Sutton SM1 . . . 218 A4
9 Wallington SM6 . . . 219 B4
7 Woodside Pk N12 . . . 29 D6
Birchdale Gdns RM6 . . . 58 D2
Birchdale Rd E7 . . . 77 C3
Birchdene Dr SE28 . . . 124 A5
Birchdown Ho 32 E3 . . . 97 D4
Birchen Cl NW9 . . . 67 B6
Birchend Cl CR2 . . . 221 B2
Birchen Gr NW9 . . . 67 B6
Birches Cl Mitcham CR4 . . 202 D6
Pinner HA5 . . . 41 A4
Birches The
2 Beckenham BR2 . . . 208 D5
Bushey WD23 . . . 8 A6
Camberwell SE5 . . . 139 C3
Greenwich SE7 . . . 143 B6
Manor Pk E12 . . . 78 A4
Orpington BR6 . . . 226 C4
Southgate N21 . . . 16 B5
South Norwood SE25 . . . 183 D1
Twickenham TW4 . . . 151 B4
Birchfield Ho 3 E14 . . . 119 C6
Birchfield St E14 . . . 119 C6
Birch Gn NW9 . . . 27 C3
Birch Gr Acton W3 . . . 110 C6
Bexley DA16 . . . 146 A1
Lewisham SE12 . . . 164 D4
Leyton E11 . . . 76 C5
Upper Halliford TW17 . . . 171 C1
Birchgrove Ho TW9 . . . 132 D5
Birch Hill CR0 . . . 222 D3
Birch Ho
New Cross Gate SE14 . . . 141 B4
Teddington TW11 . . . 175 C3
8 Tulse Hill SW2 . . . 160 C5
Birchington Cl DA7 . . . 147 D4
Birchington Ct
Crouch End N8 . . . 49 D3
2 Kilburn NW6 . . . 91 D6
Birchington Ho 1 E5 . . . 74 B3
Birchington Rd
Crouch End N8 . . . 49 D3
Kilburn NW6 . . . 91 C6
Surbiton KT5 . . . 198 B2
Birchin La EC3 . . . 242 D1
Birchlands Ave SW12 . . . 158 D4
Birch Mead BR2, BR6 . . . 226 C6
Birchmead Ave HA5 . . . 40 C5
Birchmere Bsns Pk SE2 . . 124 A4
Birchmere Lo 18 SE16 . . . 118 B1
Birchmere Row SE3 . . . 142 D3
Birchmore Wlk N5 . . . 73 A5
Birch Pk HA3 . . . 24 A3
Birch Rd Feltham TW13 . . . 172 D5
Romford RM7 . . . 59 D6
Birch Row BR2 . . . 210 C3
Birch Tree Ave BR4 . . . 224 D4
Birch Tree Ho 16 SE7 . . . 143 C6
Birch Tree Way CR0 . . . 222 B6
Birch Vale Ct NW8 . . . 236 D6
Birchway UB3 . . . 106 A5
Birch Wlk CR4 . . . 181 B2
Birchwood Ave
Beckenham BR3 . . . 207 B5
Hackbridge SM5, SM6 . . . 219 B5
Muswell Hill N10 . . . 49 A6
Sidcup DA14 . . . 168 C1
Birchwood Cl SM4 . . . 201 D5
Birchwood Ct
Burnt Oak HA8 . . . 27 A1
Edmonton N13 . . . 32 D5
Birchwood Dr NW3 . . . 69 D5
Birchwood Gr TW12 . . . 173 C4
Birchwood Rd
Orpington BR5 . . . 211 C5
Streatham SW17 . . . 181 B5
Birdbrook Rd SE3 . . . 143 C2
Birdcage Wlk SW1 . . . 115 D4 249 C1
Bird Coll DA14 . . . 168 A1
Birdham Cl BR1 . . . 210 A4
Birdhurst Ave CR2 . . . 221 B4
Birdhurst Ct SM6 . . . 219 C1
Birdhurst Gdns CR2 . . . 221 B4
Birdhurst Rd
London SW18 . . . 158 A6
Mitcham SW19 . . . 180 C4
South Croydon CR2 . . . 221 C3
Birdhurst Rise CR2 . . . 221 C3
Bird In Bush Rd SE15 . . . 140 A5
Bird-in-Hand La BR1 . . . 187 D1
Bird-In-Hand Pas SE23 . . 162 C2
Bird In Hand Yd 24 NW3 . . . 70 A4
Birdsall Ho 5 SE5 . . . 139 C2
Birdsfield La 12 E3 . . . 97 B6
Bird St W1 . . . 238 B1
Bird Wlk TW2 . . . 151 B3
Birdwood Ave 4 SE13 . . . 164 B5
Birdwood Cl TW11 . . . 174 C6
Birkbeck Ave Acton W3 . . . 111 A6
Greenford UB6 . . . 86 A6
Birkbeck Coll W1 . . 93 D1 239 C2
Birkbeck Ct W3 . . . 111 B5
Birkbeck Gdns IG8 . . . 21 A2
Birkbeck Gr W3 . . . 111 B4
Birkbeck Hill SE21 . . . 160 D3
Birkbeck Mews 5 E8 . . . 73 D3
Birkbeck Pl SE21 . . . 161 A2
Birkbeck Prim Sch DA14 . . . 168 B1
Birkbeck Rd Acton W3 . . . 111 B5
Dalston E8 . . . 73 D3
Ealing W5 . . . 109 C2
Edgware NW7 . . . 27 D5
Enfield EN2 . . . 5 B5
Hornsey N8 . . . 50 A5
Ilford IG2 . . . 57 B4
North Finchley N12 . . . 30 A5
Penge BR3 . . . 184 D1
Sidcup DA14 . . . 168 A1
Tottenham N17 . . . 33 D2
Wimbledon SW19 . . . 179 D4
Birkbeck St E2 . . . 96 B4
Birkbeck Sta SE20 . . . 206 C6
Birkbeck Univ of London WC1 . . . 93 D3 239 C6
Birkbeck Way UB6 . . . 86 B6
Birkdale Ave HA5 . . . 41 C6
Birkdale Cl
30 Bermondsey SE16 . . . 118 B1
Crofton BR6 . . . 211 B2
Erith SE28 . . . 102 D1
Birkdale Ct 3 UB1 . . . 86 A1
Birkdale Gdns CR0 . . . 222 D4
Birkdale Rd
Abbey Wood SE2 . . . 124 A2
Ealing W5 . . . 88 A3
Birkenhead Ave KT2 . . . 176 B2
Birkenhead Ho 11 N7 . . . 72 C3
Birkenhead St WC1 . . . 94 A4 233 B2
Birkhall Rd SE6 . . . 164 B2
Birkwood Cl SW12 . . . 159 D4
Birley Lo NW8 . . . 229 D4
Birley Rd N20 . . . 14 A2
Birley St SW11 . . . 137 A3
Birnam Rd N4 . . . 72 B6
Birnbeck Ct NW11 . . . 47 B4
Birnham Ho TW1 . . . 153 C4
Birrell Ho 9 SW9 . . . 138 B3
Birse Cres NW10 . . . 67 C4
Birstal Gn WD19 . . . 22 D6
Birstall Rd N15 . . . 51 C4
Birtwhistle Ho 5 E3 . . . 97 B6
Biscay Ho 11 E1 . . . 96 D3
Biscay Rd W6 . . . 112 D1
Biscoe Cl TW5 . . . 129 C6
Biscoe Ho UB2 . . . 107 D2
Biscoe Way SE13 . . . 142 B2
Biscott Ho 3 E3 . . . 97 D3
Bisenden Rd CR0 . . . 221 C6
Bisham Cl CR4 . . . 202 D1
Bisham Gdns N6 . . . 49 A1

Bishop Butt Cl BR6. . . . . 227 D5
Bishop Challoner Collegiate
  Sch 28 E1. . . . . .96 C1
Bishop Challoner Sch
  BR2. . . . . .186 B1
Bishop Ct 20 SW2. . . . . . . .160 C5
Bishop Douglass RC Sch
  N2. .48 A6
Bishop Duppa's Almshouses
  7 TW10. . . . . .154 A6
Bishop Duppas Pk
  TW17. . . . . .193 C2
Bishop Fox Way KT8 . . . .195 B5
Bishop Gilpins Prim Sch
  SW19 . . . . .179 B5
Bishop John Robinson CE
  Prim Sch SE28. . . . . 124 C6
Bishop Justus CE Sch
  BR2. . . . . .210 A2
Bishop Ken Rd HA3 . . . . . .24 D2
Bishop King's Rd
  W14. . . . . .113 A2 254 B4
Bishop Perrin CE Prim Sch
  TW2 . . . . .151 D3
Bishop Ramsey CE Sch
  (Annexe) HA4 . . . . .39 D2
Bishop Ramsey CE Sch
  (Upper) HA4 . . . . .40 A2
Bishop Rd N14. . . . . .15 B4
Bishop Ridley CE Prim Sch
  DA16. . . . . .145 C1
Bishops Ave
  Borehamwood WD6 . . . . . .10 B6
  Bromley BR1. . . . . .209 C6
  Ilford RM6 . . . . .58 C3
  Newham E13 . . . . .99 B6
Bishop's Ave SW6. . . . . . .135 A3
Bishops Ave The N2 . . . . .48 B3
Bishopsbourne Ho BR1 . .187 B3
Bishop's Bridge Rd
  W2. . . . . .92 A1 236 A2
Bishops Cl
  Acton Green W4 . . . . .111 A1
  Barnet EN5. . . . . .12 D5
  Enfield EN1. . . . . .6 B3
  New Eltham SE9. . . . . . . .167 A2
  Richmond TW10 . . . . .153 D1
  Sutton SM1. . . . . .217 C5
Bishop's Cl
  Dartmouth Pk N19 . . . . . .71 C5
  Hillingdon UB10. . . . . .82 C5
  Walthamstow E17 . . . . . . .53 D5
Bishopscourt 8 CR0. . . . .221 D6
Bishops Dr
  East Bedfont TW14. . . . . .149 B5
  Northolt UB5 . . . . .85 A6
Bishopsford Com Sch
  SM4 . . . . .202 B3
Bishopsford Ho SM4 . . . .202 C3
Bishopsford Rd SM4 . . . .202 B3
Bishopsgate EC2 . . .95 C1 243 A2
Bishopsgate Arc E1 . . . . .243 B3
Bishopsgate Churchyard
  EC2. . . . . .243 A2
Bishopsgate Inst
  EC2. . . . . .95 C2 243 B3
Bishops Gn BR1. . . . . .187 C2
Bishops Gr
  East Finchley N2. . . . . .48 C3
  Feltham TW12 . . . . .173 B6
Bishop's Hall KT1. . . . . . .175 D1
Bishophsalt Sch UB8. . . . .82 B4
Bishops Hill KT12. . . . . . .194 A2
Bishops Ho SW8. . . . . . . .270 B3
Bishops Mans SW6. . . . . .134 D3
Bishops Mead SE5. . . . . .139 A5
Bishops Park Rd SW16 . .182 A4
Bishop's Park Rd SW6 . .134 D3
Bishop's Pl SM1. . . . . .218 A3
Bishops Rd
  Fulham SW6 . . . . . . .135 B4 264 C2
  Highgate N6. . . . . .49 A3
Bishop's Rd Hanwell W7. .108 C4
  Thornton Heath CR0. . . . .204 D2
  Hayes UB3 . . . . .83 A1
Bishops Sq E1. . . . . .243 B4
Bishop St N1. . . . . .95 A6 235 A6
Bishop's Terr
  SE11. . . . . .116 C2 261 B4
Bishopsthorpe Rd SE26 . .184 D6
Bishopstone Ho 4
  SW11. . . . . .137 A3
Bishop Stopford's Sch EN1. .6 B3
Bishops View CN10 . . . . . .49 B5
Bishop's Way E2. . . . . .96 C5
Bishops Wlk
  Chislehurst BR7 . . . . .189 A2

Bishops Wlk *continued*
  South Croydon CR0, CR9. . .223 A3
Bishopswood Rd N6 . . . . .48 D2
Bishop Thomas Grant Sch
  SW16. . . . . .182 B5
Bishop Wand CE Sec Sch
  TW16 . . . . .171 D1
Bishop Wilfred Wood Cl
  SE15. . . . . .140 A3
Bishop Wilfred Wood Ct 3
  E13 . . . . .99 C5
Bishop Winnington-Ingram
  CE Prim Sch HA4 . . . . . . .39 B2
Bisley Cl KT4 . . . . .200 C1
Bisley Ho SW19 . . . . .156 D2
Bispham Ho NW10. . . . . . . .88 B4
Bissextile Ho SE13 . . . . . .141 D3
Bisson Rd E15. . . . . .98 A5
Bisterne Ave E17. . . . . .54 B6
Bittacy Bsns Ctr NW7. . . .29 A3
Bittacy Cl NW7 . . . . .28 D4
Bittacy Ct NW7 . . . . .29 A3
Bittacy Hill NW7. . . . . .28 D4
Bittacy Park Ave NW7 . . .28 D5
Bittacy Rd NW7. . . . . .28 D4
Bittacy Rise NW7 . . . . .28 D4
Bittern Cl UB4. . . . . .84 D2
Bittern Ct Chingford E4. . . .20 B4
  7 Deptford SE8. . . . . .141 C6
  Hendon NW9 . . . . .27 C1
Bittern Ho SE1. . . . . .252 A1
Bittern St SE1. . . . . .252 A1
Bittoms The KT1. . . . . .197 D6
Bixley Cl UB2. . . . . .107 B2
Blackall St EC2. . . . . .243 A6
Blackberry Cl TW17. . . . . .193 C5
Blackberry Farm Cl
  TW5. . . . . .129 A5
Blackberry Field BR5 . . . .190 A2
Blackbird Ct NW9. . . . . .67 B5
Blackbird Hill NW9 . . . . . . .67 B5
Blackborne Rd RM10. . . . . .81 D2
Black Boy La N15. . . . . .51 A4
Blackbrook La BR1, BR2 . .210 C5
Blackburn 28 NW9 . . . . .27 D1
Blackburn Ct 21 SW2. . . . .160 C5
Blackburne's Mews W1 . .248 A5
Blackburn Rd NW6. . . . . . . .69 D2
Blackburn Trad Est
  TW19. . . . . .148 B5
Blackburn Way NW4. . . . .151 A6
Blackbush Ave RM6. . . . . . .58 D4
Blackbush Cl SM2. . . . . . . .217 D1
Blackcap Ct NW9 . . . . .27 C1
Blackdown Cl N2 . . . . .30 A1
Blackdown Ho E8. . . . . .74 A4
Blackett St SW15. . . . . . . .134 D2
Black Fan Cl EN2. . . . . .5 A4
BLACKFEN. 168 A5
Blackfen Par DA15. . . . . . .168 A5
Blackfen Rd DA15. . . . . . . .168 B5
Blackfen Sch for Girls
  DA15. . . . . .168 B5
Blackford Rd WD19 . . . . . . .22 D5
Blackfriars Bridge EC4. . .251 C5
Blackfriars Ct EC4 . . . . . . .251 C6
Black Friars La
  EC4. . . . . .94 D1 241 C1
Blackfriars Pas EC4 . . . . . .251 C6
Blackfriars Pier EC4. . . . . .251 C6
Blackfriars Rd
  SE1. . . . . .116 D5 251 C3
Blackfriars Underpass
  EC4. . . . . .116 C6 251 B6
Blackham Ho SW19. . . . . .179 A4
BLACKHEATH. 142 C2
  Blackheath*★* SE3. . . . . . . .142 C4
Blackheath Ave SE3. . . . . .142 C5
Blackheath Bluecoat Sch
  SE3. . . . . .143 B5
Blackheath Bsns Est
  SE10. . . . . .142 A4
Blackheath Gr SE3 . . . . . . .142 D3
Blackheath High Jun Sch
  SE3. . . . . .142 D3
Blackheath High Sch
  SE3. . . . . .143 A5
Blackheath Hill SE10. . . . .142 A4
Blackheath Hospl SE3 . . .142 C2
BLACKHEATH PARK. 143 A1
Blackheath Pk SE3. . . . . . .143 A2
Blackheath Prep Sch
  SE3. . . . . .143 A4
Blackheath Rd SE10. . . . . .141 D4
Blackheath Rise SE13 . . . .142 A3
Blackheath Sta SE3 . . . . . .142 D2
BLACKHEATH VALE. 142 C3
Blackheath Vale SE3. . . . .142 C3
Blackheath Village SE3 . .142 D3
Black Horse Ct SE1 . . . . . .262 D6
Blackhorse La
  Croydon CR0. . . . . .206 A2
  Higham Hill E17. . . . . .34 C1
Blackhorse La Sta CR0. . .206 A2
Blackhorse Mews E17. . . . .52 D6
Black Horse Par HA5. . . . .40 B4
Blackhorse Rd
  Deptford SE8 . . . . .141 A6
  Walthamstow E17 . . . . . . .53 A5
Black Horse Rd DA14. . . . .190 A6

Blackhorse Road E17 . . . . .52 D5
Blackhorse Road Sta E17 .52 D5
Blacklands Dr UB4. . . . . . . .83 A3
Blacklands Rd SE6. . . . . . .186 A6
Blacklands Terr SW3 . . . . .257 D3
Black Lion La W6 . . . . .112 A2
Black Lion Mews 4 W6 . .112 A2
Blackmore Ave UB1. . . . . .108 B5
Blackmore Dr NW10. . . . . . .66 D1
Blackmore Ho
  Forest Hill SE23. . . . . .163 B3
  Islington N1. . . . . .233 D5
  2 Wandsworth SW18. . . . .157 D6
Blackmore's Gr TW11 . . . .175 A4
Blackmore Twr 1 W3. . . . .111 A3
Blackness La BR2. . . . . . . .225 D1
Blackpool Gdns UB4. . . . . . .83 C3
Blackpool Rd SE15. . . . . . .140 B3
Black Prince Intc DA6. . . .169 D5
Black Prince Rd SE1,
  SE11. . . . . .116 B2 260 D3
Black Rod Cl UB3. . . . . .105 C3
Black Roof Ho 9 SE5. . . . .138 D4
Blackshaw Rd SW17 . . . . .180 B5
Blacksmith Cl RM6. . . . . . . .58 C3
Blacksmiths Ho 7 E17. . . . .53 C5
Black's Rd W6. . . . . .112 C2
Blackstock Ho 2 N5. . . . . . .72 D5
Blackstock Mews N4. . . . . .72 D5
Blackstock Rd N4, N5. . . . .72 D6
Blackstone Ho
  Dulwich SE21 . . . . .161 C1
  Pimlico SW1. . . . . .259 A1
Blackstone Rd NW2. . . . . . .68 C4
Black Swan Yd SE1. . . . . . .253 A2
Blackthorn Ave UB7. . . . . .104 C3
Blackthorn Ct
  20 Camberwell SE15. . . . .139 D5
  Heston TW5 . . . . .129 A5
  4 Leyton E15. . . . . .76 B4
  5 West Norwood SW16. . .182 C5
Blackthorne Ave CR0. . . . .206 C1
Blackthorne Ct
  2 Littleton TW15. . . . . . . .171 A3
  Southall UB1. . . . . .107 D5
Blackthorne Dr E4. . . . . . . .36 B6
Blackthorn Gr DA7. . . . . . .147 A2
Blackthorn Rd IG1. . . . . . . .79 B3
Blackthorn St E3 . . . . .97 C3
Blacktree Mews 11 SW9. .138 C2
BLACKWALL. 120 B6
Blackwall Sta E14 . . . . . . .120 A6
Blackwall Trad Est E14. . . .98 B2
Blackwall Tunnel E14,
  SE10. . . . . .120 B5
Blackwall Tunnel App
  SE10. . . . . .120 C4
Blackwall Tunnel Northern
  Approach E14, E3. . . . . . .98 A3
Blackwall Way E14. . . . . . .120 A6
Blackwater Cl E7. . . . . .76 D4
Blackwater Ho NW8 . . . . .236 D4
Blackwater St SE22. . . . . .161 D6
Blackwell Cl
  10 Clapton Pk E5. . . . . . . .74 D4
  Harrow HA3 . . . . .24 B3
  Southgate N21. . . . . .16 A6
Blackwell Gdns HA8. . . . . .10 C1
Blackwell Ho 3 SW4 . . . . .159 D5
Blackwood Ho 11 E1. . . . . .96 B3
Blackwood St
  SE17. . . . . .117 B1 262 C2
Blade Ho TW1. . . . . .153 D5
Blade Mews SW15. . . . . . .135 B1
Bladen Ho 4 E1. . . . . .96 D1
Blades Ct
  4 Hammersmith W6. . . . .112 B1
  Putney SW15. . . . . .135 B1
Blades Ho 12 SE11. . . . . . .138 C6
Blades Lo 16 SW2. . . . . . . .160 C5
Bladindon Dr DA5. . . . . . . .168 D4
Bladon Ct
  Beckenham BR2. . . . . .208 C6
  Streatham SW16. . . . . . . .182 A4
Bladon Gdns HA2. . . . . .41 D3
Blagden's Cl N14. . . . . .15 D2
Blagden's La N14. . . . . .15 D2
Blagdon Ct W7. . . . . .108 C6
Blagdon Rd London SE13 . .163 D5
  New Malden KT3. . . . . . . .199 D5
Blagdon Wlk TW11. . . . . . .175 C4
Blagrove Rd 1 W10. . . . . . .91 B2
Blair Ave London NW9. . . . .45 C2
  Thames Ditton KT10. . . . .212 A6
Blair Cl Avery Hill DA15 . .167 C6
  Canonbury N1. . . . . .73 A2
  Hayes UB3 . . . . .106 A2
Blair Ct Beckenham BR3 . .185 D2
  8 Carshalton SM5. . . . . . .218 D5
  7 Catford SE6. . . . . .164 D3
  St John's Wood NW8 . . . .229 C6
Blairderry Rd SW2. . . . . . .160 A2
Blairgowrie Ct 13 E14. . . . .98 B1
Blair Ho SW9. . . . . .138 B3
Blair Peach Prim Sch
  UB1. . . . . .106 D5
Blair St E14. . . . . .98 B1
Blake Apartments N8 . . . . .50 B6
Blake Ave IG11 . . . . .101 D6
Blake Cl Bexley DA16. . . . .145 C4

Blake Cl *continued*
  Carshalton SM5 . . . . .202 C1
  Hayes SM4 . . . . .83 B5
  Blake Coll W1. . . . . .93 C2 239 A4
Blake Ct
  8 Bermondsey SE16. . . . . .118 B1
  9 Clapham SW8 . . . . .137 C3
  Croydon CR2. . . . . .220 D3
  Kilburn NW6. . . . . .91 C4
  Southgate N21. . . . . .16 B6
Blake Gdns SW6 . . .135 D4 265 C2
Blake Hall Cres E11 . . . . . . .55 A1
Blakehall Rd SM5. . . . . . . .218 D2
Blake Hall Rd E11. . . . . .55 A2
Blake Ho
  6 Beckenham BR3. . . . . . .185 D4
  2 Deptford SE8. . . . . .141 C6
  Harrow HA1 . . . . .64 C6
  Isle Of Dogs E14. . . . . . . .119 D4
  1 Kentish Town N19 . . . . .71 D3
  Lambeth SE1. . . . . .261 A6
  14 Stoke Newington N16 . .73 C4
  Blake Lo N3. . . . . .29 B1
  Blake Mews 13 TW9 . . . . .132 C4
Blakemore Rd
  Streatham SW16. . . . . . . .160 A1
  Thornton Heath CR7. . . . .204 B4
Blakemore Way DA17 . . . .125 A3
Blakeney Ave BR3. . . . . . . .185 B2
Blakeney Cl
  5 Camden Town NW1. . . . .71 C1
  4 Dalston E8. . . . . .74 A3
  Whetstone N20 . . . . .14 A3
Blakeney Ct EN2. . . . . .17 B6
Blakeney Rd BR3. . . . . .185 B2
Blakenham Ct W12. . . . . . .112 A5
Blakenham Rd SW17 . . . . .180 D6
Blaker Ct SE7. . . . . .143 C5
Blakemore Rd Croydon CR0. .221 C6
  Mitcham CR4 . . . . .202 C6
  Newham E16 . . . . .98 D3
  Wood Green N11. . . . . .31 C3
Blaker Rd E15. . . . . .98 A6
Blakes Ave KT3 . . . . .199 D3
Blakes Cl W10 . . . . .90 C2
Blake's Gn BR4 . . . . .208 A1
Blakesley Ave W5. . . . . .87 C1
Blakesley Ct W5. . . . . .87 C1
Blakesley Ho 4 E12. . . . . . . .78 C5
Blake's Rd SE15. . . . . .139 C5
Blakes Terr KT3. . . . . .200 A4
Blakesware Gdns N9. . . . . .17 B4
Blakewood Cl TW13. . . . . .172 C6
Blakewood Ct 5 SE20. . . . .184 B3
  Blanca Ho 16 N1. . . . . .95 C5
Blanchard Cl SE9 . . . . .166 A1
Blanchard Gr EN3. . . . . .7 D5
Blanchard Ho
  Chislehurst BR7. . . . . .189 A4
  7 Twickenham TW1. . . . . .153 D5
Blanchard Way E8 . . . . .74 A2
Blanch Cl SE15. . . . . .140 C5
Blanchedowne SE5. . . . . . .139 B1
Blanche Nevile Sch
  Highgate N6. . . . . .48 D3
  Muswell Hill N10. . . . . .31 A1
Blanche St E16. . . . . .98 D3
Blanchland Rd SM4 . . . . . .201 D4
Blandfield Rd SW12. . . . . .159 A4
Blandford Ave
  2 Beckenham BR3. . . . . . .185 A1
  Twickenham TW2 . . . . . . .151 D3
Blandford Cl London N2. . . .48 A5
  Romford RM7 . . . . .59 D5
  Wallington CR0. . . . . .220 A5
Blandford Cres E4 . . . . .20 A4
Blandford Ct
  Brondesbury Pk NW6. . . . . .69 A1
  6 De Beauvoir Town N1. . . .73 C1
Blandford Ho SW8 . . . . . . .270 C4
Blandford Rd Acton W4 . . .111 C3
  Ealing W5. . . . . .109 D4
  Penge BR3. . . . . .184 D1
  Southall UB2. . . . . .107 C2
  Teddington TW11. . . . . . . .174 C5
Blandford Sq NW1. . . . . . . .237 B5
Blandford St W1. . . . .93 A2 238 A3
Blandford Waye UB4. . . . . .84 C1
Bland Ho SE11. . . . . .260 D2
Bland St SE9. . . . . .143 D1
Blaney Cres E6. . . . . .100 D4
Blanmerle Rd SE9 . . . . .166 D3
Blann Cl SE9. . . . . .165 D5
Blantyre St SW10 .136 B5 266 C4
Blantyre Twr SW10 . . . . . .266 C4
Blantyre Wlk
  SW10. . . . . .136 B5 266 C4
Blashford NW3. . . . . .70 D1
Blashford St SE13. . . . . . . .164 B4
Blasker Wlk 8 E14 . . . . . . .119 D1
Blatchford Ct KT12. . . . . . .194 A1
Blatchford Ho 8 RM10. . . . .81 C5
Blawith Rd HA1. . . . . .42 D5
Blaxland Ho 12 W12. . . . . .112 B6
Blaydon Cl HA4. . . . . .39 C2
Blaydon Ct 4 UB5. . . . . .63 C2
Blaydon Wlk N17. . . . . .34 B3
Blazer Ct NW8. . . . . .229 D1

Bleak Hill La SE18. . . . . . . .145 D6
Blean Gr SE20. . . . . .184 C3
Bleak Ho SE18 . . . . .87 A5
Bleasdale Ave UB6. . . . . . . .87 A5
Blechynden Ho 17 W10. . . .90 D1
Blechynden St W10. . . . . . .112 D6
Bledlow Cl SE28 . . . . .124 C6
Bledlow Rise UB6. . . . . .86 A5
Bleeding Heart Yd EC1 . . .241 B3
Blegborough Rd SW16. . . .181 C4
Blemundsbury WC1. . . . . . .240 C4
Blendon Dr DA5. . . . . .168 D5
Blendon Path 9 BR1. . . . . .186 D3
Blendon Rd DA5. . . . . .168 D5
Blendon Terr SE18 . . . . . . .145 A6
Blendworth Point 4
  SW15. . . . . .156 B3
Blenheim 26 SW19 . . . . . . .156 D3
Blenheim Ave IG2 . . . . .56 C3
Blenheim Bsns Ctr CR4 . .180 D1
Blenheim Centre 7
  SE20. . . . . .184 D3
Blenheim Cl
  Edmonton N21. . . . . .17 A3
  Eltham SE12. . . . . .165 B3
  Greenford UB6. . . . . .86 B5
  Wallington SM6. . . . . .219 C1
  West Barnes SW20 . . . . . .200 C6
Blenheim Cres
  Notting Hill W11. . . . . .91 A1
  Notting Hill W11. . . . . .244 B6
  Ruislip HA4. . . . . .61 B6
  South Croydon CR2. . . . . .221 A1
Blenheim Ct Barnsbury N7. .72 A2
  Beckenham BR2 . . . . .208 D5
  5 Hampton TW12. . . . . . .173 C2
  Harrow HA3 . . . . .43 A3
  Hendon NW4 . . . . .46 D5
  Longlands DA14. . . . . .167 B1
  Richmond TW9 . . . . .132 B2
  17 Rotherhithe SE16. . . . .118 D5
  South Norwood SE19 . . . .183 C2
  Sutton SM2. . . . . .218 A2
  Upper Holloway N19 . . . . .72 A6
  Woodford IG8. . . . . .37 B3
Blenheim Ctr TW3 . . . . . . .129 D2
Blenheim Dr DA16. . . . . . . .145 D4
Blenheim Gdns
  Clapham Pk SW2 . . . . . . .160 B5
  Dollis Hill NW2 . . . . .68 C3
  Kingston u T KT2. . . . . . . .176 D3
  Wallington SM6 . . . . .219 C1
  Wembley HA9. . . . . .66 A5
Blenheim Gr SE15. . . . . . . .140 A3
Blenheim Ho
  6 Edmonton N9. . . . . .18 A1
  Hounslow TW3 . . . . .129 C2
  8 Woolwich SE18. . . . . . . .123 A4
Blenheim Par 2 UB10. . . . .82 D3
Blenheim Park Rd CR2 . . .221 A1
Blenheim Pas NW8 . . . . . .229 A4
Blenheim Pl TW11. . . . . . . .174 D5
Blenheim Rd Acton W4. . . .111 C3
  Bromley BR1, BR2 . . . . . .210 A5
  Harrow HA2. . . . . .41 D3
  Leyton E15. . . . . .76 C4
  Newham E6. . . . . .99 D4
  Northolt UB5. . . . . .63 D2
  Penge SE20. . . . . .184 C3
  Sidcup DA15. . . . . .168 C3
  St John's Wood
  NW8. . . . . .92 A5 229 B4
  Sutton SM1. . . . . .217 D6
  Walthamstow E17 . . . . . . .53 A6
  West Barnes SW20 . . . . . .200 C6
Blenheim Rise N15. . . . . . . .51 D5
Blenheim St W1 . . . . .238 C1
Blenheim Terr
  NW8 . . . . .92 A5 229 A4
Blenheim Way TW7 . . . . . .131 A4
Blenkarne Rd SW11. . . . . .158 D5
Bleriot 27 NW9. . . . . .27 D1
Bleriot Rd TW5. . . . . .128 C5
Blessbury Rd HA8. . . . . .27 A2
Blessed Dominic RC Sch
  NW9 . . . . .27 D1
Blessed Sacrament RC Prim
  Sch N1. . . . . .94 B6 233 C3
Blessington Cl SE13. . . . . .142 B2
Blessington Rd SE13. . . . . .142 B1
Blessing Way IG11. . . . . . .102 C5
Bletchingley Cl CR7. . . . . .204 D5
Bletchington Ct 2
  DA17. . . . . .125 C2
Bletchley Ct N1. . . . . .235 C3
Bletchley St N1. . . . .95 A5 235 B3
Bletchmore Cl UB3. . . . . . .105 B1
Bletsoe Wlk N1. . . . . .235 B4
Blewbury Ho 3 SE2. . . . . . .124 C4
Blick Ho 1 SE16. . . . . .118 C3
Bligh Ho 4 SE27. . . . . .183 A6
Blincoe Cl SW19. . . . . .156 D2
Blissett St SE10. . . . . .142 A4
Blissland Ct 5 N12. . . . . . . .30 A4
Bliss Mews 14 W10. . . . . . .91 A4
Blisworth Cl UB4. . . . . .85 A3
Blisworth Ho 12 E2. . . . . . .96 A6
Blithbury Rd RM9. . . . . .80 B2
Blithdale Rd SE2. . . . . .124 A2
Blithfield St W8. . . . . .255 C5
Blockley Rd HA0. . . . . .65 B6

Bloemfontein Ave W12 . . . 112 B5
Bloemfontein Rd W12 . . . 112 B6
Blomfield Ct
  Battersea SW11 . . . . . 266 D2
  Paddington W9 . . . . . . 236 B6
Blomfield Ho 4 E14 . . . . 119 C6
Blomfield Mans 3 W12 . . 112 C5
Blomfield Rd W9 . . 92 A2 236 A4
Blomfield St EC2 . . 95 B2 242 D3
Blomfield Villas W9 . . . . 236 A4
Blomville Rd RM8 . . . . . . 81 A5
Blondel St SW11 . . . . . . 137 A3
Blondin Ave W5 . . . . . . 109 C3
Blondin St E3 . . . . 97 C5
Bloomburg St SW1 . . . . . 259 B3
Bloomfield Cres IG2 . . . . 56 D3
Bloomfield Ct N6 . . . . 49 A3
Bloomfield Ho 19 E1 . . . . 96 A2
Bloomfield Pl W1 . . . . . 248 D6
Bloomfield Rd
  Bromley Comm BR2 . . . 209 D4
  Highgate N6 . . . . 49 A3
  Kingston u T KT1 . . . . . 198 A6
  Woolwich SE18 . . . . . . 122 D1
Bloomfield Terr
  SW1 . . . . 115 A1 258 B2
Bloom St SE27 . . . . 160 D1
Bloomhall Rd SE19 . . . . 183 B5
Bloom Park Rd SW6 . . . . 264 C3
Bloomsberg Space* . . .
  EC1 . . . . 242 D4
BLOOMSBURY 93 D2
Bloomsbury Cl
  Ealing W5 . . . . 110 B6
  Edgware NW7 . . . . 28 A3
Bloomsbury Ct
  Cranford TW5 . . . . 128 B4
  Leytonstone E11 . . . . . . 54 B1
  Pinner HA5 . . . . 41 B6
  St Giles WC1 . . . . 240 B3
Bloomsbury Ho 10 SW4 . 159 D5
Bloomsbury International
  Language Sch
  WC1 . . . . 94 A2 240 B3
Bloomsbury Pl
  London SW18 . . . . 158 A6
  St Giles WC1 . . . . 240 B3
Bloomsbury Sq
  WC1 . . . . 94 A2 240 B3
Bloomsbury St
  WC1 . . . . 93 D2 239 D3
Bloomsbury Way
  WC1 . . . . 94 A2 240 B3
Blore Cl SW8 . . . . 269 C1
Blore Ct W1 . . . . 249 C6
Blore Ho SW10 . . . . 265 D4
Blossom Cl
  Dagenham RM9 . . . . . . 103 B6
  Ealing W5 . . . . 110 A4
  South Croydon CR2 . . . . 221 D3
Blossom House Sch
  SW20 . . . . 178 C3
Blossom La EN2 . . . . 5 A4
Blossom Pl E1 . . . . 243 B5
Blossom St E1 . . . . 95 C3 243 B5
Blossom Way
  Hillingdon UB10 . . . . . . 60 B1
  West Drayton UB7 . . . . 104 C2
Blossom Waye TW5 . . . . 129 A5
Blount St E14 . . . . 97 A1
Bloxam Gdns SE9 . . . . . 166 A6
Bloxhall Rd E10 . . . . 53 B1
Bloxham Cres TW12 . . . 173 B2
Bloxworth Cl SM6 . . . . . 219 C5
Blucher Rd SE5 . . . . . . 139 A5
Blue Anchor Alley 4
  TW9 . . . . 132 A1
Blue Anchor La SE16 . . . 118 B2
Blue Anchor Yd E1 . . . . 118 A6
Blue Ball Yd SW1 . . . . . 249 A3
Bluebell Ave E12 . . . . 78 C3
Bluebell Cl
  Forest Hill SE26 . . . . . 183 D6
  Hackbridge SM6 . . . . . 203 B1
  19 Hackney E9 . . . . 96 C6
  Northolt UB5 . . . . 63 B2
  Orpington BR6 . . . . . . 227 A6
Bluebell Ct 4 N12 . . . . . . 14 A1
Bluebell Way IG1 . . . . . . 78 D2
Blueberry Cl IG8 . . . . 37 A4
Blueberry Cl Edgware HA8 . 27 A5
  3 Enfield EN2 . . . . 4 D3
Bluebird La RM10 . . . . . . 81 C1
Bluebird Way SE28 . . . . 123 B4
Bluefield Cl TW12 . . . . . 173 C5
Blue Gate Fields Jun & Inf
  Schs 22 E1 . . . . 118 C6
Bluegate Mews E1 . . . . 118 B6
Bluegates
  Stoneleigh KT17 . . . . . 216 A1
  Wimbledon SW19 . . . . . 179 A5
Bluehouse Rd E4 . . . . . . 20 C1
Blue Point Ct 3 HA1 . . . . 42 D4
Blueprint Apartments 15
  SW12 . . . . 159 B4
Blue Sch The TW7 . . . . . 131 C2
Blundell Cl E8 . . . . 74 A4
Blundell Rd HA8 . . . . 27 C3
Blundell St N7 . . . . 72 A2

Blunden Cl RM8 . . . . 58 C1
Blunt Rd CR0 . . . . 221 B3
Blunts Ave UB7 . . . . 126 C5
Blunts Rd SE9 . . . . 166 C6
Blurton Rd E5 . . . . 74 D4
Blydon Ct N21 . . . . 16 B6
Blyth Cl
  4 Cubitt Town E14 . . . . 120 B2
  Twickenham TW1 . . . . . 152 D5
Blythe Cl SE23 . . . . 163 B4
Blythe Hill Forest Hill SE6 . 163 B4
  St Paul's Cray BR5 . . . . 190 A2
Blythe Hill La SE6 . . . . . 163 B3
Blythe Ho 8 SE11 . . . . . 138 C6
Blythe Mews 2 W14 . . . 112 D3
Blythendale Ho 34 E2 . . . . 96 A5
Blythe Rd W14 . . . 113 A3 254 A5
Blythe St E2 . . . . 96 B4
Blytheswood Pl 4
  SW16 . . . . 182 B6
Blythe Vale SE6 . . . . . . 163 B3
Blythewood 5 SM1 . . . . 218 B3
Blyth Rd Bromley BR1 . . . 186 D2
  Hayes UB3 . . . . 105 C4
  Walthamstow E17 . . . . . 53 B2
  Woolwich SE28 . . . . . . 124 C6
Blyth's Wharf E14 . . . . . 119 A6
Blythswood Rd IG3 . . . . . 58 A2
Blythwood Pk 10 BR1 . . . 186 D2
Blythwood Rd London N4 . . 50 A2
  Pinner HA5 . . . . 22 D2
BMI Fitzroy Square Hospl
  W1 . . . . 93 C3 239 A5
BMI The Cavell Hospl EN2 . 4 C3
Bnois Jerusalem Girls Sch 2
  N16 . . . . 51 B2
Boades Mews 3 NW3 . . . . 70 B4
Boadicea St N1 . . . . . . 233 C5
Boardman Ave E4 . . . . . . 19 D6
Boardman Cl EN5 . . . . . . 13 A6
Boardwalk Pl E14 . . . . . 120 A5
Boarhound 25 NW9 . . . . . 27 D1
Boarley Ho SE17 . . . . . . 263 A3
Boatemah Wlk 21 SW9 . . 138 C3
Boathouse Ctr The W10 . . . 90 D3
Boathouse Wlk 24 SE15 . 139 D5
Boat Lifter Way 18 SE16 . 119 A2
Bobbin Cl SW4 . . . . 137 C2
Bob Anker Cl 1 E13 . . . . . 99 A4
Bobbington Way 11
  N16 . . . . 51 D2
Bob Thompson Ct HA9 . . . 66 D5
Bockhampton Rd KT2 . . . 176 B3
Bocking St E8 . . . . 96 B6
Boddicott Cl SW19 . . . . 157 A2
Boddington Gdns W3 . . . 110 C4
Boddington Ho 2 SE14 . . 140 C4
Bodeney Ho 10 SE5 . . . . 139 C4
Boden Ho 4 E1 . . . . 96 A2
Bodiam Cl EN1 . . . . 5 C3
Bodiam Ct
  Beckenham BR2 . . . . . 208 D5
  Sutton SM1 . . . . 218 B4
Bodiam Rd SW16 . . . . . 181 D3
Bodiam Way NW10 . . . . . 88 B4
Bodicea Mews TW4 . . . . 151 C5
Bodington Ct 2 W12 . . . 112 D4
Bodley Cl KT3 . . . . 199 C4
Bodley Manor Way
  SE24 . . . . 160 C4
Bodley Rd KT3 . . . . 199 C4
Bodmin 26 NW9 . . . . 27 D1
Bodmin Cl HA2 . . . . 63 B5
Bodmin Gr SM4 . . . . . . 201 D4
Bodmin St SW18 . . . . . 157 C3
Bodnant Gdns SW20 . . . 200 B6
Bodney Rd E5, E8 . . . . . . 74 B3
Boeing Way UB2 . . . . . . 106 B3
Boevey Path DA17 . . . . . 125 B1
Bogart Ct 18 E14 . . . . . 119 C6
Bognor Gdns WD19 . . . . . 22 C5
Bognor Rd DA16 . . . . . . 146 D4
Bograr Pl 1 E8 . . . . 74 B2
Bohn Rd E1 . . . . 97 A2
Bohun Gr EN4 . . . . 14 D5
Boileau Par W5 . . . . 88 B1
Boileau Rd Barnes SW13 . 134 B6
  Ealing W5 . . . . 88 B1
Boilerhouse SE1 . . . . . . 253 C3
Boisseau Ho 31 E1 . . . . . 96 C2
Bolden St SE8 . . . . 141 D3
Boldero Pl NW8 . . . . . . 237 A5
Bolderwood Way BR4 . . . 223 B6
Boleyn Ave EN1 . . . . 6 B4
Boleyn Ct
  Beckenham BR3 . . . . . 186 A2
  Buckhurst Hill IG9 . . . . . 21 B3
  East Molesey KT8 . . . . 196 B5
  Hayes UB3 . . . . 105 D4
  Walthamstow E17 . . . . . 53 C5
Boleyn Dr
  East Molesey KT8 . . . . 195 B6
  Ruislip HA4 . . . . 62 D6
Boleyn Gdns BR4 . . . . . 223 B6

Boleyn Ground (Upton Park)
  (West Ham Utd FC) E13,
  E6 . . . . 99 D5
Boleyn Rd Newham E6 . . . 99 D5
  Stoke Newington N16 . . . 73 C3
  Upton E7 . . . . 77 B1
Boleyn Way EN5 . . . . 2 A2
Bolina Rd SE16 . . . . . . 118 C1
Bolingbroke Gr SW11 . . 158 D5
Bolingbroke Ho
  Beckenham BR3 . . . . . 207 A4
  Catford BR3 . . . . 185 D5
Bolingbroke Rd W14 . . . 112 D3
Bolingbroke Way UB3,
  UB11 . . . . 105 B5
Bolingbroke Wlk
  SW11 . . . . 136 C4 267 A2
Bollo Bridge Rd W3 . . . . 111 A4
Bollo Ct 2 W3 . . . . 111 A3
Bollo La W3 . . . . 110 D3
Bolney Ct KT6 . . . . 197 D4
Bolney Gate SW7 . . . . . 247 A1
Bolney St SW8 . . . 138 B5 270 C3
Bolsover St W1 . . . 93 B3 238 D5
Bolstead Rd CR4 . . . . . 181 B2
Bolster Gr N22 . . . . 31 D2
Bolt Ct EC4 . . . . 241 B1
Boltmore Cl NW4 . . . . . . 46 D6
Bolton Cl
  Chessington KT9 . . . . . 214 A2
  Penge SE20 . . . . 184 A1
Bolton Cres SE5 . . . . . . 138 D5
Bolton Ct SW11 . . . . . . 268 B1
Bolton Dr SM4 . . . . 202 B2
Bolton Gdns
  Kensal Rise NW10 . . . . . 90 D5
  South Kensington
    SW5 . . . . 113 D1 255 D2
  Teddington TW11 . . . . 175 A4
Bolton Gdns Mews
  SW10 . . . . 256 A2
Bolton Ho 4 SE10 . . . . . 120 C1
Bolton Pl SW5 . . . . 256 A2
Bolton Rd
  Chessington KT9 . . . . . 214 A2
  Chiswick W4 . . . . 133 A5
  Edmonton N18 . . . . 33 D5
  Harlesden NW10 . . . . . . 89 C6
  Harrow HA1 . . . . 42 B5
  Kilburn NW8 . . . . 91 B6
  Stratford E15 . . . . 76 D2
Boltons Ct SW5 . . . . . . 255 D2
Bolton's La TW6, UB7 . . . 127 A5
Boltons The Harrow HA1 . . 42 A5
  South Kensington
    SW10 . . . . . . 114 A1 256 A2
  6 Stratford E15 . . . . . . 76 D2
  Wembley HA0 . . . . 64 D4
  Woodford IG8 . . . . 37 A6
Bolton Studios SW10 . . . 256 B1
Bolton Wlk N7 . . . . 72 B6
Bombay Ct 8 SE16 . . . . 118 C4
Bombay St SE16 . . . . . 118 B2
Bomer Cl UB7 . . . . 126 C5
Bomore Rd W11 . . 113 A6 244 A6
Bonar Pl BR7 . . . . 188 A3
Bonar Rd SE15 . . . . . . 140 A5
Bonchester Cl BR7 . . . . 188 C3
Bonchurch Cl SM2 . . . . 217 D1
Bonchurch Rd
  Ealing W13 . . . . 109 B5
  Kensal Town W10 . . . . . 91 A2
Bond Cl UB7 . . . . 82 B1
Bond Ct EC4 . . . . 242 C1
Bondfield Ave UB4 . . . . . 84 A4
Bondfield Rd 4 E6 . . . . . 100 B2
Bond Gdns SM6 . . . . . . 219 C4
Bond Ho 4 NW6 . . . . 91 B5
Bonding Yard Wlk SE16 . . 119 A3
Bond Prim Sch CR4 . . . . 180 D1
Bond Rd Mitcham CR4 . . . 180 D1
  Surbiton KT6 . . . . 214 B6
Bond St Chiswick W4 . . . 111 B2
  Ealing W5 . . . . 109 D6
  Stratford E15 . . . . 76 C3
Bond Street Sta
  W1 . . . . 93 A1 238 B1
Bondway SW8 . . . 138 A6 270 B6
Boneta Rd SE18 . . . . . . 122 B3
Bonfield Rd SE13 . . . . . 142 A1
Bonham Gdns RM8 . . . . . 80 D6
Bonham Ho W11 . . . . . 244 C4
Bonham Rd Brixton SW2 . 160 B6
  Dagenham RM8 . . . . . . 80 D5
Bonheur Rd W4 . . . . . . 111 B4
Bonhill St EC2 . . . 95 B3 242 D5
Boniface Gdns HA3 . . . . 23 D3
Boniface Rd UB10 . . . . . 60 D5
Boniface Wlk HA3 . . . . . 23 D3
Bonington Ho Enfield EN1 . 18 A6
  Pentonville N1 . . . . . . 233 C2
Bonita Mews SE15 . . . . 140 D2
Bonne Marche Terr Mews 18
  SE27 . . . . 183 C6
Bonner Hill Rd KT1 . . . . 198 C6
Bonner Ho 3 SW15 . . . . 156 A6
Bonner Prim Sch 39 E2 . . . 96 C4
Bonner Rd E2 . . . . 96 C5

Bonnersfield Cl HA1 . . . . 43 A3
Bonnersfield La
  Greenhill HA1 . . . . 42 D3
  Kenton HA1, HA3 . . . . . 43 A3
Bonner St E2 . . . . 96 C5
Bonneville Gdns SW4 . . 159 C5
Bonneville Prim Sch
  SW4 . . . . 159 C5
Bonnington Ct 14 UB5 . . . . 84 D5
Bonnington Ho 9 SM2 . . 217 D2
Bonnington Sq
  SW8 . . . . 138 B6 270 C6
Bonnington Twr BR2 . . . 210 A3
Bonny St NW1 . . . . 71 C1
Bonser Rd TW1 . . . . . . 152 D2
Bonsor Ho SW8 . . . . . . 269 B2
Bonsor St SE5 . . . . 139 C5
Bonthron Ho SW15 . . . . 134 C3
Bonus Pastor RC Sch
  BR1 . . . . 187 B5
Bonville Gdns 17 NW4 . . . 46 A5
Bonville Rd BR1 . . . . . . 186 D5
Bookbinder Cotts N20 . . . 14 D1
Booker Cl 11 E3 . . . . 97 B2
Booker Rd 5 N18 . . . . . . 34 A5
Bookham Ct CR4 . . . . . 202 B6
Boone Ct N13 . . . . 33 A5
Boones Rd SE13 . . . . . 142 C1
Boone St SE13 . . . . . . 142 C1
Boord St SE10 . . . . 120 C3
Boothby Ct E4 . . . . 20 A1
Boothby Ho 2 SW16 . . . 181 C5
Boothby Rd N19 . . . . 71 D6
Booth Cl 10 Hackney E9 . . . 96 B6
  Thamesmead SE28 . . . 124 B6
Booth Ho
  9 Brentford TW8 . . . . . 131 C5
  2 Streatham SW2 . . . . 160 C4
Booth La EC4 . . . . 252 A6
Boothman Ho HA3 . . . . . 43 D6
Booth Rd Croydon CR0 . . 220 D6
  Hendon NW9 . . . . 27 C1
Boothroyd Ho TW7 . . . . 130 D2
Booth's Pl W1 . . . . 239 B3
Boot Par HA8 . . . . 27 A4
Boot St N1 . . . . 95 C4
Bordars Rd W7 . . . . 86 D2
Bordars Wlk W7 . . . . . . 86 C2
Bordeaux Ho 1 E15 . . . . . 76 C3
Borden Ave EN1 . . . . 17 B5
Border Cres SE26 . . . . . 184 B5
Border Gate CR4 . . . . . 180 D2
Border Gdns CR0 . . . . . 223 D4
Border Rd SE26 . . . . . . 184 B5
Bordesley Rd SM4 . . . . 201 D5
Bordeston Ct 11 TW8 . . . 131 C5
Bordley Ct 4 N20 . . . . . . 14 D2
Bordon Wlk 5 SW15 . . . 156 A4
Boreas Wlk N1 . . . . 234 D3
Boreham Ave E16 . . . . . . 99 A1
Boreham Cl E11 . . . . 54 A1
Boreham Rd N22 . . . . . . 33 A1
Borgard Rd SE18 . . . . . 122 B2
Borkwood Pk BR6 . . . . . 227 D4
Borkwood Way BR6 . . . . 227 C4
Borland Rd London SE15 . 140 C1
  Teddington TW11 . . . . 175 B3
Borneo St SW15 . . . . . . 134 C2
Borough High St
  SE1 . . . . 117 B5 252 C4
Borough Hill CR0 . . . . . 220 D5
Borough Mkt*
  SE1 . . . . 117 B5 252 C3
Borough Rd
  Hounslow TW7 . . . . . . 130 D4
  7 Kingston u T KT2 . . . . 176 C3
  Lambeth SE1 . . . 116 D3 261 D6
  Mitcham CR4 . . . . 180 C5
Borough Sq SE1 . . . . . . 252 A1
Borough Sta SE1 . . 117 A4 252 B1
BOROUGH THE 117 A4
Borrett Cl SE17 . . . 117 A1 262 A1
Borrodaile Rd SW18 . . . 157 D5
Borrowdale NW1 . . . . . 232 A1
Borrowdale Ave HA3 . . . . 25 A1
Borrowdale Cl Finchley N2 . 30 A1
  Redbridge IG4 . . . . 56 A5
Borrowdale Ct EN2 . . . . . 5 A4
Borthwick Mews E15 . . . . 76 C4
Borthwick Rd Leyton E15 . . 76 C4
  London NW9 . . . . 45 D3
Borthwick St SE8 . . . . . 119 C1
Borwick Ave E17 . . . . . . 53 B6
Bosbury Rd SE6 . . . . . . 164 A1
Boscastle Rd NW5 . . . . . 71 B5
Boscobel Cl BR1 . . . . . 188 B1
Boscobel Ho 4 E8 . . . . . . 74 B2
Boscobel Pl SW1 . . . . . 258 B4
Boscobel St NW8 . . 92 B3 236 D5
Boscombe Ave E10 . . . . . 54 B2
Boscombe Circus NW9 . . . 27 B1
Boscombe Cl E5 . . . . 75 A3
Boscombe Gdns SW16 . . 182 A4
Boscombe Ho CR0 . . . . 205 B1
Boscombe Rd
  Merton SW19 . . . . 179 D2
  North Cheam KT4 . . . . 200 D1
  Shepherd's Bush W12 . . 112 A4

Boscombe Rd continued
  Streatham SW17 . . . . . 181 A4
Bose Cl N3 . . . . 29 A2
Bosgrove E4 . . . . 20 A2
Boss Ho SE1 . . . . 253 C2
Boss St SE1 . . . . 253 C2
Bostall Hill SE2 . . . . . . 124 B1
Bostall La SE2 . . . . 124 B1
Bostall Manorway SE2 . . 124 B2
Bostall Park Ave DA7 . . . 147 A5
Bostall Rd BR5 . . . . . . 190 B3
Bostock Ho TW5 . . . . . . 129 C6
Boston Bsns Pk W7 . . . . 108 C3
Boston Ct
  South Norwood SE25 . . 205 D5
  Sutton SM2 . . . . 218 A1
Boston Gdns
  Brentford TW8 . . . . . . 109 B2
  Chiswick W4 . . . . 133 C6
Boston Gr HA4 . . . . 39 C3
Boston Ho
  24 Camberwell SE5 . . . . 139 A3
  Earl's Ct SW5 . . . . . . 255 D3
  Lisson Gr NW1 . . . . . . 237 C6
Boston Lo W13 . . . . . . 109 C1
Boston Manor Ho TW8 . . 109 B2
Boston Manor Rd TW8 . . 131 B6
Boston Manor Sta TW8 . 109 A2
Boston Par W7 . . . . 109 A2
Boston Park Rd TW8 . . . 109 B2
Boston Pl NW1 . . . 92 D3 237 C5
Boston Rd Burnt Oak HA8 . 27 A3
  Ealing W7 . . . . 109 A3
  Newham E6 . . . . 100 A4
  Thornton Heath CR0 . . . 204 C3
  3 Walthamstow E17 . . . . 53 C3
Bostonthorpe Rd W7 . . . 108 C4
Boston Vale W7 . . . . . . 109 A2
Bosun Cl 22 E14 . . . . . . 119 C4
Boswell Ct
  Bloomsbury WC1 . . . . 240 B4
  9 Hammersmith W14 . . 112 D3
  Kingston u T KT2 . . . . . 176 C2
Boswell Ho
  Bloomsbury WC1 . . . . 240 B4
  5 Streatham SW16 . . . 181 C5
Boswell Rd CR7 . . . . . . 205 A5
Boswell St WC1 . . . 94 A2 240 B4
Boswood Ct TW4 . . . . . 129 B2
Bosworth Cl E17 . . . . . . 35 B2
Bosworth Ho 4 W10 . . . . 91 A3
Bosworth Rd Barnet EN5 . . 1 C2
  Dagenham RM10 . . . . . 81 C5
  Kensal Town W10 . . . . . 91 A3
  Wood Green N11 . . . . . 31 D4
Botany Bay La BR7 . . . . 189 A1
Botany Cl EN4 . . . . 2 C1
Boteley Cl E4 . . . . 20 B2
Botham Cl 6 HA8 . . . . . . 27 A3
Botha Rd E13 . . . . 99 C2
Bothwell Cl E16 . . . . 98 D1
Bothwell St 4 W6 . . . . . 134 D6
Botolph Alley EC3 . . . . . 253 A6
Botolph La EC3 . . . . . . 253 A6
Botsford Rd SW20 . . . . 179 A1
Bott's Mews W2 . . . . 91 C1
Botwell Common Rd
  UB3 . . . . 105 C6
Botwell Cres UB3 . . . . . . 83 C1
Botwell House RC Prim Sch
  UB3 . . . . 105 D4
Botwell La UB3 . . . . . . 105 C5
Boucher Cl TW11 . . . . . 174 D5
Bouchier Ho 6 N2 . . . . . . 30 B1
Bough Beech Ct EN3 . . . . 6 D6
Boughton Ave BR2 . . . . 208 D2
Boughton Ho
  Borough The SE1 . . . . 252 C2
  Bromley BR1 . . . . 188 A3
Boughton Rd SE28 . . . . 123 C3
Boulcott St E1 . . . . 96 D1
Boulevard Dr NW9 . . . . . 27 D1
Boulevard The
  Chelsea SW6 . . . . 266 B1
  4 Upper Tooting SW17 . 159 A2
Boullen Ct SM1 . . . . . . 218 A4
Boulogne Ho SE1 . . . . . 263 C6
Boulogne Rd CR0 . . . . . 205 A3
Boulter Cl BR1 . . . . . . 210 C5
Boulter Ho 4 SE14 . . . . 140 C4
Boulters Ct HA0 . . . . 65 A4
Boulton Ho TW8 . . . . . . 110 A1
Boulton Rd RM8 . . . . 81 B6
Boultwood Rd E6 . . . . . 100 B1
Bounces La N9 . . . . 18 B2
Bounces Rd N9 . . . . 18 C2
Boundaries Mans 3
  SW12 . . . . 159 A3
Boundaries Rd
  Feltham TW13 . . . . . . 150 C3
  Upper Tooting SW12 . . . 159 A3
Boundary Ave E17 . . . . . 53 C2
Boundary Bsns Ct CR4 . . 202 B6
Boundary Cl Barnet EN5 . . 1 B4
  Ilford IG3 . . . . 79 C4
  Kingston u T KT1 . . . . . 198 D6

Boundary Cl *continued*
Penge SE20 . . . .**184** A1
Southall UB2 . . . .**107** C1
Boundary Ct
3 Edmonton N18 . . . .**33** D4
9 New Southgate N11 . . . . . .**31** B6
Boundary Ho
Balham SW12 . . . .**159** B3
1 Camberwell SE5 . . . .**139** A5
Edgware HA8 . . . .**44** B6
Isleworth TW1 . . . .**153** B6
15 Notting Hill W11 . . . .**112** D5
Boundary La
Camberwell SE17 . . . .**139** A6
Newham E13, E6 . . . .**99** D3
Boundary Pas E2 . . . .**243** C6
Boundary Rd
Avery Hill DA15 . . . .**167** C6
Barking IG11 . . . .**101** A5
London N2 . . . .**30** B2
Mitcham SW19 . . . .**180** B4
Newham E13 . . . .**99** D4
Pinner HA5 . . . .**40** D2
Ponders End N9 . . . .**18** C5
St John's Wood
NW8 . . . .**92** A6 **229** B6
Tottenham N22 . . . .**33** A1
Wallington SM5, SM6 . . . . .**219** A1
Walthamstow E17 . . . .**53** C3
Boundary Road Est
NW8 . . . .**92** A6 **229** A5
Boundary Row SE1 . . . . . .**251** C2
Boundary St E2 . . . .**95** D3 **243** C6
Boundary Way CR0 . . . . . .**223** C3
Boundfield Rd SE6 . . . . . .**164** C2
Bounds Green Ct N11 . . . . .**31** D4
Bounds Green Ind Est
N11 . . . .**31** C4
Bounds Green Jun & Inf Schs
N11 . . . .**32** A3
Bounds Green Rd
London N11 . . . .**31** D4
Wood Green N22 . . . .**32** A3
Bounds Green Sta N11 . . . .**31** D3
Bourbon Ho **9** SE6 . . . . . .**186** A6
Bourchier St W1 . . . .**249** C6
Bourdillon Ct **2** SE9 . . . . .**166** A2
Bourdon Pl W1 . . . .**248** D6
Bourdon Rd SE20 . . . .**184** C1
Bourdon St W1 . . . .**115** B6 **248** D5
Bourke Cl London SW4 . . . .**160** A5
Willesden NW10 . . . .**67** C2
Bourlet Cl W1 . . . .**239** A3
Bourn Ave Hillingdon UB8 . .**82** C3
New Barnet EN4 . . . .**14** B6
West Green N15 . . . .**51** B5
Bournbrook Rd SE3, SE9 . .**143** D2
Bourne Ave Hayes UB3 . . . .**105** B3
Palmers Green N14 . . . .**16** A2
Ruislip HA4 . . . .**62** C3
Bourne Cir UB3 . . . .**105** A3
Bourne Cl
Hinchley Wood KT7 . . . .**212** D6
Isleworth TW7 . . . .**133** A2
Bourne Ct Chiswick W4 . . .**133** A6
Ruislip HA4 . . . .**62** B3
Wanstead E11 . . . .**55** A4
Woodford IG8 . . . .**37** D1
Bourne Dr CR4 . . . .**180** B1
Bourne Gdns E4 . . . .**35** D6
Bourne Hill N13 . . . .**16** B2
Bourne Ho
4 Ashford TW15 . . . .**170** C5
3 Buckhurst Hill IG9 . . . . . .**21** D1
5 Clapham SW4 . . . .**137** C1
1 Dollis Hill NW2 . . . .**68** A5
Bourne Mans N13 . . . .**32** C5
Bournemead Ave UB5 . . . . .**84** A5
Bournemead Cl UB5 . . . . . .**84** A4
Bournemead Way UB5 . . . . .**84** B5
Bourne Mews W1 . . . .**238** B1
Bournemouth Cl SE15 . . . .**140** A3
Bournemouth Ct **6**
SM1 . . . .**218** A3
Bournemouth Rd
London SE15 . . . .**140** A3
Merton SW19 . . . .**179** C2
Bourne Par DA5 . . . .**169** D4
Bourne Pl W4 . . . .**111** B1
Bourne Prim Sch HA4 . . . . .**62** C2
Bourne Rd Bexley DA5 . . . .**169** D5
Bromley BR2 . . . .**209** D5
Hornsey N8 . . . .**50** A3
Leyton E7, E11 . . . .**76** D5
Bournes Ho **4** N15 . . . . . .**51** C3
Bourneside **5** N14 . . . . . .**15** D3
Bourneside Cres **6** N14 . .**15** D3
Bourneside Gdns SE6 . . . .**186** A5
Bourne St
Belgravia SW1 . . .**115** A2 **258** A3
Croydon CR0 . . . .**220** D6
Bourne Terr W2 . . . .**91** D2
Bourne The N14 . . . .**16** A3
Bourne Vale BR2 . . . .**209** A2
Bournevale Rd SW16 . . . . .**182** A6
Bourne View UB6 . . . .**64** D3
Bourne Way Cheam SM1 . .**217** B3

Bourne Way *continued*
Coney Hall BR2, BR4 . . . . . .**224** D6
West Ewell KT19 . . . .**215** A4
Bournewood Rd SE18 . . . .**146** A5
Bournville Rd SE6 . . . .**163** C4
Bournwell Cl EN4 . . . .**2** D3
Bourton Cl UB3 . . . .**106** A5
Bousfield Prim Sch
SW10 . . . .**114** A1 **256** A2
Bousfield Rd SE14 . . . .**140** D3
Boutcher CE Prim Sch
SE1 . . . .**117** D2 **263** C4
Boutflower Rd SW11 . . . . . .**136** C1
Bouverie Ct **4** SW16 . . . . .**182** A5
Bouverie Gdns HA3 . . . .**43** D3
Bouverie Mews N16 . . . .**73** C6
Bouverie Pl W2 . . . .**236** D2
Bouverie Rd Harrow HA1 . . .**42** A3
Stoke Newington N16 . . . .**73** C6
Bouverie St EC4 . . . .**94** C1 **241** B1
Bouvier Rd EN3 . . . .**6** C5
Boveney Rd SE23 . . . .**162** D4
Bovill Rd SE23 . . . .**162** D4
Bovingdon Ave HA9 . . . .**66** C2
Bovingdon Cl **4** N19 . . . . .**71** C6
Bovingdon La NW9 . . . .**27** C2
Bovingdon Rd
SW6 . . . .**135** D4 **265** D1
Bovril Ho EN1 . . . .**5** C2
BOW **97** B5
Bowater Cl
Clapham Pk SW2 . . . .**160** A5
Kingsbury NW9 . . . .**45** B4
Bowater Gdns TW16 . . . . . .**172** C2
Bowater Ho EC1 . . . .**242** B5
Bowater Pl SE3 . . . .**143** B5
Bowater Rd
Greenwich SE18 . . . .**121** D3
Wembley HA9 . . . .**66** D5
Bow Brook The **20** E2 . . . . .**96** D5
Bow Church Sta E3 . . . .**97** C4
BOW COMMON **97** D2
Bow Common La E3 . . . .**97** B3
Bowden Cl TW14 . . . .**149** C3
Bowden Ct HA4 . . . .**62** C3
Bowden Ho **20** E3 . . . .**97** D4
Bowden St SE11 . . . .**116** C1 **261** B1
Bowdon Rd E17 . . . .**53** C2
Bowen Ct **2** N5 . . . .**72** D4
Bowen Dr SE21 . . . .**161** C1
Bowen Rd HA1 . . . .**42** A2
Bowen St E14 . . . .**97** D1
Bower Ave SE3 . . . .**142** C5
Bower Cl UB5 . . . .**84** C5
Bowerdean St SW6 . . . .**135** D3
Bower Ho SE14 . . . .**140** D4
Bowerman Ave SE14 . . . . . .**141** A6
Bowerman Ct **1** N19 . . . . . .**71** D6
Bowers Ho **5** IG11 . . . .**78** D1
Bower St E1 . . . .**96** D1
Bowers Wlk **1** E6 . . . .**100** B1
Bowery Ct **16** RM10 . . . .**81** D2
Bowes Cl DA15 . . . .**168** B5
Bowes Ho N13 . . . .**32** B5
Bowes-Lyon Hall **13**
E16 . . . .**121** A5
Bowes Lyon Ho **2**
TW10 . . . .**153** C1
BOWES PARK **32** A4
Bowes Park Sta N22 . . . .**32** A3
Bowes Prim Sch N11 . . . . . .**31** D5
Bowes Rd Acton W3 . . . . . .**111** C6
Dagenham RM8 . . . .**80** C4
New Southgate N11 . . . .**31** C5
Walton-on-T KT12 . . . .**194** B1
Bowes Rd (North Circular
Rd) N13 . . . .**32** A5
Bowfell Rd W6 . . . .**134** C6
Bowhay DA7 . . . .**147** A4
Bowhill Cl SW9 . . . .**138** C5
Bow Ho **1** E3 . . . .**97** C4
Bowie Cl SW4 . . . .**159** D4
Bow La
Barbican EC2, EC4 . .**95** A1 **242** B1
Finchley N12 . . . .**30** A3
Bowland Ho N4 . . . .**51** A2
Bowland Rd London SW4 . .**137** D1
Woodford IG8 . . . .**37** C4
Bowland Yd SW1 . . . .**247** D1
Bowl Ct EC2 . . . .**243** B5
Bowles Rd SE1 . . . .**140** A6
Bowley Cl SE19 . . . .**183** D4
Bowley Ho **5** SE16 . . . .**118** A3
Bowley La SE19 . . . .**183** D5
Bowling Cl UB10 . . . .**82** B6
Bowling Green Cl SW19 . . .**156** A4
Bowling Green Ct HA9 . . . . .**66** B6
Bowling Green Ho SW10 . .**266** C4
Bowling Green La
EC1 . . . .**94** C3 **241** B6
Bowling Green Pl SE1 . . . .**252** C2
Bowling Green Row **1**
SE18 . . . .**122** B2
Bowling Green Wlk N1 . . . . .**95** C4
Bowls Cl HA7 . . . .**25** B5
Bowman Ave E16 . . . .**120** D6

Bowman Homes W5 . . . .**109** D4
Bowman Mews
St George in t East E1 . . . . .**118** A4
Wandsworth SW18 . . . .**157** B3
Bowmans Cl W13 . . . .**109** B5
Bowmans Lea SE23 . . . . . .**162** C4
Bowman's Meadow SM6 .**219** B5
Bowman's Mews N7 . . . .**72** A5
Bowman's Pl N7 . . . .**72** A5
Bowman Trad Est NW9 . . . .**44** C5
Bowmar Lo **18** EN5 . . . .**1** D1
Bowmead SE9 . . . .**166** B2
Bowmore Wlk NW1 . . . .**71** D1
Bowness Cl **5** E8 . . . .**73** D2
Bowness Cres KT2,
SW15 . . . .**177** C5
Bowness Dr TW4 . . . .**129** A1
Bowness Ho SE15 . . . .**140** C5
Bowness Rd Catford SE6 . .**163** D4
Erith DA7 . . . .**147** D3
Bowood Rd
Clapham SW11 . . . .**159** A6
Enfield EN3 . . . .**6** D3
Bowring Gn WD19 . . . .**22** C5
Bow Road Sta E3 . . . .**97** C4
Bowrons Ave HA0 . . . .**65** D1
Bowry Ho **14** E14 . . . .**97** B2
Bow Sec Sch **19** E3 . . . .**97** C4
Bowsley Ct TW13 . . . .**150** A2
Bowsprit Point **1** E14 . . . .**119** C3
Bow St
St Giles WC2 . . . . . .**94** A1 **240** B1
Stratford E15 . . . .**76** C3
Bowstead Ct SW11 . . . .**266** D1
Bow Triangle Bsns Ctr **17**
E3 . . . .**97** C3
Bowyer Cl E6 . . . .**100** B2
Bowyer Ho Mitcham CR4 . .**202** C6
27 Shoreditch N1 . . . .**95** C6
Wandsworth SW18 . . . .**157** D5
Bowyer Pl SE5 . . . .**139** A5
Bowyer St **15** SE5 . . . .**139** A5
Boxall Rd SE21 . . . .**161** C5
Box Cnr TW2 . . . .**152** C2
Boxelder Cl HA8 . . . .**27** A5
Boxgrove Prim Sch SE2 . .**124** C3
Boxgrove Rd SE2 . . . .**124** C3
Box La IG11 . . . .**102** C5
Boxley Ho **3** E5 . . . .**74** B3
Boxley Rd SM4 . . . .**202** A5
Boxley St E16 . . . .**121** B5
Boxmoor Ho
16 Hackney E2 . . . .**96** A6
9 Shepherd's Bush W11 . . .**112** D5
Boxmoor Rd HA3 . . . .**43** B5
Boxoll Rd RM9 . . . .**81** B5
Boxshall Ho **7** SE18 . . . . . .**144** D6
Box Tree Ho SE8 . . . .**119** A1
Boxtree La HA3 . . . .**24** B3
Boxtree Rd HA3 . . . .**24** B3
Boxwood Cl UB7 . . . .**104** B4
Boxworth Cl N12 . . . .**30** B5
Boxworth Gr N1 . . . .**94** B6 **233** D6
Boyard Rd SE18 . . . .**122** D1
Boyce Ho
Streatham SW16 . . . .**181** C5
1 West Kilburn W10 . . . .**91** B4
Boyce Way E13 . . . .**99** A3
Boycroft Ave NW9 . . . .**45** A3
Boyd Ave UB1 . . . .**107** B5
Boyd Cl KT2 . . . .**176** C3
Boyd Ct SW15 . . . .**156** C5
Boydell Ct NW8 . . . .**70** B1
Boyden Ho **8** E17 . . . .**54** A6
Boyd Rd SW19 . . . .**180** B4
Boyd St E1 . . . .**96** A1
Boyfield St SE1 . . . .**116** D4 **251** D1
Boyland Rd BR1 . . . .**186** D5
Boyle Ave HA7 . . . .**25** A4
Boyle Cl UB10 . . . .**82** B5
Boyle Farm Rd KT7 . . . .**197** A3
Boyle Ho
13 Belvedere DA17 . . . .**125** C3
Wembley HA9 . . . .**66** C2
Boyle St W1 . . . .**249** A6
Boyne Ave NW4 . . . .**46** D5
Boyne Ct NW10 . . . .**68** A1
Boyne Ho **10** E5 . . . .**74** B6
Boyne Rd Dagenham RM10 . .**81** C5
Lewisham SE13 . . . .**142** B2
Boyne Terr Mews
W11 . . . .**113** B5 **244** C4
Boyson Rd **10** SE17 . . . . . .**139** B6
Boyton Cl London N8 . . . . . .**50** A6
Stepney E1 . . . .**96** D3
Boyton Ho
Kennington SE11 . . . .**261** A1
St John's Wood NW8 . . . .**229** D4
Boyton Rd N8 . . . .**50** A6
Brabant Ct EC3 . . . .**253** A6
Brabant Rd N22 . . . .**32** B1
Brabazon Ave SM6 . . . . . .**220** A1
Brabazon Rd
Heston TW5 . . . .**128** D5
Northolt UB5 . . . .**85** C5
Brabazon St E14 . . . .**97** D2
Brabner Ho **3** E2 . . . .**96** A4
Brabourne Cl **7** SE19 . . . .**183** C5
Brabourne Cres DA7 . . . . .**147** B6

Brabourne Hts NW7 . . . .**11** C1
Brabourne Rise BR3 . . . . . .**208** B4
Brabourn Gr SE15 . . . .**140** C3
Brabrook Ct SM6 . . . .**219** B3
Brabstone Ho **2** UB6 . . . . . .**86** D5
Bracer Ho **1** N1 . . . .**95** C5
Bracewell Ave UB6 . . . .**65** A2
Bracewell Rd W10 . . . .**90** C2
Bracewood Gdns CR0 . . . .**221** D5
Bracey Mews **1** N4 . . . .**72** A6
Bracey St N4 . . . .**72** A6
Bracken Ave
Balham SW12 . . . .**159** A4
Croydon CR0 . . . .**223** C5
Brackenbridge Dr HA4 . . . . .**62** D5
Brackenbury N4 . . . .**50** B1
Brackenbury Gdns W6 . . . .**112** B3
Brackenbury Prim Sch **4**
W6 . . . .**112** B3
Brackenbury Rd
East Finchley N2 . . . .**48** A6
Hammersmith W6 . . . .**112** B3
Bracken Cl
Ashford TW16 . . . .**171** D4
Newham E6 . . . .**100** B2
Twickenham TW4 . . . .**151** C4
Brackendale
Kingston u T KT1 . . . .**176** D1
Southgate N21 . . . .**16** B2
Brackendale Cl TW5 . . . . . .**129** D4
Brackendale Ct **2** BR3 . . . .**185** C3
Bracken End TW7 . . . .**152** B6
Brackenfield Cl E5 . . . .**74** B5
Bracken Gdns SW13 . . . . . .**134** A3
Bracken Hill Cl BR1 . . . . . .**186** D2
Bracken Hill La BR1 . . . . . .**186** D2
Bracken Ho **18** E3 . . . .**97** C2
Bracken Mews
Chingford E4 . . . .**20** A3
Romford RM7 . . . .**59** D3
Brackens BR3 . . . .**185** C3
Brackens The EN1 . . . .**17** C4
Bracken The E4 . . . .**20** A2
Brackenwood TW16 . . . . . .**172** A2
Brackley Ave SE15 . . . .**140** C2
Brackley Cl SM6 . . . .**220** A1
Brackley Ct NW8 . . . .**236** D6
Brackley Rd
Beckenham BR3 . . . .**185** C3
Chiswick W4 . . . .**111** C1
Brackley Sq IG8 . . . .**37** D3
Brackley St EC1 . . . .**242** B4
Brackley Terr **6** W4 . . . . . .**111** C1
Bracklyn Ct N1 . . . .**235** C4
Bracklyn St N1 . . . .**235** C4
Bracknell Cl N22 . . . .**32** C2
Bracknell Gate NW3 . . . .**69** D3
Bracknell Gdns NW3 . . . . . .**69** D4
Bracknell Way NW3 . . . .**69** D4
Bracondale KT10 . . . .**212** A3
Bracondale Rd SE2 . . . . . .**124** A2
Braconhyrst HA1 . . . .**42** C2
Bradbeer Ho **21** E2 . . . .**96** C4
Bradbourne Ct **11** SM2 . . .**217** D2
Bradbourne Rd DA5 . . . . . .**169** C4
Bradbourne St SW6 . . . . . .**135** C3
Bradbury Cl UB2 . . . .**107** B2
Bradbury Ct **4** Barnet EN5 . . .**1** D1
2 Greenwich SE3 . . . .**143** A5
Merton SW20 . . . .**178** C1
Bradbury Ho E1 . . . .**243** D2
Bradbury St **28** N16 . . . .**73** C3
Bradby Ho NW8 . . . .**91** D5
Braddock Cl TW7 . . . .**130** D3
Braddon Rd TW9 . . . .**132** B2
Braddyll St SE10 . . . .**120** C1
Bradenham **11** SE17 . . . . . .**139** B6
Bradenham Ave DA16 . . . . .**146** A1
Bradenham Cl SE17 . . . . . .**139** B6
Bradenham Rd
Harrow HA3 . . . .**43** B5
Hayes UB4 . . . .**83** C4
Braden St W9 . . . .**91** D3
Bradfield Ct **14** NW1 . . . .**71** B1
Bradfield Dr IG11 . . . .**80** A3
Bradfield Ho **15** SW8 . . . . .**137** D3
Bradfield Rd
Newham E16 . . . .**121** B4
Ruislip HA4 . . . .**63** C2
Bradford Cl Bromley BR2 . .**210** B1
Forest Hill SE26 . . . .**184** B6
Tottenham N17 . . . .**33** D4
Bradford Dr KT19 . . . .**215** D2
Bradford Ho **4** W14 . . . .**112** D2
Bradford Rd Acton W3 . . . . .**111** C4
Ilford IG1 . . . .**57** C1
Bradgate Rd SE6 . . . .**163** D5
Brading Cres E11 . . . .**77** B6
Brading Rd
Streatham SW2 . . . .**160** B4
Thornton Heath CR0 . . . .**204** B3
Brading Terr W12 . . . .**112** A3
Bradiston Rd W9 . . . .**91** B4
Bradley Cl N7 . . . .**72** B2
Bradley Ct CR0 . . . .**220** C4
Bradley Gdns W13 . . . .**87** B1
Bradley Ho
Bermondsey SE16 . . . .**118** B2

Bradley Ho *continued*
1 Bromley E3 . . . .**97** D4
Twickenham TW1 . . . .**152** D3
Woodford IG8 . . . .**37** A3
Bradley Mews SW12 . . . . . .**158** D3
Bradley Rd Enfield EN3 . . . . . .**7** A6
Upper Norwood SE19 . . . . . .**183** A4
Wood Green N22 . . . .**32** B1
Bradley's Cl N1 . . . .**234** B4
Bradley Stone Rd E6 . . . . .**100** B2
Bradlord Ho SE21 . . . .**161** C1
Bradman Row **7** HA8 . . . . . .**27** A3
Bradmead SW8 . . . .**137** C5 **269** A3
Bradmore Ct **2** EN3 . . . .**7** A2
Bradmore Park Rd W6 . . . .**112** B2
Bradon **24** NW9 . . . .**28** D3
Bradshaw Cl SW19 . . . .**179** C4
Bradshaw Dr NW7 . . . .**28** D3
Bradshawe Waye UB8 . . . . .**82** B2
Bradshaws Cl SE25 . . . . . .**206** A6
Bradsole Ho **13** BR3 . . . . . .**185** C3
Brad St SE1 . . . .**116** C5 **251** B3
Bradstock Ho E9 . . . .**75** A1
Bradstock Rd
Homerton E9 . . . .**74** D2
Stoneleigh KT17 . . . .**216** B3
Bradwell Ave RM10 . . . .**61** C5
Bradwell Cl E18 . . . .**54** D5
Bradwell Ho
8 Kilburn NW6 . . . .**91** D6
9 Walthamstow E17 . . . .**53** D6
Bradwell Mews **5** N18 . . . . .**34** A6
Bradwell Rd **24** E11 . . . .**96** C4
Brady Ct RM8 . . . .**58** D1
Brady Dr BR1 . . . .**210** C6
Brady Ho London SW4 . . . .**159** D6
South Lambeth SW8 . . . .**269** B2
Bradymead E6 . . . .**100** D1
Brady St E1 . . . .**96** B3
Braeburn Ct **1** EN4 . . . .**2** C1
Brae Ct
2 Kingston u T KT2 . . . . . .**176** C2
South Norwood SE25 . . . . . .**183** C2
Braefoot Ct SW15 . . . .**156** D6
Braemar SW15 . . . .**156** D5
Braemar Ave
Thornton Heath CR7 . . . .**204** D6
Welsh Harp NW10 . . . .**67** B6
Wembley HA0 . . . .**66** A1
Wimbledon SW18, SW19 . . .**157** C2
Wood Green N22 . . . .**32** A2
Braemar Ct
4 Brentford TW8 . . . .**131** D6
5 Catford SE6 . . . .**164** D3
Braemar Gdns
Hendon NW9 . . . .**27** B2
Longlands DA15 . . . .**167** B1
West Wickham BR4 . . . .**208** A1
Braemar Ho
Richmond TW11 . . . .**175** B5
St John's Wood W9 . . . .**229** A1
Braemar Mans W8 . . . .**255** D5
Braemar Rd
Brentford TW8 . . . .**131** D6
Newham E13 . . . .**98** D3
North Cheam KT4 . . . .**216** B5
South Tottenham N15 . . . .**51** C4
Braemore Ct EN4 . . . .**3** A1
Braeside BR3 . . . .**185** D5
Braeside Ave SW19 . . . .**179** A2
Braeside Cl HA5 . . . .**23** C3
Braeside Jun Sch IG9 . . . . .**21** C2
Braeside Rd SW16 . . . .**181** C3
Braeside Senior Sch IG9 . .**21** B3
Braes St N1 . . . .**72** D1
Braesyde Cl DA17 . . . .**125** B2
Brafferton Rd CR0 . . . .**221** A4
Braganza St
SE17 . . . .**116** D1 **261** C1
Bragg Cl RM8 . . . .**80** B2
Bragg Rd TW11 . . . .**174** D4
Braham St E1 . . . .**260** D1
Braham St E1 . . . .**243** D2
Brahma Kumaris World
Spiritual Univ NW10 . . . .**68** A1
Braid Ave W3 . . . .**89** C1
Braid Cl TW13 . . . .**151** B2
Braid Ho SE10 . . . .**142** A4
Braidwood Ho **2** CR7 . . . . .**204** D5
Braidwood Rd SE6 . . . .**164** B3
Braidwood St
SE1 . . . .**117** C5 **253** A3
Braikenridge Ho N21 . . . . . .**17** B5
Brailsford Cl SW19 . . . .**180** C3
Brailsford Rd SW2 . . . .**160** C5
Braintcroft Prim Sch
NW2 . . . .**67** D5
Brainton Ave TW14 . . . .**150** C4
Braintree Ho **6** E1 . . . .**56** A5
Braintree Ho **6** E1 . . . .**96** C3
Braintree Ind Est HA4 . . . . .**62** B4
Braintree Rd
Dagenham RM10 . . . .**81** C5
Ruislip HA4 . . . .**62** B4
Braintree St E2 . . . .**96** C4
Braithwaite Ave RM7 . . . . . .**59** C2
Braithwaite Gdns HA7 . . . . .**25** C2
Braithwaite Ho EC1 . . . .**242** C6
Braithwaite Rd EN3 . . . .**7** B2
Braithwaite Twr W2 . . . .**236** C4

Brake Shear Ho **1** EN5.... 1 B2
Bramah Gn SW9..........138 C4
Bramah Mus of Tea & Coffee
The ★ SE1...............252 B3
Bramalea Cl N6..........49 A3
Bramall Cl E15..........76 D3
Bramall Ct N7...........72 B2
Bramber WC1............233 A1
Bramber Ct TW8..........110 A2
Bramber Ho **9** KT2.....176 A2
Bramber Rd
Colney Hatch N12.........30 C5
Fulham W14.......135 B6 264 C6
Bramble Acres Cl SM2...217 C1
Bramblebury Rd SE18....123 A1
Bramble Cl
Beckenham BR3.........208 A4
Croydon CR0...........223 D4
Hillingdon UB8..........82 B1
South Tottenham N15.....52 A5
Stanmore HA7...........25 D3
Upper Halliford TW17....193 B6
Brambledown **1**......50 A2
Brambledown Cl BR2,
BR4...................208 C4
Brambledown Rd
South Croydon CR2.....221 C1
Wallington SM5, SM6....219 B4
Bramble Gdns W12.......111 D6
Bramble Ho **16** E3.....97 C2
Bramble La TW12.........173 B4
Brambles Cl TW7, TW8...131 B5
Brambles Farm Dr UB10..82 C4
Brambles The
West Drayton UB7.......104 A3
8 Wimbledon SW19....179 B5
Bramblewood Cl SM5....202 C1
Brambling Ct
25 Deptford SE8.......141 B6
South Norwood SE25....205 D5
Bramblings The E4........36 B6
Bramcote Ave CR4......202 D5
Bramcote Ct CR4........202 D5
Bramcote Gr SE16........118 C1
Bramcote Rd SW15.......134 B1
Bramdean Cres SE12.....165 A3
Bramdean Gdns SE12....165 A3
Bramerton NW6..........68 D1
Bramerton Rd BR3......207 B6
Bramerton St
SW3.............136 C6 267 A6
Bramfield Ct N4.........73 A4
Bramfield Rd SW11......158 D6
Bramford Ct N14.........15 D2
Bramford Rd SW18......136 A1
Bramham Gdns
Chessington KT9........213 D4
South Kensington
SW5............113 D1 255 D2
Bramhope Ho SE7.......143 B6
Bramlands Cl SW11.....136 C2
Bramley Ave TW17......193 C6
Bramley Cl Ilford IG2....56 C3
Nine Elms SW8...137 D5 269 D4
Bramley Ct **2** Barnet EN4..2 C1
7 Chingford E4........20 A3
Dollis Hill NW2..........68 B5
Feltham TW14...........149 C5
Hither Green SE13.......164 B6
Mitcham CR4............180 B1
Southall UB1.............108 A6
Wallington SM6.........219 C3
Welling DA16............146 B4
Bramley Gdns WD19.....22 C5
Bramley Hill CR2.........221 A4
Bramley Ho
Hounslow TW3...........129 B1
Ilford IG2................56 C3
1 Kingston u T KT2.....176 B2
19 North Kensington W10..90 D1
Roehampton SW15.......68 C3
Bramley House Ct EN2...5 B6
Bramleyhyrst CR2.......221 A3
Bramley Lo HA0..........65 D4
Bramley Rd Ealing W5...109 C3
North Kensington W10....90 D1
Southgate N14...........15 C6
Sutton SM1..............218 B3
Bramley Way
Hounslow TW4..........151 B6
West Wickham BR4......223 D6
Brampton WC1..........240 C3
Brampton Cl **14** E5.....74 B4
Brampton Coll NW4.......46 C5
Brampton Gr NW4.........46 B5
Brampton Gr Harrow HA3..43 B5
Hendon NW4.............46 C5
Wembley HA9............44 C1
Brampton La **6** NW4....46 C5
Brampton Lo DA7.......146 D5

Brampton Manor Sch E6..99 D3
Brampton Park Rd N22...50 C6
Brampton Prim Sch
Bexley DA7.............146 D3
Newham E6.............100 A4
Brampton Rd
Bexleyheath DA7........147 A4
Croydon CR0............205 D3
Harringay N15...........51 A4
Hillingdon UB10.........82 D5
Newham E6.............99 D4
Queensbury NW9........44 C5
Bramshaw Gdns WD19...22 C5
Bramshaw Rd E9........74 D2
Bramshaw Rise KT3.....199 C3
Bramshill Gdns NW5.....71 B5
Bramshot Ave SE7......143 B6
Bramshott Ct **3** KT6...198 A3
Bramshurst NW8.........91 D6
Bramston Rd
Harlesden NW10.........90 A5
Wandsworth SW17......158 A1
Bramwell Cl TW16......172 D1
Bramwell Ho
Borough The SE1.......262 B6
Chelsea SW1...........269 A6
Bramwell Mews N1......233 D6
Brancaster Dr NW7......28 A3
Brancaster Ho
22 Globe Town E1......96 D4
Islington N5..............72 D3
Brancaster Rd Ilford E12..78 B4
Newbury Pk IG2.........57 C3
Streatham SW16.........160 A1
Brancepeth Gdns IG9....21 A2
Branch Hill NW3..........70 A5
Branch Ho **13** SM1......218 A4
Branch Pl N1.......95 B6 235 D6
Branch Rd E14...........119 A6
Branch St SE15..........139 C5
Brancker Rd HA3.........43 D6
Brancroft Way EN3.......7 B4
Brandan Ho **11** HA1....42 D4
Brand Cl N4..............50 D1
Branden Lo **13** W4.....111 A1
Brandlehow Prim Sch
SW15.................135 B1
Brandlehow Rd SW15....135 B1
Brandon Ho BR3.........185 D5
Brandon Mews
Barbican EC2..........242 C4
Walworth SE17.........262 B3
Brandon Pl N8...........50 B5
Brandon Rd Barnsbury N7..72 A1
Southall UB2...........107 B1
Sutton SM1............217 D4
Walthamstow E17........54 A6
Brandon St SE17...117 A2 262 B3
Brandram Rd SE13.......142 C1
Brandrams Wharf SE16..118 C4
Brandreth Ct HA1.........42 D3
Brandreth Rd
Newham E6.............100 B1
Upper Tooting SW17.....159 B2
Brandries The SM6......219 D5
Brand St SE10..........142 A5
Brandville Gdns IG6......56 D5
Brandville Rd UB7.......104 A4
Brandy Way SM2........217 C1
Brangbourne Rd BR1....186 A5
Brangton Rd SE11......260 D1
Brangwyn Cres SW19...180 B1
Brangwyn Ct W14......254 A5
Branham Ho **1** SE18...122 C1
Branksea St SW6..135 A5 264 A3
Branksome Ave N18......33 D5
Branksome Cl
Teddington TW11........174 B6
Walton-on-T KT12......194 D1
Branksome Ct **6** N2....48 A6
Branksome Ho SW8.....270 C4
Branksome Rd
London SW2............160 A6
Merton SW19...........179 C2
Branksome Way
Harrow HA3.............44 B3
Kingston u T KT3.......177 B2
Bransby Ct **4** N16.....73 C4
Bransby Rd KT9.........214 A2
Branscombe NW1.......232 B5
Branscombe Ct BR2....208 C4
Branscombe Gdns N21...16 C4
Branscombe St SE13....141 D2
Bransdale Cl NW6........91 C6
Bransgrove Rd HA8......26 B3
Branston Cres BR5......211 B1
Branstone Ct **9** TW9..132 B4
Branstone Rd TW9......132 B4
Branston Ho N7..........72 C3
Brants Wlk W7...........86 C3
Brantwood Ave
Erith DA8..............147 D5
Isleworth TW7..........131 A1
Brantwood Cl E17........53 D6
Brantwood Gdns
Enfield EN2.............16 A6
Redbridge IG4...........56 A5
Brantwood Ho **9** SE5..139 A5
Brantwood Rd Erith DA7..147 D3

Brantwood Rd continued
Herne Hill SE24..........161 A6
Tottenham N17...........34 A4
Brasenose Dr SW13.....134 C6
Brasher Cl UB6...........64 B3
Brashley Road Cvn Site
NW10..................89 C4
Brassett Point **3** E15...98 C6
Brassey Cl TW14.........150 A3
Brassey Ho
1 Millwall E14.........119 D2
Walton-on-T KT12.......194 A1
Brassey Rd NW6.........69 B2
Brassey Sq SW11.........137 A2
Brassie Ave W3..........89 C1
Brass Talley Alley **31**
SE16..................118 D4
Brasted Cl Bexley DA6...168 D6
Forest Hill SE26..........184 C6
Brasted Lo **11** BR3....185 C3
Brathay NW1............232 B3
Brathway Rd SW18.....157 C4
Bratley St **11** E1........96 A3
Bratten Ct CR0...........205 B3
Braund Ave UB6..........85 D3
Braundton Ave DA15.....167 D3
Braunston Dr UB4........85 A3
Braunston Ho TW8.......131 C6
Bravington Cl TW17.....192 B4
Bravington Pl W9.........91 B3
Bravington Rd W9........91 B4
Brawne Ho **12** SE17...138 D6
Braxfield Rd SE4.........141 B1
Braxted Pk SW16.......182 B4
Bray NW3................70 C1
Brayard's Rd SE15.......140 B3
Braybourne Dr TW7.....130 D5
Braybrooke Gdns SE19..183 C3
Braybrook St W12........89 D1
Brayburne Ave SW4....137 C3
Braycourt Ave KT12.....194 C2
Bray Cres SE16..........118 D4
Bray Ct Chessington KT9..214 B3
Streatham SW16........182 A5
Braydon Rd N16..........52 A1
Bray Dr E16..............120 D6
Brayfield Ter N1..........72 C1
Brayford Sq **12** E1.....96 C1
Bray Pl SW3......114 D2 257 C3
Bray Rd NW7.............28 A4
Brayton Gdns EN2........3 D1
Braywick Ct **9** KT2....176 C3
Braywood Rd SE9........145 B1
Brazier Cres UB5........85 B3
Brazil Cl CR0............204 A2
Breach La RM9..........103 C4
Bread St EC2, EC4.......242 B1
Breakspeare SE21.......161 D1
Breakspear Jun & Inf Schs
UB10..................60 C6
Breakspear Rd HA4, UB9..38 D3
Breakspear Road N UB9..38 B5
Breakspear Road S UB9,
UB10..................38 C1
Breakspears Dr BR5.....190 A2
Breakspears Mews SE4..141 C3
Breakspears Rd SE4.....141 C2
Breakwell Ct **16** W10...91 A3
Bream Cl N17............52 B5
Bream Gdns E6..........100 C4
Breamore Cl SW15.......156 A3
Breamore Ct IG3.........80 A6
Breamore Ho **21** SE15..140 A5
Breamore Rd IG3.........79 D6
Bream's Bldgs
EC4..............94 C1 241 A2
Bream St E3..............75 C1
Breamwater Gdns TW10..153 B1
Brearley Cl Burnt Oak HA8..27 A3
Uxbridge UB8............60 A2
Breaside Prep Sch BR1...187 D2
Breasley Cl SW15........134 B1
Brechin Pl SW7.....114 A2 256 B3
Brecknock Prim Sch **18**
N7....................71 D2
Brecknock Rd N19.......71 D3
Breckonmead BR1......187 C1
Brecon Cl Mitcham CR4..204 A6
North Cheam KT4.......216 C6
Brecon Ct **7** Eltham SE9..166 C5
Whetstone N12..........14 A1
Brecon Gn NW9..........45 C3
Brecon Ho
Stamford Hill N16.......51 D1
Wandsworth SW18......157 C4
Brecon Rd Enfield EN3....6 C1
Fulham W6.........135 A4 264 B5
Brede Cl E6.............100 C4
Bredel Ho **1** E14.......97 C2
Bredgar SE13............163 D6
Bredgar Rd N19..........71 C6
Bredhurst Cl SE20......184 C4
Bredinghurst SE22.......162 A4
Bredinghurst Sch SE15..140 D1
Bredin Ho SW10........265 D4
Bredo Ho IG11..........102 B4
Bredon Ct HA8...........26 B6
Bredon Rd CR0..........205 D2
Breer St SW6...........135 D2
Breezer's Ct **1** E1......118 A6

Breezer's Hill E1..........118 A6
Brehon Ho NW1........232 A5
Bremans Row **1** SW18..158 A2
Brember Rd HA2.........64 A6
Bremer Mews E17.......35 D3
Bremner Rd SW7........256 B6
Brenchley Cl
Chislehurst BR7.........188 C2
Hayes BR2..............208 D3
Brenchley Gdns SE15, SE22,
SE23..................162 D5
Brenchley Rd BR5......189 D1
Bren Ct **27** EN3.........7 C6
Brenda Rd SW17.........158 B3
Brende Gdns KT8........195 D5
Brendon Ave NW10.......67 C4
Harlington UB7..........127 A5
Brendon Cl
Southall UB2............107 D2
3 London N20.........14 C2
Brendon Dr KT10.......212 A2
Brendon Gdns
Harrow HA2.............63 D4
Ilford IG2...............81 D4
Brendon Gr N2...........30 A1
Brendon Ho
Marylebone W1........238 A4
Sutton SM2............218 A2
Brendon Rd
Dagenham RM8..........59 C1
New Eltham SE9.........166 A1
Brendon St W1.......92 C1 237 B2
Brendon Villas N21........17 A3
Brendon Way EN1........17 C4
Brenley Cl CR4..........203 A6
Brenley Gdns SE9........143 D1
Brenley Ho SE1.........252 C2
Brennands Ct **14** N19..71 C5
Brent Adult Comm Education
Service Coll **9** NW10....89 B6
Brent Cl DA5...........169 A3
Brentcot Cl W13..........87 B3
Brent Cres NW10.........88 B5
Brent Cross Flyover NW2,
NW4..................46 D2
Brent Cross Gdns NW4...46 D2
Brent Cross Interchange NW2,
NW4..................46 D2
Brent Cross Sh Ctr NW4..46 C2
Brent Cross Sta NW11...46 D2
Brent Ct **5** Acton W12..111 C3
Ealing W7..............108 B6
Hendon NW11...........46 D4
Brentfield NW10.........66 D1
Brentfield Cl NW10......67 B2
Brentfield Gdns NW2.....46 D2
Brentfield Ho **7** NW10..67 B2
Brentfield Jun & Inf Sch
NW10..................67 B2
Brentfield Rd NW10......67 B2
BRENTFORD.............131 B6
Brentford Bsns Ctr TW8..131 C5
Brentford Cl UB4.........84 D3
BRENTFORD END........131 C4
Brentford Fountain L Ctr
W4....................110 C1
Brentford Ho **6** TW1...153 B4
Brentford Sch for Girls
TW8..................131 D6
Brentford Sta TW8.......131 C6
Brent Gn NW4...........46 D4
Brentham Way W5.......87 D3
Brent Ho **9** Catford BR1..186 B5
16 Hackney E9.........74 C2
Wembley HA9...........66 B3
Brenthouse Rd E9........74 C2
Brenthurst Rd NW10.....67 D2
Brent Knoll Sch **15** SE26..162 D1
Brent Lea TW8..........131 C5
Brent Mans NW4.........46 C4
Brentmead Cl W7.......108 C6
Brentmead Gdns NW10..88 B5
Brentmead Pl NW11......46 D3
Brent New Ent Ctr NW10..67 D2
Brenton Ct E9............75 A3
Brenton St E14...........97 A1
Brent Park Ind Est UB2..106 C3
Brent Park Rd NW4.......46 B2
Brent Pl EN5............13 B6
Brent Rd Brentford TW8..131 C6
Newham E16............99 A2
Southall UB2............106 C3
Woolwich SE18.........144 D5
Brentside **9** TW8......131 C6
Brentside Cl W13.........87 A3
Brentside Executive Ctr
TW8..................131 B6
Brentside High Sch W7..86 C3
Brentside Prim Sch W7..86 C3
Brent St NW4............46 D4
Brent Trad Est NW10.....67 C3
Brentvale Ave
Southall UB1...........108 B5
Wembley HA0...........88 B6
Brent View Rd NW9......46 A2
Brentwaters Bsns Pk
TW8..................131 C5

Brent Way
Brentford TW8..........131 D5
Finchley N3.............29 C4
Wembley HA9...........66 D2
Brentwick Gdns TW8....110 A2
Brentwick Cl SE9........167 A3
Brentwood Ho **2** SE18..143 A1
Brentwood Lo NW4......46 D4
Brereton Ho **4** SW2...160 C4
Brereton Rd N17.........33 D3
Bressay Dr NW7..........28 A3
Bressenden Pl
SW1..............115 C3 259 A6
Bressey Ave EN1..........6 A4
Bressey Gr E18...........36 D1
Bretherton Ct CR2......221 C2
Breton Ho
Bermondsey SE1.......263 C6
St Luke's EC2...........242 B5
Brett Cl **15** Northolt UB5..84 D4
Stoke Newington N16....73 C6
Brett Cres NW10.........89 B6
Brett Ct N9..............18 C2
Brettell St SE17.........262 D1
Brettenham Ave E17.....35 C2
Brettenham Prim Sch **10**
N18....................34 A6
Brettenham Rd
Edmonton N18...........34 A6
Walthamstow E17........35 C2
Brett Ho **1** SW15......156 D4
Brett House Cl **2** SW15..156 D4
Brettinghurst **8** SE1...118 A1
Bretton Ho N19..........50 A1
Brett Pas **28** E8........74 B3
Brett Rd Barnet EN5......12 C6
Hackney E8.............74 B3
Brewers Bldgs EC1......234 C2
Brewers Ct W2..........236 A2
Brewer's Gn SW1........259 C6
Brewers Hall Gdns EC2..242 B3
Brewers La **11** TW9....153 D6
Brewer St W1......115 C4 249 B6
Brewery Cl HA0...........65 A4
Brewery Ind Est The N1..235 B3
Brewery Mews Bsns Ctr **1**
TW7..................131 A2
Brewery Rd Islington N7..72 A2
Keston Mark BR2.......210 A1
Plumstead SE18.........123 B1
Brewery Sq
Bermondsey SE1.......253 C3
Clerkenwell EC1........241 B5
Brewhouse La
Putney SW15...........135 A2
Wapping E1.............118 B5
Brewhouse Rd **3** SE18..122 B2
Brewhouse Wlk SE16....119 A5
Brewhouse Yd EC1......241 C6
Brewood Rd RM8..........80 B2
Brewster Gdns W10......90 C2
Brewster Ho
Bermondsey SE1.......263 D4
Poplar E14............119 B6
Brewster Rd E10.........53 D1
Brian Cl N16.............31 B2
Brian Rd RM6.............58 C4
Briant Ho SE1...........260 D5
Briants Cl HA5...........23 B1
Briant St SE14..........140 D5
Briar Ave SW16.........182 B3
Briarbank Rd W13........87 A1
Briar Cl Buckhurst Hill IG9..21 D2
Edmonton N13...........17 A1
Finchley N2..............30 A1
Hampton TW12..........173 B5
Isleworth TW7..........152 D6
Briar Cres UB5...........63 D2
Briar Ct **7** Bow E3......97 C5
Cheam SM3.............216 C4
9 Dalston E8...........73 D1
Hampton TW12.........173 D5
Leytonstone E11.........54 B2
Briardale Edgware HA8...27 B6
Wandsworth SW19......157 B3
Briardale Gdns NW3......69 C5
Briar Dale Ho **12** N16...51 C1
Briarfield Ave N3.........29 D1
Briarfield Cl DA7.........147 C3
Briar Gdns BR2..........208 D1
Briaris Cl **1** N17........34 B3
Briar La CR0.............223 D4
Briar Lo E18.............37 C3
Briar Rd Cricklewood NW2..68 C4
Harrow HA3.............43 C4
Littleton TW17..........192 C4
Thornton Heath SW16...204 B6
Twickenham TW2........152 C3
Briars The SW23..........8 C4
Briarswood Way BR6....227 D3
Briar The **11** SM1......218 A4
Briarview Ct E4...........36 B4
Briar Way UB7...........104 C4
Briar Wlk Burnt Oak HA8..27 A1
Putney SW15...........134 B1
West Kilburn W10.......91 A3

Briarwood Cl
Feltham TW13 . . . . .149 C1
Kingsbury NW9 . . . . .45 A3
Briarwood Ct 5 KT4. . . . . .200 A1
Briarwood Dr HA6 . . . . .22 A1
Briarwood Rd
London SW4 . . . . .159 D6
Stoneleigh KT17 . . . . .216 A2
Briary Cl NW3 . . . . .70 C1
Briary Ct
10 Canning Town E16. . . . .98 D1
Sidcup DA14. . . . . .190 B5
Briary Gdns BR1. . . . . .187 B5
Briary Gr HA8. . . . . .26 D1
Briary La N9 . . . . .17 D1
Briary Lo BR3. . . . . .186 A2
Brickbarn Cl SW10. . . . . . . .266 B4
Brick Ct EC4 . . . . .241 A1
Brickett Cl HA4 . . . . .39 A4
Brick Farm Cl TW9 . . . . . . .132 D4
Brickfield Cl TW8 . . . . .131 C5
Brickfield Cotts SE18. . . . . .145 D6
Brickfield Farm Gdns
BR6. . . . . .227 A4
Brickfield La Edgware EN5. .11 D5
Harlington UB3. . . . . .127 B6
Brickfield Rd
South Norwood CR7,
SW16 . . . . .182 D2
Wimbledon SW19. . . . . .179 D6
Brickfields HA2. . . . . .64 B6
Brickfields Way UB7 . . . . . .104 B3
Brick La Enfield EN1. . . . . . . .9 D1
Northolt UB5 . . . . .85 B4
Shoreditch E2. . . . . .95 D4
Spitalfields E1. . . . . .95 D3 243 D5
Stanmore HA7 . . . . .25 D3
Brick Lane Mkt ★
E2. . . . . .95 D3 243 D6
Bricklayers Arms SE1 . . . . .262 D5
Brick St W1 . . . . . . .115 B5 248 C3
Brickwall La HA4 . . . . .39 D1
Brickwood Cl SE26. . . . . . . .162 B1
Brickwood Rd CR0. . . . . . . .221 C6
Brickworth Ho 26 SW9 . . . .138 C4
Brideale Cl SE15. . . . . .139 D6
Bride Ct EC4 . . . . .241 C1
Bride La EC4. . . . . . .94 D1 241 C1
Bridel Mews N1 . . . . .234 C5
Bride St N7 . . . . .72 B2
Bridewain St SE1 . . . . .263 C6
Bridewell Pl Holborn EC4. . .241 C1
20 Wapping E1. . . . . .118 B5
Bridford Mews W1. . . . . . . .238 D4
Bridge Acad The E2. . . . . . . .95 D6
Bridge App NW3 . . . . .71 A1
Bridge Ave Ealing W7 . . . . . .86 B2
Hammersmith W6 . . . . .112 C1
Bridge Avenue Mans 1
W6. . . . . .112 C1
Bridge Bsns Ctr The 2
UB2. . . . . .107 C4
Bridge Cl Enfield EN1 . . . . . . .6 B3
13 North Kensington W10 . .90 D1
Teddington TW11. . . . . .174 D6
Walton-on-T KT12. . . . . . . .193 D1
Bridge Ct
9 Blackwall E14. . . . . . . .120 B6
Leyton E10 . . . . .53 B2
2 Walton-on-T KT12. . . . .193 D1
7 Willesden NW10 . . . . . . .67 C1
Bridge Dr N13 . . . . .32 B6
Bridge End E17 . . . . .36 A2
Bridge End Cl 4 KT2. . . . . .176 C2
Bridge Field Ho 2 W2 . . . . .91 D1
Bridgefield Rd SM1. . . . . . . .217 C2
Bridgefoot SE1 . . . .116 A1 262 B1
Bridge Gate N21. . . . . .17 A4
Bridge Gdns
Canonbury N16. . . . . .73 B4
East Molesey KT8. . . . . .196 B5
Littleton TW15 . . . . .171 A3
Bridge Ho Brockley SE4 . . . .141 B4
1 Camden Town NW1. . . . . .71 A1
Ealing W7 . . . . .109 A2
Homerton E9 . . . . .74 D3
Woolwich SE28. . . . . .123 C5
Bridge Ho S TW8. . . . . .87 A1
Bridge House Quay E14 . . . .120 A5
Bridge La
Battersea SW11. . . .136 C4 267 B1
Temple Fortune NW11 . . . . . .47 B4
Bridgeland Rd E16. . . . . . . .121 A6
Bridgelands Cl BR3. . . . . . . .185 B3
Bridge L Ctr SE26 . . . . .185 B6
Bridgeman Ho 19 E9 . . . . . .74 C1
Bridgeman Rd
Islington N1. . . . . .72 B1
Teddington TW11 . . . . .175 A4
Bridgeman St
NW8 . . . . .92 C5 230 A3
Bridge Meadows SE14 . . . .140 D6
Bridgend Rd SW18. . . . . . . .136 A1
Bridgenhall Rd EN1 . . . . .5 D4
Bridgen Ho 9 E1 . . . . .96 B1
Bridgen Rd DA5 . . . . .169 A4

Bridge Par
7 Croydon CR0. . . . . .220 D5
Edmonton N21 . . . . .17 A4
Bridge Pk
7 London SW18. . . . . .157 C6
Wembley NW10 . . . . .66 D1
Bridge Pk Com L Ctr
NW10. . . . . .66 D1
Bridge Pl
Belgravia SW1 . . . . .115 B2 258 D4
Croydon CR0. . . . . .205 B1
Bridgepoint Lofts 2 E7. . . .77 C1
Bridgeport Pl 4 E1. . . . . . .118 A5
Bridge Rd
Beckenham BR3. . . . . .185 B3
Bexleyheath DA7. . . . . .147 A3
Chessington KT9 . . . . .214 A3
East Ham E6. . . . . .78 B1
East Molesey KT8. . . . . .196 C5
Isleworth TW3, TW7. . . . . . .130 B2
Southall UB2. . . . . .107 C4
Stratford Marsh E15. . . . . . . .98 B6
Sutton SM4. . . . . .217 D2
Twickenham TW1 . . . . .153 B5
Wallington SM6 . . . . .219 C3
Walthamstow E17 . . . . .53 B2
Wembley NW9. . . . . .66 C5
Willesden NW10. . . . . .67 C2
Wood Green N22 . . . . .32 A2
Bridge Row CR0 . . . . .205 B1
Bridge Sch The
Clerkenwell EC1. . . .94 D3 241 C6
Lower Holloway N7 . . . . .72 A3
Bridges Cl SW11. . . . . .136 B3
Bridges Ho 15 SE5 . . . . . . .139 B5
Bridges La CR0 . . . . .220 A5
Bridges Rd Stanmore HA7 . .24 D5
Wimbledon SW19. . . . . .179 D4
Bridges Road Mews
SW19. . . . . .179 D4
Bridge St Chiswick W4 . . . .111 B2
Pinner HA5. . . . . .41 A6
Richmond TW10 . . . . .153 D6
Walton-on-T KT12 . . . . .193 D2
Westminster SW1 . . .116 A4 250 B1
Bridge Terr E15. . . . . .76 B1
Bridge The HA3. . . . . .42 D5
Bridgetown Cl 5 SE19 . . . . .183 C5
Bridgeview 2 W6 . . . . .112 C1
Bridgewater Cl BR7. . . . . . .211 C6
Bridgewater Ct HA0. . . . . . . .65 C2
Bridgewater Gdns HA8. . . . .26 B1
Bridgewater Ho UB5. . . . . . .85 A3
Bridgewater Rd
Ruislip HA4. . . . . .62 B4
Stratford Marsh E15. . . . . . . .98 A6
Wembley HA0. . . . . .65 C1
Bridgewater Sq EC2 . . . . . .242 A4
Bridgewater St EC2. . . . . . .242 A4
Bridgeway Barking IG11. . . . .79 D1
Wembley HA0. . . . . .65 C2
Bridge Way London NW11. . .47 B4
Twickenham TW2 . . . . .152 A4
Uxbridge UB10 . . . . .60 D3
Bridgeway St
NW1 . . . . .93 C5 232 B3
Bridge Wharf 18 E2. . . . . . . .96 C5
Bridge Wharf Rd TW7. . . . .131 B2
Bridgewood Cl SE20 . . . . . .184 B3
Bridgewood Rd
North Cheam KT17, KT4. . . .216 A4
Streatham SW16 . . . . .181 D3
Bridge Yd SE1 . . . . .252 D4
Bridgford St SW17,
SW18. . . . . .158 A1
Bridgman Rd W4 . . . . .111 A3
Bridgnorth Ho 10 SE15. . . .140 A6
Bridgwater Ho W2. . . . . . . .236 A2
Bridle Cl Enfield EN3 . . . . .7 B6
Kingston u T KT1. . . . . .197 D5
Sunbury TW16 . . . . .194 A6
West Ewell KT19. . . . . .215 B3
Bridle La
Marylebone W1 . . . .115 C6 249 B6
Twickenham TW1 . . . . .153 B5
Bridle Path CR0. . . . . .220 A5
Bridle Path The IG8 . . . . . . .36 C3
Bridlepath Way TW14 . . . . .149 C3
Bridle Rd Addington CR0. . .223 C4
Claygate KT10 . . . . .213 B2
Croydon CR0. . . . . .223 C6
Pinner HA5 . . . . .40 C4
Bridle Way
Addington CR0 . . . . .223 C3
Orpington BR6 . . . . .227 A4
Bridle Way The SM6. . . . . . .219 C3
Bridlington Ho SW18. . . . . .136 A1
Bridlington Rd N9 . . . . .18 B4
Bridport SE17 . . . . .262 B1
Bridport Ave RM7. . . . . .59 D3
Bridport Ho
6 Edmonton N18. . . . . . . .34 A5
Shoreditch N1. . . . . .235 D5
Bridport Pl N1. . . . . .95 B6 235 D5
Bridport Rd Edmonton N18. .33 D5
Greenford UB6. . . . . .85 D6
Thornton Heath CR7. . . . . . .204 D6
Bridstow Pl W2 . . . . .91 C1
Brief St SE5 . . . . .138 D4
Brierfield NW1 . . . . .232 A5

Brierley CR0. . . . . .223 D2
Brierley Ave N9. . . . . .18 C3
Brierley Cl SE25 . . . . .206 A5
Brierley Ct W7. . . . . .108 C6
Brierley Rd Leyton E11 . . . . .76 B4
Upper Tooting SW12 . . . . . . .159 C2
Brierly Gdns E2. . . . . .96 C5
Brigade Cl HA2 . . . . .64 B6
Brigade St SE3 . . . . .142 D3
Brigadier Ave EN2 . . . . .5 A4
Brigadier Hill EN2 . . . . .5 A5
Briggeford Cl 5 E5. . . . . . . .74 A6
Briggs Cl CR4. . . . . .181 B2
Briggs Ho 20 E2 . . . . .95 D4
Bright Cl DA17. . . . . .124 D2
Bright Ct 8 SE28 . . . . .124 C5
Brightfield Rd SE12 . . . . . . .164 D6
Brightling Rd SE4. . . . . .163 B5
Brightlingsea Pl 5 E14. . . . .119 B6
Brightman Rd SW18 . . . . . . .158 B3
Brighton Ave E17 . . . . .53 B4
Brighton Bldgs SE1. . . . . . .263 A5
Brighton Cl UB10. . . . . .60 D1
Brighton Ct SW15. . . . . .157 B5
Brighton Dr 3 UB5. . . . . . . .63 C2
Brighton Gr SE14 . . . . .141 A4
Brighton Ho 7 SE5 . . . . . . .139 B4
Brighton Rd
Belmont SM2 . . . . .217 D1
Finchley N2. . . . . .30 A1
South Croydon CR2. . . . . . . .221 B2
Stoke Newington N16. . . . . . .73 C4
Surbiton KT6. . . . . .197 D3
Sutton SM2. . . . . .218 A1
Wallend E6. . . . . .100 C4
Brighton Terr SW9 . . . . .138 B1
Brightside Rd SE13 . . . . . . .164 B5
Brightside The EN3. . . . . .7 A4
Bright St E14 . . . . .97 D2
Brightwell Cl CR0. . . . . .204 C1
Brightwell Cres SW17. . . . . .180 D5
Brightwell Ct N7. . . . . .72 B3
Brightwells 1 SW6 . . . . . . .135 D3
Brightwen Gr HA7 . . . . .9 A2
Brig Mews SE8 . . . . .141 C6
Brigstock Ho SE5 . . . . .139 A3
Brigstock Par 1 CR7. . . . . . .204 C4
Brigstock Rd
Belvedere DA17. . . . . .125 D2
Thornton Heath CR7. . . . . . .204 D4
Brill Ho NW10 . . . . .67 B5
Brill Pl NW1. . . . . . .93 D5 232 D3
Brim Hill N2. . . . . .48 B5
Brimpsfield Cl SE2. . . . . . . .124 B3
BRIMSDOWN. 7 B3
Brimsdown Ave EN3 . . . . .7 A4
Brimsdown Ho E3 . . . . .98 A3
Brimsdown Jun & Inf Sch
EN3. . . . . .6 D2
Brimstone Ho 4 E15. . . . . . .76 C1
Brindishe Prim Sch
SE12. . . . . .164 D6
Brindle Gate DA15. . . . . . . .167 C3
Brindley Cl
Bexleyheath DA7. . . . . .147 D2
Wembley HA0. . . . . .87 D6
Brindley Ho
Carshalton SM1 . . . . .218 C3
37 Notting Hill W2 . . . . . . .91 C2
22 Streatham SW12. . . . . .160 A4
Brindley St SE14 . . . . .141 B4
Brindley Way
Bromley BR1. . . . . .187 B5
Southall UB1. . . . . .107 D6
Brindwood Rd E4. . . . . .19 C1
Brine Ct KT6. . . . . .197 D4
Brine Ho 11 E3 . . . . .97 A5
Brinkburn Cl
Abbey Wood SE2. . . . . .124 A2
Edgware HA8. . . . . .44 D6
Brinkburn Gdns HA8. . . . . . .44 C6
Brinkley 18 KT1. . . . . .176 C1
Brinkley Rd KT4. . . . . .216 B6
Brinklow Cres SE18 . . . . . . .144 D5
Brinklow Ho W2. . . . . .91 D2
Brinkworth Rd IG5. . . . . .56 A6
Brinkworth Way E9 . . . . .75 B2
Brinsdale Rd NW4 . . . . .46 D6
Brinsley Ho 17 E1. . . . . .96 C1
Brinsley Rd HA3 . . . . .24 B1
Brinsley St 35 E1. . . . . .96 B1
Brinsworth Cl TW2. . . . . . . .152 B2
Brinton Wlk SE1 . . . . .251 C1
Brion Pl E14. . . . . .98 A2
Brisbane Ave SW19 . . . . . . .179 D2
Brisbane Ct N10. . . . . .31 B3
Brisbane Ho 3 W12 . . . . . . .112 B6
Brisbane Rd Ealing W13. . . .109 A4
Ilford IG1. . . . . .57 A1
Leyton E10 . . . . .75 D6
Brisbane St SE5. . . . . .139 B5
Briscoe Cl E11. . . . . .76 D6
Briscoe Rd SW19 . . . . .180 B4
Briset Rd SE9. . . . . .143 D1
Briset St EC1. . . . . .94 D3 241 C5
Briset Way N7 . . . . .72 B6
Bristol Cl Stanwell TW19. . . .148 A5
Twickenham TW4 . . . . .151 C4
Wallington SM6 . . . . .220 A1

Bristol Ct 11 TW19 . . . . . . .148 A5
Bristol Gdns
Putney SW15 . . . . .156 C4
Westbourne Green W9. . . . . .91 D3
Bristol Ho 1 Barking IG11. .80 A1
SE11. . . . . .261 A5
Bristol Mews W9. . . . . .91 D3
Bristol Park Rd 1 E17. . . . . .53 A5
Bristol Rd Greenford UB6. . .85 D6
Morden SM4. . . . . .202 A4
Upton E7. . . . . .77 D2
Briston Gr N8. . . . . .50 A3
Briston Mews NW7 . . . . .28 A3
Bristowe Cl 24 SW2. . . . . . .160 C5
Bristow Rd
Bexleyheath DA7 . . . . .147 A4
Hounslow TW3 . . . . .130 A2
Wallington CR0. . . . . .220 A4
West Norwood SE19. . . . . . .183 C5
Britannia Building N1. . . . . .235 C2
Britannia Cl London SW4 . . .137 D1
Northolt UB5 . . . . .84 D4
Britannia Gate 1 E16. . . . . .121 A5
Britannia Ho N20 . . . . .14 A1
Britannia Junc NW1 . . . . . . .231 D6
Britannia La TW2 . . . . .152 A4
Britannia L Ctr N1. . . . . .95 C6
Britannia Rd Ilford IG1. . . . . .78 D5
23 Millwall E14. . . . . .119 C2
Surbiton KT5. . . . . .198 B2
Walham Green
SW6 . . . . .135 D5 265 C3
Whetstone N12 . . . . .14 A1
Britannia Row N1. .95 A6 235 A6
Britannia St WC1 . . .94 B4 233 C2
Britannia Village Prim Sch 17
E16. . . . . .121 B5
Britannia Way NW10 . . . . . . .88 D3
Britannia Wlk N1 . . . . .235 C2
British Coll of Osteopathic
Medicine NW3 . . . . .70 A2
British Dental Association
Mus** ★ W1. . . . . .238 C3
British Gr W4. . . . . .111 D1
British Grove Pas 2
W4. . . . . .111 D1
British Grove S 3 W4 . . . . .111 D1
British Home Tw (Hospl)
SE27. . . . . .182 D5
British Legion Rd E4. . . . . . . .20 D2
British Library Newspapers
NW9. . . . . .45 C6
British Library The ★
WC1 . . . . .93 D4 232 D2
British Mus ★
WC1. . . . . .94 A2 240 A3
British Optical Association
Mus** ★ SW1. . . . . .250 A4
British St E3. . . . . .97 B4
British Wharf Ind Est
SE14. . . . . .140 D6
Britley Ho 16 E14. . . . . .97 B1
Brit Oval The (Surrey Cnty
Crkt Club) SE11 138 C6 270 C6
BRIT Performing Arts & Tech
Sch SE25. . . . . .205 B3
Brittage Rd NW10. . . . . .67 C1
Brittain Ct SE9. . . . . .166 A3
Brittain Rd RM8. . . . . .81 B5
Brittany Ho SW15. . . . . .134 C1
Brittany Point SE11. . . . . . . .261 A3
Britten Cl Elstree WD6 . . . . . . .9 D5
Golders Green NW11. . . . . . .47 D1
Brittenden Cl 1 BR6. . . . . . .227 D2
Brittenden Par BR6. . . . . . . .227 D2
Britten Dr UB1. . . . . .85 C1
Britten Ho SW3. . . . . .257 B2
Britten St SW3. . . . .114 C1 257 A2
Britton Cl SE6 . . . . .164 B4
Britton St EC1. . . . . .94 D3 241 C5
Brixham Cres HA4. . . . . .40 A1
Brixham Gdns IG3 . . . . .79 C3
Brixham Rd DA16. . . . . .146 D4
Brixham St E16. . . . . .122 C5
BRIXTON. 138 C2
Brixton Day Coll 6
SW9 . . . . .138 A2
Brixton Hill SW2. . . . . .160 B5
Brixton Hill Ct 5 SW2. . . . . .160 B6
Brixton Hill Pl SW2. . . . . . . .160 A4
Brixton Mkt ★ SW9 . . . . . . .138 C1
Brixton Oval 2 SW2 . . . . . .138 C1
Brixton Rd SW9. . . . . .138 C4
Brixton Rec Ctr SW9 . . . . . .138 C2
Brixton Sta SW9 . . . . .138 C1
Brixton Station Rd SW9 . . . .138 C2
Brixton Water La SW2. . . . . .160 B6
Broadacre Cl UB10. . . . . .60 D5
Broadbent Cl N6. . . . . .49 B1
Broadbent St W1 . . . . .248 C6
Broadberry Ct N18. . . . . .34 B5
Broadbridge Cl SE3. . . . . . .143 A5
Broad Common Est N16. . . . .52 A1
Broadcoombe CR2. . . . . . . .222 D1
Broadcroft Ave HA7. . . . . . . .25 D1
Broadcroft Rd BR5. . . . . . . .211 B2
Broad Ct WC2. . . . . .240 B1
Broadeaves Cl CR2. . . . . . . .221 C3
Broadfield NW6 . . . . .69 D2

Broadfield Cl
Croydon CR0. . . . . .220 B6
Dollis Hill NW2 . . . . .68 C5
Broadfield Ct Bushey WD23. .8 C2
Edgware HA8 . . . . .10 D1
Broadfield La NW1. . . . . .72 A1
Broadfield Rd SE6 . . . . .164 C3
Broadfields Harrow HA2 . . . .23 D1
Thames Ditton KT8 . . . . .196 C3
Broadfields Ave
Edgware HA8. . . . . .10 D1
Southgate N21. . . . . .17 A3
Broadfields Hts HA8 . . . . . . .26 D6
Broadfields Prim Sch
HA8 . . . . .10 C2
Broadfield Sq EN1 . . . . .6 B3
Broadfields Way NW10. . . . .67 D3
Broadfield Way IG9 . . . . .21 C1
Broadford Ho 12 E1. . . . . . . .97 A3
BROADGATE. 95 C2
Broadgate Ct 2. . . . .95 C2 243 A3
Broadgate Circ
EC2 . . . . .95 C2 243 A3
Broadgate Rd E16. . . . . .99 D3
Broadgates Ave EN4 . . . . .1 D4
Broadgates Ct SE11. . . . . . .261 B1
Broadgates Rd SW18. . . . . .158 B3
Broadgate Twr The EC2. . . .243 B5
BROAD GREEN. 204 D3
Broad Green Ave CR0 . . . . . .204 D2
Broadhead Strand NW9. . . . .27 D2
Broadhead Dr BR7 . . . . .188 B5
Broadhinton Rd SW4. . . . . . .137 C2
Broadhurst Ave
Edgware HA8. . . . . .26 D6
Ilford IG3. . . . . .79 D4
Broadhurst Cl
Hampstead NW6 . . . . .70 A2
9 Richmond TW10 . . . . . .154 B6
Broadhurst Gdns
Hampstead NW6 . . . . .69 D2
Ruislip HA4. . . . . .62 C6
Broadhurst Mans NW6 . . . . .69 D2
Broad La Broadgate EC2 . . .243 A4
Hampton TW12. . . . . .173 C4
Hornsey Vale N8. . . . . .50 B4
South Tottenham N15. . . . . . .51 C5
South Tottenham N15. . . . . . .52 A5
Broadlands
Feltham TW13 . . . . .151 C1
Highgate N6 . . . . .49 A2
Broadlands Ave Enfield EN3 . .6 B2
Shepperton TW17. . . . . .193 A3
Streatham SW16. . . . . .160 A2
Broadlands Cl Enfield EN3 . . .6 C2
Highgate N6 . . . . .49 A2
Streatham SW16 . . . . .160 A2
Broadlands Ct TW9 . . . . . . .132 C5
Broadlands Lo N6 . . . . .48 D2
Broadlands Mans 2
SW16. . . . . .160 A2
Broadlands Rd
Grove Pk BR1. . . . . .187 B6
Highgate N6 . . . . .48 D2
Broadlands Way KT3 . . . . . .199 D3
Broad Lawn SE9. . . . . .166 C3
Broadlawns Ct HA3 . . . . .24 D2
Broadley St NW8. . . .92 C3 237 A4
Broadley Terr
NW1 . . . . .92 C3 237 B5
Broadmayne SE17 . . . . .262 C2
Broadmead Catford SE6. . . .163 C1
Hampton TW12. . . . . .173 C4
West Kensington W14. . . . . .254 A3
Broadmead Ave KT4 . . . . . . .200 A4
Broadmead Cl
Hampton TW12. . . . . .173 C4
Pinner HA5. . . . . .27 C6
Broadmead Ct 6 IG8. . . . . . .37 A4
Broadmead Inf Sch CR0. .205 B2
Broadmead Jun Sch
CR0. . . . . .205 B2
Broadmead Rd
Northolt UB5 . . . . .85 A3
Woodford IG8. . . . . .37 B5
Broad Oak Ashford TW16. . .171 D4
Woodford IG8. . . . . .37 B5
Broad Oak Cl Chingford E4. .35 C5
St Paul's Cray BR5. . . . . . . .190 A1
Broadoak Ct 8 SW9 . . . . . . .138 C2
Broadoak Ho 11 NW6 . . . . . .91 D6
Broadoaks BR7. . . . . .188 D4
Broadoaks KT6. . . . . .214 D6
Broadoaks Way BR2 . . . . . . .208 D4
Broadreach Coll SE28. . . . . .123 D3
Broad St Dagenham RM10. . .81 C1
Broad Sanctuary SW1. . . . . .250 A1
Broad St Dagenham RM10. . .81 C1
Teddington TW11. . . . . .174 D4
Broadstone Ho SW8 . . . . . . .270 C3
Broadstone Pl W1 . . . . .238 A3
Broad Street NHS Walk-in
Ctr RM10. . . . . .103 C6
Broadview NW9 . . . . .44 C3
Broadview Est TW19 . . . . . . .148 C4
Broadview Ho RM8 . . . . .58 D1
Broadview Rd SW16 . . . . . . .181 D3
Broadwalk Harrow HA2 . . . . .41 D4
Snaresbrook E18 . . . . .54 D6

Broadwalk Ho SW7 . . . . . **246** A1
Broadwalk La NW11 . . . . . .**47** B2
Broadwalk Sh Ctr The
HA8 . . . .**26** D4
Broadwall SE1 . . . **116** C5 **251** B4
Broadwater Farm Prim Sch
N17 . . . .**33** B1
Broadwater Gdns BR6 . . . .**227** A4
Broadwater Prim Sch
SW17 . . . .**180** C6
Broadwater Rd
Plumstead SE18 . . . .**123** B3
Tottenham N17 . . . .**33** C1
Upper Tooting SW17 . . . . .**180** C6
Broadway Barking IG11 . . .**101** A6
Bexley DA6 . . . .**147** C1
Bexleyheath DA6 . . . .**147** B1
Hanwell W7 . . . .**108** C5
Stratford E15 . . . .**76** B1
Tolworth KT6 . . . .**198** D1
West Ealing W13 . . . .**109** A5
Westminster SW1 . .**115** D3 **259** C6
Broadway Arc **3** W6 . . . . .**112** C2
Broadway Ave
Thornton Heath CR0 . . . . .**205** B4
Twickenham TW1 . . . .**153** B5
Broadway Bldgs **5** W7 . .**108** C5
Broadway Cl IG8 . . . .**37** B4
Broadway Ct
Beckenham BR3 . . . .**208** A6
Wimbledon SW19 . . . .**179** C4
Broadway Ctr The **6**
W6 . . . .**112** C2
Broadway Gdns
Mitcham CR4 . . . .**202** C5
Woodford IG8 . . . .**37** B4
Broadway Ho **2** E8 . . . . . .**96** B6
Broadway Ho **5** SW19 . . .**179** C2
Broadway Lofts SW17 . . . .**180** C6
Broadway Mans SW6 . . . .**265** B3
Broadway Market E8 . . . . . .**96** B6
Broadway Market Mews **21**
E8 . . . .**96** A6
Broadway Mews
Bowes Pk N13 . . . .**32** B5
Southgate N21 . . . .**16** D3
Stamford Hill E5 . . . .**51** D2
Broadway Mkt E8 . . . .**96** B6
Broadway Par
Chingford E4 . . . .**36** A4
Hayes UB3 . . . .**106** A5
Hornsey N8 . . . .**50** A3
West Drayton UB7 . . . . . .**104** A4
Broadway Pl SW19 . . . . . .**179** B4
Broadway Ret Pk NW2 . . . .**68** D4
Broadway Sh Ctr **5**
DA6 . . . .**147** C1
Broadway The
Barnes SW13 . . . .**133** C3
Bedington CR0 . . . .**220** A4
Cheam SM3 . . . .**217** A2
Chingford E4 . . . .**36** B4
Dagenham RM8 . . . .**81** C6
Ealing W5 . . . .**109** D6
Edgware NW7 . . . .**27** C5
Edmonton N9 . . . .**18** A1
Friern Barnet N11 . . . .**31** A5
Greenford UB6 . . . .**86** A3
Harrow HA3 . . . .**24** D1
Hornsey N8 . . . .**50** A3
Merton SW19 . . . .**179** C3
Newham E13 . . . .**99** B5
Pinner HA5 . . . .**23** B3
South Acton W3 . . . .**110** C4
Southall UB1 . . . .**107** A6
2 Southgate N14 . . . .**15** D3
Stanmore HA7 . . . .**25** C5
Sutton SM1 . . . .**218** A4
Thames Ditton KT10 . . . . .**196** C1
Tolworth KT6 . . . .**198** C1
Wembley HA9 . . . .**66** A5
Woodford IG8 . . . .**37** B4
Wood Green N22 . . . .**32** C1
Broadway Wlk **4** E14 . . . .**119** C3
Broadwell Ct TW5 . . . .**128** D4
Broadwick St W1 . . **93** C1 **239** B1
Broad Wlk
Eltham SE3, SE18 . . . . . .**144** A3
Heston TW5 . . . .**129** C4
Mayfair W1 . . . . . .**115** A5 **248** A4
Regent's Pk NW1 . .**93** A5 **231** B3
Richmond TW9 . . . .**132** B5
Southgate N21 . . . .**16** B3
Broad Wlk The
W8 . . . .**113** D5 **245** D3
Broadwood Ave HA4 . . . . . .**39** C3
Broadwood Terr W14 . . . . .**254** D4
Broad Yd EC1 . . . .**241** C5
Brocade Ct NW9 . . . .**45** D5
Brocas Cl NW3 . . . .**70** C1
Brockbridge Ho SW15 . . . .**155** D5
Brockdene Dr BR2 . . . .**225** D4
Brockdish Ave IG11 . . . .**79** D3
Brockelbank Lo RM8 . . . . . .**80** D6
Brockenhurst KT8 . . . .**195** B3
Brockenhurst Ave KT4 . . . .**199** C1
Brockenhurst Gdns
Edgware NW7 . . . .**27** C5
Ilford IG1 . . . .**79** A3

Brockenhurst Mews **9**
N18 . . . .**34** A6
Brockenhurst Rd CR0 . . . .**206** B2
Brockenhurst Way
SW16 . . . .**181** D1
Brocket Ho **16** SW8 . . . . .**137** D3
Brockham Cl SW19 . . . . . .**179** B5
Brockham Cres CR0 . . . . .**224** B1
Brockham Ct
17 Belmont SM2 . . . .**217** D1
8 South Croydon CR2 . . . .**221** A3
Brockham Dr Ilford IG2 . . . .**57** A4
Streatham SW2 . . . .**160** B4
Brockham Ho
Camden Town NW1 . . . . .**232** B5
11 Streatham SW2 . . . . . .**160** B4
Brockham St SE1 . . . .**262** B6
Brockhurst Cl HA7 . . . .**24** D4
Brockhurst Rd N4 . . . .**51** B2
Brockill Cres SE4 . . . .**163** A3
Brocklebank Ho **7** E16 . .**122** C5
Brocklebank Rd
Greenwich SE7 . . . .**121** B2
Wandsworth SW18 . . . . . .**158** A4
Brocklebank Road Ind Est
SE7 . . . .**121** A2
Brocklehurst St SE14 . . . .**140** D5
Brocklesby Rd SE25 . . . . .**206** B5
BROCKLEY **141** B1
Brockley Ave HA7 . . . .**10** A1
Brockley Cl HA7 . . . .**26** A6
Brockley Cross SE4 . . . . . .**141** B2
Brockley Cross Bsns Ctr
SE4 . . . .**141** A2
Brockley Gdns SE4 . . . . . .**141** B3
Brockley Gr SE4 . . . .**163** B6
Brockley Hall Rd SE4 . . . .**163** A6
Brockley Hill Ha7, HA8 . . . . .**9** D2
Brockley Hill Ho HA7 . . . . . .**9** C3
Brockley Ho SE17 . . . .**263** A2
Brockley Mews SE4 . . . . . .**163** A6
Brockley Pk SE23 . . . .**163** A4
Brockley Prim Sch SE4 . . .**163** B6
Brockley Rise SE23 . . . . . .**163** A4
Brockleyside HA7 . . . .**26** A6
Brockley Sta SE4 . . . .**141** A2
Brockley View SE23 . . . . . .**163** A4
Brockley Way SE4 . . . .**163** A6
Brockman Rise BR1 . . . . . .**186** B6
Brockmer Ho **6** E1 . . . . . .**118** B6
Brock Pl E3 . . . .**97** D3
Brock Rd E13 . . . .**99** B2
Brocks Dr SM3 . . . .**217** A5
Brockshot Cl **1** TW8 . . . .**131** D6
Brock St SE15 . . . .**140** C2
Brockway Cl E11 . . . .**76** C6
Brockweir **28** E2 . . . .**96** C5
Brockwell Ave BR3 . . . . . .**207** D4
Brockwell Cl BR5 . . . .**211** D4
Brockwell Ct
2 London SW2 . . . .**160** C6
Thornton Heath CR0 . . . . .**204** D2
Brockwell Ho SE11 . . . . . .**270** D6
Brockwell Lido SE24 . . . . .**160** D5
Brockwell Park ★ SE24 . . .**160** D5
Brockwell Park Gdns
SE24 . . . .**160** D4
Brockwell Park Row
SW2 . . . .**160** C5
Brockworth **8** KT2 . . . . . .**176** D2
Broderick Ho SE21 . . . . . .**161** C1
Brodia Rd N16 . . . .**73** C5
Brodick Ho **12** E3 . . . .**97** B5
Brodie Ct E10 . . . .**54** B1
Brodie Ho
Bermondsey SE1 . . . .**263** D2
7 Wallington SM6 . . . . .**219** B4
Brodie Rd Chingford E4 . . . .**20** A2
Enfield EN2 . . . .**5** A5
Brodie St SE1 . . .**117** D1 **263** D2
Brodlove La E1 . . . .**118** D6
Brodrick Gr SE2 . . . .**124** B2
Brodrick Rd SW17 . . . . . .**158** C2
Brody Ho E1 . . . .**243** C3
Brograve Gdns BR3 . . . . .**185** D1
Broken Wharf EC4 . . . .**252** A6
Brokesley St **3** **97** B4
Broke Wlk Hackney E8 . . . . .**95** D6
1 Hackney E8 . . . .**96** A6
Bromar Rd SE5 . . . .**139** C2
Bromborough Gn WD19 . . . .**22** C5
Bromefield HA7 . . . .**25** C2
Bromehead St **8** E1 . . . . . .**96** C1
Bromell's Rd SW4 . . . .**137** C1
Brome Rd SE9 . . . .**144** B2
Bromfelde Rd SW4 . . . . . .**137** D3
Bromfield Ct **20** SE16 . . .**118** A3
Bromfield St N1 . . . .**234** B4
Bromhall Rd RM8 . . . .**80** B2
Bromhedge SE9 . . . .**166** B1
Bromholm Rd SE2 . . . .**124** B3
Bromleigh Ct **1** SE21,
SE22 . . . .**162** B2
Bromleigh Ho SE1 . . . . . .**263** D6
BROMLEY BR1 . . . .**186** C2
E3 . . . .**97** D4
Bromley Ave BR1 . . . .**186** C5
Bromley-by-Bow Sta E3 . . .**98** A4
Bromley Coll BR1 . . . .**187** A2

Bromley Coll of F & H Ed
(Rookery Lane Campus)
BR2 . . . .**209** D3
Bromley Comm BR2 . . . . .**209** D4
5 Brentford TW8 . . . . . .**131** D6
Bromley Cres
Beckenham BR2 . . . .**208** D6
Ruislip HA4 . . . .**61** D4
Bromley Ct BR1 . . . .**186** D3
Bromley Gdns BR2 . . . . . .**208** D6
Bromley Gr BR2 . . . .**186** B1
Bromley Hall Rd E14 . . . . . .**98** A2
Bromley High Jun Sch
BR1 . . . .**210** C5
Bromley High Sch BR1 . . .**210** C5
Bromley High St E3 . . . .**97** C4
Bromley Hill BR1 . . . .**186** C4
Bromley Ho BR1 . . . .**187** A2
Bromley Ind Ctr BR1 . . . . .**209** D6
Bromley La BR7 . . . .**189** B3
Bromley Lo **2** W3 . . . .**89** A1
Bromley Manor Mans **3**
BR1 . . . .**209** A6
Bromley North Sta BR1 . . .**187** A2
BROMLEY PARK **186** D2
Bromley Pk **1** BR1 . . . . . .**186** D2
Bromley Pl W1 . . . .**239** A4
Bromley Rd
Beckenham BR3 . . . .**185** D2
Bromley BR2, BR3 . . . . . .**186** B1
Catford SE6 . . . .**163** D1
Chislehurst BR7 . . . .**188** D2
Edmonton N18 . . . .**17** B1
Leyton E10 . . . .**53** D3
Tottenham N17 . . . .**34** A2
Walthamstow E17 . . . .**53** C6
Bromley Road Inf Sch **5**
BR3 . . . .**185** D2
Bromley Road Ret Pk
SE6 . . . .**163** D2
Bromley Ski & Snowboard
Ctr BR5 . . . .**190** D1
Bromley South Sta BR2 . .**209** A6
Bromley St E1 . . . .**96** D1
BROMPTON **114** B3
Brompton Arc SW1 . . . . . .**247** D1
Brompton Cl
Hounslow TW4 . . . .**151** B6
Penge SE20 . . . .**184** A1
Brompton Ct **4** HA7 . . . . . .**25** C6
Brompton Gr N2 . . . .**48** C5
Brompton Ho **3** N9 . . . . . .**34** A6
Brompton Oratory
SW3 . . . .**114** C3 **257** A6
Brompton Park Cres
SW6 . . . .**135** D6 **265** C5
Brompton Pl
SW3 . . . .**114** C3 **257** B6
Brompton Rd
SW3 . . . .**114** C3 **257** A5
Brompton Sq
SW3 . . . .**114** C3 **257** A6
Bromstone Ho **16** SW9 . .**138** C4
Bromwich Ave N6 . . . .**71** A6
Bromwich Ho **3** TW10 . . .**154** A5
Bromyard Ave W3 . . . .**111** C5
Bromyard Ho Acton W3 . . .**111** C5
3 Peckham SE15 . . . . . .**140** B5
Bron Ct NW6 . . . .**91** C6
BRONDESBURY **69** A2
Brondesbury Coll for Boys **10**
NW6 . . . .**68** D2
Brondesbury Ct NW2 . . . . .**68** D2
Brondesbury Mews **11**
NW6 . . . .**69** C1
BRONDESBURY PARK **90** D6
Brondesbury Park Sta
NW6 . . . .**91** A6
Brondesbury Pk NW6 . . . . .**68** D1
Brondesbury Rd NW6 . . . . .**91** C5
Brondesbury Sta NW6 . . . . .**69** B1
Brondesbury Villas NW6 . . .**91** C5
Bronhill Terr N17 . . . .**34** A2
Bronsart Rd SW6 . .**135** A4 **264** A3
Bronson Rd SW20 . . . .**179** A1
Bronte Cl Erith DA8 . . . . . .**147** D5
1 Forest Gate E7 . . . .**77** A4
Ilford IG2 . . . .**56** C5
Bronte Ct **8** W14 . . . .**112** D3
Bronte Ho Kilburn NW6 . . . .**91** C4
5 Stoke Newington N16 . .**73** A4
Bronti Cl SE17 . . .**117** A1 **262** B2
Bronwen Ct NW8 . . . .**229** C1
Bronze Age Way DA17 . . . .**125** D4
Bronze St SE8 . . . .**141** C5
Brook Ave
Dagenham RM10 . . . .**81** D1
Edgware HA8 . . . .**26** D4
Wembley HA9 . . . .**66** C5
Brook Bank EN1 . . . .**6** B6
Brookbank Ave W7 . . . .**86** B2
Brookbank Rd SE13 . . . . . .**141** D2
Brook Cl Acton W3 . . . . . .**110** C5
Finchley N12 . . . .**29** A3
Ruislip HA4 . . . .**39** C2
Stanwell TW19 . . . .**148** B4
Upper Tooting SW17 . . . . .**159** A2
West Barnes SW20 . . . . .**200** B6
Brook Cres Chingford E4 . . .**35** D6

Brook Cres continued
Edmonton N9 . . . .**34** B6
Brook Ct Barking IG11 . . . .**101** D6
Beckenham BR3 . . . .**185** B2
5 Brentford TW8 . . . . . .**131** D6
Cheam SM3 . . . .**216** C4
Edgware HA8 . . . .**26** D5
2 Leyton E11 . . . .**76** C5
Mortlake SW14 . . . .**133** C2
Walthamstow E17 . . . .**53** A6
Brookdale N11 . . . .**31** C6
Brookdale Rd
Catford SE6 . . . .**163** D4
Lewisham SE6 . . . .**163** D5
Sidcup DA5 . . . .**169** A5
Walthamstow E17 . . . .**53** C6
Brookdales The NW4 . . . . .**47** A5
Brookdene N11 . . . .**31** C6
Brookdene Rd SE18, SE2 . .**123** D2
Brook Dr Harrow HA1 . . . . . .**42** A5
Newington SE11 . .**116** D2 **262** A4
Ruislip HA4 . . . .**39** C2
Brooke Ave Harrow HA2 . . . .**64** A5
Brooke Cl WD23 . . . .**8** A4
Brooke Ct Kilburn W10 . . . . .**91** A5
7 Kingston u T KT2 . . . . .**175** D6
Brooke Ho Bushey WD23 . . .**8** A4
4 New Cross Gate SE14 . .**141** A4
Brookehowse Rd SE6 . . . .**163** D1
Brookend Rd DA15 . . . . . .**167** C3
Brooke Rd
Shacklewell E5, N16 . . . . . .**74** A5
Walthamstow E17 . . . .**54** A5
Brookes Ct EC1 . . . .**241** A4
Brooke's Mkt EC1 . . . .**241** B4
Brooke St EC1 . . .**94** C2 **241** A3
Brooke Way WD23 . . . .**8** A4
Brookfield
Dartmouth Pk N6 . . . .**71** A5
1 Finsbury Pk N4 . . . .**72** C6
Brookfield Ave
Carshalton SM1, SM5 . . . .**218** C5
Ealing W5 . . . .**87** D3
Mill Hill NW7 . . . .**28** B4
Walthamstow E17 . . . .**54** A5
Brookfield Cl NW7 . . . .**28** B4
Brookfield Cres
Harrow HA3 . . . .**44** A4
Mill Hill NW7 . . . .**28** B4
Brookfield Ct
Greenford UB6 . . . .**86** A4
1 London N12 . . . .**29** D6
Brookfield Gdns KT10 . . . .**212** D2
Brookfield Ho **23** E2 . . . . .**96** B5
Brookfield House Sch
IG8 . . . .**36** C4
Brookfield Path IG8 . . . .**36** C4
Brookfield Pk NW5 . . . .**71** B5
Brookfield Prim Sch
Cheam SM3 . . . .**201** A1
Dartmouth Pk N19 . . . .**71** B6
Brookfield Rd Acton W4 . . .**111** B4
Edmonton N9 . . . .**18** B1
Homerton E9 . . . .**75** A2
Brookfields EN3 . . . .**6** D1
Brookfields Ave CR4 . . . . .**202** C4
Brookgate N16 . . . .**73** B6
Brook Gate W1 . .**114** D6 **247** D5
Brook Gdns
Barnes SW13 . . . .**133** D2
Chingford E4 . . . .**35** D6
Kingston u T KT2 . . . .**177** A2
Brook Gn W6 . . . .**112** D2
BROOK GREEN **112** D2
Brook Green Flats **11**
W14 . . . .**112** D3
Brookhill Cl
East Barnet EN4 . . . .**14** C6
Woolwich SE18 . . . .**122** D1
Brookhill Ct **2** EN4 . . . . . .**14** C5
Brookhill Rd
East Barnet EN4 . . . .**14** C6
Woolwich SE18 . . . .**122** D1
Brook Ho **3** Clapham Pk SW4 . . .**159** C6
Ealing W3 . . . .**110** C4
3 Edmonton N9 . . . .**18** A1
4 Hammersmith W6 . . . .**112** C2
Marylebone WC1 . . . .**239** C4
4 Twickenham TW1 . . . . .**153** A4
Brook Hos NW1 . . . .**232** D2
Brookhouse Gdns E4 . . . . .**36** C6
Brook House Sixth Form Coll
5 E5 . . . .**74** B5
Brook Ind Est UB4 . . . . . .**106** C5
Brooking Cl RM8 . . . .**80** C5
Brooking Rd E7 . . . .**77** A3
Brook La Bexley DA5 . . . . .**168** D5
Greenwich SE3 . . . .**143** B3
Plaistow BR1 . . . .**187** A4
Brook La N **3** TW8 . . . . . .**131** D6
Brookland Cl NW11 . . . . . .**47** C5
Brookland Garth NW11 . . . .**47** D5
Brookland Hill NW11 . . . . .**47** D5
Brookland Jun & Inf Schs
NW11 . . . .**47** D5
Brookland Rise NW11 . . . . .**47** D5
Brooklands Ave
New Eltham DA15 . . . . . .**167** B2
Wandsworth SW18 . . . . . .**157** D2

Brooklands Cl TW16 . . . . .**171** C2
Brooklands Cl TW15 . . . . .**170** B6
Brooklands Court
Apartments **3** NW6 . . . .**69** B1
Brooklands Ct
10 Clapham SW8 . . . . . .**137** C3
Enfield N21 . . . .**17** B6
Kingston u T KT1 . . . .**197** D5
2 London NW6 . . . .**69** B1
2 Mitcham CR4 . . . .**180** B1
Brooklands Dr UB6 . . . .**87** D6
Brooklands Ho SE3 . . . . . .**143** A4
Brooklands Pk SE3 . . . . . .**143** A4
Brooklands Pl TW12 . . . . .**173** D5
Brooklands Prim Sch
SE3 . . . .**143** A4
Brooklands Rd KT7 . . . . . .**197** A1
Brooklands The TW7 . . . . .**130** B4
Brook Lane Bsns Ctr
TW8 . . . .**109** D1
Brooklea Cl NW9 . . . .**27** C2
Brook Lo Crouch End N8 . . .**49** D3
Edgware HA8 . . . .**26** D4
Hendon NW4 . . . .**46** D4
Brooklyn SE20 . . . .**184** A3
Brooklyn Ave SE25 . . . . . .**206** B5
Brooklyn Cl SM5 . . . .**218** C6
Brooklyn Ct
Feltham TW13 . . . .**150** B2
Shepherd's Bush W12 . . . .**112** C5
Brooklyn Gr SE25 . . . .**206** B5
Brooklyn Rd
Bromley BR2 . . . .**210** A4
Croydon SE25 . . . .**206** B5
Brookmarsh Ind Est
SE10 . . . .**141** D5
Brook Mead KT19 . . . .**215** C2
Brookmead Ave BR1,
BR2 . . . .**210** B4
Brookmead Ct N20 . . . .**14** A2
Brookmead Ind Est CR4 . .**203** C3
Brook Meadow Cl IG8 . . . . .**36** C4
Brookmead Rd CR0 . . . . . .**203** C3
Brook Mews N
W2 . . . .**114** A6 **246** B6
Brookmill Rd SE8 . . . .**141** C4
Brook Park Cl N21 . . . .**16** C6
Brook Pl EN5 . . . .**13** C6
Brook Rd
Buckhurst Hill IG9 . . . .**21** A3
Dollis Hill NW2 . . . .**68** A6
Finchley N12 . . . .**30** C3
Hornsey N8 . . . .**50** A5
Ilford IG2 . . . .**57** C3
South Norwood CR7 . . . . .**205** A5
Surbiton KT6 . . . .**214** A6
Twickenham TW1 . . . .**153** A5
Wood Green N22 . . . .**50** B6
Brook Ret Pk HA4 . . . .**62** D3
Brook Road S
Brentford TW8 . . . .**109** D1
Brentford TW8 . . . .**131** D6
Brooks Ave E6 . . . .**100** B3
Brooksbank Ho **7** E9 . . . . .**74** C2
Brooksbank St **9** E9 . . . . . .**74** C2
Brooksby Ho **9** N1 . . . .**72** C1
Brooksby Mews N1 . . . .**72** C1
Brooksby St N1 . . . .**72** C1
Brooksby's Wlk E9 . . . .**74** D3
Brooks Cl SE9 . . . .**166** C2
Brookscroft E17 . . . .**53** D6
Brookscroft Rd E17 . . . .**35** D2
Brooks Ct
3 London SW4 . . . .**138** A3
Nine Elms SW8 . . . .**269** A4
Brooks Farm ★ E10 . . . . . .**53** D2
Brookshill HA3 . . . .**24** D5
Brookshiii Ave HA3 . . . .**24** D5
Brookshill Dr HA3 . . . .**24** D5
Brooks Ho **3** SW2 . . . . . .**160** C3
Brookside Broom Hill BR6 . .**211** D2
East Barnet EN4 . . . .**14** C5
Hillingdon UB10 . . . .**60** B1
Southgate N21 . . . .**16** B5
Wallington SM5 . . . .**219** A3
Brookside Cl Barnet EN5 . . .**13** A5
Feltham TW13 . . . .**150** A1
Harrow HA3 . . . .**43** D4
South Harrow HA2, HA4 . . . .**63** A4
Brookside Cres **1** KT4 . . .**200** A1
Brookside Ct SW16 . . . . . .**181** C3
Brookside Gdns EN1 . . . . . .**6** C6
Brookside Ho N1 . . . .**83** C1
Brookside Prim Sch UB4 . .**84** C4
Brookside Rd
Edmonton N9 . . . .**34** B6
Hayes UB4 . . . .**106** C6
Temple Fortune NW11 . . . .**47** B3
Upper Holloway N19 . . . . .**71** C6
Brookside S EN4 . . . .**15** A4
Brookside Way CR0 . . . . . .**206** D3
Brooks La W4 . . . .**132** C6
Brook's Mans **5** IG3 . . . . .**58** B1
Brook's Mews
W1 . . . .**115** B6 **248** C6

Brook's Par **6** IG3........58 B1
Brook Sq SE18.........144 A4
Brooks Rd W4..........110 C1
Brook's Rd E13..........99 A6
Brook St
  Bayswater W2 .... 114 B6 246 D6
  Erith DA8 ....147 D5
  Kingston u T KT1.....176 A1
  Mayfair W1......115 B6 248 C6
  7 Tottenham N17 ......33 D1
Brookstone Ct SE15....140 B1
Brooksville Ave NW6......91 A6
Brook Vale DA8........147 B4
Brookview Ct **11** EN1......11 B2
Brookview Rd SW16.....181 C5
Brookville Rd
  SW6...........135 B5 264 C3
Brookway SE3.........143 A2
Brook Wlk Burnt Oak HA8...27 B4
  Finchley N2..........30 B2
Brookwood Ave SW13...133 D3
Brookwood Cl BR2......208 D5
Brookwood Ho SE1.....251 D1
Brookwood Rd
  Hounslow TW3 ....129 D4
  Wandsworth SW18 .....157 C3
Broom Ave BR5........190 B1
Broom Cl
  Bromley Comm BR2 ....210 A3
  Teddington KT1, TW11...175 D3
Broomcroft Ave UB5.....84 C4
Broome Ct **3** TW9.......132 C4
Broome Ho **7** E5.......74 B3
Broome Rd TW12.......173 B2
Broome Way SE5.......139 B5
Broom Farm SW6.......135 C3
Broomfield
  7 Camden Town NW1....71 A1
  Sunbury TW16 ....172 A2
  Walthamstow E17 .....53 B2
Broomfield Ave N13......32 B5
Broomfield Cotts N13.....32 A5
Broomfield Ct N13.......32 A5
Broomfield Ho
  Stanmore HA7 ....9 A1
  4 St Paul's Cray BR5....190 B1
  Walworth SE17........263 A3
Broomfield House Sch
  TW9.............132 B4
Broomfield La N13.......32 B6
Broomfield Pl W13.....109 B5
Broomfield Rd
  Beckenham BR3.......207 B6
  Bexley DA6..........169 C6
  Bowes Pk N13.........32 A5
  Dagenham RM6 ....58 D2
  Ealing W13..........109 B5
  Richmond TW9 ....132 B4
  Surbiton KT5.........198 B1
  Teddington TW11 .....175 C4
Broomfields KT10......212 A3
Broomfield Sch N14 .....31 D5
Broomfield St E14.......97 D2
Broom Gdns CR0.......223 C5
Broomgrove Gdns HA8...26 C2
Broomgrove Rd SW9.....138 B3
BROOM HILL........211 D2
Broomhill Ct **2** IG8.......37 A4
Broomhill Rd
  Broom Hill BR6 ....211 D2
  Ilford IG3...........80 A6
  Wandsworth SW18 .....157 C6
  Woodford IG8.........37 A4
Broomhill Rise DA6.....169 C6
Broomhill Wlk IG8......36 D3
Broomhouse La SW6....135 C2
Broomhouse Rd SW6...135 C2
Broomleigh BR1.......187 A2
Broomloan La SM1......217 C6
Broom Lock TW11 ......175 C4
Broom Mead DA6......169 C6
Broom Pk KT1.........175 D2
Broom Rd Croydon CR0...223 C5
  Teddington TW11 .....175 C4
Broomsleigh Bsns Pk
  SE26............185 B5
Broomsleigh St NW6......69 B3
Broom Water TW11....175 C5
Broom Water W TW11...175 C5
Broomwood Cl CR0 ....206 D4
Broomwood Hall (Lower
  Sch) 5 SW12.......159 A5
Broomwood Hall Sch (Lower
  Sch) SW16........159 D1
Broomwood Hall Sch (Upper
  Sch) 3 SW12 ......159 A4
Broomwood Rd
  London SW11........159 A6
  St Paul's Cray BR5 ....190 B1
Broseley Gr SE26......185 A5
Broster Gdns SE25.....205 D6
Brougham Rd Acton W3...89 A1
  Hackney E8...........96 A6
Brougham St SW11....136 D3
Brough Cl
  Kingston u T KT2.......175 D5
  South Lambeth SW8....270 B3

Broughton Ave London N3..47 A6
  Richmond TW10 ......175 C6
Broughton Ct W13.......109 B6
Broughton Dr **19** SW9...138 D1
Broughton Gdns N6......49 C3
Broughton Ho **10** SW19...179 A3
Broughton Rd
  Ealing W13..........109 B6
  Orpington BR6........227 B6
  Sands End SW6 ....135 D3
  Thornton Heath CR7....204 C3
Broughton Road App 2
  SW6............135 D3
Broughton St SW8......137 B3
Brouncker Rd W3......111 A4
Browells La TW13......150 B2
Brown Bear Ct TW13 ...172 D6
Brown Cl SM6.........220 A1
Browne Ho
  13 Deptford SE8.......141 C5
  9 Penge SE26........184 B5
Brownfield St E14.......98 A1
Brownflete Ho SE4......141 A1
Browngraves Rd UB7...127 A5
Brown Hart Gdns W1....248 B6
Brownhill Rd SE6.......164 A4
Browning Ave
  Carshalton SM1......218 C4
  Ealing W7............86 D1
  North Cheam KT4......200 B1
Browning Cl Bexley DA16..145 C4
  Feltham TW12........173 B6
  Paddington W9........236 B5
  Walthamstow E17 .....54 A5
Browning Ct W14......264 C6
Browning Ho
  2 London SE14......141 A4
  7 Shepherd's Bush W12...90 C1
  10 Stoke Newington N16 ..73 C4
Browning Mews W1 ....238 B3
Browning Rd Enfield EN2...5 B5
  Leytonstone E11......54 D2
  Plashet E12..........78 B2
Browning St
  SE17...........117 A2 262 B3
Browning Way TW5 ....128 D4
Brownlea Gdns IG3......80 A6
Brownlow Cl EN4.......14 B6
Brownlow Ct
  2 Bowes Pk N11.......32 A4
  Hampstead Garden Suburb
  N2..............32 A4
Brownlow Ho **10** SE16...118 A4
Brownlow Lo **11** N11.....32 A4
Brownlow Mews
  WC1..........94 B3 240 D5
Brownlow Rd
  Bowes Pk N11........32 A4
  6 Ealing W13 ....109 A5
  Finchley N3..........29 D3
  3 Forest Gate E7 ......77 A4
  Hackney E8...........96 A6
  South Croydon CR0....221 D4
  Willesden NW10.......67 C1
Brownlow St WC1...94 B2 240 D3
Brownrigg Rd TW15....170 C6
Brown's Bldgs EC3.....243 B1
Brownsea Wlk NW7.....28 D4
Brownspring Dr SE9 ...166 D1
Browns Rd E17.........53 C6
Brown's Rd KT5, KT6....198 B2
Brown St W1.....92 D1 237 C2
Brownswell Rd N2......30 B1
Brownswood Rd N4......73 A6
Broxash Rd SW11......159 A5
Broxbourne Ave E18 .....55 B5
Broxbourne Ho **11** E3 ....97 D3
Broxbourne Rd
  Broom Hill BR6 ....211 D2
  Wanstead E7.........77 A5
Broxholme Cl **4** SE25...205 B5
Broxholme Ho SW6 ....265 C2
Broxholm Rd SE27,
  SW16............160 C1
Broxted Rd SE6.......163 B2
Broxwood Way
  NW8 ....92 C6 230 B5
Bruce Ave TW17......193 A3
Bruce Castle Ct N17......33 C2
Bruce Castle Mus* N17...33 C2
Bruce Castle Rd N17.....33 D2
Bruce Cl
  North Kensington W10...90 D2
  Welling DA16........146 B4
Bruce Ct DA15........189 D6
Bruce Gdns N20........14 D1
Bruce Glasier Ho **13** N19 ..49 D2
Bruce Gr N17.........33 D1
Bruce Grove N17......33 D1
Bruce Grove Prim Sch
  N17.............33 D1
Bruce Grove Sta N17....33 D1
Bruce Hall Mews SW17..181 A6
Bruce Ho
  4 Clapham Pk SW4....159 D5
  5 Greenhill HA1.......42 D4
  3 North Kensington W10 ..90 D2
  Preston HA3.........44 A2
  Putney SW15........156 B6
Bruce Lawns SW17....181 A6

Bruce Rd Barnet EN5.....1 A2
  Bromley E3..........97 D4
  Harrow HA3..........24 C1
  Mitcham CR4........181 A3
  South Norwood SE25...205 B5
  Willesden NW10.......67 B1
Bruckner St W10........91 B4
Brudenell Rd SW17....181 A6
Bruffs Meadow UB5......63 A2
Bruges Ho **16** NW1.......71 C1
Brumfield Rd KT19.....215 A3
Brune Ho E1,........243 C3
Brunei Gall* WC1......239 D4
Brunel Cl Cranford TW5...128 B5
  Northolt UB5.........85 B4
  Penge SE19..........183 D4
Brunel Ct **8** SW13......133 D3
Brunel Est W2..........91 C2
Brunel Ho Chelsea SW10 ..266 D4
  4 Gospel Oak NW5....71 B4
  Hayes UB3..........105 D3
  Millwall E14.........119 D1
  New Cross SE8.......141 B5
  25 Streatham SW2.....160 A4
Brunel Mews NW10......90 D4
Brunel Mus* SE16......118 C4
Brunel Pl **7** UB1.......85 D1
Brunel Rd Acton W3......89 C2
  Walthamstow E17 .....53 A3
  Wapping SE16.......118 C5
Brunel Science Pk UB8...82 A4
Brunel St E16..........98 D1
Brunel Univ UB8........82 A4
Brunel Wlk
  South Tottenham N15....51 C5
  Twickenham TW4 .....151 C4
Brune St E1.....95 D2 243 C3
Brunlees Ho SE1.......262 B5
Brunner Cl NW11.......48 A4
Brunner Ho **6** SE6.....186 A6
Brunner Rd Ealing W5....87 D3
  Walthamstow E17 .....53 B4
Bruno Ct **5** E8.........74 A2
Bruno Pl NW9..........67 A6
Brunswick Ave N11......15 A1
Brunswick Cl Bexley DA6. 146 D1
  Pinner HA5..........41 A3
  Thames Ditton KT7....196 D1
  Twickenham TW2 .....152 B1
Brunswick Cres N11 .....15 A1
Brunswick Ct
  Bermondsey SE1 ...117 C4 253 B2
  Finsbury EC1........234 C1
  Kingston u T KT2......175 D4
  New Barnet EN4.......14 B6
  2 Penge SE19.......184 A3
  Westminster SW1 .....259 D3
  2 Wimbledon SW19 ...179 A3
Brunswick Gdns
  Ealing W5...........88 A3
  Kensington W8....113 C5 245 B3
Brunswick Gr N11......15 A1
Brunswick Ho
  Church End N3........29 B2
  4 Haggerston E2......95 D5
  Lisson Gr NW1.......237 C6
Brunswick Lo **6** E4......20 A2
Brunswick Manor SM1..218 A4
Brunswick Mews
  Marylebone W1.......237 D2
  Streatham SW16......181 D4
BRUNSWICK PARK....15 A1
Brunswick Park Gdns
  N11.............15 A2
Brunswick Park Prim Sch
  Brunswick Pk N14 .....15 A2
  22 Camberwell SE5 ....139 B5
Brunswick Park Rd N11...15 A1
Brunswick Pk SE5......139 C4
Brunswick Pl
  Penge SE19..........184 A3
  Shoreditch N1....95 B4 235 D1
Brunswick Quay SE16...118 D3
Brunswick Rd
  Bexley DA6..........147 A1
  Ealing W5............88 A4
  Holdbrook EN3.........7 C5
  Kingston u T KT2......176 C2
  Leyton E10..........54 A1
  Poplar E14..........98 A1
  South Tottenham N15....51 C4
  South Tottenham N15....51 C5
  Sutton SM1.........217 D4
Brunswick Sh Ctr
  WC1...........94 A3 240 B6
Brunswick Sq
  St Pancras WC1 ...94 A3 240 B6
  Tottenham N17........33 D4
Brunswick St E17......54 A4
Brunswick Terr BR3....185 D2
Brunswick Villas **3** SE5 ..139 C4
Brunswick Way N11.....31 B6
Brunton Pl E14........97 A1
Brushfield St E1...95 D2 243 C4
Brushwood Lo **1** DA17...125 C2
Brussels Cl SN18........33 C5
Brussels Rd SW11.....136 B1
Bruton Cl BR7.........188 B3
Bruton La W1.....115 B6 248 B5
Bruton Pl W1.....115 B6 248 D5

Bruton Rd SM4 ....202 A5
Bruton St W1.....115 B6 248 D5
Bruton Way W13........87 A2
Brutus Ct SE11........261 C3
Bryan Ave NW10........68 B1
Bryan Ct TW16........172 A3
Bryan Cl TW1.........237 C2
Bryan Rd SE16........119 B4
Bryanston Ave TW2 ....151 D3
Bryanston Cl UB2......107 B2
Bryanston Ct SM1......237 C2
Bryanston Ct SM1......218 A5
Bryanstone Rd N8......49 D4
Bryanston Ho **12** SE15...139 D4
Bryanston Mans W1 ....237 C3
Bryanston Mews E W1 ...237 C3
Bryanston Mews W
  W1...........92 D1 237 C2
Bryanston Pl W1 ..92 D2 237 C3
Bryanston Sq W1 ..92 D1 237 C2
Bryanston St W1..92 D1 237 D1
Bryant Cl EN5..........13 B6
Bryant Rd UB5.........84 C4
Bryant St E15..........76 C1
Bryantwood Rd N5, N7 ...72 C3
Brycedale Cres N14.....15 D1
Bryce Ho **25** SE14 ....140 D6
Bryce Rd RM8..........80 C4
Brydale Ho **2** SE16 ....118 D2
Bryden Cl SE26........185 A5
Brydges Pl WC2.......250 A5
Brydges Rd E15........76 B3
Brydon Wlk N1........233 B6
Bryer Ct EC2..........242 A4
Bryett Rd N7..........72 A5
Bryher Ho W4.........111 A1
Brymay Cl E3..........97 C5
Brymon Ct W1........237 D3
Brynmaer Ho SW11....267 D1
Brynmaer Rd
  SW11...........136 D4 267 D1
Bryn-y-Mawr Rd EN1.....5 D1
Bryony Cl UB8..........82 B2
Bryony Rd W12........112 A6
Bryony Way TW16......172 A4
B Sky B Hq TW7.......131 A6
BT Twr* W1.....93 C2 239 A4
Buccleuch Ho E5........52 A2
Buchanan Cl N21........16 B6
Buchanan Ct **16** SE16...118 D2
Buchanan Gdns NW10...90 B5
Buchanan Ho
  Dulwich SE21........161 C1
  Wandsworth SW18 ....157 C4
Buchan Ho W3.........110 D4
Buchan Rd SE15......140 C2
Bucharest Rd SW18....158 A4
Buckden Cl
  Fortis Green N2........48 D5
  Lee SE12...........165 A5
Buckfast Ct W13......109 A6
Buckfast Ho N14........15 C6
Buckfast Rd SM4......201 D5
Buckfast St E2.........96 A4
Buck Hill Wlk
  W2...........114 B6 246 D5
Buckhold Rd SW18.....157 C5
Buckhurst Ave CR4, SM5 .202 D1
Buckhurst Ct **7** IG9 .....21 D2
BUCKHURST HILL.....21 C2
Buckhurst Hill Ho **3** IG9 ..21 A2
Buckhurst Hill Sta **19** IG9..21 D2
Buckhurst Ho **15** N7 .....71 D3
Buckhurst St E1........96 B3
Buckhurst Way IG9......21 D1
Buckingham Ave
  East Molesey KT8......173 D1
  Falconwood DA16......145 C1
  Feltham TW14.......150 B5
  Oakleigh Pk N20.......14 B4
  South Norwood CR7....182 C2
  St James SW1.......250 B5
  Wembley UB6.........87 A6
Buckingham Cl
  Broom Hill BR5.......211 C2
  Ealing W5............87 C2
  Enfield EN1...........5 C3
  Hampton TW12.......173 B5
Buckingham College Prep
  Sch 1 HA2.........41 C2
Buckingham College Sch
  HA1.............42 C4
Buckingham Ct
  2 Ealing W7.........86 D3
  Hendon NW4.........46 A6
  Mitcham CR4........204 A4
  Northolt UB5.........85 A6
  Wembley HA0.........65 C2
Buckingham Dr BR7....189 A5
Buckingham Gate
  SW1...........115 C3 259 B6
Buckingham Gdns
  East Molesey KT8......173 D1
  Edgware HA8.........26 B3
  South Norwood CR7....182 C1

Buckingham Ho
  1 Acton W3..........88 C1
  Finsbury Pk N4........51 A1
  Richmond TW10 ......154 C6
Buckingham La SE23....163 A4
Buckingham Lo N10 .....49 C5
Buckingham Mans NW6...69 D3
Buckingham Mews
  Harlesden NW10.......89 D5
  7 Kingsland N1.......73 C2
  Westminster SW1 .....259 A6
Buckingham Pal*
  SW1...........115 C4 249 A1
Buckingham Palace Rd
  SW1...........115 B2 258 D4
Buckingham Par **19** HA7 ..25 C5
Buckingham Pl SW1....259 A6
Buckingham Prim Sch
  TW12............173 B5
Buckingham Rd
  Edgware HA8.........26 B3
  Hampton TW12, TW13...173 B5
  Harlesden NW10.......89 D5
  Harrow HA1..........42 B4
  Ilford IG1...........79 B6
  Kingsland N1.........73 C2
  Kingston u T KT1......198 B5
  Leyton E10..........75 D5
  Mitcham CR4........204 A4
  Richmond TW10 ......153 D2
  Stratford E15.........76 D3
  Wanstead E11........55 C4
  Woodford E18.........36 D2
  Wood Green N22.......32 A2
Buckingham St WC2....250 B5
Buckingham Way SM6 ..219 C1
Buckingham Yd NW10...89 D5
Buck La NW9..........45 B4
Buckland Cl NW7.......28 A6
Buckland Cres NW3....70 B2
Buckland Ct
  6 Shoreditch N1......95 C5
  Uxbridge UB10.......61 A6
Buckland Ho **3** N1.....72 C1
Buckland Rd
  Chessington KT9.....214 B3
  Leyton E10..........76 A6
  Orpington BR6.......227 C4
Buckland Rise HA5......22 D2
Bucklands Rd TW11....175 C4
Buckland St N1....95 B5 235 D3
Buckland Way KT4....200 C1
Buckland Wlk
  2 Acton W3..........111 A4
  Morden SM4.........202 A5
Buckle Ct HA8..........27 A3
Buckleigh Ave SW20...201 B6
Buckleigh Ho SW17....180 B5
Buckleigh Rd SW16....182 A3
Buckleigh Way SE19 ...183 D3
Buckler Gdns SE9......166 B1
Buckler's Alley SW6 ....264 D4
Bucklersbury EC2, EC4...242 C1
Bucklers' Way SM5 .....218 D5
Buckles Ct DA17.......124 D2
Buckle St
  15 Whitechapel E1......96 A1
  Whitechapel E1.......243 D2
Buckley Cl SE23.......162 B4
Buckley Ct
  5 Brondesbury NW6 ....69 B1
  London N8...........49 D4
Buckley Ho SE4.......110 C5
Buckley Rd NW6........69 B1
Buckmaster Cl **1** SW9...138 C2
Buckmaster Ho **1** N7....72 B4
Buckmaster Rd SW11...136 C1
Bucknall St WC1......240 A2
Bucknall Way BR3.....208 A6
Bucknell Cl SW2.......138 B1
Buckner Rd SW2.......138 B1
Buckrell Rd E4.........20 B2
Buckridge Bldg EC1....241 A4
Buckshead Ho **19** W2....91 C2
Buck St NW1..........71 B1
Buckstone Cl SE23.....162 C5
Buckstone Rd N18.......34 A5
Buckters Rents SE16...119 A5
Buckthorne Rd SE4....163 A6
Buckthorn Ho DA15....167 D1
Buckwheat Ct DA18....124 D3
Budd Cl N12..........29 D6
Buddings Circ HA9......67 A5
Bude Cl E17...........53 B4
Budge La CR4........202 D2
Budge Row EC4.......242 C1
Budge's Wlk W2...114 A5 246 B4
Budleigh Cres DA16....146 C4
Budleigh Ho **19** SE15...140 A4
Budoch Ct IG3.........80 A6
Budoch Dr IG3.........80 A6
Buer Rd SW6.........135 A3
Bugsby's Way SE10 ...120 D2
Buick Ho **4** E3.........97 C3
Building 36 **7** SE18....123 A3
Building 47 **6** SE18....123 A3
Building 48 **5** SE18....123 A3
Building 49 **4** SE18....123 A3
Building 50 **3** SE18....123 A3

Building Crafts Coll The
  E15 . . . . 76 B1
Bulbarrow NW8 . . . . 91 D6
Bulganak Rd CR7 . . . . . . 205 A5
Bulinca St W1 . . 115 D2 259 D3
Bullace Row SE5 . . . . 139 B4
Bullard Rd TW11 . . . . 174 D4
Bullards Pl 13 E2 . . . . 96 C4
Bull Dog The (Junc)
  TW15 . . . . 148 A2
Bulleid Way SW1 . . 115 B2 258 D3
Bullen Ho 13 E1 . . . . 96 B3
Bullen St SW11 . . . . 136 C3
Buller Cl SE15 . . . . 140 A5
Buller Rd Barking IG11 . . . 79 C1
  Kensal Green NW10 . . . . . 90 D4
  South Norwood CR7 . . . . 205 B6
  Tottenham N17 . . . . 34 A1
  Wood Green N22 . . . . 32 C1
Bullers Cl DA14 . . . . 191 A5
Bullers Wood Dr BR7 . . . 188 B3
Bullers Wood Sch BR7 . . 188 A2
Bullescroft Rd HA8 . . . . . . 10 D1
Bullfinch Ct 4 SE21 . . . . 161 B2
Bullingham Mans W8 . . . 245 B2
Bull Inn Ct WC2 . . . . 250 B5
Bullivant St E14 . . . . 120 A6
Bull La Chislehurst BR7 . . 189 B3
  Dagenham RM10 . . . . 81 D5
  Edmonton N18 . . . . 33 C5
Bull Rd E15 . . . . 98 D5
Bullrush Cl
  Carshalton SM5 . . . . 218 C6
  Thornton Heath CR0 . . . . 205 C3
Bulls Alley SW14 . . . . . . 133 B3
Bulls Bridge Ind Est
  UB2 . . . . 106 B2
Bulls Bridge Rd UB2 . . . . 106 B2
Bullsbrook Rd UB4 . . . . . 106 C1
Bull's Cross EN1, EN2 . . . . 6 A6
Bull's Gdns SW3 . . . . 257 B4
Bulls Head Pas EC3 . . . . 243 A1
Bull Yd SE15 . . . . 140 A4
Bulmer Gdns HA3 . . . . 43 D2
Bulmer Mews
  W11 . . . . 113 C5 245 A4
Bulow Ct 3 SW6 . . . . . . 135 D3
Bulstrode Ave TW3 . . . . . 129 C2
Bulstrode Gdns TW3 . . . . 129 C2
Bulstrode Pl W1 . . . . 238 B3
Bulstrode Rd TW3 . . . . . . 129 C2
Bulstrode St W1 . . 93 A1 238 B2
Bulwer Court Rd E11 . . . . . 54 B1
Bulwer Ct E11 . . . . 54 B1
Bulwer Gdns EN5 . . . . 2 A1
Bulwer Rd Edmonton N18 . . 33 C4
  Leytonstone E11 . . . . 54 B1
  New Barnet EN5 . . . . 2 A1
Bulwer St W12 . . . . 112 C5
Bunbury Ho SE15 . . . . . . 140 A5
Bungalow Rd SE25 . . . . . 205 C5
Bungalows The
  Leyton E10 . . . . 54 A3
  Mitcham SW16 . . . . 181 B3
Bunhill Row EC1 . . 95 B3 242 C5
Bunhouse Pl SW1 . . . . . . 258 B2
Bunkers Hill London NW11 . . 48 A2
  North Cray DA14 . . . . . . 169 B1
Bunker's Hill DA17 . . . . . 125 C2
Bunning Ho N7 . . . . 72 A4
Bunning Way N7 . . . . 72 B1
Bunn's La NW7 . . . . 27 D4
Bunsen Ho 2 E3 . . . . 97 A5
Bunsen St 3 E3 . . . . 97 A5
Buntingbridge Rd IG2 . . . . 57 B4
Bunting Cl London N9 . . . . 18 D3
  Mitcham CR4 . . . . 202 D4
Bunting St NW9 . . . . 27 C1
Bunton St E18 . . . . 122 C3
Bunyan Rd E17 . . . . 53 A6
Buonaparte Mews SW1 . . 259 C2
Burbage Cl
  Bermondsey SE1 . . 117 B3 262 C5
  Hayes UB3 . . . . 83 B1
Burbage Ho
  18 Deptford SE14 . . . . . . 140 D6
  Shoreditch N1 . . . . 235 D5
Burbage Rd SE21, SE24 . . 161 B4
Burbage Sch 34 N1 . . . . . 95 C5
Burbank KT3 . . . . 199 D6
Burberry Cl KT3 . . . . 177 C1
Burberry Ct 8 N3 . . . . . . 29 D3
Burbidge Rd TW17 . . . . . 192 C5
Burbridge Way N17 . . . . . . 34 A1
Burcham St E14 . . . . 98 A1
Burcharbro Rd SE2 . . . . . 146 D6
Burchell Ct WD23 . . . . 8 A4
Burchell Ho SE11 . . . . . . 260 D2
Burchell Rd Leyton E10 . . . 53 D1
  London SE15 . . . . 140 B4
Burcher Gale Gr 5
  SE15 . . . . 139 D5
Burchetts Way TW17 . . . 192 D3
Burchett Way RM6 . . . . . . 59 B3
Burcote Rd SW18 . . . . . . 158 B4
Burden Cl TW8 . . . . 109 C1
Burden Ho 5 SW8 . . . . . . 270 A3
Burdenshott Ave TW10 . . 132 D1

Burden Way E11 . . . . 77 B6
Burder Cl N1 . . . . 73 C2
Burder Rd N1 . . . . 73 C2
Burdett Ave SW20 . . . . . . 178 A2
Burdett Cl 2 Ealing W7 . . 108 D3
  Sidcup DA14 . . . . 191 A5
Burdett Coutts & Townshend
  CE Prim Sch
  SW1 . . . . 115 D2 259 D3
Burdett Mews 4 W2 . . . . . 91 D1
Burdett Rd
  Richmond TW9 . . . . 132 B2
  Thornton Heath CR0 . . . . 205 B3
  Tower Hamlets E3 . . . . . . 97 B2
Burdetts Rd RM9 . . . . . . 103 B6
Burdock Cl CR0 . . . . 206 D1
Burdock Rd N17 . . . . 52 A6
Burdon Ct 8 E8 . . . . 74 A2
Burdon La SM2 . . . . 217 A1
Bure Ct 17 EN5 . . . . 13 D6
Burfield Cl SW17 . . . . . . 180 B6
Burford Cl Dagenham RM8 . . 80 C5
  Ickenham UB10 . . . . 60 A4
  Ilford IG6 . . . . 57 A5
Burford Ct SE8 . . . . 141 C6
Burford Gdns N13 . . . . 16 B1
Burford Ho
  1 Brentford TW8 . . . . . . 110 A1
  11 South Lambeth SW9 . . . 138 B3
Burford Prim Sch
  Brentford TW8 . . . . 110 A1
  Bromley BR1 . . . . 210 A5
  Forest Hill SE6 . . . . 163 B2
  Newham E6 . . . . 100 A4
  New Malden KT4 . . . . 200 A2
  5 Stratford Marsh E15 . . . 98 B6
  Sutton SM1 . . . . 217 C6
Burford Way CR0 . . . . . . 224 A2
Burford Wlk SW6 . . . . . . 265 D3
Burgate Ct 9 SW9 . . . . . 138 C2
Burges Gr SW13 . . . . 134 B5
Burges Rd E6 . . . . 78 B1
Burgess Ave NW9 . . . . 45 B3
Burgess Bsns Pk SE5 . . . 139 B5
Burgess Cl 4 TW13 . . . . . 173 A6
Burgess Ct 3 London N20 . . 14 D2
  3 Southall UB1 . . . . 85 D1
  Wallend E12 . . . . 78 C1
Burgess Hill NW2 . . . . 69 C4
Burgess Ho 3 SE5 . . . . . . 139 A5
Burgess Mews SW19 . . . . 179 D4
Burgess Park Mans NW6 . . 69 C4
Burgess Rd Leyton E15 . . . 76 C4
  Sutton SM1 . . . . 217 D4
Burgess St E14 . . . . 97 C2
Burge St SE1 . . . . 262 D5
Burgh House & Hampstead
  Mus ★ NW3 . . . . 70 D4
Burghill Rd SE26 . . . . . . 185 A6
Burghley Ave
  Borehamwood WD6 . . . . . 11 A6
  Kingston u T KT3 . . . . . . 177 B2
Burghley Ct SW19 . . . . . . 179 A5
Burghley Hall Cl SW19 . . . 157 B3
Burghley Ho SW19 . . . . . 157 A1
Burghley Pl CR4 . . . . 202 D5
Burghley Rd
  Camden Town NW5 . . . . . . 71 B4
  Leytonstone E11 . . . . 54 C1
  London N8 . . . . 50 C6
  Wimbledon SW19 . . . . . . 179 A6
Burghley Twr W3 . . . . . . 111 D6
Burgh St N1 . . . . 94 D5 234 D4
Burgon St EC4 . . . . 241 D1
Burgos Cl CR0 . . . . 220 C2
Burgos Gr SE10 . . . . 141 D4
Burgoyne Rd
  Ashford TW16 . . . . 171 D4
  Brixton SW9 . . . . 138 B2
  Harringay N4 . . . . 50 D3
  South Norwood SE25 . . . . 205 D5
Burham Cl SE20 . . . . 184 C3
Burhan Uddin Ho E1 . . . . 243 C5
Burhill Gr HA5 . . . . 23 A1
Buriton Ho 9 SW15 . . . . 156 B3
Burke Cl SW15 . . . . 133 C1
Burke Ho 1 SW11 . . . . . . 136 B1
Burke Lodge E13 . . . . 99 B4
Burke St E16 . . . . 98 D2
Burket Cl UB2 . . . . 107 B2
Burland Rd SW11 . . . . . . 158 D6
Burleigh Ave
  Bexley DA15 . . . . 167 D6
  Hackbridge SM6 . . . . . . 219 B5
Burleigh Cl RM7 . . . . 59 D5
Burleigh Coll W6 . . . . . . 112 C2
Burleigh Ct N17 . . . . 34 A4
Burleigh Gdns
  Ashford TW15 . . . . 171 A5
  Osidge N14 . . . . 15 C3
Burleigh Ho Cheam SM3 . . 201 A1
  Chelsea SW3 . . . . 266 D5
  5 North Kensington W10 . . 90 D2
Burleigh Lo 3 SW19 . . . . 179 D3
Burleigh Par N14 . . . . 15 D3
Burleigh Pl SW15 . . . . . . 156 D6
Burleigh Rd Cheam SM3 . . 201 A1
  Enfield EN1 . . . . 5 C1
  Hillingdon UB10 . . . . 82 D6
Burleigh St WC2 . . . . 250 C6

Burleigh Way EN2 . . . . 5 B2
Burleigh Wlk SE6 . . . . . . 164 A3
Burley Cl Chingford E4 . . . 35 C5
  Mitcham SW16 . . . . 181 D1
Burley Ho E1 . . . . 96 D1
Burley Rd E16 . . . . 99 C2
Burlington Apartments
  SE20 . . . . 184 B3
Burlington Arc W1 . . . . . . 249 A5
Burlington Ave
  Richmond TW9 . . . . 132 C4
  Romford RM7 . . . . 59 D3
Burlington Cl
  East Bedfont TW14 . . . . . 149 B4
  5 Newham E6 . . . . 100 A1
  Orpington BR6 . . . . 226 D6
  Paddington W9 . . . . 91 C3
  Pinner HA5 . . . . 40 B6
Burlington Ct
  Chiswick W4 . . . . 133 A5
  Highgate N6 . . . . 49 A1
Burlington Danes Acad
  W12 . . . . 90 B1
Burlington Gate SW20 . . . 179 A1
Burlington Gdns
  Acton Green W4 . . . . 111 A1
  Acton W3 . . . . 111 A5
  Dagenham RM6 . . . . 59 A2
  4 Fulham SW6 . . . . 135 A3
  Marylebone W1 . . 115 C6 249 A5
Burlington Ho 3 NW3 . . . . 70 B3
Burlington Inf Sch E17 . . . 199 D5
Burlington Jun Sch KT3 . . 199 D5
Burlington La W4 . . . . . . 133 B5
Burlington Lo BR7 . . . . . . 188 B3
Burlington Lodge SW6 . . . 135 A3
Burlington Mews
  Acton W3 . . . . 111 A5
  2 Putney SW15 . . . . 157 B6
Burlington Park Ho 6
  HA7 . . . . 25 C6
Burlington Pl
  Fulham SW6 . . . . 135 A3
  Woodford IG8 . . . . 21 A1
Burlington Rd
  Acton Green W4 . . . . 111 A1
  Enfield EN2 . . . . 5 B4
  Fulham SW6 . . . . 135 A3
  Hounslow TW7 . . . . 130 B4
  Muswell Hill N10 . . . . 49 A6
  New Malden KT3 . . . . . . 199 D5
  South Norwood CR7 . . . . 183 D1
  Tottenham N17 . . . . 34 A2
Burlington Rise EN4 . . . . . 14 D4
Burma Ho N16 . . . . 73 B4
Burmarsh 6 NW5 . . . . . . 71 A2
Burmarsh Rd SE20 . . . . . 184 C2
Burma Terr 11 SE19 . . . . 183 C5
Burmester Ho SW17 . . . . 158 A1
Burmester Rd SW17 . . . . 158 A1
Burnaby Cres W4 . . . . . . 133 A4
Burnaby St 31 SE16 . . . . 118 A4
Burnaby Gdns W4 . . . . . . 132 D6
Burnaby St SW10 . 136 A3 266 B3
Burnand Ho 3 W14 . . . . . 112 D3
Burnbrae Cl N12 . . . . 29 D4
Burnbury Rd SW12 . . . . . 159 C3
Burncroft Ave EN3 . . . . 6 C3
Burne Jones Ho W14 . . . . 254 B3
Burnell Ave
  Richmond TW10 . . . . 175 C5
  Welling DA16 . . . . 146 A3
Burnell Gdns HA7 . . . . 25 D1
Burnell Ho 18 SW2 . . . . . 160 C3
Burnell Rd SM1 . . . . 217 D4
Burnell Wlk SE1 . . . . 263 D2
Burnels Ave E6 . . . . 100 C4
Burness Cl N7 . . . . 72 B2
Burne St NW1 . . . . 237 A4
Burnett Cl E9 . . . . 74 C3
Burnett Ct SW11 . . . . . . 267 A1
Burnett Ho 6 SE13 . . . . . 142 A1
Burney Ave KT5 . . . . 198 B4
Burney Ho 3 SW16 . . . . . 181 C5
Burney St SE10 . . . . 142 A5
Burnfoot Ave
  SW6 . . . . 135 A4 264 B1
Burnham NW3 . . . . 70 C1
Burnham Ave UB10 . . . . . . 61 A4
Burnham Cl
  Bermondsey SE1 . . . . . . 263 D3
  Enfield EN1 . . . . 5 C5
  Harrow HA3 . . . . 43 A3
  Hendon NW7 . . . . 28 A3
Burnham Cres E11 . . . . . . 55 C5
Burnham Ct
  Bayswater W2 . . . . 245 D6
  Hendon NW4 . . . . 46 C6
  15 Stanmore HA7 . . . . . . 25 C5
Burnham Dr KT4 . . . . 216 D6
Burnham Est 8 E2 . . . . . . 96 C4
Burnham Gdns
  Cranford TW4 . . . . 128 B4
  Croydon CR0 . . . . 205 B2
  Hayes UB3 . . . . 105 B3
Burnham Rd
  Chingford Hatch E4 . . . . . 35 B5
  Dagenham RM9 . . . . 102 B6
  Morden SM4 . . . . 201 D5

Burnham Rd continued
  Sidcup DA14 . . . . 169 A2
Burnham St
  Bethnal Green E2 . . . . 96 C4
  Kingston u T KT2 . . . . . . 176 C2
Burnham Way
  Ealing W13 . . . . 109 B3
  Penge SE26 . . . . 185 B5
Burnhill Ho EC1 . . . . 235 A1
Burnhill Rd BR3 . . . . 185 C1
Burnley Cl WD19 . . . . 22 C5
Burnley Rd London SW9 . . 138 B3
  Willesden NW10 . . . . 68 A3
Burnsall St SW3 . . 114 C1 257 B2
Burns Ave Blackfen DA15 . . 168 B5
  Feltham TW14 . . . . 150 A5
  Ilford RM6 . . . . 58 C2
  Sidcup DA15 . . . . 168 B5
Burns Cl Bexley DA16 . . . . 145 D6
  Hayes UB4 . . . . 84 A2
  Mitcham SW17 . . . . 180 D4
  Walthamstow E17 . . . . . . 54 A5
Burns Ct Tottenham N17 . . . 34 B3
  Wallington SM6 . . . . 219 B1
Burns Ho
  18 Bethnal Green E2 . . . . 96 C4
  Bexley DA6 . . . . 146 C4
  1 Islington N7 . . . . 72 B2
  Kennington SE17 . . . . . . 261 D1
  11 Stoke Newington N16 . . 73 C4
Burn's Ho NW10 . . . . 89 C6
Burnside Ave E4 . . . . 35 B4
Burnside Cl Barnet EN5 . . . 1 C2
  Rotherhithe SE16 . . . . . . 118 D5
  Twickenham TW1 . . . . . . 153 A5
Burnside Cres HA0 . . . . . . 87 D6
Burnside Ct 11 SM6 . . . . 219 A5
Burnside Rd RM8 . . . . 58 D1
Burns Rd
  Battersea SW11 . . . . 136 D3
  Ealing W13 . . . . 109 B4
  Wembley HA0 . . . . 88 A5
Burns Way TW5 . . . . 128 D4
Burnt Ash Hill Lee SE12 . . 164 D5
Burnt Ash Hts BR1 . . . . . 187 B5
Burnt Ash La BR1, SE12 . . 187 B5
Burnt Ash Prim Sch
  BR1 . . . . 187 A5
Burnt Ash Rd SE12 . . . . . 164 D6
Burnthwaite Rd
  SW6 . . . . 135 B5 264 D3
BURNT OAK 27 B3
Burnt Oak Broadway
  HA8 . . . . 26 D3
Burnt Oak Fields HA8 . . . . 27 A2
Burnt Oak Jun Sch
  DA15 . . . . 168 A3
Burnt Oak La DA15 . . . . . 168 B3
Burnt Oak L Ctr HA8 . . . . 27 B2
Burnt Oak Sta HA8 . . . . . 27 A2
Burntwood Cl SE18 . . . . . 158 C3
Burntwood Ct SW17 . . . . 158 A1
Burntwood Grange Rd
  SW18 . . . . 158 C3
Burntwood La SW17 . . . . 158 B2
Burntwood Sch SW17 . . . 158 B2
Burntwood View
  SE19 . . . . 183 D5
Buross St E1 . . . . 96 B1
Burpham Cl UB4 . . . . 84 D2
Burrage Ct 17 SE16 . . . . 118 D2
Burrage Gr SE18 . . . . . . 123 A2
Burrage Pl SE18 . . . . 122 D1
Burrage Rd SE18 . . . . . . 123 A1
Burrard Ho 11 E2 . . . . . . 96 C5
Burrard Rd Newham E16 . . 99 B5
  West Hampstead NW6 . . . 69 C4
Burr Cl Bexleyheath DA7 . . 147 B2
  St George in t East E1 . . . 118 A5
Burrell Cl Croydon CR0 . . . 207 A3
  Edgware HA8 . . . . 10 D2
Burrell Ct HA1 . . . . 42 B2
Burrell Ho 4 TW1 . . . . . . 153 B4
Burrell Row BR3 . . . . 185 C1
Burrells 1 BR3 . . . . 185 D1
Burrell St SE1 . . . . 116 D6 251 C4
Burrell's Wharf Sq E14 . . . 119 D1
Burrhill Ct SE16 . . . . 118 D3
Burritt Rd KT1 . . . . 176 C1
Burrmead Ct NW2 . . . . 67 D5
Burroughs Gdns NW4 . . . . 46 B5
Burroughs The NW4 . . . . . 46 B5
Burrow Ho 19 SW9 . . . . . 138 B3
Burrow Rd SE22 . . . . 139 C1
Burrows Mews SE1 . . . . . 251 C2
Burrows Rd NW10 . . . . . . 90 C4
Burrow Wlk SE21 . . . . . . 161 A4
Burr Rd SW18 . . . . 157 C4
Bursar St SE1 . . . . 253 A3
Bursdon Cl DA15 . . . . . . 167 D2
Bursland Rd EN3 . . . . 6 D1
Burslem St E1 . . . . 96 A1
Bursted Wood Prim Sch
  DA7 . . . . 147 D3
Burstock Rd SW15 . . . . . 135 A1
Burston Rd SW15 . . . . . . 156 D6
Burstow Rd SW20 . . . . . . 179 A2

Burtenshaw Rd KT7 . . . . . 197 A3
Burtley Cl N4 . . . . 51 A1
Burton Bank N1 . . . . 73 B1
Burton Cl
  Chessington KT9 . . . . . . 213 D1
  South Norwood CR7 . . . . 205 B6
Burton Ct Chelsea SW3 . . 257 D2
  10 Friern Barnet N11 . . . . 30 D5
  Thames Ditton KT7 . . . . . 197 A3
Burton Dr EN3 . . . . 7 C6
Burton Gdns TW5 . . . . . . 129 B4
Burton Gr SE17 . . . . 262 C1
Burton Ho
  8 Bermondsey SE16 . . . . 118 B4
  Brixton SE5 . . . . 138 D4
  Penge SE26 . . . . 184 B5
Burtonhole Cl NW7 . . . . . . 28 C6
Burtonhole La
  Finchley NW7, NW12 . . . . 29 A6
  Mill Hill NW7 . . . . 28 D6
Burton La 3 SW9 . . . . . . 138 C3
Burton Lo 6 SW15 . . . . . 158 D3
Burton Mews SW1 . . . . . . 258 B3
Burton Pl WC1 . . . . 232 D1
Burton Rd
  7 Brixton SW9 . . . . 138 C3
  Brixton SW9 . . . . 138 D3
  Brondesbury NW6 . . . . . . 69 B1
  Kingston u T KT2 . . . . . . 176 A3
  Wanstead E18 . . . . 55 B6
Burtons Ct E15 . . . . 76 B1
Burtons Rd TW12 . . . . . . 174 A6
Burton St WC1 . . 93 D3 239 D6
Burtonwood Ho N4 . . . . . . 51 B2
Burt Rd E16 . . . . 121 C5
Burtt Ho 6 N1 . . . . 95 C4
Burtwell La SE21, SE27 . . 183 B6
Burvill Ct SW20 . . . . 178 C2
Burwash Ho SE1 . . . . 252 D1
Burwash Rd SE18 . . . . . . 123 B1
Burway Cl CR2 . . . . 221 C2
Burwell 2 KT1 . . . . 176 C1
Burwell Ave UB6 . . . . 64 C2
Burwell Cl 27 E1 . . . . 96 B1
Burwell Rd E10 . . . . 53 A1
Burwell Wlk 14 E3 . . . . . . 97 C3
Burwood Ave Hayes BR2 . . 225 B6
  Pinner HA5 . . . . 40 C4
Burwood Cl KT6 . . . . 198 C1
Burwood Ho 11 SW9 . . . . 138 D1
Burwood Lo SW9 . . . . . . 179 B6
Burwood Pl Barnet EN4 . . . 2 A4
  Paddington W2 . . . . 237 B2
Bury Ave Hayes UB4 . . . . . 83 C5
  Ruislip HA4 . . . . 39 A3
Bury Cl SE16 . . . . 118 D5
Bury Ct EC3 . . . . 243 B2
Buryfield Ct 28 SE8 . . . . 118 D2
Bury Gr SM4 . . . . 201 D4
Bury Hall Villas N9 . . . . . . 17 C4
Bury Pl WC1 . . . . 94 A2 240 B1
Bury Rd Chingford E4 . . . . 20 C6
  Dagenham RM10 . . . . 81 D3
  Hornsey N22 . . . . 50 C6
Bury St W N9 . . . . 17 C4
Buryside Cl IG2 . . . . 57 D5
Bury St Edmonton N9 . . . . 18 A3
  Ruislip HA4 . . . . 39 B3
  St James SW1 . . . . 115 C5 249 B4
  Whitechapel EC3 . . . 95 C1 243 B2
Bury Wlk SW3 . . . . 114 C1 257 A2
Burywood Ct EN3 . . . . 6 C3
Busbridge Ho 24 E14 . . . . 97 C2
Busby Ho SW16 . . . . 181 C6
Busby Mews 5 NW1 . . . . . 71 D2
Busby Pl NW5 . . . . 71 D2
Busch Cl TW7 . . . . 131 B4
Busch Cnr TW7 . . . . 131 B4
Bushbaby Cl SE1 . . . . . . 263 A5
Bushberry Rd E9 . . . . 75 A2
Bush Cl IG2 . . . . 57 B4
Bush Cotts 2 SW18 . . . . 157 C6
Bush Ct London N14 . . . . . 15 C3
  7 Shepherd's Bush W12 . . 112 C4
Bushell Cl SW2 . . . . 160 B2
Bushell Gn WD23 . . . . 8 B2
Bushell Ho 3 SE27 . . . . . 183 A6
Bushell St 18 E1 . . . . 118 A5
Bushell Way BR7 . . . . . . 188 C5
BUSHEY 8 A2
Bushey Ave Crofton BR5 . . 211 B2
  Snaresbrook E18 . . . . . . 54 D6
Bushey Cl Chingford E4 . . . 20 A1
  Ickenham UB10 . . . . 60 C6
Bushey Ct SW20 . . . . 178 B1
Bushey Down SW12 . . . . . 159 B2
Bushey Hall SE5 . . . . 139 D4
BUSHEY HEATH 8 C4
Bushey Heath Prim Sch
  WD23 . . . . 8 B3
Bushey Hill Rd SE5 . . . . . 139 D4
Bushey Ho SE20 . . . . 165 C1
Bushey La SM1 . . . . 217 D4
Bushey Lees DA15 . . . . . 167 D5
BUSHEY MEAD 200 B4
Bushey Meads Sch WD23 . . 8 A6
Bushey Rd Croydon CR0 . . 223 C6

Bushey Rd continued
Hayes UB3 . . . . 105 C2
Ickenham UB10 . . . . .60 C6
Newham E13 . . . . .99 C5
South Tottenham N15 . . . . . .51 C3
Sutton SM1 . . . . .217 C4
West Barnes SW20 . . . . . . .178 D1
Bushey Way BR3 . . . . .208 B4
Bush Fair Ct N14 . . . . .15 B5
Bushfield Cl HA8 . . . . .10 D2
Bushfield Cres HA8 . . . . . . .10 D2
Bushfield Ho N5 . . . . .73 A3
Bush Gr London NW9 . . . . . .45 A2
Stanmore HA7 . . . . .25 D2
Bushgrove Rd RM8 . . . . .80 D5
BUSH HILL 17 B5
Bush Hill N21 . . . . .17 A5
Bush Hill Par EN1 . . . . .17 C5
BUSH HILL PARK 17 C5
Bush Hill Park Prim Sch
EN1 . . . . .18 A6
Bush Hill Park Sta EN1 . . . .17 D5
Bush Hill Park Enfield EN21 . .17 B5
Harrow HA3 . . . . .44 B3
Bush Ind Est NW10 . . . . .89 B3
Bush La EC4 . . . . **117** B6 **252** C6
Bushmead Cl ⁷ N15 . . . . . . .51 C5
Bushmoor Cres SE18 . . . . .144 D5
Bushnell Rd SW17 . . . . .159 B1
Bush Rd Bermondsey SE8 . .118 D2
Hackney E8 . . . . .96 B6
Littleton TW17 . . . . .192 B4
Wanstead E11 . . . . .55 A2
Woodford IG9 . . . . .37 D6
Bushway RM8 . . . . .80 D5
Bushwood E11 . . . . .55 A1
Bushwood Dr
SE1 . . . . **117** D2 **263** D3
Bushwood Rd TW9 . . . . . . .132 C6
Bushy Ct KT1 . . . . .175 C2
Bushy Park Gdns TW12 . . .174 B5
Bushy Park Rd TW11 . . . . .175 B3
Bushy Rd TW11 . . . . .174 D3
Business Acad Bexley The
DA18 . . . . .125 A4
Business Design Ctr✶
N1 . . . . **94** C6 **234** B5
Buspace Studios ³ W10 . .91 A3
Butcher Row E1 . . . . .96 D1
Butchers Rd E16 . . . . .99 A1
Bute Ave TW10 . . . . .154 A2
Bute Ct SM6 . . . . .219 C3
Bute Gardens W SM6 . . . .219 C3
Bute Gdns
Hammersmith W6 . . . . .112 D2
Wallington SM6 ² 219 C3
Bute House Prep Sch ²
W6 . . . . .112 D2
Bute Mews NW1 . . . . .48 A4
Bute Rd Ilford IG6 . . . . .56 D4
Thornton Heath CR0 . . . . . .204 C1
Wallington SM6 . . . . .219 C4
Bute St SW7 . . . .**114** B2 **256** C4
Bute Wlk ¹⁸ N1 . . . . .73 B2
Butfield Ho ⁶ E9 . . . . .74 C2
Butler Ave HA1 . . . . .42 B2
Butler Cl HA8 . . . . .26 D1
Butler Ct Dagenham RM8 . . .81 C4
Wembley HA0 . . . . .65 A4
Butler Ho
³² Bethnal Green E2 . . . . .96 C4
⁵ Brixton SW9 . . . . .138 D4
¹¹ Poplar E14 . . . . .97 B1
Butler Pl SW1 . . . . .259 C6
Butler Rd Dagenham RM8 . . .80 B4
Harrow HA1 . . . . .42 A2
Willesden NW10 . . . . .67 D1
Butlers Cl TW3 . . . . .129 B1
Butlers & Colonial Wharf
SE1 .253 C2
Butler's Cotts DA7 . . . . . . .147 C3
Butlers Farm Cl TW10 . . . .175 D6
Butler St
³³ Bethnal Green E2 . . . . .96 C4
Hillingdon UB10 . . . . .82 D3
Butler's Wharf W SE1 . . . .253 C3
Butley Ct ⁸ E3 . . . . .97 A5
Butt Ct SM4 . . . . .202 A3
Buttercup Cl UB5 . . . . .63 B2
Butterfield Cl
¹ Bermondsey SE16 . . . . . . .118 B4
Tottenham N17 . . . . .33 A4
Twickenham TW1 . . . . .152 D5
Butterfield Ho ⁴ EN2 . . . . . . .4 D3
Butterfield Mews ¹⁵
SE18 . . . . .144 D6
Butterfields E17 . . . . .54 A4
Butterfield Sq ¹⁰ E6 . . . . . .100 B1
Butterfly Ct ¹ E6 . . . . .100 B4
Butterfly La SE9 . . . . .166 D5
Butterfly Wlk ⁴ SE5 . . . . .139 B4
Butter Hill SM5, SM6 . . . . .219 A4
Butteridges Cl RM9 . . . . . .103 B6
Buttermere NW1 . . . . .231 D2
Buttermere Cl
Bermondsey SE1 . . . . .263 C3

Buttermere Cl continued
East Bedfont TW14 . . . . . . .149 D3
Leyton E11 . . . . .76 B4
West Barnes SM4 . . . . .200 D3
Buttermere Ct NW8 . . . . . .229 C6
Buttermere Dr SW15 . . . . .157 A6
Buttermere Ho
London N12 . . . . .30 C5
¹³ Tower Hamlets E3 . . . . . . .97 B4
Buttermere Wlk ⁹ E8 . . . . .73 D2
Butterwick W6 . . . . .112 C2
Butterworth Ct SW16 . . . . .160 A1
Butterworth Gdns IG8 . . . . .37 A5
Buttery Mews N14 . . . . .16 A1
Buttesland St N1 . . . **95** B4 **235** D2
Buttfield Cl RM10 . . . . .81 D2
Buttmarsh Cl SE18 . . . . . . .122 D1
Buttsbury Rd IG1 . . . . .79 A3
Butts Cotts TW13 . . . . .151 B1
Butts Cres TW13 . . . . .151 C1
Butts Ho TW13 . . . . .151 C1
Butts Piece UB5 . . . . .84 B5
Butts Rd BR1 . . . . .186 C5
Butts The TW8 . . . . .131 D6
Buxhall Cres E9 . . . . .75 B2
Buxlow Prep Sch HA9 . . . . .66 A5
Buxted Rd
Camberwell SE22 . . . . .139 C1
Colney Hatch N12 . . . . .30 C5
Dalston E8 . . . . .73 D1
Buxton Cl London N9 . . . . . .18 C2
Woodford IG8 . . . . .37 D4
Buxton Cres SM3 . . . . .217 A4
Buxton Ct ¹ Leyton E11 . . . .54 D2
Shoreditch N1 . . . . .235 B2
Buxton Dr
Kingston u T KT3 . . . . .177 B1
Leytonstone E11 . . . . .54 C5
Buxton Gdns W3 . . . . .110 D6
Buxton Ho
Leytonstone E11 . . . . .54 C5
³ London SW11 . . . . .136 B1
Buxton Lo E11 . . . . .77 B6
Buxton Mews SW4 . . . . . . .137 D3
Buxton Rd Chingford E4 . . . .20 B4
Ilford IG2 . . . . .57 C3
Mortlake SW14 . . . . .133 C2
Newham E6 . . . . .100 A4
Stratford E15 . . . . .76 C3
Thornton Heath CR7 . . . . . .204 D4
Upper Holloway N19 . . . . . . .49 D1
Walthamstow E17 . . . . .53 A5
Willesden NW2 . . . . .68 B2
Buxton St E1 . . . . **95** D3 **243** D5
Buzzard Creek Ind Est
IG11 .102 A2
Byam Shaw Sch of Art ⁸
N19 . . . . .71 D6
Byam St SW6 . . . . .136 A3
Byards Croft SW16 . . . . . . .181 D2
Byards Ct SE16 . . . . .118 D3
Byas Ho ⁶ E3 . . . . .97 B4
Byatt Wlk TW12 . . . . .173 A6
Bychurch End ¹¹ TW11 . . . .174 D5
Bycroft Rd UB1 . . . . .85 C3
Bycroft St SE20 . . . . .184 D3
Bycullah Ave EN2 . . . . .4 D3
Bycullah Rd EN2 . . . . .4 D3
Byefield Cl SE16 . . . . .119 A4
Byegrove Ct SW19 . . . . . . .180 B4
Byegrove Rd SW19 . . . . . . .180 B4
Byelands Cl ¹² SE16 . . . . . .118 D5
Bye The W3 . . . . .89 C1
Bye Ways TW2 . . . . .151 D1
Byeways The KT5 . . . . .198 D4
Byeway The SW14 . . . . . . .133 A2
Bye Way The HA3 . . . . .24 D2
Byfeld Gdns SW13 . . . . . . .134 A4
Byfield Cl SE16 . . . . .118 D2
Byfield Rd TW7 . . . . .131 A2
Byford Cl E15 . . . . .76 C1
Bygrove CR0 . . . . .223 D1
Bygrove Prim Sch ²¹ E14. .97 D1
Bygrove St E14 . . . . .97 D1
Byland Cl
Abbey Wood SE2 . . . . .124 B3
Carshalton SM4 . . . . .202 B2
Southgate N21 . . . . .16 A4
Byne Rd Carshalton SM5 . . .218 C6
Forest Hill SE26 . . . . .184 C5
Bynes Rd CR2 . . . . .221 B1
Byng Pl WC1 . . . .**93** D3 **239** C5
Byng St E14 . . . . .119 C4
Bynon Ave DA7 . . . . .147 B2
Byre Rd N14 . . . . .15 B5
Byrne Cl ² CR0 . . . . .204 D3
Byrne Ho ¹¹ SW2 . . . . .160 B6
Byrne Rd SW12 . . . . .159 B2
Byron Ave
Borehamwood WD6 . . . . .10 C6
Cranford TW4 . . . . .128 B3
Plashet E12 . . . . .78 A2
Queensbury NW9 . . . . .44 D6
Sutton SM1 . . . . .218 B4
West Barnes KT3 . . . . .200 A4
Woodford E18 . . . . .36 D1
Byron Ave E SM1 . . . . .218 B4
Byron Cl Feltham TW12 . . . .173 B6
Forest Hill SE26 . . . . .185 A6

Byron Cl continued
Hackney E8 . . . . .96 A6
Streatham SW16 . . . . .182 A4
Thamesmead SE28 . . . . . . .124 C5
Walton-on-T KT12 . . . . .195 A1
Byron Court Prim Sch
HA0 . . . . .65 C6
Byron Ct Chelsea SW3 . . . . .257 B3
Dulwich SE21 . . . . .162 A3
Ealing W7 . . . . .109 A2
Enfield EN2 . . . . .4 D3
³ Hampstead NW6 . . . . .70 A1
Harrow HA1 . . . . .42 C3
⁴ New Barnet EN5 . . . . .2 A1
Paddington W9 . . . . .91 C3
¹ Richmond TW10 . . . . .175 D6
South Norwood CR7 . . . . . . .183 A1
St Pancras WC1 . . . . .240 C6
¹¹ Wanstead E11 . . . . .55 A5
Woodford E18 . . . . .37 B2
Byron Dr East Finchley N2 . .48 B3
Erith DA8 . . . . .147 D5
Byron Gdns SM1 . . . . .218 B4
Byron Hill Rd HA1, HA2 . . . .64 C6
Byron Ho ⁵ BR3 . . . . .185 D4
Byron Mews
Hampstead NW3 . . . . .70 C4
² Maida Vale W9 . . . . .91 C3
Byron Par UB10 . . . . .83 A3
Byron Rd Dollis Hill NW2 . . .68 B6
Ealing W5 . . . . .110 B5
Edgware NW7 . . . . .28 A5
Harrow HA1 . . . . .42 C3
Leyton E10 . . . . .53 D1
Walthamstow E17 . . . . .53 C6
Wealdstone HA3 . . . . .24 D1
Wembley HA0 . . . . .65 C5
Byron St E14 . . . . .98 A1
Byron Way Hayes UB4 . . . . .83 D3
Northolt UB5 . . . . .85 A4
West Drayton UB7 . . . . .104 B2
Bysouth Cl N15 . . . . .51 B5
Bythorn St SW9 . . . . .138 B1
Byton Rd SW17 . . . . .180 D4
Byward Ave TW14 . . . . .150 C5
Byward St EC3 . . . . . .**117** C6 **253** B5
Bywater Ho SE18 . . . . .122 A3
Bywater Pl SE16 . . . . .119 A5
Bywater St SW3 . . . . .**114** D1 **257** C2
Byway The KT19 . . . . .215 D4
Bywell Pl W1 . . . . .239 A3
Bywood Ave CR0 . . . . .206 D3
Bywood Terr CR0 . . . . .206 C3
Byworth Ho HA7 . . . . .25 C4
Byworth Wlk N19 . . . . .50 A1

C

Cabbell St NW1 . . . . .**92** C2 **237** A3
Cabinet Off SW1 . . . . .250 A2
Cabinet War Rooms &
Churchill Mus✶
SW1 . . . . **115** D4 **249** D2
Cabinet Way E4 . . . . .35 B4
Cable Ho WC1 . . . . .234 A2
Cable Pl SE10 . . . . .142 A4
Cable St E1 . . . . .118 B6
Cabot Ct SE16 . . . . .118 D3
Cabot Sq E14 . . . . .119 C5
Cabot Way ³ E6 . . . . .99 D6
Cabul Rd SW11 . . . . .136 C3
Cactus Cl SE5 . . . . .139 C3
Cactus Wlk W12 . . . . .89 D1
Cadbury Cl
Ashford TW16 . . . . .171 C3
Isleworth TW7 . . . . .131 A4
Cadbury Rd TW16 . . . . .171 C4
Cadbury Way ¹ SE16 . . . . .118 A2
Caddington Cl EN4 . . . . .14 C6
Caddington Rd NW2 . . . . . . .69 A5
Caddis Cl HA7 . . . . .24 D3
Cadell Cl E2 . . . . .95 D5
Cadell Ho ¹² E2 . . . . .95 D5
Cade Rd SE10 . . . . .142 B4
Cader Rd SW18 . . . . .158 A5
Cadet Dr SE1 . . . . . . **117** D1 **263** D2
Cade Tyler Ho ¹⁰ SE10 . . . .142 A4
Cadiz St SE17 . . . . . . **117** A1 **262** B1
Cadley Terr SE23 . . . . .162 C2
Cadman Cl SW9 . . . . .138 D5
Cadmer Cl KT3 . . . . .199 C5
Cadmore Ho ⁴ N1 . . . . .72 D1
Cadmus Cl ⁹ SW4 . . . . .137 D2
Cadmus Ct ⁶ SW9 . . . . .138 C4
Cadnam Lo E14 . . . . .120 B3
Cadnam Point ¹⁵ SW15 . . .156 B3
Cadogan Cl
Beckenham BR3 . . . . .186 B1
Hackney Wick E9 . . . . .75 B1
Harrow HA2 . . . . .63 D4
Teddington TW11 . . . . .174 C5
Cadogan Ct Chelsea SW3 . .257 C3
New Malden KT3 . . . . .199 C5
Sutton SM2 . . . . .217 D2
Cadogan Ct Gdns SW1 . . . .258 A4
Cadogan Gate
SW1 . . . . **114** D2 **257** D4
Cadogan Gdns
Chelsea SW3 . . . . **114** D2 **257** D3

Cadogan Gdns continued
Finchley N3 . . . . .29 D2
Southgate N21 . . . . .16 C6
Wanstead E18 . . . . .55 B6
Cadogan Hall✶ SW1 . . . . . . .258 A4
Cadogan Ho SW3 . . . . .266 D5
Cadogan La SW1 .**115** A3 **258** A5
Cadogan Pl SW1 . **114** D3 **257** D5
Cadogan Rd
Kingston u T KT6 . . . . .197 D4
Woolwich SE18 . . . . .122 D3
Woolwich SE18 . . . . .123 A3
Cadogan Sq
SW1 . . . . **114** D3 **257** D5
Cadogan Terr E9 . . . . .75 B1
Cadoxton Ave ³ N15 . . . . . .51 D3
Cadwallon Rd SE9 . . . . .167 A2
Caedmon Rd N7 . . . . .72 B4
Caerleon Cl
Claygate KT10 . . . . .213 B1
Sidcup DA14 . . . . .190 C5
Caerleon Terr SE2 . . . . .124 B2
Caernarfon Ho HA7 . . . . .25 A5
Caernarvon Cl CR4 . . . . . . .204 A6
Caernarvon Ct ³ KT5 . . . . . .198 B4
Caernarvon Ho W2 . . . . . . .236 A2
Caesar Ct ²⁵ E2 . . . . .96 D5
Caesar's Way TW17 . . . . . .193 B3
Caesars Wlk CR4 . . . . .202 D4
Cahill St EC1 . . . . .242 B5
Cahir St E14 . . . . .119 D2
Cain Ct ² W5 . . . . .87 C2
Caine Ho W3 . . . . .110 D4
Cain's La TW14 . . . . .149 C6
Caird St W10 . . . . .91 B4
Cairn Ave W5 . . . . .109 D5
Cairndale Cl BR1 . . . . .186 D3
Cairnfield Ave NW2 . . . . .67 D5
Cairnfield Ct NW2 . . . . .67 C5
Cairngorm Cl ³ TW11 . . . . .175 A5
Cairn Ho ³ SW19 . . . . .180 C3
Cairns Ho ³ N7 . . . . .72 B4
Cairns Mews SE18 . . . . . . .144 A4
Cairns Rd SW11 . . . . .158 C6
Cairn Way HA7 . . . . .24 D4
Cairo New Rd CR0 . . . . .220 D6
Cairo Rd E17 . . . . .53 C5
Caister Ho N7 . . . . .72 B2
Caistor Ho
¹⁰ Balham SW12 . . . . .159 B4
⁵ West Ham E15 . . . . .98 D6
Caistor Mews SW12 . . . . . .159 B4
Caistor Park Rd E15 . . . . . . .98 D6
Caistor Rd SW12 . . . . .159 B4
Caithness Gdns DA15 . . . . .167 D5
Caithness Ho N1 . . . . .233 C6
Caithness Rd
Hammersmith W14 . . . . .112 D3
Mitcham CR4 . . . . .181 B3
Calabria Rd N5 . . . . .72 D3
Calais Gate SE5 . . . . .138 D4
Calais St SE5 . . . . .138 D4
Calbourne Rd SW12 . . . . . .159 A4
Calcott Wlk SE9 . . . . .187 D6
Calcraft Ho ¹⁰ E2 . . . . .96 C5
Caldbeck Ave KT4 . . . . .200 B1
Caldecot Ct SE5 . . . . .139 A3
Caldecote ³ KT1 . . . . .176 C1
Caldecote Gdns WD23 . . . . .8 C4
Caldecote La WD23 . . . . .8 D5
Caldecot Rd SE5 . . . . .139 A3
Caldecott Way E5 . . . . .74 D5
Calder Ave UB6 . . . . .86 D5
Calder Cl EN1 . . . . .5 C2
Calder Ct SE16 . . . . .119 B5
Calder Gdns HA8 . . . . .44 C6
Calder Ho UB5 . . . . .85 A6
Calderon Ho NW8 . . . . .230 A4
Calderon Pl ²⁰ W10 . . . . . . .90 C2
Calderon Rd E11 . . . . .76 B5
Calder Rd SM4 . . . . .202 A4
Caldervale Rd SW4 . . . . . . .159 D6
Calderwood Pl EN4 . . . . .1 D4
Calderwood St SE18 . . . . . .122 C2
Caldew St NW7 . . . . .28 A3
Caldew St SE5 . . . . .139 B5
Caldicote Gn NW9 . . . . .45 C3
Caldon Ho ² UB5 . . . . .85 B3
Caldwell Rd WD19 . . . . .22 D6
Caldwell St SW9 . . **138** B5 **270** D3
Caldy Rd DA17 . . . . .125 D3
Caldy Wlk ¹⁹ N1 . . . . .73 A2
Caleb St SE1 . . . . .252 B2
Caledonia Ct
Barking IG11 . . . . .102 C5
Hendon NW4 . . . . .28 C1
Caledonia Ho ¹⁶ E14 . . . . . . .99 A1
Caledonian Cl ¹ IG3 . . . . . . .58 A1
Caledonian Ct UB5 . . . . .85 A3
Caledonian Market
SE1 . . . . **117** C3 **263** B6
Caledonian Rd
Islington N1 . . . .**94** B6 **233** C5
Lower Holloway N7 . . . . .72 B2
Caledonian Road &
Barnsbury Sta N7 . . . . .72 B2
Caledonian Sq ⁶ NW1 . . . . .71 D2

Caledonian Wharf Rd
E14 . . . . .120 B2
Caledonia Rd TW19 . . . . . . .148 A3
Caledonia St N1 . . . . .233 B3
Caledon Rd East Ham E6 . . .78 B1
Hackbridge SM5, SM6 . . . . .219 A4
Cale St SW3 . . . .**114** C1 **257** A2
Caletock Way SE10 . . . . . . .120 D1
Calgarth NW1 . . . . .232 B3
Calgary Ct ³⁰ SE16 . . . . .118 C4
Caliban Twr ⁹ N1 . . . . .95 C5
Calico Ho ⁴ SW11 . . . . .136 A2
Calico Row ⁵ SW11 . . . . . . .136 A2
Calidore Cl SW2 . . . . .160 B5
California Bldg ² SE13 . . . . .141 D4
California La WD23 . . . . .8 B3
California Rd KT3 . . . . .199 A6
Callaby Terr ¹¹ N1 . . . . .73 B2
Callaghan Cl SE13 . . . . .142 C1
Callahan Cotts ⁸ E1 . . . . . . .96 C2
Callander Rd SE6 . . . . .164 A2
Callanders The WD23 . . . . . .8 C3
Callan Sch The
W1 . . . . **93** C1 **239** B2
Callard Ave N13 . . . . .32 C6
Callcott Ct NW6 . . . . .69 B1
Callcott Rd NW6 . . . . .69 B1
Callcott St W8 . . . . .245 A4
Callendar Rd SW7 . . . . .256 C6
Callingham Cl ¹³ E14 . . . . . . .97 B2
Callingham Ho ⁴ SW4 . .138 A2
Callis Farm Cl TW19 . . . . . .148 A5
Callis Rd E17 . . . . .53 B3
Callonfield ³ E17 . . . . .53 A5
Callow St SW3 . . . . . .**136** B6 **266** C6
Calmington Rd SE5 . . . . . . .139 C6
Calmont Rd BR1 . . . . .186 C4
Calonne Rd SW19 . . . . .178 D6
Calshot Ho N1 . . . . .233 C4
Calshot Rd TW6 . . . . .126 D3
Calshot St N1 . . . .**94** B5 **233** C3
Calshot Way Enfield EN2 . . . .4 D2
Harlington TW6 . . . . .126 C3
Calstock NW1 . . . . .232 C5
Calstock Ho SE11 . . . . .261 B2
Calthorpe Gdns
Edgware HA8 . . . . .26 B5
Sutton SM1 . . . . .218 A5
Calthorpe St WC1 . . **94** B3 **240** D6
Calton Ave SE21 . . . . .161 C5
Calton Rd EN5 . . . . .14 B5
Calumet SE SW17 . . . . .180 C4
Calver ¹³ NW5 . . . . .71 B4
Calver Ct E17 . . . . .54 B6
Calverley Cl BR3 . . . . .185 D4
Calverley Cres RM10 . . . . . .81 C6
Calverley Gdns HA3 . . . . . . .43 D2
Calverley Gr N19 . . . . .49 D1
Calverley Rd KT17 . . . . .216 A2
Calvert Ave E2 . . . . .95 C4
Calvert Cl
Belvedere DA17 . . . . .125 D2
Sidcup DA14 . . . . .191 A4
Calvert Ct ¹ London N19 . . . .49 C1
⁵ Richmond TW9 . . . . .132 B1
Calvert Ho ⁹ W12 . . . . .112 B6
Calverton SE5 . . . . .139 C6
Calvert Ho ⁹ W12 . . . . .112 B6
Calverton Prim Sch E16 . . . .99 D1
Calverton Rd E6 . . . . .100 C6
Calvert Rd SE10 . . . . .120 D1
Calvert's Bldgs SE1 . . . . . .252 C3
Calvert St NW1 . . . . . .**93** A6 **231** A6
Calvin St E1 . . . .**95** D3 **243** C5
Calydon Rd SE7 . . . . .121 B1
Calypso Cres ⁸ SE15 . . . . .139 D5
Calypso Way SE8, SE16. . . .119 B2
Camac Rd TW2 . . . . .152 B3
Camarthen Grn NW9 . . . . . . .45 C3
Cambalt Ho ³ SW15 . . . . . .156 D6
Cambalt Rd SW15 . . . . .156 D6
Cambay Ho ⁷ E1 . . . . .97 A3
Cambell Jun & Inf Schs
RM9 . . . . .80 D1
Camber Ho ⁴ SE15 . . . . . . .140 C4
Camberley Ave Enfield EN1 . . .5 C1
Wimbledon SW20 . . . . .178 B1
Camberley Cl SM3 . . . . .216 D5
Camberley Ct ¹⁵ SM2 . . . . .217 D1
Camberley Ho NW1 . . . . . . .231 D3
Camberley Rd TW6 . . . . .126 C2
Cambert Way SE9 . . . . .143 B1
CAMBERWELL 139 A4
Camberwell Bsns Ctr
SE5 . . . . .139 B5
Camberwell Church St
SE5 . . . . .139 B4
Camberwell Coll of Arts
¹⁶ Camberwell SE5 . . . . . . .139 C4
²⁵ Camberwell SE15 . . . . . .139 D5
Camberwell Glebe SE5 . . .139 C4
Camberwell Gn SE5. . . . . . .139 B4
Camberwell Gr SE5 . . . . . . .139 C3
Camberwell Green SE5 . . .139 A4
Camberwell New Rd
SW9 .138 D5
Camberwell Rd SE5. . . . . . .139 A5
Camberwell Station Rd
SE5 . . . . .139 A4
Camberwell Trad Est
SE5 . . . . .139 A4

Cambeys Rd RM10 81 D3
Cambisgate SW19 179 A5
Camborne Ave W13 109 C4
Camborne Cl TW6 126 C2
Camborne Cres TW6 126 C2
Camborne Rd
Belmont SM2 217 D1
Bexley DA16 145 D3
Croydon CR0 206 A2
Harmondsworth TW6 126 C2
Sidcup DA14 168 C1
Wandsworth SW18 157 C4
West Barnes SM4 200 D4
Camborne Way
Harlington TW6 126 C2
Heston TW5 129 C4
Cambourne Ave N9 18 D4
Cambourne Mews 6 W11 91 A1
Cambrai Ct N13 32 A6
Cambray Rd
Broom Hill BR6 211 D2
Streatham SW12 159 C3
Cambria 6 BR3 185 D1
Cambria Cl
Hounslow TW3 129 C1
Sidcup DA15 167 C3
Cambria Ct TW14 150 B4
Cambria Gdns TW19 148 A4
Cambria Ho
Forest Hill SE26 184 A6
14 Limehouse E14 97 A1
Cambria Lo 3 SW15 157 B6
Cambrian Ave IG2 57 C4
Cambrian Cl SE27 160 D1
Cambrian Ct UB2 107 D2
Cambrian Gn NW9 45 C4
Cambrian Rd Leyton E10 53 C1
Richmond TW10 154 B5
Cambria Rd SE5 139 A2
Cambria St SW6 135 D5 265 D3
Cambridge Ave
Falconwood DA16 145 D1
Greenford UB6 64 D3
Kilburn NW6 91 C5
Kingston u T KT3, SW20 177 D1
Cambridge Barracks Rd 11 SE18 122 B2
Cambridge Cir WC2 93 D1 239 D1
Cambridge Cl
East Barnet EN4 15 A3
Hounslow TW4 129 A1
Walthamstow E17 53 B3
Willesden NW10 67 A5
Wimbledon SW20 178 B2
Wood Green N22 32 C2
Cambridge Cotts TW9 132 C6
Cambridge Cres
20 Bethnal Green E2 96 B5
Teddington TW11 175 A5
Cambridge Ct
4 Barnet EN5 1 B2
26 Bethnal Green E2 96 B5
7 Hammersmith W6 112 C2
2 Kilburn NW6 91 C5
Marylebone W2 237 A3
Stamford Hill N16 51 C2
Wembley HA0 65 D4
Wimbledon SW20 178 B2
Cambridge Dr Lee SE12 165 A6
Ruislip HA4 62 D6
Cambridge Gate NW1 238 C6
Cambridge Gate Mews NW1 238 D6
Cambridge Gdns
Enfield EN1 6 A3
Kilburn NW6 91 C5
Kingston u T KT1 176 C1
Muswell Hill N10 31 B2
North Kensington W10 91 A1
Southgate N21 17 B4
Tottenham N17 33 B3
Cambridge Gn SE9 166 D3
Cambridge Gr
Hammersmith W6 112 B2
Penge SE20 184 B2
Cambridge Grove Rd
13 Kingston u T KT1 176 C1
Kingston u T KT1 198 C6
Cambridge Heath Rd E1, E2 96 B4
Cambridge Heath Sta E2 96 B5
Cambridge Ho
Barking IG11 79 A1
Ealing W13 87 A1
Fulham SW6 135 A2
2 Teddington TW11 175 A5
8 Woolwich SE18 122 B2
Cambridge Mans SW11 267 C1
Cambridge Par EN1 6 A4
CAMBRIDGE PARK 153 C4
Cambridge Park Ct TW1 153 D4
Cambridge Park Rd E11 55 A2
Cambridge Pas 9 E9 74 C1
Cambridge Pk
Twickenham TW1 153 D5
Wanstead E11 55 A3
Cambridge Pl W8 245 D1
Cambridge Rd
Barking IG11 79 A1
Barnes SW13 133 D3
Battersea SW11 136 D4 267 C1
Carshalton SM5 218 C3
3 Chingford E4 20 B3
East Molesey KT8 195 B5
Hampton TW12 173 B3
Hanwell W7 108 D4
Harrow HA2 41 C4
Hounslow TW4 129 A1
Ilford IG3 57 C1
Kilburn NW6 91 C4
Kilburn NW6 91 C5
Kingston u T KT1 176 C1
Leytonstone E11 54 D3
Littleton TW15 171 A3
Mitcham CR4 203 C6
New Malden KT3 199 C5
Penge SE20 206 B6
Plaistow BR1 187 A3
Richmond TW9 132 C5
Sidcup DA14 189 C6
Southall UB1 107 B5
Teddington TW11 175 A5
Twickenham TW1 153 D5
Walton-on-T KT12 194 B3
Wimbledon SW20 178 B2
Cambridge Rd N W4 110 D1
Cambridge Rd S 3 W4 110 D1
Cambridge Row SE18 122 D1
Cambridge Sch 15 W6 112 B2
Cambridge Sq W2 92 C1 237 A2
Cambridge St SW1 115 C1 259 A2
Cambridge Terr
Edmonton N9 17 D4
Regent's Pk NW1 231 C1
Cambridge Terr Mews NW1 231 D1
Cambridge Tutors Coll CR0 221 C4
Cambstone Cl N11 15 A2
Cambus Cl UB4 85 A2
Cambus Rd E16 99 A2
Cam Ct 2 SE15 139 D6
Camdale Rd SE18 145 D5
Camden Ave
Feltham TW13 150 C3
Hayes UB4 106 D6
Camden Cl BR7 189 A2
Camden Coll of English 8 NW1 71 A1
Camden Ct 9 DA17 125 C1
Camden Gdns
Camden Town NW1 71 B1
Sutton SM1 217 D3
Thornton Heath CR7 204 D6
Camden Gr BR7 188 D4
Camden High St NW1 93 C6 232 A5
Camden Hill Rd SE19 183 C4
Camden Ho
6 Deptford SE8 119 B1
Wallington CR6 220 A5
Camdenhurst St E14 97 A1
Camden Jun Sch SM5 218 D4
Camden Lock Pl NW1 71 B1
Camden Mews NW1 71 D2
Camden Mkt* NW1 93 B6 231 D6
Camden Park Rd
Camden Town NW1 71 D2
Chislehurst West BR7 188 C3
Camden Pas* N1 94 D6 234 C5
Camden Rd
Camden Town NW1 93 B6 231 D6
Carshalton SM5 218 D4
Old Bexley DA5 169 B4
Sutton SM1 217 D3
Walthamstow E17 53 B3
Wanstead E11 55 B3
Camden Road Sta NW1 71 C1
Camden Row SE3 142 C3
Camden Sch for Girls The NW5 71 C2
Camden Sq NW1 71 D2
Camden St NW1 93 C6 232 B5
Camden Studios NW1 232 B5
Camden Terr 17 NW1 71 D2
CAMDEN TOWN 71 B1
Camden Town Sta NW1 93 B6 231 D6
Camden Way
Chislehurst West BR7 188 C3
Thornton Heath CR7 204 D6
Camden Wlk N1 234 C5
Cameford Ct 20 SW12 160 A4
Camelford NW1 232 B5
Camelford Ct 15 W11 91 A1
Camelford Ho SE1 260 B1
Camelford Wlk 13 W11 91 A1
Camel Gr KT2 175 D5
Camelia Ct IG8 36 C4
Camellia Ct 20 BR3 185 C3
Camellia Ho
Feltham TW13 150 A3
New Cross SE8 141 B5
Camellia Pl TW2 151 D4
Camellia St SW8 270 A3
Camelot Cl
Plumstead SE18 123 B4
Wimbledon SW19 179 C6
Camelot Ho 15 NW1 71 D2
Camelot Prim Sch SE15 140 B6
Camel Rd E16 121 D5
Camera Pl SW10 266 C6
Camera Press Gall The* SE1 253 C2
Cameret Ct 6 W11 112 D4
Cameron Cl
East Barnet N20 14 C2
Edmonton N18 34 B5
Cameron Cres HA8 26 D2
Cameron Ct 3 SW19 157 A3
Cameron Ho
8 Bromley BR1 186 D2
Camberwell SE5 139 A5
St John's Wood NW8 230 A4
Cameron House Sch SW10 266 D6
Cameron Lo TW3 130 A1
Cameron Pl SW16 160 C2
Cameron Rd
Bromley BR2 209 A4
Forest Hill SE6 163 B2
Ilford IG3 57 C1
Thornton Heath CR0 204 D3
Cameron Sq CR4 180 C2
Camerton Cl 8 E8 73 D2
Camfrey Ct N8 50 A5
Camgate Ctr The TW19 148 B4
Camilla Cl TW16 171 D4
Camilla Ct 12 SM2 217 C1
Camilla Rd SE16 118 B2
Camille Cl SE25 206 A6
Camlan Rd BR1 186 D6
Camlet St E2 243 C6
Camlet Way EN4 1 D4
Camley St Natural Pk* NW1 232 D5
Camley St NW1 93 D5 232 D4
Camm 23 NW9 27 D1
Camm Gdns
5 Kingston u T KT1 176 B1
Thames Ditton KT7 196 D2
Camomile Ave CR4 180 D2
Camomile St EC3 95 C1 243 B2
Camomile Way UB7 82 A1
Campaign Ct W9 91 B3
Campana Rd SW6 135 C4 265 B2
Campasps Bsns Pk TW16 193 D4
Campbell Ave IG6 57 A5
Campbell Cl Ruislip HA4 40 A3
Shooters Hill SE18 144 C4
Streatham SW16 181 D6
Twickenham TW2 152 B3
Campbell Croft HA8 26 C5
Campbell Ct
Dulwich SE21 162 A3
Ealing W7 108 C6
Kingsbury NW9 45 A3
South Kensington SW7 256 A5
Tottenham N17 33 D2
Campbell Gordon Way NW2 68 B4
Campbell Ho
Paddington W2 236 C5
Pimlico SW1 259 A1
30 Shepherd's Bush W12 112 B6
6 Wallington SM6 219 B4
Campbell Rd Bow E3 97 C4
Ealing W7 108 C6
Newham E6 100 A6
Stratford E15 76 D4
Thornton Heath CR0 204 D3
Tottenham N17 34 A2
Twickenham TW2 152 B2
Walthamstow E17 53 B5
Campbell Wlk N1 233 B6
Campdale Rd N7 71 D5
Campden Cres
Dagenham RM8 80 C4
Wembley HA0 65 B5
Campden Gr W8 113 C4 245 B2
Campden Hill W8 113 C4 245 A2
Campden Hill Ct W8 245 B2
Campden Hill Gate W8 245 A2
Campden Hill Gdns W8 245 A4
Campden Hill Mans W8 245 B4
Campden Hill Pl W14 244 D4
Campden Hill Rd W8 113 C4 245 A2
Campden Hill Sq W14 113 B5 244 D4
Campden Ho 4 NW6 70 B1
Campden Hos W8 245 A3
Campden House Cl W8 245 B2
Campden Rd
Ickenham UB10 60 B4
South Croydon CR2 221 C3
Campden St W8 113 C5 245 A3
Campden Way RM8 80 B4
Campe Ho 1 N10 31 A3
Campen Cl SW19 157 A2
Camperdown St E1 243 D1
Campfield Rd SE9 165 D4
Campion Cl Harrow HA3 44 B3
Hillingdon UB8 82 B2
Newham E6 122 B6
South Croydon CR2 221 C4
Campion Ct London N12 30 C4
10 Wembley HA0 88 A5
Campion Gdns IG8 37 A5
Campion Ho 15 N16 73 C3
Campion Pl SE28 124 B5
Campion Rd
Hounslow TW7 130 D4
Leyton E10 53 D2
Putney SW15 156 C6
Campion Terr NW2 68 D5
Campion Way HA8 27 A6
Camplin Rd HA3 44 A4
Camplin St SE14 140 D5
Camp Rd SW19 178 C5
Campsbourne Ho 3 N8 50 A5
Campsbourne Rd
Hornsey N8 50 A5
Hornsey N8 50 A6
Campsbourne Sch N8 50 A6
Campsbourne The N8 50 A5
Campsey Gdns RM9 80 B1
Campsey Rd RM9 80 B1
Campsfield Ho N8 50 A6
Campsfield Rd N8 50 A6
Campshill Pl SE13 164 A6
Campshill Rd SE13 164 A6
Camp Site The BR8 191 C3
Campton Hill Twrs W8 245 A4
Campus Rd E17 53 B3
Camp View SW19 178 B5
Cam Rd E15 98 B6
Camrose Ave
Edgware HA8 26 B2
Erith DA8 147 D6
Feltham TW13 172 C6
Camrose Cl Croydon CR0 207 A2
Morden SM4 201 C5
Camrose St SE2 124 A2
Camsey Ho 8 SW2 160 B6
Canada Ave N18 33 A4
Canada Cres W3 89 A3
Canada Gdns SE13 164 A6
Canada Rd W3 89 A2
Canada Sq E14 119 D5
Canada St SE16 118 D4
Canada Water Sta SE16 118 D3
Canada Way W12 112 B6
Canadian Ave SE6 163 D3
Canal App SE8 141 A6
Canal Bldg N1 235 A4
Canal Bridge SE15 140 A6
Canal Bvd 7 NW1 71 D2
Canal Cl Mile End E1 97 A3
North Kensington W10 90 D3
Canal Gr SE15 140 B6
Canal Head Public Sq 1 SE15 140 A4
Canal Path 22 E2 95 D6
Canalside Studios 29 N1 95 C6
Canal St SE5 139 B6
Canal Way W10 90 D3
Canal Wlk Croydon CR0 205 D3
Forest Hill SE26 184 C5
Shoreditch N1 95 B6 235 D6
CANARY WHARF 119 D5
Canary Wharf* E14 119 D5
Canary Wharf Pier (River Bus) E14 119 B5
Canary Wharf Sta E14 119 D5
Canary Wharf Sta (DLR) E14 119 C5
Canberra Cl NW4 46 A6
Canberra Dr UB4 84 C4
Canberra Ho 7 HA4 40 C1
Canberra Prim Sch W12 112 B6
Canberra Rd
Charlton SE7 143 D6
Ealing W13 109 A5
Erith DA7 146 D6
Harlington TW6 126 C2
Newham E6 100 B6
Canbury 2000 Bsns Pk 3 KT2 176 A2
Canbury Ave KT2 176 B2
Canbury Ct 3 KT2 176 A3
Canbury Mews SE26 162 A1
Canbury Park Rd KT2 176 B2
Canbury Sch KT2 176 D4
Cancell Rd SW9 138 C4
Candahar Rd SW11 136 C3
Candida Ct 9 NW1 71 B1
Candishe Ho SE1 253 C2
Candle Gr SE15 140 B2
Candlelight Ct 5 E15 76 D2
Candlemakers 24 SW11 136 B2
Candler Mews TW1 153 A4
Candler St N15 51 B3
Candover St W1 239 A3
Candy St E3 97 B6
Caney Mews NW2 68 D6
Canfield Dr HA4 62 B3
Canfield Gdns NW6 69 D1
Canfield Ho N15 51 C3
Canfield Pl NW6 70 A2
Canford Ave UB5 85 A6
Canford Cl EN2 4 C3
Canford Gdns KT3 199 C3
Canford Pl TW11 175 C4
Canford Rd SW11 159 A6
Canham Rd Acton W3 111 C4
South Norwood SE25 205 C6
Canmore Gdns SW16 181 C3
Cann Hall Prim Sch E11 76 D5
Cann Hall Rd E11 76 D4
Cann Ho W14 254 B5
Canning Cres N22 32 B2
Canning Cross SE5 139 C3
Canning Ct N22 32 B2
Canning Ho 23 W12 112 B6
Canning Pas W8 114 A3 256 A6
Canning Pl W8 114 A3 256 A6
Canning Pl Mews W8 256 A6
Canning Rd Croydon CR0 221 D6
Harrow HA3 42 D6
Highbury N5 72 D5
Walthamstow E17 53 A6
West Ham E15 98 C5
Cannington 14 NW5 71 A2
Cannington Rd RM9 80 C2
CANNING TOWN 99 B2
Canning Town E16 98 C1
Canning Town Sta E16 98 C1
Cannizaro Rd SW19 178 D5
Cannock Ho N4 51 B2
Cannock Lo EN1 17 C5
Cannonbury Ave HA5 40 D3
Cannon Cl
Hampton TW12 173 D4
West Barnes SW20 200 C6
Cannon Dr 21 E14 119 C6
Cannon Hill
Palmers Green N14 16 A1
West Hampstead NW6 69 C3
Cannon Hill La SM4, SW20 201 A5
Cannon Hill Mews N14 16 A1
Cannon Ho Lambeth SE11 260 D3
Penge SE26 184 B4
Cannon La
Hampstead NW3 70 B5
Pinner HA5 41 A3
Cannon Lane Fst & Mid Schs HA5 40 D3
Cannon Pl
Hampstead NW3 70 B5
Woolwich SE7 122 A1
Cannon Rd Erith DA7 147 B4
Palmers Green N14 16 A1
Cannon St EC4 117 A6 252 B6
Cannon Street Rd E1 96 B1
Cannon Street Sta EC4 117 B6 252 C6
Cannon Trad Est HA9 66 D4
Cannon Way KT8 195 D5
Cannon (W End of General Roy's Base Line)* TW6 126 D4
Cannon Wharf Bsns Ctr 12 SE8 119 A2
Canon Ave RM6 58 C4
Canon Barnett Prim Sch E1 95 D1 243 D2
Canon Beck Rd SE16 118 C4
Canonbie Rd SE23 162 C4
CANONBURY 73 A2
Canonbury Bsns Ctr N1 235 B6
Canonbury Cres N1 73 A1
Canonbury Ct 21 N1 72 D1
Canonbury Gr N1 73 A1
Canonbury Hts 6 N1 73 B2
Canonbury La N1 72 D1
Canonbury Pk N N1 73 A2
Canonbury Pk S N1 73 A2
Canonbury Pl N1 72 D2
Canonbury Prim Sch 4 N1 72 D2
Canonbury Rd Enfield EN1 5 C4
Islington N1 72 D1
Canonbury Sq N1 72 D1
Canonbury St N1 73 A1
Canonbury Sta N1, N5 73 A3
Canonbury Villas N1 72 D1
Canonbury Yd E 26 N1 73 A2
Canon Mohan Cl N14 15 B5
Canon Murnane Rd SE1 263 C5
Canon Palmer RC High Sch IG3 57 C1
Canon Rd BR1 209 D6
Canon Row SW1 116 A4 250 A1
Canons Cl East Finchley N2 48 B2
Edgware HA8 26 B4
Canons Cnr HA8 26 A6
Canons Ct Edgware HA8 26 B4
Leyton E15 76 C4
Canons Dr HA8 26 B4
Canons High Sch HA8 26 B1
Canons L Ctr CR4 202 D5
Canonsleigh Rd RM9 80 B1
CANONS PARK 26 A3
Canons Park Cl HA8 26 A3
Canons Park Sta HA8 26 A3
Canon St N1 95 A6 235 A5

Canon's Wlk CR0 . . . . . . 222 D5
Canopus Way
  Northwood HA6 . . . . 22 A6
  Stanwell TW19 . . . . 148 A4
Canrobert St E2 . . . . 96 B4
Cantelowes Ho EN5 . . . . . . 12 D6
Cantelowes Ho NW1 . . . . . 71 D2
Canterbury SE13. . . . . 164 A6
Canterbury Ave
  Redbridge IG1 . . . . 56 A2
  Sidcup DA15. . . . . 168 C2
Canterbury Cl
  Beckenham BR3 . . . . 185 D2
  16 Camberwell SE5 . . . 139 A3
  7 Newham E6 . . . . 100 B1
  North Cheam KT4 . . . . . 216 D6
  Southall UB6. . . . . 85 D2
Canterbury Cres SW9 . . 138 C2
Canterbury Ct Acton W3 . 111 C5
  4 Ashford TW15 . . . . . 170 B6
  Eltham SE12. . . . . 165 B1
  15 Hendon NW9. . . . . . . 27 D1
  Kilburn NW6. . . . . 91 C5
  South Croydon CR2. . . . 221 A1
  Thornton Heath CR0. . . 204 C2
Canterbury Gr SE27,
  SW16. . . . . 160 C1
Canterbury Hall KT4 . . . 200 B2
Canterbury Ho
  2 Barking IG11 . . . . 80 A1
  6 Bromley E3 . . . . 97 D4
  Lambeth SE1. . . . . 260 D6
Canterbury Ind Pk **15**
  SE15. . . . . 140 C6
Canterbury Mans NW6 . . 69 D2
Canterbury Pl SE17 . . . . 261 D3
Canterbury Rd
  Feltham TW13 . . . . 151 A2
  Harrow HA1, HA2. . . . . . 42 A4
  Kilburn NW6. . . . . 91 C5
  Leyton E10 . . . . 54 A3
  Morden SM4. . . . . 202 A3
  Thornton Heath CR0. . . 204 C2
Canterbury Terr NW6 . . . 91 C5
Cantium Ret Pk SE1. . . . 140 A6
Cantley Gdns Ilford IG2. . 57 A3
  South Norwood SE19 . . 183 D2
Cantley Rd W7. . . . . 109 A3
Canton St E14 . . . . 97 C1
Cantrell Rd E3. . . . . 97 C3
Cantwell Ho SE18 . . . . . 144 D5
Cantwell Rd SE18 . . . . . 144 D5
Canute Ct SW16 . . . . 160 C1
Canute Gdns SE16 . . . . . 118 D2
Canute Ho **1** TW8 . . . . . 131 C5
Canvey St SE1 . . . . 252 A4
Cape Cl IG11 . . . . 78 D1
Cape Henry Ct **15** E14 . 120 B6
Capel KT5 . . . . 198 B2
Capel Ave SM6. . . . . 220 B3
Capel Cl Keston Mark BR2. 210 A1
  Whetstone N20 . . . . 14 A1
Capel Cres HA7. . . . . 9 A2
Capel Ct SE2 . . . . 184 C2
Capel Gdns Ilford IG3. . . . 79 D4
  Pinner HA5. . . . . 41 B5
Capel Ho **17** Hackney E9. 74 C1
  South Oxhey WD19. . . . . 22 D6
Capella Ho **1** SE7 . . . . . 143 B6
Capel Lo
  5 Richmond TW9 . . . . . 132 B4
  12 Streatham SW2. . . . 160 B4
Capel Point E7 . . . . 77 B4
Capel Rd East Barnet EN4 . 14 C5
  Forest Gate E7, E12 . . . . . 77 C4
Capener's Cl SW1. . . . . . 248 A1
Cape Rd N17 . . . . 52 A6
Capern Rd SW18. . . . . . . 158 A3
Cape Yd **6** E1 . . . . 118 A5
Capio Nightingale Hospl
  NW1. . . . . 92 C2 237 B4
Capital Bsns Ctr
  South Croydon CR0. . . . 221 B1
  Wembley HA0. . . . . 87 B4
Capital City Acad NW10. . 90 B6
Capital East Apts **8**
  E16 . . . . 121 A6
Capital Ind Est
  Belvedere DA17 . . . . . . 125 D3
  Mitcham CR4 . . . . 202 D4
Capital Interchange Way
  TW8. . . . . 110 C1
Capital Sh Ctrs SW1 . . . 249 C1
Capital Wharf **14** E1. . . 118 A5
Capitol Ind Pk NW9 . . . . . 45 A6
Capitol Way NW9 . . . . 45 A6
Capland Ho NW8 . . . . . . 236 D6
Capland St NW8 . . 92 B3 236 D6
Caplan Est CR4 . . . . 181 C2
Caple Ho SW10 . . . . 266 B4
Caple Rd NW10 . . . . 89 D5
Capper St WC1 . . 93 C3 233 B3
Caprea Cl UB4. . . . . 84 D2
Capricorn Ctr RM8. . . . . . . 59 B2
Capri Ho E17 . . . . 35 B1
Capri Rd CR0 . . . . 205 D2
Capstan Cl RM6. . . . . 58 B3

Capstan Ho **6** E14 . . . . . 120 A2
Capstan Rd SE8. . . . . 119 B2
Capstan Ride EN2. . . . . 4 C3
Capstan Sq E14. . . . . 120 A4
Capstan Way SE16 . . . . . 119 A5
Capstone Rd BR1. . . . . . . 186 D6
Capthorne Ave HA2. . . . . . 41 B1
Capuchin Cl HA7. . . . . 25 B4
Capulet Mews **1** E16 . . . 121 A5
Capworth St E10. . . . . 53 D2
Caradoc Cl W2 . . . . 91 C1
Caradoc Evans Cl N11. . . . 31 B5
Caradoc St SE10 . . . . 120 C1
Caradon Cl **4** E11 . . . . 76 C6
Caradon Ct **7** TW1. . . . . 153 C5
Caradon Way N15. . . . . . . 51 B5
Cara Ho **10** N1 . . . . 72 C1
Caranday Villas **5** W11. . 112 C5
Caravel Cl E14. . . . . 119 C3
Caravelle Gdns **1** UB5 . . . 84 D4
Caravel Mews **14** SE8 . . 141 C6
Caraway Cl E13. . . . . 99 B2
Caraway Hts E14. . . . . . . 120 A6
Caraway Pl SM6 . . . . 219 B5
Carberry Rd **12** SE19 . . . 183 C4
Carbery Ave W3 . . . . 110 B4
Carbis Cl E4 . . . . 20 B3
Carbis Rd E14 . . . . 97 B1
Carbroke Ho **9** E9. . . . . . . 96 C6
Carburton St W1. . . 93 B3 238 D5
Cardale St **1** E14 . . . . . . 120 A3
Cardamom Ct **1** E12. . . . . 78 C4
Carden Rd SE15. . . . . 140 B2
Cardiff Ho **8** SE15 . . . . . 140 A6
Cardiff Rd Ealing W7 . . . . 109 A3
  Enfield EN3. . . . . 6 B1
Cardiff St SE18 . . . . 145 C5
Cardigan Ct **3** W7. . . . . . 86 D3
Cardigan Gdns IG3 . . . . . . 80 A6
Cardigan Rd
  Barnes SW13 . . . . 134 A3
  Bow E3 . . . . 97 B5
  Richmond TW10 . . . . . . 154 A5
  Wimbledon SW19. . . . . 180 A4
Cardigan St
  SE11 . . . . 116 C1 261 A2
Cardigan Wlk **19** N1. . . . . 73 A1
Cardinal Ave
  Kingston u T KT2. . . . . . 176 A4
  West Barnes SM4. . . . . 201 A3
Cardinal Bourne St SE1. 262 D5
Cardinal Cap Alley SE1. . 252 A5
Cardinal Cl Burnt Oak HA8 . 27 B3
  Chislehurst BR7 . . . . . . 189 B2
  West Barnes SM4. . . . . 201 A3
  Worcester Pk KT19, KT4. . 216 A4
Cardinal Cres KT3 . . . . . 177 A1
Cardinal Ct KT8. . . . . 195 B5
Cardinal Dr KT12 . . . . . . 194 D1
Cardinal Hinsley Cl
  NW10 . . . . 90 A5
Cardinal Hinsley
Mathematics & Computing
Coll NW10. . . . . 90 A6
Cardinal Pl SW15 . . . . . . 134 D1
Cardinal Pl SW1 . . 115 C3 259 A5
Cardinal Pole RC Sch
  London E9. . . . . 74 D1
  London E9. . . . . 75 A3
Cardinal Rd
  Feltham TW13 . . . . 150 B3
  Ruislip HA4. . . . . 40 D1
Cardinal Road Inf Sch **5**
  TW13 . . . . 150 B3
Cardinals Way N19. . . . . . 49 D1
Cardinal's Wlk
  Ashford TW15. . . . . 171 C4
  Hampton TW12. . . . . . . 174 A3
Cardinal Vaughan Meml Sch
  The W14 . . . . 244 A2
Cardinal Way HA3 . . . . 42 C6
Cardinal Wiseman RC Sch
  UB6. . . . . 86 A2
Cardinal Wlk SW1 . . . . . . 259 A5
Cardine Mews SE15 . . . . 140 B5
Cardington Sq TW4 . . . . . 128 D1
Cardington St
  NW1 . . . . 93 C4 232 B1
Cardozo Rd N7 . . . . 72 A3
Cardrew Ave N12 . . . . 30 B5
Cardrew Cl N12. . . . . 30 B5
Cardrew Ct **8** N12. . . . . . . 30 B5
Cardross St W6 . . . . 112 B3
Cardwell Prim Sch **22**
  SE18. . . . . 122 B2
Cardwell Rd **3** N7. . . . . . . 72 A4
Career Ct **11** SE16 . . . . . 118 D4
Carew Cl N7 . . . . 72 B6
Carew Ho
  15 Deptford SE14. . . . . 140 D6
  Ilford RM6 . . . . 58 B3
Carew Ho
  West Norwood SW16. . . 160 C1
  23 Woolwich SE18 . . . . 122 B2
Carew Manor Sch SM6 . . 219 D5
Carew Rd Ashford TW15 . . 171 A4
  Ealing W13 . . . . 109 C4
  Mitcham CR4 . . . . 181 A1
  Thornton Heath CR7. . . 204 D5
  Tottenham N17. . . . . 34 A1

Carew Rd continued
  Wallington SM6 . . . . . . 219 C2
Carew St SE5 . . . . 139 A3
  20 Camberwell SE5 . . . 139 A5
Carey Ct Bexley DA6 . . . . 169 D6
Carey Gdns SW8 . 137 D4 269 C1
Carey Ho E5 . . . . 74 B5
Carey La EC2 . . . . 242 A2
Carey Pl SW1 . . . . 259 C3
Carey Rd RM9 . . . . 81 A4
Carey St WC2 . . . . . 94 B1 240 D1
Carey Way HA9 . . . . 66 D4
Carfax Pl SW4 . . . . 137 D1
Carfax Rd UB3 . . . . 106 A2
Carfree Cl **5** N1 . . . . 72 C1
Cargill Rd SW18 . . . . 158 A3
Cargreen Pl SE25 . . . . . . 205 D5
Cargreen Rd SE25. . . . . . 205 D5
Cargrey Ho **9** HA7. . . . . . . 25 C5
Carholme Rd SE23. . . . . . 163 B3
Carillon Ct W5 . . . . 109 D6
Carinthia Ct **5** SE8 . . . . . 119 A2
Carisbrook Cl N10. . . . . . . 31 B1
Carisbrook Cl EN1 . . . . 5 D4
Carisbrooke Ave DA5. . . . 168 D3
Carisbrooke Cl
  Stanmore HA7. . . . . 25 D1
  Twickenham TW4 . . . . . 151 A4
Carisbrooke Ct
  Acton W3 . . . . 111 A4
  Belmont SM2. . . . . 217 B1
  Northolt UB5 . . . . 85 B6
  1 Streatham SW16. . . . 160 B1
Carisbrooke Gdns SE15 . 139 C5
Carisbrooke Ho
  10 Kingston u T KT2 . . . 176 A2
  Richmond TW10 . . . . . . 154 C6
Carisbrooke Rd
  Bromley BR2. . . . . 209 C5
  Mitcham CR4 . . . . 204 A5
  Walthamstow E17 . . . . . 53 A4
Carker's La
  Crouch End N19 . . . . 49 B2
  Gospel Oak NW5 . . . . . . 71 B3
Carleton Ave SM6. . . . . . 219 D1
Carleton Cl KT10. . . . . . . 196 B1
Carleton Gdns N19 . . . . . . 71 C3
Carleton Ho **4** N8. . . . . . . 50 A4
Carleton Rd N7 . . . . 71 D4
Carley Ct **6** N12 . . . . 30 B5
Carlile Cl E3 . . . . 97 B5
Carlile Ho SE1 . . . . 262 D5
Carlina Gdns IG8 . . . . 37 B5
Carling Ct TW1 . . . . 152 D4
Carlingford Dr DA14 . . . . 190 A5
Carlingford Gdns CR4 . . 181 A3
Carlingford Rd
  Hampstead NW3 . . . . . . 70 B4
  London N15 . . . . 50 D6
  West Barnes SM4. . . . . 200 D3
Carlisle Ave Acton W3. . . . 89 C1
  Whitechapel EC3 . . . . . 243 C1
Carlisle Cl
  Kingston u T KT2. . . . . . 176 C2
  Pinner HA5. . . . . 41 A6
Carlisle Gdns Harrow HA3. 43 D2
  Redbridge IG1 . . . . 56 A3
Carlisle Ho
  6 Dartmouth Pk NW5 . . 71 C5
  Redbridge IG1 . . . . 56 A3
Carlisle Inf Sch TW12 . . . 173 D4
Carlisle La SE1 . . . 116 B3 260 D6
Carlisle Lo **1** N3. . . . . 29 B1
Carlisle Pl London N11. . . . 31 B6
  Westminster SW1 115 C3 259 A5
Carlisle Rd Cheam SM1. . . 217 B2
  Finsbury Pk N4 . . . . 50 C2
  Hampton TW12. . . . . . . 173 D3
  Hendon NW9 . . . . 45 A6
  Kilburn NW6. . . . . 91 A6
  Leyton E10 . . . . 53 C1
Carlisle St W1 . . . . 93 D1 239 C1
Carlisle Way SW17 . . . . . 181 A5
Carlisle Wlk **6** E8 . . . . . . 73 D2
Carlos Pl W1 . . . . 115 B6 248 C5
Carlow St NW1 . . . . 232 A4
Carlson Ct SW15. . . . . . . 135 B1
Carlton Ave
  Feltham TW14 . . . . 150 C5
  Harrow HA3 . . . . 43 B4
  Hayes UB3 . . . . 105 C2
  South Croydon CR2. . . . 221 C1
  Southgate N14 . . . . 15 C6
Carlton Ave E HA9 . . . . . . 65 D6
Carlton Ave W HA0. . . . . . 65 B6
Carlton Cl
  Chessington KT9 . . . . . 213 D2
  Child's Hill NW3 . . . . 69 C6
  Edgware HA8 . . . . 26 C5
  Northolt UB5 . . . . 64 A3
Carlton Cres SM3. . . . . . 217 A4
Carlton Ct Brixton SW9. . . 138 C4
  Ealing W7 . . . . 108 D4
  Finchley N3. . . . . 29 C3
  Ilford IG6 . . . . 57 B6
  Kilburn NW6. . . . . 91 D5
  11 Penge SE20 . . . . . . 184 B2
  South Norwood SE19 . . 183 D2
  6 Willesden NW2. . . . . . 68 C2
Carlton Dr Ilford IG6. . . . . 57 B6

Carlton Dr continued
  Putney SW15 . . . . 157 A6
Carlton Gdns Ealing W5 . 109 C6
  St James SW1 . . . 115 D5 249 C3
Carlton Gn DA14. . . . . . . 189 D6
Carlton Gr SE15. . . . . 140 B4
Carlton Ho NW8. . 92 A5 229 A4
  Cheam SM1. . . . . 217 B2
  Edmonton N21 . . . . 17 A3
  Feltham TW14 . . . . 149 D5
  Hounslow TW4 . . . . 151 C5
  8 Kilburn NW6 . . . . 91 B5
  Kilburn NW6 . . . . 91 C5
  Marylebone W1 . . . . . . 237 D2
Carlton House Terr
  SW1. . . . . 115 D5 249 D4
Carlton Lo N4 . . . . 50 C2
Carlton Mans
  Brixton SW9 . . . . 138 C1
  Cricklewood NW2. . . . . . 68 D3
  Kensington W14 . . . . . . 244 B2
  Maida Vale W9 . . . . 91 D4
  7 South Hampstead NW6. 69 C1
  Stamford Hill N16 . . . . . . 51 D1
Carlton Par HA9 . . . . 44 A1
Carlton Park Ave SW20. . 178 D1
Carlton Prim Sch NW5 . . 71 A3
Carlton Rd Acton W4 . . . . 111 B4
  Ashford TW16. . . . . 171 D3
  Ealing W5 . . . . 87 C1
  Erith DA8. . . . . 147 D6
  Finsbury Pk N4 . . . . 50 C2
  Friern Barnet N11. . . . . . 31 A5
  Higham Hill E17 . . . . 35 A2
  Kingston u T KT3. . . . . . 177 C1
  Leytonstone E11. . . . . . . 54 D1
  Manor Pk E12. . . . . 77 D4
  Mortlake SW14 . . . . 133 A1
  Sidcup DA14. . . . . 189 D6
  South Croydon CR2. . . . 221 B1
  Walton-on-T KT12 . . . . . 194 B2
  Welling DA16 . . . . 146 B2
Carlton Sq E1 . . . . 96 D2
Carlton St SW1. . . . . 249 C5
Carltons The **5** SW15 . . 157 A6
Carlton Terr
  Edmonton N18 . . . . 33 B6
  Forest Hill SE26 . . . . . . 162 C1
  Upton E7. . . . . 77 C1
  Wanstead E11 . . . . 55 B4
Carlton Tower Pl SW1. . . 257 D6
Carlton Twrs SM5 . . . . . . 218 D5
Carlton Vale NW6 . . . . 91 C5
Carlton Vale Inf Sch **12**
  NW6. . . . . 91 B4
Carlwell St SW17 . . . . . . 180 C5
Carlyle Ave Bromley BR1. 209 D6
  Southall UB1. . . . . 107 B6
Carlyle Cl
  East Molesey KT8. . . . . 173 D1
  Hampstead Garden Suburb
  N2. . . . . 48 A3
Carlyle Gdns UB1. . . . . . 107 B6
Carlyle Ho
  4 Camberwell SE5 . . . . 139 A5
  Chelsea SW3 . . . . 266 D6
  Ealing W5 . . . . 109 D2
  East Molesey KT8. . . . . 195 C4
  12 Stoke Newington N16. . 73 C5
Carlyle Lo **6** EN5 . . . . 14 A6
Carlyle Mans SW3 . . . . . 267 A5
Carlyle Mews **24** E1. . . . 96 D3
Carlyle Pl SW15. . . . . 134 D1
Carlyle Rd Croydon CR0 . 222 A6
  Ealing W5 . . . . 109 C2
  Manor Pk E12. . . . . 78 A4
  1 Stonebridge NW10 . . . 89 B6
  Woolwich SE28 . . . . 124 C6
Carlyle's Ho ★ SW3 . . . . 267 A5
Carlyle Sq SW3 . . . 114 B1 256 D1
Carlyon Ave HA2. . . . . 63 C4
Carlyon Cl HA0 . . . . 88 A6
Carlyon Ct HA0 . . . . 88 B6
Carlyon Mans **1** HA0 . . . . 88 A5
Carlyon Rd Hayes UB4 . . . 84 C2
  Wembley HA0. . . . . 88 A6
Carlys Cl BR3. . . . . 184 D1
Carmalt Gdns SW15. . . . . 134 C1
Carmarthen Ct **4** W7 . . . . 86 D3
Carmarthen Ho **7**
  SW15. . . . . 156 C4
Carmarthen Pl SE1 . . . . . 253 A2
Carmel Ct Kensington W8. 245 C2
  Wembley Pk HA9 . . . . . . 66 D6
Carmelite Cl HA3 . . . . 24 A2
Carmelite Rd HA3. . . . . . . 24 A1
Carmelite St EC4 . . 116 C6 251 B6
Carmelite Wlk HA3 . . . . . . 24 A1
Carmelite Wlk HA3 . . . . . . 24 A2
Carmel Lo SW6 . . . . 265 A6
Carmen St E14 . . . . 97 D1
Carmichael Cl
  8 London SW11 . . . . . . 136 B2
  Ruislip HA4. . . . . 62 A4
Carmichael Ct **5** SW13 . 133 D3
Carmichael Ho
  17 Dulwich SE21 . . . . . 183 C6
  6 Poplar E14. . . . . 120 A6
Carmichael Mews SW18 . 158 A4
Carmichael Rd SE25 . . . . 206 A5

Carminia Rd SW17 . . . . . 159 B2
Carnaby St ★ W1. . . 93 C1 239 A1
Carnac St SE21, SE27 . . . 161 B1
Carna Ct TW9. . . . . 132 A2
Carnanton Rd E17 . . . . 36 B2
Carnarvon Ave EN1 . . . . . . 5 D3
Carnarvon Dr UB3 . . . . . . 105 A3
Carnarvon Rd Barnet EN5 . . 1 A2
  Leyton E10 . . . . 54 A4
  Stratford E15 . . . . 76 D2
  Woodford E18. . . . . 36 D2
Carnation St SE2 . . . . 124 B1
Carnbrook Mews SE3 . . . 143 D2
Carnbrook Rd SE3 . . . . . . 143 D2
Carnecke Gdns SE9. . . . . 166 A6
Carnegie Cl Holdbrook EN3 . . 7 D5
  Surbiton KT6. . . . . 214 B6
Carnegie Ho NW3. . . . . 70 B5
Carnegie Pl SW19. . . . . . 156 C1
Carnegie St N1 . . . . 94 B6 233 D5
Carnforth Cl KT19. . . . . . . 214 D2
Carnforth Rd SW16. . . . . . 181 D3
Carnicot Ho **9** SE15 . . . . 140 B4
Carnoustie Cl SE28 . . . . . 102 C1
Carnoustie Dr N1. . . . . 72 B1
Carnwath Ho SW6 . . . . . . 135 D2
Carnwath Rd SW6 . . . . . . 135 D2
Caroe Ct N9. . . . . 18 B3
Carol Cl NW4 . . . . 46 D5
Carole Ho **13** SE20 . . . . . 184 B2
Carolina Cl E15 . . . . 76 C3
Carolina Rd CR7 . . . . 183 A2
Caroline Cl
  Bayswater W2 . . . . 245 D5
  Hounslow TW7 . . . . 130 C5
  Muswell Hill N10. . . . . . . 31 B1
  South Croydon CR0. . . . 221 C4
  Streatham SW16 . . . . . . 160 B1
Caroline Ct
  Ashford TW15 . . . . 170 D4
  Catford SE6 . . . . 186 B6
  Stanmore HA7 . . . . 25 A4
  17 Surbiton KT6 . . . . . . 197 D2
  23 Woodside Pk N12 . . . 29 D6
Caroline Gdns E2 . . . . 95 C4
Caroline Ho
  Bayswater W2 . . . . 245 D5
  20 Hammersmith W6 . . . 112 C1
Caroline Martyn Ho **8**
  N19 . . . . 49 D2
Caroline Pl
  Bayswater W2 . . . . 245 D5
  Clapham SW11. . . . . . . 137 A3
  Harlington UB3. . . . . . . 127 C5
Caroline Pl Mews W2 . . . 245 D5
Caroline Rd SW19. . . . . . . 179 B3
Caroline St E1. . . . . 96 D1
Caroline Terr
  SW1. . . . . 115 A2 258 A3
Caroline Wlk W6. . . . . 264 A5
Carol St NW1 . . . . . 93 C6 232 A6
Carolyn Ho IG3 . . . . 58 A1
Caronia Ct **4** SE16 . . . . . 119 A2
Carpenter Gdns N21. . . . . 16 D2
Carpenter Ho
  London NW11. . . . . 48 A3
  11 Tower Hamlets E14 . . 97 C2
  5 Tufnell Pk N19 . . . . . . 71 D4
Carpenters Cl EN5 . . . . . . 13 D5
Carpenters Ct
  Camden Town NW1 . . . . 232 A6
  5 Dagenham RM10. . . . . 81 D2
  Twickenham TW2 . . . . . 152 C2
Carpenter's Pl SW4 . . . . 137 D1
Carpenters Prim Sch E15 . 98 A6
Carpenter St W1. . . . . 248 C5
Carradale Ho **2** E14 . . . . . 98 A1
Carrara Cl **18** SW9 . . . . . 138 D1
Carrara Wharf SW6 . . . . . 135 A2
Carr Cl HA7. . . . . 25 A4
Carr Gr SE18. . . . . 122 A4
Carriage Dr E
  SW11. . . . . 137 A5 268 B4
Carriage Drive E
  SW11. . . . . 137 A5 268 B4
Carriage Drive N SW11,
  SW8. . . . . 137 A6 268 B5
Carriage Dr N
  Battersea SW8,
  SW11. . . . . 136 D5 267 C4
  Battersea SW8,
  SW11. . . . . 137 A6 268 B5
Carriage Dr S
  SW11. . . . . 137 A4 268 A2
Carriage Dr W
  SW11. . . . . 136 D5 267 C3
Carriage Mews IG1 . . . . . . 79 A6
Carriage Pl **17** SW16 . . . 181 C5
Carrick Cl TW7 . . . . 131 A2
Carrick Gate KT10 . . . . . . 212 A5
Carrick Gdns N17. . . . . 33 C3
Carrick Ho Islington N7 . . . 72 B2
  Kennington SE11. . . . . . 261 C2
Carrick Mews SE8 . . . . . . 141 C6
Carrill Way DA17. . . . . . . 124 D3
Carrington Ave
  Borehamwood WD6 . . . . 10 D6
  Hounslow TW3 . . . . 151 D6
Carrington Cl Barnet EN5 . 12 A6
  Borehamwood WD6. . . . 11 A4

Carrington Cl continued
Croydon CR0. . . . . 207 A2
Carrington Ct
London SW11 . . . . 136 C1
3 New Malden KT3. . . . . . . 199 C5
Southgate N21 . . . . 16 D5
Carrington Gdns 4 E7 . . 77 A4
Carrington Ho
Mayfair W1. . . . . 248 C3
7 Merton SW19 . . . . 179 C3
Carrington Lo
3 Richmond TW10 . . . . . . 154 A6
Wembley HA9. . . . . 66 B5
Carrington Pl KT10 . . . . . . 212 A4
Carrington Rd TW10 . . . . . 132 C1
Carrington Sq HA3. . . . . . . 24 A3
Carrington St W1. . . . . . . 248 C3
Carrol Cl NW5. . . . . 71 B4
Carroll Cl IG4. . . . . 56 D3
Carroll Ct Acton W3. . . . . . 110 D3
4 Shacklewell E5 . . . . 74 A5
Carroll Ho W2 . . . . 246 C6
Carronade Pl SE18. . . . . . . 123 B3
Carron Cl E14. . . . . 97 D1
Carroun Rd SW8. .138 B5 270 C4
Carrow Rd RM9. . . . . 80 B1
Carr Rd Northolt UB5. . . . . . 64 A1
Walthamstow E17. . . . . 35 C1
Carrs La N21. . . . . 17 B6
Carr St 5 E14. . . . . 97 A1
CARSHALTON 218 C4
Carshalton Beeches Sta
SM5. . . . . 218 D2
Carshalton Coll SM5. . . . . 218 D5
Carshalton Gr SM5. . . . . . 218 D3
Carshalton High Sch for Boys
SM5. . . . . 218 C4
Carshalton High Sch for Girls
SM5. . . . . 218 C5
CARSHALTON ON THE
HILL. 219 B1
Carshalton Park Rd
SM5. . . . . 218 D3
Carshalton Pl SM5. . . . . . 219 A3
Carshalton Rd
Mitcham CR4 . . . . 203 A4
Sutton SM1, SM5. . . . . . . 218 B3
Carshalton Sta SM5. . . . . . 218 D4
Carslake Rd SW15. . . . . . . 156 C5
Carson Rd Cockfosters EN4 . . 2 D1
Dulwich SE21. . . . . 161 B2
Newham E16. . . . . 99 A2
Carstairs Rd SE6. . . . . 164 A1
Carston Cl SE12. . . . . 164 D6
Carswell Cl IG4. . . . . 55 D5
Carswell Rd SE6 . . . . 164 A4
Carter Cl NW9 . . . . 45 B3
Carter Ct EC4. . . . . 241 D1
Carteret Ho 8 W12 . . . . . 112 B6
Carteret St SW1 . . . . 249 C1
Carteret Way SE8 . . . . . . 119 A2
Carterhatch Jun & Inf Schs
EN1. . . . . 6 B4
Carterhatch La EN1 . . . . 6 B4
Carterhatch Rd EN3. . . . . . . 6 D4
Carter Ho
11 London SW2 . . . . 160 C6
Spitalfields E1 . . . . 243 C3
Carter La EC4. . . . . .94 D1 241 D1
Carter Pl SE17 . . . . . 117 A1 262 B1
Carter Rd Mitcham SW19 . .180 B4
Newham E13. . . . . 99 B6
Carters Cl
10 Kentish Town NW5 . . . . 71 D2
North Cheam KT4 . . . . 200 D1
Carters Hill Cl SE9. . . . . . . 165 C3
Carters La SE23. . . . . 163 B1
Carter St SE17 . . . . 117 A1 262 A1
Carter's Yd SW18. . . . . . . 157 C2
Carthew Rd W6. . . . . 112 B3
Carthew Villas W6. . . . . . . 112 B3
Carthusian St EC1. . . . . . . 242 A4
Cartier Circ E14 . . . . 120 A5
Carting La WC2. . . . .116 A6 250 B5
Cart La E4. . . . . 20 C3
Cartmel NW1. . . . . 232 A2
Cartmel CI N17. . . . . 34 B3
Cartmel Ct
Beckenham BR2. . . . . 186 C1
Northolt UB5. . . . . 63 A2
Cartmel Gdns SM4. . . . . . 202 A4
Cartmel Rd DA7. . . . . 147 C4
Carton Ho
4 Bermondsey SE16. . . . . 118 A3
2 Dollis Hill NW2. . . . . 68 A5
12 Shepherd's Bush W11. . 112 D6
Cartoon Mus The ★
WC1. . . . . .94 A2 240 A3
Cartwright Gdns
WC1. . . . . .94 A4 233 A1
Cartwright Ho SE1. . . . . . 262 B5
Cartwright Rd RM9. . . . . . . 81 B1
Cartwright St E1. . 117 D6 253 D5
Cartwright Way SW13. . . . 134 B5
Carvel Ho E14. . . . . 120 A1
Carver Cl 15 W4. . . . . 111 A3
Carver Rd SE24. . . . . 161 A5
Carville Cres TW8. . . . . . . 110 A2

Caryl Ho 6 SW19. . . . . . . 156 D3
Cary Rd E11. . . . . 76 C5
Carysfort Rd
Canonbury N16. . . . . 73 B4
London N8 . . . . 49 D4
Casby Ho 7 SE16. . . . . . . 118 A3
Cascade Ave N10 . . . . 49 C5
Cascade Cl IG9. . . . . 21 D2
Cascade Rd IG9 . . . . 21 D2
Cascadia Ho 22 KT1. . . . . 176 C1
Casella Rd SE14. . . . . 140 D5
Casewick Rd SE27 . . . . . . 182 D6
Casey Cl NW8. . . . . . .92 C4 230 B1
Casimir Rd E5. . . . . 74 C5
Casino Ave SE24. . . . . 161 B6
Caspian Ho 10 E1. . . . . 96 D2
Caspian St SE5. . . . . 139 B5
Caspian Wlk E16. . . . . 99 D1
Cassandra Cl UB5. . . . . 64 B4
Cassandra Ct 7 NW2. . . . . 68 C2
Cass Bsns Sch
EC1. . . . . .95 B3 242 C5
Casselden Rd NW10. . . . . . . 67 B1
Cassel Hospl TW10. . . . . . 175 D6
Cassell Ho 21 SW9 . . . . . . 138 A3
Cass Ho 23 E9 . . . . 74 D2
Cassidy Rd SW6. . . . . 265 A3
Cassilda Rd SE2. . . . . 124 A2
Cassilis Rd Millwall E14 . . . 119 C4
Twickenham TW1. . . . . 153 B5
Cassinghurst SE24. . . . . . 161 B6
Cassiobury Ave TW14 . . . . 149 D4
Cassiobury Rd E17. . . . . 53 A4
South Norwood CR7. . . . . . 205 B5
Casslee Rd SE6 . . . . 163 B4
Cassocks Sq SW17 . . . . . . 193 B2
Casson Ho 11 E1. . . . . 96 A2
Casson St E1. . . . . 96 A2
Castalia Sq 6 E14. . . . . . . 120 A4
Castellain Mans W9. . . . . . . 91 D3
Castellain Rd W9 . . . . 91 D3
Castellane Cl HA7. . . . . 24 D3
Castell Ho 11 SE8 . . . . . . 141 C5
Castello Ave SW15. . . . . . 156 C6
Castelnau SW13 . . . . 134 B5
Castelnau Gdns SW13. . . . 134 B6
Castelnau Mans SW13 . . . 134 B6
Castelnau Row SW13 . . . . 134 B6
Casterbridge Kilburn NW6. . 91 C6
3 Notting Hill W11 . . . . 91 C1
Casterbridge Rd SE3 . . . . 143 A2
Casterton St E8. . . . . 74 B2
Castile Rd SE18. . . . . 122 C2
Castillon Prim Sch SE28. . 102 C1
Castillon Rd SE6. . . . . 164 C2
Castlands Rd SE6 . . . . 163 B2
Castleacre W2. . . . . 237 A1
Castle Ave Chingford E4 . . . . 36 B5
Yiewsley UB7. . . . . 104 B6
Castlebar Ct 5 W5. . . . . . . 87 C2
Castlebar Hill W5. . . . . 87 C2
Castlebar Mews W5. . . . . . . 87 C2
Castle Bar Park Sta W7 . . . . 86 D2
Castlebar Pk W5. . . . . 87 B2
Castlebar Rd W5. . . . . 87 C1
Castlebar Sch W13. . . . . . . 87 A3
Castle Baynard St
EC4. . . . . .117 A6 252 A6
Castlebrook Cl
SE11. . . . . 116 D2 261 C4
Castle Bsns Village
TW12. . . . . 173 D2
Castle Cl 12 Acton W3. . . . 111 A4
Ashford TW16. . . . . 171 C3
Beckenham BR2. . . . . 208 C6
Homerton E9 . . . . 75 A3
South Acton W3 . . . . 110 D4
Wimbledon SW19. . . . . . . 156 D1
Castlecombe Dr SW19 . . . . 156 D4
Castlecombe Prim Sch
SE9. . . . . 188 A6
Castlecombe Rd SE9. . . . . 188 A6
Castle Ct Belmont SM2 . . . 217 C2
City of London EC3 . . . . . 242 D1
Dagenham RM9 . . . . 103 A6
Forest Hill SE26. . . . . 185 A6
Morden SM4. . . . . 202 B4
Castleden Ho NW6. . . . . . . 70 B1
Castledine Rd SE20 . . . . . 184 B3
Castle Dr IG4. . . . . 56 A3
Castleford Ave SE9 . . . . . . 166 D3
Castleford Cl N17. . . . . 33 D4
Castleford Ct NW8. . . . . . . 236 D6
Castlefrank Ho 20 N1. . . . . 95 C4
Castlegate TW9. . . . . 132 B2
CASTLE GREEN 102 C6
Castleham Ct HA8. . . . . 26 C4
Castlehaven Rd NW1. . . . . . 71 B1
Castle Hill Ave CR0. . . . . . 224 A1
Castle Hill Prim Sch
Chessington KT9. . . . . . . 214 B3
New Addington CR0 . . . . . 224 A4
Castle Ho
17 Belmont SM2. . . . . 217 C1
3 Chingford E4 . . . . 36 B5
Newington SE1. . . . . 262 A4
South Lambeth SW8. . . . . 270 A4
Castle Hts RM9 . . . . 102 B6

Castle Ind Est SE17. . . . . . 262 A4
Castle La SW1. . . . . 115 C3 259 A6
Castlelegh Ct EN2. . . . . 17 B6
Castlemaine 8 SW11. . . . . 136 D3
Castlemaine Ave CR2 . . . . 221 D3
Castlemaine St 2 E1. . . . . . 96 B2
Castle Mead SE5. . . . . 139 A5
Castle Mews
Camden Town NW1 . . . . . . 71 B2
North Finchley N12. . . . . . . 30 A5
Castle Par KT17. . . . . 216 A1
Castle Pl 8 Acton W4. . . . . 111 C2
Camden Town NW1 . . . . . . 71 B2
Castle Point 4 E13. . . . . . . 99 C5
Castle Rd
Camden Town NW1 . . . . . . 71 B2
Dagenham RM9 . . . . 102 B6
Enfield EN3. . . . . 7 A5
Isleworth TW7 . . . . 130 D3
North Finchley N12. . . . . . . 30 A5
Northolt UB5 . . . . 63 D1
Southall UB2. . . . . 107 B3
Castlereagh Ho HA7. . . . . . . 25 B4
Castlereagh St SW1 . . . . . 237 C2
Castle St E6. . . . . 99 C5
Castleton Ave HA9. . . . . 66 A4
Castleton Cl CR0. . . . . 207 A3
Castleton Ct KT5. . . . . 198 B4
Castleton Gdns HA9. . . . . . . 66 A5
Castleton Ho 3 E14 . . . . . . 120 A2
Castleton Rd
Chingford E17. . . . . 36 B1
Ilford IG3. . . . . 58 B1
Mitcham CR4 . . . . 203 D5
Mottingham SE12, SE9. . . 187 D6
Ruislip HA4. . . . . 40 D1
Castletown Rd
W14. . . . . 113 A1 254 B1
Castleview Cl N4. . . . . 73 A6
Castleview Gdns IG1. . . . . . 56 B3
Castle Way
Feltham TW13 . . . . 172 C6
Wimbledon SW19. . . . . . . 156 D1
Castle Wlk TW16. . . . . 194 C6
Castlewood Dr SE9 . . . . . . 144 B3
Castlewood Ho WC1 . . . . . 239 D2
Castlewood Rd Barnet EN4 . . 2 B2
Stamford Hill N16. . . . . 52 A3
Castle Yd Highgate N6. . . . . 49 A2
18 Richmond TW10 . . . . . . 153 D6
Castor La E14. . . . . 119 D6
Catalina Rd TW6. . . . . 126 C2
Catalpa Ct SE13. . . . . 164 B5
Caterham Rd SE13. . . . . . . 142 B2
Catesby Ho 25 E9 . . . . 74 C1
Catesby St SE17 . . . 117 B2 262 D3
CATFORD. 163 C3
Catford Br SE6. . . . . 163 B4
Catford Bridge Sta SE6. . . 163 C4
Catford Broadway SE6 . . . 163 D4
Catford Gyratory SE6 . . . . 163 D4
Catford High Sch SE6 . . . . 164 A1
Catford Hill SE6. . . . . 163 C3
Catford Rd SE6. . . . . 163 C4
Catford Sh Ctr SE6. . . . . . 163 D4
Catford Sta SE6. . . . . 163 C4
Cathall L Ctr E11. . . . . 76 C6
Cathall Rd E11. . . . . 76 B5
Cathay Ho SE16. . . . . 118 B4
Cathay St 3 SE16. . . . . . . 118 B4
Cathay Wlk UB5. . . . . 85 C5
Cathcart Dr BR6. . . . . 211 C1
Cathcart Hill N19. . . . . 71 C5
Cathcart Rd
SW10. . . . . 136 A6 266 A6
Cathcart St NW5. . . . . 71 B2
Cathedral Ct EC4 . . . . 241 D1
Cathedral Lo EC1. . . . . 242 A4
Cathedral Sch of St Saviour
& St Mary Overie Prim Sch
SE1. . . . . 117 A4 252 B2
Cathedral St SE1. . .117 B5 252 C4
Cathedral Wlk SW1 . . . . . 259 A6
Catherall Rd N5, N16. . . . . . 73 A5
Catherine Baird Ct 12
SW12. . . . . 159 B4
Catherine Ct Barnet EN5 . . . 1 D2
1 Ilford IG2 . . . . 57 A3
2 Southgate N14. . . . . 15 C6
3 Wimbledon SW19 . . . . . 179 B5
Catherine Dr
Ashford TW16. . . . . 171 D4
Wallington SM6. . . . . 219 B2
Wembley HA0. . . . . 65 D3
Whitechapel E1. . . . . 243 B2
Catherine Gdns TW3. . . . . 130 B1
Catherine Godfrey Ho
RM9. . . . . 103 B6
Catherine Gr SE10 . . . . . . 141 D4
Catherine Griffiths Ct
EC1. . . . . 241 B6
Catherine Ho
Isleworth TW7 . . . . 131 B4
16 Shoreditch N1. . . . . 95 C6
Catherine Lo E18. . . . . 37 C1
Catherine Pl Harrow HA1. . . 42 C4
Westminster SW1 . . 115 C3 259 A6
Catherine Rd Enfield EN3. . . . 7 A6
Kingston u T KT6. . . . . . . 197 D4
Catherine St
WC2. . . . . .116 B6 250 C6

Catherine Wheel Alley
E1. . . . . 243 B3
Catherine Wheel Rd
TW8. . . . . 131 D5
Catherine Wheel Yd
SW1. . . . . 249 A3
Catherwood Ct N1. . . . . . . 235 C3
Cat Hill EN4. . . . . 14 D6
Cathles Rd SW12 . . . . 159 B5
Cathnor Rd W12. . . . . 112 B4
Catisfield Rd EN3. . . . . 7 A6
Catlin Cres TW17. . . . . 193 B4
Catling Cl SE23. . . . . 162 D1
Catlin's La HA5. . . . . 40 B5
Catlin St SE16. . . . . 118 B1
Catman Ho N4. . . . . 50 B1
Caton Ct BR2. . . . . 186 C1
Cato Rd SW4 . . . . 137 D1
Cator La BR3. . . . . 185 B2
Cator Park Sch for Girls
BR3. . . . . 185 A3
Cator Rd
Penge SE20, SE26. . . . . . 184 D5
Wallington SM5 . . . . 218 D3
Cator St W1. . . . . . . .92 C1 237 B2
Catsey La WD23. . . . . 8 A4
Catsey Wood WD23. . . . . . . 8 A4
Catterick Cl N11 . . . . 31 A4
Cattistock Rd SE9. . . . . . . 188 B5
Cattley Cl EN5. . . . . 1 A1
Catton St WC1. . . . . 240 C3
Caughley Ho SE11. . . . . . . 261 A5
Caulfield Ct 15 NW1. . . . . . 71 C1
Caulfield Rd East Ham E6. . . 78 B1
London SE15. . . . . 140 C3
Causeway TW14, TW4. . . . 128 B1
Causeway The
Carshalton SM5 . . . . 219 A6
Chessington KT9 . . . . 214 A4
Claygate KT10 . . . . 212 D1
East Finchley N2. . . . . 48 C5
Teddington TW11 . . . . 174 D4
Wandsworth SW18 . . . . . . 157 D6
Wimbledon SW19. . . . . . . 178 C5
Causeyware Rd N9. . . . . 18 C4
Causton Cotts 3 E14 . . . . . 97 A1
Causton Ho SE5 . . . . 139 A5
Causton Rd N6. . . . . 49 B2
Causton Sq RM10. . . . . 81 C1
Causton St SW1 . . . 115 D1 259 D2
Cautley Ave SW4. . . . . 159 C6
Cavalier Cl RM6. . . . . 58 D5
Cavalier Gdns UB3. . . . . . . 83 B1
Cavalier Ho W5. . . . . 109 C6
Cavalry Cres TW4 . . . . 128 C2
Cavalry Gdns SW15 . . . . . 157 B6
Cavan Pl HA5. . . . . 23 B4
Cavaye Ho SW10 . . . . 266 B6
Cavaye Pl SW10. . . . . 266 B1
Cavell Ct 5 N19 . . . . 71 C6
Cavell Dr EN2. . . . . 4 C3
Cavell Ho 8 N1. . . . . 95 C6
Cavell Rd N17. . . . . 33 B3
Cavell St E1. . . . . 96 B2
Cavendish Ave Ealing W13. . 87 A1
Falconwood DA16. . . . . . . 145 D2
Finchley N3. . . . . 29 C1
Harrow HA1. . . . . 41 C4
Ruislip HA4. . . . . 62 B3
Sidcup DA15. . . . . 168 A4
St John's Wood
NW8. . . . . .92 B5 229 D3
West Barnes KT3 . . . . 200 B5
Woodford IG8. . . . . 37 B3
Cavendish Cl
Ashford TW16. . . . . 171 D4
Brondesbury NW6 . . . . 69 B2
Edmonton N18. . . . . 34 B5
Hayes UB4 . . . . 83 C2
3 Putney SW15. . . . . 157 A6
St John's Wood
NW8. . . . . .92 B4 229 D2
Cavendish Coll
WC1. . . . . .93 D2 239 C4
Cavendish Cres WD6. . . . . . 10 C6
Cavendish Ct
Ashford TW16. . . . . 171 D4
Catford SE6 . . . . 163 D3
5 Chingford E4 . . . . 20 C4
Cavendish Dr
Claygate KT10 . . . . 212 C3
Edgware HA8 . . . . 26 B4
Leytonstone E11. . . . . 54 B1
Cavendish Gdns
Barking IG11 . . . . 79 D3
Clapham Park SW4 . . . . . 159 C5
Dagenham RM6. . . . . 59 A4
Ilford IG1. . . . . 56 C1
Cavendish Ho London N12. . 30 A6
1 Muswell Hill N10. . . . . . . 31 A3
3 Richmond TW10 . . . . . . 153 C1
South Lambeth SW8. . . . . 270 A2
St John's Wood NW8 . . . . 229 D3
Twickenham TW1. . . . . 153 A5

Cavendish Jun & Inf Sch
W4 . . . . 133 C5
Cavendish Mans
2 Clapham Pk SW12. . . . . 159 C5
Hackney E5. . . . . 74 C3
Holborn EC1 . . . . 241 A5
8 West Hampstead NW6 . . 69 C3
Cavendish Mews N W1. . . . 218 A6
Cavendish Mews N W1. . . . 238 D4
Cavendish Mews S W1. . . . 238 D3
Cavendish Par
Balham SW12. . . . . 159 B5
Hounslow TW4 . . . . 129 A3
Cavendish Pl
Balham SW4 . . . . 159 B5
Bromley BR1. . . . . 210 B6
Brondesbury NW2 . . . . 68 D2
Marylebone W1 . . . . 238 D2
Cavendish Rd
Ashford TW16. . . . . 171 D4
Brondesbury NW6 . . . . 69 B1
Chingford E4 . . . . 36 A4
Chiswick W4 . . . . 133 A4
Clapham Pk SW12 . . . . . . 159 C5
Edmonton N18. . . . . 34 B5
Harringay N4 . . . . 50 D3
Mitcham SW19 . . . . 180 C3
New Malden KT3 . . . . 199 D5
Sutton SM2. . . . . 218 A1
Thornton Heath CR0. . . . . 204 D1
Cavendish Sch 14 SE16. . . 118 C2
Cavendish Sch The
NW1. . . . . .93 B6 231 D6
Cavendish Sq W1. . .93 B1 238 D2
Cavendish St N1. . . 95 B5 235 C3
Cavendish Terr
Feltham TW13 . . . . 150 A2
11 Tower Hamlets E3. . . . . 97 B4
Cavendish The NW11. . . . . . 47 D2
Cavendish Way BR4. . . . . . 207 D1
Cavenham Gdns IG1. . . . . . 79 B5
Cave Rd Newham E13 . . . . . 99 B4
Richmond TW10 . . . . 175 C6
Caverleigh Way KT4 . . . . . 200 B2
Caversham Ave
Cheam SM3 . . . . 217 A6
Palmers Green N13 . . . . . . 16 C1
Caversham Ct N11. . . . . 15 A1
Caversham Ho
7 Kingston u T KT1 . . . . . 176 A1
7 Peckham SE15. . . . . . . 140 A6
Wallington CR0. . . . . 220 A5
West Green N15. . . . . 51 A5
Caversham Lo N10. . . . . . . 31 C1
Caversham Ho
Kentish Town NW5 . . . . . . 71 C2
Kingston u T KT1. . . . . . . 176 B1
West Green N15. . . . . 51 A5
Caversham St
SW3. . . . . 136 D6 267 C6
Caverswall St W12. . . . . . . 90 C1
Caveside Cl BR7. . . . . 188 C2
Cavour Ho SE17. . . . . 261 D2
Cawdor Cres W7. . . . . 109 A2
Cawnpore St SE19 . . . . . . 183 C5
Cawston Ct 8 BR1. . . . . . . 186 D3
Caxton Gr E3. . . . . 97 C4
Caxton Hall★ SW1 . . . . . . 259 C6
Caxton Mews 9 TW8 . . . . . 131 D5
Caxton Rd
Shepherd's Bush W12 . . . . 112 D4
Southall UB2. . . . . 106 D3
Wimbledon SW19. . . . . . . 180 A5
Wood Green N22. . . . . 32 B1
Caxton St N E16 . . . . 98 D1
Caxton St SW1. . . . 115 D3 259 C6
Caxton Trad Est UB3 . . . . . 105 C5
Caxton Wlk WC2. . . . . 239 D1
Cayford Ho 4 NW3 . . . . 70 D3
Caygill Cl BR2. . . . . 208 D5
Cayley Cl SM6. . . . . 220 B5
Cayley Prim Sch 22 E14 . . . 97 A1
Cayley Rd UB2. . . . . 107 D3
Cayton Pl EC1. . . . . 235 C1
Cayton Rd UB6. . . . . 86 C5
Cayton St EC1. . . . . 235 C1
Cazenove Mans 1 N16. . . . . 74 A6
Cazenove Rd
Stoke Newington N16. . . . . 74 A6
Walthamstow E17 . . . . 35 C2
Ceasors Ct TW1. . . . . 152 D2
Cecil Ave Barking IG11 . . . . . 79 B1
Enfield EN1. . . . . 5 D1
Wembley HA9. . . . . 66 B3
Cecil Cl Chessington KT9. . . 213 D4
Ealing W5. . . . . 87 D2
Cecil Ct Chelsea SW10 . . . 266 A6
12 Croydon CR0. . . . . 221 D6
Ealing W5. . . . . 87 D2
Littleton TW15. . . . . 171 A3
South Hampstead NW6 . . . 69 D1
St James WC2. . . . . 250 A5
Cecile Pk N8. . . . . 50 A3
Cecil Ho E17. . . . . 35 C2
Cecilia Cl N2. . . . . 48 A6
Cecilia Rd E8. . . . . 74 A3

Cecil Lo KT9 . . . . 213 D4
Cecil Manning Cl UB6 . . . . .87 A6
Cecil Mans 2 SW17 . . . . 159 A2
Cecil Pk HA5 . . . . .41 A5
Cecil Pl CR4 . . . . 202 D4
Cecil Rd Acton W3 . . . . . . .89 A2
  Ashford TW15 . . . . 171 A4
  Cheam SM1, SM2 . . . . . . 217 B2
  Colindale NW9 . . . . .45 C6
  Dagenham RM6 . . . . .58 D2
  Enfield EN2 . . . . 5 B1
  Harlesden NW10 . . . . . . .89 C6
  Harrow HA3 . . . . .42 C6
  Hounslow TW3 . . . . 130 A3
  Ilford IG1 . . . . .78 D4
  Leyton E11 . . . . .76 C5
  Merton SW19 . . . . 179 D3
  Muswell Hill N10 . . . . . . .31 B1
  Newham E13 . . . . .99 A6
  Osidge N14 . . . . .15 C3
  Thornton Heath CR0 . . . 204 B3
  Walthamstow E17 . . . . . .35 C2
Cecil Rhodes Ho NW1 . . 232 C4
Cecil Rosen Ct HA0 . . . . . .65 B5
Cecil Way BR2 . . . . 209 A1
Cedar Ave Dagenham RM6 . .59 A4
  East Barnet EN4 . . . . . . .14 C4
  Enfield EN3 . . . . 6 C3
  Hayes UB3 . . . . .84 A1
  Ruislip HA4 . . . . .62 C3
  Sidcup DA15 . . . . 168 A4
  Twickenham TW2 . . . . . . 152 A5
  Yiewsley UB7 . . . . 104 B6
Cedar Cl Buckhurst Hill IG9 . .21 D2
  East Molesey KT8 . . . . . 196 C5
  Keston Mark BR2 . . . . . 226 A5
  Kingston u T KT2 . . . . . . 177 B6
  Old Ford E3 . . . . .97 B6
  Wallington SM5 . . . . 218 D2
  West Norwood SE21 . . . 161 A2
Cedar Copse BR1 . . . . . . 188 B1
Cedar Cres BR2 . . . . .35 C2
Cedarcroft Rd KT9 . . . . . . 214 B4
Cedar Ct
  7 Brentford TW8 . . . . . . 131 D6
  19 Charlton SE7 . . . . . . 143 C6
  Edgware HA8 . . . . .11 A1
  Eltham SE9 . . . . 166 A5
  Finchley N3 . . . . .29 C3
  Islington N1 . . . . .73 A1
  Marylebone W1 . . . . 237 B2
  Mortlake SW14 . . . . 133 A1
  1 Muswell Hill N10 . . . . .31 B1
  5 New Southgate N11 . . .31 C5
  Oakleigh Pk N20 . . . . . . .14 B3
  Stoneleigh KT17 . . . . . . 216 A1
  3 Sutton SM2 . . . . 218 A2
  6 Wanstead E11 . . . . . . .55 B4
  Wembley HA0 . . . . .65 B4
  Wimbledon SW19 . . . . . 156 D1
  5 Woodford E18 . . . . . . .37 A2
Cedar Dr
  Hampstead Garden Sub
  NW11 . . . . .47 C5
  London N2 . . . . .48 C5
  Pinner HA5 . . . . .23 C4
Cedar Gdns SM2 . . . . 218 A2
Cedar Gr Ealing W5 . . . . . 110 A3
  Sidcup DA5 . . . . 168 D5
  Southall UB1 . . . . .79 A4
Cedar Grange 10 EN1 . . . .17 C6
Cedar Ho Ashford TW16 . . 171 D3
  5 Cubitt Town E14 . . . . 120 A4
  Hayes UB4 . . . . .84 C3
  Kensington W8 . . . . 255 C6
  New Addington CR0 . . . . 223 D2
  New Cross Gate SE14 . . . 140 D4
  5 Richmond TW9 . . . . . 132 D4
  16 Rotherhithe SE16 . . . 118 D4
  Wood Green N22 . . . . . . .32 C2
Cedar Hts TW10 . . . . 154 A3
Cedarhurst BR1 . . . . 186 C3
Cedarhurst Dr SE9 . . . . . 165 C6
Cedar Lawn Ave EN5 . . . . .13 A6
Cedar Lo
  Brondesbury NW2 . . . . . .69 B2
  Fulham SW6 . . . . 134 D4
Cedarmore Ct BR7 . . . . . 189 A2
Cedar Mount SE9 . . . . . . 165 D3
Cedarne Rd SW6 . . 135 D5 265 C3
Cedar Park Gdns RM6 . . . .58 D2
Cedar Park Rd EN2 . . . . . . 5 A5
Cedar Pk Gdns SW19 . . . 178 B5
Cedar Pl 3 SE7 . . . . 121 C1
Cedar Rd Bromley BR1 . . 187 C1
  Cranford TW5 . . . . 128 C3
  Cricklewood NW2 . . . . . .68 C4
  Croydon CR0 . . . . 221 C6
  East Bedfont TW14 . . . . . 149 B3
  East Molesey KT8 . . . . . 196 C5
  Enfield EN2 . . . . 5 A5
  Sutton SM2 . . . . 218 A2
  Teddington TW11 . . . . . . 175 A5
  Tottenham N17 . . . . .33 D2
Cedar Rise N14 . . . . .15 A4
Cedars Ave Mitcham CR4 . 203 A6
  Walthamstow E17 . . . . . .53 C4

Cedars Cl Hendon NW4 . . . .46 D6
  Lewisham SE13 . . . . 142 B2
Cedars Ct Edmonton N9 . . .17 D2
  Putney SW15 . . . . 156 A5
Cedars Dr UB10 . . . . .82 C5
Cedars Ho
  21 London SW2 . . . . . . 138 B1
  15 Walthamstow E17 . . . .53 D6
  5 West Norwood SW27 . 182 D5
Cedars Manor Sch HA3 . . .24 A2
Cedars Mews SW4 . . . . . 137 B1
Cedars Prim Sch The
  TW5 . . . . 128 A5
Cedars Rd Barnes SW13 . . 134 A3
  Beckenham BR3 . . . . . . 185 B1
  Clapham SW4 . . . . 137 B1
  4 Lower Edmonton N9 . .18 A2
  Morden SM4 . . . . 201 C5
  Stratford E15 . . . . .76 C2
  Teddington KT8 . . . . 175 C2
  Wallington CR0 . . . . 220 A4
  Winchmore Hill N21 . . . . .16 D2
Cedars The
  Buckhurst Hill IG9 . . . . . .21 A3
  Ealing W13 . . . . .87 C1
  Hackney E9 . . . . .74 D1
  4 Kingston u T KT2 . . . 176 D2
  Teddington TW11 . . . . . 174 D4
  Wallington SM6 . . . . 219 C4
Cedar Terr
  9 Dagenham RM8 . . . . . .58 D2
  Richmond TW9 . . . . 132 A1
Cedar Tree Gr SE27 . . . . 182 D5
Cedarville Gdns SW16 . . . 182 B4
Cedar Way Ashford TW16 . 171 C3
  Camden Town NW1 . .93 D6 232 C6
Cedar Wlk KT10 . . . . 212 D2
Cedarwood BR3 . . . . 185 B3
Cedarwood Ho EN2 . . . . . . 4 D3
Cedarwood Lo HA8 . . . . . .26 B5
Cedra Ct N16 . . . . .52 A1
Cedric Chambers NW8 . . 236 C6
Cedric Rd SE9 . . . . 167 A1
Celadon Cl EN3 . . . . 7 A2
Celandine Cl E3, E14 . . . . .97 C2
Celandine Ct E4 . . . . .19 D1
Celandine Dr Dalston E8 . . 73 D1
  Woolwich SE28 . . . . 124 B5
Celandine Gr N14 . . . . . . .15 C6
Celandine Way E15 . . . . . .98 C4
Celbridge Mews W2 . . . . . .91 D1
Celestial Gdns SE13 . . . . 142 B1
Celia Blairman Ho E1 . . . 243 C4
Celia Ct 7 TW9 . . . . 132 B4
Celia Ho 10 N1 . . . . .95 C5
Celia Rd N19 . . . . .71 C4
Celtic Ave BR2 . . . . 208 C6
Celtic St E14 . . . . .97 D2
Cemetery La
  Lower Halliford TW17 . . . 192 D2
  Woolwich SE7 . . . . 144 A6
Cemetery Rd
  East Wickham SE2 . . . . . 146 B5
  Forest Gate E7 . . . . .76 D4
  Tottenham N17 . . . . .33 C3
Cenacle Cl NW3 . . . . .69 C5
Cenotaph* SW1 . . . . 250 A2
Centaurs Bsns PktTW7 . 131 A6
Centaur St SE1 . . 116 B3 260 D6
Centenary Rd EN3 . . . . 7 B1
Centennial Ave WD6 . . . . . 9 C4
Centennial CtWD6 . . . . 9 C4
Centennial PkHA7, WD6 . . . 9 C4
Central Ave
  Battersea SW11 . . 136 D5 267 D3
  East Finchley N2 . . . . . . .47 D6
  East Molesey KT8 . . . . . 195 B4
  Edmonton N9 . . . . .17 D1
  Enfield EN1 . . . . 6 B3
  Finchley N2 . . . . .30 B1
  Hayes UB3 . . . . 106 A6
  Isleworth TW3, TW7 . . . . 130 A1
  Leyton E11 . . . . .76 B6
  Pinner HA5 . . . . .41 B2
  Wallington SM6 . . . . 220 A3
  Welling DA16 . . . . 146 A3
Central Bsns Ctr NW10 . . .67 C3
Central Chambers W5 . . 109 D6
Central Cir NW4 . . . . .46 B4
Central Ct 2 SE18 . . . . . 122 D2
Centrale CtrCR0 . . . . 221 A6
Central StaCR0 . . . . 221 A6
Central Foundation Boys' Sch
  EC2 . . . . .95 B3 242 D6
Central Foundation Lower
  Girls Sch The 10 E3 . . . .97 A4
Central Foundation Upper
  Girls Sch The 27 E3 . . . .97 B4
Central Gdns SM4 . . . . . . 201 D4
Central Hill SE19 . . . . 183 B4
Central Ho Barking IG11 . . .79 A1
  Mill Meads E15 . . . . .98 A5
Central Mans
  8 London NW4 . . . . .46 B4
  1 Streatham SW16 . . . . 182 A6
Central Middlesex Hospl
  NW10 . . . . .89 A4
Central Par Croydon CR0 . 220 C4
  Ealing UB6 . . . . .87 A4

Central Par continued
  Enfield EN3 . . . . 6 C3
  Feltham TW14 . . . . 150 C4
  Harrow HA1 . . . . .42 D4
  Heston TW5 . . . . 129 C5
  Ilford IG2 . . . . .57 B3
  Penge SE20 . . . . 184 D3
  South Acton W3 . . . . . . 110 D4
  2 Streatham SW16 . . . . 182 A6
  Surbiton KT6 . . . . 198 A3
  8 Walthamstow E17 . . . .53 C5
Central Park Ave RM10 . . .81 D5
Central Park Prim Sch 7
  E6 . . . . .99 D5
Central Park Rd E6 . . . . . .99 D5
Central Par Villas BR5 . . 190 C1
Central Pk EstTW4 . . . . . 128 D1
Central Public Health
  Laboratories NW9 . . . . . .45 C6
Central Rd Finchley N2 . . .30 C2
  Morden SM4 . . . . 201 D4
  Wembley HA0 . . . . .65 B3
  Worcester Pk KT4 . . . . . 216 A6
Central St Martins Coll
  EC1 . . . . .94 C3 241 B5
Central St Martin's Coll of
  Art & Design W1 . .93 D1 239 D1
Central St Martins Coll of Art
  & Design (The London Inst)
  WC1 . . . . .94 B2 240 C3
Central Sch of Ballet
  EC1 . . . . .94 C3 241 B5
Central Sch of Speech &
  Drama NW3 . . . . .70 B1
Central Sq
  East Molesey SE15 . . . . 195 B5
  Hampstead Garden Suburb
  NW11 . . . . .47 D3
  4 Wembley HA9 . . . . . . .66 A3
Central St EC1 . . . .95 A4 235 A1
Central Terr BR3 . . . . 206 D6
Central Way
  Feltham TW14 . . . . 150 B6
  Lower Place NW10 . . . . . .89 A4
  Sutton SM5 . . . . 218 C1
  Thamesmead SE28 . . . . . 124 B6
  Centre Acad 2 SW11 . . 136 B1
  Centre Ave Acton W3 . . 111 B5
  Finchley N2 . . . . .30 C1
  Centre Bldg SE17 . . . . 262 B4
Centre Common Rd
  BR7 . . . . 189 A3
Centre Court Sh Ctr 3
  SW19 . . . . 179 B4
Centre Ct N20 . . . . .14 B2
Centre Dr E7 . . . . .77 C4
Centre Hts 5 NW3 . . . . . .70 B1
Centre Point 3 SE1 . . . . 118 A1
Centre Point Ho WC2 . . . 239 D2
Centre Rd
  Dagenham RM10 . . . . . . 103 D5
  Finchley N2 . . . . .30 C1
  Wanstead E7, E11 . . . . . .77 A6
Centre St E2 . . . . .96 B5
Centre TheTW13 . . . . 150 B3
Centre The Performing Arts
  Coll SE18 . . . . 121 D3
Centreway 4 IG1 . . . . . . .79 A6
Centre Way N9 . . . . .18 D2
Centro Ct E11 . . . . .54 C1
Centurian Sq 9 SE18 . . . 144 A4
Centurian Way DA18 . . . . 125 C3
Centurion Bldg SW8 . . . 268 C5
Centurion Cl N7 . . . . .72 B1
Centurion Ct
  Hackbridge SM6 . . . . . . 219 B6
  7 Woolwich SE18 . . . . . 122 B2
Centurion La E3 . . . . .97 B5
Centurion Lodge 2
  RM10 . . . . .81 D2
Centurion Way DA18 . . . . 125 C3
Century Cl NW4 . . . . .46 D4
Century Ho Edgware HA8 . . 26 C3
  Harrow HA3 . . . . .42 C6
  Lewisham SE13 . . . . 141 D3
  Wembley HA9 . . . . .66 B6
Century Rd E17 . . . . .53 A6
Century Yd SE23 . . . . 162 C2
Cephas Ave E1 . . . . .96 C3
Cephas Ho 9 E1 . . . . .96 C3
Cephas St E1 . . . . .96 C3
Ceres Ct 12 KT1 . . . . 176 A1
Ceres Rd SE18 . . . . 123 D2
Cerise Rd SE15 . . . . 140 A4
Cerne Cl UB4 . . . . 106 C6
Cerne Rd SM4 . . . . 202 A3
Cerney Mews W2 . . . . . . 246 C6
Cervantes Ct 12 W2 . . . . .91 D1
Cester St E2 . . . . .96 A6
Ceylon Rd
  6 Hammersmith W14 . . . 112 D3
  Kensington W14 . . . . . . 254 A5
Chabot Dr SE15 . . . . 140 B2
Chace Com Sch EN1 . . . . . 5 C4
Chadacre Ave IG5 . . . . . . .56 B6
Chadacre Ct E15 . . . . .99 A6
Chadacre Ho 10 SW9 . . . 138 B1
Chadacre Rd KT17 . . . . . 216 B3
Chadbourn St E14 . . . . . . .97 D2
Chadbury Ct NW7 . . . . . . .28 A2

Chad Cres N9 . . . . .18 C1
Chadd Dr BR1 . . . . 210 A6
Chadd Gn 2 E13 . . . . . . .99 A6
Chaddlewood EN4 . . . . 3 A1
Chadston Ho 17 N1 . . . . . .72 D1
Chadswell WC1 . . . . 233 B1
Chadview Ct 2 RM6 . . . . .58 D2
Chadville Gdns RM6 . . . . .58 C4
Chadway RM8 . . . . .58 C1
Chadwell Ave RM6 . . . . . .58 B2
CHADWELL HEATH 58 D4
Chadwell Heath Foundation
  Sch The RM6 . . . . .58 B3
Chadwell Heath Ind Pk
  RM8 . . . . .58 D1
Chadwell Heath La RM6 . .58 C3
Chadwell Heath Sta RM6 . 58 C2
Chadwell La N8 . . . . .50 B6
Chadwell Prim Sch RM6 . . 58 C2
Chadwell St EC1 . . .94 C4 234 B2
Chadwick Ave
  Chingford E4 . . . . .36 B6
  Enfield N21 . . . . 4 B1
  Wimbledon SW19 . . . . . 179 C4
Chadwick Cl 12 Ealing W7 . .86 D2
  Roehampton SW15 . . . . 156 C4
  Teddington TW11 . . . . . 175 A4
Chadwick Ct 4 SE28 . . . . 124 B5
Chadwick Pl KT6 . . . . 197 C3
Chadwick Rd
  Harlesden NW10 . . . . . . .89 D6
  Ilford IG1 . . . . .78 D5
  Leytonstone E11 . . . . . . .54 D3
  Peckham SE15 . . . . 139 D3
Chadwick St
  SW1 . . . . 115 D3 259 C5
Chadwick Way SE28 . . . . 124 D6
Chadwin Rd E13 . . . . .99 B2
Chadworth Ho
  Finsbury EC1 . . . . 235 A1
  Finsbury Pk N4 . . . . .51 A1
Chadworth Way KT10 . . . 212 B3
Chaffey Ho 6 SE7 . . . . . . 121 C1
Chaffinch Ave CR0 . . . . . 206 D3
Chaffinch Bsns Pk CR0 . . 206 D5
Chaffinch Cl
  Croydon CR0 . . . . 206 D3
  Edmonton N9 . . . . .18 D3
  Tolworth KT6 . . . . 214 C5
Chaffinch Rd BR3 . . . . . . 185 A2
Chafford Way RM6 . . . . . .58 C5
Chagford St NW1 . . . . . . 180 C3
Chagford Ho
  38 Bromley E3 . . . . .97 D4
  Marylebone NW1 . . . . . . 237 C5
Chagford St NW1 . .92 D3 237 D5
Chailey Ave EN1 . . . . 5 D3
Chailey Cl TW5 . . . . 128 C4
Chailey Ind EstUB3 . . . . . 106 A4
Chailey St E5 . . . . .74 C5
Chalbury Ho 8 SW9 . . . . 138 B1
Chalbury Wlk N1 . . . . 234 A4
Chalcombe Rd SE2 . . . . . 124 B3
Chalcot Cl SM2 . . . . 217 C1
Chalcot Cres NW1 . .92 D6 230 D6
Chalcot Gdns NW3 . . . . . .70 D2
Chalcot Mews SW16 . . . . 160 A1
Chalcot Rd NW1 . . .93 A6 231 A6
Chalcot Sch 21 NW1 . . . .71 B1
Chalcot Sq NW1 . . . . .71 A1
Chalcott Gdns KT6 . . . . . 197 C1
Chalcroft Rd SE13 . . . . . 164 C6
Chaldon Rd SW6 . .135 A5 264 B4
Chale Rd SW2 . . . . 160 A5
Chalet Cl TW15 . . . . 171 B4
Chalfont Ave HA9 . . . . . . .66 D2
Chalfont Ct
  8 Belvedere DA17 . . . . . 125 C1
  12 Harrow HA1 . . . . .42 D3
  Hendon NW9 . . . . .45 D6
  Marylebone NW1 . . . . . . 237 D5
Chalfont Gn N9 . . . . .17 C1
Chalfont Ho
  2 Bermondsey SE16 . . . 118 B3
  Willesden NW10 . . . . . . .67 B2
Chalfont Rd Edmonton N9 . .17 D1
  Hayes UB3 . . . . 106 A4
  South Norwood SE25 . . . 205 D6
Chalfont Way W13 . . . . . 109 A4
Chalfont Wlk 5 HA5 . . . . .22 C1
Chalford 7 NW3 . . . . .70 A2
Chalford Cl KT8 . . . . 195 C5
Chalford Ct Ilford IG2 . . . . .56 D4
  13 Putney SW15 . . . . . . 156 D5
Chalford Wlk IG8 . . . . .37 D3
Chalgrove Ave SM4 . . . . . 201 C4
Chalgrove Gdns N3 . . . . . .47 A6
Chalgrove Prim Sch N3 . . .47 A6
Chalgrove Rd
  Sutton SM2 . . . . 218 B1
  Tottenham N17 . . . . .34 B2
Chalice Cl SM6 . . . . 219 D2
Chalice Ct N2 . . . . .48 C5
Chalkenden Cl SE20 . . . . 184 B3
Chalkers Cnr TW9 . . . . . . 132 D2
Chalk Farm Rd NW1 . . . . .71 A1
Chalk Farm StaNW3 . . . . .71 A1
Chalkhill Prim Sch HA9 . . .66 D5

Chalkhill Rd HA9 . . . . .67 A5
Chalk Hill Rd W6 . . . . 112 D2
Chalk La EN4 . . . . 2 D1
Chalklands HA9 . . . . .67 A5
Chalkley Cl CR4 . . . . 181 A1
Chalkmill Dr EN1 . . . . 6 B2
Chalk Pk Ave BR5 . . . . . . 190 C1
Chalk Pit Way SM1 . . . . . 218 A3
Chalk Rd E13 . . . . .99 C2
Chalkstone Cl DA16 . . . . . 146 A4
Chalkwell Ho 10 E1 . . . . . .96 D1
Chalkwell Park Ave EN1 . . 5 C1
Challenge Cl NW10 . . . . . .89 C6
Challenge Ct TW2 . . . . . . 152 C4
Challenge RdTW15 . . . . . 149 B1
Challenger Ho 7 E14 . . . . 119 A6
Challice Way SE2 . . . . . . 160 B3
Challin St HA1 . . . . .43 A4
Challis Rd TW8 . . . . 109 D1
Challoner Cl N2 . . . . .30 B1
Challoner Cres W14 . . . . 254 C1
Challoner Ct BR2 . . . . . . 186 B1
Challoner Mans W14 . . . . 254 C1
Challoners Cl KT8 . . . . . . 196 B5
Challoner St
  W14 . . . . 113 B1 254 C1
Chalmers Ho
  13 London SW11 . . . . . . 136 A2
  Walthamstow E17 . . . . . .53 D4
Chalmers RdTW15 . . . . . 170 D5
Chalmers Rd E TW15 . . . . 171 A5
Chalmers Way
  Feltham TW14 . . . . 150 B6
  Isleworth TW1 . . . . 131 B1
Chalmer's Wlk 12 SE17 . . 138 D6
Chalner Ho 2 SW2 . . . . . 160 C3
Chaloner Ct SE1 . . . . 252 C2
Chalsey Lodge SE4 . . . . . 141 B1
Chalsey Rd SE4 . . . . 141 B1
Chalton Dr N2 . . . . .48 B3
Chalton St NW1 . . . .93 D5 232 C4
Chamberlain Cl Ilford IG1 . . 79 A5
  Plumstead SE18 . . . . . . 123 B3
Chamberlain Cotts SE5 . . 139 B4
Chamberlain Cres BR4 . . 207 D1
Chamberlain Dr SW13 . . . 130 A4
Chamberlain Ho 6 E1 . . . 118 C6
Chamberlain La HA5 . . . . .40 A5
Chamberlain Pl E17 . . . . . .53 A6
Chamberlain Rd
  Ealing W13 . . . . 109 A4
  Finchley N2 . . . . .30 A1
Chamberlain St 6 NW1 . . .70 D1
Chamberlain Way
  Pinner HA5 . . . . .40 B6
  Surbiton KT6 . . . . 198 A2
Chamberlain Wlk 5
  TW13 . . . . 173 A6
Chamberlayne Ave HA9 . . .66 A6
Chamberlayne Mans 3
  NW10 . . . . .90 D4
Chamberlayne Rd NW10 . .90 C6
Chambers Ave DA14 . . . . 191 A4
Chambers Bsns Pk UB7 . 126 C6
Chambers Gdns N2 . . . . . .30 B2
Chambers Ho 2 SW16 . . . 181 C6
Chambers La NW10 . . . . . .68 C1
Chambers Pl CR2 . . . . . . 221 B1
Chambers Rd N7 . . . . .72 A4
Chambers St SE16 . . . . . 118 A4
Chamber St E1 . . 117 D6 253 D6
Chambers Walk HA7 . . . . .25 B5
Chambon Pl 7 W6 . . . . . . 112 A2
Chambord St E2 . . . . .95 D4
Chambord St E2 . . . . .95 D4
Chamomile Ct E17 . . . . . .53 C3
Champa Cl N17 . . . . .33 D1
Champion Cres SE26 . . . . 185 A6
Champion Gr SE5 . . . . . . 139 B2
Champion Hill SE5 . . . . . . 139 B2
Champion Pk SE5 . . . . . . 139 B3
Champion Rd SE26 . . . . . 185 A6
Champlain Ho 28 W12 . . . 112 B6
Champness Cl 9 SE27 . . . 183 B6
Champness Cl IG11 . . . . . .79 D1
Champneys Cl SM2 . . . . . 217 B1
Champneys Ct N21 . . . . . .16 A6
Chancel Ct W1 . . . . 249 C6
Chancellor Gr SE21 . . . . . 161 A1
Chancellor Ho
  South Kensington SW7 . . 256 B6
  29 Wapping E1 . . . . 118 C6
Chancellor Pas E14 . . . . . 119 C5
Chancellor Pl NW9 . . . . . .27 D1
Chancellors' Ct WC1 . . . . 240 C4
Chancellors Loft N8 . . . . .50 A3
Chancellor's Rd W6 . . . . . 112 C1
Chancellors St W6 . . . . . . 112 C1
Chancellors Wharf 21
  W6 . . . . 112 C1
Chancelot Rd SE2 . . . . . . 124 B2
Chancel St SE1 . . 116 D5 251 C3
Chancery Bldgs 14 E1 . . . 118 C6
Chancerygate Bsns Ctr
  HA4 . . . . .63 A3
Chancery Gate Bsns Ctr
  CR4 . . . . 202 D4
Chancery Ho WC2 . . . . . . 241 A3

Chancery La
Beckenham BR3 . . . . **185** D1
Holborn EC4 . . . . **94** C1 <u>**241** A2</u>
Chancery Lane Sta
WC1 . . . . **94** C2 <u>**241** A3</u>
Chancery Mews SW17 . . . **158** C2
Chance St E2 . . . . **243** C6
Chanctonbury CI SE9 . . . **166** D1
Chanctonbury Gdns
SM2 . . . . **217** D1
Chanctonbury Way N12 . . . **29** C6
Chanderia Ct 5 CR0 . . . . **221** A5
Chand Ho 7 N12 . . . .**30** A5
Chandler Ave E16 . . . . **99** A2
Chandler CI TW2 . . . .**173** C2
Chandler Ct
Feltham TW14 . . . . **150** A5
Thornton Heath CR7 . . . . **204** D4
2 Tolworth KT5 . . . . **198** D1
8 Wallington SM6 . . . . .**219** B2
Chandlers CI
East Bedfont TW14 . . . . . .**149** D4
East Molesey KT8 . . . .**195** D4
Chandlers Field Prim Sch
KT8 . . . .**195** C4
Chandlers Mews E14 . . . .**119** C4
Chandler St E1 . . . .**118** B5
Chandlers Way 11 SE24 . .**160** C4
Chandler Way SE15 . . . . .**139** D5
Chandley Ho 26 E1 . . . . . .**96** A1
Chandon Lo SM2 . . . . **218** A1
Chandos Ave Ealing W5 . . **109** D2
New Southgate N14 . . . . . .**15** C1
Oakleigh Pk N20 . . . . **14** B3
Walthamstow E17 . . . . **35** C1
Chandos Bsns Ctr 11
SM6 . . . . **219** C2
Chandos CI IG9 . . . .**21** B2
Chandos Cres HA8 . . . .**26** C3
Chandos Ct Edgware HA8. .**26** B3
Palmers Green N14 . . . . . . **15** C2
Stanmore HA7 . . . . **25** B4
Chandos PI WC2 . .**116** A6 <u>**250** A5</u>
Chandos Rd
Cricklewood NW2 . . . .**68** C3
Finchley N2 . . . . **30** C1
Harrow HA1 . . . . **42** A4
Old Oak Comm NW10 . . . . . **89** C3
Pinner HA5 . . . . **40** D2
Stratford New Town E15 . . . **76** B3
Tottenham N17 . . . . **33** C1
Chandos St W1 . . **93** B2 <u>**238** D3</u>
Chandos Way NW11 . . . . . **47** D1
Change Alley EC3 . . . . **242** D1
Channel CI TW5 . . . .**129** C4
Channel Gate Rd NW10. . .**89** C4
Channel Ho E14 . . . . **97** A2
Channel Sea Bsns Ctr
E15 . . . . **98** B5
Channelsea Rd E15 . . . . . . **98** B6
Channing Jun Sch N6 . . . . .**49** A1
Channing Sch N6 . . . . **49** B1
Channon Ct 3 KT6 . . . . . .**198** A4
Chantress Rd SW9 . . . . . .**138** B2
Chantries The HA7 . . . . . . **25** A5
Chantry CI
2 Abbey Wood SE2 . . . . **124** C3
Edgware NW7 . . . .**11** D4
Enfield EN2 . . . .**5** A5
Harrow HA3 . . . . **44** B4
Sidcup DA14 . . . .**191** A5
Sunbury TW16 . . . .**172** A3
West Kilburn W9 . . . .**91** B3
Chantry Cres NW10 . . . . . .**67** D2
Chantry Ct SM5 . . . . **218** C5
Chantry Ct SW6 . . . .**135** A2
Chantry La BR2 . . . .**209** D4
Chantry PI HA3 . . . . **23** D2
Chantry Rd
Chessington KT9 . . . .**214** C3
Harrow HA3 . . . . **23** D2
Chantry Sch UB7 . . . .**104** A6
Chantry Sq W8 . . . .**113** D3 <u>**255** C5</u>
Chantry The NW8 . . . .**82** B4
Chantry St N1 . . . . .**94** D6 <u>**234** D5</u>
Chantry Way CR4 . . . .**202** B6
Chant Sq E15 . . . . **76** B1
Chant St E15 . . . .**76** B1
Chapel CI NW10 . . . . **67** D2
Chapel Ct
Borough The SE1 . . . .**252** C2
East Finchley N2 . . . .**48** C6
Hayes UB3 . . . .**105** D6
Chapel End Ho E17 . . . .**35** D2
Chapel End Inf Sch E17 . .**35** D2
Chapel End Jun Sch E17 . .**35** D2
Chapel Farm Sch RE9 . . .**166** B2
Chapel Hill N2 . . . . **30** C1
Chapel House St E14 . . . .**119** D2
Chapel La
5 Dagenham RM6 . . . .**58** D2
Hillingdon UB8 . . . .**82** C1
Pinner HA5 . . . . **40** D6
Chapel Mill Rd KT1 . . . . . .**198** B6
Chapel Mkt ✳ N1 . . .**94** C5 <u>**234** A4</u>
Chapel PI Islington N1 . . . **234** B4
Marylebone W1 . . . . **238** C1
12 Shoreditch EC2 . . . .**95** C4
Tottenham N17 . . . . **33** D3

Chapel Rd
Bexleyheath DA7 . . . .**147** C1
Ealing W13 . . . .**109** B5
Hounslow TW3 . . . .**129** D2
Ilford IG1 . . . .**78** D5
Twickenham TW1 . . . .**153** B4
West Norwood SE27 . . . . .**182** D6
Chapel Side W2 . . . .**113** D6 <u>**245** C5</u>
Chapel St Enfield EN2 . . . . . .**5** B2
Paddington NW1 . . . .**92** C2 <u>**237** A3</u>
Westminster SW1 . . .**115** A4 <u>**248** B1</u>
Chapel View CR2 . . . .**222** C1
Chapel Wlk NW4 . . . .**46** C5
Chapleton Ho SW2 . . . . . .**160** C6
Chaplin CI Lambeth SE1 . . .**251** C2
Wembley HA0 . . . .**65** D2
Chaplin Cres TW16 . . . . . .**171** C4
Chaplin Ho
6 London SW9 . . . .**138** C1
Sidcup DA14 . . . .**190** A6
Chaplin Rd
Dagenham RM9 . . . .**81** A1
3 Tottenham N17 . . . .**51** D6
Wembley HA0 . . . .**65** D2
West Ham E15 . . . . **98** D6
Willesden NW2 . . . . **68** A2
Chaplow CI SW6 . . . .**136** A3
Chapman CI UB7 . . . .**104** B3
Chapman Cres HA3 . . . . . .**44** B4
Chapman Gn N22 . . . .**32** C2
Chapman Ho
1 Stepney E1 . . . . **96** B1
2 West Norwood SE27 . . .**160** D1
Chapman Rd
Belvedere DA17 . . . .**125** D1
Hackney Wick E9 . . . . **75** B2
Thornton Heath CR0 . . . . .**204** C1
Chapmans End BR5 . . . . . .**191** A1
Chapman's La BR5 . . . . . .**190** D1
Chapmans Park Ind Est
NW10 . . . .**67** D2
Chapman Sq SW19 . . . . . .**156** D2
Chara PI W4 . . . .**133** B6
Chapone PI W1 . . . . **239** C1
Chapter CI Hillingdon UB10 . .**60** B1
16 South Acton W4 . . . . . .**111** A3
Chapter House & Jewel
Twr ✳ SW1 . . . . **240** A6
Chapter Rd
Kennington SE17 . .**116** D1 <u>**261** D1</u>
Willesden NW2 . . . . **68** A3
Chapter St SW1 . . . . **259** C3
Chapter Way
Hampton TW12 . . . .**173** C6
Mitcham SW19 . . . .**180** B2
Charcot Ho SW15 . . . .**155** D5
Charcroft Ct 11 W14 . . . . .**112** D4
Charcroft Gdns EN3 . . . .**6** D1
Chard Ho 7 N7 . . . . **72** B6
Chardin Ho 30 SW9 . . . . . .**138** C4
Chardin Rd 11 W4 . . . .**111** C2
Chardmore Rd N16 . . . .**52** A1
Charecroft Way W12 . . . . .**112** D4
Charfield Ct W9 . . . .**91** D3
Charford Rd E16 . . . . **99** A2
Chargeable La E13 . . . .**99** A3
Chargeable St E16 . . . .**98** D3
Chargrove CI 24 SE16 . . . .**118** D4
Charing CI BR6 . . . .**227** D4
Charing Cross
SW1 . . . .**116** A5 <u>**250** A4</u>
Charing Cross Hospl
W6 . . . .**112** D1
Charing Cross Rd
WC2 . . . .**93** D1 <u>**239** D1</u>
Charing Cross Sta
WC2 . . . .**116** A5 <u>**250** B4</u>
Charing Ct BR2 . . . .**186** C1
Charing Ho SE1 . . . . **251** B2
Chariot CI 3 E3 . . . . **97** C6
Charlbert Ct NW8 . . . . **230** A4
Charlbert St NW8 . . **92** C5 <u>**230** A4</u>
Charlbury Ave HA7 . . . .**25** D5
Charlbury Gdns IG3 . . . .**79** D6
Charlbury Gr W5 . . . .**87** C1
Charlbury Ho 1 E12 . . . . . .**78** C5
Charlbury Rd UB10 . . . .**60** B5
Charldane Rd SE9 . . . .**166** D1
Charlecote Gr 26 SE26 . . .**162** B1
Charlecote Rd RM8 . . . .**81** A5
Charlemont Rd E6 . . . .**100** C4
Charles Allen Ho EC1 . . . . **234** A2
Charles Auffray Ho 30 E1 . .**96** C2
Charles Babbage CI KT9 . .**213** C6
Charles Barry CI SW4 . . . .**137** C2
Charles Bradlaugh Ho 2
N17 . . . . **34** B3
Charles Burton Ct E5 . . . . .**75** A4
Charles CI DA14 . . . .**190** B6
Charles Cobb Gdns CR0 . .**220** C3
Charles Coveney Rd 4
SE15 . . . .**139** D4
Charles Cres HA1 . . . .**42** B2
Charles Ct 5 TW11 . . . . . .**174** C5
Charles Darwin Ho
8 Bethnal Green E2 . . . . . .**96** B4
Bromley BR1 . . . .**187** B3

Charles Dickens Ct
SE25 . . . .**206** A5
Charles Dickens Ho 1
E2 . . . . **96** B4
Charles Dickens Mus The ✳
WC1 . . . .**94** B3 <u>**240** D5</u>
Charles Dickens Prim Sch
SE1 . . . .**117** A4 <u>**252** A1</u>
Charles Edward Brooke Sch
11 SW9 . . . .**138** C4
Charles Edward Brooke Sch
(Dennen Site) SE5 . . .**138** D4
Charlesfield SE12 . . . .**165** C1
Charles Flemwell Mews 7
E16 . . . .**121** A5
Charles Goddard Ho 3
HA0 . . . . **65** D3
Charles Gr N14 . . . . **15** C3
Charles Grinling Wlk
SE18 . . . .**122** C2
Charles Haller St 23
SW2 . . . .**160** C4
Charles Harrod Ct
SW13 . . . .**134** C6
Charles Ho Southall UB2 . . .**107** C4
1 Tottenham N17 . . . .**33** D3
NW10 . . . .**67** C1
Charles Hocking Ho 8
W3 . . . .**111** A4
Charles II PI
SW3 . . . .**114** D1 <u>**257** C1</u>
Charles II St
SW1 . . . .**115** D5 <u>**249** C4</u>
Charles La NW8 . . . .**92** C5 <u>**230** A4</u>
Charles Lamb Ct N1 . . . . . **234** D4
Charles Lesser KT9 . . . . . .**213** D3
Charles Mackenzie Ho 7
SE16 . . . .**118** A2
Charlesmere Gdns SE28. .**123** C4
Charles Mills Ct SW16 . . .**182** A4
Charles PI NW1 . . . . **232** B1
Charles Rd
Dagenham RM6 . . . .**58** D3
Ealing W13 . . . .**87** A1
Merton SW19 . . . .**179** C2
Upton E7 . . . .**77** C1
Charles Rowan Ho WC1 . . **234** A1
Charles Sevright Dr NW7 . .**28** B6
Charles Sq N1 . . . . .**95** B4 <u>**235** D1</u>
Charles St Barnes SW13 . . .**133** C3
Croydon CR0 . . . .**221** A5
Enfield EN1 . . . .**17** D6
Hillingdon UB10 . . . . **82** D3
Hounslow TW3 . . . .**129** B3
Mayfair W1 . . . .**115** B5 <u>**248** C4</u>
Newham E16 . . . .**121** C5
Charles Staunton Ho 3
SE27 . . . .**183** B6
Charleston CI TW13 . . . . . .**150** A1
Charleston St SE17 . . . . . . **262** B3
Charles Townsend Ho
EC1 . . . . **241** C6
Charles Utton Ct E8 . . . .**74** A4
Charles Whincup Rd 2
E16 . . . .**121** B5
Charlesworth Ho 6 E14. . .**97** C1
Charleville Cir SE26 . . . . . .**184** A5
Charleville Ct SW5 . . . . . . **254** C1
Charleville Mans W14 . . . . **254** B1
Charleville Mews TW7 . . . .**131** B1
Charleville Rd
W14 . . . .**113** B1 <u>**254** C1</u>
Charlie Browns Rdbt E18. .**37** C1
Charlmont Rd SW17 . . . . . .**180** D4
Charlotte CI DA6 . . . .**169** A6
Charlotte Ct
Crouch End N8 . . . .**49** D3
Esher KT10 . . . .**212** A3
10 Hammersmith W6 . . . . .**112** A2
Ilford IG2 . . . .**56** C3
11 Wembley HA0 . . . .**66** A2
Charlotte Despard Ave
SW11 . . . .**137** A4 <u>**268** B1</u>
Charlotte Ho 12 W6 . . . . . .**112** C1
Charlotte Mews
Marylebone W1 . . . . **239** B4
North Kensington W10 . . . . .**90** D1
West Kensington W14 . . . . **254** A4
Charlotte Par SE23. . . . . . .**163** A2
Charlotte Park Ave BR1 . .**210** A6
Charlotte PI Kenton NW9 . . .**45** A4
Marylebone W1 . . . . **239** B3
Westminster SW1 . . . . **259** A3
Charlotte Rd
Barnes SW13 . . . .**133** D4
Dagenham RM10 . . . .**81** D2
Shoreditch EC2 . . . . .**95** C3 <u>**243** A6</u>
Wallington SM6 . . . .**219** C2
Charlotte Row SW4 . . . . . .**137** C2
Charlotte Sharman Prim Sch
SE11 . . . .**116** D3 <u>**261** C5</u>
Charlotte Sq 5 TW10 . . . . .**154** B5
Charlotte St W1 . . . .**93** D2 <u>**239** B4</u>
Charlotte Terr N1 . . .**94** B6 <u>**233** D5</u>
Charlotte Turner Prim Sch
SE8 . . . .**141** C6
CHARLTON **143** D6
171 B1
Charlton Church La SE7 . .**121** C1

Charlton CI UB10 . . . .**60** D6
Charlton Cres IG11 . . . .**101** D5
Charlton Ct Finchley N3 . . . .**29** A1
25 Hackney E2 . . . .**95** D6
17 Kentish Town N7 . . . .**71** D3
Newham E16 . . . .**100** B4
Charlton Dene SE7 . . . .**143** D5
Charlton Gate Bsns Pk
SE7 . . . .**121** C2
Charlton Ho
5 Brentford TW8 . . . .**132** A6
Charlton TW17 . . . .**171** A1
Somers Town NW1 . . . . . . **232** D2
Charlton King's Rd NW5. . .**71** D3
Charlton La
Greenwich SE7 . . . .**121** D1
Upper Halliford TW17. . . . . .**193** B5
Upper Halliford TW17. . . . . .**193** C5
Charlton Lo 1 NW11 . . . .**47** B3
Charlton Manor Prim Sch
SE7 . . . .**143** D5
Charlton Park La SE7 . . . . .**144** A6
Charlton Park Rd SE7 . . . .**143** D6
Charlton PI N1 . . . .**94** D5 <u>**234** C4</u>
Charlton Rd
Charlton TW17 . . . .**171** A1
Edmonton N9 . . . .**18** D4
Greenwich SE3, SE7 . . . . .**143** B6
Harlesden NW10 . . . .**89** C6
Harrow HA3 . . . .**43** D5
Wembley HA9 . . . .**44** B1
Charlton Sch SE7 . . . .**144** A6
Charlton Sta SE7 . . . .**121** C1
Charlton Way SE10, SE3. .**142** C4
Charlwood CI HA3 . . . .**24** C4
Charlwood Ho
Richmond TW9 . . . .**132** D5
1 Streatham SW2 . . . .**160** B3
Westminster SW1 . . . . **259** C3
Charlwood PI
SW1 . . . .**115** C2 <u>**259** B3</u>
Charlwood Rd SW15 . . . . .**134** D1
Charlwood St
SW1 . . . .**115** C1 <u>**259** B2</u>
SW15 . . . .**134** D1
Charlwood Terr 5
SW15 . . . .**134** D1
Charman Ho
18 London SW2 . . . .**160** C5
South Lambeth SW8 . . . . . **270** A4
Charmian Ave HA7 . . . .**25** D1
Charmian Ho 19 N1 . . . .**95** C5
Charminster Ave SW19 . . .**179** D1
Charminster Ct 3 KT6 . . . .**197** D2
Charminster Rd
Mottingham SE12, SE9 . . . .**187** D6
North Cheam KT4 . . . .**200** D1
Charmouth Ct TW10 . . . . . .**154** B6
Charmouth Ho SW8 . . . . . **270** C4
Charmouth Rd DA16 . . . . . .**146** C4
Charnock Ho 22 W12 . . . . .**112** B6
Charnock Rd E5 . . . .**74** B5
Charnwood Ave SW19 . . . .**179** D1
Charnwood CI KT3 . . . .**199** C5
Charnwood Dr E18 . . . .**55** B5
Charnwood Gdns E14 . . . .**119** C2
Charnwood Ho 9 E5 . . . . . .**74** B6
Charnwood PI N20 . . . .**14** A1
Charnwood Rd
Hillingdon UB10 . . . .**82** C5
South Norwood SE25 . . . . .**205** B5
Charnwood St E5 . . . .**74** B6
Charolais Ho UB4 . . . .**83** B2
Charrington Ho 42 E1. . . . .**96** C3
Charrington Rd 2 CR0 . . . .**221** A6
Charrington St
NW1 . . . .**93** D5 <u>**232** C4</u>
Charsley Rd SE6 . . . .**163** D2
Chart CI Bromley BR2 . . . . .**186** C2
Croydon CR0 . . . .**206** C3
Mitcham CR4 . . . .**202** D5
Charter Ave IG2 . . . .**57** B2
Charter Bldgs 14 SE10. . . .**141** D4
Charter Cres TW4 . . . .**129** A1
Charter Ct Finsbury Pk N4. . . .**50** C1
Kingston u T KT3 . . . .**199** C6
Marylebone W1 . . . . **237** B3
Southall UB1 . . . .**107** C5
Wood Green N22 . . . .**31** D2
Charter Dr DA5 . . . .**169** A4
Charter Ho WC2 . . . . **240** B1
Charterhouse Ave HA0 . . . . .**65** C2
Charterhouse Bldgs EC1 . .**242** A5
Charterhouse Mews EC1 . .**241** D4
Charterhouse Rd E8 . . . .**74** A3
Charterhouse Sq
EC1 . . . .**94** D2 <u>**241** D4</u>
Charterhouse Square Sch
The EC1 . . . .**94** D2 <u>**241** D4</u>
Charterhouse St EC1. . . . . **241** C3
Charterhouse Works
SW18 . . . .**136** A1
Charteris Rd
Finsbury Pk N4 . . . .**50** C1
Kilburn NW6 . . . .**91** B6
Woodford IG8 . . . .**37** B4
Charteris Sp Ctr NW6 . . . . .**91** C6
Charter Rd KT1 . . . .**198** D6
Charter Rd The IG8 . . . .**36** D4
Charter Sch SE24 . . . .**161** B6
Charters CI SE19 . . . .**183** C5

Charter Sq KT1 . . . .**176** D1
Charter Way London NW3 . . .**47** B5
Southgate N14 . . . .**15** D5
Chartes Ho SE1 . . . . **263** B6
Chartfield Ave SW15 . . . . .**156** C6
Chartfield Sq SW15 . . . . . .**156** D6
Chartham Ct 12 SW9 . . . . .**138** C2
Chartham Gr SE27 . . . .**160** D1
Chartham Ho SE1. . . . . **262** D6
Chartham Rd SE25 . . . .**206** B6
Chart Hills CI SE28 . . . .**103** A1
Chart Ho 7 SW19 . . . .**180** C1
Chart House The 5
E14 . . . .**119** D1
Chartley Ave Harrow HA7. . .**24** A4
Neasden NW2 . . . .**67** C5
Charton CI 5 DA17 . . . .**147** B6
Chartres Ct UB6 . . . .**86** B5
Chartridge SE17 . . . .**139** B6
Chartridge CI Barnet EN5 . . .**12** A6
Bushey WD23 . . . .**8** A5
Chartridge Ct 6 HA7 . . . . . .**25** C5
Chart St N1 . . . .**95** B4 <u>**235** D2</u>
Chartwell 25 SW19 . . . .**156** B4
Chartwell Bsns Ctr BR1 . .**209** D6
Chartwell CI
3 Croydon CR0 . . . .**205** B1
Greenford UB6 . . . .**85** C6
Sidcup DA14 . . . .**167** B2
Chartwell Ct 10 Barnet EN5. . .**1** A1
Dollis Hill NW2 . . . .**68** A5
2 Woodford IG8 . . . .**37** A3
Chartwell Dr BR6 . . . .**227** B3
Chartwell Gdns SM3 . . . . .**217** A4
Chartwell Lo 5 BR3 . . . . . .**185** C3
Chartwell PI Cheam SM3 . .**217** B4
Harrow HA2 . . . .**64** B6
Chartwell Way 3 SE20 . . . .**184** B2
Charville Ct 8 HA1 . . . .**42** D3
Charville La UB4 . . . .**83** C5
Charville La W UB10 . . . .**82** D4
Charville Prim Sch UB4 . . . .**83** C5
Charwood SW16 . . . .**182** C6
Chase Bridge Prim Sch
TW2 . . . .**152** C5
Chase Court Gdns EN2 . . . . .**5** A2
Chase Ct Chelsea SW3 . . . . **257** C5
Isleworth TW7 . . . .**131** A3
Merton SW20 . . . .**179** A1
Southgate N14 . . . .**15** C5
Wembley HA0 . . . .**65** D2
Chase Ctr The NW10 . . . . . .**89** B4
Chase Farm Hospl EN2. . . . . .**4** C5
Chasefield Rd SW17 . . . . . .**180** D6
Chase Gdns Chingford E4 . . .**35** C6
Twickenham TW2 . . . .**152** B4
Chase Gn EN2 . . . .**5** A2
Chase Green Ave EN2 . . . . . .**5** A3
Chase Hill EN2 . . . .**5** A2
Chase La IG6 . . . .**57** B4
Chase Lane Prim Sch E4 . .**35** B6
Chaseley Ct
Gunnersbury W4 . . . .**110** D1
Oatlands Pk KT13 . . . .**193** C1
Chaseley St E14 . . . .**97** A1
Chasemore CI CR4 . . . .**202** D2
Chasemore Gdns CR0 . . . .**220** C3
Chasemore Ho SW6. . . . . . **264** B4
Chase Rd
North Acton NW10 . . . .**89** B3
Southgate N14 . . . .**15** C5
Chase Ridings EN2 . . . .**4** C3
Chase Road Trad Est
NW10 . . . .**89** B3
Chase Side
East Barnet N14 . . . .**15** B4
Enfield EN2 . . . .**5** A3
Chase Side Ave Enfield EN2. . .**5** A3
Merton SW20 . . . .**179** A1
Chase Side Cres EN2 . . . .**5** A4
Chase Side PI EN2 . . . .**5** A3
Chase Side Prim Sch EN2 . . . .**5** A3
Chase Side Works N14 . . . . .**15** D4
Chase The Bromley BR1 . . . .**209** B6
Clapham SW4 . . . .**137** B2
Dagenham RM6 . . . .**59** A3
Eastcote HA5 . . . .**40** C3
Edgware HA8 . . . .**26** D2
Erith DA7 . . . .**147** D2
Ickenham UB10 . . . .**60** C3
Loughton IG10 . . . .**21** D4
Manor Pk E12 . . . .**77** D4
Pinner HA5 . . . .**41** B5
South Norwood SW16 . . . . .**182** C3
Stanmore HA7 . . . .**25** A4
Sunbury TW16 . . . .**172** B2
Wallington CR0, SM6 . . . . .**220** B3
Chaseville Par N21. . . . .**16** B6
Chaseville Park Rd N21 . . . .**16** B6
Chase Way N14 . . . .**15** C3
Chasewood Ave EN2 . . . .**4** D3
Chasewood Ct 4 NW7 . . . . .**27** B5
Chasewood Pk HA1 . . . .**64** C5
Chateau The 4 SM5 . . . . . .**218** D5
Chatelain Ho NW7 . . . .**28** C6
Chater Ho 6 E2 . . . .**96** D4

Chatfield Rd
London SW11 136 A2
Thornton Heath CR0 204 D1
Chatham Ave BR2 209 A2
Chatham Cl Cheam SM3 201 B2
Hampstead Garden Suburb NW11 47 C4
Woolwich SE18 122 B3
Chatham Ct SW11 158 D6
Chatham Ho
7 London SE5 139 C3
6 Wallington SM6 219 B3
21 Woolwich SE18 122 B2
Chatham Pl E9 74 C2
Chatham Rd
Clapham SW11 158 D6
Kingston u T KT1, KT2 176 C1
Walthamstow E17 53 A6
1 Woodford E18 36 D1
Chatham St SE17 117 B2 262 D4
Chatsfield Pl W5 88 A1
Chatsworth Ave
Grove Pk BR1 187 B6
Hendon NW4 28 C1
Merton SW20 179 A1
Sidcup DA15 168 A3
Wembley HA9 66 B3
Chatsworth Cl
Coney Hall BR2, BR4 224 D6
Hendon NW4 28 C1
Chatsworth Cres TW3, TW7 130 B2
Chatsworth Ct
Brondesbury NW2 68 D2
Clapton Pk E5 74 D4
Earl's Ct W8 255 A4
5 Stanmore HA7 25 C5
Thornton Heath SW16 204 B6
Chatsworth Dr EN1 18 A5
Chatsworth Est E5 74 D4
Chatsworth Gdns
Acton W3 110 D5
Harrow HA2 41 D1
New Malden KT3 199 D4
Chatsworth Ho
2 Bromley BR2 209 A5
Kingston u T KT6 197 D4
Chatsworth Inf Sch
Isleworth TW3 130 A1
Sidcup DA15 168 A3
Chatsworth Jun Sch TW3 130 A1
Chatsworth Lo
1 Chiswick W4 111 B1
West Wickham BR4 224 A6
Chatsworth Par BR5 211 A4
Chatsworth Pl
Mitcham CR4 202 D6
Teddington TW11 175 A6
Chatsworth Rd
Brondesbury NW2 68 D2
Cheam SM3 217 A4
Chiswick W4 133 A6
Clapton Pk E5 74 D4
Ealing W5 88 B3
Hayes UB4 84 B3
South Croydon CR0 221 B5
Stratford E15 76 D3
Chatsworth Rise W5 88 B3
Chatsworth Way SE27 161 A1
Chattenden Ho 8 N4 51 B2
Chatteris Ct NW4 46 D6
CHATTERN HILL 170 D6
Chattern Hill TW15 170 D6
Chattern Rd TW15 171 A6
Chatterton Ct TW9 132 B3
Chatterton Rd
Bromley Comm BR2 209 D4
Highbury N4 72 D5
Chatton Ct 5 NW9 46 A5
Chatto Rd SW11 158 D6
Chaucer Ave
Cranford TW4 128 B3
Hayes UB4 84 A2
Richmond TW9 132 C3
Chaucer Cl N11 31 D5
Chaucer Ct
14 New Barnet EN5 13 D6
17 Stoke Newington N16 73 C4
Chaucer Dr SE1 117 D2 263 D3
Chaucer Gdns SM1 217 C5
Chaucer Gn CR0 206 C2
Chaucer Ho Harrow HA2 41 D4
Pimlico SW1 259 A1
Sutton SM1 217 C5
2 West Norwood SE27 183 A6
Chaucer Rd Acton W3 111 A5
Ashford TW15 170 B6
Bexley DA16 145 D4
Chingford E17 36 A1
Herne Hill SE24 160 D6
Sidcup DA15 168 C3
Sutton SM1 217 C4
Upton E7 77 A2
Wanstead E11 55 A3
Chaucer Way SW17 180 B5
Chaulden Ho EC1 235 D1
Chauncey Cl N9 18 A1
Chaundrye Cl SE9 166 B5
Chauntler Cl E16 121 B6
Chaville Ct N11 31 A6
Cheadle Ct NW8 236 D6
Cheadle Ho 17 E14 97 B1
CHEAM 217 B3
Cheam Common Inf Sch KT4 216 B6
Cheam Common Jun Sch KT4 216 B6
Cheam Common Rd KT4 216 C5
Cheam Court Flats 1 SM3 217 A2
Cheam Fields Prim Sch SM3 217 A3
Cheam High Sch SM3 217 A4
Cheam L Ctr SM3 216 D4
Cheam Mans SM3 217 A1
Cheam Park Farm Inf Sch SM3 217 A5
Cheam Park Farm Jun Sch SM3 217 A5
Cheam Park Way SM3 217 A2
Cheam Rd
Belmont SM2, SM3 216 D1
Cheam SM1 217 C2
Cheam St 6 SE15 140 B2
Cheam Sta SM2 217 A1
Cheam Village SM3 217 A2
Cheapside
Barbican EC2 95 A1 242 B1
Edmonton N13 33 A6
Chearsley SE17 262 B4
Cheddar Cl 1 N11 31 A4
Cheddar Rd TW6 126 C3
Cheddar Waye UB4 84 B1
Cheddington Ho 9 E2 96 A6
Cheddington Rd N18 33 C6
Chedworth Cl E16 98 D1
Chedworth Ho
London N15 51 B5
2 Stoke Newington E5 74 A6
Cheeseman Cl TW12 173 A4
Cheeseman Ct UB1 107 D6
Cheesemans Terr W14 254 C1
Cheffrey Ct TW15 170 D4
Cheldon Ave NW7 28 D3
Chelford Rd BR1 186 B5
Chelmer Cres IG11 102 B5
Chelmer Ct E18 37 B2
Chelmer Rd E9 74 D3
Chelmsford Cl
Fulham W6 134 D6
Newham E6 100 B1
Chelmsford Ct N14 15 D4
Chelmsford Gdns IG1 56 B2
Chelmsford Ho 5 N7 72 B4
Chelmsford Rd
Leytonstone E11 54 B1
London N14 15 C4
Walthamstow E17 53 C3
Woodford E18 36 D2
Chelmsford Sq NW10 90 C6
CHELSEA 114 C1
Chelsea Antiques Mkt* SW3 114 C1 257 B1
Chelsea Barracks* SW1 115 A1 258 B1
Chelsea Bridge SW1 137 B6 268 C6
Chelsea Bridge Rd SW1 115 A1 258 B1
Chelsea Cl Edgware HA8 26 C1
Hampton TW12 174 A5
New Malden KT4 200 A2
Stonebridge NW10 89 B6
Chelsea Cloisters SW3 257 B3
Chelsea Coll of Art & Design SW1 116 A1 260 A2
Chelsea Cres
Brondesbury NW2 69 B2
Chelsea SW10 266 B1
Chelsea Ct Chelsea SW3 268 A6
6 Chingford E4 20 A3
Sutton SM2 217 D2
Chelsea Emb SW3 136 D6 267 C5
Chelsea Est SW3 267 A5
Chelsea Farm Ho SW10 266 D5
Chelsea Fields SW19 180 B2
Chelsea Gate SW1 258 B1
Chelsea Gdns
Cheam SM3 217 A4
Chelsea SW1 258 B1
Ealing W13 86 D2
Chelsea Harbour Design Ctr SW10 266 B2
Chelsea Harbour Dr SW10 136 A4 266 B2
Chelsea Harbour Pier SW10 266 C1
Chelsea Ind Coll SW6 256 C3
Chelsea Lo SW3 267 D6
Chelsea Manor Ct SW3 267 B6
Chelsea Manor Gdns SW3 257 B1
Chelsea Manor St SW3 114 C1 257 B1
Chelsea Manor Studios SW3 257 B1
Chelsea Mus* SW6 265 D4
Chelsea Park Gdns SW3 136 B6 266 C6
Chelsea Physic Gdn* SW1 267 C6
Chelsea Reach Twr SW10 266 C4
Chelsea Sp Ctr SW3 114 C1 257 B1
Chelsea Sq SW3 114 B1 256 D1
Chelsea Twrs SW3 267 B6
Chelsea & Westminster Hospl SW10 136 A6 266 B5
Chelsfield Ave N9 18 D4
Chelsfield Gdns SE26 162 C1
Chelsfield Gn N9 18 D4
Chelsfield Ho SE17 263 A3
Chelsfield Point 3 E9 74 D1
Chelsham Ho 1 SW4 137 D2
Chelsham Rd
London SW4 137 D2
South Croydon CR2 221 B2
Chelsiter Ct DA14 189 D6
Chelston App HA4 62 A6
Chelston Ct 2 E11 55 B4
Chelston Rd HA4 40 A1
Chelsworth Dr SE18 145 B6
Cheltenham Ave 10 TW1 153 A4
Cheltenham Cl
Kingston u T KT3 199 A6
Northolt UB5 63 D2
Cheltenham Ct 8 HA7 25 C5
Cheltenham Gdns E6 100 A5
Cheltenham Ho UB3 105 A3
Cheltenham Pl
10 Acton W3 110 D5
Acton W3 111 A4
Harrow HA3 44 A5
1 South Acton W3 110 D4
Cheltenham Rd
Leyton E10 54 A3
London SE15 162 C6
Cheltenham Terr SW3 114 D1 257 D2
Cheltenham Villas CR7 204 C3
Chelverton Ct SW15 134 D1
Chelverton Rd SW15 134 D1
Chelwood Gospel Oak NW5 71 A3
London N20 14 B2
Chelwood Cl E4 19 D5
Chelwood Ct
Battersea SW11 266 D2
9 South Croydon CR2 221 A3
Chelwood Gdns TW9 132 C3
Chelwood Ho W2 236 D1
Chelwood Lo N12 30 A4
Chenappa Cl E13 99 A4
Chenduit Way HA7 24 D5
Chene Colline Ct KT6 198 A3
Cheney Ct SE23 162 D3
Cheney Row E17 35 B2
Cheneys Rd E11 76 C5
Cheney St HA5 40 C4
Chenies Ho W2 245 C6
Chenies Mews WC1 239 C5
Chenies Pl NW1 232 D4
Chenies St WC1 93 D2 239 C4
Chenies The
Orpington BR6 211 C3
Somers Town NW1 232 D4
Cheniston Gdns W8 255 C6
Chennestone Prim Sch TW16 172 B1
Chepstow Cl SW15 157 A6
Chepstow Cres Ilford IG3 57 C3
Notting Hill W11 113 C6 245 A6
Chepstow Ct W11 245 A6
Chepstow Gdns UB1 85 B1
Chepstow Pl W2 113 C6 245 B6
Chepstow Rd
Croydon CR0 221 D6
Ealing W7 109 A3
Paddington W2 91 C1
Chepstow Rise CR0 221 C5
Chepstow Villas W11 113 C6 245 A6
Chequers IG9 21 B3
Chequers Cl London NW9 45 C6
Orpington BR5 211 D5
Chequers Ct
7 Croydon CR0 205 D1
St Luke's EC1 242 C5
Chequers Ho NW8 237 A6
Chequers La RM9 103 C5
Chequers Par
Dagenham RM9 103 C6
Edmonton N13 33 A5
Chequer St EC1 95 A3 242 B5
Chequers The HA5 40 D6
Chequers Way N13 32 D5
Cherbury Cl SE28 102 D1
Cherbury Ct N1 235 D3
Cherbury St N1 95 B5 235 D3
Cherchefells Mews HA7 25 B5
Cherimoya Gdns KT8 195 D6
Cherington Rd W7 108 D5
Cheriton Ave BR2 209 A4
Cheriton Cl Cockfosters EN4 2 D1
10 Ealing W5 87 C2
Cheriton Ct 4 Lee SE12 165 A4
South Norwood SE25 205 C4
Walton-on-T KT12 194 C1
Cheriton Dr SE18 145 B6
Cheriton Ho 9 E5 74 B3
Cheriton Sq SW17 159 A2
Cherry Ave UB1 106 D5
Cherry Blossom Cl N13 32 D5
Cherry Cl Carshalton SM5 218 D6
Ealing W5 109 D3
Merton SM4 201 A5
Ruislip HA4 61 D5
7 Streatham SW2 160 C4
Walthamstow E17 53 D4
Cherrycot Hill BR6 227 B4
Cherrycot Rise BR6 227 A4
Cherry Cres TW8 131 B5
Cherry Croft Gdns 3 HA5 23 B3
Cherry Ct Acton W3 111 C5
Hackbridge CR4 203 A1
Ilford IG6 56 D6
Pinner HA5 22 D2
5 Rotherhithe SE16 119 A5
Sidcup DA14 168 B1
Cherrydeal Ct E11 54 B2
Cherrydown Ave E4 19 C1
Cherrydown Cl E4 19 C1
Cherrydown Rd DA14 168 D2
Cherry Garden Ho 7 SE16 118 B4
Cherry Garden Sch 20 SE16 118 A2
Cherry Garden St SE16 118 B4
Cherry Garth TW8 109 D1
Cherry Gdns
Dagenham RM9 81 B3
Northolt UB5 63 D1
Cherry Gr Hayes UB3 106 B5
Hillingdon UB8 83 A2
Cherry Hill
New Barnet EN5 13 D5
Stanmore HA3 24 C4
Cherry Hill Gdns CR0 220 B4
Cherry Hills WD19 23 A5
Cherry La UB7 104 C2
Cherrylands Cl NW9 67 A6
Cherry Lane Prim Sch UB7 104 B2
Cherry Laurel Wlk SW2 160 B5
Cherry Orch
Charlton SE7 143 C6
West Drayton UB7 104 A4
Cherry Orchard Gdns
7 Croydon CR0 205 B1
East Molesey KT8 195 B6
5 South Croydon CR0 221 B6
Cherry Orchard Prim Sch SE7 143 C5
Cherry Orchard Rd
Croydon CR0 205 C1
East Molesey KT8 195 C6
Keston Mark BR2 226 A6
Cherry Rd EN3 6 C5
Cherry Tree Ave UB7 82 B1
Cherry Tree Cl
11 Hackney E9 96 C6
Wembley HA0 65 A4
Cherry Tree Ct
1 Camden Town NW1 71 C1
17 Charlton SE7 143 C6
Kingsbury NW9 45 A5
11 Peckham SE15 140 B4
3 Woodford E18 36 D1
Cherry Tree Dr SW16 160 A1
Cherry Tree Hill N6 48 D4
Cherrytree Ho 8 W10 90 D4
Cherry Tree Ho
London SE14 141 B3
Ruislip HA4 39 C1
Twickenham TW2 152 B2
Wood Green N22 32 A3
Cherry Tree Rd
London N2 48 D5
Stratford E15 76 C3
Cherry Tree Rise IG9 37 D6
Cherry Trees Sch The 22 E3 97 C4
Cherry Tree Terr SE1 253 B2
Cherry Tree Way HA7 25 B4
Cherry Tree Wlk
Beckenham BR3 207 B5
Coney Hall BR4 224 D4
St Luke's EC1 242 B5
Cherry Way
Upper Halliford TW17 193 C5
West Ewell KT19 215 B2
Cherry Wlk BR2 209 A1
Cherrywood Cl Bow E3 97 A4
Kingston u T KT2 176 C3
Cherrywood Ct 1 TW11 175 A5
Cherrywood Dr SW15 156 D6
Cherrywood La SM4, SW20 201 A5
Cherry Wood Way W5 88 C2
Chertsey Ct SW14 132 D2
Chertsey Dr SM3 217 A6
Chertsey Ho
Feltham TW13 151 C1
37 Shoreditch E2 95 D4
Chertsey Rd
Ashford TW15, TW16 171 B4
Feltham TW13, TW16 171 C6
Ilford IG1 79 B4
Leyton E11 76 B6
Lower Halliford TW17 192 C2
Shepperton TW17 192 A2
Twickenham TW2 152 B4
Chertsey St SW17 181 A5
Chervil Cl TW13 150 A1
Chervil Mews SE28 124 B5
Cherwell Ct
Teddington KT1 175 D3
West Ewell KT19 215 A4
Cherwell Ho NW8 236 D5
Cherwell Way HA4 39 A3
Cheryls Cl SW6 135 D4 265 D2
Cheseman St SE26 162 B1
Chesfield Rd KT2 176 A3
Chesham Ave BR2, BR5 210 D3
Chesham Cl SW1 258 A5
Chesham Cres SE20 184 C2
Chesham Ct SW18 158 B4
Chesham Flats W1 248 B6
Chesham Ho SW1 258 A5
Chesham Mews SW1 258 A6
Chesham Pl SW1 115 A3 258 A5
Chesham Rd
Kingston u T KT1, KT2 176 C1
Mitcham SW19 180 B4
Penge SE20 184 C2
Chesham St
Westminster SW1 115 A3 258 A5
Willesden NW10 67 B5
Chesham Terr W13 109 B4
Cheshire Cl Chingford E17 35 D2
Mitcham CR4, SW16 204 A6
Cheshire Gdns KT9 213 D2
Cheshire Ho SM4 201 D2
Cheshire Rd N22 32 B4
Cheshire St E2 95 D3 243 D6
Cheshir Ho NW4 46 C5
Chesholm Rd N16 73 C5
Cheshunt Ho Hendon NW4 46 C6
9 Kilburn NW6 91 D6
Cheshunt Rd
Belvedere DA17 125 C1
Upton E7 77 B2
Chesil Ct
17 Bethnal Green E2 96 C5
Chelsea SW3 267 B6
Chesil Ho BR7 189 B2
Chesilton Rd SW6 135 B4 264 C2
Chesil Way UB4 83 D4
Chesley Gdns E6 100 A4
Chesney Cres CR0 224 A1
Chesney Ct W9 91 C3
Chesney Ho SE13 142 B1
Chesney St SW11 268 A1
Chesnut Gr N17 51 D6
Chesnut Rd N17 51 D6
Chessell Cl CR7 204 D5
Chessholme Ct TW16 171 C3
Chessholme Rd TW15 171 A4
Chessing Ct N2 48 D6
CHESSINGTON 214 A2
Chessington Ave
Church End N3 47 B6
Erith DA7 147 A5
Chessington Cl KT19 215 A2
Chessington Com Coll KT9 213 D1
Chessington Ct London N3 47 B6
Pinner HA5 41 B5
Chessington Hall Gdns KT9 213 D1
Chessington Hill Pk KT9 214 C3
Chessington Ho 19 SW8 137 D3
Chessington Lo N3 47 B6
Chessington Mans
Leyton E10 53 C2
Leytonstone E11 54 C2
Chessington North Sta KT9 214 A3
Chessington Par KT9 213 D3
Chessington Pk KT9 214 C4
Chessington Rd KT19 215 B1
Chessington South Sta KT9 213 D1
Chessington Trade Pk KT9 214 C4
Chessington Way BR4 223 D6
Chesson Rd W14 135 B6 264 D6
Chessum Ho E8 74 A2
Chesswood Way HA5 22 D1
Chestbrook Ct 12 EN1 17 C6
Chester Ave
Richmond TW10 154 B5
Twickenham TW2 151 B3
Chester Cl Ashford TW15 171 B5
Barnes SW13 134 B2
Hayes UB8 82 D1
Knightsbridge SW1 248 C1
1 Richmond TW10 154 B5
Sutton SM1 217 C6

Chester Close N NW1 . . . **231** D2
Chester Close S NW1 . . . . . **231** D1
Chester Cres E8 . . . . .73 D3
Chester Ct 2 Acton W3 . . . . . .88 C1
  Bermondsey SE8 . . . . 118 D1
  4 Camberwell SE5 . . . . . . **139** B5
  Gospel Oak NW5 . . . . .71 A4
  Harrow HA1 . . . . .42 D3
  Regent's Pk NW1 . . . . **231** D1
Chester Dr HA2 . . . . .41 C3
Chesterfield Ct
  Ashford TW15 . . . . 170 A6
  Kingston u T KT6 . . . . 198 A4
  Lewisham SE13 . . . . 142 A2
Chesterfield Dr KT10 . . . 213 A6
Chesterfield Flats EN5 . . .12 D6
Chesterfield Gdns
  Greenwich SE10 . . . . 142 B5
  Harringay N4 . . . . .50 D4
  Mayfair W1 . . . . **248** C4
Chesterfield Gr SE22 . . 161 D6
Chesterfield Hill
  W1 . . . . **115** B5 **248** C4
Chesterfield Ho
  Highgate N6 . . . . .49 A1
  Mayfair W1 . . . . **248** B4
  6 Streatham SW16 . . . . 181 C5
Chesterfield Lo N21 . . . . . .16 B4
Chesterfield Mews
  Ashford TW15 . . . . 170 A6
  Harringay N4 . . . . .50 D4
Chesterfield Prim Sch EN3 7 A6
Chesterfield Rd
  Ashford TW15 . . . . 170 A5
  Barnet EN5 . . . . .12 D6
  Chiswick W4 . . . . 133 A6
  Enfield EN3 . . . . .7 A6
  Finchley N3 . . . . .29 C4
  Leyton E10 . . . . .54 A3
  West Ewell KT19 . . . . 215 B1
Chesterfield St W1 . . . . **248** C4
Chesterfield Way
  Hayes UB3 . . . . 106 A4
  Peckham SE15 . . . . 140 C5
Chesterford Gdns NW3 . .69 D4
Chesterford Ho 4 SE18 . 143 D5
Chesterford Rd E12 . . . . . .78 B3
Chester Gate NW1 . . . . . **231** D1
  Enfield EN3 . . . . .18 B5
  Morden SM4 . . . . 202 A3
Chester Ho 5 Barnet EN5 . . 1 D1
  Dartmouth Pk N19 . . . . . .71 B6
  1 Deptford SE8 . . . . 141 B6
  Kingston u T KT1 . . . . 176 D1
Chesterman Ct W4 . . . . . 133 C5
Chester Mews
  Belgravia SW1 . . . . **258** C6
  Walthamstow E17 . . . . . . .35 C1
Chester Pl NW1 . . . . **231** C2
Chester Rd
  Avery Hill DA15 . . . . 167 C6
  Dartmouth Pk N19 . . . . . .71 B6
  Edmonton N9 . . . . .18 B3
  Hounslow TW4 . . . . 128 B2
  Ilford IG3 . . . . .57 C2
  Newham E16 . . . . .98 C3
  Regent's Pk NW1 . . .93 A4 **231** C2
  Tottenham N17 . . . . .51 C6
  Upton E7 . . . . .77 D1
  Walthamstow E17 . . . . . . .52 D4
  Wanstead E11 . . . . .55 B3
  Wimbledon SW19, SW20 . . 178 C4
Chester Row
  SW1 . . . . **115** A2 **258** B4
Chester Sq SW1 . .**115** B2 **258** C4
Chester Sq Mews SW1 . . **258** C5
Chester St
  Bethnal Green E2 . . . . .96 A3
  Westminster SW1 .**115** A3 **258** B6
Chesters The KT3 . . . . . . 177 C2
Chester Terr NW1 . .93 B4 **231** C1
Chesterton Cl
  Greenford UB6 . . . . .85 D5
  Wandsworth SW18 . . . . . 157 C6
Chesterton Ct W3 . . . . . . 110 D3
Chesterton Dr TW19 . . . . 148 B3
Chesterton Ho
  20 Battersea SW11 . . . . . 136 B2
  3 Kensal Town W10 . . . . .91 A2
  5 Sutton SM1 . . . . 218 A4
Chesterton Prim Sch
  SW11 . . . . 137 A4 **268** A1
Chesterton Rd
  Kensal Town W10 . . . . .91 A2
  Newham E13 . . . . .99 A4
Chesterton Sq W8 . . . . . **255** A3
Chesterton Terr
  6 Kingston u T KT1 . . . . . 176 C1
  Newham E13 . . . . .99 A4
Chester Way
  SE11 . . . .**116** C2 **261** B3
Chesthunte Rd N17 . . . . . .33 A2
Chestnut Alley SW6 . . . **264** D5
Chestnut Ave
  Brentford TW8 . . . . 109 D2
  Buckhurst Hill IG9 . . . . . . .21 D1
  Coney Hall BR4 . . . . 224 C4
  Edgware HA8 . . . . .26 B4
  Forest Gate E7 . . . . .77 B4

Chestnut Ave *continued*
  Hampton TW12 . . . . 173 C3
  Hornsey N8 . . . . .50 A4
  Kingston u T KT8, KT11 . . . 174 D2
  11 Mortlake SW14 . . . . . 133 B2
  Thames Ditton KT10 . . . . 196 B1
  Wembley HA0 . . . . .65 B3
  Worcester Pk KT19 . . . . . 215 C4
  Yiewsley UB7 . . . . 104 B6
Chestnut Ave N E17 . . . . .54 B5
Chestnut Ave S E17 . . . . .54 B4
Chestnut Cl
  Buckhurst Hill IG9 . . . . . . .21 D2
  Carshalton SM5 . . . . 202 D1
  Catford SE6 . . . . 186 A6
  Chattern Hill TW15 . . . . . 170 D6
  Harlington UB7 . . . . 126 D5
  Hayes UB3 . . . . 105 C6
  New Cross Gate SE14 . . . . 141 B4
  Sidcup DA15 . . . . 168 A2
  Southgate N14 . . . . .15 D6
  1 Stoke Newington N16 . .73 B6
  Sunbury Comm TW16 . . . . 171 D4
  West Norwood SW16 . . . . 182 C6
Chestnut Ct
  Beckenham BR3 . . . . 185 C3
  7 Cheam SM3 . . . . 217 C2
  5 Croydon CR0 . . . . 221 A4
  Feltham TW13 . . . . 172 D5
  Harrow HA1 . . . . .42 C2
  Hornsey N8 . . . . .50 A4
  Hounslow TW3 . . . . 129 C2
  Kingston u T KT3 . . . . 199 C6
  Surbiton KT6 . . . . 198 A2
  Wembley HA0 . . . . .65 B3
  West Brompton SW6 . . . . **264** D6
Chestnut Dr Bexley DA7 . 147 A2
  Harrow HA3 . . . . .24 D2
  Pinner HA5 . . . . .41 A3
  Wanstead E11 . . . . .55 A3
Chestnut Gr
  Cockfosters EN4. . . . . .14 D6
  Ealing W5 . . . . 109 D3
  Isleworth TW7 . . . . 131 A1
  Kingston u T KT3 . . . . 199 B6
  Mitcham CR4 . . . . 203 D5
  Penge SE20 . . . . 184 C3
  South Croydon CR2. . . . . . 222 B1
  Upper Tooting SW12. . . . . 159 A3
  Wembley HA0. . . . . .65 B3
Chestnut Grove Sch 6
  SW12 . . . . 159 A3
Chestnut Ho
  1 Acton W4 . . . . 111 C2
  Brockley SE4. . . . . 141 B2
  3 Maitland Pk NW3 . . . . .70 D2
  West Norwood SE27 . . . . . 161 A1
Chestnut La N20 . . . . .13 A3
Chestnut Pl SE19 . . . . . . 183 D6
Chestnut Rd
  Ashford TW15 . . . . 170 D6
  Kingston u T KT2 . . . . 176 A3
  Twickenham TW2 . . . . 152 C2
  West Barnes SW20 . . . . . . 178 D1
  West Norwood SE21, SE27 . 161 A1
Chestnut Rise SE18 . . . . 123 C1
Chestnut Row N3 . . . . . . .29 C3
Chestnuts Ct 3 E17 . . . . .54 A6
Chestnuts Prim Sch N15 .54 A3
Chestnuts Royal BR7 . . . 189 B3
Chestnuts The
  Chislehurst BR7 . . . . 189 B3
  Colindale NW9 . . . . .45 C6
  East Finchley N2 . . . . .48 D4
  7 Erith DA17 . . . . 125 B1
  1 Highbury N5 . . . . .72 D4
  Penge BR3 . . . . 206 D6
  8 Pinner HA5 . . . . .23 B3
  Shooters Hill SE18 . . . . . . 144 D4
  Uxbridge UB10 . . . . .60 A1
  Walton-on-T KT12 . . . . . . 194 B1
Chestnut Way TW13 . . . . 150 B1
Chestnut Wlk
  Upper Halliford TW17. . . . . 193 C5
  Woodford IG8 . . . . .37 A5
Cheston Ave CR0 . . . . . . 207 B1
Chestwood Gr UB10 . . . . . .60 B1
Chettle Cl SE1 . . . . **262** C6
Chettle Ct N8 . . . . .50 C3
Chetwode Ho NW8 . . . . **237** A6
Chetwode Rd SW17 . . . . . 158 D1
Chetwood Wlk 13 E6 . . . . 100 A2
Chetwynd Ave EN4 . . . . . .14 D3
Chetwynd Dr UB10 . . . . . .82 B5
Chetwynd Rd NW5 . . . . . .71 B5
Cheval Cl SW15 . . . . 134 B1
Chevalier Cl HA7 . . . . .26 A6
Cheval Pl SW7 . . . .114 C3 **257** D6
Cheval St E14 . . . . 119 C3
Chevender BR7 . . . . 188 D3
Cheveney Wlk 2 BR2 . . . 209 A6
Chevening Ho BR5 . . . . . . 190 A2
Chevening Rd
  Cubitt Town SE10 . . . . . . 120 D1
  Kilburn NW6 . . . . .91 A6
  South Norwood SE19 . . . . 183 B4
Chevenings The DA14 . . . 168 C1
Cheverell Ho 25 E2 . . . . . .96 A5
Cheverton Rd N19 . . . . . . .49 D1
Chevet St E9 . . . . .75 A3

Chevington NW2 . . . . .69 B2
Cheviot 4 N17 . . . . .34 B3
Cheviot Cl Bushey WD23. . . .8 A5
  Enfield EN1. . . . . .5 B3
  Harlington UB3. . . . . 127 B5
Cheviot Ct
  16 Deptford SE14 . . . . . . 140 C5
  Enfield EN2 . . . . .5 B3
  Southall UB2. . . . . 107 D2
Cheviot Gate NW2 . . . . . . .69 A6
Cheviot Gdns
  Cricklewood NW2. . . . . . . .69 A6
  West Norwood SE27. . . . . 182 D6
Cheviot Ho N16. . . . . .51 D1
Cheviot Rd SE27 . . . . 182 D5
Cheviots Hostel EN1 . . . . . 5 B3
Cheviot Way IG2. . . . . .57 C5
Chevron Cl E16 . . . . .99 A1
Chevy Rd UB2 . . . . 108 A4
Chewton Rd E17 . . . . .53 A5
Cheylesmore Ho SW1 . . . **258** C2
Cheyne Ave
  Snaresbrook E18 . . . . .54 D6
  Twickenham TW2 . . . . 151 B3
Cheyne Cl 1 Hendon NW4. . .46 B4
  Keston Mark BR2 . . . . 226 A5
Cheyne Ct Chelsea SW3 . . **267** C6
  1 Croydon CR0 . . . . 221 D6
  Ruislip HA4. . . . . .39 C1
  4 Wallington SM6. . . . . . 219 B2
Cheyne Gdns
  SW3. . . . . .136 C6 **267** B5
Cheyne Hill KT5. . . . . 198 B5
Cheyne Mews
  SW3. . . . . .136 C6 **267** B5
Cheyne Path W7 . . . . .86 D1
Cheyne Pl SW3 . . . . **267** C6
Cheyne Rd TW15 . . . . 171 B4
Cheyne Row
  SW3. . . . . .136 C6 **267** A5
Cheyne Wlk
  Chelsea SW10 . . .136 B5 **266** C4
  Croydon CR0. . . . . 222 A6
  Hendon NW4 . . . . .46 C3
  Southgate N21 . . . . .16 D6
Cheyney Ho 2 E9 . . . . .74 D2
Cheyneys Ave HA8 . . . . . . .25 D4
Chichele Gdns CR0 . . . . . 221 C4
Chichele Ho HA8 . . . . .26 B6
Chichele Mans NW2 . . . . . .68 D3
Chichele Rd NW2 . . . . .68 D3
Chicheley Gdns HA3 . . . . . .24 A3
Chicheley Rd HA3 . . . . . . .24 A3
Chicheley St SE1. . . . . . . **250** D2
Chichester Ave HA4 . . . . . .61 B6
Chichester Cl
  Hampton TW12. . . . . 173 B4
  Kidbrooke SE3 . . . . 143 C4
  Newham E6 . . . . 100 A1
Chichester Ct Barnet EN4 . . 2 B1
  2 Camden Town NW1 . . . .71 C1
  Edgware HA8 . . . . .26 C4
  Harrow HA2 . . . . .41 B1
  Northolt UB5 . . . . .85 A6
  3 Sidcup DA5 . . . . 169 C4
  Stanmore HA7 . . . . .44 A6
  Stanwell TW19 . . . . 148 A3
Chichester Gdns IG1. . . . . .56 B2
Chichester Ho
  Kilburn NW6. . . . . .91 C5
  2 Kingston u T KT2 . . . . . 176 D2
Chichester Mews SE27. . . 182 C6
Chichester Rd
  Bayswater W2 . . . . .91 D2
  Edmonton N9 . . . . .18 A3
  Kilburn NW6. . . . . .91 C5
  Leyton E11 . . . . .76 C5
  South Croydon CR0. . . . . . 221 C5
Chichester Rents WC2 . . . **241** A2
Chichester St
  SW1 . . . .**115** C1 **259** B1
Chichester Way
  Cubitt Town E14 . . . . 120 B2
  Feltham TW14 . . . . 150 C4
Chicksand Ho 14 E1. . . . . . .96 A2
Chicksand St E1 . . . .96 A2 **243** D3
Chicksand Street E1 . . . . . .96 A2
Chiddingfold N12. . . . . . . .13 C1
Chiddingstone SE13 . . . . . 164 A6
Chiddingstone Ave DA7 . 147 B5
Chiddingstone St SW6 . . . 135 C3
Chieveley Par DA7 . . . . . . 147 D2
Chieveley Rd DA7 . . . . 147 D1
Chignell Pl W13. . . . . 109 A5
Chigwell Ct 1 E9 . . . . .75 A2
Chigwell Hill E1 . . . . 118 B6
Chigwell Hurst Ct HA5 . . . .40 D6
Chigwell Rd Wanstead E18 . .55 B6
  Woodford IG8 . . . . .37 D3
Chiham Ho 5 SE15 . . . . . 140 C6
Chilchester Ct 3 BR3. . . . 207 D6
Chilcombe Ho 5 SW15 . . 156 A4
Chilcot Cl 13 E14. . . . . .97 D1
Chilcott Rd 1 HA0 . . . . . . .65 C4
Child Ct E11 . . . . .54 B2
Childebert Rd SW17 . . . . . 159 B2
Childeric Prim Sch
  SE14. . . . . 141 A5
Childeric Rd SE14. . . . . . . 141 A5

Childerley St
  SW6. . . . .**135** A4 **264** A2
Childerly KT1. . . . . 198 C6
Childers St SE8 . . . . 141 B6
Chlld La SE10 . . . . 120 D3
Childrens House Upper Sch
  15 N1 . . . . .73 C2
  Childs Cl UB3 . . . . 106 A6
CHILD'S HILL 69 C6
Childs La 11 SE19 . . . . . . 183 C4
Child's Mews SW5. . . . . **255** B3
Child's Pl SW5. . . . . **255** B3
Child's St SW5. . . . . **255** B3
Childs Way NW11 . . . . .47 B4
Child's Wlk SW5. . . . . . . **255** B3
Chilham Cl
  Old Bexley DA5. . . . . 169 A4
  Wembley UB6. . . . . .87 A5
Chilham Ct 13 SW9 . . . . . 138 C2
Chilham Ho SE1 . . . . **262** D6
Chilham Rd SE9 . . . . 188 A6
Chilham Way BR2 . . . . 209 A2
Chillerton Rd SW17 . . . . . 181 B5
Chillingford Ho SW17 . . . . 180 A6
Chillington Dr SW11 . . . . . 136 B1
Chillingworth Gdns
  TW1. . . . . 152 D1
Chillingworth Rd N7 . . . . . .72 C3
Chilmark Gdns KT3. . . . . . 200 A3
Chilmark Rd SW16 . . . . . . 181 D2
Chiltern Ave Bushey WD23. . .8 A5
  Twickenham TW2 . . . . 151 C3
Chiltern Cl Bus WD23. . . . . . .8 A5
  Ickenham UB10 . . . . .60 C6
  North Cheam KT4 . . . . 216 C6
  South Croydon CR0. . . . . . 221 C5
Chiltern Ct
  15 Deptford SE14. . . . . . 140 C5
  East Barnet N20 . . . . .14 C2
  11 Eltham SE9 . . . . 166 C5
  Harrow HA1 . . . . .42 B4
  Hillingdon UB8 . . . . .82 D3
  Marylebone NW1 . . . . . . **237** D5
  Muswell Hill N10. . . . . .31 A1
  1 New Barnet EN5 . . . . . . .14 A6
Chiltern Dene EN2 . . . . . . .4 B1
Chiltern Dr KT5. . . . . 198 D4
Chiltern Gdns
  Beckenham BR2 . . . . 208 D5
  Cricklewood NW2. . . . . . . .68 D5
Chiltern Ho
  Camberwell SE17 . . . . . . 139 B6
  Ealing W5 . . . . .88 A2
  5 Edmonton N9. . . . . .18 A1
  Harrow HA1 . . . . .42 C1
  4 Kensal Town W10 . . . . . .91 A2
  5 Stamford Hill N16 . . . . . .51 D1
Chiltern Pl 18 E5. . . . . . . .74 B6
Chiltern Rd Bow E3. . . . . . .97 C3
  Ilford IG2 . . . . .57 C4
  Pinner HA5 . . . . .40 C4
Chilterns The BR1. . . . . . . 187 B1
Chiltern Way IG8 . . . . .21 A1
Chilthorne Cl SE6. . . . . . . 163 B4
Chilton Ave W5 . . . . 109 D2
Chilton Gr SE8. . . . . 119 A2
Chiltonian Ind Est SE12. . . 164 D5
Chilton Rd Edgware HA8. . . .26 C4
  Richmond TW9 . . . . 132 C2
Chilton St E2 . . . . . .95 D3 **243** D6
Chiltons The 1 E18 . . . . . .37 A1
Chilvers Cl TW2. . . . . 152 C2
Chilver St SE10 . . . . 120 D1
Chilwell Gdns WD19 . . . . . .22 C6
Chilworth Gdns SM1. . . . . 218 A5
Chilworth Mews
  W2. . . . . .92 B1 **236** C1
Chilworth St W2 . . . .92 A1 **236** B1
Chimes Ave N13 . . . . .32 D6
Chimes Sh Ctr The UB8. . . .60 A1
Chimney Ct 23 E1. . . . . . . 118 B5
Chimneys Ct 2 SW19 . . . . 178 C3
China Ct 1 E1. . . . . 118 B5
China Hall Mews 18
  SE16. . . . . 118 C3
China Mews 17 SW2 . . . . . 160 B4
Chinbrook Cres SE12. . . . . 165 B1
Chinbrook Rd SE12 . . . . . . 165 A1
Chinchilla Dr TW4 . . . . . . 128 C3
Chindit Ho 11 N16 . . . . . . .73 A4
Chine The London N10. . . . .49 C5
  Southgate N21 . . . . .16 D6
  Wembley HA0. . . . . .65 D6
Ching Ct Chingford E4 . . . . .20 C1
  St Giles WC2 . . . . **240** A1
Chingdale Rd E4. . . . . .20 C1
CHINGFORD 20 C1
Chingford Ave E4. . . . . . . .19 D2
Chingford CE Inf Sch 10
  E4. . . . . .20 B3
Chingford CE Jun Sch 9
  E4. . . . . .20 B3
Chingford Foundation Sch
  E4. . . . . .19 D3
CHINGFORD GREEN 20 A4
Chingford Hall Com Prim
  Sch E4 . . . . .35 B4

CHINGFORD HATCH 36 B6
Chingford Ind Ctr E4. . . . . .35 A5
Chingford La IG8 . . . . .36 D5
Chingford Mount Rd E4 . . .35 C5
Chingford Rd
  Highams Pk E4 . . . . .35 C3
  Walthamstow E17 . . . . . . .35 D1
Chingford Sta E4 . . . . .20 C4
Chingley Cl BR1. . . . . 186 C4
Ching Way E4 . . . . .35 B4
Chinnery Cl EN1 . . . . .5 C4
Chinnocks Wharf E14 . . . . 119 A6
Chinnor Cres UB6. . . . . . . .86 A5
Chipka St E14 . . . . 120 A4
Chipley St SE14 . . . . 141 A6
Chippendale Ho SW1 . . . **258** D1
Chippendale St E5 . . . . . . .74 D5
Chippenham 4 KT1 . . . . . 176 B1
Chippenham Ave HA9. . . . . .66 D3
Chippenham Cl HA5 . . . . . .39 D5
Chippenham Gdns NW6 . . .91 C4
Chippenham Mews W9 . . .91 C3
Chippenham Rd W9 . . . . . .91 C3
Chipperfield Rd BR5. . . . . 190 A3
CHIPPING BARNET 1 B1
Chipping Cl EN5 . . . . .1 A2
Chipstead Ave CR7. . . . . . 204 D5
Chipstead Cl SE19 . . . . . . 183 D3
Chipstead Gdns NW2 . . . . .68 B6
Chipstead Ho 4 SW2 . . . . 160 A3
Chipstead St SW6. . . . . . . 135 C3
Chirk Cl UB4. . . . . .85 A3
Chirk Ct SE4 . . . . 141 B3
Chisenhale Prim Sch 36
  E3. . . . . .97 A5
Chisenhale Rd E3. . . . . . . .97 A5
Chisholm Ct 1 W6 . . . . . . 112 A1
Chisholm Rd
  Croydon CR0. . . . . 221 C6
  13 Richmond TW10 . . . . . 154 B5
Chisledon Wlk E9. . . . . . . .75 B2
CHISLEHURST 189 C3
Chislehurst Ave N12 . . . . . .30 A3
Chislehurst CE Prim Sch
  BR7. . . . . 189 A3
Chislehurst High St BR7. 188 D4
Chislehurst Rd
  Bromley BR1, BR7 . . . . . . 188 A2
  Broom Hill BR6 . . . . 211 D2
  Orpington BR5, BR6, BR7 . . 211 C4
  Richmond TW10 . . . . 154 A6
  Sidcup DA14 . . . . 190 A5
Chislehurst & Sidcup Gram
  Sch DA15. . . . . 168 B2
Chislehurst Sta BR7. . . . . 188 C1
CHISLEHURST WEST 188 C4
Chislet 5 NW5 . . . . .71 A2
Chislet Cl BR3 . . . . 185 C3
Chisley Rd 5 N15. . . . . . . .51 C3
Chiswell Sq SE3 . . . . 143 B3
Chiswell St
  Barbican EC1 . . . . .95 B2 **242** C4
  Camberwell SE5 . . . . 139 B5
CHISWICK 111 D1
Chiswick & Bedford Park
  Prep Sch 15 W4 . . . . 111 C2
Chiswick Cl CR0 . . . . 220 B5
Chiswick Common Rd
  W4. . . . . 111 B2
Chiswick Com Sch W4 . . . 133 B5
Chiswick Ct HA5 . . . . .41 B6
Chiswick Green Studios 1
  W4. . . . . 111 A2
Chiswick High Rd W4 . . . 111 C2
Chiswick High Rd (North
  Circular Rd) W4. . . . . . . 110 C1
Chiswick La ★ W4 . . . . . . 133 B6
Chiswick La W4 . . . . 111 C1
Chiswick La S W4 . . . . . . 133 D6
Chiswick Mall W4. . . . . . . 111 D1
Chiswick Park Sta W4 . . . 111 A2
Chiswick Pier W4 . . . . 133 D5
Chiswick Pk W4 . . . . 110 D2
Chiswick Plaza W4 . . . . . . 133 A6
Chiswick Quay W4 . . . . . . 133 A4
Chiswick Rdbt Acton W4 . . 111 A2
  Edmonton N9 . . . . .18 A2
Chiswick Rdbt W4 . . . . . . 110 C1
Chiswick Sq W4. . . . . 133 C6
Chiswick Sta W4 . . . . 133 A5
Chiswick Staithe W4. . . . . 133 A4
Chiswick Terr 6 W4 . . . . . 111 A2
Chiswick Village W4 . . . . . 132 D6
Chiswick Wharf W4 . . . . . 133 D6
Chitterfield Gate UB7 . . . 126 C5
Chitty's La RM8 . . . . .80 D6
Chitty St W1 . . . . . .93 C2 **239** B4
Chivalry Rd SW11 . . . . 158 C2
Chivelston 2 SW19. . . . . . 156 D3
Chivenor Gr KT2 . . . . 175 D5
Chivers Rd E4 . . . . .35 C6
Chivins Ct N3. . . . . .29 C3
Choats Manor Way RM9. . 103 B4
Choats Rd IG11 . . . . 102 D4
Chobham Gdns SW19 . . . 156 D2

Chobham Rd E15.............76 B3
Cholmeley Cres N6.........49 B2
Cholmeley Ct N12..........30 A6
Cholmeley Lo N6...........49 B1
Cholmeley Pk N6...........49 B2
Cholmley Gdns NW6......69 C3
Cholmley Rd KT7.........197 B3
Cholmondeley Ave NW10..90 A5
Cholmondeley Wlk TW9..153 C6
Chopin's Ct **13** E1.........118 B5
Chopwell Ct E15...........76 B1
Chorleywood Cres BR5..190 A1
Choumert Gr SE15........140 A3
Choumert Mews SE15....140 A3
Choumert Rd SE15........139 D3
Choumert Sq **4** SE15...140 A3
Chow Sq **2** E8..............73 D3
Chrisp Ho SE10...........142 C6
Chrisp St E14...............97 D1
Christabel Cl TW7.........130 C2
Christ Church TW9........132 A2
Christchurch Ave
   Brondesbury Pk NW6....69 A1
   Finchley N12..............30 A4
   Harrow HA3................42 D5
   Harrow HA3................43 A5
   5 Teddington TW11....175 A5
   Wembley HA0..............66 A2
Christ Church Bentinck CE
   Prim Sch NW1....92 C2 **237** B4
Christ Church Brondesbury
   CE Jun & Inf Sch NW6...69 B1
Christ Church CE Jun Sch
   W5.........................109 D6
Christchurch CE Prim Sch
   SW3.........136 D6 **267** C6
Christ Church CE Prim Sch
   Battersea SW11.........136 C2
   35 Camberwell SW9....138 C4
   Cubitt Town SE10........120 C1
   6 Forest Hill SE23....162 D2
   Shooters Hill SE18......144 C4
   Surbiton KT5.............198 C3
Christ Church CE Prim Sch,
   Hampstead NW3..........70 B5
Christchurch CE Sch
   E1..............95 D2 **243** D3
   Finchley N12...............30 B3
   Mitcham SW19............180 B3
Christchurch Ct UB4.......84 C3
Christ Church Ct
   1 Brondesbury Pk NW6..69 A1
   Harlesden NW10..........89 C6
Christchurch Gdns HA3...43 A5
Christchurch Gn HA0......66 A2
Christchurch Hill NW3....70 B4
Christchurch Ho **2**
   SW2.......................160 A3
Christ Church La EN5......1 A3
Christchurch Lo EN4.......2 D1
Christ Church New Malden
   CE Prim Sch KT3........199 C6
Christchurch Pas NW3..160 B3
Christchurch Pk SM2....218 A1
Christchurch Prim Sch
   IG1.........................57 A1
Christ Church Prim Sch
   KT3........................199 B6
Christchurch Rd
   Ilford IG1..................57 A1
   Mitcham SW19...........180 B3
   Mortlake SW14..........155 A6
   Sidcup DA15.............167 D1
   Streatham SW2..........160 C3
Christ Church Rd
   1 Beckenham BR3.....185 C1
   Hornsey N8.................50 A3
   Surbiton KT5..............198 B3
Christ Church Sch
   NW1.........93 B4 **231** D2
Christchurch Sq **2** E9..96 C6
Christchurch St
   SW3.........136 D6 **267** C6
Christ Church Streatham CE
   Prim Sch **13** SW2......160 B3
Christchurch Terr SW3....267 C6
Christchurch Way SE10.120 C1
Christian Ct SE16.........119 B5
Christian Fields SW16...182 C3
Christian St E1...............96 A1
Christie Ct
   Maitland Pk NW3.........70 C3
   2 Upper Holloway N19..72 A6
Christie Dr SE25..........206 A4
Christie Gdns RM6.........58 B2
Christie Ho Bexley DA6..169 D6
   2 Cubitt Town SE10...120 D1
   Harrow HA3.................42 D6
   4 West Wickham BR4..207 D1
Christie Rd E9................75 A2
Christina Sq N4..............50 D1
Christina St EC2...........243 A6
Christine Worsley Cl N21..16 D3
Christopher Ave W7......109 A3
Christopher Boone's
   Almshouses SE13......142 B1

Christopher Cl
   Bexley DA15............167 D6
   Rotherhithe SE16......118 D4
Christopher Ct
   Ashford TW15..........170 A5
   12 Barnet EN5...........1 D1
   6 Croydon CR0.......206 A1
   Hendon NW4.............28 C1
   23 Surbiton KT6.......198 A4
   Sutton SM1.............217 C3
Christopher France Ho **1**
   E1............................97 A4
Christopher Gdns RM9...80 D3
Christopher Hatton Prim Sch
   EC1..............94 C3 **241** A5
Christopher Lo **2** N6....49 D2
Christopher Pl NW1.......232 D1
Christopher Rd UB2......106 B2
Christopher St
   EC2.............95 B3 **242** D6
Christ's Coll Finchley
   NW11........................47 D6
Christ's Sch TW10........154 C6
Christ the King RC Prim Sch
   7 N4.......................72 B6
Christ the King Sixth Form
   Coll SE13.................142 B2
Christ the Redeemer Bible
   Coll **1** E15...............76 C2
Chryssell Rd SW9.........138 C5
Chubworthy St **5** SE14..141 A6
Chudleigh **1** DA14......190 B6
Chudleigh Cres IG3........79 C4
Chudleigh Gdns SM1....218 A5
Chudleigh Rd
   Hampstead NW6..........68 D1
   London SE4...............163 C6
   Twickenham TW1, TW2..152 D4
Chudleigh St E1.............96 D1
Chudleigh Way HA4........40 A1
Chulsa Rd SE26...........184 B5
Chumleigh Gdns SE5....139 C6
Chumleigh St SE5........139 C6
Chumleigh Wlk KT5......198 B5
Church App SE21..........161 B1
Church Ave
   Beckenham BR3.........185 C2
   Camden Town NW1......71 B2
   Chingford E4...............36 B4
   Finchley N2.................30 B2
   Mortlake SW14..........133 B2
   Northolt UB5...............63 B1
   Pinner HA5..................41 B3
   Ruislip HA4..................39 B1
   Sidcup DA14.............190 B5
   Southall UB2.............107 A3
   Wanstead E12.............77 D5
Churchbank E17............53 C5
Churchbury Cl EN1..........5 C3
Churchbury La EN1.........5 C3
Churchbury Rd
   Eltham SE9...............165 D4
   Enfield EN1...................5 C3
Church Cl Edgware HA8...27 A5
   Friern Barnet N20.......14 C1
   Hayes UB4.................83 B2
   Hounslow TW4..........129 B3
   Kensington W8..........245 C2
   West Drayton UB7.....104 A3
Church Cres
   Church End N3............29 B2
   Cranley Gdns N10.......49 B5
   Friern Barnet N20.......14 C1
   Hackney E9.................74 D1
Churchcroft Cl SW12....159 A4
Church Ct East Finchley N2..48 B6
   Forest Hill SE26........185 A5
   Harmondsworth UB7...126 C6
   Holborn EC4..............241 B1
   16 Richmond TW10...153 D6
   Rotherhithe SE16......119 B4
   Ruislip HA4.................62 D5
   5 West Norwood SE27..182 D6
Churchdale Cl **1** W4..110 D1
Churchdown BR1.........186 C6
Church Dr
   Coney Hall BR4.........224 C5
   Harrow HA2................41 C3
   Welsh Harp NW9.........45 B1
Church Elm La RM10......81 C2
Church End NW4...........46 B6
Church End E17............53 D5
Church Entry EC4.........241 D1
Church Estate Almshouses **8**
   TW9........................132 B1
Church Farmhouse Mus ＊
   NW4.........................46 B6
Church Farm La SM3....217 A2
Church Farm Swimming Pool
   EN4...........................14 D4
Churchfield Ave N12.......30 B4
Churchfield Cl
   Harrow HA2................42 A5
   Hayes UB3................105 D6
Churchfield Ho W2.......236 C5
Churchfield Mans **5**
   SW6........................135 B3
Churchfield Pl TW17....192 D2

Churchfield Prim Sch N9..17 D3
Churchfield Rd
   Acton W3.................111 A5
   Ealing W13...............109 C5
   Hanwell W7..............108 C4
   Walton-on-T KT12.....194 A1
   Welling DA16............146 A2
Churchfields
   East Molesey KT8.....195 C6
   Greenwich SE10.......142 A6
   Woodford E18............37 A2
Churchfields Ave TW13..151 C1
Churchfields Jun & Inf Sch
   E18..........................37 A2
Churchfields Prim Sch
   BR3.......................206 D6
Churchfields Rd BR3....185 A1
Churchfield Way N12.....30 A4
Church Garth **4** N19....71 D6
Church Gate SW6........135 A2
Church Gdns Ealing W5..109 D4
   Wembley HA0.............65 A4
Church Gn
   4 Brixton SW9.......138 C3
   Hayes UB3.................83 D1
Church Gr London SE13..163 D6
   Teddington KT1.........175 C1
Church Hill Harrow HA1..42 C1
   Southgate N21............16 C4
   Wallington SM5.........218 D3
   Walthamstow E17........53 D5
   Wimbledon SW19......179 B5
   Woolwich SE18..........122 B3
Churchill Gardens Prim Sch
   SW1.........115 C1 **259** B1
Church Hill Prim Sch
   EN4...........................14 D4
Church Hill Rd
   Cheam SM1, SM3......217 A4
   East Barnet EN4..........14 D4
   Kingston u T KT6.......198 A4
   Walthamstow E17........53 D5
Church Hill Wood BR5..211 D4
Church Ho EC1.............241 D6
Church Hyde SE18.........145 C6
Churchill Ave Harrow HA3..43 B1
   Hillingdon UB10..........82 D4
Churchill Cl
   East Bedfont TW14.....149 D3
   Hillingdon UB10..........82 D4
Churchill Ct Ealing W5....88 B3
   Edmonton N9..............17 B3
   4 Farnborough BR6...227 A3
   Finsbury Pk N4...........50 C2
   Harrow HA2................41 D4
   7 Ilford IG1...............78 D5
   Northolt UB5...............63 C3
   Peckham SE15...........140 A3
   Willesden NW2...........68 B3
   9 Woolwich SE18.....122 B2
Churchill Gdns Acton W3...88 C1
   Pimlico SW1.....137 C6 **269** A6
Churchill Gdns Rd
   SW1.............137 C6 **269** A6
Churchill Ho
   Brentford TW8..........109 C1
   Mitcham CR4............180 D2
Churchill Lo
   Streatham SW16.......181 D5
   Woodford IG8.............36 D4
Churchill Lodge IG6........57 A5
Churchill Mews IG8........36 D4
Churchill Pl
   Canary Wharf E14.....119 D5
   Harrow HA1................42 C5
Churchill Rd Edgware HA8..26 C4
   Gospel Oak NW5.........71 B4
   Newham E16...............99 C1
   South Croydon CR2....221 A1
   Willesden NW2............68 B2
Churchill Terr E4............19 C1
Churchill Way
   Ashford TW16............172 A4
   Bromley BR1.............187 A1
Churchill Wlk E9............74 C3
Church La
   Chessington KT9......214 B2
   Chislehurst BR7.........189 A2
   Dagenham RM10.........81 D1
   Ealing W5.................109 D4
   East Finchley N2.........48 B6
   Edmonton N9...............18 A2
   Enfield EN1...................5 B2
   Harrow HA3................24 D2
   Hornsey N8.................50 B5
   Keston Mark BR2......210 A1
   Kingsbury NW9...........45 B2
   Leytonstone E11.........69 A6
   Merton SW19............179 C2
   Pinner HA5..................41 B6
   Teddington TW11.......174 D5
   Thames Ditton KT7....197 A3
   Tottenham N17............33 C2
   Twickenham TW1.......153 A3
   Upper Tooting SW17...181 A5
   Wallington SM6.........219 D5
   Walthamstow E17........53 D5
Churchlands Way **3**
   KT4........................216 D6
Churchley Rd SE26......184 B6

Churchley Villas SE26......184 B6
Church Lo UB5...............63 B1
Church Manor Way SE18,
   SE2........................124 A2
Church Mdw KT6..........213 C6
Church Mead SE5.........139 A5
Churchmead Cl EN4......14 C5
Churchmead Rd NW10...68 A2
Churchmore Rd SW16..181 D2
Church Mount N2...........48 B4
Church Paddock Ct
   SM6........................219 D5
Church Par
   5 Ashford TW15.......170 B6
   Harrow HA3...............42 C6
Church Path
   Merton SW19............179 C1
   Mitcham CR4............202 C6
   South Acton W4.........111 A3
   Walthamstow E17........53 D5
   Wanstead E11.............55 A4
Church Pl Ealing W5.....109 D4
   Mitcham CR4............202 C6
   St James SW1...........249 B5
   Uxbridge UB10...........61 A5
Church Rd Acton W3......111 A4
   Ashford TW15..........170 B6
   Barking IG11...............79 A2
   Barnes SW13............134 A4
   Beckenham BR2.........208 C6
   Bexleyheath DA7.......147 B2
   Bromley BR1, BR2......187 A1
   Buckhurst Hill IG9.......21 B3
   24 Canonbury N1.......73 A2
   Cheam SM3..............217 A2
   Claygate KT10..........212 D1
   Cranford TW5...........128 B6
   Croydon CR0............221 A5
   Ealing W7.................108 C6
   East Molesey KT8.....196 B6
   Enfield EN3.................18 C6
   Farnborough BR6.......227 B3
   Feltham TW13...........172 D5
   Hayes UB3................105 D6
   Hendon NW4...............46 C5
   Heston TW5..............129 C5
   Higham Hill E17...........35 A1
   Highgate N6................49 A3
   Hillingdon UB8...........82 A3
   Hounslow TW7...........130 C5
   Ilford IG2....................57 C3
   Keston BR2...............225 D1
   Kingston u T KT1.......176 B1
   Leyton E10.................75 C6
   Long Ditton KT6........197 C1
   Lower Halliford TW17..192 D2
   Manor Pk E12.............78 A3
   Mitcham CR4............202 C6
   Mitcham CR4, SW19...180 B1
   New Malden KT4........199 C1
   Northolt UB5...............85 A6
   Richmond TW10.........176 A6
   Richmond TW10, TW9..154 A6
   Sidcup DA14.............190 A6
   Southall UB2.............107 B3
   South Norwood SE19...183 C3
   Stanmore HA7............25 B5
   Teddington TW11.......174 D5
   Tottenham N17............33 D3
   Wallington SM6.........219 D5
   Welling DA16............146 B3
   West Drayton UB7.....104 A3
   West Ewell KT19........215 B1
   Willesden NW10..........67 C1
   Wimbledon SW19......179 A6
Church Rd N N2.............30 B2
Church Rd S N2.............30 B2
Church Rise
   Chessington KT9......214 B2
   Forest Hill SE23........162 D2
Church Row
   Chislehurst BR7........189 A2
   Hampstead NW3.........70 A4
Church Row Mews BR7..189 A3
Church St N E15.............98 C6
Church St Sta CR0.......221 A6
Church Sq TW17..........192 D2
Church St Chiswick W4..133 D6
   Croydon CR0............220 D6
   Croydon CR0............221 A6
   Dagenham RM10.........81 D2
   Edmonton N9..............17 C2
   Enfield EN2...................5 B2
   Hampton TW12..........174 A2
   Isleworth TW7..........131 B3
   Kingston u T KT1.......175 D1
   Lisson Gr NW8...92 C3 **237** A5
   Newham E16.............122 D5
   Sunbury TW16..........194 B6
   Twickenham TW1.......153 A3
   Walton-on-T KT12.....194 A2
   West Ham E15.............99 A6
Church Street Est NW8..236 D5
Church Stretton Rd
   TW3.......................152 A6
Church Studios **18** NW1..71 D2
Church Terr Hendon NW4..46 B6
   Lewisham SE13.........142 C2
   21 Richmond TW10...153 D6

Church Vale
   Forest Hill SE23.......162 D2
   Muswell Hill N2...........48 D6
Churchview Rd TW2......152 B2
Church Villa TW16........194 B6
Churchward Ho
   Camberwell SE17......138 D6
   West Kensington SW5..254 D1
Churchway NW1..........232 B2
Church Way
   Cockfosters EN4..........2 D1
   Friern Barnet N20........14 C1
Church Wlk
   Barnes SW13............134 A4
   Brentford TW8...........131 C6
   Canonbury N16............73 B4
   Child's Hill NW2..........69 B5
   Dartmouth Pk N6........71 A5
   Hayes UB3.................83 D1
   Mitcham SW16..........181 C1
   15 Richmond TW10...153 D6
   Thames Ditton KT7....196 D3
   Walton-on-T KT12.....194 A1
   Welsh Harp NW9.........67 B6
   West Barnes SW20....200 C6
Churchwood Gdns IG8....37 A6
Churchyard Row
   SE11............116 D2 **261** D4
Churnfield **2** N4..........72 C6
Churston Ave E13..........99 B6
Churston Cl **16** SW2...160 C5
Churston Dr SM4.........201 A4
Churston Gdns N11........31 C4
Churston Mans WC1....241 B6
Churton Pl Brentford W4..132 C6
   Pimlico SW1..............259 B3
Churton St SW1.....115 C2 **259** B3
Chute Ho **9** SW9.......138 C3
Chuter Ede Ho SW6......264 D5
Chyngton Cl DA15........167 D1
Chyngton Ct N11............64 C6
Cibber Rd SE23...........162 D2
Cicada Rd SW18...........158 A6
Cicely Ho NW8.............229 D3
Cicely Rd SE15............140 A4
Cinderford Way BR1......186 C6
Cinema Mus The ＊ SE11..261 C3
Cinema Par RM8.............81 B6
Cinnabar Wharf Central **16**
   E1............................118 A5
Cinnabar Wharf East **15**
   E1............................118 A5
Cinnabar Wharf West **17**
   E1............................118 A5
Cinnamon Cl
   8 Camberwell SE15...139 C5
   Thornton Heath CR0...204 A2
Cinnamon Row **3**
   SW11......................136 A2
Cinnamon St E1............118 B5
Cinnamon Wharf SE1....253 D2
Cinque Cotts SW19......178 C4
Cintra Ct SE19.............183 D4
Cintra Pk SE19............183 D3
Circle Ct HA0.................65 D4
Circle Gdns SW19........179 C1
Circle Ho **14** E14.........98 B1
Circle The
   Bermondsey SE1........253 D2
   Burnt Oak NW7...........27 B4
   Neasden NW2..............67 C5
Circuits The HA5............40 C5
Circular Rd London N2....30 B2
   Tottenham N17............51 D6
Circular Way SE18........144 C6
Circus Lo NW8.............229 C2
Circus Mews W1..........237 C4
Circus Pl EC2..............242 D3
Circus Rd NW8...92 B5 **229** C3
Circus St SE10............142 A5
Cirencester St W2..........91 D2
Cirrus **17** NW9.............27 D1
Cirrus Cl **4** SM26......220 A1
Cissbury Ho **6** SE26..162 A1
Cissbury Rd N15...........51 B4
Cissbury Ring N N12......29 C5
Cissbury Ring S N12......29 B5
Citadel Pl SE11............260 C3
Citizen Ho N7................72 C4
Citizen Rd N7...............72 C4
Citron Terr **4** SE15....140 B2
Citrus Ho **14** SE8.......119 B1
City Banking Coll
   SE1............117 B4 **252** D2
City Bsns Coll EC1..94 D4 **234** D1
City Bsns Ctr **33** SE16..118 C4
City Central Est EC1......235 A1
City Coll N1.................235 C2
City Coll of London The
   WC1.......................240 D3
City Forum EC1...95 A4 **235** A2
City Garden Row
   N1.............94 D5 **234** D3
City Gate E1.................96 C3
City & Guilds of London Art
   Sch The SE11......116 C1 **261** B1
City & Hackney Ctr for
   Mental Health (Hospl)
   E9.............................75 A3
City Hall ＊ SE1....117 C5 **253** B3

City Harbour E14 . . . . 119 D3
City & Islington 6th Form
 Coll EC1 . . . . 94 D4 234 C2
City & Islington Coll (Ctr for
 Applied Sciences)
 EC1 . . . . 94 D4 234 C2
City & Islington Coll (Ctr for
 Bsns, Arts & Technology) 6
 N7 . . . . 72 A4
City & Islington Coll (Ctr for
 Health, Social & Child Care)
 7 N7 . . . . 72 B4
City & Islington Coll (Ctr for
 Lifelong Learning) 3
 N4 . . . . 72 D6
City Law Sch The EC1 . . . 240 D3
City Lights The SE11 . . . . . 261 B1
CITY OF LONDON 117 A6
City of London Acad–
 Islington N1 . . . . . . 95 A6 235 A5
City of London Acad The
 SE1 . . . . 118 A1
City of London Bsns Coll
 N15 . . . . 52 A5
City of London Information
 Ctr* EC4 . . . . 241 C1
City of London Sch
 EC4 . . . . 117 A6 252 A6
City of London Sch for Girls
 EC2 . . . . 95 A2 242 B4
City of Westminster Coll
 W2 . . . . 92 B2 236 C4
City of Westminster Coll,
 Cosway Street Ctr
 NW1 . . . . 92 C2 237 B4
City of Westminster Coll,
 Maida Vale Ctr 1 W9 . . . . 91 D4
City of Westminster Coll,
 Queens Park Ctr 10 W9 . . 91 C4
City Prospect 5 SE19 . . . 183 C4
City Rd EC1 . . . . . 95 A4 235 B2
City Thameslink Sta
 EC4 . . . . 94 D1 241 C1
City University
 EC1 . . . . 94 D4 234 C1
City View 3 IG1 . . . . 79 A6
City Wharf Ho KT7 . . . . . . 197 B3
City Wlk SE1 . . . . 253 A1
Civic Way Ilford IG6 . . . . . . 57 A5
 Ruislip HA4 . . . . 62 D3
Civil Service Coll
 SW1 . . . . 115 C2 259 A3
Clabon Mews
 SW1 . . . . 114 D2 257 C4
Clack St SE16 . . . . 118 C4
Clacton Rd Newham E6 . . . 99 D4
 Tottenham N17 . . . . 33 D1
 Walthamstow E17 . . . . 53 A3
Claigmar Gdns N3 . . . . 29 D2
Claire Ct Brondesbury NW2 . 69 A2
 Bushey WD23 . . . . 8 B3
 4 Pinner HA5 . . . . 23 B3
 Whetstone N12 . . . . 14 A1
Claire Gdns HA7 . . . . 25 C5
Claire Pl E14 . . . . 119 C3
Clairvale Rd TW5 . . . . 129 A4
Clairview Rd SW16 . . . . . . 181 B5
Clairville Gdns W7 . . . . . . 108 C5
Clairville Point 12 SE23 . . 162 D1
Clamp Hill HA7 . . . . 24 C5
Clancarty Rd SW6 . . . . . . 135 C3
Clandon Cl
 South Acton W3 . . . . 110 D4
 Stoneleigh KT17 . . . . 216 A4
 Sutton SM2 . . . . 218 B2
Clandon Ct Plaistow BR1 . 187 A4
Clandon Gdns N3 . . . . 47 C6
Clandon Ho
 East Finchley N3 . . . . 47 C6
 12 Kingston u T KT2 . . . . 176 D4
Clandon Rd IG3 . . . . 79 C6
Clandon St SE8 . . . . 141 C3
Clanfield Ho 5 SW15 . . . . 156 A3
Clanricarde Gdns
 W2 . . . . 113 C6 245 B5
CLAPHAM 137 B2
Clapham Common* 137 B1
Clapham Common North
 Side SW4 . . . . 137 A1
Clapham Common South
 Side SW4 . . . . 159 C6
Clapham Common Sta
 SW4 . . . . 137 C1
Clapham Common West
 Side
 Clapham SW4, SW11 . . . . 136 D1
 Clapham SW11 . . . . 159 A6
Clapham Computer &
 Secretarial Coll 1
 SW4 . . . . 158 D6
Clapham Court Terr 2
 SW4 . . . . 160 A6
Clapham Cres SW4 . . . . . 137 D1
Clapham Ct 3 SW4 . . . . . 160 A6
Clapham High St SW4 . . . 137 D2
Clapham High Street Sta
 SW4 . . . . 137 D2
Clapham Junction Est
 SW11 . . . . 136 C1

Clapham Junction Sta
 SW11 . . . . 136 C1
Clapham L Ctr SW4 . . . . . 137 D2
Clapham Manor Ct 1
 SW4 . . . . 137 C2
Clapham Manor Prim Sch 8
 SW4 . . . . 137 C2
Clapham Manor St SW4 . 137 D2
Clapham Mans SW4 . . . . 159 B5
Clapham North Bsns Ctr 10
 SW4 . . . . 137 D2
Clapham North Sta
 SW4 . . . . 138 A2
CLAPHAM PARK 159 D6
Clapham Park Rd SW4 . . 137 D1
Clapham Park Terr 4
 SW2 . . . . 160 A6
Clapham Rd
 SW9 . . . . 138 B5 270 D4
Clapham South Sta
 SW4 . . . . 159 B5
Claps Gate La E6 . . . . 100 D3
Clapton Comm E5 . . . . 52 A2
Clapton Girls Tec Coll E5 . 74 C4
CLAPTON PARK 74 D4
Clapton Pas E5 . . . . 74 C3
Clapton Sq E5 . . . . 74 C3
Clapton Sta E5 . . . . 74 B6
Clapton Terr E5 . . . . 52 A1
Clapton Way E5 . . . . 74 A4
Clara Grant Ho 1 E14 . . . 119 C3
Clara Grant Prim Sch The 18
 E3 . . . . 97 C3
Clara Pl SE18 . . . . 122 C2
Clare Cl
 Borehamwood WD6 . . . . . . 10 B5
 East Finchley N2 . . . . 48 A6
Clare Cnr SE9 . . . . 166 D4
Clare Ct Chislehurst BR7 . 188 B2
 St Pancras WC1 . . . . 233 B1
 Wimbledon SW19 . . . . . . 179 A4
Claredale Ct SM2 . . . . . . 218 A1
Claredale Ho 3 E2 . . . . . . 96 B5
Claredale St E2 . . . . 96 A5
Clare Gdns Barking IG11 . . 80 A1
 Forest Gate E7 . . . . 77 A4
 Notting Hill W11 . . . . 91 A1
Clare Ho Bermondsey SE1 . 263 D2
 4 Burnt Oak HA8 . . . . 27 A1
 5 Ealing W7 . . . . 108 D5
 6 Old Ford E3 . . . . 97 B6
Clare House Prim Sch
 BR3 . . . . 186 A1
Clare La N1 . . . . 73 A1
Clare Lawn Ave SW14 . . . 155 B6
Clare Mews SW6 . . . . 265 C3
Clare Mkt WC2 . . . . 240 D1
Claremont
 1 Putney SW15 . . . . 157 A6
 Shepperton TW17 . . . . . . 192 D3
Claremont Ave
 Harrow HA3 . . . . 44 A4
 Sunbury TW16 . . . . 172 B2
 West Barnes KT3 . . . . 200 B4
Claremont Cl
 Finsbury N1 . . . . . . 94 C5 234 B3
 Newham E16 . . . . 122 C5
 Orpington BR6 . . . . 226 C4
 4 Streatham SW2 . . . . . . 160 B3
Claremont Ct 1 W9 . . . . . . 91 B5
Claremont Dr TW17 . . . . . 192 D3
Claremont Gdns
 Ilford IG3 . . . . 79 C6
 Kingston u T KT5 . . . . 198 A4
Claremont Gr
 Chiswick W4 . . . . 133 C5
 Woodford IG8 . . . . 37 C4
Claremont High Sch HA3 . . 44 A4
Claremont Ho 15 SM2 . . . 217 C1
Claremont Hts 2 . . . . 4 D1
Claremont La KT10 . . . . . 212 A3
Claremont Lo 12 SW19 . . 178 D3
Claremont Pk N3 . . . . 29 A2
Claremont Pl KT10 . . . . . . 212 D2
Claremont Prim Sch
 NW2 . . . . 68 D2
Claremont Rd
 Bromley BR1 . . . . 210 B5
 Claygate KT10 . . . . 212 C1
 Croydon CR0 . . . . 206 A1
 Ealing W13 . . . . 87 A2
 Forest Gate E7 . . . . 77 C3
 Hadley Wood EN4 . . . . 2 B6
 Harrow HA3 . . . . 24 C1
 Hendon NW2 . . . . 68 D6
 Higham Hill E17 . . . . 35 A1
 Highgate N6 . . . . 49 C2
 Kingston u T KT6 . . . . 198 A4
 Leyton E7 . . . . 76 B5
 Teddington TW11 . . . . 174 D6
 Twickenham TW1 . . . . 153 C5
 West Kilburn W9 . . . . 91 B5
Claremont Sq N1 . . 94 C5 234 A3
Claremont St
 Edmonton N18 . . . . 34 A4
 Greenwich SE10 . . . . 141 D6
 Newham E16 . . . . 122 C4
Claremont Terr KT7 . . . . . 197 B2
Claremont Way NW2 . . . . . 46 D1

Claremont Way Ind Est
 NW2 . . . . 46 C1
Clarence Ave
 Bromley BR1, BR2 . . . . . . 210 A5
 Clapham Pk SW4 . . . . 159 D5
 Ilford IG2 . . . . 56 C3
 Kingston u T KT3 . . . . 177 B1
Clarence Cl Bushey WD23 . . 8 A4
 New Barnet EN4 . . . . 14 B6
Clarence Cres
 Clapham Pk SW4 . . . . 159 D5
 Sidcup DA14 . . . . 190 A5
Clarence Ct Edgware NW7 . 27 C5
 10 Hammersmith W6 . . . . 112 B2
 5 North Finchley N12 . . . . 30 B5
Clarence Gate NW1 . . . . . 237 D6
Clarence Gate Gdns
 NW1 . . . . 237 D5
Clarence Gdns
 NW1 . . . . 93 B4 231 D1
Clarence Ho SE17 . . . . . . 139 A6
Clarence La SW15 . . . . . . 155 D5
Clarence Mews
 Balham SW12 . . . . 159 B4
 Hackney E5 . . . . 74 B3
 1 Rotherhithe SE16 . . . . . 118 D5
Clarence Pl 25 E5 . . . . 74 B3
Clarence Rd Bexley DA6 . . 147 A1
 Brentford W4 . . . . 110 C1
 Bromley BR1, BR2 . . . . . . 210 A6
 Brondesbury NW6 . . . . 69 B1
 Chislehurst SE9 . . . . 166 A2
 Enfield EN3 . . . . 18 C6
 Greenwich SE8 . . . . 141 D6
 Harringay N15 . . . . 51 A4
 Higham Hill E17 . . . . 34 D1
 Lower Clapton E5 . . . . 74 B4
 Manor Pk E12 . . . . 77 D3
 Newham E16 . . . . 98 C3
 Richmond TW9 . . . . 132 C4
 Sidcup DA14 . . . . 190 A5
 Sutton SM1 . . . . 217 D3
 Teddington TW11 . . . . 175 A4
 Thornton Heath CR0 . . . . 205 B2
 Wallington SM6 . . . . 219 B3
 Wimbledon SW19 . . . . . . 179 D4
 Wood Green N22 . . . . 32 A3
Clarence St
 Kingston u T KT1, KT2 . . . 176 A1
 5 Richmond TW9 . . . . 132 A1
 Southall UB2 . . . . 106 D3
Clarence Terr
 Hounslow TW3 . . . . 129 D1
 Lisson Gr NW1 . . . . 237 D6
Clarence Way NW1 . . . . . . 71 B1
Clarence Wlk 9 SW4 . . . . 138 A3
Clarendon Cl
 Bayswater W2 . . . . 247 A6
 38 Hackney E9 . . . . 74 C1
Clarendon Cres TW2 . . . . 152 B1
Clarendon Cross W11 . . . 244 B5
Clarendon Ct
 London N W11 . . . . 47 B5
 Mitcham SM4 . . . . 202 C4
 Paddington W9 . . . . 236 B6
 1 Richmond TW9 . . . . 132 C4
 Willesden NW2 . . . . 68 C1
Clarendon Dr SW15 . . . . . 134 C1
Clarendon Flats W1 . . . . . 238 B1
Clarendon Gdns
 Hendon NW4 . . . . 46 B6
 Paddington W9 . . . 92 A3 236 B5
 Redbridge IG1 . . . . 56 B2
 Wembley HA9 . . . . 66 A4
Clarendon Gr
 Mitcham CR4 . . . . 202 D6
 Somers Town NW1 . . . . . . 232 C2
Clarendon Ho Harrow HA2 . 42 D6
 North Finchley N12 . . . . . . 30 A5
 Somers Town NW1 . . . . . . 232 B3
 South Oxhey WD19 . . . . . . 22 D5
Clarendon Mews
 Bayswater W2 . . . . 247 A6
 Old Bexley DA5 . . . . 169 D3
Clarendon Pl W2 . 114 C6 247 A6
Clarendon Prim Sch
 TW15 . . . . 170 B6
Clarendon Rd
 Ashford TW15 . . . . 170 B6
 Croydon CR0 . . . . 220 D6
 Ealing W5 . . . . 88 A3
 Edmonton N18 . . . . 34 A5
 Harrow HA1 . . . . 42 C3
 Hayes UB3 . . . . 105 D4
 Hornsey N8 . . . . 50 B6
 Leytonstone E11 . . . . 54 B1
 Mitcham SW19 . . . . 180 C3
 Notting Hill W11 . . 113 A6 244 B6
 Wallington SM6 . . . . 219 C2
 Walthamstow E17 . . . . 53 D3
 Wanstead E18 . . . . 55 A6
 West Green N15 . . . . 51 A5
 Wood Green N22 . . . . 32 B1
Clarendon Rise SE13 . . . . 142 A1
Clarendon Specl Sch
 TW12 . . . . 173 D4
Clarendon St
 SW1 . . . . 115 B1 258 D2

Clarendon Terr W9 . . . . . . 236 B6
Clarendon Way
 Enfield N21 . . . . 17 A5
 Orpington BR5, BR7 . . . . . 211 D6
Clarendon Wlk 11 W11 . . . 91 A1
Clarens St SE6 . . . . 163 B2
Clare Pl SW15 . . . . 155 D4
Clare Point NW2 . . . . 46 D1
Clare Rd Hounslow TW4 . . 129 B2
 Leytonstone E11 . . . . 54 B3
 New Cross Gate SE14 . . . 141 B4
 Northolt UB6 . . . . 64 B2
 Stanwell TW19 . . . . 148 A4
 Willesden NW10 . . . . 68 A1
Clare St E2 . . . . 96 B5
Claret Gdns SE25 . . . . . . 205 C5
Clareville Ct SW7 . . . . 256 B3
Clareville Gr
 SW7 . . . . 114 A2 256 B3
Clareville Grove Mews
 SW7 . . . . 256 B3
Clareville Rd BR5 . . . . 227 A6
Clareville St
 SW7 . . . . 114 A2 256 B3
Clare Way DA7 . . . . 147 A4
Clarewood Ct W1 . . . . 237 C3
Clarewood Wlk SW9 . . . . 138 C1
Clarges Ho W1 . . . . 248 D4
Clarges Mews
 W1 . . . . 115 B5 248 C4
Clarges St W1 . . . . 115 B5 248 D4
Clariat Ct W3 . . . . 110 C4
Claribel Rd SW9 . . . . 138 D3
Clarice Ct NW4 . . . . 46 B6
Claridge Ct SW6 . . . . 264 C1
Claridge Rd RM8 . . . . 58 D3
Clarinet Ct HA8 . . . . 26 D3
Clarissa Ho 7 E14 . . . . . . 97 D1
Clarissa Rd RM6 . . . . 58 D2
Clarissa St E8 . . . . 95 D6
Clark Ct 17 NW10 . . . . 67 B1
Clarke Cl CR0 . . . . 205 A3
Clarke Ho
 2 London SW4 . . . . 137 C2
 5 Richmond TW10 . . . . . . 153 C1
Clarke Mans 9 IG11 . . . . . 79 D1
Clarke Mews 9 . . . . 18 B1
Clarke Path N16 . . . . 52 A1
Clarke's Ave KT4, SM3 . . . 216 D6
Clarkes Dr UB8 . . . . 82 A2
Clarkes Mews W1 . . . . . . 238 B4
Clark Gr IG3 . . . . 79 C4
Clark Ho SW10 . . . . 266 A4
Clark Lawrence Ct 10
 SW11 . . . . 136 B2
Clarks Mead WD23 . . . . 8 B4
Clarkson Rd E16 . . . . 98 D1
Clarkson Row NW1 . . . . . 232 A3
Clarkson St E2 . . . . 96 B4
Clarksons The IG11 . . . . . 101 A5
Clark's Pl EC2 . . . . 243 A2
Clark's Rd IG1 . . . . 79 B6
Clark St E1 . . . . 96 C2
Clark Way TW5 . . . . 128 D5
Classic Mans 33 E9 . . . . . . 74 C1
Classinghall Ho 14
 SW15 . . . . 156 D5
Classon Cl UB7 . . . . 104 A4
Claude Rd Leyton E10 . . . . 54 A1
 London SE15 . . . . 140 B3
 Newham E13 . . . . 99 B6
Claude St E14 . . . . 119 C2
Claudia Jones Way
 SW2 . . . . 160 A5
Claudia Pl SW19 . . . . 157 A3
Claudius Ct HA7 . . . . 9 D1
Claughton Rd E13 . . . . 99 C5
Clauson Ave UB5 . . . . 64 A3
Clavell St 8 SE10 . . . . . . 142 A6
Claverdale Rd SW2 . . . . . 160 C4
Clavering Ave SW13 . . . . 134 B6
Clavering Cl TW1 . . . . 175 A6
Clavering Ho SE13 . . . . . . 142 B1
Clavering Rd E12 . . . . 77 D6
Claverings Ind Est N9 . . . . 18 C2
Claverley Gr N3 . . . . 29 D2
Claverley Villas N3 . . . . . . 29 D3
Claverton St
 SW1 . . . . 115 C1 259 B1
Clave St E1 . . . . 118 C5
Claxton Gr W6 . . . 112 D1 254 A1
Clay Ave CR4 . . . . 181 B1
Claybank SE13 . . . . 141 D2
Claybee Ct N22 . . . . 32 B5
Claybourne Mews 2
 SE19 . . . . 183 D3
Claybridge Rd SE12 . . . . . 187 C6
Claybrook Cl N2 . . . . 48 B6
Claybrook Rd W6 . . . . 134 D6
Claybury Broadway IG5 . . . 56 A6
Clay Ct E17 . . . . 54 B6
Claydon SE17 . . . . 262 A4
Claydon Dr CR0 . . . . 220 A4
Claydon Ho NW4 . . . . 28 D1
Claydown Mews SE18 . . . 122 C1
Clayfarm Rd SE9 . . . . 167 A2
CLAYGATE 212 D1
Claygate Cres CR0 . . . . . . 224 B2
Claygate Ct SM1 . . . . 218 A5

Claygate La
 Hinchley Wood KT10 . . . . . 213 A6
 Thames Ditton KT7 . . . . . 197 A1
Claygate Lodge Cl KT10 . 212 C1
Claygate Prim Sch KT10 . 212 C1
Claygate Rd W13 . . . . 109 B3
Claygate Sta KT10 . . . . . . 212 C2
CLAYHALL 56 B6
Clayhall Ct 20 E3 . . . . 97 B5
CLAY HILL 5 A6
Clay Hill EN2 . . . . 5 B6
Clayhill Cres SE12, SE9 . . 187 D6
Clay La Bushey WD23 . . . . . 8 C4
 Stanwell TW19 . . . . 148 B4
Claylands Ct SE19 . . . . . . 183 B5
Claylands Pl SW8 . . . . . . 138 C5
Claylands Rd
 SW8 . . . . 138 B6 270 D5
Claymill Ho 3 SE18 . . . . . 123 A1
Claymore Cl SM3, SM4 . . . 201 C2
Claymore Ct 4 E17 . . . . . . 35 A2
Claypole Ct E17 . . . . 53 C4
Claypole Dr TW5 . . . . 129 A4
Claypole Rd E15 . . . . 98 A5
Claypons Ave TW8 . . . . . . 110 A4
Claypons Gdns W5 . . . . . 109 D2
Claypons Hospl W6 . . . . . 110 A4
Claypons La TW8 . . . . 110 A1
Clays Ct N16 . . . . 51 D1
Clay St W1 . . . . . . 92 D2 237 D3
Clayton 22 NW9 . . . . 27 D1
Clayton Ave HA0 . . . . 66 A1
Clayton Bsns Ctr UB3 . . . 105 C4
Clayton Cl 3 E6 . . . . 100 B1
Clayton Cres
 Brentford TW8 . . . . 109 D1
 Islington N1 . . . . 233 C1
Clayton Ct
 1 Higham Hill E17 . . . . . . 35 A1
 Stamford Hill N16 . . . . 52 A2
Clayton Field NW9 . . . . . . 27 C2
Clayton Ho 22 Hackney E9 . 74 C1
 Long Ditton KT7 . . . . 197 B1
Clayton Mews SE10 . . . . 142 B4
Clayton Rd
 Chessington KT10, KT9 . . 213 D4
 Hayes UB3 . . . . 105 C4
 Isleworth TW7 . . . . 130 C2
 Peckham SE15 . . . . 140 A4
Clayton St SE11 . . . . 138 C6
Clayton Terr UB4 . . . . 84 D2
Claytonville Terr DA17 . . . 125 D4
Clay Wood Cl BR6 . . . . . . 211 C2
Clayworth Cl DA15 . . . . . . 168 B5
Cleanthus Cl SE18 . . . . . . 144 D4
Cleanthus Rd SE18 . . . . . 144 D4
Clearbrook Way 13 E1 . . . 96 C1
Clearmont Ho UB2 . . . . . . 107 C3
Clearwater Ho BR3 . . . . . 207 D4
Clear Water Ho 9
 TW10 . . . . 154 A6
Clearwater Pl KT6 . . . . . . 197 C3
Clearwater Terr 4 W11 . . 112 D4
Clearwell Dr W9 . . . . 91 D3
Cleave Ave Hayes UB3 . . . 105 C2
 Orpington BR6 . . . . 227 C2
Cleaveland Rd KT6 . . . . . 197 D4
Cleaver Ho 6 NW3 . . . . . . 70 D1
Cleaverholme Cl SE25 . . . 206 B3
Cleaver Sq SE11 . . . 116 C1 261 B2
Cleaver St SE11 . . . 116 C1 261 B2
Cleave's Almshos 1
 KT2 . . . . 176 A1
Cleeve Ct
 East Bedfont TW14 . . . . . 149 C3
 Muswell Hill N10 . . . . 31 B3
Cleeve Hill SE23 . . . . 162 B3
Cleeve Ho 16 SE23 . . . . . . 95 C4
Cleeve Park Gdns DA14 . . 168 B2
Cleeve Park Sch DA14 . . . 168 C1
Cleeve Way Cheam SM1 . . 201 C3
 Roehampton SW15 . . . . . 155 D4
Cleeve Workshops 14 E2 . 95 C4
Clegg Ho SE3 . . . . 143 B1
Clegg St Newham E13 . . . . 99 A5
 16 Wapping E1 . . . . 118 B5
Cleland Ho 19 E2 . . . . 96 C5
Clematis Gdns IG8 . . . . . . 37 A5
Clematis St W12 . . . . 112 A6
Clem Attlee Par SW6 . . . . 264 D5
Clem Attlee Ct
 SW6 . . . . 135 B6 264 D5
Clemence St E14 . . . . 97 B2
Clement Attlee Ho NW10 . 67 D1
Clement Ave SW4 . . . . . . 137 D1
Clement Cl Acton W4 . . . . 111 B2
 Hampstead NW6 . . . . 68 C1
Clement Danes Ho 2
 W12 . . . . 90 B1
Clement Gdns UB3 . . . . . 105 C2
Clement Ho
 14 Deptford SE8 . . . . 119 A2
 17 North Kensington W10 . 90 C2
Clementhorpe Rd RM9 . . . 80 C2
Clementina Rd E10 . . . . . . 53 B1
Clementine Churchill Hospl
 The HA1 . . . . 64 D5

Clementine Cl W13 . . . . . . .109 B4
Clementine Wlk 4 IG8 . . . .37 A3
Clement Rd Penge BR3. . .184 D1
Wimbledon SW19. . . . . .179 A5
Clements Ave 1 E16. . . . .121 A6
Clements Cl 19 N12 . . . . . . .29 D6
Clements Ct
Hounslow TW4 . . . . 128 D1
5 Ilford IG1. . . . . .78 D5
Clements Ho N17. . . . . .34 A2
Clements Inn WC2 .94 B1 240 D1
Clements Inn Pas WC2 . . 240 D1
Clements La IG1. . . . . .78 D5
Clement's La EC2,
EC4 . . . . .117 B6 252 D6
Clements Pl TW8. . . . . 109 D1
Clements Rd East Ham E6 . .78 B1
Ilford IG1. . . . . .78 D5
Clement's Rd SE16. . . . . . 118 B3
Cleminson Ct DA14 . . . . . . 190 D4
Clemson Ho 9 E8 . . . . .95 D6
Clendon Way SE18. . . . . . . 123 B2
Clennam St SE1. . . . . 252 B2
Clensham Ct SM3. . . . . 217 C6
Clensham La SM1. . . . . 217 C6
Clenston Mews W1 . . . . . . 237 C2
Cleopatra Cl N16. . . . . .51 D1
Cleopatra Cl N1. . . . . .9 D1
Cleopatra's Needle ★
WC2 . . . . .116 B6 250 C5
Clephane Rd 13 N1 . . . . . . .73 A2
Clephane Rd N N1 . . . . .73 A2
Clephane Rd S N1 . . . . .73 B2
Clere Pl EC2. . . . . 242 D6
Clere St EC2 . . . . . . .95 B3 242 D6
Clerics Wlk TW17. . . . . 193 B3
CLERKENWELL 94 D3
Clerkenwell Cl
EC1. . . . . .94 C3 241 B5
Clerkenwell Gn
EC1. . . . . .94 C3 241 C5
Clerkenwell Parochial CE
Prim Sch EC1. . . .94 C4 234 A1
Clerkenwell Rd
EC1. . . . . .94 D3 241 C5
Clermont Rd E9 . . . . .96 C6
Cleveden Ct CR2. . . . . 221 C3
Cleveden Ho BR1. . . . . 188 A3
Clevedon Ct
Battersea SW11. . . . . 267 A2
Dulwich SE21. . . . . 161 B1
Clevedon Gdns
Cranford TW5. . . . . 128 B4
Hayes UB3 . . . . 105 B3
Clevedon Ho 6 SM1. . . . . 218 A4
Clevedon Mans NW5. . . . . .71 A4
Clevedon Rd
Kingston u T KT1. . . . . . . 176 C1
Penge SE20 . . . . 184 D2
Twickenham TW1 . . . . 153 D5
Cleve Ho NW6. . . . . .69 D1
Cleveland Ave
Chiswick W4. . . . . 111 D2
Hampton TW12. . . . . 173 B3
Merton SW20 . . . . 179 B1
Cleveland Cres WD6 . . . . . .11 A6
Cleveland Ct Ealing W13. . .87 B2
Marylebone W1 . . . . 239 B5
Southall UB2. . . . . 107 D2
Cleveland Gdns
Barnes SW13 . . . . 133 D3
Harringay N4, N15. . . . . . . .51 A4
Hendon NW2 . . . . .68 D6
Paddington W2 . . . . .92 A1 236 A1
Worcester Pk KT4. . . . . . . 215 D6
Cleveland Gr 39 E1. . . . . . .96 C3
Cleveland Ho 7 N2. . . . . . . .30 B1
Cleveland Inf Sch IG1. . . . .78 D5
Cleveland Jun Sch IG1. . . .78 D5
Cleveland Mans
8 Brixton SW9 . . . . 138 C5
4 Brondesbury NW6. . . . . .69 B1
Paddington W9. . . . . .91 C3
Cleveland Mews W1 . . . . . 239 A4
Cleveland Park Ave E17. .53 C5
Cleveland Park Cres E17. .53 C5
Cleveland Pk TW19 . . . . . . 148 A5
Cleveland Pl SW1. . . . . 249 B4
Cleveland Rd
Barnes SW13 . . . . 133 D3
Bexley DA16. . . . . 145 D3
Ealing W13. . . . . .87 B2
Edmonton N9. . . . . .18 B4
Ilford IG1. . . . . .78 D5
Isleworth TW7 . . . . 131 A1
Islington N1. . . . . .73 B1
New Malden KT3 . . . . 199 C5
14 South Acton W4. . . . . . 111 A3
Wanstead E18 . . . . .55 A6
Worcester Pk KT4. . . . . . . 215 C6
Cleveland Rise SM4. . . . . . 200 D2
Cleveland Row
SW1. . . . . 115 C5 249 B3
Cleveland Sq W2 . .92 A1 236 A1
Cleveland St W1. . . .93 C3 239 A5
Cleveland Terr
W2. . . . . .92 A1 236 B2

Cleveland Way E1. . . . . . . .96 C3
Cleveley Cres W5 . . . . .88 B5
Cleveley Rd E5 . . . . .74 B5
Clevely Cl SE7 . . . . 121 D2
Clevedon Cl N16. . . . . .73 D5
Cleve Rd Sidcup DA14. . . . 168 D1
South Hampstead NW6. . . .69 D1
Cleverly Cotts W12. . . . . . . 111 D5
Cleverly Est W12. . . . . 112 A6
Cleves Ct KT6. . . . . 198 A3
Cleves Prim Sch E6. . . . . . . .99 D6
Cleves Rd Newham E6. . . . .99 D5
Richmond TW10 . . . . 153 C1
Cleves Way
Ashford TW16. . . . . 171 D4
Hampton TW12. . . . . 173 B3
Ruislip HA4. . . . . .40 D1
Clewer Cres HA3. . . . . .24 B2
Clewer Ct 2 E10. . . . . .53 C1
Clewer Ho 6 SE2. . . . . 124 D4
Cley Ho SE4 . . . . 140 D1
Clichy Ho 33 E1. . . . . .96 C2
Cliftons Roundabout SE9,
SE12 . . . . 165 C5
Clifton St EC2. . . . . .95 C3 243 A5
Clifton Terr N4. . . . . .72 C6
Clifton The KT6. . . . . 214 A6
Clifton Villas W9 . . . .92 A2 236 A4
Cliftonville Ct SE12 . . . . . . 165 A3
Clifton Way
Harlington TW6 . . . . 126 D2
Peckham SE15. . . . . 140 C5
Wembley HA0. . . . . .88 A6
Climsland Ho SE1. . . . . 251 B4
Clinch Ct 11 E16. . . . . .99 A2
Cline Ho SW15. . . . . 156 A6
Cline Rd N11 . . . . .31 C4
Clinger Ct N1. . . . . .95 C6
Clink Prison Mus The ★
SE1. . . . . 252 C4
Clink St SE1 . . . . . . .117 B5 252 C4
Clinton Ave Bexley DA16 . .146 A1
East Molesey KT8. . . . . . . 196 A5
Clinton Ho
New Malden KT3 . . . . 199 B1
6 Surbiton KT6. . . . . 197 D2
Clinton Rd Bow E3. . . . . . . .97 A4
Forest Gate E7 . . . . .77 A4
West Green N15. . . . . .51 B5
Clipper Appts 12 SE10 . . . 142 A6
Clipper Cl 3 SE16. . . . . . . 118 D4
Clipper Ho E14 . . . . 120 A1
Clipper Way SE13. . . . . 142 A1
Clippesby Cl KT9. . . . . 214 B2
Clipstone Ho 10 SW15. . . .156 A6
Clipstone Mews W1. . . . . . 239 A4
Clipstone Rd TW3. . . . . 129 C2
Clipstone St W1 . . . .93 C2 239 A4
Clissold Cl N2 . . . . .48 D6
Clissold Cres N16. . . . . .73 B4
Clissold Ct N4. . . . . .73 A6
Clissold Ho 4 N16. . . . . . . .73 B6
Clissold Rd N16. . . . . .73 B5
Clitheroe Ave HA2. . . . . .41 C1
Clitheroe Rd SW9. . . . . 138 A3
Clitherow Ave W7. . . . . 109 C1
Clitherow Ave W7. . . . . 109 C1
Clitterhouse Cres NW2. . . . .46 C1
Clitterhouse Rd NW2 . . . . . .46 C1
Clive Ave N18. . . . . .33 A4
Clive Ct Paddington W9 . . . 236 B6
Streatham SW16. . . . . 181 D5
Tolworth KT6. . . . . 214 C6
Cliveden Cl N12. . . . . .30 A6
Cliveden Ho SW1. . . . . 258 A4
Cliveden Pl
Belgravia SW1 . . . . .115 A2 258 A4
Shepperton TW17. . . . . . . 193 A3
Cliveden Rd SW19 . . . . 179 B2
Clivedon Ct Ealing W13. . . .87 B2
6 New Barnet EN5 . . . . . . .2 A1
Clivedon Rd E4 . . . . .36 C5
Clive Ho
18 Clapham SW8 . . . . . . 137 D3
3 Croydon CR0. . . . . 205 D1
Greenwich SE10. . . . . 142 A6
Clive Lloyd Ho N15. . . . . . . .51 A4
Clive Lo N4. . . . . .46 D3
Clive Rd Belvedere DA17. . .125 C2
Enfield EN1. . . . . .6 A1
Feltham TW14. . . . . 150 A3
Mitcham SW19. . . . . 180 C4
Teddington TW1. . . . . 175 A6
West Norwood SE21, SE27. .161 B1
Clivesdale Dr UB3 . . . . 106 B5
Clive Way EN1 . . . . .6 A1
Cloak La EC4 . . . . . .117 B6 252 C6
Clochar Ct NW10 . . . . .89 D6
Clock Ct 2 E11. . . . . .77 A6
Clock Ho Stamford Hill N16. .51 D2
Walthamstow E17 . . . . .54 B5
Clock Ho The EN2. . . . . .5 D6
Clockhouse Ave IG11. . . . . 101 A6
Clockhouse Cl SW19 . . . . . 156 C2
Clock House Ct 11 BR3. . . .185 A1
Clockhouse Junc N13. . . . . .32 C5
Clockhouse La TW14,
TW15. . . . . 148 D2
Clockhouse Mans N13. . . . .32 C5
Clockhouse Par N13. . . . . . .32 C5
Clock House Par E11. . . . . . .55 B3

Clockhouse Pl SW15. . . . . . 157 A5
Clock House Rd BR3. . . . . . 185 A1
Clockhouse Rdbt TW14. . . .149 A3
Clock House Sta BR3. . . . . 185 A2
Clockhouse The SW19. . . . 156 C1
Clockmakers' Mus ★
EC2. . . . . .95 A1 242 B2
Clocktower Mews 6
W7 . . . . 108 C5
Clock Tower Mews
Islington N1. . . . . 235 B5
Thamesmead SE28. . . . . . 124 B6
Clock Tower Pl 1 N7. . . . . .72 A2
Clock Tower Rd TW7 . . . . . 130 D2
Clock View Cres 2 N7 . . . . .72 A2
Cloister Cl TW11. . . . . 175 B5
Cloister Gdns
Croydon SE25. . . . . 206 B3
Edgware HA8. . . . . .27 A5
Cloister Rd Acton W3. . . . . .89 A2
Child's Hill NW2 . . . . .69 B6
Cloisters Ave BR1, BR2. . . 210 B4
Cloisters Ct Erith DA7. . . . . 147 D2
Highgate N6. . . . . .49 B1
Cloisters Ho 8 SW19 . . . . 179 C3
Cloisters The 22 SW9. . . . 138 C4
Clonard Way HA5. . . . . .23 C4
Clonbrock Rd N16. . . . . .73 C4
Cloncurry St SW6. . . . . 134 D3
Clone Ct 4 W12 . . . . 111 C3
Clone The 5 KT2 . . . . 176 D3
Clonmel Cl HA2. . . . . .42 B1
Clonmel Rd N17. . . . . .51 B6
Clonmel Rd
Fulham SW6 . . . . . .135 B4 264 D2
Teddington TW11. . . . . 174 B6
Clonmore St SW18. . . . . . . 157 B3
Cloonmore Ave BR6. . . . . . 227 D4
Clorane Gdns NW3. . . . . . . .69 C5
Close The
Beckenham BR3. . . . . 207 A5
Cheam SM3. . . . . 201 B2
Chingford E4. . . . . .36 A3
Cockfosters EN4. . . . . .14 D6
Croydon SE25. . . . . 206 A3
Dagenham RM6 . . . . .59 A3
Eastcote HA5. . . . . .40 C2
Harrow HA2. . . . . .24 A1
Hillingdon UB10 . . . . .82 C6
Hounslow TW7 . . . . 130 B3
Ilford IG2. . . . . .57 C3
Kingston u T KT3. . . . . 177 A1
Lewisham SE3 . . . . 142 B3
Mitcham CR4 . . . . 202 D5
Mortlake TW9. . . . . 132 D2
Muswell Hill N10. . . . . .31 B1
1 Old Bexley DA5. . . . . . . 169 C4
Palmers Green N14 . . . . . .15 D2
Petts Wood BR5 . . . . 211 C3
Rayners La HA5. . . . . .41 B2
Sidcup DA14. . . . . 190 B5
Surbiton KT6. . . . . 198 A3
Totteridge N20 . . . . .13 B2
Wembley HA0. . . . . .66 A2
Wembley Pk HA9 . . . . .67 A5
Cloth Ct EC1. . . . . 241 D3
Cloth Fair EC1 . . . . .94 D2 241 D3
Clothier Ho SE7. . . . . 122 A1
Clothier St EC3 . . . . 243 B2
Cloth St EC1. . . . . . .95 A2 242 A4
Clothworkers Rd SE18 . . . .145 B5
Cloudesle Rd SW17. . . . . . 159 B2
Cloudesley Cl DA14 . . . . . . 189 D6
Cloudesley Mans N1. . . . . 234 B5
Cloudesley Pl N1. . . .94 C6 234 B5
Cloudesley Rd Erith DA7 . .147 B4
Islington N1. . . . . . .94 C6 234 A5
Cloudesley Sq N1. . .94 C6 234 B6
Cloudesley St N1. . . .94 C6 234 B5
Clouston Cl SM6. . . . . 220 A3
Clova Rd E7 . . . . .77 A3
Clove Cres E14 . . . . 120 B6
Clovelly Ave Colindale NW9. .45 C5
Uxbridge UB10 . . . . .61 A4
Clovelly Cl Pinner HA5 . . . . .40 C6
Uxbridge UB10 . . . . .61 A4
Clovelly Ct NW2 . . . . .68 B3
South Norwood SE19 . . . . 183 D2
Clovelly Ho W2 . . . . 236 A2
Clovelly Rd Acton W4. . . . . 111 B4
Ealing W5. . . . . 109 C4
Erith DA7. . . . . 147 A6
Hornsey N8. . . . . .49 D5
Hounslow TW3. . . . . 129 C3
Clovelly Way Harrow HA2 . .42 B6
Orpington BR6. . . . . 211 D3
Stepney E1. . . . . .96 C1
Clover Cl E11. . . . . .76 B6
Clover Ct Enfield EN3. . . . . . .7 A1
Sutton SM2. . . . . 217 D2
Cloverdale Gdns DA15 . . . .167 D5
Clover Ho Hounslow TW3. .130 A4
Southgate N21. . . . . .16 B6
Cloverleys IG10. . . . . .21 D6
Clover Mews SW3 . . . . 267 D6
Clover Way SM6 . . . . 203 A1
Clove St 9 E13. . . . . .99 A3
Clowders Rd SE6. . . . . 163 B1
Clowes Ho 3 SW4. . . . . . . 138 A1

Clowns Mus ★ E8 . . . . .95 D6
Clowser Cl 4 SM1. . . . . . . 218 A3
Cloysters Gn E1 . . . . 118 A5
Cloyster Wood HA8. . . . . . . .25 D4
Club Gardens Rd BR2. . . . . 209 A2
Club Row E2 . . . . . . .95 D3 243 C6
Clumps The TW15. . . . . 171 B6
Clunbury Ave UB2. . . . . 107 B1
Clunbury St N1. . . . . 235 D3
Clunie Ho SW1 . . . . 257 D6
Cluny Mews SW5 . . . . 255 A3
Cluny Pl SE1. . . . . . .117 C3 263 A6
Cluse Ct N1. . . . . 235 A4
Clutton St E14. . . . . .97 D2
Clydach Rd EN1. . . . . .5 D1
Clyde Cir N15. . . . . .51 C5
Clyde Ct NW1. . . . . 232 D4
Clyde Flats SW6 . . . . 264 C4
Clyde Ho 9 KT2 . . . . 175 D2
Clyde Pl E10. . . . . .53 D2
Clyde Rd Croydon CR0. . . . 221 D6
South Tottenham N15. . . . . .51 C5
Stanwell TW19 . . . . 148 A3
Sutton SM1. . . . . 217 C3
Wallington SM6 . . . . 219 C2
Wood Green N22. . . . . .31 D2
Clydesdale EN3. . . . . .6 D1
Clydesdale Ave HA7. . . . . . .43 D6
Clydesdale Cl
Borehamwood WD6. . . . . . .11 B6
Isleworth TW7 . . . . 130 D2
Clydesdale Ct N20 . . . . .14 B3
Clydesdale Gdns TW10 . . . 132 D1
Clydesdale Ho
Abbey Wood DA18 . . . . . . 125 A4
4 Notting Hill W11 . . . . . . .91 B1
Clydesdale Path WD6 . . . . .11 B6
Clydesdale Rd W11 . . . . . . .91 B1
Clyde St SE8. . . . . 141 B6
Clyde Terr SE23. . . . . 162 C2
Clyde Vale SE23. . . . . 162 C2
Clyde Works 10 SM6 . . . . . 219 C2
Clyfford Rd HA4 . . . . .61 D4
Clymping Dene TW14 . . . . 150 B4
Clynes Ho
6 Dagenham RM10. . . . . . .81 C5
3 Globe Town E2. . . . . . . .96 D4
Hayes UB4 . . . . .84 A4
Clyro Ct N4. . . . . .50 B1
Clyston St SW8 . . . . 137 C3
Clytha Ct SE27. . . . . 183 A6
Coach Ho NW10. . . . . .67 D2
Coach & Horses Yd W1. . . 249 A6
Coach House La
Highbury N5. . . . . .72 D4
Wimbledon SW19. . . . . . . 156 D1
Coach House Mews
SE23. . . . . 162 D5
Coach House Yd 5 NW3. . .70 B4
Coachmaker Mews 5
SW9. . . . . 138 A2
Coachman Lo N12. . . . . .30 A5
Coalbrook Mans 3
SW12. . . . . 159 B3
Coaldale Wlk SE21. . . . . . . 161 A4
Coalecroft Rd SW15. . . . . . 156 C6
Coalport Ho SE11. . . . . 261 A4
Coal Post Cl BR6. . . . . 227 D2
Coatbridge Ho 8 N1. . . . . . .72 B1
Coates Ave SW18 . . . . 158 C5
Coates Ct CR7 . . . . 205 A6
Coates La NW3. . . . . .70 C3
Coates Hill Rd BR1. . . . . . . 188 C1
Coates Rd WD6 . . . . .9 D4
Coate St E2 . . . . .96 A5
Coates Wlk TW8 . . . . 110 A1
Cobalt SE2. . . . . 124 A4
Cobalt Cl CR0. . . . . 206 D5
Cobb Cl WD6 . . . . .11 A6
Cobbett Rd
Kidbrooke SE9 . . . . 144 A4
Twickenham TW2 . . . . 151 C3
Cobbetts Ave IG4 . . . . .55 D4
Cobbett St SW8. . . . .138 B5 270 C3
Cobble La N1 . . . . .72 D1
Cobble Mews N4, N5 . . . . . .73 A5
Cobbler's Wlk TW11 . . . . . 174 D3
Cobblestone Pl CR0. . . . . . 205 A1
Cobbold Ct SW1 . . . . 259 C4
Cobbold Ind Est NW10. . . . .67 D2
Cobbold Mews W12. . . . . . 111 D4
Cobbold Rd
Bedford Pk W12 . . . . 111 D4
Leyton E11. . . . . .76 D5
Willesden NW10. . . . . .67 D2
Cobb's Hall 1 SW6 . . . . . . 134 D6
Cobbs Rd TW4. . . . . 129 B1
Cobb St E1 . . . . .117 C3 243 C3
Cobden Bldgs WC1 . . . . . . 233 C2
Cobden Ct Bromley BR2. . . 209 C5
9 Thamesmead SE28. . . . 124 C5
Cobden Ho
11 Bethnal Green E2 . . . . .96 A4
Regent's Pk NW1 . . . . 232 A4
Cobden Mews SE26. . . . . . 184 B5
Cobden Rd Croydon CR0. . . 206 A4
Leyton E11. . . . . .76 C6
Orpington BR6. . . . . 227 B4
Cobham 21 NW9. . . . . .27 D1
Cobham Ave KT3. . . . . 200 A4

Cobham Cl
2 Blackfen DA15 168 B5
Bromley BR2 210 A2
Clapham SW11 158 C5
Edgware HA8 26 D1
Enfield EN1 6 A2
Wallington SM6 220 A2
Cobham Ct CR4 180 B1
Cobham Ho IG11 101 A6
Cobham Mews 3 NW1 71 D1
Cobham Pl DA6 168 D6
Cobham Rd Chingford E17 36 A2
Harringay N22 50 D6
Heston TW5 128 C5
Ilford IG3 79 C5
Kingston u T KT1, KT2 176 C1
Cobland Rd SE12 187 C6
Coborn Mews 9 E3 97 B4
Coborn Rd E3 97 B4
Coborn St E3 97 B4
Cobourg Prim Sch SE5 139 D6
Cobourg Rd SE5 139 D6
Cobourg St NW1 93 C4 232 B1
Coburg Cl SW1 259 B4
Coburg Cres SW2 160 C3
Coburg Dwellings 11 E1 118 C6
Coburg Gdns IG5 37 D1
Coburg Rd N22 32 B1
Cochrane Cl NW8 229 D3
Cochrane Ct 3 E10 53 C1
Cochrane Ho 15 E14 119 C4
Cochrane Mews NW8 92 B5 229 D3
Cochrane Rd SW19 179 B3
Cochrane St NW8 92 B5 229 D3
Coci Ho W14 254 D3
Cockburn Ho SW1 259 D1
Cockerell Rd E17 53 A3
COCKFOSTERS 2 D1
Cockfosters Par EN4 3 A1
Cockfosters Rd EN4 2 D3
Cockfosters Sta EN4 3 A1
Cock Hill E1 243 B3
Cock La EC1 94 D2 241 D3
Cockpit Yd WC1 240 D4
Cocks Cres KT3 199 D5
Cocksett Ave BR6 227 C2
Cockspur Ct SW1 249 D4
Cockspur St SW1 115 D5 249 D4
Cocksure La DA14 191 C6
Coda Ctr The SW6 135 A4 264 B2
Code St E1 95 D3 243 D5
Codicote Ho 22 SE8 118 D2
Codicote Terr N4 73 A6
Codling Cl 12 E1 118 A5
Codling Way HA0 65 D4
Codrington Ct 3 SE16 119 A5
Codrington Hill SE23 163 A4
Codrington Ho 7 E1 96 B3
Codrington Mews W11 91 A1
Cody Cl Harrow HA3 43 D6
Wallington SM6 219 D1
Cody Rd E16 98 B3
Coe Ave SE25 206 A3
Coe's Alley EN5 1 A1
Coffey St SE8 141 C5
Cogan Ave E17 35 A2
Cohen Ho NW7 28 A6
Cohen Lo E5 75 A3
Coin St SE1 116 C5 251 A4
Coity Rd NW5 71 A2
Cokers La SE21 161 B3
Coke St E1 96 A1
Colab Ct N22 32 C2
Colas Mews 7 NW6 91 C6
Colbeck Mews SW5 113 D2 255 D3
Colbeck Rd HA1 42 A2
Colberg Pl N16 51 D2
Colbert 1 SE5 139 D4
Colborne Ct 8 SW19 179 D2
Colborne Ho 8 E14 119 C6
Colborne Way KT4 216 C6
Colbrook Ave UB3 105 B3
Colbrook Cl UB3 105 B3
Colburn Ave HA5 23 A4
Colburn Way SM1 218 B5
Colby Rd
Walton-on-T KT12 194 A1
West Norwood SE19 183 C5
Colchester Ave E12 78 B5
Colchester Dr HA5 40 D4
Colchester Ho 17 SW8 137 D3
Colchester Rd
Burnt Oak HA8 27 A3
Leyton E10 54 A2
Pinner HA6 22 A1
Walthamstow E17 53 C3
Colchester St E1 243 D2
Colchester Villas CR7 204 C3
Coldbath Sq EC1 241 A6
Coldbath St SE13 141 D3
Cold Blow La SE14 140 D6
Coldershaw Rd W13 109 A4
Coldfall Ave N10 31 A1
Coldfall Prim Sch N10 30 D1
Coldham Ct N22 32 D2
Coldham Gr EN3 7 A6
Coldharbour E14 120 A5
Coldharbour Crest SE9 166 C1
Coldharbour Ind Est SE5 139 A3
Coldharbour La
Brixton SW9 138 D2
Bushey WD23 8 A6
Hayes UB3 106 A5
Coldharbour Lane Ho UB3 106 A5
Coldharbour Pl SE5 139 B3
Coldharbour Rd CR0 220 C3
Coldharbour Sports Ctr SE9 166 B2
Coldharbour Way CR0 220 C3
Coldstream Gdns SW18 157 B5
Colebeck Mews N1 72 D2
Colebert Ave E1 96 C3
Colebert Ho 21 E1 96 C3
Colebrook Cl
Edgware NW7 28 D3
Putney SW19 156 D4
Colebrook Ct SW3 257 B3
Colebrooke Ave W13 87 B1
Colebrooke Ct DA14 190 B6
Colebrooke Dr E11 55 C2
Colebrooke Pl N1 234 D5
Colebrooke Row
Islington N1 233 B6
Islington N1 94 D5 234 C4
Islington N1 234 D5
Colebrook Ho 1 E14 97 D1
Colebrook Rd SW16 182 A2
Colebrook Rise BR2 186 C1
Colebrook Way N11 31 B5
Coleby Path 21 SE5 139 B5
Colechurch Ho 9 SE1 118 A1
Cole Cl SE28 124 B5
Cole Court Lo 9 TW1 153 A4
Coledale Dr HA7 25 C2
Colefax Bldg 12 E1 96 A1
Coleford Rd SW18 158 A6
Cole Gdns TW5 128 A5
Colegrave Rd E15 76 B3
Colegrave Sch E15 76 B3
Colegrove Rd SE15 139 D6
Coleherne Ct SW10 113 D1 255 D1
Coleherne Mans SW5 255 D2
Coleherne Mews SW10 113 D1 255 C1
Coleherne Rd SW10 113 D1 255 C1
Colehill Gdns SW6 264 A1
Colehill La SW6 135 A4 264 B1
Cole Ho SE1 251 B1
Coleman Cl SE25 184 A1
Coleman Ct SW18 157 C4
Coleman Fields N1 95 A6 235 B6
Coleman Mans N19 50 A2
Coleman Rd
Belvedere DA17 125 C2
Camberwell SE5 139 C5
Dagenham RM9 81 A2
Colemans Heath SE9 166 D1
Coleman St EC2 95 B1 242 C2
Coleman Street Bldgs EC2 242 C2
Colenso Dr NW7 28 A3
Colenso Rd Ilford IG2 57 C2
Lower Clapton E5 74 C4
Cole Park Gdns TW1 153 A5
Cole Park Rd TW1 153 A5
Cole Park View 2 TW1 153 A5
Colepits Wood Rd SE9 167 B6
Coleraine Park Prim Sch N17 34 B2
Coleraine Rd
Greenwich SE3 142 D6
Hornsey N8, N22 50 C6
Cole Rd TW1 153 A5
Coleridge Ave
Carshalton SM1 218 C4
Plashet E12 78 A2
Coleridge Cl SW8 137 B3
Coleridge Ct
Hammersmith W14 112 D3
15 New Barnet EN5 13 D6
2 Richmond TW10 175 D6
Coleridge Gdns NW6 70 A1
Coleridge Ho
Pimlico SW1 259 B1
Walworth SE17 262 B2
Wembley HA9 65 D6
Coleridge Prim Sch N8 49 D2
Coleridge Rd
Ashford TW15 170 B6
Crouch End N8 49 D3
Croydon CR0 206 C2
Finsbury Pk N4, N7 72 C6
North Finchley N12 30 A5
Walthamstow E17 53 B5
Coleridge Sq
Chelsea SW10 266 A4
Ealing W13 87 A1
Coleridge Way
Borehamwood WD6 10 C6
Hayes UB4 84 A1
West Drayton UB7 104 B2
Coleridge Wlk NW11 47 C5
Colerne Ct NW4 29 A1
Colesburg Rd BR3 185 B1
Coles Cres HA2 63 D6
Coles Ct SW11 266 D1
Coles Gn WD23 8 A3
Coles Green Ct NW2 68 A6
Coles Green Rd NW2 68 B6
Coleshill Flats SW1 258 B3
Coleshill Rd TW11 174 C4
Cole St SE1 117 A4 252 B1
Colestown St 4 SW11 136 C3
Coleswood N20 14 C3
Colesworth Ho 1 HA8 27 A1
Colet Cl N13 32 D4
Colet Gdns W14 112 D2
Colet Ho SE17 261 D1
Colette Ct 5 SE16 118 D4
Coley St WC1 94 B3 240 D5
Colfe & Hatchcliffe's Glebe SE13 163 D6
Colfe Rd SE23 163 A3
Colfe's Sch SE12 165 A5
Colgate Ct EN5 13 A6
Colgate Ho SE13 141 D3
Colgate Pl 10 EN3 7 C6
Colham Ave UB7 104 A5
COLHAM GREEN 82 C2
Colham Green Rd UB8 82 C2
Colham Manor Prim Sch UB8 82 C1
Colham Rd UB8 82 B3
Colina Mews N8, N15 50 D5
Colina Rd N8, N15 50 D4
Colin Blanchard Ho SE4 141 C3
Colin Cl Colindale NW9 45 C5
Coney Hall BR4 224 D5
Croydon CR0 223 B5
Colin Cres NW9 45 D5
Colin Ct Forest Hill SE6 163 B4
Hendon NW9 45 D5
Streatham SW16 159 D2
COLINDALE 45 C6
Colindale Ave NW9 45 C6
Colindale Bsns Ctr NW9 45 C6
Colindale Bsns Pk NW9 45 A6
Colindale Prim Sch NW9 45 D5
Colindale Sta NW9 45 C6
Colindeep Gdns NW4 46 A5
Colindeep La NW9, NW4 45 D5
Colin Dr NW9 45 D4
Colinette Rd SW15 134 C1
Colin Gdns NW9 45 D5
Colin Par NW9 45 C5
Colin Park Rd NW9 45 C5
Colin Pond Ct RM6 58 D6
Colin Rd NW10 68 A2
Colinsdale N1 234 C5
Colinton Rd IG3 80 B6
Colin Winter Ho 45 E1 96 C3
Coliseum Apartments N8 50 D4
Coliston Pas SW18 157 C4
Coliston Rd SW18 157 C4
Collamore Ave SW18 158 C3
Collapit Cl HA1 41 D3
Collard Pl NW1 71 B1
Collard's Almshouses 1 E17 54 A4
Collcutt Lo SW4 138 A1
Collection Point N8 50 A3
College App SE10 142 A6
College Ave HA3 24 C2
College Cl Edmonton N18 33 D5
Hackney E5 74 C3
Harrow HA3 24 C3
Twickenham TW2 152 B3
College Cres NW3 70 B2
College Cross N1 72 C1
College Ct
Chelsea SW3 114 D1 257 D1
Croydon CR0 222 A6
Ealing W5 110 A6
Enfield EN3 18 C6
3 Hammersmith W6 112 C1
Hampstead NW3 70 B2
College Dr Ruislip HA4 40 A2
Thames Ditton KT7 196 C2
College Fields Bsns Ctr SW19 180 B2
College Gdns Chingford E4 20 A3
Dulwich SE21 161 C3
Edmonton N18 34 A5
Enfield EN2 5 B4
New Malden KT3 199 D4
Redbridge IG4 56 A4
Upper Tooting SW17 158 C2
College Gn SE19 183 C3
College Gr NW1 232 C6
College Green Ct SW9 138 D2
College Hill EC4 252 B6
College Hill Rd HA3 24 C3
College La NW5 71 B4
College Mews 5 SW18 157 D6
College of North West London HA9 65 C5
COLLEGE PARK 90 B4
College Park Cl SE13 142 B1
College Park Rd N17 33 D4
College Park Sch 20 W2 91 D1
College Pl
Camden Town NW1 93 C6 232 B5
Chelsea SW10 266 A4
Walthamstow E17 54 C5
College Pt 3 E15 76 D2
College Rd
Dulwich SE19, SE21 161 C2
Ealing W13 87 B1
Enfield EN2 5 B3
Harrow HA1 42 C3
Harrow Weald HA3 24 C2
Hounslow TW7 130 D4
Kensal Green NW10 90 C5
Mitcham SW19 180 B4
Plaistow BR1 187 A3
South Croydon CR0 221 B6
Southgate N21 16 C2
Tottenham N17 33 D4
Walthamstow E17 54 A4
Wembley HA9 43 D1
College Rdbt 1 KT1 198 A6
College St EC4 117 A6 252 B6
College Terr Bow E3 97 B4
Church End N3 29 B1
College View SE9 165 D3
College Way
Ashford TW15 170 B6
Hayes UB3 106 A6
College Wlk 10 KT1 198 A6
Collent Ho 12 E9 74 C2
Collent St E9 74 C2
Collerston Ho SE10 120 D1
Colless Rd N15 51 D4
Collette Ct SE25 205 C4
Collette Ho N16 51 D1
Collett Ho SE13 141 D2
Collett Rd SE16 118 A3
Collett Way UB2 107 D4
Colley Ho 12 N7 71 D3
Collier Cl Newham E16 122 D6
West Ewell KT19 214 D2
Collier Dr HA8 26 C1
Colliers Shaw BR2 225 D3
Collier St N1 94 B5 233 C3
Colliers Water La CR7 204 C4
Colliers Wood SW19 180 B3
COLLIER'S WOOD 180 C4
Collier's Wood Sta SW19 180 B3
Collindale Ave Erith DA8 147 D6
Sidcup DA15 168 A3
Collingbourne Rd W12 112 B5
Collingham Gdns SW5 113 D2 255 D3
Collingham Pl SW5 113 D2 255 D4
Collingham Rd SW5 113 D2 255 D3
Collingham Tutors Coll SW5 113 D2 255 D3
Collings Cl N22 32 B4
Collington Ho 2 SE7 143 B6
Collington St SE10 120 B1
Collingtree Rd SE26 184 C6
Collingwood Ave
London N10 49 A5
Tolworth KT5 199 A1
Collingwood Cl
2 Penge SE20 184 B2
Twickenham TW2, TW4 151 C4
Collingwood Ct
London NW4 46 C4
New Barnet EN5 13 D6
Sutton SM1 217 C4
Collingwood Ho
27 Bethnal Green E1 96 B3
Marylebone W1 239 A4
Collingwood Rd
Hillingdon UB8 82 D3
Mitcham CR4 202 C6
South Tottenham N15 51 C5
Sutton SM1 217 C4
Collingwood Sch 7 SM6 219 B3
Collingwood St E1 96 B3
Collins Ave HA7 26 A1
Collins Ct Dalston E8 74 A2
1 Loughton IG10 21 D6
Collins Dr HA4 62 C6
Collins Ho
8 Barking IG11 78 D1
6 Cubitt Town SE10 120 D1
4 Poplar E14 120 A6
Collinson Ct
Borough The SE1 252 A1
Edgware HA8 26 B6
Collinson Ho 14 SE15 140 A5
Collinson St SE1 252 A1
Collinson Wlk SE1 252 A1
Collins Rd N5, N16 73 A4
Collins Sq SE3 142 D3
Collins St SE3 142 C3
Collins Yd N1 234 C5
Collinwood Ave EN3 6 C2
Collinwood Gdns IG5 56 C5
Collison Pl N16 51 C1
Collis Prim Sch TW11 175 B4
Coll of Arms* EC4 117 A6 252 A6
Coll of Central London The EC2 243 A6
Coll of Law The (Bloomsbury) EC1 93 D2 239 C4
Coll of Law The (Moorgate) EC1 95 B3 242 C5
Coll of North East London The N15 51 D5
Coll of NW London 15 NW6 91 C6
Coll of NW London (Willesden Centre) NW10 67 D3
Coll of Optometrists The SW1 250 A4
Coll Sharp Ct 42 E2 95 D4
Coll's Rd SE15 140 C4
Collyer Ave CR0 220 A4
Collyer Pl SE15 140 A4
Collyer Rd CR0 220 A4
Colman Ct London N12 30 A4
Stanmore HA7 25 B4
Colman Rd E16 99 C2
Colmans Wharf 5 E14 97 D2
Colmar Cl 3 E1 96 D3
Colmer Pl HA3 24 B3
Colmer Rd SW16 182 A3
Colmore Ct NW4 46 A6
Colmore Mews SE15 140 B4
Colmore Rd EN3 6 C1
Colnbrook Ct SW17 180 B6
Colnbrook St SE1 261 C6
Colne Ct Ealing W7 86 B1
West Ewell KT19 215 A4
Colne Ho Barking IG11 78 D2
Paddington NW8 236 D5
Colne Rd Clapton Pk E5 75 A4
Southgate N21 17 B4
Twickenham TW1, TW2 152 C3
Colne St E13 99 A4
COLNEY HATCH 30 C4
Colney Hatch N10 31 A3
Colney Hatch La N10 31 A3
Cologne Rd SW11 136 B1
Coloma Convent Girl's Sch CR0 222 D5
Colombo Rd IG1 57 A2
Colombo St SE1 251 C3
Colomb St SE10 120 C1
Colonades The 4 SE5 139 B4
Colonels Wlk EN2 4 D2
Colonial Ave TW2 152 A5
Colonial Dr W4 111 A2
Colonial Rd TW14 149 C4
Colonnade WC1 240 B5
Colonnade Ho SE3 142 D3
Colonnades The
Croydon CR0 220 C2
6 Hackney E8 74 B2
Colonnade The 12 SE8 119 B2
Colonnade Wlk Sh Ctr SW1 258 D4
Colorado Bldg 9 SE13 141 D4
Colosseum Ct N3 29 B1
Colosseum Ret Pk EN1 6 A1
Colosseum Terr NW1 238 D6
Colour Ho SE1 253 B1
Colroy Ct NW4 47 A4
Colson Rd CR0 221 C6
Colson Way SW16 181 C6
Colstead Ho 22 E1 96 B1
Colsterworth Rd N15 51 D5
Colston Ave SM1, SM5 218 C4
Colston Ct SM5 218 D4
Colston Rd
Mortlake SW14 133 A1
Upton E7 77 D2
Colthurst Cres N4 73 A6
Colthurst Dr N9 18 B1
Coltman Ho SE10 142 A6
Coltman St E14 97 A2
Colt Mews 5 EN3 7 C6
Coltness Cres SE2 124 B1
Colton Gdns N17 51 A6
Colton Rd HA1 42 C4
Coltsfoot Dr UB7 82 A1
Coltswood Ct N14 15 D3
Colts Yd E11 54 D2
Columba Ho SE14 141 B4
Columbas Dr NW3 48 B1
Columbia Ave
Edgware HA8 26 D2
New Malden KT4 199 D2
Ruislip HA4 40 B1
Columbia Ct Edgware HA8 26 D2
New Malden KT3 199 D2
Columbia Ho 18 E3 97 C4
Columbia Point 7 SE16 118 C3
Columbia Prim Sch 50 E2 95 D4
Columbia Rd
9 Hackney E2 96 A5
Newham E13 98 D3
Shoreditch E2 95 D4
Columbia Road Flower Mkt* E2 95 D4

Columbine Ave
Croydon CR2. . . . .**220** D1
Newham E6 . . . .**100** A4
Columbus Gdns HA6. . . .**22** A2
Colveiw Ct SE9 . . . .**165** D3
Colverson Ho 14 E1 . . .**96** C2
Colvestone Cres E8 . . . . .**73** D3
Colvestone Prim Sch E8 .**73** D3
Colville Gdns W11 . . . . . .**91** B1
Colville Ho
32 Bethnal Green E2 . . . . .**96** C5
Notting Hill W11 . . . .**91** B1
Colville Mews W11. . . . . .**91** B1
Colville Pl W1 . . . .**239** B3
Colville Prim Sch 5 W11. .**91** B1
Colville Rd Edmonton N9 . .**18** B3
Higham Hill E17 . . . .**35** A1
Leyton E11 . . . .**76** A5
Notting Hill W11 . . . .**91** B1
South Acton W3 . . . .**110** D3
Colville Sq W11. . . . .**91** B1
Colville Terr W11. . . . .**91** B1
Colvin Cl SE26 . . . .**184** C5
Colvin Gdns Chingford E4. . .**20** A4
Wanstead E11 . . . .**55** B5
Colvin Rd
Thornton Heath CR7. . . . .**204** C4
Upton Pk E6 . . . .**78** A1
Colwall Gdns IG8 . . . .**37** A5
Colwall Ho 18 SW9. . . . .**138** B3
Colwell Rd SE22 . . . .**161** D6
Colwick Cl N6 . . . .**49** D2
Colwith Rd W6 . . . .**134** C6
Colwood Gdns SW19. . . . .**180** B3
Colworth Gr SE17 . . . . . .**262** B3
Colworth Rd
Croydon CR0. . . . .**206** A1
Leytonstone E11. . . . .**54** C2
Colwyn Ave UB6 . . . .**86** D5
Colwyn Cl SW16 . . . .**181** C5
Colwyn Cres TW3 . . . . . .**130** A4
Colwyn Gn NW9 . . . .**45** C3
Colwyn Ho SE1 . . . .**261** A5
Colwyn Rd NW2 . . . .**68** B5
Colyer Cl SE2 . . . .**166** D2
Colyer Ho SE2 . . . .**124** D1
Colyton Cl Erith DA16. . . .**146** D4
Wembley HA0. . . . .**65** C2
Colyton La 14 SW16. . . . .**182** C5
Colyton Rd SE22 . . . .**162** B6
Colyton Way N18 . . . .**34** A5
Combe Ave SE3. . . . .**142** D5
Combedale Rd SE10 . . . . .**121** A1
Combe Ho
Mortlake SW14 . . . .**133** A3
20 Paddington W2 . . . .**91** C2
Combe Lane Sta CR0. . . . .**222** C3
Combemartin Rd SW18 . .**157** A3
Combe Mews 4 SE3. . . . .**142** D5
Comber Cl NW2 . . . .**68** B6
Comber Gr SE5 . . . .**139** A5
Comber Grove Prim Sch 34
SE5. . . . .**139** A5
Comber Ho SE5. . . . .**139** A5
Combermere Rd
London SW9. . . . .**138** B2
Morden SM4. . . . .**201** D4
Comberton 10 KT1. . . . . .**176** C1
Comberton Rd E5. . . . . . .**74** B6
Combeside SE18. . . . .**145** D5
Combes Rd RM9 . . . .**81** B1
Combe The NW1. . . . . . .**231** D1
Combwell Cres SE2 . . . . .**124** A3
Com Coll Hackney The 17
E8. . . . .**96** B6
Comely Bank Rd E17 . . . . .**54** A4
Comeragh Mews W14 . . .**254** B1
Comeragh Rd
W14. . . . .**113** A1 **254** B1
Comer Cres UB2. . . . .**108** A4
Comerford Rd SE4. . . . . .**141** B1
Comer Ho 10 EN5 . . . .**2** A1
Comet Cl E12. . . . .**77** D4
Comet Pl SE8. . . . .**141** C5
Comet St SE8. . . . .**141** C5
Comfort St 6 SE15 . . . . .**139** C6
Comins Ho SW4 . . . .**159** C6
Commerce Est E18 . . . .**37** C1
Commerce Pk CR0. . . . . . .**220** B6
Commerce Rd
Brentford TW8. . . . .**131** C5
Wood Green N22 . . . .**32** B2
Commerce Way CR0 . . . . .**220** B6
Commercial Rd
Edmonton N18 . . . .**33** C4
Stepney E1 . . . .**96** C1
Whitechapel E1 . . . .**96** A5
Commercial St E1 . .**95** D2 **243** C4
Commercial Way
Peckham SE15 . . . .**140** A5
Wembley NW10. . . . .**88** D5
Commerell Pl SE10 . . . . .**120** C1
Commerell St SE10 . . . . .**120** C1
Commodity Quay E1 . . . .**253** D5
Commodore Ct SE8. . . . . .**141** C4
Commodore Ho 7 E14. . .**120** A6
Commodore St E1. . . . . . .**97** A3

Commondale SW15. . . . . .**134** C2
Common La KT10 . . . .**213** A1
Common Rd
Barnes SW13 . . . .**134** A2
Claygate KT10 . . . .**213** A1
Stanmore HA7 . . . .**8** C1
Commonside BR2 . . . .**225** C4
Commonside Ct SW16 . . .**182** A4
Commonside E CR4 . . . . .**203** B6
Commonside W CR4 . . . . .**203** A6
Common The Ealing W5 . . .**110** A5
Southall UB2. . . . .**106** D2
Stanmore HA7 . . . .**8** D2
1 Stratford E15. . . . .**76** D2
Common View SW15 . . . . .**134** C2
Commonwealth Ave
Hayes UB3. . . . .**83** B1
25 Shepherd's Bush W12. .**112** B6
21 Shepherd's Bush W12. .**112** B6
Commonwealth Ho WC1 .**240** B2
Commonwealth Rd N17. . .**34** A3
Commonwealth Way
SE2 . . . .**124** C1
Community Cl
Cranford TW5. . . . .**128** B4
Uxbridge UB10 . . . .**61** A5
Community La N7 . . . .**71** D3
Community Rd
Greenford UB6. . . . .**86** A6
Stratford New Town E15. . . .**76** B3
Comodore Ho SW18 . . . . .**136** A1
Como Rd SE23. . . . .**163** A2
Compania Bldg 12 E1. . .**118** D6
Littleton TW15 . . . .**171** A3
Compass Cl Edgware HA8 . .**26** B6
Compass Ct SE1 . . . .**253** C3
Compass Hill TW10 . . . . .**153** D5
Compass Ho
Bayswater W2 . . . .**91** D1
London SE8. . . . .**141** D3
Compass Point 10 E14 . .**119** C6
Compayne Gdns NW6. . . . .**69** D1
Compton Ave Islington N1. . .**72** D2
London N6 . . . .**48** C2
Newham E6 . . . .**99** D5
Wembley HA0. . . . .**65** C4
Compton Cl
5 Burnt Oak HA8 . . . .**27** A3
Camberwell SE15 . . . . . .**139** D5
Cricklewood NW11. . . . . .**68** D5
Ealing W13 . . . .**87** A1
Esher KT10. . . . .**212** B3
Regent's Pk NW1 . . . . . .**231** D1
Compton Cres
Chessington KT9 . . . .**214** A2
Chiswick W4 . . . .**133** A6
Northolt UB5 . . . .**84** D6
Tottenham N17. . . . .**33** A3
Compton Ct London N12. . .**30** A2
Sutton SM1 . . . .**218** A4
9 West Norwood SE19 . . .**183** C5
Compton Ho SW11. . . . . .**267** A2
Compton Lo N1. . . . .**16** D3
Compton Pas EC1. . . . . . .**241** D6
Compton Pl
Bloomsbury WC1 . . . . . .**240** A6
South Oxhey WD19. . . . . .**23** A6
Compton Rd
Croydon CR0. . . . .**206** B1
Hayes UB3 . . . .**105** D6
Islington N1 . . . .**72** D2
Kensal Green NW10. . . . . .**90** D4
Southgate N21 . . . .**16** D3
Wimbledon SW19. . . . . .**179** B4
Compton Rise HA5. . . . . . .**41** B4
Compton Sch The N12 . . .**30** C4
Compton St EC1. . .**94** D3 **241** D6
Compton Terr
Islington N1 . . . .**72** D2
Southgate N21 . . . .**16** C3
Comreddy Cl EN2 . . . .**4** D4
Comus Ho SE17. . . . .**263** A3
Comus Pl SE17 . . .**117** C2 **263** A3
Comyn Rd SW11. . . . .**136** C1
Comyns Cl E16 . . . .**98** D2
Comyns Rd RM9 . . . .**81** C1
Comyns The W23 . . . .**8** A3
Conal Ct SW16 . . . .**181** D5
Conant Ho SE11 . . . .**138** D6
Conant Mews 1 E1. . . . . .**118** A6
Concanon Rd SW2, SW4 . .**138** B1
Concert Hall App
SE1 . . . .**116** B5 **250** D3
Concord Bsns Ctr W3 . . . .**88** D2
Concord Cl UB5. . . . .**85** A4
Concord Ct KT1. . . . .**198** B6
Concorde Cl
Hounslow TW3 . . . .**129** D3
Uxbridge UB10 . . . .**82** A5
Concorde Dr E6 . . . .**100** B2
Concorde Way SE16. . . . . .**118** D2
Concord Ho
Kingston u T KT3. . . . . . .**199** C6
5 Tottenham N17. . . . .**33** D3
Concordia Wharf 10
E14. . . . .**120** A5
Concord Rd Acton W3. . . . .**88** D3
Enfield EN3. . . . .**18** C6
Concord Terr HA2. . . . .**63** D6

Concourse The
32 Edgware NW9. . . . .**27** D2
7 Edmonton N9. . . . .**18** A2
Condell Rd SW8 . .**137** C4 **269** B1
Conder St E14 . . . .**97** A1
Condor Path UB5 . . . .**85** C5
Condover Cres SE18 . . . .**144** D5
Condray Pl SW11 . . . . . .**267** A3
Conduit Ct WC2. . . . .**250** A6
Conduit Ho SE10. . . . . . .**142** A6
Conduit La London N18. . . .**34** C5
South Croydon CR0. . . . .**222** A3
Conduit Mews W2 . .**92** B1 **236** C1
Conduit Pas W2 . . . .**236** C1
Conduit Pl W2 . . . .**236** C1
Conduit Rd SE18. . . . . . .**122** D1
Conduit St W1 . . .**115** C6 **249** A6
Conduit Way NW10 . . . . . .**67** A1
Conewood St N5. . . . .**72** D5
Coney Acre SE21. . . . . . .**161** A3
Coney Burrows E4. . . . . . .**20** C2
Coney Gr UB8 . . . .**82** C4
Coneygrove Path UB5. . . . .**63** A2
CONEY HALL **224** D5
Coney Hall Par BR4 . . . . .**224** C5
Coney Hall Rdbt BR4. . . . .**224** C5
Coney Hill Rd BR4 . . . . . .**224** D6
Coney Way SW8 . . . .**270** D5
Conference Cl 3 E4. . . . . .**20** A2
Conference Ho UB8. . . . . .**83** A1
Conference Rd SE2 . . . . .**124** C2
Congers Ho SE8 . . . .**141** C5
Congleton Gr SE18. . . . . .**123** A1
Congo Dr N9 . . . .**18** C1
Congo Rd SE18 . . . .**123** B1
Congress Ho WC1. . . . . . .**239** D2
Congress Rd SE2 . . . .**124** C2
Congreve Ho 10 N16. . . . .**73** C3
Congreve Rd SE9 . . . .**144** B2
Congreve St
SE17. . . . .**117** C2 **263** A3
Congreve Wlk 6 E16 . . . . .**99** D2
Conical Cnr EN2 . . . .**5** A3
Conifer Cl BR6. . . . .**227** B4
Conifer Ct Ashford TW15 . .**170** B5
Hendon NW4 . . . .**28** C1
Ilford IG1. . . . .**78** D2
23 Putney SW19. . . . . . .**156** D3
Sutton SM2. . . . .**218** B2
Conifer Gdns Enfield EN1. . .**17** C5
Streatham SW16 . . . .**160** B1
Sutton SM1. . . . .**217** D6
Conifer Ho SE4 . . . .**141** B1
Conifers Cl TW11 . . . . . .**175** C3
Conifer Way Hayes UB3 . .**106** A6
Wembley HA0. . . . .**65** C5
Coniger Rd SW6 . . . .**135** C3
Coningham Ct SW10 . . . .**266** B4
Coningham Mews W12. . .**112** A5
Coningham Rd W12. . . . . .**112** B4
Coningsby Ave NW9 . . . . . .**27** C1
Coningsby Cotts W5 . . . .**109** D4
Coningsby Ct 4 CR4. . . . .**181** A1
Coningsby Gdns E4. . . . . .**35** D4
Coningsby Rd Ealing W5 . .**109** D4
Harringay N4 . . . .**50** D2
Conington Rd SE13. . . . . .**142** A3
Conisbee Ct 3 N14. . . . . .**15** C6
Conisborough Cres SE6 . .**164** A1
Conisbrough NW1 . . . . . .**232** A5
Coniscliffe Cl BR7. . . . . .**188** C2
Coniscliffe Rd N13. . . . . . .**17** A1
Coniston NW1 . . . .**232** A2
Coniston Ave
Barking IG11. . . . .**79** C1
Ealing UB6 . . . .**87** B4
Falconwood DA16. . . . . .**145** C2
Coniston Cl Barking IG11. . .**79** C1
Barnes SW13 . . . .**133** D5
Chiswick W4 . . . .**133** A5
West Barnes SM4. . . . . .**200** D3
Whetstone N20 . . . .**14** A1
Coniston Ct
Beckenham BR3. . . . .**186** A2
Chessington KT9 . . . .**214** A5
Edgware HA8 . . . .**26** B5
4 Finchley NW7 . . . .**29** A3
Marylebone W2 . . . .**237** B1
Penge SE26. . . . .**184** B4
18 Camberwell SE5. . . . .**139** A5
Coniston Gdns
Edmonton N9 . . . .**18** C3
Kingsbury NW9 . . . .**45** B4
Pinner HA5. . . . .**40** A5
Redbridge IG4 . . . .**56** A5
Sutton SM2. . . . .**218** B2
Wembley HA9. . . . .**43** C1
Coniston Ho 14 Bow E3. . . .**97** B4
18 Camberwell SE5 . . . . .**139** A5
Catford BR1. . . . .**186** C4
Croydon CR0. . . . .**206** A2
Muswell Hill N10. . . . .**31** B1
Tottenham N17. . . . .**34** A4
Twickenham TW2 . . . . . .**151** D5
Coniston Way KT9 . . . . . .**214** A5
Coniston Wlk E9 . . . .**74** C3
Conlan St W10. . . . .**91** A3
Conley Rd NW10. . . . .**67** C2

Conley St SE10. . . . .**120** C1
Connaught Ave
Ashford TW15. . . . .**170** A6
Barnet EN4. . . . .**14** D3
Chingford E4. . . . .**20** B4
Enfield EN1. . . . .**5** C3
Hounslow TW4 . . . .**129** A1
Mortlake SW14 . . . .**133** A1
Connaught Bridge E16. . .**121** D6
Connaught Bsns Ctr
London NW9. . . . .**45** D4
Mitcham CR4 . . . .**202** D4
Wallington CR0. . . . .**220** B2
Connaught Cl
Carshalton SM1 . . . .**218** B6
Enfield EN1. . . . .**5** C3
Hillingdon UB8 . . . .**83** A3
Lea Bridge E10 . . . .**75** A6
Marylebone W2 . . . .**237** B1
Connaught Ct
7 Buckhurst Hill IG9. . . . . .**20** C4
9 Walthamstow E17. . . . . .**53** D5
Connaught Day Hospl
E11. . . . .**54** C2
Connaught Dr NW11. . . . . .**47** C5
Connaught Gdns
Cranley Gdns N10. . . . . . .**49** B4
Edmonton N13 . . . .**32** D6
Morden SM4. . . . .**202** A5
Connaught Grange N13 . .**32** D6
Connaught Ho
College Pk NW10 . . . .**90** B4
London N10 . . . .**49** B4
Mayfair W1. . . . .**248** C5
Connaught House Sch
W2. . . . .**92** C1 **237** B1
Connaught Hts UB10. . . . . .**83** A3
Connaught La IG1 . . . .**79** B6
Connaught Lo N4. . . . .**50** C2
Connaught Mans
Battersea SW11. . . . . . .**267** B1
3 Brixton SW9 . . . .**138** C1
15 Canonbury N16 . . . . . .**73** B4
Fulham SW6 . . . .**264** A2
Connaught Mews
Ilford IG1. . . . .**79** B6
Woolwich SE18. . . . .**122** C1
Connaught Pl W2. . . . . . .**237** C1
Connaught Rd Barnet EN5. .**12** D5
Carshalton SM1 . . . .**218** B6
Chingford E4. . . . .**20** C3
Ealing W13 . . . .**109** B6
Finsbury Pk N4 . . . .**50** C2
Harlesden NW10 . . . .**89** C5
Harrow HA3 . . . .**24** D2
Ilford IG1. . . . .**79** B6
Leytonstone E11. . . . .**54** B1
New Malden KT3 . . . .**199** C5
5 Richmond TW10 . . . . . .**154** B6
Teddington TW11, TW12. . .**174** B5
Walthamstow E17 . . . . . .**53** C4
Woolwich SE18. . . . .**122** C1
Connaught Sch for Girls 2
E11. . . . .**54** C1
Connaught Sch for Girls
(Annexe) 13 E11. . . . . . .**54** B1
Connaught Sq W2 . .**92** D1 **237** C1
Connaught St W2. . .**92** C1 **237** B1
Connaught Way N13. . . . . .**32** D6
Connaught Works E3. . . . .**97** A6
Connections Ho N2. . . . . . .**30** B2
Connell Cres W5. . . . .**88** B3
Connell Ct 5 SE14. . . . . .**140** D6
Connell Ho 6 SM6. . . . . .**219** C2
Connemara CI WD6 . . . . . .**11** B5
Conniffe Ct SE9. . . . .**166** D6
Connington 5 KT1. . . . . .**176** C1
Connington Cres E4 . . . . . .**20** B1
Connolly Ho SW19. . . . . .**180** A4
Connolly Ct NW2 . . . .**68** B5
Connor Cl E11 . . . .**54** C2
Connor Rd RM9 . . . .**81** B4
Connor St E9 . . . .**96** C6
Conolly Rd W7. . . . .**108** C5
Conrad Dr KT4. . . . .**200** D1
Conrad Ho
8 Limehouse SE16 . . . . .**119** A6
South Lambeth SW8. . . . .**270** A4
12 Stoke Newington N16 . .**73** C3
Conrad Twr W3 . . . .**110** D3
Conroy Ct 6 DA14 . . . . . .**190** A6
Conservatory Ct SE19 . . .**183** C3
Consfield Ave KT3. . . . . . .**200** A4
Consort Ho
Bayswater W2 . . . .**245** D5
Edgware NW7 . . . .**27** D5
Consort Lo NW8 . . . .**230** C5
Consort Mews TW7 . . . . .**152** B6
Consort Rd SE15. . . . . . .**140** B3
Cons St SE1 . . . .**251** B2
Constable Ave E16. . . . . .**121** B5
Constable Cl
12 Friern Barnet N11. . . . .**30** D5
Hampstead Garden Suburb
NW11. . . . .**47** D3
Hayes UB4 . . . .**83** A5
Constable Cres N15. . . . . .**52** A4

Constable Ct 11 SE16. . . .**118** B1
Constable Gdns
Edgware HA8 . . . .**26** C1
Isleworth TW7 . . . .**152** B6
Constable Ho Enfield EN1 . .**18** A6
25 Millwall E14. . . . .**119** C4
13 Northolt UB5. . . . .**84** D5
Primrose Hill NW3 . . . .**70** D1
Constable Mews
Bromley BR1. . . . .**187** B1
Dagenham RM8 . . . .**80** B4
Constable Wlk SE21. . . . .**161** C1
Constance Cres BR2 . . . .**208** D1
Constance Ct N10. . . . .**31** B3
Constance Rd Enfield EN1 . .**17** C5
Sutton SM1. . . . .**218** A4
Thornton Heath CR0. . . . .**204** D2
Twickenham TW2 . . . . . .**151** D4
Constance St E16. . . . . . .**122** A5
Constant Ho 26 E14. . . . .**119** D6
Constantine Ho SW2. . . . .**160** D3
Constantine Pl UB10 . . . . .**82** B6
Constantine Rd NW3. . . . .**70** C4
Constitution Hill
W1. . . . .**115** B4 **248** D2
Constitution Rise SE18. . .**144** C4
Consul Ho 5 E3. . . . .**97** C3
Content St SE17 . .**117** B2 **262** C3
Contessa Cl BR6. . . . .**227** C3
Control Tower Rd TW6. . . .**126** D2
Convair Wlk 11 UB5. . . . . .**84** C4
Convent Cl BR3. . . . .**186** A3
Convent Gdns Ealing W5 . .**109** C2
Notting Hill W11 . . . .**91** B1
Convent Hill SE19. . . . . . .**183** A4
Convent Lo TW15 . . . .**170** D5
Convent of Jesus & Mary
Language Coll NW10 . . . . .**89** D2
Convent of Jesus & Mary RC
Inf Sch 9 NW2. . . . .**68** C2
Convent Rd TW15 . . . .**170** D5
Convent Way UB2. . . . . . .**106** C2
Conway Cl HA7. . . . .**25** A4
Conway Cres
Dagenham RM6 . . . .**58** C3
Greenford UB6. . . . .**86** C5
Conway Dr Ashford TW15. .**171** A4
Hayes UB3. . . . .**105** A3
Sutton SM2. . . . .**217** D2
Conway Gdns Enfield EN2 . . .**5** C5
Mitcham CR4 . . . .**204** A5
Wembley HA9. . . . .**43** C2
Conway Gr W3. . . . .**89** B2
Conway Ho Chelsea SW3 . .**257** D1
5 Millwall E14. . . . .**119** D2
6 Streatham SW2. . . . . . .**160** A3
Conway Mews W1 . . . . . .**239** A5
Conway Prim Sch 5
SE18. . . . .**123** C2
Conway Rd Dollis Hill NW2. . .**68** C6
Feltham TW13 . . . .**172** D5
Harlington TW6 . . . .**126** D2
Harringay N15 . . . .**51** A4
Palmers Green N14 . . . . . .**16** A1
Plumstead SE18 . . . .**123** C2
Twickenham TW4 . . . . . .**151** C4
Wimbledon SW20. . . . . .**178** C2
Conway St W1 . . . .**93** C3 **239** A5
Conway Wlk TW12 . . . . . .**173** B4
Conybeare NW3 . . . .**70** C1
Conyers Cl IG8 . . . .**36** C4
Conyer's Rd SW16 . . . . . .**181** D5
Conyer St 21 E3. . . . .**97** A5
Cooden Cl BR1 . . . .**187** B3
Cookes La SM3 . . . .**217** A2
Cooke St 2 IG11 . . . .**101** A4
Cookham Cl UB2. . . . .**107** D4
Cookham Cres SE16 . . . . .**118** D4
Cookham Dene Cl BR7 . . .**189** B2
Cookham Ho E2 . . . .**243** C6
Cookham Rd BR8, DA14. . .**191** C2
Cookhill Rd SE2 . . . .**124** B3
Cooks Ferry N18. . . . .**34** D5
Cook's Hole Rd EN2. . . . . . .**5** A5
Cookson Gr DA8 . . . .**147** D5
Cook's Rd
Camberwell SE17. . . . . . .**138** C4
Stratford Marsh E15. . . . . .**97** D5
Coolfin Rd E16. . . . .**99** B1
Coolgardie Ave E4. . . . . . .**36** B5
Coolgardie Rd TW15 . . . . .**171** A5
Coolhurst Rd N8. . . . .**49** D3
Cool Oak La NW9 . . . .**45** D2
Coomassie Rd W9 . . . .**91** B3
COOMBE **177** B3
Coombe Ave CR0 . . . .**221** C4
Coombe Bank KT2, KT3 . . .**177** C2
Coombe Boys' Sch KT3. . .**200** A4
Coombe Cl Edgware HA8 . . .**26** B1
Hounslow TW3 . . . .**129** C1
Coombe Cnr N21. . . . .**16** D3
Coombe Cres TW12 . . . . .**173** A3
Coombe Ct 2 BR3. . . . . . .**185** B2
Coombe Dr HA4 . . . .**40** B1
Coombe End KT2 . . . .**177** B3
Coombefield Cl KT3. . . . . .**199** C4
Coombe Gdns
New Malden KT3 . . . .**199** D5
Wimbledon SW20. . . . . .**178** A3

Coombe Girls Sch KT3 . . .177 B1
Coombe Hill Glade KT2 . .177 C3
Coombe Hill Inf Sch
  KT2. . . . . .177 B2
Coombe Hill Jun Sch
  KT2. . . . . .177 B2
Coombe Ho 13 N7 . . . . . . .71 D3
Coombe House Chase
  KT3 . . . . .177 B2
Coombehurst Cl EN4 . . . . . . .2 D3
Coombehurst (Kingston
  University) KT2 . . . . . .177 A5
Coombe La CR0 . . . . .222 B3
Coombe Lane Flyover
  SW20 . . . . .177 D2
Coombe La W KT2 . . . . . .177 B2
Coombe Lea BR1 . . . . . . .210 A6
Coombe Lo SE7 . . . . .143 C6
Coombe Neville KT2 . . . . .177 B3
Coombe Pk KT2 . . . . .177 B5
Coombe Pl KT2 . . . . .177 A5
Coombe Ridings KT2 . . . .177 A5
Coombe Rise KT2 . . . . . . .177 A2
Coomber Way CR0 . . . . . .203 D3
Coombes Rd RM9 . . . . . . .103 B6
Coombewood Dr RM6 . . . . .59 B3
Coombe Wood Rd KT2 . . .177 A5
Coombs St N1 . . . . .234 D3
Coomer Mews SW6 . . . . .264 D5
Coomer Pl SW6 . . .135 B6 264 D5
Cooms Wlk HA8 . . . . .27 A2
Cooperage Cl 3 N17 . . . . .33 D4
Cooperage The SE1 . . . . . .253 C3
Cooper Ave E17 . . . . .35 A2
Cooper Cl SE1 . . . . .251 B1
Cooper Cres SM5 . . . . . . .218 C5
Cooper Ct SE18 . . . . .144 D6
Cooper Ho
  Hounslow TW4 . . . . .129 B2
  Paddington NW8 . . . . . .236 C5
  Upper Tooting SW17 . . . .180 B6
  7 West Norwood SW27 . . 182 D5
Cooper Rd
  Croydon CR0, CR9 . . . . . .220 D4
  Hendon NW4 . . . . .46 D3
  Willesden NW10 . . . . . . .68 A3
Coopersale Cl 3 IG8 . . . . .37 C3
Coopersale Rd E9 . . . . . . .74 D3
Coopers Cl
  Bethnal Green E1 . . . . . . .96 C3
  Dagenham RM10 . . . . . . .81 D2
Coopers Ct 8 Acton W3. . .111 A4
  4 Friern Barnet N12 . . . . .14 D1
  Isleworth TW7 . . . . .130 D3
  Tower Hamlets E3 . . . . . . .97 B3
Coopers La
  Grove Pk SE12 . . . . .165 B2
  London E10 . . . . .54 A1
  Somers Town NW1 . . . . . .232 B3
Cooper's Lane Prim Sch
  SE12 . . . . .165 B2
Coopers Lo SE1 . . . . .253 C2
Coopers Mews BR3 . . . . . .185 C1
Cooper's Rd SE1. 117 D1 263 D2
Cooper's Row
  EC3 . . . . .117 D6 253 C6
Coopers St 10 E16 . . . . . . .98 D2
Coopers Tech Sch BR7 . . .189 A2
Cooper's Yd N1 . . . . .72 D1
Cooper's Yd SE19 . . . . . . .183 C4
Coote Gdns RM8 . . . . .81 B5
Coote Rd Dagenham RM8 . .81 B5
  Erith DA7 . . . . .147 B4
Cope Ho EC1 . . . . .235 B1
Copeland Dr E14. . . . . . . .119 C2
Copeland Ho
  Lambeth SE11 . . . . .260 D5
  Upper Tooting SW17 . . . . .180 B6
Copeland Rd
  London SE15 . . . . .140 B3
  Walthamstow E17 . . . . . . .53 D3
Copelands BR3 . . . . .185 B3
Copeman Cl SE26 . . . . . . .184 C5
Copenhagen Gdns W4 . . .111 B4
Copenhagen Ho N1 . . . . . .234 A5
Copenhagen Pl E14 . . . . . .97 B1
Copenhagen Prim Sch
  N1 . . . . .94 B6 233 C5
Copenhagen St
  N1 . . . . .94 B6 233 C5
Cope Pl W8 . . . . . .113 C3 255 A5
Copers Cope Rd BR3 . . . . .185 B3
Cope St SE16 . . . . .118 D2
Copeswood Ct UB7 . . . . . .126 C5
Copford Wlk N1 . . . . .235 A6
Copgate Path SW16 . . . . .182 C4
Copinger Wlk HA8 . . . . . . .26 D2

Copland Ave HA0 . . . . . . .65 D3
Copland Cl HA0 . . . . .65 C3
Copland Ho UB1 . . . . .107 B4
Copland Mews 8 HA0 . . . .66 A2
Copland Rd HA0 . . . . .66 A2
Copland Specialist Science
  Com Coll HA9 . . . . .66 B3
Copleston Rd SE15 . . . . . .139 D2
Copley Cl
  15 Camberwell SE17 . . . .138 D6
  Ealing W7 . . . . .86 D2
Copley Dene BR1 . . . . . . .187 D2
Copley Pk SW16 . . . . .182 B4
Copley Rd HA7 . . . . .25 C5
Copley St E1 . . . . .96 D2
Coppard Gdns KT9 . . . . . .213 C2
Coppedhall 2 SE21 . . . . .161 B2
Coppelia Rd SE3 . . . . .142 D1
Coppen Rd RM8 . . . . .59 B2
Copperas St SE8 . . . . . . .141 D6
Copper Beech N6 . . . . .49 A2
Copperbeech Cl NW3 . . . . .70 B3
Copper Beech Ct N20 . . . . .14 A1
Copper Cl Penge SE19 . . . .183 D3
  Tottenham N17 . . . . .34 B3
Copperdale Rd UB3 . . . . .106 A4
Copperfield Ave UB8 . . . . .82 C3
Copperfield Ct
  Blackheath SE3 . . . . .142 D2
  Ilford IG6 . . . . .57 A6
Copperfield Dr N15 . . . . . .51 D5
Copperfield Ho 12 SE1 . .118 A4
Copperfield Mews N18. . . .33 C5
Copperfield Rd
  Stepney E3 . . . . .97 A2
  Thamesmead SE28 . . . . .102 C1
Copperfields
  5 Beckenham BR3 . . . . .186 A2
  Harrow HA1 . . . . .42 C2
Copperfield St
  SE1 . . . . .117 A4 252 A2
Copperfield Way
  Chislehurst BR7 . . . . . . .189 A4
  Pinner HA5 . . . . .41 B5
Coppergate Cl BR1 . . . . . .187 B2
Coppermead Cl NW2 . . . . .68 C5
Copper Mews 4 W4 . . . . .111 A3
Copper Mill Dr TW7 . . . . . .130 D3
Coppermill La E17 . . . . . . .52 D4
Coppermill Prim Sch E17 . .52 D4
Copper Row 4 SE1 . . . . . .253 C3
Copperwood Lo EN2 . . . . . .4 D3
Coppetts Cl N12 . . . . .30 D3
Coppetts Ctr N12 . . . . .30 D3
Coppetts Rd N10 . . . . .30 D2
Coppetts Wood Prim Sch
  N10 . . . . .31 A2
Coppice Cl
  Beckenham BR3 . . . . . . .207 D5
  Harrow HA7 . . . . .24 D4
  Ruislip HA4 . . . . .39 B3
  West Barnes SW20 . . . . .200 C6
Coppice Dr SW15 . . . . . . .156 B5
Coppice The
  Ashford TW15. . . . . .170 D4
  Enfield EN2 . . . . .4 D1
  Hillingdon UB7 . . . . .82 A1
  New Barnet EN5. . . . . . . .13 D5
Coppice Way E18 . . . . . . .54 D6
Coppice Wlk N20 . . . . . . .13 C1
Coppies Gr N11 . . . . .31 B6
Copping Cl CR0 . . . . .221 C4
Coppock Ho SW2 . . . . . . .160 D3
Coppins The
  2 Ilford RM6 . . . . .58 B2
  New Addington CR0 . . . . .223 D2
  Stanmore HA3 . . . . .24 C4
Coppock Cl SW11 . . . . . . .136 C3
Coppsfield KT8 . . . . .195 C6
Copse Ave BR4 . . . . .223 D5
Copse Cl SE7 . . . . .143 B6
Copse Ct SW15 . . . . .157 A6
Copse Glade KT6 . . . . . . .197 D1
COPSE HILL 178 B3
Copse Hill Belmont SM2 . .217 D1
  Wimbledon SW19 . . . . . . .178 C4
  Wimbledon SW20 . . . . . . .178 B3
Copsem Dr KT10 . . . . .212 A2
Copsem La KT10 . . . . .212 A1
Copsem Way KT10 . . . . . .212 A2
Copse The Chingford E4 . . .20 D3
  Muswell Hill N2. . . . . .48 D6
Copse View EN2 . . . . .223 A1
Copsewood Cl DA15 . . . . .167 C5
Coptefield Dr DA17 . . . . . .125 B3
Copthall Ave EC2 . . .95 B1 242 D2
Copthall Bldgs EC2 . . . . .242 D2
Copthall Cl EC2 . . . . .242 C2
Copthall Dr NW7 . . . . .28 A4
Copthall Gdns
  Hendon NW7 . . . . .28 A3
  Twickenham TW1 . . . . . . .152 D3
Copthall L Ctr NW4 . . . . . .28 B2
Copthall Rd E UB10 . . . . . .60 C5
Copthall Rd W UB10 . . . . . .60 C5
Copthall Sch NW7 . . . . . . .28 B3
Copthall Stadium NW4 . . .28 C2

Copthorne Ave
  Bromley BR2 . . . . .226 B6
  Streatham SW12 . . . . . . .159 D4
Copthorne Chase 3
  TW15 . . . . .170 B6
Copthorne Cl TW17 . . . . . .193 A3
Copthorne Ct SM1 . . . . . .218 A5
Copthorne Mews UB3 . . . .105 C2
Coptic St WC1 . . . . .94 A2 240 A3
Copton Ct E3 . . . . .97 C2
Copwood Cl N12 . . . . .30 B6
Coral Apts 6 E16 . . . . . . .121 A6
Coral Cl RM6 . . . . .58 C6
Coral Ho 5 E1 . . . . .97 A3
Coraline Cl UB1 . . . . .85 B4
Coralline Wlk 4 SE2 . . . . .124 C4
Coral Row 14 SW11 . . . . .136 A2
Coral St SE1 . . . . . .116 C4 251 B1
Coram Ho
  Bloomsbury WC1 . . . . . . .240 A6
  9 Chiswick W4 . . . . .111 C1
Coram Mans WC1 . . . . . . .240 C5
Coram St WC1 . . . .94 A3 240 A5
Coran Cl N9 . . . . .18 D4
Corban Rd TW3 . . . . .129 C2
Corbar Cl EN4 . . . . .2 B4
Corbden Cl SE15 . . . . . . .139 D4
Corbet Cl CR4, SM6 . . . . .219 A6
Corbet Ct EC3 . . . . .242 D1
Corbet Ho SW8 . . . . .234 A5
Corbet Pl E1 . . . . . .95 D2 243 C4
Corbett Ct SE26 . . . . .185 B6
Corbett Gr N22 . . . . .32 A3
Corbett Ho SW10 . . . . . . .266 A6
Corbett Rd
  Walthamstow E17 . . . . . . .54 A6
  Wanstead E11 . . . . .55 C3
Corbett's La SE16 . . . . . . .118 C2
Corbetts Pas 8 SE16. . . . .118 C2
Corbett Villas RM8 . . . . . .58 C1
Corbicum E11 . . . . .54 C2
Corbiere Ct SW19 . . . . . . .178 D4
Corbiere Ho 5 N1 . . . . . . .95 C6
Corbin Ho 7 E3 . . . . .97 D4
Corbin's La HA2 . . . . .63 D5
Corbridge 5 N17 . . . . . . .34 B3
Corbridge Cres E2 . . . . . . .96 B5
Corbridge Ho SE2 . . . . . . .124 C3
Corby Cres EN2 . . . . .4 A1
Corbylands Rd DA15 . . . . .167 C3
Corbyn St N4, N19 . . . . . . .50 A1
Corby Rd NW10 . . . . .89 B5
Corby Way E3 . . . . .97 C3
Cordelia Cl SE24 . . . . . . .138 D1
Cordelia Gdns TW19 . . . . .148 A4
Cordelia Ho 26 N1 . . . . . . .95 C5
Cordelia Rd TW19 . . . . . . .148 A4
Cordelia St E14 . . . . .97 D1
Cordell Ho N15 . . . . .51 D4
Cordingley Rd HA4 . . . . . .61 B6
Cording St E14 . . . . .97 D2
Cordwainers Ct 18 E9 . . . .74 C1
Cordwainers Wlk 9 E13 . . .99 A5
Cordwain Ho 7 N18 . . . . . .34 A5
Cordwell Rd SE13 . . . . . . .164 C6
Corefield Cl N11 . . . . .15 A2
Corelli Rd SE3 . . . . .144 A4
Corfe Ave HA2 . . . . .63 C4
Corfe Cl Hayes UB4 . . . . . .84 C1
  Twickenham TW4 . . . . . . .151 A3
Corfe Ho SW8 . . . . .270 C4
Corfe Lodge 15 SE21 . . . .161 B2
Corfe Twr 6 W3 . . . . .111 A4
Corfield Rd N21 . . . . .16 B6
Corfield St E2 . . . . .96 B4
Corfton Lo W5 . . . . .88 A2
Corfton Rd W5 . . . . .88 A2
Coriander Ave E14 . . . . . . .98 B1
Coriander Ct SE1 . . . . . . .253 D2
Cories Cl RM8 . . . . .80 D6
Corigan Ct 6 E11 . . . . . . .76 C6
Corinium Ct HA9 . . . . .66 B4
Corinne Rd N19 . . . . .71 C4
Corinth Ho IG3 . . . . .58 A2
Cork St Mews W1 . . . . . . .249 A5
Corkscrew Hill BR4 . . . . . .224 B5
Cork Sq E1 . . . . .118 B5
Cork St W1 . . . . . .115 C6 249 A5
Cork Tree Ho 3 SW27 . . . .182 D5
Cork Tree Ret Pk N18. . . . .35 A4
Cork Tree Way E4 . . . . . . .35 A5
Corlett St NW1 . . . . .237 A4
Cormont Rd SE5 . . . . .138 D4
Cormorant Cl E17 . . . . . . .35 A3
Cormorant Ct
  36 Deptford SE8 . . . . . . .141 B6
  13 Dulwich SE21 . . . . . . .161 B2
Cormorant Ho EN3. . . . . . .18 D6
Cormorant Pl SM1 . . . . . . .217 B3
Cormorant Rd E7 . . . . .76 D3
Cornbury Ho 5 SE8 . . . . . .141 B6
Cornbury Rd HA8 . . . . .25 D3
Cornel Ho 4 DA15 . . . . . .168 A1
Cornelia Dr UB4 . . . . .84 C3
Cornelia St N7 . . . . .72 B2
Cornelion Cotts 1 SM6 .219 B3
Cornelius Ct 4 N12 . . . . . .30 A5
Cornell Bldg 9 E1 . . . . . . .96 A1
Cornell Cl DA14 . . . . .191 A4

Cornell Ct 4 EN3 . . . . .7 A2
Cornell Ho HA2 . . . . .63 B5
Corner Fielde SW2 . . . . . .160 B3
Corner Gn SE3 . . . . .143 A3
Corner House St WC2 . . . .250 A4
Corner Mead NW9 . . . . . . .27 D2
Cornerside TW15 . . . . . . .171 A3
Cornerstone Ct 13 E1 . . . .96 A3
Cornerways Harrow HA1 . . .65 A5
  Putney SW15 . . . . .134 A1
Corney Reach Way W4 . . .133 C5
Corney Rd W4 . . . . .133 C6
Cornflower La CR0 . . . . . .206 D1
Cornflower Terr SE22 . . . .162 B5
Cornford Cl BR2 . . . . .209 A4
Cornford Gr SW12 . . . . . . .159 B2
Cornhill EC3 . . . . . .95 B1 242 D1
Cornhill Dr EN3 . . . . .7 A6
Cornick Ho 7 SE16 . . . . . .118 B3
Cornish Ct N9 . . . . .18 B4
Cornish Gr SE20 . . . . .184 B2
Cornish Ho
  Brentford TW8 . . . . .110 B1
  7 Camberwell SE17 . . . .138 D6
Cornmill La SE13 . . . . . . .142 A2
Cornmow Dr NW10 . . . . . .68 A3
Cornshaw Rd RM8 . . . . . . .58 D1
Cornthwaite Rd E5 . . . . . . .74 C5
Cornwall Ave
  Bethnal Green E2 . . . . . . .96 C4
  Claygate KT10 . . . . .212 D1
  Falconwood DA16 . . . . . .145 D2
  Finchley N3. . . . . .29 C3
  Southall UB1 . . . . .85 C2
  Wood Green N22 . . . . . . .32 A2
Cornwall Cl IG11 . . . . .79 D2
Cornwall Cres W11 . . . . . . .91 A1
Cornwall Ct 5 Ealing W7. . .86 D3
  5 Pinner HA5 . . . . .23 B3
  Upper Tooting SW17 . . . . .180 C6
Cornwall Dr BR5 . . . . .190 C3
Cornwall Flats SE1 . . . . . .251 B2
Cornwall Gdns
  Kensington SW7 . . . 113 D3 255 D5
  Willesden NW10 . . . . .68 B2
Cornwall Gdns Wlk SW7 .255 C5
Cornwall Gr W4 . . . . .111 C1
Cornwall Ho
  Marylebone NW1 . . . . . . .237 D5
  3 Putney SW15 . . . . .156 C4
Cornwallis Ave London N9 . .18 C2
  New Eltham SE9 . . . . .167 B2
Cornwallis Ct SW8 . . . . . .270 A2
Cornwallis Gr N9 . . . . .18 C2
Cornwallis Ho 24 W12. . . .112 B6
Cornwallis Rd
  Dagenham RM9 . . . . .81 A4
  Edmonton N9 . . . . .18 B2
  Upper Holloway N19 . . . . .72 A6
  Walthamstow E17 . . . . . . .52 D5
  Woolwich SE18. . . . . .122 D3
  Woolwich SE18. . . . . .123 A3
Cornwallis Sq
  3 Finsbury Park N4. . . . .72 C6
  London N19 . . . . .72 A6
Cornwallis Wlk SE9 . . . . .144 B2
Cornwall Mans
  Chelsea SW10 . . . . .266 B4
  Marylebone NW1 . . . . . . .237 D5
Cornwall Mews S SW7 . . .256 A5
Cornwall Mews W SW7 . . .255 D5
Cornwall Rd
  Belmont SM2 . . . . .217 B1
  Croydon CR0. . . . . .220 D6
  Edmonton N18 . . . . .34 A5
  Finsbury Pk N4 . . . . .50 C2
  Harrow HA1 . . . . .42 A3
  Lambeth SE1. . . . .116 C4 251 B2
  Pinner HA5 . . . . .23 B3
  Ruislip HA4 . . . . .61 D6
  Twickenham TW1 . . . . . . .153 A3
  West Green N15. . . . . .51 B4
Cornwall Sq SE11 . . . . . .261 C2
Cornwall St 4 E1 . . . . . . .118 B6
Cornwall Terr NW1 . . . . . .237 D5
Cornwall Terrace Mews
  NW1 . . . . .237 D5
Corn Way E11 . . . . .76 C5
Cornwood Cl N2 . . . . .48 B5
Cornwood Dr E1 . . . . .96 C1
Cornworthy Rd RM8 . . . . . .80 C2
Corona Rd SE12 . . . . .165 A4
Coronation Ave 1 N16. . . .73 D4
Coronation Cl
  Bexley DA5 . . . . .168 D5
  Ilford IG6 . . . . .57 A5
Coronation Ct
  19 North Kensington W10 . .90 C2
  Stratford E15 . . . . .76 D2
Coronation Rd
  Acton NW10 . . . . .88 C3
  Hayes UB3 . . . . .105 D2
  Newham E13 . . . . .99 C4
Coronet Ho 4 DA7 . . . . . .24 D4
Coronet Par 9 HA0 . . . . . .66 A2
Coronet St N1 . . . . .95 C4
Corporation Ave TW4 . . . .129 A1
Corporation Row EC1 . . . .241 B6
Corporation St
  Lower Holloway N7 . . . . . .72 A3

Corporation St continued
  West Ham E15 . . . . .98 D5
Corpus Christi RC Prim Sch
  19 Brixton SW2 . . . . . . .160 B6
  Kingston u T KT3. . . . . . .199 A6
Corrance Rd SW2, SW4 . .138 A1
Corri Ave N14 . . . . .31 D6
Corrib Ct N13. . . . . .16 B1
Corrib Dr SM1 . . . . .218 C3
Corrib Hts N8 . . . . .49 D3
Corrigan Cl NW4 . . . . .46 C6
Corringham Ct NW11 . . . . .47 C2
Corringham Ho 11 E1 . . . .96 D1
Corringham Rd
  London NW11. . . . . .47 C2
  Wembley HA9. . . . . .66 C6
Corringway Ealing W5 . . . .88 C2
  Golders Green NW11 . . . . .47 D2
Corris Gn NW9. . . . . .45 C3
Corry Dr SW9 . . . . .138 D1
Corry Ho 2 E14 . . . . .119 D6
Corsair Cl TW19. . . . . . . .148 A4
Corsair Rd TW19. . . . . . . .148 A4
Corscombe Cl KT2 . . . . . .177 A5
Corsehill St SW16. . . . . . .181 C4
Corsell Ho 5 TW8 . . . . . . .131 C5
Corsham Ho HA9 . . . . .66 C2
Corsham St N1 . . . . .95 B4 235 D1
Corsica St N5 . . . . .72 C2
Corsley Way E9 . . . . .75 B2
Cortayne Ct TW2 . . . . . . .152 C2
Cortayne Rd SW6 . . . . . . .135 B3
Cortis Rd SW15 . . . . .156 B5
Cortis Terr SW15 . . . . . . .156 B5
Corunna Rd SW8 .137 C4 269 B2
Corunna Terr SW8 . . . . . .269 A2
Corvette Sq 5 SE10. . . . . .142 B6
Corwell Gdns UB8 . . . . . . .83 A1
Corwell La UB8 . . . . .83 A1
Coryton Path W9 . . . . .91 B3
Cosbycote Ave SE24 . . . . .161 A6
Cosdach Ave SM6 . . . . . .219 D1
Cosedge Cres CR0, CR9 . .220 D3
Cosgrove Cl
  Edmonton N21 . . . . .17 A2
  Hayes UB4 . . . . .84 D3
Cosgrove Ho 11 E2 . . . . . .96 A6
Cosmo Pl WC1 . . . . .240 B4
Cosmur Cl W12 . . . . .111 D3
Cossall Wlk SE15 . . . . . . .140 B4
Cossar Mews 10 SW2 . . . .160 C6
Cosser St SE1 . . . . .116 C3 261 A6
Costa St SE15. . . . . .140 A3
Coston Prim Sch UB6 . . . .86 A4
Costons Ave UB6. . . . . . . .86 B4
Costons La UB6. . . . . .86 B4
Coston Wlk 4 SE4 . . . . . .140 D1
Cosway Ho N1 . . . . .11 A3
Cosway Mans NW1 . . . . . .237 B4
Cosway St NW1 . . . . .92 C2 237 B4
Cotall St E14 . . . . .97 C2
Coteford Cl HA5 . . . . .40 A4
Coteford Inf Sch HA5 . . . . .40 A3
Coteford Jun Sch HA5 . . . .39 D4
Coteford St SW17 . . . . . . .181 A6
Cotelands CR0 . . . . .221 C5
Cotesbach Rd E5 . . . . .74 C5
Cotes Ho NW8 . . . . .237 A5
Cotesmore Gdns RM8 . . . .80 C4
Cotford Rd CR7 . . . . .205 A5
Cotham St SE17. . . . . . . .262 B3
Cotherstone Rd SW2. . . . .160 B3
Cotleigh Ave DA5 . . . . . . .168 D2
Cotleigh Rd NW6 . . . . .69 C1
Cotman Cl London NW11. . .48 A3
  Putney SW15 . . . . .156 D6
Cotman Ct BR3 . . . . .185 B2
Cotmandene Cres BR5 . . .190 A1
Cotman Gdns HA8 . . . . . . .26 C1
Cotman Ho
  5 Northolt UB5 . . . . .84 D5
  St John's Wood NW8 . . . . .230 A4
Cotman Mews RM8 . . . . . .80 C3
Cotmans Cl UB3 . . . . .106 A5
Coton Rd DA16 . . . . .146 A2
Cotrill Gdns E8 . . . . .74 B2
Cotsford Ave KT3 . . . . . . .199 B4
Cotswold Ave WD23 . . . . . .8 A5
Cotswold Cl
  Hinchley Wood KT10. . . . .212 D6
  Kingston u T KT2. . . . . . .177 A4
Cotswold Ct London N11 . .31 A6
  St Luke's EC1 . . . . .242 A6
  3 Wembley UB6. . . . . .86 D5
Cotswold Gate NW2. . . . . .47 A1
Cotswold Gdns
  Hendon NW2 . . . . .68 D6
  Ilford IG2 . . . . .57 B2
  Newham E6 . . . . .99 D5
Cotswold Gn EN2 . . . . .4 B1
Cotswold Ho N15 . . . . .51 D1
Cotswold Mews SW11 . . . .266 C5
Cotswold Rd TW12 . . . . . .173 C4
Cotswold Rise BR6. . . . . .211 D3
Cotswold St SE27 . . . . . . .182 D6
Cotswold Way Enfield EN2. . .4 B2
  North Cheam KT4 . . . . . .216 C6

Cottage Ave BR2........210 A1
Cottage Cl Harrow HA2....64 C6
Ruislip HA4.............39 B1
Cottage Field Cl DA14...168 C3
Cottage Gn SE5.........139 B5
Cottage Gr London SW9..138 A2
Surbiton KT6...........197 D3
Cottage Pl SW3...114 C3 257 A5
Cottage Rd KT19........215 B1
Cottage St E14.........119 D6
Cottages The
  Ickenham UB10.........60 A6
  Lambeth SE1..........260 C5
  Uxbridge UB10.........60 D5
Cottage Wlk ☑ N16.....73 D5
Cottenham Dr
  London NW9...........45 D6
  Wimbledon SW20......178 B3
Cottenham Ho ☑ N19...72 A6
Cottenham Par SW20....178 B1
COTTENHAM PARK........178 B2
Cottenham Park Rd
  SW20................178 C3
Cottenham Pl SW20.....178 B3
Cottenham Rd E17.......53 B5
Cotterill Rd KT6.......198 B1
Cottesbrook St ☑ SE14.141 A5
Cottesloe Ho NW8......237 A6
Cottesloe Mews SE1....261 B6
Cottesmore Ct W8......255 C6
Cottesmore Gdns
  W8............113 D3 255 D6
Cottimore Ave KT12....194 B1
Cottimore Cres KT12...194 B2
Cottimore La KT12.....194 B2
Cottimore Terr KT12...194 B2
Cottingham Chase HA4...62 A5
Cottingham Rd
  Penge SE20...........184 D3
  South Lambeth
  SW8..........138 B5 270 D4
Cottington Rd TW13....152 D3
Cottington St SE11....261 C2
Cotton Ave W3..........89 B1
Cotton Cl Dagenham RM9..80 C1
☑ Leyton E11..........76 C6
Cotton Hill BR1.......186 B6
Cotton Ho
  Bedford Pk W12......111 D4
  ☑ Streatham SW12...160 A4
Cotton Row SW11.......136 B2
Cotton's Gdns E2.......95 C4
Cottons La SE1........252 D4
Cotton St E14.........120 A6
Cottrell Ct SE10......120 D2
Cotts Cl ☑ W7.........86 D2
Couchman Ho ☑ SW4....159 C5
Couchmore Ave KT10....212 C6
Coulgate St SE4.......141 A2
Coulsdon Ct ☑ N8......49 A4
Coulsdon Ho ☑ SW2....160 A3
Coulson Cl RM8.........58 C1
Coulson St SW3...114 D1 257 C2
Coulter Cl UB4.........85 A3
Coulter Rd W6.........112 B3
Coulthurst Ct SW16....182 A3
Coults Cres NW5........71 A5
Councillor St SE5.....139 A5
Counters Ct W14.......254 B6
Counter St SE1........253 A3
Countess Rd NW5........71 C3
Countisbury Ave EN1....17 D4
Countisbury Ho SE26...162 A1
Country Way TW13,
  TW16................172 C5
County Gate
  Longlands SE9.......167 A1
  New Barnet EN5.......13 D5
County Gr SE5.........139 A4
County Ho
  ☑ Herne Hill SE24...138 D1
  ☑ South Lambeth SW9.138 C4
County Par TW8........131 D5
County Rd Newham E6...100 D2
  South Norwood CR7...182 D1
County St SE1....117 A3 262 B5
Coupland Pl SE18......123 A1
Courcy Rd N8, N22......50 C6
Courier Ho ☑ SW2.....160 C4
Courland Gr SW8.......137 D3
Courland St
  SW8..........137 D4 269 D1
Course The SE9........166 C1
Courtauld Ho ☑ E2.....96 A5
Courtauld Inst of Art*
  WC2................250 C6
Courtauld Rd N19......50 A1
Courtaulds Cl SE28....124 A5
Court Ave DA17........125 B1
Court Cl Harrow HA3....44 A6
  Twickenham TW13, TW2...151 D1
  Wallington SM6......219 D1
Court Close Ave TW13,
  TW2................151 D1
Court Cres KT9........213 D2

Court Downs Rd BR3....185 D1
Court Dr Carshalton SM1.218 C4
  Edgware HA7..........26 A6
  Hillingdon UB10......82 C6
  Wallington CR0......220 B4
Courtenay Ave
  Harrow HA3...........24 A2
  Highgate N6..........48 C2
Courtenay Dr BR3......186 B1
Courtenay Gdns HA3.....24 A1
Courtenay Mews E17.....53 A4
Courtenay Pl E17......53 A4
Courtenay Rd Leyton E11..76 D5
  North Cheam KT4, SM3..216 C5
  Penge SE20..........184 D4
  Walthamstow E17......52 D5
Courtenay Rd HA9.......65 D5
Courtenay Sq SE11.....261 A1
Courtenay St
  SE11...........116 C1 261 A1
Courtens Mews HA7......25 C3
Court Farm Ave KT19...215 B3
Court Farm Ind Est
  TW19...............148 B5
Court Farm Rd
  Chislehurst SE9.....166 A1
  Northolt UB5.........63 C1
Courtfield W13.........87 C2
Courtfield Ave HA1.....42 D4
Courtfield Cres HA1....42 D4
Courtfield Gdns
  Ealing W13...........87 A1
  Ruislip HA4..........61 D6
  South Kensington
  SW5..........113 D2 255 D3
Courtfield Ho EC1.....241 A4
Courtfield Mews SW7...255 D3
Courtfield Rd
  Ashford TW15........170 D4
  South Kensington
  SW7..........114 A2 256 A3
Courtfield Rise BR4...224 B5
Courtgate Cl NW7......27 D4
Court Gdns N7..........72 C2
Courthill Rd SE13.....142 A1
Courthope Ho
  ☑ Rotherhithe SE16..118 C3
  South Lambeth SW8...270 A3
Courthope Rd
  Gospel Oak NW3......70 D4
  Greenford UB6........86 B5
  Wimbledon SW19......179 A5
Courthope Villas SW19.179 A3
Court House Gdns N3....29 C4
Court House Rd N12.....29 C4
Court La SE21.........161 D4
Courtland Ave
  Chingford E4.........20 D2
  Edgware NW7..........11 C1
  Redbridge IG1........78 B6
  South Norwood SW16..182 B3
Courtland Gr SE28.....124 D6
Courtland Prim Sch NW7..11 C2
Courtland Rd E6......100 A6
Courtlands
  ☑ Beckenham BR3....185 D1
  ☑ Belmont SM2......217 D1
  Chislehurst BR7.....188 D4
  Ealing W5............87 C2
  Richmond TW10.......154 C6
  ☑ Upper Clapton E5..52 B1
  Walton-on-T KT12...194 A2
Courtlands Ave
  Hampton TW12........173 B4
  Hayes BR2...........208 D1
  Lee SE12............165 B6
  Richmond TW9.......132 D3
Courtlands Cl HA4......39 D2
Courtlands Dr KT19....215 D2
Courtlands Rd KT5.....198 C2
Court Lane Gdns SE21..161 C4
Courtleet Dr DA8......147 D4
Courtleigh ☑ NW11.....47 B4
Courtleigh Ave EN4.....2 B5
Courtleigh Gdns NW11...47 A5
Court Lo ☑ DA17.......125 C1
Courtman Rd N17........33 A3
Court Mans ☑ W6......112 A2
Court Mead UB5.........85 B4
Courtmead Cl SE24....161 A5
Courtnell St W2........91 C1
Courtney Cl SE19......183 C4
Courtney Cres SM5.....218 D1
Courtney Ct N7.........72 C3
Courtney Ho
  ☑ Hendon NW4........46 C5
  Kensington W14......254 B6
Courtney Pl CR0.......220 C5
Courtney Rd
  Croydon CR0.........220 C5
  Islington N7.........72 C3
  Mitcham SW19........180 C3
Courtney Twrs IG2......57 B3
Courtney Way TW6......126 C2
Court One TW15........149 A1
Courtrai Rd SE23......163 A5
Court Rd Eltham SE9...166 B4
  Southall UB2........107 B1
  South Norwood SE25..205 D6

Court Rd continued
  Uxbridge UB10........60 D4
Court Royal SW15......157 A6
Courtside Crouch End N8..49 D3
  Forest Hill SE23....162 C1
Court St ☑ Bromley BR1..187 A1
  ☑ Stepney E1........96 B2
Courts The SW16.......182 A3
Court The London N10...49 C5
  Ruislip HA4..........63 A4
Court Three TW15......149 A1
Court Two TW15........149 A1
Courtville Ho ☑ W10...91 A4
Courtway IG8...........37 C5
Court Way Acton W3.....89 A2
  Colindale NW9........45 C5
  Ilford IG6...........57 A6
  Twickenham TW1, TW2.152 D4
Courtyard Apartments
  TW11...............174 B5
Courtyard Mews BR5....190 A3
Courtyard The
  Fulham SW6.....135 A4 264 A1
  Islington N1.........72 B1
  Keston BR2..........226 A2
  Thornton Heath CR0..204 B3
  ☑ Wandsworth SW18..136 B1
Court Yd SE9..........166 B5
Cousin La EC4....117 B6 252 C5
Cousins Cl ☑ UB7.....104 A6
Cousins Ct ☑ NW9......46 A5
Couthurst Rd SE3......143 B5
Coutts Ave KT9........214 A3
Couzens Ho ☑ E3.......97 B2
Coval Gdns SW14.......132 D1
Coval La SW14.........132 D1
Coval Pas SW14........133 A1
Coval Rd SW14.........133 A1
Covardale Ct EN3.......7 A6
Covelees Wall E6......100 C1
Covell Ct ☑ SE8......141 C5
Covent Garden Sta
  WC2...........94 A1 240 B1
Coventry Cl Kilburn NW6..91 C6
  ☑ Newham E6........100 B1
Coventry Rd
  Bethnal Green E1.....96 B3
  Croydon SE25........206 A5
  Ilford IG1...........56 D1
Coventry St W1........249 C5
Coverack Cl Croydon CR0.207 A2
  Southgate N14........15 C5
Coverdale Cl HA7.......25 B5
Coverdale Gdns CR0....221 D5
Coverdale Rd
  Brondesbury NW2.....69 A2
  Friern Barnet N11....31 A4
  Hammersmith W12....112 B4
  Hampstead NW6........68 D1
Coverdales The IG11...101 B5
Coverham Ho ☑ SE4....140 D1
Coverley Cl E1.........96 A2
Coverley Point SE11...260 C3
Coverton Rd SW17......180 C5
Coverts Rd KT10.......212 D1
Covert The BR6........211 C3
Covert Wood Cl BR5....211 D3
Covert Way EN4.........2 A3
Covey Cl SW19.........179 D1
Covey Rd KT4, SM3.....216 D6
Covington Gdns SW16...182 D3
Covington Way
  South Norwood SW16..182 C3
  South Norwood SW16..182 D3
Cowan Cl E6...........100 A2
Cowan Ct ☑ NW10......67 B1
Cowan Lo ☑ IG8........37 C4
Cowbridge La IG11......78 D1
Cowbridge Rd HA3......44 B5
Cowcross St EC1...94 D2 241 C4
Cowdenbeath Path N1...233 C6
Cowden Rd BR6........211 D2
Cowden St SE6........171 C3
Cowdray Hall Royal Coll of
  Nursing W1....93 B1 238 C2
Cowdrey Ho ☑ SE22....139 C2
Cowdrey Rd UB10.......83 A6
Cowdrey Cl EN1........5 C3
Cowdrey Rd SW19......180 A5
Cowdry Rd E9..........75 B2
Cowell Lo E4..........36 D5
Cowen Ave HA2.........64 B6
Cowen Ho ☑ SE18.....144 D6
Cowgate Rd UB6........86 B4
Cowick Rd SW17........180 D6
Cowings Mead UB5......63 A2
Cowland Ave EN3........6 C1
Cow Leaze E6.........100 C1
Cowleaze Rd KT2......176 A2
Cowley Ct ☑ E18.......37 A1
Cowley La E11.........76 C5
COWLEY PEACHY.........82 A2
Cowley Pl NW4.........46 C4
Cowley Rd Brixton SW9.138 C4
  East Acton W3.......111 D5
  ☑ Kennington SW9..138 C5
  Mortlake SW14.......133 C2
  Redbridge IG1........56 B2
  Wanstead E11.........55 B4
Cowley St SW1.........260 A5

Cowling Cl W11........244 A4
Cowper Ave Sutton SM1..218 B4
  Upton Pk E6..........78 A1
Cowper Cl Bexley DA16..168 A6
  Bromley BR2.........209 D5
Cowper Gdns
  Southgate N14........15 C5
  Wallington SM6......219 C2
Cowper Ho Pimlico SW1..259 D1
  Walworth SE17.......262 B2
Cowper Rd Acton W3....111 B5
  ☑ Belvedere DA17...125 C2
  Bromley BR2.........209 D5
  Ealing W7...........108 D6
  East Barnet N14......15 B3
  Edmonton N18.........34 A5
  Kingston u T KT2....176 B5
  Stoke Newington N16..73 C4
  Wimbledon SW19......180 A4
Cowper's Ct EC3.......242 D1
Cowper St EC1,
  EC2...........95 B3 242 D6
Cowper Terr W10........90 D2
Cowslip Cl UB10........60 A1
Cowslip Rd E18.........37 B1
Cowthorpe Rd SW8.....269 D2
Cox Cl ☑ EN4..........2 C1
Coxe Pl HA3...........43 A5
Cox Ho W6............264 A6
Cox La Chessington KT9.214 B4
  West Ewell KT19.....215 A3
Coxmount Rd SE7.......121 D1
Coxs Ave TW17........193 C6
Coxson Way SE1........253 C1
Coxwell Rd
  Plumstead SE18......123 B1
  South Norwood SE19..183 C3
Coxwold Path KT9......214 A1
Coysh Ct ☑ SW15......157 A6
Crabbs Croft ☑ BR6...227 A3
Crab Hill BR3.........186 B3
Crabtree Ave
  Dagenham RM6.........58 D5
  Wembley HA0..........88 B5
Crabtree Cl E2.........95 D5
Crabtree Ct EN5........1 D1
Crabtree Hall SW6.....134 C5
Crabtree La SW6.......134 D5
Cracknell Cl EN1.......6 B6
Craddock Rd EN1........5 D2
Craddock St NW5.......71 A2
Cradley Rd SE9.......167 B3
Cragie Ho SE1........263 D3
Craig Dr UB8..........82 D1
Craigen Ave CR0.......206 B1
Craigen Gdns IG1, IG3..79 C4
Craigerne Rd SE3......143 B5
Craig Gdns E18........36 D1
Craig Ho Ealing W13..109 B6
  Greenwich SE3.......143 B5
Craigholm SE18.......144 C4
Craigie Lea N10........31 B1
Craigieith SW15.......156 D5
Craigmuir Pk HA0.......88 B6
Craignair Rd SW2.....160 C4
Craignish Ave SW16...182 B1
Craig Park Rd N18......34 B6
Craig Rd TW10........175 C6
Craig's Ct SW1.......250 A4
Craigside KT2........176 D2
Craigton Rd SE9......144 B1
Craigweil Cl SW15.....25 D5
Craigweil Dr HA7.......25 D5
Craigwell Ave TW13....150 A1
Craik Ct NW6..........91 B5
Crail Row SE17...117 B2 262 D3
Crales Ho SE18.......122 A3
Cramer Ct KT3........199 A6
Cramer St W1.....93 A2 238 B3
Cramhurst Ho ☑ SM1..218 B3
Crammond Cl W6.......264 A5
Cramond Ct TW14......149 C3
Cramonde Ct DA16.....146 A3
Crampton Prim Sch
  SE17.........116 D1 261 D2
Crampton Rd SE20.....184 C4
Crampton St
  SE17.........117 A1 262 A2
Cranberry Cl ☑ UB5...84 D5
Cranberry La E16.......98 C3
Cranborne Ave
  Southall UB2........107 C2
  Tolworth KT6, KT9...214 C5
Cranborne Rd IG11....101 B6
Cranborne Waye
  Hayes UB4............84 C6
  Hayes UB4...........106 C1
Cranbourn Alley WC2..249 D6
Cranbourne Cl SW16...204 A6
Cranbourne Ct
  East Finchley N2.....47 D6
  ☑ Edgware HA8.......26 D5
  Finchley NW7.........29 A3
  SW11...............267 B4
  Walton-on-T KT12...194 B2
Cranbourne Dr HA5......40 D4
Cranbourne Gdns
  Ilford IG6...........57 A6
  Temple Fortune NW11..47 B4

Cranbourne Rd
  Leyton E15...........76 A4
  London N10...........31 B1
  Manor Pk E12.........78 A3
  Northwood HA6........39 D6
Cranbourn Ho ☑ SE16..118 B4
Cranbourn Pas ☑ SE16.118 B4
Cranbourn St
  WC2............115 D6 249 D6
CRANBROOK.............56 C1
Cranbrook NW1........232 B5
Cranbrook Cl BR2.....209 A3
Cranbrook Coll (Boys)
  IG1.................78 C6
Cranbrook Ct
  ☑ Brentford TW8....131 D6
  South Croydon CR2...221 C3
Cranbrook Dr
  Thames Ditton KT10..196 A1
  Twickenham TW2......151 D3
Cranbrook Ho
  ☑ Hackney E5........74 B3
  South Norwood SE19..183 B2
Cranbrook La N11.......31 B6
Cranbrook Mews E17.....53 B4
Cranbrook Pk N22......32 C2
Cranbrook Prim Sch IG1..56 B2
Cranbrook Rd
  Chiswick W4.........111 C1
  Erith DA7...........147 B4
  Hounslow TW4........129 B1
  Ilford IG1, IG2......56 C3
  New Barnet EN4.......14 B5
  South Norwood CR7...183 A1
  St Johns SE8........141 C4
  Wimbledon SW19......179 A3
Cranbrook Rise IG1.....56 B2
Cranbrook St E2........96 D5
Cranbury Rd SW6......135 D3
Crandale Ho ☑ E5......74 B3
Crandley Ct SE8.......119 A2
Crane Ave Acton W3....111 A6
  Isleworth TW7.......153 A6
Cranebank TW4..........128 B2
Cranebank Mews TW1....131 A1
Cranebrook TW2........152 A2
Crane Cl Dagenham RM10..81 C2
  Harrow HA2...........64 A5
Crane Ct ☑ Acton W12.111 C4
  Holborn EC4.........241 B1
  West Ewell KT19.....215 A4
Craneford Cl TW2......152 D4
Craneford Way TW2.....152 D4
Crane Gdns UB3........105 D2
Crane Gr N7...........72 C2
Crane Ho ☑ Bow E3.....97 A5
  ☑ Catford BR1......186 B5
  ☑ Peckham SE15.....139 D4
Crane Lodge Rd TW5....128 B6
Crane Mead SE16.......118 D2
Crane Mead Ct TW1.....152 D4
Crane Park Prim Sch
  TW13...............151 B2
Crane Park Rd TW2.....151 D2
Crane Rd Stanwell TW19.148 C5
  Twickenham TW2......152 C3
Cranesbill Cl Kenton NW9..45 B6
  Mitcham SW16........181 C1
Cranes Dr KT5.........198 B5
Cranes Park Ave KT5,
  KT6................198 B5
Cranes Park Cres KT5..198 B5
Cranes Pk KT5, KT6....198 A4
Crane St Greenwich SE10.120 B1
  ☑ Peckham SE15.....139 D4
Craneswater TW6.......127 D5
Craneswater Pk UB2....107 B1
Cranes Way WD6.........11 A4
Crane Way TW2.........152 A4
Cranfield Ct
  Marylebone NW1.....237 B3
  ☑ Woodford IG8......37 A6
Cranfield Dr NW9.......27 C3
Cranfield Ho WC1.....240 B4
Cranfield Rd SE4......141 B2
CRANFORD.............128 C4
Cranford Ave
  Bowes Pk N13........32 A5
  Stanwell TW19.......148 B4
Cranford Cl
  Stanwell TW19.......148 A4
  Wimbledon SW20......178 B3
Cranford Com Coll TW5..128 B3
Cranford Cotts ☑ E1..118 D6
Cranford Ct SM1.......218 A4
Cranford Ctry Pk TW5..128 A6
Cranford Dr UB3.......105 D2
Cranford Jun & Inf Schs
  TW4................128 B3
Cranford La
  Harlington TW6......127 D4
  Harlington UB3......127 C5
  Heston TW5..........128 C5
Cranford Lo SW19......156 D2
Cranford Mews BR2.....210 A4
Cranford Park Prim Sch
  UB3................105 D2
Cranford Park Rd UB3..105 D2
Cranford Rd TW6.......127 D4

Cranford Rise KT10 . . . . . .212 A3
Cranford St E1. . . . . 118 D6
Cranford Way N8 . . . . .50 C4
Cranhurst Rd NW2. . . . . . . .68 C3
Cranleigh W11 . . . . 244 C4
Cranleigh Cl Bexley DA5. . 169 D5
Penge SE20 . . . . .184 B1
Cranleigh Ct 1 Barnet EN5. . 1 D1
Mitcham CR4 . . . . .202 B6
Richmond TW9 . . . . 132 C2
Southall UB1. . . . . .85 B1
4 Stamford Hill N16 . . . . . .51 C1
Cranleigh Gardens Ind Est
UB1. . . . . .85 B2
Cranleigh Gdns
Barking IG11 . . . . .79 B2
Harrow HA3 . . . . .44 A4
Kingston u T KT2 . . . . . . .176 B4
Southall UB1. . . . . .85 B1
Southgate N21 . . . . .16 C6
South Norwood SE25 . . . . 205 C6
Sutton SM1. . . . . 217 D6
Cranleigh Ho SW20 . . . . . 178 B1
Cranleigh Hos NW1. . . . . . 232 B3
Cranleigh Mews SW11 . . . 136 D3
Cranleigh Rd
Feltham TW13 . . . . 171 D6
Harringay N15 . . . . .51 A4
Merton SW19 . . . . 201 C6
Thames Ditton KT10 . . . . 196 A1
Cranleigh St NW1 . . 93 C5 232 B3
Cranley Dene Ct N10 . . . . . .49 B5
Cranley Dr Ilford IG2 . . . . . .57 A2
Ruislip HA4. . . . . .61 D6
CRANLEY GARDENS 49 B5
Cranley Gdns London N10 . .49 B5
Palmers Green N13 . . . . . . .16 B1
South Kensington
SW7 . . . . 114 B1 256 C2
Wallington SM6 . . . . 219 C1
Cranley Mews
SW7 . . . . 114 A1 256 B3
Cranley Par 2 SE9. . . . . . 188 A6
Cranley Pl SW7 . . . 114 B2 256 C3
Cranley Rd Ilford IG2 . . . . . .57 A2
Newham E13 . . . . .99 B2
Cranmer Ave W13. . . . . . . 109 B3
Cranmer Cl Ruislip HA4 . . . .40 D1
Stanmore HA7 . . . . .25 C3
West Barnes SM4. . . . . . . 200 B2
Cranmer Ct Chelsea SW3. . 257 B3
Church End N3 . . . . .29 A1
Hampton TW12. . . . . 173 D5
Kingston u T KT2 . . . . . . .175 D6
Cranmere Prim Sch
KT10. . . . . 196 A1
Cranmer Farm Cl CR4 . . . . 202 D5
Cranmer Ho SW11 . . . . . . 267 A2
Cranmer Prim Sch CR4 . . . 202 D5
Cranmer Rd Brixton SW9 . . 138 C5
Croydon CR0. . . . . 221 A5
Edgware HA8 . . . . .10 D1
Forest Gate E7 . . . . .77 B4
Hampton TW12. . . . . 173 D5
Hayes UB3 . . . . .83 B1
Kingston u T KT2 . . . . . . .176 A5
Mitcham CR4 . . . . .202 D5
Cranmer Terr SW17 . . . . . . 180 B5
Cranmore Ave TW7 . . . . . . 130 A5
Cranmore Rd
Catford BR1. . . . . 164 D1
Elmstead BR7. . . . . .188 B5
Cranmore Way N10 . . . . . . .49 C5
Cranston Cl
Hounslow TW3, TW4. . . . . 129 A3
Uxbridge UB10 . . . . .61 B6
Cranston Ct 6 N20 . . . . . . .14 D2
Cranston Gdns E4 . . . . .35 D4
Cranston Rd SE23. . . . . . . 163 A2
Crantock Rd SE6. . . . . 164 A2
Cranwell Cl E3 . . . . .97 D3
Cranwell Ct Croydon CR0. . 222 D6
6 Hendon NW9. . . . . .27 D3
Cranwell Gr TW17. . . . . . . 192 B5
Cranwell Rd TW6 . . . . 126 D3
Cranwich Ave N21 . . . . .17 B4
Cranwich Rd N16. . . . . .51 C2
Cranwood St EC1. . . . . . . 235 D1
Cranworth Cres 7 E4. . . . . .20 B3
Cranworth Gdns SW9 . . . . 138 C4
Cranworth Ho 6 N7 . . . . . .72 B4
Craster Rd SW2. . . . . 160 B4
Craston Ho 2 SE5. . . . . . . 139 C3
Crathie Rd SE12 . . . . 165 B5
Crathorne Ho N2 . . . . .30 B1
Cravan Ave TW13 . . . . 150 A2
Craven Ave Ealing W5. . . . . 109 C6
Southall UB1. . . . . .85 B2
Craven Cl Hayes UB4. . . . . .84 A1
Stamford Hill N16. . . . . . . .52 A2
Craven Cottage (Fulham FC)
SW6 . . . . 134 D4
Craven Ct Dagenham RM6 . .59 A3
Edgware HA8 . . . . .26 B6
Harlesden NW10 . . . . .89 C6
Southall UB1. . . . . 107 D5
Craven Gdns
Barking IG11 . . . . 101 C5

Craven Gdns continued
Ilford IG6 . . . . .57 B6
Wimbledon SW19. . . . . . . 179 D5
Craven Hill W2 . . . . .114 A6 246 B6
Craven Hill Gdns
W2. . . . . 114 A6 246 A6
Craven Hill Mews W2 . . . . 246 B6
Craven Ho Ealing W5. . . . . 109 C6
3 Finchley N2 . . . . .30 B1
2 Mortlake SW14. . . . . . . 133 B2
Craven Lo Bayswater W2 . . 246 B6
Fulham SW6 . . . . 134 D4
Craven Mews 6 SW11 . . . 137 A2
Craven Park Mews NW10. . .89 C6
Craven Park Rd
Harlesden NW10 . . . . .89 C6
South Tottenham N15. . . . . .52 A3
Craven Pas WC2 . . . . 250 A4
Craven Pk NW10. . . . . .89 C6
Craven Rd Croydon CR0. . . 206 B1
Ealing W5 . . . . 109 C6
Kingston u T KT2. . . . . 176 B2
Paddington W2 . . . . 92 A1 236 B1
Stonebridge NW10. . . . . . . .89 B6
Craven St WC2. . . . .114 A5 250 A4
Craven Terr W2 . . . . 114 A6 246 B6
Craven Wlk E5, N16. . . . . . .52 A2
Crawford Ave HA0 . . . . .65 D3
Crawford Bldgs NW1. . . . . 237 B3
Crawford Cl TW7. . . . . 130 C3
Crawford Ct SE18. . . . . . . 146 A6
Crawford Gdns
Edmonton N13 . . . . .16 C1
Northolt UB5 . . . . .85 B4
Crawford Mews W1. . . . . . 237 C3
Crawford Pas EC1. . . . . . . 241 B5
Crawford Pl W1 . . . . 92 C2 237 B3
Crawford Place Dwellings
NW1 . . . . 237 B3
Crawford Point 4 E16 . . . . .98 D1
Crawford Prim Sch SE5 . . . 139 A4
Crawford Rd SE5 . . . . 139 A3
Crawford St
Marylebone W1 . . . . 92 D2 237 C3
16 Willesden NW10. . . . . . .67 B1
Crawley Rd Enfield EN1. . . . .17 D4
Leyton E10 . . . . .53 D1
Tottenham N22. . . . . .33 A1
Crawshay Ct SW9 . . . . 138 C4
Crawshay Ho 13 N16 . . . . . .73 B4
Crawthew Gr SE22 . . . . . . 139 D1
Cray Bldgs DA14 . . . . 190 C4
Craybrooke Rd DA14. . . . . 190 B6
Craybury End SE9. . . . . . . 167 A2
Crayfields Bsns Pk BR5 . . . 190 C2
Crayfields Ind Pk BR5. . . . . 190 C1
Crayford Cl E6. . . . . 100 A1
Crayford Ho
Bermondsey SE1 . . . . 252 D1
5 Lower Holloway N7 . . . . .72 A4
Crayford Rd N7 . . . . .72 A4
Crayke Hill KT9 . . . . 214 A1
Crayle Ho EC1 . . . . 241 D6
Crayleigh Terr DA14. . . . . . 190 C4
Crayonne Cl TW16 . . . . . . 171 C2
Cray Rd Erith DA17. . . . . . . 147 C6
Sidcup DA14 . . . . 190 C4
Crays Par The BR5. . . . . . . 190 C1
Crealock Gr IG8 . . . . .36 D5
Crealock St SW18. . . . . . . 157 D5
Creasy Est SE1. . . . . 263 A5
Crebor St SE22 . . . . 162 A5
Credenhall Dr BR2. . . . . . . 210 B1
Credenhall Ho 2 SE15. . . . 140 B5
Credenhill St SW16 . . . . . . 181 C4
Crediton Hill NW6 . . . . .69 D3
Crediton Ho EN3. . . . . .6 D2
Crediton Rd NW10 . . . . .90 D6
Crediton Way KT10. . . . . . . 213 A3
Credon Rd
Bermondsey SE16 . . . . 118 B1
Newham E13 . . . . .99 C5
Creechurch La EC3 . . . . . . 243 B1
Creechurch Pl EC3. . . . . . . 243 B1
Creed Ct 5 E1. . . . . .97 A4
Creed Ho SE15. . . . . 140 B2
Creed La EC4 . . . . 241 D1
Creek Ho W14 . . . . 254 B6
CREEKMOUTH 101 D2
Creekmouth Ind Pk
IG11. . . . . 101 D3
Creek Rd Barking IG11 . . . . 101 D4
East Molesey KT8. . . . . . . 196 C5
Greenwich SE10, SE8 . . . . 141 C5
Creekside SE8. . . . . 141 D5
Creekside Foyer SE8. . . . . 141 D6
Creek The TW16. . . . . 194 A4
Creeland Gr SE6 . . . . 163 B3
Crefeld Cl W6 . . . . 135 A6 264 A5
Creffield Rd W3, W5. . . . . . 110 C6
Creighton Ave
London N2, N10 . . . . .30 D1
Newham E6 . . . . .99 D5
Creighton Cl W12. . . . . 112 B6
Creighton Ho N2 . . . . .48 C6
Creighton Rd Ealing W5 . . . 109 D3
Kensal Rise NW6 . . . . .90 D5
Tottenham N17. . . . . .33 C3
Cremer Bsns Ctr 8 E2. . . . .95 D5

Cremer Ho 9 SE8 . . . . 141 C5
Cremer St E2 . . . . .95 D5
Cremorne Rd
SW10. . . . . 136 B5 266 C4
Creon Ct 3 SW9. . . . . 138 C4
Crescent EC3 . . . . 253 C6
Crescent Arc 1 SE10 . . . . . 142 A6
Crescent Court Bsns Ctr 1
E16 . . . . .98 B3
Crescent Ct
Clapham Pk SW4 . . . . 159 D6
Crouch End N8 . . . . .49 D3
Kingston u T KT6. . . . . 197 D4
14 Sidcup DA15 . . . . 168 A1
Crescent Dr BR5. . . . . 211 A3
Crescent E EN4 . . . . .2 A5
Crescent Gdns Ruislip HA4 . .40 B2
Wimbledon SW19. . . . . . . 157 C1
Crescent Gr London SW4 . . 137 C1
Mitcham CR4 . . . . .202 C5
Crescent Ho
London SE13. . . . . 141 D3
5 Wimbledon SW20 . . . . . 178 D2
Crescent La SW4 . . . . 159 D6
Crescent Mans
Islington N5 . . . . .72 D3
Notting Hill W11 . . . . 244 B6
Crescent Par UB10. . . . . . . .82 C4
Crescent Pl SW3 . . . . 257 B4
Crescent Rd
Beckenham BR3 . . . . 185 D1
Chingford E4. . . . . .20 C4
Church End N3 . . . . .29 B2
Crouch End N8 . . . . .49 D3
Dagenham RM10 . . . . .81 D5
East Barnet EN4 . . . . .14 C6
Edmonton N9 . . . . .18 A3
Enfield EN2. . . . . .4 D1
Friern Barnet N11 . . . . .30 D6
Harringay N15 . . . . .50 D6
Kingston u T KT2 . . . . 176 D3
Leyton E10 . . . . .75 D6
Plaistow BR1 . . . . 187 A3
Shepperton TW17. . . . . . . 193 A4
Sidcup DA15 . . . . 167 D1
Upton Pk E6 . . . . .99 C6
West Ham E13 . . . . .99 A6
Wimbledon SW20. . . . . . . 178 D2
Woodford E18. . . . . .37 C2
Wood Green N22 . . . . .31 D2
Woolwich SE18. . . . . 122 D2
Crescent Rise
East Barnet EN4 . . . . .14 C6
3 Finchley N3 . . . . .29 C2
Wood Green N22 . . . . .31 D2
Crescent Row EC1 . . . . 242 A5
Crescent St N1 . . . . .72 B1
Crescent Stables SW15 . . . 157 A6
Crescent The Acton W3 . . . . .89 C1
Ashford TW15. . . . . 170 B5
Barnes SW13 . . . . 134 A3
Barnet EN5. . . . . .1 D3
Beckenham BR3 . . . . 185 C2
Bexley DA5 . . . . 168 C4
Coombe KT3 . . . . 177 A1
Dollis Hill NW2 . . . . .68 B5
East Finchley N2 . . . . .47 D6
East Molesey KT8. . . . . . . 195 C5
Friern Barnet N11 . . . . .31 A6
Harlington UB7 . . . . 127 B5
Harrow HA2 . . . . .42 A1
Ilford IG2 . . . . .56 C3
Loughton IG10 . . . . .21 D5
Lower Halliford TW17. . . . . 193 D2
Sidcup DA14 . . . . 189 D6
Southall UB1. . . . . 107 A4
Surbiton KT6. . . . . 198 A4
Sutton SM1. . . . . 218 B3
Thornton Heath CR0. . . . . . 205 B3
Walthamstow E17 . . . . .53 A4
Wembley HA0. . . . . .65 B6
West Wickham BR4 . . . . . . 208 C3
Wimbledon SW19. . . . . . . 157 C1
Crescent View IG10 . . . . . . .21 D6
Crescent W EN4 . . . . .2 A5
Crescentway N12. . . . . .30 C4
Crescent Way
London SE4. . . . . 141 C2
Orpington BR6. . . . . 227 C3
South Norwood SW16 . . . . 182 C3
Crescent Wood Rd SE21,
SE26 . . . . 162 A1
Cresford Rd
SW6. . . . . 135 D4 265 C1
Crespigny Rd NW4 . . . . .46 B3
Cressage Cl UB1. . . . . .85 C3
Cressage Ho 9 TW8 . . . . . 132 A6
Cressall Ho 14 E14 . . . . . . 119 C3
Cresset Ho 8 E9 . . . . .74 C2
Cresset Rd E9 . . . . .74 C2
Cresset St SW4 . . . . 137 D2
Cressfield Cl NW5 . . . . .71 A3
Cressida Rd N19 . . . . .49 D1
Cressingham Ct 1
DA17 . . . . 125 C3
Cressingham Gr SM1. . . . . 218 A4
Cressingham Rd
Burnt Oak HA8 . . . . .27 B3
Lewisham SE13 . . . . 142 A2
Cressington Cl 4 N16. . . . . .73 C3

Cress Mews BR1. . . . . 186 B5
Cresswell Gdns SW5 . . . . . 256 A2
Cresswell Ho HA9. . . . . .66 A5
Cresswell Pk SE3 . . . . 142 D2
Cresswell Pl
SW10. . . . . 114 A1 256 B2
Cresswell Rd
Croydon SE25 . . . . 206 A5
Feltham TW13 . . . . 173 A6
Twickenham TW1 . . . . 153 D5
Cresswell Way N21 . . . . . . .16 C4
Cressy Ct Hammersmith W6 . . . . 112 B3
6 Stepney E1 . . . . .96 C2
38 Stepney E1 . . . . .96 C2
Cressy Ho SW13 . . . . 134 B2
Cressy Hos 7 E1. . . . . .96 C2
Cressy Pl E1 . . . . .96 C2
Cressy Rd NW3 . . . . .70 D4
Cresta Ct W5 . . . . .88 B3
Cresta Ho 7 Bow E3. . . . . . .97 B4
Hampstead NW6 . . . . .70 B1
Crestbrook Ave N13. . . . . . .16 D1
Crestbrook Pl N13 . . . . .16 D1
Crest Ct NW4 . . . . .46 C4
Crest Dr EN3 . . . . .6 C5
Crestfield St N1, WC1 . . . . 233 B2
Crest Gdns HA4. . . . . .62 C5
Crest Ho 3 TW15. . . . . 170 C5
Creston Way KT4. . . . . 200 D1
Crest Rd Dollis Hill NW2 . . . .68 A6
Hayes BR2 . . . . 208 D2
South Croydon CR2. . . . . . 222 B1
Crest Sch of English HA8. . .32 C6
CrestThe Edmonton N13 . . .32 C6
Finchley N12. . . . . .29 D4
Hendon NW4 . . . . .46 C4
Surbiton KT5. . . . . 198 C4
10 West Norwood SW27 . . 182 D5
Crestview NW5 . . . . .71 B5
CrestView HA5 . . . . .40 D5
Crest View Dr BR5. . . . . . . 211 A4
Crestway SW15. . . . . 156 B5
Crestwood Way TW4 . . . . . 151 A6
Creswell Dr BR3 . . . . 207 D4
Creswick Ct W3. . . . . 110 D6
Creswick Rd W3 . . . . 110 D6
Creswick Wlk 7 Bow E3 . . . .97 C4
Temple Fortune NW11 . . . . .47 B5
Creton St SE18. . . . . 122 C3
Crewdson Rd SW9 . . . . . . 138 C5
Crewe Pl NW10 . . . . .89 D4
Crewkerne Ct SW11 . . . . . 266 D2
Crews St E14 . . . . 119 C2
Crewys Rd Child's Hill NW2. .69 B6
London SE15. . . . . 140 B3
Crichton Ave SM6. . . . . . . 219 D4
Crichton Rd SM5. . . . . 218 D1
Crichton St SW8. . . . . 137 C3
Cricket Ct 2 E6 . . . . 100 B4
Cricketers Arms Rd EN2. . . .5 A3
Cricketers Cl
Chessington KT9 . . . . 213 D4
Oakwood N14. . . . . .15 C4
Cricketers Mews 4
SW18. . . . . 157 D6
Cricketers Terr SM5 . . . . . 218 C5
Cricketers Wlk SE26 . . . . . 184 C5
Cricketfield Rd E5 . . . . .74 B4
Cricket Gn N3 . . . . 202 D5
Cricket Green Specl Sch 1
CR4. . . . . 202 C4
Cricket Ground Rd BR7. . . . 188 D2
Cricket La BR3. . . . . 185 A4
Cricket Row N2. . . . . .48 B6
Cricklade Ave SW2. . . . . . . 160 B2
CRICKLEWOOD. 68 D4
Cricklewood Broadway
NW2 . . . . .68 D4
Cricklewood La NW2. . . . . . .69 B5
Cricklewood Sta NW2. . . . . .68 C4
Cridland St E15. . . . . .98 D6
Crieff Ct 3 TW11 . . . . 175 C3
Crieff Rd SW18 . . . . 158 A5
Criffel Ave SW2. . . . . 159 D2
Crimscott St SE1. . 117 C3 263 B5
Crimsworth Rd
SW8. . . . . 137 D5 269 D3
Crinan St N1 . . . . . 94 A5 233 B4
Cringle St SW8 . . . 137 C5 269 A4
Cripplegate St EC1. . . . . . . 242 B4
Cripps Gn UB4. . . . . .84 B3
Crispe Ho
4 Barking IG11. . . . . 101 B5
Islington N1 . . . . 233 D5
Crispen Rd TW13 . . . . 173 A6
Crispian Cl NW10 . . . . .67 C4
Crispin Cl SM6. . . . . 220 A6
Crispin Cres SM6 . . . . 219 D6
Crispin Ct SE17 . . . . 263 A3
Crispin Mews 10 NW11. . . . .47 B4
Crispin Pl E1 . . . . 243 C2
Crispin Rd HA8 . . . . .27 A4
Crispin St E1 . . . . . 95 D2 243 C3
Crispin Way UB8. . . . . .82 B3
Crisp Rd W6 . . . . 112 C1
Cristowe Rd SW6 . . . . 135 B3
Criterion Bldgs KT7. . . . . . 197 B2
Criterion Mews N19 . . . . . . .71 D6
Crittall's Cnr DA14. . . . . . . 190 C3

Crittenden Lo BR4. . . . . . . 207 C1
Crockerton Rd SW17. . . . . . 158 D2
Crockham Way SE9 . . . . . . 188 C6
Crocus Cl CR0 . . . . 206 D1
Crocus Field EN5 . . . . .13 B5
Croft Ave BR4. . . . . 208 A1
Croft Cl Edgware NW7. . . . . .11 C1
Elmstead BR7. . . . . .188 B5
Erith DA17. . . . . 125 B1
Harlington UB7 . . . . 127 A5
Hillingdon UB10 . . . . .60 C1
Croft Ct London SE13. . . . . 164 A5
Ruislip HA4. . . . . .39 D1
Croftdown Rd NW5 . . . . . . .71 B5
Croft End Cl KT9 . . . . 214 B5
Crofters Cl TW7. . . . . 152 B6
Crofters Ct 9 SE8. . . . . . . 119 A4
Crofters Way
NW1 . . . . 93 D6 232 C6
Croft Gdns Ealing W7 . . . . . 109 A4
Ruislip HA4. . . . . .39 D1
Croft Ho Putney SW15. . . . . 157 A5
Croft Lodge Cl IG8. . . . . . . .52 B4
Croft Mews 3 N12. . . . . . . .14 A1
CROFTON 227 B6
Crofton Ave Chiswick W4 . . 133 B5
Orpington BR6. . . . . 227 A6
Sidcup DA5. . . . . 168 D4
Crofton Gate Way SE4. . . . 163 A6
Crofton Gr E4 . . . . .36 B6
Crofton Inf Sch BR5. . . . . . 211 B3
Crofton Jun Sch BR5. . . . . 211 B2
Crofton La BR5, BR6 . . . . . 211 B2
Crofton Park Rd SE4 . . . . . 163 B5
Crofton Park Sta SE4 . . . . . 163 B6
Crofton Rd
Camberwell SE5 . . . . 139 C3
Locksbottom BR6 . . . . 226 C5
Newham E13 . . . . .99 B3
Crofton Roman Villa*
BR6. . . . . 227 C6
Crofton Terr Homerton E5 . . .75 A3
Richmond TW9 . . . . 132 C1
Crofton Way Enfield EN2 . . . .4 C3
New Barnet EN5. . . . . .13 D5
Croft Rd Carshalton SM1. . . 218 C3
Enfield EN3. . . . . .7 A4
Merton SW19 . . . . 180 A3
Plaistow BR1 . . . . 187 A4
South Norwood SW16 . . . . 182 C3
Crofts La N22. . . . . .32 C3
Crofts Rd HA1 . . . . .43 A4
Crofts St E1 . . . . 118 A6
Croft St SE8 . . . . 119 A2
Crofts The TW1 . . . . 193 C5
Croft The Barnet EN5. . . . . . .1 A1
Chingford E4. . . . . .20 C2
Ealing W5 . . . . .88 A2
Edgware HA8 . . . . .26 D3
Harlesden NW10 . . . . .89 D5
Heston TW5 . . . . 129 A5
New Malden KT3 . . . . 199 C4
Pinner HA5. . . . . .41 B2
Ruislip HA4. . . . . .62 C4
Wembley HA0. . . . . .65 C3
Croft Villas HA1. . . . . .43 A3
Croft Way
Richmond TW10 . . . . 153 B1
Sidcup DA15 . . . . 167 C1
Crogsland Rd NW1. . . . . . . .71 A1
Croham Cl CR2 . . . . 221 C1
Croham Manor Rd CR2. . . . 221 C2
Croham Park Ave CR2 . . . . 221 D3
Croham Rd CR2. . . . . 221 C2
Croham Valley Rd CR2. . . . . 222 B1
Croindene Rd SW16. . . . . . 182 A2
Crokesley Ho 2 HA8. . . . . . .27 A1
Cromartie Rd N19 . . . . .49 D2
Cromarty Ct 7 BR1. . . . . . . 187 C1
Cromarty Ho 8 E1. . . . . .97 A2
Cromarty Rd HA8 . . . . .10 D2
Cromberdale Ct N17 . . . . . .34 A2
Crombie Cl IG4. . . . . .56 B4
Crombie Mews 5 SW11. . . 136 C3
Crombie Rd DA15. . . . . 167 B3
Cromdale Ct N16 . . . . .51 D2
Crome Ho UB5. . . . . .85 A5
Cromer Cl UB8 . . . . .83 A1
Cromer Ct
Streatham SW16 . . . . 160 A1
Wandsworth SW18 . . . . . . 157 B5
Crome Rd NW10 . . . . .67 C3
Cromer Mans SM2 . . . . . . 217 D3
Cromer Pl 5 BR6. . . . . 211 B1
Cromer Rd Barnet EN5 . . . . . .2 A3
Croydon SE25 . . . . 206 B6
Dagenham RM6 . . . . .59 A3
Harlington TW6 . . . . 126 C3
Leyton E10 . . . . .54 B2
Streatham SW17 . . . . 181 A4
Tottenham N17. . . . . .34 A1
Woodford IG8. . . . . .37 A6
Cromer Rd W TW6 . . . . 126 C2

Cromer Road Prim Sch
EN5. .2 A2
Cromer St WC1 . . . .94 A4 233 B1
Cromer Terr Dalston E8 . . . .74 A3
🔳3 Ilford RM6. . . . . .58 B4
Cromford Cl BR6. . . . . .227 C5
Cromford Path 🔳1 E5. . . . .74 D4
Cromford Rd SW18 . . . . . .157 C6
Cromford Way KT3. . . . . . .177 B2
Cromlix Cl BR7 . . . . .188 D1
Crompton Ct SW3 . . . . . . .257 A4
Crompton Ho
  Borough The SE1. . . . . . . .262 B5
  Paddington W2. . . . . .236 C5
  South Lambeth SW8. . . . . .269 B1
Crompton Pl EN3 . . . . .7 C5
Crompton St W2. . . .92 B3 236 C5
Cromwell Ave
  Bromley BR2. . . . . .209 B5
  Hammersmith W6 . . . . .112 B2
  Highgate N6 . . . . .49 B1
  New Malden KT3. . . . . . . .199 D4
Cromwell Cl Acton W3 . . . .111 A5
  Bromley BR2. . . . . .209 B5
  East Finchley N2. . . . . .48 B5
  🔳2 Gunnersbury W4. . . . . .110 D1
  Walton-on-T KT12 . . . . . . .194 B1
Cromwell Cres
  SW5. . . . . .113 C2 255 A4
Cromwell Ct Enfield EN3 . . .18 D6
  🔳15 Kingston u T KT2 . . . . .176 C3
  Wembley HA0. . . . . .88 A5
Cromwell Ctr
  Barking IG11 . . . . .102 A4
  North Acton NW10. . . . . . . .89 B4
Cromwell Ctr The RM8. . . . .59 B2
Cromwell Est E10. . . . . .53 A1
Cromwell Gdns
  SW7. . . . . .114 B3 256 D5
Cromwell Gr W6. . . . . .112 C3
Cromwell Ho
  Battersea SW11. . . . . .268 B1
  🔳2 Croydon CR0. . . . . .220 D5
  Muswell Hill N10. . . . . .31 B3
  Putney SW15 . . . . .134 A1
Cromwell Hospl (BUPA)
  SW5. . . . . .113 D2 255 C4
Cromwell Lo Barking IG11. . .79 C3
  🔳40 Bethnal Green E1. . . . . .96 C3
Cromwell Mans SW5. . . . . .255 B4
Cromwell Mews SW7 . . . . .256 C4
Cromwell Pl
  🔳5 Acton W3. . . . . .111 A5
  Barbican EC1 . . . . .242 B4
  Highgate N6 . . . . .49 B1
  Mortlake SW14 . . . . .133 A2
  South Kensington
    SW7 . . . . .114 B2 256 D4
Cromwell Rd
  Beckenham BR3. . . . . .207 A6
  Brixton SW9 . . . . .138 D4
  Feltham TW13 . . . . .150 B3
  Finchley N3. . . . . .30 A2
  Hayes UB3 . . . . .83 B1
  Hounslow TW3 . . . . .129 C1
  Kingston u T KT2. . . . . . . .176 A2
  Muswell Hill N10. . . . . .31 A3
  South Kensington SW7. . . .256 B4
  Teddington TW11 . . . . . . .175 A4
  Thornton Heath CR0. . . . . .205 B2
  Upton E7. . . . . .77 C1
  Walthamstow E17 . . . . .54 A4
  Walton-on-T KT12 . . . . . . .194 B1
  Wembley HA0. . . . . .88 A5
  Wimbledon SW19. . . . . . . .179 D5
  Worcester Pk KT4. . . . . . . .215 C5
Cromwell St TW3 . . . . .129 C1
Cromwell Trad Ctr IG11. . . .101 C4
Cromwell Twr EC2 . . . . . . .242 B4
Crondace Rd
  SW6. . . . . .135 C4 265 B1
Crondall Ct 🔳7 N1. . . . . .95 C5
Crondall Ho SW15 . . . . . . .156 A3
Crondall Pl 🔳15 N1. . . . . .95 C5
Crondall St N1. . . . . .95 C5
Crone Ct 🔳5 NW6. . . . . .91 B5
Cronin St SE15. . . . . .139 D5
CROOKED BILLET 178 C4
Crooked Billet
  Chingford E4. . . . . .35 C3
  Wimbledon SW19. . . . . . . .178 C4
Crooked Billet Yd 🔳18 E2 . . .95 C4
Crooked Usage N3. . . . . . . .47 A6
Crooke Rd SE8. . . . . .119 A1
Crookham Rd
  SW6. . . . . .135 B4 264 C1
Crook Log DA6. . . . . .146 D1
Crook Log L Ctr DA7 . . . . .146 D2
Crook Log Prim Sch
  DA6. . . . . .146 D1
Crookston Rd SE9 . . . . . . .144 C2
Croombs Rd E16. . . . . .99 C2
Croom's Hill SE10. . . . . . . .142 B5
Croom's Hill Gr SE10. . . . . .142 A5
Cropley Ct N1 . . . . .235 C4
Cropley St N1 . . . . .95 C5 235 C4

Croppath Rd RM10. . . . . . . .81 C4
Cropthorne Ct W9 . . . . . . .229 B1
Crosbie 🔳10 NW9 . . . . .27 D1
Crosbie Ho 🔳20 E17. . . . . . . .53 D6
Crosby Cl TW13 . . . . .173 A6
Crosby Ct
  Borough The SE1. . . . . . . .252 C2
  East Finchley N2. . . . . .48 A5
  🔳7 New Southgate N11 . . . . .31 B6
Crosby Ho
  🔳18 Cubitt Town E14. . . . . .120 A3
  Forest Gate E7 . . . . .77 A2
Crosby Rd
  Dagenham RM10 . . . . .103 D6
  Upton E7. . . . . .77 A2
Crosby Row SE1 . . . .117 B4 252 C2
Crosby Sq EC3 . . . . .243 A2
Crosby Wlk 🔳3 Dalston E8 . .73 D2
  Streatham SE24. . . . . .160 C4
Crosfield Ct 🔳3 W10. . . . . . . .90 D1
Crosfield Ho W11. . . . . . . .244 A5
Crosier Cl SE3. . . . . .144 A3
Crosier Rd UB10 . . . . .61 A4
Crosier Way HA4. . . . . .61 C5
Crosland Pl 🔳5 SW11 . . . . .137 A2
Crossbow Ho Ealing W13 . .109 B5
  🔳15 Shoreditch N1. . . . . .95 C6
Crossbrook Rd SE3 . . . . . . .144 A2
Cross Cl SE15. . . . . .140 B3
Cross Ct London SE5 . . . . .139 B2
🔳1 Thamesmead SE28 . . . . . .124 B6
Cross Deep TW1. . . . . .153 A2
Cross Deep Gdns TW1. . . .152 D2
Crossfield Rd
  Hampstead NW3 . . . . .70 B2
  London N17. . . . . .51 A6
Crossfield St SE8 . . . . .141 C5
Crossford St SW9. . . . . . . .138 B3
Crossgate Edgware HA8 . . . .10 C1
  Wembley UB6. . . . . .65 B2
Crossharbour Sta E14. . . . .119 D3
Cross Ho N8. . . . . .50 B5
Cross Keys Cl
  🔳5 Edmonton N9 . . . . .18 A2
  Marylebone W1 . . . . .238 B3
Cross La
  City of London EC3 . . . . . .253 A5
  Hornsey N8. . . . . .50 B5
  Old Bexley DA5. . . . . .169 B4
Cross Lances Rd TW3 . . . . .129 D1
Crossland Rd CR7. . . . . . . .204 D3
Crosslands Ave
  Ealing W5. . . . . .110 B5
  Southall UB2. . . . . .107 B1
Crosslands Rd KT19. . . . . . .215 B2
Crosslet Ct 🔳3 New Cross SE14. . . . . .141 B5
  Streatham SW16 . . . . .181 B6
Crosslet St SE17. . . . . .262 D4
Crosslet Vale SE10 . . . . . . .141 D4
Crossley St N7. . . . . .72 C2
Crossman Hos 🔳19 SW12 . .160 A4
Crossmead SE9. . . . . .166 B3
Crossmead Ave UB6. . . . . . .85 C4
Crossmount Ho 🔳13 SE5 . .139 A5
Crossness Rd IG11. . . . . . . .101 D4
Cross Rd Belmont HA3. . . . . .25 A1
  Camberwell SE5. . . . . .139 C3
  Chingford E4. . . . . .20 C3
  Croydon CR0. . . . . .205 B1
  Enfield EN1. . . . . .5 C1
  Feltham TW13 . . . . .173 A6
  Finchley N2. . . . . .30 C1
  Friern Barnet N11 . . . . .31 B5
  Harrow HA1. . . . . .42 B4
  Ilford RM6. . . . . .58 C2
  Keston Mark BR2 . . . . .226 A6
  Kingston u T KT2. . . . . . . .176 B3
  Merton SW19 . . . . .179 C3
  Romford RM7. . . . . .59 C6
  Sidcup DA14. . . . . .190 B6
  South Harrow HA2. . . . . . . .63 D5
  Sutton SM1. . . . . .218 B3
  Wood Green N22 . . . . .32 C3
Cross St 🔳2 Edmonton N18 . .34 A5
  Hampton TW12. . . . . .174 A5
  Islington N1. . . . . .94 D6 234 D6
  Mortlake SW13 . . . . .133 C2
Crossthwaite Ave SE5,
  SE24 . . . . .139 B1
Crosstrees Ho 🔳7 E14 . . . .119 C3
Crosswall EC3 . . . . .117 D6 253 C6
Crossway Dagenham RM8. . .80 C5
  Ealing W13 . . . . .87 A3
  Enfield EN1. . . . . .17 C4
  Finchley N12. . . . . .30 B4
  Hayes UB3 . . . . .106 A5
  Hendon NW9 . . . . .45 D5
  Kingsland E8, N16 . . . . .73 C3
  Petts Wood BR5 . . . . .211 B4
  Pinner HA5. . . . . .22 B1
  Ruislip HA4. . . . . .62 C4
  Thamesmead SE28. . . . . . .102 D1
  West Barnes KT3, SW20 . . .200 C5
  Woodford IG8. . . . . .37 C6
Crossway Ct SE4. . . . . .141 A3
Crossway Par N22 . . . . .32 D3
Crossways Ashford TW16. . .171 D3
  South Croydon CR2. . . . . . .223 B1
  Sutton SM2. . . . . .218 B1

Crossways Acad SE4 . . . . .141 A3
Crossways Par CR2 . . . . . .223 B1
Crossways Rd
  Beckenham BR3 . . . . .207 C5
  Mitcham CR4 . . . . .203 B6
Crossways The
  Heston TW5. . . . . .129 B5
  Wembley HA9. . . . . .66 C6
Crossway The
  Chislehurst SE9 . . . . .165 D2
  Hillingdon UB10 . . . . .82 B5
  Tottenham N22. . . . . .32 D3
Cross Way The HA3. . . . . . .24 C1
Crosswell CT TW17. . . . . . .171 A1
Croston St E8. . . . . .96 A6
Crothall Cl N13 . . . . .16 B1
Crouch Ave IG11. . . . . .102 B5
Crouch Cl BR3. . . . . .185 C4
Crouch Croft SE9 . . . . .166 C1
CROUCH END. 49 D3
Crouch End Hill N8 . . . . .49 D2
Crouch Hall Ct N19 . . . . .50 A1
Crouch Hall Rd N8. . . . . . . .49 D2
Crouch Hill N4, N8, N19 . . . .50 A2
Crouch Hill Sta N4. . . . . . . .50 B2
Crouchmans Cl SE21,
  SE26. . . . . .162 A1
Crouch Rd NW10. . . . . .67 B1
Crowborough Ct W13 . . . . .109 C6
Crowborough Path WD19 . .22 D6
Crowborough Rd SW17 . . .181 A5
Crowden Way SE28 . . . . . .124 C6
Crowder Cl N12. . . . . .30 A3
Crowder St E1. . . . . .118 B6
Crowfield Ho N5. . . . . .73 A4
Crowfoot Cl
  Hackney Wick E9 . . . . .75 B3
  Woolwich SE28. . . . . .123 C5
Crowhurst SE25. . . . . .206 A6
Crowhurst Cl SW9 . . . . . . .138 C3
Crowhurst Ct N1. . . . . .34 B2
Crowhurst Ho 🔳21 SW9 . . .138 B3
Crow La RM7, RM8. . . . . . . .59 D2
Crowland Ave UB3 . . . . . . .105 D2
Crowland Gdns N14. . . . . . .16 A4
Crowland Ho NW8 . . . . . . .229 A5
Crowland Prim Sch N15. . . .52 A4
Crowland Rd
  South Norwood CR7. . . . . .205 B5
  South Tottenham N15 . . . . . .51 D4
Crowlands Ave RM7. . . . . . .59 D3
Crowland Terr N1 . . . . .73 B1
Crowland Wlk SM4. . . . . . .202 A3
Crowley Cres CR0. . . . . . . .220 C3
Crowline Wlk 🔳1 N1. . . . . . . .73 A2
Crowmarsh Gdns SE23 . . .162 C4
Crown Arc KT1. . . . . .175 D1
Crown Bldgs 🔳4 E4. . . . . . . .20 B3
Crownbourne Ct SM1 . . . . .217 D4
Crown Cl Bow E3. . . . . .97 C6
  Edgware NW7 . . . . .11 D2
  Hampstead NW6 . . . . .69 D2
  Hayes UB3 . . . . .105 D4
  Walton-on-T KT12 . . . . . . .194 C2
  Wood Green N22 . . . . .32 C2
Crown Close Bsns Ctr 🔳12
  E3. . . . . .97 C6
Crown Ct Bromley BR1 . . . .209 D4
  City of London EC4 . . . . . .242 B1
  Harrow HA2. . . . . .42 C1
  Lee SE12. . . . . .165 B5
  🔳11 Muswell Hill N10. . . . . . .31 A3
  🔳4 Putney SW15. . . . . .134 D1
  St Giles WC2. . . . . .240 B1
  St John's Wood NW8 . . . . .230 B1
  🔳3 Twickenham TW1. . . . . .153 B4
Crown Dale SE19 . . . . .183 A5
Crowndale Ct NW1. . . . . . .232 C4
Crowndale Rd
  NW1. . . . . .93 C5 232 B4
Crowne Ho SE1. . . . . .252 B3
Crownfield Ave IG2 . . . . . . .57 C4
Crownfield Rd E15. . . . . .76 B4
Crowngate Ho 🔳33 E3. . . . . . .97 B5
Crown Hill CR0 . . . . .221 A5
Crownhill Rd NW10. . . . . . . .89 D6
Crown Ho Ruislip HA4. . . . . .40 A1
  Wembley HA9. . . . . .66 B3
  🔳3 Woolwich SE18. . . . . . .123 A2
Crown La
  Bromley Comm BR2. . . . . .209 D4
  Chislehurst BR7 . . . . .189 A2
  Merton SM4 . . . . .201 C6
  Osidge N14. . . . . .15 C3
  South Norwood SE19,
    SW16. . . . . .182 C5
Crown Lane Gdns SE27. . . .182 C5
Crown Lane Prim Sch
  SE27. . . . . .182 D5
Crown Lane Spur BR2. . . . .209 D3
Crownleigh Ct SW2. . . . . . .160 C6
Crown Lo Chelsea SW3. . . .257 B3
  Finchley N3. . . . . .29 B1
Crownmead Way RM7. . . . . .59 D5
Crown Mews
  🔳2 Newham E13. . . . . .99 C6
  🔳9 Stepney E1. . . . . .96 D2
Crown Mill CR4. . . . . .202 C4
Crown Office Row EC4 . . . .251 A6
Crown Par London N14. . . . .15 C3

Crown Par continued
  Morden SM4. . . . . .201 D5
Crown Pas
  Kingston u T KT1. . . . . . . .175 D1
  St James SW1 . . . . .249 B3
Crown Pl Broadgate EC2. . .243 A4
  Kentish Town NW5 . . . . .71 B2
Crown Point Par SE19 . . . .182 D4
Crown Rd Enfield EN1. . . . . . .6 B2
  Ilford IG6 . . . . .57 B5
  Kingston u T KT3. . . . . . . .177 A2
  Morden SM4. . . . . .201 D5
  Muswell Hill N10. . . . . .31 A3
  Ruislip HA4. . . . . .62 D3
  Sutton SM1. . . . . .217 D4
  Twickenham TW1 . . . . .153 B5
Crown Reach SW1 . . . . . . .259 D1
Crown St Acton W3 . . . . . . .110 C5
  Camberwell SE5. . . . . .139 A5
  Dagenham RM10 . . . . .81 D2
  Harrow HA1. . . . . .42 C1
Crownstone Ct 🔳1 SW2. . .160 C6
Crownstone Rd SW2. . . . . .160 C6
Crown Terr TW9. . . . . .132 B1
Crown Trad Ctr UB3 . . . . . .105 C4
Crowntree Cl TW7 . . . . . . .130 D6
Crown Way UB7 . . . . .104 B5
Crown Wlk HA9. . . . . .66 B5
Crown Woods La SE18 . . . .144 D3
Crown Woods Sch SE9. . . .167 A6
Crown Woods Way SE9. . . .167 B6
Crown Yard TW3 . . . . .130 A2
Crowshott Ave HA7 . . . . . . .25 C2
Crows Rd Barking IG11. . . . .78 D2
  Mill Meads E3, E15. . . . . . . .98 B4
Crowther Ave TW8 . . . . . . .110 A2
Crowther Cl SW6 .135 B6 264 D5
Crowther Rd SE25. . . . . . . .206 A5
Crowthorne Cl SW18. . . . . .157 B3
Crowthorne Rd W10. . . . . . .90 D1
Croxall Ho KT12. . . . . .194 C3
Croxden Cl HA8. . . . . .44 C6
Croxden Wlk SM4. . . . . . . .202 A3
Croxford Gdns N22. . . . . . . .32 D3
Croxley Cl BR5. . . . . .190 B1
Croxley Gn BR5 . . . . .190 B2
Croxley Rd W9 . . . . .91 B4
Croxted Cl SE21. . . . . .161 A4
Croxted Rd SE21, SE24 . . .161 B3
Croxteth Ho 🔳11 SW8. . . . .137 D3
Croxton 🔳17 KT1. . . . . .176 C1
Croyde Ave Greenford UB6. .86 A4
  Hayes UB3 . . . . .105 C2
Croyde Cl DA15. . . . . .167 B4
Croyden Ct HA0. . . . . .65 D2
CROYDON. 221 B5
Croydon N17. . . . . .33 B1
Croydon Airport Ind Est
  CR0. . . . . .220 B2
Croydon Coll CR0. . . . . . . .221 B6
Croydon Coll Annexe 🔳10
  CR0. . . . . .205 B1
Croydon Coll (Selhurst
  Tertiary Ctr) SE25. . . . . . .205 B4
Croydon Flyover The
  CR0. . . . . .221 A5
Croydon Gr CR0 . . . . .204 D1
Croydon Ho Lambeth SE1. .251 B2
  Thornton Heath CR0. . . . . .204 B3
Croydon Prim Independant
  Sch 🔳8 CR0 . . . . .205 C1
Croydon Rd
  Bandonhill CR0, SM5,
    SM6 . . . . .219 C5
  Beckenham BR3 . . . . .207 A6
  Coney Hall BR2, BR4. . . . . .224 D5
  Harlington TW6 . . . . .126 D2
  Keston Mark BR2, BR4,
    BR6. . . . . .225 C5
  Mitcham CR0, CR4 . . . . . . .203 C4
  Newham E13. . . . . .98 D3
  Penge SE20 . . . . .184 C2
  Waddon CR0. . . . . .220 B4
Croydon Rd Ind Est BR3. . .206 D5
Croydon's Sports Arena
  SE25. . . . . .206 C4
Croydon Valley Trade Pk 🔳2
  CR0. . . . . .204 A2
Croyland Rd N9. . . . . .18 A3
Croylands Dr KT6. . . . . . . .198 A2
Croysdale Ave TW16. . . . . .194 A6
Crozier Ho
  Blackheath Pk SE3. . . . . . .143 B2
  South Lambeth SW8. . . . . .270 C3
Crozier Terr E9 . . . . .74 D3
Crucible Cl RM6 . . . . .58 B3
Crucifix La SE1 . . . .117 C4 253 A2
Cruden Ho 🔳15 Bow E3. . . . . .97 B5
  🔳11 Camberwell SE17 . . . . .138 D6
Cruden St N1. . . . . . .94 D6 234 D5
Cruickshank St WC1 . . . . . .234 A2
Cruikshank Ho NW8 . . . . . .230 B4
Cruikshank Rd E15. . . . . . . .76 C3
Crummock Gdns NW9 . . . . .45 C4
Crumpsall St SE2. . . . . .124 C2
Crundale Ave NW9. . . . . . . .44 C4
Crunden Rd CR2. . . . . .221 B1
Crusader Gdns CR0. . . . . . .221 C5
Crusader Ho EC1 . . . . .241 C5
Crusader Ind Est N4 . . . . . . .51 A3

Crusoe Ct E11. . . . . .76 D5
Crusoe Mews N16. . . . . .73 B6
Crusoe Rd CR4 . . . . .180 D3
Crutched Friars
  EC3. . . . . .117 C6 253 B6
Crutchfield La KT12. . . . . . .194 B1
Crutchley Rd SE6 . . . . .164 C2
Crystal Ct SE19 . . . . .183 D5
Crystal Ctr The 🔳1 HA1. . . . .42 D4
Crystal Ho SE18. . . . . .123 D1
CRYSTAL PALACE 184 A5
Crystal Palace Farm Pk★
  SE20. . . . . .184 A5
Crystal Palace Mus★
  SE19. . . . . .183 D4
Crystal Palace National
  Sports Ctr SE19. . . . . .184 A4
Crystal Palace Par SE19. . .183 D5
Crystal Palace Park Rd
  SE26. . . . . .184 B5
Crystal Palace Rd SE22. . . .162 A6
Crystal Palace Sta SE19 . . .184 A4
Crystal Palace Station Rd
  SE19. . . . . .184 A4
Crystal Terr SE19. . . . . .183 B4
Crystal View Ct BR1. . . . . . .186 B6
Crystal Way
  Dagenham RM8 . . . . .58 C2
  Harrow HA1. . . . . .42 D4
Crystal Wharf N1 . . . . .234 D3
Cuba Dr EN3. . . . . .6 C3
Cuba St E14 . . . . .119 C4
Cubitt Bldg SW1. . . . . .258 C1
Cubitt Ho 🔳4 SW4. . . . . . . .159 C5
Cubitt Sq UB2 . . . . .108 A5
Cubitt St WC1 . . . . .94 B4 233 D1
Cubitt Terr SW4. . . . . .137 C2
CUBITT TOWN. 120 A2
Cubitt Town Jun & Inf Sch
  E14. . . . . .120 A3
Cuckoo Ave W7 . . . . .86 C3
Cuckoo Dene W7 . . . . .86 B2
Cuckoo Hall La N9 . . . . .18 D4
Cuckoo Hall Prim Sch
  N9. . . . . .18 C4
Cuckoo Hill HA5 . . . . .40 C6
Cuckoo Hill Dr HA5. . . . . . . .40 C6
Cuckoo Hill Rd HA5 . . . . . . .40 D5
Cuckoo La W7 . . . . .108 C6
Cuda's Cl KT19 . . . . .215 D4
Cuddington SE17 . . . . .262 B4
Cuddington Ave KT19,
  KT4. . . . . .215 D5
Cuddington Com Prim Sch
  KT4. . . . . .215 D5
Cudham La N BR6. . . . . . . .227 C1
Cudham St SE6 . . . . .164 A4
Cudworth Ho SW8 . . . . . . .269 B1
Cudworth St E1. . . . . .96 B3
Cuff Cres SE9. . . . . .165 D5
Cuffley Ho 🔳3 W10 . . . . .90 C2
Cuff Point 🔳12 E2 . . . . .95 D4
Culand Ho SE17. . . . . .263 A3
Culford Gdns
  SW3. . . . . .114 D2 257 D3
Culford Gr N1 . . . . .73 C2
Culford Mans SW3. . . . . . .257 D3
Culford Mews N1. . . . . .73 C2
Culford Rd Kingsland N1. . . .73 C2
  Shoreditch N1. . . . . .95 C6
Culgaith Gdns EN2. . . . . .4 A1
Culham Ho
  🔳21 Paddington W2 . . . . .91 C2
  🔳33 Shoreditch E2 . . . . .95 D4
Cullen Ho W9. . . . . .91 B5
Cullen Way NW10. . . . . .89 A3
Culling Rd SE16. . . . . .118 C5
Cullington Cl HA3. . . . . .43 C5
Cullingworth Rd NW10. . . . .68 B3
Culloden Cl 🔳21 SE16. . . . . .118 A1
Culloden Prim Sch 🔳16
  E14. . . . . .98 A1
Culloden Rd EN2. . . . . .4 D3
Culloden St E14 . . . . .98 A1
Cullum St EC3 . . . . .253 A6
Culmington Mans W13. . . .109 C6
Culmington Par W13. . . . . .109 C6
Culmington Rd
  Ealing W13, W5. . . . . .109 C5
  South Croydon CR2. . . . . . .221 A1
Culmore Rd SE15 . . . . .140 C5
Culmstock Rd SW11 . . . . . .159 A6
Culpepper Cl N18. . . . . .34 B5
Culpepper Ct SE11. . . . . . .261 A4
Culross Bldgs NW1 . . . . . . .233 A4
Culross Cl N15. . . . . .51 A5
Culross St W1 . . . . .115 A6 248 A5
Culsac Rd KT6. . . . . .214 A6
Culver Ct SW18. . . . . .157 D5
Culverden Rd SW12. . . . . . .159 C2
Culver Gr HA7. . . . . .25 C1
Culverhouse WC1. . . . . . . .240 C3
Culverhouse Gdns
  SW16. . . . . .160 B1
Culverlands Cl HA7. . . . . . . .25 B6
Culverlands Ct N20 . . . . . . .14 B3
Culverley Rd SE6 . . . . .164 A3
Culvers Ave SM5. . . . . .218 D6
Culvers House Prim Sch
  CR4. . . . . .203 A1

Culvers Retreat SM5 . . . . 218 D6
Culverstone Cl BR2 . . 208 D4
Culvers Way SM5 . . . . 218 D6
Culvert Ct SW11 . . . . . 137 A3
Culverton Ct 8 DA14 . . 190 A6
Culvert Pl SW11 . . . . . 137 A3
Culvert Rd London SW11 . 136 D3
South Tottenham N15 . . . . .51 C4
Culworth Ho NW8 . . . . 230 A4
Culworth St NW8 . . . . . 230 A3
Cumber Ho SW18 . . . . . 157 C3
Cumberland Ave
Falconwood DA16 . . . . . 145 D1
Wembley NW10 . . . . .88 D4
Cumberland Bsns Pk
NW10 . . . . .88 D4
Cumberland Cl Dalston E8 .73 D2
2 Twickenham TW1 . . . . 153 B5
8 Wimbledon SW20 . . . 178 D3
Cumberland Comp Sch
E13 . . . . .99 C3
Cumberland Cres W14 . . 254 B4
Cumberland Ct
4 Croydon CR0 . . . . . . .205 B1
7 Finchley N3 . . . . .29 B1
Harrow HA1 . . . . .42 C6
Marylebone W1 . . . . . . 237 D1
Woodford IG8 . . . . .37 B3
Cumberland Dr
Chessington KT9 . . . . . .214 B5
Erith DA7 . . . . 147 A5
Hinchley Wood KT10 . . . 213 A6
Cumberland Gate
W1 . . . . 114 D6 247 D6
Cumberland Gdns
Church End NW4 . . . . . . .29 A1
Finsbury WC1 . . . . 234 A2
Cumberland Ho
Edmonton N9 . . . . .18 C3
Kingston u T KT2 . . . . . 176 D3
Paddington W2 . . . . 236 A5
1 Putney SW15 . . . . . 156 C4
Woolwich SE28 . . . . . . .123 B4
Cumberland Mans
Marylebone W1 . . . . . . 237 C2
7 West Hampstead NW6 . .69 C3
Cumberland Market
NW1 . . . . .93 B4 231 D2
Cumberland Mills Sq
E14 . . . . .120 B1
Cumberland Park Ind Est
NW10 . . . . .90 A4
Cumberland Pk W3 . . . . 111 A6
Cumberland Pl
Catford SE6 . . . . 164 D3
Regent's Pk NW1 . . . . . 231 C2
Sunbury TW16 . . . . 194 A5
Cumberland Rd
Acton W3 . . . . 111 A6
Ashford TW15 . . . . 148 A1
Barnes SW13 . . . . 134 A4
Beckenham BR2 . . . . . . 208 D6
Croydon SE25 . . . . .206 B3
Edmonton N9 . . . . .18 C3
Hanwell W7 . . . . 108 D4
Harrow HA1 . . . . .41 D4
Higham Hill E17 . . . . . . .35 A1
Manor Pk E12 . . . . .77 D4
Newham E13 . . . . .99 B3
Richmond TW9 . . . . 132 C5
Stanmore HA7, HA8 . . . . .44 B6
Wood Green N22 . . . . . . .32 B1
Cumberland St
SW1 . . . . .115 B1 258 D2
Cumberland Terr NW1 . . 231 C3
Cumberland Terrace Mews
NW1 . . . . 231 C2
Cumberland Villas W3 . . .111 A6
Cumberland Wharf 12
SE16 . . . . .118 C4
Cumberlow Ave SE25 . . .206 A4
Cumbernauld Gdns
TW16 . . . . 171 D5
Cumberton Rd N17 . . . . . .33 B2
Cumbrae Gdns KT6 . . . . 213 D6
Cumbrian Gdns NW2 . . . .69 A6
Cuming Mus ★ SE17 . . . 262 A3
Cumming St N1 . . . . . . 233 D3
Cumnor Cl 23 SW9 . . . . . 138 B3
Cumnor Gdns KT17 . . . . 216 A2
Cumnor Rd SM2 . . . . . . 218 A2
Cunard Cres N21 . . . . . . .17 B5
Cunard Pl EC3 . . . . 243 B1
Cunard Rd NW10 . . . . . . .89 B4
Cunard Wlk 3 SE16 . . . .119 A2
Cundy Rd E16 . . . . .99 C1
Cundy St SW1 . . . 115 A2 258 B3
Cunliffe Rd KT19 . . . . . . 215 D4
Cunliffe St SW16 . . . . . .181 C4
Cunningham Cl
Dagenham RM6 . . . . .58 C4
West Wickham BR4 . . . . 223 D6
Cunningham Ct
Harrow HA1 . . . . .42 B4
Paddington W2 . . . . 236 C5
Cunningham Ho 16 SE5 . .139 B5
Cunningham Pk HA1 . . . . .42 B4
Cunningham Pl
NW8 . . . . .92 B3 236 C6
Cunningham Rd N15 . . . . .52 A5

Cunnington St W4 . . . . . .111 A2
Cupar Rd SW11 . . . . . . 268 B2
Cupola Cl BR1 . . . . 187 B5
Cureton St SW1 . . 115 D2 259 D3
Curie Gdns NW9 . . . . . . .27 C1
Curie Ho 1 HA9 . . . . . . .67 C5
Curlew Cl SE28 . . . . . . 124 D6
Curlew Ct KT6 . . . . 214 C5
Curlew Ho Brockley SE4 . .141 A1
Enfield EN3 . . . . .18 D6
7 Peckham SE15 . . . . . 139 D4
Curlew St SE1 . . . 117 C4 253 D2
Curlew Way UB4 . . . . . . .84 D2
Curness St SE13 . . . . . . 142 A1
Curnick's La SE27 . . . . . .183 A6
Curran Ave Bexley DA15 . 167 D6
Hackbridge SM6 . . . . . . 219 A5
Curran Rd SW3 . . . . . . 257 A3
Currey Rd UB6 . . . . .64 B2
Curricle St W3 . . . . .111 C5
Currie Hill Cl SW19 . . . . 179 B6
Currie Ho 13 SW12 . . . . 159 D4
Curry Rise NW7 . . . . .28 A4
Cursitor St EC4 . . 94 C1 241 A2
Curtain Pl EC2 . . . . 243 B6
Curtain Rd EC2 . . 95 C3 243 B6
Curthwaite Gdns EN2 . . . .15 D6
Curtis Dr W3 . . . . .89 B1
Curtis Field Rd SW16 . . . 182 C6
Curtis Ho 7 London N11 . .31 C5
Walworth SE17 . . . . 262 C2
Curtis La HA0 . . . . .66 A3
Curtis Rd
Twickenham TW4 . . . . . .151 B4
West Ewell KT19 . . . . . . 215 A4
Curtis St SE1 . . . 117 D2 263 C4
Curtis Way
Bermondsey SE1 . . . . . . 263 C4
8 Thamesmead SE28 . .124 B6
Curtlington Ho 3 HA8 . . .27 A1
Curve Bldg The SE4 . . . .163 B6
Curve The Ealing W5 . . . 109 D4
Shepherd's Bush W12 . . . 112 A6
Curwen Ave E7 . . . . .77 B4
Curwen & New Acad Gall ★
W1 . . . . 239 C3
Curwen Prim Sch E13 . . . .99 A5
Curwen Rd W12 . . . . . . .112 A4
Curzon Ave Enfield EN3 . . .18 D6
Stanmore HA7 . . . . .25 A2
Curzon Cl BR6 . . . . 227 B4
Curzon Cres
Barking IG11 . . . . 101 D4
Willesden NW10 . . . . . . .67 C1
Curzon Ct SE9 . . . . 167 A1
Curzon Gate W1 . . . . . . 248 B3
Curzon Ho W5 . . . . .87 B3
Curzon Pl HA5 . . . . .40 C4
Curzon Rd Ealing W5 . . . .87 B3
Muswell Hill N10 . . . . . . .31 B1
Thornton Heath CR7 . . . .204 C3
Curzon Sq W1 . . . . 248 B3
Curzon St W1 . . . .115 B5 248 C4
Cusack Cl TW1 . . . . 174 D6
Custance Ho N1 . . . . . . 235 C3
Custance St N1 . . . . 235 C2
CUSTOM HOUSE 121 C6
Custom House
EC3 . . . . 117 C6 253 A5
Custom House for ExCeL Sta
E16 . . . . .121 B6
Custom House Reach
SE16 . . . . .119 B3
Cutbush Ho N7 . . . . .71 D3
Cutcombe Rd SE5 . . . . . 139 A3
Cuthberga Cl IG11 . . . . . .79 A1
Cuthbert Gdns SE25 . . . .205 C6
Cuthbert Harrowing Ho
EC1 . . . . 242 A5
Cuthbert Ho W2 . . . . . . 236 C4
Cuthbert Rd
Croydon CR0 . . . . 220 D6
8 Edmonton N18 . . . . . .34 A4
Walthamstow E17 . . . . . .54 A6
Cuthbert St W2 . . . . . . 236 C5
Cuthill Wlk 3 SE5 . . . . . 139 B4
Cutlers Gdns EC2 . . . . . 243 B2
Cutlers Gdns Arc EC2 . . . 243 B2
Cutlers Sq E14 . . . . 119 C2
Cutler St EC2 . . . . 243 B2
Cut The SE1 . . . . 116 C4 251 B2
Cutty Sark ★ SE10 . . . . 142 A6
Cutty Sark Ho 16 E14 . . . 119 D2
Cutty Sark Ret Development
SE10 . . . . .142 A6
Cutty Sark Sta SE10 . . . .142 A6
Cuxton BR5 . . . . 211 A4
Cuxton Cl DA6 . . . . 169 A6
Cuxton Ho SE17 . . . . . . 263 B2
Cyclamen Cl 4 TW12 . . . 173 C4
Cyclamen Way KT19 . . . 215 A3
Cyclops Mews 12 E14 . . . 119 C2
Cygnet Ave TW14 . . . . . 150 D4
Cygnet Cl NW10 . . . . . . .67 B3
Cygnet Cl EN3 . . . . .7 A4
Cygnet Ho Harrow HA7 . . .24 D4
St John's Wood NW8 . . . 229 A6
Cygnet Hospl Harrow
HA1 . . . . .64 C6
Cygnet House N 18 E14 . . .97 D1

Cygnet House S 19 E14 . . . .97 D1
Cygnet St E1 . . . . 243 D6
Cygnets The TW13 . . . . . 173 A6
Cygnet Way UB4 . . . . . . .84 D2
Cygnus Bsns Ctr NW10 . . .67 D2
Cymbeline Ct 6 HA1 . . . . .42 D3
Cyna Ct 5 E11 . . . . .55 A3
Cynthia St N1 . . . . 233 D3
Cyntra Pl 8 E8 . . . . .74 B1
Cypress Ave London N2 . . .47 D6
Twickenham TW2 . . . . . . 152 A4
Cypress Cl 9 E5 . . . . . . .74 A6
Cypress Ct Cheam SM1 . .217 C2
5 Leyton E11 . . . . .76 B4
7 West Norwood SW16 . . 182 C5
Cypress Gdns SE4 . . . . . 163 A6
Cypress Ho SE14 . . . . . . 140 D4
Cypress Inf Sch SE25 . . . 183 C1
Cypress Jun Sch SE25 . . . 183 C1
Cypress Lo SE25 . . . . . . 183 C1
Cypress Pl W1 . . . . 239 B5
Cypress Rd Harrow HA3 . . .24 B1
South Norwood SE25 . . . 183 C1
Cypress Tree Cl DA15 . . . 167 D3
CYPRUS 122 C6
Cyprus Ave N3 . . . . .29 A1
Cyprus Cl N4 . . . . .50 C3
Cyprus Gdns N3 . . . . . . .29 A1
Cyprus Ho 10 N3 . . . . . . .29 B1
Cyprus Pl
23 Bethnal Green E2 . . . .96 C5
Newham E6 . . . . 122 C6
Cyprus Rd Church End N3 . .29 B1
Edmonton N9 . . . . .17 D2
Cyprus St E2 . . . . .96 C5
Cyprus Sta E6 . . . . 122 C6
Cyrena Rd SE22 . . . . . . 161 D6
Cyril Jackson Prim Sch
(North Bldg) 24 E14 . . .119 B6
Cyril Jackson Prim Sch
(South Bldg) 25 E14 . . .119 B6
Cyril Lo 2 DA14 . . . . . . 190 A6
Cyril Mans SW11 . . . . . . 267 D1
Cyril Rd DA7 . . . . 147 A3
Cyril Smith Ho N13 . . . . . .32 B5
Cyril Thatcher Ho SW6 . . 265 B1
Cyrus Ho EC1 . . . . 241 C6
Cyrus St EC1 . . . . 94 D3 241 C6
Czar St SE8 . . . . 141 C6

Dairy Mews N2 . . . . .48 C5
Dabbs Hill La UB5 . . . . . .63 C3
Dabb's La EC1 . . . . 241 B5
Dabin Cres SE10 . . . . . . 142 A4
Dacca St SE8 . . . . 141 B6
Dace Rd E3 . . . . .97 C6
Dacre Cl UB6 . . . . .85 D5
Dacre Gdns
Borehamwood WD6 . . . . . .11 B6
Lewisham SE13 . . . . 142 C1
Dacre Ho SW3 . . . . 266 D5
Dacre Pk SE13 . . . . 142 C1
Dacre Pl SE13 . . . . 142 C1
Dacre Rd Leytonstone E11 . .54 D1
Newham E13 . . . . .99 B6
Thornton Heath CR0 . . . .204 A2
Dacres Rd SE23 . . . . . . 162 D5
Dacre St SW1 . . . 115 D3 259 C6
Dade Way UB2 . . . . 107 B1
Daerwood Cl BR2 . . . . . 210 B1
Daffodil Cl CR0 . . . . . . 206 D1
Daffodil Gdns IG1 . . . . . .78 D3
Daffodil Pl 7 TW12 . . . . 173 C4
Daffodil St W12 . . . . . . 111 D6
Dafforne Rd SW17 . . . . . 159 A1
DAGENHAM 81 D1
Dagenham Ave
Dagenham RM9 . . . . .81 B1
Dagenham RM9 . . . . . . 103 A6
Dagenham Dock Estate
RM9 . . . . .103 B3
Dagenham Dock Sta
RM9 . . . . .103 B5
Dagenham East Sta
RM10 . . . . .81 D3
Dagenham Heathway Sta
RM9 . . . . .81 B2
Dagenham Park Com Sch
RM10 . . . . .103 D6
Dagenham Rd
Dagenham RM10 . . . . . . .81 D4
London E10 . . . . .53 B1
Dagenham & Redbridge
Football Grd RM10 . . . . . .81 C6
Dagenham Swimming Pool
RM10 . . . . .81 C6
Dagger La WD23 . . . . .9 A6
Dagmar Ave HA9 . . . . . . .66 B4
Dagmar Ct
Cubitt Town E14 . . . . . . 120 A3
South Tottenham N15 . . . . .51 B5
Dagmar Gdns NW10 . . . . .90 D5
Dagmar Mews UB2 . . . . .107 A3
Dagmar Pas N1 . . . . 234 D6
Dagmar Rd
Camberwell SE5 . . . . . . 139 C4

Dagmar Rd continued
Finsbury Pk N4 . . . . .50 C2
4 Kingston u T KT2 . . . . 176 C3
Southall UB2 . . . . 107 A3
South Norwood SE25 . . . 205 C4
West Green N15 . . . . .51 B5
Wood Green N22 . . . . . . .31 D2
Dagmar Terr N1 . .94 D6 234 D6
Dagnall Pk SE25 . . . . . . 205 C4
Dagnall Rd SE25 . . . . . . 205 C4
Dagnall St SW11 . . 137 A4 268 A1
Dagnan Rd SW12 . . . . . 159 C4
Dagobert Ho 27 E1 . . . . . .96 C2
Dagonet Gdns BR1 . . . . . 165 A1
Dagonet Rd BR1 . . . . . . 165 A1
Dahlia Gdns Ilford IG1 . . . .78 D2
Mitcham CR4 . . . . 203 D5
Dahlia Rd SE2 . . . . 124 B2
Dahomey Rd SW16 . . . . .181 C4
Daiglen Sch IG9 . . . . .21 C2
Daimler Ho 8 E3 . . . . . . .97 C3
Daimler Way SM6 . . . . . 220 A1
Daines Cl E12 . . . . .78 B5
Dainford Cl BR1 . . . . . . 186 B5
Dainton Cl 1 BR1 . . . . . 187 B2
Dainton Ho 22 W2 . . . . . .91 C2
Daintry Cl HA3 . . . . .43 A5
Daintry Way E9 . . . . .75 B2
Dairsie Ct 3 BR1 . . . . . . 187 C1
Dairsie Rd SE9 . . . . 144 C2
Dairy Cl Bromley BR1 . . . 187 B3
South Norwood CR7 . . . . 183 A1
Willesden NW10 . . . . . . .90 A6
Dairy La SE18 . . . . 122 B2
Dairyman Cl NW2 . . . . . .69 A5
Dairy Meadow Prim Sch
UB2 . . . . .107 B3
Daisy Cl CR0 . . . . 206 D1
Daisy Dormer Ct 11
SW9 . . . . .138 B1
Daisy Ho IG3 . . . . .58 A1
Daisy La SW6 . . . . 135 C2
Daisy Rd Newham E16 . . . .98 C3
Woodford E18 . . . . .37 B1
Dakin Pl 9 E1 . . . . .97 A2
Dakota bldg 6 SE13 . . . 141 D4
Dakota Cl SM6 . . . . 220 B1
Dakota Gdns UB5 . . . . . . .85 A4
Dalberg Rd SW2 . . . . . . 160 C6
Dalberg Way SE2 . . . . . . 124 D3
Dalbury Ho 6 SW9 . . . . . 138 B1
Dalby Rd SW18 . . . . 136 A1
Dalby St NW5 . . . . .71 B2
Dalcross Rd TW4, TW5 . . 129 A3
Dale Ave Edgware HA8 . . . .26 B1
Hounslow TW4 . . . . 129 A2
Dale Cl Blackheath Pk SE3 . 143 A2
New Barnet EN5 . . . . .13 D5
Pinner HA5 . . . . .22 B2
Dale Croft N4 . . . . .73 A5
Dale Ct Cranley Gdns N8 . . .49 C5
3 Kingston u T KT2 . . . . 176 B3
Northolt UB5 . . . . .63 B1
Wembley HA0 . . . . .65 D4
Woodford E18 . . . . .37 A1
Dale Dr UB4 . . . . .83 D4
Dalefield IG9 . . . . .21 D3
Dale Gdns IG8 . . . . .37 B6
Dale Gr N12 . . . . .30 A5
Dale Green Rd N11 . . . . . .15 B1
Dalehaed NW1 . . . . 232 A3
Daleham Dr UB8 . . . . . . .82 D1
Daleham Gdns NW3 . . . . .70 B2
Daleham Mews NW3 . . . . .70 B2
Dale Ho London SE4 . . . . 141 A1
St John's Wood NW8 . . . 229 A6
Dale Lo N6 . . . . .49 C3
Dalemain Ho 8 SW8 . . . . 137 D3
Dalemain Mews 12 E16 . . 121 A5
Dale Park Ave SM5 . . . . . 218 D6
Dale Park Rd SE19 . . . . . 183 B2
Dale Rd Ashford TW16 . . . 171 D3
Camberwell SE17 . . . . . 138 D6
Cheam SM1 . . . . 217 B4
Gospel Oak NW5 . . . . . . .71 A3
Southall UB6 . . . . .85 D2
Walton-on-T KT12 . . . . . 193 D2
Dale Row W11 . . . . .91 A1
Daleside Rd
Streatham SW17 . . . . . .181 B5
West Ewell KT19 . . . . . . 215 B2
Dales Path WD6 . . . . .11 B6
Dales Rd WD6 . . . . .11 B6
Dale St W4 . . . . .111 C1
Dale The BR2 . . . . 225 D4
Dale View Ave E4 . . . . . . .20 A2
Dale View Cres E4 . . . . . .20 A1
Dale View Gdns E4 . . . . . .20 B1
Daleview Rd N15 . . . . . . .51 C3
Dalewood Gdns KT4 . . . . 216 B6
Dale Wood Rd BR6 . . . . . 211 C1
Daley Ho 6 W12 . . . . . . .90 B1
Daley St E9 . . . . .74 D2
Daley Thompson Way 7
SW8 . . . . .137 B2
Dalgarno Gdns W10 . . . . .90 C3
Dalgarno Way W10 . . . . . .90 C3
Daling Way E3 . . . . .97 A5

Dali Universe ★ SE1 . . . . 250 C2
Dalkeith Ct SW1 . . . . . . 259 D3
Dalkeith Gr HA7 . . . . .26 A5
Dalkeith Ho 6 SW9 . . . . 138 D4
Dalkeith Rd Ilford IG1 . . . .79 A5
West Norwood SE21 . . . . 161 A4
Dallas Ct SM3 . . . . 217 A2
Dallas Rd Cheam SM3 . . . 217 A2
Ealing W5 . . . . .88 B2
Forest Hill SE26 . . . . . . 162 B1
Hendon NW4 . . . . .46 A2
Dallas Terr UB3 . . . . 105 D3
Dallega Cl UB3 . . . . 105 B6
Dallinger Rd SE12 . . . . . 164 D5
Dalling Rd W6 . . . . 112 B2
Dallington Sch
EC1 . . . . .94 D3 241 D6
Dallington St EC1 . .94 D3 241 D6
Dallin Rd Bexley DA6 . . . 146 D1
Woolwich SE18 . . . . 144 D5
Dalmain Prim Sch SE23 . 163 A3
Dalmain Rd SE23 . . . . . . 162 D3
Dalmally Pas CR0 . . . . . 205 D3
Dalmally Passage CR0 . . 205 D3
Dalmally Rd CR0 . . . . . . 206 A2
Dalmeny Ave
Thornton Heath SW16 . . . 182 C1
Tufnell Pk N7 . . . . .71 D4
Dalmeny Avenue Est 3
N7 . . . . .71 D4
Dalmeny Cl HA0 . . . . . . .65 C2
Dalmeny Cres TW3 . . . . . 130 B1
Dalmeny Ct 4 SW4 . . . . 138 A3
Dalmeny Rd Erith DA8 . . . 147 D4
New Barnet EN5 . . . . .14 A5
North Cheam KT4 . . . . . . 216 B6
Tufnell Pk N7 . . . . .71 D4
Wallington SM5 . . . . 219 A1
Dalmeyer Rd NW10 . . . . . .67 D2
Dalmore Ave KT10 . . . . . 212 D2
Dalmore Rd SE21 . . . . . . 161 A2
Dalrymple Cl Barnet N20 . .14 A4
London N14 . . . . .15 D3
Dalrymple Rd SE4 . . . . . 141 A1
DALSTON 74 A2
Dalston Gdns HA7 . . . . . .26 A1
Dalston Jct E8 . . . . .73 D2
Dalston Junction Sta E8 . .73 C2
Dalston Kingsland Sta
E8 . . . . .73 D3
Dalston La E8 . . . . .74 A3
Dalton Ave CR4 . . . . 180 C1
Dalton Cl Hayes UB4 . . . . .83 B3
Orpington BR6 . . . . 227 C5
Dalton Ho
7 Balham SW12 . . . . . . 159 B4
10 Bow E3 . . . . .97 A5
19 Deptford SE14 . . . . 140 D6
Merton SW19 . . . . 180 A2
Stanmore HA7 . . . . .25 B5
Dalton St SE27 . . . . 160 D1
Daltry Ho HA1 . . . . .42 D5
Dalwood St SE5 . . . . 139 C4
Daly Ct BR1 . . . . 210 C6
Dalyell Rd SW9 . . . . 138 B2
Damascene Wlk SE21 . . . 161 A3
Damask Cres E16 . . . . . . .98 C3
Damask Ct SM1 . . . . 201 D1
Damer Ho 9 TW10 . . . . . 154 B6
Damer Terr SW10 . . . . . . 266 B3
Dames Rd E7 . . . . .77 A5
Dame St N1 . . . . . 95 A5 235 A4
Damien Ct 12 E1 . . . . . . .96 B1
Damien St E1 . . . . .96 B1
Damon Cl DA14 . . . . 168 B1
Damon Ct DA14 . . . . 168 B1
Damon Ho 2 N2 . . . . .30 B5
Damory Ho 1 SE16 . . . . . 118 C2
Damson Dr UB3 . . . . 106 A6
Damsonwood Rd UB2 . . . 107 C3
Danbrook Rd SW16 . . . . . 182 A3
Dan Bryant Ho 5 SW12 . . 159 C4
Danbury Cl RM6 . . . . .58 D6
Danbury Mans 3 IG11 . . . .78 D1
Danbury Mews SW5,
SM6 . . . . .219 B4
Danbury St N1 . . .94 D5 234 D4
Danbury Way IG8 . . . . . . .37 C4
Danby Ct EN2 . . . . .5 A2
Danby Ho 3 Hackney E9 . .74 C1
3 West Kilburn W10 . . . . .91 B4
Danby St SE15 . . . . 139 D2
Dancastle Ct 7 N3 . . . . . .29 C2
Dancer Rd
Fulham SW6 . . . . 135 B4 264 C1
Richmond TW9 . . . . 132 C2
Dando Cres SE3 . . . . 143 B2
Dandridge Cl SE10 . . . . . 120 D1
Dandridge Ho E1 . . . . . . 243 C4
Danebury
New Addington CR0 . . . . 223 D2
18 North Kensington W10 . .90 C2
Danebury Ave SW15 . . . . 155 D5
Daneby Rd SE6 . . . . 164 A2
Dane Cl Farnborough BR6 . 227 B4
Sidcup DA5 . . . . 169 C4
Danecourt Gdns CR0 . . . 221 D5

Cul–Dan 311
Dali Universe ★ SE1 . . . . 250 C2

Danecroft Rd SE24......161 B6
Daneglen Ct 18 HA7.....25 C5
Dangegrove Prim Sch
(Ridgeway Ave) EN4....14 C5
Dangegrove Prim Sch
(Windsor Dr) EN4.....14 C5
Danehill Wlk DA14......168 A1
Dane Ho 15 London SE5..139 A3
Upper Tooting SW17....180 A6
Danehurst TW8........131 C5
Danehurst Gdns IG4....56 B4
Danehurst St
SW6.........135 A4 264 A2
Daneland EN4.........14 D5
Danemead Gr UB5......63 D3
Danemere St SW15.....134 C2
Danescombe SE12......165 A3
Danescourt Cres SM1...218 A6
Danescroft Hendon NW4..46 D4
3 North Finchley N12...30 A5
Danescroft Ave NW4....46 D4
Danescroft Gdns NW4...46 D4
Danes Ct
Primrose Hill NW8.....230 C5
Wembley HA9.........66 D5
Danesdale Rd E9.......75 A2
Danesfield SE5.......139 C6
Danes Gate HA1.......42 C6
Danes Ho 10 W10......90 C2
Dane St WC1.........240 C3
Daneswood Ave SE6....164 A1
Danethorpe Rd HA0....65 D2
Danetree Cl KT19.....215 A1
Danetree Rd KT19.....215 A1
Danetree Sch KT19....215 A1
Danette Gdns RM8.....81 B6
Daneville Rd SE5......139 B4
Danford Ho 9 N11.....31 C5
Dangan Rd E11.........55 A3
Daniel Almshouse NW4..46 B5
Daniel Bolt Cl E14....97 D2
Daniel Cl London N18...34 C6
Twickenham TW4......151 B4
Upper Tooting SW17...180 C4
Daniel Ct Acton W3....111 C6
3 Beckenham BR3......185 C3
7 Edgware HA8........26 D5
10 Hendon NW9........27 C2
Daniel Gdns SE15.....139 D5
Daniel Ho 1 HA5.......22 C1
Daniell Ho N1.......235 D4
Daniell Way CR0.......204 B1
Daniel Pl NW4.........46 B2
Daniel Rd W5.........110 B6
Daniel's Rd SE15.....140 C2
Dan Leno Wlk SW6......265 C3
Dansey Pl W1........249 C6
Dansington Rd DA16...146 A1
Danson Cres DA16.....146 B2
Danson House* DA6...146 C1
Danson Intc DA5......168 C5
Danson La DA16.......146 B1
Danson Mead DA16.....146 C2
Danson Prim Sch DA16..146 A1
Danson Rd DA5........168 D6
Danson Underpass DA5..168 C5
Dante Pl SE11........261 D3
Dante Rd SE11....116 D2 261 C4
Danube Ct 13 SE15....139 D5
Danube St SW3...114 C1 257 B2
Danvers Ho 35 E1......96 A1
Danvers St N8.........49 D5
Danvers St SW3...136 B6 266 D5
Da Palma Ct SW6......265 A5
Daphne Ct Ealing W5...87 C1
Wembley HA0.........65 D3
Worcester Pk KT4.....215 C6
Daphne Gdns E4.......20 A1
Daphne Ho N22........32 C2
Daphne St SW18......158 A5
Daplyn St 6 E1........96 A2
D'arblay St W1....93 C1 239 B1
Darby Cres TW16......172 C1
Darby Gdns TW16......172 C1
Darcy Ave SM6........219 C4
Darcy Cl N20.........14 B2
D'arcy Dr HA3........43 D5
D'arcy Gdns
Dagenham RM9.......103 B6
Harrow HA3..........44 A5
Darcy Ho E8.........96 B6
D'arcy Pl BR2........209 A5
Darcy Rd Isleworth TW7.131 A4
Thornton Heath SW16..182 A1
D'arcy Rd SM3........216 D4
Dare Ct 2 E10........54 A2
Dare Gdns RM8........81 A5
Darell Prim Sch TW9...132 C2
Darell Rd TW9........132 C2

Daren Ct N7..........72 A4
Darent Ho
4 Catford BR1........186 B5
Lisson Gr NW8.......236 D4
Darenth Rd
Stamford Hill N16.....51 D1
Welling DA16.........146 A4
Darfield NW1........232 A5
Darfield Rd SE4......163 B6
Darfield Way W10......90 D1
Darfur St 2 SW15.....134 D2
Dargate Cl SE19......183 D3
Darien Ho
16 London SW11......136 B2
11 Stepney E1.........96 D2
Darien Rd SW11.......136 B2
Daring Ho 23 E3.......97 A5
Darland Ho SE17......167 B5
Darlands Dr EN5.......12 D6
Darlan Rd SW6....135 B5 264 D3
Darlaston Rd SW19....179 A3
Darley Cl CR0........207 A3
Darley Dr KT3........177 B1
Darley Gdns SM4......201 D3
Darley Ho SE11.......260 C1
Darley Rd Clapham SW11.158 D5
Edmonton N9.........17 D3
Darling Ho 12 TW1....153 D5
Darling Rd SE4.......141 C2
Darling Row E1........96 B3
Darlington Ct 8 SE6..164 D3
Darlington Ho
South Lambeth SW8....269 D3
2 Surbiton KT6.......197 D2
Darlington Rd SE27...182 D5
Darmaine Cl CR2......221 A1
Darnall Ho 4 SE10....142 A4
Darnay Ho 3 SE16....118 A3
Darndale Cl E17.......35 B1
Darnell Ho 9 SE10....142 A5
Darnley Ho 7 E14.....97 A1
Darnley Rd Hackney E9..74 C2
Woodford IG8.........37 B2
Darnley Terr 12 W11...112 D5
Darrell Ct BR2.......208 C6
Darrell Rd SE22......162 A6
Darren Cl N4.........50 B2
Darrick Wood Ho BR6...227 A5
Darrick Wood Inf Sch
BR6..............226 D5
Darrick Wood Jun Sch
BR6..............226 D4
Darrick Wood Rd BR6...227 B6
Darrick Wood Sch BR6..226 D5
Darrick Wood Sports Ctr
BR6..............227 A5
Darris Cl UB4.........85 A3
Darsley Dr 3 SW8..138 A4 270 A2
Dartford Ave N9.......18 D5
Dartford Gdns RM6....58 B4
Dartford Ho SE1......263 D4
Dartford St SE17.....139 A6
Dartington NW1......232 B5
Dartington Ho
Bayswater W2........91 D2
7 London SW8........137 D3
Dartle Ct 29 SE16....118 A4
Dartmoor Wlk 18 E14..119 C2
Dartmouth Cl W11.....91 C1
Dartmouth Ct SE10....142 A4
Dartmouth Gr SE10....142 A4
Dartmouth Hill SE10..142 A4
Dartmouth Ho
Dartmouth Pk N19.....71 B6
11 Kingston u T KT2..176 A2
Lewisham SE10.......142 A3
Thornton Heath CR0...204 D2
DARTMOUTH PARK.......71 B5
Dartmouth Park Ave
NW5..............71 B5
Dartmouth Park Hill N19.71 B6
Dartmouth Park Rd NW5..71 B5
Dartmouth Pl
Chiswick W4.........133 C6
Forest Hill SE23.....162 C2
Dartmouth Rd
Brondesbury NW2......68 D2
Forest Hill SE23, SE26..162 C1
Hayes BR2...........209 A2
Hendon NW4..........46 A3
Ruislip HA4..........62 A5
Dartmouth Row SE10...142 A4
Dartmouth St
SW1...........115 D4 249 D1
Dartmouth Terr SE10..142 B4
Dartnell Rd CR0......205 D2
Darton Ct W3.........111 A3
Dartrey Twr SW10.....266 C4
Dartrey Wlk
SW10...........136 A5 266 B4
Dart St W10..........91 B4
Darul Uloom BR7......189 C4
Darville Rd N16.......73 D5
Darwell Cl E6.........100 C5
Darwen Pl E2.........96 B6
Darwin Cl
Farnborough BR6.....227 B3
New Southgate N11....15 B1
Darwin Ct Eltham SE9..166 C5
Newham E13..........99 B4

Darwin Ct continued
Primrose Hill NW1.....231 B6
Darwin Ctr* SW7.....256 C5
Darwin Dr UB1........85 D1
Darwin Gdns WD19.....22 C5
Darwin Ho
8 London SE13.......142 A3
2 Wembley HA9........67 A5
Darwin Rd Ealing W5..109 C2
Falconwood DA16......145 D2
Tottenham N22........32 D1
Darwin St SE17....117 B2 262 D4
Daryngton Dr UB6......86 C5
Daryngton Ho SW8.....270 A3
Dashwood Cl DA6......169 C6
Dashwood Ct TW3......130 A1
Dashwood Ho SE21....161 D1
Dashwood Rd N8.......50 B3
Dassett Rd SE27......182 D2
Data Point Bsns Ctr E16..98 B3
Datchelor Pl 14 SE5..139 B4
Datchet Ho NW1......231 D2
Datchet Rd SE6.......163 B2
Datchett Ho 40 E2.....95 D4
Datchwood Ct N4......73 A5
Datchworth Ct 7 EN1..17 C6
Datchworth Ho 8 N1...72 D1
Date St SE17.....117 B1 262 C1
Daubeney Gdns N17....33 A3
Daubeney Pl TW12.....173 D1
Daubeney Prim Sch E5..75 A4
Daubeney Rd
Clapton Pk E5........75 A4
Tottenham N17........33 A3
Daubeney Twr 2 SE8..119 B1
Dault Rd SW18.......158 A5
Dauney Ho SE1.......251 C1
Dauphine Pl W4.......24 C1
Dave Adams Ho 8 E3...97 B5
Davenant Ho 20 E1.....96 A2
Davenant Rd
Croydon CR0, CR9.....220 D4
Upper Holloway N19....71 D6
Davenant St E1........96 A2
Davenport Cl TW11....175 A4
Davenport Ctr IG11...102 B5
Davenport Ho SE11....261 A5
Davenport Lo TW3.....129 A5
Davenport Mews 6
W12..............112 B5
Davenport Rd
London SE6..........164 A5
Sidcup DA14..........169 A2
Daventer Dr HA7......24 D3
Daventry Ave E17.....53 C3
Daventry St NW1...92 C2 237 A4
Dave Porter Hts SW19.157 A4
Dave Ramsey Ho SE18..123 B2
Daver Ct
Chelsea SW3.........257 B1
Ealing W5...........87 D3
Davern Cl SE10.......120 D2
Davey Cl
Bowes Pk N13........32 B5
Islington N7.........72 B2
Davey Ho HA9........67 A6
Davey Rd E9.........75 C1
Davey's Ct WC2......250 A6
Davey St SE15.......139 D6
David Ave UB6........86 C5
David Cl UB3........127 C5
David Coffer Ct DA17..125 D2
David Ct N20.........14 A1
David Devine Ho 7 E8..74 A3
David Game Coll SW7..256 C3
Davidge Ho SE1.......250 A4
Davidge St SE1...116 D4 251 D1
David Henry Waring Ct
TW14.............149 A3
David Hewitt Ho 2 E3..97 D2
David Ho
8 Putney SW15.......156 A6
South Lambeth SW8....270 A4
South Norwood SE25...206 A6
David Lee Point N15...98 C6
David Livingstone Prim Sch
CR7..............183 A2
David Mews W1.......237 D4
David Rd RM8.........81 A6
Davidson Gdns
SW8..........138 A5 270 A4
Davidson Ho 7 N19....71 C4
Davidson Lo CR0......205 C2
Davidson Prim Sch CR0.205 D3
Davidson Rd CR0......205 D3
Davidson Terrs E7.....77 B3
David's Rd SE23......162 C3
David St E15.........76 B3
David Twigg Cl KT2...176 A2
Davies Cl CR0........206 A3
Davies La E11........76 D6
Davies Laing & Dick Coll
W1............93 A1 238 B2
Davies Lane Prim Sch
E11..............76 D6
Davies Mews W1......248 C6
Davies St W1.....115 B6 248 C6
Davies Walk TW7.....130 B4
Davina Ho
Brondesbury NW2......69 B2

Davina Ho continued
14 Hackney E5........74 B3
Da Vinci Ct 12 SE16...118 B1
Davington Ct 19 SM2..217 C1
Davington Gdns RM8...80 B3
Davington Rd RM8.....80 B3
Davis Ct 1 N20........14 B2
Davis Ho 35 W12......112 B6
Davis Rd Bedford Pk W3.111 D4
Chessington KT9......214 C4
Davis St E13.........99 B5
Davisville Rd W12....112 A4
Davis Way DA14......191 A4
Davmor Ct TW4.......109 C1
Dawes Ave TW7.......131 A1
Dawe's Cl UB10.......82 A5
Dawes Ho SE17.......262 C3
Dawes Rd SW6....135 B5 264 C4
Dawe's Rd UB10......82 A5
Dawes St SE17....117 B1 262 D2
Dawley Ave UB8.......83 A1
Dawley Par UB3......105 A6
Dawley Rd
Harlington UB3.......105 C2
Hayes UB3...........105 B6
Dawlish Ave
Bowes Pk N13........32 A5
Wandsworth SW18.....157 D2
Wembley UB6.........87 A5
Dawlish Dr Ilford IG3..79 D4
Pinner HA5..........41 A3
Ruislip HA4..........62 B6
Dawlish Prim Sch E10..54 A1
Dawlish Rd
Brondesbury NW2......68 D2
Leyton E10..........76 A6
Tottenham Hale N17....52 A6
Dawnay Gdns SW18....158 B2
Dawnay Rd SW17, SW18..158 B2
Dawn Cl TW4.........129 A2
Dawn Cres E15........98 B6
Dawn Wlk BR2........186 B1
Dawpool Rd NW2......67 D6
Daws La NW7.........28 A5
Dawson Ave Barking IG11.79 D1
St Paul's Cray BR5....190 B1
Dawson Cl Hayes UB3...83 B2
Woolwich SE18.......123 A2
Dawson Gdns 10 IG11..79 D1
Dawson Ho
23 Bethnal Green E2...96 C4
5 Camberwell SE5....139 C4
Dawson Pl W2.....113 C6 245 B6
Dawson Rd
Cricklewood NW2......68 C4
Kingston u T KT1.....198 B6
Dawson St E2........95 D5
Dawson Terr N9.......18 C4
Dax Ct TW16.........194 C6
Daybrook Rd SW19....201 D6
Day Ho 2 SE5........139 A5
Daylesford Ave SW15..134 A1
Daymer Gdns HA5.....40 C5
Daynor Ho 4 NW6.....91 C6
Day's Armhouses HA8..26 B5
Daysbrook Rd SW2....160 B3
Days La DA15.........167 C4
Days Lane Prim Sch
DA15.............167 D5
Daytone Ho SW20.....178 D2
Dayton Gr SE15......140 C4
Deaconess Ct 5 N15...51 D5
Deacon Ho SE11......260 D3
Deacon Mews N1......73 B1
Deacon Rd
Kingston u T KT2.....176 B2
Willesden NW2........68 A2
Deacons Cl HA5.......22 B1
DEACONS HILL........10 C5
Deacon's Hill Rd WD6..10 C6
Deacons Hts WD6.....10 C5
Deacons Leas BR6....227 B4
Deacons Rise N2......48 B4
Deacons Wlk TW12....173 C6
Deacon Way
SE17..........117 A2 262 B4
Deal Ct 13 Hendon NW9.27 D1
7 Southall UB1.......86 A1
Deal Ho Deptford SE15.140 D6
Walworth SE17.......263 B2
Deal Porters Way SE16.118 D3
Deal Rd SW17........181 A4
Deal St E1...........96 A2
Dealtry Rd SW15.....134 C1
Deal Wlk 3 SW9......138 C5
Dean Bradley St SW1..260 A5
Dean Cl Hackney E9...74 C3
Hillingdon UB10......60 B1
Rotherhithe SE16.....118 D5
Dean Coll of London 4
N7..............72 B5
Deancross St E1......96 C1
Dean Ct Acton W3.....89 B1
Ealing W13..........109 B5
10 Kingston u T KT2..176 C3
South Lambeth SW8...270 A3
Wembley HA0.........65 B5
Dean Dr HA7.........26 A1
Deane Ave HA4........62 C5
Deane Croft Rd HA5...40 C3

Deanery Cl N2........48 C5
Deanery Mews W1.....248 B4
Deanery Rd E15......76 C2
Deanery St W1...115 A5 248 B4
Deane Way HA4........40 B3
Dean Farrar St SW1...259 D6
Deanfield Gdns CR0...221 B4
Dean Gdns E17.......54 B5
Dean Ho London SE14..141 B5
New Cross SE14.......141 B5
Ruislip HA4..........39 B1
Stamford Hill N16.....51 D1
18 Stepney E1........96 C1
Dean Rd Croydon CR0..221 B4
Hampton TW12........173 C5
Hounslow TW3........151 D6
Thamesmead SE28....124 A6
Willesden NW2........68 C2
Dean Ryle St SW1.....260 A4
Dean's Bldgs
SE17...........117 B2 262 D3
Deansbrook Cl HA8....27 A3
Deansbrook Jun & Inf Schs
NW7.............27 A4
Deansbrook Rd
Burnt Oak HA8.......27 B4
Edgware HA8.........26 D3
Deans Cl Burnt Oak HA8.27 A4
Chiswick W4.........132 D6
South Croydon CR0....221 D5
Deanscroft Ave NW9...45 A1
Deans Ct HA8.........26 D4
Dean's Ct EC4........241 D1
Deans Dr N13.........32 D4
Dean's Dr HA8........27 B5
Deansfield Prim Sch
Eltham SE9..........144 C2
Ruislip HA4..........62 D4
Deans Gate Cl SE23...162 D1
Dean's Gateway 9 SE10.141 C4
Deanshanger Ho 21 SE8.118 D2
Dean's La HA8........27 A4
Dean's Mews W1......238 D2
Deans Rd SM1........217 D5
Dean's Rd W7........108 D4
Dean St Forest Gate E7..77 A3
Soho W1.........93 D1 239 C1
Deansway East Finchley N2..48 B5
Edmonton N9.........17 C1
Deans Way HA8........27 A5
Deanswood N11.......31 D4
Dean's Yd SW1.......259 D6
Dean Trench St SW1...260 A5
Dean Way UB2........107 D4
Dean Wlk HA8.........27 B3
Deanwood Ct N14.....15 C3
Dearmer Ho 8 SW2...160 C4
Dearne Cl HA7........25 A5
De'arn Gdns CR4......202 C6
Dearsley Rd EN1......6 A2
Deason St E15.........98 A6
Deauville Ct
14 London SW4......159 C5
4 Rotherhithe SE16...118 D4
Deauville Mans 13 SW4.159 C5
De Barowe Mews
4 Highbury N5........72 D4
1 London N5.........72 D3
Debdale Ho 20 E2.....96 A6
Debden N17..........33 B1
Debden Cl
7 Edgware NW9.......27 C2
Kingston u T KT2.....175 D5
Woodford IG8.........37 D3
De Beauvoir Cres N1..95 C6
De Beauvoir Ct N1....73 B1
De Beauvoir Pl 5 N1..73 C2
De Beauvoir Prim Sch 13
N1..............73 C2
De Beauvoir Rd N1....73 C1
De Beauvoir Sq N1....73 C1
DE BEAUVOIR TOWN....73 C1
Debenham Ct Barnet EN5..12 C5
Hackney E8..........96 A6
Debham Ct NW2.......68 C5
Debnams Rd SE16.....118 C2
De Bohun Ave N14....15 B5
De Bohun Prim Sch N14..15 B6
Deborah Cl TW7......130 C4
Deborah Cres HA4.....39 B2
Deborah Ct 7 E18....55 B6
Deborah Lo HA8.......26 D2
De Broome Rd TW13...150 C3
De Burgh Ho 10 SW19.180 A3
Deburgh Rd SW19.....180 A3
Debussy 9 NW9.......27 D1
Decimal Ctr 1 UB2....107 C4
Decima St SE1....117 C3 263 A6
Decimus Cl 1 CR7....205 B5
Deck Cl SE16.........118 D5
Decoy Ave NW11......47 A5
De Crespigny Pk SE5..139 B3
Dedham Ho 1 SE6.....186 A6
Dee Ct W7...........86 B1
Deeley Rd SW8...137 D4 269 C2
Deena Cl W3.........88 B1
Deen City Farm* SW19.180 A1

Deepdale Highbury N4 . . . . .72 D5
Wimbledon SW19. . . . . . . .178 D6
Deepdale Ave BR2 . . . . . .208 D5
Deepdale Cl N11. . . . . .31 A4
Deepdene N12 . . . . .30 C6
Deepdene Ave CR0. . . . . .221 D5
Deepdene Cl E11 . . . . .55 A5
Deepdene Ct
  Beckenham BR2. . . . . . .208 C6
  Southgate N21 . . . . .16 D5
Deepdene Gdns SW2 . . . .160 B4
Deepdene Ho N16 . . . . . . .51 B1
Deepdene Lo 5 SW2 . . . .160 B4
Deepdene Mans SW6 . . . .264 C2
Deepdene Point 9
  SE26 . . . . .162 D1
Deepdene Rd
  London SE5, SE24. . . . . .139 B1
  Welling DA16 . . . . .146 A2
Deepwell Cl TW7 . . . . . . .131 A4
Deepwood La UB6 . . . . . . .86 B4
Deerbrook Rd SE24,
  SW2. . . . . .160 D3
Dee Rd TW9 . . . . .132 B1
Deerdale Rd SE24. . . . . . .139 A1
Deerfield Cl NW9 . . . . .45 D4
Deerhurst
  7 Kingston u T KT2 . . . .176 D2
  5 Streatham SW16. . . . .182 A5
Deerhurst Cl TW13 . . . . . .172 B6
Deerhurst Cres TW12 . . . .174 A5
Deerhurst Ct CR0 . . . . . . .204 D1
Deerhurst Ho 6 SE15. . . .140 A6
Deerhurst Rd
  Brondesbury NW2 . . . . . .68 D2
  Streatham SW16. . . . . . .182 B5
Deerings Ct 2 N20 . . . . . .14 B2
Deerings Dr HA5. . . . . .40 A4
Deerleap Gr E4 . . . . .19 D6
Deer Lo SW6 . . . . .135 A4
Deer Park Cl KT2 . . . . . . .176 D3
Deer Park Gdns CR4 . . . . .202 B5
Deer Park Rd SW19 . . . . .180 A1
Deer Park Way BR4 . . . . .224 D6
Deesdale Ct CR2. . . . . . . .221 B4
Deeside Rd SW17. . . . . . .158 B1
Dee St E14 . . . . .98 A1
Defence Cl SE28 . . . . .123 C5
Defiance Wlk SE18. . . . . . .122 B3
Defiant 18 NW9 . . . . .27 D1
Defiant Way SM6 . . . . . . .220 A1
Defoe Ave TW9 . . . . .132 C5
Defoe Cl SW17. . . . . .180 C4
  5 Stoke Newington N16. . .73 C5
Defoe Pl Barbican EC2. . . .242 A4
  Upper Tooting SW17. . . . .180 D6
Defoe Rd
  Rotherhithe SE16. . . . . . .119 B4
  Stoke Newington N16. . . . .73 C5
De Frene Rd SE26. . . . . . .163 A1
De Gama Pl 3 E14. . . . . . .119 C1
Degema Rd BR7 . . . . .188 D5
Dehar Cres NW9 . . . . .46 A2
De Haviland Dr 8 SE18 . .122 D1
Dehavilland Cl UB5 . . . . . .84 D4
De Havilland Rd
  Edgware HA8 . . . . .26 D1
  Heston TW5 . . . . .128 C5
De Havilland Sq 1G1 . . . . .57 B1
Dehavilland Studios E5 . . . .74 C6
De Havilland Way TW19 . .148 A5
Dekker Ho 19 SE5. . . . . . .139 B5
Dekker Rd SE21. . . . . . . .161 C5
Delacourt Rd SE3 . . . . . . .143 B5
Delafield Ho 25 E1 . . . . . . .96 A1
Delafield Rd SE7 . . . . . . .121 C1
Delaford St SW6 . .135 A6 264 B5
Delamare Cres CR0 . . . . .206 C3
Delamere Gdns NW7. . . . . .27 B4
Delamere Ho 4 N4 . . . . . .51 B2
Delamere Rd Ealing W5 . . .110 A4
  Hayes UB4 . . . . .106 D6
  Wimbledon SW20. . . . . .178 D2
Delamere St W2 . . . . .236 A3
Delamere Terr W2 . . . . . . .91 D2
Delancey Pas NW1. . . . . .231 D5
Delancey St NW1 . . .93 B6 231 D5
Delancey Studios NW1. . . .231 D5
Delany Ho SE10. . . . . . . .142 A6
Delarch Ho SE1 . . . . .251 C1
De Laune St
  SE17 . . . . .116 D1 261 C1
Delaware Rd W9 . . . . .91 D3
Delawyk Cres SE24 . .161 B5
Delcombe Ave KT4. . . . . .200 C1
Delft Ho 8 KT2. . . . . .176 B3
Delft Way 8 SE22. . . . . . .161 C6
Delhi Rd EN1 . . . . .17 D4
Delhi St N1. . . . . . .94 A6 233 B5
Delia St SW18 . . . . .157 D4
Delisle Rd SE28. . . . . . . .123 C5
Delius Cl WD6 . . . . .9 C5
Delius Gr E15. . . . . .98 A5
Dellafield N4. . . . . .72 C6
Della Path E5. . . . . .74 B5
Dellbow Rd TW14 . . . . . . .150 B6
Dell Cl Stratford Marsh E15. .98 B6
  Wallington SM6 . . . . . . .219 D4

Dell Cl continued
  Woodford IG8. . . . . .21 B1
Dellfield Cl BR3. . . . . .186 A2
Dell La KT17. . . . . .216 A3
Dellors Cl EN5 . . . . .12 C6
Dellow Cl IG2 . . . . .57 B2
Dellow Ho 6 E1 . . . . .118 B6
Dellow St E1 . . . . .118 B6
Dell Rd Enfield EN3 . . . . . . .6 C5
  Sunleigh KT17 . . . . .216 A2
  West Drayton UB7 . . . . .104 B3
Dells Cl Chingford E4 . . . . .19 D4
  Teddington TW11 . . . . . .174 D4
Dell's Mews SW1 . . . . . . .259 B3
Dell The Brentford TW8 . . .131 C6
  Feltham TW14 . . . . .150 B4
  Pinner HA5 . . . . .22 D1
  Plumstead Comm SE2 . . .124 A1
  South Norwood SE19 . . . .183 D2
  Wembley HA0. . . . . .65 B3
  Woodford IG8. . . . . .21 B1
Dell Way W13 . . . . .87 C1
Dell Wlk KT3 . . . . .177 C1
Dellwood Gdns IG5 . . . . . .56 C6
Delme Cres SE3 . . . . .143 B3
Delmey Cl CR0. . . . . .221 D5
Deloraine Ho SE8. . . . . . .141 C4
Deloraine St SE8. . . . . . . .141 C4
Delorme St W6 . . . . .134 D6
Delphian Ct 5 SW16. . . . .182 C6
Delroy Ct N20 . . . . .14 A4
Delta Bldg 7 E14. . . . . . . .98 A1
Delta Cl KT4. . . . . .215 D5
Delta Ct NW2. . . . . .68 A6
Delta Gr UB5 . . . . .84 D4
Delta Ho N1. . . . . .235 C2
Delta Pk Ind Est EN3 . . . . .7 B3
Delta Point 5 E2 . . . . .96 A4
Delta Rd KT4 . . . . .215 C5
Delta St 4 E2 . . . . .96 A4
De Lucy Prim Sch SE2. . . .124 B4
De Lucy St SE2. . . . . .124 B2
Delvan Cl SE18. . . . . .144 C5
Delverton Ho SE17. . . . . .261 D2
Delverton Rd SE17. . . . . .261 D1
Delvino Rd SW6 . .135 C4 265 B6
De Mandeville Gate EN1 . . .6 B1
Demesne Rd SM6. . . . . . .219 D4
Demeta Cl HA9. . . . . .67 A5
De Montfort Ct 1 SW16. . .160 A1
De Montfort Rd SW16. . . . .160 A2
De Morgan Rd SW6 . . . . .135 D2
Dempster Cl KT6. . . . . . . .197 C1
Dempster Rd SW18 . . . . .158 A6
Denberry Dr DA14 . . . . . .168 B1
Denbigh Cl Cheam SM1 . . .217 B3
  Ealing W7. . . . . .86 D2
  Newham E6 . . . . .99 D4
Denbigh Dr UB3 . . . . .105 A4
Denbigh Gdns TW10 . . . . .154 B6
Denbigh Ho
  Knightsbridge SW1 . . . . .257 D6
  7 Notting Hill W11 . . . . . .91 B1
  Notting Hill W11 . . . . . . .244 B6
Denbigh Mews SW1 . . . . .259 A3
Denbigh Pl SW1 . .115 C1 259 A2
Denbigh Rd Ealing W13 . . . .87 B1
  Hounslow TW3 . . . . .129 D3
  Newham E6 . . . . .99 D4
  Notting Hill W11 . .113 B6 244 B6
  Southall UB1. . . . . .85 B1
Denbigh St SW1 . .115 C1 259 A2
Denbigh Terr
  W11. . . . . .113 B6 244 B6
Denbridge Rd BR1, BR7. . .188 B1
Denbury Ho 48 E3 . . . . . . .97 D4
Denby Ct Barnet EN5. . . . . .1 D2
  Lambeth SE11. . . . . .260 D4
Dence Ho 15 E2. . . . . .96 A4
Denchworth Ho 14 SW9 . .138 C3
Den Cl BR2, BR3. . . . . . . .208 B6
Dencliffe 2 TW15 . . . . . . .170 C5
Dencora Centre The EN3 . .7 A2
Dendridge Cl EN1. . . . . . . .6 B6
Dene Ave Blackfen DA15. . .168 A4
  Hounslow TW3 . . . . .129 B2
Dene Cl Brockley SE4. . . . .141 A1
  Hayes BR2. . . . . .208 D1
  Leyton E18 . . . . .75 D6
  Worcester Pk KT4. . . . . .215 D6
Dene Ct Ealing W5. . . . . . .87 C2
  Hanwell W7 . . . . .108 D4
Dene Gdns
  Hinchley Wood KT7. . . . .213 A6
  Stanmore HA7 . . . . .25 C5
Dene Ho N14 . . . . .15 D4
Denehole Ho SE18. . . . . .124 A1
Denehurst Gdns
  Acton W3 . . . . .110 D5
  Hendon NW4 . . . . .46 C3
  Richmond TW10 . . . . . . .132 C1
  Twickenham TW2 . . . . . .152 B4
  Woodford IG8. . . . . .69 C2
Dene Mans 1 NW6 . . . . . .69 C2

Dene Rd Buckhurst Hill IG9. .21 D3
  Friern Barnet N11 . . . . . . .14 D2
Denesmead SE24 . . . . . . .161 A6
Dene The Ealing W13. . . . . .87 B2
  East Molesey KT12, KT8. .195 B4
  South Croydon CR0. . . . .222 D4
  Wembley HA9. . . . . .66 A4
Denewood EN5 . . . . .14 A6
Denewood Ho 6 SM1. . . . .218 A4
Denewood Rd N6. . . . . . . .48 D2
Dengie Wlk N1 . . . . .235 A6
Denham Cl DA16. . . . . . . .146 C2
Denham Cres CR4 . . . . . .202 D5
Denham Ct
  Forest Hill SE26 . . . . . . .162 B1
  Southall UB1. . . . . .108 A6
Denham Dr IG2. . . . . .57 A3
Denham 32 W12 . . . . .112 B6
Denham Lo W5 . . . . .88 A1
Denham Rd
  Feltham TW14 . . . . .150 C4
  Friern Barnet N20 . . . . . . .14 D1
Denham St SE10 . . . . . . .121 A1
Denham Way IG11 . . . . . .101 D6
Denholme Rd W9 . . . . .91 B4
Deniel Lo TW9 . . . . .153 C6
Denise Cl HA0. . . . . .65 C4
Denison Cl N2. . . . . .48 A6
Denison Rd Ealing W5. . . . .87 C3
  Feltham TW13 . . . . .171 D6
  Mitcham SW19. . . . . . . .180 B4
Deniston Ave DA5. . . . . . .169 A3
Denland Ho SW8 . . . . . . .270 D3
Denleigh Ct N14. . . . . .15 D4
Denleigh Gdns
  Southgate N21 . . . . .16 C4
  Thames Ditton KT7. . . . .196 C3
Denman Dr
  Ashford TW15 . . . . .170 D4
  Claygate KT10 . . . . .213 A3
  Hampstead Garden Suburb
  NW11. . . . . .47 C4
Denman Dr N NW11. . . . . .47 C4
Denman Dr S NW11. . . . . .47 C4
Denman Ho 1 N16 . . . . . . .73 C6
Denman Rd SE15 . . . . . . .139 D3
Denman St W1 . . . . .249 C5
Denmark Ave SW19 . . . . .179 A3
Denmark Ct SM4. . . . . . . .201 C4
Denmark Gdns SM5. . . . .218 D5
Denmark Gr N1. . . . . .234 A4
Denmark Hill SE5 . . . . . . .139 A3
Denmark Hill Dr NW9 . . . . .46 A6
Denmark Hill Sta SE5 . . . .139 B3
Denmark Ho 9 SE7. . . . . .122 A4
Denmark Mans 14 SE5 . . .139 A3
Denmark Pl
  2 Bromley E3 . . . . .97 C4
  Soho WC2. . . . . .239 D2
Denmark Rd
  Bromley BR1. . . . . .187 B2
  Camberwell SE5 . . . . . . .139 A3
  Carshalton SM5 . . . . . . .218 D5
  Croydon SE25 . . . . .206 B4
  Ealing W13 . . . . .109 B6
  Hornsey N8. . . . . .50 C5
  Kilburn NW6 . . . . .91 B5
  Kingston u T KT1. . . . . . .198 A6
  Twickenham TW2 . . . . . .152 B1
  Wimbledon SW19. . . . . .178 D4
Denmark St 8 Leyton E11. .76 C5
  Newham E13 . . . . .99 B2
  Soho WC2. . . . . .239 D2
  Tottenham N17 . . . . .34 B3
Denmark Terr NW2 . . . . . . .48 D6
Denmead Ho SW15 . . . . .155 D5
Denmead Rd CR0 . . . . . . .204 D1
Denmead Sch TW12. . . . .173 D3
Denmore Ct SM6 . . . . . . .219 B3
Denner Rd E4 . . . . .19 C2
Denne Terr E8 . . . . .95 D6
Dennett Rd CR0. . . . . . . .204 C2
Dennett's Gr SE14 . . . . . .140 D3
Dennett's Rd SE14 . . . . . .140 C4
Denning Ave CR0 . . . . . . .220 C3
Denning Cl
  Hampton TW12. . . . . . . .173 B5
  St John's Wood
  NW8. . . . . .92 A4 229 B1
Denning Mews SW12 . . . .159 A4
Denning Point E1. . . . . . . .243 D2
Denning Rd NW3 . . . . .70 B4
Dennington Cl 17 E5 . . . . .74 B6
Dennington Park Mansions
  12 NW6. . . . . .69 C3
Dennington Park Rd
  NW6. . . . . .69 C2
Denningtons The KT4 . . . .215 C6
Dennis Ave HA9. . . . . .66 B3
Dennis Cl TW15 . . . . .171 B3
Dennis Ct Chingford E17. . .36 B1
  Greenford UB6. . . . . .86 A1
  Lewisham SE13 . . . . . . .142 A4
Dennis Gdns HA7. . . . . . . .25 C5
Dennis Ho 4 Bow E3 . . . . .97 B5
  Sutton SM1. . . . . .217 C4
Dennis La HA7. . . . . .25 B6
Dennison Point E15. . . . . . .76 A1

Dennis Par 1 N14. . . . . . . .15 D3
Dennis Park Cres SW20 . .179 A2
Dennis Rd KT8. . . . . .196 A5
Dennis Reeve Cl CR4. . . . .180 D2
Dennis Severs' House ★
  E1. . . . . .243 B4
Dennis Way SW4. . . . . . . .137 D2
Denny Cl 15 E6 . . . . .100 A2
Denny Cres SE11. . . . . . . .261 B2
Denny Gdns RM9 . . . . .80 B1
Denny Rd N9 . . . . .18 B3
Denny St SE11 . . . .116 C1 261 B2
Den Rd BR2 . . . . .208 B6
Densham Ho NW8 . . . . . .229 D3
Densham Rd E15 . . . . .98 C6
Densole Cl BR3. . . . . .185 A2
Denstone Ho 5 SE15 . . . .140 A6
Densworth Gr N9 . . . . .18 C2
Dent Ho SE17 . . . . .263 A3
Denton NW1 . . . . .71 A2
Denton Cl EN5 . . . . .12 C6
Denton Ct BR2. . . . . .210 C2
Denton Ho N1. . . . . .72 D1
Denton Rd Bexley DA16. . .146 C3
  Edmonton N18 . . . . .33 C6
  Hornsey N8. . . . . .50 B3
  Twickenham TW1 . . . . . .153 D5
Denton St SW18 . . . . .157 D5
Denton Way E5. . . . . .74 D5
Dents Rd SW11 . . . . .158 D5
Denvale Trade Pk CR4. . . .202 B5
Denver Cl BR6. . . . . .211 C3
Denver Rd UB1. . . . . .107 B5
Denver Rd N16 . . . . .51 C2
Denwood SE23 . . . . .162 D1
Denyer Ho 1 NW5 . . . . . . .71 B4
Denyer St SW3 . . .114 C2 257 B4
Denys Bldg EC1. . . . . .241 A4
Denziloe Ave UB10. . . . . . .82 D4
Denzil Rd NW10 . . . . .67 D3
Deodar Rd SW15. . . . . . . .135 A1
Deodora Cl N20. . . . . .14 D1
Depot App NW2 . . . . .68 D4
Depot Rd
  Isleworth TW3, TW7. . . . .130 B2
  Shepherd's Bush W12 . . .112 C6
Depot St SE5 . . . . .139 B6
DEPTFORD 140 D6
Deptford Bridge SE8. . . . .141 C4
Deptford Bridge Sta
  SE8. . . . . .141 C4
Deptford Broadway SE8,
  SE14. . . . . .141 C4
Deptford Church St SE8 . .141 C5
Deptford Ferry Rd 24
  E14. . . . . .119 C2
Deptford Gn SE8. . . . . . . .141 C6
Deptford Green Sch
  SE14. . . . . .141 B5
Deptford Green Sch (Annex)
  12 SE14. . . . . .141 A5
Deptford High St SE8 . . . .141 C6
Deptford Park Prim Sch 2
  SE8. . . . . .119 A1
Deptford Sta SE8 . . . . . . .141 C5
Deptford Trad Est SE8. . . .141 A6
Deptford Wharf SE8. . . . . .119 B2
De Quincey Mews 3
  E14. . . . . .121 A5
De Quincey Rd N17. . . . . . .33 B2
Derby Ave Harrow HA3 . . . .24 B2
  North Finchley N12. . . . . .30 A5
  Romford RM7 . . . . .59 D3
Derby Ct 8 Clapton Pk E5. .74 D4
  Woodford E18. . . . . .36 D2
Derby Gate SW1 . . . . . . .250 A2
Derby Hill SE23. . . . . .162 C2
Derby Hill Cres SE23 . . . .162 C2
Derby Ho Hendon NW4 . . . .46 C6
  Lambeth SE11. . . . . .261 A4
  Pinner HA5 . . . . .22 D1
  4 Wandsworth SM6. . . . .219 B3
Derby Lo N3. . . . . .29 B1
Derby Rd
  Cheam SM1, SM2. . . . . .217 B2
  Edmonton N18 . . . . .34 C5
  Enfield EN3. . . . . .18 C6
  Greenford UB6. . . . . .85 D6
  Hounslow TW3 . . . . .129 D1
  Merton SW19 . . . . .179 D1
  Mortlake SW14 . . . . .132 D1
  South Hackney E9. . . . . . .96 D6
  Surbiton KT5, KT6. . . . . .198 C1
  Thornton Heath CR0. . . .204 D1
  Upton E7. . . . . .77 D1
  Woodford E18. . . . . .36 D2
Derby Rd Ind Est TW3. . . .129 D1
Derbyshire St E2 . . . . .96 A4
Derby St W1. . . . . .248 B3
Dereham Ho 7 SE4. . . . . .140 D1
Dereham Pl 7 E2 . . . . . . .243 B6
Dereham Rd IG11. . . . . . . .79 D3
Derek Ave
  Chessington KT19. . . . . .214 D3
  Wallington SM6 . . . . . . .219 B4
  Wembley HA9. . . . . .66 D1
Derek Cl KT19 . . . . .214 D3
Derek Walcott Cl SE24 . . .160 D6
Dericote St E8. . . . . .96 B6
Deri Dene Cl 2 TW19. . . . .148 A5

Derifall Cl E6. . . . . .100 B2
Dering Pl CR0 . . . . .221 A4
Dering Rd CR0. . . . . .221 A4
Dering St W1. . . . . .238 D1
Derinton Rd SW17. . . . . . .181 A6
Derley Rd UB2. . . . . .106 D3
Dermody Gdns SE13 . . . . .164 B6
Dermody Rd SE13. . . . . . .164 B6
Deronda Rd SE24, SW2. . .160 D3
Deroy Cl SM5. . . . . .218 D2
Derrick Gdns SE7 . . . . . . .121 C2
Derrick Ho 13 SW2. . . . . .160 C3
Derrick Rd BR3. . . . . .207 B5
Derrycombe Ho 18 W2 . . . .91 C2
Derry Ct CR0, SM6. . . . . .220 A4
Derry St W8 . . . . . .113 D4 245 C1
Dersingham Ave E12. . . . . .78 C3
Dersingham Inf Sch E12 . . .78 C3
Dersingham Rd NW2. . . . . .69 A5
Derwent NW1 . . . . .232 A1
Derwent Ave Barnet EN4 . . .14 D3
  Burnt Oak NW7. . . . . .27 B4
  Edmonton N18 . . . . .33 B5
  Hyde The NW9 . . . . .45 C4
  Kingston u T SW15. . . . .177 C6
  Pinner HA5 . . . . .23 A4
  Uxbridge UB10. . . . . .60 C5
Derwent Cl
  Claygate KT10 . . . . .212 D2
  East Bedfont TW14. . . . .149 D3
Derwent Cres
  Bexleyheath DA7. . . . . . .147 C3
  Stanmore HA7 . . . . .25 C1
  Whetstone N20 . . . . .14 A1
Derwent Ct
  2 Hammersmith W6. . . . .112 A4
  Hornsey N8. . . . . .50 A3
  8 Rotherhithe SE16 . . . . .118 D4
Derwent Dr Crofton BR5. . .211 B2
  Hayes UB4 . . . . .83 C2
Derwent Gdns
  Redbridge IG4 . . . . .56 A5
  Wembley HA9. . . . . .43 C2
Derwent Gr SE22 . . . . . . .139 D1
Derwent Ho Penge SE20. . .184 B1
  South Kensington SW7. . .256 B4
  Tower Hamlets E3 . . . . . . .97 B3
Derwent Lo
  Hounslow TW7 . . . . .130 B3
  North Cheam KT4. . . . . .216 B6
Derwent Rd Ealing W5 . . . .109 C3
  Palmers Green N13 . . . . . .16 B1
  Penge SE20 . . . . .184 B1
  Southall UB1. . . . . .85 B1
  Twickenham TW2 . . . . . .151 D5
  West Barnes SM4. . . . . .200 D3
Derwent Rise NW9. . . . . . .45 C3
Derwent St SE10 . . . . . . .120 C1
Derwentwater Mans 2
  W3. . . . . .111 A5
Derwentwater Prim Sch
  W3 . . . . .111 A5
Derwentwater Rd W3. . . . .111 A5
Derwent Wlk SM6 . . . . . . .219 B1
Derwent Yd W5 . . . . .109 C3
De Salis Rd UB10 . . . . .83 A4
Desborough Cl
  Bayswater W2 . . . . .91 D2
  Lower Halliford TW17. . . .192 C2
Desborough Ct SE25 . . . . .206 B5
Desborough Ho 11 W14 . .264 D6
Desenfans Rd SE21. . . . . .161 C5
Deseret Ho 6 CR4 . . . . . .202 D6
Desford Rd E16 . . . . .98 C3
Desford Way TW15. . . . . .148 B2
Design Mus ★ SE1 . . . . . .253 D2
Desmond Ho 4 EN4 . . . . . .14 C5
Desmond St SE14 . . . . . . .141 A6
Desmond Tutu Dr SE23 . . .163 A3
Despard Ho SW2. . . . . . . .160 C2
Despard Rd N19 . . . . .49 C1
Dessouter 19 NW9 . . . . . . .27 D1
Desvignes Dr SE14 . . . . . .164 B5
Detherick Ct TW3 . . . . . . .130 A1
Dethick Ct E3. . . . . .97 A6
Detling Ho SE17 . . . . .263 A3
Detling Rd BR1. . . . . .187 A5
Detmold Rd E5 . . . . .74 C6
Devalls Cl E6 . . . . .122 C6
Devana End SM5. . . . . . . .218 D5
Devas Rd SW20 . . . . .178 C2
Devas St E3 . . . . .97 D3
Devema Cl DA7 . . . . .188 C2
Devenay Rd E15 . . . . .76 D1
Devenish Rd SE2. . . . . . . .124 A4
Deventer Cres 8 SE22. . . .161 C6
Deveraux Cl BR3. . . . . . . .208 A4
De Vere Cl SM6 . . . . .220 A1
De Vere Cotts W8 . . . . . . .256 A6
De Vere Ct E15. . . . . .74 B5
De Vere Gdns
  Kensington W8. . . .114 A4 246 A1
  Redbridge IG1 . . . . .56 B1
Deverell St SE1 . . . .117 B3 262 C5
De Vere Mews W8. . . . . . .256 A6
Devereux Ct WC2 . . . . . . .241 A1
Devereux Ho 7 SW15. . . . .156 A6

Devereux La SW13....134 B5
Devereux Rd SW11....158 D5
Deverill Ct SE20....184 C2
Devey Ct KT2....177 B5
Devitt Ho 5 E14....119 D6
Devizes St N1....235 D5
Devon Ave TW2....152 A3
Devon Cl Chigwell IG9....21 B2
 Tottenham N17....51 D6
 Wembley UB6....87 C6
Devoncroft Gdns TW1....153 A4
Devon Ct 3 Acton W3....88 C1
 2 Ealing W7....86 D2
 Hampton TW12....173 C3
Devon Gdns N4....50 D3
Devon Ho 9 Penge SE20....184 B3
 Walthamstow E17....35 B1
 6 Wanstead E11....55 A4
Devonhurst Pl 4 W4....111 B1
Devonia Gdns N18....33 A4
Devonia Rd N1....94 D5 234 D4
Devon Mans SE1....253 B2
Devon Par HA3....43 C4
Devonport W2....237 A2
Devonport Gdns IG1....56 B3
Devonport Ho
 Greenwich SE10....142 A6
 23 Paddington W2....91 C2
Devonport Rd W12....112 B4
Devonport St E1....96 D1
Devon Rd IG11....101 C6
Devon Rise N2....48 B5
Devonshire Ave SM2....218 A1
Devonshire Cl
 Edmonton N13....32 C6
 Leyton E15....76 C4
 Marylebone W1....238 C4
Devonshire Cres NW7....28 D3
Devonshire Ct
 14 Balham SW12....159 B4
 Croydon CR0....207 C1
 Feltham TW13....150 B2
 Pinner HA5....23 B2
 6 Richmond TW9....132 B4
 Tottenham N17....33 A4
Devonshire Dr
 London SE10....141 D4
 Long Ditton KT6....213 D6
Devonshire Gdns
 Chiswick W4....133 A5
 Edmonton N21....17 A4
 Tottenham N17....33 A4
Devonshire Gr SE15....140 B6
Devonshire Hall 16 E9....74 C2
Devonshire Hill La N17....33 A4
Devonshire Hill Prim Sch
 N17....33 B4
Devonshire Ho
 Brondesbury NW6....69 B2
 Hounslow TW3....130 A2
 Newington SE1....262 A6
 Paddington W2....236 D4
 2 Putney SW15....156 C4
 10 Sutton SM2....218 A1
 Westminster SW1....259 D2
 Whetstone N12....14 A1
Devonshire House Prep Sch
 NW3....70 A3
Devonshire Mews 2
 W4....111 C1
Devonshire Mews N NW1....238 C4
Devonshire Mews S W1....238 C4
Devonshire Mews W W1....238 B4
Devonshire Pl
 Child's Hill NW2....69 C5
 Kensington W8....255 C5
 Marylebone W1....93 A2 238 B4
Devonshire Place Mews
 W1....238 B4
Devonshire Prim Sch 18
 SM2....218 A1
Devonshire Rd
 Bexley DA6....147 A1
 Chislehurst SE9....166 A2
 Chiswick W4....111 C1
 Ealing W5....109 C3
 Eastcote HA5....40 C2
 Edmonton N9....18 C3
 Feltham TW13....173 A6
 Forest Hill SE23....162 C4
 Hackbridge SM5, SM6....219 A4
 Harrow HA1....42 B3
 Hatch End HA5....23 B2
 Ilford IG2....57 C2
 Mill Hill NW7....28 D3
 Mitcham SW19....180 C3
 Newham E16....99 B1
 Palmers Green N13....32 C6
 Southall UB1....85 C2
 Sutton SM2....218 A1
 Thornton Heath CR0....205 B4
 Tottenham N17....33 A4
 Walthamstow E17....53 C3
Devonshire Rd Nat Res *
 SE23....162 D4
Devonshire Row EC2....243 B3

Devonshire Row Mews
 W1....238 D5
Devonshire Sq
 Bromley BR2....209 B5
 Whitechapel EC2....95 C1 243 B2
Devonshire St
 Chiswick W4....111 C1
 Marylebone W1....93 B2 238 C4
Devonshire Terr
 W2....92 A1 236 B1
Devonshire Way
 Croydon CR0, CR9....223 B6
 Hayes UB4....84 B1
Devons Rd E3....97 D3
Devons Road Sta E3....97 D3
Devon St SE15....140 B6
Devon Way
 Chessington KT9....213 C3
 Ewell KT19....214 D3
 Hillingdon UB10....82 B5
Devon Waye TW5....129 B5
De Walden Ho NW8....230 A4
De Walden St W1....238 B3
Dewar Ho 2 SW17....180 C1
Dewar St SE15....140 A2
Dewberry Gdns E6....100 A2
Dewberry St E14....98 A2
Dewey Rd
 Dagenham RM10....81 D2
 Islington N1....94 C5 234 A4
Dewey St SW17....180 C5
Dewhurst Rd W14....112 D3
Dewlands Ct 7 NW4....28 D1
Dewsbury Cl HA5....41 A3
Dewsbury Ct 5 W4....111 A2
Dewsbury Gdns KT4....216 A5
Dewsbury Rd NW10....68 A3
Dewsbury Terr NW1....231 D6
Dexter Ho 2 DA18....125 A3
Dexter Rd EN5....12 D5
Deyncourt Rd N17....33 A2
Deynecourt Gdns E11....55 C5
D'eynsford Rd SE5....139 B4
Dhonau Ho SE16....263 D4
Diadem Ct W1....239 C2
Dial Wlk The W8....113 D4 245 C5
Diameter Rd BR5....211 A3
Diamond Cl RM8....58 C1
Diamond Ct 8 W7....108 C5
Diamond Est SW17....158 C1
Diamond Ho 22 E3....97 A5
Diamond Rd HA4....63 A4
Diamond St
 18 London NW10....67 B1
 SE15....139 C5
Diamond Terr SE10....142 A4
Diana Cl 27 Deptford SE8....141 B6
 Sidcup DA14....169 A2
 Woodford E18....37 B2
Diana Ct SM5....219 A1
Diana Gdns KT6....214 B6
Diana Ho Barnes SW13....133 D4
 2 Brixton SW2....160 B6
Diana, Princess of Wales
 Mml Fountain *
 W2....114 C5 246 D2
Diana, Princess of Wales
 Mml Wlk W2....114 A5 246 A3
Diana Rd E17....53 B6
Dianne Ct SE12....165 A3
Dianne Way EN4....2 C1
Dianthus Cl SE2....124 B1
Dias Ho UB5....85 A6
Dibden Ho 8 SE5....139 C5
Dibden St N1....95 A5 235 A6
Dibdin Cl SM1....217 C5
Dibdin Ho W9....91 D5
Dibdin Rd SM1....217 C6
Dicey Ave NW2....68 C4
Dickens Ave Finchley N3....30 A2
 Hayes UB8....82 D1
Dickens Cl Erith DA8....147 D5
 Hayes UB3....105 C2
 Richmond TW10....154 A2
Dickens Ct
 Clerkenwell EC1....241 C5
 10 Wanstead E11....55 A5
 Wembley HA0....65 C5
Dickens Dr BR7....189 A4
Dickens Ho
 Bloomsbury WC1....240 A6
 3 Erith DA17....125 B1
 Hayes UB3....105 C2
 Kennington SE17....261 D1
 Kilburn NW6....91 C4
 Paddington NW8....236 D6
Dickens La N18....33 C5
Dickenson Cl N9....18 A3
Dickenson Ho N8....50 B3
Dickenson Rd
 Feltham TW13....172 D5
 Hornsey N8....50 A2
Dickenson's La SE25....206 A3
Dickenson's Pl SE25....206 A3
Dickens Rd E6....99 D5
Dickens Sq SE1....117 A3 262 B6
Dickens St SW8....137 B3
Dickens Wood Cl SE19....182 D3
Dickerage Hill
 Kingston u T KT3....177 A1

Dickerage Hill continued
 Kingston u T KT3....199 A6
Dickerage La KT3....199 A6
Dickerage Rd KT1, KT2, KT3....177 A1
Dickinson Ho 18 E2....96 A4
Dicksee Ho NW8....236 C5
Dick Shepherd Ct 17
 SW2....160 C5
Dickson Fold HA5....40 D5
Dickson Ho
 3 Charlton SE18....144 A4
 4 Stepney E1....96 B1
Dickson Rd SE9....144 A2
Dick Turpin Way TW14....127 D1
Didbin Ho N7....72 B6
Didsbury Cl E6....100 B6
Digby Bsns Ctr E9....74 D2
Digby Cres N4....73 A6
Digby Gdns RM10....103 C6
Digby Mans W6....112 C1
Digby Pl CR0....221 D5
Digby Rd Barking IG11....79 D1
 Homerton E9....74 D2
Digby St E2....96 C4
Diggon St E1....96 D2
Dighton Ct SE17....139 A6
Dighton Rd SW18....136 A1
Dignum St N1....234 A4
Digswell St N7....72 C2
Dilhorne Cl SE12....165 B1
Dilke St SW3....136 D6 267 D6
Dilloway Yd UB2....107 A4
Dillwyn Cl SE26....185 A6
Dilston Cl 1 UB5....84 C4
Dilston Gr SE16....118 C2
Dilton Gdns SW15....156 B3
Dilwyn Ct E17....35 A1
Dimes Pl 9 W6....112 B2
Dimmock Dr UB6....64 B3
Dimond Cl E7....77 A4
Dimsdale Dr Enfield EN1....18 A5
 Welsh Harp NW9....45 A1
Dimsdale Wlk 4 E13....99 A5
Dimson Cres E3....97 C4
Dinerman Ct NW8....229 B6
Dingle Cl EN5....11 D5
Dingle Ct 18 HA7....25 C5
Dingle Gdns E14....119 C6
Dingle Rd TW15....170 D5
Dingles Ct HA5....22 D1
Dingle The UB10....82 D4
Dingley La SW16....159 D2
Dingley Pl EC1....97 A3 235 B1
Dingley Rd EC1....95 A4 235 A1
Dingwall Ave CR0....221 A6
Dingwall Gdns NW11....47 C3
Dingwall Rd
 South Croydon CR0....221 B6
 Wandsworth SW18....158 A4
Dinmont Ho 27 E2....96 A5
Dinmont St 1 E2....96 B5
Dinmore Ho 6 E9....96 C6
Dinnington Ho 17 E1....96 B3
Dinorben Sm6....219 C1
Dinsdale Cl EN5....13 C6
Dinsdale Gdns
 New Barnet EN5....13 C6
 South Norwood SE25....205 C4
Dinsdale Rd SE3....142 D6
Dinsmore Rd SW12....159 B4
Dinton Ho NW8....237 A6
Dinton Rd
 Kingston u T KT2....176 B3
 Mitcham SW19....180 B4
Dinwiddy Ho N1....233 C3
Dionis Ho SW6....135 C3
Diploma Ave N2....48 C5
Diploma Ct N2....48 C5
Diprose Lo SW17....180 B6
Dirleton Rd E15....98 D6
Disbrowe Rd W6....135 A6 264 B5
Discovery Bsns Pk 13
 SE16....118 A3
Discovery Dock E E14....119 D4
Discovery Ho 1 E14....120 A6
Discovery Prim Sch
 SE28....123 C5
Dishforth La NW9....27 C2
Disley Ct 2 UB1....85 D1
Disney Pl SE1....252 B2
Disney St SE1....252 B2
Dison Cl EN3....6 D4
Disraeli Cl 1 Acton W4....111 B2
 Thamesmead SE28....124 C5
Disraeli Gdns SW15....135 B1
Disraeli Rd Acton NW10....89 B5
 Ealing W5....109 D5
 Putney SW15....135 A1
 Upton E7....77 A2
Diss St E2....95 D4
Distaff La EC4....252 A6
Distillery La W6....112 C1
Distillery Rd W6....112 C1
Distillery Wlk 11 TW8....132 A6
Distin St SE11....261 A3
Distin St 3 SM1....217 D3
Distin St SE11....116 C2 261 A3
District Rd HA0....65 B3
Ditchburn St E14....120 A6
Ditchfield Rd UB4....85 A3

Ditchley Ct W7....86 D2
Dittisham Rd SE9....188 A6
Ditton Cl KT7....197 A2
Dittoncroft Cl CR0....221 C4
Ditton Grange Cl KT6....197 D1
Ditton Grange Dr KT6....197 D1
Ditton Hill KT6....213 D6
Ditton Hill Rd KT6....197 C1
Ditton Ho 10 E5....74 D3
Ditton Lawn KT7....197 A1
Ditton Pl 6 SE20....184 B2
Ditton Rd Bexley DA6....169 A6
 Southall UB2....107 B1
 Surbiton KT6....198 B1
Ditton Reach KT7....197 B3
Divis Way SW15....156 B5
Dixon Cl 4 E6....100 B1
Dixon Clark Ct N1....72 C2
Dixon Ct N4....50 C3
Dixon Ho
 20 North Kensington
 NW10....90 D1
 West Heath SE2....124 C1
Dixon Pl BR4....207 D1
Dixon Rd London SE14....141 A4
 South Norwood SE25....205 D6
Dixon's Alley 10 SE16....118 B4
Dixon Way W10....67 C1
Dobbin Cl HA3....25 A1
Dobell Rd SE9....166 B6
Dobree Ave NW2....68 B1
Dobson Cl NW6....70 B1
Dobson Ho 18 SE14....140 D6
Doby Ct EC4....252 B6
Dockers Tanner Rd 26
 E14....119 C2
Dockett Eddy La KT16,
 TW17....192 B1
Dockett Moorings KT16....192 B1
Dockhead SE1....117 D4 253 D1
Dockhead Wharf SE1....253 D2
Dock Hill Ave SE16....118 D4
Docklands Ct 20 E14....97 B1
Dockland St E16....122 C5
Docklands Visitor Ctr *
 E14....120 A4
Dockley Rd SE16....118 A3
Dockley Road Ind Est 11
 SE16....118 A3
Dock Offices 12 SE16....118 C3
Dock Rd Brentford TW8....131 D5
 Canning Town E16....120 D6
Dockside Rd E16....121 D6
Dock St E1....118 A6
Dockwell Cl TW14....128 A1
Dockwell's Ind Est
 TW14....150 B6
Doctor Johnson Ho 2
 SW16....181 D6
Doctors Cl SE26....184 C5
Doctor Spurstowe
 Almshouses 9 E8....74 B2
Docura Ho N7....72 B6
Docwras Bldgs N1....73 C2
Dodbrooke Rd SE27....160 D1
Dodd Ho 18 SE16....118 B2
Doddington Gr
 SE17....116 D1 261 D1
Doddington Pl 4 SE17....138 D6
Dodsley Pl N9....18 C1
Dodson St SE1....116 C4 251 B1
Dod St E14....97 C1
Doebury Wlk SE18....146 A6
Doel Cl SW19....180 A3
Dog & Duck Yd WC1....240 C4
Doggett Rd SE6....163 C4
Doggetts Ct EN4....14 C6
Doghurst Ave UB3....126 D5
Doghurst Dr UB7....126 D5
Dog Kennel Hill SE22....139 C2
Dog Kennel Hill 28
 SE22....139 C2
Dog La NW10....67 C4
Dogrose Ct 14 NW9....46 A5
Doherty Rd E13....99 A3
Dokal Ind Est UB2....107 A4
Doland Ct SW17....180 D4
Dolben Ct SW1....259 D3
Dolben St SE1....116 D5 251 D3
Dolby Rd SW6....135 B3
Doleman Ho 19 SE10....141 D4
Dolland Ho SE11....260 D1
Dolland St SE11....260 D1
Dollar Bay E14....120 A4
Dollary Ct KT3....198 D6
Dolliffe Cl CR4....180 D1
Dollis Ave N3....29 B2
Dollis Brook Wlk EN5....13 A5
Dollis Cres UB4....40 C1
Dolliscroft NW7....29 A3
Dollis Ct N3....29 A3
DOLLIS HILL....68 B5
Dollis Hill Ave NW2....68 B5
Dollis Hill Est NW2....68 A5
Dollis Hill La NW2....68 A5
Dollis Hill Sta NW2....68 B5
Dollis Hts NW2....68 B5
Dollis Jun & Inf Schs
 NW7....28 C3
Dollis Mews N3....29 C2

Dollis Pk N3....29 B2
Dollis Rd N3, NW7....29 B3
Dollis Valley Dr EN5....13 B6
Dollis Valley Way EN5....13 B5
Dolman Cl N3....30 A1
Dolman Rd W4....111 B2
Dolman St SW4....138 B1
Dolphin Cl
 Kingston u T KT6....197 D3
 2 Rotherhithe SE16....118 D4
 Thamesmead SE28....102 D1
Dolphin Ct London NW11....47 A3
 Merton SW19....179 C3
 Tufnell Pk N7....71 C4
 2 Wallington SM6....219 B2
Dolphin Est The TW16....171 B2
Dolphin La E14....119 D6
Dolphin Rd
 Charlton TW16....171 C2
 Northolt UB5....85 B5
Dolphin Rd N TW16....171 C2
Dolphin Rd S TW16....171 C2
Dolphin Rd W TW16....171 C2
Dolphin Sch SW11....158 C6
Dolphin Sq SW1....115 C1 259 B1
Dolphin St KT2....176 A2
Dolphin Twr 21 SE8....141 B6
Dombey Ho
 13 Bermondsey SE1....118 A4
 4 Shepherd's Bush W11....112 D5
Dombey St WC1....240 C4
Dome Hill Pk SE26....183 D6
Domelton Ho SW18....157 D5
Domett Cl SE5....139 B1
Domfe Pl E5....74 C4
Domingo St EC1....242 A5
Dominica Cl 6 E6....99 D5
Dominion Bsns Pk N9....18 D2
Dominion Cl TW3....130 B3
Dominion Ind Est UB2....107 A4
Dominion Par HA1....42 D4
Dominion Rd
 Croydon CR0....205 D2
 Southall UB2....107 A3
Dominion St EC2....95 B2 242 D4
Dominion Wks RM8....59 A1
Domonic Dr SE9....166 D1
Domville Cl N20....14 B2
Donaghue Cotts 11 E14....97 A2
Donald Dr RM6....58 C4
Donald Lynch Ho CR4....180 D1
Donald Rd Newham E13....99 B6
 Thornton Heath CR0....204 B2
Donaldson Rd
 Kilburn NW6....91 B6
 Shooters Hill SE18....144 C4
Donald Woods Gdns
 KT5....215 A6
Doncaster Dr UB5....63 B3
Doncaster Gdns
 London N4....51 A3
 Northolt UB5....63 B3
Doncaster Gn WD19....22 C5
Doncaster Rd N9....18 B4
Doncel Ct E4....20 B4
Donegal Ho 2 E1....96 C3
Donegal St N1....94 B5 233 D3
Doneraile Ho SW1....258 C1
Doneraile St SW6....134 D4
Dongola Rd Newham E13....99 B4
 Tottenham N17....51 C6
 Tower Hamlets E1....97 A2
Dongola Rd W 5 E13....99 B4
Don Gratton Ho 23 E1....96 A2
Donhead Sch 7 SW19....178 D3
Donington Ave IG6....57 A4
Donkey Alley SE22....162 A5
Donkey La E1....6 A3
Donkin Ho 15 SE16....118 B2
Donne Ct SE24....161 A5
Donnefield Ave HA8....26 A3
Donne Ho
 18 Canonbury N16....73 B4
 14 Deptford SE14....140 D6
 11 Poplar E14....97 C1
Donnelly Ct SW6....264 B4
Donne Pl
 Chelsea SW3....114 C2 257 B4
 Mitcham CR4....203 B5
Donne Rd RM8....80 C6
Donnington Ct
 11 Camden Town NW1....71 B1
 Willesden NW10....68 B1
Donnington Ho 12 SW8....137 D3
Donnington Prim Sch
 NW10....90 B2
Donnington Rd
 Harrow HA3....43 D3
 Willesden Green NW10....90 B6
 Worcester Pk KT4....216 A6
Donnybrook Rd SW16....181 D3
Donoghue Bsns Pk NW2....68 D5
Donovan Ave N10....31 C1
Donovan Ct SW7....256 C1
Donovan Ho 4 E1....118 C6
Donovan Pl N21....16 B6
Don Phelan Cl SE5....139 B4
Doone Cl TW11....175 A4
Doon St SE1....116 C5 251 A4
Doradus Ct 20 SW19....156 B3

Dora Ho
- 11 Shepherd's Bush W11 . . **112** D6
- 1 Tower Hamlets E14 . . . . . **97** B1

Doral Way SM5 . . . . **218** D3
Doran Ct E6 . . . . **100** B5
Dorando Cl W12 . . . . **112** B6
Doran Gr SE18 . . . . **145** C5
Doran Manor N2 . . . . **48** D4
Dora Rd SW19 . . . . **179** C6
Dora St E14 . . . . **97** B1
Dora Way SW9 . . . . **138** C3
Dorcas Ct 9 SW18 . . . . **136** B3
Dorchester Ave
- Edmonton N13 . . . . **33** A6
- Harrow HA2 . . . . **42** A3
- Sidcup DA5 . . . . **168** D4

Dorchester Cl
- Hinchley Wood KT10 . . . . . . **212** D4
- Northolt UB5 . . . . **63** D3
- St Paul's Cray BR5 . . . . **190** B3

Dorchester Ct
- Cricklewood NW2 . . . . **68** D5
- 1 De Beauvoir Town N1 . . . **73** C1
- East Barnet N14 . . . . **15** B4
- Herne Hill SE24 . . . . **161** A6
- Knightsbridge SW1 . . . . . **257** D5
- 1 Muswell Hill N10 . . . . **49** B6
- 5 Streatham SW16 . . . . **160** A2
- 2 Woodford E18 . . . . **36** D2

Dorchester Dr
- Feltham TW14 . . . . **149** C5
- Herne Hill SE24 . . . . **161** A6

Dorchester Gdns
- Chingford E4 . . . . **35** C6
- East Finchley NW11 . . . . **47** C5

Dorchester Gr W4 . . . . **111** D1
Dorchester Ho
- Richmond TW9 . . . . **132** D5
- Wallington SM5 . . . . **218** D3

Dorchester Mews
- New Malden KT3 . . . . **199** B5
- Twickenham TW1 . . . . **153** C5

Dorchester Prim Sch
- KT4 . . . . **200** C1

Dorchester Rd
- Cheam SM4 . . . . **202** A2
- North Cheam KT4 . . . . **200** C1
- Northolt UB5 . . . . **63** D3

Dorchester Way HA3 . . . . . **44** B3
Dorchester Waye
- Hayes UB4 . . . . **84** B1
- Hayes UB4 . . . . **84** C1

Dorcis Ave DA7 . . . . **147** A3
Dordrecht Rd W3 . . . . **111** C5
Dore Ave E12 . . . . **78** C3
Doreen Ave NW9 . . . . **45** B1
Doreen Capstan Ho 5
- E11 . . . . **76** C5

Dore Gdns SM4 . . . . **201** D2
Dorell Cl UB1 . . . . **85** B2
Dorey Ho 7 TW8 . . . . **131** C5
Doria Rd SW6 . . . . **135** B3
Doric Ho 7 E2 . . . . **96** D5
Doric Way NW1 . . . **93** D4 **232** C2
Dorie Mews N12 . . . . **29** D6
Dorien Rd SW20 . . . . **178** D1
Doris Ashby Cl UB6 . . . . **87** A6
Doris Emmerton Ct
- SW18 . . . . **136** A1

Doris Rd Ashford TW15 . . . **171** B4
- Upton E7 . . . . **77** A1

Dorking Cl Deptford SE8 . . **141** B6
- North Cheam KT4 . . . . **216** D4

Dorking Ct N17 . . . . **34** A2
Dorking Ho SE1 . . . . **262** D6
Dorland Ct SW15 . . . . **157** B5
Dorlcote Rd SW18 . . . . **158** C4
Dorly Cl TW17 . . . . **193** C4
Dorleston Ct N1 . . . . **235** D6
Dorman Pl 6 N9 . . . . **18** A2
Dorman Way NW8 . **92** B6 **229** C6
Dorman Wlk NW10 . . . . **67** B2
Dorma Trad Pk E10 . . . . **52** D1
Dormay St SW18 . . . . **157** B6
Dormer Cl Barnet EN5 . . . . . **12** D6
- Stratford E15 . . . . **76** D2

Dormer's Ave UB1 . . . . **85** C1
Dormers Lo EN4 . . . . **2** D3
Dormers Rise UB1 . . . . **85** D1
DORMER'S WELLS **107** C6
Dormer's Wells High Sch
- UB1 . . . . **85** C1

Dormers Wells Ho UB4 . . . **84** C2
Dormer's Wells Inf Sch
- UB1 . . . . **107** D6

Dormer's Wells Jun Sch
- UB1 . . . . **107** D6

Dormer's Wells La UB1 . . **107** C5
Dormer's Wells L Ctr
- UB1 . . . . **107** D6

Dormer Wells L Ctr UB1 . . **85** D1
Dormstone Ho SE17 . . . . . **263** A3
Dormywood HA4 . . . . **39** D4
Dornberg Cl SE3 . . . . **143** A5
Dornberg Rd SE3 . . . . **143** B5
Dorncliffe Rd SW6 . . . . **135** A3
Dorney NW3 . . . . **70** C1
Dorney Ct SW6 . . . . **135** A2

Dorney Rise BR5 . . . . . . **211** D5
Dorney Way TW4 . . . . . . **151** A6
Dornfell St NW6 . . . . **69** B3
Dornoch Ho 26 E3 . . . . **97** B5
Dornton Rd
- South Croydon CR2 . . . . . **221** C3
- Upper Tooting SW12,
- SW17 . . . . **159** C2

Dorothy Ave HA0 . . . . **66** A1
Dorothy Barley Jun & Inf
- **Schs** RM8 . . . . **80** B3

Dorothy Charrington Ho 1
- SE22 . . . . **162** A6

Dorothy Evans Cl DA7 . . **147** D1
Dorothy Gdns RM8 . . . . **80** B4
Dorothy Pettingel Ho 1
- SM1 . . . . **217** D5

Dorothy Rd SW11 . . . . **136** D2
Dorothy Villas UB1 . . . . **107** C5
Dorrell Pl 18 SW9 . . . . **138** C2
Dorrien Wlk SW16 . . . . **159** D2
Dorrington Ct SE25 . . . . . . **183** C1
Dorrington Point 20 E3 . . . **97** D4
Dorrington St EC1 . . . . **241** A4
Dorrington Way BR3 . . . . . **208** A4
Dorrit Ho 2 W11 . . . . **112** D5
Dorrit Mews N18 . . . . **33** C5
Dorrit St SE1 . . . . **252** B2
Dorrit Way BR7 . . . . **189** A4
Dorryn Ct SE26 . . . . **184** D5
Dors Cl NW9 . . . . **45** B1
Dorset Ave
- Falconwood DA16 . . . . **145** D1
- Hayes UB4 . . . . **83** C4
- Southall UB2 . . . . **107** C2

Dorset Bldgs EC4 . . . . **241** C1
Dorset Cl Hayes UB4 . . . . . . **83** C4
- Marylebone NW1 . . . . **237** C4

Dorset Ct 3 Ealing W7 . . . . . **86** D2
- 3 London W1 . . . . **73** C1
- 4 Northolt UB5 . . . . **85** B4

Dorset Dr HA8 . . . . **26** B4
Dorset Gdns SW16 . . . . **204** B5
Dorset Hall SW19 . . . . **179** C2
Dorset Ho 1 SE20 . . . . **184** B2
Dorset Mans 2 W6 . . . . **134** D6
Dorset Mews
- Belgravia SW1 . . . . **258** C6
- Finchley N3 . . . . **29** C2

Dorset Pl E15 . . . . **76** B2
Dorset Rd Ashford TW15 . . **148** A1
- Chislehurst SE9 . . . . **166** A2
- Ealing W5 . . . . **109** D3
- Harrow HA1 . . . . **42** A3
- Merton SW19 . . . . **179** C1
- Mitcham CR4 . . . . **180** C1
- Penge BR3 . . . . **206** D6
- South Lambeth
- SW8 . . . . **138** B5 **270** C4
- Upton E7 . . . . **77** C1
- West Green N15 . . . . **51** B5
- Wood Green N22 . . . . **32** A2

Dorset Rise EC4 . . . **94** D1 **241** C1
Dorset Road Inf Sch 7
- SE9 . . . . **166** A2

Dorset Sq NW1 . . . . **92** D3 **237** C5
Dorset St W1 . . . . . . **92** D2 **237** B3
Dorset Way
- Hillingdon UB10 . . . . **82** B5
- Twickenham TW2 . . . . **152** B3

Dorset Waye TW5 . . . . **129** B5
Dorton Cl 6 SE15 . . . . **139** C5
Dorton Villas UB7 . . . . **126** C4
Dorville Cres W6 . . . . **112** B3
Dorville Rd SE12 . . . . **165** A6
Dothill Rd SE18 . . . . **145** A5
Douai Gr TW12 . . . . **174** A2
Douay Martyrs RC Sch
- **(Annexe) The** UB10 . . . . . . **60** D3

Douay Martyrs RC Sch The
- UB10 . . . . **60** D4

Doughty Ct 11 E1 . . . . **118** B5
Doughty Mews
- WC1 . . . . **94** B3 **240** C5

Doughty St WC1 . . . **94** B3 **240** C5
Douglas 20 NW9 . . . . **27** D1
Douglas Ave
- Walthamstow E17 . . . . **35** C4
- Wembley HA0 . . . . **66** A1
- West Barnes KT3 . . . . **200** B5

Douglas Bader Ho N3 . . . . . **29** D4
Douglas Bldgs SE1 . . . . . . **252** B2
Douglas Cl
- Hadley Wood EN4 . . . . **2** B5
- Stanmore HA7 . . . . **25** A5
- Wallington SM6 . . . . **220** A2

Douglas Cres UB4 . . . . **84** D3
Douglas Ct London N3 . . . . . . **29** D1
- 5 South Hampstead NW6 . . **69** C1
- 1 Upper Tooting SW17 . . . **180** C4

Douglas Dr CR0 . . . . **223** D6
Douglas Gracey Ho 1
- SW18 . . . . **157** A4

Douglas Ho
- Isleworth TW1 . . . . **153** B6
- Putney SW15 . . . . **156** A5
- Westminster SW1 . . . . **259** C3

Douglas Johnstone Ho
- SW6 . . . . **264** C5

Douglas Mews NW2 . . . . **69** A5

Douglas Path E14 . . . . . **120** A1
Douglas Rd Chingford E4 . . . **20** C3
- Hounslow TW3 . . . . **129** D2
- Ilford IG3 . . . . **58** A3
- Islington N1 . . . . **73** A1
- Kilburn NW6 . . . . **91** B6
- Kingston u T KT1 . . . . **176** D1
- 5 Newham E16 . . . . **99** A2
- Stanwell TW19 . . . . **148** A5
- Surbiton KT6 . . . . **198** B1
- Thames Ditton KT10 . . . . . **212** A6
- Welling DA16 . . . . **146** B4
- Wood Green N22 . . . . **32** C2

Douglas Rd N N1 . . . . **73** A2
Douglas Rd S N1 . . . . **73** A2
Douglas Robinson Ct
- SW16 . . . . **182** A3

Douglas Sq SM4 . . . . **201** C3
Douglas St SW1 . . **115** D2 **259** C3
Douglas Terr E17 . . . . **35** B2
Douglas Waite Ho NW6 . . . . **69** D1
Douglas Way SE8 . . . . **141** B5
Doulton Ho SE11 . . . . **260** D4
Doulton Mews 4 NW6 . . . . . **69** D2
Dounesforth Gdns
- SW18 . . . . **157** D3

Douro Pl W8 . . . . . . **113** D3 **255** D6
Douro St E3 . . . . **97** C5
Douthwaite Sq 5 E1 . . . . . . **118** A5
Dove App E6 . . . . **100** A2
Dove Ct Hendon NW7 . . . . **27** D3
Dove Ct City of London EC2 . **242** C1
- Enfield EN3 . . . . **18** B6
- Stanwell TW19 . . . . **148** A4

Dovedale Ave HA3 . . . . **43** C3
Dovedale Cl DA16 . . . . **146** A3
Dovedale Cotts 6
- SW11 . . . . **136** D3

Dovedale Ho N16 . . . . **51** B2
Dovedale Rd SE22 . . . . **162** B5
Dovedale Rise CR4 . . . . **180** D3
Dovedon Cl N14 . . . . **16** A2
Dove House Gdns E4 . . . . . . **19** C2
Dovehouse Mead IG11 . . . . **101** B5
Dovehouse St
- SW3 . . . . **114** C1 **257** A1

Dove Mews SW7 . **114** A1 **256** B2
Dove Pk HA5 . . . . **23** C3
Dover Cl NW2 . . . . **68** D6
Dovercourt Ave CR7 . . . . . . **204** C5
Dovercourt Gdns HA7 . . . . . **26** A5
Dovercourt La SM1 . . . . **218** A5
Dovercourt Rd SE22 . . . . . . **161** D5
Dover Ct Clerkenwell EC1 . . **241** C6
- 17 Greenwich SE10 . . . . . . **141** D4
- Sutton SM1 . . . . **218** B4

Dove Rd N1 . . . . **73** B2
Doverfield Rd SW2 . . . . **160** A4
Dover Flats SE1 . . . . **263** B3
Dover Gdns SM5 . . . . **218** D5
Dover Ho
- 7 Beckenham BR3 . . . . . . **185** C3
- Brixton SE5 . . . . **138** D4
- 11 Deptford SE15 . . . . **140** C6
- Edgware HA8 . . . . **26** B3
- 14 Penge SE20 . . . . **184** B2

Dover House Rd SW15 . . . . **156** B6
Doveridge Gdns N13 . . . . . . **32** D6
Dover Mans 16 SW9 . . . . . . **138** C2
Dover Row E2 . . . . **96** A6
Dover Park Dr SW15 . . . . . . **156** B5
Dover Patrol SE3 . . . . **143** C3
Dover Rd Dagenham RM6 . . . **59** A3
- Lower Edmonton N9 . . . . **18** C2
- South Norwood SE19 . . . . . **183** B4
- Wanstead E12 . . . . **77** C6
- Woolwich SE18 . . . . **145** A3

Dover St W1 . . . . . **115** C5 **249** A4
Dover Terr TW9 . . . . **132** C3
Dover Yd W1 . . . . **249** A4
Doves Cl BR2 . . . . **226** A6
Doves Yd N1 . . . . . . **94** C6 **234** A5
Dovet Ct SW8 . . . . **270** C2
Doveton Ho 7 E1 . . . . **96** C3
Doveton Rd CR2 . . . . **221** B3
Doveton St 8 E1 . . . . **96** C3
Dove Wlk SW1 . . . . **258** A2
Dovey Lo 4 N1 . . . . **72** C1
Dowanhill Rd SE6 . . . . **164** B3
Dowd Cl N11 . . . . **15** A2
Dowdeny Cl 12 NW5 . . . . **71** C3
Dowdeswell Cl SW15 . . . . . **133** C1
Dowding Ho N6 . . . . **49** A2
Dowding Pl HA7 . . . . **25** A4
Dowding Rd UB10 . . . . **60** B1
Dowe Ho SE3 . . . . **142** C2
Dowell Ho SE21 . . . . **161** D1
Dower Ho The DA14 . . . . . . **169** B1
Dowes Ho 13 SW16 . . . . . . **160** A1
Dowgate Hill EC4 . . . . **252** C6
Dowland St W10 . . . . **91** A4
Dowlas St SE5 . . . . **139** C5
Dowlen Ct 14 E14 . . . . **119** C4
Dowler Ct 2 KT2 . . . . **176** B2
Dowler Ho 32 E1 . . . . **96** A1

Dor–Dra 315

Dowson Ho 8 E1 . . . . **96** D1
Doyce St SE1 . . . . **252** A2
Doyle Gdns NW10 . . . . **90** B6
Doyle Ho W3 . . . . **110** D4
Doyle Rd SE25 . . . . **206** A5
D'Oyley St SW1 . . . . **258** A4
Doynton St N19 . . . . **71** B6
Draco St SE17 . . . . **139** A6
Dragon Ct WC2 . . . . **240** B2
Dragonfly Cl E13 . . . . **99** B4
Dragon Rd SE15 . . . . **139** C6
Dragon Yd WC1 . . . . **240** B2
Dragoon Rd SE8 . . . . **119** B1
Dragor Rd NW10 . . . . **89** A3
Drake Cl 30 SE16 . . . . **118** D4
Drake Cres SE28 . . . . **102** C1
Drake Croft N16 . . . . **51** B6
Drake Ct Dulwich SE19 . . . . **183** D5
- 5 Hammersmith W12 . . . . . **112** B4
- Kingston u T KT5 . . . . **198** B5

Drakefell Rd SE4, SE14 . . . **140** D2
Drakefield Rd SW17 . . . . . . **159** A1
Drake Hall 13 E16 . . . . **121** B5
Drake Ho
- 2 Limehouse E14 . . . . **119** A6
- 20 Stepney E1 . . . . **96** C2

Drakeley Ct N5 . . . . **72** D4
Drake Mews BR2 . . . . **209** C5
Drake Rd Brockley SE4 . . . . **141** C2
- Chessington KT9 . . . . **214** C3
- Harrow HA2 . . . . **63** B6
- Mitcham CR4 . . . . **203** A3
- Thornton Heath CR0 . . . . . . **204** B2

Drakes Ct SE23 . . . . **162** C3
Drakes Ctyd NW6 . . . . **69** B1
Drake St Enfield EN2 . . . . **5** B4
- Holborn WC1 . . . . **240** C3

Drakes Wlk E6 . . . . **100** B6
Drakewood Rd SW16 . . . . . **181** D3
Drama Ctr London
- EC1 . . . . **94** C3 **241** B5

Draper Cl
- Belvedere DA17 . . . . **125** B2
- Hounslow TW7 . . . . **130** B3

Draper Ct BR1 . . . . **210** A5
Draper Ho SE1 . . . . **261** D4
Draper Pl N1 . . . . **234** D6
Drapers Almshouses 5
- E3 . . . . **97** C4

Draper's Cottage Homes
- NW7 . . . . **28** A6

Drapers Gdns EC2 . . . . . . **242** D2
Drapers Rd Enfield EN2 . . . . . . **4** D4
- Leyton E15 . . . . **76** B4
- Tottenham N17 . . . . **51** D6

Drappers Way 8 SE16 . . . . **118** A2
Draven Cl BR2 . . . . **208** D2
Drawell Cl SE18 . . . . **123** C1
Drax Ave SW20 . . . . **178** A3
Draxmont SW19 . . . . **179** A4
Draycot Rd Tolworth KT6 . . **198** C1
- Wanstead E11 . . . . **55** B2

Draycott Ave
- Chelsea SW3 . . . . . . **114** C2 **257** B3
- Harrow HA3 . . . . **43** C3

Draycott Cl
- Camberwell SE5 . . . . **139** B5
- Cricklewood NW2 . . . . **68** D5
- Harrow HA3 . . . . **43** B3

Draycott Ct SW11 . . . . **267** A2
Draycott Ho SW3 . . . . **257** C3
Draycott Pl SW3 . **114** D2 **257** C3
Draycott Terr
- SW3 . . . . **114** D2 **257** D3

Drayford Cl W9 . . . . **91** B3
Dray Gdns SW2 . . . . **160** B6
Draymans Ct 4 SW9 . . . . . . **138** B2
Draymans Mews SE15 . . . . **139** D3
Draymans Way TW7 . . . . . . **130** D2
Drayside Mews SM3 . . . . . . **107** B4
Drayson Mews
- W8 . . . . **113** C4 **245** B1

Drayton Ave Ealing W13 . . . **109** A6
- Orpington BR6 . . . . **210** D1

Drayton Bridge Rd
- Ealing W7, W13 . . . . **108** D6
- Ealing W13 . . . . **87** A1

Drayton Cl
- Hounslow TW4 . . . . **151** B6
- Ilford IG1 . . . . **57** B1

Drayton Ct
- South Kensington SW10 . . . **256** B1
- Tolworth KT5 . . . . **214** D6
- West Drayton UB7 . . . . **104** B2

Drayton Gdns
- Ealing W13 . . . . **109** A6
- Southgate N21 . . . . **16** D4
- South Kensington
- SW10 . . . . **114** A1 **256** B1
- West Drayton UB7 . . . . **104** A4

Drayton Gn W13 . . . . **109** A6
Drayton Gr W13 . . . . **109** A6
Drayton Green Prim Sch
- W13 . . . . **109** A6

Drayton Green Rd W13 . . . **109** B6
Drayton Green Sta W7 . . . . . **86** D1

Drayton Ho
🔢 Camberwell SE5 . . . . **139** B5
Leytonstone E11 . . . . .54 B1
Drayton Lo E17 . . . . .35 D1
Drayton Manor High Sch
W7 . . . . .86 D1
Drayton Park Mews 🔢
N5 . . . . .72 C3
Drayton Park Prim Sch 🔢
N5 . . . . .72 C3
Drayton Park Sta N5 . . . . . . .72 C3
Drayton Pk N5, N7 . . . . .72 C4
Drayton Rd Croydon CR0 . .220 D6
Ealing W13 . . . . .109 B6
Harlesden NW10 . . . . .89 D6
Leytonstone E11 . . . . .54 B1
Tottenham N17 . . . . .33 C1
Drayton Waye HA3 . . . . .43 B3
DRCA Business Pk
SW11 . . . .**137** A4 **268** B1
Dreadnought Cl SW19 . . . .**180** B1
Dreadnought St SE10 . . . .**120** C3
Drenon Sq UB3 . . . . .105 D6
Dresden Cl NW6 . . . . .69 D2
Dresden Ho
🔢 Clapham SW11 . . . .**137** A3
Lambeth SE11 . . . .**260** D4
Dresden Rd N19 . . . . .49 D1
Dressington Ave SE4 . . . . .163 C5
Drew Ave NW7 . . . . .29 A4
Drewery Ct SE3 . . . . .142 C2
Drewett Ho 🔢 E1 . . . . .96 A1
Drew Gdns UB6 . . . . .64 D2
Drew Ho 🔢 SW16 . . . . .160 A1
Drew Prim Sch E16 . . . . . . .122 A5
Drew Rd E16 . . . . .122 A5
Drewstead La SW16 . . . . . .159 D2
Drewstead Rd SW16 . . . . . .159 D2
Driberg Ct RM9 . . . . .80 B2
Driffield Ct 🔢 NW9 . . . . . .27 C2
Driffield Rd E3 . . . . .97 A5
Drift The BR2 . . . . .225 D5
Driftway Ho 🔢 E3 . . . . .97 B5
Driftway The CR4 . . . . .181 A2
Drinkwater Ho 🔢 SE5 . . .139 B5
Drinkwater Rd HA2 . . . . . . .63 D6
Drive Ct HA8 . . . . .26 C5
Drive Ho CR4 . . . . .202 C5
Drive Mans 🔢 NW6 . . . . . .135 A3
Drive The Acton W3 . . . . . . .89 A1
Ashford TW15 . . . . .171 B3
Barking IG11 . . . . .79 D1
Barking IG11 . . . . .80 A2
Barnet EN5 . . . . .1 A2
Beckenham BR3 . . . . .185 C2
Bexley DA5 . . . . .168 B4
Buckhurst Hill IG9 . . . . .21 C4
Chingford E4 . . . . .20 B4
Chislehurst BR7 . . . . .189 D2
Edgware HA8 . . . . .26 C5
Enfield EN2 . . . . .5 B4
Erith DA8 . . . . .147 D6
Feltham TW14 . . . . .150 C4
Finchley N3 . . . . .29 C3
Fortis Green N6 . . . . .48 D4
Harlesden NW10 . . . . .89 D6
Harrow HA2 . . . . .41 C2
Hendon NW11 . . . . .47 A2
Hounslow TW3, TW7 . . . . . .130 B3
Ickenham UB10 . . . . .60 A5
Islington N7 . . . . .72 B2
Kingston u T KT2 . . . . .177 A3
Morden SM4 . . . . .202 B4
New Barnet EN5 . . . . .14 A5
Orpington BR6 . . . . .227 D6
Redbridge IG1 . . . . .56 B2
Sidcup DA14 . . . . .190 B6
South Norwood CR7 . . . . . .205 B5
St Paul's Cray BR7 . . . . .211 D6
Surbiton KT6 . . . . .198 A2
Thames Ditton KT10 . . . . . .196 A1
Walthamstow E17 . . . . .53 D6
Wanstead E18 . . . . .55 A6
Wembley Pk HA9 . . . . .67 A6
West Ewell KT19 . . . . .215 D2
West Wickham BR4 . . . . . . .208 B2
Wimbledon SW19, SW20 . .178 C3
Wood Green N11 . . . . .31 D4
Dr Johnson Ave SW17 . . . .159 B1
Dr Johnson's House ★
EC4 . . . .**241** B1
Droitwich Cl SE26 . . . . .162 A1
Dromey Gdns HA3 . . . . .24 D3
Dromore Rd SW15 . . . . . . .157 A5
Dronfield Gdns RM8 . . . . . .80 C3
Dron Ho E1 . . . . .96 C2
Droop St W10 . . . . .91 A3
Drovers Ct
🔢 Kingston u T KT1 . . . . . .176 A1
Lewisham SE13 . . . . .142 A2
Drovers Pl SE15 . . . . .140 B5
Drovers Rd CR2 . . . . .221 B3
Drovers Way N7 . . . . .72 A2
Dr Triplett's CE Jun & Inf Sch
UB3 .83 D1
Druce Rd SE21 . . . . .161 C5
Druid St SE1 . . . . .**117** D4 **253** C1

Druids Way BR2 . . . . .208 B5
Drumaline Ridge KT4 . . . .215 C6
Drummer Lo N7 . . . . .72 B5
Drummond Castle Ct E7 . .76 D4
Drummond Cres
NW1 . . . . .93 D4 **232** C2
Drummond Ct
Finchley N12 . . . . .30 C3
Harrow HA1 . . . . .42 C2
Drummond Ctr CR0 . . . . . .221 A6
Drummond Dr HA7 . . . . . . .24 D3
Drummond Gate SW1 . . .**259** D2
Drummond Ho
🔢 Bethnal Green E2 . . . . . . .96 A5
Finchley N2 . . . . .30 A1
Drummond Rd
Bermondsey SE16 . . . . .118 B3
Croydon CR0 . . . . .221 A6
Wanstead E11 . . . . .55 C3
Drummonds Pl TW9 . . . . . .132 A1
Drummond St
NW1 . . . . .93 C3 **239** A6
Drummonds The IG9 . . . . . .21 B2
Drum St E1 . . . .**243** D2
Drury Cres CR0 . . . . .220 C6
Drury Ho SW8 . . . .**269** A2
Drury La WC2 . . . .94 A1 **240** B1
Drury Rd HA1 . . . . .42 A2
Drury Way NW10 . . . . .67 B3
Drury Way Ind Est NW10 . .67 B3
Dryad St SW15 . . . . .134 D2
Dryburgh Gdns NW9 . . . . . .44 C6
Dryburgh Ho SW1 . . . .**258** D2
Dryburgh Mans SW15 . . . .134 C2
Dryburgh Rd SW15 . . . . . . .134 C2
Dryden Ave W7 . . . . .86 D1
Dryden Bldg 🔢 E1 . . . . . . .96 A1
Dryden Cl SW4 . . . . .159 D6
Dryden Ct Lambeth SE11 . .**261** B3
🔢 Richmond TW10 . . . . . . .175 D6
Dryden Ho
Bromley Comm BR2 . . . . . .209 D4
🔢 Camberwell SE5 . . . . . .139 C4
🔢 Stoke Newington N16 . . .73 C5
Dryden Rd Bexley DA16 . . .145 D4
Enfield EN1 . . . . .17 D5
Harrow HA1 . . . . .24 D2
Wimbledon SW19 . . . . .180 A4
Dryer Ct SW7 . . . .**240** B1
Dryer Ct 🔢 EN3 . . . . .7 C6
Dryfield Cl NW10 . . . . .67 A2
Dryfield Rd HA8 . . . . .27 A4
Dryfield Wlk 🔢 SE8 . . . . . .141 C6
Dryhill Rd DA17 . . . . .147 B6
Dryland Ave 🔢 BR6 . . . . . .227 D4
Drylands Rd N8 . . . . .50 A3
Drysdale Ave E4 . . . . .19 D5
Drysdale Flats 🔢 E8 . . . . .73 D3
Drysdale Ho 🔢 E2 . . . . .95 C4
Drysdale Pl N1 . . . . .95 C4
Drysdale St N1 . . . . .95 C4
Dublin Ave E8 . . . . .96 A6
Du Burstow Terr W7 . . . . . .108 C4
Ducal St 🔢 E2 . . . . .95 D4
Ducane Cl 🔢 W12 . . . . .90 C1
Du Cane Ct SW12 . . . . .159 A3
Du Cane Rd W12 . . . . .90 A1
Ducavel Ho SW2 . . . . .160 B3
Duchess Cl London N11 . . .31 B5
Sutton SM1 . . . . .218 A4
Duchess Gr IG9 . . . . .21 B2
Duchess Mews W1 . . . . . .**238** D3
Duchess of Bedford Ho
W8 . . . .**245** A2
Duchess of Bedford's Wlk
W8 . . . .**113** C4 **245** A1
Duchess St W1 . . . .93 B2 **238** D3
Duchy Rd EN4 . . . . .2 B5
Duchy St SE1 . . . . .116 C5 **251** B4
Ducie Ho 🔢 Charlton SE7 .143 C6
🔢 Putney SW15 . . . . .156 C6
Ducie St SW4 . . . . .138 B1
Duckett Mews N4 . . . . .50 D3
Duckett Rd N4 . . . . .50 D3
Duckett St E1 . . . . .97 A2
Duck La W1 . . . .**239** C1
Duck Lees La EN3 . . . . .7 A1
Ducks Hill Rd HA4, HA6 . . .39 A5
DUCKS ISLAND 12 D5
Duck's Wlk TW1 . . . . .153 C6
Du Cros Dr HA7 . . . . .25 D4
Du Cros Rd W3 . . . . .111 C5
DUDDEN HILL 68 A3
Dudden Hill La NW10 . . . . . .67 D3
Duddington Cl SE9 . . . . . . .187 D6
Dudley Ave HA3 . . . . .43 C6
Dudley Ct
Colney Hatch N12 . . . . .30 C5
Marylebone W1 . . . .**237** C1
St Giles WC2 . . . .**240** A2
Temple Fortune NW11 . . . . .47 B5
🔢 Wanstead E11 . . . . .55 A4
Wembley HA0 . . . . .65 D3
Dudley Dr Ruislip HA4 . . . . .62 B3
West Barnes SM4 . . . . .201 A2
Dudley Gdns Ealing W13 . .109 B4
Harrow HA2 . . . . .42 B1
Dudley Ho
🔢 Brixton SW9 . . . . .138 C3
Edgware HA8 . . . . .26 B3

Dudley Ho continued
Paddington W2 . . . .**236** C3
Dudley Mews 🔢 SW2 . . . .160 C5
Dudley Pl UB3 . . . . .105 B2
Dudley Rd Ashford TW15 . .170 B6
East Bedfont TW14 . . . . . . .149 B3
Finchley N3 . . . . .29 D1
Harrow HA2 . . . . .64 A6
Ilford IG1 . . . . .78 D4
Kilburn NW6 . . . . .91 B5
Kingston u T KT1 . . . . .198 B6
Richmond TW9 . . . . .132 B3
Southall UB2 . . . . .106 D3
Walthamstow E17 . . . . .35 C1
Walton-on-T KT12 . . . . .194 A2
Wimbledon SW19 . . . . .179 C4
Dudley St W2 . . . .**236** C3
Dudlington Rd E5 . . . . .74 C6
Dudmaston Mews SW3 . .**256** D2
Dudrich Cl N11, N12 . . . . . . .30 C4
Dudsbury Rd DA14 . . . . . . .190 B4
Dudset La TW5 . . . . .128 A4
Duett Ct TW3 . . . . .129 A5
Duffell Ho SE11 . . . .**260** D1
Dufferin Ave EC1 . . . .**242** C5
Dufferin Ct EC1 . . . .**242** C5
Dufferin St EC1 . . .95 A3 **242** B5
Duffield Cl HA1 . . . . .42 D4
Duffield Dr N15 . . . . .51 D5
Duffield Ho N4 . . . . .51 A2
Duff Miller Coll
SW7 . . . . .114 A3 **246** B5
Duff St E14 . . . . .97 D1
Dufour's Pl W1 . . . .**239** B1
Dugard Way
SE11 . . . . .116 D2 **261** C3
Dugdale Ho 🔢 N7 . . . . .71 D3
Duggan Dr BR7 . . . . .188 A4
Dugolly Ave HA9 . . . . .66 D5
Duke Humphrey Rd SE3 . .142 C3
Duke Of Cambridge Cl
TW2 . . . . .152 B5
Duke Of Edinburgh Rd
SM1 . . . . .218 B6
Duke Of Wellington Ave
SE18 . . . . .123 A3
Duke of Wellington Pl SW1,
W1 . . . .**248** B2
Duke of York's Sq
SW3 . . . . .114 D2 **257** D3
Duke of York St SW1 . . . .**249** B4
Duke Rd Chiswick W4 . . . . .111 B1
Ilford IG6 . . . . .57 B5
Duke St Hill SE1 . . . .**252** D4
Duke St St James's
SW1 . . . . .115 C5 **249** B4
Dukes Ave Edgware HA8 . . .26 B5
Finchley N3 . . . . .29 D2
Hornsey N10 . . . . .49 C6
Hounslow TW4 . . . . .129 A1
Kingston u T KT3 . . . . .199 D6
Northolt UB5 . . . . .63 A1
Rayners La HA2, HA5 . . . . . .41 B3
Richmond KT2, TW10 . . . . .175 D6
Wealdstone HA1 . . . . .42 C5
Duke's Ave W4 . . . . .111 B1
Dukes Cl Ashford TW15 . . .171 A6
Hampton TW12 . . . . .173 B5
Dukes Ct Barking E6 . . . . .100 C6
Beckenham BR3 . . . . .207 A6
Dulwich SE22 . . . . .162 A3
Ealing W13 . . . . .87 B2
East Dulwich SE22 . . . . . . .162 B6
Lewisham SE13 . . . . .142 A3
Mortlake SW14 . . . . .133 B3
Dukes Gate 🔢 W4 . . . . . . .111 A2
Dukes Green Ave TW14 . .150 A6
Dukes Head Yd N6 . . . . . . .49 B1
Duke's Ho SW1 . . . .**259** D4
Duke Shore Wharf E14 . . .119 B6
Dukes La W8 . . . . . .113 D4 **245** C2
Dukes Mews N10 . . . . .49 B6
Duke's Mews W1 . . . .**238** B2
Duke's Pl EC3 . . . . .95 C1 **243** B1
Dukes Point N6 . . . . .49 B1
Dukes Rd Acton W3 . . . . . . .88 C3
Barking E6 . . . . .100 C6
Duke's Ride UB10 . . . . .60 A4
Duke St
Marylebone W1 . . . .93 A1 **238** B1
Richmond TW10, TW9 . . . .153 D6
Sutton SM1 . . . . .218 B4
Dukesthorpe Rd SE26 . . . .184 D6
Duke Street Mans W1 . . .**238** B1
Dukes Way
Coney Hall BR4 . . . . .224 C5
Wembley HA9 . . . . .66 A3
Duke's Yd W1 . . . .**248** B6
Dulas St N4 . . . . .50 B1
Dulford St W11 . . .113 A6 **244** A6
Dulka Rd SW11 . . . . .158 D6
Dulverton NW1 . . . .**232** B5
Dulverton Ct 🔢 KT6 . . . . .198 A4
Dulverton Mans WC1 . . . .**240** D5
Dulverton Prim Sch SE9 . .167 B2
Dulverton Rd
New Eltham SE9 . . . . .167 B2
Ruislip HA4 . . . . .62 A6

DULWICH **161** C1
Dulwich Bsns Ctr SE23 . .162 D3
Dulwich Coll SE21 . . . . . .161 C2
Dulwich Coll Prep Sch
SE21 . . . . .161 C1
Dulwich Com Hospl
SE22 . . . . .139 C1
Dulwich Comm SE21 . . . . .161 C3
Dulwich Ct SE22 . . . . .162 B3
Dulwich Hamlet Jun Sch
SE21 . . . . .161 B5
Dulwich Lawn Cl SE22 . . .161 D6
Dulwich L Ctr SE22 . . . . . .140 A1
Dulwich Mead SE24 . . . . . .161 A5
Dulwich Mews
🔢 East Dulwich SE22 . . . .139 D1
East Dulwich SE22 . . . . . . .161 D6
Dulwich Oaks The SE21 . .161 D1
Dulwich Picture Gall ★
SE21 . . . . .161 C4
Dulwich Rd SE24 . . . . .160 D5
DULWICH VILLAGE 161 C4
Dulwich Village SE21 . . . .161 C5
Dulwich Village CE Inf Sch
SE21 . . . . .161 C5
Dulwich Wood Ave
SE19 . . . . .183 C5
Dulwich Wood Pk SE19 . .183 C6
Dumain Ct SE11 . . . .**261** C3
Du Maurier Ho 🔢 NW3 . . . .70 D3
Dumbarton Ct 🔢 SW2 . . .160 A4
Dumbarton Rd SW2 . . . . . .160 A5
Dumbleton Cl KT2 . . . . . . .176 D2
Dumbreck Rd SE9 . . . . . . .144 C2
Dumont Rd N16 . . . . .73 C5
Dumphreys Ho 🔢 SW4 . . .159 D4
Dumpton Pl NW1 . . . . .71 A1
Dunally Pk TW17 . . . . .193 B2
Dunbar Ave
Beckenham BR3 . . . . .207 A5
Dagenham RM10 . . . . .81 C5
Thornton Heath SW16 . . . . .182 C1
Dunbar Cl UB4 . . . . .84 A2
Dunbar Ct 🔢 London N12 . .29 D6
Sutton SM1 . . . . .218 B3
Walton-on-T KT12 . . . . .194 C1
Dunbar Gdns RM10 . . . . . . .81 D3
Dunbar Rd
New Malden KT3 . . . . .199 A5
Tottenham N22 . . . . .32 D2
Upton E7 . . . . .77 A2
Dunbar St SE27 . . . . .161 A1
Dunbar Wharf 🔢 E14 . . . .119 B6
Dunblane Cl HA8 . . . . .10 D2
Dunblane Rd SE9 . . . . .144 A3
Dunboe Pl TW17 . . . . .193 A2
Dunboyne Rd NW3 . . . . .70 D3
Dunbridge Ho SW15 . . . . .155 D5
Dunbridge St Bethnal Green E2 . . .
Bethnal Green E2 . . . . .96 B3
Duncan Cl EN5 . . . . .2 A1
Duncan Ct 🔢 London N12 . .29 D5
🔢 Poplar E14 . . . . .98 A2
Southgate N21 . . . . .16 D3
Duncan Gr W3 . . . . .89 C1
Duncan Ho Harrow HA2 . . . .64 A5
🔢 Primrose Hill NW3 . . . . . .70 D1
Duncannon Ho SW1 . . . . .**259** D1
Duncannon St WC2 . . . . . .**250** A5
Duncan Rd Hackney E8 . . . .96 B6
Richmond TW9 . . . . .132 A1
Duncan St N1 . . . . .94 D5 **234** C4
Duncan Terr N1 . . .94 D5 **234** C4
Dunch St 🔢 E1 . . . . .96 B1
Dunchurch Ho RM10 . . . . . .81 C1
Duncombe Hill SE23 . . . . .163 A4
Duncombe Ho 🔢 SW19 . . .156 D3
Duncombe Prim Sch N19 . .50 A1
Duncombe Rd N19 . . . . .49 D1
Duncrievie Rd SE13 . . . . . .164 B5
Duncroft SE18 . . . . .145 C5
Dundalk Ho 🔢 E1 . . . . .96 C1
Dundalk Rd SE4 . . . . .141 A2
Dundas Gdns KT8 . . . . . . .195 D6
Dundas Ho 🔢 E2 . . . . .96 C5
Dundas Mews 🔢 EN3 . . . . .7 C6
Dundas Rd SE15 . . . . .140 C3
Dundee Ct 🔢 E1 . . . . .118 B5
Dundee Ho W9 . . . .**229** A2
Dundee Rd Croydon SE25 . .206 B4
Newham E13 . . . . .99 B5
Dundee St E1 . . . . .118 B5
Dundee Way EN3 . . . . .7 A2
Dundee Wharf E14 . . . . . . .119 B6
Dundela Gdns KT17, KT4 . .216 B4
Dundonald Cl 🔢 E6 . . . . . .100 A1
Dundonald Prim Sch
SW19 . . . . .179 B3
Dundonald Rd
Brondesbury Pk NW10 . . . . .90 D6
Merton SW19 . . . . .179 B3
Dundonald Road Sta
SW19 . . . . .179 B3
Dundry Ho 🔢 SE26 . . . . . .162 A1
Duneaves HA1 . . . . .64 C5
Dunedin Ho E16 . . . . .122 B5
Dunedin Rd Ilford IG1 . . . . . .57 A1
Leyton E10 . . . . .75 D5
Dunedin Way UB4 . . . . .84 C3
Dunelm Gr SE27 . . . . .161 A1

Dunelm St E1 . . . . .96 C1
Dunfield Gdns SE6 . . . . . . .185 D5
Dunfield Rd SE6 . . . . .185 D5
Dunford Ct 🔢 HA5 . . . . . . .23 D3
Dunford Rd N7 . . . . .72 B4
Dungarvan Ave SW15 . . . .134 A1
Dungeness Ho SW18 . . . . .136 A1
Dunheved Ct SE27 . . . . . . .204 C3
Dunheved Rd 🔢 CR7 . . . . .204 C3
Dunheved Rd N CR7 . . . . . .204 C3
Dunheved Rd S CR7 . . . . . .204 C3
Dunheved Rd W CR7 . . . . .204 C3
Dunhill Point 🔢 SW15 . . .156 B3
Dunholme Gn N9 . . . . .17 D1
Dunholme La N9 . . . . .17 D1
Dunholme Rd N9 . . . . .17 D1
Dunkeld Ho 🔢 E14 . . . . . . .98 B1
Dunkeld Rd
Dagenham RM8 . . . . .80 C2
South Norwood SE25 . . . . .205 B5
Dunkery Rd SE9 . . . . .166 A1
Dunkirk St 🔢 SE27 . . . . . .183 A6
Dunlace Rd E5 . . . . .74 D4
Dunleary Cl TW4 . . . . .151 B4
Dunley Dr CR0 . . . . .224 A2
Dunlin Ct 🔢 SE21 . . . . . . .161 B2
Dunlin Ho 🔢 SE16 . . . . . .118 D2
Dunloe Ave N17 . . . . .51 B6
Dunloe Ct 🔢 E2 . . . . .95 D5
Dunloe St E2 . . . . .95 D5
Dunlop Pl SE16 . . . .117 D3 **263** D5
Dunmore Point 🔢 E2 . . . . .95 D4
Dunmore Rd Kilburn NW6 . .91 A6
Wimbledon SW20 . . . . .178 D2
Dunmow Cl
Dagenham RM6 . . . . .58 C4
🔢 Feltham TW13 . . . . .173 A6
Dunmow Ho
Dagenham RM9 . . . . .102 B6
Vauxhall SE11 . . . .**260** D2
Dunmow Rd E15 . . . . .76 B4
Dunmow Wlk N1 . . . .**235** A6
Dunnage Cres SE16 . . . . . .119 A2
Dunne Mews 🔢 NW5 . . . . .71 C3
Dunnet Ho 🔢 E3 . . . . .97 B5
Dunnico Ho SE17 . . . .**263** A2
Dunn Mead NW9 . . . . .27 D3
Dunnock Cl N9 . . . . .18 D3
Dunnock Ct 🔢 SE21 . . . . .161 B2
Dunnock Rd E6 . . . . .100 A1
Dunn's Pas WC1 . . . .**240** B2
Dunn St E8 . . . . .73 D3
Dunollie Pl NW5 . . . . .71 C3
Dunollie Rd NW5 . . . . .71 C3
Dunoon Gdns SE23 . . . . . .162 D4
Dunoon Ho N1 . . . .**233** C5
Dunoon Rd SE23 . . . . .162 C4
Dunraven Dr EN2 . . . . .4 C3
Dunraven Ho 🔢 TW9 . . . . .132 B4
Dunraven Rd W12 . . . . .112 A5
Dunraven Sch SW16 . . . . .182 A5
Dunraven St W1 . . .114 D6 **247** D6
Dunrobin Ct NW3 . . . . .69 D3
Dunsany Rd W14 . . . . .112 D3
Dunsfold Ct 🔢 SM2 . . . . . .217 D1
Dunsfold Ho
🔢 Kingston u T KT2 . . . . . .176 D4
🔢 Streatham SW2 . . . . . . .160 B4
Dunsfold Way CR0 . . . . . . .223 D1
Dunsford Way SW15 . . . . . .156 B5
Dunsmore Cl Bushey WD23 . .8 B5
Hayes UB4 . . . . .85 A3
Dunsmore Rd KT12 . . . . . .194 B3
Dunsmore Way WD23 . . . . . .8 B5
Dunsmure Rd N16 . . . . .51 C1
Dunstable Ct 🔢 SE3 . . . . .143 A5
Dunstable Mews W1 . . . . .**238** B4
Dunstable Rd
East Molesey KT8 . . . . .195 B5
Richmond TW10, TW9 . . . .132 A1
Dunstall Ho 🔢 SE15 . . . . .140 A4
Dunstall Rd SW19, SW20 . .178 C4
Dunstall Way KT8 . . . . .195 D6
Dunstall Welling Est
DA16 . . . . .146 B3
Dunstan Cl 🔢 N2 . . . . .48 A6
Dunstan Glade BR5 . . . . . .211 B3
Dunstan Ho SE4 . . . . .141 B3
Dunstan Rd NW11 . . . . .47 C1
Dunstan's Gr SE22 . . . . . . .162 B5
Dunstan's Rd SE22 . . . . . .162 A5
Dunster Ave SM4 . . . . .200 C1
Dunster Ct EC3 . . . .**253** B6
Dunster Dr NW9 . . . . .45 A1
Dunster Gdns NW6 . . . . . . .69 B1
Dunsterville Way SE1 . . .**252** D1
Dunster Way
Carshalton CR4 . . . . .203 A1
Harrow HA2 . . . . .63 A5
Dunston Rd
Clapham SW11 . . . . .137 A3
Hackney E8 . . . . .95 C6
Dunston St E8 . . . . .95 D6
Dunton Cl KT6 . . . . .198 A1
Dunton Ct 🔢 SE26 . . . . . . .162 B2
Dunton Ho 🔢 SW16 . . . . . .160 A1
Dunton Rd
Bermondsey SE1 . .117 D2 **263** C3

Dunton Rd *continued*
Leyton E10 . . . .**53** D2
Duntshill Rd SW18 . . . . .**157** D3
Dunvegan Cl KT8 . . . . . .**195** D5
Dunvegan Rd SE9 . . . . . .**144** B1
Dunwich Ct 2 RM6 . . . . . .**58** B4
Dunwich Rd DA7 . . . . . .**147** B4
Dunworth Mews W1 . . . . .**91** B1
Duplex Ride SW1 . . . . . .**247** D1
Dupont Rd SW20 . . . . . .**178** D1
Duppas Ave CR0 . . . . . .**220** D4
Duppas Cl TW17 . . . . . .**193** B4
Duppas Ct CR0 . . . .**220** D5
Duppas Hill La CR0 . . . . .**220** D4
Duppas Hill Rd CR0 . . . . .**220** D4
Duppas Hill Terr CR0 . . . .**220** D3
Duppas Jun Sch CR0 . . . .**220** D5
Duppas Rd CR0 . . . .**220** D5
Dupree Rd SE7 . . . .**121** B1
Dura Den Cl BR3 . . . . . .**185** D3
Durand Cl SM5 . . . .**202** D1
Durand Gdns
SW9 . . . .**138** B4 **270** D1
Durand Prim Sch
SW9 . . . .**138** B4 **270** D2
Durand Way NW10 . . . . . .**67** A1
Durants Lo EN3 . . . .**6** D2
Durants Park Ave EN3 . . . .**6** D1
Durants Rd EN3 . . . .**6** D1
Durants Sch EN3 . . . .**6** C4
Durant St E2 . . . .**96** A4
Durban Ct E7 . . . .**77** D1
Durban Ho 28 W12 . . . . .**112** B6
Durban Rd
Beckenham BR3 . . . . . .**185** B1
Ilford IG2 . . . .**57** C1
Newham E15 . . . .**98** C4
Tottenham N17 . . . .**33** D4
Walthamstow E17 . . . .**35** B2
West Norwood SE27 . . . . .**183** B6
Durbin Ho 13 N9 . . . .**18** A1
Durbin Rd KT9 . . . .**214** B4
Durdan Cotts UB5 . . . . . .**85** B1
Durdans Ho 3 NW1 . . . . .**71** C1
Durdans Park Prim Sch
UB1 . . . .**85** B2
Durdans Rd UB1 . . . .**85** B1
Durell Gdns RM9 . . . .**80** D3
Durell Rd RM9 . . . .**80** D3
Durfey Pl SE5 . . . .**139** B5
Durford Cres SW15 . . . . .**156** B3
Durham Ave
Beckenham BR2 . . . .**208** D6
Hounslow TW5 . . . .**107** B1
Woodford IG8 . . . .**37** D5
Durham Ct SW20 . . . .**178** B1
Durham Ct 2 Barnet EN5 . .**1** B2
Brockley SE4 . . . .**141** C2
4 Kilburn NW6 . . . .**91** C5
Teddington TW11 . . . .**174** C6
Durham Hill BR1 . . . .**186** D6
Durham Ho
3 Barking IG11 . . . .**80** A1
7 Dartmouth Pk NW5 . . . .**71** C5
Edgware HA8 . . . .**26** B3
Lisson Gr NW8 . . . .**230** B1
Durham House St WC2 . . .**250** B5
Durham Pl Chelsea SW3 . .**257** C1
Ilford IG1 . . . .**79** A4
Durham Rd
Beckenham BR2 . . . .**208** D6
Ealing W5 . . . .**109** D3
Edmonton N9 . . . .**18** A2
Feltham TW14 . . . .**150** C4
Harrow HA1 . . . .**41** D4
Lower Holloway N4, N7 . . . .**72** B6
Manor Pk E12 . . . .**77** D4
Muswell Hill N2 . . . .**48** D6
Newham E16 . . . .**98** C3
Sidcup DA14 . . . .**190** B5
Wimbledon SW20 . . . . . .**178** B2
Durham Rise SE18 . . . . .**123** B1
Durham Row E1 . . . .**97** A2
Durham St SE11 . .**138** B6 **270** C6
Durham Terr W2 . . . .**91** D1
Durham Wharf Dr TW8 . . .**131** C5
Durley Ave HA5 . . . .**41** A3
Durley Rd N16 . . . .**51** C2
Durlock Ho 18 SW9 . . . . .**138** C4
Durlston Rd
Kingston u T KT2 . . . .**176** A4
Stoke Newington E5 . . . . . .**74** A6
Durnford Ho SE6 . . . . . .**163** D1
Durnford St
4 Greenwich SE10 . . . . .**142** A6
South Tottenham N15 . . . . .**51** C4
Durning Rd SE19 . . . . . .**183** B5
Durnsford Ave SW18,
SW19 . . . .**157** C2
Durnsford Ct 5 EN3 . . . . . .**7** A2
Durnsford Rd London N11 . .**31** D3
Wimbledon SW18, SW19 . .**157** C1
Durnston Ct 2 SM1 . . . . .**217** D2
Durrant Ct HA3 . . . .**24** C2
Durrant Way BR6 . . . . . .**227** B3
Durrell Rd SW6 . . . .**264** C1
Durrell Way TW17 . . . . . .**193** B3
Durrels Ho W14 . . . .**254** C4
Durrington Ave SW20 . . . .**178** C3

Durrington Park Rd
SW20 . . . .**178** C2
Durrington Rd E5 . . . .**75** A4
Durrington Twr 3 SW8 . . .**137** C3
Durrisdeer Ho NW2 . . . . . .**69** B4
Dursley Cl SE3 . . . .**143** C3
Dursley Gdns SE3 . . . . . .**143** D4
Dursley Rd SE3 . . . .**143** C3
Durston NW5 . . . .**71** A3
Durston House Prep Sch
W5 . . . .**87** D1
Durston House Sch W5 . . . .**87** D1
Durward St E1 . . . .**96** B2
Durweston Mews W1 . . . .**237** D4
Durweston St W1 . . . .**237** D3
Dury Rd EN5 . . . .**1** B3
Dutch Gdns KT2 . . . .**176** D4
Dutch Yd SW18 . . . .**157** C6
Dutton Ho SW2 . . . .**160** D3
Dutton St SE10 . . . .**142** A4
Duxberry Cl BR2 . . . .**210** A4
Duxford 21 KT1 . . . .**176** C1
Duxford Ho 10 SE2 . . . . . .**124** D4
Dwight Ct 3 SW6 . . . .**135** A3
Dye Ho 19 E9 . . . .**74** D2
Dye House La E3 . . . .**97** C6
Dyer Ho Hampton TW12 . . .**173** D2
New Cross SE4 . . . .**141** A3
Dyer's Bldgs EC1 . . . .**241** A3
Dyers Hall Rd Leyton E11 . . .**76** B6
Leytonstone E11 . . . .**54** C1
Dyer's La SW15 . . . .**134** B1
Dykes Ct 11 SW2 . . . . . .**160** B3
Dykes Way BR2 . . . .**208** D6
Dylan Cl WD6 . . . .**9** D4
Dylan Rd Belvedere DA17 . .**125** C3
2 Brixton SE24 . . . .**138** D1
Dylways SE5 . . . .**138** D1
Dymchurch Cl Ilford IG5 . . .**56** C6
Orpington BR6 . . . .**227** C4
Dymchurch Ho 12 E5 . . . . .**74** B3
Dymes Path SW19 . . . . . .**156** D2
Dymock St SW6 . . . .**135** D2
Dyneley Rd SE12 . . . . . .**165** C1
Dyne Rd NW6 . . . .**69** B1
Dynevor Rd
Richmond TW10 . . . .**154** A6
Shacklewell N16 . . . .**73** D5
Dynham Rd NW6 . . . .**69** C1
Dyott St Soho WC1 . . . . . .**239** D2
St Giles WC1, WC2 . .**94** A1 **240** A2
Dysart Ave KT2, TW10 . . . .**175** C6
Dysart Sch KT6 . . . .**198** B2
Dysart St EC2 . . . . . .**95** C3 **243** A5
Wembley HA0 . . . .**65** A4
Dyson Ho 3 SE10 . . . . . .**120** D1
Dyson Rd Leytonstone E11 . .**54** C3
Stratford E15 . . . .**76** D2
Dyson's Rd N18 . . . .**34** B4

E

Eade Rd N4 . . . .**51** A2
Eagans Cl N2 . . . .**48** B6
Eagle Ave RM6 . . . .**59** A3
Eagle Cl
Bermondsey SE16 . . . . . .**118** C1
Enfield EN3 . . . .**6** C1
Wallington SM6 . . . .**220** A2
Eagle Ct 10 Dulwich SE21 . .**161** B2
Edmonton N18 . . . .**33** D4
Holborn EC1 . . . .**241** C4
6 Wanstead E11 . . . .**55** A5
Eagle Dr NW9 . . . .**27** C1
Eagle Dwellings EC1 . . . . .**235** B2
Eagle Hill SE19 . . . .**183** B4
Eagle Ho
22 Bethnal Green E1 . . . . .**96** B3
Finsbury Pk N7 . . . .**72** B5
Eagle House Sch CR4 . . . .**180** D1
Eagle Hts 19 SW11 . . . . .**168** C1
Eagle La E11 . . . .**55** A5
Eagle Lo Leytonstone E11 . . .**54** D5
London NW11 . . . .**47** B2
Eagle Mans N16 . . . .**73** D3
Eagle Mews N1 . . . .**73** C2
Eagle Pl
South Kensington
SW7 . . . .**114** A1 **256** B2
St James SW1 . . . .**249** B5
Eagle Rd Hatton TW6 . . . . .**127** D2
Wembley HA0 . . . .**65** D2
Eaglesfield Rd SE18 . . . . .**144** D4
Eagle St WC1 . . . . . .**94** B2 **240** C3
Eagle Star Ho SM1 . . . . . .**217** D4
Eagle Terr IG8 . . . .**37** B3
Eagle Trad Est CR4 . . . . .**202** D3
Eagle Wharf SE1 . . . .**253** C2
Eagle Wharf Rd
N1 . . . .**95** A5 **235** B4
Eagle Works E1 . . . .**243** D5
Eagling Cl E3 . . . .**97** C4
Ealcom Ct W5 . . . .**110** B5
Ealdham Prim Sch SE9 . . .**143** C1
Ealdham Sq SE9 . . . .**143** C1
EALING **109** D6
Ealing Broadway Ctr
W5 . . . .**109** D6

Ealing Broadway Sta
W5 . . . .**109** D6
Ealing Coll 1 W13 . . . .**87** B1
Ealing Coll of Higher Ed
W5 . . . .**109** D5
Ealing Common W5 . . . . .**110** B6
Ealing Common Sta W5 . . .**110** B5
Ealing Court Man W5 . . . .**109** D4
Ealing Gateway W5 . . . . .**109** C6
Ealing Gn W5 . . . .**109** D5
**Ealing, Hammersmith & West
London Coll**
W14 . . . . **113** A1 **254** A2
Ealing Hospl UB1 . . . . . .**108** B4
Ealing Ind Coll W5 . . . . . .**109** C6
Ealing Park Gdns W5 . . . .**109** C2
Ealing Park Lo UB6 . . . . . .**87** A5
Ealing Park Mans W5 . . . .**109** D3
Ealing Rd Brentford TW8 . . .**109** D2
Northolt UB5 . . . .**63** C1
Wembley HA0 . . . .**66** A1
Ealing Road Trad Est
W5 . . . .**109** D1
Ealing Studios * W5 . . . . .**109** D5
Ealing Village W5 . . . .**88** A1
Ealing & West London Coll
W5 . . . .**109** D5
Eamann Casey Ho 34
SW9 . . . .**138** C4
Eamont Cl HA4 . . . .**38** D2
Eamont Ct NW8 . . . .**230** B4
Eamont St NW8 . . . .**92** C5 **230** B4
Eardley Cres
SW5 . . . . **113** C1 **255** B1
Eardley Point 9 SE18 . . . .**122** D2
Eardley Rd
Belvedere DA17 . . . .**125** C1
Streatham SW16 . . . .**181** C4
Streatham SW17 . . . .**181** A4
Eardley Sch SW16 . . . . . .**181** C4
Earl Cl N11 . . . .**31** B5
Earldom Rd SW15 . . . . . .**134** C1
Earle Ho SW1 . . . .**259** D3
Earlham Gr Forest Gate E7 . .**77** A3
Wood Green N22 . . . .**32** B3
Earlham Prim Sch
Stratford E7 . . . .**76** D3
Wood Green N22 . . . .**32** C3
Earlham St WC2 . . . .**94** A1 **240** A1
Earl Ho NW1 . . . .**237** B5
Earlom Ho WC1 . . . .**234** A1
Earl Rd SW14 . . . .**133** A1
Earl Rise SE18 . . . .**123** B2
EARL'S COURT **113** C1
Earl's Court Ex Ctr *
SW5 . . . . **113** C1 **255** A1
Earl's Court Gdns
SW5 . . . . **113** D2 **255** B3
Earl's Court Rd SW5,
W8 . . . . **113** C2 **255** B4
Earl's Court Sq
SW5 . . . . **113** D1 **255** C2
Earl's Court Sta
SW5 . . . . **113** C2 **255** B3
Earls Cres HA1 . . . .**42** C5
Earlsdown Ho 6 IG11 . . . .**101** B5
Earlsferry Way N1 . . . .**72** A1
EARLSFIELD **158** A3
Earlsfield Ho 16 KT2 . . . . .**175** D2
Earlsfield Prim Sch
SW18 . . . .**158** A2
Earlsfield Rd SW18 . . . . .**158** A4
Earlsfield Sta SW18 . . . . .**158** A3
Earlshall Rd SE9 . . . .**144** C1
Earlsmead HA2 . . . .**63** B4
Earlsmead Fst & Mid Sch
HA2 . . . .**63** B4
Earlsmead Prim Sch 3
N15 . . . .**51** D5
Earlsmead Rd
Kensal Green NW10 . . . . . .**90** C4
South Tottenham N15 . . . . .**51** D4
Earl St EC2 . . . .**95** C3 **243** A4
Earls Terr W8 . . . .**254** D5
Earlsthorpe Mews 3
SW12 . . . .**159** A5
Earlsthorpe Rd SE26 . . . .**184** D6
Earlstoke St EC1 . . . .**234** C2
Earlston Gr E9 . . . .**96** B6
Earls Wlk Dagenham RM8 . . .**80** B4
Kensington W8 . . **113** C3 **255** A5
Earlswood Ave CR7 . . . . .**204** C4
Earlswood Cl 10 SE10 . . . .**120** C1
Earlswood Gdns IG5 . . . . .**56** C6
Earlswood Ho 2 SW2 . . . .**160** B3
Earlswood St SE10 . . . . . .**120** C1
Early Mews NW1 . . . .**231** D6
Earnshaw Ho EC1 . . . . . .**234** D1
Earnshaw St WC1, WC2 . . .**239** D2
Earsby St W14 . . . .**254** B4
Earth Galleries *
SW7 . . . .**114** B3
Easby Cres SM4 . . . .**201** D3
Easebourne Rd RM8 . . . . . .**80** C3
Easedale Ho TW7 . . . .**152** D2
Eashing Point 5 SW15 . . .**156** B3
Easley's Mews W1 . . . . . .**238** B2
East 10 Ent Pk E10 . . . . . .**53** A1
EAST ACTON **111** C5
East Acton Arc W3 . . . .**89** D1

East Acton Ct W3 . . . .**111** C6
East Acton La W3 . . . .**111** C6
East Acton Prim Sch
W3 . . . .**111** C6
East Acton Sta W12 . . . . . .**89** D1
East Arbour St E1 . . . .**96** D1
East Ave Croydon CR0 . . . .**220** B3
East Finchley NW2 . . . .**48** A6
Hayes UB3 . . . .**106** A5
Plashet E12 . . . .**78** A1
Southall UB1 . . . .**107** B6
Walthamstow E17 . . . .**53** D5
East Bank N16 . . . .**51** C2
Eastbank Ct 2 E17 . . . .**53** D4
Eastbank Rd TW12 . . . . . .**174** A5
EAST BARNET **14** D4
East Barnet Rd EN4 . . . . . .**2** B1
East Barnet Sch Barnet EN4 . .**2** B2
East Barnet EN4 . . . .**14** D5
East Beckton District Ctr
E6 . . . .**100** B2
EAST BEDFONT **149** C3
East Block 5 E1 . . . .**118** C6
Eastbourne Ave W3 . . . . . .**89** B1
Eastbourne Gdns SW14 . . .**133** A2
Eastbourne Mews
W2 . . . .**92** A1 **236** B2
Eastbourne Rd
Brentford TW8 . . . .**109** D1
Chiswick W4 . . . .**133** A6
Feltham TW13 . . . .**150** D2
South Tottenham N15 . . . . .**51** C3
Streatham SW17 . . . .**181** A4
Wallend E6 . . . .**100** C4
West Ham E15 . . . .**98** C6
Eastbourne Terr
W2 . . . .**92** A1 **236** B2
Eastbournia Ave N9 . . . . . .**18** B1
Eastbrook Ave N9 . . . .**18** C4
Eastbrook Rd SE3 . . . . . .**143** B4
EASTBURY **22** A5
Eastbury Ave
Barking IG11 . . . .**101** C6
Enfield EN1 . . . .**5** D4
Mo Pk HA6 . . . .**22** A5
Eastbury Comp Sch IG11 . . .**79** C2
Eastbury Ct Barking IG11 . .**101** C6
New Barnet EN4 . . . .**14** A6
Eastbury Gr W4 . . . .**111** C1
Eastbury Inf Sch IG11 . . . . .**79** D1
Eastbury Rd
Kingston u T KT2 . . . .**176** A3
Newham E6 . . . .**100** C3
Orpington BR5 . . . .**211** B3
Eastbury Sq IG11 . . . .**101** D6
Eastbury Terr E1 . . . .**96** D3
Eastcastle St W1 . . . .**93** C1 **239** B2
Eastcheap EC3 . . . .**110** C6 **253** A6
East Churchfield Rd W3 . . .**111** B5
Eastchurch Rd TW6 . . . . .**127** C2
Eastchurch Road Rdbt
TW6 . . . .**127** C3
East Cl Cockfosters EN4 . . . . .**3** A1
Ealing W5 . . . .**88** C3
Greenford UB6 . . . .**86** A5
Eastcombe Ave SE7 . . . . .**143** B6
EASTCOTE **40** C3
Eastcote BR6 . . . .**211** D1
Eastcote Ave
East Molesey KT8 . . . . . .**195** C4
Harrow HA2 . . . .**64** A6
Wembley UB6 . . . .**65** A3
Eastcote Ind Est HA4 . . . . .**40** C2
Eastcote La Harrow HA2 . . . .**63** C5
Northolt UB5 . . . .**63** B2
Eastcote La N UB5 . . . .**63** C2
Eastcote Pl HA5 . . . .**40** B3
Eastcote Prim Sch DA16 . .**145** B3
Eastcote Rd Bexley DA16 . .**145** B3
Harrow HA2 . . . .**64** A5
Pinner HA5 . . . .**40** D4
Ruislip HA4 . . . .**40** A3
Eastcote St SW9 . . . .**138** B3
Eastcote Sta HA5 . . . .**40** C2
Eastcote View HA5 . . . .**40** B4
EASTCOTE VILLAGE **40** B4
Eastcott Cl KT2 . . . .**177** A5
Eastcourt Ind Sch IG3 . . . . .**58** A1
East Cres Enfield EN1 . . . . .**17** D6
Friern Barnet N11 . . . .**30** C6
Eastcroft Rd KT19 . . . . . .**215** C1
East Cross Route Bow E3 . . .**97** C6
Hackney Wick E9 . . . .**75** B3
East Croydon Sta CR0 . . . .**221** B6
East Ct Sunbury TW16 . . . .**172** C1
Wembley HA0 . . . .**65** C4
Eastdown Ho E8 . . . .**74** A4
Eastdown Pk SE13 . . . . . .**142** B1
East Duck Lees La EN3 . . . . .**7** B1
EAST DULWICH **162** A6
East Dulwich Gr SE22 . . . .**161** C6
East Dulwich Rd SE15,
SE22 . . . .**140** A1
East Dulwich Sta SE22 . . .**139** C5
**East End Computing & Bsns
Coll 37** E1 . . . .**96** B1
East End Rd
East Finchley N2, N3 . . . . . .**48** A6
Finchley N3 . . . .**29** C1
East End Way HA5 . . . .**41** A6

East Entrance RM10 . . . . .**103** D5
Eastern Ave
Gants Hill IG1, IG2, IG4 . . . .**56** C3
Newbury Pk IG2 . . . .**57** B3
Pinner HA5 . . . .**40** D2
Wanstead E11 . . . .**55** A5
Eastern Avenue W RM7 . . . .**59** C5
Eastern Bsns Pk TW16 . . . .**127** D3
Eastern Perimeter Rd
TW14 . . . .**127** D3
Eastern Quay 15 E16 . . . .**121** B5
Fortis Green N2 . . . .**48** D5
Newham E13 . . . .**99** B5
Walthamstow E17 . . . .**54** A4
Wood Green N22 . . . .**32** A2
Easternville Gdns IG2 . . . . .**57** A3
Eastern Way SE28 . . . . . .**124** B4
East Ferry Rd E14 . . . . . .**119** D2
Eastfield Gdns RM10 . . . . .**81** C4
Eastfield Prim Sch EN3 . . . . .**6** D5
Eastfield Rd
Dagenham RM9 . . . .**81** B4
Dagenham RM10 . . . .**81** C4
Enfield EN3 . . . .**6** D5
Hornsey N8 . . . .**50** A6
Walthamstow E17 . . . .**53** C5
Eastfields HA5 . . . .**40** C4
Eastfields Ave SW18 . . . . .**135** C1
Eastfields Rd Acton W3 . . . .**89** A2
Mitcham CR4 . . . .**181** A1
Eastfield St E14 . . . .**97** A2
EAST FINCHLEY **48** B5
East Finchley Sta N2 . . . . .**48** C5
Eastgate Bsns Pk E10 . . . . .**53** A1
Eastgate Cl SE28 . . . .**102** D1
Eastgate Ct N3 . . . .**29** C1
East Gdns SW17 . . . .**180** C4
Eastglade HA5 . . . .**41** B6
EAST HAM **100** A5
Eastham Cl EN5 . . . .**13** B6
East Ham Ind Est E6 . . . . .**100** A2
East Ham L Ctr E6 . . . . . .**100** B6
East Ham Manor Way
E6 . . . .**100** C1
East Ham Meml Hospl
E7 . . . .**77** D1
East Ham Sta E6 . . . .**78** A1
East Harding St EC4 . . . . .**241** B2
East Heath Rd NW3 . . . . . .**70** B5
East Hill London SW18 . . . .**158** A6
Wembley HA9 . . . .**44** C1
Eastholm NW11 . . . .**47** D5
East India Bldgs 9 E14 . . .**119** C6
East India Ct 7 SE16 . . . . .**118** C4
East India Dock Basin *
E14 . . . .**120** C6
East India Dock Rd E14 . . .**119** D6
East India Dock Road Tunnel
18 E14 . . . .**98** B1
East India Sta E14 . . . . . .**120** B6
East India Way CR0 . . . . . .**205** D1
East La
5 Bermondsey SE16 . . . .**118** A4
Bermondsey SE16 . . . . . .**118** A4
Kingston u T KT1 . . . .**197** D6
Wembley HA0, HA9 . . . . . .**65** D5
Eastlake Ho NW8 . . . .**236** D5
Eastlake Rd SE5 . . . .**139** A3
Eastland Ct 2 BR1 . . . . . .**187** C1
Eastlands Cres SE21 . . . . .**161** D5
East Lane Bsns Pk HA9 . . . .**65** D6
Eastlea Com Sch E16 . . . . .**98** C3
Eastlea Mews E16 . . . .**98** C3
Eastleigh Ave HA2 . . . .**63** D6
Eastleigh Cl
Belmont SM2 . . . .**217** D1
Neasden NW2 . . . .**67** C5
Eastleigh Rd E17 . . . .**35** B1
Eastleigh Way TW14 . . . . .**150** A3
Eastleigh Wlk 9 SW15 . . . .**156** A4
East London Coll 14 E11 . . .**76** C6
Eastman Dental Hospl
WC1 . . . .**94** B3 **240** C6
Eastman Ho 7 SW4 . . . . . .**159** C5
Eastman Rd W3 . . . .**111** B4
East Mascalls 15 SE7 . . . .**143** C6
Eastmead IG3 . . . .**58** A2
East Mead HA4 . . . .**62** D5
Eastmead Ave UB6 . . . . . .**85** D4
Eastmead Cl BR1 . . . .**188** A1
Eastmearn Rd SE21,
SE27 . . . .**161** A2
EAST MOLESEY **196** A4
Eastmoor Rd KT10 . . . . . .**212** D6
Eastmoor Pl SE7 . . . .**121** D3
Eastmoor St SE7 . . . .**121** D3
East Mount St E1 . . . .**96** B2
Eastney Rd CR0 . . . .**204** D1
Eastney St SE10 . . . .**120** B1
Eastnor Rd SE9 . . . .**167** A3
Easton Ho 4 SE27 . . . .**160** C1
Easton St WC1 . . . .**241** A6
East Park Cl RM6 . . . .**59** A4
East Parkside SE10 . . . . . .**120** D4
East Pas EC1 . . . .**242** A4

East Pl SE27 . . . .**183** A6
East Plaza E14 . . . .**119** D5
East Point 4 SE1 . . . .**118** A1
Eastpole Cotts N14 . . . .**3** D1
East Poultry Ave EC1 . . . . .**241** C3
East Putney Sta SW15 . . . . .**157** A6
East Ramp TW6 . . . .**126** D4
East Rd Burnt Oak HA8 . . . . .**27** A2
 Chelsea SW1 . . . .**115** A1 **258** A1
 Dagenham RM6 . . . .**59** A4
 East Barnet EN4 . . . .**15** A3
 East Bedfont TW14 . . . . . .**149** B4
 Enfield EN3 . . . .**6** C5
 Finchley N2 . . . .**30** C2
 Kingston u T KT2 . . . .**176** A2
 Newham E15 . . . .**99** A6
 Shoreditch N1 . . . .**95** B4 **235** D2
 Welling DA16 . . . .**146** B3
 West Drayton UB7 . . . . . .**104** C2
 Wimbledon SW19 . . . .**180** A4
East Rochester Way DA5, DA15,
 SE9 . . . .**168** C5
East Row
 Kensal Town W10 . . . .**91** A3
 Wanstead E11 . . . .**55** A3
Eastry Ave BR2 . . . .**208** D3
Eastry Ho SW8 . . . .**270** A4
Eastry Rd DA8 . . . .**147** C5
EAST SHEEN **133** B1
East Sheen Ave SW14 . . . .**133** B1
East Sheen Prim Sch
 SW14 . . . .**133** C1
Eastside Rd NW11 . . . .**47** B5
East Smithfield
 E1 . . . .**117** D6 **253** D5
East St Barking IG11 . . . .**79** A1
 Bexleyheath DA7 . . . .**147** C1
 Brentford TW8 . . . .**131** C5
 Bromley BR1 . . . .**187** A1
 Walworth SE17 . . . .**117** B1 **262** C2
East Surrey Gr SE15 . . . . . .**139** D5
East Tenter St E1 . . .**95** D1 **243** D1
East Terr DA15 . . . .**167** C3
East Thamesmead Bsns Pk
 DA18 . . . .**125** B4
East Towers HA5 . . . .**40** D3
Eastvale W3 . . . .**111** D5
East View Barnet EN5 . . . . . .**1** B2
 Chingford E4 . . . .**36** A5
 Hampstead NW3 . . . .**70** B6
Eastview Ave SE18 . . . .**145** C5
East View Ho 13 N2 . . . .**30** B1
Eastville Ave NW11 . . . .**47** B3
Eastway Hayes BR2 . . . .**209** A2
 Merton SM4, SW20 . . . . . .**201** A5
 South Hackney E3, E9 . . . . .**97** A6
 Wallington SM6 . . . .**219** C4
 Wanstead E11 . . . .**55** B4
East Way Croydon CR0 . . . . .**223** A5
 Hayes UB3 . . . .**106** A5
 Ruislip HA4 . . . .**40** A1
Eastway Cres HA2 . . . .**63** D6
Eastwell Cl BR3 . . . .**185** A2
Eastwell Ho SE1 . . . .**262** D6
Eastwick Ct 2 SW19 . . . . .**156** D3
EAST WICKHAM **146** A5
East Wickham Inf Sch
 DA16 . . . .**145** D4
East Wickham Jun Sch
 DA16 . . . .**146** A5
East Wlk East Barnet EN4 . . .**15** A3
 Hayes UB3 . . . .**106** A5
Eastwood Cl
 2 Islington N7 . . . .**72** C3
 7 Tottenham N17 . . . .**34** B3
 Woodford E18 . . . .**37** A1
Eastwood Rd Ilford IG3 . . . .**58** A2
 Muswell Hill N10 . . . .**31** A1
 West Drayton UB7 . . . .**104** C4
 Woodford E18 . . . .**37** A1
East Woodside DA5 . . . . . .**169** A3
Eastwood St SW16 . . . .**181** C4
Eatington Rd E10 . . . .**54** B4
Eaton Cl Belgravia SW1 . .**258** A3
 Stanmore HA7 . . . .**25** B6
Eaton Ct Chislehurst BR7 . .**189** A4
 Ealing W5 . . . .**87** D1
 Edgware HA8 . . . .**26** C6
 Southall UB1 . . . .**107** B6
 Sutton SM2 . . . .**218** B2
 6 Woodford E18 . . . .**37** A1
Eaton Dr Brixton SW9 . . . . .**138** D1
 Kingston u T KT2 . . . .**176** C3
Eaton Gate SW1 . . .**115** A2 **258** A4
Eaton Gdns RM9 . . . .**81** A1
Eaton Ho Battersea SW11 . . .**266** D1
 Ealing W5 . . . .**87** D1
 23 Limehouse E14 . . . . . .**119** B6
Eaton House Sch
 SW1 . . . .**115** A2 **258** A4
Eaton House The Manor Sch
 SW4 . . . .**137** B1
Eaton La SW1 . . . .**115** B3 **258** D5
Eaton Lo SM2 . . . .**218** B2
Eaton Mans SW1 . . . .**258** A3
Eaton Mews N
 SW1 . . . .**115** A3 **258** B5

Eaton Mews S
 SW1 . . . .**115** B3 **258** C5
Eaton Mews W SW1 . . . . . .**258** B4
Eaton Park Rd N13 . . . .**16** D2
Eaton Pl SW1 . . . . .**115** A3 **258** B5
Eaton Rd Enfield EN1 . . . .**5** C1
 Hendon NW4 . . . .**46** C4
 Isleworth TW3, TW7 . . . . .**130** B1
 Sidcup DA14 . . . .**168** D2
 Sutton SM2 . . . .**218** B2
Eaton Rise Ealing W5 . . . . . .**87** D1
 Wanstead E11 . . . .**55** C4
Eaton Row SW1 . . .**115** B3 **258** C5
Eatons Mead E4 . . . .**19** C2
Eaton Sq SW1 . . . .**115** A3 **258** B5
Eaton Sq Pre-Prep Sch
 SW1 . . . .**115** B2 **258** C4
Eaton Sq Prep Sch
 SW1 . . . .**115** C2 **259** A4
Eaton Terr
 Belgravia SW1 . . . .**115** A2 **258** B4
 Bow E3 . . . .**97** A4
Eaton Terr Mews SW1 . . . .**258** A4
Eatonville Rd SW17 . . . . . .**158** D2
Eatonville Villas SW17 . . .**158** D2
Ebb Ct E16 . . . .**123** A6
Ebbisham Dr
 SW8 . . . .**138** B6 **270** C5
Ebbisham Rd KT4 . . . .**216** C6
Ebbsfleet Rd NW2 . . . .**69** A4
Ebdon Way SE13 . . . .**143** B2
Ebenezer Ho SE11 . . . .**261** C3
Ebenezer Mussel Ho 5
 E2 . . . .**96** C5
Ebenezer St N1 . . . .**235** C2
Ebenezer Wlk CR4 . . . .**181** C2
Ebley Cl SE15 . . . .**139** D6
Ebner St SW18 . . . .**157** D6
Ebony Ct NW10 . . . .**67** D2
Ebony Ho
 27 Bethnal Green E2 . . . . . .**96** A4
 10 West Hampstead NW3 . . .**69** D2
Ebor Cotts SW15 . . . .**155** C1
Ebor St E1, E2 . . . .**243** C6
Ebrington Rd HA3 . . . .**43** D3
Ebsworth St SE23 . . . .**162** D4
Eburne Rd N7 . . . .**72** A5
Ebury Bridge Rd
 SW1 . . . .**115** A1 **258** B1
Ebury Cl BR2 . . . .**226** A5
Ebury Mews
 Belgravia SW1 . . . .**115** B2 **258** C4
 West Norwood SE27 . . . . .**160** D1
Ebury Mews E SW1 . . . . . .**258** C5
Ebury Sq SW1 . . . .**258** B3
Ebury St SW1 . . . .**115** B2 **258** C4
Ecclesbourne Cl N13 . . . . . .**32** C5
Ecclesbourne Gdns N13 . . .**32** C5
Ecclesbourne Inf Sch
 CR7 . . . .**205** A4
Ecclesbourne Jun Sch
 CR7 . . . .**205** A4
Ecclesbourne Rd
 Islington N1 . . . .**73** A1
 Thornton Heath CR7 . . . . .**205** A4
Eccles Ct SE11 . . . .**260** D1
Eccleshill 8 BR2 . . . .**208** D5
Eccles Rd SW11 . . . .**136** D1
Eccleston Cl
 Cockfosters EN4 . . . .**2** D1
 Crofton BR6 . . . .**211** B1
Eccleston Cres RM6 . . . .**58** B2
Ecclestone Ct HA9 . . . .**66** A3
Ecclestone Mews HA9 . . . . .**66** A3
Ecclestone Pl HA9 . . . .**66** B3
Eccleston Ho 1 SW2 . . . . .**160** C5
Eccleston Mews
 SW1 . . . .**115** A3 **258** B5
Eccleston Pl
 SW1 . . . .**115** B2 **258** C4
Eccleston Rd W13 . . . .**109** A5
Eccleston Sq
 SW1 . . . .**115** B2 **258** D3
Eccleston Sq Mews SW1 . .**259** A3
Eccleston St
 SW1 . . . .**115** B2 **258** C4
Echelforde Dr TW15 . . . . . .**170** C6
Echelford Prim Sch The
 TW15 . . . .**170** D5
Echo Hts E4 . . . .**19** D3
Eckford St N1 . . . .**234** A4
Eckington Ho N15 . . . .**51** B3
Eckstein Rd SW11 . . . .**136** C1
Eclipse Rd E13 . . . .**99** B2
Ector Rd SE6 . . . .**164** C2
Edam Ct 11 DA14 . . . .**168** A1
Edans Ct W12 . . . .**111** D4
Edbrooke Rd W9 . . . .**91** C3
Eddisbury Ho 7 SE26 . . . . .**162** A1
Eddiscombe Rd SW6 . . . . .**135** B3
Eddison Ct N19 . . . .**72** A6
Eddy Cl RM7 . . . .**59** D3
Eddystone Rd SE4 . . . .**163** A6
Eddystone Twr SE8 . . . . . .**119** A1
Eddystone Wlk TW19 . . . . .**148** A4
Ede Cl TW4 . . . .**129** B2
Edenbridge Cl 29 SE16 . . . .**118** B1
Edenbridge Rd
 Enfield EN1 . . . .**17** C5

Edenbridge Rd continued
 Hackney E9 . . . .**74** D1
Eden Cl Child's Hill NW3 . . . .**69** C6
 Enfield EN3 . . . .**7** C5
 Kensington W8 . . . .**255** B6
 Wembley HA0 . . . .**87** D6
Edencourt W5 . . . .**88** B1
Edencourt Rd SW16 . . . . . .**181** B4
Eden Ct 3 N3 . . . .**29** B1
Edendale W3 . . . .**110** D6
Edenfield Gdns KT4 . . . . . .**215** D5
Eden Gr Islington N7 . . . .**72** B3
 Walthamstow E17 . . . .**53** D4
 Willesden NW10 . . . .**68** B2
Edenham High Sch CR0 . .**207** B2
Edenham Way W10 . . . .**91** B2
Eden High Sch 9 W6 . . . .**112** A1
Eden Ho
 15 Battersea SW11 . . . . .**136** C2
 Lisson Gr NW8 . . . .**237** A5
Edenhurst Ave SW6 . . . . . .**135** B2
Eden Ind Sch UB5 . . . .**63** B2
Eden Lodge NW6 . . . .**68** D1
Eden Mews SW17 . . . .**158** A1
EDEN PARK **207** C5
Eden Park Ave BR3 . . . . . .**207** C4
Eden Park Sta BR3 . . . .**207** C4
Eden Rd Croydon CR0 . . . . .**221** B4
 Penge BR3 . . . .**185** A2
 Walthamstow E17 . . . .**53** D4
 West Norwood SE27 . . . . .**182** D5
Edensmuir Ct SE3 . . . .**143** A5
Edensor Gdns W4 . . . .**133** C5
Edensor Rd W4 . . . .**133** C5
Eden St KT1, KT2 . . . .**176** A1
Edenvale Cl CR4 . . . .**181** A3
Edenvale Rd CR4 . . . .**181** A3
Edenvale St SW6 . . . .**136** A3
Eden Way
 Beckenham BR3 . . . .**207** C3
 Bow E3 . . . .**97** B6
Eden Wlk 5 KT1 . . . .**176** A1
 Eden Wlk Sh Ctr KT2 . . . . .**176** A1
Ederline Ave SW16 . . . . . .**182** C1
Edgar Ct KT3 . . . .**199** C6
Edgar Ho Homerton E9 . . . . .**75** A3
 South Lambeth SW8 . . . . .**270** A4
 Wanstead E11 . . . .**55** A2
Edgar Kail Way SE22 . . . . .**139** C1
Edgarley Terr SW6 . . . .**264** A1
Edgar Rd Bromley E3 . . . . . .**97** D4
 Dagenham RM6 . . . .**58** D2
 Twickenham TW4 . . . .**151** B4
 Yiewsley UB7 . . . .**104** A5
Edgar Wallace Cl 4
 SE15 . . . .**139** C5
Edgbury Ct NW9 . . . .**45** A5
Edgcott Ho 2 W10 . . . .**90** C2
Edgeborough Way BR1 . . . .**187** D2
Edge Bsns Ctr NW2 . . . .**68** B6
Edgebury BR7, SE9 . . . . . .**188** D6
Edgebury Prim Sch BR7 . . .**189** A6
Edgebury Wlk BR7 . . . .**167** A1
Edgecombe Ho
 4 London SE5 . . . .**139** C3
 Putney SW19 . . . .**157** A4
Edgecoombe CR2 . . . .**222** C1
Edgecote Cl 7 W3 . . . .**111** A5
Edgecot Gr N15 . . . .**51** C4
Edgecumbe Ct 2 CR0 . . . . .**206** A1
Edgefield Ave IG11 . . . .**79** D1
Edgefield Ct 3 IG11 . . . .**79** D1
Edge Hill
 Shooters Hill SE18 . . . . . .**144** D6
 Wimbledon SW19 . . . .**178** D3
Edgehill Ct KT12 . . . .**194** C1
Edge Hill Ct Sidcup DA14 . .**189** D6
 Wimbledon SW19 . . . .**178** D3
Edgehill Gdns RM10 . . . .**81** C4
Edgehill Ho 4 SW9 . . . . . .**138** D3
Edgehill Rd Ealing W13 . . . . .**87** C2
 Longlands BR7 . . . .**189** A6
 Mitcham CR4 . . . .**181** B2
Edgeley La SW4 . . . .**137** D2
Edgeley Rd SW4 . . . .**137** D2
Edgel St SW18 . . . .**135** D1
Edge Point Cl SE27 . . . . . .**182** D5
Edge St W8 . . . .**113** C5 **245** B4
Edgewood Dr BR6 . . . .**227** D3
Edgewood Gn CR0 . . . .**206** D1
Edgeworth Ave NW4 . . . . . .**46** A4
Edgeworth Cl NW4 . . . .**46** A4
Edgeworth Cres NW4 . . . . .**46** A4
Edgeworth Ct 10 EN4 . . . . . .**2** C1
Edgeworth Ho NW8 . . . . . .**229** A6
Edgeworth Rd Barnet EN4 . . .**2** C1
 Eltham SE9 . . . .**143** D1
Edgington Rd SW16 . . . . . .**181** D4
Edgington Way DA14 . . . . .**190** D3
Edgson Ho SW1 . . . .**258** C2
EDGWARE **26** C6
 Edgware Acad WC2 . . . . . .**240** D3
EDGWARE BURY **10** B3
Edgwarebury Ct HA8 . . . . . .**26** C5
Edgwarebury Gdns HA8 . . .**26** C5
Edgwarebury La
 Edgware Bury HA8 . . . .**10** C2
 Edgware HA8 . . . .**26** C6

Edgware Community Hospl
 HA8 . . . .**26** D3
Edgware Ct HA8 . . . .**26** C4
Edgware Jewish Prim Sch
 HA8 . . . .**26** D5
Edgware Jun & Inf Schs
 HA8 . . . .**26** C4
Edgware Rd
 Dollis Hill NW2 . . . .**68** C6
 Paddington W1, W2, NW1,
 NW8 . . . .**92** C2 **237** A3
Edgware Road Sta
 (Bakerloo) NW1 . .**92** C2 **237** A3
**Edgware Road Sta (Met,
 Distr, Circle)** NW1 . . .**237** B3
Edgware Road The Hyde
 NW9 . . . .**45** C5
Edgware Sta HA8 . . . .**26** D4
**Edgware Way (Watford By-
 Pass)** HA8 . . . .**27** A6
Edinburgh Cl
 7 Bethnal Green E2 . . . . . .**96** C5
 Pinner HA5 . . . .**41** A2
 Uxbridge UB10 . . . .**60** D4
Edinburgh Ho
 3 Acton W3 . . . .**89** B1
 Carshalton SM1 . . . .**218** B6
 Hendon NW4 . . . .**46** C6
 Maida Vale W9 . . . .**91** D4
Edinburgh Prim Sch E17 . .**53** B4
Edington 20 NW5 . . . .**71** A2
Edington Rd
 Abbey Wood SE2 . . . .**124** B3
 Enfield EN3 . . . .**6** C3
Edison Bldg 7 E14 . . . . . .**119** C4
Edison Cl
 Walthamstow E17 . . . .**53** C4
 West Drayton UB7 . . . . . .**104** B4
Edison Ct SE10 . . . .**120** D3
Edison Dr Southall UB1 . . . . .**85** D1
 Wembley HA9 . . . .**66** A6
Edison Gr SE18 . . . .**145** D5
Edison Ho Walworth SE1 . . .**262** C4
 7 Wembley HA9 . . . .**67** A5
Edison Rd Bexley DA16 . . . .**145** D4
 Brimsdown EN3 . . . .**7** B3
 Bromley BR2 . . . .**187** A1
 Crouch End N8 . . . .**49** D3
Edis St NW1 . . . . . .**93** A6 **231** B6
Editha Mans SW10 . . . . . .**266** A4
Edith Cavell Cl 2 N19 . . . . .**50** A2
Edith Cavell Way SE18 . . .**144** A4
Edith Ct TW14 . . . .**149** B5
Edith Gdns KT5 . . . .**198** D2
Edith Gr SW10 . . . .**136** A5 **266** B4
Edith Ho 6 W6 . . . .**112** C1
Edithna St SW9 . . . .**138** A2
Edith Nesbit Wlk SE9 . . . .**166** B6
Edith Neville Cotts NW1 . .**232** C2
Edith Neville Prim Sch
 NW1 . . . .**93** D5 **232** C3
Edith Ramsay Ho 2 E1 . . . .**97** A2
Edith Rd Dagenham RM6 . . . .**58** D2
 South Norwood SE25 . . . . .**205** B4
 Stratford New Town E15 . . .**76** B3
 Upton Pk E6 . . . .**77** D1
 West Kensington
 W14 . . . .**113** A2 **254** B3
 Wimbledon SW19 . . . .**179** D4
 Wood Green N11 . . . .**31** D3
Edith Row SW6 . . . .**265** D2
Edith St E2 . . . .**96** A5
Edith Summerskill Ho
 SW6 . . . .**264** C4
Edith Terr SW10 . . .**136** A5 **266** A4
Edith Villas W14 . . .**113** B1 **254** C2
Edith Yd SW10 . . . .**266** B4
Edmansons' Cl N17 . . . .**33** D2
Edmeston Cl E9 . . . .**75** A2
Edmond Ct SE14 . . . .**140** C4
Edmonscote W13 . . . .**87** A2
EDMONTON **33** D6
Edmonton Ct 5 SE16 . . . . .**118** C3
Edmonton Cty Lower Sch
 N9 . . . .**17** C3
Edmonton Cty Upper Sch
 EN1 . . . .**17** D4
Edmonton Green Sh Ctr
 N9 . . . .**18** B2
Edmonton Green Sta N9 . .**18** A2
 Edmonton Wharf N18 . . . . .**34** D4
Edmund Gr TW13 . . . .**151** B2
Edmund Halley Way
 SE10 . . . .**120** C4

Edmund Ho
 Kennington SE17 . . . .**261** D1
 New Cross Gate SE14 . . . .**141** B4
Edmund Hurst Dr E6 . . . . .**100** D2
Edmund Rd Mitcham CR4 . .**202** C6
 Welling DA16 . . . .**146** A2
Edmundsbury Ct Est 16
 SW9 . . . .**138** B1
Edmunds Cl UB4 . . . .**84** C2
Edmund St SE5 . . . .**139** B5
Edmunds Wlk N2 . . . .**48** C5
Edmund Waller Prim Sch
 SE14 . . . .**140** D3
Ednam Ho SE15 . . . .**140** A6
Edna Rd SW20 . . . .**178** D1
Edna St SW11 . . . .**136** C4 **267** A1
Edred Ho E9 . . . .**75** A4
Edrich Ho SW4 . . . .**270** A1
Edric Ho SW1 . . . .**259** D4
Edrick Rd HA8 . . . .**27** A4
Edrick Wlk HA8 . . . .**27** A4
Edric Rd SE14 . . . .**140** D5
Edridge Cl WD23 . . . .**8** A6
Edridge Ho 9 SE27 . . . . . .**160** D1
Edridge Rd CR0 . . . .**221** B5
Edward Alderton Theatre★
 DA7 . . . .**146** D2
Edward Alleyn Ho SE21 . . .**161** C4
Edward Ave Chingford E4 . . .**35** C4
 Morden SM4 . . . .**202** B4
Edward Betham CE Prim Sch
 UB6 . . . .**86** A5
 Hampton TW12 . . . .**173** C4
Edward Ct 2 Ealing W5 . . . . .**87** B3
 Harrow HA1 . . . .**64** C6
 2 Newham E16 . . . .**99** A2
Edward Dodd Ct N1 . . . . . .**235** D2
Edward Edward's Ho
 SE1 . . . .**251** C3
Edwardes Pl W8 . . . .**113** B3 **254** D5
Edwardes Sq W8 . . .**113** B3 **254** D5
Edward Friend Ho 6
 N16 . . . .**73** C5
Edward Gr EN4 . . . .**14** B6
Edward Harvey Ct DA17 . . .**125** B1
Edward Ho
 Paddington W2 . . . .**236** C5
 Vauxhall SE11 . . . .**260** D2
Edward Kennedy Ho 18
 W10 . . . .**91** A3
Edward Mann Cl 13 E1 . . . .**96** D1
Edward Mans 8 IG11 . . . . . .**79** D1
Edward Mews NW1 . . . . . .**231** D3
Edward Pauling Ho
 TW14 . . . .**149** D4
Edward Pauling Prim Sch
 TW13 . . . .**149** C2
Edward Pinner Ct 5
 KT6 . . . .**214** A6
Edward Pl SE8 . . . .**141** B6
Edward Rd Bromley BR1 . . .**187** C3
 Chislehurst BR7 . . . .**188** D5
 Croydon CR0 . . . .**205** C2
 Dagenham RM6 . . . .**59** A3
 Hampton TW12 . . . .**174** A5
 Harrow HA2 . . . .**42** A6
 Hatton TW14 . . . .**149** C6
 New Barnet EN4 . . . .**14** B6
 Northolt UB5 . . . .**84** C5
 Penge SE20 . . . .**184** D4
 Walthamstow SE17 . . . . . .**52** D4
Edward Robinson Ho 3
 SE14 . . . .**140** D5
Edward's Ave HA4 . . . .**62** C2
Edwards Cl 1 KT4 . . . .**216** D6
Edward's Cotts 11 N1 . . . . .**72** C1
Edwards Dr N11 . . . .**31** D3
Edward's Ho 7 TW10 . . . . .**153** C1
Edward's La N16 . . . .**73** C2
Edwards Language Sch 6
 W5 . . . .**110** A6
Edwards Mews
 Islington N1 . . . .**72** C1
 Marylebone W1 . . . .**93** A1 **238** A1
Edward Sq Islington N1 . . . .**233** C1
 1 Rotherhithe SE16 . . . . .**119** A5
Edwards Rd DA17 . . . .**125** C2
Edward St
 New Cross SE14 . . . .**141** B5
 10 Newham E16 . . . .**99** A3
Edward Temme Ave E15 . . .**76** D1
Edward Tyler Rd SE12 . . . .**165** C2
Edward VII Mans NW10 . . . .**90** D4
Edward Way TW15 . . . .**148** B2
Edward Wilson Prim Sch 2
 W2 . . . .**91** D2
Edwina Ct SM1 . . . .**217** D4
Edwina Gdns IG4 . . . .**56** A4
Edwin Arnold Ct DA15 . . . .**189** D6
Edwin Ave E6 . . . .**100** C5
Edwin Cl DA7 . . . .**147** B6
Edwin Ho SE15 . . . .**140** A5
Edwin Pl 10 CR0 . . . .**205** B3
Edwin Rd Burnt Oak HA8 . . . .**27** B4
 Twickenham TW1, TW2 . . .**152** C3
Edwin's Mead E9 . . . .**75** A4
Edwin St Bethnal Green E1 . . .**96** C3
 Newham E16 . . . .**99** A2
Edwin Stray Ho TW13 . . . .**151** C1

Edwin Ware Ct 4 HA5 ....22 C1
Edwy Ho E9 .....75 B4
Edwyn Cl EN5. .....12 D5
Edwin Ho SW18. ....157 D5
Eel Pie Island★ TW1 ....153 A3
Effie Pl SW6. ....**265 B3**
Effie Rd SW6. ....135 C5 **265 B3**
Effingham Ct SM2. ....217 D1
Effingham Ct SW19 ....180 C3
Effingham Ho
  37 Clapham SW8 ....137 D3
  8 Kingston u T KT2 ....176 D4
Effingham Lo 1 KT6 ....198 A4
Effingham Rd Hornsey N8 ..50 C5
  Lewisham SE12 ....164 D6
  Thames Ditton KT6, KT7 ..197 C2
  Thornton Heath CR0 ....204 B2
Effort St SW17 ....180 C5
Effra Ct SW19. ....179 D4
Effra Ct London SW2 ....160 B6
  South Norwood SE19 ....183 C3
Effra Mans SW2 ....160 C6
Effra Par SW2 ....160 C6
Effra Rd London SW2 ....160 C6
  Wimbledon SW19 ....179 D4
Effra Road Ret Pk SW2. ..160 C6
EF International Language
  Sch SE1. ....**251 B3**
Egan Way UB3. ....105 C6
Egbert Ho E9 ....75 A3
Egbert St NW1. ....93 A6 **231 A6**
Egbury Ho SW15. ....155 D5
Egerton Cl HA5. ....40 A5
Egerton Cres
  SW3. ....114 C2 **257 B4**
Egerton Ct
  5 Richmond TW10 ....154 A6
Egerton Dr SE10 ....141 D4
Egerton Gdns Ealing W13 ..87 B1
  Hendon NW4 ....46 B5
  Ilford IG3 ....79 D5
  Knightsbridge
  SW3. ....114 C3 **257 A5**
  Willesden NW10. ....90 C6
Egerton Gdns Mews
  SW3. ....**257 B5**
Egerton Ho W4 ....133 A6
Egerton Pl SW3. ....**257 B5**
Egerton Rd
  New Malden KT3 ....199 D5
  South Norwood SE25 ....205 C6
  Stamford Hill N16. ....51 D2
  Twickenham TW2 ....152 C4
  Wembley HA0. ....66 B1
Egerton Terr
  SW3. ....114 C3 **257 B5**
Egerton Way UB3 ....126 D5
Eggardon Ct UB5 ....64 A2
Egham Cl Cheam SM3 ....217 A6
  Putney SW15 ....157 A2
Egham Ct KT6 ....197 D4
Egham Cres SM3 ....217 A6
Egham Rd E13 ....99 B2
Eglantine Rd SW18 ....158 A6
Egleston Rd SM4 ....201 D3
Eglington Ct SE17 ....139 A6
Eglington Rd E4 ....20 B4
Eglinton Hill SE18. ....144 C6
Eglinton Prim Sch SE18. 144 C6
Eglinton Rd SE18 ....144 D6
Egliston Mews SW15 ....134 C2
Egliston Rd SW15 ....134 C2
Egmont Ct KT6 ....198 B1
Egmont Mews KT19 ....215 B4
Egmont Rd
  New Malden KT3 ....199 D5
  Sutton SM2. ....218 A1
  Tolworth KT6 ....198 C1
  Walton-on-T KT12 ....194 B2
Egmont St SE14. ....140 D5
Egremont Ho SE13 ....141 D3
Egremont Rd SE27 ....160 C1
Egret Ho 11 SE16 ....118 D2
Egret Way UB4. ....84 D2
Eider Cl Hayes UB4. ....84 D2
  Stratford E7 ....76 D3
Eider Ct 33 SE8 ....141 B6
Eighteenth Rd CR4. ....204 A5
Eighth Ave Hayes UB3. ..106 A5
  Ilford E12. ....78 B4
Eileen Ct BR7. ....188 C5
Eileen Rd SE25 ....205 B4
Eindhoven Cl SM5 ....203 A1
Einstein Ho HA9 ....67 A5
Eisenhower Dr E6 ....100 A2
Eisenhower Ho KT8 ....175 C2
Elaine Ct 13 NW3 ....70 D2
Elaine Gr NW5. ....71 A3
Elaine Ho N4 ....50 A1
Elam Cl SE5 ....138 C3
Elam St SE5 ....138 D3
Eland Ct E1. ....96 B2
Eland Pl CR0 ....220 D5
Eland Rd Clapham SW11. .136 D2
  Croydon CR0. ....220 D5
Elba Pl SE17 ....117 A2 **262 B4**
Elberon Ave CR0. ....203 C3
Elbe St SW6 ....136 A3
Elborough Rd SE25 ....206 A4

Elborough St SW18. ....157 C3
Elbourne Trad Est DA17. 125 D3
Elbury Dr E16. ....99 A1
Elcho St SW11. ....136 C5 **267 B3**
Elcot Ave SE15. ....140 B5
Elder Ave N8 ....50 A4
Elderberry Ct 2 EN2. ....4 D3
Elderberry Gr 10 SE27 ..183 A6
Elderberry Rd W5. ....110 A4
Elder Cl Barnet N20. ....13 D3
  Sidcup DA15. ....167 D3
  Yiewsley UB7. ....104 A6
Elder Ct WD23 ....8 C2
Elderfield Ho 4 E14 ....119 C6
Elderfield Pl SW17 ....181 B6
Elderfield Rd E5 ....74 C4
Elderflower Way E15. ....76 C1
Elder Gdns 3 SE27 ....183 A6
Elder Oak Cl SE20. ....184 B2
Elder Rd SE27 ....183 A5
Elderslie Cl BR3. ....207 D3
Elderslie Rd SE9. ....166 C4
Elder St E1. ....95 D3 **243 C5**
Elderton Rd SE26 ....185 A6
Eldertree Pl CR4. ....181 C2
Eldertree Way CR4. ....181 C2
Elder Wlk Islington N1 ..**234 D6**
  2 Lewisham SE13 ....142 A2
Elderwood Pl SE27. ....183 A5
Eldon Ave Croydon CR0. ..222 C6
  Heston TW5 ....129 C5
Eldon Ct NW6 ....91 C6
Eldon Gr NW3 ....70 B3
Eldon Ho NW9 ....138 D2
Eldon Jun & Inf Schs N9 ..33 C4
Eldon Pk SE25 ....206 B5
Eldon Rd Edmonton N9 ....33 D2
  Kensington W8. ....113 D3 **255 D5**
  Tottenham N22. ....32 D2
  Walthamstow E17 ....53 B5
Eldon St EC2 ....95 B3 **242 D3**
Eldonwall Est RM8. ....59 B1
Eldon Way NW10. ....88 D5
Eldred Rd IG11 ....101 C6
Eldrick Ct TW14. ....149 B3
Eldridge Cl TW14. ....150 A3
Eldridge Ct
  Bermondsey SE16 ....118 A3
  14 Dagenham RM10. ....81 D2
Eleanor Cl
  Rotherhithe SE16 ....118 D4
  South Tottenham N15. ....51 D6
Eleanor Cres NW7 ....28 D6
Eleanor Ct 13 E2. ....96 A6
Eleanor Gdns Barnet EN5 ..12 C3
  Dagenham RM8. ....81 B4
Eleanor Gr
  Mortlake SW13 ....133 C2
  Uxbridge UB10. ....60 D5
Eleanor Ho
  18 Hammersmith W6. ....112 C1
  8 Kentish Town NW5 ....71 C3
  6 Merton SW19 ....179 D2
Eleanor Palmer Prim Sch 12
  NW5. ....71 C4
Eleanor Rathbone Ho 1
  N6. ....49 D2
Eleanor Rd Bowes Pk N11. ..32 A4
  Hackney E8. ....74 B1
  Stratford E15 ....76 D2
Eleanor Smith Sch 2
  E13. ....99 B5
Eleanor Smith Sch (West
  Beckton Site) E16 ....99 C2
Eleanor St 3. ....97 C4
Electra Ave TW6 ....127 D2
Electra Ct 6 NW9 ....28 C2
Electric Ave SW9 ....138 C1
Electric Ho 13 Bow E3 ....97 C4
Electric La 2 SW9 ....138 C1
Electric Mans 1 SW9 ....138 C1
Electric Par Ilford IG3 ....79 C1
  Surbiton KT6. ....197 D3
  Woodford E18. ....37 A1
Elenmore Ct BR1. ....210 A5
Elephant & Castle
  Newington SE1. ....116 D3 **261 D5**
  Newington SE1. ....117 A2 **262 A4**
Elephant & Castle Sh Ctr
  SE1. ....117 A2 **262 A4**
Elephant & Castle Sta
  Lambeth SE1. ....116 D3 **261 D5**
  Newington SE1. ....117 A2 **262 A4**
Elephant La SE16. ....118 C4
Elephant Rd
  SE17. ....117 A2 **262 A4**
Elers Rd Ealing W13. ....109 C4
  Hayes UB3. ....105 B2
Eley Rd N18. ....34 D5
Eley's Est N18. ....34 D6
Elfindale Rd SE24. ....161 A6
Elfin Gr TW11 ....174 D5
Elford Cl SE9 ....143 C1
Elfort Rd N5. ....72 D1
Elfrida Cres SE6. ....185 C6
Elfrida Prim Sch SE6. ..185 C6
Elf Row E1. ....118 C6

Elfwine Rd W7. ....86 C2
Elgal Cl BR6. ....226 D3
Elgar N8 ....50 A6
Elgar Ave Ealing W5. ....110 A4
  Thornton Heath SW16 ..204 A6
  Tolworth KT5, KT6 ....198 D2
  Willesden NW10. ....67 B2
Elgar Cl Buckhurst Hill IG9 ..21 D2
  Deptford SE8 ....141 C5
  Elstree WD6 ....9 D4
  Ickenham UB10. ....60 C6
  Newham E13 ....99 C5
Elgar Ct W14 ....**254 A5**
Elgar Ho Hayes UB4. ....84 C2
  Isleworth TW2 ....152 B5
  Pimlico SW1. ....**258 D1**
  Southall UB1. ....85 C1
  South Hampstead NW6 ....73 D4
Elgar St SE16 ....119 A3
Elgin Ave Ashford TW15 ..171 A4
  Hammersmith W12 ....112 B3
  Harrow HA3 ....25 B1
  Westbourne Green W9. ....91 D3
Elgin Cl W12. ....112 B4
Elgin Cres Hatton TW6. ..127 C3
  Notting Hill W11. ....113 A6 **244 B6**
Elgin Ct 6 Croydon CR0. ..221 A4
  Westbourne Green W9. ....91 D3
Elgin Ho Northolt UB5. ....84 B5
  8 Poplar E14. ....97 D1
Elgin Mans W9 ....91 D4
Elgin Mews W11. ....91 A1
Elgin Mews N W9. ....91 A1
Elgin Mews S W9. ....91 A1
Elgin Rd Croydon CR0. ..221 D6
  Ilford IG3 ....57 C2
  Sutton SM1. ....218 A5
  Wallington SM6 ....219 C2
  Wood Green N22. ....31 C1
Elgood Ave HA6 ....22 A3
Elgood Cl W11. ....**244 A3**
Elgood Ho NW8. ....**229 D3**
Elham Cl BR1. ....187 D3
Elham Ho 13 E5. ....74 B3
Elia Mews N1. ....95 B5 **234 C3**
Elias Pl SW8. ....138 C6
Elia St N1. ....94 D5 **234 C3**
Elibank Rd SE9 ....144 C1
Elim Est SE1. ....**263 A6**
Elim St SE1. ....**263 A6**
Elim Way E13. ....98 D4
Eliot Bank SE23, SE26. ..162 B2
Eliot Bank Prim Sch
  SE26. ....162 B2
Eliot Cotts SE3. ....142 C3
Eliot Ct SW18. ....157 D5
Eliot Dr HA2. ....63 D6
Eliot Hill SE13 ....142 A4
Eliot Ho 10 TW10. ....154 B5
Eliot Mews NW8 ....**229 A3**
Eliot Pk SE13 ....142 A3
Eliot Pl SE3. ....142 C3
Eliot Rd RM9 ....80 D4
Eliot Vale SE3. ....142 B3
Elis David Almshouses
  CR0. ....220 D4
Elizabethan Ct N3 ....47 A6
Elizabeth Ave Enfield EN2 ..4 D2
  Ilford IG1 ....79 B6
  Islington N1 ....73 B1
  Shoreditch N1. ....95 A6 **235 B6**
Elizabeth Barnes Ct 5
  SW6. ....135 D3
Elizabeth Blackwell Ho
  N22. ....32 C2
Elizabeth Blount Ct 4
  E14. ....97 A1
Elizabeth Cl Cheam SM1. ..217 B4
  Paddington W9. ....**236 B5**
  12 Poplar E14. ....97 D1
Elizabeth Clyde Cl N15. ..51 C5
Elizabeth Cooper Lo
  SW12. ....159 A5
Elizabeth Cotts 5 TW9. ..132 C4
Elizabeth Ct
  Buckhurst Hill IG9 ....21 B3
  Chelsea SW10 ....**266 D5**
  East Dulwich SE22 ....140 A1
  Kingston u T KT2 ....176 A2
  Marylebone W9 ....**237 B6**
  South Croydon CR0. ....221 C5
  Sunbury TW16 ....194 C6
  13 Teddington TW11. ....174 C5
  Upper Tooting SW17. ....181 A5
  West Barnes SM4. ....201 A2
  Westminster SW1. ....**259 D5**
  6 Woodford Green E18. ....37 A2
  2 Woodford Green IG8. ....37 C3
  10 Woolwich SE18 ....122 B2
Elizabeth Finn Ho 1
  W12. ....112 A3
Elizabeth Fry Ho UB3 ....105 D2
Elizabeth Fry Pl SE18. ..144 A4
Elizabeth Garrett Anderson
  Ho 9 DA17. ....125 C3
Elizabeth Garrett Anderson
  Hospl NW1. ....93 C3 **239 B5**

Elizabeth Garrett Anderson
  Language Coll
  N1. ....94 B5 **233 D3**
Elizabeth Gdns
  East Acton W3 ....111 D5
  Isleworth TW7 ....131 A1
  Stanmore HA7 ....25 C5
  Sunbury TW16 ....194 C6
Elizabeth Ho Cheam SM3. .217 A2
  Friern Barnet N20 ....14 D1
  15 Hammersmith W6 ....112 C1
  Lambeth SE11. ....**261 B3**
  Stanmore HA7 ....25 C5
  Wembley HA9. ....66 B3
Elizabeth Ind Est SE14 ..140 D6
Elizabeth Kenny Ho N1. ...73 A2
Elizabeth Mews
  28 Hackney E2. ....96 A5
  Maitland Pk NW3 ....70 D2
Elizabeth Pl N15. ....51 B5
  South Tottenham N15. ....51 C4
Elizabeth Ride N9 ....18 B4
Elizabeth Selby Inf Sch 31
  E2. ....96 A4
Elizabeth Sq 13 SE16. ..119 A6
Elizabeth St SW1. ....115 A2 **258 B4**
Elizabeth Terr SE9 ....166 B5
Elizabeth Way
  Feltham TW13 ....172 C6
  South Norwood SE19 ....183 B3
Elkanette Mews N20. ....14 A2
Elkington Point SE11. ..**261 A3**
Elkington Rd E13 ....99 B3
Elkstone Rd W10. ....91 B2
Ella Ct BR3 ....185 C1
Ellacombe Ho 1 SW2. ..160 C4
Ellaline Rd W6. ....134 D6
Ella Mews NW3 ....70 D4
Ellanby Cres N18 ....34 B5
Elland Cl EN5. ....14 B6
Elland Ho 18 E14. ....97 B1
Elland Rd SE15 ....140 C1
Ella Rd N4, N8. ....50 A2
Ellard Ct DA16. ....146 C2
Elle Ct N3 ....29 D5
Element Cl HA5 ....40 D4
Ellena Ct N14. ....16 A1
Ellenborough H22. ....32 D2
Ellenborough Ho 5
  W12. ....112 B6
Ellenborough Pl SW15 ..134 A1
Ellenborough Rd
  Sidcup DA14. ....191 A5
  Tottenham N22. ....33 A2
Ellen Cl BR1. ....209 D6
Ellen Ct 4 Chingford E4 ....20 A3
  Lower Edmonton N9 ....18 C2
Ellen Miller Ho 2 E17. ....54 A4
Ellen St E1. ....96 A1
Ellen Webb Dr HA3. ....42 C6
Ellen Wilkinson Ho
  12 Dagenham RM10. ....81 C5
  7 Globe Town E2. ....96 D4
  West Brompton SW6. ....**264 D5**
Ellen Wilkinson Prim Sch
  E6. ....100 A2
Ellen Wilkinson Sch for Girls
  W3. ....88 B1
Elleray Rd TW11 ....174 D4
Ellerby St SW6. ....134 D4
Ellerdale Cl 15 NW3. ....70 A4
Ellerdale Rd NW3. ....70 A3
Ellerdale St SE13 ....141 D2
Ellerdine Rd TW3. ....130 B1
Ellerker Gdns TW10. ....154 A5
Ellerman Ave TW2, TW4. .151 B3
Ellerker Gdns RM9 ....80 C1
Ellerslie 6 SM6. ....219 B2
Ellerslie Gdns NW10. ....90 A6
Ellerslie Ind Est SW2. ..160 A6
Ellerslie Rd W12. ....112 B5
Ellerslie Sq SW2. ....110 D4
Ellerton Gdns RM9. ....80 C1
Ellerton Lo N3. ....29 C1
Ellerton Rd Barnes SW13 ..134 A4
  Dagenham RM9 ....80 C1
  Surbiton KT6. ....198 B1
  Wandsworth SW17, SW18. .158 B3
  Wimbledon SW20. ....178 A3
Ellery Cl 5 NW10. ....89 C5
Ellery Ho SE17 ....**262 D3**
Ellery Rd SE19 ....183 B3
Ellery St SE15. ....140 B3
Ellesborough Cl WD19 ....22 C5
Ellesmere Ave
  Beckenham BR3 ....185 D1
  Edgware NW7 ....11 B1
Ellesmere Cl
  Chiswick W4. ....133 B6
  Lewisham SE12 ....165 A3
  Penge SE20 ....184 B1
Ellesmere Gdns IG4. ....56 A3
Ellesmere Rd Bow E3. ....97 A5
  Chiswick W4. ....133 B6
  Greenford UB6. ....86 A3
  Twickenham TW1 ....153 C5

Ellesmere Rd continued
  Willesden NW10. ....68 A3
Ellesmere St E14 ....97 C1
Ellies Mews TW15. ....148 A2
Ellingfort Rd E8 ....74 B1
Ellingham Prim Sch
  KT9. ....213 D1
Ellingham Rd
  Chessington KT9. ....213 D2
  Leyton E15 ....76 B4
  Shepherd's Bush W12 ....112 A4
Ellington Ct N14. ....15 D2
Ellington Ho SE1. ....**262 B5**
Ellington Rd
  Cranley Gdns N10. ....49 B5
  Feltham TW13 ....171 D6
  Hounslow TW3 ....129 D3
Ellington St N7. ....72 C2
Elliot Cl Stratford E15 ....76 C1
  Wembley HA9. ....66 C5
  Woodford IG8. ....37 D4
Elliot Ct 6 N15. ....51 D5
Elliot Rd NW4 ....46 B3
Elliott Ave HA4 ....62 B6
Elliott Gdns TW17 ....192 C5
Elliott Ho 37 SE7. ....204 D5
Elliott Rd Acton W4 ....111 C2
  Brixton SW9 ....138 D4
  Bromley BR2. ....209 D5
  Camberwell SW9 ....138 D4
  Stanmore HA7 ....25 A4
  Thornton Heath CR7. ....204 D5
Elliott Sch SW15. ....156 C5
Elliott's Pl N1 ....**234 D5**
Elliott Sq NW3. ....70 C1
Ellis Cl Burnt Oak HA8 ....27 C4
  New Eltham SE9 ....167 A2
  Willesden NW10. ....68 C2
Elliscombe Mount 11
  SE7. ....143 C6
Elliscombe Rd SE7. ....143 C6
Ellis Ct W7 ....86 D2
Ellisfield Dr SW15. ....156 A4
Ellis Franklin Ct NW8 ..**229 A4**
Ellis Ho Walthamstow E17. ..54 A4
  Walworth SE17. ....**262 C2**
Ellison Gdns UB2. ....107 B2
Ellison Ho 1 SE13 ....142 A2
  New Malden DA15. ....167 B3
Ellison Rd Barnes SW13. .133 D3
  Streatham SW16. ....182 A3
Ellis Rd Mitcham CR4. ....202 D3
  Southall UB2. ....108 A5
Ellis St SW1. ....115 A2 **258 A4**
Elliston Ho 8 SE18 ....122 C2
Ellora Rd SW16 ....181 D5
Ellswood Ct 18 KT6 ....197 D2
Ellsworth St 13 E2 ....96 B4
Ellsworth St E2. ....96 B4
Ellwood Ct 1 W9 ....91 D3
Elmar Ct SW6. ....135 A3
Elmar Rd N15. ....51 B5
Elm Ave Ealing W5. ....110 A5
  Ruislip HA4. ....40 B2
Elmbank N14. ....16 A4
Elm Bank Dr BR1. ....187 D1
Elm Bank Gdns SW13 ....133 C3
Elm Bank Mans SW13 ....133 C3
Elmbank Way W7. ....86 B2
Elmbourne Dr DA17. ....125 D2
Elmbourne Rd SW17 ....159 B1
Elmbridge Ave KT5 ....199 A3
Elmbridge Cl HA4. ....40 A3
Elmbridge Dr HA4. ....40 A3
Elmbridge Wlk E8 ....74 A1
Elmbridge Xcel Leisure
  Complex KT12. ....194 B4
Elmbrook 3 E18. ....55 A6
Elmbrook Cl TW16 ....172 B2
Elmbrook Gdns SE9 ....144 A1
Elmbrook Rd SM1. ....217 B4
Elm Cl Buckhurst Hill IG9 ....21 C2
  Carshalton SM5. ....202 D1
  Harrow HA2. ....41 D3
  Hayes UB3. ....84 A1
  Hendon NW4 ....46 D4
  South Croydon CR2. ....221 C2
  Tolworth KT5. ....199 A2
  Twickenham TW13, TW2. .151 D2
  Upper Holloway N19 ....71 C6
  Wanstead E11 ....55 B3
  West Barnes SW20 ....200 C5
Elmcote HA5 ....40 A5
Elm Court Sch SE21, SE27. 160 D2
Elm Court Sch SE27 ....161 A2
Elm Cres Ealing W5. ....110 A4
  Kingston u T KT2. ....176 A2
Elmcroft Highgate N6 ....49 C2
  Hornsey Vale N8. ....50 B4
Elmcroft Ave
  Blackfen DA15. ....168 A5
  Enfield N9. ....18 B5
  Golders Green NW11. ....47 B2
  Wanstead E11 ....55 B5
Elmcroft Cl
  Chessington KT9. ....214 A5

Elmcroft CI continued
Ealing W5 . . . . .87 D1
Feltham TW14 . . . . .149 D5
Wanstead E11 . . . . .55 B5
Elmcroft Cres Harrow HA2 . .41 C6
Hendon NW11 . . . . .47 A2
Elmcroft Dr
Ashford TW15. . . . . .170 C5
Chessington KT9 . . . . .214 A5
Elmcroft Gdns NW9 . . . . . .44 C4
Elmcroft St E5. . . . . .74 C4
Elmcroft Terr UB8. . . . . . . .82 C1
Elm Ct 5 Ashford TW16 . .171 D3
Brixton SW9 . . . . .138 C4
Catford SE6 . . . . .163 D3
Chingford E4. . . . . .36 A4
4 Finchley N3 . . . . .29 C2
Lewisham SE13 . . . . .142 B2
Mitcham CR4 . . . . .180 D1
42 Notting Hill W2 . . . . . . .91 C2
Strand EC4 . . . . .251 A6
Elm Ct Sch SE27 . . . . .160 B4
Elmdale Rd N13 . . . . .32 B5
Elmdene KT5 . . . . .199 A1
Elmdene CI BR3. . . . . .207 B4
Elmdene Rd SE18 . . . . . . .122 D1
Elmdon Rd Hatton TW6 . . .127 D2
Hounslow TW5 . . . . .129 A3
Elm Dr Harrow HA2 . . . . . . .41 D3
Sunbury TW16 . . . . .172 C1
Elmer CI EN2 . . . . .4 B2
Elmer Ct HA1. . . . . .42 D3
Elmer Gdns Edgware HA8 . .26 D3
Isleworth TW7 . . . . .130 B2
Elmer Ho NW1. . . . . .237 A4
Elmer Rd SE6. . . . . .164 A4
Elmer's Dr TW11 . . . . .175 B4
ELMERS END 206 D6
Elmers End Rd BR3,
SE20 . . . . .206 C6
Elmers End Sta BR3. . . . . .206 D5
Elmerside Rd BR3 . . . . . . .207 A5
Elmers Rd SE25. . . . . .206 A2
Elmfield Ave London N8 . . .50 A4
1 Mitcham CR4 . . . . .181 A2
Teddington TW11 . . . . . . .174 D5
Elmfield CI HA1. . . . . .64 C6
Elmfield Ct DA16. . . . . . . .146 B4
Elmfield Ho
6 Canonbury N5 . . . . .73 A3
22 London N2. . . . . .30 B1
Paddington W9 . . . . .91 C3
Elmfield Mans 5 SW17 . .159 A2
Elmfield Pk BR1 . . . . .209 A6
Elmfield Rd Bromley BR1 . .209 A6
Chingford E4. . . . . .20 B2
East Finchley N2 . . . . .48 B6
Southall UB2. . . . . .107 A3
Upper Tooting SW17. . . . . .159 B2
Walthamstow E17 . . . . .52 D3
Elmfield Way
Paddington W9 . . . . .91 C2
South Croydon CR2. . . . . . .221 D1
Elm Friars Wlk NW1 . . . . . .71 D1
Elmgate Ave TW13 . . . . . .150 C1
Elmgate Ct HA8. . . . . .27 A5
Elmgate Gdns HA8. . . . . . . .27 B6
Elm Gdns Claygate KT10 . .212 D2
East Finchley N2 . . . . .48 A6
Enfield EN2. . . . . .5 B5
Mitcham CR4 . . . . .203 D1
Elm Gn W3 . . . . .89 C1
Elm Gr Cricklewood NW2 . . .68 D4
Harrow HA2 . . . . .41 C2
Hornsey N8. . . . . .50 A3
Kingston u T KT2. . . . . . . .176 A2
Orpington BR6 . . . . .211 D1
Peckham SE15 . . . . .140 A3
Sutton SM1. . . . . .217 D4
Wimbledon SW19. . . . . . . .179 A3
Woodford IG8. . . . . .36 D5
Yiewsley UB7 . . . . .104 B6
Elmgreen CI 8 E15 . . . . . . .98 C6
Elmgreen Sch The SE27 . .160 B2
Elmgrove Cres HA1 . . . . . . .43 A4
Elmgrove Fst & Mid Schs
HA3 . . . . .43 A5
Elmgrove Gdns HA1 . . . . . . .43 A4
Elm Grove Par SM6 . . . . . .219 A5
Elmgrove Rd
Croydon CR0. . . . . .206 B2
Harrow HA1 . . . . .42 D4
Elm Grove Rd
Barnes SW13 . . . . .134 A3
Ealing W5 . . . . .110 A4
Elm Hall Gdns E11 . . . . . . .55 B3
Elm Hatch HA5 . . . . .23 B3
Elm Ho
4 Cubitt Town E14. . . . . . .120 A4
2 Kingston u T KT2 . . . . . .176 B3
Teddington TW11 . . . . . . .175 C3
Elmhurst DA17 . . . . .147 A6
Elmhurst Ave London N2 . . .48 B6
Mitcham CR4 . . . . .181 B3
Elmhurst Cres N2. . . . . . . .48 B5
Elmhurst Ct
Carshalton SM5 . . . . .218 B6

Croydon CR0. . . . . .221 B3
Elmhurst Dr E18 . . . . .37 A1
Elmhurst Lo 3 SM2. . . . . .218 A1
Elmhurst Mans TW4 . . . . .137 D2
Elmhurst Prim Sch E7 . . . .77 B1
Elmhurst Rd
Chislehurst SE9 . . . . .166 A1
Enfield EN3. . . . . .6 C6
Tottenham N17. . . . . .33 D1
Upton E7. . . . . .77 B1
Elmhurst Sch for Boys
CR2. . . . . .221 B3
Elmhurst St SW4 . . . . .137 D2
Elmhurst Villas SE15 . . . . .140 C1
Elmington CI DA5. . . . . . . .169 D5
Elmington Rd SE5 . . . . . . .139 B5
Elmira St SE13 . . . . .141 D2
Elm La SE6 . . . . .163 B2
Elm Lawn CI UB8. . . . . .60 A1
Elmlea Dr UB3. . . . . .83 D2
Elm Lea Trad Est N17. . . . . .34 B4
Elmlee CI BR7 . . . . .188 B4
Elmley CI 12 E6 . . . . .100 A2
Elmley St SE18. . . . . .123 B2
Elm Lo SW6 . . . . .134 D4
Elmore CI HA0. . . . . .88 A5
Elmore Ho SW9 . . . . .138 D3
Elmore Rd Enfield EN3 . . . . . .6 D5
Leyton E11 . . . . .76 B5
Elmore St N1 . . . . .73 B1
Elm Park Ave N15. . . . . . . .52 A3
Elm Park Ct HA5 . . . . .40 C6
Elm Park Gdns
Chelsea SW10 . . . . .114 B1 256 C1
Hendon NW4 . . . . .46 D4
Elm Park Ho SW10 . . . . . .256 C1
Elm Park La SW3 . . .114 B1 256 C1
Elm Park Mans SW10 . . . .266 B2
Elm Park Rd
Chelsea SW3 . . . . . .136 B6 266 C6
Edmonton N21 . . . . .17 A4
Finchley N3. . . . . .29 B3
Pinner HA5. . . . . .40 D6
South Norwood SE25 . . . . .205 D6
Walthamstow E10 . . . . .53 A1
Elm Pk Stanmore HA7 . . . . .25 C5
Streatham SW2 . . . . .160 B4
Elm Pl Ashford TW15 . . . . .170 C5
SW7 . . . . .114 B1 256 C2
Elm Quay SW8. . . . . .269 C5
Elm Rd Barnet EN5. . . . . .1 B1
Beckenham BR3. . . . . .185 B1
Chessington KT9 . . . . .214 A4
Claygate KT10 . . . . .212 D2
East Bedfont TW14. . . . . . .149 B4
Hackbridge SM6. . . . . .203 A1
Kingston u T KT2 . . . . .176 B2
Leyton E11 . . . . .76 B6
Mortlake SW14 . . . . .133 A1
New Malden KT3 . . . . .199 B6
Sidcup DA14. . . . . .190 A6
South Norwood CR7 . . . . . .205 B5
Stoneleigh KT17. . . . . .215 D2
Stratford E7 . . . . .76 D2
Tottenham N22. . . . . .32 D2
Walthamstow E17 . . . . .54 A4
Wembley HA9. . . . . .66 A3
Elm Rd W SM4. . . . . .201 B2
Elm Row SW3 . . . . .70 A5
Elms Ave Hendon NW4 . . . . .46 D4
Muswell Hill N10. . . . . .49 B6
Elmscott Gdns N21 . . . . . . .17 A5
Elmscott Rd BR1. . . . . .186 D5
Elms Cotts 1 CR4 . . . . . . .180 D1
Elms Cres SW4 . . . . .159 D5
Elms Ct Merton SW19 . . . . .179 D3
Wembley HA0. . . . . .65 A4
Elmsdale Rd E17. . . . . .53 B5
Elms Gdns Dagenham RM9. . .81 A4
Wembley HA0. . . . . .65 A4
Elmshaw Rd SW15 . . . . . . .156 A6
Elmside CR0. . . . . .223 D2
Elmside Rd HA9 . . . . .66 C5
Elms La HA0. . . . . .65 A5
Elmsleigh Ave HA3. . . . . . . .43 C5
Elmsleigh Ct SM1. . . . . . . .217 D5
Elmsleigh Ho TW2 . . . . . . .152 B2
Elmsleigh Rd TW2 . . . . . . .152 B2
Elmslie Ct SE9 . . . . .166 C5
Elmslie Point 2 E3 . . . . . . .97 B2
Elms Mews W2 . . . . .246 C4
Elms Park Ave HA0. . . . . . . .65 A4
Elms Rd Clapham Pk SW4 . .159 C6
Harrow HA3 . . . . .24 C3
Elm St WC1 . . . . . . .94 B3 240 D5
ELMSTEAD. 188 A5
Elmstead Ave
Elmstead BR7. . . . . .188 B5
Wembley HA9. . . . . .66 B6
Elmstead CI
Totteridge N20. . . . . .13 C2
West Ewell KT19 . . . . .215 C3
Elmstead Crs HA4. . . . . .44 B1
Elmstead Gdns KT4 . . . . . .216 A5
Elmstead Glade BR7. . . . . .188 B4
Elmstead La BR7. . . . . .188 B5
Elmstead Rd IG3. . . . . .79 D6
Elmstead Woods Sta
BR7. . . . . .188 A4

Elmsted Cres DA16. . . . . . .146 C6
Elms The
5 Ashford TW15 . . . . .170 C5
Barnes SW13 . . . . .133 D2
Claygate KT10 . . . . .212 D1
Croydon CR0. . . . . .205 A1
3 Harlesden NW10. . . . . . .89 C5
Kingsbury NW9 . . . . .45 A3
Plashet E12 . . . . .78 A2
Wallington SM6 . . . . .219 C4
Elmstone Rd SW6 . . . . . . .265 A2
Elmsway TW15. . . . . .170 C5
Elmsworth Ave TW3 . . . . . .129 D3
Elm Terr Child's Hill NW2. . . .69 C5
3 Eltham SE9 . . . . .166 C5
Harrow HA3 . . . . .24 B2
Elm Tree CI
Ashford TW15. . . . . .170 D5
Northolt UB5 . . . . .85 B5
St John's Wood
NW8. . . . . .92 B4 229 C2
Elm Tree Ct HA4 . . . . .40 A1
Elm Tree Ct
5 Camberwell SE5 . . . . . .139 A4
18 Charlton SE7 . . . . .143 C6
St John's Wood NW8 . . . . .229 C2
Elmtree Rd TW11 . . . . .174 C5
Elm Tree Rd NW8 . .92 B4 229 C2
Elm View Ct UB2 . . . . .107 C2
Elm Way London N11 . . . . . .31 A4
North Cheam KT4. . . . . . . .216 C5
West Ewell KT19. . . . . .215 B3
Willesden NW10. . . . . .67 C4
Elm Wlk Child's Hill NW3 . . . .69 C6
Orpington BR6 . . . . .226 B5
West Barnes SW20 . . . . . .200 D5
Elmwood Ave
Bowes Pk N13. . . . . .32 A5
Feltham TW13 . . . . .150 B1
Harrow HA3 . . . . .43 B3
Elmwood CI
Hackbridge SM6. . . . . .219 A5
Stoneleigh KT17 . . . . .216 A1
Elmwood Cres NW9. . . . . . .45 A5
Elmwood Ct
Battersea SW11. . . . . .268 C2
Walthamstow E10 . . . . .53 C1
Wembley HA0. . . . . .65 A5
Elmwood Dr Sidcup DA5. . .169 A4
Stoneleigh KT17. . . . . .216 A1
Elmwood Gdns W7. . . . . . . .86 C1
Elmwood Ho Enfield EN2 . . . .4 D1
Feltham TW13. . . . . .150 B1
Elmwood Inf Sch CR0 . . . . .204 D3
Elmwood Jun Sch CR0 . . . .204 D2
Elm Wood Prim Sch
SE27. . . . . .161 B1
Elmwood Rd
Chiswick W4 . . . . .133 A6
Herne Hill SE24 . . . . .161 B6
Mitcham CR4 . . . . .202 D6
Thornton Heath CR0 . . . . .204 D2
Elmworth Gr SE21 . . . . . . .161 B2
Elnathan Mews W9 . . . . . . .91 D3
Elphinstone Ct SW16. . . . . .182 A4
Elphinstone Rd E17. . . . . . .35 B1
Elphinstone St N5 . . . . .72 C4
Elrington Rd Dalston E8. . . . .74 A2
Woodford IG8. . . . . .37 A5
Elsa Ct BR3. . . . . .185 B2
Elsa Rd DA16. . . . . .146 C3
Elsa St E1. . . . . .97 A2
Elsdale Ho 14 E9. . . . . .74 C2
Elsdale St E9. . . . . .74 C1
Elsden Mews E2. . . . . .96 C5
Elsden Rd N17. . . . . .33 D2
Elsenham Rd E12 . . . . .78 C3
Elsenham St SW18,
SW19. . . . . .157 B2
Elsfield NW5 . . . . .71 B3
Elsham Rd
Kensington W14. . . . . .113 A4 244 A1
Leyton E11 . . . . .76 C4
Elsham Terr W14. . . . . .244 A1
Elsiedene Rd N21. . . . . .17 A4
Elsie Lane Ct W2. . . . . .91 D2
Elsiemaud Rd SE4 . . . . . . .163 B6
Elsie Rd SE22 . . . . .139 D1
Elsinge Rd EN1 . . . . .6 B6
Elsinore Ave TW19 . . . . . . .148 A4
Elsinore Gdns NW2 . . . . . . .69 A5
Elsinore Ho
12 Camberwell SE5 . . . . . .139 A3
Islington N1 . . . . .234 A5
7 Woolwich SE7 . . . . .122 A2
Elsinore Rd SE23. . . . . .163 A3
Elsinore Way TW9. . . . . . . .132 D2
Elsley CI HA9 . . . . .66 D2
Elsley Prim Sch HA9 . . . . . .66 B2
Elsley Rd SW11 . . . . .137 A2
Elsley Sch 8 SW17 . . . . . .158 D2
Elspeth Rd London SW11 . .136 D1
Elsrick Ave SM4. . . . . .201 C4
Elstan Way CR0. . . . . .207 A2
Elstead Ct SM3 . . . . .201 A1
Elstead Ho 9 SW2. . . . . . . .160 B4
Elsted St SE17 . . . . .117 B2 262 D3

Elstow CI Eltham SE9 . . . . .166 B6
Ruislip HA4. . . . . .40 D2
Elstow Gdns RM9. . . . . . . .103 A6
Elstow Grange NW6. . . . . . .68 D1
Elstow Rd RM9 . . . . .103 A6
ELSTREE. 10 A5
Elstree Gdns
Abbey Wood DA17 . . . . . . .125 A2
Edmonton N9 . . . . .18 B3
Ilford IG1. . . . . .79 A3
Elstree Hill BR1. . . . . .186 C3
Elstree Hill N WD6 . . . . .9 D6
Elstree Hill S WD6 . . . . .9 D4
Elstree Ho 3 HA7. . . . . .25 C6
Elstree Pk WD6 . . . . .11 B5
Elstree Rd Bushey WD23. . . . .8 C4
Elstree WD6 . . . . .9 C4
Elswick Rd SE13 . . . . .141 D3
Elswick St SW6. . . . . .136 A3
Elsworth CI TW14 . . . . .149 C3
Elsworthy KT7. . . . . .196 C3
Elsworthy Rd
NW3 . . . . .92 C6 230 A6
Elsworthy Rise NW3. . . . . . .70 C1
Elsworthy Terr NW3 . . . . . . .70 C1
Elsynge Rd SW18 . . . . .158 B6
Elsynge Road Mans
SW18. . . . . .158 B6
ELTHAM. 166 B6
Eltham CE Prim Sch
SE9. . . . . .166 B6
Eltham Coll SE9 . . . . .165 D2
Eltham Coll Jun Sch
SE9. . . . . .165 D3
Eltham Green Rd SE9 . . . . .165 C6
Eltham Green Specialist
Sports Coll SE9. . . . . .165 D5
Eltham High St SE9 . . . . . .166 B5
Eltham Hill SE9. . . . . .166 A6
Eltham Hill Tech Coll
SE9. . . . . .166 A5
Eltham Pal* SE9 . . . . .166 A4
Eltham Palace Rd SE9 . . . .165 D5
Eltham Park Gdns SE9 . . . .144 C1
Eltham Rd SE9, SE12. . . . . .165 B6
Eltham Sta SE9 . . . . .166 B6
Elthiron Rd SW6. . . . .135 C4 265 B1
Elthorne Ave W7. . . . . .109 A4
Elthorne Ct
Feltham TW13 . . . . .150 C3
Kingsbury NW9 . . . . .45 B3
Elthorne Park High Sch
W7 . . . . .108 D3
Elthorne Park Rd W7. . . . . .109 A4
Elthorne Rd London NW9 . . .45 B2
Upper Holloway N19 . . . . . .71 D6
Elthorne Sp Ctr W7. . . . . . .108 D3
Elthorne Way NW9. . . . . . . .45 B3
Elthruda Rd SE13 . . . . .163 D2
Eltisley Rd IG1. . . . . .78 D4
Elton Ave Barnet EN5 . . . . . .13 B6
Wembley HA0. . . . . .65 B3
Wembley UB6. . . . . .64 D2
Elton CI KT1. . . . . .175 C3
Elton Ho 3 E3. . . . . .97 B6
Elton Lo 4 SW15 . . . . .110 A6
Elton PI N16. . . . . .73 C3
Elton Rd KT2 . . . . .176 C2
Elton St 11 N16. . . . . .73 C3
Eltringham St SW18. . . . . .136 A1
Elvaston Ct EN5. . . . . .12 C6
Elvaston Mews SW7 . . . . . .256 B6
Elvaston PI SW7 . . . . .114 A3 256 B5
Eveden Ho 17 SW9 . . . . . .138 D1
Eveden PI NW10 . . . . .88 C5
Eveden Rd NW10. . . . . .88 C5
Evedon Rd TW13 . . . . .149 D1
Evendon Rd N13 . . . . .32 A4
Elver Gdns 10 E2. . . . . .96 A4
Everson Rd SE8 . . . . .141 D3
Everson Rd S SE4 . . . . .141 D3
Elverton St SW1 . . . . .115 D2 259 C4
Elvin Ct NW9 . . . . .45 A2
Elvington Gn BR2. . . . . .208 D4
Elvington La NW9. . . . . .27 C2
Elvin Ho 2 E9 . . . . .74 C2
Elvino Rd SE26. . . . . .185 A5
Elvis Rd NW2 . . . . .68 C2
Elwill Way BR3. . . . . .208 B5
Elwin St E2. . . . . .96 A4
Elwood Ho N5 . . . . .72 D5
Elwood St N4, N5. . . . . .72 D5
Elworth Ho SW8 . . . . .270 D3
Elwyn Gdns SE12 . . . . .165 A4
Ely CI SW20. . . . . .177 D1
Ely Cotts SW8 . . . . .270 C3
Ely Court Flats SW6. . . . . .264 A1
Ely Ct Holborn EC1 . . . .241 B3
3 Maida Vale NW6 . . . . . . .91 C5
Ely Gdns
Borehamwood WD6 . . . . . .11 B6
Redbridge IG1 . . . . .56 A2
Ely Ho Barnet EN4 . . . . .2 C1
Northolt UB5 . . . . .85 A6
22 Peckham SE15. . . . . . .140 A5
Elyne Rd N4 . . . . .50 C3
Ely PI EC1 . . . . .94 C2 241 B3
Ely Rd Hatton TW6 . . . . . . .127 D3
Hounslow TW4 . . . . .128 C2
Leyton E10 . . . . .54 C4

Ely Rd continued
Thornton Heath CR0. . . . . .205 B4
Elysan PI CR2. . . . . .221 A1
Elysian Ave BR5. . . . . .211 D3
Elysium Gate 7 SW6. . . . . .135 B3
Elysium PI SW6. . . . . .135 B3
Elysium St SW6. . . . . .135 B3
Elystan Bsns Ctr UB4. . . . .106 C6
Elystan Ct SW15 . . . . .156 B6
Elystan PI SW3 . . . . .114 D1 257 C2
Elystan St SW3 . . . . .114 C2 257 B3
Elystan Wlk N1 . . . . .234 A5
Emanuel Ave W3. . . . . .89 A1
Emanuel Ct Acton W3. . . . . .89 B1
10 Leyton E10. . . . . .53 D2
Emanuel Dr TW12 . . . . .173 B5
Emanuel Sch SW11 . . . . . .158 C6
Embankment SW15 . . . . . .134 D3
Embankment Gdns
SW3 . . . . .136 D6 267 C6
Embankment Pier
WC2 . . . . .116 A5 250 B4
Embankment PI WC2. . . . . .250 B4
Embankment Sta
WC2 . . . . .116 A5 250 B4
Embankment The TW1 . . . .153 A3
Kingston u T KT6. . . . . . . .197 D4
Sidcup DA14. . . . . .168 B1
St John's Wood NW8 . . . . .229 D3
7 Wallington SM6 . . . . . . .219 B2
8 Wanstead E18. . . . . .55 A6
Welling DA16. . . . . .146 B2
Wood Green N11. . . . . .31 D4
Embassy Gdns BR3 . . . . . .185 B2
Embassy Ho 2 NW6. . . . . . .69 C1
Embassy Lo N3 . . . . .29 B1
Emba St SE16. . . . . .118 A4
Ember Ct BR5. . . . . .211 A2
Embercourt Rd KT10, KT7,
KT8 . . . . .196 C3
Ember Ct 2 Acton W12 . . . .111 C3
14 Hendon NW9. . . . . .27 D1
Ember Farm Ave KT8. . . . . .196 B3
Ember Farm Way KT8 . . . . .196 B4
Ember Gdns KT10, KT8. . . .196 C2
Ember Ho 8 BR1. . . . . .186 B5
Emberhurst Sch KT10 . . . . .196 B2
Ember La KT10, KT8 . . . . . .196 B2
Emberson Ho 7 E17. . . . . . .54 A5
Emberton SE5 . . . . .139 C6
Emberton Ct EC1 . . . . .234 C1
Embleton Rd SE13 . . . . . . .141 D1
Embleton Wlk TW12 . . . . . .173 B5
Embry CI HA7. . . . . .25 A6
Embry Dr HA7 . . . . .25 A4
Embry Way HA7. . . . . .25 A4
Emden CI UB7. . . . . .104 C4
Emden St SW6. . . . . .265 D2
Emerald CI E16. . . . . .100 A1
Emerald Ct N12. . . . . .30 A6
Emerald Gdns RM8. . . . . . . .59 C1
Emerald Rd NW10 . . . . .89 B6
Emerald Sq UB2 . . . . .106 D3
Emerald St WC1 . . . .94 B2 240 C4
Emerson Apartments N8. . . .50 B6
Emerson Ct 8 SW19 . . . . . .179 A4
Emerson Gdns HA3 . . . . . . .44 B3
Emerson Ho N16. . . . . .73 C3
Emerson Rd IG1. . . . . .56 C2
Emerson St SE1 . . . .117 A5 252 A4
Emerton CI DA6 . . . . .147 A1
Emery Hill St SW1 . . . . . . .259 B5
Emery St SE1 . . . . . .116 C3 261 B6
Emilia CI EN3. . . . . .8 B6
Emily St 7 E16. . . . . .98 D1
Emirates Stad (Arsenal FC)
N7. . . . . .72 C4
Emlyn Gdns 3 W12 . . . . . . .111 C3
Emlyn Rd W12. . . . . .111 D3
Emmanual Ho SE18 . . . . . .123 B1
Emmanuel CE Prim Sch
NW6. . . . . .69 C3
Emmanuel Ct 3 EN4. . . . . . .14 D1
Emmanuel Ho
Dulwich SE21. . . . . .161 B1
Lambeth SE11. . . . . .261 B4
Emmanuel Rd
Northwood HA6 . . . . .22 A3
Streatham SW12 . . . . .159 D3
Emma Rd E13 . . . . .98 D5
Emma St E2. . . . . .96 B5
Emmeline Ct KT12 . . . . . . .194 C2
Emminster NW6 . . . . .91 D6
Emmott Ave IG6. . . . . .57 A4
Emmott CI London NW11 . . . .48 A3
Mile End E1. . . . . .97 A3
Emperor's Gate
SW7. . . . . .114 A2 256 A4
Empingham Ho 20 SE8 . . . .118 C2
Empire Ave N18 . . . . .33 A4
Empire Ct HA9. . . . . .66 C5
Empire Ho Brompton SW3 . .257 A5
Edmonton N18 . . . . .33 B4
Empire Par Edmonton N18 . .33 A4
Wembley HA9. . . . . .66 C5
Empire Rd UB6 . . . . .65 C1
Empire Sq N19 . . . . .72 A5
Empire Way HA9. . . . . .66 C4
Empire Wharf E3 . . . . .97 A6

Empire Wharf Rd E14 . . . . . . .120 B2
Empress Ave Chingford E4 . . . .35 D3
  Ilford IG1 . . . . .78 C6
  Wanstead E12 . . . . .77 D6
  Woodford IG8 . . . . .36 D3
Empress Dr BR7 . . . . .188 D4
Empress Mews 36 SE5 . . . . . .139 A3
Empress Par E4 . . . . .35 C3
Empress Pl SW5 . . . . . .113 C1 255 A1
Empress St SE17 . . . . .139 A6
Empson St E3 . . . . .97 D3
Emsworth Cl N9 . . . . .18 C3
Emsworth St SW2 . . . . .160 B2
Emu Rd SW8 . . . . .137 B3
Ena Rd SW16 . . . . .204 A6
Enard Ho 28 E3 . . . . .97 B5
Enbrook St W10 . . . . .91 A4
Enclave Ct EC1 . . . . .241 C6
Endale Cl SM5 . . . . .218 D6
Endeavour Way
  Barking IG11 . . . . .102 A5
  Thornton Heath CR0 . . . . . . .204 A2
  Wimbledon SW19 . . . . .179 D6
Endell St WC2 . . . . . . .94 A1 240 A1
Enderby St SE10 . . . . .120 C1
Enderfield Ct SE7 . . . . .188 C2
Enderley Cl HA3 . . . . .24 C2
Enderley Ho SE19 . . . . .183 D2
Enderley Rd HA3 . . . . .24 C2
Endersby Rd EN5 . . . . .12 C6
Enders Cl EN2 . . . . .4 C4
Endersleigh Gdns NW4 . . . . . .46 A5
Endlebury Ct E4 . . . . .20 B2
Endlebury Rd E4 . . . . .20 A2
Endlesham Ct 2 SW12 . . . . . .159 A4
Endlesham Rd SW12 . . . . . . .159 A4
Endsleigh Gdns
  Bloomsbury WC1 . . . . .93 D3 239 C6
  Ilford IG1 . . . . .56 D1
  Kingston u T KT6 . . . . .197 C3
Endsleigh Ind Est UB2 . . . .107 B2
Endsleigh Mans 4
  SW16 . . . . .160 A1
Endsleigh Pl WC1 . . . . .239 D6
Endsleigh St Ealing W13 . . . . .109 B6
  Southall UB2 . . . . .107 A2
Endsleigh St WC1 . . . .93 D3 239 D6
Endway KT5 . . . . .198 D2
Endwell Rd SE4 . . . . .141 A3
Endymion Rd
  Harringay N4 . . . . .50 D2
  Tulse Hill SW2 . . . . .160 B5
Energen Cl NW10 . . . . .67 C2
ENFIELD 5 D2
Enfield Chase Sta EN2 . . . . .5 A2
Enfield Cloisters 7 N1 . . . .95 C4
Enfield Coll 6 C2
Enfield Cty Sch (Lower Sch)
  . . . . .5 C5
Enfield Cty Sch (Upper Sch)
  EN2 .5 C5
Enfield Gram Sch (Lower)
  EN1 .5 B3
Enfield Gram Sch (Upper)
  EN2 .5 B3
ENFIELD HIGHWAY 6 C3
Enfield Ho 24 SW9 . . . . .138 A3
ENFIELD LOCK 7 B6
Enfield Lock Sta EN3 . . . . . .7 A4
Enfield Rd
  Brentford TW8 . . . . .109 D1
  De Beauvoir Town E8, N1 . . .73 C1
  Enfield EN2 . . . . .4 A2
  Hatton TW6 . . . . .127 C3
  South Acton W3 . . . . .110 D4
Enfield Ret Pk EN1 . . . . .6 A2
Enfield Road Rdbt TW6 . . .127 C3
ENFIELD TOWN 5 B1
Enfield Town Sta EN1 . . . . . .5 A2
ENFIELD WASH 6 D5
Enfield Wlk TW8 . . . . .109 D1
Enford St W1 . . . . .92 D2 237 C4
Engadine Cl CR0 . . . . .221 D5
Engadine St SW18 . . . . .157 C3
Engate St SE13 . . . . .142 A1
Engel Pk NW7 . . . . .28 C4
Engineer Cl SE18 . . . . .144 C6
Engineers Way HA9 . . . . .66 C4
England's La NW3 . . . . .70 D2
England Way KT3 . . . . .199 A5
Englefield Bromley BR1 . . . . .188 A1
  Regent's Pk NW1 . . . . .232 A1
Englefield Cl Enfield EN2 . . . .4 C3
  Orpington BR5 . . . . .211 D5
  Thornton Heath CR0 . . . . . . .205 A3
Englefield Path BR5 . . . . . . .211 D5
Englefield Rd N1 . . . . .73 C1
Engleheart Dr TW14 . . . . . . .149 D5
Engleheart Rd SE6 . . . . .164 A4
Englewood Rd SW12 . . . . . . .159 C5
English Gardening Sch The
  SW3 . . . . .136 D6 267 C6
English Grounds SE1 . . . . .253 A3
English Martyrs RC Prim
  Sch
  Walworth SE17 . . . . . .117 B2 262 D3
  Whitechapel E1 . . . . . .95 D1 243 D1
English St E3 . . . . .97 B3
Enid St SE16 . . . . .117 D3 263 D6
Enid Stacy Ho 11 N19 . . . . .49 D2

Enmore Ave SE25 . . . . .206 A4
Enmore Ct SW14 . . . . .155 B6
Enmore Gdns SW14 . . . . . . .155 B6
Enmore Rd Croydon SE25 . . .206 A4
  Putney SW15 . . . . .156 C6
  Southall UB1 . . . . .85 C3
Ennerdale Ave HA3, HA7 . . . .43 C6
Ennerdale Cl Cheam SM1 . . .217 B4
  East Bedfont TW14 . . . . .149 D3
Ennerdale Ct E11 . . . . .55 A2
Ennerdale Dr NW9 . . . . .45 C4
Ennerdale Gdns HA3 . . . . . . .43 C1
Ennerdale Ho 6 N4 . . . . .51 B2
Ennerdale Rd Erith DA7 . . . . .147 C4
  Richmond TW9 . . . . .132 B3
Ennersdale Rd SE13 . . . . . . .164 B6
Ennis Ho 16 E14 . . . . .97 D1
Ennismore Ave
  Chiswick W4 . . . . .111 D2
  Greenford UB6 . . . . .64 C3
Ennismore Gdns
  Knightsbridge
  SW7 . . . . .114 C3 257 A6
  Thames Ditton KT7 . . . . .196 C3
Ennismore Gdns Mews
  SW7 . . . . .114 C3 257 A6
Ennismore Mews
  SW7 . . . . .114 C3 257 A6
Ennismore St
  SW7 . . . . .114 C3 257 A6
Ennis Rd London N4 . . . . .50 C1
  Shooters Hill SE18 . . . . .145 A6
Ennor Ct KT4 . . . . .216 C4
Ensbury Ho SW8 . . . . .270 C4
Ensign Cl TW19 . . . . .148 A3
Ensign Ct 12 E1 . . . . .118 A6
Ensign Dr N13 . . . . .17 A1
Ensign Ho 19 E14 . . . . .119 C4
Ensign St E1 . . . . .118 A6
Ensign Way
  Stanwell TW19 . . . . .148 A3
  2 Wallington SM6 . . . . .220 A1
Ensor Mews SW7 . . . . .256 C2
Enstone Rd Enfield EN3 . . . . . .7 A2
  Ickenham UB10 . . . . .60 B5
Enterprise Ct CR0 . . . . .204 C1
Enterprise Ho IG11 . . . . .101 D4
  Hounslow E4 . . . . .20 A4
Enterprise Ho
  36 Hackney E9 . . . . .74 C1
  Walton-on-T SE18 . . . . .194 B2
Enterprise Row N15 . . . . .51 D4
Enterprise Way
  College Pk NW10 . . . . .90 A4
  Teddington TW11 . . . . .174 D4
  Wandsworth SW18 . . . . .135 C1
Enterprise Works EN3 . . . . . .7 B4
Enterprize Way SE8 . . . . . . .119 B2
Enthoven Ho SE18 . . . . .122 D2
Enton Pl TW3 . . . . .129 D1
Enversham Ct SE23 . . . . . . .163 A1
Envoy Ave TW6 . . . . .127 D2
Epirus Mews SW6 . . . . .265 A4
Epirus Rd SW6 . . . . . .135 B5 264 D4
Epping Cl Millwall E14 . . . . . .119 C2
  Romford RM7 . . . . .59 D6
Epping Glade E4 . . . . .20 A5
Epping Ho 8 E5 . . . . .74 A4
Epping New Rd IG9 . . . . .21 B5
Epping Pl N1 . . . . .72 C2
Epping Way E4 . . . . .19 D5
Epple Rd SW6 . . . . . . .135 B4 264 D2
Epsom Cl Erith DA7 . . . . .147 D2
  Northolt UB5 . . . . .63 B3
Epsom & Ewell High Sch
  KT19 . . . . .215 A3
Epsom Ho SM1 . . . . .217 D4
Epsom Rd Croydon CR0 . . . . .220 C4
  Ilford IG3 . . . . .57 D3
  Leyton E10 . . . . .54 A3
  Morden SM3, SM4 . . . . .201 B2
Epsom Sq TW6 . . . . .127 D3
Epstein Ct N1 . . . . .234 D5
Epstein Rd SE28 . . . . .124 B5
Epworth Rd TW7, TW8 . . . . . .131 B5
Epworth St EC2 . . . . . .95 B3 242 D5
Equity Sq 29 E2 . . . . .95 D4
Erasmus St SW1 . . . . .115 D2 259 D3
Erconwald St W12 . . . . .89 D1
Erebus Dr SE28 . . . . .123 B4
Eresby Dr BR3 . . . . .207 C1
Eresby Ho SW7 . . . . .247 B1
Eresby Pl NW6 . . . . .69 C1
Erica Ct SW4 . . . . .270 B1
Erica Gdns CR0 . . . . .223 D5
Erica Ho London SE4 . . . . . . .141 B2
  6 Wimbledon SW19 . . . . . . .179 A3
  Wood Green N22 . . . . .32 C2
Erica St W12 . . . . .112 A6
Eric Cl E7 . . . . .77 A4
Eric Clarke La IG11 . . . . .101 A4
Ericcson Cl SW18 . . . . .157 C6
Eric Fletcher Ct 15 N1 . . . . .73 A1
Eric Macdonald Ho SW6 . .265 B1
Eric Rd Dagenham RM6 . . . . . .58 D2
  Forest Gate E7 . . . . .77 A4
  Willesden NW10 . . . . .67 D2

Eric Shipman Terr 2
  E13 .99 A3
Ericson Ho London SE13 . . . .142 B1
  Stamford Hill N16 . . . . .51 D1
Eric St E3 . . . . .97 B3
Eric Wilkins Ho 14 SE1 . . . .118 A1
Eridge Ho SE22 . . . . .139 D2
Eridge House Sch 13
  SW6 . . . . .135 B3
Eridge Rd W4 . . . . .111 B3
Erin Cl Bromley BR1 . . . . .186 C3
  Ilford IG3 . . . . .58 A3
Erin Ct NW2 . . . . .68 C2
Erindale SE18 . . . . .145 B6
Erindale Ct 1 BR3 . . . . .185 C2
Erindale Terr SE18 . . . . .145 B6
ERITH 147 D6
Erith Rd Belvedere DA17 . . . .125 D1
  Erith DA7 . . . . .147 D2
Erlanger Rd SE14 . . . . .140 D3
Erlesmere Gdns W13 . . . . . . .109 A3
Ermine Cl TW4 . . . . .128 C3
Ermine Ho 3 N17 . . . . .33 D3
Ermine Rd London SE13 . . . .141 D1
  South Tottenham N15 . . . . . . .51 D3
Ermine Side EN1 . . . . .18 A6
Ermington Rd SE9 . . . . .167 A2
Ernald Ave E6 . . . . .100 A5
Erncroft Way TW12 . . . . .173 C1
Ernest Ave SE27 . . . . .182 D6
Ernest Bevin Coll SW17 . . .158 C2
Ernest Cl BR3 . . . . .207 C4
Ernest Cotts KT17 . . . . .215 D1
Ernest Gdns W4 . . . . .132 D6
Ernest Gr BR3 . . . . .207 B4
Ernest Rd KT1 . . . . .176 D1
Ernest Richards Twr E17 . . .53 B3
Ernest Simmonds Ho
  SE14 . . . . .140 C3
Ernest Sq KT1 . . . . .176 D1
Ernest St E1 . . . . .96 D3
Ernle Rd SW20 . . . . .178 C3
Ernshaw Pl SW15 . . . . .157 A6
Eros Ho SE6 . . . . .163 D4
Eros (Shaftesbury Meml)★
  W1 . . . . .115 D6 249 C5
Erpingham Rd SW15 . . . . . . .134 C2
Erridge Rd SW19 . . . . .179 C1
Errington Manor 6
  SM5 . . . . .218 D5
Errington Rd W9 . . . . .91 B3
Errol Gdns Hayes UB4 . . . . . .84 B3
  West Barnes KT3 . . . . .200 A5
Errol St EC1 . . . . .95 A3 242 B5
Erskine Cl SM1 . . . . .218 C5
Erskine Cres N17 . . . . .52 B5
Erskine Hill NW11 . . . . .47 C4
Erskine Ho
  7 Charlton SE7 . . . . .143 C6
  Pimlico SW1 . . . . .259 A1
Erskine Rd
  Carshalton SM1 . . . . .218 B5
  Primrose Hill NW3 . . . . .70 D1
  Walthamstow E17 . . . . .53 B5
Erwood Rd SE7 . . . . .122 A1
Esam Way SW16 . . . . .182 C5
Escot Rd TW16 . . . . .171 C3
Escott Gdns SE9 . . . . .188 A6
Escot Way EN5 . . . . .12 C6
Escreet Gr SE18 . . . . .122 C2
Escuan Lo N5 . . . . .73 A3
ESHER 212 A4
Esher Ave Cheam SM3 . . . . .216 D5
  Walton-on-T KT12 . . . . .194 A1
Esher CE Prim Sch
  KT10 . . . . .212 A3
Esher Cl DA5 . . . . .169 A3
Esher Coll KT7 . . . . .196 C2
Esher Cres TW6 . . . . .127 D3
Esher Gdns SW19 . . . . .156 D2
Esher Ho 13 SW8 . . . . .137 D3
Esher Mews 4 CR4 . . . . .202 D6
Esher Park Ave KT10 . . . . . .212 A3
Esher Rd
  East Molesey KT8 . . . . .196 B4
  Ilford IG3 . . . . .79 C5
Esher Sta KT10 . . . . .212 B6
Eskdale Enfield EN1 . . . . .17 C6
Eskdale Ave UB5 . . . . .85 B6
Eskdale Cl HA9 . . . . .65 D6
Eskdale Rd DA7 . . . . .147 C4
Esk Ho E3 . . . . .97 B3
Eskmont Ridge SE19 . . . . . .183 C3
Esk Rd E13 . . . . .99 B3
Esmar Cres NW9 . . . . .46 A2
Esme Ho SW15 . . . . .133 D1
Esmeralda Rd SE1 . . . . .118 A2
Esmond Ct Barnet EN5 . . . . . .1 C1
  Kensington W8 . . . . .255 D6
Esmond Gdns W4 . . . . .111 B2
Esmond Rd Acton W4 . . . . . . .111 B3
  Kilburn NW6 . . . . .91 B6
Esmond St SW15 . . . . .135 A1
Esparto St SW18 . . . . .157 D4
Espirit Ct E1 . . . . .243 C3
Espirit Ho 6 SW15 . . . . .157 A6
Essan Ho W13 . . . . .87 B2
Essence Ct HA9 . . . . .66 B6

Essenden Rd
  Belvedere DA17 . . . . .125 C1
  South Croydon CR2 . . . . .221 C1
Essendine Mans W9 . . . . . . .91 C4
Essendine Prim Sch 11
  W9 . . . . .91 C4
Essendine Rd W9 . . . . .91 C4
Essex Ave TW7 . . . . .130 C2
Essex Ct Romford RM7 . . . . . .59 D5
  Ruislip HA4 . . . . .40 D1
  Walthamstow E17 . . . . .53 A5
  West Barnes SM4 . . . . .200 D2
Essex Ct Barnes SW13 . . . . .133 D3
  Hammersmith W6 . . . . .112 C3
  Holborn EC4 . . . . .241 A1
  South Norwood SE19 . . . . . . .183 B4
Essex Gdns N4 . . . . .50 D3
Essex Gr SE19 . . . . .183 B4
Essex Ho 4 Acton W3 . . . . . . .88 C1
  2 Poplar E14 . . . . .97 D1
Essex Lo 5 N10 . . . . .31 B1
Essex Mans E11 . . . . .54 B2
Essex Park Mews W3 . . . . . . .111 C5
Essex Pk N3 . . . . .29 D4
Essex Pl W4 . . . . .111 A6
Essex Place Sq 5 W4 . . . . . .111 B2
Essex Prim Sch E12 . . . . . . .78 A3
Essex Rd Acton W3 . . . . .111 A6
  Barking IG11 . . . . .79 B1
  Chingford E4 . . . . .20 C3
  Chiswick W4 . . . . .111 B2
  Enfield EN2 . . . . .5 B1
  Ilford RM6 . . . . .58 C2
  Islington N1 . . . . .94 D6 234 D6
  Leyton E10 . . . . .54 A3
  Plashet E12 . . . . .78 A2
  Romford RM7 . . . . .59 D5
  Walthamstow E17 . . . . .53 A3
  Willesden NW10 . . . . .67 C1
  Woodford E18 . . . . .37 B1
Essex Rd S E11 . . . . .54 B2
Essex Road Sta N1 . . . . .73 A1
Essex St Forest Gate E7 . . . . .77 A3
  Strand WC2 . . . . .116 C6 251 A6
Essex Twr 4 SE20 . . . . .184 B1
Essex Villas W8 . . . . . .113 C4 245 A1
Essian St E1 . . . . .97 A2
Essington SW15 . . . . .157 A5
Essoldo Way HA8 . . . . .44 B6
Estate Way E10 . . . . .53 B1
Estcourt Rd
  Croydon SE25 . . . . .206 B3
  Fulham SW6 . . . . .135 B5 264 C4
Estella Ave KT3 . . . . .200 B5
Estella Ho 15 W11 . . . . .112 D6
Estelle Rd NW3 . . . . .70 D4
Esterbrooke St SW1 . . . . . . .259 C3
Este Rd SW11 . . . . .136 C2
Esther Cl N21 . . . . .16 C4
Esther Doe Lo N21 . . . . .16 C4
Esther Rd E11 . . . . .54 C2
Estoria Cl 22 SW2 . . . . .160 C4
Estreham Rd SW16 . . . . .181 D4
Estridge Cl TW3 . . . . .129 C1
Estuary Cl IG11 . . . . .102 B4
Eswyn Rd SW17 . . . . .180 D5
Etal Ho N1 . . . . .72 D1
Etchingham Ct N12 . . . . .30 A3
Etchingham Park Rd N3 . . . .29 D3
Etchingham Rd E15 . . . . .76 A4
Eternit Wlk SW6 . . . . .134 D4
Etfield Gr DA14 . . . . .190 B5
Ethelbert Cl BR1 . . . . .209 A6
Ethelbert Gdns IG2 . . . . .56 C4
Ethelbert Ho E9 . . . . .75 A4
Ethelbert Rd
  Bromley BR1, BR2 . . . . .209 A6
  Wimbledon SW20 . . . . .178 D2
Ethelbert St SW12 . . . . .159 B3
Ethel Brooks Ho SE18 . . . . .144 D6
Ethelburga St
  SW11 . . . . .136 C4 267 B2
Ethelburga Twr SW11 . . . . .267 B2
Ethel Cotts RM6 . . . . .58 D6
Etheldene Ave N10 . . . . .49 C5
Etheldene Rd W12 . . . . .112 B5
Ethel Rankin Ct 8 SW6 . . . . .135 A4
Ethel Rd Ashford TW15 . . . . .170 A5
  Newham E16 . . . . .99 B1
Ethel St SE17 . . . . .262 B3
Ethelworth Ct 4 SW2 . . . . . .160 C4
Etheridge Rd NW2 . . . . .46 C2
Etherley Rd N15 . . . . .51 A4
Etherow St SE22 . . . . .162 A4
Etherstone Gn SW16 . . . . . .182 C6
Etherstone Rd SW16 . . . . . .182 C6
Ethnard Rd SE15 . . . . .140 B6
Ethronvi Rd DA7 . . . . .147 A2
Etienne Ho NW7 . . . . .28 C6
Etloe Ho E10 . . . . .53 D1
Etloe Rd E10 . . . . .75 C6
Eton Ave East Barnet EN4 . . . .14 C5
  Finchley N12 . . . . .30 A3
  Heston TW5 . . . . .107 B1
  New Malden KT3 . . . . .199 B5
  Primrose Hill NW3 . . . . .70 C1
  Wembley HA0 . . . . .65 C4
Eton Cl SW18 . . . . .157 D4
Eton College Rd NW3 . . . . . .70 D2
Eton Ct Hampstead NW3 . . . . .70 B1

Eton Ct continued
  Highgate N6 . . . . .49 B3
  Wembley HA0 . . . . .65 C4
Eton Garages 11 NW3 . . . . . .70 C2
Eton Gr Lewisham SE13 . . . . .142 C2
  Queensbury NW9 . . . . .44 C5
Eton Hall NW3 . . . . .70 D2
Eton Ho Hackney E9 . . . . .75 B2
  Highbury N5 . . . . .72 C4
Eton Manor Ct E10 . . . . .75 C6
Eton Pl NW1 . . . . .71 A1
Eton Rd Harlington UB3 . . . . .127 D5
  Ilford IG1 . . . . .79 B4
  Maitland Pk NW3 . . . . .70 D2
Eton Rise NW3 . . . . .70 D2
Eton St TW10 . . . . .154 A6
Eton Villas NW3 . . . . .70 D2
Etta St SE8 . . . . .141 A6
Ettrick Ho 8 E5 . . . . .74 B6
Ettrick St E14 . . . . .98 A1
Etwell Pl KT5 . . . . .198 B3
Euesden Cl N9 . . . . .18 B1
Eugene Cotter Ho SE17 . . .262 D3
Eugenia Rd SE16 . . . . .118 C2
Eugenie Mews BR7 . . . . .188 D2
Eureka Rd 8 KT1 . . . . .176 C1
Euro Bsns Ctr 3 E15 . . . . . .98 D6
Eurocentres
  SW1 . . . . .115 B2 258 D3
Euro Cl NW10 . . . . .68 A2
Eurolink Bsns Ctr SW2 . . . .160 C6
Europa Pl EC1 . . . . .235 A1
European Coll 45 E1 . . . . . . .96 A1
Europe Rd SE18 . . . . .122 B3
Eustace Bldg SW8 . . . . .268 C5
Eustace Ho SE11 . . . . .260 D4
Eustace Pl SE18 . . . . .122 B2
Eustace Rd
  Dagenham RM6 . . . . .58 D2
  Newham E6 . . . . .100 A4
  Walham Green
  SW6 . . . . .135 C5 265 A4
Euston Ct 5 HA0 . . . . .66 A2
Euston Rd
  Fitzrovia NW1 . . . . . . .93 C3 239 B6
  Thornton Heath CR0 . . . . . . .204 C1
Euston Sq NW1 . . . . .232 C1
Euston Square Sta
  WC1 . . . . .93 C3 239 B6
Euston St NW1 . . . . . . .93 C3 232 B1
Euston Sta NW1 . . . . .93 D4 232 C1
Euston Underpass NW1 . . . .239 A6
Evan Cook Cl SE15 . . . . .140 C4
Evandale Rd SW9 . . . . .138 C3
Evangelist Rd NW5 . . . . .71 B4
Evans Cl E8 . . . . .73 C2
Evans Gr TW13 . . . . .151 C2
Evans Ho
  34 Shepherd's Bush W12 . . .112 B6
  South Lambeth SW8 . . . . . . .269 D3
Evans Rd SE6 . . . . .164 C2
Evanston Ave E4 . . . . .36 A3
Evanston Gdns IG4 . . . . .56 A3
Eva Rd RM6 . . . . .58 D2
Eve Ct CR4 . . . . .181 A1
Evelina Mans 5 SE5 . . . . . . .139 B5
Evelina Rd London SE15 . . . .140 C3
  Penge SE20 . . . . .184 D3
Eveline Ct N10 . . . . .49 B4
Eveline Lowe Prim Sch 23
  SE1 . . . . .118 A1
Eveline Rd CR4 . . . . .180 D2
Evelyn Ave London NW9 . . . . .45 B5
  Ruislip HA4 . . . . .39 D2
Evelyn Cl TW12 . . . . .151 D4
Evelyn Cres TW16 . . . . .171 D2
Evelyn Ct Chislehurst SE9 . . .166 A2
  Marylebone NW9 . . . . .237 C1
  Shacklewell E8 . . . . .74 A4
  Shoreditch N1 . . . . .235 C3
Evelyn Denington Ct 2
  N1 . . . . .72 D1
Evelyn Denington Rd
  E6 .100 A3
Evelyn Dr HA5 . . . . .22 D3
Evelyn Fox Ct W10 . . . . .90 C2
Evelyn Gdns
  Richmond TW9 . . . . .132 A1
  South Kensington
  SW7 . . . . .114 B1 256 C1
  Southall UB1 . . . . .85 B1
Evelyn Gr Ealing W5 . . . . . . .110 B5
Evelyn Grace Acad SW9 . . .138 C1
Evelyn Ho
  3 Brixton SW2 . . . . .160 B6
  Harrow HA1 . . . . .42 B4
  15 Spitalfields E1 . . . . .96 A2
Evelyn Rd Acton W4 . . . . .111 B3
  Cockfosters EN4 . . . . .2 D1
  Ham TW10 . . . . .153 C1
  Newham E16 . . . . .121 B5
  Richmond TW9 . . . . .132 A2
  Walthamstow E17 . . . . .54 A5
  Wimbledon SW19 . . . . .179 D4
Evelyns Cl UB8 . . . . .82 C1
Evelyn St Greenwich SE10 . .142 A6

Evelyn St continued
SE8 . . . . 119 A1
Evelyn Terr TW9 . . . . 132 A2
Evelyn Way
Sunbury TW16 . . . . 171 D2
Wallington SM6 . . . . 219 D4
Evelyn Wlk N1 . . . 95 B5 235 C3
Evelyn Yd W1 . . . . 239 C2
Evening Hill BR3 . . . . 186 A3
Evenlode Ho 5 SE2 . . . . 124 C4
Evenwood Cl SW15 . . . 157 A6
Everard Ave BR2 . . . . 209 A1
Everard Ct N13 . . . . 16 B1
Everard Ho 33 E1 . . . . 96 A1
Everard Way HA9 . . . . 66 A5
Everatt Cl SW18 . . . . 157 B6
Eve Rd Isleworth TW7 . . . 131 A1
Leyton E11 . . . . 76 C4
Tottenham N17 . . . . 51 C6
West Ham E15 . . . . 98 C5
Everdale Ct N2 . . . . 48 C5
Everdon Rd SW13 . . . . 134 A6
Everest Ct
6 Chislehurst SE9 . . . . 166 A2
South Norwood SE19 . . . 183 C2
Everest Pl E14 . . . . 98 A2
Everest Rd Eltham SE9 . . 166 B6
Stanwell TW19 . . . . 148 A4
Everett Cl Bushey WD23 . . 8 C3
Pinner HA5 . . . . 39 D6
Everett Ho Islington N7 . . 72 C4
Walworth SE17 . . . . 262 C2
Everett Wlk DA17 . . . . 125 B1
Everglade Ho E17 . . . . 35 B1
Everglades
Beckenham BR2 . . . . 208 C6
Hounslow TW3 . . . . 130 A2
Everglade Strand NW9 . . 27 D2
Evergreen Cl 6 SM2 . . . 218 A2
Evergreen Sq 3 E8 . . . 73 D1
Evergreen Way UB3 . . . 105 D6
Everilda St N1 . . . . 233 D5
Evering Rd E5, N16 . . . 74 A5
Everington Rd N10 . . . 30 B1
Everington St W6 . . . . 134 D6
Everitt Rd NW10 . . . . 89 B4
Everleigh St N4 . . . . 50 B1
Eversfield Ct SE12 . . . 165 B2
Eversfield Gdns HA8,
NW7 . . . . 27 C3
Eversfield Rd TW9 . . . 132 B3
Evershed Ho E1 . . . . 243 D2
Evershed Wlk 11 E1 . . . . 111 B2
Eversholt Ct EN5 . . . . 14 A6
Eversholt St NW1 . . 93 D4 232 C2
Evershot Rd N4 . . . . 50 B1
Eversleigh Ct N3 . . . . 29 C3
Eversleigh Rd
Clapham SW11 . . . . 137 A3
Finchley N3 . . . . 29 B1
New Barnet EN5 . . . . 14 A6
Newham E6 . . . . 99 D6
Eversley Ave HA9 . . . . 66 C6
Eversley Cl N21 . . . . 16 B5
Eversley Cres
Hounslow TW7 . . . . 130 B4
Ruislip HA4 . . . . 61 D6
Southgate N21 . . . . 16 A5
Eversley Ho 12 E2 . . . . 96 A4
Eversley Mount N21 . . . 16 B5
Eversley Park Rd N21 . . 16 B5
Eversley Pk SW19 . . . 178 B5
Eversley Prim Sch N21 . . 16 B5
Eversley Rd
Greenwich SE7 . . . . 143 B6
Kingston u T KT5 . . . . 198 B4
South Norwood SE19 . . . 183 B3
Eversley Way CR0 . . . . 223 C5
Everthorpe Rd SE15 . . . 139 D2
Everton Bldgs NW1 . . . 232 A1
Everton Ct HA0 . . . . 65 D4
Everton Dr HA7 . . . . 44 A6
Everton Rd CR0 . . . . 206 A1
Evesham Ave E17 . . . . 35 C1
Evesham Cl Belmont SM2 . . 217 C1
Greenford UB6 . . . . 85 D5
Evesham Ct
2 Ealing W13 . . . . 109 A5
3 Richmond TW10 . . . 154 B5
Evesham Gn SM4 . . . . 201 D3
Evesham Ho
1 Bethnal Green E2 . . . 96 C5
Pimlico SW1 . . . . 258 D2
St John's Wood NW8 . . . 229 A5
Evesham Rd London N11 . . 31 D5
Morden SM4 . . . . 201 D3
Stratford E15 . . . . 76 D1
Evesham St W11 . . . . 112 D1
Evesham Way
Clapham SW11 . . . . 137 A2
Ilford IG5 . . . . 56 C6
Evesham Wlk
Brixton SW9 . . . . 138 C3
Camberwell SE5 . . . . 139 B3
Evry Rd DA14 . . . . 190 C4
Ewald Rd SW6 . . . . 135 B3

Ewanrigg Terr IG8 . . . . 37 C5
Ewart Gr N22 . . . . 32 C2
Ewart Pl 13 E3 . . . . 97 B5
Ewart Rd SE23 . . . . 162 D4
Ewe Cl N7 . . . . 72 A2
EWELL 215 C1
Ewell By-Pass KT17 . . . 216 A1
EWELL COURT 215 C3
Ewell Court Ave KT19 . . 215 C3
Ewell Park Gdns KT17 . . 216 A1
Ewell Park Way KT17 . . 216 A1
Ewell Rd
Cheam SM2, SM3 . . . . 216 D2
Surbiton KT6 . . . . 198 B2
Thames Ditton T6, KT7 . . 197 B2
Tolworth KT6 . . . . 198 D1
Ewelme Rd SE23 . . . . 162 C3
Ewen Cres SW2 . . . . 160 C4
Ewen Henderson Ct 10
SE14 . . . . 141 A5
Ewen Ho N1 . . . . 233 C5
Ewer St SE1 . . . 117 A5 252 A3
Ewhurst 19 SW15 . . . 156 D5
Ewhurst Cl E1 . . . . 96 C2
Ewhurst Ct CR4 . . . . 202 B6
Ewhurst Rd SE4 . . . . 163 B5
Exbury Ho Hackney E9 . . 74 C2
4 London SW9 . . . . 138 B1
Exbury Rd SE6 . . . . 163 C2
Excel Ct WC2 . . . . 249 D5
Excel Ex Ctr E16 . . . . 121 B6
Excelsior Cl KT1 . . . . 176 C1
Excelsior Coll N17 . . . . 33 C3
Excelsior Gdns SE13 . . . 142 A3
Excelsior Ind Est SE16. . . 140 C6
Exchange Apartments 4
BR2 . . . . 209 B5
Exchange Arc EC2 . . . . 243 B4
Exchange Ct N11 . . . . 15 A2
Exchange Ct WC2 . . . . 250 B5
Exchange Mans 2 NW11. . 47 B2
Exchange Pl EC2 . . . . 243 A4
Exchange The IG1 . . . . 78 D6
Exchange Wlk HA5. . . . 41 A2
Exeforde Ave TW15 . . . 170 C6
Exeter Cl E6 . . . . 100 B1
Exeter Ct Kilburn NW6. . . 91 C5
Kingston u T KT6 . . . . 198 A4
Mitcham SW19 . . . . 180 C3
Exeter Gdns IG1 . . . . 56 B1
Exeter Ho 7 Barking IG11 . 80 A1
Feltham TW13 . . . . 151 C2
Paddington W2 . . . . 236 A2
11 Peckham SE15 . . . . 140 A6
Putney SW15 . . . . 156 C5
Exeter Mans NW2 . . . . 69 A2
Exeter Mews Fulham SW6 . 265 A4
12 Hampstead NW6 . . . . 69 D2
Exeter Rd Bexley DA16 . . 145 D3
Brondesbury NW2 . . . . 69 A2
Croydon CR0 . . . . 205 D2
Dagenham RM10 . . . . 81 D2
East Barnet N14 . . . . 15 B4
Enfield EN3 . . . . 6 D2
Harrow HA2 . . . . 63 A6
Hatton TW6 . . . . 127 C2
Lower Edmonton N9 . . . 18 C2
Newham E16 . . . . 99 A2
Twickenham TW13 . . . 151 B1
Walthamstow E17 . . . . 53 C4
Exeter St WC2 . . . 116 B6 250 C6
Exeter Way Hatton TW6 . . 127 C3
2 New Cross SE14 . . . . 141 B5
Exford Ct SW11 . . . . 266 D2
Exford Gdns SE12 . . . . 165 B3
Exford Rd SE12 . . . . 165 B3
Exhibition Cl W12 . . . . 112 C6
Exhibition Rd
SW7 . . . . 114 B3 256 D6
Exit Rd N2 . . . . 30 B1
Exmoor Ho 25 E3 . . . . 97 A5
Exmoor St W10 . . . . 90 D2
Exmouth Ho
Clerkenwell EC1 . . . . 241 B6
6 Millwall E14 . . . . 119 D2
Exmouth Market
EC1 . . . 94 C3 241 B6
Exmouth Mews NW1 . . . 232 B1
Exmouth Pl E8 . . . . 74 B1
Exmouth Rd Bexley DA16. . 146 C5
Hayes UB4 . . . . 83 C4
Ruislip HA4 . . . . 62 C5
Walthamstow E17 . . . . 53 B4
Exmouth St E1 . . . . 96 C1
Exning Rd E16 . . . . 98 D3
Exon St SE17 . . . 117 C2 263 A3
Explorer Ave TW19 . . . 148 A3
Explorers Ct 6 E14 . . . 120 B6
Express Dr IG3 . . . . 58 B1
Express Wharf 10 E14 . . 119 C4
Exton Cres NW10 . . . . 67 A1
Exton Gdns RM8 . . . . 80 C3
Exton Rd NW10 . . . . 67 A1
Exton St SE1 . . . 116 C5 251 C3
Eyebright Cl 3 CR0 . . . 206 D1
Eyhurst Cl NW2 . . . . 68 A6
Eylewood Rd SE27 . . . 183 A5
Eynella Rd SE21 . . . . 161 D4
Eynham Rd W12 . . . . 90 C1

Eynsford Cl BR5 . . . . 211 A3
Eynsford Coll W1 . . 93 D1 239 C2
Eynsford Cres DA5 . . . 168 C3
Eynsford Ho
Borough The SE1 . . . . 252 C2
12 Deptford SE15 . . . . 140 C6
Walworth SE17 . . . . 263 A3
Eynsford Rd IG3 . . . . 79 C6
Eynsford Terr UB7 . . . 82 B1
Eynsham Dr SE2 . . . . 124 B3
Eynswood Dr DA14 . . . 190 C5
Eyot Gdns W6 . . . . 111 D1
Eyot Gn W4 . . . . 111 D1
Eyre Ct NW8 . . . . 229 C4
Eyre St Hill EC1 . . . 94 C3 241 A5
Eysham Ct 12 EN5 . . . . 13 D6
Eythorne Rd SW9 . . . . 138 C4
Ezra St E2 . . . . 95 D4

F

Faber Gdns NW4 . . . . 46 A4
Fabian Rd SW6 . . 135 B5 264 C4
Fabian St E6 . . . . 100 B3
Fabyc Ho TW9 . . . . 132 C5
Factory La Croydon CR0 . . 220 D6
Tottenham N17 . . . . 33 D1
Factory Rd E16 . . . . 122 A5
Factory Yd W7 . . . . 108 C5
Fagg's Rd TW14 . . . . 150 A6
Fairacre Hounslow TW7 . . 130 B4
Kingston u T KT3 . . . . 199 C6
Pinner HA5 . . . . 40 A5
Fairacres Putney SW15 . . 134 A1
Ruislip HA4 . . . . 39 D2
Fair Acres BR2 . . . . 209 A4
Fairbairn Gn 1 SW9 . . . 138 D4
Fairbairn Hall E13 . . . 99 A3
Fairbank Ave BR6 . . . . 226 D6
Fairbanks Rd N17 . . . . 52 A6
Fairbourne Ho UB3 . . . 105 A3
Fairbourne Rd N17 . . . 51 C6
Fairbriar Residence
SW7 . . . . 256 B4
Fairbridge Rd N19 . . . 71 D6
Fairbrook Cl N13 . . . . 32 C5
Fairbrook Rd N13 . . . . 32 C4
Fairburn Ct SW15 . . . 157 A6
Fairburn Ho
9 Stamford Hill N16 . . . 51 C1
West Kensington SW5 . . 254 D1
Fairby Ho SE1 . . . . 263 D4
Fairby Rd SE12 . . . . 165 B6
Faircharm Trad Est SE8 . . 141 D5
Fairchild Cl 6 SW11 . . . 136 B3
Fairchild Ho
13 Hackney E9 . . . . 74 C1
Pimlico SW1 . . . . 259 B3
5 Shoreditch N1 . . . . 95 C4
Fairchild Pl EC2 . . . . 243 B5
Fairchild St EC2 . . . . 243 B5
Fairclough Cl UB5 . . . . 85 B3
Fairclough St E1 . . . . 96 A1
Faircourt 14 NW3 . . . . 70 D2
Faircroft
6 Forest Hill SE26. . . . 184 C6
Stoke Newington N16. . . 51 B1
FAIR CROSS 79 D3
Fair Cross IG11 . . . . 79 C3
Faircross Ave IG11 . . . 79 A2
Faircross Par IG11 . . . 79 C3
Fairdale Gdns
Hayes UB3 . . . . 106 A4
Putney SW15 . . . . 134 B1
Fairdene Ct N7 . . . . 72 A3
Fairey Ave UB3 . . . . 105 D3
Fairfax Cl KT12 . . . . 194 B1
Fairfax Gdns SE3 . . . . 143 C4
Fairfax Ho
11 Brixton SW9 . . . . 138 C3
5 Ealing W5 . . . . 88 A4
8 Putney SW15 . . . . 156 A6
Fairfax Mews London N8 . . 50 D5
Newham E16 . . . . 121 B5
Putney SW15 . . . . 134 C1
Fairfax Pl Kensington W14 . 254 B5
South Hampstead NW6 . . 70 A1
Fairfax Rd Acton W4 . . . 111 C3
Hornsey N8 . . . . 50 C5
South Hampstead NW6 . . 70 A1
Teddington TW11 . . . . 175 B3
Fairfax Way N10 . . . . 31 A3
Fairfield
Camden Town NW1 . . . 232 A5
Oakleigh Pk N20 . . . . 14 B4
Pinner HA6 . . . . 22 A1
4 Stepney E1 . . . . 96 C2
Fairfield Ave
Edgware HA8 . . . . 26 D3
Hendon NW4 . . . . 46 B3
Ruislip HA4 . . . . 39 A2
Twickenham TW2 . . . . 151 D3
Fairfield Cl
Blackfen DA15 . . . . 167 D5
Enfield EN3 . . . . 7 A1
Mitcham SW19 . . . . 180 C3
North Finchley N12. . . . 30 A6
West Ewell KT19. . . . 215 C3
Fairfield Cres HA8 . . . . 26 D4

Fairfield Ct
Harlesden NW10 . . . . 90 A6
1 London SW18 . . . . 157 D6
Ruislip HA4 . . . . 39 B1
8 Woodford IG8 . . . . 37 A4
Fairfield Dr Harrow HA2. . . 42 A6
Wandsworth SW18 . . . 157 D6
Wembley UB6 . . . . 87 C6
Fairfield E KT1 . . . . 176 A1
Fairfield Gdns N8 . . . . 50 A4
Fairfield Gr SE7 . . . . 143 D6
Fairfield Ind Est KT1 . . . 198 B6
Fairfield N KT1, KT2 . . . 176 A1
Fairfield Path CR0 . . . . 221 B5
Fairfield Pl KT1 . . . . 198 A6
Fairfield Rd
Beckenham BR3 . . . . 185 C1
Bexleyheath DA7 . . . . 147 B3
Bow E3 . . . . 97 C5
Edmonton N18 . . . . 34 A6
Higham Hill E17 . . . . 35 A1
Hornsey N8 . . . . 50 A4
Ilford IG1 . . . . 78 D2
Kingston u T KT1 . . . . 176 A1
Petts Wood BR5 . . . . 211 B3
Plaistow BR1 . . . . 187 A3
Southall UB1 . . . . 85 B1
South Croydon CR0 . . . 221 C5
Woodford IG8 . . . . 37 A4
Yiewsley UB7 . . . . 104 A6
Fairfield S KT1 . . . . 176 B1
Fairfields SE6 . . . . 163 D4
Fairfields Cl NW9 . . . . 45 A4
Fairfields Cres NW9 . . . 45 A4
Fairfields Rd TW3 . . . . 130 A2
Fairfield St SW18 . . . . 157 D6
Fairfield W KT1 . . . . 176 A1
Fairfield Way Barnet EN5. . 13 C6
West Ewell KT19. . . . 215 C3
Fairfoot Rd E3 . . . . 97 C3
Fairford SE6 . . . . 163 C3
Fairford Ave CR0 . . . . 206 D4
Fairford Cl CR0 . . . . 207 A4
Fairford Ct SM2 . . . . 217 D1
Fairford Gdns KT4 . . . . 215 D5
Fairford Ho SE11 . . . . 261 B3
Fairgreen EN4 . . . . 2 D2
Fairgreen Ct EN4 . . . . 2 D2
Fair Green Ct 1 CR4 . . . 202 B6
Fairgreen E EN4 . . . . 2 D2
Fairgreen Rd CR7 . . . . 204 D4
Fairhall Ct KT6 . . . . 198 B2
Fairhaven Ave CR0 . . . 206 D3
Fairhaven Ct 7 CR2 . . . 221 A3
Fairhazel Gdns NW6 . . . 70 A1
Fairheathe SW15 . . . . 156 D5
Fairholme TW14 . . . . 149 C4
Fairholme Cl N3 . . . . 47 A5
Fairholme Cres UB4 . . . 84 A3
Fairholme Gdns N3 . . . 47 A5
Fairholme Ho 8 N3 . . 199 C5
Fairholme Prim Sch
TW14 . . . . 149 B3
Fairholme Rd
Ashford TW15 . . . . 170 B5
Cheam SM1 . . . . 217 B2
Harrow HA1 . . . . 42 D4
Ilford IG1 . . . . 56 C2
Thornton Heath CR0 . . . 204 C2
West Kensington
W14 . . . . 113 A1 254 B1
Fairholt Cl N16 . . . . 51 C1
Fairholt Rd N16 . . . . 51 B1
Fairholt St SW7 . . . . 257 B6
Fairhurst 4 NW6 . . . . 70 A2
Fairland Ho BR2 . . . . 209 B5
Fairland Rd E15 . . . . 76 D1
Fairlands Ave
Sutton SM1 . . . . 217 C6
Thornton Heath CR7 . . . 204 C4
Woodford IG9 . . . . 21 A2
Fairlands Ct 6 SE9 . . . 166 C5
Fairlawn SE7 . . . . 143 C6
Fairlawn Ave Acton W4 . . 111 A2
Bexley DA7 . . . . 146 D3
East Finchley N2 . . . . 48 C5
Fairlawn Cl
Claygate KT10 . . . . 212 D2
Feltham TW13 . . . . 173 B6
Kingston u T KT2 . . . . 177 A4
Southgate N14 . . . . 15 D5
Fairlawn Ct 3 W4 . . . . 111 A2
Fairlawn Dr IG8 . . . . 37 A3
Fairlawnes SM6 . . . . 219 B3
Fairlawn Gdns UB1 . . . 107 B6
Fairlawn Gr W4 . . . . 111 A2
Fairlawn Mans SE14 . . . 140 D4
Fairlawn Pk SE26 . . . . 185 A5
Fairlawn Prim Sch SE23. . 162 C4
Fairlawn Rd SW19 . . . 179 B3
Fairlawns
4 Bowes Pk N11 . . . . 32 A4
10 Chingford E4 . . . . 20 A2
Pinner HA5 . . . . 22 D1
Putney SW15 . . . . 156 D6
Sunbury TW16 . . . . 194 A6
Twickenham TW1 . . . . 153 C5
Fairlead Ho 6 E14 . . . . 119 C3
Fairlea Pl W5 . . . . 87 D3
Fair Lea Pl W5 . . . . 87 C2

Fairleas 12 BR3 . . . . 185 D1
Fairley Ct HA0 . . . . 65 D3
Fairley House Sch SW1 . . 259 D2
Fairlie Ct Bromley E3 . . . 97 D4
1 Tufnell Pk N7 . . . . 71 D4
Fairlie Gdns SE23 . . . . 162 C4
Fairlight TW12 . . . . 173 D5
Fairlight Ave Chingford E4 . 20 B2
Harlesden NW10 . . . . 89 C5
Woodford IG8 . . . . 37 A4
Fairlight Cl Cheam KT4. . . 216 C4
Chingford E4 . . . . 20 B2
Fairlight Ct Greenford UB6. . 86 B5
4 Harlesden NW10. . . . 89 C5
Fairlight Rd SW17 . . . . 180 B6
Fairline Ct BR3 . . . . 186 A1
Fairlop Ct E11 . . . . 54 C1
Fairlop Pl NW8 . . . . 229 D1
Fairlop Rd E11 . . . . 54 B2
Fairmark Cl UB10 . . . . 60 C2
Fairmead Bromley BR1 . . 210 B5
Tolworth KT5, KT6 . . . 198 D1
Fairmead Cl Bromley BR1. . 210 B5
Heston TW5 . . . . 128 C5
Kingston u T KT3 . . . . 199 B6
Fairmead Cres HA8 . . . 11 A1
Fairmead Ct
3 Chingford E4 . . . . 20 C4
Oakleigh Pk N20 . . . . 14 A4
Fairmead Gdns IG4 . . . 56 A4
Fairmead Ho E9 . . . . 75 A4
Fairmead Rd
Lower Holloway N7, N19 . . 72 A5
Thornton Heath CR0. . . 204 C2
Fairmeadside IG10 . . . 21 C6
Fairmile Ave SW16 . . . 181 D5
Fairmile Ho
St Paul's Cray BR5 . . . 190 A1
Teddington TW11 . . . . 175 A6
Fairmont Ave E14 . . . 120 B5
Fairmont Cl DA17 . . . . 125 B1
Fairmont Ho 1 E3 . . . . 97 C3
Fairmount Rd SW2 . . . 160 B5
Fairoak Cl BR5 . . . . 210 D2
Fairoak Dr SE9 . . . . 167 B6
Fairoaks Gr EN3 . . . . 6 D6
Fairseat Cl WD23 . . . . 8 C2
Fair St
Bermondsey SE1 . . 117 D4 253 C2
Hounslow TW3 . . . . 130 A2
Fairstead Lo 4 IG8 . . . 37 A4
Fairstead Wlk N1 . . . . 235 A6
Fairthorn Rd SE7, SE10 . . 121 C4
Fairview Ave HA0 . . . . 65 D2
Fairview Cl SE26 . . . . 185 A5
Fair View Cl E17 . . . . 35 A2
Fairview Cres HA2 . . . . 41 C1
Fairview Ct
Ashford TW15 . . . . 170 C5
Hendon NW4 . . . . 28 D1
Kingston u T KT2 . . . . 176 D2
Fairview Dr
Littleton TW17 . . . . 192 B4
Orpington BR6 . . . . 227 B4
Fairview Gdns IG8 . . . . 37 B2
Fairview Ho 11 SW2 . . . 160 B4
Fairview Pl SW2 . . . . 160 B4
Fairview Rd
Carshalton SM1, SM5 . . 218 C3
Enfield EN2 . . . . 4 C4
South Tottenham N15 . . 51 D3
Thornton Heath CR0 . . . 182 B2
Fairview Way HA8 . . . . 26 C6
Fairwall Ho 9 SE5 . . . 139 C4
Fairwater Ave DA16 . . . 146 A1
Fairwater Ho TW11 . . . 175 A6
Fairway Bexley DA6 . . . 169 A6
Petts Wood BR5 . . . . 211 B4
West Barnes SW20 . . . 200 C6
Woodford IG8 . . . . 37 C5
Fairway Ave NW9 . . . . 44 D6
Fairway Cl Croydon CR0 . . 207 A4
Heston TW4 . . . . 150 C6
Hounslow TW4 . . . . 150 D6
North End NW11 . . . . 48 A2
West Ewell KT19. . . . 215 A4
Fairway Ct Edgware NW7 . 11 B1
12 Eltham SE9 . . . . 166 C5
New Barnet EN5. . . . 13 D5
13 Rotherhithe SE16 . . . 118 D4
Fairway Dr Erith SE28. . . 103 A1
Greenford UB6 . . . . 63 D1
Fairway Est TW4 . . . . 150 C6
Fairway Gdns Ilford IG1. . . 79 A3
West Wickham BR3 . . . 208 B3
Fairway Prim Sch NW7 . . 11 B2
10 Chingford E4 . . . . 20 A3
4 Hounslow TW7 . . . 130 C4
Stanmore HA7 . . . . 26 A1
Teddington TW11 . . . . 175 D3
Walthamstow E17 . . . . 54 A5
Fairways Bsns Pk E10 . . 75 A6
Fairway The Acton W3 . . 89 C1
Bromley BR1, BR2 . . . 210 B4
East Molesey KT8 . . . . 195 D6
Edgware NW7 . . . . 11 B1
Edmonton N13 . . . . 17 B1
Hillingdon UB10 . . . . 82 B5
Kingston u T KT3 . . . . 177 B2

Fairway The *continued*
New Barnet EN5 13 D5
Northolt UB5 64 A2
Ruislip HA4 62 D5
Southgate N14 15 C5
Wembley HA0 65 B6
Fairweather Cl N15 51 C5
Fairweather Ct N13 32 B6
Fairweather Ho N7 72 A4
Fairweather Rd N16 52 A3
Fairwood Ct E11 54 B2
Fairwyn Rd SE26 185 A6
Faith Ct NW2 68 B2
Faithfull Ho N5 73 A3
Fakenham Cl
Hendon NW7 28 A3
5 Northolt UB5 63 C2
Fakruddin St E1 96 A3
Falcon Ave BR1 210 A5
Falconberg Ct W1 239 D2
Falconberg Mews W1 239 D2
Falconbrook Prim Sch 26
SW11 136 B2
Falcon Cl Chiswick W4 133 A6
Lambeth SE1 251 D4
Falcon Cres EN3 18 D6
Falcon Ct
9 Dulwich SE21 161 B2
Holborn EC4 241 A1
Islington N1 234 D3
New Barnet EN5 2 A1
Ruislip HA4 61 C6
6 Wanstead E18 55 B6
Falcon Dr TW19 148 A5
Falconer Ct N17 33 A3
Falconer Wlk 12 N7 72 B6
Falcon Gr SW11 136 C2
Falcon Ho
11 London SE15 139 D4
9 Merton SW19 179 D2
Falconhurst 4 KT6 198 A4
Falcon La SW11 136 C2
Falcon Lo
11 Paddington W9 91 C2
West Hampstead NW3 69 D4
Falcon Pk Ind Est NW10 67 C3
Falcon Point SE1 251 D5
Falcon Rd
Battersea SW11 136 C2
Enfield EN3 18 D6
Hampton TW12 173 B3
Falconry Ct KT1 198 A6
Falcon Sch for Girls The
W5 110 B5
Falcons Pre Prep school The
1 W4 132 D6
Falcons Prep Sch for Boys
The TW9 132 A1
Falcons Sch for Girls The
W5 110 B5
Falcon St E13 99 A3
Falcon Terr SW11 136 C2
Falcon Way
Feltham TW14 150 B6
Harrow HA3 44 A3
Hendon NW9 27 C1
Millwall E14 119 D2
Sunbury TW16 171 C1
Wanstead E11 55 A5
FALCONWOOD 145 C1
Falconwood Ave DA16 145 C3
Falconwood Ct SE3 142 D3
Falconwood Par DA16 145 D1
Falconwood Rd CR0 223 C1
Falconwood Sta SE9 145 B1
Falcourt Cl SM1 217 D3
Falkener Ct SW11 268 B1
Falkirk Ct 11 SE16 118 D5
Falkirk Gdns WD19 22 D5
Falkirk Ho W9 91 D4
Falkirk St N1 95 C5
Falkland Ave Finchley N3 29 C3
Friern Barnet N11 31 B6
Falkland Ho Catford SE6 186 A6
Kensington W8 255 C5
West Kensington W14 254 C2
Falkland Park Ave SE25 183 C1
Falkland Pl 2 NW5 71 C3
Falkland Rd Barnet EN5 1 A3
Hornsey N8 50 C5
Kentish Town NW5 71 C3
Falkner House Sch SW7 256 B2
Fallaize Ave IG1 78 D4
Falling La UB7 104 A6
Falloden Ct NW11 47 C5
Falloden Way (Barnet By-Pass) NW11 47 C5
Fallodon Ho
6 London SW8 137 D3
Paddington W11 91 B2
Fallow Court Ave N12 30 A4
Fallow Ct 20 SE16 118 A1
Fallowfield
Lower Holloway N4 72 B6
Stanmore HA7 9 A1
Fallowfield Ct HA7 9 A1
Fallow Fields IG10 21 C4
Fallowfields Dr N12 30 C4
Fallows Cl N2 30 B1
Fallsbrook Rd SW16 181 C4
Falman Cl N9 18 A3
Falmer Rd Enfield EN1 5 C1
Walthamstow E17 53 D6
West Green N15 51 B4
Falmouth Ave E4 36 C5
Falmouth Cl
London SE12 164 D6
Wood Green N22 32 B3
Falmouth Gdns IG4 55 D5
Falmouth Ho
Bayswater W2 247 A6
Kennington SE11 261 B2
15 Kingston u T KT2 175 D2
6 Pinner HA5 23 B3
Falmouth Rd SE1 117 A3 262 B5
Falmouth St E15 76 B3
Falmouth Way E17 53 B4
Falstaff Ct SE11 261 C3
Falstaff Ho 18 N1 95 C5
Falstaff Mews TW12 174 B5
Fambridge Cl SE26 185 B6
Fambridge Rd RM8 59 C1
Fane St W14 264 D6
Fan Mus The★ SE10 142 A5
Fann St EC1 95 A3 242 B5
Fanshawe Ave IG11 79 A2
Fanshawe Cres RM9 81 B3
Fanshawe Rd TW10 175 C6
Fanshaw Ho 6 E17 53 D6
Fanshaw St N1 95 C4
Fantail Cl SE28 102 C1
Fantail The BR6 226 B5
Fanthorpe St SW15 134 C2
Faraday Ave DA14 168 B2
Faraday Cl N7 72 B2
Faraday Ho
2 Balham SW12 159 B4
4 Belvedere DA17 125 C3
6 Gospel Oak NW5 71 B4
5 Hampton TW12 173 D4
Kensal Town W10 91 A2
6 Poplar E14 119 B6
Wembley HA9 67 A5
Faraday Lo SE10 120 D3
Faraday Pl KT8 195 C5
Faraday Rd Acton W3 111 A6
East Molesey KT8 195 C5
Kensal Town W10 91 A2
Southall UB1 107 D6
Stratford E15 76 D2
Welling DA16 146 A2
Wimbledon SW19 179 D4
Faraday Way
Greenwich SE18 121 D3
Thornton Heath CR0 204 B1
Fareham Ho 13 SW15 156 A3
Fareham Rd TW14 150 C4
Fareham St W1 239 C2
Farendon Ho 15 SM2 218 A2
Farewell Pl CR4 180 C2
Faringdon Ave BR2 210 C3
Faringford Rd E15 76 C1
Farjeon Ho NW6 70 B1
Farjeon Rd SE3 143 D4
Farleigh Ave BR2 209 A2
Farleigh Ct CR2 221 A3
Farleigh Ho 7 KT2 176 D4
Farleigh Pl N16 73 D4
Farleigh Rd N16 73 D4
Farleycroft 1 CR0 206 A1
Farley Croft BR2 186 C1
Farley Ct Kensington W14 254 C6
Marylebone NW1 238 A5
Farley Dr IG3 57 C1
Farley Ho SE26 162 B1
Farley Mews SE6 164 A4
Farley Pl SE25 206 A5
Farley Rd Catford SE6 164 A4
South Croydon CR2 222 B1
Farlington Pl SW15 156 B4
Farlow Rd SW15 134 D2
Farlton Rd SW18 157 D4
Farman Gr 2 UB5 84 D4
Farman Terr HA3 43 D5
Farm Ave Child's Hill NW2 69 B5
Harrow HA2, HA5 41 C3
Streatham SW16 182 A6
Wembley HA0 65 C2
Farmborough Cl HA1 42 B2
Farm Cl Barnet EN5 12 C6
Buckhurst Hill IG9 21 C1
Coney Hall BR4 224 D5
Lower Halliford TW17 192 C2
Southall UB1 107 D6
Sutton SM2 218 B1
Uxbridge UB10 60 D6
Walham Green SW6 265 B4
Farmcote Rd SE12 165 A3
Farm Cotts E17 53 A3
Farm Ct NW4 46 A6
Farmdale Rd
Greenwich SE10 121 A1
Sutton SM5 218 C1
Farm Dr CR0 223 B6
Farm End E4 20 C6
Farmer Ho 4 SE16 118 B3
Farmer Rd E10 53 D1
Farmers Mkt★
W8 113 C5 245 B4
Farmers Rd SE5 138 D5
Farmer St W8 245 A4
Farmfield Rd BR1 186 C5
Farm House Ct NW7 28 A3
Farmhouse Rd SW16 181 C3
Farmilo Rd E17 53 C2
Farmington Ave SM1 218 B5
Farm La Croydon CR0 223 B6
East Barnet N14 15 B5
Walham Green
SW6 135 C5 265 B4
Farmlands Enfield EN2 4 C4
Pinner HA5 40 A5
Farmlands The UB5 63 C2
Farmland Wlk BR7 188 D5
Farm Lane Trad Ctr
SW6 135 C6 265 B5
Farmleigh N14 15 C4
Farmleigh Ho SW9 160 D6
Farm Pl W8 245 A4
Farm Rd Edgware HA8 27 A5
Edmonton N21 17 A3
Morden SM4 201 D4
Stonebridge NW10 89 B6
Sutton SM2 218 B1
Thames Ditton KT10 195 C1
Twickenham TW4 151 A3
Farm St W1 115 B6 248 C5
Farmstead Ct 3 SM6 219 B3
Farmstead Rd
Catford SE6 185 D6
Harrow HA3 24 B1
Farm Vale DA5 169 D5
Farm View N3 47 B6
Farmway RM8 80 C5
Farm Way
Buckhurst Hill IG9 37 C6
North Cheam KT4 216 C5
Farm Wlk NW11 47 C4
Farnaby Ho 2 W10 91 B4
Farnaby Rd
Bromley BR1, BR2 186 C2
Kidbrooke SE9 143 C1
Farnan Ave E17 53 D6
Farnan Hall 6 SW16 182 A5
Farnan Rd SW16 182 A5
FARNBOROUGH 227 B3
Farnborough Ave
South Croydon CR2 223 A1
Walthamstow E17 53 A6
Farnborough Cl HA9 66 D6
Farnborough Comm
Keston Mark BR2, BR6 226 B5
Orpington BR6 226 C4
Farnborough Cres
3 Hayes BR2 208 D1
South Croydon CR2 223 A1
Farnborough Ct 2 BR6 227 A3
Farnborough Hill BR6 227 C3
Farnborough Ho 1
SW15 156 A3
Farnborough Prim Sch
BR6 227 A3
Farnborough Way BR6 227 B3
Farncombe St SE16 118 A4
Farndale Ave N13 17 A1
Farndale Cres UB6 86 A4
Farndale Ho 3 NW6 91 D6
Farnell Mews SW5 255 C2
Farnell Pl W3 110 D6
Farnell Rd TW7 130 B2
Farnell's Almshouses
TW7 130 D3
Farnfield Ho 12 SW2 160 B6
Farnham Cl N20 14 A4
Farnham Ct
2 Cheam SM3 217 A2
1 Southall UB1 86 A1
2 Stamford Hill N16 51 C1
Farnham Gdns SW20 178 B1
Farnham Green Prim Sch
IG3 58 A3
Farnham Ho
Borough The SE1 252 A3
Marylebone NW1 237 B5
Farnham Pl SE1 251 D3
Farnham Rd Bexley DA16 146 C3
Ilford IG3 57 D2
Farnham Royal
SE11 116 B1 260 D1
Farnhurst Ho 7 SW11 137 A3
Farningham Ct SW16 181 D3
Farningham Ho 9 N4 51 B2
Farningham Rd N17 34 A3
Farnley Ho 13 SW8 137 D3
Farnley Rd Chingford E4 20 C4
South Norwood SE25 205 B5
Farnsworth Ct SE10 120 D3
Farnsworth Ho 8 SW27 182 D5
Farnworth Ho 5 E14 120 B2
Faro Cl BR1 188 C1
Faroe Rd W14 112 D3
Farorna Wlk EN2 4 C4
Farquhar Rd
Dulwich SE19 183 D5
Wimbledon SW19 157 C1
Farquharson Rd CR0 205 A1
Farrance Rd RM6 59 A2
Farrance St E14 97 C1
Farrans Ct HA3 43 B2
Farrant Ave N22 32 D1
Farrant Cl BR6 227 D1
Farrant Ho 10 SW11 136 B2
Farrants Ct BR1 188 B1
Farr Ave IG11 102 A5
Farrell Ho E1 96 C1
Farren Rd SE23 163 A2
Farrer Ho SE8 141 C5
Farrer Mews N8 49 C5
Farrer Rd Harrow HA3 44 A5
Hornsey N8 49 D5
Farrer's Pl CR0 222 D4
Farrier Cl Bromley BR1 209 D6
Hillingdon UB8 82 C1
Sunbury TW16 194 A5
Farrier Pl SM1 217 D6
Farrier Rd UB5 85 C5
Farriers Ct Belmont SM2 217 A1
Wimbledon SW19 179 A3
Farriers Mews SE15 140 C2
Farrier St NW1 71 C1
Farriers Way WD6 11 B6
Farrier Wlk
SW10 136 A6 266 A6
Farringdon La
EC1 94 C3 241 B5
Farringdon Rd
EC1 94 C3 241 B5
Farringdon St EC4 94 D1 241 C2
Farringdon Sta
EC1 94 D2 241 C4
Farrington Pl BR7 189 B3
Farringtons Sch BR7 189 B3
Farrins Rents SE16 119 A5
Farrow La SE14 140 C5
Farrow Pl SE16 119 A3
Farr Rd EN2 5 B4
Farthingale Wlk E15 76 B1
Farthing Alley 8 SE1 118 A4
Farthing Ct 3 NW7 29 A3
Farthing Fields 8 E1 118 B5
Farthings Cl Chingford E4 20 C1
Pinner HA5 40 B3
Farthing St BR6 226 B1
Farthings The 1 KT2 176 C2
FARTHING STREET 226 B1
Farwell Rd DA14 190 C6
Farwig La BR1 187 A2
Fashion Retail Acad The
W1 239 C2
Fashion St E1 95 D2 243 D3
Fashion & Textile Mus★
SE1 253 A2
Fashoda Rd BR2 209 D5
Fassett Rd Dalston E8 74 A2
Kingston u T KT1 198 A5
Fassett Sq E8 74 A2
Fauconberg Ct W4 133 A6
Fauconberg Rd W4 133 A6
Faulkner Cl 6 RM8 58 D2
Faulkner Ho SW15 134 C3
Faulkner's Alley EC1 241 C4
Faulkner St SE14 140 C4
Fauna Cl Dagenham RM6 58 C3
Stanmore HA7 25 D6
Faunce Ho 1 SE17 138 D6
Faunce St SE17 116 D1 261 C1
Favart Rd SW6 135 C4 265 B2
F Ave SE18 122 D3
Faversham Ave
Chingford E4 20 D3
Enfield EN1 17 B5
Faversham Ct SE6 163 B3
Faversham Ho
Camden Town NW1 232 B5
Walworth SE17 263 A1
Faversham Rd
Beckenham BR3 185 B1
Forest Hill SE6 163 B3
Morden SM4 201 D3
Fawcett Cl London SW11 136 B3
West Norwood SW16 182 C6
Fawcett Est E5 52 A1
Fawcett Ho 25 SW9 138 A3
Fawcett Rd Croydon CR0 221 A5
Willesden NW10 67 D1
Fawcett St SW10 136 A6 266 A6
Fawcus Cl KT10 212 C2
Fawe Park Rd SW15 135 B1
Fawe St E14 97 D2
Fawkham Ho SE1 263 D3
Fawley Ct SE27 160 D2
Fawley Lo 2 E14 120 B2
Fawley Rd NW6 69 D3
Fawnbrake Ave SE24 161 A6
Fawn Rd E13 99 C5
Fawns Manor Cl TW14 149 A3
Fawns Manor Rd TW14 149 B3
Fawood Ave NW10 67 B1
Fayetville Ho 26 N19 49 D2
Faygate Cres DA6 169 C6
Faygate Ct CR2 220 D1
Faygate Rd SW2 160 B2
Fayland Ave SW16 181 C5
Fazal Laj IG1 79 A6
Fazerley Ct 49 W2 91 C2
Fearnley Cres TW12 173 B4
Fearnley Ho SE5 139 C3
Fearon St SE10 121 A1
Featherbed La CR0 223 B1
Feathers Pl SE10 142 B6
Featherstone Ave 4
SE23 162 C2
Featherstone Ct NW7 28 A3
Featherstone High Sch
UB2 107 A3
Featherstone Ho UB4 84 C2
Featherstone Ind Est
UB2 107 A3
Featherstone Prim Sch
UB2 106 C2
Featherstone Rd
Mill Hill NW7 28 B4
Southall UB2 107 A3
Featherstone St
EC1 95 B3 242 C6
Featherstone Terr UB2 107 A3
Featley Rd SW9 138 D2
Federal Rd UB6 87 C5
Federation Rd SE2 124 C2
Fee Farm Rd KT10 212 D1
Felbridge Ave HA7 25 B2
Felbridge Cl SW16 182 C6
Felbridge Ct
Croydon CR2 221 A1
Feltham TW13 150 B3
Harlington UB3 127 B6
Felbridge Ho 21 SE22 139 C2
Felbrigge Rd IG3 57 D1
Felday Rd SE13 163 D5
Felden Cl HA5 23 A3
Felden St SW6 135 B4 264 C1
Feldman Cl N16 52 A1
Feldspar Ct 6 EN3 7 A2
Felgate Mews 4 W6 112 B2
Felhampton Rd SE9 166 D1
Felhurst Cres RM10 81 D4
Feline Ct 1 EN4 14 C5
Felix Ave N8 50 A3
Felix Ct E17 53 D4
Felix La TW17 193 D3
Felix Manor BR7 189 C4
Felix Neubergh Ct EN1 5 C1
Felix Rd Ealing W13 109 A6
Walton-on-T KT12 194 A3
Felix St 19 E2 96 B5
Felixstowe Ct E16 122 D5
Felixstowe Rd
Abbey Wood SE2 124 B3
College Pk NW10 90 B4
Edmonton N9 34 A6
Tottenham N17 51 D6
Fellbrigg Rd SE22 161 D6
Fellbrigg St 21 E1 96 B3
Fellbrook TW10 153 B1
Fell Ho 11 N19 71 C5
Fellmongers Yd 1 CR0 221 A5
Fellowes Cl UB4 84 D3
Fellowes Ct UB3 127 B6
Fellowes Rd SM5 218 C6
Fellows Ct E2 95 D5
Fellows Rd NW3 70 C1
Fell Rd CR0 221 A5
Fells Haugh 6 W3 89 A1
Felltram Way SE7 121 A1
Fell Wlk HA8 26 D2
Felmersham Cl 2 SW4 137 D1
Felmingham Rd SE20 184 C1
Felnex Trad Est SM6 219 A6
Felpham Ct HA9 65 D4
Felsberg Rd SW2 160 A4
Fels Cl RM10 81 D5
Felsham Ho 5 SW15 134 D2
Felsham Mews 14 SW15 134 D2
Felsham Rd SW15 134 D2
Felspar Cl SE18 123 D1
Felstead Cl N13 32 C5
Felstead Rd E11 55 A2
Felstead St E9 75 B2
Felstead Wharf E14 120 A1
Felsted Rd E16 99 D1
FELTHAM 150 B2
Feltham Airparcs L Ctr
TW13 150 D2
Feltham Arenas TW14 150 A4
Feltham Ave KT8 196 C5
Felthambrook Ind Est
TW13 150 B1
Felthambrook Way
TW13 172 B6
Feltham Bsns Complex
TW13 150 B2
Feltham Com Sch TW13 150 C2
Feltham Corporate Ctr
TW13 150 B1
FELTHAMHILL 171 D5
Feltham Hill Jun & Inf Schs
TW13 149 D1
Feltham Hill Rd
Ashford TW15 171 A4
Feltham TW13 172 C5
Feltham Rd
Ashford TW15 171 A6
Mitcham CR4 181 A1
Feltham Sta TW13 150 B3
Felton Cl BR5 210 D3
Felton Gdns IG11 101 C5
Felton Ho Kidbrooke SE9 143 C1

Felton Ho *continued*
Shoreditch N1 235 D5
Felton Lea DA14 189 D5
Felton Rd Barking IG11 101 C5
Ealing W13 109 C4
Felton St N1 95 B6 235 D5
Fenchurch Ave
EC3 95 C1 243 A1
Fenchurch Bldgs EC3 243 B1
Fenchurch Pl EC3 253 B6
Fenchurch St
EC3 117 C6 253 B6
Fenchurch Street Sta
EC3 117 C6 253 B6
Fen Ct EC3 253 A6
Fendall Rd KT19 215 A3
Fendall St SE1 117 C3 263 B5
Fender Ct 5 SW4 138 A3
Fendt Cl 8 E16 98 D1
Fendyke Rd SE2, DA17 124 D3
Fenelon Pl W14 113 B2 254 D3
Fen Gr DA15 167 D5
Fenham Rd SE15 140 B5
Fenman Ct N17 34 B2
Fenman Gdns IG3 58 B1
Fenn Cl BR1 187 A4
Fenn Ct HA1 43 A4
Fennel Cl Croydon CR0 206 D1
Newham E16 98 C3
Fennell St SE18 144 C6
Fenner Cl SE16 118 B2
Fenner Ho 25 E1 118 B5
Fenner Sq 9 SW11 136 B2
Fenn Ho TW7 131 B4
Fenning Ct CR4 202 C5
Fenning St SE1 253 A2
Fenn St E9 74 C3
Fen St E16 120 D6
Fenstanton 3 N4 50 B1
Fenstanton Ave N12 30 B5
Fenstanton Prim Sch 20
SW2 160 C3
Fenswood Cl DA5 169 C5
Fentiman Rd
SW8 138 B5 270 C4
Fentiman Way HA2 63 D6
Fenton Cl 16 Dalston E8 73 D2
Elmstead BR7 188 B5
South Lambeth SW9 138 B3
Fenton Ct TW3 129 A5
Fenton Ho Deptford SE14 141 A5
Heston TW5 129 C6
Fenton House★ NW3 70 A5
Fenton Rd N17 33 A3
Fentons SE3 142 D5
Fenton's Ave E13 99 B5
Fenton St E1 96 B1
Fenwick Cl 16 SE18 144 C6
Fenwick Gr SE15 140 A2
Fenwick Pl Croydon CR2 220 D1
Stockwell SW9 138 A2
Fenwick Rd SE15 140 A2
Ferby Ct DA15 189 D6
Ferdinand Ho 1 NW1 71 B1
Ferdinand Pl NW1 71 A1
Ferdinand St NW1 71 A1
Ferguson Ave KT5 198 B4
Ferguson Cl BR2, BR3 208 B6
Ferguson Dr W3 89 B1
Ferguson Ho SE10 142 A4
Ferguson's Cl E14 119 C2
Fergus Rd N5 72 D3
Fermain Ct E N1 95 C6
Fermain Ct N N1 95 C6
Fermain Ct W N1 95 C6
Ferme Park Rd N4, N8 50 B3
Fermor Rd SE23 163 A3
Fermoy Rd Greenford UB6 85 D3
West Kilburn W9 91 B3
Fern Ave CR4 203 D5
Fernbank IG9 21 B3
Fernbank Ave
Walton-on-T KT12 195 A2
Wembley HA0 64 D3
Fernbank Mews SW12 159 C5
Fernbrook Cres SE13 164 C5
Fernbrook Dr HA2 41 D2
Fernbrook Rd SE13 164 C5
Fern Cl 3 N1 95 C5
Ferncliff Rd E8 74 A3
Ferncroft Ave London N12 30 D4
Ruislip HA4 62 C6
West Hampstead NW3 69 C4
Fern Ct Bexleyheath DA7 147 C1
Chingford E4 36 A4
New Cross Gate SE14 140 D3
Ferndale BR1 187 C1
Ferndale Ave
Hounslow TW4 129 A2
Walthamstow E17 54 B4
Ferndale Cl DA7 147 A4
Ferndale Com Sp Ctr
SW9 138 B1
Ferndale Ct 3 SE3 142 D5
Ferndale Ho N16 51 B1
Ferndale Rd
Ashford TW15 170 A5
Ferndale Rd *continued*
Brixton SW4, SW9 138 B1
Croydon SE25 206 B4
Enfield EN3 7 A6
Leyton E11 76 D6
South Tottenham N15 51 D4
Upton E7 77 B1
Ferndale St E6 100 D1
Ferndale Way BR6 227 B3
Ferndene NW9 45 A4
Fern Dene W13 87 B2
Ferndene Rd SE24 139 A1
Fernden Way RM7 59 D3
Ferndown
5 Kingston u T KT6 198 A4
Pinner HA6 22 A1
7 Wanstead E18 55 A6
Ferndown Ave BR6 211 B1
Ferndown Cl Pinner HA5 23 A3
Sutton SM2 218 B2
Ferndown Ct 6 UB1 86 A1
Ferndown Lo 17 E14 120 A3
Ferndown Rd
Eltham SE9 165 D4
South Oxhey WD19 22 C6
Ferney Meade Way
TW7 131 A3
Ferney Rd EN4 15 A3
Fern Gr TW14 150 B4
Fernhall N12 30 C5
Fernhall Dr IG4 55 D4
Fernham Rd CR7 205 A6
Fernhead 12 SM1 218 A4
Fernhead Rd W9 91 B4
Fernhill Ct Chingford E17 36 B1
Kingston u T KT2 175 D5
Fernhill Gdns KT2 176 A5
Fernhill Ho E5 74 A6
Fern Hill Pl 3 BR6 227 A3
Fern Hill Prim Sch KT2 176 A4
Fernhill St E16 122 B5
Fern Ho HA7 24 D4
Fernholme Rd SE15 162 D6
Fernhurst Gdns HA8 26 C4
Fernhurst Rd
Ashford TW15 171 A6
Croydon CR0 206 B1
Fulham SW6 135 A4 264 B2
Fernie Ho SE22 139 D2
Fern La TW5 107 B1
Fernlea Ho NW10 88 B4
Fernlea Rd Balham SW12 159 B3
Mitcham CR4 181 A2
Fernleigh Cl
Croydon CR0 220 C4
West Kilburn W9 91 B4
Fernleigh Ct Harrow HA2 23 D1
Wembley HA9 44 A1
Fernleigh Rd N21 16 D2
Fern Lo 13 SW16 182 C5
Fernly Cl HA5 40 A5
Fernsbury St WC1 234 A1
Fernshaw Mans SW10 266 A5
Fernshaw Rd
SW10 136 A6 266 A5
Fernside Buckhurst Hill IG9 21 B3
Golders Green NW11 47 C1
Thames Ditton KT7 197 B1
Fernside Ave
Edgware NW7 11 B1
Feltham TW13 172 B6
Fernside Ct NW4 28 D1
Fernside Rd SW12 159 A4
Ferns Rd E15 76 D2
Fern St E3 97 C3
Fernthorpe Rd SW16 181 C4
Ferntower Rd N5 73 B3
Fernways IG1 78 D4
Fern Wlk 18 SE16 118 A1
Fernwood
Wandsworth SW19 157 B3
Wood Green N22 32 A3
Fernwood Ave
Streatham SW16 181 D6
Wembley HA0 65 C2
Fernwood Cl BR1 187 C1
Fernwood Cres N20 14 D1
Fernwood Ct N14 15 D3
Ferny Hill EN4 3 A5
Ferranti Cl SE18 121 D3
Ferraro Cl TW5 129 C6
Ferrers Ave
Wallington SM6 219 D4
West Drayton UB7 104 A4
Ferrers Rd SW16 181 D5
Ferrestone Rd N8 50 B5
Ferrey Mews 19 SW9 138 C3
Ferriby Cl N1 72 C1
Ferrier Ind Est SW18 135 D1
Ferrier Point 6 E16 99 A2
Ferrier St SW18 135 D1
Ferring Cl HA2 42 A1
Ferrings SE21 161 C1
Ferris Ave CR0 223 B5
Ferris Rd SE22 140 A1
Ferron Rd E5 74 B5
Ferrour Ct N2 48 B6
Ferrybridge Ho SE11 260 D5
Ferrydale Lo 4 NW4 46 C5
Ferry Ho E5 52 B1
Ferry Island Ret Pk N17 52 A6
Ferry La Barnes SW13 133 D6
Brentford TW8 132 A6
Lower Halliford TW17 192 C1
Richmond TW9 132 B6
Tottenham Hale N17 52 B5
Ferry Lane Ind Est E17 52 D5
Ferry Lane Prim Sch N17 52 B5
Ferrymead Ave UB6 85 C5
Ferrymead Dr UB6 85 C5
Ferrymead Gdns UB6 86 A5
Ferrymoor TW10 153 B1
Ferry Quays Ctyd 13
TW8 131 D6
Ferry Rd Barnes SW13 134 A4
East Molesey KT8 195 C6
Richmond TW11 175 B5
Thames Ditton KT7 197 B3
Twickenham TW1 153 B3
Ferry Sq
1 Brentford TW8 132 A6
Lower Halliford TW17 192 D2
Ferry St E14 120 A1
Ferry Wks TW17 192 C1
Festing Rd SW15 134 D2
Festival Cl Hillingdon UB10 82 D6
Sidcup DA5 168 D3
Festival Ct Cheam SM1 201 D1
5 Dalston E8 73 D1
Festival Pier SE1 116 B5 250 C4
Festoon Way E16 121 D6
Fetherston Ct RM6 59 B3
Fetter La EC4 94 C1 241 B2
Fettes Ho NW8 229 D3
Fews Lodge RM6 58 D5
Ffinch St SE8 141 C5
Fidgeon Cl BR1 210 C6
Field Cl Bromley BR1 187 C1
Buckhurst Hill IG9 21 C1
Chessington KT9 213 C3
Chingford E4 35 D4
Cranford TW4 128 B4
East Molesey KT8 195 D4
Harlington UB7 127 A5
Ruislip HA4 39 A1
Uxbridge UB10 60 D6
Willesden NW2 68 A6
Fieldcommon La KT12 195 B1
Field Ct Hampstead NW3 70 A3
Holborn WC1 240 D3
Lower Holloway N7 72 A3
Wimbledon SW19 157 C1
Fieldend TW11 174 D6
Field End HA4 62 C2
Field End Jun & Inf Schs
HA4 62 D6
Fieldend Rd SW16 181 C2
Field End Rd HA5, HA4 40 C1
Fielders Cl 2 Enfield EN1 5 C1
Harrow HA2 42 A1
Fieldfare Rd SE28 124 C6
Fieldgate Mans 25 E1 96 A2
Fieldgate St E1 96 A2
Field Ho 4 Edmonton N9 34 A6
Kensal Green NW10 90 D4
8 Richmond TW10 153 C1
Fieldhouse Cl E18 37 B2
Fieldhouse Rd SW12 159 C3
Fielding Ave TW2 152 A1
Fielding Ho Chiswick W4 133 C6
6 Kilburn NW6 91 C4
St John's Wood NW8 229 A6
Fielding La BR2 209 C5
Fielding Mews SW13 134 B6
Fielding Prim Sch W13 109 B3
Fielding Rd Acton W4 111 C3
Hammersmith W14 112 D3
Fielding St SE17 139 A6
Fieldings The SE23 162 C3
Fielding Terr W5 110 B6
Field La Brentford TW8 131 C5
Teddington TW11 175 A5
Field Lo NW10 67 D2
Field Mead NW9, NW7 27 D3
Fieldpark Gdns CR0 207 A1
Field Pl KT3 199 D3
Field Point E7 77 A4
Field Rd Feltham TW14 150 B5
Forest Gate E7 77 A4
Fulham W6 135 A6 264 A6
Tottenham N17 51 C6
Fieldsend Rd SM3 217 A3
Fields Est E8 74 A1
Fieldside Cl BR6 227 A4
Fieldside Rd BR1 186 B5
Fields Park Cres RM6 58 D4
Field St WC1 233 C2
Fieldsway Ho N5 72 C3
Fieldview SW17, SW18 158 B3
Field View TW13 171 B6
Field View Cl RM7 59 C6
Fieldview Ct
2 Islington N5 72 D3
London NW9 44 C3
Fieldway Dagenham RM8 80 C4
Petts Wood BR5 211 B3
Field Way Greenford UB6 85 D6
New Addington CR0 223 D2
Ruislip HA4 39 A1
Willesden NW10 67 A1
Fieldway Cres N5, N7 72 C3
Fieldway Sta CR0 223 D1
Fieldwick Ho 14 E9 74 D2
Fiennes Cl RM8 58 C1
Fife Ct 5 W3 88 C1
Fifehead Cl TW15 170 A4
Fife Rd Kingston u T KT2 176 A1
Mortlake SW14 155 A6
Newham E16 99 A2
Tottenham N22 32 D3
Fife Terr N1 233 D4
Fifield Path SE23 162 D1
Fifteenpenny Fields
SE9 166 C6
Fifth Ave Hayes UB3 105 D5
Ilford E12 78 B4
West Kilburn W10 91 A4
Fifth Cross Rd TW2 152 B2
Fifth Way HA9 66 D4
Figge's Rd CR4 181 A3
Fig Tree Cl NW10 89 C6
Filanco Ct W7 108 D5
Filby Rd KT9 214 B2
Filey Ave N16 52 A1
Filey Cl SM2 218 A1
Filey Ho SW18 136 A1
Filey Waye HA4 62 B6
Filigree Ct SE16 119 B5
Fillebrook Ave EN1 5 D3
Fillebrook Rd E11 54 C1
Filmer Ho SW6 264 B2
Filmer Mews SW6 264 B2
Filmer Rd SW6 135 B5 264 C3
Filston Rd DA8 125 D1
Filton Cl NW9 27 C1
Filton Ct 14 SE14 140 C5
Finborough Rd
Upper Tooting SW17 180 D4
West Brompton
SW10 135 D6 265 D6
Finchale Rd SE2 124 A3
Fincham Cl UB10 61 A5
Finch Ave SE27 183 B6
Finch Cl Barnet EN5 13 C6
Willesden NW10 67 B2
Finch Ct DA14 168 B1
Finchdean Ho SW15 155 D4
Finch Dr TW14 150 D4
Finch Gdns E4 35 C5
Finch Ho 1 SE8 141 D5
Finchingfield Ave IG8 37 C3
Finch La EC2, EC3 242 D1
FINCHLEY 29 D3
Finchley Central Sta N3 29 C2
Finchley Ct N3 29 D4
Finchley La NW4 46 D5
Finchley Lido L Ctr N12 30 B3
Finchley Lo N12 29 D5
Finchley Meml Hospl
N12 30 A3
Finchley Pk N12 30 B6
Finchley Pl NW8 229 C4
Finchley RC High Sch
N12 13 D1
Finchley Rd
Hampstead NW3 70 A2
London NW11 47 B3
St John's Wood NW8 229 C4
Finchley Road & Frognal Sta
NW3 70 A3
Finchley Road Sta NW3 70 A2
Finchley Way N3 29 C3
Finch Lo 15 W9 91 C2
Finch Mews 3 SE15 139 D4
Finch's Ct 10 E14 119 D6
Finden Rd E7 77 C3
Findhorn Ave UB4 84 B2
Findhorn St 8 E14 98 A1
Findon Cl Harrow HA2 63 D5
Wandsworth SW18 157 C5
Findon Rd Edmonton N9 18 B3
Shepherd's Bush W12 112 A4
Fine Bush La HA4 38 D3
Fineran Ct 16 SW11 136 B1
Fingal St SE10 120 D1
Fingest Ho NW8 237 A6
Finians Cl UB10 60 B1
Finland Rd SE4 141 A2
Finland St SE16 119 A3
Finlays Cl KT9 214 C3
Finlay St SW6 134 D4
Finley Ct 21 SE5 139 A5
Finmere Ho 1 N4 51 A2
Finnemore Ho N1 235 A6
Finney La TW7 131 A4
Finn Ho N1 235 D2
Finnis St E2 96 B3
Finnymore Rd RM9 81 A1
FINSBURY 94 C4
Finsbury Ave EC2 242 D3
Finsbury Cir EC2 95 B2 242 D3
Finsbury Cotts N22 32 A3
Finsbury Ct EC2 242 C4
Finsbury Ho N22 32 A2
Finsbury L Ctr
EC1 95 A3 235 A1
Finsbury Market EC2 243 A4
Finsbury Mkt EC2 243 A5
FINSBURY PARK 72 C6
Finsbury Park Ave N4 51 A3
Finsbury Park Rd N4, N5 72 D6
Finsbury Park Sta N4 72 C6
Finsbury Pavement
EC2 95 B2 242 D4
Finsbury Rd N22 32 B2
Finsbury Sq EC2 95 B2 242 D4
Finsbury St EC2 242 C4
Finsbury Way DA5 169 B5
Finsen Rd SE5 139 A2
Finstock Rd W10 90 D1
Finton House Sch SW17 158 D2
Finucane Ct TW9 132 B2
Finucane Rise WD23 8 A2
Finwhale Ho E14 119 D3
Fiona Ct Enfield EN2 4 D2
9 Kilburn NW6 91 B5
Firbank Cl Enfield EN2 5 A1
Newham E16 99 D2
Firbank Rd SE15 140 B3
Fir Cl KT12 194 A2
Fircroft N1 94 D6 234 D6
Fircroft Gdns HA1 64 C5
Fircroft Prim Sch SW17 158 D1
Fircroft Rd
Chessington KT9 214 B4
Upper Tooting SW17 158 D1
Firdene KT5 199 A1
Fir Dene BR6 226 C5
Fire Bell Alley KT6 198 A3
Firebell Mews KT6 198 A3
Fire Brigade Cotts HA5 41 C5
Fire Brigade Pier SE1 260 B4
Firecrest Dr NW3 69 D5
Firefly 7 NW9 27 D1
Firefly Gdns E6 100 A3
Firemans Cotts N10 49 A6
Fireman's Flats N22 32 A2
Firepower (The Royal
Artillery Mus)★ SE18 122 D3
Fire Station Alley EN5 1 A3
Fire Station Flats TW7 130 C3
Fire Station Mews 4
BR3 185 D2
Firethorn Cl 4 HA8 27 A6
Fir Gr KT3 199 D3
Fir Grove Rd 25 SW9 138 C3
Firhill Rd SE6 163 C1
Fir Island NW7 28 C5
Firle Ho 7 W10 90 C2
Fir Lo SW15 134 B1
Firmans Ct E17 54 B5
Firmston Ho 9 SW14 133 B2
Fir Rd Cheam SM3 201 B1
Feltham TW13 172 D5
Firs Ave Fortis Green N10 49 A5
Friern Barnet N11 31 A4
Mortlake SW14 133 A1
Firsby Ave CR0 207 A1
Firsby Rd N16 52 A1
Firs Cl Claygate KT10 212 C2
Forest Hill SE23 163 A4
Mitcham CR4 181 B2
Muswell Hill N10 49 A6
Firscroft N13 17 A1
Firs Dr TW5 128 B5
Firs Farm Prim Sch N13 17 B1
Firs Ho N22 32 C2
Firside Gr DA15 167 D3
Firs La N21, N13 17 A2
Firs Park Ave N21 17 B3
Firs Park Gdns N21 17 B3
First Ave Bexley DA7 146 C5
Chadwell Heath RM6 58 C4
Dagenham RM10 103 D5
East Acton W3 111 D5
East Molesey KT8 195 C5
Edmonton N18 34 C6
Enfield EN1 17 D6
Hayes UB3 105 D5
Hendon NW4 46 C5
Manor Pk E12 78 A3
Mortlake SW14 133 C2
Newham E13 99 A4
Walthamstow E17 53 D4
Walton-on-T KT12 194 B3
Wembley HA9 65 D6
West Kilburn W10 91 B3
First Cl KT8 196 A6
First Cross Rd TW2 152 C2
First Dr NW10 67 A1
Firs The Belmont SM2 217 D1
Claygate KT10 212 C2
Ealing W5 87 D2
Forest Hill SE26 184 C5
Oakleigh Pk N20 14 B3
2 Penge SE26 184 B5
Sidcup DA15 167 D1
Upton Pk E6 78 A1
Wimbledon SW20 178 A3
Woodford IG8 37 C3
First St SW3 114 C2 257 B4
Firstway SW20 178 C1
First Way HA9 66 D4
Firs Wlk IG8 37 A5
Firswood Ave KT19 215 D3
Firth Gdns SW6 135 A4 264 A1
Firtree Ave CR4 181 A1
Fir Tree Ave UB7 104 C3
Fir Tree Cl Ealing W5 88 A1
Esher KT10 212 A3

Fir Tree Cl continued
⑤ Orpington BR6....... 227 D3
Streatham SW16 ...... 181 C5
Worcester Pk KT19.... 215 D4
Firtree Ct BR2....... 208 D6
Fir Tree Gdns CR0....223 C4
Fir Tree Gr SM5 ...... 218 D1
Firtree Ho SE13.......164 B4
Fir Tree Ho ⑪ SE14...140 C5
Firtree Lodge N21 ......17 A2
Fir Tree Rd TW4.......129 A1
Fir Trees Cl SE16 ......119 A5
Fir Tree Wlk EN1........5 B2
Fir Wlk KT17,SM3 ..... 216 D2
Fisher Cl Croydon CR0. 205 D1
Holdbrook EN3...........7 C6
Southall UB6...........85 C4
Fisherdene KT10.......213 A1
Fisher Ho Islington N1 . 234 A5
⑨ Shadwell E1....... 118 C6
② Tufnell Pk N19 ....71 C5
Fisherman Cl TW10....175 C6
Fishermans Dr SE16 ... 118 D4
Fishermans Wlk SE28 ..123 C4
Fisherman's Wlk E14 ...119 C5
Fisher Rd HA3..........24 D1
Fishers Cl SW16 ...... 159 D1
Fishers Ct London SE14... 140 D4
⑥ Teddington TW11.... 174 D5
Fisher's La W4.........111 B2
Fisher St Holborn WC1 . 240 C3
Newham E16 ....99 A2
Fisherton St NW8 .. 92 B3 236 D6
Fisherton Street Est
NW8............92 B3 236 D5
Fishguard Way E16 .... 122 D5
Fishlock Ct ⑥ SW4 ....138 A3
Fishponds Rd
Keston BR2........... 225 D3
Upper Tooting SW17.... 180 C6
Fish St Hill EC3 .... 252 D5
Fisk Cl TW16......... 171 D4
Fiske Ct Barking IG11 ...101 B5
① Merton SW19 .... 180 A3
Sutton SM2........... 218 A1
Tottenham N17.........34 A2
Fitch Ct London SW2....160 C6
③ Mitcham CR4....... 181 A1
Fitzalan Rd Church End N3 .. 47 B6
Claygate KT10 .... 212 C1
Fitzalan St SE11 ..116 C2 261 A4
Fitzclarence Ho W11.... 244 A2
Fitzgeorge Ave KT2,KT3 ..177 B2
Fitz-George Ave W14 ... 254 A3
Fitzgerald Ave SW14 ...133 C2
Fitzgerald Ct ① E10 ....53 D1
Fitzgerald Ho
⑱ Brixton SW9 ...... 138 C3
Hayes UB3............106 B5
⑭ Poplar E14..........97 D1
Fitzgerald Rd
Mortlake SW14 ....133 B2
Thames Ditton KT7.... 197 A3
Wanstead E11 ....55 A4
Fitzhardinge Ho
Beckenham BR3 ...... 185 D1
Marylebone W1 .... 238 A2
Fitzhardinge St W1 .... 238 A2
Fitzhugh Gr SW18......158 B5

Five Arch Bridge DA14 ...191 A6
Five Arches Bsns Pk
DA14............. 190 D4
Five Elms Prim Sch RM8 ..81 B5
Five Elms Rd
Dagenham RM9.........81 B5
Keston Mark BR2 ...... 225 C5
Five Oaks Mews BR1....165 A1
Fives Ct SE11 .... 261 C5
Fiveways Chislehurst SE9 . 186 C2
Croydon CR0.......... 220 C4
Ruislip HA4............39 B1
Five Ways Bsns Ctr
TW13.............150 B1
Five Ways Cnr NW4 .....28 A2
Fiveways Rd SW9.......138 C3
Flack Cl ⑮ E10 ....53 D2
Fladbury Rd N15........51 B3
Fladgate Rd E11........54 B4
Flag Cl CR0.......... 206 D1
Flag Wlk HA5...........40 A3
Flambard Rd HA1,HA3....43 A3
Flamborough Ho ⑫
SE15.............140 A4
Flamborough Rd HA4....62 A5
Flamborough St E14.....97 A1
Flamingo Ct ② SE8 ....141 C5
Flamingo Gdns UB5.....85 A4
Flamstead Gdns RM9 ....80 C1
Flamstead Rd RM9 .....80 C1
Flamsted Ave HA9......66 C2
Flamsteed Ct ⑱ SE13 ..141 D4
Flamsteed Ho ★ SE10 ..142 B5
Flamsteed Rd SE7 .....122 A1
Flanchford Rd W12 .....111 D3
Flanders Cres SW17 ....180 D4
Flanders Ct E17.........53 A3
Flanders Ho N16........73 C5
Flanders Rd Acton W4 ...111 C2
Wallend E6...........100 C5
Flanders Way E9........74 D2
Flandrian Cl EN3........7 D5
Flank St E1 ⑨ 118 A6
Flansham Ho ② E14 .....97 B1
Flask La EN2............5 A6
Flask Cotts ④ NW3 .....70 B4
Flask Wlk NW3 ....70 B4
Flatford Ho ② SE6......186 A6
Flather Cl ⑫ SW16.....181 C5
Flatiron Sq SE1 .... 252 B3
Flatiron Yd SE1 .... 252 B3
Flavell Mews SE10 .....120 C1
Flaxen Cl E4...........19 D1
Flaxen Rd E4...........19 D1
Flaxley Rd SM4 .... 201 D2
Flaxman Ct
⑫ Belvedere DA17 .... 125 C1
Soho W1............ 239 C1
Flaxman Ho
⑩ Chiswick W4 ...... 111 C1
Newington SE1....... 261 D6
Flaxman Rd SE5 ...... 138 D3
Flaxman Sp Ctr SE5....139 A3
Flaxman Terr
WC1...........93 D4 232 D1
Flaxman Villas N2.......48 A6
Flaxmore Ct Erith DA7 .. 147 D2
South Norwood CR7.... 183 B1
Flaxton Rd SE18 ...... 145 C5
Flecker Cl HA7..........24 D5
Flecker Ho ⑥ SE5 .....139 B5
Fleece Dr N9...........34 A6
Fleecefield Prim Sch
N18..............34 A6
Fleece Rd KT6 .... 197 C1
Fleece Wlk N7..........72 A2
Fleeming Cl E17.........35 B1
Fleeming Rd E17 ....35 B1
Fleet Cl East Molesey KT8 ..195 B4
Ruislip HA4............39 A3
Fleet Ct ① W12.........111 C3
Fleetfield WC1........ 233 B2
Fleet Ho ① Brixton SW2..160 C6
④ Limehouse E14 ..... 119 A6
Fleet Pl EC4......... 241 C2
Fleet Prim Sch ⑮ NW3...70 D3
Fleet Rd NW3..........70 D3
Fleetside KT8......... 195 C4
Fleet Sq WC1........ 233 B1
Fleet St EC4 .... 94 C1 241 B1
Fleet Street Hill ⑩ E1 ...96 A3
Fleet Terr SE6.........164 A4
Fleetway WC1........ 233 B2
Fleetway West Bsns Pk
UB6............87 B5
Fleet Wood ⑥ N16......73 C6
Fleetwood Cl
Chessington KT9 ..... 213 D1
Newham E16 ....99 D2
South Croydon CR0.... 221 D5
Fleetwood Ct
① Newham E16 ...... 100 B2
Orpington BR6....... 226 C4
⑧ Stanwell TW19 ..... 148 A5
Fleetwood Rd
Kingston u T KT3 ..... 198 D6
Willesden NW10........68 A3
Fleetwood Sq KT3 .... 198 D6
Fleetwood St N16.......73 C6

Fleetwood Way WD19 .....22 C6
Fleming Cl ④ W9........91 C3
Fleming Ct Croydon CR0...220 C4
Paddington W2........ 236 C4
Fleming Dr N21..........16 B6
Fleming Ho
⑭ Bermondsey SE16....118 A4
Finsbury Pk N4.........51 A1
⑤ Wembley HA9........67 A5
Fleming Mead CR4.....180 D3
Fleming Rd
Camberwell SE17 .....138 D6
Southall UB1..........86 A1
Fleming Way
Isleworth TW7.........130 D1
Thamesmead SE28.....124 D6
Fleming Wlk NW9.......27 C1
Flemming Ave HA4......62 B6
Flempton Rd E10 ....53 A1
Fletcher Bldgs WC2 ... 240 B1
Fletcher Cl E16 ....122 D6
Fletcher Ct ⑨ NW5.....71 B4
Fletcher Ho ⑯ N16 .....73 C4
Fletcher La E10.........54 A2
Fletcher Path ⑦ SE8....141 C5
Fletcher Rd W4........111 A3
Fletchers Cl BR2.......209 B5
Fletcher St ⑯ E1......118 A6
Fletching Rd
Charlton SE7.........143 D6
Lower Clapton E5 ......74 C5
Fletton Rd N11 ....32 A3
Fleur De Lis St E1 .... 243 C5
Fleur Gates ⑦ SW19 ...156 D4
Flexmere Rd N17 ....33 C2
Flimwell Cl BR1........186 C5
Flinders Ho ㉘ E1......118 B5
Flint Cl
⑧ Green Street Green
BR6.............227 D2
① Stratford E15........76 D1
Flint Ct CR0..........204 B3
Flint Down Cl BR5 .....190 A2
Flintmill Cres SE3,SE9...144 A3
Flinton St SE17 ....117 C1 263 B2
Flint St SE17........117 B2 262 D3
Flitcroft St WC2....... 239 D1
Flitton Ho ⑦ N1........72 D1
Floathaven Cl SE28....124 A5
Flock Mill Pl SW18....157 D3
Flockton St
⑳ Bermondsey SE16....118 A4
③ Bermondsey SE16....118 A4
Flodden Rd SE5........139 A4
Flood La ⑤ TW1........153 A3
Flood St SW3.....136 C6 267 B6
Flood Wlk SW3....136 C6 267 B6
Flora Cl Edgware HA7....10 A1
Poplar E14............97 D1
Flora Gardens Prim Sch ⑰
W6.............112 B2
Flora Gdns Dagenham RM6..58 C3
③ Hammersmith W6....112 B2
Floral St WC2....116 A6 250 A6
Flora St DA17.........125 B1
Florence Ave Enfield EN2 ...5 A2
Morden SM4..........202 A4
Florence Cl KT12 .....194 B2
Florence Ct
⑱ New Barnet EN5 .....13 C6
St John's Wood W9.... 229 B1
Wanstead E11 ....55 C5
⑤ Wimbledon SW19 ...179 A4
Florence Dr EN2 ....5 A2
Florence Elson Cl E12...78 C4
Florence Gdns
Chiswick W4 ....133 A6
Ilford RM6............58 C2
Florence Ho
⑳ Bermondsey SE16....118 B1
② Brixton SW2 .... 160 B6
Kidbrooke SE18 ......144 B4
⑤ Kingston u T KT2...176 B3
⑩ Shepherd's Bush W11...112 D6
⑦ Wandsworth SW18...136 B1
Florence Mans
Fulham SW6 .... 264 C2
④ Hendon NW4........46 B4
Florence Nightingale Ho ⑭
N1..............73 A2
Florence Nightingale Mus★
SE1..............250 D1
Florence Rd
Abbey Wood SE2......124 C2
Acton W4............111 B3
⑤ Beckenham BR3 ....185 A1
Bromley BR1..........187 A2
Ealing W5............110 A6
Feltham TW13.........150 B3
Finsbury Pk N4.........50 C2
⑥ Kingston u T KT2...176 B3
New Cross Gate SE14...141 B4
Southall UB2..........106 D3
⑦ Upton Pk E6.........99 C6
Walton-on-T KT12 ....194 B2
West Ham E13 ....99 A5
Wimbledon SW19 .....179 A4
Florence Root Ho ③ IG4..56 M4
Florence St Islington N1...72 D1
London NW4...........46 C5

Florence St continued
Newham E16 ....98 D3
Florence Terr
Kingston u T SW15 .... 155 C1
New Cross Gate SE14...141 B4
Florence Way SW12....158 D3
Florence White Ct N9 ....18 B1
Florentine Ho ③ IG1....78 D6
Flores Ho ⑬ E1.........96 D2
Florey Sq N21 ....16 B6
Florfield Rd E8.........74 B2
Florian SE5..........139 C4
Florian Ave SM1.......218 B4
Florian Rd SW15.......135 A1
Florida Cl WD23.........8 B2
Florida Ct BR2........208 D5
Florida Rd CR7........182 D2
Florida St E2...........96 A4
Florida State Univ
WC1...........93 D2 239 D3
Florin Ct Bermondsey SE1. 253 C1
Edmonton N18 ....33 C6
⑧ St George in t East SE1 . 118 A6
Floris Pl ⑦ SW4 ......137 C2
Floriston Ave UB10......61 A1
Floriston Cl HA7.......25 B2
Floriston Ct UB5.......63 D3
Floriston Gdns HA7.....25 B2
Florys Ct ⑦ SW19.....157 A3
Floss St SW11.........134 C3
Flower & Dean Wlk E1.. 243 D3
Flower La NW7.........27 D4
Flower Mews NW11......47 A3
Flowerpot Cl N15.......51 D3
Flower Pot Cl N15.......51 D3
Flowers Cl NW2........68 A5
Flowersmead SW17.....159 A2
Flowers Mews ① N19...71 C6
Flower Wlk The
SW7...........114 A4 246 B2
Floyd Rd SE7.........121 C1
Floyer Cl TW10........154 B6
Fludyer St SE13.......142 C1
Flynn Ct ⑲ E14 ....119 C6
Fogerty Cl EN3 ....7 D6
Foley Cotts KT10 ......212 D2
Foley Cl N12...........30 A5
Foley Ho ⑲ E1........96 C1
Foley Mews KT10 ......212 C2
Foley Rd KT10 ....212 C1
Foley St W1......93 C2 239 A3
Folgate St E1.....95 D2 243 C4
Foliot Ho N1..........233 C4
Foliot St W12...........89 D1
Folkestone Ct UB5.......63 D3
Folkestone Rd
Edmonton N18 ....34 A6
Wallend E6...........100 C4
Walthamstow E17 ......53 D5
Folkingham La ⑥ NW9...27 C2
Folkington Cnr N12......29 B5
Folland ⑥ NW9.........27 D1
Follett Ho SW10 ......266 C4
Follett St E14..........98 A1
Folly La Higham Hill E17...35 A4
Walthamstow E4 ....35 B3
Folly's End Christian Sch
CR2.............221 C4
Folly Wall E14 ....120 A4
Fonda Ct ⑭ E14 ......119 C6
Fontaine Ct
③ Beckenham BR3 ....185 B2
Southgate N14 ....15 D2
Fontaine Rd SW16.....182 B3
Fontarabia Rd SW11...137 A1
Fontenelle SE5........139 C4
Fontenoy Ho SE11 .... 261 C3
Fontenoy Rd SW12,
SW17.............159 C2
Fonteyne Gdns IG8......37 D1
Fonthill Cl ⑤ SE20.....184 A1
Fonthill Ct SE23.......162 C4
Fonthill Ho
Kensington W14 ...... 254 B6
Pimlico SW1......... 258 D2
Fonthill Mews N4.......72 B6
Fonthill Rd N4.........72 C6
Font Hills N2...........30 A1
Fontley Way SW15.....156 A4
Fontmell Cl TW15......170 A5
Fontmell Pk TW15......170 C5
Fontwell Cl Harrow HA3...24 C3
Northolt UB5 ....63 C2
Fontwell Dr BR2.......210 C4
Football La HA1.........42 C1
Footpath The SW15.....156 A6
FOOTS CRAY..........190 B4
Foots Cray High St
DA14.............190 D4
Foots Cray La DA14.....168 C3
Footscray Rd SE9......166 D3
Forber Ho ⑤ E2........96 C4
Forbes Cl NW2.........68 A5
Forbes Ct SE19.......183 C5
Forbes Ho ② W4 ......110 C1
Forbes St E1..........96 A1
Forbes Way HA4........62 B6
Forburg Rd N16.........52 A1
Fordbridge Ct TW15....170 A4

Fordbridge Rd
Ashford TW15.........170 B5
Lower Halliford TW16,
TW17.............193 D3
Sunbury TW16........194 A5
Fordbridge Rdbt TW15..170 A4
Ford Cl Ashford TW15....170 A4
⑫ Bow E3.............97 A5
Harrow HA1 ....42 B2
Littleton TW17........192 C4
Thornton Heath CR7....204 D4
Fordcombe ⑬ NW5.....71 A2
Forde Ave BR1........209 C6
Fordel Rd SE6.........164 B3
Ford End IG8...........37 B4
Fordham ④ KT1 ......176 C1
Fordham Cl
Cockfosters EN4........2 C2
North Cheam KT4.....200 B1
Fordham Ho ⑮ SE14...141 A5
Fordham Rd EN4.........2 C2
Fordham St ⑬ E1.......96 A1
Ford Ho
② New Barnet EN5 .....13 D6
② Woolwich SE18 .....122 D1
Fordhook Ave W5.......110 C6
Fordingley Ho W9.......91 B4
Fordington Ho ② SE26..162 B1
Fordington Rd N6.......48 D5
Fordmill Rd SE6.......163 C2
Ford Rd Ashford TW15...170 B6
Bow E3................97 B5
Dagenham RM10........81 C1
Ford's Gr N21..........17 A3
Fords Park Rd E16......99 A1
Ford Sq E1.............96 B2
Ford St Bow E3.........97 A5
Canning Town E16......98 D1
Fordwich Cl BR6......211 D2
Fordwych Ct NW2.......69 A2
Fordwych Rd NW2.......69 A3
Fordyce Ho ③ SW16...181 C6
Fordyce Rd SE13.......164 A6
Fordyke Rd RM8........81 B6
Forecastle Ct E14......119 C4
Foreign & Commonwealth
Office SW1.........250 A2
Foreland Ct NW4.......29 A2
Foreland Ho W11...... 244 A6
Foreland St SE18.......123 B2
Foreshore SE8.........119 B2
Fore St
Barbican EC2 .....95 A3 242 B3
Edmonton N18 ....34 A6
Pinner HA5............40 A4
Forest App Chingford E4...20 C4
Woodford IG8..........38 A3
Forest Ave E4.........20 C4
Forest Bsns Pk E17.....52 D2
Forest Cl
Brondesbury NW6......69 A1
Chislehurst BR7.......188 C2
Wanstead E11 ....55 A4
Woodford IG8..........37 B6
Forest Ct Chingford E4...20 D3
Leytonstone E11.......54 C5
⑭ Woodside Pk N12...29 D6
Forestdale N14.........31 D6
Forestdale Ctr The CR0..223 B1
Forestdale Prim Sch
CR0.............223 B1
Forest Dene Ct ② SM2..218 A2
Forest Dr Ashford TW16..171 D3
Chingford IG8..........36 C3
Keston Mark BR2 .....226 A4
Wanstead E12 ....77 D5
Forest Dr E E11.........54 B3
Forest Dr W E11.........54 B2
Forest Edge IG9 ....21 D1
Forester Rd SE15......140 B2
Foresters Cl SM6......219 D1
Foresters Cres DA7 ....147 D1
Foresters Dr
Wallington SM6........219 D1
Walthamstow E17 ......54 B5
Foresters Homes The
DA7.............147 D1
Foresters Prim Sch
SM6.............219 D1
FOREST GATE..........77 A3
Forest Gate NW9 ....45 C4
Forest Gate Com Sch E7 ..77 A3
Forest Gate Sta E7......77 A3
Forest Gdns N17.......33 C1
Forest Glade Chingford E4...36 C5
Leytonstone E11.......54 C5
Forest Gr E8...........73 D2
FOREST HILL..........163 A3
Forest Hill SE23.......162 C3
Forest Hill Bsns Ctr
SE23.............162 C2
Forest Hill Ct ⑥ SE26..162 C2
Forest Hill Ind Est SE23..162 C2
Forest Hill Rd SE23.....162 B2
Forest Hill Sec Sch
SE23.............162 D1
Forest Hill Sta SE23....162 C2

Forest Ho 9 E4..............20 C4
Forestholme Cl SE23.....162 C2
Forest Ho The SE23.......163 A3
Forest Hts IG9.............21 A2
Forest La E7, E15..........76 D3
Forest Lawns BR1.........187 C2
Forest Lea 3 E11..........54 D2
Forest Lo 1 SE23.........162 C1
Forest Mount Rd IG8......36 B3
Forest Point E7............77 B3
Forest Rd Dalston E8......73 D2
   Edmonton N9.............18 B3
   Feltham TW13............150 C1
   Forest Gate E7............77 A4
   Leytonstone E11..........54 B2
   Morden SM3, SM4.......201 C2
   Richmond TW9...........132 C5
   Romford RM7.............59 D6
   Walthamstow E17........53 C6
   Woodford IG8.............21 A1
Fore Street Ave EC2......242 C3
Forest Ridge
   Beckenham BR3..........207 C6
   Bromley BR2.............226 B4
Forest Rise E17............54 B5
Forest Sch E17............54 C5
Forest Side
   Buckhurst Hill IG9.........21 C3
   Chingford E4..............20 D3
   Forest Gate E7............77 B4
   New Malden KT4.........199 D1
Forest St E7...............77 A3
Forest The E11............54 C5
Forest Trad Est E17.......52 D6
Forest View Chingford E4...20 B4
   Leytonstone E11..........54 D2
Forest View Ave E10......54 B4
Forest View Rd
   Chingford E17.............36 A2
   Manor Pk E12.............78 A4
Forest Way
   Orpington BR5............211 D4
   Sidcup DA15.............167 B4
   9 Upper Holloway N19...71 C6
   Woodford IG8.............37 B6
Forest Wlk N10............31 B2
Forfar Rd
   London SW11.......137 A4 268 B2
   Tottenham N22...........32 D2
Forge Cl Harlington UB3...127 B6
   Hayes BR2...............209 A1
Forge Cotts W5............109 D5
Forge Dr KT10............213 A1
Forge La Belmont SM3.....217 A1
   Feltham TW13............173 A5
   Richmond TW10..........154 A3
   Sunbury TW16............194 A6
Forge Lane Prim Sch
   TW13....................173 A5
Forge Lo 2 TW7..........131 A2
Forge Mews
   Addington CR0...........223 C3
   Sunbury TW16............194 A6
Forge Pl NW1..............71 A2
Forlong Path UB5..........63 A2
Forman Ct TW1............152 D3
Forman Ho SE4............140 D1
Formby Ave HA3, HA7......43 C6
Formby Ct 9 N7...........72 C3
Formosa Ho 1 E1...........97 A3
Formosa St W9.............91 D3
Formunt Cl E16.............98 D2
Forres Gdns NW11.........47 C3
Forrest Ct N7..............72 C2
Forrester Path SE26.......184 C6
Forresters The HA5.........40 B3
Forrest Gdns SW16........204 B6
Forrest Ho SW15..........134 C3
Forris Ave UB3............105 D5
Forset Cl W1...............237 B2
Forset St W1.......92 C1 237 B2
Forstal Cl BR2.............209 A6
Forster Cl IG8...............36 B3
Forster Ho SE6............164 B1
Forster Park Prim Sch
   SE6.....................164 C1
Forster Rd
   Beckenham BR3..........207 A6
   Streatham SW2...........160 A4
   Thornton Heath CR0......205 A2
   Tottenham N17............51 D6
   Walthamstow E17.........53 A3
Forsters Cl RM6............59 B3
Forsters Way UB4..........84 B1
Forston St N1.......95 A5 235 B4
Forsyte Cres SE19.........183 C2
Forsyte Ct KT2............176 D2
Forsyth Ct
   13 Dagenham RM10.......81 D2
   Harrow HA1...............42 B3
   Kingston u T KT3.........177 C1
Forsythe Shades BR3......186 A2
Forsyth Gdns SE17........138 D6
Forsyth Ho 14 Hackney E9...74 C1
   Pimlico SW1..............259 B3
Forsythia Cl IG1............78 D3
Forsythia Ho SE4..........141 A2

Forsyth Pl EN1.............17 C6
Forterie Gdns IG3..........80 A4
Fortescue Ave
   1 Hackney E8.............74 B1
   Twickenham TW2.........152 A1
Fortescue Rd
   Burnt Oak HA8............27 B3
   Mitcham SW19...........180 B3
Fortess Gr NW5............71 C3
Fortess Rd NW5............71 C4
Fortess Wlk NW5...........71 B3
Forthbridge Rd SW11......137 A1
Forth Ho 30 E3.............97 B5
Forties The 9 NW5.........71 C3
Fortior Ct N6...............49 C2
Fortis Cl E16...............99 C1
Fortis Ct N10...............49 A6
Fortis Gn N2, N10...........48 D6
FORTIS GREEN.............48 D5
Fortis Green Ave N2.......48 D5
Fortis Green Cotts N2......48 D6
Fortismere Ave N10........49 A6
Fortismere Sch N10.........30 D1
Fortismere Sch (South Wing)
   N10.....................49 A6
Fortnam Rd N19............71 D6
Fortnums Acre HA7........24 D4
Fort Rd
   Bermondsey SE1...117 D2 263 D3
   Northolt UB5..............63 C1
Fortrose Cl E14.............98 B1
Fortrose Gdns SW12,
   SW2....................160 A3
Fort St Broadgate E1.......243 B3
   Newham E16.............121 B5
Fortuna Cl N7..............72 B2
Fortune Ave HA8...........26 D2
Fortune Ct Barking IG11....102 B5
   6 Dalston E8..............73 D1
Fortune Gate Rd NW10.....89 C6
Fortune Green Rd NW6.....69 C4
Fortune Ho Lambeth SE11...261 A3
   St Luke's EC1.............242 B5
Fortune La WD6.............8 A6
Fortunes Mead UB5.........63 A2
Fortune St EC1......95 A3 242 B5
Fortune Way NW10.........90 A4
Fortune Wlk 4 SE28.......123 B3
Forty Acre La E16..........99 A2
Forty Ave HA9..............66 B6
Forty Cl HA9...............66 B5
Forty Hall Mus & Gdns *
   EN2......................5 D6
FORTY HILL................5 D4
Forty Hill EN2...............5 D5
Forty Hill CE Prim Sch
   EN2......................6 A6
Forty Hill Ho EN1...........5 D5
Forty La HA9...............66 D6
Forum Cl 7 E3..............97 C6
Forumside HA8.............26 C4
Forum The KT8............195 D5
Forval Cl CR4.............202 D4
Forward Bsns Ctr The 3
   E16.....................98 B3
Forward Dr HA3............42 D5
Fosbrooke Ho SW8........270 A3
Fosbury Ho 9 SW9........138 B1
Fosbury Mews W2.........245 D5
Foscote Mews W9..........91 C2
Foscote Rd NW4............46 B3
Foskett Ho 21 N2...........30 B1
Foskett Rd SW6...........135 B3
Foss Ave CR0, CR9........220 C3
Fossdene Prim Sch 4
   SE7....................121 B1
Fossdene Rd SE7..........121 B1
Fossdyke Cl UB4...........85 A2
Fosse Way W13.............87 A2
Fossil Rd SE13............141 C2
Fossington Rd DA17......124 D2
Foss Rd SW17.............180 B6
Fossway RM8...............80 C2
Foster Ct
   6 Camden Town NW1......71 C1
   Canning Town E16........120 D6
   Hendon NW4..............46 C5
Foster Ho SE14...........141 B4
Foster La EC2.......95 A1 242 A2
Foster Rd Acton W3........111 C6
   Chiswick W4..............111 B1
   Newham E13..............99 A2
Fosters Cl Elmstead BR7...188 B5
   Woodford E18.............37 B2
Fosters Old Sch DA16.....146 B2
Foster's Prim Sch DA16...146 C2
Foster St NW4..............46 C5
Foster Wlk NW4............46 C5
Fothergill Cl E13............99 A5
Fothergill Dr N21............16 A6
Fotheringham Ct E1.........5 D1
Fotheringham Rd EN1.......5 D1
Foubert's Pl W1...........239 A1
Foulden Rd N16.............73 D4
Foulden Terr N16............73 D4
Foulis Terr SW7.......114 B1 256 D2
Foulser Rd SW17..........159 A1
Foulsham Rd CR7..........205 B6
Foundary Ho 6 E14.........97 D2
Founder Cl 2 E6..........100 D1

Founders Cl UB5............85 B4
Founders Ct EC2..........242 C2
Founders Gdns SE19......183 A3
Founders Ho SW1.........259 C2
Foundling Ct WC1.........240 A6
Foundling Mus The *
   WC1.................94 A3 240 B6
Foundry Cl SE16...........119 A5
Foundry Mews NW1.......239 B6
Foundry Pl Stepney E1......96 C2
   Wandsworth SW18.......157 D4
Fountain Cl UB8............83 A2
Fountain Ct
   Belgravia SW1...........258 C3
   Blackfen DA15...........168 B5
   New Malden KT3..........199 A5
   5 Penge SE26...........184 C4
   14 Shepherd's Bush W11...112 D4
   Strand EC4..............251 A6
Fountain Dr
   Dulwich SE19.............183 D6
   Wallington SM5..........218 D1
Fountain Green Sq 34
   SE16....................118 A4
Fountain Ho
   33 Bermondsey SE16.....118 A4
   3 Brondesbury Pk NW6....69 A1
   Mayfair W1..............248 A4
   5 Mitcham SW19.........180 D1
Fountain Mews
   1 Highbury N5.............73 A4
   Maitland Pk NW3..........70 D2
Fountain Pl SW9..........138 C4
Fountain Rd
   South Norwood CR7.......183 A1
   Upper Tooting SW17......180 B6
Fountains Ave TW13.......151 B1
Fountains Cl TW13.........151 B1
Fountains Cres N14.........16 A4
Fountains The London N3...29 B3
   Loughton IG10............21 D4
Fountayne Bsns Ctr N15...52 A5
Fountayne Rd
   South Tottenham N15......52 A5
   Stoke Newington N16......74 A6
Fount St SW8.......137 D5 269 D3
Fouracres EN3...............7 A4
Four Acres N12.............29 D6
Fourland Wlk HA8...........27 A4
Fournier St E1.......95 D2 243 D4
Fourscore Mans E8.........74 A1
Four Seasons Cl E3.........97 C5
Four Seasons Cres SM3....217 B6
Four Square Ct TW4........151 C5
Fourth Ave Hayes UB3.....105 D5
   Ilford E12.................78 B4
   West Kilburn W10.........91 A4
Fourth Cross Rd TW2......152 B2
Fourth Way Wembley HA9...66 D4
   Wembley HA9.............67 A4
Four Tubs The WD23........8 B4
Fourways 2 N7.............20 B2
Four Wents The E4..........20 B2
Fovant Ct 5 SW8..........137 C3
Fowey Ave IG4..............55 D4
Fowey Cl E1...............118 B5
Fowey Ho SE11............261 B2
Fowler Cl London SW11....136 B2
   Sidcup DA14.............191 A5
Fowler Ho
   5 Camberwell SE5........139 C3
   Islington N1........94 D6 234 D6
   South Lambeth SW8......269 D1
   West Green N15...........51 B4
Fowler Rd Forest Gate E7...77 A4
   Islington N1........94 D6 234 D6
   Mitcham CR4.............181 A1
Fowler's Wlk W5............87 D3
Fownes St SW11...........136 C2
Fox and Knot St EC1......241 D4
Foxberry Ct SE4...........141 B1
Foxberry Rd SE4..........141 A2
Foxborough Gdns SE4....163 C6
Foxbourne Rd SW17.......159 A2
Foxbury Cl BR1............187 B4
Foxbury Rd BR1...........187 B4
Fox Cl Bethnal Green E1.....96 C3
   Elstree WD6...............9 D5
   Newham E16..............99 A2
Foxcombe CR0............223 D2
Foxcombe Cl 1 E6...........99 D5
Foxcombe Rd 6 SW15......156 A3
Foxcote SE5..............263 B1
Foxcroft WC1.............233 D3
Foxcroft Rd SE18..........144 D4
Foxcroft Rd SE18..........144 D4
Foxdene Cl 12 E18..........55 B6
Foxes Dale
   Beckenham BR2...........208 B6
   Blackheath Pk SE3.......143 A2
Foxfield NW1..............231 D5
Foxfield Prim Sch SE18....123 A1
Foxfield Rd BR6............227 B6
Foxglove Cl Bexley DA15...168 A5
   Edmonton N9..............18 C3
   Southall UB1.............107 A6
Foxglove Ct 11 HA0.........88 A5
Foxglove Gdns E11..........55 C5
Foxglove La KT9...........214 C4

Foxglove Path SE28........123 C5
Foxglove St W12...........111 D6
Foxglove Way SM6.........203 B1
Fox Gr KT12...............194 B2
Foxgrove N14...............16 A1
Foxgrove Ave BR3..........185 D3
Foxgrove Path WD19........22 D5
Foxgrove Rd BR3..........186 A3
Foxham Rd N19.............71 D5
   Penge SE19..............183 D3
Fox Hill Keston BR2........225 C3
   Penge SE19..............183 D3
Fox Hill Gdns SE19.........183 D3
Fox Ho 2 London SW11....136 B1
   Northolt UB5..............85 A6
Foxhole Rd 2 SE9...........166 A6
Fox Hollow Cl 1 SE18.......123 C1
Fox Hollow Dr DA7.........146 D2
Foxhome Gdns NW10........67 A1
Foxhome Cl BR7............188 C4
Fox House Rd DA17........125 D1
Fox La Ealing W5.............88 A3
   Keston BR2..............225 C3
   Palmers Green N13........16 B1
Foxlees HA0................65 A4
Foxley Cl E8................74 A3
Foxley Ct SM2.............218 A1
Foxley Ho 4 E3.............97 C4
Foxley Rd
   Camberwell SW9..........138 D5
   Thornton Heath CR7......204 D5
Foxley Sq 3 SW9..........138 D4
Foxmead Cl EN2..............4 B2
Foxmore St SW11.........267 C1
Fox Prim Sch
   W8.................113 C5 245 A3
Fox Rd E16.................98 D2
Foxs Path CR4.............180 C1
Fox's Yd E2...............243 D6
Foxtail Ho TW3............130 A4
Foxton KT1................198 C6
Foxton Gr CR4.............180 B1
Foxton Ho E16.............122 C4
Foxwarren KT10...........212 D1
Foxwell Mews SE4.........141 A2
Foxwell St SE4............141 A2
Foxwood Cl Edgware NW7...27 C6
   Feltham TW13...........150 B1
Foxwood Green Cl EN1.....17 C5
Foxwood Rd SE3...........142 D1
Foyle Rd Greenwich SE3...142 D6
   Tottenham N17............34 A2
Fradel Lo N16..............51 B1
Framfield Cl N12............13 C1
Framfield Ct EN1...........17 C5
Framfield Rd Ealing W7......86 D1
   Islington N5...............72 D3
   Mitcham CR4.............181 A3
Framlingham Cl 2 E5........74 C6
Framlingham Cres SE9.....188 B6
Framlingham Ct 5 RM6......58 B4
Frampton NW1..............71 D1
Frampton Cl SM2...........217 C1
Frampton Ct 3 W3..........111 A4
Frampton Ho NW8..........236 D5
Frampton Park Rd E9........74 C1
Frampton Rd TW4...........151 A6
Frampton St NW8...92 B3 236 D5
Francemary Rd SE4.........163 C6
Frances Ct
   South Norwood SE25......183 D1
   Walthamstow E17..........53 C3
Frances & Dick James Ct 2
   NW7....................29 A3
Frances Rd E4..............35 C4
Frances St SE18...........122 B2
Franche Court Rd SW17....158 A1
Francis Ave
   Bexleyheath DA7..........147 C3
   Feltham TW13............150 A1
   Ilford IG1.................79 B6
Francis Barber Cl SW16....182 B6
Franciscan Prim Sch 3
   SW17...................181 A5
Franciscan Rd SW17.......181 A6
Francis Chichester Way
   SW11..............137 A4 268 B1
Francis Cl
   6 Cubitt Town E14........120 B2
   Littleton TW17...........192 C5
   West Ewell KT19.........215 B4
Francis Ct
   12 Deptford SE14........140 D6
   Ealing W5...............110 B6
   Edgware NW7.............27 D5
   Kingston u T KT5.........198 A5
Francis Gr SW19...........179 B4
Francis Ho
   Harlesden NW10..........89 D6
   11 Shoreditch N1..........95 C6
   Walham Green SW10......265 D4
Francis Holland Sch
   Belgravia SW1......115 A2 258 B3
   Marylebone NW1.....92 D3 237 C6
Francis Rd Fortis Green N2...48 D5
   Harrow HA1...............43 A4
   Hounslow TW4............128 D3
   Ilford IG1.................79 B6
   Leyton E10................76 A6
   Pinner HA5................40 C4
   Thornton Heath CR0.......204 D2

Francis Rd continued
   Wallington SM6...........219 C2
   Wembley UB6..............87 C6
Francis Snary Lo 11
   SW18..................157 C2
Francis St Ilford IG1..........79 B6
   Stratford E15.............76 C3
   Westminster SW1...115 C2 259 B4
Francis Terr N19.............71 C5
Francis Terrace Mews 16
   N19.....................71 C5
Francis Wlk N1............233 C6
Francklyn Gdns HA8........10 C1
Franconia Rd SW4.........159 D6
Frank Bailey Wlk E12........78 C2
Frank Barnes Sch 18
   NW3.....................70 B1
Frank Beswick Ho SW6....264 C5
Frank Burton Cl 5 SE7.....121 B1
Frank Dixon Cl SE21.......161 C3
Frank Dixon Way SE21....161 C3
Frankfurt Rd SE24.........161 A6
Frank Godley Ct DA14......190 B5
Frankham Ho 8 SE8........141 C5
Frankham St SE8...........141 C5
Frank Ho SW8.............270 A4
Frankland Cl
   Bermondsey SE16........118 B2
   Woodford IG8..............37 C5
Frankland Ho 4 SW12.....159 B4
Frankland Rd
   Brompton SW7......114 B3 256 C5
   Chingford E4...............35 C5
Franklin Bldg 5 E14.......119 C4
Franklin Cl
   Greenwich SE13..........141 D4
   Kingston u T KT1.........198 C6
   Oakleigh Pk N20...........14 A4
   West Norwood SE27......160 D1
Franklin Cres CR4..........203 C5
Franklin Ho
   Beckenham BR2..........208 C6
   New Cross SE4...........141 A3
   28 Wapping E1............118 B5
   West Hendon NW9.........45 D2
Franklin Ind Est SE20......184 C2
Franklin Pas SE9...........144 A2
Franklin Pl SE13...........141 D4
Franklin Rd
   Bexleyheath DA7..........147 A4
   Penge SE20..............184 C3
   Walton-on-T KT12........194 A3
Franklins Mews HA2........64 A6
Franklin Sq SW5...........254 D1
Franklin's Row
   SW3................114 D1 257 D2
Franklin St 13 Bromley E3...97 D4
   South Tottenham N15......51 C3
Franklin Way CR0.........204 A2
Franklyn Rd
   Walton-on-T KT12........194 B3
   Willesden NW10...........67 D2
Franks Ave KT3............199 A5
Franks Ho TW7............131 B1
Frank Slater Ho 4 IG3......58 B1
Frank Soskice Ho SW6.....264 D5
Frank St 5 E13.............99 A3
Frankswood Ave
   Hillingdon UB7.............82 B1
   Petts Wood BR2, BR5.....211 A4
Frank Towell Ct TW14......150 A3
Frank Welch Ct HA5.........40 C5
Frank Whymark Ho 4
   SE16...................118 C4
Franlaw Cres N13...........33 A6
Frans Ct HA4................40 A1
Fransfield Gr SE26.........162 B1
Frans Hals Ct E14..........120 B3
Franshams WD23............8 C2
Frant Cl SE20.............184 C3
Franthorne Way SE6.......163 D1
Frant Rd CR7..............204 D4
Fraserburgh Ho 29 E3......97 B5
Fraser Cl 3 E6.............100 A1
Fraser Ct Battersea SW11...267 A2
   Heston TW3..............129 A5
Fraser Ho Brentford TW8...110 B1
   40 Clapham SW8.........137 D3
   3 Woolwich SE18.........122 C2
Fraser Rd Edmonton N9......18 B1
   Walthamstow E17.........53 D3
   Wembley UB6..............87 C6
Fraser Regnart Ct 12
   NW5....................70 D3
Fraser St W4..............111 C1
Frating Cres IG8............37 B4
Frazer Ave HA4.............62 C3
Frazier St SE1.......116 C4 251 A1
Freame Ho N21.............17 B5
Frean St SE16.............118 A3
Frearson Ho WC1..........233 D2
Freda Corbett Cl 10
   SE15...................140 A5
Frederica Rd E4.............20 B4
Frederica St 4 N7...........72 B1
Frederick Blg N1.............73 C2
Frederick Bremer Sec Sch
   E17.....................54 C1
Frederick Charrington Ho 4
   E1......................96 C3

Frederick Cl Cheam SM1 . .**217** B3
Marylebone W2 . . **114** D6 **247** C6
Frederick Cres
Camberwell SW9 . . . . **138** D5
Enfield EN3 . . . . .6 C3
Frederick Ct SW6 . . . .**135** A2
Frederick Gdns
Cheam SM1 . . . .**217** B3
Thornton Heath CR0 . . . . **204** D3
Frederick Ho
Ashford TW15 . . . .**170** A6
Southall UB1 . . . .**107** B6
Woolwich SE7 . . . .**122** A3
Frederick Pl SE18 . . . .**122** D1
Frederick Rd SM1 . . . .**217** B3
Frederick's Pl
City of London EC2 . . . .**242** C1
North Finchley N12 . . . . .30 A6
Frederick Sq **11** SE16 . . . . .**119** A6
Frederick's Row EC1 . . . . .**234** C2
Frederick St WC1 . . **94** B4 **233** C1
Frederick Terr E8 . . . .**73** D1
Frederic Mews SW1 . . . . . .**248** A1
Fredora Ave UB4 . . . .**83** D3
Fred Styles Ho SE7 . . . .**143** C6
Fred Wigg Twr E11 . . . .**76** D6
Fred Tibble Ct RM9 . . . .**81** A4
Freedom Cl E17 . . . .**53** A5
Freedom Rd N17 . . . . .33 B1
Freedom St SW11 . . . .**136** D3
Freegrove Rd N7 . . . .**72** A3
Freehold Ind Ctr TW4 . . . .**150** C6
Freeland Ct W5 . . . .**110** B6
Freeland Pk N3 . . . . .29 A1
Freeland Rd W5 . . . .**110** B6
Freelands Ave UB4 . . . . . .**222** D1
Freelands Gr BR1 . . . .**187** B2
Freelands Rd BR1 . . . .**187** B2
Freeling Ho NW8 . . . .**229** C6
Freeling St **7** N1 . . . .**72** D1
Freeman Cl Northolt UB5 . . .63 A1
Upper Halliford TW17 . . . . .**193** C5
Freeman Ct SW16 . . . .**182** A1
Freeman Dr KT8 . . . .**195** B5
Freeman Ho **13** SW2 . . . . . .**160** A4
Freeman Rd SM4 . . . .**202** B4
Freemans La UB3 . . . .**105** C6
Freemantle Ave EN3 . . . . . . .18 D6
Freemantle St
SE17 . . . .**117** C1 **263** A6
Freemasons Pl **6** CR0 . .**205** C1
Freemasons Rd E16 . . . . . . .99 B1
Freemason's Rd CR0 . . . . .**205** C1
Freemens Hos **1** SW9 . . . .**138** B1
Freesia Cl BR6 . . . .**227** D3
Freethorpe Cl SE19 . . . . . .**183** C2
Freke Rd SW11 . . . .**137** A2
Fremantle Ho **14** E1 . . . . . . .96 B3
Fremantle Rd
Belvedere DA17 . . . .**125** C1
Ilford IG6 . . . . .57 A6
Fremont St E9 . . . . .96 C6
French Gdns KT12 . . . .**195** B1
French Inst The
SW7 . . . .**114** B2 **256** C4
French Pl E1 . . . .**243** B6
French St TW16 . . . .**172** C1
Frendsbury Rd SE4 . . . . . .**141** A1
Frensham Cl UB1 . . . . .85 B4
Frensham Ct
Canonbury N5 . . . . .73 A3
1 London NW9 . . . . .46 A5
Mitcham CR4 . . . .**202** B6
Frensham Dr
New Addington CR0 . . . . . .**224** A1
Roehampton SW15 . . . .**156** A2
Frensham Ho **7** KT6 . . . . . .**198** A4
Frensham Rd SE9 . . . .**167** B2
Frensham St SE15 . . . .**140** A6
Frere St **6** SW11 . . . .**136** C3
Fresham Ho BR2 . . . .**208** D6
Freshfield Ave E8 . . . . .73 D1
Freshfield Cl SE13 . . . .**142** B1
Freshfield Dr N14 . . . . .15 B4
Freshfields CR0 . . . .**207** B1
Freshford St
SW18 . . . .**158** A1
Freshwater Cl SW17 . . . . .**181** A4
Freshwater Ct UB1 . . . . . . .85 C4
Freshwater Rd
Dagenham RM8 . . . . .59 A1
Streatham SW17 . . . .**181** A4
Freshwell Ave RM6 . . . . . . .58 C5
Fresh Wharf Est IG11 . . . . .**100** D6
Fresh Wharf Rd IG11 . . . . .**100** D5
Freshwood Cl BR3 . . . .**185** D2
Freston Gdns EN4 . . . . .15 A6
Freston Pk N3 . . . . .29 B1
Freston Rd W10,W11 . . . . .**112** D6
Freswick Ho **6** SE8 . . . . . .**119** A2
Freta Rd DA6 . . . .**169** B6
Freud Mus The **1** NW3 . . . .**70** A2
Frewell Bldg EC1 . . . .**241** A4
Frewing Cl BR7 . . . .**188** C5
Frewin Rd SW18 . . . .**158** B3
Friar Mews SE27 . . . .**160** D1
Friar Rd UB4 . . . .**84** D3
Friars Ave London N20 . . . . .30 C6

Friars Ave continued
Putney SW15 . . . .**157** A6
Roehampton SW15 . . . .**155** D1
Friars Cl Chingford E4 . . . . . .20 A1
Ilford IG1 . . . . .57 B1
Lambeth SE1 . . . .**251** D3
16 Northolt UB5 . . . . .84 D4
Friars Ct
5 Wallington SM6 . . . .**219** B4
Walthamstow E17 . . . . .35 B2
Friars Gate Cl IG8 . . . . .37 A6
Friars Gdns W3 . . . . .89 B3
Friars La TW9 . . . .**153** D6
Friars Mead E14 . . . .**120** A3
Friars Mews SE9 . . . .**166** C6
Friars Place La W3 . . . .**111** B6
Friars Prim Foundation Sch
SE1 . . . .**116** D4 **251** D1
Friar's Rd E6 . . . . .99 D6
Friars Stile Pl **9** TW10 . . . .**154** A5
Friars Stile Rd TW10 . . . . .**154** A5
Friar St EC4 . . . .**241** D1
Friars Way W3 . . . . .89 B1
Friars Wlk London N14 . . . . .15 B4
West Heath SE2 . . . .**124** D1
Friary Cl N12 . . . . .30 C5
Friary La IG8 . . . . .37 A6
Friary Park Ct **12** W3 . . . . . .89 A1
Friary Rd Acton W3 . . . . . . .89 B1
London N12 . . . . .30 C6
Peckham SE15 . . . .**140** A5
Friary Way N12 . . . . .30 C6
Friday Grove Mews 11
SW12 . . . .**159** C4
FRIDAY HILL 20 C1
Friday Hill E4 . . . . .20 C1
Friday Hill E E4 . . . . .20 C1
Friday Hill W E4 . . . . .20 C2
Friday Rd CR4 . . . .**180** D3
Friday St EC4 . . . .**117** A6 **252** A6
Frideswide Pl NW5 . . . . . . .71 C3
Friendly Pl **16** SE13 . . . . . .**141** B4
Friendly St SE8 . . . .**141** C4
Friendly Street Mews
SE8 . . . .**141** C3
Friendship Way E15 . . . . . . .98 A6
Friendship Wlk UB5 . . . . . . .84 D4
Friends' Rd CR0 . . . .**221** B5
Friend St EC1 . . . . . .**94** D4 **234** C2
FRIERN BARNET 31 A6
Friern Barnet La N20 . . . . . .30 C6
Friern Barnet Rd N11 . . . . . .31 A5
Friern Barnet Sch N11 . . . . .30 D5
Friern Bridge Ret Pk N11 . .31 B4
Friern Ct N20 . . . . .14 B1
Friern Mount Dr N20 . . . . . .14 A4
Friern Pk N12 . . . . .30 B5
Friern Rd SE22 . . . .**162** A5
Friern Watch Ave N12 . . . . . .30 B6
Frigate Ho **7** E14 . . . .**120** A2
Frigate Mews SE8 . . . .**141** C6
Frimley Ave SM6 . . . .**220** B3
Frimley Cl
New Addington CR0 . . . . . .**224** A1
Putney SW19 . . . .**157** A2
Frimley Cres CR0 . . . .**224** A1
Frimley Ct DA14 . . . .**190** C5
Frimley Gdns CR4 . . . .**202** C6
Frimley Ho **1** CR4 . . . .**202** C6
Frimley Rd
Chessington KT9 . . . .**214** A3
Ilford IG3 . . . . .79 C5
Frimley Way E1 . . . . .96 D3
Frinstead Ho **1** W10 . . . . . .**112** D6
Frinton Cl W13 . . . . .87 B2
Frinton Dr IG8 . . . . .36 B3
Frinton Mews IG2 . . . . .56 C3
Frinton Rd Newham E6 . . . . .99 D4
Sidcup DA14 . . . .**169** A2
South Tottenham N15 . . . . . .51 C3
Streatham SW17 . . . .**181** A4
Friston St SW6 . . . .**135** D3
Friswell Pl **1** DA6 . . . .**147** C1
Fritham Cl KT3 . . . .**199** C3
Frith Ct NW7 . . . . .29 A4
Frith Ho Bethnal Green E2 . .96 A4
Paddington NW8 . . . .**236** D5
Frith La NW7 . . . . .29 A4
Frith Manor Cotts N12 . . . . .29 B5
Frith Manor Prim Sch
N12 . . . . .29 B5
Frith Rd Croydon CR0 . . . . .**221** A6
Leyton E11 . . . . .76 B4
Frith St W1 . . . . .**119** D2 **239** C1
Frithville Ct **2** W12 . . . . . .**112** C5
Frithville Gdns W12 . . . . . .**112** C5
Frizlands La RM10 . . . . .81 D5
Frobisher Cl HA5 . . . . .40 D2
Frobisher Cres TW19 . . . . .**148** A4
Frobisher Ct
Belmont SM2 . . . .**217** B1
6 Forest Hill SE23 . . . .**162** B2
1 Greenwich SE10 . . . . . .**142** B6
3 Shepherd's Bush W12 . .**112** C4
Frobisher Gdns TW19 . . . .**148** A4
Frobisher Ho
3 Ealing W5 . . . . .88 A4
27 Wapping E1 . . . .**118** B5
Frobisher Mews EN2 . . . . . .5 B1

Frobisher Pas E14 . . . .**119** C5
Frobisher Pl SE14 . . . .**140** C4
Frobisher Rd London N8 . . . .50 C5
Newham E6 . . . .**100** B1
Frobisher St SE10 . . . .**142** C6
Froghall Cotts EN5 . . . . . . .11 B5
Frogley Rd SE22 . . . .**139** D1
Frogmore SW18 . . . .**157** C6
Frogmore Ave UB4 . . . . . . .83 C3
Frogmore Cl SM3 . . . .**217** A5
Frogmore Ct UB2 . . . .**107** B2
Frogmore Est NW10 . . . . . . .89 A4
Frogmore Gdns
Cheam SM3 . . . .**217** A4
Hayes UB4 . . . . .83 C3
Frogmore Ind Est
Hayes UB3 . . . .**105** D4
Highbury N5 . . . . .73 A4
Frognal NW3 . . . . .70 A3
Frognal Ave Harrow HA1 . . .42 D5
Sidcup DA14 . . . .**190** A4
Frognal Cl NW3 . . . . .70 A3
Frognal Cnr BR7 . . . .**189** D4
Frognal Ct NW3 . . . . .70 A2
Frognal Gdns NW3 . . . . .70 A3
Frognal La NW3 . . . . .69 D3
Frognal Par NW3 . . . . .70 A2
Frognal Pl DA14 . . . .**190** A5
Frognal Rise NW3 . . . . .70 A4
Frognal Way NW3 . . . . .70 A4
Froissart Rd SE9 . . . .**166** A6
Frome Ho SE15 . . . .**140** C1
Frome Rd N22 . . . . .50 D6
Frome St N1 . . . . . .**95** A5 **235** A4
Fromondes Rd SM3 . . . . . .**217** A3
Fromow's Cnr **14** W4 . . . . .**111** A1
Frontenac NW10 . . . . .68 B1
Frontier Works N17 . . . . . . .33 C4
Frosbery Ct **23** EN3 . . . . .7 C5
Frostic Wlk E1 . . . .**243** D3
Froude St SW8 . . . .**137** B3
Fruen Rd TW14 . . . .**149** D4
Fryatt Rd N17 . . . . .33 B3
Frye Ct **5** E3 . . . . .97 B4
Fryent Cl NW9 . . . . .44 C3
Fryent Cres NW9 . . . . .45 C3
Fryent Ctry Park HA3, HA9,
NW9 . . . . .44 C2
Fryent Fields NW9 . . . . .45 C3
Fryent Gr NW9 . . . . .45 C3
Fryent Prim Sch NW9 . . . .45 A2
Fryent Way HA9, NW9 . . . . .44 D2
Fry Ho E6 . . . . .77 C1
Frying Pan Alley E1 . . . . . .**243** C3
Fry Rd Harlesden NW10 . . . .89 D6
Upton Pk E6 . . . . .77 D1
Fryston Ave CR0 . . . .**222** A6
Fuchsia St SE2 . . . .**124** B1
Fulbeck Dr NW9 . . . . .27 C2
Fulbeck Ho N7 . . . . .72 B2
Fulbeck Way HA2 . . . . .24 A1
Fulbourn **9** KT1 . . . .**176** C1
Fulbourne Rd E17 . . . . .36 A1
Fulbourne St E1 . . . . .96 B2
Fulbrook Rd N19 . . . . .71 C4
Fulcher Ho **40** SE8 . . . .**141** B6
Fulcher Ho
13 Deptford SE8 . . . .**119** B1
10 Shoreditch N1 . . . . .95 C6
Fulford Mans **3** N19 . . . . . .72 A5
Fulford Rd KT19 . . . .**215** B1
Fulford St SE16 . . . .**118** B4
FULHAM **134** D3
Fulham Broadway
SW6 . . . .**135** C5 **265** B3
Fulham Broadway Sh Ctr
SW6 . . . .**265** B3
Fulham Broadway Sta
SW6 . . . .**135** C5 **265** B4
Fulham Bsns Exchange
SW6 . . . .**266** B1
Fulham Cl UB10 . . . . .83 A3
Fulham Cross Girls Sec Sch
SW6 . . . .**135** A5 **264** A3
Fulham Ct SW6 . . . .**135** C5 **265** A2
Fulham High St SW6 . . . . .**135** A3
Fulham Pal* SW6 . . . .**135** A3
Fulham Palace Rd SW6,
W6 . . . .**134** D6
Fulham Park Gdns SW6 . . .**135** B3
Fulham Park Rd SW6 . . . . .**135** B3
Fulham Prep Sch
6 Fulham SW6 . . . .**135** A3
Fulham W14 . . . . . .**135** A6 **264** B6
Fulham Prim Sch
SW6 . . . .**135** C6 **265** A5
Fulham Rd
Chelsea SW10 . . . .**136** A6 **266** B6
Fulham SW6 . . . . . .**135** B4 **264** D2
Fulke Ho E6 . . . . .75 B5
Fullbrooks Ave KT4 . . . . . .**199** D1
Fuller Cl
4 Bethnal Green E2 . . . . . .96 A3
Bushey WD23 . . . . .8 B4
Orpington BR6 . . . .**227** D3
Fuller Rd RM8 . . . . .80 C4
Fullers Ave KT6 . . . .**214** B6
Fuller's Ave IG8 . . . . .36 D3
Fullers Ho **6** SW18 . . . .**157** C6
Fuller's Rd E18 . . . . .36 D3

Fuller St NW4 . . . . .46 C5
Fullers Way N KT6 . . . .**214** B5
Fullers Way S KT9 . . . .**214** A5
Fuller's Wood CR0 . . . .**223** C3
Fuller Terr IG1 . . . . .79 B3
Fullerton Ct TW11 . . . .**175** A4
Fullerton Rd
Croydon CR0 . . . .**205** D2
Wandsworth SW18 . . . .**158** A6
Fuller Way UB3 . . . .**105** D1
Fullwood Prim Sch IG6 . . . .57 A5
Fullwood's Mews N1 . . . . .**235** D2
Fulmar Ct
6 Dulwich SE21 . . . .**161** B2
10 Ealing W13 . . . . .86 D3
Surbiton KT5 . . . .**198** B3
Fulmar Ho
12 Bermondsey SE16 . . . .**118** D2
Marylebone NW8 . . . .**237** B5
Fulmead St SW6 . . . .**265** D1
Fulmer Cl TW12 . . . .**173** A5
Fulmer Rd E16 . . . . .99 D2
Fulmer Way W13 . . . .**109** B3
Fulneck **1** E1 . . . . .96 C2
Fulready Rd E10 . . . . .54 B4
Fulstone Cl TW4 . . . .**129** B1
Fulthorp Rd SE3 . . . .**143** A3
Fulton Ct EN3 . . . . .7 C5
Fulton Mews W2 . . . .**246** A6
Fulton Rd HA9 . . . . .66 C5
Fulwell Ct Southall UB1 . . .**108** A6
Teddington N1 . . . .**174** C6
Fulwell Park Ave TW2 . . . . .**152** A2
Fulwell Rd TW11, TW12 . . .**174** B6
Fulwell Sta TW11 . . . .**174** B6
Fulwood Ave HA0 . . . . .88 B5
Fulwood Cl UB3 . . . . .83 D1
Fulwood Ct Harrow HA3 . . .43 A3
Stanwell TW19 . . . .**148** A5
Fulwood Gdns TW1 . . . . . .**153** A5
Fulwood Pl WC1 . . . .**240** D3
Fulwood Wlk SW19 . . . . . .**157** A3
Furber St W6 . . . .**112** B3
Furham Field HA5 . . . . .23 C3
Furley Ho **7** SE15 . . . .**140** A5
Furley Rd SE15 . . . .**140** A5
Furlong Cl SM6 . . . .**203** B1
Furlong Rd N7 . . . . .72 C2
Furmage St SW18 . . . .**157** D4
Furneaux Ave SE27 . . . . . .**182** D5
Furness Ho SW1 . . . .**258** C2
Furness Lo **4** SW14 . . . . . .**132** C1
Furness Prim Sch NW10 . .90 A5
Furness Rd
Harlesden NW10 . . . . .90 A5
Harrow HA2 . . . . .41 D1
Morden SM4 . . . .**201** D3
Sands End SW6 . . . .**135** D3
Furnival St EC4 . . . .**94** C1 **241** A2
Furrow La E9 . . . . .74 C3
Furrows The KT12 . . . .**194** C1
Fursby Ave N3 . . . . .29 C4
Fursecroft W1 . . . .**237** C2
Further Acre NW9 . . . . .27 D1
Furtherfield Cl CR0 . . . . . .**204** C3
Further Green Rd SE6 . . . .**164** C3
Furze Cl WD19 . . . . .22 C5
Furze Ct CR0 . . . .**222** A6
FURZEDOWN **181** B6
Furzedown Dr SW17 . . . . .**181** B5
Furzedown Prim Sch
SW17 . . . .**181** A4
Furzedown Rd SW17 . . . . .**181** B5
Furzefield Cl BR7 . . . .**188** D4
Furzefield Rd SE3 . . . .**143** B5
Furzeground Way UB11 . . .**105** A5
Furzeham Rd UB7 . . . .**104** A4
Furzehill Rd WD6 . . . . .11 A6
Furzeland Ho **2** KT3 . . . . .**199** C2
Furze Rd CR7 . . . .**205** A6
Furze St E3 . . . . .97 C2
Furzewood TW16 . . . .**172** A2
Fuschia Ct IG8 . . . . .36 C4
Fuscia Ct TW13 . . . .**149** D1
Fusion Ct SW15 . . . .**155** C1
Futters Ct **1** NW10 . . . . . . .89 C5
Fyfe Way BR1 . . . .**187** A1
Fyfield N4 . . . . .72 C6
Fyfield Ct BR2, BR3 . . . . . .**208** B5
Fyfield Ct E7 . . . . .77 A2
Fyfield Ho RM9 . . . . .80 B1
Fyfield Rd
5 Brixton SW9 . . . .**138** C2
Enfield EN1 . . . . .5 C2
Walthamstow E17 . . . . .54 B6
Woodford IG8 . . . . .37 C3
Fynes St SW1 . . . .**259** C4

Fre–Gal 327

Gables Cl
Camberwell SE5 . . . .**139** C4
Lewisham SE12 . . . .**165** A3
Gables The Barking IG11 . . .79 A2
Bromley BR1 . . . .**187** B3
3 Clapham SW4 . . . .**137** C2
Ealing W13 . . . . .87 B1
Hampstead NW3 . . . . .70 B6
Heston TW5 . . . .**129** C6
Mitcham CR4 . . . .**203** B6
Muswell Hill N10 . . . . .49 A6
North Finchley N12 . . . . . . .29 D5
Wembley HA9 . . . . .66 B5
Gabriel Cl **1** TW13 . . . . . .**173** A6
Gabriel Ho SE11 . . . .**260** C4
Gabrielle Cl HA9 . . . . .66 B5
Gabrielle Ct NW3 . . . . .70 B2
Gabriel Mews NW2 . . . . . . .69 B6
Gabriel St SE23 . . . .**163** A4
Gad Cl E13 . . . . .99 B4
Gaddesden Ave HA9 . . . . . .66 B2
Gaddesden Ho EC1 . . . . . .**235** D1
Gade Cl UB3 . . . .**106** B5
Gadesden Rd KT19 . . . . . .**215** A2
Gadsbury Cl NW9 . . . . .45 D3
Gadsden Ho
6 Homerton E9 . . . . .74 D2
4 Kensal Town W10 . . . . . .91 A3
Gadwall Cl E16 . . . . .99 B1
Gadwall Way SE28 . . . . . .**123** B4
Gagarin Ho SW11 . . . .**136** B2
Gage Rd E16 . . . . .98 C2
Gage St WC1 . . . .**240** B4
Gainford Ho **18** E2 . . . . . . .96 B4
Gainford St N1 . . . . .94 C5 **234** A6
Gainsboro Gdns UB6 . . . . .64 C3
Gainsborough Ave E12 . . . .78 C3
Gainsborough Cl
Beckenham BR3 . . . .**185** C3
Thames Ditton KT10 . . . . .**196** C1
Gainsborough Ct
11 Barnet EN5 . . . . .1 D1
6 Bermondsey SE16 . . . .**118** B1
Bromley BR2 . . . .**209** C5
Dulwich SE21 . . . .**161** C2
North Finchley N12 . . . . . . .29 D5
Shepherd's Bush W12 . . . .**112** C4
Gainsborough Gdns
Edgware HA8 . . . . .26 C1
Golders Green NW11 . . . . . .47 B2
Hampstead NW3 . . . . .70 B5
Isleworth TW7 . . . .**152** B6
Gainsborough Ho
Dagenham RM8 . . . . .80 B4
Enfield EN1 . . . . .18 A6
Finsbury Pk N4 . . . . .50 B1
3 Hampstead NW3 . . . . . .70 A4
5 Limehouse E14 . . . . . .**119** A6
Westminster SW1 . . . .**259** D3
Gainsborough Lodge
HA1 . . . . .42 C4
Gainsborough Mews 5
SE26 . . . .**162** B1
Gainsborough Prim Sch
Hackney Wick E9 . . . . .75 C2
Newham E15 . . . . .98 C4
Gainsborough Rd
Bedford Pk W4 . . . .**111** D2
Dagenham RM8 . . . . .80 B5
Hayes UB4 . . . . .83 B5
Leytonstone E11 . . . . .54 C2
Newham E15 . . . . .98 C4
New Malden KT3 . . . .**199** B3
Richmond TW9 . . . .**132** B2
Gainsborough Sq DA6 . . . .**146** D3
Gainsborough St **3** E9 . . . . .75 B2
Gainsborough Studios
N1 . . . .**235** C5
Gainsborough Twr **7**
UB5 . . . . .84 D5
Gainsfield Ct **3** E11 . . . . . .76 C5
Gainsford Rd E17 . . . . .53 B5
Gainsford St SE1 . . **117** D4 **253** D2
Gairloch Ho **2** NW1 . . . . . .71 D1
Gairloch Rd SE5 . . . .**139** C3
Gaisford St NW11 . . . . .71 C2
Gaitskell Ct SW11 . . . .**136** C3
Gaitskell Ho
Camberwell SE17 . . . .**139** B6
2 Newham E6 . . . . .99 D4
3 Walthamstow E17 . . . . .53 D6
Gaitskell Rd SE9 . . . .**167** A3
Gaitskell Way SE1 . . . .**252** A2
Galahad Rd Edmonton N9 . .18 A1
Grove Pk BR1 . . . .**187** A6
Galata Rd SW13 . . . .**134** A5
Galatea Sq SE15 . . . .**140** B2
Galaxy Bldg **6** E14 . . . . . .**119** C2
Galaxy Ho EC2 . . . .**242** D6
Galba Ct **1** TW8 . . . .**131** D5
Galbraith St E14 . . . .**120** A3
Galdana Ave EN5 . . . . .2 A2
Galeborough Ave IG8 . . . . .36 B3
Gale Cl Hampton TW12 . . .**173** A4
Mitcham CR4 . . . .**202** B6

Gale Ho 10 Brixton SW2 160 B6
Carshalton SM5 218 C3
Galena Ho
5 Hammersmith W6 112 B2
Plumstead Comm SE18 123 D1
Galena Rd W6 112 B2
Galen Pl WC1 240 B3
Galesbury Rd SW18 158 A5
Gales Gdns E2 96 B4
Gale St Dagenham RM9 80 D1
Tower Hamlets E3 97 C2
Galgate Cl 4 SW19 157 A3
Gallants Farm Rd EN4 14 C3
Galleon Cl SE16 118 D4
Galleon Ho 8 E14 120 A2
Galleons Dr IG11 102 A4
Galleries of Modern London★ EC1 242 A3
Gallery Ct SW10 266 A5
Gallery Gdns UB5 84 D5
Gallery Rd SE21 161 B3
Galleywall Rd SE16 118 B2
Galleywall Road Trad Est 12 SE16 118 B2
Galleywood Ho 1 W10 90 C2
Gallia Rd N5 72 D3
Galliard Cl N9 18 C5
Galliard Cres N9 18 A4
Galliard Ct N9 18 A5
Galliard Prim Sch N9 18 A4
Galliard Rd N9 18 A5
Gallica Ct SM1 201 D1
Gallions Cl IG11 102 A4
Gallions Mount Prim Sch SE18 123 D1
Gallions Prim Sch E6 100 D1
Gallions Rd E16 123 A6
Gallions Reach Shp Pk IG11 101 A2
Gallions Reach Sta E16 122 D6
Gallions View Rd SE28 123 C4
Gallon Cl SE7 121 C2
Gallop The
South Croydon CR2 222 B1
Sutton SM2 218 A1
Gallosson Rd SE18 123 C2
Galloway Path CR0 221 B4
Galloway Rd W12 112 A5
Gallus Cl N21 16 B5
Gallus Sq SE3 143 B2
Galpin's Rd CR4, CR7 204 B5
Galsworthy Ave
Ilford RM6 58 B2
Tower Hamlets E14 97 A2
Galsworthy Cl SE28 124 B5
Galsworthy Cres SE3 143 C4
Galsworthy Ct W3 110 D3
Galsworthy Ho 4 W11 91 A1
Galsworthy Rd
Cricklewood NW2 69 A4
Kingston u T KT2 176 D2
Galton Ho SE18 144 B4
Galton St W10 91 A4
Galva Cl EN4 3 A1
Galvani Way CR0 204 B1
Galveston Ho 2 E1 97 A3
Galveston Rd SW15 157 B6
Galway Cl 28 SE16 118 B1
Galway Ho Finsbury EC1 235 B1
7 Stepney E1 96 D2
Galway St EC1 95 A4 235 B1
Galy 5 NW9 27 D1
Gambetta St 3 SW8 137 B3
Gambia St SE1 116 D5 251 D3
Gambler Ho EC1 235 B1
Gambole Rd SW17 180 C6
Games Ho 6 SE7 143 C6
Games Rd EN4 2 D2
Gamlen Rd SW15 134 D1
Gamma Ct 9 CR0 205 B1
Gamuel Cl E17 53 C3
Gander Green Cres TW12 173 C2
Gander Green La KT4, SM1, SM3 217 B5
Gandhi Cl E17 53 C3
Gandolfi St 5 SE15 139 C6
Ganley Ct 18 SW11 136 B2
Gannet Ct 5 SE21 161 B2
Gannet Ho SE15 139 D4
Ganton St W1 239 B1
Ganton Wlk WD19 22 D6
GANTS HILL 56 C3
Gants Hill IG2 56 C3
Gantshill Cres IG2 56 C4
Gants Hill Sta IG2 56 C3
Gap Rd SW19 179 D5
Garage Rd W3 88 C1
Garand Ct 2 N7 72 B3
Garbett Ho 2 SE17 138 D6
Garbutt Pl W1 238 B3
Garden Ave
Bexleyheath DA7 147 C2
Mitcham CR4 181 B3
Garden City HA8 26 C4
Garden Cl Ashford TW15 171 A4
Chingford E4 35 C5
Garden Cl *continued*
Grove Pk SE12 165 B1
Hampton TW12 173 B5
Northolt UB5 85 A6
Roehampton SW15 156 B4
Ruislip HA4 61 D6
Wallington SM6 220 A3
Garden Cotts BR5 190 C1
Garden Ct
5 Belmont SM2 217 C1
10 Eltham SE9 166 C5
Hampton TW12 173 B5
North Finchley N12 29 D5
4 Richmond TW9 132 B4
12 South Acton W4 111 A3
South Croydon CR0 221 D5
4 Stanmore HA7 25 C5
St John's Wood NW8 229 C2
Strand EC4 251 A6
Wembley HA0 65 C5
Wimbledon SW20 178 D2
Gardeners Cl SE9 166 A1
Gardeners Rd CR0 204 D1
Garden Flats SW16 160 A1
Garden Ho 2 Finchley N2 30 B1
12 South Lambeth SW9 138 A3
Garden Hospl The NW4 46 C6
Garden House Sch SW3 114 D1 257 D2
Gardenia Ct 1 BR3 185 C3
Gardenia Rd
Bromley BR1 210 C6
Enfield EN1 17 C5
Gardenia Way IG8 37 A5
Garden La Bromley BR1 187 B4
Streatham SW2 160 B3
Garden Lodge Ct N2 48 B6
Garden Mews W2 245 B5
Garden Mus★ SE1 260 C5
Garden Pl 28 E2 95 D6
Garden Prim Sch CR4 203 D6
Garden Rd Bromley BR1 187 B4
Finchley N2 30 B2
Penge SE20 184 C2
Richmond TW9 132 C2
St John's Wood NW8 92 A4 229 B2
Walton-on-T KT12 194 B2
Garden Row SE1 116 D3 261 C6
Garden Royal 16 SW15 156 D5
Garden St E1 96 D2
Gardens The
Beckenham BR3 186 A2
East Bedfont TW14 149 B5
East Dulwich SE22 140 A1
Harrow HA1, HA2 42 A3
Pinner HA5 41 B3
Stamford Hill N16 51 D2
Garden Suburb Jun & Inf Schs NW11 47 B4
Garden Terr
Knightsbridge SW7 247 B1
Pimlico SW1 259 C2
Garden Way NW10 67 A2
Garden Wlk
Beckenham BR3 185 B2
Shoreditch EC2 95 C3 243 A6
Gardiner Ave NW2 68 C3
Gardiner Cl
Chislehurst BR5 190 C1
Dagenham RM8 80 D4
Enfield EN3 18 D5
Gardiner Ct NW10 89 B6
Gardiner Ho SW11 267 A2
Gardner Cl E11 55 B3
Gardner Ct Highbury N5 73 A4
Hounslow TW3 129 C2
Tottenham N22 32 D1
Gardner Ho
Feltham TW13 151 B2
Southall UB1 106 D6
Gardner Ind Est SE26 185 B5
Gardner Pl TW14 150 B5
Gardner Rd E13 99 B3
Gardners Cl N11 15 A2
Gardners La EC4 252 A6
Gardnor Mans 14 NW3 70 A4
Gardnor Rd NW3 70 B4
Gard St EC1 234 D2
Garendon Gdns SM4 201 D2
Garendon Rd SM4 201 D2
Garenne Ct 8 E4 20 A3
Gareth Cl KT4 216 D6
Gareth Ct SW16 159 D1
Gareth Gr BR1 187 A6
Garfield Edmonton N9 18 B3
Enfield EN2 17 B6
Garfield Ho W2 237 C1
Garfield Mews 7 SW11 137 A2
Garfield Prim Sch
London N11 31 C5
Wimbledon SW19 180 A4
Garfield Rd Chingford E4 20 B3
Clapham SW11 137 A2
Enfield EN3 6 C1
Newham E13 98 D3
3 Twickenham TW1 153 A3
Wimbledon SW19 180 A4
Garford St E14 119 C6
Garganey Ct NW10 67 B2
Garganey Wlk SE28 124 C6
Garibaldi St SE18 123 C2
Garland Ct 12 E14 119 C6
Garland Dr TW3 130 A3
Garland Ho
12 Kingston u T KT2 176 A2
Stoke Newington N16 73 B5
Garland Rd
Plumstead Comm SE18 145 B5
Stanmore HA7 26 A2
Garlands Ct CR0 221 B4
Garlands Ho NW8 91 D5
Garlands La HA1 42 D1
Garlands The HA1 42 D2
Garlick Hill EC4 117 A6 252 B6
Garlies Rd SE23 163 A1
Garlinge Ho 12 SW9 138 C4
Garlinge Rd NW2 69 B2
Garman Cl N18 33 B5
Garman Rd N17 34 C3
Garnault Mews EC1 234 B1
Garnault Pl EC1 234 B1
Garnault Rd EN1 5 D5
Garner Cl RM8 58 D1
Garner Rd E17 36 A2
Garner St E2 96 A5
Garnet Ct TW13 149 C1
Garnet Ho KT4 199 B1
Garnet Rd
South Norwood CR7 205 B5
Willesden NW10 67 C2
Garnet St E1 118 C6
Garnett Cl SE9 144 B2
Garnett Ho 5 NW3 70 D3
Garnett Rd NW3 70 D3
Garnett Way 3 E17 35 A2
Garnet Wlk 8 E6 100 A2
Garnham Cl 2 N16 73 D6
Garnham St 1 N16 73 D6
Garnies Cl SE15 139 D5
Garrad's Rd SW16 159 D1
Garrard Cl
Bexleyheath DA7 147 C2
Chislehurst BR7 188 D5
Garrard Ho BR2 209 C5
Garrard Wlk NW10 67 C2
Garratt Cl CR0 220 A4
Garratt Ho 8 N16 51 C1
Garratt La
Upper Tooting SW17, SW18 180 C6
Wandsworth SW18 157 D3
Garratt Park Sec Specl Sch 6 SW18 158 A2
Garratt Rd HA8 26 C3
Garratts Rd WD23 8 A4
Garratt Terr SW17 180 C6
Garraway Ct SW13 134 C5
Garraway Ho SE21 161 D1
Garrett Cl W3 89 B2
Garrett Ho
8 Shepherd's Bush W12 90 B1
Teddington TW11 175 B4
Garrett St EC1 95 A3 242 B6
Garrick Ave NW11 47 A3
Garrick Cl Ealing W5 88 A3
1 Richmond TW9 153 D6
Wandsworth SW18 136 A1
Garrick Cres CR0 221 C6
Garrick Ct HA8 26 B6
Garrick Dr Hendon NW4 28 C1
Plumstead SE18 123 B3
Garrick Gdns KT8 195 C6
Garrick Ho Chiswick W4 133 C6
2 Kingston u T KT1 198 A5
Mayfair W1 248 C3
7 Streatham SW16 181 C5
Garrick Ind Ctr NW9 45 D4
Garrick Pk NW4 28 D1
Garrick Rd Greenford UB6 85 D3
Richmond TW9 132 C3
West Hendon NW9 45 D3
Garrick's Ait KT8 174 A1
Garricks Ho KT1 175 D1
Garrick St WC2 116 A6 250 A6
Garrick's Villa TW12 174 A1
Garrick Way NW4 46 D5
Garrick Yd WC2 250 A6
Garrison Cl
Hounslow TW4 151 B6
Shooters Hill SE18 144 C5
Garrison La KT9 214 A1
Garrowsfield EN5 13 B6
Garsdale Cl N11 31 A4
Garsdale Terr SW5 254 D2
Garside Cl
Hampton TW12 173 D4
Plumstead SE28 123 B3
Garside Ct 5 N20 14 D2
Garsington Mews SE4 141 B2
Garson Ho W2 246 C6
Garston Ho 6 N1 72 D1
Garter Way SE16 118 D4
Garth Cl Kingston u T KT2 176 B5
Ruislip HA4 40 D1
West Barnes SM4 200 D2
Garth Ct Chiswick W4 133 B6
11 Harrow HA1 42 D3
Garth Dr N9 18 A2
Garth Ho NW2 69 B6
Garthland Dr EN5 12 C6
Garth Mews W5 88 A3
Garthorne Rd SE23 162 D4
Garth Rd Child's Hill NW2 69 B6
8 Chiswick W4 111 B1
Kingston u T KT2 176 B5
West Barnes SM4 200 D2
Garth Road Ind Ctr The SM4 200 D1
Garthside TW10 176 A5
Garth The
Hampton TW12 173 D4
Harrow HA3 44 B3
North Finchley N12 29 D5
Garthway N12 30 C4
Gartmoor Gdns SW19 157 B3
Gartmore Rd IG3 79 D6
Garton Ho 6 N6 49 D2
Garton Pl SW18 158 A5
Gartons Cl EN3 6 C1
Gartons Way SW11 136 A2
Garvary Rd E16 99 B1
Garvens SE19 183 C5
Garway Rd W2 91 D1
Garwood Cl N17 34 B2
Garwood Lo N22 32 B3
Gascoigne Gdns IG8 36 C3
Gascoigne Pl 17 E2 95 D4
Gascoigne Prim Sch IG11 101 A6
Gascoigne Rd IG11 101 A5
Gascony Ave NW6 69 C1
Gascoyne Ho 2 E9 74 D1
Gascoyne Rd E9 74 D1
Gaselee St E14 120 A6
Gasholder Pl SE11 116 B1 260 D1
Gaskarth Rd
Balham SW12 159 B5
Burnt Oak HA8 27 A1
Gaskell Rd N6 48 D3
Gaskell St SW4 138 A3
Gaskin Ho N16 73 B5
Gaskin St N1 94 D6 234 C6
Gaspar Cl SW7 255 D4
Gaspar Mews SW5 255 D4
Gassiot Rd SW17 180 D6
Gassiot Way SM1 218 B5
Gasson Ho 24 SE14 140 D6
Gastein Rd W6 134 D6
Gastigny Ho EC1 235 B1
Gaston Bell Cl TW9 132 B2
Gaston Bridge Rd TW17 193 B3
Gaston Gate SW8 270 C2
Gaston Rd CR4 203 A6
Gaston Way TW17 193 B4
Gataker Ho 5 SE16 118 B3
Gataker St 6 SE16 118 B3
Gatcliff Cl SW1 258 B1
Gatcombe Ct BR3 185 C3
Gatcombe Ho 20 SE22 139 C2
Gatcombe Mews W5 110 B6
Gatcombe Rd
8 Newham E16 121 A5
Tufnell Pk N19 71 D5
Gatcombe Way EN4 2 D2
Gateacre Ct DA14 190 B6
Gate End HA6 22 A3
Gatefield Ct SE15 140 A2
Gateforth St NW8 237 A5
Gate Hill Ct W11 244 D4
Gatehill Rd HA6 22 A3
Gate Ho 4 KT6 198 A1
Gatehouse Cl KT2 177 A3
Gatehouse Sch 26 E2 96 D5
Gatehouse Sq SE1 252 B4
Gateley Ho 6 SE4 140 D1
Gateley Rd SW9 138 B2
Gate Mews SW7 114 C4 247 B1
Gater Dr EN2 5 B4
Gates 4 NW9 27 D1
Gatesborough St EC2 243 A6
Gates Ct SE17 262 A2
Gatesden WC1 233 B1
Gates Green Rd BR2, BR4 225 A4
Gateside Rd SW17 158 D1
Gate St WC2 94 B1 240 C2
Gatestone Ct 10 SE19 183 C4
Gatestone Rd SE19 183 C4
Gateway SE17 139 A6
Gateway Arc N1 234 C4
Gateway Bsns Ctr SE28 123 B3
Gateway Gdns E6 100 B4
Gateway Ho
Balham SW12 159 B5
3 Barking IG11 101 A6
3 Upper Tooting SW17 180 C4
Gateway Ind Est NW10 90 A3
Gateway Mews
Friern Barnet N11 31 C4
4 London E8 73 D3
Gateway Prim Sch NW8 92 B3 236 D6
Gateway Rd E15 75 D5
Gateway Ret Pk E6 100 D3
Gateways KT6 198 A4
Gateways Ct SM6 219 B3
Gateways The
Chelsea SW3 257 B3
Gateways The *continued*
Richmond TW9 131 D1
Gateway Trad Est NW10 89 D4
Gatfield Gr TW13 151 C2
Gatfield Ho TW13 151 C2
Gathorne Rd N22 32 C2
Gathorne St 19 E2 96 D5
Gatley Ave KT19 214 D3
Gatliff Rd SW1 115 B1 258 C1
Gatling Rd SE18, SE2 124 A1
Gatonby St SE15 139 D4
Gatting Cl HA8 27 A3
Gatting Way UB8 60 A2
Gatton Prim Sch SW17 180 C6
Gatton Rd SW17 180 C6
Gattons Way DA14 191 B6
Gatward Cl N21 16 D5
Gatward Gn N9 17 D2
Gatwick Ho 3 E14 97 B1
Gatwick Rd SW18 157 B4
Gauden Cl SW4 137 D2
Gauden Rd SW4 137 D2
Gaugin Ct 13 SE16 118 B1
Gauntlet 1 NW9 27 D1
Gauntlet Cl UB5 63 A1
Gauntlett Ct HA0 65 B3
Gauntlett Rd SM1 218 B3
Gaunt St SE1 262 A6
Gautrey Rd SE15 140 C3
Gautrey Sq 5 E6 100 B1
Gavel St SE17 262 D4
Gaven Ho N17 33 C1
Gaverick Mews 3 E14 119 C2
Gavestone Cres SE12 165 B4
Gavestone Rd SE12 165 B4
Gavestone Terr SE12 165 B4
Gaviller Pl 3 E5 74 B4
Gavina Cl SM4 202 C4
Gavin Ho 1 SE18 123 C2
Gawain Wlk N9 18 A1
Gawber St E2 96 C4
Gawsworth Cl E15 76 D3
Gawthorne Ct E3 97 C5
Gay Cl NW2 68 B3
Gaydon Ho W2 91 D2
Gaydon La NW9 27 C2
Gayfere Rd Redbridge IG5 56 B6
Stoneleigh KT17 216 A3
Gayfere St SW1 116 A3 260 A5
Gayford Rd W12 111 D4
Gay Ho N16 73 C3
Gayhurst SE17 139 B6
Gayhurst Ct 9 UB5 84 C4
Gayhurst Ho NW8 237 B6
Gayhurst Prim Sch 5 E8 74 A1
Gayhurst Rd E8 74 A1
Gaylor Rd UB5 63 B3
Gaymead NW8 91 D6
Gaynesford Rd
Forest Hill SE23 162 D2
Wallington SM5 218 D1
Gay Rd E15 98 B5
Gaysham Ave IG2 56 D4
Gaysham Hall IG5 56 D6
Gaysley Ho SE11 261 A3
Gay St SW15 134 D2
Gayton Cres NW3 70 B4
Gayton Ct 3 Harrow HA1 42 D3
New Malden KT3 199 D4
Gayton Ho E3 97 C3
Gayton Rd
Abbey Wood SE2 124 C3
Hampstead NW3 70 B4
Harrow HA1 43 A3
Gayville Rd SW11 158 D5
Gaywood Cl SW2 160 C3
Gaywood Rd E17 53 C6
Gaywood St SE1 261 D5
Gaza St SE17 116 D1 261 C1
Gaze Ho 11 E14 98 B1
Gean Ct 3 E11 76 B4
Gearies Inf Sch IG2 56 D4
Gearies Jun Sch IG2 56 D4
Geariesville Gdns IG6 56 D5
Gearing Cl SW17 181 A6
Geary Ho N7 72 B3
Geary Rd NW10 68 A3
Geary St N7 72 B3
GEC Est HA9 65 D6
Geddes Pl 3 DA6 147 C1
Gedeney Rd N17 33 A2
Gedge Ct CR4 202 C5
Gedling Ho SE22 139 D2
Gedling Pl SE1 263 D6
Geere Rd E15 98 D6
Gees Ct W1 238 B1
Gee St EC1 95 A3 242 A6
Geffrey's Ct SE9 166 A1
Geffrye Ct N1 95 C5
Geffrye Mus★ E2 95 D5
Geffrye St E2 95 D5
Geldart Rd SE15 140 B5
Geldeston Rd E5 74 A6
Gellatly Rd SE14 140 D3
Gell Cl UB10 60 B5
Gemima Ct SM1 217 C3
Gemini Bsns Ctr E16 98 B3
Gemini Gr UB5 85 A4
Gemini Ho 11 E3 97 C6
Gemma Ct BR3 185 B1

Gems Hampshire Sch (Main Sch) SW7 . . . . . . 257 A1
Gems Hampshire Sch (The Early Years) SW7 . . . . . 256 B3
General Gordon Pl SE18. 122 D2
General Wolfe Rd SE10. .142 B4
Generals Wlk The EN3. . . 7 A6
Genesis Bsns Pk NW10. . .88 D5
Genesis Cl TW19 . . . . . . 148 B3
Genesis Ho KT6. . . . . . . 197 D1
Genesta Rd SE18. . . . . . 145 A6
Geneva Cl TW17 . . . . . . 171 C1
Geneva Ct Hendon NW9 . . .45 D4
 1 Putney SW15. . . . . 156 D6
Stoke Newington N16. . . .51 B1
Geneva Dr SW9. . . . . . . 138 C1
Geneva Gdns RM6 . . . . . .59 A4
Geneva Rd
Kingston u T KT1. . . . . . 198 A5
Thornton Heath CR7. . . . 205 A4
Genever Cl E4 . . . . .35 C5
Genista Rd N18. . . . . . . .34 B5
Genoa Ave SW15. . . . . . 156 C6
Genoa Ho 19 E1 . . . . .96 D3
Genoa Rd SE20 . . . . . . .184 C2
Genotin Rd EN1. . . . . 5 B2
Genotin Terr EN1 . . . . 5 B2
Gentleman's Row EN2 . . . 5 A2
Gentry Gdns E13. . . . . . .99 A4
Geoffrey Cl SE5. . . . . . .139 A3
Geoffrey Ct SE4. . . . . . .141 B2
Geoffrey Gdns E6 . . . . . 100 A5
Geoffrey Ho SE1 . . . . . .262 D6
Geoffrey Jones Ct NW10 .90 A6
Geoffrey Rd SE4 . . . . . . 141 B2
Geoffrey Akass Ho 5
 SE18 . . . . 123 A1
George Beard Rd 11
 SE8 . . . . 119 B2
George Beare Lo 9
 SW4. . . . . 159 C6
George Belt Ho 8 E2 . . . .96 D4
George Carver Ho E7 . . . .77 A3
George Comberton Wlk 4
 E12 . . . . 78 C3
George Cres N10 . . . . . . .31 A3
George Ct
Buckhurst Hill IG9. . . . . .21 D2
St James WC2 . . . . . . .250 B5
George Davies Lodge
 IG6 . . . . 57 A4
George Downing Est N16. 73 D6
George Eliot Ho SW1. . . .259 B3
George Eliot Jun & Inf Sch
 NW8 . . . . .92 B6 229 C6
George Elliot Ho SW1. . .262 A2
George Elliston Ho 13
 SE1 . . . . 118 A1
George Eyre Ho NW8. . . .229 D3
George Gange Way HA3. .42 D6
George Green's Sch E14. 120 A1
George Groves Rd SE20 .184 A2
George Ho 8 SE26. . . . . 184 B5
George Inn Yd SE1 . . . . .252 C3
George La Hayes BR2 . . .209 B1
Lewisham SE13 . . . . . . 164 A5
Wanstead E18 . . . . .55 B6
Woodford E18. . . . . .37 A1
George Lansbury Ho
 7 Bow E3 . . . . .97 B4
 3 Willesden NW10. . . . .67 C1
Wood Green N22 . . . . . . .32 C2
George Lashwood Ct 12
 SW9. . . . . 138 B1
George Leybourne Ho 15
 E1 . . . . 118 A6
George Lindgren Ho
 SW6. . . . . 264 D4
George Loveless Ho 4
 E2 . . . . .95 D4
George Lovell Dr
Enfield EN3. . . . . 7 A6
Holdbrook EN3 . . . . 7 A6
George Mathers Rd
 SE11 . . . . 261 C4
George Mews
 27 Brixton SW9 . . . . . 138 C3
 NW1. . . . . 232 A1
George Mitchell Sch E10. .53 D1
George Parr Ho N21 . . . . .16 D4
George Peabody Ct NW1 .237 A4
George Rd Chingford E4 . .35 C4
Kingston u T KT2. . . . . . 177 A3
New Malden KT3 . . . . . 199 D4
George Row SE16. . . . . .118 A4
Georges Mead WD6. . . . .10 A5
George Spicer Prim Sch
 EN1. . . . . 5 D2
George Sq SW19. . . . . . 201 C6
George's Rd N7. . . . . . . .72 B3
George's Sq SW6 . . . . . .264 D6
George St Barking IG11 . . .79 A1
 1 Canning Town E16. . .98 D1
Ealing W7 . . . . 108 C5
Hounslow TW3, TW5. . . .129 C3
Marylebone W1 . . . .92 D1 237 D2
Richmond TW10 . . . . . . 153 D6
Southall UB2. . . . . 107 A4
South Croydon CR0. . . . .221 B6
George Street Sta CR0 . . 221 A6

George Taylor Ct N9 . . . . .18 B1
George Tingle Ho SE1. . . .263 D6
George Tomlinson Prim Sch
 E11. . . . . .54 C1
Georgetown Cl 4 SE19 . .183 C5
Georgette Pl SE10 . . . . . 142 A5
George Vale Ho 35 E2 . . .96 A5
George V Ave HA2, HA5 . . .41 C6
George V Way UB6 . . . . . .87 B6
George Walter Ho 11
 SE16 . . . . 118 C2
George Wyver Cl SW18. .157 A4
George Yd
City of London EC3 . . . .242 D1
Mayfair W1. . . . . .248 B6
Georgiana St NW1 . 93 C6 232 B6
Georgian Cl Hayes BR2. .209 B1
Ickenham UB10 . . . . . . .60 A4
Stanmore HA7 . . . . .25 A3
Georgian Ct Croydon CR0. 205 B1
 12 Hackney E9 . . . . . . .96 C6
 3 Hendon NW4. . . . . . .46 B4
Wembley HA9. . . . . .66 D2
Georgian Ho HA0 . . . . . . .65 A5
Georgian Lo HA5 . . . . . . .40 B4
Georgian Village The
 E17 . . . . .54 A6
Georgian Way HA1. . . . . .64 B6
Georgia Rd
New Malden KT3 . . . . . 199 A5
South Norwood CR7 . . . 182 D2
Georgina Ct 5 TW1. . . . .153 C5
Georgina Gdns 10 E2. . . .95 D4
Geraint Rd BR1. . . . . . . 187 A6
Geraldine Ct 6 NW6. . . . .46 A5
Geraldine Rd
Brentford W4 . . . . 132 C6
Wandsworth SW18. . . . 158 A6
Geraldine St SE11. . . . . .261 C5
Gerald Mews SW1 . . . . .258 B4
Gerald Rd
Belgravia SW1 . . . .115 A2 258 B4
Dagenham RM8 . . . . . . .59 B1
Newham E16. . . . . .98 D3
Gerard Ave TW4 . . . . . . 151 C4
Gerard Ct NW2 . . . . .68 D3
Gerard Rd Barnes SW13. .133 D4
Harrow HA1 . . . . .43 A3
Gerards Cl SE16 . . . . . . 118 C1
Gerboa Ct 6 E4 . . . . .36 B5
Gerda Rd SE9. . . . . 167 A2
Germander Way E15. . . . .98 C4
German Sch The TW10 . . 153 D3
Gernigan Ho SW18. . . . . 158 B5
Gernon Rd E3 . . . . .97 A5
Geron Way NW2 . . . . . . .68 C6
Gerrard Ave HA5 . . . . . . .40 A4
Gerrard Ho 6 SE14 . . . . 140 D5
Gerrard Pl W1 . . . . .249 D6
Gerrard Rd N1. . . . .94 D5 234 D4
Gerrards Cl N14 . . . . .15 C6
Gerrard's Ct W5 . . . . . . 109 D3
Gerrard's St W1 . . .115 D6 249 D6
Gerridge Ct SE1 . . . . . . .261 B6
Gerridge St SE1 . .116 C3 261 B6
Gerry Raffles Sq E15 . . . .76 B2
Gertrude Rd DA17 . . . . . 125 C2
Gertrude St
 SW10. . . . . . .136 A6 266 B5
Gervase Cl HA9. . . . . . . .67 A5
Gervase Rd HA8 . . . . . . .27 B2
Gervase St SE15 . . . . . . 140 B5
Getters Talmud Torah 3
 N16. . . . . .51 B2
Ghent St SE6 . . . . 163 C2
Ghent Way E8 . . . . .73 D2
Giant Arches Rd SE24 . . .161 A5
Giant Tree Hill WD23. . . . .8 B3
Gibbards Cott 1 IG11. . . .79 D1
Gibbfield Cl RM6. . . . . . . .59 A6
Gibbings Ho SE1. . . . . . .251 D1
Gibbins Rd E15 . . . . .76 A1
Gibbon Ho NW8. . . . . . .236 D5
Gibbon Rd Acton W3 . . . .111 C6
Kingston u T KT2. . . . . . 176 A3
Nunhead SE15 . . . . 140 C3
Gibbons Mews NW11 . . . .47 B4
Gibbon's Rd BR1. . . . . . . .67 C2
Gibbon's Rents SE1. . . . .253 A3
Gibbon Wlk SW15. . . . . .134 A1
Gibbs Ave SE19 . . . . . . .183 B5
Gibbs Cl SE19. . . . . 183 B5
Gibbs Gn Edgware M8 . . .27 A6
West Kensington
 W14 . . . . . . 113 B1 254 D1
Gibbs Green Rd
 W14. . . . . . . 113 B1 254 C2
Gibbs Green Specl Sch
 W14 . . . . 113 B1 254 D2
Gibbs Ho
 6 Balham SW12 . . . . .159 B4
 2 Bromley BR1. . . . . . 186 D2
Gibbs Rd N18. . . . . .34 C6
Gibbs Sq SE19 . . . . 183 B5
Gibraltar Ho NW10 . . . . . .89 C5
Gibraltar Wlk 28 E2 . . . . .99 A4
Gibson Bsns Ctr 10 N17. .33 D3
Gibson Cl
Bethnal Green E1 . . . . . .96 C3

Gibson Cl continued
Chessington KT9 . . . . . .213 C3
Isleworth TW7 . . . . 130 B2
Southgate N21 . . . . .16 C5
Gibson Ct
 9 Friern Barnet N11. . . .30 D5
Hinchley Wood KT10. . . 212 D5
Gibson Gdns N16 . . . . . . .73 D6
Gibson Ho
South Croydon CR2. . . . 221 A2
Sutton SM1 . . . . 217 C4
Gibson Rd Dagenham RM8. .58 C1
Ickenham UB10 . . . . . . .60 B4
Lambeth SE11. . . . . . . 260 D3
Sutton SM1. . . . . 217 D3
Gibson's Hill SW16. . . . .182 C3
Gibson Sq N1 . . . . .94 C6 234 B6
Gibson St SE10 . . . . 120 C1
Gideon Cl DA17 . . . . . . 125 D2
Gideon Mews W5 . . . . . 109 D4
Gideon Rd SW11 . . . . . . 137 A2
Giesbach Rd N19 . . . . . . .71 D6
Giffard Rd N18. . . . . .33 C4
Giffen Square Mkt ★
 SE8. . . . . 141 C5
Giffin St SE8 . . . . 141 C5
Gifford Gdns W7 . . . . . . .86 C2
Gifford Ho
 5 Clapham SW4 . . . . . 137 D1
Greenwich SE10 . . . . . 120 B1
Pimlico SW1 . . . . .259 A1
Gifford Prim Sch UB5 . . . .85 B5
Gifford Rd NW10 . . . . . . .67 C1
Gifford St N1. . . . . .72 A1
Gift La E15 . . . . .98 D6
Giggs Hill BR5 . . . . .190 A2
Giggs Hill Gdns KT7. . . . 197 A1
Giggs Hill Rd KT7 . . . . . 197 A2
Gilbert Cl Kidbrooke SE18. .144 B4
 1 Merton SW19 . . . . . 179 D2
Gilbert Ct W5 . . . . .88 B1
Gilbert Gr HA8. . . . . .27 B2
Gilbert Ho Barbican EC2. .242 B3
Deptford SE8 . . . . 141 C6
 5 Globe Town E2. . . . . .96 D4
South Lambeth SW8 . . .270 A4
 5 Walthamstow E17. . . .54 A6
Gilbert Pl WC1. . . .94 A2 240 A3
Gilbert Rd
Belvedere DA17 . . . . . . 125 C3
Lambeth SE11. . . .116 C2 261 B4
Merton SW19 . . . . 180 A3
Pinner HA5 . . . . .40 A5
Plaistow BR1 . . . . 187 A3
Gilbert Scott Prim Sch
 CR2. . . . . 223 A1
Gilbert Sheldon Ho W2. .236 D4
Gilbertson Ho 11 E14. . . 119 C3
Gilbert St Enfield EN3 . . . .6 C6
Hounslow TW3 . . . . . . 130 A2
Leyton E15 . . . . .76 C4
Marylebone W1 . . . .93 A1 238 B1
Gilbert White Cl UB6. . . . .87 A6
Gilbey Cl UB10. . . . . .60 D4
Gilbey Rd SW17. . . . . . .180 C5
Gilbeys Yd NW1. . . . . . . .71 A1
Gilbourne Rd SE18. . . . . 145 D6
Gilby Ho 5 E9 . . . . .74 D2
Gilda Ave EN3 . . . . .19 A6
Gilda Cres N16 . . . . .52 A1
Gilda Ct NW7 . . . . .28 A2
Gildea Cl HA5. . . . . .23 C3
Gildea St W1 . . . . .238 D3
Gilden Cres NW5 . . . . . . .71 A3
Gildersome St SE18. . . . 144 C6
Gilders Rd KT9 . . . . 214 B2
Giles Coppice SE19 . . . . 183 D6
Giles Ho
 6 Bermondsey SE16. . . 118 A3
Notting Hill W11 . . . . . . .91 C1
Gilesmead SE5 . . . . 139 B4
Gilfrid Ct UB8. . . . . .82 D1
Gilkes Cres SE21 . . . . . . 161 C5
Gilkes Pl SE21 . . . . 161 C5
Gillam Ho 9 SE16 . . . . . 118 C2
Gillan Ct SE12 . . . . 165 B1
Gillan Gn WD23. . . . . .8 A2
Gillards Mews 6 E17 . . . .53 C5
Gillards Way SW18 . . . . . .53 C5
Gill Ave E16. . . . . .99 A1
Gill Ct SE18 . . . . 123 A2
Gillender St E3 . . . . .98 A3
Gillespie Prim Sch N5 . . . .72 B5
Gillespie Rd N4, N5. . . . . .72 D5
Gillett Ave E6 . . . . 100 A5
Gillett Ho N8. . . . . .50 A6
Gillett Pl 27 E8. . . . . .73 C3
Gillett Rd CR7. . . . . 205 B5
Gillett St E8, N16. . . . . . .73 C3
Gillfoot NW1 . . . . .232 A3
Gillham Terr N17. . . . . . . .34 A3
Gillian Ho HA3. . . . . .24 C4
Gillian Park Rd SM3. . . . 201 B1
Gillian St SE13. . . . . 163 D6
Gillies Ct Sidcup DA14. . .189 C6
Southgate N21 . . . . .16 B6
Gillies St NW5 . . . . .71 A3
Gilling Ct 5 NW3 . . . . . . .70 C2

Gillingham Ho SW1 . . . .259 A4
Gillingham Mews SW1. . .259 A4
Gillingham Rd NW2. . . . . .69 A5
Gillingham Row SW1 . . .259 A4
Gillingham St
 SW1. . . . . . . .115 C2 259 A4
Gillings Ct 5 EN5. . . . . . . .1 A1
Gillison Wlk 19 SE16 . . . .118 A3
Gillman Dr E15 . . . . .98 D6
Gillman Ho 24 E2 . . . . . . .96 A5
Gillray Ho Chelsea SW10 .266 C5
 2 Sutton SM1 . . . . . . 218 B3
Gills Ct 2 EN5. . . . . .14 A6
Gill St E14 . . . . 119 B6
Gillum Cl EN4. . . . . .14 D3
Gilmore Cl UB10 . . . . . . .60 C5
Gilmore Cres TW15 . . . . 170 C4
Gilmore Ct N11 . . . . .30 D5
Gilmore Ho SW4 . . . . . . 136 D1
Gilmore Rd SE13 . . . . . . 142 B1
Gilpin Ave SW14 . . . . . . 133 B1
Gilpin Cl Mitcham CR4. . .180 C1
Paddington W2 . . . . . . 236 B4
Gilpin Cres Edmonton N18. .33 D5
Twickenham TW2 . . . . . 151 D4
Gilpin Ho 9 Edmonton N9 . .18 A1
New Malden KT3 . . . . . 199 C4
Gilpin Rd E5 . . . . .75 A4
Gilpin Way UB3. . . . . . . 127 B5
Gilray Ho W2 . . . . .246 C6
Gilsland Rd CR7 . . . . . . .205 B5
Gilson Pl N10. . . . . .30 D3
Gilstead Ho IG11 . . . . . . 102 B5
Gilstead Rd SW6. . . . . . .115 D3
Gilston Rd SW10 . .114 A1 256 B1
Gilton Rd SE6. . . . . .164 C1
Giltspur St EC1 . . . .94 D1 241 D2
Gilwell Cl E4 . . . . .7 D1
Gilwell Ct 7 E5. . . . . .74 B4
Gippeswyck Cl HA5 . . . . .22 D2
Gipsy Cnr W3 . . . . .89 B2
Gipsy Hill SE19. . . . . . . 183 C5
Gipsy Hill Sta SE19. . . . .183 C5
Gipsy La SW15 . . . . 134 B2
Gipsy Rd Bexley DA16 . . .146 D3
West Norwood SE27. . . .183 A6
Gipsy Road Gdns SE27 . .183 A6
Giralda Cl E16 . . . . .99 D2
Giraud St E14 . . . . .97 D1
Girdlers Rd W14 . . . . . . .112 D2
Girdlestone Wlk N19 . . . .71 C6
Girdwood Rd SW18,
 SW19. . . . . 157 A4
Girling Ho 9 N1. . . . . . . .95 C6
Girling Way TW14 . . . . . 128 A2
Gironde Rd SW6 . .135 B5 264 D3
Girtin Ho
 6 Belmont SM2. . . . . . 217 D1
 4 Northolt UB5. . . . . . .84 D1
Girton Ave NW9 . . . . .44 C6
Girton Cl UB5. . . . . .64 A2
Girton Gdns CR0 . . . . . . 223 C5
Girton Ho NW6 . . . . 156 D5
Girton Rd
Forest Hill SE26 . . . . . . 184 D5
Northolt UB5 . . . . .64 A2
Girton Villas 6 W10. . . . . .90 D1
Gisborne Cl SM6. . . . . . .219 D5
Gisburn Ho 23 SE15 . . . . 140 A5
Gisburn Mans N8 . . . . . . .50 B5
Gisburn Rd N8. . . . . .50 B5
Gissing Wlk N1 . . . . .72 C1
Gittens Cl BR1. . . . . 186 D6
Given-Wilson Wlk E13 . . . .98 D5
Glacier Way HA0. . . . . . . .87 D5
Gladbeck Way EN2. . . . . . 4 D1
Gladding Rd E12. . . . . . . .77 D4
Gladebury Ct 2 SW19. . . .179 B4
Glade Cl KT6 . . . . 213 D6
Glade Gdns CR0 . . . . . . 207 A2
Glade La UB2. . . . . 107 A4
Gladesdale Rd DA17 . . . .125 D2
Southgate N21 . . . . .16 B4
Gladeside Croydon CR0. .206 D3
Southgate N21 . . . . .16 B4
Gladeside Cl KT9 . . . . . . 213 D1
Gladesmore Com Sch
 N15. . . . . .52 A4
Gladesmore Rd N15. . . . . .51 D3
Glades Sh Ctr The BR1 . . 187 A1
Gladeswood Rd DA17 . . .125 D2
Glade The Bromley BR1. .187 D1
Charlton SE7 . . . . 143 C5
Croydon CR0. . . . . 206 D3
Enfield EN2. . . . . 4 C3
Hammersmith W12 . . . . 112 B4
Southgate N21 . . . . .16 A4
Stoneleigh KT17 . . . . . . 216 A2
West Wickham BR4 . . . . 223 D5
Woodford IG8. . . . . .21 B1
Gladiator St SE23. . . . . . 163 A4
Glading Terr N16. . . . . . . .73 D5
Gladioli Cl 6 TW12 . . . . .173 C4
Gladsdale Dr HA5. . . . . . .40 B5
Gladsmuir Rd Barnet EN5. . 1 A3
Upper Holloway N19 . . . .49 C1
Gladstone Ave
Feltham TW14 . . . . 150 B5
Plashet E12 . . . . .78 A1
Tottenham N22 . . . . .32 D1
Twickenham TW2 . . . . . 152 B4

Gladstone Ct
 12 Merton SW19 . . . . .179 C3
Ruislip HA4. . . . . .61 C6
Westminster SW1 . . . . .259 D3
Willesden NW2. . . . . . . .68 B3
Gladstone Gdns TW3. . . .130 A4
Gladstone Ho
 6 Mitcham SW19 . . . . 180 D1
 16 Poplar E14. . . . . . . .97 C1
Gladstone Mews
 3 Penge SE20. . . . . . 184 C3
Wood Green N22 . . . . . . .32 C1
Gladstone Par NW2. . . . . .68 C5
Gladstone Park Gdns
 NW2 . . . . .68 B5
Gladstone Park Sch
 NW10. . . . . .68 B3
Gladstone Pl KT8 . . . . . .196 C4
Gladstone Rd Acton W4. .111 B3
Buckhurst Hill IG9 . . . . . .21 C3
Farnborough BR6. . . . . .227 A3
Kingston u T KT1 . . . . . 198 C6
Merton SW19 . . . . 179 C3
Southall UB2. . . . . 107 A4
Surbiton KT6. . . . . 214 A6
Thornton Heath CR0. . . .205 B2
Gladstone St SE1 . . . . . .261 C6
Gladstone Terr SW8 . . . .268 D2
Gladstone Way HA3. . . . . .42 C6
Gladwell Rd London N8. . .50 B3
Plaistow BR1 . . . . 187 A4
Gladwin Ho NW1 . . . . . .232 B3
Gladwyn Rd SW15 . . . . . 134 D2
Gladys Aylward Sch The
 N18. . . . . .33 B6
Gladys Dimson Ho E7. . . .76 D3
Gladys Rd NW6 . . . . .69 C1
Glaisher St SE8. . . . . . . .141 C6
Glamis Cres UB3. . . . . . .105 A3
Glamis Ct W3 . . . . .110 D4
Glamis Est 3 E1. . . . . . . 118 D6
Glamis Pl E1 . . . . 118 C6
Glamis Rd E1. . . . . 118 C6
Glamis Way N20. . . . . . . .14 A2
Glamorgan Cl CR4,
 SW16. . . . . 204 A4
Glamorgan Ct 4 W7 . . . . .86 D2
Glamorgan Rd KT1. . . . . 175 C3
Glandford Way RM6. . . . . .58 B4
Glanfield Rd BR3 . . . . . .207 B5
Glanleam Rd HA7 . . . . . . .25 C5
Glanville Ho 4 SW12 . . . .159 C4
Glanville Mews HA7. . . . . .25 A5
Glanville Rd Bromley BR2. .209 B6
Clapham Pk SW2 . . . . . 160 A6
Glasbrook Ave TW2. . . . .151 B3
Glasbrook Rd SE9. . . . . .165 D4
Glasbury Ho 5 SW9 . . . .138 B1
Glaserton Rd N16. . . . . . .51 C2
Glasford St SW17 . . . . . 180 D4
Glasfryn Ct HA2. . . . . . . .64 B6
Glasgow Ho W9 . . . . .91 D5
Glasgow Rd Edmonton N18. .34 B5
Newham E13. . . . . .99 B5
Glasgow Terr
 SW1. . . . . . . .115 D1 259 A1
Glasier Ct 6 E15 . . . .76 C1
Glasse Cl W13 . . . . 109 A6
Glasshill St SE1 . . .116 D4 251 D2
Glasshouse Cl UB8. . . . . .82 D2
Glasshouse Fields E1 . . . 118 D6
Glasshouse St
 W1. . . . . .115 C6 249 B5
Glasshouse The SE13. . . .142 A1
Glasshouse Wlk
 SE11 . . . . . . .116 B1 260 C2
Glasshouse Yd EC1. . . . .242 A5
Glasslyn Rd N8 . . . . .49 D4
Glassmill La BR2. . . . . . .186 D1
Glass St 4 E2 . . . . .96 B3
Glass Yd SE18 . . . . 122 C3
Glastonbury Ave IG8. . . . .37 D4
Glastonbury Ct
 12 Deptford SE14. . . . .140 C5
 1 Ealing W13 . . . . 109 A5
Glastonbury Ho
London SE12. . . . . 164 D6
Pimlico SW1 . . . . .258 C2
Glastonbury Pl 22 E1. . . . .96 C1
Glastonbury Rd
Edmonton N9 . . . . .18 A3
Morden SM4. . . . . .201 C2
Glastonbury St NW6. . . . .69 B3
Glaston Ct W5 . . . . .109 D5
Glaucus St E3 . . . . .97 D2
Glazbury Rd W14 . .113 A1 254 B2
Glazebrook Cl SE21 . . . .161 B2
Glazebrook Rd TW11. . . .174 D3
Gleave Ct 7 N20. . . . . . . .14 D2
Glebe Ave Enfield EN2. . . . 4 D3
Harrow HA3. . . . . .44 A6
Mitcham CR4 . . . . .180 C1
Ruislip HA4. . . . . .62 B2
Uxbridge UB10. . . . . . . .61 A4
Woodford IG8. . . . . .37 A4
Glebe Cl 1 Chiswick W4. .111 C1
Uxbridge UB10. . . . . . . .61 A4

Glebe Cotts
Feltham TW13 . . . . .151 C1
Sutton SM1. . . . . .217 D4
Glebe Cres Harrow HA3 . . .44 A6
Hendon NW4 . . . . .46 C5
Glebe Ct Ealing W5 . . . . . .109 D5
Hanwell W7 . . . . .108 B6
Lewisham SE3 . . . . .142 C2
Mitcham CR4 . . . . .202 D6
Palmers Green N13 . . . .16 C1
Ruislip HA4. . . . . .39 B2
Stanmore HA7 . . . . .25 C5
Glebe Fst & Mid Sch HA3. .44 A5
Glebe Gdns KT3 . . . . . . .199 C2
Glebe Ho
8 Bermondsey SE16 . . . . .118 B3
Feltham TW13 . . . . .151 C1
7 Woolwich SE18 . . . . . .122 C2
Glebehyrst SE19 . . . . . .183 C6
Glebe House Dr BR2 . . .209 B1
Glebe La Barnet EN5 . . . .12 A5
Harrow HA3 . . . . .44 A5
Glebeland Gdns TW17 . .193 A3
Glebelands
East Molesey KT8 . . . . . .195 D5
Leyton E10 . . . . .75 D6
Mitcham CR4 . . . . .202 C6
Woodford E18 . . . . .37 A1
Glebelands Ave Ilford IG2. .57 B2
Woodford E18. . . . . .37 A1
Glebelands Cl
Camberwell SE5 . . . . . . .139 C2
Finchley N2. . . . . .30 B2
Glebelands Rd TW14 . . .150 A4
Glebe Path CR4 . . . . . . .202 D6
Glebe Pl SW3 . . . . .**136 C6 267 A6**
Glebe Prim Sch UB10 . . . .61 B4
Glebe Rd Barnes SW13 . .134 A3
Belmont SM2 . . . . .217 A1
Bromley BR1. . . . . .187 A2
Dagenham RM10 . . . . . .81 D2
Dalston E8 . . . . .73 D1
Finchley N3. . . . . .30 A2
Hayes UB3 . . . . .105 D5
Hornsey N8. . . . . .50 B5
Stanmore HA7 . . . . .25 C5
Wallington SM5 . . . . . . .218 D2
Willesden NW10. . . . . . .68 A2
Glebe Sch BR4. . . . . . . .224 B6
Glebe Side TW1. . . . . . .152 D5
Glebe Sq CR4 . . . . .202 D6
Glebe St W4 . . . . .111 C1
GlebeThe
Chislehurst BR7 . . . . . . .189 A2
Lewisham SE3 . . . . .142 C2
New Malden KT4 . . . . . .199 D1
Streatham SW16 . . . . . .181 D6
West Drayton UB7 . . . . .104 B2
Glebeway SE10 . . . . . . .37 C5
Glebe Way Feltham TW13 . .151 C1
West Wickham BR4 . . . . .224 B6
Gledhow Gdns SW5 . . . .**256 A3**
Gledstanes Rd
W14. . . . .**113 A1 254 B1**
Gledwood Ave UB4 . . . . .84 A2
Gledwood Cres UB4. . . . .83 D2
Gledwood Ct UB4. . . . . . .83 D2
Gledwood Dr UB4. . . . . . .83 D2
Gledwood Gdns UB4. . . . .84 A2
Gleed Ave WD23 . . . . .8 B2
Gleeson Dr BR6. . . . . . . .227 D4
Glegg Pl 3 SW15 . . . . .134 D1
Glenaffric Ave E14. . . . . .120 B2
Glen Albyn Rd SW19 . . . .156 D2
Glenalla Rd HA4 . . . . .39 D2
Glenalmond Ho
Ashford TW15. . . . . .148 A1
2 Putney SW15. . . . . . .156 D5
Glenalmond Rd HA3 . . . . .44 A5
Glenalvon Way 5 SE18. .122 A4
Glena Mount SM1. . . . . . .218 A4
Glenarm Coll IG1 . . . . . . .78 D6
Glenarm Rd E5 . . . . .74 D4
Glen Ave TW15. . . . . .170 C6
Glenavon Cl KT10 . . . . . .213 A1
Glenavon Ct KT4. . . . . . .216 B6
Glenavon Lo 5 E18. . . . . .55 A6
Glenavon Rd E15. . . . . . . .76 C1
Glenbarr Cl SE9. . . . . . . .144 D2
Glenbow Rd BR1. . . . . . .186 C5
Glenbrook N EN2 . . . . . . .4 B1
Glenbrook Prim Sch
SW4. . . . . .159 D5
Glenbrook Rd NW6 . . . . . .69 C3
Glenbrook S EN2 . . . . . . .4 B1
Glenbuck Ct 6 KT6. . . . .198 A3
Glenbuck Rd KT6. . . . . . .198 A3
Glenburnie Rd SW17 . . . .158 D1
Glencairn Dr W5. . . . . . . .87 C3
Glencairne Cl E16. . . . . . .99 D2
Glencairn Rd SW16 . . . . .182 A3
Glen Cl TW17 . . . . .192 C5
Glencoe Ave IG2. . . . . . . .57 C2
Glencoe Dr RM10 . . . . . . .81 C4
Glencoe Mans 6 SW9 . . .138 C1
Glencoe Rd UB4 . . . . .84 D3
Glencorse Gn WD19. . . . .22 D6
Glen Cres IG8 . . . . .37 B4

Glencroft Ct SM1 . . . . . . .217 C3
Glen Ct 6 Bromley BR1. . .186 D3
9 Penge SE20 . . . . .184 B2
Sidcup DA14 . . . . .190 A6
Glendale Ave
Edgware HA8 . . . . .26 C6
Ilford RM6 . . . . .58 C2
Wood Green N22 . . . . . .32 C3
Glendale Cl SE9 . . . . . . .144 C2
Glendale Dr SW19 . . . . . .179 B5
Glendale Gdns HA9. . . . . .44 A1
Glendale Mews BR3. . . . .185 D2
Glendale Way SE28 . . . . .124 C6
Glendall St SW9 . . . . . . .138 B1
Glendarvon St SW15 . . . .134 D2
Glendevon Cl HA8. . . . . . .10 D1
Glendish Rd N17. . . . . . . .34 B2
Glendor Gdns NW7 . . . . . .27 B6
Glendower Gdns 10
SW14. . . . . .133 B2
Glendower Pl SW7. . . . .**256 C4**
Glendower Prep Sch
SW7 . . . .**114** B2 **256 C4**
Glendower Rd
Chingford E4. . . . . .20 B3
Mortlake SW14 . . . . . . .133 B2
Glendown Ho 2 E8. . . . . .74 A3
Glendown Rd SE2. . . . . . .124 A1
Glendun Ct W3 . . . . .111 C6
Glendun Rd W3. . . . . .111 C6
Gleneagle Lo BR3. . . . . . .185 C2
Gleneagle Mews SW16. . .181 D5
Gleneagle Rd SW16. . . . . .181 D5
Gleneagles Ealing W13. . . .87 B2
Stanmore HA7 . . . . .25 B4
Gleneagles Cl
21 Bermondsey SE16. . . .118 B1
Crofton BR6 . . . . .211 B1
South Oxhey WD19. . . . .22 D6
Gleneagles Ct 4 TW11. . .175 A5
Gleneagles Gn 1 BR6. . .211 B1
Gleneagles Twr 2 UB1. . .86 A1
Gleneldon Mews SW16. . .182 A6
Gleneldon Rd SW16. . . . . .182 A6
Glenelg Rd SW2 . . . . .160 A6
Glenesk Rd SE9. . . . . . . .144 D1
Glenfarg Rd SE6. . . . . . . .164 B3
Glenfield Cres HA4. . . . . . .39 B2
Glenfield Rd
Ashford TW15. . . . . .171 A4
Ealing W13 . . . . .109 B4
Streatham SW12 . . . . . .159 C3
Glenfield Terr W13. . . . . .109 B5
Glenfinlas Way SE5 . . . . .138 D5
Glenforth St SE10. . . . . . .120 D1
Glengall Ct SE23 . . . . . . .163 A4
Glengall Gr E14. . . . . .120 A3
Glengall Pass 2 NW6. . . . .91 C6
Glengall Rd Bexley DA7. . .147 A2
Camberwell SE15. . . . . . .139 D6
Edgware HA8 . . . . .10 D1
Kilburn NW6. . . . . .91 B6
Woodford IG8. . . . . .37 B4
Glengall Terr SE15 . . . . . .139 D6
Glengarnock Ave E14. . . .120 A2
Glengarry Rd SE22. . . . . . .161 D6
Glen Gdns CR0. . . . . .220 C4
Glenham Dr IG2 . . . . .56 D4
Glenhead Cl SE9. . . . . . . .144 D2
Glenhill Cl N3 . . . . .29 C1
Glen Ho 6 Newham E16. .122 C5
Wallington SM6 . . . . . . .219 C4
Glenhouse Rd SE9. . . . . .166 C6
Glenhurst 4 BR3 . . . . . . .186 A2
Glenhurst Ave
Gospel Oak NW5 . . . . . . .71 A4
Ruislip HA4. . . . . .39 A1
Sidcup DA5. . . . . .169 B3
Glenhurst Ct 1 SE19. . . .183 D5
Glenhurst Rd
Brentford TW8 . . . . .109 C1
North Finchley N12. . . . . .30 B5
Glenhurst Rise SE19 . . . . .183 A3
Glenilla Rd NW3 . . . . .70 C2
Glenister Ho UB3 . . . . . . .106 B5
Glenister Park Rd SW16. .181 B3
Glenister Rd SE10. . . . . . .120 D1
Glenister St E16 . . . . .122 C5
Glenkerry Ho 1 E14. . . . . .98 A1
Glenlea Rd SE9 . . . . .166 C6
Glenloch Ct 2 NW3. . . . . .70 C2
Glenloch Rd Enfield EN3. . . .6 C3
Maitland Pk NW3 . . . . . . .70 C3
Glenluce Rd SE3 . . . . . . .143 A6
Glenlyon Rd SE9. . . . . . . .166 C6
Glenmead IG9 . . . . .21 C3
Glenmere Ave NW7 . . . . . .28 A4
Glenmere Row Lee SE12. .165 A5
Lewisham SE12 . . . . . . .164 D5
Glen Mews E17. . . . . .53 B4
Glenmill TW12. . . . . .173 B5
Glenmore SW15 . . . . .156 D5
Glenmore Ho 6 TW10. . . .154 A5
Glenmore Lawns W13. . . . .87 A1
Glenmore Rd
Bexley DA16. . . . . .145 D4
Maitland Pk NW3 . . . . . . .70 C2
Glenmore Way IG11 . . . . .102 A5
Glenmount Path 1
SE18 . . . . .123 A1

Glennie Ct SE21 . . . . . . .162 A3
Glennie Ho SE10 . . . . . . .142 A4
Glennie Rd SE27,SW16 . .160 C1
Glenny Rd IG11. . . . . .79 A2
Glenorchy Cl UB4. . . . . . . .85 A2
Glenpark St W13. . . . . . . .109 A6
Glenparke Rd E7. . . . . .77 B2
Glen Rd Chessington KT9. .214 A5
Newham E13 . . . . .99 C3
Walthamstow E17 . . . . . .53 B4
Glenridding NW1 . . . .**232 B3**
Glen Rise IG8. . . . . .37 B4
Glenrosa St SW6. . . . . . . .136 A3
Glenrose Ct DA14 . . . . . . .190 B5
Glenrose Ho 9 SW1 . . . . .218 A4
Glenroy St W12. . . . . .90 C1
Glensdale Rd SE4. . . . . . .141 B2
Glenshaw Mans 7 SW9. .138 C5
Glenshiel Rd SE9 . . . . . . .166 C6
Glentanner Way SW17 . . .158 B1
Glentham Gdns SW13. . . .134 B6
Glentham Rd SW13 . . . . .134 B6
Glen The Beckenham BR2 . .186 C1
Eastcote Village HA5 . . . .40 B4
Enfield EN2. . . . . .4 D1
Locksbottom BR6 . . . . . .226 C5
Rayners La HA5 . . . . .41 A2
Southall UB1. . . . . .107 B1
South Croydon CR0. . . . .222 D5
Wembley HA9 . . . . .65 D4
Glenthorpe SW15. . . . . . .134 A1
Glenthorpe Rd SM4. . . . . .200 D4
Glenton Rd SE13. . . . . . . .142 C1
Glentrammon Ave BR6. . .227 D3
Glentrammon Cl BR6 . . . .227 D3
Glentrammon Gdns BR6. .227 D2
Glentrammon Rd BR6. . . .227 D2
Glentworth Ct HA8. . . . . . .26 B5
Glentworth St
NW1. . . . .**92** D3 **237 D5**
Glenure Rd SE9. . . . . .166 C6
Glenview SE2. . . . . .146 D6
Glen View Rd BR1. . . . . . .187 D1
Glenville Ave EN2 . . . . .5 A5
Glenville Gr SE8. . . . . .141 B5
Glenville Mews SW18 . . . .157 C4
Glenville Rd KT2. . . . . . . .176 C2
Glen Wlk TW7 . . . . .152 B6
Glenwood Ave NW9 . . . . . .45 C1
Glenwood Cl HA1. . . . . . . .42 D4
Glenwood Ct
7 Sidcup DA14 . . . . .190 A6
6 Wanstead E18. . . . . . . .55 A6
Glenwood Gdns IG2. . . . . .56 C4
Glenwood Gr NW9 . . . . . . .45 A1
Glenwood Ho 3 EN5. . . . . .13 C6
Glenwood Rd
Edgware NW7 . . . . .11 C1
Forest Hill SE6 . . . . .163 C3
Harringay N15 . . . . .50 A4
Hounslow TW3 . . . . .130 B2
Stoneleigh KT17. . . . . . .216 A2
Glenwood Way CR0 . . . . .206 D3
Glenworth Ave E14 . . . . . .120 B2
Gliddon Rd W14 . . .**113** A1 **254 A2**
Glimpsing Gn DA18 . . . . . .125 A3
Glisson Rd UB10 . . . . .82 C5
Globe Acad The
SE1. . . . .**117** B3 **262 C5**
Globe Ct SE18 . . . . .145 A6
Globe Pond Rd SE16 . . . . .119 A5
Globe Prim Sch 37 E2. . . .96 C4
Globe Rd
Bethnal Green E1, E2 . . . .96 C3
Stratford E15. . . . . .76 D3
Woodford IG8. . . . . .37 C4
Globe St SE1 . . . .**117** B4 **252 C1**
Globe Terr 9 E2 . . . . .96 C4
Globe Theatre The*
SE1. . . . .**117** A5 **252 A5**
GLOBE TOWN 96 D4
Globe View EC4. . . . .**252 A6**
Globe Yd W1 . . . .**238** C1
Glossop Ho TW7 . . . . .131 A1
Gloster Rd KT3 . . . . .199 C5
Gloucester SE14 . . . .**254 D3**
Gloucester Ave
Camden Town
NW1. . . . .**93** A6 **231 B6**
Falconwood DA16. . . . . .145 D1
Sidcup DA15. . . . . .167 C2
Gloucester Cir SE10. . . . . .142 A5
Gloucester Cl
Thames Ditton KT7. . . . .197 A1
Willesden NW10. . . . . . . .67 B1

Gloucester Cres
Camden Town
NW1. . . . .**93** B6 **231 C6**
Staines TW18 . . . . .170 A4
Gloucester Ct
6 Acton W3. . . . . .88 C1
10 Belmont SM2. . . . . . . .217 C1
Borough The SE1. . . . . .**262 B6**
City of London EC3. . . . .**253 B5**
Dulwich SE22 . . . . .162 A3
5 Ealing W7 . . . . .86 D2
Golders Green NW11. . . .47 B2
Harrow HA1 . . . . .42 C6
Redbridge IG1 . . . . .56 B2
Richmond TW9 . . . . .132 C5
8 Surbiton KT6. . . . . . . .197 D2
Gloucester Dr
Finsbury Pk N4 . . . . .72 D6
London NW11. . . . . .47 C5
Gloucester Gate NW1. . .**231 C4**
Gloucester Gate Mews
NW1. . . . .**231 C4**
Gloucester Gdns
Cockfosters EN4. . . . . . . .15 A6
Golders Green NW11. . . .47 B2
Paddington W2. . . . .**236 A2**
Redbridge IG1 . . . . .56 A2
Sutton SM1. . . . . .217 D6
Gloucester Gr HA8. . . . . . .27 B2
Gloucester Ho
Kilburn NW6. . . . . .91 C5
Richmond TW10. . . . . . .154 C6
Gloucester Lo 9 CR0 . . . .221 D6
Gloucester Mews
Paddington W2. . . . .**236 B1**
Walthamstow E17 . . . . . .53 C2
Gloucester Mews W W2. .**236 B1**
Gloucester Par
Bexley DA15 . . . . .168 A6
Hayes UB3 . . . . .105 A3
Gloucester Pl SW7 . . . . .**256 A4**
Gloucester Pl W1. .**92** D2 **237 D4**
Gloucester Pl Mews
W1. . . . .**92** D2 **237 D3**
Gloucester Prim Sch
SE15. . . . . .139 C5
Gloucester Rd Acton W3 . .111 A4
Croydon CR0. . . . . .205 C2
Ealing W5 . . . . .109 C4
Edmonton N18 . . . . .33 D5
Enfield EN2. . . . . .5 A5
Erith DA17 . . . . .125 B1
Feltham TW13 . . . . .150 C3
Hampton TW12 . . . . . . .173 D3
Harrow HA1 . . . . .41 D4
Hounslow TW4 . . . . .129 A1
Ilford E12 . . . . .78 B4
Kingston u T KT1, KT2. . .176 D1
Leyton E10 . . . . .53 C2
New Barnet EN5. . . . . . . .14 A6
Richmond TW9 . . . . .132 C5
South Kensington
SW7 . . . .**114** A2 **256 A4**
Teddington TW11 . . . . . .174 C5
Tottenham N17. . . . . .51 B6
Twickenham TW2 . . . . . .152 A3
Wanstead E11 . . . . .55 C4
Gloucester Road Sta
SW7 . . . .**114** A2 **256 A4**
Gloucester Sq
6 Hackney E2. . . . . .96 A6
Paddington W2. . . .**92** C1 **237 A1**
Gloucester St
SW1. . . . .**115** C1 **259 A2**
Gloucester Terr
W2. . . . .**92** A1 **236 B1**
Gloucester Way EC1. . . .**234 B1**
Gloucester Wlk
W8. . . . .**113** C4 **245 B2**
Glover Cl SE2. . . . . .124 C2
Glover Dr N18. . . . . .34 C4
Glover Ho London SE15. . .140 B1
2 South Hampstead NW6. . .70 A1
Glover Rd HA5. . . . . .40 D3
Glovers Gr HA4. . . . . .38 D2
Glovers Lo 24 TW10. . . . .153 D6
Glowhill Ct N12. . . . . .30 A3
Gloxinia Wlk TW12. . . . . .173 C4
Glycena Rd SW11 . . . . . . .136 D2
Glyn Ave EN4 . . . . .2 B1
Glyn Cl SE25 . . . . .183 C2
Glyn Ct Stanmore HA7 . . . .25 B4
West Norwood SE27. . . .160 D1
Glyndale Grange SM2. . . .217 D2
Glyndebourne Ct 5 UB5. .84 C4
Glyndebourne Pk BR6. . . .226 D6
Glynde Mews SW3 . . . . . .**257 B5**
Glynde Rd DA7 . . . . .147 A2
Glynde Reach WC1. . . . . .**233 B1**
Glynde St SE4 . . . . .163 B5
Glyndon Rd SE18 . . . . . . .123 B2
Glyn Dr DA14 . . . . .190 B6
Glynfield Rd NW10. . . . . . .67 C1
Glyn Mans W14 . . . .**254 B4**
Glynne Rd N22. . . . . .32 C1
Glyn Rd Clapton Pk E5 . . . .74 D4
Enfield EN3. . . . . .6 C1
North Cheam KT4, SM3 . .216 D6
Glyn St SE11. . . . .**260 C1**

Glynwood Ct 7 SE23. . . .162 C2
Goater's Alley SW6 . . . . .**264** D3
Goat La EN1 . . . . .5 D5
Goat Rd CR4. . . . . .202 D2
Goat Wharf TW8 . . . . .132 A6
Godalming Ave SM6 . . . . .220 B3
Godalming Rd E14. . . . . . . .97 D2
Godbold Rd E15 . . . . .98 C4
Goddard Cl TW17 . . . . . . .192 B6
Goddard Ct HA3 . . . . .25 A1
Goddard Ho SW19 . . . . . .156 D2
Goddard Pl N19. . . . . .71 C5
Goddard Rd BR3. . . . . . . .207 A5
Goddards Way IG1. . . . . . .57 B1
Goddards Ho E17 . . . . .53 C6
Godfrey Ave Northolt UB5. .85 A4
Twickenham TW2 . . . . . .152 B4
Godfrey Hill SE18 . . . . . . .122 A2
Godfrey Ho EC1. . . . .**235** C1
Godfrey Rd SE18. . . . . . . .122 B2
Godfrey St
Chelsea SW3 . . . .**114** C1 **257 B2**
Mill Meads E15. . . . . .98 A5
Godfrey Way TW4 . . . . . . .151 B4
Goding St SE11. . . . .**116** A1 **260 B1**
Godley Rd SW18 . . . . .158 B3
Godliman St EC4. . . . .**252 A6**
Godman Rd SE15 . . . . . . .140 B3
Godolphin Cl N13. . . . . . . .32 C4
Godolphin Ho
Primrose Hill NW3 . . . . . .70 C1
7 Streatham SW2. . . . . . .160 C3
Godolphin & Latymer Sch 16
W6. . . . . .112 B2
Godolphin Pl W3 . . . . .111 B6
Godolphin Rd W12. . . . . . .112 B4
Godson Rd CR0. . . . . .220 C5
Godson St N1. . . . .**234 A4**
Godstone Ct 1 N16. . . . . . .51 C1
Godstone Ho
Borough The SE1. . . . . .**262 D6**
1 Kingston u T KT2 . . . . . .176 D4
Godstone Rd Sutton SM1. .218 A4
Twickenham TW1 . . . . . .153 B5
Godstow Rd SE2. . . . . . . .124 C4
Godwin Cl Shoreditch N1 . .**235 B4**
West Ewell KT19. . . . . . .215 A2
Godwin Ct NW1. . . . .**232 B4**
Godwin Ho
2 Haggerston E2 . . . . .95 D5
Kidbrooke SE18 . . . . . . .144 B4
Kilburn NW6. . . . . .91 D5
Godwin Jun Sch E7. . . . . .77 B4
Godwin Prim Sch RM9 . . . .81 A1
Godwin Rd
Bromley BR1, BR2 . . . . .209 C6
Forest Gate E7 . . . . .77 B4
Godwyn Ho 13 KT6. . . . . .198 A3
Goffers Ho SE3 . . . . .142 C3
Goffers Rd SE3, SE13 . . . .142 C3
Goffs Rd TW15. . . . . .171 B4
Goffton Ho 14 SW9. . . . . .138 B3
Goidel Cl SM6 . . . . .219 D4
Golborne Gdns
5 Kensal Town W10 . . . . . .91 A3
West Kilburn W10 . . . . . . .91 A3
Golborne Mews 9 W10. . . .91 A2
Golborne Rd W10. . . . . . . .91 A2
Golda Cl EN5 . . . . .12 D5
Golda Ct N3. . . . . .29 B1
Goldbeaters Gr HA8. . . . . .27 C3
Goldbeaters Prim Sch
HA8. . . . . .27 B2
Goldcliff Cl SM4 . . . . .201 C2
Goldcrest Cl Newham E16. .99 D2
Woolwich SE28. . . . . . . .124 C6
Goldcrest Mews W5 . . . . . .87 D2
Goldcrest Way
Bushey WD23 . . . . .8 A3
New Addington CR0. . . . .224 B1
Golden Cres UB3 . . . . . . .105 C5
Golden Cross Mews 2
W11. . . . . .91 B1
Golden Ct 4 Barnet EN4 . . . .2 C1
Ealing W7 . . . . .108 C6
Hounslow TW3 . . . . .130 B3
10 Richmond TW9 . . . . . .153 D6
Golden Hinde The* SE1. .**252 C4**
Golden Hind Pl 5 SE8 . . . .119 B2
Golden La EC1. . . . . .**95** A3 **242 B5**
Golden Lane Campus
EC1. . . . .**95** A3 **242 A5**
Golden Lane L Ctr
EC1. . . . .**95** A3 **242 A5**
Golden Manor W7 . . . . . . .108 C6
Golden Mews SE20 . . . . . .184 C2
Golden Par 2 E17 . . . . .54 A6
Golden Plover Cl E16 . . . . .99 A1
Golden Sq W1 . . . . .**115** C6 **249 B6**
Golders Cl HA8 . . . . .26 C5
Golders Ct NW11 . . . . .47 B2
Golders Gdns NW11. . . . . .47 B2
GOLDERS GREEN 47 B2
Golders Green Coll
NW11. . . . . .47 C1
Golders Green Cres
NW11. . . . . .47 C2
Golders Green Rd NW11. . .47 A2
Golders Green Sta NW11. .47 C1
Golders Hill Sch NW11. . . .47 C2

Golderslea NW11 . . . . .47 C1
Golders Manor Dr NW11 . .47 A3
Golders Park Cl NW11 . . . . .47 C1
Golders Rise NW4 . . . . .46 D4
Golders Way NW11 . . . . .47 B2
Golderton 2 NW4 . . . . .46 C5
Goldfinch Rd SE28 . . . . .123 B3
Goldhawk Ind Est W6 . . . .112 B3
Goldhawk Mews 2
  W12. .112 B4
Goldhawk Rd W12 . . . . .112 A3
Goldhawk Road Sta
  W12. .112 C4
Goldhaze Cl IG8 . . . . .37 D3
Gold Hill HA8 . . . . .27 B4
Goldhurst Terr NW6 . . . . . . .70 A1
Goldie Ho N19 . . . . .49 D2
Goldie Leigh Hospl SE2 . .146 C6
Golding Cl KT9 . . . . .213 C2
Golding Ct 7 IG1 . . . . .78 C5
Golding St E1 . . . . .96 A1
Goldington Cres NW1 . . . .232 C4
Goldington Ct NW1 . . . . . . .232 C5
Goldington St
  NW1. . . . . .93 D5 232 C4
Goldman Cl E2 . . . . .96 A3
Goldmark Ho SE3 . . . . .143 B2
Goldney Rd W9 . . . . .91 C3
Goldrill Dr N11 . . . . .15 A2
Goldsboro Rd
  SW8. . . . . .137 D5 269 D3
Goldsborough Cres E4 . . . .20 A2
Goldsborough Ho SW8 . . .269 D1
Goldsdown Cl EN3 . . . . .7 A3
Goldsdown Rd EN3 . . . . .7 A3
Goldsmid St 2 SE18 . . . . .123 C1
Goldsmith Ave Acton W3 . .111 B6
  Dagenham RM8 . . . . .59 C2
  Hyde The NW9 . . . . .45 C3
  Plashet E12 . . . . .78 A2
Goldsmith Cl HA2 . . . . .41 D1
Goldsmith Ct
  Edgware HA8 . . . . .26 B6
  St Giles WC1 . . . . .240 B2
Goldsmith Ho W3 . . . . .111 B6
Goldsmith La NW9 . . . . .45 A5
Goldsmith Rd Acton W3 . .111 B5
  Friern Barnet N11 . . . . .30 D5
  Higham Hill E17 . . . . .34 D1
  Leyton E10 . . . . .53 D1
  Peckham SE15 . . . . .140 A4
Goldsmiths Bldgs W3 . . . .111 B5
Goldsmiths Cl W3. . . . . . . .111 B5
Goldsmiths Coll, Univ of
  London SE14 . . . . .141 A4
Goldsmith's Ct N6 . . . . .49 B3
Goldsmith's Pl 6 NW6 . . . .91 D6
Goldsmith's Row E2 . . . . . .96 A5
Goldsmith's Sq 17 E2 . . . . .96 A5
Goldsmith St EC2 . . . . .242 B2
Goldthorpe NW1 . . . . .232 A5
Goldwell Ho SE22 . . . . .139 C1
Goldwell Rd CR7 . . . . .204 B5
Goldwin Cl SE14 . . . . .140 C4
Goldwing Cl E16 . . . . .99 A1
Golf Cl
  South Norwood SW16 . . .182 C2
  Stanmore HA7 . . . . .25 C3
Golf Club Dr KT2 . . . . .177 B3
Golfe Ho IG1 . . . . .79 B5
Golfe Rd IG1 . . . . .79 B5
Golfers View N12 . . . . .30 B6
Golf Rd Bromley BR1 . . . . .210 C6
  Ealing W5 . . . . .88 B1
Golf Side KT2 . . . . .152 B1
Golfside Cl N20 . . . . .14 C1
Golf Side Cl KT3 . . . . .177 C1
Gollogly Terr 9 SE7 . . . . . .121 C1
Gomer Pl TW11 . . . . .175 A4
Gomm Rd SE16 . . . . .118 C3
Gomshall Ave SM6 . . . . . . .220 A3
Gondar Gdns NW6 . . . . .69 B3
Gondar Mans NW6 . . . . .69 B3
Gonson St SE8 . . . . .141 D6
Gonston Cl SW19 . . . . .157 A2
Gonville Cres UB5 . . . . .63 D2
Gonville Ct 6 SW4 . . . . .14 D3
Gonville Ho 6 SW15 . . . . .156 D5
Gonville Prim Sch CR7 . . .204 B4
Gonville Rd CR7 . . . . .204 B4
Gonville St SW6 . . . . .135 A2
Gooch Ho Holborn EC1 . . .241 A4
  Lower Clapton E5 . . . . .74 B5
Goodall Ho 10 SE4 . . . . . . .140 D1
Goodall Rd E11 . . . . .76 A5
Goodbehere Ho 7 SE27. . .183 A6
Gooden Ct HA1 . . . . .64 C5
Goodenough Coll
  WC1 . . . . .94 B3 240 C6
Goodenough Rd SW19 . . .179 B3
Goodey Rd IG11 . . . . .79 D1
Goodfaith Ho 18 E14 . . . . .119 D6
Goodge Pl W1 . . . . .239 B3
Goodge St W1 . . . . .93 C2 239 B3
Goodge Street Sta
  W1 . . . . .93 D2 239 C4
Goodhall Cl HA7 . . . . .25 B4
Goodhall St NW10 . . . . .89 D4

Good Hart Pl E14 . . . . .119 A6
Goodhart Way BR4. . . . . . . .208 C3
Goodhew Rd CR0 . . . . .206 A3
Goodhope Ho 17 E14. . . . . .119 D6
Gooding Cl KT3 . . . . .199 A4
Goodinge Cl N7 . . . . .72 A2
Goodinge Rd N7. . . . . .72 A2
Gooding Ho 4 SE7 . . . . . . .121 C1
Goodison Cl WD23 . . . . .8 A6
Goodland Ho 1 KT3 . . . . . .199 C2
Goodman Cres
  Streatham SW2 . . . . .159 D2
  Thornton Heath CR0 . . . . .205 A3
Goodman Rd E10 . . . . .54 A2
Goodmans Ct HA0 . . . . .65 D4
Goodman's Stile 17 E1 . . . .96 A1
Goodman's Yd E1
  EC3 . . . . .117 D6 253 C6
GOODMAYES 58 B1
Goodmayes Ave IG3 . . . . . .58 A1
Goodmayes Hospl IG3 . . . .58 A4
Goodmayes La IG3. . . . . . . .80 A5
Goodmayes Lodge RM8. . . .80 A4
Goodmayes Prim Sch
  IG3 .58 B1
Goodmayes Rd IG3 . . . . . . .58 A1
Goodmayes Ret Pk RM6. . .58 B2
Goodmayes Sta IG3 . . . . . .58 A1
Goodrich Com Prim Sch
  SE22 . . . . .162 A5
Goodrich Ct 9 W10. . . . . . . .90 D1
Goodrich Ho
  20 Bethnal Green E2 . . . . . .96 C5
  Stamford Hill N16. . . . . . . .51 C2
Goodrich Rd SE22 . . . . . . .162 A5
Goodridge Ho E17 . . . . .36 A3
Good Shepherd RC Prim
  Sch
  Catford BR1 . . . . .186 D6
  New Addington CR0 . . . . .223 D1
Good Shepherd RC Prim Sch
  The W12 . . . . .111 D4
Goodson Ho SM4 . . . . .202 A2
Goodson Rd NW10 . . . . .67 C1
Goodson Ho 20 E14. . . . . . .119 B6
Goodway Gdns E14 . . . . . . .98 B1
Goodwill Ho 22 E14 . . . . . .119 D6
Goodwin Cl
  Bermondsey
  SE16 . . . . .117 D3 263 D5
  Mitcham CR4 . . . . .202 B6
Goodwin Ct
  East Barnet EN4 . . . . .14 C5
  Hornsey N8. . . . . .50 A6
  2 Mitcham SW19 . . . . . . .180 C3
Goodwin Dr DA14 . . . . .168 D2
Goodwin Gdns CR0, CR2 . .220 D2
Goodwin Ho Edmonton N9. .18 C3
  2 Peckham SE15. . . . . . . .140 B2
Goodwin Rd
  Croydon CR0. . . . . .220 D3
  Edmonton N9 . . . . .18 D3
  Shepherd's Bush W12 . . . .112 A4
Goodwins Ct WC2. . . . . . . .250 A6
Goodwin St N4 . . . . .72 C6
Goodwood Ave EN3 . . . . . . .6 C6
Goodwood Cl
  Morden SM4. . . . . .201 C5
  11 Stanmore HA7 . . . . .25 C5
Goodwood Ct W1 . . . . .238 D4
Goodwood Dr UB5 . . . . .63 C2
Goodwood Ho
  3 Acton Green W4 . . . . . .111 A1
  Penge SE26 . . . . .184 B4
Goodwood Lo 11 SE16 . . . .219 D5
Goodwood Mans 3
  SW9. . . . . .138 C2
Goodwood Par BR3 . . . . . . .207 A5
Goodwood Rd SE14 . . . . . .141 A5
Goodwyn Ave NW7 . . . . .27 C5
Goodwyn Sch NW7 . . . . .28 A5
Goodwyn's Vale N10 . . . . . .31 B2
Goodyear Ho 8 N2 . . . . .30 B1
Goodyers Gdns NW4 . . . . . .46 D4
Goosander Ct 34 SE8 . . . . .141 D6
Goosander Way SE18,
  SE28 . . . . .123 B3
Gooseacre La HA3 . . . . .43 D4
Goose Green Cl BR5 . . . . . .190 A1
Goose Green Prim Sch
  SE22 . . . . .139 D1
Goose Green Trad Est
  SE22 . . . . .140 A1
Gooseley La E6 . . . . .100 C4
Goose Sq 8 E6. . . . . .100 B1
Goossens Cl 1 SM1. . . . . . .218 A3
Gophir La EC4 . . . . .252 C6
Gopsall St N1. . . . . . .95 B5 235 D5
Gordon Ave Chingford E4 . . .36 C4
  Isleworth TW1 . . . . .153 B6
  Mortlake SW14 . . . . .133 C1
  Stanmore HA7 . . . . .25 A4
Gordonbrook Prim Sch
  SE4 . . . . .163 C6
Gordonbrook Rd SE4 . . . . .163 C6
Gordon Cl E17 . . . . .53 C3
Gordon Cres
  Croydon CR0. . . . . .205 D1
  Hayes UB3 . . . . .106 A2

Gordon Ct Edgware HA8. . . . .26 B5
  Hampton TW12. . . . . .174 A5
  5 Shepherd's Bush W12. . . .90 C1
  18 Wimbledon SW20 . . . . .178 D3
Gordondale Rd SW18,
  SW19. . . . . .157 C2
Gordon Dr TW17 . . . . .193 B2
Gordon Gdns HA8. . . . . .26 D1
Gordon Gr SE5. . . . . .138 D3
Gordon Hill EN2 . . . . .5 A4
Gordon Hill Sta EN2. . . . . . . .4 D4
Gordon Ho 2 Ealing W5. . . .88 A4
  Lee SE12. . . . . .165 A4
  17 Shadwell E1. . . . . .118 C6
Gordon Hospl
  SW1. . . . . .115 D2 259 C3
Gordon House Rd NW5. . . . .71 A4
Gordon Inf Sch IG1 . . . . .79 B5
Gordon Lo N16 . . . . .51 B1
Gordon Mans
  3 Dalston E8 . . . . .1 B1
  Marylebone WC1 . . . . .239 C5
Gordon Pl W8 . . . . .113 C4 245 B2
Gordon Rd Beckton SE9 . . .144 B3
  Ashford TW15. . . . . .148 A1
  Avery Hill DA15. . . . . .167 C6
  Barking IG11 . . . . .101 C6
  Beckenham BR3 . . . . .207 B6
  Chingford E4. . . . . .20 C4
  Chiswick W4 . . . . .132 D6
  Claygate KT10 . . . . .212 C1
  Dagenham RM6 . . . . .59 B3
  Ealing W13 . . . . .109 C6
  Edmonton N9 . . . . .18 B2
  Enfield EN2. . . . . .5 B3
  Finchley N3. . . . . .29 B3
  Harrow HA3 . . . . .42 C6
  Ilford IG1 . . . . .79 B5
  Isleworth TW3 . . . . .130 A1
  Kingston u T KT2. . . . . . . .176 B2
  Leyton E15. . . . . .76 A4
  Peckham SE15 . . . . .140 B3
  Richmond TW9 . . . . .132 B3
  Shepperton TW17. . . . . . .193 B3
  Southall UB2. . . . . .107 A2
  Surbiton KT5. . . . . .198 B2
  Wallington SM5 . . . . .218 D2
  Wanstead E11 . . . . .55 A3
  Woodford E18. . . . . .37 A2
  Wood Green N11 . . . . .31 D3
  Yiewsley UB7 . . . . .104 A6
Gordon Sq WC1. . . . . .93 D3 239 D6
Gordon St
  Bloomsbury WC1 . . . .93 D3 239 C6
  Newham E13 . . . . .99 A4
Gordon Way Barnet EN5. . . . .1 B1
  Bromley BR1. . . . . .187 A2
Gore Ct NW9 . . . . .44 C4
Gorefield Ho NW6 . . . . .91 C5
Gorefield Rd NW6 . . . . .91 C5
Gore Rd Hackney E9. . . . . . . .96 C6
  Merton SW20 . . . . .178 C1
Goresbrook L Ctr RM9 . . .102 D6
Goresbrook Rd RM9 . . . . . .102 D6
Gore St SW7. . . . . . .114 A3 256 B6
Gorham Ho 12 SW4 . . . . . .159 C5
Gorham Pl W11. . . . . .244 A5
Goring Gdns RM8 . . . . .80 C4
Goring Rd N11. . . . . .32 A4
Goring St EC3 . . . . .243 B2
Goring Way UB6 . . . . .86 A5
Gorleston Rd N15. . . . . .51 B4
Gorleston St
  W14. . . . . .113 A2 254 B4
Gorman Rd SE18. . . . . .122 B2
Gorringe Park Ave CR4. . . .181 A3
Gorringe Park Prim Sch
  CR4. . . . . .181 A2
Gorse Cl E16 . . . . .99 A1
Gorse Rd CR0. . . . . .223 C5
Gorse Rise SW17 . . . . .181 A5
Gorse Wlk UB7 . . . . .82 A1
Gorst Rd London SW11 . . . .158 D5
  North Acton NW10 . . . . . . .89 B3
Gorsuch Pl 1 E2 . . . . .95 D4
Gorsuch St E2 . . . . .95 D4
Gosberton Rd SW12. . . . . .159 A3
Gosbury Hill KT9. . . . . .214 A4
Gosfield Rd RM8. . . . . .59 C1
Gosfield St W1 . . . . .93 C2 239 A3
Gosford Gdns IG4. . . . . .56 B4
Gosford Ho 25 E3. . . . . .97 B5
Goshawk Gdns UB4. . . . . . .83 C5
Goslett Yd WC2 . . . . .239 D2
Gosling Cl UB6 . . . . .85 C4
Gosling Ho 2 E1 . . . . .118 C6
Gosling Way SW9 . . . . .138 C4
Gosmore Ct N9 . . . . .18 B2
Gospatric Home Ho
  SW14. . . . . .133 C2
Gospatrick Rd N17. . . . . .33 A2
GOSPEL OAK 71 A4
Gospel Oak Prim Sch
  NW5. . . . . .71 A4
Gospel Oak Sta NW5 . . . . . .71 A4
Gosport Ho 9 SW15 . . . . . .156 A3
Gosport Rd E17 . . . . .53 B4
Gosport Wlk N17 . . . . .52 B5

Gossage Rd
  Hillingdon UB10 . . . . .60 B1
  Plumstead SE18 . . . . .123 B1
Gosset St E2. . . . . .96 A4
Gosshill Rd BR7. . . . . .188 C1
Gossington Cl BR7. . . . . . . .188 D6
Gosterwood St SE8 . . . . . .141 A6
Gostling Rd TW2. . . . . .151 C3
Goston Gdns CR7. . . . . .204 C6
Goswell Pl EC1 . . . . .234 D1
Goswell Rd EC1. . . . .94 D4 234 D2
Gothic Ct
  17 Camberwell SE5 . . . . . .139 A4
  Harlington UB3 . . . . .127 B6
Gothic Rd TW2. . . . . .152 B2
Gottfried Mews NW5. . . . . . .71 C4
Goudhurst Ho 7 SE20 . . . .184 C3
Goudhurst Rd BR1 . . . . .186 D5
Gough Ho Islington N1 . . . .234 D6
  4 Kingston u T KT1 . . . . . .176 A1
Gough Rd Enfield EN1 . . . . . .6 B3
  Stratford E15 . . . . .76 D4
Gough Sq EC4. . . . . .94 C1 241 B2
Gough St WC1. . . . . .94 B3 240 C5
Gough Wlk 14 E14 . . . . .97 C1
Gould Ct SE19 . . . . .183 C5
Goulden Ho SW11 . . . . .136 C3
Goulding Gdns CR7 . . . . . . .183 A1
Gouldman Ho 33 E1. . . . . . . .96 C5
Gould Rd
  East Bedfont TW14. . . . . . .149 C4
  Twickenham TW2 . . . . .152 C3
Gould's Gn UB8. . . . . .104 D6
Gould Terr 26 E8 . . . . .74 B3
Goulston St
  E1 . . . . .95 D1 243 C2
Goulton Rd E5. . . . . .74 B4
Gourley Pl N15. . . . . .51 C4
Gourley St N15 . . . . .51 C4
Gourock Rd SE9 . . . . .166 C6
Govan St 2 E2. . . . . .96 A6
Gover Ct 8 SW4 . . . . .138 A3
Government Row EN3. . . . . . .7 C6
Govett Ave TW17 . . . . .193 A4
Govier Cl E15. . . . . .76 C1
Gowan Ave SW6 . . . .135 A4 264 A2
Gowan Ho 22 E2. . . . . .95 D4
Gowan Lea 4 E18 . . . . .55 A5
Gowan Rd NW10 . . . . .68 B2
Gower Cl SW4 . . . . .159 C5
Gower Ct WC1 . . . . .239 C6
Gower Ho 2 Barking IG11. . . .79 A1
  Hayes UB3 . . . . .105 C6
  Upper Tooting SW17. . . . . .180 B4
  12 Walthamstow E17 . . . . . .53 D6
  Walworth SE17. . . . . .262 B2
Gower House Sch NW9 . . . .67 A6
Gower Mews WC1. . . . . . . .239 D4
Gower Pl NW1,
  WC1. . . . . .93 D3 239 C6
Gower Rd Hounslow TW7. . .77 A2
  Upton E7. . . . . .77 A2
Gower Sch The 4 N7 . . . . . .72 A2
Gower St WC1. . . . . .93 D3 239 C5
Gower's Wlk E1. . . . . .96 A1
Gowland Pl BR3 . . . . .185 B1
Gowlett Rd SE15 . . . . .140 A2
Gowlland Cl CR0. . . . . .206 A2
Gowrie Rd SW11 . . . . .137 A2
Graburn Way KT8. . . . . .196 B6
Grace Ave DA7. . . . . .147 B3
Grace Bsns Ctr CR4 . . . . . .202 B3
Gracechurch St EC2, EC4. .252 D6
Grace Cl Burnt Oak HA8. . . . .27 A3
  Mottingham SE9 . . . . .165 D1
Grace Ct 5 Croydon CR0 . . .220 D5
  Twickenham TW2 . . . . .152 C2
Gracedale Rd SW16. . . . . . .181 B5
Gracedyer Ho N22 . . . . .32 A3
Gracefield Gdns SW16 . . . .160 A1
Gracehill 2 E1 . . . . .96 C2
Grace Ho
  Kennington SE11 . . . . . . .270 D6
  Penge SE26 . . . . .184 B4
Grace Jones Cl E8 . . . . .74 A2
Grace Path 2 SE26 . . . . . . .184 C6
Grace Pl E3 . . . . .97 D4
Grace Rd CR0. . . . . .205 A3
Graces Alley 14 SE1 . . . . . .118 A6
Graces Mews NW8 . . . . . . .229 B3
Grace's Mews SE5 . . . . . . .139 C3
Grace's Rd SE5 . . . . .139 C3
Grace St E3 . . . . .97 D4
Gradient The SE26. . . . . . . .184 A6
Graeme Ct UB6 . . . . .85 D4
Graeme Rd EN1 . . . . .5 C3
Graemesdyke Ave SW14. . .132 D1
Grafton 2 Ealing W13. . . . . . .87 A1
  Twickenham TW2 . . . . .151 B3
  Worcester Pk KT4. . . . . . . .215 C5
Grafton Cres NW1 . . . . .71 B2
Grafton Ct 10 Dalston E8. . . .74 A3
  East Bedfont TW14. . . . . . .149 B3
Grafton Gdns
  Dagenham RM8 . . . . .58 C5
  Harringay N4 . . . . .51 A6
Grafton Ho 18 Bow E3 . . . . .97 C4
  12 Deptford SE14 . . . . . . .119 B1
Grafton Jun & Inf Schs
  RM8 . . . . .81 B6
Grafton Mans SW4. . . . . . . .137 C1

Grafton Mews W1 . . . . .239 A5
Grafton Park Rd KT4 . . . . . .215 C6
Grafton Pl NW1. . . . . .93 D4 232 D1
Grafton Prim Sch 5 N7. . . .72 A5
Grafton Rd Acton W3 . . . . . .111 A6
  Dagenham RM8 . . . . .81 A6
  Enfield EN2. . . . . .4 B2
  Gospel Oak NW5 . . . . .71 A3
  Harrow HA1 . . . . .42 A4
  Kingston u T KT3 . . . . .199 C6
  Thornton Heath CR0. . . . . .204 C1
  Worcester Pk KT4. . . . . . . .215 C5
Grafton Sq SW4 . . . . .137 C2
Grafton St W1 . . . . .115 D6 248 D5
Grafton Terr NW5 . . . . .71 A3
Grafton Way
  East Molesey KT8. . . . . . . .195 B5
  Marylebone W1 . . . . .239 B5
Grafton Yd NW5 . . . . .71 B2
Graham Ave Ealing W13 . . .109 B4
  Mitcham CR4 . . . . .181 A2
Graham Cl CR0. . . . . .223 C6
Graham Ct Bromley BR1. . . .187 B3
  5 Deptford SE14. . . . . . . .140 D6
  Northolt UB5. . . . . .63 B3
GRAHAME PARK 27 C2
Grahame Park Way NW7,
  NW9 . . . . .27 D2
Grahame White Ho HA3 . . . .43 D6
Graham Gdns KT6 . . . . .198 A1
Graham Ho
  5 Balham SW12 . . . . .159 B4
  6 Barnet EN5 . . . . .1 D1
  Edmonton N9 . . . . .18 C3
  6 Tufnell Pk N19 . . . . .71 D4
  Woolwich SE18. . . . . .144 D5
Graham Lo Edgware HA8 . . .26 B4
  Hendon NW4 . . . . .46 B3
Graham Mans
  11 Barking IG11. . . . . .80 A1
  2 Hackney E8. . . . . .74 B2
Graham Rd Acton W4 . . . . .111 B3
  Bexleyheath DA6 . . . . .147 C1
  Dalston E8 . . . . .74 A2
  Hampton TW12. . . . . .173 C6
  Harringay N15 . . . . .50 D6
  Harrow HA3 . . . . .42 C6
  Hendon NW4 . . . . .46 B3
  Merton SW19 . . . . .179 B3
  Mitcham CR4 . . . . .181 A2
  Newham E13 . . . . .99 A3
Graham St N1 . . . . . .94 D5 234 D3
Graham Terr
  SW1. . . . . .115 A2 258 B3
Graham Twr W3. . . . . .110 D3
Grainger Cl UB5 . . . . .64 A3
Grainger Ct 22 SE5. . . . . . .139 A5
Grainger Rd
  Isleworth TW7 . . . . .130 D3
  Tottenham N22. . . . . .33 A2
Gramer Cl E11. . . . . .76 B6
Grampian Cl
  Harlington UB3. . . . . .127 B5
  Orpington BR6 . . . . .211 D3
  15 Sutton SM2 . . . . .218 A1
Grampian Gdns NW2. . . . . . .47 A1
Grampians The 10 W14 . . . .112 D4
Gramsci Way SE6 . . . . .163 D1
Granada St SW17 . . . . .180 C5
Granard Ave SW15 . . . . . . .156 B6
Granard Bsns Ctr NW7. . . . .27 C4
Granard Ho 20 E9. . . . . .74 D2
Granard Prim Sch SW15. . .156 B5
Granard Rd SW11, SW12 . .158 D4
Granary Cl N19 . . . . .18 C4
Granary Ct 3 RM6. . . . . .58 D2
Granary Mans SE28 . . . . . .123 A4
Granary Rd E1 . . . . .96 B3
Granary Sq N1. . . . . .72 C2
Granary St NW1 . . . . .93 D3 232 C5
Granary The SE8 . . . . .141 C5
Granby Ho 13 SE18 . . . . . . .122 B2
Granby Pl SE1 . . . . .251 A1
Granby Rd Eltham SE9 . . . .144 B2
  Woolwich SE18. . . . . .122 D3
Granby St
  Bethnal Green E2 . . . . .96 A3
  Shoreditch E2 . . . . .243 D6
Granby Terr NW1. . . . .93 C3 232 A3
Grand Arc N12. . . . . .30 A5
Grand Ave
  Clerkenwell EC1. . . . . .241 D4
  Fortis Green N10 . . . . .49 A5
  Tolworth KT5. . . . . .198 D3
  Wembley HA9. . . . . .66 C3
Grand Ave E HA9. . . . . .66 D3
Grand Avenue Prim Sch
  KT5. . . . . .199 A3
Grand Ct RM8 . . . . .81 A5
Grand Depot Rd SE18 . . . . .122 C1
Grand Dr London SW20. . . .178 A4
  West Barnes SM4, SW20. . .200 C5
Granden Rd SW16. . . . . . . .182 A1
Grandfield Ct W4 . . . . .133 B6
Grandison Rd
  London SW11 . . . . .158 C6
  North Cheam KT4 . . . . . . .216 C5

Grand Junction Wharf
N1 ... 235 A3
Grand Par London N4 ... 50 D3
Mortlake SW14 ... 133 A1
Tolworth KT6 ... 198 C1
Wembley HA9 ... 66 C6
Grand Union Cl W9 ... 91 B2
Grand Union Cres E8 ... 96 A6
Grand Union Ind Est
NW10 ... 88 D5
Grand Union Way UB2 .. 107 C4
Grand Vitesse Ind Est
SE1 ... 251 D3
Granfield St SW11 ... 266 D1
Grange Ave
East Barnet EN4 ... 14 D3
North Finchley N12 ... 30 A5
South Norwood SE25 ... 183 C1
Stanmore HA7 ... 25 C1
Totteridge N20 ... 13 A4
Twickenham TW2 ... 152 C2
Woodford IG8 ... 37 A3
Grange Cl
East Molesey KT8 ... 195 D5
Edgware HA8 ... 27 A5
Hayes UB3 ... 83 C2
Heston TW5 ... 129 B6
Sidcup DA15 ... 168 A1
Woodford IG8 ... 37 A3
Grangecliffe Gdns SE25 .. 183 C1
Grangecourt Rd N16 ... 51 C1
Grange Cres SE28 ... 102 C1
Grange Ct Belmont SM2 .. 217 D1
4 Finchley N12 ... 30 A4
Hackbridge SM6 ... 219 B5
Harrow HA1 ... 64 D5
Ilford IG6 ... 57 A6
Littleton TW17 ... 192 C5
Loughton IG10 ... 21 D6
Northolt UB5 ... 84 C5
Peckham SE15 ... 139 D3
Pinner HA5 ... 41 A6
Strand WC2 ... 240 D1
Wembley HA0 ... 65 C3
1 Willesden NW10 ... 67 C4
Grange Dr BR7 ... 188 B4
Grange Farm Cl HA2 ... 64 A6
Grange Farm Est TW17 .. 193 C6
Grangefield NW1 ... 72 A1
Grange Fst & Mid Schs
HA2 ... 41 D1
Grange Gdns London N14 .. 15 D3
Pinner HA5 ... 41 A5
South Norwood SE25 ... 183 C1
West Hampstead NW3 ... 69 D5
Grange Gr N1 ... 73 A2
Grange Hill Edgware HA8 .. 27 A5
South Norwood SE25 ... 183 C1
Grangehill Pl SE9 ... 144 B2
Grangehill Rd SE9 ... 144 B1
Grange Ho
6 Barking IG11 ... 101 B6
Bermondsey SE1 ... 263 C5
Willesden NW10 ... 68 B1
Grange La SE21 ... 161 D2
Grange Lo SW19 ... 178 D4
Grange Mans KT17 ... 215 D1
Grangemill 11 NW5 ... 71 B4
Grangemill Rd SE6 ... 163 C2
GRANGE MILLS ... 113 C3
Grange Mills SW12 ... 159 C3
Grangemill Way SE6 ... 163 C2
GRANGE PARK ... 16 C6
Grange Park Ave N21 ... 17 A5
Grange Park Jun & Inf Schs
UB4 ... 83 D3
Grange Park Pl SW20 ... 178 B3
Grange Park Prep Sch
N21 ... 16 D5
Grange Park Prim Sch
N21 ... 4 C1
Grange Park Rd
Leyton E10 ... 53 D1
South Norwood CR7 ... 205 B6
Grange Park Sta N21 ... 16 D5
Grange Pk W5 ... 110 A5
Grange Pl NW6 ... 69 C1
Grange Prim Sch
Bermondsey SE1 . 117 C3 263 A5
Ealing W5 ... 109 D4
Newham E13 ... 98 D4
Grange Rd Barnes SW13 .. 134 A4
Belmont SM2 ... 217 C1
Bermondsey SE1 . 117 D3 263 C5
Borehamwood WD6 ... 10 B6
Burnt Oak HA8 ... 27 B4
Chessington KT9 ... 214 A4
Ealing W5 ... 110 A5
East Molesey KT8 ... 195 D5
Greenhill HA1 ... 43 A4
Gunnersbury W4 ... 110 D1
Hayes UB3 ... 83 C1
Highgate N6 ... 49 A3
Ilford IG1 ... 79 A4
Kingston u T KT1 ... 198 A6
Leyton E10 ... 53 C1
Newham E13 ... 98 D4

Grange Rd *continued*
Orpington BR6 ... 227 A6
Roxeth HA2 ... 64 B6
Southall UB1 ... 107 A4
South Norwood SE19,
SE25 ... 183 B1
Tottenham N17 ... 34 A4
Walthamstow E17 ... 53 A4
Willesden NW10 ... 68 B2
Grange St N1 ... 235 D5
Grange The
Bermondsey SE1 . 117 D3 263 C5
Cockfosters EN4 ... 2 D2
Croydon CR0 ... 223 B6
Ealing W13 ... 87 C2
7 Gunnersbury W4 ... 110 D1
Hammersmith W12 ... 112 B3
19 Maitland Pk NW3 ... 70 D2
South Acton W3 ... 110 D4
3 Walthamstow E17 ... 53 A4
4 Wanstead E18 ... 55 A6
Wembley HA0 ... 66 C1
West Barnes KT3 ... 200 A4
West Ewell KT19 ... 215 B4
West Kensington
W14 ... 113 B2 254 C3
Wimbledon SW19 ... 178 D4
Grange Vale SM2 ... 217 D1
Grange View Rd N20 ... 14 A3
Grangeway London N12 ... 29 D6
South Hampstead NW6 ... 69 C1
Woodford IG8 ... 37 C6
Grangeway Gdns IG4 ... 56 A4
Grangeway The N21 ... 16 D5
Grange Wlk SE1 . 117 D3 263 C5
Grangewood DA5 ... 169 B3
Grangewood Cl HA5 ... 40 A4
Grangewood Ind Sch E7 .. 77 D1
Grangewood La BR3 ... 185 B4
Grangewood Sch HA5 ... 39 D4
Grangewood St E6 ... 99 D6
Grange Yd SE1 ... 117 D3 263 C5
Granham Gdns N9 ... 17 D2
Granite Apts E15 ... 76 B2
Granite St SE18 ... 123 D1
Granleigh Rd E11 ... 76 C6
Grannary The 10 SE16 ... 118 C4
Gransden Ave E8 ... 74 B1
Gransden Ho 1 SE8 ... 119 B1
Gransden Rd W12 ... 111 D4
Grantbridge St
N1 ... 94 D5 234 D4
Grantchester 12 KT1 ... 176 C1
Grantchester Cl HA1 ... 64 D5
Grant Cl London N14 ... 15 C4
Shepperton TW17 ... 192 D3
Tottenham N17 ... 33 C1
Grant Ct 2 Chingford E4 ... 20 A3
11 Hendon NW9 ... 27 D1
Grantham Cl HA8 ... 10 A1
Grantham Ct
Dagenham RM6 ... 59 B2
Kingston u T KT2 ... 175 D5
9 Rotherhithe SE16 ... 118 D4
Grantham Gdns RM6 ... 59 B2
Grantham Gn WD6 ... 11 A6
Grantham Ho
Ashford TW16 ... 171 C3
12 Peckham SE15 ... 140 A6
Grantham Pl W1 ... 248 C3
Grantham Rd
Chiswick W4 ... 133 C5
Little Ilford E12 ... 78 C4
South Lambeth SW9 ... 138 A3
Grant Ho
38 Clapham SW8 ... 137 D3
Clerkenwell EC1 ... 241 D4
Grantley Ho
2 Deptford SE14 ... 140 D6
5 Putney SW19 ... 156 D3
Grantley Pl KT10 ... 212 A3
Grantley Rd TW4, TW5 ... 128 C3
Grantley St E1 ... 96 D3
Grant Mus of Zoology*
WC1 ... 93 D3 239 C5
Grantock Rd E17 ... 36 B2
Granton Prim Sch SW16. 181 C3
Granton Rd Ilford IG3 ... 58 A1
Sidcup DA14 ... 190 C4
Streatham SW16 ... 181 C2
Grant Pl 2 CR0 ... 205 D1
Grant Rd Battersea SW11 .. 136 C2
Croydon CR0 ... 205 D1
Harrow HA3 ... 42 D6
Grants Cl NW7 ... 28 D3
Grants Cotts KT10 ... 212 B6
Grant St Islington N1 ... 234 A4
Newham E13 ... 99 A4
Grantully Rd W9 ... 91 D4
Grant Way TW7 ... 131 A6
Granville Ave
Feltham TW13 ... 150 A2
Hounslow TW3, TW4 ... 151 C6
Lower Edmonton N9 ... 18 C1
Granville Cl CR0 ... 221 C6
Granville Ct
8 Deptford SE14 ... 141 A5
Hornsey N4 ... 50 B3
Shoreditch N1 ... 235 D6

Granville Gdns
Ealing W5 ... 110 B5
South Norwood SW16 ... 182 B3
Granville Gr SE13 ... 142 A2
Granville Ho 18 E14 ... 97 C1
Granville Ind Est NW2 ... 69 B6
Granville Mans 8 W12 ... 112 C4
Granville Mews DA14 ... 190 A6
Granville Pk SE13 ... 142 B2
Granville Pl London N12 ... 30 A3
Marylebone W1 ... 93 A1 238 A1
Pinner HA5 ... 40 D6
Walham Green SW6 ... 265 C3
Granville Point NW2 ... 69 B6
Granville Rd Bexley DA16 .. 146 C2
Bowes Pk N13 ... 32 B4
Child's Hill NW2 ... 69 B6
Finchley N12 ... 30 A3
Hayes UB3 ... 105 D2
Hillingdon UB10 ... 60 D2
Hornsey N4, N8 ... 50 B3
Ilford IG1 ... 78 D6
Kilburn NW6 ... 91 C5
Merton SW19 ... 179 C3
Sidcup DA14 ... 190 B6
Tottenham N22 ... 32 D2
Walthamstow E17 ... 53 D3
Wandsworth SW18 ... 157 B4
Woodford E18 ... 37 B1
Granville Sq
3 Camberwell SE15 ... 139 C5
Finsbury WC1 ... 94 B4 233 D1
Granville St WC1 ... 233 D1
Granwood Ct 5 TW7 ... 130 C4
Grape St WC2 ... 240 A2
Grapsome Cl KT9 ... 213 C1
Grasdene Rd SE18 ... 146 A5
Grasgarth Cl W3 ... 111 A6
Grasmere NW1 ... 231 D1
Grasmere Ave Acton W3 .. 111 B6
Kingston u T SW15 ... 177 C6
Locksbottom BR6 ... 226 D5
Merton SW19 ... 201 C6
Ruislip HA4 ... 39 A2
Twickenham TW3 ... 151 D5
Wembley HA9 ... 43 D1
Grasmere Cl TW14 ... 149 D3
Grasmere Ct
Barnes SW13 ... 134 A6
Bowes Pk N22 ... 32 B4
Forest Hill SE26 ... 184 A5
7 Sutton SM2 ... 218 A2
Grasmere Gdns
Harrow HA3 ... 25 A1
Locksbottom BR6 ... 226 D5
Redbridge IG4 ... 56 B4
Grasmere Ho 20 N16 ... 73 B4
Grasmere Point 2 SE15 .. 140 C5
Grasmere Prim Sch N16 .. 73 B4
Grasmere Rd
Bromley BR1 ... 186 D3
Croydon SE25 ... 206 B4
Locksbottom BR6 ... 226 D5
Muswell Hill N10 ... 31 B2
3 Newham E13 ... 99 A5
Streatham SW16 ... 182 B5
Tottenham N17 ... 34 A4
Grasshaven Way SE28 ... 123 D5
Grassington Cl N11 ... 31 A4
Grassington Rd DA14 ... 190 A6
Grassmere Ct 6 EN1 ... 17 C6
Grassmount SE23 ... 162 B2
Grass Pk N3 ... 29 B2
Grassway SM6 ... 219 C4
Grasvenor Ave EN5 ... 13 C5
Grasvenor Avenue Inf Sch
EN5 ... 13 C5
Grateley Ho 10 SW15 ... 156 B3
Gratton Rd W14 .. 113 A3 254 A5
Gratton Terr NW2 ... 68 D5
Graveley 16 KT1 ... 176 C1
Graveley Ave WD6 ... 11 A6
Graveley Ho 7 SE8 ... 119 A2
Gravel Hill Bexley DA6 ... 169 D6
Church End N3 ... 29 B1
South Croydon CR0, CR2 ... 223 B1
Gravel Hill Cl DA6 ... 169 D5
Gravel Hill Prim Sch
DA6 ... 169 D6
Gravel Hill Sta CR0 ... 223 A2
Gravel La E1 ... 95 D1 243 C2
Gravel Rd
Keston Mark BR2 ... 226 A6
Twickenham TW2 ... 152 C3
Gravelwood Cl BR7 ... 167 A1
Gravenel Gdns 5 SW17 ... 180 C5
Graveney Gr SE20 ... 184 C3
Graveney Rd SW17 ... 180 C6
Graveney Sch SW17 ... 181 B5
Gravesend Rd W12 ... 112 A6
Graves Est DA16 ... 146 B3
Gray Ave RM8 ... 59 B1
Gray Ct 8 KT2 ... 175 D6
Grayfriars Pas EC1 ... 241 D2
Grayham Cres KT3 ... 199 B5
Grayham Rd KT3 ... 199 B5
Gray Ho SE17 ... 262 B2
Grayland Cl BR1 ... 187 D2
Grayland Ct WC1 ... 233 C1
Grayling Cl E16 ... 98 C3

Grayling Ct Ealing W5 ... 109 D5
Tottenham Hale N17 ... 52 B5
Grayling Rd N16 ... 73 B6
Grayling Sq E2 ... 96 A4
Grays Cotts UB9 ... 38 C1
Grays Court Com Hospl
RM10 ... 81 D1
Grayscroft Rd SW16 ... 181 D3
Grays Farm Prim Sch
BR5 ... 190 B2
Grays Farm Production
Village BR5 ... 190 B2
Grays Farm Rd BR5 ... 190 B2
Grayshott Ct 10 SM2 ... 217 D1
Grayshott Rd SW11 ... 137 A2
Gray's Inn* WC1 ... 94 B2 240 D4
Gray's Inn Pl WC1 ... 240 D3
Gray's Inn Rd WC1 . 94 B3 240 D6
Gray's Inn Sq WC1 . 94 C2 241 A4
Grays La TW15 ... 170 D6
Grayson Ho EC1 ... 235 B1
Gray's Rd UB10 ... 60 A1
Gray St SE1 ... 116 C4 251 B1
Grayswood Gdns SW20 ... 178 B1
Grayswood Point 14
SW15 ... 156 A3
Gray's Yd W1 ... 238 B2
Graywood Ct N12 ... 30 A3
Grazebrook Rd N16 ... 73 B6
Grazeley Ct SE19 ... 183 C5
Great Amwell La N8 ... 50 B6
Great Arthur Ho EC1 ... 242 A5
Great Bell Alley EC2 ... 242 C2
Great Benty UB7 ... 104 A2
Great Brownings SE21 .. 183 D6
Great Bushey Dr N20 ... 13 D3
Great Cambridge Ind Est
EN1 ... 18 B6
Great Cambridge Junction
N13, N18 ... 33 B6
Great Cambridge Rd
Edmonton N9, N18 ... 17 C3
Enfield EN1 ... 6 A3
Great Castle St W1 ... 239 A2
Great Central Ave HA4 ... 62 C3
Great Central St
NW1 ... 92 D2 237 C4
Great Central Way NW10 .. 67 B4
Great Chapel St
W1 ... 93 D1 239 C2
Great Chart St SW11 ... 136 A1
Great Chertsey Rd
Chiswick SW14, W4 ... 133 B4
Feltham TW13, TW2 ... 151 C1
Great Church La W6 ... 112 D1
Great College St
SW1 ... 116 A3 260 A6
Great Croft WC1 ... 233 B1
Great Cross Ave SE3 ... 142 C5
Great Cumberland Mews
W1 ... 237 C1
Great Cumberland Pl
W1 ... 92 D1 237 D1
Great Dover St
SE1 ... 117 B3 262 C6
Greatdown Rd W7 ... 86 D2
Great Eastern Bldgs 10
E8 ... 74 B2
Great Eastern Ent Ctr
E14 ... 119 D4
Great Eastern Pier E14 .. 119 C1
Great Eastern Rd E15 ... 76 B2
Great Eastern St
EC2 ... 95 C3 243 A6
Great Eastern Wharf
SW11 ... 267 B3
Great Elms Rd BR2 ... 209 C5
Great Field Hendon NW9 ... 27 D2
7 Kentish Town NW5 ... 71 C3
Greatfield Ave E6 ... 100 B3
Greatfield Cl London SE4 .. 141 C1
4 Tufnell Pk N19 ... 71 C4
Greatfields Dr UB8 ... 82 C2
Greatfields Rd IG11 ... 101 B5
Great Fleete Way IG11 ... 102 C5
Great Galley Cl IG11 ... 102 C4
Great Gatton Cl CR0 ... 207 A2
Great George St
SW1 ... 116 A4 250 A1
Great Guildford Bsns Sq
SE1 ... 252 A3
Great Guildford St
SE1 ... 117 A5 252 A3
Great Hall The 1 E11 ... 55 B5
Greatham Wlk 8 SW15 .. 156 A3
Great Harry Dr SE9 ... 166 C1
Great James St WC1 ... 240 C4
Great Marlborough St
W1 ... 93 C1 239 A1
Great Maze Pond
SE1 ... 117 B4 252 D2
Great Newport St WC2 .. 250 A6
Great North Rd Barnet EN5 .. 1 A2
East Finchley N2 ... 48 C5
New Barnet EN5 ... 13 D6
Great North Way (Barnet By-
Pass) NW4 ... 46 D6
Greatorex Ho 13 E1 ... 96 A2
Greatorex St E1 ... 96 A2

Great Ormond St Hospl for
Children WC1 ... 94 B3 240 C5
Great Ormond St
WC1 ... 94 B3 240 C5
Great Percy St
WC1 ... 94 C4 234 A2
Great Peter St
SW1 ... 115 D3 259 D5
Great Portland St
W1 ... 93 B2 238 D4
Great Portland Street Sta
W1 ... 93 B3 238 D5
Great Pulteney St W1 ... 249 B6
Great Queen St
WC2 ... 94 A1 240 B2
Great Russell Mans WC1 240 A3
Great Russell St
WC1 ... 94 A2 240 A3
Great St Helen's EC3 ... 243 A2
Great St Thomas Apostle
EC4 ... 252 B6
Great Scotland Yd SW1,
WC2 ... 116 A5 250 A4
Great Smith St
SW1 ... 115 D3 259 D6
Great South West Rd TW6,
TW14, TW4 ... 148 B6
Great South-West Rd
TW5 ... 128 B2
Great Spilmans SE22 ... 161 C6
Greatstone Ho 10 SE20 ... 184 C3
Great Strand NW9 ... 27 D1
Great Suffolk St
SE1 ... 116 D5 251 D3
Great Sutton St
EC1 ... 94 D3 241 D5
Great Swan Alley EC2 ... 242 C2
Great Thrift BR5 ... 211 A5
Great Titchfield St
W1 ... 93 C2 239 A3
Great Tower St
EC3 ... 117 C6 253 A6
Great Trinity La EC4 ... 252 B6
Great Turnstile WC2 ... 240 D3
Great Western Ind Pk UB1,
UB2 ... 108 A4
Great Western Rd W2,
W9 ... 91 B2
Great West Ho TW8 ... 131 C6
Great West Rd
Brentford TW7, TW8 ... 131 B6
Chiswick W4, W6 ... 133 B6
Heston TW5, TW7 ... 129 B4
Hounslow TW5, TW7 ... 130 B5
Great West Road Cedars Rd
W4 ... 133 A6
Great West Road Hogarth La
W4 ... 133 C6
Great West Trad Est
TW8 ... 131 B6
Great Winchester St
EC2 ... 95 B1 242 D2
Great Windmill St
W1 ... 115 D6 249 C6
Greatwood BR7 ... 188 C3
Great Yd SE1 ... 253 B2
Greaves Cl IG11 ... 79 C1
Greaves Cotts 10 E14 ... 97 A2
Greaves Ct N8 ... 50 C5
Greaves Pl SW17 ... 180 C6
Greaves Twr SW10 ... 266 B4
Grebe 3 NW9 ... 27 D1
Grebe Ave UB4 ... 84 D1
Grebe Cl Barking IG11 ... 102 A3
Higham Hill E17 ... 35 A3
Stratford E7 ... 76 D3
Grebe Ct Cheam SM1 ... 217 B3
16 Cubitt Town E14 ... 120 A4
Grebe Terr 4 KT1 ... 198 A6
Grecian Cres SE19 ... 182 D4
Greek Ct W1 ... 239 D1
Greek Sch of London
W3 ... 110 D6
Greek Sec Sch of London
N22 ... 32 B2
Greek St W1 ... 93 D1 239 D1
Greenacre Cl Barnet EN5 ... 1 B5
Northolt UB5 ... 63 B3
Greenacre Ct E8 ... 74 A3
Greenacre Gdns E17 ... 54 A5
Greenacre Pl SM6 ... 219 B6
Greenacres Bushey WD23 ... 8 B2
Church End N3 ... 29 A1
Eltham SE9 ... 166 C5
Green Acres Hayes UB4 ... 84 B3
Sidcup DA14 ... 189 D6
South Croydon CR0 ... 221 D5
Greenacres Ave UB10 ... 60 C5
Greenacres Cl BR6 ... 227 A4
Greenacres Dr HA7 ... 25 B3
Greenacres Prim Sch
SE9 ... 166 C2
Greenacre Sq 26 SE16 ... 118 D4
Greenacre Wlk N14 ... 15 D1
Green Arbour Ct EC1 ... 241 C2
Green Ave Ealing W13 ... 109 B3
Edgware NW7 ... 27 C6
Greenaway Gdns NW3 ... 69 D4
Greenaway Ho
Finsbury WC1 ... 234 A1

Greenaway Ho continued
St John's Wood NW8 . . . . . **229** A6
Greenaway Terr TW19 . . . . **148** A3
Green Bank London N12 . . . .**29** C6
Wapping E1 . . . . **118** B5
Greenbank Ave HA0 . . . .**65** A3
Greenbank Cl E4 . . . .**20** A2
Greenbank Cres NW4 . . . . . .**47** A5
Greenbank Lo 2 BR7 . . . . **188** C2
Greenbanks HA1 . . . .**64** C4
Greenbay Rd SE7 . . . . **143** D5
Greenberry St NW8 . . . . . **230** A3
Greenbrook Ave EN4 . . . .**2** A4
Green CE Prim Sch The 14
N17 . . . .**51** D6
Green CE Sch Holy Trinity
(Inf Annexe) The 10
N15 . . . .**51** D5
Green Cl Beckenham BR2 . .**208** C6
Carshalton SM5 . . . . **218** D6
Feltham TW13 . . . . **173** A5
Kingsbury NW9 . . . .**45** A3
North End NW11 . . . .**48** A2
Greencoat Pl
SW1 . . . . **115** C2 **259** B4
Greencoat Row SW1 . . . . . **259** B5
Greencourt Ave HA8 . . . .**26** D2
Green Court Ave CR0 . . . . . **222** B6
Green Court Gdns CR0 . . . . **222** B6
Greencourt Ho 25 E1. . . . .**96** D3
Greencourt Rd BR5 . . . . . . **211** C4
Greencroft HA8. . . . .**27** A5
Greencroft Ave HA4 . . . .**62** C6
Greencroft Cl E16. . . . .**99** D2
Greencroft Gdns
Enfield EN1. . . . .**5** C2
South Hampstead NW6 . . . . .**70** A1
Greencroft Rd TW5 . . . . . . **129** B4
Green Ct Ashford TW16 . . . **171** D4
2 Willesden NW10 . . . .**67** C4
Greendale NW7. . . . .**27** C6
Green Dale SE2 . . . . **161** C6
Greendale Cl SE22 . . . . **161** C6
Greendale Ct CR2 . . . . **221** C4
Green Dr UB1. . . . . **107** C5
Green Dragon Ct SE1 . . . . . **252** C3
Green Dragon Ho WC1 . . . . **240** B2
Green Dragon La
Brentford TW8 . . . . **110** B1
Southgate N21 . . . .**16** D5
Green Dragon Prim Sch
TW8 . . . . **132** A6
Green Dragon Yd 24 E1. . .**96** A2
Greene Ct 20 SE14 . . . . . . **140** D6
Green Elms IG6. . . . .**57** A6
Greene Ho SE1 . . . . **262** C5
Green End
Chessington KT9 . . . . **214** A4
Edmonton N21 . . . .**16** D2
Greenend Rd W4 . . . . **111** C4
Greener Ct 28 SE16 . . . .**7** C6
Greener Ho 3 SW4 . . . . . . **137** D2
Green Farm Cl BR6 . . . . . . **227** D3
Greenfield Mans SE8 . . . . . **141** D6
Greenfield Ave KT5 . . . . . . **198** D3
Greenfield Ct SE9 . . . . **166** A1
Greenfield Dr
Bromley BR1 . . . . **187** C1
Fortis Green N2 . . . .**48** D5
Greenfield Gdns
Cricklewood NW2. . . . .**69** A5
Crofton BR5 . . . . **211** B2
Dagenham RM9 . . . . **102** D6
Greenfield Ho 28 SW19. . **156** D3
Greenfield Rd
Dagenham RM9 . . . . **102** C6
South Tottenham N15 . . . . . .**51** C4
Whitechapel E1 . . . .**96** A1
Greenfields UB1 . . . .**85** C1
Greenfields Prim Sch
WD19 . . . .**22** C5
Greenfield Way HA2 . . . .**41** D6
GREENFORD **86** A4
Greenford Ave Ealing W7 . . .**86** C1
Southall UB1. . . . . **107** B6
Greenford Gdns UB6. . . . . . .**86** A4
Greenford High Sch UB6 . . .**85** C4
Greenford Rd
Greenford UB6 . . . .**86** A3
Sudbury HA1, UB6 . . . .**64** C3
Sutton SM1. . . . . **217** D4
Greenford Rdbt UB6 . . . .**86** B5
Greenford Sp Ctr UB1 . . . . .**85** C4
Greenford Sta UB6. . . . .**86** B6
Greengate UB6 . . . .**65** B2
Greengate St E13 . . . .**99** B4
Green Gdns BR6 . . . . **227** A3
Greenhalgh Wlk N2 . . . .**48** A5
Greenham Cl SE1 . . . . **251** A1
Greenham Cres E4 . . . .**35** B4
Greenham Ho
5 Hackney E9 . . . .**96** C6
Isleworth TW7 . . . . **130** B2
Greenham Rd N10 . . . .**31** A1
Greenhaven Dr SE28 . . . . . **102** B1
Greenheath Bsns Ctr 3
E2. . . . .**96** B3
Green Hedges 8 TW1 . . . . **153** C5
Greenheys Dr E18. . . . .**54** D6
GREENHILL **42** D1

Greenhill
Buckhurst Hill IG9 . . . .**21** C3
Hampstead NW3 . . . .**70** B4
Sutton SM1. . . . . **218** A6
Wembley Pk HA9 . . . .**66** D6
Green Hill SE18 . . . . **122** B1
Greenhill Cts SE7 . . . . **122** B1
Greenhill Gdns UB5. . . . .**85** B5
Greenhill Gr E12. . . . .**78** A4
Greenhill Par EN5 . . . .**13** D6
Greenhill Pk
Harlesden NW10 . . . .**89** C6
New Barnet EN5 . . . .**13** D6
Greenhill Rd
Harlesden NW10 . . . .**89** C6
Harrow HA1 . . . .**42** C3
Greenhill's Rents EC1 . . . . **241** C4
Greenhills Terr 16 N1 . . . . .**73** B2
Greenhill Terr
Northolt UB5 . . . .**85** B5
Woolwich SE18 . . . . **122** B1
Greenhill Way
Harrow HA1 . . . .**42** C3
Wembley Pk HA9 . . . .**66** D6
Greenhithe Cl DA15. . . . . . **167** C4
Green Ho TW7 . . . . **130** D3
Greenholm Rd SE9 . . . . . . **166** B6
Green Ho The 5 SW19 . . . **157** A3
Green Hundred Rd SE15. . **140** A6
Greenhurst Rd SE27. . . . . . **182** C5
Greening Ho SE13 . . . . **142** B1
Greening St SE2 . . . . **124** C2
Green La Ashford TW16. . . . **171** D4
Chessington KT9 . . . . **214** A1
Chislehurst SE9 . . . . **166** D1
Dagenham RM8 . . . .**81** B6
East Molesey KT8. . . . . **195** D4
Edgware HA8 . . . .**26** C5
Feltham TW13 . . . . **173** A5
Hanwell W7 . . . . **108** C4
Hendon NW4 . . . .**46** D4
Hillingdon UB8 . . . .**83** A2
Hounslow TW4 . . . . **128** C1
Ilford IG1, IG3 . . . .**79** C6
Morden SM4. . . . . **201** D3
New Malden KT3 . . . . **199** A4
New Malden KT4 . . . . **200** A1
Penge SE20 . . . . **184** D3
Shepperton TW17. . . . . **193** A4
South Norwood CR7,
SW16 . . . . **182** C2
Stanmore HA7 . . . .**25** B5
Greenland Cres UB2 . . . . . **106** D3
Greenland Ho
4 Mile End E1. . . . .**97** A3
Bermondsey SE8 . . . . **118** D1
Greenland Mews SE8 . . . . **118** D1
Greenland Pl NW1 . . . . **231** D6
Greenland Quay SE16 . . . . **118** D2
Greenland Rd Barnet EN5 . . .**12** C5
Camden Town NW1 . .**93** C6 **232** A6
Greenlands
Borehamwood WD6 . . . .**11** B5
Chessington KT19 . . . . **214** D3
Greenland St NW1 . . . . **231** D6
Greenland Way CR0. . . . . . **203** D2
Green Lane Bsns Pk
SE9 . . . . **166** C2
Green Lane Cotts HA7. . . . . .**25** B6
Green Lane Gdns CR7. . . . . **183** A1
Green Lane Mews SM4 . . . **201** D3
Green Lane Prim Sch
KT4 . . . . **200** B2
Green Lanes
London N4, N8, N15 . . . .**50** D2
Palmers Green N13 . . . .**16** C1
West Ewell KT19. . . . . **215** C1
Greenlaw Ct W5 . . . .**87** D1
Greenlaw Gdns KT3. . . . . . **199** D2
Greenlawn La TW8. . . . . **109** D2
Greenlawns N12. . . . .**29** D4
Green Lawns Ruislip HA4 . . . .**40** C1
8 Woolwich SE18 . . . . **122** C2
Greenlaw St SE18 . . . . **122** C3
Green Leaf Ave SM6 . . . . . . **219** D4
Greenleaf Cl 8 SW2 . . . . . **160** C4
Greenleaf Ct N20 . . . .**14** B3
Greenleafe Dr IG6 . . . .**56** D6
Greenleaf Prim Sch E17. . . .**53** B6
Greenleaf Rd
5 Newham E6 . . . .**99** C6
Walthamstow E17 . . . .**53** B6
Greenleaf Way HA3 . . . .**42** D6
Greenlea Pk SW19. . . . . . . **180** C2
Green Leas
Ashford TW15 . . . . **171** D4
Kingston u T KT1. . . . . **198** A6
Green Leas Cl TW16. . . . . . **171** D4
Greenleaves Ct TW15 . . . . **170** D4
Green Link Wlk TW9 . . . . . **132** D4
Green Man Gdns W13 . . . . **109** A6
Green Man Intc E11 . . . .**54** D2
Green Man La
Ealing W13 . . . . **109** A5
Hatton TW14 . . . . **128** A1
Greenman St N1. . . .**95** A6 **235** A6
Greenmead Cl SE25. . . . . . **206** A4
Greenmead Prim Sch
SW15 . . . . **156** B6
Green Moor Link N21 . . . . . .**16** D4

Greenmoor Rd EN3 . . . .**6** C3
Greenoak Pl EN4 . . . .**2** D3
Green Oaks UB2 . . . . **106** D2
Greenoak Way SW19 . . . . . **178** D6
Greenock Rd
Mitcham SW16 . . . . **181** D2
11 South Acton W3. . . . . . **111** A3
Greeno Cres TW17. . . . . . . **192** C4
Green Park ★ SW1,
W1 . . . . **115** B4 **248** D2
Greenpark Ct HA0 . . . .**65** C1
Green Park Sta
W1 . . . . **115** C5 **249** A4
Green Park Way UB6 . . . .**86** C6
Eltham SE9 . . . . **165** D6
Sunbury TW16 . . . . **194** A5
Green Pond Cl E17. . . . .**53** B6
Green Pond Rd E17 . . . .**53** A6
Green Pt E15 . . . .**76** C2
Green Rd East Barnet N14. . . .**15** B5
Whetstone N20 . . . .**14** A1
Green Ride IG10, E4 . . . .**21** A6
Greenroof Way SE10 . . . . . **120** D3
Green Sch (Girls) The
TW7 . . . . **131** A4
Greens Ct Soho W1 . . . . . . **249** C6
Wembley HA9. . . . .**65** D5
Green's Ct W11 . . . . **244** C3
Greens End SE18 . . . . **122** D2
Greenshank Cl E17 . . . .**35** A3
Greenshaw High Sch
SM1 . . . . **218** A6
Greenshields Ind Est
E16 . . . . **121** B5
Greenside Dagenham RM8. . .**58** C1
Sidcup DA5 . . . . **169** A3
Greenside Cl Catford SE6. . **164** B2
Whetstone N20 . . . .**14** B2
Greenside Prim Sch
W12 . . . . **112** A4
Greenside Rd
Shepherd's Bush W12 . . . . **112** A4
Thornton Heath CR0. . . . . . **204** C2
Greenslade Prim Sch
SE18. . . . . **145** B6
Greenslade Rd IG11. . . . .**79** B1
Greensleeves Ho 2 SE17 . **107** D2
Greensleeves Manor
SM2. . . . . **217** D2
Green St Enfield EN3 . . . .**6** D3
Mayfair W1. . . . .**115** A6 **248** A6
Newham E13. . . . .**99** C6
Sunbury TW16 . . . . **172** A1
Upton E7. . . . .**77** C1
Greenstead Ave IG8 . . . .**37** C4
Greenstead Cl IG8 . . . .**37** C4
Greenstead Gdns
Putney SW15 . . . . **156** B6
Woodford IG8. . . . .**37** C4
Greenstone Mews E11 . . . . .**55** A3
GREEN STREET GREEN . .**227** C2
Green Street Green Prim Sch
BR6. . . . . **227** D2
Greenstreet Hill SE14 . . . . **140** D2
Greensward Ho SW6 . . . . . **136** A3
Green Terr EC1 . . . . **234** B1
Green The Acton W3 . . . .**89** C1
Buckhurst Hill IG9 . . . .**21** B3
Chingford E4. . . . .**20** B3
Claygate KT10 . . . . **212** D2
Ealing W5 . . . . **109** D6
Edmonton N9 . . . .**18** A2
Erith DA7 . . . . **147** C4
Falconwood DA16. . . . . **145** C1
Feltham TW13 . . . . **150** B2
Grove Pk BR1. . . . . **165** A1
Hackbridge SM6. . . . . **219** A6
Hayes BR2 . . . . **209** A2
Heston TW5 . . . . **129** C6
Kingston u T KT3. . . . . **177** A1
Merton SM4 . . . . **201** A5
Palmers Green N14 . . . .**15** D1
Richmond TW9 . . . . **131** D1
7 Richmond TW9 . . . . **153** D6
Sidcup DA14 . . . . **190** A5
Southall UB2. . . . . **107** B4
Southgate N14 . . . .**16** C4
St Paul's Cray BR5. . . . . . . **190** B3
Stratford E15 . . . .**76** D2
Sutton SM1 . . . . **217** D5
Tottenham N17. . . . .**33** A4
Twickenham TW2 . . . . **152** C2
Upper Halliford TW17 . . . . . **193** C5
Uxbridge UB10 . . . .**61** A6
Wallington SM5 . . . . **219** A4
Wanstead E11 . . . .**55** B3
Wembley HA0. . . . .**65** A6
Wimbledon SW19. . . . . **178** D5
Woodford IG8. . . . .**37** A5
Green Vale Bexley DA6 . . . . **168** D6
Ealing W5 . . . .**88** B1
Greenvale Rd SE9 . . . . **144** C1
Greenvale Sch SE23. . . . . . **164** C1
Green Verges HA7. . . . .**25** D3
Green View KT9. . . . . **214** B1
Greenview Ave CR0 . . . . . . **207** A3
Greenview Cl W3 . . . . **111** C5
Greenview Ct
Ashford TW15. . . . . **170** B6
East Dulwich SE22 . . . . **140** A1
Oakleigh Pk N20. . . . .**14** A4
Wandsworth SW18 . . . . **158** C4

Greenway
Chislehurst BR7 . . . . **188** D5
Dagenham RM8 . . . .**58** C1
Harrow HA3 . . . .**44** A4
Hayes UB4 . . . .**84** B3
Palmers Green N14 . . . .**16** A2
Pinner HA5 . . . .**22** B1
Totteridge N20 . . . .**13** C2
Wallington SM6 . . . . **219** C4
West Barnes SW20 . . . . . . **200** C5
Woodford IG8. . . . .**37** C5
Green Way
Bromley Comm BR2 . . . . . **210** A3
Eltham SE9 . . . . **165** D6
Sunbury TW16 . . . . **194** A5
Greenway Ave E17 . . . .**54** B5
Greenway Cl
Finsbury Pk N4 . . . .**73** A6
Friern Barnet N11 . . . .**31** A4
Hendon NW9 . . . .**27** B1
2 South Tottenham N15 . . . .**51** D5
Totteridge N20 . . . .**13** C2
Greenway Ct Hayes UB4. . . .**84** B3
Ilford IG1 . . . .**56** D1
2 Newham E15 . . . .**98** C5
Greenway Gdns
Croydon CR0. . . . . **223** B5
Greenford UB6 . . . .**85** D4
Hendon NW9 . . . .**27** B1
Green Way Gdns HA3 . . . . . .**24** C1
Greenways
Beckenham BR3 . . . . **185** C1
5 Forest Hill SE26. . . . . . **184** C6
Hinchley Wood KT10. . . . . . **212** C4
Greenways The 1 TW1. . . **153** A5
Greenway The
Harrow HA3 . . . .**24** C2
Hendon NW9 . . . .**27** B1
Hounslow TW4 . . . . **129** B1
Pinner HA5 . . . .**41** B3
Uxbridge UB8 . . . .**82** A5
West Ruislip UB10 . . . .**61** A6
Greenwell St W1. . . . . **238** D5
GREENWICH **142** C6
Greenwich Acad SE10 . . . . **141** D5
Greenwich Borough Mus ★
SE10 . . . . **141** D5
Greenwich Bsns Ctr
SE10 . . . . **142** A6
Greenwich Bsns Pk
SE10 . . . . **141** D5
Greenwich Church St
SE10 . . . . **142** A6
Greenwich Coll 17 SE10 . . **142** A5
Greenwich Com Coll
Plumstead Ctr SE18. . . . . . **123** A2
Greenwich Cres E6 . . . . . . **100** A3
Greenwich Ct 11 E1. . . . . . .**96** B1
Greenwich Heritage Ctr ★
SE18 . . . . **122** D3
Greenwich High Rd
SE10 . . . . **141** D5
Greenwich Ho SE13 . . . . . . **164** B5
Greenwich Hts SE18 . . . . . **144** A5
Greenwich Ind Est SE10. . **141** D5
Greenwich London Coll 15
SE18 . . . . **122** C2
Greenwich Mkt 2 SE10 . . . **142** A6
Greenwich Mkt ★ SE10 . . . **142** A6
Greenwich Park ★ SE10 . . **142** C5
Greenwich Park St SE10. . **142** B6
Greenwich Quay SE8. . . . . **141** D6
Greenwich Sh Pk SE7 . . . . **121** B2
Greenwich South St
SE10 . . . . **142** A4
Greenwich Sta SE10 . . . . . **141** D5
Greenwich View Pl E14. . . **119** D3
Green Wlk
Bermondsey SE1 . . . . **263** A5
Hampton TW12. . . . . **173** B4
Hendon NW4 . . . .**46** D4
Ruislip HA4. . . . .**39** D1
Southall UB2. . . . . **107** C1
Green Wlk The E4. . . . .**20** B3
Greenwood
8 Putney SW19. . . . . **156** D4
3 Woodford IG8 . . . .**37** C5
Green Wood NW5. . . . .**71** C3
Greenwood Ave
Dagenham RM10 . . . .**81** D4
Enfield EN3. . . . .**7** A4
Greenwood Cl
Bushey WD23 . . . .**8** C3
Merton SM4 . . . . **201** A5
Orpington BR5 . . . . **211** C3
Sidcup DA15 . . . . **168** A2
Thames Ditton KT7. . . . . . . **197** A1
Greenwood Dr E4. . . . .**36** B5
Greenwood Gdns N13. . . . . .**16** D1
Greenwood Ho
Finsbury WC1. . . . . **234** A1
8 Nunhead SE4 . . . . **140** D1
Wood Green N22 . . . .**32** C2
Greenwood La TW12 . . . . . **173** D6
Greenwood Mans 9
IG11 . . . .**80** A1
Greenwood Pk KT2 . . . . . . **177** C3
Greenwood Pl NW5. . . . .**71** B3
Greenwood Prim Sch
UB5. . . . .**64** A3

Greenwood Rd Dalston E8. .**74** A2
Hinchley Wood KT7. . . . . . **213** A6
Isleworth TW7 . . . . **130** D2
Mitcham CR4 . . . . **203** D6
Thornton Heath CR0. . . . . . **205** A4
West Ham E13 . . . .**98** D5
Greenwoods The HA2 . . . . . .**64** B5
Greenwood Terr NW10 . . . . .**89** B5
Green Wrythe Cres SM5. . . **202** C1
Green Wrythe La SM5 . . . . **202** C2
Green Wrythe Prim Sch
SM5 . . . . **202** B3
Green Yd WC1 . . . . **240** D6
Greer Rd HA3. . . . .**24** A2
Greet Ho SE1 . . . . **251** B1
Greet St SE1 . . . . **116** C5 **251** B3
Greg Cl E10. . . . .**54** A3
Gregor Mews SE3. . . . . **143** A5
Gregory Cres SE9 . . . . **165** D4
Gregory Ho SE3. . . . . **143** B3
Gregory Pl W8. . . . . **245** C2
Gregory Rd
Dagenham RM6. . . . .**58** D5
Southall UB2. . . . . **107** C3
Greig City Acad 6 N8. . . . . .**50** A5
Greig Cl N8. . . . .**50** A4
Greig Ho 9 TW10 . . . . **153** C1
Greig Terr SE17 . . . . **137** D6
Grenaby Ave CR0 . . . . **205** B2
Grenaby Rd CR0 . . . . **205** B2
Grenada Ho 18 E14 . . . . . . **119** B6
Grenada Rd SE7 . . . . **143** C5
Grenade St E14 . . . . **119** B6
Grenadier St E16 . . . . **122** C5
Grena Gdns TW9 . . . . **132** B1
Grena Rd TW10, TW9. . . . . **132** B3
Grenard Cl SE15 . . . . **140** A5
Grendon Gdns HA9 . . . .**66** C6
Grendon Ho
29 Hackney E9 . . . .**74** C1
Pentonville N1 . . . . **233** C3
Grendon St NW8 . .**92** C3 **237** A6
Grenfell Ct NW7 . . . .**28** B4
Grenfell Gdns Harrow HA3 . .**44** A2
Ilford IG2. . . . .**57** D4
Grenfell Ho SE5. . . . . **139** A5
Grenfell Rd
Mitcham CR4, SW17. . . . . . **180** C4
Shepherd's Bush W11 . . . . **112** D6
Grenfell Twr 5 W11. . . . . . **112** D6
Grenfell Wlk 4 W11 . . . . . **112** D6
Grengate Lodge 2 E13 . . . .**99** B4
Grenier Apartments 11
SE15 . . . . **140** B5
Grennell Cl SM1 . . . . **218** B6
Grennell Rd SM1. . . . . **218** A6
Grenoble Gdns N13 . . . .**32** C4
Grenville Ct
3 Dulwich SE19 . . . . **183** D5
Ealing W13 . . . .**87** B2
Edgware HA8 . . . .**26** D6
Grenville Gdns IG8 . . . .**37** C3
Grenville Ho 26 Bow E3 . . . .**97** A5
4 Deptford SE8. . . . . **141** C6
Grenville Lo N6. . . . .**49** C2
Grenville Mans WC1 . . . . . **240** A6
Grenville Mews
Hampton TW12. . . . . **173** D5
South Kensington SW7. . . . **256** A3
Grenville Pl
Burnt Oak NW7. . . . .**27** B5
South Kensington
SW7 . . . . **114** A2 **256** A4
Grenville Rd N19. . . . .**50** A1
Grenville St WC1. . . . . **240** B5
Gresham Almshouses 3
SW9. . . . . **138** B1
Gresham Ave N20. . . . .**30** D6
Gresham Cl Enfield EN2 . . . . .**5** A2
Sidcup DA5 . . . . **169** B5
Gresham Coll EC1 . .**94** C2 **241** B3
Gresham Dr RM6 . . . .**58** B3
Gresham Gdns NW11 . . . . . .**47** A1
Gresham Ho
4 Teddington TW11. . . . . . **174** D5
3 Thames Ditton KT7 . . . . **197** A2
West Barnes KT3 . . . . **200** B5
Gresham Lo E17 . . . .**53** D4
Gresham Pl 2 N19. . . . .**71** D2
Gresham Rd
Beckenham BR3 . . . . **185** A1
Brixton SW9 . . . . **138** C2
Canning Town E16 . . . .**99** B1
Croydon CR25 . . . . **206** A5
East Ham E6 . . . . **100** B5
Edgware HA8 . . . .**26** B4
Hampton TW12. . . . . **173** C4
Hillingdon UB10 . . . .**82** C5
Hounslow TW3, TW5. . . . . . **130** A4
Willesden NW10 . . . .**89** C5
Gresham St EC2 . . . .**95** A1 **242** B2
Gresham Way SW19. . . . . . **157** C1
Gresham Way West SW19 . **157** D1
Gresley Cl London N15 . . . . .**51** B5

Gresley Cl *continued*
Walthamstow E17 ... 53 A3
Gresley Ho SW8 ... 269 D2
Gresley Rd N19 ... 49 C2
Gressenhall Rd SW18 ... 157 B4
Gressenham Ct 7 HA7 ... 25 C6
Gresse St W1 ... 93 D1 239 C2
Gresswell Cl DA14 ... 168 A1
Greswell St SW6 ... 134 D4
Greta Ho SE3 ... 142 D6
Gretton Ho 2 E2 ... 96 C4
Gretton Rd N17 ... 33 D3
Greville Cl TW1 ... 153 B4
Greville Ct Harrow HA1 ... 64 C4
3 Lower Clapton E5 ... 74 B5
Greville Hall NW6 ... 91 D5
Greville Ho Harrow HA2 ... 42 B1
Knightsbridge SW1 ... 258 A6
Putney SW15 ... 134 D2
Greville Lo
5 Bayswater W2 ... 91 D1
16 London N12 ... 29 D6
Greville Mews 5 NW6 ... 91 D6
Greville Pl W9 ... 91 D5
Greville Rd Kilburn NW6 ... 91 D5
Richmond TW10 ... 154 B5
Walthamstow E17 ... 54 A5
Greville St EC1 ... 94 C2 241 B4
Grey Cl NW11 ... 48 A3
Grey Coat Hospital The
SW1 ... 115 D2 259 C3
SW1 ... 115 D3 259 C5
Greycoat Pl SW1. 115 D3 259 C5
Greycoat St SW1. 115 D3 259 C5
Greycot Rd BR3 ... 185 C5
Grey Court Sch TW10 ... 153 C1
Grey Eagle St E1 ... 95 D3 243 D5
Greyfell Cl HA7 ... 25 B5
Greyfriars 16 SE26 ... 162 A1
Greyfriars Ho SE3 ... 142 D6
Grey Ho 27 W12 ... 112 B6
Greyhound Ct WC2 ... 251 A6
Greyhound Hill NW4 ... 46 B6
Greyhound La SW16 ... 181 D4
Greyhound Rd
College Pk NW10 ... 90 B4
Fulham W6 ... 135 A6 264 A6
Sutton SM1 ... 218 A3
Tottenham N17 ... 51 C6
Greyhound Terr SW16 ... 181 C2
Greyladies Gdns SE10 ... 142 A3
Greys Park Cl BR2 ... 225 D3
Greystead Rd SE23 ... 162 C4
Greystoke Ave HA5 ... 41 C6
Greystoke Ct W5 ... 88 B3
Greystoke Dr HA4 ... 38 D3
Greystoke Gdns Ealing W5 ... 88 B3
Enfield EN2 ... 3 D1
Greystoke Ho Ealing W5 ... 88 A3
Peckham SE15 ... 140 A6
Greystoke Lo W5 ... 88 B3
Greystoke Park Terr W5 ... 88 A4
Greystoke Pl EC4 ... 241 B2
Greystone Gdns HA3 ... 43 C3
Greystones TW2 ... 152 A2
Greyswood St SW16 ... 181 B4
Greytiles TW11 ... 174 D4
Grey Turner Ho W12 ... 90 A1
Grice Ct N1 ... 73 A2
Grierson Ho SW16 ... 181 C6
Grierson Rd
Forest Hill SE23 ... 162 D4
Forest Hill SE23 ... 163 A5
Griffin Cl NW10 ... 68 B3
Griffin Ct
8 Brentford TW8 ... 132 A6
Chiswick W4 ... 111 D1
Shepherd's Bush W12 ... 112 B5
Griffin Ctr TW14 ... 150 B5
Griffin Ctr The KT1 ... 175 D1
Griffin Gate 1 SW15 ... 134 D2
Griffin Lo N12 ... 30 A6
Griffin Manor Way SE28 ... 123 B3
Griffin Park (Brentford FC)
TW8 ... 131 D6
Griffin Rd
Plumstead SE18 ... 123 B1
Tottenham N17 ... 33 C1
Griffins Cl N21 ... 17 B4
Griffin Way
Sunbury TW16 ... 172 A1
Woolwich SE28 ... 123 C3
Griffith Cl RM8 ... 58 C1
Griffiths Cl KT4 ... 216 B6
Griffiths Ho 2 SE18 ... 144 D6
Griffiths Rd SW19 ... 179 D3
Griffon Ho 3 SW11 ... 136 C2
Griggs App IG1 ... 79 A6
Griggs Cl IG1 ... 79 C4
Grigg's Pl SE1 ... 263 B5
Griggs Rd E10 ... 54 A3
Grilse Cl N9 ... 34 B6
Grimaldi Ho N1 ... 233 C4
Grimsby Gr E16 ... 122 D5
Grimsby St
8 Bethnal Green E2 ... 96 A3
Shoreditch E2 ... 243 D6
Grimsdell Mill Hill Pre Prep
Sch NW7 ... 28 B5
Grimsdyke Fst & Mid Sch
HA5 ... 23 B4
Grimsdyke Rd HA5 ... 23 A3
Grimsel Path SE5 ... 138 D5
Grimshaw Cl N6 ... 49 A2
Grimston Rd SW6 ... 135 B3
Grimthorpe Ho EC1 ... 241 C6
Grimwade Ave CR0 ... 222 A5
Grimwade Cl SE15 ... 140 C2
Grimwood Rd TW1 ... 152 D4
Grindall Cl CR0 ... 220 D4
Grindall Ho 26 E1 ... 96 B3
Grindal St SE1 ... 251 A1
Grindleford Ave N11 ... 15 A2
Grindley Gdns CR0 ... 205 D3
Grindley Ho 3 E3 ... 97 B2
Grinling Gibbons Prim Sch
42 SE8 ... 141 B6
Grinling Ho 6 SE18 ... 122 C2
Grinling Pl SE8 ... 141 C6
Grinstead Rd SE8 ... 119 A1
Grisedale NW1 ... 232 A2
Grittleton Ave HA9 ... 66 D2
Grittleton Rd W9 ... 91 C3
Grizedale Terr 8 SE23 ... 162 B2
Grogan Cl TW12 ... 173 B4
Groombridge Cl DA16 ... 168 A6
Groombridge Ho 1
SE20 ... 184 D3
Groombridge Rd E9 ... 74 D1
Groom Cl BR2 ... 209 B5
Groom Cres SW18 ... 158 B4
Groome Ho SE11 ... 260 D3
Groomfield Cl SW17 ... 181 A6
Groom Pl SW1 ... 115 A3 258 B6
Grooms Dr HA5 ... 40 A4
Grosmont Rd SE18 ... 123 D1
Grosse Way SW15 ... 156 B5
Grosslea SM4 ... 202 B4
Grosvenor Ave
Canonbury N5 ... 73 A3
Harrow HA2 ... 41 D3
Hayes UB4 ... 83 D5
Mortlake SW14 ... 133 C2
Richmond TW10 ... 154 A6
Wallington SM5, SM6 ... 219 A2
Grosvenor Bridge
SW1 ... 137 B6 268 D6
Grosvenor Cotts SW1 ... 258 A4
Grosvenor Court Mans
W2 ... 237 C1
Grosvenor Cres
Hillingdon UB10 ... 82 D6
Queensbury NW9 ... 44 C5
Westminster SW1 ... 115 A4 248 B1
Grosvenor Cres Mews
SW1 ... 248 A1
Grosvenor Ct
4 Acton W3 ... 110 C5
Brondesbury Pk NW6 ... 90 D6
3 Ealing W5 ... 110 A6
3 Edgware NW7 ... 27 B5
Gunnersbury W4 ... 110 D1
Leyton E10 ... 53 D1
Morden SM4 ... 201 C5
Oakwood N14 ... 15 C4
Penge SE19 ... 183 D4
22 Poplar E14 ... 97 B1
Putney SW15 ... 157 A6
1 Sutton SM2 ... 218 A2
Teddington TW11 ... 175 A4
3 Wanstead E11 ... 55 B4
2 Wimbledon SW19 ... 179 A4
Grosvenor Gdns
Cricklewood NW2 ... 68 C3
Hornsey N10 ... 49 C6
Kingston u T KT2 ... 175 D4
Mortlake SW14 ... 133 C2
Newham E6 ... 99 D4
Southgate N14 ... 15 D6
Temple Fortune NW11 ... 47 B4
Wallington SM6 ... 219 C1
Westminster SW1 ... 115 B3 258 D5
Woodford IG8 ... 37 B4
Grosvenor Gdns Mews E
SW1 ... 258 D6
Grosvenor Gdns Mews N
SW1 ... 258 C5
Grosvenor Gdns Mews S
SW1 ... 258 D5
Grosvenor Hill
Mayfair W1 ... 115 B6 248 C6
Wimbledon SW19 ... 179 A4
Grosvenor Hill Ct W1 ... 248 C6
Grosvenor Ho
5 Sutton SM1 ... 217 D3
Upper Clapton E5 ... 52 A1
Grosvenor Hts E4 ... 20 C4
Grosvenor Lo London N20 ... 14 A1
4 Woodford E18 ... 36 D1
Grosvenor Par 1 W5 ... 110 C5
Grosvenor Park SE5 ... 139 A5
Grosvenor Park Rd E17 ... 53 D4
Grosvenor Pier SW1 ... 269 C6
Grosvenor Pk SE5 ... 139 A6
Grosvenor Pl
SW1 ... 115 B4 248 C1
Grosvenor Rd
Acton Green W4 ... 111 A1
Bexley DA6 ... 169 A6
Brentford TW8 ... 131 D6
Croydon SE25 ... 206 A5
Dagenham RM8 ... 59 B1
Ealing W7 ... 109 A5
Edmonton N9 ... 18 B3
Erith DA17 ... 147 C6
Finchley N3 ... 29 C3
Hounslow TW3, TW4 ... 129 B2
Ilford IG1 ... 79 A5
Leyton E10 ... 54 A1
Muswell Hill N10 ... 31 B2
Newham E6 ... 99 D6
Orpington BR6 ... 211 C3
Pimlico SW1 ... 137 C6 269 B6
Richmond TW10 ... 154 A6
Southall UB2 ... 107 B3
Twickenham TW1 ... 153 A3
Upton E7 ... 77 B2
Wallington SM6 ... 219 B3
Wanstead E11 ... 55 B4
West Wickham BR4 ... 223 D6
Grosvenor Residences 1
W14 ... 112 D3
Grosvenor Rise E E17 ... 53 D4
Grosvenor Sq
W1 ... 115 A6 248 B6
Grosvenor St W1 ... 115 B6 248 C6
Grosvenor Terr SE5 ... 139 A6
Grosvenor The NW11 ... 47 D2
Grosvenor Vale HA4 ... 61 D6
Grosvenor Way E5 ... 74 C6
Grosvernor Wharf Rd
E14 ... 120 B2
Grote's Bldgs SE3 ... 142 C3
Grote's Pl SE3 ... 142 C3
Groton Rd SW18 ... 157 D2
Grotto Ct SE1 ... 252 A2
Grotto Pas W1 ... 238 A4
Grotto Rd TW1 ... 152 D2
Grove Ave Cheam SM1 ... 217 C2
Ealing W7 ... 86 C1
Finchley N3 ... 29 C3
Pinner HA5 ... 41 A5
Twickenham TW1 ... 152 D3
Wood Green N10 ... 31 C1
Grovebury Ct Bexley DA6 ... 169 D6
Southgate N14 ... 15 D4
Grovebury Rd SE2 ... 124 B4
Grove Cl Forest Hill SE23 ... 163 A3
Hayes BR2 ... 225 A6
Ickenham UB10 ... 60 C3
Kingston u T KT1 ... 198 B5
Grove Cres
Feltham TW13 ... 173 A6
Kingsbury NW9 ... 45 B5
Kingston u T KT1 ... 198 A6
Walton-on-T KT12 ... 194 B2
Woodford E18 ... 36 D1
Grove Crescent Rd E15 ... 76 B2
Grove Ct Barnet EN5 ... 1 B2
Camberwell SE5 ... 139 C3
Clapham SW4 ... 137 C2
Ealing W5 ... 110 A5
East Molesey KT8 ... 196 B4
3 Forest Hill SE26 ... 185 A6
Hounslow TW3 ... 129 C1
8 Kingston u T KT1 ... 198 A6
New Malden KT3 ... 199 C6
Penge SE20 ... 184 B3
Seething Wells KT6 ... 197 D4
South Kensington SW10 ... 256 B1
St John's Wood NW8 ... 229 C2
Grovedale Rd N19 ... 71 D6
Grove Dwellings E1 ... 96 C2
Grove End
Gospel Oak NW5 ... 71 B4
Woodford E18 ... 36 D1
Grove End Gdns NW8 ... 229 B3
Grove End Ho NW8 ... 229 C1
Grove End La KT10 ... 196 B1
Grove End Rd
NW8 ... 92 B4 229 C1
Grove Farm Ct CR4 ... 202 D4
Grovefield 1 N11 ... 31 B6
Grove Footpath KT5 ... 198 A5
Grove Gdns Enfield EN3 ... 6 D5
Hendon NW4 ... 46 A5
Lisson Gr NW8 ... 92 C4 230 B1
Teddington TW11 ... 175 A6
Grove Glade Shop Hall
W13 ... 109 A5
Grove Green Rd E11 ... 76 B6
Grove Hall Ct Bow E3 ... 97 C5
St John's Wood
NW8 ... 92 A4 229 B2
Grove Hill Harrow HA1 ... 42 C2
Woodford E18 ... 36 D1
Grovehill Ct BR1 ... 186 D4
Grove Hill Rd
Camberwell SE5 ... 139 C2
Harrow HA1 ... 42 D2
Grove Ho Blackheath SE3 ... 142 D3
Chelsea SW3 ... 267 B6
Hendon N3 ... 46 D6
Grove House Rd N8 ... 50 A5
Grove La Camberwell SE5 ... 139 C2
Hillingdon UB8 ... 82 B3
Grove La *continued*
Kingston u T KT1 ... 198 A5
Groveland Ave SW16 ... 182 B3
Groveland Ct EC4 ... 242 B1
Groveland Rd BR3 ... 207 B6
Grovelands
East Molesey KT8 ... 195 C5
Kingston u T KT1 ... 197 D5
Grovelands Cl
Camberwell SE5 ... 139 C3
Harrow HA2 ... 63 D5
Grovelands Ct N14 ... 15 D4
Grovelands Rd
Palmers Green N13 ... 16 B1
South Tottenham N15 ... 52 A3
St Paul's Cray BR5 ... 190 A3
Grovelands Sch KT12 ... 194 B3
Groveland Way KT3 ... 199 B4
Grove Lane Terr SE5 ... 139 B3
Groveley Ho 7 N4 ... 51 A2
Groveley Rd TW13,
TW16 ... 171 D5
Grove Lo Clapham SW4 ... 137 C1
Cranley Gdns N10 ... 49 C5
Grove Mans London SW4 ... 136 D1
2 Shepherd's Bush W6 ... 112 C4
3 Stamford Hill N16 ... 52 A1
Grove Market Pl SE9 ... 166 B5
Grove Mews W6 ... 112 C3
Grove Mill CR4 ... 202 C4
Grove Mill Pl SM5 ... 219 A5
GROVE PARK SE9 ... 165 B1
W4 ... 133 A4
Grove Park Ave E4 ... 35 D3
Grove Park Bridge W4 ... 133 A5
Grove Park Gdns W4 ... 133 A5
Grove Park Mews W4 ... 133 A5
Grove Park Prim Sch
W4 ... 133 A6
Grove Park Rd
Chiswick W4 ... 132 D5
Mottingham SE9, SE12 ... 165 D2
South Tottenham N15 ... 51 C5
Grove Park Sch NW9 ... 45 A5
Grove Park Sta SE12 ... 165 B1
Grove Park Terr W4 ... 132 D6
Grove Pk Camberwell SE5 ... 139 C3
Kingsbury NW9 ... 45 B5
Wanstead E11 ... 55 B4
Grove Pl Acton W3 ... 111 A5
Balham SW12 ... 159 B5
Hampstead NW3 ... 70 B5
Grove Prim Sch RM6 ... 58 C4
Grover Ct SE13 ... 141 D3
Grove Rd Acton W3 ... 111 A5
Barnes SW13 ... 133 D3
Belmont SM2 ... 217 C2
Bow E3 ... 97 A5
Brentford TW8 ... 109 C1
Chingford E4 ... 20 A1
Cockfosters EN4 ... 2 C2
Dagenham RM6 ... 58 C3
Ealing W5 ... 109 D6
East Molesey KT8 ... 196 B5
Edgware HA8 ... 26 C4
8 Erith DA17 ... 147 B6
Friern Barnet N11 ... 31 B5
Hounslow TW3 ... 129 C1
Kingston u T KT6 ... 197 D4
Leytonstone E11 ... 54 D2
Merton SW19 ... 180 A3
Mitcham CR4 ... 181 B1
North Finchley N12 ... 30 B5
Pinner HA5 ... 41 B4
Richmond TW10 ... 154 B5
Shepperton TW17 ... 193 A3
South Tottenham N15 ... 51 C4
Spring Gr TW7 ... 130 C4
Thornton Heath CR7 ... 204 C5
Twickenham TW2 ... 152 B1
Uxbridge UB8 ... 60 A1
Walthamstow E17 ... 53 D4
Willesden NW2 ... 68 C2
Woodford E18 ... 36 D1
Grove Rd Prim Sch TW3 ... 129 C1
Grove Rd W EN3 ... 6 C6
Grover Ho
4 London SW4 ... 159 C6
Vauxhall SE11 ... 260 D1
Groves Ho UB4 ... 84 B4
Groveside Cl Acton W3 ... 88 C1
Carshalton SM5 ... 218 C6
Groveside Ct SW11 ... 136 B3
Groveside Rd E4 ... 20 C1
Grove St Deptford SE8 ... 119 B1
Edmonton N18 ... 33 D4
Grovestile Waye TW14 ... 149 B4
Grove Terr
Gospel Oak NW5 ... 71 B4
Southall UB1 ... 107 C6
Teddington TW11 ... 175 A6
Grove Terrace Mews
NW5 ... 71 B5
Grove The Bexley DA6 ... 146 D1
Dulwich SE21 ... 162 A3
Ealing W5 ... 110 A5
Edgware HA8 ... 26 D6
Edmonton N13 ... 32 C6
Enfield EN2 ... 4 C3
Finchley N3 ... 29 C3
Grove The *continued*
Hendon NW11 ... 47 A2
Highgate N6 ... 49 A1
Hornsey N8 ... 49 D4
Hounslow TW7 ... 130 C4
Ickenham UB10 ... 60 C3
Kingsbury NW9 ... 45 B4
Sidcup DA14 ... 191 A6
Southall UB6 ... 86 A1
Stratford E15 ... 76 C2
Stroud Green N4 ... 50 B2
Teddington TW11 ... 175 A6
1 Twickenham TW1 ... 153 B5
Walton-on-T KT12 ... 194 B2
West Wickham BR4 ... 224 A6
Grove Vale
Chislehurst West BR7 ... 188 C4
East Dulwich SE22 ... 139 D1
Groveway Dagenham RM8 ... 80 D4
South Lambeth
SW9 ... 138 B4 270 D1
Grove Way
Thames Ditton KT10 ... 196 A1
Wembley HA9 ... 67 A3
Grovewood 9 TW9 ... 132 C4
Grove Wood Cl BR1 ... 210 C6
Grovewood Ct 6 TW7 ... 130 C4
Grovewood Ho NW2 ... 69 B6
Grummant Rd SE15 ... 139 D4
Grundy St E14 ... 97 D1
Gruneisen Rd N3 ... 29 D3
Guardian Angels RC Prim
Sch 9 E3 ... 97 A4
Guardian Ct SE12 ... 164 C6
Guards Mus The★
SW1 ... 115 C4 249 B1
Gubyon Ave SE24 ... 160 D6
Gudden Dr E5 ... 74 B4
Guerin Sq E3 ... 97 B4
Guernsey Cl TW5 ... 129 C5
Guernsey Gr SE24 ... 161 A4
Guernsey Ho
10 Canonbury N1 ... 73 A2
Enfield EN3 ... 6 D5
Guernsey Rd
11 Canonbury N1 ... 73 A2
Leytonstone E11 ... 54 B1
Guibal Rd SE12 ... 165 B3
Guildersfield Rd SW16 ... 182 A3
Guildford Ave TW13 ... 150 A2
Guildford Gr SE10 ... 141 D4
Guildford Ho 23 SE5 ... 139 A3
Guildford Rd
Chingford E17 ... 36 A2
Ilford IG3 ... 79 C6
Newham E6 ... 100 B1
South Lambeth
SW8 ... 138 A4 270 B2
Thornton Heath CR0 ... 205 B3
Guildford Way SM6 ... 220 A3
Guildhall Art Gall★
EC2 ... 95 A1 242 B2
Guildhall Ho EC2 ... 242 C2
Guildhall Sch Music & Drama
EC2 ... 95 A2 242 B4
Guildhall Yd EC2 ... 242 B2
Guild Ho SW19 ... 179 B4
Guildhouse St
SW1 ... 115 C2 259 A3
Guildown Ave N12 ... 29 D6
Guild Rd SE7 ... 143 D6
Guildsway E17 ... 35 B2
Guilford Ave KT5 ... 198 B4
Guilford Pl WC1 ... 240 C5
Guilford St WC1 ... 94 A3 240 B5
Guilfoyle 2 NW9 ... 27 D1
Guillemot Ct 28 SE8 ... 141 B6
Guinness Cl Hayes UB3 ... 105 B3
Homerton E9 ... 75 A1
Guinness Ct Chelsea SW3 ... 257 C3
6 Croydon CR0 ... 221 D6
Finsbury EC1 ... 235 B1
Primrose Hill NW8 ... 230 B5
Whitechapel E1 ... 243 D1
Guinness Sq SE1 ... 263 A4
Guinness Trust Bldgs
Bermondsey SE1 ... 253 A2
7 Bethnal Green E2 ... 96 A5
Chelsea SW3 ... 257 C3
Hammersmith W6 ... 112 C1
Kennington SE11 ... 261 C2
Guion Rd SW6 ... 135 B3
Gujarat Ho 1 N16 ... 73 C5
Gulland Cl WD23 ... 8 A6
Gulland Wlk 21 N1 ... 73 A2
Gullane Ho 24 E3 ... 97 B5
Gull Cl SM6 ... 220 A1
Gulliver Cl UB5 ... 85 B6
Gulliver Ct CR2 ... 220 D1
Gulliver Rd DA15 ... 167 C2
Gulliver St SE16 ... 119 B3
Gulston Wlk SW3 ... 257 D3
Gumleigh Rd W5 ... 109 C2
Gumley Gdns TW7 ... 131 A2
Gumley House Convent Sch
(Girls) TW7 ... 131 A2
Gumping Rd BR5 ... 227 A6
Gundulph Rd BR2 ... 209 C6
Gunmakers La E3 ... 97 A6
Gunnel Cl SE20 ... 184 A6

Gunnell Cl SE25. . . . . .206 A3
Gunnell Ct 3 CR4. . . . . .180 C2
Gunnels Ct & Hastingwood
Ct 6 IG9. . . . . .21 C2
Gunner Dr 9 EN3. . . . . .7 C6
Gunner La SE18. . . . . .122 C1
GUNNERSBURY. 110 D2
Gunnersbury Avenue (North
Circular Rd) W3. . . . . .110 C3
Gunnersbury Cl 8 W4 . .110 B3
Gunnersbury Cres W3. . . . . . .110 C3
Gunnersbury Ct 8 W3 . .110 D4
Gunnersbury Dr W5. . . . . . . .110 B4
Gunnersbury Gdns W3. . . . . .110 C4
Gunnersbury La W3. . . . . . . .110 C4
Gunnersbury Manor W5. . .110 B5
Gunnersbury Mews 6
W4. .110 D1
Gunnersbury Park W3 . .110 C3
Gunnersbury Park Mus★
W3 .110 C3
Gunnersbury RC Sch
TW8. . . . . .109 C1
Gunnersbury Sta W4. . . .110 D1
Gunnersbury Triangle Nat
Res★ W12. . . . . .111 A2
Gunners Gr E4. . . . . .20 A1
Gunners Rd SW18. . . . . .158 B2
Gunnery Terr SE18. . . . . . . .123 A3
Gunning St SE18. . . . . .123 C2
Gunpowder Sq EC4. . . . .241 B2
Gun St E1 . . . . .243 C3
Gunstor Rd N16. . . . . .73 C4
Gunter Gr
Chelsea SW6 . . . .136 A5 266 A4
Hendon HA8. . . . . .27 B2
Gunterstone Rd
W14. . . . . . . .113 A1 254 B2
Gunthorpe St E1. . .95 D1 243 D2
Gunton Rd
Streatham SW17 . . . . .181 A4
Upper Clapton E5 . . . . .74 B6
Gunwhale Cl SE16 . . . . .118 D5
Gun Wharf Old Ford E3 . . . . .97 A6
Wapping E1 . . . . .118 C5
Gurdon Ho 7 E14 . . . . .97 C1
Gurdon Rd SE7 . . . . .121 A1
Gurnell Gr W13. . . . . .86 D3
Gurnell L Ctr W13. . . . . .86 D4
Gurney Cl Barking IG11. . . . . .78 D2
Higham Hill E17 . . . . .34 D2
Stratford E15 . . . . .76 C3
Gurney Cres CR0. . . . . .204 B1
Gurney Dr N2. . . . . .48 A5
Gurney Ho
3 Bayswater W2. . . . . .91 D1
14 Bethnal Green E2 . . . . . .96 A5
Hayes UB3 . . . . .105 C2
Gurney Rd London SW6 . . .136 A2
Northolt UB5 . . . . .84 C4
Stratford E15 . . . . .76 C3
Wallington SM5 . . . . .219 A4
Guru Nanak Sikh Prim & Sec
Schs UB4 . . . . .106 C5
Guthrie Ct SE1. . . . . .251 B1
Guthrie St SW3 . . . . .257 A2
Gutter La EC2. . . .95 A1 242 B2
Guyatt Gdns CR4. . . . . .181 A1
Guy Barnett Gr SE3 . . . . . .143 A2
Guy Rd SM6. . . . . .219 D5
Guyscliff Rd SE13. . . . . .164 A6
Guy's Hosp SE1 . . .117 B4 252 D2
Guy's Retreat IG9. . . . . .21 C4
Guy St SE1 . . . . . .117 B4 252 D2
Gwalior Ho N14. . . . . .15 C5
Gwalior Rd SW15 . . . . .134 D2
Gwendolen Ave SW15. . . . .156 D6
Gwendolen Cl SW15 . . . . . .156 D6
Gwendolen Ho TW19. . . . . .148 A3
Gwendoline Ave E13 . . . . . . .99 B6
Gwendoline Ct TW15. . . . . .170 A6
Gwendwr Rd
W14. . . . . . . .113 A1 254 B2
Gwent Ct 13 SE16. . . . . . . .118 D5
Gwillim Cl DA15. . . . . .186 A5
Gwilym Maries Ho 11 E2 . .96 B4
Gwydor Rd BR3. . . . . .206 D6
Gwydyr Rd BR2. . . . . .208 D6
Gwyn Cl SW6 . . . .136 A5 266 A3
Gwyn Jones Prim Sch
E11. . . . . .54 B2
Gwynne Ave CR0. . . . . .206 D2
Gwynne Cl W4. . . . . .133 D6
Gwynne Ho Finsbury WC1. .234 A1
6 Streatham SW2. . . . . . .160 B3
3 Wanstead E11. . . . . .55 A4
Whitechapel E1. . . . . .96 B4
Gwynne Pl WC1. . . . . . . .233 D1
Gwynne Rd SW11. . . . . . . .136 D1
Gye Ho 3 SW4 . . . . .138 A1
Gylcote Cl SE5. . . . . .139 B1
Gyles Pk HA7. . . . . .25 C2
Gyllyngdune Gdns IG3 . . .79 D5

H

Haarlem Rd 12 W14. . . . . . .112 D3
Haberdasher Pl 4 N1. . . . . . .95 C4
Haberdashers' Aske's
Hatcham Coll SE4 . . . . . .141 A3
Haberdashers' Aske's Knights
Acad BR1. . . . . .187 A6
Haberdasher St
N1. . . . . .95 B4 235 D2
Haccombe Rd SW19 . . . . . .180 A4
HACKBRIDGE. 219 B6
Hackbridge Park Gdns
SM5. . . . . .218 D6
Hackbridge Prim Sch
SM5. . . . . .203 A1
Hackbridge Rd SM5,
SM6. . . . . .219 A6
Hackbridge Sta SM6 . . . . . .219 B6
Hackford Rd
SW9. . . . . .138 B4 202 D2
Hackford Wlk SW9. . . . . . . .138 C4
Hackforth Cl EN5 . . . . .12 B6
Hackington Cres BR3 . . . . .185 C4
HACKNEY. 74 B2
Hackney Central Sta E8 . . . . .74 B2
Hackney Cl WD6 . . . . .11 B6
Hackney Com Coll 33 N1. . .95 C4
Hackney Downs Sta E8. . . . . .74 B3
Hackney Empire E8. . . . . .74 B2
Hackney Free & Parochial CE
Sec Sch 18 E9. . . . . .74 C2
Hackney Gr E8. . . . . .74 B2
Hackney Rd E2. . . . . .96 A5
HACKNEY WICK. 75 C2
Hackney Wick E9. . . . . .75 B2
Hackney Wick Sta E9 . . . . . . .75 C2
Hackworth Point 24 E9. . . . .97 D4
Hacon Sq 12 E8. . . . . .74 B1
Hadar Cl N20 . . . . .13 D3
Haddenham Ct SW17 . . . . .180 B6
Hadden Rd SE28. . . . . .123 C3
Hadden Way UB6 . . . . .64 B2
Haddington Rd BR1. . . . . . .186 B6
Haddo Ho Gospel Oak NW5. .71 B4
Greenwich SE10. . . . . .141 D6
Haddon Cl Enfield EN1 . . . . . .18 A3
New Malden KT3 . . . . .199 D4
Haddon Ct
East Acton W3 . . . . .111 D6
Hendon NW4 . . . . .46 C6
Haddon Gr DA15. . . . . .168 A4
Haddon Rd SM1. . . . . .217 D4
Haddo St SE10. . . . . .142 A6
Haden Ct N4. . . . . .72 C6
Hadfield Cl UB1. . . . . .85 B4
Hadfield Ho Edgware NW7. .28 C6
37 Whitechapel E1. . . . . . . .96 A1
Hadleigh Cl
17 Bethnal Green E1 . . . . . .96 C3
Merton SW20. . . . . .179 B1
Hadleigh Ct 8 E4. . . . . .20 C4
Hadleigh Ho 16 E1. . . . . . . .96 C3
Hadleigh Lo 5 IG8 . . . . .37 A4
Hadleigh Rd N9. . . . . .18 B4
Hadleigh St E2 . . . . .96 C4
Hadleigh Wlk 1 E6. . . . . . .100 A1
HADLEY. 1 B2
Hadley Cl
Borehamwood WD6. . . . . . .10 B5
Southgate N21. . . . . .16 C5
Hadley Ct 1 London N3 . . . . .29 D3
Stamford Hill N16. . . . . .52 A1
Hadley Gdns
Chiswick W4. . . . . .111 B1
Southall UB2. . . . . .107 B1
Hadley Gn W EN5 . . . . .1 A3
Hadley Gr EN5 . . . . .1 A3
Hadley Green Rd EN5 . . . . . .1 B3
Hadley Hall N21. . . . . .16 C3
Hadley Highstone EN5 . . . . . .1 B4
Hadley Ho BR5. . . . . .189 D1
Hadley Hts EN5. . . . . .1 D2
Hadley Rd Barnet EN5. . . . . . .1 D2
Belvedere DA17. . . . . .125 B2
Enfield EN2. . . . . .4 A5
Mitcham CR4. . . . . .203 D5
Hadley Ridge EN5. . . . . .1 B2
Hadley St NW1. . . . . .71 B2
Hadleyvale Ct EN5. . . . . .1 D1
Hadley View 9 EN5 . . . . .1 D1
Hadley Way N21. . . . . .16 C5
HADLEY WOOD. 2 B5
Hadley Wood Prim Sch
EN4. .2 A5
Hadley Wood Rd
Barnet EN4. . . . . .2 A3
Barnet EN5. . . . . .1 C3
Hadley Wood Sta EN4. . . . . . .2 A4
Hadlow Coll (Mottingham
Ctr) SE12. . . . . .165 C3
Hadlow Ho SE17. . . . . . . .263 B2
Hadlow Pl SE19. . . . . .184 A3
Hadlow Rd Bexley DA16. . . .146 C5
Sidcup DA14. . . . . .190 A6
Hadrian Cl 3 Old Ford E3. . .97 B5
Stanwell TW19. . . . . .148 A4
Hadrian Ct Barnet EN5 . . . . . .1 D1
11 Belmont SM2. . . . . .217 D1

Hadrian Ct continued
Brockley SE4. . . . . .141 C2
Hadrian Est 33 E2. . . . . .96 A5
Hadrian's Ride EN1. . . . . . . .17 D6
Hadrian St SE10. . . . . .120 C1
Hadrian Way TW19. . . . . . . .148 A4
Hadstock Ho NW1. . . . . .232 D2
Hadyn Park Ct 13 W12. . . . .112 A4
Hadyn Park Rd W12. . . . . . .112 A4
Hafer Rd SW11. . . . . .136 D1
Hafton Rd SE6. . . . . .164 C2
Haggard Rd TW1. . . . . .153 B4
Hagger Ct E17. . . . . .54 B6
Haggerston Rd E8. . . . . .95 D5
Haggerston Sch 15 E2 . . . . .95 D5
Haggerston Sta E2. . . . . .95 D6
Haggerston Studios 30
E8. .95 D6
Hague Prim Sch 21 E2 . . . . .96 B3
Hague St 30 E2. . . . . .96 A4
Ha-Ha Rd SE7, SE18. . . . . .144 B6
Haig Ct SE7. . . . . .188 D5
Haig Ho 4 E2 . . . . .96 A5
Haig Pl SM4 . . . . .201 C3
Haig Rd E13 . . . . .99 C5
Haig Rd W E13. . . . . .99 C4
Haigville Gdns IG6. . . . . .56 D5
Hailes Cl SW19 . . . . .180 A4
Haileybury Ave EN1. . . . . . . .17 D5
Hailey Rd DA18. . . . . .125 C4
Hailey Rd Bsns Pk DA18. . .125 C4
Hailing Mews BR2. . . . . . . .209 B6
Hailsham Ave SW2. . . . . . . .160 B2
Hailsham Cl KT6 . . . . .197 D2
Hailsham Dr HA1. . . . . .42 B6
Hailsham Rd SW17. . . . . . . .181 A4
Hailsham Terr N18. . . . . .33 B5
Haimo Prim Sch SE9. . . . . .165 D6
Haimo Rd SE9 . . . . .165 D6
Hainault Bldgs E10. . . . . . . .54 A1
Hainault Bridge Par 5
IG1. .78 D6
Hainault Ct E17. . . . . .54 B5
Hainault Gore RM6. . . . . . . .59 A4
Hainault Rd
Dagenham RM6. . . . . .59 B3
Ilford RM6 . . . . .58 B6
Leytonstone E11. . . . . .54 B2
Hainault St Ilford IG1. . . . . . .78 D6
New Eltham SE9 . . . . .166 D3
Haines Wlk SM4 . . . . .201 D2
Hainford Cl SE4. . . . . .140 D1
Haining Cl 3 W4 . . . . .110 C1
Hainthorpe Rd SE27. . . . . . .182 D6
Hainton Cl E1 . . . . .96 B1
Halberd Mews E5. . . . . .74 B6
Halbutt Gdns RM9 . . . . .81 B5
Halbutt St RM9 . . . . .81 B4
Halcomb St N1. . . . . .95 C6
Halcot Ave DA6. . . . . .169 D6
Halcroft Ct SM1. . . . . .218 B4
Halcrow St E1. . . . . .96 B2
Halcyon Ho 3 EN1. . . . . .17 C6
Haldane Cl Holbrook EN3 . . . .7 D5
Muswell Hill N10. . . . . .31 B3
Haldane Pl SW18 . . . . .157 D3
Haldane Rd
Fulham SW6 . . . .135 B6 264 D5
Newham E6 . . . . .100 A4
Southall UB1. . . . . .86 A1
Thamesmead SE28. . . . . . .124 D6
Haldan Rd E4. . . . . .36 A4
Haldon Rd SW18. . . . . .157 B5
Hale Cl Chingford E4 . . . . . . .20 A1
Edgware HA8 . . . . .27 A5
Orpington BR6 . . . . .227 A4
Hale Ct HA8 . . . . .27 A5
Hale Dr NW7 . . . . .27 B4
HALE END. 36 C4
Hale End Cl HA4 . . . . .40 A3
Hale End Rd E17. . . . . .36 B2
Halefield Rd N17. . . . . .34 B2
Hale Gdns Acton W3 . . . . . .110 C5
Tottenham Hale N17. . . . . . .52 A6
Hale Grove Gdns NW7. . . . . .27 C5
Hale Ho Enfield EN3. . . . . . . .6 D5
Westminster SW1 . . . . . .259 D2
Hale La N7, HA8 . . . . .27 B5
Hale Lo HA1. . . . . .42 C2
Hale Rd Newham E6. . . . . . .100 A3
Tottenham Hale N17. . . . . . .52 A6
Hales Ct 6 TW11. . . . . .175 A5
Hales Ho 3 SW12. . . . . . . .159 B4
Halesowen Rd SM4. . . . . . .201 D2
Hales Prior N1. . . . . .233 C3
Hales St SE8. . . . . .141 C5
Hale St E14. . . . . .119 D6
Halesworth Cl 3 E5. . . . . . .74 C6
Halesworth Rd SE13. . . . . . .141 D2
Hale The Chingford E4 . . . . . .36 B3
Tottenham Hale N17. . . . . . .52 A6
Haley Rd NW4 . . . . .46 C3
Halfacre 14 HA7. . . . . .25 C5
Half Acre Brentford TW8. . . .131 D6
2 Wanstead E18. . . . . .55 A6
Half Acre Mews TW8. . . . . .131 D6

Half Acre Rd W7. . . . . .108 C5
Half Moon Cres N1 . . . .233 D4
Half Moon Ct EC1. . . . . .242 A3
Half Moon La SE24. . . . . . . .161 A5
Halfmoon Pas E1. . . . . . .243 D1
Half Moon St
W1. . . . . .115 B5 248 D3
Halford Cl HA8. . . . . .26 C1
Halford Ct KT9. . . . . .214 A1
Halford Ho 9 SW15. . . . . . .156 D6
Halford Rd Ickenham UB10. .60 C3
Leyton E10. . . . . .54 B4
Richmond TW10. . . . . .154 A6
West Brompton
SW6 . . . . .135 C6 265 A5
Halfway St DA15. . . . . .167 C3
Haliburton Rd TW1,TW7. . .131 A2
Haliday Ho N1. . . . . .73 B2
Haliday Wlk 4 N1. . . . . .73 B2
Halidon Cl E9. . . . . .74 C3
Halifax 8 NW9. . . . . .27 D1
Halifax Cl TW11. . . . . .175 A4
Halifax Rd Enfield EN2. . . . . . .5 B3
Greenford UB6. . . . . .85 D6
Halifax St SE26 . . . . .182 B1
Halifield Dr DA17. . . . . .125 A3
Haling Gr CR2. . . . . .221 A1
Haling Manor High Sch
CR2. . . . . .220 D1
Haling Park Gdns CR2. . . . .220 D2
Haling Park Rd
Croydon CR2. . . . . .220 D3
South Croydon CR2. . . . . . .221 A2
Haling Rd CR2. . . . . .221 B2
Haliwell Ho 10 NW6. . . . . . .91 D6
Halkett Ho 1 E2 . . . . .96 C6
Halkin Arc SW1. . . .114 D3 257 D6
Halkin Mews SW1 . . . . . .258 A6
Halkin Pl SW1. . . . . .258 A6
Halkin St SW1. . . .115 A4 248 B1
Hallam Cl BR7. . . . . .188 B5
Hallam Ct N1. . . . . .238 D4
Hallam Gdns HA5. . . . . .23 A3
Hallam Ho
17 London SW9. . . . . .138 C4
Pimlico SW1. . . . . .259 B1
Hallam Mews W1. . . . . . .238 D4
Hallam Rd Barnes SW13. . . .134 B2
Harringay N15. . . . . .50 D5
Hallam St W1. . . . .93 B2 238 D4
Hallane Ho SE27. . . . . .183 A5
Hall Cl W5. . . . . .88 A2
Hall Ct TW11. . . . . .174 D5
Hall Dr Ealing W7 . . . . .86 C1
Forest Hill SE26 . . . . .184 C5
Halley Gdns SE13 . . . . .142 B1
Halley Ho
16 Bethnal Green E2 . . . . . .96 A5
8 Cubitt Town SE10. . . . . .120 D1
Halley Prim Sch E14 . . . . . . .97 A2
Halley Rd E7, E12. . . . . .77 D2
Halley St E14 . . . . .97 A2
Hall Farm Cl HA7. . . . . .25 B6
Hall Farm Dr TW2. . . . . .152 B4
Hallfield Jun & Inf Schs 21
W2. . . . . .91 D1
Hallgate SE3 . . . . .143 A2
Hall Gate NW8. . . . .92 A4 229 B2
Hall Gdns E4 . . . . .35 B6
Halliards The KT2. . . . . .194 A3
Halliday Ho 40 E1. . . . . .96 A1
Halliday Sq UB2 . . . . .108 B5
Halliford Cl TW17 . . . . .193 C6
Halliford Rd
Sunbury TW16. . . . . .194 A5
Upper Halliford TW16,
TW17. . . . . .193 D5
Halliford Sch TW17 . . . . . . .193 A2
Halliford St N1. . . . . .73 B1
Hallingbury Ct 1 E17. . . . . .53 D6
Halling Ho SE1. . . . . .252 D1
Hallings Wharf Studios 2
E15. . . . . .98 B6
Halliwell Ct 4 SE22. . . . . . .162 A6
Halliwell Rd SW2. . . . . .160 B5
Halliwick Court Par 2
N12. . . . . .30 D5
Halliwick Rd 1 N12. . . . . . .30 D5
Halliwick Rd N21. . . . . .17 B5
Halliwick Rd N10. . . . . .31 A2
Hall La Chingford Hatch E4. . .35 B5
Harlington UB3. . . . . .127 B5
Hendon NW4 . . . . .28 A1
Hall Lane E4. . . . . .35 A5
Hallmark Trad Ctr HA9 . . . . .67 A4
Hallmead Rd SM1. . . . . . . .217 D5
Hall Oak Wlk NW6 . . . . .69 B2
Hallowell Ave CR0. . . . . . . .220 A4
Hallowell Cl CR4. . . . . .203 A6
Hallowfield Way CR4. . . . . .202 C6
Hallows Gr TW16. . . . . .171 D5
Hall Pl W2 . . . . . . .92 B3 236 C5
Hall Pl Dagenham RM6. . . . . .58 D3
Isleworth TW7. . . . . .152 B6
Leyton E10. . . . . .76 B4
Newham E6. . . . . .100 B6
St John's Wood
NW8. . . . . .92 A4 229 B2
Halls Bsns Ctr UB3. . . . . . .106 A3
Hall Sch SW20. . . . . .178 D2

Hall Sch The NW3. . . . . .70 B2
Hall Sch Wimbledon
SW15 . . . . .156 A1
Hallside Rd EN1 . . . . .5 D5
Hall St
Finsbury EC1 . . . . .94 D4 234 D2
North Finchley N12. . . . . . . .30 A5
Halls Terr UB10. . . . . .82 D3
Hallsville Prim Sch E16. . . . . .99 A1
Hallsville Rd E16. . . . . .98 D1
Hallswelle Par 1 NW11. . . .47 B4
Hallswelle Rd NW11. . . . . . .47 B4
Hall The SE3. . . . . .143 A2
Hall Twr W2 . . . . .236 D4
Hall View SE9. . . . . .165 D2
Hallywell Cres E6. . . . . .100 B3
Halons Rd SE9. . . . . .166 C4
Halpin Pl SE17. . . .117 B2 262 D3
Halsbrook Rd SE3. . . . . . . .143 D2
Halsbury Cl HA7. . . . . .25 B6
Halsbury Ct HA7. . . . . .25 B6
Halsbury Ho 4 N7. . . . . . . .72 B4
Halsbury Rd W12. . . . . .112 B5
Halsbury Rd E UB5. . . . . . . .64 A4
Halsbury Rd W UB5. . . . . . .63 D3
Halsend UB3. . . . . .106 B5
Halsey St SW3 . . . .114 D3 257 C4
Halsham Cres IG11. . . . . . . .79 D3
Halsmere Rd SE5 . . . . .138 C4
Halstead Cl 2 CR0. . . . . . . .221 A5
Halstead Ct
Shoreditch N1. . . . . .235 D3
Walthamstow E17 . . . . .53 B2
Halstead Gdns N21. . . . . . . .17 B3
Halstead Rd
Edmonton N21. . . . . .17 B3
Enfield EN1. . . . . .5 C1
Wanstead E11. . . . . .55 B4
Halston Cl SW11. . . . . .158 D5
Halstow 12 NW5. . . . . .71 A2
Halstow Prim Sch 5
SE10. . . . . .121 A1
Halstow Rd
Greenwich SE3, SE10. . . . .121 A1
Kensal Green NW10. . . . . . .90 D4
Halsway UB3. . . . . .106 A5
Halter Cl WD6. . . . . .11 B6
Halton Cl N11. . . . . .31 A4
Halton Cross St
N1. . . . . .94 D6 234 D6
Haltone Ho 1 SW4 . . . . . . .137 D3
Halton Ho 22 N1 . . . . .72 D1
Halton Mans N1. . . . . .72 D1
Halton Pl N1. . . . . .235 A6
Halton Rd N1. . . . . . .94 D6 234 D6
Halt Robin La DA17. . . . . . .125 D2
Halt Robin Rd DA17. . . . . . .125 D2
Halyard Ho E14. . . . . .120 A3
HAM. 153 C1
Hamara Ghar 4 E13. . . . . . .99 C6
Hambalt Rd SW4. . . . . .159 C6
Hamble Cl HA4. . . . . .61 C6
Hamble Ct KT1. . . . . .175 D3
Hambledon SE17 . . . . .139 B6
Hambledon Chase N4. . . . . .50 A2
Hambledon Cl UB8. . . . . . . .82 D3
Hambledon Ct
5 Ealing W5. . . . . .110 A6
9 Wallington SM6. . . . . . . .219 B6
Hambledon Gdns SE25. . . .205 D6
Hambledon Ho
2 Kingston u T KT2 . . . . . .176 D2
Lower Clapton E5. . . . . .74 B4
Hambledon Pl SE21. . . . . . .161 D3
Hambledon Rd SW18 . . . . .157 B4
Hambledown Rd DA15. . . . .167 C4
Hamble St SW6. . . . . .135 D2
Hambleton Cl KT4. . . . . . . .216 C6
Hambie Wlk UB5. . . . . .85 C5
Hambley Ho 5 SE16. . . . . .118 B2
Hamblin Ho UB1. . . . . .107 A6
Hambly Mans SW16. . . . . .182 A4
Hamblyn Ct N16. . . . . .51 D2
Hambridge Way SW2. . . . . .160 C4
Hambro Ave BR2. . . . . .209 A1
Hambrook Ct 12 NW5. . . . . .71 B4
Hambrook Rd SE25. . . . . . .206 B6
Hambro Rd SW16. . . . . .181 D5
Hambrough Ho UB4. . . . . . . .84 C2
Hambrough Prim Sch
UB1. . . . . .107 B5
Hambrough Rd UB1. . . . . . .107 A5
Ham Cl TW10. . . . . .153 C1
Ham Comm TW10. . . . . . . .153 D1
Ham Croft Cl TW13. . . . . . .150 A1
Ham Ct 12 NW9. . . . . .27 D1
Hamden Cres RM10. . . . . . .81 D5
Hamel Cl HA3. . . . . .43 D5
Hamers Ho 10 SW2. . . . . . .160 C4
Hameway E6 . . . . .100 C3
Ham Farm Rd KT2,TW10. . .176 A6
Hamfrith Rd E15. . . . . .76 D2
Ham Gate Ave TW10. . . . . .176 A6
Ham Ho★ TW10. . . . . .153 C2
Hamilton Ave
Cheam SM3. . . . . .217 A6
Edmonton N9. . . . . .18 A4

Hamilton Ave continued
Ilford IG6 . . . . **57** A4
Tolworth KT6, SM3 . . . **214** C6
Hamilton Cl
Ashford TW13 . . . . **171** D5
Cockfosters EN4 . . . . **2** D1
Rotherhithe SE16 . . . . . **119** A4
St John's Wood
NW8 . . . . **92** B4 **229** C1
Teddington TW11 . . . . . **175** B4
Tottenham N17 . . . . **51** D6
Hamilton Cres
Edmonton N13 . . . . **32** C6
Harrow HA2 . . . . **63** B5
Hounslow TW3 . . . . . . **151** D6
Hamilton Ct
9 Catford SE6 . . . . **164** D3
Croydon CR0 . . . . **206** A1
Ealing W5 . . . . **110** B6
St John's Wood W9 . . . . **229** A2
Hamilton Gdns
NW8 . . . . **92** A4 **229** B2
Hamilton Hall
NW8 . . . . **92** A5 **229** A3
Hamilton Ho 23 Bow E3 . . . **97** B4
Chiswick W4 . . . . **133** C6
Kensington W8 . . . . **245** C2
Oakleigh Pk N20 . . . . **14** A4
1 Poplar E14 . . . . **119** B6
9 Richmond TW9 . . . . . **132** C4
St John's Wood NW8 . . . **229** C2
Hamilton La N5 . . . . **72** D4
Hamilton Mews **248** C2
Hamilton Par TW13 . . . . . **172** A6
Hamilton Pk N5 . . . . **72** D4
Hamilton Pk W N5 . . . . . . **72** D4
Hamilton Pl
Mayfair W1 . . . . . . **115** A5 **248** B3
Sunbury TW16 . . . . **172** B3
Tottenham N17 . . . . **33** D1
Hamilton Rd Acton W4 . . . **111** C4
Barnet EN4 . . . . **2** C1
Bexleyheath DA7 . . . . . **147** A3
Brentford TW8 . . . . **131** D6
Ealing W5 . . . . **110** A6
East Finchley N2 . . . . **48** A6
Edmonton N9 . . . . **18** A4
Feltham TW13 . . . . **171** D6
Harrow HA1 . . . . **42** C4
Hayes UB3 . . . . **106** B6
Hendon NW11 . . . . **47** A2
Higham Hill E17 . . . . **35** A1
Ilford IG1 . . . . **78** D4
Merton SW19 . . . . **179** D3
Newham E15 . . . . **98** C4
Sidcup DA15 . . . . **190** A6
Southall UB1 . . . . **107** B5
South Norwood CR7 . . . **205** B6
Twickenham TW2 . . . . . **152** C3
West Norwood SE27 . . . **183** B6
Willesden NW10 . . . . **68** A3
Hamilton Road Ind Est
SE27 . . . . **183** B6
Hamilton Road Mews 1
SW19 . . . . **179** D3
Hamilton Sq
Bermondsey SE1 . . . . . . **252** D2
Finchley N12 . . . . **30** A4
Hamilton St SE8 . . . . **141** C6
Hamilton Terr
NW8 . . . . **92** A4 **229** B2
Hamilton Way
Edmonton N13 . . . . **32** C6
Finchley N3 . . . . **29** C4
Hamlea Cl SE12 . . . . **165** A6
Hamlet Cl SE13 . . . . **142** C1
Hamlet Ct 14 Enfield EN1 . . **17** C6
1 Hammersmith W6 . . . **112** A4
Kennington SE11 . . . . . . **261** C2
Hamlet Gdns W6 . . . . . . **112** A2
Hamlet Ho SE9 . . . . **166** C6
Hamlet Ind Ctr E9 . . . . . . **75** C1
Hamleton Terr RM9 . . . . . **80** C1
Hamlet Rd SE19 . . . . **184** A3
Hamlet Sq NW2 . . . . **69** A5
Hamlets Way E3 . . . . **97** B3
Hamlet The SE5 . . . . **139** B2
Hamlet Way SE1 . . . . **252** D2
Hamlin Cres HA5 . . . . **40** C4
Hamlyn Cl HA8 . . . . **10** A1
Hamlyn Gdns SE19 . . . . . **183** C3
Hamlyn Ho 3 TW13 . . . . **150** B3
Hammelton Ct 4 BR1 . . . **186** D2
Hammelton Gn 2 SW9 . . **138** D4
Hammelton Rd BR1 . . . . . **187** A2
Hammers La NW7 . . . . . . **28** A6
Hammersley Ho 8
SE14 . . . . **140** C5
HAMMERSMITH **112** C2
Hammersmith Bridge Rd W6,
SW13 . . . . **112** C1
Hammersmith Broadway
Hammersmith W6 . . . . **112** C1
5 Hammersmith W6 . . . **112** C2

Hammersmith Flyover
W6 . . . . **112** C1
Hammersmith Gr W6 . . . . **112** C3
Hammersmith Hospl
W12 . . . . **90** B1
Hammersmith Rd
Hammersmith W6 . . . . **112** C2
Kensington W14 . . . . . . **254** B4
Hammersmith Sta W6 . . . **112** C2
Hammersmith Terr 6
W6 . . . . **112** A1
Hammet Cl UB4 . . . . **84** D2
Hammett St EC3 . . . . **253** C6
Hammond Ave CR4 . . . . . **181** B1
Hammond Cl Barnet EN5 . . **13** B6
Greenford UB6 . . . . **64** B3
Hampton TW12 . . . . **173** C2
Hammond Ct
1 Leyton E10 . . . . **75** D6
1 Walthamstow E17 . . . . **53** A4
Hammond Ho
10 Deptford SE14 . . . . . **140** C5
Millwall E14 . . . . **119** D3
Hammond Lo 6 W9 . . . . . **91** C2
Hammond Rd Enfield EN1 . . **6** B3
Southall UB2 . . . . **107** A3
Hammonds Cl RM8 . . . . . . **80** C5
Hammonds Ho TW9 . . . . **148** B3
Hammond St NW5 . . . . . . **71** C2
Hammond Way 2 SE28 . . **124** B6
Hamonde Cl HA8 . . . . **10** D2
Hamond Sq N1 . . . . **95** C5
Ham Park Rd E15 . . . . **76** D1
Hampden Ave BR3 . . . . . **185** A1
Hampden Cl NW1 . . . . . . **232** D4
Hampden Ct Harrow HA1 . . **42** A5
10 Muswell Hill N10 . . . . **31** A3
Hampden Gurney CE Prim
Sch W1 . . . . . . **92** C1 **237** B2
Hampden Gurney St W1 . . **237** C1
Hampden La N17 . . . . **34** A2
Hampden Rd
Beckenham BR3 . . . . . . **185** A1
Harrow HA3 . . . . **24** A1
Hornsey N8 . . . . **50** C5
Kingston u T KT1 . . . . . . **198** C6
Muswell Hill N10 . . . . **31** A3
Tottenham N17 . . . . **34** A2
Upper Holloway N19 . . . . **71** D6
Hampden Sq N14 . . . . **15** B3
Hampden Way N14 . . . . . . **15** B2
Hampshire Cl N18 . . . . **34** B5
Hampshire Ct
6 Barnes SW13 . . . . . . **133** D3
Hendon NW4 . . . . **46** D4
Hampshire Ho HA8 . . . . . . **26** B3
Hampshire Hog La
3 Hammersmith W6 . . . **112** B1
11 Hammersmith W6 . . . **112** B2
Hampshire Rd N22 . . . . . . **32** B3
Hampshire St NW5 . . . . . . **71** D2
Hampson Way
SW8 . . . . **138** B4 **270** C2
HAMPSTEAD **70** A3
Hampstead Cl SE28 . . . . . **124** B5
Hampstead Coll of Fine Arts
& Humanities 12 NW3 . . **70** C2
Hampstead Com Mkt★
NW3 . . . . **70** B4
HAMPSTEAD GARDEN
SUBURB **47** D4
Hampstead Gate NW3 . . . . **70** A3
Hampstead Gdns NW11 . . **47** C3
Hampstead Gn NW3 . . . . . **70** C3
Hampstead Gr NW3 . . . . . **70** A5
Hampstead Heath★ NW3 . . **70** B4
Hampstead Heath Pre Prep
Sch NW3 . . . . **70** D4
Hampstead Heath Sta
NW3 . . . . **70** C4
Hampstead High Sch 3
NW3 . . . . **70** A3
Hampstead High St NW3 . . **70** B4
Hampstead Hill Gdns
NW3 . . . . **70** C4
Hampstead Hill Sch 1
NW3 . . . . **70** C3
Hampstead Hts N2 . . . . **48** A6
Hampstead La N6 . . . . **48** C2
Hampstead Parochial CE
Prim Sch 30 NW3 . . . . . . **70** A4
Hampstead Rd
NW1 . . . . **93** C4 **232** A2
Hampstead Sq 1 NW3 . . . . **70** A5
Hampstead Sta NW3 . . . . . **70** A4
Hampstead Way NW11 . . . **47** A3
Hampstead West NW6 . . . . **69** C2
Hampstead Wlk 1 E3 . . . . . **97** B6
HAMPTON **173** C1
Hampton Cl
Borehamwood WD6 . . . . **11** A6
Friern Barnet N11 . . . . . . **31** B5
Kilburn NW6 . . . . **91** C4
Wimbledon SW20 . . . . . **178** C3
Hampton Com Coll
TW12 . . . . **173** C5
Hampton Court Ave KT8 . . **196** C3
Hampton Court Cres
KT8 . . . . **196** B6

Hampton Court Landing
Stage KT8 . . . . **196** C6
Hampton Court Pal★
KT8 . . . . **196** D6
Hampton Court Par KT8 . . **196** C5
Hampton Court Rd KT1,
KT8 . . . . **197** B6
Hampton Court Sta KT8 . . **196** C5
Hampton Court Way KT10, KT7,
KT8 . . . . **196** C3
Hampton Ct
Hampton Ct KT8 . . . . . . **196** C6
1 Islington N1 . . . . **72** D2
19 Rotherhithe SE16 . . . **118** D5
Wood Green N22 . . . . . . **31** C2
Hampton Ct House Sch
KT8 . . . . **174** C1
Hampton Farm Ind Est
TW13 . . . . **151** A1
HAMPTON HILL **174** A5
Hampton Hill Bsns Pk
TW12 . . . . **174** A5
Hampton Hill Jun Sch
TW12 . . . . **174** A5
Hampton Ho DA7 . . . . . . **147** D3
Hampton Inf Sch TW12 . . **173** C3
Hampton Jun Sch TW12 . . **173** C2
Hampton La TW13 . . . . . . **173** A6
Hampton Pool (Open Air)
TW12 . . . . **174** A3
Hampton Rd
Chingford Hatch E4 . . . . . **35** B5
Forest Gate E7 . . . . **77** C3
Ilford IG1 . . . . **79** A4
Leytonstone E11 . . . . **54** B1
North Cheam KT4 . . . . . **216** B6
Teddington TW11, TW12 . **174** C5
Thornton Heath CR0 . . . **205** A3
Twickenham TW2 . . . . . **152** B1
Hampton Rd E TW13 . . . . **151** B1
Hampton Rd W TW13 . . . . **151** A1
Hampton Rise HA3 . . . . . . **44** A3
Hampton Road Ind Pk
CR0 . . . . **205** A3
Hampton Sch TW12 . . . . **173** C5
Hampton St SE1 . . **116** D2 **261** D3
Hampton Sta TW12 . . . . . **173** C2
HAMPTON WICK **175** D3
Hampton Wick Inf Sch
TW11 . . . . **175** D3
Hampton Wick Sta KT1 . . **175** C2
Ham Ridings TW10 . . . . . **176** B5
Ham Shades Cl 1 DA15 . . **168** A1
Hamson Ct HA2 . . . . **64** B6
Ham St TW10 . . . . **153** C1
Hamstead Gates 11 NW5 . . **71** B2
Ham The TW8 . . . . **131** C5
Ham View CR0 . . . . **207** A3
Ham Yd W1 . . . . **249** C6
Hanameel St E16 . . . . . . **121** B5
Hana Mews E5 . . . . **74** B4
Hanbury Cl NW4 . . . . **46** C6
Hanbury Ct HA1 . . . . **42** D3
Hanbury Dr 2 Leyton E11 . . **54** D2
Southgate N21 . . . . **16** B6
Hanbury Ho
8 Bethnal Green E1 . . . . . **96** A2
South Lambeth SW8 . . . **270** B5
Hanbury Mews N1 . . . . . . **235** B5
Hanbury Rd
South Acton W3 . . . . . . **110** D4
Tottenham N17 . . . . **34** C2
Hanbury St E1 . . . **95** D2 **243** D4
Hancock Ho 7 E1 . . . . **53** D6
Hancock Nunn Ho 1
NW3 . . . . **70** D1
Hancock Rd Bromley E3 . . . **98** A4
South Norwood SE19 . . . **183** B4
Handa Wlk 3 N1 . . . . **73** A2
Handcroft Rd CR0 . . . . . . **204** D1
Hand Ct WC1 . . . . **240** D3
Handel Cl HA8 . . . . **26** B4
Handel Ho 7 NW3 . . . . . **152** B5
Handel Mans
Barnes SW13 . . . . **134** C5
Bloomsbury WC1 . . . . . . **240** B6
Handel Par HA8 . . . . **26** C3
Handel Pl NW10 . . . . **67** B2
Handel St WC1 . . . **94** A3 **240** B6
Handel Way HA8 . . . . **26** C3
Handen Rd SE12 . . . . **164** D6
Handforth Rd
Brixton SW9 . . . . **138** C5
6 Ilford IG1 . . . . **78** D5
Handley Gr NW2 . . . . **68** D5
Handley Page Rd SM6 . . . **220** B1
Handley Rd E9 . . . . **96** C6
Handowe Cl NW4 . . . . **46** A5
Handside Cl KT4 . . . . **200** D1
Hands Wlk E16 . . . . **99** A1
Handsworth Ave E4 . . . . . . **36** B4
Handsworth Prim Sch E4 . . **36** B4
Handsworth Rd N17 . . . . . **51** B6
Handtrough Way IG11 . . . **100** D5
Hanford Cl SW18 . . . . . . **157** C3
Hanford Row SW19 . . . . . **178** C4
Hanger Ct W5 . . . . **88** C3
Hanger Gn W5 . . . . **88** C3

Hanger Lane Sta W5 . . . . . **88** A4
Hanger La (North Circular
Rd) W5 . . . . **88** B2
Hanger Vale La W5 . . . . . . **88** B1
Hanger View Way W3 . . . . **88** C2
Hangmans Cnr BR7 . . . . . **188** D2
Hankey Pl SE1 . . . **117** B4 **252** D1
Hankins La NW7 . . . . **11** C1
Hanley Ct N4 . . . . **50** B1
Hanley Gdns N4 . . . . **50** B1
Hanley Pl BR3 . . . . **185** C3
Hanley Rd N4, N19 . . . . . . **50** A1
Hanmer Wlk N7 . . . . **72** B6
Hannah Cl
Beckenham BR3 . . . . . . **208** A6
Wembley NW10 . . . . **67** A4
Hannah Ct
Palmers Green N13 . . . . . **16** B2
5 Sutton SM1 . . . . **217** D2
Wimbledon SW19 . . . . . **178** D3
Hannah Mary Way 17
SE1 . . . . **118** A2
Hannah Mews SM6 . . . . . **219** C1
Hannay La N8 . . . . **49** D2
Hannay Wlk SW16 . . . . . . **159** D2
Hannell Rd SW6 . . **135** A5 **264** B4
Hannen Ho SE5 . . . . **139** B2
Hannen Rd SE27 . . . . **160** D1
Hannibal Rd
Stanwell TW19 . . . . **148** A4
Stepney E1 . . . . **96** C2
Hannibal Way CR0 . . . . . **220** B2
Hanning Lo TW3 . . . . **130** A1
Hannington Rd SW4 . . . . **137** B2
Hanno Cl SM6 . . . . **219** D1
Hanover Ave
Feltham TW13 . . . . **150** A2
Newham E16 . . . . **121** A5
Hanover Circ UB3 . . . . **83** B1
11 Pinner HA5 . . . . **23** B3
Shepherd's Bush W12 . . **112** A5
Stamford Hill N16 . . . . . . **51** D2
Hanover Dr BR7 . . . . **189** A6
Hanover Gate Mans
NW1 . . . . **237** B6
Hanover Gdns SE11 . . . . . **138** C6
Hanover Ho
1 New Barnet EN5 . . . . . . **2** A1
St John's Wood NW8 . . . **230** A3
Tolworth KT6 . . . . **198** C1
Hanover Lo N21 . . . . **16** D6
Hanover Mans 1 SW2 . . . **160** C6
Hanover Mead NW11 . . . . **47** A3
Hanover Pk SE15 . . . . **140** A4
Hanover Pl 16 Bow E3 . . . . **97** B4
St Giles WC2 . . . . **240** B1
Hanover Prim Sch
N1 . . . . **95** A5 **235** A4
Hanover Rd
Merton SW19 . . . . **180** A3
South Tottenham N15 . . . **51** D5
Willesden NW10 . . . . **90** C6
Hanover Sq W1 . . . **93** B1 **238** D1
Hanover St Croydon CR0 . . **220** D5
Marylebone W1 . . . **93** B1 **238** D1
Hanover Stps W2 . . . . **237** B1
Hanover Terr
Isleworth TW7 . . . . **131** A4
Lisson Gr NW1 . . . . **92** D4 **230** C1
Hanover Terrace Mews
NW1 . . . . **92** C4 **230** C1
Hanover Way DA6 . . . . . . **146** D2
Hanover West Ind Est
NW10 . . . . **89** B4
Hanover Yd N1 . . . . **235** A4
Hansard Mews W14 . . . . **112** D4
Hansart Way EN2 . . . . **4** C4
Hanscomb Mews SW4 . . . **137** C1
Hans Cres SW1 . . . **114** D3 **257** C6
Hanselin Cl HA7 . . . . **24** D5
Hansen Dr N21 . . . . **16** B6
Hanshaw Dr HA8 . . . . **27** B2
Hansler Ct 14 SW19 . . . . . **157** A3
Hansler Gr KT8 . . . . **196** B5
Hansler Rd SE22 . . . . **161** D6
Hansol Rd DA6 . . . . **169** A6
Hanson Cl Balham SW12 . . **159** B4
Beckenham BR3 . . . . . . **185** D4
Mortlake SW14 . . . . **133** A2
West Drayton UB7 . . . . . **104** B3
Hanson Ct E17 . . . . **53** D3
Hanson Gdns UB1 . . . . . . **107** A4
Hanson Ho 2 E1 . . . . . . **118** A6
Hanson St W1 . . . . **93** C2 **239** A4
Hans Pl SW1 . . . . . **114** D3 **257** C6
Hans Rd SW3 . . . . **114** D3 **257** C6
Hans St SW1 . . . . . **114** D3 **257** D5
Hanway E 25 SW9 . . . . . . **138** C4
Hanway Pl W1 . . . . **239** C2
Hanway Rd W7 . . . . **108** C5
Hanway St W1 . . . . **239** C2
HANWELL **108** D5
Hanwell Sta W7 . . . . **108** C6
HANWORTH **172** D6
Hanworth Ho SE5 . . . . . . **138** D5

Hanworth Rd
Ashford TW16 . . . . **172** A3
Feltham TW13 . . . . **150** B3
Hampton TW12 . . . . **173** C5
Hounslow TW3, TW4 . . . **129** D1
Twickenham TW4 . . . . . **151** B4
Hanworth Terr TW3 . . . . . **129** D1
Hanworth Trad Est
TW13 . . . . **151** A1
Hapgood Cl UB6 . . . . **64** B3
Harben Rd NW6 . . . . **70** A1
Harberson Rd
Balham SW12 . . . . **159** B3
West Ham E15 . . . . **98** C6
Harberton Rd N19 . . . . **49** C1
Harbet Rd Highams Pk N18 . **35** A4
Paddington W2 . . . . **92** B2 **236** D3
Harbex Cl DA5 . . . . **169** D4
Harbinger Prim Sch 11
E14 . . . . **119** D2
Harbinger Rd E14 . . . . . . **119** D2
Harbin Ho 5 SW2 . . . . . . **160** C3
Harbledown Ho SE1 . . . . . **252** C1
Harbledown Rd SW6 . . . . **265** A2
Harbord Cl
Camberwell SE15 . . . . . **139** C4
London SE5 . . . . **139** B3
Harbord Ho 5 SE16 . . . . . **118** D2
Harbord St SW6 . . . . **134** D4
Harborne Cl WD19 . . . . **22** C5
Harborough Ave DA15 . . . **167** D4
Harborough Rd SW16 . . . **182** B6
Harbour Ave
SW10 . . . . **136** A4 **266** B3
Harbour Cl 2 CR4 . . . . . . **181** A2
Harbour Exchange Sq
E14 . . . . **119** D4
Harbour Rd SE5 . . . . **139** A2
Harbridge Ave SW15 . . . . **156** A4
Harbury Rd SM5 . . . . **218** C1
Harbut Rd SW11 . . . . **136** B1
Harcombe Rd N16 . . . . **73** C5
Harcourt Ave
Edgware HA8 . . . . **11** A1
Little Ilford E12 . . . . **78** B3
Sidcup DA15 . . . . **168** C4
Wallington SM6 . . . . **219** B4
Harcourt Cl TW7 . . . . **131** A2
Harcourt Field SM6 . . . . . **219** B4
Harcourt Ho
5 Chingford E4 . . . . **36** B5
27 Clapham SW8 . . . . . . **137** D3
Marylebone W1 . . . . **238** C2
4 Willesden NW10 . . . . . **68** C2
Harcourt Lo 2 SM6 . . . . . **219** B4
Harcourt Rd Bexley DA6 . . **147** A1
Brockley SE4 . . . . **141** B2
Bushey WD23 . . . . **8** A6
Merton SW19 . . . . **179** C3
Thornton Heath CR7 . . . **204** C3
Wallington SM6 . . . . **219** B4
West Ham E15 . . . . **98** D5
Wood Green N22 . . . . . . **31** C2
Harcourt St W1 . . . **92** C2 **237** B3
Harcourt Terr
SW10 . . . . **113** D1 **255** D1
Hardcastle Cl SE25 . . . . . **206** A4
Hardcastle Ho
3 New Cross Gate SE14 . . **141** A4
8 Peckham SE15 . . . . . . **140** A4
Hardcourts Cl BR4 . . . . . . **223** D5
Hard Ct IG8 . . . . **37** C4
Hardel Rise SW2 . . . . **160** D3
Hardel Wlk SE24, SW2 . . . **160** C4
Harden Ct 1 SE7 . . . . **122** A2
Harden Ho SE5 . . . . **139** C3
Harders Rd SE15 . . . . **140** B3
Hardess St SE24 . . . . **139** A2
Hardham Ho 5 SW2 . . . . **160** C5
Hardie Cl NW10 . . . . **67** B3
Harding Cl
Camberwell SE17 . . . . . **139** A6
South Croydon CR0 . . . . **221** D5
Harding Ct SE25 . . . . **183** D1
Hardinge Cl UB8 . . . . **82** D1
Hardinge Cres SE18 . . . . **123** A3
Hardinge Rd
Edmonton N18 . . . . **33** C4
Willesden NW10 . . . . **90** C6
Hardinge St Stepney E1 . . . **96** C1
Woolwich SE18 . . . . **122** D3
Harding Ho Barnes SW13 . **134** B6
Hayes UB3 . . . . **84** B1
14 Woolwich SE18 . . . . . **122** B2
Harding Pl SE23 . . . . **163** A4
Harding Rd DA7 . . . . **147** B3
Hardings Cl KT2 . . . . **176** B2
Hardings La SE20 . . . . . . **184** D4
Hardington 2 NW1 . . . . . . **71** A1
Hardman Rd
Greenwich SE7 . . . . **121** B1
Kingston u T KT2 . . . . . . **176** A1
Hardwick Cl 7 HA7 . . . . . . **25** C5
Hardwick Ct 3 E11 . . . . . . **55** A3
Hardwicke Ave TW5 . . . . **129** C4
Hardwicke Ho 14 E3 . . . . . **97** D4
Hardwicke Mews WC1 . . . **233** D1
Hardwicke Rd Acton W4 . . **111** B2
Bowes Pk N13 . . . . **32** A4
Richmond TW10 . . . . . . **175** C6

Hardwicke St IG11 . . . . . . .101 A6
Hardwick Gn W13 . . . . .87 B2
Hardwick Ho
　🔟 London SW8 . . . . 137 D3
　Marylebone NW8 . . . . 237 B6
Hardwick St EC1 . . 94 C4 234 B1
Hardwick's Way SW18 . . . . .157 C6
Hardwidge St SE1 . . . . 253 A2
Hardy Ave
　🔒 Newham E16 . . . . 121 A5
　Ruislip HA4 . . . . .62 B3
Hardy Cl Barnet EN5 . . . . . . .13 A6
　Pinner HA5 . . . . .40 D2
　Rotherhithe SE16 . . . . . . .118 D4
Hardy Cotts 🔢 SE10 . . . . . . 142 B6
Hardy Ct Greenwich SE3 . . 142 D6
　🔟 Wanstead E11 . . . . .55 A5
Hardyng Ho 🔢 E17 . . . . .53 A5
Hardy Pas N22 . . . . .32 C1
Hardy Rd Greenwich SE3 . . 142 D6
　Merton SW19 . . . . 179 D3
　Walthamstow E4 . . . . .35 B4
Hardys Mews KT8 . . . . .196 C5
Hardy Way EN2 . . . . .4 C4
Hare and Billet Rd SE3 . . . 142 B3
Harebell Dr E6 . . . . 100 C2
Harecastle Cl UB4 . . . . .85 A3
Harecourt Rd N1 . . . . .73 A2
Hare Ct EC4 . . . . 241 A1
Haredale Ho 🔢 SE16 . . . . .118 A4
Haredale Rd SE24 . . . . .139 A1
Haredon Cl SE23 . . . . .162 D4
Harefield KT10 . . . . .212 C5
Harefield Cl EN2 . . . . .4 C4
Harefield Ct 🔢 SW19 . . . . .179 C3
Harefield Mews SE4 . . . . . .141 B2
Harefield Rd
　Brockley SE4 . . . . .141 B2
　Hornsey N8 . . . . .49 D4
　Sidcup DA14 . . . . .168 D1
　South Norwood SW16 . . . .182 B3
　Uxbridge UB8 . . . . .60 A3
Hare La KT10 . . . . .212 C2
Hare Marsh E2 . . . . .96 A3
Harenc Sch DA14 . . . . 190 C5
Harepit Cl CR2 . . . . .220 D1
Hare Pl EC4 . . . . 241 B1
Hare Row E2 . . . . .96 B5
Haresfield Rd RM10 . . . . . . .81 C2
Hare St SE18 . . . . 122 C3
Harestone Ct CR2 . . . . 221 C2
Hare Wlk N1 . . . . .95 C5
Harewood Ave
　Lisson Gr NW1 . . . .92 C3 237 B5
　Northolt UB5 . . . . .63 B1
Harewood Cl UB5 . . . . .63 B1
Harewood Ct HA3 . . . . .24 C2
Harewood Pl W1 . . . . 238 D1
Harewood Rd
　Hounslow TW7 . . . . 130 D4
　Mitcham SW19 . . . . 180 C4
　South Croydon CR2 . . . . . 221 C2
Harewood Row NW1 . . . . . 237 B4
Harewood Terr UB2 . . . . . .107 B2
Harfield Gdns 🔢 SE5 . . . . .139 C2
Harfield Rd TW16 . . . . 172 D1
Harfleur Ct SE11 . . . . 261 C3
Harford Cl E4 . . . . .19 D4
Harford Ho
　Camberwell SE5 . . . . 139 A6
　Notting Hill W11 . . . . .91 B2
Harford Mews 🔢 N19 . . . . .71 D5
Harford Rd E4 . . . . .19 D4
Harford St E1 . . . . .97 A3
Harford Wlk N2 . . . . .48 B5
Hargood Cl HA3 . . . . .44 A3
Hargood Rd SE3 . . . . .143 C4
Hargrave Mans 🔢 N19 . . . . .71 C6
Hargrave Park Prim Sch 🔢
　N19 . . . . .71 C6
Hargrave Pk N19 . . . . .71 C6
Hargrave Pl N7 . . . . .71 C6
Hargrave Rd N19 . . . . .71 C6
Hargraves Ho 🔢 W12 . . . . .112 B6
Hargwyne St SW9 . . . . 138 B2
Haringey Pk N8 . . . . .50 A3
Haringey Rd N8 . . . . .50 A5
Haringey Sixth Form Ctr
　N17 . . . . .33 D4
Harington Terr N18 . . . . .17 B1
Harkett Cl HA3 . . . . .24 D1
Harkett Ct HA3 . . . . .24 D1
Harkness Ct SM1 . . . . .201 D1
Harkness Ho 🔢 E1 . . . . .96 A1
Harland Ave Sidcup DA15 . .167 C2
　South Croydon CR0 . . . . .222 A5
Harland Cl SW19 . . . . .201 D6
Harland Rd SE12 . . . . .165 A3
Harlands Gr BR6 . . . . .226 D4
Harlech Ct 🔢 SE23 . . . . . .162 C3
Harlech Gdns TW5 . . . . . . .128 C5
Harlech Rd N14 . . . . .16 A1
Harlech Twr 🔢 W3 . . . . . . .111 A4
Harlequin Ave TW8 . . . . . . .131 A6
Harlequin Cl Hayes UB4 . . . .84 D2
　Isleworth TW7 . . . . 152 C6
Harlequin Ct
　Croydon CR2 . . . . 221 A1
　Ealing W5 . . . . .109 C6
　Willesden NW10 . . . . .67 B2

Harlequin Ho 🔳 DA18 . . .125 A3
Harlequin Rd TW11 . . . . . . .175 B3
Harlescott Rd SE15 . . . . . . 140 D1
HARLESDEN 89 C6
Harlesden Gdns NW10 . . . . .89 D6
Harlesden Plaza 🔢
　NW10 . . . . .89 D5
Harlesden Prim Sch
　NW10 . . . . .89 C5
Harlesden Rd NW10 . . . . . . .90 A6
Harlesden Sta NW10 . . . . . .89 B5
Harleston Cl 🔢 E5 . . . . .74 C6
Harley BR7 . . . . .189 B2
Harley Cl HA0 . . . . .65 D2
Harley Cres HA1 . . . . .42 B5
Harley Ct Harrow HA1 . . . . . .42 B5
　Wanstead E11 . . . . .55 A2
　Whetstone N20 . . . . .14 A1
Harley Ct 🔢 BR1 . . . . .187 C2
Harleyford Ct
　Kennington SW8 . . . . 270 C6
　Wembley HA0 . . . . .65 A4
Harleyford Manor 🔢
　W3 . . . . .111 A5
Harleyford Rd
　SE11 . . . . .138 B6 270 C6
Harleyford St SE11 . . . . . . .138 C6
Harley Gdns
　Orpington BR6 . . . . 227 C4
　South Kensington
　SW10 . . . . .114 A1 256 B1
Harley Gr E3 . . . . .97 B4
Harley Ho Leytonstone E11 . .54 B2
　Marylebone NW1 . . . . 238 B5
Harley Pl W1 . . . . .93 B2 238 C3
Harley Rd Hampstead NW3 . .70 B1
　Harlesden NW10 . . . . .89 C5
　Harrow HA1 . . . . .42 B5
Harley St W1 . . . . .93 B2 238 C3
Harley Villas NW10 . . . . .89 C5
Harling Ct 🔢 SW11 . . . . . .136 D3
Harlinger St SE18 . . . . 122 A3
HARLINGTON 127 A6
Harlington Cl UB7 . . . . .127 A5
Harlington Cnr UB3 . . . . . . .127 B4
Harlington Com Sch
　UB3 . . . . .105 B2
Harlington Rd
　Bexley DA7 . . . . 147 A2
　Hillingdon UB8 . . . . .82 C3
Harlington Rd E TW13,
　TW14 . . . . .150 C3
Harlington Rd W TW14 . . . .150 B5
Harlowe Ho 🔢 E8 . . . . .95 D6
Harlow Mans 🔢 IG11 . . . . . .78 D1
Harlow Rd N13 . . . . .17 B1
Harlyn Dr HA5 . . . . .40 B6
Harlyn Prim Sch HA5 . . . . . .40 B6
Harlynwood 🔢 SE5 . . . . . .139 A5
Harman Ave IG8 . . . . .36 D4
Harman Cl
　🔟 Bermondsey SE1 . . . . .118 A1
　Chingford E4 . . . . .36 B6
　Cricklewood NW2 . . . . . . .69 A5
Harman Dr
　Blackfen DA15 . . . . 167 C5
　Cricklewood NW2 . . . . . . .69 A4
Harman Rd EN1 . . . . .17 D6
HARMONDSWORTH 126 A6
Harmondsworth La UB7 . .126 B6
Harmondsworth Rd
　UB7 . . . . .104 A2
Harmon Ho 🔢 SE8 . . . . . . .119 B2
Harmony Cl NW11 . . . . .47 A4
Harmony Way
　Bromley BR1 . . . . 187 A1
　Hendon NW4 . . . . .46 C5
Harmood Gr 🔢 NW1 . . . . . .71 B1
Harmood Ho 🔢 NW1 . . . . . .71 B1
Harmood St NW1 . . . . .71 B1
Harmsworth St
　SE17 . . . . .116 D1 261 C1
Harmsworth Way N20 . . . . .13 C3
Harnage Ho TW8 . . . . .110 A1
Harney Ct SE14 . . . . .141 A4
Harold Ave Erith DA17 . . . .125 B3
　Hayes UB3 . . . . 105 D3
Harold Ct
　🔟 Rotherhithe SE16 . . . . .118 D4
　🔢 Teddington TW11 . . . . .174 C5
Harold Est SE1 . . . . 263 B5
Harold Gibbons Ct 🔢
　SE7 . . . . .143 C6
Harold Ho 🔢 E2 . . . . .96 D5
Harold Laski Ho EC1 . . . . . 234 D1
Harold Maddison Ho
　SE17 . . . . 261 D2
Harold Rd Chingford E4 . . . . .20 A1
　Hornsey N8 . . . . .50 B5
　Leytonstone E11 . . . . .54 C1
　Newham E13 . . . . .99 B6
　North Acton NW10 . . . . . . .89 B4
　South Norwood SE19 . . . .183 B3
　South Tottenham N15 . . . . .51 D4
　Sutton SM1 . . . . 218 B4
　Woodford IG8 . . . . .37 A2
Haroldstone Rd E17 . . . . . . .53 A4
Harold Wilson Ho SW6 . . . 264 D5
Haronton Ct E10 . . . . .76 A6
Harp Alley EC4 . . . . 241 C2

Harp Bsns Ctr The NW2 . . . .68 A6
Harpenden Rd
　Wanstead E12 . . . . .77 C6
　West Norwood SE27,
　SW16 . . . . .160 D2
Harpenmead Point NW2 . . . .69 B6
Harper Cl N14 . . . . .15 C6
Harper Ho 🔢 SW9 . . . . . . .138 D2
Harper Mews SW17 . . . . . .158 A1
Harper Rd
　Bermondsey SE1 . .117 A3 262 B6
　Newham E6 . . . . 100 B1
Harper's Yd N17 . . . . .33 D2
Harp Island Cl NW10 . . . . . . .67 B5
Harp La EC3 . . . . 253 A5
Harpley Sq E1 . . . . .96 D3
Harpour Rd IG11 . . . . .79 A2
Harp Rd W7 . . . . .86 D3
Harpsden St SW11 . . . . 268 A1
Harpur Mews WC1 . . . . 240 C4
Harpur St WC1 . . . . .94 B2 240 C4
Harraden Rd SE3 . . . . .143 C4
Harrier Ave E11 . . . . .55 B3
Harrier Ct TW4 . . . . .129 A3
Harrier Ho 🔢 SW11 . . . . . .136 C2
Harrier Mews SE28 . . . . . . .123 B4
Harrier Rd NW9 . . . . .27 C1
Harriers Cl W5 . . . . .110 A6
Harrier Way E6 . . . . .100 B2
Harriescourt Ho E8 . . . . .96 A6
Harriet Cl E8 . . . . .96 A6
Harriet Gdns CR0 . . . . .222 A6
Harriet Ho
　Walham Green SW6 . . . . . 265 D3
　🔟 Walthamstow E17 . . . . .53 D4
Harriet Mews DA16 . . . . . .146 B3
Harriet St SW1 . . . .114 D4 247 D3
Harriet Tubman Cl 🔢
　SW2 . . . . .160 C4
Harriet Way WD23 . . . . .8 B4
Harriet Wlk SW1 . .114 D4 247 D3
HARRINGAY 50 D4
Harringay Gdns N8 . . . . .50 D5
Harringay Green Lanes Sta
　N4 . . . . .50 D3
Harringay Rd N15 . . . . .50 D5
Harringay Sta N4 . . . . .50 C3
Harrington Cl
　Wallington CR0 . . . . 220 A6
　Willesden NW10 . . . . .67 B5
Harrington Ct
　🔢 South Croydon CR0 . . . 221 B6
　South Kensington SW7 . . . 256 D4
　🔢 West Kilburn W9 . . . . . .91 B4
Harrington Gdns
　SW7 . . . . .114 A2 256 A3
Harrington Hill E5 . . . . .52 B1
Harrington Hill Prim Sch
　E5 . . . . .52 B1
Harrington Ho
　🔢 Bromley BR1 . . . . 187 A2
　Regent's Pk NW1 . . . . 232 A2
　Upper Clapton E5 . . . . . . .52 C1
　Westminster SW1 . . . . . . 259 D2
Harrington Rd
　Croydon SE25 . . . . .206 B5
　Leytonstone E11 . . . . .54 C1
　South Kensington
　SW7 . . . . .114 B2 256 C4
Harrington Road Sta
　SE25 . . . . 206 C6
Harrington Sq
　NW1 . . . . .93 C5 232 A3
Harrington St
　NW1 . . . . .93 C4 232 A2
Harrington Way SW18 . . . . 121 D3
Harriott Cl SE10 . . . . .120 D2
Harriott Ho 🔢 E1 . . . . .96 C1
Harris Acad at Peckham
　SE15 . . . . .139 D4
Harris Acad Bermondsey
　SE1 . . . . .117 D2 263 D4
Harris Acad Falconwood
　DA16 . . . . .145 C1
Harris Acad Merton Sch
　CR4 . . . . .203 D6
Harris Acad South Norwood
　SE25 . . . . .205 D6
Harris City Acad Crystal
　Palace SE19 . . . . .183 D2
Harris Cl Enfield EN2 . . . . . . .4 D4
　Heston TW5 . . . . .129 C4
Harris Cotts 🔢 E15 . . . . . . .98 D6
Harris Girl's Acad SE15 . . .162 C6
Harris Ho 🔟 Bow E3 . . . . . . .97 C4
　🔢 Brixton SW9 . . . . 138 C2
Harris Lo SE6 . . . . .164 A3
Harrison Cl N20 . . . . .14 C3
Harrison Dr BR1 . . . . .210 D5
Harrison Ho SE17 . . . . 262 C2
Harrison Rd
　Dagenham RM10 . . . . .81 D2
　Stonebridge NW10 . . . . . . .89 B6
Harrisons Ct 🔢 SE14 . . . . .140 D6
Harrison's Rise CR0 . . . . . 220 D5
Harrison St WC1 . . .94 A4 233 B1
Harrison Way TW17 . . . . . .192 D4
Harris Rd Dagenham RM9 . . .81 B3
　Erith DA7 . . . . .147 B4

Harris St Camberwell SE5 . . .139 B5
　Walthamstow E17 . . . . .53 B2
Harris Way TW16 . . . . .171 C2
Harrodian Sch The
　SW13 . . . . .133 D5
Harrods Gn HA8 . . . . .26 C5
Harrogate Ct
　🔢 Forest Hill SE26 . . . . . .162 A1
　🔢 New Southgate N11 . . . . .31 A4
Harrold Ho 🔟 NW3 . . . . .70 A1
Harrold Rd RM8 . . . . .80 B3
Harrovian Bsns Village 🔢
　HA1 . . . . .42 C2
HARROW 42 B3
Harrow Arts Ctr ★ HA5 . . . .23 C3
Harrow Ave EN1 . . . . .17 D5
Harroway Rd SW11 . . . . . . .136 B3
Harrowby St W1 . . . .92 C1 237 B2
Harrow Coll HA1 . . . . .42 C2
Harrow Coll (Harrow Weald
　Campus) HA3 . . . . .24 C4
Harrowdene Cl HA0 . . . . . . .65 D4
Harrowdene Ct SW19 . . . . .179 A5
Harrowdene Gdns
　TW11 . . . . .175 A3
Harrowdene Rd HA0 . . . . . . .65 D4
Harrow Dr N9 . . . . .17 D3
Harrowes Meade HA8 . . . . . .10 C1
Harrow Fields Gdns HA1 . . . .64 C5
Harrowgate Ho 🔢 E9 . . . . . .74 D2
Harrowgate Rd E9 . . . . .75 A1
Harrow Gn E11 . . . . .76 C5
Harrow High Sch HA1 . . . . . .43 A3
Harrow La E14 . . . . .120 A6
Harrow Lo SM2 . . . . .218 B3
Harrow Manor Way SE2 . . .124 C3
Harrow Mus & Her Ctr ★
　HA2 . . . . .42 A6
HARROW ON THE HILL 42 C1
Harrow-on-the-Hill Sta
　HA1 . . . . .42 C3
Harrow Pk HA1 . . . . .64 C6
Harrow Rd Ashford TW15 . .148 C2
　Barking IG11 . . . . .101 C6
　Carshalton SM5 . . . . 218 C2
　Ilford IG1 . . . . .79 A4
　Leyton E11 . . . . .76 D5
　Little Venice W2 . . . .92 A2 236 B3
　🔢 Newham E6 . . . . 100 A6
　Sudbury HA0 . . . . .65 A4
　Tokyngton HA9 . . . . .66 C2
　Wembley HA0 . . . . .65 D3
　Westbourne Green W2, W9 . .91 C3
Harrow Sch HA1 . . . . .42 C1
Harrow St NW1 . . . . 237 A4
Harrow View
　Harrow HA1, HA2 . . . . .42 B5
　Hayes UB3 . . . . .84 A1
　Hillingdon UB10 . . . . .83 A4
Harrow View Rd W5 . . . . . . .87 B3
Harrow Way
　Charlton TW17 . . . . 171 A1
　South Oxhey WD19 . . . . . . .23 A6
HARROW WEALD 24 B2
Harrow Weald Pk HA3 . . . . . .24 B4
Harrow & Wealdstone Sta
　HA1 . . . . .42 C5 256 C4
Harry Cl CR7 . . . . .205 A5
Harry Ct 🔢 NW3 . . . . .46 A5
Harry Gosling Prim Sch 🔢
　E1 . . . . .96 A1
Harry Hinkins Ho SE17 . . . 262 B1
Harry Lambourn Ho 🔟
　SE15 . . . . .140 B5
Harston 🔢 KT1 . . . . .176 C1
Harston Dr EN3 . . . . .7 C5
Hart Ct E12 . . . . .78 C1
Harte Rd TW3 . . . . .129 B3
Hartfield Ave
　Borehamwood WD6 . . . . . . .10 C6
　Northolt UB5 . . . . .84 B5
Hartfield Cl WD6 . . . . .10 C6
Hartfield Cres
　Coney Hall BR4 . . . . .225 A5
　Merton SW19 . . . . .179 B3
Hartfield Ct CR2 . . . . .220 D1
Hartfield Gr SE20 . . . . .184 C2
Hartfield Ho UB5 . . . . .84 B5
Hartfield Rd
　Chessington KT9 . . . . . . .213 D3
　Hayes BR4 . . . . .225 A4
　Merton SW19 . . . . .179 C3
Hartfield Terr E3 . . . . .97 C5
Hartford Ave HA3 . . . . .43 B6
Hartford Rd
　Old Bexley DA5 . . . . .169 C5
　West Ewell KT19 . . . . . . .214 D2
Hart Gr Ealing W5 . . . . .110 C5
　Southall UB1 . . . . .85 C2
Hartgrove Ct SW9 . . . . .45 A5
Hart Grove Ct 🔢 W5 . . . . . .110 C5
Hartham Cl
　Isleworth TW7 . . . . 131 A4
　Lower Holloway N7 . . . . . .72 A3
Hartham Rd
　Isleworth TW7 . . . . 131 A4
　Lower Holloway N7 . . . . . .72 A3
　Tottenham N17 . . . . .33 D1

Hart Ho Hayes UB4 . . . . . . .83 B2
　Streatham SW2 . . . . .160 C3
Harting Rd SE9 . . . . .166 A1
Hartington Cl
　Farnborough BR6 . . . . . . 227 A3
　Harrow HA1 . . . . .64 C4
Hartington Ct
　Chiswick W4 . . . . .132 D5
　South Lambeth SW8 . . . . . 270 A2
Hartington Rd
　Chiswick W4 . . . . .133 A4
　Ealing W13 . . . . .109 B6
　Newham E16 . . . . .99 B1
　Southall UB2 . . . . .107 A3
　South Lambeth
　SW8 . . . . .138 A5 270 A3
　Twickenham TW1 . . . . . . .153 B5
　Walthamstow E17 . . . . .53 A3
Hartismere Rd
　SW6 . . . . .135 B5 264 D4
Hartlake Rd E9 . . . . .75 A2
Hartland NW1 . . . . .71 C1
Hartland Cl Edgware HA8 . . . .10 C2
　Enfield N21 . . . . .17 A5
Hartland Ct 🔢 N11 . . . . .30 D5
Hartland Dr Edgware HA8 . . .10 C2
　Ruislip HA4 . . . . .62 B4
Hartland Rd
　Camden Town NW1 . . . . . . .71 B1
　Cheam SM4 . . . . .201 D2
　Friern Barnet N11 . . . . . . .30 D5
　Hampton TW12 . . . . .173 D6
　Isleworth TW7 . . . . 131 A2
　Kilburn NW6 . . . . .91 B6
　Stratford E15 . . . . .76 D1
Hartlands Cl DA5 . . . . .169 B5
Hartlands The TW5 . . . . . . .128 C3
Hartland Way
　Croydon CR0 . . . . 223 A6
　Morden SM4 . . . . .201 B2
Hartlepool Ct E16 . . . . .122 D5
Hartley Ave Edgware NW7 . .27 D5
　Newham E6 . . . . 100 A6
Hartley Cl Bickley BR1 . . . .188 B1
　Edgware NW7 . . . . .27 D5
Hartley Ho 🔢 SE1 . . . . 263 D4
　Finchley N3 . . . . .29 D4
　Putney SW15 . . . . 156 A6
Hartley Prim Sch 🔢 E6 . . . 100 A6
Hartley Rd Bexley DA16 . . .146 C5
　Leytonstone E11 . . . . .54 D1
　Thornton Heath CR0 . . . . .205 A2
Hartley St E2 . . . . .96 C4
Hart Lo EN5 . . . . .1 A2
Hartmoor Mews EN3 . . . . . . .6 D6
Hartnoll Ho 🔢 N7 . . . . .72 C3
Hartnoll St N7 . . . . .72 B3
Harton Cl BR1 . . . . .187 D2
Harton Lodge 🔢 SE8 . . . . .141 C4
Harton Rd N9 . . . . .18 B2
Harton St SE8 . . . . .141 C4
Hartopp Ct 🔢 N16 . . . . .73 C5
Hartopp Point SW6 . . . . . . 264 B4
Hartsbourne Ave WD23 . . . . .8 B2
Hartsbourne Cl WD23 . . . . . .8 B2
Hartsbourne Ct 🔢 UB1 . . . .86 A1
Hartsbourne Pk WD23 . . . . . .8 B2
Hartsbourne Prim Sch
　WD23 . . . . .8 B2
Hartsbourne Rd WD23 . . . . . .8 B2
Harts Gr IG8 . . . . .37 A5
Hartshill Cl UB10 . . . . .60 D2
Hartshorn Alley EC3 . . . . . 243 B1
Hartshorn Gdns E6 . . . . . . .100 C3
Harts La IG11 . . . . .78 D2
Hart's La SE14 . . . . .141 A4
Hartslock Dr SE2 . . . . .124 D4
Hartsmead Rd SE9 . . . . . . .166 B2
Hart Sq SM4 . . . . .201 C3
Hart St EC3 . . . . 253 B6
Hartsway EN3 . . . . .6 C1
Hartswood Gdns W12 . . . . .110 A3
Hartswood Ho 🔢 SW2 . . . .160 A3
Hartswood Rd W12 . . . . . . .111 D3
Hartsworth Cl E13 . . . . .98 D5
Hartville Rd SE18 . . . . .123 C2
Hartwell Cl 🔢 SW2 . . . . . .160 B3
Hartwell Dr E4 . . . . .36 A4
Hartwell Ho 🔢 SE7 . . . . . .121 B1
Hartwell St E8 . . . . .73 D2
Hartwell St E8 (dup)
Harvard Ct
　🔢 Eltham SE9 . . . . 166 C5
　West Hampstead NW6 . . . .69 D3
Harvard Hill W4 . . . . .132 C6
Harvard Ho
　🔢 Camberwell SE17 . . . . 138 D6
　Putney SW15 . . . . 156 D5
Harvard Mans 🔢 SW11 . . .136 B1
Harvard Rd
　🔢 Acton Green W4 . . . . . 111 A1
　Gunnersbury W4 . . . . 110 D1
　Hounslow TW7 . . . . 130 C4

Harvard Rd continued
Lewisham SE13 . . . . 164 A6
Harvel Cres SE2 . . . . 124 D1
Harvel Ct SE2 . . . . 125 A1
Harvest Bank Rd BR4 . . 225 A5
Harvest Ct
Beckenham BR3 . . . . 185 C3
Littleton SW17 . . . . 192 C5
Harvesters Cl TW7 . . . . . 152 B6
Harvest La Loughton IG10. . . 21 C4
Thames Ditton KT7 . . . . 197 A3
Harvest Rd TW13 . . . . . . 150 A1
Harvey Ct Battersea SW11 **267** B2
Walthamstow E17 . . . . . . 53 C4
Harvey Dr TW12 . . . . . . 173 C2
Harvey Gdns
Greenwich SE7 . . . . 121 C1
Leytonstone E11 . . . . 54 D1
Harvey Ho
1 Barking IG11 . . . . 79 A1
10 Bethnal Green E1 . . . . 96 B3
Brentford TW8 . . . . 110 A1
Dagenham RM6 . . . . 58 D5
Hornsey N8 . . . . 50 A6
Pimlico SW1 . . . . 259 D1
Shoreditch N1 . . . . 235 D5
Wembley Pk HA9 . . . . . . 66 D6
Harvey Lo 8 W9 . . . . 91 C2
Harvey Mews N8 . . . . 50 B4
Harvey Point 7 E16 . . . . 99 A2
Harvey Rd
15 Camberwell SE5 . . . . 139 B4
Hillingdon UB10 . . . . 82 C5
Hornsey Vale N8 . . . . 50 B4
Ilford IG1 . . . . 78 D3
Leytonstone E11 . . . . 54 D1
Ruislip UB5 . . . . 62 C1
Twickenham TW4 . . . . . . 151 B4
Walton-on-T KT12 . . . . . 194 A2
Harvey St N1 . . . . **235** D5
Harvill Rd
Newyears Green UB9 . . . . 38 A2
Sidcup DA14 . . . . 191 A5
Harvil Rd UB9, UB10 . . . . 38 A2
Harvington Sch W5 . . . . . 87 D1
Harvington Wlk E8 . . . . . 74 A1
Harvist Rd NW6 . . . . 91 A5
Harwell Cl HA4 . . . . 39 B1
Harwood Ave
Bromley BR1 . . . . 187 B1
Mitcham CR4 . . . . 202 C6
Harwood Cl London N12. . . 30 C4
Wembley HA0 . . . . 65 D4
Harwood Ct
Putney SW15 . . . . 134 C1
Shoreditch N1 . . . . 235 D5
Harwood Dr UB10 . . . . . . 82 B6
Harwood Point SE16 . . . 119 B4
Harwood Rd
SW6 . . . . 135 D5 265 C3
Harwoods Yd N21 . . . . 16 C4
Harwood Terr
SW6 . . . . 135 D4 265 C2
Hascombe Ho 11 SW15. . . 156 B3
Hascombe Terr 2 SE5 . . 139 B3
Haselbury Rd N9 . . . . 17 C1
Haseley End SE23 . . . . . . 162 C4
Haselrigge Rd SW4 . . . . . 137 D1
Haseltine Prim Sch
SE26 . . . . 185 B6
Haseltine Rd SE26 . . . . . 185 B6
Haselwood Dr EN2 . . . . 4 D1
Haskard Rd RM9 . . . . 80 D4
Hasker St SW3 . . . 114 C2 257 B4
Haslam Ave N22 . . . . 201 A1
Haslam Cl Islington N1 . . . 72 C1
Uxbridge UB10 . . . . 61 A6
Haslam Ct N11 . . . . 31 B6
Haslam Ho 12 N1 . . . . 73 A1
Haslam St SE15 . . . . 139 D4
Haslemere Ave
Barnet EN4 . . . . 14 D3
Cranford TW5 . . . . 128 C3
Ealing W13 . . . . 109 A3
Hendon NW4 . . . . 46 D3
Mitcham CR4, SW19 . . . . 180 B1
Wandsworth SW18 . . . . . 157 D2
Haslemere Bsns Ctr EN1 . . 18 B6
Haslemere Cl
Hampton TW12 . . . . 173 B5
Wallington SM6 . . . . 220 A3
Haslemere Ct 5 N16 . . . . . 51 C1
Haslemere Gdns N3 . . . . . 47 B5
Haslemere & Heathrow Est
The TW4 . . . . 128 B3
Haslemere Ind Est
Feltham TW14 . . . . 150 A6
Wandsworth SW18 . . . . . 157 D2
Haslemere Prim Sch
CR4. . . . . 180 B1
Haslemere Rd
Bexleyheath DA7 . . . . . . 147 C3
Hornsey N8 . . . . 50 A2
Ilford IG3 . . . . 79 D6
Southgate N21 . . . . 16 D3
Thornton Heath CR7 . . . 204 D4
Hasler Cl SE28 . . . . 124 C6

Hasler Ct E12 . . . . 78 A4
Haslett Rd TW17 . . . . . . 171 C1
Hasluck Gdns EN5 . . . . . . 14 A5
Hasmonean High Sch (Boys)
NW4 . . . . 28 D1
Hasmonean High Sch (Girls)
NW7 . . . . 28 A2
Hasmonean Prim Sch 1
NW4 . . . . 46 D4
Hassard St E2 . . . . 95 D5
Hassendean Rd SE3 . . . . . 143 B5
Hassett Rd E9 . . . . 75 A2
Hassocks Cl SE23, SE26 . . 162 B1
Hassocks Rd SW16 . . . . . 181 D2
Hassock Wood BR2 . . . . . 225 D4
Hassop Rd NW2 . . . . 68 D4
Hassop Wlk SE9 . . . . 188 A6
Hasted Rd SE7 . . . . 121 D1
Hasting Ct TW11 . . . . 174 B5
Hastings Ave IG6 . . . . 57 A5
17 Peckham SE15. . . . . . 140 A5
Wembley HA0. . . . . 65 C4
Hastings Cl New Barnet EN5. . . 2 A1
18 Shepherd's Bush W12. . . 112 B6
Tottenham N17 . . . . 34 A2
6 Woolwich SE18 . . . . . 122 B2
Hastings Hos WC1 . . . . . . 233 A1
Hastings Pl 1 CR0. . . . . . 205 D1
Hastings Rd Croydon CR0. . . 205 D1
Ealing W13 . . . . 109 B6
Keston Mark BR2 . . . . . . 226 A6
Tottenham N17 . . . . 51 B6
Wood Green N11 . . . . 31 D5
Hastings St
St Pancras WC1 . . . . 94 A4 233 A1
Woolwich SE18 . . . . 123 A1
Hastingwood Ct
1 Newham E6 . . . . 100 B5
Walthamstow E17 . . . . . . 53 D4
Hastingwood Trad Est
N18. . . . . 35 A4
Hastoe Cl UB4 . . . . 85 A3
Hasty Cl CR4 . . . . 181 A2
Hatcham Mews Bsns Ctr
SE14. . . . . 140 D4
Hatcham Park Mews
SE14. . . . . 140 D4
Hatcham Park Rd SE14 . . 140 D4
Hatcham Rd SE15. . . . . . . 140 C6
Hatchard Rd N19 . . . . 72 A6
Hatchcroft NW4 . . . . 46 B6
HATCH END 23 A3
Hatch End High Sch HA3 . . 23 D2
Hatch End Sta HA5. . . . . . . 23 C3
Hatchers Mews SE1 . . . . **253** B1
Hatchett Rd TW14. . . . . . 149 A3
Hatchfield Ho 8 N15 . . . . 51 C3
Hatch Gr RM6 . . . . 59 A5
Hatch Ho
9 Muswell Hill N10. . . . . 31 A3
14 Richmond TW10 . . . . 153 C1
Hatch La E4 . . . . 20 C1
Hatch Pl KT2 . . . . 176 B5
Hatch Rd SW16 . . . . 182 A1
Hatch The EN3 . . . . 6 D4
Hatchwoods IG8 . . . . 36 D6
Hatcliffe Almshouses 8
SE10 . . . . 120 C1
Hatcliffe Cl SE3 . . . . 142 D2
Hatcliffe St SE10. . . . . . . 120 D1
Hatfield Cl Deptford SE14. 140 D5
Ilford IG6 . . . . 56 D6
Mitcham CR4 . . . . 202 B5
Hatfield Ct
Greenwich SE3 . . . . 143 A5
8 Northolt UB5 . . . . 84 C4
Hatfield Ho
16 Kingston u T KT6 . . . 198 A4
Leytonstone E11. . . . . 54 D2
St Luke's EC1 . . . . 242 A5
Hatfield Mead SM4 . . . . . 201 C4
Hatfield Mews RM9 . . . . . 81 A1
Hatfield Prim Sch SM4 . . 201 A3
Hatfield Rd Acton W4 . . . 111 B4
Dagenham RM9 . . . . 81 A1
10 Ealing W13, W7 . . . . . 109 A5
Stratford E15 . . . . 76 C3
Hatfields SE1. . . . . . 116 C5 **251** B4
Hathaway Cl
Bromley BR2. . . . . 210 B1
Ruislip HA4 . . . . 61 D4
Stanmore HA7 . . . . 25 A5
Hathaway Cres E12 . . . . . . 78 C2
Hathaway Gdns
Ealing W13 . . . . 87 A2
Ilford RM6 . . . . 58 D4
Hathaway Ho 3 N1 . . . . . . 95 C4
Hathaway Prim Sch W13 . . 86 D2
Hathaway Rd CR0 . . . . 204 D2
Hatherleigh Cl 7 Barnet EN4 . . . 1 D4
Chessington KT9 . . . . . . 213 D3
Edgware NW7 . . . . 28 D3
Morden SM4 . . . . 201 C5
Hatherleigh Ho NW1. . . . . 201 C5
Hatherleigh Rd HA4. . . . . . 62 A6
Hatherley Cres DA14 . . . . 168 A2
Hatherley Ct 6 W2 . . . . 91 D1

Hatherley Gdns
London N8 . . . . 50 A3
Newham E6 . . . . 99 D4
Hatherley Gr W2 . . . . 91 D1
Hatherley Ho 2 E17 . . . . . . 53 C5
Hatherley Mews E17 . . . . . 53 C5
Hatherley Rd
Richmond TW9 . . . . 132 B4
Sidcup DA14 . . . . 168 A1
Walthamstow E17 . . . . . . 53 C5
Hatherley St SW1 . . . . . . **259** B3
Hathern Gdns SE9 . . . . . . 188 C6
Hatherop Rd TW12 . . . . . 173 B3
Hathersage Ct N1 . . . . 73 B3
Hathersley Ho 3 SW2 . . . 160 C4
Hathorne Cl 3 SE15 . . . . . 140 B3
Hathway Ho 3 SE15 . . . . . 140 C3
Hathway St 4 SE15 . . . . . 140 C3
Hatley Ave IG6. . . . . 57 A5
Hatley Cl N11 . . . . 30 D5
Hatley Rd N4, N7 . . . . 72 B6
Hat & Mitre Ct EC1 . . . . . **241** D5
Hatstone Ct 3 NW3 . . . . . . 70 A3
Hatteraick St 6 SE16 . . . . 118 C4
Hattersfield Cl DA17 . . . . 125 B2
HATTON 127 D1
Hatton Cl SE18 . . . . 145 B5
Hatton Cross Rdbt TW6 . . 127 D2
Hatton Cross Sta TW6 . . . 127 D1
Hatton Ct BR7 . . . . 188 B3
Hatton Gdn EC1 . . . . . 94 C2 **241** B4
Hatton Gdns CR4 . . . . 202 D4
Hatton Gn TW14 . . . . 128 A1
Hatton Ho 17 E1 . . . . 118 A6
Hatton Pl EC1 . . . . **241** B4
Hatton Rd
Hatton TW14, TW6 . . . . 149 C6
Thornton Heath CR0 . . . 204 C1
Hatton Row NW8 . . . . 236 D5
Hatton Sch IG8 . . . . 55 D6
Hatton St NW8 . . . . 236 D5
Hatton Wall EC1 . . . . 94 C2 **241** B4
Haughmond 4 N12 . . . . 29 A5
Haunch of Venison Yd
W1 . . . . **238** C1
Hauteville Court Gdns 2
W6 . . . . 111 D3
Havana Rd SW18, SW19 . . 157 C2
Havannah St E14 . . . . 119 C4
Havant Rd E17 . . . . 54 A6
Havelock Ct 13 W12 . . . . . 112 B6
Havelock Ct
8 Peckham SE15. . . . . . 140 B5
Southall UB2 . . . . 107 B3
Havelock Hall 8 CR0 . . . . 205 D1
Havelock Ho
4 Croydon CR0 . . . . . . 205 D1
Forest Hill SE23 . . . . 162 C3
Havelock Pl HA1 . . . . 42 C3
Havelock Prim Sch UB2 . . 107 B3
Havelock Rd
Belvedere DA17 . . . . 125 B2
Bromley BR2. . . . . 209 C5
Croydon CR0. . . . . 221 D6
Harrow HA3 . . . . 42 C6
Southall UB2 . . . . 107 C3
Tottenham N17 . . . . 34 A1
Wimbledon SW19 . . . . . . 180 A5
Havelock St Ilford IG1 . . . 78 D6
10 Richmond TW10 . . . . 153 C1
Islington N1 . . . . 94 A6 **233** B6
Havelock Terr
SW8. . . . . 137 B5 **268** C3
Havelock Wlk SE23 . . . . . **162** C2
Haven Cl Chislehurst SE9 . . 166 B1
Hayes UB4 . . . . 83 C3
Hinchley Wood KT10. . . . 212 C6
Sidcup DA14 . . . . 190 C4
Wimbledon SW19 . . . . . . 156 D1
Haven Ct Beckenham BR3. . 186 A1
Hinchley Wood KT10. . . . 212 C6
Thornton Heath CR7 . . . 204 C6
Haven Gn W5 . . . . 87 D1
Haven Green Ct W5 . . . . . . 87 D1
Havenhurst Rise EN2 . . . . . . 4 C3
Haven La W5 . . . . 88 A1
Haven Lo 15 Enfield EN1 . . . 17 C6
Temple Fortune NW11 . . . 47 B4
7 Woolwich SE18 . . . . . 122 D2
Haven Pl Ealing W5 . . . . . 109 D6
Hinchley Wood KT10. . . . 212 C6
Havenpool NW8 . . . . 91 D6
Haven Rd TW15 . . . . 148 D1
Haven St 18 NW1 . . . . 71 B1
Havenswood Ct 14 KT2. . . 176 D4
Haven The Ashford TW16. . 172 A3
East Barnet N14 . . . . 15 B5
Richmond TW9 . . . . 132 C2
Havenwood HA9 . . . . 66 D5
Havercourt 3 NW3 . . . . . . 70 C2
Haverfield Gdns TW9 . . . . 132 C5
Haverfield Rd E3 . . . . 97 A4
Haverford Way HA8 . . . . . . 26 B2
Havergal Villas N15 . . . . . . 50 D6
Haverhill Rd Chingford E4 . . 20 A3
Streatham SW12 . . . . 159 C3
Havering 8 NW1 . . . . 71 B1
Havering Gdns RM6. . . . . . 58 D4
Havering Ho N4 . . . . 51 A2
Havering St E1 . . . . 96 D1
Havering Way IG11 . . . . . . 102 B4

Haverley 15 SW20. . . . . . . 178 D3
Haversham Cl TW1. . . . . . 153 D5
Haversham Ct UB6. . . . . . . 64 D2
Haversham Lo NW2. . . . . . . 68 D3
Haversham Pl N6 . . . . 70 D6
Haverstock Ct 2 BR5 . . . . 190 B1
Haverstock Hill NW3 . . . . . 70 D2
Haverstock Rd NW5. . . . . . 71 A3
Haverstock Sch 22 NW1. . . 71 A2
Haverstock St N1 . . 94 D5 **234** D3
Haverthwaite Rd BR6 . . . . 227 B5
Havilland Ct HA8. . . . . 26 B6
Havil St SE5 . . . . 139 C4
Havisham Ho 25 SE16 . . . . 118 A4
Havisham Pl SW16. . . . . . . 182 D3
Hawarden Gr SE24. . . . . . . 161 A4
Hawarden Hill NW2. . . . . . . 68 A5
Hawarden Rd E17. . . . . 52 D5
Hawberry Lo N7 . . . . 72 A2
Hawbridge Rd E11 . . . . 54 B1
Hawes Down Inf Sch
BR4. . . . . 208 B3
Hawes Down Jun Sch
BR4. . . . . 208 B3
Hawes La BR4 . . . . 224 C6
Hawes Rd Bromley BR1. . . 187 B2
Edmonton N18 . . . . 34 B4
Hawes St N1 . . . . 72 D1
Haweswater Ho TW1. . . . . 152 D6
Hawfinch 29 NW9. . . . . 27 D2
Hawgood St E3. . . . . 97 C2
Hawkdene E4 . . . . 20 A5
Hawke Ct UB4 . . . . 84 C3
Hawkdale Inf Sch
TW16 . . . . 193 D6
Hawke Ho 2 E1 . . . . 96 D3
Hawke Park Rd N22. . . . . . . 50 D6
Hawke Pl 29 SE16 . . . . . . 118 D4
Hawker 28 NW9. . . . . 27 D2
Hawker Ct 14 KT2. . . . . . . 176 C3
Hawker Ctr The KT2. . . . . 175 D5
Hawke Rd SE19. . . . . 183 C4
Hawker Pl E4. . . . . 36 A1
Hawkesbury Rd SW15. . . . 156 B6
Hawkesdown House Sch
W2 . . . . 113 C5 **245** B3
Hawkesfield Rd SE23. . . . . **163** B2
Hawkesley Cl TW1. . . . . . . 175 A6
Hawkes Rd
Feltham TW14 . . . . 150 A4
Mitcham CR4 . . . . 180 D2
Hawkesworth Ho 5
SW4. . . . . 159 C5
Hawke Twr 4 SE14. . . . . . . 141 A6
Hawkewood Rd TW16 . . . . 194 A6
Hawkfield Ct TW7. . . . . . . 130 C3
Hawk Ho 7 SW11. . . . . 136 C2
Hawkhurst Gdns KT9. . . . . 214 A4
Hawkhurst Rd SW16 . . . . . 181 D2
Hawkhurst Way
New Malden KT3 . . . . . . 199 B4
West Wickham BR4 . . . . . 223 D6
Hawkinge N17. . . . . 33 B1
Hawkins Cl Burnt Oak NW7 . . 27 B5
Harrow HA1 . . . . 42 B2
Hawkins Ho
3 Deptford SE8. . . . . . . 141 C6
10 Richmond TW10 . . . . 153 C1
Hawkins Rd
Teddington TW11 . . . . . . 175 B4
Willesden NW10. . . . . 67 C1
Hawkins Way SE6. . . . . . . 185 C5
Hawkley Gdns SE27 . . . . . 160 D2
Hawkridge 19 NW5 . . . . . . 71 A2
Hawkridge RM6. . . . . 58 C3
Hawksbrook La BR3 . . . . . 208 A3
Hawkshaw Cl 28 SW2 . . . . 160 A4
Hawkshead N4 . . . . 232 A2
Hawkshead Cl BR1. . . . . . . 186 C3
Hawkshead Rd
Acton W4 . . . . 111 C4
Willesden NW10. . . . . 67 D1
Hawkslade Rd SE15 . . . . . 162 D6
Hawksley Rd N16 . . . . 73 C5
Hawks Mews 10 SE10 . . . . 142 A5
Hawksmoor Cl
2 Newham E6 . . . . 100 A1
Plumstead Comm SE18 . . 123 C1
Hawksmoor Mews E1. . . . . 118 B6
Hawksmoor Pl 2 E2. . . . . . 96 A3
Hawksmoor Prim Sch
SE28 . . . . 124 B6
Hawksmoor St 5 W6 . . . . . 134 D6
Hawksmouth E4. . . . . 20 A4
Hawks Rd KT1. . . . . 176 B1
Hawkstone Rd SE16. . . . . . 118 C2
Hawkwell Ct E4. . . . . 20 A1
Hawkwell Ho RM8 . . . . 81 C6
Hawkwell Wlk N1 . . . . **235** B6
Hawkwood Cres E4 . . . . . . 19 D5
Hawkwood La BR7. . . . . . . 189 A2
Hawkwood Mount 1 E5 . . . . 52 B1
Hawlands Dr HA5. . . . . 41 A2
Hawley Cl TW12. . . . . 173 B4
Hawley Cres NW1. . . . . 71 B1
Hawley Inf Sch 23 NW1. . . . 71 B1
Hawley Mews 4 NW1. . . . . . 71 B1
Hawley Rd
3 Camden Town NW1. . . . 71 B1

Hawley Rd continued
London N18 . . . . 34 D5
Hawley St NW1 . . . . 71 B1
Hawley Way TW15 . . . . . . 170 D5
Haworth Ho 7 SW2. . . . . . 160 C5
Hawstead Rd SE6 . . . . 163 D5
Hawsted IG9 . . . . 21 B4
Hawthorn Ave
Bowes Pk N13. . . . . 32 A5
South Norwood CR7 . . . . 182 D2
Hawthorn Cl
Cranford TW5 . . . . 128 B5
Hampton TW12. . . . . 173 C5
Petts Wood BR5 . . . . 211 B3
Hawthorn Cres SW17 . . . . 181 A5
Hawthorn Ct
Littleton TW15 . . . . 171 A3
2 Pinner HA5 . . . . 22 C1
Putney SW15 . . . . 134 B2
Redbridge IG5 . . . . 56 B6
Richmond TW9 . . . . 132 D4
Sutton SM1. . . . . 217 C4
8 West Norwood SW16 . . 182 C5
Hawthorn Ctr HA1. . . . . . . 43 A4
Hawthornden Cl N12. . . . . 30 C4
Hawthorndene Cl BR2. . . . 225 A6
Hawthorndene Rd BR2. . . . 225 A6
Hawthorn Dr
Coney Hall BR4 . . . . 224 C4
Harrow HA2 . . . . 41 C3
Hawthorne Ave
Harrow HA3 . . . . 43 A3
Mitcham CR4 . . . . 180 B1
Old Ford E3. . . . . 97 B6
Ruislip HA4. . . . . 40 B2
Wallington SM5 . . . . 219 A1
Hawthorne Cl
Bickley BR1. . . . . 210 B6
Kingsland N1 . . . . 73 C2
Sutton SM1. . . . . 218 A6
Hawthorne Cres UB7. . . . . 104 B4
Hawthorne Ct
Chingford E4. . . . . 35 D4
Ealing W5 . . . . 110 A5
Pinner HA6. . . . . 22 A1
Hawthorne Gr NW9 . . . . . . 45 A2
Hawthorne Ho SW1. . . . . . **259** B1
Hawthorne Mews UB6 . . . . 86 A1
Hawthorne Rd
Bickley BR1. . . . . 210 B6
Edmonton N18 . . . . 33 D5
Walthamstow E17 . . . . . . 53 C6
Hawthorne Way N9 . . . . . . 17 D2
Hawthorn Farm Ave UB5. . . 85 A6
Hawthorn Gdns W5 . . . . . . 109 D3
Hawthorn Gr
Edgware EN5 . . . . 11 D5
Enfield EN2 . . . . 5 B5
Penge SE20 . . . . 184 B2
Hawthorn Hatch TW8 . . . . 131 B5
Hawthorn Ho SE14. . . . . . . 141 B4
Hawthorn Mews NW7. . . . . 29 A2
Hawthorn Pl UB3 . . . . 105 D6
Hawthorn Rd
Bexleyheath DA6 . . . . . . 147 B1
Brentford TW8 . . . . 131 B5
Carshalton SM1 . . . . 218 C2
Feltham TW14 . . . . 150 A3
Hornsey N8. . . . . 50 A6
Wallington SM5, SM6 . . . 219 B1
Willesden NW10. . . . . 68 A1
Woodford IG9. . . . . 37 D6
Hawthorns IG8 . . . . 21 A1
Hawthorns The
2 Cheam SM2. . . . . 217 C2
Edgware NW7 . . . . 27 B4
Stoneleigh KT17 . . . . . . 216 A1
Hawthorn Terr DA15 . . . . 167 D2
Hawthorn Way TW17. . . . . 193 B5
Hawthorn Wlk W10 . . . . . . 91 A3
Hawtrey Ave UB5 . . . . 84 D5
Hawtrey Dr HA4 . . . . 40 A2
Hawtrey Rd NW3. . . . . 70 C2
Haxted Rd BR1. . . . . 187 B2
Haybridge Ho 1 E5. . . . . . . 74 C4
Hay Cl E15. . . . . 76 D1
Haycroft Gdns NW10. . . . . . 90 B6
Haycroft Mans NW10. . . . . . 90 A6
Haycroft Rd London SW2 . . 160 A6
Surbiton KT6. . . . . 214 A6
Hay Currie St E14. . . . . 97 C1
Hayday Rd E16. . . . . 99 A2
Hayden Piper Ho SW3. . . . **267** C6
Hayden's Pl W11. . . . . 91 B1
Haydock Ave UB5. . . . . 63 C2
Haydock Gn UB5. . . . . 63 C2
Haydock Green Flats 2
UB5 . . . . 63 C2
Haydock Lo 2 SM6 . . . . . . 219 D5
Haydon Cl Enfield EN1. . . . 17 C6
Kingsbury NW9 . . . . 45 A5
Haydon Ct NW9. . . . . 45 A5
Haydon Dr HA5. . . . . 40 A5
Haydon Ho W7 . . . . 108 D5
Haydon Park Rd SW19 . . . 179 D5
Haydon Rd RM8. . . . . 80 C6
Haydon Sch HA5. . . . . 39 D6
Haydon's Rd SW19. . . . . . . 180 A4
Haydons Road Sta
SW19 . . . . 180 A5

Haydon St E1,
  EC3 . . . . 117 D6 253 C6
Haydon Way SW11 . . . . 136 B1
Haydon Wlk E1 . . . . 243 D1
HAYES BR2 . . . . 209 A2
  UB3 . . . . 83 C1
Hayes Bridge Ret Pk
  UB4 . . . . 106 D6
Hayes Chase BR4 . . . . 208 C3
Hayes Cl BR2 . . . . 225 A6
Hayes Cres Cheam SM3 . . . 216 D4
  Temple Fortune NW11 . . . . 47 B4
Hayes Ct
  23 Camberwell SE5 . . . . . . 139 A5
  Streatham SW12 . . . . 160 A3
  Wimbledon SW19 . . . . 179 A4
HAYES END 83 B3
Hayes End Cl UB4 . . . . 83 B2
Hayes End Dr UB4 . . . . 83 B3
Hayesend Ho SW17 . . . . . . 180 A6
Hayes End Rd UB4 . . . . 83 B3
Hayesford Park Dr BR2 . . . . 208 D4
Hayes Gdn BR2 . . . . 209 A1
Hayes Gr SE15, SE22 . . . . . 139 D1
Hayes & Harlington Sta
  UB3 . . . . 105 D3
Hayes Hill BR2 . . . . 208 C1
Hayes Hill Rd BR2 . . . . 208 D1
Hayes La
  Beckenham BR2, BR3 . . . . 208 B5
  Hayes BR2 . . . . 209 A4
Hayes Mead Rd BR2 . . . . . . 208 C1
Hayes Park Sch UB4 . . . . 83 D3
Hayes Pl NW1 . . . . 237 B5
Hayes Rd Bromley BR2 . . . . 209 A5
  Southall UB2 . . . . 106 B2
Hayes Sch BR2 . . . . 225 B6
Hayes St BR2 . . . . 209 B1
Hayes Sta BR2 . . . . 208 D1
Hayes Stadium Sp Ctr
  UB3 . . . . 83 B1
HAYESTOWN 106 B5
Hayes Way BR3 . . . . 208 B5
Hayes Wood Ave BR2 . . . . . 209 B1
Hayfield Pas E1 . . . . 96 C3
Hayfield Yd 43 E1 . . . . 96 C3
Hayford Ct NW2 . . . . 68 D5
Haygarth Pl 2 SW19 . . . . . 178 D5
Haygreen Cl KT2 . . . . 176 D4
Hay Hill W1 . . . . . 115 B6 248 D5
Hayhurst N1 . . . . 234 D6
Hay La NW9 . . . . 45 B5
Hayland Cl NW9 . . . . 45 B5
Hay Lane Sch NW9 . . . . 45 A5
Hayles Bldgs SE11 . . . . 261 D4
Hayles St SE11 . . . . 116 D2 261 C4
Haylett Gdns KT1 . . . . 197 D5
Hayley Ho DA17 . . . . 147 C6
Hayling Ave TW13 . . . . 150 A1
Hayling Ct 20 N16 . . . . 73 C3
Hayling Ct SM3 . . . . 216 C4
Haymaker Cl UB10 . . . . 60 B1
Haymans Point SE11 . . . . . . 260 C2
Haymeads Dr KT10 . . . . 212 A2
Haymer Gdns KT4 . . . . 216 A5
Haymerle Ho 6 SE15 . . . . . 140 A5
Haymerle Rd SE15 . . . . 140 A6
Haymerle Sch 15 SE15 . . . . 140 A6
Haymill Cl UB6 . . . . 86 D4
Haymills Ct W5 . . . . 88 B3
Hayne Ho W11 . . . . 244 A4
Hayne Rd BR3 . . . . 185 B2
Haynes Cl
  Friern Barnet N11 . . . . 15 A1
  Lewisham SE3 . . . . 142 C2
  Tottenham N17 . . . . 34 B3
Haynes Dr N9 . . . . 18 B1
Haynes Ho 6 E9 . . . . 74 D2
Haynes La SE19 . . . . 183 C4
Haynes Rd HA0 . . . . 106 C2
Hayne St EC1 . . . . 94 D2 241 D4
Haynt Wlk SW20 . . . . 201 A6
Hay's Galleria* SE1 . . . . . 253 A6
Hay's La SE1 . . . . 253 A4
Haysleigh Gdns SE20 . . . . . 184 A1
Haysleigh Ho SE20 . . . . 184 B1
Hay's Mews W1 . . . 115 B5 248 C4
Hay St E2 . . . . 96 A6
Haystall Cl UB4 . . . . 83 C5
Hayter Ct E11 . . . . 77 B6
Hayter Ho W12 . . . . 112 A6
Hayter Rd SW2 . . . . 160 B6
Haythorn Ho
  SW11 . . . . 136 B4 266 D1
Hayton Cl 11 E8 . . . . 73 D2
Hayward Cl SW19 . . . . 179 D2
Hayward Ct
  14 London SW4 . . . . 138 A3
  Mitcham CR4 . . . . 180 B1
Hayward Gallery*
  SE1 . . . . 116 B5 250 D4
Hayward Gdns SW15 . . . . . 156 D3
Hayward Ho Islington N1 . . 234 A4
  Lower Clapton E5 . . . . 74 B5
Hayward Rd London N20 . . . 14 A2
  Thames Ditton KT7 . . . . . . 196 D1
Haywards Cl RM6 . . . . 58 C4

Haywards Pl EC1 . . . . 241 C6
Hayward's Pl EC1 . . . . 241 C6
Haywood Ct HA5 . . . . 22 D1
Haywood Ct N11 . . . . 31 D4
Haywood Lo 23 N7 . . . . 71 D3
Haywood Rd BR2 . . . . 209 D5
Haywood Rise BR6 . . . . 227 C3
Hazel Ave UB7 . . . . 104 C3
Hazelbank KT5 . . . . 199 A1
Hazel Bank SE25 . . . . 183 C1
Hazelbank Rd SE6 . . . . 164 C2
Hazelbourne Rd SW12 . . . . 159 B5
Hazelbury Cl SW19 . . . . 179 C1
Hazelbury Inf Sch N9 . . . . . . 17 C1
Hazelbury Jun Sch N9 . . . . . . 17 C1
Hazelbury La N9 . . . . 17 C1
Hazel Cl Brentford TW8 . . . . 131 B5
  Croydon CR0 . . . . 206 D1
  Edmonton N13 . . . . 17 B1
  Hendon NW9 . . . . 27 C1
  Mitcham CR4 . . . . 203 D5
  Peckham SE15 . . . . 140 A3
  Twickenham TW2 . . . . 152 A4
  Upper Holloway N19 . . . . . . 71 C6
Hazelcroft HA5 . . . . 23 D4
Hazelcroft Cl UB10 . . . . 60 B1
Hazel Ct Ealing W5 . . . . 110 A6
  8 Rotherhithe SE16 . . . . . 119 A5
  9 West Norwood SW16 . . . 182 C5
Hazeldean Rd NW10 . . . . 67 B1
Hazeldene Dr HA5 . . . . 40 C6
Hazeldene Gdns UB10 . . . . . 83 A6
Hazeldene Rd
  Bexley DA16 . . . . 146 C3
  Ilford IG3 . . . . 80 B6
Hazel Gdns HA8 . . . . 26 D6
Hazel Gr Dagenham RM6 . . . 59 A6
  Enfield EN1 . . . . 18 A5
  Feltham TW14 . . . . 150 A3
  Forest Hill SE26 . . . . 184 D6
  Orpington BR6 . . . . 226 D6
  Wembley HA0 . . . . 88 A6
Hazelgreen Cl N21 . . . . 16 D3
Hazel Ho London SE4 . . . . . 141 B2
  12 Maitland Pk NW3 . . . . . 70 D2
Hazelhurst BR3 . . . . 186 B2
Hazelhurst Ct SE6 . . . . 186 A5
Hazelhurst Rd SW17 . . . . . . 180 B6
Hazellville Rd N19 . . . . 49 D1
Hazel Mead EN5 . . . . 12 B6
Hazelmere Cl
  Feltham TW14 . . . . 149 C5
  Northolt UB5 . . . . 85 B5
Hazelmere Ct 10 SW2 . . . . . 160 B3
Hazelmere Dr UB5 . . . . 85 B5
Hazelmere Rd
  Kilburn NW6 . . . . 91 B6
  Northolt UB5 . . . . 85 B5
  Petts Wood BR5 . . . . 211 B5
Hazelmere Way BR2 . . . . . . 209 A3
Hazelmere Wlk UB5 . . . . 85 B5
Hazel Rd
  Kensal Green NW10 . . . . . . 90 C4
  Stratford E15 . . . . 76 C3
Hazeltree La UB5 . . . . 85 A4
Hazel Way
  Bermondsey SE1 . . . . 263 C4
  Walthamstow E4 . . . . 35 B4
Hazel Wlk BR2 . . . . 210 C3
Hazelwood IG10 . . . . 21 D6
Hazelwood Ave SM4 . . . . . . 201 D5
Hazelwood Ct
  Clapton Pk E5 . . . . 75 A5
  Ealing W5 . . . . 110 A4
  Harrow HA2 . . . . 41 D5
Hazelwood Cres N13 . . . . . . 32 C6
Hazelwood Ct
  1 Edmonton N13 . . . . 32 C6
  Surbiton KT6 . . . . 198 A3
  1 Willesden NW10 . . . . . . 67 C5
Hazelwood Dr HA5 . . . . 22 B1
Hazelwood Ho
  Beckenham BR2 . . . . 208 C6
  Chingford E4 . . . . 20 B4
  11 Deptford SE8 . . . . 119 A2
  Edmonton N13 . . . . 32 C6
  2 Sutton SM1 . . . . 218 A4
Hazelwood Jun & Inf Schs
  N13 . . . . 32 C6
Hazelwood La N13 . . . . 32 C6
Hazelwood Lo BR4 . . . . 208 A2
Hazelwood Mans 264 C2
Hazelwood Rd Enfield EN1 . . 17 D3
  Walthamstow E17 . . . . 53 A4
Hazlebury Rd SW6 . . . . 135 D3
Hazledean Rd CR0 . . . . 221 B6
Hazledene Rd W4 . . . . 133 A6
Hazlemere 3 DA14 . . . . 190 A6
Hazlemere Gdns KT4 . . . . . 200 A1
Hazlewell Rd SW15 . . . . . . 156 C6
Hazlewood Cres W10 . . . . . . 91 A3
Hazlewood Twr W10 . . . . . . 91 B3
Hazlitt Cl TW13 . . . . 173 A6
Hazlitt Ct 4 SE28 . . . . 124 C5
Hazlitt Mews W14 . . . . 126 A1
Hazlitt Rd W14 . . . 113 A3 254 A5
Heacham Ave UB10 . . . . 61 A5
Headbourne Ho SE1 . . . . . . 262 D6

Headcorn 10 NW5 . . . . 71 A2
Headcorn Pl CR7 . . . . 204 B5
Headcorn Rd
  Plaistow BR1 . . . . 187 A5
  Thornton Heath CR7 . . . . . 204 B5
  Tottenham N17 . . . . 33 D3
Headfort Pl SW1 . . 115 A4 248 B1
Headingley Dr BR3 . . . . 185 C4
Headington Rd SW18 . . . . . 158 A2
Headlam Rd SW4 . . . . 159 D4
Headlam St E1 . . . . 96 B3
Headley App IG2 . . . . 56 D4
Headley Ct London CR0, SM6 . 220 B3
Headley Cl KT19 . . . . 214 C2
Headley Ct SE26 . . . . 184 C5
Headley Dr Ilford IG2 . . . . . . 56 D3
  New Addington CR0 . . . . . 224 A1
Headley Ho 6 BR5 . . . . 190 B1
Heads Mews W11 . . . . 91 C1
Head St E1 . . . . 96 D1
Headstart Montessori Sch
  SW17 . . . . 180 A6
HEADSTONE 41 D5
Headstone Dr HA1, HA3 . . . . 42 C6
Headstone Gdns HA2 . . . . . . 42 A5
Headstone La
  Harrow HA2, HA3 . . . . 23 D2
  Headstone HA2 . . . . 41 D5
Headstone Lane Sta HA3 . . . 23 D2
Headstone Manor* HA2 . . . . 42 A6
Headstone Rd HA1 . . . . 42 C3
Headway CT10 . . . . 175 C6
Heald St SE8, SE14 . . . . 141 C4
Healey Ho RM6 . . . . 59 A5
Healey St NW1 . . . . 71 B2
Healy Ct EN5 . . . . 12 D5
Healy Dr 1 BR6 . . . . 227 D4
Healy Ho
  12 Kennington SW9 . . . . . 138 C5
  2 Tower Hamlets E3 . . . . . . 97 C3
Heanor Ct 4 E5 . . . . 74 D4
Hearne Rd W4 . . . . 132 C6
Hearn Rise UB5 . . . . 84 D6
Hearn's Bldgs SE17 . . . . . . 262 D3
Hearnshaw St 1 E14 . . . . . . 97 A1
Hearn St EC2 . . . . . 95 C3 243 B5
Hearnville Rd SW12 . . . . . . 159 A3
Heart Hospl The
  W1 . . . . 93 A2 238 B3
Heart Raido W11 . . . . 112 D6
Heart The KT12 . . . . 193 D1
Heatham Pk TW2 . . . . 152 D4
Heath Ave DA7 . . . . 146 D6
Heathbourne Rd WD23 . . . . . 8 D3
Heathbrook Prim Sch 11
  SW4 . . . . 137 C3
Heath Brow NW3 . . . . 70 A5
Heath Bsns Ctr The
  TW3 . . . . 130 A1
Heath Cl Croydon CR2 . . . . . 220 D2
  Ealing W5 . . . . 88 B3
  Golders Green NW11 . . . . . 47 D2
  Harlington UB3 . . . . 127 B5
Heathcote Gr E4 . . . . 20 A2
Heathcote Point 25 E9 . . . . 74 D2
Heathcote Rd TW1 . . . . 153 B6
Heathcote St WC1 . . . . 20 C2
Heathcroft Ealing W5 . . . . . . 88 B3
  Golders Green NW11 . . . . . 47 D1
Heathcroft Ave TW16 . . . . . 171 D3
Heathcroft Gdns E4 . . . . 36 B2
Heath Ct Carshalton SM5 . . 218 B6
  Eltham SE9 . . . . 167 A3
  2 Hampstead NW3 . . . . . . 70 A2
  Leytonstone E11 . . . . 54 D3
  Stoke Newington N16 . . . . . 51 B1
  Uxbridge UB8 . . . . 60 A1
Heathdale Ave TW4 . . . . . . 129 A2
Heathdene N1 . . . . 14 C4
Heathdene Dr DA17 . . . . . . 125 D2
Heathdene Rd
  South Norwood SW16 . . . . 182 B3
  Wallington SM5, SM6 . . . . 219 B1
Heath Dr
  West Barnes SW20 . . . . . . 200 C5
  West Hampstead NW3 . . . . 69 D4
Heathedge SE23, SE26 . . . . 162 B2
Heath End Rd WD23 . . . . 8 C2
Heatherbank
  Chislehurst BR7 . . . . 188 C1
  Eltham SE9 . . . . 144 B3
Heather Cl Clapham SW8 . . 137 B2
  Hampton TW12 . . . . 173 B2
  Hillingdon UB8 . . . . 82 B2
  Hither Green SE13 . . . . . . 164 B4
  Isleworth TW7 . . . . 152 B6
  Newham E6 . . . . 100 C1
Heather Ct
  South Lambeth SW4 . . . . . 270 B1
  6 West Norwood SW16 . . . 182 C6
Heatherdale Cl KT2 . . . . 176 D3
Heatherdene Cl
  London N12 . . . . 30 A2
  Mitcham CR4 . . . . 202 C5
Heatherdene Ct CR4 . . . . . . 202 B5
Heatherdene Mans 2
  TW1 . . . . 153 D5
Heather Dr EN2 . . . . 4 D3

Heatherfold Way HA5,
  HA6 . . . . 39 D6
Heather Gdns
  Belmont SM2 . . . . 217 C2
  Hendon NW11 . . . . 47 A3
Heather Ho 11 E14 . . . . 98 A1
Heather La UB7 . . . . 82 A1
Heatherlands TW16 . . . . . . 172 A4
Heatherlea Gr KT4 . . . . 200 B1
Heatherley Ct N16 . . . . 74 A5
Heatherley Dr IG5 . . . . 56 B6
Heatherley Sch of Fine Art
  SW10 . . . . 266 B3
Heather Lo N16 . . . . 51 C1
Heather Park Dr HA0 . . . . . . 66 C1
Heather Park Par HA0 . . . . . . 66 C1
Heather Rd Dollis Hill NW2 . . 67 D6
  Lewisham SE12 . . . . 165 A3
  Walthamstow E4 . . . . 35 B4
Heatherset Cl KT10 . . . . 212 A3
Heatherset Gdns SW16 . . . . 182 B3
Heatherside Rd
  Sidcup DA14 . . . . 168 C1
  West Ewell KT19 . . . . 215 B1
Heathers The TW19 . . . . . . 148 B4
Heather Way HA7 . . . . 24 D4
Heather Wlk Edgware HA8 . . 26 D5
  Twickenham TW4 . . . . 151 C4
  West Kilburn W10 . . . . 91 A3
Heatherwood Cl E12 . . . . . . 77 C6
Heatherwood Dr UB4 . . . . . . 83 B5
Heathfield Chingford E4 . . . . 20 A1
  Chislehurst BR7 . . . . 189 A4
Heathfield Ave SW18 . . . . . 158 B4
Heathfield Cl Keston BR2 . . 225 C3
  Newham E16 . . . . 99 D2
Heathfield Ct
  Ashford TW15 . . . . 148 A1
  3 Bow E3 . . . . 97 C5
  5 Chiswick W4 . . . . 111 B1
  Penge SE20 . . . . 184 C3
  Sidcup DA14 . . . . 190 B5
  8 Sutton SM2 . . . . 218 A2
  Wandsworth SW18 . . . . . . 158 B4
Heathfield Dr CR4 . . . . 180 C2
Heathfielde N2 . . . . 48 A4
Heathfield Gdns
  Acton Green W4 . . . . 111 A1
  Blackheath SE3 . . . . 142 C3
  Croydon CR0 . . . . 221 B4
  Hendon NW11 . . . . 46 D3
  Wandsworth SW18 . . . . . . 158 B5
Heathfield House Sch 15
  W4 . . . . 111 A1
Heathfield Inf Sch TW2 . . . . 151 C3
Heathfield Jun Sch
  TW2 . . . . 151 C3
Heathfield La BR7 . . . . 189 A4
Heathfield N TW1, TW2 . . . . 152 D4
Heathfield Park Dr RM6 . . . . 58 B4
Heathfield Pk NW2 . . . . 68 C2
Heathfield Rd
  Bexleyheath DA6 . . . . 147 B1
  Bromley BR1 . . . . 186 D3
  Croydon CR0 . . . . 221 B4
  Keston BR2 . . . . 225 D3
  South Acton W3 . . . . 110 D4
  Wandsworth SW18 . . . . . . 158 B5
Heathfield Rise HA4 . . . . 39 A2
Heathfield S TW1, TW2 . . . . 152 D4
Heathfield Sch HA5 . . . . 40 D2
Heathfield Sq SW18 . . . . . . 158 B4
Heathfield Terr
  Chiswick W4 . . . . 111 A1
  Plumstead Comm SE18 . . . 145 D6
Heathfield Vale CR2 . . . . . . 223 A4
Heathgate NW11 . . . . 47 D3
Heathgate Pl NW3 . . . . 70 D4
Heath Gdns TW1 . . . . 152 D2
Heath Gr Ashford TW16 . . . . 171 D3
  Penge SE20 . . . . 184 C3
Heath Ho
  Thornton Heath CR7 . . . . . 204 C4
  Uxbridge UB10 . . . . 60 D4
Heath House Prep Sch 1
  SE8 . . . . 142 D3
Heath Hurst Rd NW3 . . . . . . 70 C4
Heath La SE3 . . . . 142 B3
Heathland Rd N16 . . . . 51 C1
Heathland Sch The TW4 . . . 151 B5
Heathlands Cl
  Sunbury TW16 . . . . 172 A1
  Twickenham TW1 . . . . 152 D3
Heathlands Ct
  Hounslow TW4 . . . . 151 A6
  Mitcham CR4 . . . . 203 A6
Heathlands Way TW4 . . . . . 151 A6
Heathlee Rd SE3 . . . . 142 D1
Heathley End BR7 . . . . 189 A4
Heath Lo WD23 . . . . 8 B3
Heath Mans
  5 Hampstead NW3 . . . . . . 70 A4
  Putney SW15 . . . . 156 D5
Heathman's Rd
  SW6 . . . . 135 B4 264 D1
Heath Mead SW19 . . . . 156 D1
Heathmere Prim Sch
  SW15 . . . . 156 A3
Heath Park Dr BR1 . . . . 210 A6

Heath Park Gdns NW3 . . . . . 69 D5
Heath Park Ind Est RM8 . . . . 59 A1
Heathpool Ct 8 E1 . . . . 96 B3
Heath Rd Clapham SW8 . . . 137 B3
  Dagenham RM6 . . . . 59 A2
  Harrow HA1 . . . . 42 A2
  Hillingdon UB10 . . . . 83 A3
  Isleworth TW3, TW7 . . . . . 130 A1
  South Norwood CR7 . . . . . 205 A6
  Twickenham TW1 . . . . 152 D3
Heath Rise Hayes BR2 . . . . 209 A3
  Putney SW15 . . . . 156 D5
Heathrow Airport London
  TW6 . . . . 126 D3
Heathrow Bvd UB7 . . . . 126 B5
Heathrow Causeway Est
  TW4 . . . . 128 B2
Heathrow International Trad
  Est TW4 . . . . 128 B2
Heathrow Prim Sch
  UB7 . . . . 126 B6
Heathrow Terminal 4 Sta
  TW6 . . . . 149 A5
Heathrow Terminals 1, 2, 3
  Sta TW6 . . . . 126 D2
Heath Royal SW15 . . . . 156 D5
Heath's Cl EN1 . . . . 5 C3
Heathshott 8 TW10 . . . . . . 154 A5
Heathside Hampstead NW3 . 70 B4
  Hinchley Wood KT10 . . . . 212 C5
  Twickenham TW4 . . . . 151 B4
Heathside Ave DA7 . . . . 147 A3
Heathside Cl
  Hinchley Wood KT10 . . . . 212 C5
  Ilford IG2 . . . . 57 B4
Heathside Prep Sch 32
  NW3 . . . . 70 A4
Heath St NW3 . . . . 70 A5
Heathstan Rd W12 . . . . 90 A1
Heath Terr RM6 . . . . 58 D2
Heath The W7 . . . . 108 C5
Heath View
  Gospel Oak NW5 . . . . 71 A4
  London N2 . . . . 48 A5
Heath View Cl N2 . . . . 48 A5
Heathview Ct SW19 . . . . . . 156 D2
Heathview Dr SE2 . . . . 146 D6
Heathview Gdns SW15 . . . . 156 C4
Heathview Rd CR7 . . . . 204 C5
Heath Villas
  Hampstead NW3 . . . . 70 B5
  Plumstead Comm SE18 . . . 123 D1
Heathville Rd N4, N19 . . . . . 50 A2
Heathwall St SW11 . . . . 136 D2
Heathway Croydon CR0 . . . . 223 B5
  Dagenham RM10 . . . . 81 C2
  Dagenham RM10 . . . . 103 C6
  Greenwich SE3 . . . . 143 A5
  Woodford IG8 . . . . 37 C5
Heathway Ct NW3 . . . . 69 C6
Heathway Ind Est RM10 . . . . 81 D4
Heathwood Ct
  1 Hounslow TW3 . . . . 129 D1
  Streatham SW12 . . . . 159 C3
Heathwood Gdns SE7 . . . . . 122 A1
Heathwood Point 7
  SE26 . . . . 162 D1
Heaton Cl E4 . . . . 20 A1
Heaton Ct 3 N20 . . . . 14 D2
Heaton Ho Chelsea SW10 . . 266 B6
  6 Peckham SE15 . . . . 140 B3
Heaton Rd London SE15 . . . 154 A3
  Mitcham CR4 . . . . 181 A3
Heaven Tree Cl N1 . . . . 73 A3
Heaver Rd 23 SW11 . . . . . . 136 B2
Heavers Farm Prim Sch
  SE25 . . . . 205 D4
Heavitree Cl SE18 . . . . 123 B1
Heavitree Rd SE18 . . . . 35 D2
Heavitree Rd 2 SE18 . . . . . 123 B1
Hebble Ho UB5 . . . . 85 A6
Hebden Ct 24 E2 . . . . 95 D6
Hebden Terr N17 . . . . 33 C4
Hebdon Rd SW17 . . . . 158 C1
Hebe St SW1 . . . . 218 A4
Heber Prim Sch SE22 . . . . . 161 D5
Heber Rd
  Cricklewood NW2 . . . . 68 D4
  East Dulwich SE22 . . . . . . 161 D5
Hebron Rd W6 . . . . 112 B3
Hecham Cl E17 . . . . 35 A2
Heckfield Pl
  SW6 . . . . 135 C5 265 A3
Heckford Ho E14 . . . . 97 D1
Heckford St E1 . . . . 118 D6
Hector 3 NW6 . . . . 27 D2
Hector Cl 8 N9 . . . . 18 A2
Hector Ct
  1 London SW9 . . . . 138 C4
  Putney SW15 . . . . 156 D6
Hector Ho 14 E2 . . . . 96 B5
Hector St SE18 . . . . 123 C2
Heddington Gr N7 . . . . 72 B3
Heddon Cl TW7 . . . . 131 A1
Heddon Court Ave EN4 . . . . 14 D6
Heddon Court Par EN4 . . . . . 15 A6

Heddon Ct EN4 . . . . .15 A6
Heddon Rd EN4 . . . . .14 D6
Heddon St W1 . . . . 249 A6
Hedge Hill EN2 . . . . .4 D4
Hedge La N13 . . . . .17 A1
Hedgeley IG4 . . . . .56 B5
Hedgemans Rd RM9 . . . . .81 A1
Hedgemans Way RM9 . .81 A2
Hedgemoor Ct ■ E4 . . . . .36 B5
Hedgerley Gdns UB6 . . . .86 A5
Hedgerow La EN5 . . . . .12 B6
Hedger's Gr E9 . . . . .75 A2
Hedger St SE11 . . . . 261 C4
Hedge Wlk SE6 . . . . 185 D6
Hedgewood Gdns IG5 . . .56 C4
Hedgewood Sch UB4 . . .83 C4
Hedgley Mews SE12 . . . 164 D6
Hedgley St SE12 . . . . 164 D6
Hedingham Cl ■ N1 . . . .73 A1
Hedingham Ho ■ KT2 . .176 A2
Hedingham Rd RM8 . . . . .80 B3
Hedley Cl SW15 . . . . 156 D5
Hedley Ho E14 . . . . 120 A3
Hedley Rd TW4 . . . . .151 C4
Hedley Row N5, N16 . . . .73 B3
Hedsor Ho E2 . . . . 243 C4
Heenan Cl IG11 . . . . .79 A2
Heene Rd EN2 . . . . .5 B4
Heidegger Cres SW13 . .134 B5
Heigham Rd E6 . . . . .78 A1
Heighton Gdns CR0 . . . 220 D3
Heights Cl SW20 . . . . . . .178 B3
Heights The
  Beckenham BR3 . . . . . . .186 A3
  Greenwich SE7 . . . . .121 C1
  Hampstead NW3 . . . . . . .70 A4
  Northolt UB5 . . . . .63 C3
  Stroud Green N4 . . . . . . .50 C3
Heiron St SE17 . . . . .138 D6
Helby Rd SW4 . . . . .159 D5
Heldar Ct SE1 . . . . 252 D1
Helder Gr SE12 . . . . 164 D4
Helder St CR2 . . . . .221 B2
Heldmann Cl TW7 . . . . . .130 B1
Helegan Cl TW6 . . . . .227 D4
Helena Cl EN4 . . . . .2 B2
Helena Ct W5 . . . . .87 D2
Helena Pl ■ E9 . . . . .96 C6
Helena Rd Ealing W5 . . . .87 D2
  Newham E13 . . . . .99 A5
  Walthamstow E17 . . . . . .53 C4
  Willesden NW10 . . . . .68 B3
Helena Sq ■ SE16 . . . . .119 A6
Helen Ave TW14 . . . . . . .150 B4
Helen Cl East Finchley N2 . .48 A6
  East Molesey KT8 . . . . . .195 D5
Helen Clare Ct EN2 . . . . . .4 D2
Helen Ct N3 . . . . .47 A6
Helen Gladstone Ho SE1 251 C2
Helen Ho ■ E2 . . . . .96 B5
Helen Mackay Ho ■ E14 . .98 B1
Helen Peele Cotts ■
  SE16 . . . . .118 C3
Helenslea Ave NW11 . . . .47 C1
Helen's Pl E2 . . . . .96 C4
Helen St SE18 . . . . 122 D2
Helen Taylor Ho ■
  SE16 . . . . .118 A2
Helen Way WD19 . . . . .22 D6
Helford Cl HA4 . . . . .61 C6
Helgiford Gdns TW16 . .171 C3
Helios Rd CR4 . . . . 203 A1
Heliport Ind Est SW11 . .136 B3
Helix Ct ■ W11 . . . . .112 D5
Helix Gdns SW2 . . . . .160 B5
Helix Ho TW7 . . . . .131 B3
Helix Rd SW2 . . . . .160 B5
Helix The SW19 . . . . .156 D2
Hellings St E1 . . . . .118 A5
Helme Cl SW19 . . . . .179 B5
Helmet Row EC1 . . . . . . 242 B6
Helmore Rd IG11 . . . . .79 D1
Helmsdale Cl UB4 . . . . . . .85 A3
Helmsdale Ho NW6 . . . . .91 D5
Helmsdale Rd SW16 . . .181 D2
Helmsley St ■ E18 . . . . . .55 A6
Helmsley Pl E8 . . . . .74 B1
Helmsley St ■ E8 . . . . . . .74 B1
Helperby Rd NW10 . . . . . .67 C1
Helsby Ct NW8 . . . . 236 C6
Helsinki Sq SE16 . . . . . . .119 A3
Helston NW1 . . . . 232 B4
Helston Cl HA5 . . . . .23 B3
Helston Ct N15 . . . . .51 C4
Helston Ho SE11 . . . . . . 261 B2
Helvetia St SE6 . . . . .163 B2
Helwys Ct E4 . . . . .36 A4
Hemans Est SW8 137 D5 269 D3
Hemans St SW8 . 137 D5 269 D3
Hemberton Rd SW9 . . . .138 A2
Hemery Rd UB6 . . . . .64 B3
Hemingford Cl N12 . . . . . .30 B5
Hemingford Rd
  Cheam SM3 . . . . 216 C4
  Islington N1 . . . . 94 B6 233 D6
Heming Rd HA8 . . . . .26 D3
Hemington Ave N11 . . . . .30 D5

Hemlock Cl SW16 . . . . . .181 D1
Hemlock Rd W12 . . . . . . .111 D6
Hemmen La UB3 . . . . .83 D1
Hemming Cl ■ TW12 . . .173 C2
Hemmings Cl DA14 . . . . .168 B2
Hemmings Ct HA8 . . . . . . .27 A3
Hemmings Mead KT19 . .215 A2
Hemming St E1 . . . . .96 A3
Hemmingway Cl NW5 . . .71 A4
Hempstead Cl IG9 . . . . . . .21 A2
Hempstead Rd E17 . . . . . .36 B1
Hemp Wlk SE17 . . . . 262 D4
Hemsby Rd KT9 . . . . .214 B2
Hemstal Rd NW6 . . . . .69 C1
Hemswell Dr NW9 . . . . . . .27 C2
Hemsworth Ct N1 . . . . . . .95 C5
Hemsworth St N1 . . . . . . .95 C5
Hemus Pl ■ SW3 . . . . . . 257 B1
Henchman St W12 . . . . . .89 D1
Hendale Ave NW4 . . . . . . .46 B6
Hendale Ho ■ SE16 . . . . .74 B6
Henderson Cl NW10 . . . . .67 A2
Henderson Ct
  ■ Deptford SE14 . . . . . .140 D6
  Hampstead NW3 . . . . . . .70 B3
  Wandsworth SW18 . . . .158 C4
  Woodside Pk N12 . . . . . . .29 D6
Henderson Dr
  NW8 . . . . 92 B3 236 C6
Henderson Ho ■ RM10 . .81 C5
Henderson Rd
  Edmonton N9 . . . . .18 B3
  Forest Gate E7 . . . . .77 C2
  Hayes UB4 . . . . .84 A4
  Thornton Heath CR0 . . . .205 B3
  Wandsworth SW18 . . . .158 C4
Hendfield Ct ■ SM6 . . . .219 B2
Hendham Rd SW17 . . . . .158 D2
HENDON 46 C3
Hendon Ave N3 . . . . .29 A2
Hendon Central NW4 . . . .46 B4
Hendon Central Sta NW4 . .46 B4
Hendon Hall Ct NW4 . . . .46 D6
Hendon Ho N4 . . . . .46 D4
Hendon La N3 . . . . .29 B1
Hendon L Ctr NW2 . . . . . .46 D2
Hendon Lo NW4 . . . . .46 D4
Hendon Park Mans NW4 . .46 C4
Hendon Park Row NW11 . .47 B3
Hendon Pk Cotts NW7 . . .11 D2
Hendon Prep Sch NW4 . .46 D6
Hendon Rd N9 . . . . .18 A2
Hendon Sch NW4 . . . . . . .46 D4
Hendon Sta NW4 . . . . . . .46 A3
Hendon Terr TW15 . . . . .171 B4
Hendon Way NW2, NW4 . .46 C3
Hendon Wood La NW7 . . .12 A3
Hendre Ho SE1 . . . . 263 B3
Hendren Cl UB6 . . . . .64 B3
Hendre Rd SE1 . .117 C2 263 B3
Hendrick Ave SW12 . . . .158 D4
Heneage La EC3 . . . . 243 B1
Heneage Pl EC3 . . . . 243 B1
Heneage St E1 . . .95 D2 243 D4
Henfield Cl London N19 . . .49 C1
  Old Bexley DA5 . . . . .169 C5
Henfield Rd SW19 . . . . . .179 B2
Hengelo Gdns CR4 . . . . .202 B5
Hengist Rd Eltham SE12 .165 B4
  Erith DA8 . . . . .147 D5
Hengist Way
  Beckenham BR2, BR3 . .208 C5
  Wallington SM6 . . . . .219 D1
Hengrave Rd SE23 . . . . .162 D4
Hengrove Ct DA5 . . . . . . .169 A3
Henley Ave SW3 . . . . . . .217 A5
Henley Cl Greenford UB6 . .86 A5
  Hounslow TW7 . . . . .130 D4
  Rotherhithe SE16 . . . . . .118 C4
Henley Ct
  Brondesbury NW2 . . . . . .68 D2
  Hendon NW4 . . . . .46 A6
  Ilford IG1 . . . . .78 D4
  Mitcham CR4 . . . . 203 A6
  Oakwood N14 . . . . .15 C4
  Peckham SE15 . . . . .140 A2
  Sidcup DA5 . . . . .169 B4
Henley Dr
  Bermondsey SE1 . 117 D2 263 D4
  Kingston u T KT2 . . . . . .177 D3
Henley Gdns
  Dagenham RM6 . . . . .59 A4
  Pinner HA5 . . . . .40 B6
Henley Ho London N12 . . .30 B5
  Shoreditch E2 . . . . 243 D6
Henley Lo
  South Norwood SE25 . . .205 D5
  Walthamstow E17 . . . . . .53 B4
Henley Prior N1 . . . . 233 C3
Henley Rd Edmonton N18 . .33 C6
  Ilford IG1 . . . . .79 B4
  Newham E16 . . . . .122 B4
  Willesden NW10 . . . . .90 C6
Henleys Cnr NW11 . . . . . .47 B5
Henleys Rdbt TW5 . . . . .128 C3
Henley St SW11 . . . . .137 A3
Henley Way TW13 . . . . . .172 D5
Henlow Pl TW10 . . . . .153 D2
Hennel Cl SE23 . . . . .162 C1
Hennessy Rd N9 . . . . .18 C2

Henniker Gdns E6 . . . . . .100 A4
Henniker Mews SW3 . . . 266 C6
Henniker Point E15 . . . . .76 C3
Henniker Rd E15 . . . . .76 B3
Henningham Rd N17 . . . . .33 B2
Henning St
  SW11 . . . . .136 C4 267 A1
Henrietta Barnett Sch
  NW11 . . . . .47 D3
Henrietta Cl SE8 . . . . . . .141 C6
Henrietta Ho
  ■ Hammersmith W6 . . . .112 C1
  ■ New Barnet EN5 . . . . . .2 A1
  ■ South Tottenham N15 . .51 C3
Henrietta Mews WC1 . . .240 B6
Henrietta Pl W1 . .93 B1 238 C2
Henrietta St
  Strand WC2 . . . . .116 A6 250 B6
  Stratford New Town E15. . .76 A3
Henriques St E1 . . . . .96 A1
Henry Addlington Cl E6 .100 D2
Henry Cavendish Prim Sch ■
  SW12 . . . . .159 C3
Henry Cl EN2 . . . . .5 C5
Henry Compton Sch
  SW6 . . . . .135 A4 264 A2
Henry Cooper Way
  SE12 . . . . .187 D6
Henry Darlot Dr NW7 . . . .29 A5
Henry Dent Cl SE5 . . . . .139 B2
Henry Dickens Ct W11 . .244 A4
Henry Doulton Dr SW17 .181 B6
Henry Fawcett Prim Sch ■
  SE11 . . . . .138 C6
Henry Green Prim Sch
  RM8 . . . . .80 D6
Henry Hatch Ct SM2 . . . .218 A1
Henry Ho Lambeth SE1 . .251 B3
  South Lambeth SW8 . . . .270 A4
  St John's Wood NW8 . . . 230 A4
Henry Jackson Ho ■
  SW15. . . . . .134 D2
Henry Jackson Rd
  SW15. . . . . .134 D2
Henry Macaulay Ave ■
  KT2 . . . . .175 D2
Henry Maynard Inf Sch
  E17 . . . . .54 A4
Henry Maynard Jun Sch
  E17 . . . . .54 A4
Henry Peters Dr TW11 . . .174 C5
Henry Rd London N4 . . . . .51 A1
  New Barnet EN4 . . . . .14 B6
  Newham E6 . . . . .100 A5
Henry's Ave IG8 . . . . .36 C5
Henryson Rd SE4 . . . . . .163 C6
Henry St BR1 . . . . .187 B2
Henry Tate Mews SW16 .182 C5
Henry Wise Ho SW1 . . . 259 B3
Henshall Point ■ E3 . . . . .97 D4
Henshall St N1 . . . . .73 B2
Henshaw St SE17 .117 B2 262 C4
Hensley Point ■ E9 . . . . .74 D2
Henslowe Rd SE22 . . . . .162 A6
Henslow Ho ■ SE15 . . . .140 A5
Henson Ave NW2 . . . . . . .68 C3
Henson Ct ■ BR6 . . . . . .226 D6
Henson Ct ■ N5 . . . . .73 A4
Henson Path HA3 . . . . . . .43 D6
Henson Pl UB5 . . . . .84 C6
Henstridge Pl NW8 . . . . 230 A5
Henty Cl SW11 . . .136 C4 267 B2
Henty Wlk SW15 . . . . . . .156 B6
Henville Rd BR1 . . . . .187 B2
Henwick Prim Sch SE9 . .144 A2
Henwick Rd SE9 . . . . .144 A2
Hepburn Gdns BR2 . . . . .208 D1
Hepburn Mews SW11 . . .158 D6
Hepple Cl TW7 . . . . .131 B3
Hepplestone Cl SW15 . .156 B5
Hepscott Rd E9 . . . . .75 C1
Hepworth Ct Barking IG11. .80 A3
  Cheam SM3 . . . . 201 C1
  Chelsea SW1 . . . . 258 C1
  Islington N1 . . . . 234 C6
Hepworth Gdns IG11 . . . .80 A3
Hepworth Ho IG8 . . . . . . .21 A1
Hepworth Rd SW16 . . . . .182 A3
Hepworth Way KT12 . . . .193 D1
Heracles St NW9 . . . . .27 D2
Heracles Cl SM6 . . . . . . .220 A1
Hera Ct ■ E14 . . . . .119 C2
Herald Gdns SM6 . . . . . .219 B5
Heralds Pl SE11 . . . . 261 C4
Herald St ■ E2 . . . . .96 B3
Herbal Hill EC1 . . . . 241 B5
Herbert Chapman Ct N5 . .72 D4
Herbert Cres SW1 . . . . . 257 D6
Herbert Ct ■ KT5 . . . . . .198 B3
Herbert Gdns
  Chiswick W4 . . . . .132 D6
  Dagenham RM6 . . . . .58 D2
  Willesden Green NW10 . . .90 B5
Herbert Ho ■ E1 . . . . . . 243 C2
Herbert Mews ■ SW2 . . .160 C5
Herbert Morrison Ho
  SW6. . . . . 264 C5
Herbert Morrison Prim Sch
  SW8 . . . . .138 A5 270 A3

Herbert Pl
  Hounslow TW3 . . . . .130 B3
  Shooters Hill SE18 . . . . .144 D6
Herbert Rd
  Bexleyheath DA7 . . . . . .147 A3
  Bromley BR2 . . . . .210 A4
  Hendon NW9 . . . . .46 A3
  Ilford IG3 . . . . .79 C6
  Kingston u T KT1 . . . . . .198 B6
  Manor Pk E12 . . . . .78 A4
  Merton SW19 . . . . .179 B3
  Shooters Hill SE18 . . . . .144 D6
  Southall UB1 . . . . .107 B5
  South Tottenham N15 . . . .51 C4
  Walthamstow E17 . . . . . .53 B2
  Wood Green N11 . . . . . . .32 A3
Herbert St
  Camden Town NW5 . . . . .71 A2
  Newham E13 . . . . .99 A5
Herbrand Est WC1 . 94 A3 240 A6
Herbrand St WC1 . .94 A3 240 A6
Hercies Rd UB10 . . . . .60 C2
Hercules Ct ■ SE14 . . . .141 A6
Hercules Pl N7 . . . . .72 A5
Hercules Rd SE1 . .116 B3 260 D5
Hercules St N7 . . . . .72 A5
Hereford Ave EN4 . . . . . . .14 D3
Hereford Bldgs SW3 . . . 266 D6
Hereford Ct
  ■ Belmont SM2 . . . . . . .217 C1
  ■ Croydon CR0 . . . . . . .205 D1
  ■ Ealing W7 . . . . .86 D2
  Harrow HA1 . . . . .42 C6
Hereford Gdns
  London SE13 . . . . .164 C6
  Pinner HA5 . . . . .41 A4
  Redbridge IG1 . . . . .56 A2
  Twickenham TW2 . . . . . .152 A3
Hereford Ho ■ Acton W3 . .88 C1
  ■ Brixton SW2 . . . . .138 C1
  ■ Camberwell SE5 . . . . .139 A3
  Edgware HA8 . . . . .26 B3
  Knightsbridge SW3 . . . . 257 B6
  Walham Green SW10 . . . 265 C4
Hereford Mans ■ W2 . . . .91 C1
Hereford Mews ■ W2 . . . .91 C1
Hereford Pl SE14 . . . . . . .141 B5
Hereford Rd Acton W3 . . .111 A6
  Bayswater W2 . . . .113 C6 245 B6
  Ealing W5 . . . . .109 C3
  Feltham TW13 . . . . .150 C3
  Wanstead E11 . . . . .55 B4
Hereford Retreat ■
  SE15 . . . . .140 A5
Hereford Sq
  SW7 . . . . .114 A2 256 B3
Hereford St E2 . . . . .96 A3
Hereford Way KT9 . . . . . .213 D3
Herent Dr IG5 . . . . .56 B6
Hereward Gdns N13 . . . . .32 C5
Hereward House Sch
  NW3 . . . . .70 B2
Hereward Rd SW17 . . . . .180 D6
Herga Ct HA1 . . . . .64 C6
Herga Rd HA3 . . . . .42 D5
Heriot Ave E4 . . . . .19 C2
Heriot Rd NW4 . . . . .46 C4
Heriots Cl HA7 . . . . .25 A6
Heritage Ave NW9 . . . . . . .27 D1
Heritage Cl London SW9. .138 D2
  Sunbury TW16 . . . . .172 A2
Heritage Ct SE8 . . . . .118 D1
Heritage Hill BR2 . . . . . . .225 C3
Heritage Ho
  ■ Putney SW19. . . . . . . .156 D3
  ■ Twickenham TW1 . . . .153 A4
Heritage View HA1 . . . . . .64 D5
Herlwyn Ave HA4 . . . . .61 C5
Herlwyn Gdns SW17 . . . .180 D5
Herm Cl TW7 . . . . .130 A5
Hermes Cl ■ W9 . . . . .91 C3
Hermes Ct ■ SW9 . . . . .138 C4
Hermes Ho BR3 . . . . .185 A2
Hermes St N1 . . . . 234 A3
Hermes Wlk UB5 . . . . .85 C5
Herm Ho EN3 . . . . .6 D5
Hermiston Ave N8 . . . . . . .50 A4
Hermiston Ct
  ■ Hornsey N8 . . . . .50 A4
  ■ North Finchley N12 . . . .30 B5
Hermitage Cl
  Abbey Wood SE2 . . . . .124 C3
  Claygate KT10 . . . . .213 A2
  Enfield EN2 . . . . .4 D3
  Littleton TW17 . . . . .192 C5
  Snaresbrook E18 . . . . . . .54 D5
Hermitage Ct
  ■ Child's Hill NW2 . . . . . .69 C5
  Colney Hatch N11 . . . . . .30 D4
  ■ Wanstead E18 . . . . .55 A5
  ■ Wapping E1 . . . . .118 A5
Hermitage Gdns
  Child's Hill NW2 . . . . .69 C5
  South Norwood SE19 . . .183 A3
Hermitage La
  Child's Hill NW2 . . . . .69 C5
  Croydon CR0 . . . . .206 A3
  South Norwood SW16 . .182 B3
Hermitage Prim Sch ■
  E1 . . . . .118 A5

Hermitage Rd
  London N4, N15 . . . . .51 A3
  South Norwood SE19 . . .183 B4
Hermitage Row ■ E8 . . . .74 A3
Hermitage St W2 . . . . . . 236 C3
Hermitage The
  Barnes SW13 . . . . .133 D4
  Feltham TW13 . . . . .149 D1
  Forest Hill SE23 . . . . . . .162 C3
  Kingston u T KT1 . . . . . .197 D5
  Richmond TW10 . . . . . . .154 A6
  Uxbridge UB8 . . . . .60 A2
Hermitage Villas SW6 . . 265 B6
Hermitage Wall E1 . . . . . .118 A5
Hermitage Way HA7 . . . . .25 A2
Hermitage Wlk E18 . . . . . .54 D5
Hermit Pl NW6 . . . . .91 D6
Hermit Rd E16 . . . . .98 D3
Hermit St EC1 . . . . 234 C2
Hermon Gr UB3 . . . . .106 A5
Hermon Hill E11 . . . . .55 A5
Herndon Rd SW18 . . . . . .158 A6
Herne Cl Hayes UB3 . . . . .83 D1
  Willesden NW10 . . . . .67 B3
Herne Ct WD23 . . . . .8 A4
HERNE HILL 161 A6
Herne Hill SE24 . . . . .139 A1
Herne Hill Ho SE24 . . . . .139 A1
Herne Hill Mans SE24 . . .161 A5
Herne Hill Rd SE24 . . . . .139 A1
Herne Hill Sch SE24 . . . .161 A6
Herne Hill Sta SE24 . . . .160 D5
Herne Hill Velodrome
  SE24. . . . . .161 B5
Herne Mews N18 . . . . .34 A6
Herne Pl SE24 . . . . .160 D6
Herne Rd KT6 . . . . .214 A6
Heron Cl Buckhurst Hill IG9. .21 A3
  Cheam SM1 . . . . .217 B3
  Walthamstow E17 . . . . . .35 B1
  Willesden NW10 . . . . .67 C2
Heron Cres DA14 . . . . . . .189 C6
Heron Ct Bromley BR2 . . .209 C5
  ■ Cubitt Town E14. . . . . .120 A3
  ■ Dulwich SE21 . . . . . . .161 B2
  ■ Forest Hill SE23 . . . . .162 C3
  Ilford IG1 . . . . .78 D6
  ■ Kingston u T KT1 . . . . .198 A6
  Merton SW20 . . . . .178 C1
  Mitcham CR4 . . . . .180 C2
  Ruislip HA4 . . . . .61 B6
  Stanwell TW19 . . . . .148 A3
Herondale Ave SW18 . . .158 C3
Heron Dr N4 . . . . .73 A6
Herongate N1 . . . . 235 B6
Herongate Rd E12 . . . . . . .77 C6
Heron Hill DA17 . . . . .125 B2
Heron Ho Battersea SW11 267 B2
  Ealing W13 . . . . .87 A3
  Peckham SE15 . . . . .139 D4
  Sidcup DA14 . . . . .168 B1
  St John's Wood NW8 . . . 230 A3
  Teddington KT1 . . . . .175 C2
Heron Mead EN3 . . . . .7 C5
Heron Mews IG1 . . . . .78 D6
Heron Pl Marylebone W1. . 238 C2
  Rotherhithe SE16 . . . . . .119 A5
Heron Quays E14 . . . . . . .119 C5
Heron Quays Sta E14. . . .119 C5
Heron Rd Croydon CR0 . .221 C6
  Herne Hill SE24 . . . . . . .139 A1
  Isleworth TW1 . . . . .131 B1
Heronsforde W13 . . . . . . .87 C1
Heronsgate HA8 . . . . .26 C5
Heronsgate Prim Sch
  SE28. . . . . .123 B3
Heron's Lea N6 . . . . .48 D3
Heronslea Dr HA7 . . . . . . .26 A5
Herons Pl TW1 . . . . .131 B2
Herons Sq ■ TW10 . . . . .153 D6
Herons Rise EN4 . . . . .2 C1
Herons The E11 . . . . .54 D3
Heron Trad Est W3 . . . . . .88 D2
Heronway IG8 . . . . .37 C6
Heron Way Hatton TW14. . .128 A1
  Wallington SM6 . . . . . . .219 D1
Herrick Ct ■ TW10 . . . . .175 D6
Herrick Ho
  ■ Camberwell SE5 . . . . .139 B5
  ■ Canonbury N16 . . . . . . .73 B4
Herrick Rd N5 . . . . .73 A5
Herrick St SW1 . . . 115 D2 259 D3
Herries St W10 . . . . .91 A5
Herringham Rd SE7 . . . . .121 C3
Herrongate Cl EN1 . . . . . . .5 D3
Hersant Cl NW10 . . . . .90 A6
Herschell Rd SE23 . . . . .163 A4
Herschell's Mews SE5 . .139 A2
Hersham Cl SW15 . . . . . .156 A4
Hersham Rd KT12 . . . . . .194 A1
Hershell Ct ■ SW14 . . . .132 D1
Hertford Ave EN4 . . . . .2 B2
Hertford Ct
  ■ London SW11 . . . . . . .136 C2
  Newham E6 . . . . .100 B4
  Palmers Green N13 . . . . .16 C1
Hertford Ho ■ UB5 . . . . . .85 B3
Hertford Lo ■ SW19 . . . .157 A3
Hertford Pl W1 . . . . 239 B5

Hertford Rd Barking IG11...78 D1
Barnet EN4..............2 A2
East Finchley N2...........48 C6
Edmonton N9.............18 B3
Enfield EN3..............6 C5
Ilford IG2...............57 C3
Shoreditch N1............95 C6
Hertford Rd High St EN3..18 C6
Hertford St W1.....115 B5 248 C3
Hertford Way CR4.........204 A5
Hertford Wlk 13 DA17.....125 C1
Hertmitage The 5 SE13..142 A3
Hertslet Rd N7............72 B5
Hertsmere Rd E14.........119 C6
Hertswood Ct 1 EN5.......1 A1
Hervey Cl N3.............29 C2
Hervey Park Rd E17.......53 A5
Hervey Rd SE3...........143 B4
Hesa Rd UB3.............106 A6
Hesewall Cl SW4.........137 C3
Hesketh Pl W11..........244 A5
Hesketh Rd E7............77 A5
Heslop Ct 1 SW12........159 A3
Heslop Rd SW12..........158 D3
Hesper Mews
  SW5...........113 D2 255 C3
Hesperus Cres E14.......119 D2
Hessel Rd W13...........109 B4
Hessel St E1.............96 B1
Hestercombe Ave
  SW6...........135 A4 264 B1
Hester Ct SW16..........181 C5
Hesterman Way CR0.......204 B1
Hester Rd
  Battersea SW11..136 C5 267 A4
  Edmonton N18.........34 A5
Hester Terr TW9.........132 C2
HESTON.................129 B5
Heston Ave TW5.........129 A5
Heston Com Sch TW5.....129 C5
Heston Ctr The TW5......106 C1
Heston Grange TW5.......129 A4
Heston Grange La TW5....129 B6
Heston Ho
  Gunnersbury W4.......110 D1
  5 St Johns SE8.......141 C4
Heston Ind Est TW5.......129 B5
Heston Inf Sch TW5.......129 B5
Heston Jun Sch TW5......129 C5
Heston Phoenix Distribution
  Pk TW5..............128 C6
Heston Rd TW5..........129 C5
Heston St SE14..........141 C4
Hetherington Rd
  Charlton TW17.........171 A1
  Stockwell SW2, SW4....138 A1
Hetherington Way UB10...60 A4
Hethpool Ho W2.........236 C5
Hetley Gdns 1 SE19.....183 D3
Hetley Rd W12..........112 B4
Heton Gdns NW4..........46 A5
Hetty Rees Ct 6 N19....50 A2
Hevelius Cl SE10........120 D1
Hever Croft SE9.........188 C6
Heverfield Ct CR4.......180 D3
Hever Gdns BR1.........188 C1
Heversham Rd SE18......123 C2
Hever Ho SE15..........140 D6
Heversham Ho DA7.......147 C4
Hevingham Dr RM6........58 C4
Heward Ct SE13.........142 A3
Hewens Rd UB4...........83 A3
Hewer Ho 6 SW4.........159 C6
Hewer St W10............90 D2
Hewes Ho E17............52 D5
Hewett Cl HA7............25 B6
Hewett Ho Putney SW15..134 C3
  7 Woolwich SE18......122 D1
Hewett Rd RM8...........80 D4
Hewetts Quay 5 IG11...101 A6
Hewish Rd N18...........33 C6
Hewison St E3............97 B5
Hewitt Ave N22..........32 D1
Hewitt Cl CR0..........223 C5
Hewitt Ho 2 E4..........36 B5
Hewitt Rd N8............50 D4
Hewlett Rd E3............97 A5
Hewling Ho 1 N16........73 C3
Hexagon Bsns Ctr UB4...106 C4
Hexagon The N6..........48 D1
Hexal Rd SE6...........164 C1
Hexham Gdns TW7........131 A5
Hexham Rd Barnet EN5....1 D1
  Cheam SM4...........201 D1
  West Norwood SE27....161 A2
Hexton Ct N4.............73 A6
Heybourne Rd N17........34 B3
Heybridge 9 NW1.........71 B2
Heybridge The W5.......182 B4
Heybridge Dr IG6.........57 B6
Heybridge Way E10.......53 B1
Heydon Ct BR4..........224 C6
Heydon Ho 3 SE14......140 C4
Heyford Ave
  Merton SW20.........201 B6

Heyford Ave continued
  South Lambeth
  SW8...........138 A5 270 B4
Heyford Rd CR4.........180 C1
Heyford Terr SW8.......270 B4
Heygate St SE17...117 A2 262 B4
Heylyn Sq E3............97 B4
Heynes Rd RM8...........80 C4
Heysham Dr WD19.........22 D5
Heysham La NW3..........69 D5
Heysham Rd N15.........51 B3
Heythorp St SW18.......157 B2
Heythrop Coll
  W8...........113 D3 255 C6
Heythrop Dr UB10........60 B4
Heyward Ct SM2.........217 C2
Heywood Ave NW9........27 C2
Heywood Ct 2 HA7.......25 C5
Heywood Ho
  11 Deptford SE14.....140 D6
  6 Tulse Hill SW2.....160 C5
Heyworth Rd
  Lower Clapton E5.....74 B4
  Stratford E15........76 D4
Hibbert Ho 13 E14.....119 C3
Hibbert Rd Harrow HA3..24 C1
  Walthamstow E17......53 B2
Hibbert St SW11........136 B2
Hibernia Gdns TW3......151 C4
Hibernia Point 9 SE2..124 D4
Hibernia Rd TW3........129 C1
Hibiscus Cl 18 HA8......27 A6
Hibiscus Lo 5 E15.......76 C1
Hichisson Rd SE15......162 C6
Hicken Rd SW2..........160 B6
Hickes Ho 6 NW6.........70 B1
Hickey's Almshouses 7
  TW9.................132 B1
Hickin Cl SE7..........121 D2
Hickin St 2 E14........120 A3
Hickleton NW1..........232 B5
Hickling Ho IG1.........78 D3
Hickling Rd IG1.........78 D3
Hickman Ave E4..........36 A4
Hickman Cl E16..........99 D2
Hickman Rd RM6.........58 C2
Hickmore Wlk SW4......137 C2
Hickory Cl N9............18 A4
Hicks Ave UB6...........86 C4
Hicks Cl SW11..........136 C2
Hicks Ct RM10...........81 D5
Hicks St SE8...........119 A1
Hidaburn Ct 7 SW16....181 C6
Hidcote Gdns SW20......200 B6
Hidcote Ho 11 SM2.....218 A1
Hide E6................100 C1
Hide Pl SW1.....115 D2 259 C3
Hider Ct SE3...........143 C5
Hide Rd HA1.............42 B5
Hide Twr SW1...........259 C3
Hieover SE21...........161 A2
Higgins Ho 7 N1.........95 C6
Higginson Ho 2 NW3.....70 D1
Higgins Wlk TW12.......173 A4
Higgs Ind Est 9 SE24..138 D2
High Acre EN2............4 D2
High Bridge 8 SE7......121 D2
2 Kingston u T KT5....198 B4
Highbury Ave HA0........88 C6
Highbury Gdns NW11.....47 B3
Highbury Point E17......35 D2
High Cross N19..........50 A2
High Cross Rd N17........52 A6
Highcross Way 4 SW15..156 A3
Highdaun Dr SW16......204 B5
High Dene EN2...........4 D2
Highdown KT4..........215 D6
Highdown Rd SW15......156 B5
High Dr KT2, KT3.......177 A1
Higham's Lodge Bsns Ctr
  E17.................52 B6
HIGHAMS PARK...........36 A3
Highams Park Sch E4....36 B4
Highams Park Sta E4.....36 B4
Higham St E17...........53 A6
Higham Station Ave E4...35 D4
Highams The E17.........36 A2
High Ashton 11 KT2....176 D3
Highbanks Cl DA16.....146 B5
Highbanks Rd HA5........23 D4
Highbank Way N8........50 C3
HIGH BARNET............1 B2
High Barnet Sta EN5.....1 C1
Highbarrow Rd CR0.....206 A1
High Beech
  South Croydon CR2....221 C1
  Southgate N21........16 B5
High Beeches DA14.....191 A5
High Birch Ct 7 EN4....2 C1
Highbridge Ct 13 SE14..140 C5
Highbridge Rd IG11....100 D6
High Bridge Wharf SE10.120 B1
Highbrook Rd SE3.......143 D2
High Broom Cres BR4...224 C6
Highbury Mans 24 N1....72 D1
HIGHBURY...............72 D4
Highbury Ave CR7......182 D1
Highbury Cl
  New Malden KT3......199 A4
  West Wickham BR4....223 D4
Highbury Cnr N5.........72 D2
Highbury Corner N5......72 D2
Highbury Cres N5........72 C3

Highbury Fields Sch 4
  N5.................72 D3
Highbury Gdns IG3.......79 C6
Highbury Gr N5..........72 D3
Highbury Grange N5......73 A4
Highbury Grove Ct N5....72 D2
Highbury Grove Sch 7
  N5.................73 A3
Highbury Hill N5.........72 D4
Highbury & Islington Sta
  N1.................72 D2
Highbury New Pk N5.....73 A4
Highbury Pk N5.........72 D4
Highbury Pl N5.........72 D3
Highbury Pool N5.......72 D2
Highbury Quadrant N5...73 A5
Highbury Quadrant Prim Sch
  N5.................73 A4
Highbury Rd SW19......179 A5
Highbury Station Rd N1..72 C2
Highbury Terr N5.......72 D3
Highbury Terrace Mews
  N5.................72 D3
High Cedar Dr SW20....178 B3
Highclears 6 IG9.........21 B2
Highclere Rd KT3.......199 B6
Highclere St SE26......185 A6
Highcliffe
  Beckenham BR3......185 D6
  Ealing W13...........87 B2
Highcliffe Dr SW15.....155 D5
Highcliffe Gdns IG4......56 A4
Highcombe SE7.........143 B6
Highcombe Cl SE9......166 A3
High Coombe Pl KT2....177 B3
Highcroft Highgate N6...49 A3
  Hyde The NW9.........45 C4
Highcroft Ave HA0.......88 C6
Highcroft Gdns NW11....47 B3
Highcroft Point E17......35 D2
High Cross Ctr The N15..52 A5
High Cross Rd N17.......52 A6
Highdown Rd SW15......156 B5
Highfield Ave Erith DA8..147 D6
  Greenford UB6........64 D3
  Hendon NW11.........47 A2
  Kingsbury NW9........45 A4
  Orpington BR6.......227 D3
  Pinner HA5...........41 B4
  Wembley HA9..........66 B5
Highfield Cl
  Hither Green SE13....164 B5
  Kingsbury NW9........45 A4
  Long Ditton KT6......197 C1
  Wood Green N22.......32 C2
Highfield Ct 7 Barnet EN5..1 C1
  Hendon NW11.........47 A3
  Mitcham CR4.........202 C5
  Southgate N14........15 C5
  Wanstead E12..........77 C6
Highfield Dr
  Beckenham BR2......208 D5
  Ickenham UB10........60 A5
  West Ewell KT19.....215 D2
  West Wickham BR4....224 A5
Highfield Gdns NW11....47 A3
Highfield Hill SE19....183 C3
Highfield Ho N21........16 D3
Highfield Inf Sch BR2..208 C5
Highfield Jun Sch BR2..208 C5
Highfield Mews NW6.....69 D1
Highfield Prim Sch
  Edmonton N21.........17 A3
  Hillingdon UB10......82 D4
Highfield Rd Acton W3...89 A2
  Bexley DA6..........169 B6
  Bromley BR1.........210 B5
  Carshalton SM1......218 C3
  Edmonton N21.........16 D2
  Feltham TW13........150 A2
  4 Feltham TW13......150 B3
  Hendon NW11..........47 A3
  Hounslow TW7........130 D4
  Orpington BR5, BR7..211 D6
  St Paul's Cray BR5, BR7..211 D6
  Tolworth KT5........199 A2
  Upper Halliford TW16..193 D4
  Walton-on-T KT12....194 A1
Highfields SM1.........217 C6
Highfields Gr N6........48 D1
High Foleys KT10......213 B1
High Gables
  Beckenham BR2......186 C1
  Loughton IG10........21 D6
High Garth KT10.......212 A2
HIGHGATE...............49 A2
Highgate Archway N6...49 C1

Highgate Ave N6.........49 B2
Highgate Cemetery★
  N19.................71 B6
Highgate Cl N6..........49 A2
High Gate Edge N2.......48 C4
Highgate High St N6....49 B1
Highgate Hill N19......49 B1
Highgate Ho 11 SE26...162 A1
Highgate Hts N6........49 C3
Highgate Pre-Prep & Jun
  Sch N6.............48 D2
Highgate Prim Sch N6...48 D3
Highgate (Private) Hospl
  N6.................48 D3
Highgate Rd NW5.......71 B4
Highgate Sch N6.........49 A2
Highgate Spinney N8....49 D3
Highgate Sta N6.........49 B3
Highgate West Hill
  Highgate N6..........49 A1
  London N6............71 A6
Highgate Wlk SE23.....162 C2
Highgate Wood Sch N8...49 D3
High Gr Bromley BR1....187 D2
  Woolwich SE18.......145 B4
Highgrove Cl London N11..31 A5
  Widmore BR7........188 A2
Highgrove Ct BR3......185 C3
Highgrove Ho HA4........40 A3
Highgrove Mews SM5....218 D5
Highgrove Point 2 NW3..70 A4
Highgrove Rd RM8........80 C4
Highgrove Way HA4......40 A2
High Hill Ferry 3 E5....52 B1
High Holborn
  WC1................94 B2 240 C3
High Holborn Ho WC1...240 D3
High La W7..............86 B1
Highland Ave W7........86 C1
Highland Cotts SM6....219 C4
Highland Croft BR3.....185 D4
Highland Ct E18.........37 B2
Highland Dr WD19.......8 A4
Highland Lo 3 SE19...183 D3
Highland Pk TW13......171 D6
Highland Rd Bexley DA6..147 C1
  Bromley BR1.........186 D2
  Pinner HA6...........22 A1
  West Norwood SE19...183 C4
Highlands N20...........14 B2
Highlands Ave Acton W3..111 A6
  Southgate N21.......16 B6
Highlands Cl Hornsey N4..50 A2
  Hounslow TW3........129 D4
Highlands Ct SE19.....183 C4
Highlands Gdns IG1......56 B1
Highlands Heath SW15..156 C4
Highlands Prim Sch IG1..56 B1
Highlands Rd EN5.......13 C6
Highlands Sch N21......4 C1
Highlands The Barnet EN5..1 D1
  Edgware HA8..........26 D1
Highlawn Hall HA1......64 C5
Highlea Cl NW9..........27 C2
High Level Dr SE26.....184 A6
Highlever Rd W10........90 C2
High Limes 2 SE19....183 C4
High London 5 N6......49 D2
Highmead
  9 Edmonton N18......34 A5
  Plumstead Comm SE18..145 D5
Highmead Cres HA0......66 B1
High Meadow Cl HA5.....40 C5
High Meadow Cres NW9..45 B4
High Meads Rd E16.......99 D1
Highmore Rd SE3.......142 C5
High Mount Hendon NW4..46 A3
  11 Hornsey N4........50 A2
High Oaks EN2...........4 B5
High Oaks Lo 6 E18.....37 A1
High Park Ave TW9.....132 C4
High Park Rd TW9......132 C4
High Par The TW16......150 A3
High Path SW19........180 A2
Highpoint EN5..........14 A6
High Point
  Chislehurst SE9.....166 D1
  Highgate N6..........49 A2
High Range SW20......178 C3
High Rd
  Buckhurst Hill IG9, IG10..21 C5
  Bushey WD23..........8 B3
  Chadwell Heath RM6...58 C2
  East Finchley N2.....48 C6
  Finchley N2, N12.....30 A3
  Friern Barnet N11....31 B5
  Harrow HA3...........24 C3
  Ilford IG1...........78 D6
  Leyton E10...........53 D3
  Oakleigh Pk N20......14 A4
  Seven Kings IG1, IG3..79 C6
  South Tottenham N15, N17..51 D5
  Tottenham N17........33 D2
  Wembley HA0, HA9.....66 A3
  Willesden NW10........68 A2
  Woodford E18.........37 A2
  Wood Green N22.......32 B3
HIGHGATE...............49 A2
Highgate Archway N6...49 C1

Highridge Pl EN2.........4 B5
High Road Buckhurst Hill
  IG9.................21 B2
High Road Eastcote HA5..40 B4
High Road, Ickenham
  UB10...............61 A6
High Road Leyton E10...75 D6
High Road Leytonstone
  E11.................76 C6
High Road Woodford Gn
  IG8.................37 A6
High St Mews SW19....179 A5
High St N Newham E6...100 A6
  Plashet E12..........78 A2
High St S E6..........100 B4
High Sheldon N6.........48 D3
Highshore Rd SE15.....139 D3
Highshore Sch 16 SE15..139 D4
High Silver IG10.........21 D6
High St Acton W3.......110 D5
  Barnet EN5...........1 B1
  Beckenham BR3......185 C1
  Brentford TW8.......132 A6
  Bromley BR1.........187 A1
  Cheam SM1, KT17.....217 A2
  Claygate KT10.......212 D2
  Cranford TW5........128 B5
  Croydon CR0.........221 A5
  Ealing W5...........109 D6
  East Molesey KT8....195 C5
  Edgware HA8..........26 C4
  Elstree WD6..........9 D5
  Farnborough BR6.....227 A3
  Feltham TW13........150 A2
  Green Street Green BR6..227 D2
  Hampton TW12.......174 A4
  Harlington UB3.......127 B6
  Harrow on t H HA1....42 C1
  Hornsey N8...........50 B5
  Hounslow TW3........129 D2
  Ilford IG6...........57 A6
  Kingston u T KT1....175 D2
  Kingston u T KT1....197 D6
  Mill Hill NW7........28 B5
  Newham E13...........99 A5
  New Malden KT3......199 C5
  Palmers Green N14....15 D2
  Penge SE20..........184 D3
  Pinner HA5...........41 A6
  Ruislip HA4..........39 C1
  Shepperton TW17.....193 A3
  Sidcup DA14.........190 A6
  Southall UB1........107 B5
  South Norwood CR7...205 B5
  South Norwood SE25..206 A5
  Stratford Marsh E15..98 A6
  Sutton SM1..........217 D4
  Sutton SM1, SM2.....217 D3
  Teddington TW11.....175 A5
  Thames Ditton KT7...197 A3
  Twickenham TW2......152 A4
  Wallington SM5......219 A4
  Walthamstow E17......53 B5
  Walton-on-T KT12....194 A1
  Wanstead E11.........55 A4
  Wealdstone HA3.......24 C1
  Wealdstone HA3......42 C6
  Wembley HA9..........66 B4
  West Wickham BR4....207 D1
  Wimbledon SW19......179 D5
  Yiewsley UB7........104 A6
Highstone Ave E11.......55 A3
Highstone Ct E11.......54 D3
High Street Collier's Wood
  SW17, SW19.........180 B4
High Street Harlesden
  NW10...............89 D5
High Street Harlington
  TW6................127 B5
High Street Kensington Sta
  W8............113 D4 245 C1
High The SW16.........160 A1
High Timber St EC4.....252 A6
High Tor Ct BR1.......187 B3
High Tor View SE28....123 C5
High Trees Cheam SM3..201 B2
  Croydon CR0.........207 A1
  East Barnet EN4......14 C6
  Streatham SW2.......160 C3
  Uxbridge UB10........61 A6
  Whetstone N20.......14 A1
Hightrees B W7........108 C6
Hightrees Ho SW12....159 A5
Highview Crouch End N6..49 C3
  Hornsey N8...........50 A2
  Northolt UB5.........85 A4
  Woolwich SE18.......144 D5
High View
  6 Penge SE19........183 D3
  Pinner HA5...........40 C6
Highview Ave HA8.......27 C6
High View Ave CR0, SM6..220 B3
High View Cl
  Loughton IG10........21 C6
  South Norwood SE19..183 D1
Highview Ct 2 SW19...157 A3
High View Ct HA3.......24 C1

Highview Gdns
Edgware HA8 . . . . **27** A6
Hendon N3 . . . . **47** A6
New Southgate N11 . . . . . **31** C5
Highview Ho
1 Buckhurst Hill IG9 . . . . **21** D1
2 Buckhurst Hill IG9 . . . . **21** D1
High View Ho RM6 . . . . . **59** A5
High View Par 1 IG4 . . . . **56** B4
High View Prim Sch
1 London SW11 . . . . . **136** B1
Wallington SM6 . . . . . . **220** A3
Highview Rd Ealing W13 . . **87** A1
Sidcup DA14 . . . . **190** B6
High View Rd London N10 . . **30** D2
Snaresbrook E18 . . . . . . **54** D6
South Norwood SE19 . . . . **183** B4
Highway Bsns Pk The 7
E1 . . . . **118** D6
Highway The
Shadwell E1 . . . . **118** C6
Stanmore HA7 . . . . **25** A3
Highway Trad Ctr The 6
E1 . . . . **118** D6
High Wigsell TW11 . . . . . **175** A5
Highwood IG8 . . . . **36** D6
Highwood Ave N12 . . . . . **30** A6
Highwood Cl
Dulwich SE22 . . . . **162** A3
Orpington BR6 . . . . **227** A6
Highwood Ct Barnet EN5 . . **13** C6
Whetstone N12 . . . . **14** A1
Highwood Dr BR6 . . . . . . **227** A6
Highwood Gdns IG5 . . . . . **56** B5
Highwood Gr NW7 . . . . . . **27** B5
Highwood Hill NW7 . . . . . **11** D2
Highwood Rd N19 . . . . . . **72** A5
High Worple HA4 . . . . . . **41** B1
Highworth Rd N11 . . . . . **31** D5
Highworth St NW1 . . . . . **237** B4
Hilary Ave CR4 . . . . . . **203** A6
Hilary Cl Bexley DA8 . . . **147** D4
Walham Green SW6 . . . . . **265** C4
Hilary Ct N9 . . . . **18** D3
Hilary Rd W12 . . . . . . **111** D6
Hilbert Rd SM3 . . . . . . **216** D5
Hilborough Cl SW19 . . . . **180** A3
Hilborough Ct 1 E8 . . . . **95** D6
Hilborough Rd 1 E8 . . . . **73** D1
Hilborough Way BR6 . . . . **227** B3
Hilda Rd Newham E16 . . . . **98** C3
Upton Pk E6 . . . . **77** D1
Hilda Terr 2 SW9 . . . . . **138** C3
Hilda Vale Cl BR6 . . . . . **226** D4
Hilda Vale Rd BR6 . . . . . **226** D4
Hildenborough Gdns
BR1 . . . . **186** D4
Hildenbrough Ho BR3 . . . . **185** B3
Hildenlea Pl BR2 . . . . . **186** C1
Hilditch Ho 7 TW10 . . . . **154** B5
Hildreth St 6 SW12 . . . . **159** B3
Hildreth Street Mews 2
SW12 . . . . **159** B3
Hildyard Rd SW6 . . . . . . **265** B6
Hiley Rd NW10 . . . . **90** C4
Hilfield La WD23 . . . . . . **8** C6
Hilgrove Rd NW6 . . . . . . **70** A1
Hiliary Gdns HA7 . . . . . **25** C1
Hillary Cres KT12 . . . . . **194** C1
Hillary Ct
3 Chislehurst SE9 . . . . **166** A2
13 Shepherd's Bush W12 . . **112** C4
Stanwell TW19 . . . . . . **148** A3
Hillary Dr TW7 . . . . . . **152** D6
Hillary Rd UB2 . . . . . . **107** C3
Hillary Rise EN5 . . . . . . **1** C1
Hillbeck Cl
Deptford SE15 . . . . . . **140** C5
Deptford SE15 . . . . . . **140** C6
Hillbeck Way UB6 . . . . . . **86** B6
Hillborne Cl UB3 . . . . . **106** A1
Hillboro Ct
Leytonstone E11 . . . . . . **54** B2
1 Woodford E18 . . . . . **36** D2
Hillborough Ct HA1 . . . . . **42** C2
Hillbrook Prim Sch
SW17 . . . . **181** A6
Hillbrook Rd SW17 . . . . . **181** A6
Hillbrow Kingston u T KT3 . . **199** D6
7 Richmond TW10 . . . . . **154** A5
Hill Brow BR1 . . . . **187** D2
Hillbrow Ct KT10 . . . . . **212** A4
Hillbrow Rd Catford BR1 . . **186** C4
Esher KT10 . . . . **212** A4
Hill Bunker's DA17 . . . . . **125** C2
Hillbury Ave HA3 . . . . . . **43** B4
Hillbury Rd SW17 . . . . . **159** B1
Hill Cl Barnet EN5 . . . . . **12** C6
Chislehurst BR7 . . . . . **188** D5
Dollis Hill NW2 . . . . . . **68** B5
Hampstead Garden Suburb
NW11 . . . . **47** C3
Harrow HA1 . . . . **64** C5
Stanmore HA7 . . . . **25** B6
Hillcote Ave SW16 . . . . . **182** C3
Hillcourt N6 . . . . **49** C3

Hillcourt Ave N12 . . . . . **29** D4
Hillcourt Rd SE22 . . . . . **162** B5
Hill Cres Harrow HA1 . . . . **43** A4
Kingston u T KT5 . . . . . **198** B4
North Cheam KT4 . . . . . **216** C6
Totteridge N20 . . . . . . **13** D2
Hillcrest
Camberwell SE24 . . . . . **139** B1
Highgate N6 . . . . **49** A2
Notting Hill W11 . . . . . **244** C5
Southgate N21 . . . . **16** C4
Hill Crest DA15 . . . . . . **168** B4
Hillcrest Ave
Edgware HA8 . . . . **26** D6
Pinner HA5 . . . . **40** D5
Temple Fortune NW11 . . . . **47** B4
Hillcrest Cl
Beckenham BR3 . . . . . . **207** B3
Forest Hill SE26 . . . . . **184** A6
Hillcrest Ct
Brondesbury NW2 . . . . . . **69** A3
8 Edgware HA8 . . . . . . **26** D5
Lewisham SE6 . . . . **164** B4
Sutton SM2 . . . . **218** B2
Hillcrest Gdns
Dollis Hill NW2 . . . . . . **68** A5
Hendon N3 . . . . **47** A5
Hinchley Wood KT10 . . . . **212** D5
Hillcrest Hts W5 . . . . . . **88** A3
Hillcrest Rd Acton W3 . . . **110** D5
Chingford E17 . . . . **36** B1
Ealing W5 . . . . **88** A2
Grove Pk BR1 . . . . **187** A6
Loughton IG10 . . . . **21** D5
Woodford E18 . . . . **37** A1
Hillcrest View BR3 . . . . . **207** B3
Hillcroft Ave HA5 . . . . . **41** B3
Hillcroft Coll KT6 . . . . . **198** A3
Hillcroft Cres Ealing W5 . . **87** D1
Ruislip HA4 . . . . **62** D5
Wembley HA9 . . . . **66** B4
Hillcroft Rd E6 . . . . . . **100** D2
Hillcroome Rd SM2 . . . . . **218** B2
Hillcross Ave SM4 . . . . . **201** A4
Hillcross Prim Sch SM4 . . . **201** B5
Hill Ct Barnet EN4 . . . . . **2** C1
Ealing W5 . . . . **88** B3
Hampstead NW3 . . . . **70** C4
9 Norbiton KT2 . . . . . **176** D3
Northolt UB5 . . . . **63** C3
Putney SW15 . . . . **156** D6
14 Surbiton KT6 . . . . . **198** A4
Wembley HA0 . . . . **65** A4
Hillsborough SW19 . . . . . **179** A4
Hilldale Rd SM1 . . . . . . **217** B4
Hilldown Ct SW16 . . . . . **182** A3
Hilldown Rd Hayes BR2 . . . **208** D1
South Norwood SW16 . . . . **182** B3
Hill Dr London NW9 . . . . . **45** A1
Thornton Heath SW16 . . . **204** B6
Hilldrop Cres N7 . . . . . . **71** D3
Hilldrop La N7 . . . . **71** D3
Hilldrop Rd Bromley BR1 . . **187** B4
Kentish Town N7 . . . . . . **71** D3
Hill End Orpington BR6 . . . **227** D6
Shooters Hill SE18 . . . . **144** C4
Hillersdon Ave
Barnes SW13 . . . . **134** A3
Edgware HA8 . . . . **26** B5
Hillersdon Ho SW1 . . . . . **258** C2
Hillery Cl SE17 . . . . . . **262** D3
Hill Farm Rd W10 . . . . . . **90** D2
Hillfield Ave
Colindale NW9 . . . . **45** C5
Hornsey N8 . . . . **50** A5
Mitcham SM4 . . . . **202** C4
Wembley HA0 . . . . **66** B1
Hillfield Cl HA2 . . . . . . **42** A5
Hillfield Ct NW3 . . . . . . **70** C3
Hillfield Ho N5 . . . . . . **73** A3
Hillfield La WD23 . . . . . . **8** D5
Hillfield Lo SW17 . . . . . **180** D5
Hillfield Mans NW3 . . . . . **70** C3
Hillfield Par SM4 . . . . . **202** B3
Hillfield Park Mews N10 . . . **49** B5
Hillfield Pk London N10 . . . **49** B5
Southgate N21 . . . . **16** C2
Hillfield Rd
Hampton TW12 . . . . **173** B2
West Hampstead NW6 . . . . **69** C3
Hillgate Pl Balham SW12 . . **159** B4
Kensington W8 . . . . **113** C5 **245** A4
Hillgate St W8 . . . . **245** A4
Hill Gate Wlk N6 . . . . . . **49** C3
Hill Gr TW13 . . . . **151** B2
Hill Ho Southall UB1 . . . . **85** C1
Stanmore HA7 . . . . **9** A1
Upper Clapton E5 . . . . . **52** B1
Woolwich SE28 . . . . . . **123** C5
Hill House Ave HA7 . . . . . **24** D3
Hill House Cl N21 . . . . . **16** C4
Hill House Dr TW12 . . . . . **173** C2
**Hill House International Jun
Sch** SW1 . . . . **114** D3 **257** D5
Hill House Mews BR2 . . . . **182** B5
Hilliard Ct SM6 . . . . . . **219** D2
Hilliard Ho 15 E1 . . . . . **118** B5
Hilliard's Ct E1 . . . . . **118** C5
Hillier Cl EN5 . . . . **13** D5
Hillier Gdns CR0 . . . . . . **220** C3

Hillier Ho 1 NW1 . . . . . . **71** D1
Hillier Lo TW12 . . . . . . **174** B5
Hillier Pl KT9 . . . . . . **213** D2
Hillier Rd SW11 . . . . . . **158** D5
Hilliers Ave UB8 . . . . . . **82** C4
Hillier's La CR0, SM6 . . . . **220** A5
HILLINGDON **82** D5
Hillingdon Ave TW19 . . . . **148** A3
Hillingdon Circus UB10 . . . **60** D2
HILLINGDON HEATH **82** D2
Hillingdon Hill UB10 . . . . **82** B4
Hillingdon Hospl UB8 . . . . **82** B2
Hillingdon Manor Sch
UB8 . . . . **82** D2
Hillingdon Manor Upper Sch
UB3 . . . . **83** D1
Hillingdon Par 6 UB10 . . . **82** D3
Hillingdon Prim Sch
UB10 . . . . **82** D4
Hillingdon Rd UB10 . . . . . **82** A5
Hillingdon St SE17 . . . . . **138** D6
Hillingdon Sta UB10 . . . . **60** D3
Hillington Gdns IG8 . . . . **37** D1
Hill La HA4 . . . . **39** A1
Hill Lo SW11 . . . . **136** B1
Hillman Cl UB8 . . . . **60** A3
Hillman Dr 12 NW10 . . . . . **90** C3
Hillman St E8 . . . . **74** B2
Hillmarton Rd N7 . . . . . . **72** A3
Hillmead Dr SW9 . . . . . . **138** D1
Hill Mead Prim Sch 23
SW9 . . . . **138** D1
Hillmont Rd KT10 . . . . . . **212** C5
Hillmore Ct SE13 . . . . . . **142** B2
Hillmore Gr SE26 . . . . . . **185** A5
Hill Rd Carshalton SM5 . . . **218** C2
Finchley N10 . . . . **30** D2
Harrow HA1 . . . . **43** A4
Mitcham CR4 . . . . **181** B3
Pinner HA5 . . . . **41** A3
St John's Wood
NW8 . . . . . . **92** A5 **229** B3
Sutton SM1 . . . . **217** D3
Wembley HA0 . . . . **65** B5
Hillreach SE7, SE18 . . . . **122** B1
Hillrise KT12 . . . . **193** D2
Hill Rise
East Finchley NW11 . . . . **47** D5
Enfield N9 . . . . **18** B5
Forest Hill SE23 . . . . . **162** B3
Greenford UB6 . . . . **86** A6
Hinchley Wood KT10 . . . . **213** B6
Richmond TW10 . . . . . . **153** D6
Ruislip HA4 . . . . **39** B1
Hillrise Mans N19 . . . . . **50** A2
Hillrise Rd N19 . . . . . . **50** A2
Hillsboro Rd SE22 . . . . . **161** C6
Hillsborough Ct 13 NW6 . . . **91** D6
Hillside 6 SM1 . . . . . . **218** B3
Hillsgrove Cl DA16 . . . . . **146** C5
Hillsgrove Prim Sch
DA16 . . . . **146** C5
Hillside Barnet EN5 . . . . **14** A6
Crouch End N8 . . . . **49** D3
Greenwich SE10 . . . . . . **142** B5
Kingsbury NW9 . . . . **45** B5
Stonebridge NW10 . . . . . **89** B6
Wimbledon SW19 . . . . . . **178** D4
Hillside Ave London N11 . . **30** D4
Wembley HA9 . . . . **66** B4
Woodford IG8 . . . . **37** C5
Hillside Cl Merton SM4 . . . **201** A5
St John's Wood NW8 . . . . **91** B5
Woodford IG8 . . . . **37** C5
Hillside Cres Enfield EN2 . . **5** B5
Harrow HA2 . . . . **42** A1
Northwood HA6 . . . . **22** A2
Hillside Ct
Hampstead NW3 . . . . **69** D3
7 Kingston u T KT2 . . . **176** D3
Hillside Dr HA8 . . . . . . **26** C5
Hillside Gdns
Chipping Barnet EN5 . . . . **1** A1
Edgware HA8 . . . . **26** B6
Friern Barnet N11 . . . . . **31** C4
Harrow HA3 . . . . **44** A2
Highgate N6 . . . . **49** B3
Northwood HA6 . . . . **22** B2
Streatham SW2 . . . . . . **160** C2
Wallington SM6 . . . . . . **219** C1
Walthamstow E17 . . . . . . **54** B6
Hillside Glen CR0 . . . . . **220** B4
Hillside Gr Hendon NW7 . . . **28** A3
Southgate N14 . . . . **15** D4
Hillside Ho CR0 . . . . . . **220** B4
Hillside Jun & Inf Schs
HA6 . . . . **22** A3
Hillside La BR2 . . . . . . **224** D6
Hillside Mans EN5 . . . . . . **1** B1
Hillside Rd
Beckenham BR2 . . . . . . **208** D6
Belmont SM2 . . . . **217** B1
Croydon CR0 . . . . **220** D4
Ealing W5 . . . . **88** A2
Northwood HA6, HA5 . . . . **22** B3
Southall UB1 . . . . **85** C3
South Tottenham N15 . . . . **51** C3
Streatham SW2 . . . . . . **160** C2
Surbiton KT5 . . . . **198** C4

Hillside Rise HA6 . . . . . . **22** A3
Hillsleigh Rd
W14 . . . . . . **113** B5 **244** D4
Hillsley DA14 . . . . **190** A6
Hills Mews 2 W5 . . . . . . **110** A6
Hills Pl W1 . . . . **239** A1
Hill's Rd IG9 . . . . **21** B3
Hill St Mayfair W1 . . **115** B5 **248** C4
Richmond TW10 . . . . . . **153** D6
Hillstone Ct 5 E3 . . . . . **97** D3
Hillstowe St E5 . . . . . . **74** C5
Hilltop 7 E17 . . . . **53** D6
Hill Top Cheam SM3 . . . . . **201** B2
East Finchley NW11 . . . . **47** D5
Hilltop Ave NW10 . . . . . . **67** A1
Hilltop Ct
12 London SW18 . . . . . **136** B1
South Hampstead NW8 . . . . **70** A1
South Norwood SE19 . . . . **183** B2
Hilltop Gdns Hendon NW4 . . **28** B1
Orpington BR6 . . . . **227** C6
Hilltop Ho 7 N6 . . . . . . **49** D2
Hilltop Rd NW6 . . . . **69** C1
Hilltop Way HA7 . . . . **9** A1
Hillview SW20 . . . . **178** B3
Hill View Mitcham CR4 . . . **204** A5
Primrose Hill NW1 . . . . . **230** D6
Hillview Ave HA3 . . . . . . **44** A4
Hillview Cl Pinner HA5 . . . **23** B4
Wembley HA9 . . . . **66** B6
Hillview Cres
Orpington BR6 . . . . . . **211** D1
Redbridge IG1 . . . . **56** B3
Hillview Ct SE19 . . . . . . **183** C6
Hill View Dr Bexley DA16 . . **145** C3
Woolwich SE28 . . . . . . **123** C5
Hillview Gdns Harrow HA2 . . **41** C5
Hendon NW4 . . . . **46** D5
Hill View Gdns NW9 . . . . . **45** B4
Hillview Rd
Carshalton SM1 . . . . . . **218** B5
Chislehurst BR7 . . . . . **188** D6
Mill Hill NW7 . . . . **28** D6
Pinner HA5 . . . . **23** B4
Hill View Rd
Claygate KT10 . . . . . . **213** A1
Orpington BR6 . . . . **227** D6
Twickenham TW1 . . . . . . **153** A5
Hillway Highgate N6 . . . . **71** A6
London NW9 . . . . **45** C1
Hill Wood Ho NW1 . . . . . . **232** C3
Hillworth 7 BR3 . . . . . . **185** D1
Hillworth Rd SW2 . . . . . . **160** C4
Hillyard Rd W7 . . . . **86** C2
Hillyard St SW9 . . . . . . **138** C4
Hillyfield E17 . . . . **35** A1
Hillyfield Cl E9 . . . . . . **75** A3
Hillyfield Prim Sch E17 . . . **53** A6
Hilly Fields Cres SE4 . . . **141** C2
Hilly Mead SW19 . . . . . . **179** A3
Hilsea Point 7 SW15 . . . . **156** B3
Hilsea St E5 . . . . **74** C4
Hilton Ave N12 . . . . **30** B5
Hilton Ho 4 Ealing W13 . . . **87** C1
12 Finchley N2 . . . . . . **30** B1
Lower Holloway N7 . . . . . **72** A4
9 Nunhead SE4 . . . . . . **140** D1
Hilversum Cres 10 SE22 . . . **161** C6
Himley Rd SW17 . . . . . . **180** D4
Hinchley Manor KT10 . . . . **212** D5
Hinchley Cl KT10 . . . . . . **212** D5
Hinchley Dr KT10 . . . . . . **212** D5
Hinchley Way KT10 . . . . . **213** A5
HINCHLEY WOOD **213** A6
Hinchley Wood Prim Sch
KT10 . . . . **213** A6
Hinchley Wood Sch
KT10 . . . . **212** D5
Hinckley Rd SE15 . . . . . . **140** A1
Hind Ct EC4 . . . . **241** B1
Hinde Mews W1 . . . . **238** B2
Hindes Rd HA1 . . . . **42** C4
Hinde St W1 . . . . . . **93** A1 **238** B2
Hind Gr E14 . . . . **97** C1
Hindhead Cl UB8 . . . . . . **82** D2
Hindhead Gdns UB5 . . . . . **85** A6
Hindhead Gn WD19 . . . . . . **22** C5
Hindhead Point 6
SW15 . . . . **156** B3
Hindhead Way SM6 . . . . . . **220** A3
Hind Ho
13 Deptford SE14 . . . . . **140** D6
Islington N7 . . . . **72** C4
Hindhurst Ct NW9 . . . . . . **45** A5
Hindle Ho E8 . . . . **73** D3
Hindley Ho N7 . . . . **72** B5
Hindlip Ho SW8 . . . . **269** C1
Hindmans Rd SE22 . . . . . . **162** A6
Hindmans Way RM9 . . . . . **103** B3
Hindmarsh Cl E1 . . . . . . **118** A6
Hindrey Rd E5 . . . . **74** B6
Hindsley's Pl SE23 . . . . . **162** C2
Hines Ct HA1 . . . . **43** A4
Hinkler Rd HA3 . . . . **43** D6
Hinksey Path SE2 . . . . . . **124** D3
Hinstock NW6 . . . . **91** D6
Hinstock Rd SE18 . . . . . . **145** A5
Hinton Ave TW4 . . . . . . **128** D1

Hinton Cl SE9 . . . . **166** A3
Hinton Ct 3 E10 . . . . . . **75** D6
Hinton Rd Brixton SE24 . . . **138** D2
Edmonton N18 . . . . **33** C6
Wallington SM6 . . . . . . **219** C2
Hippisley Ct TW7 . . . . . . **130** D2
Hippodrome Mews W11 . . . . **244** B5
Hippodrome Pl W11 . . . . . **244** B5
Hirst Cres HA9 . . . . **66** A5
Hirst Ct SW1 . . . . **258** C1
Hispano Mews 17 EN3 . . . . . **7** C6
Hitcham Rd E17 . . . . **53** B2
Hitchcock Cl TW17 . . . . . **192** B6
Hitchin Sq E3 . . . . **97** A5
Hithe Gr 15 SE16 . . . . . **118** C3
Hitherbroom Rd UB3 . . . . . **106** A6
Hither Farm Rd SE3 . . . . . **143** C2
Hitherfield Prim Sch
SW16 . . . . **160** C2
Hitherfield Rd
Dagenham RM8 . . . . **81** A6
Streatham SW16, SW27 . . . **160** C1
HITHER GREEN **164** C5
Hither Green La SE13 . . . . **164** B5
Hither Green Prim Sch
SE13 . . . . **164** B5
Hither Green Sta SE13 . . . **164** C5
Hitherlands SW12 . . . . . . **159** B2
Hitherwell Dr HA3 . . . . . **24** B2
Hitherwood Ct SE21 . . . . . **183** D6
Hitherwood Dr SE19 . . . . . **183** D6
Hive Cl WD23 . . . . **8** B2
Hive Rd WD23 . . . . **8** C2
Hive Wood Ho E7 . . . . **77** A2
**HM Prison Wormwood
Scrubs** W12 . . . . **90** A1
HMS Belfast* SE1 . . . . . . **253** B4
Hoadly Rd SW16 . . . . . . **159** D2
Hobart Cl East Barnet N20 . . **14** C2
Hayes UB4 . . . . **84** D3
Hobart Ct Harrow HA1 . . . . **42** C2
Woodford IG8 . . . . **36** D6
Hobart Dr UB4 . . . . **84** D3
Hobart Gdns CR7 . . . . . . **205** B6
Hobart Ho 24 KT6 . . . . . . **198** A4
Hobart La UB4 . . . . **84** D3
Hobart Pl
Richmond TW10 . . . . . . **154** B4
Westminster SW1 . . **115** B3 **258** C6
Hobart Rd Dagenham RM9 . . . **80** D4
Hayes UB4 . . . . **84** D3
North Cheam KT4 . . . . . **216** B5
Hobbayne Prim Sch W7 . . . . **86** D1
Hobbayne Rd W7 . . . . **86** B1
Hobbes Wlk SW15 . . . . . . **156** B6
Hobb's Ct SE1 . . . . **253** D2
Hobbs Gn N2 . . . . **48** A6
Hobbs Mews IG3 . . . . **79** D6
Hobbs' Pl N1 . . . . **95** C6
Hobbs Rd 5 SE27 . . . . . . **183** A6
Hobby St EN3 . . . . **18** D6
Hobday St E14 . . . . **97** D1
Hobhouse Ct SW1 . . . . . . **249** D5
Hoblands End BR7 . . . . . . **189** C4
Hobsons Pl 7 E1 . . . . . . **96** A2
Hobury St SW10 . . **136** B6 **266** C5
Hockenden La BR5, BR8 . . . **191** D1
Hocker St E2 . . . . **95** D4
Hockett Cl SE8 . . . . . . **119** B2
Hockington Ct 7 EN5 . . . . **13** D6
Hockley Ave E6 . . . . . . **100** A5
Hockley Ct 2 E18 . . . . . . **37** A2
Hockley Ho 4 E9 . . . . . . **74** C2
Hockley Mews IG11 . . . . . **101** C5
Hockliffe Ho 5 W10 . . . . . **90** C2
Hockney Ct 1 SE16 . . . . . **118** B1
Hockworth Ho 7 N16 . . . . . **51** C1
Hocroft Ave NW2 . . . . . . **69** B5
Hocroft Ct NW2 . . . . **69** B5
Hocroft Rd NW2 . . . . **69** B5
Hocroft Wlk NW2 . . . . . . **69** B5
Hodder Dr UB6 . . . . **86** D5
Hoddesdon Rd DA17 . . . . . **125** C1
Hodford Lo NW11 . . . . . . **69** C6
Hodford Rd NW11 . . . . . . **47** B1
Hodgkins Cl SE28 . . . . . . **124** D6
Hodgkins Mews HA7 . . . . . **25** B5
Hodister Cl 26 SE5 . . . . . **139** A5
Hodnet Gr SE16 . . . . . . **118** C2
Hodson Cl HA2 . . . . **63** B5
Hodson Pl EN3 . . . . **7** C5
Hoecroft Ct EN3 . . . . **6** C5
Hoe La EN1 . . . . **6** B5
Hoe St E17 . . . . **53** C4
Hoffman Gdns CR2 . . . . . . **222** B1
Hoffman Sq N1 . . . . **235** D2
Hofland Rd W14 . . . **113** A3 **254** A6
Hogan Mews W2 . . . . **236** C4
Hogan Way E5 . . . . **74** A6
Hogarth Ave TW15 . . . . . **171** A4
Hogarth Bsns Pk W4 . . . . . **133** C6
Hogarth Ct Ealing W5 . . . . **88** A2
Newham E16 . . . . **99** D2
Hogarth Cres
Mitcham SW19 . . . . . . **180** B2
Thornton Heath CR0 . . . . **205** A4
Hogarth Ct
8 Camden Town NW1 . . . . **71** C2
City of London EC3 . . . . **253** B6

Hogarth Ct continued
Dulwich SE19 . . . . 183 D6
Heston TW5 . . . . 129 A5
24 Whitechapel E1 . . . . 96 A1
Hogarth Gdns TW5 . . . . . . 129 C5
Hogarth Hill NW11 . . . . 47 B5
Hogarth Ho Enfield EN1 . . . 18 A6
12 Northolt UB5 . . . . 84 D5
1 Sutton SM1 . . . . 218 B3
Westminster SW1 . . . . 259 D3
6 West Norwood SE27 . . 183 A6
Hogarth Ind Est NW10. . . . 90 A3
Hogarth La W4 . . . . 133 C6
Hogarth Pl SW5 . . . . 255 C3
Hogarth Rd Barking RM8 . . . 80 B3
Earl's Ct SW5 . . . . 113 D2 255 C3
Edgware HA8 . . . . 26 C1
Hogarth Roundabout
W4. . . . . 133 C6
Hogarth's House ★ W4 . . 133 C6
Hogarth Way TW12. . . . . . 174 A2
Hogsmill Way KT19 . . . . . 215 A4
Holbeach Cl 8 NW9 . . . . . . 27 C2
Holbeach Gdns DA15. . . . . 167 D5
Holbeach Mews 1
SW12. . . . . 159 B3
Holbeach Prim Sch SE6 . 163 C4
Holbeach Rd SE6 . . . . 163 D4
Holbeck Row SE15. . . . . . 140 A5
Holbein Ho Chelsea SW1 . 258 A2
10 Stanmore HA7. . . . . 25 C5
Holbein Mews
SW1. . . . . 115 A1 258 A2
Holbein Pl SW1 . . . 115 A2 258 A3
Holberry Ho 5 SE21 . . . . . 183 C6
Holberton Gdns NW10 . . . . 90 B4
HOLBORN 94 C2
Holborn EC1 . . . . . . 94 C2 241 B3
Holborn Cir EC1 . . 94 C2 241 B3
Holborn Coll SE18 . . . . . . 121 D2
Holborn Ho 1 W12 . . . . 90 B1
Holborn Pl WC1 . . . . 240 C3
Holborn Rd E13. . . . . 99 B3
Holborn Sta WC1 . . 94 D2 240 C3
Holborn Viaduct
EC1. . . . . 94 D2 241 C3
Holborn Way CR4 . . . . . . 180 D1
Holbrook Cl Enfield EN1 . . . . 6 A5
Highgate N19 . . . . 49 B1
Holbrook Ct W7 . . . . 108 C6
Holbrooke Ct N7. . . . . 72 A4
Holbrook Ho 25 SW10 . . . 153 D6
Chislehurst BR7 . . . . 189 B2
5 Streatham SW2. . . . . . . 160 B3
Holbrook La BR7. . . . . 189 B3
Holbrook Rd E15. . . . . 98 D5
Holbrook Way BR2. . . . . . 210 B4
Holburne Cl SE3 . . . . 143 C4
Holburne Gdns SE3 . . . . . 143 D4
Holburne Rd SE3 . . . . 143 D4
Holcombe Hill NW7. . . . . . . 12 A1
Holcombe Ho SW9. . . . . . 138 A2
Holcombe Pl SE4 . . . . 141 A2
Holcombe Rd Ilford IG1. . . 156 C2
Tottenham Hale N17. . . . . . . 52 A6
1 Tottenham N17. . . . . 51 D6
Holcombe St W6. . . . . 112 B2
Holcote Cl DA17 . . . . 125 A3
Holcroft Ct W1 . . . . 239 A4
Holcroft Ho
Battersea SW11. . . . . 136 B2
Lewisham SE10 . . . . 142 A4
Holcroft Rd E9. . . . . 74 C1
Holden Ave
North Finchley N12. . . . . . . 29 D5
Welsh Harp NW9 . . . . 45 A1
Holdenby Rd SE4 . . . . 163 A6
Holden Cl RM8. . . . . 80 B5
Holden Ho
12 Deptford SE8. . . . . 141 C4
Islington N1 . . . . 235 A5
Holden Hts N12. . . . . 13 D1
Holdenhurst Ave N12 . . . . 30 A3
Holden Lo N11. . . . . 31 C5
Holden Point E15. . . . . 76 B2
Holden Rd East Barnet N11 . 13 B1
London N12 . . . . 29 D6
Holden St SW11 . . . . 137 A3
Holdernesse Rd
Isleworth TW7 . . . . 131 A4
6 Upper Tooting SW17 . . . 159 A2
Holderness Ho SE5 . . . . . 139 C2
Holderness Way SE27 . . . 182 D5
Holders Hill Ave NW4. . . . . 46 D6
Holders Hill Cres NW4 . . . . 28 D1
Holders Hill Dr NW4 . . . . . . 28 D1
Holders Hill Gdns NW4. . . . 29 A2
Holders Hill Par NW7 . . . . . 29 A2
Holders Hill Rd
Church End NW4. . . . . 29 A2
Hendon NW4 . . . . 28 D1
Holdsworth Ho 5 SW2. . . 160 C4
Holford Ho
6 Bermondsey SE16. . . . . 118 B2
Finsbury WC1 . . . . 233 D2
Holford Pl WC1 . . . . 233 D2
Holford Rd NW3 . . . . 70 A5
Holford St WC1 . . . . 234 A2
Holford Yd WC1 . . . . 234 A3

Holgate Ave SW11 . . . . . . 136 B2
Holgate Ct HA8 . . . . 26 B6
Holgate Gdns RM10 . . . . . . 81 C2
Holgate Rd RM10 . . . . 81 C3
Holgate St SE7 . . . . 121 D3
Holkham Ho 6 EN5. . . . . 1 A2
Hollam Ho N8 . . . . 50 B5
Holland Ave
Belmont SM2 . . . . 217 C1
Wimbledon SW20. . . . . . . 177 D2
Holland Cl
Coney Hall BR2. . . . . 224 D6
New Barnet EN5. . . . . 14 B4
Stanmore HA7 . . . . 25 B5
Holland Ct Ashford TW15. . 170 B4
Hendon NW7 . . . . 28 A4
6 Walthamstow E17 . . . . . . 54 A5
Holland Dr SE23 . . . . 163 A1
Holland Gdns
Brentford TW8 . . . . 132 A6
Kensington W14. . . . . 254 B6
Holland Gr SW9 . . . . 138 C5
Holland Ho E4 . . . . 36 A6
Holland House Sch SA8 . . . 26 D6
Holland Park
W11. . . . . 113 B5 244 C3
Holland Park Ave
Ilford IG3 . . . . 57 D4
Notting Hill W11. . . . 113 A5 244 B3
Holland Park Ct W14. . . . . 244 B2
Holland Park Gdns
W14. . . . . 113 A4 244 A2
Holland Park Mews
SW11. . . . . 113 B5 244 C3
Holland Park Pre Prep Sch
W14 . . . . 113 B3 254 C5
Holland Park Rd
W14. . . . . 113 B3 254 D5
Holland Park Rdbt W12 . . 112 D4
Holland Park Sch
W8 . . . . 113 B4 244 D2
Holland Park Sta
W11. . . . . 113 B5 244 C3
Holland Pas N1. . . . . 235 A6
Holland Pl W8 . . . . 245 C2
Holland Rd Croydon SE25. 206 A4
Newham E15 . . . . 98 C4
Wallend E6 . . . . 78 C1
Wembley HA0. . . . . 65 D2
West Kensington
W14 . . . . 113 A3 254 B6
Willesden Green NW10 . . . . 90 B5
Holland Rise Ho SW9 . . . . 270 D3
Holland St
Kensington W8. . . . . 113 C4 245 B2
Lambeth SE1. . . . . . 116 D3 251 D4
Hollands The
Feltham TW13 . . . . 172 D6
New Malden KT4 . . . . 199 D1
Holland Villas Rd
W14. . . . . 113 A4 244 A1
Holland Way BR2. . . . . . . 224 D6
Holland Wlk
Kensington W14. . . . 113 B4 244 D1
Stanmore HA7 . . . . 25 A5
Upper Holloway N19 . . . . . . 49 D1
Hollar Rd N16 . . . . 73 D5
Hollen St W1 . . . . 239 C2
Holles Cl TW12 . . . . 173 C5
Holles Ho 8 SW9. . . . . 138 C3
Holles St W1 . . . . . 93 B1 238 D2
Holley Rd W3. . . . . 111 C4
Hollickwood Ave N12 . . . . . 30 D4
Hollickwood JMI Sch
N10. . . . . 31 B3
Holliday Sq 6 SW11 . . . . . 136 B2
Hollidge Way RM10 . . . . . . 81 D1
Hollies Ave DA15. . . . . . . 167 D3
Hollies Cl
South Norwood SW16 . . . 182 C4
Twickenham TW1 . . . . 152 D2
Hollies End NW7. . . . . 28 B5
Hollies Rd W5 . . . . 109 C2
Hollies The Harrow HA3 . . . 43 A5
Oakleigh Pk N20. . . . . 14 B3
Upper Tooting SW12 . . . . . 159 C2
9 Wanstead E11. . . . . 55 A4
Wood Green N11 . . . . 31 D4
Hollies Way 1 SW12 . . . . 159 A4
Holligrave Rd BR1. . . . . . . 187 A2
Hollingbourne Ave DA7 . . 147 B4
Hollingbourne Gdns W13 . 87 B2
Hollingbourne Rd SE24 . . 161 A6
Hollingsworth Ct 7
KT6 . . . . 197 D2
Hollingsworth Rd CR0 . . . 222 B2
Hollington Cres KT3 . . . . . 199 D3
Hollington Ct BR7. . . . . . . 188 D4
Hollington Rd
Newham E6 . . . . 100 B4
Tottenham N17. . . . . 34 A1
Hollingworth Cl KT8 . . . . . 195 B5
Hollingworth Rd BR2,
BR5. . . . . 210 D2
Hollins Ho N7. . . . . 72 A4
Hollisfield WC1 . . . . 233 B1
Hollman Gdns SW16 . . . . . 182 D4
Holloway Ho 7 UB7. . . . . . 104 A1
Holloway La UB7. . . . . 104 B1
Holloway Rd Leyton E11. . . 76 B5

Holloway Rd continued
Lower Holloway N7 . . . . 72 B4
Newham E6 . . . . 100 B4
Upper Holloway N19 . . . . . . 71 D6
Holloway Road Sta N7 . . . 72 B3
Holloway Sch N7 . . . . 71 D3
Holloway St TW3. . . . . 129 D2
Hollow Combe SE20 . . . . . 184 B6
Hollowfield Wlk UB5. . . . . . 63 A2
Hollow The IG8 . . . . 36 D6
Holly Ave London N2 . . . . . 47 D6
Stanmore HA7 . . . . 26 A1
Walton-on-T KT12 . . . . 194 D1
Hollybank Cl TW12. . . . . . . 173 C5
Holly Berry La 8 NW3 . . . . . 70 A4
Hollybrake Cl BR7 . . . . 189 B3
Hollybush Cl Harrow HA3 . . 24 C2
Wanstead E11. . . . . 55 A4
Hollybush Gdns E2 . . . . 96 B4
Hollybush Hill E11. . . . . 54 D3
Holly Bush Hill NW3 . . . . . . 70 A4
Hollybush Ho 23 E2. . . . . . . 96 B4
Holly Bush La TW12 . . . . . 173 C3
Hollybush Pl E2 . . . . 96 B4
Hollybush Rd KT2. . . . . . . 176 A4
Hollybush St E13 . . . . 99 B4
Holly Bush Steps 6 NW3 . . 70 A4
Holly Bush Vale 10 NW3 . . 70 A4
Holly Cl Beckenham BR3 . . 208 A5
Buckhurst Hill IG9 . . . . 21 D1
Feltham TW13 . . . . 173 A5
Wallington SM6 . . . . 219 B1
Willesden NW10. . . . . 67 C1
Holly Cottage Mews UB8 . 82 C2
Holly Cotts KT7 . . . . 197 A1
Holly Cres
Beckenham BR3 . . . . 207 B4
Chingford IG8. . . . . 36 B3
Hollycroft Ave
Child's Hill NW3 . . . . 69 C5
Wembley HA9. . . . . 66 B5
Hollycroft Cl
Harmondsworth UB7 . . . . 126 C6
South Croydon CR2. . . . . 221 C3
Hollycroft Gdns UB7 . . . . 126 C6
Holly Ct 16 Belmont SM2. . 217 C1
Catford SE6 . . . . 164 A1
South Tottenham N15. . . . . 51 C5
Hollydale Cl UB5. . . . . 63 D4
Hollydale Dr BR2. . . . . 226 B5
Hollydale Prim Sch 7
SE15. . . . . 140 C3
Hollydale Rd SE15 . . . . . . 140 C3
Hollydene Bromley BR1 . . . 186 D2
Hither Green SE13. . . . . . . 164 B5
5 Peckham SE15. . . . . 140 B4
Hollydown Way E11. . . . . . . 76 B5
Holly Dr E4 . . . . 19 D4
Holly Farm Rd UB2. . . . . . 107 A1
Hollyfield Ave N11. . . . . 30 D5
Hollyfield Rd KT5 . . . . 198 B2
Hollyfield Sch & Sixth Form
Ctr The KT6 . . . . 198 A4
Holly Gdns UB7 . . . . 104 B4
Holly Gr Kingsbury NW9 . . . . 45 A2
Peckham SE15 . . . . 140 A3
Pinner HA5 . . . . 23 A2
Hollygrove WD23 . . . . 8 B4
Hollygrove Cl TW3. . . . . . . 129 B1
Hollyhedge Ho SE3 . . . . . . 142 B3
Holly Hedge Terr SE13. . . . 164 B6
Holly Hill Hampstead NW3 . 70 A4
Southgate N21 . . . . 16 B5
Holly Hill Rd DA8, DA17 . . 125 D1
Holly Ho Brentford TW8. . . 131 C6
Ilford IG3 . . . . 58 A1
Holly House (Private) Hospl
IG9 . . . . 21 B2
Holly Lo
Cottenham Pk SW20. . . . . 178 B1
Harrow HA1 . . . . 42 B4
Kensington W8. . . . . 245 A2
Southgate N21 . . . . 16 C3
4 Wimbledon SW19 . . . . . 179 A4
Holly Lodge
Lewisham SE13 . . . . 142 B1
Southall UB2. . . . . 107 B2
Holly Lodge Gdns N6 . . . . . 49 A1
Holly Lodge Mans N6 . . . . . 71 A6
Hollymead SM5. . . . . 218 D5
Holly Mews SW10 . . . . 256 B1
Holly Mount NW3 . . . . 70 A4
Hollymount Cl 9 SE10 . . . . 142 A4
Hollymount Sch SW20 . . . 178 C2
Holly Park Est N4 . . . . 50 B2
Holly Park Gdns N3 . . . . . . 47 C6
Holly Park JMI Sch N11 . . . 31 A5
Holly Park Rd Ealing W7. . . 108 C5
Friern Barnet N11 . . . . 31 A5
Holly Pk East Finchley N3 . . 47 C6
Hornsey N4. . . . . 50 B2
Holly Pl NW3 . . . . 70 A4
Holly Rd 6 Chiswick W4. . . 111 B2
Hampton TW12 . . . . 174 A4
Hounslow TW3 . . . . 129 D1
Leytonstone E11. . . . . 54 D2
Twickenham TW1 . . . . 153 A3
Holly St E8 . . . . 73 D1
Holly Terr N6 . . . . 49 A1

Hollytree SW19 . . . . 156 D3
Holly Tree Ho SE4 . . . . 141 B2
Holly Tree Lo EN2 . . . . 4 D3
Hollyview CN W4. . . . . 46 A3
Holly Village N6 . . . . 71 B6
Holly Way CR4 . . . . 203 D6
Holly Wlk Enfield EN2 . . . . . 5 B2
Hampstead NW3 . . . . 70 A4
Hollywood CW5. . . . . 175 A4
Hollywood Gdns UB4. . . . . 84 B1
Hollywood Lofts E1. . . . . . 243 C5
Hollywood Mews SW10 . . 266 A6
Hollywood Rd
Chelsea SW10 . . 136 A6 266 A6
Highams Pk E4 . . . . 35 A5
Hollywood Way IG8. . . . . . . 36 B6
Holman Ho 2 E2. . . . . 96 D4
Holman Hunt Ho W14 . . . . 254 A1
Holman Rd London SW11 . 136 B3
West Ewell KT19. . . . . 215 A3
Holmbank Dr TW17. . . . . . 193 C5
Holmbridge Gdns EN3 . . . . . 6 D1
Holmbrook NW1. . . . . 232 B3
Holmbrook Dr NW4. . . . . . . 46 D4
Holmbury Cl WD23. . . . . 8 C2
Holmbury Ct
Mitcham SW19. . . . . 180 C3
Upper Tooting SW17. . . . . 158 D1
Holmbury Gdns UB3 . . . . . 105 D5
Holmbury Gr CR0. . . . . 223 B1
Holmbury Ho SW9 . . . . . . 160 D6
Holmbury Manor 9
DA14. . . . . 190 A6
Holmbury Pk BR7. . . . . 188 A3
Holmbury View 2 E5. . . . . . 52 B1
Holmbush Ct NW4 . . . . 46 D4
Holmbush Rd SW15. . . . . . 157 A5
Holmcote Gdns N5 . . . . 73 A3
Holmcroft Ho 10 E17. . . . . . 53 D5
Holmcroft Way BR2. . . . . . 210 B4
Holm Ct SE12. . . . . 165 B1
Holmdale Gdns NW4. . . . . . 46 D4
Holmdale Rd
Chislehurst BR7 . . . . 189 A5
South Hampstead NW6 . . . . 69 C3
Holmdale Terr N15. . . . . 51 C3
Holmdene N12 . . . . 29 D5
Holmdene Ave
Harrow HA2 . . . . 41 D6
Hendon NW7 . . . . 28 A4
Herne Hill SE24 . . . . 161 A6
Holmdene Ct BR3. . . . . 186 A1
Holmdene Ho BR1. . . . . . . 210 A6
Holmead Rd
SW6. . . . . 135 D5 265 D3
Holme Ct 12 TW7 . . . . 131 A2
Holmefield Ct 4 NW3. . . . . . 70 C2
Holmefield Ho W10 . . . . 91 A3
Holme Lacey Rd SE12 . . . . 164 D5
Holmeleigh Ct EN3 . . . . 6 C1
Holme Rd E6 . . . . 100 A4
Holmes Ave Mill Hill NW7 . . 29 A5
Walthamstow E17 . . . . 53 B6
Holmes Cl SE22. . . . . 140 A1
Holmes Ct Chingford E4 . . . 20 B2
18 South Acton W4. . . . . . 111 A3
18 South Lambeth SW4 . . 138 A3
Holmesdale Ave SW14 . . . 132 C5
Holmesdale Cl SE25 . . . . . 205 B4
Holmesdale Ho 12 NW6 . . . 91 C6
Holmesdale Rd
Bexley DA7. . . . . 146 D3
Highgate N6 . . . . 49 B2
Richmond TW9 . . . . 132 B4
South Norwood SE25 . . . . 205 C5
Teddington TW11 . . . . 175 C4
Thornton Heath CR0. . . . . 205 B4
Holmesley Rd SE23 . . . . . 163 A5
Holmes Pl SW10 . . . . 266 B6
Holmes Rd
Kentish Town NW5 . . . . 71 B3
Merton SW19. . . . . 180 A3
Twickenham TW1 . . . . 152 D2
Holmes Terr SE1. . . . . 251 A2
Holmeswood 1 SM2. . . . . 217 D1
Holmeswood Ct 3 N22 . . . . 32 C1
Holme Way HA7 . . . . 24 D4
Holmewood Gdns SW2. . . 160 B4
Holmewood Rd
South Norwood SE25 . . . . 205 C6
Streatham SW2 . . . . 160 B4
Holmfield Ave NW4 . . . . 46 D4
Holmfield Ho E17 . . . . 54 B5
Holm Gr UB10 . . . . 60 C1
Holmhurst London SE13 . . 164 B5
Wimbledon SW19. . . . . . . 178 C3
Holmhurst Rd DA17. . . . . . 125 D1
Holmlea Ct CR0 . . . . 220 D5
Holmleigh Prim Sch N16. . 51 C1
Holmleigh Rd N16 . . . . 51 C1
Holm Oak Cl SW15 . . . . . . 157 B5
Holmoaks Ho BR3 . . . . 186 A1
Holmsbury Ho 6 N7. . . . . . . 71 D3
Holmsdale Ho
6 London N11. . . . . 31 B6
24 Poplar E14. . . . . 119 D6
Holmshaw Cl SE26. . . . . . . 185 A6
Holmside Ct SW12 . . . . . . 159 A5
Holmside Rd SW12. . . . . . 159 A5
Holmsley Cl KT3 . . . . 199 D2

Hog–Hol 343

Holmsley Ho SW15. . . . . . 155 D4
Holmstall Ave HA8 . . . . 27 A1
Holmstall Par HA8 . . . . 27 A1
Holm Wlk SE3 . . . . 143 A3
Holmwood 2 KT5 . . . . 198 B3
Holmwood Cl
Cheam SM2 . . . . 216 D1
Harrow HA2 . . . . 42 A6
Northolt UB5 . . . . 63 D2
Holmwood Ct
Kingston u T KT3. . . . . 199 B6
Sidcup DA14. . . . . 189 D5
3 Stamford Hill N16 . . . . . . 51 D2
Holmwood Gdns
London N3 . . . . 29 C1
Wallington SM6 . . . . 219 B2
Holmwood Gr NW7 . . . . 27 B5
Holmwood Mans W3. . . . . 110 C5
Holmwood Rd
Chessington KT9 . . . . 214 A3
Ilford IG3 . . . . 79 C6
Holne Chase London N2. . . 48 A3
Morden SM4. . . . . 201 C3
Holne Lo N6. . . . . 49 C3
Holness Rd E15. . . . . 76 D2
Holocaust Meml Gdn ★
W2 . . . . 114 D3 247 D2
Holroyd Rd SW15 . . . . 156 C6
Holsgrove Ct W3. . . . . 111 C5
Holstein Way 6 DA18. . . . . 125 A3
Holst Mans SW13 . . . . 134 C5
Holstock Rd IG1 . . . . 79 A6
Holsworth Cl HA2 . . . . 42 A4
Holsworthy Ho 49 E3. . . . . . 97 D4
Holsworthy Sq WC1. . . . . 240 D5
Holsworthy Way KT9. . . . . 213 C3
Holt Cl London N10. . . . . . . 49 A5
Sidcup DA14. . . . . 191 A6
Woolwich SE28. . . . . 124 C6
Holt Ct SE10. . . . . 142 A6
Holt Ho SW2. . . . . 160 C5
Holtoake Ct 1 W5. . . . . 87 C3
Holtoake Ho 3 W5 . . . . 87 C3
Holt Rd Newham E16. . . . . 122 A5
Wembley HA0. . . . . 65 C5
Holt The Morden SM4 . . . . 201 C5
Wallington SM6 . . . . 219 C4
Holtwhite Ave EN2. . . . . 5 A3
Holtwhite's Hill EN2 . . . . . . 4 D4
Holwell Pl HA5 . . . . 41 A5
Holwood Park Ave BR2,
BR6. . . . . 226 B4
Holwood Pl 7 SW4 . . . . . . 137 D1
Holybourne Ave SW15 . . . 156 A4
Holy Cross Prep Sch
KT2. . . . . 177 A2
Holy Cross Prim Sch
SW6 . . . . 135 C4 265 A2
Holy Cross RC Prim Sch
SE6 . . . . 164 A3
Holy Cross Sch The 4
KT3. . . . . 199 C4
Holy Family RC Prim Sch
Kidbrooke SE9 . . . . 143 C1
28 Poplar E14. . . . . 119 C6
Holy Family Tech Coll
E17. . . . . 54 A5
Holy Ghost RC Prim Sch 4
SW12 . . . . 159 A4
Holyhead Cl Bow E3. . . . . . 97 C4
3 Newham E6. . . . . 100 B2
Holyhead Ct KT1. . . . . 197 D5
Holy Innocents RC Prim Sch
BR6. . . . . 227 D5
Holyoake Ct SE16. . . . . . . 119 B4
Holyoake Wlk Ealing W5 . . . 87 C2
East Finchley N2. . . . . 48 A6
Holyoak Rd SE11. 116 D2 261 D3
Holyport Rd SW6 . . . . 134 D5
Holyrood Ave HA2 . . . . 63 B4
Holyrood Gdns HA8. . . . . . . 26 D1
Holyrood Ho N4 . . . . 51 A1
Holyrood Mews
6 Greenwich SE7 . . . . 121 A1
10 Newham E16. . . . . 121 A5
Holyrood Rd EN5. . . . . 14 B5
Holyrood St SE1 . . 117 C5 253 A3
Holy Trinity CE Jun Sch 1
SM6 . . . . 219 C4
Holy Trinity CE Prim Sch
Belgravia SW1 . . . . 115 A2 258 A4
Dalston E8 . . . . 73 D2
East Finchley N2. . . . . 48 B6
10 Forest Hill SE26. . . . . . 162 C2
12 Hampstead NW3. . . . . . 70 A2
Richmond TW10 . . . . 132 C1
Streatham SW2 . . . . 160 B4
Wimbledon SW19. . . . . . . 179 D4
Holy Trinity Coll Prep Sch
BR1. . . . . 187 C2
Holy Trinity Lamorbey CE
Prim Sch DA15 . . . . 168 A4
Holy Trinity & Saint Silas CE
Prim Sch 22 NW1. . . . . 71 B1
Holywell Cl
35 Bermondsey SE16. . . . 118 B1

Holywell Cl continued
2 Greenwich SE3 . . . . 143 A6
Stanwell TW19 . . . . 148 A3
Holywell La EC2 . . . . **243 B6**
Holywell Lo EN2 . . . . 4 B5
Holywell Row EC2 . .95 C3 **243 A5**
Holywell Way TW19 . . . . . .148 A3
Homan Ct N12. . . . . 30 A6
Homan Ho 6 SW4 . . . . . . 159 D4
Homebush Ho E4 . . . . .19 D4
Homecedars Ho WD23 . . . . . 8 B3
Home Cl Carshalton SM5. . 218 D6
Northolt UB5 . . . . 85 B4
Homecoppice Ho 1
BR1. . . . . 186 D3
Homecroft Rd
Forest Hill SE26 . . . . . . 184 C5
Tottenham N22. . . . . 33 A2
Homecross Ho 7 W4 . . . . 111 B2
Homedale Ho SM1. . . . . . 217 D4
Home Ct KT6 . . . . 197 D4
Homefarm Rd W7. . . . . . . .86 D1
Homefield SM4. . . . . 201 C5
Home Field EN5 . . . . .13 B6
Homefield Ave IG2. . . . . . . 57 C4
Homefield Cl Hayes UB4. . .84 D3
Willesden NW10. . . . . 67 A2
Homefield Ct NW4 . . . . . . 46 C5
Homefield Gdns
London N2 . . . . 48 B6
Mitcham CR4, SW19. . . . 180 B1
Homefield Ho SE23 . . . . . 162 D1
Homefield Pk SM1, SM2. . 217 D2
Homefield Pl 4 SW19. . . . 178 D5
Homefield Prep Sch
SM1. . . . . 217 C3
Homefield Rd
Bromley BR1. . . . . 187 C2
Burnt Oak HA8 . . . . 27 B4
Chiswick W4 . . . . 111 D1
Walton-on-T KT12 . . . . . 195 A2
Wembley HA0. . . . . 65 B4
Wimbledon SW19. . . . . . 179 A4
Homefield St 14 N1. . . . . . 95 C5
Homefirs Ho HA9 . . . . 66 B5
Homeheather Ho 5 IG4 . .56 B4
Homelands Dr SE19. . . . . 183 C3
Home Lea BR6. . . . . 227 D3
Homeleigh Ct 8 SW16. . . 160 A1
Homeleigh Rd SE15. . . . . 162 D6
Homemead SW12. . . . . . . .159 B2
Home Mead HA7. . . . . 25 C2
Homemead Rd
Bromley BR2. . . . . 210 B4
Wallington CR0. . . . . 203 C3
Home Office SW1. . . . . . . .259 D5
Home Park Rd SW19. . . . . 157 B1
Home Park Terr KT1. . . . . 175 D1
Home Park Wlk KT1. . . . . 197 D5
Home Rd SW11. . . . . .136 C3
Homer Dr E14 . . . . 119 C2
Homer Rd Croydon CR0. . . 206 D3
Homerton E9 . . . . 75 A2
Homer Row W1. . . . . .237 B3
Homersham Rd KT1. . . . . 176 D1
Homer St W1. . . . . .92 C2 **237 B3**
HOMERTON 74 D1
Homerton Ct 2 EN4 . . . . . 14 D3
Homerton Gr E9. . . . . 74 D3
Homerton High St E9 . . . . 74 D3
Homerton Ho E9. . . . . 75 B3
Homerton Row E9 . . . . 74 C3
Homerton Sta E9. . . . . 74 D2
Homerton Terr E9. . . . . 74 C3
Homerton University Hospl
E9. . . . . 74 D3
Homesdale Cl E11. . . . . . . 55 A4
Homesdale Rd
Bromley BR1, BR2. . . . . 209 C6
Orpington BR5. . . . . 211 C2
Homesfield NW11 . . . . .47 C4
**Homes Of Rest (CE
Temperance Society)**
IG1. . . . . 79 B5
Homestall Rd SE22. . . . . . .162 C6
Homestead Ct EN5. . . . . . .13 C6
Homestead Gdns KT10 . . 212 C3
Homestead Paddock N14 .15 B6
Homestead Pk NW2. . . . . . .67 D5
Homestead Rd
Dagenham RM8 . . . . .81 B6
Fulham SW6 . . . . 135 B5 **264 D3**
Homesteads The BR3 . . . . 185 D4
Homestead The N11. . . . . .31 A3
Homewalk Ho 1 SE26 . .184 C6
Homewaters Ave TW16. . . 171 D2
Homewillow Cl N21. . . . . . .16 D5
Homewood Cl TW12 . . . . . 173 B4
Homewood Cres BR7 . . . . 189 C4
Homewood Gdns SE25 . . . 205 C4
Homewoods 2 SW12 . . . . 159 C4
Homildon Ho 10 SE26 . . .162 A1

Homington Ct KT2. . . . . . . .176 A3
Honduras St EC1. . . . .**242 A6**
Honeybourne Rd NW6. . . . .69 D3
Honeybourne Way BR5. . .211 B1
Honeybrook Rd SW12,
SW4. . . . . 159 C4
Honey Cl RM10 . . . . .81 D2
Honeycroft Hill UB10. . . . . .60 A1
Honeyden Rd DA14 . . . . . . 191 A4
Honeyfield N4. . . . . .72 C6
Honey Hill UB10 . . . . .60 B1
Honey La EC2. . . . .**242 B1**
Honey Lane Ho SW10 . . . .**265 D6**
Honeyman Cl NW6. . . . . . . .68 D1
Honeypot Bsns Ctr HA7 . . .26 A2
Honeypot Cl NW9. . . . . .44 B5
Honeypot La
Stanmore HA3, HA7, NW9 . .44 B6
Stanmore HA7 . . . . .25 D3
Honeysett Rd 3 N17. . . . . .33 D1
Honeysuckle Cl UB1 . . . . . 107 A6
Honeysuckle Ct Ilford IG1. .78 D2
2 Lee SE12. . . . . 165 A4
6 Sutton SM2. . . . . 217 D2
Honeysuckle Gdns CR0. . . 206 D1
Honeywell Jun & Inf Schs 3
SW11. . . . . 158 D5
Honeywell Rd SW11. . . . . . 158 D5
Honeywood Ho 5 SE15 . .140 A4
Honeywood Rd
Harlesden NW10. . . . . . . .89 D5
Isleworth TW7 . . . . 131 A1
Honeywood Wlk SM5 . . . . 218 D4
Honister Cl HA7 . . . . .25 B2
Honister Gdns HA7 . . . . . . .25 B2
Honister Pl HA7 . . . . .25 B2
Honiton Gdns
Edgware NW7 . . . . .28 D3
1 Nunhead SE15. . . . . . 140 C3
Honiton Ho 29 SE5. . . . . . 139 A3
Honiton Rd Bexley DA16. . 145 D3
Kilburn NW6. . . . . .91 B5
Honley Rd SE6. . . . . 163 D4
Honnor Gdns TW7 . . . . 130 B3
HONOR OAK 162 C6
Honor Oak Park Sta
SE23. . . . . 162 D5
Honor Oak Pk SE23 . . . . . 162 D5
Honor Oak Rd SE23 . . . . . 162 C4
Honor Oak Rise SE23. . . . 162 C5
Honwell Ho 20 W2. . . . . . . .91 C2
Hood Ave East Barnet N14 . .15 B5
Mortlake SW14 . . . . 155 A6
Hood Cl CR0. . . . . 204 D1
Hoodcote Gdns N21 . . . . . .16 D4
Hood Ct N7. . . . . .72 B5
Hood Ho 17 SE5. . . . . 139 B5
Hood Lo E11. . . . . .77 B6
Hood Rd SW20. . . . . 177 D3
HOOK. 214 A4
Hook KT6 . . . . 214 A5
Hooke Ct SE10. . . . . 142 A4
Hooke Ho 32 E3. . . . . .97 A5
Hooker's Rd E17 . . . . .52 B6
Hook Farm Rd BR2. . . . . . 209 D4
Hookham Ct SW8. . . . .**269 C2**
Hook Ho 8 SW27. . . . . . . 182 D5
Hooking Gn HA2. . . . . .41 D4
Hook La DA16. . . . . 146 A1
Hook Lane Prim Sch
DA16. . . . . 146 A2
Hook Rd KT19, KT17 . . . . . 215 A1
Hook Rise N
Surbiton KT6. . . . . 214 A5
Tolworth KT6 . . . . 214 D6
Hook Rise S KT6, KT9 . . . . 214 D6
Hook Rise S Ind Est KT6. . 214 C5
Hook Rise South KT6. . . . . 214 A5
KT6. . . . . 214 C5
Hooks Cl SE15 . . . . 140 B4
Hookstone Way IG8. . . . . . .37 D3
Hook The EN5 . . . . .14 B5
Hook Underpass KT6. . . . . 214 A5
Hook Wlk HA8. . . . . .27 A4
Hooper Dr UB8 . . . . .82 D2
Hooper Ho 9 SW18. . . . . . 157 B6
Hooper Rd E16 . . . . .99 A1
Hooper's Ct SW1 . . . .**247 C1**
Hooper's Mews 4 W3 . . . 111 A5
Hooper St E1. . . . . .96 A1
Hoop La NW11. . . . . .47 C2
Hoover Ho 6 SE6. . . . . . . 186 A6
Hope Cl
2 Brentford TW8 . . . . . . 110 A1
Canonbury N1. . . . . .73 A2
Dagenham RM8. . . . . . . .58 D5
Grove Pk SE12 . . . . 165 B1
Sutton SM1. . . . . 218 A3
1 Woodford IG8. . . . . . . .37 C4
Hope Ct 5 SE1. . . . . 118 A1
Hopedale Rd SE7 . . . . 143 B6
Hopefield 3 W7. . . . . 108 D5
Hopefield Ave NW6 . . . . . . .91 A5
Hope Gdns 10 W3. . . . . . . 110 D4
Hope Pk BR1. . . . . 186 D3
Hopes Cl TW5 . . . . 129 C6
Hope St SW11 . . . . 136 B2
Hopetown St E1. . . . .**243 D1**

Hopewell Sch IG11. . . . . . . .79 B2
Hopewell St SE5. . . . . 139 B5
Hop Gdns WC2. . . . .**250 A5**
Hopgood St 5 W12 . . . . . . 112 C5
Hopkins Cl N10. . . . . .31 A3
Hopkins Ho 17 E14. . . . . . .97 C1
Hopkins Mews E15 . . . . . . .98 D6
Hopkinson's Pl NW1 . . . . .**231 A6**
Hopkins Rd E10. . . . . .53 D2
Hopkins St W1. . . . . .93 D1 **239 C1**
Hopley Ho W13 . . . . 109 B6
Hoppers Rd N21. . . . . .16 C2
Hoppett Rd E4. . . . . .20 C2
Hopping La N1. . . . . .72 D2
Hoppingwood Ave KT3. . . 199 C6
Hoppner Rd UB4. . . . . .83 B5
Hop St SE10 . . . . 120 D2
Hopton Ct BR2. . . . . 209 A1
Hopton Gdns KT3. . . . . 200 A3
Hopton Ho 5 SW9. . . . . . . 138 D3
Hopton Par 2 SW16 . . . . . 182 A5
Hopton Rd
Streatham SW16. . . . . . 182 A5
Woolwich SE18. . . . . . . 122 D3
Hopton's Gdns SE1 . . . . . .**251 D2**
Hopton St SE1. . . 116 D5 **251 D4**
Hoptree Cl N12. . . . . .29 D6
Hopwood Cl SW17 . . . . . . 158 A1
Hopwood Rd SE17 . . . . . . 139 B6
Hopwood Wlk E8. . . . . .74 A1
Horace Rd Forest Gate E7. . .77 B4
Ilford IG6 . . . . 57 A6
Kingston u T KT1. . . . . . 198 B6
Horatio Ho
13 Haggerston E2 . . . . . .95 D5
4 Merton SW19 . . . . . . 179 D3
Horatio Pl
9 Canary Wharf E14 . . . 120 A5
Merton SW19 . . . . 179 C2
Horatio St 11 E2. . . . . .95 D5
Horatius Way CR0. . . . . . . .220 D2
Horbury Cres
W11. . . . . .113 C6 **245 A5**
Horbury Lo TW12 . . . . 173 C3
Horbury Mews
W11. . . . . .113 B6 **244 D5**
Horder Rd SW6. . .135 A4 **264 B1**
Hordle Prom E 15 SE15 . . 139 C5
Hordle Prom N 4 SE15. . . 139 C5
Hordle Prom S 7 SE15. . . 139 D5
Horizon Bldg 22 E14 . . . . .119 C6
Horizon Ind Est SE15. . . . 140 A5
Horizon Sch N16. . . . . .73 C4
Horle Wlk SE5. . . . . 138 D3
Horley Cl DA6 . . . . 169 C6
Horley Rd SE9 . . . . 188 A6
Hormead Rd W9 . . . . .91 B3
Hornbeam Cl
Barking IG11 . . . . .102 B3
Buckhurst Hill IG9 . . . . . .21 D1
Edgware NW7 . . . . .11 D1
Ilford IG1. . . . . .79 B3
Lambeth SE11. . . . .**261 A4**
Northolt UB5 . . . . .63 B3
Hornbeam Cres TW8 . . . . . 131 B5
Hornbeam Gdns KT3. . . . . 200 A3
Hornbeam Gr E4. . . . . .20 D1
Hornbeam Ho
1 Buckhurst Hill IG9. . . . .21 D1
2 Maitland Pk NW3 . . . . .70 D2
6 Penge SE20. . . . . 184 D3
5 Sidcup DA15 . . . . 168 A1
Hornbeam La E4. . . . . .20 C6
Hornbeam Rd
Buckhurst Hill IG9 . . . . . .21 D1
Hayes UB4. . . . . .84 C2
Hornbeam Sq 8 E3. . . . . . .97 B6
Hornbeams Rise N11. . . . . .31 A4
Hornbeam Terr SM5. . . . . . 202 C1
Hornbeam Way BR2. . . . . . 210 C3
Hornblower Cl 2 SE16 . . .119 A2
Hornbuckle Cl HA2 . . . . . . .64 B6
Hornby Cl NW3 . . . . .70 B1
Hornby Ho
6 Kennington SE11. . . . 138 C6
13 Richmond TW10 . . . . 153 C1
Horncastle Cl SE12. . . . . . 165 A4
Horncastle Rd SE12. . . . . . 165 A4
Hornchurch N17. . . . . .33 B1
Hornchurch Cl KT2 . . . . . . 175 D6
Horndean Cl 3 SW15. . . . 156 A3
Horne Ho 4 SE18. . . . . . . 144 A4
Horner Ct E11 . . . . .76 B5
Horne Rd TW17 . . . . 192 C5
Horner La 3 CR4 . . . . 180 B1
Horne Way SW15 . . . . 134 C3
Hornfair Rd SE7 . . . . 143 D5
Horniman Dr SE23. . . . . . . 162 C4
Horniman Grange 7
SE23. . . . . 162 C3
Horniman Mus & Gdns★
SE23. . . . . 162 B3
Horniman Prim Sch
SE23. . . . . 162 B3
Horning Cl SE9 . . . . 188 A6
Horn La Acton W3 . . . . .89 A1
Greenwich SE10. . . . . . 121 A2
Woodford IG8. . . . . .37 A3

Horn Link Way SE10. . . . . 121 A2
Horn Park Cl SE12 . . . . . . 165 B6
Horn Park La SE12. . . . . . . 165 B5
Horn Park Prim Sch
SE12. . . . . 165 B4
Hornsby House Sch 7
SW12 . . . . 159 A3
Horns Croft IG11 . . . . .79 C1
Hornscroft Cl IG11. . . . . . . .79 C1
Horns End Pl HA5. . . . . .40 C4
HORNSEY. 50 A5
Hornsey La N6. . . . . .49 C2
Hornsey Lane Gdns N6. . . .49 C2
Hornsey Park Rd N8. . . . . . .50 B6
Hornsey Rd N7, N19 . . . . . .72 B6
Hornsey Rise Gdns N19 . . .50 A2
Hornsey Sch for Girls N8. .50 B4
Hornsey St N7 . . . . .72 B3
Hornsey Sta N8. . . . . .50 B5
HORNSEY VALE. 50 B4
Hornshay St SE15. . . . . . . 140 C6
Horns Rd IG2, IG6. . . . . . . .57 A4
Hornton Ct W8. . . . .**245 B1**
Hornton Pl W8. . . . .**245 B1**
Hornton St W8 . . . .113 C4 **245 B2**
Horrocks Ho SW15. . . . . . . 156 B6
Horsa Rd Eltham SE12. . . . 165 C4
Erith DA8 . . . . 147 D5
Horsebridge Cl RM9 . . . . . 103 A6
Horsecroft Rd HA8. . . . . . . .27 B3
Horse & Dolphin Yd W1 . .**249 D6**
Horse Fair KT1 . . . . 175 D1
Horseferry Pl SE10. . . . . . 142 A6
Horseferry Rd
Limehouse E14. . . . . . . 119 A6
Westminster SW1 115 D2 **259 D4**
Horseferry Rd Est SW1. . .**259 C5**
Horse Guards Ave
SW1. . . . . .116 A5 **250 A3**
Horse Guards Par★
SW1. . . . . .115 D5 **249 D3**
Horse Guards Rd
SW1. . . . . 115 D4 **249 D2**
Horse Leaze E6. . . . . 100 C1
Horsell Rd Islington N5. . . .72 C3
St Paul's Cray BR5 . . . . 190 B2
Horselydown La
SE1 . . . . .117 D5 **253 C3**
Horselydown Mans 1 . . . .**253 C2**
Horsemongers Mews
SE1 . . . .**252 B1**
Horsenden Ave UB6. . . . . . .64 D3
Horsenden Cres UB6. . . . . .64 D3
Horsenden La N UB6. . . . . .64 D1
Horsenden La S UB6 . . . . . .87 A6
Horsenden Prim Sch
UB6. . . . . .64 C2
Horsendon Ho 11 N7. . . . . .71 D3
Horseshoe Cl
Cubitt Town E14 . . . . . . 120 A1
Dollis Hill NW2 . . . . .68 B6
Horse Shoe Cres UB5 . . . . .85 C5
Horseshoe Dr UB8 . . . . .82 C1
Horse Shoe Gn SM1. . . . . . 217 D6
Horseshoe La Barnet N20 . .12 D3
Enfield EN2. . . . . .5 A2
Horse Yd N1. . . . .**234 D6**
Horsfall Gdns 1 SE9 . . . . 166 A6
Horsfeld Rd SE9 . . . . 165 D6
Horsford Rd SW2 . . . . 160 B6
Horsham Ave N12. . . . . .30 C5
Horsham Ct N17. . . . . .34 A2
Horsham Rd Bexley DA6. . 169 C6
East Bedfont TW14. . . . . 149 A5
Horsley Ct SW1. . . . .**259 D3**
Horsley Dr
Kingston u T KT2 . . . . . . 175 D5
New Addington CR0. . . . 224 A1
Horsley Ho 11 SE4 . . . . . . 140 D1
Horsley Rd Bromley BR1. . 187 B2
Chingford E4. . . . . .20 A2
Horsley St 3 SE17. . . . . . 139 B6
Horsman Ho SE5. . . . . 139 A6
Horsman St SE5. . . . . 139 A6
Horsmonden Cl BR6 . . . . . 211 D2
Horsmonden Rd SE4. . . . . 163 B5
Horston Ho N4 . . . . .51 A2
Hortensia Ho SW10 . . . . . .**266 A4**
Hortensia Rd
SW10. . . . . 136 A5 **266 A4**
Horticultural Pl 6 W4 . . . 111 B1
Horton Ave NW2. . . . . .69 A4
Horton Bridge Rd UB7 . . . 104 B5
Horton Cl UB7. . . . . 104 B5
Horton Ctry Pk KT19 . . . . . 214 C1
Horton Ho
13 Deptford SE15. . . . . 140 C6
South Lambeth SW8. . . . .**270 C4**
West Kensington W14 . . .**254 A1**
Horton Ind Pk UB7. . . . . . . 104 B5
Horton La KT19 . . . . 215 A1
Horton Par UB7. . . . . 104 A5
Horton Rd Hackney E8 . . . .74 B2
Yiewsley UB7 . . . . 104 B5
Horton Road Ind Est
UB7. . . . . 104 B5
Horton St SE13. . . . . 141 D2
Horton Way CR0. . . . . 206 D4
Hortus Rd Chingford E4. . . .20 A2

Hortus Rd continued
Southall UB2. . . . . 107 B4
Horwood Ho
24 Bethnal Green E2. . . .96 B4
Marylebone NW8. . . . . . .**237 B6**
Hosack Rd SW12, SW17. . 159 A2
Hoser Ave SE12. . . . . 165 A2
Hosier La EC1. . . . . .94 D2 **241 D3**
Hoskins Cl UB3 . . . . 105 D1
Hoskin's Cl E16. . . . . .99 C1
Hoskins St SE10 . . . . 120 B1
Hospital Bridge Rd TW2. . 151 D3
Hospital Bridge Rdbt
TW2. . . . . 151 D2
**Hospital of the Holy Trinity
(Almshouses)** 5 CR0. . .221 A6
Hospital Rd
Hounslow TW3 . . . . 129 C2
Leytonstone E10, E11. . . .54 B4
Hospital Way SE13. . . . . . 164 B4
Hospl for Tropical Diseases
NW1. . . . . .93 C3 **239 B5**
**Hospl of St John & St
Elizabeth** NW8 . .92 B5 **229 C3**
Hotham Cl KT8. . . . . 195 C6
Hotham Prim Sch SW15. . 134 D1
Hotham Rd Merton SW19. . 180 A3
Putney SW15. . . . . 134 C2
Hotham Road Mews 12
SW19. . . . . 180 A3
Hotham St E15 . . . . .98 C6
Hothfield Pl SE16 . . . . 118 C3
Hotspur Ind Est N17 . . . . . .34 B4
Hotspur Rd UB5 . . . . .85 C5
Hotspur St SE11 . .116 C1 **261 A2**
Houblon Rd TW10. . . . . 154 A6
Houghton Cl
10 Dalston E8. . . . . .73 D2
Hampton TW12. . . . . 173 A4
Houghton Rd N15. . . . . .51 D5
Houghton Sq SW9 . . . . . . 138 A2
Houghton St WC2. . . . .**240 D1**
Houlder Cres CR0. . . . . . . .220 D2
Houndsden Rd N21. . . . . . . .16 C5
Houndsditch EC3. .95 C1 **243 B2**
Houndsfield Prim Sch N9 .18 B4
Houndsfield Rd N9. . . . . . . .18 B4
HOUNSLOW. 129 C3
Hounslow Ave TW3 . . . . . . 151 D6
Hounslow Bsns Pk TW3 . . 129 C1
Hounslow Central Sta
TW3. . . . . 129 D2
Hounslow Ctr The TW3. . . 129 D2
Hounslow East Sta TW3. . 130 A3
Hounslow Gdns TW3. . . . . 151 D6
**Hounslow Heath Jun & Inf
Schs** TW4. . . . . 129 A2
**Hounslow Heath Nature
Reserve** TW4. . . . . 151 A5
Hounslow Manor Sch
TW3. . . . . 130 A2
Hounslow Rd
Feltham TW14. . . . . 150 B4
Hanworth TW13 . . . . . . 151 A2
Twickenham TW2, TW3. . 152 A5
Hounslow Sta TW3. . . . . . . 151 D6
Hounslow Town Prim Sch
TW3. . . . . .130 B2
Hounslow Urban Farm★
TW14. . . . . 150 A6
HOUNSLOW WEST 128 D2
Hounslow West Sta
TW3. . . . . 129 A3
Household Cavalry Mus★
SW1. . . . .**250 A3**
Houseman Way 20 SE5. . . 139 B5
House Mill The★ E3. . . . . . .98 A4
Houses of Parliament★
SW1. . . . . .116 A3 **260 B6**
Houston Ct 3 CR0. . . . . . . 205 C1
Houston Pl KT10. . . . . 196 C1
Houston Rd
Forest Hill SE23. . . . . . . 163 A1
Thames Ditton KT6. . . . . 197 B3
Houstoun Ct TW5 . . . . 129 B5
Hove Ave E17. . . . . .53 B4
Hoveden Rd NW2 . . . . .69 A3
Hove Gdns SM1. . . . . 201 D1
Hovenden Ho 6 SE21. . . . 183 C6
Hoveton Rd SE28. . . . . 102 C1
Howard Ave DA5. . . . . 168 C4
Howard Bldg SW8 . . . .**268 C5**
Howard Cl Acton W3. . . . . . .88 D1
Ashford TW16. . . . . 171 D4
Brunswick Pk N11 . . . . . .15 A2
Bushey WD23 . . . . .8 C4
Cricklewood NW2. . . . . . .69 A4
Hampton TW12. . . . . 174 A4
Howard Ct
12 Barking IG11. . . . . . . 101 B6
Beckenham BR3. . . . . . . 186 A1
Lewisham SE10 . . . . 142 A4
Peckham SE15 . . . . 140 A2
Howard Ho
6 Brixton SW9 . . . . 138 C2
14 Deptford SE8. . . . . . . 141 B6
Fitzrovia W1 . . . .**238 D5**
Penge SE20 . . . . 184 C2
6 Upper Clapton E5. . . . .74 C6
Howard Mans E17 . . . . .53 D6

Howard Mews N5.........72 D4
Howard Prim Sch CR0.. 221 A4
Howard Rd Barking IG11 .101 B6
Cricklewood NW2......68 D4
Croydon SE25......206 A3
Ilford IG1......78 D4
Isleworth TW7......130 D2
Leyton E11......76 C5
Newham E6......100 B5
New Malden KT3......199 D5
Penge SE20......184 C2
Plaistow BR1......187 A3
Southall UB1......85 D1
South Tottenham N15....51 C3
Surbiton KT5......198 B3
Walthamstow E17......53 D6
Howards Cl N......22 B1
Howards Crest Cl BR3..186 A1
Howard's La SW15......134 C1
Howard's Rd E13......99 A4
Howard St KT7......197 B3
Howard Way EN5......12 D6
Howarth Rd SE2......124 A2
Howberry Cl HA8......25 D4
Howberry Rd
South Norwood CR7......183 B1
Stanmore HA7, H8......25 D4
Howbury Rd SE15......140 C2
Howcroft Cres N3......29 C3
Howcroft Ho E3......97 B4
Howcroft La UB6......86 B4
Howden Cl SE28......124 D6
Howden Ct SE25......183 D1
Howden Rd SE25......183 D1
Howden St SE15......140 A2
Howell Cl RM6......58 D4
Howell Ct E10......53 D2
Howell Ho N7......71 D3
Howell Wlk SE1......261 D1
Howe Lo TW1......153 A4
Howerd Way SE18......144 A4
Howes Cl N3......47 C6
Howeth Ct N11......31 A4
Howfield Pl SE6......51 D6
Howgate Rd SW14......133 B2
Howick Mans SE18......122 A3
Howick Pl SW1......115 C3 259 B3
Howie St SW11......136 C5 267 A3
Howitt Cl Maitland Pk NW3....70 C2
Stoke Newington N16......73 C4
Howitt Rd NW3......70 C2
Howland Ho SW16......160 A1
Howland Mews E W1......239 A4
Howland St W1......93 C2 239 B4
Howland Way SE16......119 A4
Howletts La HA4......39 A3
Howletts Rd SE24......161 A1
Howley Pl W2......92 A2 236 B4
Howley Rd CR0......221 A5
Howmic Ct TW1......153 C5
Howsman Rd SW13......134 A6
Howson Rd SE4......141 A1
Howson Terr TW10......154 A5
How's St E2......95 D5
Howton Pl WD23......8 B3
HOXTON......95 C5
Hoxton Mkt N1......95 C4
Hoxton Point EC1......95 C4
Hoxton Sq N1......95 C4
Hoxton St N1......95 C5
Hoxton Sta E2......95 D5
Hoylake Cres UB10......60 D6
Hoylake Gdns
Mitcham CR4......203 C6
Ruislip HA4......40 B1
South Oxhey WD19......22 D6
Hoylake Rd W3......89 C1
Hoyland Cl SE15......140 B5
Hoyle St SW17......180 C5
Hoy St E16......98 D1
Hubbard Dr KT9......213 D2
Hubbard Rd SE27......183 A6
Hubbards Cl UB8......82 D1
Hubbard St E15......98 C6
Hub Buildings The
SW12......159 B3
Hub E15 E15......97 D5
Huberd Ho SE1......262 D6
Hubert Gr SW9......138 A2
Hubert Ho NW8......237 A5
Hubert Rd E6......99 D4
Hucknall Ct NW8......236 C6
Huddart St E3......97 B2
Huddleston Cl E2......96 C5
Huddleston Rd
Forest Gate E7......76 C4
Willesden NW2......68 B2
Huddleston Rd N7......71 C4
Hudson NW9......24 D7
Hudson Cl Newham E15....99 A6
Shepherd's Bush W12....112 B6
Hudson Ct Croydon SE25..206 A5
Isle Of Dogs E14......119 C1
Merton SW17......179 D3
Hudson Ho Chelsea SW10 266 A4
Notting Hill W11......91 A1
Hudson Pl SE18......123 A1

Hudson Rd Erith DA7....147 B4
Harlington UB7......127 B6
Hudsons Ho N1......235 D1
Hudson's Pl SW1..115 C2 259 A4
Hudson Way N9......18 C2
Huggin Ct EC4......252 B6
Huggin Hill EC4......252 B6
Huggins Ho E3......97 C4
Huggins Pl SW2......160 B3
Hughan Rd E15......76 B3
Hugh Astor Ct SE1......261 D6
Hugh Clark Ho W13....109 A5
Hugh Dalton Ave SW6....264 C5
Hughenden Ave HA3......43 B4
Hughenden Gdns UB5....84 C4
Hughenden Ho NW8......237 A6
Hughenden Rd KT4......200 A2
Hughendon EN5......1 D1
Hughendon Terr E15......76 A4
Hughes Cl N12......30 A5
Hughes Ho Bethnal Green E2....96 C4
Camberwell SE5......139 A4
Deptford SE8......141 C6
Newington SE17......261 D3
Hughes Mans E1......96 A3
Hughes Rd Ashford TW15..171 A4
Hayes UB3......106 B6
Hughes Terr E16......98 D2
Hughes Wlk CR0......205 A2
Hugh Gaitskell Cl SW6....264 C5
Hugh Gaitskell Ho
Stoke Newington N16....73 D6
Willesden NW10......67 D1
Hugh Herland KT1......198 A6
Hugh Mews SW1......258 D3
Hugh Morgan Ho
SW4......137 D2
Hugh Myddelton Prim Sch
EC1......94 C4 234 B1
Hugh Platt Ho E2......96 B5
Hugh St SW1......115 B2 258 D3
Hugo Ho SW1......257 D6
Hugon Rd SW6......135 D2
Hugo Rd N19......71 C4
Huguenot Ct E1......96 A2
Huguenot Pl
London SW18......158 A6
Spitalfields E1......243 D4
Huguenot Sq SE15......140 B2
Hullbridge Mews N1......235 C6
Hull Cl SE16......118 D5
Hull Ct SE5......139 B3
Hull Pl E16......123 A5
Hull St EC1......235 A1
Hulme Pl SE1......252 B1
Hulse Ave IG11......79 C2
Humber Ct W7......86 B1
Humber Dr W10......90 D3
Humber Rd Dollis Hill NW2..68 B3
Greenwich SE3......142 D6
Humberstone Rd E13....99 C4
Humberton Cl E9......75 A3
Humber Trad Est NW2....68 B6
Humbolt Rd W6......135 A6 244 A4
Hume Ct N1......72 D1
Hume Ho W11......112 D5
Humes Ave W7......108 D4
Hume Terr E16......99 B1
Hume Way HA4......40 A3
Humphrey Ct SW11......266 D1
Humphrey St
SE1......117 D1 263 C2
Humphries Cl RM9......81 B4
Humphry Ho SW15......156 D6
Hundred Acre NW9......27 D1
Hungerdown E4......20 A3
Hungerford Bridge WC2..250 C4
Hungerford Ho SW1......269 B6
Hungerford La WC2......250 B4
Hungerford Prim Sch
N7......71 D2
Hungerford Rd
Camden Town N7......71 D2
Lower Holloway N7......72 A3
Hungerford St E1......96 B1
Hunsdon Cl RM9......81 A2
Hunsdon Ho E5......74 B5
Hunsdon Rd SE14......140 D5
Hunstanton Ho NW1......237 B4
Hunston Rd SM4......201 D1
Hunt Cl W11......112 D5
Hunt Ct London N14......15 B4
Northolt UB5......84 D5
Hunter Cl Borehamwood WD6....11 A6
Borough The SE1......262 D5
Upper Tooting SW12....159 A3
Wallington SM6......220 A1
Huntercombe-Roehampton
Hospl The SW15......156 A4
Huntercrombe Gdns
WD19......22 C5
Hunter Ct London SE5....139 B1
Streatham SW2......160 C4
Wanstead E11......55 A4
Hunter Ho Bloomsbury WC1....240 B6
Feltham TW14......150 A3

Hunter Ho continued
Lambeth SE1......251 D1
South Lambeth SW8....269 D3
Tufnell Pk N19......71 C5
West Brompton SW5....255 B1
Hunterian Mus★
WC2......94 B1 240 D2
Hunter Lo W9......91 C2
Hunter Rd
South Norwood CR7....205 B6
Wimbledon SW20......178 C2
Hunters Cl SW9......153 D6
Hunters Gr Harrow HA3....43 C5
Hayes UB3......106 A4
Hunter's Gr BR6......227 A4
Hunters Hall Prim Sch
RM10......81 D3
Hunters Hall Rd RM10....81 D3
Hunters Hill HA4......62 D5
Hunters Lo
Edgware HA8......26 D5
Sidcup DA15......168 A1
Hunters Mdw SE19......183 C6
Hunters Rd
Chessington KT9......214 A4
Ilford IG1......78 D3
Hunters Sq RM10......81 C4
Hunter St WC1......94 A3 240 B6
Hunters The E3......186 A2
Hunters Way Enfield EN2....4 C4
South Croydon CR0....221 C4
Hunter Wlk
Borehamwood WD6......11 B6
Newham E13......99 A5
Huntingdon Cl
Mitcham CR4, SW16....204 A5
Northolt UB5......63 C2
Huntingdon Ct
Barnet EN5......1 B2
Mortlake SW14......133 A2
Huntingdon Gdns
Chiswick W4......133 A5
North Cheam KT4......216 C5
Huntingdon Ho NW5....255 B4
Huntingdon Rd
East Finchley N2......48 C6
Edmonton N9......18 C3
Huntingdon St
Canning Town E16......98 D1
Islington N1......72 B1
Huntingfield CR0......223 B1
Huntingfield Rd SW15....156 A6
Huntingford Ho SW15....134 C3
Hunting Gate Cl EN2......4 C2
Hunting Gate Dr KT9....214 A1
Hunting Gate Mews
Sutton SM1......217 D5
Twickenham TW2......152 C3
Huntings Farm IG1......79 C6
Huntings Rd RM10......81 C2
Huntington Ho NW2......68 C2
Huntley Cl TW19......148 A4
Huntley Ho SE21......183 C6
Huntley St WC1......93 D3 239 C5
Huntley Way SW20......178 A1
Huntly Dr N3......29 C4
Huntly Rd SE25......205 C5
Hunton St E1......96 A2
Hunt Rd UB2......107 C3
Hunts Cl SE3......143 A3
Hunt's Ct WC2......249 D5
Huntshaw Ho E3......97 D4
Hunt's La E15......98 A5
Huntsman Cl TW13......172 B6
Huntsman St SE17......263 A3
Hunts Mead EN3......6 D2
Hunts Medde Cl BR7....188 B3
Huntsmoor Rd KT19....215 B3
Huntspill St SW17......158 A1
Hunts Slip Rd SE21......161 C2
Huntsworth Ct SE6......163 C3
Huntsworth Mews
NW1......92 D3 237 C5
Huon Ct N20......14 C2
Hurdwick Ho NW1......232 A4
Hurdwick Pl NW1......232 A4
Hurleston Ho SE8......119 B1
Hurley Cres SE16......118 D4
Hurley Ct S1......87 C1
Hurley Ho Lambeth SE11....261 B3
Shoreditch E2......95 D4
Hurley Lo SE22......162 C5
Hurley Rd UB6......85 D2
Hurlingham Bsns Pk
SW6......135 C2
Hurlingham & Chelsea Sec
Sch SW6......135 C2
Hurlingham Court Mans
SW6......135 C3
Hurlingham Ct SW6......135 B2
Hurlingham Gdns SW6....135 B2
Hurlingham Rd
Erith DA7......147 B5
Fulham SW6......135 B3
Hurlingham Sch SW15....135 B1
Hurlingham Sq SW6....135 D2
Hurlock St N5......72 D5
Hurlstone Rd SE25......205 C4
Hurn Court Rd TW5......128 D3

Hurn Ct TW5......128 D3
Huron Cl BR6......227 D2
Huron Rd SW17......159 A1
Hurren Cl SE3......142 C2
Hurricane Rd SM6......220 B1
Hurricane Trad Ctr NW9...28 A2
Hurry Cl E15......76 C1
Hursley Ct KT6......197 D2
Hurst Ave Chingford E4....19 C1
Highgate N6......49 C3
Hurstbourne KT10......212 D2
Hurstbourne Cotts DA5...169 D4
Hurstbourne Gdns IG11...79 C2
Hurstbourne Ho SW15....155 D5
Hurstbourne Priors CR2..221 C2
Hurstbourne Rd SE23....163 A3
Hurst Cl Chessington KT9...214 C3
Chingford E4......19 C1
Hampstead Garden Suburb
NW11......47 D3
Hayes BR2......208 D1
Northolt UB5......63 B3
Hurstcombe IG9......21 A2
Hurstcourt Rd SM1......217 D6
Hurst Ct Beckenham BR3..185 C3
Newham E6......99 D2
South Norwood SE25....205 D5
Woodford IG8......37 B4
Hurstdene Ave BR2......208 D1
Hurstdene Gdns N15......51 C2
Hurstfield BR2......209 A4
Hurstfield Cres UB4......83 C2
Hurstfield Rd KT8......195 C6
Hurst Gr KT12......193 C1
Hurst Ho Penge SE26......184 B1
Pentonville WC1......233 D2
West Hampstead SE2....124 D1
Hurst La
East Molesey KT8......196 A6
West Heath SE2......124 D1
Hurst Lo SW9......91 C1
Hurst Lo Hounslow N8....49 D3
Wembley HA0......66 B1
Hurstmead Ct HA8......26 D6
Hurstmere Foundation Sch
DA15......168 C3
HURST PARK......174 A1
Hurst Park Prim Sch
KT8......195 C6
Hurst Pl Erith SE2......146 D6
Woolwich SE2......124 C1
Hurst Pool The KT8......195 C6
Hurst Prim Sch DA5......168 D3
Hurst Rd Buckhurst Hill IG9..21 D3
Croydon CR0......221 B3
East Molesey KT8, KT12...195 C6
Sidcup DA5, DA15......168 C3
Southgate N21......16 C3
Walthamstow E17......53 D6
Walton-on-T KT8&KT12...194 D5
Hurst Rise EN5......1 C2
Hurst Springs DA5......169 A3
Hurst St SE24......160 D5
Hurst View Grange CR2...220 D1
Hurst View Rd CR2......221 C1
Hurst Way CR2......221 C2
Hurstway Wlk W11......112 D6
Hurstwood Ave
Sidcup DA5......169 A3
Wanstead E18......55 B5
Hurstwood Ct
Colney Hatch N12......30 C4
Temple Fortune NW11....47 B1
Hurstwood Dr BR1......210 B6
Hurstwood Rd NW11......47 B5
Hurtwood Rd KT12......195 B2
Husbourne Ho SE8......119 A2
Huson Cl NW3......70 C1
Hussain Cl HA1......64 D4
Hussars Ct TW4......129 A2
Husseywell Cres BR2....209 A4
Hutchings St E14......119 C4
Hutching's Wharf
E14......119 C4
Hutchings Wlk NW11......47 D5
Hutchins Cl E15......76 A1
Hutchins Ho SW4......159 D4
Hutchinson Ct RM6......58 D5
Hutchinson Ho SE14....140 D5
Hutchinson Terr HA9......65 D5
Hutchins Rd SE28......124 A5
Hutton Cl Greenford UB6...64 B3
Woodford IG8......37 B4
Hutton Ct Ealing W5......87 C2
Edmonton N9......16 D6
Finsbury Pk N4......50 B1
Hutton Gdns HA3......24 A3
Hutton Gr N12......29 D5
Hutton Ho E2......96 A4
Hutton La HA3......24 A3
Hutton Row HA8......27 A3
Hutton St EC4......241 B1
Hutton Wlk HA3......24 A3
Huxbear St SE4......163 B6
Huxley Cl UB5......85 A6
Huxley Dr RM6......58 B2
Huxley Gdns NW10......88 B5
Huxley Ho
London SW9......138 B3
Paddington NW8......236 D5

Huxley Ho continued
West Heath SE2......124 D1
Huxley Par N18......33 B5
Huxley Pl N13......16 D1
Huxley Rd Edmonton N18...33 C6
Falconwood DA16......145 D2
Leyton E10......76 A6
Huxley Sayze N18......33 B5
Huxley South N18......33 B5
Huxley St W10......91 A4
Hyacinth Cl
Hampton TW12......173 C4
Ilford IG1......78 D2
Hyacinth Ct HA5......40 C6
Hyacinth Dr UB10......60 A1
Hyacinth Rd SW15......156 A3
Hyde Ashford TW16......171 C4
Barnet EN5......1 B2
Newham E13......99 A5
Hyde Cres NW9......45 C4
Hyde Ct Forest Hill SE23...163 A2
Hounslow TW4......151 B6
Kingsbury NW9......45 B2
Whetstone N20......14 B1
Hyde Estate Rd NW9......45 D4
Hyde Farm Mews SW12...159 D3
Hydefield Cl N21......17 B3
Hydefield Ct N9......17 C2
Hyde Ho Ealing W13......109 A5
Hounslow TW3......130 A2
Hyde Ind Est The NW9....45 D4
Hyde La SW11......136 C4 267 A2
Hyde Park★ W2......114 D5 247 C3
Hyde Park Ave N21......17 B3
Hyde Park Cnr SW1......248 B5
Hyde Park Corner Sta
SW1......115 A4 248 B2
Hyde Park Cres
W2......92 C1 237 A1
Hyde Park Gate Mews
SW7......246 B1
Hyde Park Gdns
Bayswater W2......114 B6 246 D6
Edmonton N21......17 A3
Hyde Park Gdns Mews
W2......114 C6 247 A6
Hyde Park Mans NW1....237 A3
Hyde Park Pl W2......247 B6
Hyde Park Sq W2..92 C1 237 A1
Hyde Park Square Mews
W2......237 A1
Hyde Park St W2..92 C1 237 A1
Hyde Park Twrs W2......246 A5
Hyderabad Way E15......76 C1
Hyde Rd Bexleyheath DA7..147 B3
Richmond TW10......154 B6
Shoreditch N1......95 C6
Hyde Sch The NW9......45 D4
Hydeside Gdns N9......17 D2
Hyde's Pl N1......72 D1
Hyde St SE8......141 C6
Hyde Terr TW15, TW16...171 C4
HYDE THE......45 D4
Hydethorpe Ave N9......17 D2
Hydethorpe Rd SW12....159 C3
Hyde Vale SE10......142 A5
Hyde Way Edmonton N9....17 D2
Hayes UB3......105 D2
Hyde Wlk SM4......201 C2
Hydon Ct N11......30 D5
Hyh Ho E17......35 D2
Hyland House Sch E17....36 B1
Hylands Rd E17......36 B1
Hylda Ct NW5......71 A5
Hylton St SE18......123 D2
Hyndewood SE23......162 D1
Hyndman Ho
Dagenham RM10......81 C5
Tufnell Pk N19......71 D4
Hyndman St SE15......140 B6
Hynton Rd RM8......80 C6
Hyperion Ho Bow E3......97 A5
Streatham SW2......160 B4
Hyrstdene CR0......220 D4
Hyrst The CR0......207 A1
Hyson Rd SE16......118 B1
Hythe Ave DA7......147 B5
Hythe Cl N18......34 A6
Hythe Ho London SE16....118 C4
South Norwood CR7....183 A1
Hythe Road Ind Est
NW10......90 A3
Hyver Hill NW7......11 B4

I

Ian Ct SE23......162 C2
Ian Hamilton Ho NW1....232 C2
Ianson Ct SE23......6 D1
Ian Sq EN3......6 D1
Ibberton Ho
Kensington W14......254 B5
South Lambeth SW8....270 C4
Ibbotson Ave E16......98 D1
Ibbott St E1......96 C3

Iberia Ho **17** N19..........49 D2
Iberian Ave CR0, SM6....220 A4
Ibex Ho E15...............76 C3
Ibis Ct **16** SE8..........141 B6
Ibis Ho E12................78 B4
Ibis La W4................133 A4
Ibis Way UB4..............84 D1
Ibrox Ct **3** IG9..........21 C2
Ibsley Gdns SW15.........156 A3
Ibsley Way EN4.............2 C1
Ibstock Place Sch SW15. 155 C5
Icarus Ho **21** E3.........97 B4
Iceland Rd E3.............97 C6
Iceland Wharf SE16.......119 A2
Iceni Ct **22** Bow E3......97 B6
  Buckhurst Hill IG9........21 B3
Ice Wharf NW1............**233** B4
Ickburgh Est E5...........74 B6
Ickburgh Rd E5............74 B6
Ickburgh Sch E5...........74 B5
ICKENHAM................60 C4
Ickenham Cl HA4..........61 B6
Ickenham Rd HA4.........39 B1
Ickenham St UB10..........61 A4
Icknield Dr IG2............56 D4
Ickworth Park Rd E17.....53 A5
Icough Ct SE3............143 B5
Idaho Bldg **7** SE13....141 D4
Ida Rd N15................51 B5
Ida St E14.................98 A1
Iden Cl BR2...............208 C6
Identity & Passport Office
  SW1..............**115** B2 **258** D4
Idlecombe Rd SW17.......181 A4
Idmiston Rd
  New Malden KT4.........199 D2
  Stratford E15.............76 D3
  West Norwood SE21, SE27. 161 A2
Idmiston Sq KT4...........199 D2
Idol La EC3.........**117** C6 **253** A5
Idonia St SE8.............141 C5
Iffley Ho **47** E2.........95 D4
Iffley Rd W6..............112 B3
Ifield Ho SE17............**263** B2
Ifield Rd SW10.....135 D6 **265** D6
Ifor Evans Pl E1..........96 D3
Ightham Ho
  Beckenham BR3...........185 B3
  Walworth SE17...........**263** A3
Ightham Rd DA8...........147 C5
Ikon Ho **21** E1..........118 C6
Ilbert St W10..............91 A4
Ilchester Gdns W2........**245** C6
Ilchester Mans W8........**255** A6
Ilchester Pl W14...113 B3 **254** D6
Ilchester Rd RM8..........80 C3
Ildersly Gr SE21..........161 B2
Ilderton Prim Sch **16**
  SE16....................118 C1
Ilderton Rd SE15, SE16....140 C6
Ilex Cl TW16..............172 C1
Ilex Rd NW10..............67 D2
Ilex Way SW16............182 C5
ILFORD...................78 D6
Ilford Chambers **10** IG1. 78 C5
Ilford Hill IG1.............78 C5
Ilford Ho **14** N1.........73 B2
Ilford Interchange IG1.....78 C5
Ilford Jewish Prim Sch
  IG6.....................57 B6
Ilford La IG1..............78 D4
Ilford Mus★ IG1...........78 D5
Ilford Prep Sch IG3........58 A1
Ilford Ret Pk IG1..........79 A6
Ilford Sta IG1.............78 D6
Ilford Ursuline High Sch
  IG1.....................78 D6
Ilford Ursuline Prep Sch **7**
  IG1.....................78 B6
Ilfracombe Flats SE1......**252** B2
Ilfracombe Gdns RM6......58 B2
Ilfracombe Rd BR1.........164 D1
Iliffe St SE17......116 D1 **261** D2
Iliffe Yd SE17......116 D1 **261** D2
Ilkeston Ct **7** E5........74 D4
Ilkley Cl SE19............183 B4
Ilkley Ct N11.............31 A4
Ilkley Rd Newham E16......99 C2
  South Oxhey WD19.........22 D5
Illingworth Cl CR4........202 B6
Illingworth Way EN1.......17 C6
Ilmington Rd HA3..........43 D3
Ilminster Gdns SW11......136 C1
Ilsley Ct **8** SW8........137 C3
Iman Zakaria Acad **2** E7..77 C3
Imber Court N14..........115 C4
  Thames Ditton KT7.......196 B1
Imber Court Trad Est
  KT8....................196 B3
Imber Cross KT7..........196 D3
Imber Ct **4** SE9.........166 C5
Imber Gr KT10............196 B2
Imber Park Rd KT10.......196 B1
Imber St N1..............**235** C5
Immanuel CE Prim Sch
  SW16..................182 A4

Immanuel Coll WD23.......8 C4
Impact Ct SE20...........184 B1
Imperial Ave **5** N16.....73 C4
  Wallington SM6.........219 D1
Imperial Cl Harrow HA2....41 C3
  Willesden NW2............68 B3
Imperial College London
  (Charing Cross) W6 ...112 D1
Imperial College London
  (Chelsea & Westminster)
  SW10...........**136** A6 **266** B5
Imperial College London
  (Hammersmith) W12.....90 B1
Imperial College London
  (Northwick Park) HA1...43 A1
Imperial College London
  (Royal Brompton)
  SW3............114 C1 **257** A2
Imperial College London
  (South Kensington)
  SW7............114 B3 **256** C6
Imperial College London (St
  Mary's) W2....92 B1 **236** D2
Imperial College Rd
  SW7............114 B3 **256** C6
Imperial Cres SW6........136 A3
Imperial Ct
  Chislehurst BR7.........188 D4
  Harrow HA2..............41 C2
  St John's Wood NW8......**230** B4
  Wembley HA9.............66 C5
  Whetstone N20...........14 A1
Imperial Dr HA2...........41 C3
Imperial Gdns CR4........203 B6
Imperial Ho **1** Bow E3...97 A4
  2 Poplar E14.........119 B6
  Strand WC2.............**240** C1
Imperial Mews **5** E6.....99 D5
Imperial Pl BR7..........188 C2
Imperial Rd
  East Bedfont TW14.......149 C4
  Walham Green SW6.......**265** D1
  Wood Green N22..........32 A2
Imperial Sq SW6..........**265** D2
Imperial St E3.............98 A4
Imperial Twrs **3** NW3....70 A2
Imperial War Mus★ SE1,
  SE11...........116 C3 **261** B5
Imperial Way
  Croydon CR0, CR9.......220 C2
  Harrow HA3..............44 A3
  Longlands BR7..........167 A1
Imperial Wharf Sta
  SW10...........**136** A4 **266** B1
Impington **19** KT1......176 C1
Imre Cl W12..............112 B5
Inca Dr SE9..............166 D4
Ince Terr **3** N15.........50 D6
Inchbald Sch of Design
  (Garden Design)
  SW1............**115** B2 **258** D3
Inchbald Sch of Design
  (Interior Design)
  SW1............**115** A2 **258** A4
Inchmery Rd SE6..........164 A3
Inchwood BR4, CR0.......223 D4
Independant Jewish Day Sch
  2 NW4...............46 D4
Independence Ho **4**
  SW19..................180 B2
Independent Ind Est
  UB7...................104 C5
Independent Pl E8.........73 D3
Independents Rd SE3......142 D2
Inderwick Rd N8...........50 B4
Indescon Ct E14..........119 D4
Indiana Bldg **7** SE8.....141 C4
India St EC3.............**243** C1
India Way W12............112 B6
Indigo Ct TW13...........149 D1
Indigo Mews N16...........73 B5
Indoor Go Karting Arena
  (The Raceway) SE7....121 C3
Indoor Sports Arena
  E14...................120 A5
Indus Ct **16** SE15......139 D5
Indus Rd SE7.............143 C5
Ingal Rd E13..............99 A3
Ingate Pl SW8...137 B2 **268** D1
Ingatestone Rd
  Croydon SE25...........206 B5
  Wanstead E12............55 C1
  Woodford IG8.............37 B3
Ingelow Ho W8...........**245** C2
Ingelow Rd SW8..........137 A3
Ingersoll Rd Enfield EN3....6 C5
  Shepherd's Bush W12.....112 B5
Ingestre Pl W1...........**239** B1
Ingestre Rd Forest Gate E7..77 A4
  Gospel Oak NW5.........71 B4
Ingham Rd NW6............69 C4
Inglebert St EC1...94 C4 **234** A2
Ingleborough EN2..........4 C3
Ingleborough St SW9.....138 C3
Ingleby Ct N21...........16 D3
Ingleby Dr HA1...........64 B5
Ingleby Rd
  Dagenham RM10..........81 D2
  Ilford IG1................56 D1
  Lower Holloway N7.......72 A5

Ingleby Way
  Chislehurst West BR7...188 C5
  Wallington SM6.........219 D1
Ingle Cl HA5..............41 B6
Ingledew Rd SE18.........123 B1
Inglefield Sq **12** E1.....118 B5
Ingle Ho **3** SW12.......159 D3
Inglehurst Gdns IG4.......56 B4
Inglemere Ct CR4, SW17 . 180 C3
Inglemere Rd
  Forest Hill SE23.........162 D1
  Mitcham CR4, SW17......180 D3
Inglesham Wlk E9..........75 B2
Ingleside Cl BR3..........185 C3
Ingleside Gr SE3.........142 D6
Inglethorpe Ho **5**......65 A6
  E5.....................74 A6
Inglethorpe St SW6.......134 D4
Ingleton Ave DA16........168 A6
Ingleton Rd N18...........34 A4
Ingleton St SW9..........138 C3
Ingleway N12..............30 C4
Inglewood BR7............189 B4
Inglewood Cl E14.........119 C2
Inglewood Copse BR1......188 B1
Inglewood Ct BR1.........186 D6
Inglewood Mans **11** NW6..69 C3
Inglewood Mews **11** NW6..69 C3
Inglewood Rd NW6.........69 C3
Inglis Ct W5..............110 B6
Inglis St SW15...........156 C6
Inglis Rd Croydon CR0....205 D1
  Ealing W5...............110 B6
Inglis St SE5.............138 D4
Ingram Ave NW11..........48 A2
Ingram Cl Lambeth SE11...**260** D4
  Stanmore HA7............25 C5
Ingram Ct EN1.............17 D5
Ingram Ho **7** Harrow HA1..42 D4
  Old Ford E3..............97 A6
  Teddington KT8..........175 C2
Ingram Lo **8** SW4.......159 D5
Ingram Rd London N2......48 C5
  South Norwood CR7......183 A2
Ingram Way UB6...........86 B6
Ingrave Ho RM9...........102 B6
Ingrave St SW11..........136 C2
Ingrebourne Ct E4.........19 D2
Ingrebourne Ho
  2 Catford BR1.......186 B5
  Lisson Gr NW8..........**236** D4
Ingress St **4** W4........111 C1
Inigo Jones Rd SE7........144 A5
Inigo Pl WC2............**250** A6
Inkerman Rd NW5..........71 B2
Inkerman Terr W8.........**255** B5
Inks Gn E4................36 A5
Inkster Ho **8** SW11......136 C2
Inkwell Cl N12.............14 A1
Inman Rd Harlesden NW10..89 C6
  Wandsworth SW18........158 A4
Inmans Row IG8............37 A4
Innellan House Sch HA5....41 A6
Inner Circ NW1...**93** A4 **231** A2
Inner Park Rd SW19.......156 D2
Inner Ring E TW6.........126 D2
Inner Ring W TW6.........126 C2
Innes Cl SW20............179 A1
Innes Gdns SW15.........156 B5
Innes Lo SE23............162 D1
Innes Yd CR0.............221 A5
Innisfree Ho NW2..........68 D2
Innis Ho SE17............**263** A2
Inniskilling Rd E13........99 C5
Innova Bsns Pk EN3........7 B3
Innovation Cl HA0.........88 A6
Inskip Cl E10..............75 D6
Inskip Rd RM8.............58 D1
Insley Ho **13** E3.........97 D4
Institute of Cancer Research
  The SW7........114 A1 **256** B2
Institute Pl **31** E8.......74 B3
Institute The N2...........48 C5
Inst of Child Health
  WC1............94 B3 **240** C5
Inst of Neurology
  Bloomsbury WC1...94 A2 **240** B4
  St Pancras WC1...94 A3 **240** B4
Int Coll of Accountancy The
  SW17..................158 D1
Integer Gdns E11..........54 B2
Interchange The
  Kentish Town NW5.......71 B3
  Thornton Heath CR0.....204 D2
International Ave TW5....106 C1
International Com Sch
  W1.............93 A3 **238** B5
International House
  Language Sch
  WC2...........94 A1 **240** B2
International Sch of Bsns
  Studies HA2.............41 C2
International Sch of London
  W3....................110 C2
International Trad Est
  UB2...................106 B3
International Univ of
  America (London Campus)
  15 SE18.............122 D2

International Way TW16. .171 C2
Inverary Pl SE18.........145 B6
Inver Cl E5...............74 C6
Inverclyde Gdns RM6......58 D5
Inver Ct **11** Bayswater W2..91 D1
  4 Hammersmith W6....112 A3
Inveresk Gdns KT4........216 A5
Inverey Ho **2** N12.......29 D5
Inverforth Cl NW3.........70 A6
Inverforth Ho NW3........70 A6
Inverforth Rd N11.........31 B5
Invergarry Ct **11** EN5....13 D6
Invergarry Ho NW6.........91 D5
Inverine Rd SE7...........121 B1
Invermead Cl W6..........112 A2
Invermore Pl SE18........123 A2
Inverness Ave EN1..........5 C4
Inverness Ct **8** Acton W3..88 C1
  16 Catford SE6.......164 D3
Inverness Gdns W8........**245** C3
Inverness Mews
  Bayswater W2...........**245** D6
  Newham E16............122 D5
  North Woolwich E16.....123 A5
Inverness Pl W2..........**245** D6
Inverness Rd
  Edmonton N18...........34 B5
  Hounslow TW3...........129 C1
  North Cheam KT4........200 D1
  Southall UB2...........107 A2
Inverness St NW1.........**231** D6
Inverness Terr
  W2............113 D6 **245** D6
Inverton Rd SE15.........140 D1
Invicta Cl
  Chislehurst West BR7...188 C5
  East Bedfont TW14......149 D3
  21 Tower Hamlets E3..97 C2
Invicta Ct KT9...........214 B3
Invicta Ctr The IG11......102 A6
Invicta Gr UB5............85 B4
Invicta Plaza SE1........**251** C4
Invicta Prim Sch SE3.....143 A5
Invicta Rd SE3, SE7.......143 A6
Inville Rd SE17....117 B1 **262** D1
Inwen Ct SE8.............119 A1
Inwood Ave Acton W3.....130 A2
  Hounslow TW3..........129 D1
Inwood Bsns Pk TW3......129 C1
Inwood Cl CR0............223 A6
Inwood Ct **2** NW1.......71 C1
Inwood Ho **19** SE22.....139 C2
Inwood Rd TW3...........130 A1
Inworth St SW11..........136 C3
Inworth Wlk N1..........**235** A6
  lo Ctr Barking IG11......101 D3
Iona Cl Catford SE6.......163 C4
  Morden SM4............201 D2
Ion Ct **8** E2.............96 A5
Ionian Bldg **19** E14......119 A6
Ionian Ho **22** E1.........96 D3
Ipsden Bldgs SE1.........**251** B2
Ipswich Ho SE4...........162 D6
Ipswich Rd SW17.........181 A4
Iqra Ind Sch SW9.........138 C2
Irby Ho SW2..............160 C5
Ireland Cl E6.............100 B2
Ireland Pl N22.............32 A3
Ireland Yd EC4...........**241** D1
Irene Rd Broom Hill BR6 . 211 D2
  Parsons Green
  SW6............135 C4 **265** B1
Ireton Ho **22** SW9......138 C3
Ireton St **12** E3.........97 C3
Iris Ave DA5.............169 A5
Iris Cl Croydon CR0.......206 D1
  Newham E6.............100 A3
  Surbiton KT6...........198 B2
Iris Cres DA7............147 B6
Iris Ct Dagenham IG11......80 B1
  8 Peckham SE15.......140 B3
  4 Pinner HA5..........40 C6
Iris Rd KT19.............214 D3
Iris Way E4...............35 B4
Iris Wlk **1** HA8.........27 A6
Irkdale Ave N1.............5 D4
Iroko Ho **7** NW3........69 D2
Iron Bridge Cl
  Southall UB2...........108 A5
  Willesden NW10..........67 C3
Iron Bridge Ho NW3.......70 D1
Iron Bridge Rd N UB11...104 C5
Iron Bridge Rd S UB7....104 C4
Irongate Ho EC3..........**243** B2
Iron Mill Pl SW18.........157 D5
Iron Mill Rd SW18........157 D5
Ironmonger La
  EC2............95 B1 **242** C1
Ironmonger Pas EC1......**235** B1
Ironmonger Row
  EC1............95 A4 **235** B1
Ironmonger Row Baths
  EC1...................**235** B1
Ironmongers Pl E14......119 C2
Ironmonger's Pl **22** E14..119 C2
Ironside Cl SE16.........118 D4
Ironside Ho E9............75 A4
Ironworks **1** E3.........97 C6
Irvine Ave HA3............43 B6

Irvine Cl N20.............14 C2
Irvine Ct Marylebone W1...**239** B5
  Thornton Heath CR7.....204 C3
Irvine Ho N7..............72 B2
Irvine Way BR6...........211 D2
Irving Ave UB5............84 D6
Irving Ct SW9............138 B3
Irving Gr SW9............138 B3
Irving Ho SE17...........**261** C1
Irving Mews N1............73 A2
Irving Rd W14............112 D3
Irving St WC2............**249** D5
Irwell Est **31** SE16......118 C4
Irwin Ave SE18...........145 C5
Irwin Gdns UB10...........60 C5
Irwin Gdns NW10..........90 B6
Isabel Hill Cl TW12......173 C2
Isabella Cl N14...........15 C4
Isabella Ct **8** TW10.....154 B5
Isabella Dr BR6...........227 A4
Isabella Ho
  19 Hammersmith W6...112 C1
  Kennington SE11........**261** C2
Isabella Mews **11** E8.....73 C2
Isabella Pl KT2..........176 B5
Isabella Rd E9............74 C3
Isabel St SW9............**270** D2
Isambard Mews E14.......120 A3
Isambard Pl SE16.........118 C5
Iseldon Ct N7.............72 A4
Isel Way **4** SE22.......161 C6
Isham Rd SW16...........182 A1
Isis Cl Putney SW15......134 C1
  Ruislip HA4..............39 A3
Isis Ct W4...............132 D5
Isis Ho **2** Edmonton N18..33 D4
  Paddington NW8.........**236** D5
Isis St SW18.............158 A2
Islamia Girls' High Sch
  NW6....................91 A6
Islamia Prim Sch NW6.....91 A6
Islamic Coll for Advanced
  Studies **2** NW10.......68 B2
Islamic Shaksiyah
  Foundation Sch N15.....51 B4
Island Centre Way **16** EN3 . 7 C6
Island Farm Ave KT8......195 B4
Island Farm Rd KT8.......195 C4
Island Gardens Sta E14 . .120 A1
Island Ho Bromley E14.....98 A4
  Morden SW19...........202 A5
Island Rd Deptford SE16...118 D2
  Mitcham CR4...........180 D3
Island Row E14............97 B1
Isla Rd SE18.............145 A6
Islay Gdns TW4...........150 D6
Islay Wlk **17** N1.........73 A2
Isleden Ho N1...........**235** A6
Isledon Rd N4, N7.........72 C5
Islehurst Cl BR7.........188 C2
ISLE OF DOGS............120 A2
ISLEWORTH.............131 B2
Isleworth Bsns Complex
  TW7...................130 D3
Isleworth Sta TW7.......130 D3
Isleworth & Syon Sch for
  Boys TW7..............130 C5
Isleworth Town Prim Sch
  TW7...................131 A3
ISLINGTON..............72 D2
Islington Arts & Media Sch
  6 N4................50 B1
Islington Bsns Ctr N1....**235** B6
Islington Est N1...95 A6 **235** A6
Islington Gn N1...94 D6 **234** C5
Islington High St
  N1.............94 D5 **234** C4
Islington Mus★
  WC1...........94 D4 **234** C1
Islington Park Mews **1**
  N1.....................72 D1
Islington Park St N1......72 D1
Islington Tennis Ctr N7...72 A2
Islip Gdns Burnt Oak HA8 . 27 B3
  Northolt UB5............63 A1
Islip Manor Rd UB5........63 A1
Islip St NW5..............71 C3
Ismailia Rd E7............77 B1
Isobel Ho
  10 Ashford TW16.....171 D3
  Harrow HA1..............42 D4
Isokon Flats **3** NW3.....70 D3
Isom Cl E13...............99 B4
Issac Way SE1...........**252** B2
Issa Rd TW3.............129 B1
Italia Conti Acad of Theatre
  Arts EC1...............**242** A5
Ithell Ct HA0..............65 D3
Ivanhoe Dr HA3...........25 B1
Ivanhoe Ho
  11 Balham SW12.....159 B4
  34 Bow E3............97 A5
Ivanhoe Rd
  Hounslow TW4...........128 D2
  Peckham SE5...........139 D2
Ivatt Pl W14......113 B1 **254** D1
Ivatt Way N17............50 D6
Ivax Quays E16...........123 A6
Iveagh Ave NW10..........88 C3

Iveagh Cl Ealing NW10 . . . . .88 C5
South Hackney E9. . . . . . . .96 D6
Iveagh Ct
4 Beckenham BR3 . . . . . . 207 D6
Whitechapel EC3 . . . . . . 243 C1
Iveagh Ho
2 Brixton SW9 . . . . 138 D3
Chelsea SW10 . . . . 266 B4
Ivebury Ct 9 W10. . . . . .90 C1
Ivedon Rd DA16. . . . . .146 C3
Ive Farm Cl E10. . . . . .75 C6
Ive Farm La E10. . . . . .75 C6
Iveley Rd SW4 . . . . .137 C3
Iver Ct N1. . . . . .73 A2
Iverhurst Cl DA6. . . . . .168 D6
Iverna Ct W8 . . . . 255 B6
Iverna Gdns Hatton TW14. .149 B6
Kensington W8. . . . . .113 C3 255 B6
Iverson Rd NW6 . . . . .69 C2
Ivers Way CR0 . . . . 223 D1
Ives Rd E16. . . . . .98 C2
Ives St SW3 . . . . . . .114 C2 257 B4
Ivestor Terr SE23. . . . . . . .162 C4
Ivimey Ct E2 . . . . .96 A4
Ivinghoe Cl EN1. . . . . .5 C4
Ivinghoe Ho 1 N7 . . . . .71 D3
Ivinghoe Rd Barking RM8. . .80 B3
Bushey WD23. . . . . .8 B4
Ivor Ct Hendon N3 . . . . .47 A6
Hornsey N8. . . . . .50 A3
Lisson Gr NW1 . . . . 237 C6
Ivor Gr SE9 . . . . .166 D3
Ivor Ho DA14 . . . . .190 C5
Ivories The N1. . . . . .73 A1
Ivor Mayor Lo SW12 . . . . .159 A5
Ivor Pl NW1 . . . . . . .92 D3 237 C5
Ivor St NW1 . . . . .71 C1
Ivory Ct TW13. . . . . .150 A3
Ivorydown BR1. . . . . .187 A6
Ivory Ho 9 Shadwell NW11. .136 A2
St George in t East E1. . . 253 D4
Ivory Sq 15 SW18 . . . . . . .136 A2
Ivybridge Cl
2 Twickenham TW1 . . . . .153 A4
Uxbridge UB8 . . . . .82 A4
Ivybridge Ct 1 BR7 . . . . . .188 C2
Ivybridge Ho 1 SE22. . . . . .139 C2
Ivybridge La WC2 . . . . . . 250 B5
Ivybridge Prim Sch
TW1. . . . . .152 D5
Ivybridge Ret Pk TW7 . . . .152 D6
Ivychurch Cl SE20. . . . . . . .184 C3
Ivy Church La SE1, SE17. . 263 C2
Ivy Cl Harrow HA2. . . . . . . .63 B4
Pinner HA5. . . . . .40 C2
Sunbury TW16 . . . . .172 C1
Ivy Cotts UB10 . . . . .82 C4
Ivy Cres W4. . . . . .111 A2
Ivy Ct
19 Bermondsey SE16. . . . .118 A1
Lewisham SE3 . . . . .142 D1
Ivydale Prim Sch SE15 . . .140 D1
Ivydale Rd
Carshalton SM5 . . . . . . .218 D6
Nunhead SE15 . . . . .140 D1
Ivyday Gr SW16 . . . . .160 B1
Ivydene Cl SM1. . . . . .218 A4
Ivy Gdns London N8. . . . . . .50 A3
Mitcham CR4 . . . . .203 D6
Ivy Ho Croydon CR0 . . . . .206 D1
6 Upper Clapton E5 . . . . .52 B1
Ivyhouse Rd RM9 . . . . .81 A2
Ivy House Rd UB10 . . . . . . .60 D5
Ivy La TW4. . . . . .129 B1
Ivy Lo W8. . . . . 245 A4
Ivymount Rd SE27. . . . . . . .160 C1
Ivy Rd Brockley SE4 . . . . . .141 C1
Cricklewood NW2. . . . . . .68 C4
Hounslow TW3 . . . . .129 D1
Newham E16 . . . . .99 A1
Southgate N14. . . . . .15 D4
Tolworth KT6 . . . . .198 C1
Upper Tooting SW17. . . .180 C5
Walthamstow E17 . . . . . .53 C3
Ivy St N1 . . . . .95 C5
Ivy Terr 2 IG2 . . . . .57 A3
Ivy Wlk RM9 . . . . .81 A2
Ixworth Pl SW3 . . . . 114 C2 257 A3
Izane Rd DA6 . . . . .147 B1

J

Jacaranda Cl KT3. . . . . . . .199 C6
Jacaranda Gr E8. . . . . .73 C1
Jack Ashley Ct 5 NW9 . . . .27 C2
Jackass La BR2. . . . . .225 C2
Jack Barnett Way N22. . . . . .32 B1
Jack Clow Rd E15. . . . . .98 C5
Jack Cook Ho 9 IG11. . . . . .78 D1
Jack Cornwell St E12 . . . . . .78 C4
Jack Dash Gdns E6 . . . . . .100 A3
Jack Goodchild Way
KT3. . . . . .198 D6
Jack & Jill Sch
Hampton TW12. . . . . . . .173 C4
1 Twickenham TW2. . . . .152 C2
Jack Jones Way RM9. . . . .103 B5

Jacklin Gn IG8 . . . . .37 A6
Jackman Ho 24 E1. . . . . . . .118 B5
Jackman Mews NW2. . . . . . .67 C5
Jackman St E8 . . . . .96 B6
Jackson Cl Hackney E9. . . . .74 D1
Uxbridge UB10. . . . . .60 A1
Jackson Ct Forest Gate E7 . .77 B2
Wanstead E11 . . . . .55 B1
Jackson Ho
15 London SW11 . . . . . . .136 B2
13 New Southgate N11 . . . .31 C5
Jackson Rd Barking IG11. . .101 B6
Bromley BR2. . . . . .226 B6
East Barnet EN4 . . . . . . .14 C5
Lower Holloway N7 . . . . . .72 B4
Uxbridge UB10. . . . . .60 A1
Jackson's La N6 . . . . .49 B2
Jackson's Pl CR0 . . . . .205 C1
Jackson St SE18 . . . . .144 C6
Jackson's Way CR0 . . . . . .223 C5
Jackson Way UB2. . . . . . . .107 D4
Jack Taylor Sch
NW8. . . . . .92 A6 229 A6
Jack Tizard Sch W12. . . . . .112 B5
Jack Walker Ct N5 . . . . .72 D4
Jacob Ho 14 DA18. . . . . . . .124 D4
Jacobin Lo N7. . . . . .72 A3
Jacob Mans 15 E1 . . . . .96 B1
Jacobs Cl RM10. . . . . .81 D4
Jacobs Ho E13. . . . . .99 C4
Jacobson Ct SW11. . . . . . . 267 B1
Jacobson Ho E1 . . . . 243 C2
Jacob St SE1 . . . . .118 A4
Jacob's Well Mews W1. . . . 238 B2
Jacotts Ho N10. . . . . .90 C3
Jacqueline Cl UB5. . . . . .85 A6
Jacqueline Ho 4 E1. . . . . . . .96 D2
Jacques Prevert Sch 3
W6 . . . . .112 D2
Jade Cl Dagenham RM8. . . . .58 C1
Hendon NW2 . . . . .46 D2
Newham E16 . . . . .99 D1
Jaffe Rd IG1. . . . . .57 B1
Jaffray Rd BR2 . . . . .209 D5
Jaggard Way SW12 . . . . . .158 D4
Jagger Ho SW11. . . . . 267 C2
Jago Cl SE18 . . . . .145 A6
Jago Wlk SE5. . . . . .139 B5
Jamahirya Sch
SW3 . . . . 136 C6 267 A6
Jamaica Rd
Bermondsey SE1. . . . . . 253 D1
Bermondsey SE16. . . . . .118 B3
Thornton Heath CR7. . . .204 D3
Jamaica St E1 . . . . .96 C2
James Allen's Girls' Sch 12
SE22. . . . . .161 B5
James Allen's Pre-Prep Sch
SE21. . . . . .161 B5
James Allen's Prep Sch 13
SE22. . . . . .161 C5
James Anderson Ct 29
E2 . . . . .95 C5
James Ave
Cricklewood NW2. . . . . . .68 C3
Dagenham RM8 . . . . .59 B1
James Bedford Cl HA5 . . . . .22 C1
James Boswell Cl 1
SW16. . . . . .182 C6
James Brine Ho 6 E2. . . . . .95 D4
James Campbell Ho 2
E2 . . . . .96 C5
James Cl London NW11. . . . .47 A3
8 Newham E13. . . . . .99 A5
James Collins Cl W9 . . . . . .91 B3
James Ct Chingford E4 . . . . .20 B2
Finchley N12. . . . . .30 C3
Hendon NW9 . . . . .27 C1
3 Woodford E18 . . . . .37 B1
James Dixon Prim Sch
SE20. . . . . .184 A2
James Docherty Ho 4
E2 . . . . .96 C5
James Dudson Ct NW10. . . .67 A1
James Est CR4. . . . . .180 D1
James Gdns N22. . . . . .32 D3
James Hammett Ho 9
E2 . . . . .95 D5
James Ho Mile End E1. . . . . .97 A3
33 Rotherhithe SE16. . . . .118 D4
James Joyce Wlk 7
SE24 . . . . .138 C1
James La E10, E11. . . . . . . .54 B3
James Lee Sq EN3 . . . . .7 C5
James Leicester Hall of
Residence N7. . . . . .72 A2
James Lind Ho 6 SE8. . . . .119 B2
James Middleton Ho 20
E2 . . . . .96 B4
James Newman Ct SE9. . . .166 C1
James Oglethorpe Prim Sch
RM14. . . . . .100 A4
Jameson Ct 6 E2. . . . . .96 C5
Jameson Ho SE11. . . . . . . 260 C2
Jameson Lo N6. . . . . .49 C3
Jameson Pl 11 W3 . . . . . . .111 A4
Jameson St W8. . . . . 245 B4
James Pl N17. . . . . .33 D2
James's Cotts TW9. . . . . . .132 C5
James St Barking IG11. . . . .79 A1

James St continued
Enfield EN1. . . . . .17 D6
Hounslow TW3 . . . . .130 B2
Marylebone W1 . . . .93 A1 238 B1
Strand WC2 . . . . . . .116 A6 250 B6
James Stewart Ho NW6 . . . .69 B1
James Stroud Ho SE17 . . . 262 B1
Jamestown Rd
NW1. . . . . .93 B6 231 C6
Jamestown Way E14. . . . . .120 B6
James Voller Way 30 E1. . . .96 C1
James Way WD19 . . . . .22 D6
James Wolfe Prim Sch 16
SE10. . . . . .142 A5
Jamiatul Ummah Sch 40
E1. . . . . .96 B1
Jamieson Ho TW4. . . . . . . .151 B5
Jamuna Cl E14 . . . . .97 A2
Jane Austen Hall 14 E16. . .121 B5
Jane St E1 . . . . .96 B1
Janet Ct
4 Bexleyheath DA7. . . . . .147 C1
Wood Green N22 . . . . . . .32 B2
Janet St E14. . . . . .119 C3
Janeway Pl 2 SE16 . . . . . .118 B4
Janeway St SE16. . . . . .118 A4
Janice Mews 3 IG1 . . . . . . .78 D5
Jansen Ho 5 SW15. . . . . . .156 A6
Jansen Wlk SW11. . . . . . . .136 B1
Janson Cl Stratford E15. . . . .76 C3
Willesden NW10. . . . . . . .67 C5
Janson Rd E15. . . . . .76 C3
Jansons Rd N15 . . . . .51 C6
Japan Cres N4. . . . . .50 B1
Japanese Sch The W3. . . . .110 C6
Japan Rd RM6 . . . . .58 D3
Jaquets Ct DA5 . . . . .169 C2
Jardine Ho HA1. . . . . .42 C2
Jardine Rd E1 . . . . .118 D6
Jarman Ho
Bermondsey SE16 . . . . . .118 D2
16 Stepney E1 . . . . .96 C2
Jarrett Cl SW2. . . . . .160 D3
Jarrow Cl SM4. . . . . .201 D4
Jarrow Rd
Bermondsey SE16 . . . . . .118 C1
Dagenham RM6. . . . . . . .58 C3
Tottenham Hale N17. . . . .52 B5
Jarrow Way E9. . . . . .75 A4
Jarvis Cl 1 Barking IG11. . .101 B6
Barnet EN5. . . . . .12 D6
Jarvis Ho 3 SE15. . . . . . . .140 A4
Jarvis Rd London SE22 . . . .139 C1
South Croydon CR2. . . . .221 B2
Jasmin SE1. . . . . 253 D3
Jasmine Cl Ilford IG1. . . . . . .78 D3
Orpington BR6 . . . . .226 D6
Southall UB1. . . . . .107 A6
Jasmine Ct Lee SE12. . . . . .165 A5
11 Wallington SM6. . . . . .219 B2
Wimbledon SW19. . . . . .179 C5
Jasmine Gdns
Harrow HA2. . . . . .63 C6
West Wickham CR0 . . . . .223 D5
Jasmine Gr SE20. . . . . .184 B2
Jasmine Sq 15 E3. . . . . .97 B6
Jasmine Terr UB7 . . . . .104 C4
Jasmine Way KT7 . . . . .196 C5
Jasmin Ho SE4 . . . . .141 B2
Jasmin Lo 17 SE16. . . . . . .118 B1
Jasmin Rd KT19 . . . . .214 D3
Jason Ct 2 London SW9. . . .138 C4
Marylebone W1 . . . . 238 B2
Jason Ho UB5 . . . . .85 A6
Jason Wlk SE9 . . . . .188 C6
Jasper Cl EN3 . . . . .6 C5
Jasper Ho KT4. . . . . .199 B1
Jasper Rd Newham E16 . . . .99 D2
Penge SE19. . . . . .183 D4
Jasper Wlk N1. . . . . 235 C2
Java Wharf SE1. . . . . 253 D2
Javelin Ct HA7. . . . . .25 B5
Javelin Way UB5. . . . . .84 D4
Jawahar Bagh SW16. . . . . .182 D4
Jaycroft EN2 . . . . .4 C4
Jay Gdns BR7. . . . . .188 B6
Jay Ho SW15 . . . . .134 C3
Jay Mews SW7 . . . . 114 A4 246 B1
Jayson Ct 7 CR0 . . . . .206 A1
Jazzfern Terr HA0. . . . . .65 A3
Jean Batten Cl SM6 . . . . . .220 B1
Jean Darling Ho SW10 . . . .266 C5
Jean Ho 3 SW17. . . . . .180 C5
Jean Humbert Ho 2
SE27. . . . . .183 B6
Jean Pardies Ho 23 E1. . . . .96 C2
Jebb Ave SW2. . . . . .160 A5
Jebb St E3 . . . . .97 C5
Jedburgh Rd E13. . . . . .99 C4
Jedburgh St SW11. . . . . . . .137 A1
Jeddo Mews W12. . . . . .111 D4
Jeddo Rd W12. . . . . .111 D4
Jefferies Ho 13 NW10. . . . . .67 B1
Jefferson Bldg 3 E14. . . . . .119 C4
Jefferson Cl Ealing W13. . . .109 B3
Ilford IG2. . . . . .56 D4
Jefferson Wlk 13 SE18 . . . .144 C6
Jeffrey Row SE12. . . . . . . .165 B6
Jeffrey's Ct 2 SW4 . . . . . . .138 A3
Jeffrey's Pl NW1. . . . . .71 C1

Jeffreys Rd EN3. . . . . .7 B1
Jeffrey's Rd SW4 . . . . .138 A3
Jeffrey's St NW1. . . . . .71 C1
Jeffs Cl TW12. . . . . .173 D4
Jeffs Rd SM1 . . . . .217 B4
Jeff Wooller Coll
WC1. . . . . .94 A2 240 B4
Jefton Ct SM6. . . . . .219 C3
Jeger Ave E2 . . . . .95 D6
Jeken Rd SE9. . . . . .143 C1
Jelf Rd SW2 . . . . .160 C6
Jellicoe Ct E4 . . . . .36 B4
Jellicoe Gdns HA7. . . . . . . .25 A4
Jellicoe Ho
5 Bethnal Green E2 . . . . .96 A5
Fitzrovia NW1. . . . . 238 D5
11 Putney SW15. . . . . . . .156 D6
Jellicoe Rd
4 Newham E13. . . . . .99 A3
Tottenham N17. . . . . .33 B3
Jemmett Ct KT2 . . . . .176 D2
Jemotts Ct 9 SE14 . . . . . . .140 B6
Jem Paterson Ct HA1. . . . . .64 C4
Jengar Cl SM1. . . . . .217 D4
Jenkins Ho SW8 . . . . 269 C2
Jenkins La IG11. . . . . .101 A4
Jenkinson Ho 12 E2. . . . . . .96 B4
Jenkins Rd E13 . . . . .99 B3
Jenner Ave W3 . . . . .89 B2
Jenner Cl DA14. . . . . .190 A6
Jenner Ct N21. . . . . .16 A6
Jenner Ho
5 Belvedere DA17 . . . . . .125 C3
Greenwich SE3. . . . . . . .142 C6
Jenner Pl SW13. . . . . .134 B6
Jenner Rd N16 . . . . .73 D5
Jennett Rd CR0. . . . . .220 C5
Jennifer Ho SE11 . . . . 261 B3
Jennifer Rd BR1 . . . . .164 D1
Jennings Cl KT6. . . . . .197 C2
Jennings Ho SE10 . . . . .120 B1
Jennings Rd SE22. . . . . . . .161 D5
Jenny Hammond Cl E11. . . .76 D5
Jenny Hammond Prim Sch
E11. . . . . .76 C4
Jensen Ho 10 E3. . . . . .97 C3
Jenson Way SE19 . . . . .183 D3
Jenton Ave DA7. . . . . .147 A3
Jephson Ct 17 SW4. . . . . . .138 A3
Jephson Ho SE17 . . . . .138 D6
Jephson Rd E7 . . . . .77 C1
Jephson St SE5. . . . . .139 B4
Jephtha Rd SW18. . . . . . . .157 C5
Jeppo's La CR4 . . . . .202 D5
Jerdan Pl SW6. . . . . .265 A4
Jeremiah St E14 . . . . .97 D1
Jeremy Bentham Ho 24
E2 . . . . .96 A4
Jeremy's Gn N18 . . . . .34 C6
Jermyn St SW1 . . . . 115 C5 249 B4
Jerningham Ct SE14 . . . . . .141 A4
Jerningham Rd SE14. . . . . .141 A4
Jerome Cres NW8 .92 C3 237 A6
Jerome Ct 2 N11. . . . . .31 C5
Jerome Ho
Kingston u T KT1. . . . . . .175 D1
Lisson Gr NW1 . . . . 237 B4
Jerome Pl KT1. . . . . .175 D1
Jerome St E1 . . . . . . .95 D3 243 C5
Jerome Twr 5 W3. . . . . . . .110 D4
Jerrard St SE13 . . . . .141 D2
Jerrold Lo SW15. . . . . .134 C2
Jerrold St 24 N1. . . . . .95 C5
Jersey Ave HA7. . . . . .107 B3
Jersey Ct UB2 . . . . .107 B3
Jersey Dr BR5 . . . . .211 B3
Jersey Ho
15 Canonbury N1. . . . . . . .73 A2
Enfield EN3. . . . . .6 D5
Jersey Rd Canonbury N1. . . .73 A2
Ealing W7 . . . . .109 A4
Hounslow TW5, TW7. . . .130 B5
Ilford IG1. . . . . .78 D4
Leytonstone E11. . . . . . . .54 B1
Mitcham SW17. . . . . . . .181 B4
Newham E16 . . . . .99 C1
Jersey St E2. . . . . .96 B4
Jerusalem Pas EC1. . . . . . 241 C5
Jervis Bay Ho 9 E14. . . . . . .98 B1
Jervis Ct
9 Dagenham RM10. . . . . .81 D2
2 Greenwich SE10 . . . . .142 A4
Marylebone W1 . . . . 238 D1
Jerviston Gdns SW16. . . . . .182 C4
Jesmond Ave HA9. . . . . .66 B2
Jesmond Cl CR4 . . . . .203 B6
Jesmond Ct HA9. . . . . .66 C2
Jesmond Rd CR0 . . . . .205 D2
Jesmond Way HA7. . . . . . . .26 A5
Jessam Ave E5 . . . . .52 B1
Jessamine Rd W7. . . . . .108 D5
Jessel Ho St Pancras WC1. 233 A1
Westminster SW1 . . . . . 259 D4
Jesse Rd E10 . . . . .54 D1
Jessica Rd SW18. . . . . .158 A6
Jessie Blythe La 4 N19. . . . .50 A2
Jessie Duffett Ho 11
SE5. . . . . .139 A5
Jessie's Cotts E17 . . . . .53 A3
Jessiman Terr TW17. . . . . .192 C4

Jesson Ho SE17. . . . . 262 C3
Jessop Ave UB2. . . . . .107 B2
Jessop Ct N1. . . . . 234 D3
Jessop Ho 9 W4 . . . . .111 B2
Jessop Pl CR4 . . . . .202 C5
Jessop Sq E14 . . . . .119 C5
Jessops Way CR0 . . . . .203 C3
Jessops Wharf 4 TW8 . . . .131 C5
Jessup Cl SE18 . . . . .123 A2
Jeston Ho 10 SE27 . . . . . . .160 D1
Jethou Ho 16 N1. . . . . .73 A2
Jetstar Way UB5. . . . . .85 A4
Jevington Way SE12 . . . . . .165 B3
Jevons Ho 9 NW8. . . . . .70 B1
Jewell Ho 3 SW12. . . . . . . .159 C4
Jewel Rd E17. . . . . .53 C6
Jewish Free Sch HA3. . . . . .44 C3
Jewish Mus The*
NW1. . . . . .93 B6 231 D5
Jewry St EC3 . . . . . . .95 D1 243 C1
Jews Row SW18 . . . . .136 A1
Jews Wlk SE26 . . . . .184 B6
Jeymer Ave NW2 . . . . .68 C3
Jeymer Dr UB6 . . . . .86 A6
Jeypore Rd SW18. . . . . . . .158 A5
Jillian Cl TW12. . . . . .173 C3
Jim Bradley Cl 10 SE18. . . .122 C2
Jim Griffiths Ho SW6. . . . . 264 D5
Jimis Coll HA9. . . . . .65 C5
Jim Veal Dr 3 N17. . . . . .72 A2
Joan Cres SE9 . . . . .165 D4
Joan Gdns RM8. . . . . .81 A6
Joanna Ho 7 W6 . . . . .112 C1
Joanne Ct EN1. . . . . .17 C5
Joan Rd RM8. . . . . .81 A6
Joan St SE1 . . . . 116 D5 251 D5
Joan Villas IG2. . . . . .57 A2
Jocelin Ho N1. . . . . 233 D5
Jocelyn Rd TW9 . . . . .132 A2
Jocelyn St SE15. . . . . .140 A4
Jockey's Fields
WC1. . . . . .94 B2 240 D4
Jodane St SE8 . . . . .119 B2
Jodrell Cl TW7. . . . . .131 A4
Jodrell Rd E3. . . . . .75 B1
Joe Hunte Ct 2 SW27. . . . .182 D5
Joel St HA5, HA6. . . . . .40 A4
Johanna Prim Sch
SE1. . . . . .116 C4 251 A1
Johanna St SE1. . . . . .251 A1
John Adam St
WC2. . . . . .116 A6 250 B5
John Aird Ct W2 . . . .92 A2 236 B4
John Aldis Ho N22 . . . . .32 B1
John Archer Way SW18 . . .158 B5
John Ashby Cl SW2. . . . . . .160 A5
John Austin Cl KT2. . . . . . .176 B2
John Baird Ct SE26 . . . . . .184 D6
John Baird Ho 11 SE20 . . . .184 C3
John Ball Prim Sch SE3 . . .142 C3
John Barker Ct NW6 . . . . . .69 A1
John Barker Ho IG1. . . . . . .79 B6
John Barnes Wlk E15 . . . . . .76 D2
John Barter Ho TW3 . . . . . .129 B3
John Betts' Ho W12. . . . . . .112 A3
John Betts Prim Sch
W6 . . . . .112 B3
John Bond Ho 2 E3 . . . . . . .97 B5
John Bradshaw Rd N14 . . . .15 D3
John Brent Ho 8 SE8 . . . . .118 D2
John Buck Ho NW10 . . . . . .89 D6
John Burns Dr IG11. . . . . . .79 C1
John Burns Prim Sch 17
SW11. . . . . .137 A3
Johnby Cl EN3. . . . . .7 A6
John Campbell Rd 26
N16. . . . . .73 C3
John Carpenter St EC4. . . . 251 C6
John Cartwright Ho 7
E2 . . . . .96 B4
John Chilton Sch UB5. . . . . .63 A1
John Clifford Ho N8 . . . . . . .50 A3
John Clynes Ct SW15. . . . .134 B1
John Conwey Ho 23
SW2. . . . . .160 C5
John Cornwell VC Ho 6
E12 . . . . .78 C4
John Day Ho TW7. . . . . . . .131 B2
John Dee Ho 3 SW14. . . . .133 B2
John Donne Prim Sch 13
SE15. . . . . .140 B4
John Drinkwater Cl E11. . . . .54 C2
John Dwight Ho SW6 . . . . .135 D2
John Fearon Wlk 5 W10. . . .91 A4
John Felton Rd 19 SE16. . . .118 A4
John Fielden Ho 10 E2. . . . .96 B4
John Fisher St E1. . . . . .118 A6
John F Kennedy Specl Sch
E15. . . . . .98 B6
John Gooch Dr EN2 . . . . . . .4 D4
John Harris Ho SE15. . . . . .140 A2
John Harrison Way
SE10. . . . . .120 D3
John Hunt Ct 5 SE9 . . . . . .166 A2
John Islip St
SW1. . . . . .116 A2 260 A3

John Kaye Ct TW17 . . . . . . .192 C4
John Keall Ho **3** SW15 . .134 D2
John Keats Ho N22 . . . . .32 B2
John Keats Lo EN2 . . . . .5 B4
John Keble CE Prim Sch
   NW10 . . . . .89 D6
John Kelly Tech Colls
   NW2 . . . . .67 D5
John Kennedy Ct **1** N1 . .73 B2
John Kennedy Ho **1**
   SE16 . . . . .118 D2
John Kennedy Lo **2** N1 . . .73 B2
John King Ct **5** N19 . . . .71 D6
John Kirk Ho
   21 Battersea SW11 . . . . . .136 B2
   Beckenham BR3 . . . . .207 A5
   5 Streatham SW16 . . . . . .160 A1
John Knight Lo SW6 . . . . .265 B4
John Lamb Ct HA3 . . . . .24 C2
John Loughborough Sch **9**
   N17 .33 D1
John Lyon Sch The HA2 . . .42 B1
John McDonald Ho **3**
   E14 . . . . .120 A3
John McKenna Wlk **17**
   SE16 . . . . .118 A3
John Masefield Ho N15 . . .51 B3
John Maurice Cl
   SE17 . . . . .117 B2 262 C4
John Nettleford Ho **14**
   E2 . . . . .96 B4
John Newton Ct DA16 . . .146 B2
John Orwell Sports Ctr
   E1 .118 B5
John Parker Cl RM10 . . . . . .81 C1
John Parker Sq **7**
   SW11 . . . . .136 B2
John Parry Ct **28** N1 . . . .95 C5
John Paul II Sch **9**
   SW19 . . . . .156 A4
John Penn Ho SE8 . . . . . . .141 B5
John Penn St SE13 . . . . . . .141 D4
John Perrin Pl HA3 . . . . . . .44 A2
John Perryn Prim Sch
   W3 .89 C1
John Prince's St W1 . . . . .238 D2
John Pritchard Ho **16** E1 . .96 A3
John Ratcliffe Ho **8**
   NW6 . . . . .91 C4
John Rennie Wlk **1** E1 . .118 C5
John Roan Sch SE3 . . . . . . .142 C5
John Roll Way SE16 . . . . . .118 A3
John Ruskin Coll CR2 . . . .223 A1
John Ruskin Prim Sch
   SE5 . . . . .139 A6
John Ruskin St SE5 . . . . . .139 A6
Johns Cl TW5 . . . . .171 A6
John Scurr Ho **18** E14 . . . .97 A1
John Scurr Prim Sch **46**
   E1 . . . . .96 C3
John Silkin La SE8 . . . . . . .118 D1
Johns La SM4 . . . . .202 A4
John's Mews WC1 . . .94 B3 240 D5
John Smith Ave
   SW6 . . . . .135 B5 264 C4
John Smith Mews E14 . . . .120 B6
Johnson Cl E8 . . . . .96 A6
Johnson Ct Hendon NW4 . . .46 A6
   10 Wandsworth SW18 . . . .136 B1
Johnson Ho
   Belgravia SW1 . . . . .258 B3
   23 Bethnal Green E2 . . . . . .96 A4
   Somers Town NW1 . . . . . .232 B3
   South Lambeth SW8 . . . . .269 D3
Johnson Lo **12** W9 . . . . . .91 C2
Johnson Rd
   Bromley Comm BR2 . . . . .209 D4
   Heston TW5 . . . . .128 C5
   Stonebridge NW10 . . . . . . .89 B6
   Thornton Heath CR0 . . . . .205 B2
Johnson's Cl SM5 . . . . .218 D5
Johnsons Ct EC4 . . . . .241 B1
Johnsons Dr TW12 . . . . . . .174 A2
Johnson's Ind Est UB3 . .106 A3
Johnson's Pl
   SW1 . . . . .115 C1 259 A1
Johnson St Southall UB2 . .106 D3
   Stepney E1 . . . . .96 C1
Johnsons Way NW10 . . . . . .88 D3
John Spencer Sq N1 . . . . . .72 D2
John's Pl E1 . . . . .96 B1
John St Croydon SE25 . . . .206 A5
   Enfield EN1 . . . . .17 D6
   Finsbury WC1 . . . . . .94 B3 240 D5
   Hounslow TW3, TW5 . . . . .129 A3
   West Ham E15 . . . . .98 D6
John Stainer Prim Sch
   SE4 . . . . .141 A2
John's Terr CR0 . . . . .205 C1
Johnston Cl SW9 . . . . .270 D1
Johnstone Ho SE13 . . . . . .142 B2
Johnstone Rd E6 . . . . .100 B4
Johnston Rd IG8 . . . . .37 A5
John Strachey Ho SW6 . .264 D5
John Strype Ct E10 . . . . . . .53 D1
John Trundle Ct EC4 . . . . .242 A4

John Tucker Ho **3** E14 . . .119 C3
John Walsh Twr E11 . . . . . . .76 D6
John Wesley Cl **4** E6 . . .100 B4
John Wesley Cl **6** TW1 . .153 A3
John Wesley's House & Mus
   of Methodism★ EC1 . . . .242 D6
John Wheatley Ho
   14 London N19 . . . . .49 D2
   West Brompton SW6 . . . . .264 D5
John William Cl **12** KT2 . .175 D2
John Williams Cl SE14 . . . .140 D3
John Wilson St SE18 . . . . .122 C2
John Wooley Cl SE13 . . . . .142 C1
Joiners Arms Yd **1** SE5 .139 B4
Joiners Ct **5** N20 . . . . . . .14 D1
Joiner St SE1 . . . . .252 D3
Joiners Yd N1 . . . . .233 B3
Joint Rd N10 . . . . .30 C2
Jolles Ho **9** E3 . . . . .97 D4
Jollys La Harrow HA2 . . . . . .42 B1
   Hayes UB4 . . . . .84 D2
Jonathan Ct **9** W4 . . . . . .111 C2
Jonathan St
   SE11 . . . . .116 B1 260 C2
Jones Ho
   4 South Bromley E14 . . . . .98 B1
   Stamford Hill N16 . . . . .51 C1
Jones Rd E13 . . . . .99 B3
Jones St W1 . . . . .248 C5
Jones Wlk **6** TW10 . . . . .154 B5
Jonquil Gdns **5** TW12 . .173 C4
Jonson Cl Hayes UB4 . . . . . .84 A2
   Mitcham CR4 . . . . .203 B6
Jonson Ho
   Borough The SE1 . . . . . . .262 D5
   18 Canonbury N16 . . . . . . .73 B4
Jordan Cl HA2 . . . . .63 B5
Jordan Ct SW15 . . . . .134 D1
Jordan Ho N10 . . . . .30 C2
Jordan Ho
   12 London SE4 . . . . .140 D1
   Shoreditch N1 . . . . .235 D1
Jordan Lo SW17 . . . . .180 C5
Jordan Rd UB6 . . . . .87 C6
Jordans Cl
   Dagenham RM10 . . . . .81 D4
   Hounslow TW7 . . . . .130 C4
Jordans Ho NW8 . . . . .237 A5
Jordans Mews TW11 . . . . .152 C2
Jo Richardson Com Sch
   RM9 . . . . .102 D6
Joscoyne Ho **5** E1 . . . . . .96 A6
Josef Perrin Ho **1** SE27 .183 B6
Joseph Ave W3 . . . . .89 B1
Joseph Clarke Specl Sch
   E4 . . . . .36 B4
Joseph Conrad Ho SW1 . .259 B3
Joseph Ct N16 . . . . .51 C2
Joseph Hardcastle Cl
   SE14 . . . . .140 D5
Joseph Hood Prim Sch
   SW20 . . . . .201 A6
Josephine Ave SW2 . . . . . .160 B6
Joseph Irwin Ho **11** E14 .119 B6
Joseph Lister Ct E7 . . . . . . .77 A1
Joseph Lister Lo E11 . . . . . .55 B1
Joseph Powell Cl **1**
   SW12 . . . . .159 C5
Joseph Priestley Ho **12**
   E2 .96 B4
Joseph Ray Rd E11 . . . . .76 C6
Joseph St E3 . . . . .97 B3
Joseph Trotter Cl EC1 . . . .234 B1
Joshua Cl Croydon CR2 . . .220 D1
   Muswell Hill N10 . . . . .31 B3
Joshua St E14 . . . . .98 A1
Joslings Cl W12 . . . . .112 A6
Joslyn Cl EN3 . . . . .7 C5
Josseline Ct **9** E3 . . . . . .97 A5
Joubert Mans SW3 . . . . . .257 B2
Joubert St SW11 . . . . .136 D3
Jowett Ho **27** SW9 . . . . .138 A3
Jowett St SE15 . . . . .139 D5
Joyce Ave N18 . . . . .33 C5
Joyce Butler Ho N22 . . . . . .32 B2
Joyce Dawson Way
   SE28 . . . . .124 A6
Joyce Lattimore Ct N9 . . . .18 B1
Joyce Page Cl SE7 . . . . . . .143 D6
Joy Ct NW2 . . . . .68 D5
Joydon Dr RM6 . . . . .58 B3
Joyner Ct UB1 . . . . .107 B6
Joyners Ct RM9 . . . . .81 B4
Joystone Ct **8** EN4 . . . . . .2 C1
Jubb Powell Ho N15 . . . . . .51 C3
Jubet Ho **9** N16 . . . . .73 D4
Jubilee Ave Chingford E4 . . .36 A4
   Romford RM7 . . . . .59 D4
   Twickenham TW2 . . . . .152 A3
Jubilee Bldgs NW8 . . . . . .229 C4
Jubilee Cl
   4 Harlesden NW10 . . . . . . .89 D5
   Kingsbury NW9 . . . . .45 B3
   Pinner HA5 . . . . .22 C1
   Romford RM7 . . . . .59 D4
   Teddington KT1 . . . . .175 C4
Jubilee Cres
   Cubitt Town E14 . . . . .120 A3
   Edmonton N9 . . . . .18 A3

Jubilee Ct continued
   Hounslow TW3 . . . . .129 D2
   Islington N1 . . . . .233 B6
   Muswell Hill N10 . . . . .49 A6
   12 Sutton SM2 . . . . .218 A2
   Thornton Heath CR7 . . . . .204 C5
Jubilee Dr HA4 . . . . .63 A4
Jubilee Gdns UB1 . . . . .85 C1
Jubilee Ho
   3 Hampton TW12 . . . . . . .173 C2
   Lambeth SE11 . . . . .261 B3
Jubilee Hts NW2 . . . . .69 B2
Jubilee JMI Sch N16 . . . . . .52 A1
Jubilee Lo HA7 . . . . .25 A5
Jubilee Mans **10** E1 . . . . .96 C1
Jubilee Par IG8 . . . . .37 C4
Jubilee Park Ctry Pk
   BR2 . . . . .210 C4
Jubilee Pl SW3 . . . . .114 C1 257 B2
Jubilee Prim Sch
   London SW2 . . . . .160 C5
   Woolwich SE28 . . . . .124 C6
Jubilee Rd Cheam SM3 . . .216 D1
   Wembley UB6 . . . . .87 B6
Jubilee St E1 . . . . .96 C2
Jubilee The **2** SE10 . . . .141 D5
Jubilee Villas KT10 . . . . . .196 C1
Jubilee Way
   East Bedfont TW14 . . . . . .150 A3
   Merton SW19 . . . . .179 D2
   Sidcup DA14 . . . . .168 A2
   Tolworth KT4, KT9 . . . . . . .214 D5
Jubilee Wks SW19 . . . . . . .180 A1
Jubilee Wlk WD19 . . . . .22 B6
Jubilee Yd SE1 . . . . .253 C2
Judd St WC1 . . . . . .94 A4 233 A1
Jude St E16 . . . . .98 D1
Judge Heath La UB3 . . . . . .83 B1
Judges' Wlk NW3 . . . . .70 A5
Judge Wlk KT10 . . . . .212 C2
Juer St SW11 . . . . . .136 C5 267 B3
Jules Thorn Ave EN1 . . . . . . .6 A1
Julia Ct E17 . . . . .53 D4
Julia Garfield Mews **4**
   E16 . . . . .121 B5
Julia Gdns IG11 . . . . .102 C5
Juliana Cl N2 . . . . .48 A6
Julian Ave W3 . . . . .110 D6
Julian Cl EN5 . . . . .1 D2
Julian Ct SW13 . . . . .133 D4
Julian Hill HA1 . . . . .64 C6
Julian Ho SE21 . . . . .183 C6
Julian Pl E14 . . . . .119 D1
Julian's Prim Sch SW16 . .182 C6
Julian Taylor Path **7**
   SE23 . . . . .162 B2
Julia St NW5 . . . . .71 A3
Julien Rd W5 . . . . .109 C3
Juliet Ho **11** N1 . . . . .95 C5
Juliette Rd E13 . . . . .99 A5
Julius Caesar Way **7** 9 D1
Julius Ct TW8 . . . . .132 A5
Julius Ho **8** E14 . . . . .98 B1
Julius Nyerere Cl N1 . . . .233 C5
Junction App
   Battersea SW11 . . . . .136 C2
   Lewisham SE13 . . . . .142 A2
Junction Mews W2 . . . . . .237 A2
Junction Pl W2 . . . . .236 D2
Junction Rd
   Ashford TW15 . . . . .171 B5
   Brentford TW8 . . . . .109 D2
   Croydon CR2 . . . . .221 B3
   Dartmouth Pk N19 . . . . .71 C5
   Edmonton N9 . . . . .18 A3
   Harrow HA1 . . . . .42 C3
   Newham E13 . . . . .99 B5
   Tottenham Hale N17 . . . . . .52 A6
Junction Rd E RM6 . . . . . . .59 A2
Junction Rd W RM6 . . . . . .59 A2
Junction Wembley Ret Pk
   The HA9 . . . . .66 D4
Juniper Cl Barnet EN5 . . . . .12 C6
   Chessington KT9 . . . . .214 B3
   Wembley HA9 . . . . .66 C3
Juniper Cres NW1 . . . . .71 A1
Juniper Ct Dagenham RM6 . .58 C3
   Harrow HA3 . . . . .24 C2
   Hounslow TW3 . . . . .129 D1
   Stoke Newington N16 . . . . .73 B6
   Thornton Heath CR0 . . . . .204 C3
Juniper Dr SW18 . . . . .136 A1
Juniper Gdns
   Ashford TW16 . . . . .171 A1
   Streatham CR4 . . . . .181 C2
Juniper Ho **12** Ealing W5 . .87 C2
   6 Peckham SE14, SE15 . .140 C5
   9 Richmond TW9 . . . . . . .132 D4
Juniper La E6 . . . . .100 A2
Juniper Rd IG1 . . . . .78 D4
Juniper St **16** E1 . . . . . . .118 C6
Juniper Way UB3 . . . . .105 C6
Juno Ct **11** SW9 . . . . . . .138 C5
Juno Ho **2** E3 . . . . .97 C6
Juno Way SE14 . . . . .140 D6
Juno Way Ind Est SE14 . . .140 D6
Jupiter Ct
   10 Brixton SW9 . . . . .138 C5
   8 Northolt UB5 . . . . .84 D4

Jupiter Hts UB10 . . . . .82 B6
Jupiter Way N7 . . . . .72 B2
Jupp Rd E15 . . . . .76 B1
Jupp Rd W E15 . . . . .98 B6
Jura Ho SE16 . . . . .119 A2
Jurston Ct SE1 . . . . .251 B1
Justice Wlk SW3 . . . . .267 A5
Justin Cl TW8 . . . . .131 D5
Justin Ct **3** CR7 . . . . .204 C4
Justines Pl E2 . . . . .96 D4
Justin Plaza CR4 . . . . .202 C5
Justin Rd E4 . . . . .35 B4
Jute La EN3 . . . . .7 A2
Jutland Cl N19 . . . . .50 A1
Jutland Ho
   4 London SE5 . . . . .139 A3
   10 Woolwich SE7 . . . . . . .122 A2
Jutland Rd Catford SE6 . . .164 A4
   Newham E13 . . . . .99 A3
Jutsums Ave RM7 . . . . .59 D3
Jutsums Ct RM7 . . . . .59 D3
Jutsums La RM7 . . . . .59 D2
Juxon Cl HA3 . . . . .23 D2
Juxon St SE11 . . . . .116 B2 260 C4
JVC Bsns Pk NW2 . . . . .46 A1

K

Kaduna Cl HA5 . . . . .40 B4
Kaine Pl CR0 . . . . .207 A2
Kaizen Prim Sch E13 . . . . . .99 B3
Kale Rd DA18 . . . . .125 A4
Kambala Rd SW11 . . . . . . .136 B2
Kangley Bridge Ctr
   SE26 . . . . .185 B5
Kangley Bridge Rd SE26 . .185 B5
Kaplan Dr N21 . . . . .16 B6
Karachi Ho E15 . . . . .76 C2
Kara Way NW2 . . . . .68 D4
Karen Ct Bromley BR1 . . . .186 D2
   2 Camberwell SE5 . . . . . .139 C2
   Forest Hill SE23 . . . . .163 A5
Karen Ho **7** N16 . . . . .73 B4
Karens Ct EN3 . . . . .6 D6
Karen Terr Ilford IG2 . . . . . . .57 B4
   Leyton E11 . . . . .76 D6
Karenza Ct HA9 . . . . .43 C2
Kariba Cl N9 . . . . .18 C1
Karman Ct HA3 . . . . .42 C6
Karma Way HA2 . . . . .41 C1
Karoline Gdns UB6 . . . . . . .86 B5
Karyatis Ct EN1 . . . . .17 D6
Kashgar Rd SE18 . . . . .123 D2
Kashmir Rd SE7 . . . . .143 D5
Kasmin Ct NW10 . . . . .68 A1
Kassala Rd
   SW11 . . . . .136 D4 267 D1
Katella Trad Est IG11 . . . . .101 C4
Kates Cl EN5 . . . . .12 A6
Katharine Rd **1** TW1 . . . .153 A3
Katharine St CR0 . . . . .221 A5
Katherine Cl **3** SE16 . . . .118 D5
Katherine Ct
   17 Forest Hill SE23 . . . . .162 C3
   Penge SE20 . . . . .184 C2
Katherine Gdns SE9 . . . . .143 D1
Katherine Ho
   15 Kensal Town W10 . . . . .91 A3
   6 South Croydon CR0 . . . .221 A5
   South Norwood SE19 . . . . .183 C4
Katherine Rd E6, E7 . . . . . . .77 C1
Katherine Sq W11 . . . . . . .244 A4
Kathleen Ave Acton W3 . . . .89 A2
   Wembley HA0 . . . . .66 A1
Kathleen Ferrier Ct **4**
   N17 . . . . .33 D3
Kathleen Godfree Ct
   SW19 . . . . .179 C5
Kathleen Moore Ct BR4 . .224 A6
Kathleen Rd SW11 . . . . . . .136 D2
Katrine Ct NW2 . . . . .68 C5
Kayemoor Rd SM2 . . . . . . .218 C2
Kay Rd SW9 . . . . .138 B3
Kays Ct EN3 . . . . .6 D1
Kay St E2 . . . . .96 A5
Keadby Ho **2** UB5 . . . . . . .85 B4
Kean Ho **5** SE17 . . . . . . .138 D6
Kean St WC2 . . . . . .94 B1 240 C1
Keates Est N16 . . . . .73 D6
Keatley Gn E4 . . . . .35 B4
Keats Ave E16 . . . . .121 B5
Keats Cl Bermondsey SE1 . .263 C3
   Enfield EN3 . . . . .18 C6
   Hampstead NW3 . . . . .70 C4
   Hayes UB4 . . . . .84 A2
   Mitcham SW19 . . . . .180 B4
   Wanstead E11 . . . . .55 B4
Keats Gr NW3 . . . . .70 C4
Keats Ho
   7 Beckenham BR3 . . . . . .185 D4
   22 Bethnal Green E2 . . . . . .96 C4
   30 Camberwell SE5 . . . . .139 A5
   Chelsea SW1 . . . . .269 B6
   Harrow HA2 . . . . .64 C6
Keats House Mus★ NW3 . .70 C4
Keats Par **3** N9 . . . . .18 A2
Keats Pl EC2 . . . . .242 C3
Keats Rd DA16 . . . . .145 D4

Keats Way Croydon CR0 . . .206 C3
   Southall UB6 . . . . .85 D2
   West Drayton UB7 . . . . . . .104 B2
Kebbell Terr E7 . . . . .77 B3
Keble Cl New Malden KT4 . .199 D1
   Northolt UB5 . . . . .64 A3
Keble Ct SW19 . . . . .179 C4
Keble Ho **4** SW15 . . . . . .156 D5
Keble Pl SW13 . . . . .134 B6
Keble Prep Sch N21 . . . . . . .16 C4
Keble St SW17 . . . . .180 A6
Kechill Gdns BR2 . . . . .209 A2
Kedelston Ct E5 . . . . .75 A4
Kedeston Ct SM1 . . . . .201 D1
Kedge Ho E14 . . . . .119 C3
Kedleston Dr BR5 . . . . .211 D4
Kedleston Wlk **4** E2 . . . . .96 B4
Kedyngton Ho **5** HA8 . . . .27 A1
Keeble Cl SE18 . . . . .144 D6
Keedonwood Rd BR1 . . . . .186 D5
Keel Cl Barking IG11 . . . . . .102 C5
   Rotherhithe SE16 . . . . .118 C5
Keel Ct **8** E14 . . . . .120 B6
Keeley Rd CR0 . . . . .221 A6
Keeley St WC2 . . . . .94 B1 240 C1
Keeling Ct **2** TW1 . . . . . .174 C5
Keeling Ct CR0 . . . . .220 D4
Keeling Ho **4** E2 . . . . .96 B5
Keeling Rd SE9 . . . . .165 D6
Keelson Ho **9** E14 . . . . . .119 C3
Keely Cl EN4 . . . . .14 C6
Keemor Cl SE18 . . . . .144 C5
Keens Cl SW16 . . . . .181 D5
Keen's Rd CR0 . . . . .221 A4
Keen's Yd N1 . . . . .72 D2
Keepers Ct **4** CR2 . . . . . .221 A3
Keepers Mews TW11 . . . . .175 C4
Keeper Wharf E1 . . . . .118 D6
Keepier Wharf **1** E14 . . . .119 C6
Keep The Forest Hill SE6 . .163 C3
   Kidbrooke SE3 . . . . .143 A3
   Kingston u T KT2 . . . . .176 B3
Keeton's Rd SE16 . . . . .118 B3
Keevil Dr SW19 . . . . .157 A4
Keighley Cl N7 . . . . .72 A4
Keightley Dr SE9 . . . . .167 A3
Keilder Cl UB10 . . . . .82 C5
Keildon Rd SW11 . . . . .136 D1
Keir Hardie Ho
   6 Belvedere DA17 . . . . . .125 C3
   Fulham W6 . . . . .134 D6
   15 Upper Holloway N19 . . .49 D2
   Willesden NW10 . . . . .67 D1
Keir Hardie Way
   Barking IG11 . . . . .80 A1
   Hayes UB4 . . . . .84 A4
Keir Hardy Prim Sch **13**
   E16 . . . . .99 A2
Keirin Rd E20 . . . . .99 A3
Keir The SW19 . . . . .178 C5
Keith Connor Cl **5** SW8 . .137 B2
Keith Gr W12 . . . . .112 A5
Keith Ho NW6 . . . . .91 D5
Keith Park Rd UB10 . . . . . . .60 B1
Keith Rd Barking IG11 . . . . .101 B5
   Hayes UB3 . . . . .105 C3
   Walthamstow E17 . . . . .35 B2
Keith Sutton Ho **3** SE9 . .167 A2
Kelbrook Rd SE3 . . . . .144 A2
Kelby Ho N7 . . . . .72 B2
Kelceda Cl NW2 . . . . .68 A6
Kelf Gr UB3 . . . . .83 D1
Kelfield Ct **1** W10 . . . . . . .90 D1
Kelfield Gdns W10 . . . . .90 D1
Kelfield Mews W10 . . . . . . .90 D1
Kelham Ho **10** SE18 . . . .144 D6
Kelland Cl **1** N8 . . . . .49 D4
Kelland Rd E13 . . . . .99 A3
Kellaway Rd SE3 . . . . .143 D3
Keller Cres E12 . . . . .77 D4
Kellerton Rd SE13 . . . . .164 C6
Kellett Ho N1 . . . . .235 D5
Kellett Rd SW2 . . . . .138 C1
Kelling Gdns CR0 . . . . .204 D2
Kellino St SW17 . . . . .180 D6
Kellner Rd SE28 . . . . .123 D3
Kellow Ho SE1 . . . . .252 C2
Kell St SE1 . . . . . . .116 D3 261 D6
Kelly Ave SE15 . . . . .139 D4
Kelly Cl
   Upper Halliford TW17 . . . . .171 C1
   Willesden NW10 . . . . .67 B5
Kelly Ct **18** E14 . . . . .119 C6
Kelly Mews **4** W9 . . . . . . .91 B3
Kelly Rd NW7 . . . . .29 A4
Kelly St NW1 . . . . .71 B2
Kelly Way RM6 . . . . .59 A3
Kelman Cl SW4 . . . . .137 D3
Kelmore Gr SE22 . . . . .140 A1
Kelmscott **5** SE23 . . . . . .162 D1
Kelmscott Cl E17 . . . . .35 B2
Kelmscott Ct **2** HA7 . . . . .25 C6
Kelmscott Gdns W12 . . . . .112 A3
Kelmscott House★ W6 . . .112 B2
Kelmscott L Ctr E17 . . . . . . .53 B3
Kelmscott Rd SW11 . . . . . .158 D6
Kelmscott Sch E17 . . . . . . .53 B3
Kelross Rd N5 . . . . .73 A4
Kelsall Cl SE3 . . . . .143 B3
Kelsall Mews TW9 . . . . . . .132 C4

Kelsey Gate **8** BR3 . . . . . 185 D1
Kelsey La BR3 . . . . . . 207 C6
Kelsey Park Ave BR3 . . . 185 D1
Kelsey Park Man BR3 . . 207 D6
Kelsey Park Rd BR3 . . . 185 C1
Kelsey Park Sp Coll
BR3 . . . . 207 C6
Kelsey Rd BR5 . . . . 190 B1
Kelsey Sq BR3 . . . . 185 C1
Kelsey St E2 . . . . 96 A3
Kelsey Way BR3 . . . . . . 207 C6
Kelshall St E4 . . . . .73 A6
Kelso Ct SE20 . . . . 184 B3
Kelso Lo E18 . . . . 37 B1
Kelson Ho E14 . . . . 120 A3
Kelso Pl W8 . . . . 113 D3 255 D6
Kelso Rd SM5 . . . . 202 A2
Kelvedon Cl KT2 . . . . . . 176 C4
Kelvedon Cl HA4 . . . . 62 C4
Kelvedon Ho SW8 . . . . 270 B2
Kelvedon Rd
SW6 . . . . 135 B5 264 D3
Kelvin Ave N13 . . . . 32 B4
Kelvinbrook KT8 . . . . . . 195 D6
Kelvin Cl KT19 . . . . 214 C2
Kelvin Cres HA3 . . . . 24 C3
Kelvin Ct Chiswick W4 . . 133 A5
Harrow HA2 . . . . 42 A1
Isleworth TW7 . . . . . . 130 C3
Notting Hill W11 . . . . 245 A5
7 Penge SE20 . . . . . . 184 B2
8 Twickenham TW1 . . . 153 B5
Kelvin Dr TW1 . . . . 153 B5
Kelvin Gdns Southall UB1 . .85 C1
Thornton Heath CR0 . . 204 A2
Kelvin Gr Forest Hill SE26 .162 B1
Surbiton KT6 . . . . 214 A5
Kelvin Grove Prim Sch **7**
SE26 . . . . 162 B1
Kelvington Cl CR0 . . . . 207 A2
Kelvington Rd SE15 . . . 162 D6
Kelvin Ho Southall UB2 . . . .85 C2
Kelvin Ind Est UB6 . . . . . .85 D6
Kelvin Par BR6 . . . . 211 C1
Kelvin Rd Highbury N5 . . . .73 A4
Welling DA16 . . . . 146 A2
Kelyway Ho **20** SW2 . . . . 160 C4
Kember St N1 . . . . 72 B1
Kemble Dr BR2 . . . . 226 A5
Kemble Ho Isleworth SW9 . 138 D2
Stanmore HA7 . . . . .24 D5
Kemble Rd Croydon CR0 . . 220 D5
Forest Hill SE23 . . . . . 162 D3
Tottenham N17 . . . . 34 B2
Kemble St WC2 . . . . 94 B1 240 C1
Kemerton Rd
Beckenham BR3 . . . . . 185 D1
Camberwell SE5 . . . . . 139 A2
Croydon CR0 . . . . 205 D2
Kemey's St E9 . . . . .75 A3
Kemnal Rd BR7 . . . . 189 B5
Longlands BR7, SE9 . . 167 B1
Kemnal Tech Coll DA14 . . 190 B3
Kemnal Warren BR7 . . . 189 B4
Kemp **24** SW8 . . . . .27 D2
Kemp Ct SW9 . . . . 270 A3
Kempe Ho SE1 . . . . 262 D5
Kempe Rd NW6 . . . . 90 D5
Kemp Gdns CR0 . . . . . . 205 A3
Kemp Ho Finsbury EC1 . . 235 C1
1 Globe Town E2 . . . . . .96 D5
Wallend E6 . . . . .78 C2
Kempis Way **5** SE22 . . 161 C6
Kemplay Rd NW3 . . . . . . .70 B4
Kemp Rd RM8 . . . . .58 D1
Kemps Ct NW2 . . . . .68 D5
Kemp's Ct W1 . . . . 239 C1
Kemps Dr E14 . . . . 119 C6
Kempsford Gdns
SW5 . . . . 113 C1 255 B1
Kempsford Rd
Lambeth SE11 . . . . . . 261 B1
Newington SE11 . . . . . 261 C1
Kemps Gdns SE13 . . . . 164 A6
Kempshott Rd SW16 . . 182 A3
Kempson Rd
SW6 . . . . 135 C5 265 B3
Kempthorne Rd SE8 . . . 119 B2
Kempton Ave
Northolt UB5 . . . . .63 C3
Sunbury TW16 . . . . . . 172 B2
Kempton Cl UB10 . . . . . .61 A4
Kempton Ct Stepney E1 . . .96 B2
Sunbury TW16 . . . . . . 172 B2
Kempton Ho **13** N1 . . . . .95 C6
Kempton Lo **3** NW9 . . 219 D5
Kempton Park Race Course
TW16 . . . . 172 C3
Kempton Park Sta
TW16 . . . . 172 B2
Kempton Rd E6 . . . . 100 B6
Kempton Wlk CR0 . . . . 207 A3
Kempt St SE18 . . . . 144 C6
Kemsing Cl
Coney Hall BR2 . . . . . . 224 D6
Sidcup DA5 . . . . 169 A4
South Norwood CR7 . . 205 A5
Kemsing Ho SE1 . . . . . . 252 D1
Kemsing Rd SE10 . . . . . 121 A1
Kemsley SE13 . . . . 163 D6

Kemsley Ct Ealing W13 . . 109 C5
St Paul's Cray BR5 . . . . 190 B2
Kenbrook Ho
Kensington W14 . . . . . 254 D5
5 Kentish Town NW5 . . . 71 C3
Kenbury Cl UB10 . . . . 60 C5
Kenbury Gdns **10** SE5 . . 139 A3
Kenbury Mans **15** SE5 . . 139 A3
Kenbury St SE5 . . . . 139 A3
Kenchester Cl
SW8 . . . . 138 A5 270 B3
Kencot Cl DA18 . . . . 125 B4
Kencot Way DA18 . . . . . 125 B4
Kendal NW1 . . . . 231 D2
Kendal Ave Acton W3 . . . .88 D2
Barking IG11 . . . . 101 C6
Edmonton N18 . . . . .33 B6
Kendal Cl
Camberwell SE5 . . . . . 138 D5
East Barnet N20 . . . . . . .14 C2
East Bedfont TW14 . . . 149 D3
Hayes UB4 . . . . .83 C5
Woodford IG8 . . . . .20 C2
Kendal Ct Acton W3 . . . . .88 C2
Brondesbury NW2 . . . . .69 A3
9 Chingford E4 . . . . 20 A3
Kendale Rd BR1 . . . . . . 186 C5
Kendal Gdns
Edmonton N18 . . . . . . .33 B6
Sutton SM1 . . . . 218 A6
Kendal Ho Edgware HA8 . . 27 A6
Forest Hill SE23 . . . . . 163 B3
32 Hackney E9 . . . . .74 C1
Islington N1 . . . . 233 D4
Penge SE20 . . . . 184 B1
Kendall Ave BR3 . . . . . . 185 A1
Kendall Ct
3 London SE22 . . . . . . 162 A6
Mitcham SW19 . . . . . . 180 B4
5 Penge SE19 . . . . . . 183 D3
Sidcup DA15 . . . . 168 A1
Kendall Ho SE12 . . . . . . 164 D4
Kendall Lo **5** BR1 . . . . 187 B2
Kendall Pl W1 . . . . 238 A3
Kendall Rd
Beckenham BR3 . . . . . 185 A1
Isleworth TW7 . . . . . . 131 A3
Kidbrooke SE18 . . . . . 144 A4
Kendalmere Cl N10 . . . . .31 B2
Kendal Par N18 . . . . .33 B6
Kendal Pl SW15 . . . . . . 157 B6
Kendal Rd NW10 . . . . . . .68 A4
Kendal Stps W2 . . . . . . 237 B1
Kendal St W2 . . . . 92 C1 237 B1
Kender Prim Sch SE14 . . 140 C4
Kender St SE14 . . . . 140 C4
Kendoa Rd **1** SW4 . . . . 137 D1
Kendon Cl E11 . . . . .55 B4
Kendon Ho E15 . . . . .76 B1
Kendra Ct CR2 . . . . 220 D1
Kendra Hall Rd CR2 . . . 220 D1
Kendrey Gdns TW2 . . . . 152 C4
Kendrick Ct **12** SE15 . . 140 B4
Kendrick Mews SW7 . . . 256 C3
Kendrick Pl SW7 . . . . . . 256 C3
Kenelm Cl HA1 . . . . .65 A5
Kenerne Dr EN1 . . . . .13 A6
Kenilford Rd SW12 . . . . 159 B4
Kenilworth Ave
Harrow HA2 . . . . .63 B4
Walthamstow E17 . . . . .53 C6
Wimbledon SW19 . . . . 179 C6
Kenilworth Cres EN1 . . . . 5 C4
Kenilworth Ct
7 Chingford E4 . . . . . . 20 A3
Fulham SW6 . . . . 135 A2
Twickenham TW2 . . . . 152 C2
Kenilworth Gdns
Hayes UB4 . . . . .83 D2
Ilford IG3 . . . . .79 D6
Southall UB1 . . . . .85 B4
South Oxhey WD19 . . . .22 C5
Woolwich SE18 . . . . . . 144 D3
Kenilworth Ho HA7 . . . . .25 B3
Kenilworth Rd
Ashford TW15, TW19 . . . 148 A1
Bow E3 . . . . .97 A5
Ealing W5 . . . . 110 A5
Edgware HA8 . . . . .11 A1
Kilburn NW6 . . . . .91 B6
Orpington BR5 . . . . . . 211 A3
Penge SE20 . . . . 184 D2
Stoneleigh KT17 . . . . . 216 A3
Kenilworth Terr **3** SM2 . 217 C1
Kenley N17 . . . . .33 B1
Kenley Cl Barnet EN4 . . . . 2 C1
Chislehurst BR7 . . . . . 188 A4
St Paul's Cray BR7 . . . 211 C6
Kenley Gdns CR7 . . . . . 204 D5
Kenley Ho
5 Croydon CR0 . . . . . 206 A3
6 St Paul's Cray BR5 . . 190 B1
Kenley Rd
Kingston u T KT1, KT3 . . 176 D1
Merton SW19 . . . . 201 C6
Twickenham TW1 . . . . 153 B5
Kenley Wlk Cheam SM3 . . 216 D4
Notting Hill W11 . . . . . 244 A5
Kenlor Ct **6** HA8 . . . . 26 D5

Kenlor Rd SW17 . . . . . . 180 B5
Kenmare Ct **5** HA7 . . . . .25 C6
Kenmare Dr
Mitcham CR4 . . . . 180 D3
1 Tottenham N17 . . . . . .33 D1
Kenmare Gdns N13 . . . . .33 A6
Kenmare Rd CR7 . . . . . . 204 C3
Kenmere Gdns HA0 . . . . .88 C6
Kenmere Rd DA16 . . . . . 146 C3
Kenmont Gdns NW10 . . .90 B4
Kenmont Prim Sch NW10 . .90 B4
Kenmore Ave HA3 . . . . . .43 A6
Kenmore Cl TW9 . . . . . . 132 C5
Kenmore Cres UB4 . . . . .83 D4
Kenmore Ct NW6 . . . . . .69 C1
Kenmore Gdns HA8 . . . . 26 D1
Kenmore Park Fst & Mid
Schs HA3 . . . . .44 A6
Kenmore Rd HA3 . . . . . . .43 D5
Kenmure Mans W5 . . . . .87 C3
Kenmure Rd E8 . . . . .74 B3
Kenmure Yd E8 . . . . .74 B3
Kennacraig Cl **6** E16 . . 121 A5
Kennard Ho **12** SW11 . . 137 A3
Kennard Mans **1** E16 . . . .30 D5
Kennard Rd London N11 . . 30 D5
Stratford E15 . . . . .76 B1
Kennard St
9 London SW11 . . . . . 137 A3
Newham E16 . . . . 122 B5
Kennedy Ave EN3 . . . . . .18 C5
Kennedy Cl Crofton BR5 . 211 B1
1 Mitcham CR4 . . . . . . 181 A1
Newham E13 . . . . .99 A5
Pinner HA5 . . . . .23 B4
Kennedy Cox Ho **9** E16 . .98 D2
Kennedy Ct
Ashford TW15 . . . . 171 A5
Bushey WD23 . . . . .8 B2
Kennedy Ho SE11 . . . . . 260 C2
Kennedy Path W7 . . . . . .86 D3
Kennedy Rd
Barking IG11 . . . . 101 C6
Ealing W7 . . . . .86 C2
Kennedy Wlk SE17 . . . . 262 D3
Kennet Cl SW11 . . . . . . 136 B1
Kennet Ct **1** W2 . . . . . . .91 C2
Kennet Dr UB4 . . . . .85 A2
Kennet Ho NW8 . . . . . . 236 D6
Kennet Rd Isleworth TW7 . 130 D2
West Kilburn W9 . . . . . .91 B3
Kennet Sq CR4 . . . . 180 C2
Kennet St E1 . . . . 118 A5
Kennett Ho HA1 . . . . . . .64 D6
Kennett Rd RM6 . . . . . . .59 A2
Kennett Wharf La EC4 . . 252 B6
Kenninghall **15** 34 C5
Kenninghall Rd
London N18 . . . . .34 C5
Lower Clapton E5 . . . . .74 B5
Kenning Ho **6** N1 . . . . . .95 C6
Kenning St **18** SE16 . . . 118 C4
Kennings Way
SE11 . . . . 116 C1 261 B2
KENNINGTON 116 C1
Kennington Ent Ctr SE17 261 C1
Kennington La
SE11 . . . . 116 B1 260 D1
Kennington Oval
SE11 . . . . 138 B6 270 D4
Kennington Palace Ct
SE11 . . . . 261 A2
Kennington Park Gdns
SE17 . . . . 138 D6
Kennington Park Ho
SE11 . . . . 261 B1
Kennington Park Pl
SE11 . . . . 138 D6
Kennington Park Rd
SE11 . . . . 116 D1 261 C2
Kennington Rd
SE17 . . . . 116 C2 261 A3
Kennington Sta
SE17 . . . . 116 D1 261 C2
KENNOLDES SE21 . . . . . 161 B2
Kennylands Ct NW4 . . . . .46 B3
Kenrick Pl W1 . . . . 238 A3
KENSAL GREEN 90 C4
Kensal Green Cemy (All
Souls)★ NW10 . . . . . . .90 C4
Kensal Green Sta NW10 . . 90 C3
Kensal Ho W10 . . . . .90 D3
Kensal Rd W10 . . . . .91 A3
KENSAL RISE 90 D5
Kensal Rise Prim Sch
NW6 . . . . .90 D5
Kensal Rise Sta NW10 . . .90 D5
KENSAL TOWN 91 A3

KENSINGTON 113 C4
Kensington Acad SW6 . . 256 C3
Kensington Ave
Plashet E12 . . . . .78 B2
South Norwood CR7 . . 205 A4
Kensington Avenue Prim Sch
CR7 . . . . 182 C2
Kensington & Chelsea Coll
Chelsea SW10 . . . 136 A5 266 A4
14 Kensal Town W10 . . .91 A2
Kensington Church Ct
W8 . . . . 245 C4
Kensington Church St
W8 . . . . 113 C5 245 B3
Kensington Church Wlk
W8 . . . . 245 C4
Kensington Cl N11 . . . . . .31 A4
Kensington Court Mans
W8 . . . . 245 D4
Kensington Court Mews
W8 . . . . 255 D6
Kensington Court Pl
W8 . . . . 113 D3 255 D6
Kensington Ct
2 Burnt Oak NW7 . . . . .27 B5
Enfield EN2 . . . . 5 C1
Hendon NW4 . . . . .28 C1
Kensington W8 . . 113 D3 245 D1
Kensington Ct Gdns W8 . 255 D6
Kensington Dr IG8 . . . . . .37 D1
Kensington Gardens★
W2 . . . . 114 A5 246 B3
Kensington Gate
W8 . . . . 114 A3 256 A6
Kensington Gdns
Kingston u T KT1 . . . . . 197 D6
Redbridge IG1 . . . . .56 B1
Kensington Gdns Sq W2 . .91 D1
Kensington Gore
SW7 . . . . 114 B4 246 C1
Kensington Hall Gdns
W14 . . . . 254 C2
Kensington High St
W8 . . . . 113 C3 255 B6
Kensington Ho **3** NW5 . . .71 C3
Kensington Hts
Harrow HA1 . . . . .42 D1
Kensington W8 . . . . . . 245 A3
Kensington L Ctr
W11 . . . . 113 A6 244 A6
Kensington Lodge UB5 . . .85 C5
Kensington Mall W8 . . . 245 B4
Kensington Mans SW5 . . 255 B2
Kensington Olympia Sta
W14 . . . . 113 A3 254 A6
Kensington Pal★
W8 . . . . 113 D5 245 D5
Kensington Palace Gdns
W8 . . . . 113 D5 245 C4
Kensington Park Gdns
W11 . . . . 113 B6 244 D5
Kensington Park Mews
W11 . . . . .91 B1
Kensington Park Rd
W11 . . . . 113 B6 244 D6
Kensington Pl
W8 . . . . 113 C5 245 A4
Kensington Prep Sch
SW6 . . . . 135 B4 264 D2
Kensington Prim Sch E12 .78 B2
Kensington Rd
Kensington SW7 . . 114 A4 246 B1
Northolt UB5 . . . . .85 C5
Kensington Sq
W8 . . . . 113 D4 245 C1
Kensington Terr CR2 . . . 221 B1
Kensington Village
W14 . . . . 113 B2 254 D3
Kensington W W14 . . . . 254 A4
Kensit Meml Coll N3 . . . .29 A1
Kensworth Ho EC1 . . . . 235 C1
Kent Ave Bexley DA16 . . . 167 D6
Dagenham RM9 . . . . . 103 C3
Ealing W13 . . . . .87 B2
Kent Cl
Mitcham CR4, SW16 . . 204 A5
Orpington BR6 . . . . . . 227 C2
Kent Ct Acton W3 . . . . . .88 B1
3 Haggerston E2 . . . . . .95 D5
Hendon NW9 . . . . .27 C1
Kent Dr Cockfosters EN4 . . 15 A6
Teddington TW11 . . . . 174 C5
Kent Gate Way CR0 . . . . 223 D3
Kent Gdns Ealing W13 . . .87 B2
Ruislip HA4 . . . . .40 B5
Kent Ho Camberwell SE1 . 263 D1
13 Chiswick W4 . . . . . 111 C1
Edgware HA8 . . . . .26 B3
Marylebone W1 . . . . . 239 A2
Pimlico SW1 . . . . 259 C1
Richmond TW10 . . . . . 154 C6
Kent House La BR3 . . . . 185 A5
Kent House Rd BR3 . . . . 185 A5
Kent House Sta BR3 . . . 185 A2
Kent House Station App
BR3 . . . . 184 D2
Kentish Bldgs SE1 . . . . 252 C3
Kentish Rd DA17 . . . . . . 125 C4
KENTISH TOWN 71 C3

Kentish Town CE Prim Sch
NW5 . . . . .71 C3
Kentish Town City Farm★
NW5 . . . . .71 A3
Kentish Town Rd NW1 . . .71 B2
Kentish Town Sta NW5 . . .71 C3
Kentish Town West Sta
NW5 . . . . .71 B2
Kentish Way BR1, BR2 . . 209 B6
Kentlea Rd SE28 . . . . . . 123 C4
Kent Lo **9** SW19 . . . . . . 156 D3
Kentmere Ho SE15 . . . . 140 C6
Kentmere Rd SE18 . . . . 123 C2
KENTON 43 C3
Kenton Ave Harrow HA1 . . .42 D2
Southall UB1 . . . . 107 C6
Sunbury TW16 . . . . . . 173 A1
Kenton Ct
2 Forest Hill SE26 . . . 185 A6
Harrow HA3 . . . . .43 B3
3 Richmond TW10 . . . 153 D5
West Kensington W14 . . 254 C5
Kenton Gdns HA3 . . . . . .43 C4
Kenton Grove Ho HA3 . . .44 B4
Kenton Ho
20 Globe Town E1 . . . . .96 C3
Highbury N5 . . . . .72 C5
Kenton La Harrow HA3 . . .24 D3
Kenton HA3 . . . . .43 D5
Kenton Park Ave HA3 . . . .43 D5
Kenton Park Cl HA3 . . . . .43 C4
Kenton Park Cres HA3 . . .43 D5
Kenton Park Mans HA3 . . 43 C4
Kenton Park Par HA3 . . . .43 D4
Kenton Park Rd HA3 . . . . 43 C5
Kenton Rd Harrow HA3 . . . 43 C4
Homerton E9 . . . . .74 D2
Kenton St WC1 . . . . 240 D1
Kenton Twr HA3 . . . . . . .43 B3
Kenton Way Hayes UB4 . . .83 C4
Kent Pas NW1 . . . . 237 C6
Kent Pk Ind Est SE15 . . . 140 B6
Kent Rd Dagenham RM10 . 81 D3
East Molesey KT8 . . . . 196 A5
Kingston u T KT1 . . . . . 197 D6
Richmond TW9 . . . . . . 132 C5
South Acton W4 . . . . . 111 A3
Southgate N21 . . . . . . .17 B4
West Wickham BR4 . . . 207 D1
Kent St Haggerston E2 . . . 95 D5
Newham E13 . . . . .99 B4
Kent Terr NW1 . . . . 92 C4 230 B1
Kent View Gdns IG3 . . . . .79 C6
Kent Way KT6 . . . . 214 B6
Kentwell Cl SE4 . . . . 141 A1
Kentwins N14 . . . . .15 B6
Kentwode Gn SW13 . . . . 134 A5
Kent Yard SW7 . . . . 247 B1
Kenver Ave N12 . . . . .30 B4
Ken Way HA9 . . . . .67 B2
Kenway Rd SW5 . . 113 D2 255 C3
Ken Wilson Ho **15** E2 . . . .96 A5
Kenwood Ave N14 . . . . . .15 D6
Kenwood Cl
North End NW3 . . . . . . .48 B1
Sipson UB7 . . . . 126 C6
Kenwood Ct NW9 . . . . . .45 A5
Kenwood Dr BR3 . . . . . 208 A6
Kenwood Gdns Ilford IG2 . .56 C4
2 Wanstead E18 . . . . . .55 B6
Kenwood Ho
16 Brixton SW9 . . . . . 138 D1
Enfield EN1 . . . . .17 C5
Kenwood Ho★ NW3 . . . . .48 C1
Kenwood Rd Edmonton N9 . 18 A3
Highgate N6 . . . . .48 B3
Kenworthy Rd E9 . . . . . .75 A2
Kenwrick Ho N1 . . . . . . 233 D5
Kenwyn Dr NW2 . . . . . . .67 D5
Kenwyn Rd
Clapham SW4 . . . . 137 D1
Wimbledon SW20 . . . . 178 C2
Kenya Rd SE7 . . . . 143 D5
Kenyngton Dr TW16 . . . . 172 C3
Kenyngton Manor Prim Sch
TW16 . . . . 172 A4
Kenyngton Pl HA3 . . . . . .43 C4
Kenyon Ho **31** SE5 . . . . 139 A5
Kenyon St SW6 . . . . 134 C4
Keogh Rd E15 . . . . .76 D2
Kepler Ho **9** SE10 . . . . . 120 D1
Kepler Rd SW2, SW4 . . . 138 A1
Keppel Ho Brompton SW3 257 A3
5 Deptford SE8 . . . . . 119 B1
Keppel Rd Dagenham RM9 . 81 A5
Newham E6 . . . . 100 B6
Keppel Row SE1 . . . . . . 252 A3
Keppel St WC1 . . . . 239 D4
Kerala Ct N17 . . . . .33 D2
Kerbela St **3** E2 . . . . . . .96 A3
Kerbey St E14 . . . . .97 D1
Kerem Sch N2 . . . . .48 B4
Kerfield Cres SE5 . . . . . 139 B4
Kerfield Pl SE5 . . . . 139 B4
Kerridge Ct **10** N1 . . . . . .73 C2

Kerrier Ho SW10. . . . . . . 266 B3
Kerrington Ct **7** W12. . . 112 C4
Kerrison Pl W5 . . . . 109 D5
Kerrison Rd
　Battersea SW11. . . . . . 136 C2
　Ealing W5 . . . . 109 D5
　Mill Meads E15. . . . . . . 98 B6
Kerrison Villas W5 . . . 109 D5
Kerry N7 . . . . 72 A2
Kerry Ave HA7 . . . . 25 D6
Kerry Cl Newham E16 . . . 99 B1
　Palmers Green N13 . . . 16 B2
Kerry Ct HA7 . . . . 25 D6
Kerry Ho **5** E1. . . . . 96 C1
Kerry Path SE8 . . . . . . 141 B6
Kerry Rd SE8 . . . . 141 B6
Kerscott Ho **30** E3. . . . . . 97 D4
Kersey Gdns SE9 . . . . . 188 A6
Kersfield Ho SW15 . . . . 156 D5
Kersfield Rd SW15 . . . . 156 D5
Kershaw Cl SW18 . . . . . 158 B5
Kershaw Ho **7** SE27 . . . 160 D1
Kershaw Rd RM10. . . . . . 81 C3
Kersley Mews SW11 . . . 267 C1
Kersley Rd N16 . . . . 73 C5
Kersley St SW11 . . . . . . 136 D3
Kerstin Cl UB3. . . . . . . 105 D6
Kerswell Cl N15. . . . . 51 C4
Kerwick Cl **1** N7 . . . . 72 B1
Keslake Mans NW10 . . . . 90 D5
Keslake Rd NW6 . . . . 90 D5
Kessock Cl N17. . . . . 52 B4
Kestlake Rd DA5. . . . . . 168 C5
KESTON. 225 D4
Keston Ave BR2. . . . . . . 225 C3
Keston CE Prim Sch
　BR2. . . . . 225 D3
Keston Cl Bexley DA16 . . 146 C5
　Edmonton N18 . . . . 17 B1
Keston Ct DA5. . . . . 169 B4
Keston Gdns BR2. . . . . . 225 C4
Keston Ho SE17. . . . . . . 263 B2
KESTON MARK. 225 D6
Keston Mark BR2 . . . . . 226 A5
Keston Park Cl BR2 . . . . 226 B5
Keston Rd
　East Dulwich SE15 . . . . 140 A2
　Thornton Heath CR7. . . 204 C3
　West Green N17. . . . . . . 51 B5
Kestrel Ave East Ham E6 . . 100 A2
　Herne Hill SE24 . . . . . . 161 A6
Kestrel Cl
　Grahame Pk NW9. . . . . . 27 C1
　Kingston u T KT2. . . . . . 175 D6
　Neasden NW10 . . . . 67 B3
Kestrel Ct Higham Hill E17. . 34 D1
　Ruislip HA4. . . . . 61 B6
　South Croydon CR2. . . . 221 A4
　Wallington SM6 . . . . . . 219 C3
Kestrel Ho
　4 Battersea SW11. . . . 136 C2
　Enfield EN3. . . . . 19 A6
　Finsbury EC1. . . . . 235 A2
Kestrel Pl SE14 . . . . 141 A6
Kestrel Way UB3. . . . . . 105 B4
Keswick Apartments 4
　N17. . . . . 51 D6
Keswick Ave
　Kingston u T KT2, SW15. . 177 C5
　Merton SW19. . . . . 179 C1
　Upper Halliford TW17. . . 193 C6
Keswick Broadway **1**
　SW15. . . . . 157 B6
Keswick Cl SM1. . . . . . . 218 A4
Keswick Ct
　13 Catford SE6. . . . . . 164 D3
　2 East Dulwich SE22 . 162 A6
Keswick Dr EN3. . . . . 6 C6
Keswick Gdns
　Redbridge IG4 . . . . 56 A5
　Ruislip HA4. . . . . 39 B3
　Wembley HA9. . . . . 66 A4
Keswick Ho **8** SE5. . . . 139 A4
Keswick Hts **5** SW15 . . 157 A6
Keswick Lo E8. . . . . 73 D2
Keswick Mews W5. . . . . 110 A5
Keswick Rd
　Bexleyheath DA7 . . . . . 147 C4
　Broom Hill BR6. . . . . . . 211 D1
　Putney SW15. . . . . 157 A6
　Twickenham TW2 . . . . . 152 A5
　West Wickham BR4 . . . . 224 C6
Kettering Ct CR7. . . . . . 205 A5
Kettering Rd EN3 . . . . 6 D6
Kettering St SW16 . . . . . 181 C4
Kett Gdns SW2 . . . . 160 B6
Kettlebaston Rd E10 . . . . 53 B1
Kettleby Ho SW9. . . . . . 138 D2
Kettlewell Cl N11. . . . . . . 31 A4
Ketton Ho **11** W10. . . . . . 90 C3
Kevan Ct **6** E17. . . . . . . 53 D5
Kevan Ho SE5. . . . . 139 A5
Kevelioc Rd N17. . . . . . . 33 A2
Kevin Cl TW4 . . . . 128 D3
Kevington Cl BR5. . . . . . 211 D5
Kevington Dr BR5, BR7. . . 211 D5
KEW. 132 C6

Kew Bridge TW8 . . . . . . 110 B1
Kew Bridge Ct W4. . . . . 110 C1
Kew Bridge Distribution Ctr
　TW8. . . . . 110 B1
Kew Bridge Rd TW8 . . . . 110 B1
Kew Bridge Sta TW8 . . . 110 B1
Kew Bridge Steam Mus ★
　TW8. . . . . 110 B1
Kew Coll TW9. . . . . 132 C5
Kew Cres SM3 . . . . 217 B5
Kew Ct KT2. . . . . 176 A2
Kew Foot Rd TW9 . . . . . 132 C4
Kew Gardens (Royal
　Botanic) ★ TW9. . . . 132 A4
Kew Gardens Sta TW9. . . 132 C4
Kew Gn TW9. . . . . 132 B6
Kew Green TW9. . . . . . . 132 C6
Kew Green Prep Sch
　TW9 . . . . 132 B6
Kew Lo **11** TW9 . . . . 132 B4
Kew Obsy ★ TW9 . . . . . . 131 C2
Kew Pal ★ TW9. . . . . 132 A5
Kew Pier TW9. . . . . 132 C6
Kew Rd Finchley N2 . . . . . 30 C2
　Richmond TW9, W4. . . . 132 B4
Kew Ret Pk TW9 . . . . . . 132 D3
Kew Riverside Prim Sch
　TW9 . . . . 132 D3
Key Cl E1. . . . . 96 B3
Keyes Ct SE22 . . . . 162 A6
Keyes Rd NW2 . . . . 68 D3
Keyham Ho **31** W2 . . . . . . 91 C2
Key Ho **9** SE11 . . . . . . 138 C6
Keymer Rd SW2 . . . . . . 160 B2
Keynes Ct N2 . . . . 48 D6
Keynes Ct **9** SE28 . . . . 124 B6
Keynsham Ave IG8. . . . . . 36 C6
Keynsham Gdns SE9 . . . 166 A6
Keynsham Ho **2** N4. . . . . 51 A2
Keynsham Rd
　Cheam SM4. . . . . 201 B4
　Eltham SE9. . . . . 166 A6
Keynsham Wlk SM4. . . . 201 D1
Keysham Ave TW5 . . . . . 128 A4
Keysham Ct HA9 . . . . 66 A6
Keystone Cres N1. . . . . . 233 B3
Keywood Dr TW16 . . . . . 172 A4
Keyworth Cl E5. . . . . 75 A4
Keyworth Pl SE1. . . . . . 261 D6
Keyworth Prim Sch
　SE17. . . . . 116 D1 261 C2
Keyworth St SE1. . 116 D3 261 D6
Kezia St SE8. . . . . 119 A1
Khalsa Coll London HA1. . 42 B3
Khalsa Ct N22 . . . . 32 D2
Khama Rd SW17. . . . . . 180 C6
Khartoum Rd Ilford IG1. . . 78 D3
　Newham E13. . . . . 99 B4
　Upper Tooting SW17. . . 180 B6
Khyber Rd SW11. . . . . . 136 C3
Kibworth St SW8 . . 138 B5 270 C3
KIDBROOKE. 143 C3
Kidbrooke Gdns SE3 . . . 143 A4
Kidbrooke Gr SE3 . . . . . 143 B4
Kidbrooke Interchange
　SE3 . . . . 143 C2
Kidbrooke La SE9. . . . . . 144 A1
Kidbrooke Park Cl SE3 . . 143 B4
Kidbrooke Park Prim Sch
　SE3 . . . . 143 C4
Kidbrooke Park Rd SE12,
　SE3. . . . . 143 B2
Kidbrooke Sch SE3 . . . . 143 D3
Kidbrooke Sta SE3 . . . . 143 B2
Kidbrooke Way SE3 . . . . 143 B3
Kiddens BR8 . . . . 191 D1
Kidderminster Pl CR0. . . 204 D1
Kidderminster Rd CR0 . . 205 A2
Kidderpore Ave NW3. . . . 69 C4
Kidderpore Gdns NW3 . . . 69 C4
Kidd Ho RM9. . . . . 81 B4
Kidd Pl SE7. . . . . 122 A1
Kidlington Way NW9. . . . . 27 C2
Kidspace Indoor Adventure
　Pk ★ CR0. . . . . 220 C2
Kierbeck Bsns Complex
　E16. . . . . 121 B4
Kiffen St EC2 . . . . 242 D6
Kilberry Cl TW7. . . . . . . 130 B4
Kilbrennan Ho **9** E14. . . . 98 A1
KILBURN. 91 C6
Kilburn Bridge **14** NW6. . . 91 C6
Kilburn Gate NW6 . . . . . . 91 D5
Kilburn High Rd NW6 . . . . 91 C6
Kilburn High Road Sta
　NW6. . . . . 91 D6
Kilburn Ho **11** W9 . . . . . . 91 B4
Kilburn La W10. . . . . 91 A5
Kilburn Park Rd NW6 . . . . 91 D5
Kilburn Park Sch **10** NW6. . 91 B5
Kilburn Park Sta NW6. . . . 91 C5
Kilburn Pl NW6. . . . . 91 D6
Kilburn Priory NW6 . . . . . 91 D6
Kilburn Sq NW6 . . . . 91 C6
Kilburn Sta NW2. . . . . . . 69 B2
Kilburn Vale NW6. . . . . . . 91 D6
Kilburn Vale Est **13** NW6. . . 91 C6
Kilby Ct SE10 . . . . 120 D3
Kildare Cl HA4. . . . . 40 C1

Kildare Ct W2 . . . . 91 C1
Kildare Gdns W2. . . . . . . 91 C1
Kildare Rd E16. . . . . 99 A2
Kildare Terr W2. . . . . 91 C1
Kildare Wlk E14 . . . . 97 C1
Kildoran Rd SW2 . . . . . 160 A6
Kildowan Rd IG3 . . . . . . 58 A1
Kilgour Rd SE23 . . . . . . 163 A5
Kilkie St SW6. . . . . 136 A3
Killarney Rd SW18 . . . . 158 A5
Killburns Mill Cl SM6. . . 219 B6
Killearn Rd SE6. . . . . . . 164 B3
Killester Gdns KT17, KT4. . 216 B4
Killick Ho SW1. . . . . . . 217 D4
Killick Mews **6** SM3 . . . 217 A2
Killick St N1. . . . . . 94 B5 233 C3
Killieser Ave SW2 . . . . . 160 A2
Killigrew Ho TW16. . . . . 171 C3
Killip Cl E16. . . . . 98 D1
Killoran Ho **9** E14. . . . . 120 A3
Killowen Ave UB5. . . . . . 64 A3
Killowen Rd E9. . . . . 74 D2
Killyon Rd SW8 . . . . . . 137 C3
Kilmaine Rd
　SW6. . . . . 135 A5 264 B3
Kilmarnock Gdns RM8 . . . 80 C5
Kilmarnock Rd WD19 . . . . 22 C6
Kilmarsh Rd W6. . . . . . . 112 C2
Kilmartin Ave SW16. . . . 204 C6
Kilmartin Rd IG3. . . . . . . 80 A6
Kilmington Rd SW13. . . . 134 A6
Kilmiston Ave TW17. . . . 193 A3
Kilmiston Ho TW17. . . . . 193 A3
Kilmore Ho **17** E14 . . . . . 97 D1
Kilmorey Gdns TW1 . . . . 131 B1
Kilmorey Rd TW1. . . . . . 131 B1
Kilmorie Prim Sch SE23 . . 163 A2
Kilmorie Rd SE23 . . . . . 163 A2
Kilmuir Ho SW1 . . . . . . 258 B3
Kiln Cl UB3 . . . . 127 B6
Kiln Ct E14. . . . . 119 B6
Kilner Ho **3** SE11. . . . . 138 C6
Kilner St E14. . . . . 97 C2
Kiln Mews SW17. . . . . . 180 B5
Kiln Pl NW5 . . . . 71 A3
Kilnsey Ct **8** N11. . . . . . 31 A4
Kilnside KT10. . . . . 213 A1
Kiloh Ct **1** SW11. . . . . . 136 C2
Kilpatrick Ct N16. . . . . . . 51 D1
Kilpatrick Way UB4 . . . . . 85 A2
Kilpeck Ho **3** N4. . . . . . . 51 A2
Kilravock Ho SE25 . . . . . 205 C6
Kilravock St W10 . . . . . . 91 A4
Kilronan **5** W3 . . . . 89 B1
Kilross Rd TW14 . . . . . . 149 C3
Kilsby Wlk RM9. . . . . 80 B2
Kilsha Rd KT12 . . . . 194 C3
Kilvinton Dr EN2. . . . . 5 B5
Kimbell Gdns
　SW6. . . . . 135 A4 264 A1
Kimbell Pl SE3. . . . . . . 143 C1
Kimber Ctr The SW18 . . . 157 C4
Kimber Ho **11** SE18. . . . . 144 D6
Kimberley Ave Ilford IG2. . 57 C2
　Newham E6 . . . . 100 A5
　Nunhead SE15 . . . . . . 140 C2
Kimberley Ct
　Belvedere DA17. . . . . . 125 B2
　Kilburn NW6. . . . . 91 A6
Kimberley Dr DA14. . . . . 168 D2
Kimberley Gate **3** BR1. . 186 D3
Kimberley Gdns
　Enfield EN1. . . . . 5 D2
　Harringay N4 . . . . 50 D4
Kimberley Ho **7** E14. . . . 120 A3
Kimberley Ind Est E17. . . 35 B2
Kimberley Rd
　Chingford E4. . . . . 20 C3
　Edmonton N18 . . . . 34 B4
　Kilburn NW6. . . . . 91 A6
　Leyton E11. . . . . 76 B6
　Newham E16 . . . . 98 D3
　Penge BR3. . . . . 184 D1
　Stockwell SW9 . . . . . . 138 A2
　Thornton Heath CR0. . . 204 D3
　Tottenham N17. . . . . . . 34 A1
　Walthamstow E17 . . . . . 35 B2
Kimberley Way E4. . . . . . 20 C3
Kimberley Wlk KT12 . . . 194 B2
Kimber Pl SW18. . . . . . 157 C4
Kimber Rd SW18. . . . . . 157 D4
Kimble Cres WD23 . . . . . . 8 A4
Kimble Ho Lisson Gr NW8. . 237 B6
　1 Lower Holloway N7. . 72 A3
Kimble Rd SW17. . . . . . 180 B4
Kimbolton Cl SE12. . . . . 164 D5
Kimbolton Row SW3 . . . 257 A3
Kimmeridge Gdns 3
　SE9 . . . . 188 A6
Kimmeridge Rd SE9 . . . 188 A6
Kimm Ho **16** E17. . . . . . . 53 D6
Kimpton Ct **12** SE5. . . . . 139 B4
Kimpton Ho SW15 . . . . . 156 A4
Kimpton Link Bsns Ctr
　SM3. . . . . 217 B6
Kimpton Park Way SM3. . 217 B6
Kimpton Rd
　Camberwell SE5. . . . . . 139 B4
　Cheam SM3. . . . . 217 B6

Kimpton Trade & Bsns Ctr
　SM3. . . . . 217 B6
Kinburn St SE16 . . . . . . 118 D4
Kincaid Rd SE15 . . . . . . 140 B5
Kincardine Gdns W9 . . . . 91 C3
Kinch Gr HA3, HA9. . . . . . 44 B2
Kindell Ho **4** SW14 . . . . 133 B2
Kinder Cl SE28. . . . . . . 124 D6
Kinder Ho N1. . . . . 235 D4
Kindersley Ho **38** E1. . . . . 96 A1
Kinder St **19** E1. . . . . 96 B1
Kinderton Cl N14. . . . . . . 15 C3
Kinefold Ho N7. . . . . 72 A2
Kinfauns Rd Ilford IG3 . . . 58 B1
　Streatham SW2. . . . . . 160 C2
King Alfred Ave
　Catford SE6 . . . . 163 C1
　Catford SE6 . . . . 185 C6
King Alfred Sch NW11. . . . 47 D1
King Arthur Cl SE15. . . . 140 C5
King Athelstan Prim Sch
　KT1. . . . . 198 B6
King Charles Cres KT5 . . 198 B2
King Charles Ct **16** SE17. . 138 D6
King Charles Ho SW6 . . . 265 D4
King Charles' Rd KT5,
　KT6. . . . . 198 B3
King Charles St
　SW1. . . . . 116 A4 250 A2
King Charles Terr **11** E1. . 118 B6
King Charles Wlk **6**
　SW19. . . . . 157 A3
King Ct **16** SE10 . . . . 53 D2
King Cup Cl CR0. . . . . . 206 D1
King David La E1. . . . . . 118 C6
Kingdom St W2. . . 92 A2 236 A3
Kingdom Ho **8** E14. . . . . 120 A3
Kingdom Rd NW6 . . . . . . 69 C2
Kingdown Cl W10. . . . . . . 90 D1
King Edward Dr KT6. . . . 214 A5
King Edward Mans **12** E8. . 96 B6
King Edward Mews
　SW13. . . . . 134 A4
King Edward Rd
　Barnet EN5 . . . . 1 D1
　Leytonstone E10. . . . . . 54 A1
　Walthamstow E17 . . . . . 53 A6
King Edward St EC1. . . . 242 A2
King Edward The Third Mews
　11 SE16. . . . . 118 B4
King Edward VII Hospl for
　Officers W1. . . . . 93 A2 238 B4
King Edward Wlk
　SE1. . . . . 116 C3 261 B6
King Fahad Acad The
　W5 . . . . 109 C2
King Fahed Acad W3. . . . 111 D6
Kingfield Rd W5 . . . . 87 D3
Kingfield St E14. . . . . . . 120 A2
Kingfisher Ave E11. . . . . . 55 B3
Kingfisher Cl Harrow HA3. . 24 D3
　Woolwich SE28. . . . . . 124 C6
Kingfisher Ct
　11 Battersea SW11. . . . 136 C2
　Cheam SM1. . . . . 217 B3
　17 Cubitt Town E14. . . 120 A4
　East Molesey KT8. . . . . 196 C5
　Enfield EN2 . . . . 4 B5
　Hounslow TW3. . . . . . . 151 D6
　Merton SW19. . . . . 179 B3
　Putney SW19. . . . . 157 A2
　Spring Gr TW3. . . . . . . 130 B3
Kingfisher Dr TW10 . . . . 175 B6
Kingfisher Ho
　16 Battersea SW18. . . . 136 A2
　Peckham SE15 . . . . . . 139 D4
　West Kensington W14. . . 254 D2
Kingfisher L Ctr E14. . . . 176 A1
Kingfisher Lo TW11. . . . . 175 A6
Kingfisher Mews SE13 . . 163 D6
Kingfisher Sq **19** SE8. . . . 141 B6
Kingfisher St E6 . . . . . . 100 A2
Kingfisher Way
　Croydon CR0. . . . . 206 D4
　Neasden NW10 . . . . 67 B3
Kingfisher Wlk NW9 . . . . . 27 C1
King Frederick IX Twr
　SE16. . . . . 119 B3
King Garth Mews SE23. . 162 C2
King Gdns CR0. . . . . . . 220 D3
King George Ave
　Ilford IG2. . . . . 57 B3
　Newham E16 . . . . 99 D1
　Walton-on-T KT12 . . . . 194 D1
King George Cl TW16. . . 171 D5
King George Hospl IG3 . . 58 A4
King George Sq TW10 . . 154 B5
King George St SE10 . . . 142 A5

King George's Trad Est
　KT9. . . . . 214 C4
King George VI Ave CR4. . 202 D5
King George V Sta E16 . . 122 C5
Kingham Cl
　3 Shepherd's Bush W11. . 112 C4
　Wandsworth SW18 . . . . 158 A4
Kingham Ind Est NW10. . . 89 B4
King Harolds Way DA7. . . 147 A3
King Henry Mews
　Harrow HA2. . . . . 42 C1
　7 Orpington BR6. . . . . 227 D3
King Henry's Mews EN3 . . 7 C1
King Henry's Rd
　Kingston u T KT1, KT3. . 198 D6
　Primrose Hill NW3 . . . . . 70 C1
King Henry's Reach W6 . . 134 C6
King Henry St N16. . . . . . 73 C3
King Henry's Wlk N1. . . . . 73 C2
King Henry's Yd **5** N16. . . 73 C3
King Henry Terr **10** E1 . . . 118 B6
King Ho **5** W12. . . . . 90 B1
Kinghorn St EC1. . . . . . 242 A3
King James Ct SE1. . . . 251 D1
King James St
　SE1. . . . . 116 D4 251 D1
King John Ct EC2. . . . . . 243 B6
King John St E1 . . . . 96 D1
King John's Wlk SE9 . . . 166 A5
Kinglake St SE17. . 117 C1 263 B2
Kinglet Cl E7 . . . . 77 A2
Kingly Ct W1 . . . . 249 B6
Kingly St W1 . . . . 115 C6 249 A6
King & Queen Cl **4** SE9 . . 188 A6
King & Queen St
　SE17. . . . . 117 A1 262 B2
Kingsand Rd SE12 . . . . . 165 A2
King's Arbour UB2. . . . . 107 A1
King's Arms Ct **1** E1. . . . . 96 A2
King's Arms Yd EC2. . . . 242 C2
Kingsash Dr UB4. . . . . . . 85 B2
Kings Ave Bromley BR1. . . 186 D4
　Clapham Pk SW4 . . . . . 160 A5
　Dagenham RM6 . . . . . . 59 B3
　Ealing W5 . . . . 87 C1
　Muswell Hill N10. . . . . . 49 A6
　New Malden KT3 . . . . . 199 D5
　Wallington SM5 . . . . . . 218 D1
King's Ave Ashford TW16. . 171 D4
　Buckhurst Hill IG9 . . . . . 21 D2
　Hounslow TW3, TW5. . . 129 D4
　Southall UB1. . . . . 85 D1
　Southgate N21. . . . . . . 16 D3
　Woodford IG8. . . . . 37 C5
Kings Avenue Sch SW4. . 160 A4
King's Bench St
　SE1. . . . . 116 D4 251 D2
King's Bench Wlk EC4. . . 241 B1
Kingsbridge N16 . . . . 51 C5
Kingsbridge Ave W3 . . . . 110 B4
Kingsbridge Cres UB1. . . 85 B2
Kingsbridge Ct
　Edmonton N21 . . . . 16 D2
　Millwall E14 . . . . 119 C2
Kingsbridge Dr NW7. . . . 28 D3
Kingsbridge Ho **10** SE20. . 184 B2
Kingsbridge Ind Est
　IG11. . . . . 101 C4
Kingsbridge Rd
　Barking IG11. . . . . 101 B5
　North Kensington W10. . . 90 C1
　Southall UB2. . . . . 107 B2
　Walton-on-T KT12 . . . . 194 B2
　West Barnes SM4. . . . . 200 C4
Kingsbridge Way UB4. . . . 83 C4
KINGSBURY. 45 B3
Kingsbury Green Prim Sch
　NW9 . . . . 44 D4
Kingsbury High Sch (Lower
　Sch) NW9. . . . . 45 A5
Kingsbury High Sch (Upper
　Sch) NW9. . . . . 44 D5
Kingsbury Rd
　Kingsbury NW9 . . . . 44 D4
　Kingsland N1. . . . . 73 C2
Kingsbury Sta NW9. . . . . 44 C4
Kingsbury Terr N1. . . . . . 73 C2
Kingsbury Trad Est NW9. . 45 B3
Kings Chase KT8. . . . . . 196 A6
Kings Chase View EN2. . . . 4 C3
Kings Cl Hendon NW4. . . . 46 D5
　Walthamstow E17. . . . . 53 D2
　Walton-on-T KT12 . . . . 194 B1
King's Cl KT7 . . . . 197 A2
Kingsclere Cl SW15 . . . . 156 A4
Kingsclere Ct
　Colney Hatch N12. . . . . . 30 C5
　New Barnet EN5. . . . . . . 14 A6
Kingsclere Gdns SW19. . 157 B3
Kingscliffe Gdns SW19. . 157 B3
King's Coll SE24. . . . . . 161 B5
King's Coll Hospl CR7. . . 204 C1
King's College NW3. . . . . 70 C1
King's College Hospl
　SE5. . . . . 139 B3
Kings College Rd
　Primrose Hill NW3 . . . . . 70 B1
　Ruislip HA4 . . . . 39 D3
King's Coll Jun Sch
　SW19 . . . . 178 D4

King's Coll London (Denmark Hill Campus) SE5. . . . . 139 A2
King's Coll London School of Medicine SE1 . . . 117 B5 252 D3
King's Coll London (Strand Campus) WC2. . . 116 B6 250 D6
King's Coll London (St Thomas' Campus) SE1. . . . . 116 B3 260 C5
King's Coll London (Waterloo Campus) SE1. . . 116 B3 251 A3
King's Coll Sch SW19 . . . 178 D4
Kingscote Rd
　Bedford Pk W4. . . . . .111 B3
　Croydon CR0. . . . . 206 B2
　Kingston u T KT3. . . . . . . .199 B6
Kingscote St EC4 . . . . 251 C6
Kings Court Mews KT8. . .156 A4
Kingscourt Rd SW16 . . . . .160 A1
King's Court S SW3 . . . . . .257 A1
King's Cres N4, N5 . . . . . . .73 A5
Kingscroft SW4. . . . . .160 A5
Kingscroft Rd NW2 . . . . . .69 B2
KING'S CROSS 94 A5
King's Cross WC1. . . .94 A4 233 B2
King's Cross Bridge WC1 233 B2
King's Cross Rd
　WC1 . . . . .94 B4 233 D1
King's Cross, St Pancras N1 . . . . .94 A4 233 A2
King's Cross Sta N1 . . . . .94 A5 233 B3
Kings Ct 6 Barnsbury N7 . .72 B1
　2 Buckhurst Hill IG9. . . . .21 D2
　Chiswick W6. . . . . .112 A2
　East Dulwich SE22 . . . . . .140 A1
　16 Kingston u T KT2 . . . . .176 C3
　Newham E13 . . . . .99 B6
　Primrose Hill NW8 . . . . . .230 C5
　10 Putney SW15. . . . . . . .156 A4
　3 Wallington SM6 . . . . . .219 B2
　Wembley Pk HA9 . . . . . . .66 D6
King's Ct Beckenham BR3 . 207 D6
　9 Ealing W5 . . . . .87 C2
　Wimbledon SW19. . . . . . .179 C4
Kingsdale Ct EN4 . . . . .2 D3
Kingsdale Gdns W11. . . . .112 D5
Kingsdale Rd
　Penge SE20 . . . . .184 D3
　Plumstead Comm SE18 . . .145 D6
　Kingsdale Sch SE21. . . . . .161 C1
Kingsdown SW19 . . . . . . .178 D3
Kingsdown Ave
　East Acton W3 . . . . .111 C6
　West Ealing W13 . . . . . . .109 B4
Kingsdown Cl
　26 Deptford SE16. . . . . . .118 B1
　8 Notting Hill W11 . . . . . .91 A1
Kingsdown Ct SW11 . . . . .158 C5
Kingsdowne Rd KT6. . . . . .198 B2
Kingsdown Ho 1 E8 . . . . .74 A3
Kingsdown Rd
　Cheam SM3 . . . . .217 A3
　Leyton E11. . . . . .76 C5
　4 Upper Holloway N19 . . .72 A4
Kingsdown Way BR2 . . . . .209 A3
Kings Dr Edgware HA8 . . . .26 B6
　Surbiton KT5 . . . . .198 C3
　Wembley Pk HA9 . . . . . . .66 D6
King's Dr KT7. . . . . .197 B2
Kingsend HA4 . . . . .39 C1
Kingsend Ct HA4. . . . . .39 C1
Kings Farm E17. . . . . .35 D2
Kings Farm Ave HA1, HA2 .42 A4
Kingsfield Ave HA1, HA2 . .42 A4
Kingsfield Ct HA1. . . . . . . .42 B2
Kingsfield Ho
　Mottingham SE9. . . . . . . .165 D1
　7 Muswell Hill N10. . . . . .31 A3
　18 Stoke Newington N16 . .73 C5
Kingsfield Rd HA1 . . . . . . .42 B2
Kingsfield Com Sch E6. . . .100 B4
Kingsford St NW5. . . . . . . .70 D3
Kingsford Way E6. . . . . . . .100 B2
Kingsgate HA3 . . . . .67 A5
Kingsgate Ave N3. . . . . . . .47 C6
Kingsgate Bsns Ctr KT2 . .176 A2
Kingsgate Cl Erith DA7. . . .147 A4
　Sidcup BR5 . . . . .190 C1
Kingsgate Est N1 . . . . .73 C2
Kingsgate Ho 29 SW9 . . . .138 C4
Kingsgate Par SW1 . . . . . .259 B5
Kingsgate Pl NW6 . . . . . . .69 C1
Kingsgate Prim Sch NW6 .69 C1
Kingsgate Rd
　Hampstead NW6 . . . . .69 C1
　Kingston u T KT2 . . . . . . .176 A2
Kings Gdns IG1. . . . . .57 B1
King's Gdns 6 NW6 . . . . . .69 C1
King's Gr Peckham SE15 . . .140 B4
　Peckham SE15 . . . . .140 B5
Kings Grange HA4 . . . . . . .39 D1
Kingsground SE9 . . . . .166 A5
Kingshall Mews SE13 . . . .142 A2
Kings Hall Rd BR3. . . . . . . .185 A2
Kings Head Hill E4. . . . . . . .19 D4
King's Head Yd SE1 . . . . . .252 C3
King's Highway SE18. . . . .145 D6

Kingshill SE17 . . . . .262 B4
Kingshill Ave Harrow HA3 . .43 B5
　Hayes UB4 . . . . .83 D4
　New Malden KT4 . . . . . . .200 B2
　Northolt UB5 . . . . .84 B4
Kingshill Cl UB4, UB5. . . . .84 A4
Kingshill Ct 8 EN5. . . . . . . .1 A1
Kingshill Dr HA3 . . . . .43 B6
Kings Ho
　19 Limehouse E14 . . . . . .119 B6
　South Lambeth SW8. . . . .270 A4
Kingshold Rd E9 . . . . .74 C1
Kingsholm Gdns SE9. . . . .144 A1
King's House Sch TW10 . .154 B6
King's House Sch (Jun) TW10 . . . . .154 B6
Kingshurst Rd SE12 . . . . . .165 A4
Kings Keep KT6. . . . . .198 A5
King's Keep 6 SW15. . . . . .156 D6
King's La SM1 . . . . .218 B3
Kingsland NW8 . . . .92 C6 230 B5
Kingsland Gn 1 E8, N1 . . .73 C2
Kingsland High St E8 . . . . .73 D3
Kingsland Pas 2 E8 . . . . . .73 C2
Kingsland Rd Hoxton E2 . . .95 C5
　Newham E13 . . . . .99 B6
Kingsland Sh Ctr 12 E8. . . .73 D2
Kingslawn Cl SW15. . . . . .156 B6
Kingslee Ct 4 SM2 . . . . . .217 D1
Kingsleigh Cl TW8 . . . . . . .131 D6
Kingsleigh Pl CR4. . . . . . . .202 D6
Kingsleigh Wlk BR2 . . . . . .208 D5
Kingsley Ave Ealing W13 . .87 A1
　Hounslow TW3 . . . . .130 A3
　Southall UB1. . . . . .107 C6
　Sutton SM1 . . . . .218 B4
Kingsley Cl
　Dagenham RM10 . . . . .81 D4
　East Finchley N2. . . . . .48 A4
Kingsley Ct Bexley DA6. . .147 C1
　Edgware HA8 . . . . .10 D2
　Snaresbrook E11 . . . . .54 D3
　1 Thamesmead SE28 . . .124 C5
　Willesden NW2. . . . . .68 B2
　Wood Green N22 . . . . . . .32 B3
　Worcester Pk KT4. . . . . . .215 D6
Kingsley Dr KT4 . . . . .215 D6
Kingsley Flats SE1 . . . . . . .263 B3
Kingsley Gdns E4 . . . . .35 C5
Kingsley Grange 1 E11 . . .55 A4
Kingsley High Sch HA3. . . .24 A3
Kingsley Ho Chelsea SW3 .266 D5
　3 Clapham SW4 . . . . . . .137 D3
　East Finchley NW11 . . . . .48 A3
　8 Kingston u T KT6 . . . . .198 A4
Kingsley Mews
　Chislehurst West BR7. . . .188 D4
　Dagenham RM9 . . . . .80 D4
　4 Ilford IG1 . . . . .78 D6
　Kensington W8. . . . . .255 D5
　15 St George in t East E1 . .118 B6
Kingsley Pl N6. . . . . .49 A2
Kingsley Prim Sch CR9. . . .204 C1
Kingsley Rd Chingford E17 . .36 A1
　Edmonton N13 . . . . .32 D6
　Harrow HA2 . . . . .64 A5
　Hounslow TW3 . . . . .130 A3
　Kilburn NW6. . . . . .91 B6
　Orpington BR6 . . . . .227 D1
　Pinner HA5 . . . . .41 B5
　Thornton Heath CR0. . . . .204 C1
　Upton E7. . . . . .77 A1
　Wimbledon SW19. . . . . . .179 D5
Kingsley St SW11 . . . . . . .136 D2
Kingsley Way N2. . . . . .48 A4
Kingsley Wood Dr SE9 . . .166 B1
Kings Lo HA4 . . . . .39 C1
Kingslyn Cres SE19 . . . . . .183 C2
Kings Mall Sh Ctr W6 . . . .112 C2
King's Mans SW3 . . . . .267 A5
Kingsman St SE18 . . . . . . .122 B3
Kingsmead Barnet EN5. . . . .1 C1
　Richmond TW10 . . . . .154 B5
Kingsmead Ave
　Edmonton N9 . . . . .18 B3
　Kingsbury NW9 . . . . .45 B2
　Mitcham CR4 . . . . .203 C6
　North Cheam KT4 . . . . . .216 B5
　Sunbury TW16 . . . . .172 C1
　Tolworth KT6 . . . . .214 C6
Kingsmead Cl
　Sidcup DA15. . . . . .168 A2
　Teddington TW11 . . . . . . .175 B4
　West Ewell KT19. . . . . . . .215 B1
Kingsmead Cotts BR2. . . .210 A1
Kingsmead Ct
　Bromley BR1. . . . . .186 D3
　Crouch End N6 . . . . .49 D2
Kingsmead Dr UB5. . . . . . .63 D1
Kingsmead Ho E9. . . . . . . .75 A4
Kingsmead Lo
　9 Chingford E4 . . . . .20 A2
　Sutton SM2. . . . . .218 B4
Kings Mead Pk KT10 . . . . .212 C1
Kingsmead Prim Sch E9 . .75 A4
Kingsmead Rd SW2. . . . . .160 C2
Kingsmead Sch EN1 . . . . . .6 A2
King's Mead Way E5, E9 . .75 A4

Kingsmere Catford SE6. . . .163 D3
　Widmore BR7. . . . . .188 A2
Kingsmere Cl 13 SW15. . . .134 D2
Kingsmere Ct NW9. . . . . . .44 D1
Kingsmere Pk NW9 . . . . . . .45 A1
Kingsmere Pl N16 . . . . .51 B1
Kingsmere Rd SW19 . . . . .156 D2
King's Mews
　1 Clapham Pk SW4. . . . . .160 A6
　Gray's Inn WC1. . . .94 B3 240 D5
Kingsmill NW8 . . . . .92 B5 229 D4
Kingsmill Bsns Pk KT1 . . .198 B6
Kingsmill Gdns RM9. . . . . .81 B3
Kingsmill Rd RM9. . . . . . . .81 B3
Kingsmill Terr
　NW8 . . . . .92 B5 229 D4
Kingsmount Ct SM1. . . . . .217 D4
Kingsnorth Ho 17 W10. . . .90 D1
Kingsnympton Pk KT2 . . .176 D4
Kings Oak RM7 . . . . .59 C6
Kings Oak Hospl (Private)
　The EN2. . . . . .4 C5
King Solomon Acad
　NW1. . . . . .92 C2 237 A4
King's Orch SE9 . . . . .166 A5
King's Paddock TW12 . . . .174 A2
King's Par
　3 Hammersmith W12. . . .112 A3
　Willesden NW10. . . . . . . .90 C6
Kingspark Bsns Ctr KT3 . .199 A6
Kingspark Ct E18 . . . . .55 A6
King's Penny Ho 4 KT2 . .176 A3
Kings Pl Acton Green W4. .111 A2
　Buckhurst Hill IG9 . . . . . . .21 D2
Kings Pl 1 N1 . . . . .94 A5 233 B4
Kings Pl IG10. . . . . .21 D4
King's Pl SE1 . . . . .252 A1
King's Quay SW10 . . . . . . .266 B2
Kings Rd Ealing W5 . . . . . . .87 D2
Feltham TW13 . . . . .150 C3
Harrow HA2 . . . . .63 B6
Mitcham CR4 . . . . .203 A6
Orpington BR6 . . . . .227 D4
Richmond TW10, TW9. . . .154 B6
Walton-on-T KT12 . . . . . . .194 B1
West Drayton UB7 . . . . . . .104 B4
Willesden NW10. . . . . .68 B1
Wood Green N22 . . . . .32 B2
Chelsea SW3 . . . . .257 B1
Chelsea SW10 . . . .136 B6 266 C5
Chingford E4. . . . . .20 B3
Edmonton N18 . . . . .34 A6
Kingston u T KT2. . . . . . . .176 B3
Leytonstone E11. . . . . .54 C2
Long Ditton KT6. . . . . .197 C1
Mortlake SW14 . . . . .133 B2
Newham E6 . . . . .99 C6
South Norwood SE25 . . . .206 A6
Teddington TW11, TW12 . . .174 B5
Tottenham N17 . . . . .33 D2
Twickenham TW1 . . . . .153 B1
Wimbledon SW19. . . . . . . .179 C4
Kings Ride Gate TW10 . . .132 C1
Kingsridge SW19 . . . . .157 A2
Kings Road Bglws HA2 . . . .63 B5
King's Scholars' Pas
　SW1. . . . . .259 A4
King St Acton W3 . . . . .111 A4
　East Finchley N2. . . . . . . .48 B6
　Hammersmith W6 . . . . . . .112 A2
　Newham E13 . . . . .98 D3
　Newham E13 . . . . .99 A3
　Richmond TW9 . . . . .153 D6
　Southall UB2. . . . . .107 A3
　St James SW1 . . . .115 C5 249 B4
　Strand WC2 . . . . .250 A6
　Tottenham N17. . . . . .33 D2
　Twickenham TW1 . . . . . . .153 A3
　Whitechapel EC2. . . .95 A1 242 B1
King Stairs Cl SE16. . . . . . .118 B4
King's Terr
　Camden Town
　　NW1. . . . . .93 C6 232 A5
　10 Isleworth TW7 . . . . . . .131 A2
Kingsthorpe Rd SE26. . . . .184 D6
Kingston Ave
　Cheam SM3 . . . . .217 A5
　Feltham TW14 . . . . .149 D5
　Yiewsley UB7 . . . . .104 A6
Kingston Bsns Ctr KT9 . . .214 B5
Kingston Gram Sch KT2 . .176 B1
Kingston Hall Rd KT1 . . . .197 D6
Kingston Hill KT2 . . . . . . .177 A5
Kingston Hill Ave RM6. . . .59 A6
Kingston Hill Pl KT2,
　TW10. . . . . .177 A6

Kingston Ho 4 NW6 . . . . . . .69 A1
Kingston Ho E SW7 . . . . . .247 A1
Kingston Ho N SW7 . . . . . .247 A1
Kingston Ho S SW7 . . . . . .247 A1
Kingston Hospl KT2. . . . . .176 D2
Kingston House Est KT6. .197 B3
Kingston La
　Teddington TW11 . . . . . . .175 B4
　Uxbridge UB8. . . . . .82 A4
　West Drayton UB7 . . . . . .104 B4
Kingston Lo 2 KT3 . . . . . .199 C5
Kingston Mus★ KT1 . . . . .176 A1
Kingston Pl HA3 . . . . .24 D3
Kingston Rd
　Ashford TW15. . . . . .170 A4
　Ashford TW15. . . . . .170 B4
　Edmonton N9 . . . . .18 A2
　Ewell KT17 . . . . .215 D1
　Ilford IG1 . . . . .79 A4
　Kingston u T KT1, KT3. . . .199 A5
　Merton SW19, SW20. . . . .179 B1
　New Barnet EN4. . . . . . . .14 B6
　Roehampton SW15, SW19 .156 B3
　Southall UB2. . . . . .107 B4
　Teddington TW11 . . . . . . .175 B4
Kingston Sq SE19 . . . . . . .183 B5
Kingston Sta KT2 . . . . . . .176 A2
Kingston Univ (Kingston Hill)
　KT2. . . . . .177 B5
Kingston Univ (Knights Park)
　KT1. . . . . .198 A6
Kingston Univ (Penrhyn Road) KT1. . . . . .198 A6
Kingston Univ (Roehampton Vale) SW15. . . . . .155 D1
KINGSTON UPON THAMES. 197 C6
KINGSTON VALE 177 B6
Kingston Vale SW15. . . . . .155 C1
Kingston St
　NW1 . . . . .93 A6 231 A6
King Street Cloisters 8
　W6. . . . . .112 B2
King Street Coll 10 W12. .112 C2
King Street Par 7 TW1. . .153 A3
Kings View Ct 1 SW20 . . .178 D3
Kingswater Pl SW11 . . . . .267 A3
Kingsway Coney Hall BR4 . .224 D5
　Enfield EN3 . . . . .18 B6
　Hayes UB3 . . . . .83 A2
　Mortlake SW14, TW9 . . . .132 C2
　North Finchley N12. . . . . .30 A4
　Petts Wood BR5 . . . . .211 B4
　Stanwell TW19. . . . . .148 A3
　St Giles WC2. . . . . .94 B1 240 C2
　Wembley HA9. . . . . .66 A4
　West Barnes KT3 . . . . . . .200 C4
　Woodford IG8. . . . . .37 C5
Kings Way Croydon CR0 . . .220 B3
　Harrow HA1. . . . . .42 C5
Kingsway Bsns Pk TW12. .173 B2
Kingsway Coll 12 NW5 . . .71 B2
Kingsway Cres HA2 . . . . . .42 A5
Kingsway Est N18. . . . . . . .34 D4
Kingsway Mans WC1 . . . . .240 C4
Kingsway Pl EC1. . . . . .241 C6
Kingsway Rd SM3 . . . . . . .217 A1
Kingswear Ho 5 SE23 . . .162 C2
Kingswear Rd
　Dartmouth Pk NW5 . . . . .71 B5
　Ruislip HA4 . . . . .62 A6
Kings Well 25 NW3. . . . . . .70 A4
Kings Wlk Sh Mall
　SW3 . . . . .114 D1 257 C5
Kingswood 31 E2. . . . . . . .96 C5
Kingswood Ave
　Beckenham BR2, BR3. . . .208 C5
　Belvedere DA17 . . . . .125 B2
　Hampton TW12 . . . . .173 D4
　Hounslow TW3, TW5. . . . .129 B3
　Kensal Rise NW6 . . . . . . .91 A5
　Thornton Heath CR7 . . . . .204 C4
Kingswood Cl
　Ashford TW15. . . . . .171 B5
　Crofton BR6 . . . . .211 B2
　East Barnet N20. . . . . . . .14 A4
　Enfield EN1 . . . . .17 D6
　New Malden KT3 . . . . . . .199 D3
　South Lambeth SW8. . . . .270 B3
　Surbiton KT6. . . . . .198 A2
Kingswood Ct
　Chingford E4. . . . . .35 C5
　Hither Green SE13 . . . . . .164 B5
　7 Richmond TW10 . . . . . .154 B6
Kings Wood Ct 4 NW6 . . . .69 C1
Kingswood Dr
　Carshalton SM5 . . . . .202 D1
　Dulwich SE19, SE21 . . . . .183 D6
Kingswood Ho 3 KT2. . . . .176 D4
Kingswood Mans 14
　SM2. . . . . .217 C1
Kingswood Pk N3. . . . . . . .29 B1
Kingswood Pl SE13 . . . . . .142 C1
Kingswood Prim Sch
　SE27. . . . . .183 B5
Kingswood Rd
　Beckenham BR2 . . . . .208 C6
　Ilford IG3 . . . . .58 A2
　Leytonstone E11. . . . . . . .54 C2
　Merton SW19. . . . . .179 B2

Kingswood Rd continued
　Penge SE20 . . . . .184 C4
　South Acton W4 . . . . .111 A3
　Streatham SW2 . . . . .160 A4
　Wembley HA9. . . . . .66 C5
Kingswood Terr W4. . . . . .111 A3
Kingswood Way SM6. . . . .220 A3
Kingsworth Ct BR3. . . . . . .207 A4
Kingsworthy Cl KT1. . . . . .198 B6
Kings Yd E15 . . . . .75 C2
Kingthorpe Rd NW10. . . . .67 B1
Kingthorpe Terr 2 NW10. .67 B1
Kington Ho 18 NW6 . . . . . .91 D6
Kingward Ho E1 . . . . .96 A2
Kingwell Rd EN4. . . . . .2 B5
Kingweston Cl NW2. . . . . .69 A5
King William IV Gdns
　SE20. . . . . .184 C4
King William La 3 SE10. .120 C1
King William St
　EC4 . . . . .117 B6 252 D6
King William Wlk SE10 . .142 A6
Kingwood Rd
　SW6. . . . . .135 A5 264 A3
Kinlet Rd SE18. . . . . .145 A4
Kinloch Dr NW9 . . . . .45 C2
Kinloch St N7 . . . . .72 B5
Kinloss Ct NW3. . . . . .47 B5
Kinloss Gdns NW3 . . . . . . .47 B5
Kinloss Rd SM5 . . . . .202 A2
Kinnaird Ave
　Bromley BR1. . . . . .186 D4
　Chiswick W4 . . . . .133 A5
Kinnaird Cl BR1. . . . . .186 D4
Kinnear Ct 3 SW20 . . . . . .178 D2
Kinnear Rd W12 . . . . .111 D4
Kinnerton Pl N SW1. . . . . .247 D1
Kinnerton Pl S SW1 . . . . . .247 D1
Kinnerton St
　SW1. . . . . .115 A4 248 A1
Kinnerton Yd SW1 . . . . . . .248 A1
Kinnoull Mans 10 E5 . . . . .74 B4
Kinnoull Rd W6 . . . .135 A6 264 A6
Kinross Ave KT4 . . . . .216 A6
Kinross Cl Ashford TW16 .171 D5
　Edgware HA8 . . . . .10 D2
　Harrow HA3 . . . . .44 B4
Kinross Ct 1 SE6 . . . . .164 D2
Kinross Dr TW16. . . . . .171 D5
Kinross Ho N1 . . . . .233 C6
Kinross Terr E17. . . . . .35 B1
Kinsale Grange 10 SM2. . .218 A2
Kinsale Rd SE15 . . . . .140 A2
Kinsella Gdns SW19. . . . . .178 B5
Kinsey Ho SE21. . . . . .183 C6
Kinsham Ho 5 E2 . . . . .96 A3
Kintore Way SE1 . . . . .263 C4
Kintyre Cl SW16 . . . . .204 B6
Kintyre Ct 3 SW2. . . . . . . .160 A4
Kintyre Ho 6 E14. . . . . . . .120 A5
Kinveachy Gdns SE7 . . . . .122 A1
Kinver Ho N4 . . . . .51 B2
Kinver Rd SE26 . . . . .184 C6
Kipling Ct W7 . . . . .108 D6
Kipling Dr SW17 . . . . .180 B4
Kipling Ho 29 SE5 . . . . . . .139 A5
Kipling Pl HA7. . . . . .24 D4
Kipling Rd DA7 . . . . .147 B3
Kipling St SE1 . . . .117 B4 252 D2
Kipling Terr N9 . . . . .17 B2
Kipling Twr 3 W3. . . . . . . .111 A3
Kippington Dr SE9. . . . . . .165 D3
Kirby Cl KT19 . . . . .215 D3
Kirby Est SE16 . . . . .118 B4
Kirby Gr SE1 . . . . . .117 C4 253 A4
Kirby St EC1 . . . . . .94 C2 241 B4
Kirby Way Hillingdon UB8 . .82 B3
　Walton-on-T KT12 . . . . . .194 C3
Kirchen Rd W13 . . . . .109 B6
Kirkby Cl N11. . . . . .31 A4
Kirkdale SE26 . . . . .162 B1
Kirkdale Rd E11 . . . . .54 C2
Kirkeby Bldg EC1 . . . . .241 A4
Kirkfield Cl W13 . . . . .109 B5
Kirkham Rd E6 . . . . .100 A1
Kirkham St SE18 . . . . .145 C6
Kirk Ho HA9 . . . . .66 A5
Kirk La SE18 . . . . .145 A6
Kirkland Cl DA15. . . . . . . .167 C5
Kirkland Dr EN2 . . . . .5 A4
Kirkland Terr BR3. . . . . . . .185 C4
Kirkland Wlk 4 E8 . . . . . . .73 D2
Kirkleas Rd KT6. . . . . .198 A1
Kirklees Rd
　Dagenham RM8 . . . . .80 C3
　Thornton Heath CR7. . . . .204 C4
Kirkley Ho N16 . . . . .51 C1
Kirkley Rd SW19 . . . . .179 C2
Kirkman Ho W1. . . . . .239 C3
Kirkman Pl W1 . . . . .239 C3
Kirkmichael Rd E14. . . . . .98 A1
Kirk Rd E17. . . . . .53 B3
Kirk Rise SM1 . . . . .217 D5
Kirkside Rd SE3 . . . . .143 A6
Kirk St WC1 . . . . .240 D5
Kirkstall Ave N17. . . . . . . .51 B5
Kirkstall Gdns SW2 . . . . . .160 A3

Kirkstall Ho SW1 . . . . **258** C2
Kirkstall Rd SW2 . . . . 160 A3
Kirkstead Ct E5 . . . . 75 A4
Kirksted Rd SM4 . . . . 201 D1
Kirkstone NW1 . . . . **232** A2
Kirkstone Way BR1 . . . . 186 C3
Kirkton Rd N15 . . . . 51 C5
Kirkwall Pl E2 . . . . 96 C4
Kirkwood Rd SE15 . . . . . 140 B3
Kirn Rd W13 . . . . 109 B6
Kirrane Cl KT3 . . . . 199 D4
Kirtley Ho SW8 . . . . **269** B2
Kirtley Rd SE26 . . . . 185 A6
Kirtling St SW8 . . . . 137 C5 **269** A4
Kirton Cl W4 . . . . 111 B2
Kirton Gdns 23 E2 . . . . 95 D4
Kirton Rd E13 . . . . 99 C5
Kirton Wlk HA8 . . . . 27 A3
Kirwin Way SE5 . . . . 138 D5
Kisharon Sch NW11 . . . . . 47 B3
Kismul Sch KT6 . . . . 213 C6
Kitcat Terr E3 . . . . 97 C4
Kitchener Rd
   Dagenham RM10 . . . . .81 D2
   East Finchley N2 . . . . .48 C6
   South Norwood CR7 . . . . 205 B6
   Tottenham N17 . . . . .51 C6
   Upton E7 . . . . .77 B2
   Walthamstow E17 . . . . .35 D2
Kite Ho 5 SW11 . . . . 136 C2
Kite Pl 9 E2 . . . . 96 A4
Kitley Gdns SE19 . . . . . . 183 D2
Kitson Rd Barnes SW13 . .134 A4
   Camberwell SE5 . . . . 139 A5
Kittiwake Ct 28 SE8 . . . . 141 B6
Kittiwake Pl SM1 . . . . 217 B3
Kittiwake Rd UB5 . . . . .84 D4
Kittiwake Way UB4 . . . . . .84 D2
Kitto Rd SE14 . . . . 140 D3
KITTS END 1 A5
Kitt's End Rd EN5 . . . . 1 A6
Kiver Rd N19 . . . . 72 A6
Klea Ave SW4 . . . . 159 C5
Kleffens Ct 2 SE3 . . . . . 142 D5
Kleine Wharf 30 N1 . . . . . .95 C6
Knaggs Ho 1 TW11 . . . . 174 C5
Knapdale Cl SE23 . . . . . . 162 B2
Knapmill Rd SE6 . . . . 163 D2
Knapmill Way SE6 . . . . . 163 D2
Knapp Cl NW10 . . . . .67 C2
Knapp Rd Ashford TW15 . .170 B6
   Bow E3 . . . . .97 C3
Knapton Mews SW17 . . . 181 A4
Knaresborough Dr
   SW18 . . . . 157 D3
Knaresborough Ho 4 N4 .51 A2
Knaresborough Pl
   SW5 . . . . 113 D2 **255** C4
Knatchbull Rd
   Brixton SE5 . . . . 138 D4
   Stonebridge NW10 . . . . . . .89 B6
Knebworth Ave E17 . . . . . .35 C2
Knebworth Cl EN5 . . . . 1 D1
Knebworth Ho
   South Lambeth SW8 . . . . **269** D1
   2 Stoke Newington N16 . .73 C4
   Walthamstow E17 . . . . .35 C4
Knebworth Rd 8 N16 . . . .73 C4
Knee Hill SE2 . . . . 124 C1
Knee Hill Cres SE2 . . . . . 124 C2
Kneller Gdns TW7 . . . . . . 152 B5
Kneller Ho 9 SW8 . . . . . 137 D3
Kneller Rd Brockley SE4 . .141 A1
   Isleworth TW2 . . . . 152 B5
   New Malden KT3 . . . . 199 C2
Knevett Terr TW3 . . . . . . 129 C1
Knight Cl RM8 . . . . .80 C6
Knight Ct N15 . . . . .51 C4
Knighten St E1 . . . . 118 B5
Knighthead Point 28
   E14 . . . . 119 C4
Knight Ho Walworth SE17 . 263 A3
   Worcester Pk KT4 . . . . . . 216 A6
Knightland Ho E5 . . . . .74 B6
Knightland Rd E5 . . . . .74 B6
Knightleas Ct NW2 . . . . . .68 C2
Knightleys Ct E10 . . . . . . .53 A1
Knighton Cl Croydon CR2 . 220 D1
   Woodford IG8 . . . . .37 B6
Knighton Dr IG8 . . . . .37 B6
Knighton Gn IG9 . . . . .21 B2
Knighton La IG9 . . . . .21 D2
Knighton Park Rd SE26 . .184 D5
Knighton Rd E7 . . . . .77 A4
Knightrider Ct EC4 . . . . . **252** A6
Knightrider St EC4 . . . . . **251** D6
Knights Arc SW1 . . . . **247** C1
Knight's Ave W5 . . . . 110 A4
KNIGHTSBRIDGE 114 C4
Knightsbridge SW1,
   SW7 . . . . 114 D4 **247** C1
Knightsbridge Ct SW1 . . **247** B1
Knightsbridge Gn SW1 . **247** C1
Knightsbridge Mews
   BR7 . . . . 188 B2
Knightsbridge Sch
   SW11 . . . . 114 D3 **257** C5

Knightsbridge Sta
   SW1 . . . . 114 D4 **247** C1
Knightsbridge Under Sch
   SW7 . . . . **256** B3
Knights Cl
   East Molesey KT8 . . . . . . 195 B4
   Lower Clapton E9 . . . . .74 C3
   11 Friern Barnet N11 . . . . .30 D5
   Kingston u T KT1 . . . . 198 A6
   Penge BR3 . . . . 185 A2
Knight's Ct BR1 . . . . 164 D1
Knightshayes Ho 8 NW4 . .28 D1
Knight's Hill SE19, SE27 . .182 B6
Knight's Hill Sq SE27 . . . 182 B6
Knights Ho
   Bermondsey SE1 . . . . **253** C2
   South Lambeth SW8 . . . . **270** B3
   West Kensington SW5 . . . **254** C2
Knight's Ho SW10 . . . . . **266** A4
Knight's Pk KT1 . . . . 198 A6
Knight's Pl TW2 . . . . 152 C3
Knights Rd Newham E16 . .121 A4
   Stanmore HA7 . . . . .25 C6
Knight's Wlk SE11 . . . . . **261** C3
Knightswood Cl HA8 . . . . .11 A2
Knightswood Ct N6 . . . . . .49 D2
Knightswood Ho N12 . . . .30 A4
Knightwood Cres KT3 . . .199 C3
Knivet Rd SW6 . . . 135 C6 **265** A5
Knockholt Rd SE9 . . . . . 165 D6
Knole Cl CR0 . . . . 206 C3
Knole Ct UB5 . . . . .84 C4
Knole Gate DA15 . . . . . . 167 C1
Knole The SE9 . . . . 188 C6
Knoll Ct Dulwich SE19 . . .183 D5
   Orpington BR6 . . . . 227 D6
Knoll Dr N14 . . . . .15 A4
Knoll Ho NW8 . . . . **229** A4
Knoll Lo E5 . . . . .14 A6
Knollmead KT5 . . . . 199 A1
Knollmead Prim Sch
   KT5 . . . . 215 A6
Knollmead KT5 . . . . 199 A1
Knollys Gdns
   Croydon CR0 . . . . 206 D1
   Edmonton N21 . . . . .17 A2
Knollys Gr
   Edmonton N21 . . . . .17 A2
   Hounslow TW3 . . . . 129 B1
   Kingsbury NW9 . . . . .45 A2
   Kingston u T KT3 . . . . 177 B1
   Ruislip HA4 . . . . .39 B3
   Southall UB1 . . . . .85 B3
Knollys Ho
   Dagenham RM10 . . . . .81 C6
   New Cross SE14 . . . . 141 B3
   6 Stoke Newington N16 . .73 B6
Knollys Rd SW16 . . . . . . 182 B6
Knolly's Cl SE27, SW16 . .160 C1
Knolly's Rd SE27, SW16 . .160 C1
Knottisford St E2 . . . . .96 C4
Knotts Green Mews E10 . .54 A3
Knotts Green Rd E10 . . . . .54 A3
Knowlden Ho 6 E1 . . . . . 118 C6
Knowle Ave DA7 . . . . 147 B5
Knowle Cl SW9 . . . . 138 C2
Knowledge Point Sch 6
   N7 .72 B2
Knowle Lo BR7 . . . . 188 B4
Knowle Rd Bromley BR2 . .226 A6
   Twickenham TW2 . . . . 152 C3
Knowles Cl UB7 . . . . 104 A5
Knowles Hill Cres SE13 . .164 B6
Knowles Ho
   Wandsworth SW18 . . . . . 157 D5
   Willesden Green NW10 . . . .90 A6
Knowles Wlk SW4 . . . . . . 137 C2
Knowl Pk WD6 . . . . .10 A6
Knowles Ave UB1 . . . . . . 107 D5
Knowlton Gn 1 BR2 . . . . 208 D4
Knowlton Ho 32 SW9 . . . 138 C4
Knowl Way WD6 . . . . .10 B6
Knowsley Ave UB1 . . . . . 107 D5
Knowsley Rd SW11 . . . . . 136 D3
Knox Ct 16 SW4 . . . . 138 A3
Knox Ho SW15 . . . . 134 C3
Knox Rd E7 . . . . .77 A2
Knox St W1 . . . . . . .92 D2 **237** C4
Knoyle Ho W14 . . . . **254** B6
Knoyle St SE14 . . . . 141 A6
Kobi Nazrul Prim Sch 43
   E1 .96 A1
Koblenz Ho N8 . . . . .50 A6
Kohat Rd SW19 . . . . 179 D5
Korda Cl TW17 . . . . 192 B6
Kossuth St SE10 . . . . . . 120 C1
Kotree Way 16 SE1 . . . . . 118 A2
Kramer Mews SW5 . . . . . **255** C1
Kreedman Wlk 8 E8 . . . . .74 A3
Kreisel Wlk TW9 . . . . 132 B6
Krishna Avanti Prim Sch
   HA8 . . . . .26 C2
Kristina Ct 5 SM2 . . . . . 217 C2
Kuala Gdns SW16 . . . . . 182 B2
Kubrick Bsns Est E7 . . . . .77 B4
Kuhn Way E7 . . . . .77 A3
Kwesi Johnson Ct 4
   N22 . . . . .32 C1
Kydbrook Cl BR5 . . . . . . 211 A2
Kyle Ho TW12 . . . . 174 A2
Kylemore Cl 3 E6 . . . . . . .99 D5
Kylemore Ct 4 W12 . . . . 112 A4
Kylemore Rd NW6 . . . . . . .69 C1
Kylestrome Ho SW1 . . . . **258** B3
Kymberley Rd HA1 . . . . . .42 C3

Kynance Gdns HA7 . . . . . . .25 C2
Kynance Mews
   SW7 . . . . 113 D3 **255** D5
Kynance Pl SW7 . . . . **256** A5
Kynaston Ave CR7 . . . . . 205 A4
Kynaston Cl HA3 . . . . .24 B3
Kynaston Cres CR7 . . . . 205 A4
Kynaston Ho 7 SW2 . . . . 160 B3
Kynaston Rd Enfield EN2 . . . 5 A4
   Plaistow BR1 . . . . 187 A5
   Stoke Newington N16 . . . . .73 C5
   Thornton Heath CR7 . . . . 205 A4
Kynaston Wood HA3 . . . . .24 B3
Kynersley Cl 1 SM5 . . . . 218 D5
Kynoch Rd N18 . . . . .34 C6
Kyrle Rd SW11 . . . . 159 A5
Kyverdale Rd N16 . . . . . . .51 D1

L

Laburnam Ct 12 SW16 . . .182 C5
Laburnham Ct
   Child's Hill NW2 . . . . .69 B6
   Sutton SM1 . . . . 217 C3
Laburnam Pl SE9 . . . . . . 166 C6
Laburnum Ave
   Carshalton SM1 . . . . 218 C5
   Edmonton N9 . . . . .17 D2
   Tottenham N17 . . . . .33 B3
   Yiewsley UB7 . . . . 104 B6
Laburnum Cl
   Friern Barnet N11 . . . . .31 A4
   5 Nunhead SE15 . . . . 140 C5
   Walthamstow E4 . . . . .35 B4
   Wembley HA0 . . . . .88 C6
Laburnum Cres TW16 . . . 172 B2
Laburnum Ct
   26 Haggerston E2 . . . . .95 D6
   Harrow HA1 . . . . .41 D3
   5 Mitcham CR4 . . . . 181 A1
   Stanmore HA7 . . . . .25 C6
Laburnum Gdns
   Croydon CR0 . . . . 206 D1
   Edmonton N21 . . . . .17 A2
Laburnum Gr
   Edmonton N21 . . . . .17 A2
   Hounslow TW3 . . . . 129 B1
   Kingsbury NW9 . . . . .45 A2
   Kingston u T KT3 . . . . 177 B1
   Ruislip HA4 . . . . .39 B3
   Southall UB1 . . . . .85 B3
Laburnum Ho
   Dagenham RM10 . . . . .81 C6
   New Cross SE14 . . . . 141 B3
   6 Stoke Newington N16 . .73 B6
Laburnum Lo 2 N3 . . . . . .29 B1
Laburnum Rd Hayes UB3 . 105 D2
   Merton SW19 . . . . 180 A3
   Mitcham CR4 . . . . 181 A1
Laburnum St 2 E2 . . . . . . .95 D6
Laburnums The E6 . . . . . 100 A3
Laburnum Way
   Southborough BR2 . . . . . . 210 D2
   Stanwell TW19 . . . . 148 B3
Lacebark Cl DA15 . . . . . . 167 D4
Lacewing Cl E13 . . . . .99 A4
Lacey Cl N9 . . . . .18 A2
Lacey Dr Dagenham RM8 . .80 C5
Lacey Ho 7 SE13 . . . . . . 142 A3
Lacey Mews 9 E3 . . . . . . .97 C5
Lacine Ct 12 SE16 . . . . . 118 D4
Lacock Cl SW19 . . . . 180 A4
Lacock Ct 3 W13 . . . . . . 109 A5
Lacon Rd SE22 . . . . 140 A1
Lacrosse Way SW16 . . . . 181 D2
Lacy Rd SW15 . . . . 134 D1
Ladas Rd SE27 . . . . 183 A5
Ladbroke Cres W11 . . . . .91 A1
Ladbroke Gdns
   W11 . . . . 113 B6 **244** C6
Ladbroke Gr
   Kensal Town W10 . . . . .91 A2
   Notting Hill W11 . . . 113 B6 **244** C6
Ladbroke Grove Ho W11 . 244 C6
Ladbroke Grove Sta W10 . .91 A1
Ladbroke Ho E1 . . . . **243** D3
Ladbroke Mews W11 . . . . 244 B3
Ladbroke Rd Enfield EN1 . .17 D5
   Notting Hill W11 . . . 113 B5 **244** C5
Ladbroke Sq
   W11 . . . . 113 B6 **244** D5
Ladbroke Terr
   W11 . . . . 113 B5 **244** D4
Ladbroke Wlk
   W11 . . . . 113 B5 **244** D4
Ladbroke Cl HA5 . . . . .41 B4
Ladbrooke Cres DA14 . . .168 D1
Ladbrook Rd SE25 . . . . . 205 B5
Ladderstile Ride KT2,
   TW10 . . . . 176 D5
Ladderswood Way N11 . . .31 C5
Ladlands SE22 . . . . 162 A4
Lady Alesford Ave HA7 . . .25 B5

Lady Bankes Jun & Inf Schs
   HA4 . . . . .62 A6
Lady Booth Rd 7 KT1 . . .176 A1
Ladybower Ct 6 E5 . . . . . .74 D4
Ladycroft Gdns 8 BR6 . . 227 A3
Ladycroft Rd SE13 . . . . . 141 D2
Ladycroft Way BR6 . . . . . 227 A3
Ladycroft Wlk HA7 . . . . . .25 D1
Lady Eleanor Holles Sch (Jun
   Girls) The TW12 . . . . . . 173 D5
Lady Eleanor Holles Sch
   (Senior Girls) The
   TW12 . . . . 173 D5
Lady Elizabeth Ho SW14 . 133 A2
Ladyfern Ho 19 E3 . . . . . .97 C2
Lady Florence Ctyd 15
   SE8 . . . . 141 C5
Ladygate La HA4 . . . . .39 A3
Lady Hay KT4 . . . . 215 D6
Lady Helen Seymour Ho 14
   E13 . . . . .99 A5
Lady Margaret Prim Sch
   UB1 . . . . .85 B2
Lady Margaret Rd
   Kentish Town NW5 . . . . . . .71 C3
   Southall UB1 . . . . .85 B2
Lady Margaret Sch
   SW6 . . . . 135 C4 **265** A1
Lady Shaw Ct N13 . . . . . . .16 B1
Ladysmith Ave Ilford IG2 . .57 C2
   Newham E6 . . . . 100 A5
Ladysmith Cl NW7 . . . . . . .28 A3
Ladysmith Rd
   Edmonton N18 . . . . .34 B5
   Eltham SE9 . . . . 166 C5
   Enfield EN1 . . . . 5 D3
   Harrrow HA3 . . . . .24 C1
   Newham E16 . . . . .98 D4
   Tottenham N17 . . . . .34 A1
Lady Somerset Rd NW5 . .71 B4
LADYWELL 163 C6
Ladywell Cl SE4 . . . . 141 C1
Ladywell Arena SE13 . . . 163 D5
Ladywell Ho 7 SE7 . . . . . 190 B1
Ladywell Hts SE4 . . . . . . 163 B5
Ladywell Rd SE13 . . . . . 163 B6
Ladywell Rise 4 E15 . . . . .98 D6
Ladywell Sta SE13 . . . . . 163 D6
Ladywell Water Twr
   SE4 . . . . 163 C6
Ladywood Ave BR5 . . . . . 211 C4
Ladywood Rd KT6 . . . . . 214 C6
Lafitte Ho 22 N19 . . . . . . .49 D2
Lafone Ave TW13 . . . . . . 150 C2
Lafone Ho 11 SW2 . . . . . 160 A4
Lafone St SE1 . . . 117 D4 **253** C2
Lagado Mews SE16 . . . . 118 D5
Lagonda Ho 11 E3 . . . . . .97 C3
Lagonier Ho EC1 . . . . . . **235** B1
Laidlaw Dr N21 . . . . .16 B6
Laindon Ho 6 N16 . . . . . .51 D1
Laing Dean UB5 . . . . .84 C6
Laing Ho SE5 . . . . 139 A5
Laings Ave CR4 . . . . 180 A5
Laings Cnr CR4 . . . . 180 D2
Lainlock Pl TW3 . . . . 129 D4
Lainson St SW18 . . . . . . 157 C4
Lairdale Cl SE21 . . . . 161 A4
Laird Ho SE5 . . . . 139 A5
Lairs Cl N7 . . . . .72 A2
Lait Ho 3 BR3 . . . . 185 D2
Laitwood Rd SW12 . . . . . 159 B3
Lakanal 14 SE5 . . . . 139 C4
Lake Ave BR1 . . . . 187 A4
Lake Bsns Ctr N17 . . . . . .34 A3
Lake Cl Dagenham RM8 . . .80 C5
   6 Wimbledon SW19 . . . . 179 B5
Lakedale Ct IG11 . . . . . . 102 A3
Lakedale Rd SE18 . . . . . 123 C1
Lake Dr WD23 . . . . 8 B2
Lake Farm Ctry Pk UB3 . .105 C5
Lakefield Cl SE20 . . . . . . 184 B3
Lakefield Rd N22 . . . . .32 D1
Lake Gdns
   Dagenham RM10 . . . . .81 C3
   Hackbridge SM6 . . . . 219 B5
   Richmond TW10 . . . . 153 B2
Lakehall Gdns CR7 . . . . . 204 D4
Lakehall Rd CR7 . . . . 204 D4
Lake Ho Borough The SE1 . **252** A1
   4 West Norwood SW27 . .182 D5
Lake House Rd E11 . . . . . .77 A6
Lakehurst Rd KT19 . . . . . 215 C3
Lakeland Cl HA3 . . . . .24 B4
Lakeman Ct CR7 . . . . 183 A1
Lakenham N14 . . . . .15 C6
Laker Ct SW4 . . . . 138 A3
Lake Rd Croydon CR0 . . . 223 B6
   Dagenham RM6 . . . . .58 D5
   Wimbledon SW19 . . . . . . 179 B5
Laker Pl SW15 . . . . 157 A5
Lakeside Beckenham BR3 . 207 D6
   Deacons Hill WD6 . . . . .10 C6
   Ealing W13 . . . . .87 C1
   Enfield EN2 . . . . 4 B2
   Finchley N3 . . . . .29 D1
   10 Kingston u T KT2 . . . . 176 D3
   Wallington SM6 . . . . 219 B4
   West Ewell KT19 . . . . 215 C2

Lakeside Ave
   Redbridge IG4 . . . . .55 D5
   Thamesmead SE28 . . . . . 124 A5
Lakeside Cl Ruislip HA4 . . .39 B5
   Sidcup DA15 . . . . 168 C6
   South Norwood SE25 . . . . 184 A1
Lakeside Complex The
   SE2 . . . . 124 D5
Lakeside Cres EN4 . . . . . .14 D6
Lakeside Ct N4 . . . . .51 A1
Lakeside Dr Acton NW10 . .88 B4
   Esher KT10 . . . . 212 A2
   Keston Mark BR2 . . . . . . 226 A5
Lakeside Lo NW4 . . . . . . .47 A5
Lakeside Rd
   Brook Green W14 . . . . 112 D3
   Palmers Green N13 . . . . . .16 B1
Lakeside Way HA9 . . . . . .66 C4
Lakes Rd BR2 . . . . 225 C3
Lakeswood Rd BR5 . . . . . 211 A3
Lake The WD23 . . . . 8 B3
Lakeview 23 E3 . . . . .96 C5
Lake View HA8 . . . . .26 B5
Lakeview Ct E4 . . . . .36 B4
Lakeview Ct SW1 . . . . . . **258** D6
Lakeview Rd
   Bexley DA16 . . . . 146 B1
   West Norwood SE27 . . . . 182 D5
Lake View Terr N18 . . . . . .33 D6
Lakis Cl NW3 . . . . .70 A4
Laleham Ave NW7 . . . . . . .11 B1
Laleham Ho E2 . . . . **243** C6
Laleham Rd Catford SE6 . .164 A4
   Littleton TW17 . . . . 192 C4
Lalor St SW6 . . . . 135 A3
Lambarde Ave SE9 . . . . . 188 C6
Lambard Ho 4 SE10 . . . . 142 A5
Lamb Cl UB5 . . . . .85 A4
Lamb Ct 19 E14 . . . . 119 A6
Lamberhurst Ho 14
   SE15 . . . . 140 C6
Lamberhurst Rd
   Dagenham RM8 . . . . .59 B1
   West Norwood SE27 . . . . 182 C5
Lambert Ave TW9 . . . . . . 132 D2
Lambert Ho
   16 Brixton SW9 . . . . 138 C3
   19 Crouch End N19 . . . . . .49 D2
Lambert Lo TW8 . . . . 109 D1
Lambert Rd
   Clapham Pk SW2 . . . . . . 160 A6
   Newham E16 . . . . .99 B1
   North Finchley N12 . . . . . .30 B5
Lambert's Pl CR0 . . . . . . 205 B1
Lambert's Rd KT6 . . . . . . 198 B4
Lambert St N1 . . . . .72 C1
Lambert Way N12 . . . . . . .30 A5
Lambert Wlk HA9 . . . . . . .65 D5
LAMBETH 116 B4
Lambeth Acad SW4 . . . . 159 C6
Lambeth Coll SW16 . . . . 160 A1
Lambeth Coll (Brixton Ctr)
   SW2 . . . . 160 A6
Lambeth Coll (Clapham Ctr)
   SW4 . . . . 159 C6
Lambeth Coll (Vauxhall Ctr)
   SW8 . . . . 137 D4 **269** C2
Lambeth Ct 8 SW18 . . . 157 C6
Lambeth High St
   SE1 . . . . 116 B2 **260** C4
Lambeth Hill EC4 . . . . . . **252** A6
Lambeth Hospl SW9 . . . . 138 B2
Lambeth North Sta
   SE1 . . . . 116 C3 **261** A6
Lambeth Pal ★ 261 A6
Lambeth Palace Rd
   SE1 . . . . 116 B3 **260** C5
Lambeth Pier SE1 . . . . . **260** B5
Lambeth Prospect SE19 . 183 B4
Lambeth Rd
   Lambeth SE1 . . . . 116 C3 **261** A5
   Thornton Heath CR0 . . . . 204 D1
Lambeth Twrs SE11 . . . . **261** A5
Lambeth Wlk
   SE11 . . . . 116 B2 **260** D6
Lambfold Ho N7 . . . . .72 A2
Lamb Ho
   28 Camberwell SE5 . . . . . 139 A5
   11 Camberwell SE5 . . . . . 139 B4
   Greenwich SE10 . . . . 142 A6
Lamb La E8 . . . . .74 B1
Lamb St NW5 . . . . .71 A4
Lambley Rd RM9 . . . . .80 B2
Lamb Office Ct WC1 . . . . **240** C4
Lambolle Pl NW3 . . . . . . .70 C2
Lambolle Rd NW3 . . . . . . .70 C2
Lambourn Cl
   Hanwell W7 . . . . 108 C2
   9 Kentish Town NW5 . . . . .71 C4
Lambourne Ave SW19 . . . 179 B6
Lambourne Ct 5 IG8 . . . . .37 C3
Lambourne Gdns
   5 Barking IG11 . . . . .79 D1
   Chingford E4 . . . . .19 C2
   Enfield EN1 . . . . 5 D3
Lambourne Gr
   Deptford SE16 . . . . 118 D1
   Kingston u T KT1 . . . . 176 D1
Lambourne Ho NW8 . . . . **236** D4

Lambourne Pl SE3 . . . . 143 B4
Lambourne Rd
  Barking IG11 . . . . 79 D1
  Ilford IG3 . . . . 79 C6
  Leytonstone E11 . . . . 54 A2
Lambourn Ho BR1 . . . . 188 A3
Lambourn Rd SW4 . . . . . . 137 B2
Lambrook Ho 13 SE15 . . . 140 A4
Lambrook Terr
  SW6 . . . . 135 A4 264 A2
Lamb's Bldgs EC1 . . . . . . 242 C5
Lamb's Cl N9 . . . . 18 A2
Lamb's Conduit Pas
  WC1 . . . . 240 C4
Lamb's Conduit St
  WC1 . . . . 94 B3 240 C4
Lambscroft Ave SE9,
  SE12 . . . . 165 D1
Lambs Mdw IG8 . . . . 37 D1
Lamb's Mews N1 . . . . 234 C5
Lamb's Pas EC1 . . . . 95 B3 242 C5
Lamb St E1 . . . . 95 D2 243 C4
Lamb'sTerr N9 . . . . 17 B2
Lambs Wlk EN2 . . . . 5 A3
Lambton Ct 2 N19 . . . . 50 A1
Lambton Mews 4 N19 . . . . 50 A1
Lambton Pl W11 . . . . 244 D6
Lambton Rd
  Finsbury Pk N19 . . . . 50 A1
  Wimbledon SW20 . . . . . . 178 C2
Lamb Wlk SE1 . . . . 253 A1
Lamerock Rd BR1 . . . . 186 D6
Lamerton Rd SE23 . . . . . . 165 D1
Lamerton St 8 SE8 . . . . . 141 C6
Lamford Cl N17 . . . . 33 B3
Lamington St 3 W6 . . . . . 112 B2
Lamlash St SE11 . . . . 261 C4
Lamley Ho SE10 . . . . 141 D5
Lammas Ave CR4 . . . . 181 A1
Lammas Gn SE26 . . . . 162 B1
Lammas Park Gdns W5 . . . 109 C5
Lammas Park Rd W5 . . . . 109 D4
Lammas Rd Homerton E9 . . 74 D1
  Richmond TW10 . . . . 175 C6
  Walthamstow E10 . . . . 53 A1
Lammas Sch E10 . . . . 53 B1
Lammermoor Rd SW12 . . . 159 B4
Lamont Rd SW10 . 136 B6 266 C5
Lamont Rd Pas SW10 . . . . 266 C5
Lamorbey Cl DA15 . . . . . . 167 D2
Lamorna Cl E17 . . . . 36 A2
Lamorna Gr HA7 . . . . 25 D1
Lampard Gr N16 . . . . 51 D1
Lampern Sq 8 E2 . . . . 96 A4
Lampeter Cl NW9 . . . . 45 C3
Lampeter Sq W6 . . . . 264 A5
Lamplighter Cl 34 E1 . . . . 96 C3
Lampmead Rd SE12 . . . . . 142 D1
Lamport Cl SE18 . . . . 122 B2
Lampson Ho 6 N19 . . . . . . 71 C4
LAMPTON 129 C4
Lampton Ave TW5 . . . . . . 129 C4
Lampton Ct TW5 . . . . 129 C4
Lampton House Cl
  SW19 . . . . 178 D6
Lampton Park Rd TW3 . . . 129 D3
Lampton Rd TW3,TW5 . . . 129 D3
Lampton Sch TW5 . . . . . . 129 C4
Lampton Sp Ctr TW5 . . . . 129 C4
Lanacre Ave NW9 . . . . 27 C2
Lanadron Cl 5 TW7 . . . . . 130 D3
Lanain Ct SE12 . . . . 164 D4
Lanark Cl W5 . . . . 87 C2
Lanark Ct UB5 . . . . 63 C3
Lanark Ho 12 SE1 . . . . . . 118 A1
Lanark Mans
  Paddington W9 . . . . 236 B6
  15 Shepherd's Bush W12 . . 112 C2
Lanark Mews NW8 . . . . . . 229 B1
Lanark Pl W9 . . . . . . 92 A3 236 A6
Lanark Rd W9 . . . . . . 92 A4 229 A1
Lanark Sq E14 . . . . 119 D3
Lanata Wlk UB4 . . . . 84 D3
Lanbury Rd SE15 . . . . 140 D1
Lancashire Ct W1 . . . . . . 248 D6
Lancaster Ave
  Barking IG11 . . . . 101 C6
  Croydon CR4 . . . . 204 A5
  Hadley Wood EN4 . . . . 2 B5
  Wanstead E18 . . . . 55 B5
  West Norwood SE21, SE27 . 161 A2
  Wimbledon SW19 . . . . . . 178 D5
Lancaster Cl
  Ashford TW15 . . . . 170 A6
  Beckenham BR2 . . . . 208 D5
  10 De Beauvoir Town N1 . . 73 C1
  Grahame Pk NW9 . . . . 27 D3
  Kensington W2 . . . . 245 C5
  Kingston u T KT2 . . . . 175 D5
  New Malden KT4 . . . . 200 B2
  Stanwell TW19 . . . . 148 A5
  Tottenham N17 . . . . 34 A3
Lancaster Cotts 1
  TW10 . . . . 154 A5
Lancaster Ct
  Bayswater W2 . . . . 246 B6
  1 Belmont SM2 . . . . 217 C1
  Parsons Green SW6 . . . . . 264 C5
  Stanwell TW19 . . . . 148 A3
  Walton-on-T KT12 . . . . . . 194 B2

Lancaster Ct *continued*
  West Norwood SE27 . . . . . 160 D2
Lancaster Dr
  Canary Wharf E14 . . . . . . 120 A5
  Maitland Pk NW3 . . . . 70 C2
Lancaster Gate
  W2 . . . . 114 A6 246 B6
Lancaster Gate Sta
  W2 . . . . 114 B6 246 C6
Lancaster Gdns
  Bromley BR1 . . . . 210 A4
  Kingston u T KT2 . . . . 175 D5
  West Ealing W13 . . . . 109 B4
  Wimbledon SW19 . . . . . . 179 A5
Lancaster Gr NW3 . . . . 70 C2
Lancaster hall 14 E16 . . . 121 A5
Lancaster Ho Enfield EN2 . . . 5 B4
  Putney SW15 . . . . 134 C3
  Stanmore HA7 . . . . 9 A1
Lancaster Ho SW1 . . . . . . 249 A2
Lancaster Lo 2 W11 . . . . . 91 A1
Lancaster Mews
  Bayswater W2 . . . . 114 A6 246 B6
  2 Richmond TW10 . . . . . 154 A5
  3 Wandsworth SW18 . . . . 157 D6
Lancaster Pk TW10 . . . . . . 154 A6
Lancaster Pl
  Hounslow TW5 . . . . 128 D3
  Ilford IG1 . . . . 79 A4
  Strand WC2 . . . . . 116 B6 250 C5
  Twickenham TW1 . . . . . . 153 A4
  1 Wimbledon SW19 . . . . 178 D5
Lancaster Rd
  Bowes Pk N11 . . . . 31 D4
  Dudden Hill NW10 . . . . . . 68 A3
  Edmonton N18 . . . . 33 D5
  Enfield EN2 . . . . 5 B4
  Finsbury Pk N4 . . . . 50 C2
  Harrow HA2 . . . . 41 C4
  Higham Hill E17 . . . . 34 D1
  Leytonstone E11 . . . . 76 C6
  New Barnet EN4 . . . . 14 B6
  Northolt UB5 . . . . 64 A2
  Notting Hill W11 . . . . 91 A1
  Southall UB1 . . . . 107 A6
  South Norwood SE25 . . . . 206 A6
  Upton E7 . . . . 77 A1
  Wimbledon SW19 . . . . . . 178 D5
Lancaster Road Ind Est 2
  EN4 . . . . 14 B6
Lancaster St SE1 . 116 D4 251 D1
Lancaster Stables 10
  NW3 . . . . 70 C2
Lancaster Terr
  W2 . . . . 114 B6 246 C6
Lancaster Wlk Hayes UB3 . . 83 A1
  Knightsbridge W2 . 114 A5 246 B4
Lancastrian Rd SM6 . . . . . 220 B1
Lancefield Ho SE15 . . . . . 140 B2
Lancefield St W10 . . . . 91 B4
Lancell St N16 . . . . 73 C6
Lancelot Ho HA0 . . . . 65 D4
Lancelot Cres HA0 . . . . . . 65 D4
Lancelot Gdns EN4 . . . . . . 15 A4
Lancelot Ho SM5 . . . . 202 C1
Lancelot Pl SW7 . 114 D4 247 D1
Lancelot Rd
  Welling DA16 . . . . 146 A2
  Wembley HA0 . . . . 65 D3
Lance Rd HA1 . . . . 42 A2
Lancer Sq W8 . . . . 245 C2
Lancey Cl SE7 . . . . 122 A2
Lanchester Ct W2 . . . . . . 237 C1
Lanchester Rd N6 . . . . 48 D4
Lanchester Way SE14 . . . . 140 D4
Lancing Gdns N9 . . . . 17 D3
Lancing Rd Ealing W13 . . . 109 B6
  Feltham TW13 . . . . 149 D2
  Ilford IG2 . . . . 57 B2
  Thornton Heath CR0 . . . . 204 B2
Lancing St NW1 . . . . 232 C1
Lancresse Ct N1 . . . . 95 C6
Landale Ct SE10 . . . . 142 A4
Landale Ho 13 SE16 . . . . 118 C3
Landau Ct 11 CR2 . . . . . . 221 A3
Landcroft Rd SE22 . . . . . . 161 D5
Landells Rd SE22 . . . . . . 162 A5
Lander Ct EN5 . . . . 14 A6
Landford Rd SW15 . . . . . . 134 C2
Landgrove Rd SW19 . . . . . 179 C5
Landin Ho 1 E14 . . . . 97 C1
Landleys Field 21 N7 . . . . . 71 D3
Landmann Ho 16 SE16 . . . 118 B2
Landmann Way SE14 . . . . 118 D1
Landmark Commercial Ctr
  N18 . . . . 33 C4
Landmark Hts E5 . . . . 75 A4
Landon Pl SW1 . . . . 257 C6
Landons Cl E14 . . . . 120 A5
Landon Way TW15 . . . . . . 170 C4
Landon Wlk 16 E14 . . . . . 119 D6
Landor Ct N16 . . . . 73 C3
Landor Ho 7 SE5 . . . . 139 B5
Landor Rd SW9 . . . . 138 A2
Landor Wlk 11 W12 . . . . . 112 A4
Landra Gdns N21 . . . . 16 D5
Landrake NW1 . . . . 232 B5

Landridge Dr EN1 . . . . 6 B5
Landridge Rd SW6 . . . . . . 135 B3
Landrock Rd N8 . . . . 50 B3
Landscape Rd IG8 . . . . 37 B3
Landsdown Cl 9 EN5 . . . . . 2 A1
Landseer Ave E12 . . . . 78 C3
Landseer Cl Edgware HA8 . . 26 C1
  Mitcham SW19 . . . . 180 B2
Landseer Ct Hayes UB4 . . . 83 B5
  10 Upper Holloway N19 . . . 72 A6
Landseer Ho
  Battersea SW11 . . . . 268 B1
  16 Northolt UB5 . . . . 84 D5
  Paddington NW8 . . . . 236 D6
  Westminster SW1 . . . . . . 259 D3
Landseer Rd Cheam SM1 . . 217 C2
  Enfield EN1 . . . . 18 A6
  New Malden KT3 . . . . 199 B2
  Upper Holloway N19 . . . . . 72 A6
Lands' End WD6 . . . . 9 D5
Landstead Rd SE18 . . . . . 145 B5
Landulph Ho SE11 . . . . . . 261 B2
Landward Ct W1 . . . . 237 B2
Lane Cl NW2 . . . . 68 B5
Lane End DA7 . . . . 147 D2
Lane Gdns
  Bushey Heath WD23 . . . . . 8 C4
  Claygate KT10 . . . . 212 D1
Lanercost Cl SW2 . . . . . . 160 C2
Lanercost Gdns N14 . . . . . 16 A4
Lanercost Rd SW2 . . . . . . 160 C2
Laneside Chislehurst BR7 . 189 A5
  Edgware HA8 . . . . 27 A5
Laneside Ave RM8 . . . . . . 59 B2
Lane The
  Blackheath Pk SE3 . . . . . 143 A2
  St John's Wood
  NW8 . . . . 92 A5 229 A3
Laneway SW15 . . . . 156 B6
Laney Bldg EC1 . . . . 241 A4
Lanfranc Ct HA1 . . . . 64 D5
Lanfranc Rd E3 . . . . 97 A5
Lanfrey Pl W14 . . . . 254 C1
Langbourne Ct E17 . . . . . . 53 A3
Langbourne Ho 7 SW2 . . 160 C6
Langbourne Mans N6 . . . . 71 A6
Langbourne Pl E14 . . . . . . 119 D1
Langbourne Prim Sch
  SE21 . . . . 161 C1
Langbourne Way KT10 . . . 213 A2
Langbrook Rd SE3 . . . . . . 143 D3
Langcroft Cl SM5 . . . . 218 D5
Langdale NW1 . . . . 232 A2
Langdale Ave CR4 . . . . . . 202 D6
Langdale Cl
  Camberwell SE17 . . . . . . 139 A6
  Dagenham RM8 . . . . 58 C1
  Locksbottom BR6 . . . . . . 226 D5
  Mortlake SW14 . . . . 132 D1
Langdale Cres DA7 . . . . . . 147 C4
Langdale Ct 3 Ealing W5 . . 87 C2
  Ruislip HA4 . . . . 62 B3
Langdale Dr UB4 . . . . 83 C5
Langdale Gdns UB6 . . . . . . 87 B4
Langdale Ho SW1 . . . . . . 259 A1
Langdale Par 8 CR4 . . . . . 202 D6
Langdale Rd
  Greenwich SE10 . . . . 142 A5
  Thornton Heath CR7 . . . . . 204 C5
Langdale St 15 E1 . . . . 96 B1
Langdon Cres E6 . . . . 100 C5
Langdon Ct Finsbury EC1 . 234 D3
  Harlesden NW10 . . . . 89 C6
Langdon Dr NW9 . . . . 45 A1
Langdon Ho 3 E14 . . . . . . 98 A1
Langdon Park Rd N6 . . . . . 49 C2
Langdon Park Sch E14 . . . . 98 A1
Langdon Park Sta E14 . . . . 97 D1
Langdon Pk TW11 . . . . . . 175 C3
Langdon Pk L Ctr E14 . . . . 98 A1
Langdon Pk Sta E3 . . . . . . 97 D2
Langdon Pl SW14 . . . . . . 133 A2
Langdon Rd Barking E6 . . . 100 C6
  Bromley BR2 . . . . 209 B6
  Morden SM4 . . . . 202 A4
Langdon Sch E6 . . . . 100 D6
Langdons Ct UB2 . . . . 107 C3
Langdon Shaw DA14 . . . . 189 D5
Langdon Way 18 SE1 . . . . 118 A2
Langdon Wlk SM4 . . . . . . 202 A4
Langford Cl
  Shacklewell E8 . . . . 74 A3
  7 South Tottenham N15 . . 51 C3
  St John's Wood NW8 . . . . 229 B4
Langford Cres EN4 . . . . . . 2 D1
Langford Ct NW8 . . . . . . 229 B3
Langford Gn SE5 . . . . 139 C2
Langford Ho 5 SE8 . . . . . 141 C6
Langford Pl Sidcup DA14 . 168 A1
  St John's Wood
  NW8 . . . . 92 A5 229 B4
Langford Prim Sch SW6 . . 135 D3
Langford Rd
  Cockfosters EN4 . . . . 2 D1
  4 Sands End SW6 . . . . . 135 D3
  Woodford IG8 . . . . 37 C4

Langfords IG9 . . . . 21 D2
Langham Cl 1 N15 . . . . . . 50 D6
Langham Ct Hendon NW4 . . 46 D4
  Merton SW20 . . . . 178 C1
  4 Putney SW15 . . . . 156 D6
  Ruislip HA4 . . . . 62 B3
  12 Twickenham TW1 . . . 153 C5
Langham Dr RM6 . . . . 58 B3
Langham Gdns
  Burnt Oak HA8 . . . . 27 A3
  Ealing W13 . . . . 109 B6
  Richmond TW10 . . . . 175 C6
  Southgate N21 . . . . 16 D6
  Wembley HA0 . . . . 65 C6
Langham Ho
  Clapham Pk SW4 . . . . . . 159 C6
  3 Wanstead E11 . . . . 55 B5
Langham House Cl
  TW10 . . . . 175 D6
Langham Mans SW5 . . . . 255 C1
Langham Park Pl BR2 . . . . 208 D5
Langham Pl Chiswick W4 . 133 C6
  Fitzrovia W1 . . . . . 93 B2 238 D3
  Noel Pk N15 . . . . 50 D6
Langham Rd
  Burnt Oak HA8 . . . . 27 A4
  Teddington TW11 . . . . . . 175 B4
  West Green N15 . . . . 51 A6
  Wimbledon SW20 . . . . . . 178 C2
Langham St W1 . . . 93 B2 238 D3
Langhedge Cl N18 . . . . 33 D4
Langhedge La N18 . . . . 33 D4
Langhedge Lane Ind Est
  N18 . . . . 33 D4
Lang Ho
  South Lambeth SW8 . . . . 270 A3
  Stanwell TW19 . . . . 148 A3
  3 Tufnell Pk N19 . . . . 71 C5
Langholm Cl SW12 . . . . . 159 D4
Langholme WD23 . . . . 8 A3
Langhorn Dr TW2 . . . . . . 152 C4
Langhorne Ct 10 NW8 . . . . 70 B1
Langhorne Ho 5 SE7 . . . . 143 C6
Langhorne Rd RM10 . . . . . 81 C1
Langhurst Ho 10 SW11 . . 137 A3
Langland Cres HA7 . . . . . . 25 D1
Langland Dr HA5 . . . . 23 A3
Langland Gdns
  Croydon CR0 . . . . 223 B6
  West Hampstead NW3 . . . . 69 D3
Langland Ho 10 SE5 . . . . 139 B5
Langland Mans NW3 . . . . . 69 D3
Langler Rd NW10 . . . . 90 C5
Langley Ave
  North Cheam KT4, SM3 . . 216 D6
  Ruislip HA4 . . . . 62 B6
  Surbiton KT6 . . . . 198 A1
Langley Cres
  Dagenham RM9 . . . . 80 D1
  Edgware HA8 . . . . 11 A1
  Harlington UB3 . . . . 127 D5
  Wanstead E11 . . . . 55 C2
Langley Ct
  South Lambeth SW8 . . . . 270 A2
  Strand WC2 . . . . 250 A6
  13 Sutton SM2 . . . . 218 A2
Langley Dr
  South Acton W3 . . . . 110 D4
  Wanstead E11 . . . . 55 B2
Langley Gdns
  Bromley BR2 . . . . 209 C5
  Dagenham RM9 . . . . 80 D1
  Southborough BR5 . . . . . 225 D2
Langley Gr KT3 . . . . 177 C1
Langley Ho
  11 Lower Clapton E5 . . . . 74 B3
  36 Paddington W2 . . . . . . 91 D2
Langley La SW8 . . 138 A4 270 B6
Langley Lawns SM2 . . . . . 218 B1
Langley Manor BR3 . . . . . 208 A4
Langley Mans 4 . . . . 270 B6
Langley Park Rd SM1,
  SM2 . . . . 218 A1
Langley Park Sch for Boys
  BR3 . . . . 207 D3
Langley Park Sch for Girls
  BR3 . . . . 208 A3
Langley Pk NW7 . . . . 27 C4
Langley Pl 4 KT4 . . . . 216 D6
Langley Rd
  Beckenham BR3 . . . . 207 A5
  Isleworth TW7 . . . . 130 D3
  Merton SW19 . . . . 179 C2
  Surbiton KT6 . . . . 198 A2
  West Heath DA16 . . . . . . 146 C6
Langley Row EN5 . . . . 1 B4
Langley St WC2 . . . 94 A1 240 A1
Langley Way BR4 . . . . 208 C2
Langmead Dr WD23 . . . . . . 8 B3
Langmead Ho 34 E3 . . . . . 97 D4
Langmead St 27 SE27 . . . 183 A6
Langmore Ct DA6 . . . . . . 146 D2
Langmore Ho 39 E1 . . . . . 96 A1
Langport Ct KT12 . . . . . . 194 C1
Langport Ho 1 SW9 . . . . . 138 D3
Langridge 15 NW5 . . . . . . 71 A2
Langridge Mews TW12 . . . 173 B4
Langroyd Rd SW17 . . . . . 158 D2
Langside Ave SW15 . . . . . 134 A1

Langside Cres N14 . . . . . . 15 D1
Lang St E1 . . . . 96 C3
Langstone Way NW7 . . . . . 28 D3
Langston Hughes Cl 5
  SE24 . . . . 138 D1
Langthorn Ct EC2 . . . . . . 242 D2
Langthorne Ct 3 SE6 . . . . 186 A6
Langthorne Ho UB3 . . . . . 105 C2
Langthorne Lo 80 SW2 . . 160 C4
Langthorne Rd E11 . . . . . . 76 B5
Langthorne St SW6 . . . . . 134 D5
Langton Ave
  Oakleigh Pk N20 . . . . 14 B4
  Wallend E6 . . . . 100 C4
Langton Cl W1 . . . . 94 B3 240 D6
Langton Ct SW15 . . . . 157 B5
Langton Ho Harrow HA2 . . . 64 C6
  Lambeth SE11 . . . . 260 D4
  5 Streatham SW16 . . . . . 181 C6
Langton Pl SW18 . . . . 157 C3
Langton Rd
  Camberwell SW9 . . . . 138 D5
  Cricklewood NW2 . . . . 68 C5
  East Molesey KT8 . . . . . . 196 A5
  Harrow Weald HA3 . . . . . . 24 A3
Langton Rise SE22 . . . . . . 162 B4
Langton St SW10 . 136 A6 266 B5
Langton Way
  Greenwich SE3 . . . . 143 A5
  South Croydon CR0 . . . . . 221 C4
Langtry Ho BR1 . . . . 187 B3
Langtry Pl SW6 . . . . 265 B6
Langtry Rd Northolt UB5 . . . 84 D5
  Paddington NW8 . . . . 91 D6
Langtry Wlk NW8 . 92 A6 229 A6
Langwood Chase TW11 . . 175 C4
Langworth Dr UB4 . . . . . . 84 B1
Langworthy HA5 . . . . 23 C4
Lanherne Ho 7 SW19 . . . 178 D3
Lanhill Rd W9 . . . . 91 C3
Lanier Rd SE13 . . . . 164 B5
Lanigan Dr TW3 . . . . 151 D6
Lankaster Gdns N2 . . . . . . 30 B2
Lankers Dr HA2 . . . . 41 B3
Lankton Cl BR3 . . . . 186 A2
Lanner Ho 2 SW11 . . . . . 136 C2
Lannock Ct 2 SW17 . . . . 180 C4
Lannock Rd UB3 . . . . 105 D5
Lannoy Point SW6 . . . . . . 264 B4
Lannoy Rd SE9 . . . . 167 A3
Lanrick Rd E14 . . . . 98 C1
Lanridge Rd SE2 . . . . 124 D3
Lansan Ct E11 . . . . 76 D6
Lansbury Ave
  Barking IG11 . . . . 80 A1
  Dagenham RM6 . . . . 59 A4
  Edmonton N18 . . . . 33 C5
  Feltham TW14 . . . . 150 B5
Lansbury Cl NW10 . . . . . . 67 A3
Lansbury Ct 4 SE28 . . . . 124 B6
Lansbury Dr UB4 . . . . 83 D3
Lansbury Gdns 1 E14 . . . . 98 B1
Lansbury Ho 5 DA17 . . . . 125 B1
Lansbury Lawrence Prim Sch
  20 E14 . . . . 97 C1
Lansbury Rd EN3 . . . . 6 D4
Lansbury Way N18 . . . . . . 33 C5
Lanscombe Wlk SW8 . . . 270 A3
Lansdell Ho 5 SW2 . . . . . 160 C5
Lansdell Rd CR4 . . . . 181 A1
Lansdown Cl KT12 . . . . . . 194 C1
Lansdowne Ave
  Orpington BR6 . . . . 210 D1
  West Heath DA7 . . . . 146 D5
Lansdowne Cl
  Tolworth KT5 . . . . 214 D6
  Twickenham TW1 . . . . . . 152 D3
  Wimbledon SW20 . . . . . . 178 D3
Lansdowne Coll W2 . . . . . 245 C5
Lansdowne Copse 1
  KT4 . . . . 216 A6
Lansdowne Cres
  W11 . . . . 113 A6 244 B5
Lansdowne Dr
  Redbridge IG5 . . . . 56 A6
  2 Worcester Pk KT4 . . . . 216 A6
Lansdowne Dr E8 . . . . 74 A1
Lansdowne Gdns
  SW8 . . . . 138 A4 270 A2
Lansdowne Gr NW10 . . . . . 67 C4
Lansdowne Hill SE27 . . . . 160 D1
Lansdowne Ho
  19 Belmont SM2 . . . . . . 217 D1
  Enfield EN2 . . . . 4 C3
  Notting Hill W11 . . . . 244 C4
Lansdowne La SE7 . . . . . . 121 C1
Lansdowne Mews
  Greenwich SE7 . . . . 121 D1
  Notting Hill W11 . . . . 244 C4
Lansdowne Pl
  Borough The SE1 . . . . . . 262 D6
  Penge SE19 . . . . 183 D1
Lansdowne Rd
  Chingford E4 . . . . 19 C2
  Croydon CR0 . . . . 205 B1
  Finchley N3 . . . . 29 C3
  Harrow HA1 . . . . 42 C1

Lansdowne Rd continued
Hayes UB8 . . . .**83** A1
Hounslow TW3 . . . .**129** D2
Ilford IG3 . . . .**57** D2
Leytonstone E11. . . . .**76** D6
Muswell Hill N10. . . . .**31** C1
Notting Hill W11. . . .**113** A6 **244** B5
Stanmore HA7 . . . .**25** C4
Sundridge BR1. . . . .**187** B3
Tottenham N17. . . . .**34** A2
Walthamstow E17 . . . .**53** C3
Wanstead E18 . . . .**55** A6
West Ewell KT19. . . . . . .**215** B1
Wimbledon SW19, SW20 . .**178** C3
Lansdowne Rise
W11. . . . .**113** A6 **244** B5
Lansdowne Row W1 . . .**248** D4
Lansdowne Sch **5** SW9 . .**138** B2
Lansdowne Terr WC1. . .**240** B5
Lansdowne Way SW4,
SW8. . . . .**138** A4 **270** B1
Lansdowne Wlk
W11. . . . .**113** B5 **244** C4
Lansdowne Wood Cl **11**
SE27 . . . .**160** D1
Lansdowne Workshops
SE7 . . . .**121** D1
Lansdown Ho **28** SE5. . . .**139** A3
Lansdown Rd
Sidcup DA14. . . . .**168** B1
Upton E7. . . . .**77** C1
Lansfield Ave N18. . . . . .**34** A6
Lanson Ho HA8 . . . .**26** C4
Lantern Cl Orpington BR6. .**226** D4
Putney SW15 . . . .**134** A1
Wembley HA0. . . . .**65** D3
Lantern Ct Southgate N14. . .**15** D3
4 Wimbledon SW20 . . .**178** D2
Lantern Ho Millwall E14 . .**119** C4
Woolwich SE18. . . . . . .**122** C1
Lantern of Knowledge Boys
Sec Sch **1** E10 . . . .**76** A6
Lanterns Ct E14. . . . . . .**119** C3
Lanterns The N12 . . . . . .**29** D4
Lantern Way UB7 . . . . . .**104** B4
Lant Ho SE1 . . . .**252** A1
Lantry Ct 1 W3. . . . . . .**110** D5
Lanvanor Rd SE15. . . . .**140** B2
Lanyard Ho 4 SE8 . . . . .**119** B2
Lapford Cl W9 . . . .**91** B3
Lapponum Wlk UB4. . . . .**84** D2
Lapsang SE1 . . . .**253** D3
Lapse Wood Wlk SE22. . .**162** B3
Lapstone Gdns HA3. . . . .**43** C3
Lapwing Ct
Grahame Pk NW9. . . . . . .**27** C1
Tolworth KT6 . . . .**214** C5
Lapwing Terr E7 . . . .**77** D3
Lapwing Twr 31 SE8. . . .**141** B6
Lapwing Way UB4 . . . . . .**84** D1
Lapworth 2 N11 . . . .**31** B6
Lapworth Ct W2 . . . .**91** D2
Lara Lo SM1 . . . .**217** C3
Larbert Rd SW16. . . . . .**181** C3
Larch Ave W3. . . . .**111** C5
Larch Cl Balham SW12 . . .**159** B2
Colney Hatch N11. . . . . . .**31** A3
15 Deptford SE8. . . . . .**141** B6
10 Newham E13 . . . . . .**99** C3
10 Upper Holloway N19 . .**71** C6
Larch Cres Hayes UB4. . . .**84** D2
West Ewell KT19. . . . . .**214** D2
Larch Ct 41 W2 . . . .**91** C2
Larch Dene BR6 . . . . . .**226** C6
Larches Ave SW14 . . . . .**133** B1
Larches The
Edmonton N13 . . . .**17** A1
Hillingdon UB10 . . . .**82** D5
Larchfield Ho 2 N5. . . . . .**73** A3
Larch Gn NW9 . . . .**27** C2
Larch Gr DA15 . . . .**167** D3
Larch Ho Hayes UB4. . . . .**84** C2
23 Rotherhithe SE16 . . .**118** C4
Larchmont HA4. . . . .**39** B2
Larchmore Ct N19 . . . . . .**72** A6
Larch Rd Criclewood NW2. . .**68** C4
Leyton E10 . . . .**75** C6
Larch Tree Way CR0 . . . .**223** C5
Larchvale Ct 20 SM2 . . . .**217** D1
Larch Way BR2 . . . .**210** C2
Larchwood Rd SE9. . . . .**166** D2
Larcombe Cl CR0 . . . . . .**221** D4
Larcom St SE17. . . . .**117** A2 **262** B3
Larden Rd W3 . . . .**111** C4
La Retraite RC Girls Sch
SW12. . . . .**159** C4
Largewood Ave KT6. . . . .**214** C6
Larissa St SE17 . . . .**262** D3
Larix Ct NW10 . . . .**90** A6
Larkbere Rd SE26. . . . . .**185** A6
Larken Cl WD23 . . . .**8** A3
Larken Dr WD23 . . . .**8** A3
Larkfield Ave HA3. . . . . . .**43** B6
Larkfield Cl BR2 . . . .**225** A6

Larkfield Rd
Longlands DA14. . . . . . .**167** D1
Richmond TW9 . . . .**132** A1
Larkhall La SW4 . .**138** A4 **270** A1
Lark Hall Prim Sch SW4. .**137** D3
Larkhall Rise SW4 . . . . .**137** D3
Larkham Cl TW13 . . . . . .**149** C1
Lark Row E2 . . . .**96** C6
Larksfield Gr EN1. . . . .**6** B4
Larks Gr IG11. . . . .**79** C1
Larkshall Bsns Ctr E4. . . .**20** B2
Larkshall Cres E4. . . . . . .**36** A6
Larkshall Ct E4. . . . .**36** A5
Larkshall Rd E4. . . . .**36** B6
Larkspur Cl
Kingsbury NW9 . . . .**44** D4
4 Newham E6. . . . . . .**100** A2
Ruislip HA4. . . . .**39** A2
Tottenham N17. . . . .**33** B3
Larkspur Ct SM6. . . . . . .**219** B1
Larkspur Gr HA8 . . . .**27** A6
Larkspur Way KT19 . . . . .**215** A3
Larkswood Ct E4 . . . .**36** B5
Larkswood L Ctr E4. . . . . .**36** A6
Larkswood Prim Sch E4. . .**35** D6
Larkswood Rd E4 . . . .**35** D6
Larkswood Rise HA5. . . . .**40** C5
Lark Way SM5 . . . .**202** C2
Larkway Cl NW9 . . . .**45** B3
Larmenier & Sacred Heart
RC Prim Sch **4** W6 . . .**112** D2
Larnaca Ho SE1. . . . . . .**263** C6
Larnach Rd W6 . . . .**134** D6
Larne Rd HA4. . . . .**39** D2
Larpent Ave SW15 . . . . .**156** C6
Larwood Cl UB6. . . . .**64** B3
La Saint Union RC Sec Sch
NW5 . . . .**71** A5
Lascelles Ave HA1 . . . . . .**42** B2
Lascelles Cl E11 . . . .**76** B6
Lascelles Ho NW1 . . . . .**237** B5
Lascott's Rd N22. . . . .**32** B4
Laseron Ho 1 N15. . . . . .**51** D5
Lashford Ho HA8. . . . .**27** A4
Lassa Rd SE9 . . . .**166** B6
Lassell St SE10 . . . .**120** B1
Lasseter Pl SE3 . . . .**142** D6
Latchett Rd E18. . . . .**37** B2
Latchingdon Ct E17. . . . . .**52** D5
Latchmere Cl KT2, TW10 . .**176** A5
Latchmere La KT2, TW10 . .**176** B5
Latchmere L Ctr SW11 . . .**136** D3
Latchmere Prim Sch
KT2. . . . .**176** B4
Latchmere Rd
Battersea SW11 . . . .**136** D3
Kingston u T KT2. . . . . . .**176** B4
Latchmere St 5 SW11 . . .**136** D3
Lateward Rd TW8 . . . . . .**131** D6
Latham Cl Newham E6 . . . .**100** A1
6 Twickenham TW1. . . .**153** A4
Latham Ct
7 Bowes Pk N11. . . . . . .**32** A4
9 Northolt UB5. . . . .**84** D4
Latham Ho Stepney E1 . . . .**96** D1
18 Walthamstow E17 . . . .**53** D6
Latham Rd
Bexleyheath DA6 . . . . . .**169** C6
Twickenham TW1 . . . . . .**152** D4
Latham's Way CR0. . . . . .**220** B6
Lathkill Cl EN1. . . . .**18** A4
Lathkill Ct BR3. . . . .**185** B2
Lathom Jun Sch E6. . . . . .**78** A1
Lathom Rd E6 . . . .**78** B1
Lathwood Ho 6 SE26. . . .**184** B5
Latimer SE17 . . . .**263** A1
Latimer Ave E6 . . . .**100** B6
Latimer Cl
North Cheam KT4. . . . . .**216** B4
Pinner Green HA5. . . . . . .**22** C2
Latimer Gdns HA5 . . . . . .**22** C2
Latimer Ho
11 Homerton E9. . . . . . .**74** D2
Notting Hill W11 . . . .**244** D5
Latimer Ind Est **1** NW10 . .**90** C1
Latimer Pl W10 . . . .**90** C1
Latimer Rd Barnet EN5 . . . . .**1** D2
1 Croydon CR0 . . . . . .**220** D5
Forest Gate E7 . . . .**77** B4
North Kensington W10 . . . .**90** C1
South Tottenham N15. . . . .**51** C3
Teddington TW11 . . . . . .**174** D5
Wimbledon SW19. . . . . .**179** D4
Latimer Road Sta W10 . . .**112** D6
Latitude Ct E16. . . . .**123** A6
Latitude Ho NW1 . . . .**231** C5
Latona Rd SE15. . . . . . .**140** A6
La Tourne Gdns BR6. . . . .**227** A5
Lattimer Pl W4. . . . .**133** C6
Latton Cl KT12. . . . .**195** A2
Latvia Ct SE17 . . . .**262** B1
Latymer All Saints CE Prim
Sch N9. . . . .**17** D2
Latymer Ct W6. . . . .**112** D2
Latymer Rd N9 . . . .**17** D3
Latymer Sch The N9 . . . . .**17** C2
Latymer Upper Sch 14
W6 . . . .**112** A2
Latymer Way N9. . . . .**17** C1
Laubin Cl TW1 . . . .**131** B1

Lauder Cl UB5 . . . .**84** D5
Lauder Ct N14. . . . .**16** A4
Lauderdale Dr TW10 . . . .**153** D1
Lauderdale Mans W9 . . . .**91** D4
Lauderdale Rd W9. . . . . . .**91** D4
Lauderdale Twr EC2. . . . .**242** A4
Laud St Croydon CR0 . . . .**221** A5
Vauxhall SE11. . . . .**116** B1 **260** C2
Laughton Ho 11 SW2. . . .**160** C5
Laughton Rd UB5 . . . .**84** D6
Launcelot Prim Sch
BR1. . . . .**187** A6
Launcelot Rd BR1, SE12. . .**187** A6
Launcelot St SE1 . . . . . .**251** A1
Launceston Ct CR7. . . . . .**204** C3
Launceston Gdns UB6. . . .**65** C1
Launceston Pl
W8. . . . .**114** A3 **256** A5
Launceston Rd UB6. . . . . .**87** C6
Launch St E14. . . . .**120** A3
Laundress La N16. . . . . . .**74** A5
Laundry La 7 N1 . . . .**73** A1
Laundry Mews SE23. . . . .**162** D4
Laundry Rd W6 . . . .**135** A6 **264** A5
Launton Dr DA6 . . . .**146** D1
Laura Cl Enfield EN1 . . . . .**17** C6
Wanstead E11. . . . .**55** C4
Laura Ct HA2 . . . .**24** A1
Lauradale Rd N2. . . . .**48** D5
Laura Pl E5. . . . .**74** C4
Laurel Ave TW1 . . . .**152** D3
Laurel Bank Gdns 3
SW6. . . . .**135** B3
Laurel Bank Rd EN2. . . . . .**5** B4
Laurel Cl Sidcup DA14. . . . .**168** A1
8 Upper Holloway N19 . .**71** C6
Upper Tooting SW17. . . . .**180** C5
Laurel Cres CR0. . . . . . .**223** C5
Laurel Ct Dalston E8 . . . . . .**73** D1
2 Putney SW15. . . . . . .**156** D6
9 Rotherhithe SE16 . . . .**119** A5
South Norwood SE25 . . . .**205** C4
9 Wembley HA0 . . . .**88** A5
Laurel Dr N21 . . . .**16** C4
Laurel Gdns Bromley BR1. .**210** A5
Chingford E4. . . . .**19** D4
Ealing W7 . . . .**108** C5
Edgware NW7 . . . .**11** B1
Hounslow TW4 . . . .**129** A1
Laurel Gr Forest Hill SE26. .**185** A6
Penge SE20 . . . .**184** C3
Laurel Ho Brentford W5 . . .**109** C2
9 Deptford SE8. . . . . . .**141** B6
5 Hamstead NW3 . . . . . .**69** D2
Morden SM4 . . . .**201** D4
Laurel La UB7. . . . .**104** A2
Laurel Manor SM2 . . . . . .**218** A1
Laurel Mead Ct 8 E18 . . . .**37** A2
Laurel Pk HA3 . . . .**24** D3
Laurel Rd Barnes SW13 . . .**134** A3
Teddington TW12 . . . . . .**174** B5
Wimbledon SW20. . . . . .**178** B2
Laurel St E8 . . . .**73** D2
Laurels The
8 Belvedere DA17 . . . . .**125** C1
2 Buckhurst Hill IG9 . . . .**21** C3
Bushey WD23 . . . .**8** C2
Finchley N3. . . . .**29** D4
Shortlands BR2. . . . . . .**209** A5
Sundridge BR1 . . . .**187** B2
Laurel View N12 . . . .**13** D1
Laurel Way
Snaresbrook E18 . . . .**54** D5
Woodside Pk N20 . . . . . .**13** C1
Laurence Ct E10 . . . .**53** D2
Laurence Mews 2 W12 . . .**112** A4
Laurence Pountney Hill
EC4 . . . .**252** C6
Laurence Pountney La
EC4. . . . .**252** D6
Laurie Gr SE14. . . . .**141** A4
Laurie Ho Newington SE1 . .**261** D5
Notting Hill W8 . . . .**113** C5 **245** A3
Laurie Rd W7. . . . .**86** C2
Laurier Rd Croydon CR0 . . .**205** D2
Dartmouth Pk NW5 . . . . . .**71** B5
Laurimel Cl HA7 . . . .**25** B4
Laurino Pl WD23 . . . .**8** A2
Lauriston Apartments 6
N17 . . . .**51** D6
Lauriston Ho 6 E9. . . . . . .**74** D1
Lauriston Lo N6. . . . .**69** B2
Lauriston Prim Sch **6**
E9. . . . .**96** D6
Lauriston Rd Homerton E9. .**74** D1
Wimbledon SW19. . . . . .**178** D4
Lausanne Rd Hornsey N8. . .**50** C5
St Johns SE15. . . . .**140** C4
Lavehham Ho E17 . . . .**35** D2
Lavell St N16 . . . .**73** B4
Lavender Ave
Mitcham CR4 . . . .**180** D2
North Cheam KT4, SM3 . . .**216** C5
Welsh Harp NW9 . . . .**45** A1
Lavender Cl
Bromley Comm BR2 . . . .**210** A3
Chingford E4. . . . .**35** C6
South Kensington SW3. . . .**266** D5
Wallington SM5 . . . .**219** B4

Lavender Ct
Colney Hatch N12. . . . . . .**30** C4
East Molesey KT8. . . . . .**195** D6
Edgware HA8 . . . .**27** A5
Feltham TW14 . . . .**150** B5
South Lambeth SW4. . . . .**270** B1
Sutton SM2. . . . .**218** A1
Lavender Gdns
Clapham SW11 . . . .**136** D1
Enfield EN2. . . . .**4** D4
Stanmore HA3 . . . .**24** C4
Lavender Gr Dalston E8 . . . .**74** A1
Mitcham CR4 . . . .**180** C2
Lavender Hill
Clapham SW11 . . . .**137** A2
Enfield EN2. . . . .**4** D4
Lavender Ho
8 Richmond TW9 . . . . .**132** D4
14 Rotherhithe SE16 . . . .**118** D5
Lavender Pl IG1 . . . .**78** D3
Lavender Prim Sch EN2. . . .**5** C5
Lavender Rd
Battersea SW11 . . . . . .**136** B2
Enfield EN2. . . . .**5** B4
Hillingdon UB8 . . . .**82** B2
Rotherhithe SE16 . . . . . .**119** A5
Sutton SM1. . . . .**218** B4
Thornton Heath CR0. . . . .**204** B3
Wallington SM5 . . . .**219** A4
West Ewell KT19. . . . . .**214** D2
Lavender Rise UB7. . . . . .**104** C4
Lavender St E15 . . . .**76** C2
Lavender Sweep SW11. . .**136** D1
Lavender Terr 12 SW11 . . .**136** C2
Lavender Vale SM6. . . . . .**219** D2
Lavender Way CR0 . . . . . .**206** D3
Lavender Wlk SW11. . . . .**136** D1
Lavendon Ho NW8 . . . . .**237** B6
Lavengro Rd SE27 . . . . . .**161** A2
Lavenham Rd SW18. . . . .**157** C3
Lavernock Rd DA7 . . . . . .**147** C3
Lavers Rd N16 . . . .**73** C5
Laverstoke Gdns SW15. . .**156** A4
Laverton Mews SW5 . . . .**255** D3
Laverton Pl SW5 . . . .**255** D3
Lavidge Rd SE9 . . . .**166** B2
Lavina Gr N1. . . . .**233** C4
Lavington Cl E9. . . . .**75** B2
Lavington Rd Ealing W13 . .**109** B5
Wallington CR0. . . . . . .**220** B4
Lavington St SE1 . .**116** D5 **251** D3
Lavinia Ct BR1. . . . .**186** C3
Lavisham Ho BR1. . . . . . .**187** B5
Lawdale Jun Sch 32 E2. . .**96** A4
Lawdon Gdns CR0. . . . . .**220** D4
Lawford Rd Chiswick W4 . .**133** A5
De Beauvoir Town N1 . . . . .**73** C1
Kentish Town NW5 . . . . . .**71** C2
Lawfords Wharf 18 NW1. . .**71** C1
Law Ho IG11. . . . .**102** A5
Lawless Ho 5 E14. . . . . .**120** A6
Lawless St 12 E14. . . . . .**119** D6
Lawley Ho 11 TW1. . . . . .**153** D5
Lawley Rd N14. . . . .**15** B4
Lawley St E5. . . . .**74** C4
Lawman Ct 2 TW9. . . . . .**132** B4
Lawn Cl Edmonton N9 . . . . .**17** C4
Kingston u T KT3. . . . . .**177** C1
Ruislip HA4. . . . .**61** D5
Sundridge BR1 . . . .**187** B3
Lawn Cres TW9 . . . .**132** C3
Lawn Farm Gr RM6 . . . . . .**59** A5
Lawnfield Ct NW6. . . . . . .**68** D1
Lawn Gdns W7 . . . .**108** C5
Lawn House Cl E14 . . . . . .**120** A4
Lawn La SW8 . . . . .**138** B6 **270** C6
Lawn Mans EN5. . . . .**1** B1
Lawn Rd Beckenham BR3 . .**185** B3
Maitland Pk NW3 . . . .**70** D3
Lawns Ct HA9. . . . .**66** C6
Lawnside SE3 . . . .**142** D1
Lawns The Belmont SM2. . .**217** A1
Blackheath SE3. . . . . . .**142** D2
Chingford E4. . . . .**35** C5
Harrow HA5 . . . .**23** D3
Sidcup DA14. . . . .**190** B6
South Norwood SE19 . . . .**183** B2
Stoke Newington N16. . . . .**73** C3
11 Wimbledon SW19 . . . .**179** B5
Lawn Terr SE3 . . . .**142** C2
Lawn The UB2 . . . .**107** C1
Lawn Vale HA5. . . . .**23** A1
Lawrence Ave
Edmonton N13 . . . .**32** D6
Higham Hill E17 . . . .**34** D2
Little Ilford E12. . . . .**78** C4
Mill Hill NW7 . . . .**27** D6
New Malden KT3 . . . . . .**199** C2
Stonebridge NW10. . . . . .**89** B6
Lawrence Bldgs 1 N16 . . .**73** D5
Lawrence Camp Cl N20 . . .**14** B1
Lawrence Cl 2 Bow E3. . . .**97** C5
6 Shepherd's Bush W12. .**112** B6
West Green N15. . . . . . .**51** C5
Lawrence Cres
Dagenham RM10 . . . .**81** D5
Edgware HA8 . . . .**26** C1
Lawrence Ct Hornsey N10 . .**49** C6
Mill Hill NW7. . . . .**27** C5
4 South Acton W3. . . . .**111** A3

Lawrence Ct continued
Stoke Newington N16. . . . .**73** D5
5 Woodford IG8 . . . .**37** C4
Lawrence Dr UB10 . . . . . .**61** A4
Lawrence Est TW4 . . . . .**128** C1
Lawrence Gdns NW7 . . . . .**11** D1
Lawrence Hall E13. . . . . . .**99** B3
Lawrence Hill E4 . . . .**19** C2
Lawrence Ho
Bowes Pk N22. . . . .**32** B4
20 Camden Town NW1. . .**71** B1
Westminster SW1 . . . . . .**259** D3
Lawrence La EC2 . . . . . .**242** B2
Lawrence Mans SW3. . . . .**267** A5
Lawrence Pl N1 . . . .**233** B6
Lawrence Rd
Coney Hall BR4. . . . . . .**225** A4
Ealing W5 . . . .**109** D2
Edmonton N18 . . . .**34** B6
Erith DA8 . . . .**147** D5
Hampton TW12. . . . . . .**173** B3
Hillingdon UB4 . . . .**83** A5
Hounslow TW4 . . . .**128** C1
Pinner HA5 . . . .**40** D4
Richmond TW10 . . . . . .**175** C6
South Norwood SE25 . . . .**205** D5
Tottenham N15. . . . .**51** C5
Upton Pk E6 . . . .**100** A6
West Ham E13 . . . .**99** B6
Lawrence St
Canning Town E16 . . . . . .**98** D2
Chelsea SW3 . . . .**136** C6 **267** A5
Mill Hill NW7. . . . .**27** D6
Lawrence Trad Est SE10 . .**120** C2
Lawrence Univ SW7 . . . . .**256** B3
Lawrence Way NW10. . . . .**67** B5
Lawrence Weaver Cl
SM4. . . . .**201** C3
Lawrence Yd N15 . . . .**51** C5
Lawrie Park Ave SE26. . . .**184** B5
Lawrie Park Cres SE26 . . .**184** B5
Lawrie Park Gdns SE26. . .**184** B5
Lawrie Park Rd SE26. . . . .**184** C5
Laws Cl SE25 . . . .**205** B5
Lawson Cl Ilford IG1. . . . . .**79** B3
Newham E16 . . . .**99** C2
Wimbledon SW19. . . . . .**156** D1
Lawson Ct
1 Finsbury Pk N4 . . . . . .**50** B1
13 Surbiton KT6. . . . . . .**197** D2
Lawson Gdns HA5 . . . . . .**40** B6
Lawson Ho
17 Shepherd's Bush W12. .**112** B6
1 Woolwich SE18. . . . .**144** C6
Lawson Rd Enfield EN3. . . . .**6** C4
Southall UB1. . . . .**85** C3
Law St SE1 . . . . . .**117** B3 **262** D6
Lawton Rd Barnet EN4 . . . . .**2** C1
Bow E3. . . . .**97** A4
Leytonstone E10. . . . . . .**54** A1
Laxcon Cl NW10 . . . .**67** B3
Laxey Rd BR6 . . . .**227** D2
Laxfield Ct E8 . . . .**96** A6
Laxley Cl SE5 . . . .**138** D5
Laxmi Ct N3 . . . .**29** B2
Laxton Ct CR7 . . . .**205** A5
Laxton Path 1 SE4 . . . . .**140** D1
Laxton Pl NW1. . . . .**238** D6
Layard Rd Enfield EN1. . . . . .**5** D4
Rotherhithe SE16 . . . . . .**118** B2
South Norwood CR7. . . . .**183** B1
Layard Sq SE16 . . . .**118** B2
Laybourne Ho 18 E14 . . . .**119** C4
Laycock Prim Sch **5** N1 . . .**72** D2
Laycock St N1. . . . .**72** D2
Layer Gdns W3 . . . .**110** C6
Layfield Cl NW4. . . . .**46** B2
Layfield Cres NW4 . . . . . .**46** B2
Layfield Ho 1 SE10 . . . . .**121** A1
Layfield Rd NW4. . . . .**46** B2
Laymarsh Cl DA17 . . . . . .**125** B3
Laymead Cl UB5 . . . .**63** A2
Laystall Ct EC1. . . . .**241** A5
Laystall St EC1. . . . .**241** A5
Layton Cres CR0. . . . . . .**220** D3
Layton Ct TW8 . . . .**109** D1
Layton Pl TW9 . . . .**132** C4
Layton Rd Brentford TW8 . .**109** D1
Hounslow TW3 . . . .**129** D1
Layton's La TW16 . . . . . .**171** D1
Layzell Wlk SE9. . . . .**165** D3
Lazar Wlk 2 N7 . . . .**72** B6
Leabank Cl HA1. . . . .**64** C5
Leabank Sq E9 . . . .**75** C2
Leabank View N15 . . . . . .**52** A3
Leabourne Rd N16. . . . . . .**52** A2
LEA BRIDGE **74** D5
Lea Cl TW2 . . . .**151** B4
Lea Cotts 10 CR4. . . . . .**181** A1
Lea Cres HA4 . . . .**61** D4
Leacroft Ave SW12 . . . . .**158** D4
Leacroft Cl Southgate N21. . .**16** D2
3 Yiewsley UB7 . . . . . .**104** A6
Lea Ct 3 Bedford Pk W12 . .**111** C4
1 Chingford E4. . . . .**20** A2
3 Hillingdon UB10 . . . . .**82** D3
2 Newham E13. . . . .**99** A4
Leadale Ave E4 . . . .**19** C2

Leadale Rd N16. . . . . .52 A3
Leadbeaters Cl **8** N11. . . . .30 D5
Leadbetter Ct **12** NW10. . . .67 B1
Leadenhall Mkt★ EC3. . . .243 A1
Leadenhall Pl EC3. . . . . . . .243 A1
Leadenhall St EC3 . .95 C1 243 A1
Leadenham Ct **15** E3. . . . . . .97 C3
Leader Ave E12. . . . . .78 C3
Leadings The HA9. . . . . .67 A5
Leaf Cl KT7, KT8. . . . . .196 C4
Leaf Gr SE27. . . . . .182 C5
Leaf Ho Barnet EN5 . . . . .1 D1
  9 Harrow HA1. . . . . .42 D4
Leafield Cl SW16. . . . . .182 D4
Leafield La DA14. . . . . .169 B1
Leafield Rd
  Merton SW19, SW20. . . . .201 B6
  Sutton SM1. . . . . .217 C6
Leafy Gr BR2. . . . . .225 C3
Leafy Oak Rd SE12. . . . . . .165 C1
Leafy Way CR0. . . . . .221 D6
Lea Gdns HA9. . . . . .66 B4
Leagrave St E5. . . . . .74 C5
Lea Hall Gdns E10. . . . . . . .53 C1
Lea Hall Rd E10. . . . . .53 C1
Lea Ho **2** Edmonton N9. . . . .18 A1
  Lisson Gr NW8. . . . . .237 A5
  Upper Clapton E5. . . . . . . .52 C1
Leaholme Waye HA4. . . . . . .39 A3
Leahurst Rd SE13. . . . . . . .164 B6
Lea Int E9. . . . . .75 C3
Leake St Lambeth SE1. . . . .251 A1
  South Bank SE1 . . .116 B4 250 D1
Lealand Rd N15. . . . . .51 D3
Leamington Ave
  Bromley BR1. . . . . .187 C5
  Farnborough BR6. . . . . . .227 C4
  Merton SM4. . . . . .201 B5
  Walthamstow E17. . . . . . . .53 C4
Leamington Cl
  Bromley BR1. . . . . .187 C5
  Hounslow TW3. . . . . .152 A4
  Plashet E12. . . . . .78 A3
Leamington Cres HA2. . . . . .63 B5
Leamington Ct
  4 Forest Hill SE26. . . . . .162 A1
  North Acton W3 . . . . .28 B3
Leamington Gdns IG3. . . . . .79 D6
Leamington Ho
  Edgware HA8 . . . . .26 B5
  4 Kensal Town W11 . . . . .91 B2
Leamington Pk W3. . . . . . . .89 B2
Leamington Pl UB4. . . . . . . .83 D3
Leamington Rd UB2. . . . . . .106 D2
Leamington Rd Villas
  W11. . . . . .91 B2
Leamington Villas SE13. . . .164 C6
Leamore St W6. . . . . .112 C2
Leamouth Rd
  Newham E6 . . . . .100 A2
  South Bromley E14. . . . . . . .98 B1
Leander Ct
  11 Edgware NW9. . . . . . . .27 C2
  27 Hackney E9. . . . . .74 C1
  St Johns SE8. . . . . .141 C4
  5 Surbiton KT6. . . . . . . .197 D2
Leander Rd Northolt UB5 . . . .85 C5
  Thornton Heath CR7. . . . . .204 B5
  Tulse Hill SW2. . . . . .160 C5
Lea Park Trad Est E10 . . . . . .53 B1
Lea Rd
  2 Beckenham BR3 . . . . . .185 C1
  Enfield EN2. . . . . .5 B4
  Southall UB2. . . . . .107 A2
Learner Dr HA2. . . . . .63 C6
Learoyd Gdns E6 . . . . .122 C6
Leary Ho SE11. . . . . .260 D1
Leas Cl KT9. . . . . .214 B1
Leas Dale SE9. . . . . .166 C1
Leas Gn BR7. . . . . .189 D4
Leaside Ave N10. . . . . .49 A5
Leaside Bsns Ctr EN3 . . . . . . .7 B3
Leaside Ct UB10. . . . . .82 D4
Leaside Ho **4** E5. . . . . .52 B1
Leaside Mans N10. . . . . .49 A6
Leaside Rd E5. . . . . .52 C1
Leasowes Rd E10. . . . . .53 C1
Lea Sq **22** E3. . . . . .97 B6
Leas The SE18 . . . . .144 C4
Leatherbottle Gn DA18. . . .125 B3
Leather Cl CR4 . . . . .181 A1
Leatherdale St
  32 Bethnal Green E1. . . . . .96 C3
  18 Globe Town E1. . . . . . .96 D4
Leather Gdns E15. . . . . .98 C6
Leatherhead Cl N16. . . . . . . .51 D1
Leatherhead Rd KT9. . . . . . .213 D1
Leather La **1** E1. . .94 C2 241 B4
Leather La Mkt★
  EC1. . . . . .94 C2 241 B4
Leathermarket Ct SE1. . . . .253 A1
Leathermarket St
  SE1. . . . . .117 C4 253 A1
Leather Rd SE16. . . . . .118 D2
Leathersellers Cl **5** EN5 . .1 A2
Leathsale Rd HA2. . . . . .63 D5
Leathwaite Rd SW11. . . . . .158 D6
Leathwell Rd SE8. . . . . .141 D4
Lea Valley Athletics Stad
  N9. . . . . .18 D3

Lea Valley Prim Sch N17. . .34 A3
Lea Valley Rd EN3. . . . . .19 B5
Lea Valley Technopark
  N17. . . . . .52 A6
Lea Valley Trad Est N18. . . .34 D5
Leaveland Cl BR3. . . . . . . .207 C5
Leaver Gdns UB6. . . . . .86 C5
Leavesden Rd HA7. . . . . . . .25 A4
Lea View Ho E5. . . . . .52 B1
Lebanon Ave TW13. . . . . . .172 D5
Lebanon Ct **10** TW1. . . . . .153 B4
Lebanon Gdns SW18. . . . . .157 C5
Lebanon Park Mans
  TW1. . . . . .153 B4
Lebanon Pk TW1. . . . . .153 B4
Lebanon Rd Croydon CR0. . .205 C1
  Wandsworth SW18 . . . . . .157 C6
Lebanon Road Sta CR0. . . .221 C6
Lebrun Sq SE3. . . . . .143 B2
Lebus Ho SW8. . . . . .230 A3
Le Chateau CR0. . . . . .221 B5
Lechmere App IG8. . . . . .37 D1
Lechmere Ave IG8. . . . . .37 D1
Lechmere Rd NW2. . . . . .68 B2
Leckford Rd SW18. . . . . . . .158 A3
Leckhampton Pl **23**
  SW2. . . . . .160 C4
Leckwith Ave DA7. . . . . . . .147 A6
Lecky Ho NW2. . . . . .68 B4
Lecky St SW7. . . . .114 B1 256 C2
Leclair Ho SE3. . . . . .143 B2
L'Ecole des Petits Sch
  SW6. . . . . .135 D3
Leconfield Ave SW13,
  SW15. . . . . .133 D2
Leconfield Ho SE5 . . . . . . .139 C2
Leconfield Rd N5. . . . . .73 B4
Lector Ct EC1. . . . . .241 B5
Leda Ave EN3. . . . . .6 D5
Leda Ct **9** SW9. . . . . .138 C5
Ledalle Ho NW2. . . . . .68 B5
Ledam Bldg EC1. . . . . .241 A4
Ledbury Ho **12** SE22. . . . . .139 C2
Ledbury Mews W W11 . . . .245 A6
Ledbury Mews N W11 . . . . .91 C1
Ledbury Pl **10** CR0 . . . . . . .221 A4
Ledbury Rd Croydon CR0. . .221 B4
  Kensington W11. . . . . .91 C1
Ledbury St SE15. . . . . .140 A5
Ledo Ho **1** N16. . . . . .73 B4
Ledrington Rd SE19. . . . . . .184 A4
Ledway Dr HA9 . . . . .44 B2
LEE. 164 D5
Lee Ave RM6. . . . . .59 A3
Leechcote Rd DA15. . . . . . .167 D6
Leechcroft Rd SM6. . . . . . .219 A5
Lee Church St SE13. . . . . . .142 C1
Lee Cl Higham Hill E17. . . . . .34 C2
  New Barnet EN5. . . . . .2 A1
Lee Conservancy Rd E9 . . . .75 B3
Leecroft Rd EN5. . . . . .1 A1
Lee Ct SE13. . . . . .142 B1
Leeds Ct
  7 Carshalton SM5. . . . . .218 D5
  Catford SE6. . . . . .163 D1
  Clerkenwell EC1. . . . . . . .241 C6
Leeds Rd IG1. . . . . .57 B1
Leeds St N18. . . . . .34 A5
Leegate SE12. . . . . .164 B6
Leegate Sh Ctr SE12. . . . . .164 D6
Lee Green SE12. . . . . .142 D1
Lee High Rd SE12, SE13. . .142 C1
Lee Ho
  3 Kentish Town N19 . . . . .71 D3
  Wimbledon SW19. . . . . . . .179 D4
Leeke St WC1. . . . . . .94 B4 233 C2
Leeland Mans **15** W13. . . .109 A5
Leeland Rd W13. . . . . .109 A5
Leeland Terr W13 . . . . .109 A5
Leeland Way NW10. . . . . . . .67 D4
Lee Manor Prim Sch
  SE13. . . . . .164 C5
Lee Mews BR3. . . . . .207 A6
Lee Park Way N9, N18. . . . . .19 A1
Lee Pk SE3. . . . . .142 D2
Lee Rd Enfield EN1. . . . . .18 A5
  Lewisham SE3 . . . . .142 D1
  Merton SW19. . . . . .179 D2
  Mill Hill NW7. . . . . .28 D3
  Wembley UB6. . . . . .87 C6
Leerdam Dr E14. . . . . .120 A3
Lees Ct W1 . . . . .248 A6
Lees Ho SE17. . . . . .262 D1
Leeside EN5. . . . . .13 A5
Leeside Cres NW11. . . . . . . .47 C3
Leeside Ind Est N17. . . . . . .34 B3
Leeside Rd N17. . . . . .34 B4
Leeside Trad Est N17. . . . . .34 C3
Leeside Works N17. . . . . . . .34 C3
Leeson Ho **7** TW1. . . . . . . .153 B4
Leeson Rd SE24 . . . . .138 C1
Leesons Hill BR5, BR7. . . . .211 D6
Leesons Way BR5. . . . . . . .189 D1
Lees Par UB10. . . . . .82 D3
Lees Pl W1. . . . . . . .115 A6 248 A6
Lee Rd UB8. . . . . .82 D3
Lee St E8. . . . . .95 D6
Lee Sta SE12. . . . . .165 A5
Lees The CR0. . . . . .223 B6

Leet Ct N16. . . . . .73 B4
Lee Terr SE3. . . . . .142 C2
Lee Valley Athletics Ctr
  N9. . . . . .18 D3
Lee Valley Country Pk EN3. . .7 C4
Lee Valley Ice Ctr E10 . . . . .74 D6
Lee Valley Leisure Complex
  N9. . . . . .19 A3
Lee Valley Riding Ctr
  E10. . . . . .52 D1
Leeve Ho **7** W9 . . . . .91 B4
Lee View Ho E2 . . . . .4 D4
Leeview Ct **5** E4. . . . . .20 A3
Leeward Ct **3** E1. . . . . . . .118 A5
Leeward Gdns SW19. . . . . .179 B5
Leeway SE8. . . . . .119 B1
Leeway Cl HA5. . . . . .23 B3
Leewood Cl SE12. . . . . .165 A5
Lefevre Wlk E3. . . . . .97 C6
Leffern Rd W12. . . . . .112 A4
Leff Ho NW6. . . . . .69 A1
Lefroy Ho SE1. . . . . .252 A1
Lefroy Rd W12. . . . . .111 D4
Legard Rd N5. . . . . .72 D5
Legat Ct N4. . . . . .51 A4
Legatt Rd SE9. . . . . .165 D6
Legge St SE13. . . . . .164 A6
Leghorn Rd
  Plumstead SE18. . . . . . . .123 B1
  Willesden Green NW10 . . . .90 A5
Legion Cl N1. . . . . .72 C1
Legion Ct SM4. . . . . .201 C3
Legion Rd UB6. . . . . .86 A5
Legion Terr E3. . . . . .97 C6
Legion Way N12. . . . . .30 C3
Legrace Ave TW4, TW5. . . .128 D3
Leicester Ave CR4 . . . . . . .204 A5
Leicester Cl KT4 . . . . .216 C4
Leicester Ct
  46 Paddington W2 . . . . . . .91 C2
  St James WC2 . . . . .249 D6
  1 Twickenham TW1. . . . .153 D5
Leicester Gdns IG3. . . . . . . .57 C2
Leicester Ho
  4 Brixton SW9 . . . . .138 D2
  Carshalton SM5. . . . . . . .218 C5
  5 Putney SW15. . . . . . . .156 C4
  2 Thames Ditton KT7. . .197 A2
Leicester Mews N2. . . . . . . .48 C6
Leicester Pl WC2 . . . . .249 D6
Leicester Rd Barnet EN5 . . . .1 D1
  Croydon CR0. . . . . .205 C2
  East Finchley N2. . . . . .48 C6
  Stonebridge NW10. . . . . . . .67 B1
  Wanstead E11. . . . . .55 B4
Leicester Sq★
  WC2 . . . . .115 D6 249 D5
Leicester Square Sta
  WC2. . . . . .115 D6 249 D6
Leicester St WC2. . . . . .249 D6
Leigham Ave SW16. . . . . . .160 A1
Leigham Cl
  5 Streatham SW16. . . . .160 B1
  Streatham SW16 . . . . .182 B6
  9 Wallington SM6. . . . . .219 C2
Leigham Court Rd
  SW16. . . . . .182 C6
Leigham Dr TW7. . . . . .130 C5
Leigham Hall **1** SW16. . . . .160 A1
Leigham Hall Par **2**
  SW16. . . . . .160 A1
Leigham Vale SE27, SW16,
  SW1. . . . . .160 C2
Leigh Ave IG4. . . . . .55 D5
Leigh Cl KT3. . . . . .199 B5
Leigh Cl Ind Est KT3. . . . . .199 B5
Leigh Close Ind Est KT3 . . .199 B5
Leigh Cres CR0. . . . . .223 D1
Leigh Ct Harrow HA2. . . . . . .42 C1
  22 Tulse Hill SW2. . . . . .160 C5
  3 Woodford E18 . . . . .37 A1
Leighfield Ho **5** N4. . . . . . .51 A2
Leigh Gdns NW10. . . . . .90 C5
Leigh Ho
  4 Kingston u T KT2 . . . . .176 D4
  5 Putney SW15. . . . . . . .156 A6
Leigh Hunt Dr N14. . . . . .15 D3
Leigh Orchard Cl SW16. . . .160 B1
Leigh Pl Feltham TW13 . . . .150 C3
  Holborn EC1. . . . . .241 A4
  Welling DA16. . . . . .146 A3
Leigh Rd Highbury N5. . . . . .72 D4
  Isleworth TW3 . . . . .130 B1
  Leytonstone E10. . . . . .54 A2
  Wallend E6. . . . . .78 C2
Leigh St WC1. . . . . . .94 A4 233 A4
Leigh The KT2 . . . . .177 C3
Leighton Ave
  Little Ilford E12. . . . . .78 C3
  Pinner HA5. . . . . .41 A4
Leighton Cl HA8. . . . . .26 C1
Leighton Cres NW5. . . . . . . .71 C3
Leighton Ct NW7 . . . . .28 D3
Leighton Gdns
  Thornton Heath CR0. . . . . .204 D1
  Willesden Green NW10. . . . .90 C5
Leighton Gr NW5 . . . . .71 C3
Leighton Ho **6** KT6. . . . . . .198 A3

Leighton House (Art Gall &
  Mus)★ W14 . . . . .254 D6
Leighton Pl NW5. . . . . .71 C3
Leighton Rd Ealing W13. . . .109 A4
  Enfield EN1. . . . . .18 A6
  Harrow HA3. . . . . .24 B1
  Kentish Town NW5. . . . . . . .71 C3
Leighton St CR0. . . . . .204 D1
Leila Parnell Pl **14** SE7. . . .143 C6
Leinster Ave SW14. . . . . . . .133 A1
Leinster Gdns
  W2. . . . . .114 A6 246 A6
Leinster Mews
  7 Barnet EN5. . . . . .1 A2
  Bayswater W2 . . . . .246 A6
Leinster Pl W2. . . . . .236 A1
Leinster Rd N10 . . . . .49 B5
Leinster Sq W2 . . . . .91 D1
Leinster Terr W2. . . . . .246 A6
Leisure Way N12. . . . . .30 B3
Leitch Ho **8** NW8. . . . . .70 B1
Leith Cl NW9. . . . . .45 B1
Leithcote Gdns SW16. . . . .182 B6
Leithcote Path SW16. . . . . .160 B1
Leith Hill BR5. . . . . .190 A2
Leith Hill Gn BR5. . . . . .190 A2
Leith Ho
  7 Kentish Town N7 . . . . .71 D3
  13 Streatham SW2. . . . . .160 B4
Leith Mans W9. . . . . .91 D4
Leith Rd N22. . . . . .32 D2
Leith Towers **1** SM2. . . . .217 D1
Leith Yd **3** NW6. . . . . .91 C6
Lela Ave TW4, TW5. . . . . . .128 C3
Lelitia Cl E8. . . . . .96 A6
Lely Ho **3** UB5. . . . . .84 D5
Leman St E1. . . . . .96 A1
Lemark Cl HA7. . . . . .25 C4
Le May Ave SE12. . . . . .165 B1
Lemmon Rd SE10 . . . . .142 C6
Lemna Ct E11. . . . . .54 C2
Lemna Rd E11. . . . . .54 C2
Le Moal Ho SE1. . . . . .96 C2
Lemon Gr TW14. . . . . .150 A3
Lemonwell Ct SE9. . . . . . . .167 A6
Lemonwell Dr SE9. . . . . . . .167 A6
Lemsford Cl N15. . . . . .52 A4
Lemsford Ct N4. . . . . .73 A6
Lena Cres N9. . . . . .18 C2
Lena Gardens Prim Sch
  W6 . . . . .112 C3
Lena Gdns W6. . . . . .112 C3
Lena Kennedy Cl E4. . . . . . .36 A4
Lenanton Cl W13. . . . . .109 C5
Len Clifton Ho **12** SE18. . . .122 B2
Lendal Terr **7** SW4. . . . . . .137 D2
Lenelby Rd KT6. . . . . .198 C1
Len Freeman Pl SW6. . . . . .264 C5
Lenham Ho SE1. . . . . .252 D1
Lenham Rd Erith DA7. . . . . .147 B6
  Lewisham SE12 . . . . .142 D1
  South Norwood CR7. . . . . .183 B1
  Sutton SM1. . . . . .218 A3
Lennard Ave BR4. . . . . .224 C6
Lennard Cl BR4. . . . . .224 C6
Lennard Rd Bromley BR2 . .210 B1
  Croydon CR0. . . . . .205 A1
  Penge BR3. . . . . .185 A4
Lennon Rd NW2 . . . . .68 C2
Lennox Gdns
  Croydon CR0. . . . . .220 D4
  Knightsbridge
  SW1. . . . . .114 D3 257 C5
  Redbridge IG1 . . . . .56 B1
  Willesden NW10. . . . . .67 D4
Lennox Gdns Mews SW1 . .257 C4
Lennox Ho
  7 Belvedere DA17. . . . . .125 C3
  10 Hackney E9. . . . . .74 C2
  4 Twickenham TW1. . . . .153 D5
Lennox Rd
  Finsbury Pk N4, N7. . . . . . .72 C6
  Walthamstow E17. . . . . . . .53 C3
Lenor Cl DA6. . . . . .147 A1
Lensbury Way SE2. . . . . . . .124 D3
Lens Rd E7 . . . . .77 C1
Lenthall Ho SW1. . . . . .259 B1
Lenthall Rd E8. . . . . .96 A5
Lenthorp Rd SE10. . . . . . . .120 D2
Lentmead Rd BR1. . . . . . . .164 D1
Lenton Rise TW9. . . . . .132 A2
Lenton St SE18. . . . . .123 B2
Leo Ct **4** TW8. . . . . .131 D5
Leof Cres SE6. . . . . .185 D5
Leominster Rd SM4. . . . . . .202 A3
Leominster Wlk SM4. . . . . .202 A3
Leonard Ave SM4. . . . . . . .202 A4
Leonard Ct
  Bloomsbury WC1 . . . . . . .240 A6
  Harrow HA3 . . . . .24 C3
  Kensington W8. . . . . .255 A6
Leonard Day Ho **3** NW5. . . .71 B2
Leonard Ho **10** E17. . . . . . .54 A5
Leonard Pl **6** N16. . . . . .73 C4
Leonard Rd Chingford E4. . . .35 C4
  Edmonton N9. . . . . .18 A1
  Forest Gate E7 . . . . .77 A4
  Mitcham CR4, SW16. . . . . .181 C2

Lea–Lev 355

Leonard Rd continued
  Southall UB2. . . . . .106 D2
Leonard Robbins Path **3**
  SE28 . . . . .124 B6
Leonard St
  Broadgate EC2. . . .95 B3 242 D6
  Newham E16. . . . . .122 A5
Leonora Ho W9. . . . . .236 A6
Leontine Cl SE15. . . . . .140 A5
Leopards Ct EC1. . . . . .241 A4
Leopold Ave SW19. . . . . . . .179 B5
Leopold Bldgs **14** E2. . . . . . .95 D4
Leopold Ct **12** SW19. . . . . .179 B5
Leopold Mews E9. . . . . .96 C6
Leopold Prim Sch NW10 . . . .67 D1
Leopold Rd Ealing W5. . . . .110 B5
  East Finchley N2 . . . . .48 B6
  Edmonton N18 . . . . .34 B5
  Walthamstow E17. . . . . . . .53 C4
  Willesden NW10. . . . . .67 C1
  Wimbledon SW19. . . . . . . .179 B5
Leopold St E3 . . . . .97 B2
Leopold Terr SW19. . . . . . .179 C5
Leopold Wlk SE11. . . . . . . .260 C1
Leo St SE15. . . . . .140 B5
Leo Yd EC1 . . . . .241 D5
Leppoc Rd SW4. . . . . .159 D6
Leroy St SE1. . . . . . .117 C2 263 A4
Lerry Cl W14. . . . . .264 D6
Lerwick Ct **4** EN1. . . . . .17 C6
Lerwick Ho SW18 . . . . .136 A1
Lescombe Cl SE23 . . . . . . .163 A1
Lescombe Rd SE23, SE6. . .163 A1
Lesley Cl DA5. . . . . .169 D4
Lesley Ct
  8 Wallington SM6. . . . . .219 B4
  Westminster SW1 . . . . . . .259 C5
Leslie Gdns SM2. . . . . .217 C1
Leslie Gr CR0. . . . . .205 C1
Leslie Grove Pl CR0. . . . . . .205 C1
Leslie Park Rd CR0. . . . . . . .205 C1
Leslie Prince Ct **8** SE5. . .139 B5
Leslie Rd East Finchley N2. . .48 B6
  Leyton E11. . . . . .76 B4
  Newham E16. . . . . .99 B1
Leslie Smith Sq **7** SE18 . .144 C6
Lessar Ave SW4. . . . . .159 C5
Lessar Ct SW4. . . . . .159 C5
Lessingham Ave
  Ilford IG5 . . . . .56 C6
  Upper Tooting SW17. . . . . .181 A6
Lessing St SE23. . . . . .163 A4
Lessness Ave DA7. . . . . . . .146 D5
LESSNESS HEATH. 125 D1
Lessness Heath Prim Sch
  DA17. . . . . .125 C1
Lessness Pk DA17. . . . . . . .125 C1
Lessness Rd
  Belvedere DA17. . . . . .125 C1
  Morden SM4. . . . . .202 A4
Lester Ave E16. . . . . .98 C3
Lester Ct **42** E3 . . . . .97 D4
Lester Ho IG8. . . . . .36 B3
Lestock Cl **2** SE25. . . . . . .206 A6
Lestock Ho SE3. . . . . .143 D4
Lestor Ct TW7 . . . . .130 D2
Leswin Pl N16. . . . . .73 D5
Leswin Rd N16. . . . . .73 D5
Letchford Gdns NW10. . . . . .90 A4
Letchford Mews NW10. . . . . .90 A4
Letchmore Ho **7** W10. . . . . .90 C3
Letchworth Ave TW14. . . . .149 D4
Letchworth Cl
  Bromley BR2. . . . . .209 A4
  South Oxhey WD19. . . . . . .22 D5
Letchworth Dr BR2 . . . . . . .209 A4
Letchworth St SW17. . . . . .180 D6
Lethaby Ho **13** SW4 . . . . . .138 B1
Lethbridge Cl SE13. . . . . . .142 A3
Letterstone Rd SW6. . . . . . .264 C3
Lettice St SW6. . . . .135 B4 264 D1
Lett Rd E15. . . . . .76 B1
Lettsom St SE5. . . . . .139 C3
Lettsom Wlk **1** E13. . . . . . .99 A5
Leucha Rd E17. . . . . .53 A4
Levana Cl SW19. . . . . .157 A3
Levant Ho **17** E1. . . . . .96 D3
Levehurst Ho SE27. . . . . . . .183 A5
Levehurst Way SW4,
  SW9. . . . . .138 A3
Leven Cl WD19. . . . . .22 D5
Levendale Rd SE23. . . . . . .163 B2
Leven Rd E14. . . . . .98 B1
Leven Way UB3. . . . . .83 C1
Lever Ct **15** E9. . . . . .74 D2
Leverett St SW3. . . . . .257 B4
Leverholme Gdns SE9. . . . .166 C1
Leverington Pl N1. . . . . .235 D1
Leverson St SW16. . . . . . . .181 C4
Lever St EC1. . . . . . .95 A4 235 A1
Leverstock Ho SW3 . . . . . . .257 B2
Leverton Pl NW5. . . . . .71 C3
Leverton St NW5. . . . . .71 C3
Levett Gdns IG3. . . . . .80 A5
Levett Ho **8** SW16. . . . . . . .181 C5
Levine Gdns IG11. . . . . .102 D5

Levison Way **2** N19.........49 D1
Levita Ho NW1.............232 D2
Levyne Ct EC1............241 A6
Lewes Cl UB5..............63 C2
Lewes Ct **3** CR4.........202 D6
Lewesdon Cl **13** SW19...156 D3
Lewes Ho
  Bermondsey SE1........253 B2
  Peckham SE15..........94 B2
Lewes Rd Bromley BR1....187 D1
  Colney Hatch N12.......30 C5
Leweston Pl N16...........51 D2
Lewey Ho E3..............97 B3
Lewgars Ave NW9..........45 A3
Lewin Ct
  4 Plumstead SE18.....123 C2
  Streatham SW16.......182 A4
Lewing Cl BR6...........211 C1
Lewington Ct EN3..........6 D6
Lewin Rd Bexley DA6......147 A1
  Mortlake SW14........133 B2
  Streatham SW16.......181 D4
Lewin Terr TW14.........149 B4
Lewis Ave E17............35 C2
Lewis Cl N14.............15 C4
Lewis Cres NW10.........67 B3
Lewis Ct **5** SE16.......118 B1
Lewis Gdns London N2.....30 B1
  South Tottenham N15, N16..51 D3
Lewis Gr SE13...........142 A2
LEWISHAM.............142 A1
Lewisham Bridge Prim Sch
  3 SE13.............141 D2
Lewisham Bsns Ctr
  SE14.................140 D6
Lewisham Coll (Deptford
  Campus) **12** SE8......141 C4
Lewisham Coll (Lewisham
  Way Campus) SE4.......141 C3
Lewisham Ct EN3..........7 C5
Lewisham Ctr SE13.......142 A2
Lewisham High St SE13..163 D6
Lewisham Hill SE13......142 A3
Lewisham Hospl SE13....163 D6
Lewisham Pk SE13.......164 A5
Lewisham Rd SE13.......142 A3
Lewisham St SW1........249 D1
Lewisham Sta SE13......142 A2
Lewisham Way SE4,
  SE14.................141 B4
Lewis Ho **2** E4.........35 C5
Lewis King Ho BR1......187 B3
Lewis Pl E8..............74 A3
Lewis Rd Bexley DA16....146 C2
  Mitcham CR4..........180 C1
  19 Richmond TW10....153 D6
  Sidcup DA14...........168 C1
  Southall UB1..........107 A4
  Sutton SM1...........217 D4
Lewis Silkin Ho **3** SE15..140 C6
Lewis Sports & L Ctr
  SE19.................183 D2
Lewis St NW1............71 B2
Lewiston Cl KT4........200 B2
Lewis Way RM10..........81 D2
Lexden Dr RM6...........58 B3
Lexden Rd Acton W3.....110 D5
  Mitcham CR4..........203 D5
Lexdon Ct RM6...........58 B3
Lexfield Ho N5...........73 A4
Lexham Ct UB6...........86 B6
Lexham Gardens Mews
  W8..................255 D5
Lexham Gdns
  W8...............113 D2 255 C4
Lexham Ho **9** IG11.....101 B6
Lexham Mews
  W8...............113 C2 255 B4
Lexham Wlk W8.........255 D5
Lexington Pl KT1........175 D2
Lexington St W1....115 C6 249 B6
Lexton Gdns SW12.......159 D3
Leyborne Ave W13.......109 C4
Leyborne Pk TW9........132 C4
Leybourne Cl BR2.......209 A3
Leybourne Ct **1** SE25...206 A6
Leybourne Ho **20** SE15..140 C6
Leybourne Rd
  17 Camden Town NW1...71 B1
  Hillingdon UB10........83 A6
  Leytonstone E11........54 D1
  Queensbury NW9........44 C4
Leybourne St **5** NW1...71 B1
Leybridge Ct SE12......165 A6
Leyburn Cl E17...........53 D5
Leyburn Gdns CR0......221 C6
Leyburn Gr N18..........34 A4
Leyburn Rd N18..........34 B4
Leyden Mans **7** N19.....50 A2
Leyden St E1......95 D2 243 C3
Leydon Cl
  Rotherhithe SE16.......118 D5
  SE16.................118 D5
Leyes Rd E16............99 D1
Leyfield KT4............199 D1
Ley Ho SE1.............252 A1
Leyland Ave EN3..........7 A3

Leyland Ct **8** N11.......31 B6
Leyland Gdns IG8.........37 C5
Leyland Ho
  6 Canary Wharf E14...119 D6
  12 Richmond TW10....153 C1
Leyland Rd SE12........165 A6
Leylands SW18..........157 B5
Leyland St **4** SE14.....140 D5
Leys Cl Finchley N12......30 C3
  Harrow HA1............42 B4
Leys Ct **9** SW9.........138 C3
Leysdown **9** NW5........71 A2
Leysdown Ho SE17.......263 B2
Leysdown Rd SE9.......166 B2
Leysfield Rd W12.......112 A4
Leys Gdns EN4............15 A6
Leyspring Rd E11.........54 D1
Leys Rd E EN3............7 A4
Leys Rd W EN3............7 A4
Ley St Ilford IG1.........78 D6
  Newbury Pk IG1, IG2....57 B1
Leys The East Finchley N2..48 A5
  Harrow HA3............44 B3
Leyswood Dr IG2.........57 C4
Leythe Rd W3...........111 A4
LEYTON...............76 B5
Leyton Bsns Ctr E10......75 C6
Leyton Ct SE23.........162 C3
Leyton Grange E10.......53 C1
Leyton Green Rd E10......54 A3
Leyton Green Twrs E10....54 A3
Leyton Ind Village E10....52 D2
Leyton Leisure Lagoon
  E10.................54 A2
Leyton Link Est E10......53 A2
Leyton Midland Road Sta
  E10.................54 A1
Leyton Mill Ret Pk E10....76 A4
Leyton Mills E10.........76 A4
Leyton Park Rd E10.......76 A5
Leyton Rd Merton SW19..180 A3
  Stratford E15..........76 B2
Leyton Sixth Form Coll
  E10.................54 B3
Leyton Sta E11...........76 A5
LEYTONSTONE..........54 D1
Leytonstone High Road Sta
  E11.................76 C6
Leytonstone Rd E15.......76 C3
Leytonstone Sch E11......54 C3
Leytonstone Sta E11......54 C1
Leyton Town Ctr E10......76 A5
Leywick St E15...........98 C5
Lezayre Rd BR6.........227 D2
Liardet St SE14.........141 A6
Liberia Rd N5............72 D2
Libert Cl N18............33 D6
Liberty Ave SW19.......180 B2
Liberty Cl KT4.........200 C1
Liberty Ct IG11.........102 C5
Liberty Ctr HA0..........88 B6
Liberty Ho **11** E1.......118 A6
Liberty Mews
  Balham SW12..........159 B5
  Orpington BR6........227 D6
  Wood Green N22........32 D2
Liberty Sch CR4.........180 C1
Liberty St SW9....138 B4 270 D2
Libra Ct **7** Bow E3......97 B5
  Newham E13............99 A5
Library Mans **4** W12...112 C4
Library Par NW10........89 C6
Library Pl E1..........118 B6
Library St SE1....116 D4 251 D1
Library Way **1** TW2....152 A4
Libro Ct E4..............35 C6
Lichen Ct IG6............56 D6
Lichfield Cl EN4..........2 D1
Lichfield Ct
  Kingston u T KT6.......198 A4
  Richmond TW9.........132 A1
Lichfield Gdns TW10,
  TW9.................154 A6
Lichfield Gr N3..........29 C1
Lichfield Ho **27** SE5....139 A3
Lichfield Rd
  Dagenham RM8..........80 C5
  Edmonton N9...........18 A2
  Hounslow TW4.........128 C2
  Mile End E3............97 A4
  Newham E6.............99 D4
  Northwood HA6.........40 A6
  Richmond TW9.........132 B4
  West Hampstead NW2....69 A4
  Woodford IG8...........36 C6
Lichfield Terr **1** TW9...154 A6
Lichlade Cl **7** BR6.....227 D4
Lickey Ho W14..........264 D6
Lidbury Rd NW7..........29 A4
Lidcote Gdns **22** SW9..138 B3
Liddall Way UB7........104 B5
Liddell Cl HA3...........43 D6
Liddell Gdns NW10.......90 C5
Liddell Rd NW6..........69 C2
Lidding Rd HA3..........43 D4
Liddington Rd E15.......98 D6
Liddlesdale Ho E **6**
  KT2.................176 D2

Liddlesdale Ho W **5**
  KT2.................176 D2
Liddon Rd Bromley BR1...209 D6
  Newham E13...........99 B4
Liden Cl E10, E17........53 B1
Lidfield Rd N16..........73 B4
Lidgate Rd **22** SE15...139 D5
Lidiard Rd SW18.......158 A2
Lidlington Pl NW1.......232 B3
Lido Sq N17..............33 B1
Lido The ★ W2....114 A4 247 A3
Lidyard Rd N19..........49 C1
Liffey Ct Edmonton N9....18 C1
  Willesden NW10........68 A1
Liffler Rd SE18.........123 C1
Liffords Pl SW13.......133 D3
Lifford St SW15.........134 D1
Lightcliffe Rd N13.......16 C1
Lighted Lady ★ IG11......78 D1
Lighter Ct **16** SE16...119 A2
Lighterman Mews **15** E1..96 D1
Lighterman's Rd E14.....119 D4
Lighterman's Wlk SW18..135 C1
Lightfoot Rd N8...........50 A4
Light Horse Ct SW1......258 A1
Lightley Cl Wembley HA0...66 B1
  Wembley HA0...........88 B6
Ligonier St E2..........243 C6
Lilac Cl E4...............35 B4
Lilac Ct Colney Hatch N12..30 C4
  3 Newham E13.......99 C6
  Teddington N11.........174 D6
Lilac Gdns Croydon CR0..223 C5
  Ealing W5.............109 D3
  Hayes UB3.............83 C1
Lilac Ho SE4............141 B2
Lilac Pl
  Vauxhall SE11....116 B2 260 C3
  Yiewsley UB7..........104 B6
Lilac St W12............112 A6
Lilah Mews BR2..........186 D1
Lilburne Gdns SE9......166 A6
Lilburne Rd SE9........166 A6
Lilburne Wlk NW10.......67 A2
Lile Cres W7.............86 C2
Lilestone Est NW8......236 D5
Lilestone Ho NW8.......236 D5
Lilestone St NW8...92 C3 237 A6
Lilford Ho **21** SE5.....139 A3
Lilford Rd SE5..........138 D3
Lilian Barker Cl SE12...165 A6
Lilian Baylis Ho N1......73 A2
Lilian Baylis Tech Sch
  SE11.............116 B1 260 D1
Lilian Board Way UB6....64 B3
Lilian Gdns IG8..........37 B2
Lilian Rd SW16.........181 C2
Lilian Rolfe Ho **5** SE27..183 B6
Lillechurch Rd RM8.......80 C2
Lilleshall Rd SM4......202 B3
Lilley Cl E1...........118 A5
Lillian Ave W3..........110 C4
Lillian Cl **14** N16.....73 C5
Lillian Rd SW13........134 B6
Lillie Ho N5............72 C3
Lillie Rd SW6......135 B6 264 C5
Lillie Road Mans SW6...264 B5
Lillieshall Rd SW4......137 C2
Lillie Yd SW6.....135 C6 265 A6
Lillington Ho N7.........72 C4
Lilliput Ave UB5.........85 B6
Lillywhite **21** NW9......27 D2
Lily Albon Ct RM9........81 B4
Lily Cl W14............112 D2
Lily Gdns HA0............87 C5
Lily Ho **7** HA9.........66 A3
Lily Pl EC1.............241 B4
Lily Rd E17..............53 C3
Lilyville Rd SW6..135 B4 264 C2
Limavady Ho **12** SE18..122 C2
Limborough Ho **5** E14..97 C2
  Thornton Heath CR7....204 B4
Limburg Rd SW11.......136 C1
Lime Ave UB7...........104 B6
Limeburner La
  EC4...............94 D1 241 C2
Lime Cl Bromley BR1.....210 A5
  Buckhurst Hill IG9......21 D2
  Carshalton SM5.......218 D6
  Harrow HA3............25 A1
  Pinner HA5.............39 D6
  Wapping E1...........118 A5
Lime Cres TW16.........172 C1
Limecroft Cl KT19......215 B1
Lime Ct **9** Harrow HA1...42 D3
  Hendon NW4...........28 C1
  Kingston u T KT3.......198 D6
  9 Leyton E11........76 C6
  Mitcham CR4..........180 B1
  Putney SW15..........134 B2
Limedene Cl HA5..........22 D2
Lime Gr Barnet N20.......13 B3
  Blackfen DA15.........167 D5
  Hayes UB3............105 B6
  Kingston u T KT3.......199 C6
  Orpington BR6........226 D6
  Ruislip HA4............40 B2
  Shepherd's Bush W12...112 C4
  Twickenham TW1.......153 A5
  Walthamstow E4........35 B4

Limeharbour E14........119 D4
Lime Ho **7** TW9........132 D4
LIMEHOUSE............119 A6
Limehouse Cswy E14.....119 B6
Limehouse Ct **5** E14....97 C1
Limehouse Ct **23** E14....97 B1
Limehouse Cut **4** E14...97 D2
Limehouse Fields Est **14**
  E14.................97 A2
Limehouse Link (Tunnel)
  E14.................119 B6
Limehouse Sta E14.......97 A1
Lime Kiln Dr SE7........143 B6
Limekiln Pl SE19.......183 D3
Limekiln Wharf **21** E14..119 B6
Limeleaf Ct HA8..........27 A6
Lime Lo **3** TW16.......171 D3
Limerick Cl SW12.......159 C4
Limerick Ct **1** SW12...159 C4
Lime Row DA18..........125 B3
Limerston St
  SW10.............136 A6 266 B5
Lime St Pas EC3.........253 A6
Limes Ave Barnes SW13..133 D3
  Carshalton SM5.......202 D1
  Croydon CR0..........220 C5
  Edgware NW7...........27 C4
  Golders Green NW11....47 A2
  North Finchley N12.....30 A6
  Penge SE20...........184 B3
  Wanstead E11..........55 B5
Limes Ave The N11........31 C5
  3 Friern Barnet N11...31 C5
Limes Ct Beckenham BR3..185 D1
  Willesden NW6.........68 D1
Limesdale Gdns HA8.......27 A1
Limes Field Rd SW14....133 C2
Limesford Rd SE15......140 D1
Limes Gdns SW18.......157 C5
Limes Gr SE13..........142 A1
Limes Rd Beckenham BR3..185 D1
  Thornton Heath CR0....205 B2
Limes Row BR6.........226 D3
Lime St Walthamstow E17..53 A5
  Whitechapel EC3...95 C1 243 A1
Limes The
  Camberwell SE5........139 C2
  3 Cheam SM2........217 C2
  East Molesey KT8......195 D5
  Kensington W2.........245 B5
  Keston Mark BR2......226 A6
  Stanmore HA7...........9 B2
Limes Wlk Ealing W5.....109 D4
  Nunhead SE15.........140 C1
Lime Terr W7...........108 C6
Lime Tree Ave KT10, KT7..196 C5
Limetree Cl SW2........160 B3
Lime Tree Cl E11.........55 C5
Limetree Ct HA5..........23 C3
Lime Tree Ct
  East Barnet EN4........14 C6
  East Finchley N2........47 D6
  14 Poplar E3........97 C2
  South Croydon CR2....221 A2
Lime Tree Gr CR0.......223 B5
Limetree Pl CR4........181 B2
Lime Tree Rd TW5.......129 D4
Limetree Wlk **2** SW17..181 A5
Lime Tree Wlk
  Bushey WD23............8 C2
  Coney Hall BR4........224 D4
  Enfield EN2.............5 A5
Lime Wlk **11** E15........98 C6
Limewood Cl
  Beckenham BR3........208 A4
  Ealing W13.............87 B1
Limewood Ct IG4..........56 B4
Limpsfield Ave
  Putney SW19..........156 D2
  Thornton Heath CR7....204 B4
Limscott Ho **35** E3......97 D4
Linacre Cl SE15........140 B2
Linacre Ct W6...........112 D1
Linacre Rd NW2...........68 B2
Linale Ho N1...........235 C3
Linberry Wlk **3** SE8....119 B2
Linchmere Rd SE12......164 D4
Lincoln Ave Osidge N14...15 C2
  Twickenham TW2.......152 A2
  Wimbledon SW19.......156 D1
Lincoln Cl Croydon CR25..206 B3
  Greenford UB6..........86 A6
  Harrow HA2............41 B4
Lincoln Cres EN1.........17 D6
Lincoln Ct
  Borehamwood WD6.......11 B6
  Enfield EN2.............5 B1
  Grove Pk SE12........165 C1
  Hampton TW12.........173 B5
  Hendon NW4............46 B5
  Mitcham CR4..........204 A4
  Redbridge IG1..........56 B2
  5 South Croydon CR2..221 A3
  Stoke Newington N16....51 B2
Lincoln Gdns IG1.........56 A2
Lincoln Green Rd BR5...211 D4

Lincoln Ho
  Bloomsbury WC1.......240 D3
  9 Dartmouth Pk NW5..71 C5
  2 Islington N1.......73 A1
  Knightsbridge SW1.....247 C5
Lincoln Lo **10** BR3.....185 D1
Lincoln Mews NW6........91 B6
Lincoln Rd Croydon SE25..206 B6
  East Finchley N2........48 C6
  Enfield EN1, EN3........17 D6
  Harrow HA2, HA5........41 B4
  Kingston u T KT3.......199 A6
  Mitcham CR4..........204 A4
  Newham E13............99 B3
  North Cheam KT4......200 B1
  Northwood HA6.........39 D6
  Plashet E7.............77 D2
  Sidcup DA14...........190 B5
  Twickenham TW13......151 B1
  Wembley HA0...........65 D2
  Woodford IG8...........37 A2
Lincoln's Inn ★
  WC2...............94 B1 240 D2
Lincoln's Inn Fields
  WC2...............94 B1 240 D2
Lincoln St Chelsea SW3...257 C3
  Leyton E11.............76 C6
LincoIns The NW7.........11 D1
Lincoln Terr **4** SM2...217 C1
Lincoln Way
  Charlton TW16........171 C2
  Enfield EN1............18 B6
Lincombe Rd BR1........164 D1
Linda Ct KT9...........213 D4
Lindal Cres EN2...........4 B1
Lindal Ct **1** E18........37 A2
Lindale SW19...........157 A2
Lindales The N17.........33 D4
Lindal Rd SE4..........163 B6
Lindbergh Rd SM6.......220 A1
Linden Ave Enfield EN1.....6 A4
  Hounslow TW3.........151 C6
  Kensal Rise NW10.......90 D5
  Ruislip HA4............40 A1
  Thornton Heath CR7....204 D5
  Wembley HA9............66 A6
Linden Bridge Sch KT4...215 C5
Linden Cl Ruislip HA4.....40 A1
  Southgate N14.........15 C5
  Stanmore HA7...........25 B5
  Thames Ditton KT7.....197 A2
Linden Cotts **6** SW19..179 A4
Linden Cres
  Kingston u T KT1.......176 B1
  Wembley UB6...........64 D2
  Woodford IG8...........37 B4
Linden Ct
  8 Battersea SW18...136 B1
  1 Beckenham BR3....207 D6
  2 Bromley BR1.......186 D3
  Edgware NW7...........27 B5
  Penge SE20...........184 B3
  1 Shepherd's Bush W12..112 C5
  Sidcup DA14..........189 C6
  11 Sutton SM2.......218 A2
Lindenfield BR7.........188 D1
Linden Gate SW20......200 C6
Linden Gdns
  Chiswick W4...........111 B1
  Enfield EN1.............6 A4
  Notting Hill W2....113 C6 245 B5
Linden Gr
  Kingston u T KT3.......199 C6
  Nunhead SE15.........140 C2
  Penge SE20...........184 C4
  Teddington TW11.......174 D5
Linden Ho Bromley BR1...187 B3
  10 Deptford SE8......141 B6
  Hampton TW12.........173 D4
  Walthamstow E17.......35 B1
Linden Lawns HA9.........66 B4
Linden Lea N2............48 A4
Lindenlea Ct E17.........53 B5
Linden Leas BR4........224 B6
Linden Lo N21............10 A6
Linden Lodge Sch SW19..157 A3
Linden Mans N6..........49 B1
Linden Mews
  Kensington W2.........245 B5
  Stoke Newington N1.....73 B3
Linden Pl CR4..........202 C5
Linden Rd
  Brunswick Pk N11.......15 A2
  Cranley Gdns N10.......49 B5
  Hampton TW12.........173 C2
  Tottenham N15..........51 A3
Lindens The
  Chiswick W4...........133 A4
  New Addington CR0....224 A2
  North Finchley N12......30 B5
  5 Walthamstow E17...53 D5
Linden Way
  Shepperton TW17......193 A4
  Southgate N14..........15 C5
Lindeth Cl HA7...........25 B4
Lindfield Gdns NW3......70 A3
Lindfield Hts NW3........70 A3
Lindfield Rd
  Croydon CR0..........205 D3
  Ealing W5..............87 C3

Lindfield St E14. . . . . .97 C1
Lindhill Cl EN3. . . . . .6 D3
Lindholme Ct 3 NW9 . . . .27 C2
Lindisfarne Rd
 Dagenham RM8 . . . . .80 C5
 Wimbledon SW20. . . . . . .178 A3
Lindisfarne Way E9 . . . . .75 A4
Lindley Ct KT1. . . . . .175 C2
Lindley Ho
 13 Peckham SE15 . . . . . .140 A5
 9 Stepney E1 . . . . .96 C2
Lindley Pl TW9. . . . . .132 C4
Lindley Rd E10. . . . . .76 A6
Lindley St E1 . . . . .96 C2
Lindon Bennett Sch The
 TW13 . . . . .172 C5
Lindop Ho 8 E1. . . . . .97 A3
Lindore Rd SW11 . . . . . .136 D1
Lindores Rd SM5. . . . . . . .202 A1
Lindo St SE15. . . . . .140 C3
Lind Rd SM1. . . . . .218 A3
Lindrop St SW6 . . . . .136 A3
Lindsay Cl KT9. . . . . .214 A1
Lindsay Ct
 Battersea SW11. . . . . . . .266 C1
 Sutton SM1. . . . . .217 C3
Lindsay Dr Harrow HA3 . . .44 B4
 Shepperton TW17. . . . . . .193 B3
Lindsay Ho 2 SE18 . . . . .122 C2
Lindsay Rd
 Hampton TW12. . . . . . . .173 D6
 North Cheam KT4. . . . . . .216 B6
Lindsay Sq SW1. 115 D1 259 D2
Lindsell St SE10 . . . . .142 A4
Lindsey Cl Bickley BR1. . . .210 A6
 Mitcham CR4, SW16. . . . .204 A5
Lindsey Ct N13. . . . . .16 C1
Lindsey Gdns TW14 . . . . .149 B4
Lindsey Ho SW10 . . . . . .109 D2
Lindsey Ho* SW10 . . . . . .266 D4
Lindsey Mews 18 N1 . . . . .73 A1
Lindsey Rd RM8. . . . . .80 C5
Lindsey St EC1. . . . .94 D2 241 D4
Lindum Rd SW13. . . . . . .175 C3
Lindums The BR3. . . . . . .185 B4
Lindway SW17. . . . . .182 D5
Lindwood Cl 8 E6. . . . . .100 B2
Linear View HA9 . . . . .66 D6
Linfield WC1. . . . . .233 C1
Linfield Cl NW4 . . . . .46 C5
Linford Christie Stadium The
 W12. . . . . .90 B2
Linford Ct 1 CR4 . . . . . .180 C2
Linford Ho 17 E2. . . . . .96 A6
Linford Rd E17 . . . . .54 B6
Linford St SW8 . . .137 C4 269 A1
Linford Street Bsns Est
 SW8 . . . . .269 A2
Lingard Ho 11 E14. . . . . .120 A3
Lingards Rd SE13. . . . . . .142 A1
Lingey Cl DA15 . . . . .167 D2
Lingfield Ave KT1, KT5 . . . .198 A5
Lingfield Cl EN1. . . . . .17 C5
Lingfield Cres SE9 . . . . . .145 B1
Lingfield Rd Northolt UB5. . .85 C5
 Wimbledon SW19. . . . . . .178 D4
Lingfield Gdns N9 . . . . . . .18 B4
Lingfield Ho
 5 Acton Green W4 . . . . .111 A1
 Lambeth SE1. . . . . .251 D1
 Penge SE26 . . . . .184 B4
Lingfield Rd
 North Cheam KT4. . . . . . .216 C5
 Wimbledon SW19. . . . . . .178 D4
Lingham St SW9 . . . . . . .138 B3
Lingholm Way EN5. . . . . . .12 D6
Ling Rd E16 . . . . .99 A2
Lingrove Gdns IG9. . . . . . .21 B2
Ling's Coppice SE21 . . . . .161 B2
Lingwell Rd SW17. . . . . . .158 C1
Lingwood DA7. . . . . .147 D3
Lingwood Gdns TW7 . . . . .130 C5
Lingwood Rd E5 . . . . .52 A2
Linhope St NW1. . . .92 D3 237 C5
Link Day Prim Sch The
 CR0. . . . . .220 A4
Linkenholt Mans 3 W6 . .111 D2
Linkfield KT8 . . . . .195 D6
Link Field BR2. . . . . .209 A3
Linkfield Rd TW7 . . . . . . .130 D3
Link La SM6 . . . . .220 A2
Linklea Cl NW9 . . . . .27 C6
Link Rd Dagenham RM9. . . .103 D5
 East Bedfont TW14. . . . . .149 D4
 Friern Barnet N11 . . . . . .31 A4
 Hackbridge SM6. . . . . . . .203 A1
Links Ave SM4 . . . . .201 C5
Linkscroft Ave TW15 . . . . .170 D4
Links Ct N20. . . . . .14 B1
Links Dr N20 . . . . .13 D3
Link Sec Sch The CR0 . . . .220 B4
Links Gdns SW16. . . . . . .182 C3
Linkside Finchley N12 . . . . .29 C4
 Kingston u T KT3. . . . . . .177 C1
Linkside Cl EN2 . . . . .4 C2
Linkside Gdns EN2. . . . . . .4 B1
Links Ind EstTW13 . . . . . .151 A1
Links Prim Sch SW17 . . . . .181 A4
Links Rd Acton W3. . . . . . .88 C1

Links Rd continued
 Ashford TW15. . . . . .170 A5
 Mitcham SW16, SW17 . . . .181 A4
 West Wickham BR4 . . . . .208 A1
 Willesden NW2. . . . . .67 D6
 Woodford IG8. . . . . .37 A5
Links Side EN2 . . . . .4 C2
Link St E9 . . . . .74 C3
Links The E17. . . . . .53 A5
Linksview N2. . . . . .48 D4
Links View Finchley N3 . . . .29 B3
 Shooters Hill SE18 . . . . . .144 D4
Links View Cl HA7. . . . . . .25 A4
Links View Rd
 Croydon CR0. . . . . .223 C5
 Hampton TW12. . . . . . . .174 A6
Linksway NW4. . . . . .28 D1
Links Way
 Beckenham BR3. . . . . . . .207 C3
 Streatham SW17 . . . . . . .181 A4
Links Yd 10 Spitalfields E1. . .96 A2
 Spitalfields E1. . . . . .243 D4
Link The Acton W3 . . . . . . .88 D1
 Chislehurst SE9 . . . . . . .166 C1
 Enfield EN3. . . . . .7 A4
 Hendon NW2. . . . . .46 A1
 Northolt UB5. . . . . .63 B3
 Pinner HA5. . . . . .40 C2
 Teddington TW11 . . . . . . .174 D4
 Wembley HA0. . . . . .43 C1
Linkway Dagenham RM8 . . .80 C4
 Pinner HA5. . . . . .22 D2
 Stoke Newington N4. . . . . .51 A2
 West Barnes SW20 . . . . . .200 B5
Link Way Bromley BR2. . . .210 A2
 Richmond TW10 . . . . . . .153 B2
Linkway The EN5. . . . . . . .13 C5
Linkway Dagenham RM8 . . .71 D1
Linley Cres RM7 . . . . .59 D6
Linley Ct
 1 Dulwich SE21 . . . . . .183 C6
 Sutton SM1. . . . . .218 A4
Linley House Sch KT5. . . . .198 B3
Linley Rd N17. . . . . .33 C1
Linnell Cl NW11. . . . . .47 D3
Linnell Dr NW11 . . . . .47 D3
Linnell Ho Spitalfields E1 . .243 C4
 St John's Wood NW8 . . . .229 A6
Linnell Rd
 Camberwell SE5. . . . . . . .139 C3
 Edmonton N18. . . . . .34 A5
Linnet Cl Bushey WD23 . . . .8 A3
 Lower Edmonton N9. . . . . .18 D3
 Woolwich SE28. . . . . . . .124 C6
Linnet Ct CR4. . . . . .180 C2
Linnet Mews SW12. . . . . .159 A4
Linnett Cl E4 . . . . .36 A6
Linom Rd SW4. . . . . .138 A1
Linscott Rd E5. . . . . .74 C4
Linsdell Rd IG11. . . . . . . .101 A6
Linsey St
 Bermondsey SE16 . . . . . .118 A2
 Bermondsey SE16 . . . . . .118 A3
Linslade Cl
 Hounslow TW4 . . . . .151 A6
 Pinner HA5. . . . . .40 B6
Linslade Ho
 10 Hackney E2. . . . . .96 A4
 Marylebone NW8 . . . . . . .237 B6
Linstead St 1 NW6 . . . . . .69 C1
Linstead Way SW18,
 SW19. . . . . .157 A4
Linsted Ct SE9 . . . . .167 C5
Linster Gr W10 . . . . .11 A6
Lintaine Cl W6. . . . . .264 B5
Linthorpe Ave HA0 . . . . . . .65 C2
Linthorpe Rd
 Cockfosters EN4. . . . . . . .2 C2
 Stamford Hill N16. . . . . . .51 C2
Linton Cl Carshalton CR4. . .202 D2
 2 Greenwich SE7 . . . . . .121 C1
 Welling DA16 . . . . .146 B4
Linton Gdns E6 . . . . .100 A1
Linton Gr SE27. . . . . .183 A5
Linton Ho
 Lower Holloway N7 . . . . . .72 B4
 2 Tower Hamlets E3 . . . . .97 C2
Linton Mead Prim Sch
 SE28. . . . . .124 B6
Linton Rd IG11. . . . . .79 A1
Linton St N1 . . . . . .95 A6 235 B5
 Finchley N3. . . . . .29 B2
Linver Rd SW6. . . . . .135 C3
Linwood Cl SE5. . . . . .139 D3
Linwood Cres EN1 . . . . . . .6 A4
Linzee Rd N8 . . . . .50 A5
Lion Ave TW1 . . . . .152 D3
Lion Cl Ladywell SE4 . . . . .163 C5
 Littleton TW17 . . . . .192 A6
Lion Ct 12 NW9 . . . . .46 A5
Lion Ctr The TW13 . . . . . .151 A1
Lionel Gdns SE9 . . . . .165 D6
Lionel Ho Bowes Pk N22 . . .32 B4
 5 Kensal Town W10 . . . . .91 A2
Lionel Mans 14 W14. . . . . .112 D3
Lionel Mews 19 W10 . . . . . .91 A2
Lionel Rd SE9. . . . . .165 D6
Lionel Road N TW8. . . . . .110 A2

Lionel Road Prim Sch
 TW8 . . . . .110 A2
Lionel Road S TW8. . . . . .110 B1
Lion Gate Gdns TW9 . . . . .132 B2
Lion Gate Mews SW18 . . . .157 C4
Lion House Sch SW15. . . . .134 D1
Lion Mills 36 E2. . . . . .96 A5
Lion Park Ave KT9. . . . . . .214 C4
Lion Rd Bexleyheath DA6. . .147 B1
 Edmonton N9. . . . . .18 A2
 Newham E6. . . . . .100 B2
 Thornton Heath CR0. . . . .205 A4
 Twickenham TW1, TW2. . . .152 D3
Lions Cl SE12. . . . . .165 D1
Lion Way TW8 . . . . .131 D5
Lion Wharf Rd TW7 . . . . . .131 B2
Lion Yd SW4 . . . . .137 D1
Liphook Cres SE23 . . . . . .162 C4
Liphook Rd WD19 . . . . . . .22 C6
Lipton Cl SE28. . . . . .124 C6
Lipton Ct N14. . . . . .15 C4
Lipton Rd 9 E1. . . . . .96 D1
Lisa Lo 5 EN5 . . . . .13 D6
Lisbon Ave TW2. . . . . . . .152 A2
Lisbon Cl E17. . . . . .35 B1
Lisburne Rd NW3 . . . . . . .70 D4
Lisford St SE15 . . . . .139 D4
Lisgar Terr W14. . . .113 B2 254 C4
Liskeard Cl BR7. . . . . .189 A4
Liskeard Gdns SE3 . . . . . .143 A4
Liskeard Ho SE11 . . . . . . .261 B2
Lisle Cl SW17 . . . . .181 B6
Lisle Ct NW2. . . . . .69 A5
Lisle St WC2. . . . . . .119 C5 249 D6
Lismirrane Ind Pk WD6. . . . .9 B5
Lismore 9 SW19 . . . . . . .179 B5
Lismore Cir NW5 . . . . .71 A3
Lismore Cl TW7. . . . . .131 A3
Lismore Rd
 South Croydon CR2. . . . . .221 C2
 Tottenham N17. . . . . .51 B6
Lismore Wlk 4 N1. . . . . . . .73 A2
Lissant Cl KT6 . . . . .197 D2
Lisselton Ho 3 NW4 . . . . . .46 D5
Lissenden Gdns NW5 . . . . .71 A4
Lissenden Mans NW5 . . . . .71 A4
Lisson Cotts NW1. . . . . . .237 B4
Lisson Gr NW1,
 NW8 . . . . .92 C3 237 A6
LISSON GROVE 92 B3
Lisson Ho NW1 . . . . .237 A4
Lisson St NW1 . . . . .92 C2 237 A4
Lister Cl Dagenham W3. . . . .89 B2
 Mitcham SW19. . . . . .180 C2
Lister Com Sch 1 E13 . . . . .99 B5
Lister Cotts WD6. . . . . .9 A6
Lister Ct Hendon NW9 . . . . .27 C1
 Stoke Newington N16. . . . .73 C6
Lister Gdns N18 . . . . .33 A5
Lister Ho Greenwich SE3. . .142 C6
 Hayes UB3 . . . . .105 C2
 Marylebone W1 . . . . .238 C2
 Spitalfields E1. . . . . .96 A2
 6 Wembley HA9 . . . . . . .67 A5
Lister Hospl SW1 .115 B1 258 C1
Lister Mews N7 . . . . .72 B4
Lister Rd E11. . . . . .54 D1
Lister Wlk SE28 . . . . .124 D6
Liston Ho N21 . . . . .16 B6
Liston Rd Clapham SW4 . . .137 C2
 Tottenham N17. . . . . .34 A2
Liston Way 1 IG8 . . . . .37 C3
Listowel Cl 2 SW9. . . . . .138 C5
Listowel Rd RM10. . . . . . . .81 C5
Listria La N16 . . . . .73 D6
Listria Pk N16 . . . . .73 D6
Litcham Ho 23 E1. . . . . . . .96 D4
Litchfield Ave
 Morden SM4. . . . . .201 B2
 Stratford E15. . . . . .76 C2
Litchfield Ct 1 E17 . . . . . . .53 C3
Litchfield Gdns NW10. . . . . .68 A2
Litchfield Rd SM1. . . . . . .218 A4
Litchfield St WC2. . . . . . .249 D6
Litchfield Way NW11. . . . . .48 A4
Lithgow's Rd TW14, TW6 . .127 D1
Lithos Rd NW3. . . . . .70 A2
Little Acre BR3 . . . . .207 C6
Little Albany St NW1. . . . . .238 D6
Little Argyll St W1 . . . . . . .239 A1
Little Birches DA15 . . . . . .167 C2
Little Boltons The SW10 . . .255 D1
Little Bornes SE21. . . . . . .183 C6
Littlebourne 2 SE13. . . . . .164 C4
Littlebrook Cl CR0 . . . . . . .206 D3
Little Brownings SE23. . . . .162 B2
Littleburg Rd SW4 . . . . . . .137 D2
Little Bury St N9. . . . . .17 C4
Little Bushey La WD23. . . . .8 B5
Little Cedars N12 . . . . .30 A4
Little Chelsea Ho SW10 . . .266 B5
Little Chester St SW1 . . . . .258 C6
Little Cloisters SW1. . . . . .260 A6
Little College St SW1 . . . . .260 A6
Little Combe Cl 13
 SW15. . . . . .156 D5

Little Common HA7. . . . . . . .9 A1
Littlecote Cl SW19 . . . . . . .157 A4
Littlecote Pl HA5 . . . . .23 B2
Little Ct WC2 . . . . .144 C2
Little Ct Harrow HA1 . . . . . .42 C2
 West Wickham BR4 . . . . .224 C6
Littledale SE2. . . . . .146 A6
Little David's Sch CR0 . . . .32 D1
Little Deans Yd SW1. . . . . .260 A6
Little Dell Lo 8 N3 . . . . . . .29 B1
Little Dimocks SW12. . . . . .159 B2
Little Dorrit Ct SE1 . . . . . . .252 B2
Little Ealing La W5. . . . . . .109 C2
Little Ealing Prim Sch 2
 W5 . . . . .109 C3
Little Edward St NW1 . . . . .231 D2
Little Elms UB3. . . . . .127 B5
Little Essex St WC2. . . . . .251 A6
Little Ferry Rd TW1 . . . . . .153 B3
Littlefield Cl
 9 Kingston u T KT1 . . . . .176 A1
 Tufnell Pk N19. . . . . .71 C4
Littlefield Ct UB7 . . . . . . .126 A5
Littlefield Ho KT1. . . . . . . .176 A1
Littlefield Rd HA8. . . . . . . .27 A3
Little Friday Rd E4 . . . . . . .20 C2
Little Gearies IG6. . . . . . . .56 D5
Little George St SW1. . . . . .250 A1
Little Gn TW9 . . . . .131 D1
Little Grange UB6. . . . . . . .87 A4
Little Green St NW5 . . . . . .71 B4
Littlegrove EN4 . . . . .14 C5
Littlegrove Ct 3 EN4. . . . . .14 C5
Little Halliards KT12 . . . . . .194 A3
Little Heath Ilford RM6. . . . .58 B5
LITTLE HEATH 58 B5
Little Heath DA7 . . . . .147 B5
Little Heath Sch RM6 . . . . .58 B5
Little Holt N11 . . . . .16 A4
Little Holt 10 E11 . . . . .55 A4
Little Ilford La E12 . . . . . . .78 B4
Little Ilford Sch E12. . . . . . .78 B3
Littlejohn Rd W7. . . . . .86 D1
Little Larkins EN5 . . . . .13 A5
Little London UB8 . . . . . . .82 D2
Little Marlborough St
 W1. . . . . .239 A1
Littlemead KT10 . . . . .212 B4
Littlemede SE9. . . . . .166 B1
Littlemoor Rd IG1 . . . . .79 B5
Littlemore Rd SE2 . . . . . . .124 A4
Little Moss La HA5. . . . . . .23 A1
Little Newport St WC2. . . . .249 D6
Little New St EC4 . . . . . . .241 B2
Little Oak Cl TW17 . . . . . .192 B5
Little Orchard Cl
 Esher KT10. . . . . .212 A5
 Pnr HA5 . . . . .23 A1
Little Oxhey La WD19. . . . . .23 A6
Little Park Dr TW13 . . . . . .151 A2
Little Park Gdns EN2 . . . . . .5 B2
Little Pluckett's Way IG9. . . .21 D3
Little Portland St W1. . . . . .239 A2
Little Potters WD23. . . . . . .8 C4
Little Queens Rd TW11 . . . .174 D4
Little Rd UB3 . . . . .105 A4
Little Redlands BR1. . . . . .188 A1
Littlers Cl SW19. . . . . . . .180 B2
Little Russell St WC1. . . . . .240 A1
Little St James's St SW1. . .249 A3
Little St Leonards SW14 . . .133 A2
Little Sanctuary SW1. . . . . .250 A1
Little Smith St SW1 . . . . . .259 D6
Little Somerset St E1 . . . . .243 C1
LITTLE STANMORE. 26 B2
Little Stanmore Fst & Mid
 Sch HA8 . . . . .26 B2
Littlestone Cl BR3. . . . . . .185 C4
Little Strand NW9. . . . . . . .27 D1
Little Thrift BR5. . . . . .211 A5
Little Titchfield St W1. . . . . .239 A3
LITTLETON. 192 C6
Littleton Ave E4 . . . . .20 D3
Littleton CE Inf Sch
 TW17 . . . . .192 C6
LITTLETON COMMON. 171 B3
Littleton Cres HA1. . . . . . . .64 D6
Littleton Ho 11. . . . . .171 A3
Littleton La TW17, TW18. . . .192 A4
Littleton Rd Harrow HA1 . . . .64 D6
 Littleton TW15, TW17 . . . .171 A3
Littleton St SW18 . . . . . . .158 A2
Little Trinity La EC4 . . . . . .252 B6
Little Turnstile WC1 . . . . . .240 C3
LITTLE VENICE. 92 A2
Little Venice*
 W9. . . . . .92 A2 236 A4
Littlewood SE13. . . . . .164 A5
Littlewood Cl W13. . . . . . .109 B3
Little Wood Cl BR5. . . . . . .190 A2
Littleworth Ave KT10. . . . . .212 B3
Littleworth Common Rd
 KT10 . . . . .212 B5
Littleworth La KT10 . . . . . .212 B5
Littleworth Pl KT10. . . . . . .212 B4
Littleworth Rd KT10. . . . . .212 C5
Livermere Ct 3 E8. . . . . . .95 D6

Livermere Rd E8. . . . . .95 D6
Liverpool Gr
 SE17. . . . . .117 B1 262 C1
Liverpool Ho N7 . . . . .72 C2
Liverpool Rd Ealing W5 . . . .109 D4
 Islington N1 . . . . .234 B5
 Islington N1, N7 . . . . .72 C1
 Kingston u T KT2. . . . . . .176 C3
 Leytonstone E10. . . . . . . .54 A3
 Newham E16 . . . . .98 C2
 South Norwood CR7 . . . . .205 A6
Liverpool St EC2. . . .95 C2 243 A3
Liverpool Street Sta
 EC2. . . . . .95 C2 243 A3
Livesey Cl
 Kingston u T KT1. . . . . . .198 B6
 Woolwich SE28. . . . . . . .123 A3
Livesey Pl SE15 . . . . .140 A6
Livingstone Ct
 Leytonstone E10. . . . . . . .54 A3
 Stanwell TW19 . . . . .148 A3
Livingstone Ho 18 SE5 . . . .139 A5
Livingstone Lo
 13 Paddington W9 . . . . . .91 C2
 Walthamstow E17 . . . . . . .35 C1
Livingstone Pl E14 . . . . . .120 A1
Livingstone Prim Sch EN4. . .2 B2
Livingstone Rd
 13 Battersea SW11. . . . . .136 B2
 Bowes Pk N13. . . . . .32 A5
 Hounslow TW3 . . . . .130 A1
 Mill Meads E15. . . . . .98 A6
 Southall UB1. . . . . .106 D6
 South Norwood CR7 . . . . .183 B1
 Walthamstow E17 . . . . . . .53 D3
Livity Sch The SW2. . . . . .160 A6
Livonia St W1. . . . . .239 B1
Lizard St EC1. . . . . .95 A4 235 B1
Lizban St SE3 . . . . .143 B5
Llandovery Ho 1 E14 . . . . .120 A4
Llanelly Rd NW2 . . . . .69 B6
Llanover Rd
 Shooters Hill SE18. . . . . .144 C5
 Wembley HA9. . . . . .65 D4
Llanthony Rd SM4 . . . . . . .202 B4
Llanvanor Rd NW2 . . . . . . .69 B6
Llewellyn Ct SE20 . . . . . . .184 C2
Llewellyn Ho 10 N19 . . . . . .71 C5
Llewellyn St SE16 . . . . . . .118 A4
L'Ile aux Enfants NW5. . . . .71 A3
Lloyd Ave SW16 . . . . .182 A2
Lloyd Baker St
 WC1. . . . . .94 C4 234 A1
Lloyd Ct Ladywell SE13 . . . .163 D6
 Pinner HA5. . . . . .24 A6
 6 West Norwood SE27 . . .160 D1
Lloyd Ho
 3 Beckenham BR3. . . . . .185 D4
 Bromley BR1. . . . . .187 B5
 Stoke Newington N16. . . . .73 B5
Lloyd Mews EN3 . . . . .7 C5
Lloyd Park Ave CR0 . . . . . .221 C4
Lloyd Park Ho E17 . . . . . . .53 C6
Lloyd Park Sta CR0. . . . . .221 D4
Lloyd Rd Dagenham RM9. . . .81 B1
 Newham E6 . . . . .100 B3
 North Cheam KT4, SM3 . . .216 D5
 Walthamstow E17 . . . . . . .52 D5
Lloyd's Ave EC3. . . . . . . .243 B1
Lloyd's Bldg* EC3. 95 C1 243 A1
Lloyd's Pl SE3. . . . . .142 C3
Lloyd Sq WC1. . . . . .94 C4 234 A2
Lloyd's Row EC1. . . .94 D4 234 C1
Lloyd St WC1. . . . . .94 C4 234 A2
Lloyds Way BR3. . . . . .207 B4
Lloyd Villas SE4 . . . . .141 C3
Lloyd Williamson Sch 17
 W10 . . . . .91 A2
Loampit Hill SE13 . . . . . . .141 D3
Loampit Vale SE13 . . . . . .142 A2
Loanda Ct 17 E8 . . . . .95 D6
Loats Rd SW2. . . . . .160 A5
Lobelia Cl E6 . . . . .100 A2
Locarno Cl 15 SW16. . . . . .181 C5
Locarno Rd 6 Acton W3 . . .111 A1
 Greenford UB6. . . . . .86 B3
Lochaber Rd SE13 . . . . . . .142 C1
Lochaline St W6 . . . . .134 C6
Lochan Cl UB4. . . . . .85 A3
Lochbie 9 N4 . . . . .50 A2
Lochinvar St SW12. . . . . . .159 B4
Lochleven Ho 9 N2. . . . . . .30 B1
Lochmere Cl DA8 . . . . . . .147 D6
Lochmore Ho SW1. . . . . . .258 B3
Lochnagar St E14. . . . . . . .98 A2
Lockbridge Ct 3 W9. . . . . .91 C2
Lock Chase SE3. . . . . . . .142 C2
Lock Cl UB2 . . . . .108 A4
Locke Ho Nine Elms SW8. . .269 D2
 Stamford Hill N16. . . . . . .51 D1
Lockesfield Pl E14 . . . . . . .119 D1
Lockesley Dr BR5. . . . . . . .211 D3
Lockesley Sq KT6 . . . . . . .197 D3
Locket Rd HA3 . . . . .24 D1
Locket Rd Ms HA3 . . . . . . .42 C6
Lockfield Ave EN3. . . . . . . .7 B4
Lockgate Cl E9 . . . . .75 B3

Lockhart Cl Barnsbury N7 . . . . **72** B2
　Enfield EN3 . . . . **18** B6
Lockhart Lo 4 E4 . . . . **20** C4
Lockhart St E3 . . . . **97** B3
Lockhurst St E5 . . . . **74** D4
Lockier Wlk HA9 . . . . **65** D5
Lockington Rd
　SW8 . . . . **137** B4 **268** D2
Lockmead Rd
　Lewisham SE13 . . . . **142** A2
　South Tottenham N15 . . . . . . **52** A3
Lock Mews 9 NW1 . . . . **71** D2
Lock Rd TW10 . . . . **175** C6
LOCKSBOTTOM **226** D5
Lockside E17 E14 . . . . **119** A6
Lock's La CR4 . . . . **181** A1
Locksley St E14 . . . . **97** B2
Locksmeade Rd TW10 . . . . . **175** C6
Lock View Ct 9 E14 . . . . **119** A6
Lockwell Rd RM10 . . . . **81** C5
Lockwood Cl Barnet EN4 . . . . **2** D1
　Forest Hill SE26 . . . . **184** D6
Lockwood Ct KT3 . . . . **199** A5
Lockwood Ho 10 SE11 . . . **138** C6
Lockwood Ind Pk N17 . . . . . **52** B6
Lockwood Pl E4 . . . . **35** C4
Lockwood Sq SE16 . . . . **118** B3
Lockwood Way
　Chessington KT9 . . . . **214** C3
　Higham Hill E17 . . . . **34** D1
Lockyer Cl EN3 . . . . **7** D5
Lockyer Est SE1 . . . . **252** D1
Lockyer Ho
　7 Greenwich SE10 . . . . . . **120** D1
　10 Putney SW15 . . . . **134** D2
　South Lambeth SW8 . . . . . . **270** A4
Lockyer St SE1 . . . . **252** D1
Locomotive Dr TW14 . . . . . **150** A4
Locton Gn 4 E3 . . . . **97** B6
Lodden Lo 13 SM2 . . . . **218** A1
Loddiges Ho 5 E9 . . . . **74** C1
Loddiges Rd E9 . . . . **74** C1
Loddon Ho NW8 . . . . **236** D5
Loder St SE15 . . . . **140** C5
Lodge Ave
　Borehamwood WD6 . . . . **10** B6
　Croydon CR0 . . . . **220** C5
　Dagenham RM8, RM9, IG11 . . **80** B3
　Harrow HA3 . . . . **44** A5
　Mortlake SW14 . . . . **133** C2
Lodge Cl Edgware HA8 . . . . . **26** C4
　Edmonton N18 . . . . **33** A4
　Hackbridge SM6 . . . . **203** A1
　Isleworth TW7 . . . . **131** B4
Lodge Ct 3 HA0 . . . . **66** A3
Lodge Dr N13 . . . . **32** C6
Lodge Gdns BR3 . . . . **207** B4
Lodge Hill
　East Wickham DA16 . . . . . . **146** B5
　Redbridge IG4 . . . . **56** A5
Lodgehill Park Cl HA2 . . . . . . **63** D6
Lodge La Bexley DA5 . . . . . . **168** D5
　New Addington CR0 . . . . . . **223** D1
　North Finchley N12 . . . . **30** A5
Lodge Mead Ct 5 N3 . . . . . . **29** D2
Lodge Pl SM1 . . . . **217** D3
Lodge Rd Bromley BR1 . . . . . **187** C3
　Hendon NW4 . . . . **46** C5
　Lisson Gr NW8 . . . . . **92** C4 **230** A1
　Sutton SM1 . . . . **217** D3
　Thornton Heath CR0 . . . . . . **204** D2
　Wallington SM6 . . . . **219** B3
Lodge The
　9 Chiswick W4 . . . . **111** C3
　1 Sutton SM1 . . . . **218** A4
Lodge Villas IG8 . . . . **36** D4
Lodge Way
　Charlton TW17 . . . . **171** A1
　Stanwell TW15 . . . . **148** A2
Lodore Gdns NW9 . . . . **45** C4
Lodore Gn UB10 . . . . **60** A5
Lodore St E14 . . . . **98** A1
Lodsworth Ho SW11 . . . . . . **268** A1
Lofthouse Pl KT9 . . . . **213** C2
Loftie St SE16 . . . . **118** A4
Lofting Ho 8 N1 . . . . **72** C1
Lofting Rd N1 . . . . **72** C1
Lofts on the Park 24 E9 . . . . **74** D2
Loftus Rd Barking IG11 . . . . . . **79** A2
　Shepherd's Bush W12 . . . . . **112** B5
Loftus Rd (Queens Park
　Rangers FC) W12 . . . . **112** B5
Logan Cl Enfield EN3 . . . . **6** D4
　Hounslow TW4 . . . . **129** B2
Logan Mews W8 . . . . **255** A4
Logan Pl W8 . . . . . **113** C2 **255** A4
Logan Rd Edmonton N9 . . . . . **18** B2
　Wembley HA9 . . . . **66** A4
Loggetts SE21 . . . . **161** C2
Logs Hill BR1, BR7 . . . . **188** A4
Logs Hill Cl BR7 . . . . **188** A2
Lohmann Ho 9 SE11 . . . . . . **138** C6
Lois Dr TW17 . . . . **192** D4
Lolesworth Cl E1 . . . . **243** D3
Lolland Ho 8 SE7 . . . . **122** A2
Lollard St SE11 . . . . **116** C2 **261** A3
Lollards Twr SE1 . . . . **260** C5

Loman St SE1 . . . . **116** D4 **251** D2
Lomas Cl CR0 . . . . **224** A1
Lomas Dr 10 E8 . . . . **73** D1
Lomas St E1 . . . . **96** A2
Lombard Ave Enfield EN3 . . . . **6** C4
　Ilford IG3 . . . . **57** C1
Lombard Bsns Pk
　Merton SW19 . . . . **179** D1
　Thornton Heath CR0 . . . . . . **204** B2
Lombard Ct 14 Acton W3 . . **110** D5
　City of London EC3 . . . . **252** D6
Lombard La EC4 . . . . **241** B1
Lombard Rd
　Battersea SW11 . . . . **136** B3
　Friern Barnet N11 . . . . **31** B5
　Merton SW19 . . . . **179** D1
Lombard Rdbt CR0 . . . . **204** B2
Lombard St EC3 . . . **95** B1 **242** D1
Lombard Trad Est SE7 . . . . . **121** B2
Lombard Wall SE7 . . . . **121** B2
Lombardy Pl W2 . . . . **245** D5
Lombardy Ret Pk UB3 . . . . . **106** B6
Lomley Ho 10 SW2 . . . . **160** C5
Lomond Cl Tottenham N15 . . **51** C4
　Wembley HA0 . . . . **66** B1
Lomond Ct HA3 . . . . **42** D6
Lomond Gdns CR2 . . . . **223** A1
Lomond Gr SE5 . . . . **139** B5
Lomond Ho 10 SE5 . . . . **139** B4
Loncroft Rd SE5 . . . . **139** C6
Londesborough Ho 1
　N16 . . . . **73** C4
Londesborough Rd N16 . . . . . **73** C4
London Academy UB4 . . . . . **26** B6
London Acad for Higher
　Education The E15 . . . . **98** B6
London Acad of Computing
　& Electronics SW17 . . . . . **158** D1
London Bridge EC4,
　SE1 . . . . **117** B5 **252** D5
London Bridge City Pier
　SE1 . . . . **117** C5 **253** A4
London Bridge Experience
　The SE1 . . . . **252** D4
London Bridge Hospl
　SE1 . . . . **252** D4
London Bridge St
　SE1 . . . . **117** B5 **252** D5
London Bridge Sta
　SE1 . . . . **117** B5 **252** D5
London Bridge Wlk SE1 . . . . **252** D4
London Britannia Coll
　N1 . . . . **95** B4 **235** C2
London Business Sch
　NW1 . . . . **92** D3 **237** C6
London Canal Mus *
　N1 . . . . **94** A3 **233** B4
London Central Mosque *
　NW8 . . . . **92** C4 **230** B1
London Chest Hospl E2 . . . . **96** C5
London Christian Sch
　SE16 . . . . **118** C3
London City Airport E16 . . . **122** B5
London City Airport Sta
　E16 . . . . **122** A5
London City Sh Ctr EC1 . . . **242** B5
London Clinic (Hospl)
　NW1 . . . . **93** A3 **238** B5
London Coll of Advanced
　Studies SE1 . . . . **252** C2
London Coll of Beauty
　Therapy W1 . . . . . **93** C1 **239** B1
London Coll of Bsns &
　Computer Studies 12
　SW4 . . . . **137** D1
London Coll of
　Communication (Sch of
　Printing & Publishing)
　SE11 . . . . **116** D3 **261** D6
London Coll of Economics &
　Science NW10 . . . . **89** A3
London Coll of Fashion
　(Curtain Rd) EC2 . **95** C3 **243** B6
London Coll of Fashion
　(Davies St) W1 . . . . **238** C1
London Coll of Fashion
　(Golden La) EC1 . **95** A3 **242** A5
London Coll of Fashion
　(John Prince's St) W1 . **238** D2
London Coll of Fashion
　(Lime Grove) 18 W6 . . **112** C4
London Coll of Fashion
　(Mare St) E8 . . . . **74** C1
London Coll of International
　Business Studies WC1 . **240** B3
London Coll of Tech IG2 . . **56** C3
London Ct 3 SW18 . . . . **157** C6
London Dungeon The *
　SE1 . . . . **117** B5 **252** D4
London Electronics Coll
　SW5 . . . . **113** D1 **255** C2
London Eye (Millennium
　Wheel) * SE1 . . . **116** B4 **250** C2
London Fields East Side
　E8 . . . . **74** B1
London Fields Prim Sch 16
　E8 . . . . **96** B6
London Fields Sta E8 . . . . . . **74** B1
London Fields West Side
　E8 . . . . **74** A1

London Fire Brigade Mus *
　SE1 . . . . **252** A2
London Glassblowing
　Workshop SE1 . . . . **253** A1
London Group Bsns Pk
　NW2 . . . . **46** A1
London Ho Edgware HA8 . . **26** A6
　13 Hammersmith W6 . . . . **112** A2
　London Ho TW9 . . . . **132** B2
London Ho NW8 . . . . **230** B4
London Hospital Dental Inst
　5 E1 . . . . **96** B2
London Independent Hospl
　The E1 . . . . **96** D2
London Inst The SW17 . . . . **181** B5
London International Film
　Sch WC2 . . . . **94** A1 **240** A1
London Irish Rifles Mus *
　SW9 . . . . **139** A4
London Jewish Girls High
　Sch NW4 . . . . **46** C4
London La Bromley BR1 . . . **186** D3
　Hackney E8 . . . . **74** B1
London Meridian Coll 2
　N7 . . . . **72** B5
London Metrocity Coll 21
　E3 . . . . **97** E3
London Metropolitan Univ
　Islington N7 . . . . **72** C3
　Whitechapel E1 . . . **95** D1 **243** C1
　Whitechapel E1 . . . **95** D1 **243** C2
London Metropolitan Univ
　(Central Ho) 44 E1 . . . . . . **96** A1
London Metropolitan Univ
　(Commercial Rd) 42 E1 . . **96** A1
London Metropolitan Univ
　(Ladbrook Ho) 5 N5 . . . **72** D3
London Metropolitan Univ
　(Moorgate) EC2 . . **95** B2 **242** D3
London Metropolitan Univ
　(Tower Hill) EC3 . . . . **253** C6
London Metropolitan Univ
　(Spring Ho) 1 N7 . . . . **72** C2
London Mews W2 . . . . **236** D2
London Motorcycle Mus *
　UB6 . . . . **86** A4
London Nautical Sch
　SE1 . . . . **116** C5 **251** B4
London Oratory Sch The
　SW6 . . . . **135** C3 **265** B4
London Oratory The *
　SW7 . . . . **114** C3 **257** A5
London Rd
　Ashford TW15, TW18, TW19,
　TW14 . . . . **148** B2
　Brentford TW7, TW8 . . . . . **131** B4
　Bromley BR1 . . . . **186** D3
　Carshalton CR4 . . . . **203** A2
　Enfield EN2 . . . . **5** B1
　Forest Hill SE22, SE23 . . . **162** C3
　Hackbridge SM6, CR4 . . . . **219** B6
　Harrow HA1 . . . . **64** C6
　Hounslow TW3, TW7, TW1,
　TW8 . . . . **130** B3
　Kingston u T KT1, KT2 . . . . **176** B1
　Lambeth SE1 . . . . . **116** D3 **261** D6
　Mitcham CR4 . . . . **180** D2
　Morden SM4 . . . . **201** C5
　Newham E13 . . . . **99** A5
　Romford RM7, RM8 . . . . **59** C5
　Stanmore HA7 . . . . **25** D6
　Stoneleigh KT17, KT4, SM3 . **216** B3
　Thornton Heath CR0, CR7,
　SW16 . . . . **204** C3
　Twickenham TW1 . . . . **153** A4
　Wembley HA9 . . . . **66** A2
London Road Rdbt TW1 . . . **153** A5
London Sch of Economics &
　Political Science
　WC2 . . . . **94** B1 **240** D1
London Sch of Jewish
　Studies 5 NW4 . . . . **46** D5
London South Bank Univ
　SE1 . . . . **116** D3 **261** D6
London St
　City of London EC3 . . . . . . **253** B6
　Paddington W2 . . . . **92** B1 **236** C1
London Stile 4 W4 . . . . **110** C1
London Stock Exchange *
　EC2 . . . . **242** D3
London Stone Bsns Est 15
　SW11 . . . . **137** A3
London Terr 1 E2 . . . . **96** A5
London Tottenham Coll 12
　N17 . . . . **33** D3
London Transport Mus *
　WC2 . . . . **250** B6
London Trocadero * W1, SE1
London Wall EC2 . . **95** B2 **242** D3
London Wall Bldgs EC2 . . **242** D3
London Wetland Ctr *
　SW13 . . . . **134** B4
London Wetland Visitor Ctr *
　SW13 . . . . **134** B4
London Wharf 4 E2 . . . . **96** B5
London Zoo *
　NW1 . . . . **93** A5 **231** A4
Lonesome Prim Sch
　CR4 . . . . **181** B1
Lonesome Way CR4 . . . . . **181** C2

Long Acre WC2 . . . . **94** A1 **240** B1
Long Acre Ct W13 . . . . **87** A2
Longacre Pl SM5 . . . . **219** A2
Longacre Rd E17 . . . . **36** B2
Longbeach Rd SW11 . . . . . . **136** D2
Longberrys NW2 . . . . **69** B5
Longboat Row UB1 . . . . **85** B1
Longbridge Ho RM8 . . . . **80** B4
Longbridge Rd
　Barking IG11 . . . . **79** C3
　Dagenham RM8 . . . . **80** B4
Longbridge Way SE13 . . . . **164** A6
Longbury Dr BR5 . . . . **190** B1
Longchamp Ct 13 HA7 . . . . **25** C5
Longcliffe Ho SW18 . . . . . . **157** D6
Longcroft SE9 . . . . **166** C1
Longcrofte Rd HA8 . . . . **25** D3
Long Deacon Rd E4 . . . . **20** C3
LONG DITTON **197** C1
Long Ditton City Inf Sch
　KT6 . . . . **197** C1
Longdon Wood BR2 . . . . . . **226** A4
Longdown Rd SE6 . . . . **185** C6
Long Dr Dagenham W3 . . . . . **89** C1
　Greenford UB6 . . . . **85** D6
　Ruislip HA4 . . . . **62** D4
Long Elmes HA3 . . . . **24** A2
Longfellow Rd
　North Cheam KT4 . . . . **200** B1
　Walthamstow E17 . . . . **53** B3
Longfellow Way SE1 . . . . . **263** D3
Longfield
　3 Bromley BR1 . . . . **186** D2
　Loughton IG10 . . . . **21** C6
Long Field NW9 . . . . **27** D3
Longfield Ave Ealing W5 . . . **109** C6
　Enfield EN3 . . . . **6** C5
　Hackbridge SM6 . . . . **203** A1
　Hendon NW7 . . . . **28** A3
　Walthamstow E17 . . . . **53** A5
　Wembley HA9 . . . . **44** A1
Longfield Cres SE23,
　SE26 . . . . **162** C1
Longfield Ct 4 N2 . . . . **48** A6
Longfield Dr
　Mitcham SW19 . . . . **180** C2
　Mortlake SW14 . . . . **154** D6
Longfield Est SE1 . . . . **263** D3
Longfield Fst & Mid Schs
　HA2 . . . . **41** C3
Longfield Ho Ealing W5 . . . . **109** C6
　Walthamstow E17 . . . . **53** B4
Longfield Rd W5 . . . . **87** C1
Longfield St SW18 . . . . **157** C4
Longford Ave
　Feltham TW14 . . . . **149** D5
　Southall UB1 . . . . **107** D6
　Stanwell TW19 . . . . **148** A3
Longford Cl
　Feltham TW13 . . . . **151** A1
　Hampton TW12 . . . . **173** C6
　Hayes UB4 . . . . **106** D6
Longford Com Sch
　TW14 . . . . **149** D4
Longford Ct
　1 Bedford Pk W12 . . . . . . **111** C4
　2 Clapton Pk E5 . . . . **74** D4
　Hampton TW12 . . . . **173** C6
　9 Hendon NW4 . . . . **46** C5
　Southall UB1 . . . . **107** C5
　West Ewell KT19 . . . . **215** A4
Longford Gdns
　Hayes UB4 . . . . **106** D6
　Sutton SM1 . . . . **218** A6
Longford Ho
　1 Catford BR1 . . . . **186** B5
　Hampton TW12 . . . . **173** C6
　7 Stepney E1 . . . . **96** C1
Longford Ind Est TW12 . . . **173** D4
Longford Rd TW2 . . . . **151** D3
Longford St NW1 . . . **93** B3 **238** D6
Longford Way TW19 . . . . . . **148** A3
Longford Wlk 9 SW2 . . . . . **160** C4
Longhayes Ave RM6 . . . . **58** D5
Longhayes Ct RM6 . . . . **58** D5
Longheath Gdns CR0 . . . . . **206** C4
Longhedge Ho SE26 . . . . . **184** A6
Longhedge St SW11 . . . . . . **137** A3
Longhill Rd SE6 . . . . **164** B1
Long Ho SM5 . . . . **218** C6
Longhook Gdns UB5 . . . . . . **84** B4
Longhope Cl SE15 . . . . **139** B6
Longhurst Ho 8 W9 . . . . **91** B4
Longhurst Rd
　Croydon CR0 . . . . **206** B3
　Lewisham SE13 . . . . **164** C6
Long La
　Bermondsey SE1 . . **117** B4 **252** D1
　Croydon CR0 . . . . **206** C3
　East Finchley N2 . . . . **48** B6
　Erith DA7 . . . . **147** B4
　Finchley N3 . . . . **29** D2
　Hillingdon UB10 . . . . **82** B4
　Holborn EC1 . . . . . . **94** D2 **241** D4
　Stanwell TW15, TW19 . . . . **148** B3

Longlands Ct
　Higham Hill E17 . . . . **35** A2
　Mitcham CR4 . . . . **181** A2
　Notting Hill W11 . . . . **244** D6
　Sidcup DA15 . . . . **167** D1
Longlands Park Cres
　DA15 . . . . **167** C2
Longlands Prim Sch
　DA15 . . . . **167** C1
Longlands Rd DA15 . . . . **167** C1
Longleat Ct 3 DA6 . . . . **147** A1
Longleat Ho SW1 . . . . **259** C2
Longleat Rd EN1 . . . . **17** C6
Longleat Way TW14 . . . . . . **149** B4
Longleigh Ho 8 SE5 . . . . . . **139** C4
Longleigh La SE2, DA7 . . . . **146** C6
Longlents Ho 3 NW10 . . . . . **89** B6
Longley Ave HA0 . . . . **88** B6
Longley Ho 5 N19 . . . . **71** C4
Longley Rd Harrow HA1 . . . . **42** B5
　Thornton Heath CR0 . . . . . . **204** D2
　Upper Tooting SW17 . . . . . **180** D4
Long Leys E4 . . . . **36** A4
Longley St SE1 . . . . **118** A2
Longley Way NW2 . . . . **68** C5
Longman Ho
　9 Globe Town E2 . . . . **96** D5
　10 Shoreditch E8 . . . . **95** D6
Long Mark Rd 5 E16 . . . . . . **99** D2
Longmarsh La SE28 . . . . . . **123** C5
Longmead BR7 . . . . **188** C1
Long Mead NW9 . . . . **27** D2
Longmead Dr DA14 . . . . **168** D2
Longmead Ho SE27 . . . . **183** A5
Long Meadow 20 N7 . . . . . . **71** D3
Long Meadow Cl BR3,
　BR4 . . . . **208** A2
Longmeadow Rd DA15 . . . . **167** C3
Longmead Prim Sch
　UB7 . . . . **104** A2
Longmead Rd
　Hayes UB3 . . . . **105** D6
　Thames Ditton KT7 . . . . . . **196** D2
　Upper Tooting SW17 . . . . . **180** D5
Longmoor Point 14
　SW15 . . . . **156** B3
Longmore Ave EN4, EN5 . . . **14** B5
Longmore St
　SW1 . . . . **115** C2 **259** A3
Longnor Rd E1 . . . . **96** D4
Long Pond Rd SE3 . . . . **142** C4
Long Rd SW4 . . . . **137** C1
Longreach Ct IG11 . . . . **101** B5
Long Reach Rd IG11 . . . . . . **101** D3
Longridge Ho SE1 . . . . **262** B5
Longridge La UB1 . . . . **85** D1
Longridge Rd
　SW5 . . . . **113** C2 **255** B3
Long Ridges N2 . . . . **49** A6
Longs Ct 2 TW9 . . . . **132** B1
Long's Ct W1 . . . . **249** D5
Longshaw Prim Sch E4 . . . . **20** B1
Longshaw Rd E4 . . . . **20** B1
Longshore SE8 . . . . **119** B2
Long St E2 . . . . **95** D4
Longstaff Cres SW18 . . . . . **157** C4
Longstaff Rd SW18 . . . . **157** C5
Longstone Ave NW10 . . . . . . **89** C6
Longstone Rd SW17 . . . . . . **181** B5
Longthorne Ho 18 E3 . . . . . . **97** B4
Longthornton Rd SW16 . . . **181** D1
Longthorpe Ct 9 W6 . . . . . . **112** A2
Longton Ave SE26 . . . . **184** A6
Longton Gr SE26 . . . . **184** B6
Longville Rd SE11 . . . . **261** D4
Longwalk Rd UB11 . . . . **104** D5
Long Wlk Bermondsey SE1 . **263** D3
　Kingston u T KT3 . . . . **199** A6
　Shooters Hill SE18 . . . . **144** D6
Longwood Bsns Pk
　TW16 . . . . **193** D4
Longwood Dr SW15 . . . . . . **156** A5
Longwood Gdns IG2, IG6,
　IG5 . . . . **56** C6
Longwood Par RM6 . . . . **56** D6
Longworth Cl SE28 . . . . **102** D1
Long Yd WC1 . . . . . **94** B3 **240** C5
Loning The Enfield EN3 . . . . . **6** C5
　Hyde The NW9 . . . . **45** D5
Lonsdale Ave
　Newham E6 . . . . **100** A3
　Wembley HA9 . . . . **66** A4
Lonsdale Cl Edgware HA8 . . . **26** B5
　Hillingdon UB8 . . . . **83** A2
　Mottingham SE12 . . . . **165** D1
　Newham E6 . . . . **100** A3
　Pinner HA5 . . . . **23** A2
Lonsdale Cres IG2 . . . . **56** D3
Lonsdale Dr EN2 . . . . **16** A6
Lonsdale Dr N EN2 . . . . **4** A1
Lonsdale Gdns CR7,
　SW16 . . . . **204** C3
Lonsdale Ho
　Fulham SW6 . . . . **135** C2
　4 Stoke Newington N4 . . . **51** A2
Lonsdale Mews
　Notting Hill W11 . . . . **91** B1
　4 Richmond TW9 . . . . **132** C4
Lonsdale Pl N1 . . . . **72** C1

Lonsdale Rd
Barnes SW13 . . . . 133 D5
Bexley DA7 . . . . 147 B3
Chiswick W4 . . . . 111 D2
Croydon SE25 . . . . 206 B5
Kilburn NW6 . . . . 91 B6
Leytonstone E11 . . . . 54 D2
Notting Hill W11 . . . . 91 B1
Southall UB2 . . . . 106 D3
Lonsdale Sq Islington N1 . . 72 C1
Islington N1 . . . . **234 B6**
Loobert Rd N15 . . . . 51 C6
Looe Gdns IG6 . . . . 56 D6
Loop Rd BR7 . . . . 189 A4
Lopen Rd N18 . . . . 33 C6
Lopen Works N18 . . . . 33 C6
Lopez Ho 4 SW9 . . . . 138 A2
Lorac Ct 13 SM2 . . . . 217 C1
Loraine Cl EN3 . . . . 18 C6
Loraine Ct BR7 . . . . 188 D5
Loraine Ho 1 SM5 . . . . . . 219 B4
Loraine Ho Chiswick W4 . . 132 D6
Islington N7 . . . . 72 B4
Lord Ave IG5 . . . . 56 B6
Lord Chancellor Wlk
KT2 . . . . 177 A2
Lord David Pitt Ho 8
SE24 . . . . 138 C1
Lordell Pl SW19 . . . . 178 C4
Lorden Wlk 13 E2 . . . . 96 A4
Lord Gdns IG5 . . . . 56 B5
Lord Hills Rd W2 . . . . 91 D2
Lord Holland La 5 SW9 . . 138 C3
Lord Knyvetts Ct 3
TW19 . . . . 148 A5
Lord Napier Pl W6 . . . . . . 112 A1
Lord North St SW1 . . . . . . 260 A5
Lord Roberts Mews SW6 265 C3
Lord Roberts Terr SE18 . . 122 C1
Lords Cl Feltham TW13 . . . 151 A2
West Norwood SE21 . . . . . 161 A2
Lord's Cricket Mus★
NW8 . . . . 92 B4 **229 D1**
Lords Ct 3 HA8 . . . . 27 A3
Lordship Gr N16 . . . . 73 B6
Lordship Ho 3 N16 . . . . . . 73 B6
Lordship La
Dulwich Village SE22 . . . . 161 D5
Tottenham N22 . . . . 33 B2
Lordship Lane Prim Sch 1
N22 . . . . 33 A2
Lordship Park Mews N16 . 73 A6
Lordship Pk N16 . . . . 73 B6
Lordship Pl SW3 . . . . **267 A5**
Lordship Rd Northolt UB5 . 63 A1
Stoke Newington N16 . . . . 73 B6
Lordship Terr N16 . . . . 73 B6
Lord's Indoor Cricket Sch
NW8 . . . . **230 A2**
**Lord's (MCC & Middlesex Cty
Cricket Ground)★**
NW8 . . . . 92 B4 **229 D2**
Lordsmead Rd N17 . . . . 33 C1
Lord St E16 . . . . 122 A5
Lord's View NW8 . . . . **229 D1**
Lord Warwick St SE18 . . . 122 B3
Loreburn Rd N7 . . . . 72 B4
Lorenzo St N1, WC1 . . . . . **233 C2**
Loretto Gdns HA3 . . . . 44 A5
Lorian Cl N12 . . . . 29 D6
Loring Rd East Barnet N20 . 14 C2
Isleworth TW7 . . . . 130 D3
Loris Rd W6 . . . . 112 C3
Lorn Ct SW9 . . . . 138 C3
Lorne Ave CR0 . . . . 206 D2
Lorne Cl NW8 . . . . . 92 C4 **230 B1**
Lorne Ct Harrow HA1 . . . . . 42 C2
Putney SW15 . . . . 156 D5
Lorne Gdns Croydon CR0 . 206 D2
5 Hammersmith W11 . . . . 112 D4
Wanstead E11 . . . . 55 C5
Lorne Ho
Friern Barnet N11 . . . . 31 B5
Hornsey N4 . . . . 50 B2
7 Tower Hamlets E1 . . . . . 97 A2
Lorne Rd Finsbury Pk N4 . . 50 B1
Forest Gate E7 . . . . 77 C4
Harrow HA3 . . . . 24 D1
3 Richmond TW10 . . . . . 154 B6
Walthamstow E17 . . . . 53 C4
Lorn Rd SW9 . . . . 138 C3
Lorraine Ct
Beckenham BR3 . . . . 186 A2
5 Belmont SM2 . . . . 217 C1
10 Camden Town NW1 . . . 71 B1
Lorraine Pk HA3 . . . . 24 C3
Lorrimore Rd SE17 . . . . . . 138 D6
Lorrimore Sq SE17 . . . . . . 138 D6
Lorton Ho 10 NW6 . . . . . . 91 C6
Loseberry Rd KT10 . . . . . . 212 B3
Lostock Ho 10 SW8 . . . . . 137 D3
Lothair Rd W5 . . . . 109 D4
Lothair Rd N N4 . . . . 50 D3
Lothair Rd S N4 . . . . 50 D2
Lothbury EC2 . . . . . 95 B1 **242 C2**
Lothian Ave UB4 . . . . 84 B2
Lothian Cl HA0 . . . . 65 A5
Lothian Rd SW9 . . . . 138 D4
Lothrop St W10 . . . . 91 A4
Lots Rd SW10 . . . . . 136 A5 **266 B3**

Loubet St SW17 . . . . 180 D4
Loudoun Ave IG6 . . . . 56 D4
Loudoun Rd NW8 . . 92 A6 **229 B5**
Loudwater Cl TW16 . . . . . . 194 A5
Loudwater Rd TW16 . . . . . 194 A5
Loughborough Ct 7
SW9 . . . . 138 D2
Loughborough Junction Sta
SW9 . . . . 138 D2
Loughborough Pk SW9 . . . 138 D1
Loughborough Prim Sch
SW9 . . . . 138 D3
Loughborough Rd SE5,
SW9 . . . . 138 D3
Loughborough St
SE11 . . . . 116 B2 **260 D1**
Lough Rd N7 . . . . 72 B2
LOUGHTON 21 D5
Loughton Way IG9 . . . . 21 D3
Louie Black Ho 4
SW19 . . . . 179 A3
Louisa Ct E9 . . . . 96 D6
Louisa Ct
Twickenham TW2 . . . . 152 C2
Wood Green N11 . . . . 31 D3
Louisa Gdns E1 . . . . 96 D3
Louisa Ho SW15 . . . . 133 D1
Louisa St E1 . . . . 96 D3
Louis Ct 3 EN1 . . . . 81 D2
Louise Bennett Cl 9
SE24 . . . . 138 D1
Louise Ct Bexley DA6 . . . . 147 A1
4 Wanstead E11 . . . . 55 B4
Wood Green N22 . . . . 32 C2
Louise De Marillac Ho 26
E1 . . . . 96 C2
Louise Graham Ho 5
IG11 . . . . 101 B6
Louise Rd E15 . . . . 76 C2
Louise White Ho 1 N19 . . 49 D1
Louis Gdns BR7 . . . . 188 B6
Louis Mews N10 . . . . 31 B2
Louisville Rd SW17 . . . . . . 159 A1
Lousada Lo N14 . . . . 15 C5
Louvaine Rd SW11 . . . . . . 136 B1
Lovage App E6 . . . . 100 A2
Lovat Cl NW2 . . . . 67 D5
Lovat Ct E3 . . . . **253 A5**
Lovatt Cl HA8 . . . . 26 D4
Lovatt Ct SW12 . . . . 159 B3
Lovatt Dr HA4 . . . . 39 D4
Lovatt Wlk TW5 . . . . 129 A5
Loveday Ho 2 SW2 . . . . . 160 C3
Loveday Rd W13 . . . . 109 B5
Lovegrove St SE1 . . . . 140 A6
Lovegrove Wlk E14 . . . . . . 120 A5
Lovekyn Cl KT2 . . . . 176 B1
Love La Cheam SM3 . . . . . 217 A2
City of London EC2 . . 95 A1 **242 B2**
Croydon SE25 . . . . 206 B6
Long Ditton KT6 . . . . 213 D6
Mitcham SW19 . . . . 202 C6
Morden SM4 . . . . 201 D2
Old Bexley DA5 . . . . 169 C5
Pinner HA5 . . . . 41 A6
Tottenham N17 . . . . 33 D3
Woolwich SE18 . . . . 122 D2
Lovelace Gdns
Barking IG11 . . . . 80 A4
Surbiton KT6 . . . . 197 D2
Lovelace Gn SE9 . . . . 144 B2
Lovelace Ho 12 E8 . . . . 95 D6
Lovelace Prim Sch KT9 . . . 213 C3
Lovelace Rd
East Barnet EN4 . . . . 14 C4
Surbiton KT6 . . . . 197 D2
West Norwood SE21 . . . . . 161 A3
Loveland Mans 7 IG11 . . . 79 D1
Lovel Ave DA16 . . . . 146 A3
Lovelinch Cl SE15 . . . . 140 C6
Lovell Ho Hackney E8 . . . . 96 A6
4 Merton SW19 . . . . 180 A2
Lovell Pl SE16 . . . . 119 A3
Lovell Rd Richmond TW10 . 153 C1
Southall UB1 . . . . 85 D1
Loveridge Mews NW6 . . . . 69 B2
Loveridge Rd NW6 . . . . . . 69 B2
Lover's Wlk W1 . . . . 115 A5 **248 A3**
Lovett Dr SM5 . . . . 202 B2
Lovette Ho 4 E3 . . . . 97 C4
Lovetts Pl SW18 . . . . 135 D1
Lovett Way NW10 . . . . 67 A3
Love Wlk SE5 . . . . 139 B3
Lovibonds Ave
Hillingdon UB7 . . . . 82 B1
Locksbottom BR6 . . . . . . 226 D5
Lowbrook Rd IG1 . . . . 78 D4
Low Cross Wood La
SE21 . . . . 161 D1
Lowdell Cl UB7 . . . . 82 A1
Lowden Rd Edmonton N9 . . 18 B3
Herne Hill SE24 . . . . 139 A1
Southall UB1 . . . . 107 A6
Lowder Ho 6 E1 . . . . 118 B5
Lowe Ave E16 . . . . 99 A2
Lowell Ho 10 SE5 . . . . 139 A5
Lowell St E14 . . . . 97 A1
Lower Addiscombe Rd
CR0 . . . . 205 C1

Lower Addison Gdns
W14 . . . . 113 A4 **244 A1**
Lower Belgrave St
SW1 . . . . 115 B3 **258 C5**
Lower Boston Rd W7 . . . . . 108 C4
Lower Broad St RM10 . . . . 103 C6
Lower Camden BR7 . . . . . . 188 B2
Lower Church St CR0 . . . . 220 D6
LOWER CLAPTON 74 C4
Lower Clapton Rd E5 . . . . . 74 C4
Lower Clarendon Wlk 9
W11 . . . . 91 A1
Lower Comm S SW15 . . . . 134 B2
Lower Coombe St CR0 . . . 221 A4
Lower Downs Rd SW20 . . . 178 D2
LOWER EDMONTON 18 B1
LOWER FELTHAM 149 D1
Lower Fosters NW4 . . . . . . 46 C4
Lower George St 13
TW10 . . . . 153 D6
Lower Gn W CR4 . . . . 202 C6
Lower Gravel Rd BR2 . . . . 210 B1
LOWER GREEN 195 C1
Lower Green Gdns KT4 . . . 200 A1
Lower Green Rd KT10 . . . . 212 A6
Lower Grosvenor Pl
SW1 . . . . 115 B3 **258 D6**
Lower Grove Rd TW10 . . . . 154 B6
LOWER HALLIFORD 193 C3
Lower Hall La E4 . . . . 35 A6
Lower Hampton Rd TW12,
TW16 . . . . 172 D1
Lower Ham Rd KT2 . . . . . . 175 D4
LOWER HOLLOWAY 72 A3
Lower James St W1 . . . . . . **249 B6**
Lower John St W1 . . . . **249 B6**
Lower Kenwood Ave EN2 . . 16 A6
Lower Kings Rd KT2 . . . . . 176 A3
Lower Lea Crossing E14,
E16 . . . . 120 C6
Lower Maidstone Rd N11 . . 31 C4
Lower Mall W6 . . . . 112 B1
Lower Marsh
SE1 . . . . 116 C4 **251 A1**
Lower Marsh La KT1,
KT5 . . . . 198 C5
Lower Merton Rise NW3 . . 70 C1
LOWER MORDEN 201 A2
Lower Morden La SM4 . . . . 201 A2
Lower Mortlake Rd TW9 . . 132 B2
Lower Park Rd
Belvedere DA17 . . . . 125 C2
Friern Barnet N11 . . . . 31 C5
2 Loughton IG10 . . . . 21 D6
Putney SW15 . . . . 156 D6
5 Putney SW15 . . . . 89 A5
LOWER PLACE 89 A5
Lower Place Bsns Ctr
NW10 . . . . 89 A5
Lower Queen's Rd IG9 . . . . 21 D2
Lower Rd
Belvedere DA17 . . . . 125 D3
Finchley N2 . . . . 30 B2
Harrow HA2 . . . . 42 B1
Rotherhithe SE16 . . . . 118 C4
Sutton SM1 . . . . 218 A4
Lower Richmond Rd
Mortlake SW14, TW9 . . . . 132 D2
Putney SW15 . . . . 134 C3
Lower Robert St WC2 . . . . **250 B5**
Lower Sand Hills KT6 . . . . 197 C2
Lower Sloane St
SW1 . . . . 115 A1 **258 A2**
Lower Sq TW7 . . . . 131 B2
Lower Strand NW9 . . . . 27 D1
Lower Sunbury Rd
TW12 . . . . 173 C1
LOWER SYDENHAM 185 A6
Lower Sydenham Sta
SE26 . . . . 185 B5
Lower Teddington Rd
KT1 . . . . 175 D2
Lower Terr NW3 . . . . 70 A5
Lower Thames St
EC3 . . . . 117 C6 **253 A5**
Lower Tub WD23 . . . . 8 B4
Lowerwood Ct W11 . . . . . . 91 A1
Lower Wood Rd KT10 . . . . 213 B2
Lowestoft Cl 5 E5 . . . . 74 C6
Lowestoft Mews E16 . . . . . 122 D4
Loweswater Cl HA9 . . . . . . 65 D6
Loweswater Ho 8 E3 . . . . . 97 B3
Lowfield Rd
Dagenham W3 . . . . 89 A1
Hampstead NW6 . . . . 69 C1
Low Hall Cl E4 . . . . 19 D4
Low Hall La E17 . . . . 53 A3
Lowick Rd HA1 . . . . 42 C4
Lowland Gdns RM7 . . . . . . 59 D3
Lowlands NW3 . . . . 70 C2
Lowlands Ct NW7 . . . . 27 D5
Lowlands Rd Harrow HA1 . . 42 C2
Pinner HA5 . . . . 40 C3
Lowman Rd N7 . . . . 72 B4
Lowndes Cl SW1 . . . . **258 B5**
Lowndes Ct
Knightsbridge SW1 . . . . . **257 D6**
Marylebone W1 . . . . **239 A1**
Lowndes Lo Barnet EN5 . . . 1 D2
Lowndes Pl
SW1 . . . . **257 D6**

Lowndes Pl SW1 . . 115 A3 **258 A5**
Lowndes Sq
SW1 . . . . 114 D4 **247 D1**
Lowndes St SW1 . . 115 A3 **258 A6**
Lownds Ct BR1 . . . . 187 A1
Lowood Ct SE19 . . . . 183 D5
Lowood Ho 12 E1 . . . . 118 C6
Lowood St E1 . . . . 118 B6
Lowry Cres CR4 . . . . 180 C1
Lowry Ct 3 SE16 . . . . 118 B1
Lowry Ho 1 N17 . . . . 33 D2
Lowry Lo 1 HA0 . . . . 65 D3
Lowry Rd RM8 . . . . 80 B3
Lowther Cl WD6 . . . . 10 B6
Lowther Dr EN2 . . . . 4 A1
Lowther Hill SE23 . . . . 163 A4
Lowther Ho Pimlico SW1 . . **259 B1**
11 Shoreditch E8 . . . . 95 D6
Lowther Prim Sch
SW13 . . . . 134 A6
Lowther Rd
Barnes SW13 . . . . 133 D4
Higham Hill E17 . . . . 35 A1
Islington N7 . . . . 72 C3
Kingston u T KT2 . . . . 176 B2
Stanmore HA7 . . . . 44 B6
Lowth Rd SE5 . . . . 139 A3
Lowton Lo E17 . . . . 53 A6
LOXFORD 79 A3
Loxford Ave E6 . . . . 99 D5
Loxford Ho SW1 . . . . **258 B3**
Loxford La IG1 . . . . 79 B3
Loxford Rd IG11 . . . . 78 D2
**Loxford Sch of Science &
Tech** IG1 . . . . 79 B3
Loxham Rd E4 . . . . 35 D3
Loxham St WC1 . . . . **233 B1**
Loxley Cl SE26 . . . . 184 D5
Loxley Hall E11 . . . . 54 C2
Loxley Ho HA9 . . . . 66 A5
Loxley Rd Feltham TW12 . . 173 B6
Wandsworth SW18 . . . . . 158 B3
Loxton Rd SE23 . . . . 163 A3
Loxwood Cl TW14 . . . . 149 B3
Loxwood Rd N17 . . . . 51 C6
Loyola Prep Sch IG9 . . . . . 21 C3
LTC Coll London W1 . . . . . **239 A2**
Lubavitch Boys Prim Sch 6
E5 . . . . 51 D2
Lubavitch Girls Prim Sch 8
N16 . . . . 51 D2
**Lubavitch House Sch (Jun
Boys) 9** E5 . . . . 51 D2
Lubbock Ct BR7 . . . . 188 B3
Lubbock Ho
21 Canary Wharf E14 . . . . 119 D6
Orpington BR6 . . . . 227 C6
Lubbock Rd BR7 . . . . 188 B3
Lubbock St SE14 . . . . 140 C5
Lucan Ho N1 . . . . 73 C1
Lucan Pl SW3 . . . . 114 C2 **257 B3**
Lucan Rd EN5 . . . . 1 A2
Lucas Ave Harrow HA2 . . . . 63 C6
Newham E13 . . . . 99 B6
Lucas Ct Battersea SW11 . . **268 B1**
Forest Hill SE26 . . . . 185 A5
Lucas Gdns N2 . . . . 30 A1
Lucas Ho
2 Clapham SW8 . . . . 137 C3
Walham Green SW10 . . . . **265 D4**
Lucas Rd SE20 . . . . 184 C4
Lucas Sq NW11 . . . . 47 C3
Lucas St SE4, SE8 . . . . . . 141 C4
Lucas Vale Prim Sch 10
SE8 . . . . 141 C4
Lucerne Cl N14 . . . . 16 A1
Lucerne Ct
5 Abbey Wood DA18 . . . . 125 A3
8 Beckenham BR3 . . . . . 185 C3
Lucerne Gr E17 . . . . 54 B5
Lucerne Mews W8 . . . . . . **245 B4**
Lucerne Rd Highbury N5 . . . 72 D4
Orpington BR6 . . . . 211 D3
South Norwood CR7 . . . . 205 A5
Lucey Rd SE16 . . . . 118 A3
Lucey Way SE16 . . . . 118 A3
Lucie Ave TW15 . . . . 170 D4
Lucien Rd
Upper Tooting SW17 . . . . 181 A6
Wandsworth SW18 . . . . . 157 D2
Lucille Ho SE26 . . . . 184 B4
Lucknow St SE18 . . . . 145 C5
Lucorn Cl SE12 . . . . 164 D5
Lucraft Ho 12 SW2 . . . . . . 160 A4
Luctons Ave IG9 . . . . 21 C3
Lucy Ashe Ho SE17 . . . . . . **261 D3**
Lucy Brown Ho SE1 . . . . . . **252 B3**
Lucy Cres W3 . . . . 89 A3
Lucy Gdns RM8 . . . . 81 A5
Luddesdon Rd DA8 . . . . . . 147 C5
Ludford Cl Croydon CR0 . . 220 D4
Edgware NW9 . . . . 27 C2
Ludgate Broadway EC4 . . . **241 D1**
Ludgate Cir EC4 . . . 94 D1 **241 C1**
Ludgate Hill EC4 . . . 94 D1 **241 D1**
Ludgate Ho EC4 . . . . **241 C1**
Ludgate Sq EC4 . . . . **241 D1**
Ludgrove Ct EN4 . . . . 2 C1
Ludgrove Hall EN4 . . . . 2 D2
Ludham NW5 . . . . 70 D3

Ludham Cl SE28 . . . . 102 C1
Lud Lo TW15 . . . . 148 A2
Ludlow Cl Bromley BR2 . . . 209 A6
Harrow HA2 . . . . 63 B4
Ludlow Ct Acton W3 . . . . . 111 A4
East Barnet EN4 . . . . 14 C6
Ludlow Rd Ealing W5 . . . . . 87 C3
Feltham TW13 . . . . 172 A6
Ludlow St EC1 . . . . **242 A6**
Ludlow Way N2 . . . . 48 A5
Ludovick Wlk SW15 . . . . . 133 C1
Ludwell Ho W14 . . . . **254 B6**
Ludwick Mews SE14 . . . . . 141 A5
Luffield Rd SE2 . . . . 124 B3
Luffman Rd SE12 . . . . 165 B1
Lugard Ho 2 W12 . . . . 112 B5
Lugard Rd SE15 . . . . 140 B4
Lugg App E12 . . . . 78 C5
Luke Ho 32 E1 . . . . 96 B1
Lukes Ct N3 . . . . 47 C5
Luke St EC2 . . . . . . 95 C3 **243 A6**
Lukin Cres E4 . . . . 20 B1
Lukin St E1 . . . . 96 C1
Lullingstone Cl BR5 . . . . . 190 B3
Lullingstone Cres BR5 . . . 190 B3
Lullingstone Ho 21 SE15 . 140 C6
Lullingstone La SE13 . . . . 164 B5
Lullingstone Rd 3
Belvedere DA17 . . . . 125 C1
DA17 . . . . 147 B6
Lullington Garth
Borehamwood WD6 . . . . . 10 D6
Bromley BR1 . . . . 186 C3
Finchley N12 . . . . 29 B5
Lullington Rd
Dagenham RM9 . . . . 81 A1
Penge SE20 . . . . 184 A3
Lulot Gdns N19 . . . . 71 B6
Lulworth
Camden Town NW1 . . . . . 71 C1
Walworth SE17 . . . . **262 C2**
Lulworth Ave
Hounslow TW5, TW7 . . . . 130 A5
Wembley HA9 . . . . 43 C2
Lulworth Cl HA2 . . . . 63 B5
Lulworth Cres CR4 . . . . . . 180 C5
Lulworth Ct N14 . . . . 16 A1
Lulworth Dr HA5 . . . . 41 A2
Lulworth Gdns HA2 . . . . . . 63 B6
Lulworth Ho SW8 . . . . **270 C6**
Lulworth Rd Bexley DA16 . 145 D3
Chislehurst SE9 . . . . 166 A2
Peckham SE15 . . . . 140 B3
Lulworth Waye UB4 . . . . . . 84 B1
Lumen Rd HA9 . . . . 65 D6
Lumiere Bldg The E7 . . . . . 77 D3
Lumiere Ct 7 SW17 . . . . . 159 A2
Lumina Bldg 1 E14 . . . . . . 120 A5
Lumley Cl DA17 . . . . 125 C1
Lumley Ct WC2 . . . . **250 B5**
Lumley Flats SW1 . . . . **258 A2**
Lumley Gdns SM3 . . . . . . 217 A3
Lumley Ho KT3 . . . . 199 B1
Lumley Rd SM1, SM3 . . . . . 217 A3
Lumley St W1 . . . . **238 B1**
Lumsdon NW8 . . . . 91 D6
Luna Ho 6 SE16 . . . . 118 A4
Lunan Ho 14 E3 . . . . 97 B5
Luna Rd CR7 . . . . 205 A6
Lundin Wlk WD19 . . . . 22 D3
Lundy Dr UB3 . . . . 105 C2
Lunham Rd SE19 . . . . 183 C4
Luntley Pl E1 . . . . 96 A2
Lupin Cl Croydon CR0 . . . . 206 D1
Streatham SW2 . . . . 160 D2
Lupin Cres IG11 . . . . 78 D2
Lupino Ct SE11 . . . . **260 D4**
Lupin Point SE1 . . . . **253 D1**
Lupton Cl SE12 . . . . 187 B6
Lupton St NW5 . . . . 71 C4
Lupus Ct SE19 . . . . 183 B2
Lupus St SW1 . . . . 115 C1 **259 B1**
Luralda Gdns E14 . . . . 120 B1
Lurgan Ave W6 . . . . 134 D6
Lurline Gdns
SW11 . . . . 137 A4 **268 B2**
Luscombe Ct BR2 . . . . 186 C1
Luscombe Ho SW18 . . . . . 157 B6
Luscombe Way
SW8 . . . . 138 A5 **270 A4**
Lusher Ho SW15 . . . . 156 D5
Lushington Ho KT12 . . . . . 194 C3
Lushington Rd
Catford SE6 . . . . 185 D5
Willesden Green NW10 . . . 90 B5
Lushington Terr 11 E8 . . . . 74 A3
Lutea Ho SM2 . . . . 218 A1
Luther Cl HA8 . . . . 11 A2
Luther King Cl E17 . . . . 53 A3
Luther Mews 2 TW11 . . . . 174 D5
Luther Rd TW11 . . . . 174 D5
Luton Pl SE10 . . . . 142 A5
Luton Rd Newham E13 . . . . 99 A3
Sidcup DA14 . . . . 168 C1
Walthamstow E17 . . . . . . 53 B5
Luton St NW8 . . . . . 92 B3 **236 D5**
Luttrell Ave SW15 . . . . 156 B6

Lutwyche Rd SE6 . . . . **163** B2
Lutyens Ho SW1 . . . . **259** A1
Luxborough Ho W1 . . . . **238** A4
Luxborough St
 W1 . . . .**93** A2 **238** A4
Luxborough Twr W1 . . . . **238** A4
Luxembourg Mews 2
 E15 . . . .**76** C3
Luxemburg Gdns W6 . . . **112** D2
Luxfield Rd SE9 . . . . **166** A3
Luxford St SE16 . . . . **118** D2
Luxmore St SE4 . . . . **141** B4
Luxor St SE5 . . . . **139** A2
Lyall Ave SE21 . . . . **183** D6
Lyall Mews SW1 . . **115** A3 **258** A5
Lyall Mews W SW1 . . . . **258** A5
Lyall St SW1 . . . **115** A3 **258** A5
Lyal Rd E3 . . . .**97** A5
Lycett Ho 10 SW2 . . . . . . **160** A4
Lycett Pl 3 W12 . . . . **112** A4
Lychgate Ct 4 N12 . . . . . .**30** B5
Lychgate Manor HA1 . . . .**42** C2
Lych Gate Wlk UB3. . . . **105** D6
Lyconby Gdns CR0 . . . . **207** A2
Lycott Gr SE22 . . . . **161** D6
Lydd Cl DA14 . . . . **167** C1
Lydden Ct SE9 . . . . **167** C5
Lydden Gr SW18 . . . . . . **157** B4
Lydden Rd SW18 . . . . . . **157** D4
Lydeard Rd E6 . . . .**78** B1
Lydford NW1 . . . . **232** B5
Lydford Cl 22 N16 . . . .**73** C3
Lydford Rd
 Brondesbury NW2 . . . .**68** D2
 Paddington W9 . . . .**91** B3
 Tottenham N15. . . . .**51** B4
Lydgate Ho 8 N6. . . . .**73** C3
Lydhurst Ave SW2 . . . . . **160** B2
Lydia Ct 2 N12 . . . .**30** A4
Lydia Lodge HA1. . . . .**64** C4
Lydney Cl
 Camberwell SE15. . . . . . . **139** C5
 Putney SW19 . . . . **157** A2
Lydon Rd SW4 . . . . **137** C2
Lydstep Rd BR7 . . . . **188** C6
Lydwell Ho 29 SW8. . . . . **137** D3
Lyford Rd SW18 . . . . **158** C3
Lyford St SE18 . . . . **122** A2
Lygoe Ho 18 N6. . . . .**49** D2
Lygoe Rd N2 . . . .**30** B2
Lygon Ho 2 E2. . . . .**96** A4
Lygon Pl SW1. . . . . **258** C5
Lyham Cl SW2 . . . . **160** A5
Lyham Rd SW2 . . . . **160** A5
Lyle Cl CR4 . . . . **203** A2
Lyle Ct SM4. . . . . **202** B3
Lyle Pk SW15 . . . . **156** D5
Lyly Ho SE1. . . . . **262** D5
Lyme Farm Rd SE12. . . . **143** B1
Lyme Gr E9. . . . .**74** C1
Lyme Grove Ho 2 E9 . . . .**74** C1
Lymer Ave SE19. . . . . . . **183** D5
Lyme Rd DA16 . . . . **146** B4
Lymescote Gdns SM1 . . **217** C6
Lyme St NW1 . . . .**93** C6 **232** A6
Lyminge Cl DA14 . . . . . . **189** D6
Lyminge Gdns SW17,
 SW18. . . . . **158** C3
Lymington Ave N22 . . . . .**32** D1
Lymington Cl
 Mitcham SW16 . . . . **181** D1
 2 Newham E6. . . . . **100** B2
Lymington Ct SM1 . . . . . **218** A5
Lymington Dr HA4 . . . . . .**61** B6
Lymington Gdns KT19 . . **215** D3
Lymington Mans NW6. . . .**69** D2
Lymington Rd
 Dagenham RM8 . . . .**58** D1
 Hampstead NW6 . . . .**69** D2
Lyminster Cl UB4 . . . .**85** A2
Lympne N17. . . . .**33** B1
Lympstone Gdns SE15. . **140** A5
Lynbridge Gdns N13 . . . .**32** D6
Lynbrook Gr SE15. . . . . . **139** C5
Lynchen Cl TW5 . . . . **128** B4
Lynch Wlk 2 SE8. . . . . . . **141** B6
Lyncott Cres SW4. . . . . . **137** B1
Lyncourt SE3 . . . . **142** B3
Lyncroft Ave HA5 . . . .**41** A4
Lyncroft Gdns
 Ealing W13 . . . . **109** C5
 Hampstead NW6 . . . .**69** D2
 Hounslow TW3 . . . . **152** A6
Lyncroft Mans 4 NW6 . . .**69** C3
Lyndale NW2 . . . .**69** B5
Lyndale Ave NW2 . . . .**69** B5
Lyndale Cl SE3. . . . . **142** D6
Lyndean Ind Est SE2 . . . **124** C3
Lynde Ho
 2 Clapham SW4 . . . . **137** D2
 Walton-on-T KT12 . . . . . . **194** C3
Lynden Gate SW15 . . . . . **156** B4
Lyndenhurst SE3 . . . . . . **142** D2
Lynden Hyrst CR0. . . . . . **221** D6
Lyndhurst BR7. . . . . **188** D4

Lyndhurst Ave
 Colney Hatch N12. . . . .**30** D4
 Edgware NW7 . . . .**27** C4
 Mitcham SW16 . . . . **181** D1
 Pinner HA5 . . . .**22** B2
 Southall UB1. . . . . **107** D5
 Sunbury TW16 . . . . **194** A6
 Tolworth KT5 . . . . **198** D1
 Twickenham TW2, TW4. . . **151** C3
Lyndhurst Cl
 Bexleyheath DA7 . . . . **147** D2
 Neasden NW10 . . . .**67** B5
 Orpington BR6 . . . . **226** D4
 South Croydon CR0. . . . . . **221** D5
Lyndhurst Ct
 8 Belmont SM2. . . . . **217** C1
 11 Woodford E18 . . . .**37** A2
Lyndhurst Dr
 Leytonstone E10. . . . .**54** A2
 New Malden KT3 . . . . **199** D2
Lyndhurst Gdns
 Barking IG11 . . . .**79** C2
 Enfield EN1 . . . .**5** C1
 Hampstead NW3 . . . .**70** B3
 Hendon N3 . . . .**29** A2
 Ilford IG2 . . . .**57** B3
 Pinner HA5 . . . .**22** B2
Lyndhurst Gr SE5, SE15 . **139** D3
Lyndhurst Ho 2 SW15 . . **156** A4
Lyndhurst House Prep Sch
 NW3 . . . .**70** B3
Lyndhurst Lo 3 E14 . . . . **120** B2
Lyndhurst Rd
 Bexleyheath DA7 . . . . **147** D2
 Chingford E4. . . . .**36** A3
 Edmonton N18 . . . .**34** A6
 Greenford UB6. . . . .**85** D3
 Hampstead NW3 . . . .**70** B3
 Thornton Heath CR7 . . . . . **204** C5
 Tottenham N22. . . . .**32** C4
Lyndhurst Sch SE5. . . . . **139** B3
Lyndhurst Sq SE15. . . . . **139** D4
Lyndhurst Terr NW3. . . . . .**70** B3
Lyndhurst Way
 Belmont SM2 . . . . **217** C1
 Camberwell SE15. . . . . . . **139** D3
Lyndon Bexley DA15 . . . **167** D6
 Hackbridge SM6. . . . . **219** A5
 Pinner HA5 . . . .**23** A4
Lyndon Rd DA17 . . . . **125** C2
Lyndon Yd SW17 . . . . . . **179** D6
Lyndum N22 . . . .**32** C2
Lyne Cres E17 . . . .**35** B2
Lyne Ct NW9. . . . .**45** B2
Lynegrove Ave TW15 . . . **171** A5
Lyneham Wlk Hackney E5 . .**75** A3
 Pinner HA5 . . . .**39** D6
Lynette Ave SW4 . . . . . . **159** C5
Lynfield Ct SE23 . . . . **162** D4
Lynford Cl
 Barnet Gate EN5. . . . .**11** D6
 Burnt Oak HA8 . . . .**27** A2
Lynford French Ho SE17. **262** A2
Lynford Gdns
 Edgware HA8 . . . .**10** D1
 Ilford IG3 . . . .**79** D6
Lynford Terr N9. . . . .**17** D3
Lyngham Ct 10 N4 . . . . . .**50** A2
Lynhurst Cres UB10 . . . . .**61** B1
Lynhurst NW8. . . . . **229** C5
Lynhurst Rd UB10. . . . . . .**61** A1
Lynmere Rd DA16 . . . . . . **146** B3
Lyn Mews 12 E3 . . . .**97** B4
Lynmouth Ave Enfield EN1. .**17** D5
 West Barnes SM4. . . . . . . **200** D2
Lynmouth Dr HA4 . . . .**62** B5
Lynmouth Gdns
 Heston TW5. . . . . **128** C4
 Wembley UB6. . . . .**65** B1
Lynmouth Rd
 Fortis Green N2 . . . .**48** D5
 Stamford Hill N16. . . . .**51** D1
 Walthamstow E17 . . . .**53** A4
 Wembley UB6. . . . .**87** B6
Lynn Cl Ashford TW15 . . . **171** B5
 Harrow HA3 . . . .**24** B1
Lynn Ct SW16. . . . . **181** D5
Lynne Cl 7 BR6 . . . . **227** D2
Lynne Ct Forest Hill SE23. **163** B4
 Hampstead NW6 . . . .**69** D1
 South Croydon CR2. . . . . . **221** C4
 Wimbledon SW20. . . . . . . **178** B2
Lynnett Ct E9 . . . .**75** A2
Lynnett Rd RM8. . . . .**58** D1
Lynne Way UB5 . . . .**84** D5
Lynne Wlk KT10. . . . . . . **212** A3
Lynn Ho SE15. . . . . **140** A6
Lynn Mews E11. . . . .**76** C6
Lynn Rd Balham SW12. . . **159** B4
 Ilford IG2 . . . .**57** B2
 Leyton E11 . . . .**76** C5
Lynn St EN2 . . . .**5** A3
Lynsted Cl Bexley DA6. . . **169** D6
 Bromley BR1. . . . . **187** C1
Lynsted Ct 4 BR3. . . . . . . **185** A1
Lynsted Gdns SE9. . . . . . **143** D2
Lynton KT7. . . . . **197** A2
Lynton Ave Ealing W13 . . .**87** A1
 Hyde The NW9 . . . .**45** D5
 North Finchley N12. . . . . . .**30** B6

Lynton Cl
 Chessington KT9 . . . . **214** A4
 Isleworth TW7 . . . . **130** D1
 Willesden NW10. . . . .**67** D3
Lynton Cres IG2 . . . .**56** D3
Lynton Ct Bowes Pk N13 . .**32** A5
 9 Dagenham W3. . . . .**89** A1
 Penge SE20 . . . . **184** B2
 Sutton SM2. . . . . **218** A2
Lynton Est SE1. . . . . **118** A2
Lynton Gdns Enfield EN1 . .**17** C4
 Friern Barnet N11 . . . .**31** D4
Lynton Grange N2 . . . .**48** D6
Lynton Ho 16 W2. . . . .**91** D1
Lynton Lo N5 . . . .**72** D3
Lynton Mans SE1 . . . . . . **261** A6
Lynton Mead N20. . . . .**13** D2
Lynton Rd Acton W3 . . . . **110** D6
 Bermondsey SE1 . . . . **117** D2
 Chingford E4. . . . .**35** D5
 Harrow HA2 . . . .**63** A6
 Hornsey N8. . . . .**50** A4
 New Malden KT3 . . . . **199** B4
 Paddington NW6 . . . .**91** B5
 Thornton Heath CR0. . . . . **204** C3
Lynton Terr 4 W3. . . . .**89** A1
Lynton Wlk UB4 . . . .**83** C4
Lynwood Harrow HA2 . . . .**63** A5
 Woodford E18. . . . .**37** C2
Lynwood Cl TW15. . . . . . . **170** D5
Lynwood Dr KT4. . . . . **216** A6
Lynwood Gdns
 Southall UB1. . . . .**85** B1
 Wallington CR0. . . . . **220** B4
Lynwood Gr
 Orpington BR6 . . . . **211** C1
 Southgate N21 . . . .**16** C3
Lynwood Rd Ealing W5. . . .**88** A3
 Thames Ditton KT7 . . . . . **196** D1
 Upper Tooting SW17 . . . . . **180** D6
Lynx Terr SW19 . . . . **157** C1
Lynx Way E16. . . . . **121** D6
Lyon Bsns Pk IG11 . . . . . **101** C5
Lyon Cl HA4 . . . .**39** D1
Lyon Ho NW8. . . . . **237** A5
Lyon Meade HA7. . . . .**25** C2
Lyon Park Ave HA0. . . . . . .**66** B2
Lyon Park Jun & Inf Schs
 HA0 . . . .**66** B1
Lyon Rd Harrow HA1 . . . . .**42** D3
 Merton SW19 . . . . **180** A2
Lyonsdown Ave EN5. . . . . .**14** A5
Lyonsdown Ct EN5. . . . . . .**14** A5
Lyonsdown Rd EN5 . . . . . .**14** A6
Lyonsdown Sch EN5 . . . . .**14** A6
Lyons Pl NW8. . . . .**92** B3 **236** C5
Lyon St N1 . . . .**72** B1
Lyons Wlk W14 . . . . **254** A4
Lyon Way UB6. . . . .**86** C6
Lyoth Rd BR5. . . . . **227** A6
Lyric Dr UB6. . . . .**85** D3
Lyric Mews SE26. . . . . . . **184** C6
Lyric Rd SW13 . . . . **133** D4
Lysander 20 NW9. . . . .**27** D2
Lysander Ct 8 EN5. . . . . . .**13** C6
Lysander Gdns KT5 . . . . . **198** B3
Lysander Gr N19 . . . .**49** D1
Lysander Ho 10 E2. . . . . . .**96** B5
Lysander Mews N19 . . . . .**49** C1
Lysander Rd Ruislip HA4 . . .**61** B6
 Wallington CR0. . . . . **220** B2
Lysander Way BR6. . . . . . **227** A5
Lysia Ct SW6 . . . . **134** D5
Lysias Rd SW12 . . . . **159** B5
Lysia St SW6 . . . . **134** D5
Lysons Wlk SW15 . . . . . . **156** A6
Lytchet Rd BR1 . . . . **187** B3
Lytchet Way EN3. . . . .**6** C4
Lytchgate Cl CR2 . . . . . . **221** C1
Lytcott Dr KT8 . . . . **195** B6
Lytham Ave WD19. . . . . . .**22** C5
Lytham Cl SE28 . . . . **103** A1
Lytham Ct 5 UB1. . . . .**85** D1
Lytham Gr W5 . . . .**88** B4
Lytham St SE17. . . .**117** B1 **262** C1
Lyttelton Cl NW3. . . . .**70** C1
Lyttelton Ct N2 . . . .**48** A4
Lyttelton Rd
 Hampstead Garden Suburb
 N2. . . . .**48** A4
 Leyton E10 . . . .**76** A5
Lytten Ct 6 W12. . . . . **112** A4
Lyttleton Cl UB4 . . . .**84** C3
Lyttleton Ho 10 E9 . . . .**74** C1
Lyttleton Rd N8. . . . .**50** C6
Lytton Ave Enfield EN3 . . . .**7** A5
 Southgate N13 . . . .**16** C2
Lytton Cl
 Hampstead Garden Suburb
 N2. . . . .**48** B4
 Northolt UB5 . . . .**63** B1
Lytton Ct WC1. . . . . **240** B3
Lytton Gdns SM6. . . . . . . **219** D4
Lytton Gr SW15 . . . . **157** A5
Lytton Ho 3 TW12 . . . . . . **173** D4
Lytton Rd Leytonstone E11. .**54** C2
 New Barnet EN5. . . . .**2** A1
 Pinner HA5 . . . .**23** A3
Lytton Strachey Path 8
 SE28 . . . . **124** B6

Lyveden Rd
 Greenwich SE3. . . . . **143** B5
 Mitcham SW17, SW19 . . . **180** D4

M

Mabbett Ho 2 SE18. . . . . **144** C6
Mabel Crout Ct SE9 . . . . **145** B1
Mabel Evetts Ct UB3 . . . **106** B6
Mabel Thornton Ho 12
 N16. . . . .**73** B4
Maberley Cres SE19. . . . . **184** A5
Maberley Ct SE19 . . . . . . **184** A3
Maberley Rd SE19 . . . . . . **182** C2
Mabledon Pl NW1, WC1 . . **232** D1
Mablethorpe Rd SW6 . . . **264** A3
Mabley St E9 . . . .**75** A3
Mablin Lo 3 IG9 . . . .**21** C3
Mcadam Dr EN2 . . . .**4** D3
Macallister Ho 8 SE18 . . **144** D6
Macaret Cl N20. . . . .**14** A4
Macarthur Cl London E7. . .**77** A2
 Wembley HA9 . . . .**66** D2
MacArthur Ho 4 SW2. . . **160** A4
Macartney Ho SE10 . . . . **142** B5
Macaulay Ave KT10 . . . . **212** C6
Macaulay CE Prim Sch
 SW4 . . . . **137** B1
Macaulay Ct SW4 . . . . . . **137** B2
Macaulay Ho
 2 Kensal Town W10 . . . . . .**91** A2
 10 Stoke Newington N16 . . .**73** C5
Macaulay Rd
 Clapham SW4. . . . . **137** B2
 Newham E6. . . . .**99** C5
Macaulay Sq SW4. . . . . . **137** B1
Macaulay Way 2 SE28 . . **124** B5
McAuley Cl Eltham SE9. . . **166** C6
 Lambeth SE1. . . . . .**116** C3 **261** A6
Macauley Mews SE13 . . . **142** A3
McAusland Ho 5 E3. . . . . .**97** B5
Macbean St SE18 . . . . . . **122** D3
Macbeth Ho 4 N1. . . . .**95** C5
Macbeth St W6 . . . . **112** B1
McBride Ho 6 E3. . . . .**97** B5
McCall Cl SW4. . . . . **138** A3
McCall Cres SE7 . . . . **122** A1
McCall Ho N7 . . . .**72** A4
Mccarthy Ct SW11 . . . . . **267** B1
McCarthy Rd TW13. . . . . . **172** D5
Macclesfield Rd
 Croydon SE25. . . . . **206** C4
 Shoreditch EC1. . . . . .**95** A4 **235** A2
Macclesfield St w1 . . . . . **249** D6
McClintock Pl EN3 . . . .**7** D6
McCoid Way SE1. . . . . . . **252** A1
Mcconnell Ho SW8 . . . . . **269** C1
McCormick Ho 9 SW2. . . **160** C3
McCrone Mews 3 NW3 . . .**70** B2
McCullum Rd E3. . . . .**97** B6
McDermott Cl SW11 . . . . **136** C2
McDermott Rd SE15 . . . . **140** A2
Macdonald Ave RM10 . . . .**81** D5
Macdonald Ct TW3. . . . . . **130** A1
McDonald Ho 1 KT2. . . . . **176** B3
Macdonald Ho 2 SW11 . . **137** A3
Macdonald Rd
 Chingford E4. . . . .**36** A1
 Dartmouth Pk N19 . . . .**71** C6
 Forest Gate E7 . . . .**77** A4
 Friern Barnet N11 . . . .**30** D5
McDonough Cl KT9 . . . . . **214** A4
McDougall Ct TW9 . . . . . . **132** C3
Mcdougall Ho E2 . . . .**96** A4
McDowall Cl E16 . . . .**98** D2
McDowall Rd SE5. . . . . . . **139** A4
Macduff Rd
 SW11 . . . .**137** A4 **268** B2
Mace Cl E1. . . . . **118** B5
Mace Ho 2 E17 . . . .**53** D6
McEntee Ave E17 . . . .**35** A2
Mace St E2. . . . .**96** D5
McEwan Way E15. . . . .**98** B6
Macey Ho
 10 Battersea SW11. . . . . . **267** A1
 2 Greenwich SE10 . . . . . . **142** A6
Macfarlane La TW7 . . . . . **131** A6
Macfarlane Rd W12 . . . . . **112** C5
Macfarren Ho 7 W10. . . . .**91** A4
MacFarren Pl NW1. . . . . . **238** B5
McGlashon Ho 19 E1. . . . .**96** A3
McGrath Rd E15 . . . .**76** D2
McGregor Ct 8 N1. . . . . . .**95** C4
McGregor Rd W11 . . . .**91** B2
Macgregor Rd E16. . . . . . .**99** C2
Mcguffie Ct E17 . . . .**53** B6
Machell Rd SE15. . . . . **140** C2
McIndoe Ct N1. . . . . **235** C6
McIntosh Cl SM6. . . . . . . **220** A1
McIntosh Ho 14 SE16. . . . **118** C2
McIntyre Ct 19 SW4. . . . . **138** A3
Mackay Ho 33 W12. . . . . . **112** B6
McKay Rd SW20 . . . . **178** A3
Mackay Rd SW4 . . . . **137** B2
McKellar Ct WD23. . . . .**8** A2
McKenna Ho 3 E3. . . . . . .**97** B5
Mackennal St
 NW8 . . . .**92** C5 **230** B4

Mackenzie Cl 7 W12 . . . . **112** B6
Mackenzie Ho
 5 Dollis Hill NW2 . . . .**68** A5
 1 Hornsey N8. . . . .**50** A5
Mackenzie Rd
 Barnsbury N7 . . . .**72** B2
 Penge BR3 . . . . **184** D1
Mackenzie Wlk E14 . . . . . **119** C5
McKerrell Rd SE15. . . . . . **140** A4
Mackeson Rd NW3. . . . . . .**70** D4
Mackie Ho 18 SW2. . . . . . **160** C4
Mackie Rd SW2. . . . . **160** C4
McKiernan Ct 2 SW11. . . **136** C3
Mc Killop Way DA14. . . . . **190** C3
McKinlay Ct
 Beckenham BR3. . . . . **185** B1
 Bexley DA16. . . . . **146** C2
McKinnon Wood Ho 16
 E2 . . . .**96** A4
Mackintosh La E9. . . . .**74** D3
Macklin Ho SE3. . . . . **162** B2
Macklin St WC2. . . . .**94** A1 **240** B2
Mackonochie Ho EC1. . . . **241** A4
Mackrow Wlk 11 E14. . . . **120** A6
Macks Rd SE16 . . . . **118** A2
Mackworth Ho NW1 . . . . . **232** A2
Mackworth St NW1 . . . . . **232** A2
Mac Laren Mews SW15. . **134** C1
Maclean Rd SE23 . . . . . . **163** A5
Mcleod Ct SE21. . . . . **162** A3
McLeod Ho 3 SE23. . . . . **162** C2
McLeod Rd SE2 . . . . **124** B2
Macleod Rd N21. . . . .**16** A6
McLeod's Mews
 SW7. . . . .**113** D2 **255** D4
Macleod St SE17. . .**117** A1 **262** B1
Maclise Rd W14 . . . .**113** A3 **254** A5
McManus Ho 2 SW11 . . . **136** B2
McMillan Ct 2 SE6 . . . . . **164** D3
Mcmillan Ho SE4 . . . . **141** A2
Macmillan Ho
 Cricklewood NW4. . . . .**68** B4
 Lisson Gr NW8 . . . . **230** B1
McMillan St SE8 . . . . **141** C6
Macmillan Way SW17. . . . **181** B6
Mcmorran Ho 4 N7 . . . . . .**72** A4
McNair Rd UB2 . . . . **107** C3
Macnamara Ho SW10 . . . **266** C4
Mcneil Rd SE5 . . . . **139** C3
McNicol Dr NW10. . . . .**89** A5
Macoma Rd SE18 . . . . . . **145** B6
Macoma Terr SE18 . . . . . **145** B6
Maconochies Rd 9 E14. . **119** D1
Macquarie Way E14. . . . . **119** D2
McRae La CR4 . . . . **202** D2
Macready Ho W1 . . . . **237** B3
Macready Pl 2 N7. . . . . . .**72** A4
Macroom Ho W9. . . . .**91** B4
Macroom Rd W9. . . . .**91** B4
Mac's Pl EC4 . . . . **241** B2
Madame Tussaud's *
 NW1. . . . .**93** A3 **238** A5
Madani Girls Sch 36 E1 . . .**96** B1
Mada Rd BR6 . . . . **226** D5
Maddams St E3. . . . .**97** D3
Madderfields Ct N11. . . . . .**31** D2
Maddison Cl Finchley N2 . . .**30** A1
 Teddington TW11 . . . . **174** D4
Maddison Ct NW4 . . . .**28** C1
Maddocks Cl DA14. . . . . . **191** A5
Maddocks Ho 3 E1. . . . . **118** B6
Maddock Way SE17 . . . . . **138** D6
Maddox Ct 1 E4. . . . .**20** B3
Maddox St W1. . . . . **248** D6
Madeira Ave BR1 . . . . **186** C3
Madeira Gr IG8. . . . .**37** C4
Madeira Rd Edmonton N13. .**16** D1
 Leytonstone E11. . . . .**54** C1
 Mitcham CR4 . . . . **202** D5
 Streatham SW16 . . . . **182** A5
Madeleine Cl RM6 . . . .**58** C3
Madeleine Ct RM6 . . . .**58** C3
Madeley Ct W5 . . . .**88** A1
Madeley Rd W5. . . . .**88** A1
Madeline Gr IG1. . . . .**79** B3
Madeline Rd SE20 . . . . . . **184** A2
Madge Gill Way 4 E6. . . . **100** A6
Madge Hill W7. . . . . **108** C6
Madinah Rd 7 Dalston E8. .**74** A2
 London E8. . . . .**74** A3
Madingley 11 KT1. . . . . . . **176** C1
Madingley Ct TW1 . . . . . . **153** C6
Madison Apartments
 N11 . . . .**31** D3
Madison Cl SM2 . . . . **218** B1
Madison Cres DA7 . . . . . . **146** C5
Madison Ct 8 RM10 . . . . . .**81** D2
Madison Gdns
 Beckenham BR2. . . . . **208** D6
 Bexley DA7. . . . . **146** C5
Madison Ho E3 . . . .**98** A4
Madras Ho IG1 . . . .**78** D4
Madras Pl N7. . . . .**72** C2
Madras Rd IG1 . . . .**78** D4
Madrid Rd SW13. . . . . **134** A5
Madron St SE17. . . .**117** C1 **263** B2
Mafeking Ave
 Brentford TW8 . . . . **132** A6
 Ilford IG2 . . . .**57** B2

Mafeking Ave *continued*
Newham E6 . . . . **100** A5
Mafeking Rd Enfield EN1 . . . **5** D2
Newham E16 . . . .**98** D3
Tottenham N17 . . . .**34** A1
Magdala Ave N19 . . . .**71** C6
Magdala Rd
Isleworth TW7 . . . . **131** A2
South Croydon CR2 . . . . . .**221** B1
Magdalen Ct SE25 . . . . . .**206** A4
Magdalene Cl **7** SE15. . . .**140** B3
Magdalene Gdns
7 East Barnet N11 . . . .**14** D3
Newham E6 . . . . **100** C3
Magdalene Ho **7** SW15. .**156** D5
Magdalene Rd TW17 . . . . .**192** B6
Magdalen Pas E1 . . . .**253** D6
Magdalen Rd SW18 . . . . . .**158** B3
Magdalen St SE1 . . . .**253** A3
Magee St SE11 . . . .**138** C6
Magellan Bvd E16 . . . .**123** A6
Magellan Ct **11** NW10 . . . .**67** B1
Magellan Ho **16** E1 . . . . . .**96** D3
Magellan Pl **25** E14 . . . . .**119** C2
Magna Ct UB6 . . . .**86** B4
Magnaville Rd WD23 . . . .**8** D4
Magnetic Cres EN3 . . . .**7** B6
Magnet Rd HA9 . . . .**65** D6
Magnin Pl **5** E8 . . . .**96** A6
Magnolia Cl
Kingston u T KT2 . . . .**176** D4
Leyton E10 . . . .**75** C6
Magnolia Ct
13 Belmont SM2 . . . . . .**217** D1
Feltham TW14 . . . .**150** A3
2 Finchley N12 . . . .**29** D6
Forest Hill SE26 . . . .**184** C5
Harrow HA3 . . . .**44** B2
Hillingdon UB10 . . . .**60** D2
Northolt UB5 . . . .**85** A3
Richmond TW9 . . . .**132** D4
Wallington SM6 . . . .**219** B3
Wandsworth SW11 . . . . . .**158** D5
Magnolia Gdns HA8 . . . . . .**27** A6
Magnolia Ho **13** SE8 . . . .**141** B6
Magnolia Lo E4 . . . .**19** D1
Magnolia Pl
Clapham Pk SW4 . . . .**160** A6
Ealing W5 . . . .**87** D2
Magnolia Rd W4 . . . .**132** D6
Magnolia Way KT19 . . . . .**215** A3
Magnolia Wharf W4 . . . . .**132** D6
Magpie Cl Edgware NW9 . . .**27** C1
Enfield EN1 . . . .**6** A4
Forest Gate E7 . . . .**76** D3
Magpie Cl **1** BR2 . . . .**210** A3
Magpie Hall La BR2 . . . . .**210** B3
Magpie Hall Rd WD23 . . . . .**8** C2
Magpie Ho **7** E3 . . . .**97** B6
Magpie Pl SE14 . . . .**141** A6
Magri Wlk **22** E1 . . . .**96** C2
Maguire St SE1 . . . . .**117** C4 **253** D2
Mahatma Gandhi Ind Est **1**
SE24 . . . .**138** D1
Mahlon Ave HA4 . . . .**62** B2
Mahogany Cl SE16 . . . .**119** A5
Mahon Cl EN1 . . . .**5** D4
Mahoney Ho SE14 . . . .**141** B4
Maida Ave Chingford E4 . . . .**19** D4
Little Venice W2 . . . . .**92** A3 **236** B5
Maida Rd DA17 . . . .**125** C3
MAIDA VALE **91** D4
Maida Vale W9 . . . .**92** A4 **229** A1
Maida Vale Sta W9 . . . .**91** D4
Maida Way E4 . . . .**19** D4
Maiden Erlegh Ave DA5 . .**169** A3
Maiden La
Borough The SE1. . .**117** A5 **252** B4
Camden Town NW1 . . . . . .**71** D1
Strand WC2 . . . .**116** A6 **250** B6
Maiden Rd E15 . . . .**76** C1
Maidenstone Hill SE10 . .**142** A4
Maidstone Bldgs SE1 . . . .**252** C2
Maidstone Ct N11 . . . .**31** D1
Maidstone Ho **4** E14 . . . . .**97** D1
Maidstone Rd
Friern Barnet N11 . . . .**31** D4
Ruxley DA14 . . . .**191** C3
Mail Coach Yd **28** E2 . . . . .**95** C4
Main Ave EN1 . . . .**17** D6
Main Dr HA9 . . . .**65** D5
Main Rd Chislehurst BR5 . .**190** C1
Sidcup DA14 . . . .**167** C1
Main St TW13 . . . .**172** D2
Mainridge Rd BR7, SE9 . .**188** C6
Main Yd **1** E9 . . . .**75** C2
Mainwaring Ct **3** CR4 . . .**181** A1
Mais Ho SE26 . . . .**162** B2
Maismore St SE15 . . . .**140** A6
Maison Alfort HA3 . . . .**24** C2
Maisonettes The SM1 . . . .**217** B3
Maitland Cl
3 Greenwich SE10 . . . .**141** D5
Hounslow TW4 . . . .**129** B2
Maitland Ct W2 . . . .**246** C6
Maitland Ho Chelsea SW1 .**269** A6
1 South Hackney E2 . . . . .**96** C5

MAITLAND PARK. **70** D2
Maitland Park Rd NW3 . . . .**70** D2
Maitland Park Villas
NW3 . . . .**70** D2
Maitland Pl **5** **74** C4
Maitland Rd Penge SE26 . .**184** D4
Stratford E15 . . . .**76** D2
Majendie Rd SE18 . . . .**123** B1
Majestic Ct N4 . . . .**50** D1
Majestic Way CR4 . . . .**180** D1
Major Cl SW9 . . . .**138** D2
Majorie Mews **6** E1 . . . . . .**96** D1
Major Rd
22 Bermondsey SE16 . . .**118** A3
Stratford New Town E15 . . .**76** B3
Makepeace Ave N6 . . . .**71** A6
Makepeace Mans N6. . . . . .**71** A6
Makepeace Rd
Northolt UB5 . . . .**85** A6
Wanstead E11 . . . .**55** A5
Makinen Ho **5** IG9 . . . .**21** C3
Makins St SW3 . . . .**257** B3
Malabar Ct **20** W12 . . . . . .**112** B6
Malabar St E14 . . . .**119** C4
Malam Ct SE11 . . . .**261** A3
Malam Gdns **3** E14 . . . . .**119** D6
Malatia CR2 . . . .**221** A2
Malay Ho **2** E1 . . . .**118** C5
Malborough Ho **3** N20. . . .**14** D1
Malbrook Rd SW15 . . . . . .**134** B1
Malbury Rd N22 . . . .**32** A3
Malcolm Cl SE20 . . . .**184** C3
Malcolm Cres NW4 . . . .**46** A3
Malcolm Ct Ealing W5. . . . . .**88** B3
Hendon NW4 . . . .**46** A3
Stanmore HA7 . . . .**25** C5
Stratford E7 . . . .**76** D2
Malcolm Ho **13** N1 . . . .**95** C5
Malcolm Pl E2 . . . .**96** C3
Malcolm Prim Sch SE20. .**184** C3
Malcolm Rd
Bethnal Green E1 . . . .**96** C3
Croydon SE25 . . . .**206** A3
Ickenham UB10 . . . .**60** B4
Penge SE20 . . . .**184** C3
Wimbledon SW19 . . . .**179** A4
Malcolmson Ho SW1 . . . . .**259** D1
Malcolms Way N14 . . . .**15** C6
Malcolm Way E11 . . . .**55** A5
Malden Ave
Croydon SE25 . . . .**206** B6
Northolt UB6 . . . .**64** C2
Malden Cres NW1 . . . .**71** A2
Malden Ct
Stoke Newington N4 . . . . . .**51** A3
West Barnes KT3 . . . .**200** B6
Malden Ctr The KT3 . . . . .**199** D5
Malden Green Ave KT4 . .**200** A1
Malden Hill KT3 . . . .**199** D6
Malden Hill Gdns KT3 . . .**199** D6
Malden Junc KT3 . . . .**199** D4
Malden Manor Prim Sch
KT3 . . . .**199** C2
Malden Manor Sta KT3 . .**199** C2
Malden Parochial Prim Sch
KT4 . . . .**199** C1
Malden Pk KT3 . . . .**199** D3
Malden Pl **1** NW5 . . . .**71** A3
Malden Rd
Camden Town NW5 . . . . . .**71** A2
Cheam KT4, SM3 . . . .**216** D4
New Malden KT3, KT4 . . .**199** D2
Malden Way **3** **200** A5
Malden Way (Kingston By-
Pass) KT3, KT5 . . . .**199** C4
Maldon Cl
Camberwell SE5 . . . .**139** C2
Shoreditch N1 . . . .**235** B6
Stratford New Town E15 . . .**76** B3
Maldon Ct Barking E6 . . . .**100** C6
Wallington SM6 . . . .**219** C3
Maldon Rd Acton W3. . . . . .**111** A6
Edmonton N9 . . . .**17** D1
Wallington SM6 . . . .**219** B3
Maldon Wlk IG8 . . . .**37** C4
Malet Pl WC1 . . . .**239** C5
Malet St WC1 . . . .**93** D2 **239** D4
Maley Ave SE27 . . . .**160** D2
Malford Ct E18 . . . .**37** A1
Malford Gr E18 . . . .**54** D6
Malfort Rd SE5 . . . .**139** C2
Malham Cl N11 . . . .**31** A4
Malham Rd SE23 . . . .**162** D3
Malham Road Ind Est
SE23 . . . .**162** D3
Malindi Ct N8 . . . .**49** D4
Malins Cl EN5 . . . .**12** C6
Malins Ct SW12 . . . .**159** A5
Mallaig Cl HA8 . . . .**26** D2
Mallams Mews **1** SW9. . .**138** D2
Mallard Cl **1** Hackney E9 . . .**75** B2
Hanwell W7 . . . .**108** C4
Kilburn NW6 . . . .**91** C6
New Barnet EN5 . . . .**14** B5
Twickenham TW4 . . . .**151** C4
Mallard Ct Chingford E4 . . . .**20** B4
Ilford IG1 . . . .**79** A6
Kingsbury NW9 . . . .**45** A3
Little Ilford E12. . . . .**78** B3

Mallard Ct *continued*
16 Richmond TW10 . . . . .**153** D5
Walthamstow E17 . . . .**54** B6
Mallard Ho
8 Camberwell SE15 . . . .**139** D4
St John's Wood NW8 . . . . .**230** A3
Mallard Path **3** SE28 . . . .**123** B3
Mallard Pl TW1 . . . .**153** A1
Mallard Point **2** E3. . . . . . .**97** C4
Mallards E11 . . . .**55** A2
Mallards Rd
Barking IG11 . . . .**102** A3
Woodford IG8. . . . .**37** B3
Mallard Way NW9 . . . .**45** A2
Mallard Wlk BR3 . . . .**206** D4
Sidcup DA14 . . . .**190** C4
Mall Ct W5 . . . .**110** A6
Mallet Dr UB5 . . . .**63** B3
Mallet Ho **11** SW15 . . . . . .**156** A6
Mallet Rd SE13 . . . .**164** B5
Mall Galleries * SW1. . . . .**249** D4
Malling SE13 . . . .**163** D6
Malling Ct CR0. . . . .**206** C3
Malling Gdns SM4 . . . .**202** A3
Malling Ho **9** BR3. . . . . . .**185** C3
Malling Way BR2 . . . .**208** D2
Mallinson Ct **2** E11 . . . . . .**76** C6
Mallinson Rd
Wallington SM6 . . . .**219** D5
Wandsworth SW11 . . . . . .**158** D6
Mallinson Sp Ctr N6 . . . . . .**48** D2
Mallon Gdns E1 . . . .**243** D5
Mallord St SW3 . .**136** B6 **266** D6
Mallory Cl London SE4. . . .**141** A1
South Bromley E14 . . . .**98** C3
Mallory Gdns EN4. . . . .**14** A4
Mallory Ho **1** SW8 . .**92** C3 **237** B6
Mallow Cl CR0 . . . .**206** D1
Mallow Ct
Colney Hatch N12. . . . .**30** C4
Lewisham SE13 . . . .**142** A3
Mallow Mead NW7 . . . .**29** A3
Mallow St EC1 . . . .**242** C6
Mallows The UB10 . . . .**60** D5
Mall Rd W6 . . . .**112** B1
Mall Sh Ctr The RM10 . . . . .**81** C2
Mall Studios **3** NW3 . . . . . .**70** D3
Mall The **6** Bexley DA6 . . .**147** C1
Brentford TW8 . . . .**131** D6
4 Bromley BR1 . . . .**209** A6
Ealing W5 . . . .**110** A6
Harrow HA3 . . . .**44** B3
Kingston u T KT6 . . . .**197** D4
Mortlake SW14 . . . .**155** A6
Palmers Green N14 . . . .**16** A1
St James SW1 . . . .**115** D3 **249** C3
Mall The N22 . . . .**32** C1
Mall The (Sch) TW2 . . . . .**152** B1
Malmains Cl BR3 . . . .**208** B5
Malmains Way BR3 . . . . . .**208** B5
Malmesbury **30** E2 . . . .**96** C5
Malmesbury Cl HA5. . . . . . .**40** A5
Malmesbury Prim Sch
Morden SM4. . . . .**202** A3
25 Tower Hamlets E3 . . . .**97** B4
Malmesbury Rd Bow E3. . . .**97** B5
Morden SM4. . . . .**202** A3
Newham E16 . . . .**98** C2
Woodford E18. . . . .**36** D2
Malmesbury Terr E16 . . . . . .**98** D2
Malmsey Ho SE11. . . . .**260** D1
Malmstead Ho **9** **75** A3
Malorees Jun & Inf Schs
NW6. . . . .**68** D1
Malory Cl BR3 . . . .**185** A1
Malpas Dr HA5 . . . .**40** B6
Malpas Rd Dagenham RM9. .**80** D2
Hackney E8. . . . .**74** B2
New Cross SE4 . . . .**141** B3
Malta Rd E10 . . . .**53** C2
Malta St EC1. . . . .**241** D6
Maltby Dr EN1 . . . .**6** B5
Maltby Rd KT9 . . . .**214** C2
Maltby St SE1 . . . . . .**117** D3 **263** C6
Maltham Terr N18. . . . .**34** B4
Malthouse Dr
Chiswick W4 . . . .**133** D6
Feltham TW13 . . . .**172** D5
Malthouse Pas SW13. . . . .**133** C3
Malthus Path **7** SE28 . . . .**124** C5
Malting Ho E14 . . . .**119** B6
Maltings W4 . . . .**110** C1
Maltings **3** Barnes SW13. .**133** C3
South Bromley E3 . . . .**98** C3
Maltings Lo W4 . . . .**133** C5
Maltings Pl
Bermondsey SE1 . . . .**253** B2
Parsons Green SW6 . . . . .**265** D1
Maltings The BR6 . . . .**211** D1
Malting Way TW7 . . . .**130** D2
Malt Mill SE1 . . . .**253** C3
Malton Ho SE25. . . . .**205** D5
Malton Mews
1 Notting Hill W10 . . . . . .**91** A1
Plumstead Comm SE18 . . .**145** C6
Malton Rd W10 . . . .**91** A1
Malton St SE18 . . . .**145** C6
Maltravers St WC2 . . . .**251** A6

Malt St SE1 . . . .**140** A6
Malva Cl SW18 . . . .**157** D6
Malvern Ave Chingford E4 . .**36** B3
Erith DA7 . . . .**147** A5
Harrow HA2 . . . .**63** B5
Malvern Cl Bushey WD23 . . .**8** A5
Ickenham UB10 . . . .**60** C6
Mitcham CR4 . . . .**203** C6
Notting Hill W10 . . . .**91** B2
Penge SE20 . . . .**184** A1
Surbiton KT6 . . . .**198** A1
Malvern Ct Belmont SM2 . .**217** C1
5 East Barnet N20 . . . . . .**14** C2
15 Shepherd's Bush W12. .**112** A4
South Kensington SW7 . . .**256** D4
3 Surbiton KT6 . . . .**198** A1
Malvern Dr
Feltham TW13 . . . .**172** D5
Ilford IG3 . . . .**79** D4
Woodford IG8. . . . .**37** C6
Malvern Gdns
Cricklewood NW2. . . . .**69** A6
Harrow HA3 . . . .**44** A5
Malvern Ho London N16. . . .**51** D1
SE17. . . . .**262** B1
Malvern Lo N12. . . . .**30** B6
Malvern Mews NW6. . . . . . .**91** B4
Malvern Pl NW6 . . . .**91** B4
Malvern Rd Dalston E8 . . . . .**74** A1
Enfield EN3. . . . .**7** A6
Hampton TW12. . . . .**173** C3
Harlington UB3. . . . .**127** C5
Hornsey N8. . . . .**50** C6
Leytonstone E11. . . . .**76** D6
Maida Vale NW6 . . . .**91** C4
Newham E6 . . . .**100** A6
Surbiton KT6. . . . .**198** A1
Thornton Heath CR7. . . . . .**204** C5
Tottenham Hale N17. . . . . . .**52** A6
Upper Holloway N19 . . . . . .**49** D1
Malvern Terr
Edmonton N9 . . . .**17** D3
Islington N1 . . . .**234** A6
Malvern Way W13. . . . .**87** B2
Malwood Rd SW12 . . . .**159** B5
Malyons Rd SE13 . . . .**163** D6
Malyons Terr SE13 . . . .**163** D6
Malyons The TW17 . . . .**193** B3
Managers St **8** E14 . . . . .**120** A5
Manaton Cl SE15. . . . .**140** B2
Manaton Cres UB1. . . . .**85** C1
Manbey Gr E15 . . . .**76** C2
Manbey Park Rd E15 . . . . . .**76** C2
Manbey Rd E15 . . . .**76** C2
Manbey St E15 . . . .**76** C2
Manbre Rd W6 . . . .**134** C6
Manbrough Ave E6 . . . .**100** C4
Manchester Ct E16 . . . .**99** B1
Manchester Dr W10. . . . .**91** A3
Manchester Gr E14 . . . . . .**120** A1
Manchester Ho SE17. . . . .**262** B2
Manchester Mans N19 . . . .**49** D2
Manchester Mews N1 . . . .**238** A3
Manchester Rd
Cubitt Town E14 . . . .**120** A3
South Norwood CR7 . . . . .**205** A6
Tottenham N15. . . . .**51** B3
Manchester Sq
W1. . . . .**93** A1 **238** B2
Manchester St
W1. . . . .**93** A2 **238** A3
Manchester Way RM10. . . . .**81** D4
Manchuria Rd SW11 . . . . . .**159** A5
Manciple St SE1 . . . .**117** B3 **262** D6
Mandalay Ho **6** N16. . . . . .**73** B4
Mandalay Rd SW4 . . . .**159** C6
Mandarin Ct
6 Deptford SE8. . . . .**141** C6
Willesden NW10. . . . .**67** B2
Mandarin Way UB4. . . . .**84** D1
Mandela Cl
36 Shepherd's Bush W12. .**112** B6
Stonebridge NW10. . . . .**67** A1
Mandela Ho
Plumstead Comm SE18 . . .**145** B6
18 Spitalfields E2 . . . .**95** D4
Mandela Rd E16 . . . .**99** A1
Mandela St
Camden Town
NW1. . . . .**93** C6 **232** B3
Kennington SW9. . . . .**138** C5
Mandela Way
SE1 . . . .**117** C2 **263** B4
Manderville Ho SE1. . . . . .**263** D2
Mandeville Cl
5 Greenwich SE3 . . . . . .**142** D5
Merton SW19. . . . .**179** A2
Mandeville Ct
Hampstead NW3 . . . .**69** D3
Highams Pk E4 . . . .**35** A6
Mandeville Ctyd SW11 . . .**268** A1
Mandeville Dr KT6 . . . .**197** D1
Mandeville Ho **8** SW4 . . . .**159** C6
Mandeville Pl W1 . . . .**238** B2
Mandeville Prim Sch E5 . . .**74** D5
Mandeville Rd Enfield EN3. . .**7** A6
Isleworth TW7 . . . .**131** A3
Littleton TW17 . . . .**192** C4
Northolt UB5 . . . .**63** C1

Mandeville Rd *continued*
Osidge N14. . . . .**15** C2
Mandeville Sch UB5 . . . . . .**63** B2
Mandeville St E5 . . . .**75** A5
Mandrake Rd SW17 . . . . . .**158** D1
Mandrake Way **3** E15. . . . .**76** C1
Mandrell Rd SW2. . . . .**160** A6
Manesty Ct N14. . . . .**15** D4
Manette St W1 . . . .**239** D1
Manfred Ct **7** SW15. . . . .**157** B6
Manfred Rd SW15. . . . .**157** B6
Manger Rd N7. . . . .**72** A2
Mangold Way **4** DA18 . . .**125** A3
Manilla St E14 . . . .**58** B3
Manilla St E14 . . . .**119** C4
Manister Rd SE2. . . . .**124** A3
Manitoba Ct **29** SE16 . . . .**118** C4
Manitoba Gdns **6** BR6. . .**227** D2
Manley Ct N16. . . . .**73** D5
Manley Ho SE11 . . . .**261** A2
Manley St NW1 . . . .**231** A6
Manly Dixon Dr EN3. . . . . . .**7** A6
Mann Cl **3** CR0. . . . .**221** A5
Manneby Prior N1. . . . .**233** D3
Mannering Ho **16** SW2 . . .**160** B6
Manning Ct **3** SE28. . . . . .**124** B5
Manningford Cl EC1 . . . . .**234** C2
Manning Gdns
Croydon CR0. . . . .**206** B2
Harrow HA3 . . . .**43** D2
Manning Ho
3 Notting Hill W11 . . . . . .**91** A1
6 Walthamstow E17 . . . . .**54** A6
Manning Pl TW10 . . . .**154** B5
Manning Rd
Dagenham RM10. . . . .**81** C1
Walthamstow E17 . . . .**53** A4
Manningtree Cl SW19. . . . .**157** A3
Manningtree Rd HA4. . . . . . .**62** B4
Manningtree St **2** E1. . . . . .**96** A2
Mannin Rd RM6. . . . .**58** B2
Mannock Cl NW9 . . . .**45** B6
Mannock Mews IG8 . . . .**37** B2
Mannock Rd N22 . . . .**50** D6
Mann's Cl TW7. . . . .**152** D6
Manns Rd HA8. . . . .**26** C4
Manny Shinwell Ho SW6 .**264** D5
Manoel Rd TW2. . . . .**152** A2
Manor Ave
Hounslow TW4 . . . .**128** D3
New Cross SE4 . . . .**141** B3
Northolt UB5 . . . .**63** B1
Manorbrook SE12, SE3. . . .**143** A1
Manor Circus TW9 . . . .**132** C2
Manor Cl Barnet EN5. . . . . . .**1** A1
Edgware NW7 . . . .**27** B5
Higham Hill E17 . . . .**35** A1
Kingsbury NW9 . . . .**44** D4
New Malden KT4 . . . .**199** C1
Ruislip HA4. . . . .**39** D1
Thamesmead SE28 . . . . . .**102** C1
Manor Cottages App N2. . . .**30** A1
Manor Cotts N2 . . . .**30** A1
Manor Court Lo **12** E18 . . .**37** A2
Manor Court Rd W7. . . . . . .**108** C6
Manor Cres KT5 . . . .**198** C3
Manor Croft HA8 . . . .**26** C4
Manor Ct **4** Barking IG11 . .**79** D1
1 Brixton SW2 . . . .**160** B6
Camberwell SE15 . . . .**139** D4
Chingford E4. . . . .**20** C3
Fortis Green N2 . . . .**48** D4
Friern Barnet N20 . . . .**14** D1
Gunnersbury W3 . . . .**110** C2
5 Hackbridge SM6 . . . . .**219** A5
Harrow HA1. . . . .**42** D3
Kingston u T KT2. . . . .**176** C2
Osidge N14. . . . .**15** D2
Parsons Green SW6. . . . . .**265** D1
Streatham SW16 . . . .**160** A4
Surbiton KT5. . . . .**198** C3
8 Sutton SM1 . . . .**218** A4
Twickenham TW2 . . . .**152** A2
Walthamstow E10 . . . .**53** D1
5 Wembley HA9 . . . .**66** A3
Manordene Ct N17. . . . .**197** A1
Manordene Rd SE28 . . . . .**102** D1
Manor Dr East Barnet N14 . .**15** B3
Edgware NW7 . . . .**27** B5
Feltham TW13 . . . .**172** D5
Friern Barnet N20 . . . .**14** D1
Hinchley Wood KT10. . . . .**213** A5
Sunbury TW16 . . . .**172** A1
Surbiton KT5. . . . .**198** C3
Wembley HA9. . . . .**66** B4
West Ewell KT19. . . . .**215** C2
Manor Dr N KT3, KT4 . . . . .**199** B2
Manor Dr The KT4. . . . .**199** D1
Manor Farm Ave TW17 . . .**192** D3
Manor Farm Cl KT4 . . . . . .**199** C1
Manor Farm Ct E6 . . . .**100** B4
Manor Farm Dr E4. . . . .**20** C1
Manor Farm Rd
Thornton Heath CR7,
SW16. . . . .**182** C1
Wembley HA0. . . . .**87** D5
Manorfield Cl **3** N19 . . . . .**71** C4

Manorfield Prim Sch [8]
E14..........................97 D2
Manorfields Cl BR7....211 D6
Manor Gate UB5...........63 A1
Manorgate Rd KT2....176 C2
Manor Gdns
[8] Chiswick W4.........111 C1
Clapham SW4...........137 C3
Gunnersbury W3........110 C2
Hampton TW12..........174 A3
Merton SW20............179 B1
Richmond TW10, TW9..132 B1
Ruislip HA4................62 C3
South Croydon CR2.....221 D2
Sunbury TW16...........172 A1
Upper Holloway N7.......72 A5
Manor Gr
Beckenham BR3........185 D1
Deptford SE15..........140 C6
Richmond TW9..........132 C2
Manor Gt SW15........157 A6
Manor Hall Ave NW4....28 D1
Manor Hall Dr NW4.....28 D1
Manor Hall Gdns E10...53 C1
Manor Ho Brentford TW8..109 C1
Manor Pk E12............77 D4
Osidge N14................15 D3
Paddington NW1.......237 B4
Twickenham TW2.......152 C2
Wallington SM6.........219 B3
Manor Ho The
Bexley DA5...............169 D3
Chislehurst SE9.........188 A5

Manor House Ct
Lower Halliford TW17...192 D2
Paddington W9.........236 A5
Manor House Dr NW6...68 D1
Manor House Est HA7...25 B5
Manor House Gdns E11..55 B3
Manor House Sta N4...205 A6
Manor House Way TW7..131 B2
Manor Jun & Inf Schs
IG11.......................79 D2
Manor La Feltham TW13..150 A2
Harlington UB3...........127 B6
Hither Green SE12.....164 C5
Sunbury TW16...........172 B1
Sutton SM1...............218 A4
Manor Lane Terr SE13..164 C6
Manor Lo NW2...........68 D2
Manor Mans
[7] Hampstead NW3......70 C2
Tufnell Pk N7.............72 A5
Manor Mead Sch TW17..192 D4
Manor Mews
New Cross SE4..........141 B3
Paddington NW6.........91 C5
Manor Mount SE23....162 C3
Manor Oak Mans SE22..162 B5
Manor Par Harrow HA1..42 D3
Stoke Newington N16..73 D6
MANOR PARK...........78 A4
Manor Park Cl BR4....207 D1
Manor Park Cres HA8...26 C4
Manor Park Dr HA2.....41 D6
Manor Park Gdns HA8..26 C4
Manor Park Par SE13..142 D4
Manor Park Prim Sch [8]
SM1........................218 A3
Manor Park Rd
Chislehurst BR7.........189 B2
Dagenham NW10.........89 D6
East Finchley N2.........48 B6
Manor Pk E12............77 D4
Sutton SM1...............218 A3
West Wickham BR4.....207 D1
Manor Park Sta E12....77 D4
Manor Pk
Chislehurst BR7.........189 B2
Lewisham SE13.........164 C6
Richmond TW9..........132 B1
Manor Pl Chislehurst BR7..189 B1
East Bedfont TW14.....150 A3
Mitcham CR4............203 C6
Newington SE17......117 A1 262 A2
Sutton SM1...............217 D4
Walton-on-T KT12.....194 A2
Manor Prim Sch E15...98 D5
Manor Rd Ashford TW15..170 C5
Barking IG11.............79 D2
Barnet EN5.................1 A1
Beckenham BR3........185 D1
Belmont SM2............217 B1
Bowes Pk N22............32 A4
Dagenham RM6..........58 D3
Ealing W13...............109 A6
East Molesey KT8......196 B5
Enfield EN2..................5 B3
Harrow HA1...............43 A3
Hayes UB3.................84 A1
Higham Hill E17.........35 A1
Loughton IG10............21 B5
Merton SW20............179 B1
Mitcham CR4............203 C6
Newham E15, E16.......98 C4
Old Bexley DA5.........169 D3
Richmond TW10, TW9..132 B1

Manor Rd continued
Ruislip HA4.................39 B1
Sidcup DA15.............168 A1
South Norwood SE25..206 A6
Stamford Hill N16........51 C1
Teddington TW11......175 B5
Tottenham N17...........34 B2
Twickenham TW2.......152 B2
Wallington SM5, SM6..219 B3
Walthamstow E10.......53 C2
Walton-on-T KT12.....193 D2
West Wickham BR4....223 D6
Manor Rd N
Hinchley Wood KT7....213 A6
Wallington SM5, SM6..219 B4
Manor Rd S KT10.......212 C4
Manorside EN5...........1 A1
Manorside Cl SE2.....124 D2
Manorside Prim Sch N3..30 A2
Manor Specl Sch NW10..90 C6
Manor Sq RM8............80 C6
Manor Street Est SW3..267 B6
Manor The Dulwich SE23..162 C4
Mayfair W1...............248 C5
Manor Vale TW8......109 C1
Manor View N3...........29 D1
Manorway Enfield EN1..17 C4
Woodford IG8............37 C5
Manor Way
Beckenham BR3........207 C6
Bromley BR2............210 A3
Chingford E4..............36 B6
Colindale NW9...........45 C5
Greenwich SE3..........143 A1
Gunnersbury W3.......110 C2
Harrow HA2...............41 D5
Mitcham CR4............203 C6
New Malden KT4........199 D1
Orpington BR5..........211 A5
Ruislip HA4................39 D1
Sidcup DA5..............169 C3
Southall UB2............106 D2
South Croydon CR2....221 D2
Manor Waye UB8.......82 A6
Manor Way The SM6..219 B4
Manpreet Ct E12........78 B3
Manray Ct [2] N8.........50 A4
Manresa Rd SW3..114 C1 257 A1
Mansard Beeches SW17..181 A5
Mansard Cl HA5..........40 D6
Mansard Manor [4] SM2..218 A1
Manse Cl UB3...........127 B6
Manse Ct DA14........190 C5
Mansel Ct SW11........267 B1
Mansel Gr E17...........35 C2
Mansell Ho SW8.......269 B2
Mansell Rd Acton W3..111 B4
Southall UB6..............85 D2
Mansell St E1....95 D1 243 D1
Mansel Rd SW19......179 B4
Manse Rd N16............73 D5
Mansergh Cl SE18....144 A5
Mansfield Ave
East Barnet EN4.........15 A5
Ruislip HA4................40 B1
Tottenham N15...........51 B5
Mansfield Cl N9..........18 A5
Mansfield Ct [27] E2....95 D6
Mansfield Dr HA5.......83 C3
Mansfield Hill E4........19 D3
Mansfield Ho SW15...156 D5
Mansfield Hts N2.......48 D4
Mansfield Mews W1..238 C3
Mansfield Pl NW3........70 A4
Mansfield Rd Acton W3..88 D3
Chessington KT9........213 D3
Ilford IG1....................78 C6
South Croydon CR2...221 B2
Walthamstow E17.......53 B5
Wanstead E11............55 B3
Mansfield St W1..93 B2 238 C3
Manship Rd CR4.......181 A2
Mansion Cl SW9........138 C4
Mansion Gdns NW3....69 C5
Mansion Ho * EC4....242 C1
EC4........................242 C1
Mansion House Pl EC3,
EC4........................242 C1
Mansion House St EC2..242 C1
Mansion House Sta
EC4........117 A6 252 B6
Mansions The NW6.....69 B3
Manson Mews
SW7.............114 B2 256 C3
Manson Pl SW7...114 B2 256 C3
Manstead Gdns RM6...58 C2
Manston
Camden Town NW1.....71 C1
Tottenham N17...........33 B1
Manston Ave UB2.....107 C2
Manston Cl SE20......184 C2
Manstone Rd NW2......69 A3
Manston Gr KT2.......175 D5
Manston Ho W14......254 B5
Mantell Ho SW4.......159 C6
Manthorpe Rd SE18..123 A1
Mantilla Rd SW17.....181 A6
Mantle Rd SE4..........141 A2

Mantlet Cl SW16.......181 C3
Mantle Way E15..........76 C1
Manton Ave W7.........109 A4
Manton Cl UB3..........105 C6
Manton Ho N16...........73 B5
Manton Rd Holdbrook EN3..7 C5
Plumstead SE2..........124 A2
Mantua St [2] SW11..136 B2
Mantus Cl
Bethnal Green E1........96 C3
[19] Stepney E1...........96 C3
Mantus Rd E1............96 C3
Manville Gdns SW17..159 B1
Manville Rd SW17.....159 B1
Manwood Rd SE4.....163 B5
Manwood St E16......122 B5
Manygate La TW17..193 A3
Many Gates SW12....159 B2
Mapesbury Ct NW2....69 A3
Mapesbury Mews [1]
NW9.......................46 A3
Mapesbury Rd NW2....69 A2
Mapeshill Pl NW2......68 C2
Mapes Ho [7] NW6.....69 A1
Mape St E2................96 B3
Maple Ave East Acton W3..111 C5
Harrow HA2................63 D6
Walthamstow E4.........35 B4
Yiewsley UB7............104 B6
Maple Cl
Buckhurst Hill IG9........21 D1
Clapham Pk SW4.......159 D5
Finchley N3................29 C4
Hampton TW12..........173 B4
Hayes UB4..................84 D4
Mitcham CR4............181 B2
Petts Wood BR5........211 B4
Ruislip HA4................40 B3
South Tottenham N16..52 A3
Maple Cres DA15.....168 A5
Maplecroft Cl E6.......100 A1
Maple Ct Ashford TW15..171 B3
Catford SE6..............163 D3
[2] Croydon CR0........221 A4
[7] Dagenham RM8......58 D2
Kingston u T KT3.......199 B6
Newham E6...............100 C2
[8] Pinner HA5.............22 C1
Sidcup DA14............190 B5
[11] West Norwood SW16..182 C5
[8] Willesden NW2........68 D4
Mapledale Ave CR0..222 A5
Mapledene BR7........189 A5
Mapledene Est E8.......74 A1
Mapledene Rd E8........74 A1
Mapledown Sch NW2..46 C2
Mapledurham Ct [3] N13..32 C6
Maple Gdns
Grahame Pk HA8........27 C3
Stanwell TW19..........148 A2
Maple Gr Brentford TW8..131 B5
Ealing W5.................109 D3
Kingsbury NW9...........45 A2
Southall UB1..............85 B2
Maple Gr Bsns Ctr TW4..128 C1
Maple Ho
[2] Kingston u T KT6....198 A4
[3] Maitland Pk NW3.....70 D2
[5] New Cross SE8.....141 B5
[4] Richmond TW9.....132 D4
Teddington KT1..........175 C3
[13] Walthamstow E17...53 D6
Maple House Ind Montessori
Sch [3] SE26.............205 A6
Maplehurst [2] BR2...186 C1
Maplehurst Cl KT1....198 A5
Maple Ind Est TW13..150 A1
Maple Inf Sch KT6....197 D4
Maple Leaf Dr DA15..167 D3
Mapleleafe Gdns IG6..56 D6
Maple Leaf Sq [27] SE16..118 D4
Maple Lo
Buckhurst Hill IG9........21 D3
Putney SW15............157 A5
Welsh Harp NW9........67 B6
Maple Mews
Paddington NW6.........91 D5
Streatham SW16.......182 B5
Maple Pl Marylebone W1..239 B5
[3] Tottenham N17.......34 A3
Yiewsley UB7............104 B6
Maple Rd Hayes UB4....84 D4
Kingston u T KT6.......197 D4
Leytonstone E11.........54 C3
Penge SE20..............184 C2
Maples Pl E1..............96 B2
Maple St
[5] Bethnal Green E2....96 B5
Fitzrovia W1.....93 C3 239 B5
Maplestead Rd
Dagenham RM9.........102 B6
Streatham SW2.........160 B4
Maples The [4] KT1...175 C3
Maplethorpe Rd CR7..204 D5
Mapleton Cl BR2......209 A3
Mapleton Cres Enfield EN3..6 C5
Wandsworth SW18....157 D5
Mapleton Rd Chingford E4..20 A1
Enfield EN1..................6 B3

Mapleton Rd continued
Wandsworth SW18....157 D5
Maple Tree Pl [7] SE3..144 A4
Maple Way TW13.....150 B1
Maple Wlk W10..........90 D3
Maplin Cl N21.............16 B5
Maplin Ho [7] SE2.....124 D4
Maplin Rd E16............99 B1
Maplin St E3...............97 B4
Mapperley Cl [3] E11...55 A3
Mapperley Dr IG8........36 C3
Marabou Cl E12........178 A3
Marada Ho NW6..........69 A1
Marais W4................133 A5
Maran Way DA18......124 D3
Marathon Way SE28..123 D4
Marban Rd W9............91 B4
Marble Arch *
W1.............114 D6 247 D6
Marble Arch Sta
W1.............92 D1 237 D1
Marble Cl W3............110 D5
Marble Dr NW2...........46 D2
Marbleford Ct [4] N6....49 D2
Marble Hill Cl TW1....153 B4
Marble Hill Gdns TW1..153 B4
Marble Hill House *
TW1........................153 C4
Marble Ho Paddington W9..91 B3
Plumstead Comm SE18..123 D1
Marble Quay SE1......118 A5
Marbrook Ct SE12....165 C1
Marcella Rd SW9.....138 C3
Marcellina Way BR6..227 D5
March [23] NW9...........27 D2
Marchant Cl NW7.......27 C3
Marchant Ho [13] SW2..160 B6
Marchant Rd E11........76 B6
Marchant St SE14....141 A6
Marchbank Rd
W14.............135 B6 264 D6
March Ct SW15.........134 B1
Marchmont Ho [10] SW16..181 C5
Marchmont Rd
Richmond TW10........154 B6
Wallington SM6.........219 C1
Marchmont St
WC1.............94 A3 240 A6
March Rd [7] TW1......153 A4
Marchside Cl TW5....128 D4
Marchwood Cl [7] SE5..139 C5
Marchwood Cres W5..87 D1
Marcia Rd SE1....117 C2 263 B3
Marcilly Rd SW18....158 B6
Marcol Ho W1..........238 D2
Marcon Ct [29] E8.......74 B3
Marconi Pl N11...........31 B6
Marconi Rd E10..........53 C1
Marconi Way UB1.......85 D1
Marcon Pl E8..............74 B3
Marco Rd W6............112 C3
Marcourt Lawns W5...88 A3
Marcus Ct Brentford TW8..132 A5
Newham E15...............98 C6
Marcus Garvey Mews
SE22......................162 B6
Marcus Garvey Way [9]
SE24......................138 C1
Marcus Ho [14] SE15..139 D4
Marcus St
Wandsworth SW18....157 D5
West Ham E15.............98 D6
Marcus Terr SW18....157 D5
Mardale Cl NW7..........28 A3
Mardale Dr NW9..........45 B4
Mardell Rd CR0........206 D4
Marden Ave BR2......209 A3
Marden Cres CR0.....204 B3
Marden Ho [6] E8........74 B3
Marden Rd
Thornton Heath CR0..204 B3
Tottenham N17............33 C1
Marden Sq SE16......118 B3
Marder Rd W13.........109 A4
Mardon HA5...............23 B3
Mardyke Ho SE17.....262 D4
Marechal Niel Ave DA15..167 B1
Marechal Niel Par DA15..167 B1
Maresby Ho E4...........19 D2
Maresfield CR0.........221 C5
Maresfield Gdns NW3..70 A2
Mare St E8..................74 B1
Marey Ct [10] CR2....221 A3
Marfleet Cl SM5.......218 C6
Margaret Ave E4........19 D5
Margaret Bondfield Ave
IG11.........................80 A1
Margaret Bondfield Ho
[5] Bow E3..................97 A5
[22] Kentish Town N7....71 D3
Margaret Ct Barnet EN4..2 B1
Marylebone W1.........239 A2
Margaret Gardner Dr
SE9........................166 B2
Margaret Herbison Ho
SW6.......................264 D5
Margaret Hill Ho [1] N8..50 A4
Margaret Ho
[16] Hammersmith W6..112 C1
[2] Sutton SM1..........217 D5

Margaret Ingram Cl
SW6.......................264 C5
Margaret Lockwood Cl
KT5........................198 B1
Margaret Mcmillan Ho [10]
N19..........................49 D2
Margaret Rd Barnet EN4..2 B1
Bexley DA5...............168 D5
Stamford Hill N16.......51 D1
Margaret Rutherford Pl [3]
SW12......................159 C1
Margarets Ct HA8......26 D5
Margaret's Ct E11.......54 B2
Margaret St W1...93 C1 239 A2
Margaretta Terr
SW3.............136 C6 267 B6
Margaretting Rd E12...55 C1
Margaret Way IG4......56 A3
Margaret White Ho NW1..232 C2
Margate Rd SW2.......160 A6
Margery Fry Ct N7.......72 A5
Margery Park Rd E7.....77 A2
Margery Rd RM8.........80 D5
Margery St WC1....94 C4 234 A1
Margin Dr SW19.......178 D6
Margravine Gdns
Hammersmith W6.......112 D1
West Kensington W14..254 A2
Margravine Rd
W6.............135 A6 264 A6
Marham Dr [17] NW9....27 C2
Marham Gdns
Morden SM4..............202 A3
Wandsworth SW17, SW18..158 C3
Mar Ho [4] SE7.........143 C6
Maria Cl [13] SE1......118 A2
Maria Fidelis Convent Sch
(Lower) NW1.....93 C4 232 B1
Maria Fidelis Convent Sch
(Upper) NW1.....93 D4 232 C2
Marian Cl UB4............84 D3
Marian St Hackney E9..74 C3
[1] Sutton SM1............217 D3
Marian Lo [5] SW20..178 D3
Marian Pl E2...............96 B5
Marian Rd SW16.......181 C2
Marian Sq E2..............96 B5
Marian St [2] E2..........96 B5
Marian Vian Prim Sch
BR3........................207 A4
Marian Way NW10......67 D1
Maria Terr E1..............96 D3
Maria Theresa Cl KT3..199 B4
Maribor [18] SE10......142 A5
Maricas Ave HA3.........24 B2
Marie Curie SE5........139 D4
Marie Lloyd Ct [13] SW9..138 B1
Marie Lloyd Gdns [1] N19..50 A2
Marie Lloyd Ho N1....235 C3
Marien Ct E4...............36 B5
Marie Stopes Ct [3] N19..50 A2
Marigold Cl UB1........107 A6
Marigold Rd N17.........34 C3
Marigold St SE16......118 B4
Marigold Way CR0....206 D1
Marilea Ct W5..........109 D4
Marillic Ho NW7..........28 C6
Marina App UB4..........85 A2
Marina Ave KT3.........200 B4
Marina Cl [1] BR2.....209 A6
Marina Ct [12] Bow E3..97 C4
Greenford UB6.............85 D5
Marina Dr DA16........145 C3
Marina Gdns RM7.......59 D4
Marina Pl KT1...........175 D2
Marina Point [4] E14..119 D3
Marina Way TW11.....175 D3
Marine Dr Barking IG11..102 B4
[5] Woolwich SE18....122 B2
Marinefield Rd SW6..135 D3
Marinel Ho [25] SE5...139 A5
Mariner Gdns TW10..153 C1
Mariner Rd E12..........78 C4
Mariners Mews E14..120 B2
Marine St SE16........118 A3
Marine Twr [29] SE8..141 B6
Marion Ave TW17.....192 D4
Marion Cl [4] SW17..180 C5
Marion Gr IG8.............36 C6
Marion Rd Mill Hill NW7..28 A5
Thornton Heath CR0..205 B4
Marion Richardson Prim Sch
[17] E1.....................96 D1
Marischal Rd SE13...142 B2
Maritime Greenwich Coll [18]
SE8........................141 C4
Maritime Ho
[5] Clapham SW4......137 C2
[14] Woolwich SE18...122 D2
Maritime Ind Est SE7..121 B2
Maritime Quay [5] E14..119 C1
Maritime St E3............97 B3
Marius Mans [3] SW17..159 A2
Marius Rd SW17.......159 A2
Marjorie Gr SW11.....136 D1
Marjorie McClure Sch
BR7........................189 A2
Marjory Kinnon Sch
TW14.......................149 C6
Markab Rd HA6...........22 D4

Mark Ave E4. . . . . .19 D5
Mark Cl Bexleyheath DA7. .147 A4
Keston Mark BR2. . . . . . .226 A4
Southall UB1. . . . . .107 D5
Markeston Gn WD19 . . . . . .22 D6
Market Ct W1. . . . .**239 A2**
Market Ctr The UB2. . . . . .106 B2
Market La Burnt Oak HA8 . . .27 A2
Shepherd's Bush W12 . . . .112 C4
Market Mews
W1. . . . . .115 B5 **248 C3**
Market Par Croydon SE25. .206 A5
Edmonton N9. . . . . .18 A2
Feltham TW13 . . . . .151 A2
Leyton E10. . . . . .53 D3
Walthamstow E17 . . . . . .53 B6
Market Pavilion E10 . . . . . .75 C5
Market Pl Acton W3. . . . . .111 A5
Bermondsey SE16. . . . . .118 B2
Bexleyheath DA6. . . . . . .147 C1
Brentford TW8 . . . . .131 C5
East Finchley N2. . . . . . . .48 C6
Enfield EN2. . . . . .5 B2
Kingston u T KT1. . . . . . .175 D1
Marylebone W1 . . . .**239 A2**
Market Pl The NW11 . . . . .47 D5
Market Rd Barnsbury N7. . .72 A2
Richmond TW9. . . . . . . .132 C2
Market Sq Bromley BR1 . . .187 A1
Poplar E14. . . . . .97 D1
Market Sq The N9. . . . . . . .18 B2
Market St Spitalfields E1. . .**243 C4**
Wallend E6. . . . . .100 C5
Woolwich SE18. . . . . . . .122 C2
Market Studios **14** W12. .112 C4
Market The SM1, SM5 . . . .202 A1
Market Way Poplar E14. . . .97 C1
Wembley HA0 . . . . .66 A3
Market Yd Mews SE1. . . . .**263 A6**
Markfield Beam Engine &
Mus* N15. . . . . .52 A4
Markfield Gdns E4. . . . . . . .19 D4
Markfield Ho N15. . . . . . . .52 A4
Markfield Rd N15. . . . . . . .52 A4
Markham Ct NW4. . . . . . . .46 C6
Markham Ho
Dagenham RM10. . . . . . . .81 C5
Dulwich SE21. . . . . .183 C6
Markham Pl SW3 . . . .**257 C2**
Markham Sq
SW3. . . . . .114 D1 **257 C2**
Markham St
SW3. . . . . .114 C1 **257 B2**
Mark Ho **3** E2. . . . . .96 D5
Markhole Cl TW12 . . . . . .173 B3
Markhouse Ave E17. . . . . .53 A3
Markhouse Pas E17. . . . . .53 B3
Markhouse Rd E17. . . . . . .53 B3
Mark La EC3. . . . . . .117 C6 **253 B6**
Markland Ho W10. . . . . . .112 D6
Mark Lo **9** EN4. . . . . .2 C1
Markmanor Ave E17. . . . . .53 B2
Mark Mans W12 . . . . .112 A4
Marksbury Ave TW9. . . . . .132 C2
Marks Gate Jun & Inf Schs
RM6. . . . . .59 A6
Mark Sq EC2. . . . .**243 A6**
Mark St Broadgate EC2. . .**243 A6**
Stratford E15. . . . . .76 C1
Markstone Ho SE1. . . . . . .**251 C1**
Mark Wade Cl E12 . . . . . . .55 D1
Markway The TW16 . . . . . .172 C1
Markwell Cl SE26 . . . . . . .184 B6
Markyate Ho **6** W10. . . . . .90 C3
Markyate Rd RM8. . . . . . . .80 B3
Marland Ho SW1. . . . .**257 D6**
Marlands Rd IG5 . . . . .56 B6
Marlang Ct BR3. . . . . . . .186 B2
Marlborough
Putney SW19. . . . . . . .156 D3
St John's Wood W9. . . . .**229 A2**
Marlborough Ave
Edgware HA8 . . . . .10 D1
Hackney E8. . . . . .96 A6
New Southgate N14 . . . .15 C1
Ruislip HA4. . . . . .39 B3
Marlborough Cl
Broom Hill BR6. . . . . . . .211 D3
Friern Barnet N20 . . . . . .14 D1
Mitcham SW19. . . . . . . .180 C4
Newington SE17. . . . . . .**261 D3**
Marlborough Cres
Bedford Pk W4. . . . . . . .111 C3
Harlington UB3. . . . . . . .127 B5
Marlborough Ct
Beckenham BR3. . . . . . .185 C2
Bromley BR1. . . . . .186 D3
Buckhurst Hill IG9. . . . . .21 C2
Harrow HA1. . . . . .42 B5
Kensington W8. . . . .**255 A4**
Wallington SM6 . . . .**219 C1**
Marlborough Dr IG5. . . . . .56 A6
Marlborough Flats SW3. .**257 B4**
Marlborough Fst & Mid Sch
HA1. . . . . .42 C5
Marlborough Gdns
Friern Barnet N20 . . . . . .14 D1
Surbiton KT6. . . . . .197 D2

Marlborough Gr SE1 . . . .118 A1
Marlborough Hill
Harrow HA1. . . . . .42 C5
St John's Wood
NW8. . . . . .92 A6 **229 B5**
Marlborough Ho
Marylebone NW1 . . . . . .**238 D6**
Richmond TW10 . . . . . . .154 C6
Stoke Newington N4. . . . .51 A1
Marlborough Ho SW1 . . . .**249 B3**
Marlborough Ho SW19. . .156 D1
Marlborough La SE7 . . . .**143 C5**
Marlborough Lo
Stepney E1. . . . . .96 C3
St John's Wood NW8 . . .**229 A3**
Marlborough Mans **5**
NW6 . . . . .69 C3
Marlborough Mews **18**
SW2. . . . . .138 B1
Marlborough Par **1**
UB10 . . . . .82 D3
Marlborough Park Ave
DA15 . . . . .168 A3
Marlborough Pl
NW8 . . . . .92 A5 **229 B4**
Marlborough Prim Sch
Chelsea SW3 . . . . . .114 C2 **257 B3**
Isleworth TW7 . . . . .131 A4
Marlborough Rd
Acton Green W4. . . . . . .111 A1
Ashford TW15. . . . . . . .170 A5
Bexley DA7. . . . . .146 D2
Bowes Pk N22. . . . . .32 B4
Brentford TW7 . . . . .131 B5
Bromley BR2. . . . . .209 C5
Chingford E4. . . . . .35 D4
Dagenham RM8 . . . . . . .80 C4
Ealing W5 . . . . .109 D4
Edmonton N9. . . . . .18 A3
Feltham TW13 . . . . .150 D2
Hampton TW12 . . . . . . .173 C4
Hillingdon UB10 . . . . . . .82 D4
Leyton E15. . . . . .76 C4
Mitcham SW19. . . . . . . .180 C4
Richmond TW10 . . . . . . .154 B5
Romford RM7. . . . . .59 D5
Southall UB2. . . . . .106 C3
South Croydon CR2. . . . .221 A1
St James SW1 . . . . .115 C5 **249 B3**
Sutton SM1. . . . . .217 C6
Upper Holloway N19 . . . .72 A6
Upton E7 . . . . .77 C1
Wanstead E18. . . . . .55 A4
Woolwich SE18. . . . . . .123 A3
Marlborough Sch DA15 . . .168 A4
Marlborough St
SW3. . . . . .114 C2 **257 B3**
Marlborough Trad Est
TW9 . . . . .132 C4
Marlborough Yd N19. . . . . .71 D6
Marlbury NW8. . . . . .91 D6
Marler Rd SE23. . . . . . . .163 B3
Marlesford Ct SM6. . . . . .219 C4
Marlex Lo N3. . . . . .29 D2
Marley Ave DA7. . . . . . . .146 B4
Marley Ct
Southall UB5. . . . . .85 C4
Marley Ho **14** W11 . . . . . .112 D6
Marley Wlk NW2 . . . . .68 C3
Marlfield Cl KT4 . . . . .200 A1
Marlfield Ct KT3 . . . . .199 D2
Marlin Cl TW16. . . . . .171 C4
Marlin Ct **5** DA14. . . . . . .190 A6
Marling Ct TW12. . . . . . . .173 B4
Marlingdene Cl TW12 . . . .173 C4
Marlings Cl BR7 . . . . .211 A4
Marlings Park Ave BR7. . .211 C6
Marlin Ho SW15 . . . . .157 A6
Marlins Cl **3** SM1. . . . . . .218 A3
Marloes Ct HA0 . . . . .65 D4
Marloes Rd W8. . . .113 D3 **255 C5**
Marlow Cl SE20. . . . . . . .206 B6
Marlow Cres TW1 . . . . . .152 D5
Marlow Ct Colindale NW9. .45 D6
Ealing W7 . . . . .108 C5
Finchley N3. . . . . .29 C2
Harrow HA1. . . . . .42 A3
Osidge N14. . . . . .15 C4
Willesden NW6. . . . . . . .68 D1
Marlow Dr SM3. . . . . .216 D5
Marlowe Bsns Ctr **2**
SE14. . . . . .141 A5
Marlowe Cl BR7. . . . . . . .189 B4
Marlowe Ct Chelsea SW3. .**257 B3**
Dulwich SE19. . . . . .183 D5
Kingston u T KT2 . . . . . .175 D6
Marlowe Gdns SE9. . . . . .166 C5
Marlowe Ho
Kingston u T KT1. . . . . . .197 D5
Stoke Newington N16. . .73 C4
Marlowe Lo CR0. . . . . . . .223 A6
Marlowe Rd E17. . . . . .54 A5
Marlowe Sq CR4. . . . . . . .203 C5
Marlowes The
NW8 . . . . .92 B6 **229 C6**
Marlow Ho
Bermondsey SE1. . . . . . .**263 C6**
Kensington W2. . . . . . . .91 D1

Marlow Ho *continued*
Spitalfields E2. . . . . . . .95 D4
Teddington TW11. . . . . .175 A6
Wallington CR0. . . . . . . .220 A5
Marlow Rd Newham E6. . .100 B4
Penge SE20. . . . . .184 B1
Southall UB2. . . . . .107 B3
Marlow Studio Workshops **43**
E2. . . . . .95 D4
Marlow Way SE16. . . . . . .118 D4
Marl Rd SW18 . . . . .136 A1
Marlston NW1. . . . .**231 D1**
Marlton St SE10 . . . . . . .120 D1
Marlwood Cl DA15. . . . . .167 C2
Marmadon Rd SE18, SE2. .123 D2
Marmara Apts **4** E16 . . .121 A6
Marmion App E4 . . . . .35 C6
Marmion Ave E4. . . . . . . .35 B6
Marmion Cl E4. . . . . .35 B6
Marmion Ho **13** SW12 . .159 B4
Marmion Mews **4**
SW11. . . . . .137 A2
Marmion Rd SW11 . . . . . .137 A1
Marmont Rd SE15. . . . . . .140 A5
Marmora Ho E1 . . . . .97 A2
Marmora Rd SE22. . . . . . .162 C5
Marncrest Ct KT5. . . . . . .198 B4
Marne Ave
Friern Barnet N11 . . . . . .31 B6
Welling DA16 . . . . .146 A2
Marnell Way TW4 . . . . . . .128 D2
Marner Prim Sch **6** E3. . . .97 D3
Marne St W10. . . . . .91 A4
Marney Rd SW11 . . . . . . .137 A1
Marnfield Cres SW2. . . . . .160 B3
Marnham Ave NW2 . . . . . .69 A4
Marnham Cres UB6. . . . . .85 D5
Marnham Ct HA0 . . . . .65 C3
Marnie Ct **11** E11 . . . . . . .76 C6
Marnock Ho SE17. . . . . . .**262 C2**
Marnock Rd SE4. . . . . . . .163 B6
Maroon St E14. . . . . .97 A2
Maroons Way SE6. . . . . . .185 C5
Marquee Twrs **1**
SW16. . . . . .182 B3
Marquess Rd N1. . . . . .73 B2
Marquis Cl HA0 . . . . .66 B1
Marquis Ct Barking IG11 . .79 C3
Finsbury Pk N4. . . . . . . .50 B1
Kingston u T KT1 . . . . . .198 A5
Stanwell TW19 . . . . . . .148 A3
Marquis Rd Bowes Pk N22. .32 B4
Finsbury Pk N4. . . . . . . .50 C1
Kentish Town NW1 . . . . .71 D2
Marrabon Cl DA15. . . . . . .168 A3
Marrick Cl SW15. . . . . . . .134 A1
Marrick Ho **19** NW6. . . . . .91 D6
Marrilyne Ave EN3 . . . . . . .7 B5
Marriner Ct UB3. . . . . . . .105 C6
Marriott Cl TW14. . . . . . . .149 B5
Marriott Ho **8** SE6. . . . . .186 A6
Marriott Rd Finsbury Pk N4. .50 B1
Newham E15. . . . . .98 C6
Marriotts Cl NW9. . . . . . . .45 D3
Marryat Cl TW3 . . . . .129 B1
Marryat Ct **12** W6 . . . . . .112 B2
Marryat Ho SW1 . . . .**259 A1**
Marryat Pl SW19. . . . . . . .179 A6
Marryat Rd SW19. . . . . . .179 A6
Marryat Sq SW6 . . . .**264 A2**
Marryatt Ct W5 . . . . .88 B1
Marryfields Way SE6. . . . .163 D4
Marsala Rd SE13. . . . . . . .141 D1
Marsalis Ho **3** E3 . . . . . . .97 C4
Marsden Rd
Camberwell SE15. . . . . .139 D2
Edmonton N9. . . . . .18 B2
Marsden St NW5. . . . . . . .71 A2
Marsden Way **2** BR6. . . .227 D4
Marshall Cl
Brunswick Pk N11 . . . . . .15 B1
Harrow HA1. . . . . .42 B2
Hounslow TW4 . . . . .151 B6
Wandsworth SW18 . . . . .158 A5
Marshall Ct SW4. . . . .**270 B1**
Marshall Dr UB4. . . . . .83 D2
Marshall Ho
New Malden KT3. . . . . . .199 C5
Paddington NW6 . . . . . .91 B5
Shoreditch N1. . . . .**235 D4**
Walworth SE17. . . . .**262 C2**
Marshall Path **10** SE28. . .124 B6
Marshall Rd Leyton E10. . .75 D4
Tottenham N17. . . . . . . .33 A2
Marshall St L Ctr
SE1. . . . . .117 A4 **252 B2**
Marshall St
SW1. . . . . .93 C1 **239 B1**
Marshalls Gr SE18. . . . . .122 A2
Marshall's Pl SE16 . . . . . .**263 D5**
Marshall's Rd SM1. . . . . .217 D4
Marshall St W1. . .93 C1 **239 B1**
Marshalsea Rd
SE1. . . . . .117 A4 **252 B2**
Marsham Cl BR7. . . . . . . .188 D5
Marsham Ct
Putney SW15. . . . . .156 D3
Westminster SW1 . . . . .**259 D1**
Marsham St
SW1. . . . . .115 D2 **259 D1**

Marsh Ave CR4. . . . . .181 A1
Marshbrook Cl SE3 . . . . . .143 D2
Marsh Cl NW7. . . . . .11 D1
Marsh Ct Dalston E8 . . . . . .74 A2
Merton SW19 . . . . .180 A2
Marsh Dr NW9. . . . . .45 D3
Marsh Farm Rd TW2 . . . .152 D3
Marshfield St E14. . . . . . .120 A3
Marsh Gate Bsns Ctr E15. .98 A5
Marshgate Sch TW10 . . . .154 B6
Marsh Green Prim Sch
RM10. . . . . .103 C5
Marsh Green Rd RM10. . . .103 C6
Marsh Hall HA9. . . . . .66 B5
Marsh Hill E9. . . . . .75 A3
Marsh Ho Nine Elms SW8 . .**269 B2**
Pimlico SW1. . . . .**259 D1**
Marsh La Edgware NW7 . . .11 C6
Leyton E10. . . . . .75 C6
Stanmore HA7. . . . . .25 C4
Tottenham N17. . . . . . . .34 B2
Marsh Point HA5. . . . . . . .41 B5
Marsh Rd Pinner HA5 . . . . .41 A5
Wembley HA0. . . . . .87 D5
Marshside Cl N9. . . . . .18 C3
Marsh St E14. . . . . .119 D2
Marsh Wall E14. . . . . .119 D2
Marshwood Ho **10** NW6 . .91 C6
Marsland Cl SE17 . . . .**261 D1**
Marsom Ho N1 . . . .**235 C3**
Marston SE17. . . . .**262 B4**
Marston Ave
Chessington KT9. . . . . .214 A2
Dagenham RM10. . . . . . .81 C5
Marston Cl
Dagenham RM10. . . . . . .81 C5
South Hampstead NW6 . .70 A1
Marston Ct Barnet EN5. . . .13 A1
Sidcup DA14. . . . . .189 D6
Walton-on-T KT12. . . . . .194 C1
Marston Ho **23** SW9. . . . .138 C3
Marston Rd TW11. . . . . . .175 B5
Marston Way SE19. . . . . .183 A3
Marsworth Ave HA5. . . . . .22 D2
Marsworth Cl UB4. . . . . . . .85 A2
Marsworth Ho **8** E2 . . . . .96 A6
Martaban Rd N16. . . . . . . .73 D6
Martello St E8. . . . . .74 B1
Martello Terr E8. . . . . .74 B1
Martell Rd SE21. . . . . . . .161 B1
Martel Pl E8. . . . . .73 D2
Marten Rd E17. . . . . .35 C1
Martens Ave DA7. . . . . . .147 D1
Martham Cl SE28. . . . . . .124 D6
Martha Rd E15. . . . . .76 C2
Martha's Bldgs EC1. . . . . .**242 C6**
Martha St E1 . . . . .96 C1
Marthorne Cres HA3. . . . . .24 B1
Martin Bowes Rd SE9 . . . .144 B2
Martinbridge Trad Est
EN1. . . . . .18 A6
Martin Cl
Lower Edmonton N9. . . . .18 D3
Uxbridge UB10 . . . . .82 A5
Martin Cres CR0. . . . . . . .204 C1
Martin Ct
Cubitt Town E14. . . . . . .120 A4
Lewisham SE12. . . . . . . .164 D4
Merton SW19 . . . . .179 C3
Southall UB2. . . . . .107 B4
Martindale SW14 . . . . . . .155 A6
Martindale Ave **2** E16. . .121 A6
Martindale Ho **23** E14. . .119 D6
Martindale Rd
Balham SW12. . . . . .159 B4
Hounslow TW4 . . . . .129 A2
Martin Dene DA6. . . . . . . .169 B6
Martin Dr UB5. . . . . .63 B3
Martineau Cl KT10. . . . . . .212 B4
Martineau Dr TW1. . . . . . .131 B1
Martineau Ho SW1. . . . . .**259 A1**
Martineau Mews N5. . . . . .72 D4
Martineau Rd N5. . . . . . . .72 D4
Martingale Cl TW16. . . . . .194 A5
Martingales Cl TW10. . . . .153 D1
Martin Gdns RM8. . . . . . . .80 D4
Martin Gr SM4. . . . . .201 C6
Martin Ho Newington SE1. .**262 B5**
New Malden KT3. . . . . . .199 C5
South Lambeth SW8. . . . .**270 A4**
Martin La EC4. . . . .**252 D6**
Martin Prim Sch N2. . . . . . .30 C1
Martin Rd RM8. . . . . .80 D4
Martin Rise DA6. . . . . . . .169 B6
Martins Cl BR4. . . . . .224 B6
Martins Mount EN5 . . . . . .1 D1
Martin's Pl SE28. . . . . . . .123 C5
Martin's Rd BR2. . . . . . . .186 D1
Martin St SE28. . . . . .123 C5
Martins The Penge SE26. .184 B5
Wembley HA9. . . . . .66 B5
Martins Wlk
Muswell Hill N10. . . . . . .31 A2
Woolwich SE28. . . . . . . .123 C5
Martin Way SW20, SM4. . .201 B6
Martlesham N17. . . . . .33 C1
Martlesham Wlk NW9. . . . .27 C2
Martlet Gr **5** UB5. . . . . . .84 D4
Martlett Ct WC2 . . . .**240 B1**

Martlett Lo NW3. . . . . .69 D4
Martley Dr IG2. . . . . .56 D4
Martley Ho SW8 . . . .**269 B2**
Martock Cl HA3. . . . . .43 A5
Martock Ct **10** SE15. . . . .140 B4
Martock Gdns N11. . . . . . .31 A5
Marton Cl SE6. . . . . .163 C1
Marton Rd **2** N16. . . . . . .73 C5
Martyn Cl HA8. . . . . .26 B6
Martyn Ho SE2. . . . . .146 D6
Martynside **22** NW9 . . . . .27 D2
Marvel Ho **6** SE5 . . . . . . .139 B5
Marvell Ave UB4 . . . . .84 A2
Marvels Cl SE12. . . . . . . .165 B2
Marvels La SE12 . . . . .165 C1
Marvels Lane Prim Sch
SE12. . . . . .187 C6
Marville Rd SW6. . . .135 B5 **264 C3**
Marvin Ho **9** SE18. . . . . .144 D6
Marvin St E8. . . . . .74 B2
Marwell Cl BR4 . . . . .224 D6
Marwell Ct SE3. . . . . .142 B3
Marwick Rd UB2. . . . . . . .104 B4
Marwood Cl DA16. . . . . . .146 B2
Marwood Ct N3. . . . . .29 D3
Marwood Dr NW7. . . . . . . .28 D3
Mary Adelaide Cl
Kingston u T SW15. . . . .155 C1
Kingston u T SW15. . . . .177 C6
Mary Adelaide Ho **2** W2. .**236 D4**
Mary Ann Bldgs SE8 . . . . .141 C6
Maryatt Ave HA2. . . . . . . .63 D6
Marybank SE18 . . . . .122 B2
Mary Cl HA7. . . . . .44 B5
Mary Datchelor Cl SE5 . . .139 B4
Mary Dine Ct SW8 . . . . . .**270 D3**
Mary Gn NW8. . . . . .91 D6
Marygold Ho TW3. . . . . . .130 A4
Mary Ho
Hammersmith W6. . . . . .112 C1
Stockwell SW9 . . . . .138 B3
Mary James Ho **32** E2. . . .96 A5
Mary Jones Ho **20** E14. . .119 C6
Maryland Ct KT1. . . . . . . .176 D1
Maryland Pk E15 . . . . .76 C3
Maryland Point E15. . . . . .76 C3
Maryland Prim Sch E15. . .76 C3
Maryland Rd
Paddington W9. . . . . . . .91 C3
South Norwood CR7. . . .182 D2
Stratford New Town E15. .76 B3
Tottenham N22. . . . . . . .32 C4
Marylands Ind Est E15. . . .76 C3
Maryland Sq E15 . . . . .76 C3
Maryland St E15. . . . . .76 C3
Maryland Sta E15. . . . . . . .76 C2
Maryland Way TW16 . . . . .172 A1
Maryland Wlk N1 . . . .**235 A6**
Mary Lawrenson Pl **1**
SE3 . . . . .143 A5
MARYLEBONE. 93 B1
Marylebone Ct **3** HA0 . . . .66 A2
Marylebone Flyover
NW1 . . . . .92 C2 **237 A3**
Marylebone High St
W1. . . . . .93 A3 **238 B4**
Marylebone La
W1. . . . . .93 A1 **238 B2**
Marylebone Mews W1 . . .**238 C3**
Marylebone Pas W1 . . . . .**239 B2**
Marylebone Rd
NW1 . . . . .92 D2 **237 D4**
Marylebone St
W1. . . . . .93 A2 **238 B3**
Marylebone Sta
NW1 . . . . .92 D3 **237 C5**
Marylee Way
SE11. . . . . .116 B2 **260 D2**
Mary McArthur Ho **12**
N19 . . . . .49 D2
Mary Macarthur Ho
Belvedere DA17. . . . . . .125 C3
Dagenham RM10. . . . . . .81 C5
Globe Town E2. . . . . . . .96 D4
W14 . . . .**264 A6**
Marymount International Sch
KT2. . . . . .177 A3
Maryon Gr SE7. . . . . .122 A4
Maryon Mews NW3 . . . . . .70 C4
Maryon Rd SE7. . . . . .122 A4
Mary Peters Dr UB6. . . . . .64 B3
Mary Pl W11. . . . . .113 A6 **244 A5**
Mary Rose Cl TW12. . . . . .173 C2
Mary Rose Mall E6. . . . . .100 B2
Maryrose Way N20. . . . . . .14 B3
Mary's Ct NW8. . . . .**237 B6**
Mary Seacole Villas **19**
NW10 . . . . .67 B1
Mary Secole Cl **21** E8. . . . .95 D6
Mary Smith Ct SW5 . . . . .**255 B5**
Mary St
Canning Town E16. . . . . .98 D2
Shoreditch N1. . . . .95 A6 **235 B5**
Mary's Terr TW1. . . . . . . .153 A4
Mary Tates Cotts CR4. . . .202 D5
Mary Terr NW1. . . . .**232 A5**

Maryville DA16 . . . . 145 D3
Mary Way WD19 . . . . .22 C6
Mary Wharrie Ho 4
  NW3 . . . . .70 D1
Marzena Ct TW2 . . . . . . .152 A6
Masbro' Rd W14 . . . . 112 D3
Mascalls Ct SE7 . . . . . . .143 C6
Mascalls Rd SE7 . . . . . . .143 C6
Mascotte Rd 2 SW15 . . . .134 D1
Mascotts Cl NW2 . . . . .68 B5
Masefield Ave
  Borehamwood WD6 . . . . . .10 D6
  Southall UB1. . . . . .107 C6
  Stanmore HA7. . . . . .24 D5
Masefield Cres N14 . . . . . .15 C5
Masefield Ct
  New Barnet EN5 . . . . .2 A1
  Stoke Newington N5. . . . . .73 B3
  19 Surbiton KT6. . . . . . . .197 D2
Masefield Gdns E6. . . . . .100 C3
Masefield Ho 4 NW6 . . . . .91 C4
Masefield La UB4 . . . . . . .84 C3
Masefield Rd TW13 . . . . .173 B6
Masefield View BR6. . . . . .227 A5
Masefield Way TW19 . . . .148 B3
Masham Ho 19 DA18 . . . .124 D4
Mashie Rd W3 . . . . .89 C1
Maskall Cl SW2. . . . . . . .160 C3
Maskani Wlk SW16 . . . . .181 C3
Maskell Rd SW17 . . . . . .158 A1
Maskelyne Cl
  SW11. . . . . .136 C4 267 B2
Mason Cl
  Bermondsey SE16 . . . . . .118 A1
  Bexleyheath DA7 . . . . . . .147 D2
  Hampton TW12 . . . . .173 B2
  Newham E16 . . . . .121 A6
  Wimbledon SW20. . . . . . .178 D2
Mason Ct 4 Penge SE19 . 183 D3
  Wembley HA9. . . . . .66 C6
Mason Ho
  15 Bermondsey SE1. . . . . .118 A2
  8 Friern Barnet N11. . . . . .31 C5
  16 Hackney E9 . . . . .74 C1
Mason Rd Sutton SM1. . . .217 D3
  Woodford IG8. . . . . .36 C6
Mason's Arms Mews W1 248 D6
Masons Ave HA3. . . . . . . .42 D5
Mason's Ave
  City of London EC2 . . . . . 242 C2
  Croydon CR0. . . . . 221 A5
  13 Woolwich SE18 . . . . . .122 D2
13 Masons Ho NW9 . . . . . .44 D4
Mason's Pl Finsbury EC1. 235 A2
  Mitcham CR4 . . . . .180 D2
Mason St SE17. . . .117 B2 262 D4
Mason's Yd Finsbury EC1. 234 D2
  St James SW1 . . . . 249 B4
  Wimbledon SW19. . . . . . .178 D5
Massey Cl N11. . . . . .31 B5
Massey Ct 6 E6 . . . . .99 C6
Massie Rd E8. . . . . .74 A2
Massingberd Way SW17. .181 B6
Massinger St SE1, SE17 . 263 A3
Massingham St E1. . . . . . .96 D3
Masson Ave HA4. . . . . . . .62 C2
Mast Ct 17 SE16. . . . . . . .119 A2
Master Gunner's Pl 1
  SE18 . . . . .144 A4
Masterman Ho 1 SE5. . . .139 B5
Masterman Rd E6 . . . . . .100 A4
Masters Cl SW16. . . . . . .181 C4
Masters Ct HA4. . . . . .61 C6
Masters Dr SE16 . . . . . . .118 B1
Masters Lo 24 E1 . . . . . . .96 C1
Master's St 18 E1 . . . . . . .96 D2
Mast House Terr E14 . . . .119 C2
Mastin Ho SW18 . . . . . . .157 C3
Mastmaker Rd E14. . . . . .119 C4
Maswell Park Cres TW3. .152 A6
Maswell Park Rd TW3 . . .130 A1
Matara Mews SE17. . . . . 262 A1
Matcham Rd E11 . . . . .76 D5
Matching Ct 14 E3 . . . . . .97 C4
Matchless Dr SE18. . . . . .144 C5
Matchroom Stadium
  (Brisbane Rd) (Leyton
  Orient FC) E10 . . . . .75 D5
Matfield Cl BR2. . . . . . . .209 A4
Matfield Rd DA17 . . . . . .147 C6
Matham Gr SE22. . . . . . .139 D1
Matham Rd KT8 . . . . . . .196 B4
Mathart Ct E4 . . . . .36 B4
Matheson Lang Ho SE1. . 251 A1
Matheson Rd
  W14. . . . . .113 B2 254 C3
Mathews Ave E6. . . . . . .100 C5
Mathews Park Ave E15. . .76 D2
Mathews Yd WC2 . . . . . 240 A1
Mathieson Ct SE1. . . . . . 251 D1
Mathieson Ho 10 E4 . . . . .20 C4
Mathilda Marks-Kennedy
  Jewish Prim Sch 5
  NW7. . . . . .27 B5
Mathison Ho SW10. . . . . 266 A4
Matilda Ct SE19. . . . . . . .183 B3

Matilda Gdns 10 E3 . . . . . .97 C5
Matilda Ho E1. . . . . .118 A5
Matilda St N1. . . . . .94 B6 233 D6
Matlock Cl Barnet EN5 . . . .12 C6
  Herne Hill SE24 . . . . .139 A1
Matlock Cres SM3 . . . . . .217 A4
Matlock Ct
  7 Herne Hill SE5. . . . . . . .139 B1
  St John's Wood NW8 . . . . 229 A4
  Woodford IG8. . . . . .36 D2
Matlock Gdns SM1, SM3 . .217 A4
Matlock Pl SM1, SM3 . . . .217 A4
Matlock Rd E10. . . . . .54 A3
Matlock St E14 . . . . .97 A1
Matlock Way KT3 . . . . . . .177 B2
Maton Ho SW6 . . . . 264 C4
Matson Ct IG8. . . . . .36 C3
Matson Ho
  9 Bermondsey SE16. . . . . .118 B3
  16 Homerton E9. . . . . .74 D2
Matthew Cl W10 . . . . .90 D3
Matthew Ct Mitcham CR4. 203 D4
  4 Walthamstow E17 . . . . . .54 A6
Matthew Parker St SW1. . . 249 D1
Matthews Ct. 73 A4
Matthews Ho 3 E14 . . . . . .97 C2
Matthews Rd UB6. . . . . . . .64 B3
Matthews St SW11. . . . . .136 D3
Matthias Ho 2 N16 . . . . . .73 C3
Matthias Rd N16. . . . . . . .73 C3
Mattingly Way 3 SE15 . . .139 D5
Mattison Rd N4. . . . . .50 D3
Mattock La W5, W13. . . . .109 C5
Maud Cashmore Way
  SE18 . . . . .122 B3
Maude Ho 3 E2 . . . . .96 A5
Maude Rd
  Camberwell SE5 . . . . .139 C4
  Walthamstow E17 . . . . . . .53 A4
Maudesville Cotts W7. . . .108 C5
Maude Terr E17. . . . . .53 A5
Maud Gdns Barking IG11 . 101 D5
  Newham E13 . . . . .98 D5
Maudlins Grn E1 . . . . . . .118 A5
Maud Rd Leyton E10 . . . . .76 A5
  Newham E13 . . . . .98 D5
Maudslay Rd SE9 . . . . . .144 B2
Maudsley Ho TW8. . . . . . .110 A1
Maudsley Hospl SE5. . . . .139 B3
Maud St E16. . . . . .98 D2
Maud Wilkes Cl 10 NW5 . .71 C3
Maugham Ct 5 W3 . . . . . .111 A3
Mauleverer Rd SW2. . . . .160 A6
Maundeby Wlk NW10 . . . . .67 C2
Maunder Rd 4 W7 . . . . . .108 D5
Maunsel St SW1 . .115 D2 259 C4
Maureen Campbell Ct
  TW17. . . . . .192 D4
Maurer Ct 2 SE10 . . . . . .120 D3
Mauretania Bldg 11 E1. . .118 D6
Maurice Ave N22 . . . . . . .32 D2
Maurice Browne Cl NW7. .28 D4
Maurice Ct
  3 Brentford TW8. . . . . . . .131 D5
  4 Mile End E1. . . . . .97 A4
  Wood Green N22 . . . . .32 C2
Maurice Ho
  Hither Green SE12. . . . . . .164 D5
  1 Stockwell SW9. . . . . . . .138 B3
Maurice St W12 . . . . .90 B1
Maurice Wlk NW11 . . . . . .48 A5
Maurier Cl UB5. . . . . .84 C6
Mauritius Rd SE10 . . . . . .120 C2
Maury Rd N16 . . . . .74 A5
Mausoleum Rd N2. . . . . . .30 C2
Mauveine Gdns TW3 . . . .129 C1
Mavelstone Cl BR1. . . . . .188 A2
Mavelstone Rd BR1. . . . . .188 A2
Maverton Rd E3 . . . . .97 C6
Mavery Ct 5 BR1. . . . . . .186 D3
Mavis Ave KT19 . . . . .215 C3
Mavis Cl KT19 . . . . .215 C3
Mavis Ct 33 NW9 . . . . . . .27 D1
Mavis Wlk 9 E6 . . . . .100 A2
Mavor Ho N1. . . . . 233 D5
Mawbey Ho SE1 . . . . . . 263 D1
Mawbey Pl SE1. . . 117 D1 263 D1
Mawbey Rd SE1 . . . . . . 263 D1
Mawbey St SW8 . . . . . . 270 A3
Mawdley Ho SE1. . . . . . . 251 B1
Mawney Cl RM7 . . . . .59 D6
Mawney Rd RM7. . . . . . . .59 D6
Mawson Cl SW20 . . . . . .179 A1
Mawson Ct N1. . . . . 235 D5
Mawson Ho EC1. . . . . . . 241 A4
Mawson La W4 . . . . .133 D6
Maxden Ct SE15. . . . . . . .140 A2
Maxey Gdns RM9 . . . . . . .81 A4
Maxey Rd Dagenham RM9. .81 A4
  Plumstead SE18. . . . . . . .123 A2
Maxilla Gdns 4
  BR2. . . . . .209 B5
Maxim Rd N21. . . . . .16 C5
Maxted Pk HA1 . . . . .42 C2
Maxted Rd SE15 . . . . . . .139 D2
Maxwell Cl Croydon CR0. .204 A1
  Hayes UB3 . . . . .106 A6

Maxwell Ct SE21 . . . . . . .162 A3
Maxwell Gdns BR6. . . . . .227 D5
Maxwell Ho Bowes Pk N22. .32 B4
  Chislehurst BR7 . . . . .188 D3
  12 Shooters Hill SE18. . . .144 D6
Maxwell Rd
  Ashford TW15. . . . . .171 A4
  Fulham SW6. . . . . . 135 D5 265 D3
  Welling DA16 . . . . .146 A2
  West Drayton UB7 . . . . . . .104 B2
Maxwelton Ave NW7 . . . . .27 B5
Maxwelton Cl NW7 . . . . . .27 B5
Maya Angelou Ct E4 . . . . .36 A6
Maya Cl SE15. . . . . .140 B3
Mayall Cl EN3. . . . . .7 C5
Mayall Rd SE24 . . . . .160 D6
Maya Pl N11. . . . . .31 D3
Maya Rd N2. . . . . .48 A5
Maybank Ave
  Wembley HA0. . . . . .65 A3
  Woodford E18. . . . . .37 B1
Maybank Gdns HA5. . . . . .40 A4
Maybank Rd E18. . . . . . . .37 C2
May Bate Ave KT2. . . . . . .175 D2
Maybells Commercial Est
  IG11. . . . . .102 D5
Mayberry Pl KT5. . . . . . . .198 B2
Mayberry Ct SE26 . . . . . .184 B5
Maybourne Grange CR0. .221 C6
Maybrook Ct E11 . . . . .77 B6
Maybury Cl Enfield EN1. . . . .6 B5
  Petts Wood BR5 . . . . .210 D4
Maybury Ct
  Beckenham BR3. . . . . . . .185 B3
  Croydon CR2. . . . . .220 D3
  Harrow HA1. . . . . .42 B3
  Marylebone W1 . . . . 238 B3
Maybury Gdns NW10. . . . .68 B2
Maybury Mews N6. . . . . . .49 C2
Maybury Rd
  Barking IG11 . . . . .102 A5
  Newham E13 . . . . .99 C3
Maybury St SW17. . . . . . .180 C5
Maychurch Cl HA7 . . . . . . .25 D3
May Cl KT9 . . . . .214 B2
Maycroft 2 Hayes BR2. . .208 D1
  Pinner HA5. . . . . .22 B1
Maycross Ave SM4. . . . . .201 C5
May Ct 2 SW19. . . . . . . .180 A2
Mayday Gdns SE3. . . . . . .144 A3
Mayday Rd CR0, CR7. . . .204 D3
Mayday University Hospl
  CR7. . . . . .204 D3
Maydeb Ct RM6. . . . . .59 B3
Maydew Ho SE16 . . . . . . .118 C2
Maydwell Ho 6 E14 . . . . . .97 C2
Mayerne Rd SE9 . . . . . . .165 D6
Mayesbrook Rd
  Barking IG11 . . . . .101 D6
  Dagenham RM8, IG3 . . . . . .80 B5
Mayesford Rd RM6. . . . . . .58 C2
Mayespark Prim Sch IG3. .80 A5
Mayes Rd N22 . . . . .32 B1
Mayeswood Rd SE12. . . . .187 C6
MAYFAIR. 115 B6
Mayfair Ave Bexley DA7 . .146 D4
  Dagenham RM6. . . . . .58 D3
  Ilford IG1. . . . . .56 C1
  New Malden KT4 . . . . . . .200 A1
  Twickenham TW2 . . . . . . .152 A4
Mayfair Cl
  Beckenham BR3. . . . . . . .185 D2
  Surbiton KT6. . . . . .198 A1
Mayfair Ct
  2 Beckenham BR3. . . . . . .185 D2
  7 Croydon CR0 . . . . .221 D6
  Edgware HA8 . . . . .26 B5
  13 Wimbledon SW19 . . . .179 A3
Mayfair Gdns
  Tottenham N17. . . . . .33 B4
  Woodford IG8. . . . . .37 A3
Mayfair Ho 11 SE1 . . . . . .118 A2
Mayfair Pl W1 . . . . 248 D4
Mayfair Terr N14. . . . . .15 C4
Mayfield DA7. . . . . .147 B2
Mayfield Ave
  Broom Hill BR6. . . . . .211 D2
  Chiswick W4. . . . . .111 C2
  Harrow HA3. . . . . .43 B4
  North Finchley N12. . . . . . .30 B6
  Osidge N14. . . . . .15 D2
  West Ealing W13 . . . . . . .109 B4
  Woodford IG8. . . . . .37 A4
Mayfield Cl
  Ashford TW15. . . . . .170 D4
  Clapham Pk SW4 . . . . . . .159 D6
  Dalston E8 . . . . .73 D2
  Hillingdon UB10 . . . . .82 D4
  Long Ditton KT7 . . . . .197 B1
  Penge SE20 . . . . .184 B2
Mayfield Cres Enfield N9 . .18 B5
  Thornton Heath CR7. . . . .204 B4
Mayfield Ct SM2 . . . . . . .218 A1
Mayfield Dr HA5. . . . . .41 B5
Mayfield Gdns Ealing W7. .86 C2
  Hendon NW4 . . . . .46 D3
Mayfield Ho
  31 Bethnal Green E2 . . . . . .96 B5
  Stamford Hill N16. . . . . . . .51 C2
Mayfield Mans SW15. . . .157 B6

Mayfield Prim Sch W7 . . . .86 B1
Mayfield Rd Acton W3 . . . .110 D6
  Bedford Pk W12 . . . . .111 C4
  Bromley BR1. . . . . .210 A4
  Chingford E4. . . . . .20 B2
  Dagenham RM8 . . . . .58 C1
  Dalston E8 . . . . .73 D1
  Enfield EN3. . . . . .6 D3
  Higham Hill E17 . . . . .35 A1
  Hornsey Vale N8. . . . . .50 B3
  Merton SW19 . . . . .179 B2
  Newham E13 . . . . .98 D3
  South Croydon CR2. . . . . .221 B1
  Sutton SM2. . . . . .218 B2
  Thornton Heath CR7. . . . .204 B4
Mayfields HA9. . . . . .66 C6
Mayfields Sch & Coll RM8 .58 C1
Mayfields Cl HA9 . . . . .66 C6
Mayfield Villas DA14 . . . .190 C4
Mayflower Cl
  Bermondsey SE16 . . . . . . .118 D2
  Ruislip HA4. . . . . .39 A3
Mayflower Ho 2 IG11 . . . .101 B6
Mayflower Lo Hendon N3. .47 B6
  Muswell Hill N10. . . . . .31 A2
Mayflower Prim Sch 22
  E14 . . . . .97 D1
Mayflower Rd SW9 . . . . . .138 A2
Mayflower St 1 SE16. . . . .118 C4
Mayfly Cl HA5 . . . . .40 C2
Mayfly Gdns 12 UB5. . . . . .84 D4
Mayford NW1. . . . . 232 B4
Mayford Cl Balham SW12. .158 D4
  Penge BR3 . . . . .206 D6
Mayford Rd SW12. . . . . . .159 A4
May Gdns Elstree WD6 . . . .9 D5
  Wembley HA0. . . . . .78 D6
Maygood Ho N1. . . . . . . 234 A4
Maygood St N1 . . .94 C5 234 A4
Maygrove Rd NW6. . . . . . .69 B2
Mayhew Cl E4. . . . . .19 C1
Mayhew Ct 2 SE5 . . . . . .139 B1
Mayhill Rd Barnet EN5 . . . .13 A5
  Greenwich SE7. . . . . .143 B6
Mayland Mans 4 IG11. . . .78 D1
Maylands Dr DA14 . . . . . .168 D1
Maylands Ho SW3 . . . . . 257 B3
Maylands Rd WD19 . . . . . .22 C6
Maylie Ho 4 SE16 . . . . . .118 B4
Maynard Cl
  Fulham SW6. . . . . . 135 D5 265 D3
  Tottenham N15. . . . . .51 C4
Maynard Ct EN3 . . . . .7 C5
Maynard Ho Mile End E1. . . .97 A4
  2 Plumstead SE18 . . . . . .123 A2
Maynard Rd E17 . . . . .54 A4
Maynards Quay E1. . . . . .118 C6
Mayne Ct E8. . . . . .74 A4
Maynooth Gdns CR4 . . . .202 D2
Mayo Ct W13 . . . . .109 B3
Mayo Ho 10 E1 . . . . .96 C2
Mayola Rd E5. . . . . .74 C4
Mayo Rd
  Thornton Heath CR0. . . . . .205 B4
  Walton-on-T KT12 . . . . . . .194 A2
  Willesden NW10. . . . . .67 C2
Mayow Rd SE23, SE26. . . .184 D6
Mayplace Cl DA7 . . . . . . .147 D2
Mayplace La SE18. . . . . . .144 D6
Mayplace Rd W DA7 . . . . .147 C1
Maypole Ct UB2 . . . . .107 B4
May Rd Chingford E4 . . . . .35 C4
  Newham E13 . . . . .99 A5
  Twickenham TW2 . . . . . . .152 C3
Mayroyd Ave KT6. . . . . . .214 C6
May's Buildings Mews
  SE10 . . . . .142 B5
Mays Ct WC2 . . . . 250 A5
May's Ct SE10 . . . . .142 B5
May's Hill Rd BR2. . . . . . .208 C6
May's La EN5 . . . . .12 C5
Maysoule Rd SW11 . . . . .136 B1
Mays Rd TW11, TW12. . . .174 B5
May St W14. . . . . 254 D1
Maystocks E18 . . . . .36 C4
Mayston Mews 3 SE10 . . .121 A1
May Terr IG1 . . . . .78 D4
Maythorne Cotts SE13. . . .164 B5
Mayton St N7. . . . . .72 B5
Maytree Cl HA8. . . . . .11 A1
Maytree Ct Mitcham CR4. .203 A6
  Northolt UB5. . . . . .85 A4
May Tree Ho SE4. . . . . . . .141 B2
Maytree La HA7. . . . . .24 D3
Maytree Wlk SW2. . . . . . .160 C2
Mayville Prim Sch E11 . . . .76 C6
Mayville Rd Ilford IG1. . . . .78 D3
  Leyton E11 . . . . .76 C6
Mayward Ho 7 SE5. . . . . .139 C4
May Wlk E13 . . . . .99 B5
Maywood Cl BR3. . . . . . . .185 D3
May Wynne Ho E16 . . . . . .99 B1
Maze Hill SE10, SE3. . . . .142 C6
Maze Hill Lodge 7
  SE10 . . . . .142 B6
Maze Hill Sta SE10. . . . . .142 C6
Mazenod Ave NW6. . . . . . .69 C1
Maze Rd TW9 . . . . .132 C5
Mead Cl
  3 Camden Town NW1. . . . .71 A1

Mead Cl continued
  Harrow HA3. . . . . .24 B2
Mead Cres
  Carshalton SM1 . . . . .218 C4
  Chingford E4. . . . . .36 A6
Meadcroft Rd 4 KT3. . . . .199 C2
Meadcroft Rd SE17 . . . . .138 D6
Mead Ct NW9. . . . . .45 B4
Meade Cl W4 . . . . .132 C6
Meader Ct SE14. . . . . . . .140 D5
Meadfield HA8 . . . . .10 D2
Mead Field HA2 . . . . .63 B5
Meadfield Gn HA8 . . . . . . .10 D2
Meadfoot Rd SW16 . . . . .181 C2
Mead Gr RM6. . . . . .58 D6
Mead Ho W11 . . . . 244 C4
Mead House La UB4. . . . . .83 B3
Meadhurst Club TW16. . . .171 D5
Meadhurst Pk TW16. . . . .171 C4
Mead Inf Sch The KT19. . .215 D4
Meadlands Dr TW10. . . . .153 D2
Meadlands Prim Sch
  TW10 . . . . .175 C6
Mead Lo W4. . . . . .111 B4
Meadow Ave CR0 . . . . . . .206 D3
Meadowbank
  Lewisham SE3. . . . . .142 D2
  Primrose Hill NW3 . . . . . . .70 D1
  Southgate N21. . . . . .16 B5
  Surbiton KT5. . . . . .198 B3
Meadow Bank 8 SW15 . . .157 B6
Meadowbank Cl SW6 . . . .134 C5
Meadowbank Gdns TW5. .128 B4
Meadowbank Rd NW9 . . . .45 B2
Meadowbanks EN5 . . . . . .12 A6
Meadowbrook Ct TW7 . . . .130 D2
Meadow Cl Barking IG11 . . .80 A1
  Barnet EN5. . . . . .13 B5
  Bexley DA5. . . . . .169 B6
  Catford SE6. . . . . .185 C5
  Chingford E4. . . . . .19 D3
  Chislehurst BR7. . . . . .188 D5
  Enfield EN3. . . . . .7 A5
  Hackney E9. . . . . .75 B3
  Hinchley Wood KT10. . . . .212 D5
  Hounslow TW4 . . . . .151 C5
  Northolt UB5. . . . . .85 C5
  Richmond TW10 . . . . .154 A3
  Ruislip HA4. . . . . .39 D3
  Sutton SM1. . . . . .218 A6
  West Barnes SW20 . . . . . .200 C5
Meadowcourt Rd SE3. . . .142 D1
Meadowcroft 8 W4 . . . . .110 C1
Meadow Croft BR1. . . . . .210 B6
Meadowcroft Rd N13. . . . .16 C2
Meadow Dr Hendon NW4. .28 C1
  Muswell Hill N10. . . . . .49 B6
Meadowford Cl SE28. . . . .124 A6
Meadow Garth NW10 . . . . .67 B2
Meadow Gate HA2 . . . . . .63 D5
Meadowgate Cl NW7. . . . .27 D5
Meadowgate Sch SE4. . . .141 A2
Meadow Gdns HA8. . . . . .27 A4
Meadow High Sch UB8. . . .82 A4
Meadow Hill KT3 . . . . . . .199 C3
Meadow La SE12. . . . . . . .165 B1
Meadow Mews SW8 . . . . 270 C5
Meadow Pl Chiswick W4. .133 C5
  South Lambeth
  SW8 . . . . .138 A5 270 B4
Meadow Rd
  Ashford TW15. . . . . .171 B5
  Barking IG11 . . . . .80 A1
  Beckenham BR2 . . . . .186 C1
  Carshalton SM1. . . . . .218 C3
  Claygate KT10 . . . . .212 C2
  Dagenham RM9 . . . . .81 B2
  Feltham TW13 . . . . .151 A2
  Merton SW19 . . . . .180 A3
  Pinner HA5. . . . . .41 A5
  Southall UB1. . . . . .107 B6
  South Lambeth
  SW8 . . . . .138 B5 270 C4
Meadow Row SE1. . . . . . 262 A5
Meadows Cl E10. . . . . .75 C6
Meadows Ct DA14 . . . . . .190 B4
Meadows End TW16. . . . .172 A2
Meadowside Eltham SE9 . .143 C1
  Twickenham TW1 . . . . . . .153 D4
Meadow Stile CR0. . . . . . .221 A5
Meadowsweet Cl
  3 Newham E16. . . . . .99 D2
  West Barnes KT3. . . . . . . .200 C5
Meadow The BR7 . . . . . . .189 A4
Meadowview W17 . . . . . .193 A2
Meadow View
  Blackfen DA15 . . . . .168 B4
  Harrow HA1. . . . . .42 C1
Meadow View Rd
  Catford SE6. . . . . .185 C5
  Sidcup DA5. . . . . .169 B5
  West Ewell KT19. . . . . . . .215 C1
Meadow View Rd
  Hayes UB4 . . . . .83 B3
  Thornton Heath CR7. . . . .204 D4
Meadow Way
  Kingsbury NW9 . . . . .45 B4
  Locksbottom BR6. . . . . . . .226 C5
  Ruislip HA4. . . . . .40 B3
  Wembley HA9. . . . . .65 D4

Meadow Waye TW5 . . . . .129 A5
Meadow Way The HA3. . . . .24 C2
Meadow Wlk
 Dagenham RM9 . . . . .81 B2
 Hackbridge SM6. . . . . . . .219 B5
 Wanstead E18 . . . . .55 A5
 West Ewell KT17, KT19. . .215 D1
Meadow Wood Sch WD23 . .8 A6
Mead Pl Croydon CR0 . . . .205 A1
 Hackney E9. . . . . .74 C2
Mead Plat NW10. . . . . . . .67 A2
Mead Rd Chislehurst BR7 .189 A4
 Edgware HA8. . . . . .26 C4
 Richmond TW10 . . . . . . .153 C1
Mead Road Inf Sch BR7 . .189 A4
Mead Row SE1 . . .116 C3 261 A6
Meads Ct E15. . . . . .76 D2
Meadside Cl BR3 . . . . . . .185 A2
Meads La IG3. . . . . .57 D2
Meads Rd Enfield EN3 . . . . .7 A4
 Tottenham N22. . . . . .32 D1
Meads The Cheam SM3. . .217 A3
 Edgware HA8. . . . . .27 B4
 Hillingdon UB8. . . . . .82 A3
Mead The
 Beckenham BR3 . . . . .186 A2
 Ealing W13 . . . . .87 B2
 Finchley N2. . . . . .30 A1
 Ickenham UB10 . . . . .60 C6
 Wallington SM6 . . . . .219 D2
 West Wickham BR4 . . . . .208 B1
Meadvale Rd
 Croydon CR0. . . . . .206 A3
 Ealing W5 . . . . .87 C3
Meadway Ashford TW15. .170 C6
 Barnet EN5 . . . . .1 C1
 Beckenham BR3 . . . . .186 A2
 Enfield EN3. . . . . .6 D6
 Esher KT10. . . . . .212 A1
 Hampstead Garden Suburb
  NW11. . . . . .47 D3
 Ilford IG3. . . . . .79 C4
 Palmers Green N14 . . . . . .16 A2
 Tolworth KT5 . . . . .199 A1
 Twickenham TW2 . . . . . .152 B3
 West Barnes SW20 . . . . .200 C5
 Woodford IG8. . . . . .37 C5
Mead Way Croydon CR0 . .223 A6
 Hayes BR2 . . . . .209 A3
 Ruislip HA4. . . . . .39 B3
Meadway Cl Barnet EN5. . . .1 C1
 Hampstead Garden Suburb
  NW11. . . . . .47 D3
 Pinner HA5. . . . . .23 D4
Meadway Ct
 Dagenham RM8 . . . . .81 B6
 Ealing W5 . . . . .88 B2
 Hampstead Garden Suburb
  NW11. . . . . .47 D3
Meadway Gate NW11 . . . . .47 C3
Meadway Gdns HA4. . . . . .39 B3
Meadway The
 Buckhurst Hill IG9 . . . . . .21 D3
 Lewisham SE3 . . . . .142 B3
Meaford Way SE20 . . . . . .184 B3
Meakin Est SE1 . . . . .263 A6
Meakin Ho N7 . . . . .72 B3
Meanley Rd E12 . . . . .78 A3
Meard St W1 . . . . .239 C1
Meath Cres E1, E2. . . . . . . .96 D4
Meath Ho SE24 . . . . .160 D5
Meath Rd Ilford IG1 . . . . . .79 A5
 Newham E15 . . . . .98 D5
Meath St SW11 . . .137 B4 268 C2
Mecklenburgh Pl WC1 . . . .240 C4
Mecklenburgh Sq
 WC1. . . . . .94 B3 240 C6
Mecklenburgh St WC1 . . . .240 C4
Medburn St NW1 . . . . .232 C4
Medcalf Rd EN3 . . . . .7 B6
Medcroft Gdns SW14 . . . .133 A1
Mede Ho BR1. . . . . .187 B5
Medebourne Cl SE3. . . . . .143 A4
Medesenge Way N13. . . . . .32 D4
Medfield St SW15. . . . . . . .156 B4
Medhurst Cl 19 E3 . . . . . . .97 A5
Medhurst Dr BR1 . . . . . . .186 C5
Median Rd E5 . . . . .74 C3
Medici Cl IG3. . . . . .58 A3
Medina Ave KT10 . . . . . . .212 C5
Medina Gr N7 . . . . .72 C5
Medina Rd N7 . . . . .72 C5
Medina Ho SE15 . . . . .140 C1
Medlar Cl 1 UB5 . . . . .84 D5
Medlar Ho 3 DA15 . . . . . .168 A1
Medlar St SE5 . . . . .139 A4
Medley Rd NW6 . . . . .69 C2
Medora Rd SW2 . . . . .160 B4
Medresco Ho NW3 . . . . . . .70 B3
Medusa Ho SE6, SE13 . . . .163 D5
Medway Bldgs E3. . . . . . . .97 A5
Medway Cl Croydon CR0. .206 C3
 Ilford IG1. . . . . .79 A3
Medway Dr UB6 . . . . .86 D5
Medway Gdns HA0. . . . . . .65 A4

Medway Ho
 Bermondsey SE1 . . . . . . .252 D1
 6 Kingston u T KT2 . . . .175 D2
 Paddington NW8 . . . . . . .237 A4
 Stoke Newington N16. . . . .73 B4
Medway Mews 35 E3. . . . . .97 A5
Medway Par 1 UB6. . . . . . .86 D5
Medway Rd E3 . . . . .97 A5
Medway St SW1 . .115 D3 259 D5
Medwin St SW4. . . . . .138 B1
Meecham Ct 1 SW11 . . . .136 C3
Meerbrook Rd SE3. . . . . . .143 C2
Meers Ct SW20 . . . . .178 C2
Meeson Rd E15 . . . . .76 D1
Meeson St E5 . . . . .75 A4
Meeting House Alley 7
 E1. . . . . .118 B5
Meeting House La SE15 . .140 B5
Mehetabel Rd E9 . . . . .74 C3
Meister Cl IG1 . . . . .57 B1
Melanda Cl BR7 . . . . .188 B5
Melanie Cl DA7 . . . . .147 A4
Melba Way SE13 . . . . .141 D4
Melbourne Ave
 Bowes Pk N13. . . . . .32 B4
 Ealing W13 . . . . .109 A5
 Pinner HA2, HA5. . . . . . . .41 D6
Melbourne Cl
 Broom Hill BR6. . . . . .211 C2
 Ickenham UB10 . . . . .60 C4
 Wallington SM6 . . . . .219 C3
Melbourne Ct Hackney E5. .75 A4
 Muswell Hill N10. . . . . . . .31 B3
 Paddington W9 . . . . .236 B6
 Penge SE20 . . . . .184 A3
 Twickenham TW2 . . . . . .152 B3
Melbourne Gdns RM6. . . . .59 A4
Melbourne Gr SE22 . . . . .139 D1
Melbourne Ho Hayes UB4. .84 C3
 Kensington W8. . . . . .245 A3
 South Norwood SE25 . . . .205 D5
Melbourne Mews
 Brixton SW9 . . . . .138 C4
 Catford SE6 . . . . .164 A4
Melbourne Pl WC2. . . . . . .240 D1
Melbourne Rd Ilford IG1. . .56 D1
 Leyton E10 . . . . .53 D2
 Merton SW19 . . . . .179 C2
 Newham E6 . . . . .100 B5
 Teddington TW11 . . . . . .175 C4
 Wallington SM6 . . . . .219 C3
 Walthamstow E17 . . . . . . .53 A5
Melbourne Sq 21 SW9 . . .138 C4
Melbourne Way EN1 . . . . . .17 D5
Melbray Mews 11 SW6. . . .135 B3
Melbreak Ho 11 SE22 . . . .139 C2
Melbury Ave UB2 . . . . . . .107 D3
Melbury Cl Claygate KT10. .213 B2
 Elmstead BR7 . . . . .188 B4
Melbury Ct W8 . . . .113 B3 254 D6
Melbury Dr SE5. . . . . .139 C5
Melbury Gdns SW20 . . . . .178 B2
Melbury Grange BR1. . . . .188 A2
Melbury Ho
 South Lambeth SW8. . . . .270 C4
 Twickenham TW2 . . . . . .152 B3
Melbury Rd Harrow HA3. . . .44 B4
 Kensington W14. . .113 B3 254 D6
Melchester 5 W11 . . . . . . .91 B1
Melchester Ho 1 N19 . . . . .71 D5
Melcombe Ct NW1. . . . . . .237 C4
Melcombe Gdns HA3. . . . . .44 B3
Melcombe Ho SW8 . . . . . .270 C3
Melcombe Pl NW1 . . . . . . .237 C4
Melcombe Prim Sch 6
 W6 . . . . .134 D6
Melcombe St
 NW1 . . . . .92 D3 237 D5
Meldex Cl NW7 . . . . .28 C4
Meldon Cl SW6. . . . . .265 D2
Meldone Cl KT3. . . . . .199 B1
Meldon Rd KT5. . . . . .198 D3
Meldrum Rd IG3. . . . . .80 A6
Melfield Gdns SE6 . . . . . . .186 A5
Melford Ave IG11 . . . . .79 D2
Melford Cl KT9 . . . . .214 B3
Melford Ct
 Bermondsey SE1 . . . . . . .263 B6
 Dulwich SE22 . . . . .162 A4
 Hackney E5. . . . . .74 B5
 2 Sutton SM2. . . . . .218 A1
Melford Rd
 Dulwich SE21, SE22 . . . . .162 A3
 Ilford IG1. . . . . .79 B6
 Leyton E11 . . . . .76 C6
 Newham E6 . . . . .100 B4
 Walthamstow E17 . . . . . . .53 B5
Melfort Ave CR7 . . . . .204 D6
Melfort Rd CR7 . . . . .204 D6
Melgund Rd N5. . . . . .72 C3
Melina Cl UB3 . . . . .83 B2
Melina Ct Putney SW15. . . .134 A2
 St John's Wood NW8 . . . . .229 C1
Melina Pl NW8. . . . .92 B4 229 C1
Melina Rd W12 . . . . .112 B4
Melior Cl N6 . . . . .49 C3
Melior Pl SE1. . . . . .263 A2
Melior St SE1. . . . .117 C4 253 A2
Meliot Rd SE6 . . . . .164 B2
Melisa Ct N6 . . . . .49 D2

Meller Cl SM6 . . . . .220 A5
Mellifont Cl SM5. . . . . . . .202 B2
Melling Dr EN1 . . . . .6 A4
Melling St SE18. . . . . .145 C6
Mellington Ct 2 N16 . . . . . .74 A5
Mellis Ave TW9 . . . . .132 D4
Mellish Cl IG11 . . . . .101 D6
Mellish Ct SE18. . . . . .198 A3
Mellish Flats E10 . . . . .53 C2
Mellish Gdns IG8 . . . . .37 A5
Mellish Ho 2 E1. . . . . .96 B1
Mellish Ind Est SE18 . . . . .121 D3
Mellish St E14 . . . . .119 C3
Mellison Rd SW17 . . . . . . .180 C5
Mellitus St W12. . . . . .89 D1
Mellor Cl KT12. . . . . .195 B2
Mellor Ct SW19 . . . . .180 A3
Mellor Ho 2 SE21 . . . . . . .183 C6
Mellow La E UB4. . . . . .83 A3
Mellow Lane Sch UB4. . . . .83 A3
Mellow La W UB10. . . . . . .83 A3
Mellows Rd Redbridge IG5. .56 B6
 Wallington SM6 . . . . .219 D3
Mells Cres SE9. . . . . .188 B6
Mell St 6 SE10 . . . . .120 C1
Melody La N5 . . . . .73 A3
Melody Rd SW18. . . . . . . .158 A6
Melon Pl W8 . . . . .245 B2
Melon Rd Leyton E11. . . . . .76 C5
 Peckham SE15 . . . . .140 A4
Melrose Ave
 Borehamwood WD6 . . . . . .10 D6
 Cricklewood NW2. . . . . . . .68 C3
 Greenford UB6. . . . . .85 D5
 Mitcham CR4 . . . . .181 B3
 Thornton Heath SW16 . . .204 C6
 Tottenham N22. . . . . .32 D2
 Twickenham TW2 . . . . . .151 D4
 Wimbledon SW19. . . . . . .157 C1
Melrose Cl Greenford UB6. .85 D5
 Grove Pk SE12 . . . . .165 B3
 Hayes UB4 . . . . .84 C3
Melrose Cres BR6. . . . . . . .227 B3
Melrose Ct
 5 Ealing W13 . . . . .109 A5
 Wandsworth SW18 . . . . .157 B5
Melrose Dr UB1 . . . . .107 C5
Melrose Gdns
 Edgware HA8 . . . . .26 D1
 Hammersmith W6 . . . . . .112 C3
 Kingston u T KT3 . . . . . . .199 B6
Melrose Ho
 Maida Vale NW6. . . . . .91 C4
 Pimlico SW1 . . . . .258 D2
Melrose Rd
 1 Barnes SW13 . . . . . . .133 D3
 Merton SW19 . . . . .179 C2
 Pinner HA5. . . . . .41 B5
 Wandsworth SW18 . . . . .157 B5
Melrose Specl Sch 2
 CR4. . . . . .202 C6
Melrose Terr W6 . . . . .112 C3
Melrose Tudor SM6 . . . . . .220 A3
Melsa Rd SM4 . . . . .202 A3
Melthorne Dr HA4 . . . . .62 C5
Melthorpe Gdns SE3 . . . . .144 A4
Melton Cl HA4. . . . . .40 C1
Melton Ct
 11 Croydon CR0 . . . . . . .221 D6
 South Kensington SW7. . .256 D3
 Sutton SM2. . . . . .218 A1
 2 Twickenham TW1. . . . .153 B4
Melton Ho E5. . . . . .74 A6
Melton St NW1 . . . .93 D4 232 C1
Melville Ave
 Greenford UB6. . . . . .64 D3
 South Croydon CR2. . . . . .221 D3
 Wimbledon SW20. . . . . . .178 A3
Melville Cl UB10. . . . . .61 B5
Melville Court Flats 8
 W12. . . . . .112 B4
Melville Ct
 4 Brentford W4 . . . . .110 C1
 Rotherhithe SE8 . . . . .119 A4
Melville Gdns N13 . . . . .32 D5
Melville Ho
 Lewisham SE10 . . . . .142 A4
 New Barnet EN5. . . . . .14 B5
Melville Pl 4 N1. . . . . .73 A1
Melville Rd Barnes SW13. .134 A4
 Sidcup DA14. . . . . .168 C2
 Stonebridge NW10. . . . . . .67 B1
 Walthamstow E17 . . . . . . .53 B6
Melville Villas Rd W3. . . . .111 B5
Melvin Rd SE20 . . . . .184 C2
Melyn Cl N7 . . . . .71 C4
Memel Ct EC1 . . . . .242 A5
Memel St EC1 . . . . .242 A5
Memess Path 4 SE18. . . . .144 C6
Memorial Ave E15 . . . . .98 C4
Memorial Cl TW5 . . . . .129 B6
Memorial Hospl SE18. . . . .144 C3
Memorial Hts IG2. . . . . .57 C5
Menai Pl 2 E3 . . . . .97 C5
Menard Ct EC1 . . . . .235 B1
Mendham Ho SE1. . . . . . . .263 A6
Mendip Cl
 Forest Hill SE26 . . . . .184 C4

Mendip Cl continued
 Harlington UB3. . . . . .127 B5
 North Cheam KT4. . . . . . .216 C6
Mendip Ct
 12 Battersea SW11 . . . . .136 A2
 Deptford SE14 . . . . .140 C6
 1 East Barnet N20 . . . . . .14 C2
Mendip Dr NW2. . . . . .69 A6
Mendip Ho Harrow HA3 . . . .43 A3
 2 Stoke Newington N4 . . .51 B2
Mendip Hos 12 E2 . . . . .96 C4
Mendip Rd
 Battersea SW11. . . . . . . .136 A2
 Bushey WD23 . . . . .8 B2
 Ilford IG2. . . . . .57 C4
Mendora Rd
 SW6. . . . . .135 B5 264 C4
Menelik Rd NW2. . . . . .69 B4
Menin Wks CR4. . . . . .180 D1
Menlo Gdns SE19 . . . . . . .183 B3
Menlo Ho Harrow HA3 . . . .43 A3
Menlo Rd SE18 . . . . .144 B4
Mennis Ho SM5. . . . . .218 C6
Menon Dr N9 . . . . .18 B1
Menorah Foundation Sch 8
 HA8 . . . . .27 A3
Menorah Gram Sch HA8 . . .27 A3
Menorah High Sch for Girls
 NW2. . . . . .68 A5
Menorah Prim Sch NW11 . .47 A2
Menotti St 6 E2. . . . . .96 A3
Menteath Ho 9 E14 . . . . . .97 C1
Mentmore Cl HA3. . . . . . . .43 C3
Mentmore Terr E8 . . . . .74 B1
Mentone Ct SW8. . . . . . . .270 B2
Meon Ct TW7 . . . . .130 C3
Meon Rd W3 . . . . .111 A4
Meopham Rd CR4, SW16. .181 C2
Mepham Cres HA3 . . . . . . .24 A3
Mepham Gdns HA3 . . . . . . .24 A3
Mepham St SE1. . .116 C5 251 A3
Mera Dr DA7 . . . . .147 D1
Merantun Way SW19 . . . . .180 A2
Merbury Cl
 Lewisham SE13 . . . . .164 B6
 Woolwich SE28. . . . . .123 B5
Merbury Rd SE28 . . . . .123 C4
Mercator Pl 4 E14 . . . . . . .119 C1
Mercator Rd SE13. . . . . . . .142 B1
Mercer Cl KT7 . . . . .196 D2
Merceron Ho 3 E2 . . . . . . .96 C4
Merceron St E1. . . . . .96 B3
Mercer Pl HA5. . . . . .22 C1
Mercer's Cotts 8 E3. . . . . .97 A1
Mercers Mews N7 . . . . .71 D4
Mercers Pl W6. . . . . .112 D2
Mercers Rd N19 . . . . .71 D5
Mercer St WC2 . . .94 A1 240 A1
Merchant Ct E1. . . . . .118 C5
Merchants Cl SE25 . . . . . .206 A5
Merchants Ho SE10 . . . . . .120 B1
Merchants Lo 6 E17 . . . . . .53 C5
Merchant Sq W2 . . . . .236 C3
Merchant St E3. . . . . .97 B4
Merchant Taylors'
 Almshouses SE13 . . . . . .142 C1
Merchant Taylors' Hall *
 EC3. . . . . .242 D1
Merchiston Rd SE6 . . . . . .164 B2
Merchland Rd SE9 . . . . . . .167 A3
Merchon Ho N7 . . . . .71 C4
Mercia Gr SE13 . . . . .142 A1
Mercia Ho
 9 Camberwell SE5 . . . . .139 A3
 Charlton TW15 . . . . .171 A2
Mercie Ct SE22 . . . . .162 A3
Mercier Rd SW15. . . . . . . .157 A6
Mercury 25 NW9 . . . . .27 D2
Mercury Ct
 8 Brixton SW9 . . . . .138 C4
 10 Millwall E14. . . . . . . .119 C2
 Mercury Ctr TW14 . . . . . .150 A6
Mercury Ho
 Brentford TW8 . . . . .109 D1
 6 Old Ford E3 . . . . .97 C6
Mercury Rd 2 TW8 . . . . . .109 C1
Mercury Way SE14 . . . . . .140 D6
Mercy Terr SE13 . . . . .163 D6
Merebank La CR0, SM6. . . .220 B3
Mere Cl Orpington BR6 . . .226 D6
 Putney SW15, SW19. . . . .156 D4
Meredith Ave NW2. . . . . . . .68 C3
Meredith Cl HA5. . . . . .22 D3
Meredith Ho 17 N16. . . . . . .73 C3
Meredith Mews SE4. . . . . .141 B1
Meredith St Finsbury EC1. .234 C1
 Newham E13 . . . . .99 A4
Meredyth Rd SW13 . . . . . .134 A3
Mere End CR0 . . . . .206 D2
Mereside BR6. . . . . .226 C6
Mereside Pk TW15 . . . . . . .171 A6
Meretone Cl SE4. . . . . .141 A1
Mereton Mans 6 SE8 . . . . .141 C4
Merevale Cres SM4 . . . . . .202 A3
Mereway Industry TW2. . . .152 C4
Mereway Rd TW2 . . . . .152 C3
Merewood Cl BR1. . . . . . . .188 C1

Mea – Mer 365

Merewood Gdns CR0. . . . .206 D2
Mereworth Cl BR2 . . . . . . .208 D4
Mereworth Dr SE18 . . . . . .145 A5
Mereworth Ho 3 SE15 . . .140 C6
Merganser Ct 17 SE8. . . . .141 B6
Merganser Gdns SE28. . . . .123 B3
Meridan Ct SE13 . . . . .142 B1
Meriden Cl BR1. . . . . .187 D3
Meriden Ct SW3 . . . . .257 A1
Meriden Ho 4 Barnet EN5 . .1 A1
 5 Hoxton N1. . . . . .95 C6
Meridian Building *
 SE10. . . . . .142 B5
Meridian Cl NW7 . . . . .27 B6
Meridian Ct
 4 Bermondsey SE16. . . . .118 A4
 4 Catford SE6. . . . . .164 D3
 Croydon CR0. . . . . .220 C4
Meridian Ho SE10. . . . . . . .120 C2
Meridian Pl E14 . . . . .120 A4
Meridian Prim Sch 9
 SE10. . . . . .142 B6
Meridian Rd SE7. . . . . .143 D5
Meridian Sq E15 . . . . .76 B1
Meridian Trad Est SE7. . . .121 B2
Meridian Way Enfield N9, N18. .18 A5
 Lower Edmonton N9, N18. .18 D1
Meridian Wlk N17 . . . . .33 C4
Merifield Rd SE9 . . . . .143 C1
Merino Cl E11 . . . . .55 C5
Merino Pl DA15. . . . . .168 A6
Merioneth Ct 7 W7. . . . . . . .86 D2
Merivale Rd Harrow HA1 . . .42 A1
 Putney SW15 . . . . .135 A1
Merlewood Dr BR7 . . . . . .188 B2
Merley Ct NW9 . . . . .45 A1
Merlin 26 NW9. . . . . .27 D2
Merlin Cl Mitcham CR4 . . .202 C6
 4 Northolt UB5. . . . . .84 C4
 South Croydon CR0. . . . . .221 C4
 Wallington SM6 . . . . .220 B2
Merlin Cres HA8 . . . . .26 B2
Merlin Ct
 Beckenham BR2 . . . . .208 D5
 6 Ealing W7. . . . . .86 D3
 Mitcham CR4 . . . . .180 C2
 Ruislip HA4. . . . . .61 B6
 Stanmore HA7 . . . . .25 B5
 Wood Green N22 . . . . .32 C2
Merling Cl KT9 . . . . .213 D3
Merlin Gdns BR1. . . . . .165 A1
Merlin Gr BR3 . . . . .207 C4
Merlin Ho
 7 Chiswick W4 . . . . .111 B1
 Enfield EN3. . . . . .18 D6
 West Hampstead NW3. . . . .69 D4
Merlin Prim Sch BR1. . . . .165 A1
Merlin Rd Bexley DA16 . . .146 A1
 Wanstead E12 . . . . .77 D6
Merlin Rd N DA16. . . . . . . .146 A1
Merlins Ave HA2 . . . . .63 B5
Merlin Sch The 11
 SW15. . . . . .157 A6
Merlins Ct WC1 . . . . .234 A1
Merlin St EC1. . . . . .94 C4 234 A1
Mermaid Ct
 Bermondsey SE1 . .117 B4 252 C2
 Rotherhithe SE16. . . . . . .119 B5
 Stroud Green N4 . . . . .50 C3
Mermaid Ho 8 E14 . . . . . .120 A4
Mermaid Twr 22 SE8 . . . . .141 B6
Meroe Ct N16. . . . . .73 C6
Merredene St SE24. . . . . . .160 B5
Merriam Ave 2 E9. . . . . . . .75 B2
Merriam Cl E4 . . . . .36 A5
Merrick Rd UB2. . . . . .107 B3
Merricks Ct 5 SW14. . . . . .132 D1
Merrick Sq SE1 . . .117 B3 262 C6
Merridale SE12 . . . . .164 D6
Merridene N21. . . . . .16 D5
Merrielands Cres RM9 . . . .103 B5
Merrielands Ret Pk
 RM9 . . . . .103 B5
Merrilands Rd KT4. . . . . . .200 C1
Merrilees Rd DA15. . . . . . .167 C4
Merrilyn Cl KT10. . . . . . . .213 A2
Merriman Rd SE3 . . . . .143 C4
Merrington Rd SW6. . . . . .265 B6
Merrion Ave HA7 . . . . .25 D5
Merritt Gdns KT9 . . . . .213 C2
Merritt Rd SE4. . . . . .163 B6
Merrivale
 Camden Town NW1 . . . . .232 B5
 Southgate N14 . . . . .15 D6
Merrivale Ave IG4 . . . . .55 D5
Merrow Ct CR4 . . . . .180 B1
Merrow St SE17 . . .117 B1 262 C1
Merrow Way CR0 . . . . .224 A2
Merrow Wlk SE17. . . . . . . .262 D2
Merrydown Way BR7. . . . .188 B2
Merry Fiddlers RM8. . . . . . .81 B6
Merryfield SE3 . . . . .142 D3
Merryfield Gdns HA7. . . . . .25 C5
Merryfield Ho SE12 . . . . . .165 C1
Merryhill Cl E4 . . . . .19 D4
Merry Hill Rd WD23 . . . . . . .8 A3
Merryhills Ct N14 . . . . .15 C4

Merryhills Dr EN2 . . . . 4 A1
Merryhills Prim Sch EN2 . . . 4 B1
Merryweather Ct
 🔟 Dartmouth Pk N19 . . . . 71 C5
 🔟 New Malden KT3 . . . . . 199 C4
Mersea Ho IG11 . . . . 78 D2
Mersey Ct 🔟 KT2 . . . . . 175 D2
Mersey Ho 🔟 N7 . . . . 72 C3
Mersey Rd E17 . . . . 53 B6
Mersey Wlk UB5 . . . . 85 C5
Mersham Dr NW9 . . . . 44 D4
Mersham Pl Penge SE20 . . 184 B2
 South Norwood CR7 . . . . 183 B1
Mersham Rd CR7 . . . . 183 B1
Merstone Ho SW18 . . . . . . 157 D5
Merten Rd RM6 . . . . 59 A2
Merthyr Terr SW13 . . . . . . 134 B6
MERTON 179 C2
Merton Abbey Mills Mkt★
 SW19 . . . . 180 A2
Merton Abbey Prim Sch
 SW19 . . . . 179 C2
Merton Ave Chiswick W4 . 111 D2
 Hillingdon UB10 . . . . 60 D1
 Northolt UB5 . . . . 64 A3
Merton Coll SM4 . . . . 201 B4
Merton Court Prep Sch
 DA14 . . . . 190 C6
Merton Ct Barnet EN5 . . . . . 1 D1
 Welling DA16 . . . . 146 B3
Merton Gdns BR5 . . . . 210 D4
Merton Hall Gdns SW20 . 179 A2
Merton Hall Rd SW19 . . . . 179 A2
Merton High St SW19 . . . . 180 A3
Merton Ho SW18 . . . . 157 C3
Merton Ind Pk SW19 . . . . 180 A2
Merton La N6 . . . . 70 D6
Merton Lo New Barnet EN5 . 14 A6
 🖸 Streatham SW16 . . . . . 182 A5
Merton Mans SW20 . . . . . 178 D1
MERTON PARK 179 C1
Merton Park Par SW19 . . 179 B2
Merton Park Prim Sch
 SW19 . . . . 179 C1
Merton Park Sta SW19 . . 179 C2
Merton Pl 🖸 SW19 . . . . . . 180 A3
Merton Rd Barking IG11 . . . . 79 D1
 Croydon CR0 . . . . 205 D3
 Croydon SE25 . . . . 206 A4
 Enfield EN2 . . . . 5 B5
 Harrow HA2 . . . . 42 A1
 Ilford IG3 . . . . 57 D2
 Leytonstone E17 . . . . 54 A3
 Merton SW19 . . . . 179 D3
 Wandsworth SW18 . . . . 157 C4
Merton Rise NW3 . . . . 70 C1
Merton Road Ind Est
 SW18 . . . . 157 C4
Merton Way
 East Molesey KT8 . . . . . 196 A6
 Hillingdon UB10 . . . . 60 D1
Merttins Rd SE15 . . . . 162 D6
Meru Cl NW5 . . . . 71 A3
Mervan Rd SW2 . . . . 138 C1
Mervyn Ave SE9 . . . . 167 A2
Mervyn Ct SE18 . . . . 145 C6
Mervyn Rd
 Brentford W13 . . . . 109 A3
 Shepperton TW17 . . . . . 193 A2
Mervyn Stockwood Ho 🔟
 SE9 . . . . 167 A2
Messaline Ave W3 . . . . 89 A1
Messent Rd SE9 . . . . 165 D6
Messer Ct CR0 . . . . 220 D4
Messeter Pl SE9 . . . . 166 C5
Messina Ave NW6 . . . . 69 C1
Messiter Ho N1 . . . . 233 D5
Met Appts The SE12 . . . . 164 D6
Metcalfe Ho 🟨 SW8 . . . . . 137 D3
Metcalfe Wlk 🟦 TW13 . . . 173 A6
Metcalf Rd TW15 . . . . 170 D5
Meteor St SW11 . . . . 137 A1
Meteor Way SM6 . . . . 220 A1
Metford Cres EN3 . . . . 7 C5
Metherell Ho N21 . . . . 17 B5
Metheringham Way NW9 . 27 C2
Methley Ho 🟦 N7 . . . . 72 B6
Methley St SE11 . . 116 C1 261 B1
Methodist Central Hall★
 SW1 . . . . 115 D4 249 D1
Methuen Cl HA8 . . . . 26 C3
Methuen Pk N10 . . . . 49 B6
Methuen Rd
 Belvedere DA17 . . . . 125 D2
 Bexleyheath DA6 . . . . . . 147 B1
 Edgware HA8 . . . . 26 C3
Methwold Rd W10 . . . . 90 D2
Metro Bsns Ctr The
 SE26 . . . . 185 B5
Metro Ctr UB4 . . . . 106 C6
Metro Ho E7 . . . . 77 B2
Metro Ind Ctr TW7 . . . . . . 131 B2
Metropolis Apartments 🖸
 SW12 . . . . 159 B3
Metropolitan Benefit
 Societies Almshouses 🖸
 N1 . . . . 73 C2

Metropolitan Bsns Ctr 🟦
 N1 . . . . 73 C1
Metropolitan Ct 🟥 E14 . . 97 C2
Metropolitan Ctr The
 UB6 . . . . 85 D6
Metro Trad Ctr HA9 . . . . . . 66 D4
Meudon Ct KT6 . . . . 197 D4
Mews Pl IG8 . . . . 37 A6
Mews St E1 . . . . 118 A5
Mews The
 Beckenham BR3 . . . . 185 C2
 Hampton TW12 . . . . 174 A4
 Hornsey N8 . . . . 50 C5
 Redbridge IG4 . . . . 55 D4
 Shoreditch N1 . . . . 235 B6
 Thornton Heath SW16 . . 182 B2
 Tottenham N15 . . . . 51 C5
 Woolwich SE18 . . . . 122 D1
Mexborough NW1 . . . . . . 232 A5
Mexfield Rd SW15 . . . . . . 157 B6
Meyer Gn EN1 . . . . 6 A5
Meyer Ho 🔟 SW12 . . . . . . 159 B4
Meymott St SE1 . 116 D5 251 C3
Meynell Cres E9 . . . . 74 D1
Meynell Gdns E9 . . . . 74 D1
Meynell Rd E9 . . . . 74 D1
Meyrick Ct CR7 . . . . 204 C3
Meyrick Ho 🟦 E14 . . . . . . 97 C2
Meyrick Rd
 Battersea SW11 . . . . 136 C2
 Willesden NW10 . . . . 68 A2
Miah Terr 🟦 E1 . . . . 118 A5
Miall Wlk SE26 . . . . 185 A6
Micawber Ave UB8 . . . . . . 82 C3
Micawber Ct N1 . . . . 235 B2
Micawber Ho 🟦 SE16 . . . 118 A4
Micawber St N1 . . 95 A4 235 B2
Michael Cliffe Ho EC1 . . 234 B1
Michael Faraday Ho
 SE17 . . . . 262 D1
Michael Faraday Prim Sch
 SE17 . . . . 118 B1 262 D1
Michael Gaynor Cl W7 . . 108 D5
Michael Manley Ind Est 🟦
 SW8 . . . . 137 C3
Michael Marshall Ho 🟦
 SE9 . . . . 167 A2
Michaelmas Cl SW20 . . . 200 C6
Michael Rd
 Leytonstone E11 . . . . 54 D1
 Parsons Green
 SW6 . . . . 135 D4 265 D2
 South Norwood SE25 . . 205 C6
Michaels Cl SE13 . . . . . . 142 C1
Michael Sobell Sinai Sch
 HA3 . . . . 44 C3
Michaelson Ho 🟦 SE21 . 183 C6
Michael Tippett Sch The
 SE24 . . . . 139 A1
Michelangelo Ct 🟦
 SE16 . . . . 118 B1
Micheldever Rd SE12 . . . 164 D5
Micheldever Rd SE12 . . . 164 D5
Michelham Gdns TW1 . . . 152 D1
Michelle Ct Acton W3 . . . 111 B6
 North Finchley N12 . . . . . . 30 A5
Michell Ho TW1 . . . . 152 D3
Michels Almshouses 🔟
 TW10 . . . . 154 A6
Michelsdale Dr 🟦 TW9 . . 132 A1
Michelson Ho SE11 . . . . . 260 D3
Michel's Row 🟦 TW9 . . . 132 A1
Michel Wlk SE18 . . . . 122 D1
Michigan Ave E12 . . . . 78 B4
Michigan Ho E14 . . . . 119 C3
Mickleham Down N12 . . . 29 B6
Mickledore NW1 . . . . 232 B3
Micklefield Ct CR0 . . . . . 204 D3
Mickleham Cl BR5 . . . . . . 190 A1
Mickleham Gdns SM3 . . . 217 A2
Mickleham Rd BR5 . . . . . 190 A1
Mickleham Way CR0 . . . . 224 B1
Micklethwaite Rd
 SW6 . . . . 135 C6 265 B5
Mickleton Ho 🟩 W2 . . . . . 91 C2
Midas Bsns Ctr RM10 . . . . 81 D4
Midas Metro Ctr SM4 . . . 200 D2
Midcroft HA4 . . . . 39 C1
Middle Dene NW7 . . . . 11 B1
Middlefield NW8 . 92 B6 229 C6
Middlefielde W13 . . . . 87 B2
Middlefield Gdns IG2 . . . . 56 D3
Middle Green Cl 🟦 KT5 . 198 B3
Middleham Gdns N18 . . . . 34 A4
Middleham Rd N18 . . . . . . 34 A4
Middle La Hornsey N8 . . . . 50 A4
 Teddington TW11 . . . . . . 174 D4
Middle Lane Mews N8 . . . 50 A4
Middle Park Ave SE9 . . . . 165 D4
Middle Park Prim Sch
 SE9 . . . . 165 D4
Middle Rd East Barnet EN4 . 14 C5
 Finchley N10 . . . . 30 C2
 Harrow HA2 . . . . 42 B1
 Mitcham SW16 . . . . 181 D1
 🟦 Newham E13 . . . . 99 A5
Middle Row W10 . . . . 91 A3
Middle Row Prim Sch 🟥
 W10 . . . . 91 A3

Middlesborough Rd N18 . . 34 A4
Middlesex Bsns Ctr UB2 . 107 B4
Middlesex Cl UB6 . . . . 85 D3
Middlesex Ct
 🖸 Chiswick W4 . . . . 111 D2
 🔟 Harrow HA1 . . . . 42 D4
Middlesex Cty Cricket Sch
 N3 . . . . 29 D1
Middlesex Ho
 Marylebone W1 . . . . 239 B4
 🟦 Penge SE20 . . . . 184 C3
 Wembley HA0 . . . . 87 D6
Middlesex Pas EC1 . . . . . 241 D3
Middlesex Rd 🔟 E9 . . . . . 74 C2
Middlesex Rd CR4 . . . . . . 204 A4
Middlesex Sch of
 Complementary Medicine
 HA7 . . . . 26 A1
Middlesex St E1 . . 95 D1 243 C2
Middlesex Univ (Archway
 Campus) 🖬 N19 . . . . . . 71 C6
Middlesex Univ (Cat Hill)
 EN4 . . . . 15 A6
Middlesex Univ (Chase Farm
 Hospl) EN2 . . . . 4 C5
Middlesex Univ (Hendon
 Campus) NW4 . . . . 46 B5
Middlesex Univ (Trent Park)
 EN4 . . . . 3 C3
Middle St Croydon CR0 . . 221 A5
 Holborn EC1 . . . . 242 A4
Middle Temple★ EC4 . . . . 251 A6
Middle Temple La
 EC4 . . . . 116 C6 251 A6
Middleton Ave
 Chingford Green E4 . . . . . 19 B1
 Greenford UB5 . . . . 86 B5
 Sidcup DA14 . . . . 190 C5
Middleton Cl E4 . . . . 19 B1
Middleton Ct
 Bromley BR1 . . . . 187 B3
 New Barnet EN5 . . . . 2 A1
Middleton Dr
 Bermondsey SE16 . . . . . 118 D4
 Pinner HA5 . . . . 40 A6
Middleton Gdns IG2 . . . . . 56 D3
Middleton Gr N7 . . . . 72 A3
Middleton Ho Dalston E8 . . 73 D1
 Newington SE1 . . . . 262 C5
Middleton Mews N7 . . . . . 72 A3
Middleton Pl W1 . . . . 239 A3
Middleton Rd
 Carshalton CR4, SM5 . . . 202 B2
 Dalston E8 . . . . 73 D1
 Golders Green NW11 . . . . 47 C2
 Hayes UB3 . . . . 83 B2
Middleton St E2 . . . . 96 B4
Middleton Way SE13 . . . 142 B1
Middleway NW11 . . . . 47 D4
Middle Way Hayes UB4 . . . 84 C3
 Mitcham SW16 . . . . 181 D1
Middle Way The HA3 . . . . . 24 D1
Middlewich Ho 🟦 UB5 . . . 85 B3
Middle Yd SE1 . . . . 253 A4
Midfield Prim Sch BR5 . . . 190 A3
Midfield Way BR5 . . . . 190 B2
Midford Ho 🔟 NW4 . . . . . . 46 D5
Midford Pl W1 . . . . 239 B5
Midholm
 East Finchley NW11 . . . . . 47 D5
 Wembley HA9 . . . . 44 C1
Midholm Cl NW11 . . . . 47 D5
Midholm Rd CR0 . . . . 223 A6
Midhope Ho WC1 . . . . 233 B1
Midhope St WC1 . . . . 233 B1
Midhurst 🔟 SE26 . . . . . . 184 C4
Midhurst Ave
 Muswell Hill N10 . . . . 49 A6
 Thornton Heath CR0 . . . 204 C2
Midhurst Ct N8 . . . . 50 A2
Midhurst Gdns UB10 . . . . . 61 A1
Midhurst Hill DA6 . . . . . . 169 C6
Midhurst Ho 🟦 E14 . . . . . 97 B1
Midhurst Par N10 . . . . 49 A6
Midhurst Rd W13 . . . . 109 A3
Midhurst Way E5 . . . . 74 A4
Midland Pl E14 . . . . 120 A1
Midland Rd
 Leytonstone E10 . . . . 54 A2
 St Pancras NW1 . . . 94 A4 233 A2
Midland Terr NW10 . . . . . . 89 C3
Midlea Ho EN3 . . . . 6 C4
Midleton Rd KT3 . . . . 177 A1
Midlothian Ho NW2 . . . . . . 68 B4
Midlothian Rd E3 . . . . 97 B3
Midmoor Rd
 Merton SW19 . . . . 179 A2
 Streatham SW12 . . . . . . 159 C3
Midship Cl SE16 . . . . 118 D5
Midship Point E14 . . . . . . 119 C4
Midstrath Rd NW10 . . . . . . 67 C4
Midsummer Apartments 🟦
 SM2 . . . . 217 C1
Midsummer Ave TW4 . . . 129 B1
Midsummer Ct
 Blackheath Pk SE12 . . . . 143 A1
 Edgware HA8 . . . . 10 D1
 Harrow HA1 . . . . 42 B4
Midway SM3 . . . . 201 B2
Midway Ho EC1 . . . . 234 D2

Midwinter Cl 🟦 DA16 . . . 146 A2
Midwood Cl NW2 . . . . 68 B5
Mighell Ave IG4 . . . . 55 D4
Milan Ct N11 . . . . 31 D2
Milan Rd UB1 . . . . 107 B4
Milborne St SE20 . . . . . . 256 B1
Milborne Ho 🔟 E9 . . . . . . 74 C2
Milborne St E9 . . . . 74 C2
Milborough Cres SE12 . . 164 C5
Milbourne La KT10 . . . . . 212 A3
Milbourne Lodge Jun Sch
 KT10 . . . . 212 A2
Milbourne Lodge Sch
 KT10 . . . . 212 B2
Milbrook KT10 . . . . 212 A2
Milbrook Ct NW3 . . . . 48 A1
Milburn Dr 🔟 UB7 . . . . . 104 A6
Milburn Ho SW20 . . . . 178 B1
Milcote St SE1 . . . . 251 D1
Mildenhall Rd E5 . . . . 74 C5
Mildmay Ave N1 . . . . 73 B2
Mildmay Ct N1 . . . . 73 B3
Mildmay Gr N N1 . . . . 73 B3
Mildmay Gr S N1 . . . . 73 B3
Mildmay Ho 🟦 SW15 . . . 156 C6
Mildmay Mission Hospl
 E2 . . . . 95 D4
Mildmay Pk N1 . . . . 73 B3
Mildmay Rd Ilford IG1 . . . . 78 D5
 Stoke Newington N1 . . . . 73 C3
Mildmay St N1 . . . . 73 B2
Mildon Ho EN3 . . . . 6 C3
Mildred Ave Hayes UB3 . . 105 B3
 Northolt UB5 . . . . 63 D3
Mildura Ct N8 . . . . 50 B5
MILE END 97 A3
Mile End Hospl E2 . . . . 96 D4
Mile End Park L Ctr & Stad
 E3 . . . . 97 B2
Mile End Pl E1 . . . . 96 D3
Mile End Rd E1, E3 . . . . . . 96 D3
Mile End Sta E3 . . . . 97 B4
Mile End The E17 . . . . 34 C2
Mile Rd Hackbridge SM6 . . 203 A1
 Wallington CR0, CR4, CR9 . 203 D1
Miles Bldgs NW1 . . . . 237 A4
Miles Cl SE28 . . . . 123 B5
Miles Coverdale Prim Sch 🔟
 W12 . . . . 112 C4
Miles Ct Croydon CR0 . . . 220 D6
 Stepney E1 . . . . 96 B1
Miles Dr SE28 . . . . 123 C5
Miles Ho 🖸 SE10 . . . . 120 C1
Miles Lo Harrow HA1 . . . . . 42 B4
 Stratford New Town E15 . . 76 B3
Milespit Hill NW7 . . . . 28 C5
Miles Pl NW8 . . . . 236 D4
Miles Rd Hornsey N8 . . . . . 50 A6
 Mitcham CR4 . . . . 202 C6
Miles St SW8 . . . . . 138 A6 270 B5
Milestone Cl Edmonton N9 . 18 A2
 Sutton SM2 . . . . 218 B1
Milestone Ct TW7 . . . . . . 131 A4
Milestone Green SW14 . . 133 B1
Milestone Ho KT1 . . . . . . 197 D5
Milestone Rd SE19 . . . . . 183 D4
Miles Way N20 . . . . 14 C2
Milfoil St W12 . . . . 112 A6
Milford Cl SE2 . . . . 147 A6
Milford Ct Southall UB1 . . 107 C5
 🖸 Stamford Hill N16 . . . . . 51 C1
Milford Gdns
 Croydon CR0 . . . . 206 D4
 Edgware HA8 . . . . 26 C3
 Wembley HA0 . . . . 65 D3
Milford Gr SM1 . . . . 218 A4
Milford La WC2 . . 116 C6 251 A6
Milford Mews SW16 . . . . 160 B1
Milford Rd Ealing W13 . . . 109 B5
 Southall UB1 . . . . 107 C6
Milk St Bromley BR1 . . . . . 187 B4
 City of London EC2 . . 95 A1 242 B2
 Newham E16 . . . . 122 D5
Milkwell Gdns IG8 . . . . 37 B3
Milkwell Yd 🟦 SE5 . . . . . 139 A4
Milkwood Rd SE24 . . . . . 138 D1
Milk Yd E1 . . . . 118 C6
Millais Ave E12 . . . . 78 C3
Millais Cres KT19 . . . . . . 215 C3
Millais Ct 🟦 UB5 . . . . 84 D5
Millais Ho SW1 . . . . 259 D3
Millais Rd Enfield EN1 . . . . 17 C6
 Leyton E11 . . . . 76 B4
 New Malden KT3 . . . . . . 199 C2
Millais Way KT19 . . . . 215 A4
Milland Ho SW15 . . . . 156 A3
Millard Cl 🟦 N16 . . . . 73 C3
Millard Rd SE8 . . . . 119 B1
Millard Terr RM10 . . . . 81 C2
Millars Meadow Cl SE12 . 165 A6
Millbank Wallington SM6 . 219 D3
 Westminster SW1 . 116 A2 260 A3
Millbank Ho KT6 . . . . 198 B2
Millbank Prim Sch
 SW1 . . . . 115 D2 259 D3
Millbank Way SE12 . . . . . 165 A6
Millbourne Rd TW13 . . . . 173 A6
Mill Bridge EN5 . . . . 13 B5
Millbrook 🔟 E18 . . . . 55 A6
Millbrook Ave DA16 . . . . . 145 B1

Millbrooke Ct 🟦 SW15 . . 157 A6
Millbrook Gdns RM6 . . . . . 59 A3
Millbrook Ho 🟦 SE15 . . . 140 A6
Millbrook Pl NW1 . . . . 232 A4
Millbrook Rd
 Brixton SW9 . . . . 138 D2
 Edmonton N9 . . . . 18 B3
Mill Cl SM5 . . . . 219 A6
Mill Cnr EN5 . . . . 1 B4
Millcroft Ho SE6 . . . . 185 D6
Mill Ct Hendon NW7 . . . . . . 29 A2
 Leyton E10 . . . . 76 B6
 🟦 Thamesmead SE28 . . . 124 B6
Millender Wlk SE16 . . . . . 118 C2
Millennium Bridge★ SE1,
 EC4 . . . . 252 A5
Millennium Bsns Ctr
 NW2 . . . . 68 B6
Millennium City Acad
 W1 . . . . 238 D3
Millennium Cl E16 . . . . 99 B1
Millennium Dr E14 . . . . . . 120 B2
Millennium Harbour
 E14 . . . . 119 C4
Millennium Ho E17 . . . . . . 52 D4
Millennium Pl 🟦 E2 . . . . . 96 B5
Millennium Prim Sch The
 SE10 . . . . 120 D3
Millennium Sq SE1 . . . . . 253 D2
Millennium Way SE10 . . . 120 C3
Miller Ave EN3 . . . . 7 C5
Miller Cl Bromley BR1 . . . 187 B5
 Carshalton CR4 . . . . 202 D2
 Pinner HA5 . . . . 22 C1
Miller Ct
 Bexleyheath DA7 . . . . . . 147 D2
 🔟 Hammersmith W6 . . . . 46 A5
Miller Ho Harringay N15 . . . 50 D5
 🖸 Streatham SW2 . . . . . 160 A4
Miller Rd Mitcham SW19 . . 180 B4
 Thornton Heath CR0 . . . 204 C1
Miller's Ave E8, N16 . . . . . . 73 D3
Millers Ct NW7 . . . . 28 A6
Millers Ct 🟦 HA0 . . . . 88 A5
Miller's Ct 🔟 W4 . . . . 111 D1
Millers Green Cl EN2 . . . . . 4 D2
Millers Mead Ct SW19 . . 180 B3
Miller St NW1 . . . . 232 A4
Miller's Terr 🟦 E8 . . . . 73 D3
Miller's Way W6 . . . . 112 C4
Millers Wharf Ho E1 . . . . 118 A5
Millers Yd N3 . . . . 29 D3
Miller Wlk SE1 . . . . 251 B3
Millet Rd UB6 . . . . 85 D5
Mill Farm Ave TW16 . . . . 171 C3
Millfarm Bsns Pk TW4 . . 151 A4
Mill Farm Cl HA5 . . . . 22 C1
Mill Farm Cres TW4 . . . . 151 A3
Millfield Charlton TW16 . . 171 B2
 Finsbury Pk N4 . . . . 72 C6
 Kingston u T KT1 . . . . . . 198 B6
Millfield Ave E17 . . . . 35 B2
Millfield La N6 . . . . 70 D6
Millfield Pl N6 . . . . 71 A6
Millfield Rd Hendon HA8 . . 27 A1
 Twickenham TW4 . . . . . . 151 B3
Millfields Com Sch E5 . . . 74 C4
Millfields Rd E5 . . . . 74 C5
Mill Gdns SE26 . . . . 162 B1
Mill Gn CR4 . . . . 203 A2
Mill Green Bsns Pk CR4 . 203 A2
Mill Green Rd CR4 . . . . . . 203 A2
Millgrove St 🟦 SW11 . . . 137 A3
Millharbour E14 . . . . 119 D4
Millhaven Cl RM6 . . . . 58 B3
MILL HILL 28 B5
Mill Hill SW13 . . . . 134 A2
Mill Hill Broadway Sta
 NW7 . . . . 27 C4
Mill Hill Circus NW7 . . . . . 27 D5
Mill Hill Cty High Sch
 NW7 . . . . 11 C3
Mill Hill East Sta NW7 . . . 29 A3
Mill Hill Gr 🟦 W3 . . . . . . 110 D5
Mill Hill Ind Est NW7 . . . . 27 D4
Mill Hill Rd Barnes SW13 . 134 A3
 South Acton W3 . . . . 110 D4
Mill Hill Sch NW7 . . . . 28 B6
Mill Hill Terr 🟦 W3 . . . . . 110 D5
Mill Ho
 🟨 Lewisham SE13 . . . . . 142 A2
 Morden SM4 . . . . 202 A5
 Woodford IG8 . . . . 36 D5
Millhouse Pl SE27 . . . . . . 182 B6
Millicent Fawcett Ct N17 . 33 D2
Millicent Gr N13 . . . . 32 D5
Millicent Preston Ho 🟦
 IG11 . . . . 101 B6
Millie Ho E10 . . . . 53 B1
Milligan Ho SE23 . . . . 163 B3
Milligan St E14 . . . . 119 B6
Milliners Ho SW18 . . . . . . 135 C1
Milling Rd HA8 . . . . 27 B3
Millington Ho N16 . . . . 73 B5
Millington Rd UB3 . . . . . . 105 C3
Mill La Brondesbury NW6 . . 69 B3
 Carshalton SM5 . . . . 219 A5
 Croydon CR0 . . . . 220 C5
 Dagenham RM6 . . . . 59 A3
 Sewardstone E4 . . . . 7 D2

Mill La continued
Woodford IG8. . . . . .36 D5
Woolwich SE18. . . . . . .122 C1
Mill Lane Trad Est CR0 . 220 B5
Millman Ct
Bloomsbury WC1 . . . . . 240 C5
Greenwich SE3 . . . . . . 143 B5
Millman Mews WC1 . . . 240 C5
Millman PI WC1 . . . . . . 240 D5
Millman St WC1 . . 94 B3 240 C5
Millmark Gr SE14 . . . . .141 A3
Millmarsh La EN3 . . . . . . .7 B3
Millmead Bsns Ctr N17. .52 B6
Millmead Ind Ctr N17 . . .52 B6
Mill Mead Rd N17 . . . . .52 B6
MILL MEADS 98 B5
Millner Ct SE4 . . . . . . .141 B3
Mill PI Chislehurst BR7. .188 D2
Kingston u T KT1 . . . . .198 B6
Limehouse E14 . . . . . . .97 A1
Mill Plat TW7 . . . . .131 A3
Mill Plat Ave TW7 . . . . .131 A3
Mill Pond Cl
SW8. . . . . 137 D5 269 D3
Millpond Est SE16 . . . . .118 B4
Millpond PI 2 SM6 . . . . .219 A5
Mill Rd Ilford IG1 . . . . . .78 C5
Merton SW19 . . . . .180 A3
Newham E16 . . . . .121 B5
Twickenham TW2 . . . . .152 A2
Mill Ridge HA8 . . . . . . .26 C5
Mill River Trad Est EN3 . . .7 A1
Mill Row N1 . . . . .95 C6
Mills Cl UB10 . . . . .82 C5
Mills Ct 9 Leyton E11 . . .76 C5
Shoreditch EC2. . . . . . .95 C4
Mills Gr Hendon NW4 . . .46 D6
1 South Bromley E14 . . .98 A2
Mills Ho Nine Elms SW8. .269 B2
Walthamstow E17 . . . . .54 B6
Millshott Cl SW6. . . . . .134 C4
Millside SM5 . . . . .218 D6
Millside PI TW7 . . . . . .131 B3
Millson Cl N20. . . . . . . .14 B2
Mills Row W4 . . . . .111 B2
Mill St
Bermondsey SE1 . 117 D4 253 D2
Kingston u T KT1. . . . . .198 A6
Mayfair W1 . . . . 249 A6
Millstone Ct E15 . . . . . .76 B2
Millstream Cl N13 . . . . .32 C5
Millstream Ho 14 SE16 . .118 B4
Millstream Rd
SE1 . . . . .117 D4 253 C1
Mill Trad Est NW10 . . . .89 A4
Mill Vale BR2 . . . . .186 D1
Mill View Cl KT17. . . . . .215 D1
Mill View Gdns CR0 . . . 222 D5
MILLWALL 119 C3
Millwall Dock Rd E14 . . .119 C3
Mill Way Edgware NW7 . . .27 C5
Feltham TW14 . . . . . . .150 B6
Millway Gdns UB5 . . . . .63 A3
Millwood Rd TW3, TW7. .152 A6
Millwood St 10 W10. . . .91 A2
Mill Yd E1 . . . . .118 A6
Milman Cl HA5 . . . . .40 D6
Milman Rd NW6 . . . . . .91 A5
Milman's Ho SW10. . . . 266 C5
Milman's St
SW10. . . . . . . .136 B6 266 C5
Milne Ct Enfield EN2 . . . . .4 C3
4 Woodford E18 . . . . . .37 A2
Milne Field HA5 . . . . . .23 C3
Milne Gdns SE9. . . . . . .166 A6
Milne Ho 18 SE18 . . . . .122 B2
Milner Bldg N16. . . . . . .73 B5
Milner Dr TW2 . . . . . . .152 B4
Milner Ho
1 Battersea SW11 . . . . .136 B2
Hayes UB4 . . . . .84 B4
Milner PI N1. . . . . 94 C6 234 B6
Milner Rd Dagenham RM8 . .80 C6
Kingston u T KT1 . . . . .197 D6
Merton SW19 . . . . .179 D2
Morden SM4. . . . . .202 B4
Newham E15 . . . . .98 C4
South Norwood CR7 . . . .205 B6
Milner Sq N1 . . . . .72 C1
Milner St SW3 . . . 114 D2 257 C4
Milnthorpe Rd W4 . . . . .133 B6
Milo Rd SE22 . . . . .161 D5
Milroad Ho 6 5 E1. . . . . .96 D2
Milroy Wlk SE1. . . . . . . 251 C4
Milson Rd W14 . . .113 A3 254 A6
Milsted Ho 23 E5 . . . . . .74 B3
Milton Ave Barnet EN5 . . .13 B6
Becontree NW10 . . . . . .89 B6
Carshalton SM1 . . . . . .218 C4
Crouch End N6 . . . . . . .49 C2
Kingsbury NW9 . . . . . . .45 A6
Plashet E6 . . . . .78 A1
Stonebridge NW10. . . . . .89 A6
Thornton Heath CR0. . . . 205 B2
Milton Cl
Bermondsey SE1 . 117 D2 263 C3
Carshalton SM1 . . . . . . .218 B5
Hampstead Garden Suburb
N2. . . . . .48 A3

Milton Cl continued
Hayes UB4 . . . . .84 A1
Milton Court Rd SE14 . . .141 A4
Milton Cres IG2 . . . . . . .57 A3
Milton Ct Fulham SW6. . .135 A2
Ilford RM6 . . . . .58 C2
Kingston u T KT2 . . . . .176 A6
St Luke's EC2 . . . . 242 C4
Twickenham TW2 . . . . .152 C1
Uxbridge UB10 . . . . . . .60 D5
9 Wandsworth SW18 . . .157 C6
Milton Dr
Borehamwood WD6 . . . . .10 D6
Littleton TW17 . . . . . . .192 A5
Milton Gdns TW19 . . . . .148 B3
Milton Gr
Friern Barnet N11 . . . . .31 D5
Stoke Newington N16. . . .73 C4
Milton Ho
12 Beckenham BR3 . . . . .185 C3
19 Bethnal Green E2 . . . . .96 C4
2 Camberwell SE5 . . . . .139 B5
5 Kingston u T KT2 . . . .176 D4
Sutton SM1 . . . . .217 C5
Milton House Mans E8 . .73 D4
Milton Lo
4 Sidcup DA14 . . . . . . .190 A6
Southgate N21 . . . . . . .16 D3
Twickenham TW1 . . . . .152 D4
Milton Pk N6 . . . . .49 C2
Milton PI 8 N7 . . . . .72 C3
Milton Rd Acton W3. . . .111 B5
Belvedere DA17 . . . . . .125 C2
Bexley DA16 . . . . .145 D4
Crouch End N6 . . . . . . .49 C2
Ealing W7 . . . . .108 D6
Hampton TW12 . . . . . .173 C3
Harrow HA1 . . . . .42 C5
1 Hendon NW9 . . . . . . .46 A2
Mill Hill NW7 . . . . .28 A5
Mitcham CR4 . . . . .181 A3
Mortlake SW14 . . . . . . .133 B2
Sutton SM1 . . . . .217 C4
Thornton Heath CR0 . . . .205 B2
Tottenham N15 . . . . . . .50 D6
Tulse Hill SE24 . . . . . .160 D6
Uxbridge UB10 . . . . . . .60 D4
Wallington SM6 . . . . . .219 D2
Walthamstow E17 . . . . .53 C5
Wimbledon SW19 . . . . .180 A4
Milton St EC1, EC2. . 95 B2 242 C4
Milton Way UB7 . . . . . .104 B2
Milverton Dr UB10 . . . . .61 A4
Milverton Gdns IG3 . . . .79 D6
Milverton Ho SE23 . . . . .163 A1
Milverton Rd NW6 . . . . .68 C1
Milverton St
SE11 . . . . .116 C1 261 B1
Milverton Way SE9. . . . .188 C6
Milward St E1 . . . . .96 B2
Milward Wlk 14 SE18. . . .144 C6
Mimosa N15. . . . . .51 B4
Mimosa Ct
Colney Hatch N12. . . . . .30 C4
South Lambeth SW4. . . . 270 B1
Mimosa Ho UB4 . . . . . .84 C2
Mimosa Rd UB4 . . . . . .84 C2
Mimosa St SW6. . . .135 B4 264 D1
Mina Rd Merton SW19. . .179 C2
Walworth SE17. . .117 C1 263 B2
Minard Rd SE6 . . . . . . .164 C3
Minchenden Cres N14 . .15 D1
Minchenden Ct N14. . . . .15 D2
Minchin Ho 10 E14. . . . . .97 C1
Mincing La EC3 . . .117 C6 253 A6
Minden Rd Cheam SM3. .217 B6
Penge SE20 . . . . .184 B2
Minehead Ct HA2 . . . . . .63 C6
Minehead Rd Harrow HA2 . .63 C5
Streatham SW16 . . . . . .182 B5
Mineral Cl EN5 . . . . . . .12 C6
Mineral St SE18. . . . . . .123 C2
Minera Mews SW1. . . . . 258 B4
Minerva Cl
Kennington SW9. . . . . . .138 C5
Sidcup DA14 . . . . .189 C6
Minerva Rd
Becontree NW10 . . . . . .89 B4
Chingford E4. . . . . .35 D3
Kingston u T KT1 . . . . .176 B1
Minerva St E2 . . . . .96 B5
Minerva Wlk EC1 . . . . . 241 D2
Minet Ave NW10 . . . . . .89 C5
Minet Ctry Pk UB2, UB3,
UB4. . . . . .106 C5
Minet Dr UB3 . . . . .106 A5
Minet Gdns
Dagenham NW10 . . . . . .89 C5
Hayes UB3 . . . . .106 B5
Minet Ho 20 E1. . . . . . . .96 A1
Minet Jun & Inf Schs
UB3. . . . . .106 B5
Minet Rd SE5, SW9 . . . .138 D3
Minetta Ct 15 EN5. . . . . .13 A1
Minford Gdns W14 . . . .112 D4
Mingard Wlk N7 . . . . . .72 C5
Ming St E14 . . . . .119 C6
Minimax Cl TW14 . . . . .150 A5
Ministry Way SE9 . . . . .166 B2

Mink Ct TW4. . . . . .128 C3
Minnie Bennett Ho SE3 . .143 C5
Minniedale N15. . . . . . .198 B4
Minnow Wlk SE17. . . . . 263 B3
Minories EC3 . . .117 D6 253 C6
Minshaw Ct DA14 . . . . .189 D6
Minshull PI 28 BR3. . . . .185 C3
Minshull St SW8. . . . . . 269 C1
Minson Rd E9 . . . . .96 D6
Minstead Gdns SW15 . . .155 D4
Minstead Way KT3. . . . .199 C3
Minster Ave SM1. . . . . .217 C6
Minster Ct EC3 . . . . . . 253 B6
Minster Dr CR0 . . . . . . .221 C4
Minster Gdns KT8. . . . . .195 B5
Minsterley Ave TW16,
TW17. . . . . .193 C5
Minster Rd Bromley BR1. .187 B3
Brondesbury NW2 . . . . .69 A3
Minster Wlk N8. . . . . . . .50 A5
Minstrel Ct HA3. . . . . . .24 C1
Minstrel Gdns KT5. . . . .198 B5
Mint Bsns Pk 12 E16. . . . .99 A2
Mint Cl UB10 . . . . .82 D4
Mintern Cl N13. . . . . . . .16 D1
Minterne Ave UB2 . . . . .107 C2
Minterne Rd HA3 . . . . . .44 B4
Minterne Waye UB4. . . . .84 C1
Mintern St N1 . . .95 B5 235 D4
Minton Ho SE11 . . . . . . 261 A4
Minton Mews 3 NW6. . . .69 D2
Mint Rd SM5, SM6. . . . .219 B4
Mint St SE1. . . . . 252 B2
Mint Wlk CR0. . . . . . . .221 A5
Mirabel Rd SW6 . .135 B5 264 D4
Mirage Ctr The HA9 . . . .66 D4
Miranda Cl 19 E1 . . . . . .96 C2
Miranda Ct W3 . . . . .88 B1
Miranda Ho
6 Belvedere DA17 . . . . .125 C1
17 Hoxton N1 . . . . .95 C5
Miranda Rd N19 . . . . . . .49 C1
Mirfield Ct SE20 . . . . . .184 A1
Mirfield St SE7 . . . . . . .121 D3
Miriam Ct DA14. . . . . . .190 B6
Miriam Rd SE18. . . . . . .123 C1
Mirravale Ct 11 IG9 . . . . .21 C2
Mirravale Trad Est RM8. . .59 A2
Mirren Cl HA2 . . . . .63 B5
Mirror Path SE12 . . . . . .165 C1
Misbourne Rd UB10. . . . .82 C6
Missenden SE17 . . . . . . 262 D1
Missenden Cl TW14 . . . .149 D3
Missenden Gdns SM4 . . .202 A3
Missenden Ho NW8 . . . . 237 A6
Mission Gr E17 . . . . .53 A4
Mission Grove Prim Sch
E17. . . . . .53 B5
Mission PI SE15. . . . . . .140 A4
Mission Sq 13 TW8 . . . . .132 A6
Mission The
13 Bermondsey SE16. . . .118 B4
6 Poplar E14. . . . . .97 B1
Missouri Ct HA5 . . . . . . .40 C3
Misterton Ct SW11. . . . . 266 D2
Mistletoe Cl CR0. . . . . . .206 D1
Mistley Thorn IG1. . . . . .56 C2
Mistral SE5 . . . . .139 C4
Mistral Ct E4 . . . . .19 D1
Mistys Field KT12. . . . . .194 C1
Mitali Pas 21 E1 . . . . . . .96 A1
MITCHAM 202 D5
Mitcham Eastfields Sta
CR4. . . . . .181 A1
Mitcham Garden Village
CR4. . . . . .203 A4
Mitcham Ho 9 SE5 . . . . .139 A4
Mitcham Ind Est CR4. . . .181 A2
Mitcham Junction Sta
CR4. . . . . .203 A4
Mitcham La SW16. . . . . .181 C5
Mitcham Pk CR4 . . . . . .202 C5
Mitcham Rd Ilford IG3. . . .57 D2
Newham E6 . . . . .100 A4
Upper Tooting SW17. . . .180 D5
Thornton Heath CR4 . . . .181 D2
Mitchell 19 New E9 . . . . .74 B1
Mitchell Brook Prim Sch
NW10. . . . . .67 C2
Mitchellbrook Way NW10 . 67 B2
Mitchell Cl
Abbey Wood SE2. . . . . .124 C4
Belvedere DA17 . . . . . .125 D3
Mitchell Ct SW14. . . . . .133 C1
Mitchell Ho
Gunnersbury W4 . . . . . .110 D1
6 Islington N1 . . . . .72 C1
31 Shepherd's Bush W12. .112 B6
Mitchell Rd Edmonton N13. .33 A5
Orpington BR6 . . . . . . .227 D4
Mitchell's PI SE21. . . . . .161 C4
Mitchell St EC1 . . . .95 A3 242 B6
Mitchell Way
1 Bromley BR1. . . . . . . .187 A2
Tokyngton NW10 . . . . . .67 A2
Mitchell Wlk E6 . . . . . . .100 B2
Mitchison Rd N1. . . . . . .73 B2
Mitchley Rd N17. . . . . . .52 A6
Mitford Cl KT9. . . . . . . .213 C2
Mitford Rd N19 . . . . . . .72 A4

Mitre Bridge Ind Pk W10 . .90 B3
Mitre Cl
Shepperton TW17. . . . . .193 B3
Sutton SM2. . . . . .218 B1
Mitre Ct Belvedere DA17 . .125 C1
1 Ilford RM6 . . . . .58 B2
9 Woodford E18 . . . . . . .37 A2
Mitre Ho RM7. . . . . .59 D5
Mitre Rd
Lambeth SE1. . . .116 C4 251 B2
Newham E15 . . . . .98 C5
Mitre Sq EC3 . . . . 243 B1
Mitre St EC3 . . . . 95 C1 243 B1
Mitre The 9 E14. . . . . . .119 B6
Mitre Way W10 . . . . . . .90 B2
Mizzen Ct E14 . . . . .119 C4
Moatbridge Sch SE9 . . . .165 D5
Moat Ct BR6 . . . . .227 D2
Moat Cres N3. . . . . .47 D6
Moat Croft DA16. . . . . . .146 C2
Moat Ct Eltham SE9 . . . .166 B5
Sidcup DA15 . . . . .167 D1
Moat Dr Harrow HA1 . . . .42 B5
5 Newham E13 . . . . .99 C5
Ruislip HA4 . . . . .39 C2
Moat Farm Rd UB5. . . . . .63 B1
Moatfield NW6 . . . . .69 A1
Moat Lodge The HA1. . . . .64 C6
Moat PI Acton W3. . . . . .88 D1
Stockwell SW9. . . . . . . .138 B2
Moat Sch The 7 SW6 . . . .135 A3
Moat Side Enfield EN3. . . . .6 D1
Feltham TW13 . . . . .172 C6
Moat The KT3. . . . . .199 C3
Moberly Rd SW4. . . . . . .159 D4
Mobey St SW8 . . . . 270 A1
Moby Dick RM6. . . . . . . .59 B5
Mocatta Ho 6 E1 . . . . . . .96 B3
Modbury Gdns NW5 . . . .71 A2
Modder PI SW15. . . . . . .134 D1
Model Cotts SW14 . . . . .133 A2
Model Farm Cl SE9 . . . . .166 A1
Modling Ho 8 E2. . . . . . .96 D5
Modoc Ho EN3 . . . . .18 D6
Moelwyn Hughes Ct N7. . .71 D3
Moelyn Mews HA1. . . . . .43 A4
Moffat Ct
Upper Tooting SW17 . . . .180 C6
Wimbledon SW19. . . . . .179 C5
Moffat Ho 24 SE5 . . . . . .139 A5
Moffat Rd Bowes Pk N13. . .32 A4
South Norwood CR7. . . . .183 B1
Upper Tooting SW17. . . .180 D6
Mogden La TW7. . . . . . .152 D6
Mohammedi Pk Complex
UB5. . . . . .85 C6
Mohawk Ho 33 E3. . . . . .97 A5
Mohmmad Khan Rd E11. .54 D1
Mohr Ct N22. . . . . .32 B3
Moidart Ct HA8 . . . . . . .10 D2
Moineau 18 NW9 . . . . . . .27 D2
Moira Cl N17. . . . . .33 C1
Moira Ct SW17. . . . . . . .159 A2
Moira Ho 13 SW9 . . . . . .138 C4
Moira Rd SE9 . . . . .144 B1
Molasses Ho 1 SW11. . . .136 A2
Molasses Row 2 SW11 . .136 A2
Mole Abbey Gdns KT8. . .195 D6
Mole Ct
2 Bedford Pk W12 . . . . .111 C4
West Ewell KT19. . . . . . .215 A4
Mole Ho NW8. . . . . 236 D5
Molember Ct KT7. . . . . . .196 C5
Molember Rd KT8. . . . . .196 C4
Molescroft SE9 . . . . . . .167 A1
Molesey Ave KT12, KT8. .195 B4
Molesey Bsns Ctr KT8. . .195 B4
Molesey Dr SM3 . . . . . .217 A5
Molesey Ho E2 . . . . 243 C6
Molesey Hospl KT8 . . . . .195 C4
Molesey Park Ave KT8. . .195 D4
Molesey Park Cl KT8 . . . .196 A4
Molesey Park Rd KT8 . . .195 A2
Molesford Rd SW6 . . . . . 265 A1
Molesham Cl KT8. . . . . . .195 D6
Molesham Way KT8. . . . .195 D6
Molesworth Ho 9 SE17 . .138 D6
Molesworth St SE13 . . . .142 A2
Moliner Ct 4 BR3. . . . . . .185 C3
Mollie Davis Ct SE19 . . . .183 D4
Mollison Ave EN3 . . . . . . .7 B5
Mollison Dr SM6. . . . . . .220 A1
Mollison Sq SM6. . . . . . .219 D1
Mollison Way HA8 . . . . . .26 C1
Molly Huggins Cl SW12 . .159 C4
Molton Ho N1 . . . . 233 D5
Molvic Ct BR3 . . . . .185 B1
Molyneux Dr SW17. . . . .181 B6
Molyneux Ho W1 . . . . . . 237 B2
Molyneux St W1 . . 92 C2 237 B3
Monarch Cl
Coney Hall BR4. . . . . . .224 D4
East Bedfont TW14 . . . . .149 C4
Monarch Ct Ealing W5 . . .87 C2
Hampstead Garden Suburb
N2. . . . . .48 A4
Monarch Dr E16. . . . . . . .99 D2
Monarch Mews
Walthamstow E17. . . . . . .53 D3

Monarch Mews continued
West Norwood SW16. . . .182 C5
Monarch Par CR4. . . . . .180 D1
Monarch PI
Buckhurst Hill IG9 . . . . .21 C2
Sutton SM1. . . . . .218 B3
Monarch Rd DA17. . . . . .125 C3
Monarchs Ct
1 Edgware NW7 . . . . . . .27 B5
Harrow HA2 . . . . .41 C2
Monarchs Way HA4 . . . . .39 C1
Monarch Way IG2 . . . . . .57 B3
Mona Rd SE15 . . . . .140 C3
Mona St E16. . . . . .98 D2
Monastery Gdns EN2. . . . .5 B3
Monaveen Gdns KT8. . . .195 D6
Monck's Row SW18 . . . .157 B5
Monck St SW1 . . . 115 D3 259 D5
Monckton Ct W14. . . . . . 254 C6
Monclar Rd SE5 . . . . . . .139 B1
Moncorvo Cl
SW7. . . . . .114 C4 247 A1
Moncrieff Cl 4 E6. . . . . . .100 A1
Moncrieff St SE15 . . . . . .140 A3
Mondial Way UB7. . . . . .127 A5
Mondragon Ho 9 SW8 . . . 270 B2
Monega Prim Sch E12 . . . .77 D2
Monega Rd E7, E12. . . . . .77 D2
Monet Ct 15 SE16 . . . . . .118 B1
Moneyer Ho N1. . . . . . . 235 C2
Monica Ct SW16. . . . . . .181 D4
Monica James Ho 12
DA14. . . . . .168 A1
Monica Shaw Ct NW1 . . . 232 D3
Monier Rd E3. . . . . .75 C1
Monivea Rd BR3. . . . . . .185 B3
Monkbretton Ho E2. . . . . .96 A4
Monk Ct W12. . . . . .112 A5
Monk Dr E16 . . . . .121 A6
MONKEN HADLEY. 1 A3
Monken Hadley CE Prim Sch
EN4. . . . . .1 C4
Monkfrith Ave N14. . . . . .15 B5
Monkfrith Cl N14 . . . . . .15 B4
Monkfrith Prim Sch N14. .15 A4
Monkfrith Way N14 . . . . .15 A4
Monkham's Ave IG8 . . . . .37 B5
Monkham's Dr IG8 . . . . . .37 B5
Monkham's La IG8. . . . . .37 B6
Monkleigh Rd SM4,
SW20. . . . . .201 A5
Monkridge 3 N8 . . . . . . .49 D2
Monks Ave
East Molesey KT8. . . . . .195 B4
New Barnet EN5. . . . . . .14 A5
Monks Cl
Abbey Wood SE2. . . . . .124 D2
Enfield EN2. . . . . .5 A3
Harrow HA2 . . . . .63 D6
Ruislip HA4 . . . . .62 D4
Monks Cres KT12 . . . . . .194 B1
Monksdene Gdns SM1 . .217 D5
Monks Dr W3. . . . . .88 C1
Monksfield N4 . . . . .72 C6
Monks Hill Sp Ctr CR2. . .222 D1
MONKS ORCHARD 207 A3
Monks Orchard Rd BR3,
CR0. . . . . .207 C2
Monks Orchard Sch
CR0. . . . . .206 D4
Monks Park Gdns HA9 . . .66 D1
Monks Pk HA9. . . . . .67 A2
Monks Rd EN2 . . . . .5 A3
Monk St SE18. . . . . .122 C2
Monks Way
Beckenham BR3 . . . . . .207 C3
Crofton BR5 . . . . .211 B1
Harmondsworth UB7 . . . .126 A6
Temple Fortune NW11 . . .47 B5
Monkswell Ct N10. . . . . .31 A4
Monkswell Ho E2 . . . . . . .96 A4
Monkswood Gdns
Borehamwood WD6 . . . . .11 B6
Ilford IG5. . . . . .56 C6
Monk Terr SE23. . . . . . . .163 B2
Monkton Ho
32 Bermondsey SE16. . . .118 D4
22 Hackney E5 . . . . .74 B3
Monkton Rd DA16. . . . . .145 D3
Monkton St SE11 . 116 C2 261 B4
Monkville Ave NW11. . . . .47 B5
Monkwell Sq EC2. . . . . . 242 B3
Monmouth Ave
Teddington KT1. . . . . . . .175 C3
Wanstead E18 . . . . .55 B6
Monmouth Cl
Bedford Pk W4 . . . . . . .111 B3
Bexley DA16 . . . . .146 A1
Mitcham CR4, SW16. . . .204 A5
Wallington SM6 9 W7 . . . .86 D2
Monmouth Gr TW8. . . . . .110 A2
Monmouth Ho
5 Camden Town NW5. . . .71 B2
Wandsworth SW18 . . . . .157 C5
Monmouth PI W2. . . . . . .91 D1

Monmouth Rd
Dagenham RM9 . . . . .81 B3
Hayes UB3 . . . . 105 D2
Lower Edmonton N9. . . . . . .18 C2
Newham E6 . . . . .100 B4
Notting Hill W2 . . . . .91 C1
Monmouth St
WC2. . . . . .94 A1 <u>240 A1</u>
Monnery Rd N19. . . . . .71 C5
Monnow Rd SE1. . . . . .118 A2
Mono La TW13. . . . . .150 B2
Monoux Almshouses E17. .53 D5
Monoux Gr E17 . . . . .35 C2
Monroe Cres EN1 . . . . .6 B4
Monroe Dr SW14 . . . . .154 D6
Monroe Ho
16 Crouch End N19. . . . . . . .49 D2
Lisson Gr NW8 . . . .<u>230 B1</u>
Monro Gdns HA3 . . . . .24 C3
Monro Ho
18 Hampstead NW3. . . . . . .70 A4
Putney SW15 . . . . .156 B6
Monro Way E5. . . . . .74 A4
Monsal Ct E5 . . . . .75 A4
Monsell Ct 4 N4 . . . . .72 D5
Monsell Rd N4, N5 . . . . .72 D5
Monson Rd
Deptford SE14 . . . . .140 D5
Willesden Green NW10. . . . .90 B5
Mons Way BR2. . . . . .210 A3
Montacute Rd
Bushey WD23 . . . . .8 C4
Carshalton SM4 . . . . .202 B3
Forest Hill SE6. . . . . .163 B4
Montagu Cres N18. . . . . . . .34 B6
Montagu Ct W1. . . . .<u>237 D3</u>
Montague Ave
Brockley SE4. . . . . .141 C1
Ealing W7 . . . . .108 D5
Montague Cl 4 Barnet EN5 . .1 B1
Borough The SE1. . . . .<u>252 C4</u>
Walton-on-T KT12 . . . . . . .194 A2
Montague Fell HA0 . . . . . . .64 D4
Montague Gdns W3. . . . . . .110 D4
Montague Pl WC1. .93 D2 <u>239 D4</u>
Montague Rd Ealing W13. . . .87 B1
Hanwell W7 . . . . .108 A4
Hornsey Vale N8. . . . . .50 B4
Hounslow TW3 . . . . .129 D2
Leytonstone E11. . . . . .76 D6
Merton SW19 . . . . .179 D3
Richmond TW10 . . . . .154 A5
Shacklewell E8 . . . . .74 A3
Southall UB2. . . . . .107 A2
Thornton Heath CR0. . . . . .204 D1
Tottenham Hale N15. . . . . . .52 A5
Uxbridge UB8 . . . . .60 A1
Montague Sq SE15. . . . . . .140 C5
Montague St
Bloomsbury WC1 . . .94 A2 <u>240 A2</u>
City of London EC1 . . . .<u>242 A3</u>
Montague Terr 1 BR2. . . . . .209 A4
Montague Waye UB2. . . . . .107 A3
Montague Works HA0. . . . . .88 B5
Montagu Gdns
Edmonton N18. . . . . .34 B6
Wallington SM6 . . . . .219 C4
Montagu Ind Est N18. . . . . .34 C6
Montagu Mans
W1. . . . . .92 D2 <u>237 D3</u>
Montagu Mews N W1 . . . . .<u>237 D3</u>
Montagu Mews S W1 . . . . .<u>237 D2</u>
Montagu Mews W W1 . . . . .<u>237 D2</u>
Montagu Pl W1. . . . .92 D2 <u>237 D3</u>
Montagu Rd Hendon NW4 . . .46 A3
Lower Edmonton N9, N18. . .18 C1
Montagu Row W1. . . . .<u>237 D3</u>
Montagu Sq W1 . . . .92 D1 <u>237 D2</u>
Montagu St W1. . . . .92 D1 <u>237 D2</u>
Montaigne Cl SW1. . . . .<u>259 D3</u>
Montalt Ho IG8. . . . . .36 D6
Montalt Rd IG8. . . . . .36 D5
Montana Bldg 4 SE13 . . . .141 D4
Montana Rd
Upper Tooting SW17. . . . . .159 A1
Wimbledon SW20. . . . . . . .178 C2
Montbelle Prim Sch
SE9. . . . . .188 C6
Montbelle Rd SE9. . . . . . . .188 C6
Montcalm Cl Hayes BR2. . . .209 A3
Yeading UB4 . . . . .84 B4
Montcalm Ho E14. . . . . . . .119 C3
Montcalm Rd SE7. . . . . . . .143 D5
Montclair Ct 21 N12. . . . . . .29 B4
Montclare St E2 . . .95 D3 <u>243 C6</u>
Monteagle Ave IG11 . . . . . . .79 A2
Monteagle Ct
Barking IG11 . . . . .79 A1
27 Hoxton N1 . . . . .95 C5
Monteagle Prim Sch
RM9 . . . . .102 B6
Monteagle Way
Nunhead SE15 . . . . .140 B2
Shacklewell E5 . . . . .74 A5

Montefiore Ct 2 N16 . . . . . . .51 D1
Montefiore St 2 SW8. . . . .137 B3
Montego Cl 10 SW2 . . . . . . .138 C1
Montem Prim Sch 5 N7 . .72 B5
Montem Rd
Forest Hill SE23. . . . . .163 B4
New Malden KT3 . . . . .199 C5
Montem St N4. . . . . .50 B1
Montenotte Rd N8. . . . . .49 C4
Monteray Studios W10. . . . . .91 A5
Monterey NW7 . . . . .27 C5
Montesole Ct 7 HA5. . . . . . .22 C1
Montesquieu Terr 3 E16. .98 C1
Montford Pl
Kennington SE11 . . . . .138 C6
Kennington SE11 . . . .<u>261 A1</u>
Montford Rd TW16. . . . . . . .194 A5
Montfort Ho
4 Bethnal Green E2 . . . . . .96 C4
Cubitt Town E14 . . . . .120 A3
Montfort Pl SW19 . . . . .156 D3
Montgolfier Wlk UB5 . . . . . .85 A4
Montgomerie Ct 2 BR3. .185 C2
Montgomery Ave KT10 . . . .212 C6
Montgomery Cl
Blackfen DA15. . . . . .167 D5
Mitcham CR4 . . . . .204 A5
Montgomery Ct W4. . . . . . .133 A4
Montgomery Gdns SM2. .218 B1
Montgomery Ho 5
SW14. . . . . .133 B2
Montgomery Lo 38 E1. . . . . .96 C3
Montgomery Rd
Acton W4 . . . . .111 A2
Edgware HA8 . . . . .26 B4
Montgomery St E14. . . . . . .119 D5
Montholme Rd SW11. . . . . .158 D5
Monthope Rd 1 E1 . . . . . . .96 A2
Montolieu Gdns SW15 . . . . .156 B6
Montpelier Ave Ealing W5. . .87 C2
Sidcup DA5. . . . . .168 D4
Montpelier Cl UB10. . . . . . . .82 C6
Montpelier Ct
5 Beckenham BR2. . . . . . .208 D5
Ealing W5 . . . . .87 D2
Montpelier Gdns
Ilford RM6 . . . . .58 C2
Newham E6 . . . . .99 D4
Montpelier Gr NW5. . . . . . . .71 C3
Montpelier Mews SW7. . . . .<u>257 B6</u>
Montpelier Pl
Knightsbridge SW7 . . . .<u>257 B6</u>
21 Stepney E1. . . . . .96 C1
Montpelier Prim Sch W5. .87 D2
Montpelier Rd Ealing W5. . . .87 D2
Finchley N3. . . . . .30 A2
Peckham SE15 . . . . .140 B4
Sutton SM1. . . . . .218 A4
Montpelier Rise
Golders Green NW11. . . . . . .47 A2
Wembley HA9. . . . . .43 D1
Montpelier Row
Blackheath Vale SE3. . . . . .142 D5
Twickenham TW1 . . . . .153 C4
Montpelier Sq
SW7. . . . . .114 C4 <u>247 B1</u>
Montpelier St
SW7. . . . . .114 C3 <u>257 B6</u>
Montpelier Terr SW7 . . . . . .<u>247 B1</u>
Montpelier Vale SE3. . . . . . .142 D3
Montpelier Wlk
SW7. . . . . .114 C3 <u>257 B6</u>
Montpellier Ct KT12. . . . . . .194 B3
Montrave Rd SE20. . . . . . . .184 C3
Montreal Ho Catford SE6 . . .163 D3
Hayes UB4 . . . . .84 B4
Montreal Pl WC2. . . . .<u>250 C6</u>
Montreal Rd IG1. . . . . .57 A2
Montrell Rd SW2. . . . . .160 A3
Montrose Ave
Falconwood DA16. . . . . . . .145 C2
Hendon HA8. . . . . .27 B2
Kensal Rise NW6 . . . . .91 A5
Sidcup DA15. . . . . .168 A4
Twickenham TW2 . . . . .151 D4
Montrose Cl
Ashford TW15. . . . . .171 A5
Falconwood DA16. . . . . . . .145 D2
Woodford IG8. . . . . .37 A6
Montrose Cres
Finchley N12. . . . . .30 A4
1 Wembley HA0. . . . . .66 A2
Montrose Ct
2 Catford SE6. . . . . .164 D2
Hendon NW9 . . . . .27 A1
Knightsbridge
SW7 . . . . .114 B4 <u>246 D1</u>
Temple Fortune NW11. . . . . .47 B5
Montrose Gdns
Mitcham CR4 . . . . .180 D1
Sutton SM1. . . . . .217 D6
Montrose Ho
Belgravia SW1. . . . .<u>248 B1</u>
Millwall E14 . . . . .119 C3
Twickenham TW2 . . . . .151 D4
Montrose Pl
SW1. . . . . .115 A4 <u>248 B1</u>
Montrose Rd
East Bedfont TW14. . . . . . . .149 B5

Montrose Rd *continued*
Harrow HA3. . . . . .24 D1
Montrose Villas 5 W6. . . . .112 A1
Montrose Way SE23. . . . . . .162 D3
Montserrat Ave IG8. . . . . . . .36 B3
Montserrat Cl SE19. . . . . . .183 B5
Montserrat Rd SW15. . . . . .135 A1
Montway Hts SW19 . . . . . . .179 D3
Monument★ EC3 . . . .<u>252 D6</u>
Monument Gdns SE13. . . . .164 A6
Monument St
EC3 . . . . .117 B6 <u>252 D6</u>
Monument Sta
EC3 . . . . .117 B6 <u>252 D6</u>
Monument Way N17 . . . . . . .51 D6
Monza Bldg The E1 . . . . . . .118 C6
Monza St E1. . . . . .118 C6
Moodkee St SE16. . . . . .118 C3
Moody Rd SE15. . . . . .139 D4
Moody St E1. . . . . .96 D4
Moolinock Pl EN3. . . . . .7 D6
Moon Ct SE12. . . . . .143 A1
Moon Ho HA1 . . . . .42 D5
Moon La EN5 . . . . .1 B2
Moon St N1. . . . . .94 D6 <u>234 C6</u>
Moorcroft HA8. . . . . .26 D2
Moorcroft Rd SW16 . . . . . . .29 B1
Moorcroft Gdns BR1. . . . . .210 A4
Moorcroft La UB8. . . . . .82 C2
Moorcroft Rd SW16. . . . . . .160 A1
Moorcroft Sch UB8. . . . . . . .82 B1
Moorcroft Way HA5. . . . . . . .41 A4
Moordown SE18. . . . . .144 D4
Moore Cl Mitcham CR4 . . . .181 B1
Mortlake SW14 . . . . .133 A2
Wallington SM6 . . . . .220 A1
Moore Cres RM9. . . . . .102 B6
Moore Ct N1. . . . . .234 C5
Moorefield Rd N17. . . . . . . .33 D1
Moorehead Way SE3. . . . . .143 B2
Moore Ho
16 Bethnal Green E2 . . . . . .96 C4
5 Greenwich SE10 . . . . . . .120 D1
Hornsey N8. . . . . .50 A5
7 Shadwell E1. . . . . .118 C6
Wandsworth SW17 . . . . . . .158 B1
1 West Norwood SE27 . . . .183 A6
Mooreland Rd BR1. . . . . . . .187 A2
Moore Park Ct SW6. . . . . . .265 D4
Moore Park Rd
SW6. . . . . .135 D5 <u>265 C3</u>
Moore Rd SE19. . . . . .183 A4
Moore St SW3 . . . . .114 D2 <u>257 C4</u>
Moore Wlk E7. . . . . .77 A4
Moorey Cl 2 E15. . . . . .98 D6
Moorfield Ave W5. . . . . .87 D3
Moorfield Rd
Chessington KT9. . . . . .214 A3
Enfield EN3. . . . . .6 C4
Moorfields EC2. . . . . .95 B2 <u>242 C3</u>
Moorfields Ct 4 N1 . . . . .29 B1
Moorfields 6 SW16. . . . . . .181 C6
Moorfields Eye Hospl
EC1. . . . . .95 B4 <u>235 C1</u>
Moorfields Highwalk
EC2. . . . .<u>242 C3</u>
Moorgate EC2. . . . . .95 B2 <u>242 C3</u>
Moorgate Pl EC2. . . . .<u>242 C2</u>
Moorgate Sta EC2. . .95 B2 <u>242 C3</u>
Moorgreen Ho EC1. . . . .<u>234 C2</u>
Moorhouse Moorgate EC2. .<u>242 C3</u>
17 NW9 . . . . .27 D2
Moorhouse Rd
Harrow HA3. . . . . .43 D6
Notting Hill W2 . . . . .91 C1
Moorings Ho 3 TW8. . . . . .131 C5
Moorings The 5 E16. . . . . . .99 C2
Moor La
Broadgate EC2. . . . . .95 B2 <u>242 C3</u>
Chessington KT9. . . . . .214 A3
Moorland Cl TW4. . . . . .151 C4
Moorland Ct N21. . . . . .16 B5
Moorland Rd SW9. . . . . . . .138 D1
Moorlands
Chislehurst BR7. . . . . .188 D3
Northolt UB5 . . . . .85 A6
17 Wallington SM6. . . . . . .219 B2
Moorlands Ave NW7 . . . . . . .28 A4
Moormead Dr KT19 . . . . . . .215 C3
Moor Mead Rd TW1. . . . . . .153 A5
Moor Park Gdns KT2. . . . . . .177 C3
Moor Park Ho N21. . . . . . . .16 D4
Moor Pl EC2. . . . . .242 C3
Moorside Ct W13. . . . . .109 C5
Moorside Rd BR1. . . . . .186 D6
Moor St W1. . . . .<u>239 D1</u>
Moortown Rd WD19. . . . . . .22 C4
Moot Ct NW9 . . . . .44 C4
Morant Ho SW9. . . . . .138 B3
Morant Pl N22. . . . . .32 B2
Morant St E14. . . . . .119 C6
Mora Prim Sch NW2. . . . . . .68 C4
Mora Rd NW2. . . . . .68 C4
Mora St EC1. . . . . . .95 A4 <u>235 B1</u>
Morat St SW9. . . . . .138 B4 <u>270 D2</u>
Moravian Cl SW3. . . . .<u>266 D5</u>
Moravian Pl
SW10. . . . . .136 B6 <u>266 D5</u>
Moravian St 10 E2. . . . . . . .96 C4
Moray Ave UB3. . . . . .105 D5
Moray Cl HA8. . . . . .10 D2

Moray Ho
11 Kingston u T KT6 . . . . . .198 A4
9 Mile End E1. . . . . .97 A3
Moray Mews N4, N7. . . . . . .72 B6
Moray Rd N4, N7 . . . . .72 B6
Mordaunt Gdns RM9 . . . . . .81 A1
Mordaunt Ho
4 Becontree NW10. . . . . . .89 B6
34 Clapham SW8 . . . . .137 D3
Mordaunt Rd NW10 . . . . . . .89 B6
Mordaunt St SW9. . . . . .138 B2
MORDEN 201 D3
Morden Court Par SM4. . . .201 D5
Morden Ct SM4 . . . . .201 D5
Morden Gdns
Greenford UB6. . . . . .64 D3
Mitcham CR4 . . . . .202 B5
Morden Hall SW19 . . . . . . .201 D6
Morden Hall Rd SM4. . . . . .202 A5
Morden Hill SE13 . . . . .142 A3
Morden La SE13 . . . . .142 A4
Morden Lo BR2. . . . . .186 B1
Morden Mount Prim Sch 1
SE13. . . . . .141 D3
MORDEN PARK 201 A3
Morden Park Pools SM4 .201 B4
Morden Prim Sch SM4. .201 C4
Morden Rd
Dagenham RM6. . . . . .59 A2
Kidbrooke SE3 . . . . .143 A3
Merton SW19 . . . . .179 D1
Mitcham CR4, SM4. . . . . . .202 B5
Morden Road Mews
SE3 . . . . .143 A3
Morden Road Sta SW19 . . .179 D1
Morden South Sta SM4. . . .201 C4
Morden St SE13. . . . . .141 D4
Morden Sta SW19. . . . . . . .201 D6
Morden Way SM3. . . . . .201 C2
Morden Wharf Rd SE10 . . . .120 C3
Mordern Ho NW1 . . . .<u>237 B5</u>
Mordon Rd IG3. . . . . .57 D2
Mordred Rd SE6. . . . . .164 C2
Morecambe Cl 3 E1. . . . . . .96 D2
Morecambe Gdns HA7 . . . . .25 D6
Morecambe St
SE17. . . . . .117 A1 <u>262 B2</u>
Morecambe Terr N18. . . . . . .33 B4
More Cl Canning Town E16. .98 D1
West Kensington
W14 . . . . .113 A2 <u>254 A3</u>
Morecoombe Cl KT2. . . . . . .176 D3
Morecroft TW2 . . . . .152 A2
Moredown Ho 3 E8. . . . . . . .74 A3
Moree Way N18. . . . . .34 A6
More House Sch
SW1. . . . . .114 D3 <u>257 D5</u>
Moreland Ct 3 NW2. . . . . . .69 C5
Moreland Prim Sch
EC1. . . . . .94 D4 <u>234 D1</u>
Moreland St EC1. . . .94 D4 <u>234 D2</u>
Moreland Way E4. . . . . .20 A1
Morella Rd SW11, SW12. . . .158 D4
Morell Ho 5 SW9. . . . . .138 B3
Morello Ave UB8. . . . . .82 D2
Morello Ct HA9 . . . . .66 B5
More London Pl SE1. . . . . .253 A3
Moremead Rd SE6 . . . . . . .185 C6
Morena St SE6. . . . . .163 D4
Moresby Ave KT5 . . . . .198 D2
Moresby Rd E5 . . . . .52 B1
Moresby Wlk 6 SW8. . . . . .137 B3
More's Gdn SW3 . . . .<u>266 D5</u>
Moreton Ave SW7. . . . . . . .130 C4
Moreton Cl Mill Hill NW7 . . . .28 C4
Stoke Newington N15. . . . . .51 B3
Upper Clapton E5 . . . . .52 C1
Moreton Ho SE16. . . . . .118 D3
Moreton Pl SW1 . .115 C1 <u>259 B2</u>
Moreton Rd Croydon CR2. . .221 B3
North Cheam KT4. . . . . . . .216 B6
Tottenham N15. . . . . .51 B3
Moreton St SW1 . .115 D1 <u>259 C2</u>
Moreton Terr
SW1. . . . . .115 C1 <u>259 B2</u>
Moreton Terr Mews N
SW1. . . . .<u>259 B2</u>
Moreton Terr Mews S
SW1. . . . .<u>259 B2</u>
Moreton Twr 3 W3 . . . . . . .110 D5
Morford Cl HA4. . . . . .40 B2
Morford Way HA4. . . . . .40 B2
Morgan Ave E17. . . . . .54 B5
Morgan Cl RM10. . . . . .81 C1
Morgan Ct Ashford TW15. . .170 D5
5 Battersea SW11. . . . . . .136 B3
Carshalton SM5 . . . . .218 D4
Morgan Ho
Nine Elms SW8 . . . .<u>269 B2</u>
Pimlico SW1 . . . .<u>259 B3</u>
Morgan Rd Islington N7 . . . . .72 C3
Notting Hill W10 . . . . .91 B2
Plaistow E13 . . . . .187 A3
Morgans La SE1 . . . . .253 A2
Morgan's La UB3. . . . . .83 D2

Morgan St
Canning Town E16. . . . . . . .98 D2
Globe Town E3 . . . . .96 D4
Morgan's Wlk SW11. . . . . . .267 A3
Morgan Terr RM6 . . . . .58 C4
Moriah Jewish Day Sch
HA5. . . . . .41 A1
Moriarty Cl BR1. . . . . .210 D5
Moriarty Cl N7. . . . . .72 A4
Morie St SW18. . . . . .157 D6
Morieux Rd E10. . . . . .53 B1
Moring Rd SW17. . . . . .181 A6
Morkyns Wlk SE21. . . . . . . .161 C1
Morland Ave CR0 . . . . .205 C1
Morland Cl
Golders Green NW11. . . . . . .47 D1
Hampton TW12. . . . . .173 B5
Mitcham CR4 . . . . .202 C6
Morland Ct W12 . . . . .112 B4
Morland Est E8 . . . . .74 A1
Morland Gdns
Southall UB1. . . . . .107 D5
Stonebridge NW10. . . . . . . .67 B1
Morland Ho Kilburn NW6 . . . .91 C6
Notting Hill W11 . . . . .91 A1
Somers Town NW1 . . . .<u>232 B3</u>
Westminster SW1 . . . .<u>260 A4</u>
Morland Mews N1 . . . . .72 C1
Morland Rd Croydon CR0 . . .205 C1
Dagenham RM10 . . . . .81 C1
Harrow HA3. . . . . .44 A5
Ilford IG1 . . . . .78 D6
Penge SE20 . . . . .184 D4
Sutton SM1. . . . . .218 A3
Walthamstow E17 . . . . .52 D4
Morley Ave Chingford E4. . . .36 B3
Edmonton N18. . . . . .34 A6
Tottenham N22. . . . . .32 D1
Morley Cl BR6 . . . . .226 D6
Morley Coll SE1 . .116 C3 <u>261 B6</u>
Morley Cres Edgware HA8 . .11 A2
Ruislip HA4. . . . . .62 C6
Morley Cres E HA7 . . . . .43 D6
Morley Cres W HA7 . . . . . . .43 C6
Morley Ct Bromley BR3. . . . .186 B2
Chingford Hatch E4 . . . . . . .35 B5
Lewisham SE13 . . . . .142 A1
Shortlands BR2. . . . . .208 D5
Morley Hill EN2. . . . . .5 B5
Morley Ho
Stoke Newington N16. . . . . .74 A6
Streatham SW2 . . . . .160 A4
W1 . . . .<u>238 D2</u>
Morley Rd Barking IG11 . . . .101 B6
Cheam SM3 . . . . .201 B1
Chislehurst BR7 . . . . .189 A2
Dagenham RM6. . . . . .59 A4
Lewisham SE13 . . . . .142 A1
Leytonstone E10. . . . . .54 A1
Newham E15 . . . . .98 D5
Twickenham TW1 . . . . .153 D5
Morley St SE1 . . .116 C4 <u>261 B1</u>
Morna Rd SE5 . . . . .139 A3
Morning La E9. . . . . .74 C2
Morningside Prim Sch 17
E9. . . . . .74 C2
Morningside Rd KT4 . . . . . .216 C6
Mornington Ave
Bromley BR1. . . . . .209 D6
Ilford IG1 . . . . .56 C2
West Kensington
W14 . . . . .113 B2 <u>254 C3</u>
Mornington Avenue Mans
W14. . . . .<u>254 C3</u>
Mornington Cl IG8. . . . . .37 A6
Mornington Cres
Camden Town
NW1. . . . . .93 C5 <u>232 A4</u>
Cranford TW5. . . . . .128 A2
NW1. . . . .<u>232 A4</u>
Mornington Crescent Sta
NW1. . . . . .93 C5 <u>232 A4</u>
Mornington Ct NW1. . . . . . .<u>232 A4</u>
Mornington Gr E3 . . . . .97 A4
Mornington Lo EN1 . . . . . . .17 C6
Mornington Mews 2
SE5. . . . . .139 A4
Mornington Pl
4 New Cross SE8. . . . . . . .141 B5
Regent's Pk NW1 . . . .<u>232 A4</u>
Mornington Rd
Ashford TW15. . . . . .171 A5
Chingford E4. . . . . .20 B4
Greenford UB6. . . . . .85 D3
Leytonstone E11. . . . . .54 C1
New Cross SE14, SE8. . . . .141 B5
Woodford IG8. . . . . .36 C4
Mornington St
NW1. . . . . .93 B5 <u>231 D4</u>
Mornington Terr
NW1. . . . . .93 B5 <u>231 D4</u>
Mornington Wlk TW10 . . . .175 C6
Morocco St SE1 . .117 C4 <u>253 A3</u>
Morpeth Gr E9 . . . . .96 C6
Morpeth Rd E9 . . . . .96 C6
Morpeth Sch E2. . . . . .96 C4
Morpeth St E2. . . . . .96 D4
Morpeth Terr
SW1. . . . . .115 C2 <u>259 A4</u>
Morpeth Wlk N17. . . . . .34 B3

Morphou Rd NW7. . . . . .29 A5
Morrab Gdns IG3 . . . . . .79 D5
Morrel Cl EN5 . . . . 2 A2
Morrel Ct **11** E2. . . . . .96 A5
Morris Ave E12 . . . . .78 B3
Morris Blitz Ct **2** N16. . .73 D4
Morris Cl Croydon CR0 . . .207 A4
Orpington BR6 . . . . .227 C5
Morris Ct Chingford E4 . . . .19 D1
Croydon CR0. . . . . .220 D4
3 Herne Hill SE5. . . . . . .139 B1
Morris Gdns SW18 . . . . . .157 C4
Morris Ho
17 Bethnal Green E2 . . . . .96 C4
Lisson Gr NW8 . . . . .237 A5
1 Stockwell SW4 . . . . . . .138 A1
10 Tufnell Pk N19 . . . . . . .71 C4
Morrish Rd SW2. . . . . . . .160 A4
Morrison Ave
Chingford E4. . . . . .35 C4
Tottenham N17. . . . . .51 C6
Morrison Bldgs **5** E1 . .96 A1
Morrison Ct **7** Barnet EN5 . . .30 C3
Finchley N12. . . . . .30 C3
Morrison Ho SW2. . . . . . .160 C3
Morrison Rd
Barking IG11 . . . . .103 A5
24 Brixton SW9 . . . . . . .138 C3
Hayes UB4 . . . . .84 B4
Morrison St SW11 . . . . . .137 A2
Morrison Yd N17. . . . . . . .33 D1
Morris Pl N4 . . . . .72 C1
Morris Rd Bow Comm E14. .97 D2
Dagenham RM8 . . . . .81 B6
Isleworth TW7 . . . . .130 D2
Leyton E15 . . . . .76 C4
Morriss Ho
6 Bermondsey SE16. . . .118 B4
5 Upper Clapton E5 . . . .74 B6
Morris St E1. . . . . .96 B1
Morris Stephany Ho **4**
SE27 . . . . .182 D6
Morriston Cl WD19. . . . . . .22 C5
Morritt Ho **2** HA0. . . . . . .65 D3
Morse Cl E13 . . . . .99 A4
Morshead Mans W9 . . . . . .91 C4
Morshead Rd W9 . . . . .91 C4
Morson Rd EN3 . . . . .19 A5
Morston Gdns SE9 . . . . . .188 B6
Mortain Ho **9** SE16 . . . .118 B2
Morten Cl SW4 . . . . .159 D5
Morteyne Rd N17. . . . . . . .33 B2
Mortgramit Sq SE18 . . . .122 C3
Mortham St E15 . . . . .98 C6
Mortimer Cl
1 Child's Hill NW2 . . . . .69 B5
Streatham SW16 . . . . . . .159 D2
Mortimer Cres
Paddington NW6 . . . . .91 D6
Worcester Pk KT4. . . . . . .215 B4
Mortimer Ct
St John's Wood NW8 . . . .229 B3
4 Whetstone N20 . . . . . . .14 A2
Mortimer Dr EN1 . . . . .17 C6
Mortimer Est NW6 . . . . . . .91 D6
Mortimer Ho
6 Shepherd's Bush W11. .112 D5
West Kensington W14 . . . .254 B3
Mortimer Lo **11** SW19 . .157 A3
Mortimer Market WC1 . . . .239 B5
Mortimer Pl NW6 . . . . .91 D6
Mortimer Rd
De Beauvoir Town N1 . . . .73 C1
Ealing W13 . . . . .87 C1
Kensal Green NW10. . . . . .90 C4
Mitcham CR4 . . . . .180 D2
Newham E6 . . . . .100 B4
Mortimer Sq W11. . . . . . . .112 D6
Mortimer St W1 . . . .93 C2 239 B3
Mortimer Terr NW5 . . . . . .71 B4
MORTLAKE 133 A2
Mortlake Cl CR0 . . . . .220 A5
Mortlake Dr CR4 . . . . .180 C2
Mortlake High St SW14. . .133 B2
Mortlake Ho **7** SW4 . . . .111 A2
Mortlake Rd Ilford IG1. . . . .79 B4
Newham E16 . . . . .99 B1
Mortlake Sta SW14 . . . . . .133 A2
Mortlake Terr TW9 . . . . . .132 C5
Mortlock Cl SE15 . . . . . . .140 B4
Mortlock Ct E12 . . . . .77 D4
Morton Cl Hillingdon UB8 . . .82 B3
29 Stepney E1 . . . . .96 C1
Wallington SM6 . . . . .220 B1
Morton Cres N14 . . . . .31 D6
Morton Ct UB5. . . . . .64 A3
Morton Gdns SM6 . . . . . .219 C3
Morton Ho
Kennington SE17 . . . . . . .138 D6
West Norwood SE27. . . . .183 B6
Morton Mews SW5 . . . . . .255 C3
Morton Pl SE1. . . . . .261 A5
Morton Rd Islington N1 . . . .73 A1
Morden SM4. . . . . .202 B4
Stratford E15 . . . . .76 D1
Morton Way N14. . . . . .31 D6
Morvale Cl DA17. . . . . . . .125 B2
Morval Rd SW2. . . . . .160 C6
Morven Rd SW17 . . . . . . .158 D1

Morville Ho SW18. . . . . . .158 A5
Morville St E3. . . . . .97 C5
Morwell St WC1 . . . . .239 D3
Moscow Pl W2 . . . . .245 C6
Moscow Rd W2. . . 113 D6 245 C6
Mosedale NW1. . . . . .231 D1
Moseley Row SE10 . . . . . .120 D2
Moselle Ave N22. . . . . .32 C1
Moselle Cl N8 . . . . .50 B6
Moselle Ho **2** N17. . . . . . .33 D3
Moselle Pl N17 . . . . .33 D3
Moselle Sch (Upper) N17 .51 A6
Moselle Specl Sch N17. . . .33 C1
Moselle St N17 . . . . .33 D3
Mosque Tower **26** E1 . . . .96 A2
Mosquito Cl **5** SM6. . . . .220 A1
Mossborough Cl N12. . . . . .29 D4
Mossbourne Com Acad
E8. . . . . .74 A3
Mossbury Rd SW11 . . . . . .136 C2
Moss Cl Pinner HA5. . . . . . .23 A1
Spitalfields E1. . . . . .96 A2
Mossdown Cl DA17. . . . . .125 C2
Mossford Cl IG6. . . . . .56 D6
Mossford Gn IG6 . . . . .57 A6
Mossford St E3 . . . . .97 B3
Moss Gdns
Feltham TW13 . . . . .150 A2
South Croydon CR2. . . . .222 D1
Moss Hall Cres N12 . . . . . .30 A4
Moss Hall Ct N12 . . . . .29 D4
Moss Hall Gr N12 . . . . .29 D4
Moss Hall Inf Sch **1** N12 . .29 D4
Moss Hall Jun Sch N3. . . . .29 D4
Mossington Gdns SE16. . .118 C2
Moss La HA5 . . . . .23 A1
Mosslea Rd
Bromley Comm BR2. . . . .209 D4
Orpington BR6 . . . . .227 A5
Penge SE20 . . . . .184 C4
Mossop St SW3. . . . 114 C2 257 B4
Moss Rd RM10. . . . . .81 C1
Mossville Gdns SM4 . . . . .201 B5
Mosswell Ho **4** N10 . . . . .31 A3
Moston Cl UB3. . . . . .105 D1
Mostyn Ave HA9 . . . . .66 B3
Mostyn Gdns NW10. . . . . .90 D5
Mostyn Gr E3. . . . . .97 C5
Mostyn Lo N5 . . . . .73 A4
Mostyn Rd Brixton SW9 . . .138 C4
Bushey WD23. . . . . .8 A6
Grahame Pk HA8 . . . . . . .27 C3
Merton SW19 . . . . .179 B1
Mosul Way BR2. . . . . .210 A3
Motcomb St
SW1. . . . . .115 A3 258 A6
Moth Cl HA8. . . . . .220 A1
Mothers Sq The **13** E5 . . .74 B4
Motley Ave EC2 . . . . .243 A6
Motley St SW8. . . . . .137 C3
MOTSPUR PARK 200 A3
Motspur Park Sta KT3. . . .200 B4
Motspur Pk KT3 . . . . .200 A3
MOTTINGHAM 165 D2
Mottingham Ct SE9 . . . . . .166 B3
Mottingham Gdns SE9 . . .165 D3
Mottingham La SE9 . . . . . .165 C3
Mottingham Nature
Reserve★ SE12. . . . . . . .165 C3
Mottingham Prim Sch
SE9 . . . . .166 B1
Mottingham Rd
Chislehurst SE9 . . . . .166 B1
Ponders End N9 . . . . .18 D4
Mottingham Sta SE9 . . . . .166 B3
Mottisfont Rd SE2 . . . . . . .124 B2
Moules Ct SE5 . . . . .139 A5
Moulins Rd E9. . . . . .74 C1
Moulsford Ho
5 Lower Holloway N7. . . .72 A3
32 Paddington W2 . . . . . .91 C2
Moulton Ave TW5. . . . . . .129 B3
Moundfield Rd N16. . . . . . .52 A3
Mound The SE9. . . . . .166 C1
Mounsey Ho **13** W10 . . . . .91 A4
Mountacre Cl SE26. . . . . .183 D6
Mount Adon Pk SE21,
SE22 . . . . .162 A4
Mountague Pl **2** E14 . . . .120 A6
Mountain Ho SE11 . . . . . .260 C2
Mountaire Ct NW9 . . . . . . .45 B4
Mount Angelus Rd
SW15. . . . . .155 C4
Mount Ararat Rd TW10 . . .154 A6
Mount Arlington **3** BR2. .186 C1
Mount Ash Rd SE26 . . . . .162 B1
Mount Ave Chingford E4. . . .19 D1
Ealing W5 . . . . .87 D2
Southall UB1. . . . . .85 C1
Mountbatten Cl
Plumstead Comm SE18 . .145 C6
6 West Norwood SE19. .183 C5
Mountbatten Ct **8** IG9. . .21 D2
Mountbatten Gdns BR3 . .207 A5
Mountbatten Ho N6. . . . . . .49 A2
Mountbatten Mews
SW18. . . . . .158 A3
Mountbel Rd HA7 . . . . .25 A1
Mount Carmel **3** N7. . . . .72 B3

Mount Carmel RC Tech Coll
for Girls **6** N19. . . . . . . .49 D1
Mount Cl Bromley BR1 . . . .188 A2
Cockfosters EN4. . . . . .3 A1
Ealing W5. . . . . .85 A5
Mountcombe Cl KT6 . . . . .198 A2
Mountcombe Ho SW17. . . .180 B5
Mount Ct
6 Kingston u T KT2 . . . .176 D3
West Wickham BR4 . . . . .224 C6
Mount Culver Ave DA14 . .190 D4
Mount Dr Bexley DA6 . . . . .169 A6
Harrow HA2, HA5. . . . . . . .41 B4
Welsh Harp HA9. . . . . . . .67 A6
Mountearl Gdns SW16,
SW2. . . . . .160 B1
Mount Eaton Ct W5 . . . . . .87 C2
Mount Echo Ave E4 . . . . . .19 D3
Mount Echo Dr E4 . . . . . . .19 D3
Mount Ephraim La
SW16. . . . . .159 D1
Mount Ephraim Rd
SW16. . . . . .159 D1
Mount Felix KT12 . . . . . . .193 D1
Mountfield NW2. . . . . .69 B6
Mountfield Cl SE6 . . . . . . .164 B4
Mountfield Ct SE13 . . . . . .164 B5
Mountfield Rd Ealing W5. . .88 A1
East Finchley N3. . . . . . . .47 C6
Wallend E6 . . . . .100 C4
Mountfield Way W5. . . . . . .88 A1
Mount Ford St E1. . . . . . . .96 A1
Mountfort Cres N1. . . . . . . .72 C1
Mountfort Terr **1** N1. . . . . .72 C1
Mount Gdns SE26 . . . . . . .162 B1
Mount Gr HA8 . . . . .27 B6
Mountgrove Rd N5 . . . . . . .73 A5
Mount Holme KT7 . . . . . . .197 B2
Mounthurst Rd BR2. . . . . .208 D2
Mountnessing
Mountington Park Cl
HA3. . . . . .43 D3
Mountjoy Cl SE2 . . . . .124 B4
Mountjoy Ho EC2. . . . . . . .242 A3
Mount Lo N6 . . . . .49 C3
Mount Lodge SW4 . . . . . .137 D1
Mount Mews TW12 . . . . . .173 D2
Mount Mills EC1 . . . . .234 D1
Mount Nod Rd SW16,
SW2. . . . . .160 B1
Mount Olive Ct W7 . . . . . .108 C4
Mount Par EN4 . . . . 2 C1
Mount Park Ave HA1. . . . . .64 C6
Mount Park Cres W5. . . . . .87 D1
Mount Park Rd Ealing W5. .87 D1
Harrow HA1. . . . . .64 B5
Pinner HA5. . . . . .40 A4
Mount Pl **7** W3. . . . . . . .110 D5
Mount Pleasant
Cockfosters EN4. . . . . 2 D1
Finsbury WC1. . . . . . 94 C3 241 A5
Ilford IG1 . . . . .79 A3
Ruislip HA4. . . . . .62 D6
Wembley HA0. . . . . .88 B6
West Norwood SE27. . . . .183 A6
Mount Pleasant Cotts
Osidge N14. . . . . .15 D4
Southall UB1. . . . . .85 C1
Mount Pleasant Cres N4 . .50 B2
Mount Pleasant Hill E5. . . .74 C4
Mount Pleasant La E5. . . . .52 B1
Mount Pleasant Pl SE18. .123 B2
Mount Pleasant Rd
Ealing W5 . . . . .87 C3
Higham Hill E17 . . . . .35 A1
Kingston u T KT3 . . . . . . .199 A6
Lewisham SE13 . . . . .164 A5
Tottenham N17. . . . . .33 C1
Willesden NW10. . . . . .90 C6
Mount Pleasant Villas N4. .50 B2
Mount Prim Sch The
KT3. . . . . .199 A6
Mount Rd Bexley DA6 . . . . .169 A6
Chessington KT9 . . . . . . .214 B3
Dagenham RM8 . . . . .59 B1
Dollis Hill NW2 . . . . .68 C5
East Barnet EN4. . . . . .14 C6
Feltham TW13 . . . . .151 A1
Hayes UB3 . . . . .106 A4
Hendon NW4 . . . . .46 C6
Kingston u T KT3. . . . . . .199 B6
Mitcham CR4 . . . . .180 C1
South Norwood SE19 . . . .183 B4
Wimbledon SW18, SW19 . .157 D2
Mount Row W1. . . 115 B6 248 C5
Mount Sch The NW7 . . . . . .28 C5
Mountside HA7 . . . . .25 A2
Mounts Pond Rd SE3,
SE13 . . . . .142 B3
Mount Sq The **3** NW3. . . .70 A5
Mount St W1 . . . . .115 A6 248 B5
Mount Stewart Ave HA3. . .43 D2
Mount Stewart Jun & Inf
Schs HA3 . . . . .43 D2
Mount Terr E1 . . . . .96 B2
MountThe Bexley DA6 . . . .169 D6
Mulberry Cres
Brentford TW8 . . . . .131 C5
West Drayton UB7 . . . . . .104 C4
Mulberry Ct Barking IG11 . .79 D1
Bexley DA16. . . . . .145 D3
Finchley N2. . . . . .48 C6
Finsbury EC1. . . . . .234 D1

MountThe continued
Hampstead NW3 . . . . .70 A5
Harrow HA1. . . . . .64 C6
Kensington W8 . . . . .245 A3
Kingston u T KT3. . . . . . .199 D6
North Cheam KT4 . . . . . .216 B4
Northolt UB5 . . . . .63 D3
6 South Croydon CR2. . .221 A3
Upper Clapton E5 . . . . . . .74 B6
Welsh Harp HA9. . . . . . . .67 A6
Whetstone N20 . . . . .14 A2
Mount Tyndal NW3. . . . . . .48 B1
Mount Vernon NW3 . . . . . .70 A4
Mountview Edgware NW7 . .11 B1
Northwood HA6 . . . . .22 A4
5 Streatham SW16. . . . .160 B1
Mount View Ealing W5 . . . .87 D3
Enfield EN2. . . . . .4 B5
Southall UB2. . . . . .106 D2
Mountview W11 . . . . .48 A1
Mountview Cotts EN5 . . . .11 D5
Mountview Ct
Harringay N8 . . . . .50 D5
3 Whetstone N20. . . . . . .14 A2
Mount View Rd
Chingford E4. . . . . .20 B1
Claygate KT10 . . . . .213 B1
Hornsey Vale N4. . . . . . . .50 B3
Kingsbury NW9 . . . . .45 B4
Mount Villas SE27 . . . . . .160 D1
Mountwood KT8 . . . . .195 D6
Mountwood Ho W3 . . . . . . .87 D3
Mourne Ho NW3 . . . . .70 A2
Movers La IG11. . . . . .101 C6
Movers Lane (Flyover)
IG11 . . . . .101 C5
Moviem The★ SE11 . . . . .250 C2
Mowat St KT4 . . . . .215 D6
Mowatt Cl N19. . . . . .49 D1
Mowbray Ct
South Norwood SE19 . . . .183 D2
Wood Green N22 . . . . .32 C2
Mowbray Gdns UB5 . . . . . .85 C6
Mowbray Ho **5** N2 . . . . . .30 B1
Mowbray Rd
Brondesbury NW6 . . . . . . .69 A1
Edgware HA8 . . . . .26 C6
New Barnet EN5 . . . . .14 A6
Richmond TW10 . . . . .153 C1
South Norwood SE19 . . . .183 D2
Mowlem Prim Sch **36** E2 . .96 C5
Mowlem St E2. . . . . .96 B5
Mowlem Trad Est N17. . . . .34 C3
Mowll St SW9 . . . . .138 C5
Moxon Cl E13. . . . . .98 D5
Moxon St Barnet EN5 . . . . . 1 B2
Marylebone W1 . . . .93 A2 238 A3
Moye Cl **10** E2 . . . . .96 A5
Moyers Rd E10 . . . . .54 A2
Moylan Rd W6. . . .135 A6 264 B5
Moyle Ho **1** SW8 . . . . . . .138 D1
Moyne Ho **16** SW9 . . . . . .138 D1
Moyne Pl NW10. . . . . .88 C5
Moynihan Dr N21. . . . . . . .16 A6
Moys Cl CR0. . . . . .204 A3
Moyser Rd SW16. . . . . . . .181 B5
Mozart St W10 . . . . .91 B4
Mt Carmel RC Prim Sch **1**
W5 . . . . .109 C3
Muchelney Rd SM4. . . . . .202 A3
Muchelney Ho **1**
E14. . . . . .120 A2
Muchute Pk & Farm★
E14. . . . . .120 A2
Mudchute Sta E14. . . . . . .119 D2
Mudie Ho **6** SW2. . . . . . .160 A4
Mudlarks Blvd **3** SE10. . .120 D3
Muggeridge Cl CR2. . . . . .221 A2
Muggeridge Rd RM10. . . . .81 D4
Muirdown Ave SW14 . . . . .133 B1
Muir Dr SW18 . . . . .158 C5
Muirfield W3 . . . . .89 C1
Muirfield Cl
23 Bermondsey SE16. . .118 B1
South Oxhey WD19. . . . . .22 C6
Muirfield Cres E14 . . . . . . .119 D3
Muirfield Gn WD19. . . . . . .22 C6
Muirfield Rd WD19. . . . . . .22 C6
Muirhead Quay SE16 . . . .101 A5
Muirkirk Rd SE6 . . . . .164 A3
Muir Rd E5 . . . . .74 A5
Muir St E16. . . . . .122 A5
Mulbarton Ct BR7. . . . . . .189 B4
Mulberry Ave TW19 . . . . . .148 A3
Mulberry Bsns Ctr SE16. .118 C4
Mulberry Cl Barnet EN4 . . . 2 B1
Charlton SE7. . . . . .143 D6
Chelsea SW3 . . . . .266 D5
Chingford E4. . . . . .19 C2
East Dulwich SE22 . . . . . .162 A5
Hampstead NW3 . . . . .70 B4
Hendon NW4 . . . . .46 C6
Hornsey N8. . . . . .50 A4
Northolt UB5 . . . . .85 A5
Streatham SW16 . . . . . . .181 C6

Mulberry Ct continued
Islington N5 . . . . .72 D3
1 Leyton E11. . . . . .76 B4
10 Paddington W9 . . . . . .91 B4
4 Surbiton KT6. . . . . . . .197 D2
Twickenham TW1 . . . . . . .152 D1
Willesden NW10. . . . . .67 B2
Mulberry Ho
8 Bethnal Green E2 . . . . .96 C4
8 Deptford SE8. . . . . . . .141 B6
Mulberry House Sch
NW2. . . . . .69 A3
Mulberry La CR0. . . . . . . .205 D1
Mulberry Mews
New Cross SE14 . . . . . . .141 B4
2 Wallington SM6 . . . . .219 C2
Mulberry Par UB7. . . . . . .104 C4
Mulberry Pl Chiswick W6 . .112 A1
Greenwich SE9 . . . . .143 D1
Mulberry Prim Sch N17 . . .34 A1
Mulberry Rd E8. . . . . .73 D1
Mulberry Sch for Girls
39 Stepney E1. . . . . .96 B1
16 St George in E East E1 . .118 B6
Mulberry Trees **7** E1. . . . .96 A1
Mulberry Trees TW17. . . . .193 B2
Mulberry Way Ilford IG6. . . .57 A5
Woodford E18. . . . . .37 B1
Mulberry Wlk
SW3. . . . . .136 B6 266 D6
Mulgrave Chambers
SM2. . . . . .217 D2
Mulgrave Hall SM2. . . . . .217 D2
Mulgrave Ho **19** SE18. . .122 B2
Mulgrave Manor SM2 . . . .217 D2
Mulgrave Prim Sch
SE18. . . . . .122 C2
Mulgrave Rd
Belmont SM2. . . . . .217 C2
Ealing W5 . . . . .87 D3
Harrow HA1. . . . . .65 A6
South Croydon CR0. . . . .221 B5
West Kensington W14 . . . .264 C6
Willesden NW10. . . . . .67 D4
Woolwich SE18. . . . . .122 C2
Mulholland Cl CR4. . . . . . .181 B1
Mulkern Rd N19 . . . . .49 D1
Mullard Ho WC1 . . . . .239 C4
Mullards Cl CR4 . . . . .202 D1
Mullens Ho **7** SW15. . . . .156 C6
Mullen Twr EC1 . . . . .241 A5
Muller Ho SE18 . . . . .122 C1
Muller Rd SW4 . . . . .159 D5
Mullet Gdns **7** E2 . . . . . . .96 A4
Mulletsfield WC1 . . . . .233 B1
Mull Ho **17** E3 . . . . .97 B5
Mullins Path SW14. . . . . . .133 B2
Mullion Cl HA3 . . . . .23 D2
Mullion Wlk WD19 . . . . . . .22 C6
Mulready St NW8 . . . . . . .237 A5
Multi Way W3 . . . . .111 C4
Multon Ho E9 . . . . .74 C1
Multon Rd SW18. . . . . . . .158 B4
Mulvaney Way SE1. . . . . .252 D1
Mumford Rd SE24. . . . . . .160 D4
Muncaster Cl TW15 . . . . . .170 C6
Muncaster Rd
Ashford TW15. . . . . .170 D5
Balham SW11. . . . . .159 A6
Muncies Mews SE6 . . . . . .164 A2
Mundania Ct SE22 . . . . . .162 B5
Mundania Rd SE22. . . . . .162 C5
Munday Ho SE1. . . . . .262 C5
Munday Rd E16 . . . . .121 A6
Munden Ho **5** E3. . . . . . . .97 D4
Munden St W14. . . .113 A2 254 A4
Mundford Rd E5. . . . . .74 C6
Mundon Gdns IG1 . . . . . . .57 B1
Mundsley Cl WD19. . . . . . .22 C6
Mund St W14 . . . . .113 B1 254 D1
Mundy Ho **6** W10. . . . . . . .91 A4
Mundy St N1 . . . . .95 C4
Mungo-Park Cl WD23. . . . . .8 A2
Munnery Way BR6 . . . . . .226 D6
Munning Ho **12** E16 . . . . .121 B5
Munnings Gdns TW7 . . . . .152 B6
Munro Dr N11 . . . . .31 C4
Munro Ho
Bermondsey SE1 . . . . . . .252 D1
Lambeth SE1. . . . . .251 A1
Munro Mews W10 . . . . .91 A2
Munro Rd WD23 . . . . .8 A6
Munslow Gdns SM1. . . . . .218 B4
Munstead Ct **12** SM2. . . .218 A4
Munster Ave TW4 . . . . . . .151 A6
Munster Ct Fulham SW6 . . .135 B3
Teddington TW11 . . . . . . .175 C4
Munster Gdns N13. . . . . . .33 A6
Munster Ho N17 . . . . .33 C3
Munster Rd
Fulham SW6 . . . . .135 A5 264 B4
Teddington TW11 . . . . . . .175 C4
Munster Residences
SW6. . . . . .264 B2
Munster Sq NW1. . . .93 B3 238 D6
Munton Rd SE1,
SE17 . . . . .117 A2 262 B4

Murchison Ave DA5 . . . . .169 A3
Murchison Ho **1** W10 . . . .91 A2
Murchison Rd E10 . . . . .76 A6
Murdoch Ho **4** SE16 . . . .118 C3
Murdock Cl E16 . . . . .98 D1
Murdock St SE15 . . . . .140 B6
Murfett Cl SW19 . . . . .157 A2
Muriel Ct **18** E10 . . . . .53 D2
Muriel St N1 . . . . . . .94 B6 233 D6
Murillo Rd SE13 . . . . .142 C1
Murley Ct N21 . . . . .17 A4
Murphy Ho SE1 . . . . .261 D6
Murphy St SE1 . . . .116 C4 251 A1
Murray Ave Bromley BR1 . .187 B1
 Hounslow TW3 . . . . .151 D6
Murray Cl SE28 . . . . .123 C5
Murray Ct **5** Harrow HA1 . . .42 D3
 Southall TW7 . . . . .108 C3
 Twickenham TW2 . . . . .152 A2
Murray Gr N1 . . . . . .95 B5 235 C3
Murray Grey Ho UB4 . . . . . .83 B2
Murray Ho
 1 North Finchley N12 . . . .30 B5
 20 Woolwich SE18 . . . . . . .122 B7
Murray Mews NW1 . . . . . . .71 D1
Murray Rd Brentford W5. . . .109 C2
 Richmond TW10 . . . . .153 C2
 Wimbledon SW19 . . . . . . .178 D4
Murray Sq E16 . . . . .121 B6
Murray St NW1 . . . . .71 D1
Murray Terr NW3 . . . . .70 B4
Musard Rd W6. . . .135 A6 264 B6
Musbury St E1 . . . . .96 C1
Muscal W6 . . . . .264 A6
Muscatel Pl SE5 . . . . .139 C4
Muschamp Prim Sch
 SM5 . . . . .218 C6
Muschamp Rd
 Camberwell SE15 . . . . . . .139 D2
 Carshalton SM5 . . . . .218 C6
Muscott Ho **15** E2 . . . . .96 A6
Muscovy Ho DA18. . . . . . . .125 A4
Muscovy St EC3 . . . . .253 B6
Museum & Galleries of
 Modern Art★ EC2 . 242 A2
Museum Ho **7** E2 . . . . .96 C4
Museum La SW7 . . . . .256 C5
Museum Mans WC1 . . . . . .240 A3
Museum of Brands,
 Packaging & Advertising★
 W11 . . . . .91 B1
Museum of Childhood
 (V&A)★ E2 . . . . .96 C4
Museum of Culinary History
 & Alimentation★
 NW1 . . . . .93 C5 232 B4
Museum of Domestic Design
 & Architecture (MoDA)★
 EN4. . . . . .15 A6
Museum of Instruments★
 SW7 . . . . .256 C6
Museum of London★
 EC2 . . . . .95 A2 242 A3
Museum of London
 Docklands★ E14 . . . .119 C6
Museum of Richmond★
 TW10 . . . . .153 D6
Museum of the Great Eastern
 Rly★ E16. . . . . .122 C4
Museum of the Order of St
 John★ EC1. . . . . .94 D3 241 C5
Museum St WC1 . . .94 A1 240 A2
Museum Way W3 . . . . .110 C4
Musgrave Cl EN4 . . . . .2 A4
Musgrave Cres
 SW6. . . . . .135 C4 265 B2
Musgrave Ct SW11 . . . . . . .267 A2
Musgrave Rd TW7 . . . . . . .130 D4
Musgrove Ho **1** E9 . . . . . .74 D2
Musgrove Rd SE14 . . . . . . .141 A4
Musical Mus The★ TW8 . .132 B6
Musjid Rd SW11 . . . . .136 B3
Muslim Coll The W5. . . . . . .110 C6
Mus of the Royal
 Pharmaceutical Society★
 SE1. . . . . .260 C4
Musquash Way TW4. . . . . .128 C3
Muston Rd E5 . . . . .74 B6
Mustow Pl **2** SW6 . . . . . .135 B3
Muswell Ave N10 . . . . .31 B1
MUSWELL HILL 49 A6
Muswell Hill N10 . . . . .49 C6
Muswell Hill Broadway
 N10 . . . . .49 B6
Muswell Hill Pl N10 . . . . . . .49 B5
Muswell Hill Prim Sch
 N10. . . . . .49 B6
Muswell Hill Rd N10 . . . . . .49 A4
Muswell Mews N10 . . . . . . .49 B6
Muswell Rd N10 . . . . .31 B1
Mutrix Rd NW6 . . . . .91 C6
Mutton Pl NW1 . . . . .71 A2
Muybridge Rd KT3 . . . . . . .177 A1
Myatt Garden Prim Sch
 SE4 . . . . .141 B3
Myatt Ho SE5 . . . . .138 D3

Myatt Rd SW9 . . . . .138 D4
Myatts Field Ct SE5 . . . . . .139 A4
Mycenae Rd SE3. . . . . .143 A6
Mychell Ho **8** SW19 . . . . .180 A3
Myddelton Ave EN1 . . . . . . .5 C5
Myddelton Cl EN1. . . . . .5 D4
Myddelton Gdns N21. . . . . .17 A4
Myddelton Ho N8. . . . . .50 A6
Myddelton Pas
 EC1. . . . . .94 C4 234 B2
Myddelton Pk N20 . . . . .14 B2
Myddelton Rd N8. . . . . .50 A5
Myddelton Sq EC1. .94 C4 234 B2
Myddelton St EC1. . .94 C4 234 B2
Myddleton Ave N4 . . . . .73 A6
Myddleton Cl HA7 . . . . .9 A2
Myddleton Ho **14** N22 . . . .30 B1
Myddleton Mews N22. . . . . .32 A3
Myddleton Rd N22. . . . . . . .32 B3
Myers Ho **5** SE5. . . . . . . .139 A5
Myers La SE14 . . . . .140 D6
Myherin Ct SE23 . . . . .163 B2
Mylis Cl SE26 . . . . .184 B6
Mylius Cl SE14 . . . . .140 C4
Mylne Cl W6. . . . . .112 A1
Mylne Ho N21 . . . . .17 B5
Mylne St EC1 . . . . .234 A3
Mynterne Ct **16** SW19 . . . .156 D3
Myra St SE2 . . . . .124 A2
Myrdle Ct **14** E1. . . . . .96 A1
Myrdle St E1 . . . . .96 A1
Myrna Cl SW19 . . . . .180 C3
Myron Pl SE13 . . . . .142 A2
Myrtle Alley SE18 . . . . .122 C3
Myrtle Ave Hatton TW4 . . . .149 C6
 Ruislip HA4 . . . . .40 B2
Myrtle Cl Barnet EN4. . . . . .14 D3
 Hillingdon UB8 . . . . .82 B2
 West Drayton UB7 . . . . . . .104 B3
Myrtledene Rd SE2 . . . . . . .124 A1
Myrtle Gdns W7 . . . . .108 C5
Myrtle Gr Enfield EN2 . . . . .5 B5
 Kingston u T KT3. . . . . . . .177 A1
Myrtle Rd SE14 . . . . .140 D4
Myrtle Rd Acton W3. . . . . . .111 A5
 Croydon CR0. . . . . .223 C5
 Edmonton N13 . . . . .17 B1
 Hampton TW12. . . . . .174 A4
 Hounslow TW3 . . . . .130 A3
 Ilford IG1 . . . . .78 D6
 Newham E6 . . . . .100 A6
 Sutton SM1. . . . . .218 A3
 Walthamstow E17 . . . . .53 A3
Myrtle Wlk **20** N1 . . . . . . .95 C5
Mysore Rd SW11. . . . . .136 D1
Myton Rd SE21 . . . . .161 B1
Mytton Ho SW8 . . . . .270 C3

N

N1 Shopping Ctr
 N1. . . . . .94 C5 234 B4
Nacton Ct **2** RM6. . . . . . . .58 C4
Nadine St SE7 . . . . .121 C1
Nadir Ct E11. . . . . .55 A2
Naffenton Rise IG10 . . . . . .21 D6
Nagle Cl E17. . . . . .36 B1
Nags Head Ct EC1. . . . . . . .72 B4
Nags Head Ho **1** EC1. . . .242 B5
Nag's Head La DA16. . . . . .146 B2
Nags Head Rd EN3. . . . . . .6 D1
Nags Head Sh Ctr The
 N7. . . . . .72 B4
Naima Jewish Prep Sch **4**
 NW6 . . . . .91 D5
Nainby Ho SE11. . . . . .261 A3
Nairn Ct
 3 Wallington SM6. . . . . .219 C2
 Wimbledon SW19 . . . . . . .179 D4
Nairne Gr SE5, SE24 . . . . . .139 B1
Nairn Rd HA4 . . . . .62 C2
Nairn St E14 . . . . .98 A2
Naish Ho SW19 . . . . .201 D6
Naldera Gdns SE3 . . . . . . .143 A6
Nallhead Rd TW13 . . . . . . .172 C5
Nalton Ho **4** NW6 . . . . . . .70 A1
Namba Roy Cl SW16 . . . . .182 B6
Namco Sta★ SE1 . . . . .250 C2
Namton Dr CR7, SW16. . . .204 B5
Nan Clark's La NW7 . . . . . .11 D2
Nancy Reuben Prim Sch **8**
 NW4 . . . . .46 D5
Nankin St E14 . . . . .97 C1
Nansen Ct **1** E11 . . . . .76 C6
Nansen Ho **8** NW10 . . . . . .67 B1
Nansen St SW11 . . . . .137 A2
Nansen Village **5** N12 . . . .29 D6
Nant Ct NW2 . . . . .69 B6
Nantes Cl SW18. . . . . .136 A1
Nant Rd NW2 . . . . .69 B6
Nant St E2. . . . . .96 B4
Naomi Watts Ho **11**
 SW19. . . . . .179 A3
Naoroji St WC1 . . . . .234 A1
Napier **15** NW9 . . . . .27 D2
Napier Ave Deptford E14 . .119 C1
 Fulham SW6. . . . . .135 B2
Napier Cl
 New Cross SE14, SE8. . . . .141 B5

Napier Cl continued
 West Drayton UB7 . . . . . . .104 B3
 West Kensington W14 . . . .254 C6
Napier Ct
 13 Croydon CR0 . . . . . . .221 D6
 Fulham SW6. . . . . .135 B2
 Grove Pk SE12 . . . . .165 B1
 Hayes UB4. . . . . .84 C3
 Shoreditch N1. . . . . .235 C4
 1 Surbiton KT6. . . . . . . .197 D2
 12 Wallington SM6. . . . . .219 B2
 Wembley HA0. . . . . .65 D2
Napier Gr N1 . . . . . .95 A5 235 B4
Napier Ho Eltham SE12 . . .165 B1
 Kennington SE17 . . . . .138 D6
Napier Lo TW15. . . . . .171 B4
Napier Pl W14. . . . . .113 B3 254 C5
Napier Rd Ashford TW15. . .171 B3
 Belvedere DA17 . . . . .125 B2
 Bromley BR2. . . . . .209 B5
 College Pk NW10 . . . . .90 B4
 Croydon SE25. . . . . .206 B5
 Enfield EN3 . . . . .18 D6
 Isleworth TW7 . . . . .131 A1
 Kensington W14 . . . .113 B3 254 C5
 Leyton E11 . . . . .76 C5
 Newham E15 . . . . .98 C5
 South Croydon CR2. . . . . .221 B1
 Tottenham N17. . . . . .51 C6
 Wallend E6 . . . . .100 C5
 Wembley HA0. . . . . .65 D2
Napier Terr N1. . . . . .72 D1
Napier Wlk TW15 . . . . .171 B3
Napoleon Rd Hackney E5. . .74 A5
 Twickenham TW1 . . . . .153 B4
Napton Cl UB4. . . . . .85 A3
Narbonne Ave SW4 . . . . . . .159 C6
Narborough Cl UB10. . . . . .61 A6
Narborough St SW6. . . . . .135 D3
Narcissus Rd NW6 . . . . . . .69 C3
Nardini **12** NW9. . . . . .27 D2
Naresby Fold HA7. . . . . . . .25 C4
Narford Rd E5 . . . . .74 A6
Narrow Boat Cl SE28 . . . . .123 B4
Narrow St **6** Acton W3. . . .110 D5
 Limehouse E14. . . . . .119 A6
Narrow Way BR2. . . . . .210 A3
Nascot St W12. . . . . .90 C1
Naseby Cl Hounslow TW7 . .130 C4
 South Hampstead NW6 . . . .70 A1
Naseby Ct DA14. . . . . .189 D6
Naseby Rd
 Dagenham RM10 . . . . .81 C5
 South Norwood SE19 . . . . .183 B4
NASH 225 A2
Nash Cl SM1. . . . . .218 B5
Nash Coll of FE BR4. . . . . .224 D4
Nash Ct HA3. . . . . .43 B3
Nashe Ho SE1 . . . . .262 C5
Nash Gn BR1. . . . . .187 A4
Nash Ho **5** Millwall E14 . . .119 C3
 Pimlico SW1. . . . . .258 D1
 1 Walthamstow E17. . . . . .53 D5
Nash La BR2. . . . . .225 A2
Nash Rd Brockley SE4 . . . .163 A6
 Dagenham RM6 . . . . .58 D5
 Lower Edmonton N9. . . . . . .18 C2
Nash St NW1 . . . . .231 D2
Nash Way HA3 . . . . .43 B3
Nasmyth St W6. . . . . .112 B3
Nassau Path **6** SE28 . . . .124 C5
Nassau Rd SW13 . . . . .133 D4
Nassau St W1. . . . . .239 A3
Nassington Rd NW3. . . . . . .70 D4
Natalie Cl TW14. . . . . .149 B4
Natalie Mews TW2 . . . . . . .152 B1
Natal Rd Bowes Pk N11. . . .32 A4
 Ilford IG1 . . . . .78 D4
 South Norwood CR7 . . . . .205 B6
 Streatham SW16 . . . . .181 D4
Nathan Cl N9. . . . . .18 C4
Nathan Ho SE11 . . . . .261 B3
Nathaniel Cl E1. . . . . .243 D3
Nathaniel Ct E17. . . . . .53 A3
Nathans Rd HA0 . . . . .65 C6
Nathan Way SE28, SE18 . . .123 D3
National Archives The
 TW9 . . . . .132 D5
National Army Mus★
 SW3 . . . . .136 D6 267 D6
National Construction Coll &
 National Skills Acad
 E16. . . . . .123 A5
National Gallery★
 W1 . . . . .115 D6 249 D5
National Hospl for Neurology
 & Neurosurgery
 WC1 . . . . .94 A3 240 B5
National Maritime Mus★
 SE10. . . . . .142 B6
National Physical Laboratory
 TW11 . . . . .174 C4
National Portrait Gallery★
 W1 . . . . .249 D5
National Portrait Gallery
 (Annexe)★ SW1 . . . .249 D4
National Theatre★
 SE1. . . . . .116 B5 250 D4
National Wks TW4. . . . . . . .129 B2
Nation Way E4. . . . . .20 A3

Natural History Mus★
 SW7 . . . . .114 B3 256 C5
Nautilus Bldg The EC1. . . .234 B2
Naval Row E14. . . . . .120 A6
Navarino Gr E8 . . . . .74 A2
Navarino Mans E8 . . . . .74 A2
Navarino Rd E8. . . . . .74 A2
Navarre Rd E6. . . . . .100 A5
Navarre St E2 . . . . .243 C6
Naveby Wlk **13** E3 . . . . . . .97 C3
Navestock Cl E4. . . . . .20 A1
Navestock Cres IG8. . . . . . .37 C3
Navestock Ho IG11 . . . . . .102 B5
Navigation Ct E16. . . . . . . .123 A6
Navigator Dr UB2. . . . . . . .108 A4
Navy St SW4. . . . . .137 D2
Naxos Bldg **9** E14 . . . . . .119 C4
Nayland Ho SE6 . . . . .186 A6
Naylor Bldg W **4** E1 . . . . .96 A1
Naylor Gr EN3 . . . . .18 D6
Naylor Ho
 33 Clapham SW8 . . . . . .137 D3
 Walworth SE17. . . . . .262 D2
 5 West Kilburn W10 . . . . .91 B4
Naylor Rd Peckham SE15 . .140 B5
 Whetstone N20 . . . . .14 A2
Nayor Bldg E **6** E1. . . . . . .96 A1
Nazareth Cl SE15 . . . . .140 B3
Nazrul St E2 . . . . .95 D4
Neal Ave UB1 . . . . .85 B3
Neal Cl HA6 . . . . .22 A2
Nealden St SW9 . . . . .138 B2
Neale Cl N2 . . . . .48 A6
Neale Ct Dagenham RM9. . .80 B2
 Muswell Hill N10. . . . . .31 B3
Neal St WC2. . . . . . .94 A1 240 A1
Neal's Yd WC2 . . . . .240 A1
Near Acre NW9 . . . . .27 D2
NEASDEN 67 B4
Neasden Cl NW10. . . . . . . .67 C3
Neasden Junc NW10 . . . . . .67 C4
Neasden La
 Church End NW10 . . . . . . .67 C3
 Neasden NW10 . . . . .67 B5
Neasden La N NW10 . . . . . .67 C5
Neasden Sta NW10 . . . . . . .67 C3
Neasham Rd RM8. . . . . .80 B3
Neath Gdns SM4. . . . . .202 A3
Neathouse Pl SW1 . . . . . . .259 A4
Neats Acre HA4. . . . . .39 B2
Neatscourt Rd E16. . . . . . . .99 D2
Nebraska Bldg **11** E13 . . .141 D4
Nebraska St SE1. . . .117 B4 252 C1
Neckinger SE16 . . . .117 D3 263 D6
Neckinger Est SE16 . . . . . .263 D6
Neckinger St SE1. . . . . . . .263 D6
Nectarine Way SE13 . . . . . .141 D3
Nedahall Ct **4** NW11. . . . . .47 B2
Needham Ct **20** EN3. . . . . .7 C6
Needham Ho SE11 . . . . . . .261 A3
Needham Rd W11. . . . . .91 C1
Needham Terr NW2 . . . . . . .68 D5
Needleman St SE16 . . . . . .118 D4
Needwood Ho N4. . . . . .51 A1
Neela Cl UB10 . . . . .60 D4
Neeld Cres Hendon NW4 . . .46 B4
 Wembley HA9. . . . . .66 C3
Neeld Ct HA9 . . . . .66 C3
Neeld Par HA9 . . . . .66 B3
Neil Cl TW15. . . . . .171 A5
Neilson-Terry Ct **9**
 SW9. . . . . .138 B1
Neil Wates Cres **17** SW2 . .160 C3
Nelgarde Rd SE6. . . . . .163 C4
Nella Rd W6 . . . . .134 D6
Nelldale Rd SE16 . . . . .118 C2
Nellgrove Rd UB10. . . . . . . .82 D3
Nell Gwynn Ave TW17 . . . .193 B3
Nell Gwynn Ho SW3. . . . . .257 B3
Nello James Gdns SE27 . . .183 B6
Nelson Ct
 East Bedfont TW14. . . . . . .149 D3
 Hillingdon UB10 . . . . .82 D4
 2 Paddington NW6 . . . . .91 C4
 Thornton Heath CR0. . . . . .204 D1
 Walton-on-T KT12 . . . . . . .194 B1
Nelson Ct
 5 Carshalton SM5. . . . . .218 D5
 Rotherhithe SE16. . . . . . . .119 B5
Nelson Docks SE16 . . . . . .119 B5
Nelson Gdns
 Bethnal Green E2 . . . . .96 A4
 Twickenham TW3, TW4. . . .151 C5
Nelson Grove Rd SW19 . . .180 A2
Nelson Ho **1** W5 . . . . .88 A4
Nelson Hospl SW20 . . . . . .179 B1
Nelson La UB10 . . . . .82 D4
Nelson Mandela Cl N10 . . . .31 A1
Nelson Mandela Rd SE3. . .143 C2
Nelson Pas EC1. . . . . .235 B2
Nelson Pl N1 . . . . .234 D3
Nelson Prim Sch
 Twickenham TW2 . . . . .151 D5
 Wallend E6 . . . . .100 C5
Nelson Rd Ashford TW15 . . .170 A5
 Bromley BR2. . . . . .209 C6
 Chingford E4. . . . . .35 D4
 Edmonton N9 . . . . .18 B2
 Enfield EN3 . . . . .18 D5
 Erith DA17 . . . . .125 B1

Nelson Rd continued
 Greenwich SE10. . . . . . . .142 A6
 Harmondsworth TW6. . . . .126 B4
 Harrow HA1 . . . . .42 C1
 Hillingdon UB10 . . . . .82 D4
 Hornsey Vale N8. . . . . .50 B3
 Merton SW19 . . . . .180 A3
 New Malden KT3 . . . . .199 B4
 Sidcup DA14. . . . . .190 A6
 Stanmore HA7 . . . . .25 C4
 Tottenham N15. . . . . .51 C5
 Twickenham TW2, TW4. . . .151 C5
 Wanstead E11 . . . . .55 B5
Nelson's Monument★
 WC2 . . . . .116 A5 250 A4
Nelson Sq SE1. . . . .116 D4 251 C2
Nelsons Row SW4 . . . . . . .137 D1
Nelson St Barking E6. . . . . .100 C6
 Canning Town E16 . . . . . . .120 D6
 Newham E6 . . . . .100 B5
 Stepney E1. . . . . .96 B1
Nelsons Yd NW1 . . . . .232 A4
Nelson Terr N1 . . . . .234 D3
Nelson Trad Est SW19 . . . .179 D2
Nemoure Rd W3. . . . . .111 A6
Nene Gdns TW13. . . . . .151 B2
Nene Rd TW6, UB7. . . . . . .126 D4
Nene Road Rdbt TW6 . . . . .126 D4
Nepaul Rd **17** SW11. . . . .136 C2
Nepean St SW15 . . . . .156 A4
Neptune Ct
 Dagenham IG11 . . . . .102 B4
 13 Millwall E14. . . . . . . .119 C2
Neptune Ho
 2 Rotherhithe SE16. . . . .118 C3
 14 Stoke Newington N16. .73 C3
Neptune Rd
 Harlington TW6 . . . . .127 A4
 Harrow HA1 . . . . .42 B3
Neptune St SE16. . . . . .118 C3
Nero Ct **6** TW8 . . . . .131 D5
Nesbit Cl SE3 . . . . .142 C2
Nesbit Rd SE9 . . . . .143 D1
Nesbitt Ho DA6 . . . . .169 D6
Nesbitt Sq SE19. . . . . .183 C3
Nesham Ho **14** N1. . . . . . . .95 C6
Nesham St E1 . . . . .118 A5
Ness St **9** SE16. . . . . .118 A3
Nesta Rd IG8 . . . . .36 D4
Nestle's Ave UB3. . . . . . . .105 D3
Nestor Ave N21 . . . . .16 D5
Nestor Ho **13** E2 . . . . .96 B5
Netheravon Rd
 Chiswick W4 . . . . .111 D1
 Ealing W7 . . . . .108 D5
Netheravon Rd S W4 . . . . .111 D1
Netherbury Rd W5. . . . . . . .109 D3
Netherby Gdns EN2 . . . . . . .4 A1
Netherby Ho **23** SW8 . . . .137 D3
Netherby Rd SE23. . . . . . . .162 C4
Nether Cl N3 . . . . .29 C3
Nethercombe Ho **1**
 SE3 . . . . .143 A6
Nethercott Ho **27** E3. . . . . .97 D4
Nethercourt Ave N3. . . . . . .29 C4
Netherfield Gdns IG11 . . . . .79 B1
Netherfield Rd
 Finchley N12. . . . . .29 D5
 Upper Tooting SW17. . . . . .159 A1
Netherford Rd SW4 . . . . . .137 C3
Netherhall Gdns NW3. . . . . .70 A3
Netherhall Int Coll NW3. . . .70 A2
Netherhall Way NW3. . . . . .70 A3
Netherlands Rd EN5 . . . . . .14 B5
Netherleigh Cl N6. . . . . .49 B1
Nether St Finchley N3 . . . . .29 D4
 North Finchley N12. . . . . . .30 A5
Netherton Gr
 SW10. . . . . .136 A6 266 B5
Netherton Ho **1** UB5. . . . . .85 B4
Netherton Rd
 Isleworth TW1 . . . . .153 B6
 Tottenham N15. . . . . .51 B3
Netherwood **24** N2. . . . . . .30 B1
Netherwood Rd W14 . . . . . .112 D4
Netherwood St NW6 . . . . . .69 C2
Nethewode Ct DA17. . . . . . .125 D3
Netley **18** SE5. . . . . .139 C4
Netley Cl Cheam SM3 . . . . .216 D3
 New Addington CR0 . . . . . .224 A1
Netley Ct IG2. . . . . .57 B4
Netley Dr KT12. . . . . .195 B2
Netley Gdns SM4 . . . . .202 A2
Netley Prim Sch
 NW1 . . . . .93 C4 232 A1
Netley Rd Brentford TW8. . .132 A6
 Cheam SM4 . . . . .202 A2
 Ilford IG2. . . . . .57 B4
 Walthamstow E17 . . . . .53 B4
Netley St NW1 . . . . .93 C4 232 A1
Nettlecombe Ho N1 . . . . . . .71 D1
Nettleden Ho SW3 . . . . . . .257 B3
Nettlefold Pl SE27 . . . . . . .160 D1
Nettlestead Ct **16** BR3. . . .185 C3
Nettleton Rd
 Harlington TW6 . . . . .126 D4
 Ickenham UB10 . . . . .60 B4
 New Cross Gate SE14. . . . .140 D4
Nettlewood Rd SW16 . . . . .181 D3

Neuchatel Rd SE6....163 B2
Nevada Cl KT3....199 A5
Nevada St SE10....142 A6
Nevena Ct 3 SW2....160 C6
Nevern Mans SW5....255 A2
Nevern Pl SW5....113 C2 255 B3
Nevern Rd SW5....255 A3
Nevern Sq SW5....113 C2 255 B3
Nevil Ho 7 SW9....138 D3
Nevill Ct SW10....266 A4
Neville Ave KT3....177 B2
Neville Cl Acton W3....111 A4
  Hounslow TW3....129 D3
  Leyton E11....76 D5
  Paddington NW6....91 B5
  Peckham SE15....140 A4
  Sidcup DA15....189 D6
  Somers Town NW1....232 A4
Neville Ct 10 SW12....159 C4
Neville Dr N2....48 A3
Neville Gdns RM8....80 D5
Neville Gill Cl SW18....157 C5
Neville Ho
  Friern Barnet N11....31 A6
  5 Twickenham TW1....153 A4
Neville Pl N22....32 B2
Neville Rd Dagenham RM8....80 D5
  Ealing W5....87 D3
  Forest Gate E7....77 B1
  Kingston u T KT1....176 C1
  Paddington NW6....91 B5
  Richmond TW10....153 C2
  Thornton Heath CR0....205 B2
Neville's Ct NW2....68 A5
Neville St SW7....114 B1 256 C2
Neville Terr SW7....256 C2
Neville Wlk SM5....202 C2
Nevill Rd N16....73 C5
Nevin Dr E4....19 D3
Nevin Ho UB3....105 A3
Nevinson Cl SW18....158 B5
Nevis Rd SW17....159 A2
Nevitt Ho N1....235 D3
New Acres Rd SE28....123 C5
NEW ADDINGTON....224 B1
Newall Ho SE1....262 B6
Newall Rd TW6....127 A4
Newark Cres NW10....89 B4
Newark Ct KT12....194 C1
Newark Ho 3 SW9....138 D3
Newark Knok E6....100 C2
Newark Rd CR2....221 B2
Newark St E1....96 B2
Newark Way NW4....46 A6
New Ash Cl N2....48 B6
New Atlas Wharf E14....119 C3
New Barn Cl SM6....220 B2
NEW BARNET....14 A6
  New Barnet Sta EN5....14 B6
New Barns Ave CR4....203 D5
New Barn St E13....99 B3
NEW BECKENHAM....185 A4
  New Beckenham Sta
  BR3....185 B3
New Belmont Ho 4
  SE23....162 C3
New Bentham Ct 10 N1....73 A1
Newbery Ho N1....73 A1
Newbiggin Path WD19....22 C6
Newbold Cotts 4 E1....96 C1
Newbolt Ave SM3....216 D3
Newbolt Ho SE17....262 C2
Newbolt Rd HA7....24 D5
New Bond St W1....115 B6 248 D6
Newborough Gn KT3....199 B5
Newborough Ho SW19....180 B3
New Brent St NW4....46 C4
Newbridge Ct SW17....180 A6
Newbridge Point 3
  SE23....162 D1
Newbridge Sch RM6....58 B4
New Bridge St
  EC4....94 D1 241 C1
New Broad St EC2....95 C2 243 A3
New Broadway
  Ealing W5....109 C6
  7 Hillingdon UB10....82 D3
  Teddington TW12....174 B5
New Bsns Ctr The NW10....89 D4
Newburgh Rd W3....111 A5
Newburgh St W1....239 B1
New Burlington Mews
  W1....249 A6
New Burlington Pl W1....249 A6
New Burlington St W1....249 A6
Newburn Ct N12....30 A3
Newburn Ho SE11....260 D2
Newburn St
  SE11....116 B1 260 D2
Newbury Ave EN3....7 B6
Newbury Cl UB5....63 B2
Newbury Cotts 3 IG2....57 A3
Newbury St Hackney E5....75 A3
  Sidcup DA14....189 D6
  7 Wanstead E11....55 A5
Newbury Gdns KT9....215 D4
Newbury Ho Barnet EN4....2 B1
  Brixton SW9....138 D3
  14 Kensington W2....91 D1
  Wood Green N22....32 A2

Newbury Mews NW5....71 A2
NEWBURY PARK....57 B3
  Newbury Park Prim Sch
  IG2....57 B3
  Newbury Park Sta IG2....57 B3
Newbury Rd
  Bromley BR2....209 A6
  Chingford E4....36 A4
  Harmondsworth TW6....126 B4
  Ilford IG2....57 C3
Newbury St EC1....242 A4
Newbury Way UB5....63 B2
New Butt La SE8....141 C5
Newby NW1....232 A2
Newby Cl EN1....5 C3
Newby Pl E14....120 A6
Newby St SW8....137 B2
New Caledonian Mkt*
  SE1....117 C3 263 B6
New Caledonian Wharf
  SE16....119 B3
New Campden Ct 9
  NW3....70 A4
Newcastle Cl EC4....241 C2
Newcastle Ct EC4....252 B6
Newcastle Ho W1....238 A4
Newcastle Pl W2....92 B2 236 D4
Newcastle Row EC1....241 B5
New Cavendish St
  W1....93 B2 238 C3
New Change EC4....95 A1 242 A1
New Chapel Sq TW13....150 B3
New Charles St EC1....234 D2
NEW CHARLTON....121 C2
New Church Ct 3 SE19....184 A3
New Church Rd
  32 Camberwell SE5....139 A5
  Camberwell SE5....139 B6
New City Prim Sch E13....99 C4
New City Rd E13....99 C4
New Cl Feltham TW13....173 A5
  Morden SW19....202 A6
New Colebrooke Ct
  SM5....219 A1
New College Ct 9 NW3....70 A2
New College Mews 7
  N1....72 C1
New College Par 1 NW3....70 B1
Newcombe Gdns TW3....129 B1
Newcombe Pk
  Edgware NW7....27 C5
  Wembley HA0....88 B6
Newcombe Rise UB7....82 A1
Newcombe St W8....245 B4
Newcome Gdns SW16....182 A6
Newcome Ho E5....74 B5
New Comen Ho 5 NW5....71 B4
Newcomen Rd
  Battersea SW11....136 B2
  Leyton E11....76 D5
Newcomen St
  SE1....117 B4 252 C2
New Compton St
  WC2....94 A1 240 A1
New Concordia Wharf
  SE1....253 D2
Newcourt Ho 26 E2....96 B4
Newcourt St NW8....92 C1 230 A3
New Covent Garden Flower
  Market* SW8....138 A6 270 A5
New Covent Garden Fruit &
  Vegetable Mkt*
  SW8....137 D5 269 C3
New Crane Pl E1....118 C5
New Crescent Yd 1
  NW10....89 D5
Newcroft Cl UB8....82 B2
Newcroft Ho 10 NW10....67 B1
NEW CROSS....141 B4
  New Cross Sta SE14....141 B5
NEW CROSS GATE....140 D4
  New Cross Gate Sta
  SE14....141 A5
New Cross Rd SE14....141 A4
  New Cross Sta SE14....141 B5
New Ct City of London EC4....241 A1
  26 Hampstead NW3....70 A4
  Northolt UB5....63 D3
  Stoke Newington N16....7 C3
Newdales Cl N9....18 A2
Newdene Ave UB5....84 D5
New Den (Millwall FC) The
  SE16....118 C1
Newdigate Ho
  6 Kingston u T KT2....176 D4
  5 Poplar E14....97 B1
Newell St E14....97 B1
NEW ELTHAM....167 A2
  New Eltham Sta SE9....166 C3
New End NW3....70 A5
  New End Prim Sch 33
  NW3....70 A4
New End Sq NW3....70 B4
New England Est IG11....101 A5
Newent Cl
  Camberwell SE15....139 C1
  Carshalton SM5....202 D1
New Farm Ave BR2....209 A5

New Ferry App SE18....122 C3
New Fetter La EC4....94 C1 241 B2
Newfield Cl TW12....173 C2
Newfield Prim Sch NW10....67 D1
Newfield Rise NW2....68 B5
Newgale Gdns HA8....26 B2
New Garden Dr UB7....104 A4
Newgate CR0....205 A1
Newgate Cl TW13....151 A1
Newgate St Chingford E4....20 C1
  Holborn EC1....94 D1 241 D2
New Globe Wlk SE1....252 A4
New Goulston St E1....243 C2
New Green Pl SE19....183 C4
NEWHAM....98 D4
Newham Acad of Music 8
  E6....100 A6
Newham City Farm* E6....99 D1
Newham Coll of FE 3
  E6....100 B5
Newham Coll of FE
  (Stratford Campus) E15....76 C1
Newham Ctr for Mental
  Health E13....99 D3
Newham Gn N22....32 C2
Newham L Ctr E13....99 C2
Newham Sixth Form Coll
  E13....99 B3
Newham Sixth Form Coll
  (Stratford Site) 7 E15....76 B1
Newham's Row SE1....253 B1
Newham Training & Ed Ctr
  E15....76 C2
Newham University Hospl
  E13....99 C3
Newham Way Beckton E6....100 B3
  Canning Town E13....99 B2
Newhaven Cl UB3....105 D2
Newhaven Cres TW15....171 B5
Newhaven Gdns SE9....143 D1
Newhaven La 3 E16....99 A2
Newhaven Rd SE25....205 B4
New Heston Rd TW5....129 B5
New Hope Christian Sch 1
  SE22....139 D1
New Horizons Ct TW8....131 A4
Newhouse 5 KT3....199 C2
Newhouse Ave RM6....58 D6
Newhouse Cl KT3....199 C2
Newhouse Wlk SM4....202 A2
Newick Cl DA5....169 D5
Newick Rd E5....74 C5
Newing Gn BR1....187 D3
NEWINGTON....116 D2
Newington Barrow Way
  N7....72 B5
Newington Butts SE1,
  SE11....116 D2 261 D3
Newington Cswy
  SE1....117 A3 262 A6
Newington Gn N16....72 C3
Newington Green Mans
  N16....73 B3
Newington Green Prim Sch
  1 N16....73 B3
Newington Green Rd N1....73 B3
Newington Ind Est SE17....262 A3
New Inn Broadway EC2....243 B6
New Inn Ct The KT8....196 B4
New Inn Sq EC2....243 B6
New Inn St EC2....243 B6
New Inn Yd EC2....95 C3 243 B6
New James Ct SE15....140 B2
New Jubilee Ct 1 IG8....37 A3
New Kelvin Ave TW11....174 C4
New Kent Rd
  SE1....117 A2 262 B4
New King's Prim Sch 12
  SW6....135 B3
New King's Rd
  SW6....135 C4 265 B1
New King St SE8....141 C6
Newland Cl HA5....23 B4
Newland Ct St Luke's EC1....242 C6
  Wembley HA9....66 C6
Newland Dr EN1....6 B4
Newland Gdns W13....109 A4
Newland Ho
  17 Deptford SE14....140 D6
  Hornsey N8....50 A6
Newland House Sch
  TW1....174 D6
Newland N8....50 A6
Newlands 11 NW1....232 A2
Newlands Ave KT7....196 C1
Newlands Cl Edgware HA8....10 A1
  Southall UB2....107 A1
  Wembley HA0....65 C2
Newlands Croft SE20....184 D4
Newlands Ct
  8 Eltham SE9....166 C5
  6 Penge SE26....184 C4
  Streatham SW16....182 A5
Newlands Pk SE26....184 D5
Newlands Quay E1....118 C6
Newlands Rd
  Thornton Heath SW16....182 A1
  Woodford IG8....20 D2

Newlands The
  Thames Ditton KT7....196 C1
  Wallington SM6....219 D1
Newlands Way KT9....213 C3
New Life Christian Sch
  CR0....220 D6
Newling Cl E6....100 B1
New London St EC3....253 B6
New Lydenburg Commercial
  Est SE7....121 C3
New Lydenburg St SE7....121 C3
Newlyn NW1....232 B5
Newlyn Cl Hillingdon UB8....82 C2
  Orpington BR6....227 D4
Newlyn Gdns HA2....41 B2
Newlyn Ho 7 Pinner HA5....23 B3
  7 Sutton SM1....218 A4
Newlyn Rd Barnet EN5....1 B1
  Bexley DA16....145 D3
  Tottenham N17....33 D2
NEW MALDEN....199 D5
  New Malden Sta KT3....199 C6
Newman Ct
  3 Bromley BR1....187 A2
  8 Finchley N3....29 C2
Newman Ho UB3....106 B6
Newman Pas W1....239 B3
Newman Rd Bromley BR1....187 A2
  Harmondsworth UB7....126 C4
  Hayes UB3....106 B6
  Newham E13....99 B4
  Thornton Heath CR0....204 B1
  Walthamstow E17....52 D4
Newman's Ct EC3....242 D1
Newmans La 15 KT6....198 A3
Newman's Row WC2....240 D3
Newman St W1....93 C2 239 B3
Newman's Way EN4....2 A4
Newman Terr 9 CR4....202 D6
Newmarket Ave UB5....63 D3
Newmarket Gn SE9....165 D4
Newmarsh Rd SE28....123 D5
Newmill Ho E3....98 A3
New Mill Rd BR5....190 C2
Newminster Rd SM4....202 A3
Newmount NW3....70 B3
New Mount St E15....76 B1
Newnes Path SW15....134 B1
Newnham Ave HA4....40 C1
Newnham Cl
  Loughton IG10....21 D5
  Northolt UB5....64 A2
  South Norwood CR7....183 A1
Newnham Gdns UB5....64 A2
Newnham Ho
  Catford SE6....164 A1
  Loughton IG10....21 D5
  9 Putney SW15....156 D5
Newnham Jun & Inf Schs
  HA4....40 C1
Newnham Lo 10 DA17....125 C1
Newnham Mews N22....32 C2
Newnham Rd N22....32 C2
Newnhams Cl BR1....210 B6
Newnham Terr SE1....261 A6
Newnham Way HA3....44 A4
New North Com Sch
  N1....95 A6 235 A6
New North Pl EC2....243 A6
New North Rd N1....95 B6 235 C5
New North Road Bridge
  N1....235 C5
New North St
  WC1....94 B2 240 C4
New Oak Rd N2....30 A1
New Oxford St
  WC1....94 B2 240 A2
New Palace Yd
  SW1....116 A4 250 A1
New Par Ashford TW15....170 B6
  Yiewsley UB7....104 A5
New Park Ave N13....17 B1
New Park Cl UB5....63 A2
New Park Ct 26 SW2....74 A6
New Park Ho N13....32 B6
New Park Par 14 SW2....160 A4
New Park Rd
  Ashford TW15....171 A5
  Streatham SW2....160 A4
New Pl SE16....223 C2
New Place Sq SE16....118 B3
New Plaistow Rd E15....98 C6
New Pond Par HA4....62 A5
Newport Ave
  Blackwall E14....120 B6
  Newham E13....99 B3
Newport Cl EN3....7 A6
Newport Ct WC2....249 D6
Newport Ho 2 E3....97 A4
Newport Lo 2 EN1....17 C6
Newport Mead WD19....22 D6
Newport Pl WC2....249 D6
Newport Rd
  Barnes SW13....134 A4
  Harmondsworth TW6....126 C4
  Hayes UB4....83 B2
  Leyton E10....76 B6
  Walthamstow E17....53 A5
Newport Sch E10,E11....76 A6

Newport St SE11....116 B2 260 D4
New Priory Ct 9 NW6....69 C1
New Providence Wharf
  E14....120 B5
Newquay Cres HA2....63 A6
Newquay Ho SE11....261 A2
Newquay Rd SE6....164 A2
New Quebec St W1....237 D1
New Rd Brentford TW8....109 D1
  Carshalton CR4....203 A1
  Chingford E4....36 A6
  Dagenham RM10....103 D5
  East Bedfont TW14....149 B5
  East Molesey KT8....195 C6
  Edmonton N9....18 B2
  Elstree WD6....9 D5
  Esher KT10....212 A4
  feltham TW14....150 B3
  Finchley N10....30 C2
  Hanworth TW13....173 A5
  Harlington TW6,UB7....127 A5
  Harrow HA1....64 D4
  Hendon NW7....29 A3
  Hillingdon UB8....83 A2
  Hornsey N8....50 A4
  Hounslow TW3....129 D1
  Ilford IG3....79 C6
  Kingston u T KT2....176 C3
  Littleton TW17....192 D6
  Richmond TW10....175 C6
  Stepney E1....96 B2
  Tottenham N22....33 A2
  Welling DA16....146 B3
  West Heath SE2....124 D1
New River Ave N8....50 B6
New River Cres N13....32 D6
New River Ct N5....73 B4
New River Stad N22....32 D3
New River Way N4....51 B2
New Row WC2....116 A6 250 A6
New Rush Hall Sch IG1....79 A6
Newry Rd TW1....153 A6
New St Sq EC4....94 C1 241 B2
New Scotland Yard*
  SW1....115 D3 259 C6
New Shepherd's Bush Mkt*
  6 W12....112 C4
Newsholme Dr N21....16 B4
NEW SOUTHGATE....31 C6
  New Southgate Ind Est 10
  N11....31 C5
  New Southgate Sta N11....31 B5
New Spitalfields Mkt E10....75 C5
New Spring Gdns Wlk
  SE11....260 B1
New Sq
  East Bedfont TW14....149 A3
  St Giles WC2....94 B1 240 D2
New Square Pas WC2....241 A2
New St EC2....95 C2 243 B3
Newstead Ave BR6....227 C6
Newstead Cl N12....30 C4
Newstead Ct UB5....85 A4
Newstead Ho
  Edmonton N9....17 D1
  Islington N1....234 B4
Newstead Rd SE12....164 D4
Newstead Way SW19....178 D6
Newstead Wlk SM5....202 A2
Newstead Wood Sch for Girls
  BR6....227 B5
New Street Hill BR1....187 C5
Newton Ave Acton W3....111 A4
  Muswell Hill N10....31 B2
Newton Cl Harrow HA2....63 C6
  Walthamstow E17....53 A3
Newton Farm Ecology Pk
  HA2....63 B6
Newton Farm Fst & Mid Sch
  HA2....63 B6
Newton Gr W4....111 C2
Newton Ho
  22 Clapham SW8....137 D3
  Paddington NW8....91 D6
  1 Stepney E1....118 B6
  10 Walthamstow E17....54 A6
  Newton Ind Est RM6....58 D5
Newton Pl E14....119 C2
Newton Point 1 E16....98 D1
Newton Prep Sch
  SW8....137 B4 268 D2
Newton Rd Acton W3....111 A4
  Cricklewood NW2....68 C2
  Harmondsworth UB7....126 B4
  Harrow HA3....24 C1
  Isleworth TW7....130 D3
  Kensington W2....91 D1
  South Tottenham N15....52 A4
  Stratford New Town E15....76 B3
  Welling DA16....146 A2
  Wembley HA0....66 B1
  Wimbledon SW19....179 A3
Newton St WC2....94 A1 240 B2
Newton's Yd 14 SW18....157 C6
Newton Terr BR2....209 D3
Newton Way N18....33 A5

Newton Wlk HA8 . . . . .26 D2
New Tower Bldgs 21 E1. . .118 B5
Newtown Ct
  Battersea SW11. . . . .**268** C1
  Clapham SW4. . . . . .159 B6
New Trinity Hosp 1 N2. . . . .30 B1
New Union Cl E14. . . . . .120 A3
New Union St EC2 . . . . **242** C3
New Victoria Hospl KT3 . .**177** C2
New Wanstead E11 . . . . .55 A3
New Way Rd NW9. . . . . .45 C1
New Wharf Rd N1. . **94** A5 **233** B4
New Woodlands Sch
  BR1. .186 C6
NEWYEARS GREEN 38 B3
Newyears Green La UB9. . .38 B3
New Zealand Ave KT12. .193 D1
Nexus St E11 . . . . .54 C2
Niagara Ave W5 . . . . .109 C2
Niagara Cl N1 . . . .**235** B4
Niagara Ct 6 SE16. . . . . . . .118 C3
Niagara Ho W5. . . . . .109 C2
Nibthwaite Rd HA1 . . . . .42 C4
Nicholas Cl UB6 . . . . .85 D5
Nicholas Ct Chiswick W4 . .133 C5
  Golders Green NW11 . . . . . . .47 C2
  Lewisham SE12 . . . . .165 A3
  Newham E13 . . . . .99 B4
Nicholas Gdns NW5 . . . . . .109 D4
Nicholas Ho Ealing W13. . . .87 C1
  Penge SE26 . . . . .184 B4
  2 Putney SW15. . . . . .156 A6
Nicholas La EC2, EC4 . . . . .**252** D6
Nicholas Pas EC3 . . . .**252** D6
Nicholas Rd
  Bethnal Green E1 . . . . .96 C3
  Borehamwood WD6 . . . . .10 B6
  Dagenham RM8 . . . . .81 B5
  20 Shepherd's Bush W11. . .112 D6
  Wallington CR0. . . . . .220 A4
Nicholas Stacey Ho 3
  SE7 .121 B1
Nicholay Rd N19. . . . . .49 D1
Nichol Cl N14. . . . . .15 D3
Nicholes Rd TW3 . . . . .129 C1
Nichol La BR1 . . . . .187 A3
Nicholl Ho N4 . . . . .51 A1
Nicholls Almshouses
  NW7 . . . . .28 B5
Nicholls Ave UB8 . . . . .82 C3
Nicholls Point 4 E15 . . . . . .99 A6
Nicholl St E2 . . . . .96 A6
Nichols Cl
  Chessington KT9 . . . . .213 C2
  Finsbury Pk N4 . . . . .50 C1
Nichols Ct E2. . . . . .95 D5
Nichols Gn W5. . . . . .88 A2
Nicholson Ct 9 N17 . . . . .51 D6
Nicholson Ho SE17. . . . .**262** C2
Nicholson Mews KT1. . . . . .198 A5
Nicholson Rd CR0. . . . . .205 D1
Nicholson St SE1 . . . .**251** C3
Nickelby Cl SE28. . . . . .102 C1
Nickleby Cl UB8 . . . . .82 D1
Nickleby Ho
  18 Bermondsey SE1. . . . . .118 A4
  7 Shepherd's Bush W11. . .112 D5
Nickols Wlk SW18 . . . . .135 D1
Nicola Cl Harrow HA3. . . . . . .24 B1
  South Croydon CR2. . . . . . .221 A2
Nicola Terr DA7 . . . . .147 A4
Nicol Cl 6 TW1. . . . . .153 B5
Nicole Ho SE25 . . . . .206 A6
Nicoll Ct Dagenham NW10 . .89 C6
  Muswell Hill N10. . . . . .31 B3
Nicoll Pl NW4 . . . . .46 B2
Nicoll Rd NW10. . . . . .89 C6
Nicoll Way WD6. . . . . .11 B6
Nicolson 14 NW9 . . . . .27 D2
Nicolson Dr WD23 . . . . .8 A2
Nicosia Rd SW18. . . . . .158 C4
Niederwald Rd SE26 . . . . . .185 A6
Nield Rd UB3 . . . . .105 D4
Nigel Bldg EC1 . . . .**241** A4
Nigel Cl UB5. . . . . .85 A6
Nigel Ct N3. . . . . .29 D3
Nigel Fisher Way KT9 . . . .213 D1
Nigel Mews IG1 . . . . .78 D3
Nigel Playfair Ave W6. . . .112 B1
Nigel Rd Forest Gate E7. . . .77 C3
  Peckham SE15 . . . . .140 A2
Nigeria Rd SE7 . . . . .143 D5
Nighthawk 16 NW9 . . . . .27 D2
Nightingale Ave
  Chingford E4. . . . . .36 C5
  Harrow HA1 . . . . .43 B1
Nightingale Cl
  Carshalton SM5 . . . . .219 A6
  Chingford E4. . . . . .36 C6
  Chiswick W4. . . . . .133 A6
  Pinner HA5. . . . . .40 C4
Nightingale Ct
  14 Cubitt Town E14. . . . . . .120 A3
  Finsbury Pk N4 . . . . .72 B6
  1 Harrow HA1 . . . . .42 D3
  Penge SE19 . . . . .183 D4
  Sutton SM1. . . . . .218 A3

Nightingale Ct continued
  1 Wanstead E11. . . . . .55 B4
Nightingale Dr KT19 . . . . .214 D2
Nightingale Gr SE13. . . . . .164 B6
Nightingale Ho
  Hayes UB3 . . . . .105 D2
  21 Hoxton E1 . . . . .95 C6
  4 North Kensington W12 . . . .90 C1
  7 St George in t East E1 . .118 A5
  Woolwich SE18. . . . . .122 C1
Nightingale La
  Balham SW11, SW12 . . . . .159 A5
  Bromley BR1. . . . . .187 D1
  Hornsey N8. . . . . .50 A6
  Richmond TW10 . . . . .154 A4
  Wanstead E11 . . . . .55 B4
Nightingale Lo
  Edgware HA8 . . . . .27 A4
  5 Paddington W9 . . . . .91 C2
Nightingale Mans 4
  SW12. . . . . .159 A5
Nightingale Mews
  1 Bow E3 . . . . .97 A5
  Newington SE11. . . . .**261** C4
  8 Wanstead E11 . . . . .55 B4
Nightingale Pl
  Shooters Hill SE18 . . . . .144 D6
  West Brompton
    SW10 . . . .**136** A6 **266** B6
Nightingale Prim Sch
  Shacklewell E5. . . . . .74 A4
  Wanstead E18 . . . . .55 C5
  Wood Green N22 . . . . .32 B2
  Woolwich SE18. . . . . .122 D1
Nightingale Rd
  22 Canonbury N1 . . . . .73 A2
  Carshalton SM5 . . . . .219 A6
  Dagenham NW10 . . . . .89 D5
  Ealing W7 . . . . .108 D5
  East Molesey KT8. . . . . .195 D4
  Hackney E5. . . . . .74 B5
  Hampton TW12. . . . . .173 C4
  Orpington BR5 . . . . .211 A3
  Ponders End N9 . . . . .18 C4
  Walton-on-T KT12 . . . . .194 B2
  Wood Green N22 . . . . .32 B3
Nightingale Sch SW17 . . .158 C2
Nightingale Sq SW12 . . . .159 A4
Nightingales The TW19 . .148 B3
Nightingales Vale SE18 . .144 C6
Nightingale Way E6. . . . . .100 A2
Nightingale Wlk SW18,
  SW4. . . . . .159 B5
Nile Cl N16 . . . . .73 D5
Nile Ct N12. . . . . .30 C4
Nile Dr N9. . . . . .18 C2
Nile Ho N1 . . . .**235** C2
Nile Path 6 SE18 . . . . .144 C6
Nile Rd E13. . . . . .99 C5
Nile St N1. . . . . . . .95 B4 **235** C2
Nile Terr SE1,
  SE15 . . . . .117 D1 **263** D1
Nimegen Way 8 SE22. . . . .161 C6
Nimmo Dr WD23 . . . . .8 B4
Nimrod 12 NW9. . . . . .27 C2
Nimrod Cl UB5. . . . . .84 D4
Nimrod Pas 4 N1 . . . . .73 C2
Nimrod Rd SW16. . . . . .181 B5
Nina Mackay Cl E15 . . . . . .98 C6
Nine Acres Cl Hayes UB3. .105 A3
  London E12. . . . . .78 A3
NINE ELMS 137 C5
Nine Elms Cl TW14. . . . . . . .149 D3
Nine Elms La
  SW8. . . . . .137 D6 **269** C5
Nineteenth Rd CR4 . . . . . .204 A5
Ninhams Wood BR6. . . . . . .226 C4
Ninth Ave UB3 . . . . .106 A6
Nisbet 13 NW9 . . . . .27 C2
Nisbet Ho E9. . . . . .74 D3
Nisbett Wlk DA14. . . . . .190 A6
Nita Ct SE12 . . . . .165 A3
Nithdale Rd SE18 . . . . .145 A5
Nithsdale Gr UB10 . . . . .61 A5
Niton Cl EN5. . . . . .12 D5
Niton Rd TW9. . . . . .132 C2
Niton St SW6 . . . . .134 D5
No 1 St SE18. . . . . .122 D3
No 2 Willow Rd＊ NW3 . . . .70 C4
Noam Prim Sch HA9 . . . . . . .66 B5
Nobel Dr TW6 . . . . .127 C5
Nobel Ho 8 SE5 . . . . .139 A3
Nobel Rd N18. . . . . .34 C6
Noble Cnr TW5 . . . . .129 C4
Noble Ct Mitcham CR4. . . . .180 B1
  Stepney E1. . . . . .118 B6
Noblefield Hts N2. . . . . .48 D4
Noble Ho 18 E1 . . . . .118 A6
Noble St EC2 . . . . . .95 A1 **242** A2
Noel 13 NW9 . . . . .27 D2
Noel Baker Ct 5 E11. . . . . . .76 C6
Noel Coward Ho SW1 . . . .259 B3
Noel Ct TW4 . . . . .129 B2
Noel Dene W5 . . . . .109 C1
Noel Ho 3 NW3 . . . . .70 B1
NOEL PARK 32 D1
Noel Park Prim Sch N22 . .32 C1
Noel Park Rd N22. . . . . .32 C1
Noel Rd Acton W3 . . . . .88 D1
  Islington N1. . . . . . . .94 D5 **234** D4

Noel Rd continued
  Newham E6 . . . . .100 A3
Noel Sq RM8 . . . . .80 C4
Noel St W1 . . . . .93 C1 **239** B1
Noel Terr Forest Hill SE23 .162 C2
  Sidcup DA14. . . . . .190 B6
Noko NW10. . . . . .90 D4
Nolan Way E5. . . . . .74 A4
Noll Ho N7 . . . . .72 B6
Nolton Pl HA8 . . . . .26 B2
Nonsuch Ct SM3 . . . . .217 A2
Nonsuch High Sch for Girls
  SM3 .216 D1
Nonsuch Ho 5 SW19 . . . . . .157 B6
Nonsuch Prim Sch KT17. .216 B3
Nook The SW19. . . . . .180 A1
Noor Ul Islam Prim Sch
  E10. . . . . .76 A6
Nora Gdns NW4 . . . . .46 D5
NORBITON 176 C1
Norbiton Ave KT1, KT2 . . .176 C1
Norbiton Common Rd KT1,
  KT3 .198 D6
Norbiton Hall KT2 . . . . .176 B1
Norbiton Rd E14. . . . . .97 B1
Norbiton Sta KT1 . . . . .176 C2
Norbreck Gdns NW10. . . . . .88 B4
Norbreck Par NW10. . . . . . . .88 B4
Norburn St W10 . . . . .91 A2
NORBURY 182 C2
Norbury Ave
  Isleworth TW3 . . . . .130 B1
  Thornton Heath CR7,
    SW16. . . . . .182 C1
Norbury Cl SW16 . . . . .182 D2
Norbury Court Rd SW16. .182 A1
Norbury Cres SW16. . . . . . .182 C1
Norbury Cross SW16. . . . . .204 A6
Norbury Ct N12. . . . . .30 A6
Norbury Fst & Mid Sch
  HA1 . . . . .42 C4
Norbury Gdns RM6. . . . . . . .58 D4
Norbury Gr NW7. . . . . .11 C1
Norbury Hill SW16 . . . . .182 D3
Norbury Manor Bsns &
  Enterprise Coll For Girls
  CR7. . . . . .182 C2
Norbury Manor Prim Sch
  SW16. . . . . .182 A2
Norbury Rd Chingford E4 . . . .35 C5
  Feltham TW13 . . . . .149 D1
  South Norwood CR7. . . . . . .205 A6
Norbury Rise SW16 . . . . . . .204 A6
Norbury Sta SW16. . . . . . . .182 B2
Norbury Trad Est SW16. . .182 B1
Norcombe Gdns HA3. . . . . . .43 C4
Norcombe Ho 2 N19 . . . . . .71 D5
Norcott Cl UB4 . . . . .84 C3
Norcott Rd N16. . . . . .74 A5
Norcroft Gdns SE22 . . . . . .162 A4
Norcutt Rd TW2. . . . . .152 C3
Norden Ho 25 E2. . . . . .96 B4
Norden Point N22 . . . . .46 C1
Nore Ct NW10 . . . . .88 A5
Norfolk Ave Edmonton N13. .32 C4
  South Tottenham N15. . . . . . .51 C4
Norfolk Cl Cockfosters EN4 . . .3 A1
  East Finchley N2 . . . . .48 C6
  Edmonton N13. . . . . .32 D4
  5 Twickenham TW1. . . . . . .153 B5
Norfolk Cres
  Paddington W2. . . . . .92 C1 **237** B2
  Sidcup DA15. . . . . .167 A4
Norfolk Ct 5 Barnet EN5. . . . .1 A1
  4 Ilford RM6. . . . . .58 B4
  Surbiton KT5. . . . . .198 B3
  Wembley NA6. . . . . .65 C2
Norfolk Gdns DA7. . . . . .147 B4
Norfolk Ho 13 Acton W3. . . . .88 C1
  Beckenham BR2 . . . . .208 D5
  City of London EC4 . . . .**252** A6
  Edgware HA8 . . . . .26 B3
  Greenwich SE3. . . . . .142 C6
  11 Merton SW19 . . . . .180 A3
  Penge SE20 . . . . .184 C2
  4 Putney SW15. . . . . .156 C4
  Richmond TW10 . . . . .154 C6
  Shacklewell E8. . . . . .73 D4
  2 South Croydon CR0 . . . . .221 B6
  3 Stanmore HA7. . . . . .25 C5
  St Johns SE8. . . . . .141 C4
  Westminster SW1 . . . . .259 D4
Norfolk House Rd SW16 . .160 A1
Norfolk House Sch N10 . . . .31 B1
Norfolk Mans
  Battersea SW11. . . . .**267** D1
  10 Wandsworth SW18 . . . .157 C6
Norfolk Mews 12 W10 . . . . .91 A2
Norfolk Pl
  Paddington W2. . . . . .92 B1 **236** D2
  Welling DA16. . . . . .146 A3
Norfolk Rd Barking IG11. . . .79 C1
  Barnet EN5. . . . . .1 C2
  Claygate KT10 . . . . .212 C3
  Dagenham RM10 . . . . .81 D3
  Enfield EN3. . . . . .18 B6
  Feltham TW13 . . . . .150 C3
  Harrow HA1 . . . . .41 D4
  Higham Hill E17 . . . . .34 D1

Norfolk Rd continued
  Ilford IG3. . . . . .57 C2
  Mitcham SW19. . . . . .180 C4
  Newham E6 . . . . .100 B6
  South Norwood CR7. . . . . . .205 A6
  St John's Wood
    NW8. . . . . .92 B6 **229** D5
  Willesden NW10. . . . . .67 C1
Norfolk Row SE1,
  SE11 . . . . .116 B2 **260** C4
Norfolk Sq W2. . . . . .92 B1 **236** D1
Norfolk Sq Mews W2. . . . .**236** D1
Norfolk St E7 . . . . .77 A3
Norgrove St SW12 . . . . .159 A4
Norhyrst Ave SE25 . . . . . . .205 D6
Norland Ho 13 W11 . . . . . . .112 D5
Norland Pl W11. . . . .113 A5 **244** B3
Norland Place Sch
  W11 . . . . .113 A5 **244** A3
Norland Rd 16 W11 . . . . . . .112 D5
Norlands Cres BR7. . . . . . . .188 D2
Norland Sq W11 . . .113 A5 **244** B3
Norley Vale SW15. . . . . .156 A3
Norlington Rd E10, E11. . . . .54 B1
Norlington Sch E10. . . . . . . .54 B1
Norman Ave
  Feltham TW13 . . . . .151 B2
  Southall UB1. . . . . .107 A6
  Tottenham N22. . . . . .33 A2
  Twickenham TW1. . . . . .153 C4
Norman Butler Ho 10
  W10. .91 A3
Normanby Cl SW15. . . . . . .157 B6
Normanby Rd NW10. . . . . . . .67 D4
Norman Cl
  Orpington BR6 . . . . .227 A5
  Tottenham N22. . . . . .33 A2
Norman Cres
  Heston TW5 . . . . .128 D5
  Pinner HA5. . . . . .22 C2
Norman Ct Dulwich SE22 . .162 A4
  5 Finchley N3 . . . . .29 C2
  Finsbury Pk N4 . . . . .50 C2
  8 Hampton TW12 . . . . .173 C2
  Ilford IG2. . . . . .57 B2
  West Norwood SW16. . . . . .182 C5
  Willesden NW10. . . . . .68 A1
  Woodford IG8. . . . . .37 B5
Normand Croft Com Sch
  W14 . . . . .135 B6 **264** D6
Normand Mews W14. . . . . .**264** B6
Normand Rd
  W14. . . . . .135 B6 **264** C6
Normanby Ave EN5 . . . . .1 B1
Normandy Cl SE26 . . . . . . .163 A1
Normandy Dr UB3 . . . . .83 A1
Normandy Ho
  6 Cubitt Town E14. . . . . . . .120 A4
  4 Hendon NW4. . . . . .28 D1
Normandy Rd SW9. . . . . . . .138 C4
Normandy Terr E16 . . . . . . .99 B1
Norman Gr E3 . . . . .97 A5
Norman Hay Trad Est
  UB7. . . . . .126 B4
Norman Ho
  1 Cheam SM1. . . . . .217 C2
  Feltham TW13 . . . . .151 B2
  7 Leyton E11. . . . . .76 C6
  Lower Halliford TW17. . . . . .192 C2
  South Lambeth SW8. . . . . . .**270** A4
Normanhurst TW15 . . . . . . .170 C5
Normanhurst Ave DA7 . . . .146 D4
Normanhurst Dr TW1 . . . . .153 B6
Normanhurst Rd
  St Paul's Cray BR5 . . . . . . .190 B1
  Streatham SW2 . . . . .160 B2
  Walton-on-T KT12 . . . . .194 D1
Normanhurst Sch E4 . . . . . .20 B4
Norman Par DA14. . . . . .168 D2
Norman Rd
  Ashford TW15. . . . . .171 B4
  Belvedere DA17. . . . . .125 D3
  Greenwich SE10 . . . . .141 D5
  Ilford IG1. . . . . .78 D3
  Leyton E11. . . . . .76 C6
  Merton SW19 . . . . .180 A3
  Newham E6 . . . . .100 B3
  South Tottenham N15. . . . . . .51 D4
  Sutton SM1. . . . . .217 C3
  Thornton Heath CR7. . . . . . .204 D4
Normans Cl Hillingdon UB8 .82 A2
  Willesden NW10. . . . . .67 B2
Normansfield Ave KT1,
  KT8 .175 C3
Normanshire Dr E4 . . . . .35 D6
Normans Mead NW10. . . . . .67 B2
Norman St EC1 . . . . .95 A4 **235** B1
Normanton Ave SW18,
  SW19. . . . . .157 C2
Normanton Ct CR2. . . . . . . .221 C3
Normanton Ho SW4. . . . . . .159 C5
Normanton Pk E4. . . . . .20 C2
Normanton Rd CR2 . . . . . . .221 C2
Normanton St SE23 . . . . . .162 D2
Norman Way Acton W3. . . . . .88 D1
  Palmers Green N14 . . . . .16 A2
Normington Cl SW16. . . . . .182 C5
Norrice Lea N2. . . . . .48 B4
Norris 11 NW9 . . . . .27 D2
Norris Ho 12 Hoxton N1. . . . .95 C6

Norris Ho continued
  18 South Hackney E9 . . . . . .96 C6
Norris St SW1 . . . .**249** C5
Norroy Rd SW15 . . . . .134 D1
Norrys Cl EN4 . . . . .2 D1
Norrys Rd EN4 . . . . .2 D1
Norse Ho 13 SE5 . . . . .139 A3
Norseman Cl 3 IG3 . . . . .58 B1
Norseman Way UB6. . . . . . . .85 B6
Norstead Pl SW15 . . . . .156 A2
North Access Rd E17. . . . . .52 D3
North Acre NW9 . . . . .27 C2
NORTH ACTON 89 B4
North Acton Rd NW10. . . . . .89 B4
North Acton Sta W3. . . . . . . .89 B2
Northala Fields UB5. . . . . . .85 B6
Northampton Gr N1 . . . . . . .73 B3
Northampton Pk N1 . . . . . . .73 B2
Northampton Rd
  Croydon CR0. . . . . .222 A6
  Enfield EN3. . . . . .7 A1
  Finsbury EC1 . . . . . . .94 C3 **241** B6
Northampton Sq
  EC1 . . . . .94 D4 **234** C1
Northampton St N1. . . . . . . .73 A1
Northanger Rd SW16 . . . . .182 A4
North Audley St
  W1. . . . . .115 A6 **248** A6
North Ave Ealing W13 . . . . . .87 B2
  Edmonton N18. . . . . .34 A6
  Harrow HA2. . . . . .41 D3
  Hayes UB3 . . . . .106 A6
  8 Richmond TW9 . . . . .132 C4
  Southall UB1. . . . . .107 B6
  Wallington SM5 . . . . .219 A1
Northaw Ho 4 W10 . . . . .90 C3
North Bank NW8. . . . .92 C4 **230** A1
Northbank Rd E17. . . . . .36 A1
North Beckton Prim Sch
  E6. .100 B2
North Birkbeck Rd E11. . . .76 B5
North Block 19 E1 . . . . .118 C6
Northborough Rd SW16. . .182 A1
Northbourne BR2. . . . . .209 A2
Northbourne Ho
  21 Hackney E5. . . . . .74 B3
  Osidge N14. . . . . .15 D4
Northbourne Rd SW4 . . . . .159 D6
North Bridge House Sch 13
  NW3. .70 A2
North Bridge House Senior
  Sch NW1. . . . . . .93 B6 **231** C5
Northbrook CE Sch
  SE12. . . . . .164 B6
Northbrook Rd
  Barnet EN5 . . . . .13 A5
  Ilford IG1. . . . . .78 C6
  Lewisham SE13 . . . . .164 C6
  Thornton Heath CR0. . . . . . .205 B4
  Wood Green N22 . . . . .32 A3
Northburgh St
  EC1 . . . . .94 D3 **241** D6
Northbury Inf & Jun Schs
  IG11. .79 A2
North Carriage Dr
  W2. . . . . .114 C6 **247** B6
NORTH CHEAM 216 C6
Northchurch SE17 . . . .**262** D2
Northchurch Ho 19 E2 . . . . .96 A6
Northchurch Rd
  De Beauvoir Town N1. . . . . . .73 B1
  Wembley HA9. . . . . .66 C2
Northchurch Terr N1. . . . . . .73 C1
North Circular Rd
  Edmonton N13. . . . . .32 C5
  Finchley N2. . . . . .30 B2
  Highams Pk E17. . . . . .35 D2
  Ilford IG1, E12. . . . . .78 C4
  Neasden NW2, NW10. . . . . . .67 C3
  Temple Fortune N3, NW2,
    NW4. . . . . .47 A4
  Woodford E18. . . . . .37 C1
North Cl Barnet EN5 . . . . . . .12 C6
  Bexley DA6 . . . . .146 D1
  Dagenham RM10 . . . . .103 C6
  East Bedfont TW14. . . . . . . .149 B5
  Merton SM4 . . . . .201 A5
Northcliffe Cl KT4 . . . . .215 C5
Northcliffe Dr N20. . . . . .13 B3
North Colonnade The
  E14 .119 D5
North Common Rd
  Ealing W5. . . . . .110 A6
  Uxbridge UB8 . . . . .60 A3
Northcote 3 HA5. . . . . .22 C1
Northcote Ave Ealing W5. .110 A6
  Isleworth TW7 . . . . .153 A6
  Southall UB1. . . . . .107 A6
  Tolworth KT5. . . . . .198 D2
Northcote Ho UB4 . . . . .84 D2
Northcote Lodge Sch
  SW11 . . . . .158 D5
Northcote Rd
  Isleworth TW7 . . . . .153 A6
  Kingston u T KT3. . . . . .199 B6
  Sidcup DA14. . . . . .189 C6
  Thornton Heath CR0. . . . . . .205 B3
  Walthamstow E17 . . . . .53 A5
  Wandsworth SW11 . . . . . . .158 D6
  Willesden NW10. . . . . .67 C1

Northcott Ave N22 . . . . .32 A2
North Countess Rd E17 . . .35 B2
Northcourt W1 . . . . .239 B4
NORTH CRAY 169 B1
North Cray Rd DA14 . . . .191 A5
North Cres Finchley N3 . . . . .29 B1
Marylebone WC1 . . . . . .239 C4
Newham E16 . . . . .98 B3
Northcroft Ct 8 W12 . . . .112 A4
Northcroft Rd
Brentford W13 . . . . .109 B3
West Ewell KT19 . . . . . .215 C1
North Crofts SE21 . . . . . .162 B3
North Cross Rd
East Dulwich SE22 . . . . .162 A6
Ilford IG6 . . . . .57 A5
North Ct SW1 . . . . .260 A5
North Dene Edgware NW7 . . .11 B1
Hounslow TW5 . . . . .129 D4
Northdene Gdns N15 . . . . .51 B3
Northdown Cl HA4 . . . . . .61 D5
Northdown Gdns IG2 . . . .57 C4
Northdown Rd DA16 . . . .146 C3
Northdown St N1 . . 94 B5 233 C3
North Dr Beckenham BR3 . .207 D5
Hounslow TW3, TW7 . . . .130 A3
Orpington BR6 . . . . .227 C4
Ruislip HA4 . . . . .39 C2
Streatham SW16 . . . . . .181 C6
North Dulwich Sta SE21 . .161 B6
North Ealing Prim Sch
W5 . . . . .87 B3
North Ealing Sta W3 . . . . .88 B1
NORTH END 70 A6
North End
Buckhurst Hill IG9 . . . . . .21 C4
Croydon CR0 . . . . .221 A6
North End NW3 . . . . .70 A6
North End Ave NW3 . . . . .70 A6
North End Cres
W14 . . . . .113 B2 254 C3
North End Ho
W14 . . . . .113 A2 254 B3
Northend Lodge E5 . . . .40 D6
North End Par W14 . . . . .254 B3
North End Rd
Golders Green NW11 . . . .47 D1
Wembley HA9 . . . . .66 D5
West Kensington
W14 . . . . .113 B1 254 D1
North End Way NW3 . . . .70 A6
Northern Ave N9 . . . . .17 C2
Northernhay Wlk SM4 . . .201 A5
Northern Hts 49 D2
Northern Perimeter Rd
TW6 . . . . .127 C4
Northern Perimeter Rd (W)
TW6 . . . . .126 B4
Northern Rd E13 . . . . .99 B5
Northern Relief Rd IG11 . . .79 A2
Northern Star Ho N11 . . . .31 B5
Northesk Ho 6 E1 . . . . . .96 B5
North Eyot Gdns 5 W6 . . .111 D1
Northey St E14 . . . . .119 A6
NORTH FELTHAM 150 B6
North Feltham Trad Est
TW14 . . . . .128 B1
Northfield IG10 . . . . .21 D6
Northfield Ave Pinner HA5 . .40 D5
West Ealing W13, W5 . . .109 B4
Northfield Cl
Bromley BR1 . . . . .188 A2
Hayes UB3 . . . . .105 D3
Northfield Cres SM3 . . . .217 A4
Northfield Gdns RM9 . . . .81 B4
Northfield Hall N6 . . . . . .49 A2
Northfield Ho
2 Newham E13 . . . . . . .99 C5
3 Peckham SE15 . . . . .140 A6
Northfield Ind Est HA0 . . .88 C6
Northfield Path RM9 . . . .81 B4
Northfield Pk UB3 . . . . . .105 D3
Northfield Rd
Cockfosters EN4 . . . . . . .2 C2
Dagenham RM9 . . . . . . .81 B4
Enfield EN3 . . . . .18 B6
Heston TW5 . . . . .128 D5
Plashet E6 . . . . .78 B1
Stamford Hill N16 . . . . . .51 C2
West Ealing W13 . . . . . .109 B4
Northfields SW18 . . . . . .135 C1
Northfields Prospect
SW18 . . . . .135 C1
Northfields Rd W3 . . . . . .89 A2
Northfields Sta W5 . . . . .109 C3
NORTH FINCHLEY 30 A6
Northfleet Ho SE1 . . . . . .252 C2
North Flower Wlk
W2 . . . . .114 B6 246 C5
North Gate NW8 . . .92 C5 230 A3
Northgate Bsns Ctr EN1 . . .6 B1
Northgate Ct 14 SW9 . . . .138 C2
North Gdns SW19 . . . . . .180 B3
North Glade The DA5 . . . .169 B3
North Gn NW9 . . . . .27 C3

North Gower St
NW1 . . . . .93 C4 232 B1
North Gr Highgate N6 . . . . .49 A2
Tottenham N15 . . . . .51 B4
North Greenwich Sta
SE10 . . . . .120 C4
North Harringay Prim Sch
N8 . . . . .50 C5
NORTH HARROW 41 D2
North Harrow Sta HA2 . . . .41 D4
North Hill N6 . . . . .49 A3
North Hill Ave N6 . . . . . . .48 D3
North Hill Ct N6 . . . . .49 A2
NORTH HILLINGDON 61 A2
North Ho 3 SE8 . . . . . . .119 B1
NORTH HYDE 107 A1
North Hyde Gdns UB2,
UB3 . . . . .106 A3
North Hyde La UB2 . . . . .107 A1
North Hyde Rd UB3 . . . . .105 D3
Northiam Finchley N12 . . . .29 C6
St Pancras WC1 . . . . . . .233 B1
Northiam St E9 . . . . .96 B6
Northington St
WC1 . . . . .94 B3 240 D5
NORTH KENSINGTON 90 D2
North Kingston Ctr KT2 . .176 A4
North La TW11 . . . . .174 D4
Northlands 4 BR1 . . . . . .187 C1
Northlands Ave BR6 . . . . .227 C4
Northlands St SE5 . . . . . .139 A3
Northleigh Ho 36 E3 . . . . .97 C4
North Lo Clapham SW4 . . .137 B1
Muswell Hill N22 . . . . . . .31 D1
New Barnet EN5 . . . . . . .14 A6
North Lodge Cl SW15 . . . .156 D6
North London Bsns Pk
N11 . . . . .15 A1
North London Coll 13 . . . .51 D6
North London Collegiate Sch
HA7, HA8 . . . . .26 A5
North London Int Sch (IB
Diploma Ctre) 15 N11 . .30 D5
North London Int Sch
(Lower Sch)
5 North Finchley N12 . .14 A1
24 North Finchley N12 . . .29 C6
North London Int Sch (Lower
School) 24 N12 . . . . . . .29 D6
North London Int Sch (Upper
Sch) 14 N11 . . . . .30 D5
North London Rudolf Steiner
Sch 7 N8 . . . . .49 C4
North London Science Ctr 12
N1 . . . . .72 C1
North Mall The N9 . . . . . .18 B2
North Mews WC1 . .94 B3 240 D5
North Middlesex University
Hospl N18 . . . . .33 C5
Northmoor 4 SE23 . . . . .162 D1
North Mount N20 . . . . . . .14 A2
Northmuir HA8 . . . . .27 B6
Northolme Gdns HA8 . . . .26 C2
Northolme Rd N5 . . . . . . .73 A4
Northolme Rise BR6 . . . .227 C6
NORTHOLT 63 C1
Northolt N17 . . . . .33 C1
Northolt Aerodrome HA4 . .61 D3
Northolt Ave UB6 . . . . . . .62 B3
Northolt Gdns UB6 . . . . . .64 D3
Northolt High Sch UB5 . . .63 B2
Northolt Park Sta HA2 . . . .63 D4
Northolt Rd HA2 . . . . .64 A5
Northolt Sta UB5 . . . . . . .63 C2
Northolt Trad Est UB5 . . . .63 D1
Northover BR1 . . . . .164 D1
North Par
Chessington KT9 . . . . . .214 B3
Edgware HA8 . . . . .26 C1
Southall UB1 . . . . .85 C1
North Pas SW18 . . . . . . .157 C2
North Pk SE9 . . . . .166 C5
North Pl Mitcham SW19 . .180 D3
Teddington TW11 . . . . . .174 D4
Northpoint BR1 . . . . .187 A2
North Point HA1 . . . . . . .104 A5
Northpoint Cl SM1 . . . . . .218 A5
Northpoint Sq 8 NW1 . . . .71 D2
North Pole La BR2 . . . . . .225 A2
North Pole Rd W10 . . . . . .90 C2
Northport St N1 . . . . .235 D5
North Prim Sch UB1 . . . .107 B6
North Rd Barnsbury N7 . . .72 A2
Brentford TW8 . . . . .132 A6
Bromley BR1 . . . . .187 B2
Dagenham RM6 . . . . . . .59 A4
Ealing W5 . . . . .109 D3
East Bedfont TW14 . . . .149 B5
Edgware HA8 . . . . .26 D2
Edmonton N9 . . . . .18 B3
Erith DA17 . . . . .125 D4
Finchley N2 . . . . .30 C2
Hayes UB3 . . . . .83 B2
Highgate N6 . . . . .49 A2
Ilford IG3 . . . . .79 C6
Plumstead SE18 . . . . . .123 C2
Richmond TW9 . . . . . . .132 C3
Southall UB1 . . . . .107 C6

North Rd continued
Surbiton KT6 . . . . .197 D3
West Drayton UB7 . . . . .104 B3
1 West Wickham BR4 . .207 D1
Wimbledon SW19 . . . . .180 A4
North Residence IG3 . . . . .58 B4
North Ride W2 . . . . .114 C6 247 A5
North Rise W2 . . . . .237 B1
Northrop Rd TW6 . . . . . .127 C4
North Row W1 . . .115 A6 248 A6
NORTH SHEEN 132 C3
North Sheen Sta TW10 . .132 C1
Northside Prim Sch N12 . .30 A5
Northside Rd BR1 . . . . . .187 A2
North Side Wandsworth
Comm SW18 . . . . .158 B6
Northspur Rd SM1 . . . . . .217 C5
North Sq Edmonton N9 . . . .18 B2
Hampstead Garden Suburb
NW11 . . . . .47 C4
North St Barking IG11 . . . .79 A1
Bexleyheath DA7 . . . . . .147 C1
Bromley BR1 . . . . .187 A2
Carshalton SM5 . . . . . . .218 D4
Clapham SW4 . . . . .137 C2
Hendon NW4 . . . . .46 C4
Isleworth TW7 . . . . .131 A2
Newham E13 . . . . .99 B5
Northstead Rd SW2 . . . .160 C2
North Tenter St E1 . . . . .243 D1
North Terr SW3 . . . . .257 A5
Northumberland Alley
EC3 . . . . .243 B1
Northumberland Ave
Enfield EN1 . . . . .6 B4
Falconwood DA16 . . . . .145 C2
Hounslow TW7 . . . . . . .130 D4
Wanstead E12 . . . . .55 C1
Westminster WC2 116 A5 250 A4
Northumberland Cl
TW19 . . . . .148 A5
Northumberland Cres
TW14 . . . . .149 C5
Northumberland Ct
3 Hounslow TW3 . . . . .129 D1
South Croydon CR2 . . . .221 C3
Northumberland Gdns
Brentford TW7 . . . . .131 A5
Bromley BR1 . . . . .210 C5
Edmonton N9 . . . . .17 D1
Mitcham CR4 . . . . .203 D4
Northumberland Gr N17 . .34 B3
Northumberland Heath Prim
Sch DA8 . . . . .147 D5
Northumberland Ho
Finchley N12 . . . . .29 D4
Kentish Town NW5 . . . . .71 C2
Northumberland Mans
E5 . . . . .74 C4
Northumberland Park Com
Sch 2 N17 . . . . .34 A3
Northumberland Park Ind Est
N17 . . . . .34 B3
Northumberland Park
Resource Ctr N17 . . . . .34 A4
Northumberland Park Sta
N17 . . . . .34 B3
Northumberland Pk
Erith DA8 . . . . .147 D5
Tottenham N17 . . . . .34 A3
Northumberland Pl
Notting Hill W2 . . . . .91 C1
26 Richmond TW10 . . . .153 D6
Northumberland Rd
Harrow HA2 . . . . .41 C4
New Barnet EN5 . . . . . . .14 A4
Newham E6 . . . . .100 A1
Walthamstow E17 . . . . .53 C2
Northumberland St WC2 .250 A4
Northumbria Ct 10 TW9 . .132 A1
Northumbria St E14 . . . . .97 C1
North Verbena Gdns 2
W6 . . . . .112 A1
Northview 1 N7 . . . . .72 A5
North View Ealing W5 . . . .87 C3
Pinner HA5 . . . . .40 C2
Wimbledon SW19 . . . . .178 C5
Northview Cres NW10 . . . .67 D4
Northview Dr IG8 . . . . .37 D1
Northview Prim Sch
NW10 . . . . .67 D4
North View Rd N8 . . . . . . .49 D6
North Villas NW1 . . . . . . .71 D2
Northway
Hampstead Garden Suburb
NW11 . . . . .47 D4
Merton SM4 . . . . .201 A5
Wallington SM6 . . . . . . .219 C4
North Way
Friern Barnet N11 . . . . . .31 C4
Lower Edmonton N9 . . . .18 D2
Pinner HA5 . . . . .40 D5
Queensbury NW9 . . . . . .44 D6
Uxbridge UB10 . . . . .60 A1
Northway Cres NW7 . . . . .27 C6
Northway Rd
Camberwell SE5 . . . . . .139 A2
Croydon CR0 . . . . .205 D2

Northway Sch NW7 . . . . . .11 B1
Northways Par 2 NW3 . . . .70 B1
North Weald La KT2 . . . . .175 D5
NORTH WEMBLEY 65 C6
North Wembley Sta HA0,
HA9 . . . . .65 D5
North Western Ave (Tylers
Way) WD23 . . . . .8 C3
North Western Ave (Watford
By-Pass) WD6 . . . . .9 B4
North Wharf Rd
W2 . . . . .92 B2 236 C3
Northwick Ave HA3 . . . . . .43 B3
Northwick Circ HA3 . . . . . .43 C3
Northwick Cl Harrow HA1 . .43 A3
Lisson Gr NW8 . . . .92 B3 236 C6
Northwick Ho NW8 . . . . .236 B6
Northwick Park Hospl
HA1 . . . . .43 A4
Northwick Park Rd HA1 . . .43 D2
Northwick Park Sta HA3 . .43 B2
Northwick Rd
South Oxhey WD19 . . . . .22 C6
Wembley HA0 . . . . .87 D6
Northwick Terr
NW8 . . . . .92 B3 236 C6
North Wlk
Bayswater W2 . . . .114 A6 246 A5
New Addington CR0 . . . .224 A3
Northwold Dr HA5 . . . . . .40 C6
Northwold Prim Sch E5 . . .74 A6
Northwold Rd E5, N16 . . . .74 A6
NORTHWOOD 22 A3
Northwood Gdns
Greenford UB6 . . . . .64 D3
Ilford IG5 . . . . .56 C5
North Finchley N12 . . . . .30 B5
NORTHWOOD HILLS 22 A1
Northwood Hills Cir HA6 . .22 A2
Northwood Hills Sta HA6 . .22 A1
North Wood Lo NW3 . . . . .69 D4
Northwood Pl DA18 . . . . .125 B3
Northwood Prim Sch
DA18 . . . . .125 B3
Northwood Rd
Forest Hill SE23 . . . . . . .163 B3
Highgate N6 . . . . .49 B2
South Norwood CR7 . . . .183 A1
Wallington SM5 . . . . . . .219 A2
Northwood Sch HA6 . . . . .22 A2
Northwood Twr 1 E17 . . . .54 A5
Northwood Way
Northwood HA6 . . . . .22 A2
1 West Norwood SE19 .183 C4
NORTH WOOLWICH 122 D4
North Woolwich Rd E16 . .121 B5
North Woolwich Rdbt
E16 . . . . .121 D5
North Worple Way
SW14 . . . . .133 B2
Norton Ave KT5 . . . . .198 D2
Norton Cl Chingford E4 . . .35 D5
Enfield EN1 . . . . .6 B3
Norton Ct
Beckenham BR3 . . . . . . .185 B2
Ilford IG2 . . . . .57 B3
Norton Folgate E1 . . . . . .243 B4
Norton Gdns SW16 . . . . .182 A1
Norton Ho
14 Globe Town E2 . . . . .96 D5
6 Holloway N1 . . . . .72 C4
30 Stepney E1 . . . . .96 B1
16 Stockwell SW9 . . . .138 B3
Norton Rd
Walthamstow E10 . . . . . .53 B1
Wembley HA0 . . . . .65 C1
Norval Gn 1 SW9 . . . . . .138 C3
Norval Rd HA0 . . . . .43 B1
Norvic Ho 5 SE5 . . . . . .139 A3
Norway Gate SE16 . . . . . .119 A3
Norway Pl E14 . . . . .97 B1
Norway St SE10 . . . . . . .141 D6
Norwegian Sch The 6
SW20 . . . . .178 C3
Norwich Cres RM6 . . . . . .58 B4
Norwich Ho 6 E14 . . . . . .97 C1
Norwich Mews IG3 . . . . . .58 A1
Norwich Rd
Forest Gate E7 . . . . .77 A3
Greenford UB6 . . . . .85 D6
Northwood HA6 . . . . .39 D6
South Norwood CR7 . . . .205 A6
Norwich St EC4 . . .94 C1 241 A2
Norwich Wlk HA8 . . . . . . .27 A3
Norwood Ave HA0 . . . . . .88 B5
Norwood Cl
Cricklewood NW2 . . . . . .69 A5
Southall UB2 . . . . .107 C5
Twickenham TW2 . . . . . .152 B2
Norwood Dr HA2 . . . . . . .41 C3
Norwood Gdns Hayes UB4 .84 C3
Southall UB2 . . . . .107 C5
NORWOOD GREEN 107 C2
Norwood Green Inf Sch
UB2 . . . . .107 B1
Norwood Green Jun Sch
UB2 . . . . .107 A1

Norwood Green Rd UB2 . .107 C2
Norwood Heights Sh Ctr 13
SE19 . . . . .183 C4
Norwood High St SE27 . .183 A6
Norwood Ho 25 E14 . . . .119 D6
Norwood Junction Sta
SE25 . . . . .206 A5
NORWOOD NEW
TOWN 183 A4
Norwood Park Rd SE27 . .183 A5
Norwood Rd
Southall UB2 . . . . .107 C2
West Norwood SE24, SE27 . .160 D3
Norwood Sch SE19 . . . . .183 A5
NorwoodTerr UB2 . . . . . .107 D2
Notley St SE5 . . . . .139 B5
Notre Dame RC Girls Sch
SE1 . . . . .116 D3 261 D5
Notre Dame RC Prim Sch
SE18 . . . . .144 D6
Notson Rd SE25 . . . . . . .206 B5
Notting Barn Rd W10 . . . . .90 D3
Nottingdale Sq W11 . . . . .244 A4
Nottingham Ave E6 . . . . . .99 C1
Nottingham Ct WC2 . . . . .240 A1
Nottingham Ho
33 Camberwell SE5 . . .139 A4
Stoke Newington N4 . . . . .51 A1
Nottingham Pl
W1 . . . . .93 A2 238 A4
Nottingham Rd
Croydon CR2 . . . . .221 A3
Isleworth TW7 . . . . .130 D3
Leytonstone E10 . . . . . . .54 A3
Upper Tooting SW17 . . . .158 D3
Nottingham St W1 . . . . . .238 A4
Nottingham Terr NW1 . . . .238 A5
NOTTING HILL 113 B6
Notting Hill & Ealing High
Sch W13 . . . . .87 B2
Notting Hill Gate
W11 . . . . .113 C5 245 A6
Notting Hill Gate Sta
W11 . . . . .113 C5 245 A4
Notting Hill Prep Sch 17
W11 . . . . .91 A1
Nottingwood Ho W11 . . .244 A6
Nova Bldg 1 E14 . . . . . . .119 C2
Nova Ct E 3 E14 . . . . . .120 A5
Nova Ct W 2 E14 . . . . . .120 A5
Nova Mews SM4 . . . . . . .201 A2
Novar Cl BR6 . . . . .211 D2
Novar Ho CR0 . . . . .205 A2
Novar Rd SE9 . . . . .167 A3
Novello St SW6 . . .135 C4 265 A2
Nowell Rd SW13 . . . . . . .134 A6
Nower Ct HA5 . . . . .41 B5
NOWER HILL 41 B6
Nower Hill HA5 . . . . .41 B5
Nower Hill High Sch HA5 . .41 C5
Noyna Rd SW17 . . . . . . .158 D1
Nubia Way SE6 . . . . .164 C1
Nucleus NW10 . . . . .89 A4
Nuding Cl SE13 . . . . .141 C2
Nuffield Ct TW5 . . . . .129 C3
Nuffield 14 W9 . . . . .91 C2
Nugent Ct
Streatham SW16 . . . . . .181 C6
3 Upper Holloway N19 . .50 A1
Nugent Rd
Finsbury Pk N19 . . . . . . .50 A1
South Norwood SE25 . . .205 D6
Nugents Ct HA5 . . . . .23 A2
Nugent's Pk HA5 . . . . . . .23 B2
Nugent Terr NW8 . .92 A5 229 B3
Numa Ct TW8 . . . . .131 D5
Nun Ct EC2 . . . . .242 C2
Nuneaton Rd RM9 . . . . . .81 A1
Nuneham SW16 . . . . . . .181 D6
NUNHEAD 140 C1
Nunhead Cres SE15 . . . .140 B2
Nunhead Gn SE15 . . . . . .140 B2
Nunhead Gr SE15 . . . . . .140 C2
Nunhead La SE15 . . . . . .140 B2
Nunhead Sta SE15 . . . . .140 C3
Nunnington Cl SE9 . . . . .166 A1
Nunn's Rd EN2 . . . . .5 A3
Nupton Dr EN5 . . . . .12 C5
Nurse Cl HA8 . . . . .27 A2
Nursery Ave
Bexleyheath DA7 . . . . . .147 B2
Croydon CR0 . . . . .222 D6
Finchley N3 . . . . .30 A1
Nursery Cl
Broom Hill BR6 . . . . . . .211 D2
Croydon CR0 . . . . .222 D6
Dagenham RM6 . . . . . . .58 D3
Enfield EN3 . . . . .6 D4
Feltham TW14 . . . . .150 B4
New Cross SE4 . . . . . . .141 B3
Putney SW15 . . . . .134 D1
Woodford IG8 . . . . .37 B5
Nursery Ct Ealing W13 . . .87 A2
8 Tottenham N17 . . . . . .33 D3
Nursery Gdns
Chislehurst BR7 . . . . . . .188 D4
Enfield EN3 . . . . .6 D4

Nursery Gdns continued
Hampton TW13 . . . .**173** B6
Hounslow TW4 . . . .**151** B6
Sunbury TW16 . . . .**171** D1
Nursery La Forest Gate E7 . .**77** A2
North Kensington W10 . . . . . .**90** C2
Shoreditch E2 . . . .**95** D6
Nurserymans Rd N11 . . . . .**15** A2
Nursery Rd Finchley N2. . . . .**30** B2
Hackney E9. . . . .**74** C2
Loughton IG10 . . . .**21** C6
Merton SW19 . . . .**179** D1
Mitcham CR4 . . . .**202** C6
Osidge N14. . . . .**15** C4
Pinner HA5 . . . .**40** C6
South Norwood CR7 . . . . .**205** B5
Stockwell SW9 . . . .**138** B1
Sunbury TW16 . . . .**171** D1
Sutton SM1 . . . .**218** A4
Wimbledon SW19 . . . .**179** A3
Nursery Row SE17 . . . . . .**262** C3
Nursery St N17 . . . .**33** D3
Nursery Walk Ct NW4 . . . .**46** B6
Nursery Wlk NW4 . . . .**46** C6
Nurstead Rd DA8 . . . .**147** C5
Nutborn Ho SW19. . . . . . .**178** D4
Nutbourne St W10 . . . .**91** A4
Nutbrook St SE15 . . . .**140** A2
Nutbrowne Rd RM9 . . . . .**103** B6
Nutchford EN1. . . . .**17** C5
Nutcroft Rd SE15 . . . .**140** B5
Nutfield Cl
Carshalton SM5 . . . .**218** C5
Edmonton N18 . . . .**34** A4
Nutfield Gdns Ilford IG3 . . .**80** A6
Northolt UB5 . . . .**84** C5
Nutfield Pl 1 CR7 . . . .**204** D5
Nutfield Rd Dollis Hill NW2. . .**68** A5
East Dulwich SE22 . . . .**139** D1
Leyton E15 . . . .**76** A4
Thornton Heath CR7. . . . . .**204** D5
Nutfield Way BR6 . . . .**226** D6
Nutford Pl W1 . . . .**92** D1 **237** C2
Nuthatch Cl TW19. . . . . . .**148** B3
Nuthatch Gdns SE28 . . . . .**123** B4
Nuthurst Ave SW2 . . . . . .**160** B2
Nutkin Wlk UB8. . . . .**60** A1
Nutley Terr NW3 . . . .**70** B2
Nutmeg Cl E16 . . . .**98** C3
Nutmeg La E14 . . . .**98** B1
Nuttall St N1 . . . .**95** C5
Nutter La E11. . . . .**55** C4
Nutt Gr HA8 . . . .**9** D2
Nutt St SE15 . . . .**139** D5
Nutty La TW17 . . . .**193** A6
Nutwell St SW17 . . . .**180** C5
Nuxley Rd DA17. . . . .**125** C1
Nyanza St SE18 . . . .**145** B6
Nye Bevan Est E5 . . . .**74** D5
Nye Bevan Ho SW6. . . . . .**264** C4
Nye's Wharf SE1, SE15. . . .**140** A6
Nylands Ave TW9 . . . .**132** C3
Nymans Gdns SW20. . . . . .**200** B6
Nynehead St SE14 . . . . . .**141** A5
Nyon Gr SE6. . . . .**163** B2
Nyton Cl N19 . . . .**50** A1

O

O2 Ctr NW6 . . . .**70** A2
O2 Millennium Dome The★
SE10. . . . .**120** C5
Oak Apple Ct SE12 . . . . . .**165** A3
Oak Ave Croydon CR0. . . .**223** D6
Enfield EN2. . . . .**4** B5
Hampton TW12, TW13 . . . .**173** A4
Heston TW5 . . . .**129** A5
Hornsey N8. . . . .**50** A5
Muswell Hill N10. . . . .**31** B3
Tottenham N17. . . . .**33** C3
Uxbridge UB10 . . . .**60** D6
West Drayton UB7 . . . . . .**104** C3
Oak Bank CR0 . . . .**224** A2
Oakbank Ave KT12 . . . . . .**195** B2
Oakbank Gr SE24 . . . .**139** A1
Oakbark Ho 10 TW8 . . . . .**131** C5
Oakbrook 3 BR3 . . . .**185** D1
Oakbrook Cl BR1 . . . .**187** B6
Oakbury Rd SW6. . . . .**135** D3
Oak Cl East Barnet N14 . . . .**15** B4
Sutton SM1 . . . .**218** A6
Oakcombe Cl KT3. . . . . . .**177** C2
Oak Cottage Cl 11 SE6. . .**164** D3
Oak Cotts W7. . . . .**108** C4
Oakcourt 17 SE15 . . . .**139** D5
Oak Cres E16 . . . .**98** C2
Oakcroft SE12 . . . .**165** B1
Oakcroft Bsns Ctr KT9 . . .**214** B4
Oakcroft Cl HA5 . . . .**22** B1
Oakcroft Ct SE3. . . . .**143** A4
Oakcroft Ho 3 KT3 . . . . . .**199** C2
Oakcroft Rd
Chessington KT9 . . . .**214** B4
Lewisham SE13 . . . .**142** B4
Oakcroft Villas KT9. . . . . .**214** B4
Oak Ct Bickley BR1. . . . . . .**188** B1

Oak Ct continued
Chingford E4. . . . .**35** D4
Oakdale Beckenham BR3. . .**186** A1
East Barnet N14. . . . .**15** B3
Oakdale Ave Harrow HA3. . .**44** A4
Pinner HA6. . . . .**22** A1
Oakdale Cl WD19 . . . .**22** C6
Oakdale Ct Chingford E4. . . .**36** A5
Upper Holloway N19 . . . . . .**72** A6
Oakdale Gdns E4 . . . .**36** A5
Oakdale Inf Sch E18 . . . . . .**37** B1
Oakdale Jun Sch E18 . . . . .**37** B1
Oakdale Lo NW4 . . . .**29** A2
Oakdale Rd Leyton E11. . . . .**76** B6
Nunhead SE15 . . . .**140** C2
South Oxhey WD19 . . . .**22** C6
Streatham SW16 . . . .**182** A5
Tottenham N4. . . . .**51** B3
Upton E7. . . . .**77** B1
Woodford E18. . . . .**37** B1
Oakdale Way CR4 . . . .**203** A2
Oakdene Ealing W13 . . . . . .**87** B2
3 Peckham SE15. . . . .**140** B4
1 West Norwood SE19 . . . .**183** C5
Oakdene Ave
Chislehurst West BR7. . . . .**188** C5
Thames Ditton KT7. . . . . . .**197** A1
Oakdene Cl HA5 . . . .**23** B3
Oakdene Ct
Feltham TW12 . . . .**173** B6
1 Streatham SW16. . . . . .**182** A5
Oakdene Dr KT5 . . . .**198** A1
Oakdene Ho Enfield EN2. . . .**4** D2
11 Stamford Hill N16 . . . . . .**51** C1
Oakdene Lo 3 SE20 . . . . .**184** B4
Oakdene Mews SM3 . . . . .**201** B1
Oakdene Pk N3. . . . .**29** B3
Oakdene Rd
Hillingdon UB10 . . . .**82** D5
Orpington BR5 . . . .**211** D4
Oakden St SE11. . . .**116** C2 **261** B4
Oakeford Ho W14. . . . .**254** B5
Oakend Ho N4 . . . .**51** B2
Oaken Dr KT10. . . . .**212** D2
Oakenholt Ho 1 SE2. . . . .**124** D4
Oaken La KT10. . . . .**212** C3
Oakenshaw Cl KT6. . . . . . .**198** A2
Oakes Cl E6 . . . .**100** B1
Oakeshott Ave N6. . . . .**71** A6
Okey La SE1 . . . .**261** A6
Oak Farm WD6 . . . .**11** A6
Oak Farm Jun & Inf Schs
UB10. . . . .**82** D6
Oakfield E4 . . . .**35** D5
Oakfield Ave HA3 . . . .**43** B6
Oakfield Cl
New Malden KT3. . . . .**199** D4
Ruislip HA4 . . . .**39** D3
Oakfield Ct
Clapham Pk SW4 . . . .**160** A5
2 Ealing W5 . . . .**110** C5
Finchley N3. . . . .**29** D2
Finsbury Pk N8 . . . .**50** A2
Hendon NW2 . . . .**46** D2
South Croydon CR2. . . . . .**221** A2
Oakfield Gdns
Beckenham BR3 . . . .**207** C4
Carshalton SM5 . . . .**202** D1
Edmonton N18 . . . .**33** C6
Greenford UB6. . . . .**86** B4
3 West Norwood SE19 . . . .**183** C5
Oakfield Ho 2 IG1. . . . .**78** D5
Oakfield La BR2 . . . .**225** C4
Oakfield Lo 8 IG1. . . . .**78** D5
Oakfield Prep Sch SE21 . .**161** B3
Oakfield Rd
Ashford TW15. . . . .**170** D5
Croydon CR0. . . . .**205** A1
Finchley N3. . . . .**29** D2
Finsbury Pk N4 . . . .**50** C2
Higham Hill E17 . . . .**35** A1
Ilford IG1. . . . .**78** D5
Newham E6 . . . .**100** A6
Palmers Green N14 . . . .**16** A2
Penge SE20 . . . .**184** B3
Wimbledon SW19. . . . . . .**156** D1
Oakfield Road Ind Est 11
SE20. . . . .**184** B3
Oakfields KT12 . . . .**194** A1
Oakfields Rd NW11 . . . .**47** A3
Oakfield St
SW10. . . . .**136** A6 **266** A6
Oakford Rd NW5. . . . .**71** C4
Oak Gdns Croydon CR0 . . .**223** C6
Hendon HA8 . . . .**27** A1
Oak Gr Ruislip HA4 . . . .**40** B1
Sunbury TW16 . . . .**172** B3
West Hampstead NW2. . . . .**69** A4
West Wickham BR4 . . . . . .**208** A1
Oak Grove Rd SE20. . . . . .**184** C1
Oakhall Ct Ashford TW16 . .**171** D5
Wanstead E11 . . . .**55** B3
Oakhall Dr TW16. . . . .**171** D5
Oak Hall Rd E11 . . . .**55** B3
Oakham Cl Cockfosters EN4. . .**2** D2
Forest Hill SE6 . . . .**163** B2
Oakham Dr BR2. . . . .**208** D5
Oakham Ho 5 W10 . . . .**90** C3
Oakhampton Rd NW7 . . . . .**28** D3
Oakhill KT10. . . . .**213** A2

Oak Hill Chingford IG8. . . . .**36** C3
Surbiton KT6. . . . .**198** A2
Oakhill Ave Pinner HA5. . . . .**23** A1
West Hampstead NW3. . . . .**69** D4
Oak Hill Cl IG8. . . . .**36** B3
Oak Hill Cres
Chingford IG8. . . . .**36** C3
Surbiton KT6. . . . .**198** A2
Oakhill Ct
Honor Oak SE23 . . . .**162** C5
Putney SW15 . . . .**157** B6
8 Surbiton KT6. . . . .**198** A3
Wimbledon SW19. . . . . . .**178** D3
Oak Hill Cl IG8. . . . .**36** C3
Oak Hill Gdns E4. . . . .**36** C2
Oak Hill Gr KT6 . . . .**198** A3
Oakhill Ho BR5 . . . .**190** A2
Oakhill Mans EN4 . . . .**14** C5
Oak Hill Park Mews NW3. .**70** A4
Oak Hill Pk NW3 . . . .**69** D4
Oakhill Pl SW15. . . . .**157** C6
Oakhill Prim Sch IG8 . . . . .**36** C4
Oakhill Rd
Beckenham BR3 . . . .**186** A1
Orpington BR6 . . . .**227** D6
Putney SW15 . . . .**157** B6
Sutton SM1 . . . .**218** A5
Thornton Heath SW16 . . . .**182** B2
Oak Hill Rd KT6. . . . .**198** A3
Oak Hill Theological Coll
N14. . . . .**15** A5
Oak Hill Way NW3. . . . .**70** A4
Oak Ho
13 Cubitt Town E14. . . . . .**120** A4
11 Finchley N2. . . . .**30** B1
8 Maitland Pk NW3 . . . . . .**70** D2
Penge SE20 . . . .**184** B1
7 Richmond TW9 . . . .**132** D4
13 Sidcup DA15. . . . .**168** A1
9 Stoke Newington N16 . . .**73** B6
Teddington TW11 . . . .**175** C4
Wood Green N22 . . . .**32** A3
Oakhouse Rd DA6. . . . . . .**169** C6
Oak Hts Ind Sch 1 TW3 . .**129** D2
Oakhurst Ave
East Barnet EN4 . . . .**14** C4
Erith DA7 . . . .**147** A5
Oakhurst Cl
Chislehurst BR7 . . . .**188** B2
Snaresbrook E17 . . . .**54** C5
4 Teddington TW11. . . . . .**174** C5
Oakhurst Ct E17 . . . .**54** C5
Oakhurst Gdns
Chingford E4. . . . .**20** D3
Erith DA7 . . . .**147** A5
Snaresbrook E11, E17 . . . . .**54** C5
Oakhurst Gr SE22 . . . .**140** A1
Oakhurst Rd KT19. . . . . . .**215** B2
Oakington 14 KT1. . . . . . .**176** C1
Oakington Ave
Harrow HA2. . . . .**41** C2
Hayes UB3 . . . .**105** B2
Wembley HA9. . . . .**66** B5
Oakington Cl TW16 . . . . . .**172** C1
Oakington Ct 1 EN2. . . . . . .**4** D3
Oakington Dr TW16. . . . . .**172** C1
Oakington Manor Dr HA9 . .**66** C3
Oakington Manor Sch
HA9 . . . .**66** D3
Oakington Rd W9. . . . .**91** C3
Oakington Way N8. . . . .**50** A2
Oak La Finchley N2. . . . .**30** B1
Friern Barnet N11 . . . .**31** D4
Isleworth TW7 . . . .**130** C1
Limehouse E14. . . . .**119** B6
Twickenham TW1 . . . .**153** A4
Woodford IG8. . . . .**36** C6
Oakland Pl IG9 . . . .**21** A2
Oakland Rd E15. . . . .**76** C4
Oaklands Chislehurst BR7. .**189** B4
Croydon CR0. . . . .**220** D3
Ealing W13 . . . .**87** A2
Southgate N21. . . . .**16** B2
Twickenham TW2 . . . .**152** A4
Oaklands Ave Enfield N9 . . .**18** B5
Hounslow TW7 . . . .**130** D6
Sidcup DA15. . . . .**167** D4
Thames Ditton KT10. . . . . .**196** B1
Thornton Heath CR7. . . . . .**204** C5
West Wickham BR4 . . . . . .**223** D5
Oaklands Cl Bexley DA6 . .**169** B6
Chessington KT9 . . . .**213** C4
Orpington BR5 . . . .**211** C3
Oaklands Ct
Beckenham BR3 . . . .**186** A1
Dagenham NW10. . . . .**89** C6
Orpington BR6 . . . .**227** A6
5 Shepherd's Bush W12. . .**112** B5
Wembley HA0. . . . .**65** D3
Oaklands Dr TW2 . . . .**152** A4
Oaklands Gr W12. . . . .**112** A5
Oaklands Ho SE4 . . . .**141** B2
Oaklands Mews 1 NW2. . . .**68** D4
Oaklands Park Ave IG1. . . .**79** A6
Oaklands Pas NW2. . . . . . .**68** D4
Oaklands Pl 8 SW4. . . . . .**137** D1
Oaklands Prim Sch W7. . .**108** D4
Oaklands Rd Barnet N20 . . .**13** B4
Bexley DA6 . . . .**169** B6

Oaklands Rd continued
Bromley BR1. . . . .**186** C3
Cricklewood NW2. . . . .**68** D4
Ealing W7 . . . .**108** D4
Mortlake SW14 . . . .**133** B2
West Ealing W7, W13 . . . .**109** A4
Oaklands Sch
Hounslow TW5 . . . .**130** B2
Loughton IG10 . . . .**21** D6
Oaklands Sec Sch 31 E2. . .**96** B4
8 Surbiton KT6. . . . .**198** A3
Oaklands Way SM6 . . . . . .**219** D1
Oakland Way KT19 . . . . . .**215** C2
Oaklawn Ct HA7 . . . .**25** B4
Oakleafe Gdns IG6. . . . . . .**56** D6
Oaklea Pas KT1. . . . .**197** D6
Oakleigh Ave
East Barnet N20 . . . .**14** C3
Edgware HA8 . . . .**26** D2
Tolworth KT6. . . . .**214** D6
Oakleigh Cl N20 . . . .**14** D1
Oakleigh Cres N20. . . . .**14** C1
Oakleigh Ct
East Barnet EN4 . . . .**14** C5
Hendon HA8 . . . .**27** A1
7 Penge SE20. . . . .**184** B3
Southall UB1. . . . .**107** B5
Surbiton KT6. . . . .**214** B6
Oakleigh Gdns
Edgware HA8 . . . .**26** B5
Oakleigh Pk N20. . . . .**14** B3
Orpington BR6 . . . .**227** C4
Oakleigh Lodge IG3 . . . . . .**80** A5
Oakleigh Mews 2 N20. . . . .**14** A2
OAKLEIGH PARK. **14** B3
Oakleigh Park Ave BR7. . .**188** C2
Oakleigh Park Sta EN4 . . . .**14** C4
Oakleigh Pk N N20. . . . .**14** B3
Oakleigh Pk S N20 . . . .**14** C3
Oakleigh Rd
Hillingdon UB10 . . . .**61** A1
Pinner HA5. . . . .**23** B4
Oakleigh Rd N N20. . . . .**14** C2
Oakleigh Rd S N11 . . . .**31** A6
Oakleigh Sch N20. . . . .**14** D1
Oakleigh Way
Mitcham CR4 . . . .**181** D2
1 Tolworth KT6. . . . .**198** D1
Oakley Ave Barking IG11 . . .**79** D1
Ealing W5 . . . .**110** C6
Wallington CR0. . . . .**220** A4
Oakley Cl Chingford E4 . . . .**20** A1
Ealing W7 . . . .**108** C6
Hounslow TW7 . . . .**130** B4
7 Newham E6. . . . .**100** A1
Oakley Cres EC1. . . . .**234** D3
Oakley Ct Carshalton CR4 .**203** A2
Harlington UB7 . . . .**127** A5
Wembley HA0. . . . .**65** A4
Oakley Dr
Keston Mark BR2 . . . .**226** A5
Lewisham SE13 . . . .**164** B5
New Eltham SE9 . . . .**167** B3
Oakley Gdns
Chelsea SW3 . . . . .**136** C6 **267** B6
Hornsey Vale N8. . . . .**50** B4
Oakley Ho Chelsea SW1 . .**257** C4
Ealing W5 . . . .**110** C6
Oakley Pk DA5. . . . .**168** C4
Oakley Pl SE1. . . .**117** D1 **263** C1
Oakley Rd Croydon SE25. .**206** B4
De Beauvoir Town N1. . . . . .**73** B1
Harrow HA1. . . . .**42** C3
Keston Mark BR2 . . . .**226** A6
Oakley Sq NW1 . . .**93** C5 **232** B4
Oakley St SW3 . . .**136** C6 **267** A6
Oakley Wlk W6 . . . .**134** D6
Oak Lo 4 Ashford TW16. . .**171** D3
Southgate N21. . . . .**16** B5
10 Sutton SM1 . . . .**218** A4
Wanstead E11 . . . .**55** A2
6 Wembley HA0. . . . .**65** D3
Oak Lodge 14 SE21. . . . . .**161** B2
Oak Lodge Cl HA7. . . . .**25** C5
Oak Lodge Dr BR4 . . . . . .**207** D2
Oak Lodge Prim Sch
BR4. . . . .**207** D2
Oak Lodge Sch
Balham SW12. . . . .**159** A4
East Finchley N2. . . . .**48** A5
Oaklodge Way NW7. . . . . . .**27** D4
Oakman Ho 29 SW19. . . . .**156** D3
Oakmead HA5 . . . .**64** B5
Oakmead Ave BR2 . . . . . .**209** A3
Oakmead Ct HA7 . . . .**25** C6
Oakmeade HA5. . . . .**23** C4
Oakmead Gdns HA8. . . . . . .**27** B6
Oakmead Pl CR4 . . . .**180** C2
Oakmead Rd
Balham SW12. . . . .**159** B2
Wallington CR0. . . . .**203** D3
Oakmere Rd SE2 . . . .**146** A6
Oakmont Pl 6 BR6 . . . .**211** B1
Oak Park Gdns SW19. . . . .**156** D3
Oak Park Mews N16 . . . . . .**73** D5
Oak Rd Ealing W5. . . . .**109** D6
Kingston u T KT3. . . . .**177** B1
Oakridge Dr N2. . . . .**48** B6
Oakridge La BR1. . . . .**186** B5
Oakridge Rd BR1 . . . .**186** C6
Oak Rise IG9 . . . .**21** D1

Oak Row CR4 . . . .**181** C1
Oaks Ave Feltham TW13 . . .**151** A2
North Cheam KT4 . . . .**216** B4
West Norwood SE19. . . . . .**183** C5
Oaksford Ave SE26. . . . . .**162** B3
Oaks Gr E4 . . . .**20** C2
Oakshade Rd BR1. . . . . . .**186** B6
Oakshaw Rd SW18 . . . . . .**157** D4
Oakshott Ct NW1 . . . .**232** C2
Oaks La Ilford IG2 . . . .**57** C5
South Croydon CR0. . . . . .**222** C5
Oaks Park High Sch IG2. . .**57** C4
Oaks Rd CR0. . . . .**222** C4
Oaks Sh Ctr The W3. . . . .**111** A5
Oaks The
Brondesbury Pk NW6 . . . . .**68** D1
Chingford IG8. . . . .**36** C3
Enfield EN2. . . . .**4** D2
Finchley N12. . . . .**29** D6
Hayes UB4 . . . .**83** A5
Long Ditton KT6. . . . .**213** C5
Ruislip HA4. . . . .**39** C2
Southborough BR2 . . . . . .**210** C3
Wallington SM6 . . . .**219** C4
Willesden NW10. . . . .**68** B1
Wimbledon SW19. . . . . . .**179** A4
Woolwich SE18. . . . .**123** A1
Oaks Way Surbiton KT6. . .**197** D1
Wallington SM5 . . . .**218** D1
Oakthorpe Ct N13 . . . .**33** A5
Oakthorpe Prim Sch N13. .**33** A5
Oakthorpe Rd N13 . . . .**32** C5
Oaktree Ave N13. . . . .**16** D1
Oak Tree Ave N2 . . . .**47** D6
Oak Tree Cl Ealing W5 . . . . .**87** C1
Stanmore HA7 . . . .**25** C3
Oak Tree Ct Acton W3 . . . .**110** D6
8 Clapham Pk SW4. . . . . .**160** A6
Elstree WD6 . . . .**9** D5
Oak Tree Dell NW9 . . . .**45** B4
Oak Tree Dr N20 . . . .**13** D3
Oak Tree Gdns BR1. . . . . .**187** B5
Oaktree Gr IG1. . . . .**79** B3
Oak Tree Ho W9. . . . .**91** D3
Oak Tree Rd NW8 . . .**92** C4 **230** A1
Oaktree Sch EN4 . . . .**15** A5
Oaktrees Hostel HA8. . . . . .**11** A2
Oakview Gdns N2. . . . .**48** B5
Oakview Gr CR0. . . . .**207** A1
Oakview Lo NW11. . . . .**47** B2
Oakview Rd SE6 . . . .**185** D5
Oak Village NW5. . . . .**71** A4
Oakway Beckenham BR2 . .**186** B1
West Barnes SW20 . . . . . .**200** C5
Oak Way Croydon CR0. . . .**206** D3
East Acton W3 . . . .**111** C5
East Barnet N14. . . . .**15** B4
East Bedfont TW14. . . . . .**149** C3
Oakway Cl DA5 . . . .**169** A5
Oakways SE9 . . . .**166** D5
Oakwell Ho 24 SW8 . . . . .**137** D3
Oak Wlk CR4 . . . .**203** A1
OAKWOOD **15** D6
Oakwood Ave
Beckenham BR2, BR3. . . .**186** A1
Bromley BR2. . . . .**209** B6
Chessington KT9 . . . .**214** B1
Mitcham CR4 . . . .**180** B1
Osidge N14. . . . .**15** D4
Southall UB1. . . . .**107** C6
Oakwood Cl
Chislehurst West BR7. . . . .**188** C4
Lewisham SE13 . . . .**164** B5
Southgate N14 . . . .**15** C5
Oakwood Cres
Southgate N21. . . . .**16** B5
Wembley UB6. . . . .**65** B2
Oakwood Ct
Beckenham BR3 . . . .**186** A1
6 Chingford E4. . . . .**20** C4
Kensington W14. . . . .**113** B3 **254** C6
1 Newham E16. . . . .**100** A6
17 Sutton SM1 . . . .**218** A4
Oakwood Dr
Burnt Oak HA8 . . . .**27** A4
West Norwood SE19. . . . . .**183** C4
Oakwood Gdns Ilford IG3 . .**79** D6
Orpington BR6 . . . .**227** A6
Sutton SM1. . . . .**217** C6
Oakwood La
W14. . . . .**113** B3 **254** C6
Oakwood Park Rd N14 . . . .**16** A3
Oakwood Pl CR0. . . . .**204** C3
Oakwood Rd
Hampstead Garden Suburb
NW11. . . . .**47** A2
Orpington BR6 . . . .**227** A6
Pinner HA5. . . . .**22** B1
Thornton Heath CR0. . . . .**204** C3
Wimbledon SW20. . . . . . .**178** A2
Oakwood Sta N14. . . . .**15** C6
Oakwood View N14. . . . . . .**15** D4
Oakworth Rd W10 . . . .**90** D2
Oarsman Pl KT8. . . . .**196** C5
Oasis The 6 BR1. . . . .**187** C1
Oast Ct 8 E14. . . . .**119** B6
Oast Lo W4. . . . .**133** C5
Oates Cl BR2 . . . .**208** B6
Oatfield Ho 1 N15. . . . .**51** C3
Oatfield Rd BR6. . . . .**211** D1

Oat La EC2 . . . . . . 95 A1 242 B2
Oatland Rise E17 . . . . 35 A1
Oatlands Cl 3 SW19 . . . 156 D3
Oatlands Dr KT13 . . . . 193 C1
Oatlands Rd EN3 . . . . 6 C4
Oatwell Ho SW3 . . . . . . 257 B3
Oban Cl E13 . . . . 99 C3
Oban Ct HA8 . . . . 10 D2
Oban Ho 5 Barking IG11 . 101 B5
 South Bromley E14 . . . . 98 B1
Oban Rd Newham E13 . . . 99 C4
 South Norwood SE25 . . . 205 B5
Oban St E14 . . . . 98 B1
Oberon Ho 6 N1 . . . . . . 95 C5
Oberon Way TW17 . . . . 192 A6
Oberstein Rd 15 SW11 . 136 B1
Oborne Cl SE24 . . . . . . 160 D6
O'Brian Ho 10 E1 . . . . . 96 D4
Observatory Gdns W8. . . 245 B2
Observatory Mews E14.. 120 B2
Observatory Rd
 Kensington SW7. . . . . . 256 C5
 Mortlake SW14 . . . . . . 133 A1
Occupation La
 Brentford W5 . . . . 109 D2
 Shooters Hill SE18 . . . . 144 D4
Occupation Rd
 Newington SE17. . 117 A1 262 A2
 West Ealing W13 . . . . . 109 B4
Ocean St E1 . . . . 96 D2
Ocean Wharf E14 . . . . . 119 C4
Ochre Ct TW13 . . . . . . 149 D1
Ockbrook 3 E1 . . . . 96 C2
Ockendon Rd N1 . . . . . . 73 B2
Ockham Dr BR5 . . . . . . 190 A3
 Greenford UB6. . . . . . . 64 B1
Ockley Ct Sidcup DA14 . . 167 C1
 Sutton SM1. . . . . 218 A4
Ockley Ho 8 KT2 . . . . . 176 D4
Ockley Rd
 Streatham SW16 . . . . . 160 A1
 Thornton Heath CR0. . . . 204 B2
Octagon Arc EC2. . . . . . 243 A3
Octagon The NW3. . . . . 69 C4
Octavia Cl CR4. . . . . . . 202 C4
Octavia Ho Catford SE6 . 163 D4
 Kensal Town W10 . . . . . 91 A3
Octavia Mews 1 W9 . . . 91 B3
Octavia Rd TW7 . . . . . . 130 D2
Octavia St SW11 . . 136 C4 267 B1
Octavia Way 12 SE28 . . . 124 B6
Octavius St SE8 . . . . . . 141 C5
October Ct BR2 . . . . . . 208 D6
October Pl NW4 . . . . . . 46 D6
Odard Rd KT8 . . . . 195 C5
Odell Cl IG11 . . . . 79 D1
Odell Wlk SE13 . . . . . . 142 A2
Odeon Ct Dagenham NW10.. 89 C6
 1 Newham E16 . . . . . . 99 A2
Odeon Par Eltham SE9 . . 144 A1
 Wembley HA9. . . . . . . 65 B2
Odeon The IG11 . . . . . . 79 B1
Odessa Inf Sch E7 . . . . 77 A3
Odessa Rd Leyton E7. . . . 76 D4
 Willesden Green NW10 . . 90 A5
Odessa St SE16 . . . . . . 119 B3
Odette Ct N20 . . . . 14 A1
Odette Duval Ho 20 E1 . . 96 C2
Odette Ho 6 SE27 . . . . 183 B6
Odger St SW11 . . . . . . 136 D3
Odhams Wlk WC2. . . . . . 240 B1
Odin Ho 8 SE5 . . . . . . 139 A3
O'Donnell Ct WC1. . . . . . 240 B6
O'Driscoll Ho 4 W12 . . . 90 B1
Odyssey Bsns Pk HA4 . . . 62 B3
Offa's Mead E9 . . . . . . 75 A4
Offenbach Ho 12 E2. . . . 96 D5
Offenham Rd BR7, SE9. . . 188 B6
Offers Ct KT1. . . . . 198 B6
Offham Ho SE17 . . . . . . 263 A3
Offham Slope N12 . . . . . 29 B5
Offley Ho 10 E9 . . . . . . 74 D2
Offley Pl TW7 . . . . 130 B3
Offley Rd SW9 . . . . 138 C5
Offord Cl N17. . . . . 34 A4
Offord Rd N1. . . . . 72 B1
Offord St N1. . . . . 72 B1
Ogden Ho TW13 . . . . . . 173 A6
Ogilby St SE18 . . . . . . 122 B2
Ogilvie Ho 12 E1 . . . . . 96 D1
Oglander Rd SE15 . . . . . 139 D2
Ogle St W1. . . . . . 93 C2 239 A4
Oglethorpe Rd RM10. . . . 81 C5
O'Gorman Ho SW10. . . . . 266 B4
O'Grady Ct 17 W13 . . . 109 A5
O'Grady Ho 17 E17 . . . . 53 D6
Ohio Bldg 13 SE13 . . . . 141 D4
Ohio Rd E13 . . . . 98 D3
Oil Mill La W6 . . . . 112 A1
Okeburn Rd SW17 . . . . . 181 A5
Okehampton Cl N12 . . . . 30 B5
Okehampton Cres DA16 .. 136 C4
Okehampton Rd NW10. . . 90 D6
Okeover Manor SW4. . . . 137 B1
Olaf Palme Ho TW13 . . . 150 B1
Olaf St W11. . . . . 112 D6
Old Bailey EC4. . . . 94 D1 241 D1
Old Bailey (Central Criminal
 Court)★ EC4. . . . . 94 D1 241 D2

Old Barn Cl SM2 . . . . . . 217 A1
Old Barrack Yd SW1. . . . 248 A1
Old Barrowfield 7 E15. . . 98 C6
Old Bellgate Wharf E14 . 119 C3
Oldberry Rd HA4. . . . . . 62 B2
Old Bethnal Green Rd E2.. 96 B4
OLD BEXLEY 169 D4
Old Bexley Bsns Pk DA5 . 169 D4
Old Bexley CE Prim Sch
 DA5. . . . . 169 B3
Old Billingsgate Wlk
 EC3 . . . . 253 A5
Old Bldgs WC2. . . . . . . 241 A4
Old Bond St W1. . 115 C6 249 A5
Oldborough Rd HA0. . . . . 65 C5
Old Brewery Mews NW3.. 70 B4
Old Bridge Cl UB5. . . . . 85 C5
Old Bridge St KT1. . . . . 175 D1
Old Broad St EC2 . . 95 B1 242 C1
Old Bromley Rd BR1. . . . 186 B5
Old Brompton Rd SW5,
 SW7. . . . . 114 A2 256 B3
Old Burlington St
 W1. . . . . 115 C6 249 A5
Oldbury Ct E9 . . . . 75 A3
Oldbury Pl W1. . . . 93 A2 238 B4
Oldbury Rd EN1. . . . . . . 6 A3
Old Castle St E1 . . 95 D1 243 D2
Old Cavendish St W1. . . . 238 C1
Old Change Ct EC4. . . . . 242 A1
Old Chapel Pl 2 N10. . . . 49 B6
Old Charlton Rd TW17. . . 193 A4
Old Chiswick Yd W4. . . . 133 C6
Old Church Ct N11. . . . . 31 B5
Old Church La Ealing UB6.. 87 A4
 Stanmore HA7. . . . . . . 25 C4
 Welsh Harp NW9 . . . . . 67 B6
Old Church Path KT10. . . 212 A4
Old Church Rd
 Chingford E4. . . . . 19 C1
 Stepney E1. . . . . 96 D1
Old Church St SW3. . . . . 256 C1
Old Claygate La KT10. . . 213 A3
Old Clem Sq 12 SE18 . . . 144 C6
Old College Ct DA17 . . . 125 D1
Old Compton St
 W1. . . . . 93 D1 239 C1
Old Cople La SE26 . . . . . 184 A5
Old Cote Dr TW5 . . . . . 129 C6
Old Court (Mus & Liby)★
 HA0 . . . . 65 C3
Old Court Pl W8 . . 113 D4 245 C1
Old Covent Gdn★
 WC2. . . . . 116 A6 250 B6
Old Ctyd The BR1 . . . . . 187 B2
Old Cty H★ SE1. . . . . . 250 C2
Old Dairy Mews
 5 Balham SW12. . . . . . 159 A3
 4 Camden Town NW5. . . . 71 B2
Old Dairy Sq The N21. . . . 16 C4
Old Deer Park Gdns
 TW9. . . . . 132 A2
Old Devonshire Rd
 SW12. . . . . 159 B4
Old Dock Cl TW9. . . . . . 132 C6
Old Dover Rd SE3 . . . . . 143 B5
Oldegate Ho 11 E6 . . . . 99 D6
Old Farm Ave Osidge N14 . 15 C4
 Sidcup DA15. . . . . 167 C2
Old Farm Cl TW4. . . . . . 129 B1
Old Farm Ct UB2. . . . . . 107 D2
Old Farm Rd
 Hampton TW12. . . . . . 173 C4
 London N2 . . . . 30 B2
Old Farm Rd E DA15. . . . 168 A2
Old Farm Rd W DA15. . . . 167 D2
Oldfield Cl Bromley BR1. . 210 B5
 Greenford UB6. . . . . . . 64 C2
 Stanmore HA7. . . . . . . 25 A5
Oldfield Farm Gdns UB6.. 86 B6
Oldfield Gr SE16 . . . . . . 118 D2
Oldfield Ho
 14 Chiswick W4. . . . . . 111 C1
 Streatham SW16 . . . . . 181 B6
Oldfield House Specl Sch
 TW12. . . . . 173 B2
Oldfield La N UB6. . . . . . 64 B1
Oldfield La S UB6. . . . . . 86 A4
Oldfield Mews N6 . . . . . 49 C2
Oldfield Prim Sch UB6. . . 86 B5
Oldfield Rd
 Bedford Pk W3, W12. . . . 111 D4
 Bexleyheath DA7. . . . . . 147 A3
 Bromley BR1. . . . . 210 B5
 Hampton TW12. . . . . . 173 B2
 Stoke Newington N16. . . 73 C5
 Willesden NW10. . . . . . 67 D1
 Wimbledon SW19. . . . . 179 A4
Oldfields Cir UB5. . . . . . 64 A2
Oldfields Rd SM1, SM3.. 217 C6
Oldfields Trad Est SM1 . 217 C5
Old Fire Station The
 SE18. . . . . 144 D5
Old Fish St Hill EC4 . . . . 252 A6
Old Fleet La EC4 . . . . . . 241 C2
Old Fold Cl EN5. . . . . . . 1 B4
Old Fold La EN5. . . . . . . 1 B4
OLD FORD 97 B6
Old Ford Ho CR0. . . . . . 220 A5

Old Ford Prim Sch 38 E3 . 97 B5
Old Ford Rd E2, E3. . . . . 96 D5
Old Ford Trad Est E3 . . . . 97 C6
Old Forge Cl HA7 . . . . . . 25 A6
Old Forge Cres TW17. . . 192 D3
Old Forge Mews W12 . . . 112 B4
Old Forge Rd Enfield EN1. . 5 D5
 Upper Holloway N19 . . . . 71 D6
Old Forge Way DA14 . . . 190 B6
Old Gloucester St
 WC1. . . . . 94 A2 240 B4
Old Hall Cl HA5. . . . . . . 23 A2
Old Hall Dr HA5. . . . . . . 23 A2
Oldham Ho 10 SE21 . . . . 183 C6
Oldham Terr W3 . . . . . . 111 A5
Old Hatch Manor HA4. . . 40 A2
Old Hill Chislehurst BR7. . 188 C2
 Orpington BR6. . . . . . . 227 C2
Oldhill St N16 . . . . 52 A1
Old Homesdale Rd BR2. . 209 C5
Old Hospital Cl SW12,
 SW17. . . . . 158 D3
Old Ho The BR7. . . . . . . 189 B2
Old House Gdns 9 TW1. . 153 C5
Old Howlett's La HA4 . . . 39 B3
Olding Ho 6 SW12. . . . . 159 C4
Old Jamaica Bsns Est 23
 SE16. . . . . 118 A3
Old Jamaica Rd SE16. . . 118 A3
Old James St SE15. . . . . 140 B2
Old Jewry EC2. . . 95 B1 242 C1
Old Kenton La NW9. . . . . 44 D4
Old Kent Rd
 Deptford SE1, SE15. . . . 140 B6
 Walworth SE1. . . . 117 C1 263 B2
Old Kingston Rd KT4. . . . 215 A5
Old Laundry The 14
 SW18. . . . . 136 B1
Old Lodge Pl 7 TW1. . . . 153 B5
Old Lodge Way HA7. . . . . 25 A5
Old London Rd KT2. . . . . 176 A1
Old Maidstone Rd BR8,
 DA14. . . . . 191 B3
OLD MALDEN. 199 C1
Old Malden La KT4. . . . . 215 C6
Oldman Ct SE12 . . . . . . 165 B2
Old Manor Ct NW8. . . . . 229 B4
Old Manor Dr TW7 . . . . . 152 A5
Old Manor House Mews
 TW17. . . . . 192 C6
Old Manor Rd UB2. . . . . 106 D2
Old Manor Way BR7, SE9. 188 B5
Old Manor Yd SW5. . . . . 255 C3
Old Market Ct SM1. . . . . 217 D4
Old Market Sq 11 E2. . . . 95 D4
Old Marylebone Rd
 NW1. . . . . 92 C2 237 B3
Oldmead Ho 8 RM10. . . . 81 D2
Old Mill Ct E18 . . . . 55 C6
Old Mill Rd SE18 . . . . . 145 B6
Old Mitre Ct EC4. . . . . . 241 B1
Old Montague St E1 . . . . 96 B2
Old Nichol St E2 . . 95 D3 243 C6
Old North St WC1 . . . . . 240 C4
Old Nursery Pl TW15 . . . 170 D5
OLD OAK COMMON 89 D3
Old Oak Common La
 NW10. . . . . 89 C3
Old Oak La NW10 . . . . . 89 D4
Old Oak Prim Sch W12. . 89 D1
Old Oak Rd W3. . . . . . . 111 D6
Old Orch TW16. . . . . . . 172 C1
Old Orchard Cl
 Hadley Wood EN4 . . . . . 2 B5
 Hillingdon UB8. . . . . . . 82 C1
Old Orch The NW3. . . . . 70 D4
Old Palace La TW9. . . . . 153 C6
Old Palace of John Whitgift
 Sch (Juniors) CR2. . . . 221 D3
Old Palace of John Whitgift
 Sch (Seniors) 11 CR9 . 220 D5
Old Palace Prim Sch 51
 E3. . . . . 97 D4
Old Palace Rd CR0. . . . . 221 A5
Old Palace Terr 8 TW9. . 153 C6
Old Palace Yd 7 TW9 . . 153 D6
Old Paradise St
 SE11. . . . . 116 B2 260 C4
Old Park Ave
 Balham SW12. . . . . . . 159 A5
 Enfield EN2. . . . . 5 A1
Old Park Gr EN2 . . . . . . 5 A1
Old Park Ho N13. . . . . . 32 B6
Old Park La W1. . . 115 D5 248 C5
Old Park Mews TW5. . . . 129 B5
Old Park Rd Enfield EN2. . 4 D2
 Palmers Green N13 . . . . 32 B6
 Plumstead Comm SE2 . . 124 A1
Old Park Rd S EN2. . . . . 4 D1
Old Park Ridings N21. . . . 17 A6
Old Park View EN2 . . . . . 4 A2
Old Pearson St SE10 . . . 141 D5
Old Perry St BR7. . . . . . 189 C3
Old Post Office La SE3. . 143 B2
Old Pound Ct TW7 . . . . . 131 A4
Old Priory UB9. . . . . . . 38 D2
Old Pye St SW1. . . . . . . 259 C6
Old Pye Street Est SW1.. 259 C5
Old Quebec St W1. . . . . 237 D1

Old Queen St
 SW1. . . . . 115 D4 249 D1
Old Rd Enfield EN3. . . . . 6 C4
 Lewisham SE13 . . . . . . 142 C1
Old Rectory Gdns HA8 . . 26 C4
Old Redding HA3 . . . . . . 24 A6
Oldridge Rd SW12. . . . . 159 B4
Old Royal Free Pl N1 . . . 234 B5
Old Royal Free Sq
 N1. . . . . 94 C6 234 B5
Old St Andrews Mans
 NW9. . . . . 67 B6
Old School Cl
 3 Beckenham BR3. . . . . 185 A1
 Merton SW19 . . . . 179 C1
Old School Cres E7 . . . . 77 A2
Old School Ct 6 N17. . . . 51 D6
Old School Ho CR4. . . . . 202 C6
Old School Ho The EN2.. 4 D2
Old School Pl CR0 . . . . . 220 C4
Old School Sq UB8. . . . . 82 B3
Old School Sq
 12 Poplar E14. . . . . . . 97 C1
 Thames Ditton KT7. . . . 196 D3
Old School The
 Bloomsbury WC1 . . . . . 240 D4
 Merton SW19 . . . . 179 C1
Old Seacoal La EC4. . . . 241 C1
Old South Cl HA5 . . . . . 22 D2
Old South Lambeth Rd
 SW8. . . . . 138 A3 270 B4
Old Spitalfields Mkt★
 E1. . . . . 95 D2 243 D4
Old Sq WC2. . . . . 241 A2
Old St
 Broadgate EC1. . . 95 B3 242 D6
 Newham E13 . . . . 99 C4
Old Stable Mews N5. . . . 73 A5
Old Station Rd UB3 . . . . 105 D3
Old Station Yard The 11
 E17. . . . . 54 A5
Oldstead Rd BR1. . . . . . 186 B6
Old Street Sta
 EC1. . . . . 95 B3 242 D6
Old Studio Cl CR0. . . . . 205 B2
Old Sun Wharf E14. . . . . 119 A6
Old Swan Wharf SW11. . 266 C2
Old Swan Yd SM5 . . . . . 218 D4
Old Theatre Ct SE1. . . . . 252 B4
Old Town Clapham SW4. . 137 C2
 Croydon CR0. . . . . 220 D5
Old Tramyard SE18. . . . . 123 C2
Old Twelve Cl W7 . . . . . 86 C3
Old Vicarage Sch 13
 TW10. . . . . 154 A5
Old Vicarage The CR4. . . 202 C6
Old Woolwich Rd SE10. . 120 B1
Old York Rd SW18. . . . . 157 D6
Oleander Cl BR6. . . . . . 227 B3
O'Leary Sq E1 . . . . 96 C2
Oleaster Ct IG5. . . . . . . 56 A6
Olga Prim Sch 87 E3 . . . 97 A5
Olga St 20 E3. . . . . 97 A5
Olinda Rd N16. . . . . 51 D3
Oliphant St W10. . . . . . 91 A4
Olive Blythe Ho 12 W10.. 91 A3
Oliver Ave SE25. . . . . . . 205 D6
Oliver Cl W4. . . . . 132 D6
Oliver Ct Isleworth TW7 . 130 D2
 2 Penge SE26. . . . . . . 184 C4
 Plumstead SE18. . . . . . 123 A2
Olive Rd Cricklewood NW2 . 68 C4
 Ealing W5. . . . . 109 A3
 3 Merton SW19. . . . . . 180 A3
 Newham E13. . . . . 99 C4
Oliver Gdns E6 . . . . 100 A1
Oliver Goldsmith Prim Sch
 18 Camberwell SE5 . . . 139 C4
 Kingsbury NW9 . . . . . . 45 B4
Oliver Gr SE25 . . . . 205 D5
Oliver Ho
 22 Bermondsey SE16. . . 118 A4
 Notting Hill W11 . . . . . 244 A5
 South Lambeth SW8. . . . 270 A4
Oliver House Prep Sch 1
 SW4. . . . . 159 B5
Oliver Mews SE15. . . . . . 140 A3
Oliver Rd
 Kingston u T KT3 . . . . . 177 A1
 Leyton E10 . . . . 75 D5
 Sutton SM1. . . . . 218 B4
Oliver's Yd EC1. . . . . . . 242 D6
Olive Tree Ho
 7 Deptford SE15. . . . . . 140 C6
 Stroud Green N4. . . . . . 50 C4
Olive Tree Sch The
 SE13. . . . . 163 D5
Olivette St 1 SW15. . . . 134 D1
Olive Waite Ho NW6 . . . . 69 D1
Olivia Ct 1 EN5. . . . . . . 1 B1
Ollard's Gr IG10 . . . . . . 21 B6
Ollerton Gn E3. . . . . . . 97 B6
Ollerton Rd N11 . . . . . . 31 D5
Olley Cl SM6. . . . . 220 A2
Ollgar Cl W12 . . . . 111 D5
Olliffe St E14. . . . . 120 A3
Olmar St SE1 . . . . 140 A6

Olney Ho NW8 . . . . 237 B6
Olney Rd SE17 . . . . 139 A6
Olron Cres DA6 . . . . . . 169 A6
Olven Rd SE18 . . . . 145 A6
Olveston Wlk SM5 . . . . . 202 B3
Olwen Mews HA5 . . . . . 22 D1
Olyffe Ave DA16. . . . . . 146 A3
Olyffe Dr BR3. . . . . 186 A2
Olympia Ex Ctr★
 W14. . . . . 113 A3 254 B5
Olympia Ind Est N22 . . . 50 B6
Olympian Ct 8 E14 . . . . 119 C2
Olympia Way
 W14. . . . . 113 A3 254 B5
Olympia Yd W2 . . . . . . 245 D5
Olympic Ho 10 W10 . . . . 90 C1
Olympic Ret Pk HA9. . . . 66 D4
Olympic Way
 Greenford UB6. . . . . . . 85 D6
 Wembley HA9. . . . . . . 66 C4
Olympus Gr N22. . . . . . 32 C2
Olympus Sq E5 . . . . . . 74 A5
Oman Ave NW2 . . . . . . 68 C4
Oman Ct NW4 . . . . 68 B4
Ombersley Ho N4. . . . . . 51 A2
Omeara St SE1 . . . . 252 B3
Omega Cl E14 . . . . 119 C3
Omega Ho SW10. . . . . . 266 B4
Omega Pl N1. . . . . 233 B3
Omega St SE14 . . . . . . 141 C4
Omega Works E3. . . . . . 75 C1
Ommaney Rd SE14. . . . . 141 A4
Omnibus Bsns Ctr N7 . . 72 A3
Omnibus Way E17. . . . . 35 C1
Ondine Rd SE15. . . . . . 139 D1
Onedin Point 10 E1 . . . . 118 A6
Onega Gate SE16 . . . . . 119 A3
O'Neill Ho NW8 . . . . . . 229 D3
O'Neill Path 11 SE18. . . . 144 C6
One Tree Cl SE23 . . . . . 162 C5
Ongar Cl RM6. . . . . 58 C4
Ongar Ho 15 N1. . . . . . 73 B2
Ongar Rd SW6. . . . 135 C6 265 B6
Onra Rd E17. . . . . 53 C2
Onslow Ave TW10. . . . . 154 A6
Onslow Avenue Mans 10
 TW10. . . . . 154 A6
Onslow Cl Chingford E4. . . 20 B2
 Notting Hill W9 . . . . . . 91 B4
 Thames Ditton KT7. . . . 196 C1
Onslow Cres BR7 . . . . . 188 D2
Onslow Ct SW10 . . . . . . 256 B1
Onslow Dr DA14 . . . . . . 168 D2
Onslow Gdns
 Chelsea SW7 . . . 114 B1 256 C2
 Cranley Gdns N10. . . . . 49 B4
 Southgate N21 . . . . . . 16 C6
 Thames Ditton KT7. . . . 196 C1
 Wallington SM6 . . . . . . 219 C1
 Wanstead E18 . . . . . . 55 C6
Onslow Ho 1 KT2 . . . . . 176 B2
Onslow Lo 28 SW2 . . . . 160 C4
Onslow Mews E SW7 . . . 256 C3
Onslow Mews W SW7 . . 256 C3
Onslow Par N14 . . . . . . 15 B3
Onslow Rd
 Richmond TW10 . . . . . . 154 A5
 Thornton Heath CR0. . . . 204 C1
 West Barnes KT3. . . . . . 200 A5
Onslow Sq SW7 . . 114 B2 256 D3
Onslow St EC1. . . . . . . 241 B5
Onslow Way KT7 . . . . . . 196 C1
Ontario St SE1 . . . 116 D3 261 D6
Ontario Way E14 . . . . . . 119 C6
Onyx Ct N11. . . . . 31 D3
Onyx Ho KT4. . . . . 199 B1
Onyx Mews 4 E15 . . . . . 76 D2
Opal Cl E16 . . . . 99 D1
Opal Ct N11. . . . . 31 D3
Opal Ho KT4 . . . . 199 B1
Opal Mews 2 IG1 . . . . . 78 D6
Opal St SE11. . . . 116 D2 261 C2
Open Air Theatre, Regent's
 Pk★ NW1 . . . . 231 A1
Openshaw Rd SE2 . . . . . 124 B2
Openview SW17, SW18.. 158 B2
Opera Ct 7 N19 . . . . . . 71 D5
Operating Theatre Mus &
 Herb Garret The★
 SE1. . . . . 117 B5 252 D3
Ophelia Gdns NW2. . . . . 69 A5
Ophir Terr SE15 . . . . . . 140 A4
Opie Ho NW8 . . . . 230 B4
Opossum Way TW4. . . . . 128 C2
Oppenheim Rd SE13 . . . 142 A3
Oppidan Apartments
 NW6. . . . . 69 C2
Oppidans Rd NW3 . . . . . 70 D1
Opus Studios E13. . . . . . 99 A5
Orange Gr E11. . . . . 76 C5
Orange Hill Rd HA8 . . . . 27 A3
Orange Pl SE16 . . . . . . 118 C3
Orangery Gallery The★
 W8. . . . . 113 B4 244 C1
Orangery La SE9. . . . . . 166 B6
Orangery The TW10. . . . 153 C2
Orange Sq SW1. . . . . . . 258 C3
Orange St WC2 . . 115 D6 249 D5

Orange Yd WC2 . . . . **239** D1
Oransay Rd **25** N1 . . . . .73 A2
Oratory La SW3 . . . . **256** D2
Oratory RC Prim Sch
  SW3 . . . . 114 C1 **257** A2
Orbain Rd SW6 . .135 A5 **264** B3
Orbel St SW11 . . . .136 C4 **267** A1
Orb St SE17 . . . . . .117 B2 **262** C3
Orchard Ave
  Ashford TW15. . . . . .171 A4
  Carshalton CR4. . . . . . . .203 A1
  Croydon CR0. . . . . .207 A1
  East Finchley N3. . . . . . . .47 C6
  Erith DA17 . . . . .147 B6
  Hatton TW14. . . . . .149 B6
  Heston TW5. . . . . .129 A5
  Hinchley Wood KT7. . . . .213 A6
  Kingston u T KT3. . . . . . .199 C6
  Osidge N14. . . . . .15 C4
  Southall UB1. . . . . .107 B5
  Whetstone N20. . . . . .14 B2
Orchard Bsns Ctr SE26 . .185 B5
Orchard Cl Ashford TW15 . .171 A4
  Bexleyheath DA7. . . . . . .147 A4
  Bushey WD23. . . . . .8 B3
  Chingford E4. . . . . .35 C6
  Dollis Hill NW2. . . . . .68 A5
  Edgware HA8. . . . . .26 A4
  Honor Oak SE23 . . . . . . .162 C5
  21 Islington N1. . . . . .73 A1
  Kensal Town W10 . . . . . . .91 A2
  Northolt UB5 . . . . .64 A2
  Ruislip HA4. . . . . .39 A2
  Thames Ditton KT7. . . . .197 B2
  Walton-on-T KT12 . . . . .194 B2
  Wanstead E11 . . . . .55 B5
  Wembley HA0. . . . . .88 A6
  West Barnes SW20 . . . . .200 C5
  West Ewell KT19. . . . . . .214 D2
Orchard Cotts
  Chislehurst BR7. . . . . . . .189 C4
  Hayes UB3 . . . . .105 C4
Orchard Cres
  Edgware HA8 . . . . .27 A5
  Enfield EN1. . . . . .5 D4
Orchard Ct Barnes SW13 . .133 D2
  Barnet EN5 . . . . .1 D2
  Croydon BR3. . . . . .207 C1
  Edgware HA8 . . . . .26 B5
  Hounslow TW7. . . . . . . .130 B5
  Marylebone W1 . . . . **238** A2
  New Malden KT4 . . . . . . .200 A1
  Penge SE26 . . . . .184 D5
  Southgate N14. . . . . .15 C5
  Wallington SM6 . . . . . . .219 B3
  Walthamstow E10 . . . . . . .53 D1
  1 Walton-on-T KT12. . . .193 D1
  Wood Green N22 . . . . .32 A3
Orchard Dr
  Blackheath Vale SE3. . . . .142 C3
  Edgware HA8 . . . . .26 B5
  Upper Halliford TW17. . . .193 C6
Orchard Gate
  Colindale NW9 . . . . .45 C5
  Thames Ditton KT10. . . . .196 B1
  Wembley UB6. . . . . .65 B2
Orchard Gdns
  Chessington KT9 . . . . . . .214 A4
  Sutton SM1. . . . . .217 C3
Orchard Gn Bromley BR1 . .187 C2
  Orpington BR6 . . . . .227 C6
Orchard Gr BR6. . . . . . . .227 D6
  Croydon CR0. . . . . .207 A2
  Edgware HA8 . . . . .26 D2
  Harrow HA3 . . . . .44 B4
  Orpington BR6 . . . . .211 D1
  Penge SE20 . . . . .184 A3
Orchard Hill SE13 . . . . . .141 D4
Orchard Hill Coll **18**
  SM6 . . . . .219 B2
Orchard Ho
  Camberwell SE5 . . . . . . .139 A4
  11 Rotherhithe SE16. . . . .118 C3
  Shepherd's Bush W12 . . . .112 A5
Orchard House Sch **15**
  W4 . . . . .111 C2
Orchard La
  Thames Ditton KT8. . . . .196 B3
  Wimbledon SW20. . . . . .178 B2
  Woodford IG8. . . . . .37 C6
Orchardleigh Ave EN3. . . . .6 C3
Orchard Lo N12. . . . . .14 A1
Orchard Mead Ho NW11. . .69 C6
Orchardmede N21. . . . . . .17 B5
Orchard Mews N1 . . . . . . .73 B1
Orchard Pl
  Canning Town E14 . . . . . .120 C6
  Tottenham N17. . . . . .33 D3
Orchard Prim Sch DA14. .190 B5
  41 London E9 . . . . .74 C1
Orchard Prim Sch The
  TW3 . . . . .151 C6
Orchard Rd Barnet EN5 . . . .1 B1
  Belvedere DA17. . . . . . . .125 C2
  Brentford TW8. . . . . .131 C6
  Bromley BR1. . . . . .187 C2
  Carshalton CR4. . . . . . . .203 A1

Orchard Rd continued
  Chessington KT9 . . . . . . .214 A4
  Dagenham RM10 . . . . . . .103 C6
  Enfield EN3. . . . . .18 C6
  Farnborough BR6. . . . . . .226 D3
  Feltham TW14 . . . . .150 A3
  Hampton TW12. . . . . . . .173 B3
  Hayes UB3 . . . . .106 A6
  Highgate N6. . . . . .49 B2
  Hounslow TW4 . . . . .151 C6
  Isleworth TW1 . . . . .153 B6
  Kingston u T KT1. . . . . . .176 A1
  Richmond TW9 . . . . .132 C2
  Sidcup DA14. . . . . .189 C6
  Sunbury TW16 . . . . .172 B3
  Sutton SM1. . . . . .217 C4
  Welling DA16 . . . . .146 B2
Orchard Rise
  Croydon CR0. . . . . .207 B1
  Kingston u T KT2. . . . . . .177 A2
  Mortlake TW10. . . . . . . .132 D1
  Pinner HA5. . . . . .39 D6
Orchard Rise E DA15 . . . . .167 D6
Orchard Rise W DA15 . . . . .167 C6
Orchard Sch HA3 . . . . .44 B4
Orchard Sch The KT8. . . . .196 B5
Orchardson Ho NW8 . . . . **236** D5
Orchardson St
  NW8 . . . . .92 B3 **236** D5
Orchard Sq W14 . . . . **254** C1
  Marylebone W1 . . . . **238** B2
  Walthamstow E17 . . . . . . .53 A5
Orchard Terr EN1 . . . . .18 A5
Orchard The
  Acton Green W4 . . . . . . .111 B2
  Ealing W5. . . . . .87 D2
  East Barnet N14. . . . . . . .15 B6
  Edgware HA8 . . . . .26 C5
  Enfield N21. . . . . .17 B5
  Ewell KT17 . . . . .215 D1
  Hampstead Garden Suburb
  NW11. . . . . .47 C4
  Hounslow TW3 . . . . .130 A3
  Lewisham SE3 . . . . .142 B3
  Totteridge N20. . . . . .13 D3
Orchard Villas BR7. . . . . . .189 C6
Orchard Way
  Ashford TW15. . . . . .148 B2
  Croydon BR3, CR0. . . . . .207 A3
  Enfield EN1. . . . . .5 C2
  Esher KT10. . . . . .212 A2
  Sutton SM1. . . . . .218 B4
Orchard Way Prim Sch
  CR0. . . . . .207 A2
Orchestra Ct HA8 . . . . .26 D3
Orchid Cl
  Chessington KT9 . . . . . . .213 C1
  Lewisham SE13 . . . . .164 B6
  1 Newham E6. . . . . .100 A2
  Southall UB1. . . . . .85 A1
Orchid Ct Catford BR1. . . . .164 B1
  Harrow HA3 . . . . .24 C2
  Wembley HA9. . . . . .66 A6
Orchid Gdns TW3 . . . . . . .129 B1
Orchid Grange N14 . . . . . . .15 C4
Orchid Lo N14. . . . . .15 C4
Orchid Rd N14. . . . . .15 C4
Orchid St W12. . . . . .112 A6
Orch Sch The **16** SW2 . . . .160 B3
Orde **6** NW9 . . . . .27 D2
Orde Hall St WC1 . . .94 B2 **240** C4
Orde Ho **10** N16. . . . . .73 B4
Ordell Ct **36** E3 . . . . .97 B5
Ordell Rd E3. . . . . .97 B5
Ordnance Ct TW13 . . . . . . .150 A2
Ordnance Cres SE10 . . . . . .120 C4
Ordnance Hill
  NW8 . . . . .92 B6 **229** D5
Ordnance Mews NW8 . . . . **229** D4
Ordnance Rd
  Canning Town E16 . . . . . . .98 D2
  Enfield EN3. . . . . .7 B6
  Shooters Hill SE18 . . . . . .144 C6
Oregano Cl UB7 . . . . .104 B6
Oregano Dr E14 . . . . .98 B1
Oregon Ave E12 . . . . .78 A4
Oregon Bldg **5** SE13. . . . . .141 D4
Oregon Cl KT3. . . . . .199 A5
Oregon Sq BR6 . . . . .211 B1
Orestes Ct **9** E18. . . . . . . .55 A6
Orestes Mews **11** NW6 . . . .69 C3
Orford Ct Stanmore HA7. . . .25 C4
  Wallington SM6 . . . . .219 C3
  West Norwood SE27. . . . .160 D2
Orford Gdns TW1 . . . . . . .152 D2
Orford Rd Catford SE6. . . . .163 D1
  Walthamstow E17 . . . . . . .53 D4
  Wanstead E18 . . . . .55 B6
Organ Crossroads KT17 . .216 A1
Oriana Ct CR0 . . . . .221 B1
Oriana Ho **3** E14 . . . . .119 B6
Oriel Cl CR4 . . . . .203 D6
Oriel Ct **6** Croydon CR0 . . .205 B1
  Hampstead NW3 . . . . .70 A4
Oriel Dr SW13 . . . . .134 C6
Oriel Gdns IG5 . . . . .56 B6
Oriel Prim Sch TW13. . . . . .151 A1
Oriel Rd Hackney E9 . . . . . . .75 A2
  Homerton E9 . . . . .75 A2

Oriel Way UB5 . . . . .63 D1
Oriental Rd E16. . . . . .121 D5
Orient Ind Pk E10. . . . . . . .75 C6
Orient St SE11 . . . . 116 D2 **261** C4
Orient Way Lea Bridge E5 . . .74 D5
  Leyton E10 . . . . .75 B6
Oriole Way SE28 . . . . .124 B6
Orion Bsns Ctr SE14. . . . . .118 D1
Orion Ct **10** HA8. . . . . .26 D5
  Orion Ctr The CR0. . . . . .220 A6
Orion Ho **20** E1 . . . . .96 B3
Orion Mews SM4 . . . . . . .201 C5
Orion Point **5** E14. . . . . . .119 C2
Orion Prim Sch The NW9 . .27 C3
Orion Rd N11. . . . . .31 A4
Orion Way HA6 . . . . .22 A6
Orissa Rd SE18 . . . . .123 C1
Orkney Ho N1 . . . . **233** C6
Orkney St SW11 . . . . .137 A3
Orlando Rd SW4 . . . . .137 C2
Orleans Cl KT10. . . . . .212 B6
Orleans Ct **9** TW1 . . . . . . .153 B4
Orleans House Gallery★
  TW1. . . . . .153 B3
Orleans Inf Sch TW1 . . . . . .153 B4
Orleans Park Sch TW1 . . . . .153 B4
Orleans Rd
  South Norwood SE19 . . . .183 B4
  Twickenham TW1 . . . . . . .153 C4
Orleston Mews N7. . . . . . . .72 C2
Orleston Rd N7. . . . . .72 C2
Orley Farm Rd HA1 . . . . . . .64 C5
Orley Farm Sch HA1 . . . . . .64 B5
Orlop St SE10. . . . . .120 C1
Ormanton Rd SE26. . . . . . .184 A6
Orme Ct W2 . . . . . . 113 D6 **245** C5
  Orme Ct Mews W2. . . . . . **245** C5
Orme Ho **8** E8. . . . . .95 D6
  Orme La W2. . . . . . 113 D6 **245** C5
Ormeley Rd SW12. . . . . . . .159 B3
Orme Rd
  Kingston u T KT1, KT3. . . .176 D1
  Sutton SM1. . . . . .217 D2
Ormerod Gdns CR4 . . . . . .181 A2
Ormerod Ho **3** SW9 . . . . . .138 A2
Ormesby Cl SE28 . . . . .124 D6
Ormesby Way HA3 . . . . . . .44 B4
  Orme Sq W2. . . . . **245** C5
Ormiston Gr W12 . . . . .112 B5
Ormiston Rd SE10 . . . . . . .121 A1
Ormond Ave
  Hampton TW12. . . . . . . .173 D2
  23 Richmond TW10 . . . . .153 D6
Ormond Cl WC1. . . . . **240** B4
Ormond Cres TW12 . . . . . .173 D2
Ormond Dr TW12 . . . . . . .173 D3
Ormonde Ave BR6. . . . . . . .227 A6
  Hendon NW4 . . . . .46 D6
  Putney SW15 . . . . .134 C1
Ormonde Gate
  SW3. . . . . 114 D1 **257** D1
Ormonde Mans WC1. . . . . **240** B4
Ormonde Pl SW1 . . . . **258** B3
Ormonde Rd SW14. . . . . . .133 A2
Ormonde Rise IG9 . . . . .21 C3
Ormonde Terr
  NW8 . . . . .92 D6 **230** C5
Ormond Ho **7** N16. . . . . . . .73 B6
Ormond Mans WC1 . . . . . **240** C5
Ormond Mews WC1. . . . . . **240** B5
Ormond Rd
  Finsbury Pk N4, N19. . . . . .50 A1
  Richmond TW10 . . . . . . .153 D6
Ormond Yd SW1 . . . . **249** B4
Ormrod Ct W11. . . . . .91 B1
Ormsby SM2. . . . . .217 D1
Ormsby Gdns UB6 . . . . .86 A5
Ormsby Lo **7** W4 . . . . .111 C3
Ormsby Pl N16. . . . . .73 D5
Ormsby Point **6** SE18. . . . .122 D2
Ormsby St E2. . . . . .95 D5
Ormside St SE15. . . . . .140 C6
Ormskirk Rd WD19. . . . . . . .22 D5
Ornan Rd NW3. . . . . .70 C3
Orpen Ho N5 . . . . **255** B3
Orpen Wlk N16. . . . . .73 C5
Orpheus Ho **25** N19 . . . . . . .49 D2
Orpheus St SE5. . . . . .139 B4
ORPINGTON 227 D6
Orpington Gdns N18. . . . . . .17 C1
Orpington Hospl BR6 . . . . .227 D4
Orpington Mans N21. . . . . .16 C3
Orpington Rd
  Southgate N21. . . . . .16 D3
  St Paul's Cray BR7 . . . . . .211 C6
Orpington Sta BR6. . . . . . .227 C6
Orpwood Cl TW12. . . . . . . .173 B4
Orsett Mews W2. . . .92 A1 **236** A2
Orsett St SE11 . . . . 116 D2 **260** D2
Orsett Terr
  Bayswater W2. . . . . .92 A1 **236** A2
  Woodford IG8. . . . . .37 C3
Orsman Rd N1. . . . . .95 C6
Orton Gr EN1 . . . . .6 A4
Orton St E1. . . . . .118 A5
Orville Rd SW11 . . . . .136 B3
Orwell Cl UB3 . . . . .105 C6
Orwell Ct Hackney E8 . . . . . .96 A6
  Highbury N5 . . . . .73 A4
  Northolt UB5 . . . . .85 A6

Orwell Ho W12 . . . . .112 A6
Orwell Lo **2** E18. . . . . .55 A5
Orwell Rd E13 . . . . .99 C6
Osbaldeston Rd N16. . . . . . .52 A1
Osberton Rd SE12. . . . . . . .165 A6
Osbert St SW1. . . . . **259** C3
Osborne Ave TW19. . . . . . .148 B3
Osborne Cl
  Beckenham BR3 . . . . . . .207 A5
  Cockfosters EN4. . . . . .2 D2
  Feltham TW13 . . . . .172 D5
Osborne Ct Ealing W5. . . . . .88 A2
  6 Surbiton KT6 . . . . .198 A3
  17 Walthamstow E10 . . . . .53 D2
Osborne Gdns CR7. . . . . . .183 A1
Osborne Gr E17. . . . . .53 B5
Osborne Mews E17. . . . . . . .53 B5
Osborne Pl SM1 . . . . .218 B3
Osborne Rd
  Buckhurst Hill IG9 . . . . . . .21 B3
  Dagenham RM9 . . . . .81 B3
  Enfield EN3. . . . . .7 A3
  Erith DA17. . . . . .147 B6
  Finsbury Pk N4 . . . . .50 C1
  Forest Gate E7 . . . . .77 B3
  Hackney E9. . . . . .75 B2
  Hounslow TW3, TW4. . . . .129 B2
  Kingston u T KT2. . . . . . .176 A3
  Leyton E10 . . . . .75 D6
  Palmers Green N13 . . . . . .16 C1
  South Acton W3 . . . . .110 D4
  Southall UB1. . . . . .86 A1
  South Norwood CR7 . . . . .183 A1
  Walton-on-T KT12 . . . . . .194 A1
  Willesden NW2. . . . . .68 B2
Osborne Sq RM9. . . . . .81 B4
Osborne Terr **1** SW17. . . . .181 A5
  South Wembley HA9. . . . .214 B3
Osborn Gdns NW7 . . . . .28 D3
Osborn La SE23. . . . . .163 A4
Osborn Rd E6. . . . . .100 A1
Osborn St E1. . . . . . .95 D2 **243** D4
Osborn Terr SE3 . . . . .142 D1
Osbourne Ct HA2 . . . . .41 D5
Osbourne Ho
  Richmond TW10 . . . . . . .154 C6
  Twickenham TW2 . . . . . . .152 A2
Oscar Faber Pl **8** N1. . . . . . .73 C1
Oscar St SE8. . . . . .141 C3
Oseney Cres NW5. . . . . .71 D2
Osgood Ave BR6 . . . . .227 D3
Osgood Gdns **1** BR6. . . . . .227 D3
OSIDGE 15 B2
Osidge Ct N14. . . . . .15 B3
Osidge La N14. . . . . .15 B3
Osidge Prim Sch N14 . . . . . .15 C3
Osier Cres N10 . . . . .30 D2
Osier Ct E1. . . . . .96 D3
Osier La SE10. . . . . .120 D3
Osier Mews W4. . . . . .133 D6
Osier St **3** KT1 . . . . .175 D2
Osiers Rd SW18. . . . . .135 C1
Osier St E1. . . . . .96 C3
Osier Way Leyton E10 . . . . . .75 D5
  Mitcham CR4 . . . . .202 D4
Oslac Rd SE6 . . . . .185 D5
Oslo Ct Mitcham SW19. . . . .180 B3
  St John's Wood NW8 . . . . **230** A3
Oslo Ho **2** SE5 . . . . .139 A3
Oslo Sq SE16 . . . . .119 A3
Oslow Cl W10. . . . . .91 B4
Osman Cl N15 . . . . .51 B3
Osman Prim Sch E1. . . . . . . .96 A2
Osman Rd Edmonton N9 . . . .18 A1
  Hammersmith W6 . . . . . .112 C3
Osmington Ho SW8 . . . . . . **270** D3
Osmond Cl HA2 . . . . .64 A6
Osmond Gdns SM6. . . . . . .219 C3
Osmund St W12 . . . . .89 D2
Osnaburgh St
  NW1 . . . . .93 B3 **238** D6
Osnaburgh Terr NW1. . . . . **238** D6
Osney Ho **4** SE2 . . . . .124 D4
Osney Wlk SM5 . . . . .202 B3
Osprey **7** NW9 . . . . .27 D2
Osprey Cl Cheam SM1. . . . .217 B3
  Higham Hill E17 . . . . .35 A3
  Keston Mark BR2 . . . . . . .210 A1
  Newham E6 . . . . .100 A2
  Wanstead E11 . . . . .55 A5
Osprey Ct **7** Ealing W7. . . . . .86 D3
  Hampstead NW3 . . . . .69 D3
  Thornton Heath SW16 . . . .182 B1
Osprey Ho
  Camberwell SE15 . . . . . . .139 D4
  Isleworth TW7 . . . . .131 B2
  3 Limehouse E14 . . . . . .119 A6
  Walthamstow E4 . . . . .35 B4
Osprey Mews EN3. . . . . . . .18 B6
Ospringe Cl **6** SE20. . . . . .184 C3
Ospringe Ct SE9. . . . . .167 B5
Ospringe Ho SE1. . . . . **251** B3
Ospringe Rd NW5. . . . . .71 C4
Osram Ct W6 . . . . .112 C3
Osram Rd HA9. . . . . .65 D5
Osric Path **8** N1. . . . . .95 C5
Ossian Mews N4. . . . . .50 B2
Ossian Rd N4. . . . . .50 B2
Ossie Garvin Rdbt UB4. . . .106 C6

Ossington Bldgs W1 . . . . **238** A3
Ossington Cl W2. . . . . **245** C5
Ossington St W2. . 113 D6 **245** C5
Ossory Rd SE1. . . . . .140 A6
Ossulston St NW1. . .93 D5 **232** D4
Ossultan Pl N2 . . . . .48 A6
Ossulton Way N2 . . . . .48 A5
Ostade Rd SW2. . . . . .160 B4
Ostell Cres EN3. . . . . .7 C5
Osten Mews
  SW7. . . . . 113 D3 **255** D5
OSTERLEY. 130 B5
Osterley Ave TW7. . . . . . . .130 B5
Osterley Cl BR5. . . . . .190 A2
Osterley Cres TW7 . . . . . . .130 C4
Osterley Ct
  Hounslow TW7 . . . . .130 B4
  7 Northolt UB5. . . . . .84 C4
Osterley Gdns
  Southall UB2. . . . . .108 A4
  South Norwood CR7. . . . .183 A1
Osterley Ho **5** E14. . . . . . . .97 C1
Osterley La
  Isleworth TW7 . . . . .108 C1
  Southall UB2, TW7. . . . . .107 D1
Osterley Lo **6** TW7. . . . . . .130 C4
Osterley Park★ TW7. . . . . . .108 B3
Osterley Park Rd UB2 . . . . .107 B3
Osterley Park View Rd
  W7. . . . . .108 C4
Osterley Rd
  Hounslow TW7 . . . . .130 C4
  Stoke Newington N16. . . . .73 C4
Osterley Sta TW7 . . . . .130 B5
Osterley Views UB2 . . . . . .108 B4
Osterly Lodge UB2. . . . . . .107 B3
Oster Terr E17 . . . . .52 D4
Ostlers Dr TW15 . . . . .171 A5
Ostliffe Rd N13 . . . . .33 A5
Oswald Bldg SW8 . . . . . . **268** C5
Oswald's Mead E9. . . . . .75 A4
Oswald St E5 . . . . .74 D5
Oswald Terr NW2 . . . . .68 C5
Osward Pl N9 . . . . .18 B2
Osward Rd SW12, SW17. . . .158 D2
Oswell Ho **9** E1. . . . . .118 B5
Oswin St SE11 . . . . . 116 D2 **261** D4
Oswyth Rd SE5. . . . . .139 C3
Otford Cl Bexley DA5. . . . . .169 D5
  Bromley BR1. . . . . .210 C6
  Penge SE20 . . . . .184 C2
Otford Cres SE4. . . . . .163 B5
Otford Ho
  Bermondsey SE1. . . . . . . **252** D1
  6 Deptford SE15. . . . . . .140 C6
Otha Ho **13** SW9. . . . . .138 A3
Othello Cl SE11 . . . . **261** C2
Otho Ct **5** TW8 . . . . .131 D5
Otis St E3 . . . . .98 A4
Otley App IG2 . . . . .56 D3
Otley Ct N11. . . . . .31 A4
Otley Dr IG2. . . . . .56 D3
Otley Ho N5 . . . . .72 D5
Otley Rd E16. . . . . .99 C1
Otley Terr E5 . . . . .74 D5
Ottawa Ho **4** HA4 . . . . .40 C1
Ottaway Ct E5 . . . . .74 A5
Ottaway St E5 . . . . .74 A5
Otterbourne Rd
  Chingford E4. . . . . .20 B1
  1 Croydon CR0. . . . . . . .221 A6
Otterburn Gdns TW7 . . . . .131 A5
Otterburn Ho **12** SE5. . . . . .139 A5
Otterburn St SW17. . . . . . .180 D4
Otter Cl E15 . . . . .98 A6
Otterden Cl BR6 . . . . .227 C4
Otterden St SE6 . . . . .185 C6
Otterfield Rd UB7. . . . . . . .104 A6
Otter Rd UB6. . . . . .86 A3
Ottershaw Ho BR5 . . . . . . .190 B2
Otto Cl SE26. . . . . .162 B1
Ottoman Ct W5 . . . . .109 D2
Otto St SE17. . . . . .138 D6
Otway Ct N4. . . . . .50 B3
Otway Gdns WD23. . . . . .8 C4
Oulton Cl Erith SE28 . . . . . .102 C1
  Upper Clapton E5. . . . . . . .74 C6
Oulton Cres IG11. . . . . .79 D3
Oulton Rd N15. . . . . .51 B4
Oulton Way WD19. . . . . . . .23 B6
Oundle Ave WD23. . . . . .8 A5
Our Lady Immaculate RC
  Prim Sch KT6. . . . . .198 D1
Our Lady of Dolours RC Prim
  Sch **7** W2 . . . . .91 D2
Our Lady of Grace RC Inf Sch
  NW2. . . . . .68 C6
Our Lady of Grace RC Jun
  Sch NW2. . . . . .68 B5
Our Lady of Grace RC Prim
  Sch **4** SE7 . . . . .143 B6
Our Lady of Lourdes RC
  Prim Sch
  1 Finchley N12. . . . . . . .30 A2
  Friern Barnet N11 . . . . . . .31 C5
  1 Lewisham SE13. . . . . .142 B2
  London NW10. . . . . .89 A6
Our Lady of Lourds RC Prim
  Sch E11. . . . . .55 A3

Our Lady of Muswell Prim
Sch N10. . . . . 49 A6
Our Lady of Muswell RC Prim
Sch N10. . . . . 31 A1
Our Lady of the Rosary RC
Prim Sch DA15 . . . . 167 C5
Our Lady of the Visitation RC
Combined Prim Sch
UB6 . . . . 86 A3
Our Lady of Victories RC
Prim Sch
7 Putney SW15 . . . . 134 D1
South Kensington
SW7 . . . . 114 A2 256 B3
Our Lady Queen of Heaven
RC Prim Sch **10** SW19 . 156 D4
Our Lady RC Prim Sch
Camden Town
NW1 . . . . 93 C6 232 B6
28 Poplar E14. . . . . 97 B1
Our Lady & St John's RC Jun
& Inf Sch **4** TW8 . . . . 109 C1
Our Lady & St Joseph RC
Prim Sch **14** N1 . . . . 73 C2
Our Lady & St Philip Neri RC
Infants Sch **15** SE23 . . 162 D1
Our Lady & St Philip Neri RC
Prim Sch **6** SE26 . . . . 185 A6
Our Lady's Convent RC High
Sch **3** N15 . . . . 51 C2
Ouseley Rd SW12 . . . . . 158 D3
Outer Circ NW8. . . . . . 92 D5 230 D3
Outgate Rd NW10. . . . . 67 D1
Outram Pl N1 . . . . . . 94 A6 233 B6
Outram Rd Croydon CR0. . 221 D6
Muswell Hill N22. . . . . 31 D2
Newham E6 . . . . 100 A6
Outwich St EC3 . . . . 243 B2
Outwood Ho **3** SW2. . . . 160 B4
Oval Ct Burnt Oak HA8. . . . 27 A3
8 Teddington TW11. . . . 174 D5
Oval Mans SE11. . . . . 270 D6
Oval Pl SW8 . . . . 138 B3 270 D4
Oval Prim Sch CR0. . . . . 205 C1
Oval Rd
Camden Town
NW1. . . . . 93 B6 231 C6
Croydon CR0. . . . . 205 C1
Oval Rd N RM10. . . . . 103 D6
Oval Rd S RM10. . . . . 103 D5
Oval Sta SE11. . . . . 138 C6
Oval The Hackney E2 . . . . 96 B5
Sidcup DA15. . . . . 190 C6
Oval Way SE11. . . . . 116 B1 260 D1
Overbrae BR3 . . . . 185 C5
Overbrook Wlk HA8. . . . . 26 C3
Overbury **1** BR3. . . . . . . 208 A6
Overbury Ave BR3 . . . . . 208 A6
Overbury Ho **3** E5 . . . . . 74 D4
Overbury Rd N4, N15. . . . . 51 B3
Overbury St E5 . . . . 74 D4
Overcliff Rd SE13 . . . . . 141 C2
Overdale Ave KT3. . . . . . 177 B1
Overdale Rd W5 . . . . 109 C3
Overdown Rd SE6. . . . . . 185 D6
Overhill Rd SE21, SE22. . 162 A4
Overhill Way BR3 . . . . . 208 B4
Overlea Rd E5 . . . . 52 A2
Overmead DA15. . . . . . . 167 B4
Oversley Ho **17** W2. . . . . . 91 C2
Overstand Cl BR3. . . . . . 207 C4
Overstone Gdns CR0. . . 207 B2
Overstone Ho **19** E14. . . . 97 C1
Overstone Rd W6. . . . . . 112 C2
Overstrand Mans SW11 . 268 A1
Overton Cl
1 Hounslow TW7 . . . . . 130 D4
Tokyngton NW10 . . . . 67 A2
Overton Ct E11. . . . . 55 A2
Overton Dr Ilford RM6 . . . 58 C2
Wanstead E11 . . . . 55 B2
Overton Grange Sch
SM2 . . . . 217 D1
Overton Ho SW15. . . . . . 155 D4
Overton Rd
Abbey Wood SE2. . . . . . 124 D3
Belmont SM2 . . . . 217 C1
Brixton SW9. . . . . 138 C3
Southgate N14. . . . . 16 A6
Walthamstow E10 . . . . 53 A1
Overton's Yd CR0. . . . . . 221 A5
Overy Ho SE1. . . . . 251 C1
Ovesdon Ave HA2. . . . . . 41 B1
Ovett Cl SE19 . . . . 183 C4
Ovex Cl E14. . . . . 120 A4
Ovington Ct SW3 . . . . . . 257 B5
Ovington Gdns SW3. . . . 257 B5
Ovington Mews SW3. . . 257 B5
Ovington Sq
SW3. . . . . 114 C1 257 B5
Ovington St SW3. . 114 C1 257 B4
Owen Cl Hayes UB4. . . . . . 84 B4
Northolt UB5. . . . . 63 A2
Thamesmead SE28. . . . . 124 C5
Thornton Heath CR0. . . 205 B3
Owen UB4 . . . . 84 B4
Owen Ho Feltham TW14. . 150 A4

Owen Ho continued
11 Tufnell Pk N19 . . . . 71 C4
5 Twickenham TW1. . . . . 153 B4
Owenite St SE2. . . . . 124 B2
Owen Rd Edmonton N13 . . 33 A5
Hayes UB4. . . . . 84 B4
Owen's Ct EC1. . . . . 234 C2
Owens Mews **10** E11. . . . . 76 C6
Owen's Row EC1. . . . . . 234 C2
Owen St EC1. . . . . 234 C3
Owens Way SE23. . . . . . 163 A4
Owen Way NW10. . . . . 67 A3
Owen Wlk **7** SE20. . . . . . 184 A3
Owgan Cl SE5. . . . . 139 B5
Oxberry Ave SW6. . . . . . 135 A3
Oxbridge Ct **4** W4. . . . . 110 D1
Oxendon St SW1,
W1. . . . . 115 D6 249 C5
Oxenford St SE15. . . . . . 139 D2
Oxenham Ho **13** SE8. . . . 141 C6
Oxenholme N1. . . . . 232 B3
Oxenpark Ave HA9. . . . . . 44 A2
Oxestalls Rd SE8. . . . . . 119 A1
Oxford Ave
Harlington TW6 . . . . 127 D5
Hounslow TW5 . . . . 107 C1
Merton SW20. . . . . 179 A1
Southgate N14. . . . . 15 C3
Oxford & Cambridge Mans
NW1. . . . . 237 B3
Oxford Cir W1 . . . . 93 C1 239 A1
Oxford Circus Ave W1. . 239 A1
Oxford Circus Sta
W1. . . . . 93 C1 239 A1
Oxford Cl Edmonton N9. . . 18 B2
Littleton TW15, TW17. . . 171 A3
Mitcham CR4 . . . . 203 C6
Oxford Cres KT3 . . . . . . 199 B3
Oxford Ct **16** Acton W3. . . 88 C1
City of London EC4 . . . . 252 C6
8 Ealing W7. . . . . 86 D2
Gunnersbury W4 . . . . . . 110 D1
17 Kingston u T KT6. . . . 198 A4
48 Paddington W2. . . . . . 91 C2
Sidcup DA14. . . . . 189 D6
Oxford Dr
Bermondsey SE1. . . . . . 253 A3
Ruislip HA4. . . . . 62 C6
Oxford Gardens Prim Sch **21**
W10 . . . . 90 D1
Oxford Gate W6 . . . . . . 112 D2
Oxford Gdns
Brentford W4 . . . . 132 C6
Edmonton N21. . . . . 17 A4
North Kensington W10. . . 90 D1
Oakleigh Pk N20 . . . . 14 B3
Oxford Ho N4. . . . . 50 C1
Oxford Mews DA15. . . . 169 C4
Oxford Rd
Carshalton SM5 . . . . . . 218 C3
Ealing W5. . . . . 109 D6
Edmonton N9. . . . . 18 B2
Enfield EN3. . . . . 18 B6
Finsbury Pk N4. . . . . 50 C1
Harrow HA1. . . . . 42 A3
Ilford IG1. . . . . 79 A3
Paddington NW6 . . . . 91 C5
Putney SW15 . . . . 135 A1
Sidcup DA14. . . . . 190 B5
South Norwood SE19. . . 183 B4
Stratford E15. . . . . 76 B2
Teddington TW11, TW12. . 174 B5
Wallington SM6 . . . . 219 C3
Wealdstone HA3. . . . . . . 42 C6
Woodford IG8. . . . . 37 D5
Oxford Rd N W4 . . . . . . 110 D1
Oxford Rd S W4. . . . . . . 110 D1
Oxford Sq W1. . . . . 237 B1
Oxford St W1. . . . . . 93 B1 238 D1
Oxford Wlk TW13 . . . . . 172 D6
Oxford Wlk UB1. . . . . . . 107 B5
Oxgate Cl NW2 . . . . 68 A6
Oxgate Ct Par NW2 . . . . . 68 A6
Oxgate Ctr NW2 . . . . 68 A6
Oxgate Gdns NW2 . . . . . . 68 B6
Oxgate La NW2. . . . . 68 B6
Oxhawth Cres BR2. . . . . 210 D3
Oxhey Dr WD19 . . . . 22 B6
Oxhey Dr S HA6. . . . . 22 B5
Oxhey La HA5. . . . . 23 C5
Oxhey Ridge Cl HA6. . . . . 22 B5
Oxhey Wood Prim Sch
WD19. . . . . 22 C6
Oxleas E6 . . . . 100 D1
Oxleas Cl DA16. . . . . 145 B3
Oxleay Rd HA2. . . . . 41 C1
Oxleigh Cl KT3. . . . . 199 C4
Oxley Cl SE1. . . . . 118 A1
Oxleys Rd NW2 . . . . 68 B5
Oxlip Cl **2** CR0 . . . . 206 D1
Oxlow La RM10. . . . . 81 C4
Oxonian St SE22. . . . . . 139 D1
Oxo Tower Wharf SE1 . . 251 B5
Oxo Twr★ SE1. . . . . 251 B5
Oxted Cl CR4 . . . . 202 B6
Oxted Ct N16. . . . . 232 D4
Oxtoby Way SW16. . . . . 181 D2
Oyster Catchers Cl E16. . 99 B1
Oyster Catcher Terr IG5. . 56 C6
Oyster Row E1. . . . . 96 C1

Ozolins Way E16. . . . . 99 A1

P

Pablo Neruda Cl **4**
SE24 . . . . 138 D1
Pace Pl E1. . . . . 96 B1
Pacific Cl TW14. . . . . . . 149 D3
Pacific Ho **15** E1. . . . . 96 D3
Pacific Hts BR3. . . . . . . 185 C3
Pacific Rd E16. . . . . 99 A1
Pacific Wharf IG11. . . . . . 78 D1
Pacific Wharf SE16. . . . 118 D5
Packenham Ho
24 Crouch End N19. . . . . . 49 D2
21 Spitalfields E2. . . . . . . 95 D4
Packham Ct E1. . . . . 216 C5
Packington Sq N1 . 95 A6 235 A6
Packington St N1. . 94 D6 234 D5
Packmores Rd SE9. . . . 167 B6
Padbury SE17. . . . . 263 B1
Padbury Cl TW14. . . . . . 149 B3
Padbury Ct E2. . . . . 95 D4
Padbury Ho NW8 . . . . . . 237 B6
Padden Ct NW7. . . . . 28 D3
Paddenswick Ct **2** W6. . 112 B3
Paddenswick Rd W6. . . 112 A3
PADDINGTON. 92 A2
Paddington Acad **7** W9. . 91 C3
Paddington Cl UB4. . . . . . 84 D3
Paddington Ct
10 Ealing W7. . . . . 86 D2
7 Wembley HA0 . . . . 66 A2
Paddington Gn
W2. . . . . 92 B2 236 C4
Paddington Green Prim Sch
NW8. . . . . 92 B3 236 C5
Paddington St W1. . . . . 238 A4
Paddington Sta
W2. . . . . 92 B1 236 C2
Paddock Cl
Forest Hill SE26. . . . . . . 184 D6
Kidbrooke SE3. . . . . 143 A3
New Malden KT4. . . . . . 199 C1
Northolt UB5. . . . . 85 C5
Orpington BR6. . . . . 226 D4
Paddock Ct SW20. . . . . 200 C5
Paddock Gdns SE19. . . 183 C4
Paddock Lo **13** EN1. . . . . 17 C6
Paddock Prim Sch
SW11. . . . . 137 A1
Paddocks Cl HA2. . . . . . . 63 D4
Paddocks Gn NW9. . . . . . 44 D1
Paddocks The
Addington CR0. . . . . 223 C2
Cockfosters EN4. . . . . 2 D1
Preston HA9. . . . . 66 D6
Paddock The
Muswell Hill N10. . . . . . . 49 B6
Uxbridge UB10. . . . . 60 D4
Paddock Way
Chislehurst BR7. . . . . . . 189 B3
11 Putney SW15. . . . . . . 156 C1
Padelford La HA7. . . . . 9 A2
Padfield Cl HA9. . . . . 66 B5
Padfield Rd SE5. . . . . . . 139 A2
Padley Cl KT9. . . . . 214 B3
Padnall Ct RM6. . . . . 58 D6
Padnall Rd RM6. . . . . 58 D5
Padstone Ho **50** E3. . . . . . 97 D4
Padstow Cl DA6. . . . . . . 227 D4
Padstow Ho **12** E14. . . . . 119 B6
Padstow Rd EN2 . . . . 4 D4
Padstow Wlk TW14. . . . 149 D3
Padua Rd SE20 . . . . 184 C2
Pagden St SW8. . . . . . . 268 D2
Pageant Ave NW9. . . . . . . 27 C2
Pageant Cres SE16. . . . 119 B5
Pageantmaster Ct EC4. . 241 C1
Pageant Wlk CR0. . . . . . 221 C5
Page Cl Dagenham RM9. . . 81 A3
Hampton TW12. . . . . 173 A4
Harrow HA3. . . . . 44 B3
Page Cres CR0. . . . . 220 D3
Page Ct NW7. . . . . 28 A3
Page Green Rd N15. . . . . 52 A4
Page Green Terr N15. . . . 51 D4
Page Heath La BR1. . . . 209 D6
Page Heath Villas BR1. . 209 D6
Page Ho SE10 . . . . 142 A6
Pagehurst Rd CR0. . . . . 206 B2
Page Mdw NW7. . . . . 28 A3
Page Rd TW14. . . . . 149 B5
Page's Ct N10. . . . . 31 A1
Page's Hill N10. . . . . 31 A1
Page's La N10. . . . . 31 A1
Page St Hendon NW7. . . . 28 A3
Westminster SW1 . 115 D2 259 D4
Page's Wlk SE1. . . . 117 C3 263 B5
Page's Yd W4. . . . . 133 C6
Paget Ave SM1. . . . . 218 B5
Paget Cl TW12. . . . . 174 B6
Paget Ct UB7. . . . . 104 A4
Paget Gdns BR7. . . . . . . 188 D2

Paget Ho **15** E2. . . . . 96 C5
Paget La TW7. . . . . 130 C2
Paget Pl Kingston u T KT2 . 177 A4
Thames Ditton KT7. . . . . 196 D1
Paget Rd Hillingdon UB10. . 83 A3
Ilford IG1. . . . . 78 D4
Stoke Newington N16. . . . 51 B1
Paget Rise SE18. . . . . . . 144 C5
Paget St EC1. . . . . 234 C2
Paget Terr SE18. . . . . . . 144 D6
Pagham Ho **8** W10 . . . . . . 90 C3
Pagin Ho N15. . . . . 51 C4
Pagitts Gr EN4. . . . . 1 D4
Pagnell St SE14. . . . . . . 141 B5
Pagoda Ave TW9. . . . . . 132 B2
Pagoda Gdns SE3. . . . . 142 B3
Pagoda Gr SE27. . . . . . . 161 A2
Paignton Rd Ruislip HA4. . 62 A5
Tottenham N15. . . . . 52 A5
Paine Ct SE3 . . . . 142 D6
Paines Cl HA5. . . . . 41 A6
Paine's La HA5 . . . . 23 A1
Pain's Cl CR4. . . . . 181 B1
Painsthorpe Rd **3** N16. . 73 C5
Painswick Ct **1** SE15 . . 139 D5
Painters Mews SE16. . . 118 A2
Painters Rd IG2, RM6. . . 58 A6
Paisley Rd
Carshalton SM5 . . . . . . 202 B1
Tottenham N22. . . . . 32 C2
Paisley Terr SM5. . . . . . 202 B2
Pakeman Ho SE1. . . . . . 251 D2
Pakeman Prim Sch **1**
N7. . . . . 72 B5
Pakeman St N7. . . . . 72 B5
Pakenham Cl SW12. . . . 159 A3
Pakenham St WC1 . 94 B3 240 D6
Pakington Ho **22** SW9. . 138 A3
Palace Ave W8 . . . 113 D4 245 D2
Palace Cl **4** E9. . . . . 78 D1
Palace Court Gdns N10 . . 49 C6
Palace Ct Bromley BR1 . . 187 B2
Eltham SE9 . . . . 166 B5
Hampstead NW3 . . . . 69 D3
Harrow HA3. . . . . 44 A3
Kensington W2. . . . 113 D6 245 C5
2 South Norwood CR7. . 205 B5
Streatham SW2 . . . . 160 C2
Palace Exchange EN2. . . . 5 B1
Palace Garden Mews
W8. . . . . 245 B4
Palace Gate
Hampton KT8 . . . . 196 C6
Knightsbridge W8. . 114 A4 246 A1
Palace Gate Mews **4** N8 . 50 A5
Palace Gates Rd N22. . . . 31 D2
Palace Gdns IG9. . . . . 21 D3
Palace Gdns Mews
W8. . . . . 113 D5 245 D3
Palace Gdns Sh Ctr EN2. . 5 B1
Palace Gn
Kensington W8. . . . 113 D5 245 C5
New Addington CR0. . . . 223 B1
Palace Gr Bromley BR1. . 187 B2
Penge SE19 . . . . 183 D3
Palace Mans W14. . . . . . 254 B4
Palace Mews
Belgravia SW1. . . . . 258 B3
Fulham SW6. . . . . 264 D4
1 Walthamstow E17. . . . 53 B5
Palace of Ind HA9. . . . . . . 66 C4
Palace Par **1** E17. . . . . . 53 C5
Palace Pl SW1 . . . . 259 A6
Palace Rd Bromley BR1. . 187 B2
East Molesey KT8. . . . . . 196 B6
Hornsey N8. . . . . 49 D4
Kingston u T KT1. . . . . . . 197 D5
Penge SE19 . . . . 183 D3
Ruislip HA4. . . . . 63 A4
Streatham SE27, SW16,
SW2 . . . . 160 C2
Wood Green N11 . . . . 32 A3
Palace Sq SE19. . . . . . . 183 D3
Palace St SW1. . . . . 115 C3 259 A6
Palace View
Bromley BR1. . . . . 209 B6
Croydon CR0. . . . . 223 B4
Grove Pk SE12. . . . . 165 A2
Palace View Rd E4 . . . . . 35 D5
Palamos Rd E10. . . . . 53 C1
Palatine Ave N16. . . . . . . 73 C4
Palatine Rd N16. . . . . 73 C4
Palazzo Apartments **11**
N1 . . . . 73 C1
Palemead Cl SW6. . . . . 134 D4
Palermo Rd NW10 . . . . . . 90 A5
Palestine Gr SW19 . . . . 180 B2
Palewell Cl BR5. . . . . . . 190 B1
Palewell Common Dr
SW14. . . . . 155 B6
Palewell Pk SW14 . . . . . 133 B1
Palfrey Pl SW8. . . . 138 B5 270 D4
Palgrave Ave UB1. . . . . 107 C6
Palgrave Gdns
NW1 . . . . 92 C3 237 B6
Palgrave Ho
7 Camberwell SE5. . . . 139 A5
4 Maitland Pk NW3 . . . . 70 D3
Twickenham TW2 . . . . . . 152 A4
Palgrave Rd W12 . . . . . . 111 D3

Palissy St **35** E2. . . . . 95 D4
Palladino Ho **6** SW17. . 180 C5
Pallant Ho SE1. . . . . 262 D5
Pallant Way BR6. . . . . . . 226 C5
Pallester Ct NW11. . . . . . 47 A1
Pallet Way SE18 . . . . . . 144 A4
Palliser Ct W14 . . . . 254 A1
Palliser Ho
3 Greenwich SE10 . . . 142 B6
21 Stepney E1. . . . . 96 D3
Palliser Rd W14. . . 113 A1 254 A1
Pallister Terr SW15 . . . . 155 D2
Pall Mall SW1 . . . . 115 D5 249 C3
Pall Mall E SW1. . . 115 D5 249 C3
Pall Mall Pl SW1. . . . . . 249 B3
Palmar Cres DA7. . . . . . 147 C3
Palmar Rd DA7 . . . . 147 C3
Palm Ave DA14. . . . . 190 D4
Palm Cl E10 . . . . 75 C5
Palm Ct Beckenham BR3. . 207 B6
18 Camberwell SE15. . . 139 D5
Stoke Newington N16. . . . 73 B6
Wood Green N22 . . . . 32 B3
Palmeira Rd DA7 . . . . . . 146 D2
Palmer Ave Heston TW5. . 129 C4
Northolt UB5. . . . . 63 A2
West Wickham BR4 . . . . 224 B6
Palmer Cres KT1. . . . . . 198 A6
Palmer Gdns EN5 . . . . . . 12 D6
Palmer Ho
6 Deptford SE14. . . . . 140 D5
5 Kentish Town NW5. . . 71 C4
5 Tufnell Pk N19 . . . . . . 71 C5
Palmer Pl N7 . . . . 72 C3
Palmer Rd Dagenham RM8. . 58 D1
Newham E13 . . . . 99 B3
Palmer's Ct **11** N11 . . . . . 31 C5
Palmers Gr KT8. . . . . . . 195 C5
PALMERS GREEN 16 A1
Palmers Green High Sch
N21. . . . . 16 C2
Palmers Green Sta N13 . . 32 B6
Palmers La EN3. . . . . 6 C4
Palmers Rd Globe Town E2. . 96 C5
Mortlake SW14 . . . . 133 A2
Thornton Heath SW16. . 182 B1
Palmer's Rd N11. . . . . . . 31 C5
Palmer St SW1. . . . . 259 C6
Palmerston Cres
Bowes Pk N13. . . . . 32 B5
Woolwich SE18. . . . . . . 145 A6
Palmerston Ct
2 Buckhurst Hill IG9. . . . 21 C2
6 Globe Town E3. . . . . . 96 C5
9 Surbiton KT6. . . . . . . 197 D2
7 Sutton SM1. . . . . 218 A3
Walthamstow E17 . . . . . . 53 B5
Palmerston Ctr HA3 . . . . 42 D6
Palmerston Gr **11** SW19 . 179 C3
Palmerston Ho
Battersea SW11 . . . . . . 268 B1
Kensington W8. . . . . 245 A3
Palmerston Rd
Acton Green W3 . . . . . . 111 A3
Bowes Pk N22. . . . . 32 B4
Brondesbury NW6 . . . . . . 69 B1
Buckhurst Hill IG9 . . . . . 21 C3
Farnborough BR6. . . . . . 227 A3
Hampstead NW6 . . . . 69 C1
Harrow HA3. . . . . 42 B6
Hounslow TW3 . . . . 130 A4
Merton SW19 . . . . 179 C3
Mortlake SW14 . . . . 133 A1
Sutton SM1. . . . . 218 A3
Thornton Heath CR0. . . 205 B4
Twickenham TW2 . . . . . 152 C5
Upton E7. . . . . 77 B2
Wallington SM5 . . . . 219 A4
Walthamstow E17 . . . . . . 53 B5
Palmerston Way SW8. . . 268 D3
Palm Gr W5. . . . . 110 A3
Palm Tree Ct **5** N17. . . . . 33 D1
Palm Tree Ho **2** SE14 . . 140 D5
Pamela Ct Finchley N12. . 29 D4
Willesden NW10. . . . . 68 A1
Pamela Gdns HA5. . . . . . 40 B4
Pamela Ho **14** E8 . . . . . . 95 D6
Pamir Ct **10** SM2. . . . . . 217 D2
Pamlion Ct N4. . . . . 50 A2
Pams Way KT19. . . . . . . 215 B3
Panama Ho **6** E1. . . . . . . 96 D2
Panbro Ho SE18 . . . . . . 144 B4
Pancras La EC2. . . . . . . 242 C1
Pancras Rd NW1. . . 93 D5 232 D4
Pancras Way Bow E3. . . . 98 C5
Old Ford E3. . . . . 97 C5
Pandian Way **4** NW5. . . . 71 D2
Pandora Ct **4** KT6. . . . . 198 A3
Pandora Rd NW6. . . . . . . 69 C2
Panfield Mews IG2. . . . . . 56 C3
Panfield Rd SE2. . . . . . . 124 A3
Pangbourne NW1. . . . . . 232 A1
Pangbourne Ave W10 . . . 90 C2
Pangbourne Ct
Oakleigh Pk N20. . . . . . . 14 A4
Upper Tooting SW17. . . 180 A6

Pangbourne Dr HA7 . . . . . . .26 A5
Pangbourne Ho **4** N7 . . . .72 A3
Panhard Pl UB1 . . . . .107 D6
Pank Ave EN5 . . . . .14 A6
Pankhurst Ave **8** E16 . . .121 B5
Pankhurst Cl
  7 Deptford SE14 . . . . .140 D5
  Isleworth TW7 . . . . .130 D2
Pankhurst Ho
  2 Kensington NW10 . . . . . . .90 C1
  Streatham SW16 . . . . .181 D5
Pankhurst Rd KT12 . . . . . .194 C2
Panmuir Rd SW20 . . . . . . .178 B2
Panmure Cl N5 . . . . .72 D4
Panmure Ct **11** UB1 . . . . . .86 A1
Panmure Rd SE26 . . . . .162 B1
Panorama Ct N6 . . . . .49 C3
Pan Penisula Sq E14 . . . . .119 D4
Pansy Gdns W12 . . . . .112 A6
Panther Dr NW10 . . . . .67 B3
Pantiles Cl N13 . . . . .32 D5
Pantiles The Bickley BR1 . .210 A6
  Bushey WD23 . . . . .8 B3
  Erith DA7 . . . . .147 B5
  Temple Fortune NW11 . . . . .47 B4
Panton Cl CR0 . . . . .204 D1
Panton St SW1 . . . . .249 C5
Panyer Alley EC2 . . . . .242 A2
Papermill Cl SM5 . . . . .219 A4
Paper Mill Wharf E14 . . . .119 A6
Papillons Wlk SE3 . . . . . . .143 A2
Papworth Gdns N7 . . . . .72 B3
Papworth Way SW2 . . . . . .160 C4
Parade Mans
  19 Camberwell SE5 . . . . .139 A3
  2 Hendon NW4 . . . . .46 B4
Parade Mews SE27, SW2 . 160 D2
Parade The
  Ashford TW16 . . . . .171 D3
  Battersea SW11 . . 136 D5 267 D4
  Claygate KT10 . . . . .212 C2
  Ilford IG2 . . . . .57 B3
  Thornton Heath CR0 . . . . .204 A3
  Thornton Heath CR7 . . . . .204 C6
  Waddon CR0 . . . . .220 B3
  Wembley UB6 . . . . .65 B3
Paradise Pas N7 . . . . .72 C3
Paradise Pl **15** SE7 . . . . . .122 A2
Paradise Rd
  Richmond TW10 . . . . .154 A6
  South Lambeth SW4 . . . . .138 A3
Paradise Row E2 . . . . .96 B4
Paradise St SE16 . . . . .118 B4
Paradise Wlk
  SW3 . . . . 136 D6 267 D6
Paragon N8 . . . . .50 C5
Paragon Christian Acad
  E5 . . . . .74 D4
Paragon Cl E16 . . . . .99 A1
Paragon Ct NW4 . . . . .29 A2
Paragon Gr KT5 . . . . .198 B3
Paragon Ho SE3 . . . . .142 D3
Paragon Mews SE1 . . . . . .262 D4
Paragon Pl
  Blackheath Vale SE3 . . . . .142 D3
  Surbiton KT5 . . . . .198 B3
Paragon Rd E9 . . . . .74 C2
Paragon The
  Kidbrooke SE3 . . . . .143 A3
  Walworth SE17 . . . . .262 D4
Paramount Bldg EC1 . . . . .241 C6
Paramount Ct WC1 . . . . . . .239 B5
Paramount Ho **10** E11 . . . .76 C5
Parbury Rd SE23 . . . . .163 A5
Parbury Rise KT9 . . . . .214 A2
Parchmore Rd CR7 . . . . . . .205 A6
Parchmore Way CR7 . . . . .182 D1
Pardes House Gram Sch **11**
  N3 . . . . .29 B1
Pardes House Prim Sch **12**
  N3 . . . . .29 B1
Pardoner St SE1 . .117 B3 262 D6
Pardon St EC1 . . . . .241 D6
Parfett St E1 . . . . .96 A1
Parfew Ct **2** SE22 . . . . . .162 B2
Parfitt Cl NW11 . . . . .48 A1
Parfrey St W6 . . . . .134 C6
Pargraves Ct HA9 . . . . .66 C6
Parham Dr IG2 . . . . .56 D4
Paris Gdn SE1 . . . 116 D5 251 C4
Parish CE Prim Sch BR1 . .187 A3
Parish Church CE Inf Sch **10**
  CR0 . . . . .220 D5
Parish Church CE Jun Sch **9**
  CR0 . . . . .220 D5
Parish Ct KT6 . . . . .198 A3
Parish Gate Dr DA15 . . . . .167 C5
Parish La SE20 . . . . .184 D3
Paris Ho **12** E2 . . . . .96 B5
Parish Wharf **6** SE7 . . . . .122 A2
Park App DA16 . . . . .146 B1
Park Ave Barking IG11 . . . . .79 A2
  Bromley BR6 . . . . .226 C6
  Edmonton N18 . . . . .34 A6
  Enfield EN1 . . . . .17 C5
  Finchley N3 . . . . .29 D2
  Golders Green NW11 . . . . . .47 D1

Park Ave continued
  Ilford IG1 . . . . .56 C1
  Mitcham CR4 . . . . .181 B3
  Mortlake SW14 . . . . .133 B1
  Palmers Green N13 . . . . . . .16 C1
  Plaistow BR1 . . . . .187 A4
  Ruislip HA4 . . . . .39 C3
  Southall UB1 . . . . .107 C5
  Stratford E15 . . . . .76 C2
  Twickenham TW3 . . . . . . .151 D5
  Upper Halliford TW17 . . . .193 C6
  Wallend E6 . . . . .100 C5
  Wallington SM5 . . . . .219 A2
  West Wickham BR4 . . . . . .224 A6
  Willesden NW2 . . . . .68 C2
  Woodford IG8 . . . . .37 B5
  Wood Green N22 . . . . .32 B2
Park Ave E KT17 . . . . .216 A2
Park Ave N
  Dudden Hill NW10 . . . . . . .68 B3
  Hornsey N8 . . . . .49 D5
Park Avenue Mews CR4 . .181 B3
Park Avenue Rd N17 . . . . . .34 B3
Park Ave S N8 . . . . .49 D5
Park Ave W KT17 . . . . .216 A2
Park Chase HA9 . . . . .66 B4
Park Cl Dollis Hill NW2 . . . . .68 B5
  Ealing NW10 . . . . .88 B4
  Hampton TW12 . . . . .174 A2
  Harrow HA3 . . . . .24 C2
  Isleworth TW3, TW7 . . . . .152 A6
  Kensington W14 . . 113 B3 254 D6
  Kingston u T KT2 . . . . . . .176 C2
  Knightsbridge SW1 . . . . . .247 C1
  North Finchley N12 . . . . . . .30 B6
  13 South Hackney E9 . . . .96 C6
  Wallington SM5 . . . . .218 D2
Park Cotts **10** TW1 . . . . . .153 B5
Park Cres Enfield EN2 . . . . . .5 B1
  Finchley N3 . . . . .30 A3
  Harrow HA3 . . . . .24 C2
  Regent's Pk W1 . . . 93 B3 238 C5
  Twickenham TW2 . . . . . . .152 B3
Park Crescent Mews E
  W1 . . . . .238 D5
Park Crescent Mews W
  W1 . . . . .238 C5
Park Croft HA8 . . . . .27 A2
Parkcroft Rd SE12 . . . . . . .164 D4
Park Ct Battersea SW11 . . .268 C2
  2 Beckenham BR3 . . . . .207 D6
  2 Chingford E4 . . . . .20 A2
  Clapham Pk SW4 . . . . . . .159 D6
  Dulwich SE21 . . . . .161 B1
  12 Hammersmith W6 . . . .112 A2
  New Barnet EN5 . . . . .14 B4
  New Malden KT3 . . . . .199 B5
  North Finchley N12 . . . . . . .30 B5
  Teddington KT1 . . . . .175 C2
  Twickenham TW1 . . . . . . .151 D6
  Upper Tooting SW12 . . . . .159 A3
  Wallington SM6 . . . . .220 A3
  Walthamstow E17 . . . . .53 D4
  Wembley HA9 . . . . .66 A3
  Wood Green N11 . . . . .31 D3
Parkdale N11 . . . . .31 D4
Parkdale Cres KT4 . . . . . . .215 B5
Parkdale Rd SE18 . . . . .123 C1
Park Dr Acton W3 . . . . .110 C3
  Enfield N21 . . . . .17 A5
  Golders Green NW11 . . . . . .47 D1
  Harrow HA2 . . . . .41 C2
  Mortlake SW14 . . . . .133 B1
  Stanmore HA3 . . . . .24 C4
  Woolwich SE7 . . . . .144 A6
Park Dwellings **7** NW3 . . .70 D3
Park End Bromley BR1 . . . .186 D2
  Hampstead NW3 . . . . .70 C4
Parker Cl Newham E16 . . . .122 A5
  Wallington SM6 . . . . .218 D2
Parker Ct Shoreditch N1 . . .235 B6
  South Lambeth SW4 . . . . .270 A1
  Wimbledon SW19 . . . . . . .179 A3
Parke Rd Barnes SW13 . . . .134 A4
  Sunbury TW16 . . . . .194 A5
Parker Ho **4** SE18 . . . . . . .122 D1
Parker Mews WC2 . . . . . . .240 B2
Parker Rd CR0 . . . . .221 A4
Parkers Rd N10 . . . . .30 C2
Parkers Row **15** SE16 . . . .118 A4
Parker's Row SE1 . . . . .253 D1
Parker St Newham E16 . . . .122 A5
  St Giles WC2 . . . . 94 A1 240 B2
Park Farm Cl
  East Finchley N2 . . . . .48 A6
  Pinner HA5 . . . . .40 B4
Park Farm Ct UB3 . . . . . . .105 C6
Park Farm Rd
  Bromley BR1 . . . . .187 D2
  Kingston u T KT2 . . . . .176 A3
Parkfield **3** TW7 . . . . .130 C4
Parkfield Ave
  Feltham TW13 . . . . .150 A1
  Harrow HA2 . . . . .24 A1
  Hillingdon UB10 . . . . .82 D4
  Mortlake SW14 . . . . .133 C1
Parkfield Cl Edgware HA8 . . .26 D4
  Northolt UB5 . . . . .85 A5

Parkfield Cres
  Feltham TW13 . . . . .150 A1
  Harrow HA2 . . . . .24 A1
  Ruislip HA4 . . . . .63 A5
Parkfield Ct SE14 . . . . .141 B4
Parkfield Dr UB5 . . . . .84 D5
Parkfield Gdns HA2 . . . . . . .41 D6
Parkfield Ho HA2 . . . . .23 D2
Parkfield Par TW13 . . . . . .150 A1
Parkfield Prim Sch NW4 . . .46 B2
Parkfield Rd
  Feltham TW13 . . . . .150 A1
  Harrow HA2 . . . . .64 A5
  New Cross SE14 . . . . .141 B4
  Northolt UB5 . . . . .85 A5
  Uxbridge UB10 . . . . .60 D6
  Willesden NW10 . . . . .68 B1
Parkfields Croydon CR0 . . .207 B1
  Putney SW15 . . . . .134 C1
Parkfields Ave
  Welsh Harp NW9 . . . . .45 B1
  Wimbledon SW20 . . . . . . .178 B1
Parkfields Cl SM5 . . . . .219 A4
Parkfields Rd KT2 . . . . .176 B5
Parkfield St N1 . . . 94 C5 234 B4
Parkfield Way BR2 . . . . . . .210 B4
Park Flats N6 . . . . .48 C2
Parkgate SE3 . . . . .142 D2
Park Gate Ealing W5 . . . . . .87 D2
  East Finchley N2 . . . . .48 B6
  Southgate N21 . . . . .16 B4
Parkgate Ave EN4 . . . . .2 A4
Parkgate Cl KT2 . . . . .176 D4
Parkgate Cres EN4 . . . . .2 A4
Park Gate Ct TW12 . . . . . . .174 A5
Parkgate Gdns SW14 . . . . .155 B6
Parkgate House Sch
  SW11 . . . . .137 A1
Parkgate Mews N6 . . . . .49 C2
Parkgate Rd
  Battersea SW11 . . .136 C5 267 B6
  Wallington SM5, SM6 . . . .219 B3
Park Gates HA2 . . . . .63 C4
Park Gdns
  Kingston u T KT2 . . . . .176 B5
  Queensbury NW9 . . . . .44 D6
Park Gr Bromley BR1 . . . . . .187 B2
  Edgware HA8 . . . . .26 B5
  Newham E15 . . . . .99 A6
  Wood Green N11 . . . . .31 D3
Park Grove Rd E11 . . . . .76 C6
Park Hall SE10 . . . . .142 B5
Park Hall Rd
  Dulwich SE21 . . . . .161 B1
  East Finchley N2 . . . . .48 C5
Park Hall Road Trad Est
  SE21 . . . . .161 B1
Parkham Ct BR2 . . . . .186 C1
Parkham St
  SW11 . . . . .136 C4 267 A1
Parkham Way N10 . . . . .31 C1
Park Heights Ct **21** E14 . . .97 B1
Park High Sch HA7 . . . . .25 C1
Park Hill Bromley BR1 . . . . .210 B5
  Clapham Pk SW4 . . . . . . .159 D6
  Ealing W5 . . . . .87 D2
  Forest Hill SE23 . . . . .162 C3
  Loughton IG10 . . . . .21 D6
  Richmond TW10 . . . . .154 B5
  Wallington SM5 . . . . .218 D2
Park Hill Cl SM5 . . . . .218 C3
Park Hill Ct Croydon CR0 . .221 C6
  Ealing W5 . . . . .87 D2
  Upper Tooting SW17 . . . . .158 D1
Parkhill Ho **7** SW16 . . . . .182 C5
Parkhill Inf Sch IG5 . . . . . . .56 C6
Park Hill Inf Sch CR0 . . . . .221 C5
Parkhill Jun Sch IG5 . . . . . .56 C6
Park Hill Jun Sch CR0 . . . .221 C5
Parkhill Rd Chingford E4 . . . .20 A4
  Maitland Pk NW3 . . . . .70 D3
  Old Bexley DA5 . . . . .169 B4
  Sidcup DA15 . . . . .167 C1
Park Hill Rd
  Beckenham BR2 . . . . .186 C1
  South Croydon CR0 . . . . . .221 C5
  Wallington SM6 . . . . .219 B1
Park Hill Rise CR0 . . . . .221 D5
Park Hill St **17** KT2 . . . . . .176 C3
Park Hill Wlk **10** NW3 . . . .70 D3
Park Ho
  8 Camberwell SE5 . . . . .139 B4
  Finsbury Pk N4 . . . . .72 D6
  Forest Hill SE26 . . . . .184 A5
  35 Hackney E9 . . . . .74 C1
  Richmond TW10 . . . . .154 A5
  Sidcup DA15 . . . . .190 A5
  Southgate N21 . . . . .16 B4
Parkholme Rd E8 . . . . .74 A2
Park House Gdns TW1 . . . .153 C6
Parkhouse St SE5 . . . . .139 B5
Park Hts NW4 . . . . .46 B6
Parkhurst Ct N7 . . . . .72 A4
Parkhurst Gdns **2** DA5. . .169 C4
Parkhurst Rd
  Bowes Pk N22 . . . . .32 B4
  Friern Barnet N11 . . . . .31 A5
  Little Ilford E12 . . . . .78 C4
  Lower Holloway N7 . . . . . . .72 A4

Parkhurst Rd continued
  Sidcup DA5 . . . . .169 C4
  Sutton SM1 . . . . .218 B4
  Tottenham N17 . . . . .34 A1
  Walthamstow E17 . . . . .53 A5
Parkin Ho SE20 . . . . .184 D3
Parkinson Ct Finsbury N1. .235 C1
  Shoreditch EC1 . . . . .235 D2
Parkinson Ho **6** E9 . . . . . .74 C1
Park La Cheam SM3 . . . . . .217 A2
  Cranford TW5 . . . . .128 A5
  Dagenham RM6 . . . . .58 D3
  Edmonton N9 . . . . .17 D1
  Harrow HA2 . . . . .63 D5
  Hayes UB4 . . . . .83 C3
  Mayfair W1 . . . . . 115 A6 248 A5
  Mill Meads E15 . . . . .98 B6
  Richmond TW9 . . . . .131 D1
  South Croydon CR0 . . . . . .221 B5
  Stanmore HA7 . . . . .9 A1
  Teddington TW11 . . . . .174 D4
  Tottenham N17 . . . . .34 A3
  Wallington SM5, SM6 . . . .219 A3
  Wembley HA9 . . . . .66 A4
Parkland Ct
  Kensington W14 . . . . .244 A2
  Stratford E15 . . . . .76 C3
Parkland Gdns **12** SW19. .156 D3
Parkland Gr
  Ashford TW15. . . . . .170 C6
  Hounslow TW7 . . . . .130 D4
Parkland Mead BR1 . . . . . .210 D6
Parkland Rd
  Ashford TW15. . . . . .170 C6
  Woodford IG8 . . . . .37 B3
  Wood Green N22 . . . . .32 B1
Parklands Bushey WD23 . . . .8 A5
  East Dulwich SE22 . . . . . .162 B6
  Highgate N6 . . . . .49 B2
  Kingston u T KT5 . . . . .198 B4
  5 Whetstone N20 . . . . . . .14 A2
Parklands Cl
  Hadley Wood EN4 . . . . .2 B5
  Ilford IG2 . . . . .57 A2
  Mortlake SW14 . . . . .155 A6
Parklands Ct TW5 . . . . .128 D3
Parklands Dr N3 . . . . .47 A6
Parklands Par TW5 . . . . . . .128 D3
Parklands Pl HA8 . . . . .26 B6
Parklands Rd SW16 . . . . . .181 B5
Parklands Way KT4 . . . . . . .215 C6
Park Lane Cl N17 . . . . .34 A3
Park Lane Mans CR0 . . . . .221 B5
Park Lane Prim Sch HA9 . . .66 A4
PARK LANGLEY 208 B4
Park Lawn CR7 . . . . .183 A1
Parklea Cl NW9 . . . . .27 C2
Park Lea N16 . . . . .51 C2
Parkleigh Ct SW19 . . . . . . .179 D1
Parkleigh Rd SW19 . . . . . .179 D1
Parkleys KT2, TW10 . . . . . .175 D6
Parklife Oxford St W1 . . . . .238 A1
Park Lo **3** Ealing W5 . . . . . .87 B3
  North Finchley N12 . . . . . . .30 A5
  11 South Hampstead NW8 . .78 D3
  10 Wapping E1 . . . . .118 B5
  Willesden NW2 . . . . .68 C4
Park Lodge Ave UB7 . . . . .104 B4
Park Lofts **9** SW4 . . . . . . .160 A6
Park Lorne **8** 230 B1
Park Mans
  Battersea SW11 . . . . .267 C1
  Bedford Pk W6 . . . . .111 D3
  Forest Hill SE26 . . . . .162 C1
  Fulham SW6 . . . . .264 B1
  5 Hendon NW4 . . . . .46 B4
  Knightsbridge SW1 . . . . . .247 C1
  St John's Wood NW8 . . . . .230 A3
  Vauxhall SW8 . . . . .270 B6
Parkmead SW15 . . . . .156 B5
Park Mead Blackfen DA15 . .168 B5
  Harrow HA2 . . . . .63 D5
Parkmead Gdns NW7 . . . . . .27 D4
Park Mews
  Chislehurst BR7 . . . . .188 D4
  Greenwich SE10 . . . . .120 D1
  Hornsey N8 . . . . .50 A3
  Kensal Rise W10 . . . . .91 A5
  Stanwell TW19 . . . . .148 B4
Parkmore BR7 . . . . .188 D3
Park Nook Gdns EN2 . . . . . .5 B6
Park Par Acton W3 . . . . . . .110 C3
  Dagenham NW10 . . . . .89 D6
  Hayes UB3 . . . . .83 C1
  Kingsbury NW9 . . . . .45 B6
Park Piazza **3** SE13 . . . . .164 B5
Park Pl Canary Wharf E14 . .119 C5
  Ealing W5 . . . . .109 D5
  Gunnersbury W3 . . . . .110 C2
  Hampton TW12 . . . . .174 A4
  Shoreditch N1 . . . . .235 D6
  St James SW1 . . . 115 C5 249 A4
  Wembley HA9 . . . . .66 B4
Park Place Dr W3 . . . . .110 C3
Park Place Villas W2 . . . . . .236 B4
Park Prim Sch E15 . . . . .76 D1
Park Rd Ashford TW15 . . . . .170 D5
  Beckenham BR3 . . . . .185 C3

Park Rd continued
  Bromley BR1 . . . . .187 B2
  Cheam SM3 . . . . .217 A2
  Chipping Barnet EN5 . . . . . .1 B1
  Chislehurst BR7 . . . . .188 D4
  Chiswick W4 . . . . .133 B6
  Cockfosters EN4 . . . . .2 C1
  Dagenham NW10 . . . . .89 C6
  Ealing W7 . . . . .108 D6
  East Finchley N2 . . . . .48 B6
  East Molesey KT8 . . . . . . .196 A5
  Edmonton N18 . . . . .34 A6
  Feltham TW13 . . . . .172 D6
  Hackbridge SM6 . . . . .219 B6
  Hampton TW12 . . . . .174 A5
  Hampton Wick KT1 . . . . . .175 C2
  Harringay N8, N15 . . . . . . .50 D5
  Hayes UB4 . . . . .83 C2
  Hendon NW4 . . . . .46 A3
  Hornsey N8 . . . . .49 D4
  Hounslow TW3, TW7 . . . . .152 A6
  Ilford IG1 . . . . .79 B5
  Isleworth TW7 . . . . .131 B3
  Kingsbury NW9 . . . . .45 B2
  Kingston u T KT2, TW10 . . .176 C3
  Leyton E10 . . . . .53 C1
  Lisson Gr NW1,
    NW8 . . . . 92 C3 237 B6
  Lower Halliford TW17. . . . .192 C1
  Mitcham SW19 . . . . .180 C4
  Newham E15 . . . . .99 A6
  New Malden KT3 . . . . .199 B5
  Osidge N14 . . . . .15 D4
  Richmond TW10 . . . . .154 B5
  South Norwood SE25 . . . . .205 C5
  Sunbury TW16 . . . . .172 B3
  Teddington TW11 . . . . .174 D4
  Twickenham TW1 . . . . . . .153 C5
  Upton Pk E6 . . . . .99 C6
  Uxbridge UB8 . . . . .60 A2
  Wallington SM6 . . . . .219 B3
  Walthamstow E17 . . . . .53 B4
  Wanstead E12 . . . . .77 B6
  Wembley HA0 . . . . .66 A2
  Wood Green N11 . . . . .31 D3
Park Rd E Acton W3 . . . . . .111 A4
  Uxbridge UB10 . . . . .82 A5
Park Rd N Chiswick W4 . . . .111 B1
  South Acton W3 . . . . .110 D4
Park Ridings N8 . . . . .50 C6
Park Rise Forest Hill SE23. .163 A4
  Harrow HA3 . . . . .24 C2
Park Rise Rd SE23 . . . . . . .163 A4
Park Road E **11** W3. . . . . .110 D4
Park Road Ho **3** KT2 . . . . .176 C3
Park Row SE10 . . . . .142 B6
PARK ROYAL 88 D4
Park Royal NW10 . . . . .88 D6
Park Royal Bsns Ctr
  NW10 . . . . .89 A3
Park Royal Metro Ctr
  NW10 . . . . .88 D3
Park Royal Rd NW10, W3. . .89 A3
Park Royal Sta W5 . . . . .88 C3
Park S SW11 . . . . .268 A1
Park St James NW8 . . . . . .230 C5
Park Sch for Girls IG1. . . . . .56 D1
Park Sheen **3** SW14 . . . . .132 D1
Parkshot TW9 . . . . .132 A1
Parkside
  1 Beckenham BR3 . . . . .185 D1
  Cheam SM3 . . . . .217 A2
  Ealing W5 . . . . .110 A6
  East Acton W3 . . . . .111 C5
  Finchley N3 . . . . .29 D3
  Greenwich SE3 . . . . .142 D5
  Hampton TW12 . . . . .174 A5
  Hayes UB3 . . . . .105 C6
  Hendon NW7 . . . . .28 A4
  Sidcup DA14 . . . . .168 B2
  Wimbledon SW19 . . . . . . .179 A5
Park Side Chigwell IG9 . . . . .21 B2
  Dollis Hill NW2 . . . . .68 B4
Parkside Ave
  Bromley BR1 . . . . .210 A5
  Wimbledon SW19 . . . . . . .178 D5
Parkside Bsns Est SE8 . . . .141 A6
Parkside Cl SE20 . . . . .184 C3
Parkside Cres
  Highbury N7 . . . . .72 C5
  Tolworth KT5 . . . . .199 A3
Parkside Ct Bowes Pk N22 . .32 B4
  2 Wanstead E11 . . . . .55 A3
Parkside Dr HA8 . . . . .10 C1
Parkside Est E9 . . . . .96 D6
Parkside Gdns
  East Barnet EN4 . . . . .15 A4
  Wimbledon SW19 . . . . . . .178 D6
Parkside Lo DA17 . . . . .125 D1
Parkside Prep Sch **2**
  N17 . . . . .33 C2
Parkside (Private) Hospl
  SW19 . . . . .156 D1
Parkside Rd
  Belvedere DA17 . . . . .125 D2
  Hounslow TW3 . . . . .151 D6
Parkside St SW11 . . . . .268 A1
Parkside Terr N18 . . . . .33 B6
Parkside Way HA2 . . . . .42 A5
Park Sq E NW1 . . . 93 B3 238 D6

Park Square Mews NW1. **238 C5**
Park Sq W NW1....93 B3 **238 C5**
Park St
Borough The SE1...**117** A5 **252 B4**
Croydon CR0.........**221** A6
Mayfair W1.....**115** A6 **248 A5**
Teddington TW11.....**174** C4
Parkstead Rd SW15....**156 B6**
Parkstone Ave N18......**33** D5
Parkstone Rd
5 Peckham SE15......**140 A3**
Walthamstow E17......**54 A6**
Park Stps W2.............**247 B6**
Park Terr Carshalton SM5 . **218 C5**
Enfield EN3...........**7** A5
New Malden KT4......**200 A1**
Park The Ealing W5.....**109 D5**
Forest Hill SE23......**162 C3**
Golders Green NW11....**47** D1
Highgate N6...........**49** A3
Sidcup DA14..........**190 A5**
Wallington SM5......**218 D3**
Parkthorne Cl HA2.......**41** D3
Parkthorne Dr HA2......**41** D3
Parkthorne Rd SW12...**159 D4**
Park Twrs W1...........**248 C3**
Parkview UB6..........**87** A4
Park View Dagenham W3 . **89** A2
Highbury N5.........**73** A4
Kingston u t KT3......**199 D6**
Morden SM4.........**202 B4**
Pinner HA5...........**23** B2
Southgate N21........**16** B4
Wembley HA9.........**66** D3
Willesden NW2.......**68** C4
Yiewsley UB7.........**104 A6**
Park View Acad N15....**51** A5
Park View Cl SM5......**219 A1**
Parkview Cres KT4......**200 C1**
Park View Cres N11.....**31** B6
Parkview Ct Fulham SW6 . **135** A3
Harrow HA3..........**24** C3
Ilford IG2............**57** C3
Penge SE20..........**184 B2**
Twickenham TW1.....**153** C4
Park View Ct
Colney Hatch N12......**30** C6
Kingsbury NW9........**45** A5
Wandsworth SW18....**157** C5
Park View Dr CR4......**180 B1**
Park View Gdns
Hendon NW4.........**46** D4
Redbridge IG4........**56** B5
Wood Green N22......**32** C2
Park View Ho
Chingford E4.........**35** C5
Hampton TW12.......**174** A5
Streatham SE24......**160 D5**
Parkview Lo BR3.......**207 D6**
Park View Mans N4....**50** D2
Park View Mews **24**
SW9................**138 B3**
Parkview Rd
Bexley DA16.........**146** C2
Ealing W5............**88** A3
Finchley N3...........**29** D2
Hillingdon UB8.......**82** C1
Pinner HA5...........**22** B3
Southall UB1.........**107** C5
Tottenham N17.......**34** A1
Tottenham N17.......**34** B2
Willesden NW10......**67** D4
Park Village E
NW1...........93 B5 **231 D3**
Park Village W
NW1...........93 B5 **231 C4**
Park Villas RM6.......**58** D3
Parkville Rd SW6 .**135** B5 **264 C3**
Park Vista SE10........**142 B6**
Park Vista Apartments
E13................**98** D4
Park Walk Prim Sch
SW10 ....**136 B6 266 C5**
Parkwat Cres E15......**76** A3
Parkway
Abbey Wood DA18......**125** A3
Camden Town NW1 .**93 B6 231** C5
Hillingdon UB10......**60** D1
Ilford IG3............**79** D5
Palmers Green N14....**16** A2
West Barnes SW20.....**200** D5
Woodford IG8.........**37** C5
Park Way
East Molesey KT8.....**195** D6
Edgware HA8.........**26** D2
Enfield EN2...........**4** C3
Feltham TW14.......**150** B4
Friern Barnet N20.....**30** D6
Gunnersbury W3......**110** C2
Ruislip HA4..........**40** A1
Temple Fortune NW11 . . **47** A4
Park Way Ct HA4......**39** D1
Parkway SW14..........**133** B1
Parkway Prim Sch DA18. **125** A3
Parkway The
Cranford TW5..........**128** B5

Parkway The continued
Hayes UB2, UB3, UB4,
TW5................**106** B3
Yeading UB4...........**84** D2
Parkway Trad Est TW5. . **128** C6
Park West W2.....92 C1 **237 B1**
Park West Pl W1,
W2............92 C1 **237 B2**
Park Wlk
Chelsea SW10 .**136 B6 266 C6**
Highgate N6............**49** A2
Parkwood
Beckenham BR3.......**185** C3
Primrose Hill NW8......**230** C5
Parkwood Ave KT10...**196** A1
Parkwood Gr TW16.....**194** A6
Parkwood Mews N6......**49** B3
Parkwood Prim Sch **1**
N4...................**72** D6
Parkwood Rd
Hounslow TW7.......**130** D4
Old Bexley DA5.......**169** B4
Wimbledon SW19.....**179** B5
Parliament Ct NW3.....**70** C4
Parliament Hill NW3....**70** C4
Parliament Hill Mans
NW5................**71** A4
Parliament Hill Sch NW5. **71** A4
Parliament Mews SW14. **133** A3
Parliament Sq*
SW1............**116** A4 **250 A1**
Parliament St
SW1...........**116** A4 **250 A1**
Parliament View Apartments
SE11...............**260** C4
Parma Cres SW11......**136** D1
Parminter Ind Est **21** E2 . **96** B5
Parmiter St E2..........**96** B5
Parmoor Ct EC1........**242** A6
Parnall Ho **11** SE19....**183** C6
Parnell Cl Edgware HA8 . . **27** A6
Hammersmith W12.....**112** B3
Parnell Ho WC1.......**239** D2
Parnell Rd E3..........**97** B6
Parnham Cl BR1.......**210** D6
Parnham St E14........**97** A1
Parolles Rd N19.......**49** C1
Paroma Rd DA17......**125** C3
Parr Cl N9............**34** B6
Parr Ct Feltham TW13...**172** C6
Shoreditch N1.........**235** C4
Parrington Ho **11** SW4 . **159** D5
Parr Pl W4...........**111** D2
Parr Rd Newham E6.....**99** D6
Stanmore HA7........**26** A2
Parr's Pl TW12........**173** C3
Parr St N1.......95 B5 **235** C4
Parry Ave E6..........**100** B1
Parry Cl KT17.........**216** A1
Parry Ho **32** E1.........**118** B5
Parry Pl SE18.........**122** D2
Parry Rd
South Norwood SE25 . . . . **205** C6
West Kilburn W10......**91** A4
Parry St SW8....**138** A6 **270 B6**
Parsifal Coll **1** NW3 . . **69** C4
Parsifal Ho NW3.......**69** C4
Parsifal Rd NW6.......**69** C3
Parsley Gdns CR0.....**206** D1
Parsloes Ave RM9......**81** A3
Parsloes Prim Sch RM9 . **81** B2
Parsonage Ct UB3......**83** D1
Parsonage Ct WD6......**11** A6
Parsonage Gdns EN2 . . . . **5** A3
Parsonage La Enfield EN2 . **5** A3
Sidcup DA14........**191** B6
Parsonage Manorway
DA17...............**147** C6
Parsonage St E14......**120** A2
Parsons Cl SM1.......**217** D5
Parsons Cres HA8......**10** C1
Parsons Gn SW6 .**135** C4 **265** A2
PARSONS GREEN......**135** C4
Parsons Green La
SW6...........**135** C4 **265 A2**
Parsons Green Sta
SW6...........**135** C4 **265** A1
Parsons Hill SE18.....**122** C3
Parsons Ho
Paddington W2.......**236** C5
21 Streatham SW12...**160** A4
Parsons Lo NW6.......**69** D1
Parsons Mead KT8.....**196** A6
Parson's Mead CR0....**204** D1
Parsons Rd Edgware HA8 . . **10** C1
Newham E13..........**99** C5
Parson St NW4........**46** C4
Parthenia Rd
SW6...........**135** C4 **265 B1**
Partingdale La NW7....**28** D5
Partington Cl N19......**49** D1
Parton Lo **14** E8........**78** C3
Partridge Cl Barnet EN5 . **12** C5
Bushey WD23.........**8** A3
1 Newham E16.......**99** D2
Stanmore HA7........**26** A4
Partridge Ct EC1.......**241** C6
Partridge Dr BR6.....**227** A5
Partridge Gn SE9.....**166** C1
Partridge Ho **22** E3.....**97** B5

Partridge Rd
8 Hampton TW12....**173** C4
Sidcup DA14.........**189** C6
Partridge Sq **3** E6....**100** A2
Partridge Way N22.....**32** A2
Pasadena Cl UB3......**106** B4
Pascall Ho SE17........**139** A6
Pascals Coll BR3.......**185** C1
Pascal St SW8... **137** D5 **269** D4
Pascoe Rd SE13......**164** B6
Pasley Cl SE17........**262** A1
Pasquier Rd E17........**53** A6
Passey Pl SE9.........**166** B5
Passfield Dr E14.......**97** D2
Passfield Ho SE18.....**123** B2
Passfield Path **13** SE28. **124** B6
Passfields Catford SE6 . . **164** A1
West Kensington W14 . . . **254** C1
Passing Alley EC1......**241** D5
Passingham Ho TW5...**129** C6
Passmore Edwards Ho
N11................**31** D3
Passmore Gdns N11...**31** D4
Passmore Ho **12** N9....**18** A1
Passmore St
SW1..........**115** A1 **258** A2
Pasters Ct EN1........**17** D5
Pasteur Cl NW9.......**27** C1
Pasteur Gdns N18.....**33** A5
Paston Cl SM6.......**219** C5
Paston Cres SE12.....**165** B4
Pastor Ct N6..........**49** C3
Pastor St E1,
SE1...........**116** D2 **261** D4
Pasture Cl Bushey WD23. **8** A4
Wembley HA0........**65** B5
Pasture Rd Catford SE6 . **164** D3
Dagenham RM9.......**81** B3
Wembley HA0.........**65** B5
Pastures Mead UB10...**60** C2
Pastures Path E11......**54** C1
Pastures The N20.......**13** B3
Patcham Terr SW8.....**268** D2
Patch Cl UB10..........**82** B6
Patching Way UB4......**85** A2
Pat Drew Ho BR1.....**187** C2
Patent Ho E14..........**97** D2
Paternoster La
EC4..............**94** D1 **241** D2
Paternoster Sq
EC4..............**94** D1 **241** D2
Pater St W8 ...**113** C3 **255** A5
Pates Manor Dr TW14. **149** B4
Pathfield Rd SW16.....**181** D4
Path The SW19........**179** D2
Pathway Ho SW17.....**180** D4
Pathway Lo CR4.......**180** D2
Patience Rd SW11....**136** C3
Patience Villas SE13...**142** B2
Patio Cl SW4.........**159** D5
Patmore Ho **9** N16....**73** C3
Patmore St SW8...**137** C4 **269** B2
Patmos Rd SW9.......**138** D4
Paton Cl E3............**97** C4
Paton Ho **3** SW9......**138** B3
Paton St EC1.........**235** A1
Patricia Ct
Chislehurst BR7......**189** B2
Woolwich DA16......**146** B5
Patrick Coman Ho EC1. **234** C1
Patrick Connolly Gdns **41**
E3.................**97** B4
Patrick Rd E13........**99** C4
Patriot Sq E2...........**96** B5
Patrol Pl SE6.........**163** D5
Pat Shaw Ho **2** E1.....**96** D3
Patshull Pl NW5.......**71** C2
Patshull Rd NW5.......**71** C2
Patson Cl E5...........**74** D5
Pattenden Rd SE6.....**163** B3
Patten Ho N4..........**51** A1
Patten Rd SW18......**158** C4
Patterdale NW1........**231** D1
Patterdale Cl BR1.....**186** C4
Patterdale Rd SE15...**140** C5
Patterson Ct SE19....**183** D4
Patterson Rd SE19....**183** D4
Pattina Wlk SE16.....**119** A5
Pattison Point **10** E16. **99** A2
Pattison Ho
Borough The SE1.....**252** B2
1 Stepney E1........**96** D1
Pattison Rd NW2......**69** C5
Pattison Wlk SE18....**123** A1
Pat Williams Ho SE27. **161** A1
Paul Byrne Ho **3** N2....**48** A6
Paul Cl E15............**76** C1
Paul Ct **7** Edmonton N18 . **34** A6
Hendon N3...........**29** A1
Paul Daisley Ct **2** NW6 . **69** A1
Paulet Rd SE5.........**138** D4
Paul Gdns CR0.......**221** D6
Paulhan Rd HA3.......**43** D5
Paul Ho **18** W10........**91** A3
Paulin Dr N21.........**16** C4
Pauline Cres TW2.....**152** A3
Pauline Ho **21** E1......**96** A2
Paulinus Cl BR5......**190** C1
Paul Julius Cl E14....**120** B6
Paul Robeson Cl E6...**100** C4

Paulson Ho **7** IG11.....**78** D1
Paul St
Broadgate EC2.....**95** C3 **243** A6
Newham E15...........**98** C6
Paultons Ho SW3......**266** D6
Paultons Sq SW3 .**136 B6 266** D6
Paultons St SW3 .**136 B6 266** D6
Pauntley Ho **6** N19....**49** C1
Pauntley St **4** N19.....**49** C1
Pavan Ct **29** E2........**96** C4
Paved Ct **9** TW9.......**153** D6
Paveley Ct NW7........**28** D3
Paveley Dr SW11. .**136** C5 **267** A3
Paveley Ho N1........**233** C3
Paveley St NW8.....**92** C3 **237** B6
Pavement Mews **1** RM6 . **58** D2
Pavement Sq CR0....**206** A1
Pavement The
Brentford W5........**110** A3
Clapham SW4........**137** C1
Leytonstone E11......**54** A1
11 West Norwood SE27 . . **183** A6
Pavet Cl RM10.........**81** D2
Pavilion Ct
Dagenham RM9......**103** A6
7 Hampstead NW3....**70** A4
Hampstead NW3......**70** B3
3 Paddington NW6....**91** C4
5 South Norwood SW16...**182** B3
3 Wimbledon SW19....**179** A3
Pavilion L Ctr The BR1. **187** A1
Pavilion Lo HA2.......**42** B1
Pavilion Mans **10** SW9. **138** B1
Pavilion Mews N3.......**29** C1
Pavilion Rd
Knightsbridge
SW1..............**114** D3 **257** D5
Redbridge IG1........**56** B2
Pavilion Sq SW17.....**158** D1
Pavilion St SW1.......**257** D5
Pavilions The BR3.....**185** C4
Pavilion Terr Ilford IG2. . **57** C4
8 North Kensington W12 . . **90** C1
Pavilion Way
Burnt Oak HA8.......**27** A3
Ruislip HA4..........**62** C6
Pavillion Ct SW1......**268** C6
Pavitt Ct NW10.......**68** A1
Pawleyne Cl SE20....**184** C3
Pawsey Cl E13.........**99** A6
Pawson's Rd CR0.....**205** A4
Paxford Rd HA0........**65** B6
Paxton Cl Richmond TW9 . **132** B3
Walton-on-T KT12....**194** C2
Paxton Ct
1 Forest Hill SE26....**185** A6
Grove Pk SE9........**165** C1
Mitcham CR4........**180** D1
Paxton Ho SE17.......**262** B2
Paxton Pl SE27.......**183** C6
Paxton Prim Sch **14**
SE19...............**183** C4
Paxton Rd Chiswick W4. **133** C6
Forest Hill SE23......**163** A1
Plaistow BR1........**187** A3
Tottenham N17.......**34** A3
Paxton Terr SW1......**268** D6
Paymal Ho **33** E1.......**96** C2
Payne Cl IG11.........**79** D1
Payne Ho N1.........**233** D5
Paynell Ct SE3........**142** C2
Payne Rd E3...........**97** D5
Paynesfield Ave SW14. **133** B2
Paynesfield Rd WD23 . . . **8** D4
Payne St SE8.........**141** B6
Paynes Wlk W6 ..**135** A6 **264** A5
Payzes Gdns IG8.......**36** D5
Peabody Ave
SW1..............**115** B1 **258** D1
Peabody Bldgs
6 Camberwell SE5....**139** B4
Walworth SE17.......**262** C3
Peabody Cl Croydon CR0. **206** C1
SW1................**268** D6
Peabody Cotts N17.....**33** C2
Peabody Ct
9 Camberwell SE5....**139** B4
25 Enfield EN3........**7** C6
St Luke's EC1.......**242** B5
Peabody Est
18 Bethnal Green E2 . . . **96** B5
Borough The SE1.....**252** A3
Fulham SW6 . .**135 B6 264** D6
17 Hammersmith W6...**112** C1
Holborn EC1.........**241** B5
Lambeth SE1.........**251** B3
North Kensington W10...**90** C2
1 Ratcliff E1.........**118** D6
7 St George in t East E1 . . **118** A6
St Luke's EC1.......**242** B5
Strand WC2..........**240** C1
Streatham SE24......**161** A4
Westminster SW1.....**259** B4
Peabody Hill SE21....**161** A3
Peabody Sq SE1......**251** C1
Peabody Twr EC1.....**242** B5
Peabody Yd N1......**235** A6
Peace Cl East Barnet N14. **15** B6
Greenford UB6........**86** B6
South Norwood SE25 . . **205** C5

Peace Ct **10** NW9......**46** A5
Peace Gr HA9..........**66** D5
Peacehaven Ct **8** N10. . **31** A3
Peace Pagoda* SW3 . **267** D4
Peace St SE18........**144** C6
Peach Ct E4...........**35** C6
Peaches Cl SM2......**217** A1
Peaches Ct SM2......**217** A1
Peach Gr E11..........**76** B5
Peach Rd Feltham TW14 . **150** A3
London W10..........**91** A4
Peach Tree Ave UB7....**82** B1
Peachum Rd SE3......**142** D6
Peach Walk Mews **24** E3 . **96** C5
Peacock Ave TW14...**149** B3
Peacock Cl
Dagenham RM8......**80** C6
Finchley NW7.........**29** A5
Walthamstow E4.......**35** B3
Peacock Cl EN1........**17** C5
Peacock Ind Est N17....**33** D3
Peacock St SE17 . .**116** D2 **261** D3
Peacock Wlk E16......**99** B1
Peacock Yd SE17.....**261** D3
Peaketon Ave IG4......**55** D4
Peak Hill SE26.......**184** C6
Peak Hill Ave SE26...**184** C6
Peak Hill Gdns SE26..**184** C6
Peak Ho N4...........**51** A1
Peak The SE26.......**162** C1
Peal Gdns W13.........**87** A3
Peall Rd CR0.........**204** B3
Peall Rd Ind Est CR0 . . **204** B3
Pearce Cl **2** CR4......**181** A1
Pearcefield Ave **5** SE23. **162** C3
Pearce Ho
Camden Town N19.....**71** C5
1 Streatham SW2.....**160** A4
Westminster SW1.....**259** D3
Pear Cl Kingsbury NW9 . . **45** B5
New Cross Gate SE14....**141** A5
Pearcroft Rd E11......**76** B6
Peardon St SW8......**137** B3
Peareswood Gdns HA7. . **25** D2
Pearfield Ho **1** N5......**73** A3
Pearfield Rd SE23....**163** A1
Pearing Cl **2** KT4.....**216** D6
Pearl Cl Hendon NW2...**46** D2
Newham E6.........**100** C1
Pearl Ct **18** NW9.......**46** A5
Pearl Rd E17..........**53** C6
Pearl St E1...........**118** B5
Pearlstones Ct RM10... **103** C5
Pearmain Cl TW17....**192** D4
Pearmain Ho **9** SE13 . . **142** A3
Pearman St SE1 ..**116** C4 **251** B1
Pear Pl SE1..........**251** A2
Pear Rd E11...........**76** C5
Pears Ave TW17......**193** C6
Pearscroft Ct
SW6..........**135** D4 **265** D1
Pearscroft Rd
SW6..........**135** D4 **265** D1
Pearse St **3** SE15.....**139** C6
Pearson Cl Barnet EN5 . . **1** D2
4 Camberwell SE5....**139** A4
Pearson Ct SM4......**201** D4
Pearson Ho SW15....**134** C3
Pearson's Ave SE8, SE14 . **141** C4
Pearson St E2.........**95** D5
Pearson Way CR4....**181** A2
Pears Rd TW3........**130** A2
Peartree Ave SW17...**158** A1
Pear Tree Ave UB7.....**82** B1
Peartree Cl BR2......**209** D4
Pear Tree Cl
Chessington KT9.....**214** C3
Mitcham CR4........**180** C1
23 Shoreditch E2......**95** D6
Pear Tree Ct Holborn EC1. **241** B5
Putney SW15........**134** B1
Woodford IG8.........**37** B2
Peartree Gdns RM8....**80** B4
Pear Tree Ho
Brockley SE4........**141** B1
Hayes UB8...........**83** A1
Peartree La E1.......**118** C6
Peartree Rd EN1.......**5** C2
Pear Tree Rd TW15....**171** A5
Peartree St EC1....**95** A3 **242** A6
Peartree Way SE10...**121** A2
Peary Ho **4** NW10.....**67** B1
Peary Pl E2............**96** C4
Peaslake Ct SM2......**218** A1
Peas Mead Terr E4......**36** A6
Peatfield Cl DA15....**167** C1
Pebworth Lo
2 Belmont SM2......**217** D1
South Norwood SE25 . . **205** D5
Pebworth Rd HA1......**65** A6
Peckarmans Wood SE21,
SE26..............**162** A1
Peckett Sq **3** N5.......**72** D4
Peckford Pl SW9.....**138** C3
PECKHAM............**140** A4
Peckham Gr SE15....**139** C5

Peckham High St SE15....140 A4
Peckham Hill St SE15....140 A5
Peckham Park Prim Sch 28
  SE15....140 A5
Peckham Park Rd SE5....139 C4
Peckham Rye
  East Dulwich SE22....140 A1
  Peckham SE15, SE22....140 A4
Peckham Rye Sta SE15....140 A3
Peckwater Ho 2 NW5....71 C2
Peckwater St NW5....71 C3
Pedlars Wlk N7....72 A3
Pedley Rd RM8....58 C1
Pedley St E1....95 D3 243 D5
Pedro St E5....74 D4
Pedworth Gdns 4 SE16....118 C2
Peebles Ct SE1....86 A1
Peek Cres SW19....178 D5
Peel Centre (Metropoliton
  Police Training
  Establishment) NW9....45 D6
Peel Cl Chingford E4....19 D2
  Edmonton N9....18 A1
Peel Ct UB6....86 A4
Peel Dr Colindale NW9....45 D6
  Redbridge IG5....56 A6
Peel Gr E2....96 C5
Peel Pass W8....245 A3
Peel Pl IG5....37 D1
Peel Prec NW6....91 C5
Peel Rd Farnborough BR6....227 A3
  Harrow HA3....42 D6
  Wembley HA0, HA9....65 D5
  Woodford E18....36 D2
Peel St W8....113 C5 245 A3
Peel Way UB8....82 A2
Peel Yates Ho 13 SE7....122 A2
Peerglow Est EN3....18 C6
Peerless St EC1....95 B4 235 C1
Pegamoid Rd N18....18 C1
Pegasus Ct N16....73 B4
Pegasus Ct 11 Acton W3....89 A1
  Brentford TW8....110 B1
  6 Buckhurst Hill IG9....21 D2
  College Pk NW10....90 B4
  Edmonton N21....17 A4
  Harrow HA3....43 D4
  Kingston u T KT1....197 D6
  Sutton SM1....217 D6
Pegasus Ho 9 E1....96 D3
Pegasus Lo N21....17 A4
Pegasus Pl 2 SE11....138 C6
Pegasus Rd CR0, CR9....220 C2
Pegasus Way N11....31 B4
Peggotty Way UB8....82 D1
Pegg Rd TW5....128 D5
Peggy Quirke Ct 2 HA0....66 A2
Pegley Gdns SE12....165 A2
Pegwell Ho 19 E5....74 B3
Pegwell St SE18....145 C5
Pekin St E14....97 C1
Pekoe SE1....253 D3
Peldon Ct TW10....154 B6
Pele Ct N17....33 B3
Pelham Ave IG11....101 D6
Pelham Cl SE5....139 C2
Pelham Cotts DA7....169 D3
Pelham Cres SW7....257 A3
Pelham Ct SW3....257 A3
Pelham Ho W14....254 C2
Pelham Pl Chelsea SW7....257 A3
  8 Ealing W7....86 D3
Pelham Prim Sch
  Bexleyheath DA7....147 C2
  15 Merton SW19....179 C3
Pelham Rd
  Bexleyheath DA7....147 C2
  Ilford IG1....79 B6
  Merton SW19....179 C3
  Penge BR3, SE20....184 C1
  Tottenham N15....51 D5
  Wanstead E18....55 B6
  Wood Green N22....32 C1
Pelham St SW7....114 B2 256 D4
Pelican Ho 8 SE8....119 B2
Pelican Pas 3 E1....96 C5
Pelier St SE17....139 A6
Pelinore Rd SE6....164 C2
Pella Ho SE11....260 D2
Pellant Rd SW6....135 A5 264 B4
Pellatt Gr N22....32 C2
Pellatt Rd
  East Dulwich SE22....161 D6
  Wembley HA9....66 A6
Pellerin Rd N16....73 C3
Pellew Ho 15 E1....96 B3
Pellings Cl BR2....208 C6
Pelling St E14....97 C1
Pellipar Cl N13....16 C1
Pellipar Gdns SE18....122 B1
Pellipar Rd SE18....122 B1
Pellow Cl EN5....13 B5
Pelly Ct 4 E17....54 A5
Pelly Rd E13....99 A5
Pelter St E2....95 D4
Pelton Ct CR2....221 A2

Pelton Rd SE10....120 C1
Pembar Ave E17....53 A6
Pemberley Chase KT19....214 D3
Pemberley Cl KT19....214 D3
Pemberley Ho KT19....214 D3
Pember Rd NW10....90 D4
Pemberton Cl TW19....148 A3
Pemberton Ct 18 E1....96 D4
Pemberton Gdns
  Camden Town N19....71 C5
  Dagenham RM6....59 A4
Pemberton Ho SE26....184 A6
Pemberton Pl
  Esher KT10....212 A5
  2 Hackney E8....74 B1
Pemberton Rd
  East Molesey KT8....196 A5
  Harringay N4....50 D4
Pemberton Row EC4....241 B2
Pemberton Terr N19....71 C5
Pembridge Ave TW4....151 B3
Pembridge Cres
  W11....113 C6 245 A6
Pembridge Gdns
  W2....113 C6 245 A5
Pembridge Hall Prep Sch for
  Girls W2....113 C6 245 B5
Pembridge Mews
  W11....113 C6 245 A6
Pembridge Pl
  Notting Hill W2....113 C6 245 B6
  1 Wandsworth SW15....157 C6
Pembridge Rd
  W11....113 C6 245 A6
Pembridge Sq
  W2....113 C6 245 A5
Pembridge Villas
  W11....113 C6 245 A6
Pembroke W14....254 D3
Pembroke Ave Enfield EN1....6 B4
  Harrow HA3....43 B6
  Islington N1....94 A6 233 B6
  Surbiton KT5....198 D4
Pembroke Bldgs NW10....90 A4
Pembroke Cl SW1....248 B1
Pembroke Ct 11 W7....86 D2
Pembroke Gdns
  Dagenham RM10....81 D5
  West Kensington
  W8....113 B2 254 D4
Pembroke Gdns Cl W8....255 A5
Pembroke Hall NW4....46 C6
Pembroke Ho Acton W3....111 A4
  Chelsea SW1....258 A5
  5 Clapham Pk SW2....160 A6
  17 Kensington W2....91 D1
  Putney SW15....156 A6
  Upper Tooting SW17....180 B5
Pembroke Lo 2 SW16....160 B1
Pembroke Mews
  8 Bow E3....97 A4
  Kensington W8....255 A5
  Muswell Hill N10....31 A2
Pembroke Pl
  Edgware HA8....26 C3
  Isleworth TW7....130 C3
  Kensington W8....255 A5
Pembroke Rd
  Bromley BR1....187 D1
  Edmonton N13....17 A1
  Greenford UB6....85 D3
  Hornsey N8....50 A5
  Ilford IG3....57 D2
  Kensington W8....113 C2 255 A4
  Mitcham CR4....181 A1
  Muswell Hill N10....31 A3
  Newham E6....100 B2
  Ruislip HA4....39 D1
  South Norwood SE25....205 C5
  South Tottenham N15....51 D4
  Walthamstow E17....53 D4
  Wembley HA9....65 D5
Pembroke Sq
  W8....113 C3 255 A4
Pembroke St N1....94 A6 233 B6
Pembroke Studios W8....254 C5
Pembroke Terr NW8....229 C5
Pembroke Villas
  Kensington W8....255 A4
  Richmond TW9....131 D1
Pembroke Way UB3....105 A3
Pembroke Wlk W8....255 A4
Pembry Cl SW9....138 C4
Pembury Ave KT4....200 A2
Pembury Cl 3 Hackney E5....74 B3
  Hayes BR2....208 D2
Pembury Cres DA14....169 A2
Pembury Ct UB3....127 B6
Pembury Ho
  Camberwell SE5....139 C3
  Keston Mark BR2....210 A1
Pembury Pl 19 E5, E8....74 B3
Pembury Rd
  Croydon SE25....206 A5
  Erith DA7....147 A6
  Hackney E5....74 B3
  Tottenham N17....33 D1
Pemdevon Rd CR0....204 C2
Pemell Cl 30 E1....96 C3
Pemell Ho 31 E1....96 C3

Pemerich Cl UB3....105 D1
Pempath Pl HA9....65 D6
Penair Lodge HA1....64 C5
Penally Pl N1....235 D6
Penang St E1....118 B5
Penard Rd UB2....107 D3
Penarth Ct SM2....218 A1
Penarth Ctr The SE15....140 C6
Penarth St SE15....140 C6
Penates KT10....212 B4
Penberth Rd SE6....164 A3
Penbury Rd UB2....107 B1
Penceat Ct SE20....184 C1
Pencombe Mews W11....244 D6
Pencraig Way SE15....140 B6
Pendall Cl EN4....2 C1
Penda Rd DA8....147 D5
Pendarves Rd SW20....178 C2
Penda's Mead E9....75 A4
Pendell Ave UB3....127 C5
Pendennis Ho 15 SE8....119 A2
Pendennis Rd
  Streatham SW16....182 A6
  Tottenham N17....51 B6
Penderel Rd TW3....151 C6
Penderry Rise SE6....164 B2
Penderyn Way N7....71 D4
Pendlebury Ho 5 SE18....144 A4
Pendle Ho 13 SE26....162 A1
Pendle Rd SW16....181 B5
Pendlestone Rd E17....53 D4
Pendlewood Ct 13 W5....87 C2
Pendley Ho 18 E2....96 A6
Pendolino Way NW10....66 D1
Pendragon Rd BR1....165 A1
Pendragon Sch BR1....165 A1
Pendragon Wlk NW9....45 C3
Pendrell Ho WC2....239 D1
Pendrell Rd SE4....141 A3
Pendrell St SE18....145 B6
Pendula Dr UB4....84 D3
Penelope Ho 20 SW9....138 C4
Penerley Rd SE6....163 D3
Penfield Lo 7 W9....91 C2
Penfields Ho N7....72 A2
Penfold Cl CR0....220 C5
Penfold Ct 7 Mitcham CR4....181 A1
Penfold Ho 14 SE18....144 D6
Penfold La DA5....168 D3
Penfold Pl NW1....92 C2 237 A4
Penfold Rd N9....18 D3
Penfold St NW8....92 B3 236 D5
Penford Gdns SE9....143 D2
Penford St SE5....138 D3
Pengarth Rd DA5....168 D5
PENGE....184 D4
Penge East Sta SE20....184 C4
Penge La SE20....184 D3
Penge Rd Newham E13....99 C6
  South Norwood SE25....206 A6
Penge West Sta SE20....184 B4
Penhall Rd SE7....121 D2
Penhill Rd DA5....168 C4
Penhurst Mans SW6....264 C2
Penifather La UB6....86 B4
Peninsula Ct E14....119 D3
Peninsular Cl TW14....145 C5
Peninsular Park Rd SE7....121 A2
Penistone Rd SW16....182 A3
Penketh Dr HA1....64 B5
Penmayne Ho SE11....261 B2
Penmon Rd SE2....124 A3
Pennack Rd SE15....139 D6
Penn Almshouses 1
  SE10....142 A4
Pennant Mews
  W8....113 D2 255 C4
Pennant Terr E17....35 B1
Pennard Mans 5 W12....112 C4
Pennard Rd W12....112 C4
Pennards The TW16....194 C6
Penn Cl Greenford UB6....85 D5
  Harrow HA3....43 C5
Penn Ct NW9....45 B6
Pennefather Ho N1....73 B2
Pennells Ct TW5....129 C6
Penner Cl SW19....157 A2
Penners Gdns KT6....198 A2
Pennethorne Cl E9....96 C6
Pennethorne Ho N1....136 B2
Pennethorne Rd SE15....140 B5
Penn Gdns BR7....188 D1
Penn Ho 7 Edmonton N9....18 A1
  Lisson Gr NW8....237 A5
Pennine Dr NW2....68 D6
Pennine La NW2....69 A6
Pennine Mans NW2....69 A6
Pennine Par NW2....69 A6
Pennine Way UB7....127 B5
Pennington Cl 10 SE27....183 B6
Pennington Ct
  4 Rotherhithe SE16....119 A5
  31 St George in East E1....118 A6
Pennington Dr N21....16 A4
Pennington Lo 18 KT5....198 A4
Pennington St E1....118 B6
Pennington Way SE12....165 B2
Penniston Cl N17....33 A1
Penniwell Cl HA8....26 B6
Penn La Bexley DA5....168 D5

Penn La continued
  Sidcup DA5....169 A5
Penn Rd N7....72 A4
Penn St N1....95 B6 235 D6
Penny Ct SW10....266 B6
Pennyfields E14....119 C6
Pennyford Ct NW8....236 C6
Penny La TW17....193 C2
Penny Mews SW12....159 B4
Pennymore Wlk W9....91 B3
Penny Rd NW10....88 D4
Penny Royal SM6....219 D2
Pennyroyal Ave E6....100 C1
Penpoll Rd E8....74 B2
Penpool La DA16....146 B2
Penray EN5....1 A2
Penrhyn Ave E17....35 C2
Penrhyn Cres
  Mortlake SW14....133 A1
  Walthamstow E17....35 C2
Penrhyn Gdns KT1....197 D5
Penrhyn Gr E17....35 C2
Penrhyn Rd KT1....198 A6
Penrith Cl
  Beckenham BR3....185 D2
  Putney SW15....157 A6
Penrith Pl SE27....160 D2
Penrith Rd
  New Malden KT3....199 B5
  South Norwood CR7....183 A1
  Tottenham N15....51 B4
Penrith St SW16....181 C4
Penrose Gr SE17....117 A2 262 A1
Penrose Ho
  Camberwell SE17....262 A1
  Southgate N21....16 B6
Penrose St SE17....117 A2 262 A1
Penryn Ho SE11....261 C2
Penryn St NW1....93 D5 232 C4
Penry St SE1....263 B3
Pensbury Pl SW8....137 C3
Pensbury St SW8....137 C3
Pensford Ave TW9....132 C3
Penshurst 2 NW5....71 A2
Penshurst Ave DA15....168 A5
Penshurst Ct
  Croydon CR2....220 D1
  1 Edgware HA8....26 C5
Penshurst Gdns HA8....26 D5
Penshurst Gn BR2....208 D4
Penshurst Ho 1 SE15....140 C6
Penshurst Rd Erith DA7....147 B4
  Homerton E9....74 D1
  Thornton Heath CR7....204 D4
  Tottenham N17....33 D3
Penshurst Way SM2....217 C1
Penshurst Wlk 4 BR2....208 D4
Pensilver Cl EN4....2 C1
Penstemon Cl N3....29 C4
Pentavia Retail Pk NW7....27 D3
Pentelow Gdns TW14....150 A5
Pentire Rd E17....36 B2
Pentland Ave
  Edgware HA8....10 D2
  Littleton TW17....192 C4
Pentland Cl
  Cricklewood NW11....69 A6
  Lower Edmonton N9....18 C2
Pentland Gdns SW18....158 A5
Pentland Ho
  17 Camden Town NW5....71 A2
  7 Stamford Hill N16....51 D1
Pentland Pl UB5....85 A6
Pentland Rd Bushey WD23....8 A5
  1 Maida Vale NW6....91 C4
Pentlands BR3....186 A2
Pentlands Cl CR4....203 B6
Pentland St SW18....158 A5
Pentlow St SW15....134 C2
Pentney Rd
  5 Chingford E4....20 B3
  Merton SW19, SW20....179 A2
  Streatham SW12....159 C3
Penton Gr N1....234 A3
Penton Ho
  3 Abbey Wood SE2....124 D4
  Islington N1....234 A3
  Sutton SM2....218 A1
Penton Pl SE17....116 D1 261 D2
Penton Rise WC1....94 B4 233 D2
Penton St N1....94 C5 234 A3
PENTONVILLE....94 B5
Pentonville Rd
  WC1....94 B5 233 C3
Pentrich Ave EN1....6 A5
Pentridge St SE15....139 D5
Pentyre Ave N18....33 B5
Penwerris Ave TW5,
  TW7....129 A5
Penwerris Ct TW7....130 A5
Penwith Rd SW18....157 D2
Penwood Ct HA5....41 B5
Penwood Ho SW15....155 D5
Penwortham Ct 1 N22....32 C1
Penwortham Prim Sch
  SW17....181 B4
Penwortham Rd SW16....181 C4
Penylan Pl HA8....26 C3

Penywern Rd
  SW5....113 C1 255 B2
Penzance Ho SE11....261 B2
Penzance Pl
  W11....113 A5 244 B4
Penzance St
  W11....113 A5 244 B4
Peony Ct IG8....36 C3
Peony Gdns W12....112 A6
Peperfield WC1....233 C1
Pepler Ho 17 W10....91 A3
Pepler Mews SE1....263 C1
Peploe Rd NW6....90 B5
Pepper Cl E6....100 B2
Peppercorn Cl CR7....183 B1
Peppermead Sq SE13....163 C6
Peppermint Cl CR0....204 A2
Peppermint Pl 7 E11....76 C5
Pepper St
  Borough The SE1....252 A2
  Millwall E14....119 D3
Peppie Cl N16....73 C6
Pepys Cl UB10....60 D4
Pepys Cres Barnet EN5....12 C6
  2 Newham E16....121 A5
Pepys Ct SW20....178 C1
Pepys Ent Ctr 13 SE8....119 B2
Pepys Ho
  14 Bethnal Green E2....96 C4
  Clapham Pk SW4....159 D6
Pepys Rd
  New Cross Gate SE14....140 D3
  Wimbledon SW20....178 C2
Pepys Rise BR6....211 D3
Pepys St EC3....117 C6 253 B6
Perak Ct KT5....199 A2
Peralte Terr CR4....204 A5
Perceval Ave NW3....70 C3
Perceval Ct UB5....63 C3
Percheron Cl TW7....130 D2
Percheron Ct 3 SW9....138 B2
Percheron Rd WD6....11 B5
Perch St E8....73 D4
Percival Ct N17....33 D3
Percival Gdns RM6....58 C3
Percival Ho 3 IG8....37 A6
Percival Rd Enfield EN1....5 D1
  Feltham TW13....149 D2
  Mortlake SW14....133 A1
  Orpington BR6....226 D6
Percival St EC1....94 D4 234 D1
Percival Way KT19....215 B4
Percy Ave TW15....170 C5
Percy Bilton Ct TW5....129 D4
Percy Bryant Rd TW16....171 C3
Percy Bush Rd UB7....104 B3
Percy Cir WC1....94 B4 233 D2
Percy Ct 1 KT5....198 B3
Percy Gdns Enfield EN3....18 D5
  Hayes UB4....83 C4
  5 Isleworth TW7....131 A2
  New Malden KT4....199 C1
Percy Ho 4 SW16....181 C6
Percy Laurie Ho 6
  SW15....134 D1
Percy Mews W1....239 C3
Percy Pas W1....239 C3
Percy Rd
  Bexleyheath DA7....147 A3
  Carshalton CR4....203 A2
  Croydon SE25....206 A4
  Edmonton N21....17 A4
  Hampton TW12....173 C3
  Ilford IG3....58 A2
  Isleworth TW7....131 A1
  Leytonstone E11....54 C2
  Newham E16....98 C2
  North Finchley N12....30 A5
  Penge SE20....184 D2
  Romford RM7....59 D6
  Shepherd's Bush W12....112 A4
  Twickenham TW2....152 A3
Percy St W1....93 D2 239 C3
Percy Way TW2....152 A3
Peregrine Cl NW10....67 B3
Peregrine Ct
  Bexley DA16....145 D4
  Streatham SW16....182 B6
Peregrine Gdns CR0....223 A6
Peregrine Ho
  6 Battersea SW11....136 C2
  Finsbury EC1....234 D2
Peregrine Rd
  Sunbury TW16....171 D1
  Tottenham N17....33 B3
Peregrine Way SW19,
  SW20....178 C2
Perham Rd W14....113 A1 254 B1
Peridot St E6....100 A2
Perifield SE21....161 A3
Perimeade Rd UB6....87 C5
Period Wks E10....53 A1
Periton Rd SE9....143 D1
PERIVALE....87 B5
Perivale Gdns W13....87 B3
Perivale Grange UB6....87 A4
Perivale Ind Pk UB6....87 B5
Perivale La UB6....87 A4

Perivale Lo UB6 . . . . 87 A4
Perivale New Bsns Ctr
UB6. . . . . 87 C5
Perivale Pk Athletics Tk
UB6. . . . . 86 C4
Perivale Prim Sch UB6 . . . . 87 C5
Perivale Sta UB6. . . . . 87 A5
Periwood Cres UB6. . . . . . . 87 A6
Perkin Cl Hounslow TW3 . . 129 D1
Wembley HA0 . . . . 65 B3
Perkins Ct TW15 . . . . 170 B5
Perkins Ho E5 E14 . . . . 97 B2
Perkins Rd IG2 . . . . 57 B4
Perkins Rents SW1 . . . . 259 C5
Perkins Sq SE1 . . . . 252 B4
Perks Cl SE3. . . . . 142 C2
Perley Ho E3 . . . . 97 B2
Perpins Rd SE9 . . . . 167 C5
Perotti Ho SW6 . . . . 135 D2
Perran Rd SE24, SW2 . . . . 160 D2
Perren St NW5 . . . . 71 B2
Perrers Rd W6 . . . . 112 B2
Perrin Cl TW15 . . . . 170 B5
Perrin Ct TW15 . . . . 170 C6
Perring Est E3 . . . . 97 C2
Perrin Grange HA9 . . . . 66 B6
Perrin Rd HA0. . . . . 65 B4
Perrins Ct HA3. . . . . 44 B2
Perrin's Ct 20 NW3. . . . . . . 70 A4
Perrin's La NW3 . . . . 70 A4
Perrin's Wlk NW3 . . . . 70 A4
Perronet Ho SE1. . . . . . . 261 D5
Perry Ave W3. . . . . 89 B1
Perry Cl UB8. . . . . 82 D1
Perry Ct
    Isle of Dogs E14 . . . . 119 C1
    2 Kingston u T KT2 . . . . . 176 A1
    Sutton SM1. . . . . 217 C3
    2 Tottenham N15 . . . . 51 C3
Perryfield Way
    Richmond TW10 . . . . 153 B2
    West Hendon NW9. . . . . . . 45 D3
Perry Garth UB5 . . . . 84 C6
Perry Gdns N9. . . . . 17 C1
Perry Hall Prim Sch
BR6. . . . . 211 D3
Perry Hill SE6 . . . . 163 B1
Perry Ho 24 SW2. . . . . . . 160 A4
Perry How KT4 . . . . 199 D1
Perryman Ho
    Barking IG11 . . . . 101 A6
    Tottenham N17. . . . . 34 B3
Perrymans Farm Rd IG2 . . 57 B4
Perry Mead Bushey WD23 . . 8 A5
    Enfield EN2. . . . . 4 D3
Perrymead St
SW6. . . . . 135 D4 265 C1
Perrymount Prim Sch 5
SE23. . . . . 162 D2
Perryn Ct 1 TW1 . . . . . . 153 A4
Perryn Ho W3 . . . . 111 C6
Perryn Rd Acton W3 . . . . . 111 B6
    1 Bermondsey SE16. . . . . 118 B3
Perry Rd RM9. . . . . 103 B2
Perry Rise SE23 . . . . 163 A1
Perry's Pl W1. . . . . 239 C2
Perry St BR7. . . . . 189 C4
Perry Street Gdns BR7 . . 189 C4
Perry Vale SE23 . . . . 162 D2
Perryvale Ho 17 E5 . . . . . 74 B3
Persant Rd SE6. . . . . 164 C2
Perseverance Pl SW9 . . 138 C5
Perseverance Works 17
E2 . . . . 95 C4
Pershore Cl IG2 . . . . 56 D4
Pershore Gr SM5 . . . . 202 B3
Pershore Ho 11 W13 . . . . 109 A5
Pert Cl N10 . . . . 31 B4
Perth Ave Hayes UB4. . . . . 84 C3
    Kingsbury NW9 . . . . 45 B2
Perth Cl Northolt UB5 . . . . 63 C3
    Wimbledon SW20. . . . . . . 178 A1
Perth Ct 5 SE5 . . . . 139 B1
Perth Ho 12 Acton W3. . . . 88 C1
    Barnsbury N1. . . . . 72 B1
Perth Rd Barking IG11. . . 101 B6
    Beckenham BR3 . . . . 186 A1
    Finsbury Pk N4 . . . . 50 C1
    Ilford IG2 . . . . 56 D3
    Newham E13 . . . . 99 B5
    Tottenham N22. . . . . 32 D2
    Walthamstow E10 . . . . . . 53 B1
Perth Terr IG2. . . . . 57 A2
Perwell Ave HA2. . . . . 41 B1
Perystreete SE23 . . . . . . 162 C2
Petavel Rd TW11. . . . . . . 174 C4
Petchey Acad The E8. . . . 73 D3
Peter Ave W10 . . . . 68 B1
Peter Best Ho 1 E1. . . . . . 96 B1
Peterboat Cl SE10 . . . . . 120 C2
Peterborough Ct EC4 . . 241 B1
Peterborough Gdns IG1. . 56 A2
Peterborough Mews
SW6. . . . . 135 C3
Peterborough Rd
    Carshalton SM5 . . . . 202 C3
    Fulham SW6 . . . . 135 C2
    Harrow HA1. . . . . 42 D2
    Leytonstone E10. . . . . 54 B3

Peterborough & St
    Margarets High Sch HA7. . 8 C1
Peterborough Villas
SW6. . . . . 265 C2
Peter Bradley Ct RM9 . . . . 81 B1
Peter Butler Ho 9 SE1. . 118 A4
Peterchurch Ho SE15 . . 140 B6
Peter Fagan Ho UB3 . . . . 105 C3
Petergate SW11 . . . . 136 A1
Peterhead Ct 12 UB1. . . . 86 A1
Peter Heathfield Ho 4
E15 . . . . 98 B6
Peter Hills Ho 6 SE16. . 118 A4
Peter Hills Sch 28 SE16. . 118 D5
Peter Ho SW8 . . . . 270 A4
Peter James Bsns Ctr
UB3. . . . . 106 A4
Peter James Ent Ctr
NW10. . . . . 89 A4
Peter Kennedy Ct CR0. . . 207 B3
Peterley Bsns Ctr 21 E2 . . 96 B5
Peter Lyell Ct HA4 . . . . 62 B6
Peters Cl Bexley DA16. . . 145 C3
    Dagenham RM8 . . . . 58 D1
    Stanmore HA7 . . . . 25 D4
Peter's Ct 9 SW4 . . . . 91 D1
Peter's Cl SW4 . . . . 160 A5
Petersfield Cl N18 . . . . 33 A3
Petersfield Rd W3 . . . . . . 111 A4
Petersfield Rise SW15 . . 156 B3
PETERSHAM. 154 A3
Petersham Cl
    Richmond TW10 . . . . 153 D2
    Sutton SM1. . . . . 217 C3
Petersham Dr BR5. . . . . . 190 A1
Petersham Gdns BR5 . . 189 D1
Petersham Ho SW7 . . . . 256 A6
Petersham La SW7. . . . . 256 A6
Petersham Mews
    SW7. . . . . 114 A3 256 B6
Petersham Pl
    SW7. . . . . 114 A3 256 B6
Petersham Rd TW10 . . . . 154 A3
Petersham Terr CR0. . . . . 220 A5
Peter's La EC1. . . . . 241 D4
Peter's Lo HA8 . . . . 26 B4
Peter's Path SE26. . . . . . 184 B6
Peter St W1 . . . . 115 D6 249 C6
Peterstone Rd SE2. . . . . 124 B4
Peterstow Cl SW19 . . . . 157 A2
Peterwood Pk CR9. . . . . . 220 B6
Peterwood Way CR0 . . . . 220 B6
Petherton Ct
    Brondesbury Pk NW10. . . . 90 D6
    10 Harrow HA1. . . . . 42 D3
Petherton Ho N4 . . . . 51 A1
Petherton Rd N5 . . . . 73 A3
Petiver Cl 28 E9. . . . . 74 C1
Petley Rd W6 . . . . 134 D5
Peto Pl NW1 . . . . 238 D6
Peto St N E16. . . . . 98 D1
Petrel Ct 8 SE21 . . . . 161 B2
Petrie Cl NW2. . . . . 69 A2
Petrie Ho 3 SE18. . . . . . . 144 C6
Petrie Mus of Egyptian
    Archaeology ★
WC1 . . . . 93 D3 239 C5
Petros Gdns 1 NW3 . . . . . 70 A2
Pettacre Cl SE28. . . . . . . 123 A3
Petticoat Lane Mkt ★
EC2 . . . . 95 D2 243 C3
Petticoat Sq 1 . . . . 243 C2
Petticoat Twr E1. . . . . . . 243 C2
Pettit's Pl RM10. . . . . 81 C3
Pettit's Rd RM10. . . . . 81 C3
Pettiward Cl SW15 . . . . . 134 C1
Pettman Cres SE18, SE28. . 123 B3
Pettsgrove Ave HA0. . . . . 65 C3
Pett's Hill UB5. . . . . 63 D3
Petts Hill Prim Sch UB5 . . 63 D3
Petts La TW17 . . . . 192 C5
Pett St SE18 . . . . 122 A2
PETTS WOOD 211 B5
Petts Wood Rd BR5. . . . . 211 B4
Petts Wood Sta BR5. . . . 211 A4
Petty France
    SW1. . . . . 115 D3 259 C6
Petty Wales EC3 . . . . . . 253 B5
Petworth Cl UB5. . . . . 63 B1
Petworth Gdns
    Hillingdon UB8 . . . . 83 A6
    West Barnes SW20 . . . . . 200 B6
Petworth Ho 16 SE22 . . . 139 C2
Petworth Rd Bexley DA6. . 169 C6
    Colney Hatch N12. . . . . . . 30 C5
Petworth St
    SW11. . . . . 136 C4 267 B2
Petyt Pl SW3 . . . . . . 136 C6 267 A6
Petyward SW3. . . . . . 114 C2 257 B3
Pevensey Ave Enfield EN1 . . 5 C3
    Friern Barnet N11. . . . . 31 C5
Pevensey Cl TW7 . . . . . . 130 A5
Pevensey Ct
    4 South Acton W3. . . . . . 110 D4
    West Norwood SW16 . . . . 160 C1
    10 Woodford E18 . . . . 37 A2
Pevensey Ho 5 E1. . . . . . . 97 A2
Pevensey Rd
    Feltham TW13 . . . . 151 A3
    Forest Gate E7 . . . . 77 A4

Pevensey Rd continued
    Upper Tooting SW17. . . . . 180 B6
Peveril E6 . . . . 100 C1
Peveril Ho RM10 . . . . 81 C6
Peverett Cl N11. . . . . 31 B5
Peveril Ho SE1. . . . . 262 D5
Pewsey Cl E4. . . . . 35 C5
Pewsham Ho N4. . . . . 51 A1
Pewterers Ct N3. . . . . 29 B2
Peyton Ho N11 . . . . 31 A6
Peyton Pl SE10 . . . . 142 A5
Pharamond NW2. . . . . 68 D2
Pharaoh Cl CR4. . . . . 202 D2
Pheasant Cl E16 . . . . 99 B1
Phelps Ho 15 SW15 . . . . 134 D2
Phelp St SE17 . . . . 139 B6
Phelps Way UB3 . . . . 105 D2
Phene St SW3 . . . . . 136 C6 267 B6
Philadelphia Ct SW10 . . 266 B3
Philbeach Gdns
    SW5. . . . . 113 C1 255 A2
Phil Brown Pl 3 SW8 . . . 137 B2
Philchurch Pl 36 E1. . . . . . 96 A1
Philia Ho 4 NW1 . . . . 71 C1
Philimore Cl SE18. . . . . . 123 C1
Philip Blairman Ho E1 . . 243 C5
Philip Ct Enfield EN2 . . . . . 5 B4
    Paddington W2 . . . . 236 C4
Philip Gdns CR0. . . . . . . 223 B6
Philip Ho East Barnet N20. . 14 D2
    12 Paddington NW6. . . . . . 91 B6
Philip La N15. . . . . 51 C6
Philpot Almshouse SE9. . 166 B5
Philpot Path SE9. . . . . . . 166 B5
Philippa Gdns SE9 . . . . . 165 D6
Philips Cl CR4. . . . . 203 A1
Philip St E13 . . . . 99 A3
Philip Turner Est 28 E9 . . . 74 C1
Philip Wlk SE15. . . . . 140 A2
Phillimore Cl W8 . . . . . . 245 B1
Phillimore Gardens Cl
    W8. . . . . 113 C4 255 A6
Phillimore Gdns
    Kensington W8. . . . 113 C4 245 A1
    Willesden NW10. . . . . 90 C6
Phillimore Pl
    W8. . . . . 113 C4 245 A1
Phillimore Terr W8. . . . . 255 B6
Phillimore Wlk
    W8. . . . . 113 C3 255 B6
Phillip Ho E1. . . . . 243 D1
Phillipp St N1. . . . . 95 C6
Phillips Ct Edgware HA8. . . 26 C4
    Hayes UB4. . . . . 84 B4
Phillipson Ho 6 N12. . . . . 29 D5
Philpot La EC3. . . . . 253 A6
Philpot Sq SW6. . . . . 135 D2
Philpot St E1 . . . . 96 B1
Philson Mans 13 E1. . . . . . 96 B1
Phineas Pett Rd SE9 . . . 144 A2
Phipp's Bridge Rd CR4,
    SW19. . . . . 202 B6
Phipps Bridge Sta CR4 . . 202 B6
Phipps Hatch La EN2. . . . . 5 A5
Phipps Ho
    1 Greenwich SE7 . . . . . . 121 B1
    16 Shepherd's Bush W12. . 112 B6
Phipp St EC2 . . . . . . 95 C3 243 A6
Phoebeth Rd SE4. . . . . . 163 C6
Phoenix Acad 2 E4. . . . . . 20 A1
Phoenix Bsns Ctr 22 E3 . . 97 C2
Phoenix Ct
    18 Shoreditch E8 . . . . 95 C6
    Walthamstow E17. . . . . . . 35 B1
    West Wickham BR4 . . . . . 224 C6
Phoenix Ctr
    4 Brentford TW8 . . . . 110 A1
    Chingford E4. . . . . 19 D1
    Croydon SE25 . . . . 206 A4
    2 Deptford SE14. . . . . . . 141 A6
    Enfield EN3. . . . . 6 C5
    Feltham TW13 . . . . 171 C6
    8 New Barnet EN5. . . . . . . 2 A1
Phoenix Ctr The 1 SM6 . . 220 A1
Phoenix Dr BR2. . . . . 225 D5
Phoenix High Sch W12. . . 112 A6
Phoenix Ho Chelsea SW1. . 258 A4
    Kingston u T KT3. . . . . . . 199 D6
Phoenix Ind Est HA1 . . . . 42 D5
Phoenix Lodge Mans 1
    W6. . . . . 112 C2
Phoenix Pk NW2. . . . . 68 A6
Phoenix Pl WC1. . . 94 B3 240 D6
Phoenix Rd Penge SE20 . . 184 C4
    Somers Town NW1. . . 93 D4 232 C2
Phoenix Sch The 12 NW3. . 70 A2
Phoenix Sec & Prim Sch 26
    E3. 97 B4
Phoenix St WC2. . . . . . . 239 D1
Phoenix Trad Est UB6. . . . 87 D6
Phoenix Trad Pk TW8. . . . 109 D1
Phoenix Way TW5. . . . . . 111 A6
Phoenix Wharf Rd SE1. . 253 D1
Phyllis Ave KT3 . . . . 200 B4
Phyllis Ho CR0. . . . . 220 D4
Phyllis Hodges Ho
    NW1. . . . . 93 D5 232 C3
Physic Pl SW3 . . . . 136 D6 267 C6

Picador Ho 1 RM10 . . . . . 81 D2
Picardy Manorway
    DA17. . . . . 125 D4
Picardy Rd DA17. . . . . . . 125 C2
Picardy St DA17. . . . . 125 C3
Piccadilly W1. . . . . . 115 C5 249 A4
Piccadilly Arc SW1. . . . . 249 A4
Piccadilly Cir ★
    W1. . . . . 115 D6 249 C5
Piccadilly Circus Sta
    SW1 . . . . 115 D6 249 C5
Piccadilly Ct 5 N7. . . . . . . 72 B2
Piccadilly Pl W1. . . . . . . 249 B5
Pickard Cl N14. . . . . 15 D3
Pickard St EC1. . . . . 234 D2
Pickering Ave E6 . . . . . . 100 C4
Pickering Cl E9. . . . . 74 D1
Pickering Ct N22 . . . . 32 D2
Pickering Gdns
    Croydon SE25. . . . . 205 D3
    Friern Barnet N11. . . . . . . 31 A4
Pickering Ho
    Brentford W5 . . . . 109 C2
    18 Kensington W2 . . . . 91 D1
    Stoke Newington N4. . . . . . 51 B2
    4 Woolwich SE18 . . . . . . 122 C2
Pickering Mews 9 W2. . . . 91 D1
Pickering Pl SW1 . . . . . . 249 B3
Pickering St N1. . . . . 234 D6
Pickets Cl WD23 . . . . 8 C3
Pickets St SW12 . . . . 159 B4
Pickett Croft HA7. . . . . . . 25 D2
Pickett's Lock La N9 . . . . . 18 D2
Pickford Cl DA7 . . . . 147 A3
Pickford La DA7. . . . . . . 147 A2
Pickford Rd DA7. . . . . . . 147 A2
Pickfords Wharf N1. . . . . 235 A3
Pickhurst Gn BR2 . . . . . . 208 D2
Pickhurst Inf Sch BR2. . . 208 D3
Pickhurst Jun Sch BR2. . 208 D3
Pickhurst La BR2, BR3,
    BR4 . . . . 208 C2
Pickhurst Mead BR2 . . . . 208 D2
Pickhurst Pk BR2 . . . . . . 208 D4
Pickhurst Rise BR4 . . . . . 208 B1
Pickwick Cl TW4 . . . . 151 A6
Pickwick Ct SE9 . . . . 166 B3
Pickwick Ho
    21 Bermondsey SE16. . . . 118 A4
    3 Shepherd's Bush W11. . 112 D5
Pickwick Mews N18 . . . . . 33 C5
Pickwick Pl HA1. . . . . 42 C2
Pickwick Rd SE21. . . . . . 161 A4
Pickwick St SE1 . . . . . . 252 A1
Pickwick Way BR7 . . . . . 189 A4
Pickworth Cl SW8 . . . . . 270 B3
Picton Ho 1 SW4. . . . . . . 160 A4
Picton Pl Marylebone W1 . . 238 B1
    Tolworth KT6 . . . . 198 C1
Picton St SE5 . . . . 139 B5
Picture Ho 6 SW16. . . . . 160 A2
Pied Bull Ct WC1. . . . . . 240 B3
Pied Bull Yd WC1 . . . . . . 240 B3
Piedmont Rd SE18. . . . . . 123 B1
Field Heath Ave UB8. . . . 82 C3
Field Heath Rd UB8. . . . . 82 B3
Field Heath Sch UB8. . . . 82 A3
Pier Head E1 . . . . 118 B5
Pierhead Wharf 37 E1. . . 118 B5
Pier Ho SW3 . . . . 267 B5
Piermont Pl BR1. . . . . . . 188 A1
Piermont Rd SE22 . . . . . 162 B6
Pier Par 3 E16 . . . . 122 C5
Pierpoint Bldg 4 E14. . . 119 C4
Pier Rd Feltham TW14 . . . 150 B6
    Newham E16 . . . . 122 C4
Pierrepoint SE25 . . . . . . 205 C6
Pierrepoint Ho 3 . . . . . . 110 D6
Pierrepoint Rd W3. . . . . . 234 C4
Pierrepoint Row N1. . . . . 234 C4
Pierson Ho 12 SE19 . . . . 183 C6
Pier St E14. . . . . 120 A2
Pier Terr SW18 . . . . 136 A1
Pier Way SE18 . . . . 123 B3
Pigeon Ct E4 . . . . 36 A4
Pigeon La TW12 . . . . 173 C6
Piggott Ho 2 E2. . . . . 96 D5
Pigott St E14 . . . . 97 C1
Pike Cl Bromley BR1. . . . . 187 B5
    Hillingdon UB10 . . . . 82 B6
Pike Rd NW7 . . . . 27 B6
Pike's End HA5 . . . . 40 B5
Pikestone Cl UB4 . . . . 85 A3
Pikethorne SE23 . . . . . . 162 D2
Pilgrimage St
    SE1 . . . . 117 B4 252 C1
Pilgrim Cl SM4 . . . . 201 D2
Pilgrim Hill SE27. . . . . . . 183 A6
Pilgrim Ho SE1 . . . . 262 D5
Pilgrims Cl Northolt UB5 . . 64 A3
    Palmers Green N13 . . . . . 32 B6
Pilgrims Cloisters 10
    SE5 . . . . 139 C5
Pilgrims Ct Enfield EN1. . . 5 B3
    Greenwich SE3 . . . . 143 A4
Pilgrim's La NW3. . . . . 70 B4
Pilgrims Mews 12 E14. . . 120 B6
Pilgrim's Pl 6 NW3. . . . . . 70 B4
Pilgrim's Rise EN4. . . . . . 14 C6
Pilgrim St EC4. . . . . 241 C1

Per–Pin 381

Pilgrims Way
    5 Newham E6. . . . . 100 A6
    Upper Holloway N19. . . . . 49 D1
    Wembley HA9. . . . . 44 D1
Pilgrim's Way CR2 . . . . . 221 D3
Pilgrims Way Prim Sch 7
    SE15. . . . . 140 C6
Pilkington Ct 1 NW9 . . . . 46 A5
Pilkington Rd
    Orpington BR6 . . . . 227 A6
    4 Peckham SE15. . . . . . . 140 B3
Pillions La UB4 . . . . 83 B3
Pilot Ind Ctr NW10. . . . . . 89 C3
Pilsden Cl SW19 . . . . 156 D3
Piltdown Rd WD19 . . . . . . 22 D6
Pilton Est The CR0 . . . . . 220 D6
Pilton Pl SE17 . . . . 262 B2
Pimento Ct W5 . . . . 109 D3
Pimlico Sta
    SW1 . . . . 115 D1 259 C2
PIMLICO. 115 C1
Pimlico Acad
    SW1 . . . . 115 C1 259 B1
Pimlico Rd SW1 . . . 115 A1 258 B2
Pimlico Wlk 1 N1. . . . . . . 95 C4
Pinchbeck Rd BR6 . . . . . 227 D2
Pinchin St E1. . . . . 118 A6
Pincombe Ho SE17. . . . . 262 C2
Pincott Pl SE4 . . . . 140 D2
Pincott Rd
    7 Bexley DA6. . . . . 147 C1
    Merton SW19 . . . . 180 A3
Pindar St EC2. . . . . . 95 C2 243 A4
Pindock Mews W9 . . . . 91 D3
Pine Apple Ct SW1. . . . . 259 A6
Pine Ave
    Stratford New Town E15. . . 76 B3
    West Wickham BR4 . . . . . 207 D1
Pine Cl
    11 Dartmouth Pk N19. . . . 71 C6
    London E10. . . . . 75 D6
    Osidge N14. . . . . 15 C4
    3 Penge SE20 . . . . 184 C2
    Stanmore HA7 . . . . 25 B6
Pine Coombe CR0 . . . . . 222 D4
Pinecrest Gdns BR6. . . . 226 D4
Pinecroft
    East Wickham DA16. . . . . 146 A5
    Harrow HA4. . . . . 44 B4
Pinecroft Cres EN5 . . . . . . 1 A1
Pine Ct UB5 . . . . 85 A4
Pinedene 2 SE15. . . . . . 140 B4
Pinefield Cl E14 . . . . 119 C6
Pine Gdns Ruislip HA4. . . 62 B6
    Surbiton KT5. . . . . 198 C3
Pine Glade BR6 . . . . 226 B4
Pine Gr
    Finsbury Pk N4, N19. . . . . 72 B6
    Totteridge N20. . . . . 13 C3
    Wimbledon SW19. . . . . . . 179 B5
Pine Ho Bow E3 . . . . 97 A6
    21 Rotherhithe SE16. . . . . 118 C4
Pinehurst
    Chislehurst BR7 . . . . 188 D4
    Stanmore HA7 . . . . 25 A5
Pinehurst Ct 6 W11. . . . . 91 B1
Pinehurst Wlk 4 BR6. . . 211 B1
Pinelands Cl 7 SE3. . . . . 142 D5
Pine Lo SW15. . . . . 157 A5
Pinemartin Cl NW2 . . . . . 68 C5
Pine Pl UB4 . . . . 83 D3
Pine Rd Brunswick Pk N11. . 15 A2
    Cricklewood NW2. . . . . . . 68 D4
Pine Ridge SM5. . . . . 219 A1
Pines Cl 1 SW19 . . . . . . 156 D3
Pines Rd BR1 . . . . 188 A1
Pine St EC1 . . . . 94 C3 241 A6
Pines The Southgate N14 . . 15 C6
    South Norwood SE19 . . . . 182 D4
    Sunbury TW16 . . . . 194 A6
    Surbiton KT6. . . . . 214 A5
    Woodford IG8. . . . . 21 A1
Pine Tree Ho 14 SE14. . . 140 D5
Pine Tree Ho SE14. . . . . 140 D5
Pine Tree Lo BR2. . . . . . . 208 D5
Pine Trees Dr UB10. . . . . 60 A4
Pine Tree Way 1 SE13. . . 141 D2
Pineview Ct 3 E4 . . . . 20 A3
Pine Wlk KT5. . . . . 198 C3
Pinewood BR7. . . . . 188 C4
Pine Wood TW16. . . . . . 172 A2
Pinewood Ave
    Hillingdon UB8 . . . . 82 B1
    Pinner HA5. . . . . 23 D4
    Sidcup DA15. . . . . 167 C3
Pinewood Cl Crofton BR6. . 227 D2
    Croydon CR0. . . . . 223 A5
    Pinner HA5. . . . . 23 D4
    South Oxhey HA6. . . . . 22 B5
Pinewood Ct
    Clapham Pk SW4 . . . . . . 159 D5
    Enfield EN2. . . . . 4 D2
    Merton SW19 . . . . 179 D3
Pinewood Dr BR6. . . . . . 227 C3
Pinewood Gr W5. . . . . 87 C1
Pinewood Lo WD23 . . . . . . 8 B3
Pinewood Pl KT19 . . . . . 215 B4

Pinewood Rd
Bromley BR2 209 A5
Feltham TW13 150 B1
West Heath SE2 146 D6
Pinfold Rd SW16 182 A6
Pinglestone Cl UB7 126 A5
Pinkcoat Cl TW13 150 B1
Pinkerton Ct KT2 176 D1
Pinkerton Pl SW16 181 D6
Pinkham Mans W4 110 C1
Pinkham Way (North Circular Rd) N12 31 A4
Pinkwell Ave UB3 105 B2
Pinkwell La UB3 105 B2
Pinkwell Prim Sch UB3 105 A2
Pinley Gdns RM9 102 B6
Pinnace Ho E14 120 A3
Pinnacle Hill DA7 147 D1
Pinnacle Hill N DA7 147 D1
Pinnacle Ho EC3 253 A5
Pinnacle The
Dagenham RM6 59 A3
7 Kingsland N1 73 B2
Pinnata Cl EN2 5 A4
Pinnell Rd SE9 143 D1
PINNER 41 A6
Pinner Ct NW8 236 C6
Pinner Gn HA5 22 C1
Pinner Gr HA5 41 A4
PINNER GREEN 22 C1
Pinner Hill HA5 22 B3
Pinner Hill Rd HA5 22 C1
Pinner Ho
30 Camberwell SE5 139 A3
Pinner HA5 41 A6
Pinner Park Ave HA2 24 A1
Pinner Park Fst & Mid Schs HA5 41 D6
Pinner Park Gdns HA2 24 A1
Pinner Rd
Harrow HA1, HA2 42 A3
Northwood HA6 22 A1
Pinner HA2, HA5 41 C5
Pinner Sta HA5 41 A5
Pinner View HA1, HA2 42 A4
PINNERWOOD PARK 22 C3
Pinner Wood Sch HA5 22 C2
Pinn Way HA4 39 C2
Pintail Cl E6 100 A2
Pintail Ct 39 SE8 141 B6
Pintail Rd IG8 37 B3
Pintail Way UB4 84 D2
Pinter Ho 30 SW9 138 A3
Pinto Cl WD6 11 B5
Pinto Way SE3 143 B1
Pioneer Cl
10 Bow Comm E14 97 D2
London W12 90 B1
Pioneers Ind Pk CR0 204 A1
Pioneer St SE15 140 A4
Pioneer Way W12 90 C1
Piper Cl N7 72 B3
Piper Rd KT1 198 C6
Pipers Gdns CR0 207 A2
Pipers Gn NW9 45 A4
Pipers Green La HA8 10 A1
Pipers Ho SE10 120 B1
Piper Way IG1 57 B1
Pipewell Rd SM5 202 C3
Pippenhall SE9 166 D5
Pippin Cl Croydon CR0 207 B1
Dollis Hill NW2 68 B5
Pippin Ct 5 EN4 2 C1
Pippin Ho 17 W10 112 D6
Pippins Ct TW15 170 D4
Piquet Rd SE20 184 C1
Pirate Castle The★ NW1 71 A1
Pirbright Cres CR0 224 A2
Pirbright Ho 11 KT2 176 D4
Pirbright Rd SW18 157 C3
Pirie St 6 E16 121 B5
Pitcairn Cl RM7 59 C5
Pitcairn Ct CR4 180 D3
Pitcairne Ct N21 16 B6
Pitcairn Ho 1 E9 74 C1
Pitcairn Rd CR4 180 D3
Pitchford St E15 76 C1
Pitfield Cres SE28 124 A5
Pitfield Ho N5 73 A3
Pitfield St N1 95 C5
Pitfield Way Enfield EN3 6 C4
Tokyngton NW10 67 A2
Pitfold Cl SE12 165 B5
Pitfold Rd SE12 165 A4
Pit Ho NW10 67 B5
Pitlake CR0 220 D6
Pitman Ho Southgate N21 16 B6
4 St Johns SE8 141 C4
Pitman St SE5 139 A5
Pitmaston Ho 2 SE13 142 A3
Pitsea Pl E1 96 D1
Pitsea St E1 96 D1
Pitshanger Ct 2 W5 87 C3
Pitshanger La W5 87 C3
Pitt Cres SW19 179 D6
Pitt Ho 4 SW11 136 B1
Pittman Gdns IG1 79 A3
Pitt Rd Harrow HA2 64 A6
Orpington BR6 227 A4
Thornton Heath CR0, CR7 205 A4
Pitt's Head Mews W1 248 B3
Pittsmead Ave BR2 209 A2
Pitt St W8 113 C4 245 B2
Pittville Gdns SE25 206 A6
Pitzhanger Manor House & Gallery★ W5 109 D5
Pixfield Ct BR2 186 D1
Pixham Ct 5 SW19 179 B5
Pixley St E14 97 B1
Pixton 14 NW9 27 C2
Pixton Way CR2 223 B1
Place Farm Ave BR5, BR6 211 B1
Plains The 7 E4 20 C4
PLAISTOW BR1 187 A4
E13 99 B4
Plaistow Gr Bromley BR1 187 B3
West Ham E15 98 D6
Plaistow La BR1 187 C2
Plaistow Park Rd E13 99 B5
Plaistow Prim Sch E13 99 B5
Plaistow Rd E13, E15 98 D5
Plaistow Sta E13 98 D5
Plane St SE26 162 B1
Plane Tree Cres TW13 150 B1
Planetree Ct W6 112 D2
Plane Tree Ho
Deptford SE8 141 A6
Greenwich SE7 121 D1
Plane Tree Wlk 4 SE19 183 C4
Plantagenet Cl KT19 215 B4
Plantagenet Gdns RM6 58 D2
Plantagenet Ho SE18 122 B3
Plantagenet Pl RM6 58 D2
Plantagenet Rd EN5 2 A1
Plantain Gdns E11 76 B5
Plantain Pl SE1 252 C2
Plantation La EC3 253 A6
Plantation The SE3 143 A3
Plasel Ct E13 99 B6
PLASHET 78 A2
Plashet Gr E6 77 D1
Plashet Rd E13 77 B1
Plashet Sch E6 78 A1
Plassy Rd SE6 163 D4
Platehouse The 3 E14 119 D1
Platina St EC2 242 D6
Platinum Ct RM7 59 D6
Plato Pl 1 SW6 135 B3
Plato Rd SW2 138 A1
Platt Halls (a) 35 NW9 27 D1
Platt Halls (b) 37 NW9 27 D1
Platt Halls (c) 38 NW9 27 D1
Platt's Eyot TW12 173 C1
Platt's La NW3 69 C5
Platts Rd EN3 6 C4
Platt St NW1 232 C4
Plaxdale Ho SE17 263 A3
Plaxtol Cl BR1 187 C2
Plaxtol Rd DA8 147 C5
Plaxton Ct E11 76 D5
Playfair St W6 112 C1
Playfield Cres SE22 161 D6
Playfield Rd HA8 27 A1
Playford Rd
Finsbury Pk N4 72 B6
Finsbury Pk N4 72 C6
Playgreen Way SE6 185 C6
Playground Cl BR3 184 D1
Playhouse Yd EC4 241 C1
Plaza Bsns Ctr EN3 7 B3
Plaza Hts E10 76 A5
Plaza Sh Ctr W1 93 C1 239 B2
Plaza Wlk NW9 45 A6
Pleasance Rd
Putney SW15 156 B6
St Paul's Cray BR5 190 B1
Pleasance The SW15 134 B1
Pleasant Gr CR0 223 B5
Pleasant Pl N1 72 D1
Pleasant Row NW1 231 D5
Pleasant View BR6 227 A3
Pleasant View Pl BR6 227 A3
Pleasant Way HA0 87 C5
Pleasaunce Ct SE9 144 B1
Plender Ct NW1 232 B5
Plender St NW1 93 C6 232 B5
Pleshey Rd N7 71 D4
Plevna Cres N15 51 C3
Plevna Ho 1 N9 18 A1
Plevna Rd Edmonton N9 18 B1
Hampton TW12 173 D2
Plevna St E14 120 A3
Pleydell Ave
Chiswick W6 111 D2
Penge SE19 183 D3
Pleydell Ct EC4 241 B1
Pleydell Gdns SE19 183 D4
Pleydell St EC4 241 B1
Plimsoll Cl E14 97 D1
Plimsoll Rd N4 72 D5
Plough Ct EC3 252 D6
Plough Farm Cl HA4 39 B3
Plough La
Dulwich Village SE22 161 D5
7 Teddington TW11 175 A5
Wallington CR0, SM6 220 A3
Plough La *continued*
Wimbledon SW17, SW19 180 A6
Plough Lane Cl CR0, SM6 220 A3
Ploughmans Cl NW1 232 C6
Ploughmans End TW7 152 B6
Plough Mews 19 SW11 136 B1
Plough Pl EC4 241 B2
Plough Rd
Battersea SW11 136 B1
West Ewell KT19 215 B1
Plough St 16 E1 96 A1
Plough Terr SW11 136 B1
Plough Way SE16 119 A2
Plough Yd EC2 243 B5
Plover Ho 4 SW9 138 C5
Plover Way Hayes UB4 84 D2
Rotherhithe SE16 119 A3
Plowman Cl N18 33 B5
Plowman Ho SW19 156 D2
Plowman Way RM8 58 C1
Plumbers Row E1 96 A1
Plumbridge St 7 SE10 142 A4
Plum Cl TW14 150 A3
Plumcroft Prim Sch SE18 145 A6
Plume Ho SE10 141 D6
Plum Garth TW8 109 D2
Plum La SE18 145 A5
Plummer Ct SE13 163 D5
Plummer La CR4 180 D1
Plummer Rd SW4 159 D4
Plumpton Cl UB5 63 C2
Plumpton Ct SE23 163 A4
Plumpton Lo E5 74 D5
Plumpton Way SM5 218 C5
PLUMSTEAD 123 C2
PLUMSTEAD COMMON 145 D6
Plumstead Common Rd SE18 145 A6
Plumstead High St SE18, SE2 123 C2
Plumstead Manor Sch SE18 145 B6
Plumstead Rd SE18, SE28 123 A2
Plumstead Road Covered Mkt★ SE18 122 D2
Plumstead Sta SE18 123 B2
Plumtree Cl
Dagenham RM10 81 D2
Wallington SM6 219 D1
Plumtree Ct EC4 241 C2
Plymen Ho KT8 195 C4
Plymouth Ho
10 Barking IG11 80 A1
20 Lewisham SE10 141 D4
Plymouth Rd
Bromley BR1 187 B2
Newham E16 99 A2
Plymouth Wharf E14 120 B2
Plympton Ave NW6 69 B1
Plympton Cl 8 DA17 125 A3
Plympton Pl NW1 237 A5
Plympton Rd NW6 69 B1
Plympton St NW8 237 A5
Plymstock Rd DA16 146 C5
Pocklington Cl NW9 27 C1
Pocklington Ct SW15 156 A3
Pocklington Lo 6 W12 112 A3
Pocock Ave UB7 104 B3
Pocock St SE1 116 D4 251 D2
Podmore Rd SW18 136 A1
Poets Cnr★ SW1 260 A6
Poets Mews 3 SE24 160 D6
Poet's Rd N5 73 B3
Poets Way HA1 42 C5
Pointalls Cl N3 30 A1
Point Cl SE10 142 A4
Pointer Cl SE28 102 D1
Pointer Sch The SE3 143 A5
Pointers Cl E14 119 D1
Point Hill SE10 142 A4
Point Ho SE10 142 A4
Point Pl HA9 66 D1
Point Pleasant SW18 135 C1
Point Terr E7 77 B3
Point The HA4 62 A4
Point Wharf La TW8 132 A5
Poland Ho 3 E15 98 B6
Poland St W1 93 C1 239 B1
Polaris Ct EN4 14 B6
Polebrook Rd SE3 143 C2
Polecroft La SE6 163 B2
Polehamptons The TW12 174 A2
Pole Hill Rd Chingford E4 20 A4
Hillingdon UB4 83 A4
Polesden Gdns SW20 178 B1
Polesworth Ho 16 W2 91 C2
Polesworth Rd RM9 80 D1
Polish Inst & Sikorski Mus★ SW7 246 D1
Polish Univ Abroad 16 W6 112 A2
Polish War Meml HA4 62 C2
Pollard Cl Islington N7 72 B4
Newham E16 121 A6
Pollard Ct SM4 202 C4
Pollard Ho Cheam KT4 216 C4
Pollard Ho *continued*
Islington N1 233 C3
Pollard Rd
East Barnet N20 14 C2
Morden SM4 202 B4
Pollard Row E2 96 A4
Pollards Cl IG10 21 C6
Pollards Cres SW16 204 A6
Pollards Hill E SW16 204 B6
Pollards Hill N SW16 204 B6
Pollards Hill S SW16 204 B6
Pollards Hill W SW16 204 B6
Pollard St E2 96 A4
Pollards Wood Rd SW16 204 A6
Pollard Wlk DA14 190 C4
Pollen St W1 238 D1
Pollitt Dr NW8 92 B3 236 D6
Pollock Ho W10 91 A3
Pollock's Toy Mus★ W1 239 B4
Polperro Cl BR6 211 D3
Polperro Mans 3 NW6 69 C3
Polperro Mews SE11 261 C4
Polsted Rd SE6 163 B4
Polsten Mews 2 EN3 7 C6
Polthorne Gr SE18 123 B2
Polworth Rd SW16 182 A5
Polygon Rd NW1 93 D5 232 C3
Polygon The
1 Clapham SW4 137 C1
St John's Wood NW8 229 D6
Polytechnic St SE18 122 C2
Pomell Way E1 243 D2
Pomeroy Cl TW1 131 B1
Pomeroy Ct W11 91 A1
Pomeroy Ho 5 E2 96 D5
Pomeroy St SE14 140 C4
Pomfret Rd SE5 138 D2
Pomoja La N19 72 A6
Pomona Ho 10 SE8 119 A2
Pond Cl Colney Hatch N12 30 C4
Kidbrooke SE3 143 A3
Pond Cottage La BR3, BR4 207 C1
Pond Cotts SE21 161 C3
PONDERS END 18 D6
Ponders End Ind Est EN3 19 A6
Ponders End Sta EN3 19 A6
Ponder St 5 N7 72 B1
Pond Farm Est E5 74 C5
Pondfield End IG10 21 C4
Pondfield Ho
4 Islington N5 73 A3
West Norwood SE27 183 A5
Pondfield Rd
Dagenham RM10 81 D3
Locksbottom BR6 226 D5
West Wickham BR2 208 C1
Pond Gn HA4 61 C6
Pond Hill Gdns SM3 217 A2
Pond Ho Chelsea SW3 257 A3
Stanmore HA7 25 B4
Pond Mead SE21 161 B5
Pond Path BR7 188 D4
Pond Pl SW3 114 C2 257 A3
Pond Rd
Blackheath Vale SE3 142 D3
Newham E15 98 C5
Pondside Ave KT4 200 C1
Pondside Cl UB3 127 B6
Pond Sq N6 49 A1
Pond St NW3 70 C3
Pond Way TW11 175 C4
Pondwood Rise BR6 211 C2
Ponler St E1 96 B1
Ponsard Rd NW10 90 B4
Ponsford St E9 74 C2
Ponsonby Ho 13 E2 96 C5
Ponsonby Pl SW1 115 D1 259 D2
Ponsonby Rd SW15 156 B4
Ponsonby Terr SW1 259 D2
Pontefract Ct UB5 63 D3
Pontefract Rd BR1 186 D5
Ponton Ho SW2 160 C3
Ponton Rd SW8 137 D6 269 D5
Pontoon Dock Sta E16 121 C5
Pont St Mews SW1 257 C5
Pont St SW1 114 D3 257 D5
Pontypool Pl SE1 251 C2
Pool Cl Beckenham BR3 185 C5
East Molesey KT8 195 B4
Pool Ct SE6 163 C2
Poole Cl HA4 61 C6
Poole Court Rd TW5 129 A3
Poole Ct
De Beauvoir Town N1 73 C1
Hounslow TW5 129 A3
Poole Ho SE11 260 D5
Pool End Cl TW17 192 C4
Poole Rd Homerton E9 74 D2
West Ewell KT19 215 B2
Pooles Bldgs EC1 241 A5
Pooles Ct IG3 80 A5
Pooles La SW10 266 A3
Pooles Park Prim Sch 16 N4 72 B6
Pooles Pk N4 72 C6
Poole St N1 95 B6 235 C5
Poole Way UB4 83 C4
Pooley Ho E1 96 D4
Pool Ho NW8 236 D4
Poolmans St SE16 118 D4
Pool Rd
East Molesey KT12, KT8 195 B4
Harrow HA1 42 B2
Poolsford Rd NW9 45 C5
Poonah St E1 96 C1
Pope Cl
East Bedfont TW14 149 D3
Mitcham SW17, SW19 180 B4
Pope Ct 10 KT2 175 D6
Pope Ho
7 Bermondsey SE16 118 B2
3 Camberwell SE5 139 B5
Pope John Prim Sch W12 112 B6
Pope Rd BR2 209 D4
Pope's Ave TW2 152 C2
Popes Ct TW2 152 C2
Popes Dr N3 29 C2
Popes Gr CR0 223 B5
Pope's Gr TW1, TW2 152 D2
Pope's Head Alley EC3 242 D1
Pope's La W5 110 A3
Pope's Rd SW9 138 C2
Pope St SE1 253 B1
Pope Street Ct SE9 166 B3
Popham Cl TW13 151 B1
Popham Ct N16 73 C5
Popham Gdns TW9 132 D2
Popham Rd N1 95 A6 235 A6
Popham St Islington N1 234 D6
Shoreditch N1 95 A6 235 A6
Pop In Bsns Ctr HA9 66 D3
POPLAR 97 C1
Poplar Ave Mitcham CR4 180 D2
Orpington BR6 226 D6
Southall UB2 107 D3
Yiewsley UB7 104 B6
Poplar Bath St 11 E14 119 D6
Poplar Bsns Pk E14 120 A6
Poplar Cl Hackney E9 75 B3
Pinner HA5 22 D2
Poplar Cres KT19 215 A2
Poplar Ct Chingford E4 35 D4
Northolt UB5 84 C5
4 Streatham SW16 160 B1
13 Twickenham TW1 153 C5
Wimbledon SW19 179 C5
Poplar Farm Cl KT19 215 A2
Poplar Gdns KT3 177 B1
Poplar Gr
Friern Barnet N11 31 A4
Hammersmith W6 112 C4
Kingston u T KT3 199 B6
Wembley HA9 67 A5
Poplar High St E14 119 D6
Poplar Ho Brockley SE4 141 B1
19 Rotherhithe SE16 118 D4
Poplar La BR3 207 D4
Poplar Mews 4 W12 112 C5
Poplar Mount DA17 125 D2
Poplar Pl Hayes UB3 106 A6
Kensington W2 113 D6 245 D6
Woolwich SE28 124 C6
Poplar Prim Sch SW19 201 C6
Poplar Rd Ashford TW15 171 A5
Cheam SM3 201 B1
Herne Hill SE24 139 A1
Merton SW19 179 C1
Poplar Rd S SW19 201 C6
Poplars Cl HA4 39 C1
Poplars Ho 14 E17 53 D6
Poplars Rd E17 53 D3
Poplar Sta E14 119 D6
Poplars The
East Barnet N14 15 B6
Kentish Town NW5 71 C3
Poplar View HA9 65 D6
Poplar Way
Feltham TW13 150 B1
Ilford IG6 57 A5
Poplar Wlk Croydon CR0 205 A1
Herne Hill SE24 139 A1
Poppins Ct EC4 241 C1
Poppleton Rd E11 54 C3
Poppy Cl Belvedere DA17 125 D4
Hackbridge SM6 203 A1
Northolt UB5 63 B2
Poppy Ct HA3 42 C6
Poppy La CR0 206 C1
Porchester Ct W2 91 D1
Porchester Gate W2 246 A5
Porchester Gdn Mews W2 91 D1
Porchester Gdns W2 113 D6 245 D6
Porchester Ho 3 E1 96 B1
Porchester Mead BR3 185 D4
Porchester Mews W2 91 D1
Porchester Pl W2 237 B1
Porchester Rd
Kensington W2 91 D1
Kingston u T KT1 176 D1
Porchester Sq W2 91 D1
Porchester Terr W2 114 A6 246 A6
Porchester Terr N W2 91 D1
Porch Way N20 14 D1

Porcupine Cl SE9 . . . . .166 A2
Porden Rd SW2 . . . . .138 B1
Porland Ct SE1 . . . . 262 C6
Porlock Ave HA1, HA2 . . . . . . .42 A1
Porlock Ho 5 SE26 . . . . .162 A1
Porlock Rd EN1 . . . . .17 D4
Porlock St SE1 . . . . . .117 B4 252 D2
Porrington Cl BR7 . . . . .188 C2
Porson Ct SE13 . . . . .141 D2
Portal Cl Hillingdon UB10 . . . .14 A1
  Ruislip HA4 . . . . .62 B4
  West Norwood SE27 . . . . . . .160 C1
Portal Way W3 . . . . .89 B2
Portbury Cl 17 SE15 . . . . .140 A4
Portchester Cl SE24 . . . . .139 B1
Port Cres E13 . . . . .99 B3
Portcullis Lodge Rd EN1 . . . . .5 B2
Porte 10 NW9 . . . . .27 D2
Portelet Ct 1 N1 . . . . .95 C6
Portelet Rd E1 . . . . .96 D4
Porten Hos W14 . . . . 254 A5
Porten Rd W14 . . . . 254 A5
Porter Rd E6 . . . . .100 B1
Porters Ave RM8, RM9 . . . . . .80 C3
Porter Sq N19 . . . . .50 A1
Porter St
  Borough The SE1 . . . .117 A5 252 B4
  Marylebone W1 . . . . 237 D4
Porters & Walters
  Almshouses N22 . . . . .32 B3
Porters Way UB7 . . . . .104 B4
Porteus Rd W2 . . . . 236 B4
Portfleet Pl 34 N1 . . . . .95 C6
Portgate SW7 . . . . .91 B3
Porthallow Cl BR6 . . . . .227 D4
Porthcawe Rd SE26 . . . . .185 B6
Porthkerry Ave DA16 . . . . . . .146 A1
Port Ho 6 SW11 . . . . .136 A2
Port House The 6 E14 . . .119 D1
Portia St SE1 . . . . .80 A1
Portia Way E3 . . . . .97 B3
Porticos The SW3 . . . . 266 C5
Portinscale Rd SW15 . . . . . . .157 B6
Portished Ho 29 W2 . . . . .91 C2
Portland Ave
  Blackfen DA15 . . . . .168 A5
  New Malden KT3 . . . . .199 D2
  Stamford Hill N16 . . . . .51 D2
Portland Cl
  Dagenham RM6 . . . . .59 A4
  New Malden KT4 . . . . .200 B2
Portland Commercial Est
  IG11 . . . . .102 C2
Portland Cotts
  Feltham TW13 . . . . .173 A5
  Wallington CR0 . . . . .203 D2
Portland Cres
  1 Chislehurst SE9 . . . . .166 A2
  Feltham TW13 . . . . .171 B6
  Southall UB6 . . . . .86 A2
  Stanmore HA7 . . . . .42 A4
Portland Cres W HA7 . . . . . . .43 D6
Portland Ct
  7 De Beauvoir Town N1 . . . .73 C1
  8 Deptford SE14 . . . . .141 A6
  1 Sutton SM2 . . . . .217 D2
Portland Dr EN2 . . . . .5 C5
Portland Gdns
  Harringay N4 . . . . .50 D3
  Ilford RM6 . . . . .58 D4
Portland Gr SW8 . .138 B4 270 C2
Portland Ho 19 SW2 . . . . . . .160 C3
Portland Hospl for Women &
  Children The W1 . . . . 238 D5
Portland Mans SE25 . . . . . . .206 D4
Portland Mews W1 . . . . 239 B1
Portland Pl
  Croydon SE25 . . . . .206 A5
  Marylebone W1 . . . .93 B2 238 D3
Portland Place Sch
  W1 . . . . .93 B2 238 D4
Portland Rd
  Ashford TW15 . . . . .148 A1
  Bromley BR1 . . . . .187 C5
  Chislehurst SE9 . . . . .166 A2
  Croydon SE25 . . . . .206 B4
  Hayes UB4 . . . . .83 C4
  Kingston u T KT1 . . . . .198 B5
  Kingston u T KT1 . . . . .198 B6
  Mitcham CR4 . . . . .180 C1
  Notting Hill W11 . . . .113 A5 244 B4
  Notting Hill W11 . . . .113 A6 244 A5
  Southall UB2 . . . . .107 B3
  Tottenham N15 . . . . .51 D5
Portland Rise N4 . . . . .51 A1
Portland Sq 4 E1 . . . . .118 B5
Portland St SE17 . . . .117 B1 262 C1
Portland Terr
  Edgware HA8 . . . . .26 C3
  Richmond TW9 . . . . .131 D1
Portland Village W6 . . . . .112 C3
Portman Ave SW14 . . . . .133 B2
Portman Cl Bexley DA7 . . . . .147 A2
  Marylebone W1 . . . .93 A1 238 A2
Portman Dr IG8 . . . . .37 D1
Portman Gate NW1 . . . . 237 B5
Portman Gdns
  Hendon NW9 . . . . .27 B1
  Hillingdon UB10 . . . . .60 C1
Portman Hall HA3 . . . . .24 B5

Portman Hts 1 NW3 . . . . . .69 C5
Portman Lo N21 . . . . .16 D6
Portman Mews S W1 . . . . . . 238 A1
Portman Pl E2 . . . . .96 C4
Portman Rd KT1 . . . . .176 B1
Portman Sq W1 . . . . .93 A1 238 A2
Portman St W1 . . . . .93 A1 238 A1
Portman The NW1 . . . . .47 C2
Portman Twrs W1 . . . . 237 D2
Portmeadow Wlk SE2 . . . . . .124 D4
Portmeers Cl E17 . . . . .53 C3
Portnall Rd W9 . . . . .91 B4
Portobello Ct Est W11 . . . . . . .91 B1
Portobello Ho 6 SW27 . .182 D5
Portobello Mews W11 . . . . . 245 A5
Portobello Rd
  W11 . . . . .113 B6 244 D6
Portobello Road Mkt★
  W10 .91 A2
Porton Ct KT6 . . . . .197 C3
Portpool La EC1 . . . .94 C2 241 A4
Portree Cl N22 . . . . .32 B3
Portree St E14 . . . . .98 B1
Port Royal Pl 3 N16 . . . . . . .73 C3
Portrush Ct 9 UB1 . . . . .86 A1
Portsdown HA8 . . . . .26 C5
Portsdown Ave NW11 . . . . . . .47 B3
Portsdown Mews NW11 . . . . .47 B3
Portsea Hall W2 . . . . 237 B1
Portsea Ho 3 SW15 . . . . . . .156 B3
Portsea Mews W2 . . . . 237 B1
Portsea Pl W2 . . . . 237 B1
Portslade Rd SW8 . . . . .137 C3
Portsmouth Ave KT7 . . . . . . .197 A2
Portsmouth Mews 16
  E16 .121 B5
Portsmouth Rd
  Esher KT10 . . . . .212 A5
  Putney SW15 . . . . .156 C4
  Thames Ditton KT6, KT7 . . .197 C3
Portsmouth St WC2 . . . . 240 D1
Portsoken St E1, EC3 . . . . . 253 C6
Portswood Pl SW15 . . . . .155 D5
Portugal Gdns TW2 . . . . .152 A2
Portugal St WC2 . . . .94 B1 240 D1
Portway E15 . . . . .98 D6
Portway Gdns SE18 . . . . .143 D5
Portway Prim Sch 7 E13 . .99 A6
Poseidon Ct
  Dagenham IG11 . . . . .102 B4
  9 Millwall E14 . . . . .119 C2
Postern Gn EN2 . . . . .4 C2
Postern The EC2 . . . . 242 B3
Post La TW2 . . . . .152 B3
Postmasters Lodge HA5 . . . . .41 A1
Postmill Cl CR0 . . . . .222 D5
Post Office App E7 . . . . .77 B3
Post Office Way
  SW8 . . . . .137 D5 269 C4
Post Rd UB2 . . . . .107 D3
Postway Mews 1 IG1 . . . . . .78 D5
Potier St SE1 . . . . .262 D5
Potter Cl CR4 . . . . .181 B1
Potteries The EN5 . . . . .13 C6
Potterill Ct TW11 . . . . .175 B3
Potterne Cl 5 SW19 . . . . . . .156 D4
Potters Cl
  5 Camberwell SE15 . . . . . .139 C5
  Croydon CR0 . . . . .207 A1
Pottersfield EN1 . . . . .5 C1
Potters Fields
  SE1 . . . . .117 C5 253 B3
Potters Gr KT3 . . . . .199 A5
Potters Heights HA5 . . . . .22 B3
Potter's La Barnet EN5 . . . . . . .1 C1
  Streatham SW16 . . . . .181 D4
Potters Lo E14 . . . . .120 A1
Potters Mews WD6 . . . . .9 D5
Potters Rd SW6 . . . . .136 A3
Potter's Rd EN5 . . . . .1 D1
Potter St HA5 . . . . .22 B2
Potter Street Hill HA5 . . . . . .22 B3
Pottery La 11 W11 . .113 A5 244 B4
Pottery Rd TW8 . . . . .132 A6
Pottery St SE16 . . . . .118 B4
Pott St E2 . . . . .96 B4
Poulett Gdns TW1 . . . . .153 A3
Poulett Rd E6 . . . . .100 B5
Poullett Ho SW2 . . . . .160 D3
Poulters Wood BR2 . . . . .225 D3
Poulton Ave SM1 . . . . .218 B5
Poulton Cl E8 . . . . .74 B2
Poultry EC2 . . . . .95 B1 242 C1
Pound Cl Long Ditton KT6 . .197 C1
  Orpington BR6 . . . . .227 B6
Pound Court Dr BR6 . . . . . . .227 B6
Pound Farm Cl KT10 . . . . . . .196 B1
Pound Green 4 DA5 . .169 C4
Pound La NW10 . . . . .68 A2
Pound Park Rd SE7 . . . . .121 D2
Pound Pl SE9 . . . . .166 C5
Pound St SM5 . . . . .218 D3
Pountney Rd SW11 . . . . .137 A2
Poverest Rd BR5 . . . . .211 D4
Povey Ho Tulse Hill SW2 . . . .160 C5
  Walworth SE17 . . . . 263 A3
Powder Mill La TW2,
  TW4 . . . . .151 C3
Powell Cl
  Chessington KT9 . . . . .213 D4

Powell Cl continued
  Edgware HA8 . . . . .26 B4
  Wallington SM6 . . . . .220 A1
Powell Ct Croydon CR2 . . . . .221 A4
  19 Walthamstow E17 . . . . . .53 D6
Powell Gdns RM10 . . . . .81 C4
Powell Ho 10 SW19 . . . . . . .179 A4
Powell Rd
  Buckhurst Hill IG9 . . . . .21 C4
  Hackney E5 . . . . .74 B5
Powell's Wlk W4 . . . . .133 D6
Powell Terr CR4 . . . . .204 A5
Powergate Bsns Pk
  NW10 . . . . .89 B4
Power Ho 13 TW9 . . . . .132 C4
Power Ho The W4 . . . . .111 D2
Power Rd W4 . . . . .110 C2
Powerscroft Rd
  Lower Clapton E5 . . . . .74 C4
  Sidcup DA14 . . . . .190 C4
Powers Ct TW1 . . . . .153 D4
Powis Gdns
  Golders Green NW11 . . . . . . .47 B2
  Notting Hill W11 . . . . .91 B1
Powis Ho WC2 . . . . 240 B2
Powis Mews W11 . . . . .91 B1
Powis Pl WC1 . . . . . .94 A3 240 B5
Powis Rd E3 . . . . .97 C4
Powis Sq W11 . . . . .91 B1
Powis St SE18 . . . . .122 C2
Powis Terr W11 . . . . .91 B1
Powlesland Ct 21 E14 . . . . . .97 A1
Powle Terr IG1 . . . . .79 B3
Powlett Ho NW1 . . . . .71 B2
Powlett Pl NW1 . . . . .71 B1
Pownall Gdns TW3 . . . . .129 D1
Pownall Rd Hackney E8 . . . . . .96 A6
  Hounslow TW3 . . . . .129 D1
Pownsett Terr IG1 . . . . .79 A3
Powrie Ho 4 SW11 . . . . .136 B3
Powster Rd BR1 . . . . .187 B5
Powys Cl DA7 . . . . .146 D6
Powys Ct N11 . . . . .32 A5
Powys La Bowes Pk N13 . . . . .32 A5
  Palmers Green N14 . . . . .32 A6
Poynder Ct 3 N7 . . . . .72 A3
Poynder Lo TW7 . . . . .131 A4
Poynders Ct 9 SW4 . . . . . . .159 C5
Poynders Gdns SW4 . . . . . . .159 C4
Poynders Rd SW12, SW4 . . .159 D4
Poynings Rd N19 . . . . .71 C5
Poynings Way N12 . . . . .29 C5
Poyntell Cres BR7 . . . . .189 B2
Poynter Ct 11 UB5 . . . . .84 D5
Poynter Ho
  Paddington NW8 . . . . 236 C6
  10 Shepherd's Bush W11 . .112 D5
Poynter Rd EN1 . . . . .18 A6
Poynton Rd N17 . . . . .34 A1
Poyntz Rd SW11 . . . . .136 D3
Poyser St E2 . . . . .96 B5
Praed Mews W2 . . . . 236 D2
Praed St W2 . . . . . . .92 B1 236 D2
Pragel St E13 . . . . .99 C5
Pragnell Rd SE12 . . . . .165 B2
Prague Pl SW2 . . . . .160 A6
Prah Rd N4 . . . . .72 C6
Prairie St SW8 . . . . .137 B3
Pratt Mews NW1 . . . . 232 A5
Pratt St NW1 . . . . . . .93 C6 232 A6
Pratt Wlk SE1,
  SE11 . . . . .116 B2 260 D6
Prayle Gr NW2 . . . . .46 D1
Preachers Ct EC1 . . . . 241 D5
Prebend Gdns W4, W6 . . . . . .111 D2
Prebend Mans 4 W4 . . . . .111 D2
Prebend St N1 . . . . .95 A6 235 A6
Precinct Rd UB3 . . . . .106 A6
Precincts The SM4 . . . . .201 C3
Precinct The Islington N1 . .235 A5
  Islington N5 . . . . .72 D3
Premier Corner NW6 . . . . .91 B5
Premier Ct EN3 . . . . .6 D5
Premier Ho 25 N1 . . . . .72 D1
Premier Lo N3 . . . . .29 C2
Premier Park Rd NW10 . . . . . .88 D5
Premier Pk NW10 . . . . .88 D5
Premier Pl 17 E14 . . . . .119 C6
Prendergast Ho 4 SW4 . . . .159 D4
Prendergast Ladywell Fields
  Coll SE4 . . . . .163 C5
Prendergast Rd SE3 . . . . .142 C2
Prendergast Sch SE4 . . . . . . .141 C1
Prentice Ct 2 SW19 . . . . . . .179 B5
Prentis Rd SW16 . . . . .181 D6
Prentiss Ct SE7 . . . . .121 D2
Presburg Rd KT3 . . . . .199 C4
Prescelly Pl HA8 . . . . .26 B6
Prescot St E1 . . . . . . .117 D6 253 D6
Prescott Ave BR5 . . . . .210 D3
Prescott Ho Croydon CR0 . . .220 C5
  13 Kennington SE17 . . . . . .138 D6
Prescott Pl SW4 . . . . .159 D4
Presentation Mews
  SW2 . . . . .160 B3
Preshaw Cres CR4 . . . . .202 C4
President Dr E1 . . . . .118 B5
President Ho EC1 . . . . 234 D1

President St EC1 . . . . 235 A2
Prespa Cl N9 . . . . .18 C2
Press Ho NW10 . . . . .67 B5
Press Rd NW10 . . . . .67 B5
Prestage Way 13 E14 . . .120 A6
Prestbury Rd E7 . . . . .77 C1
Prestbury Sq SE9 . . . . .188 B6
Prested Rd SW11 . . . . .136 C1
PRESTON 44 A1
Preston Ave E4 . . . . .36 B4
Preston Cl
  Twickenham TW2 . . . . .152 C1
  Walworth SE1 . . . . 263 A4
Preston Ct
  5 New Barnet EN5 . . . . .2 A1
  Northwood Hills HA6 . . . . . . .22 A1
  Sidcup DA14 . . . . .189 D6
  Walton-on-T KT12 . . . . .194 C1
Preston Dr Bexley DA7 . . . . . .146 D4
  Wanstead E11 . . . . .55 C4
  West Ewell KT19 . . . . .215 D2
Preston Gdns Enfield EN3 . . . . .7 A6
  Redbridge IG1 . . . . .56 A3
  Willesden NW10 . . . . .67 C2
Preston Hill HA3 . . . . .44 B3
Preston Ho
  Bermondsey SE1 . . . . 263 C6
  3 Dagenham RM10 . . . . . . .81 C5
  Walworth SE1 . . . . 263 A4
  1 Woolwich SE18 . . . . .122 C2
Preston Manor High Sch
  HA9 . . . . .66 B6
Preston Park Prim Sch
  HA9 . . . . .43 D1
Preston Pl
  Richmond TW10 . . . . .154 A6
  Willesden NW2 . . . . .68 A2
Preston Rd
  Leytonstone E11 . . . . .54 C3
  Littleton TW17 . . . . .192 C4
  South Norwood SE19 . . . . . .182 D4
  Wembley HA3, HA9 . . . . .66 A6
  Wimbledon SW20 . . . . .177 D3
Preston Road Sta HA3 . . . . . .44 A1
Prestons Rd BR2 . . . . .225 A6
Preston's Rd E14 . . . . .120 A5
Preston Waye HA3 . . . . .44 A3
Prestwich Terr SW4 . . . . .159 D6
Prestwick Ct UB2 . . . . .107 A1
Prestwick Ct
  Southall UB1 . . . . .108 A6
  Tottenham N17 . . . . .34 A3
Prestwick Rd WD19 . . . . .22 D6
Prestwood Ave HA3 . . . . .43 B5
Prestwood Cl
  East Wickham SE18 . . . . . . .146 A6
  Harrow HA3 . . . . .43 B5
Prestwood Gdns CR0 . . . . . .205 A2
Prestwood Ho 3 SE16 . . . . .118 B3
Prestwood St N1 . . . . 235 B3
Pretoria Ave E17 . . . . .53 A5
Pretoria Cres E4 . . . . .20 A3
Pretoria Ho 3 HA4 . . . . .40 C1
  Ilford IG1 . . . . .78 D3
  Leytonstone E11 . . . . .54 B1
  Newham E16 . . . . .98 D3
  Streatham SW16 . . . . .181 C5
  Tottenham N17 . . . . .33 D4
Pretoria Rd N N18 . . . . .33 D4
Pretty Cnr HA6 . . . . .22 A5
Prevost Rd N11 . . . . .15 A2
Priam Ho 17 E2 . . . . .96 B5
Price Cl Finchley NW7 . . . . . . .29 A4
  Upper Tooting SW17 . . . . . . .158 D1
Price Ct HA1 . . . . .43 A4
Price Ho N1 . . . . 235 A5
Price Rd CR0 . . . . .220 D3
Prices St SE1 . . . . .136 B2
Price St SE1 . . . . .251 D4
Price's Yd N1 . . . . 233 D5
Price Way TW12 . . . . .173 A4
Prichard Ct
  Battersea SW11 . . . . .266 D1
  Islington N7 . . . . .72 B3
Pricklers Hill EN5 . . . . .13 D5
Prickley Wood BR2 . . . . .208 D1
Priddy's Yd 4 CR0 . . . . .221 A6
Prideaux Ho WC1 . . . . 233 D2
Prideaux Pl Acton W3 . . . . . .111 B6
  St Pancras WC1 . . . . .94 B4 233 D2
Prideaux Rd SW9 . . . . .138 A2
Pride Ct N1 . . . . 234 B4
Pridham Rd CR7 . . . . .205 B5
Priestfield Rd SE23 . . . . .163 A1
Priestlands Park Rd
  DA15 . . . . .167 D1
Priestley Cl N16 . . . . .51 D2
Priestley Gdns RM6 . . . . .58 B3
Priestley Ho
  2 Camden Town NW5 . . . . .71 B2
  St Luke's EC1 . . . . 242 B6
  3 Wembley HA9 . . . . .67 A5
Priestley Rd CR4 . . . . .181 A1
Priestley Way
  Hendon NW2 . . . . .46 A1
  Walthamstow E17 . . . . .52 B6
Priestman Point 25 E3 . . .97 D4
Priestmead Fst & Mid Schs
  HA3 .43 B6

Priest Park Ave HA2 . . . . .63 C6
Priests Bridge SW14 . . . . . . .133 C2
Priest's Ct EC2 . . . . 242 A2
Prima Rd SW9 . . . . .138 C5
Primrose Ave Enfield EN2 . . . . .5 C4
  Ilford RM6 . . . . .58 B2
Primrose Cl 6 Bow E3 . . . . .97 C5
  Catford SE6 . . . . .186 A5
  Finchley N3 . . . . .29 D1
  Hackbridge SM6 . . . . .203 B1
  Harrow HA2 . . . . .63 B5
Primrose Ct
  2 Child's Hill NW2 . . . . .69 B5
  New Malden KT4 . . . . .200 A2
  Thornton Heath NW8 . . . . . .230 C5
  11 Streatham SW12 . . . . . .159 D4
Primrose Gdns
  Hampstead NW3 . . . . .70 C2
  Ruislip HA4 . . . . .62 C3
PRIMROSE HILL 70 D1
Primrose Hill EC4 . . . . 241 B1
Primrose Hill Ct NW3 . . . . . . .70 D1
Primrose Hill Rd
  Primrose Hill NW3 . . . . .70 D1
  Primrose Hill NW1, NW3 . . .230 C6
Primrose Hill Sch
  NW1 . . . . .93 A6 231 B6
Primrose Hill Studios
  NW1 . . . . 231 A6
Primrose Ho
  7 Peckham SE15 . . . . .140 A4
  1 Richmond TW9 . . . . .132 B4
Primrose Mans SW11 . . . . . .268 A2
Primrose Mews 9 NW1 . .70 D1
Primrose Pl 4 TW7 . . . . .130 D3
Primrose Rd
  Walthamstow E10 . . . . .53 D1
  Woodford E18 . . . . .37 B1
Primrose Sq E9 . . . . .96 C6
Primrose St EC2 . . . .95 C2 243 B4
Primrose Way HA0 . . . . .87 D5
Primrose Wlk
  Ewell KT17 . . . . .215 C1
  6 New Cross Gate SE14 . . .141 A5
Primula St W12 . . . . .90 A1
Prince Albert Ct
  Primrose Hill NW8 . . . . .230 C5
  Sunbury TW16 . . . . .171 C3
Prince Albert Rd
  NW8 . . . . .92 D6 230 C5
Prince Arthur Ct 18 NW3 .70 A4
Prince Arthur Mews 17
  NW3 .70 A4
Prince Arthur Rd NW3 . . . . . .70 A3
Prince Charles Dr NW2 . . .46 C2
Prince Charles Rd SE3 . . . . .142 D4
Prince Charles Way
  SM6 .203 B1
Prince Consort Dr BR7 . . . . .189 B2
Prince Consort Ho SE1 . . . . .260 B2
Prince Consort Rd
  SW7 . . . . .114 B3 256 C6
Princedale Rd
  W11 . . . . .113 A5 244 B4
Prince Edward Mans
  W2 . . . . 245 B6
Prince Edward Rd E9 . . . .75 B2
Prince George Ave N14 . . .15 D6
Prince George Rd N16 . . . .73 C4
Prince George's Ave
  SW20 . . . . .178 C3
Prince Georges Rd
  SW19 . . . . .180 B2
Prince Henry Rd SE7 . . . . . . .143 D5
Prince Imperial Rd
  Chislehurst BR7 . . . . .188 D3
  Kidbrooke SE18 . . . . .144 B4
Prince John Rd SE9 . . . . .166 A6
Princelet St E1 . . . . . .95 D2 243 D4
Prince of Orange La 3
  SE10 . . . . .142 A5
Prince Of Wales Cl NW4 . .46 B5
Prince Of Wales Dr
  SW11 . . . . .137 A4 268 A2
Prince Of Wales Mans
  Battersea SW11 . . . . .268 B2
  Clapham SW4 . . . . .159 B6
Prince Of Wales Pas
  NW1 . . . . 232 A1
Prince Of Wales Prim Sch
  EN3 . . . . .7 B6
Prince of Wales Rd
  Blackheath Vale SE3 . . . . . .142 D4
  Camden Town NW5 . . . . .71 A2
  Newham E16 . . . . .99 C1
Prince Of Wales' Rd
  SM1 .218 B6
Prince Of Wales Terr
  Chiswick W4 . . . . .111 C1
  Kensington W8 . . . . 245 D1
Prince Rd SE25 . . . . .205 C4
Prince Regent Ho E16 . . . .99 C2
Prince Regent Ct 2
  SE16 . . . . .119 A5
Prince Regent La E13 . . . .99 C3

Prince Regent Mews
NW1 . . . . 232 A1
Prince Regent Rd TW3 . . 130 A2
Prince Regent Sta E16 . . 121 C6
Prince Rupert Rd SE9 . . 144 B1
Princes Arc SW1. . . . . . 249 B4
Princes Ave Acton W3 . . 110 C3
Edmonton N13 . . . . 32 C5
Finchley N3 . . . . 29 D2
Muswell Hill N10. . . . . . . 49 B6
Orpington BR5 . . . . 211 C4
Queensbury NW9 . . . . . . 44 D5
Tolworth KT6 . . . . 214 C6
Wallington SM5 . . . . . . 218 D1
Woodford IG8. . . . . 37 C6
Wood Green N22 . . . . . . 31 D2
Prince's Ave UB1 . . . . . . 85 D1
Princes Cir WC2 . . 94 A1 240 A2
Princes Cl Edgware HA8. . 26 C5
Finsbury Pk N4 . . . . 50 D1
Queensbury NW9. . . . . . 44 C5
Sidcup DA14. . . . . 168 D1
Prince's Cl TW11, TW12 . 174 B6
Princes Coll WC1 . . . . . 240 A2
Princes Court Bsns Ctr [14]
E1. . . . . 118 B6
Princes Ct
Brondesbury NW2 . . . . . . 69 A3
Hampstead NW3 . . . . 70 B4
Kingston u T KT3. . . . . . 199 D6
Stepney E1. . . . . 118 B6
Wembley HA9. . . . . 66 A3
Prince's Ct SE16 . . . . . . 119 B3
Princes Dr HA1 . . . . 42 C6
Princes Gate
SW7. . . . . 114 B4 246 D1
Prince's Gate
SW7. . . . . 114 C4 247 A1
Princes Gate Ct SW7 . . . 246 D1
Princes Gate Mews
SW7. . . . . 114 B3 256 D6
Princes Gdns Acton W3 . . 88 C2
Brompton SW7. . . 114 B3 256 D6
Ealing W5 . . . . 87 C3
Princes Ho W11 . . . . . . 245 A5
Princes La N10 . . . . 49 B6
Princes Mews TW3. . . . 129 C1
Prince's Mews
[1] Hammersmith W6. . . . 112 B1
Kensington W2. . . 113 D6 245 C6
Princes Par NW11 . . . . . 47 A3
Princes Park Ave
Hayes UB3 . . . . 105 B6
Temple Fortune NW11 . . . 47 A4
Princes Park Circ UB3 . . 105 B6
Princes Park Cl UB3 . . . 105 B6
Princes Park La UB3 . . . 105 B6
Princes Park Par UB3 . . 105 B6
Princes Pl
Notting Hill W11. . . 113 A5 244 A4
St James SW1 . . . . 249 B4
Prince's Plain BR2 . . . . 210 A1
Princes Plain Prim Sch
BR2. . . . . 210 A2
Princes Rd Ashford TW15. 170 B5
Buckhurst Hill IG9 . . . . . 21 C2
Ealing W13 . . . . 109 B5
Edmonton N18 . . . . 34 C6
Feltham TW13 . . . . 149 D1
Ilford IG6 . . . . 57 B5
Kew TW9 . . . . 132 B4
Kingston u T KT2 . . . . . 176 C3
Penge SE20 . . . . 184 D4
Richmond TW10 . . . . . . 154 B6
Prince's Rd
Mortlake SW14 . . . . . . 133 B2
Teddington TW11, TW12 . 174 B6
Wimbledon SW19 . . . . . 179 C4
Princes Rise SE13. . . . . 142 A3
Princes Riverside Rd [7]
SE16 . . . . 118 D5
Princessa Ct EN2 . . . . . 17 B6
**Princess Alexandra School of
Nursing The** [6] E1 . . . . 96 B2
Princess Alice Ho [1]
W10. . . . . 90 C3
Princess Alice Way
SE28 . . . . 123 B4
Princess Ave HA9 . . . . . 66 A6
Princess Beatrice Ho
SW10. . . . . 255 C1
Princess Cl SE28 . . . . . 102 D1
Princess Cres N4 . . . . . 72 D6
Princess Ct Catford BR1. 186 C4
[3] Croydon CR0 . . . . . . 221 D6
Hampstead NW6 . . . . . . 69 D1
Hounslow TW4. . . . . . . 128 C2
Kensington W2. . . . . . . 245 D6
Marylebone W1 . . . . 237 C3
[11] Wimbledon SW19 . . . 178 D3
**Princess Frederica CE Jun &
Inf Sch** NW10. . . . . 90 C5
Princess Grace Hospl The
W1 . . . . 93 A3 238 A5
Princess La HA4 . . . . . . 39 C1
Princess Louise Cl W2 . . 236 D4
Princess Mary Ho SW1. . 259 D3

Princess May Prim Sch [6]
N16. . . . . 73 D4
Princess May Rd N16 . . . 73 C4
Princess Mews
Hampstead NW3 . . . . 70 B2
Kingston u T KT1 . . . . . 198 B6
Princess Par
Dagenham RM10 . . . . . . 103 C5
Locksbottom BR6 . . . . . . 226 C5
Princess Park Manor
N11 . . . . 31 A5
Prince's Sq W2 . . 113 D6 245 C6
Princess Rd
Camden Town
NW1. . . . . 93 A6 231 B6
Paddington NW6 . . . . 91 C5
Thornton Heath CR0 . . . . 205 A3
**Princess Royal University
Hospl** BR6. . . . . 226 C5
Princess St Bexley DA7. . 147 B2
Newington SE1. . . . . . . 261 D5
Princes St
Bexleyheath DA7 . . . . . 147 B1
Marylebone W1 . . . . 238 D1
Sutton SM1. . . . . 218 B4
Tottenham N17. . . . . 33 C4
Prince's St
City of London EC2. . 95 B1 242 C1
Richmond TW10, TW9. . . 154 A6
Prince St SE8. . . . . 141 B6
Prince's Terr E13 . . . . . . 99 B6
Prince's Way Acton W3 . . 110 C3
Buckhurst Hill IG9 . . . . . 21 C2
Coney Hall BR4. . . . . . . 224 D5
Croydon CR0. . . . . 220 B3
Putney SW15, SW19. . . . 157 A3
Ruislip HA4. . . . . 63 A4
Princes Yd W11 . . . . . . 244 B3
Princethorpe Ho W2. . . . 91 D2
Princethorpe Rd SE26. . 184 D6
Princeton Ct [12] SW15. . 134 D2
Princeton Mans WC1. . . 240 C3
Princeton Mews [3] KT2 . 176 C2
Princeton St WC1. . 94 B2 240 C4
Prince William Ct TW15 . 170 B5
Principal Cl N14 . . . . . . 15 C3
Principal Sq E9 . . . . 74 D3
Pringle Gdns SW16 . . . . 181 C6
Pringle Ho N21 . . . . 16 B6
Printers Mews E3. . . . . . 97 A6
Printer St EC4 . . . . 241 B2
Printinghouse La UB3. . . 105 C4
Printing House Yd [16] E2. . 95 C4
Print Village Ind Est
SE15 . . . . 139 D3
Priolo Rd SE7. . . . . 121 C1
Prior Ave SM2, SM5. . . . 218 C1
Prior Bolton St N1 . . . . . 72 D2
Prioress Ho [2] E3. . . . . . 97 D4
Prioress Rd SE27 . . . . . 160 D1
Prioress St SE1. . . . . . . 262 D5
Prior Rd IG1. . . . . 78 C5
Priors Croft E17 . . . . . . 35 B1
Priors Field UB5. . . . . . . 63 A2
Priors Gdns HA4. . . . . . 62 C3
Priors Lo [4] TW10. . . . . 154 A5
Priors Mead EN1. . . . . . . 5 C4
Prior St SE10 . . . . 142 A5
Priors Wood KT10 . . . . . 212 D6
Prior Weston Prim Sch
EC1. . . . . 95 B3 242 C6
Priory Ave
Bedford Pk W4 . . . . 111 C3
Cheam SM3 . . . . 216 D4
Chingford E4. . . . . 19 C1
Hornsey N8. . . . . 49 D5
Petts Wood BR5 . . . . . . 211 B3
Walthamstow E17 . . . . . . 53 C4
Wembley HA0. . . . . 64 D4
Priory CE Prim Sch
SW19 . . . . 179 D5
Priory Cl Ashford TW16. . 172 A3
Barnet N20. . . . . 13 B4
Beckenham BR3 . . . . . . 207 A6
Chingford Green E4. . . . . 19 B1
Chislehurst BR7 . . . . 188 B2
East Barnet N14. . . . . . . 15 B6
Finchley N3. . . . . 29 B2
Hampton TW12. . . . . . . 173 B2
Hayes UB3 . . . . 106 B6
[3] Merton SW19 . . . . . . 179 D2
Ruislip HA4. . . . . 39 D1
Stanmore HA7 . . . . 8 D1
Wembley HA0. . . . . 64 D4
Woodford E18. . . . . 37 A2
Priory Cres Cheam SM3 . 216 D4
South Norwood SE19 . . . 183 A3
Wembley HA0. . . . . 65 A5
Priory Ct Bushey WD23. . . 8 A3
Cheam SM3 . . . . 217 A4
City of London EC4. . . . . 241 D1
Hampton TW12. . . . . . . 173 C3
Highgate N6. . . . . 49 B3
Homerton E9 . . . . 74 D3
Hounslow TW3 . . . . 129 D2
Ilford RM6 . . . . 58 B3
Newham E6 . . . . 99 D6
Nunhead SE15 . . . . 140 C1
Roehampton SW15. . . . . 133 D1

Priory Ct continued
South Lambeth
SW8 . . . . 137 D4 269 D2
Walthamstow E17 . . . . . . 35 B1
[4] Wembley HA0. . . . . . 88 A5
Priory Dr Stanmore HA7 . . 8 D1
West Heath SE2 . . . . . . 124 D1
Priory Field Dr HA8 . . . . 26 D6
Priory Gdns
Ashford TW15. . . . . 171 B5
Barnes SW13 . . . . 133 D2
[6] Chiswick W4 . . . . . . 111 C2
Ealing W5 . . . . 88 A4
Hampton TW12. . . . . . . 173 B2
Highgate N6. . . . . 49 B3
South Norwood SE25 . . . 205 D5
Wembley HA0. . . . . 65 A4
Priory Gn N1 . . . . 234 C4
Priory Gr Barnet EN5. . . . 13 C6
South Lambeth
SW8 . . . . 138 A3 270 A1
Priory Grange N2. . . . . . 48 D6
Priory Hill HA0 . . . . 65 A4
Priory Ho
[3] Charlton SE7 . . . . . . 143 C6
Clerkenwell EC1. . . . . . 241 C6
Pimlico SW1. . . . . 259 C2
Spitalfields E1. . . . . 243 C4
**Priory Hospl Grange
Roehampton** SW15 . . . . 133 D1
**Priory Hospl Hayes Grove
The** BR2. . . . . 225 A6
**Priory Hospl North London
The (Grovelands)** N14 . . 16 A3
Priory House Ct SE6 . . . 163 D3
Priory Hts N1. . . . . 233 D4
Priory La
East Molesey KT8. . . . . 195 D5
Roehampton SW15. . . . 155 D6
Priory Leas SE9. . . . . . 166 A3
Priory Lo
[7] Brentford W4 . . . . . . 110 C1
Coney Hall BR4. . . . . . . 224 C5
Ealing W5 . . . . 87 C1
Priory Mans
[17] Maitland Pk NW3 . . . 70 D2
South Kensington SW10. . 256 B1
Priory Park Rd
Kilburn NW6. . . . . 91 B6
Wembley HA0. . . . . 65 A4
Priory Pk SE3. . . . . 142 D2
Priory Rd Barking IG11. . . 79 B1
Bedford Pk W4 . . . . 111 B3
Cheam SM3 . . . . 216 D4
Chessington KT9 . . . . . . 214 A5
Hampstead NW6 . . . . 69 D1
Hampton TW12. . . . . . . 173 C3
Hornsey N8. . . . . 49 D5
Hounslow TW3 . . . . 152 A6
Mitcham SW19. . . . . . . 180 B3
Newham E6 . . . . 99 C5
Richmond TW9 . . . . 132 C5
Thornton Heath CR0 . . . . 204 C2
Priory Ret Pk SW19 . . . . 180 B3
Priory Specl Sch SE25. . 205 D5
Priory St [16] E3 . . . . 97 D4
Priory Terr NW6 . . . . 91 D6
Priory The Croydon CR0 . 220 C5
Hornsey N8. . . . . 49 D5
[21] Kingston u T KT6 . . 198 A4
Lambeth SE1. . . . . 251 C1
Lewisham SE3 . . . . 142 D1
Priory View WD23. . . . . . 8 C4
Priory Villas N11. . . . . . 30 D5
Priory Way
Harmondsworth UB7. . . 126 A6
Harrow HA2. . . . . 41 D5
Southall UB2. . . . . 106 D3
Priory Wlk
South Kensington
SW10 . . . . . . 114 A1 256 B1
Sunbury TW16 . . . . 172 A3
Priscilla Cl N15. . . . . 51 A4
Priscilla Ho [8] TW16 . . . 171 D3
Pritchard Ho [38] E2. . . . 96 A5
Pritchard's Rd E2. . . . . . 96 A5
Pritchett Cl [13] EN3. . . . . 7 C6
Priter Rd SE16. . . . . . . 118 A3
Priter Road Hostel [14]
SE16 . . . . 118 A3
Private Rd EN1. . . . . 17 C6
Probert Rd SW2 . . . . . . 160 C6
Probyn Ho SW1. . . . . . . 259 D4
Probyn Rd SW2 . . . . . . 160 D2
Procter Ho [12] SE5 . . . . 139 B5
Procter St WC1 . . 94 B2 240 C3
Proctor Cl CR4. . . . . . . 181 A2
Proctor Ho [5] SE1 . . . . 118 A1
Proctors Cl TW14 . . . . . 150 A3
Prodger [8] NW9 . . . . 27 D2
Progress Bsns Pk CR9. . 220 B6
Progress Way
Croydon CR0. . . . . 220 B6
Enfield EN1. . . . . 18 A6
Wood Green N22 . . . . . . 32 C2
Prologis Pk
Hounslow TW4. . . . . . . 128 C1
Wallington CR0. . . . . . . 203 D2
Prome Ho [3] N16. . . . . . 73 B4

Promenade Approach Rd
W4. . . . . 133 C5
Promenade Mans HA8 . . 26 C5
Promenade The W4. . . . 133 C4
Pronto Trad Est UB4. . . . 83 C2
Prospect Cl
Belvedere DA17. . . . . . 125 C2
Bushey WD23. . . . . 8 B4
Forest Hill SE26 . . . . . . 184 B6
Hounslow TW5. . . . . . . 129 B4
Ruislip HA4. . . . . 40 D2
Prospect Cotts SW18. . . 135 C1
Prospect Cres TW2. . . . 152 A5
Prospect Hill E17 . . . . . . 53 D5
Prospect Ho
[1] Dalston E8. . . . . 73 D2
Islington N1 . . . . 234 A3
[3] Mitcham SW19 . . . . 180 B2
Newington SE1. . . . . . . 261 D5
[14] North Kensington W10. 90 D1
[9] Walthamstow E17 . . . 54 A6
Prospect House Sch [11]
SW15 . . . . 156 D4
Prospect Pl Bromley BR2. 209 B6
[5] Child's Hill NW2. . . . . 69 B5
[2] Chiswick W4 . . . . . . 111 B1
[6] Deptford SE8. . . . . . 141 B6
East Finchley N2. . . . . . . 48 B5
[12] Hampstead NW3. . . . 70 A4
[7] Lower Holloway N7. . . 72 A4
Tottenham N17. . . . . 33 C3
Wapping E1 . . . . 118 C5
Wimbledon SW20. . . . . 178 B3
Prospect Quay SW18. . . 135 C1
Prospect Rd Barnet EN5. . 1 D1
Child's Hill NW2 . . . . 69 C5
Kingston u T KT6. . . . . . 197 C3
Woodford IG8. . . . . 37 C5
Prospect Ring N2. . . . . . 48 B6
Prospect St SE16 . . . . . 118 B4
Prospect Vale SE18. . . . 122 A2
Prospect Wharf E1. . . . . 118 C6
Prospero Ho [7] DA17 . . 125 C1
Prospero Rd N19 . . . . . . 49 D1
Protea Cl E16. . . . . 98 D3
Protheroe Ho [11] N17. . . 51 D6
Prothero Gdns NW4. . . . 46 B4
Prothero Ho [15] NW10 . . 67 B1
Prothero Rd
SW6. . . . . 135 B5 264 C4
Proud Ho [16] E1. . . . . . 96 B1
Prout Gr NW10 . . . . 67 D4
Prout Rd E5 . . . . 74 B5
Provence St N1. . . . . . . 235 A4
Providence Ave HA2 . . . 41 C1
Providence Cl E9 . . . . . . 96 D6
Providence Ct
Harlington UB3. . . . . . . 127 B5
Islington N1 . . . . 234 C5
Mayfair W1. . . . . 248 B6
Providence La UB3. . . . . 127 B5
Providence Pl N1. . . . . . 234 C5
Providence Rd UB7. . . . 104 B5
Providence Row N1. . . . 234 C3
Providence Row Cl [30] E1. . 96 B4
Providence Sq [36] SE1. . 118 A4
Providence Yd [1] E2. . . . 96 A4
Provident Ind Est UB3. . . 106 A4
Provincial Terr [2] SE20. . 184 D3
Provost Ct NW3. . . . . . . 70 D2
Provost Rd NW3 . . . . . . 70 D1
Provost St N1 . . . 95 B4 235 C2
Prowse Ave WD23. . . . . . 8 A2
Prowse Pl NW1 . . . . 71 C1
Prudence La BR6 . . . . . 226 C4
Pruden Cl N14. . . . . 15 C2
Prudent Pas EC2. . . . . . 242 B1
Prusom's Island [8] E1. . 118 C5
Prusom St E1. . . . . 118 B5
Pryors The NW3 . . . . . . 70 B5
Puccinia Ct TW19 . . . . . 148 A3
Pudding La EC3. . . . . . . 252 D6
Pudding Mill La E15. . . . 97 D6
Pudding Mill-Lane Sta
E15. . . . . 97 D6
Puddle Dock
EC4 . . . . 116 D6 251 D6
Puffin Cl Barking IG11. . . 102 B4
Beckenham BR3 . . . . . . 206 D4
Puffin Ct [9] W13. . . . . . 86 D3
Puffin Terr IG5. . . . . 56 C6
Puget Ct N12. . . . . 30 A5
Pugin Ct N1 . . . . 72 C1
Pulborough Rd SW18 . . 157 B4
Pulborough Way TW4. . . 128 C1
Pulford Rd N15 . . . . 51 B3
Pulham Ave N2. . . . . . . 48 B5
Pulham Ho SW8 . . . . . . 270 C3
Puller Rd EN5. . . . . 1 A3
Pulleyns Ave E6 . . . . . . 100 A4
Pullman Ct SW2 . . . . . . 160 B3
Pullman Gdns SW15. . . 156 C5
Pullman Mews SE12. . . 165 B1
Pullman Pl SE9 . . . . 166 A6
Pulross Rd SW9. . . . . . 138 B2
Pulteney Cl
[3] Isleworth TW7 . . . . . 131 A2
[20] Old Ford E3 . . . . 97 B6
Pulteney Gdns [9] E18. . . 55 B6

Pulteney Rd E18. . . . . . . 55 B6
Pulteney Terr N1. . 94 B6 233 D6
Pulton Ho SE4 . . . . 141 A1
Pulton Pl SW6. . . 135 C5 265 A3
Puma Ct E1 . . . . 243 C4
Puma Trade Pk CR4 . . . 202 B5
Pump Alley [8] TW8 . . . . 131 D5
Pump Cl UB5. . . . . 85 C5
Pump Ct EC4 . . . . 241 A1
Pump House Cl
Bromley BR2. . . . . 186 D1
Rotherhithe SE16. . . . . 118 C4
**Pumphouse Educational Mus
The*** SE16. . . . . 119 A5
Pump House Gall*
SW11 . . . . 137 A5 268 A3
Pumping Ho [3] E14. . . . 120 B6
Pumping Station Rd
W4. . . . . 133 C6
Pump La Deptford SE14. . 140 C5
Hayes UB3 . . . . 106 A4
Pump Pail N CR0. . . . . . 221 A5
Pump Pail S CR0. . . . . . 221 A5
Punchard Cres EN3 . . . . . 7 D5
Punderson's Gdns E2. . . 96 B4
Puran Ho E13. . . . . 99 C5
Purbeck Ave KT3 . . . . . 199 D3
Purbeck Ct [2] N20. . . . . 14 C2
Purbeck Dr NW2. . . . . . . 68 D6
Purbeck Ho SW8 . . . . . 270 C3
Purbrook Est SE1. . . . . 253 B1
Purbrook Ho [3] SW15. . 156 B3
Purbrook St SE1. . . . . . 263 B6
Purcell Cres
SW6. . . . . 135 C5 264 A4
Purcell Ho Chelsea SW10. 266 C5
Isleworth TW2 . . . . 152 B5
Southall UB1. . . . . 85 C1
Purcell Mews [2] NW10. . 67 C1
Purcell Rd UB6 . . . . 85 B2
Purcells Ave HA8 . . . . . . 26 C5
Purcell St N1. . . . . 95 C5
Purchese St NW1. . 93 D5 232 D3
Purday Ho [4] W10 . . . . . 91 B4
Purdey Ct [3] KT4 . . . . . 200 A1
Purdon Ho [11] SE15. . . . 140 A4
Purdy St E3 . . . . 97 D3
Purkis Cl UB3. . . . . 105 A6
Purland Cl RM8. . . . . . . 59 B1
Purland Rd SE28, SE18. . 123 D4
Purley Ave NW2 . . . . . . 69 A6
Purley Oaks Prim Sch
CR2. . . . . 221 B1
Purley Pl N1. . . . . 72 D1
Purley Rd Edmonton N9. . 17 C1
South Croydon CR2. . . . 221 B1
Purley View Terr CR2. . . 221 B1
Purley Way
Croydon CR0, CR9. . . . . 220 C3
Thornton Heath CR0. . . . 204 B1
Purley Way Cres CR0. . . 204 B2
Purneys Rd SE9. . . . . . 143 C1
Purrett Rd SE18. . . . . . 123 D1
Purser Ho [3] SW2 . . . . 160 C5
Pursers Cross Rd
SW6. . . . . 135 B4 264 D2
Pursewardens Cl W13. . 109 C5
Pursley Rd NW7 . . . . . . 28 B3
Purves Rd NW10. . . . . . 90 C5
Purvis Ho CR0 . . . . 205 B2
Pusey Ho [20] E14. . . . . 97 C1
Puteaux Ho [6] E2. . . . . . 96 D5
PUTNEY. 156 C6
Putney Bridge App SW6. 135 A2
Putney Bridge Rd SW15. 135 B1
Putney Bridge Sta SW6. 135 B2
Putney Comm SW15. . . 134 C2
**Putney Exchange Shopping
Ctr** SW15. . . . . 134 D1
Putney Gdns RM6. . . . . 58 B4
PUTNEY HEATH. 156 C4
Putney Heath SW15. . . 156 C5
Putney Heath La SW15. . 156 D5
Putney High Sch SW15. . 156 D6
Putney High St SW15. . . 135 A1
Putney Hill
[12] Putney SW15. . . . . 156 C4
Putney SW15. . . . . 156 C6
Putney L Ctr SW15. . . . 134 C1
Putney Park Ave SW15. . 134 A1
Putney Park La SW15. . . 156 B6
Putney Park Sch SW15. . 134 B1
Putney Pier SW15. . . . . 135 A2
**Putney School of Art &
Design** SW15. . . . . 135 A1
Putney Sta SW15. . . . . 135 A1
PUTNEY VALE. 156 A1
Putney Wharf Twr
SW15. . . . . 135 A2
Pycombe Cnr N12. . . . . . 29 B6
Pycroft Way N9. . . . . 34 A6
Pykewell Lo [13] E8. . . . . 74 A3
Pylbrook Rd SM1. . . . . . 217 D5
Pylon Trad Est E16. . . . . 98 B2
Pylon Way CR0 . . . . 204 A1
Pym Cl EN4. . . . . 14 B6
Pymers Mead SE21 . . . . 161 A3
Pymmes Brook Dr EN4. . . 2 C1
Pymmes Brook Ho [3]
N10. . . . . 31 A3

Pymmes Cl Bowes Pk N13 . . **32** B5
Tottenham N17. . . . . **34** B2
Pymmes Gdns N N9 . . . .**17** D1
Pymmes Gdns S N9 . . . .**17** D1
Pymmes Green Rd N11. . . . .**15** C1
Pymmes Mews N13 . . . . **32** A5
Pymmes Rd N13 . . . . **32** A5
Pynchester Cl UB10. . . . . . .**60** C6
Pyne Rd KT6. . . . .**198** C1
Pynfolds SE16 . . . .**118** B4
Pynham Cl SE2 . . . .**124** B3
Pynnacles Cl HA7. . . . .**25** B5
Pynnersmead SE24 . . . .**161** A6
Pyramid Ho N12 . . . .**30** A6
Pyrford Ho 12 SW9. . . . . . .**138** D1
Pyrland Rd
  Richmond TW10 . . . .**154** B5
  Stoke Newington N5. . . . . .**73** B3
Pyrmont Gr SE27 . . . .**160** D1
Pyrmont Rd W4. . . . .**132** C6
Pytchley Cres SE19 . . . . . .**183** A4
Pytchley Rd SE22 . . . .**139** C2

Q

Quadrangle Cl SE1. . . . . . . **263** A4
Quadrangle Ho The E15 . . .**76** C2
Quadrangle Lo SW19. . . . . .**179** C4
Quadrangle The
  Chelsea SW10 . . . . **266** B2
  Fulham W6. . . . . **264** A3
  Herne Hill SE24 . . . . **161** A6
  3 North Kensington W12 . . .**90** C1
  Paddington W2. . . . . **237** A2
  Stanmore HA7 . . . .**25** C3
  Walthamstow E17 . . . .**35** B1
Quadrant Arc W1. . . . . **249** B5
Quadrant Bsns Ctr NW6 . . .**91** A6
Quadrant Cl NW4 . . . .**46** B4
Quadrant Gr NW5. . . . .**70** D3
Quadrant Ho E15 . . . .**98** C4
Quadrant Rd Finchley N2 . .**30** C2
  Richmond TW9 . . . .**131** D1
  Thornton Heath CR7. . . . . .**204** D5
Quadrant The
  4 Kensal Green W10 . . . . . .**90** D4
  Richmond TW9 . . . . **132** A1
  Sutton SM2. . . . . **218** A2
  West Heath DA7 . . . . **146** D5
  Wimbledon SW20. . . . . . . **179** A2
Quad Rd HA9 . . . .**65** D5
Quaggy Wlk SE3 . . . . **143** A1
Quainton Hall Sch HA1. . . .**42** C4
Quainton St NW10 . . . .**67** B5
Quaker St EC1 . . . . **242** B6
Quaker La UB2. . . . . **107** C3
Quakers Course NW9 . . . . .**27** D2
Quakers La TW7 . . . . **131** A4
Quaker St E1 . . . . **95** D3 **243** C5
Quakers Wlk N21 . . . .**17** B5
Quality Ct WC2 . . . . **241** A2
Quantock Cl UB3 . . . . **127** B5
Quantock Ct
  4 East Barnet N20 . . . .**14** C2
  Greenford UB6 . . . .**64** C3
Quantock Dr KT4 . . . .**216** C6
Quantock Gdns NW2 . . . . . .**68** D6
Quantock Ho N16 . . . .**51** D1
Quantock Mews 3
  SE15 . . . .**140** A3
Quarles Park Rd RM6 . . . . .**58** C3
Quarrendon St SW6. . . . . . **135** C3
Quarr Rd SM5 . . . . **202** C3
Quarry Park Rd SM1 . . . . .**217** B2
Quarry Rd SW18 . . . . **158** A5
Quarry Rise SM1 . . . .**217** B2
Quarterdeck The E14. . . . . **119** C4
Quartermain Ho SM4 . . . . **202** A4
Quartermile La E10 . . . .**75** D4
Quayside Ct 6 SE16 . . . . . **118** D5
Quay West St TW11 . . . . . .**175** B5
Quebec & Crown Wharves
  E14. . . . .**97** B1
Quebec Ind Est SE16 . . . . **119** A3
Quebec Mews W1 . . . . **237** D1
Quebec Rd Hayes UB4 . . . .**84** C1
  Ilford IG1 . . . .**57** A2
Quebec Way SE16. . . . . . . **119** A4
Quebec Wharf 32 E8 . . . . . .**95** C6
Quedgeley Ct 3 SE15 . . . . **139** D6
Queen Adelaide Ct SE20. .**184** C4
Queen Adelaide Rd
  SE20 . . . . **184** C4
Queen Alexandra Mans
  WC1. . . . . **233** A4
Queen Alexandra's Ct
  SW19. . . . . **179** B5
Queen Anne Ave BR2. . . . **208** D6
Queen Anne Dr KT10. . . . **212** C1
Queen Anne Gate DA7 . . .**146** D2
Queen Anne Mews W1 . . . **238** D3
Queen Anne Rd E9. . . . .**74** D2
Queen Annes Cl TW2. . . . .**152** B1
Queen Anne's Gate
  SW1. . . . . . . **115** D4 **249** C1
Queen Anne's Gdns
  Bedford Pk W4 . . . . **111** C3
  Ealing W5 . . . . **110** A4

Queen Anne's Gdns continued
  Enfield EN1. . . . .**17** C5
  Mitcham CR4 . . . .**202** D6
Queen Anne's Gr
  Bedford Pk W4 . . . . **111** C3
  Ealing W5 . . . . **110** A4
  Enfield EN1. . . . .**17** C5
Queen Anne's Pl EN1 . . . . .**17** C5
Queen Anne St
  W1. . . . . **93** B2 **238** C3
Queen Anne Terr 9 E1. . .**118** B6
Queenborough Gdns
  Chislehurst BR7 . . . .**189** B4
  Ilford IG2 . . . .**56** C5
Queen Caroline St W6 . . . **112** C1
Queen Charlotte's & Chelsea
  Hospl W12 . . . .**90** A1
Queen Ct WC1 . . . . **240** B5
Queen Elizabeth Ct
  Barnet EN5 . . . .**1** B1
  5 Kingsland N1. . . . .**73** B2
Queen Elizabeth Gdns
  SM4 . . . . **201** C5
Queen Elizabeth Hall &
  Purcell Room* SE1 . . **250** D4
Queen Elizabeth Ho
  SW12. . . . . **159** A4
Queen Elizabeth Hospl
  SE18. . . . . **144** A5
Queen Elizabeth II Con Ctr
  SW1 . . . . **249** D1
Queen Elizabeth II Jubilee
  Sch 5 W9 . . . .**91** B3
Queen Elizabeth II Pier
  SE10 . . . . **120** D5
Queen Elizabeth Rd
  Kingston u T KT2. . . . .**176** B1
  Walthamstow E17 . . . .**53** A6
Queen Elizabeth's Cl N16 .**73** B6
Queen Elizabeth's Coll 15
  SE10 . . . . **142** A5
Queen Elizabeth's Dr N14. **16** A3
Queen Elizabeth's Girls Sch
  EN5. . . . .**1** B1
Queen Elizabeth's Hunting
  Lodge Mus* E4 . . . .**20** D4
Queen Elizabeth St
  SE1 . . . . **117** D4 **253** C2
Queen Elizabeth's Wlk
  Stoke Newington N16. . . . . .**73** B6
  Wallington SM6 . . . .**219** D4
Queen Elizabeth Wlk
  SW13. . . . . **134** B4
Queenhithe EC4 . . . . **252** B6
Queen Margaret Flats 22
  E2 . . . .**96** B4
Queen Margarets Ct N1 . .**73** C3
Queen Margaret's Gr N1 . .**73** C3
Queen Mary Ave SM4 . . . **200** B4
Queen Mary Cl KT9 . . . . .**214** C5
Queen Mary Ct TW19. . . .**148** A3
Queen Mary Rd
  Charlton TW17 . . . . **171** A1
  South Norwood SE19 . . . . .**182** D4
Queen Mary's Ave SM5. . .**218** D1
Queen Mary's Gdns*
  NW1. . . . . **231** A1
Queen Mary's Hospl
  DA14. . . . . **190** A4
Queen Mary's Univ Hospl
  SW15 . . . . **156** A5
Queen Mary, Univ of London
  E1. . . . .**97** A3
Queen Mother Sp Ctr
  SW1 . . . . **259** A4
Queen of Denmark Ct
  SE16 . . . . **119** B3
Queens Acre SM3. . . . . . . **217** A1
Queen St Pl EC4 . . . . **252** B6
Queens Ave
  Feltham TW13 . . . . **172** C6
  Muswell Hill N10. . . . .**49** B6
  Stanmore HA7 . . . .**25** C1
  Whetstone N20 . . . .**14** B2
Queen's Ave Finchley N3 . .**30** A2
  Southall UB1. . . . .**86** A1
  Southgate N21. . . . .**16** D3
  Woodford IG8. . . . .**37** B5
Queensberry Ho 6
  TW9. . . . . **153** D6
Queensberry Mews W
  SW7. . . . . **256** C4
Queensberry Pl
  Chelsea SW7 . . .**114** B2 **256** C4
  Plashet E12 . . . .**78** A3
Queensberry Way SW7. . . **256** C4
Queensborough Ct N3 . . .**47** B5
Queensborough Mews
  W2. . . . . **246** A6
Queensborough Pas W2 . **246** A6
Queensborough Terr
  W2. . . . . **113** D6 **246** A6
Queensbridge Ho 1 E2. . . .**95** D5
Queensbridge Inf Sch 11
  E8. . . . .**73** D1
Queensbridge Pk TW7 . . .**152** C6
Queensbridge Rd
  Dalston E8 . . . .**73** D1
  Shoreditch E2, E8. . . . .**95** D6
QUEENSBURY. **44** B6

Queensbury IG9 . . . .**21** B3
Queensbury Circ Par
  HA3 . . . .**44** A6
Queensbury Ct CR7 . . . . . .**183** A1
Queensbury Rd
  Kingsbury NW9 . . . .**45** B2
  Wembley HA0. . . . .**88** A5
Queensbury St 22 N1 . . . . .**73** A1
Queensbury Sta HA7, HA8. .**44** B6
Queensbury Station Par
  HA8. . . . .**44** B6
Queen's CE Prim Sch The
  TW9 . . . . **132** C5
Queen's Cir
  SW11. . . . . **137** B5 **268** C3
Queen's Cl Edgware HA8 . .**26** C5
  Wallington SM6 . . . .**219** B3
Queen's Club Gdns
  W14. . . . .**135** A6 **264** B6
Queen's Club The
  W14 . . . . **113** A1 **254** B1
Queen's Coll W1. . . **93** B2 **238** C3
Queen's Coll Prep Sch
  W1 . . . . **238** C4
Queenscourt HA9. . . . .**66** A4
Queens Cres TW10 . . . . . . **154** B6
Queen's Cres NW5. . . . .**71** A2
Queenscroft Rd SE9 . . . . . **165** D5
Queens Ct
  Battersea SW11. . . . . **268** C2
  Beckenham BR3 . . . . **185** D3
  Camberwell SE5 . . . . **139** C3
  Leyton E10 . . . .**53** C2
  4 Limehouse E14 . . . .**119** B6
  Sidcup DA14. . . . . **190** A6
  Stanmore HA7 . . . .**25** C1
  8 Temple Fortune NW11. . . .**47** B4
  Walthamstow E17 . . . .**53** C4
Queen's Ct Barnes SW13 . .**134** A2
  Beckenham BR3 . . . . **185** C2
  Croydon CR2. . . . . **221** A3
  8 Ealing W5 . . . .**87** C2
  Hampstead Garden Suburb
  NW11. . . . .**47** C4
  Kensington W2 . . . . **245** D5
  1 Kingston u T KT2 . . . . . .**176** C3
  Leytonstone E11. . . . .**54** C2
  3 Richmond TW10 . . . .**154** B5
  St John's Wood NW8 . . . . .**229** C4
  Thornton Heath CR7. . . . . .**204** C4
Queensdale W11 . . . . **112** D5
Queensdale Cres W11. . . . **112** D5
Queensdale Wlk W11 . . . . **244** A3
Queensdale Rd
  Notting Hill W11. . . . . **112** D5
  Notting Hill W11 . . . .**113** A5 **244** A3
Queensdown Rd E5. . . . . . .**74** B4
Queens Dr Surbiton KT5. .**198** C3
  Walthamstow E10 . . . .**53** C2
Queen's Dr Acton W3 . . . . .**88** C1
  Finsbury Pk N4 . . . .**72** D6
  Thames Ditton KT7 . . . . . .**197** A3
Queen's Elm Par SW3 . . . **256** D2
Queen's Elm Sq SW3 . . . . **256** D1
Queensferry Wlk N17 . . . . . .**52** B5
Queensfield Ct SM3 . . . . .**216** C4
Queen's Gallery*
  SW1 . . . . **115** B4 **248** D1
Queens Gate IG4 . . . .**56** B5
Queen's Gate
  SW7. . . . . **114** A3 **256** B5
Queensgate Ct N12 . . . . . .**29** D5
Queensgate Gdns SW15. . **134** B1
Queens Gate Gdns BR7. . .**189** B2
Queen's Gate Gdns
  SW7. . . . . **114** A3 **256** B5
Queensgate Ho 34 E3 . . . .**97** B5
Queen's Gate Jun Sch
  SW7 . . . . **256** C4
Queen's Gate Mews
  SW7. . . . . **114** A3 **256** B5
Queensgate Pl 10 NW6. . . .**69** C1
Queen's Gate Pl
  SW7. . . . . **114** A3 **256** B5
Queen's Gate Pl Mews
  SW7. . . . . **114** A3 **256** B5
Queen's Gate Terr
  SW7. . . . . **114** A3 **256** B5
Queens Gate Villas E9 . . . .**75** A1
Queens Gdns NW4 . . . .**46** C4
Queen's Gdns
  Bayswater W2 . . . **114** A6 **246** A6
  Ealing W5 . . . .**87** C3
  Heston TW5. . . . . **129** A4
Queen's Gr NW8 . . . **229** D5
Queen's Grove Rd E4 . . . . .**20** B3
Queen's Head Pas EC2 . .**242** A2
Queen's Head St
  N1 . . . . **86** D4 **234** D5
Queen's Head Yd SE1 . . . **252** C3
Queens Ho 1 SE17 . . . . . .**139** B6
Queen's Ho N1 . . . .**174** D4
Queen's House The*
  SE10 . . . . **142** B6
Queens Keep 10 TW1. . . .**153** C5
Queens La
  2 Ashford TW15. . . . . **170** A6
  Muswell Hill N10. . . . .**49** B6

Queensland Ave
  Edmonton N18 . . . .**33** A4
  Merton SW19 . . . . **179** D2
Queensland Cl E17. . . . .**35** B1
Queensland Ct N10 . . . .**31** B3
Queensland Ho 2 E16 . . . **122** C5
Queensland Rd N7. . . . .**72** C4
Queens Lo HA7 . . . .**25** A5
Queens Manor Sch
  SW6. . . . . **134** C5
Queens Mans
  Hampstead NW6 . . . .**69** D3
  Hendon NW4 . . . .**46** B4
Queen's Mans
  Brook Green W6. . . . . **112** D2
  Muswell Hill N10. . . . .**49** A6
Queensmead
  Ashford TW15. . . . . **170** B5
  St John's Wood
  NW8 . . . .**92** B6 **229** D6
Queens Mead HA8 . . . .**26** B4
Queen's Mead Rd BR2 . . . **186** D1
Queensmead Sch HA4. . . . .**62** D3
Queensmead Sp Ctr HA4 . .**62** D3
Queensmere 4 SW1. . . . . **217** D3
Queensmere Cl SW19 . . . **156** C2
Queensmere Ct SW13 . . . **134** A6
Queensmere Rd SW19 . . . **156** D2
Queens Mews 5 IG9 . . . . . .**21** C2
Queen's Mews
  W2. . . . . **113** D6 **245** C6
Queensmill Rd SW6. . . . . . **134** D5
Queensmill Sch SW6. . . . . **135** C3
Queen's Mkt* E13. . . . .**99** C6
Queens Par Ealing W5 . . . .**88** B1
  7 Hendon NW4. . . . .**46** B4
  8 Willesden NW2 . . . .**68** C2
Queen's Par
  3 Friern Barnet N11. . . . . . .**30** D5
  Wood Green N11 . . . .**32** A3
Queens Parade Cl N11 . . . .**30** D5
Queens Park Com Sch
  NW6. . . . .**90** D6
Queens Park Ct 5 W10 . . . .**90** D6
Queens Park Gdns
  TW13. . . . . **149** D1
Queen's Park Prim Sch 20
  W10 . . . .**91** A3
Queen's Park Sta NW6 . . . .**91** B5
Queen's Pas BR7 . . . . **188** D4
Queen's Pl SM4 . . . .**201** C5
Queen's Quay EC4 . . . . **252** B6
Queen's Rd Hayes UB3 . . .**83** C1
  Morden SM4 . . . . **201** C5
  Twickenham TW1 . . . . **153** A3
  West Drayton UB7 . . . . **104** B4
Queen's Rd Barking IG11 . . .**79** A2
  Beckenham BR3 . . . . **185** A1
  Bowes Pk N11. . . . .**32** A4
  Bromley BR1. . . . . **187** A1
  Buckhurst Hill IG9 . . . .**21** C2
  Chislehurst BR7 . . . . **188** D4
  Ealing W5 . . . .**88** A1
  Edmonton N9 . . . .**18** B2
  Enfield EN1. . . . .**5** C1
  Feltham TW13 . . . . **150** B3
  Finchley N3. . . . .**30** A2
  Hampton TW12. . . . . **173** D6
  Hendon NW4 . . . .**46** C4
  Hounslow TW3 . . . . **129** D2
  Kingston u T KT2. . . . .**176** C3
  Leytonstone E11. . . . .**54** C2
  Mitcham CR4 . . . .**202** B6
  Mortlake SW14 . . . .**133** B2
  New Cross Gate SE14,
  SE15. . . . . **140** C4
  Newham E13 . . . .**99** C6
  New Malden KT3 . . . . **199** D4
  Richmond KT2, TW10 . . . .**176** C5
  Richmond TW10 . . . . **154** B5
  Southall UB2. . . . . **107** A4
  Teddington TW11 . . . . **174** D4
  Thames Ditton KT7 . . . . . .**196** D4
  Thornton Heath CR0. . . . . **205** A3
  Wallington SM6 . . . .**219** B3
  Walthamstow E17 . . . .**53** C3
  Welling DA16 . . . .**146** B3
  Wimbledon SW19. . . . . . . **179** C4
Queen's Rd W E13 . . . .**99** B5
Queens Reach KT8. . . . . . .**196** C5
Queen's Ride SW13 . . . . . **134** B2
Queen's Rise SW10 . . . . . **154** B5
Queen's Road Sta SE15 . .**140** C4
Queen's Row SE17 . . . . . . **139** B6
Queen St
  Bexleyheath DA7 . . . . **147** B2
  City of London
  EC4. . . . . **117** A6 **252** B6
  Croydon CR0. . . . . **221** A4
  Mayfair W1. . . . . . **115** B5 **248** C4
  Tottenham N17 . . . .**33** C4
Queens Terr Harrow HA3 . .**24** C1
  Newham E13 . . . .**99** B6
  St John's Wood
  NW8 . . . .**92** B5 **229** C4
Queen's Terr TW7 . . . . **131** A1
Queen's Terr Cotts W7 . . . **108** C4
Queensthorpe Rd SE26. . .**184** D6
Queenstown Mews SW8 . **268** C1

Queenstown Rd
  SW8. . . . . **137** B5 **268** C4
Queenstown Road
  (Battersea) Sta
  SW8 . . . . **137** B4 **268** D2
Queensville Rd SW12,
  SW4. . . . . **159** D4
Queens Walk Ho W5 . . . . . .**87** C2
Queensway
  Coney Hall BR4. . . . . **224** D4
  Croydon CR0. . . . . **220** B3
  Enfield EN3. . . . .**6** C1
  Kensington W2 . . . **113** D6 **245** D6
  Orpington BR5 . . . . **211** A3
  Sunbury TW16 . . . . **172** B1
Queens Way
  Feltham TW13 . . . . **172** C6
  Hendon NW4 . . . .**46** C4
Queensway Bsns Ctr EN3. . .**6** C1
Queensway Sta
  W2 . . . . **113** D6 **245** D5
Queens Well Ave N20 . . . . .**30** C6
Queenswell Jun & Inf Scts
  N20. . . . .**14** B2
Queens Wlk
  Ashford TW15. . . . . **170** A6
  Chingford E4. . . . .**20** B3
  Harrow HA1. . . . .**42** C5
  Ruislip HA4. . . . .**62** C5
  Welsh Harp NW9 . . . .**67** A6
Queen's Wlk Ealing W5 . . . .**87** C2
  St James SW1 . . . **115** C5 **249** A3
Queenswood Ave
  Chingford E17. . . . .**36** A2
  Hampton TW12. . . . . **173** D4
  Hounslow TW3, TW5. . . . . **129** B3
  Thornton Heath CR7. . . . . .**204** C4
  Wallington CR0, SM6 . . . . **219** D4
Queenswood Ct
  7 Clapham Pk SW4. . . . . **160** A6
  11 West Norwood SE27 . . .**183** B6
Queenswood Gdns E11 . . .**55** B1
Queenswood Pk N3. . . . . . .**29** A2
Queenswood Rd
  Blackfen DA15 . . . . **167** D5
  Forest Hill SE23 . . . . **163** A1
Queen's Wood Rd N6 . . . . .**49** B3
Queens Yd E9 . . . .**75** C2
Queen's Yd W1 . . . . **239** B5
Queen Victoria Ave HA0 . . .**65** D1
Queen Victoria Meml*
  SW1. . . . . **249** A2
Queen Victoria St
  EC4 . . . . **117** A6 **252** A6
Queen Victoria Terr 12
  E1 . . . . **118** B6
Quelch Ho 2 N19. . . . .**71** D3
Quemerford Rd N7 . . . .**72** B3
Quendon Ho 9 W10 . . . .**90** C3
Quenington Ct 5 SE15 . . . **139** D6
Quenington Mans SW6. . . **264** C2
Quennel Ho 7 SW12. . . . . .**159** C4
Quentin Pl SE13 . . . . **142** C2
Quentin Rd SE13 . . . . **142** C2
Quernmore Cl BR1. . . . . . .**187** A4
Quernmore Rd
  Plaistow BR1 . . . . **187** A4
  Stroud Green N4. . . . .**50** C3
Querrin St SW6. . . . .**136** A3
Quested Ct 27 E8 . . . .**74** B3
Quex Mews NW6. . . . .**91** C6
Quex Rd NW6. . . . .**91** C6
Quick Rd W4 . . . . **111** C1
Quicks Rd SW19 . . . . **179** D3
Quick St N1 . . . . . **94** D5 **234** D3
Quick Street Mews N1 . . . **234** C3
Quickswood NW3. . . . .**70** C1
Quiet Nook BR2. . . . . **225** D5
Quill La SW15. . . . . **134** D1
Quill St Ealing W5. . . . .**88** A5
  Highbury N4 . . . .**72** C5
Quilp St SE1. . . . . **252** A2
Quilters Pl SE9 . . . . **167** A3
Quilter St
  Bethnal Green E2 . . . .**96** A4
  Plumstead Comm SE18 . . **123** D1
Quilting Ct 23 SE16. . . . . . **118** D4
Quince Ho TW13 . . . . **150** A3
Quince Rd SE13. . . . . **141** D3
Quinnel Ct SE18. . . . . **123** D1
Quinta Dr EN5 . . . .**12** C6
Quintin Ave SW20. . . . . . . **179** B2
Quintin Cl HA5. . . . .**40** B4
Quintin Ct W4 . . . . **133** A5
Quintin Kynaston Sch
  NW8 . . . .**92** B6 **229** C5
Quintock Ho 2 TW9 . . . . . **132** C4
Quinton Cl
  Beckenham BR3 . . . . **208** A6
  Cranford TW5. . . . . **128** B5
  Wallington SM6 . . . .**219** B4
Quinton Ho SW8 . . . . **270** A4
Quinton Rd KT7. . . . . **197** A1
Quinton St SW18 . . . . **158** A2
Quixley St 1 E14 . . . . **120** B6
Quorn Rd SE22 . . . . **139** C4

Quwwatul Islam Girls Sch
E7 . . . . .77 B2

R

Rabbit Row W8 . . . . .245 B4
Rabbits Rd E12 . . . . .78 A4
Rabbs Farm Prim Sch
UB7 . . . . .104 A6
Rabinal Ho EN3 . . . . .18 D6
Rabournmead Dr UB5 . . . .63 A3
Raby Rd KT3 . . . . .199 B5
Raby St E14 . . . . .97 A1
Raccoon Way TW4 . . . . . .128 C3
Rachel Cl IG6 . . . . .57 B6
Rachel Ct SM2 . . . . .218 B1
Racine 15 SE5 . . . . .139 C4
Rackham Cl DA16 . . . . . . .146 B3
Rackham Mews SW16 . . .181 C4
Racs Flats 9 SE1 . . . . .118 A2
Racton Rd SW6 . . . .135 C6 265 A5
Radbourne Ave W5 . . . . . .109 C2
Radbourne Cl E5 . . . . .74 C4
Radbourne Cres E17 . . . . . .36 B1
Radbourne Ct HA3 . . . . .43 B3
Radbourne Rd SW12 . . . . .159 D3
Radcliff Bldg EC1 . . . . . . .241 A4
Radcliffe Ave Enfield EN2 . . .5 A4
Willesden Green NW10 . . . .90 A5
Radcliffe Coll
Marylebone W1 . . . . .93 C1 239 A1
Soho W1 . . . . .93 D1 239 C2
Radcliffe Gdns SM5 . . . . .218 C1
Radcliffe Ho 10 SE16 . . . .118 B2
Radcliffe Path 5 SW8 . . . .137 B3
Radcliffe Rd
Bermondsey SE1 . . . . .263 B6
Harrow HA3 . . . . .25 A1
South Croydon CR0 . . . . . .221 D5
Southgate N21 . . . . .16 D3
Radcliffe Sq SW15 . . . . . .156 D5
Radcliffe Way UB5 . . . . . . .84 D4
Radcliff Mews TW12 . . . . .174 A5
Radcot Point 2 SE23 . . . . .162 D1
Radcot St SE11 . . . . .261 B1
Raddington Rd W10 . . . . . .91 A2
Radfield Way DA15 . . . . . .167 B4
Radford Ho
7 Bow Comm E14 . . . . .97 D2
Islington N7 . . . . .72 B3
Radford Rd SE13 . . . . .164 A5
Radford Way IG11 . . . . . . .101 D4
Radipole Rd
SW6 . . . . .135 B4 264 C2
Radius Pk TW6 . . . . .127 D1
Radland Rd E16 . . . . .99 A1
Radlet Ave SE23 . . . . .162 B2
Radlett Cl E7 . . . . .76 D4
Radlett Pl NW8 . . . .92 C6 230 A6
Radley Ave IG3 . . . . .80 A4
Radley Cl TW3 . . . . .111 A4
Radley Ct 4 Catford BR1 . .186 A6
25 Rotherhithe SE16 . . . . .118 D4
Radley Gdns HA3 . . . . .44 A5
Radley Ho
11 Abbey Wood SE2 . . . . . .124 D4
Marylebone NW1 . . . . .237 C6
Radley Lo 30 SW19 . . . . . .156 D3
Radley Mews W8 . . . . .255 B5
Radley Rd N17 . . . . .33 C1
Radley's La E18 . . . . .37 A1
Radleys Mead RM10 . . . . . .81 D2
Radley Sq E5 . . . . .74 C6
Radley Terr 1 E16 . . . . .98 D2
Radlix Rd E10 . . . . .53 C1
Radnor Ave Bexley DA16 . .168 B6
Harrow HA1 . . . . .42 C4
Radnor Cl
Chislehurst BR7 . . . . .189 C4
Mitcham CR4 . . . . .204 A5
Radnor Cres
Redbridge IG4 . . . . .56 B4
Woolwich SE18 . . . . .146 A5
Radnor Ct Ealing W7 . . . . . .86 D1
6 Forest Hill SE23 . . . . . . .162 D1
Harrow HA2 . . . . .24 D2
Radnor Gdns Enfield EN1 . . .5 C4
Twickenham TW1 . . . . .152 D2
Radnor Gr UB10 . . . . .82 C5
Radnor Ho
East Molesey KT8 . . . . . . .196 B5
Thornton Heath SW16 . . . .182 B1
Radnor Lo W2 . . . . .236 D1
Radnor Mews W2 . .92 B1 236 D1
Radnor Pl W2 . . . . . .92 C1 237 A1
Radnor Rd Harrow HA1 . . . .42 C4
Kensal Rise NW6 . . . . .91 A6
Peckham SE15 . . . . .140 A5
Twickenham TW1 . . . . .152 D2
Radnor St EC1 . . . . .95 A4 235 B3
Radnor Terr W14 . . .113 B2 254 C4
Radnor Way NW10 . . . . . . .88 D3
Radnor Wlk
Chelsea SW3 . . . . . .114 D1 257 C1
Croydon CR0. . . . . .207 A3
21 Millwall E14 . . . . .119 C2

Radstock Ave HA3 . . . . .43 B6
Radstock Cl N11 . . . . .31 A4
Radstock St SW11 . . . . . . .267 A3
Radway Ho 38 W2 . . . . .91 C2
Radwell Ho W2 . . . . .160 C6
Raebarn Ct 6 SW16 . . . . .160 A1
Raeburn Gdns EN5 . . . . . . .12 B6
Raeburn Ave KT5 . . . . .198 D3
Raeburn Cl
Hampstead Garden Suburb
NW11 . . . . .48 A3
Teddington KT1 . . . . .175 D3
Raeburn Ho
5 Belmont SM2 . . . . .217 D1
2 Northolt UB5 . . . . .84 D5
Raeburn Rd Edgware HA8 . .26 C2
Hayes UB4 . . . . .83 B5
Sidcup DA15 . . . . .167 C5
Raeburn St SW2 . . . . .138 A1
Raffles Ct HA8 . . . . .26 B6
Raffles Ho NW4 . . . . .46 B5
Rafford Way BR1 . . . . .209 B6
RAF Mus ★ NW9 . . . . .28 A1
Ragged School Mus ★ E3. .97 A2
Ragglesswood BR7 . . . . . .188 C2
Raglan Cl TW4 . . . . .151 B6
Raglan Ct Brixton SW9 . . .138 C2
Croydon CR0, CR2. . . . . . .220 D3
Lee SE12. . . . . .165 A6
Wembley HA9. . . . . .66 C5
Raglan Jun & Inf Schs
EN1. .17 C4
Raglan Prim Sch BR2 . . . .209 D5
Raglan Rd
Belvedere DA17 . . . . .125 B2
Bromley BR2. . . . . .209 C5
Enfield EN1. . . . . .17 D4
Walthamstow E17 . . . . .54 B4
Woolwich SE18. . . . . .123 A1
Raglan St NW5 . . . . .71 B2
Raglan Terr HA2 . . . . .63 D4
Raglan Way UB5 . . . . .64 A2
Ragley Cl W3 . . . . .111 A4
Rahere Ho EC1 . . . . .235 A2
Railey Mews NW5. . . . . . . .71 C3
Railshead Rd TW1, TW7 . .131 B1
Railton Rd SE24. . . . . .160 D6
Railway App
Bermondsey SE1 . . . . .252 D4
Harrow HA1, HA3. . . . . .42 D5
Stroud Green N4. . . . . .50 C3
Wallington SM6 . . . . .219 B3
Railway Ave SE16 . . . . . . .118 C4
Railway Cotts
Hammersmith W6 . . . . .112 C4
Ilford IG6 . . . . .57 B6
Railway Gr SE14 . . . . .141 B5
Railway Pl DA17 . . . . .125 C3
Railway Rd TW11 . . . . . . .174 D6
Railway Rise SE22 . . . . . . .139 C1
Railway Side SW13 . . . . . .133 C2
Railway St Ilford RM6 . . . . . .58 C2
King's Cross N1 . . . . .233 B3
Railway Terr
Chingford E17. . . . . .36 A2
Feltham TW13, TW14 . . . . .150 A3
Ladywell SE13 . . . . .163 D6
Rainborough Cl NW10 . . . . .67 A2
Rainbow Ave E14 . . . . .119 D1
Rainbow Ct 3 SE14. . . . . .141 A6
Rainbow Ind Est SW20 . . .178 B1
Rainbow Montessori Sch
NW6. . . . . .69 D1
Rainbow Quay SE16 . . . . .119 A3
Rainbow Sch 5 SW17 . . . .158 A2
Rainbow St SE5. . . . . .139 C5
Rainbow Terr 4 IG8 . . . . . .37 A6
Rainbow Works N15 . . . . . . .52 A4
Raine Gdns 4 IG8 . . . . .37 A6
Raines Ct N16 . . . . .73 D6
Raine's Foundation Lower
Sch 32 E2 . . . . .96 B4
Raine's Foundation Sch 34
E2 . . . . .96 C5
Rainford Ho 9 N7 . . . . .72 B6
Rainham Cl Sidcup SE9 . . .167 C5
Wandsworth SW11 . . . . . . .158 C5
Rainham Ho NW1 . . . . .232 B5
Rainham Rd NW10 . . . . .90 C4
Rainham Rd N RM10 . . . . . .81 D6
Rainham Rd S RM10. . . . . .81 D4
Rainhill Way E3. . . . . .97 C4
Rainsborough Ave SE8 . . .119 A2
Rainsford Cl HA7 . . . . .25 C5
Rainsford Ct NW10 . . . . . . .88 D5
Rainsford Ho 14 SW2 . . . . .160 B6
Rainsford Rd NW10 . . . . . . .88 D5
Rainsford St W2 . . . . .237 A2
Rainstar Est N18 . . . . .34 C6
Rainton Rd SE7 . . . . .121 A1
Rainville Rd W6 . . . . .134 C6
Raisins Hill HA5 . . . . .40 C6
Raith Ave N14 . . . . .15 D1
Raleigh Ave Hayes UB4 . . . .84 B2
Wallington SM6 . . . . .219 D4
Raleigh Cl Hendon NW4 . . . .46 C4
Pinner HA5 . . . . .40 D2
Ruislip HA4. . . . . .61 D6

Raleigh Ct
Beckenham BR3 . . . . .185 D2
4 Dulwich SE19 . . . . .183 D5
Ealing W13 . . . . .87 B2
7 Hammersmith W12 . . . . .112 B4
2 Rotherhithe SE16 . . . . . .118 D5
Wallington SM6 . . . . .219 B2
Raleigh Dr
East Barnet N20 . . . . .14 C1
Esher KT10. . . . . .212 B3
Tolworth KT5 . . . . .199 A1
Raleigh Gdns
Mitcham CR4 . . . . .202 B6
Tulse Hill SW2. . . . . .160 B5
Raleigh Ho
30 Clapham SW8 . . . . .137 D3
Isle of Dogs E14 . . . . .119 D4
1 Thames Ditton KT7 . . . .197 A2
Raleigh Mews
Islington N1 . . . . .234 D5
6 Orpington BR6. . . . . . . .227 D3
Raleigh Rd Enfield EN2 . . . . .5 B1
Feltham TW13 . . . . .149 D2
Finchley N10. . . . . .30 C2
Hornsey N8. . . . . .50 C5
Penge SE20 . . . . .184 D3
Richmond TW9 . . . . .132 B2
Southall UB2. . . . . .107 A1
Raleigh St N1 . . . . .94 D6 234 D5
Raleigh Way
Feltham TW13 . . . . .172 C5
Southgate N14 . . . . .16 A3
Ralph Ct 8 W2 . . . . .91 D1
Ralph Perring Ct BR3 . . . .207 C5
Ralston St SW3 . . . . .257 C1
Ramac Ind Est SE7 . . . . . .121 B1
Rama Cl SW16 . . . . .182 A3
Rama Ct HA1 . . . . .64 C6
Ramac Way SE7 . . . . .121 B1
Rama La SE19 . . . . .183 D3
Ramar Ho 12 E1 . . . . .96 A2
Rambler Cl SW16 . . . . .181 C6
Rambler Ct 11 NW9 . . . . . .46 A5
Rame Cl SW17. . . . . .181 A5
Ramilles Cl SW2 . . . . .160 A5
Ramilles Ho SW1 . . . . .239 B1
Ramillies Pl W1. . . .93 C1 239 A1
Ramillies Rd
Bedford Pk W4 . . . . .111 B3
Blackfen DA15 . . . . .168 B5
Edgware NW7 . . . . .11 C2
Ramillies St W1 . . . . .239 A1
Ramney Dr EN3 . . . . .7 A6
Rampart St E1. . . . . .96 B1
Rampayne St SW1 . . . . . . .259 C2
Rampton Cl E4 . . . . .19 C1
Ramsay Ho NW8 . . . . .230 A4
Ramsay Rd Acton W3 . . . . .111 A4
Leyton E7 . . . . .76 D4
Ramscroft Cl N9 . . . . .17 C4
Ramsdale Rd SW17 . . . . . .181 A5
Ramsdean Ho 1 SW15. . . .156 B3
Ramsden Rd
Balham SW12. . . . . .159 A4
Friern Barnet N11 . . . . .30 C5
Ramsey Cl Greenford UB6. . .64 B3
West Hendon NW9. . . . . . . .45 D3
Ramsey Ct Croydon CR0 . . .220 D6
Hornsey N8. . . . . .49 D4
Putney SW15 . . . . .156 C5
6 Upper Holloway N19 . . . .71 D6
Ramsey Ho
5 Battersea SW11 . . . . . . .136 B1
14 Kennington SW9 . . . . .138 C5
7 Merton SW19 . . . . .179 D2
Ramsey Rd CR7. . . . . .204 B3
Ramsey St E2. . . . . .96 A3
Ramsey Way N14 . . . . .15 C4
Ramsey Wlk N1. . . . . .73 B2
Ramsfort Ho 4 SE16. . . . . .118 B2
Ramsgate Cl 10 E16. . . . . .121 B5
Ramsgate St E8 . . . . .73 D2
Ramsgill App IG2. . . . . .57 D5
Ramsgill Dr IG2 . . . . .57 D5
Rams Gr RM6 . . . . .59 A5
Ram St SW18. . . . . .157 D6
Ramulis Dr UB4. . . . . .84 D3
Ramus Wood Ave BR6. . . .227 C3
Rance Ho 12 SE7. . . . . .122 A2
Rancliffe Gdns SE9 . . . . . .144 A1
Rancliffe Rd E6. . . . . .100 A5
Randal Cremer JMI Sch 16
E2 . . . . .95 D5
Randall 9 NW9. . . . . .27 D2
Randall Ave NW2 . . . . .67 D5
Randall Cl SW11 . . .136 C4 267 A2
Randall Ct NW7. . . . . .28 A3
Randall Pl SE10. . . . . .142 A5
Randall Rd SE11 . . .116 B2 260 C3
Randall Row SE11. . . . . . . .260 C3
Randell's Rd N1 . . . .94 A6 233 B6
Randisbourne Gdns SE6. . .163 D1
Randle Rd TW10 . . . . .175 C6
Randlesdown Rd SE6 . . . . .163 D1
Randmore Ct 6 BR3. . . . . .185 C3
Randolf Ct
Paddington NW6 . . . . .91 D5
St John's Wood NW8 . . . . .229 A5

Randolph App E16. . . . . . . .99 C1
Randolph Ave W9. . .92 A4 229 A1
Randolph Cl KT2. . . . . .177 A5
Randolph Cres
W9. . . . . .92 A3 236 A6
Randolph Ct HA5 . . . . .23 C3
Randolph Gdns NW6. . . . . .91 D5
Randolph Gr RM6. . . . . .58 C4
Randolph Mews
W9. . . . . .92 A3 236 B5
Randolph Rd
Paddington W9. . . . .92 A3 236 B5
Southall UB1. . . . . .107 B4
Walthamstow E17 . . . . .53 D4
Randolph St NW1. . . . . .71 C1
Randon Cl HA2 . . . . .23 D1
Ranelagh Ave
Barnes SW13 . . . . .134 A3
Fulham SW6. . . . . .135 B2
Ranelagh Cl HA8. . . . . .26 C6
Ranelagh Cl HA8 . . . . .26 C6
Ranelagh Dr Edgware HA8. .26 C6
Twickenham TW1 . . . . .153 C6
Ranelagh Gardens Mans
SW6. . . . . .135 B2
Ranelagh Gardens (site of
Chelsea Flower Show) ★
SW1 . . . . .115 A1 258 B1
Ranelagh Gdns
3 Bedford Pk W6 . . . . .111 B3
Chiswick W4. . . . . .133 A5
Fulham SW6. . . . . .135 B2
Ilford IG1 . . . . .56 C1
Wanstead E11 . . . . .55 C4
Ranelagh Gr
SW1. . . . . .115 A1 258 B2
Ranelagh Ho SW3 . . . . . . .257 C2
Ranelagh Mans 4 SW6 . . .135 B3
Ranelagh Pl KT3. . . . . .199 C4
Ranelagh Prim Sch E15. . . .98 C5
Ranelagh Rd
Dagenham NW10. . . . . .89 D5
Ealing W5 . . . . .109 D4
Leyton E11 . . . . .76 C4
Newham E15 . . . . .98 C5
Pimlico SW1. . . . . . .115 C1 259 B1
Southall UB1. . . . . .106 D5
Tottenham N17. . . . . .51 C6
Wallend E6 . . . . .100 C5
Wembley HA0. . . . . .65 D2
Wood Green N22 . . . . .32 B2
Ranfurly Rd SM1. . . . . .217 C6
Rangdon St EC3 . . . . .243 C1
Rangefield Prim Sch
BR1. . . . . .186 C5
Rangefield Rd BR1. . . . . . .186 D5
Rangemoor Rd N15. . . . . . .51 D4
Ranger's House (The
Wernher Collection) ★
SE10. . . . . .142 B4
Ranger's Rd
Buckhurst Hill IG9, IG10. . . .21 A4
Chingford E4. . . . . .20 D4
Rangers Sq SE10. . . . . . . .142 B4
Range Villas TW17 . . . . . . .192 A2
Range Way TW17 . . . . .192 C2
Rangeworth Pl DA15 . . . . .167 D1
Rangoon Ho 6 N16. . . . . . . .73 B4
Rankin Cl NW9 . . . . .45 C6
Rankine Ho SE1 . . . . .262 A5
Ranleigh Gdns DA7 . . . . . .147 B5
Ranmere St SW12. . . . . . . .159 B3
Ranmoor Cl HA1. . . . . .42 B5
Ranmoor Gdns HA1. . . . . . .42 C5
Ranmore Ave CR0. . . . . . . .221 D5
Ranmore Ct
Kingston u T KT6. . . . . .197 D4
3 Wimbledon SW20 . . . . .178 D2
Rann Ho 1 SW14 . . . . .133 B2
Rannoch Cl HA8 . . . . .10 D2
Rannoch Ct 9 KT6. . . . . . . .198 A4
Rannoch Rd W6 . . . . .134 D6
Rannock Ave NW9 . . . . .45 C2
Ransford Ho 16 SE21. . . . .183 C6
Ransomes Dock Bsns Ctr
SW11. . . . . .267 B3
Ransomes Mews SW11. . . .267 B4
Ransom Rd 1 SE7. . . . . . .121 C1
Ranston St NW1 . . . . .237 A4
Ranulf Rd NW2 . . . . .69 B4
Ranwell Cl 18 E3. . . . . .97 B6
Ranwell Ho 17 E3 . . . . .97 B6
Ranworth Rd N9. . . . . .18 C2
Ranyard Cl KT9. . . . . .214 B5
Raphael Ct 9 SE16 . . . . . .118 B1
Raphael Dr KT7. . . . . .196 D2
Raphael St SW7 . . . . .247 C1
Rapide 15 NW9 . . . . .27 C2
Rapley Ho 14 E2 . . . . .96 A4
Rashleigh Ct 8 SW8 . . . . .137 B2
Rashleigh Ho WC1. . . . . . . .233 A1
Rasper Rd N20. . . . . .14 A2
Rastell Ave SW12 . . . . .159 D3
RATCLIFF 118 D6
Ratcliffe Cl SE12. . . . . .165 A6
Ratcliffe Cross St E1. . . . . . .96 D1
Ratcliffe Ho 10 E14 . . . . . . .97 A1
Ratcliffe La 16 E14 . . . . . . .97 A1
Ratcliffe Orch 9 E1. . . . . . .118 D6
Ratcliff Rd E7 . . . . .77 C3

Rathbone Ho
5 Canning Town E16. . . . . . .98 D1
Kilburn NW6. . . . . .91 C6
10 Wimbledon SW19 . . . . .178 D3
Rathbone Mkt ★ 3 E16 . . . .98 D2
Rathbone Pl W1 . . . .93 D1 239 C2
Rathbone St
Canning Town E16. . . . . .98 D1
Fitzrovia W1. . . . . . .93 C2 239 B3
Rathcoole Ave N8. . . . . .50 B4
Rathcoole Gdns N8. . . . . . . .50 B4
Rathfern Prim Sch SE6. . . .163 B3
Rathfern Rd SE6 . . . . .163 B3
Rathgar Ave W13 . . . . .109 C5
Rathgar Cl N3 . . . . .29 B1
Rathgar Rd SW9 . . . . .138 D2
Rathmell Dr SW4 . . . . .159 D5
Rathmore Rd SE7 . . . . .121 B1
Ratier 16 NW9 . . . . .27 C2
Rattray Ct 3 SE6 . . . . .164 D2
Rattray Rd SW2. . . . . .160 C6
Raul Rd SE15 . . . . .140 A4
Raveley St NW5. . . . . .71 C4
Raven Cl NW9 . . . . .27 C1
Ravendale Rd TW16. . . . . . .171 D1
Ravenet Ct
Battersea SW11. . . . . .268 C1
Clapham SW4. . . . . .159 B6
Ravenet St SW11 . . .137 B4 268 C1
Ravenfield Rd SW17 . . . . .158 D1
Ravenhill Rd E13. . . . . .99 C5
Raven Ho 10 SE16 . . . . . . .118 D2
Ravenings Par IG3. . . . . . . .58 A1
Ravenna Rd SW15 . . . . . . .156 D6
Ravenor Ct UB6. . . . . .85 D3
Ravenor Park Rd UB6 . . . . .86 A4
Ravenor Prim Sch UB6. . . .85 C4
Raven Rd E18. . . . . .37 C1
Raven Row E1. . . . . .96 B2
Ravensbourne Ave
Bromley BR2, BR3 . . . . . . .186 C2
Catford BR2. . . . . .186 B3
Stanwell TW19 . . . . .148 A3
Ravensbourne Bsns Ctr
BR2. . . . . .225 D4
Ravensbourne Coll of Design
& Communication BR7. .188 B5
Ravensbourne Ct SE6. . . . .163 C4
Ravensbourne Gdns W13. . .87 B2
Ravensbourne Ho
10 Catford BR1. . . . . .186 B5
Paddington NW8 . . . . .237 A4
3 Twickenham TW1. . . . . .153 C5
Ravensbourne Mans 9
SE8 .141 C6
Ravensbourne Park Cres
SE6 .163 B4
Ravensbourne Pk SE6. . . . .163 C4
Ravensbourne Pl SE13 . . .141 D3
Ravensbourne Rd
Bromley BR1, BR2 . . . . . . .209 A6
Forest Hill SE23 . . . . .163 B3
Twickenham TW1 . . . . .153 C5
Ravensbourne Sch The
BR2. . . . . .209 B5
Ravensbourne Sta BR3. . . .186 B3
Ravensbury Ave SM4. . . . . .202 A4
Ravensbury Ct CR4 . . . . . .202 B5
Ravensbury Gr CR4 . . . . . .202 A5
Ravensbury La CR4. . . . . . .202 B5
Ravensbury Rd
Orpington BR5 . . . . .211 D5
Wandsworth SW18 . . . . . . .157 D2
Ravensbury Terr SW18 . . . .157 D2
Ravenscar NW1. . . . . .232 A5
Ravenscar Lo 14 SW19 . . .178 D3
Ravenscar Rd
Catford BR1. . . . . .186 C6
Surbiton KT6. . . . . .214 B6
Ravens Cl Bromley BR2. . . .186 D1
Enfield EN1. . . . . .5 C3
Kingston u T KT1. . . . . .197 D5
Kingston u T KT6. . . . . .197 D3
Ravenscourt
1 Shacklewell N16 . . . . .74 A5
Sunbury TW16 . . . . .171 D2
Ravenscourt Ave W6. . . . . .112 A2
Ravenscourt Cl HA4. . . . . . .39 A2
Ravenscourt Gdns W6 . . . .112 A2
Ravenscourt Ho 18 W6 . . .112 B2
Ravenscourt Park Mans 1
W6. .112 B3
Ravenscourt Park Prep Sch
W6 .112 A2
Ravenscourt Park Sta
W6 .112 B2
Ravenscourt Pk W6. . . . . . .112 A2
Ravenscourt Pl W6 . . . . . . .112 B2
Ravenscourt Rd
Hammersmith W6 . . . . .112 B2
St Paul's Cray BR5 . . . . . . .190 B1
Ravenscourt Sq W6. . . . . . .112 A2
Ravenscourt Theatre Sch 14
W6 .112 B2
Ravenscraig Rd N11 . . . . . .31 C6
Ravenscroft Ave
Golders Green NW11. . . . . .47 B2
Wembley HA9. . . . . .44 B2
Ravenscroft Cl 4 E16. . . . . .99 A2
Ravenscroft Cres SE9 . . . .166 B5

Rav–Reg 387

Ravenscroft Ct NW11 ... 47 B2
Ravenscroft Pk EN5 ... 1 A1
Ravenscroft Point 26 E9 ... 74 D2
Ravenscroft Prim Sch 12
E16 ... 99 A3
Ravenscroft Rd
Acton W4 ... 111 A2
Newham E16 ... 99 A2
Penge BR3 ... 184 D1
Ravenscroft Sch N20 ... 13 B4
Ravenscroft St E2 ... 95 D4
Ravensdale Ave N12 ... 30 B6
Ravensdale Commercial Est
N16 ... 52 A3
Ravensdale Gdns
Hounslow TW4 ... 129 A2
South Norwood SE19 ... 183 B3
Ravensdale Mans N8 ... 50 A3
Ravensdale Rd
Hounslow TW4 ... 129 A2
South Tottenham N16 ... 51 D3
Ravensdon St
SE11 ... 116 C1 261 B1
Ravensfield Cl RM9 ... 80 D4
Ravensfield Gdns KT19 ... 215 C4
Ravenshaw St NW6 ... 69 B3
Ravenshill BR7 ... 188 D2
Ravens Ho KT1 ... 175 D1
Ravenshurst Ave NW4 ... 46 C5
Ravenside KT6 ... 197 D4
Ravenside Cl N18 ... 34 D5
Ravenside Ret Pk N18 ... 34 D5
Ravenslea Rd SW11,
SW12 ... 158 D4
Ravensleigh Gdns BR1 ... 187 B5
Ravensmead Rd BR2 ... 186 B3
Ravensmede Way W4 ... 111 D2
Ravensroost SE19 ... 183 B2
Ravenstone SE17 . 117 C1 263 B1
Ravenstone Prim Sch
SW12 ... 159 A2
Ravenstone Rd
Hornsey N8 ... 50 C6
West Hendon NW9 ... 45 D3
Ravenstone St SW12 ... 159 A3
Ravensview Ct KT6 ... 197 D4
Ravens Way SE3, SE12 ... 165 A6
Ravenswood
Bowes Pk N22 ... 32 B4
Sidcup DA5 ... 169 A3
Ravenswood Ave
Tolworth KT6 ... 214 C6
West Wickham BR4 ... 208 A1
Ravenswood Cres
Harrow HA2 ... 63 B6
West Wickham BR4 ... 208 A1
Ravenswood Gdns TW7 ... 130 C4
Ravenswood Ind Est 5
E17 ... 54 A5
Ravenswood Pk HA6 ... 22 A4
Ravenswood Rd
Balham SW12 ... 159 B4
Croydon CR0 ... 220 D5
Walthamstow E17 ... 54 A5
Ravens Wood Sch BR2 ... 225 D5
Ravensworth Ct SW6 ... 265 A3
Ravensworth Rd
Chislehurst SE9 ... 188 B6
College Pk NW10 ... 90 B4
Raven Wharf SE1 ... 253 C2
Ravey St EC2 ... 95 C3 243 A6
Ravine Gr SE18 ... 145 C6
Rav Pinter Cl N16 ... 51 C2
Rawlings Cl
Beckenham BR3 ... 208 A4
3 Orpington BR6 ... 227 D3
Rawlings Cres HA9 ... 66 D5
Rawlings St SW3 114 D2 257 C4
Rawlins Cl Hendon N3 ... 47 A6
South Croydon CR2 ... 223 B1
Rawlinson Ct NW2 ... 46 C2
Rawlinson Ho SE13 ... 142 B1
Rawlinson Point 8 E16 ... 98 D2
Rawnsley Ave CR4 ... 202 C4
Rawreth Wlk N1 ... 235 B6
Rawson Ct SW11 ... 268 B1
Rawson St SW11 .. 137 B4 268 C1
Rawsthorne Cl E16 ... 122 B5
Rawstone Wlk 5 E13 ... 99 A5
Rawstorne Pl EC1 ... 234 C2
Rawstorne St EC1 .. 94 D4 234 C2
Raybell Ct TW7 ... 130 D3
Rayburne Ct
1 Buckhurst Hill IG9 ... 21 C3
West Kensington W14 ... 254 A6
Ray Cl KT9 ... 213 C2
Ray Ct Ealing W13 ... 109 B5
Stanmore HA7 ... 25 B5
Woodford IG8 ... 37 D4
Raydean Rd EN5 ... 13 D6
Raydons Gdns RM9 ... 81 A3
Raydons Rd RM9 ... 81 A3
Raydon St N19 ... 71 B6
Rayfield Cl BR2 ... 210 A3
Rayford Ave SE12 ... 164 D4
Ray Gdns Barking IG11 ... 102 A5
Stanmore HA7 ... 25 B5
Ray Ho
7 North Kensington W10 ... 90 D1
Shoreditch N1 ... 235 D5
Rayleas Cl SE18 ... 144 D4
Rayleigh Ave TW11 ... 174 C4
Rayleigh Cl N13 ... 17 B1
Rayleigh Ct
2 Kingston u T KT1 ... 176 B1
Tottenham N22 ... 33 A2
Rayleigh Rd Edmonton N13 . 17 B1
Merton SW19 ... 179 B2
5 Newham E16 ... 121 B5
Woodford IG8 ... 37 C3
Rayleigh Rise CR2 ... 221 C2
Ray Lodge Prim Sch IG8 ... 37 D4
Ray Lodge Rd IG8 ... 37 D4
Ray Massey Way 3 E6 ... 100 A6
Raymead Ave CR7 ... 204 C4
Raymede Twr 2 W10 ... 90 D2
Raymere Gdns SE18 ... 145 C5
Raymond Ave
Brentford W13 ... 109 A3
Woodford E18 ... 36 D1
Raymond Bldgs WC1 ... 240 D4
Raymond Cl SE26 ... 184 C5
Raymond Ct N10 ... 31 A3
Raymond Postgate Ct 5
SE28 ... 124 B6
Raymond Rd
Beckenham BR3 ... 207 A5
Ilford IG2 ... 57 B2
Newham E13 ... 99 C6
Wimbledon SW19 ... 179 A4
Raymond Way KT10 ... 213 A2
Raymouth Rd SE16 ... 118 B2
Raynald Ho 15 SW16 ... 160 A1
Rayne Ct Bermondsey SE1. 253 C2
Snaresbrook E18 ... 54 D5
Rayne Ho
1 Balham SW12 ... 159 A5
Paddington W9 ... 91 D3
Rayner Ct 10 W12 ... 112 C4
Rayners Cl HA0 ... 65 D3
Rayners Cres UB5 ... 84 B4
Rayners Gdns UB5 ... 84 B4
Rayners La Harrow HA2 ... 63 D6
Pinner HA5 ... 41 B3
RAYNERS LANE ... 41 B1
Rayners Lane Sta HA5 ... 41 B2
Rayner's Rd SW15 ... 157 A6
Rayner Twrs E10 ... 53 C2
Raynes Ave E11 ... 55 C2
Raynes Ct NW2 ... 69 A4
Raynesfield SW20 ... 200 C6
RAYNES PARK ... 200 C6
Raynes Park High Sch
SW20 ... 200 B6
Raynes Park Sta SW20 ... 178 C1
Raynham W2 ... 237 A2
Raynham Ave N18 ... 34 A5
Raynham Ho 1 E1 ... 96 D3
Raynham Prim Sch N18 ... 34 A5
Raynham Rd
Edmonton N18 ... 34 A5
Hammersmith W6 ... 112 B2
Raynham Terr N18 ... 34 A5
Raynor Cl UB1 ... 107 B5
Raynor Pl
23 Canonbury N1 ... 73 A1
N1 ... 235 B6
Raynton Cl Harrow HA2 ... 41 A2
Hayes UB4 ... 83 D3
Raynton Dr Hayes UB4 ... 83 C5
Hayes UB4 ... 83 D3
Raynton Rd EN3 ... 6 D6
Ray Rd KT8 ... 195 D4
Rays Ave N18 ... 34 C6
Rays Rd Edmonton N18 ... 34 C6
West Wickham BR4 ... 208 A2
Ray St EC1 ... 241 B5
Ray Wlk N7 ... 72 B6
Raywood Cl UB7 ... 127 A5
Reachview Cl 17 NW1 ... 71 C1
Read Cl KT7 ... 197 A2
Read Ct E17 ... 53 D3
Reade Ct 6 W3 ... 111 A3
Reade Wlk 5 NW10 ... 67 C1
Read Ho Friern Barnet N11 ... 30 D6
4 Kennington SE11 ... 138 C6
Reading Ho
Paddington W2 ... 236 A1
Peckham SE15 ... 140 A6
Reading La E8 ... 74 B2
Reading Rd Northolt UB5 ... 64 A3
Sutton SM1 ... 218 A3
Reading Way NW7 ... 29 A5
Readman Ct 8 SE20 ... 184 B2
Reads Cl IG1 ... 78 D5
Reapers Cl NW1 ... 232 C6
Reapers Way TW7 ... 152 B6
Reardon Ho 5 E1 ... 118 B5
Reardon Path 31 E1 ... 118 B5
Reardon St E1 ... 118 B5
Reaston St SE14 ... 140 D5
Reay Prim Sch
SW9 ... 138 B5 270 D3
Rebecca Ct
3 Beckenham BR3 ... 185 C2
Sidcup DA14 ... 190 B6
Rebecca Ho 12 N12 ... 29 D6
Reckitt Rd W4 ... 111 C1
Record St SE16 ... 140 C6
Recovery St SW17 ... 180 C5
Recreation Rd
Bromley BR2 ... 186 D1
Forest Hill SE26 ... 184 D6
Southall UB2 ... 107 A2
Recreation Way CR4,
SW16 ... 204 A6
Rector St N1 ... 95 A6 235 A5
Rectory Bsns Ctr 5
DA14 ... 190 B6
Rectory Cl Chingford E4 ... 19 C1
Finchley N3 ... 29 B2
Littleton TW17 ... 192 C6
Long Ditton KT6 ... 197 C1
Sidcup DA14 ... 190 B6
Stanmore HA7 ... 25 B5
West Barnes SW20 ... 200 C6
Rectory Cres E11 ... 55 C3
Rectory Ct Cranford TW5 ... 128 C3
Feltham TW13 ... 172 C6
Leyton E11 ... 76 D5
Wallington SM6 ... 219 C4
West Drayton UB7 ... 104 A4
Woodford E18 ... 36 D2
Rectory Field Cres SE7 ... 143 C5
Rectory Gdns
Beckenham BR3 ... 185 C2
6 Clapham SW4 ... 137 C2
Hornsey N8 ... 50 A5
Northolt UB5 ... 85 B6
Rectory Gn BR3 ... 185 B2
Rectory Gr Clapham SW4 ... 137 C2
Croydon CR0 ... 220 D6
Hampton TW12, TW13 ... 173 B6
Rectory La Edgware HA8 ... 26 C4
Long Ditton KT6 ... 197 C1
Sidcup DA14 ... 190 C6
Stanmore HA7 ... 25 B5
Upper Tooting SW17 ... 181 A5
Wallington SM6 ... 219 C4
Rectory Orch SW19 ... 179 A6
Rectory Park Ave UB5 ... 85 B4
Rectory Pl SE18 ... 122 C2
Rectory Rd Barnes SW13 ... 134 A3
Beckenham BR3 ... 185 C2
Cranford TW5 ... 128 C3
Dagenham RM10 ... 81 D1
Hayes UB3 ... 84 A1
Keston BR2 ... 225 D1
Little Ilford E12 ... 78 B3
1 London W3 ... 111 A5
Shacklewell N16 ... 73 D5
Southall UB2 ... 107 B3
Sutton SM1 ... 217 D5
Walthamstow E17 ... 53 D5
Rectory Road Sta N16 ... 73 D5
Rectory Sq E1 ... 96 D2
Rectory Way UB10 ... 60 D5
Reculver Ho 2 SE15 ... 140 C6
Reculver Mews N18 ... 34 A6
Reculver Rd SE16 ... 118 D1
Red Anchor Cl SW3 ... 267 A5
Redan Pl W2 ... 91 D1
Redan St W14 ... 112 D3
Redan Terr SE5 ... 138 D3
Red Barracks Rd 4
SE18 ... 122 B2
Redberry Gr SE23, SE26 ... 162 C1
Redbourne Ave N3 ... 29 C2
Redbourne Dr SE28 ... 102 D1
Redbourne Ho
Finchley N3 ... 29 C2
7 Poplar E14 ... 97 B1
Redbourn Ho 10 W10 ... 90 C3
REDBRIDGE ... 55 C3
Redbridge Coll RM6 ... 58 B4
Redbridge Ct IG1 ... 55 D3
Redbridge Ent Ctr IG1 ... 79 A6
Redbridge Foyer IG1 ... 79 A6
Redbridge Gdns SE5 ... 139 C5
Redbridge La E IG4 ... 56 A4
Redbridge La W E11 ... 55 C3
Redbridge Prim Sch IG4 ... 56 A4
Redbridge Rdbt IG4 ... 55 D3
Redbridge Sta IG4 ... 55 D3
Redburn St SW3 . 136 D6 267 C6
Redburn Trad Est EN3 ... 18 D5
Redcar Cl UB5 ... 63 D2
Redcar Ho SE26 ... 184 B4
Redcar St SE5 ... 139 A5
Redcastle Cl E1 ... 118 C6
Red Cedars Rd BR6 ... 211 C2
Redchurch St E2 ... 95 D3 243 C6
Redcliffe Cl SW5 ... 255 C1
Redcliffe Ct 2 E5 ... 74 B5
Redcliffe Gdns
Chiswick W4 ... 132 D5
Fulham SW10 ... 135 D6 265 D6
Ilford IG1 ... 56 C1
Redcliffe Mews SW10 ... 255 D1
Redcliffe Pl SW10 ... 266 A5
Redcliffe Rd
SW10 ... 136 A6 266 B6
Redcliffe Sch
SW10 ... 136 A6 266 A6
Redcliffe Sq
SW10 ... 113 D1 255 D1
Redcliffe St SW10 ... 265 D6
Redclose Ave SM4 ... 201 C4
Redclyffe Rd E6 ... 99 C6
Redclyffe Terr 2 SM2 ... 217 C1
Redclyf Ho 13 E1 ... 96 C3
Redcroft 5 NW6 ... 69 C2
Redcroft Rd UB1 ... 86 A1
Red Cross Cotts SE1 ... 252 B2
Redcross Way
SE1 ... 117 A5 252 B3
Reddiford Sch HA5 ... 41 A5
Redding Ho SE18 ... 122 A3
Reddings Ave WD23 ... 8 A6
Reddings Cl NW7 ... 27 D6
Reddings The NW7 ... 11 D1
Reddins Rd SE15 ... 140 A6
Reddons Rd BR3 ... 185 A3
Rede Pl W2 ... 113 C6 245 B6
Redesdale Gdns TW7 ... 131 A5
Redesdale St SW3 ... 267 C6
Redfern Ave TW2, TW4 ... 151 C4
Redfern Ho 6 E13 ... 98 D6
Redfern Rd Catford SE6 ... 164 A4
Willesden NW10 ... 67 C1
Redfield La SW5. 113 D2 255 C4
Redfield Mews SW5 ... 255 B4
Redfiff Est SE16 ... 119 B3
Redford Ave
Thornton Heath CR7 ... 204 B5
Wallington SM6 ... 220 A2
Redford Cl TW13 ... 149 D2
Redford Wlk N1 ... 235 A6
Redgate Dr BR2 ... 225 B6
Red Gates Sch CR9 ... 220 C3
Redgate Terr SW15 ... 156 D5
Redgrave Cl SE25 ... 205 D3
Redgrave Rd SW15 ... 134 D2
Red Hill BR7 ... 188 D5
Redhill Ct SW2 ... 160 C2
Redhill Dr HA8 ... 27 A1
Red Hill Prim Sch BR7 ... 188 D5
Redhill St NW1 ... 93 B4 231 D2
Red House★ DA6 ... 147 A1
Red House La DA6 ... 147 A1
Red House Rd CR0 ... 203 D3
Red House Sq 20 N1 ... 73 A1
Redif Ho RM10 ... 81 D4
Redington Gdns NW3 ... 69 D4
Redington Ho N1 ... 233 D4
Redington Rd NW3 ... 69 D4
Redknap Ho TW10 ... 153 C1
Red La KT10 ... 213 A2
Redland Gdns KT8 ... 195 B5
Redlands
Teddington TW11 ... 175 A4
Tottenham N15 ... 51 B5
Redlands Ct BR1 ... 186 D3
Redlands Prim Sch 35 E1 . 96 C2
Redlands Rd EN3 ... 7 A4
Redlands The 5 BR3 ... 185 D1
Redlands Way SW2 ... 160 B4
Redleaf Cl DA17 ... 147 C6
Redleaves Ave TW15 ... 170 D4
Redlees Cl TW7 ... 131 A1
Red Leys UB8 ... 60 A1
Red Lion Bsns Ctr KT6 ... 214 B5
Red Lion Cl 9 SE17 ... 139 B6
Red Lion Ct Holborn EC4 ... 241 B1
Hounslow TW3 ... 129 D2
Red Lion Hill N2 ... 30 B1
Red Lion La SE18 ... 144 C4
Red Lion Pl SE18 ... 144 C4
Red Lion Rd KT6 ... 214 C6
Red Lion Row SE17 ... 139 A6
Red Lion Sq WC1 ... 94 B2 240 C3
Red Lion St
Gray's Inn WC1 ... 94 B2 240 C3
Richmond TW10 ... 153 D6
Red Lion Yd W1 ... 248 B4
Red Lo Ealing W5 ... 88 A2
West Wickham BR4 ... 208 A2
Red Lodge Rd BR3, BR4 ... 208 B2
Redlynch Ct W14 . 113 A4 244 B1
Redlynch Ho 27 SW9 ... 138 C4
Redman Bldg EC1 ... 241 A4
Redman Cl UB5 ... 84 C5
Redman Ho SE1 ... 252 B1
Redman's Rd E1 ... 96 C2
Redmayne Ho 15 SW9 ... 138 B3
Redmead La E1 ... 118 A5
Redmead Rd UB3 ... 105 C2
Redmill Ho 24 E1 ... 96 B3
Redmond Ho N1 ... 233 D5
Redmore Rd W6 ... 112 B2
Red Oak Cl BR6 ... 226 D6
Redo Ho 3 E12 ... 78 C3
Red Pl W1 ... 248 A6
Redpoll Way DA18 ... 124 D3
Red Post Hill SE21, SE24 ... 161 B6
Red Post Ho E6 ... 77 D1
Redriffe Rd E13 ... 98 D6
Redriff Prim Sch SE16 ... 119 A4
Redriff Rd SE16 ... 119 A3
Redroofs Cl BR3 ... 185 D2
Redrose Trad Ctr 1 EN4 ... 14 B6
Red Rover SW13 ... 134 A2
Redrup Ho 21 SE14 ... 140 D6
Redruth Cl N22 ... 32 B3
Redruth Gdns KT10 ... 212 D1
Redruth Ho SM2 ... 217 D1
Redruth Rd E9 ... 96 C6
Red Sq The N16 ... 73 B5
Redstart Cl
New Cross Gate SE14 ... 141 A5
Redstart Cl *continued*
Newham E6 ... 100 A2
Redston Rd N8 ... 49 D5
Redvers Rd N22 ... 32 C1
Redvers St E2 ... 95 C4
Redwald Rd E5 ... 74 D4
Redway Dr TW2 ... 152 A4
Redwing Path SE28 ... 123 B4
Redwing Rd SM6 ... 220 B1
Redwood Cl 4 Bow E3 ... 97 C5
Chigwell IG9 ... 21 B2
Hillingdon UB10 ... 82 D5
Osidge N14 ... 15 D4
Rotherhithe SE16 ... 119 A5
Sidcup DA15 ... 168 A3
South Oxhey WD19 ... 22 D6
Redwood Ct
Brondesbury NW6 ... 69 A1
Crouch End N19 ... 49 D2
Northolt UB5 ... 85 A4
10 Surbiton KT6 ... 197 D2
Redwood Est TW5 ... 128 B6
Redwood Gdns E4 ... 19 D5
Redwood Gr W5 ... 109 B2
Redwood Mews
Ashford TW15 ... 171 B3
2 Clapham SW4 ... 137 B2
Redwoods SW15 ... 156 A3
Redwood Way EN5 ... 12 D6
Redwood Wlk KT6 ... 197 D1
Reece Mews SW7 ... 256 C4
Reed Ave BR6 ... 227 C5
Reed Cl Lee SE12 ... 165 A6
Newham E16 ... 99 A2
Reede Gdns RM10 ... 81 D3
Reede Rd RM10 ... 81 D2
Reede Way RM10 ... 81 D2
Reedham Cl N17 ... 52 B5
Reedham St SE15 ... 140 A2
Reed Ho SW15 ... 156 A5
Reedholm Villas N16 ... 73 B4
Reed Mans 6 E11 ... 55 A3
Reed Pl Battersea SW11 ... 136 C1
Clapham SW4 ... 137 D1
Lower Halliford TW17 ... 192 B1
Reed Rd N17 ... 33 D1
Reedsfield Cl TW15 ... 148 D1
Reedsfield Rd TW15 ... 170 D6
Reed's Pl NW1 ... 71 C1
Reedworth St
SE11 ... 116 C2 261 B3
Reef Ho E14 ... 120 A3
Reenglass Rd HA7 ... 25 D6
Rees Dr HA7 ... 26 A6
Rees Gdns CR0 ... 205 D3
Rees Ho 6 N17 ... 33 D3
Reesland Cl E12 ... 78 C2
Rees St N1 ... 95 A6 235 B5
Reets Farm Cl NW9 ... 45 C3
Reeves Ave NW9 ... 45 B2
Reeves Cnr CR0 ... 220 D6
Reeves Cnr Sta CR0 ... 220 D6
Reeves Ho Lambeth SE1 ... 251 A1
Mayfair W1 ... 248 A5
Reeves Mews
W1 ... 115 A6 248 B5
Reeves Rd Bromley E3 ... 97 D3
Shooters Hill SE18 ... 144 D6
Reflection Ho 9 E2 ... 96 A3
Reflection The E16 ... 122 D4
Reflex Apartments 1
BR2 ... 209 B5
Reform Row N17 ... 33 D1
Reform St SW11 ... 136 D3
Regal Cl Ealing W5 ... 87 D2
Spitalfields E1 ... 96 A2
Regal Cres SM6 ... 219 B5
Regal Ct Edmonton N18 ... 33 D5
2 Mitcham CR4 ... 202 D6
Wembley HA0 ... 65 D4
Regal Dr N11 ... 31 B5
Regal Ho IG2 ... 57 B3
Regal Int Coll HA9 ... 66 A3
Regal La NW1 ... 231 B5
Regal Pl
8 Tower Hamlets E3 ... 97 B4
Walham Green SW6 ... 265 D3
Regal Way HA3 ... 44 A3
Regan Ho 1 N18 ... 33 D4
Regan Way N1 ... 95 C5
Regatta Ho TW11 ... 175 A6
Regatta Point TW8 ... 132 B6
Regel Ct NW7 ... 29 A2
Regency Cl Ealing W5 ... 88 A1
Hampton TW12 ... 173 B5
Regency Cres 3 NW4 ... 28 D1
Regency Ct 9 Bow E3 ... 97 B5
Enfield EN1 ... 17 B6
4 Kingston u T KT5 ... 198 B4
4 Penge SE19 ... 184 A3
14 South Hackney E9 ... 96 C6
Sutton SM1 ... 217 D5
Wimbledon SW19 ... 179 B3
7 Woodford E18 ... 37 A1
Regency Dr HA4 ... 39 C1
Regency Gdns KT12 ... 194 C1
Regency Ho Finchley N3 ... 29 B1

Regency Ho continued
Marylebone NW1 . . . . **238** D6
Regency Lo
1 Buckhurst Hill IG9 . . . . .21 D2
Harrow HA3 . . . . .42 C6
South Hampstead NW3 . . .**70** B1
Regency Mews
Beckenham BR3 . . . . 186 A2
Camberwell SW9 . . . . . . 138 D5
Isleworth TW7 . . . . 152 C6
1 Willesden NW10 . . . . . .**68** A2
Regency Pl SW1 . . . . **259** C4
Regency St SW1 . . 115 D2 **259** D3
Regency Terr SW7 . . . . . **256** C2
Regency Way DA6 . . . . . **147** A2
Regency Wlk
Croydon CR0 . . . . **207** B3
8 Richmond TW10 . . . . . **154** A6
Regeneration Rd SE16 . . 118 D1
Regent Ave UB10 . . . .**60** D1
Regent Bsns Ctr UB3 . . . 106 A4
Regent Cl Cranford TW4 . .**128** B4
Harrow HA3 . . . . .44 A3
North Finchley N12 . . . . .**30** A5
Regent Ct 4 Finchley N3 . .29 D3
Lisson Gr NW8 . . . . **230** A1
South Norwood SE19 . . . .**182** D4
1 Stamford Hill N16 . . . .51 D2
Regent Gdns IG3 . . . .**58** A2
Regent Ho W14 . . . . **254** A4
Regent Pl Croydon CR0 . . 205 D1
St James W1 . . . . **249** B6
Wimbledon SW19 . . . . . .180 A5
Regent Rd Surbiton KT5 . .**198** C4
Tulse Hill SE24 . . . . 160 D6
Regents Ave N13 . . . .**32** C5
Regents Bridge Gdns
SW8 . . . . **270** B4
Regents Canal Ho 19 E14 . .**97** A1
Regents Cl Hayes UB4 . . . .**83** C2
South Croydon CR2 . . . . . 221 C2
Regent's Coll
NW1 . . . . .93 A3 **238** A6
Regents Ct
22 Beckenham BR3 . . . . . 185 C3
Bromley BR1 . . . . 186 D3
Edgware HA8 . . . . .26 A6
Hackney E8 . . . . .96 A6
1 Kingston u T KT2 . . . . 176 A2
Regent's Dr BR2 . . . . . . 225 D3
Regents Gate Ho 20 E14 . .**119** A6
Regents Lo 9 SW2 . . . . . 160 B3
Regents Mews
NW8 . . . . .92 A5 **229** B4
REGENT'S PARK **93** B4
Regent's Park*
NW1 . . . . .93 A5 **231** A3
Regent's Park Barracks
NW1 . . . . **231** D3
Regent's Park Rd
Camden Town
NW1 . . . . .93 A6 **231** A6
Hendon N3 . . . .**47** B6
Primrose Hill NW3 . . . . . .**71** A1
Regent's Park Sta
NW1 . . . . .93 B3 **238** C5
Regent's Park Terr NW1 . .**231** C6
Regents Pl IG10 . . . . . . .21 D4
Regent's Pl SE3 . . . . **143** A5
Regents Plaza 2 NW6 . . . .**91** D5
Regent Sq
Belvedere DA17 . . . . **125** D2
23 Bromley E3 . . . .**97** D4
St Pancras WC1 . . . .94 A4 **233** B1
Regent's Row E8 . . . .**96** A6
Regent St Brentford W4 . .110 C1
7 Kensal Green NW10 . . .**90** D4
Mayfair W1 . . . . . 115 C6 **249** A6
Regents Wharf
3 Hackney E2 . . . .**96** B6
Islington N1 . . . . **233** C4
Regina Coeli RC Prim Sch
CR2 . . . . **220** D1
Regina Ct TW11 . . . . **174** C5
Reginald Ct BR3 . . . . 186 A2
Reginald Pl 6 SE8 . . . . . 141 C5
Reginald Rd
Deptford SE8 . . . . 141 C5
Forest Gate E7 . . . .**77** A2
Reginald Sorenson Ho
E11 . . . .**54** B2
Reginald Sq SE8 . . . . . . 141 C5
Regina Point SE16 . . . . . 118 C3
Regina Rd Ealing W13 . . .109 A5
Finsbury Pk N4 . . . .**50** B1
Southall UB2 . . . . 107 A2
South Norwood SE25 . . . 206 A6
Regina Terr W13 . . . . . . 109 B5
Regis Ct
East Bedfont TW14 . . . . . **149** B5
Hornsey N8 . . . . .50 B5
Marylebone NW1 . . . . . . **237** C4
Mitcham SW19 . . . . 180 C2
Regis Pl 17 SW2 . . . . 138 B1
Regis Rd NW5 . . . .**71** B3
Regnart Bldgs NW1 . . . . **232** B1

Regnolruf Ct KT12 . . . . . .**194** A2
Reid Cl Hayes UB3 . . . . . .**83** C1
Pinner HA5 . . . . .40 A5
Reid Ct SW14 . . . .**133** A3
Reidhaven Rd SE18 . . . . . 123 C2
Reigate Ave SM1 . . . . . . 201 D1
Reigate Rd Catford BR1 . . 164 D1
Grove Pk BR1, SE12 . . . . 165 A2
Ilford IG3 . . . .**79** D6
Reigate Way SM6 . . . . . . **220** A3
Reighton Rd E5 . . . .**74** A6
Reinckendorf Ave SE9 . . .167 A5
Reindeer Cl 5 E13 . . . . . .**99** A6
Reizel Cl N16 . . . . .51 D1
Relay Rd W12 . . . . **112** C5
Relf Rd SE15 . . . . **140** A2
Reliance Sq E2 . . . . **243** B6
Relko Gdns SM1 . . . . **218** B3
Relton Ct W3 . . . .**110** C4
Relton Mews SW7 . . . . . . **257** B6
Rembrandt Cl E14 . . . . . .**120** B3
Rembrandt Ct
10 Bermondsey SE16 . . . .**118** B1
Harrow HA3 . . . . .43 A3
West Ewell KT19 . . . . . . **215** D2
Rembrandt Rd
Edgware HA8 . . . .**26** C1
Lewisham SE13 . . . . 142 C1
Rembrant Cl SW1 . . . . . . **258** A3
Remembrance Ave N2 . . . .**47** D6
Remington Rd
Newham E6 . . . . 100 A1
Tottenham N15 . . . .**51** B3
Remington St N1 . . **94** D5 **234** D3
Remnant St WC2 . . . . . . **240** C2
Remsted Ho 7 NW6 . . . . .**91** D6
Remus Rd E3 . . . .**75** C1
Renaissance Ct SM1 . . . . **202** A1
Renaissance Wlk 4
SE10 . . . . **120** D3
Renbold Ho 5 SE10 . . . . .**142** A4
Rendlebury Ho 17 SE18 . . **122** B2
Rendle Cl CR0 . . . . **206** A4
Rendlesham Ho 3 E5,
N16 . . . .**74** A5
Rendlesham Rd Enfield EN2 . .**4** D1
Shacklewell E5 . . . .**74** A5
Renforth St SE16 . . . . . . **118** C4
Renfree Way TW17 . . . . . **192** C2
Renfrew Cl E6 . . . . **122** C6
Renfrew Ct TW5 . . . . **129** A3
Renfrew Ho
Paddington NW6 . . . .**91** D5
Walthamstow E17 . . . . . .**35** B1
Renfrew Rd
Hounslow TW5 . . . . 129 A3
Kingston u T KT2 . . . . . . 177 A3
Newington SE11 . . 116 D2 **261** C3
Renmuir St SW17 . . . . . . **180** D4
Rennell Ho 18 E9 . . . .**74** D2
Rennell St SE13 . . . . **142** A2
Renness Rd E17 . . . .**53** A6
Rennets Cl SE9 . . . . **167** C6
Rennets Wood Ho SE9 . . .167 B6
Rennets Wood Rd SE9 . . .167 B6
Rennie Cotts 29 E1 . . . . . .**96** C3
Rennie Ct Holdbrook EN3 . . .**7** C5
Lambeth SE1 . . . . **251** C4
Rennie Ho 5 SE1 . . . . . . **262** A5
Rennie St SE1 . . . . **116** D5 **251** C4
Renoir Ct 7 SE16 . . . . . . **118** B1
Renovation The E16 . . . . **122** D4
Renown Cl CR0 . . . . **204** D1
Rensburg Rd E17 . . . .**52** D3
Rensburg Villas E17 . . . . .**52** D4
Renshaw Cl 7 DA17 . . . . .**147** B6
Renshaw Cnr CR4 . . . . . .**181** A2
Renshaw Ct SW19 . . . . . 179 A6
Renshaw Ho 11 SW27 . . . **182** D5
Renters Ave NW4 . . . .**46** C3
Renton Cl SW2 . . . . 160 B5
Renwick Rd IG11 . . . . . . **102** B4
Repens Way UB4 . . . .**84** D3
Rephidim St SE1 . . . . . . **263** A5
Reporton Rd
SW6 . . . . **135** A5 **264** B3
Repository Rd SE7, SE18 . .**122** B1
Repton Ave Hayes UB3 . . .**105** B2
Wembley HA0 . . . .**65** C4
Repton Cl SM5 . . . . **218** C3
Repton Ct
Beckenham BR3 . . . . 185 D2
Southgate N11 . . . .**16** C3
Repton Ho SW1 . . . . **259** B3
Repton Rd Harrow HA3 . . .44 B5
Orpington BR6 . . . . 227 D5
Repton St E14 . . . .**97** A1
Reserve Ct N2 . . . .**30** C2
Reservoir Cl 3 CR7 . . . . . **205** B5
Reservoir Rd
New Cross Gate SE4 . . . . 141 A3
Ruislip HA4 . . . . .39 B5
Southgate N14 . . . . .15 C4
Reservoir Studios 14 E1 . .**96** D1
Resham Cl UB2 . . . . **106** C3
Resolution Way 18 SE8 . . **141** C5
Resolution Wlk SE18 . . . **122** B3
Restell Cl SE3 . . . . **142** C6
Restmor Way SM5, SM6 . .**219** A6

Reston Pl SW7 . . . . **246** A1
Restons Cres DA15, SE9 . .**167** C5
Restoration Sq SW11 . . . **266** D1
Restormel Cl TW3 . . . . . . **151** C6
Retcar Pl N19 . . . .**71** B6
Retford St E2 . . . .**95** C5
Retingham Way E4 . . . . . .**19** D2
Retlas Ct HA1 . . . .**42** B2
Retreat Cl HA3 . . . .**43** C4
Retreat Cvn Site The IG9 . .**21** A3
Retreat Ho 5 E9 . . . .**74** C2
Retreat Pl E9 . . . .**74** C2
Retreat Rd TW9 . . . . **153** D6
Retreat The Harrow HA2 . .41 C2
Kingsbury NW9 . . . .**45** B4
Mortlake SW14 . . . . 133 C2
North Cheam KT4 . . . . . . 216 B6
South Norwood CR7 . . . . 205 B5
Reunion Row E1 . . . . **118** B6
Reveley Sq SE16 . . . . **119** A4
Revell Rd Cheam SM1 . . . **217** B2
Kingston u T KT1 . . . . . . 176 D2
Revell Rise SE18 . . . . **145** D6
Revelon Rd SE4 . . . . **141** A2
Revelstoke Rd SW18,
SW19 . . . . **157** C2
Reventlow Rd SE9 . . . . . . **167** A3
Reverdy Rd SE1 . . . . **118** A2
Reverend Cl HA2 . . . .**63** D5
Revesby Rd SM5 . . . . **202** C3
Review Lo RM10 . . . . **103** D5
Review Rd
Dagenham RM10 . . . . . . 103 D6
Willesden NW2 . . . .**67** D6
Rewell St SW6 . . . **136** A5 **266** A3
Rewley Rd SM4 . . . . **202** B3
Rew Lo 25 N2 . . . .**30** B1
Rex Ave TW15 . . . . **170** C5
Rex Ho TW13 . . . . **151** A1
Rex Par 2 IG8 . . . .**37** C4
Rex Pl W1 . . . . . . **115** A5 **248** B4
Reydon Ave E11 . . . .**55** C3
Reygate Ct N4 . . . .**51** A3
Reynard Cl Brockley SE4 . .**141** A2
Bromley BR1 . . . . 210 C6
Reynard Dr SE19 . . . . . . **183** D3
Reynard Mills Trad Est
TW8 . . . . **109** C1
Reynard Pl SE14 . . . . **141** A6
Reynardson Rd N17 . . . . .**33** A3
Reynardson's Ct 10 N17 . .**51** D6
Reynola Gdns SE7 . . . . . **121** B1
Reynolds Ave
Chessington KT9 . . . . . . 214 A1
Ilford RM6 . . . .**58** C2
Little Ilford E12 . . . .**78** C3
Reynolds Cl
Carshalton SM5 . . . . **202** D1
Golders Green NW11 . . . .47 D2
Mitcham SW19 . . . . 180 B2
Reynolds Ct Ilford RM6 . . .**58** D6
Leyton E11 . . . .**76** D5
Reynolds Dr HA8 . . . .**44** B6
Reynolds Ho Enfield EN1 . .**18** A6
Finsbury Pk N4 . . . . .50 A1
18 South Hackney E2 . . . .96 C5
St John's Wood NW8 . . . . **229** D3
Westminster SW1 . . . . . . **259** D3
Reynolds Pl
Greenwich SE3 . . . . **143** B5
12 Richmond TW10 . . . . **154** B5
Reynolds Rd
Acton Green W4 . . . . **111** A3
Hayes UB4 . . . . .84 C3
New Malden KT3 . . . . . . 199 B2
Nunhead SE15 . . . . 140 C1
Reynolds Sp Ctr W3 . . . . **110** C4
Reynolds Way CR0 . . . . . **221** C4
Rfrra Rd Ret Pk SW2 . . . . **160** C6
Rheidol Mews N1 . . . . . . **235** A4
Rheidol Terr N1 . . . **95** A6 **235** A5
Rhein Ho N8 . . . .**50** A6
Rheola Cl N17 . . . .**33** D2
Rhizotron & Xstrata Treetop
Walkway* TW9 . . . . **132** A4
Rhoda St E2 . . . . . **95** D3 **243** D6
Rhodes Ave N22 . . . .**31** C2
Rhodes Avenue Prim Sch
N22 . . . .**31** C2
Rhodes Ho
Shepherd's Bush W12 . . . **112** B5
Shoreditch N1 . . . . **235** C2
Rhodesia Rd Leyton E11 . .**76** B6
Stockwell SW9 . . . . 138 A3
Rhodes-Moorhouse Ct
SM4 . . . . **201** C3
Rhodes St N7 . . . .**72** B3
Rhodeswell Rd E14 . . . . . .**97** B1
Rhodrons Ave KT9 . . . . . **214** A3
Rhondda Gr E3 . . . .**97** B4
Rhyl Prim Sch 21 NW5 . . .**71** A2
Rhyl Rd UB6 . . . .**86** D5
Rhyl St NW5 . . . .**71** A2
Rhys Ave N11 . . . .**31** D3
Rialto Rd CR4 . . . . **181** A1
Ribble Cl IG8 . . . .**37** C4
Ribblesdale Ave
Friern Barnet N11 . . . . . .**31** A4
Northolt UB5 . . . .**63** D2

Ribblesdale Ho 11 NW6 . . .**91** C6
Ribblesdale Rd
Hornsey N8 . . . .**50** B5
Streatham SW16 . . . . . . 181 B5
Ribbon Dance Mews
SE5 . . . . **139** B4
Ribchester Ave UB6 . . . . .**86** D4
Ribston Cl BR2 . . . . **210** B1
Ribstone Ho 12 E9 . . . . . .**74** D2
Ricardo Path 5 SE28 . . . . **124** C5
Ricardo St E14 . . . .**97** D1
Ricards Lodge High Sch
SW19 . . . . **179** B5
Ricards Rd SW19 . . . . . . **179** B5
Riccall Ct 2 NW9 . . . .**27** C2
Riceyman Ho WC1 . . . . . . **234** A1
Richard Alibon Prim Sch
RM10 . . . .**81** C3
Richard Anderson Ct 1
SE14 . . . . **140** D5
Richard Atkins Prim Sch 29
SW2 . . . . **160** A4
Richard Burbidge Mans
SW13 . . . . **134** C6
Richard Burton Ct 4 IG9 . .**21** C2
Richard Challoner Sch
KT3 . . . . **199** B2
Richard Cl SE18 . . . . **122** A2
Richard Cloudesley Sch
(Prim Dept) EC1 . .**95** A3 **242** B5
Richard Cloudesley Sch
(Secondary Dept)
EC1 . . . .**95** A3 **242** A5
Richard Cobden Prim Sch
NW1 . . . .**93** C6 **232** B5
Richard Ct Ashford TW15 . .**170** B5
1 Barnet EN5 . . . .**1** A2
Richard Fell Ho 3 E12 . . . .**78** C4
Richard Fox Ho N4 . . . . . .**73** A5
Richard Ho 10 SE16 . . . . **118** C2
Richard House Dr E16 . . . **100** A1
Richard Knight Ho SW6 . . **265** B2
Richard Neale Ho 2 E1 . . .**118** B6
Richard Neve Ho 2
SE18 . . . . **123** C2
Richards Cl Bushey WD23 . .**8** A4
Harlington UB3 . . . . 127 B6
Harrow HA1 . . . . .43 A4
Hillingdon UB10 . . . . . . .82 C6
Richards Ct BR3 . . . . **184** D2
Richard Sharples Ct 16
SM2 . . . . **218** A1
Richardson Cl 19 E8 . . . . .**95** D6
Richardson Ct 20 SW4 . . .**138** A3
Richardson Gdns 12
RM10 . . . .**81** D2
Richardson Ho
Isleworth TW7 . . . . 130 D2
10 Poplar E14 . . . .**97** C2
Richardson Rd E15 . . . . . .**98** C5
Richardson's Mews W1 . . **239** A5
Richards Pl E17 . . . .**53** C6
Richard's Pl SW3 . . . . . . **257** B4
Richard St 20 E1 . . . .**96** B1
Richbell WC1 . . . . **240** B4
Richbell Pl WC1 . . . . **240** C4
Richborne Terr
SW8 . . . . **138** B5 **270** D4
Richborough Ho
10 Deptford SE15 . . . . . **140** C6
14 Hackney E5 . . . .**74** B4
Richborough Rd NW2 . . . .**69** A4
Richbourne Ct W1 . . . . . **237** B2
Richens Cl TW3 . . . . **130** B3
Riches Rd IG1 . . . .**79** A6
Richfield Ct
4 Beckenham BR3 . . . . . **185** B2
Wembley HA0 . . . .**66** A2
Richfield Rd WD23 . . . .**8** A4
Richford Gate W6 . . . . . . **112** C3
Richford Rd E15 . . . .**98** D6
Richford St W6 . . . . **112** C3
Richill Lodge TW2 . . . . . **151** C5
Rich Ind Est SE15 . . . . . . **140** B6
Richings Ho BR5 . . . . **190** A2
Rich La SW5 . . . . **255** C2
Richland Ho 4 SE15 . . . . **140** A4
Richlands Ave KT17 . . . . . **216** A4
Richman Ho 10 SE8 . . . . . **119** B1
RICHMOND **131** C1
Richmond Adult Com Coll
TW9 . . . . **131** D1
Richmond American Int Univ
in London TW10 . . . . . . **154** A4
Richmond Ave
Chingford E4 . . . .**36** B5
Feltham TW14 . . . . 149 C5
Hillingdon UB10 . . . . . . .60 D2
Islington N1 . . . . . **94** B6 **233** D6
Willesden NW10 . . . . . . .68 C2
Wimbledon SW20 . . . . . . 179 A2
Richmond Bldgs 1 . . . . . **239** C1
Richmond Bridge TW1 . . .**153** D5
Richmond Bridge Mans 1
TW1 . . . . **153** D5
Richmond Circus TW9 . . . **132** A1
Richmond Cl
Borehamwood WD6 . . . . . .**11** B6
Walthamstow E17 . . . .**53** B3

Richmond Coll
W8 . . . . **113** D3 **255** D6
Richmond Cres
Chingford E4 . . . .**36** B5
Edmonton N9 . . . .**18** A3
Islington N1 . . . . . **94** C6 **234** A6
Richmond Ct
Bromley BR1 . . . . **187** B3
12 Kingston u T KT2 . . . . **176** C3
Knightsbridge SW1 . . . . . **247** D1
Mitcham CR4 . . . . **202** B6
4 New Southgate N11 . . . .**31** A4
Wembley HA9 . . . . .66 B6
Wimbledon SW20 . . . . . . 178 B1
Richmond Dr TW17 . . . . . **193** B3
Richmond Gate TW10 . . . **154** B4
Richmond Gdns
Harrow HA3 . . . .**24** D3
Hendon NW4 . . . .**46** A4
Richmond Gn CR0 . . . . . **220** A5
Richmond Gr Islington N1 . .**72** C1
Surbiton KT5 . . . . 198 B3
Richmond Healthcare
Hamlet Hospl TW9 . . . . . **132** A2
RICHMOND HILL **154** A5
Richmond Hill TW10 . . . . **154** A5
Richmond Hill Ct 5
TW10 . . . . **154** A5
Richmond Ho
12 Forest Hill SE26 . . . . **162** A1
Regent's Pk NW1 . . . . . . **231** B3
Walworth SE17 . . . . **262** C2
Richmond Ho (Hampton Com
Coll) TW12 . . . . **173** B5
Richmond International Bsns
Ctr 9 TW9 . . . . **132** B1
Richmond Mans
Earl's Ct SW5 . . . . **255** C2
Putney SW15 . . . . 135 A2
13 Twickenham TW1 . . . . 153 D5
Richmond Mews W1 . . . . **239** C1
Richmond Park* TW10 . . . **155** A4
Richmond Park Rd
Kingston u T KT2 . . . . . . 176 A3
Mortlake SW14 . . . . 133 B1
Richmond Pk IG10 . . . . . .**21** D4
Richmond Pl SE18 . . . . . **123** A2
Richmond Rd
Bowes Pk N11 . . . .**32** A4
Chingford E4 . . . . .20 B3
Dalston E8 . . . . .74 A1
Ealing W5 . . . . 110 A4
Finchley N2 . . . . .30 A1
Forest Gate E7 . . . . .77 B3
Ilford IG1 . . . . .79 A5
Isleworth TW7 . . . . 131 A2
Kingston u T KT2 . . . . . . 176 A4
Leyton E11 . . . . .76 B6
New Barnet EN5 . . . . .14 A6
Thornton Heath CR7 . . . . 204 D5
Tottenham N15 . . . . .51 C3
Twickenham TW1 . . . . . . 153 C4
Wallington CR0 . . . . 220 A5
Wimbledon SW20 . . . . . . 178 B2
Richmond St E13 . . . .**99** A5
Richmond Sta TW9 . . . . . **132** A1
Richmond Terr
SW1 . . . . **116** A4 **250** A2
Richmond upon Thames Coll
TW2 . . . . **152** C4
Richmond Way
Hammersmith W12, W14 . . **112** D4
Wanstead E11 . . . .**77** A6
Richmount Gdns SE3 . . . . **143** A2
Rich St E14 . . . . **119** B6
Rickard Cl Hendon NW4 . . .**46** A5
Streatham SW2 . . . . 160 C3
Rickards Cl KT6 . . . . **214** A6
Rickett St SW6 . . . . **265** B6
Rickman Ho 23 E2 . . . . . .**96** C3
Rickman St 24 E1 . . . .**96** C3
Rickmansworth Rd HA5 . . .**22** C1
Rick Roberts Way E15 . . . .**98** B5
Rickthorne Rd 7 N19 . . . .**72** A6
Rickyard Path SE9 . . . . . **144** A1
Riddell Ct SE1 . . . . **263** C2
Riddell Lo EN2 . . . .**4** D3
Ridding La UB6 . . . .**64** D3
Riddons Rd SE12 . . . . . . **187** C6
Rideout St SE18 . . . . **122** B2
Rider Cl DA15 . . . . **167** C5
Ride The Brentford TW8 . . **109** C1
Enfield EN3 . . . . .6 D2
Ridgdale St E3 . . . .**97** D5
Ridge Ave N21 . . . .**17** B4
Ridgebrook Rd SE3, SE9 . .**143** D2
Ridge Cl Hendon NW4 . . . .**28** D1
Kingsbury NW9 . . . . .45 B5
Plumstead SE28 . . . . 123 B4
Ridge Crest EN2 . . . .**4** B5
Ridge Hill NW11 . . . .**47** A1
Ridge Ho 4 KT2 . . . . **176** D3
Ridgeleigh Ct 3 EN5 . . . . . .**1** A2
Ridgemead Cl N13, N14 . . .**16** A2
Ridgemont Gdns HA8 . . . .**27** A6
Ridgemount Ave CR0 . . . . **222** D6
Ridgemount Cl 4 SE20 . . .**184** B3
Ridgemount Gdns EN2 . . . .**4** D3
Ridgeon Ct N22 . . . .**32** B4
Ridge Rd Cheam SM3 . . . **201** B4

Ridge Rd *continued*
Child's Hill NW2 . . . . **69** B5
Edmonton N21 . . . . **17** B3
Hornsey Vale N8 . . . . **50** B3
Mitcham CR4 . . . . **181** B3
Ridges The E4 . . . . **35** C6
Ridge's Yd 3 CR0 . . . . **220** D5
Ridge Terr N21 . . . . **17** A4
Ridge The Barnet EN5 . . . . **13** B6
Old Bexley DA5 . . . . **169** B4
Orpington BR6 . . . . **227** B6
Surbiton KT5 . . . . **198** C4
Twickenham TW2 . . . . **152** B4
Ridgeview Cl EN5 . . . . **12** D5
Ridgeview Ct EN4 . . . . **15** C6
Ridgeview Rd N20 . . . . **14** A1
Ridgeway Hayes BR2 . . . . **225** A6
11 Richmond TW10 . . . . . **154** A5
Walton-on-T KT12 . . . . **193** D1
Woodford IG8 . . . . **37** C6
Ridge Way Feltham TW13 . . . **151** A1
7 West Norwood SE19 . . . **183** C4
Ridgeway Ave EN4 . . . . **14** D5
Ridgeway Cres BR6 . . . . **227** C5
Ridgeway Crescent Gdns
BR6 . . . . **227** C5
Ridgeway Dr Acton W3 . . . . . **110** C3
Grove Pk BR1 . . . . **187** B6
Ridgeway E DA15 . . . . **167** D6
Ridgeway Gdns
Crouch End N6 . . . . **49** C2
Redbridge IG4 . . . . **56** A4
Ridgeway Rd TW7 . . . . **130** C4
Ridgeway Rd N TW7 . . . . **130** C5
Ridgeway The Acton W3 . . . . **110** C3
Chingford E4 . . . . **20** A3
1 Chingford E4 . . . . **20** A3
Enfield EN2 . . . . **4** B5
Finchley N3 . . . . **29** D3
Friern Barnet N11 . . . . **30** D6
Golders Green NW11 . . . . . . **47** B1
Kenton HA3 . . . . **43** C3
Kingsbury NW9 . . . . **45** B5
Mill Hill NW7 . . . . **28** B6
North Harrow HA2 . . . . **41** D3
Palmers Green N14 . . . . **16** A2
Pinner HA2 . . . . **41** B4
Ruislip HA4 . . . . **40** A2
Stanmore HA7 . . . . **25** C4
Wallington CR0 . . . . **220** B5
Ridgeway W DA15 . . . . **167** C6
Ridgeway Wlk UB5 . . . . **63** A2
Ridgewell Cl
Dagenham RM10 . . . . **103** D6
Forest Hill SE26 . . . . **185** B6
Shoreditch N1 . . . . **235** B6
Ridgmount Gdns
WC1 . . . . **93** D2 **239** C4
Ridgmount Pl WC1 . . . . **239** C4
Ridgmount Rd SW18 . . . . . . **157** D6
Ridgmount St
WC1 . . . . **93** D2 **239** C4
Ridgway SW19, SW20 . . . . . **178** D4
Ridgway Ct SW19 . . . . **178** D4
Ridgway Gdns SW19 . . . . . . **178** D3
Ridgway Pl SW19 . . . . **179** A4
Ridgway Rd SW9 . . . . **138** D2
Ridgway The SM2 . . . . **218** B1
Ridgwell Rd E16 . . . . **99** C2
Riding House St
W1 . . . . **93** C2 **239** A3
Ridings Ave N21 . . . . **17** A4
Ridings Cl N6 . . . . **49** C2
Ridings The Ealing W5 . . . . . . **88** B3
Oakleigh Pk EN4 . . . . **14** B4
Sunbury TW16 . . . . **172** A2
Surbiton KT5 . . . . **198** C4
Riding The NW11 . . . . **47** B2
Ridler Rd EN1 . . . . **5** C5
Ridley Ave W13 . . . . **109** B3
Ridley Cl IG11 . . . . **79** D1
Ridley Ct Orpington BR6 . . . . **227** A4
Streatham SW16 . . . . **182** A4
Ridley Ho 14 SW11 . . . . **136** C2
Ridley Rd
Beckenham BR2 . . . . **208** D6
Dalston E8 . . . . **73** D3
Forest Gate E7 . . . . **77** C4
Merton SW19 . . . . **179** D3
Welling DA16 . . . . **146** B4
Willesden Green NW10 . . . . **90** A5
Ridley Road Mkt★ E8 . . . . . **73** D3
Ridsdale Rd SE20 . . . . **184** B2
Riefield Rd SE9 . . . . **167** A6
Riesco Dr CR0 . . . . **222** C4
Riffel Rd NW2 . . . . **68** C3
Rifle Ct SE11 . . . . **138** C6
Rifle Pl W11 . . . . **112** D5
Rifle St E14 . . . . **97** D2
Riga Ho 12 E1 . . . . **96** D2
Rigault Rd SW6 . . . . **135** A3
Rigby Cl CR0 . . . . **220** C5
Rigby Ho 2 N17 . . . . **51** D6
Rigby La UB3 . . . . **105** A4
Rigby Mews IG1 . . . . **78** C6
Rigby Pl 8 EN3 . . . . **7** C6
Rigden St E14 . . . . **97** D1
Rigeley Rd NW10 . . . . **90** A4
Rigg App E10 . . . . **53** A1
Rigge Pl SW4 . . . . **137** D1

Rigg Ho 2 SW4 . . . . **160** A4
Riggindale Rd SW16 . . . . . . **181** D6
Rignold Ho 6 SE5 . . . . **139** C3
Riley Ho 9 Bow E3 . . . . **97** C3
Chelsea SW10 . . . . **266** C5
1 Streatham SW4 . . . . . . **159** D4
Riley Rd
Bermondsey SE1 . **117** D3 **263** C6
Enfield EN3 . . . . **6** C5
Riley St SW10 . . . . **136** B5 **266** C4
Rill Ho 16 SE5 . . . . **139** C5
Rimini Ct SW12 . . . . **158** D3
Rinaldo Rd SW12 . . . . **159** B4
Ring Cl BR1 . . . . **187** B3
Ringcroft St N7 . . . . **72** C3
Ringer's Rd BR1 . . . . **209** A6
Ringford Ho SW18 . . . . **157** B6
Ringford Rd SW18 . . . . **157** C5
Ring Ho 15 E1 . . . . **118** C6
Ringlet Cl E16 . . . . **99** B2
Ringlewell Cl EN1 . . . . **6** B3
Ringmer Ave
SW6 . . . . **135** A4 **264** B1
Ringmer Gdns 3 N19 . . . . . . **72** A6
Ringmer Ho 13 SE22 . . . . . . **139** C2
Ringmer Pl N21 . . . . **17** B6
Ringmer Way BR1 . . . . **210** B4
Ringmore Rise SE23 . . . . . . **162** B4
Ring Rd W12 . . . . **112** C5
Ringsfield Ho SE17 . . . . **262** B1
Ringslade Rd N22 . . . . **32** B1
Ringstead Bldgs SE6 . . . . . **163** D4
Ringstead Ct SM1 . . . . **218** B3
Ringstead Rd
Catford SE6 . . . . **163** D4
Sutton SM1 . . . . **218** B3
Ringway UB2 . . . . **107** A1
Ring Way N11 . . . . **31** C4
Ringwold Cl BR3 . . . . **185** A3
Ringwood Ave
Muswell Hill N2 . . . . **48** D6
Thornton Heath CR0 . . . . . **204** A2
Ringwood Cl HA5 . . . . **40** C6
Ringwood Gdns
17 Millwall E14 . . . . **119** C2
Roehampton SW15 . . . . . . **156** A3
Ringwood Rd E11 . . . . **53** B3
Ringwood Way
Hampton TW12 . . . . **173** C6
Southgate N21 . . . . **16** D4
Ripley Cl Bromley BR1 . . . . . **210** B4
New Addington CR0 . . . . . . **224** A2
Ripley Ct 1 CR4 . . . . **180** B1
Ripley Gdns
Mortlake SW14 . . . . **133** B2
Sutton SM1 . . . . **218** A4
Ripley Ho
13 Kingston u T KT2 . . . . . **176** D4
Mortlake SW14 . . . . **133** C2
Nine Elms SW8 . . . . **269** A6
5 Penge SE26 . . . . **184** B5
Ripley Mews E11 . . . . **54** C3
Ripley Rd
Belvedere DA17 . . . . **125** C2
Enfield EN2 . . . . **5** A4
Hampton TW12 . . . . **173** C3
Ilford IG3 . . . . **79** D6
Newham E16 . . . . **99** C1
Ripley's Believe It or Not!★
SW1 . . . . **249** C5
Riplington Ct SW15 . . . . **156** B4
Ripon Cl UB5 . . . . **63** C2
Ripon Ct 10 N11 . . . . **31** A4
Ripon Gdns
Chessington KT9 . . . . **213** D3
Redbridge IG1 . . . . **56** A2
Ripon Rd Edmonton N9 . . . . . **18** B4
Shooters Hill SE18 . . . . . . **144** D6
Tottenham N17 . . . . **51** B6
Ripon Way NW6 . . . . **11** B6
Rippersley Rd DA16 . . . . **146** A4
Ripple Ct 10 IG11 . . . . **101** B6
Ripple Jun & Inf Schs
IG11 . . . . **79** C1
Ripple Rd Barking IG11 . . . . . **79** A1
Barking IG11 . . . . **101** C4
Castle Green RM9 . . . . **102** A6
Rippleside Commercial Est
IG11 . . . . **102** C5
Ripplevale Gr N1 . . . . **72** B1
Rippolson Rd SE18 . . . . **123** D1
Ripston Rd TW15 . . . . **171** B5
Risborough SE17 . . . . **262** A4
Risborough Cl N10 . . . . **49** B6
Risborough Ct 5 N10 . . . . . . **49** B6
Risborough Dr KT4 . . . . **200** A2
Risborough Ho NW8 . . . . . . **237** B6
Risborough St SE1 . . . . **251** D2
Risdon Ho 28 SE16 . . . . **118** C4
Risdon St 27 SE16 . . . . **118** C4
Risedale Rd DA7 . . . . **147** D2
Riseholme Ct E9 . . . . **75** B2
Riseholme Ho 14 SE22 . . . . **139** C2
Riseldine Rd SE23 . . . . **163** A4
Rise The
Borehamwood WD6 . . . . . . **10** B6
Buckhurst Hill IG9 . . . . **21** D4
Chingford E4 . . . . **20** C3
Edgware HA8 . . . . **26** C5
Edmonton N13 . . . . **32** C6

Rise The *continued*
Harrow HA2 . . . . **24** A1
Hendon NW7 . . . . **27** D4
Hillingdon UB10 . . . . **82** B5
Neasden NW10 . . . . **67** B5
Sidcup DA5 . . . . **168** C4
Wanstead E11 . . . . **55** A4
Wembley HA0, UB6 . . . . **65** A3
Risinghill St N1 . . . . **234** A4
Risingholme Cl HA3 . . . . **24** C1
Risingholme Rd HA3 . . . . **24** C1
Risings The E17 . . . . **54** B5
Risley Ave N17 . . . . **33** B2
Risley Avenue Prim Sch 1
N17 . . . . **33** C2
Risley Ho 7 E9 . . . . **74** D2
Rita Rd SW8 . . . . **138** B5 **270** C4
Ritches Rd N15 . . . . **51** A4
Ritchie Ho Crouch End N19 . . **49** D2
8 Rotherhithe SE16 . . . . . **118** C3
12 South Bromley E14 . . . . **98** B1
Ritchie Rd CR0 . . . . **206** B4
Ritchie St N1 . . . . . **94** C5 **234** B4
Ritchings Ave E17 . . . . **53** A5
Ritherdon Rd SW17 . . . . **159** B2
Ritson Ho N1 . . . . **233** C5
Ritson Rd E8 . . . . **74** A2
Ritter St SE18 . . . . **144** C6
Ritz Par W5 . . . . **88** B3
Rivaz Pl E9 . . . . **74** C2
Riven Ct 10 W2 . . . . **91** D1
Rivenhall Gdns E11, E18 . . . **54** D5
Riverains The SW11 . . . . . . **266** C1
River Ave Southgate N13 . . . . **16** D1
Thames Ditton KT7 . . . . . . **197** A2
Riverbank KT8 . . . . **196** C5
River Bank Edmonton N21 . . . **17** A4
Thames Ditton KT7 . . . . . . **196** D4
Riverbank Rd BR1 . . . . **165** A1
Riverbank Way TW8 . . . . **131** C6
River Barge Cl E14 . . . . **120** A4
River Brent Bsns Pk W7 . . . **108** C3
River Cl Ruislip HA4 . . . . **39** D3
Wanstead E11 . . . . **55** C3
River Cotts BR5 . . . . **190** C1
Rivercourt Rd W6 . . . . **112** B1
River Crane Way TW13 . . . . **151** B2
River Ct Kingston u T KT6 . . . **197** D4
Lambeth SE1 . . . . **251** C5
Shepperton TW17 . . . . **193** A2
Wanstead E11 . . . . **55** C3
Riverdale Cl IG11 . . . . **102** B3
Riverdale Ct N21 . . . . **17** B6
Riverdale Dr SW18 . . . . **157** D3
Riverdale Gdns TW1 . . . . . . **153** C6
Riverdale Rd Erith DA8 . . . . . **125** D1
Feltham TW13 . . . . **173** B6
Plumstead SE18 . . . . **123** D1
Sidcup DA5 . . . . **169** B5
Twickenham TW1 . . . . **153** C5
Riverdene HA8 . . . . **11** A1
Riverdene Rd IG1 . . . . **78** D5
Riverfleet WC1 . . . . **233** B2
Riverford Ho 28 W2 . . . . **91** C2
River Front EN1 . . . . **5** C2
River Gdns
Carshalton SM5 . . . . **219** A5
Feltham TW14 . . . . **150** B6
River Gdns Bsns Ctr
TW14 . . . . **128** B1
River Grove Pk BR3 . . . . **185** B2
Riverhead Cl E17 . . . . **34** D1
Riverhill Mews KT4 . . . . **215** B5
River Ho Barnes SW13 . . . . . **133** C3
1 Forest Hill SE26 . . . . . . **162** B1
Riverholme KT8 . . . . **196** C6
River House Montessori Sch
E14 . . . . **119** D4
Riverine Lo HA7 . . . . **25** A5
River La TW10 . . . . **153** D3
Riverleigh Ct E4 . . . . **35** A5
Riverly Prim Sch E10 . . . . **53** C1
Rivermead
East Molesey KT8 . . . . **196** A6
Kingston u T KT6 . . . . **197** D4
Rivermead Cl TW11 . . . . **175** B5
Rivermead Ct Ealing UB6 . . . **87** A4
Fulham SW6 . . . . **135** B2
Rivermead Ho Hackney E9 . . . **75** A3
Sunbury TW16 . . . . **194** C6
River Meads Ave TW13,
TW2 . . . . **151** D1
River Mole Bsns Pk
KT10 . . . . **195** C1
River Mount KT12 . . . . **193** D2
Rivernook Cl KT12 . . . . **194** C4
River Park Gdns BR2 . . . . . . **186** B3
River Park Rd N22 . . . . **32** B1
River Pl N1 . . . . **73** A1
River Plate Ho EC2 . . . . **242** D3
River Rd Barking IG11 . . . . . **101** D3
Buckhurst Hill IG9 . . . . **21** D1
River Road Bsns Pk
IG11 . . . . **101** D4
Riversdale Gdns N22 . . . . . . **32** C2

Riversdale Prim Sch
SW18 . . . . **157** C3
Riversdale Rd
Highbury N5 . . . . **73** A5
Thames Ditton KT7 . . . . . . **197** A3
Riversdene N5 . . . . **73** A5
Riversfield Rd EN1 . . . . **5** C2
Rivers Ho 10 TW8 . . . . **110** C1
Riverside Battersea SW11 . . **267** B4
Forest Hill SE6 . . . . **185** B6
Greenwich SE7 . . . . **121** B3
Hendon NW4 . . . . **46** B2
Oatlands Pk TW17 . . . . **193** C2
Sunbury TW16 . . . . **193** D6
11 Rotherhithe SE16 . . . . . **118** C4
St Pancras WC1 . . . . **233** B2
Sunbury TW16 . . . . **172** D1
Twickenham TW1 . . . . **153** B2
Riverside Apartments
N13 . . . . **32** B4
Riverside Ave KT8 . . . . **196** B4
Riverside Bsns Ctr
SW18 . . . . **157** D3
Riverside Bsns Pk SW19 . . . **180** A2
Riverside Cl
Chislehurst BR5 . . . . **190** C1
Ealing W7 . . . . **86** C3
Hackbridge SM6 . . . . **219** B5
Kingston u T KT1 . . . . **197** D5
Upper Clapton E5 . . . . **74** C6
Riverside Ct Chingford E4 . . . **19** D5
Lewisham SE12 . . . . **142** D1
Nine Elms SW8 . . . . **269** D6
Richmond TW10 . . . . **175** C5
Riverside Dr
Chiswick W4 . . . . **133** C4
Mitcham CR4 . . . . **202** C4
Richmond TW10 . . . . **153** B1
Temple Fortune NW11 . . . . **47** A3
Riverside Est EN3 . . . . **19** A5
Riverside Gdns Enfield EN2 . . . **5** A3
Hammersmith W6 . . . . **112** B1
Hendon N3 . . . . **47** A6
Wembley HA0 . . . . **88** A5
Riverside Health & Racquets
Club Chiswick The W4 . . **133** C4
Riverside Ho Finchley N12 . . . **29** D6
Morden SW19 . . . . **202** A5
30 Richmond TW10 . . . . . **153** D6
Riverside Ind Est IG11 . . . . . **102** A4
Riverside Mans 4 E1 . . . . . . **118** C5
Riverside Pl
New Southgate N11 . . . . . . **15** C1
Stanwell TW19 . . . . **148** A5
Riverside Prim Sch 37
SE16 . . . . **118** A4
Riverside Rd
Mill Meads E15 . . . . **98** A5
Sidcup DA14 . . . . **169** A2
South Tottenham N15 . . . . . **52** A3
Stanwell TW19 . . . . **148** A5
Wandsworth SW17, SW19 . . **158** A1
Riverside Sch BR5 . . . . **190** C1
Riverside The KT8 . . . . **196** B6
Riverside Wlk
Isleworth TW7 . . . . **130** C2
3 West Wickham BR4 . . . **207** D1
Riverside Wlk Mkt★
WC2 . . . . **116** B5 **250** D4
Riverside Works IG11 . . . . . . **78** D1
Riverside Workshops
SE1 . . . . **252** B4
River St EC1 . . . . . . **94** C4 **234** A2
Riverstone Cl HA2 . . . . **64** B6
Riverstone Ct KT2 . . . . **176** B2
Riverston Sch SE12 . . . . . . **165** A6
River Terr London W6 . . . . . . **112** C1
St James SW1 . . . . **250** C5
Riverton Cl W9 . . . . **91** B4
Riverview TW17 . . . . **193** B2
River View EN2 . . . . **5** B3
Riverview CE Prim Sch
KT19 . . . . **215** B4
Riverview Ct 14 DA17 . . . . . **125** C1
Riverview Gdns SW13 . . . . . **134** B6
River View Gdns TW1 . . . . . **152** D2
Riverview Gr W4 . . . . **132** C6
Riverview Hts SE18 . . . . **144** D5
Riverview Lo NW9 . . . . **67** B6
Riverview Pk SE6 . . . . **163** C2
Riverview Rd
Chiswick W4 . . . . **132** C6
West Ewell KT19 . . . . **215** B4
Riverway N13 . . . . **32** C6
River Way
Canning Town SE10 . . . . . **120** D3
Twickenham TW13, TW2 . . **151** D2
West Ewell KT19 . . . . **215** D3
River Wlk KT12 . . . . **194** A3
Riverwood La BR7 . . . . **189** B2
Rivet Ho SE1 . . . . **263** D2
Rivington Ave IG8 . . . . **37** D1
Rivington Cres NW7 . . . . **27** D3
Rivington Ct
17 Dagenham RM10 . . . . . **81** D2
Willesden Green NW10 . . . . **90** A6
Rivington Pl EC2 . . . . **95** C4
Rivington St EC2 . . . . **95** C4
Rivington Wlk 4 E8 . . . . **96** A6

Rivulet Rd N17 . . . . **33** A3
Rixon Ho SE18 . . . . **144** D6
Rixon St N7 . . . . **72** C5
Rixsen Rd E12 . . . . **78** A3
Roach Rd E3 . . . . **75** C1
Roads Pl N19 . . . . **72** A6
Robart Ho 2 N12 . . . . **30** A5
Robarts Cl HA5 . . . . **40** B4
Robbins Hall EN3 . . . . **18** D5
Robb Rd HA7 . . . . **25** A4
Robert Adam St W1 . . . . . . **238** A2
Roberta St E2 . . . . **96** A4
Robert Bell Ho 2 SE16 . . . . . **118** A2
Robert Blair Prim Sch
N7 . . . . **72** A2
Robert Browning Prim Sch
SE17 . . . . **117** B1 **262** C2
Robert Burns Ho N17 . . . . **34** B3
Robert Cl Barking IG11 . . . . . . **79** A2
Paddington W9 . . . . **236** B5
Robert Clack Sch
Dagenham RM8 . . . . **59** C1
Dagenham RM8 . . . . **81** B6
Robert Dashwood Way
SE17 . . . . **262** A3
Robert Gentry Ho W14 . . . . **254** B1
Robert Gerard Ho 7
SE27 . . . . **183** B6
Robert Ho 12 HA1 . . . . **42** D4
Robert Jones Ho 3
SE16 . . . . **118** A2
Robert Keen Cl 18 SE15 . . . **140** A4
Robert Lowe Cl SE14 . . . . . **140** D5
Roberton Dr BR1 . . . . **187** C2
Robert Owen Ho
Fulham SW6 . . . . **134** D4
8 Spitalfields E2 . . . . **95** D4
Robert Owen Lo 4 E5 . . . . . . **74** B4
Robertsbridge Rd SM5 . . . . **202** B2
Roberts Cl Cheam SM3 . . . . . **216** D1
Dagenham RM10 . . . . **81** C2
New Eltham SE9 . . . . **167** B3
South Norwood CR7 . . . . . **205** B6
Yiewsley UB7 . . . . **104** A5
Roberts Ct
Chessington KT9 . . . . **213** D3
Ealing W5 . . . . **88** A1
Islington N1 . . . . **234** D5
Penge SE20 . . . . **184** C2
Willesden NW10 . . . . **67** C2
Roberts Ho
Dagenham RM10 . . . . **81** D1
Friern Barnet N11 . . . . **31** B5
6 Kidbrooke SE18 . . . . . **144** A4
5 West Norwood SE27 . . **160** D1
Roberts Mews SW1 . . . . . . **258** A5
Robertson Ho
Kidbrooke SE18 . . . . **144** B4
11 Lewisham SE10 . . . . . **142** A4
1 Upper Tooting SW17 . . **180** C5
Robertson St SW8 . . . . **137** B3
Robert's Pl EC1 . . . . **241** B6
Roberts Rd
Belvedere DA17 . . . . **125** C1
Finchley NW7 . . . . **29** A4
Highams Pk E17 . . . . **35** C2
Robert St Croydon CR0 . . . . **221** A5
Newham E16 . . . . **122** D5
Plumstead SE18 . . . . **123** B2
Regent's Pk NW1 . . . **93** B4 **231** D1
Strand WC2 . . . . **250** B5
Robert Sutton Ho 20 E1 . . . . **96** C1
Robeson St 4 E3 . . . . **97** B2
Robina Cl DA6 . . . . **146** D1
Northwood HA6 . . . . **22** A2
Robin Cl Edgware NW7 . . . . . . **11** C1
Hampton TW12 . . . . **173** A5
Robin Cres E16 . . . . **99** D2
Robin Ct
16 Cubitt Town E14 . . . . . **120** A3
Wallington SM6 . . . . **219** C2
Wood Green N22 . . . . **32** B3
Robin Gr Brentford TW8 . . . . **131** C6
Dartmouth Pk N6 . . . . **71** A6
Harrow HA3 . . . . **44** B3
Highgate N6 . . . . **71** A6
Robin Hill Dr BR7 . . . . **188** A4
Robin Ho NW8 . . . . **230** A3
Robin Hood SW15 . . . . **155** C1
Robinhood Cl CR4 . . . . **203** C6
Robin Hood Ct 2 SM1 . . . . . **217** D3
Robin Hood Dr HA3 . . . . **24** C1
Robin Hood Gdns 12
E14 . . . . **120** A6
Robin Hood Jun Sch 8
SM1 . . . . **217** D3
Robinhood La CR4 . . . . **203** C6
Robin Hood La
Bexley DA6 . . . . **169** A6
Blackwall E14 . . . . **120** A6
Kingston u T SW15 . . . . . . **177** C6
Sutton SM1 . . . . **217** D3
Robin Hood Prim Sch
Kingston u T SW15 . . . . . . **177** C5
Sutton SM1 . . . . **217** D3

Robin Hood Way
Kingston u T SW15 . . . . . . **177** C5
Wembley UB6. . . . .**64** D2
Robin Hood Way (Kingston By-Pass) KT2, SW15,
SW20. . . . . **177** C5
Robinia Cl SE20. . . . .**184** A2
Robinia Cres E10 . . . .**75** D6
Robin La NW4 . . . .**46** D6
Robinscroft Mews 18
SE10 . . . . **141** D4
Robins Ct Grove Pk SE12. . .**165** C1
Richmond TW10 . . . .**154** A5
South Croydon CR2. . . . . . .**221** C4
Robin's Ct
Beckenham BR3. . . . .**186** B1
Clapham Pk SW4 . . . .**160** A5
Robinsfield Inf Sch
NW8 . . . .**92** C5 **230** A4
Robins Gr BR4 . . . .**225** A5
Robinson Cl Enfield EN2. . . . .**5** A2
11 Leyton E11 . . . .**76** C5
Robinson Cres WD23. . . . .**8** A3
Robinson Ct
5 Barnet EN4 . . . .**14** D3
Islington N1 . . . . **234** D6
4 Richmond TW9 . . . .**132** B1
Thornton Heath CR0. . . . . .**204** D3
Robinson Ho
4 North Kensington W10 . . .**90** D1
12 Tower Hamlets E14 . . . . .**97** C2
Robinson Rd
Dagenham RM10 . . . .**81** C4
Mitcham SW19. . . . .**180** C4
South Hackney E2 . . . .**96** C5
Robinson's Cl W13 . . . .**87** A2
Robinson St SW3 . . . .**267** C6
Robinswood Mews 6 N5 .**72** D3
Robinwood Gr UB8 . . . .**82** B3
Robinwood Pl SW15 . . . . . .**177** B6
Robsart St SW9. . . . .**138** C3
Rob Pascoe La RM9 . . . .**103** A4
Robson Ave NW10 . . . .**68** A3
Robson Cl Enfield EN2. . . . . . .**4** D3
Newham E6 . . . .**100** A1
Robson Ct N12 . . . .**30** A5
Robson Rd SE21, SE27 . . . .**161** A1
Roby Ho EC1 . . . .**242** A6
Roch Ave HA8 . . . .**26** B1
Rochdale 8 SE19 . . . .**183** C4
Rochdale Rd
Abbey Wood SE2. . . . .**124** B2
Walthamstow E17 . . . .**53** C2
Rochdale Way 4 SE8 . . . .**141** C5
Roche Ho 15 E14. . . . .**119** B6
Rochelle Cl SW11 . . . .**136** B1
Rochelle Ct
Beckenham BR3 . . . .**185** D3
14 Stepney E1 . . . .**96** C1
Rochelle St 9 E2 . . . .**95** D4
Rochemont Wlk 2 E8 . . . .**96** A6
Roche Rd SW16 . . . .**182** B2
Roche Sch The 15 SW18. .**157** C6
Rochester Ave
Bromley BR1 . . . .**187** B1
Feltham TW13 . . . .**149** D2
Newham E13 . . . .**99** C6
Rochester Cl
1 Blackfen DA15 . . . .**168** B5
Enfield EN1. . . . .**5** C4
Streatham SW16 . . . .**182** A3
Rochester Ct
1 Bethnal Green E2 . . . . .**96** B3
9 Camden Town NW1. . . . .**71** C1
Finchley N3. . . . .**29** A1
Kingsbury NW9 . . . .**45** B4
South Norwood SE25 . . . . .**184** A1
Rochester Dr
Old Bexley DA5. . . . .**169** C5
Pinner HA5. . . . .**40** D4
Rochester Gdns
Redbridge IG1 . . . .**56** B2
South Croydon CR0. . . . . . .**221** C5
Rochester Ho
Bermondsey SE1 . . . .**252** D1
13 Deptford SE15. . . . . . .**140** C6
Rochester Par TW13 . . . . .**150** A1
Rochester Mews NW1. . . . .**71** C1
Rochester Pl NW1 . . . .**71** C1
Rochester Rd
Carshalton SM5 . . . .**218** D4
Kentish Town NW1 . . . .**71** C2
Northwood HA6 . . . .**39** D6
Rochester Row
SW1. . . . .**115** C2 **259** B4
Rochester Sq NW1 . . . .**71** C1
Rochester St SW1 . . . . . .**259** C5
Rochester Terr NW1 . . . . . .**71** C2
Rochester Way
Eltham SE9 . . . .**144** C2
Kidbrooke SE3, SE9 . . . . . .**143** D2
Rochester Wlk SE1 . . . . .**252** C4
Roche Wlk SM5. . . . .**202** B3
Rochford N17. . . . .**33** C1
Rochford Ave RM6 . . . .**58** C4
Rochford Cl 2 E6. . . . .**99** D5
Rochford Way CR0 . . . .**204** A3

Rochford Wlk 3 E8. . . . . .**74** A1
Rochfort Ho 4 SE8 . . . . . .**119** B1
Rock Ave 13 SW14 . . . . . .**133** B2
Rockbourne Rd SE23. . . . .**162** D3
Rock Cl CR4 . . . .**180** B1
Rockell's Pl SE22 . . . .**162** B5
Rockfield Ho
Greenwich SE10 . . . .**142** A6
2 Hendon NW4 . . . .**46** D5
Rockford Ave UB6 . . . .**87** B5
Rock Gdns RM10. . . . .**81** D3
Rock Grove Way SE16 . . . .**118** A2
Rockhall Rd NW2 . . . .**68** D4
Rockhampton Cl 4
SE27 . . . .**182** C6
Rockhampton Rd
South Croydon CR2. . . . . . .**221** C2
West Norwood SE27,
SW16. . . . .**182** C6
Rock Hill SE19 . . . .**183** B6
Rockingham Cl SW15 . . . .**133** D1
Rockingham St 19 BR3. . .**185** C3
Rockingham Gate WD23. . . . .**8** A5
Rockingham St
SE1 . . . .**117** A3 **262** A5
Rockland Rd SW15. . . . . . .**135** A1
Rocklands N3 . . . .**29** B3
Rocklands Dr HA7 . . . .**25** C1
Rockley Ct 9 W14 . . . .**112** D4
Rockley Rd W14 . . . .**112** D4
Rockliffe Manor Prim Sch
SE18. . . . .**145** D6
Rockmount Prim Sch
SE19 . . . .**183** B4
Rockmount Rd
Plumstead Comm SE18,
SE2. . . . .**123** D1
South Norwood SE19 . . . . .**183** B4
Rocks La SW13. . . . .**134** A2
Rock St N4 . . . .**72** C6
Rockstraw Ho 5 NW3 . . . .**70** D1
Rockware Ave UB6. . . . .**86** C6
Rockware Bsns Ctr UB6 . .**86** B6
Rockways EN5. . . . .**11** C5
Rockwell Gdns SE19 . . . . .**183** C6
Rockwell Rd RM10. . . . .**81** D3
Rockwood Ct N16. . . . .**52** A2
Rocliffe St N1 . . . . . .**94** D5 **234** D3
Rocombe Cres SE23 . . . . .**162** C4
Rocque Ho SW6 . . . .**264** C6
Rocque La SE3 . . . .**142** D2
Rodborough Rd NW11 . . . .**47** C1
Rodd Est TW17 . . . .**193** B4
Roden Gdns CR0. . . . .**205** C3
Rodenhurst Rd SW4 . . . . .**159** D6
Rodenhurst Rd SW4 . . . . .**159** D5
Roden St Ilford IG1 . . . .**78** C5
Upper Holloway N7 . . . .**72** B5
Roderick Ho 3 SE16. . . . . .**118** C2
Roderick Rd NW3. . . . .**70** D4
Rodgers Cl WD6 . . . .**9** D5
Rodgers Ho 4 SW4 . . . . . .**159** D4
Rodin Ct N1 . . . .**234** C5
Roding Ct 6 W12. . . . .**111** C4
Roding Ho N1 . . . .**234** A5
Roding La IG9 . . . .**21** D3
Roding La N IG8 . . . .**37** D1
Roding La S IG4 . . . .**55** D5
Roding Lo IG1 . . . .**55** D3
Roding Mews E1. . . . .**118** A5
Roding Prim Sch RM8. . . . . .**80** C3
Roding Rd Hackney E5 . . . .**75** A3
Newham E6 . . . .**100** D2
Rodings Row EN5. . . . .**1** A1
Rodings The 1 IG8 . . . . . .**37** C4
Roding Valley Sta IG9 . . . . .**37** D6
Roding View IG9. . . . .**21** D3
Rodmarton St W1. . . .**92** D2 **237** D3
Rodmell WC1. . . . .**233** B1
Rodmell Cl UB4. . . . .**85** A3
Rodmell Slope N12 . . . .**29** B5
Rodmere St SE10 . . . .**120** C1
Rodney Cl
New Malden KT3 . . . .**199** C4
Pinner HA5. . . . .**41** A2
Thornton Heath CR0. . . . . .**204** D1
Walton-on-T KT12 . . . .**194** C1
Rodney Ct NW8 . . . .**236** B6
Rodney Gdns Hayes BR4 . . .**225** A4
Pinner HA5. . . . .**40** C4
Rodney Ho
4 Cubitt Town E14. . . . . .**119** D2
Islington N1 . . . .**233** D3
Notting Hill W11 . . . .**245** A6
Rodney Pl Merton SW19. . . .**180** A2
Newington SE17. . . . .**117** A2 **262** B4
Walthamstow E17 . . . .**35** B1
Rodney Rd Mitcham CR4. . . .**202** C6
New Malden KT3 . . . .**199** C4
Twickenham TW4 . . . .**151** C4
Walton-on-T KT12 . . . .**194** C1
Walworth SE17. . . . . .**117** B2 **262** C4
Wanstead E11 . . . .**55** B5
Rodney St N1. . . . . .**94** B5 **233** D3
Rodwall Pl HA8 . . . .**26** C3
Rodway Rd Bromley BR1. . .**187** B2
Putney SW15 . . . .**156** A4
Rodwell Cl 2 HA4 . . . .**40** C1
Rodwell Rd SE22. . . . .**161** D5

Roe 5 NW9 . . . .**27** D2
Roebourne Way E16 . . . . .**122** C4
Roebuck Cl
Feltham TW13 . . . .**172** B6
Tottenham N17. . . . .**33** D4
Roebuck Ct Chingford E4. . .**36** A3
2 New Malden KT3 . . . . .**199** C4
Roebuck Hts IG10 . . . .**21** C4
Roebuck Rd KT9. . . . .**214** C3
Roedean Ave EN3. . . . .**6** C5
Roedean Cl EN3 . . . .**6** C4
Roedean Cres SW15 . . . . .**155** C6
Roe End NW9. . . . .**45** A5
Roe Gn NW9. . . . .**45** A4
Roe Green Jun & Inf Schs
NW9. . . . .**44** D1
ROEHAMPTON. **155** C4
Roehampton Church Sch
SW15 . . . .**156** B4
Roehampton Cl SW15. . . . .**134** A1
Roehampton Dr SW13. . . . .**134** A2
Roehampton Dr BR7 . . . . . .**189** A4
Roehampton Gate
SW15. . . . .**155** C5
Roehampton High St
SW15. . . . .**156** A4
Roehampton La
Putney SW15 . . . .**156** A5
Roehampton SW15. . . . . . .**156** B3
Roehampton Univ (Digby Stuart Coll) SW15 . . . . .**156** A4
Roehampton Univ (Froebel Coll) SW15 . . . .**155** D5
Roehampton Univ (Southlands Coll)
SW15 . . . .**156** A4
Roehampton Univ (Whitelands Coll)
SW15 . . . .**156** A4
Roehampton Vale SW15 . . .**155** D2
Roe La NW9 . . . .**45** A5
Roe Rd SM6. . . . .**220** A1
Roe Way SM6. . . . .**220** A2
Roffey Ct 3 NW9 . . . .**46** A5
Roffey St E14. . . . .**120** A4
Rogate Ho E5. . . . .**74** A5
Roger Ascham Prim Sch
E17. . . . .**35** B2
Roger Dowley Ct 8 E2. . .**96** C5
Roger's Almshouses 2
SW9. . . . .**138** B1
Rogers Ct 16 E14 . . . .**119** C6
Rogers Est 28 E2. . . . .**96** C4
Rogers Gdns RM10. . . . . . .**81** C3
Rogers Ho
9 Dagenham RM10. . . . . . .**81** C4
Westminster SW1 . . . .**259** D4
Rogers Rd
Canning Town E16 . . . .**98** D1
Dagenham RM10 . . . .**81** C3
Upper Tooting SW17. . . . . .**180** C6
Roger St WC1 . . . . .**94** B3 **240** D5
Roger Stone Ct NW10 . . . .**67** B4
Rogers Wlk N12 . . . .**13** D1
Rohan Pl 4 IG4 . . . .**56** B4
Rojack Rd SE23 . . . .**162** D3
Rokeby Gdns IG8 . . . .**37** A2
Rokeby Ho
9 Balham SW12 . . . .**159** B4
Bloomsbury WC1 . . . .**240** C5
Rokeby Pl SW20 . . . .**178** B3
Rokeby Rd SE4 . . . .**141** B3
Rokeby Sch
Kingston u T KT2. . . . .**177** A3
Stratford E15. . . . .**76** B1
Rokeby St E15 . . . .**98** C6
Rokeland Ho SE4 . . . .**141** A1
Rokell Ho BR3 . . . .**185** D5
Roker Park Ave UB10. . . . . .**60** A4
Rokesby Cl DA16 . . . .**145** B3
Rokesby Pl HA0. . . . .**65** D3
Rokesly Ave N8 . . . .**50** A4
Rokesly Jun & Inf Schs 5
N8. . . . .**50** A4
Roland Ct SE19 . . . .**183** D2
Roland Gdns
SW7. . . . .**114** A1 **256** B2
Roland Ho SW7. . . . .**256** B2
Roland Mews 1 E1. . . . . . .**96** D2
Roland Rd E17. . . . .**54** B5
Roland Way
South Kensington
SW7. . . . .**114** A1 **256** B2
Walworth SE17. . . . .**262** D1
Worcester Pk KT4. . . . .**215** D6
Roles Gr RM6 . . . .**59** A5
Rolfe Cl EN4 . . . .**2** C1
Rolfe Ho N11 . . . .**30** D6
Rolinsden Way BR2 . . . . . .**225** D4
Rolland Ho W7 . . . .**86** C2
Rollesby Rd KT19, KT9 . . . .**214** C2
Rollesby Way SE28. . . . . . .**102** C6
Rolleston Ave BR5 . . . .**210** D3
Rolleston Cl BR5 . . . .**210** D2
Rolleston Rd CR2 . . . .**221** B1
Roll Gdns IG2 . . . .**56** C5
Rollins St SE15 . . . .**140** C6
Rollit Cres TW3 . . . .**151** C6
Rollit Ho N7 . . . .**72** C3

Rollit St N7. . . . .**72** C3
Rollo Ct SW11 . . . .**268** C1
Rolls Bldgs EC4. . . . .**241** B2
Rolls Ct The E4 . . . .**36** A5
Rolls Park Ave E4. . . . .**35** D5
Rolls Park Rd E4. . . . .**35** D5
Rolls Pas EC4. . . . .**241** A2
Rolls Rd SE1. . . . . .**117** D1 **263** D2
Rolt St SE8 . . . .**141** A6
Rolvenden Gdns BR1. . . . .**187** D3
Rolvenden Pl N17. . . . .**34** A2
Roman Cl Feltham TW14. . . .**150** C6
South Acton W3 . . . .**110** D4
Roman Ct 4 N7 . . . .**72** B2
Romanfield Rd SW2. . . . . . .**160** B4
Romanhurst Ave BR2 . . . . .**208** C5
Romanhurst Gdns BR2,
BR3 . . . .**208** C5
Roman Ind Est CR0 . . . . . .**205** C2
Roman Lo 6 IG9 . . . .**21** C3
Roman Rd Chiswick W4. . . . .**111** D2
Elstree WD6 . . . .**9** D5
Finchley N12. . . . .**30** C2
Globe Town E2, E3 . . . .**96** D5
Ilford IG1 . . . .**78** D2
Muswell Hill N10. . . . .**31** B3
Newham E6 . . . .**100** A3
25 Old Ford E3 . . . .**97** B6
Willesden NW2. . . . .**68** C5
Roman Rise SE19 . . . .**183** B4
Roman Road Mkt ★ 1 E3. .**97** B5
Roman Road Prim Sch
E6. . . . .**99** D3
Roman Sq SE28. . . . .**124** A5
Roman Way Barnsbury N7 . .**72** B2
Croydon CR0. . . . .**220** D6
4 Deptford SE15. . . . . . .**140** C5
Enfield EN1. . . . .**17** D6
Romany Gdns
Cheam SM3 . . . .**201** C2
1 Higham Hill E17. . . . . . .**35** A2
Romany Ho 8 N9 . . . .**18** A1
Romany Prospect SE19 . . .**183** B4
Romany Rise BR5. . . . .**211** A1
Roma Read Cl SW15 . . . . .**156** B4
Romayne Ho SW4. . . . .**137** D2
Romberg Rd SW17 . . . .**159** A1
Romborough Gdns SE13 .**164** A6
Romborough Way SE13 . . .**164** A6
Romeland WD6 . . . .**9** D5
Romeland Ct WD6 . . . .**9** D5
Romer Ho 9 SW2 . . . .**160** B6
Romero Cl SW9 . . . .**138** B2
Romero Sq SE9 . . . .**143** C1
Romeyn Rd SW16 . . . .**160** B1
ROMFORD. **59** D4
Romford Ho 17 N1 . . . .**73** B2
Romford Rd
Forest Gate E7, E12 . . . . . .**77** C3
Stratford E15. . . . .**76** D2
Romford St E1. . . . .**96** B2
Romilly Dr WD19. . . . .**23** A6
Romilly Rd N4 . . . .**72** D2
Romilly St W1 . . . .**249** D6
Romily Ct 2 SW6 . . . .**135** A3
Rommany Ct SE27 . . . .**183** B6
Rommany Rd SE27. . . . . . .**183** B6
Romney Cl Ashford TW15 . .**171** A5
Chessington KT9 . . . .**214** A4
7 Deptford SE14. . . . . . .**140** C5
Harrow HA2. . . . .**41** C2
North End NW11. . . . .**48** A1
Tottenham N17. . . . .**34** B2
Romney Ct
9 Hammersmith W12. . . . .**112** C4
8 Hampstead NW3. . . . . . .**70** C2
15 Northolt UB5. . . . .**84** D5
Romney Dr Bromley BR1. . .**187** D3
Harrow HA2. . . . .**41** C2
Romney Gdns DA7. . . . . . .**147** B4
Romney Ho
2 Blackwall E14. . . . .**120** B6
Enfield EN1. . . . .**18** A6
Sutton SM2. . . . .**217** D2
Romney Mews W1 . . . . . .**238** A4
Romney Par UB4. . . . .**83** B5
Romney Rd
Greenwich SE10 . . . .**142** B6
Hayes UB4 . . . .**83** B1
New Malden KT3 . . . .**199** B3
10 Woolwich SE18 . . . . . .**123** A3
Romney Row NW2 . . . .**68** D6
Romney St SW1. . . . .**116** A3 **260** A5
Romola Rd SE24, SW2 . . . .**160** D3
Romsey Cl BR6 . . . .**226** D4
Romsey Gdns RM9 . . . . . .**102** D6
Romsey Rd
Dagenham RM9 . . . .**102** D6
Ealing W13 . . . .**109** A6
Romulus Ct 7 TW8 . . . . . .**131** D5
Ronald Ave E15. . . . .**98** C4
Ronald Cl BR3. . . . .**207** B4
Ronald Ct EN5 . . . .**1** D2
Ronald Ho Eltham SE9. . . . .**143** C1
4 Sutton SM1 . . . .**218** B3
Ronald Ross Prim Sch 6
SW19 . . . .**157** A4
Ronaldshay N4 . . . .**50** C1

Ronalds Rd Bromley BR1 . .**187** A2
Islington N5. . . . .**72** C3
Ronald St E1 . . . .**96** C1
Ronaldstone Rd DA15. . . . .**167** C5
Rona Rd NW3. . . . .**71** A4
Ronart St HA3 . . . .**42** D6
Rona Wlk 20 N1 . . . .**73** B2
Rondu Rd NW2 . . . .**69** A3
Ronelean Rd KT6. . . . .**214** B5
Ron Leighton Way E6 . . . .**100** A6
Ronnie La E12. . . . .**78** C4
Ron Todd Cl RM10. . . . . . .**103** C6
Ronver Lo E4. . . . .**20** C1
Ronver Rd SE12. . . . .**164** D3
Rood La EC3. . . . . .**117** C6 **253** A6
Rookby Ct N21. . . . .**16** D2
Rook Cl HA9. . . . .**66** D5
Rookeries Cl TW13. . . . . . .**150** C1
Rookery Cl NW9 . . . .**45** D4
Rookery Cotts EN4 . . . .**3** B2
Rookery Cres RM10 . . . . . .**81** D1
Rookery Dr BR7. . . . .**188** C2
Rookery La BR2. . . . .**209** D3
Rookery Rd SW4. . . . .**137** C1
Rookery Way NW9 . . . .**45** D4
Rooke Way SE10 . . . .**120** C1
Rookfield Ave N10. . . . .**49** C5
Rookfield Cl N10. . . . .**49** C5
Rook Lo IG1. . . . .**55** D3
**Rooks Heath Coll Bsns &
Enterprise** HA2. . . . .**63** C5
Rooksmead Rd TW16. . . . .**172** A2
Rooks Terr UB7. . . . .**104** A4
Rookstone Rd SW17 . . . . .**180** D5
Rook Wlk E6. . . . .**100** A1
Rookwood Ave
Wallington SM6. . . . .**219** D4
West Barnes KT3 . . . .**200** A5
Rookwood Gdns E4 . . . .**20** D2
Rookwood Ho 2 IG11 . . . . .**101** B5
Rookwood Rd N16. . . . .**52** A2
Roosevelt Ct 15 SW19 . . . .**157** A3
Rootes Dr W10 . . . .**90** D2
Ropemaker Rd SE16 . . . . .**119** A3
Ropemaker's Fields 7
E14 . . . .**119** B6
Ropemaker St
EC2 . . . .**95** B2 **242** C4
Roper Ho 13 SE21. . . . . . .**183** C6
Roper La SE1 . . . . . .**117** C4 **253** B1
Ropers Ave E4. . . . .**36** A5
Roper's Orch SW3 . . . . . .**267** A5
Roper St 1 SE9. . . . .**166** C5
Ropers Wlk 13 SE24. . . . .**160** C4
Roper Way CR4 . . . .**181** A1
Ropery Bsns Pk SE7. . . . . .**121** C2
Ropery St E3 . . . .**97** B3
Rope St SE16 . . . .**119** A3
Ropewalk Gdns 18 E1 . . . .**96** A1
Ropley St 6 E2. . . . .**96** A5
Rosa Alba Mews N5. . . . . . .**73** A4
Rosa Ave TW15 . . . .**170** C6
Rosa Freedman Ctr NW2 . .**46** C1
Rosalind Ct 6 IG11. . . . . . .**80** A1
Rosalind Ho 25 N1 . . . .**95** C5
Rosaline Rd SW6 . . . .**135** A5 **264** B3
Rosaline Terr SW6 . . . . . .**264** B3
Rosamond St SE26 . . . . . .**162** B1
Rosamund Cl CR2. . . . .**221** B4
Rosamun St UB2. . . . .**107** A2
Rosa Parks Ho 8 SW9 . . . .**138** B3
Rosary Cl TW3, TW5. . . . . .**129** A3
Rosary Ct 17 E1. . . . .**96** D2
Rosary Gdns
Ashford TW15 . . . .**170** D6
Bushey WD23 . . . .**8** C4
South Kensington
SW7 . . . .**114** A2 **256** B3
Rosary RC Inf Sch TW5 . . .**129** C6
Rosary RC Jun Sch TW5 . .**129** C6
Rosary RC Prim Sch NW3 .**70** C3
Rosaville Rd
SW6. . . . .**135** B5 **264** C3
Rosbury SW15 . . . .**157** A5
Roscastle Rd SE4 . . . .**163** A6
Roscoe St EC1. . . . . .**95** A3 **242** B5
Roscoff Cl HA8 . . . .**27** B2
Roscommon Ho 2 NW3. . . .**70** B3
Roseacre Cl Ealing W13 . . . .**87** B2
Littleton TW17 . . . .**192** C4
Roseacre Lo E1. . . . .**6** C1
Roseacre Rd DA16. . . . . . .**146** B2
Rose Alley
Borough The SE1. . . . .**252** B4
Broadgate EC2 . . . .**243** B3
Rose Ave Mitcham CR4. . . .**180** D2
Morden SM4. . . . .**202** A4
Woodford E18. . . . .**37** B1
Rosebank
2 Hammersmith W3. . . . . .**89** B1
Fulham SW6. . . . .**134** C4
Penge SE20 . . . .**184** B3
Rosebank Ave HA0. . . . .**64** D4
Rosebank Cl
Colney Hatch N12. . . . .**30** C5
Teddington TW11. . . . .**175** A4
Rosebank Gdns Bow E3. . . .**97** B5
1 Dagenham W3. . . . .**89** B1
Rosebank Gr E17. . . . .**53** B6

Rosebank Rd
Hanwell W7 . . . .**108** C4
Walthamstow E17 . . . .**53** D3
Rosebank Villas E17 . . . .**53** C5
Rosebank Way W3 . . . . . .**89** B1
Rose Bates Dr NW9 . . . . .**44** C5
Rosebay Ho 20 E3 . . . . .**97** C2
Roseberry Gdns
Harringay N4 . . . .**50** D3
Orpington BR6 . . . .**227** C5
Roseberry Pl E8 . . . .**73** D2
Roseberry St SE16 . . . . .**118** B2
Rosebery Ave
Finsbury EC1 . . . . .**94** C4 **234** B1
Harrow HA2 . . . .**63** B4
Kingston u T KT3 . . . . . .**199** D6
Plashet E12 . . . .**78** B2
Sidcup DA15 . . . .**167** C4
South Norwood CR7 . . . . .**183** A1
Tottenham N17 . . . .**34** A1
Rosebery Ct SM4 . . . . . .**200** D3
Rosebery Ct
Chessington KT9 . . . .**214** B3
Holborn EC1 . . . .**241** A6
Mayfair W1 . . . .**248** C4
Rosebery Gdns
Ealing W13 . . . .**87** A1
Hornsey N8 . . . .**50** A4
Sutton SM1 . . . .**217** D4
Rosebery Ho 21 E2 . . . . .**96** C5
Rosebery Ind Pk N17 . . . .**34** B1
Rosebery Mews N10 . . . .**31** C1
Rosebery Rd
Cheam SM1, SM2 . . . . . .**217** B2
Clapham SW2 . . . .**160** A5
Isleworth TW3, TW7 . . . . .**152** A6
Kingston u T KT1 . . . . . .**176** D1
Muswell Hill N10 . . . .**31** B3
Rosebery Sq Holborn EC1.**241** A5
Kingston u T KT1 . . . . . .**176** D1
Rosebine Ave TW2 . . . . .**152** B4
Rosebriars KT10 . . . . . .**212** A3
Rose Bruford Coll DA15 .**168** B3
Rosebury Ct SW16 . . . . .**182** B2
Rosebury Rd SW6 . . . . .**135** D3
Rosebury Vale HA4 . . . . .**62** A6
Rose Bush Ct NW3 . . . . .**70** D3
Rose Cotts KT10 . . . . . .**212** B3
Rosecourt Rd CR0 . . . . .**204** B3
Rosecroft Ave NW3 . . . . .**69** C5
Rosecroft Gdns
Dollis Hill NW2 . . . .**68** A5
Twickenham TW2 . . . .**152** B3
Rosecroft Rd UB1 . . . . . .**85** D3
Rosecroft Wlk Pinner HA5. .**40** D4
Wembley HA0 . . . .**65** D3
Rose & Crown Ct EC2 . . .**242** A2
Rose & Crown Yd SW1 . .**249** B3
Rose Ct 7 Dalston E8 . . .**73** D1
Harrow HA2 . . . .**64** A6
Ilford IG1 . . . .**78** D2
Islington N1 . . . .**234** C5
Muswell Hill N10 . . . .**31** B3
3 Pinner HA5 . . . .**40** C6
Spitalfields E1 . . . .**243** D3
7 Wembley HA0 . . . .**88** A5
10 Wimbledon SW19 . . . .**179** B5
Rose Dale BR6 . . . .**226** D6
Rosedale Ave UB3 . . . . .**83** B2
Rosedale Cl
Abbey Wood SE2 . . . . . .**124** B3
Hanwell W7 . . . .**108** D4
Stanmore HA7 . . . .**25** B4
Rosedale Cnr BR7 . . . . .**188** B2
Rosedale Coll UB3 . . . . .**83** C1
Rosedale Ct N5 . . . .**72** D4
Rosedale Dr RM9 . . . . . .**80** B1
Rosedale Gdns RM9 . . . . .**80** B1
Rosedale Ho N16 . . . .**51** B1
Rosedale Lo N14 . . . .**15** B4
Rosedale Pl CR0 . . . . . .**206** D2
Rosedale Rd
Dagenham RM9 . . . .**80** B1
Forest Gate E7 . . . .**77** C3
Richmond TW9 . . . .**132** A1
Stoneleigh KT17 . . . .**216** A3
Rosedale Terr W6 . . . . . .**112** B3
Rosedene NW6 . . . .**90** D6
Rosedene Ave
Morden SM4 . . . .**201** C4
Southall UB6 . . . .**85** C4
Streatham SW16 . . . .**160** B1
Thornton Heath CR0 . . . . .**204** A2
Rosedene Ct HA4 . . . . . .**39** C1
Rosedene Gdns IG2 . . . . .**56** C5
Rosedene Terr E10 . . . . . .**75** D6
Rosedew Rd W6 . . . .**134** D6
Rose End KT4 . . . .**200** D1
Rosefield Cl SM5 . . . . . .**218** C3
Rosefield Ct EN4 . . . .**2** D1
Rosefield Gdns E14 . . . .**119** C6
Roseford Ct 16 W12 . . . .**112** D4
Rose Garden Cl HA8 . . . .**26** A4
Rosegate Ho 32 E3 . . . . .**97** B5
Rose Gdns Ealing W5 . . .**109** D3
Feltham TW13 . . . .**150** A2

Rose Gdns continued
Southall UB1 . . . .**85** C3
Rose Glen NW9 . . . .**45** B5
Rosehart Mews 8 W11 . . .**91** C1
Rosehatch Ave RM6 . . . . .**58** D6
Roseheath Rd TW4 . . . . .**151** B6
ROSEHILL **202** A1
Rosehill Claygate KT10 . .**213** A2
Hampton TW12 . . . .**173** C2
Rose Hill
Carshalton SM4, SM5 . . . .**202** A2
Cheam SM1 . . . .**201** D1
Rosehill Ave SM1, SM5 . .**202** A1
Rosehill Ct SM4 . . . .**202** A2
Rosehill Gdns
Greenford UB6 . . . .**64** D3
Sutton SM1 . . . .**218** A6
Rose Hill Park W SM1 . . .**218** A6
Rosehill Rd SW18 . . . . . .**158** A6
Rose Joan Mews NW6 . . .**69** C4
Rose La RM6 . . . .**59** A5
Roseland Cl N17 . . . .**33** B3
Roseland Ho SW6 . . . . . .**135** A2
Rose Lawn WD23 . . . .**8** A3
Roseleigh Ave N5 . . . .**72** D4
Roseleigh Cl 15 TW1 . . . .**153** D5
Roselle Ct W5 . . . .**88** A1
Rosemary Ave
East Finchley NW2 . . . .**47** D5
East Molesey KT8 . . . . . .**195** C5
Edmonton N9 . . . .**18** B3
Enfield EN2 . . . .**5** C4
Finchley N3 . . . .**29** D1
Hounslow TW4 . . . .**128** D3
Rosemary Branch Bridge
N1 . . . .**235** D6
Rosemary Cl
Hillingdon UB8 . . . .**82** C2
Thornton Heath CR0 . . . . .**204** A3
Rosemary Cotts 4
SW19 . . . .**178** C3
Rosemary Ct 35 SE8 . . . .**141** B6
Rosemary Dr
Redbridge IG4 . . . .**55** D4
16 South Bromley E14 . . . .**98** B1
Rosemary Gdns
Chessington KT9 . . . .**214** A4
Dagenham RM8 . . . .**59** B1
Mortlake SW14 . . . .**133** A2
Rosemary Ho
Shoreditch N1 . . . .**235** D5
Willesden NW10 . . . .**90** B6
Rosemary La SW14 . . . . .**133** A2
Rosemary Rd
Bexley DA16 . . . .**145** D4
Camberwell SE15 . . . . . .**139** D5
Wandsworth SW17 . . . . .**158** A1
Rosemary St N1 . . . .**235** D6
Rosemary Works Sch
N1 . . . .**95** B6 **235** D5
Rosemead NW9 . . . .**46** A2
Rosemead Ave
Feltham TW13 . . . .**149** D2
Mitcham CR4 . . . .**181** C1
Wembley HA9 . . . .**66** A3
Rosemead Prep Sch
SE27 . . . .**161** A2
Rose Mews N18 . . . .**34** B6
Rosemont Ave N12 . . . . . .**30** A4
Rosemont Mans 11 NW3 . .**69** D2
Rosemont Rd Acton W3 . .**110** D6
Kingston u T KT3 . . . . . .**199** A6
Richmond TW10 . . . .**154** A5
South Hampstead NW3 . . . .**70** A2
Wembley HA0 . . . .**88** A4
Rosemoor Ho 14 W13 . . .**109** A5
Rosemoor St
SW3 . . . .**114** D2 **257** D2
Rosemount Ct
2 Acton W3 . . . .**110** D5
South Norwood SE25 . . . .**205** C6
Rosemount Dr BR1 . . . . .**210** B5
Rosemount Lo W3 . . . . . .**110** D6
Rosemount Point 10
SE23 . . . .**162** D1
Rosemount Rd W13 . . . . .**87** A1
Rosemount Twrs 5
SM6 . . . .**219** C2
Rosenau Cres SW11 . . . .**267** C1
Rosenau Rd
SW11 . . . .**136** D4 **267** C2
Rosendale Prim Sch
SE21 . . . .**161** A4
Rosendale Rd SE21,
SE24 . . . .**161** A3
Roseneath Ave N21 . . . . . .**16** D3
Roseneath Pl 2 SW16 . . .**182** B6
Roseneath Rd SW11 . . . .**159** A5
Roseneath Wlk EN1 . . . . . .**5** C1
Rosens Wlk HA8 . . . .**10** D1
Rosenthal Ho SE6 . . . . . .**163** D5
Rosenthal Rd SE6 . . . . . .**164** A5
Rosenthorpe Rd SE15 . . .**162** D6
Roserton St E14 . . . .**120** A4
Rosethorne Ct CR0 . . . . .**206** D3
Rose Sq SW7 . . . .**256** C6
Rose Walton Beckton E4 . .**241** D2
Strand WC2 . . . .**116** A6 **250** A6
Roses The IG8 . . . .**36** D5
Rose Theatre SE1 . . . . . .**252** A4

Rosethorn Cl SW12 . . . . .**159** D4
Rosetree Pl TW12 . . . . . .**173** C4
Rosetta Cl SW8 . . . .**270** B3
Rosetta Ct SE19 . . . .**183** C5
Rosetta Prim Sch E16 . . .**99** B2
Rosetti Terr RM8 . . . .**80** B4
Roseveare Rd SE12 . . . . .**187** C6
Roseville N21 . . . .**16** C3
Roseville Ave TW3, TW4 . .**151** C6
Roseville Rd UB3 . . . . . .**106** A2
Rosevine Rd SW20 . . . . .**178** C2
Rosewall Ct SW19 . . . . . .**179** D5
Roseway 7 Edgware HA8 . .**27** A6
London SE21 . . . .**161** B5
Rose Way Edgware HA8 . . .**27** A6
Lee SE12 . . . .**165** A6
Rosewell Cl SE20 . . . . . .**184** B3
Rose Wlk Surbiton KT5 . . .**198** D4
West Wickham BR4 . . . . .**224** B6
Rosewood Ave UB6 . . . . .**65** A2
Rosewood Cl DA14 . . . . .**168** C1
Rosewood Ct
Bromley BR1 . . . .**187** D2
Dagenham RM6 . . . .**58** C4
Kingston u T KT2 . . . . . .**176** C3
2 Leyton E11 . . . .**76** B4
Rosewood Dr TW17 . . . . .**192** B4
Rosewood Gdns SE13 . . .**142** A3
Rosewood Gr SM1 . . . . . .**218** A4
Rosewood Ho 9 NW3 . . . . .**69** D2
Rosewood Sq W12 . . . . . .**90** A1
Rosher Cl E15 . . . .**76** B1
Roshni Ho SW17 . . . .**180** C4
Rosh Pinah Prim Sch
HA8 . . . .**10** D1
Rosina Ct SW17 . . . .**180** C5
Rosina St E9 . . . .**74** D2
Roskeen Ct 1 SW19 . . . . .**178** C3
Roskell Rd SW15 . . . . . .**134** D2
Roskild Ct HA9 . . . .**66** B4
Roslin Ho 2 E1 . . . .**118** D6
Roslin Rd W3 . . . .**110** D3
Roslin Way BR1 . . . .**187** A5
Roslyn Cl CR4 . . . .**180** B1
Roslyn Rd N15 . . . .**51** C4
Rosmead Rd
W11 . . . .**113** A6 **244** B6
Rosoman Pl EC1 . . . .**241** B6
Rosoman St EC1 . . . .**234** B1
Rossal Ct SE20 . . . .**184** B3
Rossall Cres NW10 . . . . . .**88** B4
Rossanne Ho N3 . . . .**29** D3
Ross Ave RM8 . . . .**59** B1
Ross Cl Harrow HA3 . . . . .**24** A3
Hayes UB3 . . . .**105** B2
Northolt UB5 . . . .**84** B2
Ross Ct Chislehurst BR7 . .**188** B3
Colindale NW9 . . . .**45** C6
Ealing W13 . . . .**87** B2
Hackney E5 . . . .**74** B4
2 Putney SW15 . . . .**156** D4
South Croydon CR2 . . . . .**221** A2
Rossdale SM1 . . . .**218** C3
Rossdale Dr
Ponders End N9 . . . .**18** C5
South Harp NW9 . . . .**45** A1
Rossdale Rd SW15 . . . . .**134** C1
Rosse Gdns SE13 . . . . . .**164** B5
Rosse Mews SE3 . . . . . .**143** B4
Rossendale Cl EN1 . . . .**4** D6
Rossendale Ho 7 E5 . . . . .**74** B4
Rossendale St E5 . . . .**74** B6
Rossendale Way
NW1 . . . .**93** C6 **232** B6
Rossendon Ct 1 SM6 . . . .**219** C2
Rossetti Ct WC1 . . . .**239** C4
Rossetti Gdns Mans
SW3 . . . .**267** C6
Rossetti Ho SW1 . . . .**259** D3
Rossetti Mews NW8 . . . . .**229** D5
Rossetti Rd SE16 . . . . . .**118** B1
Rossetti Studios SW3 . . .**267** B6
Ross Ho
2 Kidbrooke SE18 . . . . . .**144** A4
Twickenham TW2 . . . .**151** D2
18 Wapping E1 . . . .**118** B5
Rossignol Gdns SM5 . . . .**219** A6
Rossindel Rd TW3 . . . . . .**151** C6
Rossington Cl EN1 . . . .**6** B5
Rossington St E5 . . . .**74** A6
Rossiter Cl SE19 . . . .**183** A3
Rossiter Fields EN5 . . . . .**13** B5
Rossiter Rd SW12 . . . . . .**159** B3
Rossland Cl DA6 . . . .**169** D6
Rosslyn Ave
Barnes SW13 . . . .**133** D2
Chingford E4 . . . .**20** D2
Dagenham RM8 . . . .**59** C2
East Barnet EN4 . . . .**14** C5
Feltham TW14 . . . .**150** A5
Rosslyn Ashford TW16 . . .**171** C4
Coney Hall BR4 . . . .**224** D5
Hayes UB3 . . . .**83** B2
Rosslyn Cres Harrow HA1 . .**42** D5
Wembley HA9 . . . .**66** A4
Rosslyn Ct NW3 . . . .**70** C3
Rosslyn Hill NW3 . . . .**70** B3
Rosslyn Ho 8 TW9 . . . . .**132** B4

Rosslyn Mans
8 Hampstead NW3 . . . . . .**70** A2
South Hampstead NW6 . . . .**70** A2
Rosslyn Mews 7 NW3 . . . .**70** B4
Rosslyn Park Mews NW3 . .**70** B3
Rosslyn Rd Barking IG11 . .**79** B1
Twickenham TW1 . . . . . .**153** C5
Walthamstow E17 . . . .**54** A5
Rossmore Cl EN3 . . . .**6** D1
Rossmore Ct NW1 . . . . . .**237** C6
Rossmore Rd
NW1 . . . .**92** C3 **237** B6
Ross Par SM6 . . . .**219** B2
Ross Rd
South Norwood SE25 . . . .**205** C6
Twickenham TW2 . . . . . .**152** A3
Wallington SM6 . . . .**219** C3
Ross Way SE9 . . . .**144** A2
Rossway Dr WD23 . . . .**8** B6
Rosswood Gdns SM6 . . . .**219** C2
Rosswood Ho 13 SM6 . . .**219** B2
Rosswood Lo CR0 . . . . . .**222** D6
Rostella Rd SW17 . . . . . .**180** B6
Rostrevor Ave N15 . . . . . .**51** D3
Rostrevor Gdns UB2 . . . .**107** A3
Rostrevor Mans SW6 . . . .**264** C2
Rostrevor Mews SW6 . . . .**264** C1
Rostrevor Rd
Fulham SW6 . . . . . .**135** B4 **264** C2
Wimbledon SW19 . . . . . .**179** C5
Rotary Ct KT8 . . . .**196** C6
Rotary Lo 12 SE27 . . . . .**160** D1
Rotary St SE1 . . . .**261** D6
Rothay NW1 . . . .**231** D2
Rothbury Gdns TW7 . . . . .**131** A5
Rothbury Rd E9 . . . .**75** C1
Rothbury Wlk N17 . . . .**34** A3
Rotheley Ho 39 E9 . . . . . .**74** C1
Rotherfield Ct
De Beauvoir Town N1 . . . . .**73** B1
Shoreditch N1 . . . . .**95** B6 **235** C6
Rotherfield Prim Sch
N1 . . . .**95** A6 **235** B6
Rotherfield Rd Enfield EN3 . .**6** D6
Wallington SM5 . . . .**219** A3
Rotherfield St
Islington N1 . . . .**73** A1
Shoreditch N1 . . . . .**95** A6 **235** B6
Rotherham Wlk SE1 . . . . .**251** C3
Rotherhill Ave SW16 . . . .**181** D4
ROTHERHITHE **118** D3
Rotherhithe Bsns Est 6
SE16 . . . .**118** C2
Rotherhithe New Rd
SE16 . . . .**118** B1
Rotherhithe Old Rd
SE16 . . . .**118** D2
Rotherhithe Prim Sch 24
SE16 . . . .**118** C4
Rotherhithe St SE16 . . . .**118** C4
Rotherhithe Sta SE16 . . .**118** C4
Rotherhithe Tunnel
SE16 . . . .**118** D5
Rother Ho SE15 . . . .**140** B1
Rotherwick Hill W5 . . . . . .**88** B3
Rotherwick Rd NW11 . . . .**47** C2
Rotherwood Cl SW20 . . . .**179** A4
Rotherwood Rd SW15 . . .**134** D2
Rothery St N1 . . . .**234** D6
Rothesay Ave
Merton SW20 . . . .**179** A1
Mortlake SW14, TW10 . . .**132** D1
Northolt UB6 . . . .**64** B2
Rothesay Ct
4 Catford SE6 . . . .**164** D2
Grove Pk SE12 . . . .**165** B1
13 Kennington SE11 . . . .**138** C6
Rothesay Rd SE25 . . . . .**205** C5
Rothley Ct NW8 . . . .**236** C6
Rothsay Rd E7 . . . .**77** C2
Rothsay St SE1 . . . .**117** C3 **263** A5
Rothsay Wlk 19 E14 . . . .**119** C2
Rothschild Rd W4 . . . . . .**111** A3
Rothschild St SE27 . . . . .**182** D6
Rothwell Ct
2 Bromley BR1 . . . .**187** B2
4 Harrow HA1 . . . .**42** D4
Rothwell Gdns RM9 . . . . .**102** C6
Rothwell Ho TW5 . . . . . .**129** C6
Rothwell Rd RM9 . . . . . .**102** C6
Rothwell St
10 Hampstead NW1 . . . . . .**70** D1
Primrose Hill NW1 . . . . . .**230** D6
Roth Wlk N7 . . . .**72** B6
Rotten Row SW1 . .**114** D4 **247** C2
Rotterdam Dr E14 . . . . . .**120** A3
Rouel Rd
Bermondsey SE16 . . . . . .**118** A2
Bermondsey SE16 . . . . . .**118** B1
Rougemont Ave SM4 . . . .**201** C3
Roundabout Ho HA6 . . . . .**22** A2
Roundacre SW19 . . . . . .**156** D2
Roundel Cl SE4 . . . .**141** B1
Roundell Ho 14 SE21 . . . .**183** C6
Rounders Ct 7 RM10 . . . . .**81** D2
Round Gr CR0 . . . .**206** D2
Roundhay Cl SE23 . . . . . .**162** D2
Roundhedge Way EN2 . . . . .**4** B5
Round Hill SE23 . . . .**162** C1

Ros–Row **391**

Roundhill Dr EN2 . . . .**4** B1
ROUNDSHAW **220** B1
Roundshaw Ctr SM6 . . . .**220** A1
Roundtable Rd BR1 . . . . .**164** D1
Roundtree Rd HA0 . . . . . .**65** B3
Roundways HA4 . . . .**61** D5
Roundway The
Claygate KT10 . . . .**212** D2
Tottenham N17 . . . .**33** B2
Roundwood BR7 . . . .**188** D1
Roundwood Ave UB11 . . .**105** A5
Roundwood Cl HA4 . . . . . .**39** D2
Roundwood Rd NW10 . . . . .**67** D1
Rounton Rd E3 . . . .**97** C3
Rountree Ct 9 UB1 . . . . . .**85** D1
Roupell Ho 7 KT2 . . . . . .**176** B3
Roupell Rd SW2 . . . .**160** B3
Roupell St SE1 . . . . .**116** D5 **251** B3
Rousden St NW1 . . . .**71** C1
Rouse Gdns SE21 . . . . . .**183** C6
Routemaster Cl E13 . . . . .**99** B4
Routh Ct TW14 . . . .**149** B3
Routh Rd SW18 . . . .**158** C4
Routh St E6 . . . .**100** B2
Rover Ho 26 N1 . . . .**95** C6
Rowallan Ct 3 SE6 . . . . .**164** D3
Rowallan Rd
SW6 . . . .**135** A5 **264** A3
Rowallen Par RM8 . . . . . .**58** C1
Rowan N10 . . . .**31** B1
Rowan Ave E4 . . . .**35** B4
Rowan Cl Ealing W5 . . . . .**110** A4
Harrow HA7 . . . .**24** D4
Kingston u T KT3 . . . . . .**177** C1
Streatham SW16 . . . .**181** C2
Wembley HA0 . . . .**65** A5
Rowan Cres SW16 . . . . . .**181** C2
Rowan Ct
19 Camberwell SE15 . . . .**139** D5
Forest Hill SE26 . . . .**184** C6
11 Kingston u T KT2 . . . .**176** C3
Newham E13 . . . .**99** B5
Twickenham TW4 . . . . . .**151** D6
Wandsworth SW11 . . . . .**158** D5
Wimbledon SW20 . . . . . .**178** B1
Rowan Dr NW9 . . . .**46** A6
Rowan Gdns CR0 . . . . . .**221** D5
Rowan Ho 9 Bow E3 . . . . .**97** B6
Dagenham NW10 . . . .**89** C3
East Bedfont TW14 . . . . .**149** B6
Ilford IG1 . . . .**79** B3
5 Maitland Pk NW3 . . . . . .**70** D2
Sidcup DA14 . . . .**167** D1
Rowan Pl UB3 . . . .**105** D6
Rowan Pre Prep Sch
KT10 . . . .**212** C1
Rowan Prep Sch KT10 . . .**212** D1
Rowan Rd Brentford TW8 . .**131** B5
Brook Green W6 . . . .**112** D2
DA7 . . . .**147** A2
Mitcham SW16 . . . .**181** C1
West Drayton UB7 . . . . . .**104** A2
Rowans Sch The SW20 . .**178** A3
Rowans The
Ashford TW16 . . . .**171** D5
Edmonton N13 . . . .**17** A1
2 Sutton SM2 . . . .**217** D2
Rowan Terr W6 . . . .**112** D2
Rowantree Cl N21 . . . .**17** B3
Rowantree Rd
Edmonton N21 . . . .**17** B3
Enfield EN2 . . . .**4** D3
Rowan Way RM6 . . . .**58** C6
Rowan Wlk BR2 . . . .**226** B5
7 Dartmouth Pk N19 . . . . .**71** C6
Hampstead Garden Suburb
N2 . . . .**48** A4
Kensal Town W10 . . . .**91** A3
1 New Barnet EN5 . . . . . .**13** D6
Rowanwood Ave DA15 . . .**168** A3
Rowanwood Mews EN2 . . . .**4** D3
Rowberry Cl N20 . . . .**13** D3
Rowcross St SE1 . .**117** D1 **263** D2
Rowdell Rd UB5 . . . .**85** C6
Rowden Par E4 . . . .**35** C4
Rowden Park Gdns E4 . . . .**35** C4
Rowden Rd
Beckenham BR3 . . . .**185** B2
Chingford E4 . . . .**35** C4
West Ewell KT19 . . . .**215** A4
Rowditch La SW11 . . . . . .**137** A3
Rowdowns Rd RM9 . . . . . .**81** B1
Rowe Gdns IG11 . . . .**102** A5
Rowe Ho E9 . . . .**74** C2
Rowe La E9 . . . .**74** C3
Rowena Cres SW11 . . . . .**136** C3
Rowe Wlk HA2 . . . .**63** C5
Rowfant Rd SW12, SW17 . .**159** A2
Rowhill Mans 11 E5 . . . . .**74** B4
Rowhill Rd E5 . . . .**74** B4
Rowington Cl W2 . . . .**91** D2
Rowland Ave HA3 . . . .**43** C6
Rowland Ct E16 . . . .**98** D3
South Croydon CR0 . . . . .**221** C6

Rowland Gr SE26 . . . . .162 B1
Rowland Hill Almshouses **7**
TW15. . . . . .170 C5
Rowland Hill Ave N17 . . . .33 B4
Rowland Hill Ho SE1 . . . .251 C2
Rowland Pl St NW3. . . . . .70 C3
Rowlands Ave HA5. . . . . . .23 D4
Rowlands Cl Hendon NW7 . .28 A3
Highgate N6. . . . . .49 A3
Rowlands Rd RM8 . . . . . . .81 B6
Rowland Way
Ashford TW15. . . . . . . .171 B3
Merton SW19. . . . . .179 D2
Rowley Ave DA15 . . . . . .168 B4
Rowley Cl HA0. . . . . .66 B1
Rowley Ct EN1. . . . . .17 C6
Rowley Gdns N4 . . . . .51 A2
Rowley Green Rd EN5. . . .12 A6
Rowley Ho SE8 . . . . .141 C6
Rowley Ind Pk W3 . . . . . .110 D3
Rowley La EN5. . . . . .11 D6
Rowley Rd N15 . . . . .51 A4
Rowley Way NW8 . . . . . .229 A6
Rowlheys Pl UB7. . . . . . .104 A3
Rowls Rd KT1. . . . . .198 B6
Rowney Gdns RM9 . . . . . .80 C2
Rowney Rd RM9 . . . . .80 B2
Rowntree Cl NW6. . . . . . . .69 C2
Rowntree Clifford Cl **7**
E13 . . . . .99 B4
Rowntree Path **1** SE28. .124 B5
Rowntree Rd TW2. . . . . . .152 C3
Rowse Cl E15. . . . . .98 A6
Rowsham Ct HA1. . . . . . . .64 C5
Rowsley Ave NW4. . . . . . .64 C6
Rowstock **1** NW5 . . . . . .71 D2
Rowstock Gdns N7 . . . . . .71 D3
Rowton Rd SE18. . . . . . . .145 A5
ROXETH. 64 A6
Roxeth Ct **6** TW15 . . . . .170 C5
Roxeth Fst & Mid Sch
HA2 . . . . .64 B6
Roxborough Ave
Harrow HA1. . . . . .42 C2
Hounslow TW7 . . . . . . .130 D5
Roxborough Pk HA1 . . . . .42 C2
Roxborough Rd HA1 . . . . .42 B3
Roxbourne Cl UB5 . . . . . .62 D2
Roxbourne Fst & Mid Schs
HA2 . . . . .63 A6
Roxburgh Rd SE27 . . . . .182 D5
Roxburn Way HA4. . . . . . .61 D5
Roxby Pl SW6. . . . .135 C6 265 B6
ROXETH. 64 A6
Roxeth Ct **6** TW15 . . . . .170 C5
Roxeth Fst & Mid Sch
HA2 . . . . .64 B6
Roxeth Gr HA2. . . . . .63 D4
Roxeth Green Ave HA2 . . .63 D6
Roxeth Hill HA2. . . . . .64 C6
Roxeth Manor Fst & Mid
Schs HA2 . . . . .63 C5
Roxeth Mead Sch HA2 . . .64 B6
Roxford Cl TW17 . . . . . . .193 C4
Roxford Ho **2** E3 . . . . . .97 D3
Roxley Rd SE13 . . . . .163 D5
Roxton Gdns CR0. . . . . . .223 C3
Roxwell **10** NW1 . . . . . . .71 D2
Roxwell Rd Barking IG11 . .102 A5
Shepherd's Bush W12 . . .112 A4
Roxwell Trad Pk E10 . . . . .53 A2
Roxwell Way IG8 . . . . .37 C3
Roxy Ave RM6 . . . . .58 C2
Royal Academy of Dramatic
Art★ WC1 . . . . . . .93 D2 239 C4
Royal Acad of Arts★
W1 . . . . .115 C6 249 A5
Royal Acad of Dance
SW11 . . . . .266 D1
Royal Acad of Music
NW1. . . . . .238 B5
Royal Albert Hall★
SW7 . . . . .114 B4 246 C1
Royal Albert Sta E16 . . . .122 A6
Royal Albert Way E6 . . . .122 B6
Royal Arc W1 . . . . .249 A5
Royal Armouries The★
E1 . . . . .253 C5
Royal Ave SW3 . . . .114 D1 257 C2
Worcester Pk KT4. . . . .215 C6
Royal Avenue Ho SW3★ . .257 C2
Royal Ballet Sch (White
Lodge) The TW10 . . . . .155 B3
Royal Ballet Upper Sch The
WC2 . . . . .94 A1 240 B6
Royal Brompton Hospl
Chelsea SW3 . . . .114 B1 256 C2
Chelsea SW3 . . . .114 C1 257 A2
Royal Cir SE27 . . . . .160 D1
Royal Cl Deptford SE8 . . .141 B6
Hillingdon UB7 . . . . . . .82 B1
Ilford IG3 . . . . .58 A2
Locksbottom BR6 . . . . .226 D4
Putney SW19 . . . . .156 D2
Stamford Hill N16. . . . . .51 C1
Worcester Pk KT4. . . . .215 C6
Royal College of Physicians
Liby NW1 . . . . . .93 B3 238 D6
Royal College St
NW1 . . . . .93 C6 232 B6

Royal Coll of Anaesthetists
WC1 . . . . .240 C3
Royal Coll of Art
SW7 . . . . .114 B4 246 C1
Royal Coll of Art Sculpture
Sch SW11 . . . . .136 C5 267 A3
Royal Coll of Midwives
W1 . . . . .93 B2 238 C3
Royal Coll of Music
SW7 . . . . .114 B3 256 C6
Royal Coll of Obstetricians &
Gynaecologists
NW1. . . . . .92 D3 230 C1
Royal Coll of
Ophthalmologists NW1 238 A5
Royal Coll of Paediatrics &
Child Health W1. . . . . . .240 D4
Royal Coll of Pathologists
SW1 . . . . .115 D5 249 C3
Royal Coll of Physicians
NW1. . . . . .93 B3 238 D6
Royal Coll of Radiologists
W1 . . . . .238 D4
Royal Coll of Science
SW7 . . . . .114 B3 256 C6
Royal Coll of Speech
Language Therapists
SE1. . . . . .252 C2
Royal Coll of Surgeons
WC2 . . . . .94 B1 240 D2
Royal Coll of Veterinary
Surgeons SW1 . .116 A3 260 A5
Royal Connaught Apts
E16 . . . . .121 D5
Royal Courts of Justice
WC2 . . . . .94 C1 241 A1
Royal Cres Ilford IG2 . . . . .57 B3
Ruislip HA4. . . . . .39 D1
W11 . . . . .113 A5 244 A3
Royal Crescent Mews
W11. . . . . .112 D5
Royal Crest Ho SM2★ . . .217 A1
Royal Ct
City of London EC3 . . . .242 D1
Enfield EN1. . . . . .17 C5
9 Kingston u T KT2 . . .176 D3
Mottingham SE9 . . . . . .166 B3
Rotherhithe SE16 . . . . .119 B3
Ruislip HA4. . . . . .40 A2
Royal Dock Com Sch The
E16. . . . . .99 C1
Royal Docks Rd E6. . . . . .100 D2
Royal Dr N11 . . . . .31 A5
Royal Duchess Mews **18**
SW12. . . . . .159 B4
Royal Exchange★ EC3 . . .242 D1
Royal Exchange Bldgs
EC3 . . . . .242 D1
Royal Festival Hall★
SE1. . . . . .116 B5 250 D3
Royal Free Hospl NW3 . . . .70 D4
Royal Fusiliers Mus★ E1 .253 C5
Royal Gdns W7 . . . . .109 A3
Royal Geographical Society
SW7 . . . . .246 D1
Royal Hill SE10 . . . . .142 A5
Royal Hill Ct **2** SE10 . .142 A5
Royal Horticultural Society
(Lawrence Hall & Conf Ctr)
SW1 . . . . .259 C5
Royal Horticultural Society
(Lindley Hall) SW1. . . . .259 C4
Royal Hospital Chelsea The★
SW1 . . . . .115 A1 258 A1
Royal Hospital Rd
SW3. . . . . .114 D1 257 D1
Royal Hospl for Neuro-
Disability The SW15. . . .157 A5
Royal Hospl Mus★ SW3 . .257 D1
Royal Institute of British
Architects W1. . . .93 B2 238 D4
Royal Institution Mus The★
SW1 . . . . .249 A5
Royal La Hillingdon UB7. . .82 B1
Hillingdon UB8 . . . . . . .82 B3
Royal Langford Apartments
3 NW6 . . . . .91 D5
Royal London Est N17. . . . .34 B4
Royal London Est The
NW10 . . . . .89 B5
Royal London Homeopathic
Hospl WC1 . . . . .94 A2 240 B4
Royal London Hospl Mus★
E1. . . . . .96 B2
Royal London Hospl
(Whitechapel) The E1 . . .96 B2
Royal Marsden Hospl
SW3 . . . . .114 B1 256 C2
Royal Mews KT8 . . . . . . .196 C6
Royal Mews The★
SW1 . . . . .115 B3 258 D6
Royal Military Sch of Music
(Kneller Hall) TW2. . . . .152 B5
Royal Mint Pl **6** E1 . . . .118 A6
Royal Mint St E1. . .117 D3 253 D6
Royal National Orthopaedic
Hospl
Regent's Pk W1 . . .93 B3 238 D5
Stanmore HA7 . . . . .9 C2

Royal National TNE Hospl
The WC1 . . . . . . .94 B4 233 C2
Royal Naval St SE14. . . . .141 B5
Royal Oak Ct
Dagenham RM8 . . . . . . .80 C6
9 Shoreditch N1 . . . . . .95 C4
Royal Oak Mews **9**
TW11. . . . . .175 A5
Royal Oak Pl SE22. . . . . .162 B5
Royal Oak Rd Bexley DA6. .147 C1
DA6. . . . . .169 B6
5 Hackney E8. . . . . . . .74 B2
Royal Oak Sta W2. . . . . . .91 D2
Royal Oak Yd SE1 . . . . . .253 A1
Royal Observatory The★
SE10. . . . . .142 B5
Royal Opera Arc SW1 . . .249 C4
Royal Orchard Cl SW18. . .157 A4
Royal Par
Blackheath Vale SE3. . . .142 D3
Chislehurst BR7 . . . . . .189 A3
11 Dagenham RM10. . . .81 D2
Ealing W5. . . . . .88 A4
Fulham SW6 . . . . .264 A4
12 Richmond TW9 . . . .132 C4
Royal Park Prim Sch
DA14. . . . . .169 A1
Royal Pl **11** SE10 . . . . .142 A5
Royal Rd
Kennington SE17 . . . . . .138 D6
Newham E16 . . . . .99 D1
Sidcup DA14. . . . . .168 D1
Teddington TW11 . . . . .174 B5
Royal Route N9. . . . . .66 B4
Royal Russell Sch CR0 . . .222 B3
Royal Sch Hampstead The **8**
NW3. . . . . .70 B4
Royal St SE1 . . . .116 B3 260 D6
Royal Tower Lo **3** SE1. .118 A6
Royalty Ho W1. . . . . .239 C1
Royalty Mews W1. . . . . . .239 C1
Royalty Studios W11 . . . . .91 A1
Royal United Services Mus★
SW1 . . . . .250 A3
Royal Veterinary Coll
NW1. . . . . .93 D6 232 C5
Royal Victoria Pl **7** E16 .121 B5
Royal Victoria Sq E16 . . . .121 B5
Royal Victoria Sta E16. . . .121 A6
Royal Victor Pl E3. . . . . . .96 C5
Royal Wlk SW6 . . . . .219 B5
Roycraft Ave IG11 . . . . . .101 D5
Roycraft Cl
Streatham SW2 . . . . . . .160 C3
Woodford E18. . . . . .37 B2
Roydene Rd SE18 . . . . . .123 C1
Roydon Cl **7** SW11 . . . .136 D3
Roy Gdns IG2. . . . . .57 D4
Roy Gr TW12. . . . . .173 D4
Royle Cres W13 . . . . .87 A3
Roymount Ct TW2. . . . . . .152 C1
Roy Ridley Ho **6** SW4 . .137 D2
Roy Sq E14. . . . . .119 A6
Royston Ave
Carshalton SM1 . . . . . .218 B5
Chingford E4. . . . . .35 D5
Wallington SM6 . . . . . . .219 D4
Royston Cl Cranford TW5 . .128 B4
Walton-on-T KT12 . . . . .194 A1
Royston Ct
Hinchley Wood KT10. . . .212 D6
New Cross SE4. . . . . . . .141 B3
1 Newham E13. . . . . . . .99 A6
Redbridge IG1. . . . . . . .55 D3
3 Richmond TW9 . . . .132 B4
Ruislip HA5. . . . . .40 C2
Tolworth KT6 . . . . .214 C6
Royston Gdns IG1 . . . . . . .55 D3
Royston Gr HA5. . . . . .23 C4
Royston Ho
Friern Barnet N11 . . . . . .31 A4
14 SE15. . . . . .140 A6
Royston Lo SW19 . . . . . .180 A4
Royston Par IG1 . . . . .55 D3
Royston Park Rd HA5 . . . .23 C5
Royston Prim Sch SE20 . .184 D2
Royston Rd Penge SE20 . .184 D2
Richmond TW10 . . . . . .154 A6
Royston St **24** E2. . . . . . .96 C5
Roystons The KT5. . . . . . .198 D4
Rozel Ct **3** N1. . . . . .95 C6
Rozelle Ct **1** CR7. . . . . .204 C3
Rozel Rd SW4 . . . . .137 C2
Rubastic Rd UB2. . . . . . . .106 C3
Rubens Rd UB5. . . . . .84 D5
Rubens St SE6. . . . . .163 B2
Rubin Pl **14** EN3. . . . . . . .7 C6
Ruby Ct TW13. . . . . .149 D1
Ruby Rd E17. . . . . .53 C6
Ruby St SE15. . . . . .140 B6
Stonebridge NW10. . . . .67 A1
Ruby Triangle SE15. . . . . .140 B6
Ruckholt Cl E10. . . . . .75 D5
Ruckholt Rd London E10. . .75 D5
Temple Mills E9, E10. . . .75 C4
Rucklidge Ave NW10. . . . .90 A5
Rudall Cres NW3. . . . . . . .70 B4
Rudbeck Ho **11** SE15 . .140 A5
Ruddington Cl E5. . . . . . . .75 A4
Ruddock Cl HA8 . . . . .27 A3

Ruddstreet Cl SE18 . . . . .123 A2
Rudge Ho **1** SE16 . . . . .118 A3
Rudgwick Terr
NW8 . . . . .92 C6 230 B5
Rudhall Ho **4** SW2 . . . .160 C5
Rudland Rd DA7 . . . . .147 D2
Rudloe Rd SW12 . . . . . . .159 C4
Rudolf Pl SW8 . . . . .270 B5
Rudolph Ct SE22 . . . . . . .162 B4
Rudolph Rd E13 . . . . .98 D5
Paddington NW6 . . . . . .91 C5
Rudstone Ho **10** E3 . . . . .97 D4
Rudyard Ct SE1. . . . . . . .252 D1
Rudyard Gr NW7 . . . . .27 A4
Ruegg Ho **5** SE18 . . . . .144 C6
Ruffetts Cl CR2 . . . . .222 B1
Ruffetts The CR2. . . . . . .222 B1
Ruffle Cl UB7 . . . . .104 B4
Rufford Cl HA3 . . . . .43 A3
Rufford St N1. . . . . .94 A6 233 B6
Rufford Street Mews N1 . .72 A1
Rufford Twr **5** W3 . . . . .110 D5
Rufforth Ct **1** NW9 . . . . .27 C2
Rufus Bsns Ctr SW18. . . .157 D2
Rufus Cl HA4 . . . . .63 A5
Rufus Ho SE1. . . . . .263 D6
Rufus St N1. . . . . .95 C4
Rugby Ave Edmonton N9. . .17 D3
Northolt UB6 . . . . .64 B2
Wembley HA0. . . . . .65 C4
Rugby Cl HA1. . . . . .42 C5
Rugby Gdns RM9 . . . . . . .80 C2
Rugby Mans W14 . . . . . .254 B4
Rugby Rd Bedford Pk W4. . .111 C4
Dagenham RM9 . . . . . . .80 C2
Queensbury NW9 . . . . . .44 D5
Twickenham TW1, TW2,
TW7 . . . . .152 C5
Rugby St WC1 . . . . .94 B3 240 C5
Rugg St E14 . . . . .119 C6
Rugless Ho **2** E14 . . . . .120 A4
Rugmere **4** NW1 . . . . . . .71 A1
RUISLIP 39 B2
Ruislip Cl UB6 . . . . .85 B3
RUISLIP COMMON 39 B4
Ruislip Ct HA4. . . . . .61 D6
RUISLIP GARDENS 61 D5
Ruislip Gardens Prim Sch
HA4 . . . . .61 D4
Ruislip Gardens Sta HA4 . .62 A4
Ruislip High Sch HA4 . . . .62 A5
Ruislip Lido★ HA4, HA5. . .39 B5
Ruislip Lido Rly★ HA4. . . .39 B5
RUISLIP MANOR 40 A1
Ruislip Manor Sta HA4 . . . .40 A1
Ruislip Rd UB6, UB5. . . . .85 C4
Ruislip Rd E
Ealing UB6, W7 . . . . . . .86 D3
Greenford UB6. . . . . . . .86 B3
Ruislip St SW17 . . . . .180 D6
Ruislip Sta HA4. . . . . .39 D1
Rumball Ho **14** SE5. . . .139 C5
Rumbold Rd
SW6. . . . . .135 D5 265 D3
Rum Cl E1. . . . . .118 C6
Rumford Ho SE1. . . . . . . .262 A5
Rumsey Cl TW12 . . . . . . .173 B4
Rumsey Rd SW9 . . . . . . .138 B2
Runacres Ct SE17 . . . . . .262 A1
Runbury Circ NW9 . . . . . .67 B6
Runcorn Cl N17. . . . . .52 B5
Runcorn Pl W11 . . . . .244 A6
Rundell Cres NW4 . . . . . .46 B4
Rundell Twr SW8. . . . . . .270 C2
Runes Cl CR4 . . . . .202 C5
Runnelfield HA1 . . . . .64 C5
Running Horse Yd **12**
TW8. . . . . .132 A6
Runnymede SW19 . . . . . .180 B2
Runnymede Cl TW2 . . . . .151 D4
Runnymede Cres SW16 . .182 A2
Runnymede Ct
Roehampton SW15. . . . .156 A3
1 Wallington SM6. . . . .219 B2
Runnymede Gdns
Greenford UB6. . . . . . . .86 C5
Twickenham TW2 . . . . .151 D4
Runnymede Ho
Hackney E9. . . . . .75 A4
Richmond TW10 . . . . . .154 A6
Runnymede Rd TW2 . . . .151 D5
Runway The HA4. . . . . . . .62 C3
Rupack St **3** SE16 . . . . .118 C4
Rupert Ave HA9 . . . . .66 A3
Rupert Ct W1. . . . . .249 C6
Rupert Gdns SW9. . . . . . .138 D3
Rupert Ho SE11. . . . . . . .261 B3
8 Upper Holloway N19 . . .71 D5
Rupert Rd Bedford Pk W4. .111 C3
Paddington NW6 . . . . . .91 B5
Upper Holloway N19 . . . .71 D6
Rupert St W1 . . . . .115 D4 249 C6
Rural Way SW16 . . . . . . .181 B3
Rusbridge Cl E8 . . . . .74 A3
Ruscoe Ho **12** SW27 . . .182 D5
Ruscoe Rd E16 . . . . .98 D1
Ruscombe Way TW14 . . .149 D4
Rusham Rd SW12 . . . . . .158 D4
Rushbridge Cl CR0. . . . . .205 A3
Rushbrook Cres E17 . . . . .35 B2

Rushbrook Ho **20** SW8 . . .137 D3
Rushbrook Rd SE9 . . . . . .167 A2
Rushbury Ct **4** TW12. . . .173 C2
Rushby Ct SW4 . . . . .270 A1
Rush Common Mews **18**
SW2. . . . . .160 B4
Rushcroft Rd
Brixton SW2, SW9 . . . . .138 C1
Chingford E4. . . . . .35 D3
Rush Croft Sch E4 . . . . . . .35 D3
Rushcutters Ct **18** SE16. .119 A2
Rushden Cl SE19. . . . . . .183 B3
Rushdene SE2. . . . . .124 D3
Rushdene Ave EN4. . . . . .14 C4
Rushdene Cl UB5 . . . . . . .84 C5
Rushdene Cres UB5. . . . . .84 C4
Rushdene Rd HA5 . . . . . . .40 D3
Rushden Gdns Ilford IG5. . .56 C6
Mill Hill NW7. . . . . .28 C4
Rushen Wlk SM5. . . . . . .202 B1
Rushet Rd BR5. . . . . .190 A1
Rushett Cl KT7. . . . . .197 B1
Rushett Rd KT7 . . . . .197 B2
Rushey Cl KT3 . . . . .199 B5
Rushey Gn SE6 . . . . .163 D4
Rushey Green Prim Sch
SE6. . . . . .163 D3
Rushey Hill EN2. . . . . .4 B1
Rushey Mead SE4. . . . . .163 C6
Rushford Rd SE4. . . . . . .163 B5
Rush Green Rd RM7, RM8,
RM10. . . . . .59 D1
Rushgrove Ave NW9. . . . . .45 D5
Rushgrove Ct NW9. . . . . . .45 C4
Rushgrove St SE18. . . . . .122 B2
Rush Hill Mews **3**
SW11. . . . . .137 A2
Rush Hill Rd SW11 . . . . . .137 A2
Rushlake Ho **3** SW11 . . .137 A3
Rushley Cl BR2 . . . . .226 A4
Rushman Villas KT3 . . . . .199 D5
Rushmead
5 Bethnal Green E2 . . . .96 B4
Richmond TW10 . . . . . .153 B1
Rushmead Cl CR0. . . . . . .221 D4
Rushmere Ct KT4 . . . . . .216 A6
Rushmere Ho **2** SW15 . .156 A3
Rushmere Pl SW19 . . . . .178 D5
Rushmon Pl SM3 . . . . . . .217 A2
Rushmoor Cl HA5. . . . . . .40 B5
Rushmore Cl BR1. . . . . . .210 A6
Rushmore Cres **9** E5 . . .74 D4
Rushmore Ho
9 Kentish Town N7 . . . .71 D3
W14 . . . . .254 B5
Rushmore Prim Sch **12**
E5. . . . . .74 D4
Rushmore Rd
Clapton Pk E5. . . . . . . .74 D4
Hackney E5. . . . . .75 A4
Rusholme Ave RM10 . . . . .81 C5
Rusholme Gr SE19 . . . . .183 C5
Rusholme Rd SW15 . . . . .157 A5
Rushout Ave HA3. . . . . . . .43 B3
Rush The SW20 . . . . .179 B2
Rushton Ho **26** SW8 . . . .137 D3
Rushton St N1 . . . .95 B5 235 D4
Rushworth St
SE1 . . . . .116 D4 251 D1
Rushy Meadow La SM5. . .218 C5
Rushy Meadow Prim Sch
SM5. . . . . .218 C5
Ruskin Ave DA16. . . . . . .146 A3
Feltham TW14 . . . . .149 D5
Plashet E12. . . . . .78 A2
Richmond TW9 . . . . . . .132 C5
Ruskin Cl NW11. . . . . .47 D3
Ruskin Ct Herne Hill SE5. . .139 B2
SE9. . . . . .166 B5
Southgate N21 . . . . .16 B4
Ruskin Dr
North Cheam KT4 . . . . .216 C6
Orpington BR6 . . . . . . .227 C5
Welling DA16 . . . . .146 A2
Ruskin Gdns Ealing W5. . . .87 D3
Harrow HA3. . . . . .44 B5
Ruskin Gr DA16. . . . . . . .146 A3
Ruskin Ho SW1. . . . . . . .259 D3
Ruskin Par CR0. . . . . . . .221 B3
Ruskin Park Ho SE5. . . . .139 B2
Ruskin Rd
Belvedere DA17. . . . . . .125 C2
Croydon CR0. . . . . .220 D6
Isleworth TW7 . . . . .130 D2
Southall UB1. . . . . .107 A6
Tottenham N17. . . . . . . .33 D2
Wallington SM5 . . . . . .219 A3
Ruskin Way SW19. . . . . .180 B2
Ruskin Wlk BR2 . . . . .210 B3
Edmonton N9 . . . . .18 A2
Herne Hill SE24 . . . . . .161 A6
Rusland Ave BR6. . . . . . .227 B5
Rusland Hts HA1. . . . . . . .42 C5
Rusland Park Rd HA1 . . . .42 C5
Rusper Cl
Cricklewood NW2. . . . . .68 C5
Stanmore HA7 . . . . .25 C6
Rusper Ct SW9 . . . . .138 A3
Rusper Rd Dagenham RM9. .80 C2
Tottenham N17, N22. . . . .51 A4

Russel Cl BR3. . . . . .208 A6
Russel Ct N14 . . . . .15 D6
Russell Ave N22 . . . . .32 D1
Russell Cl
Bexleyheath DA7 . . . . . . .147 C1
Chiswick W4. . . . . .133 D6
Greenwich SE7. . . . . .143 C5
Ruislip HA4. . . . . .62 C6
Stonebridge NW10. . . . . . .67 A1
Russell Ct
Battersea SW11. . . . . . . .268 B1
Bloomsbury WC1 . . . . . . .240 A5
Bromley BR1. . . . . .186 D3
12 New Barnet EN5 . . . . .2 A1
5 Peckham SE15. . . . . . . .140 B3
St James SW1 . . . . .249 B3
Streatham SW16 . . . . . . .182 B5
Surbiton KT6. . . . . .198 A2
Wallington SM6 . . . . .219 C3
4 Walthamstow E10. . . . . .53 D2
Wembley HA0. . . . . .66 A1
Russell Gdns
East Barnet N20. . . . . .14 C2
Ilford IG2 . . . . .57 B2
Richmond TW10 . . . . .153 C2
Temple Fortune NW11. . . . .47 A3
W14 . . . . .113 A3 254 A6
West Drayton UB7 . . . . . .104 C1
Russell Gdns Mews
W14. . . . . .113 A3 254 A6
Russell Gr
33 Brixton SW9 . . . . .138 C4
Edgware NW7 . . . . .27 C6
Russell Ho 21 Poplar E14 . .97 C1
SW1 . . . . .259 A2
Russell Kerr Cl W4. . . . . .133 A5
Russell La N20. . . . . .14 D2
Russell Lo 5 Chingford E4. .20 A4
SE1 . . . . .262 C6
Russell Mans WC1 . . . . . .240 B4
Russell Mead HA3 . . . . . . .24 D2
Russell Par NW11. . . . . . . .47 A3
Russell Pickering Ho 2
SW4. . . . . .138 A2
Russell Pl Hampstead NW3 .70 C3
Rotherhithe SE16. . . . . . . .119 A3
Russell Prim Sch The
TW10 . . . . .153 D3
Russell Rd Bowes Pk N13 . .32 B4
Buckhurst Hill IG9 . . . . . . .21 C3
Chingford Hatch E4 . . . . . . .35 B6
Crouch End N8 . . . . .49 D3
East Barnet N20. . . . . .14 C2
Enfield EN1. . . . . .5 D5
Leyton E10 . . . . .53 D3
Merton SW19 . . . . .179 C3
Mitcham CR4 . . . . .202 C6
Newham E16 . . . . .99 B1
Northolt UB5 . . . . .64 A3
Shepperton TW17. . . . . . . .193 A2
Tottenham N15. . . . . .51 C4
Twickenham TW1, TW2. . . .152 D5
W14 . . . . .113 A3 53 B6
Walthamstow E17 . . . . .53 C3
Walton-on-T KT12 . . . . . . .194 A3
West Hendon NW9. . . . . . . .45 D3
Russell Sq WC1 . . . . .94 A3 240 A5
Russell Square Ho WC1 . .240 A5
Russell Square Mans
WC1. . . . . .240 B4
Russell Square Sta
WC1. . . . . .94 A3 240 A5
Russell St WC2 . . . .116 A6 250 B6
Russell's Wharf 2 W9 . . . .91 B3
Russell Way SM1. . . . . . . .217 D3
Russell Wlk 4 TW10 . . . . .154 B5
Russell Yd SW15 . . . . .135 A1
Russet Ave TW16, TW17 . .193 C6
Russet Cres N7 . . . . .72 B1
Russet Ct 6 Barnet EN4. . . .2 C1
Dollis Hill NW2 . . . . .68 B5
Feltham TW13 . . . . .149 C1
Russet Dr CR0. . . . . .207 A1
Russet Ho TW3 . . . . .129 B1
Russet House Sch EN1 . . . . .6 B4
Russets Cl E4. . . . . .36 B6
Russettings 1 HA5 . . . . . . .23 B3
Russett Way SE13. . . . . . . .141 D3
Rusthall Ave W4 . . . . .111 B3
Rusthall Cl CR0. . . . . .206 C3
Rusthall Mans 3 W4. . . . .111 B2
Rustic Ave SW16. . . . . . . .181 B3
Rustic Pl HA0. . . . . .65 D4
Rustic Wlk E16 . . . . .99 B1
Rustington Wlk SM4 . . . . .201 B2
Ruston Ave KT5. . . . . .198 D2
Ruston Gdns N14 . . . . .15 A5
Ruston Mews W11 . . . . . . .91 A1
Ruston Rd SE18. . . . . .122 A3
Ruston St E3 . . . . .97 B6
Rust Sq SE5 . . . . .139 B5
Rutford Rd SW16 . . . . . . .182 A5
Ruth Cl HA7 . . . . .44 B5
Ruth Ct 16 E3. . . . . .97 A5

Rutherford Cl
Hillingdon UB8 . . . . .82 B3
Sutton SM2. . . . . .218 B2
Rutherford Ct
Mitcham SW19. . . . . .180 B3
Southgate N21. . . . . .16 B6
Rutherford Ho
12 Bethnal Green E1 . . . . . .96 B3
Teddington TW11. . . . . . . .174 D5
4 Wembley HA9 . . . . .67 A5
Rutherford Sch CR2. . . . . .221 D3
Rutherford St
SW1. . . . . .115 D2 259 C4
Rutherford Twr 8 UB1. . . .85 D1
Rutherford Way
Bushey WD23 . . . . .8 C3
Wembley HA9. . . . . .66 C4
Rutherglen Rd SE2. . . . . . .146 A6
Rutherwyke Cl KT17. . . . . .216 A2
Ruth Ho W10 . . . . .91 A3
Ruthin Cl NW9. . . . . .45 C3
Ruthin Rd SE3 . . . . .143 A6
Ruthven St E9 . . . . .96 D6
Rutland Ave DA15. . . . . . .168 A4
Rutland Cl
Chessington KT9 . . . . .214 B2
DA5. . . . . .168 D3
Mitcham SW19. . . . . .180 C3
Mortlake SW14. . . . . .133 A2
Rutland Ct 15 Acton W3. . .88 C1
Chislehurst BR7 . . . . .188 C2
Enfield EN3. . . . . .18 B6
Herne Hill SE5 . . . . .139 B1
Sidcup SE9 . . . . .167 A2
SW7 . . . . .247 B1
Twickenham TW2 . . . . .152 C1
Richmond TW10 . . . . .154 A3
Rutland Gate
Beckenham BR2 . . . . .208 D5
Belvedere DA17 . . . . .125 D1
SW7 . . . . .114 C4 247 B1
Rutland Gate Mews SW7 247 A1
Rutland Gdns
Dagenham RM8 . . . . .80 C3
Ealing W13 . . . . .87 A2
South Croydon CR0. . . . . .221 C4
Stoke Newington N4. . . . . . .51 A3
SW7 . . . . .114 C4 247 B1
Rutland Gdns Mews
SW7 . . . . .247 B1
Rutland Gr W6. . . . . .112 B1
Rutland Ho Edgware HA8. . .26 B4
6 Northolt UB5 . . . . .63 C2
10 Penge SE20. . . . . .184 C2
10 Putney SW15. . . . . . . .156 C4
Tolworth KT6 . . . . .198 C1
W8 . . . . .255 C5
15 Woolwich SE18. . . . . . .122 B2
Rutland Lo
Forest Hill SE6 . . . . .163 B2
Teddington TW11. . . . . . . .174 C5
Rutland Mews 21 NW8 . . . .91 D6
Rutland Mews E SW7 . . . .257 B6
Rutland Mews S SW7 . . . .257 A6
Rutland Mews W SW7 . . . .257 A6
Rutland Park Gdns 1
NW2 . . . . .68 C2
Rutland Park Mans 2
NW2 . . . . .68 C2
Rutland Pk
Forest Hill SE6 . . . . .163 B2
Willesden NW2. . . . . .68 C2
Rutland Pl Bushey WD23 . . . .8 B3
EC1. . . . . .241 D4
Rutland Rd Forest Gate E7 . .77 D1
Harrow HA1. . . . . .42 A3
Hayes UB3 . . . . .105 B2
Ilford IG1. . . . . .78 D5
Mitcham SW19. . . . . .180 C3
South Hackney E9. . . . . . . .96 D6
Twickenham TW2 . . . . .152 B2
Walthamstow E17 . . . . .53 C3
Wanstead E11 . . . . .55 B4
Rutland St SW7 . . . . .257 B6
Rutland Studios NW10 . . . . .90 A4
Rutland Wlk SE6. . . . . . . .163 B2
Rutley Cl SE11. . . . . .138 D6
Rutlish Rd SW19 . . . . .179 C2
Rutlish Sch SW20. . . . . . . .179 B1
Rutter Gdns CR4 . . . . .202 B5
Rutters Cl UB7. . . . . .104 C4
Rutt's Terr SE14. . . . . .140 D4
Rutts The WD23 . . . . .8 B3
Ruvigny Gdns SW15. . . . . .134 D2
Ruvigny Mans 7 SW15. . . .134 D2
Ruxbury Ct TW15 . . . . .148 A1
RUXLEY 191 A3
Ruxley Cl
Chessington KT19 . . . . . . .214 D3
Sidcup DA14. . . . . .191 A4
Ruxley Cnr DA14. . . . . . . .191 A4
Ruxley Corner Ind Est
DA14. . . . . .190 D4
Ruxley Cres KT10. . . . . . . .213 B1
Ruxley Ct KT15. . . . . .215 A3
Ruxley Gdns TW17. . . . . . .193 A4
Ruxley La KT19 . . . . .215 B3
Ruxley Mews KT19 . . . . . .214 D3

Ruxley Ridge KT10. . . . . . .213 A1
Ryall's Ct N20 . . . . .14 D1
Ryan Cl Ruislip HA4. . . . . . .40 B1
SE9. . . . . .143 C1
Ryan Ct SW16. . . . . .182 A3
Ryan Dr TW8 . . . . .131 A6
Ryan Ho 8 HA1. . . . . .42 D4
Ryarsh Cres BR6. . . . . . . .227 C4
Rycott Path SE22 . . . . . . .162 A4
Rycroft Way N17. . . . . .51 D6
Rycullf Sq SE3. . . . . .142 D3
Rydal Cl NW4. . . . . .29 A2
Rydal Cres UB6. . . . . .87 C5
Rydal Ct Edgware HA8. . . . .26 B5
Wembley HA9. . . . . .44 A2
Rydal Dr DA7 . . . . .147 C4
West Wickham BR4 . . . . . .224 C6
Rydal Gdns
Kingsbury NW9 . . . . .45 C4
Kingston u T SW15 . . . . . .177 C5
Twickenham TW2, TW3. . . .151 D5
Wembley HA9. . . . . .43 C1
Rydal Ho 23 SW8. . . . . . . .137 D3
Rydal Lo N17. . . . . .34 A3
Rydal Rd SW16 . . . . .181 D6
Rydal Water NW1. . . . . . . .232 A1
Rydal Way Enfield EN3 . . . . .18 C5
Ruislip HA4. . . . . .62 C4
Ryde Ho N1. . . . . .91 C6
Rydens Ho SE9. . . . . .165 C1
Rydens Rd KT12 . . . . .194 D1
Ryde Pl TW1. . . . . .153 D5
Ryder Cl BR1. . . . . .187 B5
Ryder Ct Leyton E10. . . . . .75 D6
SW1 . . . . .249 B4
Ryder Dr SE16. . . . . .118 B1
Ryder St SW1. . . . . .249 B4
Ryder's Terr NW8 . . . .92 A5 229 A4
Ryderd Yd SW1. . . . . .249 B4
Ryde Vale Rd SW12. . . . . .159 C2
Rydon Mews SW19. . . . . . .178 C3
Rydons Cl SE9 . . . . .144 A2
Rydon St N1. . . . . .235 B6
Rydston Cl 2 N7 . . . . .72 B1
Rye Cl DA5. . . . . .169 D5
Ryecotes Mead SE21. . . . .161 C3
Ryecroft Ave TW2 . . . . . . .151 D3
Ryecroft Cres EN5 . . . . . . .12 B6
Ryecroft Rd BR5. . . . . .211 B3
Lewisham SE13 . . . . .164 A6
South Norwood SW16. . . . .182 C4
Ryecroft St SW6 . . . .135 D4 265 C1
Rye Ct BR3 . . . . .185 B2
Ryedale SE22 . . . . .162 B5
Ryedale Ct 7 TW12 . . . . . .173 C2
Ryefield Ave UB10 . . . . .60 D1
Ryefield Cres HA5, HA6 . . . .22 A1
Ryefield Ct HA6. . . . . .22 A1
Ryefield Jun & Inf Sch
UB10. . . . . .83 B6
Ryefield Path 7 SW15 . . . .156 A3
Ryefield Rd SE19. . . . . . . .183 A4
Ryegates 2 SE15 . . . . .140 B3
Ryehill Ct 3 SW13 . . . . . . .199 D2
Rye Hill Pk SE15 . . . . .140 C5
Rye Ho 17 SE16 . . . . .118 C4
Rye La SE15. . . . . .140 A3
Ryeland Cl UB7. . . . . .82 A1
Ryelands Cres SE12 . . . . . .165 C5
Ryelands Ct SE25 . . . . . . .206 B4
Rye Lane Mkt* SE15. . . . . .140 A3
Rye Oak Sch 7 SE15. . . . . .140 B2
Rye Rd SE15. . . . . .140 B6
Rye The N14 . . . . .15 C4
Rye Way HA8 . . . . .26 B4
Rye Wlk SW15 . . . . .156 C6
Ryfold Rd SW19. . . . . .157 C1
Ryhope Rd N11. . . . . .31 B6
Ryland Cl TW13 . . . . .171 D6
Rylandes Rd NW2. . . . . . . .68 A5
Ryland Ho 11 SW16 . . . . . .181 C5
Ryland Rd NW5. . . . . .71 B2
Rylett Cres W12 . . . . .111 D3
Rylett Rd W12 . . . . .111 D3
Rylston Rd Edmonton N13. . .17 B1
SW6. . . . . .135 B6 264 C5
Rylton Ho KT12 . . . . .194 A1
Rymer Rd CR0 . . . . .205 C2
Rymer St SE24 . . . . .160 D5
Rymill St E16 . . . . .122 C5
Rysbrack St SW1 . . . . .257 C6
Rythe Cl Chessington KT9 . .213 C1
Claygate KT10. . . . . .212 C3
Rythe Ct KT7 . . . . .197 A2
Rythe Ho 7 BR1. . . . . .186 B5
Rythe Rd KT10. . . . . .212 C3

S

Saatchi Gallery Duke of
York's HQ*
SW3 . . . . .114 D1 257 D2
Sabah Ct TW15 . . . . .170 C6
Sabbarton St 9 E16 . . . . . . .98 D1
Sabella Ct E3. . . . . .97 B5
Sabine Rd SW11 . . . . .137 A2

Sable Cl TW4. . . . . .128 C2
Sable Ct 3 KT3. . . . . .199 C4
Sable St N1 . . . . .72 C1
Sach Rd E5. . . . . .74 B6
Sacketts Ho 24 SW9 . . . . .138 C4
Sackville Cl HA2. . . . . .64 B5
Sackville Gdns IG1 . . . . . . .56 B1
Sackville Ho Hornsey N8 . . .50 A5
18 Streatham SW16. . . . . .160 A1
Sackville Rd SM2 . . . . .217 C1
Sackville St W1 . . . . .115 C6 249 B5
Sacred Heart High Sch 9
W6 . . . . .112 C2
Sacred Heart Language Coll
HA3 . . . . .24 C1
Sacred Heart Prim Sch,
Battersea SW11 . . . . .136 C3
Sacred Heart RC Prim Sch
East Barnet N20. . . . . .14 C2
Putney SW15. . . . . .156 A6
Ruislip HA4. . . . . .61 C6
Teddington TW11. . . . . . . .175 B3
West Barnes KT3 . . . . . . .200 A5
Sacred Heart RC Sec Sch 10
SE5. . . . . .139 A4
Sacred Heart Sch N7 . . . . .72 B3
Saddlebrook Pk TW16. . . . .171 C3
Saddlers 21 Barnet EN5 . . . .11 B5
Borehamwood WD6 . . . . . .11 B5
Pinner HA5. . . . . .23 C5
Saddlers Mews SW8 . . . . .270 B2
Teddington KT1. . . . . .175 C2
Wembley HA0. . . . . .64 D4
Saddlers Path WD6 . . . . . . .11 B6
Saddlescombe Way N12 . . .29 C5
Sadler Ho 17 Bromley E3 . . .97 B4
EC1. . . . . .234 C2
Sadlers Ho EN1. . . . . .17 C6
Sadlers Ride KT8. . . . . . . .174 A1
Saffron Ave E14 . . . . .120 B6
Saffron Cl
East Bedfont TW14. . . . . . .149 A4
10 Kingsland N1. . . . . .73 B2
Stratford E15 . . . . .98 C5
Saffron Hill EC1 . . . . .94 C2 241 B4
Saffron Ho 6 TW9 . . . . . . .132 D4
Saffron St EC1. . . . . .241 B4
Saffron Way KT6. . . . . .197 D1
Saffron Wharf 7 . . . . .253 D2
Sage Cl 7 E6. . . . . .100 B2
Sage Mews SE22. . . . . . . .161 D6
Sage St E1. . . . . .118 C6
Sage Way WC1. . . . . .233 C1
Sage Yd KT6. . . . . .198 B1
Sahara Ct UB1. . . . . .107 A6
Saigasso Cl E16. . . . . .99 D1
Sailacre Ho 10 SE10. . . . . .120 D1
Sail Ct 10 E14. . . . . .120 B6
Sailmakers Ct SW6 . . . . . .136 A2
Sail St SE11 . . . . . .116 B2 260 D4
Saimet 3 NW9. . . . . .27 D2
Sainfoin Rd SW17. . . . . . . .159 A2
Sainsbury Rd SE19. . . . . . .183 C5
St Agatha's Dr KT2 . . . . . .176 B4
St Agatha's Gr SM5 . . . . . .202 D1
St Agatha's RC Prim Sch
KT2. . . . . .176 B4
St Agnes Ct E9. . . . . .96 C6
St Agnes Pl SE11. . . . . . . .138 D6
St Agnes RC Prim Sch
15 E3 . . . . .97 D4
London NW2. . . . . .69 A5
St Aidan Ct IG11 . . . . .102 B5
St Aidan's Prim Sch N4 . . . .50 C2
St Aidan's RC Prim Sch
IG1. . . . . .57 B1
St Aidan's Rd
East Dulwich SE22 . . . . . .162 B6
West Ealing W13 . . . . .109 B4
St Aidan's Ct W13. . . . . . .109 C4
St Albans Ave
Bedford Pk W4 . . . . .111 B3
Feltham TW13 . . . . .172 D5
St Alban's Ave E6. . . . . . . .100 B1
St Alban's CE Prim Sch
EC1. . . . . .94 C2 241 A4
St Alban's Cl NW11. . . . . . .47 C1
St Albans Cres N22 . . . . . . .32 A2
St Albans Gdns TW11. . . . .175 A5
St Alban's Gr
Carshalton SM5 . . . . .202 D1
W8 . . . . .113 D3 255 D6
St Albans Ho 2 SW16. . . . .182 C6
St Albans La NW11. . . . . . .47 C1
St Albans Mans W8 . . . . . .255 D6
St Alban's Pl N1 . . . . .94 D6 234 C5
St Alban's RC Aided Prim Sch
KT8. . . . . .196 A4
St Albans Rd Barnet EN5 . . .1 A3
Cheam SM1 . . . . .217 B4
Ilford IG3 . . . . .57 D2
Kingston u T KT2. . . . . . . .176 A4
St Alban's Rd
Dagenham RM10 . . . . .89 C6

St Alban's Rd *continued*
Dartmouth Pk NW5 . . . . . . .71 B5
Woodford IG8. . . . . .37 A3
St Alban's St SW1. . . . . . .249 C5
St Albans Studios W8 . . . .255 D6
St Albans Terr W6 . . . . . . .264 A6
St Alfege Pas SE10. . . . . . .142 A6
St Alfege Rd SE7. . . . . . . .143 D1
St Alfege with St Peter's CE
Prim Sch SE10. . . . . .142 A6
St Aloysius Convent
NW1. . . . . .93 D4 232 C2
St Aloysius RC Coll 9
N19. . . . . .49 C1
St Aloysius RC Inf Sch
NW1. . . . . .93 D4 232 C2
St Aloysius RC Jun Sch
NW1. . . . . .93 D4 232 C2
St Alphage Ct NW9. . . . . . .45 B6
St Alphage Gdn EC2. . . . . .242 B3
St Alphage Highwalk
EC2. . . . . .242 B3
St Alphage Wlk HA8. . . . . . .27 A1
St Alphege Rd N9. . . . . .18 C4
St Alphonsus Rd SW4 . . . .137 D1
St Amunds Cl SE6. . . . . . .185 C4
St Andrew & St Francis CE
Prim Sch 6 NW2. . . . . . . .68 A2
St Andrews Ave HA0. . . . . .65 A4
St Andrew's (Barnsbury)
Prim Sch N1 . . . . .94 B6 233 D6
St Andrew's CE Prim Sch
Enfield EN1. . . . . .5 C3
Osidge N14. . . . . .15 D1
St Andrew's CE VA Prim Sch
N20. . . . . .13 B2
St Andrews Chambers
W1. . . . . .239 B2
St Andrews Cl
25 Bermondsey SE16. . . . .118 B1
Erith SE28. . . . . .102 D1
Long Ditton KT7 . . . . .197 B1
Ruislip HA4. . . . . .62 D6
Stanmore HA7 . . . . .25 C1
Wimbledon SW19 . . . . . . .179 D4
St Andrew's Cl
Dollis Hill NW2 . . . . .68 B5
2 Hounslow TW7 . . . . . . .130 C4
North Finchley N12. . . . . . .30 A6
Upper Halliford TW17. . . . .193 B5
St Andrews Ct W4 . . . . . . .133 A4
St Andrew's Ct
Carshalton SM5 . . . . .218 C5
2 Clapham Hill E17. . . . . . .35 A1
Kingston u T KT3. . . . . . . .199 D6
2 Wandsworth SW18 . . . . .158 A2
St Andrew's Dr HA7 . . . . . .25 C2
St Andrew's Gr N16. . . . . . .51 B1
St Andrew's Greek Sch
NW1. . . . . .71 C2
St Andrew's High Sch
CR0. . . . . .220 D4
St Andrew's Hill
EC4. . . . . .94 D1 241 D1
St Andrews Ho
11 Bermondsey SE16. . . . .118 B3
Bromley BR1. . . . . .187 A6
St Andrews Mans 9 E5 . .74 B4
St Andrew's Mans W1. . . . .238 A3
St Andrews Mews
Greenwich SE3 . . . . .143 A5
4 Streatham SW12. . . . . . .159 D3
St Andrew's Mews N16. . . . .51 C1
St Andrew's Pl NW1. . . . . .238 D6
St Andrew's Prim Sch 33
SW9 . . . . .138 A3
St Andrews RC Prim Sch
SW16 . . . . .182 A5
St Andrews Rd
Carshalton SM5 . . . . .218 C5
DA14. . . . . .168 D1
Dagenham W3 . . . . .89 C1
Higham Hill E17 . . . . .35 A1
Ponders End N9 . . . . .18 C4
Uxbridge UB10 . . . . .60 B1
Welsh Harp NW9 . . . . .45 B1
St Andrew's Rd
3 Croydon CR0. . . . . .221 A4
Enfield EN1. . . . . .5 B2
Hanwell W7 . . . . .108 C4
Hillingdon UB10 . . . . .82 B6
Leytonstone E11. . . . . .54 C3
Newham E13 . . . . .99 B4
Redbridge IG1 . . . . .56 B2
Surbiton KT6. . . . . .197 D3
Temple Fortune NW11. . . . .47 B3
W14 . . . . .264 B6
Willesden NW2. . . . . .69 A3
St Andrew's & St Mark's CE
Jun Sch KT1. . . . . .197 D4
St Andrew's Sq
Notting Hill W11 . . . . .91 A1
Surbiton KT6. . . . . .197 D3
St Andrew St EC4 . . . . . . .241 B3
St Andrew's Terr WD19. . . . .22 C5
St Andrew's Twr UB1. . . . .108 A6

St Andrews Way E3 . . . .**97** D3
St Andrew's Wharf SE1. . **253** D2
St Angela's & St
Bonaventure's Sixth Form
Ctr E7 . . . .**77** B2
St Angela's Ursuline Sch
E7 . . . .**77** B2
St Anna Rd EN5 . . . .**12** D6
St Anne RC Prim Sch 18
E1 . . . .**96** A3
St Annes Catholic High Sch
N13 . . . .**32** C6
St Anne's CE Prim Sch 6
SW18 . . . .**157** B3
St Annes Cl WD19 . . . .**22** C2
St Anne's Cl N6 . . . .**71** A5
St Annes Ct 8 SM2 . . . .**217** D2
St Anne's Ct
Kensal Rise NW6 . . . .**91** A6
W1 . . . .**239** C1
St Anne's Flats NW1 . . . . . .**232** C2
St Annes Gdns NW10 . . . .**88** B4
St Anne's Independent PRU
CR0 . . . .**205** B3
St Anne's Pas E14. . . . .**97** B1
St Anne's RC High Sch for
Girls EN2. . . . .**5** B1
St Anne's RC Prim Sch
SE11. . . . .**138** B6 **270** C6
St Anne's Rd Leyton E11. . . . .**76** B6
Wembley HA0. . . . .**65** D3
St Anne's Row E14. . . . .**97** B1
St Anne St E14. . . . .**97** B1
St Anne's Trad Est 28 E14. .**97** B1
St Ann's IG11. . . . .**101** A6
St Ann's CE Prim Sch
N15. . . . .**51** B4
St Ann's Cres SW18 . . . .**158** A5
St Ann's Ct NW4 . . . .**46** B6
St Ann's Ctr HA1. . . . .**42** C3
St Ann's Gdns NW5 . . . .**71** A2
St Ann's Hill SW18 . . . .**158** A5
St Ann's Ho WC1. . . . .**234** A1
St Ann's Hospl N4, N15 . . . .**51** A4
St Ann's La SW1 . . . .**259** C5
St Ann's Park Rd SW18. . . .**158** A5
St Anns Rd Barnes SW13 . . .**133** D4
Shepherd's Bush W11 . . . . .**112** D6
St Ann's Rd
1 Barking IG11. . . . .**101** A6
Edmonton N9 . . . .**17** D3
Harrow HA1. . . . .**42** C3
Tottenham N15. . . . .**51** B4
St Ann's Sch 9 W7 . . . .**108** C5
St Ann's Specl Sch SM4 . . .**201** D6
St Ann's Terr NW8. . . **92** B5 **229** D4
St Ann's Villas
W11. . . . .**113** A4 **244** A3
St Ann's Way CR2. . . . .**220** D2
St Anselm RC Prim Sch
UB2. . . . .**107** B3
St Anselm's Ct SW16 . . . . . .**182** A5
St Anselm's Pl W1 . . . .**248** C6
St Anselm's RC Prim Sch
Harrow HA1. . . . .**42** C2
Upper Tooting SW17. . . . . . .**159** A1
St Anselms Rd UB3 . . . .**105** D4
St Anthony's Ave IG8. . . . . . .**37** C3
St Anthonys Cl 5 SW17 . .**158** C2
St Anthony's Cl 8 E1 . . . .**118** A5
5 Hackney Wick E9 . . . .**75** B2
St Anthony's Ct
2 Balham SW12. . . . .**159** A5
Orpington BR6 . . . .**226** D6
Upper Tooting SW17. . . . . . .**159** A2
St Anthony's Flats NW1 . .**232** C3
St Anthony's Hospl SM3. .**200** D1
St Anthony's RC Prim Sch
East Dulwich SE22 . . . .**162** A5
4 Penge SE20. . . . .**184** C2
Upton E7. . . . .**77** B1
St Anthony's Sch 8 NW3. .**70** B3
St Anthony's Way TW14 . .**127** D1
St Antony's RC Prim Sch
IG8. . . . .**37** A6
St Antony's Rd E7. . . . .**77** B1
St Arvans Cl CR0. . . . .**221** C5
St Asaph Ct SE4. . . . .**140** C2
St Asaph Rd SE4 . . . .**140** D2
St Aubins Ct N1. . . . .**235** D6
St Aubyns E18 . . . .**54** D5
St Aubyn's Ave
Hounslow TW3, TW4. . . . . .**151** C6
Wimbledon SW19. . . . .**179** B5
St Aubyns Cl BR6 . . . .**227** D5
St Aubyn's Ct SW19 . . . .**179** A4
St Aubyns Gdns BR6 . . . . . .**227** D6
St Aubyn's Rd SE19 . . . .**183** D4
St Aubyn's Sch IG8. . . . .**36** D3
St Audrey Ave DA7 . . . .**147** C3
St Augustine's Ave
BR1, BR2. . . . .**210** A4
Ealing W5 . . . .**88** A4
South Croydon CR2. . . . .**221** A1
Wembley HA9. . . . .**66** A5

St Augustine's CE High Sch
5 NW6 . . . .**91** C5
St Augustine's CE Prim Sch
DA17. . . . .**125** B2
St Augustines Ct
Beckenham BR3. . . . .**185** A1
4 New Barnet EN5 . . . .**14** A6
St Augustine's Ct E11 . . . . . .**54** D1
St Augustine's Ho NW1 . . .**232** C2
Upper Tooting SW17. . . . . . .**180** D6
St Augustine's Prim Sch 5
NW6 . . . .**91** D5
St Augustines Priory Sch
W5 . . . .**88** B2
St Augustine's RC Prim Sch
Catford SE6 . . . .**186** A5
1 Ilford IG2. . . . .**56** D4
W6 . . . .**135** A6 **264** B5
St Augustine's Rd
Camden Town NW1 . . . .**71** D1
DA17. . . . .**125** B2
St Austell Cl HA8. . . . .**26** B1
St Austell Rd SE13 . . . .**142** B3
St Awdry's Rd IG11 . . . .**79** B1
St Barnabas CE Prim Sch
SW1 . . . .**115** A1 **258** B2
St Barnabas Cl
Beckenham BR3. . . . .**186** A1
11 Dulwich Village SE21 . .**161** C6
St Barnabas Ct HA3 . . . .**24** A2
St Barnabas' Gdns KT8 . . .**195** C4
St Barnabas Ho CR4. . . . . . .**181** A3
St Barnabas Rd
Mitcham CR4 . . . .**181** A3
Sutton SM1. . . . .**218** B3
Walthamstow E17 . . . .**53** C3
Woodford IG8. . . . .**37** C3
St Barnabas & St Philip CE
Prim Sch W8 . . . .**113** C3 **255** A5
St Barnabas St SW1. . . . . . .**258** B2
St Barnabas Terr E9. . . . .**74** D3
St Barnabas Villas
SW8. . . . .**138** A4 **270** B2
St Bartholomew's CE Prim
Sch SE26. . . . .**184** C6
St Bartholomew's Cl
SE26. . . . .**184** C6
St Bartholomews Ct 6
E6 . . . .**100** A6
St Bartholomew's Hospl
EC1. . . . .**94** D2 **241** D3
St Bartholomew's Mus *
EC1. . . . .**241** D3
St Bartholomew's Rd E6 .**100** B5
St Bede's RC Inf Sch
SW12 . . . .**159** D3
St Bede's RC Prim Sch
RM6 . . . .**58** C4
St Benedict's Cl SW17. . . . .**181** A5
St Benedict's Jun Sch 15
W5 . . . .**87** C2
St Benedict's Sch W5 . . . . . .**87** D2
St Benets Cl 8 SW17. . . . . .**158** C2
St Benet's Gr SM5 . . . .**202** A2
St Benet's Pl EC3 . . . .**252** D6
St Bernadette RC Jun Sch 12
SW12 . . . .**159** D3
St Bernadette's Fst & Mid
Sch HA3 . . . .**44** B5
St Bernadette's RC Prim Sch
UB10. . . . .**82** D6
St Bernard Ho 6 E14 . . . . .**120** A3
St Bernards CR0. . . . .**221** C5
St Bernards Cl 8 SE27. . . . .**183** B6
St Bernards Ho 1 KT6 . . . .**214** A6
St Bernard's Rd E6. . . . .**99** D6
St Blaise Ave BR1. . . . .**187** B1
St Bonaventure's Sch E7. .**77** A1
St Boniface RC Prim Sch 1
SW17 . . . .**180** D5
St Botolph St E1,
EC3 . . . .**95** D1 **243** C2
St Brelades Ct N1. . . . .**235** D6
St Bride's EC4 . . . .**241** C1
St Bride's Ave EC4 . . . .**241** C1
Edgware HA8 . . . .**26** B2
St Brides Cl DA18. . . . .**124** D4
St Bride's Pas EC4 . . . .**241** C1
St Bride St EC4 . . . . . .**94** D1 **241** C2
St Catherines Cl
Chessington KT9 . . . .**213** D2
7 Upper Tooting SW17. . . .**158** C2
St Catherines Ct TW13 . . . .**150** A3
St Catherine's Ct 8 W4 . .**111** C3
St Catherine's Dr SE14 . . .**140** D3
St Catherines Farm Ct
HA4 . . . .**39** A3
St Catherines Mews
SW3. . . . .**257** C4
St Catherine's RC Sch EN5 . .**1** C1
St Catherine's RC Sch for
Girls DA6. . . . .**169** D6
St Catherines Rd
Chingford E4. . . . .**19** C2
Ruislip HA4. . . . .**39** B3
St Catherine's Sch TW1 . . .**153** A2
St Catherines Twr 5 E10 .**53** D2
St Cecilia's CE Sch
SW18 . . . .**157** B3
St Cecilia's Cl SM3. . . . .**201** A1

St Cecilia's RC Prim Sch
SM3 . . . .**216** D6
St Chads Cl KT6. . . . .**197** C2
St Chad's Gdns RM6 . . . .**59** A2
St Chad's Pl WC1 . . . .**233** C2
St Chad's RC Prim Sch
SE25. . . . .**205** C4
St Chad's Rd RM6. . . . .**59** A2
St Chad St WC1 . . . .**233** B2
St Charles' Hospl W10 . . . . . .**90** D2
St Charles Pl W10 . . . .**91** A2
St Charles RC Prim Sch 7
W10 . . . .**90** D2
St Charles RC Sixth Form
Coll 8 W10 . . . .**90** D2
St Charles Sq W10 . . . .**90** D2
St Christina's RC Prep Sch
NW8 . . . . **92** C5 **230** B4
St Christopher's Cl TW7 . .**130** C4
St Christophers Ct 15
N19 . . . .**71** C5
St Christophers Dr UB3 . .**106** B6
St Christophers Gdns
CR7. . . . .**204** C5
St Christopher's Ho NW1 .**232** C3
St Christopher's Mews
SM6. . . . .**219** C3
St Christopher's Pl W1 . . .**238** B2
St Christopher's Sch
Beckenham BR3 . . . .**186** A1
5 Hampstead NW3. . . . .**70** B3
Wembley HA9. . . . .**66** B5
St Clair Dr KT4. . . . .**216** B4
St Clair Ho 17 E3. . . . .**97** B4
St Clair Rd E13 . . . .**99** B5
St Clair's Rd CR0. . . . .**221** C6
St Clare Bsns Pk TW12 . . . .**174** A4
St Clare St EC3 . . . .**243** C1
St Clement Danes CE Prim
Sch WC2 . . . .**94** B1 **240** C1
St Clement & St James CE
Prim Sch W11. . . . . . .**113** A1 **244** A4
St Clements Ct
Barnsbury N7 . . . .**72** B2
7 SE14. . . . .**140** D6
8 Shepherd's Bush W11. .**112** D6
St Clement's Ct EC3. . . . . . .**252** D6
St Clements Ho E1. . . . .**243** C3
Walton-on-T KT12 . . . .**194** A2
St Clement's Hts SE26. . . .**184** A6
St Clement's La WC2. . . . . .**240** D1
St Clements Mans 3
SW6. . . . .**134** D6
St Clements St N7 . . . .**72** C1
St Cloud Rd SE27 . . . .**183** B6
St Columba's Cl E15 . . . .**76** C4
St Columba Ho 2 E17. . . . . .**53** D5
St Columba's RC Boys Sch
DA6. . . . .**169** D6
St Columb's Ho 11 W10 . . . .**91** A2
St Crispin's Cl NW3. . . . .**70** C4
St Crispin's Cl UB1. . . . .**85** B1
St Crispins Ct 1 UB1. . . . . . .**85** B1
St Cross St EC1 . . . . . .**94** C2 **241** B4
St Cuthberts Gdns 2
HA5 . . . .**23** B3
St Cuthberts Rd N13 . . . .**32** C4
St Cuthbert's Rd NW2. . . . . . .**69** B2
St Cuthbert with St Matthias
CE Prim Sch
SW5 . . . .**113** D1 **255** C2
St Cyprian's Greek Orthodox
Prim Sch CR7 . . . .**183** A2
St Cyprian's St SW17 . . . . .**180** D6
St Davids Cl
27 Bermondsey SE16. . . . .**118** B1
Wembley HA9. . . . .**67** A5
St David's Cl BR4 . . . .**207** D2
St David's Coll BR4 . . . .**207** D2
St Davids Ct 5 E11 . . . .**55** B4
St David's Ct
Bromley BR1. . . . .**210** D6
8 Southall UB1. . . . .**86** A1
1 Walthamstow E17. . . . . . .**54** A6
St David's Dr HA8. . . . .**26** B2
St David's Pl NW4. . . . .**46** B2
St David's Sch TW15 . . . . . .**148** B1
St David's Sq E14 . . . .**119** D1
St Denis Rd SE27. . . . .**183** B6
St Dionis Rd Fulham SW6. .**135** B3
Wanstead E12 . . . .**78** A5
St Domingo Ho SE18. . . . . .**122** B3
St Dominic RC Prim Sch 14
NW5. . . . .**70** D3
St Dominics Ct 6
E9. . . . .**75** A2
St Dominic's Sixth Form Coll
HA1 . . . .**64** C6
St Donatt's Rd
London SE14. . . . .**141** B4
New Cross Gate SE4. . . . . .**141** B3
St Dunstan Ave W3 . . . .**111** B6
St Dunstan Gdns W3 . . . . . .**111** B6
St Dunstans SM1. . . . .**217** B2
St Dunstan's Alley EC3 . . .**253** A5
St Dunstan's CE Prim Sch 2
SM3 . . . .**217** A1
St Dunstans Cl UB3 . . . . . .**105** D2
St Dunstan's Coll SE6. . . . .**163** C3
St Dunstan's Ct EC4. . . . . .**241** B1

St Dunstan's Hill
Cheam SM1, SM3 . . . .**217** A3
EC3. . . . .**253** A5
St Dunstans Rd E7 . . . .**77** C2
St Dunstan's Rd
Cranford TW5. . . . .**128** B3
Feltham TW13 . . . .**149** D1
Hammersmith W6 . . . .**112** D1
Hanwell W7 . . . .**108** C4
South Norwood SE25 . . . . .**205** D5
St Edmunds Ave **39** B3
St Edmunds Cl DA18 . . . . .**124** D4
3 Upper Tooting SW17. . . .**158** C2
St Edmund's Cl NW8 . . . . .**230** C5
St Edmund's Ct NW8. . . . . .**230** C5
St Edmund's Dr HA7 . . . .**25** A2
St Edmund's La TW2 . . . . . .**151** D4
St Edmunds RC Prim Sch
E14. . . . .**119** C2
St Edmund's RC Prim Sch
1 Edmonton N9 . . . .**18** B3
Twickenham TW2 . . . .**151** D4
St Edmunds Rd N9. . . . .**18** A4
St Edmund's Rd IG1 . . . .**56** B3
St Edmund's Sq SW13. . . .**134** C6
St Edmund's Terr
NW8 . . . .**92** D6 **230** C5
St Edward's CE Comp Sch
RM7 . . . .**59** C3
St Edward's Cl NW11. . . . . . .**47** C3
St Edwards Ct 3 E10. . . . . . .**54** A2
St Edward's Ct NW11. . . . . . .**47** C3
St Edwards RC Prim Sch 10
E6. . . . .**99** C6
St Edward's RC Prim Sch
NW1. . . . .**92** C3 **237** B5
St Egberts Way E4 . . . .**20** A3
St Elizabeth Ct
North Finchley N12. . . . .**30** A6
9 Walthamstow E10 . . . . . .**53** D2
St Elizabeth RC Prim Sch 33
E2. . . . .**96** C5
St Elizabeth's RC Prim Sch
TW10 . . . .**154** B5
St Elmo Rd W12. . . . .**111** D4
St Elmos Rd SE16 . . . .**119** A4
St Elphege's RC Sch
SM6. . . . .**220** A2
SS Peter & Paul's Prim Sch
CR4. . . . .**202** D5
SS Peter & Paul's RC Prim
Sch IG1. . . . .**79** B5
St Erkenwald Mews
IG11 . . . .**101** B6
St Erkenwald Rd IG11 . . . .**101** B6
St Ermin's Hill SW1 . . . .**259** C6
St Ervan's Rd W10 . . . .**91** B2
St Eugene de Mazenod RC
Prim Sch 12 NW6. . . . .**69** C1
St Faith's CE Prim Sch 1
SW18 . . . .**158** A6
St Faith's Cl EN2. . . . .**5** A4
St Faith's Rd SE24 . . . .**160** D3
St Fillans Rd SE6. . . . .**164** A4
St Francesca Cabrini RC
Prim Sch SE23 . . . .**162** C5
St Francis Cl BR5 . . . .**211** C3
St Francis de Sales RC Jun &
Inf Sch 12 N17. . . . .**33** D3
St Francis' Ho NW1 . . . .**232** C3
St Francis Lodge HA0. . . . . .**64** D5
St Francis of Assisi Prim Sch
19 W11. . . . .**112** D6
St Francis Pl SW12. . . . .**159** B5
St Francis RC Prim Sch
26 SE15. . . . .**140** A5
Stratford E15 . . . .**76** C3
St Francis Rd SE22. . . . .**139** C1
St Francis Way IG1 . . . .**79** B4
St Francis Xavier Coll
SW12 . . . .**159** B5
St Frideswides Mews 5
E14 . . . .**98** A1
St Gabriel's CE Prim Sch
SW1 . . . .**115** C1 **259** A1
St Gabriels Cl 3 E14. . . . . .**97** D2
St Gabriel's Cl E11 . . . .**55** B1
St Gabriels Ct N1. . . . .**31** D3
St Gabriel's Rd NW2 . . . .**68** D3
St George Ho SW11 . . . . . .**268** B1
ST GEORGE IN THE
EAST **118** A6
St George's Ave
Ealing W5 . . . .**109** D4
Kingsbury NW9 . . . .**45** B5
Southall UB1. . . . .**107** B6
Tufnell Pk N7. . . . .**71** D4
Upton E7. . . . .**77** B1
St George's Bldgs SE11 .**261** D5
St Georges Cath RC Prim
Sch SE1. . . . .**116** D3 **261** C6
St George's CE Prim Sch
BR1. . . . .**187** D1
18 SE5 . . . .**139** C5
SW8 . . . .**137** C5 **269** B3

St George's Circ
SE1 . . . .**116** D3 **261** C6
St Georges Cl Erith SE28 . .**102** D1
Nine Elms SW8 . . . .**269** B2
Wembley HA0. . . . .**65** A5
St George's Cl NW11. . . . . . .**47** B3
St Georges Coll N7 . . . .**72** C5
St Georges Ct
Harrow HA3 . . . .**43** A3
Newham E6 . . . .**100** B3
Penge SE20. . . . .**184** B2
Putney SW15 . . . .**135** B1
Walthamstow E17 . . . .**54** B4
St George's Ct
Brompton SW3. . . . .**257** A4
Kensington SW7. . . . .**256** A5
Newington SE1 . . . .**261** C5
St George's Dr
Ickenham UB10. . . . .**60** B6
South Oxhey WD19. . . . .**23** A6
SW1 . . . .**115** C1 **259** A2
St George's Field
W2. . . . .**92** C1 **237** B1
St George's Gdns KT6. . . .**214** D6
St George's Gr SW17. . . . . .**158** B1
St Georges Hanover Sq Sch
W1 . . . .**115** A6 **248** B5
St George's Ho NW1 . . . . . .**232** B3
St George's Hospl SW17 .**180** B5
St Georges Ind Est N12. . . . .**32** D3
St George's Ind Est KT2 . . .**175** D5
St George's La EC3. . . . .**253** A6
St Georges Lo N10. . . . .**49** C5
St Georges Mews 11
NW1 . . . .**70** D1
St George's Mews
2 Rotherhithe SE8 . . . .**119** B2
SE1 . . . .**261** B6
St George's Pl 7 . . . .**91** D4
St George's Pools E1 . . . . .**118** B6
St George's RC Cath
SE1. . . . .**116** C3 **261** B6
St George's RC Prim Sch
Enfield EN2. . . . .**5** B3
Harrow HA1. . . . .**64** D5
St George's RC Sec Sch
W9 . . . .**91** D5
St Georges Rd Acton W4 . .**111** B4
Bickley BR1. . . . .**210** B6
Dagenham RM9 . . . .**81** A4
Petts Wood BR5 . . . .**211** B3
St George's Rd
Beckenham BR3. . . . .**185** D2
Ealing W7 . . . .**108** D5
Enfield EN1. . . . .**5** D5
Feltham TW13 . . . .**172** D6
Isleworth TW1. . . . .**153** B6
2 Kingston u T KT2 . . . . . .**176** C3
Leyton E10 . . . .**76** A5
Mitcham CR4 . . . .**203** B6
Newington SE1. . . . . .**116** D3 **261** C5
Palmers Green N13 . . . .**16** B2
Redbridge IG1 . . . .**56** B2
Richmond TW9 . . . .**132** B2
Sidcup DA14. . . . .**190** D4
Temple Fortune NW11. . . . . .**47** B3
Upton E7. . . . .**77** B2
Wallington SM6 . . . .**219** B3
Wimbledon SW19. . . . .**179** B4
St Georges Rd Ctr RM9 . . . . .**81** B4
St Georges Rd W BR1 . . . .**188** A1
St George's Residences 4
SW2. . . . .**160** C6
St George's Sch E14. . . . . . .**241** C2
St George's Sh Ctr HA1 . . . .**42** C3
St Georges Sq 1 E14 . . . .**119** A4
St George's Sq
Kingston u T KT3 . . . .**199** C6
Rotherhithe SE8 . . . .**119** B2
SW1 . . . .**115** D1 **259** C1
Upton E7. . . . .**77** B1
St George's Square Mews
SW1. . . . .**259** C1
St George St W1 . . . . .**115** B6 **248** D6
St Georges Terr
Hampstead NW1 . . . .**70** D1
NW1 . . . .**230** D6
St Georges Univ of London
SW17 . . . .**180** B5
St George's Way SE15. . . .**139** C4
St George's Wlk CR0 . . . . .**221** A5
St George the Martyr CE
Prim Sch WC1. . . . . . .**94** B3 **240** D5
St George Wharf SW8. . . . .**270** A6
St Gerards Cl SW4 . . . .**159** C6
St German's Pl SE3 . . . .**143** A4
St German's Rd SE23. . . . . .**163** A3
St Gildas' RC Jun Sch 13
N8. . . . .**50** A2
ST GILES **94** A1
St Giles Ave
Dagenham RM10 . . . .**81** D6
Uxbridge UB10. . . . .**61** A4
St Giles Cir WC1 . . . . .**93** D1 **239** D2
St Giles Ct BR6. . . . .**227** B3
Dagenham RM10 . . . .**81** D1
Heston TW5 . . . .**129** A5
St Giles Coll Highgate N6. . .**49** C3
WC1 . . . .**94** A2 **240** B4
St Giles Ct Ealing W13. . . . .**109** C5

St Giles Ct *continued*
WC2 . . . . **240** A2
St Giles High St
WC2 . . . .**93** D1 **239** D2
St Giles Ho
🏢 New Barnet EN5 . . . . **2** A1
Streatham SW16 . . . . **160** A1
St Giles Pas WC2 . . . . **239** D1
St Giles Pl SE5 . . . . **139** C4
St Giles' Specl Sch CR2 . **220** D2
St Giles Terr EC1 . . . . **242** B3
St Giles Twr 🖪 SE5 . . . . **139** C4
St Gilles Ho 🖪 E2 . . . . **96** D5
St Gothard Rd SE21,
SE27 . . . . **183** B6
St Gregor High Sch HA3. . . **43** D4
St Gregory Ct HA4 . . . . **62** C4
St Gregory's RC Prim Sch 🖪
W5 . . . . **87** D2
St Helena Ho WC1 . . . . **234** A1
St Helena Pier TW9 . . . . **153** D6
St Helena Rd SE16 . . . . **118** D2
St Helena St WC1 . . . . **234** A1
St Helena Terr 🖪 TW9 . . . . . **153** D6
St Helens KT7 . . . . **196** D2
St Helens Coll UB10 . . . . . . **60** C1
St Helen's Cres SW16 . . . . . **182** B2
St Helens Gdns W10 . . . . . . **90** D1
St Helen's Pl E10 . . . . **53** A2
St Helen's Pl EC3 . . . . **243** C1
St Helen's RC Inf Sch E17 . **54** A4
St Helen's RC Prim Sch
E13 . . . . **99** A3
St Helen's RC Sch 🖪
SW9 . . . . **138** C2
St Helens Rd 🖪 DA18 . . . . . **124** D4
St Helen's Rd Ealing W13. . **109** C5
Redbridge IG1 . . . . **56** B3
Thornton Heath SW16 . . . . **182** B2
ST HELIER **202** B2
St Helier Ave SM4 . . . . **202** A3
St Helier Ct 🖪 N1 . . . . **95** C6
St Helier Hospl SM5 . . . . . **202** A1
St Heliers Ave TW3, TW4 . . **151** C4
St Helier's Rd E10 . . . . **54** A3
St Helier Sta SM4 . . . . **201** C3
St Hilary's Ct BR1 . . . . **210** D6
St Hilda's Ct TW15 . . . . **170** A5
St Hildas Cl 🖪 SW17 . . . . . . **158** C2
St Hilda's Ct N16 . . . . **68** D1
St Hilda's Rd SW13 . . . . **134** B6
St Hildas Wharf E1 . . . . **118** C1
St Hubert's Ho 🖪 E14. . . . . . **119** C3
St Hughes Cl 🖪 SW17 . . . . . **158** C2
St Hugh's Rd SE20 . . . . **184** B3
St Ignatius Coll EN1 . . . . **6** B6
St Ignatius RC Prim Sch
TW16 . . . . **172** A2
St Ignatius' RC Prim Sch
N15 . . . . **51** D3
St Ives TN N2 . . . . **69** A2
St Ivian Ct 🖪 N10 . . . . **31** B1
ST JAMES **115** C5
St James Apartments 🖪
E17 . . . . **53** A4
St James Ave
East Barnet N20 . . . . **14** C1
Sutton SM1 . . . . **217** C3
St James' Ave W13. . . . . . . **109** A5
St James' CE Jun & Inf Sch
🖪 SE16 . . . . **118** A3
St James CE Jun Sch E7 . . **77** A3
St James CE Prim Sch
EN3. . . . . **6** C3
St James Cl Barnet EN4 . . . . **2** B1
East Barnet N20 . . . . **14** C1
St James' Cl
New Malden KT3 . . . . **199** D4
Ruislip HA4 . . . . **62** C6
St James Ct
🖪 Bethnal Green E2 . . . . . . **96** A4
🖪 Brentford W4 . . . . **110** C1
🖪 Bromley BR2 . . . . **187** A1
Forest Hill SE23 . . . . **163** A3
SE3 . . . . **143** B4
Thornton Heath CR0. . . . . **204** D2
Wanstead E12 . . . . **77** C6
St James' Ct
Bedford Pk W4 . . . . **111** B3
🖪 Kingston u T KT1 . . . . . . **198** A6
SW1 . . . . **259** B6
St James Gate IG9 . . . . **21** C3
St James Gdns IG6 . . . . **58** B5
St James' Gdns HA0. . . . . . . **66** A1
St James Ho E15 . . . . **72** C3
St James Hts 🖪 SE18 . . . . . **123** A1
St James Independent Schs
W14 . . . . **113** A2 **254** B4
St James Ind Mews 🖪
SE1 . . . . **118** A1
St James Ind Sch for Boys
TW1 . . . . **153** A2
St James' Mans NW6. . . . . . **69** C1
St James Mews E14. . . . . . . **120** C3
St James' RC High Sch
NW9 . . . . **27** D2
St James RC Prim Sch
BR5. . . . . **210** D4
St James Rd
Carshalton SM5 . . . . **218** C4

St James Rd *continued*
Kingston u T KT1. . . . . **175** D1
Sutton SM1, SM2 . . . . **217** C3
St James' Rd Edmonton N9 . **18** B2
Forest Gate E15 . . . . **76** D3
Mitcham CR4 . . . . **181** A3
Surbiton KT6. . . . . **197** D3
Sutton SM1 . . . . **217** C2
St James's SE14 . . . . **141** A4
St James & St Michael's CE
Prim Sch W2 . . . . **114** A6 **246** B6
St James's App EC2 . . . . . . **243** A5
St James's Ave
Beckenham BR3 . . . . **207** A6
Hampton TW12 . . . . **174** A5
South Hackney E2. . . . . **96** C5
St James's CE Prim Sch
Cranley Gdns N10. . . . . **49** A5
London SE14. . . . . **141** A4
St James School Flats 🖪
N7 . . . . **72** C3
St James's Cl NW8. . . . . **230** C5
Upper Tooting SW17. . . . . **158** D2
Woolwich SE18. . . . . **123** A1
St James's Cloisters 🖪
SE22 . . . . **139** D1
St James's Cotts 🖪
TW10. . . . . **153** D6
St James's Cres SW9 . . . . . **138** C2
St James's Ct
🖪 Edmonton N18 . . . . **34** A5
Harrow HA1 . . . . **43** A3
St James's Dr
Balham SW12 . . . . **158** D4
Upper Tooting SW17. . . . . **158** D3
St James's Gdns
W11. . . . . **113** A5 **244** A4
St James's Gr SW11. . . . . . **136** D3
St James's La N10 . . . . **49** B5
St James's Market SW1 . . **249** C5
St James's Mews E17 . . . . . **53** A4
St James's Pal ★
SW1 . . . . **115** C5 **249** B3
St James's Park Sta
SW1 . . . . **115** D3 **259** C6
St James's Pas EC3 . . . . . . **243** B1
St James's Pk ★ SW1. . . . . **249** C2
St James's Pk EC3. . . . . . . **205** A2
St James's Pl
SW1. . . . . **115** C5 **249** A3
St James's RC Prim Sch
TW2 . . . . **152** C1
St James's Rd
Bermondsey SE1, SE16 . . . **118** A2
Hampton TW12 . . . . **173** D5
Peckham SE1 . . . . **140** A6
Thornton Heath CR0. . . . . **205** B2
St James's Sq
SW1. . . . . **115** C5 **249** B4
St James's St
SW1 . . . . **115** C5 **249** A4
Walthamstow E17 . . . . **53** A4
St James's Terr NW8 . . . . . **230** C6
🖪 Upper Tooting SW12 . . . **159** A3
St James's Terrace Mews
NW8 . . . . **230** C6
St James Street Sta E17. . . **53** A4
St James The Great RC
Prim Sch
🖪 Camberwell SE15 . . . . . **139** D4
South Norwood CR7 . . . . . **182** D1
St James Way DA14 . . . . . . **191** A5
St James Wlk EC1. . . . . **241** C6
St Jerome's Gr UB3 . . . . **83** A1
St Joachim's RC Prim Sch 🖪
E16. **99** C1
St Joan of Arc RC Prim Sch
N5. . . . . **73** A4
St Joan's Rd N9 . . . . **17** D2
St John Baptist CE Prim Sch
BR1. . . . . **186** A6
St John Fisher RC Fst & Mid
Sch HA5 . . . . **41** C5
St John Fisher RC Prim Sch
DA18. . . . . **125** A3
Wembley HA0. . . . . **87** C5
West Barnes SW20 . . . . . . **200** D4
St John of Jerusalem CE
Prim Sch 🖪 E9 . . . . **74** C1
ST JOHN'S **141** C3
St John & St James CE Prim
Sch
Edmonton N18 . . . . **33** D5
🖪 Hackney E9 . . . . **74** C3
St John's Angell Town CE
Prim Sch SW9 . . . . **138** C3
St John's Ave
Dagenham NW10. . . . . **89** D6
Friern Barnet N11 . . . . **30** D5
Putney SW15 . . . . **156** D6
St John's CE First Sch
HA7 . . . . **25** A6
St John's CE Prim Sch
Buckhurst Hill IG9 . . . . **21** B3
Croydon CR0. . . . . **222** D5
Enfield EN2 . . . . **4** D6
🖪 Kingston u T KT1. . . . . . **198** A6
London N11 . . . . **30** D1
🖪 Penge SE20 . . . . **184** C3

St John's CE Prim Sch
continued
🖪 South Hackney E2 . . . . . . **96** C5
Whetstone N20 . . . . **14** A2
St John's CE Sch HA7 . . . . . **25** A6
St John's CE Walham Green
Prim Sch SW6 . . . . **135** A4 **264** B2
St John's Church Rd E9 . . . . **74** C3
St Johns CE N14 . . . . **15** C5
St John's Cl SW6 . . . . **265** A4
Wembley HA9. . . . . **66** A3
St John's Concert Hall ★
SW1 . . . . **246** A5
St John's Cotts 🖪 SE20 . . . **184** C3
St John's Cres SW9 . . . . . . **138** C2
St Johns Ct 🖪 E1 . . . . **118** B5
St John's Ct
Buckhurst Hill IG9 . . . . **21** B3
Finsbury Pk N4 . . . . **72** D6
Hammersmith W6 . . . . **112** B2
🖪 Harrow HA1 . . . . **42** D3
Isleworth TW7 . . . . **130** D3
Kingston u T KT1. . . . . **198** A5
Lewisham SE13 . . . . **142** A3
Leytonstone E11. . . . . **54** D1
🖪 South Hampstead NW3. . **70** A2
Saint John's Ct N5. . . . . **72** D4
St Johns Dr KT12 . . . . **194** C1
St John's Dr SW18 . . . . **157** D3
St John's Est SE1 . . . . **253** C1
St John's Gdns
W11. . . . . **113** B6 **244** C5
St John's Gr
🖪 Barnes SW13 . . . . **133** D3
🖪 Richmond TW9 . . . . **132** A1
Upper Holloway N19 . . . . . . **71** C6
St John's Highbury Vale CE
Prim Sch N5 . . . . **72** D5
St John's Hill SW11 . . . . . . **136** B1
St John's Hill Gr SW11 . . . . **136** B1
St Johns Ho 🖪 SE17 . . . . . **139** B6
Streatham SW16 . . . . **182** A4
St John's Ho 🖪 E14 . . . . . . **120** A2
St John's La EC1. . . . **94** D2 **241** D4
St John's Lodge 🖪 SE8 . . . **141** C4
St John's Mans N5 . . . . **74** C3
St John's Par Ealing W13. . **109** B5
🖪 Sidcup DA14 . . . . **190** B6
St John's Park Mans N19. . **71** C5
St John's Path EC1. . . . . . . **241** C5
St John's Pk SE3 . . . . **143** A5
St John's Pl EC1 . . . . **241** C5
St John's Prim Sch W13. . . **109** A6
St John's RC Prim Sch
SE16 . . . . **119** A4
St Johns Rd Ilford IG2 . . . . . **57** C2
🖪 Kingston u T KT3. . . . . . **199** A6
St John's Rd
Barking IG11 . . . . **101** C6
Battersea SW11. . . . . **136** C1
Canning Town E16 . . . . **99** A1
Carshalton SM5 . . . . **218** C5
Chingford E4. . . . . **35** D6
Croydon CR0. . . . . **220** D5
DA16. . . . . **146** B2
East Ham E6 . . . . **100** A6
East Molesey KT8. . . . . . . **196** B5
Feltham TW13 . . . . **173** B6
Harrow HA1 . . . . **42** D3
Isleworth TW7 . . . . **130** D3
Orpington BR5. . . . . **211** C3
Penge SE20 . . . . **184** C4
Richmond TW9 . . . . **132** A1
Sidcup DA14 . . . . **190** B6
Southall UB2. . . . . **107** A3
Sutton SM1. . . . . **217** D6
Teddington KT1. . . . . **175** C1
Temple Fortune NW11 . . . . **47** B3
Tottenham N17 . . . . **51** C3
Walthamstow E17 . . . . **36** A1
Wembley HA9 . . . . **66** A3
Wimbledon SW19. . . . . **179** A4
St John's & St Clements CE
Jun & Inf Sch 🖪 SE15. . **140** A2
St John's Sch HA6. . . . . **22** A4
St John's Sq EC1. . . . **94** D3 **241** C5
St Johns Sta SE8. . . . . **141** C3
St John St EC1. . . . . . **94** D3 **241** C6
St John's Terr Enfield EN2 . . **5** A6
North Kensington W10 . . . . **90** D3
SE18. . . . . **145** B6
Upton E7. . . . . **77** B2
St John's Therapy Ctr
SW11 . . . . **136** B1
St Johnstone Ho 🖪 N12. . . **29** D6
St John's Upper Holloway CE
Prim Sch 🖪 N19. . . . . **71** D6
St John's Villas
🖪 Friern Barnet N11. . . . . . **30** D5
Upper Holloway N19 . . . . . . **71** D6
W8 . . . . **255** D5
St John's Walworth CE Prim
Sch SE17. . . . . **117** A2 **262** B3
St John's Way N19 . . . . **49** D1
ST JOHN'S WOOD. **92** B5
St John's Wood Ct NW8. . . **229** D1
St John's Wood High St
NW8 . . . . **92** C5 **230** A3

St John's Wood Park
NW8 . . . . **92** B6 **229** C6
St John's Wood Pre-Prep
Sch NW8 . . . . **92** C4 **230** A2
St John's Wood Rd
NW8 . . . . **92** B4 **229** D1
St John's Wood Sta
NW8 . . . . **92** B5 **229** C6
St John's Wood Terr
NW8 . . . . **92** C5 **230** A4
St John the Baptist CE Jun
Sch KT1 . . . . **175** D3
St John the Baptist VA CE
Prim Sch N1 . . . . . . **95** B5 **235** D3
St John the Divine CE Jun &
Inf Sch SE5 . . . . **138** D5
St John the Evangelist RC
Prim Sch N1 . . . . . . **94** D5 **234** C4
St John Vianney RC Prim Sch
🖪 N8 . . . . **50** D5
St Josephs Cl BR6 . . . . **227** D4
St Joseph's Cl W10 . . . . **91** A2
St Joseph's Convent Sch 🖪
E11 . . . . **55** A3
St Josephs Ct
🖪 Dagenham NW10 . . . . . . **89** D5
🖪 Walthamstow E10 . . . . . **53** D2
St Joseph's Ct E4 . . . . **20** B4
St Joseph's Dr UB1 . . . . **107** B5
St Joseph's Flats NW1 . . . . **232** A2
St Joseph's Gr NW4 . . . . **46** B5
St Joseph's Ho W6 . . . . **112** D2
St Joseph's Hospice E9,
E8. . . . . **96** B6
St Joseph's RC Coll
SW16 . . . . **182** B6
St Joseph's RC Fst & Mid Sch
HA3 . . . . **25** A1
St Joseph's RC Inf & Jun
Schs
Hendon NW4 . . . . **46** B5
🖪 SE5 . . . . **139** A5
St Joseph's RC Inf Sch
Leyton E10 . . . . **75** C6
South Norwood SE19 . . . . **183** A4
St Joseph's RC Jun & Inf
Schs HA9 . . . . **66** B3
St Joseph's RC Jun Sch
South Norwood SE19 . . . . **183** A4
Walthamstow E10 . . . . **53** D1
St Josephs RC Prim Sch 🖪
W7 . . . . **108** C5
St Joseph's RC Prim Sch
Barking IG11 . . . . **101** A6
🖪 Bermondsey SE16. . . . . **118** A4
Bromley BR1. . . . . **187** B3
Chelsea SW3 . . . . . . **114** D2 **257** C3
Dagenham RM9 . . . . **81** B4
🖪 Deptford SE8 . . . . **141** C5
🖪 Greenwich SE10 . . . . . . **120** C1
Kingston u T KT1. . . . . **176** B2
Paddington W9. . . . . **92** A4 **229** A1
St Giles WC2 . . . . . . **94** A1 **240** B2
Upper Holloway N19 . . . . . . **49** B1
🖪 Wandsworth SW18 . . . . **157** C6
🖪 Willesden NW10 . . . . . . **67** C1
St Joseph's Rd N9 . . . . **18** C3
St Joseph's St SW8 . . . . . . **268** D2
St Joseph's Vale SE3 . . . . . **142** B2
St Jude & St Paul's CE Prim
Sch 🖪 N1. . . . . **73** C2
St Jude's CE Prim Sch
🖪 London SE24. . . . . **160** D6
SE1. . . . . **116** D3 **261** C5
St Judes Ho 🖪 W10 . . . . **91** B4
St Jude's Rd E2 . . . . **96** B5
St Jude St N16. . . . . **73** C3
St Julian's Cl SW16 . . . . . . **182** C6
St Julian's Farm Rd SE27,
SW16 . . . . **182** D6
St Julian's Rd NW6 . . . . **91** C6
St Katharine's Ho N1. . . . . . **234** A4
St Katharine's Prec NW1 **231** C4
St Katharine's Way
E1 . . . . **117** D5 **253** D4
St Katherines Rd DA18 . . . . **124** D4
St Katherine's Row EC3 . . **243** B1
St Katherine's Wlk 🖪
W11. . . . . **112** D5
St Keverne Rd SE9 . . . . **188** A4
St Kilda Rd BR6. . . . . **211** D1
Ealing W13. . . . . **109** A4
St Kilda's Rd Harrow HA1. . . **42** C3
Stamford Hill N16. . . . . **51** C1
St Kitts Terr SE19. . . . . **183** C5
St Laurence's Cl NW6 . . . . . **90** D6
St Lawrence Bsns Ctr
TW13 . . . . **150** B2
St Lawrence Cl HA8. . . . . **26** B5
St Lawrence Ct N1 . . . . **235** D6
St Lawrence Dr HA5 . . . . **40** B4
St Lawrence Ho SE1 . . . . . . **263** B6
St Lawrence Jun Sch
KT8. . . . . **196** B5
St Lawrence RC Prim Sch
TW13 . . . . **150** B2
St Lawrence St E14 . . . . **120** A5
St Lawrence Terr W10 . . . . . **91** A2
St Lawrence Way SW9 . . . . **138** C3

St Leonards Ave HA3 . . . . . . **43** C4
St Leonard's Ave E4. . . . . **36** B4
St Leonard's CE Prim Sch
SW16 . . . . **181** D5
St Leonards Cl 🖪 DA16. . . **146** A2
St Leonards Ct SW14 . . . . . **133** A2
St Leonard's Ct N1. . . . . . . **235** D2
St Leonards Gdns IG1. . . . . **79** A3
St Leonard's Gdns TW5. . . **129** A4
St Leonards Hospl N1 . . . . . **95** C5
St Leonards Rd SW14 . . . . . **133** A2
St Leonard's Rd
Becontree NW10 . . . . **89** B3
Claygate KT10 . . . . **212** D2
Croydon CR0. . . . . **220** D5
Ealing W13 . . . . **109** C6
Kingston u T KT6. . . . . **197** D4
South Bromley E14. . . . . . . **98** A2
Thames Ditton KT7. . . . . . **197** A2
St Leonards Rise BR6 . . . . . **227** C4
St Leonard's Sq
Camden Town NW5 . . . . . . **71** A2
Kingston u T KT6. . . . . **197** D4
St Leonard's St E3 . . . . **97** D4
St Leonard's Terr
SW3. . . . . **114** D1 **257** D1
St Loo Ave SW3 . . . . **136** C6 **267** B6
St Loo Ct SW3 . . . . **267** C6
St Louis Rd SE27 . . . . **183** B6
St Loy's Rd N17 . . . . **51** D6
St Lucia Dr E15 . . . . **98** D6
St Luke Prim CE Sch 🖪
E16. **98** D1
ST LUKE'S **95** A3
St Luke's Ave
Clapham SW4. . . . . **137** D1
Enfield EN2 . . . . **5** B5
Ilford IG1 . . . . **78** D3
St Luke's CE Prim Sch
🖪 Cubitt Town E14. . . . . . **120** B2
Kingston u T KT2. . . . . **176** B2
Paddington W9 . . . . **91** B4
Shoreditch EC1. . . . . **95** A4 **235** A1
West Norwood SE27. . . . . **183** A5
St Luke's Cl
Croydon SE25 . . . . **206** B3
St Luke's EC1. . . . . . **95** A3 **242** B6
St Lukes Ct 🖪 E10 . . . . **53** D2
St Luke's Ct N11. . . . . **91** B1
St Luke's Mews W11 . . . . **91** B1
St Luke's Path 🖪 IG1 . . . . . . **78** D3
St Luke's RC Sixth Form Coll
DA14. . . . . **189** C5
St Luke's Rd
Notting Hill W11. . . . . **91** B2
Uxbridge UB10 . . . . **60** A1
St Luke's Sq E16. . . . . **98** D1
St Luke's St SW3. . . . . **257** B2
St Luke's Woodside Hospl
N10. **49** A5
St Malo Ave N9 . . . . **18** C1
St Margaret Clitherow RC
Prim Sch
Neasden NW10 . . . . **67** B4
Woolwich SE28. . . . . **124** B5
St Margaret Lee CE Prim Sch
SE13. . . . . **142** C1
ST MARGARETS **153** A5
St Margarets IG11 . . . . **101** B6
St Margarets Ave
Ashford TW15. . . . . **170** D5
DA15. . . . . **167** B1
Hillingdon UB8 . . . . **82** C3
Whetstone N20 . . . . **14** A3
St Margaret's Ave
Cheam SM3 . . . . **217** A5
Harringay N8, N15. . . . . **50** D5
Harrow HA2 . . . . **64** A3
St Margarets Bsns Ctr 🖪
TW1 . . . . **153** B5
St Margaret's CE Prim Sch
Barking IG11 . . . . **79** A1
Woolwich SE18. . . . . **123** A1
St Margaret's Cres
SW15 . . . . **156** B6
St Margaret's Ct
Leyton E15 . . . . **76** C4
Putney SW15 . . . . **134** B1
SE1. . . . . **252** C3
🖪 Twickenham TW1 . . . . . **153** B5
St Margaret's Dr TW1 . . . . . **153** B6
St Margaret's Gr
Leyton E11 . . . . **76** D5
SE18. . . . . **145** A6
Twickenham TW1 . . . . **153** A5
St Margaret's La
W8. . . . . **113** D3 **255** C5
St Margarets Lo W3 . . . . . . **110** D4
St Margaret's Pass SE13. . **142** C2
St Margaret's Path 🖪
SE18 . . . . **123** A1
St Margarets Rd
Edgware HA8 . . . . **26** D5
Ruislip HA4. . . . . **39** B3
St Margaret's Rd
Brockley SE4. . . . . **141** B1

St Margaret's Rd *continued*
Hanwell W7 . . . . 108 C4
Isleworth TW1 . . . . .153 B6
Kensal Green NW10 . . . . . . .90 C4
Tottenham N17. . . . . .51 C6
Wanstead E12 . . . . .77 C6
St Margarets Rdbt TW1. .153 B6
St Margaret's Sch NW3 . . .69 D4
St Margaret's Sta TW1 . . .153 B5
St Margaret St SW1. . . . . 250 A1
St Margaret's Terr SE18 . .123 A1
St Margret's Ct N11. . . . . .31 A6
St Mark's CE Acad CR4. . .181 B1
St Mark's CE Prim Sch
Bromley BR2. . . . . 209 A6
3 Croydon SE25 . . . . . . 206 A5
Kennington SE11 . 138 B6 270 C6
St Marks Cl 5 SE10 . . . . .142 A5
Harrow HA1. . . . . .43 B1
St Mark's Cres
NW1 . . . . 93 A6 231 B6
St Mark's Ct Hanwell W7 .108 C4
8 Walthamstow E10. . . . . .53 D2
St Marks Gate E9 . . . . . . .75 B1
St Mark's Gr
SW10. . . . . 135 D5 265 D4
St Marks Ho 6 SE17 . . . . .139 B6
St Mark's Ho 8 E17. . . . . .54 A5
St Mark's Hospl HA1. . . . . .43 B2
St Mark's Hts 25 KT6 . . . .198 A4
St Marks Ind Est E16. . . . .121 D5
St Mark's Mans 14 N4. . . . .72 B6
St Marks Pl RM10 . . . . . . .81 D2
St Mark's Pl
Notting Hill W11. . . . . .91 A1
Wimbledon SW19. . . . . . . .179 B4
St Mark's Prim Sch
Hanwell W7 . . . . 108 C4
8 Mitcham CR4. . . . . . . .180 D1
11 Upper Holloway N19 . . . .72 A6
St Mark's RC Sch TW3. . . .129 C2
St Marks Rd
15 North Kensington
NW10. . . . . .90 D1
North Kensington W10. . . . . .90 D2
St Mark's Rd
Bromley BR2. . . . . 209 B6
Croydon SE25 . . . . 206 A5
Ealing W5 . . . . 110 A5
Enfield EN1. . . . . .17 D6
Hanwell W7 . . . . 108 C4
Mitcham CR4 . . . . .181 A1
Notting Hill W11. . . . . .91 A1
Teddington TW11 . . . . .175 B3
St Mark's Rise E8. . . . . . .73 D3
St Mark's Sq NW1. . . . . . .231 A5
St Mark St E1. . . . 95 D1 243 D1
St Martha's Convent Jun Sch
11 EN5 . . . . .1 A1
St Martha's Senior Sch
EN4. . . . . .1 C4
**St Martin-in-the-Fields High
Sch 21** SW2 . . . . 160 C3
St Martin of Porres Prim Sch
N11. . . . . .31 C4
St Martin's Almshouses
NW1 . . . . 232 A6
St Martins App HA4 . . . . . .39 C2
St Martin's Ave E6 . . . . . . .99 D5
St Martins Cl DA18. . . . . . 124 D4
South Oxhey WD19. . . . . . . .22 C6
St Martin's Cl Enfield EN1. . .6 B4
NW1 . . . . 232 A6
St Martins Ct N1. . . . . . . .95 C6
West Norwood SE27. . . . . . 160 D2
St Martins La BR3. . . . . . 207 D4
St Martin's La
WC2. . . . . . . .116 A6 250 A5
St Martin's Le Grand
EC1 . . . . 242 A2
St Martin's Pl WC2 . . . . . . 250 A5
St Martin's Rd
Edmonton N9 . . . . .18 B2
Finchley N2. . . . . .30 B2
Stockwell SW9 . . . . .138 B3
St Martin's Sch NW7. . . . . .27 B5
St Martin's Way SW17. . . . .158 A1
St Mary Abbots CE Prim Sch
W8 . . . . .113 D4 245 C1
St Mary Abbot's Ct W14. . . 254 C5
St Mary Abbot's Pl W8 . . . 254 D5
St Mary Abbots Terr
W14. . . . . 254 D5
St Mary at Hill
EC3 . . . . .117 C6 253 A5
St Mary Ave SM6. . . . . . . 219 B5
St Mary Axe EC3 . . 95 C1 243 B2
St Marychurch St SE16. . . .118 C4
St Mary Graces Ct E1 . . . . 253 D6
St Marylebone CE Sch The
W1. . . . . 93 A2 238 B4
St Mary le Bow Church★
EC2 . . . . 242 B1

St Mary- le-Park Ct
SW11. . . . . 267 B3
St Mary Magdalene Acad
N7. . . . . .72 C2
**St Mary Magdalene CE Prim
Sch**
3 Paddington W2 . . . . . . .91 D2
10 Peckham SE15. . . . . . .140 B3
16 Woolwich SE18 . . . . . . 122 C2
**St Mary Magdalene's RC
Prim Sch**
Brockley SE4 . . . . 141 A1
14 Mortlake SW14. . . . . . .133 B2
**St Mary Magdelen's RC Jun
Sch 1** NW2 . . . . .68 B2
St Mary Newington Cl
SE17 . . . . 263 B2
**St Mary of the Angels RC
Prim Sch** W2. . . . . .91 C1
St Mary RC Prim Sch 22
W10. . . . . .91 A3
St Mary Rd E17. . . . . .53 D5
St Marys IG11. . . . . .101 B6
**St Mary & St Michael Prim
Sch 27** E1. . . . . .96 C1
**St Mary & St Pancras CE
Prim Sch** NW1. . . .93 D5 232 C3
St Mary's App E12 . . . . . . .78 B3
St Marys Ave UB2 . . . . . . 107 D2
St Mary's Ave
Beckenham BR2. . . . . 208 C4
Finchley N3. . . . . .29 B1
Teddington TW11 . . . . .174 D4
Wanstead E11 . . . . .55 B2
**St Mary's Bryanston Square
CE Sch** W1 . . . . . .92 D2 237 C3
St Mary's CE High Sch
NW4. . . . . .46 C6
St Mary's CE Inf Sch 3
N8. . . . . .50 B5
St Mary's CE Jun Sch 5
N8. . . . . .50 A5
St Mary's CE Prim Sch
Chessington KT9 . . . . .214 A2
East Barnet EN4 . . . . .14 C5
Finchley N3. . . . . .29 B3
Islington N1. . . . . . .94 D6 234 D6
London SE13. . . . . 163 D6
15 Putney SW15. . . . . . . .134 D2
Walthamstow E17 . . . . .53 D5
Willesden NW10. . . . . .67 C2
St Mary's CE Prim Sch (Inf)
12 TW1. . . . . .153 A4
St Mary's CE Prim Sch (Jun)
TW1 . . . . .153 B4
St Mary's Church Ho 11
E17. . . . . .53 D5
St Mary's Cl BR5. . . . . . . .190 B1
Chessington KT9 . . . . .214 B1
Ewell KT17 . . . . 215 D1
Sunbury TW16 . . . . 194 A5
Tottenham N17. . . . . .34 A2
St Mary's Coll TW1. . . . . . .152 D1
St Mary's Cres
Hayes UB3 . . . . 105 D6
Hendon NW4 . . . . .46 B6
Hounslow TW7 . . . . 130 C5
St Marys Ct
Abbey Wood SE2. . . . . 124 D2
Newham E6 . . . . 100 B3
SE7 . . . . 143 D5
St Mary's Ct
Bedford Pk W6 . . . . 111 D3
Ealing W5 . . . . 109 D4
Finchley N12. . . . . .30 A3
Kingston u T KT3. . . . . 199 C6
Leytonstone E11. . . . . .54 D1
Wallington SM6 . . . . 219 C4
St Mary's Dr TW14 . . . . . . .149 A4
St Mary's Est 2 SE16 . . . . .118 C4
St Mary's Flats NW1 . . . . . 232 C2
St Mary's Gate W8 . . . . . . 255 C5
St Mary's Gdns SE11 . . . . . 261 B4
St Mary's Gn 1 N2. . . . . . . .48 A6
St Mary's Gr
Barnes SW13. . . . . .134 B2
Chiswick W4 . . . . .132 D6
Islington N1. . . . . .72 D2
Richmond TW10, TW9. . . . . .132 B1
St Mary's Ho Ealing W5 . . . 109 D3
N1. . . . . 234 D6
St Mary's Hospl
W2 . . . . 92 B1 236 D2
St Mary's Hospl Medical Sch
W2 . . . . 92 B1 236 D2
**St Mary's Kilburn CE Prim
Sch 10** NW6. . . . . .91 C6
St Mary's Lo E11. . . . . .55 B3
St Mary's Mans
Dagenham NW10. . . . . .89 C6
Paddington W2. . . . . .92 B2 236 C4
St Mary's Mews NW6. . . . . .69 D1
St Mary's Path N1 . . . . 234 D6
St Mary's Pl Ealing W5 . . . 109 D4
Eltham SE9. . . . . .166 C5
Kensington W8. . . . .113 D3 255 C5
St Mary's RC High Sch
CR0. . . . . 205 A1

St Mary's RC Inf Sch
SM5 . . . . 218 D4
St Mary's RC Jun & Inf Schs
Croydon CR0. . . . . 205 B1
London N15 . . . . .51 B4
St Mary's RC Jun Sch
Wallington SM5 . . . . 218 D3
Walthamstow E17 . . . . .54 A6
St Mary's RC Prim Sch
Beckenham BR3 . . . . 186 A3
8 Chingford E4. . . . . .20 B3
Chiswick W4. . . . . 133 C6
10 Clapham Pk SW4. . . . . 159 C6
Clapham SW8. . . . 137 B4 268 C2
Enfield EN3. . . . . .6 D1
Hammersmith W14 . . . . 112 D3
13 Isleworth TW7 . . . . 131 A2
Merton SW19 . . . . 179 C3
Paddington NW6 . . . . .91 C5
SE9 . . . . 166 C6
St Mary's Rd IG1 . . . . .79 B6
Ealing W5. . . . . 109 D5
East Barnet EN4. . . . . .14 D4
East Molesey KT8. . . . . .196 B4
Finchley N2. . . . . .30 B2
Golders Green NW11 . . . . . . .47 A2
Harlesden NW10 . . . . .89 C6
Hayes UB3 . . . . 105 D6
Hornsey N8. . . . . .50 A5
Leyton E10 . . . . .76 A6
Long Ditton KT6 . . . . 197 C1
Lower Edmonton N9. . . . . . . .18 C3
Newham E13 . . . . .99 B5
Nunhead SE15 . . . . 140 C3
South Norwood SE25 . . . . . . 205 C6
Surbiton KT6. . . . . 197 D3
Wimbledon SW19. . . . . 179 B5
Worcester Pk KT4. . . . . 215 C6
**St Mary's & St John's CE
Prim Sch** NW4. . . . . .46 B4
**St Mary's & St Peter's CE
Prim Sch 12** TW11 . . . . . . 174 D5
St Mary's Sch Hampstead
NW3. . . . . .70 B3
St Mary's Sq Ealing W5. . . . 109 D4
W2 . . . . 236 C4
**St Mary's Stoke Newington
CE Prim Sch 2** N16. . . . . . .73 C6
St Mary St SE18. . . . . . . .122 C2
St Mary's Terr W2 . . . . . . 236 C4
St Mary's Twr EC1. . . . . . . 242 B5
St Marys View HA3 . . . . . . .43 A4
St Mary's Wlk Hayes UB3. . .105 D6
SE11. . . . . 261 B4
St Matthew Acad SE3 . . . . . 142 C2
St Matthew's Ave KT6 . . . . .198 B1
St Matthew's CE Prim Sch
Enfield EN3. . . . . .18 C6
Surbiton KT6. . . . . 198 A2
Wimbledon SW20. . . . . 178 A4
Yiewsley UB7 . . . . 104 A5
St Matthews CE Sch
SW1 . . . . 115 D3 259 D6
St Matthews Ct
Muswell Hill N10. . . . . .31 A1
SE1. . . . . 262 A5
2 Stratford E15. . . . . . . .76 D1
7 Walthamstow E10. . . . . .53 D2
St Matthew's Ct 1
TW15. . . . . 170 C5
St Matthews Dr BR1. . . . . . 210 B4
St Matthew's Ho 8
SE17 . . . . 139 B6
St Matthew's Lo NW1 . . . . . 232 B4
St Matthew's Rd
Clapham Pk SW2 . . . . 160 B6
Ealing W5 . . . . 110 A5
St Matthew's Row E2 . . .96 A3
St Matthew St SW1 . . . . . 259 C5
St Matthias CE Prim Sch
E2 . . . . 95 D3 243 D6
St Matthias CI NW9 . . . . . . .45 D4
St Matthias's CE Prim Sch 32
N16. . . . . .73 C4
St Mauritius Ho SE13. . . . . 164 A6
St Maur Rd SW6 . . .135 B4 264 D1
St Mellion Cl SE28 . . . . . . 102 D1
St Merryn Cl SE17 . . . . . . .145 B5
St Merryn Ct BR3 . . . . .185 C3
**St Michael & All Angels CE
Acad 35** SE5. . . . . 139 A3
**St Michael-at-Bowes CE Jun
Sch** N13. . . . . .32 C4
**St Michael & St Martin RC
Prim Sch 1** TW4 . . . . . . .129 B2
St Michael's Alley EC3 . . . . 242 D1
St Michaels Ave N9 . . . . . . .18 C4
St Michael's Ave HA9 . . . . . .66 C2
St Michael's CE Prim Sch
Camden Town
NW1. . . . . 93 C6 232 A6
DA16. . . . . .146 C4
Enfield EN2. . . . . .5 A4
5 Forest Hill SE26. . . . . . .185 A6
Highgate N6. . . . . .49 A2
Wandsworth SW18 . . . . .157 B4
Wood Green N22 . . . . .32 B2
St Michaels Cl BR1. . . . . . 210 A6
4 Newham E16. . . . . .99 D2
Worcester Pk KT4. . . . . 215 D6

St Michael's Cl
Colney Hatch N12. . . . . .30 C5
DA18. . . . . .124 D4
Finchley N3. . . . . .29 B1
St Michael's Cres HA5. . . . . .41 A3
St Michaels Ct 2 E14 . . . .98 A2
St Michael's Ct
Brunswick Pk N11 . . . . .15 A1
Golders Green NW11. . . . . . . .47 B2
St Michael's Flats NW1. . . . 232 C3
St Michael's Gdns W10. . . . .91 A2
St Michaels Ho SE26. . . . . 185 B6
St Michael's Hospl EN2 . . . .5 B4
St Michael's RC Gram Sch 8
N12. . . . . .30 A5
St Michaels RC Prim Sch
TW15. . . . . 170 C5
St Michael's RC Prim Sch 4
E6. . . . . 100 B5
St Michael's RC Sec Sch 38
SE16. . . . . .118 A4
St Michaels Rd TW15. . . . . 170 C5
St Michael's Rd
Cricklewood NW2. . . . . .68 C4
Croydon CR0. . . . . 205 A1
DA16. . . . . .146 B2
Stockwell SW9 . . . . 138 B3
Wallington SM6 . . . . 219 C2
St Michael's Rise DA16. . . . 146 B4
St Michael's St
W2. . . . . 92 C1 237 A2
St Michael Steiner Sch The
18 SW18. . . . . 157 C6
St Michael's Terr N22 . . . . . .32 A2
St Mildred's Ct EC2 . . . . . . 242 C1
St Mildreds Rd SE12,
SE6 . . . . 164 D4
St Mirren Ct 8 EN5. . . . . . .14 A6
St Monica's RC Prim Sch
Palmers Green N14 . . . . .16 A1
24 Shoreditch N1. . . . . . .95 C4
St Monica's CE Prim Sch
TW17 . . . . 192 D3
St Nicholas Cl WD6 . . . . . . .9 D5
St Nicholas Ct E4. . . . . . . .36 A4
St Nicholas Ctr 7 SM1. . 217 D3
St Nicholas' Flats NW1. . . . 232 C3
St Nicholas Glebe SW17. . . .181 A4
St Nicholas Ho SE8 . . . . . . 141 C6
St Nicholas Mans SW17 . . . 158 D2
St Nicholas Rd
Plumstead SE18. . . . . 123 D2
Sutton SM1. . . . . 217 D3
Thames Ditton KT7. . . . . . . 196 D3
St Nicholas Sch Elst WD6 . . .9 D5
London NW9. . . . . .67 A6
St Nicholas St SE8 . . . . . . .141 C4
St Nicholas Way SM1. . . . . 217 D3
St Nicolas La BR7 . . . . 188 A2
St Ninian's Ct N20 . . . . .14 D1
St Norbert Gn SE4. . . . . . . 141 A1
St Norbert Rd SE4 . . . . 141 A1
St Olaf's Rd SW6. . .135 A5 264 B3
St Olaves Ct W2. . . . . 245 C5
St Olave's Ct EC2 . . . . 242 C1
St Olave's Est SE1. . . . . . . 253 B2
St Olave's Gdns SE11. . . . . 261 A4
St Olave's Mans SE11 . . . . . 261 A4
St Olaves Prep Sch SE9 . . . 166 D2
St Olav's Sq 32 SE16. . . . . .118 C4
St Osmund's RC Prim Sch
SW13. . . . . 133 D4
St Oswald's Pl
SE11 . . . . 116 B1 260 C1
St Oswald's Rd SW16. . . . . 182 D2
St Oswulf St SW1. . . . . . . 259 D3
St Owen Ho SE1 . . . . 263 B6
ST PANCRAS. 94 A4
St Pancras Almshouses 13
NW5 . . . . .70 D3
St Pancras Commercial Ctr
NW1. . . . . 232 B6
6 Wembley HA0. . . . . . . .66 A2
St Pancras Ct Finchley N2 . . .30 B1
St Pancras Hospl
NW1. . . . . .93 D6 232 C5
St Pancras International Sta
WC1. . . . . .94 A4 233 A2
St Pancras Way
NW1 . . . . .93 D6 232 C6
St Patrick's Coll
W1. . . . . .93 D1 239 C2
St Patricks Ct IG8. . . . . . . .36 C3
St Patrick's RC Prim Sch
Camden Town NW5 . . . . .71 B3
Plumstead SE18 . . . . 123 B2
6 Walthamstow E17. . . . . .53 A5
St Paul's Acad SE2. . . . . . 146 A6
**St Paul's & All Hallows CE
Jun & Inf Schs 1** N17. . . .34 A3
St Paul's Ave Harrow HA3 . . .44 B5
Rotherhithe SE16. . . . . .118 D5
Willesden NW2. . . . . .68 C2
St Paul's Cath★
EC4. . . . . 95 A1 242 A1
St Paul's Cath Sch
EC4. . . . . 95 A1 242 A1

St Paul's CE Jun Sch 18
KT2. . . . . 176 C3
St Pauls CE Prim Sch
14 Brentford TW8 . . . . . . .131 D6
1 Friern Barnet N11. . . . . .31 B5
St Paul's CE Prim Sch
Chessington KT9 . . . . .214 A4
24 E1. . . . . 118 A6
1 Friern Barnet N11. . . . . .31 B5
23 Hammersmith W6. . . . . .112 C1
Hampstead NW3 . . . . .70 D1
Mill Hill NW7. . . . . .28 B6
SE17. . . . . 117 A1 262 A2
Southgate N21. . . . . .16 A3
St Pauls Church Yd
EC4. . . . . 95 A1 242 A1
St Pauls Cl Ealing W5 . . . . .110 B4
Hayes UB3. . . . . .105 B1
St Paul's Cl
Ashford TW15. . . . . 171 A5
Borehamwood WD6 . . . . .11 A6
Carshalton SM5 . . . . 202 C1
Chessington KT9 . . . . .213 D4
Greenwich SE7 . . . . 121 D1
Hounslow TW3, TW4. . . . . . .129 A3
ST PAUL'S CRAY. 190 A1
St Paul's Cray Rd BR7. . . . .189 B2
St Pauls Cres NW1 . . . . . . .71 D1
St Paul's Ct
Clapham SW4. . . . . 137 D1
Hounslow TW4 . . . . 129 A2
6 Upper Holloway N19 . . . .72 A6
St Paul's Dr E15 . . . . .76 B3
St Paul's Girls' Sch 1
W6 . . . . .112 D2
St Pauls Ho N17 . . . . .34 A3
St Pauls Mews NW1. . . . . . .71 D1
St Paul's Pl N1 . . . . .73 B2
St Paul's RC Coll TW16. . . . 172 A2
St Paul's RC Prim Sch
Thames Ditton KT7. . . . . . . 196 C2
2 Wood Green N22. . . . . . .32 B1
St Pauls Rd Barking IG11. . . 101 A6
Richmond TW9 . . . . 132 B2
St Paul's Rd
Brentford TW8 . . . . 131 D6
Canonbury N1. . . . . .73 A2
South Norwood CR7. . . . . . . 205 A6
Tottenham N17. . . . . .34 A2
St Pauls Rise N13. . . . . . . .32 D4
St Paul's Sch SW13 . . . . . . 112 A1
St Paul's Sq BR2. . . . . 187 A1
St Pauls Sta EC2 . . .95 A1 242 A2
St Pauls Steiner Sch 22
N1. . . . . .73 B2
St Paul St N1 . . . . 235 B5
St Paul's Terr SE17 . . . . . . 138 D6
St Paul's Twr 14 E10. . . . . . .53 D2
St Pauls View WC1 . . . . . . 234 A1
St Paul's Way Finchley N3 . . .29 D3
Tower Hamlets E3 . . . . .97 C2
St Paul's Way Com Sch 28
E3. . . . . .97 C2
**St Paul's with St Michael's
Prim Sch 28** E8 . . . . .96 A6
St Paul's Wood Hill BR5. . . .189 D1
**St Paul with St Luke CE Prim
Sch 18** E3 . . . . .97 B2
St Peter Chanel RC Prim Sch
DA14. . . . . .190 C5
St Peter in Chains RC Inf Sch
N8. . . . . .50 A4
St Peter & Paul RC Prim Sch
BR5. . . . . 189 C1
**St Peter & St Paul RC Prim
Sch** EC1. . . . . .94 D3 241 D6
St Peter & St Paul RC Sch
CR4. . . . . 202 D5
St Peter's Alley EC3 . . . . . . 242 D1
St Peters Ave N12. . . . . . . .30 C3
St Peter's Ave
Edmonton N18 . . . . .34 A6
37 Hackney E2. . . . . .96 A5
Walthamstow E17 . . . . .54 C5
St Petersburgh Mews
W2 . . . . 245 C6
St Petersburgh Pl
W2 . . . . 113 D6 245 C5
St Peter's CE Prim Sch
15 Chiswick W6 . . . . .112 A2
9 E1. . . . . .118 C5
6 Paddington W9 . . . . .91 C1
SE17. . . . . 117 B1 262 C1
SW1 . . . . 115 D3 258 D5
St Peter's Church Ct N1. . . . 234 D6
St Peters Cl BR7. . . . . .189 B3
Ilford IG2. . . . . .57 D5
1 Upper Tooting SW17. . . . 158 C2
St Peter's Ct Barnet EN5. . . .12 B6
Bushey WD23. . . . . .8 B3
Hackney E2. . . . . .96 A5
Ruislip HA4. . . . . .62 D6
St Peters Ct
East Molesey KT8. . . . . 195 C5
New Cross SE4. . . . . 141 B3
28 Stepney E1. . . . . .96 C3
St Peter's Ct SE Hendon NW4. .46 C4
Lewisham SE12 . . . . 164 C6
St Peter's Gdns SE27. . . . . .160 C1
St Peter's Gr W6. . . . . 112 A2

St Peters Ho
Tottenham Hale N15.......52 A5
WC1...........................233 B1
St Peter's Ho 4 SE17...139 B6
Stamford Hill N16.........51 C2
St Peters La BR5...........190 A1
St Peters Mews N4.........50 D4
St Peter's Pl W9...........91 D3
St Peter's Prim Sch CR2. 221 C2
St Peter's RC Prim Sch
Dagenham RM9..........103 B6
Woolwich SE18...........122 D2
St Peters Rd KT1.........176 C1
St Peter's Rd
Chiswick W6............112 A4
Croydon CR0............221 B4
East Molesey KT8......195 C5
Edmonton N9..............18 B3
Isleworth TW1..........153 B6
Southall UB1.............85 C2
St Peter's Sq
Chiswick W6............111 D1
Hackney E2................96 A5
St Peter's St
Croydon CR2............221 B3
Islington N1.....94 D6 234 D5
St Peter's Street Mews
N1.........................234 D4
St Peter's Terr SW6.....264 B3
St Peter's Villas 5 W6..112 A2
St Peters Way UB3......105 B1
St Peter's Way
De Beauvoir Town N1.....73 C1
Ealing W5..................87 D2
St Peter's Wharf 8 W6..112 A1
St Philip Ho WC1........234 A1
St Philip's Ave KT4......216 B4
St Philips Gate KT4.....216 B6
St Philip St 1 SW8......137 B3
St Philip's Rd Dalston E8..74 A2
Surbiton KT6..............197 D3
St Philip's Sch
Chessington KT9........213 D2
SW7...............114 A2 256 B3
St Philip St SW8........137 B3
St Philip's Way N1......235 B5
St Philomena's RC High Sch
SM5.......................218 C3
St Quentin Ave W10....158 B5
St Quentin Rd DA16....145 D2
St Quintin Ave W10......90 D2
St Quintin Gdns 21 W10..90 C2
St Quintin Rd E13........99 B5
St Raphaels Ho W13.....109 C5
St Raphael's RC Prim Sch
UB5........................84 B5
St Raphael's Way NW10..67 A3
St Regis Cl N10...........31 B1
St Regis Hts NW3.........69 D5
St Richards Ct TW10....153 B1
St Richard's Ho NW1....232 C2
St Richard's with St Andrew's
CE Prim Sch TW10....153 B1
St Robert Southwell RC Prim
Sch NW9...................45 A3
St Ronan's 2 N3...........29 C2
St Ronans Cl EN4...........2 B5
St Ronans Cres IG8........37 A3
St Rule St SW8............137 C3
St Savior's CE Inf Sch 3
W5.........................109 D6
St Saviours SW4.........137 B1
St Saviour & St Olaves CE
Sch SE1........117 B3 262 D5
St Saviour's CE Jun Sch
TW1......................153 B5
St Saviour's CE Prim Sch
Paddington W2...........91 C2
17 Shepherd's Bush W12. 112 C4
2 St Johns SE8..........141 C3
SW8..............138 B5 270 C4
St Stephens Cl E17.......53 D4
St Stephen's Cl
Maitland Pk NW5.........70 D3

St Stephen's Cl continued
NW8.......................230 B5
Southall UB1..............85 C2
St Stephen's Cres
Notting Hill W2...........91 C1
Thornton Heath CR7...204 C6
St Stephens Ct
Ealing W13................87 B1
Enfield EN1................17 C5
Hornsey Vale N8..........50 B3
St Stephen's Gdns
Notting Hill W2...........91 C1
4 Putney SW15.........157 B6
Twickenham TW1.......153 C5
St Stephen's Gr SE13...142 A2
St Stephens Ho 7 SE17..139 B6
St Stephen's Mews 34
W2.........................91 C2
St Stephens Par E6.......77 C1
St Stephens Prim Sch E6..77 C1
St Stephen's RC Prim Sch
DA16.....................146 A3
St Stephens Rd
Barnet EN5................12 D6
Upton E6...................77 C1
Walthamstow E17........53 D4
St Stephen's Rd Bow E3..97 B5
Ealing W13................87 C1
Enfield EN1.................6 D6
Hounslow TW3, TW4...151 C6
Yiewsley UB7............104 A5
St Stephen's Row EC4...242 C1
St Stephen's Terr SW8..270 C3
St Stephen's Wlk SW7..256 A4
St Swithin's La
EC4.............117 B6 252 C6
St Swithun's Rd SE13...164 B6
St Swithun Wells RC Prim
Sch HA4...................62 D5
St Teresa's RC Fst & Mid Sch
HA4........................24 A2
St Teresa's RC Prim Sch
SM4.......................202 B3
St Teresa's RC Prim Sch The
RM8........................80 C4
St Theresa Ct E4..........20 B4
St Theresas Ct E9.........75 C4
St Theresa's RC Prim Sch
N3..........................47 D6
St Theresa's Rd TW14...127 C1
St Thomas à Beckett RC Prim
Sch SE2..................124 A3
St Thomas Becket RC Prim
Sch 4 SE25.............206 A3
St Thomas' CE Prim Sch 23
W10........................91 A3
St Thomas' Cl KT6.......198 B1
St Thomas Ct
14 Camden Town NW1...71 C1
Sidcup DA5..............169 C4
11 Walthamstow E10.....53 D2
St Thomas' Ct HA5........23 A2
St Thomas' Dr BR5.......211 A1
Pinner HA5.................23 A2
St Thomas Gdns IG1......79 A2
St Thomas Ho 2 E1.......96 D1
St Thomas More Language
Coll SW3......114 C2 257 C6
St Thomas More RC Prim
Sch
Bexley DA7..............147 B3
SE9........................144 A2
St Thomas More RC Sch
SW6.............166 C5
Wood Green N22..........32 C3
St Thomas of Canterbury
RC Prim Sch
Mitcham CR4............203 A6
SW6.............135 B5 264 C4
St Thomas Rd
Newham E16...............99 A1
Osidge N14.................15 D4
St Thomas' Rd W4.......133 A6
Highbury N4, N5..........72 C5
St Thomas's Rd E9........74 C1
St Thomas Sq
SE1.............117 B5 252 D3
St Thomas's Way
SW6.............135 B5 264 D4
St Thomas the Apostle Coll
SE15.......................140 C4
St Timothy's Mews 3
BR1.......................187 B2
St Ursula Gr HA5..........41 A4
St Ursula Rd UB1..........85 C1
St Ursula's Convent Sch
SE10......................142 B5
St Vincent Cl SE27.......182 D5
St Vincent De Paul Ho 24
E1.........................96 C2
St Vincent De Paul RC Prim
Sch SW1......115 C3 259 B6
St Vincent Ho SE1.......263 C6
St Vincent Rd TW2......152 A5

St Vincents La NW7......28 C6
St Vincent's Nursing Home
HA5........................39 D6
St Vincents RC Prim Sch
SE9........................188 A6
St Vincent's RC Prim Sch
Acton W3.................110 D6
Dagenham RM8...........80 C6
London NW7................28 C5
Marylebone W1....93 A2 238 B3
St Vincent St W1........238 B3
St Wilfrid's Cl EN4........14 C6
St Wilfrid's Rd EN4........14 C6
St William of York Prim Sch
SE23......................163 A3
St Winefride's Ave E12...78 B3
St Winefride's RC Prim Sch
E12........................78 B3
St Winifred's RC Inf Sch
SE12......................164 C6
St Winifred's RC Jun Sch
SE12......................164 D4
St Winifred's Rd TW11..175 B4
Sakura Dr N22..............31 D2
Sala Ho SE3...............143 B1
Salamanca Pl SE1.......260 C3
Salamanca St SE1,
SE11...........116 B2 260 C3
Salamander Cl KT2......175 C5
Salamander Quay KT1..175 D2
Salcombe Dr
Dagenham RM6...........59 B3
North Cheam SM4......200 D1
Salcombe Gdns
Clapham SW4............137 B1
Mill Hill NW7...............28 C4
Salcombe Ho 6 SE23...162 C2
Salcombe Lo NW5.........71 A4
Salcombe Pk IG10........21 D6
Salcombe Prep Sch (Infant
Dept) N14...................15 B6
Salcombe Prep Sch (Junior
Dept) 1 N14...............15 B4
Salcombe Rd
Ashford TW15...........148 A1
23 Stoke Newington N16. 73 C3
Walthamstow E17........53 B2
Salcombe Villas 13
TW10.....................154 A6
Salcombe Way Hayes UB4. 83 C4
Ruislip HA4................62 A6
Salcot N4....................72 B6
Salcott Rd
Wallington CR0.........220 B4
Wandsworth SW11.....158 D6
Salehurst Cl HA3..........44 A4
Salehurst Rd SE4.......163 B5
Salem Ho 13 E9..........74 D2
Salem Pl CR0.............221 A5
Salem Rd W2....113 D6 245 D6
Sale Pl W2........92 C1 237 A2
Salesian Coll
SW11.........136 C4 267 A1
Sale St E2...................96 A3
Salford Ho 5 E14........120 A2
Salford Rd SW12, SW2. 159 D3
Salhouse Cl SE28.......102 C1
Salisbury Ave
Barking IG11...............79 C1
Cheam SM1, SM2......217 B2
Hendon N3.................47 B6
Salisbury Cl SE17.......262 C4
Worcester Pk KT4......215 D5
Salisbury Ct
15 Bermondsey SE16...118 A3
Chiswick W4.............111 C2
EC4........................241 C1
Edgware HA8..............26 B6
Enfield EN2.................5 B1
Finchley N3................29 B1
Hackney E9................75 A3
Northolt UB5...............63 D3
Salisbury Gdns
5 Buckhurst Hill IG9.....21 D2
Wimbledon SW19......179 A3
Salisbury Hall Gdns E4...35 C4
Salisbury Ho
2 Islington N1............72 D2
Islington N1..............234 C6
3 Poplar E14...............97 D1
1 Ruislip HA4..............40 C1
Stanmore HA7............25 A4
5 Wallington SM6......219 B3
Westminster SW1......259 D2
Wimbledon SW19......156 D1
Salisbury Lower Sch N9..18 C4
Salisbury Mans
Edmonton N9..............18 A1
Harringay N4, N15.......50 D4
Salisbury Mews
Bromley Comm BR2....210 A4
Fulham SW6..............264 C3
Salisbury Pl
Camberwell SW9.......138 D5
Marylebone W1.........237 C4
Salisbury Prim Sch 1
E12.........................78 A3
Salisbury Rd Barnet EN5..1 A2
Bromley Comm BR2....210 A4
Chingford E4...............19 C1

Salisbury Rd continued
Croydon SE25............206 A3
Dagenham RM10.........81 D2
East Bedfont TW6......149 A5
Enfield EN3..................7 B6
Feltham TW13..........150 C3
Forest Gate E7............77 A2
Harringay N4...............50 D4
Harrow HA1................42 B4
Hounslow TW4..........128 C2
Ilford IG3...................79 C6
Kingston u T KT3.......199 B6
Leyton E10..................76 A6
Old Bexley DA5..........169 C3
Pinner HA5.................40 C3
Plashet E12................77 D3
Richmond TW9..........132 A1
Southall UB2.............107 A2
Tottenham N22............32 D1
Wallington SM5.........218 D2
Walthamstow E17........54 A4
West Ealing W13.......109 B4
Wimbledon SW19......179 A3
Worcester Pk KT4......215 C5
Salisbury Sq EC4........241 B1
Salisbury St
10 Acton W3..............111 A4
NW8.......................237 A5
Salisbury Terr SE15....148 C2
Salisbury Upper Sch N9..18 C4
Salisbury Wlk N19........71 C6
Salix Cl TW16............172 B3
Salix Ct N18................80 C3
Salliesfield TW2.........152 B5
Sally Murray Cl E12......78 C4
Salmen Rd E13.............98 D5
Salmon Cl HA7.............25 A4
Salmon La E14.............97 A1
Salmon Rd DA17........125 C1
Salmons Brook Ho EN2....4 D2
Salmons Rd
Chessington KT9.......214 A2
Edmonton N9..............18 A3
Salmon St Kingsbury NW9..45 A2
13 Poplar E14.............97 B1
Salomons Rd 2 E13......99 C2
Salop Rd E17...............52 D3
Saltash Cl SM1............217 B4
Saltash Rd DA16.........146 C4
Saltcoats Rd W4.........111 C4
Saltcroft Cl HA9...........44 D1
Saltdene N4.................50 B1
Salter Cl HA2...............63 B4
Salterford Rd SW17....181 A4
Salter Ho 8 SW16.......181 C6
Saltern Ct IG11...........102 B4
Salter Rd
Rotherhithe SE16.......118 D5
SE16......................119 A5
Salters' Hall Ct EC4.....252 C6
Salter's Hill SE19.......183 B5
Salters Rd
North Kensington W10...90 D3
Walthamstow E17........54 B5
11 Poplar E14............119 C6
Salterton Rd N7...........72 B5
Salt Hill Cl UB8............60 A3
Saltley Cl E6...............100 A1
Saltoun Rd SW2, SW9. 138 C1
Saltram Cl N15.............51 D5
Saltram Cres W9...........91 C4
Saltwell St E14............119 C6
Saltwood Gr SE17.......262 C1
Saltwood Ho 19 SE15...140 C6
Salusbury Prim Sch NW6. 91 B6
Salusbury Rd NW6........91 A6
Salutation Rd SE10.....120 C2
Salvador SW17..........180 D5
Salvatorian Coll HA3....24 C1
Salvia Gdns UB6...........87 A5
Salvin Rd SW15..........134 D2
Salway Cl IG8..............37 A3
Salway Ho E10.............75 D6
Salway Pl E15..............76 C2
Salway Rd E15.............76 B2
Salween Ho 2 N16........73 B4
Samantha Cl E17..........53 B2
Samantha Ct E11..........54 C2
Sam Bartram Cl SE7.....121 C1
Sambrook Ho 25 E1......96 C2
Sambruck Mews SE6....163 D3
Samels Ct W6.............112 A1
Samford Ho N1...........234 B1
Samford St NW8.........237 A5
Samira Cl 1 E17............53 C2
Sam Manners Ho 7
SE10......................120 C1
Sam March Ho 5 E14.....98 B1
Samos Rd SE20..........184 B1
Sampson Ave EN5........12 C6
Sampson Cl DA17........125 A3
Sampson Ct TW17......193 A4
Sampson St E1............118 A5
Samson Ct 5 DA17......125 C2
Samson Ho SE18.........123 A4
Samson St E13.............99 C5
Samuel Cl Bushey HA7...9 A2
SE14......................140 D6

St P–San 397

Samuel Cl continued
Shoreditch E8..............95 D6
Woolwich SE18..........122 A2
Samuel Ct
Beckenham BR3........207 D6
Shoreditch N1.............95 D6
Samuel Gray Gdns KT2. 175 D2
Samuel Ho
15 Shoreditch E8........95 D6
3 West Norwood SE27. 182 D6
Samuel Johnson Cl
SW16......................182 B6
Samuel Jones Ind Est 7
SE15......................139 C5
Samuel Lewis Bldgs N1..72 C2
Samuel Lewis Trust
Dwellings
6 Camberwell SE5......139 A4
Chelsea SW3............257 A3
Walham Green
SW6.............135 C5 265 B4
West Kensington W14...254 B4
Samuel Lewis Trust Est
N15........................51 C3
Samuel Lo N3..............29 B1
Samuel Rhodes Sch
N1...............94 C6 234 A6
Samuel Richardson Ho
W14......................254 C3
Samuel's Cl 2 W6........112 C2
Samuel St SE15...........139 D5
Woolwich SE18..........122 B2
Sancroft Cl NW2...........68 B5
Sancroft Ct SW11.......267 B2
Sancroft Ho SE11.......260 D2
Sancroft Rd HA3...........25 A1
Sancroft St SE11.116 B1 260 D2
Sanctuary Mews 15 E8..73 D2
Sanctuary Rd TW19,
TW6......................148 C5
Sanctuary St SE1........252 B2
Sanctuary The
Morden SM4.............201 C3
Sidcup DA5...............168 D5
35 Wapping E1...........118 B5
Westminster SW1.115 D3 259 D6
Sandale Cl N16.............73 B5
Sandall Cl W5...............88 A3
Sandall Ho 7 E3............97 A5
Sandall Rd Ealing W5.....88 A3
Kentish Town NW5.......71 C2
Sandal Rd Edmonton N18..34 A5
New Malden KT3........199 C5
Sandal St E15...............98 C6
Sandalwood Cl
Borehamwood EN5.......11 D6
11 E1.......................97 A3
Sandalwood Dr HA4......39 A2
Sandalwood Ho N15.....167 D1
6 Hampstead NW3........69 D2
Sandalwood Rd TW13..150 B1
Sandbach Pl SE18.......123 A1
Sandbourne
4 Kensington W11.......91 C1
14 Paddington NW8.....91 D6
Sandbourne Ave SW19. 179 D1
Sandbourne Rd SE4.....141 A4
Sandbrook Cl NW7........27 B4
Sandbrook Rd N16........73 C5
Sandby Ct BR3...........185 B2
Sandby Gn SE9...........144 A2
Sandby Ho
11 Camberwell SE5....139 C4
6 Kilburn NW6............91 C6
Sandcroft Cl N13..........32 D4
Sandells Ave
Ashford TW15...........171 A6
Ashford TW15...........171 A6
Sandell St SE1............251 A2
Sanderling Ct 20 SE8...141 B6
Woolwich SE28..........124 C6
Sanders Cl TW12........174 A5
Sanders Ho
Streatham SW16.......182 A4
WC1.......................234 A2
Sanders La NW7..........28 C3
Sanderson Cl NW5........71 B4
Sanderson Ho 7 SE8....179 B1
Sanderson Sq BR1......210 C6
Sandersted Ave NW2.....69 A6
Sandersted Cl SW12....159 C4
Sandersted Rd
South Croydon CR2.....221 B1
Walthamstow E10.......53 B6
Sanders Way 3 N19.......49 D1
Sandfield WC1............233 B1
Sandfields Gdns CR7...204 D6
Sandfield Pl CR7.........205 A6
Sandfield Rd CR7........204 D6
Sandford Ave N22.........33 A2
Sandford Cl E6...........100 B3
Sandford Ct Barnet EN5..1 D2
Stamford Hill N16.........51 C1
Sandford Rd Bexley DA7. 147 A2
BR2.......................209 A5
Newham E6...............100 B4

Sandford Row SE17 .... **262** D2
Sandford St SW6 ...... **265** D3
Sandgate Ho
  14 Beckenham BR3 ..... **185** C3
  Ealing W5 .... **87** C2
  15 Hackney E5 .... **74** B4
Sandgate La SW17,
  SW18 .... **158** C3
Sandgate Rd DA16 ..... **146** C5
Sandgate St SE15 ..... **140** B6
Sandgate Trad Est SE15 .. **140** B6
Sandham Ct SW4 .... **270** B1
Sandham Point 10 SE18 . **122** D2
Sandhills CR0, SM6 .... **219** D4
Sandhills Mdw TW17 ... **193** A2
Sandhills The SW10 .... **266** B6
Sandhurst Ave
  Harrow HA2 .... **41** D3
  Tolworth KT5 .... **198** D2
Sandhurst Cl
  Queensbury NW9 .... **44** C6
  South Croydon CR2 ... **221** C1
Sandhurst Ct SW2 ..... **138** A1
Sandhurst Dr IG3 ...... **79** D4
Sandhurst Ho 12 E1 .... **96** C2
Sandhurst Jun & Inf Schs
  SE6 .... **164** C3
Sandhurst Mkt SE6 .... **164** A3
Sandhurst Rd
  Bexley DA5 .... **168** D6
  Catford SE6 .... **164** B3
  DA15 .... **168** A1
  Ponders End N9 .... **18** D5
  Queensbury HA8, NW9 .. **44** C6
Sandhurst Way CR2 .... **221** C1
Sandifer Dr NW9 .... **68** D5
Sandiford Rd SM3 ..... **217** B6
Sandiland Cres BR2 ... **224** D4
Sandilands CR0 .... **222** A5
Sandilands Rd
  SW6 .... **135** D4 **265** C1
Sandilands Sta CR0 .... **221** D6
Sandison St SE15 ..... **140** A2
Sandland St WC1 ...... **240** D3
Sandlings Cl SE15 ..... **140** B3
Sandlings The
  Tottenham N22 .... **50** D6
  5 Wood Green N22 .... **32** C1
Sandmartin Way CR4 ... **203** A1
Sandmere Rd SW4 ...... **138** A1
Sandon Cl KT10 .... **196** B1
Sandon Ct IG3 .... **80** A5
Sandon Ho 5 SW2 ...... **160** A4
Sandow Commercial Est
  UB3 .... **105** D3
Sandow Cres UB3 ...... **105** D3
Sandown Ave KT10 ..... **212** A3
Sandown Cl TW5 .... **128** A4
Sandown Gate KT10 .... **212** B5
Sandown Ho
  2 Acton Green W4 .... **111** A1
  Esher KT10 .... **212** A4
  Penge SE26 .... **184** B4
Sandown Park KT10 .... **212** A6
Sandown Rd
  Croydon SE25 .... **206** B4
  Esher KT10 .... **212** A4
Sandown Way UB5 ...... **63** B3
Sandpiper Cl
  Higham Hill E17 .... **34** D3
  Rotherhithe SE16 ..... **119** B4
Sandpiper Ct
  13 Cubitt Town E14 ... **120** A3
  1 SE8 .... **141** C5
Sandpiper Rd SM1 ..... **217** B3
Sandpiper Terr IG5 .... **56** D6
Sandpit Pl SE7 .... **122** A1
Sandpit Rd BR1 .... **186** C5
Sandpits Rd
  Richmond TW10 .... **153** D2
  South Croydon CR0 ... **222** D4
Sandra Cl Hounslow TW3 . **151** D6
  Tottenham N17 .... **33** A2
Sandra Ho KT8 .... **196** B4
Sandridge Cl
  Hadley Wood EN4 ...... **2** C6
  Harrow HA1 .... **42** C5
Sandridge St 3 N19 .... **71** C6
Sandringham Ave SW20 .. **179** A1
Sandringham Cl
  Enfield EN1 .... **5** C3
  Ilford IG6 .... **57** A6
  1 Putney SW19 .... **156** D3
Sandringham Cres HA2 .. **63** D6
Sandringham Ct
  3 Beckenham BR3 ..... **186** A2
  Edgware HA8 .... **26** D6
  Hillingdon UB10 ...... **83** A3
  Kingston u T KT2 ..... **176** A2
  Marylebone W1 .... **239** B1
  Putney SW15 .... **156** D5
  18 Rotherhithe SE16 .. **118** D5
  St John's Wood W9 ... **229** B1
  2 Twickenham TW1 ... **153** A3

Sandringham Dr
  Ashford TW15 .... **170** A6
  DA16 .... **145** C3
Sandringham Flats WC2. **249** D6
Sandringham Gdns
  Cranford TW5 .... **128** A4
  East Molesey KT8 ..... **195** C5
  Finchley N12 .... **30** B4
  Hornsey Vale N8 ...... **50** A3
  Ilford IG6 .... **57** A6
Sandringham Ho
  Richmond TW10 .... **154** C6
  W14 .... **254** A4
Sandringham Lo BR6 ... **226** C4
Sandringham Mews
  1 Ealing W5 .... **109** D6
  Hampton TW12 .... **173** B2
Sandringham Prim Sch 1
  E7 .... **77** C3
Sandringham Rd
  Barking IG11 .... **79** D2
  BR1 .... **187** A5
  Dalston E8 .... **73** D3
  Forest Gate E7 .... **77** C3
  Golders Green NW11 .. **47** A2
  Leytonstone E10 ...... **54** B3
  Northolt UB5 .... **63** C1
  Stanwell TW19, TW6 .. **148** A6
  Thornton Heath CR0 .. **205** A4
  Tottenham N22 .... **33** A1
  Willesden NW2 .... **68** B2
  Worcester Pk KT4 .... **216** A5
Sandrock Pl CR0 .... **222** D4
Sandrock Rd SE13 ..... **141** C2
SANDS END **136** A2
Sands End La
  SW6 .... **135** D4 **265** D2
Sandstone TW9 .... **132** C5
Sandstone La E16 ...... **121** B6
Sandstone Pl N19 ...... **71** B6
Sandstone Rd SE12 .... **165** B2
Sandtoft Rd SE7 .... **143** B6
Sandways 6 TW9 .... **132** C4
Sandwell Cres 2 NW6 .. **69** C2
Sandwell Mans 3 NW6 .. **69** C2
Sandwich Ho
  15 Rotherhithe SE16 .. **118** C4
  WC1 .... **233** A1
Sandwich St WC1 .. **94** A4 **233** A1
Sandwick Cl NW7 .... **28** A3
Sandy Bury BR6 .... **227** B5
Sandycombe Ctr TW9 .. **132** C2
Sandycombe Rd
  East Bedfont TW14 .... **150** A3
  Richmond TW9 .... **132** C3
Sandycoombe Rd TW1 .. **153** C5
Sandycroft SE2 .... **146** A6
Sandy Dr TW14 .... **149** C3
Sandy Hill Ave SE18 ... **122** D2
Sandy Hill La SE18 ..... **122** D2
Sandyhill Rd IG1 .... **78** D4
Sandy Hill Rd SE18 ..... **122** D1
Sandy La Belmont SM2 .. **217** A1
  BR5 .... **190** D2
  Bushey HA6 .... **22** A6
  Harrow HA3 .... **44** C3
  Mitcham CR4 .... **181** A2
  Richmond TW10 .... **153** D2
  Teddington KT8, TW11 . **175** B3
  Walton-on-T KT12 .... **194** C3
Sandy Lane N SM6 ...... **219** D3
Sandy Lane S SM6 ...... **219** C1
Sandy Lo N6 .... **49** C2
Sandymount Ave HA7 ... **25** D5
Sandy Rd NW3 .... **69** D6
Sandy Ridge BR7 .... **188** C4
Sandy's Row E1 .... **243** B3
Sandy Way Croydon CR0 . **223** B5
  Walton-on-T KT12 .... **193** D1
Sanford La 3 N16 .... **73** D6
Sanford St SE14, SE8 .. **141** A6
Sanford Terr N16 .... **73** D5
Sanford Wlk SE14 ...... **141** A6
  4 Stoke Newington N16 . **73** D6
Sangam Cl UB2 .... **107** A3
Sanger Ave KT9 .... **214** B4
Sangley Rd Catford SE6 . **164** A3
  South Norwood SE25 .. **205** C5
Sangora Rd 17 SW11 ... **136** B1
San Ho 29 E9 .... **74** D2
Sankey Ho 22 E2 .... **96** C5
Sansom Rd E11 .... **76** D6
Sansom St
  Camberwell SE5 .... **139** B4
  SE5 .... **139** B5
Sans Wlk EC1 ...... **94** A3 **241** C6
Santana SE18 .... **144** D5
Santley Ho SE1 .... **251** B1
Santley St SW4 .... **138** B1
Santos Rd SW18 .... **157** C6
Sapcote Trad Ctr NW10 . **67** D2
Saperton Wlk SE11 .... **260** D4
Sapperton Ct EC1 ...... **242** A6
Sapphire Cl
  Dagenham RM8 .... **58** C1
  Newham E6 .... **100** C1
Sapphire Ct 13 E1 ...... **118** A6
Sapphire Rd
  Rotherhithe SE8 ...... **119** A2

Sapphire Rd continued
  Willesden NW10 .... **67** A1
Saracen Cl CR0 .... **205** B3
Saracen's Head Yd EC2. **243** B1
Saracen St E14 .... **97** C1
Sarah Bonnell Sch E15 .. **76** C2
Sarah Ct UB5 .... **85** B6
Sarah Ho
  Roehampton SW15 .... **133** D1
  8 Stepney E1 .... **96** B1
Sarah Swift Ho SE1 .... **252** D2
Sarah Turnbull Ho 2
  SE18 .... **122** B2
Sara Lane Ct 31 N1 ..... **95** C5
Saratoga Rd E5 .... **74** C4
Sardeson Ho 13 SW27 .. **182** D5
Sardinia Ho WC2 .... **240** C1
Sardinia St WC2 .... **240** C2
Sargents Hill 7 .... **30** C2
Sarita Cl HA3 .... **24** B1
Sarjant Path SW19 ..... **156** D2
Sark Cl TW5 .... **129** C5
Sark Ho 3 Canonbury N1 . **73** A2
  Enfield EN3 .... **6** D5
Sark Twr SE28 .... **123** A4
Sark Wlk E16 .... **99** B1
Sarnesfield Ho SE15 ... **140** B6
Sarnes Ct 4 N11 .... **31** B6
Sarnesfield Rd EN2 ...... **5** B2
Sarratt Ho 6 W10 ...... **90** C2
Sarre Rd NW2 .... **69** B3
Sarsden Bldgs W1 ..... **238** B1
Sarsen Ave TW3 .... **129** C3
Sarsfeld Rd SW12, SW17 . **158** D3
Sarsfield Rd UB6 .... **87** C5
Sartor Rd SE15 .... **140** D1
Sarum Hall Sch NW3 .... **70** C1
Sarum Ho W11 .... **244** D5
Sarwan Ho 1 E7 .... **77** C1
Sassoon 4 NW9 .... **27** D2
Sassoon Ho SE15 ...... **140** C3
Satanita Cl E16 .... **99** D1
Satchell Mead NW9 .... **27** D2
Satchwell Rd 17 E2 .... **96** A4
Satin Ct NW9 .... **45** D5
Saturn Ho 4 E3 .... **97** C6
Satyr Ho SE15 .... **139** D6
Sauls Gn E11 .... **76** C5
Saunders Cl Ilford IG1 ... **57** B1
  14 Limehouse E14 ..... **119** B6
Saunders Ho 11 SW2 ... **160** C3
Saunders Ness Rd E14 .. **120** B2
Saunders Rd
  Hillingdon UB10 .... **82** B6
  Plumstead Comm SE18 . **123** D1
Saunders St SE11 ...... **261** A4
Saunders Way SE28 .... **124** B6
Saunderton Rd HA0 ..... **65** B3
Saunton Ave UB3 ...... **127** D5
Saunton Ct UB1 .... **108** A6
Savage Gdns EC3 ...... **253** B6
  Newham E6 .... **100** B1
Savana N16 .... **73** C6
Savannah Cl 9 SE15 .... **139** D5
Savera Cl UB2 .... **106** C3
Savernake Ct HA7 ...... **25** B4
Savernake Ho N4 .... **51** B2
Savernake Rd Enfield N9 . **18** A5
  Maitland Pk NW3 ...... **70** D4
Savery Dr KT6 .... **197** C2
Savile Cl New Malden KT3 . **199** C4
  Thames Ditton KT7 .... **197** A1
Savile Gdns CR0 .... **221** D6
Savill Gdns SW20 ...... **200** A6
Savill Ho 2 SW4 .... **159** D5
Savill Row IG8 .... **36** D4
Savin Lo 7 SM2 .... **218** A1
Savona Cl SW19 .... **178** D3
Savona Ct SW20 .... **178** D2
Savona St SW8 ... **137** C5 **269** A3
Savoy Ave UB3 .... **105** C1
Savoy Circus W3 ...... **111** D6
Savoy Cl Edgware HA8 ... **26** C5
  Newham E15 .... **98** C6
Savoy Ct Earl's Ct SW5 .. **255** B4
  Strand WC2 .... **250** B5
Savoy Hill WC2 .... **250** C5
Savoy Mews SW9 ...... **138** A2
Savoy Par EN1 .... **5** C2
Savoy Pier WC2 .... **250** C5
Savoy Pl WC2 ... **116** B6 **250** C5
Savoy Row WC2 .... **250** C6
Savoy St WC2 ... **116** B6 **250** C6
Savoy Stps WC2 .... **250** C5
Savoy Way WC2 .... **250** C5
Sawbill Cl UB4 .... **84** D2
Sawkins Cl SW19 ...... **157** A2
Sawley Rd W12 .... **112** A5
Sawmill Yd E3 .... **97** A6
Sawtry Cl SM5 .... **202** C2

Sawyer Cl N9 .... **18** A2
Sawyer Ho 16 SE21 .... **183** C6
Sawyer's Hill TW10 .... **154** B4
Sawyers Lawn W13 ...... **87** A1
Sawyer St SE1 ... **117** A4 **252** A2
Saxby Rd SW2 .... **160** A4
Saxham Rd IG11 .... **101** D5
Saxlingham Rd E4 .... **20** B1
Saxon Ave TW13 .... **151** B2
Saxon Bsns Ctr SW19 .. **180** A2
Saxonbury Ave TW16 ... **172** B1
Saxonbury Cl CR4 ...... **202** B6
Saxonbury Ct
  16 Kentish Town N7 ... **71** D3
  2 Lower Holloway N7 .. **72** A3
Saxonbury Gdns KT6 ... **197** C1
Saxon Cl Hillingdon UB8 .. **82** A2
  Surbiton KT6 .... **197** D3
  Walthamstow E17 ..... **53** C2
Saxoncroft Ho SW16 ... **159** D1
Saxon Ct Colney Hatch N12 . **30** C5
  4 Edgware HA8 .... **26** D5
Saxon Dr W3 .... **88** D2
Saxonfield Cl SW2 ...... **160** B4
Saxon Gdns UB1 .... **107** A6
Saxon Hall W2 .... **245** C5
Saxon Ho
  4 Clapham SW4 .... **137** D3
  Feltham TW13 .... **151** B2
Saxon Prim Sch TW17 .. **192** C4
Saxon Rd Ashford TW15 . **171** B4
  Bow E3 .... **97** B5
  Bromley BR1 .... **186** D3
  Ilford IG1 .... **78** D3
  Kingston u T KT2 ..... **176** A2
  Newham E6 .... **100** B3
  Southall UB1 .... **107** A6
  South Norwood SE25 .. **205** B4
  Tottenham N22 .... **32** D2
  Wembley HA9 .... **67** A5
Saxon Terr SE6 .... **163** B2
Saxon Way N14 .... **15** D5
Saxon Wlk DA14 .... **190** C4
Saxony Par UB3 .... **83** A2
Saxton Cl SE13 .... **142** B2
Saxville Rd BR5 .... **190** B1
Sayer Ho SE4 .... **141** A1
Sayers Ho 4 N2 .... **30** B1
Sayer's Wlk TW10 ..... **154** B4
Sayesbury La N18 ...... **34** A5
Sayes Court Rd SE8 .... **141** B6
Sayes Ct SE8 .... **141** B6
Sayline Ct CR0 .... **221** B5
Scadbury Gdns BR5 .... **190** A1
Scadbury Park ★ BR7 .. **189** D4
Scads Hill Cl BR6 ...... **211** D3
Scafell NW1 .... **232** A2
Scala St W1 .... **239** B4
Scales Rd N17 .... **52** A6
Scampston Mews 5
  W10 .... **90** D1
Scandrett St 38 E1 ..... **118** B5
Scarba Wlk N1 .... **73** B2
Scarborough Rd
  East Bedfont TW6 ..... **149** A5
  Finsbury Pk N4 .... **50** C1
  Leytonstone E11 ...... **54** B1
  Ponders End N9 .... **18** C4
Scarborough St E1 ..... **243** D1
Scarbrook Rd CR0 ...... **221** A5
Scardale Ho 12 E5 ...... **74** B6
Scarle Rd HA0 .... **65** D2
Scarlet Rd SE6 .... **164** C1
Scarlette Manor Wlk 10
  SE24 .... **160** C4
Scarsbrook Ho 2 SW2 .. **160** C5
Scarsbrook Rd SE3 ..... **143** D2
Scarsdale Pl W8 .... **255** C6
Scarsdale Rd HA2 ...... **64** A5
Scarsdale Villas
  W8 .... **113** C3 **255** B5
Scarth Rd SW13 .... **133** D2
Scawen Cl SM5 .... **219** A4
Scawen Rd SE8 .... **119** A1
Scawfell St E2 .... **95** D5
Scaynes Link N12 ...... **29** C6
Sceptre Ho 10 E1 .... **96** C3
Sceptre Rd E2 .... **96** C4
Schiller International Univ
  SE1 .... **116** C3 **251** A3
Schofield Wlk SE3 ...... **143** A5
Sch of Pharmacy
  WC1 .... **94** A3 **240** B6
Sch of the Islamic Republic
  of Iran The 6 NW6 ..... **91** C5
Scholars Cl EN5 .... **1** A1
Scholars Ct 5 N19 ...... **49** D1
Scholars Ho 6 E4 .... **20** B3
Scholars Rd Chingford E4. **20** B3
  Streatham SW12 ...... **159** C3
Scholefield Rd N19 ..... **71** D6
Scholey Ho SW11 ...... **136** C2
Schomberg Ho SW1 .... **259** D4
Schonfeld Sq N16 ...... **51** B1
School App 21 E2 .... **95** C4
Schoolbank Rd SE10 ... **120** D2
School Bell Cloisters 17
  E3 .... **97** A5
Schoolbell Mews 18 E3 . **97** A5

School Cotts
  Bromley BR1 .... **187** A3
  Sidcup DA14 .... **190** C5
School Flats SW8 ...... **270** A1
School Ho SE1 .... **263** A4
Schoolhouse La E1 ..... **118** D6
School House La TW11 .. **175** C3
Schoolhouse Yd 9
  SE18 .... **122** D1
School La
  Lower Halliford TW17 .. **192** D2
  Pinner HA5 .... **41** A5
  Surbiton KT6 .... **198** B1
  Teddington KT1 .... **175** C2
School Pas
  3 Kingston u T KT1 ... **176** B1
  Southall UB1 .... **107** B6
School Rd Ashford TW15 . **170** D4
  Becontree NW10 ...... **89** B3
  BR7 .... **189** A3
  Dagenham RM10 ...... **103** D6
  East Molesey KT8 ..... **196** B5
  Hampton TW12 .... **174** A4
  Hounslow TW3 .... **130** A2
  Ilford E12 .... **78** B4
  Littleton TW15 .... **170** D3
  Teddington KT1 .... **175** C2
School Road Ave TW12 .. **174** A4
School Sq SE10 .... **120** D3
Schoolway N12 .... **30** B4
School Way RM8 .... **80** C5
School Wlk TW16 .... **193** D6
Schooner Cl
  Barking IG11 .... **102** B4
  Cubitt Town E14 ...... **120** B3
  1 Rotherhithe SE16 ... **118** D4
Schubert Rd Elstree WD6 . **9** D5
  Putney SW15 .... **157** B6
Science Mus ★
  SW7 .... **114** B3 **256** C5
Scilly Isles KT10 .... **212** C6
Sclater St E1 .... **243** D6
Scoles Cres SW2 ...... **160** C3
Scope Way KT1 .... **198** A5
Scoresby St SE1 .... **251** C3
Scoresdale SE19 .... **183** C2
Scorton Ave UB6 .... **87** A5
Scorton Ho 2 N1 .... **95** C5
Scotch Comm W13 ...... **87** B2
Scotch Ho SW1 ... **114** D4 **247** C1
Scoter Cl IG8 .... **37** B3
Scoter Ct 23 SE8 ...... **141** B6
Scot Gr HA5 .... **22** D3
Scotia Bldg 10 E1 ...... **118** D6
Scotia Ct 3 SE16 ...... **118** C3
Scotia Rd 24 SW2 ...... **160** C4
Scotland Gn N17 .... **33** D1
Scotland Green Rd EN3 .. **18** C6
Scotland Green Rd N EN3 .. **7** A1
Scotland Pl SW1 .... **250** A3
Scotland Rd IG9 .... **21** C3
Scotney Cl BR6 .... **226** C4
Scotney Ho E9 .... **74** C2
Scots Cl TW19 .... **148** A3
Scotsdale Cl
  Belmont SM3 .... **217** A1
  BR5 .... **211** C5
Scotsdale Rd SE12 ..... **165** B6
Scotson Ho SE11 ...... **261** A3
Scotswood St EC1 . **94** C3 **241** B6
Scotswood Wlk N17 .... **34** A3
Scott Ave SW15, SW18 .. **157** A5
Scott Cl
  Thornton Heath SW16 . **182** B2
  West Drayton UB7 .... **104** B2
  West Ewell KT19 ...... **215** A3
Scott Ct Acton W4 ...... **111** B4
  4 Clapham SW11 ...... **137** B3
  17 Stoke Newington N16 . **73** C5
Scott Ellis Gdns
  NW8 .... **92** B4 **229** C1
Scottes La RM8 .... **58** D1
Scott Farm Cl KT7 ..... **197** B1
Scott Gdns TW5 .... **128** D5
Scott Ho 2 Barnsbury N7. . **72** B2
  3 Edmonton N18 ...... **34** A5
  4 Erith DA17 .... **125** B1
  Islington N1 .... **235** C6
  Lisson Gr NW8 .... **237** A5
  12 Millwall E14 .... **119** C4
  6 Newham E13 .... **99** A5
  Richmond TW10 .... **153** C2
  3 Stonebridge NW10 .. **67** B1
Scott Lidgett Cres SE16 . **118** A4
Scott Rd HA8 .... **26** D1
Scott's Ave
  Ashford TW16 .... **171** C3
  Beckenham BR2 ...... **186** B1
Scotts Cl 6 W12 .... **112** B4
Scotts Dr TW12 .... **173** D3
Scotts Farm Rd KT19 .. **215** A2
Scotts Ho DA16 .... **146** C4
Scott's La BR2, BR3 .... **186** B1
Scotts Park Prim Sch
  BR1 .... **187** C2
Scotts Rd BR1 .... **187** A3
  Southall UB2 .... **106** D3
Scott's Rd Leytonstone E10. **54** A1
  Shepherd's Bush W12 . **112** B4

Scott's Sufferance Wharf
  SE1. . . . . **253** D1
Scott St E1. . . . . .96 B3
Scott's Way TW16. . . . .**171** C3
Scott's Yd EC4. . . . . **252** C6
Scott Trimmer Way
  TW3. . . . . .129 A3
Scottwell Dr NW9. . . . . .45 D4
Scott Wilkie Prim Sch
  E16. . . . . .99 C1
Scoulding Ho **12** E14. . . . .119 C3
Scoulding Rd E16. . . . . .99 A1
Scouler St E14. . . . . .120 B6
Scout App NW10. . . . . .67 C4
Scout La SW4. . . . . .137 C2
Scout Way NW7. . . . . .27 B6
Scovell Cres SE1. . . . . **252** A1
Scovell Rd SE1. . . . . **252** A1
Scratchwood Nature Trail★
  NW7. . . . . .11 B4
Scrattons Terr IG11. . . . . . .103 A5
Scriven Ct **2** E8. . . . . .95 D6
Scriven St E8. . . . . .95 D6
Scrooby St SE6. . . . . .163 D5
Scrope Bldg EC1. . . . . **241** A4
Scrubs La NW10,W10,
  W12. . . . . .90 B3
Scrutton Cl SW12. . . . . . . .159 D4
Scrutton St EC2. . . . .95 C3 **243** A4
Scudamore La NW9. . . . . . . .45 A5
Scutari Rd SE22. . . . . .162 C6
Scylla Cres TW6&TW14. . . .148 B4
Scylla Rd
  East Bedfont TW14,TW6 . . 148 D5
  Nunhead SE15. . . . . .140 B2
Seabright St **2** E2. . . . . . .96 B4
Seabrook Dr BR4. . . . . . . .224 C6
Seabrook Gdns RM7. . . . . . .59 C2
Seabrook Rd RM8. . . . . .80 D5
Seacole Cl W3. . . . . .89 B2
Seacole Ct N15. . . . . .51 D4
Seacole Lo N21. . . . . .16 B6
Seacon Twr **8** E14. . . . . . .119 C4
Seacroft Gdns WD19. . . . . . .22 D6
Seafield Cl HA4. . . . . .61 B6
Seafield Rd N11. . . . . .31 D6
Seaford Cl HA4. . . . . .61 B6
Seaford Ho **13** SE16. . . . . .118 C4
Seaford Rd Ealing W13. . . . .109 B5
  Enfield EN1. . . . . .5 C1
  Tottenham N15. . . . . .51 C4
  Walthamstow E17. . . . . .53 D6
Seaford St WC1. . . . . **233** B1
Seaforth Ave KT3. . . . . . . .200 B5
Seaforth Cres N5. . . . . .73 A3
Seaforth Gdns
  Southgate N21. . . . . .16 C3
  Woodford IG8. . . . . .37 C5
  Worcester Pk KT19. . . . . . .215 D3
Seaforth Lo **2** SW13. . . . . .133 D3
Seaforth Pl SW1. . . . . .259 B6
Seagrave Lo SW6. . . . . **265** B6
Seagrave Rd
  SW6. . . . . .135 C6 **265** B6
Seagrove Cl E1. . . . . .96 D2
Seagry Rd E11. . . . . .55 B2
Seagull Cl IG11. . . . . .102 A4
Seagull La E16. . . . . .121 A6
Sealand Rd TW6. . . . . .148 C5
Sealand Wlk UB5. . . . . .85 A4
Seal Ho SE1. . . . . **252** C1
Sea Life London Aquarium★
  SE1. . . . . **250** C1
Seal St E8. . . . . .73 D4
Searle Ct **2** CR4. . . . . . . .180 C2
Searle Pl N4. . . . . .50 B1
Searles Cl SW11. . . .136 C5 **267** B3
Searles Dr E6. . . . . .100 D2
Searles Rd SE1. . . . . .262 D4
Searson Ho SE17. . . . . **261** D3
Sears St SE5. . . . . .139 B5
Seasalter Ho **10** SW9. . . . .138 C4
Seasprite Cl **10** UB5. . . . . .84 D4
Seath Ho **4** SE26. . . . . . . .184 B5
Seaton Ave IG3. . . . . .79 D3
Seaton Cl Isleworth TW2 . .152 B3
  6 Newham E13. . . . . .99 A3
  Roehampton SW15. . . . . . .156 B4
Seaton Dr TW15. . . . . .148 A2
Seaton Gdns HA4. . . . . .62 A6
Seaton Point E5. . . . . .74 A4
Seaton Rd Bexley DA16. . . . .146 C5
  Hayes UB3. . . . . .105 A3
  Mitcham CR4. . . . . .180 C1
  Twickenham TW2. . . . . . . .152 A5
  Wembley HA0. . . . . .88 A5
Seaton Sq NW7. . . . . .28 D3
Seaton St N18. . . . . .34 A5
Seavington Ho **3** SE5. . . . .139 C2
Sebastian Ct **11** IG11. . . . . .79 D1
Sebastian Ho **21** N1. . . . . . .95 C5
Sebastian St EC1. . . .94 D4 **234** D1
Sebastopol Rd N9. . . . . .34 A6
Sebert Rd E7. . . . . .77 B4
Sebbon St N1. . . . . .72 D1
Sebergham Gr NW7. . . . . . . .28 A3
Sebright Ho **22** E2. . . . . . . .96 A5
Sebright Pas **29** E2. . . . . . . .96 A5
Sebright Rd EN5. . . . . .1 A2

Sebright Sch **39** E2. . . . . . .96 A5
Secker Cres HA3. . . . . .24 A2
Secker Ho SW9. . . . . .138 D3
Secker St SE1. . . . . **251** A1
Second Ave
  Chadwell Heath RM6. . . . . .58 C4
  Dagenham RM10. . . . . . . .103 D5
  East Acton W3. . . . . .111 D5
  Edmonton N18. . . . . .34 C6
  Enfield EN1. . . . . .17 D6
  Hayes UB3. . . . . .105 D5
  Hendon NW4. . . . . .46 D5
  Kensal Town W10. . . . . . . .91 A3
  Manor Pk E12. . . . . .78 A3
  Mortlake SW14. . . . . .133 C2
  Newham E13. . . . . .99 A4
  Walthamstow E17. . . . . .53 C4
  Walton-on-T KT12. . . . . . .194 B3
  Wembley HA9. . . . . .65 D6
Second Cl KT8. . . . . .196 A5
Second Cross Rd TW2. . . . .152 C2
Second Way HA9. . . . . .66 D4
Secrett Ho **6** TW10. . . . . .153 C1
Sedan Way SE17. . . .117 C1 **263** A2
Sedcombe Cl DA14. . . . . . . .190 C6
Sedcote Rd EN3. . . . . .18 D6
Sedding St SW1. . . . . **258** A4
Seddon Ho EC2. . . . . **242** A4
Seddon Rd SM4. . . . . .202 B4
Seddon St WC1. . . . .94 B4 **233** D1
Sedgebrook Rd SE3. . . . . . .143 D2
Sedgecombe Ave HA3. . . . . .43 C4
Sedgefield Ct UB5. . . . . .63 D3
Sedgeford Rd W12. . . . . . . .111 D5
Sedgehill Rd SE6. . . . . .185 D5
Sedgehill Sch SE6. . . . . . . .185 D5
Sedgemere Ave N2. . . . . . . .48 A6
Sedgemere Rd SE2. . . . . . . .124 C3
Sedgemoor Dr RM10. . . . . . .81 C4
Sedge Rd N17. . . . . .34 C3
Sedgeway SE6. . . . . .164 D3
Sedgewick Ho SW19. . . . . .156 D2
Sedgewood Cl BR2. . . . . . .208 D2
Sedgley Ho N4. . . . . .72 B6
Sedgmoor Pl SE5. . . . . .139 C5
Sedgwick Ave UB10. . . . . . . .60 D1
Sedgwick Rd E10. . . . . .76 A6
Sedgwick St E9. . . . . .74 D3
Sedleigh Rd SW18. . . . . . . .157 B5
Sedlescombe Rd
  SW6. . . . . .135 C6 **265** A6
Sedley Cl EN1. . . . . .5 A6
Sedley Ct SE26. . . . . .162 B2
Sedley Ho SE11. . . . . **260** D2
Sedley Pl W1. . . . . **238** C1
Sedum Cl NW9. . . . . .44 D4
Seeley Dr SE21. . . . . .183 C6
Seely Rd SW17. . . . . .181 A4
Seely Rd SW17. . . . . .181 A4
Seething La EC3. . . . .117 C6 **253** B6
SEETHING WELLS. 197 C3
Seething Wells Halls of
  Residence KT6. . . . . .197 C3
Seething Wells La KT6 . . . .197 C3
Sefton Ave Edgware NW7. . . .27 B5
  Harrow HA3. . . . . .24 B2
Sefton Cl BR5. . . . . .211 D5
Sefton Ct TW5. . . . . .129 D4
Sefton Lo **2** SW11. . . . . . .153 C5
Sefton Rd Croydon CR0. . . .206 A1
  Orpington BR5. . . . . .211 D5
Sefton St SW15. . . . . .134 C2
Segal Cl SE23. . . . . .163 A4
Sekforde St EC1. . . .94 D3 **241** C6
Sekhon Terr TW13. . . . . . . .151 C1
Selan Gdns UB4. . . . . .84 B2
Selbie Ave NW10. . . . . .67 D3
Selborne Ave **2** SW11. . . . .137 A2
Selborne Ave DA5. . . . . . . .169 A3
  Little Ilford E12. . . . . .78 C4
  Walthamstow E17. . . . . .53 B5
Selborne Gdns
  Hendon NW4. . . . . .46 A5
  Wembley UB6. . . . . .87 A5
Selborne Ho SE1. . . . . **252** C1
Selborne Prim Sch UB6. . . . .86 D5
Selborne Rd
  1 Camberwell SE5. . . . . .139 B3
  Ilford IG1. . . . . .78 C6
  Kingston u T KT3. . . . . . . .177 C1
  Palmers Green N14. . . . . . . .16 A1
  Sidcup DA14. . . . . .190 B6
  South Croydon CR0. . . . . .221 D5
  Walthamstow E17. . . . . .53 C4
  Wood Green N22. . . . . .32 B2
Selborne Wlk E17. . . . . .53 B5
Selborne Wlk Sh Ctr E17. . . .53 B5
Selbridge Ct SW19. . . . . . .179 C4
Selby Chase HA4. . . . . .62 B6
Selby Cl BR7. . . . . .188 C4
  Chessington KT9. . . . . . . .214 A1
  14 Newham E6. . . . . .100 A2
Selby Ct TW2. . . . . .152 B2
Selby Gdns UB1. . . . . .85 C3
Selby Gn SM5. . . . . .202 C2
Selby Ho **10** SW4. . . . . . . .159 C5
Selby Rd Ashford TW15. . . . .171 A4
  Carshalton SM5. . . . . .202 C2
  Ealing W5. . . . . .87 C3

Selby Rd continued
  Leyton E11. . . . . .76 C5
  Newham E13. . . . . .99 B2
  Penge SE20. . . . . .184 A1
  Tottenham N17. . . . . .33 C4
Selby Sq **1** W10. . . . . .91 A4
Selby St E1. . . . . .96 A3
Selden Ho **2** SE15. . . . . . .140 C3
Selden Rd SE15. . . . . .140 C3
Selden Wlk N7. . . . . .72 B6
Seldon Ho Nine Elms SW8 . . **269** A3
  Pimlico SW1. . . . . **259** A1
Selena Ct N20. . . . . .14 D1
SELHURST. 205 B4
Selhurst Cl SW19. . . . . .156 D3
Selhurst New Ct SE25. . . . .205 C3
Selhurst New Rd SE25. . . . .205 B3
Selhurst Park (Crystal Palace
  FC) SE25. . . . . .205 C5
Selhurst Pl SE25. . . . . .205 C3
Selhurst Rd Edmonton N9. . . .17 C1
  South Norwood SE25. . . . .205 C5
Selhurst Sta SE25. . . . . . . .205 C4
Selina Ho NW8. . . . . **236** D6
Selinas La RM8. . . . . .59 B2
Selkirk Ct N17. . . . . .33 C1
Selkirk Ho N1. . . . . **233** C6
  4 Stoke Newington N16 . . . .73 C5
Selkirk Rd
  Twickenham TW2. . . . . . . .152 A3
  Upper Tooting SW17. . . . . .180 C6
Sellers Hall Cl N3. . . . . .29 C3
Sellincourt Prim Sch
  SW17. . . . . .180 C4
Sellincourt Rd SW17. . . . . .180 C4
Sellindge Cl BR3. . . . . .185 B3
Sellons Ave NW10. . . . . .89 D6
Sellsby St SW17. . . . . .31 B5
Sellwood Dr EN5. . . . . .12 D6
Selma Ho **7** W12. . . . . .90 B1
Selman Ho **3** E9. . . . . .75 A2
SELSDON. 223 A1
Selsdon Ave CR2. . . . . .221 B2
Selsdon Cl KT6. . . . . .198 A4
Selsdon High Sch CR2 . . . .222 D1
Selsdon Park Rd CR0,
  CR2. . . . . .223 B1
Selsdon Rd Newham E13. . . . .99 C5
  Wanstead E11. . . . . .55 A2
  West Norwood SE27. . . . . .182 D6
  Willesden NW2. . . . . .67 D6
Selsdon Road Ind Est
  CR2. . . . . .221 B2
Selsdon Way E14. . . . . .119 D3
Selsea Pl N16. . . . . .73 C3
Selsey Cres DA16. . . . . .146 D4
Selsey St E14. . . . . .97 C2
Selvage La NW7. . . . . .27 B6
Selway Cl HA5. . . . . .40 B6
Selway Ho SW8. . . . . **270** B2
Selwood Ho
  Chislehurst BR7. . . . . .189 A4
  1 Stoke Newington N4 . . . .51 B2
Selwood Pl SW7. . . .114 B1 **256** C2
  Cheam SM3. . . . . .201 B1
  Chessington KT9. . . . . . . .213 D4
  Croydon CR0. . . . . .206 B1
Selwood Terr SW7. . . . . **256** C2
Selworthy Cl E11. . . . . .55 A4
Selworthy Ho SW11. . . . . . . **266** D2
Selworthy Rd SE6. . . . . .163 B1
Selwyn Ave Chingford E4 . . . .36 A4
  Ilford IG3. . . . . .57 D3
  Richmond TW9. . . . . .132 B2
Selwyn Cl W14. . . . . .129 A1
Selwyn Cres DA16. . . . . . . .146 B1
Selwyn Ct Edgware HA8 . . . .26 D3
  Lewisham SE3. . . . . .142 D2
  8 Richmond TW10. . . . . . .154 B6
  Walthamstow E17. . . . . .53 C4
  Wembley HA9. . . . . .67 A5
Selwyn Ho **3** SW15. . . . . . .156 D5
Selwyn Prim Sch
  Chingford E4. . . . . .36 A4
  6 Newham E13. . . . . .99 A6
Selwyn Rd Bow E3. . . . . .97 B5
  Newham E13. . . . . .99 B6
  New Malden KT3. . . . . . . .199 B4
  Willesden NW10. . . . . .67 C1
Semley Gate E9. . . . . .75 B2
Semley Ho SW1. . . . . **258** A3
Semley Pl SW1. . . .115 B2 **258** C3
  Thornton Heath SW16. . . . .182 B1
Semley Rd SW16. . . . . .182 A1
Senate St SE15. . . . . .140 C3
Senators Lo **31** E3. . . . . . . .97 A5
Senator Wlk **2** SE28. . . . . .123 B3
Sencler Ho SE2. . . . . .146 D6
Sendall Ct **12** SW11. . . . . .136 B2
Seneca Rd CR7. . . . . .205 A5
Senga Rd SM6. . . . . .203 A1
Senhouse Rd SM3. . . . . . . .216 D5
Senior St W2. . . . . .91 D2
Senlac Rd SE12. . . . . .165 B3
Sennen Rd EN1. . . . . .17 D4
Sennen Wlk SE9. . . . . .166 A1
Senrab St E1. . . . . .96 D1
Sentinel Cl UB5. . . . . .85 A1
Sentinel Ho NW4. . . . . .46 C5

Sentinel Sq NW4. . . . . .46 C5
September Ct UB1. . . . . . . .107 D5
September Way HA7. . . . . . . .25 B4
Sequoia Cl WD23. . . . . .8 B3
Sequoia Gdns BR6. . . . . . . .211 D2
Sequoia Pk HA5. . . . . .23 D4
Seraph Ct EC1. . . . . .95 A4 **235** A2
Serbin Cl E10. . . . . .54 A2
Serenaders Rd **20** SW9. . . .138 C3
Sergeant Ind Est The
  SW18. . . . . .157 D5
Serica Ct **2** SE10. . . . . . . .142 A5
Serjeants' Inn EC4. . . . . **241** B1
Serlby Ct W14. . . . . **254** C6
Serle St WC2. . . . . . .94 B1 **240** D2
Sermon La EC4. . . . . **242** A1
Serpentine Ct **10** SE16. . . . .118 D4
Serpentine Gallery★
  W2. . . . . .114 B4 **246** D2
Serpentine Rd
  W2. . . . . .114 D5 **247** C3
Serpentine The★
  W2. . . . . .114 C5 **247** B3
Service Route No 1 E15. . . . .76 B1
Service Route No 2 **1**
  E15. . . . . .76 B1
Service Route No 3 **2**
  E15. . . . . .76 B1
Serviden Dr BR1. . . . . .187 D2
Servite Ho
  Beckenham BR3. . . . . .185 B2
  Bromley BR1. . . . . .188 B1
  East Barnet N14. . . . . .15 B6
  Lewisham SE13. . . . . .141 D4
  Penge SE26. . . . . .184 C4
  Worcester Pk KT4. . . . . . . .215 D6
Servite RC Prim Sch
  SW10. . . . . .136 A6 **266** A6
Servius Ct **2** TW8. . . . . . .131 D5
Sessions Terr CR4. . . . . . . .180 D2
Setchell Rd SE1. . . . .117 D2 **263** C4
Setchell Way SE1. . . . . **263** C4
Seth St **25** SE16. . . . . .118 C4
Seton Ct **3** NW9. . . . . .46 A5
Seton Gdns RM9. . . . . .80 C1
Settle Point **11** E13. . . . . . .99 A5
Settlers Ct **11** E14. . . . . . . .120 B6
Settles St E1. . . . . .96 A1
Settrington Rd SW6. . . . . . .135 D3
Seven Acres
  Carshalton SM5. . . . . .218 C6
  Northwood HA6. . . . . .22 A4
Seven Dials WC2. . . .94 A1 **240** A1
Seven Islands L Ctr
  SE16. . . . . .118 C3
SEVEN KINGS. 57 D2
Seven Kings High Sch
  IG2. . . . . .79 D6
Seven Kings Rd IG3. . . . . . . .79 D6
Seven Kings Sta IG3. . . . . . .57 C1
Seven Kings Way KT2. . . . . .176 A2
Seven Mills Prim Sch **27**
  E14. . . . . .119 C4
Sevenoaks Cl DA7. . . . . . . .147 D1
Sevenoaks Rd BR6. . . . . . . .227 D4
  Catford SE4. . . . . .163 B5
Sevenoaks Way BR5. . . . . . .190 C1
Seven Seas Rd TW6. . . . . . .149 A5
Seven Sisters N15. . . . . .51 D4
Seven Sisters Prim Sch
  N15. . . . . .51 B4
Seven Sisters Rd
  Finsbury Pk N4. . . . . .72 D6
  Stoke Newington N4,N7,
  N15. . . . . .51 A2
Seven Sisters Sta N15. . . . . .51 C4
Seven Stars Cnr W12. . . . . .112 A3
Seven Stars Yd E1. . . . . **243** D4
  Seventh Ave Hayes UB3 . . .106 A5
  Ilford IG2. . . . . .78 B4
Seven Ways Par IG2. . . . . . . .56 C4
Severnake Cl E14. . . . . .119 C2
Severn Ave **2** W10. . . . . . . .91 A4
Severn Ct **11** KT2. . . . . . . .175 D2
Severn Dr Enfield EN1. . . . . . .6 A5
  Hinchley Wood KT10. . . . . .213 A6
Severn Way NW10. . . . . .67 D3
Severus Rd SW11. . . . . .136 C1
Seville Ho **10** E1. . . . . .118 A5
Seville Mews N1. . . . . .73 C1
Seville St SW1. . . . . **247** D1
Sevington Rd NW4. . . . . .46 B3
Sevington St W9. . . . . .91 D3
Seward Rd Penge BR3. . . . . .184 D1
  West Ealing W7. . . . . .109 B6
Seward St EC1. . . . . .95 A4 **235** A1
SEWARDSTONEBURY. 20 C6
Sewardstone Gdns E4. . . . . . .19 D6
Sewardstone Rd
  Chingford E4. . . . . .19 C6
  South Hackney E2. . . . . .96 C5
Sewdley St E5. . . . . .74 D5
Sewell Ho **7** N16. . . . . .73 C3
Sewell Rd SE2. . . . . .124 B4
Sewell St E13. . . . . .99 A4
Sextant Ave E14. . . . . .120 B2
Sexton Ct **7** E14. . . . . .120 B6
Sexton's Ho **5** SE13. . . . . .142 A6
Seychelle Ct BR3. . . . . .185 D3

Sco–Sha 399

Seymour Ave
  Tottenham N17. . . . . .34 A1
  West Barnes SM4. . . . . . . .200 D2
Seymour Cl
  East Molesey KT8. . . . . . . .196 A4
  Pinner HA5. . . . . .23 B2
Seymour Ct Chingford E4. . . .20 D2
  Dollis Hill NW2. . . . . .68 B6
  Muswell Hill N10. . . . . .31 A1
  Putney SW15. . . . . .134 B1
  Southgate N21. . . . . .16 B5
  Upper Clapton N16. . . . . . . .52 A1
Seymour Dr BR2. . . . . .210 B1
Seymour Gdns
  Brockley SE4. . . . . .141 A2
  Feltham TW13. . . . . .172 C6
  Kingston u T KT5. . . . . . . .198 B4
  Redbridge IG1. . . . . .56 B1
  Ruislip HA4. . . . . .40 C1
  Twickenham TW1. . . . . . . .153 B4
Seymour Ho
  Bloomsbury WC1. . . . . **240** A6
  1 Clapham SW8. . . . . . . .137 C3
  Ruislip HA4. . . . . .40 A5
  Somers Town NW1. . . . . . . **232** D1
Seymour Lo **14** KT1. . . . . . .175 D2
Seymour Mews **1**. **238** A2
Seymour Pl
  Croydon SE25. . . . . .206 B5
  Paddington W1. . . . .92 D1 **237** C2
Seymour Rd Acton W4. . . . . .111 A2
  Carshalton CR4. . . . . .203 A2
  Chingford E4. . . . . .19 D3
  East Molesey KT8. . . . . . . .196 A4
  Edmonton N9. . . . . .18 B2
  Finchley N3. . . . . .29 C3
  Hampton TW12. . . . . .174 A5
  Harringay N8. . . . . .50 D4
  Newham E6. . . . . .99 D6
  Teddington KT1. . . . . .175 D2
  Wallington SM5. . . . . .219 A3
  Walthamstow E10. . . . . .53 B1
  Wandsworth SW18. . . . . . .157 B5
  Wimbledon SW19. . . . . . . .156 D1
Seymour St
  Paddington W1. . . . .92 D1 **237** D1
  Woolwich SE18. . . . . .123 A3
Seymour Terr SE20. . . . . . . .184 B2
Seymour Villas SE20. . . . . .184 A2
Seymour Way TW16. . . . . . .171 C3
Seymour Wlk
  SW10. . . . . .136 A6 **266** A6
Seyssel St E14. . . . . .120 A2
Shaa Rd W3. . . . . .111 B6
Shabana Ct **3** W12. . . . . . .112 B5
Shacklegate La TW11. . . . . .174 C6
Shackleton Cl SE23. . . . . . .162 B2
Shackleton Ct
  3 Dulwich SE21. . . . . . . .161 B2
  2 Isle of Dogs E14. . . . . .119 C1
  4 Shepherd's Bush W12. . .112 A2
  7 Stanwell TW19. . . . . . .148 A5
Shackleton Ho
  5 Stonebridge NW10. . . . .67 B1
  1 Wapping E1. . . . . .118 C5
Shackleton Lo SW16. . . . . .181 D5
Shackleton Rd UB1. . . . . . .107 B6
SHACKLEWELL. 73 D4
Shacklewell Ho **3** E8. . . . . .73 D4
Shacklewell La E8. . . . . .73 D4
Shacklewell Prim Sch **5**
  E8. . . . . .73 D4
Shacklewell Rd N16. . . . . . . .73 D4
Shacklewell Row E8. . . . . . . .73 D4
Shacklewell St **30** E2. . . . . .95 D4
Shadbolt Ave E4. . . . . .35 A5
Shadbolt Cl KT4. . . . . .215 D6
Shad Thames
  SE1. . . . . .117 D4 **253** D2
SHADWELL. 118 C6
Shadwell Ct UB5. . . . . .85 B5
Shadwell Dr UB5. . . . . .85 B4
Shadwell Gdns E1. . . . . . . .118 C6
Shadwell Pierhead E1. . . . . .118 C6
Shadwell Pl **1** E1. . . . . . . .118 C6
Shadwell Sta E1. . . . . .118 B6
Shady Bush Cl WD23. . . . . . .8 A4
Shaef Way TW11. . . . . .175 A3
Shaftesbury Ave
  Enfield EN3. . . . . .6 D3
  Feltham TW14. . . . . .150 A5
  Kenton HA3. . . . . .44 A3
  New Barnet EN5. . . . . .2 A1
  Southall UB2. . . . . .107 C3
  W1. . . . . .115 D6 **249** D6
  West Harrow HA1,HA2. . . . .42 A1
Shaftesbury Circ HA2. . . . . .42 A1
Shaftesbury Ctr NW10. . . . . .90 D3
Shaftesbury Ct
  Borough The SE1. . . . . **262** C6
  1 Herne Hill SE5. . . . . . .139 B1
  Ilford RM6. . . . . .58 C2
  Newham E6. . . . . .100 C1
  Shoreditch N1. . . . . **235** C3
  Streatham SW16. . . . . .159 D1
  3 Thamesmead SE28. . . . .124 C5
Shaftesbury Gdns NW10. . . . .89 C3

Shaftesbury High Sch
HA3 . . . . .23 D2
Shaftesbury Ho
11 Canning Town E16 . . . . . . .98 D1
Croydon SE25 . . . . 206 A3
13 Stoke Newington N16 . . . .73 C5
Upper Tooting SW17 . . . . .180 B6
W2 . . . . .245 D6
Shaftesbury Lo 9 E14 . . . . .97 D1
Shaftesbury Mews
2 Clapham Pk SW4 . . . . . .159 C6
W8 . . . . .255 B5
Shaftesbury Park Chambers
1 SW11 . . . . .137 A2
Shaftesbury Point E13 . . . . .99 B5
Shaftesbury Prim Sch E7. .77 C1
Shaftesbury Rd
Beckenham BR3 . . . . .185 B1
Carshalton SM5 . . . . .202 C2
Chingford E4 . . . . .20 B3
Edmonton N18 . . . . .33 D4
Finsbury Pk N4, N19 . . . . . .50 A1
Leyton E10 . . . . .53 C1
Richmond TW9 . . . . .132 A2
Upton E7 . . . . .77 C1
Walthamstow E17 . . . . .53 D3
Shaftesbury St N1 . . . . . .235 C3
Shaftesburys The IG11 . . .101 A5
Shaftesbury Way TW13 . . .152 B1
Shaftesbury Waye UB4 . . .84 C1
Shafteswood Ct SW17. . . .158 D1
Shafto Mews SW1 . . . . . .257 D5
Shafton Rd E9 . . . . .96 D6
Shaftsbury Park Prim Sch 16
SW11 . . . . .137 A3
Shafts Ct EC3 . . . . .243 A1
Shahjalal Ho 18 E2. . . . . . .96 A5
Shakespeare Ave
7 Becontree NW10 . . . . . .89 B6
Feltham TW14 . . . . .150 A5
Friern Barnet N11 . . . . .31 C5
Hayes UB4 . . . . .84 B2
Shakespeare Cl HA3 . . . . .44 C2
Shakespeare Cres E12 . . . .78 B2
Shakespeare Ct EN5 . . . . . . .1 D2
Shakespeare Dr HA3 . . . . .44 C2
Shakespeare Gdns N2 . . . .48 D5
Shakespeare Ho
1 Erith DA17. . . . . .125 B1
3 Hackney E9 . . . . .74 C1
Osidge N14. . . . . .15 D2
Shakespeare Rd
Acton W3 . . . . .111 A5
Brixton SE24. . . . . .138 D1
DA7. . . . . .147 A4
Ealing W7 . . . . .108 D6
Finchley N3. . . . . .29 C2
Higham Hill E17 . . . . .34 D1
Mill Hill NW7. . . . . .28 A6
Stonebridge NW10. . . . . . .89 B6
Shakespeare's Globe Theatre
(site of)* SE1. . . . . .252 B4
Shakespeare Twr EC2 . . . .242 B4
Shakespeare Way TW13 . .172 C6
Shakspeare Mews 7
N16 . . . . .73 C4
Shakspeare Wlk N16. . . . . .73 C4
Shalbourne Sq E9 . . . . . . .75 B2
Shalcomb St
SW10. . . . . .136 A6 266 B5
Shalden Ho SW15. . . . . . .155 D5
Shaldon Dr Ruislip HA4. . . .62 C5
West Barnes SM4. . . . . . . .201 A4
Shaldon Rd HA8 . . . . .26 B1
Shalfleet Dr W10 . . . . . . .112 D6
Shalford
Willesden Green NW10 . . . .90 A6
3 Woodford IG8 . . . . .37 C4
Shalford Cl BR6. . . . . .227 A4
Shalford Ct N1. . . . . .234 C4
Shalford Ho SE1 . . . . .262 D6
Shalimar Gdns W3 . . . . . .111 A6
Shalimar Lo W3 . . . . .111 A6
Shalimar Rd W3 . . . . .111 A6
Shallons Rd SE9 . . . . .188 D6
Shalstone Rd SW14,
TW9. . . . . .132 D2
Shalston Villas KT5, KT6. .198 B3
Shamrock Ct E7 . . . . .77 D3
Shamrock Ho
East Barnet N14 . . . . .15 B4
Forest Hill SE26 . . . . .184 A6
Shamrock Rd CR0 . . . . . . .204 B3
Shamrock St SW4 . . . . . . .137 D2
Shamrock Way N14 . . . . . .15 B3
Shandon Ct SE4 . . . . .141 A3
Shandon Rd SW4 . . . . . . .159 C5
Shand St SE1 . . . . . . .117 C4 253 B2
Shandy St E1 . . . . .96 D3
Shane Ct EN2. . . . . .5 A3
Shan Ho WC1. . . . . .240 C5
Shanklin Gdns WD19. . . . .22 C6
Shanklin Ho E17. . . . . .35 B1
Shanklin Rd Hornsey N8. . . .49 D4
Tottenham Hale N15. . . . . .52 A5
Shannon Cl UB2. . . . . . . .106 D1
Shannon Cnr KT3. . . . . . . .200 A5

Shannon Cnr Ret Pk
KT3. . . . . .200 A5
Shannon Commercial Ctr
KT3. . . . . .200 A5
Shannon Ct Croydon CR0 . .205 A1
11 Peckham SE15. . . . . . .139 D5
Stoke Newington N16. . . . .73 C5
Willesden NW10. . . . . .68 A2
Shannon Gr SW9 . . . . . . .138 B1
Shannon Pl NW8. . . . .92 C5 230 B4
Shannon Way BR3 . . . . . .185 D4
Shanti Ct SW18 . . . . .157 C3
Shap Cres SM5 . . . . .202 D1
Shapland Way N13. . . . . . .32 B5
Shapla Prim Sch 25 E1. . .118 A6
Shapwick Cl N11 . . . . .30 D5
Shardcroft Ave SE24 . . . .160 D6
Shardeloes Rd SE14. . . . .141 B3
Shard's Sq SE15 . . . . .140 A6
Sharebourne Ho SW2. . . .160 C6
Sharland Cl CR7 . . . . .204 C3
Sharman Ct DA14. . . . . . .190 A6
Sharman Ho 13 E14. . . . . .98 A1
Sharnbrooke Cl DA16. . . .146 C2
Sharnbrook Ho W6 . . . . . .265 A6
Sharon Cl KT6. . . . . .197 C1
Sharon Ct 1 N12 . . . . . . .30 A4
Sharon Gdns 96 C6
Sharon Rd Chiswick W4 . .111 B1
Enfield EN3. . . . . .7 A3
Sharpe Cl W7. . . . . .86 D2
Sharp Ho SW8 . . . . .137 B2
Sharples Hall St 8 NW1. . .70 D1
Sharpness Cl UB4. . . . . . . .85 A2
Sharpness Ct 2 SE15 . . . .139 D5
Sharps La HA4. . . . . .39 B2
Sharratt St SE15. . . . . . . .140 C6
Sharsted St SE17 . . .116 D1 261 C1
Sharvel La UB5 . . . . .84 B6
Sharwood WC1. . . . . .233 D3
Shaver's Pl SW1. . . . . . . .249 C5
Shaw Ave IG11 . . . . .103 A5
Shawbrooke Rd SE9 . . . . .143 D1
Shawbury Cl 9 NW9. . . . . .27 C2
Shawbury Ct SE22 . . . . . .161 D6
Shawbury Rd SE22 . . . . . .161 D6
Shaw Cl Bushey WD23. . . . . .8 C2
Woolwich SE28. . . . . .124 B5
Shaw Cotts SE23 . . . . . . .163 A1
Shaw Cres 6 E14 . . . . . . .97 A1
Shaw Ct
8 Acton Green W3 . . . . . .111 A3
11 Battersea SW11 . . . . . .136 B2
Cheam SM4 . . . . .202 A2
Upper Holloway N19 . . . . .72 A6
Shaw Dr KT12 . . . . .194 C2
Shawfield Ct UB7 . . . . . . .104 A3
Shawfield Pk BR1. . . . . . .187 D1
Shawfield St
SW3. . . . . .114 C1 257 B1
Shawford Ct 8 SW15. . . .156 A4
Shawford Rd KT19 . . . . . .215 B2
Shaw Gdns IG11 . . . . .103 A5
Shaw Ho 6 Erith DA17. . . .125 B1
5 Newham E16. . . . . . . .122 C5
Shaw Path BR1 . . . . .164 D1
Shaw Rd
Camberwell SE22 . . . . . . .139 C1
Catford BR1 . . . . .164 D1
Enfield EN3. . . . . .6 D4
Shaw Sq E17 . . . . .35 A2
Shaws Wood Cotts EN4 . . . .3 C3
Shaw Way SM6 . . . . .220 A1
Shearing Dr SM4 . . . . . . .202 A2
Shearling Way N7 . . . . . . .72 A2
Shearman Rd SE3. . . . . . .142 D2
Shears Ct TW16. . . . . .171 C3
Shearsmith Ho 19 E1. . . . .118 A6
Shears The TW16 . . . . . . .171 C3
Shears Way TW16. . . . . . .171 C2
Shearwater Cl IG11. . . . . .102 A4
Shearwater Ct 24 SE8. . . .141 B6
Shearwater Rd SM1. . . . .217 B3
Shearwater Way UB4 . . . .84 D1
Sheaveshill Ave NW9. . . . .45 C5
Sheaveshill Ct NW9. . . . . .45 C5
Sheaveshill Par NW9. . . . .45 C5
Sheba Ct N17. . . . . .34 A4
Sheba Pl E1. . . . . .243 D5
Sheen Common Dr SW14,
TW10. . . . . .154 C6
Sheen Court Rd TW10 . . .132 C1
Sheen Ct TW10 . . . . .132 C1
Sheendale Rd TW9. . . . . .132 B1
Sheenewood SE26. . . . . . .184 B6
Sheen Gate Gdns SW14 . .133 A1
Sheengate Mans SW14. . .133 B1
Sheen Gr N1 . . . . . .94 C6 234 A6
Sheen La SW14. . . . . .133 A1
Sheen Mount Prim Sch
SW14 . . . . .154 D6
Sheen Pk TW10, TW9. . . .132 A1
Sheen Rd Orpington BR5. .211 D5
Richmond TW10, TW9. . . .132 B1
Sheen Way SM6 . . . . .220 B3
Sheen Wood SW14. . . . . .155 A6
Sheepcote Cl TW5 . . . . . .128 A5
Sheepcote La SW11. . . . .136 D3
Sheepcote Rd HA1. . . . . . .42 D3
Sheepcotes Rd RM6 . . . . .59 A5

Sheephouse Way KT3 . . . .199 C2
Sheep La E8. . . . . .96 B6
Sheepwalk TW17 . . . . . . .192 B3
Sheep Walk Mews 7
SW19. . . . . .179 A4
Sheerness Mews E16 . . . .122 C4
Sheerwater Rd E16 . . . . . .99 D2
Sheffield Ho 15 SE15. . . . .139 C4
Sheffield Rd TW14, TW6. .149 A6
Sheffield Sq 2 E3 . . . . . . .97 B4
Sheffield St WC2. . . . . . . .240 C1
Sheffield Terr
W8. . . . . .113 C5 245 B3
Sheffield Way TW14,
TW6. . . . . .149 B6
Shefton Rise HA6. . . . . . . .22 A3
Shelbey Ct BR1. . . . . .186 D2
Shelbourne Cl HA5 . . . . . .41 B6
Shelbourne Ho 20 N19 . . . .49 D2
Shelbourne Rd N17. . . . . . .34 B2
Shelburne Ct SW15 . . . . .156 D6
Shelburne Dr TW4 . . . . . .151 C5
Shelburne Ho 9 SW16. . . .181 C5
Shelburne Rd N7 . . . . .72 B4
Shelbury Cl DA14. . . . . . .168 A1
Shelbury Rd SE22. . . . . . .162 B6
Sheldon Ave N6 . . . . .48 D3
Sheldon Cl Penge SE20. . .184 B2
SE12. . . . . .165 B6
Sheldon Ct Barnet EN5. . . . .1 D1
SW8 . . . . .270 A3
Sheldon Ho Chingford E4 . .36 C4
9 Homerton E9. . . . . .74 D2
Teddington TW11 . . . . . . .175 A4
Sheldon Pl E2 . . . . .96 B5
Sheldon Rd
Cricklewood NW2. . . . . . . .68 D4
DA7. . . . . .147 B4
Dagenham RM9 . . . . .81 A1
Edmonton N18 . . . . .33 C6
Sheldon Sq W2. . . . . .236 B3
Sheldon St CR0. . . . . .221 A5
Sheldrake Cl E16 . . . . . . .122 B5
Sheldrake Ho 15 SE16. . . .118 D2
Sheldrake Pl W8. .113 C4 245 A2
Sheldrick Cl CR4. . . . . . . .180 B1
Shelduck Cl E15. . . . . .76 D3
Shelduck Ct 37 SE8. . . . . .141 B6
Sheldwich Terr BR2. . . . . .210 A3
Shelford 20 KT1. . . . . . . .176 C1
Shelford Ct 7 E5. . . . . . . .52 B1
Shelford Pl N16. . . . . .73 B5
Shelford Rd EN5. . . . . .12 C5
Shelford Rise SE19. . . . . .183 D3
Shelgate Rd SW11 . . . . . .158 D6
Shell Cl BR2 . . . . .210 A3
Shell Ctr SE1 . . . . .250 D3
Shellduck Cl NW9 . . . . . . .27 C1
Shelley N8 . . . . .50 A6
Shelley Ave Greenford UB6 . .86 B4
Plashet E12 . . . . .78 A2
Shelley Cl BR6. . . . . .227 C5
Edgware HA8 . . . . .26 C6
Greenford UB6. . . . . .86 B4
Hayes UB4 . . . . .84 A2
Peckham SE15. . . . . .140 B3
Shelley Cres
Heston TW5 . . . . .128 D4
Southall UB1. . . . . .85 B1
Shelley Ct Finsbury Pk N4 . .50 B1
9 Kingston u T KT2 . . . . .175 D6
SW3 . . . . .267 D6
13 Walthamstow E10. . . . .53 D2
8 Wanstead E11. . . . . . . .55 A5
Wembley HA0. . . . . .65 C4
West Barnes KT3 . . . . . . .200 A4
Shelley Dr DA16 . . . . .145 C4
Shelley Gdns HA0. . . . . . . .65 C6
Shelley Ho
21 Bethnal Green E2. . . . . .96 C4
Chelsea SW1 . . . . .269 A6
3 Stoke Newington N16 . . .73 C4
Walworth SE17. . . . . .262 B2
Shelley Rd NW10. . . . . . . .89 B6
Shelley Way SW17 . . . . . .180 B4
Shellgrove Rd 31 N16. . . . .73 C3
Shellness Rd E5 . . . . .74 B3
Shell Rd SE13. . . . . .141 D2
Shellwood Rd SW11 . . . . .136 D3
Shelly Lo EN2. . . . . .5 B4
Shelmerdine Cl E3. . . . . . .97 C2
Shelson Ave TW13 . . . . . .171 D6
Shelton Ct N21 . . . . .16 C4
Shelton Rd SW19 . . . . . . .179 C2
Shelton St WC2. . . . .94 A1 240 A1
Shene Bldg EC1 . . . . .241 A4
Shene Sch SW14. . . . . . . .133 C1
Shenfield Ho 3 SE18 . . . .143 D5
Shenfield Rd IG8 . . . . .37 B3
Shenfield St N1. . . . . .95 C5
Shenley Ave HA4. . . . . .39 D1
Shenley Ho 3 SW16. . . . .182 B6
Shenley Rd
Camberwell SE5. . . . . . . .139 C4
Heston TW5 . . . . .129 A4
Shenstone W13. . . . . .109 C5
Shenstone Gdns IG2. . . . .57 D4
Shenstone Ho SW16 . . . .181 C5
Shepard Ho 17 SW11. . . .136 B2
Sheperdess Pl N1. . . . . . .235 B2

Shepherd Cl
Feltham TW13 . . . . .173 A6
W1 . . . . .248 A6
Shepherdess Wlk
N1 . . . . .95 A5 235 B3
Shepherd Ho
Barnsbury N1 . . . . .72 A2
10 Poplar E14. . . . . .97 D1
Shepherd Mkt W1 . . . . . .248 C3
SHEPHERD'S BUSH 112 B5
Shepherd's Bush Gn
W12. . . . . .112 C4
Shepherd's Bush Market
W12. . . . . .112 C4
Shepherd's Bush Mkt Sta
W12. . . . . .112 C4
Shepherd's Bush Overground
Sta W12. . . . . .112 D4
Shepherd's Bush Pl
W12. . . . . .112 D4
Shepherd's Bush Rd W6. .112 C3
Shepherd's Bush Sta
W12. . . . . .112 D4
Shepherds Cl
Dagenham RM6 . . . . .58 D5
Orpington BR6. . . . . .227 D5
Shepperton TW17. . . . . . .192 D3
Stanmore HA7. . . . . .25 A5
Shepherd's Cl N6. . . . . . . .49 B3
Shepherds Ct
8 Hammersmith W12. . . .112 D4
13 Harrow HA1 . . . . .42 D3
Shepherds Gn BR7. . . . . .189 B3
Shepherd's La E9 . . . . . . .74 D2
Shepherds La SE28 . . . . .123 C5
Shepherd's La E9. . . . . . . .74 D2
Shepherds Leas SE9 . . . .145 B1
Shepherds Path UB5. . . . .63 A2
Shepherds Pl W1 . . . . . . .248 A6
Shepherd St W1 . .115 B5 248 C5
Shepherds Way CR2 . . . . .222 D1
Shepherds Wlk
Bushey WD23. . . . . .8 B2
Dollis Hill NW2. . . . . .68 A6
Shepherd's Wlk NW3 . . . .70 B4
Shepiston La UB3. . . . . . .105 A1
Shepley Cl SM5 . . . . .219 A5
Shepley Ct SW16. . . . . . .181 C6
Shepley Mews EN3. . . . . . . .7 C6
Sheppard Cl Enfield EN1. . . . .6 B5
Kingston u T KT6 . . . . . . .198 A5
Sheppard Dr SE16 . . . . . .118 B1
Sheppard Ho
31 Hackney E2 . . . . .96 A5
8 Streatham SW2. . . . . .160 C3
Sheppard St E16. . . . . .98 D3
Shepperd's Ct
Harrow HA1. . . . . .42 C2
Wembley UB6. . . . . .64 D2
Sheppard St E16. . . . . .98 D3
SHEPPERTON. 193 A3
Shepperton Bsns Park
TW17 . . . . .193 A4
Shepperton Court Dr
TW17. . . . . .192 D4
Shepperton Ct TW17. . . . .192 D3
SHEPPERTON GREEN . . .192 D5
Shepperton Rd
Littleton TW17, TW16. . . .192 A5
Orpington BR5 . . . . .211 A3
Shoreditch N1. . . . . .95 B6 235 C6
Shepperton Sta TW17. . . .193 A4
Shepperton Studios
TW17. . . . . .192 B6
Sheppey Gdns RM9 . . . . . .80 C1
Sheppey Ho 16 E5 . . . . . . .74 B4
Sheppey Rd RM9. . . . . . . .80 C1
Shepton Ct SW11 . . . . . . .266 D2
Shepton Hos 11 E2. . . . . . .96 C4
Sherard Ct N19 . . . . .72 A5
Sherard Ho 24 E9 . . . . . . .74 C1
Sherard Rd SE9. . . . . .166 A6
Sheraton Bsns Ctr UB6. . .87 C5
Sheraton Cl WD6 . . . . .10 B6
Sheraton Ho SW1. . . . . . .268 D6
Sheraton Lo HA3 . . . . .42 C6
Sheraton St W1. . . . . .239 C1
Sheraton The 22 E16 . . . .198 A4
Sherborne Ave Enfield EN3 . .6 C3
Southall UB2. . . . . .107 C2
Sherborne Cl UB4 . . . . . . .84 C1
Sherborne Cres SM5 . . . .202 C2
Sherborne Ct SE20. . . . . .184 C1
Sherborne Gdns
Ealing W13 . . . . .87 B2
Queensbury NW9. . . . . . . .44 C6
Sherborne Ho
Pimlico SW1. . . . . .258 D2
South Lambeth SW8. . . . .270 C3
Sherborne La EC4 . . . . . .252 D6
Sherborne Rd BR5. . . . . . .211 D4
Cheam SM3 . . . . .201 C1
Chessington KT9 . . . . . . .214 A3
East Bedfont TW14. . . . . .149 B3
Sherborne St N1. . . . .95 B6 235 C6
Sherboro Rd 1 N15 . . . . . .51 D3
Sherbourne Ct
1 Hampton TW12. . . . . . .173 C2
8 Sutton SM2 . . . . .218 A2
SW5 . . . . .255 C4
Sherbourne Gdns TW17. .193 C2

Sherbourne Pl HA7 . . . . . . .25 A4
Sherbrooke Cl DA7. . . . . .147 C1
Sherbrooke Ho 9 E2. . . . . .96 C5
Sherbrooke Rd
SW6. . . . . .135 A5 264 B3
Sherbrooke Terr SW6 . . . .264 B3
Sherbrooke Way KT4. . . . .200 B2
Sherbrook Gdns N21. . . . .16 A4
Sherbrook Ho 2 N3 . . . . . .29 D3
Shere Cl KT9 . . . . .213 D3
Sheredan Rd E4 . . . . .36 C5
Shere Ho SE1. . . . . .262 C6
Shere Lo 1 SW19. . . . . . .180 C3
Shere Rd IG2. . . . . .56 C4
Sherfield Cl KT3 . . . . .198 D5
Sherfield Gdns SW15 . . . .155 D5
Sheridan N8. . . . . .50 C5
Sheridan Bldgs WC2 . . . .240 B1
Sheridan Cl UB10. . . . . . . .83 A3
Sheridan Cres BR7. . . . . .188 D1
Sheridan Ct Ealing W7 . . .108 D6
Earl's Ct SW5 . . . . .255 C3
Harrow HA1 . . . . .42 B3
Hounslow TW4 . . . . .151 A6
South Hampstead NW6. . . .70 A1
South Lambeth SW9. . . . .270 D1
Sheridan Gdns HA3 . . . . . .43 D3
Sheridan Ho SE11 . . . . . .261 B3
7 Stoke Newington N16. . .73 C5
Sheridan Lo Barnet EN5 . . . .1 D1
Bromley BR2. . . . . .209 C5
East Barnet N14. . . . . .15 B4
Sheridan Mews E11. . . . . .55 B3
Sheridan Pl
Barnes SW13. . . . . .133 D2
Bromley BR1. . . . . .187 D1
Hampton TW12. . . . . .174 A2
Harrow HA1 . . . . .42 C2
Sheridan Rd
Belvedere DA17. . . . . .125 C2
DA7. . . . . .147 A2
Leyton E7 . . . . .76 D5
Little Ilford E12. . . . . .78 B3
Merton SW19 . . . . .179 B2
Richmond TW10 . . . . .153 C1
Sheridan St 34 E1. . . . . . .96 B1
Sheridan Terr UB5. . . . . . .63 A3
Sheridan Way 5 BR3 . . . .185 B2
Sheridan Wlk
Golders Green NW11. . . . . .47 C3
Wallington SM5 . . . . .218 D3
Sheringdale Prim Sch
SW18. . . . . .157 B3
Sheringham NW8. . . . . . . .229 D6
Sheringham Ave
Feltham TW13 . . . . .150 A1
Little Ilford E12. . . . . .78 B3
Southgate N14 . . . . .15 D5
Twickenham TW2 . . . . . . .151 C3
Sheringham Ct 1 N3 . . . . .29 C2
Sheringham Dr IG11. . . . . .80 A3
Sheringham Ho NW1 . . . .237 B4
Sheringham Jun Sch E12 . .78 B4
Sheringham Mews 4
SW18. . . . . .158 A2
Sheringham Rd
Islington N7 . . . . .72 C2
Penge SE20. . . . . .206 C6
Sheringham Twr UB1. . . . .107 D6
Sherington Ave HA5 . . . . .23 C3
Sherington Prim Sch 3
SE7. . . . . .143 B6
Sherington Rd SE7. . . . . .143 B6
Sheriton Ct SM1. . . . . . . .217 C5
Sherland Rd TW1 . . . . . . .152 D3
Sherleys Ct HA4 . . . . .61 C6
Sherlies Ave BR6 . . . . . . .227 C6
Sherlock Ct NW6. . . . . .69 C2
Sherlock Ct 1 NW8. . . . . .229 C6
Sherlock Holmes Mus*
NW1. . . . . .92 D3 237 D5
Sherlock Mews W1 . . . . . .238 A4
Sherman Gdns RM6. . . . . .58 C3
Sherman Rd BR1 . . . . . . .187 A2
Shernhall St E17. . . . . .54 A5
Sherwood Ho 1 E18. . . . . .55 A5
Sherrard Rd E7, E12 . . . . .77 C2
Sherrards Way EN5 . . . . . .13 C5
Sherren Ho 35 E1. . . . . . . .96 C3
Sherrick Green Rd NW10. .68 B3
Sherriff Ct NW6. . . . . .69 C2
Sherriff Rd NW6 . . . . .69 C2
Sherringham Ave N17. . . . .34 A1
Sherrin Rd E10 . . . . .75 D4
Sherrock Gdns NW4 . . . . .46 A5
Sherry Mews IG11. . . . . . .79 B1
Sherston Ct Finsbury N1 WC1 234 A1
Newington SE1. . . . . .261 D4
Sherwin Ho 1 SE11. . . . . .138 C6
Sherwin Rd SE14 . . . . . . .140 D4
Sherwood 3 Barnet EN5. . . .1 D1
Brondesbury NW6. . . . . . . .69 A1
Long Ditton KT6. . . . . . . .213 D6
Sherwood Ave
Greenford UB6. . . . . .64 C4
Hayes UB4 . . . . .84 B3
Mitcham SW16. . . . . .181 D2
Ruislip HA4. . . . . .39 C3
Wanstead E18 . . . . .55 B6
Sherwood Cl
Barnes SW13. . . . . .134 B2

Sherwood Cl continued
DA5.............................168 C5
Ealing W13....................109 B5
Walthamstow E17...........35 B1
Sherwood Ct
11 Battersea SW11........136 A2
Colney Hatch N12...........30 C5
2 South Croydon CR2....221 A3
St Johns SE13................141 D3
Sutton SM1...................217 C3
W1..............................237 C3
6 West Wickham BR4....207 D1
Sherwood Gdns
Barking IG11...................79 B1
Bermondsey SE16.........118 B1
Millwall E14..................119 C2
Sherwood Hall 7 N2...48 A6
Sherwood Ho N4..........51 A2
Sherwood Park Ave
DA15............................168 B5
Sherwood Park Prim Sch
DA15............................168 B5
Sherwood Park Rd
Mitcham CR4.................203 D5
Sutton SM1...................217 C3
Sherwood Park Sch
SM6.............................219 D5
Sherwood Rd
Croydon CR0.................206 B1
DA16............................145 C2
Hampton TW12.............174 A5
Harrow HA2....................64 A6
Hendon NW4...................46 C6
Ilford IG6.......................57 B5
Merton SW19................179 B3
Sherwood Sch CR4.....203 C5
Sherwood St W1........249 B6
Whetstone N20..............14 B1
Sherwood Terr N20.....14 B1
Sherwood Way BR4....224 A6
Shetland Cl NW6.........11 B5
Shetland Rd Bow E3....97 B5
East Bedfont TW6..........149 A5
Shield Dr TW8............131 A6
Shieldhall St SE2.......124 C2
Shield Rd TW15..........171 B6
Shifford Path SE23....162 D1
Shillaker Ct W3.........111 D5
Shillibeer Ct N18........34 B5
Shillibeer Pl W1.........237 B3
Shillingford Cl NW7....28 D3
Shillingford Ho 40 E3...97 B4
Shillingford St 23 N1...72 D1
Shilling Pl TW8..........109 A5
Shillingstone Ho W14...254 B5
Shine Ho 3 N3............29 D3
Shinfield St W12..........90 C1
Shinglewell Rd DA8....147 C5
Shinners Cl SE25.......206 A4
Shipka Rd SW12.........159 B3
Ship La SW14............133 A3
Shiplake Ct SW17......180 B6
Shiplake Ho 45 E2.......95 D4
Shipley Ho 32 SW8....137 D3
Shipman Rd
Forest Hill SE23............162 D2
Newham E16...................99 C1
Ship & Mermaid Row
SE1..............................253 A2
Ship St SE8...............141 C4
Ship Tavern Pas EC3...253 A6
Shipton Cl RM8............80 C5
Shipton Ho
7 Camden Town NW5.....71 A2
14 Haggerston E2............95 D5
Shipton Rd UB8..........60 B4
Shipton St E2...............95 D4
Shipwright Rd SE16....119 A4
Shipwright Yd SE1......253 A3
Shirburn Cl SE23.......162 C4
Shirbutt St E14..........119 D6
Shirebrook Rd SE3.....143 D2
Shire Ct DA18............124 D3
Ewell KT17...................215 D1
Shirehall Cl NW4.........46 D3
Shirehall Gdns NW4....46 D3
Shirehall La NW4.........46 D3
Shirehall Pk NW4.........46 D3
Shire Ho E11................76 D5
Shire Horse Way TW7...130 D2
Shire La BR6..............227 B2
Shiremeade WD6..........10 B6
Shire Mews TW2.........152 A5
Shire Pl
12 Brentford TW8..........131 C5
Wandsworth SW18.........158 A4
Shires The TW10........176 A6
Shirland Mews W9.......91 B4
Shirland Rd W9............91 C3
SHIRLEY......................206 C1
Shirley Ave
Carshalton SM1.............218 C4
Croydon CR0.................206 D1
DA5.............................168 C6
Shirley Church Rd CR0..223 A5
Shirley Cl Hounslow TW3..152 A6
Walthamstow E17...........53 D4
Shirley Cres BR3.........207 A5
Shirley Ct 8 Ealing W13..109 A5

Shirley Ct continued
Ilford IG2.......................57 B4
Kingsbury NW9...............45 B4
2 South Norwood SW16..182 B3
Thornton Heath SW16....204 B6
Shirley Dr TW3...........152 A6
Shirley Gdns Barking IG11..79 C2
Ealing W7.....................108 D5
Shirley Gr Clapham SW11..137 A2
Ponders End N9...............18 D4
Shirley High Sch CR0...222 B5
Shirley Hills Rd CR0....222 D3
Shirley Ho 18 SE5......139 B5
Shirley House Dr SE7...143 C5
Shirley Hts 6 SE18.....147 A1
Shirley Lo 4 SE26......185 A6
Shirley Oaks...............207 A1
Shirley Oaks Hospl CR0..206 C2
Shirley Oaks Rd CR0...222 D6
Shirley Park Rd CR0....206 C5
Shirley Rd Acton W4...111 B4
Croydon CR0.................206 B1
Enfield EN2......................5 A2
Sidcup DA15.................167 C1
Stratford E15..................76 C1
Shirley St E16..............98 D1
Shirley Way CR0.........223 B5
Shirlock Rd NW3..........70 D4
Shirwell Cl NW7...........28 D3
Shobden Rd N17...........33 B2
Shobroke Cl NW2.........68 C5
Shoebury Rd E6...........78 B1
Shoe La EC4.........94 C1 241 B2
Shoelands Ct NW9.......45 B6
Shona Ho E16...............99 C2
Shooters Ave HA3.......43 C5
Shooters Hill..............145 A4
Shooters Hill Rd SE18...144 B4
Shooters Hill Post 16
Campus SE18................144 C4
Shooters Hill Rd
Blackheath Vale SE3,
SE10............................142 C4
SE18, SE3, SE7............143 D5
Shoot-Up Hill NW2.......69 A2
Shopstop SW11..........136 C1
Shore Bsns Ctr 31 E9....74 C1
Shore Cl Feltham TW14...150 A4
Hampton TW12.............173 A5
Shorediche Ct UB10.....60 B5
SHOREDITCH................95 B5
Shoreditch Ct 8 E8.......73 D1
Shoreditch High St Sta
E2........................95 D3 243 C5
Shoreditch High St
E2........................95 C3 243 B6
Shoreditch Ho N1........235 D1
Shore Gr TW13...........151 C2
Shoreham Cl
Croydon CR0.................206 D3
DA5.............................168 D3
Wandsworth SW18........157 D6
Shoreham Rd BR5.......190 B1
Shoreham Rd (E) TW6..148 A6
Shoreham Rd (W) TW6..148 A6
Shoreham Way BR2....209 A3
Shore Ho SW8............137 B2
Shore Mews 30 E9.......74 C1
Shore Pl E9..................74 C1
Shore Point 2 IG9........21 B2
Shore Rd E9.................74 C1
Shore Way 26 SW9.....138 C3
Shorncliffe Rd
SE1..................117 D1 263 C2
Shorndean St SE6.......164 A3
Shorne Cl 3 DA15......168 B5
Shornefield Rd E11......210 C6
Shornells Way SE2......124 C1
Shorrolds Rd
SW6..................135 B5 264 D4
Shortcroft Mead Ct
NW10.............................68 A3
Shortcroft Rd KT17......215 D1
Shortcrofts Rd RM9....101 A2
Shorter St EC3...117 D6 253 D6
Shortgate N12..............29 B6
Short La TW15, TW19...148 B3
SHORTLANDS..............208 C6
Shortlands
Brook Green W6............112 D2
Harlington UB3.............127 B6
Shortlands Cl DA17.....125 B3
Edmonton N18.................17 B1
Shortlands Gdns BR2..186 C1
Shortlands Gr BR2......208 B6
Shortlands Rd
Beckenham BR2, BR3....208 C6
Kingston u T KT2..........176 B3
Walthamstow E10............53 D2
Shortlands Sta BR2....186 C1
Short Path SE18..........144 D6
Short Rd Chiswick W4..133 C4
Leyton E11.....................76 C6
Stanwell TW19..............148 A5
Shorts Croft NW9........44 D5
Shorts Gdns WC2..94 A1 240 A1
Shorts Rd SM5............218 C3
Short St 7 Hendon NW4..46 C5
SE1..............................251 B2

Shortway SE9.............144 A2
Short Way
Colney Hatch N12..........30 C4
Twickenham TW2...........152 A4
Shotfield SM6............219 B2
Shott Cl SM1...............218 A3
Shottendane Rd
SW6..................135 C4 265 A2
Shottery Cl SE9..........166 A1
Shotfield Ave SW14....133 C1
Shottsford 1 W11........91 C1
Shoulder of Mutton Alley 10
E14..............................119 A6
Shouldham St W1..92 C2 237 B3
Showers Way UB3......106 A5
Shrapnel Cl SE18........144 A5
Shrapnel Rd SE9.........144 B2
Shreveport Ho 23 N19..49 D2
Shrewsbury Ave
Harrow HA3.....................44 A5
Mortlake SW14..............133 B1
Shrewsbury Cl KT6......214 A6
Shrewsbury Cres NW10..89 B6
Shrewsbury Ho
Chelsea SW3.................267 A5
Kennington SE11...........270 D5
Shrewsbury House Sch
KT6..............................214 A6
Shrewsbury La SE18...144 D4
Shrewsbury Mews 33 W2..91 C2
Shrewsbury Rd
Beckenham BR3............207 A6
Carshalton SM5............202 C2
Friern Barnet N11...........31 D4
Harlington TW14, TW6...149 B5
Notting Hill W2................91 C1
Plashet E7.......................77 D2
Shrewsbury St W10......90 C3
Shrewsbury Wlk 9
TW7..............................131 A2
Shri Swaminarayan Mandir✱
NW10.............................67 B2
Shroffold Rd BR1.........164 D1
Shropshire Cl CR4......204 A5
Shropshire Ct W7.........86 D1
Shropshire Ho WC1....239 B5
Shropshire Rd N22.......32 B3
Shroton St NW1...92 C2 237 B4
Shrubberies The
Ilford IG2........................57 D4
Woodford E18..................37 A1
Shrubbery Cl N1.........235 B5
Shrubbery Gdns N21....16 D4
Shrubbery Rd
Edmonton N9...................18 A1
Southall UB1.................107 C5
Streatham SW16............182 A6
Shrubbery The
2 Surbiton KT6..............198 A1
7 Wanstead E11.............55 B4
Shrub Ct 5 SM2..........218 A2
Shrubland Gr KT4........216 C5
Shrubland Rd Hackney E8..96 A6
Leyton E10......................53 C2
Walthamstow E17...........53 C4
Shrublands Ave CR0....223 C4
Shrublands Cl
Forest Hill SE26............162 C1
Whetstone N20................14 B2
Shrubsall Cl SE9.........166 A3
Shrubs Ho SW1...........259 D3
Shrubland Ave GS15...139 D5
Shurland Ave EN4.......14 B5
Shurland Gdns SE15...139 D5
Shurlock Dr BR6.........227 A4
Shuters Sq W14..........254 C1
Shuttle Cl DA15..........167 D4
Shuttlemead DA5........169 B4
Shuttle St E1................96 A3
Shuttleworth Rd SW11..136 C3
Siamese Mews 11 N3...29 C2
Sibella Rd SW4...........137 D3
Sibford Ct 5 CR4.........202 D6
Sibley Cl Bexley DA6...169 A6
Bromley BR1.................210 A4
Sibley Ct Beckenham BR3..186 C1
Hillingdon UB8................83 A2
Sibley Gr E12................78 A1
Sibthorpe Rd SE12......165 C4
Sibthorp Rd 2 CR4......180 D1
Sibton Rd SM5............202 C2
Sicilian Ave WC1........240 B3
Sidbury St SW6...135 A4 264 A2
SIDCUP.......................190 A5
Sidcup By-Pass Rd
Sidcup DA14.................189 C6
St Paul's Cray BR5, BR7,
DA14............................190 B3
Sidcup Hill DA14.........190 B5
Sidcup Hill Gdns DA14..190 C5
Sidcup Pl DA14...........190 A5
Sidcup Rd SE9.............166 A3
Sidcup Sta DA15.........168 A2
Sidcup Tech Ctr DA14..190 D4
Siddeley Dr TW4.........129 A3
Siddons La NW1..92 D3 237 D5
Siddons Ho 8 NW3.......70 D3
Siddons La NW1..92 D3 237 D5
Siddons Rd Croydon CR0..220 D5
Forest Hill SE23............163 A2

Siddons Rd continued
Tottenham N17................34 A2
Side Rd E17.................53 B4
Sidewood Rd SE9........167 B3
Sidford Ho SE1............260 D5
Sidford Pl SE1...116 B3 260 D5
Sidgwick Ho 26 SW9...138 A3
Sidi Ct 2 N15................50 D6
Sidings Mews N7..........72 C4
Sidings The E11............54 A1
Sidlaw Ho N16..............51 D1
Sidmouth Ave TW7......130 C3
Sidmouth Dr HA4..........62 A5
Sidmouth Ho
18 Camberwell SE15.....140 A5
Marylebone W1.............237 B2
26 Streatham SW2.......160 C4
Sidmouth Mews WC1...233 C1
Sidmouth Par NW2.......68 C1
Sidmouth Rd
Bexley DA16.................146 C5
Leyton E10......................76 A5
Willesden NW2................68 C1
Sidmouth St WC1..94 B4 233 C1
Sidney Ave N13.............32 B5
Sidney Boyd Ct NW6....69 C1
Sidney Elson Way E6...100 C5
Sidney Gdns TW8........131 D6
Sidney Godley (VC) Ho 31
E2..................................96 C4
Sidney Gr EC1.............234 C3
Sidney Ho
4 Globe Town E2............96 D5
SE18..............................144 B4
Sidney Miller Ct 8 W3..110 D5
Sidney Rd
Beckenham BR3............185 A1
Croydon SE25...............206 A4
Harrow HA2.....................42 A6
Stockwell SW9..............138 B3
Twickenham TW1..........153 B5
Walton-on-T KT12.........194 B1
Wanstead E7...................77 A5
Wood Green N22.............32 B3
Sidney Sq E1................96 C2
Sidney St E1.................96 C2
Sidworth St 6 E8..........74 B1
Siebert Rd SE3............143 A6
Siedle Ho 9 SE18.........144 C6
Siege Ho 14 E1.............96 B1
Siemens Rd SE18........121 D3
Sienna Cl KT9..............213 D2
Sienna St SE28............123 D3
Sienna CT SW13...........149 D1
Sierra Dr RM9, RM10...103 D5
Sigdon Rd E8.................74 A3
Sigers The HA5.............40 B3
Signal Ho 8 London E8..74 A1
SE1..............................252 A1
Signmakers Yd NW1...231 D5
Sigrist Sq 4 KT2.........176 A2
Silbury Ave CR4..........180 C2
Silbury Ho 9 SE26.......162 A1
Silbury St N1...............235 C2
Silchester Ct
Stanwell TW15..............148 A2
Thornton Heath CR7......204 C5
Silchester Rd W10........90 D1
Silecroft Rd DA7.........147 C4
Silesia Bldgs E8...........74 B1
Silex St SE1........116 D4 251 D1
Silicone Bsns Ctr UB6...87 C5
Silk Cl SE12................165 A5
Silkfield Rd NW9...........45 C4
Silk Ho NW9.................45 B6
Silkin Mews 24 SE15...140 A5
Silk Mews SE11..........261 B1
Silk Mills Path SE13....142 A2
Silk Mills Sq E9............75 B2
Silks Ct E11..................54 C1
Silk St EC2.........95 A4 242 B4
Silkstream Par HA8......27 A2
Silkstream Rd HA8........27 A2
Sillitoe Ho N1..............235 D5
Silsoe Ho NW1............231 D3
Silsoe Rd N22..............50 B6
Silverbell Ct 1 N12.......29 C5
Silver Birch Ave E4......35 B4
Silver Birch Cl
Forest Hill SE6..............163 B1
Friern Barnet N11...........31 A4
Ickenham UB10...............60 A4
SE28............................124 A5
Silver Birch Ct EN3.......18 C6
Silver Birch Gdns E6...100 B3
Silverbirch Wlk 1 NW3..71 A2
Silver Cl Harrow HA3....24 B3
SE14............................141 A5
Silvercliffe Gdns EN4..2 C1
Silver Cres W4.............110 D2
Silver Ct N19.................71 C5
Silverdale Enfield EN2....4 A1
Forest Hill SE26............184 C6
NW1............................232 A2
Silverdale Ave IG3........57 D4
Silverdale Cl Cheam SM1..217 B4
1 Ealing W7..................108 D5
Northolt UB5....................63 B3
Silverdale Ct EC1........241 D6

She–Sin 401

Silverdale Dr
Chislehurst SE9............166 A2
Sunbury TW16..............172 B1
Silverdale Factory Ctr
UB3.............................106 A3
Silverdale Gdns UB3...106 A4
Silverdale Ind Est UB3..106 A4
Silverdale Par IG3........57 D4
Silverdale Rd
Bexleyheath DA7...........147 D3
Chingford E4..................36 B4
Hayes UB3...................106 A4
Petts Wood BR5............211 A5
Silverhall St TW7........131 A2
Silverholme Cl HA3......44 A2
Silver Ind Est N17.........33 D1
Silver Jubilee Way TW4..128 B3
Silver La BR4...............224 B6
Silverland St E16.........122 B5
Silverleigh Rd CR7......204 B4
Silvermere 7 E18..........37 A2
Silvermere Rd SE6......163 D5
Silver Pl W1.................249 B6
Silver Rd
Shepherd's Bush W12...112 D6
St Johns SE13..............141 D2
Silvers 4 IG9..................21 C3
Silver Spring Cl DA8...147 D6
Silver St Edmonton N18..33 C6
Enfield EN1......................5 B2
Silverstone Ct 3 BR1...187 C1
Silverston Way HA7.....25 C4
Silver Street Sta N18....33 D5
Silverthorn 17 NW6.......91 D6
Silverthorne Lo EN1......17 C6
Silverthorne Rd SW8...137 B3
Silverthorn Gdns E4....19 C2
Silverton Lo SE19........183 C3
Silverton Rd W6...........134 D6
SILVERTOWN...............121 B4
Silvertown Way E16....121 A5
Silvertree La UB6..........86 B4
Silver Way Hillingdon UB10..82 D5
Romford RM7..................59 D6
Silver Wing Ind Est CR0..220 B2
Silver Wlk SE16...........119 B5
Silverwood Cl BR3.......185 C3
Silvester Ho
27 Bethnal Green E2.......96 C4
1 Notting Hill W11..........91 B1
Pinner HA5.....................40 A5
8 Stepney E1..................96 B1
Silvester Rd SE22.......161 D6
Silvester St SE1...........252 C1
Silwex Ho E1...............243 C5
Silwood St SE16..........118 C1
Simba Cl TW1..............152 D3
Simla Ho SE1..............252 D1
Simmil Rd KT10...........212 D3
Simmonds Ct SW5......255 C3
Simmons Cl
Chessington KT9...........213 C2
East Barnet N20..............14 C3
Simmons Dr RM8..........81 A5
Simmons Gate KT10....212 A3
Simmons Ho
20 Bethnal Green E2.......96 A4
Finsbury Pk N7................72 B6
Simmons La E4..............20 B2
Simmons Rd SE18.......122 D1
Simmons' Way N20......14 C2
Simms Cl SM5.............218 C6
Simms Ct SW6............135 A2
Simms Gdns N2.............30 A1
Simms Rd SE1.............118 A2
Simnel Rd SE12...........165 B4
Simon Cl W11.....113 B6 244 D6
5 Woolwich SE28...........124 B5
Simonds Rd E10...........75 C6
Simone Cl BR1............187 D2
Simon Lo 51 SW19......156 D3
Simon Marks Jewish Prim
Sch 8 N16.......................73 D6
Simons Wlk E15...........76 B3
Simpson Cl Southgate N21..16 B6
Thornton Heath CR0......205 A3
Simpson Dr W3..............89 B1
Simpson Ho
Lisson Gr NW8..............230 A1
Vauxhall SE11...............260 C2
Wembley HA9..................65 D6
Simpson Rd
Hounslow TW4..............151 B5
Richmond TW10............175 C6
Simpson's Rd BR2......209 A6
Poplar E14....................119 D6
Simpson St SW11.......136 C3
Simpson Way KT6.......197 C3
Sim's Cotts KT10.........212 D2
Sims Ho SE3...............142 D1
Sinclair Ct
21 Beckenham BR3.......185 C3
Canonbury N5..................73 A2
5 Croydon CR0..............221 D6
Sinclair Gdns W14......112 D4
Sinclair Gr NW11..........46 D3

Sinclair Ho Harrow HA7 . . . .24 D4
3 South Norwood SW16 . .182 B3
1 Streatham SW12. . . . . .159 D3
Sinclair Mans **13** W12 . . .112 D4
Sinclair Pl SE4. . . . . .163 C5
Sinclair Rd
  Chingford Hatch E4 . . . . . . .35 B5
  W14 . . . . .113 A3 254 A6
Sinclairs Ho **18** E3 . . . . . . .97 B5
Sinclare Cl EN1 . . . . .5 D4
Singapore Rd W13 . . . . . .109 A5
Singer St EC2. . . . . .235 D1
Singlegate Prim Sch
  SW19 . . . . .180 B3
Singleton Cl
  Mitcham SW17 . . . . .180 D3
  Thornton Heath CR0. . . . .205 A2
Singleton Rd RM9 . . . . . . .81 B3
Singleton Scarp N12. . . . . .29 C5
Sinnott Rd E17 . . . . .34 D2
Sion Ct TW1 . . . . .153 B2
Sion Ho SE13 . . . . .142 A1
Sion-Manning RC Sch for
Girls
  16 Kensal Town W10 . . . . . .91 A2
  6 North Kensington W10 . .90 D2
Sion Rd TW1. . . . . .153 B3
Sippetts Ct IG1 . . . . .57 B1
SIPSON 126 C6
Sipson Cl UB3, UB7 . . . . .126 C6
Sipson La UB3, UB7 . . . . .126 D6
Sipson Rd
  Harmondsworth UB7 . . . . .126 C6
  West Drayton UB7 . . . . . .104 B2
  West Drayton UB7 . . . . . .104 C1
Sipson Way UB7 . . . . . . .126 C5
Sir Abraham Dawes Cotts
  SW15. . . . . .135 A1
Sir Alexander Cl W3 . . . . .111 D5
Sir Alexander Rd W3 . . . .111 D5
Sir Arthur Bliss Ct **4**
  SW19. . . . . .180 D1
Sir Cyril Black Way **2**
  SW19. . . . . .179 C3
Sirdar Rd Mitcham CR4 . . .181 A4
  Tottenham N22. . . . . .33 A1
  W11 . . . . .113 A6 244 A5
Sir Francis Drake Prim Sch
  1 SE8 . . . . .119 A1
Sir George Monoux Coll
  E17. . . . . .35 D1
Sir Henry Floyd Ct HA7. . . .9 B2
Sirinham Point SW8 . . . .270 D5
Sirius Bldg **13** E1 . . . . . . .118 D6
Sir James Barrie Prim Sch
  SW8 . . . . .137 C4 269 B1
Sir John Cass Foundation &
Redcoat CE Sec Sch **19**
  E1. . . . . .96 D2
Sir John Cass's Foundation
  Prim Sch EC3. . . .95 C1 243 B1
Sir John Heron Prim Sch
  E12. . . . . .78 B4
Sir John Kirk Cl **33** SE5. .139 A5
Sir John Lillie Prim Sch
  SW6 . . . . .128 A6 264 B5
Sir John Soane's Mus★
  WC2. . . . . .94 B1 240 C2
Sir Martin Bowes Ho **9**
  SE18 . . . . .122 C2
Sir Oswald Stoll Foundation
The SW6. . . . . .265 C4
Sir Thomas Abney Prim Sch
  N16. . . . . .51 B1
Sir Thomas More Est
  SW3. . . . . .136 B6 266 D5
Sirus Rd HA6 . . . . .22 A5
Sir William Burrough Prim
  Sch **27** E14 . . . . .97 B1
Sir William Powell's Almshos
  SW6. . . . . .135 A2
Sise La EC4 . . . . .242 C1
Siskin Ho Edmonton N9. . . .18 D3
  14 Rotherhithe SE16 . . . .118 D2
Sisley Rd IG11 . . . . .101 D6
Sispara Gdns SW18 . . . . .157 B5
Sissinghurst Cl BR1. . . . .186 C5
Sissinghurst Ho **17** SE15. .140 C6
Sissinghurst Rd CR0 . . . .206 A2
Sissulu Ct **8** E6 . . . . .99 C6
Sister Mabel's Way **13**
  SE15. . . . . .140 A5
Sisters Ave SW11 . . . . . . .60 C3
Sisters of St Marcellina Sch
  34 NW3 . . . . .70 A4
Sistova Rd SW12. . . . . . . .159 B3
Sisulu Pl SW9 . . . . .138 C2
Sitarey Ct **4** W12 . . . . . . .112 B5
Site of Changing of the
  Guard★ SW1. . . . . .249 A1
Sittingbourne Ave EN1. . . .17 B5
Sitwell Gr HA7. . . . . .24 D5
Sivill Ho **9** E2 . . . . .95 D4
Siverst Cl UB5. . . . . .63 D2
Siviter Way RM10 . . . . . . .81 D1
Siward Rd Bromley BR2 . .209 C6
  Tottenham N17. . . . . .33 B2

Siward Rd continued
  Wandsworth SW17 . . . . . .158 A1
Six Bridges Ind Est **15**
  SE1. . . . . .118 A1
Sixpenny Ct IG11 . . . . .79 A2
Sixth Ave Hayes UB3 . . . .105 D5
  Ilford E12. . . . . .78 B4
  West Kilburn W10. . . . . . . .91 A4
Sixth Cross Rd TW2 . . . . .152 A1
Skardu Rd 69 A3
Skeena Hill SW18, SW19 . .157 A4
Skeffington Rd E6 . . . . . .100 B6
Skeffington St SE18. . . . . .123 A3
Skeggs Ho **3** E14 . . . . . .120 A3
Skegness Ho **3** N7 . . . . . .72 B1
Skelbrook St SW18. . . . . .158 A2
Skelgill Rd SW15. . . . . . . .135 B1
Skelley Rd E15. . . . . .76 D1
Skelton Cl **7** E8 . . . . .73 D2
Skelton Ho N16. . . . . .73 C3
Skelton Rd E7 . . . . .77 A2
Skeltons La E10. . . . . .53 D2
Skelwith Rd W6. . . . . .134 C6
Skenfrith Ho SE15 . . . . . .140 B6
Skerne Rd KT2. . . . . .175 D2
Skerne Wlk KT2. . . . . .175 D2
Sketchley Gdns SE16. . . . .118 D1
Sketty Rd EN1 . . . . .5 D2
Skiers St E15. . . . . .98 C6
Skiffington Cl SW2. . . . . .160 C3
Skillen Lodge HA5. . . . . . . .22 D2
Skinner Ct E17 . . . . .53 C4
Skinner Pl SW1 . . . . .258 A3
Skinners Almshouses
  N13. . . . . .16 C1
Skinners Company Sch
  (Upper) **10** N16. . . . . .51 D2
Skinner's Company's Lower
  Sch **8** E5 . . . . .52 B1
Skinners La EC4 . . . . .252 B6
  Hounslow TW5 . . . . .129 C4
Skinner St EC1 . . . .94 C3 241 B6
Skip La UB9 . . . . .38 A1
Skipper Ct **5** IG11 . . . . . .101 A6
Skipsea Ho SW18 . . . . . .158 B5
Skipton Cl N11. . . . . .31 A4
Skipton Dr UB3 . . . . .105 A3
Skipton Ho SE14 . . . . . . .141 A1
Skipwith Bldg EC1. . . . . . .241 A4
Skipworth Rd E9. . . . . .96 C6
Skua Ct **33** SE8. . . . . .141 B6
Skyline Ct SE1. . . . . .263 C5
Skyline Plaza Bldg **19** E1. .96 A1
Skylines E14. . . . . .120 A4
Sky Peals Rd IG8 . . . . .36 B3
Sky Studios E16 . . . . .122 C4
Sladebrook Rd SE3 . . . . . .143 D2
Slade Ct Barnet EN5 . . . . . .1 D2
  Brondesbury NW2 . . . . . . .69 A3
  Muswell Hill N10. . . . . .31 B3
Sladedale Rd SE18. . . . . .123 C1
Slade Ho TW4 . . . . .151 B5
Sladen Pl **12** E5. . . . . .74 B4
Slades Cl EN2 . . . . .4 C2
Slades Dr BR7 . . . . .189 A6
Slades Gdns EN2. . . . . .4 C2
Slades Hill EN2 . . . . .4 C2
Slades Rise EN2 . . . . .4 C2
Slade The SE18. . . . . .145 C6
Slade Twr E10 . . . . .75 C6
Slade Way CR4 . . . . .181 A2
Slagrove Pl SE13. . . . . . . .163 D6
Slaidburn St
  SW10. . . . . .136 A6 266 B5
Slaithwaite Rd SE13. . . . . .142 A1
Slaney Ct NW10. . . . . .68 C1
Slaney Pl **1** N7 . . . . .72 C3
Slater Cl **13** SE18. . . . . . .122 C2
Slatter **1** NW9 . . . . .27 D2
Slattery Rd TW13 . . . . . . .150 C3
Sleaford Ho **16** E3. . . . . . .97 C3
Sleaford Ind Est
  SW8 . . . . .137 C5 269 B3
Sleaford St SW8 . .137 C5 269 B3
Sleat Ho **11** E3. . . . . .97 B5
Sledmere Ct TW14 . . . . . .149 C3
Slievemore Ct **8** SW4. . . .137 D2
Sligo Ho **8** E1. . . . . .96 D3
Slingsby Pl WC2 . . . . .250 A6
Slippers Pl SE16. . . . . . . .118 B3
Slipway Ho **1** E14 . . . . . .119 D1
Sloane Ave SW3 . .114 C2 257 B3
Sloane Avenue Mans
  SW3. . . . . .257 C3
Sloane Ct E SW3 . . . . . . .258 A2
Sloane Ct W SW3 . . . . . . .258 A2
Sloane Gate Mans SW1 . .258 A4
Sloane Gdns
  Belgravia SW1 . . .115 A2 258 A3
  Orpington BR6. . . . . .227 A5
Sloane Ho **7** E9 . . . . .74 C1
Sloane Hospl BR3. . . . . . . .186 B2
Sloane Sq SW1 . . . . .257 D3
Sloane Square Sta
  SW1 . . . . .115 A2 258 A3
Sloane St SW1 . . .114 D3 257 D5
Sloane Terr SW1 . . . . . . .258 A4
Sloane Terr Mans SW1 . . .258 A4
Sloane Wlk CR0 . . . . .207 B3

Sloan Ho RM10 . . . . .81 D1
Slocum Cl SE28 . . . . .124 C6
Slough La NW9 . . . . .45 A3
Sly St **17** E1. . . . . .96 B1
Smaldon Cl UB7 . . . . .104 C3
Smallberry Ave TW7 . . . . .130 D3
Smallberry Green Prim Sch
  TW7. . . . . .131 A3
Smallbrook Mews W2. . . .236 C1
Smallbugh Mans HA0 . . . . .65 B4
Smalley Cl N16 . . . . .73 D5
Smallwood Prim Sch
  SW17 . . . . .180 B6
Smallwood Rd SW17 . . . .180 B6
Smarden Cl DA17 . . . . . . .125 C1
Smarden Gr SE9 . . . . .188 B6
Smart's Pl Edmonton N18. .34 A5
  WC1, WC2 . . . . .240 B2
Smart St E2 . . . . .96 C4
Smeaton Cl KT9 . . . . .213 D2
Smeaton Ct SE1. . . . . . . .262 A5
Smeaton Rd Holdbrook EN3. . .7 C1
  Wandsworth SW18 . . . . . .157 C4
Smeaton St E1. . . . . .118 B5
Smedley St SW4 . . . . .137 D3
Smeed Rd E3. . . . . .75 C1
Smiles Pl SE13. . . . . .142 A3
Smith Cl SE16. . . . . .118 D5
Smithers Ho **3** SE20. . . . .184 D3
Smithfield Mkt★
  EC1. . . . . .94 D2 241 D3
Smithfield St EC1 . .94 D2 241 C3
Smithies Rd SE2. . . . . . . .124 B2
Smith's Ct W1 . . . . .249 C6
Smithson Rd N17. . . . . .33 B2
Smiths Point E13 . . . . .99 A6
Smith Sq SW1 . . .116 A3 260 A5
Smith St Surbiton KT5 . . . .198 B3
  SW3 . . . . .114 D1 257 C1
Smith's Yd
  7 Croydon CR0. . . . . . . .221 A5
  Wandsworth SW18 . . . . . .158 A2
Smith Terr SW3 . .114 D1 257 C1
Smithy St E1 . . . . .96 C2
Smithwood Cl SW19 . . . . .157 A2
Smithy Street Sch **34** E1. .96 C2
Smock Wlk CR0. . . . . .205 A3
Smoothfield TW3 . . . . .129 C1
Smythe Cl N9. . . . . .18 A2
Smugglers Way SW18. . . .135 D1
Smyrk's Rd SE17. .117 C1 263 B1
Smyrna Mans **8** NW6. . . . .69 C1
Smyrna Rd NW6 . . . . .69 C1
Smythe St E14. . . . . .119 D6
Snakes La EN4, N14. . . . . . .3 C1
Snakes La E IG8. . . . . .37 C4
Snakes La W IG8. . . . . .37 B4
Snakey La TW13 . . . . .172 B6
SNARESBROOK. 54 D6
Snaresbrook Coll Prep Sch
  10 E18 . . . . .37 A1
Snaresbrook Dr HA7 . . . . . .26 A6
Snaresbrook Hall **12** E18 . .55 A4
Snaresbrook Ho E18 . . . . . .54 D5
Snaresbrook Prim Sch
  E18 . . . . .55 A5
Snaresbrook Rd E11 . . . . . .54 D5
Snaresbrook Sta E11. . . . . .55 A4
Snarsgate St W10. . . . . . . .90 C2
Sneath Ave NW11 . . . . .47 B2
Snell's Pk N18. . . . . .33 D4
Sneyd Rd NW2. . . . . .68 C4
Snowberry Cl E11. . . . . .76 B4
Snowbury Rd **6** SW6 . . . .135 D3
Snow Ct **4** HA0. . . . . .65 D3
Snowden Ave UB10 . . . . . .82 D5
Snowden St EC2. . .95 C3 243 A5
Snowdon Cres UB3 . . . . . .105 A3
Snowdon Dr NW9. . . . . . . .45 C3
Snowdon Rd TW6. . . . . . . .149 A5
Snowdown Cl SE20 . . . . . .184 D2
Snowdrop Cl **2** TW12 . . . .173 C4
Snowe Ho SE27. . . . . .160 D1
Snowman Ho NW6. . . . . . . .91 D6
Snowsfields SE1. .117 B4 252 D2
Snowsfields Prim Sch
  SE1. . . . . .117 C4 253 A2
Snowshill Rd E12 . . . . .78 A3
Snowy Fielder Waye
  TW7. . . . . .131 B3
Soames St SE15 . . . . .139 D2
Soames Wlk KT3. . . . . . . .177 C2
Soane Cl W5 . . . . .109 D4
Soane Ct **10** NW1 . . . . . . .71 C1
Soane Ho SE17 . . . . .262 D1
Soaphouse La TW8. . . . . . .132 A5
Sobell L Ctr N7 . . . . .72 B5
Soham Rd EN3. . . . . .7 B6
SOHO 105 D4
Soho★ W1 . . . . . . .93 D1 239 C2
Soho Mills SM6. . . . . .203 B1
Soho Parish CE Prim Sch
  W1 . . . . .115 D6 249 C6
Soho Sq W1 . . . . . .93 D1 239 C2
Soho St W1. . . . . .239 C2
Sojourner-Truth Cl **11** E8 .74 B2
Sola Ct **8** CR0. . . . . .205 B1
Solander Gdns
  13 Shadwell E1. . . . . . . .118 C6

Solander Gdns continued
  Stepney E1. . . . . .118 B6
Solar Ct N3. . . . . .29 D3
Soldene Ct N7. . . . . .72 B2
Solebay St E1 . . . . .97 A3
Solent Ct SW16. . . . . .182 B1
Solent Ho **1** E1. . . . . .97 A2
Solent Rd NW6 . . . . .69 C3
Solent Rise E13. . . . . .99 A4
Soley Mews WC1 . . . . . . .234 A2
Solidarity Ho **5** NW10 . . . .68 C2
Solna Ave SW15 . . . . .156 C6
Solna Rd N21. . . . . .17 B4
Solomon Ave N9. . . . . .34 A6
Solomons Ct N12. . . . . .30 A3
Solomon's Pas SE15 . . . . .140 B1
Soion New Rd SW4. . . . . .138 A1
Soion Rd SW2. . . . . .138 A1
Solway Ct **1** TW4. . . . . . . .129 A2
Solway Ho **12** E1. . . . . .96 D3
Solway Rd
  East Dulwich SE22 . . . . . .140 A1
  Tottenham N22. . . . . .32 D2
Somaford Gr EN4 . . . . .14 B5
Somali Rd NW2. . . . . .69 B3
Somborne Ho **11** SW15. . .156 A4
Sombrook Ho SE11 . . . . . .261 A3
Somerby Rd IG11. . . . . .79 B1
Somercoates Cl EN4 . . . . . .2 C2
Somer Ct SW6. . . . . .265 A5
Somerfield Rd N4 . . . . .72 D6
Somerfield St SE16 . . . . . .118 D1
Somerford Cl HA5 . . . . .40 A5
Somerford Gr
  Shacklewell N16. . . . . .73 D4
  Tottenham N17. . . . . .34 A3
Somerford Grove Est
  N16 . . . . .73 D4
Somerford St E1. . . . . .96 B3
Somerford Way SE16. . . . .119 A4
Somerhill Ave DA15. . . . . .168 B4
Somerhill Rd DA16. . . . . . .146 B3
Somerleyton Rd SW9 . . . . .138 C1
Somersby Est SE20 . . . . . .184 C3
Somersby Gdns IG4. . . . . . .56 B4
Somers Cl NW1. . . . . .232 C4
Somers Cres W2. . . . . . . .237 A1
Somerset Ave
  Chessington KT9 . . . . .213 D4
  DA16. . . . . .145 D1
  Wimbledon SW20. . . . . . . .178 B1
Somerset Cl
  New Malden KT3. . . . . . . .199 C3
  North Cheam KT4. . . . . . . .216 C5
  Tottenham N17. . . . . .33 B1
  Woodford IG8. . . . . .37 A2
Somerset Ct
  10 Buckhurst Hill IG9. . . . .21 C2
  Ealing W7 . . . . .86 D1
  2 Hampton TW12 . . . . . .173 C2
Somerset Gdns
  Highgate N6 . . . . .49 A2
  St Johns SE13 . . . . .141 D3
  Teddington TW11 . . . . . . .174 C5
  Thornton Heath SW16 . . . .204 B6
  Tottenham N17. . . . . .33 C3
Somerset Ho N17. . . . . .33 C3
Somerset Ho
  WC2 . . . . .116 B6 250 D6
Somerset Ho SW19 . . . . . .157 A1
Somerset Lo
  9 Brentford TW8 . . . . . . .131 D6
  5 New Barnet EN5 . . . . . .14 A6
  Putney SW15 . . . . .134 B1
Somerset Rd
  Bedford Pk W4 . . . . .111 B3
  Brentford TW8 . . . . .131 C6
  Ealing W13 . . . . .109 C5
  Edmonton N18. . . . . .33 D5
  Harrow HA1. . . . . .42 A4
  Hendon NW4 . . . . .46 C5
  Holdbrook EN3 . . . . .7 C5
  Kingston u T KT1. . . . . . . .176 B1
  New Barnet EN5. . . . . .14 A6
  Southall UB1. . . . . .85 C2
  Teddington TW11 . . . . . . .174 C5
  Tottenham N17. . . . . .33 B1
  Walthamstow E17 . . . . .53 C3
  Wimbledon SW19. . . . . . . .157 A1
Somerset Sq
  W14. . . . . .113 B4 244 C1
Somerset Waye TW5 . . . . .129 A5
Somersham Rd DA7. . . . . .147 A3
Somers Pl SW2 . . . . .160 B4
Somers Rd
  Tulse Hill SW2. . . . . .160 B5
  Walthamstow E17 . . . . .53 B5
SOMERSTOWN. 93 D4
Somers Town Est
  NW1 . . . . .93 C5 232 B3
Somers Way WD23. . . . . . . .8 A4
Somerton Ave TW9 . . . . . .132 D2
Somerton Rd
  Cricklewood NW2. . . . . . . .69 A5
  Nunhead SE15 . . . . .140 B1
Somertrees Ave SE12 . . . .165 B2
Somervell Rd HA2 . . . . .63 C3
Somerville Ave SW14 . . . .134 C6
Somerville Cl SW9 . . . . . . .138 B3
Somerville Ct SW16. . . . . .181 D4

Somerville Ho **10** SW15 . .156 D5
Somerville Point SE16 . . . .119 B4
Somerville Rd
  Dagenham RM6. . . . . .58 C4
  Penge SE20 . . . . .184 D3
Sonderling Rd **13** N7. . . . .72 B6
Sondes St SE17 . . . . .139 B6
Songhurst Cl CR0. . . . . . . .204 B3
Sonia Ct Edgware HA8. . . . .26 B3
  North Finchley N12. . . . . . .30 A6
Sonia Gdns Heston TW5 . .129 C5
  North Finchley N12. . . . . . .30 A6
  Willesden NW10. . . . . .67 D4
Sonning Ct CR0. . . . . .222 A6
Sonning Gdns TW12. . . . . .173 A4
Sonning Ho **32** E2. . . . . . .95 D4
Sonning Rd CR0 . . . . .206 A3
Soper Cl
  Chingford Hatch E4. . . . . . .35 B5
  4 Forest Hill SE23. . . . . .162 D2
Soper Mews EN3 . . . . .7 C5
Sophia Cl N7 . . . . .72 B2
Sophia Ho
  10 Hammersmith W6. . . . .112 C1
  Tottenham N15. . . . . .51 D5
Sophia Rd Newham E13 . . . .99 B2
  Walthamstow E10 . . . . .53 D1
Sophia Sq **14** SE16 . . . . . .119 A6
Sopwith **2** NW9 . . . . .27 D2
Sopwith Ave KT9. . . . . . . .214 A3
Sopwith Cl KT2 . . . . .176 B5
Sopwith Rd TW5 . . . . .128 C5
Sopwith Way
  Battersea SW8 . . .137 B5 268 C4
  Kingston u T KT2. . . . . . . .176 A2
Sorbus Ct EN2 . . . . .4 D3
Sorensen Ct **2** E10 . . . . . . .75 D6
Sorrel Cl SE28 . . . . .124 A5
Sorrel Gdns E6 . . . . .100 A2
Sorrel Ho TW3 . . . . .130 A4
Sorrel La **17** E14 . . . . .98 B1
Sorrell Cl **6** Brixton SW9 . .138 C3
  SE14. . . . . .141 A5
Sorrento Rd SM1 . . . . .217 D5
Soseki Mus★ SW4 . . . . . .137 B2
Sotheby Rd N5 . . . . .73 A4
Sotheran Cl E8 . . . . .96 A6
Sotheron Pl SW6 . . . . .265 D3
Soudan Rd SW11 .136 D4 267 C1
Souldern Rd **10** W14 . . . . .112 D3
South Acre NW9 . . . . .27 D1
Southacre Way HA5. . . . . . .22 C2
SOUTH ACTON. 110 D3
South Acton Sta W3, W4. .111 A3
South Africa Rd W12. . . . . .112 B6
SOUTHALL. 107 A5
Southall Ct UB1. . . . . .107 B6
Southall Ent Ctr UB2. . . . .107 C4
Southall La TW5 . . . . .106 B1
Southall Norwood Hospl
  UB2. . . . . .107 B3
Southall Pl SE1. . . . . .252 C1
Southall Sp Ctr UB1. . . . . .107 B5
Southall Sta UB1 . . . . .107 B4
Southall & West London Coll
  UB1. . . . . .107 A5
Southam Ho **9** W10 . . . . . .91 A3
Southampton Bldgs
  WC2. . . . . .241 A3
Southampton Gdns CR4. . .204 A4
Southampton Mews
  E16 . . . . .121 B5
Southampton Pl WC1 . . . .240 B3
Southampton Rd
  Maitland Pk NW5 . . . . .70 D3
  Stanwell TW19, TW6. . . . .148 A5
Southampton Rd E TW6 . .148 B5
Southampton Rd W
  TW6 . . . . .148 B5
Southampton Row
  WC1. . . . . .94 A2 240 B4
Southampton St WC2 . . . .250 B6
Southampton Way SE5. . . .139 C5
Southam St W10 . . . . .91 A3
South Audley St
  W1. . . . . .115 A5 248 B4
South Ave Chingford E4. . . .20 A4
  East Finchley N11 . . . . .47 D5
  Richmond TW9 . . . . .132 C3
  Southall UB1. . . . . .107 B6
  Wallington SM5 . . . . .219 A1
South Avenue Gdns
  UB1. . . . . .107 B6
Southbank KT7. . . . . .197 B2
SOUTH BANK 116 B4
South Bank KT6. . . . . .198 A3
South Bank Bsns Ctr
  SW8 . . . . .137 D6 269 D5
Southbank International Sch
  14 NW3 . . . . .70 A2
Southbank International Sch
  (Westminster Campus)
  W1 . . . . .93 B2 238 C4
Southbank Int Sch
  W11 . . . . .113 C6 245 A5
South Bank Lo **2** KT6. . . .198 A3
South Bank Terr KT6 . . . . .198 A3
South Bank Univ
  SW8 . . . . .137 D4 269 D2

South Bank University (Erlang House) SE1 116 D4 251 C1
SOUTH BEDDINGTON 219 C2
South Bermondsey Sta SE16 118 C1
South Birkbeck Rd E11 76 B5
South Black Lion La 7 W6 112 A1
South Bldg SW1 259 B6
South Block 20 E1 118 C6
South Bolton Gdns SW10 255 D2
SOUTHBOROUGH BR2 210 B3
KT6 197 D1
Southborough Cl KT6 197 D1
Southborough Ho SE17 263 B2
Southborough La BR1, BR2 210 B4
Southborough Prim Sch BR2 210 C4
Southborough Rd
Bromley BR1, BR2 210 A5
South Hackney E9 96 D6
Surbiton KT6 198 A1
Southborough Rd (The Lane) KT6 198 A1
Southborough Sch KT6 214 A5
Southbourne BR2 209 A2
Southbourne Ave NW9 27 B1
Southbourne Cl HA5 41 A2
Southbourne Cres NW4 47 A5
Southbourne Ct NW9 27 A1
Southbourne Gdns
Ilford IG1 79 A3
Ruislip HA4 40 B1
SE12 165 B6
Southbridge Pl CR0 221 A4
Southbridge Rd CR0 221 A4
Southbridge Way UB2 107 A4
SOUTH BROMLEY 98 B2
Southbrook Mews SE12 164 D5
Southbrook Rd
Hither Green SE12 164 D5
Thornton Heath SW16 182 A2
South Building★ SE10 142 B5
Southbury NW8 229 B6
Southbury Ave EN1 6 A1
Southbury Prim Sch EN3 6 C1
Southbury Rd Enfield EN1 5 D2
Enfield EN1, EN3 6 B1
Southbury Sta EN3 6 B1
South Camden Com Sch NW1 93 D5 232 C4
South Carriage Dr SW1, SW7 114 D4 247 C2
South Chelsea Coll 22 SW9 138 B1
Southchurch Ct
Bowes Pk N13 32 B5
Newham E6 100 B5
Southchurch Rd E6 100 B5
South Cl Barnet EN5 1 B2
DA6 146 D1
Dagenham RM10 103 C6
Highgate N6 49 B3
Morden SM4 201 C3
Pinner HA5 41 B2
Twickenham TW2 151 C1
West Drayton UB7 104 C3
South Colonnade The E14 119 D5
Southcombe St W14 254 A4
South Common Rd UB8 60 A2
Southcote Ave
Feltham TW13 150 A2
Tolworth KT5 198 D2
Southcote Rd
Croydon SE25 206 B3
Tufnell Pk N19 71 C4
Walthamstow E17 53 A4
Southcote Rise HA4 39 B2
Southcott Ho
31 Bromley E3 97 D4
W9 236 B5
South Countess Rd E17 53 B6
South Cres Newham E16 98 B3
WC1 239 C3
Southcroft
Carshalton SM1 218 C3
8 Stonebridge NW10 89 B6
Southcroft Ave DA16 145 C2
West Wickham BR4 224 A6
Southcroft Rd BR6 227 C5
Streatham SW17 181 A4
South Cross Rd IG6 57 A4
South Croxted Rd SE21 183 B6
SOUTH CROYDON 221 B1
South Croydon Sta CR2 221 B3
South Ct 17 SW15 156 D5
Southdean Gdns SW19 157 B2
South Dene NW7 11 B1
Southdene Ct N11 15 C1
Southdown N7 72 A2
Southdown Ave W7 109 A3
Southdown Cres
Harrow HA2 42 A1
Ilford IG2 57 C4
Southdown Dr SW20 178 D3
Southdown Rd SW20 178 D2
South Dr Orpington BR6 227 C3
Ruislip HA4 39 C1
South Ealing Cemy W5 109 D2
South Ealing Rd W5 109 D3
South Ealing Sta W5 109 D3
South Eastern Ave N9 17 D1
South Eastern Univ 3 N7 72 B5
South Eaton Pl SW1 115 A2 258 B4
South Eden Park Rd BR3 207 D4
South Edwardes Sq W8 255 A5
SOUTHEND 186 B6
South End Croydon CR0 221 A4
W8 113 D3 255 D6
Southend Cl SE9 166 D5
South End Cl NW3 70 C4
Southend Cres SE9 166 D5
South End Gn NW3 70 C4
Southend Ho SE9 166 C4
Southend La SE6 185 C6
Southend Rd
Beckenham BR3 185 C2
Plashet E6 78 B1
Woodford IG8 37 D1
South End Rd NW3 70 C4
Southend Road (North Circular Rd) E17, E18 36 B2
South End Row W8 113 D3 255 D6
Southern Ave
East Bedfont TW14 150 A3
South Norwood SE25 205 D6
Southerngate Way SE14 141 A5
Southern Gr E3 97 B3
Southernhay IG10 21 D6
Southern Perimeter Rd
Hatton TW14, TW6 149 B6
West Bedfont TW19, TW6 148 C5
Southern Rd
Fortis Green N2 48 D5
Newham E13 99 B5
Southern Road Prim Sch E13 99 B5
Southern Row W10 91 A3
Southern St N1 233 C4
Southern Way
Greenwich SE10 120 D3
Romford RM7 59 C3
Southerton Rd W6 112 C2
South Esk Rd E7 77 C2
Southey Ho SE17 262 B2
Southey Mews E16 121 A5
Southey Rd Brixton SW9 138 C4
Merton SW19 179 C3
Tottenham N15 51 C4
Southey St SE20 184 D3
Southfield EN5 12 D5
Southfield Cl UB8 82 C4
Southfield Cotts W7 108 D4
Southfield Ct E11 76 D5
Southfield Gdns TW1, TW2 174 D6
Southfield Lo W4 111 B4
Southfield Pk HA2 41 D5
Southfield Prim Sch W4 111 C4
Southfield Rd Acton W4 111 B4
Enfield EN3 18 C5
St Paul's Cray BR7 211 D6
SOUTHFIELDS 157 D3
Southfields Hendon NW4 46 B6
Thames Ditton KT8 196 C3
Southfields Ave TW15 170 D4
Southfields Com Coll SW18 157 C3
Southfields Ct SM3 217 C6
Southfields Rd SW18 157 C5
Southfields Sta SW18 157 B3
Southfleet Rd BR6 227 C4
SOUTHGATE 16 B4
South Gate Ave TW13 171 B6
Southgate Cir 3 N14 15 D3
Southgate Coll N14 15 D2
Southgate Ct N1 73 B1
Southgate Gr N1 73 B1
Southgate Ho 7 E17 54 A6
Southgate Rd N1 95 B6 235 D6
South Gate Rd E12 77 D5
Southgate Sch EN4 15 B6
Southgate Sta N14 15 D3
Southgate Way N2 30 C2
South Gdns
Mitcham SW19 180 B3
Wembley HA9 66 C6
South Gipsy Rd DA16 146 D2
South Glade The DA5 169 B3
South Gn NW9 27 C2
South Gr Highgate N6 49 A1
Tottenham N15 51 B4
Walthamstow E17 53 B4
South Greenford Sta UB6 86 C4
South Grove Ho N6 49 A1
South Grove Prim Sch E17 53 B3
SOUTH HACKNEY 96 C6
SOUTH HAMPSTEAD 70 A1
South Hampstead High Sch 11 NW3 70 B2
South Hampstead Sta NW8 70 A1
South Harringay Jun & Inf Schs 1 N4 50 D4
SOUTH HARROW 63 D5
South Harrow Sta HA2 64 A5
South Hill BR7 188 B4
South Hill Ave HA1, HA2 64 B5
South Hill Gr HA1 64 C4
South Hill Pk NW3 70 C4
South Hill Pk Gdns NW3 70 C4
South Hill Rd
Beckenham BR2 208 C5
6 Beckenham BR2 208 D5
Southholme Cl SE19 183 C2
Southill La HA5 40 B5
Southill Rd BR7 188 B3
Southill St E14 97 D1
South Island Pl SW9 138 C5
SOUTH KENSINGTON 114 A1
South Kensington Sta SW7 114 B2 256 D4
South Kensington Station Arc SW7 256 D4
South Kenton Sta HA9 43 C1
South La
Kingston u T KT1 197 D6
New Malden KT3 199 B3
SOUTH LAMBETH 138 A4
South Lambeth Pl SW8 270 B6
South Lambeth Rd SW8 138 A5 270 B4
Southland Rd SE18 145 D5
Southlands Ave BR6 227 C3
Southlands Ct BR2 209 D5
Southlands Dr SW19 156 D2
Southlands Gr BR1 210 A6
Southlands Rd BR1, BR2 209 D5
Southland Way TW7 152 B6
South La W KT3 199 B5
South Lo
6 New Barnet EN5 13 D6
NW8 229 C2
Twickenham TW2 152 A5
South Lodge Ave CR4, CR7, SW16 204 A5
South Lodge Cres EN2 3 D1
South Lodge Dr N14 15 D6
South London Gall★ SE5 139 C4
South London Montessori Sch SW11 267 A1
South Mall The N9 18 A1
South Mead
Grahame Pk NW9 27 D2
West Ewell KT19 215 D1
Southmead Prim Sch 16 SW19 157 A3
Southmead Rd SW19 157 A3
South Merton Sta SW20 201 B6
South Molton La W1 93 B1 238 C1
South Molton Rd E16 99 A1
South Molton St W1 93 B1 238 C1
Southmont Rd KT10 212 C5
Southmoor Way E9 75 B3
South Mount N20 14 A2
SOUTH NORWOOD 205 C6
South Norwood Ctry Pk★ SE25 206 C5
South Norwood Hill SE19, SE25 183 D1
South Norwood Pools & L Ctr SE25 206 B4
South Norwood Prim Sch SE25 206 A5
South Oak Rd SW16 182 B6
Southold Rise SE9 166 B1
Southolm St SW11 137 B4 268 D1
South Ordnance Rd EN3 7 C5
Southover BR1 187 A5
Finchley N12 29 C6
SOUTH OXHEY 22 B6
South Par
Acton Green W4 111 B2
Edgware HA8 26 C1
Wallington SM6 219 C2
South Parade SW3 114 B1 256 D2
South Park Bsns Ctr IG3 79 C6
South Park Cres
Catford SE6 164 D3
Ilford IG1 79 C5
Southpark Ct SW19 179 C4
South Park Ct 24 BR3 185 C3
South Park Dr IG3 79 C4
South Park Gr KT3 199 A5
South Park Hill Rd CR2 221 B4
South Park Mews SW6 135 D2
South Park Prim Sch IG3 79 C5
South Park Rd Ilford IG1 79 B5
Wimbledon SW19 179 D4
South Park Terr IG1 79 C5
South Park Villas IG3 79 C4
South Park Way HA4 62 C3
South Pl
Broadgate EC2 95 B2 242 D3
Enfield EN3 18 C6
South Pl *continued*
Surbiton KT5 198 B2
South Pl Mews EC2 242 D3
Southport Rd SE18 123 B2
South Quay Plaza E14 119 D4
South Quay Sta E14 119 D4
South Rd Brentford W5 109 D2
Edgware HA8 26 D2
Edmonton N9 18 A3
Feltham TW13 172 D5
Forest Hill SE23 162 D2
Hampton TW12 173 B4
Heston TW5 128 D6
Mitcham SW19 180 B4
Southall UB1 107 B5
Twickenham TW2 152 B1
West Drayton UB7 104 C3
South Residence IG3 58 B4
South Ridge BR2 209 C5
Southridge Pl SW20 178 D3
South Rise W2 247 B6
South Rise Prim Sch 3 SE18 123 B1
South Rise Way SE18 123 B2
South Row SE3 142 D3
SOUTH RUISLIP 62 D4
South Ruislip Sta HA4 62 C3
Southsea Rd KT1 198 A5
South Sea St SE16 119 B3
Southside N7 71 D4
South Side W6 111 D3
Southside Comm SW19 178 D4
Southside Ind Est SW8 269 A2
Southside Quarter 4 SW11 136 D3
Southside Sh Ctr SW18 157 D5
Southspring DA15 167 B4
South Sq
Hampstead Garden Suburb NW11 47 D3
WC1 241 A3
South St Bromley BR1 187 A1
Enfield EN3 18 D6
Isleworth TW7 131 A2
Mayfair W1 115 A5 248 B4
South Tenter St E1 95 D1 243 D1
South Terr
Muswell Hill N22 31 D1
Surbiton KT6 198 A3
SW7 114 C2 257 A4
South Thames Coll (Putney Ctr) 12 SW15 156 D6
South Thames Coll (Roehampton Ctr) SW15 156 A5
South Thames Coll (Tooting Ctr) 7 SW17 180 C5
South Thames Coll (Wandsworth Ctr) 7 SW18 157 D6
SOUTH TOTTENHAM 51 D3
South Tottenham Sta N15 51 D4
South Vale Harrow HA1 64 C4
West Norwood SE19 183 C4
Southvale Rd SE3 142 C3
South View BR1 187 C1
Wimbledon SW19 178 D4
Southview Ave NW10 67 D3
Southview Cl SW17 181 A5
South View Cl DA5 169 B5
South View Cres IG2 56 D3
South View Ct
8 Forest Hill SE23 162 C3
South Norwood SE19 183 A3
Southview Dr E18 55 B6
Southview Gdns SM6 219 C1
Southview Rd BR1 186 B6
South View Rd
Hornsey N8 50 A6
Pinner HA5 22 B4
South Villas NW1 71 D2
Southville
London SW8 137 D4 269 D1
South Lambeth SW8 137 A4
Southville Cl
East Bedfont TW14 149 C3
West Ewell KT19 215 B1
Southville Cres TW14 149 C3
Southville Jun & Inf Schs TW14 149 D3
Southville Rd
East Bedfont TW14 149 C4
Thames Ditton KT7 197 B2
SOUTHWARK 117 B5
Southwark Bridge SE1, EC4 117 A6 252 B5
Southwark Bridge Rd SE1 117 A5 252 B3
Southwark Cath★ SE1 117 B5 252 C4
Southwark Coll SE1 116 D4 251 C2
Southwark Coll (Blackfriars Ctr) SE1 251 C3
Southwark Coll (Camberwell Ctr) 17 SE5 139 C5
Southwark Coll (Grange Ctr) SE1 263 B5
Southwark Coll (Surrey Docks Ctr) 12 SE16 118 B3
Southwark Park Est 11 SE16 118 B2
Southwark Park Prim Sch 19 SE16 118 B2
Southwark Park Rd SE16 118 A2
Southwark Pk Sports Complex SE16 118 C2
Southwark Pl BR1 210 B6
Southwark St SE1 117 A5 252 A3
Southwark Sta SE1 116 D5 251 C3
Southwater Cl
Beckenham BR3 185 D3
8 Poplar E14 97 B1
Southway
Hampstead Garden Suburb NW11 47 D4
Hayes BR2 209 A2
Totteridge N20 13 C2
Wallington SM6 219 C4
West Barnes SW20 200 D5
South Way Croydon CR0 223 A5
Friern Barnet N11 31 C4
Harrow HA2 41 C5
Lower Edmonton N9 18 C2
Wembley HA9 66 C3
Southway Cl 9 W12 112 B4
Southwell Ave UB5 63 C2
Southwell Gdns SW7 256 A3
Southwell Grove Rd E11 76 C6
Southwell Ho
8 Bermondsey SE16 118 B2
13 Stoke Newington N16 73 C3
Southwell Rd
Camberwell SE5 139 A2
Harrow HA3 43 D3
Thornton Heath CR0 204 C3
South Western Rd TW1 153 B5
Southwest Rd E11 54 B1
South Wharf Rd W2 92 B1 236 D2
Southwick Mews W2 236 D2
Southwick Pl W2 237 A1
Southwick St W2 92 C1 237 A2
Southwick Yd W2 237 A1
SOUTH WIMBLEDON 179 D4
South Wimbledon Sta SW19 179 D3
South Wlk
Coney Hall BR4 224 C5
Hayes UB3 83 B2
Southwold Dr IG11 80 A3
Southwold Mans W9 91 C4
Southwold Prim Sch E5 74 B6
Southwold Rd DA5 169 D5
Upper Clapton E5 74 C6
Southwood Ave
Highgate N6 49 B2
Kingston u T KT2, KT3 177 A2
Southwood Cl BR1 210 B5
North Cheam KT4 200 D1
Southwood Ct EC1 234 C1
Hampstead Garden Suburb NW11 47 D4
Southwood Dr KT5 199 A1
South Woodford 10 E18 37 A1
South Woodford Sta E18 37 B1
Southwood Gdns
Hinchley Wood KT10 213 A5
Ilford IG2 56 D5
Southwood Hall N6 49 B3
Southwood Ho
New Eltham SE9 166 D2
Notting Hill W11 244 A6
Southwood Hts N6 49 B2
Southwood La N6 49 A2
Southwood Lawn Rd N6 49 B2
Southwood Mans N6 49 B3
Southwood Park N6 49 A2
Southwood Prim Sch RM9 81 A4
Southwood Rd SE9 166 D2
Woolwich SE28 124 B5
Southwood Smith Ho 4 E2 96 B4
Southwood Smith St N1 234 C5
South Worple Ave SW14 133 C2
Southwyck Ho SW9 138 C1
South Yd EC1 242 C4
Sovereign Bsns Ctr EN3 7 B2
Sovereign Cl Ealing W5 87 C2
Ruislip HA4 39 C1
Stepney E1 118 B6
Sovereign Cres SE16 119 A6
Sovereign Ct BR2 210 B3
East Molesey KT8 195 B5
Harlington UB7 126 D5
3 Richmond TW9 132 B1
13 Stepney E1 118 B6
Sovereign Gr HA0 65 D5
Sovereign Ho
Ashford TW15 170 A6

Sovereign Ho continued
23 Bethnal Green E1 . . . . . .96 B3
Chislehurst BR7 . . . . .189 B3
Edgware NW7 . . . . .27 B6
3 Wimbledon SW19 . . . . .179 A4
Woolwich SE18 . . . . .122 B3
Sovereign Mews
Barnet EN4 . . . . .2 D2
6 Haggerston E2 . . . . . . .95 D5
Sovereign Pk NW10 . . . . . .88 D3
Sovereign Pl HA1 . . . . .42 D4
Sovereign Rd IG11 . . . . . .102 C4
Sovreign Ct HA6 . . . . .22 A2
Sowerby Cl SE9 . . . . .166 B6
Spa at Beckenham The
BR3 . . . . .185 A2
Space Apartments N22 . . .32 B3
Space Bsns Pk NW10 . . . . .88 D4
Spa Central 1 SW16 . . . .182 A3
Space Waye TW14 . . . . . .150 B6
Spa Cl SE19 . . . . .183 C2
Spa Ct
12 Bermondsey SE16 . . . .118 A3
Streatham SW16 . . . . . . .182 B6
Spafield St EC1 . . . . .241 A6
Spa Hill CR7, SE19 . . . . . .183 B2
Spalding Cl HA8 . . . . .27 C3
Spalding Ct HA8 . . . . .26 B6
Spalding Ho SE4 . . . . . . .163 A6
Spalding Rd Hendon NW4 . .46 C3
Streatham SW17 . . . . . . .181 B5
Spanby Rd E3 . . . . .97 C3
Spangate SE3 . . . . .142 D2
Spaniards Cl NW11 . . . . . .48 B1
Spaniards End NW3 . . . . . .48 B1
Spaniards Rd NW3 . . . . . . .70 A6
Spanish Billingual Sch
W10 . . . . .91 A2
Spanish Pl W1 . . . . .238 B2
Spanish Rd SW18 . . . . . . .158 A6
Spanswick Lo 2 N15 . . . . .50 D5
Spa Rd SE16 . . . . .117 D3 263 D5
Sparkbridge Rd HA1 . . . . . .42 C5
Sparkes Cl BR2 . . . . .209 B5
Sparke Terr 2 E16 . . . . . . .98 D1
Sparkford Gdns N11 . . . . .31 A5
Sparkford Ho SW11 . . . . .266 D2
Sparks Cl Acton W3 . . . . . .89 B1
Dagenham RM8 . . . . .80 D6
Hampton TW12 . . . . .173 A4
Sparrow Ct TW12 . . . . . . .173 A4
Sparrow Ct E4 . . . . .36 A4
Sparrow Dr BR5 . . . . .211 B1
Sparrow Farm Com Jun Sch
KT17 . . . . .216 B4
Sparrow Farm Dr TW14 . .150 C4
Sparrow Farm Inf Sch
TW14 . . . . .150 C4
Sparrow Farm Jun Sch
TW14 . . . . .150 C4
Sparrow Farm Rd KT17,
KT4 . . . . .216 B4
Sparrow Gn RM10 . . . . .81 D5
Sparrows Herne WD23 . . . .8 A4
Sparrows La SE9 . . . . . . .167 A3
Sparrows Way WD23 . . . . .8 A4
Sparsholt Rd
Barking IG11 . . . . .101 C6
Finsbury Pk N19 . . . . .50 B1
Sparta St SE10 . . . . .142 A4
Spa Sch SE1 . . . . .118 A2
Spa View 6 SW16 . . . . . .160 B1
Speakers' Corner ★
W1 . . . . .114 D6 247 D6
Speaker's Ct 3 CR0 . . . . .205 B1
Speakman Ho SE4 . . . . . .141 A2
Spearman St 8 SE18 . . . .144 C6
Spear Mews
SW5 . . . . .113 C2 255 B3
Spearpoint Gdns IG2 . . . . .57 D5
Spears Rd N19 . . . . .50 A1
Speart La TW5 . . . . .129 A5
Spectacle Works E13 . . . . .99 C4
Spectrum Ho NW5 . . . . . . .71 A4
Spectrum Twr 1 IG1 . . . . .79 A6
Spedan Cl NW3 . . . . .70 A5
Speechly Mews E8 . . . . . .73 D3
Speed Ho EC2 . . . . .242 C4
Speedwell Ct 9 N12 . . . . .29 D6
Speedwell Ho 11 N12 . . . .29 D6
Speedwell St 8 SE8 . . . . .141 C5
Speedy Pl WC1 . . . . .233 A1
Speer Rd KT7 . . . . .196 D3
Speirs Cl KT3 . . . . .199 D3
Spekehill SE9 . . . . .166 B1
Speke Rd CR7 . . . . .183 B1
Speldhurst Ct 2 BR2 . . . .208 D4
Speldhurst Rd
Bedford Pk W4 . . . . .111 B3
Homerton E9 . . . . .74 D1
Spellbrook Wlk N1 . . . . . .235 B6
Spelman Ho 15 E1 . . . . . .96 A2
Spelman St E1 . . . . .96 A2
Spelthorne TW16 . . . . . . .171 D3
Spelthorne Inf Sch
TW15 . . . . .171 B4

Spelthorne Jun Sch
TW15 . . . . .171 B4
Spelthorne La TW15,
TW17 . . . . .171 A2
Spelthorne Sports Club
TW16 . . . . .171 B3
Spence Cl SE16 . . . . .119 B4
Spencer Ave
Bowes Pk N13 . . . . .32 B4
Hayes UB4 . . . . .84 A2
Spencer Cl BR6 . . . . .227 D6
Church End N3 . . . . .29 C1
Ealing NW10 . . . . .88 B4
Woodford IG8 . . . . .37 C5
Spencer Ct 5 BR6 . . . . . .227 A3
6 Finchley N3 . . . . .29 D3
Wimbledon SW20 . . . . . . .178 B2
Spencer Dr N2 . . . . .48 A3
Spencer Gdns SW14 . . . . .155 A6
Spencer Hill SW19 . . . . . .179 A3
Spencer Hill Rd SW19 . . . .179 A3
Spencer Ho
31 Clapham SW8 . . . . . .137 D3
Hendon NW4 . . . . .46 B4
24 Putney SW19 . . . . . . .156 D3
Vale of Health NW3 . . . . . .70 B5
Wimbledon SW19 . . . . . . .156 D1
Spencer House Mus ★
SW1 . . . . .115 C5 249 A3
Spencer Mews
Fulham W6 . . . . .264 A6
South Lambeth SW9 . . . . .270 C1
Spencer Park Ct SW18 . . .158 B6
Spencer Pk
East Molesey KT8 . . . . . . .196 A4
Wandsworth SW18 . . . . . .158 B6
Spencer Pl
16 Islington N1 . . . . .72 D1
SW1 . . . . .259 B5
Thornton Heath CR0 . . . . .205 B2
Spencer Rd Acton W3 . . . .111 A5
Bromley BR1 . . . . .186 D3
Carshalton CR4 . . . . .203 A2
Chingford E17 . . . . .36 A1
Chiswick W4 . . . . .133 A5
East Molesey KT8 . . . . . . .196 A4
Friern Barnet N11 . . . . . . .31 B6
Harrow HA3 . . . . .24 C1
Hornsey Vale N8 . . . . .50 B4
Hounslow TW5, TW7 . . . . .130 A4
Ilford IG3 . . . . .57 D1
Mitcham CR4 . . . . .203 A6
Newham E6 . . . . .99 D6
South Croydon CR2 . . . . . .221 C3
Tottenham N17 . . . . .34 A2
Twickenham TW2 . . . . . . .152 C2
Wandsworth SW18 . . . . . .158 B6
Wembley HA0 . . . . .65 C6
Wimbledon SW20 . . . . . . .178 B2
Spencer Rise NW5 . . . . . . .71 B5
Spencer St
Finsbury EC1 . . . . . .94 D4 234 C1
Southall UB2 . . . . .106 D4
Spencer Way 35 E1 . . . . . .96 B1
Spencer Wlk
23 Hampstead NW3 . . . . .70 A4
Putney SW15 . . . . .134 D1
Spenlow Ho 2 SE16 . . . . .118 A3
Spenlow Ho 4 SW10 . . . . .175 D6
Spenser Ct 5 TW10 . . . . .175 D6
Spenser Gr N16 . . . . .73 C4
Spenser Mews SE21 . . . . .161 B3
Spenser Rd SE24 . . . . . . .160 D6
Spenser St SW1 . . . . .259 B6
Spens Ho WC1 . . . . .240 C5
Spensley Wlk N16 . . . . . . .73 B5
Speranza St SE18 . . . . . .123 D1
Sperling Rd N17 . . . . .33 C1
Spert St E14 . . . . .119 A6
Speyside N14 . . . . .15 C5
Spey St E14 . . . . .98 A2
Spezia Rd NW10 . . . . .90 A5
Spice Ct
10 Battersea SW11 . . . . .136 A2
2 St George in t East E1 . .118 A5
Spice Quay Htss SE1 . . . .253 D3
Spicer Cl
Brixton SE5, SW9 . . . . . . .138 D3
Walton-on-T KT12 . . . . . . .194 C3
Spicer Ct EN1 . . . . .5 C2
Spicer Ho E2 . . . . .96 A4
Spices Yd CR0 . . . . .221 A4
Spigurnell Rd N17 . . . . . . .33 B2
Spikes Bridge Rd UB1 . . .107 A6
Spilsby Cl NW9 . . . . .27 C1
Spindle Cl SE18 . . . . .122 A3
Spindle Ho 8 DA15 . . . . . .168 A1
Spindlewood Gdns CR0 . . .221 C4
Spindrift Ave E14 . . . . . . .119 D2
Spinel Cl SE18 . . . . .123 D1
Spinnaker Cl IG11 . . . . . . .102 B4
Spinnaker Ct 2 KT1 . . . . .175 D2
Spinnaker Ho 21 E14 . . . . .119 C4
Spinnells Rd HA2 . . . . .41 B1
Spinney Cl
Beckenham BR3 . . . . .207 B5
New Malden KT3 . . . . .199 C4
Worcester Pk KT4 . . . . . . .215 D6
Yiewsley UB7 . . . . .104 A6
Spinney Dr TW14 . . . . . . .149 A4

Spinney Gdns
Dagenham RM9 . . . . .81 A3
Dulwich SE19 . . . . .183 D5
Spinney Oak BR1 . . . . . . .188 A1
Spinneys The BR1 . . . . . . .188 B1
Spinney The
Barnes SW13 . . . . .134 B6
Barnet EN5 . . . . .1 D3
Cheam SM3 . . . . .216 C4
DA14 . . . . .191 A5
Edgware HA7 . . . . .26 A6
Southgate N21 . . . . .16 C4
Streatham SW16 . . . . .159 D1
Sunbury TW16 . . . . .172 A2
Wembley HA0 . . . . .65 A5
Spire Bushey Hospl WD23 . .8 D3
Spire Ct 10 TW10 . . . . . . .154 A5
Spire Ho W2 . . . . .246 B6
Spire Roding Hospl IG4 . . . .55 D6
Spires The EN5 . . . . .1 A2
Spirit Quay E1 . . . . .118 B5
SPITALFIELDS 95 C2
Spital Sq E1 . . . . . .95 C2 243 B4
Spital St E1 . . . . .96 A2
Spital Yd E1 . . . . .243 B4
Spitfire Bsns Pk CR0 . . . .220 C2
Spitfire Est The TW5 . . . . .106 C1
Spitfire Rd SM6 . . . . .220 A1
Spitfire Way TW5 . . . . . . .106 C1
Splendour Wlk SE16 . . . . .118 C1
Spode Ho SE11 . . . . .261 A5
Spode Wlk NW3 . . . . .69 D3
Spondon Rd N15 . . . . .52 A5
Spoonbill Way UB4 . . . . . . .84 D2
Spooner 8 NW9 . . . . .27 D3
Spooner Ho TW5 . . . . .129 C6
Spooner Wlk SM6 . . . . . . .219 D3
Sporle Ct 5 SW11 . . . . . .136 B2
Sportsbank St SE6 . . . . . .164 A4
Spottons Gr N17 . . . . .33 A2
Spout Hill CR0 . . . . .223 C3
Spratt Hall Rd E11 . . . . . . .55 A3
Spray St SE18 . . . . .122 D2
Spreighton Rd KT8 . . . . . .195 D5
Sprewell SW15 . . . . .157 A5
Spriggs Ho 14 N1 . . . . . . .72 D1
Sprimont Pl
SW3 . . . . .114 D1 257 C2
Springall St 9 SE15 . . . . .140 B5
Springalls Wharf 2
SE16 . . . . .118 A4
Springbank N21 . . . . .16 B5
Springbank Rd SE13 . . . . .164 C5
Springbank Wlk NW1 . . . . .71 D1
Springbourne Ct BR3 . . . .186 A2
Spring Bridge Rd W5 . . . .109 D6
Spring Cl Barnet EN5 . . . . .12 C6
Dagenham RM8 . . . . .58 D1
Springclose La SM3 . . . . .217 A2
Spring Cnr TW13 . . . . .149 D1
Spring Cott 10 W12 . . . . .112 A4
Spring Cotts KT6 . . . . .197 D4
Spring Court Rd EN2 . . . . . .4 C5
Springcroft Ave N2 . . . . . . .48 D5
Spring Ct
Brondesbury NW2 . . . . .69 B2
Ealing W7 . . . . .108 B6
Edgware HA8 . . . . .26 B5
10 Wanstead E18 . . . . . . .55 B6
Spring Ct Rd EN2 . . . . .4 B5
Springdale Rd N16 . . . . . . .73 B4
Spring Dr HA5 . . . . .40 A3
Springett Ho 15 SW2 . . . .160 B6
Springfield Bushey WD23 . . .8 B3
South Norwood SE25 . . . . .206 A6
Upper Clapton E5 . . . . .52 B1
Springfield Ave
Hampton TW12 . . . . .173 D4
Hornsey N10 . . . . .49 C6
Merton SW20 . . . . .201 B6
Springfield Christian Sch
SE6 . . . . .163 B1
Springfield Cl
Finchley N12 . . . . .29 D5
Stanmore HA7 . . . . .9 A1
Springfield Com Prim Sch
N16 . . . . .52 A3
Springfield Ct
7 Dagenham W3 . . . . . . .89 A1
1 Friern Barnet N20 . . . . .14 D1
Hampstead NW3 . . . . .70 C1
2 Ilford IG1 . . . . .78 D3
9 Kingston u T KT1 . . . . .198 A6
Upper Clapton E5 . . . . .52 B1
Wallington SM6 . . . . .219 B3
Springfield Dr IG2 . . . . . . .57 A3
Springfield Gdns BR1 . . . .210 B5
Kingsbury NW9 . . . . .45 B4
Ruislip HA4 . . . . .40 B1
Upper Clapton E5 . . . . .52 B1
West Wickham BR4 . . . . . .223 D6
Woodford IG8 . . . . .37 C3
Springfield Gr SE7 . . . . . .143 C6
Sunbury TW16 . . . . .172 A2
Springfield Ho Acton W3 . .111 A5
1 Camberwell SE5 . . . . .139 C3
13 Dalston E8 . . . . .73 D2
Springfield La NW6 . . . . . .91 D6
Springfield Mount NW9 . . . .45 C4

Springfield Par Mews 4
N13 . . . . .32 C6
Springfield Pl KT3 . . . . . . .199 A5
Springfield Prim Sch
TW16 . . . . .171 D1
Springfield Rd
Ashford TW15 . . . . .170 B5
Bexleyheath DA7 . . . . .147 D1
Bromley BR1 . . . . .210 B5
Chingford E4 . . . . .20 C4
Ealing W7 . . . . .108 C5
Friern Barnet N11 . . . . . . .31 C5
Harrow HA1 . . . . .42 C3
Hayes UB4 . . . . .106 C5
Kingston u T KT1 . . . . .198 A6
Newham E15 . . . . .98 C4
Penge SE26 . . . . .184 B5
Plashet E6 . . . . .78 B1
South Norwood CR7 . . . . . .183 A2
St John's Wood
NW8 . . . . .92 A6 229 B5
8 Teddington TW11 . . . . .175 A5
Tottenham Hale N15 . . . . . .52 A5
Twickenham TW2 . . . . . . .151 C3
Wallington SM6 . . . . .219 B3
Walthamstow E17 . . . . .53 B3
Welling DA16 . . . . .146 B2
Wimbledon SW19 . . . . . . .179 B5
Springfield Rise SE26 . . . .162 B1
Springfields 18 EN5 . . . . . .13 D6
Springfield University Hospl
SW17 . . . . .158 C1
Springfield Wlk 3 BR6 . . .211 B1
Paddington NW6 . . . . .91 D6
Spring Gdns
East Molesey KT8 . . . . . . .196 A5
Islington N5 . . . . .73 A3
SW1 . . . . .116 A5 250 A4
Wallington SM6 . . . . .219 C3
Woodford IG8 . . . . .37 C3
Spring Gr Brentford W4 . . .132 C6
Hampton TW12 . . . . .173 D2
Loughton IG10 . . . . .21 D5
Mitcham CR4 . . . . .181 A2
SPRING GROVE 130 C3
Spring Grove Cres TW3,
TW5 . . . . .130 A4
Spring Grove Prim Sch
TW7 . . . . .130 B3
Spring Grove Rd
Hounslow TW3, TW5,
TW7 . . . . .130 A4
Richmond TW10 . . . . .154 B6
Springhallow Sch W13 . . . .87 A1
Spring Hill
Forest Hill SE26 . . . . .184 C6
Upper Clapton E5 . . . . .52 A2
Springhill Cl SE5 . . . . . . .139 B2
Spring Ho Merton SW19 . . .179 B2
WC1 . . . . .234 A1
Springhurst Cl CR0 . . . . . .223 B4
Spring La Croydon SE25 . . .206 B3
Muswell Hill N10 . . . . .49 A6
Upper Clapton E5 . . . . .52 B1
Spring Lake HA7 . . . . .25 B6
Spring Mews W1 . . . . . . .237 D4
SPRING PARK 223 B5
Spring Park Ave CR0 . . . . .222 D6
Springpark Dr
Beckenham BR3 . . . . .208 A6
Stoke Newington N4 . . . . . .51 A1
Spring Park Prim Sch
CR0 . . . . .223 C5
Spring Park Rd CR0 . . . . . .222 D6
Spring Pl Barking IG11 . . . .101 A5
Camden Town NW5 . . . . . . .71 B3
Church End N3 . . . . .29 C1
Springpond Rd RM9 . . . . . .81 A3
Spring Rd TW13 . . . . .149 D1
Springrice Rd SE13 . . . . . .164 B5
Spring Shaw Rd BR5 . . . . .190 A2
Spring St W2 . . . . . .92 B1 236 C1
Spring Terr TW10 . . . . . . .154 A6
Springtide Cl 10 SE15 . . . .140 A4
Spring Vale DA7 . . . . .147 D1
Springvale Ave TW8 . . . . .110 A1
Springvale Ct SE12 . . . . . .143 A1
Springvale Terr 5 W14 . . .112 D3
Springville Rd HA8 . . . . . . .26 C3
Springwater WC1 . . . . . . .240 C4
Springwater Cl SE18 . . . . .144 C4
Springway HA1 . . . . .42 B2
Springwell Ave NW10 . . . . .89 D6
Springwell Cl SW16 . . . . . .182 B6
Springwell Ct TW5 . . . . . .128 D3
Springwell Jun & Inf Schs
TW5 . . . . .129 A5
Springwell Rd
Heston TW5 . . . . .128 D4
West Norwood SW16 . . . . .182 C5
Spring Wlk E1 . . . . .96 A2
Springwood Cl 8 E3 . . . . . .97 C5
Springwood Cres HA8 . . . .11 A2
Springwood Ct CR2 . . . . . .221 C4
Sproggit Ind Est TW19 . . .148 B5
Sprowston Mews E7 . . . . . .77 A3
Sprowston Rd E7 . . . . .77 A3
Spruce Ct W5 . . . . .110 A3
Sprucedale Gdns CR0 . . . .222 D4
Spruce Hills Rd E17 . . . . . .36 A1

Spruce Ho
2 Brentford TW8 . . . . . . .131 C5
15 Rotherhithe SE16 . . . .118 D4
Spruce Pk BR2 . . . . .208 D5
Sprules Rd SE4 . . . . .141 A3
Spurfield KT8 . . . . .195 D6
Spurgeon Ave SE19 . . . . .183 B2
Spurgeon Rd SE19 . . . . . .183 B3
Spurgeon's Coll SE25 . . . .183 C1
Spurgeon St SE1 . .117 B3 262 C6
Spur Ho 10 SW19 . . . . . . .179 D2
Spurling Rd
Dagenham RM9 . . . . .81 B2
East Dulwich SE22 . . . . . .139 D1
Spur Rd Brentford TW7 . . . .131 B5
Edgware HA8 . . . . .26 A6
Feltham TW14 . . . . .128 B1
SE1 . . . . .116 C4 251 A2
Tottenham N15 . . . . .51 B5
Wallend IG11 . . . . .101 A4
Spurstowe Rd E8 . . . . .74 B2
Spurstowe Terr E8 . . . . . . .74 B3
Spurway Par 2 IG2 . . . . . . .56 B4
Square Rigger Row 7
SW11 . . . . .136 A2
Square The
Hammersmith W6 . . . . . . .112 C1
Hayes UB11 . . . . .105 B5
Ilford IG1 . . . . .56 C2
Leyton E10 . . . . .76 A5
12 Richmond TW10 . . . . .153 D6
SW6 . . . . .265 A1
Wallington SM5 . . . . .219 A3
Woodford IG8 . . . . .37 A5
Squarey St SW17 . . . . . . .158 A5
Squire Ct 2 CR0 . . . . .205 C1
Squire Gdns NW8 . . . . . . .229 C1
Squire's Almshouses 7
E17 . . . . .53 D5
Squires Bridge Rd KT17 . .192 B5
Squires Ct Finchley N3 . . . .30 A2
SW4 . . . . .270 A2
Wimbledon SW19 . . . . . . .179 C6
Squires Ho 3 SE18 . . . . . .144 D6
Squires La N3 . . . . .30 A2
Squire's Mount NW3 . . . . . .70 B5
Squire's Rd TW17 . . . . . . .192 C5
Squires The RM7 . . . . .59 D3
Squires Wlk TW15 . . . . . .171 B3
Squires Wood Dr BR7 . . . .188 B3
Squirrel Cl TW4 . . . . .128 C2
Squirrel Mews W13 . . . . . .109 A6
Squirrels Cl
Hillingdon UB10 . . . . .60 C1
North Finchley N12 . . . . . . .30 A6
Orpington BR6 . . . . .211 C1
Squirrels Ct KT4 . . . . .215 D6
Squirrels Gn KT4 . . . . .216 A6
Squirrel's La IG9 . . . . .21 D1
Squirrels The Bushey WD23 . .8 B5
Lewisham SE13 . . . . .142 B2
Pinner HA5 . . . . .41 B6
Squirrels Trad Est UB3 . . .105 D3
Squirries St E2 . . . . .96 A4
Stable Cl
Kingston u T KT2 . . . . .176 B4
Northolt UB5 . . . . .85 C5
Stable Ct 4 SM6 . . . . .219 A5
Stable Ho 9 SE16 . . . . . . .118 C4
Stable La DA5 . . . . .169 D2
Stable Mews
Twickenham TW1 . . . . .152 D3
West Norwood SE27 . . . . . .183 A5
Stables End BR6 . . . . .227 A5
Stables The IG9 . . . . .21 C4
Stables Way
SE11 . . . . .116 C1 261 A2
Stable Way W10 . . . . .90 C1
Stable Wlk N2 . . . . .30 B2
Stable Yd Rd
SW1 . . . . .115 C4 249 B2
Staburn Ct HA8 . . . . .27 A1
Stacey Ave N18 . . . . .34 C6
Stacey Cl E10 . . . . .54 B4
Stacey St Highbury N7 . . . .72 C5
Soho WC2 . . . . .93 D1 239 C1
Stack Ho SW1 . . . . .258 B3
Stackhouse St SW1 . . . . .257 C6
Stacy Path 18 SE5 . . . . . .139 C5
Staddon Ct BR3 . . . . .207 A5
Stadium Bsns Ctr HA9 . . . .66 D5
Stadium Rd Hendon NW2 . . .46 C2
SE7, SE18 . . . . .144 B6
Stadium Rd E NW2 . . . . . . .46 C2
Stadium Ret Pk HA9 . . . . . .66 C5
Stadium St SW10 . .136 A5 266 B3
Stadium Way HA9 . . . . .66 C4
Staffa Rd E10 . . . . .53 A1
Stafford Cl Cheam SM3 . . .217 A2
Maida Vale NW6 . . . . .91 C4
Southgate N14 . . . . .15 C6
Walthamstow E17 . . . . .53 B3
Stafford Cripps Ho
30 Bethnal Green E2 . . . . .96 C4
SW6 . . . . .264 D5
Stafford Cross CR0 . . . . . .220 B3
Stafford Cross Bsns Pk
CR0 . . . . .220 B3
Stafford Ct Croydon CR0 . . .220 C4
Ealing W7 . . . . .86 D1

Stafford Ct continued
Kensington W8 . . . . **255** B6
South Lambeth SW8 . . . . . **270** A2
Stafford Gdns CR0 . . . . **220** B3
Stafford Ho SE1 . . . . **263** D2
Stafford Mans
  13 Hammersmith W14 . . . . **112** D3
  14 Stockwell SW4 . . . . . . **138** A1
  SW11 . . . . **267** C3
Stafford Morris Ho 9
  E15 . . . . **.98** C6
Stafford Pl
  Richmond TW10 . . . . **154** B4
  SW1 . . . . **115** C3 **259** A6
Stafford Rd Bow E3 . . . . **.97** B5
  Harrow HA3 . . . . **.24** A3
  Kingston u T KT3 . . . . **199** A6
  Maida Vale NW6 . . . . **.91** C4
  Plashet E7 . . . . **.77** D2
  Ruislip HA4 . . . . **.61** D4
  Sidcup DA14 . . . . **189** C6
  Wallington CR0, SM6 . . . . **220** A3
Staffordshire Ho N3 . . . . . . **.47** A6
Staffordshire St
  Peckham SE15 . . . . **140** A4
  Peckham SE15 . . . . **140** B4
Stafford St W1 . . . . **249** A4
Stafford Terr
  W8 . . . . **113** C3 **255** A6
Stag Cl HA8 . . . . **.27** A1
Stag Ct 16 SM6 . . . . **219** B2
Stagg Hill EN4 . . . . **.2** C6
Stag Hts 1 IG9 . . . . **.21** B2
Stag La Chigwell IG9 . . . . . **.21** B2
  Edgware HA8, NW9 . . . . . . **.45** A6
  Roehampton SW15 . . . . . **155** D2
Stag Lane Fst & Mid Schs
  HA8 . . . . **.26** C1
Stags Ct KT7 . . . . **197** A2
Stagshaw Ho 17 SE22 . . . **139** C2
Stags Way TW7 . . . . **130** D6
Stainbank Rd CR4 . . . . **203** B6
Stainby Cl UB7 . . . . **104** A3
Stainby Rd N15 . . . . **.51** D5
Staincliffe Ho 5 SM1 . . . . **218** A4
Stainer Ho SE9 . . . . **143** C1
Stainer St SE1 . . . . **252** D3
Staines Ave SM3 . . . . **216** D6
Staines By-Pass TW15 . . . **170** A4
Staines Rd
  East Bedfont TW14 . . . . . . **149** B4
  Feltham TW14, TW3 . . . . . **150** C6
  Hounslow TW3 . . . . **129** C1
  Ilford IG1 . . . . **.79** B4
  Twickenham TW2 . . . . . . **152** A1
  Twickenham TW3, TW2 . . **151** D1
Staines Rd E TW12,
  TW16 . . . . **172** C2
Staines Rd W TW15 . . . . . **171** B3
Staines Wlk DA14 . . . . **190** C4
Stainford Cl TW15 . . . . . . **171** B5
  Walthamstow E17 . . . . **.53** C5
Staining La EC2 . . . . **242** B2
Stainmore Cl BR7 . . . . **189** B2
Stainsby St E25 . . . . **.96** C5
Stainsby Rd E14 . . . . **.97** C1
Stainton Rd Enfield EN3 . . . . **.6** C4
  Lewisham SE13 . . . . **164** B4
Stalbridge Flats W1 . . . . . **238** B1
Stalbridge Ho NW1 . . . . . . **232** A3
Stalbridge St NW1 . . . . . . **237** B4
Stalham St SE16 . . . . **118** C3
Stambourne Ho SW8 . . . . . **270** B2
Stambourne Way
  Penge SE19 . . . . **183** D3
  West Wickham BR4 . . . . . **224** A5
Stambourne Woodland Wlk
  7 SE19 . . . . **183** D3
**Stamford Bridge Stadium
  (Chelsea FC)**
  SW6 . . . . **135** D5 **265** C4
Stamford Brook Ave
  W6 . . . . **111** D3
Stamford Brook Gdns 1
  W6 . . . . **111** D3
Stamford Brook Mans 2
  W6 . . . . **111** D2
Stamford Brook Rd W6 . . . **111** D3
Stamford Brook Sta W6 . . **111** D2
Stamford Cl Harrow HA3 . . **.24** C3
  2 London NW3 . . . . **.70** A5
  Southall UB1 . . . . **107** C6
  Tottenham Hale N15 . . . . . **.52** A6
Stamford Cotts SW10 . . . . **265** D4
Stamford Ct Chiswick W6 . . **112** A2
  Edgware HA8 . . . . **.26** B6
Stamford Dr BR2 . . . . **208** D5
Stamford Gdns RM9 . . . . . **.80** C1
Stamford Gr E 1 N16 . . . . **.52** A1
Stamford Gr W 4 N16 . . . . **.52** A1
STAMFORD HILL . . . . **.51** C1
Stamford Hill N16 . . . . **.51** D1
Stamford Hill Mans 1
  N16 . . . . **.51** D1
Stamford Hill Prim Sch
  N15 . . . . **.51** B2
Stamford Hill Sta N16 . . . . **.51** C2
Stamford N N15 . . . . **.52** A4
Stamford Lo 2 N16 . . . . . . **.51** D2

Stamford Mans 2 N16 . . . . **.52** A1
Stamford Rd
  Dagenham RM9 . . . . **.80** C1
  Kingsland N1 . . . . **.73** C2
  Newham E6 . . . . **100** A6
  South Tottenham N15 . . . . **.52** A4
Stamford St SE1 . . **116** C5 **251** B4
Stamp Pl E2 . . . . **.95** B4
Stanard Cl N16 . . . . **.51** C2
Stanborough Cl TW12 . . . . **173** B4
Stanborough Ho 4 E3 . . . . **.97** D3
Stanborough Pas E8 . . . . . **.73** D2
Stanborough Rd TW3,
  TW7 . . . . **130** B2
Stanbridge Mans SW15 . . **134** C2
Stanbridge Pl N21 . . . . **.16** D2
Stanbridge Rd SW15 . . . . **134** C2
Stanbrook Ct W1 . . . . **249** A4
Stanbrook Rd SE2 . . . . . . **124** B4
Stanburn Fst & Mid Schs
  HA7 . . . . **.25** C3
Stanbury Ct 16 NW3 . . . . . **.70** D2
Stanbury Rd
  Nunhead SE15 . . . . **140** C3
  Peckham SE15 . . . . **140** B3
Stancroft NW9 . . . . **.45** C4
Standale Gr HA4 . . . . **.39** A4
Standard Ind Est E16 . . . . **122** B4
Standard Pl 13 EC2 . . . . . . **.95** C4
Standard Rd
  Becontree NW10 . . . . **.89** B3
  Belvedere DA17 . . . . **125** C1
  DA6 . . . . **147** A1
  Enfield EN3 . . . . **.7** A6
  Hounslow TW4 . . . . **129** A2
Standen Rd SW18 . . . . **157** C4
Standfield Gdns RM10 . . . . **.81** C2
Standfield Rd RM10 . . . . . . **.81** C2
Standish Ho
  6 Chiswick W6 . . . . **112** A2
  SE9 . . . . **143** B1
Standish Rd W6 . . . . **112** A2
Standlake Point 1
  SE23 . . . . **162** D1
Standor Ho 7 CR4 . . . . . . **202** D6
Stane Cl SW19 . . . . **179** D3
Stanedge Ct SW16 . . . . . . **182** A5
Stane Gr SW4 . . . . **138** A3
Stanesgate Ho SE15 . . . . . **140** A5
Stanetta Ct 3 RM6 . . . . . . **.58** B2
Stane Way SE18 . . . . **144** A5
Stanfield Ho
  8 Northolt UB5 . . . . **.84** D3
  NW8 . . . . **236** D6
Stanfield Rd 14 E3 . . . . . . **.97** A5
Stanford Cl
  Hampton TW12 . . . . **173** B4
  Romford RM7 . . . . **.59** D3
  Ruislip HA4 . . . . **.39** A3
Stanford Ct
  Friern Barnet N11 . . . . **.31** A5
  Kensington W8 . . . . **255** D5
  Walham Green SW6 . . . . . **265** D1
Stanford Ho IG11 . . . . **102** B5
Stanford Pl SE1 . . **117** C2 **263** A3
Stanford Prim Sch
  SW16 . . . . **181** D2
Stanford Rd
  Friern Barnet N11 . . . . **.30** D5
  Thornton Heath SW16 . . . **182** A1
  W8 . . . . **113** D3 **255** D6
Stanford St SW1 . . . . **259** C3
Stanford Way SW16 . . . . . **181** D1
Stangate SE1 . . . . **260** D6
Stangate Cres WD6 . . . . . . **.11** C6
Stangate Gdns HA7 . . . . . . **.25** B6
Stangate Lo N21 . . . . **.16** B4
Stangate Mansi TW1 . . . . **152** D1
Stanger Rd SE25 . . . . **206** A5
Stanhope Ave Harrow HA3 . **.24** B2
  Hayes BR2 . . . . **209** A1
  Hendon N3 . . . . **.47** B6
Stanhope Cl 23 SE16 . . . . **118** D4
Stanhope Ct N3 . . . . **.29** B1
Stanhope Gate W1 . . . . . . **248** B4
Stanhope Gdns
  Crouch End N6 . . . . **.49** C3
  Dagenham RM8 . . . . **.81** B5
  Edgware NW7 . . . . **.27** D5
  Redbridge IG1 . . . . **.56** B1
  Stoke Newington N4 . . . . . **.51** A3
  SW7 . . . . **114** A2 **256** B4
Stanhope Ho
  Crouch End N6 . . . . **.49** C3
  5 Friern Barnet N11 . . . . **.31** B6
  4 Putney SW15 . . . . **156** C6
  SE8 . . . . **141** B5
Stanhope Mews E
  SW7 . . . . **114** A2 **256** B4
Stanhope Mews S SW7 . . . **256** B3
Stanhope Mews W
  SW7 . . . . **114** A2 **256** B4
Stanhope Par NW1 . . . . . . **232** A2
Stanhope Park Rd UB6 . . . **.86** A3
Stanhope Pl W2 . . . . **237** C1
Stanhope Prim Sch UB6 . . . **.86** A3
Stanhope Rd Barnet EN5 . . . **.12** C5
  Crouch End N6 . . . . **.49** C2
  DA7 . . . . **147** A3

Stanhope Rd continued
  Dagenham RM8 . . . . **.81** B5
  North Finchley N12 . . . . . . **.30** A5
  Sidcup DA15 . . . . **190** A6
  Southall UB6 . . . . **.86** A2
  South Croydon CR0 . . . . . **221** C5
  Wallington SM5 . . . . **219** A1
  Walthamstow E17 . . . . **.53** D4
Stanhope Row W1 . . . . . . **248** C3
Stanhope St NW1 . . **93** C4 **232** A1
Stanhope Terr
  W2 . . . . **114** B6 **246** D6
Stanier Cl SW5 . . . . **254** C1
Stanlake Mews 7 W12 . . . **112** C5
Stanlake Rd W12 . . . . **112** C5
Stanlake Villas 8 W12 . . . . **112** C5
Stanley Ave Barking IG11 . . **101** D5
  Beckenham BR2, BR3 . . . . **208** A6
  Dagenham RM8 . . . . **.59** B2
  Greenford UB6 . . . . **.86** A6
  Wembley HA0 . . . . **.66** A1
  West Barnes KT3 . . . . **200** A4
Stanley Cl Eltham SE9 . . . . **167** A3
  SW8 . . . . **270** C5
  Wembley HA0 . . . . **.66** A1
Stanley Cohen Ho EC1 . . . **242** A5
Stanley Cres
  W11 . . . . **113** B6 **244** C6
Stanleycroft Cl TW7 . . . . . **130** C4
Stanley Ct Belmont SM2 . . **217** D1
  11 Ealing W5 . . . . **.87** C2
  Wallington SM5 . . . . **219** A1
  Wimbledon SW19 . . . . . . **179** C4
Stanley Gardens Rd
  TW11 . . . . **174** C5
Stanley Gdns
  Bedford Pk W3 . . . . **111** C4
  Cricklewood NW2 . . . . **.68** C3
  Mitcham CR4 . . . . **181** A4
  W3 . . . . **244** C6
  Wallington SM6 . . . . **219** C2
Stanley Glynn Ct BR7 . . . . **188** C5
Stanley Gr
  Clapham SW11 . . . . **137** A3
  Thornton Heath CR0 . . . . . **204** C3
Stanley Ho
  35 Clapham SW8 . . . . . . **137** D3
  Leytonstone E11 . . . . **.54** C3
  12 Poplar E14 . . . . **.97** C1
  Wembley HA0 . . . . **.66** A1
Stanley Holloway Ct E16 . . **.99** A1
Stanley Inf Sch KT11 . . . . . **174** C6
Stanley Jun Sch KT11 . . . . **174** C6
Stanley Mans SW10 . . . . . **266** B6
  Upper Tooting SW17 . . . . . **158** D2
Stanley Park Dr HA0 . . . . . **.88** B6
Stanley Park High Sch
  SM5 . . . . **219** A2
Stanley Park Inf Sch
  SM5 . . . . **218** D1
Stanley Park Jun Sch
  SM5 . . . . **218** D1
Stanley Park Rd SM5,
  SM6 . . . . **219** A1
Stanley Rd
  Acton Green W3 . . . . **111** A3
  Ashford TW15 . . . . **170** A5
  Belmont SM2 . . . . **217** D1
  BR6 . . . . **211** D1
  Bromley BR2 . . . . **209** C5
  Chingford E4 . . . . **.20** B3
  East Finchley N2 . . . . **.48** B6
  Edmonton N9 . . . . **.17** D2
  Enfield EN1 . . . . **.5** C2
  Friern Barnet N11 . . . . **.31** D5
  Harringay N15 . . . . **.50** D5
  Harrow HA2 . . . . **.64** A6
  2 Hendon NW9 . . . . **.46** A2
  Ilford IG1 . . . . **.79** B6
  Isleworth TW3 . . . . **130** A1
  Mill Meads E15 . . . . **.98** B6
  Mitcham CR4 . . . . **181** A3
  Morden SM4 . . . . **201** C5
  Mortlake SW14 . . . . **132** D1
  Muswell Hill N10 . . . . **.31** B3
  Northwood HA6 . . . . **.22** A2
  Plashet E12 . . . . **.78** A3
  Sidcup DA14 . . . . **168** A1
  Southall UB1 . . . . **107** A6
  Teddington TW11, TW2 . . . **174** C5
  Thornton Heath CR0 . . . . . **204** C3
  Twickenham TW2 . . . . . . **152** B1
  Wallington SM5 . . . . **219** A1
  Walthamstow E10 . . . . **.53** D3
  Wembley HA9 . . . . **.66** B2
  Wimbledon SW19 . . . . . . **179** C4
  Woodford E18 . . . . **.36** D2
Stanley St SE14, SE8 . . . . **141** B5
Stanley Studios SW10 . . . **266** B6
Stanley Terr 8 N19 . . . . . . **.72** A6
Stanliff Ho 8 E14 . . . . **119** C3
Stanmer St SW11 . . . . **136** C3
STANMORE . . . . **.25** A5
Stanmore Coll HA7 . . . . . . **.25** C4
Stanmore Gdns
  Richmond TW9 . . . . **132** A2
  Sutton SM1 . . . . **218** A5
Stanmore Hill HA7 . . . . **.25** A6
Stanmore Ho 21 SW8 . . . . **137** D3
Stanmore Pl NW1 . . . . **231** D6
Stanmore Rd
  Harringay N15 . . . . **.50** D5
  Leytonstone E11 . . . . **.54** D1
  Richmond TW9 . . . . **132** B2
Stanmore St N1 . . **94** B6 **233** C6
Stanmore Sta HA7 . . . . . . **.25** D6
Stanmore Terr 3 BR3 . . . . **185** C5
Stanmuir Lo NW9 . . . . **.45** A4
Stannard Cotts 27 E1 . . . . **.96** C3
Stannard Ct SE6 . . . . **163** D3
Stannard Mews E8 . . . . . . **.74** A2
Stannard Rd E8 . . . . **.74** A2
Stannary Pl SE11 . . . . **261** B1
Stannary St SE11 . . **116** C5 **261** B1
Stannet Way SM6 . . . . **219** C4
Stansfeld Rd SE6 . . . . **263** D3
Stansfeld Rd E6 . . . . **.99** D1
Stansfield Rd
  Cranford TW4, TW5 . . . . . **128** B3
  Stockwell SW9 . . . . **138** B2
Stansgate Rd RM10 . . . . . . **.81** C5
Stanstead Cl BR2 . . . . **208** D3
Stanstead Gr SE23 . . . . . . **163** B3
Stanstead Ho E3 . . . . **.98** A3
Stanstead Manor SM1 . . . **217** C2
Stanstead Rd
  Forest Hill SE23, SE6 . . . . **163** A3
  Wanstead E11 . . . . **.55** B4
Stansted Cres DA5 . . . . . . **168** D3
Stansted Express Terminal
  EC2 . . . . **243** A4
Stansted Rd TW6 . . . . **148** B5
Stanswood Gdns SE5 . . . . **139** C5
Stanthorpe Cl SW16 . . . . . **182** A5
Stanthorpe Rd SW16 . . . . **182** A5
Stanton Ave TW11 . . . . . . **174** C4
Stanton Cl
  Chessington KT19 . . . . . . **214** D3
  North Cheam KT4 . . . . . . **200** D1
  Finchley N3 . . . . **.88** B1
  Stoke Newington N16 . . . . **.51** B2
Stanton Ho 9 SE10 . . . . . . **142** A6
Stanton Ct DA15 . . . . **168** A1
Stanton Rd Barnes SW13 . . **133** D3
  Thornton Heath CR0 . . . . . **205** A2
  Wimbledon SW20 . . . . . . **178** D2
Stanton Sq SE26 . . . . **185** B6
Stanton Way SE26 . . . . . . **185** B6
Stanway Ct 28 N1 . . . . **.95** C5
Stanway Gdns Acton W3 . . **110** C5
  Edgware HA8 . . . . **.27** A5
Stanway St N1 . . . . **.95** C5
STANWELL **148** A3
Stanwell Fields CE Prim Sch
  TW19 . . . . **148** A4
Stanwell Rd
  Ashford TW15 . . . . **170** A6
  East Bedfont TW14, TW19,
  TW6 . . . . **148** D4
  Stanwell TW15 . . . . **148** A1
Stanwick Rd
  W14 . . . . **113** B2 **254** C3
Stanworth Ct TW5 . . . . **129** C5
Stanworth St SE1 . . . . **253** D1
Stanyhurst SE23 . . . . **163** A3
Stapenhill Rd HA0 . . . . **.65** B5
Staplefield Cl Pinner HA5 . . **.23** A3
  3 Streatham SW2 . . . . . **160** A3
Stapleford Ave IG2 . . . . . . **.57** C4
Stapleford Cl Chingford E4 . **.20** A1
  Kingston u T KT1 . . . . **198** C6
  Putney SW19 . . . . **157** A4
Stapleford Rd HA0 . . . . **.65** D1
Stapleford Way IG11 . . . . . **102** B4
Staplehurst Cl SE11 . . . . . **158** D5
Staplehurst Ho 18 E5 . . . . **.74** B3
Staplehurst Rd
  Lewisham SE13 . . . . **164** C6
  Sutton SM5 . . . . **218** C1
Staple Inn WC2 . . . . **241** A3
Staple Inn Bldgs WC2 . . . . **241** A3
Staples Cl SE16 . . . . **119** A5
Staples Corner Bsns Pk
  NW2 . . . . **.46** B1
Staples Corner (East)
  NW2 . . . . **.46** B1
Staples Corner Ret Pk
  NW20 . . . . **.46** B1
Staples Corner (West)
  NW2 . . . . **.46** B1
Staple St SE1 . . . . **117** B4 **252** D1
Stapleton Gdns CR0 . . . . . **220** C3
Stapleton Hall N4 . . . . **.50** B2
Stapleton Hall Rd N4 . . . . . **.50** B2
Stapleton Ho 19 E2 . . . . . . **.96** B4
Stapleton Rd DA7 . . . . **147** B6
  Orpington BR6 . . . . **227** D5
  Upper Tooting SW17 . . . . . **159** A1
Stapley Rd DA17 . . . . **125** C1
Stapylton Rd EN5 . . . . **1** A2
Star Alley EC3 . . . . **253** B6
Star and Garter Hill
  TW10 . . . . **154** A4
Starboard Way E14 . . . . . . **119** C3
Starbuck Cl SE9 . . . . **166** C4
Star Cl EN3 . . . . **18** C5
Starcross St NW1 . . **93** C4 **232** B1

Stanmore Pl NW1 . . . . **231** D6
Stardome * NW1 . . . . **238** A5
Starfield Rd W12 . . . . **112** A4
Star & Garter Mans 8
  SW15 . . . . **134** D2
Starks Field Prim Sch N9 . **.17** C2
Star La EC1 . . . . **98** C3
Starliner Ct N7 . . . . **.72** C2
Starling Cl
  Beckenham BR3 . . . . **207** A3
  Buckhurst Hill IG9 . . . . **.21** A3
  Pinner HA5 . . . . **.40** C6
Starling Ct E13 . . . . **.99** B6
Starling Ho NW8 . . . . **230** A4
Starling Wlk TW12 . . . . . . **173** A5
Starmans Ct RM9 . . . . **103** A6
Star Path UB5 . . . . **.85** C5
Star Pl E1 . . . . **118** A6
Star Prim Sch E16 . . . . . . **.98** C3
Star Rd Hillingdon UB10 . . . **.83** A3
  Hounslow TW7 . . . . **130** B3
  W14 . . . . **113** B1 **254** C1
Star St W2 . . . . . . **92** C1 **237** A2
Starts Cl BR6 . . . . **226** C5
Starts Hill Ave BR6 . . . . . . **226** D4
Starts Hill Rd BR6 . . . . **226** D4
Starveall Cl UB7 . . . . **104** B3
Star Works NW10 . . . . **.90** A4
Star Yd WC2 . . . . . **94** C1 **241** A2
State Farm Ave BR6 . . . . . **227** A4
Stateland Ct 10 N11 . . . . . . **.31** B6
Staten Gdns TW1 . . . . **152** D3
Statham Ct N7 . . . . **.72** A5
Statham Gr Edmonton N18 . **.33** C5
  Stoke Newington N16 . . . . **.73** B5
Statham Ho SW8 . . . . **269** A2
Station App
  Ashford TW15 . . . . **170** B6
  Belmont SM2 . . . . **217** A1
  Bexleyheath DA7 . . . . **147** A3
  Chislehurst BR7 . . . . **188** C1
  Dagenham NW10 . . . . **.89** D4
  Elmstead BR7 . . . . **188** A4
  20 Finchley N12 . . . . **.29** C6
  Forest Gate E7 . . . . **.77** B4
  Friern Barnet N11 . . . . **.31** B5
  Fulham SW6 . . . . **135** A2
  Greenford UB6 . . . . **.64** B1
  Hampton TW12 . . . . **173** C2
  Harrow HA1 . . . . **.42** C2
  Hayes BR2 . . . . **209** A1
  Hayes Town UB3 . . . . **105** D3
  Hinchley Wood KT10 . . . . . **212** D2
  4 Kingston u T KT1, KT2 . . **176** C2
  Lewisham SE3 . . . . **143** B2
  Mottingham SE9 . . . . **166** B3
  New Barnet EN5 . . . . **2** A1
  6 New Malden KT4 . . . . . **200** A4
  Orpington BR6 . . . . **227** D6
  Penge SE26 . . . . **185** B5
  Pinner HA5 . . . . **.41** A6
  Richmond TW9 . . . . **132** C4
  Ruislip HA4 . . . . **.39** D1
  Shepperton TW17 . . . . . . **193** A4
  1 South Croydon CR0 . . . **221** B6
  South Ruislip HA4 . . . . **.62** B3
  Streatham SW16 . . . . **181** D5
  Sunbury TW16 . . . . **172** A2
  1 Surbiton KT6 . . . . **198** A3
  Walthamstow E17 . . . . **.53** C4
  Wanstead E11 . . . . **.55** A4
  Welling DA16 . . . . **146** A3
  Wembley HA0 . . . . **.65** B2
  2 Woodford E18 . . . . **.37** B1
  Woodford IG8 . . . . **.37** B4
  Woodford IG9 . . . . **.37** D6
  Worcester Pk KT19 . . . . . . **216** A3
  Yiewsley UB7 . . . . **104** A5
Station Approach Rd
  W4 . . . . **133** A5
Station Ave
  5 Brixton SW9 . . . . **138** D2
  Kingston u T KT3 . . . . **199** C6
  14 Richmond TW9 . . . . . **132** C4
  West Ewell KT19 . . . . **215** D1
Station Bldgs
  Catford SE6 . . . . **163** C4
  Merton SW20 . . . . **178** C1
Station Blgs W5 . . . . **110** B5
Station Cl Finchley N3 . . . . . **.29** C2
  Hampton TW12 . . . . **173** D2
Station Cres
  Ashford TW15 . . . . **170** A6
  Greenwich SE3 . . . . **121** A1
  Tottenham N15 . . . . **.51** B5
  Wembley HA0 . . . . **.65** B2
Station Cl Mitcham CR4 . . . **202** C5
  5 Nunhead SE15 . . . . . . **140** C3
  South Tottenham N15 . . . . **.51** D4
  Wembley HA9 . . . . **.43** C1
Stationers Hall Ct EC4 . . . **241** D1
Station Est BR3 . . . . **206** D3
Station Est E 11 . . . . **.37** B1
Station Estate Rd TW14 . . **150** B3
Station Gdns W4 . . . . **133** A5
Station Gr HA0 . . . . **.66** A2
Station Hill BR2 . . . . **209** B1

Station House Mews N9...**34** A6
Station Mans 9 N3....**29** C2
Station Mews Terr 4
SE3...............**121** A1
Station Par Acton W3....**88** C1
1 Ashford TW15......**170** B6
Barking IG11...........**79** A1
Belmont HA3...........**25** A1
Cockfosters EN4........**3** A1
Cricklewood NW2.......**68** C2
Dagenham RM10........**81** C2
Ealing W5.............**110** B5
Edgware HA8...........**26** A3
Feltham TW14..........**150** B4
Northolt UB5...........**63** D4
4 Osidge N14..........**15** D3
Richmond TW9.........**132** C4
Ruislip HA4............**61** B6
South Harrow HA2......**63** D4
4 Upper Tooting SW12..**159** A3
2 Wanstead E11........**55** A4
Woodford IG9..........**37** D6
Station Pas
New Cross Gate SE15...**140** C4
Woodford E18..........**37** B1
Station Pl N4..........**72** C6
Station Rd Ashford TW15..**170** B6
Barkingside IG6........**57** B6
Barnes SW13..........**133** D3
Beckenham BR2........**186** C1
Belvedere DA17.......**125** C3
Bexleyheath DA7......**147** A2
Bromley BR1..........**187** A2
Camden Town N19......**71** C5
Carshalton SM5........**218** D4
Chadwell Heath RM6....**58** D2
Chessington KT9.......**214** A3
Chingford E4...........**20** B3
Church End N3.........**29** C1
Claygate KT10.........**212** C3
Croydon CR0..........**205** A1
Edgware HA8..........**26** C4
Edgware NW7..........**27** C4
Esher KT10............**212** B6
Forest Gate E7.........**77** A4
Friern Barnet N11.......**31** B5
Greenhill HA1..........**42** D4
Hampton TW12.........**173** D2
Hampton Wick KT1....**175** D2
Hanwell W7...........**108** C5
Harlesden NW10.......**89** D5
Hayes UB3............**105** C2
Hendon NW4...........**46** A4
Hounslow TW3.........**129** D1
Ilford IG1.............**78** D5
Kingston u T KT2.......**176** C2
Lewisham SE13.........**142** A2
Leyton E10............**76** A5
Manor Pk E12..........**78** A4
Merton SW19..........**180** A2
New Barnet EN5........**13** D4
North Harrow HA1, HA2...**41** D4
Orpington BR6........**227** D6
Penge SE20...........**184** C4
Shepperton TW17......**193** A4
Sidcup DA14, DA15......**168** A1
Southgate N21.........**16** D3
South Norwood SE25....**205** D5
Sunbury TW16.........**172** A3
Teddington TW11.......**175** A4
Thames Ditton KT7.....**196** D2
Tottenham Hale N17.....**52** A6
Twickenham TW1.......**152** D4
Walthamstow E17.......**53** A4
West Acton W5........**88** B1
West Barnes KT3.......**200** B4
West Drayton UB7......**104** A4
West Wickham BR4.....**208** A1
Wood Green N22.......**32** B1
Station Rd N DA17....**125** D3
Station Rise SE27.....**160** D2
Station Sq BR5........**211** A4
Station St Newham E16..**122** D5
Stratford E15..........**76** B1
Station Terr
Camberwell SE5.......**139** A4
Kensal Rise NW10......**90** D5
Station View UB6.....**86** B6
Station Way
Cheam SM2, SM3......**217** A1
Claygate KT10........**212** C2
Woodford IG9.........**37** D6
Station Yd TW1.......**153** A4
Staton Ct 1 E10......**53** D2
Staunton Ho SE17....**263** A3
Staunton Rd KT2.....**176** B3
Staunton St SE8.....**141** B6
Staveley NW1.......**232** A2
Staveley Cl Hackney E9..**74** C3
Lower Holloway N7.....**72** A4
New Cross Gate SE15...**140** C4
8 Peckham SE15........**140** B4
Staveley Ct 4 E11....**55** A4
Staveley Gdns W4....**133** B4
Staveley Ho SE4.....**163** A6
Staveley Rd
Ashford TW15.........**171** B4

Staveley Rd continued
Chiswick W4...........**133** B5
Stavers Ho 31 E3.......**97** B5
Staverton Rd NW2.....**68** C1
Stave Yard Rd SE16....**119** A5
Stavordale Lo W14.....**254** D6
Stavordale Rd
Carshalton SM5........**202** A2
Highbury N5...........**72** D4
Stayner's Rd E1.......**96** D3
Stayton Rd SM1......**217** C5
Steadfast Rd KT1.....**175** D2
Steadman Ct EC1.....**242** B6
Steadman Ho 4 RM10..**81** C5
Stead St SE17......**117** B2 **262** C3
Steam Farm La TW14...**127** D1
Stean St E8...........**95** D6
Stebbing Ho 8 W11...**112** D5
Stebbing Way IG11...**102** A5
Stebondale St E14....**120** A2
Stebon Prim Sch 26 E14..**97** C2
Stedham Pl WC1.....**240** A2
Stedman Cl UB10.....**60** C5
Steedman St
SE17.........**117** A2 **262** A3
Steeds Rd N10........**30** D2
Steel App IG11.......**102** B5
Steele Rd
Acton Green W4.......**111** A3
Becontree NW10.......**89** A5
Isleworth TW7.........**131** A1
Leyton E11............**76** C4
Tottenham N17........**51** C6
Steele's Mews N NW3..**70** D2
Steele's Mews S NW3..**70** D2
Steele Wlk DA8......**147** D5
Steel's La 23 E1.......**96** C1
Steen Way 7 SE22....**161** C6
Steep Cl BR6.........**227** D2
Steep Hill
South Croydon CR0....**221** C4
Streatham SW16......**159** D1
Steeple Cl Fulham SW6..**135** A3
Wimbledon SW19......**179** A5
Steeple Ct
19 Bethnal Green E1....**96** B3
Wimbledon SW19......**179** A5
Steeplestone Cl N18...**33** A5
Steepleton Ct E11....**54** A1
Steeple Wlk N1.......**235** B6
Steerforth St SW18...**158** A2
Steering Cl N9........**18** C3
Steers Mead CR4.....**180** D2
Steers Way SE16.....**119** A4
Steetley Ct 14 SE18...**218** A1
Steinman Ct TW7.....**130** D2
Stelfax Ho WC1......**233** D2
Stella Cl UB8.........**82** D2
Stella Rd SW17......**180** D4
Stellar Ho 4 N17......**33** D4
Stellman Cl E5.......**74** A5
Stembridge Rd SE20..**184** B1
Sten Cl 12 EN3........**7** C6
Stephan Cl E8........**96** A6
Stephen Cl BR6.......**227** D5
Stephen Ct 18 SW19..**156** D3
Stephendale Rd SW6..**136** A3
Stephen Fox Ho 7 W4..**111** C1
Stephen Hawking Sch 23
E14..................**97** A1
Stephen Mews W1....**239** C3
Stephen Pl SW4......**137** C2
Stephen Saunders Ct
SW11.................**158** C2
Stephens Collection The★
N3...................**29** C1
Stephens Ct
Brockley SE4..........**141** A2
E16...................**98** D3
Stephens Lo N12.....**14** A1
Stephenson Ct SM2...**217** B1
Stephenson Ho
2 Gospel Oak NW5....**71** B4
6 Maitland Pk NW3....**70** D3
Newington SE1........**262** A6
West Heath SE2.......**124** D1
Stephenson Rd Ealing W7..**86** D1
Twickenham TW4......**151** C4
Walthamstow E17.....**53** A4
Stephenson St
Dagenham NW10......**89** D4
Newham E16...........**98** C2
Stephenson Way
NW1.........**93** C3 **239** B6
Stephen's Rd E15.....**98** C6
Stephen St W1......**239** C3
STEPNEY.............**96** D2
Stepney City E1......**96** C2
Stepney Cswy E1.....**96** D1
Stepney Gn E1.......**96** D2
Stepney Greencoat CE Prim
Sch The **26** E14.......**97** B1
Stepney Green Ct 4 E1..**96** D2
Stepney Green Maths &
Computing Coll **18** E1..**96** D2
Stepney Green Sta E1...**96** D3
Stepney High St E1....**96** D2
Stepney Way
Mitcham CR4.........**181** A2

Stepney Way continued
Stepney E1............**96** C2
Stepping Stones Farm★
E1...................**96** D2
Sterling Ave HA8.......**26** B6
Sterling Cl NW10.......**68** A1
Sterling Gdns SE14...**141** A6
Sterling Ho SE9......**143** B1
Sterling Pl W5.......**110** A2
Sterling Rd EN2.......**5** B5
Sterling St SW7......**257** B6
Sterling Way (North Circular
Rd) N18..............**33** C5
Stern Cl IG11.........**102** C5
Sterndale Rd W14....**112** D3
Sterne St W12.......**112** D4
Sternhall La SE15....**140** A2
Sternhold Ave SW12,
SW2..................**159** D2
Sterry Cres RM10.....**81** C3
Sterry Dr
Thames Ditton KT7....**196** C3
Worcester Pk KT19....**215** C4
Sterry Gdns RM10....**81** C2
Sterry Rd Barking IG11..**101** D6
Dagenham RM10......**81** C3
Sterry St SE1........**252** C1
Steucers La SE23....**163** A3
Stevanne Ct 1 DA17..**125** C1
Steve Biko Ct W10....**90** D3
Steve Biko La SE6....**185** C6
Steve Biko Lodge 13 E13..**99** A5
Steve Biko Rd N7.....**72** C5
Steve Biko Way TW3..**129** C2
Stevedale Rd DA16...**146** C3
Stevedore St 3 E1....**118** B5
Stevenage Rd
Fulham SW6..........**134** D4
Wallend E6............**78** C2
Stevens Ave E9......**74** C2
Stevens Cl
Beckenham BR3......**185** C4
Hampton TW12.......**173** B4
Pinner HA5............**40** C4
Stevens Ct BR3......**185** C4
Stevens Gn WD23.....**8** A3
Stevens Ho KT1......**175** D1
Stevens' La KT10.....**213** A2
Stevenson Cl EN5.....**14** B4
Stevenson Cres SE16..**118** B1
Stevenson Ho
1 Battersea SW11....**136** D3
6 Clapham Pk SW2....**160** A6
NW8..................**229** A6
Wembley HA9..........**65** D6
Stevens Rd RM8.....**80** C5
Stevens St SE1......**263** B6
Steventon Rd W12...**111** D6
Stewards Holte Wlk 3
N11...................**31** B6
Stewart Ave TW17....**192** C5
Stewart Cl BR7.......**188** D6
Hampton TW12.......**173** A4
Kingsbury NW9........**45** A3
Stewart Fleming Prim Sch
SE20.................**206** C6
Stewart Headlam Prim Sch
28 E1................**96** B3
Stewart Ho SE1......**263** A5
Stanmore HA7.........**25** B5
Stewart Quay UB3....**105** C4
Stewart Rainbird Ho 1
E12...................**78** C3
Stewart Rd E15.......**76** B4
Stewartsby Cl N18....**33** A5
Stewart's Gr
SW3.........**114** C1 **257** A2
Stewart's Rd
SW8.........**137** C4 **269** A2
Stewart St E14.......**120** A4
Stew La EC4.........**252** A6
Steyne Ho 13 Acton W3...**110** D5
11 Acton W3..........**111** A5
Steyne Rd W3........**110** D5
Steyne Gr SE9.......**188** B6
Steynings Way N12...**29** C5
Steyning Way TW4...**128** C1
Steynton Ave DA5....**168** D2
Stickland Rd DA17....**125** C2
Stickleton Cl UB6....**85** D4
Stifford Ho E1........**96** C2
Stilecroft Gdns HA0...**65** B5
Stile Hall Gdns W4...**110** C1
Stile Hall Par 6 W4...**110** C1
Stileman Ho 4 E3.....**97** B2
Stile Path TW16.....**194** A5
Stiles Cl BR2.........**210** B3
Erith DA8.............**125** D1
Stillingfleet Rd SW13..**134** A6
Stillington St
SW1.........**115** C2 **259** B4
Stillness Jun & Inf Schs
SE23.................**163** A5
Stillness Rd SE23....**163** B5
Stilwell Dr UB8........**82** B3
Stilwell Rdbt UB8....**104** D6
Stipularis Dr UB4.....**84** D3
Stirling Ave Pinner HA5..**41** A2
Upper Halliford TW17...**193** C6

Stirling Ave continued
Wallington SM6......**220** A1
Stirling Cl Sidcup DA14..**189** D6
Streatham SW16.....**181** C2
Stirling Cnr EN5, WD6....**11** B5
Stirling Ct
Clerkenwell EC1......**241** C6
Ealing W13...........**109** B6
Strand WC2..........**240** C1
Stirling Gr TW3......**130** A3
Stirling Ho 5 SE18...**122** D1
Stirling Ind Ctr WD6....**11** B6
Stirling Lo 7 EN5.....**14** A6
Stirling Mans NW6....**70** A2
Stirling Rd Harrow HA3..**42** D6
Hayes UB3............**106** B6
Newham E13..........**99** B5
South Acton W3.......**110** D3
Stanwell TW19, TW6...**148** B5
Stockwell SW9.......**138** A3
Tottenham N17........**34** A2
Twickenham TW2.....**151** D4
Walthamstow E17.....**53** A6
Wood Green N22......**32** D2
Stirling Ret Pk WD6....**11** B5
Stirling Way
Borehamwood WD6....**11** B6
Thornton Heath CR0...**204** A2
Stiven Cres HA2.......**63** B5
Stoatley Ho 10 SW15..**156** A3
Stockbeck NW1......**232** B3
Stockbridge Ho EN2....**4** D3
Stockbury Rd CR0....**206** C3
Stockdale Rd RM8....**81** B6
Stockdove Way UB6...**86** D4
Stocker Gdns RM9....**80** C1
Stockfield Rd
Claygate KT10........**212** C3
Streatham SW16.....**160** B1
4 Stratford E15.......**76** D1
Stockford Ave NW7...**28** D3
Stockholm Ho E1....**118** A6
Stockholm Rd SE16..**118** C1
Stockholm Way E1...**118** A5
Stockhurst Cl SW15..**134** D3
Stockingswater La EN3...**7** B2
Stockleigh Hall NW8..**230** B4
Stockley Acad UB8....**82** B1
Stockley Cl UB7.......**104** D4
Stockley Ctry Pk UB7..**104** C6
Stockley Farm Rd UB7..**104** D3
Stockley Park Bsns Pk
UB11.................**105** A5
Stockley Rd UB7, UB8,
UB11.................**104** D4
Stock Orchard Cres N7...**72** B3
Stock Orchard St N7...**72** B3
Stockport Rd SW16..**181** D2
Stocks Ct 5 E1........**96** D3
Stocksfield Rd E17....**54** A6
Stocks Pl Hillingdon UB10..**82** C6
16 Limehouse E14......**119** B6
Stock St E13.........**99** A5
Stockton Cl EN5.......**2** A1
Stockton Gdns
Edgware NW7........**11** C1
Tottenham N17........**33** A3
Stockton Ho 16 E2....**96** B4
Harrow HA2...........**41** C1
Stockton Rd
Edmonton N18........**34** B4
Tottenham N17........**33** A3
STOCKWELL........**138** A2
Stockwell Ave SW9..**138** B2
Stockwell Cl BR1....**187** B1
Stockwell Gdns
SW9.........**138** B4 **270** C1
Stockwell Gn SW9...**138** B3
Stockwell La SW9...**138** B3
Stockwell Park Cres
SW9.................**138** B4
Stockwell Park Rd
SW9.........**138** B4 **270** D1
Stockwell Park Sch
SW9.........**138** B4 **270** C1
Stockwell Park Wlk
SW9.................**138** C2
Stockwell Prim Sch 6
SW9.................**138** B2
Stockwell Rd SW9...**138** B3
Stockwell St SE10...**142** A6
Stockwell Sta SW4...**138** A3
Stockwell Terr SW9..**270** C1
Stodart Rd SE20....**184** C2
Stoddart Ho SW8....**270** D5
Stodmarsh Ho 28 SW9..**138** C4
Stofield Gdns SE9...**165** D1
Stoford Cl 4 SW19...**157** A4
Stokenchurch St
SW6.........**135** D4 **265** C1
STOKE NEWINGTON..**73** C6
Stoke Newington Church St
N16..................**73** C6
Stoke Newington Comm
N16..................**73** D6
Stoke Newington High St
N16..................**73** D5
Stoke Newington Rd N16..**73** D4
Stoke Newington Sch
N16..................**73** B5

Stoke Newington Sta
N16...................**73** D6
Stoke Pl NW10........**89** D4
Stoke Rd KT2.........**177** A3
Stokesby Rd KT9....**214** B2
Stokes Ct N2..........**48** C5
Stokesley St W12.....**89** D1
Stokes Rd Croydon CR0...**206** A3
Newham E6...........**100** A3
Stokley Ct N8.........**50** A5
Stoll Cl NW2..........**68** C5
Stoms Path SE6.....**185** C5
Stonard Rd
Dagenham RM8.......**80** B4
Palmers Green N13....**16** C1
Stondon Pk SE23....**163** A5
Stondon Wlk 4 E6....**99** D5
Stonebanks KT12....**194** A2
Stone Bldgs WC2..**94** B2 **240** D3
STONEBRIDGE.......**89** A6
Stonebridge Ct 9 NW10..**67** B1
Stonebridge Ctr 6 NW10..**89** B6
Stonebridge Ctr The N15..**52** A4
Stonebridge Park HA9...**66** D1
Stonebridge Park Sta
NW10.................**66** D1
Stonebridge Pk NW10..**67** B1
Stonebridge Prim Sch
NW10.................**89** B6
Stonebridge Rd N15...**51** D2
Stonebridge Way HA9...**66** D2
Stonechat Sq 6 E6...**100** A2
Stone Cl Clapham SW4...**137** C3
Dagenham RM8.......**81** B6
Yiewsley UB7.........**104** B5
Stonecot Cl SM3.....**201** A1
Stonecot Hill SM3....**201** A1
Stone Cres TW14.....**149** D4
Stonecroft Way CR0..**204** A2
Stonecrop Cl NW9....**45** B6
Stonecutter St EC4..**241** C2
Stonefield N4.........**72** B6
Stonefield Cl DA7....**147** C2
Ruislip HA4...........**63** A3
Stonefield Mans N1...**234** A5
Stonefield St N1...**94** C6 **234** B6
Stonefield Way
Ruislip HA4...........**63** A3
SE7...................**143** D5
Stonegate 8 NW5.....**71** A2
Stone Gr HA8.........**26** B5
Stone Grove Ct HA8...**26** B5
Stonegrove Gdns HA8..**26** A5
Stonegrove Ho HA8...**26** A5
Stonehall Ave IG1....**56** A3
Stone Hall Rd N11....**16** C4
Stoneham Rd N11....**31** C5
Stonehaven BR3.....**185** D1
Stonehill Bsns Pk N18..**34** C1
Stonehill Cl SW14....**155** B6
Stonehill Ct E4........**19** D4
Stonehill Rd
Brentford W4.........**110** C1
Mortlake SW14.......**155** B6
Stonehills Ct SE21...**161** C1
Stonehill's Mans 3
SW16.................**160** A2
Stonehill Woods Pk
DA14.................**191** D4
Stonehorse Rd EN3....**18** C6
Stonehouse NW1....**232** B5
Stonehouse Ct EC2...**243** B2
Stonehouse Ho 27 W2..**91** C2
Stone Lake Ind Pk SE7..**121** C2
Stone Lake Ret Pk SE7..**121** C2
STONELEIGH.........**216** A3
Stoneleigh Ave Enfield EN1..**6** B4
North Cheam KT17, KT4...**216** A5
Stoneleigh Broadway
KT17.................**216** B4
Stoneleigh Cres KT19..**215** D3
Stoneleigh Ct
Redbridge IG5.........**56** A6
6 Tottenham N17.....**33** D1
Stoneleigh Fst Sch
KT17.................**216** B4
Stoneleigh Lo 13 TW9..**132** A1
Stoneleigh Mews 15 E3..**97** A5
Stoneleigh Park Ave
CR0..................**206** D3
Stoneleigh Park Rd KT19,
KT4..................**216** A3
Stoneleigh Pl W11....**112** D6
Stoneleigh Rd
Bromley BR1..........**210** D6
Carshalton SM5......**202** C2
Redbridge IG5.........**56** B6
Tottenham N17........**33** D1
Stoneleigh St W11...**112** D6
Stoneleigh Sta KT19..**216** A3
Stoneleigh Terr N19....**71** B6
Stonell's Rd SW11...**158** D6
Stonemasons Cl N15..**51** B5
Stonenest St N4......**50** B1
Stone Park Ave BR3..**207** D5
Stone Pl KT4.........**216** A6
Stone Rd BR2.......**208** D4
Stones End St SE1...**252** A1

Stonewall E6 . . . . .100 C2
Stoneworth Ct SE25 . . . . . .206 A3
Stoneyard La E14 . . . . .119 D6
Stoneycroft Cl SE12 . . . . . .164 D4
Stoney Deep TW11 . . . . . .175 A6
Stoneydown E17 . . . . .53 A5
Stoneydown Ave E17 . . . . . .53 A5
Stoneydown Ho **2** E17 . . . .53 A5
Stoneydown Park Sch **5**
 E17 . . . . .53 A5
Stoneyfields Gdns HA8 . . .27 A6
Stoneyfields La HA8 . . . . .27 A6
Stoney La EC3 . . . . .243 B2
 Penge SE19 . . . . .183 D4
Stoney St SE1 . . . . .117 B5 252 C4
Stonhouse St SW4 . . . . . .137 D1
Stonor Rd W14 . . . .113 B2 254 C3
Stonycroft Cl EN3 . . . . .7 A3
Stopes St SE15 . . . . .139 D5
Stopford Rd Newham E13 . .99 A6
 SE17 . . . . .261 D1
Stopher Ho SE1 . . . . .251 D1
Storace Ho **5** SW4 . . . . . .138 A1
Store Rd E16 . . . . .122 C4
Storers Quay E14 . . . . .120 B2
Store St
 Bloomsbury WC1 . . .93 D2 239 C4
 Stratford New Town E15 . . .76 B3
Storey Ct NW8 . . . . .229 C1
Storey Ctr The E16 . . . . . . .122 C5
Storey Ho **13** E14 . . . . . . .119 D6
Storey Rd Highgate N6 . . . . .48 D3
 Walthamstow E17 . . . . .53 B5
Storey's Gate
 SW1 . . . . .115 D4 249 D1
Storey St E16 . . . . .122 C4
Stories Rd SE5 . . . . .139 C2
Stork Rd E7 . . . . .77 A2
Storksmead Rd HA8 . . . . . .27 C3
Storks Rd SE16 . . . . .118 A3
Stormont House Sch E5. . .74 B4
Stormont Rd
 Clapham SW11 . . . . .137 A1
 Highgate N6 . . . . .48 D2
Stormont Way KT9 . . . . . .213 C3
Stormount Dr UB3 . . . . . . .105 A4
Storrington WC1 . . . . .233 B1
Storrington Rd CR0 . . . . . .205 D1
Story St N1 . . . . .72 B1
Stotfold BR1 . . . . .188 A2
Stothard Ho **25** E1 . . . . . . .96 C3
Stothard Pl E2 . . . . .243 B4
Stothard St **12** E1 . . . . . . .96 C3
Stott Cl SW18 . . . . .158 B5
Stoughton Ave SM3 . . . . . .217 A3
Stoughton Cl
 Roehampton SW15 . . . . . . .156 A3
 SE11 . . . . .260 D3
Stour Ave UB2 . . . . .107 C3
Stourbridge Ho **8** UB5 . . .85 B3
Stour Cl BR2 . . . . .225 C4
Stourcliffe Cl W1 . . . . .237 C2
Stourcliffe St W1 . . . . .237 C1
Stour Ct UB1 . . . . .86 B1
Stourhead Cl SW19 . . . . . .169 C4
Stourhead Gdns SW20 . . .200 A6
Stour Rd Dagenham RM10 . .81 C6
 Hackney Wick E3 . . . . .75 C1
Stourton Ave TW13 . . . . . .173 B6
Stowage SE8 . . . . .141 D6
Stow Cres E17 . . . . .35 A3
Stowe Cres HA4 . . . . .39 A3
Stowe Gdns N9 . . . . .17 D3
Stowe Ho
 Hampstead Garden Suburb
 NW11 . . . . .48 A3
 11 Stoke Newington N16 . .73 C5
Stowell Ho **2** N8 . . . . .50 A5
Stowe Rd W12 . . . . .112 B4
Stowford Coll SM2 . . . . . . .218 A1
Stowting Rd BR6 . . . . .227 C4
Stox Mead HA3 . . . . .24 B2
Stracey Rd
 Becontree NW10 . . . . .89 B6
 Forest Gate E7 . . . . .77 A4
Strachan Pl SW19, SW20 . .178 C4
Stradbroke Gr
 Buckhurst Hill IG9 . . . . .21 D3
 Redbridge IG5 . . . . .56 C6
Stradbroke Rd N5 . . . . .73 A4
Stradbrook Cl HA2 . . . . . . .63 B5
Stradella Rd SE24 . . . . . . .161 A5
Straffan Lo **8** NW3 . . . . . .70 C2
Strafford Ho **9** SE8 . . . . .119 B1
Strafford Rd Acton W3 . . . .111 A4
 Barnet EN5 . . . . .1 A2
 Hounslow TW3 . . . . .129 B2
 Twickenham TW1 . . . . .153 A4
Strafford St E14 . . . . .119 C4
Strahan Rd E3 . . . . .97 A4
Straightsmouth SE10 . . . . .142 A5
Straight The UB2 . . . . .107 A4
Strait Rd E6 . . . . .122 B6
Straker's Rd SE15 . . . . .140 B1
Strale Ho **17** N1 . . . . .95 C6
STRAND 116 B6
Strand
 Strand WC2 . . . . .116 B6 250 C6
 Strand WC2 . . . . .240 D1
 Strand SE18. . . . . .123 D1

Strand Dr TW9 . . . . .132 D5
Strandfield Cl SE18 . . . . . .123 C1
Strand Ho SE28 . . . . .123 B5
Strand La WC2 . . . . .250 D6
STRAND ON THE
 GREEN 132 C6
Strand-on-the-Green
 W4 . . . . .132 C6
Strand-on-the-Green Schs
 5 W4 . . . . .132 C6
Strand Pl N18 . . . . .33 C6
Strang Ho N1 . . . . .235 A5
Strangways Terr W14 . . . . .254 C5
Stranraer Way
 Barnsbury N1 . . . . .72 A1
 1 Stanwell TW6 . . . . . . .148 A5
Strasburg Rd
 SW11 . . . . .137 B4 268 C1
Stratfield Ho SE12 . . . . . . .165 A2
Stratfield Park Cl N21 . . . . .16 D4
STRATFORD 76 A2
Stratford Ave UB10 . . . . . . .82 B5
Stratford Bus Sta E15 . . . . .76 B1
Stratford Cl IG11 . . . . .80 A1
Stratford Coll (Newham 6th
 Form Coll) E15 . . . . .76 B2
Stratford Ct SE11 . . . . .199 B5
Stratford Gr SW15 . . . . . . .134 D1
Stratford House Ave
 BR1 . . . . .210 A6
Stratford International Sta
 E15 . . . . .76 A2
STRATFORD MARSH 97 D6
STRATFORD NEW
 TOWN 76 A3
Stratford Office Village The
 1 E15 . . . . .76 C1
Stratford Pl W1 . . . . .238 C1
Stratford Rd
 Harlington TW6 . . . . .149 A6
 Hayes UB4 . . . . .84 B3
 Hendon NW4 . . . . .46 D5
 Newham E13 . . . . .99 A6
 Southall UB2 . . . . .107 A2
 Thornton Heath CR7 . . . . .204 D6
 W8 . . . . .113 C3 255 B5
 Stratford Sch E7 . . . . .77 A1
 Stratford Sh Ctr E15 . . . . . .76 B1
 Stratford Sta E15 . . . . .76 B1
Stratford Studios W8 . . . . .255 C5
Stratford Villas NW1 . . . . . .71 D1
Stratford Workshops E15 . .98 B6
Strathan Cl SW18 . . . . .157 A5
Strathaven Rd SE12 . . . . . .165 B5
Strathblaine Rd SW11 . . . .136 B1
Strathbrook Rd SW16 . . . .182 B3
Strathcona Rd HA9 . . . . . . .65 C6
Strathdale SW16 . . . . .182 B5
Strathdon Dr SW17 . . . . . .158 B1
Strathearn Ave
 Harlington UB3 . . . . .127 D5
 Twickenham TW2 . . . . .152 A3
Strathearn Ho **2** W2 . . . . .247 A6
Strathearn Pl
 W2 . . . . .114 C6 247 A6
Strathearn Rd
 Sutton SM1 . . . . .217 C3
 Wimbledon SW19 . . . . .179 C6
Stratheden Par SE3 . . . . . .143 A5
Stratheden Rd SE3 . . . . . . .143 A5
Strathfield Gdns IG11 . . . . .79 B2
Strathleven Rd SW2 . . . . . .160 A6
Strathmore Ct NW8 . . . . . .230 A2
Strathmore Gdns
 Edgware HA8 . . . . .26 D1
 Finchley N3 . . . . .29 D2
 W8 . . . . .245 B4
Strathmore Rd
 Teddington TW11, TW2 . . . .174 C6
 Thornton Heath CR0 . . . . .205 B2
 Wimbledon SW19 . . . . .157 C1
 Strathmore Sch TW10 . . . .153 D2
Strathnairn St SE1 . . . . . . .118 A2
Strathray Gdns NW3 . . . . . .70 C2
Strath Terr SW11 . . . . .136 C1
Strathville Rd SW18 . . . . . .157 D2
Strathyre Ave SW16 . . . . . .204 C6
Stratton Ave EN2 . . . . .5 B6
Stratton Cl DA7 . . . . .147 A2
 Edgware HA8 . . . . .26 B4
 Heston TW5 . . . . .129 C4
 Merton SW19 . . . . .179 C1
 Walton-on-T KT12 . . . . . . .194 C1
Stratton Ct
 4 De Beauvoir Town N1 . . .73 C1
 10 Kingston u T KT6 . . . . .198 A4
 10 Pinner HA5 . . . . .23 B3
Strattondale St E14 . . . . . .120 A3
Stratton Dr IG11 . . . . .79 D2
Stratton Gdns UB1 . . . . . . .85 C1
Stratton Ho HA8 . . . . .26 B6
Stratton Lo **10** EN5 . . . . . . .1 D1
Stratton Rd DA7 . . . . .147 A2
 Merton SW19 . . . . .179 C1
 Sunbury TW16 . . . . .171 D1
Stratton St W1 . . . . .115 B5 248 D4
Strauss Rd W4 . . . . .111 B4
Strawberry Fields BR6 . . . .226 D3
STRAWBERRY HILL 152 D1
Strawberry Hill Cl TW1 . . 152 D1

Strawberry Hill Rd TW1 . 152 D1
Strawberry Hill Sta
 TW2 . . . . .152 D1
Strawberry La SM5 . . . . . .219 A5
Strawberry Terr N10 . . . . . .30 D2
Strawberry Vale
 Finchley N2 . . . . .30 B2
 Twickenham TW1 . . . . .153 A1
Strayfield Rd EN2 . . . . .4 D6
Streakes Field Rd NW2 . . . .68 A6
Streamdale SE2 . . . . .146 B6
Stream La HA8 . . . . .26 D5
Streamline Mews SE22 . . .162 A3
Streamside Cl BR2 . . . . . . .209 A5
 Edmonton N9 . . . . .17 D3
Stream Way DA17 . . . . . . .147 C6
Streatfeild Ave E6 . . . . . . .100 B6
Streatfield Rd HA3, HA7 . . .43 D6
STREATHAM 182 A4
Streatham & Clapham High
 Sch SW16 . . . . .159 D1
Streatham Common N
 SW16 . . . . .182 B5
Streatham Common S
 SW16 . . . . .182 B4
Streatham Common Sta
 SW16 . . . . .181 D3
Streatham Ct SW16 . . . . . .160 A1
Streatham High Rd SW16,
 SW2 . . . . .182 A5
Streatham Hill & Clapham
 High Sch **14** SW2 . . . . . .160 B3
Streatham Hill Sta SW2 . . .160 A3
Streatham L Ctr & Ice Arena
 SW16 . . . . .181 D5
STREATHAM PARK 181 C6
Streatham Pl SW2 . . . . . . .160 A4
Streatham Rd CR4 . . . . . . .181 A2
Streatham St WC1 . . . . . . .240 A2
Streatham St SW16 . . . . . .181 D5
STREATHAM VALE 181 D3
Streatham Vale SW16 . . . . .181 D3
Streathbourne Rd SW17 . .159 A1
Streatham Wells Prim Sch
 SW2 . . . . .160 C2
Streatleigh Par **4**
 SW16 . . . . .160 A2
Streatley Pl
 27 Hampstead NW3 . . . . .70 A4
 Hampstead NW3 . . . . .70 B4
Streatley Rd NW6 . . . . .69 B1
Streeters La SM6 . . . . .219 D5
Streetfield Mews SE3 . . . . .143 A2
Streimer Rd E15 . . . . .98 A5
Strelley Way W3 . . . . .111 C6
Stretton Lo W13 . . . . .109 B6
Stretton Mans **15** SE8 . . .141 C6
Stretton Rd Croydon CR0 . .205 C2
 Richmond TW10 . . . . .153 C2
Strickland Ct SE15 . . . . . . .140 A2
Strickland Ho **26** E2 . . . . . .95 D4
Strickland Row SW18 . . . . .158 B4
Strickland St SE8 . . . . .141 C4
Strickland Way **4** BR6 . . .227 D4
Stride Rd E13 . . . . .98 D5
Strimon Cl N9 . . . . .18 C2
Stringer Hos **19** N1 . . . . . .95 C6
Strode Cl N10 . . . . .31 A3
Strode Ho **3** SW2 . . . . . . .160 C3
Strode Rd Forest Gate E7 . .77 A4
 NW10 . . . . .135 A5 264 A4
 NW17 . . . . .33 C1
 Willesden NW10 . . . . .68 A2
Strome Ho NW6 . . . . .91 D5
Strone Rd E7, E12 . . . . .77 D2
Strone Way UB4 . . . . .85 A3
Strongbow Cres SE9 . . . . .166 B6
Strongbow Rd SE9 . . . . . . .166 B6
Strongbridge Cl HA2 . . . . . .41 C1
Stronsa Rd W12 . . . . .111 D4
Strood Ho
 9 Penge SE20 . . . . .184 C3
 SE1 . . . . .252 D1
Stroud Cres SW15 . . . . . . .156 A1
Stroudes Cl KT4 . . . . .199 D2
Stroud Field UB5 . . . . .63 A2
Stroud Gate HA2 . . . . .63 D4
STROUD GREEN 50 C3
Stroud Green Gdns CR0 . .206 C2
Stroud Green Prim Sch
 N4 . . . . .50 C1
Stroud Green Rd N4 . . . . . . .50 C1
Stroud Green Way CR0 . . .206 C3
Stroudley Ho SW8 . . . . . . .269 B2
Stroudley Wlk E3 . . . . .97 D4
Strouds Cl RM6 . . . . .58 B4
Stroud Way TW15 . . . . .171 A4
Strout's Pl **2** E2 . . . . .95 D4
Struan Ho **3** E11 . . . . .55 A4
Strudwick Ct SW4 . . . . . . .270 B1
Strutton Ground
 SW1 . . . . .115 D3 259 C5
Strype St E1 . . . . .243 C3
Stuart Ave Ealing W5 . . . . .110 B4

Stuart Ave continued
 Harrow HA2 . . . . .63 B5
 Hayes BR2 . . . . .209 A1
 Hendon NW9 . . . . .46 A2
 Walton-on-T KT12 . . . . . . .194 B1
Stuart Cl UB10 . . . . .60 C2
Stuart Cres Croydon CR0 . .223 B5
 Hayes UB3 . . . . .83 A1
 Wood Green N22 . . . . .32 B2
Stuart Ct Chingford E4 . . . . .20 D2
 6 Croydon CR0 . . . . .220 D5
 2 Elstree WD6 . . . . .9 D5
Stuart Evans Cl DA16 . . . . .146 C2
Stuart Gr TW11 . . . . .174 C5
Stuart Ho
 Hammersmith W6 . . . . .112 C3
 1 Homerton E9 . . . . .74 D1
 Queensbury NW9 . . . . .44 C5
 5 Stockwell SW4 . . . . . . .138 A1
 W14 . . . . .254 A4
Stuart Lo SE25 . . . . .183 C1
Stuart Mill Ho N1 . . . . .233 C3
Stuart Pl DF14 . . . . .180 D2
Stuart Rd Acton W3 . . . . . .111 A5
 Barking IG11 . . . . .79 D1
 DA16 . . . . .146 B4
 East Barnet EN4 . . . . .14 D4
 Harrow HA3 . . . . .42 D6
 Maida Vale NW6 . . . . .91 C4
 Nunhead SE15 . . . . .140 C1
 Richmond TW10 . . . . .153 B1
 South Norwood SE27 . . . . .205 A5
 Wimbledon SW19 . . . . .157 C1
Stubbs Cl NW9 . . . . .45 A4
Stubbs Dr SE16 . . . . .118 B1
Stubbs Ho Finsbury Pk N4 . .50 B1
 1 Globe Town E2 . . . . .96 D4
Stubbs Mews RM8 . . . . .80 B4
Stubbs Point E13 . . . . .99 B3
Stubbs Way SW19 . . . . . . .180 B2
Stucley Pl **19** NW1 . . . . . . .71 B1
Stucley Rd TW5, TW7 . . . . .130 A5
Studdridge St SW6 . . . . . . .135 C3
Studd St N1 . . . . . . .94 D6 234 C6
Studholme Ct NW3 . . . . . . .69 C4
Studholme St SE15 . . . . . .140 B5
Studio Mews **5** NW4 . . . . .46 C5
Studio Pl SW1 . . . . .247 D1
Studios NW8 . . . . .229 A4
Studios Rd TW17 . . . . .192 B6
Studios The
 4 Clapham SW4 . . . . . . .137 C1
 SW8 . . . . .269 D1
Studland SE17 . . . . .262 C2
Studland Cl DA15 . . . . .167 D1
Studland Ho E14 . . . . .97 A1
Studland Rd Ealing W7 . . . . .86 C1
 Forest Hill SE26 . . . . .184 D5
 Kingston u T KT2 . . . . .176 A4
Studland St W6 . . . . .112 B2
Studley Ave E4 . . . . .36 B3
Studley Cl E5 . . . . .75 A3
Studley Ct
 13 Blackwall E14 . . . . . .120 B6
 DA14 . . . . .190 B5
 Redbridge IG4 . . . . .55 D3
Studley Dr IG4 . . . . .55 C3
Studley Grange Rd W7 . . . .108 D4
Studley Rd Dagenham RM9 . .80 D1
 South Lambeth SW4 . . . . . .138 A3
 Upton E7 . . . . .77 B2
Sturdee Ho **7** E2 . . . . .96 A5
Sturdy Ho **28** E3 . . . . .97 A5
Sturdy Rd SE15 . . . . .140 B3
Sturge Ave E17 . . . . .35 D1
Sturgeon Rd
 SE17 . . . . .117 A1 262 A1
Sturges Field BR7 . . . . . . .189 B4
Sturgess Ave NW4 . . . . .46 B2
Sturge St SE1 . . . . . .117 A4 252 A2
Sturmer Way N7 . . . . .72 B3
Sturminster Cl UB4 . . . . . . .84 C1
Sturminster Ho SW8 . . . . .270 D3
Sturrock Cl N15 . . . . .51 B5
Sturry St E14 . . . . .97 D1
Sturt St N1 . . . . .235 B3
Stutfield St E1 . . . . .96 A1
Stuttle Ho **14** E1 . . . . .96 A3
Styles Gdns SW9 . . . . .138 D2
Styles Ho SE1 . . . . .251 C3
Styles Way BR3 . . . . .208 A5
Stylus Apartments **21** E1 . .96 C1
Sudbourne Prim Sch **18**
 SW2 . . . . .160 B6
Sudbourne Rd SW2 . . . . . .160 B6
Sudbrooke Rd SW12 . . . . .159 A5
Sudbrook Gdns TW10 . . . .154 A1
Sudbrook La TW10 . . . . . . .154 A2
SUDBURY 65 A4
Sudbury E6 . . . . .100 C1

Sudbury Ave HA0 . . . . .65 D4
Sudbury Court Dr HA1 . . . . .65 A5
Sudbury Court Rd HA1 . . . . .65 A5
Sudbury Cres BR1 . . . . . . .187 A5
 Wembley HA0 . . . . .65 B3
Sudbury Croft HA0 . . . . . . .64 D4
Sudbury Ct **1** Ilford RM6 . .58 B4
 SW8 . . . . .269 D2
Sudbury Gdns CR0 . . . . . . .221 C4
Sudbury & Harrow Road Sta
 HA0 . . . . .65 B3
Sudbury Heights Ave
 UB6 . . . . .65 A3
Sudbury Hill HA1 . . . . .64 C5
Sudbury Hill Cl HA0 . . . . . .64 D5
Sudbury Hill Harrow Sta
 HA1 . . . . .64 C4
Sudbury Hill Sta HA1 . . . . .64 C4
Sudbury Ho SW18 . . . . . . .157 D6
Sudbury Prim Sch HA0 . . . .65 B4
Sudbury Rd IG11 . . . . .79 D3
Sudbury Town Sta UB6 . . . .65 B2
Sudeley St N1 . . . . .94 D6 234 D3
Sudlow Rd SW18 . . . . .157 C6
Sudrey St SE1 . . . . .252 A1
Suez Ave UB6 . . . . .86 D5
Suez Rd EN3 . . . . .7 A2
Suffah Prim Sch TW3 . . . .129 B1
Suffield Ho SE17 . . . . .261 D2
Suffield Rd Chingford E4 . . . .35 D6
 Penge SE20 . . . . .184 C1
 2 South Tottenham N15 . . .51 D4
Suffolk Cl WD6 . . . . .11 B6
Suffolk Ct
 3 Dagenham RM6 . . . . . . .58 C4
 Ilford IG3 . . . . .57 C3
 3 West Norwood SW16 . .182 C6
Suffolk Ho **11** Acton W3 . . . .88 C1
 Beckenham BR2 . . . . .208 D5
 3 Dartmouth Pk NW5 . . . . .71 C5
 Edgware HA8 . . . . .26 B4
 Penge SE20 . . . . .184 C2
 4 South Croydon CR0 . . . .221 B6
Suffolk La EC4 . . . . .252 C6
 Barnes SW13 . . . . .134 A5
 Dagenham RM10 . . . . .81 D3
 Enfield EN3 . . . . .18 B6
 Harrow HA2 . . . . .41 C4
 Ilford IG3 . . . . .57 C3
 4 Newham E13 . . . . .99 A4
 Sidcup DA14 . . . . .190 C4
 South Norwood SE25 . . . . .205 D5
 Tottenham N15 . . . . .51 B3
 Willesden NW10 . . . . .67 C1
 Worcester Pk KT4 . . . . .215 D6
Suffolks Prim Sch EN1 . . . . .6 B3
Suffolk St Forest Gate E7 . . .77 A4
 SW1 . . . . .115 D5 249 D4
Sugar House La E15. . . . . . .98 A5
Sugar Loaf Wlk **6** E2 . . . . .96 C4
Sugden Rd
 Clapham SW11 . . . . .137 A1
 Long Ditton KT7 . . . . .197 B1
Sugden Way IG11 . . . . .101 D5
Sulby Ho SE4 . . . . .141 A1
Sulgrave Gdns **11** W6 . . . .112 C4
Sulgrave Rd W6 . . . . .112 C3
Sulina Rd SW2 . . . . .160 A4
Sulivan Ct SW6 . . . . .135 C3
Sulivan Ent Ctr SW6 . . . . . .135 C2
Sulivan Prim Sch SW6 . . . .135 C3
Sulivan Rd SW6 . . . . .135 C2
Sulkin Ho **11** E2 . . . . .96 D4
Sullivan Ave E16 . . . . .99 D2
Sullivan Cl
 Battersea SW11 . . . . .136 C2
 Hayes UB4 . . . . .84 C2
Sullivan Ct
 4 Croydon CR0 . . . . .206 A1
 Stamford Hill N16 . . . . .51 D1
 SW5 . . . . .255 B4
Sullivan Ho Chelsea SW1 . .268 D6
 Isleworth TW2 . . . . .152 B5
 Vauxhall SE11 . . . . .260 D3
Sullivan Rd SE11 . . .116 C3 261 B4
Sullivans Reach KT12 . . . .193 D2
Sullivan Way WD6 . . . . .9 C5
Sultan Ho SE1 . . . . .118 A1
Sultan Rd E11 . . . . .55 B5
Sultan St Penge BR3 . . . . .184 D1
 SE5 . . . . .139 A5
Sumal Ct E9 . . . . .76 B6
Sumatra Rd NW6 . . . . .69 C2
Sumburgh Rd SW12 . . . . . .159 A5
Summer Ave KT8 . . . . .196 C4
Summercourt Rd E1 . . . . . . .96 C1
Summer Crossing KT7 . . . .196 C4
Summerene Cl SW16 . . . . .181 C3
Summerfield **6** BR1 . . . . .187 B2
Summerfield Ave
 Colney Hatch N12 . . . . .30 C4
 Kensal Rise NW6 . . . . .91 A5
Summerfield Ho RM9 . . . . . .80 D4

Summerfield La KT6....213 D6
Summerfield Rd
　Ealing W5........87 B3
　Loughton IG10....21 D5
Summerfield St SE12...164 D4
Summer Gdns KT8....196 C4
Summer Gr WD6.......9 D5
Summer Hill
　Borehamwood WD6.....10 C6
　BR7............188 C1
Summerhill Cl BR6....227 C5
Summerhill Gr EN1....17 C5
Summerhill Rd N15....51 B5
Summerhill Villas BR7...188 D2
Summerhill Way CR4...181 A2
Summer Ho SE13......142 B1
Summerhouse Ave TW5.129 A4
Summerhouse Rd N16...73 C6
Summerland Gdns N10..49 B6
Summerland Grange N10.49 B6
Summerlands Ave W3...111 A6
Summerlands Lo BR6....24 D5
Summerlee Ave N2.....48 D5
Summerlee Gdns N2....48 D5
Summerley St SW18....157 D2
Summer Rd
　East Molesey KT8.....196 B4
　Thames Ditton KT7, KT8..196 D4
Summersby Rd N6......49 B3
Summers Cl
　Belmont SM2.......217 C1
　Wembley HA9.......44 D1
Summersell Rd SE27...183 B5
Summerside Prim Sch
　N12.............18 B2
Summerskille Cl N9....30 B3
Summers La N12.......30 B3
Summers Row N12.....30 C4
Summers St EC1.......241 A5
SUMMERSTOWN........158 A1
Summerstown SW17....180 A6
Summerswood Prim Sch
　WD6.............10 D6
Summerton Way SE28...102 D1
Summer Trees TW16...172 B2
Summerville Gdns SM1.217 B2
Summerwood Rd TW1,
　TW7...........152 D5
Summit Ave NW9......45 B4
Summit Bsns Pk TW16.172 A3
Summit Cl Edgware HA8..26 C3
　Kingsbury NW9.....45 B5
　Osidge N14........15 C2
Summit Ct 5 Barnet EN5..1 B2
　Brondesbury NW2....69 A3
Summit Dr IG8.......37 D1
Summit Est N16......52 A2
Summit Rd Northolt UB5..63 C1
　Walthamstow E17....53 D5
Summit Way
　Brunswick Pk N14....15 B2
　South Norwood SE19..183 C3
Sumner Ave SE15.....139 D4
Sumner Bldgs SE1.....252 A4
Sumner Cl BR6.......227 A4
Sumner Ct SW8.......270 A2
Sumner Gdns CR0.....204 C1
Sumner Ho 1 E3......97 D2
Sumner Pl SW7...114 B2 256 D3
Sumner Place Mews
　SW7............256 D3
Sumner Rd Harrow HA1..42 A2
　SE15............139 D5
　Thornton Heath CR0..204 D1
Sumner Rd S CR0.....204 C1
Sumner St SE1...117 A5 252 A4
Sumpter Cl NW3......70 A2
Sun Alley 6 TW9.....132 A1
Sun Alliance Ho WC2..241 A2
Sunbeam Cres W10....90 C3
Sunbeam Rd NW10....89 B3
SUNBURY............194 B6
Sunbury Ave
　Edgware NW7......27 B6
　Mortlake SW14.....133 A1
Sunbury Cl KT12......194 A3
SUNBURY COMMON....171 D3
Sunbury Court Island
　TW16...........194 D6
Sunbury Court Mews
　TW16...........172 D1
Sunbury Court Rd TW16.172 C1
Sunbury Cres TW13....171 D6
Sunbury Cross TW16..172 A3
Sunbury Cross Ctr 9
　TW16...........171 D3
Sunbury Ct 3 Barnet EN5..1 B2
　3 SE14.........140 D6
　Sunbury TW16.....172 D1
Sunbury Ct (Con Ctr)
　TW16...........172 D1
Sunbury Gdns NW7....27 B5
Sunbury Ho 38 E2.....95 D4
Sunbury Int Bsns Ctr
　TW16...........171 C2
Sunbury La
　Battersea SW11..136 B4 266 D2

Sunbury La continued
　Walton-on-T KT12....194 A3
Sunbury L Ctr TW16...171 D2
Sunbury Manor Sch
　TW16...........171 D2
Sunbury Rd Cheam SM3.217 A5
　Feltham TW13.....171 D6
Sunbury St SE18......122 B3
Sunbury Sta TW16....172 A2
Sunbury Walled Gdn*
　TW16...........194 B6
Sunbury Way TW13....172 C5
Sunbury Workshops 39
　E2.............95 D4
Suncroft Pl SE26.....162 C1
Sun Ct EC3..........242 D1
Sundeala Cl TW16.....172 A3
Sunderland Ct
　Dulwich SE22......162 A4
　12 Stanwell TW19..148 A5
Sunderland Ho 28 W2..91 C2
Sunderland Mount
　SE23...........162 D2
Sunderland Point E16..123 A5
Sunderland Rd
　Ealing W5........109 D3
　Forest Hill SE23....162 D2
Sunderland Terr W2....91 D1
Sunderland Way E12...77 D6
Sundew Ave W12......112 A6
Sundew Ct 9 HA0.....88 A5
Sundial Ave SE25.....205 D6
Sundial Ct KT5.......214 D6
Sundorne Rd SE7.....121 C1
Sundown Rd TW15....171 A5
Sundra Wlk 26 E1.....96 D3
SUNDRIDGE..........187 C4
Sundridge Ave
　Bromley BR1, BR7...188 A3
　DA16...........145 B2
Sundridge Ho
　4 Homerton E9.....74 D1
Sundridge Par BR1....187 B3
Sundridge Park Sta BR1.187 B3
Sundridge Pl 8 CR0...206 A1
Sundridge Rd CR0....206 A1
Sunfields Pl SE3......143 B5
Sun in the Sands SE3..143 B5
Sunken Rd CR0.......222 C3
Sun La SE3..........143 B5
Sunland Ave DA6.....147 A1
Sunleigh Ct HA0......88 A6
Sunleigh Rd HA0.....88 A6
Sunley Gdns UB6.....87 A6
Sunley Ho E1........243 D3
Sun Life Trad Est TW14.128 A2
Sunlight Cl SW19.....180 A4
Sunlight Sq 29 E2.....96 B4
Sunmead Rd TW16....194 A6
Sunna Gdns TW16....172 B1
Sunna Lo TW16.......171 D3
Sunnholme Ct CR2....221 A3
Sunningdale Ave
　Barking IG11......79 B1
　East Acton W3.....111 C6
　Feltham TW13.....151 A2
　Ruislip HA4.......40 C1
Sunningdale Cl
　22 Bermondsey SE16..118 B1
　Erith SE28........103 A1
　3 Newham E6.....100 B4
　Stanmore HA7......25 A3
　3 Surbiton KT6....214 A6
Sunningdale Ct
　13 Kingston U KT2..176 C3
　13 Southall UB1....86 A1
Sunningdale Gdns
　Kingsbury NW9.....45 A4
　W8.............255 B5
Sunningdale Lo HA8....26 B5
Sunningdale Rd
　BR1, BR2........210 A4
　Cheam SM1.......217 B4
Sunningfields Cres NW4.28 B1
Sunningfields Rd NW4..46 B6
Sunninghill 3 W3.....111 A4
Sunninghill Gdns IG2...57 D4
Sunninghill Rd SE13...141 D3
Sunny Bank SE25.....206 A6
Sunny Cres NW10.....67 A1
Sunnycroft Rd
　Hounslow TW3.....129 D3
　Southall UB1......85 C2
　South Norwood SE25..206 A6
Sunnydale BR6.......226 C6
Sunnydale Gdns NW7..27 C4
Sunnydale Rd SE12...165 B6
Sunnydene Ave
　Chingford E4......36 B5
　Ruislip HA4.......62 A6
Sunnydene Gdns HA0..65 C2
Sunnydene St SE26...185 A6
Sunnyfield NW7......27 D6
Sunnyfields Prim Sch
　NW4...........46 B6
Sunny Gardens Par NW4.28 B1
Sunny Gardens Rd NW4.46 C6

Sunny Hill NW4.......46 B6
Sunnyhill Cl E5......75 A4
Sunny Hill Ct NW4....28 B1
Sunnyhill Prim Sch
　SW16...........182 B6
Sunnyhill Rd SW16...182 A6
Sunnyhurst Cl SM1....217 C5
Sunnymead Ave CR4..203 D6
Sunnymead Ct W5....109 D6
Sunnymead Rd
　Kingsbury NW9.....45 B2
　Putney SW15......156 B6
Sunnymede Ave KT19..215 C1
Sunnymede Dr IG6....56 D5
Sunny Nook Gdns CR2.221 B2
Sunny Pl NW4........46 C5
Sunny Rd The EN3......6 C1
Sunnyside
　4 Child's Hill NW2...69 B5
　Walton-on-T KT12..194 C4
　Wimbledon SW19...179 A4
Sunnyside Dr E4......20 A4
Sunnyside Ho 3 NW2..69 B5
Sunnyside Pl SW19...179 A4
Sunnyside Rd
　Crouch End N19....49 D2
　Ealing W5........109 D5
　Ilford IG1........79 B5
　Teddington TW11...174 B6
　Walthamstow E10...53 C1
Sunnyside Rd E N9....18 A1
Sunnyside Rd N N9....18 A1
Sunnyside Rd S N9....18 A1
Sunny View NW9......45 B4
Sunny Way N12.......30 C3
Sun Pas 8 SE16......118 A3
Sunray Ave BR2......210 B3
　Herne Hill SE5, SE24..139 B1
　Tolworth KT5......214 D6
Sun Rd W14...113 B1 254 C1
Sunrise Cl TW13......151 B1
Sunrise Sch N17......34 A4
Sunrise View NW7....27 D4
Sun St Pas EC2...95 C2 243 A3
Sunset Ave Chingford E4..19 D3
　Woodford IG8......36 D6
Sunset Ct 4 IG8......37 C3
Sunset Gdns SE25....183 D1
Sunset Ho 4 HA3.....42 C6
Sunset Rd Herne Hill SE5.139 B1
　SE28...........124 A5
　Wimbledon SW19...178 B5
Sunset View EN5.......1 A3
Sunshine Way CR4....180 D1
Sun St EC2......95 B2 242 D4
Sunwell Cl SE15......140 B4
Superior Dr 4 BR6....227 D2
Suraj Ho 6 N22......32 C1
SURBITON...........198 A2
Surbiton Boys Prep Sch 26
　KT6............198 A4
Surbiton Cres KT1, KT6..198 A5
　Surbiton Ct KT6.....197 D3
Surbiton Ct Mews KT6..197 D3
Surbiton Hall Cl KT1...198 A3
Surbiton High Sch Jun Girls
　Sch 3 KT1........198 A5
Surbiton High Senior Sch 4
　KT1............198 A5
Surbiton Hill Pk KT5..198 C5
Surbiton Hill Rd KT6..198 A4
Surbiton Hospl KT6...198 A3
Surbiton Par 11 KT6..198 A3
Surbiton Rd KT1.....198 A5
Surbiton Sta KT6.....198 A3
Surcot Ho 2 SW4.....137 D3
Surlingham Cl SE28...124 D6
Surma Cl E1.........96 A3
Surmans Ct RM9.....102 C6
Surrendale Pl W9.....91 C3
Surrey Canal Rd SE14,
　SE8............140 D6
Surrey Cl N3.........47 A6
Surrey Cres 1 W4.....110 C1
Surrey Ct 15 SM6.....219 B2
Surrey Docks Farm*
　SE16...........119 B4
Surrey Docks Watersports
　Ctr SE8..........119 B2
Surrey Gdns N4......51 A3
Surrey Gr Carshalton SM1.218 B5
　SE17...........263 A1
Surrey Ho Edgware HA8..26 B4
　8 Rotherhithe E6...118 D5
Surrey La SW11..136 C4 267 B1
Surrey Lo SW20......178 C1
Surrey Mews SE27...183 C6
Surrey Mount SE23...162 B3
Surrey Quays Rd SE16..118 D4
Surrey Quays Sh Ctr
　SE16...........118 D3
Surrey Quays Sta SE16..118 D2
Surrey Rd Barking IG11..79 C1
　Dagenham RM10...81 D3
　Harrow HA1.......42 A4
　Honor Oak SE15....162 D6
　West Wickham BR4..207 D1
Surrey Row SE1..116 D4 251 D2
Surrey Sq SE17...117 C1 263 B2

Surrey Square Inf Sch
　SE17.......117 C1 263 A2
Surrey Square Jun Sch
　SE17.......117 C1 263 A2
Surrey St Croydon CR0..221 A5
　4 Newham E13.....99 B4
　WC2........116 B6 250 D6
Surrey Terr SE17.....263 B2
Surrey Water Rd SE16.118 D5
Surrey Wharf SE1....140 A6
Surridge Ct 15 SW9...138 A3
Surridge Gdns SE19...183 B4
Surr St N7..........72 A3
Sury Basin KT2......176 A2
Susan Constant Ct 18
　E14............120 B6
Susan Lawrence Ho 4
　E12............78 C4
Susannah St E14......98 A1
Susan Rd SE3........143 B3
Susan Wood BR7.....188 C2
Sussex Ave TW7......130 C2
Sussex Cl
　New Malden KT3...199 C5
　Redbridge IG4......56 B4
　4 Twickenham TW1..153 B5
　Upper Holloway N19..72 A6
Sussex Cres UB5......63 C2
Sussex Ct
　4 Barnes SW13....133 D3
　Greenwich SE10....142 A6
　Mitcham CR4......204 A4
　Paddington W2.....236 C1
Sussex Gate N6......48 D4
Sussex Gdns
　Chessington KT9...213 D2
　Fortis Green N6....48 D4
　Harringay N4......51 A4
　Paddington W2..92 B1 236 D1
Sussex Ho Edgware HA8..26 B4
　Hampstead NW3....70 C2
　Richmond TW9.....132 B3
Sussex House Sch
　SW3...........114 D2 257 C4
Sussex Lo W2........236 D1
Sussex Mans
　South Kensington SW7..256 C3
　Strand WC2.......250 B6
Sussex Mews SE6.....163 C3
Sussex Mews E W2....236 D1
Sussex Mews W W2...246 D6
Sussex Pl
　22 Hammersmith W6..112 C1
　Lisson Gr NW1...92 D3 237 C6
　New Malden KT3...199 C5
　Paddington W2..92 B1 236 D1
Sussex Rd Barking E6..100 C6
　Erith DA8........147 D5
　Harrow HA1.......42 A4
　Mitcham CR4......204 A4
　New Malden KT3...199 C5
　Sidcup DA14......190 B5
　Southall UB2......106 D3
　South Croydon CR2..221 B2
　Uxbridge UB10.....61 A3
　Wallington SM5....218 D2
　2 West Wickham BR4.207 D1
Sussex Ring N12......29 C5
Sussex St Newham E13..99 B4
　SW1............258 D2
Sussex Way
　Cockfosters EN4....15 B6
　Upper Holloway N7..72 B5
　Upper Holloway N7, N19..72 A6
　Upper Holloway N19..49 D1
Sutcliffe Cl NW11....47 D4
Sutcliffe Ho UB3......84 A1
Sutcliffe Rd Bexley DA16.146 C3
　SE18...........145 C6
Sutherland Ave
　Ealing W13.......87 B1
　Falconwood DA16...145 C1
　Hayes UB3.......106 A2
　Orpington BR5.....211 D4
　Paddington W9..92 A3 236 A6
　Sunbury TW16.....171 D1
Sutherland Cl EN5......1 A1
Sutherland Ct
　Kingsbury NW9.....44 D4
　3 Paddington W9...91 C3
　Stoke Newington N16..73 B5
Sutherland Dr SW19...180 B2
Sutherland Gdns
　Mortlake SW14....133 C2
　North Cheam KT4...200 B1
　Sunbury TW16.....171 D1
Sutherland Gr
　Putney SW18, SW19..157 B4
　Teddington TW11...174 C5
Sutherland Ho
　Ealing W13.......109 A6
　Kensington W8.....255 C5
　7 Putney SW15....156 C4
　Richmond TW10....153 C2
　9 South Hampstead NW6..70 A2
Sutherland Pl W2.....91 C1
Sutherland Rd
　Belvedere DA17.....125 C3

Sutherland Rd continued
　Chiswick W4......133 C6
　Ealing W13........87 A1
　Edmonton N9......18 B3
　Enfield EN3.......18 D6
　Southall UB1......85 B1
　Thornton Heath CR0..204 C2
　Tottenham N17.....34 A2
　Walthamstow E17...53 A6
Sutherland Row SW1..258 D2
Sutherland Sq
　SE17.......117 A1 262 A1
Sutherland St
　SW1.........115 B1 258 D2
Sutherland Wlk SE17...262 B1
Sutlej Rd SE7.......143 C5
Sutterton St N7.......72 B2
SUTTON.............218 B1
Sutton Arena L Ctr SM5..202 B2
Sutton Cl
　Beckenham BR3....185 D2
　Pinner HA5.......40 A4
Sutton Coll of Learning for
　Adults 10 SM1.....217 D2
Sutton Common Rd
　Cheam SM3.......201 C1
　Sutton SM1, SM3...217 D6
Sutton Common Sta
　SM1............217 D6
Sutton Courtenay Ho
　SW17...........180 B6
Sutton Court Mans W4.133 A6
Sutton Court Rd
　Chiswick W4......133 A6
　Hillingdon UB10....82 D6
　Newham E13.......99 C4
　Sutton SM1.......218 A2
Sutton Cres EN5......12 C6
Sutton Ct Chiswick W4.133 A6
　Ealing W5........110 A5
　East Molesey KT8...195 B4
　8 Hackney E5......74 B4
　Penge SE19.......183 D3
　Sutton SM2.......218 A2
Sutton Dene TW3....129 D4
Sutton Est The 8 W10..90 C2
Sutton Gdns
　Barking IG11......101 C5
　Croydon CR0......205 D4
Sutton Gn IG11......101 C6
Sutton Gr SM1.......218 B3
Sutton Gram Sch For Boys 8
　SM1............218 A3
Sutton Hall Rd TW5...129 C5
Sutton High Sch SM1..217 D2
Sutton Ho N21.......16 B6
Sutton House* E9.....74 C3
Sutton Hts SM2......218 B1
Sutton La EC1.......241 B3
　Hounslow TW3, TW4, TW5..129 B3
Sutton La N W4......111 A1
Sutton La S W4......133 A6
Sutton Par NW4......46 C5
Sutton Park Rd SM1,
　SM2............217 D2
Sutton Pl E9........98 C6
Sutton Rd Barking IG11..101 C6
　E13............98 D3
　Heston TW5......129 C4
　Higham Hill E17....34 D2
　Muswell Hill N10....31 A2
Sutton Row W1......239 D2
Sutton Sq Hackney E9..74 C3
　Hounslow TW5.....129 B4
Sutton St E1........96 C1
Sutton Sta SM2......218 A2
Suttons Way EC1.....242 B1
Sutton Way
　Hounslow TW5.....129 B4
　North Kensington W10..90 C2
Sutton Wlk SE1...116 B5 250 D3
Swaby Rd SW17, SW18.158 A2
Swaffham Ct 1 RM6...58 C4
Swaffield Prim Sch
　SW18...........158 A4
Swaffield Rd SW18...158 A4
Swain Cl SW16......181 B4
Swain Ho CR4.......180 D3
Swain Rd CR7.......205 A4
Swains Cl UB7.......104 A4
Swain's La N6.......71 B6
Swainson Ho N7.....72 C4
Swainson Rd W3.....111 D4
Swains Rd CR4, SW17..180 D3
Swain St NW8....92 C3 237 A6
Swakeleys Dr UB10...60 C3
Swakeleys Rd UB10...60 C5
Swakeleys Rdbt UB8,
　UB10...........60 D5
Swakeleys Sch UB10..82 D5
Swaledale Cl N11.....31 A4
Swallands Rd SE6....163 C1
Swallowbrook Bsns Ctr
　UB4...........106 D5
Swallow Cl Bushey WD23..8 A3
　New Cross Gate SE14...140 D4
Swallow Ct Chingford IG8..36 B3
　Ilford IG2........56 D4
　4 Paddington W9...91 C2

Swallow Ct *continued*
5 Ruislip HA4 40 C1
1 SE12 165 A4
Swallow Dr Northolt UB5 85 C5
Willesden NW10 67 B2
Swallowfield NW1 231 D1
Swallowfield Rd SE7 121 B1
Swallowfield Way UB3 105 B4
Swallow Gdns SW16 181 D5
Swallow Ho Hornsey N8 50 B6
NW8 230 A4
Swallow Pk KT6 214 B5
Swallow Pl 24 Poplar E14 97 B1
W1 238 D1
Swallows Ct 5 SE20 184 D3
Swallow St Newham E6 100 A2
W1 115 C6 249 B5
Swaminarayan Sch The
NW10 67 B2
Swanage Ct 5 N1 73 C1
Swanage Ho SW8 270 C3
Swanage Rd Chingford E4 36 A3
Wandsworth SW18 158 A5
Swanage Waye UB4 84 C1
Swan And Pike Rd EN3 7 C5
Swan App E6 100 A2
Swanbourne SE17 262 A3
Swanbourne Ho NW8 237 A6
Swanbridge Rd DA7 147 C4
Swan Bsns Ctr 8 W4 111 B2
Swan Cl Croydon CR0 205 C2
Feltham TW13 173 A6
Higham Hill E17 35 A3
Swan Ct Chelsea SW3 257 B1
Parsons Green SW6 265 A3
Poplar E14 97 B1
Whetstone N20 14 A2
Swan Ctr SW17 158 A1
Swandon Way SW18 135 D1
Swan Dr NW9 27 C1
Swanfield St E2 95 D4
Swan Ho
De Beauvoir Town N1 73 B1
Enfield EN3 18 C6
Swan La EC4 117 B6 252 D5
Loughton IG10 21 C4
Whetstone N20 14 A1
Swan Lane Pier
EC4 117 B6 252 C5
Swanlea Sch E1 96 B3
Swanley Ho SE17 263 B2
Swanley Rd DA16 146 C4
Swan Mead SE1 117 C3 263 A5
Swan Mews
Stockwell SW9 138 B3
SW6 265 A2
Swanmore Ct SW18 158 A5
Swann Ct 8 TW7 131 A2
Swanne Ho 12 SE10 142 A5
Swan Pas 5 E1 118 A6
Swan Pl SW13 133 D3
Swan Rd Feltham TW13 173 A6
Greenwich SE18 121 D3
Rotherhithe SE16 118 C4
Southall UB1 85 D1
West Drayton UB7 104 A4
Swanscombe Ho 1 BR5 190 B1
11 Shepherd's Bush W11 112 D5
Swanscombe Point 7
E16 98 D2
Swanscombe Rd
5 Chiswick W4 111 C1
Shepherd's Bush W11 112 D5
Swansea Ct E16 122 D5
Swansea Rd Enfield EN3 6 C1
Harlington TW14, TW6 149 B5
Swansland Gdns 2 E17 35 A2
Swan St Isleworth TW7 131 B2
SE1 117 A4 252 B1
Swanston Ct TW1 152 D4
Swan The BR4 224 A6
Swanton Gdns SW19 156 D3
Swanton Rd DA8 147 D5
Swan Way EN3 6 D3
Swanwick Cl SW15 155 D4
Swan Wlk
Oatlands Pk TW17 193 C2
SW3 136 D6 267 C6
Swan Yd N1 72 D2
Swaton Rd E3 97 C3
Swaylands Rd DA17 147 C6
Swaythling Cl N18 34 B6
Swaythling Ho SW15 155 D5
Swedenborg Gdns E1 118 B6
Sweden Gate SE16 119 A2
Swedish Quays SE16 119 A3
Swedish Sch The SW13 134 A6
Sweeney Cres SE1 253 D1
Sweet Briar Gn N9 17 D1
Sweet Briar Gr N9 17 D1
Sweet Briar Wlk N18 33 D6
Sweetcroft La UB10 60 C1
Sweetmans Ave HA5 40 D6
Sweets Way N20 14 B2
Swell Ct E17 53 D3
Swetenham Wlk SE18 123 A1
Swete St E13 99 A5
Sweyn Pl SE3 143 A3
Swift Cl Harrow HA2 63 D6
Hayes UB3 83 D1

Swift Cl *continued*
Higham Hill E17 35 A3
Thamesmead SE28 124 B6
Swift Ct SM2 217 D1
Swift Ctr CR0 220 B1
Swift Ho 16 Stepney E1 96 C1
15 Stoke Newington N16 73 C5
1 SW9 138 C5
8 Wanstead E18 55 B6
Swift Rd Feltham TW13 173 A6
Southall UB2 107 B3
Swiftsden Way BR1 186 C4
Swift St SW6 135 B4 264 C2
Swinbrook Rd W10 91 A2
Swinburne Cres CR0 206 C3
Swinburne Ct 4 SE5 139 B1
Swinburne Ho 15 E2 96 C4
Swinburne Rd SW15 134 A1
Swinderby Rd HA0 66 A2
Swindon Cl IG3 57 C1
Swindon Rd TW6 149 A6
Swindon St W12 112 C5
Swinfield Cl TW13 173 A6
Swinford Gdns SW9 138 D2
Swingate La SE18 145 C5
Swingfield Ct BR2 209 D4
Swingfield Ho 4 E9 96 C6
Swinley Ho NW1 231 D2
Swinnerton St E9 75 A3
Swinson Ho 12 N11 31 C5
Swinton Cl HA9 44 D1
Swinton Ho 21 E2 96 A4
Swinton Pl WC1 233 C2
Swinton St WC1 94 B4 233 C2
Swires Shaw BR2 225 D4
Swiss Cottage NW3 70 B1
Swiss Cottage L Ctr NW3 70 B1
Swiss Cottage Sch
14 South Hampstead NW3 70 B1
St John's Wood
NW8 92 B6 229 D6
Swiss Cottage Sta NW3 70 B1
Swiss Ct SW1 249 D5
Swiss Re Building*
EC2 95 C1 243 B2
Swiss Terr 7 NW3 70 B1
Switch Ho 4 E14 120 B6
Swithland Gdns SE9 188 C6
Swyncombe Ave W5 109 B2
Swynford Gdns 7 NW4 46 A5
Sybil Elgar Sch UB2 107 B3
Sybil Mews N4 50 D3
Sybil Phoenix Cl SE8 118 D1
Sybil Thorndike Casson Ho
SW5 255 B1
Sybil Thorndike Ho 12
N1 73 A2
Sybourn Inf Sch E17 53 B2
Sybourn Inf Sch (Annexe)
E10 53 A1
Sybourn St E17 53 B2
Sycamore Ave DA15 167 D5
Ealing W5 109 D3
East Finchley N3 47 D6
Hayes UB3 105 C6
Old Ford E3 97 B6
Sycamore Cl
Carshalton SM5 218 D4
Chislehurst SE9 166 A2
East Acton W3 111 C5
2 Edgware HA8 27 A6
Edmonton N9 34 A6
Feltham TW13 150 A1
New Barnet EN4 14 B5
Newham E16 98 C3
Northolt UB5 85 A6
South Croydon CR2 221 C3
Yiewsley UB7 104 B6
Sycamore Ct
4 Beckenham BR3 185 C2
Forest Gate E7 77 A2
8 Forest Hill SE26 184 C6
Golders Green NW11 47 A3
Hendon NW4 28 C1
Hillingdon UB8 82 C3
Hounslow TW4 129 A1
Kilburn NW6 91 C6
Surbiton KT6 198 A2
Tufnell Pk N19 71 D5
10 West Norwood SW16 182 C5
Sycamore Gdns
Hammersmith W6, W12 112 B3
Mitcham CR4 180 B1
Tottenham N15 51 D5
Sycamore Gr
Kingsbury NW9 45 A2
Kingston u T KT3 199 C6
Lewisham SE6 164 A5
Penge SE20 184 A2
Sycamore Hill N11 31 A4
Sycamore Ho
4 Buckhurst Hill IG9 21 D2
23 Finchley N2 30 B1
10 Maitland Pk NW3 70 D2
Penge SE20 184 D4
17 Rotherhithe SE16 118 D4
3 Shepherd's Bush W6 112 B4
2 Stoke Newington N16 73 B6
Teddington TW11 175 C3
Twickenham TW1 152 D2

Sycamore Lo
7 Ashford TW16 171 D3
Putney SW15 134 B2
Sycamore Lodge HA2 64 B6
Sycamore Mews 4
SW4 137 C2
Sycamore Rd SW19,
SW20 178 C4
Sycamore St EC1 242 A5
Sycamore Way TW11 175 C4
Sycamore Wlk Ilford IG6 57 A5
1 Kensal Town W10 91 A3
Sydcote SE21 161 A3
Sydenham Ave
Penge SE26 184 B5
Southgate N21 16 B6
Sydenham Girls Sch
SE26 162 B1
Sydenham High Sch Jun
Dept SE26 184 B6
Sydenham High Sch (Sec) 13
SE26 184 B5
Sydenham Hill SE21, SE22, SE23,
SE26, SE19 162 A1
Sydenham Hill Sta SE21 161 D1
Sydenham Hill Wood Nature
Reserve SE26 162 A1
Sydenham Ho 16 KT6 197 D2
Sydenham Ind Est SE26 185 B5
Sydenham Park Mans 2
SE26 162 C1
Sydenham Park Rd SE23,
SE26 162 C1
Sydenham Pk SE26 162 C1
Sydenham Rd
Forest Hill SE26 185 A6
Thornton Heath CR0 205 B2
Sydenham Rise SE23 162 B2
Sydenham Sta SE26 184 C6
Sydenham Station App 4
SE26 184 C6
Sydmons Ct SE23 162 C4
Sydner Mews N16 73 D4
Sydner Rd N16 73 D4
Sydney Chapman Way EN5 1 B3
Sydney Cl SW3 256 D3
Sydney Cotts KT10 212 D2
Sydney Cres TW15 170 D4
Sydney Ct Hayes UB4 84 C3
Surbiton KT6 214 A6
Sydney Gr NW4 46 C4
Sydney Ho
4 Chiswick W4 111 C2
Muswell Hill N10 31 B3
Sydney Mews SW3 256 D3
Sydney Pl SW7 257 A3
Sydney Rd
Abbey Wood SE2 124 D3
Bexley DA6 146 D1
Ealing W13 109 A4
East Bedfont TW14 150 A3
Hornsey N8 50 C5
Muswell Hill N10 31 B3
Richmond TW10, TW9 132 A1
Sidcup DA14 189 C6
Sutton SM1 217 C4
Teddington TW11 174 D5
Wanstead E11 55 B3
West Barnes SW20 178 D1
Woodford IG8 37 A6
Sydney Russell Sch The
RM9 80 D3
Sydney St SW3 114 C1 257 A2
Sydney Terr KT10 212 D2
Sylva Cotts 3 SE8 141 C4
Sylva Ct 3 SW15 156 D4
Sylvana Cl UB10 82 B6
Sylvan Ave Church End N3 29 C1
Dagenham RM6 59 B3
Edgware NW7 27 D4
Wood Green N22 32 C3
Sylvan Ct Finchley N12 29 D6
1 Kilburn NW6 91 D6
South Croydon CR2 221 A2
Sylvan Gdns KT6 197 D2
Sylvan Gr Hampstead NW2 68 D4
SE15 140 B6
Sylvan Hill SE19 183 C2
Sylvan Ho N21 16 B6
Sylvan Rd Ilford IG1 79 A6
South Norwood SE19 183 D2
Upton E7 77 B2
Walthamstow E17 53 C4
Wanstead E11 55 A4
Sylvan Way
Coney Hall BR4 224 C4
Dagenham RM8 80 B5
Sylvan Wlk BR1 210 B6
Sylverdale Rd CR0 220 D5
Sylvester Ave BR7 188 B4
Sylvester Ct HA0 65 D3
Sylvester Ho 7 E8 74 B2
Sylvester Path 8 E8 74 B2
Sylvester Rd Finchley N2 30 B1
Hackney E8 74 B2
Walthamstow E17 53 B2
Wembley HA0 65 C3
Sylvestrus Cl KT1 176 C1
Sylvia Ave HA5 23 B4
Sylvia Ct N1 235 C3

Sylvia Ct *continued*
Wembley HA9 66 D1
Sylvia Gdns HA9 66 D1
Sylvia Lawla Ct N22 32 B1
Sylvia Pankhurst Ho
10 Dagenham RM10 81 C5
14 Globe Town E2 96 D4
Sylvia Young Theatre Sch
NW1 92 C3 237 B5
Symes Mews NW1 232 A4
Symington Ho SE1 262 C5
Symington Mews E9 74 D3
Symister Mews N1 95 C4
25 Shoreditch N1 95 C4
Symons Cl 6 SE15 140 C3
Symons St SW3 114 D2 257 D3
Symphony Cl HA8 26 D3
Symphony Mews 15 W10 91 A4
Syon Gate Way TW7,
TW8 131 B5
Syon Ho & Pk* TW8 131 C4
Syon La
Brentford TW7, TW8 131 B5
Hounslow TW7 130 D6
Syon Lane Sta TW7 131 A5
Syon Lo 6 SE12 165 A4
Syon Park Cotts TW8 131 C4
Syon Park Gdns TW7 130 D5
Syracuse Univ
W11 113 B6 244 C5
Syringa Ho SE4 141 B2

T

Tabard Ct 6 E14 98 A1
Tabard Ho SE1 262 D6
Teddington KT1 175 C2
Tabard St SE1 117 B3 262 C6
Tabernacle Ave 7 E13 99 A3
Tabernacle St EC2 95 B3 242 D6
Tableer Ave SW4 159 D6
Tabley Rd N7 72 A4
Tabor Ct 3 SM3 217 A2
Tabor Gdns SM2, SM3 217 B1
Tabor Gr SW19 179 B3
Tabor Rd W6 112 B3
Tachbrook Est
SW1 115 D1 259 D1
Tachbrook Mews SW1 259 A4
Tachbrook Rd
East Bedfont TW14 149 D4
Southall UB2 106 D2
Tachbrook St
SW1 115 C2 259 B3
Tack Mews SE4 141 C2
Tadbourne Ct 1 HA8 27 A3
Tadema Ho NW8 236 D5
Tadema Rd
SW10 136 A5 266 B3
Tadlow KT1 198 C6
Tadmor Cl TW16 193 D5
Tadmor St W12 112 D5
Tadworth Ave KT3 199 D4
Tadworth Ct 5 N11 31 A4
Tadworth Ho SE1 251 C1
Tadworth Rd NW2 68 A6
Taeping St E14 119 D2
Taffrail Ho 2 E14 119 D1
Taffy's How CR4 202 C6
Taft Way 44 E3 97 D4
Taggs Ho KT1 175 D1
Tailors Ct 9 SW16 181 C6
Tailworth St 16 E1 96 A2
Tait 7 NW9 27 D3
Tait Ct 16 Old Ford E3 97 B6
SW8 269 D2
Tait Ho SE1 251 B3
2 Tufnell Pk N19 71 C4
Tait Rd CR0 205 C2
Tait Rd Ind Est CR0 205 C2
Takhar Mews SW11 136 C3
Talacre Com Sp Ctr NW5 71 B2
Talacre Rd NW5 71 A2
Talbot Ave N2 48 B6
Talbot Cl N15 51 D5
Talbot Cres NW4 46 A4
Talbot Ct EC3 252 D6
Neasden NW9 67 B5
Talbot Gdns IG3 80 A6
Talbot Grove Ho 10 W11 91 A1
Talbot Ho Highbury N7 72 C5
Poplar E14 97 D1
Talbot Pl SE3 142 C3
Talbot Rd Ashford TW15 170 A5
Camberwell SE22 139 C1
Dagenham RM9 81 B1
Ealing W13 109 A5
Forest Gate E7 77 A4
Harrow HA3 24 D1
Highgate N6 49 A3
Isleworth TW1, TW7 131 A1
Notting Hill W2 91 C1
Notting Hill W11 91 B1
Southall UB2 107 A2
South Norwood CR7 205 B5
Tottenham N15 51 D5
Twickenham TW2 152 D3
Wallend E6 100 C5
Wallington SM5 219 A3

Talbot Rd *continued*
Wembley HA0 65 D2
Wood Green N22 31 C2
Talbot Sq W2 92 B1 236 C1
Talbot Wlk
Notting Hill W11 91 A1
Willesden NW10 67 C2
Talbot Yd SE1 252 C3
Talcott Path 12 SW2 160 C3
Talehangers Cl DA6 146 D1
Talfourd Pl SE15 139 D4
Talfourd Rd SE15 139 D4
Talgarth Rd
Hammersmith W6 112 C1
W14 113 A1 254 B2
Talgarth Wlk NW9 45 C4
Talia Ho E14 120 A3
Talisman Cl 2 IG3 58 B1
Talisman Sq SE26 184 A6
Talisman Way HA9 66 B5
Tallack Cl HA3 24 C3
Tallack Rd E10 53 B1
Tall Elms Cl BR2 208 D4
Talleyrand Ho SE5 139 A3
Tallis Cl E16 99 B1
Tallis Gr SE7 143 B6
Tallis St EC4 251 B6
Tallis View NW10 67 B2
Tallow Cl RM9 81 A2
Tallow Rd TW8 131 C5
Tall Trees SW16 204 B6
Talma Gdns TW2 152 C4
Talmage Cl SE23 162 C4
Talman Gr HA7 25 D4
Talma Rd SW2 138 C1
Talmud Torah Machzikei
Hadass Sch E5 52 A2
Talmud Torah Tiferes
Shlomo 1 NW11 47 A2
Talmud-Torah Yetev-Lev 6
N16 52 A1
Talwin St E3 97 D4
Tamar Cl 24 E3 97 B6
Tamar Ho
10 Cubitt Town E14 120 A4
SE11 261 B2
Tamarind Ct 8 W3 89 A1
Tamarind Ho 4 SE15 140 A5
Tamarind Yd 5 E1 118 A5
Tamarisk Sq W12 111 D6
Tamar Sq IG8 37 B4
Tamar St SE7 122 A2
Tamar Way N17 52 A6
Tame Ho 3 UB5 85 B4
Tamesa Ho TW17 192 C2
Tamesis Gdns KT4 215 C6
Tamian Ind Est TW4 128 C1
Tamian Way TW4 128 C1
Tamil Ho SE6 163 C2
Tamworth N7 72 A2
Tamworth Ave IG8 36 C4
Tamworth La CR4 203 B6
Tamworth Pk CR4 203 B6
Tamworth Pl 3 CR0 221 A6
Tamworth Rd CR0 221 A6
Tamworth St
SW6 135 C6 265 A5
Tancred Rd N4 50 D3
Tandem Ctr SW19 180 B2
Tandridge Ct SM2 217 D2
Tandridge Dr BR6 211 B1
Tandridge Pl 2 BR6 211 B1
Tanfield Ave NW2 67 D5
Tanfield Rd CR0 221 A4
Tangier Rd TW10 132 D2
Tangleberry Cl BR1 210 B5
Tangle Tree Cl N3 29 D1
Tanglewood Cl
Hillingdon UB10 82 C3
South Croydon CR0 222 C5
Stanmore HA7 8 C2
Tanglewood Lo HA8 27 A4
Tanglewood Way TW13 150 B1
Tangley Gr SW15 155 D4
Tangley Park Rd TW12 173 B4
Tanglyn Ave TW17 192 D4
Tangmere Tottenham N17 33 B1
WC1 233 C1
Tangmere Gdns UB5 84 C5
Tangmere Gr KT2 175 D5
Tangmere Way NW9 27 C1
Tanhurst Ho 27 SW2 160 A4
Tanhurst Wlk SE2 124 D3
Tankerton Rd KT6 214 B6
Tankerton St WC1 233 B1
Tankerton Terr CR0 204 B3
Tankerville Rd SW16 182 A3
Tankridge Rd NW2 68 B6
Tanner Ho
1 Merton SW19 180 A2
SE1 253 B1
Tanner Point 3 E13 99 A6
Tanners Cl KT12 194 B3
Tanners End La N18 33 C5
Tanner's Hill SE8 141 C4
Tanners La IG6 57 A6
Tanners Mews SE8 141 B4

Tanner St Barking IG11......79 A2
SE1................117 C4 253 B1
Tanners Yd 33 E2.........96 B5
Tannery Cl
  Beckenham BR3, CR0...206 D4
  Dagenham RM10.........81 D5
Tannery Ho 22 E1.........96 A2
Tannington Terr N5.......72 C5
Tannsfeld Rd SE26......184 D5
Tansley Cl N7.............71 D3
Tanswell St SE1.........251 A1
Tantallon Rd SW12......159 A3
Tant Ave E16.............98 D1
Tanworth Gdns HA5.....22 C1
Tanyard Ho 8 TW8.......131 C5
Tan Yard La DA5.........169 C4
Tanza Rd NW3............70 D4
Tapestry Cl SM2.........217 D1
Tapley Ho 11 SE1.......118 A4
Taplow NW3..............70 B1
Taplow Ct CR4..........202 C5
Taplow Ho 38 E2.........95 D4
Taplow Rd N13............33 A6
Taplow St N1......95 A5 235 B3
Tappesfield Rd SE15...140 C2
Tapping Cl 5 KT2.......176 C3
Tapp St E1................96 B3
Tapster St EN5............1 B2
Tara Ct 4 BR3...........185 D1
Tara Mews N8.............50 A3
Taranto Ho 14 E1.........96 D2
Tarati Ct HA0.............65 D1
Tarbert Rd SE22........161 C6
Tarbert Wlk E1..........118 C6
Target Cl TW14.........149 C5
Target Ho W13..........109 B5
Target Rdbt UB5.........85 B6
Tariff Rd N17............34 A4
Tarleton Ct 2 N22.......32 C1
Tarleton Gdns SE23....162 B3
Tarling Cl DA14........168 B1
Tarling Rd
  Canning Town E16.......98 D1
  Finchley N2.............30 A1
Tarling St E1.............96 C1
Tarnbank EN2............16 A6
Tarnbrook Ct SW1......258 A3
Tarn St SE1......117 A3 262 A5
Tarns The NW1.........232 A2
Tarnwood Pk SE9......166 B3
Tarplett Ho 22 SE14...140 D6
Tarquin Ho SE26.......184 A6
Tarragon Cl SE14......141 A5
Tarragon Gr SE26......184 D4
Tarranbrae NW6.........69 A1
Tarrant Ho E2............96 C4
Tarrant Pl W1..........237 C3
Tarrantt Ho W14.......254 A6
Tarriff Cres SE8........119 B2
Tarrington Cl SW16....159 D1
Tartan Ho 12 E14.......98 A1
Tarver Rd SE17...116 D1 261 D2
Tarves Way SE10......141 D5
Tashbar of Edgware Prim
  Sch HA8...............26 C6
Tash Pl N11..............31 B5
Tasker Cl UB7..........127 A5
Tasker Ho
  3 Barking IG11.......101 B5
  17 Poplar E14.........97 B2
Tasker Lo W8...........245 A2
Tasker Rd NW3...........70 D3
Tasman Ct Ashford TW16..171 C3
  9 Cubitt Town E14....119 D2
Tasman Ho 17 E1......118 B5
Tasmania Terr N18......33 A4
Tasman Rd SW9........138 A2
Tasman Wlk E16........99 D1
Tasso Rd W6.....135 A6 264 A6
Tasso Yd W6............264 A5
Tatam Rd NW10..........67 B1
Tatchbury Ho SW15...155 D5
Tate Britain ★
  SW1..............116 A2 260 A3
Tate Gdns WD23.........8 C4
Tate Ho 13 E2............96 D5
Tate Modern ★
  EC4.............116 D5 251 D4
  Sutton SM1...........217 C3
Tatham Pl NW8....92 B5 229 D4
Tatnell Rd SE23........163 A5
Tattersall Cl SE9......166 A6
Tatton Cres E5, N16.....51 D2
Tatum St SE17....117 B2 262 D3
Tauheed Cl N4...........73 A6
Taunton Ave
  Hounslow TW3........130 A3
  Wimbledon SW20......178 B1
Taunton Cl SM3.........201 C1
Taunton Dr Enfield EN2...4 C2
  Finchley N2............30 A1
Taunton Ho W2.........236 A1
Taunton Mews NW1....237 C5
Taunton Pl NW1...92 D3 237 C6

Taunton Rd
  Greenford UB6.........85 D6
  Lewisham SE12.......164 D6
Taunton Way HA7........26 A1
Tavern Cl SM5..........202 C2
Tavern Ct SE1..........262 B5
Taverner Ho N16.........73 B5
Taverners Cl W11......244 A3
Taverners Ct HA9.......66 B6
Taverners Lo E14........15 A6
Taverner Sq 4 N5.......73 A4
Taverners Way E4.......20 C3
Tavern La SW9..........138 C3
Tavistock Ave
  Mill Hill NW7...........28 D3
  Walthamstow E17.......53 A6
  Wembley UB6...........87 A5
Tavistock Cl
  Mitcham CR4..........204 A5
  Notting Hill W11........91 B2
Tavistock Ct
  1 Croydon CR0........205 B1
  WC1..................239 C6
Tavistock Gdns IG3......79 C4
Tavistock Gr CR0.......205 B2
Tavistock Ho 3 W11....91 B1
Tavistock Mews 3 W11..91 B1
Tavistock Pl
  Bloomsbury WC1...94 A3 240 A6
  East Barnet N14........15 B5
Tavistock Rd
  4 Beckenham BR2....208 D5
  Carshalton SM5......202 B1
  Croydon CR0..........205 B1
  DA16................146 C4
  Dagenham NW10........89 D5
  Edgware HA8...........26 C2
  Leyton E7.............76 D4
  Notting Hill W11........91 B2
  Stratford E15..........76 D2
  Tottenham N4, N15......51 B3
  Uxbridge UB10.........61 A3
  Wanstead E18..........55 A6
Tavistock Sq WC1..93 D3 239 D6
Tavistock St
  WC2..............116 A6 250 B6
Tavistock Terr N19......71 D5
Tavistock Twr SE16....119 A3
Tavistock Wlk SM5.....202 B1
Taviton St WC1...93 D3 239 C6
Tavy Bridge SE2.......124 C4
Tavy Cl SE11..........261 B2
Tawhid Boys Sch N16...73 D6
Tawney Rd SE28.......124 B6
Tawny Cl Ealing W13...109 B5
  Feltham TW13.........150 A1
Tawny Way SE16.......118 D2
Tayben Ave TW2.......152 C5
Taybridge Rd SW11....137 A1
Tayburn Cl E14..........98 A1
Tayfield Cl UB10.........61 A5
Tay Ho 10 E3.............97 B5
Tayler Ave TW9........132 D3
Taylor Ct Deptford SE8..141 B6
  Hampton TW12.........174 A5
  Hounslow TW3........130 A4
  3 Orpington BR6......227 D4
  Tottenham N17.........34 A3
Taylor Ho
  Carshalton SM5.......218 C6
  10 Streatham SW2....160 C3
Taylor Rd Mitcham CR4..180 C3
  Wallington SM6.......219 B3
Taylor's Bldgs SE18...122 D2
Taylors Ct DA14.......167 D1
Taylors Ct TW13.......150 A2
Taylor's Gn W3..........89 C1
Taylor's La Barnet EN5...1 B4
  Forest Hill SE26......184 B6
  Willesden NW10........67 C1
Taylorsmead NW7.......28 A5
Taymount Grange 2
  SE23................162 C2
Taymount Ri SE23.....162 B2
Taymount Rise SE23...162 C2
Tayport Cl N1............72 A1
Tayside Ct 6 SE5.......139 B1
Tayside Dr HA8..........10 C2
Taywood Rd UB5.........85 B3
Tayyibah Girls Sch 5 E5..52 B1
Teak Cl SE16..........119 A5
Tealby Ct N7.............72 B2
Teal Cl Enfield EN3.......6 C1
  Newham E16...........99 D2
Teal Ct 30 SE8.........141 B6
  Wallington SM6.......219 C3
  Willesden NW10........67 B2
Teale St E2..............96 A4
Tealing Dr KT19.......215 B4
Teal Pl SM1............217 B3
Teal St 1 SE10.........120 D3
Teasel Cl CR0..........206 D1
Teasel Cres SE28......123 C5
Teasel Way E15..........98 C4
Teather St 12 SE5.....139 C5
Tebbs Ho 14 SW2......160 C4

Tebworth Rd N17.........33 D3
Technology Pk NW9......45 C6
Teck Cl TW7............131 A3
Tedder 5 NW9............27 D3
Tedder Cl
  Chessington KT9......213 C3
  Hillingdon UB10........60 B1
  Ruislip HA4.............62 B3
Tedder Rd CR2.........222 D1
TEDDINGTON...........175 C5
Teddington Bsns Pk
  TW11.................174 D4
Teddington Meml Hospl
  TW11.................174 C4
Teddington Park Rd
  TW11.................174 D6
Teddington Pk TW11...174 D5
Teddington Sch TW11..175 C4
Teddington Sta TW11...175 A4
Ted Hennem Ho RM10...81 D5
Tedman Ct SE13........142 A1
Ted Roberts Ho 25 E2...96 B5
Tedworth Gdns SW3....257 C1
Tedworth Sq
  SW3..........114 D1 257 C1
Tees Ave UB6............86 D5
Tees Ct W7..............86 B1
Teesdale Ave TW7......131 A4
Teesdale Cl E2...........96 B5
Teesdale Gdns
  Isleworth TW7........131 A4
  South Norwood SE25..183 C1
Teesdale Rd E11.........54 D2
Teesdale St E2...........96 B5
Teesdale Yd 34 E2.......96 B5
Teeswater Ct DA18.....124 D3
Tee The W3..............89 C1
Teevan Cl CR0..........206 A2
Teevan Rd CR0.........206 A2
Tegan Cl SM2..........217 C1
Teign Mews SE9........166 A2
Teignmouth Cl
  6 Clapham SW4.......137 D1
  Edgware HA8...........26 B1
Teignmouth Gdns UB6...87 A4
Teignmouth Par UB6....87 B5
Teignmouth Rd
  Bexley DA16..........146 C3
  Brondesbury NW2......68 D2
Tejas Ct W3.............47 A5
Tej Ct E7................77 D3
Telcote Way HA4.......40 C2
Telegraph Hill NW3......69 D5
Telegraph La KT10.....212 D3
Telegraph Mews IG3.....58 A1
Telegraph Pl E14......119 D2
Telegraph Rd SW15....156 C4
Telegraph St EC2......242 C2
Telemann Sq SE3......143 B2
Telephone Pl SW6.....264 D6
Teign Mews SE9........166 A2
Telfer Cl 4 W3..........111 A4
Telfer Ho
  8 Dulwich SE21......183 C6
  EC1..................234 D1
Telferscot Prim Sch 5
  SW12................159 D3
Telferscot Rd SW12...159 D3
Telford Ave SW12, SW2..160 A3
Telford Avenue Mans 7
  SW2.................160 A3
Telford Cl Penge SE19..183 D4
  Walthamstow E17......53 A2
Telford Ct EN5...........13 C6
Telford Dr KT12........194 C2
Telford Ho
  2 Belvedere DA17....125 C3
  6 Kensal Town W10....91 A2
  SE1..................262 A6
Telford Parade Mans 8
  SW2.................160 A3
Telford Rd
  3 Hendon NW9........46 A3
  Kensal Town W10......91 A2
  Sidcup SE9...........167 B2
  Southall UB1...........85 D1
  Twickenham TW4.....151 C4
Telford Rd (North Circular
  Rd) N11...............31 C5
Telford's Yd 21 SE1....118 A6
Telford Terr SW1.......269 A6
Telford Way
  Dagenham W3.........89 C2
  Hayes UB4.............85 A2
Telham Rd E6...........100 C5
Tell Gr SE22............139 D1
Tellson Ave SE18......144 A4
Telscombe Cl BR6.....227 C6
Telscombe Ho SW11....268 A1
Temair Ho 1 SE10.....142 A5
Temeraire Pl TW8......110 B1
Temeraire St SE16.....118 C4
Tempelhof Ave NW2.....46 C2
Temperley Rd SW12...159 A4
Templar Ct RM7.........59 D5
Templar Dr SE28.......102 D1
Templar Ho
  Hampstead NW2.......69 B2
  7 Upper Clapton E5...74 C6
Templars Ave NW11.....47 B3

Templars Cres N3........29 C1
Templars Dr HA3.........24 B4
Templar St SE5.........138 D3
Temple Ave Croydon CR0..223 B5
  Dagenham RM8.........59 C1
  EC4..........116 C6 251 B6
  Oakleigh Pk N20.......14 B4
Temple Bar ★ EC4....241 D1
Temple Cl Finchley N3...29 B1
  Leytonstone E11........54 C2
  Woolwich SE18.......123 A3
Templecombe 8 E9.....96 C6
Templecombe Way SM4..201 A4
Templecroft TW15.....171 B4
Temple Ct Stepney E1...96 D2
  SW8.................270 A3
Templedene BR2......186 B1
Temple Dwellings 7 E2..96 B5
TEMPLE FORTUNE........47 A4
Temple Fortune Ct 9
  NW11................47 B4
Temple Fortune Hill
  NW11................47 C4
Temple Fortune Ho 3
  NW11................47 B4
Temple Fortune La NW11..47 C3
Temple Fortune Par 5
  NW11................47 B4
Temple Gdns
  Dagenham RM8.........80 D5
  Edmonton N21.........16 D2
  Temple Fortune NW11...47 B3
  Golders Green NW11....47 C3
Temple Gr Enfield EN2...4 D2
  Golders Green NW11....47 C3
Temple Gr Hatcham Sch
  SE14................141 A3
Temple Hall Ct E4.......20 B2
Temple Ho
  13 Battersea SW11...136 C2
  4 Tufnell Pk N7.......71 C5
  11 Walthamstow E17...53 D6
Temple La EC4.....94 C1 241 B1
Temple Lo E5...........74 C6
Temple Mead NW1......86 D2
Templemead Cl W3......89 C1
Temple Mead Cl HA7....25 B4
Templemead Ho E9......75 A4
TEMPLE MILLS...........75 D3
Temple Mills La
  London E10, E15........76 A4
  Stratford E15..........75 D4
Temple Mills Rd E9......75 C4
Templemore DA14.....190 B5
Temple Par EN5.........14 B4
Temple Pk UB8..........82 C4
Temple Pl WC2....116 B6 250 D6
Temple Rd
  Acton Green W4.......111 A3
  Cricklewood NW2......68 C5
  Croydon CR0..........221 B4
  Ealing W5.............109 D3
  Hornsey N8............50 B5
  Isleworth TW3........130 A1
  Newham E6...........100 A6
  Richmond TW9.........132 B2
Temple Sheen SW14...155 A6
Temple Sheen Rd SW14..133 A1
Temple St E2............96 B5
Temple Sta WC2..116 C6 251 A6
Temple Terr N22.........32 C1
Templeton Ave E4.......35 D6
Templeton Cl
  South Norwood SE19..183 B2
  25 Stoke Newington N16..73 C3
Templeton Ct Enfield EN3..6 C5
  Walthamstow E10.......53 D1
Templeton Pl
  SW5............113 C2 255 B3
Templeton Rd N4, N15...51 B3
Temple Way SM1.......218 B5
Temple West Mews
  SE11................261 C5
Templewood W13.......87 B2
Templewood Ave NW3...69 D5
Templewood Gdns NW3..69 D5
Templewood Point NW2..69 B6
Tempsford Cl EN2........5 A2
Tempsford Ct HA1........42 D3
Temsford HA2...........24 A1
Ten Acre Wood Nature
  Reserve UB4............83 D6
Tenbury Cl E7............77 D3
Tenbury Ct SW12......159 D3
Tenby Ave HA3...........25 B1
Tenby Cl Dagenham RM6..59 A3
  Tottenham N15.........51 D5
Tenby Ct E17............53 A4
Tenby Gdns UB5.........63 C2
Tenby Ho Hayes UB3...105 A3
  Islington N7............72 C4
  W2..................236 A1
Tenby Rd DA16.........146 D4
  Dagenham RM6.........59 A3
  Edgware HA8...........26 B1
  Enfield EN3..............6 C1
  Walthamstow E17.......53 A4
Tench St E1............118 B5
Tenda Rd SE16.........118 B2
Tendring Ho SW2......160 C5
Tendring Way RM6......58 C4

Tenham Ave SW2.......159 D2
Tenison Ct W1.........249 A6
Tenison Way SE1......251 A3
Tenniel Cl W2..........245 D6
Tennison Ave WD6.......10 C6
Tennison Rd SE25......205 D4
Tennis St SE1.....117 B4 252 C2
Tenniswood Rd EN1......5 C4
Tennyson Ave
  Kingsbury NW9.........45 A6
  Plashet E12............78 A1
  Twickenham TW1.....152 D3
  Wanstead E11..........55 A2
  West Barnes KT3.....200 B4
Tennyson Ct DA16......145 C4
  Enfield EN3.............18 D6
  Feltham TW14........150 A5
Tennyson Ct 3 TW10...175 D6
Tennyson Ho
  2 Erith DA17.........125 B1
  SE17................262 B2
  Southall UB1...........85 C1
Tennyson Rd
  Ashford TW15.........170 A5
  Ealing W7............108 D6
  Hounslow TW3........130 A3
  Kilburn NW6...........91 B6
  Leyton E10............75 D6
  Mill Hill NW7...........28 A5
  Penge SE20...........184 D3
  Stratford E15..........76 C1
  Walthamstow E17.......53 B3
  Wimbledon SW19......180 A4
Tennyson St SW8......137 B3
Tensing Ct TW19.......148 A3
Tensing Ho N1............72 D2
Tensing Rd UB2........107 C3
Tentelow La UB2.......107 C3
Tenterden Cl
  Hendon NW4............46 D6
  SE9..................188 B6
Tenterden Dr NW4.......46 D6
Tenterden Gdns
  Croydon CR0..........206 A2
  Hendon NW4............46 D6
Tenterden Gr NW4.......46 D6
Tenterden Ho SE17....263 B2
Tenterden Rd
  Croydon CR0..........206 A2
  Dagenham RM8.........81 B6
  Tottenham N17.........33 D3
Tenterden St W1.......238 D1
Tenter Ground E1......243 C3
Tent Peg La BR5........211 A4
Tent St E1...............96 B3
Tenzing Ct 4 SE9......166 A2
Terborch Way 6 SE22..161 C6
Tercelet Terr NW3.......70 A4
Teredo St SE16........118 D3
Terence Ct 6 DA17....147 B6
Teresa Mews E17.......53 C5
Teresa Wlk N10.........49 B4
Terling Cl E11...........76 D5
Terling Ho 9 W10.......90 C2
Terling Rd RM8..........81 C6
Terling Wlk N1.........235 A6
Terminal Four Rdbt
  TW6.................149 A5
Terminus Pl SW1......258 D5
Tern Ho 9 SE15........139 D4
Terrace Gdns SW13...133 D3
Terrace Ho 2 N20.......14 A1
Terrace La TW10......154 A5
Terrace Rd Hackney E9..74 C1
  Newham E13............99 B6
  Walton-on-T KT12....194 B3
Terraces The 6 SW20..178 D3
Terrace The
  Barnes SW13, SW14...133 C3
  Chingford E4...........20 C1
  Cranley Gdns N2........49 A5
  EC4..................241 B1
  Kilburn NW6...........91 C6
  10 Rotherhithe SE8...119 B2
  1 Woodford IG8........37 A4
Terrace Wlk RM9.........81 A3
Terral Apartments 7
  N17..................51 D6
Terrano Ho 1 TW9.....132 D4
Terrapin Ct SW17......159 B1
Terrapin Rd SW17.....159 B1
Terrapins KT6.........197 D2
Terrence McMillan Stad
  E13..................99 C3
Terrick Rd N22..........32 A2
Terrick St W12..........90 B1
Terrilands HA5...........41 B6
Territorial Ho SE11....261 B3
Terront Rd N15..........51 A5
Terry Ct 8 SM6........219 C2
Terry Ho SW2..........160 C3
Terry Lodge 2 CR7....204 C4
Tersha St TW9.........132 B1
Tessa Sanderson Pl 6
  SW8.................137 B2
Tessa Sanderson Way
  UB6..................64 B3
Testerton Wlk 3 W11..112 D6
Testwood Ct W7.......108 C5

Tet–Tho 411

Tetcott Rd SW10 . . 136 A5 266 A3
Tetherdown N10 . . 49 A6
Tetherdown Prim Sch N10 . . 49 A5
Tetty Way BR1, BR2 . . 187 A1
Teversham La SW8 . . 138 A4 270 B2
Teviot Cl DA16 . . 146 B4
Teviot St E14 . . 98 A2
Tewkesbury Ave
Forest Hill SE23 . . 162 B4
Pinner HA5 . . 41 A4
Tewkesbury Cl Barnet EN4 . . 2 B1
Tottenham N15 . . 51 B3
Tewkesbury Ct N11 . . 31 D4
Tewkesbury Gdns NW9 . . 44 D6
Tewkesbury Rd
Carshalton SM5 . . 202 B1
Ealing W13 . . 109 A6
Tottenham N15 . . 51 B3
Tewkesbury Terr N11 . . 31 D4
Tewson Rd SE18 . . 123 C1
Teyham Ct 2 SW11 . . 158 D5
Teynham Ave EN1 . . 17 B5
Teynham Ct N12 . . 30 A6
Teynham Gn BR2 . . 209 A4
Teynham Ho SE9 . . 167 B5
Teynton Terr N17 . . 33 A2
Thackeray Ave N17 . . 34 A1
Thackeray Cl Hayes UB8 . . 82 D1
Isleworth TW7 . . 131 A3
Wimbledon SW19 . . 178 D3
Thackeray Ct
Chelsea SW3 . . 257 C2
Ealing W5 . . 88 B1
West Kensington W14 . . 254 A5
Thackeray Dr RM6 . . 58 B2
Thackeray Ho
College Pk NW10 . . 90 A4
WC1 . . 240 A6
Thackeray Manor SM1 . . 218 A3
Thackeray Mews 6 E8 . . 74 A2
Thackeray Rd
Clapham SW8 . . 137 B3
Newham E6 . . 99 D5
Thackeray's Almshouses SE6 . . 163 D5
Thackeray St W8 . . 255 D6
Thackery Lo TW14 . . 149 B5
Thackrah Cl N2 . . 30 A1
Thakeham Cl SE26 . . 184 B5
Thalia Cl SE10 . . 142 B6
Tham Cl 10 SE24 . . 138 D2
Thame Rd SE16 . . 118 D4
Thames Ave
Dagenham RM9 . . 103 D3
North Cheam KT4 . . 200 C1
Sands End SW10 . . 136 A4 266 B2
Wembley UB6 . . 86 D5
Thames Bank SW14 . . 133 A3
Thamesbank Pl SE28 . . 102 C1
Thames Barrier Visitor Ctr* SE18 . . 121 D3
Thames Christian Coll 25 SW11 . . 136 B2
Thames Circ E14 . . 119 C2
Thames Cl TW12 . . 173 D1
Thames Cnr TW16 . . 194 C6
Thames Cres W4 . . 133 C5
Thames Ct Ealing W7 . . 86 C1
Edmonton N9 . . 18 C1
10 SE15 . . 139 D5
West Molesey KT8 . . 173 D1
THAMES DITTON . . 197 B2
Thames Ditton Inf Sch KT7 . . 196 D3
Thames Ditton Island KT7 . . 197 A3
Thames Ditton Jun Sch KT7 . . 196 D2
Thames Ditton Sta KT7 . . 196 D2
Thames Dr HA4 . . 39 A3
Thames Eyot 8 TW1 . . 153 A3
Thamesfield Ct TW17 . . 193 A2
Thamesfield Ho TW17 . . 193 A2
Thamesfield Mews TW17 . . 193 A2
Thamesgate Cl TW10 . . 175 B6
Thames Gateway Pk RM9 . . 103 B4
Thames Haven KT6 . . 197 D4
Thames Hts SE1 . . 253 C2
Thameside TW11 . . 175 D3
Thameside Ctr TW8 . . 132 B6
Thameside Ind Est E16 . . 121 D4
Thameside Pl KT1 . . 175 D2
Thames Link Ho 7 TW9 . . 132 A1
Thames Mdw KT12, TW17 . . 193 C1
THAMESMEAD . . 124 A5
Thames Mead KT12 . . 194 A3
Thames Meadow KT8 . . 195 C6
Thamesmead Sch TW17 . . 193 B3
Thamesmead Sh Ctr SE28 . . 124 A6
Thamesmere Dr SE28 . . 124 A6
Thames Pl SW15 . . 134 D2
Thamespoint TW11 . . 175 D3
Thames Quay
Millwall E14 . . 119 D4
Thames Quay *continued*
SW10 . . 266 B1
Thames Rd Barking IG11 . . 102 A4
Chiswick W4 . . 132 D6
Newham E16 . . 121 D5
Thames Reach
Fulham W6 . . 134 C6
Woolwich SE28 . . 123 C4
Thames Road Ind Est E16 . . 121 D4
Thames Row TW9 . . 132 B6
Thames Side
Teddington KT1 . . 175 D2
Thames Ditton KT7 . . 197 B3
Thames St
Hampton TW12 . . 173 D1
Kingston u T KT1, KT2 . . 175 D1
SE10 . . 141 D6
Sunbury TW16 . . 194 B6
Walton-on-T KT12 . . 193 D2
Thamesvale Cl TW3 . . 129 C3
Thames Valley Univ W5 . . 109 D5
Thames Valley Univ (Ealing Campus) W5 . . 109 D5
Thames Valley Univ (Walpole House) W5 . . 109 C6
Thames View 2 IG1 . . 79 A6
Thames View Ho TW12 . . 194 A3
Thames View Inf Sch IG11 . . 102 A5
Thames View Jun Sch IG11 . . 101 D5
Thames View Lo IG11 . . 101 C4
Thames Village W4 . . 133 A4
Thames Wlk SW11 . . 136 C5 267 A4
Thane Mans N7 . . 72 B5
Thanescroft Gdns CR0 . . 221 C5
Thanet Ct 14 W3 . . 88 C1
Thanet Dr BR2 . . 225 D5
Thanet Ho WC1 . . 233 A1
1 West Norwood SE27 . . 160 D1
Thanet Lo NW2 . . 69 A2
Thanet Pl CR0 . . 221 A4
Thanet Rd DA5 . . 169 C4
Thanet St WC1 . . 94 A4 233 A1
Thane Villas N7 . . 72 B5
Thane Works N7 . . 72 B5
Thanington Ct DA15 . . 167 C5
Thant Cl E10 . . 75 D5
Tharp Rd SM6 . . 219 D3
Thatcham Ct N20 . . 14 A4
Thatcham Gdns N20 . . 14 A4
Thatcher Cl UB7 . . 104 A4
Thatchers Way TW7 . . 152 B6
Thatches Gr RM6 . . 59 A5
Thavies Inn EC4 . . 241 B2
Thaxted Ct N1 . . 235 D3
Thaxted Ho
Bermondsey SE16 . . 118 C2
Dagenham RM10 . . 81 D1
Thaxted Lo 3 E18 . . 55 B6
Thaxted Pl 9 SW20 . . 178 D3
Thaxted Rd
Buckhurst Hill IG9 . . 21 D4
SE9 . . 167 A2
Thaxton Rd W14 . . 135 B6 264 D6
Thayers Farm Rd BR3 . . 185 A2
Thayer St W1 . . 93 A1 238 B2
Theatre Royal* E10 . . 76 B2
Theatre Sq E15 . . 76 B2
Theatre St SW11 . . 136 D2
Theberton St N1 . . 94 D6 234 C6
Theed St SE1 . . 116 C5 251 B3
Thelbridge Ho 28 E3 . . 97 D4
Thelma Gdns SE3 . . 144 A4
Thelma Gr TW11 . . 175 A4
Theobald Cres HA3 . . 24 A2
Theobald Rd
Croydon CR0 . . 220 D6
Walthamstow E17 . . 53 C2
Theobalds Ave N12 . . 30 A6
Theobalds Ct N4 . . 73 A6
Theobalds Park Rd EN2 . . 4 D6
Theobald's Rd WC1 . . 94 B2 240 C4
Theobald St SE1 . . 262 C5
Theodora Way HA5 . . 39 D6
Theodore Ct SE13 . . 164 B5
Theodore Ho 1 SW15 . . 156 A6
Theodore Rd SE13 . . 164 B5
Therapia La
Thornton Heath CR0 . . 204 A2
Thornton Heath CR0 . . 204 A3
Wallington CR0 . . 203 D2
Therapia Lane Sta CR0 . . 204 A2
Therapia Rd SE22 . . 162 C5
Theresa Rd W6 . . 112 A2
Therfield Ct N4 . . 73 A6
Thermopylae Gate E14 . . 119 D2
Theseus Ho
2 South Bromley E14 . . 98 B1
2 E14 . . 98 B1
Theseus Wlk N1 . . 234 D3
Thesiger Rd SE20 . . 184 D3
Thessaly Ho SW8 . . 269 A3
Thessaly Rd SW8 . . 137 C4 269 B2
Thetford Cl N13 . . 32 D4
Thetford Ct
3 Dulwich SE21 . . 162 B2
Thetford Ct *continued*
New Malden KT3 . . 199 C4
Thetford Gdns RM9 . . 103 A6
Thetford Ho SE1 . . 263 C6
Thetford Rd
Ashford TW15 . . 148 A1
Dagenham RM9 . . 80 D1
New Malden KT3 . . 199 C4
Thetis Terr TW9 . . 132 C6
Theydon Gr IG8 . . 37 C4
Theydon Rd E5 . . 74 C6
Theydon St E17 . . 53 B2
Thicket Cres SM1 . . 218 A4
Thicket Ct 14 SM1 . . 218 A4
Thicket Gr Dagenham RM9 . . 80 C2
Penge SE20 . . 184 A3
Thicket Rd Penge SE20 . . 184 B3
Sutton SM1 . . 218 A4
Thicket The UB7 . . 82 A1
Third Ave
Chadwell Heath RM6 . . 58 C3
Dagenham RM10 . . 103 D5
East Acton W3 . . 111 D5
Enfield EN1 . . 17 D6
Hayes UB3 . . 105 D5
Little Ilford E12 . . 78 B3
3 Newham E13 . . 99 A4
Walthamstow E17 . . 53 C4
Wembley HA9 . . 65 D6
West Kilburn W10 . . 91 A4
Third Cl KT8 . . 196 A5
Third Cross Rd TW2 . . 152 B2
Thirleby Rd Hendon HA8 . . 27 B2
SW1 . . 115 C3 259 B5
Thirlestane Ct N10 . . 31 A1
Thirlestane Ho TW12 . . 173 D6
Thirlmere NW1 . . 231 D2
Thirlmere Ave UB6 . . 87 C4
Thirlmere Gdns HA9 . . 43 D1
Thirlmere Ho
Isleworth TW1 . . 152 D6
19 Stoke Newington N16 . . 73 B4
Thirlmere Rd
Muswell Hill N10 . . 31 B2
Streatham SW16 . . 181 D6
Thirlmere Rise BR1 . . 186 D4
Thirsk Cl UB5 . . 63 C2
Thirsk Rd Clapham SW11 . . 137 A1
Mitcham CR4 . . 181 A3
South Norwood SE25 . . 205 B5
Thistlebrook SE2 . . 124 C3
Thistlebrook Ind Est SE2 . . 124 C4
Thistlecroft Gdns HA7 . . 25 D1
Thistle Ct N17 . . 52 B5
Thistledene KT7 . . 196 C3
Thistledene Ave HA2 . . 63 A5
Thistledown Ct SE25 . . 205 C6
Thistlefield Cl DA5 . . 168 D3
Thistle Gr SW7 . . 256 B1
Thistle Ho 10 E14 . . 98 A1
Thistlemead BR7 . . 188 D1
Thistlewaite Rd E5 . . 74 B5
Thistlewood Cl 3 N7 . . 72 B6
Thistleworth Cl TW7 . . 130 B5
Thistley Cl N12 . . 30 C4
Thistly Ct SE8 . . 141 D6
Thomas a' Beckett Cl HA0 . . 64 D4
Thomas Arnold Prim Sch RM9 . . 81 B1
Thomas Baines Rd SW11 . . 136 B2
Thomas Burt Ho 9 E2 . . 96 B4
Thomas Buxton Jun & Inf Sch 17 E1 . . 96 A3
Thomas Cribb Mews E6 . . 100 B1
Thomas Crowell Ct 29 N1 . . 73 C3
Thomas Ct RM8 . . 80 C6
Thomas Dean Rd SE26 . . 185 B6
Thomas Dinwiddy Rd SE12 . . 165 B2
Thomas Doyle St SE1 . . 261 D6
Thomas Fairchild Com Sch N1 . . 95 A5 235 B4
Thomas Gamuel Prim Sch E17 . . 53 C3
Thomas Hardy Ho N22 . . 32 B2
Thomas Hewlett Ho HA1 . . 64 C4
Thomas Ho
9 Belmont SM2 . . 217 D1
3 Hackney E9 . . 74 C2
4 Stockwell SW4 . . 138 A1
Thomas Hollywood Ho 3 E2 . . 96 C5
Thomas Jacomb Pl 2 E17 . . 53 B5
Thomas Jones Prim Sch 16 W11 . . 91 A1
Thomas Knyvett Coll TW15 . . 148 A1
Thomas' La SE6 . . 163 C4
Thomas Lo E17 . . 53 D4
Thomas London Ind Day Sch W8 . . 113 D3 255 D6
Thomas Milner Ho 8 SE15 . . 140 A5
Thomas More Bldg The HA4 . . 39 C1
Thomas More Ho EC2 . . 242 A3
Thomas More Sq E1 . . 118 A6
Thomas More St E1 . . 118 A5
Thomas More Way N2 . . 48 A6
Thomas Neal's Ctr WC1 . . 94 A1 240 A1
Thomas North Terr 4 E16 . . 98 D2
Thomas Pl W8 . . 255 C5
Thomas Pooley Ct KT6 . . 198 A2
Thomas Rd E14 . . 97 C2
Thomas Road Ind Est 2 E14 . . 97 C1
Thomas Shearley Ct DA5 . . 169 D4
Thomas's Prep Sch Clapham SW11 . . 158 D6
Thomas's Prep Schs SW11 . . 136 B4 266 D1
Thomas St SE18 . . 122 D2
Thomas Tallis Sch SE3 . . 143 B2
Thomas Wall Cl SM1 . . 217 D3
Thomas Watson Cottage Homes The EN5 . . 13 A6
Thompson Ave
Richmond TW9 . . 132 C2
6 SE5 . . 139 A5
Thompson Cl Ilford IG1 . . 79 A6
Morden SM3 . . 201 C1
Thompson Ho
11 Kensal Town W10 . . 91 A3
SE14 . . 140 D6
Southall UB1 . . 107 A6
Thompson Rd
Dagenham RM9 . . 81 B5
Dulwich Village SE22 . . 161 D5
Hounslow TW3 . . 129 D1
Uxbridge UB10 . . 60 A1
Thomson Cres CR0 . . 204 C1
Thomson Ct 4 E8 . . 74 A2
Thomson Ho Pimlico SW1 . . 259 D1
Walworth SE17 . . 263 A3
Thomson Rd HA3 . . 42 C6
Thorburn Ho SW1 . . 248 A1
Thorburn Sq SE1 . . 118 A2
Thorburn Way SW19 . . 180 B2
Thoresby Ho N16 . . 73 B5
Thoresby St N1 . . 95 A4 235 B2
Thorkhill Gdns KT7 . . 197 B1
Thorkhill Rd KT7 . . 197 B2
Thornaby Gdns N18 . . 34 B5
Thornaby Ho 15 E2 . . 96 B4
Thorn Ave WD23 . . 8 A3
Thornbill Ho 1 SE15 . . 140 A5
Thornbridge Ct 10 EN5 . . 13 D6
Thornbury 3 NW4 . . 46 C5
Thornbury Ave TW7 . . 130 B5
Thornbury Cl
Edgware NW7 . . 28 D3
Stoke Newington N16 . . 73 C3
Thornbury Ct
Croydon CR2 . . 221 B3
Hounslow TW7 . . 130 C5
W11 . . 245 A6
Thornbury Ho N6 . . 49 C1
Thornbury Lo EN2 . . 4 D2
Thornbury Rd
Clapham Pk SW2 . . 160 A5
Hounslow TW7 . . 130 B4
Thornbury Sq N6 . . 49 C1
Thornby Rd E5 . . 74 C5
Thorn Cl BR2 . . 210 C3
Northolt UB5 . . 85 B4
Thorncliffe Ct SW2 . . 160 A5
Thorncliffe Rd
Clapham Pk SW2 . . 160 A5
Southall UB2 . . 107 B1
Thorncombe Rd SE22 . . 161 C6
Thorncroft HA2 . . 64 A5
Thorncroft Rd SM1 . . 217 D4
Thorncroft St SW8 . . 138 A5 270 A3
Thorndale BR7 . . 188 B3
Thorndale Ho 10 N16 . . 51 C1
Thorndean St SW18 . . 158 A2
Thorndene Ave N11 . . 15 A3
Thorndike Ave UB5 . . 84 D6
Thorndike Cl SW10 . . 136 A5 266 A4
Thorndike Ho SW1 . . 259 C2
Thorndike Rd 21 N1 . . 73 B2
Thorndike St SW1 . . 115 D2 259 C3
Thorndon Cl BR5 . . 189 D1
Thorndon Gdns KT19 . . 215 C4
Thorndon Rd BR5 . . 189 D1
Thorndyke Ct HA5 . . 23 B3
Thorne Cl Claygate KT10 . . 213 A1
DA8 . . 147 D6
Leyton E11 . . 76 C4
Littleton TW15 . . 171 A3
Newham E16 . . 99 A1
Thorne Ho
34 Bethnal Green E2 . . 96 C4
4 Cubitt Town E14 . . 120 A3
Thorneloe Gdns CR0, CR9 . . 220 D3
Thorne Pas 7 SW13 . . 133 D3
Thorne Rd SW8 . . 138 A5 270 B3
Thorne's Cl BR3 . . 208 A6
Thorness Ct SW18 . . 158 A5
Thorne St SW13, SW14 . . 133 C2
Thornet Wood Rd BR1 . . 210 C6
Thornewill Ho 8 E1 . . 118 C6
Thorney Cres SW11 . . 136 B5 266 D3
Thorneycroft Cl KT12 . . 194 C3
Thorneycroft Dr EN3 . . 7 C6
Thorneycroft Ho 11 W4 . . 111 C1
Thorney Ct W8 . . 246 A1
Thorney Hedge Rd W4 . . 110 D2
Thorney St SW1 . . 116 A2 260 A4
Thornfield Ave NW7 . . 29 A2
Thornfield Ct NW7 . . 29 A2
Thornfield Ho 5 E14 . . 119 C6
Thornfield Par NW7 . . 29 A3
Thornfield Rd W12 . . 112 B4
Thornford Rd SE13 . . 164 A6
Thorngate Rd W9 . . 91 C3
Thorngrove Rd E13 . . 99 B6
Thornham Gr E15 . . 76 B3
Thornham Ho SE1 . . 262 D6
Thornham St SE10 . . 141 D6
Thornhaugh St WC1 . . 239 D5
Thornhill Ave SE18 . . 145 C5
Surbiton KT6 . . 214 A6
Thornhill Bridge Wharf N1 . . 233 C5
Thornhill Cres N1 . . 72 B1
Thornhill Ct N8 . . 49 D3
Thornhill Gdns
Barking IG11 . . 79 C1
Leyton E10 . . 75 D6
Thornhill Gr N1 . . 72 C1
Thornhill Ho
12 Chiswick W4 . . 111 C1
Islington N1 . . 72 C1
Thornhill Mews SW15 . . 135 B1
Thornhill Prim Sch 11 N1 . . 72 C1
Thornhill Rd
Ickenham UB10 . . 60 C4
Islington N1 . . 94 C6 234 A6
Leyton E10 . . 75 D6
Surbiton KT6 . . 214 B6
Thornton Heath CR0 . . 205 A2
Thornhill Sq N1 . . 72 B1
Thornhill Way TW17 . . 192 C4
Thornicroft Ho 12 SW9 . . 138 B3
Thornlaw Rd SE27 . . 182 D6
Thornley Cl N17 . . 34 A3
Thornley Dr HA2 . . 63 D6
Thornley Pl 2 SE10 . . 120 C1
Thornsbeach Rd SE6 . . 164 A2
Thornsett Pl SE20 . . 184 B1
Thornsett Rd Penge SE20 . . 184 B1
Wandsworth SW18 . . 157 D3
Thornsett Terr SE20 . . 184 B1
Thornton Ave
Chiswick W4 . . 111 C2
Streatham SW2 . . 159 D3
Thornton Heath CR0 . . 204 B3
West Drayton UB7 . . 104 B3
Thornton Cl UB7 . . 104 B3
Thornton Ct
Lower Holloway N7 . . 72 A3
West Barnes SW20 . . 200 D4
Thornton Dene BR3 . . 185 C1
Thornton Gdns SW12 . . 159 D3
Thornton Gr HA5 . . 23 C4
THORNTON HEATH . . 204 D3
Thornton Heath L Ctr CR7 . . 205 A5
Thornton Heath Pond CR7 . . 204 C4
Thornton Heath Sta CR7 . . 205 A5
Thornton Hill SW19 . . 179 A3
Thornton Ho SE17 . . 263 A3
7 Wanstead E11 . . 55 A3
Thornton Lo
South Norwood CR7 . . 205 A6
8 Wimbledon SW19 . . 179 A3
Thornton Pl W1 . . 237 D4
Thornton Rd Barnet EN5 . . 1 A2
Belvedere DA17 . . 125 D2
BR1 . . 187 A5
Carshalton SM5 . . 202 B1
Ilford IG1 . . 78 D4
Leyton E11 . . 76 B6
Lower Edmonton N18 . . 18 C1
Mortlake SW14 . . 133 B2
Streatham SW12, SW2 . . 159 D3
Thornton Heath CR0, CR7 . . 204 B3
Wimbledon SW19 . . 178 D3
Thornton Rd E SW19 . . 178 D4
Thornton Rd Ind Est CR0 . . 204 B3
Thornton Row CR7 . . 204 C4
Thornton St SW9 . . 138 C3
Thornton Way NW11 . . 47 D4
Thorntree Ct W5 . . 88 A2
Thorntree Prim Sch SE7 . . 121 D1
Thorntree Rd SE7 . . 121 D1
Thornville Gr CR4 . . 180 B1
Thornville St SE8 . . 141 C4

Thornwell Ct W7. . . . . . . .108 C4
Thornwood Cl E18. . . . . . .37 B1
Thornwood Gdns W8. . . .245 A2
Thornwood Lo W8. . . . . .245 A2
Thornwood Rd SE13. . . .164 C6
Thornycroft Ct TW9. . . . .132 B3
Thorogood Gdns E15. . . .76 C3
Thorold Ho SE1. . . . . . . .252 A2
   6 Streatham SW2. . . . .160 A4
Thorold Rd Ilford IG1. . . . .57 A1
   Wood Green N22. . . . . . .32 A3
Thorparch Rd
   SW8. . . . . .137 D5 269 D3
Thorpebank Rd W12. . . .112 A5
Thorpe Cl BR6. . . . . .227 C6
   Forest Hill SE26. . . . . .184 D6
   Notting Hill W10. . . . . . .91 A1
Thorpe Coombe Hospl
   E17. . . . . .54 A6
Thorpe Cres E17. . . . . . . .35 B1
Thorpe Ct Enfield EN2. . . . .4 D2
   Upper Tooting SW17. . . .180 C6
Thorpedale Gdns IG6. . . .56 D5
Thorpedale Rd N4. . . . . . .50 B1
Thorpe Hall W5. . . . . .87 D2
Thorpe Hall Prim Sch
   E17. . . . . .36 B2
Thorpe Hall Rd E17. . . . . .36 A2
Thorpe Ho N1. . . . . .233 D5
Thorpe Rd Barking IG11. . . .79 B1
   Chingford E17. . . . . .36 A1
   Kingston u T KT2. . . . . .176 A3
   Leyton E7. . . . . .76 D4
   Newham E6. . . . . .100 B6
   Tottenham N15. . . . . . . .51 C3
Thorpewood Ave SE23,
   SE26. . . . . .162 B2
Thorpland Ave UB10. . . . .61 A5
Thorsden Way 2 SE19. . .183 C5
Thorverton Rd NW2. . . . . .69 A5
Thoydon Rd E3. . . . . .97 A5
Thrale Almshouses
   SW16. . . . . .182 A5
Thrale Rd SW16. . . . . . .181 C5
Thrale St SE1. . . . . .252 B3
Thrasher 20 E8. . . . . .95 D6
Thrawl St E1. . . . .95 D2 243 D3
Thrayle Ho 2 SW9. . . . . .138 B2
Threadgold Ho 8 N1. . . . .73 B2
Threadneedle St EC2,
   EC3. . . . . .95 B1 242 D1
Three Bridges Bsns Ctr
   UB2. . . . . .108 A4
Three Bridges Prim Sch
   UB2. . . . . .107 D3
Three Colts La E2. . . . . . .96 B3
Three Colt St E14. . . . . .119 B6
Three Corners DA7. . . . . .147 D3
Three Cups Yd WC1. . . . .240 D3
Three Kings Yd W1. . . . . .248 C6
Three Meadows Mews
   HA7. . . . . .24 D2
Three Mill La E3. . . . . . . .98 A4
Three Mills Studios *
   E14. . . . . .98 A4
Three Nun Ct EC2. . . . . .242 B2
Three Oak La SE1. . . . . .253 C2
Three Oaks Cl UB10. . . . .60 B5
Threshers Pl W11. . . . . .244 A6
Thriffwood SE23, SE26. . .162 D1
Thrigby Rd KT9. . . . . . . .214 B2
Thring Ho 2 SW9. . . . . .138 B3
Throckmorten Rd E16. . . .99 B1
Throgmorton Ave
   EC2. . . . . .95 B1 242 D2
Throgmorton St
   EC2. . . . . .95 B1 242 D2
Throwley Cl SE2. . . . . . .124 C3
Throwley Rd SM1. . . . . .217 D3
Throwley Way SM1. . . . .217 D3
Thrupp Cl CR4. . . . . .181 B1
Thrush Gn N4. . . . . .41 C5
Thrush St SE17. . . . . . . .262 A2
Thunderer Rd RM9. . . . . .103 B3
Thurbarn Rd SE6. . . . . . .185 D5
Thurbin Ho UB4. . . . . . . .83 B2
Thurland Ho 3 SE16. . . .118 B2
Thurland Rd SE16. . . . . .118 A3
Thurlby Cl HA1. . . . . .43 A3
Thurlby Croft NW4. . . . . .46 C6
Thurlby Rd Wembley HA0. . .65 D2
   West Norwood SE27. . . .182 C6
Thurleigh Ave SW12. . . . .159 A5
Thurleigh Ct SW12. . . . . .159 A5
Thurleigh Rd SW12. . . . .159 A5
Thurleston Ave SM4. . . . .201 A4
Thurlestone Ave
   Colney Hatch N12. . . . . .30 D4
   Ilford IG3. . . . . .79 D4
Thurlestone Cl TW17. . . . .193 A3
Thurlestone Ct 1 UB1. . . .85 D1
Thurlestone Par TW17. . . .193 A3
Thurlestone Rd SE27. . . .182 C6
Thurloe Cl SW7. . . . . . . .257 A4
Thurloe Ct SW3. . . . . . . .257 A3
Thurloe Pl SW7. . . .114 B2 256 D4

Thurloe Place Mews
   SW7. . . . . .256 D4
Thurloe Sq SW7. . .114 C2 257 A4
Thurloe St SW7. . . .114 B2 256 D4
Thurlow Cl E4. . . . . .35 C4
Thurlow Ct 5 E11. . . . . . .55 A4
Thurlow Gdns HA0. . . . . .65 D3
Thurlow Hill SE21. . . . . .161 A2
Thurlow Ho 17 SW16. . . .160 A1
Thurlow Park Rd SE21,
   SE24. . . . . .161 A2
Thurlow Rd
   Hampstead NW3. . . . . . .70 B3
   West Ealing W7. . . . . . .109 A4
Thurlow St SE17. . .117 C1 263 A1
Thurlow Terr NW5. . . . . . .71 A3
Thurlow Twrs SE27. . . . .160 C1
Thurlow Wlk SE17. . . . . .263 A1
Thurlston Rd HA4. . . . . . .62 A5
Thurnby Ct TW2. . . . . . .152 C1
Thurnscoe NW1. . . . . . .232 A5
Thursland Rd DA14. . . . .191 A5
Thursley Cres CR0. . . . .224 B1
Thursley Gdns SW19. . . .156 D2
Thursley Ho
   3 Kingston u T KT2. . . .176 D3
   10 Streatham SW2. . . . .160 B4
Thursley Rd SE9. . . . . . .166 B1
Thurso Ho NW6. . . . . . . .91 D5
Thurso St SW17. . . . . . .180 B6
Thurstan Rd SW20. . . . .178 B3
Thurston Ho 4 BR3. . . . .185 D4
Thurston Ind Est E13. . . .141 D2
Thurston Rd Southall UB1. . .85 B1
   St Johns SE8, SE13. . . .141 D3
Thurtle Rd E2. . . . . .95 D5
Thurza Ct 3 TW7. . . . . .130 D3
Thyer Cl BR6. . . . . .227 A4
Thyme Cl SE3. . . . . .143 C2
Thyme Ct NW7. . . . . .29 A3
Thyra Gr N12. . . . . .29 D4
Tibbatt's Rd E3. . . . . .97 D3
Tibbenham Pl SE6. . . . . .163 C2
Tibbenham Wlk E13. . . . .98 D5
Tibberton Sq N1. . . . . . .235 A6
Tibbets Cl SW19. . . . . . .156 D3
Tibbet's Corner SW19. . .156 D4
Tibbet's Ride SW19. . . . .156 D4
Tiber Cl 10 E3. . . . . .97 C6
Tiber Gdns N1. . . . . .233 B5
Ticehurst Cl BR5. . . . . . .190 A3
Ticehurst Rd SE23. . . . . .163 A2
Tickford Cl SE2. . . . . . . .124 C4
Tickford Ho NW8. . . . . . .230 A1
Tidal Basin Rd E16. . . . .120 D6
Tidbury Ct SW8. . . . . . . .269 A3
Tide Cl 3 CR4. . . . . .181 A2
Tideham Ho SE28. . . . . .123 B5
Tidelock Ho SE28. . . . . .123 B5
Tidemill Prim Sch 20
   SE8. . . . . .141 C5
Tidenham Gdns CR0. . . .221 C5
Tideside Ct SE18. . . . . . .122 A3
Tideslea Path SE28. . . . .123 B5
Tideslea Twr SE28. . . . . .123 A4
Tideswell 10 NW5. . . . . . .71 B4
Tideswell Rd
   Croydon CR0. . . . . . . .223 C5
   Putney SW15. . . . . . . .134 C1
Tideway Cl TW10. . . . . . .175 C6
Tideway Ct 9 SE16. . . . .118 D5
Tideway Ho E14. . . . . . .119 C4
Tideway Ind Est
   SW8. . . . . .137 C6 269 B5
Tideway Wharf SW13. . . .133 C3
Tideway Yd SW13. . . . . .133 C3
Tidey St E3. . . . . .97 C2
Tidford Rd DA16. . . . . . .145 D3
Tidworth Ho 13 SE22. . . .139 C2
Tidworth Rd E3. . . . . .97 C3
Tiepigs La BR2, BR4. . . . .208 D1
Tierney Ct 4 CR0. . . . . . .221 D6
Tierney Rd SW2. . . . . . .160 A3
Tierney Terr SW2. . . . . . .160 A3
Tiffin Girls' Sch KT2. . . . .176 A4
Tiffin Sch KT2. . . . . .176 B1
Tiger Ho WC1. . . . . .232 D1
Tiger La BR2. . . . . .209 B3
Tiger Way E5. . . . . .74 B4
Tignel Ct W3. . . . . .110 C4
Tilbrook Rd SE3. . . . . . .143 C2
Tilbury Cl
   14 Camberwell SE15. . . .139 D5
   12 Pinner HA5. . . . . . . .23 B3
   St Paul's Cray BR5. . . . .190 B1
Tilbury Ho 4 SE14. . . . . .140 D6
Tilbury Rd Leytonstone E10 .54 A2
   Newham E6. . . . . .100 B5
Tildesley Rd SW15. . . . .156 C5
Tile Farm Rd BR6. . . . . .227 B5
Tilehurst NW1. . . . . .231 D1
Tilehurst Point 2 SE2. . .124 C4
Tilehurst Rd Cheam SM3. . .217 A3
   Wandsworth SW17, SW18. .158 D3
Tile Kiln La Edmonton N13 .33 A5
   Harefield UB9. . . . . .38 D2
   Upper Holloway N6. . . . .49 C1
Tileyard Rd N7. . . . . .72 A1
Tilford Ave CR0. . . . . . . .224 A1

Tilford Gdns SW19. . . . .156 D3
Tilford Ho 8 SW2. . . . . .160 B4
Tilia Cl SM1. . . . . .217 B3
Tilia Rd E5. . . . . .74 B4
Tilia Wlk 31 SW9. . . . . . .138 D1
Tiller Ho 28 N1. . . . . .95 C6
Tiller L Ctr E14. . . . . . . .119 C3
Tiller Rd E14. . . . . .119 C3
Tillet Sq SE16. . . . . .119 A4
Tillett Cl NW10. . . . . .67 A2
Tillett Way 6 E2. . . . . . . .96 A4
Tilley Rd TW14. . . . . . . .150 A3
Tillingbourne Gdns N3. . . .47 B6
Tillingbourne Way N3. . . .47 B5
Tillingham Way N12. . . . . .29 C6
Tilling Ho 1 SE15. . . . . .140 B2
Tilling Rd NW2. . . . . .46 C2
Tilling Way HA9. . . . . .65 C6
Tillman Ho 8 SW2. . . . . .160 B3
Tillman St E1. . . . . .96 B1
Tilloch St 9 N1. . . . . .72 B1
Tillotson Ct SW8. . . . . . .269 D3
Tillotson Rd Edmonton N9 . .17 D2
   Harrow HA3. . . . . .23 D3
   Ilford IG1. . . . . .56 C2
Tilney Ct EC1. . . . . .242 B6
   Kingston u T KT6. . . . . .197 D4
Tilney Dr IG9. . . . . .21 A2
Tilney Gdns 12 N1. . . . . . .73 B2
Tilney Rd Dagenham RM9. . .81 B2
   Southall UB2. . . . . .106 C2
   Woodford IG9. . . . . .21 A2
Tilney St W1. . . . . .248 B4
Tilson Cl 2 SE5. . . . . . . .139 C5
Tilson Gdns SW2, SW4. . .160 A4
Tilson Ho SW2. . . . . . . .160 A4
Tilson Rd N17. . . . . .34 A2
Tilston Cl 11 E11. . . . . . . .76 D5
Tilton St SW6. . . . . .264 B5
Tiltwood The W3. . . . . . .111 A6
Tilt Yard App SE9. . . . . . .166 B5
Timber Cl BR7. . . . . .188 C1
Timberwharf Rd N16. . . . .52 A3
Time Sq E8. . . . . .73 D3
Times Sq SM1. . . . . . . .217 D3
Times Sq Sh Ctr SM1. . .217 D3
Timms Ct E1. . . . . .210 B5
Timor Ct UB1. . . . . .107 D5
Timothy Cl Bexley DA6. . .169 A6
   1 Clapham Pk SW4. . . .159 C6
Timothy Ho DA18. . . . . .125 A4
Timsbury Wlk 5 SW15. . .156 A3
Tina Ct Forest Hill SE6. . .163 B4
   West Norwood SW16. . . .160 C1
Tindal St SW9. . . . . .138 D4
Tinniswood Cl N5. . . . . . .72 C3
Tinsley Cl SE25. . . . . . . .206 B6
Tinsley Rd E1. . . . . .96 C2
Tintagel Cres SE22. . . . .139 D1
Tintagel Ct EC1. . . . . . . .241 C6
Tintagel Dr HA7. . . . . . . .25 D6
Tintern Ave NW9. . . . . . . .44 D6
Tintern Cl Putney SW15. . .157 A6
   Wimbledon SW19. . . . . .180 A4
Tintern Ct W13. . . . . . . .109 A6
Tintern Gdns N14. . . . . . .16 A4
Tintern Ho Belgravia SW1 .258 C3
   Regent's Pk NW1. . . . . .231 D3
Tintern Path NW9. . . . . . .45 C3
Tintern Rd
   Carshalton SM5. . . . . . .202 B1
   Tottenham N22. . . . . . . .33 A2
Tintern St SW4. . . . . . . .138 A1
Tintern Way HA2. . . . . . . .41 D1
Tinto Rd E16. . . . . .99 A3
Tinwell Mews WD6. . . . . .11 B6
Tinworth St SE11. . .116 A1 260 B2
Tippett Ct 2 E6. . . . . . . .100 B5
Tippetts Cl EN2. . . . . .5 A4
Tipthorpe Rd SW11. . . . .137 A2
Tipton Dr CR0. . . . . .221 C4
Tiptree 7 NW1. . . . . .71 B1
Tiptree Cl E4. . . . . .20 A1
Tiptree Cres IG5. . . . . . . .56 C6
Tiptree Ct EN2. . . . . .5 B1
Tiptree Dr EN2. . . . . .5 B1
Tiptree Rd HA4. . . . . .62 B4
Tirlemont Rd CR2. . . . . . .221 A1
Tirrell Rd CR0. . . . . .205 A3
Tisbury Ct W1. . . . . .249 C6
Tisbury Rd SW16. . . . . . .182 A1
Tisdall Pl SE17. . . .117 B2 262 D3
Tissington Ct 16 SE16. . .118 D2
Titan Bsns Est 3 SE8. . .141 C5
Titan Ct TW8. . . . . .110 B1
Titchborne Row W2. . . . .237 B1
Titchfield Rd
   Carshalton SM5. . . . . . .202 B1

Titchfield Rd continued
   Enfield EN3. . . . . .7 A6
   Paddington NW8. . . .92 D6 230 C6
Titchfield Wlk SM5. . . . . .202 B2
Titchwell Rd SW18. . . . . .158 B3
Tite St SW3. . . . . .136 D6 267 C6
Tithe Barn Cl KT2. . . . . .176 B2
Tithe Barn Way UB5. . . . . .84 B5
Tithe Cl Hayes UB4. . . . . .83 D2
   Hendon NW7. . . . . .28 A2
   Walton-on-T KT12. . . . . .194 B3
Tithe Ct NW4. . . . . .28 A2
Tithe Farm Ave HA2. . . . . .63 C5
Tithe Farm Cl HA2. . . . . . .63 C5
Tithe Wlk NW7. . . . . .28 A2
Titian Ave WD23. . . . . .8 C4
Titley Cl E4. . . . . .35 C5
Titmus Cl UB8. . . . . .83 A1
Titmuss Ave SE28. . . . . .124 B6
Titmuss St W12. . . . . . . .112 C4
Tivendale NE. 50 A6
Tiverton Ave IG5. . . . . . . .56 C6
Tiverton Cl CR0. . . . . . . .205 D2
Tiverton Dr SE9. . . . . . . .167 A3
Tiverton Prim Sch N15. . . .51 B3
Tiverton Rd
   Brondesbury Pk NW6,
   NW10. . . . . .90 D6
   Edgware HA8. . . . . .26 B1
   Edmonton N18. . . . . . . .33 C5
   Hounslow TW3. . . . . . . .130 A3
   Ruislip HA4. . . . . .62 A5
   Tottenham N4, N15. . . . .51 B3
   Wembley HA0. . . . . .88 A5
Tiverton St SE1. . . .117 A3 262 A6
Tiverton Way
   Chessington KT9. . . . . .213 D3
   Edgware NW7. . . . . .28 D3
Tivoli Ct SE16. . . . . .119 B5
Tivoli Gdns 11 SE18. . . . .122 A2
Tivoli Rd Hornsey N8. . . . .49 D4
   Hounslow TW4. . . . . . . .129 A1
   West Norwood SE27. . . .183 A5
Toad La TW4. . . . . .129 B1
Tobago St 12 E14. . . . . . .119 C4
Tobin Cl NW3. . . . . .70 C1
Toby Ct N9. . . . . .18 C4
Toby La E1. . . . . .97 A3
Toby Way KT5, KT6. . . . . .214 D6
Todber Ho W14. . . . . . . .254 A6
Todd Ho 3 N2. . . . . .30 B1
Todds Wlk N7. . . . . .72 B6
Tokenhouse Yd EC2. . . . .242 C2
Token Yd SW15. . . . . . . .135 A1
TOKYNGTON. 66 D2
Tokyngton Ave HA9. . . . . .66 C2
Toland Sq SW15. . . . . . .156 A6
Tolcairn Ct 2 DA17. . . . .125 C1
Tolcarne Dr HA5. . . . . . . .40 B6
Tolchurch 2 W11. . . . . . .91 C1
Toldos Sch N16. . . . . .51 C1
Toley Ave HA3, HA9. . . . . .44 A2
Tolhurst Dr 4 W10. . . . . .91 A4
Tollbridge Cl W10. . . . . . .91 A3
Tollesbury Gdns IG6. . . . .57 B6
Tollet St E1. . . . . .96 D3
Tollgate Dr Dulwich SE21 .161 C2
   Hayes UB4. . . . . .106 D6
Tollgate Gdns 1 NW6. . . .91 D5
Tollgate Prim Sch E13. . . .99 C3
Tollgate Rd E6. . . . . .100 A2
Tollhouse Way N19. . . . . .71 C6
Tollington Ct N4. . . . . . . .72 B6
Tollington Ho 4 N19. . . . .72 A5
Tollington Pk N4. . . . . . . .72 B6
Tollington Pl N4. . . . . . . .72 B6
Tollington Rd N7. . . . . . . .72 B4
Tollington Way N7. . . . . . .72 A5
Tolmers Sq NW1. . . .93 C3 239 B6
Tolpaide Ho SE11. . . . . .261 A3
Tolpuddle Ave 1 E13. . . . .99 C6
Tolpuddle St N1. . . .94 C5 234 A4
Tolsford Rd E5. . . . . .74 B3
Tolson Ho 4 TW7. . . . . . .131 A2
Tolson Rd TW7. . . . . . . .131 A2
Tolverne Rd SW20. . . . . .178 C2
TOLWORTH. 214 C6
Tolworth Cl KT6. . . . . . . .198 D1
Tolworth Gdns RM6. . . . . .58 D4
Tolworth Girls' Sch KT6. . .214 B5
Tolworth Hospl KT6. . . . .214 C6
Tolworth Inf Sch KT6. . . . .198 B1
Tolworth Jun KT6. . . . . . .214 D6
Tolworth Jun Sch KT6. . . .198 B1
Tolworth Par RM6. . . . . . .59 A4
Tolworth Park Rd KT6. . . .214 B6
Tolworth Rd KT6. . . . . . .214 A6
Tolworth Rise N KT5. . . . .198 D1
Tolworth Rise S KT5. . . . .198 D1
Tolworth Sta KT5. . . . . . .214 D6
Tolworth Underpass KT5,
   KT6. . . . . .214 D6
Tomahawk Gdns 4 UB5. . .84 D4
Tom Blau Gallery * SE1 .250 C2
Tom Coombs Cl SE9. . . .144 A1
Tom Cribb Rd SE18,
   SE28. . . . . .123 B3
Tom Groves Cl E15. . . . . .76 B3
Tom Hood Cl E15. . . . . . .76 B3

Tom Hood Sch E11. . . . . .76 D5
Tom Jenkinson Rd 5
   E16. . . . . .121 A5
Tomkyns Ho SE11. . . . . .261 A3
Tomline Ho SE1. . . . . . . .252 A3
Tomlin's Gr E3. . . . . .97 C4
Tomlinson Cl
   5 Gunnersbury W4. . . . .110 D1
   Spitalfields E2. . . . . .95 D4
Tomlins Orch IG11. . . . . .101 A6
Tomlin's Terr E14. . . . . . .97 A1
Tomlins Wlk 4 N7. . . . . . .72 B6
Tom Mann Cl IG11. . . . . .101 C6
Tom Nolan Cl E15. . . . . . .98 C5
Tompion Ho EC1. . . . . . .241 D6
Tompion St EC1. . . . . . . .234 D1
Tom Smith Cl SE10. . . . .142 C6
Tom Smith Ho 3 E17. . . . .54 A4
Tomson Ho SE1. . . . . . . .263 C6
Tom Williams Ho SW6. . . .264 C5
Tonbridge Cres HA3. . . . . .44 A5
Tonbridge Hos WC1. . . . .233 A1
Tonbridge Rd KT12, KT8. . .195 B5
Tonbridge St WC1. .94 A4 233 A1
Toneborough 16 NW8. . . .91 D6
Tonfield Rd SM3. . . . . . . .201 B1
Tonge Cl BR3. . . . . .207 C4
Tonsley Hill SW18. . . . . .157 D6
Tonsley Pl SW18. . . . . . .157 D6
Tonsley Rd SW18. . . . . . .157 D6
Tonsley St SW18. . . . . . .157 D6
Tonstall Rd CR4. . . . . . . .181 A1
Tony Law Ho SE12. . . . . .165 A6
Tooke Cl HA5. . . . . .23 A2
Tookey Cl HA3. . . . . .44 B2
Took's Ct EC4. . . . . .241 A2
Tooley St SE1. . . . .117 C5 253 A3
Toorack Rd HA3. . . . . . . .24 B1
Tooting Bec Gdns SW16. .181 D6
Tooting Bec Lido SW16. . .181 C6
Tooting Bec Rd
   Furzedown SW17. . . . . .181 B6
   Streatham SW16. . . . . .181 C5
Tooting Bec Sta SW17. . .159 A1
Tooting Broadway
   SW17. . . . . .180 C5
Tooting Broadway Sta
   SW17. . . . . .180 C5
TOOTING GRAVENEY. . .180 B5
Tooting High St SW17,
   SW19. . . . . .180 C5
Tooting L Ctr SW17. . . . .180 B6
Tooting Mkts * SW17. . . .180 D6
Tooting Sta SW17. . . . . . .180 D4
Tootswood Rd BR2, BR3. .208 C5
Topaz Ct TW13. . . . . . . .149 D1
Topaz Ho KT4. . . . . .199 B1
Topaz Wlk NW2. . . . . .46 D2
Topcliffe Dr BR6. . . . . . . .227 B4
Topham Ho 8 SE10. . . . .142 A5
Topham Sq N17. . . . . .33 A2
Topham St EC1. . . . . . . .241 A6
Top House Rise E4. . . . . .20 A4
Topiary Sq TW9. . . . . . . .132 B2
Topley St SE9. . . . . .143 D1
Topmast Point 23 E14. . . .119 C4
Top Pk BR3. . . . . .208 C4
Topsfield Cl N8. . . . . .49 D4
Topsfield Par N8. . . . . . . .50 A3
Topsfield Rd N8. . . . . .50 A4
Topsham Rd SW17. . . . . .181 A6
Tora Ct 9 IG9. . . . . .21 C2
Torah Vodaas N11. . . . . . .47 B1
Tora Temimah Prim Sch
   NW2. . . . . .68 B4
Torbay Ct 13 NW1. . . . . . .71 B1
Torbay Mans NW6. . . . . . .91 B6
Torbay Rd
   Brondesbury NW6. . . . . .69 B1
   Harrow HA2. . . . . .63 A6
Torbay St 15 NW1. . . . . . .71 B1
Torbitt Way IG2. . . . . .57 D4
Torbridge Cl HA8. . . . . . . .26 A3
Torbrook Cl DA5. . . . . . .169 A5
Torcross Dr SE23. . . . . .162 C2
Torcross Rd HA4. . . . . . . .62 C5
Tor Ct W8. . . . . .245 B2
Torfell 5 E18. . . . . .36 D1
Tor Gdns W8. . . . . .113 C4 245 A2
Tor Gr SE28. . . . . .123 C5
Tor Ho N6. . . . . .49 B3
Tormead Cl SM1. . . . . . .217 C2
Tormount Rd SE18. . . . . .145 C6
Tornay Ho Hackney E9. . . .74 C1
   N1. . . . . .233 C4
Toronto Ave E12. . . . . . . .78 B4
Toronto Rd IG1. . . . . .57 A1
Torquay Gdns IG4. . . . . . .55 D5
Torquay Ho 1 SM6. . . . . .219 D3
Torquay St W2. . . . . .91 D2
Tor Rd DA16. . . . . .146 C4
Torrence Ho 6 N19. . . . . .71 C6
Torrens Ct SE5. . . . . . . .139 B2
Torrens Rd
   Clapham Pk SW2. . . . . .160 B6
   Stratford E15. . . . . .76 D2
Torrens Sq E15. . . . . .76 D2
Torrens St EC1. . . .94 D5 234 C3
Torres Sq E14. . . . . .119 C1

Torre Wlk SM5.........202 C1
Torrey Dr SW9.........138 C3
Torriano Ave NW5.........71 D3
Torriano Cotts NW5.........71 C3
Torriano Jun & Inf Schs 24
  NW5.........71 C3
Torriano Mews NW5.........71 C3
Torridge Gdns SE15.........140 C1
Torridge Rd CR7.........204 D4
Torridon Ct HA8.........10 D2
Torridon Ho NW6.........91 D5
Torridon Jun & Inf Schs
  SE6.........164 B2
Torridon Rd SE13, SE6 ...164 B3
Torrington Ave N12.........30 B5
Torrington Cl
  Claygate KT10.........212 C2
  North Finchley N12.........30 B6
Torrington Ct
  Forest Hill SE26.........184 A5
  Harrow HA2.........63 D5
  North Finchley N12.........30 B6
Torrington Dr HA2.........63 D5
Torrington Gdns
  Friern Barnet N11.........31 C4
  Wembley UB6.........65 C1
Torrington Gr N12.........30 C5
Torrington Pk N12.........30 B6
Torrington Pl
  Bloomsbury WC1 ...93 D2 239 C4
  St George in t East E1.........118 A5
Torrington Rd
  Claygate KT10.........212 C2
  Dagenham RM8.........59 B1
  Ruislip HA4.........62 A5
  Wanstead E18.........55 A6
  Wembley UB6.........87 C6
Torrington Sq
  Bloomsbury WC1 ...93 D3 239 D5
  Thornton Heath CR0.........205 B2
Torrington Vlls SW4 ...201 C3
Torr Rd SE20.........184 D3
Tortington Ho 1 SE15 ...140 B5
Torver Rd HA1.........42 C5
Torver Way BR6.........227 B5
Torwood Rd SW15.........156 A6
Totham Ho SW20.........178 B2
Tothill Ho SW1.........259 D4
Tothill St SW1.... 115 D4 249 D1
Totland Ho SW18.........157 D5
Totnes Rd DA16.........146 C5
Totnes Villas N11.........31 C5
Totnes Wlk N2.........48 B5
Tottan Terr E1.........96 D1
Tottenhall 5 NW1.........71 A1
Tottenhall Inf Sch N13 ...32 C4
Tottenhall Rd N13.........32 C4
TOTTENHAM.........33 D1
Tottenham Court Rd
  W1.........93 C2 239 B4
Tottenham Court Road Sta
  W1.........93 D1 239 D2
Tottenham Gn E 3 N15 ...51 D5
Tottenham Gn E South Side
  4 N15.........51 D5
Tottenham Gn L Ctr N17...51 B5
TOTTENHAM HALE.........52 A6
Tottenham Hale N15.........52 A5
Tottenham Hale Ret Pk
  N15.........52 A5
Tottenham Hale Sta N17 ..52 B5
Tottenham La N8.........50 B2
Tottenham Mews W1 ...239 B4
Tottenham Rd N1.........72 B2
Tottenham St W1 ..93 C2 239 B4
Totterdown St SW17 ...180 D5
TOTTERIDGE.........13 C3
Totteridge Comm N20 ...12 C3
Totteridge Gn N20.........13 C2
Totteridge Ho Barnet N20...13 B3
  Battersea SW11.........136 B3
Totteridge La N20.........13 D3
Totteridge Pk N20.........12 D3
Totteridge Rd EN3.........6 D6
Totteridge Village N20.........13 C3
Totteridge & Whetstone Sta
  N20.........14 A2
Totternhoe Cl HA3.........43 C4
Totton Rd CR7.........204 C6
Toucan Cl NW10.........88 C4
Touchard Ho N1.........235 D1
Toulmin St SE1 ...117 A4 262 A3
Toulon Ct SE5.........139 A5
Toulouse Ct 2 SE16.........118 B1
Tournay Rd SW6 ...135 B5 264 D4
Toussaint Wlk 18 SE16 ...118 A3
Tovil Cl SE20.........184 B1
Tovy Ho 6 SE1.........118 A1
Towcester Rd E3.........98 A3
Tower 42 ★ EC2...95 C1 243 A2
Tower Bldgs 22 E1.........118 B5
Tower Br App E1, EC3...253 C5
Tower Bridge ★ E1, EC3,
  SE1.........117 D5 253 C4
Tower Bridge Bsns Complex
  SE16.........118 B3
Tower Bridge Bsns Sq
  SE16.........118 B2
Tower Bridge Ex ★ E1 ...253 C4

Tower Bridge Mews HA0 ...64 D4
Tower Bridge Piazza
  SE1.........253 C3
Tower Bridge Prim Sch
  SE1.........117 D4 253 C2
Tower Bridge Rd
  SE1.........117 C4 253 A1
Tower Bridge Sq SE1 ...253 C2
Tower Bridge Wharf
  SE1.........118 A5
Tower Cl Hampstead NW3...70 B3
  Orpington BR6.........227 D5
  Penge SE20.........184 B3
Tower Ct Brockley SE4.........141 A1
  Stamford Hill E5.........51 D2
  St Giles WC2.........240 A1
  St John's Wood NW8 ...230 B4
Tower Gardens Rd N17 ...33 B2
Towergate SE1.........263 A4
Towergate Cl UB8.........60 A1
Towergate Ho 35 E3.........97 B5
Tower Gateway Sta
  EC3.........117 D6 253 C5
Tower Gdns KT10.........213 A1
Tower Gr KT13.........193 C1
TOWER HAMLETS.........97 B2
Tower Hamlets Coll
  25 Poplar E14.........97 D1
  27 Poplar E14.........119 D6
  18 Stepney E1.........96 D1
Tower Hamlets Rd
  Forest Gate E7.........76 D3
  Walthamstow E17.........53 C6
Tower Hill E3...117 D6 253 D5
Tower Hill Sta
  EC3.........117 D6 253 C6
Tower House Sch SW14 .133 A1
Tower La HA9.........65 D5
Tower Mans SE1.........263 C5
Tower Mews Hackney E5 ...75 A3
  Walthamstow E17.........53 C5
Tower Millennium Pier
  EC3.........117 C5 253 D4
Tower Mill Rd
  7 Camberwell SE15 ...139 C6
  1 SE15.........139 C5
Tower Pl E EC3.........253 B5
Tower Pl W EC3.........253 B5
Tower Rd DA7.........147 D1
  Orpington BR6.........227 D5
  Twickenham TW1, TW2...152 D1
  Willesden NW10.........68 A1
Tower Rise TW9.........132 A2
Tower Royal EC4.........252 C6
Towers Ave UB10.........83 A4
Towers Bsns Pk HA9 ...66 D4
Towers Ct UB10.........83 A4
Towers Pl TW10.........154 A6
Towers Rd Pinner HA5 ...23 A2
  Southall UB1.........85 C3
Tower St WC2.........240 A1
Towers The
  Dartmouth Pk NW5.........71 B5
  1 Richmond TW9.........132 B1
  Wood Green N22.........32 B1
Tower The ★ EC3...117 D6 253 C5
Towerview SE13.........163 C6
Tower View Bushey WD23...8 C4
  Croydon CR0.........207 A2
Tower Wharf SE1.........253 C2
Tower Wlk SE1.........263 A4
Towncourt Cres BR5.........211 B5
Towncourt La BR5.........211 B2
Towncourt Path N4.........51 A1
Townend Ct 6 BR1.........186 D2
Towney Mead UB5.........85 B5
Towney Mead Ct UB5 ...85 B5
Townfield Rd UB3.........105 C5
Townfield Sq UB3.........105 D6
Town Field Way TW7 ...131 A3
Town Hall Approach Rd
  N15.........51 D5
Townhall Ave 3 W4.........111 B1
Town Hall Rd SW11 ...136 D2
Townholm Cres W7.........108 D3
Town Hos EC1.........241 D5
Town La TW19.........148 A2
Townley Ct E15.........76 D2
Townley Gram Sch for Girls
  DA6.........169 B6
Townley Rd DA6.........169 B6
  Dulwich Village SE22 ...161 C6
Townley St SE17 ...117 B1 262 C2
Townmead Bsns Ctr
  SW6.........136 A2
Town Meadow TW8.........131 D5
Townmead Rd
  Richmond TW9.........132 D3
  Sands End SW6.........136 A3
Town Quay IG11.........100 D5
Town Quay Wharf IG11...100 D5
Town Rd N9.........18 B2
Townsend Ave N14.........31 D6
Townsend Ho 14 SE1.........118 A2
Townsend Ind Est NW10...89 A3
Townsend La NW9.........45 B3

Townsend Mews 3
  SW18.........158 A2
Townsend Prim Sch
  SE17.........117 C2 263 A4
Townsend Rd
  Ashford TW15.........170 A5
  Regents Park NW8...92 C5 230 B4
  Southall UB1.........107 A5
  South Tottenham N15.........51 D4
Townsend St SE1,
  SE17.........117 C2 263 A4
Townsend Way HA6.........22 A3
Townsend Yd N6.........49 B1
Townshend Cl DA14.........190 C4
Townshend Ct NW8 ...230 B4
Townshend Est
  NW8.........92 C5 230 A4
Townshend Ho 16 SE18...122 B2
Townshend Rd
  Chislehurst BR7.........188 D5
  Primrose Hill NW8 ..92 C6 230 A5
  Richmond TW9.........132 B1
Townshend Terr TW9.........132 B1
Towns Ho 4 SW4.........137 D2
Townson Ave UB5.........84 B5
Townson Way UB5.........84 A5
Town The EN2.........5 B2
TownTree Rd TW15.........170 C5
Towpath TW17.........192 B1
Towpath Way CR0.........205 D4
Towpath Wlk E9.........75 B3
Towton Rd SE27.........161 A2
Toxteth Ho N4.........51 A2
Toynbec Cl BR7.........188 D6
Toynbee Rd SW19, SW20...179 A2
Toynbee St E1...111 A3 243 C3
Toynbee Studios ★ E1...243 B3
Toyne Way N6.........48 D3
Tracey Ave NW2.........68 C3
Tracy Ct HA7.........25 C3
Tracy Ho 15 E3.........97 B4
Trade Cl N13.........32 C6
Trader Rd E6.........100 D1
Tradescant Ho 15 E9.........74 C1
Tradescant Rd
  SW8.........138 A5 270 B3
Trade Twr 3 SW11 ...136 A2
Trade Winds Ct 1 E1...118 A5
Trading Estate Rd NW10...89 A3
Traemore Ct SW16.........160 C1
Trafalgar Ave
  North Cheam KT4, SM3,
  SM4.........200 D1
  SE15.........139 D6
  Tottenham N17.........33 C4
Trafalgar Bsns Ctr IG11...101 D3
Trafalgar Cl 1 SE16.........119 A2
Trafalgar Ct Barking E6.........100 C6
  Hounslow TW3.........129 B2
  West Barnes KT3.........200 B6
Trafalgar Gdns
  Stepney E1.........96 D2
  W8.........255 D6
Trafalgar Gr SE10.........142 B6
Trafalgar Ho
  Barking IG11.........102 B4
  SE17.........262 B2
Trafalgar Inf Sch TW2...152 B2
Trafalgar Jun Sch TW2...152 B2
Trafalgar Mews E9.........75 B2
Trafalgar Pl Edmonton N18...34 A5
  Wanstead E11.........55 A5
Trafalgar Point 2 N1.........73 B1
Trafalgar Rd
  Greenwich SE10.........120 C1
  Merton SW19.........180 A3
  Twickenham TW2.........152 B2
Trafalgar Sq ★
  SW1.........115 D5 249 D4
Trafalgar St
  SE17.........117 B1 262 D2
Trafalgar Terr HA1.........42 C1
Trafalgar Trad Est EN3 ...7 A1
Trafalgar Way
  Canary Wharf E14.........120 A5
  Croydon CR0.........220 C6
Trafford Ho N1.........235 D4
Trafford Rd CR7.........204 B4
Trafford Villas CR0.........204 B4
Tragail SW15.........157 A6
Traherne Lo 6 TW11...174 D5
Trahorn Cl E1.........96 B3
Traitors Gate ★
  EC3.........117 D5 253 C4
Tralee Ct 31 SE16.........118 B1
Tramsheds Ind Est The CR0,
  CR4.........203 D2
Tramway Ave
  Ponders End N9.........18 C4
  Stratford E15.........76 B1
Tramway Cl SE20.........184 C2
Tramway Path CR4.........202 C5
Trance Way W3.........110 C3
Tranmere Ct 5 SM2.........218 A1
Tranmere Ho 7 N7.........72 C3
Tranmere Rd
  Edmonton N9.........17 D4
  Twickenham TW2.........151 D4
  Wandsworth SW17, SW18. 158 A2
Tranquil Pas SE3.........142 D3

Tranquil Vale SE3 ....142 C3
Transept St NW1.........237 B3
Transmere Cl BR5.........211 A3
Transmere Rd BR5.........211 A3
Transom Cl SE16.........119 A2
Transom Sq E14.........119 D1
Transport Ave TW8.........131 B6
Tranton Rd SE16.........118 B3
Trappes Ho 2 SE16.........118 B2
Traps La KT2, KT3.........177 C2
Travellers Way TW5.........128 C3
Travers Cl E17.........34 D2
Travers Ho 6 SE10.........142 B6
Travers Rd N7.........72 C5
Travis Ho SE10.........142 A4
Treacy Cl WD23.........8 A3
Treadgold Ho 7 W11.........112 D6
Treadgold St W11.........112 D6
Treadway St E2.........96 B5
Treasury Bldgs SW1.........250 A2
Treasury Cl SM6.........219 D3
Treaty Ctr TW3.........129 D2
Treaty St N1.........94 B6 233 C4
Trebeck St W1.........248 C3
Treborough Ho W1.........238 A4
Trebovir Rd SW5...113 C2 255 B3
Treby St E3.........97 B3
Trecastle Way 2 N7.........71 D4
Tredegar Mews 10 E3.........97 B4
Tredegar Rd Bow E3.........97 B5
  Wood Green N11.........31 D3
Tredegar Sq E3.........97 B4
Tredegar Terr E3.........97 B4
Trederwen Rd E8.........96 A6
Tredown Rd SE26.........184 C5
Tredwell Cl BR2.........210 A5
Tredwell Rd SE27.........182 D6
Tree Cl TW10.........153 D3
Treehouse Sch N10.........49 A5
Treen Ave SW13.........133 D2
Tree Rd E16.........99 C1
Trees The N16.........51 B2
Tree Tops 1 IG8.........37 A6
Treetops Cl SE2.........125 A1
Treetops Ct CR7.........205 A4
Treetops View IG10.........21 D4
Treeview Cl SE19.........183 C2
Treewall Gdns BR1.........187 B6
Trefgarne Rd RM10.........81 C6
Trefil Wlk N7.........72 A4
Trefoil Ho DA18.........125 A4
Trefoil Rd SW18.........158 A6
Trefusis Ct TW5.........128 B4
Tregaron Ave N8.........50 A3
Tregaron Gdns KT3.........199 C5
Tregarvon Rd SW11.........137 A1
Tregenna Ave HA2.........63 C4
Tregenna Cl 1 N14.........15 C5
Tregenna Ct HA2.........63 C4
Trego Rd E9.........75 C1
Tregothnan Rd SW9.........138 A2
Tregunter Rd
  SW10.........114 A1 256 A1
Treherne Ct Brixton SW9 .138 C4
  Upper Tooting SW17.........181 A6
Trehern Rd 12 SW14.........133 B2
Trehurst St E5.........75 A3
Trelawney Cl E17.........53 D5
Trelawney Est E9.........74 C2
Trelawney Ho SE1.........252 A2
Trelawn Rd Leyton E10...76 A5
  Tulse Hill SW2.........160 C6
Trellis Ho SW19.........180 A3
Trellis Sq 1 E3.........97 B4
Treloar Gdns SE19.........183 B4
Tremadoc Rd SW4.........137 D1
Tremaine Cl SE4.........141 C3
Tremaine Rd SE20.........184 B1
Trematon Ho SE11.........261 B2
Trematon Pl TW11.........175 C3
Tremlett Gr N19.........71 C5
Tremlett Mews 17 N19...71 C5
Trenance Gdns IG3.........80 A5
Trenchard Ave HA4.........62 B4
Trenchard Cl
  Grahame Pk NW9.........27 C2
  Stanmore HA7.........25 B4
Trenchard Ct SM4.........201 C3
Trenchard St SE10.........120 B1
Trenchold St
  SW8.........138 A6 270 A5
Trendell Ho 8 E14.........97 C1
Trenholme Cl SE20.........184 B3
Trenholme Ct CR7.........205 B3
Trenholme Rd SE20.........184 B3
Trenholme Terr SE20.........184 B3
Trenmar Gdns NW10.........90 B4
Trent Ave W5.........109 C3
Trent CE Prim Sch EN4.........2 D1
Trent Ct
  1 South Croydon CR2 ...221 A3
  Wanstead E11.........55 A4
Trent Ctry Pk ★ EN4.........3 A3
Trent Gdns N14.........15 B5
Trentham St SW18.........157 D3
Trentham Lo 8 EN1.........17 C6
Trent Ho
  4 Kingston u T KT2 ...175 D2
  SE15.........140 C1

Trent Rd Buckhurst Hill IG9...21 B3
  Clapham Pk SW2.........160 B6
Trent Way Hayes UB4.........83 C4
  North Cheam KT4.........216 C5
Trentwood Side EN2.........4 B2
Treport St SW18.........157 D4
Tresco Cl BR1.........186 C4
Trescoe Gdns HA2.........41 A2
Tresco Gdns IG3.........80 A6
Tresco Ho SE11.........261 A2
Tresco Rd SE15.........140 B1
Tresham Cres
  NW8.........92 C3 237 A6
Tresham Rd IG11.........79 D1
Tresham Wlk E9.........74 C3
Tresidder Ho 10 SW4.........159 D4
Tresilian Ave N21.........16 B6
Tressel Cl 20 N1.........72 D1
Tressillian Cres SE4.........141 C2
Tressillian Rd SE4.........141 C2
Trestis Cl UB4.........84 D2
Treswell Rd RM9.........103 A6
Tretawn Gdns NW7.........11 C1
Tretawn Pk NW7.........27 C6
Trevallyn Lo 1 KT2.........176 D2
Trevanion Rd W14.........254 B2
Treve Ave HA1.........42 B2
Trevelyan Ave E12.........78 B4
Trevelyan Cres HA3.........43 D2
Trevelyan Ct KT3.........199 D2
Trevelyan Gdns NW10.........90 C6
Trevelyan Ho
  16 Globe Town E2.........96 D4
  SE5.........138 D5
  6 Twickenham TW1.........153 C5
Trevelyan Rd Leyton E15...76 D4
  Upper Tooting SW17.........180 D4
Trevenna Ho 13 SE23.........162 D1
Trevera Ct EN3.........19 A6
Treveris St 1 SE1.........251 D3
Treversh Ct 7 BR1.........186 D2
Treverton St W10.........90 D3
Treverton Twr 1 W10.........90 D2
Treves Cl N21.........16 B6
Treves Ho E1.........96 A3
Treville St SW15.........156 B4
Treviso Rd SE23.........163 A2
Trevithick Ho
  13 Bermondsey SE16.........118 B2
  3 Gospel Oak NW5.........71 B4
  SW8.........269 C2
Trevithick St SE8.........141 C6
Trevone Gdns HA5.........41 A3
Trevor Cl Harrow HA3 ...24 D3
  Hayes BR2.........209 A2
  Isleworth TW7.........152 D6
  New Barnet EN4.........14 B5
  Northolt UB5.........84 C5
Trevor Cres HA4.........61 D4
Trevor Gdns Hendon HA8...27 B2
  Northolt UB5.........84 C5
  Ruislip HA4.........62 A4
Trevor Pl SW7 ...114 C4 247 B3
Trevor Rd Hayes UB3.........105 C3
  Hendon HA8.........27 B2
  Wimbledon SW19.........179 A3
  Woodford IG8.........37 A3
Trevor Roberts Sch NW8...70 B1
Trevor Sq SW7 ...114 C4 247 B3
Trevor St SW7 ...114 C4 247 B3
Trevose Ho SE11.........260 D2
Trevose Rd E17.........36 B2
Trewenna Dr KT9.........213 D3
Trewince Rd SW20.........178 C2
Trewint St SW18.........158 A2
Trewsbury Ho 2 SE2.........124 D4
Trewsbury Rd SE26.........184 D5
Triandra Way UB4.........84 D2
Triangle Ct
  4 Newham E16.........99 C2
  SE1.........252 B3
Triangle Ctr UB1.........108 B5
Triangle Est The SE11 ...261 A1
Triangle Ho SE1.........253 C2
Triangle Pl SW4.........137 D1
Triangle The 7 E8.........96 B6
Triangle The Barking IG11 ...79 A2
  Crouch End N19.........49 D2
  EC1.........241 D6
  16 Hackney E8.........96 B6
  Kingston u T KT3.........177 A1
Tribune Ct 18 NW9.........46 A5
Tricorn Ho SE7.........123 B5
Trident Bsns Ctr SW17 ...180 D5
Trident Gdns 6 UB5.........84 D4
Trident Ho
  14 South Bromley E14.........98 A1
  Woolwich SE28.........123 B5
Trident St SE16.........118 D2
Trident Way UB2.........106 B3
Trieste Ct SW12.........158 D3
Trig La EC4.........252 A6
Trigon Rd SW8...138 B5 270 D4
Trilby Rd SE23.........162 D2
Trillington Ho W12.........112 A5
Trillo Ct IG1.........57 C2

Trimdon NW1 ... 232 B5
Trimmer Ct TW7 ... 130 D2
Trimmer Wlk [11] TW8 ... 132 A6
Trim St SE8 ... 141 B6
Trinder Gdns N19 ... 50 A1
Trinder Mews [10] TW11 ... 175 A5
Trinder Rd Barnet EN5 ... 12 C6
  Finsbury Pk N4, N19 ... 50 A1
Tring Ave Ealing W5 ... 110 B5
  Southall UB1 ... 85 B1
  Wembley HA9 ... 66 C2
Tring Cl IG2 ... 57 B4
Tring Ct TW1 ... 175 A6
Trinidad Ho [17] E14 ... 119 B6
Trinidad St E14 ... 119 B6
Trinity Ave
  East Finchley N2 ... 48 B6
  Enfield EN1 ... 17 D5
Trinity Church Rd SW13 ... 134 B6
Trinity Church Sq
  SE1 ... 117 A3 262 B6
Trinity Cl
  [3] Clapham SW4 ... 137 C1
  Hounslow TW4 ... 129 A1
  Keston Mark BR2 ... 210 A1
  Lewisham SE13 ... 142 B1
  Leyton E11 ... 76 C6
Trinity Coll London
  SE1 ... 116 A1 260 B1
Trinity Coll of Music
  SE10 ... 142 B6
Trinity Cotts TW9 ... 132 B2
Trinity Cres SW17 ... 159 A2
Trinity Ct [8] Chingford E4 ... 20 A2
  Edmonton N18 ... 33 D4
  Eltham SE9 ... 166 D5
  Finsbury WC1 ... 240 C6
  Forest Hill SE23 ... 162 C1
  Greenwich SE7 ... 121 D2
  [2] Hoxton N1 ... 95 C6
  Rotherhithe SE16 ... 119 A4
  Southgate N21 ... 16 D3
  Thornton Heath SE25 ... 205 C3
  Twickenham TW2 ... 152 C2
  Wallington SM6 ... 219 C1
  Willesden NW2 ... 68 C3
  Wimbledon SW19 ... 179 C4
Trinity Dr UB8 ... 83 A1
Trinity Gdns E16 ... 98 D2
  Stockwell SW2, SW9 ... 138 B1
  [11] Wanstead E18 ... 55 B6
Trinity Gn E1 ... 96 C2
Trinity Gr [8] SE10 ... 142 A4
Trinity Ho SE1 ... 262 B6
  [5] Walthamstow E17 ... 53 D6
Trinity Homes [14] SW2 ... 138 B1
Trinity Mews Penge SE20 ... 184 B2
  SE9 ... 167 B5
  Wandsworth SW18 ... 157 C3
Trinity Par TW3 ... 129 D2
Trinity Pl
  Bexleyheath DA6 ... 147 B1
  City of London EC3 ... 253 C5
Trinity RC High Sch (Lower)
  IG8 ... 37 A6
Trinity RC High Sch (Upper)
  IG8 ... 37 A6
Trinity RC High Sch (Upper
  Sch) IG8 ... 36 D6
Trinity Rd East Finchley N2 ... 48 B6
  Ilford IG6 ... 57 A6
  Richmond TW9 ... 132 B2
  Southall UB1 ... 85 B1
  Wandsworth SW17, SW18 ... 158 C4
  Wimbledon SW19 ... 179 C4
  Wood Green N22 ... 32 A3
  Wood Green N22 ... 32 A3
Trinity Rise SE24, SW2 ... 160 D4
Trinity St Mary's Prim Sch [8]
  SW12 ... 159 A3
Trinity Sch Croydon CR0 ... 222 C6
  Dagenham RM10 ... 81 C4
Trinity Sq EC3 ... 117 C6 253 B6
Trinity St Enfield EN2 ... 5 A3
  [9] Newham E16 ... 99 A2
  SE1 ... 117 B3 262 C6
Trinity Terr IG9 ... 21 B4
Trinity Way
  East Acton W3 ... 111 D6
  Walthamstow E4 ... 35 B4
Trio Pl SE1 ... 117 A4 252 B1
Triscott Ho UB3 ... 106 A5
Tristan Ct [34] SE8 ... 141 B6
Tristan Sq SE3 ... 142 C2
Tristram Cl E17 ... 54 B6
Tristram Dr N9 ... 18 A1
Tristram Rd BR1 ... 186 D6
Triton Ct EC2 ... 242 D5
  Woodford IG8 ... 21 A2
Triton Ho [2] E14 ... 119 D2
Tritton Ave CR0 ... 220 A4
Tritton Ho N1 ... 17 B5
Tritton Rd SE21, SE27 ... 161 B1
Triumph Cl UB7 ... 127 A4
Triumph Ho IG11 ... 102 A4
Triumph Rd E6 ... 100 B1
Triumph Trad Est N17 ... 34 A4

Trocette Mans SE1 ... 263 B6
Trojan Ct
  Brondesbury NW6 ... 69 A1
  [9] Ealing W7 ... 109 A5
Trojan Ind Est NW10 ... 67 D2
Trojan Way CR0 ... 220 B5
Troon Cl
  [34] Bermondsey SE16 ... 118 B1
  Erith SE28 ... 102 D1
Troon Ct UB1 ... 108 A6
Troon Ho [9] E14 ... 97 A1
Troon St E1 ... 97 A1
Tropical Ct [2] W10 ... 90 D4
Trosley Rd DA17 ... 147 C6
Trossachs Rd SE22 ... 161 C6
Trothy Rd SE1 ... 118 A2
Trotman Ho [1] SE14 ... 140 C4
Trott Rd N10 ... 31 A3
Trott St SW11 ... 136 C4 267 A1
Trotwood Ho [3] SE16 ... 118 B4
Troubridge Ct [12] W4 ... 111 A1
Troughton Rd SE7 ... 121 B1
Troutbeck NW1 ... 231 D1
Troutbeck Rd SE14 ... 141 A4
Trouville Rd SW4 ... 159 C5
Trowbridge Est [6] E15 ... 75 B2
Trowbridge Rd E9 ... 75 B2
Trower Ho [5] E9 ... 75 A2
Trowlock Ave TW11 ... 175 C4
Trowlock Island TW11 ... 175 D4
Trowlock Way TW11 ... 175 D4
Troy Ct W8 ... 255 A6
  [5] Woolwich SE18 ... 122 D2
Troyes Ho NW3 ... 70 D3
Troy Rd SE19 ... 183 B4
Troy Town N15 ... 140 A2
Troy Town Flats SE15 ... 140 A2
Trubshaw Rd UB2 ... 107 D3
Trulock Ct N17 ... 34 A3
Trulock Rd N17 ... 34 A3
Truman Cl [2] HA8 ... 27 A3
Truman's Rd [24] N16 ... 73 C3
Trumpers Way W7 ... 108 D3
Trumpeters Inn TW9 ... 153 C6
Trumpington Rd E7 ... 76 D4
Trump St EC2 ... 242 B1
Trundlers Way WD23 ... 8 C3
Trundle St SE1 ... 252 A2
Trundleys Rd SE8 ... 141 A6
Trundley's Rd SE8 ... 118 D1
Trundley's Terr SE8 ... 118 D2
Truro Ct [2] N8 ... 49 D4
Truro Gdns IG1 ... 56 A2
Truro Ho
  [25] Paddington W2 ... 91 C2
  Pinner HA5 ... 40 A5
Truro Rd Walthamstow E17 ... 53 B5
  Wood Green N22 ... 32 B3
Truro St NW5 ... 71 A2
Truro Way UB4 ... 83 C4
Truscott Ho [3] CR7 ... 204 C3
Trusedale Rd E6 ... 100 B1
Truslove Rd SE27 ... 182 D5
Trussley Rd W6 ... 112 C3
Trust Wlk SE21 ... 160 D3
Tryfan Cl IG4 ... 55 C4
Tryon Cres E9 ... 96 C6
Tryon St SW3 ... 114 D1 257 C2
Trystings Cl KT10 ... 213 A2
Tuam Rd SE18 ... 145 B6
Tubbenden Cl BR6 ... 227 C5
Tubbenden Dr BR6 ... 227 B4
Tubbenden Jun & Inf Schs
  BR6 ... 227 B4
Tubbenden La BR6 ... 227 C5
Tubbenden La S BR6 ... 227 B3
Tubbs Rd NW10 ... 89 D5
Tudor Ave
  Hampton TW12 ... 173 C3
  North Cheam KT4 ... 216 B4
Tudor Cl Ashford TW15 ... 170 A6
  BR7 ... 188 B2
  Cheam SM3 ... 217 A2
  Chessington KT9 ... 214 A3
  Crouch End N6 ... 49 C2
  Hampstead NW3 ... 70 C2
  Hampton TW12 ... 174 A5
  Hendon NW7 ... 28 A4
  Pinner HA5 ... 40 A4
  Tulse Hill SW2 ... 160 B5
  Wallington SM6 ... 219 C1
  Welsh Harp NW9 ... 67 A6
  Woodford IG8 ... 37 B5
Tudor Coll WC1 ... 233 A1
Tudor Court N HA9 ... 66 C3
Tudor Court S HA9 ... 66 C3
Tudor Cres EN2 ... 5 A4
Tudor Ct [2] Barnet EN5 ... 1 B1
  [3] Ealing W13 ... 87 C1
  Feltham TW13 ... 172 C6
  Kingsland N1 ... 73 C2
  [5] Rotherhithe SE16 ... 118 D5
  Sidcup DA14 ... 168 A1
  South Acton W5 ... 110 C4
  [4] Stanwell TW19 ... 148 A5
  Teddington TW11 ... 174 D4
  Walthamstow E17 ... 53 B2
Tudor Dr
  Kingston u T KT2 ... 176 A5
  Walton-on-T KT12 ... 194 D1

Tudor Dr continued
  West Barnes SM4 ... 201 A3
Tudor Ent Pk HA3 ... 42 B6
Tudor Est NW10 ... 88 D5
Tudor Gables NW7 ... 27 D6
Tudor Gdns Acton W3 ... 88 C1
  Harrow HA3 ... 24 B1
  Mortlake SW14 ... 133 C2
  Twickenham TW1 ... 152 D3
  Welsh Harp NW9 ... 67 A6
  West Wickham BR4 ... 224 A5
Tudor Gr E9 ... 74 C1
Tudor Ho
  Brook Green W14 ... 112 D2
  Feltham TW13 ... 172 C6
  [34] Newham E6 ... 74 C1
  Mitcham CR4 ... 181 A2
  Queensbury NW9 ... 44 C5
  [6] Muswell Hill N10 ... 31 A3
  Tolworth KT6 ... 198 C1
Tudor Lo [4] N12 ... 29 D5
Tudor Mews
  Walthamstow E17 ... 53 B5
  [2] Willesden NW10 ... 68 A2
Tudor Par Dagenham RM6 ... 58 D2
  SE9 ... 144 A1
Tudor Pl SW19 ... 180 C3
Tudor Prim Sch
  Finchley N3 ... 30 A2
  Southall UB1 ... 107 A6
Tudor Rd Ashford TW15 ... 171 B4
  Barking IG11 ... 101 D6
  Barnet EN5 ... 1 D2
  Beckenham BR3 ... 208 A6
  Chingford E4 ... 35 D4
  Croydon SE25 ... 206 B4
  Hackney E9 ... 96 B6
  Hampton TW12 ... 173 C3
  Harrow HA3 ... 24 B1
  Hayes UB3 ... 83 B1
  Isleworth TW3 ... 130 B1
  Kingston u T KT2 ... 176 C3
  Newham E6 ... 99 C6
  Penge SE19 ... 183 D3
  Pinner HA5 ... 22 C1
  Ponders End N9 ... 18 C4
  Southall UB1 ... 107 A6
Tudor Sq UB3 ... 83 B2
Tudor St EC4 ... 116 C6 251 B6
Tudors The [2] BR3 ... 185 D1
Tudor Way BR5 ... 211 B3
  Hillingdon UB10 ... 60 C2
  Osidge N14 ... 15 D3
  South Acton W3 ... 110 C4
Tudor Well Cl HA7 ... 25 B5
Tudor Wlk DA5 ... 169 A5
Tudway Rd SE3, SE9 ... 143 C1
Tufnell Ct [3] E3 ... 97 B6
Tufnell Mans [7] N7 ... 71 D4
TUFNELL PARK ... 71 B4
Tufnell Park Mans [2] N7 ... 72 A5
Tufnell Park Prim Sch
  N7 ... 71 C4
Tufnell Park Rd N19, N7 ... 71 D4
Tufnell Park Sta N19 ... 71 C4
Tufton Ct SW1 ... 260 A5
Tufton Gdns KT8 ... 173 D1
Tufton Rd E4 ... 35 C6
Tufton St SW1 ... 116 A3 260 A5
Tugboat St SE28 ... 123 C4
Tugela Rd CR0 ... 205 B3
Tugela St SE6 ... 163 B2
Tugmutton Cl BR6 ... 226 D4
Tuke Sch SE15 ... 140 B4
Tulip Cl Croydon CR0 ... 206 D1
  Hampton TW12 ... 173 B4
  [5] Newham E6 ... 100 B2
  Southall UB2 ... 108 A4
Tulip Ct [1] HA5 ... 40 C6
Tulip Gdns Chingford E4 ... 20 B1
  Ilford IG1 ... 78 D2
Tullis Ho [12] E9 ... 74 C1
Tull St CR4 ... 202 D2
Tulse Cl BR3 ... 208 A6
TULSE HILL ... 160 D4
Tulse Hill Tulse Hill SW2 ... 160 C4
  Tulse Hill SW27 ... 160 D2
Tulse Hill Sta SE27 ... 160 D2
Tulse Ho SW2 ... 160 C5
Tulsemere Rd SE21,
  SE27 ... 161 A2
Tumbling Bay KT12 ... 194 A3
Tummons Gdns SE25 ... 183 C1
Tump Ho SE28 ... 123 C5
Tunbridge Ct [1] SE26 ... 162 A1
Tunbridge Ho EC1 ... 234 C2
Tuncombe Rd N18 ... 33 C6
Tunis Rd W12 ... 112 B5
Tunley Gn [12] E14 ... 97 B2
Tunley Rd
  Dagenham NW10 ... 89 C6
  Upper Tooting SW12,
  SW17 ... 159 A2
Tunmarsh La E13 ... 99 C4
Tunnan Leys E6 ... 100 C1
Tunnel Avenue Trad Est
  SE10 ... 120 B4
Tunnel Gdns N11 ... 31 C3
Tunnel Link Rd TW6 ... 148 C5
Tunnel Rd SE16 ... 118 C4

Tunnel Rd E TW6 ... 126 D3
Tunnel Rd W TW6 ... 126 D4
Tunstall Cl BR6 ... 227 C4
Tunstall Ct [14] TW9 ... 132 B4
Tunstall Rd Croydon CR0 ... 205 C1
  Stockwell SW9 ... 138 B1
Tunstall Wlk [10] TW8 ... 132 A6
Tunstock Way DA17 ... 125 A3
Tunworth Cl NW9 ... 45 A3
Tunworth Cres SW15 ... 155 D5
Tun Yd SW8 ... 137 B2
Tupelo Rd E10 ... 75 D6
Tupman Ho [28] SE16 ... 118 A4
Tuppy St SE28 ... 123 A3
Turberville Ho [1] SW9 ... 138 B2
Turenne Cl SW18 ... 136 A1
Turin Gr Sch N9 ... 18 C4
Turin Rd N9 ... 18 C4
Turin St E2 ... 96 A4
Turkey Oak Cl SE19 ... 183 C2
Turkey St EN1, EN3 ... 6 C6
Turkey Street Sta EN3 ... 6 C6
Turks Cl UB8 ... 82 C4
Turk's Head Yd EC1 ... 241 C4
Turks Row SW3 ... 114 D1 257 D2
  Thornton Heath SW16 ... 182 A1
Turle Rd Finsbury Pk N4 ... 72 B2
Turlewray Cl N4 ... 50 B1
Turley Cl E15 ... 98 C6
Turnagain La EC4 ... 241 C2
Turnage Rd RM8 ... 59 A1
Turnant Rd N17 ... 33 A2
Turnberry Cl
  [24] Bermondsey SE16 ... 118 B1
  Hendon NW4 ... 28 D1
Turnberry Quay [1] E14 ... 119 D3
Turnberry Way BR6 ... 211 B1
Turnbull Ho N1 ... 234 D6
Turnbury Cl SE28 ... 102 D1
Turnchapel Mews [1]
  SW4 ... 137 B2
Turner Ave Mitcham CR4 ... 180 D2
  Tottenham N15 ... 51 C5
  Twickenham TW2 ... 152 A1
Turner Cl [7] Brixton SW9 ... 138 D2
  Hampstead Garden Suburb
  NW11 ... 47 D3
  Hillingdon UB4 ... 83 A4
  Wembley HA0 ... 65 D2
Turner Cres CR7 ... 205 A3
Turner Ct
  [9] Herne Hill SE5 ... 139 B1
  [24] Rotherhithe SE16 ... 118 C4
Turner Dr NW11 ... 47 D3
Turner Ho Finsbury Pk N4 ... 50 B1
  [24] Millwall E14 ... 119 C4
  St John's Wood NW8 ... 230 A4
  Strand WC2 ... 250 B5
  [6] Twickenham TW1 ... 153 D5
  Westminster SW1 ... 259 D3
Turner Lo [10] SW19 ... 156 D3
Turner Mews SM2 ... 217 D1
Turner Pl SW11 ... 158 C6
Turner Rd Edgware HA8 ... 26 B1
  New Malden KT3 ... 199 B2
  Walthamstow E17 ... 54 A6
Turners Cl N20 ... 14 D1
Turners Ct Leyton E15 ... 76 A4
  New Barnet EN5 ... 13 D5
  Tottenham N15 ... 51 B4
Turners Meadow Way
  BR3 ... 185 B2
Turner's Rd E3 ... 97 B2
Turner St
  Canning Town E16 ... 98 D1
  Stepney E1 ... 96 B2
Turners Way CR0 ... 220 C6
Turneville Rd
  W14 ... 135 B6 264 C6
Turney Rd SE21 ... 161 B4
Turney Sch SE21 ... 161 A4
Turnham Green Sta W4 ... 111 C2
Turnham Green Terr
  W4 ... 111 C2
Turnham Ho SE4 ... 141 A1
Turnham Prim Sch [1]
  SE4 ... 141 A1
Turnham Rd SE4 ... 141 A1
Turnmill Ho [8] SW2 ... 160 C6
Turnmill St EC1 ... 94 D2 241 C4
Turnour Ho [31] E1 ... 96 B1
Turnpike Cl SE8 ... 141 B5
Turnpike Ho DA6 ... 146 D1
Turnpike Ho EC1 ... 234 D2
Turnpike La Hornsey N8 ... 50 C6
  Sutton SM1 ... 218 A3
  Uxbridge UB10 ... 82 A5
Turnpike Lane Sta N15 ... 50 D6
Turnpike Link CR0 ... 221 C6
Turnpike Mews N8 ... 50 C6
Turnpike Way TW7 ... 131 A4
Turnstone Cl
  Edgware NW9 ... 27 C1
  Newham E13 ... 99 A4
  Uxbridge UB10 ... 60 D3
Turnstone Terr [11] W13 ... 86 D3
Turpentine La
  SW1 ... 115 B1 258 D1
Turpin Cl [15] EN3 ... 7 C6

Turpington Cl BR2 ... 210 A2
Turpington La BR2 ... 210 A3
Turpin Ho SW11 ... 268 C2
Turpin Rd TW14 ... 149 C5
Turpin Way
  Upper Holloway N19 ... 49 D1
  Wallington SM6 ... 219 B1
Turquand St SE17 ... 262 B3
Turret Gr SW4 ... 137 C2
Turret Ho KT2 ... 176 A4
Turton Ho [5] SE18 ... 144 D6
Turton Rd HA0 ... 66 A3
Turville Ho NW8 ... 237 A6
Turville St E2 ... 243 C6
Tuscan Ho [36] E2 ... 96 C4
Tuscan Rd SE18 ... 123 B1
Tuscany Ho E17 ... 35 B1
Tuskar St SE10 ... 120 C1
Tuttlebee La IG9 ... 21 A2
Tuttle Ho SW1 ... 259 D1
Tweed Ct W7 ... 86 C1
Tweeddale Gr UB10 ... 61 A5
Tweeddale Prim Sch
  SM5 ... 202 B2
Tweeddale Rd SM5 ... 202 B1
Tweed Ho E14 ... 98 A3
Tweedmouth Rd E13 ... 99 B5
Tweedy Cl EN1 ... 17 D6
Tweedy Rd BR1 ... 187 A2
Tweezer's Alley WC2 ... 251 A6
Twelve Acre Ho [5] E12 ... 78 C5
Twelvetrees Bsns Pk E16 ... 98 B3
Twelvetrees Cres E3 ... 98 A3
Twentyman Cl IG8 ... 37 A5
TWICKENHAM ... 152 D4
Twickenham Bridge
  TW9 ... 153 C6
Twickenham Cl CR0 ... 220 B5
Twickenham Gdns
  Harrow HA3 ... 24 C3
  Wembley UB6 ... 65 A3
Twickenham Mus The*
  TW1 ... 153 A3
Twickenham Pl KT7 ... 212 D6
Twickenham Prep Sch
  TW12 ... 174 A2
Twickenham Rd
  Isleworth TW1, TW7 ... 131 A2
  Leyton E11 ... 76 B6
  Richmond TW1, TW9 ... 131 C1
  Teddington TW11 ... 175 A6
  Twickenham TW3 ... 151 B1
Twickenham Sta TW1 ... 153 A4
Twickenham Stad (Rugby
  Football Union)* TW2 ... 152 C5
Twickenham Stoop Stadium
  TW2 ... 152 D4
Twickenham Trad Ctr
  TW1 ... 152 D5
Twickenham Trad Est
  TW1 ... 152 D5
Twig Folly Cl [21] E2 ... 96 D5
Twilley St SW18 ... 157 D4
Twine Cl IG11 ... 102 B4
Twine Ct E1 ... 118 C6
Twineham Gn N12 ... 29 C6
Twining Ave TW2 ... 152 B1
Twinings Mus* WC2 ... 241 A1
Twinn Rd NW7 ... 29 A4
Twin Tumps Way SE28 ... 124 A6
Twisden Rd NW5 ... 71 B4
Twiss Ho [6] SE18 ... 122 D1
Twist Ho E10 ... 75 D6
Two Bridges Ind Est
  CR0 ... 221 B2
Twybridge Way NW10 ... 67 A1
Twycross Mews SE10 ... 120 C2
Twyford Abbey Rd NW10 ... 88 B4
Twyford Ave Acton W3 ... 110 C6
  Muswell Hill N2 ... 48 D6
Twyford CE High Sch
  W3 ... 110 D5
Twyford Cres W3 ... 110 C5
Twyford Ct Acton W3 ... 110 C6
  Muswell Hill N10 ... 49 A6
  [6] Wembley HA0 ... 88 A5
Twyford Ho Highbury N5 ... 72 D5
  [6] Tottenham N15 ... 51 C3
Twyford Par KT6 ... 198 C1
Twyford Pl
  Carshalton SM5 ... 202 B1
  Harrow HA2 ... 41 D2
  Ilford IG1 ... 79 A3
Twyford Sp Ctr W3 ... 110 D5
Twyford St N1 ... 94 B6 233 C6
Twynholm Mans SW6 ... 264 A4
Tyas Rd E16 ... 98 D3
Tybenham Rd SW19 ... 201 C6
Tyberry Rd EN3 ... 6 C2
Tyburn La HA1 ... 42 D2
Tyburn Tree (site of)*
  W2 ... 247 C6
Tyburn Way W1 ... 247 C6
Tye La BR6 ... 227 A3
Tyer's Est SE1 ... 253 A2
Tyers Gate SE1 ... 117 C4 253 A1
Tyers Ho [1] SW16 ... 181 C5
Tyers St SE11 ... 116 B1 260 C2
Tyers Terr SE11 ... 116 B1 260 D1
Tyeshurst Cl SE2 ... 125 A1

Tylecroft Rd SW16 . . . . . . .182 A1
Tylehurst Gdns IG1 . . . . . . .79 A3
Tyler Cl Erith DA8 . . . . . .147 D5
 Haggerston E2 . . . . .95 D5
Tyler Ho SE3 . . . . .142 B3
Tyler Rd UB2 . . . . .107 D3
Tylers Ct
 4 Walthamstow E17 . . . . . . .53 C5
 5 Wembley HA0 . . . . .88 A5
Tylers Gate HA3 . . . . .44 A3
Tylers Path SM5 . . . . .218 D4
Tyler St Greenwich SE10 . . . .120 C1
 SE10 . . . . .142 C6
Tylney Ave SE19 . . . . .183 D5
Tylney Ho 10 E1 . . . . .96 B1
Tylney Rd BR1 . . . . .187 D1
 Forest Gate E7 . . . . .77 C4
Tymperley Ct SW19 . . . . . .157 A3
Tynamara KT1 . . . . .197 D5
Tynan Cl TW14 . . . . .150 A3
Tyndale La N1 . . . . .72 D1
Tyndale Mans N1 . . . . .72 D1
Tyndale Terr 13 N1 . . . . .72 D1
Tyndall Gdns E10 . . . . .76 A6
Tyndall Rd DA16 . . . . .145 D2
 Leyton E10 . . . . .76 A6
Tyne Ct W7 . . . . .86 C1
Tyneham Cl 10 SW11 . . . . . .137 A4
Tyneham Rd SW11 . . . . . . .137 A4
Tyne Ho 8 KT2 . . . . .175 D2
Tynemouth Cl E6 . . . . .100 D1
Tynemouth Dr EN1 . . . . .6 A5
Tynemouth Rd
 Mitcham CR4 . . . . .181 A3
 Plumstead Comm SE18 . . . .123 C1
 Tottenham N15 . . . . .51 D5
Tynemouth St SW6 . . . . . . .136 A3
Tynemouth Terr 9 N15 . . . . .51 D5
Tyne St E1 . . . . .243 D2
Tynsdale Rd NW10 . . . . .67 C2
Tynte Ct E9 . . . . .75 A3
Tynwald Ho 14 SE26 . . . . . .162 A1
Type St E2 . . . . .96 D5
Tyrawley Rd SW6 . . . . .265 C2
Tyrell Cl HA1 . . . . .64 C4
Tyrell Ct SM5 . . . . .218 D4
Tyrells Ct 3 SE15 . . . . .140 B2
Tyrols Rd SE23 . . . . .162 D3
Tyrone Ct SW16 . . . . .181 D5
Tyrone Rd E6 . . . . .100 B4
Tyron Way DA14 . . . . .189 D5
Tyrrell Ave DA16 . . . . .168 B6
Tyrrell Ho Catford BR3 . . . . .185 D5
 SW1 . . . . .269 B6
Tyrrell Rd SE22 . . . . .140 A1
Tyrrell Sq CR4 . . . . .180 C2
Tyrrel Way NW9 . . . . .46 A2
Tyrwhitt Rd SE4 . . . . .141 C2
Tysoe Ave EN3 . . . . .7 B6
Tysoe St EC1 . . . . .234 B1
Tyson Rd SE23 . . . . .162 C4
Tyssen Com Prim Sch
 N16 . . . . .52 A1
Tyssen Rd N16 . . . . .73 D5
Tyssen St Dalston E8 . . . . . .73 D2
 Hoxton N1 . . . . .95 C5
Tyson Ho E9 . . . . .75 A1
Tytherton 29 E2 . . . . .96 C5
Tytherton Rd N19 . . . . .71 D5

U

Uamvar St E14 . . . . .97 D2
Uckfield Gr CR4 . . . . .181 A2
Uckfield Rd EN3 . . . . .6 D6
Udall St SW1 . . . . .259 B3
Udimore Ho 11 W10 . . . . . . .90 C2
Udney Park Rd TW11 . . . . . .175 A4
Uffington Rd
 West Norwood SE27 . . . . . .182 C6
 Willesden Green NW10 . . . . . .90 B6
Ufford Cl HA3 . . . . .23 D3
Ufford Rd HA3 . . . . .23 D3
Ufford St SE1 . . . . . . .116 C4 251 B2
Ufton Gr UB5 . . . . .84 D4
Ufton Gr N1 . . . . .73 B1
Ufton Rd N1 . . . . .73 C1
Uhura Sq N16 . . . . .73 C5
 Streatham SW16 . . . . .182 A6
Ujima Ct Finsbury Pk N19 . . . .50 A1
Ujima Ho SW16 . . . . .182 A6
UK Coll of Bsns & Computing
 IG2 . . . . .56 C3
Uk Cotts UB3 . . . . .105 B4
Ullathorne Rd SW16 . . . . . .181 C6
Ulleswater Rd N14 . . . . .16 B1
Ullin St E14 . . . . .98 A2
Ullswater SW15 . . . . .156 D5
Ullswater Cl
 Bromley BR1 . . . . .186 C3
 Hayes UB4 . . . . .83 C5
 Kingston u T KT2, SW15 . . . .177 B6
Ullswater Cres SW15 . . . . .177 B6
Ullswater Ct Harrow HA2 . . . .41 C2
 2 Woodford E18 . . . . .37 A1
Ullswater Ho SE15 . . . . . . .140 C6
Ullswater Rd
 Barnes SW13 . . . . .134 A5

Ullswater Rd continued
 West Norwood SE27,
 SW16 . . . . .160 D2
Ulster Ct KT2 . . . . .175 D4
Ulster Gdns N13 . . . . .33 A6
Ulster Pl NW1 . . . . .238 C5
Ulster Terr NW1 . . . . .238 C6
Ulundi Rd SE3 . . . . .142 C6
Ulva Rd SW15 . . . . .134 D1
Ulverscroft Rd SE22 . . . . . .162 A6
Ulverstone Rd SE27 . . . . . .160 D2
Ulverston Rd E17 . . . . .36 B1
Ulysses Rd NW6 . . . . .69 B3
Umberston St E1 . . . . .96 B1
Umbria St SW15 . . . . .156 A5
Umfreville Rd N4 . . . . .50 D3
Umoja Ho N22 . . . . .32 B1
Una Ho 7 NW5 . . . . .71 B2
Undercliff SE10 . . . . .142 A4
Undercliff Rd SE13 . . . . . . .141 D2
UNDERHILL 13 C6
Underhill EN5 . . . . .13 C6
Underhill Ct EN5 . . . . .13 C6
Underhill Ho 7 E14 . . . . . . .97 C2
Underhill Jun & Inf Schs
 EN5 . . . . .13 A6
Underhill Pas NW1 . . . . . . .231 D6
Underhill Rd SE21, SE22 . . .162 B4
Underhill St NW1 . . . . .231 D5
Underne Ave N14 . . . . .15 B2
Undershaft EC3 . . . . . .95 C1 243 A1
Undershaw Rd BR1 . . . . . . .164 D1
Underwood CR0 . . . . .224 A3
Underwood Ct 3 E10 . . . . . .53 D1
Underwood Ho
 East Molesey KT8 . . . . .195 C4
 Hammersmith W6 . . . . .112 B3
Underwood Rd
 Bethnal Green E1 . . . . .96 A3
 Chingford E4 . . . . .35 D5
 Woodford IG8 . . . . .37 D3
Underwood Row N1 . . . . . . .235 B2
Underwood St N1 . . .95 A4 235 B2
Underwood The SE9 . . . . . .166 B2
Undine Rd E14 . . . . .119 D2
Undine St SW17 . . . . .180 D5
Uneeda Dr UB6 . . . . .86 B6
Unicorn Bldg 14 E1 . . . . . . .118 C6
Unicorn Prim Sch BR3 . . . . .207 D4
Unicorn Sch TW9 . . . . .132 B4
Unicorn Works N17 . . . . . . .34 C3
Union Cl E11 . . . . .76 B4
Union Ct
 45 Paddington W2 . . . . .91 C2
 2 Richmond TW10 . . . . . . .154 A6
 South Lambeth SW4 . . . . . . .138 A3
 Whitechapel EC2 . . . . .243 A2
Union Dr E1 . . . . .97 A3
Union Gr SW8 . . . . .137 D3
Union Mews 32 SW9 . . . . . .138 A3
Union Pk 11 SE10 . . . . .120 D1
Union Rd BR2 . . . . .209 D4
 Clapham SW8 . . . . .137 D3
 Friern Barnet N11 . . . . .31 D4
 Northolt UB5 . . . . .85 C5
 Thornton Heath CR0 . . . . . .205 A2
 Wembley HA0 . . . . .66 A2
Union Sq N1 . . . . . .95 A6 235 B5
Union St Barnet EN5 . . . . .1 A2
 Kingston u T KT1 . . . . .175 D1
 Mill Meads E15 . . . . .98 B6
 SE1 . . . . .117 A5 252 A1
Union Terr HA2 . . . . .41 C1
Union Wharf N1 . . . . .235 B4
Union Wlk E2 . . . . .95 C4
Union Yd W1 . . . . .238 D1
United International Coll
 W1 . . . . .238 D3
Unity Cl
 West Norwood SE19 . . . . . .183 A5
 Willesden NW10 . . . . .68 A2
Unity Mews NW1 . . . . .232 C4
Unity Rd RI3 . . . . .6 C6
Unity Terr HA2 . . . . .63 D6
Unity Way SE18 . . . . .121 D3
Univ Coll Jun Sch 31
 NW3 . . . . .70 A4
Univ Coll London
 Bloomsbury WC1 . . .93 D3 239 C6
 Bloomsbury WC1 . . .94 A3 240 B6
Univ Coll London (Windeyer
 Inst) W1 . . . . .93 C2 239 A4
Univ Coll London (Wolfson
 Ho) NW1 . . . . .93 C4 232 B1
University Cl NW7 . . . . .27 D3
University Coll Hospl
 WC1 . . . . .93 C3 239 B6
University Coll Sch NW3 . .70 A3
University Gdns DA5 . . . . . .169 B4
University Mans 9
 SW15 . . . . .134 D2
University Pl DA8 . . . . .147 D5
University Rd SW19 . . . . . .180 B4
University St WC1 . .93 C3 239 B5
University Way E16 . . . . . . .122 D6
Univ of California
 WC1 . . . . .93 D2 239 D3
Univ of East London
 Barking RM8 . . . . .80 A4
 Newham E16 . . . . .122 C4

Univ of East London continued
 Stratford E15 . . . . .76 C2
Univ of East London (Duncan
 Ho) 7 E15 . . . . .98 B6
Univ of East London
 (Holbrook Ctr) E15 . . . . . . .98 D5
Univ of Greenwich SE10 . .142 B6
Univ of Greenwich Avery Hill
Campus Mansion Site
 SE9 . . . . .167 A5
Univ of Greenwich Avery Hill
Campus Southwood Site
 SE9 . . . . .167 B4
Univ of London
 WC1 . . . . .93 D3 239 D5
Univ of London (King's Coll
 Hall) SE5 . . . . .139 B2
Univ of London Obsy
 NW7 . . . . .27 D4
Univ of London (Queen Mary
 & Westfield Coll) E1 . . . . . .97 A3
Univ of Notre Dame
 SW1 . . . . .115 D6 249 D5
Univ of Notre Dame
 SW1 . . . . .249 D4
Univ of Westminster
 (Cavendish Campus)
 W1 . . . . .93 C2 239 A4
Univ of Westminster (Harrow
 Campus) HA1 . . . . .43 A2
Univ of Westminster
 (Marylebone Campus)
 W1 . . . . .93 A2 238 A4
Univ of Westminster (Regent
 Campus) W1 . . . . . .93 C2 239 A3
Univ of Westminster (Regent
 Campus, Univ HQ)
 W1 . . . . .93 B1 238 D2
Univ of Westminster
 (Wigram House Halls of
 Residence)
 SW1 . . . . .115 C3 259 B5
Uno Apartments 4 BR1 . .187 A2
Unwin Ave TW14 . . . . .149 B6
Unwin Cl SE15 . . . . .140 A6
Unwin Rd Isleworth TW7 . . .130 C2
 SW7 . . . . .114 B3 256 C6
Upbrook Mews
 W2 . . . . .92 A1 236 B1
Upcerne Rd
 SW10 . . . . .136 A5 266 B3
Upchurch Cl 8 SE20 . . . . . .184 B3
Upcott Ho 33 Bromley E3 . . . .97 D4
 4 Hackney E9 . . . . .74 C1
Upcroft Ave HA8 . . . . .27 B6
Updale Rd DA14 . . . . .189 D6
Upfield CR0 . . . . .222 B5
Upfield Rd W7 . . . . .86 D2
Upgrove Manor Way 12
 SE24 . . . . .160 C4
Uphall Prim Sch IG1 . . . . . . .78 D3
Uphall Rd IG1 . . . . .78 D3
Upham Park Rd W4 . . . . . . .111 C2
Uphill Dr Edgware NW7 . . . . .27 C5
 Kingsbury NW9 . . . . .45 A4
Uphill Gr NW7 . . . . .27 C6
Uphill Rd NW7 . . . . .27 C6
Upland Ct SE23 . . . . .162 C2
Upland Prim Sch DA7 . . . . .147 B2
Upland Rd Croydon CR2 . . .221 B3
 DA7 . . . . .147 B2
 East Dulwich SE22 . . . . . . .162 A5
 8 Newham E13 . . . . .99 A3
 Sutton SM2 . . . . .218 B1
Uplands Beckenham BR3 . .185 C1
 Woolwich SE18 . . . . .122 D1
Uplands Ave E17 . . . . .34 D1
Uplands Bsns Pk E17 . . . . . .52 D6
Uplands Cl SW14 . . . . .154 D6
Uplands Ct N21 . . . . .16 C4
Uplands Park Rd EN2 . . . . . . .4 C3
Uplands Rd
 East Barnet EN4 . . . . .15 A3
 Hornsey Vale N8 . . . . .50 B4
 Ilford RM6 . . . . .58 D6
 Woodford IG8 . . . . .37 D3
Uplands The HA4 . . . . .40 A1
Uplands Way N21 . . . . .16 C6
Upnall Ho 16 SE15 . . . . . . .140 C6
Upney Ct 2 IG11 . . . . .79 D1
Upney La IG11 . . . . .79 D1
Upney Sta IG11 . . . . .79 D1
Upnor Way SE17 . . . . .263 B2
Uppark Dr IG2 . . . . .57 A3
Upper Abbey Rd DA17 . . . .125 C2
Upper Addison Gdns
 W14 . . . . .113 A4 244 A2
Upper Bank St E14 . . . . . . .119 C5
Upper Bardsey Wlk 7
 N1 . . . . .73 A2
Upper Belgrave St
 SW1 . . . . .115 A3 258 B6
Upper Berkeley St
 W1 . . . . .92 D1 237 A2
Upper Beulah Hill SE19 . . .183 C2
Upper Brighton Rd KT6 . . . .198 A2
Upper Brockley Rd SE4 . . . .141 B3
Upper Brook St
 W1 . . . . .115 A6 248 A6
Upper Butts TW8 . . . . .131 C6

Upper Caldy Wlk 18 N1 . . . .73 A2
Upper Camelford Wlk 14
 W10 . . . . .91 A1
Upper Cavendish Ave N3 . . .47 C6
Upper Cheyne Row
 SW3 . . . . .136 C6 267 A6
UPPER CLAPTON 52 B1
Upper Clapton Rd E5 . . . . . .74 B6
Upper Clarendon Wlk 12
 W11 . . . . .91 A1
Upper Dengie Wlk N1 . . . . .235 A6
UPPER EDMONTON 34 B5
UPPER ELMERS END 207 B3
Upper Elmers End Rd
 BR3 . . . . .207 A4
Upper Farm Rd KT8 . . . . . . .195 B5
Upper Fosters NW4 . . . . . . .46 C5
Upper Gn W CR4 . . . . .180 D1
Upper Gr SE25 . . . . .205 D5
Upper Grosvenor St
 W1 . . . . .115 A6 248 A6
Upper Grotto Rd TW1 . . . . .152 D2
Upper Ground
 SE1 . . . . .116 C5 251 A4
Upper Grove Rd DA17 . . . . .147 B6
Upper Gulland Wlk 23
 N1 . . . . .73 A2
UPPER HALLIFORD 193 B5
Upper Halliford Rd
 TW17 . . . . .193 C6
Upper Halliford Sta
 TW16 . . . . .171 C1
Upper Hampstead Wlk 29
 NW3 . . . . .70 A4
Upper Ham Rd KT2,
 TW10 . . . . .175 D2
Upper Handa Wlk 2 N1 . . . .73 A2
Upper Harley St NW1 . . . . .238 B5
Upper Hawkwell Wlk N1 . . .235 B6
UPPER HOLLOWAY 71 C6
Upper Holloway Sta N19 . . .71 C6
Upper Holly Hill Rd
 DA17 . . . . .125 D1
Upper James St W1 . . . . . . .249 B6
Upper John St W1 . . . . .249 B6
Upper Lismore Wlk 8
 N1 . . . . .73 A2
Upper Lodge Mews
 TW12 . . . . .174 A4
Upper Mall W6 . . . . .112 B1
Upper Marsh
 SE1 . . . . .116 B3 260 D6
Upper Montague St
 W1 . . . . .92 D2 237 C3
Upper Mulgrave Rd
 SM2 . . . . .217 A1
Upper North St E3, E14 . . . .97 C2
UPPER NORWOOD 183 C3
Upper Park Rd
 Belvedere DA17 . . . . .125 D2
 BR1 . . . . .187 C2
 Friern Barnet N11 . . . . .31 C5
 Kingston u T KT2 . . . . .176 C4
 Maitland Pk NW3 . . . . .70 D3
Upper Phillimore Gdns
 W8 . . . . .113 C4 245 A1
Upper Pk IG10 . . . . .21 D6
Upper Ramsey Wlk 19 N1 . .73 B2
Upper Rawreth Wlk N1 . . . .235 B6
Upper Rd Finchley N2 . . . . . .30 C2
 Newham E13 . . . . .99 A4
 Wallington SM6 . . . . .219 D3
Upper Richmond Rd
 SW15 . . . . .134 C1
Upper Richmond Rd W TW10,
 SW14, SW15 . . . . .133 A1
UPPER RUXLEY 191 C3
Upper St Martin's La
 WC2 . . . . .250 A6
Upper Selsdon Rd CR2 . . . .221 D1
Upper Sheridan Rd 3
 DA17 . . . . .125 C2
UPPER SHIRLEY 222 D4
Upper Shirley Rd CR0 . . . . .222 D5
Upper Sq TW7 . . . . .131 A2
Upper St N1 . . . . . . .94 D6 234 C5
Upper Sunbury Rd
 TW12 . . . . .173 C2
Upper Sutton La TW5 . . . . .129 C4
UPPER SYDENHAM 184 A6
Upper Tachbrook St
 SW1 . . . . .259 B4
Upper Talbot Wlk 7
 W10 . . . . .91 A1
Upper Teddington Rd KT1,
 KT8 . . . . .175 C2
Upper Terr NW3 . . . . .70 A5
Upper Thames St
 EC4 . . . . .117 A6 252 B6
Upper Tollington Pk N4 . . . .50 C1
Upperton Rd DA14 . . . . . . .189 D5
Upperton Rd E E13 . . . . .99 C4
Upperton Rd W E13 . . . . . . .99 C4
UPPERTOOTING 158 D1
Upper Tooting Park Mans 1
 SW17 . . . . .159 A2
Upper Tooting Pk SW17 . . .158 D2
Upper Tooting Rd SW17 . . .158 D1
Upper Town Rd UB6 . . . . . . .85 D3
Upper Tulse Hill SW2 . . . . .160 B3

Upper Vernon Rd SM1 . . . . .218 B3
UPPER WALTHAMSTOW . .54 C6
Upper Walthamstow Rd
 E17 . . . . .54 B6
Upper Wickham La
 DA16 . . . . .146 B4
Upper Wimpole St
 W1 . . . . .93 A2 238 B4
Upper Woburn Pl NW1,
 WC1 . . . . .93 D4 232 D1
Uppingham Ave HA7 . . . . . .25 C1
Upsdell Ave N13 . . . . .32 C4
Upshire Ho E17 . . . . .35 B1
Upstall St SE5 . . . . .138 D4
UPTON 77 B1
Upton Ave E7 . . . . .77 A1
Upton Cl Cricklewood NW2 . .69 A5
 Sidcup DA5 . . . . .169 B5
Upton Cross E13 . . . . .99 A6
Upton Cross Prim Sch
 E13 . . . . .99 B6
Upton Ct Penge SE20 . . . . .184 C3
 Southall UB1 . . . . .107 D5
 4 Wimbledon SW19 . . . . . .178 D3
Upton Day Hospl DA6 . . . . .147 A1
Upton Dene SM2 . . . . .217 D1
Upton Gdns HA3 . . . . .43 C3
Upton Hts E7 . . . . .77 A1
Upton La E7 . . . . .77 A1
Upton Lo E7 . . . . .77 A2
Upton Lodge Cl WD23 . . . . . .8 A4
UPTON PARK 99 D6
Upton Park Rd E7 . . . . .77 B1
Upton Park Sta E13 . . . . . . .99 C6
Upton Prim Sch DA5 . . . . . .169 B6
Upton Rd Bexley DA6 . . . . . .169 A6
 Edmonton N18 . . . . .34 A5
 Hounslow TW3 . . . . .129 C2
 SE18 . . . . .145 A6
 South Norwood CR7 . . . . . .183 B1
Upton Rd S DA5 . . . . .169 B5
Upton Villas 4 DA6 . . . . . . .147 A1
Upway N12 . . . . .30 C4
Upwood Rd SE12 . . . . .165 A5
 Thornton Heath SW16 . . . . .182 A2
Urban Mews N4 . . . . .50 D2
Urlwin St SE5 . . . . .139 A6
Urlwin Wlk SW9 . . . . .138 D4
Urmston Dr SW19 . . . . .157 A3
Urmston Ho 4 E14 . . . . . . .120 A2
Urquhart Ct BR3 . . . . .185 B3
Ursula Lo DA14 . . . . .190 B5
Ursula Mews N4 . . . . .51 A1
Ursula St SW11 . . . . .136 C4 267 A3
Ursuline High Sch
 SW20 . . . . .178 D2
Ursuline Prep Sch 20
 SW19 . . . . .178 D3
Urswick Gdns RM9 . . . . .81 A1
Urswick Rd
 Dagenham RM9 . . . . .81 A1
 Hackney E5, E9 . . . . .74 C3
Usborne Mews SW8 . . . . . .270 D4
Usher Hall NW4 . . . . .46 B5
Usher Rd E3 . . . . .97 B5
Usk Rd SW11 . . . . .136 A1
Usk St E2 . . . . .96 D4
Utah Bldg 3 SE13 . . . . . . .141 D4
Utopia Ho 3 NW2 . . . . .68 A2
Utopia Village
 NW1 . . . . .93 A6 231 A6
Uvedale Rd
 Dagenham RM10 . . . . .81 C5
 Enfield EN2 . . . . .17 B6
Uverdale Rd
 SW10 . . . . .136 A5 266 B3
UXBRIDGE 82 A6
Uxbridge Coll Hayes UB3 . .106 A4
 Uxbridge UB8 . . . . .60 A2
Uxbridge High Sch UB8 . .82 A5
Uxbridge Rd
 Acton W3, W5 . . . . .110 C5
 Ealing W13 . . . . .109 C6
 Feltham TW13 . . . . .150 D2
 Hampton TW12, TW13 . . . .173 D5
 Hayes UB4 . . . . .106 C6
 Hillingdon UB10, UB4 . . . . . .83 C2
 Kingston u T KT1, KT6 . . . .197 D4
 Shepherd's Bush W12 . . . . .112 B5
 Southall UB1, UB2, UB5,
 W7 . . . . .108 B5
 Stanmore HA7 . . . . .25 A4
Uxbridge Road (Harrow
 Weald) HA3 . . . . .24 B3
Uxbridge Road (Hatch End)
 HA5 . . . . .23 B3
Uxbridge Road (Pinner)
 HA5 . . . . .22 D1
Uxbridge St W8 . . . . .113 C5 245 A4
Uxendon Cres HA3, HA9 . . . .44 A1
Uxendon Hill HA9 . . . . .44 B2
Uxendon Manor JMI Sch
 HA3 . . . . .44 A4

V

Vadnie Bish Ho NW5 . . . . .71 C2
Vaine Ho 4 E9 . . . . .75 A2
Valance Ave E4 . . . . .20 D3
Valan Leas BR2 . . . . .208 C6
Vale Ave WD6 . . . . .10 D6
Vale Cl Muswell Hill N2. . . . . .48 D6
　Orpington BR6 . . . . .226 C4
　St John's Wood W9. . .92 A4 229 A1
　Twickenham TW1 . . . . .153 A1
Vale Cres SW15 . . . . .177 C6
　Pinner HA5 . . . . .41 A4
Vale Ct Barnet EN5 . . . . .1 D1
　East Acton W3 . . . . .111 D5
　St John's Wood W9. . .92 A4 229 A1
　Wembley HA0. . . . . .65 C5
Vale Dr EN5 . . . . .13 C6
Vale End SE22 . . . . .139 D1
Vale Est The W3. . . . . .111 C5
Vale Farm Sports Ctr
　HA0 . . . . .65 B4
Vale Gr Acton W3 . . . . .111 B5
　Stoke Newington N4. . . . . .51 A2
Vale La W3 . . . . .88 C2
Vale Lo SE23. . . . . .162 C2
Valence Ave RM8 . . . . .80 D6
Valence Cir RM8 . . . . .81 A5
Valence House Mus ★
　RM8 . . . . .81 A6
Valence Prim Sch RM8 . . . . .80 D6
Valence Wood Rd RM8 . . . . .81 A5
Valencia Rd HA7 . . . . .25 C6
Valens Ho 1 SW2. . . . . .160 C3
Valentia Pl SW9 . . . . .138 C1
Valentine Ave DA5 . . . . .169 A3
Valentine Ct Elstree WD6. . . . . . . .9 D5
　3 Forest Hill SE23. . . . . .162 D2
Valentine Ho
　11 Clapham Pk SW4. . . . . .159 C5
　26 Old Ford E3 . . . . .97 B6
Valentine Pl SE1. . .116 D4 251 C2
Valentine Rd Harrow HA2. . . . . . .64 A5
　Homerton E9 . . . . .74 D2
Valentine Row SE1. . . . . .251 C1
Valentines High Sch IG2. . .56 C3
Valentines Rd IG1 . . . . .56 D1
VALE OF HEALTH. 70 B5
Vale of Health NW3 . . . . .70 B5
Vale Rd BR1 . . . . .188 C1
　Claygate KT10 . . . . .212 D1
　Mitcham CR4 . . . . .203 D5
　Stoke Newington N4. . . . . .51 A2
　Sutton SM1. . . . . .217 D4
　Upton E7 . . . . .77 B2
　Worcester Pk KT19, KT4.. . . . . .215 D5
Vale Rd N N K T6 . . . . .214 A6
Vale Rd S KT6 . . . . .214 A6
Valerian Way E15 . . . . .98 C4
Valerian Wlk N11 . . . . .15 A2
Valerie Ct Belmont SM2. . . . . . . .217 D1
　Bushey WD23. . . . . .8 A4
Vale Rise NW11 . . . . .47 B1
Vale Row N5. . . . . .72 D5
Vale Royal N7 . . . . .72 A1
Valery Pl TW12. . . . . .173 C3
Vale Sch The SW7. . . . . .256 A5
Valeside Ct 2 EN5 . . . . .1 D1
Valeswood Rd BR1. . . . . .186 D5
Vale Terr N4 . . . . .51 A3
Vale The Ashford TW16. . . . . . . .172 A4
　Cricklewood NW11. . . . . .69 A6
　Croydon CR0. . . . . .222 D6
　East Acton W3 . . . . .111 C5
　Feltham TW14. . . . . .150 B5
　Heston TW5 . . . . .129 A6
　Muswell Hill N10. . . . . .31 A2
　Ruislip HA4. . . . . .62 C4
　Southgate N14 . . . . .16 A4
　SW3 . . . . .136 B6 266 D6
　Woodford IG8. . . . . .37 A3
Valetta Gr E13 . . . . .99 A5
Valetta Rd W3 . . . . .111 D4
Valette Ct N10 . . . . .49 B5
Valette Ho E9. . . . . .74 C2
Valette St E8 . . . . .74 C2
Valiant Cl 13 UB5 . . . . .84 D4
Valiant Ho
　9 Cubitt Town E14. . . . . .120 A4
　5 Greenwich SE7 . . . . .121 C1
　SW11 . . . . .266 D1
Valiant Way E6 . . . . .100 B2
Vallance Rd
　Bethnal Green E1 . . . . .96 A3
　Muswell Hill N22. . . . . .31 C1
Valley Ave N12 . . . . .30 B6
Valley (Charlton Athletic FC)
　The SE7. . . . . .121 C1
Valley Cl HA5 . . . . .22 B1
Valley Ct IG8 . . . . .37 B3
Valley Dr NW9 . . . . .44 D3
Valleyfield Rd SW16. . . . . .182 B5

Valley Gdns
　Mitcham SW19. . . . . .180 B3
　Wembley HA0. . . . . .66 B1
Valley Gr SE7 . . . . .121 C1
Valley Ho 4 Edmonton N9 . . .18 A1
　Upper Clapton E5 . . . . .52 C1
Valleylink Est EN3 . . . . .19 A5
Valley Mews TW1 . . . . .153 A2
Valley Pl KT6 . . . . .198 A3
Valley Point Ind Est CR0. .204 A2
Valley Prim Sch BR2 . . . . .186 D1
Valley Prospect 3 SE19 . .183 C4
Valley Rd
　Beckenham BR2 . . . . .186 C1
　BR5. .190 B2
　Streatham SW16. . . . . .182 B6
　Uxbridge UB10. . . . . .82 A5
Valleyside SE7. . . . . .121 D1
Valley Side E4 . . . . .19 C3
Valley Side Par E4 . . . . .19 C2
Valley View EN5. . . . . .13 A5
Valley Wlk CR0 . . . . .222 C6
Valliere Rd NW10 . . . . .90 A4
Valliers Wood Rd DA15. . .167 C3
Vallis Way
　Chessington KT9 . . . . .213 D4
　Ealing W13 . . . . .87 A2
Val McKenzie Ave N7 . . . . .72 C5
Valmar Rd SE5. . . . . .139 A4
Valmar Trad Est SE5. . . . . . .139 A4
Valnay St SW17 . . . . .180 D5
Valognes Ave E17. . . . . .35 A2
Valois Ho SE1. . . . . .263 C6
Valonia Gdns SW18 . . . . .157 B5
Vambery Rd SE18 . . . . .145 A6
Vanbern Ho NW5. . . . . .71 A2
Vanborough Ct 4 SM2. . .218 A2
Vanbrough Cres UB5. . . . . .84 C6
Vanbrugh Ct SE11. . . . . .261 B3
Vanbrugh Dr KT12 . . . . .194 C3
Vanbrugh Fields SE3 . . . . .142 D4
Vanbrugh Hill SE10, SE3 . .142 D6
Vanbrugh Ho 8 E9 . . . . .74 C1
Vanbrugh Mews KT12 . . . . .194 C2
Vanbrugh Park SE3 . . . . .142 D5
Vanbrugh Park Rd W
　SE3 . . . . .142 D5
Vanbrugh Pk SE3 . . . . .142 D5
Vanbrugh Rd W4 . . . . .111 B3
Vanbrugh Terr SE3 . . . . .142 D4
Vanburgh Cl
　2 Newham E16. . . . . .99 C2
　Orpington BR6 . . . . .211 C1
Vanburgh Ct 6 EN5. . . . . .1 A1
Vanburgh Ho 1 E1 . . . . .243 C4
Vancouver Rd
　Edgware HA8 . . . . .26 D2
　Forest Hill SE23 . . . . .163 B2
　Hayes UB4. . . . . .84 B3
　Richmond TW10 . . . . .175 C6
Vancover Ho 33 E1. . . . . .118 B5
Vanderbilt Rd SW18. . . . . .158 A3
Vanderbilt Villas 1
　W12. .112 D4
Vanderville Gdns N2. . . . . .30 B1
Vandome Cl E16. . . . . .99 B1
Vandon Ct SW1. . . . . .259 B6
Vandon Pas SW1. . . . . .259 B6
Vandon St SW1. . . . . .259 B6
Van Dyck Ave KT3. . . . . .199 B2
Vandyke Cl SW15 . . . . .156 D5
Vandyke Cross SE9. . . . . .166 A6
Vandy St EC2 . . . . .243 A5
Vane Cl Hampstead NW3. . . .70 B4
　Harrow HA3. . . . . .44 B3
Vane Ho 18 N2. . . . . .30 B1
Vanessa Cl DA17. . . . . .125 C1
Vane St SW1. . . . . .259 B4
Vanfame Ct KT3 . . . . .199 D6
Vange Ho 12 W10 . . . . .90 C2
Van Gogh Cl 11 TW7. . . . . .131 A2
Van Gogh Ct E14. . . . . .120 B3
Vanguard Bldg 6 E14. . . . .119 C4
Vanguard Ct 7 Newham E16 . .99 B2
　Thornton Heath CR0. . . . . .204 D1
Vanguard Ho
　11 Hackney E8 . . . . .74 B1
　7 Merton SW19 . . . . .180 A3
　6 Stanwell TW19 . . . . .148 A5
Vanguard St SE8 . . . . .141 C4
Vanguard Way
　Hatton TW6 . . . . .127 C3
　Wallington SM6. . . . . .220 A1
Van Lang Ho EN3 . . . . .18 D6
Vanneck Sq SW15. . . . . .156 A6
Vanner Point 27 E9 . . . . .74 D2
Vanoc Gdns BR1. . . . . .187 A6
Vanquish Cl TW2. . . . . .151 C4
Vansittart Rd E7 . . . . .77 A4
Vansittart St 1 SE14 . . .141 A5
Vanston Pl SW6. . .135 C5 265 B4
Vantage Ct
　Haringun UB3. . . . . .127 C5
　4 South Norwood SW16. . . . . . .182 B3
Vantage Mews 7 E14. . . . .120 A5
Vantage Pl W8 . . . . .255 B5
Vant Rd SW17 . . . . .180 D5
Vantrey Ho SE11. . . . . .261 A3
Varcoe Rd SE16. . . . . .118 C1
Vardens Rd SW11. . . . . .136 B1

Varden St E1 . . . . .96 B1
Vardon Cl W3. . . . . .89 B1
Vardon Ho SE10. . . . . .142 A4
Vardy Ho HA7. . . . . .25 B5
Varey Ho E1. . . . . .97 A4
Varley Ho 6 NW6. . . . . .91 C6
Varley Par NW9 . . . . .45 C5
Varley Rd E16. . . . . .99 B1
Varley Way CR4. . . . . .180 B1
Varma Ct SE3 . . . . .143 A4
Varna Rd Hampton TW12. . . .173 D2
　SW6. . . . . .135 B5 265 A2
Varndell St NW1. . . . . . .93 C4 232 A2
Varnishers Yard N1 . . . . . . .233 B3
Varsity Dr TW1, TW7 . . . . . .152 D5
Varsity Row SW14. . . . . .133 A3
Vartry Rd N15 . . . . .51 C3
Vascroft Est NW10. . . . . .88 D3
Vassall Ho 3 E3. . . . . .97 A4
Vassall Rd SW9. . . . . .138 C5
Vat Ho SW8. . . . . .270 B4
Vauban Est SE16. . . . . .263 D5
Vauban St SE16. . .117 D3 263 D5
Vaudeville Ct N4. . . . . .72 C6
Vaughan Almshouses
　TW15. . . . . .170 D5
Vaughan Ave
　Chiswick W6. . . . . .111 D2
　Hendon NW4 . . . . .46 A4
Vaughan Cl TW12. . . . . .173 A4
Vaughan Est 3 E2. . . . . .95 D4
Vaughan Fst & Mid Sch
　HA1 . . . . .42 A3
Vaughan Gdns IG1. . . . . .56 B2
Vaughan Ho SE1. . . . . .251 C2
Vaughan Rd
　Camberwell SE5. . . . . .139 A2
　DA16. .145 D3
　Harrow HA1. . . . . .42 B3
　Stratford E15 . . . . .76 D2
　Thames Ditton KT7. . . . . .197 B2
Vaughan St SE16. . . . . .119 B4
Vaughan Way E1. . . . . .118 A5
Vaughan Williams Cl
　SE8 . . . . .141 C5
VAUXHALL. 116 A1
Vauxhall Bridge Rd
　SW1. . . . . .115 C2 259 B3
Vauxhall City Farm ★
　SE1 . . . . .260 C1
Vauxhall Cross SE1,
　SW8. . . . . .116 A1 260 B1
Vauxhall Gdns CR2. . . . . .221 A2
Vauxhall Gr SW8. . .138 B6 270 C6
Vauxhall Prim Sch
　SE11. . . . . .116 D2 260 D2
Vauxhall St SE11. .116 B1 260 D2
Vauxhall Sta
　SE11. . . . . .116 A1 260 B1
Vauxhall Wlk SE11. . . . . .260 C2
Vawdrey Cl E1. . . . . .96 C3
Vaynor Ho N7. . . . . .72 A4
Veals Mead CR4. . . . . .180 C2
Vectis Ct SW18. . . . . .157 D5
Vectis Gdns SW17. . . . . .181 B4
Vectis Rd SW17. . . . . .181 B4
Veda Rd SE13. . . . . .141 C1
Vega Cres HA6. . . . . .22 A5
Vega Rd WD23. . . . . .8 A4
Veitch Cl TW14. . . . . .149 D4
Veldene Way HA2. . . . . .63 B5
Velde Way 1 SE22. . . . . .161 C6
Vellacott Ho 3 W12. . . . . .90 B1
Velletri Ho 17 E2. . . . . .96 D5
Vellum Dr SM5. . . . . .219 A5
Velocity Way EN3 . . . . .7 B6
Venables Cl RM10. . . . . .81 D4
Venables St NW8 . . .92 B2 236 D4
Vencourt Pl W6. . . . . .112 A2
Venetian Rd SE5. . . . . .139 A3
Venetia Rd Ealing W5 . . . . . .109 D4
　Harringay N4 . . . . .50 D3
Venice Ct 14 SE5. . . . . .139 A5
Venita Manor SE27. . . . . .182 C5
Venmead Ct 7 DA17. . . . . .125 C2
Venner Rd SE26. . . . . .184 C5
Venn Ho N1. . . . . .233 D5
Venn St SW4. . . . . .137 C1
Ventnor Ave HA7. . . . . .25 B1
Ventnor Dr N20. . . . . .13 D2
Ventnor Gdns IG11. . . . . .79 C2
Ventnor Mans IG11. . . . . .79 C2
Ventnor Rd Belmont SM2. . .217 D1
　SE14. .140 D5
Ventnor Terr N15. . . . . .52 A5
Ventura Ho 12 SW2. . . . . .138 A1
Venture Cl DA5. . . . . .169 A4
Venture Ct 3 SE12. . . . . .165 A4
Venue St E14. . . . . .98 A2
Venus Ho 7 Millwall E14. . . .119 C2
　8 Old Ford E3 . . . . .97 C6
Venus Mews CR4. . . . . .202 C6
Venus Rd SE18. . . . . .122 B3
Vera Ave N21. . . . . .16 C6
Vera Ct 1 Kensington W2. . . .91 D1
　Tottenham N22. . . . . .32 D2
Vera Lynn Cl 5 E7. . . . . .77 A4
Vera Rd SW6 . . . . .135 A4 264 B2
Verbena Cl E16. . . . . .98 D3
Verbena Gdns 4 W6. . . . . .112 A1

Verdant Ct 3 SE6. . . . . .164 C4
Verdant La SE6. . . . . .164 C3
Verdayne Ave CR0. . . . . .222 D6
Verdun Rd Barnes SW13. . . .134 A5
　SE18. .146 A6
Vere Bank SW19. . . . . .157 B3
Vereker Dr TW16. . . . . .194 A6
Vereker Rd W14 . . . . .254 B1
Vere St W1 . . . . .93 B1 238 C1
Verity Cl W11. . . . . .91 A1
Verity Ct N9. . . . . .18 D3
Verity Ho 20 E3. . . . . .97 B4
Vermeer Ct E14. . . . . .120 B3
Vermillion Ct TW13. . . . . .149 D1
Vermont Cl EN2. . . . . .4 D1
Vermont Ho E17. . . . . .35 B1
Vermont Rd Sutton SM1. . . .217 D5
　Wandsworth SW18. . . . . .157 D5
　West Norwood SE19. . . . . .183 C4
Verne Ct 9 W3. . . . . .111 A3
Verneer Gdns SE15. . . . . .140 C1
Verney Gdns RM9. . . . . .81 A4
Verney Ho
　Isleworth TW3. . . . . .130 A1
　Lisson Gr NW8 . . . . .237 A6
　South Kensington SW10. . . .266 A6
Verney Rd
　Bermondsey SE16. . . . . .118 B1
　Dagenham RM9 . . . . .81 A4
Verney St NW10. . . . . .67 B5
Verney Way SE16. . . . . .118 B1
Vernham Rd SE18. . . . . .145 A6
　West Barnes SW20. . . . . .178 D1
　Woodford IG8. . . . . .37 B3
Vernon Cl Stanwell TW19 . .148 A3
　West Ewell KT19. . . . . .215 A2
Vernon Cres EN4. . . . . .15 A5
Vernon Ct Child's Hill NW2 . .69 B5
　Ealing W5 . . . . .109 C6
　Stanmore HA7 . . . . .25 B2
Vernon Dr HA7. . . . . .25 A2
Vernon Ho Hyde The NW9 . . .45 D4
　SE11. .260 D1
Vernon House Specl Sch
　NW10. .67 B3
Vernon Mews W14. . . . . .254 B3
Vernon Pl WC1. . . . . .240 B3
Vernon Rd Bow E3. . . . . .97 B5
　Feltham TW13. . . . . .149 D2
　Hornsey N8. . . . . .50 C6
　Ilford IG3. . . . . .57 D1
　Leytonstone E11. . . . . .54 C1
　Mortlake SW14. . . . . .133 B2
　Stratford E15 . . . . .76 C1
　Sutton SM1. . . . . .218 B3
　Walthamstow E17. . . . . .53 B4
Vernon Rise
　Greenford UB6. . . . . .64 B3
　WC1. .233 D2
Vernon Sq WC1. . . . . .233 D2
Vernon St W14. . . . . . . .113 B2 254 B3
Vernon Yd W11 . . . . .113 B6 244 C6
Veroan Rd DA7. . . . . .147 A3
Verona Ct Chiswick W4 . . . . .111 C1
　10 SE14. . . . . .140 D6
Verona Dr KT6. . . . . .214 A6
Verona Rd E7. . . . . .77 A1
Veronica Gdns CR4,
　SW16. . . . . .181 C2
Veronica Ho
　Brockley SE4. . . . . .141 B2
　46 Bromley E3. . . . . .97 D4
Veronica Rd SW17. . . . . .159 B2
Veronique Gdns IG6. . . . . .57 A4
Verran Rd SW12. . . . . .159 B4
Versailles Rd SE20. . . . . .184 A3
Verulam Ave E17. . . . . .53 B2
Verulam Bldgs WC1. . . . . . . .240 D4
Verulam Ct Hendon NW9 . . . .46 A2
　4 Southall UB1. . . . . .86 A1
Verulam Ho 1 W6. . . . . .112 C4
Verulam Rd UB6. . . . . .85 C3
Verulam St EC1. . . . . .94 C2 241 A4
Vervain Ho 2 SE15. . . . . .140 A5
Verwood Dr EN4. . . . . .2 D2
Verwood Ho SW8. . . . . .270 D3
Verwood Lo 1 E14. . . . . .120 B2
Verwood Rd HA2. . . . . .24 A1
Veryan Ct 3 N8 . . . . .49 D4
Vesage Ct EC1. . . . . .241 B3
Vesey Path 15 E14 . . . . .97 D1
Vespan Rd W12. . . . . .112 A4
Vesta Ct SE1. . . . . .253 A1
Vesta Ho 3 E3. . . . . .97 C6
Vesta Rd SE4, SE14. . . . . .141 A3
Vestris Rd SE23. . . . . .162 D2
Vestry House (Mus) ★
　E17. . . . . .53 D5
Vestry Mews 12 SE5. . . . . .139 C4
Vestry Rd
　Camberwell SE5. . . . . .139 C4
　Walthamstow E17 . . . . .53 D5
Vestry St N1. . . . . .95 B4 235 C2
Vevey St SE23, SE6. . . . . .163 B2
Veysey Gdns RM10. . . . . .81 C5
Viaduct Pl 28 E2. . . . . .96 B4
Viaduct Rd N2. . . . . .30 C1
Viaduct St E2. . . . . .96 B4
Viaduct The Harrow HA2. . . .64 A5

Viaduct The continued
　Woodford E18. . . . . .37 B1
Vian St SE13. . . . . .141 D2
Vibart Gdns SW2. . . . . .160 B4
Vibart Wlk N1. . . . . .233 B6
Vicarage Ave SE3 . . . . .143 A5
Vicarage Cl
　New Malden KT4. . . . . .199 C1
　Northolt UB5. . . . . .63 B1
　Ruislip HA4. . . . . .39 B2
Vicarage Cres
　SW11. . . . . .136 B4 266 C1
Vicarage Ct
　Beckenham BR3. . . . . .207 A6
　East Bedfont TW14. . . . . .149 A4
　Finchley N12. . . . . .29 D5
　7 Putney SW15. . . . . .156 A4
　W8 . . . . .245 C2
Vicarage Dr Barking IG11. . . .79 A1
　Beckenham BR3. . . . . .185 C2
　Mortlake SW14. . . . . .133 B2
Vicarage Farm Ct TW5. . . . .129 B5
Vicarage Farm Rd TW3, TW4,
　TW5. .129 A4
Vicarage Fields KT12. . . . . .194 C3
Vicarage Field Sh Ctr The
　IG11. . . . . .79 A1
Vicarage Gate
　W8. . . . . .113 D5 245 C3
Vicarage Gdns
　Mitcham CR4. . . . . .202 C6
　Mortlake SW14. . . . . .155 B6
　W8 . . . . .245 C3
Vicarage Gr SE5 . . . . .139 B4
Vicarage Ho 1 KT1. . . . . .176 B1
Vicarage La Ilford IG1. . . . . . .57 B1
　Stratford E15 . . . . .76 D1
　Wallend E6 . . . . .100 C4
Vicarage Mans N15. . . . . .51 A5
Vicarage Pk SE18. . . . . .123 A1
Vicarage Prim Sch 5
　E6. . . . . .100 B4
Vicarage Rd
　Ashford TW16. . . . . .171 D4
　Croydon CR0. . . . . .220 C5
　DA5. . . . . .169 D3
　Dagenham RM10. . . . . .81 D1
　Hampton Wick KT1. . . . . .175 C2
　Hendon NW4 . . . . .46 A3
　Kingston u T KT1. . . . . .175 D1
　Mortlake SW14. . . . . .155 B6
　Old Bexley DA5. . . . . .169 D2
　Stratford E15 . . . . .76 D1
　Sutton SM1. . . . . .217 D5
　Teddington TW11. . . . . .175 A5
　Tottenham N17. . . . . .34 A2
　Walthamstow E10. . . . . .53 D1
　Woolwich SE18. . . . . .123 A1
Vicarage The N8. . . . . .50 B3
Vicarage Way Harrow HA2. . .41 C2
　Neasden NW10 . . . . .67 B5
Vicarage Wlk
　SW11. . . . . .136 B4 266 D2
Vicars Bridge Cl HA0. . . . . .88 A5
Vicar's Cl Enfield EN1 . . . . . .5 C3
　Newham E15. . . . . .99 A4
　South Hackney E9. . . . . .96 C6
Vicar's Green Prim Sch
　HA0. . . . . .87 C5
Vicars Hill SE13. . . . . .141 D1
Vicar's Moor La N21. . . . . .16 D4
Vicars Oak Rd SE19. . . . . .183 C4
Vicar's N NW5 . . . . .71 A3
Vicar's Wlk RM8. . . . . .80 B5
Viceroy Cl N2. . . . . .48 C6
Viceroy Ct
　5 Croydon CR0. . . . . .205 B1
　NW8 .230 B4
Viceroy Lo 6 KT6. . . . . .198 A4
Viceroy Par N2 . . . . .48 C6
Viceroy Rd SW8. . . . . .138 A4 270 A2
Vic Johnson Ho 21 E3. . . . .97 B6
Vickers Cl SM6. . . . . .220 B1
Vickers Ct 10 TW19. . . . . .148 A5
Vickery Ct EC1. . . . . .242 B6
Vickery Ho 13 SW4. . . . . .138 A1
Vickery's Wharf 8 E14. . . . .97 C1
Victor Cazalet Ho N1. . . . . . .234 C6
Victor Gr HA0. . . . . .66 A1
Victor Ho 2 N20. . . . . .14 D1
Victoria & Albert Mus ★
　SW7 . . . . .114 B3 256 D5
Victoria Arc SW1. . . . . .258 C5
Victoria Ave Barnet EN4. . . . .2 B1
　East Molesley KT8. . . . . .195 D6
　EC2. .243 B3
　Finchley N3. . . . . .29 B2
　Hackbridge SM5, SM6 . . . . .219 A5
　Hillingdon UB10 . . . . .60 D1
　Hounslow TW3, TW4. . . . . .151 C6
　Newham E6. . . . . .99 D6
　Surbiton KT6. . . . . .197 D3
　Wembley HA9. . . . . .66 D2
Victoria Bglws DA14. . . . . . .191 B3
Victoria Bldgs 13 E8. . . . . . .96 B6
Victoria Bsns Ctr DA16. . . .146 B3
Victoria Chambers EC2. . . .243 A6
Victoria Cl Barnet EN4. . . . . .2 B1
　East Molesley KT8. . . . . .195 C6
　Harrow HA1. . . . . .42 D3

Victoria Cl continued
Hayes UB3 . . . . .83 B1
Victoria Coach Sta
SW1 . . . . 115 B2 **258 C3**
Victoria Coll WC2 . . . . . **241 A2**
Victoria Cotts Ilford IG6 . .57 A4
Muswell Hill N10. . . . . . .31 A1
7 Richmond TW9 . . . . 132 C4
3 Spitalfields E1 . . . . . .96 A2
Victoria Cres
Tottenham N15. . . . . . . .51 C4
West Norwood SE19. . . 183 C4
Victoria Ct
5 Clapham Pk SW4. . . . 159 D5
3 Penge SE26. . . . . . . 184 C4
South Acton W3 . . . . . 110 C4
4 St George in t East E1 . 118 A6
1 Wanstead E18. . . . . . .55 B6
Wembley HA9. . . . . . . .66 C2
Victoria Dock Rd E16 . . 121 B6
Victoria Dr SW19 . . . . . 156 D3
Victoria Emb
WC2. . . . . . . 116 C6 **251 A5**
Victoria Gdns
Heston TW5 . . . . .129 A4
W11 . . . . . . 113 C5 **245 A4**
Victoria Gr
North Finchley N12. . . . . 30 B5
W8 . . . . 114 A3 **256 A6**
Victoria Gr Mews W2 . . **245 C5**
Victoria Hall 15 E16 . . . 121 A5
Victoria Ho
6 Clapham Pk SW4. . . . 159 D5
Edgware HA8 . . . . .26 D4
2 Shepherd's Bush W12 . 112 A4
SW1 . . . . **258 C2**
Victoria Ind Est W3 . . . . .89 C2
Victoria Jun Sch TW13 . . 150 B3
Victoria La Barnet EN5 . . . 1 B1
Hayes UB3 . . . . 105 B1
Victoria Lo 5 SW19 . . . 178 C3
Victoria Mans
8 Islington N7 . . . . . . .72 C3
Willesden NW10. . . . . . .68 B1
Victoria Mews
Kilburn NW6 . . . . .91 C6
Wandsworth SW18 . . . . 158 A3
Victoria Mills 1 E15 . . . . 98 B6
Victorian Gr N16. . . . . . .73 C5
Victorian Hts 7 SW8. . . 137 B3
Victorian Rd N16 . . . . . .73 D5
Victoria Park Ct 11 E9 . . . 74 C1
Victoria Park Ind Ctr E9 . 75 B1
Victoria Park Lofts E9. . . .96 D6
Victoria Park Rd E9 . . . . .74 D1
Victoria Park Sq E2 . . . . .96 C4
Victoria Pas NW8 . . . . . **236 C6**
Victoria Pl 17 TW10 . . . 153 D6
Victoria Place Sh Ctr
SW1 . . . . 115 B2 **258 D4**
Victoria Point 10 E13. . . . .99 A5
Victoria Rd Barking IG11 . .78 D2
Barnet EN4 . . . . 2 B1
Bexley DA6 . . . . 147 C1
Bromley Comm BR2 . . . 209 D4
Buckhurst Hill IG9 . . . . .21 D2
Chingford E4. . . . . . . .20 C3
Chislehurst West BR7. . . 188 C5
Dagenham RM10 . . . . . .81 D3
Ealing W5 . . . . .87 B2
Edgware NW7 . . . . 27 D5
Edmonton N9 . . . . .17 D1
Feltham TW13 . . . . . . 150 B3
Finsbury Pk N4 . . . . . . .50 B1
Hendon NW4 . . . . .46 D5
Kensington W8 . . . 114 A3 **256 A6**
Kilburn NW6. . . . . .91 B6
Kingston u T KT1. . . . . 176 B1
Leyton E11 . . . . .76 C4
Mitcham CR4 . . . . 180 D3
Mortlake SW14 . . . . . . 133 B2
Muswell Hill N22. . . . . . 31 D2
Newham E13 . . . . .99 A5
North Acton NW10 . . . . .89 C3
Ruislip HA4. . . . . .62 B4
Sidcup DA15. . . . . . . .168 A1
Southall UB2. . . . . . . .107 B3
Surbiton KT6. . . . . . . 197 D3
Sutton SM1. . . . . 218 B3
Teddington TW11 . . . . 175 A4
Tottenham Hale N15. . . . .52 A5
Twickenham TW1 . . . . .153 B4
Walthamstow E17 . . . . . 36 A1
Wanstead E18 . . . . 55 B5
Victoria Ret Pk HA4. . . . .62 D3
Victoria Rise SW4. . . . . 137 B2
Victoria Sq SW1 . . . . . **258 C3**
Victoria St Erith DA17 . . 125 B1
Stratford E15. . . . . . . .76 C1
SW1 . . . . 115 C3 **259 B5**
Victoria Sta SW1. 115 B2 **258 D4**
Victoria Terr
Dagenham NW10. . . . . .89 C3
Finsbury Pk N4 . . . . . . .50 C1
Harrow HA1. . . . . .42 C1
Victoria (Underground)
SW1 . . . . 115 B3 **258 D5**
Victoria Villas TW9 . . . . 132 B1
Victoria Way SE7 . . . . . 143 C6
Victoria Wharf E14. . . . .119 A6

Victoria Yd 28 E1. . . . . . .96 A1
Victor Mills Cotts BR8. . . 191 C3
Victor Rd College Pk NW10. .90 B4
Harrow HA2 . . . . .42 A6
Penge SE20 . . . . 184 D3
Teddington TW11 . . . . . 174 C6
Victors Dr TW12 . . . . . 173 A4
Victor Seymour Inf Sch 6
SM5 . . . . 219 A5
Victors Way EN5 . . . . . . .1 B2
Victor Villas N9 . . . . . . .17 B1
Victory Ave SM4 . . . . . 202 A4
Victory Bsns Ctr TW7. . . 130 D1
Victory Cl TW19. . . . . . 148 A3
Victory Ct IG11 . . . . . . 102 B4
Victory Pl
6 Limehouse E14 . . . . 119 A6
SE17 . . . . . . 117 B2 **262 C4**
West Norwood SE19 . . . 183 C4
Victory Prim Sch
SE17 . . . . . . 117 A2 **262 B4**
Wanstead E11 . . . . 55 B5
Victory Rd Merton SW19. . 180 A3
Wanstead E11 . . . . 55 B5
Victory Road Mews 5
SW19 . . . . 180 A3
Victory Way
Hounslow TW5 . . . . . . 106 C1
Rotherhithe SE16 . . . . . 119 A4
Video Ct N1 . . . . .50 A2
Vidler Cl KT9 . . . . 213 C2
Vienna Cl IG5. . . . . 37 D1
Vietory Day Sch 3 CR7 . 205 A6
View Cl Harrow HA1. . . . .42 B5
Highgate N6. . . . . 48 D2
View Cres N4 . . . . .49 D4
Viewfield Cl HA3. . . . . . .44 A2
Viewfield Rd DA5. . . . . 168 C3
Wandsworth SW18 . . . . 157 B5
Viewland Rd SE18. . . . . 123 D1
Viewpoint Ealing W5 . . . 110 B6
3 Islington N5 . . . . . . .72 D3
View Point N20 . . . . . . .14 A4
Viewpoint Ct 8 HA5 . . . . 22 C1
View Rd N6 . . . . .48 D3
Viewside Lo N6. . . . . . . 49 C3
View The SE2 . . . . 125 A1
Viga Rd N21. . . . . .16 C5
Vigilant Cl SE26. . . . . . 184 A6
Vignoles Rd RM7. . . . . .59 C2
Vigo St W1 . . . . . 115 C6 **249 A5**
Vi & John Rubens Ho
IG2 . . . . .56 C3
Viking Cl 13 E3. . . . . . .97 A5
Viking Ct Hampton TW12. . 173 D2
New Barnet EN4 . . . . . .14 B6
Viking Gdns E6 . . . . . . 100 A3
Viking Ho
3 Camberwell SE5 . . . . 139 A3
3 Woolwich SE18 . . . . 122 A2
Viking Pl E10 . . . . .53 B1
Viking Prim Sch UB5. . . . .84 C4
Villacourt Rd SE18 . . . . 146 A6
Village Arc The 2 E4. . . . 20 B3
Village Cl 2 Chingford E4. . 36 A5
Hampstead NW3 . . . . . .70 B3
Village Ct Blackheath SE3. . 142 C2
Walthamstow E17 . . . . . 53 D4
Village Gate TW17 . . . . 192 D4
Village Home The IG6 . . . 57 A6
Village Hts IG8 . . . . . . .36 D5
Village Inf Sch RM10. . . . .81 C1
Village Mount 11 NW3 . . .70 A4
Village Park Cl EN1 . . . . .17 C5
Village Rd Enfield EN1. . . .17 C6
Hendon N3 . . . . .29 A1
Village Row SM2. . . . . . 217 C1
Village School The NW3 . . .70 D2
Village The
Battersea SW11. . . . . . 136 D2
SE7 . . . . 143 D6
Village Way
Ashford TW15. . . . . . . 170 A5
Beckenham BR3 . . . . . 207 C6
Dulwich Village SE21. . . 161 B5
Ilford IG6 . . . . .57 A6
Pinner HA5 . . . . .41 B2
Willesden NW10. . . . . . .67 B4
Village Way E HA2 . . . . .41 C2
Villa Rd SW9. . . . . 138 C2
Villas On The Heath NW3 . .70 A5
Villas Rd SE18 . . . . . . 123 A2
Villa St SE17 . . . . . 117 B1 **262 D1**
Villiers Ave
Kingston u T KT5 . . . . . 198 B5
Twickenham TW2 . . . . . 151 B3
Villiers Cl
Kingston u T KT5 . . . . . 198 B5
Leyton E10 . . . . .75 C6
Villiers Ct Oakleigh Pk N20 . .14 A4
SW11 . . . . **267 B2**
Villiers High Sch UB1 . . . 107 B5
Villiers Ho W5 . . . . 109 D6
Villiers Rd Isleworth TW7 . 130 C3
Kingston u T KT1 . . . . . 198 B6
Penge BR3. . . . . 184 D1
Southall UB1. . . . . . . .107 B5
Willesden NW2. . . . . . . 68 A2
Villiers St WC2 . . . . . . **250 B4**

Vimy Cl TW4 . . . . 151 B6
Vincam Cl TW2 . . . . . . 151 C4
Vince Ct N1 . . . . **235 D1**
Vincent Ave KT5 . . . . . . 215 A6
Vincent Cl
Avery Hill DA15. . . . . . 167 C3
Barnet EN5 . . . . 1 D2
Bromley BR2. . . . . 209 B5
Harmondsworth UB7. . . 126 C6
Vincent Ct Finsbury Pk N4. .50 A1
Hendon NW4 . . . . .46 D5
Marylebone W1 . . . . . . **237 C2**
Ruislip HA4. . . . . .62 B3
South Lambeth SW8 . . . **270 D1**
Vincent Dr Hillingdon UB10. .82 B6
Upper Halliford TW17. . . 193 C6
Vincent Gdns NW2. . . . . .67 D5
Vincent Ho KT3 . . . . . . 199 D5
Vincent Mews 1 E3 . . . . .97 C5
Vincent Rd
Acton Green W3 . . . . . . 111 A3
Chingford E4. . . . . . . .36 B4
Croydon CR0. . . . . . . 205 C2
Dagenham RM9 . . . . . . .81 A1
Hounslow West TW4. . . . 128 C2
Kingston u T KT1. . . . . . 198 C6
Osterley TW7 . . . . 130 B4
Tottenham N15. . . . . . . 51 A5
Wembley HA0. . . . . . . .66 B1
Wood Green N22 . . . . . .32 C1
Woolwich SE18. . . . . . 122 D2
Vincent Row TW12 . . . . 174 A5
Vincent St SE16. . . . . . 119 A4
Vincents Path UB5 . . . . . 63 A2
Vincent Sq SW1 . . 115 D2 **259 C4**
Wood Green N22 . . . . . .32 C1
Vincent St
Canning Town E16 . . . . . 98 D2
Westminster SW1 . . 115 D2 **259 D4**
Vince St EC1. . . . . . 95 B4 **235 D1**
Vine Cl Shacklewell E5 . . . 74 A4
Surbiton KT5. . . . . . . 198 B3
Sutton SM1. . . . . 218 A5
West Drayton UB7 . . . . 104 C2
Vine Cotts 1 Ealing W7 . . 108 C5
Spitalfields E1. . . . . . . .96 A2
Vine Ct Harrow HA3 . . . . .44 A3
Spitalfields E1. . . . . . . .96 A2
Vine Gr UB10 . . . . .60 C1
Vine Hill EC1 . . . . **241 A5**
Vine La Hillingdon UB10. . .82 B6
SE1. . . . . . . 117 C5 **253 B3**
Uxbridge UB10 . . . . . . .60 B1
Vine Lo N12 . . . . .30 A4
Vine Pl Ealing W5 . . . . . 110 A5
Hounslow TW3 . . . . . . 129 D1
Vine Rd Barnes SW13. . . 133 D2
BR6. . . . . 227 D2
East Molesey KT8. . . . . 196 A5
Stratford E15. . . . . . . .76 D1
Vineries Bank NW7 . . . . . 28 B5
Vineries Cl Dagenham RM9 . 81 B2
Harmondsworth UB7. . . 126 C6
Vineries The Enfield EN1. . . 5 C2
Southgate N14. . . . . . . 15 C5
Viners Cl KT2 . . . . 194 C3
Vine St Bridge EC1. . . . **241 B5**
Vines Ave N3 . . . . .29 D2
Vine Sq W14 . . . . **254 D1**
Vine St W1 . . . . **249 B5**
Whitechapel EC3 . . 95 D1 **243 C1**
Vinewood Ct E17 . . . . . . 54 B4
Vineyard Ave NW7 . . . . .29 A3
Vineyard Cl
Forest Hill SE6 . . . . . . 163 C3
Kingston u T KT1. . . . . . 198 B6
Vineyard Gr N3 . . . . . . .29 D2
Vineyard Hill Rd SW19 . . 179 C6
Vineyard Path SW14 . . . 133 B2
Vineyard Prim Sch The
TW10 . . . . 154 A5
Vineyard Rd TW13. . . . . 150 A1
Vineyard Row KT1, KT8 . . 175 C2
Vineyards The TW13. . . . 150 A1
Vineyard Studios 3 E7. . . .77 C1
Vineyard Wlk EC1. . . . . **241 A6**
Viney Ct 9 SW4 . . . . . . 159 D5
Viney Rd SE13 . . . . 141 D2
Vining St SW2, SW9. . . . 138 C1
Vinlake Ave UB10 . . . . . . 60 C5
Vinson Ho N1. . . . . **235 D3**
Vinter Ct TW17. . . . . . . 192 C4
Vintners Ct EC4 . . . . . . **252 B6**
Vintry Mews 3 E17 . . . . . 53 C5
Viola Ave Feltham TW14 . . 150 C5
SE2 . . . . 124 B1
Stanwell TW19 . . . . . . 148 A3
Viola Ct HA8 . . . . .26 D3
Viola Sq W12 . . . . 111 D6
Violet Ave Enfield EN2. . . . 5 B5
Hillingdon UB8 . . . . . . .82 B2
Violet Cl Cheam SM3 . . . 201 A1
Hackbridge SM6. . . . . . 203 A1
Newham E16 . . . . .98 C3

Violet Cl continued
32 SE8 . . . . 141 B6
Violet Ct 2 E15. . . . . . . .76 C1
Violet Gdns CR0 . . . . . . 220 D3
Violet Hill NW8 . . . 92 A5 **229 A3**
Violet Hill Ho NW8 . . . . **229 A3**
Violet La CR0 . . . . 220 D3
Violet Rd Bromley E3. . . . . 97 D3
Walthamstow E17 . . . . . 53 C3
Woodford E18. . . . . . . .37 B1
Violet St E2. . . . . .96 B3
Violet Terr 82 C2
SE27 . . . . 183 B6
VIP Trad Est SE7 . . . . . 121 C2
Virgil Pl W1 . . . . **237 C3**
Virgil St SE1. . . . . 116 B3 **260 D6**
Virginia Cl
Beckenham BR2 . . . . . 208 C6
New Malden KT3 . . . . . 199 A5
Virginia Ct Ashford TW15 . 170 A6
7 Rotherhithe SE16 . . . 118 D4
Virginia Ho
3 Blackwall E14 . . . . . 120 A6
Teddington TW11 . . . . . 175 A5
Virginia Prim Sch 48 E2. . .95 D4
Virginia Rd
South Norwood CR7. . . . 182 D2
19 Spitalfields E2 . . . . .95 D4
Virginia St E1. . . . . 118 A6
Virginia Wlk SW2 . . . . . 160 B5
Virgo Fidelis Convent Senior
Sch SE19 . . . . 183 B4
Virgo Fidelis Prep Sch
SE19. . . . . 183 B4
Viridian Ct TW13 . . . . . 149 D1
Viscount Ct N11 . . . . . . .31 B5
Viscount Ct
9 Kensington W11 . . . . .91 C1
1 Littleton TW15. . . . . 171 A3
Viscount Dr E6 . . . . . . 100 B2
Viscount Gr 3 UB5 . . . . . 84 C4
Viscount Point 6 SW19 . . 179 C3
Viscount Rd TW19. . . . . 148 A3
Viscount St EC1. . . . . . **242 A4**
Viscount Way TW6 . . . . 127 C1
Vision Coll of Theology
E9 . . . . .75 C2
Vista Ave EN3 . . . . 6 D3
Vista Bldgs 19 E3 . . . . . .97 B4
Vista Bldg The 14 SE18 . . 122 C2
Vista Dr IG4 . . . . .55 D4
Vista Ho 2 SW19 . . . . . 180 B2
Vista The Chingford E4. . . .20 B4
SE9. . . . . 166 B5
Sidcup DA14. . . . . . . .189 D5
Vista Way HA3 . . . . 44 A3
Vitae Apartments 7
W6. . . . . 112 A3
Vita Et Pax Sch N14 . . . . 15 B6
Vittoria Ho N1. . . . . **233 D5**
Vittoria Prim Sch
N1. . . . . 94 C5 **234 A4**
Viveash Cl UB3 . . . . . . 105 D3
Vivian Ave Hendon NW4 . . 46 B4
Wembley HA9. . . . . . . .66 C2
Vivian Comma Cl 3 N4 . . .72 D5
Vivian Ct Finchley N12. . . .29 D5
Paddington NW6 . . . . . .91 D5
Vivian Gdns Wembley HA9. . 66 C3
Vivian Ho N4 . . . . 51 B2
Vivian Mans 1 NW4 . . . . 46 B4
Vivian Rd E3. . . . . .97 A5
Vivian Sq SE15. . . . . . . 140 B2
Vivian Way N2 . . . . 48 B4
Vivien Ct KT9 . . . . 214 A1
Vivienne Cl TW1 . . . . . 153 D5
Voce Rd SE18. . . . . . . 145 B5
Voewood Cl KT3 . . . . . 199 D3
Vogans Mill SE1 . . . . . **253 D2**
Vogler Ho 6 E1 . . . . 118 C6
Vogue Ct 8 BR1. . . . . . 187 B2
Vollasky Ho 5 E1. . . . . . .96 A2
Volta Ct N12 . . . . .18 C1
Voltaire
2 Camberwell SE5 . . . . 139 D4
15 Richmond TW9 . . . . 132 B4
Voltaire Ct 13 SW11 . . . 137 A3
Voltaire Rd SW4 . . . . . . 137 D2
Voltaire Way UB3 . . . . . 105 C6
Volt Ave NW10 . . . . 89 C4
Volta Way CR0 . . . . . . 204 B1
Voluntary Pl E11 . . . . . . 55 A3
Vora Ho HA0. . . . . .65 D2
Vorley Rd N19 . . . . .71 C6
Voss St SW16 . . . . 182 A4
Voss St E2. . . . . 96 A4
Voyager Bsns Est 10
SE16. . . . . 118 A3
Voyagers Cl IG11 . . . . . 102 C1
Voysey Cl N3 . . . . 47 A6
Vulcan Cl E6. . . . . 100 C1
Vulcan Gate EN2. . . . . . . 4 C3
Vulcan Ho 8 E15 . . . . . .76 B5
Vulcan Rd SE4 . . . . . . 141 B3
Vulcan Sq E14 . . . . 119 C2
Vulcan Terr SE4 . . . . . . 141 B3
Vulcan Way N7 . . . . 72 B2
Vyne Ho SM5 . . . . 218 D2
Vyner Ct E5 . . . . .74 A6

Vyner Rd W3 . . . . .111 B6
Vyners Sch UB10 . . . . . .60 B4
Vyner St E2. . . . . .96 B6
Vyners Way UB10 . . . . . .60 C3
Vyne The DA7. . . . . . . 147 D2
Vyvyan Ho SE18. . . . . . 144 C4

W

Wadbrook St KT1 . . . . . 175 D1
Wadcroft Ct SE4 . . . . . 141 B2
Waddesdon Lo HA3 . . . . .43 A3
Wadding St SE17 . 117 B2 **262 C3**
Waddington Cl EN1 . . . . . 5 C1
Waddington Rd E15. . . . .76 B2
Waddington St E15 . . . . .76 B2
Waddington Way SE19 . . 183 B2
WADDON 220 C4
Waddon Cl CR0 . . . . . . 220 C5
Waddon Court Rd CR0 . . 220 C5
Waddon Inf Sch CR0 . . . 220 C3
Waddon Marsh Sta CR0 . 220 C4
Waddon Marsh Way
CR0. . . . . 204 B1
Waddon New Rd CR0. . . 220 C4
Waddon Park Ave CR0 . . 220 C5
Waddon Rd CR0 . . . . . . 220 D5
Waddon Sta CR0 . . . . . 220 C4
Waddon Way CR0, CR2,
CR9 . . . . 220 D2
Wade Ct Muswell Hill N10 . . 31 B3
Wembley HA0. . . . . . . .65 D5
Wade Ho
16 Bermondsey SE1. . . 118 A4
1 Enfield EN1. . . . . . . .17 C6
Wade's Gr N21. . . . . . . .16 C4
Wade's Hill N21 . . . . . . .16 C4
Wade's La TW11 . . . . . 175 A5
Wadeson St E2 . . . . . . .96 B5
Wade's Pl E14 . . . . 119 D6
Wadeville Ave E17 . . . . . 59 B2
Wadeville Cl DA17 . . . . 125 C1
Wadham Ave E17 . . . . . . 35 D3
Wadham Cl TW17 . . . . . 193 A2
Wadham Gdns
Greenford UB6. . . . . . .64 B2
Primrose Hill NW3 . . 92 C6 **230 A6**
Wadham Ho N1. . . . . . . .33 D5
Wadham Rd Chingford E4. . 36 A2
Highams Pk E17 . . . . . . 35 D2
Putney SW15 . . . . 135 A1
Wadhurst Cl SE20. . . . . 184 B1
Wadhurst Ct E6. . . . . . 100 C5
Wadhurst Rd W4. . . . . . 111 B3
Wadley Rd E11 . . . . 54 C2
Wadsworth Bsns Ctr UB6 . .87 C5
Wadsworth Cl Enfield EN3. . 18 D6
Wembley UB6. . . . . . . .87 C5
Wadsworth Ct E10 . . . . . 54 A3
Wadsworth Rd UB6 . . . . . 87 C5
Wager St E3 . . . . .97 B3
Waggoners Rdbt TW5 . . . 128 B4
Waggon Mews N14 . . . . . 15 C3
Waghorn Rd EN4 . . . . . . 2 B6
Harrow HA3. . . . . .43 C6
Newham E13 . . . . .99 C6
Waghorn St SE15 . . . . . 140 A2
Wagner St SE15. . . . . . 140 C5
Wagon Rd EN4, EN5 . . . . 1 D6
Wagstaff Gdns RM9. . . . . 80 C1
Wagtail Cl Enfield EN1. . . . 6 B4
NW9 . . . . .27 C1
Wagtail Wlk BR3. . . . . . 208 A4
Waights Ct KT2 . . . . . . 176 A2
Waikato Lo IG9 . . . . 21 C3
Wainford Cl SW19 . . . . . 156 D3
Wainwright Gr TW7 . . . . 130 B1
Wainwright Ho 3 E1 . . . . 118 C5
Waite Davies Rd SE12 . . 164 D4
Waitelands Ho KT3 . . . . 199 B5
Waite St SE15. . . . . 139 D6
Waithman St EC4 . . . . . **241 C1**
Wakefield Ct 4 SE26. . . . 184 C4
Wakefield Gdns
Redbridge IG1 . . . . 56 A3
South Norwood SE19 . . . 183 C3
Wakefield Ho
Dulwich SE22. . . . . . . 162 B3
6 Peckham SE15. . . . . 140 A4
Wakefield Mews WC1 . . . **233 B1**
Wakefield Rd
Friern Barnet N11 . . . . . 31 D5
20 Richmond TW10 . . . 153 D6
South Tottenham N15. . . . 51 D4
Wakefield St
Edmonton N18 . . . . 34 A5
Newham E6 . . . . 100 A6
St Pancras WC1 . . . 94 A4 **233 B1**
Wakeford Cl
London SW4 . . . . 159 C6
Sidcup OP5. . . . . 168 D3
Wakehams Hill HA5. . . . . 41 B6
Wakeham St 9 N1. . . . . . 73 B2
Wakehurst Rd SW11 . . . 158 D6
Wakeling Ct E7 . . . . 77 C2
Wakeling Ho 8 SE27. . . . 160 D1

Wakeling La HA0.........65 B5
Wakeling Rd W7.........86 D2
Wakeling St 11 E14.......97 A1
Wakelin Ho
  Forest Hill SE23........163 A4
  19 Islington N1..........72 D1
Wakelin Rd E15..........98 C5
Wakeman Ho HA8........26 A6
Wakeman Rd NW10.......90 D4
Wakemans Hill Ave NW9..45 B4
Wakering Rd IG11.......179 A4
Wakerley Ct 6 E6.......100 B1
Wakley St EC1......94 D4 234 C2
Walberswick St SW4....270 B3
Walbrook EC4...........252 C6
  10 Wanstead E18........55 A6
Walbrook Ct 32 N1.......95 C5
Walbrook Ho N9..........18 C2
Walbrook Wharf EC4.....252 C6
Walburgh St E1...........96 B1
Walcorde Ave SE17......262 B3
Walcot Cl CR0..........222 A6
Walcot Gdns SE11.......261 A4
Walcot Ho 9 SE22......139 C2
Walcot Rd EN3............7 B3
Walcot Sq SE11.....116 C2 261 A4
Walcott St SW1.........259 B4
Waldair Ct E16..........122 D4
Waldeck Gr SE27........160 D1
Waldeck Rd
  Brentford W4..........132 C6
  Ealing W13............87 B1
  Mortlake SW14........133 A2
  Tottenham N15.........50 D6
Waldeck Terr SW14......133 A2
Waldegrave Ct
  11 Barking IG11........101 B6
  1 Teddington TW11.....174 D5
Waldegrave Gdns TW1...152 D1
Waldegrave Girls Sch
  TW2...................152 B1
Waldegrave Ho 5
  SW15..................156 C6
Waldegrave Pk TW1.....174 D6
Waldegrave Rd BR1.....210 B5
  Dagenham RM8........80 C6
  Ealing W5.............110 B6
  Hornsey N8.............50 C6
  Penge SE19............183 D3
  Teddington TW11.......174 D6
Waldegrove CR0........221 D5
Waldemar Ave
  Ealing W13............109 C5
  Fulham SW6...........135 A3
Waldemar Avenue Mans
  SW6...................264 A1
Waldemar Rd SW19.....179 C5
  Edmonton N13.........33 A6
Walden Ave BR7.......188 B6
Walden Cl DA17........125 B1
Walden Ct SW8........269 D2
Walden Gdns CR7, SW16..204 B5
Walden Ho Barnet EN4....2 C1
  8 Clapham SW11......137 A3
  SW1...................258 B3
Walden Rd BR7........188 B4
  Tottenham N17.........33 B2
Waldenshaw Rd SE23...162 C3
Walden St E1............96 B1
Walden Way NW7.......28 D4
Waldo Cl SW4...........159 C6
Waldo Ind Est BR1.....209 D6
Waldo Pl SW19.........180 C3
Waldo Rd BR1..........209 D6
  College Pk NW10.......90 B4
Waldorf Cl CR2.........220 D1
Waldorf Sch of S W London
  SW16..................159 A2
Waldram Cres SE23.....162 C3
Waldram Park Rd SE23..162 D3
Waldram Pl 6 SE23.....162 C2
Waldrist Way DA18......125 B4
Waldron Gdns BR2......208 A6
Waldron Ho 17 SW2....160 B6
Waldronhyrst CR0, CR2..220 D4
Waldron Mews SW3....266 D6
Waldron Rd
  Harrow HA1, HA2.......42 C1
  Wandsworth SW18.....158 A1
Waldrons The CR0......221 A4
Waldron's Yd HA2........64 B6
Waldstock Rd SE28......124 A6
Waleran Cl HA7..........24 D4
Waleran Rd SE13........142 A3
Waleran Flats SE1......263 A4
Wales Ave SM5..........218 C3
Wales Cl SE15..........140 B6
Wales Farm Rd W3.......89 B2
Waleton Acres SM6.....219 C2
Waley St 1 E1...........97 A2
Walfield Ave N20........13 D4
Walfield Ho N20.........14 A4
Walford Rd 28 E1.........96 B1
Walford Rd N16..........73 C4
Walfrey Gdns RM9........81 A1
Walham Ct 18 NW3......70 D2
Walham Gr SW6...135 C5 265 A4

WALHAM GREEN........135 D5
Walham Green Arc SW6..265 B4
Walham Rise 1 SW19....179 A4
Walham Yd SW6........265 A4
Walkden Rd BR7........188 C5
Walker Cl Ealing W7....108 C5
  East Bedfont TW14.....149 D4
  Friern Barnet N11.......31 C6
  Hampton TW12........173 B4
  Plumstead SE18........123 A2
Walker Ho NW1.........232 C3
Walker Mews 9 SW2....160 D4
Walker Prim Sch N14....15 D2
Walkerscroft Mead
  SE21..................161 A3
Walker's Ct W1........249 C6
Walkers Lo 18 E14......120 A4
Walker's Pl SW15.......135 A1
Walkinshaw Ct 9 N1.....73 A1
Walks The N2............48 B6
Walk The Ashford TW16..171 D3
  Palmers Green N13.....16 C1
Walkynscroft 1 SE15...140 B3
Wallace Cl SE28........124 D6
  Upper Halliford TW17...193 B5
  Uxbridge UB10.........82 A5
Wallace Collection ★
  W1...................238 A2
Wallace Cres SW11.....218 D3
Wallace Ct 19 Enfield EN3..7 C6
  NW1...................237 B3
Wallace Ho N7..........72 B2
Wallace Lo N4...........50 C1
Wallace Rd N1, N5.......73 A2
Wallasey Cres UB10.....60 C5
Wallbrook Bsns Ctr
  TW4...................128 B2
Wallbutton Rd SE4......141 A3
Wallcote Ave NW2.......46 D1
Wall Ct N4..............50 B1
Walled Garden Cl BR3..207 D5
WALLEND...............100 C6
Wall End Ct E6..........100 C6
Wall End Rd E6..........78 C1
Waller Dr HA6...........22 A2
Waller Rd SE14.........140 D3
Wallers Ct RM9.........103 B6
Wallett Ct 11 NW1.......71 C1
Wallflower St W12......111 D6
Wallgrave Rd SW5......255 C3
Wallingford Ave W10....90 D1
WALLINGTON...........219 A2
Wallington Cl HA4.......39 A3
Wallington Ct 10 SM6...219 B2
Wallington Cty Gram Sch
  SM6...................219 B5
Wallington Green SM6...219 B4
Wallington Rd IG3.......57 D2
Wallington Sq 4 SM6....219 C2
Wallington Sta SM6.....219 B2
Wallis Alley SE1........252 B2
Wallis Ct SW11.........136 B2
Wallis Ho
  5 New Cross Gate SE14..141 A4
  Ruislip HA4............39 A1
  Ruislip HA4............39 B1
Wallis Rd Hackney Wick E9..75 C2
  Southall UB1..........85 D1
Wallman Pl N22.........32 B2
Wallorton Gdns SW14...133 B1
Wallside EC2...........242 B3
Wall St N1..............73 B2
Wallwood Rd E11.......54 B2
Wallwood St E14........97 B2
Walmar Cl EN4...........2 B4
Walmer Cl BR6.........227 B4
  Chingford E4...........19 D2
Walmer Gdns W13......109 A4
Walmer Ho
  8 North Kensington W10..90 D1
  7 Penge SE20.........184 C3
Walmer Pl W1..........237 C4
Walmer Rd
  North Kensington W10..90 C1
  W11..............113 A6 244 A5
Walmgate Rd UB6.......87 B6
Walmington Fold N12....29 C4
Walm La NW2............68 C2
Walmsley Ho 1 SW16...181 C6
Walney Wlk 6 N1........73 A2
Walnut Ave UB7.........104 C3
Walnut Cl Hayes UB3...105 C6
  Ilford IG6..............57 A5
  SE8...................141 B6
  Wallington SM5.......218 D3
Walnut Ct 2 E17.........54 A5
Walnut Gdns E15........76 C3
Walnut Gr EN1..........17 B6
Walnut Ho 11 E3.........97 B6
Walnut Mews SM2.....218 A1
Walnut Rd E10..........75 D6
Walnut Tree Ave CR4...202 C6
Walnut Tree Cl
  Barnes SW13..........133 D4
  Chislehurst BR7.......189 A2
Walnut Tree Cotts
  SW19..................179 A5
Walnut Tree Ho SW10..265 D6

Walnut Tree Rd
  Brentford TW8........132 A6
  Charlton TW17.........171 A1
  Dagenham RM8........81 A6
  Greenwich SE10.......120 C1
  Heston TW5...........129 B6
Walnut Tree Walk Prim Sch
  SE11...........116 C2 261 A4
Walnut Tree Wlk
  SE11...........116 C2 261 A4
Walnut Way
  Buckhurst Hill IG9.......21 D1
  Ruislip HA4............62 C2
Walpole Ave W9........132 B3
Walpole Cl Pinner HA5...23 C4
  West Ealing W13......109 C4
Walpole Cres 10 TW11..174 D5
Walpole Ct Ealing W5...109 D5
  7 Hammersmith W14..112 D3
  South Hampstead NW6..70 A1
  Twickenham TW2......152 C2
  2 Wallington SM6.....219 B3
Walpole Gdns
  Acton Green W4.......111 A1
  Twickenham TW2......152 C1
Walpole Ho
  Chislehurst BR7.......189 B2
  East Molesey KT8......195 C4
Walpole Lo W13........109 C5
Walpole Mews NW8....229 C5
Walpole Pl
  9 Teddington TW11....174 D5
  3 Woolwich SE18......122 D2
Walpole Rd BR2........209 D4
  Mitcham SW19.........180 B4
  South Croydon CR0....221 B6
  Surbiton KT6..........198 A3
  Teddington TW11......174 D5
  Tottenham N17.........33 A1
  Tottenham N17.........51 A6
  Twickenham TW2......152 C2
  Upton E6...............77 C1
  Walthamstow E17.......53 A5
  Woodford E18..........36 D2
Walpole St SW3...114 D1 257 D2
Walrond Ave HA9........66 A3
Walsham Cl SE28.......124 D6
  Upper Clapton N16.....52 A1
Walsham Ho
  New Cross Gate SE14..140 D3
  SE17..................262 C2
Walsham Rd
  Feltham TW14..........150 B4
  New Cross Gate SE14..140 D3
Walsh Lodge HA4........40 B3
Walsingham NW8.......229 D6
Walsingham Gdns KT19..215 D3
Walsingham Ho
  Chingford E4...........20 B4
  Twickenham TW2......152 B2
Walsingham Lo SW13...134 A4
Walsingham Mans SW6..265 D4
Walsingham Pk BR7....189 B1
Walsingham Pl SW4,
  SW11..................159 A5
Walsingham Rd BR5....190 B2
  Ealing W13.............109 A5
  Enfield EN2............17 B6
  Mitcham CR4..........202 D4
  Shacklewell E5.........74 A5
Walsingham Wlk DA17..147 C6
Walter Besant Ho 20 E1..96 D4
Walter Ct 3 W3..........89 A1
Walter Green Ho SE15..140 C4
Walter Ho SW10........266 C4
Walter Hurford Par 5
  E12...................78 C4
Walter Northcott Ho 2
  NW6...................69 C3
Walter Rodney Cl 6 E6..78 B2
Walter Savill Twr 7 E17..53 C3
Walters Cl Hayes UB3...105 D4
  SE17..................262 B3
Walters Ho
  3 Camberwell SE5.....139 C3
  Islington N1...........234 D6
  10 Kennington SE17...138 D6
Walter Sickert Hall N1..235 A3
Walters Rd EN3...........6 C1
Walter's Rd SE25.......205 C5
Walter St Globe Town E2..96 D4
  2 Kingston u T KT2....176 A2
Walters Way SE23......162 D5
Walters Yd BR1.........187 A1
Walterton Rd W9........91 C3
Walter Wlk HA8..........27 A4
Waltham Ave Hayes UB3..105 B3
  Preston NW9............44 C6
Waltham Ct Chingford E17..36 A2
  Whetstone N20.........14 B1
Waltham Dr HA8..........44 C6
Waltham Forest Coll E17..35 D1
Waltham Forest Pool & Tk
  E17...................35 D1
Waltham Gdns EN3.......6 C6
Waltham Green Ct SW6..265 C3
Waltham Ho NW8.......229 A6
  10 Stockwell SW9......138 B3

Waltham Park Way E17...35 C3
Waltham Pk E17.........35 C2
Waltham Rd
  Carshalton SM5........202 C1
  Southall UB2..........107 A3
WALTHAMSTOW........53 D6
  Walthamstow Acad E17..35 B2
  Walthamstow Ave E4....35 C3
Walthamstow Ave (North
  Circular Rd) E4.......35 B4
Walthamstow Bsns Ctr
  E17...................36 A1
Walthamstow Central Sta
  E17...................53 C4
Walthamstow Marshes
  Country Pk E10........52 C1
Walthamstow Mkt ★ E17..53 C5
Walthamstow Queens Road
  Sta E17...............53 C4
Walthamstow Sch for Girls
  E17...................53 D5
Waltham Way E4.........19 C2
Waltheof Ave N17........33 B2
Waltheof Gdns N17......33 B2
Walton Ave Cheam SM3..217 B5
  Harrow HA2.............63 B4
  New Malden KT3.......199 D5
  Wembley HA9...........66 D5
Walton Bridge Rd KT12,
  TW17..................193 C2
Walton Cl Dollis Hill NW2..68 B6
  Harrow HA1............42 B5
  Lea Bridge E5..........74 D5
  SW8..............138 A5 270 B4
Walton Croft HA1........64 C4
Walton Ct EN5...........14 A6
Walton Dr Harrow HA1...42 B5
  Willesden NW10........67 B2
Walton Gdns Acton W3..88 D2
  Feltham TW13.........171 D6
  Wembley HA9...........66 A6
Walton Gn CR0.........224 A1
Walton Ho E2...........243 D6
  Ealing W5..............109 D2
  1 Edmonton N9.........34 A6
  1 Kingston u T KT2....176 A3
  Upper Holloway N7......72 B5
  10 Walthamstow E17....53 D6
  Wandsworth SW18.....157 C5
Walton La
  Oatlands Pk KT13, TW17..193 B1
  Shepperton TW17......193 B2
Walton Oak Sch KT12..194 C1
WALTON-ON-THAMES..194 C2
Walton Pl SW3..........257 C6
Walton Rd
  East Molesey KT8, KT12..195 C5
  Harrow HA1............42 B5
  Little Ilford E12.........78 C4
  Newham E13...........99 C5
  Sidcup DA14...........168 C1
  Tottenham N15.........51 D5
  Walton-on-T KT12&KT8..194 D4
Walton St Enfield EN2....5 B4
  SW3..............114 C3 257 B5
Walton Way Acton W3...88 D2
  Mitcham CR4..........203 C5
Walt Whitman Cl 6
  SE24..................138 D1
WALWORTH.............117 B1
Walworth Acad (Lower
  School) SE17...117 B1 262 D2
Walworth Acad (Upper
  School) SE17...117 C1 263 B1
Walworth Pl
  SE17..................117 A1 262 B1
Walworth Rd
  SE17..................117 A1 262 B4
Walwyn Ave BR1.......209 D6
Wanborough Dr SW15..156 B3
Wanderer Dr IG11......102 C4
Wandle Bank
  Mitcham SW19.........180 B3
  Wallington CR0........220 A5
Wandle Court Gdns CR0..220 A5
Wandle Cl
  4 Bedford Pk W12....111 C4
  Wallington CR0........220 A5
  West Ewell KT19.......215 A4
Wandle Ho
  6 Catford BR1.........186 B5
  NW8..................237 A4
  Wandsworth SW18.....157 D4
Wandle Ind Mus ★ CR4..202 D6
Wandle Lo CR0.........220 A5
Wandle Lodge SM6.....219 B6
Wandle Pk Sta CR0.....220 C6
Wandle Rd Croydon CR0..221 A5
  Hackbridge SM6.......219 B6
  Morden SM4...........202 B4
  Upper Tooting SW17...158 C2
  Wallington CR0........220 A5
Wandle Side
  Hackbridge SM6.......219 B5
  Wallington CR0........220 A5
Wandle Tech Pk CR4...202 D2
Wandle Trad Est CR4...202 D2
Wandle Valley Sch SM5..202 C2
Wandle Way
  Mitcham CR4..........202 D4

Wandle Way continued
  Wandsworth SW18.......157 D3
Wandon Rd SW6..135 D5 265 D3
WANDSWORTH.........157 C6
Wandsworth Bridge Rd
  SW6...........135 D4 265 C1
Wandsworth Common Sta
  SW12..................158 D4
Wandsworth Common West
  Side SW18...........158 A6
Wandsworth Gyratory
  SW18..................157 D6
Wandsworth High St
  SW18..................157 D6
Wandsworth Plain
  SW18..................157 D6
Wandsworth Rd
  SW8..............138 A5 270 A3
Wandsworth Road Sta
  SW4...................137 C3
Wandsworth Town Sta
  SW18..................135 D1
Wangey Rd RM6..........58 D2
Wangford Ho 13 SW9...138 D1
Wanless Rd SE24.......139 A2
Wanley Rd SE5..........139 B1
Wanlip Rd E13...........99 B3
Wansbeck Ct EN2.........4 D2
Wansbeck Rd E3, E9......75 B1
Wansdown Pl
  SW6...........135 D5 265 C4
Wandsworth Riverside
  Quarter Pier SW6......135 C2
Wansey St SE17....117 A2 263 A3
Wansford Rd IG8.........37 C2
WANSTEAD.............55 C3
Wanstead CE Prim Sch
  E11...................55 A4
Wanstead Cl BR1.......187 C1
Wanstead High Sch E11..55 C3
Wanstead Hts 8 E11.....55 A4
Wanstead La IG1.........56 A3
Wanstead L Ctr E11.....55 C3
Wanstead Park Ave E12..77 D6
Wanstead Park Rd IG1..56 A1
Wanstead Park Sta E7...77 B4
Wanstead Pl E11.........55 A4
Wanstead Rd BR1.......187 C1
Wanstead Sta E11.......55 B3
Wantage Rd SE12.......164 D6
Wantz Rd RM10..........81 D3
WAPPING..............118 B5
Wapping Dock St 19 E1..118 B5
Wapping High St E1.....118 B5
Wapping La E1..........118 B5
Wapping Sta E1.........118 C5
Wapping Wall E1........118 C5
Warbank La KT2.........177 D3
Warbeck Rd W12........112 B4
Warberry Rd N22.........32 B1
Warboys App KT2........176 D4
Warboys Cres E4.........36 A5
Warboys Rd KT2........176 D4
Warburg Ho E2..........96 A4
Warburton Cl
  6 Kingsland N1........73 C2
  Stanmore HA3..........24 B4
Warburton Ct
  Peckham SE15.........140 A2
  Ruislip HA4.............62 A6
Warburton Ho 5 E8.....96 B6
  8 Hackney E8..........96 B6
  Twickenham TW2......151 D3
Warburton St 6 E8.......96 B6
Warburton Terr E17......35 D1
Wardalls Ho 12 SE8....141 B6
Ward Cl CR2............221 C3
Wardell Cl NW7..........27 C3
Wardell Ct N2...........48 B6
Wardell Field 16 NW9..27 C2
Wardell Ho 7 SE10......142 A4
Warden Ave HA2.........41 B1
Warden Rd NW5..........71 A2
Wardens Field Cl 2
  BR6...................227 D2
Wardens Gr SE1........252 A3
Wardle St E9............74 D3
Wardley Lo E11..........54 D3
Wardley St SW18........157 D4
Wardlow 8 NW5..........71 B4
Wardo Ave SW6....135 A4 264 A2
Wardour Mews W1......239 B1
Wardour St W1....93 D1 239 C1
Ward Point SE11........261 A3
Ward Rd
  Camden Town N19......71 C5
  Mill Meads E15.........98 B6
Wardrew Ct 9 EN5......14 A6
Wardrobe Pl EC4.......241 D1
Wardrobe Terr EC4.....251 D6
Wardrobe The 3 TW9..153 D6
Wards Cotts TW19.....148 B4
Wards Rd IG2...........57 B2
Wards Wharf App E16..121 D4
Ware Ct Cheam SM1...217 B4
  Edgware HA8...........26 A6
Wareham Cl TW3.......129 D1
Wareham Ct 2 N1.......73 C1
Wareham Ho SW8......270 C4

Warehouse W E16 . . . . .121 B6
Waremead Rd IG2 . . . . .56 D4
Ware Point Dr SE28 . . . . . .123 B4
Warfield Rd
East Bedfont TW14. . . . . .149 C4
Hampton TW12. . . . . . . .173 D2
Kensal Green NW10. . . . . .90 D4
Warfield Yd **5** NW10. . . . .90 D4
Wargrave Ave N15 . . . . . . .51 D3
Wargrave Ho **46** E2 . . . . . .95 D4
Wargrave Rd HA2. . . . . . . .64 A5
Warham Rd Croydon CR2 . .221 A3
Harringay N4 . . . . .50 D4
Harrow HA3 . . . . .24 D1
Warham St SE5 . . . . .138 D5
Waring Cl BR6 . . . . .227 D2
Waring Dr BR6. . . . . .227 D2
Waring Ho **25** E2. . . . . . . .96 A4
Waring Rd DA14 . . . . .190 C4
Waring St SE27 . . . . .183 A6
Warkworth Gdns TW7 . .131 A5
Warkworth Rd N17 . . . . . .33 B3
Warland Rd SE18 . . . . . . .145 C5
Warley Ave
Dagenham RM8 . . . . . . .59 B2
Hayes UB4 . . . . .84 A1
Warley Cl E10 . . . . .53 B1
Warley Ho N1 . . . . .73 B2
Warley Rd Hayes UB4. . . . .84 A2
Lower Edmonton N9. . . . . .18 C2
Woodford IG8. . . . . .37 B3
Warley St E2 . . . . .96 D4
Warlingham Rd CR7 . . . . .204 D5
Warlock Rd W9 . . . . .91 C3
Warlters Cl N7. . . . . .72 A4
Warlters Rd N7 . . . . .72 A4
Warltersville Mans N19 . .50 A2
Warltersville Rd N4, N8,
N19 . . . . .50 A2
War Meml Homes W4 . .133 B5
Warming Cl E5 . . . . .74 D5
Warmington Rd SE24 . .161 A5
Warmington St **3** E13 . . .99 A3
Warminster Gdns SE25. .184 A1
Warminster Rd SE25 . . .184 A1
Warminster Sq SE25 . . .184 A1
Warminster Way CR4 . . .181 B1
Warmsworth NW1 . . . .232 A6
Warmwell Ave NW9 . . . . .27 C2
Warndon St SE16 . . . . . .118 C2
Warneford Rd HA3 . . . . . .44 A6
Warneford St E9 . . . . .96 B6
Warne Pl **4** DA15. . . . . . .168 B5
Warner Ave SM3 . . . . . . .217 A4
Warner Cl Hadley Wood EN4 . .2 C6
Hampton TW12. . . . . . . .173 B3
Harlington UB3. . . . . . . .127 B5
Hendon NW9 . . . . .46 A2
Stratford E15 . . . . .76 C3
Warner Ct SM3 . . . . .217 A6
Warner Ho
1 Beckenham BR3 . . . . .185 D4
Harrow HA1 . . . . .42 B2
4 Homerton E9 . . . . . . .74 D2
Lewisham SE13 . . . . . . .141 D4
NW8 . . . . .229 A2
Warner Pl E2 . . . . .96 A4
Warner Rd Bromley BR1 . .186 D3
Camberwell SE5 . . . . . . .139 A4
Hornsey N8. . . . . .49 D5
Walthamstow E17 . . . . . .53 A5
Warners Cl IG8 . . . . .37 A5
Warner St EC1 . . . . .94 C3 241 A4
Warner Yd EC1. . . . . .241 A5
Warnford Ho SW15 . . . . .155 C5
Warnford Ind Est UB3. . .105 C4
Warnford Rd BR6 . . . . . . .227 D3
Warnham WC1 . . . . .233 C1
Warnham Court Rd
SM5. . . . . .218 D1
Warnham Ho **6** SW2. . . .160 B4
Warnham Rd N12 . . . . . . .111 C4
Warple Mews W3. . . . . . .111 C4
Warple Way W3, W12 . . . .111 C4
Warren Ave Bromley BR1 . .186 C3
Leyton E11 . . . . .76 B5
Mortlake SW14, TW10 . . .132 C4
Orpington BR6 . . . . .227 D3
South Croydon CR2 . . . . .222 D1
Warren Cl DA6. . . . . .169 C6
Esher KT10. . . . . .212 A4
Hayes UB4 . . . . .84 C2
Ponders End N9 . . . . . . .18 D4
Wembley HA9. . . . . .65 D6
West Norwood SE21. . . .161 A4
Warren Comp Sch RM6 . .59 B4
Warren Cres N9 . . . . .17 D4
Warren Ct
17 Beckenham BR3 . . . . .185 C3
5 Croydon CR0 . . . . . . .205 C1
6 Ealing W5 . . . . .87 C2
Greenwich SE7. . . . . . . .143 C6
N1. . . . . .234 A4
Tottenham Hale N17. . . . .52 A6
Warren Cutting KT2. . . . .177 B3
Warrender Prim Sch
HA4 . . . . .39 D2
Warrender Rd N19 . . . . . .71 C4
Warrender Way HA4 . . . . .40 A2

Warren Dr Greenford UB6. . .86 A3
Ruislip HA4. . . . . .40 D2
Warren Dr N KT5, KT6. . .198 D1
Warren Dr S KT5. . . . . . . .199 A1
Warren Dr The E11. . . . . . .55 C2
Warren Farm Cotts RM6. .59 B5
Warren Fields HA7. . . . . . .25 C6
Warren Gdns E15 . . . . . . .76 B3
Warren Hill IG10. . . . . . . .21 C6
Warren Ho **21** E3. . . . . . . .97 C4
Warren Jun Sch RM6. . . . .59 B4
Warren La Stanmore HA7 . . .9 A2
Woolwich SE18. . . . . . . .122 D3
Warren La Gate SE18. . . .122 D3
Warren Mews W1. . . . . . .239 A5
Warren Park Rd SM1. . . .218 C2
Warren Pk KT2. . . . . .177 A4
Warren Pond Rd E4. . . . . .20 D4
Warren Rd Ashford TW15. .171 C3
Bexleyheath DA6 . . . . . .169 C6
Bushey WD23. . . . . .8 B3
Chingford E4. . . . . .20 A2
Croydon CR0. . . . . .205 D1
Hayes BR2. . . . . .225 A6
Ickenham UB10 . . . . . . .60 B4
Ilford IG6 . . . . .57 B4
Isleworth TW7 . . . . .152 B5
Kingston u T KT3. . . . . . .177 A4
Leyton E10 . . . . .76 A5
Mitcham SW19 . . . . . . .180 C4
Sidcup DA14. . . . . .168 C1
Wanstead E11 . . . . .55 C2
Willesden NW2. . . . . . . .67 D6
Warren Rise KT3. . . . . . . .177 B2
Warren Road Prim Sch
BR6. . . . . .227 D4
Warrens Shawe La HA8 . .10 C3
Warren St W1 . . . . .93 C3 239 A5
Warren Street Sta
NW1. . . . . .93 C3 239 A5
Warren Terr RM6. . . . . . . .58 D3
Warren The Hayes UB4. . . .84 A1
Heston TW5 . . . . .129 B5
Manor Pk E12. . . . . .78 A4
Worcester Pk KT19. . . . .215 B5
Warren Way HA8. . . . . . . .26 D1
Warren Wlk **1** SE7. . . . . .143 C6
Warren Wood Cl BR2. . . .225 A6
Warriner Dr N9 . . . . .18 A1
Warriner Gdns
SW11. . . . . .137 A4 268 A1
Warrington Cres
W9. . . . . .92 A3 236 A6
Warrington Ct
4 Croydon CR0. . . . . . .220 D5
13 Merton SW19 . . . . . .179 C3
Warrington Gdns W9 . .236 A5
Warrington Rd
Croydon CR0. . . . . .220 D5
Dagenham RM8 . . . . . . .81 A6
Harrow HA1 . . . . .42 C4
22 Richmond TW10 . . . . .153 D6
Warrington Sq RM8. . . . . .80 D6
Warrior Cl SE28. . . . . . . .123 C5
Warrior Sq E12 . . . . .78 C4
Warsaw Cl HA4 . . . . .62 B2
Warspite Ho **3** E14 . . . .119 D2
Warspite Rd SE18 . . . . . .122 A3
Warton Rd E15 . . . . .98 A6
Warwall E6. . . . . .100 D1
Warwick W14. . . . . .113 B2 254 D3
Warwick Ave
Edgware HA8 . . . . .11 A1
Harrow HA2 . . . . .63 B4
Paddington W9 . . . . .92 A3 236 A5
Warwick Avenue Sta
W9. . . . . .92 A3 236 A5
Warwick Bldg SW8 . . . . .268 C5
Warwick Chambers W8. .255 A6
Warwick Cl Bushey WD23. . .8 C4
DA5. . . . . .169 B4
Hampton TW12. . . . . . . .174 A3
New Barnet EN4. . . . . . .14 B6
Warwick Cres Hayes UB4. .83 D3
Little Venice W9 . . . .92 A2 236 A4
Warwick Ct
1 Beckenham BR2 . . . . .186 C1
Ealing W7 . . . . .86 D1
5 East Finchley N2 . . . . .48 A6
Friern Barnet N11 . . . . . .31 D4
Harrow HA1 . . . . .42 C6
Merton SW19 . . . . .179 B2
13 New Barnet EN5 . . . . .13 D6
Northolt UB5 . . . . .63 C3
3 Upper Clapton E5 . . . . .74 B6
WC1 . . . . .240 D3
Warwick Dene SW15. . . .110 A5
Warwick Dr SW15. . . . . .134 B2
Warwick Gdns
Harringay N4 . . . . .51 A4
Ilford IG1. . . . . .56 D1
Thames Ditton KT7. . . . .196 D4
Thornton Heath CR7. . . .204 C5
W14 . . . . .113 B2 254 D4
Warwick Gr Surbiton KT5. .198 B2
Upper Clapton E5 . . . . . .52 B1
Warwick Ho **9** Acton W3. .88 C1
10 Brixton SW9 . . . . . . .138 C3
6 Kingston u T KT2 . . . . .176 A2

Warwick Ho continued
6 Putney SW15. . . . . . . .156 C4
Stoke Newington N4. . . . .51 A1
5 Wimbledon SW19 . . . .179 A3
Warwick House St SW1 . .249 D6
Warwick La EC4 . . .94 D1 241 D1
Warwick Lo
Brondesbury NW2 . . . . . .69 A3
Cheam SM1 . . . . .217 B4
Twickenham TW2 . . . . . .151 D1
Warwick Mans SW5 . . . .255 A4
Warwick Par HA7 . . . . . . .25 B1
Warwick Pas EC4 . . . . . .241 D2
Warwick Pl Ealing W5. . . .109 D4
Little Venice W9 . . . .92 A2 236 A4
Warwick Pl N SW1. . . . . .259 A3
Warwick Rd
Ashford TW15. . . . . . . .170 A5
Barnet EN5. . . . . .1 D1
Bexley DA16. . . . . .146 C2
Chingford E4. . . . . .35 C5
Ealing W5 . . . . .110 A5
Edmonton N18 . . . . .33 D6
Enfield EN3. . . . . .7 B6
Friern Barnet N11 . . . . . .31 D4
Hounslow TW4 . . . . .128 B2
Kingston u T KT3. . . . . . .199 A6
Penge SE20 . . . . .206 B6
Plashet E12 . . . . .78 A3
Sidcup DA14. . . . . .190 B5
Southall UB1. . . . . .107 B3
Stratford E15 . . . . .76 C2
Sutton SM1. . . . . .218 A3
Teddington KT1. . . . . . .175 C2
Thames Ditton KT7. . . . .196 D4
Thornton Heath CR7. . . .204 C6
Twickenham TW2 . . . . . .152 C3
Walthamstow E17 . . . . . .35 B1
Wanstead E11 . . . . .55 B4
West Kensington W14,
SW5 . . . . .113 B2 254 D4
Yiewsley UB7 . . . . .104 A5
Warwick Row
SW1. . . . . .115 B3 258 D6
E17. . . . . .54 A5
Warwick Sch for Boys
E17. . . . . .54 A5
Warwickshire Path SE8 . .141 B5
Warwick Sq Holborn EC4 . .241 D2
Pimlico SW1 . . . .115 C1 259 A2
Warwick Sq Mews SW1 . .259 A3
Warwick St W1 . . . .115 C6 249 B6
Warwick Terr
Leytonstone E17 . . . . . . .54 B4
SE18. . . . . .145 B6
Warwick Way
SW1. . . . . .115 B2 258 D6
Warwick Yd EC1. . . . . . . .242 B5
Wasdale NW1 . . . . .231 D1
Washbourne Ct N9 . . . . . .18 A2
Washbrook Ho SW2. . . . .160 C5
Washington Ave E12. . . . .78 B4
Washington Bldg **1**
SE13 . . . . .141 D4
Washington Cl **43** E3. . . . .97 D4
Washington Ct SW17 . . .180 D4
Washington Ho SW1 . . . .247 C1
Walthamstow E17 . . . . . .35 B1
Washington Rd
Barnes SW13 . . . . .134 A5
Kingston u T KT1. . . . . . .176 C1
North Cheam KT4. . . . . .200 B1
Upton E6. . . . . .77 C1
2 Woodford IG8 . . . . . . .36 D1
Wastdale Rd SE23. . . . . .162 D3
Watchfield Ct **7** W4 . . . .111 A1
Watcombe Cotts TW9. . .132 C6
Watcombe Rd SE25 . . . .206 B4
Waterbank Rd SE6. . . . . .186 A6
Waterbeach Rd RM9. . . . .80 C2
Water Brook La NW4. . . . .46 C4
Waterdale Rd SE2. . . . . .146 A6
Waterden Rd E15. . . . . . . .75 C2
Waterer Ho **7** SE6. . . . . .186 A6
Waterer Rise SM6. . . . . .219 D2
Waterfall Cl N14 . . . . .15 C1
Waterfall Cotts SW19 . . .180 B4
Waterfall Rd
Mitcham SW19 . . . . . . .180 B4
New Southgate N11, N14. . .15 C1
Waterfall Terr SW17 . . . .180 C4
Waterfield Cl
Belvedere DA17 . . . . . . .125 C3
Woolwich SE28. . . . . . . .124 B5
Waterfield Gdns SE25. . .205 C4
Waterford Ct **18** W13. . . .109 A5
Waterford Rd
SW6. . . . . .135 D5 265 C3
Waterford Way NW10. . . .68 A3
Watergardens The
Kingston u T KT2 . . . . . .177 A4
Woodford IG8. . . . . .37 A5
Water Gardens The
W2. . . . . .92 C1 237 B2
Watergate EC4 . . . . .251 C6
Watergate Ho **5** SE18. . .122 C2
Watergate Sch SE6 . . . . .185 D5
Watergate St SE8 . . . . . .141 C6
Watergate Wlk WC2. . . . .250 B4
Water Gdns HA7. . . . . . . .25 B4

Waterglade Ctr The W5 . .109 D6
Waterhall Ave E4 . . . . . . .36 C6
Waterhall Cl E17. . . . . . . .34 D2
Waterhead NW1 . . . . . . .232 A2
Waterhedge Mews EN1 . .17 D6
Waterhouse Cl
Hammersmith W6 . . . . . .112 D1
Hampstead NW3 . . . . . .70 B3
Newham E16 . . . . .99 D2
Waterhouse Ct **7** TW11. .174 D5
Waterhouse Sq EC1. . . . .241 A3
Wateridge Cl E14. . . . . . .119 C3
Wateringbury Cl BR5. . . .190 B1
Water La
16 Camden Town NW1 . . .71 B1
Edmonton N9 . . . . .18 B1
Ilford IG3. . . . . .79 D5
Richmond TW10, TW9. . .153 D6
SE14. . . . . .140 C5
Sidcup DA14. . . . . .169 B2
Stratford E15 . . . . .76 C2
Teddington KT1. . . . . . .175 D2
Twickenham TW1 . . . . . .153 A3
Water Lane Ho **23** TW10. .153 D6
Water Lily Cl UB2. . . . . . .108 A4
Waterloo Bridge SE1,
WC2. . . . . .116 B6 250 D5
Waterloo Cl
East Bedfont TW14. . . . .149 D3
Hackney E9. . . . . .74 C3
Stratford E15 **4** HA0. . . . .66 A2
Waterloo East Sta
SE1. . . . . .116 C5 251 B3
Waterloo Gdns
26 Islington N1. . . . . .72 D1
South Hackney E2. . . . . .96 C5
Waterloo Millennium Pier
SE1. . . . . .250 C2
Waterloo Pl Kew TW9. . . .132 C6
9 Richmond TW9 . . . . . .132 A5
SW1 . . . . .115 D5 249 C4
Waterloo Rd
Dollis Hill NW2. . . . . . . .68 A6
Forest Gate E7 . . . . .76 D3
SE1. . . . . .116 C4 251 B2
Sutton SM1. . . . . .218 B3
Walthamstow E10 . . . . . .53 C2
Waterloo Sta
SE1. . . . . .116 C4 251 A2
Waterloo Terr N1 . . . . . . .72 D1
Waterlow Ct NW11. . . . . .47 D2
Waterlow Rd N19 . . . . . . .49 C1
Waterman Bldg **2** E14. .119 C4
Watermans Arts Ctr *
TW8 . . . . .132 A6
Watermans Ct
1 Brentford TW8 . . . . . .131 D6
2 Brentford TW8 . . . . . .132 A6
Watermans Mews **1**
W5. . . . . .110 A6
Waterman St SW15 . . . .134 D2
Waterman Way E1 . . . . . .118 B5
Watermark Ct RM6. . . . . .58 B3
Watermead TW14. . . . . .149 C3
Watermead Ho E9 . . . . . .75 B3
Watermead La SW4 . . . . .136 A3
Watermeadow Ho SE6 . .186 A6
Watermead Rd SE6 . . . . .186 A6
Water mead Way N17. . . . .34 B1
Watermen's Sq **1** SE20. .184 C3
Water Mews SE15. . . . . .140 C5
Watermill Business Ctr EN3 . . .7 B3
Watermill Cl TW10 . . . . . .153 C1
Watermill La N18 . . . . . . .33 C5
Watermill Way SW19. . . .180 A2
Water Mill Way TW13. . . .151 C2
Watermint Quay N16. . . . .52 A2
Water Rd HA0 . . . . .88 B6
Watersedge KT19. . . . . .215 A4
Water's Edge SW6 . . . . .134 C4
Watersfield Way HA8 . . . .26 A3
Waters Gdns RM10. . . . . .81 C3
Watershipdown Ho **4**
E11. . . . . .54 D2
Waterside
11 Beckenham BR3 . . . . .185 C2
N1. . . . . .235 A3
Walthamstow E17 . . . . . .52 C3
Waterside Ave BR3. . . . .207 D4
Waterside Bsns Ctr
TW7 . . . . .131 B1
Waterside Cl Barking IG11. . .80 A4
30 Bermondsey SE16. . . . .118 A4
Northolt UB5 . . . . .85 B4
Old Ford E3. . . . . .97 B6
Surbiton KT6. . . . . .214 A6
Woolwich SE28. . . . . . . .123 D5
Waterside Ct
3 Hackbridge SM6 . . . . .219 A5
Lewisham SE13 . . . . . . .142 B1
Waterside Dr KT12. . . . . .194 B4
Waterside Pl NW1 . . . . . .231 B6
Waterside Point SW11 . .267 B4
Waterside Prim Sch
SE18. . . . . .123 B1
Waterside Rd UB2. . . . . .107 C3
Waterside Trad Ctr W7 . .108 C3
Waterside Way SW17 . . .180 A5

Watersmeet Way SE28 . .102 D1
Waterson St E2. . . . . .95 D4
Waters Pl SW15. . . . . . . .134 C3
Watersplash Cl KT1. . . . .198 A6
Watersplash La
Hayes UB3 . . . . .106 A2
Southall TW5 . . . . .106 B1
Watersplash Rd
Littleton TW17 . . . . .192 C5
Littleton TW17 . . . . .192 C6
Waters Rd Catford SE6 . .164 C1
Kingston u T KT1. . . . . . .176 D1
Waters Sq KT1. . . . . .198 D6
Water St WC2. . . . . .251 A6
Water Tower Cl UB8 . . . . .60 A3
Water Tower Hill CR0. . . .221 B4
Water Tower Pl N1 . . . . . .234 C5
Water View Cl DA6. . . . . .168 D6
Waterview Ho **13** E14 . . . .97 A2
Waterville Lo **6** N12. . . . .30 A5
Waterway Ave **2** SE13. .141 D2
Waterways Bsns Ctr EN3 . . .7 C5
Waterworks Cnr E17. . . . .36 C1
Waterworks Ctr * E10. . . .75 A6
Waterworks La E5 . . . . . .74 D6
Waterworks Nature Reserve
E10. . . . . .75 A6
Waterworks Rd SW2. . . .160 B5
Waterworks Yd **4** CR0. . .221 A5
Watery La DA14. . . . . . . .190 B4
Hayes UB3 . . . . .105 B1
Merton SW19, SW20. . . .179 B1
Northolt UB5 . . . . .84 C5
Wates Way CR4 . . . . . . .202 D3
Wateville Rd N17 . . . . . . .33 A2
Watford Cl SW11. . . . . . .267 B2
Watford Rd Elstree WD6. . .9 C5
Harrow HA1 . . . . .43 A1
Newham E16 . . . . .99 A2
Northwood HA6 . . . . . . .22 A4
Sudbury HA0, HA1 . . . . . .65 B4
Watford Way NW4 . . . . . .46 A5
Watford Way (Barnet By-
Pass) NW4. . . . . .27 D3
Watkin Mews **18** EN3. . . . .7 C6
Watkin Rd HA9 . . . . .66 D5
Watkins Ho
11 Cubitt Town E14. . . . .120 A4
Harrow HA1 . . . . .42 D4
Watkinson Rd N7 . . . . . . .72 B2
Watling Ave HA8. . . . . . . .27 B2
Watling Ct EC4 . . . . .242 B1
1 Elstree WD6 . . . . .9 D5
Watling Gate NW9 . . . . . .45 C5
Watling Gdns NW2. . . . . .69 A2
Watling Ho **10** SE18 . . . .144 C6
Watlings Cl CR0. . . . . . . .207 A3
Watling St
Bexleyheath DA7 . . . . . .147 D1
4 Camberwell SE15 . . . .139 C6
City of London EC4 . .95 A1 242 B1
Elstree WD6 . . . . .9 D6
Watlington Gr SE26 . . . . .185 A5
Watney Cotts SW14 . . . .133 A2
Watney Mkt * E1 . . . . . . .96 B1
Watney Rd SW14 . . . . . .133 A2
Watneys Rd CR4 . . . . . . .203 D4
Watney St E1 . . . . .96 B1
Watson Ave Cheam SM3 . .217 A6
Wallend E6. . . . . .78 C1
Watson Cl Mitcham SW19. .180 C3
Stoke Newington N16. . . .73 B3
Watson Ho **3** SW2. . . . .160 A4
Watsons Lo **4** RM10. . . .81 D2
Watsons Mews W1. . . . . .237 B3
Watsons Rd N22 . . . . . . .32 B2
Watson's St SE8 . . . . . . .141 C5
Watson St E13 . . . . .99 B5
Wattisfield Rd E5 . . . . . . .74 C5
Watts Cl N15 . . . . .51 C4
Wattsdown Cl E13 . . . . . .99 A6
Watts Gr E3 . . . . .97 D2
Watts Ho **5** W10. . . . . . .91 A2
Watt's La Chislehurst BR7. .189 A2
Teddington TW11 . . . . . .175 A5
Watts Rd KT7. . . . . .197 A2
Watts St E15. . . . . .139 D4
Wapping E1 . . . . .118 B5
Wat Tyler Ho N8 . . . . .50 A6
Wat Tyler Rd SE10. . . . . .142 B4
Wauthier Cl N13. . . . . . . .32 D5
Wavel Ct
7 Streatham SW16. . . . .160 A1
7 Wapping E1. . . . . . . .118 C5
Wavell Dr DA15. . . . . . . .167 C5
Wavell Ho N6. . . . . .49 A3
Wavel Mews
Hampstead NW6 . . . . . .69 D1
Hornsey N8. . . . . .49 D5
Wavel Pl SE26 . . . . .183 D6
Wavendon Ave W4. . . . . .111 B1
Waveney Ave SE15. . . . .140 B1
Waveney Cl E1 . . . . .118 A5
Waveney Ho **20** E1. . . . .118 A5
Waveney Ho SE15. . . . . .140 B1
Waverley Ave
Chingford Hatch E4 . . . . .35 B6

Waverley Ave continued
Sutton SM1. . . . .**217** D6
Tolworth KT5 . . . . **199** A3
Twickenham TW2, TW4. . . **151** C3
Walthamstow E17 . . . . . . **54** B6
Wembley HA9. . . . . **66** B3
Waverley Cl BR2. . . . . . **209** D4
East Molesey KT8. . . . . . **195** C4
Hayes UB3 . . . . **105** B2
Woodford E18. . . . . **37** C1
Waverley Cres SE18. . . . **123** B1
Waverley Ct
🖪 Brondesbury NW6 . . . . . **69** A1
Enfield EN2 . . . . **5** A2
North Finchley N12. . . . . . **30** B6
W1 . . . . **238** B4
Waverley Gdns
Barking IG11 . . . . **101** C5
Ealing NW10. . . . . **88** B5
Ilford IG6 . . . . **57** B6
Newham E6 . . . . **100** A2
Northwood HA6 . . . . . . **22** A2
Waverley Gr N3. . . . . . **47** A6
Waverley Ind Pk HA1. . . **42** B6
Waverley Pl
Finsbury Pk N4 . . . . **50** D1
St John's Wood
NW8. . . . . **92** B5 **229** C4
Waverley Rd
Croydon SE25. . . . . **206** B6
Enfield EN2 . . . . **4** D2
Finsbury Pk N8 . . . . **50** A2
Harrow HA2 . . . . **41** A1
Plumstead SE18. . . . . . . **123** B1
Southall UB1. . . . . **107** C6
Stoneleigh KT17, KT4. . . . **216** B3
Tottenham N17. . . . . **34** B3
Walthamstow E17 . . . . . . **54** A6
Woodford E18. . . . . **37** C2
Waverley Sch SE18 . . . . . **6** C1
Waverley Way SM5. . . . **218** C2
Waverly Ct NW3 . . . . . . **70** D2
Waverton Ho 🛚 E3. . . . . **97** B6
Waverton Rd SW18 . . . . **158** A4
Waverton St W1 . . . **115** B5 **248** C4
Wavertree Ct 🗐 SW2. . . . **160** A3
Wavertree Rd
Streatham SW2 . . . . . . **160** B3
Woodford E18. . . . . **37** A1
Waxham NW5 . . . . **70** D3
Waxlow Cres UB1. . . . . . **85** C1
Waxlow Ho UB4. . . . . . . **84** C2
Waxlow Rd NW10. . . . . . **89** B5
Waxlow Way UB5. . . . . . **85** B3
Waxwell Cl HA5. . . . . . . **22** D1
Waxwell La HA5 . . . . . . **22** D1
Wayatt Point 🛘 SE28. . . **123** A3
Wayborne Gr HA4. . . . . . **39** A3
Waye Ave TW5 . . . . **128** A4
Wayfarer Rd UB5 . . . . . . **85** A4
Wayfield Link SE9. . . . . **167** B5
Wayford St SW11 . . . . . **136** C3
Wayland Ave E8 . . . . **74** A3
Wayland Ho 🗩 SW9. . . . **138** C3
Waylands UB3 . . . . **83** B2
Waylands Ct IG1. . . . . . . **79** B4
Waylands Mead BR3 . . . **185** D2
Waylett Ho SE11 . . . . . . **261** A1
Waylett Pl Wembley HA0. . . **65** D4
West Norwood SE27. . . . . **160** D1
Wayman Ct E8. . . . . **74** B2
Wayne Cl BR6. . . . . **227** D5
Waynflete Ave CR0. . . . **220** D5
Waynflete Sq
🛚 North Kensington W10 . . . **90** D1
🛗 Shepherd's Bush W10. . . **112** D6
Waynflete St SW18. . . . **158** A2
Wayside Chislehurst BR7. . **189** B2
Golders Green NW11. . . . . **47** A1
Mortlake SW14 . . . . . . **155** A6
New Addington CR0 . . . . . **223** D2
Wayside Ave WD23. . . . . . **8** B5
Wayside Cl N14. . . . . . . **15** C5
Wayside Commercial Est
IG11. . . . . **102** A5
Wayside Ct
Isleworth TW7 . . . . **130** C3
Twickenham TW1 . . . . . **153** C5
Wembley HA9. . . . . **66** C5
Wayside Gr BR7, SE9. . . . **188** B6
Wayside Mews IG2 . . . . . **56** C4
Weald Cl
🛗 Bermondsey SE16. . . . . **118** B1
BR2. . . . . **226** A6
Weald Fst & Mid Schs
HA3 . . . . **24** D3
Weald La HA3 . . . . **24** B2
Weald Rd UB10 . . . . **82** C5
Weald Rise HA3. . . . . . . **24** D2
Weald Sq E5. . . . . **74** B6
WEALDSTONE **42** D6
Wealdstone Rd SM3. . . . **217** B6
Weald The BR7 . . . . **188** B4
Weald Way Hayes UB4 . . . **83** C4
Romford RM7. . . . . **59** D3
Wealdwood Gdns HA5 . . . **23** D4

Weale Rd E4. . . . . **20** B1
Weall Ct HA5 . . . . **41** A5
Weardale Ct EN5. . . . . . . **12** C6
Weardale Gdns EN2. . . . . . **5** B4
Weardale Ho N4. . . . . **51** A2
Weardale Rd SE13. . . . . . **142** B1
Wearmouth Ho 🛘 E1 . . . . **97** B2
Wear Pl 🛯 E2. . . . . **96** B4
Wearside Rd SE13 . . . . . **141** D1
Weatherbury 🗍 W2. . . . . . **91** C1
Weatherbury Ho 🛐 N19. . . **71** D5
Weatherill Ct SE25. . . . . **206** B3
Weatherley Cl E3 . . . . **97** B2
Weathersfield St SE9 . . . **166** B5
South Croydon CR0. . . . . **221** D4
Weaver Ct 🛘 E2. . . . . **96** B3
Weaver Ho
🛚 Bethnal Green E1. . . . . . **96** A3
🛘 Northolt UB5. . . . . **85** B3
Weavers Cl TW7 . . . . . . **130** C1
Weavers Ho 🖪 E11. . . . . . **55** A3
Weaver's La SE1 . . . **117** C5 **253** B3
Weaver St E1. . . . . **96** A3
Weavers Way
🛘 Camden Town NW1. . . . . **71** D1
NW1. . . . . **232** C6
Weaver Wlk SE27 . . . . . . **182** D6
Webb Cl W10. . . . . **90** C3
Webb Ct 🛚 SE28. . . . . . **124** B6
South Acton W3 . . . . . . **110** D4
Webber Cl WD6. . . . . **9** D5
Webber Ho 🛚 IG11 . . . . . **78** D1
Webber Row
SE1 . . . . **116** D4 **251** C1
Webber St SE1. . . . **116** D4 **251** C1
Webb Est E5. . . . . **52** A2
Webb Gdns 🛘 E13. . . . . . **99** A3
Webb Ho
🛘 Dagenham RM10. . . . . . **81** C5
Feltham TW13 . . . . **151** A1
SW8 . . . . **269** D3
Webb Pl NW10. . . . . **89** D4
Webb Rd SE3 . . . . **142** D6
Webbscroft Rd RM10. . . . . **81** D4
Webbs Rd UB4. . . . . **84** B4
Webb's Rd SW11. . . . . . **158** D6
Webb St SE1. . . . . **117** C3 **263** A5
Webheath 🛘 NW6. . . . . . **69** B1
Webley Ct 🛛 EN3. . . . . **7** C6
Webster Gdns W5. . . . . . **109** D5
Webster Ho 🛗 N16 . . . . . . **73** C3
Webster Rd
Bermondsey SE16 . . . . . **118** A3
Leyton E11. . . . . **76** A5
Weddell Ho 🛚 E1. . . . . . . **96** D3
Wedderburn Rd
Barking IG11 . . . . **101** C6
Hampstead NW3 . . . . **70** B3
Wedgewood Ct
🛘 Beckenham BR2 . . . . . **208** D5
DA5. . . . . **169** B4
Wedgewood Ho SW1 . . . **259** A1
Thames Ditton KT7. . . . . **196** D1
Wedgewood Mews W1. . **239** D1
Wedgewood Wlk NW3. . . **69** D3
Wedgwood Ho
🛗 Globe Town E2. . . . . **96** D4
SE11. . . . . **261** A5
Wedgwood Way SE19. . . **183** A3
Wedlake St W10. . . . . . . **91** A3
Wedmore Gdns N19. . . . . **71** D6
Wedmore Mews N19. . . . . **71** D5
Wedmore Rd UB6. . . . . . . **86** B4
Wedmore St N19. . . . . . . **71** D5
Weech Rd NW6. . . . . **69** C4
Weedington Rd NW5. . . . . **71** A3
Weedon Ho W12. . . . . **90** A1
Weekley Sq SW11. . . . . . **136** B2
Weeks Ho TW10. . . . . . . **175** C6
Weigall Rd SE12, SE3 . . . **143** A1
Weighhouse St W1 . . . . . **238** B1
Weighton Rd Harrow HA3 . . **24** B2
Penge SE20. . . . . **184** B1
Weihurst Ct SM1. . . . . . **218** C3
Weihurst Gdns SM1. . . . **218** B3
Weimar St SW15. . . . . . **135** A2
Weir Hall Ave N18. . . . . . **33** B4
Weir Hall Gdns N18. . . . . **33** B5
Weir Hall Rd N18 . . . . . . **33** B4
Weir Ho 🛘 SW12. . . . . . **159** C4
Weir Rd Sidcup DA5. . . . . **169** D4
Streatham SW12 . . . . . . **159** C4
Walton-on-T KT12. . . . . **194** A3
Wimbledon SW18, SW19. . **157** D1
Weiss Rd SW15. . . . . . . **134** D2
Welbeck Ave
Grove Pk BR1. . . . . **187** B6
Hayes UB4 . . . . **84** B3
Sidcup DA15. . . . . **168** A3
Welbeck Cl
New Malden KT3 . . . . . . **199** D4
North Finchley N12. . . . . . **30** B5
Stoneleigh KT17 . . . . . . **216** A1
Welbeck Ct Hayes UB4. . . . **84** B3
W14. . . . . **254** C4
Welbeck Mans 🛘 NW6. . . . **69** C3
Welbeck Rd
Carshalton SM1 . . . . . . **218** A6

Welbeck Rd continued
Carshalton SM5 . . . . . . **202** C1
East Barnet EN4 . . . . **14** C5
Harrow HA2 . . . . **41** D1
Newham E6 . . . . **99** D4
Welbeck St W1 . . . **93** B1 **238** C2
Welbeck Villas N21. . . . . . **17** A3
Welbeck Way W1 . . . . . . **238** C2
Welbeck Wlk SM5 . . . . . **202** B1
Welbourne Prim Sch 🛛
N17. . . . . **52** A6
Welbury Ct E8 . . . . **73** C1
Welby Ho N19 . . . . **49** D2
Welby St SE5 . . . . **138** D4
Welch Pl HA5. . . . . **22** C2
Welcome Ct E17. . . . . **53** C2
Weldon Ct Southgate N21. . . **16** B6
St Johns SE8 . . . . **141** C3
🛗 Sutton SM1. . . . . **218** B3
Thornton Heath CR7. . . . **204** D4
Weldon Dr KT8 . . . . **195** B5
Weld Pl N11 . . . . **31** B5
Welfare Rd E15. . . . . **76** C1
Welford Cl E5. . . . . **74** D5
Welford Ct
🛗 Camden Town NW1. . . . . **71** B1
🛛 Clapham SW8 . . . . **137** C3
Welford Ho 🛮 UB5. . . . . . **85** B3
Welford Pl SW19. . . . . . **179** A6
Welham Rd SW16, SW17. . **181** B4
Welhouse Rd SM5 . . . . . **202** C1
Wellacre Rd HA3. . . . . . . **43** B3
Wellan Cl DA15, DA16. . . . **168** B6
Welland Ct SE6 . . . . **163** B2
Welland Gdns UB6. . . . . . **86** D5
Welland Ho SE15 . . . . . . **140** C1
Welland Mews 🛛 E1. . . . **118** A5
Welland St SE10 . . . . . . **142** A6
Wellands Cl BR1. . . . . . . **188** B1
Well App EN5. . . . . **12** C6
Wellbrook Rd BR6. . . . . . **226** C4
Wellby Cl N9 . . . . **18** A3
Wellby Ct 🛘 E13 . . . . **99** C5
Well Cl Ruislip HA4. . . . . . **63** A5
Streatham SW16 . . . . . . **182** B6
Wellclose Sq E1. . . . . . . **118** A6
Wellclose St 🛛 E1. . . . . **118** A6
Well Cottage Cl E11. . . . . **55** C2
Well Ct EC4. . . . . **242** B1
Wellday Ho 🛛 E9 . . . . **75** A2
Welldon Cres HA1 . . . . . . **42** C3
Welldon Ct Harrow HA1. . . . **42** C4
🛘 West Dulwich SE21. . . . **161** B2
Welldon Park Fst Sch
HA2. . . . . **64** A4
Welldon Park Mid Sch
HA2. . . . . **64** A4
Weller Ho 🛛 SE16. . . . . . **118** A4
Weller Mews 🛘 BR2. . . . **209** B5
Weller St SE1. . . . . **252** A2
Welles Ct 🛗 E14. . . . . . . **119** C6
Wellesley Ave W6. . . . . . **112** B3
Wellesley Cl 🛛 SE7 . . . . **121** C1
Wellesley Court Rd 🛘
CR0. . . . . **221** B6
Wellesley Cres TW2. . . . **152** C1
Wellesley Ct Cheam SM3. . **201** A1
St John's Wood W9. . **92** A4 **229** A2
Twickenham TW2 . . . . . **152** C1
Wellesley Gr CR0. . . . . . **221** B6
Wellesley Ho NW1 . . . . . **232** C1
🛛 Wimbledon SW19 . . . . **179** A3
Wellesley Park Mews EN2. . **4** D3
Wellesley Pl
Camden Town NW5 . . . . . **71** A3
NW1. . . . . **232** C1
Wellesley Rd
Croydon CR0. . . . . **205** A1
Gospel Oak NW5 . . . . **71** A3
Gunnersbury W4 . . . . . . **110** D1
Harrow HA1 . . . . **42** C4
Ilford IG1 . . . . **57** A1
Sutton SM2. . . . . **218** A2
Twickenham TW2 . . . . . **152** C1
Walthamstow E17 . . . . . . **53** C3
Wanstead E11 . . . . **55** A4
Wood Green N22 . . . . **32** C1
Wellesley Road Sta CR0. . **221** B6
Wellesley St E1. . . . . **96** D2
Wellesley Terr N1. . . **95** A4 **235** B2
Wellfield Ave N10. . . . . . **49** B6
Wellfield Rd SW16 . . . . . **182** B6
Wellfit St 🛚 SE24 . . . . . **138** D2
Wellgarth UB6. . . . . **65** B2
Wellgarth Rd NW11. . . . . **47** D1
Well Gr N20. . . . . **14** B3
Wellgrove Sch N20 . . . . . **14** B3
Well Hall Par SE9 . . . . . . **144** B1
Well Hall Pleasance ★
SE9. . . . . **144** A1
Well Hall Rd SE9. . . . . . . **144** B1
Well Ho 🛘 N9 . . . . **18** A1
Wellhouse Rd BR3 . . . . . **207** C5
Wellhurst Cl BR6. . . . . . **227** D4
WELLING **146** B2
Wellingfield Ct DA16. . . . **146** A2
Welling High St DA16. . . . **146** B2
Welling Sch DA16. . . . . . **146** B4
Wellings Ho UB3. . . . . . **106** B5

Welling Sta DA16 . . . . . **146** A3
Wellington
🛘 Grahame Pk NW9 . . . . . **27** D3
Hornsey N8. . . . . **50** A5
Wellington Arch★ SW1 . . **248** B2
Wellington Ave
Chingford E4. . . . . **19** D2
DA15. . . . . **168** A5
Edmonton N9 . . . . **18** B1
Hounslow TW3, TW4. . . . **151** C6
North Cheam KT4. . . . . . **216** C5
Pinner HA5 . . . . **23** B2
South Tottenham N15. . . . . **52** A3
Wellington Bldgs
🛗 Bow E3 . . . . **97** C4
SW1 . . . . **258** B1
Wellington Cl
Kensington W11 . . . . **91** C1
New Cross Gate SE14. . . . **140** D4
Walton-on-T KT12 . . . . . **193** D1
Wellington Cres KT3 . . . . **199** A6
Wellington Ct
Ashford TW15. . . . . **170** A6
Knightsbridge SW1 . . . . **247** C1
Stanwell TW19 . . . . **148** A4
St John's Wood NW8 . . . . **229** D3
Strand WC2 . . . . **250** A6
🛘 Surbiton KT6. . . . . **198** A3
🛗 Teddington TW12 . . . . **174** B5
🛗 Upper Tooting SW17. . . **180** C4
Wandsworth SW18 . . . . . **158** C6
Wellington Gdns
Greenwich SE7. . . . . . . **121** C1
Teddington TW12, TW2. . . **174** B6
Wellington Gr SE10 . . . . **142** B5
Wellington Ho
🛚 Ealing W5 . . . . **88** A4
🛗 Maitland Pk NW3 . . . . . **70** D2
Northolt UB5. . . . . **63** C1
🛙 Ruislip HA4 . . . . **40** C1
Stanmore HA7 . . . . **9** A1
Wellington Hospl The
NW8. . . . . **92** B5 **229** D3
Wellington Mans
Shacklewell N16. . . . . . . **73** D4
🛘 Walthamstow E10 . . . . . **53** C1
Wellington Mews
East Dulwich SE22 . . . . . **140** A1
🛘 Islington N7. . . . . **72** B2
SE7. . . . . **143** C6
Streatham SW16 . . . . . . **159** D1
Wellington Par DA15. . . . **168** A6
Wellington Park Est NW2. **68** A6
Wellington Pas 🛛 E11 . . . . **55** A4
Wellington Pl
East Finchley N2. . . . . . . **48** C1
St John's Wood
NW8. . . . . **92** B4 **229** D2
Wellington Prim Sch
🛛 Bow E3 . . . . **97** C4
Chingford E4. . . . . **19** D2
Hounslow TW3. . . . . . . **129** B3
Wellington Rd
Ashford TW15. . . . . **170** A5
Bexley DA5. . . . . **168** D6
Brentford W5 . . . . **109** C3
Bromley BR2. . . . . **209** C5
Enfield EN1 . . . . **17** C6
Erith DA17 . . . . **125** B1
Harrow HA3 . . . . **42** C6
Hatton TW14 . . . . **149** C6
Kensal Green NW10. . . . . . **90** D4
Leyton E7. . . . . **76** D4
Newham E6 . . . . **100** B5
Pinner HA5 . . . . **23** B2
St John's Wood
NW8. . . . . **92** B5 **229** D3
Teddington TW12, TW2. . . **174** B6
Thornton Heath CR0. . . . **204** D2
Walthamstow E10 . . . . . . **53** A1
Walthamstow E17 . . . . . . **53** A5
Wanstead E11 . . . . **55** A4
Wimbledon SW19. . . . . . **157** C2
Wellington Rd N TW4. . . **129** B2
Wellington Rd S TW4. . . . **151** B2
Wellington Row E2 . . . . . **96** A4
Wellington Sq
Islington N1. . . . . **233** B6
SW3 . . . . **114** D1 **257** C2
Wellington St
WC2 . . . . **116** B6 **250** C6
Woolwich SE18. . . . . . . **122** C2
Wellington Terr
Harrow HA1 . . . . **42** B1
🛛 Wapping E1. . . . . **118** B5
Wellington Way E3 . . . . . **97** C4
Welling Way DA16 . . . . . **145** B2
Well La SW14 . . . . **155** A6
Wellmead IG3 . . . . **58** A2
Wellmeadow Rd
Brentford W7 . . . . **109** A2
Catford SE13, SE6. . . . . **164** C3
Wellow Wlk SM5. . . . . . **202** B1
Well Rd Barnet EN5 . . . . . . **12** C6
Vale of Health NW3 . . . . . **70** B5
Wells Cl 🛘 Northolt UB5. . . **84** C4
South Croydon CR2. . . . . **221** C3
Wells Ct
🛛 Hampstead NW3. . . . . . **70** A4
🛘 Mitcham CR4. . . . . . . **180** C2

Wells Ct continued
🛘 Paddington NW6. . . . . . **91** C5
Stoke Newington N1. . . . . **73** C3
Wells Dr NW9. . . . . **45** B1
Wells Gdns
Dagenham RM10 . . . . . . **81** D3
Redbridge IG1 . . . . **56** A2
Wells Ho 🛮 Barking IG11. . . **80** A1
Ealing W5 . . . . **109** D6
Finsbury EC1 . . . . **234** C2
🛚 Kensal Town W10 . . . . . **91** A3
New Cross Gate SE4. . . . . **141** A3
Plaistow BR1. . . . . **187** B5
🛛 Rotherhithe SE16 . . . . **118** C3
Wells Ho The 🛛 NW3. . . . **70** B4
Wells House Rd NW10. . . . **89** C2
Wellside Gdns SW14 . . . . **155** A6
Wells Mews W1. . . . . . . **239** B2
Wellsmoor Gdns BR1 . . . **210** C6
Wells Park Ct SE26. . . . . **184** B6
Wells Park Rd SE26 . . . . **184** B6
Wells Pl SW18 . . . . **158** A4
Wells Prim Sch IG8 . . . . . **37** A4
Wellspring Cres HA9 . . . . **66** D5
Wells Rd BR1. . . . . **188** B1
Hammersmith W12 . . . . . **112** C4
Wells Rise NW8. . . . **92** B6 **230** C5
Wells Sq WC1. . . . . **233** D1
Wells St W1 . . . . . **93** C1 **239** B2
Well St Hackney E9. . . . . . **74** C1
Stratford E15. . . . . **76** C2
Wellstead Ave N9 . . . . . . **18** D4
Wellstead Rd E6 . . . . . . **100** C5
Wells Terr N4 . . . . **72** C6
Wells The N14. . . . . **15** D4
Wells Way
Brompton SW7. . . . **114** B3 **256** C6
Camberwell SE5. . . . . . **139** C6
Well Wlk NW3 . . . . **70** B5
Wellwood Ct SW15. . . . . **134** C1
Wellwood Rd IG3. . . . . . . **58** A2
Welmar Works SW4 . . . . **137** D1
Welsby St W5. . . . . **87** C2
Welsford St SE1. . . . . . . **118** A2
Welsh Cl E13 . . . . **99** A1
Welsh Harp Field Centre
NW9. . . . . **45** B1
Welsh Ho 🛚 E1. . . . . **118** B5
Welshpool Ho 🛛 E8. . . . . **96** A6
Welshpool St 🛘 E8 . . . . . **96** B6
Welshside NW9. . . . . **45** C3
Welshside Wlk NW9 . . . . . **45** C3
Welstead Ho 🛚 E1. . . . . . **96** B1
Welstead Way W4 . . . . . **111** D2
Weltje Rd W6. . . . . **112** A1
Welton Ct SE5 . . . . **139** C4
Welton Ho E1. . . . . **96** D2
Welton Rd SE18. . . . . . . **145** C5
Welwyn Ave TW14. . . . . **149** D5
Welwyn St E2. . . . . **96** C4
Welwyn Way UB4 . . . . . . **83** C3
WEMBLEY. **65** D2
Wembley HA0 . . . . **65** D2
Wembley Arena HA9 . . . . **66** C4
Wembley Central Sta
HA9. . . . . **66** A3
Wembley Commercial Ctr
HA9. . . . . **65** D6
Wembley Conference Ctr
HA9. . . . . **66** C4
Wembley Exhibition Halls
HA9. . . . . **66** C4
Wembley High Tech Coll
HA0. . . . . **66** B4
Wembley Hill Rd HA9 . . . . **66** B4
Wembley Mkt
🛘 Wembley HA0. . . . . **66** A3
🛘 Wembley Pk HA9. . . . . . **66** C4
WEMBLEY PARK. **66** C5
Wembley Park Bsns Ctr
Wembley HA9. . . . . **66** D5
Wembley HA9. . . . . **66** D5
Wembley Park Dr HA9. . . . **66** C5
Wembley Park Sta HA9. . . **66** C5
Wembley Prim Sch HA9 . . **66** A5
Wembley Rd TW12. . . . . **173** C2
Wembley Stadium HA9. . . **66** C3
Wembley Stadium Ind Est
HA9. . . . . **66** B3
Wembley Stadium Sta
HA9. . . . . **66** B3
Wembley Way HA9. . . . . **66** D2
Wemborough Rd HA7 . . . . **25** C3
Wembury Mews N6 . . . . . **49** C2
Wembury Rd N6 . . . . **49** B2
Wemyss Rd SE3. . . . . . . **142** D3
Wendela Ct HA1 . . . . **64** C6
Wendell Park Prim Sch
W12. . . . . **111** D4
Wendell Rd W12. . . . . . . **111** D4
Wenderholme CR2. . . . . . **221** B3
Wendle Ct SW8 . . . . **270** A5
Wendling NW5 . . . . **70** D3
Wendling Rd SM1. . . . . . **218** B6
Wendon Ct 🛛 SE6. . . . . . . **219** C2
Wendon St E3 . . . . **97** B6
Wendover SE17. . . . **117** C1 **263** A1
Wendover Cl UB4. . . . . . . **85** A3
Wendover Ct Acton W3. . . . **88** D3
Becontree W3. . . . . **89** A3

Wendover Ct *continued*
Bromley BR2. . . . . .209 B6
4 Child's Hill NW2 . . . . . .69 C5
W1 . . . . .238 A3
Wendover Dr KT3. . . . . . .199 D3
Wendover Ho
Bowes Pk N22. . . . . .32 B5
W1 . . . . .238 A3
Wendover Lo NW9 . . . . . .45 D3
Wendover Rd
Blackheath SE9. . . . . .143 D2
Bromley BR1, BR2 . . . . . .209 B6
Dagenham NW10. . . . . . . .89 D5
Wendover Way
Bexley DA16. . . . . .146 A1
Bushey WD23 . . . . .8 A5
Wendy Cl EN1 . . . . .17 D5
Wendy Ho 3 N12 . . . . .30 B5
Wendy Way HA0. . . . . .88 A6
Wengham Ho W12 . . . . . .112 A6
Wenham Ho SW8 . . . . . . .269 A3
Wenlake Ho EC1. . . . . . . .242 A6
Wenlock Ct N1. . . . . .235 D3
Wenlock Gdns 13 NW4. . . .46 A5
Wenlock Rd
Burnt Oak HA8 . . . . .27 A4
Shoreditch N1. . . . . .95 B5 235 B3
Wenlock St N1 . . . . .95 B5 235 C3
Wennington Rd E3. . . . . . . .96 C5
Wensdale Ho E5. . . . . .74 A6
Wensley Ave IG8. . . . . .37 A3
Wensley Cl 6 Barnet N11 . .31 A4
SE9. . . . . .166 B5
Wensleydale Gdns
TW12. . . . . .173 D3
Wensleydale Ho 8 N4 . .51 A2
Wensleydale Rd TW12. . . .173 D3
Wensley Rd N18 . . . . .34 B4
Wentland Cl SE6. . . . . .164 B2
Wentland Rd SE6. . . . . . . .164 B2
Wentway Ct W13. . . . . .87 A3
Wentwood Ho 1 E5 . . . . . .74 B6
Wentworth Ave
Borehamwood WD6 . . . . . .10 B6
Finchley N3. . . . . .29 C3
Wentworth Cl
Ashford TW15. . . . . .170 D6
Finchley N3. . . . . .29 D3
Hayes BR2. . . . . .225 A6
Long Ditton KT6 . . . . . . .213 D6
Morden SM4. . . . . .201 C2
Orpington BR6 . . . . .227 C3
Thamesmead SE28. . . . . .102 D1
Wentworth Cres
Hayes UB3 . . . . .105 B3
SE15. . . . . .49 C3
Wentworth Ct Barnet EN5 . . .1 A2
7 Chingford E4 . . . . .36 B5
20 Kingston u T KT6 . . . . .198 A4
Southall UB2. . . . . .106 C2
2 Surbiton KT6 . . . . .214 A6
Twickenham TW2 . . . . . . .152 C1
W6 . . . . .264 A5
Wandsworth SW18 . . . . . .157 D5
Wentworth Dr Pinner HA5 . .40 A4
South Oxhey WD19. . . . . .22 D5
Wentworth Dwellings
E1 . . . . .243 C2
Wentworth Gdns N13 . . . .16 D1
Wentworth Hall NW7. . . . .28 C5
Wentworth Hill HA9. . . . . .44 B1
Wentworth Ho
Enfield EN1. . . . . .17 C5
4 Greenwich SE3 . . . . . .143 A5
Wentworth Lo N3. . . . . . . .29 D3
Wentworth Mews E3. . . . . .97 B4
Wentworth Pk N3. . . . . . . .29 D3
Wentworth Pl HA7 . . . . . . .25 B4
Wentworth Rd
Manor Pk E12 . . . . .77 D4
Southall UB2. . . . . .106 D2
Temple Fortune NW11 . . . .47 B3
Thornton Heath CR0. . . . .204 C2
Wentworth St E1 . .95 C2 243 D3
Wentworth Tutorial Coll
NW11. . . . . .46 D3
Wentworth Way HA5. . . . . .41 A5
Wepham Cl UB4 . . . . .84 D2
Wenvoe Ave DA2. . . . . . . .147 D3
Werndee Rd SE25. . . . . . . .206 A5
Werneth Hall Rd IG5. . . . . .56 C6
Werrington St
NW1 . . . . .93 C5 232 B3
Werter Rd SW15. . . . . .135 A1
Wesleyan Pl NW5 . . . . .71 B4
Wesley Ave
Becontree NW10 . . . . .89 B4
Hounslow TW3 . . . . .129 B3
Newham E16 . . . . .121 B4
Wesley Cl Finsbury Pk N7 . .72 B6
Harrow HA2 . . . . .64 A6
SE17. . . . . .261 D3
Wesley Ct W1. . . . . .238 B3
Wesley Ho SE24. . . . . .161 B5
Wesley Rd
Becontree NW10 . . . . .89 A6
Finchley N10. . . . . .30 C2
Hayes UB3 . . . . .84 A1
Leytonstone E10. . . . . .54 A2

Wesley Sq W11. . . . . .91 A1
Wesley St W1. . . . . .238 B3
Wessex Ave SW19. . . . . . .201 C6
Wessex Cl
Hinchley Wood KT10,
KT7. . . . . .212 D6
Ilford IG3 . . . . .57 C3
Kingston u T KT1, KT2. . . .176 D2
Wessex Ct Putney SW15 . . .156 D6
5 Stanwell TW19 . . . . . . .148 A5
Wembley HA9. . . . . .66 B6
Wessex Dr HA5 . . . . .23 A3
Wessex Gardens Prim Sch
NW11. . . . . .47 A1
Wessex Gdns NW11. . . . . .47 A1
Wessex Ho SE1. . . . . .263 D1
4 Tufnell Pk N19 . . . . . . .71 D5
Wessex La UB6. . . . . .86 B5
Wessex St E2. . . . . .96 C4
Wessex Way NW11. . . . . . .47 A1
Wesson Ho 3 CR0. . . . . . . .206 A1
West 12 Sh Ctr W12. . . . . .112 D4
Westacott Cl N19 . . . . .49 D1
WEST ACTON 88 C1
West Acton Prim Sch
W3 . . . . .88 D1
West Acton Sta W3 . . . . . . .88 C1
West App BR5. . . . . .211 A4
West Arbour St E1 . . . . . . .96 D1
West Ave East Finchley N2. .47 D6
Finchley N3. . . . . .29 C4
Hayes UB3 . . . . .105 D6
Hendon NW4 . . . . .46 D4
Pinner HA5 . . . . .41 B2
Southall UB1. . . . . .107 B6
Wallington SM6 . . . . .220 A3
Walthamstow E17 . . . . . . .53 D4
West Avenue Rd E17. . . . . .53 D5
West Bank Barking IG11. . . .100 D6
Enfield EN2. . . . . .5 A3
Stamford Hill N16. . . . . . .51 C2
Westbank Rd TW12. . . . . . .174 A4
WEST BARNES 200 C4
West Barnes La KT3,
SW20. . . . . .200 B5
WEST BEDFONT 148 B4
Westbeech Rd N22. . . . . . .50 C6
Westbere Ct HA7 . . . . .25 D5
Westbere Dr HA7 . . . . .25 D5
Westbere Rd NW2 . . . . .69 A3
West Block 18 SE1 . . . . . . .118 C6
Westbourne Ave
Cheam SM3 . . . . .217 A6
Dagenham W3 . . . . .89 B1
Westbourne Cl UB4 . . . . . .84 C3
Westbourne Cres W2 . . . . .246 C6
Westbourne Ct
Cheam SM3 . . . . .217 A6
W2 . . . . .236 A2
Westbourne Dr SE23. . . . . .162 D2
Westbourne Gdns W2. . . . .91 D1
Westbourne Gr
Notting Hill W2, W11. . . . .91 C1
W11 . . . . .113 B6 244 D6
WESTBOURNE GREEN . . .91 D3
Westbourne Gr Mews 7
W11. . . . . .91 C1
Westbourne Gr Terr W2 . . .91 D1
Westbourne Ho
Heston TW5 . . . . .129 C6
SW1 . . . . .258 C2
8 Twickenham TW1. . . . . .153 B6
Westbourne Par 4 UB10. . .82 D3
Westbourne Park Rd
Notting Hill W2 . . . . .91 C1
Notting Hill W11 . . . . .91 B1
Westbourne Park Sta
W11 . . . . .91 B2
Westbourne Park Villas
W2. . . . . .91 D2
Westbourne Pl N9 . . . . .18 B1
Westbourne Prim Sch
SM1 . . . . .217 C5
Westbourne Rd
Barnsbury N7. . . . . .72 B2
Croydon CR0. . . . . .205 D3
DA7. . . . . .147 A5
Feltham TW13 . . . . .149 D1
Hillingdon UB8 . . . . .82 D3
Penge SE26 . . . . .184 D4
Westbourne St
W2. . . . . .114 B6 246 C6
Westbourne Terr
W2. . . . . .92 A1 236 B2
Westbourne Terrace Mews
W2. . . . . .236 A2
Westbourne Terrace Rd
W2. . . . . .92 A1 236 A3
Westbridge Cl W12. . . . . . .112 A5
Westbridge Prim Sch
SW11. . . . . .267 A2
Westbridge Rd
SW11. . . . . . . .136 C4 244 A2
WEST BROMPTON 135 D6
West Brompton Sta
SW5. . . . . .113 C1 255 B1
Westbrook Ave TW12. . . . .173 B3
Westbrook Cl EN4 . . . . .2 B1
Westbrook Cres EN4 . . . . . .2 B1

Westbrook Ct SE3. . . . . . . .143 B4
Westbrooke Cres DA16. . . .146 C2
Westbrooke Rd
Bexley DA16. . . . . .146 C2
DA15. . . . . .146 C2
Westbrooke Sch DA16. . . .146 D2
Westbrook Ho
5 Bethnal Green E2 . . . . . .96 C4
5 Clapham SW4. . . . . . . .159 C6
Westbrook Rd
Heston TW5 . . . . .129 B5
SE3. . . . . .143 B4
South Norwood CR7. . . . .183 B1
Westbrook Sq SE4 . . . . .2 B2
West Brow BR7. . . . . .188 D5
Westbury Ave
Claygate KT10. . . . . .212 D2
Southall UB1. . . . . .85 C3
Tottenham N22. . . . . .32 D1
Wembley HA0. . . . . .66 A1
Westbury Cl Ruislip HA4. . . .40 A2
Shepperton TW17. . . . . . .192 D3
Westbury Ct
3 Barking IG11. . . . . .101 B6
Beckenham BR3. . . . . .185 D2
1 Buckhurst Hill IG9. . . . . .21 C2
Clapham SW4. . . . . .159 B5
11 New Barnet EN5 . . . . . .14 A6
Tottenham N22. . . . . .33 A1
Westbury Gr N12. . . . . .29 C4
Westbury Ho
1 Walthamstow E17. . . . . .53 C5
6 Willesden NW10. . . . . . .67 C1
Westbury House Sch
KT3. . . . . .199 B4
Westbury La IG9. . . . . .21 C2
Westbury Lodge Cl HA5. . . .40 D6
Westbury Pl 2 TW8. . . . . . .131 D6
Westbury Rd
Barking IG11. . . . . .101 B6
Beckenham BR3. . . . . .207 A6
Bowes Pk N11. . . . . .32 A4
Bromley BR1. . . . . .187 D2
Buckhurst Hill IG9. . . . . . .21 C3
Ealing W5 . . . . .88 A1
Feltham TW13 . . . . .150 D3
Finchley N12. . . . . .29 D5
Ilford IG1 . . . . .78 C6
New Malden KT3 . . . . . . .199 B4
Penge SE20 . . . . .184 D2
Thornton Heath CR0. . . . .205 B3
Upton E7. . . . . .77 B2
Walthamstow E17 . . . . . . .53 C5
Wembley HA0. . . . . .66 A1
Westbury Terr E7. . . . . .77 B2
Westbush Ct 1 W12 . . . . . .112 B4
West Carriage Dr
W2. . . . . .114 C5 247 A4
West Central St WC1 . . . . . .240 A2
West Chantry HA3 . . . . . . .23 D2
Westchester Ct NW4 . . . . . .46 D6
Westchester Dr NW4. . . . . .46 D6
West Cl Ashford TW15. . . . .170 A6
Barnet EN5. . . . . .12 B6
Cockfosters EN4. . . . . .3 A1
Edmonton N9 . . . . .17 D1
Greenford UB6. . . . . .86 A5
Hampton TW12. . . . . .173 A4
Wembley HA9. . . . . .44 B1
Westcliff Ho 13 N1. . . . . . . .73 B2
Westcombe Ave CR0. . . . . .204 B2
Westcombe Ct 1 SE3. . . . . .142 D5
Westcombe Dr EN5 . . . . . . .13 C6
Westcombe Hill SE3,
SE10. . . . . .143 A6
Westcombe Lodge Dr
UB4. . . . . .83 B2
Westcombe Park Rd
SE3 . . . . .142 D5
Westcombe Park Sta
SE3. . . . . .121 A1
West Common Rd BR2. . . . .225 B5
Westcoombe Ave SW20 . . .177 D2
Westcote Rd SW16. . . . . . .181 C5
Westcote Rise HA4. . . . . . . .39 A2
Westcott Cl BR1. . . . . .210 A4
2 South Tottenham N15. . . .51 D3
Westcott Cres W7. . . . . . . .86 C2
Westcott Ho 1 E14. . . . . . .119 C6
Westcott Ho SE17. . . . . . . .138 D6
West Cotts NW6 . . . . .69 C3
Westcroft Cl Enfield EN3. . . .6 C1
West Hampstead NW2. . . . .69 A4
Westcroft Ct
3 Chiswick W6 . . . . .112 A2
Kingsbury NW9 . . . . .44 D4
Westcroft Gdns SM4. . . . . .201 B5
Westcroft Ho 2 SE3. . . . . . .219 A4
Westcroft L Ctr SM5. . . . . .219 A4
Westcroft Rd SM5, SM6. . . .219 A4
Westcroft Sq W6. . . . . .112 A2
Westcroft Way NW2. . . . . . .69 A4
West Cromwell Rd
W14. . . . . .113 B1 254 D2
West Cross Ctr TW8. . . . . . .131 B6
West Cross Route W10,
W11. . . . . .112 D6
West Cross Way TW8. . . . . .131 B6

West Croydon Sta CR9. . . .205 A1
West Ct Hounslow TW7. . . .130 A5
Sunbury TW16 . . . . .172 B1
Walthamstow E17 . . . . . . .53 D5
Wembley HA0. . . . . .65 C6
Westdale Rd SE18. . . . . . . .144 D6
Westdean Ave SE12. . . . . .165 C3
Westdean Cl SW18. . . . . . .157 D5
Westdown Rd
Catford SE6 . . . . .163 C4
Leyton E15. . . . . .76 A4
West Dr Stanmore HA3. . . . .24 B4
Streatham SW16 . . . . .181 C6
WEST DRAYTON 104 B4
West Drayton Park Ave
UB7. . . . . .104 A3
West Drayton Prim Sch
UB7. . . . . .104 A4
West Drayton Rd UB8. . . . . .82 D1
West Drayton Sta UB7. . . . .104 A5
West Drive Gdns HA3 . . . . .24 B4
WEST DULWICH 161 B3
West Dulwich Sta SE21. . . .161 B3
WEST EALING 109 B5
West Ealing Bsns Ctr
W13 . . . . .109 A6
West Ealing Sta W13. . . . . .109 B6
West Eaton Pl SW1. . . . . . .258 A4
West Eaton Pl Mews
SW1. . . . . .258 A4
West Ella Rd NW10. . . . . . .67 C1
West End Ave
Leytonstone E10. . . . . .54 B4
Pinner HA5. . . . . .40 D5
West End Cl
Stonebridge NW10. . . . . . .67 A1
Willesden NW10. . . . . .67 A1
West End Ct
Hampstead NW6 . . . . .69 D1
Pinner HA5. . . . . .40 D5
West End Gdns UB5. . . . . . .84 C5
West End La
Hampstead NW6 . . . . .69 D2
Harlington UB7. . . . . .127 A5
Pinner HA5. . . . . .40 D5
West End Rd
Ruislip HA4, UB5. . . . . . . .62 A4
Ruislip UB5. . . . . .62 C1
Southall UB1. . . . . .107 A5
Westerdale Ct N5. . . . . . . .72 D4
Westerdale Rd 2 SE10. . . .143 B1
Westerfield Rd 1 N15. . . . . .51 D4
Westergate W5. . . . . .88 A2
Westergate Rd SE2 . . . . . . .147 A6
Westerham
13 Kingston u T KT6 . . . . .198 A4
NW1. . . . . .232 A5
Westerham Ave N9 . . . . . . .17 C1
Westerham Dr DA15. . . . . .168 C5
Westerham Lo 10 BR3. . . . .185 C3
Westerham Rd
Keston BR2. . . . . .225 D2
Walthamstow E17 . . . . . . .53 D4
Westerley Cres SE26. . . . . .185 B5
Westerley Ct HA4. . . . . . . .62 B3
Western Ave
Dagenham W3 . . . . .89 B1
Hendon NW11 . . . . .46 D3
Hillingdon HA4, UB4, UB5,
UB10 . . . . .61 C1
Northolt UB5, UB6. . . . . . .85 B6
Ruislip UB8, UB9, UB10. . . .60 B3
Wembley UB6. . . . . .87 C4
Western Avenue Bsns Pk
W3 . . . . .88 D3
Western Beach Apts
E16 . . . . .121 A5
Western Ct
4 Dagenham W3. . . . . . . .89 B1
Finchley N3. . . . . .29 C4
5 Kilburn W9. . . . . .91 B5
Southall UB2. . . . . .107 A3
Western Dr TW17 . . . . .193 B3
Western Eye Hospl The
NW1. . . . . .92 D2 237 C4
Western Gateway E16. . . . .121 A6
Western Gdns W5. . . . . . . .110 C6
Western Ho 3 W9 . . . . .91 B3
Western Hts SM1 . . . . .217 C3
Western International
Market UB2. . . . . .106 B2
Western La SW12 . . . . .159 A4
Western Mews W9. . . . . . . .91 B3
Western Par EN5 . . . . .13 C6
Western Pl 19 SE16. . . . . . .118 C4
Western Rd
Becontree NW10. . . . . .89 A3
Brixton SW9 . . . . .138 C2
Ealing W5 . . . . .109 A5
Fortis Green N2 . . . . .48 D5
Mitcham CR4, SW19. . . . . .180 C1
Newham E13 . . . . .99 C5
Southall UB2. . . . . .106 A2
Sutton SM1. . . . . .217 C3
Walthamstow E17 . . . . . . .54 A4
Wood Green N22 . . . . .32 B1
Western Terr 3 W6 . . . . . . .112 A1
Western View 1 . . . . .105 D4
Westernville Gdns IG2. . . . .57 A2

Western Way
New Barnet EN5. . . . . .13 D5
Plumstead SE28 . . . . .123 C4
Western Wharf 2 SE15 . . . .140 A6
WEST EWELL 215 C1
West Ewell Inf Sch KT19. . .215 B3
West Farm Ct EN4 . . . . .2 D2
Westferry Cir E14. . . . . . . .119 C5
Westferry Rd E14. . . . . . . .119 C6
Westferry Sta E14 . . . . . . .119 C6
Westfield 1 BR6 . . . . .227 A3
Loughton IG10 . . . . .21 C6
West Hampstead NW3. . . . .69 C4
Westfield Cl Cheam SM1 . . .217 B4
Enfield EN3. . . . . .7 A2
Kingsbury NW9 . . . . .45 A6
SW10 . . . . .266 A3
Westfield Ct
1 Kensal Green W10 . . . . .90 D4
Kingston u T KT6 . . . . . . .197 D4
Westfield Dr HA3 . . . . .43 D5
Westfield Gdns
Harrow HA3 . . . . .43 D5
Ilford RM6 . . . . .58 C3
Westfield Ho 6 SE16. . . . . .118 D2
Westfield La HA3 . . . . .43 D5
Westfield London Sh Ctr
W12 . . . . .112 D5
Westfield Pk HA5 . . . . .23 B3
Westfield Rd
Beckenham BR3. . . . . .185 B1
Cheam SM1 . . . . .217 B4
Croydon CR0. . . . . .220 D6
Dagenham RM9 . . . . .81 B4
Ealing W13 . . . . .109 A5
Edgware NW7 . . . . .11 C1
Kingston u T KT6 . . . . . . .197 D4
Mitcham CR4. . . . . .180 D1
Walton-on-T KT12 . . . . . . .195 A2
Westfields SW13. . . . . .133 D2
Westfields Ave SW13. . . . . .133 C2
Westfields Rd W3. . . . . .88 D2
Westfield St SE18 . . . . .121 D6
Westfield Way
Mile End E1. . . . . .97 A3
Ruislip HA4. . . . . .61 D5
West Finchley Sta N3 . . . . .29 D4
West Garden Pl W2 . . . . . . .237 B1
West Gate W5 . . . . .88 A4
Westgate Bsns Ctr
2 Kensal Town W10 . . . . . .91 A3
North Kensington W10. . . . .90 D4
Westgate Ct
6 Beckenham BR3 . . . . . .186 A2
15 Brixton SW9 . . . . .138 C2
Lewisham SE12 . . . . .165 A3
Westgate Est TW14 . . . . . .148 D3
Westgate Rd
Beckenham BR3 . . . . .186 A2
Croydon SE25. . . . . .206 B5
Westgate St E8 . . . . .96 B6
Westgate Terr
SW10. . . . . .135 D6 265 D6
West Gdns
Mitcham SW19 . . . . .180 C4
Stepney E1 . . . . .118 B6
Westglade Ct HA3 . . . . .43 D4
West Gr Lewisham SE10. . . .142 B4
Woodford IG8. . . . . .37 C5
WEST GREEN 51 A5
West Green Pl UB6. . . . . . . .86 B6
West Green Prim Sch
N15. . . . . .51 A5
West Green Rd N15 . . . . . .51 B5
Westgrove La SE10. . . . . . .142 A4
West Grove Prim Sch
N14. . . . . .15 D4
West Halkin St
SW1. . . . . .115 A3 258 A6
West Hallowes SE9. . . . . . .166 A3
West Hall Rd TW9. . . . . . . .132 D4
WEST HAM 99 B6
West Ham Church Prim Sch
7 E15. . . . . .98 D6
West Ham La E15. . . . . .76 C1
WEST HAMPSTEAD 69 C4
West Hampstead Mews
NW6. . . . . .69 D2
West Hampstead Sta
NW6. . . . . .69 D2
West Hampstead Thameslink
Sta NW6. . . . . .69 C2
West Ham Sta E15. . . . . . . .98 C4
West Harding St EC4. . . . . .241 B2
WEST HARROW 42 A3
West Harrow Sta HA1 . . . . .42 A3
West Hatch Manor HA4 . . .39 D2
Westhaven SM1 . . . . .217 C3
Westhay Gdns SW14 . . . . .154 D6
WEST HEATH 146 D6
West Heath Ave NW11. . . . .47 C1
West Heath Cl NW3 . . . . . .69 C4
West Heath Ct NW11. . . . . .47 C1
West Heath Dr NW11. . . . . .47 C1
West Heath Gdns NW3. . . . .69 C5
West Heath Rd SE2, DA7. . .146 D6
West Hampstead NW3. . . . .69 D5

WEST HENDON **45** D3
WEST HILL **157** B5
West Hill Harrow HA2 . . . . . **64** C6
Putney SW15 . . . . **157** A5
South Croydon CR2. . . . . **221** C1
Wembley HA9 . . . . **44** B1
Westhill Ct W11 . . . . **244** D6
West Hill Lt N6 . . . . **71** A5
West Hill Hall HA2 . . . . **64** C6
Westhill Pk
Dartmouth Pk N6 . . . . . . **71** A6
Highgate N6 . . . . **70** D6
West Hill Prim Sch 17
SW18 . . . . **157** C6
West Hill Rd SW18 . . . . . . **157** B5
West Hill Way N20 . . . . **13** D3
West Ho Barking IG11 . . . . **78** D2
4 Penge SE20. . . . . **184** D3
9 Streatham SW12. . . . . **159** C4
Westholm N11 . . . . **47** D5
Westholme BR6 . . . . **211** D6
Westholme Gdns HA4 . . . . **40** A1
Westhope Ho 28 E2 . . . . . . **96** A4
Westhorne Ave SE9,
SE12 . . . . **165** C5
Westhorpe Gdns NW4 . . . . **46** C6
Westhorpe Rd SW15 . . . . . **134** C2
West House Cl SW19 . . . . . **157** A3
Westhurst Dr BR7 . . . . **188** D5
West India Ave E14 . . . . . . **119** C5
West India Dock Rd E14 . . **119** C6
West India Ho 1 E14 . . . . . **119** C6
West India Quay Sta
E14 . . . . **119** C6
WEST KENSINGTON **113** A2
West Kensington Ct
W14 . . . . **254** C2
West Kensington Mans
W14 . . . . **254** C1
West Kensington Sta
W14 . . . . **113** B1 **254** C2
WEST KILBURN **91** A4
West La SE16 . . . . **118** B4
Westlake 12 SE16 . . . . **118** B4
Westlake Cl Hayes UB4 . . . **85** A3
Palmers Green N13 . . . . . **16** C1
Westlake Rd HA9 . . . . **65** D6
Westland Cl TW19 . . . . **148** A5
Westland Ct 9 UB5 . . . . . . **84** D4
Westland Dr BR2, BR4 . . . **224** D6
Westland Ho 1 E16 . . . . . . **122** C5
Westland Lo 1 BR1 . . . . . . **187** C1
Westland Pl N1 . . . . **235** C2
Westlands Cl UB3 . . . . **106** A2
Westlands Ct KT8 . . . . **196** C5
Westlands Terr 3
SW12. . . . . **159** C5
Westlea Rd W7 . . . . **109** A3
West Lea Sch N9. . . . . **17** C1
Westleigh Ave SW15 . . . . . **156** C6
Westleigh Ct Finchley N12 . . **29** D4
16 Wanstead E11 . . . . **55** A4
Westleigh Dr BR1 . . . . **188** A2
Westleigh Gdns HA8 . . . . . **26** C1
West Links HA0 . . . . **87** D4
Westlinton Cl NW7 . . . . **29** A4
West Lodge Ave W3 . . . . . **110** C5
West Lodge Ct W3 . . . . . . **110** C5
West Lodge Fst & Mid Schs
HA5 . . . . **40** D5
West Lodge Sch DA15 . . . . **168** A1
West London Acad
Northolt UB5 . . . . **63** A1
Northolt UB5 . . . . **85** A4
West London Shooting Sch
UB5. . . . . **84** B6
Westly Ct NW2 . . . . **68** D2
Westly Ho N9 . . . . **18** B3
Westmacott Dr TW14. . . . . **149** D3
Westmacott Ho NW8. . . . . **236** D5
West Mall N11 . . . . **245** B4
Westmark Point 13
SW15. . . . . **156** B3
Westmead SW15. . . . . **156** B3
West Mead Ruislip HA4. . . . **62** C4
West Ewell KT19 . . . . . . **215** C2
Westmead Cnr SM5. . . . . . **218** C4
Westmead Rd SM1. . . . . . **218** B4
Westmeath Ho NW2 . . . . . . **68** A5
Westmere Dr NW7 . . . . **11** B1
West Mersea Cl 9 E16 . . . **121** B5
West Mews NW1 . . . . **259** A3
West Middlesex Univ Hosp
TW7 . . . . **131** A3
Westmill Ct N4 . . . . **73** A6
WESTMINSTER **115** C4
Westminster Abbey★
SW1 . . . . **116** A3 **260** A6
Westminster Abbey Choir
Sch SW1 . . . . . **115** D3 **259** D6
Westminster Acad w2 . . . . **91** C2
Westminster Acad (Sch of
English) W1. . . . **93** C1 **239** B2
Westminster Ave CR7 . . . . **182** D1
Westminster Boating Base
SW1 . . . . **269** C6

Westminster Bridge SE1,
SW1 . . . . **116** A4 **250** B1
Westminster Bridge Rd
SE1 . . . . **116** B4 **250** C1
Westminster Cath★
SW1 . . . . **115** C3 **259** A2
Westminster Cath Choir Sch
SW1 . . . . **115** C2 **259** B4
Westminster Cath RC Prim
Sch SW1 . . . . . **115** D3 **259** D2
Westminster City Hall
SW1 . . . . **259** B6
Westminster City Sch
SW1 . . . . **259** B6
Westminster Cl
East Bedfont TW14. . . . . **150** A3
Teddington TW11 . . . . . . **175** A5
Westminster Coll
W1 . . . . **115** D6 **249** C6
Westminster Ct
22 Rotherhithe SE16 . . . . **118** D5
South Norwood CR7 . . . . **183** A1
5 Wandsworth SW18 . . . . **157** C6
Wanstead E11 . . . . **55** B3
Westminster Dr N13 . . . . . . **32** A5
Westminster Dragoons
Mus★ SW6 . . . . **135** A2
Westminster Gdns
Barking IG11 . . . . **101** C5
Chingford E4. . . . . **20** C3
SW1 . . . . **260** A4
Westminster Ind Est
SE18 . . . . **121** D3
Westminster Kingsway Coll
(King's Cross Centre)
WC1 . . . . **94** B4 **233** C1
Westminster Kingsway Coll
(Regent's Park Ctr)
NW1 . . . . **93** D3 **239** A6
Westminster Kingsway Coll
(Victoria Centre)
SW1 . . . . **115** D2 **259** C4
Westminster Pier SW1 . . . . **250** B1
Westminster Rd
Carshalton SM1 . . . . **218** B6
Ealing W7 . . . . **108** C5
Edmonton N9 . . . . **18** B3
Westminster Sch
SW1 . . . . **116** A3 **260** A6
Westminster Sta
SW1 . . . . **116** A4 **250** B1
Westminster Under Sch
SW1 . . . . **115** D2 **259** C3
Westmoat Cl BR3 . . . . **186** A3
Westmont Rd KT10. . . . . . . **212** C6
Westmoor Gdns EN3 . . . . . . **6** D3
Westmoor Rd EN3 . . . . **6** D3
Westmoor St SE7 . . . . **121** D3
Westmore Ct SW15 . . . . . . **157** A6
Westmoreland Ave
DA16 . . . . **145** C1
Westmoreland Dr SM2 . . . **217** D1
Westmoreland Ho NW10 . . **90** A4
Westmoreland Pl
5 Bromley BR1 . . . . **209** A6
Ealing W5 . . . . **87** D2
Pimlico SW1 . . . . **258** D1
Westmoreland Rd
Barnes SW13 . . . . **134** A4
Beckenham BR2, BR3 . . **208** D5
Bromley BR2. . . . . **209** A5
Camberwell SE17 . . . . . **139** B6
Queensbury NW9. . . . . . . **44** B5
Westmoreland St W1 . . . . **238** B3
Westmoreland Terr
10 Penge SE20. . . . . . . **184** B4
SW1 . . . . **115** B1 **258** D1
Westmorland Cl
3 Twickenham TW1 . . . . **153** B5
Wanstead E12 . . . . **77** D6
Westmorland Ct
12 Surbiton KT6. . . . . . . **197** D2
Sutton SM1 . . . . **218** A5
Westmorland Rd BR2 . . . . **209** A5
Harrow HA1 . . . . **41** D4
Walthamstow E17 . . . . . . **53** C3
Westmorland Way CR4 . . **203** D4
Westmount Ct W5 . . . . **88** B2
Westmount Rd SE9 . . . . . . **144** C1
WEST NORWOOD **161** A1
West Norwood Sta
SE27. . . . . **160** D1
West Oak BR3 . . . . **186** B2
Westoe Rd N9 . . . . **18** B2
Weston A?e
East Molesey KT8. . . . . . **195** B5
Thames Ditton KT10, KT7 . . **196** C2
Westonbirt Ct 6 SE15. . . . **139** D6
Weston Ct Highbury N4. . . . **73** A5
3 Kingston u T KT1 . . . . **198** A6
Oakleigh Pk N20 . . . . **14** A4
Weston Dr HA7 . . . . **25** B2
West One Ho W1 . . . . **239** A3
Westone Mans 6 IG11 . . . **79** D1
West One Sh Ctr
W1 . . . . **93** B1 **238** C1
Weston Gdns TW7 . . . . **130** C4
Weston Gn Dagenham RM9 . . **81** B4
Thames Ditton KT7. . . . . **196** C1

Weston Gr 1 BR1. . . . . **186** D2
WESTON GREEN **196** D1
Weston Green Rd KT7. . . . . **196** C2
Weston Green Sch KT7. . . . **196** C1
Weston Ho
6 Brondesbury NW6 . . . . . **69** A1
8 South Hackney E9 . . . . . **96** C6
Weston Lo KT7 . . . . **196** D1
Weston Park Cl KT7. . . . . . **196** C1
Weston Park Prim Sch
N8. . . . . **50** B4
Weston Pk
Hornsey Vale N8. . . . . **50** B3
Kingston u T KT1 . . . . . . **176** A1
Thames Ditton KT10, KT7. . **196** C1
Weston Rd
Acton Green W4 . . . . **111** A3
Bromley BR1. . . . . **186** D3
Dagenham RM9 . . . . **81** A4
Enfield EN2. . . . . **5** B1
Thames Ditton KT7 . . . . . **196** C1
Weston Rise N1,
WC1 . . . . **94** B4 **233** D2
Weston St SE1. . . . . **117** B4 **252** D2
Weston Wlk 3 E8, E9. . . . . **74** B1
Westover Hill NW3. . . . . **69** C6
Westover Rd SW18. . . . . . . **158** A5
Westow Hill SE19 . . . . **183** C4
Westow St SE19 . . . . **183** C4
Westpark W5 . . . . **87** D1
West Park Ave TW9 . . . . . . **132** D4
West Park Cl
Heston TW5. . . . . **129** B6
Ilford RM6 . . . . **58** D4
West Park Rd
Richmond TW9 . . . . **132** C4
Southall UB2. . . . . **108** B5
West Parkside
Greenwich SE10. . . . . . . **120** D3
Greenwich SE10. . . . . . . **121** A2
West Pk SE9 . . . . **166** A3
West Pl SW19. . . . . **178** C5
West Plaza E14 . . . . **119** D5
Westpoint
Beckenham BR2 . . . . . . **208** B6
Putney SW15 . . . . **156** D5
West Point 2 SE1 . . . . **118** A1
Westpoint Apartments
N8 . . . . **50** B5
Westpoint Trad Est W3 . . . **88** D2
Westpole Ave EN4 . . . . **3** B1
Westport Ct UB4 . . . . **84** C3
Westport Rd E13. . . . . **99** B3
Westport St E1 . . . . **96** D1
West Poultry Ave EC1 . . . . **241** C3
West Quarters W12 . . . . **90** A1
West Quay Dr UB4 . . . . **85** A2
West Ramp TW6 . . . . **126** C4
West Rd
Chelsea SW3 . . . . . **136** D6 **267** D6
Clapham Pk SW4 . . . . . . **159** D6
Dagenham RM6 . . . . **59** A3
Ealing W5 . . . . **88** A2
East Barnet EN4. . . . . **15** A3
East Bedfont TW14. . . . . **149** B4
Finchley N2. . . . . **30** B2
Tottenham N17. . . . . **34** B4
West Drayton UB7 . . . . . **104** B3
West Ham E15 . . . . **98** D6
West Ridge Gdns UB6 . . . . **86** A5
Westrow SW15 . . . . **156** C5
West Row W10. . . . . **91** A3
Westrow Dr IG11 . . . . **80** A2
Westrow Gdns IG3 . . . . **79** D5
WEST RUISLIP **61** B6
West Ruislip Ct HA4. . . . . . . **61** B6
West Ruislip Elementary Sch
UB10. . . . . **61** A5
West Ruislip Sta HA4. . . . . . **61** A6
West Sheen Vale TW9 . . . . **132** B1
Westside
11 Hammersmith W6. . . . **112** A2
Hendon NW4 . . . . **28** B1
Muswell Hill N2. . . . . **48** D6
West Side Comm SW19 . . **178** C5
Westside Ct 1 W9 . . . . **91** C3
West Silvertown Sta
E16. . . . . **121** A5
West Smithfield
EC1 . . . . **94** D2 **241** D3
West Sq SE11. . . . . . **116** D3 **261** C5
West St
30 Bethnal Green E2 . . . . . **96** B5
Bexleyheath DA7 . . . . . . **147** B2
Bromley BR1. . . . . **187** A1
Carshalton SM5 . . . . **218** D4
Croydon CR0. . . . . **221** A4
Harrow HA1 . . . . **42** C1
Leyton E11 . . . . **76** C5
Soho WC2. . . . . . . **93** D1 **239** D1
Sutton SM1. . . . . **217** D3
Walthamstow E17 . . . . . . **53** D4
West Street La SM5 . . . . . . **218** D4
West Street Pl 1 CR0. . . . . **221** A4
West Surrey Est TW15. . . . **171** A2
West Sutton Sta SM1. . . . . **217** C4
West Temple Sheen
SW14. . . . . **154** D6

West Tenter St
E1. . . . . **95** D1 **243** D1
West Terr DA15 . . . . **167** C3
West Thames Coll TW7 . . . **130** C4
West Thamesmead Bsns Pk
SE28. . . . . **123** D3
West Thornton Prim Sch
CR0. . . . . **204** B3
West Towers HA5 . . . . **40** D3
West Twyford Prim Sch
NW10 . . . . **88** C5
Westvale Mews W3 . . . . . . **111** C4
Westview W7 . . . . **86** C1
West View Dagenham RM6 . . **58** C4
East Bedfont TW14. . . . . **149** A4
Westview Cl
North Kensington W10. . . . **90** C1
Willesden NW10. . . . . **67** D3
Westview Cres N9 . . . . **17** C4
Westview Ct
3 Elstree WD6 . . . . **9** D5
1 Whetstone N20. . . . . . . **14** A2
Westview Dr IG8. . . . . **37** D1
West View Gdns WD6. . . . . . **9** D5
Westville Rd
Shepherd's Bush W12 . . . **112** A4
Thames Ditton KT7 . . . . . **197** A2
Westward Rd E4 . . . . **35** B5
Westward Way HA3 . . . . **44** A3
West Warwick Pl SW1. . . . **259** A3
Westway
Shepherd's Bush W10,
W12 . . . . **112** A6
West Barnes SW20 . . . . . **200** C5
West Way BR5 . . . . **211** B4
Burnt Oak HA8 . . . . **27** A4
Croydon CR0. . . . . **223** A5
Edmonton N18 . . . . **33** B6
Hounslow TW5 . . . . **129** B4
Neasden NW10 . . . . **67** B5
Pinner HA5 . . . . **40** D5
Ruislip HA4. . . . . **39** D1
Shepperton TW17. . . . . . **193** B3
West Wickham BR4 . . . . **208** C3
Westway Cl SW20 . . . . **200** B6
Westway Ct UB5 . . . . **85** C6
Westway (Elevated Rd)
W10. . . . . **91** B2
West Way Gdns CR0. . . . . **222** D6
Westway Lo 35 W2 . . . . **91** C2
Westways KT19 . . . . **215** D4
West Ways HA6 . . . . **22** A1
Westwell 4 NW5 . . . . **71** A2
Westwell Rd SW16 . . . . . . **182** A4
Westwell Road App
SW16. . . . . **182** A4
Westwick 7 KT1. . . . . **176** C1
Westwick Gdns
Cranford TW4, TW5 . . . . **128** B3
Hammersmith W14 . . . . . **112** D4
WEST WICKHAM **224** C6
West Wickham Sta BR3 . . **208** A2
West Wimbledon Prim Sch
SW20 . . . . **200** B6
West Wlk East Barnet EN4. . . **15** A3
Hayes UB3 . . . . **106** A5
Westwood Ave
Harrow HA2 . . . . **63** D4
South Norwood SE19 . . . **183** A2
Westwood Bsns Ctr
NW10 . . . . **89** C3
Westwood Cl BR1 . . . . **209** D6
Esher KT10. . . . . **212** A5
Ruislip HA4. . . . . **38** D3
Westwood Ct Enfield EN1. . **17** C5
3 Forest Hill SE23. . . . . **162** C3
7 Wimbledon SW19 . . . . **179** B5
Westwood Gdns SW13 . . . **133** D2
Westwood Hill SE26. . . . . . **184** B6
Westwood Ho
6 Shepherd's Bush W12. . **112** C5
5 Stoke Newington N4 . . . **51** B2
Westwood La DA16 . . . . . . **145** D1
Westwood Language College
for Girls SE19. . . . . **183** B3
Westwood Lo N12 . . . . **30** C5
Westwood Park Trad Est
W3 . . . . **88** D3
Westwood Pk SE23 . . . . . . **162** B4
Westwood Pl SE26 . . . . . . **184** A6
Westwood Rd
Barnes SW13 . . . . **133** D2
Ilford IG3 . . . . **58** A2
Westwood Sch WD23 . . . . . . **8** B2
West Woodside DA5 . . . . . **169** A3
Wetheral Ct SW17 . . . . . . **180** B6
Wetheral Dr HA7. . . . . **25** C1
Wetherby Cl UB5 . . . . **63** D2
Wetherby Ct SE25. . . . . . . **183** C1
Wetherby Gdns
SW5. . . . . **114** A2 **256** A3
Wetherby Mans SW5. . . . . **255** C2
Wetherby Mews SW5 . . . . **255** D2
Wetherby Pl
SW7. . . . . **114** A2 **256** B3
Wetherby Prep Sch
W11 . . . . **113** C6 **245** A6
Wetherby Rd EN2. . . . . **5** A4
Wetherby Way KT9. . . . . . **214** A1
Wetherden St E17 . . . . **53** B2

Wetherell Rd E9 . . . . **96** D6
Wetherill Rd N10 . . . . **31** A2
Wevco Wharf SE15. . . . . . **140** B6
Wexford Ho 11 E1. . . . . **96** C2
Wexford Rd SW12. . . . . . . **158** D4
Weybourne St SW18 . . . . . **158** A2
Weybridge Ct 19 SE16 . . . **118** B1
Weybridge Ho N4. . . . . **51** A2
Weybridge Point 11
SW11 . . . . **136** D3
Weybridge Rd CR7 . . . . . . **204** C5
Wey Ct KT19 . . . . **215** A4
Weydown Cl SW19 . . . . . . **157** A3
Weyhill Ho 20 SE5. . . . . . . **139** A3
Weyhill Rd 11 E1. . . . . **96** A1
Wey Ho 6 Northolt UB5 . . . **85** B3
NW8. . . . . **236** D5
Weylands Cl KT12. . . . . . . **195** B1
Weylond Rd RM8. . . . . **81** B5
Weyman Rd SE3 . . . . **143** C4
Weymarks The N17 . . . . . . **33** B4
Weymouth Ave
Brentford W5 . . . . **109** C3
Edgware NW7 . . . . **27** C5
Weymouth Cl 1 E6. . . . . . **100** D1
Weymouth Ct
Belmont SM2 . . . . **217** C1
5 Haggerston E2 . . . . **95** D5
15 Streatham SW2. . . . . **160** B4
Weymouth Ho
Bromley BR2. . . . . **186** D1
Edgware HA8 . . . . **26** B4
Fitzrovia W1. . . . . **238** D4
South Lambeth SW8. . . . **270** C3
Weymouth Mews
W1 . . . . **93** B2 **238** C4
Weymouth Rd UB4. . . . . **83** C4
Weymouth St W1 . . . **93** B2 **238** C4
Weymouth Terr E2 . . . . **95** D5
Weymouth Wlk HA7. . . . . . . **25** A4
Whadcoat St N4 . . . . **72** C6
Whaddon Ho
10 Camberwell SE5 . . . . **139** C2
SW1 . . . . **247** D1
Whalebone Ave RM6 . . . . . . **59** B3
Whalebone Gr RM6 . . . . **59** B3
Whalebone La E15. . . . . **76** C1
Whalebone Lane N RM6. . . . **59** A6
Whalebone Lane S RM6,
RM8. . . . . **59** B2
Whales Yd E15. . . . . **76** C1
Wharfdale Cl N11. . . . . **31** A4
Wharfdale Rd N1. . . . **94** A5 **233** B4
Wharfedale Ct 5 E5. . . . . . . **74** D4
Wharfedale Gdns CR7,
SW16. . . . . **204** B6
Wharfedale St SW10 . . . . . **255** C1
Wharf La 19 Poplar E14. . . . **97** B1
Twickenham TW1 . . . . . . **153** A3
Wharf Pl E2 . . . . **96** B6
Wharf Rd Enfield EN3 . . . . . **19** A5
King's Cross NW1. . . **93** D6 **232** D5
Shoreditch N1. . . . . **95** A5 **235** A3
Wharf Road NW1 . . **94** A5 **233** A4
Wharfside HA0 . . . . **88** A6
Wharfside Rd E16. . . . . **98** C2
Wharf St E16 . . . . **98** C2
Wharf View Ct 15 E14 . . . . . **98** A1
Wharncliffe Dr UB1. . . . . . **108** B5
Wharncliffe Gdns SE25. . . **183** C1
Wharncliffe Ho 3
SW15. . . . . **156** C6
Wharncliffe Rd SE25 . . . . . **183** C1
Wharton Cl NW10. . . . . **67** C2
Wharton Ho SE1 . . . . **263** C6
Wharton Rd BR1. . . . . **187** B2
Wharton St WC1. . . . **94** B4 **233** D1
Whateley Ho
East Dulwich SE22 . . . . . **161** D6
Penge SE20 . . . . **184** D3
Whatley Ave SW20 . . . . . . **201** A6
Whatman Ho 10 E14 . . . . . . **97** B1
Whatman Rd SE23 . . . . . . **162** D4
Wheatcroft Ct SM1 . . . . . . **201** D1
Wheatfields Enfield EN3. . . . . **7** A3
Newham E6 . . . . **100** D1
Wheatfield Way KT1 . . . . . **176** A1
Wheathill Rd SE20. . . . . . . **184** B1
Wheathill Rd SE20. . . . . . . **206** B6
Wheat Ho TW19. . . . . **148** A3
Wheatland Ho 7 SE22 . . . . **139** C2
Wheatlands TW5 . . . . **129** C6
Wheatlands Rd SW17 . . . . **159** A1
Wheatley Cl NW4 . . . . **28** A1
Wheatley Cres UB3 . . . . . . **106** A6
Wheatley Gdns N9 . . . . **17** C2
Wheatley Ho
Gospel Oak NW5 . . . . **71** B4
3 Putney SW15. . . . . . . **156** A4
Wheatley Mans 8 IG11 . . . **81** A4
Wheatley Rd TW7 . . . . **130** D2
Wheatley St W1 . . . . **238** B3
Wheatsheaf Cl UB5 . . . . **63** A3
Wheat Sheaf Cl E14. . . . . . **119** D2
Wheatsheaf La
Fulham SW6 . . . . **134** C5
SW8 . . . . **270** C4
Wheatsheaf Par 7 BR4. . . **207** D1
Wheatsheaf Terr SW6 . . . . **264** D3
Wheatstone Cl SW19. . . . . **180** C2

Wheatstone Ho 7 W10 . . .91 A2
Wheatstone Rd W10 . . . . .91 A2
Wheeler 2 NW9. . . . . .27 D3
Wheeler Ct 4 SW11 . . . .136 B2
Wheeler Gdns N1. . . . . . . 233 B6
Wheeler Ho E1. . . . . 243 C4
Wheeler PI 2 BR2. . . . . . 209 B5
Wheelers Cross IG11 . . . .101 B5
Wheelers Dr HA4. . . . . . . .39 A3
Wheeler's St SM1. . . . . . . 217 C5
Wheelhouse The 4 E14. .119 D1
Wheelock Cl HA8 . . . . . . .147 D5
Wheelwright St N7 . . . . . . .72 B1
Whelan Way SM6 . . . . . . .219 D5
Wheldon Ct SE1 . . . . 253 C2
Wheler Ho E1 . . . . 243 C5
Wheler St E1 . . . .95 D3 243 C5
Whellock Rd W4. . . . . . . .111 C3
Whernside Cl SE28. . . . . .124 C6
WHETSTONE 14 A2
Whetstone Cl N20 . . . . . . .14 B2
Whetstone Park
WC2. . . . . .94 B1 240 C2
Whetstone Rd SE3. . . . . .143 D4
Whewell Rd N19. . . . . .72 A6
Whichcote St SE1. . . . . . 251 A3
Whidborne Bldgs WC1. . .233 A1
Whidborne St SE8. . . . . .141 C3
Whidborne WC1. . . . . 233 A1
Whimbrel Cl SE28. . . . . . .124 C6
Whimbrel Way UB4. . . . . .84 D2
Whinchat Rd SE18, SE28 .123 B3
Whinfell Cl SW16 . . . . . . .181 D5
Whinyates Rd SE9 . . . . . .144 A2
Whippendell Cl BR5 . . . . .190 B2
Whippendell Way BR5. . . .190 B2
Whippingham Ho 22 E3 . . .97 B4
Whipps Cross E17 . . . . . . .54 B4
Whipps Cross Ho E17 . . . .54 B4
Whipps Cross Hospl E10,
E11. . . . . .54 B3
Whipps Cross Rd E11. . . . .54 C3
Whiskin St EC1 . . . . .94 D4 234 D3
Whisperwood Cl HA3 . . . . .24 C3
Whistler Gdns HA8. . . . . . .26 B1
Whistler Mews
Dagenham RM8 . . . . . . .80 B3
23 SE15 . . . . .139 D5
Whistlers Ave
SW11. . . . . . .136 B5 266 D3
Whistler St N5. . . . . .72 D3
Whistler Twr SW10 . . . . . 266 A3
Whistler Wlk SW10 . . . . . 266 B4
Whiston Ho 18 N1 . . . . . . .72 D1
Whiston Rd E2 . . . . .96 A6
Whitakers Lo EN2. . . . . .5 B4
Whitbread Cl N17. . . . . . . .34 A2
Whitbread Ctr EC1. . . . . . 242 C5
Whitbread Rd SE4 . . . . . .141 B1
Whitburn Rd SE13 . . . . . .142 A1
Whitby Ave NW10 . . . . . . .88 D4
Whitby Ct
6 Lower Holloway N7 . . .72 A4
3 New Southgate N11 . . .31 A4
Whitby Gdns
Carshalton SM1 . . . . . . .218 B6
Queensbury NW9 . . . . . . .44 C6
Whitby Ho NW8. . . . . 229 A5
Whitby Par HA4. . . . . .62 C6
Whitby Rd
Carshalton SM1 . . . . . . .218 B6
Harrow HA2 . . . . .64 A5
Ruislip HA4. . . . . .62 C6
Woolwich SE18. . . . . . . .122 B2
Whitby St E1 . . . . 243 C6
Whitcher Cl SE14 . . . . . . .141 A6
Whitcher Pl NW1 . . . . .71 C2
Whitchurch Ave HA8. . . . . .26 B3
Whitchurch Cl HA8 . . . . . . .26 B4
Whitchurch Ct SW17 . . . .180 A6
Whitchurch Fst Sch HA7 . .25 D3
Whitchurch Gdns HA8 . . . .26 B4
Whitchurch Ho
Catford SE6 . . . . .164 A1
16 North Kensington W10 .90 D1
Whitchurch La HA8 . . . . . . .26 B3
Whitchurch Par HA8 . . . . . .26 C3
Whitchurch Rd W11. . . . . .112 D6
Whitcomb Ct W1 . . . . 249 D5
Whitcomb St
WC2. . . . . .115 D6 249 D5
Whitcome Mews TW9 . . . .132 D4
Whiteacre Mews SE11 . . . 261 B1
Whiteadder Way E14. . . . .119 D2
Whitear Wlk E15. . . . . .76 B2
Whitebeam Ave BR2 . . . . .210 C3
Whitebeam Cl SW9 . . . . . 270 D3
Whitebeam Ho 3 NW3. . . .70 D2
White Bear Pl 1 NW3. . . . .70 B4
White Bear Yd EC1. . . . . . 241 A5
White Bridge Ave CR4. . . .202 B6
White Bridge Cl TW14. . . .149 D5
White Butts Rd HA4. . . . . .62 D5
WHITECHAPEL 95 D1
Whitechapel Bell Foundry *
E1. . . . . .96 A2
Whitechapel Gall* E1 . . 243 C2
Whitechapel High St
E1. . . . . .95 D1 243 D2

Whitechapel Mkt* E1 . . . .96 A2
Whitechapel Rd E1. . . . . . .96 B2
Whitechapel Sta E1. . . . . . .96 B2
Whitechurch La 3 E1. . . . .96 A1
Whitechurch Pas 1 E1. . . .96 A1
White City W10 . . . . .90 C1
White City Cl W12. . . . . . .112 C6
White City Est W12 . . . . . .112 B6
White City Rd W12 . . . . . .112 C6
White City Sta W12 . . . . . .112 C6
Whitecliff Ho SW18 . . . . . .157 D5
White Conduit St N1 . . . . 234 B4
Whitecote Rd UB1 . . . . . . .86 A1
White Craig Cl HA5 . . . . . .23 C5
Whitecroft Cl BR3 . . . . . . .208 B5
Whitecroft Way BR3. . . . . .208 B5
Whitecross Pl EC2 . . . . . . 242 D4
Whitecross St EC1 . .95 A3 242 B5
White Cube The, Art
Gallery* N1. . . . . .95 C4
Whitefield Ave NW2. . . . . . .46 C1
Whitefield St SW15 . . . . . .157 A5
Whitefield Sch NW2 . . . . . .46 D2
Whitefield Sch & Ctr E17 . .36 A1
Whitefoot La BR1. . . . . . . .164 B1
Whitefoot Terr BR1. . . . . . .164 B1
Whitefriars Ave HA3 . . . . . .24 C1
Whitefriars Ct 9 N12. . . . . .30 B5
Whitefriars Dr HA3 . . . . . . .24 C1
Whitefriars Fst & Mid Sch
HA3 . . . . .24 C1
Whitefriars St EC4 .94 C1 241 B1
Whitefriars Trad Est HA3 . .24 B1
White Gate Gdns HA3 . . . . .24 D3
Whitegates 4 EN5. . . . . . .13 D6
White Gates 5 KT7 . . . . . .197 A2
White Gdns RM10. . . . . . . .81 C2
Whitehall SW1 . . . . 250 A2
Whitehall Cres KT9 . . . . . .213 B3
Whitehall Ct
SW1. . . . . .116 A5 250 B3
Whitehall Gdns
Acton W3 . . . . .110 C5
Chingford E4. . . . . .20 C3
Chiswick W4. . . . . .132 D6
SW1. . . . . 250 A3
Whitehall La IG9. . . . . .21 A2
Whitehall Lo
Muswell Hill N10. . . . . . . .49 A6
Woodford IG8. . . . . .21 A1
Whitehall Mans 3 N19. . . .49 C1
Whitehall Park Rd W4. . . .132 D6
Whitehall Pk N19 . . . . .49 C1
Whitehall Pl
Wallington SM5 . . . . . . .219 B4
WC2, SW1 . . . . .116 A5 250 A3
Whitehall Prim Sch E4. . . .20 C2
Whitehall Rd
Bromley BR2. . . . . .209 D5
Chingford E4. . . . . .20 C2
Harrow HA1. . . . . .42 C2
Thornton Heath CR7. . . . .204 C4
West Ealing W7 . . . . .109 A4
Woodford IG8. . . . . .21 A1
Whitehall St N17 . . . . .33 D3
White Hart Ave SE28,
SE18 . . . . .123 D3
White Hart Ct EC2 . . . . . . 243 A3
White Hart La
Mortlake SW13 . . . . . . .133 C2
Willesden NW10. . . . . . . .67 D2
White Hart Lane Sta N17 . .33 D3
White Hart Lane (Tottenham
Hotspur FC) N17 . . . . . .34 A3
Whitehart Lo SW19 . . . . . .180 A4
White Hart Rd SE18 . . . . .123 C2
White Hart Rdbt UB5. . . . . .84 D5
White Hart St
Holborn EC4 . . . . 241 D1
Kennington SE11 . .116 C1 261 B2
White Hart Terr N17. . . . . . .33 D3
White Hart Yd SE1 . . . . . . 252 C3
Whitehaven Cl BR2. . . . . .209 A5
Whitehaven Ct 5 DA6 . . . .147 A1
Whitehaven St NW8. . . . . 237 A5
Whitehead Cl
Edmonton N18 . . . . .33 B5
Wandsworth SW18 . . . . .158 A4
Whitehead Ho 8 SW15 . . .156 D6
Whitehead's Gr
SW3. . . . . .114 C2 257 B3
White Heart Ave UB8. . . . . .83 A2
Whiteheath Ave HA4 . . . . . .39 A4
Whiteheath Inf Sch HA4. . . .39 A3
Whiteheath Jun Sch HA4. . .39 A2
White Heron Mews
TW11. . . . . .174 D4
White Ho
2 Battersea SW11. . . . . .136 B3
Lower Edmonton N9. . . . .18 C2
3 Streatham SW4. . . . . .159 D4
Whitehorn Ho 6 E1 . . . . . .118 D5
White Horse Hill BR7,
SE9 . . . . .188 C6
Whitehorse La SE25. . . . . .205 C5
White Horse La E1. . . . . . . .96 D2

Whitehorse Manor Inf Sch 6
CR7. . . . . .205 B5
Whitehorse Manor Jun Sch
5 CR7 . . . . .205 B5
Whitehorse Mews SE1 . . . 261 C6
Whitehorse Rd
South Norwood CR0, CR7. .205 B3
Tower Hamlets E1 . . . . . .97 A2
White Horse Rd
Limehouse E1. . . . . .97 A1
Newham E6 . . . . .100 B4
White Horse St
W1. . . . . .115 B5 248 D3
White Horse Yd EC2 . . . . . 242 C2
White Ho The NW1. . . . . . 238 D6
Whitehouse Est E10 . . . . . .54 A3
White House La EN2 . . . . . . .5 A4
White House Prep Sch
SW12 . . . . .159 D3
Whitehouse Way N14. . . . .15 B1
White Kennett St E1 . . . . . 243 B2
Whitelands Cres SW18. . . .157 A4
Whitelands Ho SW3. . . . . 257 D2
Whiteledges W13. . . . . . . .87 C1
Whitelegg Rd E13 . . . . .98 D5
Whiteley Ho 9 SW4 . . . . . .159 D4
Whiteley Rd SE19 . . . . . . .183 B5
Whiteleys Ctr 19 W2 . . . . . .91 D1
Whiteleys Ho TW13 . . . . . .151 C1
Whiteleys Par 5 UB10 . . . .82 D3
Whiteleys Way TW13. . . . . .151 C1
White Lion Ct EC3. . . . . . . 243 A1
White Lion Hill
EC4 . . . . .116 B2 251 D6
White Lion St N1 . .94 C5 234 B3
White Lo 7 Ealing W5 . . . . .87 C2
Golders Green NW11. . . . . .47 B1
South Norwood SE19 . . . . .182 D3
Whitelock Ho 21 E9 . . . . . .74 D2
White Lodge Cl
Hampstead Garden Suburb
N2. . . . . .48 B3
Isleworth TW7 . . . . .131 A3
Sutton SM2. . . . . .218 A1
White Lodge Ct TW16 . . . .172 C2
White Lyon Ct EC2 . . . . . . 242 A4
Whiteness Ho 18 SW9. . . . .138 C4
White Oak Dr BR3. . . . . . . .186 A1
White Oak Gdns DA15. . . . .167 D4
Whiteoak Ho SE19 . . . . . .183 A3
Whiteoaks La UB6. . . . . . . .86 B5
White Orchards
Barnet N20. . . . . .13 B3
Stanmore HA7 . . . . .25 A5
White Post La E9 . . . . .75 C2
White Post St SE14,
SE15 . . . . .140 C5
White Rd Broadgate EC2. . 243 A3
London E15. . . . . .76 C1
Whites Ave IG2 . . . . .57 C3
Whites Dr BR2. . . . . .208 D2
White's Grounds
SE1 . . . . .117 C4 253 B2
White's Grounds Est SE1 . 253 B2
White's Mdw BR1. . . . . . . .210 C5
White's Row E1. . . . .95 D2 243 C3
White's Sq SW4 . . . . .137 D1
White St UB1 . . . . .106 D4
Whitestile Rd TW8 . . . . . . .109 D1
Whitestone La NW3. . . . . . .70 A5
Whitestone Wlk NW3 . . . . .70 A5
Whitethorn Gdns
Croydon CR0. . . . . .222 B6
Enfield EN2. . . . . .17 B6
Whitethorn Pl UB7. . . . . . .104 B5
Whitethorn St E3 . . . . .97 C2
White Twr Way E1. . . . . . . .97 A2
Whiteways N4 . . . . .46 D5
Whitewebbs Way BR5. . . . .189 D2
Whitfield Ct
3 Dulwich SE21 . . . . . . .183 C6
Redbridge IG1. . . . . .56 B2
SW4. . . . . 270 A1
West Barnes SW20 . . . . .178 D1
Whitfield Gdns NW1 . . . . . 239 B4
Whitfield Ho NW8 . . . . . . 237 A5
Whitfield Pl W1. . . . . 239 B5
Whitfield Rd DA7 . . . . .147 B5
Upton E6. . . . . .77 C1
Whitfield St W1. . . .93 C2 239 B4
Whitford Gdns CR4 . . . . . .202 D6
Whitgift Ave CR2. . . . . . . .221 A3
Whitgift Ctr CR2. . . . . . . .221 A3
Whitgift Ctr CR0. . . . . . . .221 B3
Whitgift Ho
Battersea SW11. . . . . . . 267 A2
Croydon CR2. . . . . .221 A3
Lambeth SE11. . . . . 260 C4
Whitgift Sch CR2 . . . . . . .221 A5
Whitgift St Croydon CR0. . .221 A3
SE11. . . . . .116 B2 260 C4

Whiting Ave IG11 . . . . .78 D1
Whitings Hill Prim Sch
EN5. . . . . .12 C6
Whitings Rd EN5. . . . . .12 C6
Whitings The IG2 . . . . .57 C4
Whitings Way E6 . . . . .100 C2
Whitington Ave EC3. . . . . . 243 A1
Whitland Rd SM5. . . . . . . .202 B3
Whitley Cl TW19 . . . . .148 A5
Whitley Ho SW1 . . . . 269 B6
Whitley Rd N17. . . . . .33 C1
Whitlock Dr SW19 . . . . . . .157 A3
Whitman Ho 20 E2 . . . . . . .96 C4
Whitman Rd E3. . . . . .97 A3
Whitmead Cl CR2. . . . . . . .221 C2
Whitmore Cl N11 . . . . .31 B5
Whitmore Gdns NW10 . . . . .90 C5
Whitmore High Sch HA1,
HA2. . . . . .42 A1
Whitmore Ho
Friern Barnet N11 . . . . . . .30 D6
20 Hoxton E1. . . . . .95 C6
Whitmore Prim Sch
N1. . . . . .95 B6 235 D5
Whitmore Rd
Beckenham BR3. . . . . . . .207 B6
Harrow HA1. . . . . .42 A2
Hoxton N1. . . . . .95 C6
Whitnell Ct 7 SW15 . . . . . .156 D6
Whitnell Way SW15 . . . . . .156 D6
Whitney Ave IG4 . . . . .55 D5
Whitney Ho 6 SE6. . . . . . .139 C2
Whitney Rd E10. . . . . .53 D2
Whitney Wlk DA14 . . . . . . .191 A4
Whitstable Cl
Beckenham BR3. . . . . . . .185 B2
Ruislip HA4. . . . . .61 C6
Whitstable Ho 11 W10. . . . .90 D1
Whitstable Pl 9 CR0. . . . . .221 A4
Whitsters Ho 7 SE1. . . . . . 253 C2
Whitstone La BR3. . . . . . . .207 D4
Whittaker 3 NW9 . . . . .27 D3
Whittaker Ave TW10,
TW9. . . . . .153 D6
Whittaker Ct SW4. . . . . . . 270 B1
Whittaker Pl 28 TW10 . . . .153 D6
Whittaker Rd
Cheam SM3 . . . . .217 B5
Forest Gate E6 . . . . .77 D1
Whittaker St SW1 . . . . 258 A3
Whittaker Way 19 SE1. . . .118 A2
Whittam Ho SE27. . . . . . . .183 A5
Whitta Rd E12. . . . . .77 D4
Whittell Gdns SE26 . . . . . .162 C1
Whitten Lo N12. . . . . .30 C6
Whittingham 6 N17. . . . . .34 B3
Whittingham Com Prim Sch
E17 . . . . .35 A2
Whittingham Ct W4. . . . . . .133 C5
Whittingstall Mans SW6. . .264 D1
Whittingstall Rd
SW6. . . . . .135 B4 264 D1
Whittington Ave UB4. . . . . .83 D2
Whittington Ct
Fortis Green N2 . . . . .48 D4
Penge SE20 . . . . .184 B1
Whittington Hospl The
N19. . . . . .71 C6
Whittington Mews N12. . . . .30 A6
Whittington Rd N22. . . . . . .32 A3
Whittington Way HA5 . . . . .41 A4
Whittle 4 NW9 . . . . .27 D3
Whittlebury Cl SM5. . . . . . .218 D1
Whittlebury Ho N4. . . . . . . .51 A2
Whittle Cl Southall UB1. . . .85 D1
Walthamstow E17 . . . . . .53 A2
Whittle Rd Heston TW5. . . .128 C5
Southall UB2. . . . . .107 D4
Whittlesea Cl HA3 . . . . .24 A3
Whittlesea Path HA3 . . . . . .24 A2
Whittlesea Rd HA3. . . . . . . .24 A2
Whittlesey St
SE1. . . . . .116 C5 251 B3
WHITTON 152 A4
Whitton N3. . . . . .70 D1
Whitton Ave W UB5, UB6. . .64 B3
Whitton Cl UB6. . . . . .65 B2
Whitton Dene TW3, TW7. . .152 B6
Whitton Dr UB6. . . . . .65 C2
Whitton Manor Rd TW7 . . .152 A5
Whitton Rd
Hounslow TW3. . . . . .151 D6
Twickenham TW1 . . . . . .153 A4
Whitton Road Rdbt
TW1. . . . . .152 D5
Whitton Sch TW2 . . . . . . .151 D2
Whitton Sta TW2. . . . . . . .152 A4
Whitton Waye TW2, TW3 . .151 C5
Whitton Wlk E3. . . . . .97 C4
Whitwell Ho 11 E5 . . . . . . .74 B6
Whitwell Rd E13. . . . . .99 A4
Whitworth Cres 1 EN3. . . . .7 C6
Whitworth Ho SE1 . . . . . . 262 B5
Whitworth Rd SE18 . . . . . .144 C5
South Norwood SE25 . . . . .205 D5
Whitworth St SE10. . . . . . .120 C1
Whorlton Rd SE15 . . . . . . .140 B2
Whychcote Point NW2. . . . .46 C2
Whymark Ave N22. . . . . . . .50 D6
Whytecroft TW5 . . . . .128 D5

Whyte Mews 5 SM3 . . . . .217 A2
Whyteville Ho E7 . . . . .77 B2
Whyteville Rd E7 . . . . .77 B2
Whytlaw Ho 10 E3 . . . . . . .97 B2
Wickersley Rd SW11 . . . . .137 A3
Wickers Oake SE19 . . . . . .183 D6
Wicker St 24 E1. . . . . .96 B1
Wicket Rd UB6. . . . . .87 A4
Wickets The TW15. . . . . . .170 A6
Wicket The CR0. . . . . .223 C3
Wickfield Ho 32 SE16. . . . .118 A4
Wickford St E1. . . . . .96 C3
Wickford St E1 . . . . .96 C3
Wickford Way E17 . . . . .52 D5
Wickham Ave
Cheam KT4, SM3 . . . . . .216 C3
Croydon CR0. . . . . .207 A1
Wickham Chase BR4. . . . .208 C2
Wickham Cl Enfield EN3 . . . .6 C2
New Malden KT3 . . . . . . .199 D4
Stepney E1. . . . . .96 C2
Wickham Common Prim Sch
BR4. . . . . .225 A4
Wickham Court BR4 . . . . .224 A6
Wickham Court Sch
BR4. . . . . .224 B4
Wickham Cres BR4 . . . . . .224 A6
Wickham Ct DA16. . . . . . . .145 C3
Wickham Gdns SE4 . . . . . .141 B2
Wickham Ho SW15. . . . . . .156 D5
Wickham La SE2. . . . . .146 A6
Wickham Mews SE4 . . . . .141 B3
Wickham Rd
Beckenham BR3. . . . . . . .207 D6
Brockley SE4. . . . . .141 B2
Chingford E4. . . . . .36 A3
Croydon CR0. . . . . .207 B1
Harrow HA3 . . . . .24 B1
Wickham St Bexley DA16. .145 C3
Vauxhall SE11. . . .116 B1 260 C2
Welling DA16 . . . . .146 A4
Wickham Way BR3. . . . . . .208 A4
Wick Ho 1 KT1. . . . . .175 D2
Wick La
Stratford Marsh E3. . . . . .97 C6
Wickliffe Ave N3. . . . . .29 A1
Wickliffe Gdns HA9 . . . . . . .66 B6
Wicklow St WC1 SE26. . . . .184 C5
Wicklow Ho N16. . . . . .51 D1
Wicklow St WC1 . . .94 B4 233 C2
Wick Rd Hackney E9 . . . . . .75 A2
Hackney E9. . . . . .75 A2
Teddington TW11 . . . . . .175 C3
Wicks Cl SE12. . . . . .187 D6
Wickstead Ho TW8. . . . . . .110 B1
Wicksteed Ho SE1 . . . . . . 262 B5
Wick Village 7 E15 . . . . . . .75 B2
Wickway Ct 7 SE15. . . . . .139 C6
Wickwood St SE5. . . . . . . .138 C3
Widdenham Rd N7. . . . . . . .72 B4
Widdicombe Ave HA2. . . . . .63 A6
Widdin St E15. . . . . .76 C1
Widecombe Ct N2 . . . . .48 B4
Widecombe Gdns IG4. . . . . .56 A3
Widecombe Ho 32 SE5. . . .139 A3
Widecombe Rd SE9 . . . . . .166 A1
Widecombe Way N2 . . . . . .48 B5
Widegate St E1. . . . . 243 B3
Widenham Cl HA5. . . . . . . .40 C4
Wide Way CR4 . . . . .203 D6
Widewing Cl TW11. . . . . . .175 B3
Widford 8 NW1. . . . . .71 B2
Widford Ho N1 . . . . 234 C3
Widgeon Cl E16 . . . . .99 B1
Widgeon Path SE28. . . . . .123 B3
Widley Rd W9 . . . . .91 C3
Widmer Ct TW5. . . . . .129 A3
WIDMORE 188 A1
Widmore Lodge Rd BR1. . .187 D1
Widmore Rd BR1 . . . . .187 C1
Hillingdon UB8. . . . . .82 D3
Widnes Ho 6 N7 . . . . .72 C3
Wieland Rd HA6. . . . . .22 A3
Wigeon Way UB4 . . . . .84 D1
Wiggins La TW10 . . . . .153 C2
Wiggins Mead NW9. . . . . . .27 D3
Wigginton Ave HA9. . . . . . .66 D2
Wigham Ho IG11 . . . . .78 A1
Wightman Rd N4, N8 . . . . . .50 C4
Wighton Mews SW7. . . . . .130 C3
Wigley Rd TW13. . . . . .150 D3
Wigmore Ct W13. . . .109 A5
Wigmore Hall* W1. . . . . . 238 C2
Wigmore Pl W1. . . . .93 B1 238 C2
Wigmore Rd SM5 . . . . .202 C1
Wigmore St W1 . . . .93 A1 238 B2
Wigmore Wlk SM5 . . . . . . .218 B6
Wigram Ct SW11. . . . . 267 A2
Wigram Ho 7 E14 . . . . . . .119 D6
Wigram Rd E11. . . . . .55 C3
Wigram Sq E17 . . . . .54 A4
Wigston Cl N18. . . . . .33 C5
Wigston Rd E13. . . . . .99 B3
Wigton Gdns HA7. . . . . . . .26 A3
Wigton Pl SE11. . . . . 261 B1
Wigton Rd E17. . . . . .35 B2

Wilberforce Ct
Edgware HA8 . . . . .26 B6
2 SE28 . . . . 124 C5
Wilberforce Ho 3
SW11. . . . . .136 B2
Wilberforce Mews 9
SW4. . . . . 137 D1
Wilberforce Prim Sch
W10 . . . . .91 A4
Wilberforce Rd
Finsbury Pk N4 . . . . .72 D6
Hendon NW9 . . . . .46 A3
Highbury N4, N5 . . . . .73 A5
Wilberforce Way SW19 . .178 D4
Wilbraham Ho SW8 . . . . . 270 A3
Wilbury Prim Sch N18 . . .33 B5
Wilbury Way N18 . . . . .33 B5
Wilby Mews W11 . .113 B5 244 D4
Wilcox Cl SW8 . . . . 270 B4
Wilcox Gdns TW17 . . . . . .192 B6
Wilcox Ho **5** E3 . . . . .97 B2
Wilcox Pl SW1 . . . . 259 B5
Wilcox Rd Sutton SM1 . . . .217 D4
SW8 . . . . 138 A5 270 A4
Teddington TW11 . . . . .174 B6
Wildcroft Gdns HA8 . . . . . .25 D4
Wildcroft Manor SW15 . .156 C4
Wildcroft Rd SW15 . . . . . .156 C4
Wild Ct WC2 . . . . . . 94 B1 240 C2
Wilde Cl E8 . . . . .96 A6
Wilde Pl Edmonton N13 . . . .32 D4
Wandsworth SW18 . . . . . .158 B4
Wilder Cl HA4 . . . . .40 B1
Wilde Rd DA8 . . . . .147 D5
Wilderness Mews SW4 . .137 B1
Wilderness Rd BR7 . . . . . .188 D3
Wilderness The
East Molesey KT8 . . . . . . .196 A4
Hampton TW12 . . . . .173 D6
Wilderton Rd N16 . . . . .51 C2
Wildes Cotts SM3 . . . . . . .217 A2
Wildfell Rd SE6 . . . . .163 D4
Wild Goose Dr SE14 . . . . .140 C4
Wild Hatch NW11 . . . . .47 C3
Wilding Ho **17** E9 . . . . .74 D2
Wild Marsh Ct EN3. . . . . . .7 A6
Wild's Rents SE1. .117 C3 263 A6
Wild St WC2 . . . . . . 94 B1 240 C1
Wildwood Cl SE12 . . . . . . 164 D4
Wildwood Gr NW3 . . . . . . .48 A1
Wildwood Rd NW11 . . . . . .48 A2
Wildwood Rise NW11 . . . .48 A1
Wildwood Terr NW3,
NW11 . . . . .48 A1
Wilford Cl EN2 . . . . .5 B2
Wilford Ho **3** SE18 . . . . . .122 D1
Wilford Rd CR0 . . . . .205 A2
Wilfred Fienburgh Ho
N7 .71 D4
Wilfred Owen Cl SW19 . .180 A4
Wilfred St SW1 . .115 C3 259 A6
Wilfrid Gdns W3 . . . . .89 A2
Wilkes Rd **3** TW8 . . . . . . .132 A6
Wilkie Ho SW1 . . . . 259 D2
Wilkin St Mews NW1 . . . . .71 B2
Wilkins Cl Hayes UB3 . . . .105 D1
Mitcham CR4 . . . . .180 C2
Wilkins Ho SW1 . . . . 269 A6
Wilkinson Cl UB10 . . . . . . .83 A6
Wilkinson Ct SW17 . . . . . .180 B6
Wilkinson Gdns CR7 . . . .183 C2
Wilkinson Ho
Isleworth TW7 . . . . .130 D2
N1. . . . . 235 D3
Twickenham TW2 . . . . .152 B2
Wilkinson Rd E16 . . . . .99 C1
Wilkinson St
SW8. . . . . .138 B5 270 C3
Wilkinson Way W4 . . . . . . .111 B4
Wilkin St NW5 . . . . .71 B2
Wilks Gdns CR0 . . . . .207 A1
Wilks Pl N1 . . . . .95 C5
Willan Rd N17 . . . . .33 C1
Willan Wall E16 . . . . .120 D6
Willard St SW8 . . . . .137 B2
Wilbury Ho **4** N7 . . . . .71 D3
Willcocks Cl KT9 . . . . .214 A1
Willcott Rd W3 . . . . .110 D5
Will Crooks Gdns SE9 . . .143 D1
Willenfield Rd NW10 . . . . . .89 A5
Willenhall Ave EN5 . . . . . .14 A5
Willenhall Ct EN5 . . . . .14 A5
Willenhall Dr UB3 . . . . . . .105 C6
Willenhall Rd SE18 . . . . . .122 D1
Willersley Ave
Blackfen DA15 . . . . .167 D4
Orpington BR6 . . . . .227 B5
Willersley Cl DA15 . . . . . . .167 D3
WILLESDEN 67 D1
Willesden Community Hospl
The NW10. . . . . .68 A1
WILLESDEN GREEN 90 B6
Willesden Green Sta
NW2. . . . . .68 C2

Willesden Junction Sta
NW10. . . . . .89 D4
Willesden La NW2, NW6 . .68 D2
Willesden Sports Ctr
W10 . . . . .90 B6
Willes Rd NW5. . . . . .71 B2
Willett Cl BR5 . . . . .211 C3
3 Northolt UB5. . . . . .84 C4
Willett Ho **7** Newham E13 . .99 A5
Stockwell SW9 . . . . .138 A2
Willett Pl CR7. . . . . .204 C4
Willett Rd CR7. . . . . .204 C4
Willett Way BR5 . . . . .211 C3
William Allen Ho HA8 . . . .26 B3
William Ash Cl RM9 . . . . . .80 B2
William Atkinson Ho N7 . .33 C3
William Banfield Ho 10
SW6. . . . . .135 B3
William Bellamy Jun & Inf
Schs RM10 . . . . .81 C6
William Blake Ho 2
SE15 . . . . .140 A3
William Bonney Est 10
SW4. . . . . .137 D1
William Booth Meml Training
Coll SE5. . . . . .139 B3
William Booth Rd SE20 . .184 A2
William Brown Ct SE27. . .160 D2
William Byrd Sch UB7 . . . .127 A6
William Carey Way HA1 . .42 C3
William Caslon Ho **28** E2 . .96 B5
William Channing Ho 6
E2 .96 B4
William C Harvey Specl Sch
N17. . . . . .33 B1
William Cl **26** Finchley N2. . .30 B1
Lewisham SE13 . . . . .142 A2
Southall UB2. . . . . .108 A4
William Covell Cl EN2 . . . . .4 B5
William Ct
4 Belvedere DA17 . . . . . .125 C2
4 Ealing W5 . . . . .87 C2
Ilford IG2 . . . . .57 B5
William Davies Prim Sch
E7 .96 A3
William Davis Prim Sch 19
E2 .96 A3
William Dr HA7 . . . . .25 B5
William Dromey Ct NW6. . .69 B1
William Dunbar Ho NW6 . .91 B5
William Dyce Mews 1
SW16. . . . . .181 D6
William Ellis Sch NW5 . . . .71 A5
William Ellis Way 16
SE16 . . . . .118 A3
William Evans Ho 9
SE8 . . . . .118 D2
William Ford CE Jun Sch
RM10 . . . . .81 C1
William Foster La DA16 . .146 A2
William Gdns SW15 . . . . . .156 B6
William Guy Gdns **47** E3 . . .97 D4
William Harvey Ho 1
SW19. . . . . .157 A3
William Ho N13. . . . . .32 D4
William Hogarth Sch The 15
W4 . . . . .111 C1
William Hunt Mans
SW13. . . . . .134 C6
William IV St
WC2. . . . . .116 A6 250 A1
William Margrie Cl 1
SE15 . . . . .140 A3
William Marsden Ho 2
SE27 . . . . .182 D6
William Mews
SW1. . . . . .114 D4 247 D1
William Morley Cl E6. . . . . .99 D6
William Morris Acad
W6 . . . . .112 D1
William Morris Cl E17. . . . .53 B6
William Morris Gallery★
E17. . . . . .53 C6
William Morris Ho W6 . . .134 D6
William Morris Prim Sch
CR4. . . . . .203 D6
William Morris Sch E17 . . .35 A2
William Morris Way
SW6. . . . . .136 A3
William Patten Prim Sch 9
N16. . . . . .73 D6
William Perkin Ct UB6 . . . .64 C2
William Pl **37** E3 . . . . .97 B5
William Rainbird Ho 9
N17. . . . . .33 D3
William Rathbone Ho 3
E2 .96 B4
William Rd
Regent's Pk NW1 . . .93 C4 232 A1
Sutton SM1. . . . . .218 A3
Wimbledon SW19. . . . . . . .179 A3
William Rushbrooke Ho 4
SE16 . . . . .118 A2
Williams Ave E17 . . . . .35 B2
William Saville Ho 2
NW6 . . . . .91 B5
William's Bldgs **1** E2 . . . . .96 C3
Williams Cl SW6 . .135 A5 264 D1

Williams Coll EC1. . . . . 241 B3
Williams Dr TW3. . . . . . . .129 C1
Williams Gr
Kingston u T KT6. . . . . . . .197 C3
Wood Green N22 . . . . .32 C2
Williams Ho **10** Bow E3 . . . .97 C4
9 Hackney E9 . . . . .96 B6
14 Streatham SW2. . . . . . .160 C3
7 Tottenham N17. . . . . .33 D3
Willesden NW2. . . . . .68 C5
Williams La Morden SM4 . .202 A4
Mortlake SW14 . . . . .133 A3
William Smith Ho 10
DA17. . . . . .125 C3
Williamson Cl SE10 . . . . .120 D1
Williamson Ct SE17 . . . . . 262 A1
Williamson Rd N4 . . . . .50 D3
Williamson St N7 . . . . .72 A4
Williams Rd UB2. . . . . . . .107 A2
William's Rd W13. . . . . . . .109 A5
William St Barking IG11 . . .79 A1
Carshalton SM5 . . . . .218 D5
SW1 . . . . .114 D4 247 D1
Tottenham N17. . . . . .33 D3
Walthamstow E10 . . . . .53 D3
Williams Terr CR0. . . . . . .220 C2
William Torbitt Prim Sch
IG2. . . . . .57 D5
William Tyndale Prim Sch 27
N1. .72 D1
William Wilberforce Ho 1
SE27 . . . . .182 D6
William Winter Ct 29
SW2. . . . . .160 C4
William Wood Ho 3
SE26 . . . . .162 C1
Willfield Way NW11 . . . . . .47 C4
Willingale Cl IG8 . . . . .37 C4
Willingdon Rd N22 . . . . . . .32 D1
Willingham Cl **4** NW5 . . . . .71 C3
Willingham Terr NW5 . . . . .71 C3
Willingham Way KT1. . . . .176 C1
Willington Ct E5. . . . . .75 A5
Willington Rd SW9 . . . . . .138 A2
Willington Sch **13** SW19 . .179 B5
Willis Ave SM2, SM5 . . . . .218 C2
Willis Ct CR7 . . . . .204 C3
Willis Ho **2** Ilford E12 . . . . .78 C5
8 Poplar E14. . . . . .119 D6
Willis Rd E15 . . . . .98 D5
Thornton Heath CR0. . . . . .205 A2
Willis St E14. . . . . .97 D1
Willis Yd N14. . . . . .15 D4
Willows The CR0 . . . . .223 A6
Will Miles Ct **9** SW19 . . . .180 A3
Willmore End SW19. . . . . .179 D1
Willoughby Ave CR0 . . . . .220 B4
Willoughby Gr N17. . . . . . .34 B3
Willoughby Ho EC2 . . . . . 242 C3
34 Wapping E1. . . . . .118 B5
Willoughby La N17. . . . . . .34 B3
Willoughby Mews N17. . . .34 B3
Willoughby Park Rd N17 . .34 B3
Willoughby Rd
Hampstead NW3 . . . . .70 B4
Hornsey N8. . . . . .50 C5
Kingston u T KT2. . . . . . . .176 B2
Twickenham TW1 . . . . .153 D6
Willoughby St WC1 . . . . . 240 A1
Willoughbys The SW14 . .133 C1
Willoughby Way SE7 . . . .121 B2
Willow Ave Barnes SW13 . .133 D3
DA15. . . . . .168 A5
Yiewsley UB7 . . . . .104 B6
Willowbank SW6 . . . . .135 A2
Willowbank TW10 . . . . . . .153 B1
Willowbank Rd SE15 . . . . .139 D6
Willowbay Cl EN5. . . . . . . .12 D5
Willow Bridge Rd N1. . . . . .73 A2
Willow Brook Prim Sch
E10. . . . . .53 C1
Willow Cotts
Carshalton SM4 . . . . .202 D2
Feltham TW13 . . . . .151 A1
Richmond TW9 . . . . .132 C6
Willowcourt Ave HA3 . . . . .43 B4
Willowcroft SE3 . . . . .142 D1
Willow Ct Ashford TW16. . .171 C3
5 Beckenham BR3 . . . . . .185 C2
Brixton SW9 . . . . .138 C4
Chiswick W4 . . . . .133 C5
8 Dagenham RM8. . . . . . . .58 D2
EC2 . . . . 243 A6
Edgware HA8 . . . . .26 A6
6 Finchley N12. . . . . .29 D6
Harrow HA2. . . . . .24 D2
Headstone HA2. . . . . .24 A1
Ilford IG1. . . . . .79 A3
Islington N7 . . . . .72 B3

Willow Ct continued
Kingston u T KT3. . . . . . . .198 D6
8 London E11 . . . . .76 C6
Mitcham CR4 . . . . .202 C5
40 Paddington W2 . . . . .91 C2
3 Streatham SW16. . . . . . .160 B1
Thornton Heath CR7. . . . . .205 B4
Willow Ctr The CR4 . . . . .202 D3
Willow Dean HA5 . . . . .22 D1
Willowdene Highgate N6 . .48 D2
1 Peckham SE15. . . . . . . .140 B4
5 SE15 . . . . .140 B5
Willow Dene WD23. . . . . . . .8 C4
Willowdene Cl TW2. . . . . . .152 A4
Willowdene Ct N20 . . . . . . .14 A4
Willow Dene Sch SE18 . . .145 C4
Willow Dr EN5 . . . . .1 A1
Willow End
Northwood HA6 . . . . .22 A4
Surbiton KT6. . . . . .198 A1
Totteridge N20 . . . . .13 C2
Willow Farm La SW15 . . . .134 B2
Willowfield Sch E17 . . . . . .52 D6
Willowfields Cl SE18 . . . . .123 C1
Willow Gdns
Heston TW5. . . . . .129 C4
Ruislip HA4. . . . . .61 D6
Willow Gn
Borehamwood WD6 . . . . . .11 B6
Grahame Pk NW9 . . . . .27 C2
Willow Gr BR7. . . . . .188 D6
Newham E13 . . . . .99 A5
Ruislip HA4. . . . . .39 D1
Willow Hall NW3. . . . . .70 B4
Willowhayne Dr KT12 . . . .194 B2
Willowhayne Gdns KT4. . .216 C4
Willow Ho TW14 . . . . .150 B6
Willow Ho **17** Finchley N2. . .30 B1
9 Maitland Pk NW3 . . . . . .70 D2
North Kensington W10 . . . .90 D3
Teddington TW11 . . . . .175 C3
Willow La Mitcham CR4. . .202 D3
Woolwich SE18. . . . . .122 C2
Willow Lo
6 Ashford TW16. . . . . . . .171 D3
Fulham SW6 . . . . .134 D4
New Barnet EN5. . . . . .14 A6
Putney SW15 . . . . .134 B2
Willow Lodge UB8 . . . . . . .137 B2
Willow Manor SM1. . . . . . .217 B4
Willowmead CI W5 . . . . . . .87 D2
Willowmere Esher KT10. . .212 A4
Ladywell SE13 . . . . .163 D6
Willow Mount CR0 . . . . . . .221 C5
Willow Pl SW1. . . . .115 C2 259 B4
Willow Rd Dagenham RM6 . .59 A3
Ealing W5 . . . . .110 A4
Enfield EN1. . . . . .5 C3
Hampstead NW3 . . . . .70 B4
New Malden KT3 . . . . .199 A5
Wallington SM6 . . . . .219 B1
Willows Ave SM4 . . . . .201 D4
Willows Cl HA5 . . . . .22 C1
Willows Ct **3** SW19 . . . . . .179 C3
Willows Sch The UB4. . . . . .84 D3
Willow St
Broadgate EC2 . . . . .95 C3 243 A6
Chingford E4. . . . . .20 B4
Willows Terr NW10. . . . . . . .89 D5
Willows The
Beckenham BR3 . . . . .185 C2
Claygate KT10 . . . . .212 C2
Loughton IG10 . . . . .21 D6
Wallend E12. . . . . .78 C1
Whetstone N20 . . . . .14 A1
Willowtree Cl UB10 . . . . . . .61 A5
Willow Tree Cl Hayes UB4 . .84 C3
Northolt UB5 . . . . .63 A2
14 Old Ford E3 . . . . .97 B6
Wandsworth SW18 . . . . . .157 D3
Willow Tree Ct DA14. . . . . .189 D5
5 Wembley HA0 . . . . .65 D3
Willow Tree La UB4 . . . . . . .84 C3
Willow Tree Prim Sch
UB5. . . . . .63 A2
Willow Tree Rd UB4. . . . . . .84 D2
Willowtree Way SW16 . . . .182 C2
Willow Tree Wlk BR1. . . . .187 B2
Willow Vale BR7 . . . . .188 D4
Shepherd's Bush W12 . . . .112 A5
Willow View SW19 . . . . . . .180 B2
Willow Way Finchley N3 . . .29 C3
Forest Hill SE26 . . . . .162 C1
9 Shepherd's Bush W11. . .112 D6
Sunbury TW16 . . . . .194 A5
Twickenham TW2 . . . . .151 D2
Wembley HA0. . . . . .65 A5
West Kenton KT19. . . . . . . .215 B2
Willow Wlk
Bermondsey SE1 . .117 D2 263 C4
Cheam SM1, SM3 . . . . . . .217 B5
15 Finchley N2. . . . . .30 B1
Harringay N15 . . . . .50 D5
Lockesbottom BR6 . . . . . . .226 D5
Southgate N21. . . . . .16 B5
Walthamstow E17 . . . . .53 B4
Willow Wood Cres SE25 . .205 C3
Willridge Ct E11. . . . . .54 B2
Willrose Cres SE2. . . . . . .124 B1
Willsbridge Ct **1** SE15 . . . .139 D6

Wills Cres TW3 . . . . .151 D5
Wills Gr NW7 . . . . .28 B5
Will Thorne Pav The
E16. . . . . .100 A1
Wilman Gr E8 . . . . .74 A1
Wilmar Cl UB4. . . . . .83 B3
Wilmar Gdns BR4. . . . . . .207 D1
Wilmcote Ho W2 . . . . .91 D2
Wilment Ct NW2. . . . . .68 C5
Wilmer Cl KT2. . . . . .176 B5
Wilmer Cres KT2. . . . . . . .176 B5
Wilmer Gdns **22** N1 . . . . . . .95 C6
Wilmer Ho **6** E3. . . . . .97 A5
Wilmer Lea Cl E15 . . . . . . .76 B1
Wilmers Ct **5** NW10 . . . . . .89 B6
Wilmer Way N14. . . . . .31 D5
Wilmington Ave W4. . . . . .133 B5
Wilmington Ct SW16. . . . . .182 A3
Wilmington Gdns IG11. . . .79 C1
Wilmington Sq
WC1. . . . . .94 C4 234 A1
Wilmington St WC1 . . . . . 234 A1
Wilmot Cl Finchley N2. . . . .30 A1
SE15 . . . . .140 A5
Wilmot Ho **14** SM2 . . . . . . .218 A2
Wilmot Pl
Camden Town NW1 . . . . . . .71 C1
Ealing W7 . . . . .108 C5
Wilmot Rd Leyton E10. . . . . .75 D6
Tottenham N17. . . . . .51 B6
Wallington SM5 . . . . .218 D3
Wilmot St E2 . . . . .96 B3
Wilmount St SE18. . . . . . . .122 D2
Wilna Rd SW18 . . . . .158 A4
Wilnett Ct **3** RM6. . . . . .58 B2
Wilnett Villas **5** RM6. . . . . .58 B2
Wilsham St W11 . . .113 A5 244 A4
Wilshaw Cl NW4. . . . . .46 A6
Wilshaw Ho **10** SE8 . . . . . .141 C5
Wilshaw St SE14. . . . . . . .141 C4
Wilsmere Dr Harrow HA3. . .24 C3
Northolt UB5. . . . . .63 A3
Wilson Ave CR4. . . . . .180 C2
Wilson Cl Croydon CR2 . . .221 B3
Wembley HA9. . . . . .44 B2
Wilson Ct **9** SE28. . . . . . . .123 A3
Wilson Dr HA9. . . . . .44 B2
Wilson Gdns HA1 . . . . .42 A2
Wilson Gr SE16 . . . . .118 B4
Wilson Ho
39 Clapham SW8 . . . . . . .137 D3
2 SE7 . . . . .143 C6
South Hampstead NW6 . . . .70 A1
Wilson Rd
Camberwell SE5 . . . . .139 C4
Chessington KT9 . . . . .214 B2
Newham E6 . . . . .99 D4
Redbridge IG1. . . . . .56 B2
Wilson's Ave **4** N17 . . . . . . .33 D1
Wilson's Pl E14. . . . . .97 B1
Wilson's Rd W6. . . . . .112 D1
Wilson's Sch SM6. . . . . . .220 A2
Wilson St
Broadgate EC2 . . . . .95 B2 242 D4
Southgate N21. . . . . .16 C4
Walthamstow E17 . . . . .54 A4
Wilstone Cl UB4 . . . . .85 A3
Wiltern Ct NW2. . . . . .69 A2
Wilthorne Gdns RM10. . . . .81 D1
Wilton Ave W4. . . . . .111 C1
Wilton Cres
Merton SW19. . . . . .179 B2
SW1 . . . . .115 A4 248 A1
Wilton Ct **3** Edgware HA8 . .26 D5
Muswell Hill N10. . . . . .31 A1
4 Richmond TW10 . . . . . .154 A6
7 Stepney E1. . . . . .96 B1
7 Woodford IG8. . . . . .37 A4
Wilton Est E8. . . . . .74 A2
Wilton Gdns
East Molesey KT8 . . . . . . .195 C6
Walton-on-T KT12 . . . . . . .194 D1
Wilton Gr Merton SW19 . . .179 B2
New Malden KT3 . . . . .199 D3
Wilton Ho
8 Camberwell SE22 . . . . .139 C2
Chislehurst BR7 . . . . .189 B2
Ealing W13 . . . . .109 B6
Wilton Mews
SW1. . . . . .115 A3 258 B6
Wilton Par TW13. . . . . .150 B2
Wilton Pl
2 Beckenham BR3 . . . . . .208 A6
4 Harrow HA1. . . . . .42 D1
SW1 . . . . .115 A4 248 A1
Wilton Rd
Abbey Wood SE2. . . . . . . .124 C2
Cockfosters EN4. . . . . .2 D1
Hounslow TW4 . . . . .128 D2
Mitcham SW19. . . . . .180 C3
Muswell Hill N10. . . . . .31 A1
Westminster SW1 . .115 C2 259 A4
Wilton Row SW1. . . . . 248 A1
Wilton Sq N1 . . . . . . 95 B6 235 C6
Wilton St SW1 . . . . .115 A3 258 C6
Wilton Terr SW1 . . . . 258 A6
Wilton Villas N1. . . . . 235 C5
Wilton Way E8. . . . . .74 A2
Wiltshire Cl Edgware NW7. . .27 C5

Wiltshire Cl *continued*
  SW3 . . . . **257** C3
Wiltshire Ct Barking IG11 . . 79 A2
  2 Finsbury Pk N4 . . . . 50 B1
Wiltshire Gdns
  Stoke Newington N4 . . . . . . 51 A3
  Twickenham TW2 . . . . 152 A3
Wiltshire Rd Brixton SW9 . **138** C2
  Thornton Heath CR7 . . . . . 204 C6
Wiltshire Row N1 . . 95 B6 **235** D5
Wilverley Cres KT3 . . . . **199** C3
Wimbart Rd SW2 . . . . 160 B4
WIMBLEDON 179 B4
Wimbledon Bridge
  SW19 . . . . 179 B4
Wimbledon Central
  SW19 . . . . 179 B4
Wimbledon Chase Prim Sch
  2 SW20 . . . . 179 A2
Wimbledon Chase Sta
  SW20 . . . . 179 A1
Wimbledon Cl **1** SW20 . . 178 D3
Wimbledon Coll SW19 . . . . 178 D3
Wimbledon Common*
  SW19 . . . . 178 D3
Wimbledon Common Prep
  Sch SW19 . . . . 178 D3
Wimbledon High Sch
  SW19 . . . . 179 A4
Wimbledon Hill Rd
  SW19 . . . . 179 B4
Wimbledon Lawn Tennis
  Mus* SW19 . . . . 157 A1
Wimbledon L Ctr SW19 . . . 179 D4
Wimbledon Mus*
  SW19 . . . . 179 A4
Wimbledon Park Ct
  SW19 . . . . 157 B3
Wimbledon Park Montessori
  Sch SW18 . . . . 157 C2
Wimbledon Park Prim Sch
  SW19 . . . . 157 D2
Wimbledon Park Rd SW18,
  SW19 . . . . 157 B3
Wimbledon Park Side
  SW19 . . . . 156 D3
Wimbledon Park Sta
  SW19 . . . . 157 C1
Wimbledon Rd SW17 . . . . 180 A6
Wimbledon Sch of Art **1**
  SW19 . . . . 179 A2
Wimbledon Sch of Art
  Annexe **14** SW19 . . . . . 179 C3
Wimbledon Sta SW19 . . . . 179 B4
Wimbledon Stad SW17 . . 180 A6
Wimbledon Stadium Bsns Ctr
  SW17 . . . . 157 D1
Wimbledon Windmill Mus*
  SW19 . . . . 156 C1
Wimbolt St E2 . . . . 96 A4
Wimborne **2** DA14 . . . . 190 B6
Wimborne Ave Hayes UB4 . 84 B1
  Southall UB2 . . . . 107 C2
  St Paul's Cray BR5, BR7 . . 211 D5
Wimborne Ct
  Buckhurst Hill IG9 . . . . 21 C2
  Lewisham SE12 . . . . 164 D6
  North Cheam KT4 . . . . . . 200 C1
Wimborne Ct **1** UB5 . . . . . 63 C2
Wimborne Dr Pinner HA5 . . 41 A2
  Queensbury NW9 . . . . 44 C6
Wimborne Gdns W13 . . . . 87 B2
Wimborne Ho
  Canning Town E16 . . . . . . 120 D6
  Croydon CR0 . . . . 206 C4
  Marylebone NW1 . . . . **237** B5
  South Lambeth SW8 . . . . **270** D3
  Upper Tooting SW12 . . . . 159 C1
Wimborne Rd
  Edmonton N9 . . . . 18 A2
  Tottenham N17 . . . . 33 C1
Wimborne Way BR3 . . . . . 207 A5
Wimbourne Ct
  Mitcham SW19 . . . . 180 B3
  N1 . . . . **235** C4
  South Croydon CR2 . . . . . 221 C4
Wimbourne St N1 . 95 B5 **235** C4
Wimbush Ho **3** N12 . . . . . 29 D5
Wimpole Cl Bromley BR2 . 209 C5
  1 Kingston u T KT1 . . . 176 C1
Wimpole Mews
  W1 . . . . 93 B2 **238** C3
Wimpole St W1 . . 93 B1 **238** C2
Wimshurst Cl CR0 . . . . 204 A1
Winans Wlk SW9 . . . . 138 C3
Winant Ho **19** E14 . . . . . . 119 D6
Wincanton Cres UB5 . . . . . 63 C3
Wincanton Ct **2** N11 . . . . 31 A4
Wincanton Gdns IG6 . . . . . 56 D6
Wincanton Rd SW18 . . . . 157 B4
Winchcombe Rd SM5 . . . . 202 C1
Winchcomb Gdns SE9 . . . 143 D2
Winchelsea Ave DA7 . . . . . 147 B5
Winchelsea Cl SW15 . . . . . 156 D6
Winchelsea Ho **16** SE16 . 118 C4
Winchelsea Rd
  Becontree NW10 . . . . 89 B6
  Forest Gate E7 . . . . 77 A4

Winchelsea Rd *continued*
  Tottenham N17 . . . . 51 C6
Winchelsea Rise CR2 . . . . 221 D2
Winchendon Rd
  Fulham SW6 . . . . . 135 B4 **264** D2
  Teddington TW11, TW12 . . 174 B6
Winchester Ave
  Brondesbury NW6 . . . . 69 A1
  Heston TW5 . . . . 129 B6
  Queensbury NW9 . . . . 44 C6
Winchester Cl
  Beckenham BR2 . . . . 208 D6
  Enfield EN1 . . . . 17 C6
  Kingston u T KT2 . . . . 176 D3
  11 Newham E6 . . . . . . 100 B1
  SE17 . . . . **261** D3
Winchester Ct
  15 Belvedere DA17 . . . 125 C1
  5 Higham Hill E17 . . . . . 35 C4
  Richmond TW9 . . . . 132 B2
  W8 . . . . **245** C2
Winchester Dr HA5 . . . . . . 40 D4
Winchester Ho
  5 Barking IG11 . . . . 80 A1
  Bayswater W2 . . . . **236** A1
  Chelsea SW3 . . . . **266** D5
  1 Greenwich SE18 . . . . 143 D5
  24 Tower Hamlets E3 . . . 97 B4
  Twickenham TW1 . . . . . . 153 C4
Winchester Mews KT4 . . . 216 D6
Winchester Pal* SE1 . . . . **252** C4
Winchester Pk BR2 . . . . . 208 D6
Winchester Pl
  6 Dalston E8 . . . . 73 D3
  Highgate N6 . . . . 49 B1
Winchester Rd
  Beckenham BR2 . . . . 208 D6
  Bexley DA7 . . . . 146 D3
  Chingford E4 . . . . 36 A3
  Edmonton N9 . . . . 18 A3
  Harlington UB3 . . . . 127 C5
  Harrow HA3 . . . . 44 A5
  Highgate N6 . . . . 49 B1
  Ilford IG1 . . . . 79 B5
  Northwood HA6 . . . . 40 A6
  South Hampstead NW3 . . . 70 B1
  St Margarets TW1 . . . . . . 153 B5
  Twickenham TW13 . . . . . 151 B1
  Walton-on-T KT12 . . . . . . 194 A1
Winchester Sq SE1 . . . . . **252** C4
Winchester St Acton W3 . . 111 A4
  SW1 . . . . 115 B1 **258** D2
Winchester Wlk SE1 . . . . . **252** C4
Winchet Wlk CR0 . . . . **206** C3
Winchfield Cl HA3 . . . . 43 C3
Winchfield Ho SW15 . . . . 155 D5
Winchfield Rd SE26 . . . . . 185 B4
Winch Ho
  Isle of Dogs E14 . . . . 119 D3
  SW10 . . . . **266** B4
Winchilsea Cres KT8 . . . . 174 A1
Winchilsea Ho NW8 . . . . . **229** D1
WINCHMORE HILL 16 D4
Winchmore Hill Rd N14,
  N21 . . . . 16 A4
Winchmore Hill Sta N21 . . 16 D4
Winchmore Sch N21 . . . . . 17 A2
Winchmore Villas N21 . . . . 16 B4
Winchstone Cl TW17 . . . . 192 B5
Winckley Cl HA3 . . . . 44 B4
Wincott St SE11 . . 116 C2 **261** B3
Wincrofts Dr SE9 . . . . 145 B1
Windall Cl SE20 . . . . 184 A2
Windborough Rd SM5 . . . 219 A1
Windcott Ct HA3 . . . . 43 C2
Windermere NW1 . . . . **231** D2
  12 Putney SW15 . . . . . 156 D5
Windermere Ave
  Golders Green N3 . . . . 47 C6
  Kensal Rise NW6 . . . . 91 A6
  Merton SW19 . . . . 201 D6
  Ruislip HA4 . . . . 40 D2
  Wembley HA9 . . . . 43 C1
Windermere Cl BR6 . . . . . 226 D5
  East Bedfont TW14 . . . . . 149 D3
  Stanwell TW19 . . . . 148 A2
Windermere Ct
  Barnes SW13 . . . . 133 C6
  Barnet EN5 . . . . 1 D1
  Carshalton SM5 . . . . 219 A5
  Wembley HA9 . . . . 43 C1
Windermere Gdns IG4 . . . . 56 A4
Windermere Gr HA9 . . . . . . 43 C1
Windermere Hall HA8 . . . . 26 B5
Windermere Ho
  Isleworth TW1 . . . . 152 D6
  Tower Hamlets E3 . . . . 97 B3
Windermere Point **3**
  SE15 . . . . 140 C5
Windermere Rd
  Brentford W5 . . . . 109 C4
  Croydon CR0 . . . . 205 D1
  Kingston u T SW15 . . . . . 177 C5
  Mitcham SW19 . . . . 181 D1
  Muswell Hill N10 . . . . 31 B2
  Southall UB1 . . . . 85 B2
  Upper Holloway N19 . . . . . 71 C6
  West Wickham BR4 . . . . . 224 C6
Windermere Way UB7 . . . 104 B5
Winders Rd SW11 . . . . . . 136 C3

Windfield Cl SE26 . . . . 184 D6
Windham Rd TW9 . . . . 132 B2
Winding Way RM8 . . . . 80 C5
Windlass Pl SE8 . . . . 119 A2
Windlesham Gr SW19 . . . . 156 D3
Windley Cl SE23 . . . . 162 C2
Windmill WC1 . . . . **240** C4
Windmill Alley **7** W4 . . . 111 C2
Windmill Ave UB2 . . . . 108 A4
Windmill Bridge Ho **1**
  CR0 . . . . 205 C1
Windmill Bsns Ctr UB2 . . 108 A5
Windmill Bsns Village
  TW16 . . . . 171 C2
Windmill Cl
  Ashford TW16 . . . . 171 C3
  12 Bermondsey SE1 . . 118 A2
  Kingston u T KT6 . . . . 197 C2
  4 Lewisham SE13 . . . . 142 A3
Windmill Ct
  Brentford W5 . . . . 109 C2
  Brondesbury NW2 . . . . 69 A2
  Bushey WD23 . . . . 8 B3
Windmill Dr
  Clapham SW4 . . . . 159 B6
  Cricklewood NW2 . . . . 69 A5
Windmill Gdns
  Brixton SW9 . . . . 160 B5
  Enfield EN2 . . . . 4 C2
Windmill Gr CR0 . . . . 205 A3
Windmill Hill Enfield EN2 . . 5 A2
  1 Hampstead NW3 . . . . 70 A4
  Hampstead NW3 . . . . 70 A5
  Ruislip HA4 . . . . 39 D1
Windmill Ho
  4 Millwall E14 . . . . 119 C2
  SE1 . . . . **251** B3
Windmill La
  Barnet Gate EN5 . . . . 11 D5
  BR2 . . . . 225 C4
  Bushey WD23 . . . . 8 C3
  Greenford UB6 . . . . 86 A2
  Isleworth TW7, UB2, W7 . 108 C2
  Southall UB2 . . . . 108 A4
  Stratford E15 . . . . 76 B2
  Thames Ditton KT7 . . . . . 197 B2
Windmill Lo TW16 . . . . . . 171 C2
Windmill Pas **10** W4 . . . 111 C2
Windmill Pl UB1 . . . . 108 A5
Windmill Rd
  Brentford TW8, W5 . . . . . 109 C1
  Charlton TW16 . . . . 171 C2
  Chiswick W4 . . . . 111 C2
  Edmonton N18 . . . . 33 B6
  Hampton TW12 . . . . 174 A5
  Mitcham CR4 . . . . 203 C5
  Roehampton SW19 . . . . . 156 B1
  Thornton Heath CR0 . . . . 205 A2
  Wandsworth SW18 . . . . . 158 B5
  W WandTd WTW16 . . . . . 171 C1
Windmill Rise KT2 . . . . . . 176 D3
Windmill Row SE11 . . . . . **261** A1
Windmill St
  Bloomsbury W1 . . . 93 D2 **239** C3
  Bushey WD23 . . . . 8 C3
Windmill Terr TW17 . . . . . 193 C2
Windmill Trad Est CR4 . . . 203 C5
Windmill Way HA4 . . . . 39 D1
Windmill Wlk SE1 . . . . . . **251** B2
Windmore Cl HA0 . . . . 65 A3
Windover Ave NW9 . . . . . . 45 B5
Windrose Cl SE16 . . . . . . 118 D4
Windrush KT3 . . . . 199 A5
Windrush Cl
  Battersea SW11 . . . . 136 B1
  Chiswick W4 . . . . 133 A5
  4 Hackney E8 . . . . 74 A1
  Ickenham UB10 . . . . 60 B4
  Tottenham N17 . . . . 33 C2
Windrush Ho NW10 . . . . . . 89 B6
Windrush La SE23 . . . . . . 162 D1
Windrush Prim Sch
  SE28 . . . . 124 B5
Windrush Rd NW10 . . . . . . 89 B6
Windrush Sq SW9 . . . . . . 138 C1
Windsock Cl **1** SE16 . . . 119 B2
Windsor Ave Cheam SM3 . 217 A5
  East Molesey KT8 . . . . . . 195 C6
  Edgware HA8 . . . . 10 D1
  Higham Hill E17 . . . . 35 A1
  Hillingdon UB10 . . . . 60 D1
  Merton SW19 . . . . 180 A2
  New Malden KT3 . . . . 199 A4
Windsor Cl
  Brentford W5 . . . . 131 B6
  Chislehurst BR7 . . . . 188 D5
  Harrow HA2 . . . . 63 C5
  Hendon N3 . . . . 29 A1
  Pinner HA6 . . . . 22 A1
  West Norwood SE27 . . . . 183 A6
Windsor Cres Harrow HA2 . 63 C5
  Wembley HA9 . . . . 66 D5
Windsor Ct
  Battersea SW11 . . . . 136 B3
  Bayswater W2 . . . . **245** A6
  Bickley BR1 . . . . 210 A6
  Bushey WD23 . . . . 8 A3
  Chelsea SW3 . . . . **257** B2
  2 Clapham SW4 . . . . . 137 C1
  Edgware HA8 . . . . 26 B3

Windsor Ct *continued*
  Friern Barnet N11 . . . . 30 D5
  Fulham SW6 . . . . 135 A2
  Northolt UB5 . . . . 63 B3
  Osidge N14 . . . . 15 C4
  20 Rotherhithe SE16 . . 118 D5
  South Norwood SE19 . . . 183 C2
  Sunbury TW16 . . . . 172 A3
  Temple Fortune NW11 . . . 47 A3
  Walthamstow E17 . . . . 53 B6
  4 Wandsworth SW18 . . 157 C4
  West Hampstead NW3 . . . 69 C4
  5 West Wickham BR4 . . 207 D1
Windsor Ctr The SE27 . . . 183 A6
Windsor Dr EN4 . . . . 14 D5
Windsor Gdns
  Hayes UB3 . . . . 105 B3
  Paddington W9 . . . . 91 C3
  Wallington CR0 . . . . 220 A5
Windsor Gr SE27 . . . . 183 A6
Windsor Hall **11** E16 . . . 121 B5
Windsor Ho
  4 Acton Green W4 . . . . 111 A1
  Brondesbury NW2 . . . . 69 A2
  4 Globe Town E2 . . . . . . 96 D4
  7 Hendon NW4 . . . . 28 D1
  7 Northolt UB5 . . . . 63 C2
  Queensbury NW9 . . . . 44 C5
  Regent's Pk NW1 . . . . . . **231** D2
  Shoreditch N1 . . . . **235** B4
  Stanmore HA7 . . . . 25 B3
  Stoke Newington N4 . . . . . 51 A1
Windsor Lo KT3 . . . . 199 A4
Windsor Mews
  Catford SE6 . . . . 164 A3
  Forest Hill SE23 . . . . 163 A6
Windsor Park Rd UB3 . . . 127 D5
Windsor Pl SW1 . . . . **259** B4
Windsor Rd
  Ashford TW16 . . . . 172 A4
  Barnet EN5 . . . . 12 D5
  Chingford E4 . . . . 35 D6
  Cranford TW4, TW5 . . . . 128 C3
  DA6 . . . . 147 A1
  Dagenham RM8 . . . . 81 A5
  Ealing W5 . . . . 110 A6
  Forest Gate E7 . . . . 77 C3
  Harrow HA3 . . . . 24 B2
  Hendon N3 . . . . 29 A1
  Ilford IG1 . . . . 79 A4
  Kingston u T KT2 . . . . 176 A3
  Leyton E10 . . . . 75 D6
  Palmers Green N13 . . . . . 16 C1
  Richmond TW9 . . . . 132 B3
  Southall UB2 . . . . 107 B3
  South Norwood CR7 . . . . 182 D1
  Teddington TW11 . . . . . . 174 B5
  Tottenham N17 . . . . 34 A1
  Upper Holloway N7 . . . . . . 72 A5
  Wanstead E11 . . . . 77 A6
  Willesden NW2 . . . . 68 B2
  Worcester Pk KT4 . . . . . . 216 A6
Windsor St N1 . . . . 96 D6 **234** D6
Windsor Terr N1 . . 95 A4 **235** B2
Windsor Way
  W14 . . . . 113 A2 **254** A4
Windsor Wharf E9 . . . . 75 B3
Windsor Wlk
  Camberwell SE5 . . . . 139 B3
  Walton-on-T KT12 . . . . . . 194 D1
Windspoint Dr SE15 . . . . . 140 B6
Windus Rd N16 . . . . 51 D1
Windus Wlk N16 . . . . 51 D1
Windy Ridge BR1 . . . . 188 A2
Windy Ridge Cl SW19 . . . 178 D5
Wine Cl E1 . . . . 118 C6
Wine Office Ct EC4 . . . . . **241** B2
Winery La KT1 . . . . 198 B6
Winey Cl KT9 . . . . 213 C1
Winfield Ho **3** SW11 . . . 136 B3
Winford Ct **18** SE15 . . . 140 A4
Winford Ho E3 . . . . 75 B1
Winford Par **6** UB1 . . . . . 85 D1
Winforton St SE10 . . . . . . 142 A4
Winfrith Rd SW18 . . . . . . 158 A3
Wingate Cres CR0 . . . . . . 204 A3
Wingate Ho
  26 Bromley E3 . . . . 97 D4
  8 Stoke Newington N16 . 73 B4
Wingate Rd
  Hammersmith W6 . . . . . . 112 B3
  Ilford IG1 . . . . 78 D3
  Sidcup DA14 . . . . 190 C4
Wingate Trad Est **17** N17 . 33 D3
Wingfield Ho
  5 Blackwall E14 . . . . . 120 B6
  Sidcup DA15 . . . . 167 D3
Wingfield Mews SE15 . . . 140 A2
Wingfield Prim Sch SE3 . 143 B2
Wingfield Rd
  Kingston u T KT2 . . . . 176 C4
  Leyton E15 . . . . 76 C4
  Walthamstow E17 . . . . 53 D4
Wingfield St SE15 . . . . . . 140 A2
Wingfield Way HA4 . . . . . . 62 B2
Wingford Rd SW2 . . . . . . 160 A5

Wingham **3** NW5 . . . . . . 71 A2
Wingham Ho **3** SE26 . . . 184 B5
Wingmore Rd SE24 . . . . . 139 A2
Wingrad Ho **1** E1 . . . . 96 C2
Wingrave SE17 . . . . **262** C3
Wingrave Rd W6 . . . . 134 C6
Wingreen **15** NW8 . . . . . . 91 D6
Wingrove Ho E4 . . . . 19 D4
Wingrove Rd SE6 . . . . 164 C2
Wings Cl SM1 . . . . 217 C4
Winicotte Ho W2 . . . . **236** D4
Winifred Cl EN5 . . . . 11 D5
Winifrede Paul Ho **7**
  NW5 . . . . 71 B4
Winifred Pl N12 . . . . 30 A5
Winifred Rd
  Dagenham RM8 . . . . 59 A1
  Hampton TW12 . . . . 173 C6
  Merton SW19 . . . . 179 C2
Winifred St E16 . . . . 122 B5
Winifred Terr Enfield EN1 . 17 D4
  15 Newham E13 . . . . . . 99 A5
Winkfield Rd Newham E13 . 99 B5
  Wood Green N22 . . . . 32 C2
Winkley Ct
  Cranley Gdns N10 . . . . . . 49 B5
  Harrow HA2 . . . . 63 C5
Winkley St **6** E2 . . . . . . 96 B5
Winkworth Cotts **14** E1 . 96 C3
Winlaton Rd BR1 . . . . 186 B6
Winmill Rd RM8 . . . . 81 B5
Winn Bridge Cl IG8 . . . . . . 37 D2
Winn Common Rd SE18 . 145 C6
Winnett St W1 . . . . **249** C6
Winningales Ct IG5 . . . . . . 56 A6
Winnings Wlk UB5 . . . . . . 63 A2
Winnington Cl N2 . . . . 48 B3
Winnington Ho
  19 Kensal Town W10 . . 91 A3
  8 SE5 . . . . 139 A5
Winnington Rd Enfield EN3 . 6 C6
Hampstead Garden Suburb
  N2 . . . . 48 B3
Winnipeg Dr **3** BR6 . . . . 227 D2
Winnipeg Ho W4 . . . . 84 B3
Winn Rd SE12 . . . . 165 B3
Winns Ave E17 . . . . 53 B6
Winns Mews N15 . . . . 51 C5
Winns Prim Sch E17 . . . . . 35 B1
Winns Terr E17 . . . . 53 C6
Winsbeach E17 . . . . 36 B1
Winscombe Cres W5 . . . . . 87 D3
Winscombe St N19 . . . . . . 71 B6
Winscombe Way HA7 . . . . 25 A5
Winsford Rd SE6 . . . . 163 B1
Winsford Terr N18 . . . . 33 B5
Winsham Gr SW11 . . . . . . 159 A6
Winsham Ho NW1 . . . . . . **232** D2
Winslade Ho **4** E8 . . . . . . 74 B6
Winslade Rd SW2 . . . . . . 160 A6
Winslade Way SE6 . . . . . . 163 D4
Winsland Mews W2 . . . . . **236** C2
Winsland St W2 . . . 92 B1 **236** C2
Winsley St W1 . . . . **239** B2
Winslow SE17 . . . . **263** A1
Winslow Cl
  2 Neasden NW10 . . . . . 67 C5
  Pinner HA5 . . . . 40 B3
Winslow Gr E4 . . . . 20 C2
Winslow Rd W6 . . . . 134 C6
Winslow Way TW13 . . . . . 151 A1
Winsmoor Ct EN2 . . . . 4 D2
Winsor Prim Sch E6 . . . . 100 C1
Winsor Terr E6 . . . . 100 C2
Winstanley Rd SW11 . . . . 136 B2
Winston Ave NW9 . . . . 45 C2
Winston Churchill Britain at
  War Experience* SE1 . **253** A3
Winston Cl Harrow HA3 . . . 24 D4
  Romford RM7 . . . . 59 D5
Winston Ct **7** BR1 . . . . . 187 B2
  Harrow HA3 . . . . 23 D3
Winston Ho WC1 . . . . **239** D6
Winston House Prep Sch
  E18 . . . . 37 A1
Winston Rd N16 . . . . 73 B4
Winston Way IG1 . . . . 79 A5
Winston Way Prim Sch
  IG1 . . . . 78 D5
Winston Wlk **2** W4 . . . . . 111 B2
Winter Ave E6 . . . . 100 A2
Winterberry Ct **22** N12 . . 29 D6
Winterborne Ave BR6 . . . 227 B5
Winterbourne Ho W11 . . **244** A6
Winterbourne Inf Sch
  CR7 . . . . 204 C5
Winterbourne Jun Boys' Sch
  CR7 . . . . 204 C5
Winterbourne Jun Girls' Sch
  CR7 . . . . 204 C5
Winterbourne Rd
  Dagenham RM8 . . . . 80 C6
  Forest Hill SE6 . . . . 163 B3
  Thornton Heath CR7 . . . . 204 C5
Winter Box Wlk TW10 . . . 154 B6
Winterbrook Rd SE24 . . . 161 A5

Winterburn Cl N11. . . . .**31** A4
Winterfold Cl SW19. . . . . .**157** A2
Wintergreen Cl **7** E6. . . .**100** A2
Winterleys **7** NW6. . . . .**91** B5
Winter Lo **17** SE16. . . . .**118** A1
Winter's Ct E4. . . . .**35** A4
Winterslow Ho **20** SE5. . .**139** A3
Winters Rd KT7. . . . .**197** B2
Winterstoke Gdns NW7. . .**28** A5
Winterstoke Rd SE6. . . . .**163** B3
Winterton Ct KT1. . . . . . .**176** C1
Winterton Ho **15** E1. . . . . . .**96** C1
Winterton Pl SW10. . . . . .**266** B6
Winterwell Rd SW2. . . . . .**160** A6
Winthorpe Rd SW15. . . . .**183** A4
Winthrop Ho **10** W12. . . . .**112** B6
Winthrop St E1. . . . .**96** B2
Winthrop Wlk HA9. . . . . . .**66** A5
Winton Ave N11. . . . .**31** C3
Winton Ct N9. . . . .**18** D4
Winton Ct **15** KT6. . . . . .**197** D2
Winton Gdns HA8. . . . .**26** B3
Winton Prim Sch
N1. . . . . **94** B5 **233** C3
Winton Rd BR6. . . . .**226** D4
Winton Way SW16. . . . . . .**182** C5
Wintour Ho HA9. . . . .**65** D6
Wirrall Ho **15** SE26. . . . . .**162** A1
Wirral Wood Cl BR7. . . . .**188** C4
Wisbeach Rd CR0. . . . . . .**205** B4
Wisbech **5** N4. . . . .**50** B1
Wisdom Ct **7** TW7. . . . . .**131** A2
Wisdom Sch **1** N15. . . . . . .**51** B5
Wisdons Cl RM7, RM9. . . . .**59** A3
Wise La NW7. . . . .**28** A4
Wiseman Ct **12** SE19. . . .**183** C5
Wiseman Rd E10. . . . .**75** C6
Wise Rd E15. . . . .**98** B6
Wiseton Rd SW17. . . . . . .**158** D3
Wishart Rd SE3. . . . .**143** D3
Wishaw Wlk N13. . . . .**32** A4
Wisley Ho SW1. . . . .**259** C2
Wisley Rd Balham SW11. .**159** A6
St Paul's Cray BR5. . . . . .**190** B3
Wistaria Cl BR6. . . . .**226** D6
Wisteria Cl Edgware NW7. .**27** D4
Ilford IG1. . . . .**78** D3
Wisteria Ho SE4. . . . .**141** A2
Wisteria Rd SE13. . . . . . .**142** B1
Wistow Ho **14** E2. . . . .**96** A6
Witanhurst La N6. . . . .**49** A1
Witan St E2. . . . .**96** B4
Witchwood Ho **10** SW9. .**138** C2
Witcombe Point **14**
SE15. . . . .**140** A4
Witechapel Sp Ctr E1. . . . .**96** C2
Witham Ct Leyton E10. . . . .**75** D5
Upper Tooting SW17. . . . .**158** D1
Witham Ho **34** SE5. . . . . .**139** A3
Witham Rd
Dagenham RM10. . . . .**81** C3
Ealing W13. . . . .**109** B5
Hounslow TW7. . . . .**130** B4
Penge SE20. . . . .**206** C6
Witherby Cl CR0. . . . .**221** C4
Witherington Rd N5. . . . . .**72** C3
Withers Cl KT9. . . . .**213** C2
Withers Mead NW9. . . . . . .**27** D2
Withers Pl EC1. . . . .**242** B6
Witherston Way SE9. . . . .**166** C1
Withington Rd N2. . . . .**30** C2
Withycombe Rd SW19. . .**156** D4
Withy Ho **4** E1. . . . .**96** D3
Withy La HA4. . . . .**39** A4
Withy Mead E4. . . . .**20** B1
Witley Cres CR0. . . . .**224** A2
Witley Ct Southall UB2. . .**107** B2
WC1. . . . .**240** A5
Witley Gdns UB2. . . . .**107** B2
Witley Ho **2** SW2. . . . . . .**160** B4
Witley Ind Est UB2. . . . . .**107** B2
Witley Point **8** SW15. . .**156** B3
Witley Rd N19. . . . .**71** C6
Witney Cl Ickenham UB10. .**60** B4
Pinner HA5. . . . .**23** B4
Witney Path SE23. . . . . . .**162** D1
Wittenham Way E4. . . . . . .**20** B1
Witten Ho KT3. . . . .**199** B1
Wittering Cl KT2. . . . .**175** D5
Wittering Ho **9** SW11. . .**136** D3
Wittersham Rd BR1. . . . . .**186** D5
Witts Ho KT2. . . . .**198** B6
Wivenhoe Cl SE15. . . . . . .**140** B2
Wivenhoe Ct TW4. . . . . . .**129** B1
Wivenhoe Rd IG11. . . . . . .**102** B5
Wiverton Rd SE26. . . . . . .**184** C5
Wixom Ho SE9. . . . .**143** C1
Wix Prim Sch SW4. . . . . .**137** B1
Wix Rd RM9. . . . .**102** D6
Wix's La SW4. . . . .**137** B1
Woburn W13. . . . .**87** B2
Woburn Cl Bushey WD23. . . .**8** A5
SE28. . . . .**102** D1
Wimbledon SW19. . . . . . .**180** A4
Woburn Ct
32 Bermondsey SE16. . . . .**118** B1

Woburn Ct continued
Croydon CR0. . . . .**205** A1
1 DA6. . . . .**147** A1
Richmond TW9. . . . .**132** B2
4 Woodford E18. . . . .**37** A1
Woburn Pl WC1. . . **94** A3 **240** A5
Woburn Rd
Carshalton SM5. . . . .**202** C1
Croydon CR0. . . . .**205** A1
Woburn Sq WC1. . . .**93** D3 **239** D5
Woburn Twr **14** UB5. . . . .**84** D4
Woburn Wlk WC1. . . . . . .**232** D1
Wodeham Gdns **1** E1. . . .**96** B2
Wodehouse Ave SE15. . .**139** D4
Wodehouse Ct **10** W3. . .**111** A3
Woffington Cl KT1, KT8. .**175** C2
Woking Cl SW15. . . . .**133** D1
Wolcot Ho NW1. . . . .**232** B3
Woldham Pl BR2. . . . .**209** C5
Woldham Rd BR2. . . . . . .**209** C5
Wolds Dr BR6. . . . .**226** C4
Wolfe Cl Hayes BR2. . . . .**209** A3
Yeading UB4. . . . .**84** B4
Wolfe Cres
Greenwich SE7. . . . .**121** D1
34 Rotherhithe SE16. . . .**118** D4
Wolfe Ho **19** W12. . . . . . .**112** B6
Wolferton Rd E12. . . . .**78** B4
Wolffe Gdns **2** E15. . . . . .**76** D2
Wolf Fields Prim Sch
UB2. . . . .**107** B2
Wolfington Rd SE27. . . . .**182** D6
Wolfram Cl SE13. . . . . . .**164** C6
Wolfson Ct **4** Barnet EN4. .**14** D3
Golders Green NW11. . . . .**47** A2
SE1. . . . .**253** D2
Wolfson Hillel Prim Sch
N14. . . . .**15** D5
Wolftencroft Cl SW11. . .**136** B2
Wollaston Cl SE1. . . . . . .**262** A4
Wollotan Ho N1. . . . .**234** B4
Wolmer Cl HA8. . . . .**26** D6
Wolmer Gdns HA8. . . . . . .**10** C1
Wolmer Rd HA8. . . . .**26** D6
Wolseley Ave SW18,
SW19. . . . .**157** C2
Wolseley Gdns W4. . . . . .**132** D6
Wolseley Rd Acton W4. . .**111** A2
Carshalton CR4. . . . .**203** A2
Harrow HA3. . . . .**42** C6
Hornsey N8. . . . .**49** D4
Upton E7. . . . .**77** B1
Wood Green N22. . . . .**32** B2
Wolseley St SE1. . **117** D4 **253** D1
Wolsey Ave
Thames Ditton KT7. . . . .**196** D4
Wallend E6. . . . .**100** C4
Walthamstow E17. . . . .**53** B6
Wolsey Cl Isleworth TW3. .**130** A1
Kingston u T KT2. . . . . . .**176** D2
Southall UB2. . . . .**108** A3
Wimbledon SW20. . . . . . .**178** B3
Worcester Pk KT19, KT4. .**216** A4
Wolsey Cres SM4. . . . . . .**201** B2
Wolsey Ct Bromley BR1. .**186** D3
SE9. . . . .**166** B5
South Hampstead NW6. . .**70** A1
Wolsey Dr
Kingston u T KT2. . . . . . .**176** A4
Walton-on-T KT12. . . . . .**194** D1
Wolsey Gr HA8. . . . .**27** B3
Wolsey Ho
2 Hampton TW12. . . . . .**173** D4
3 Kentish Town NW5. . . .**71** D2
Wolsey Inf Sch CR0. . . . .**224** A1
Wolsey Jun Sch CR0. . . .**224** A1
Wolsey Mews
Kentish Town NW5. . . . . .**71** C2
Orpington BR6. . . . .**227** D3
Wolsey Rd Ashford TW15. .**170** B6
East Molesey KT8. . . . . .**196** B5
Enfield EN1. . . . .**6** B3
Hampton TW12. . . . .**174** A4
Stoke Newington N1. . . . .**73** B3
Sunbury Comm TW16. . . .**171** D4
Wolsey St E1. . . . .**96** C2
Wolsey Way KT9. . . . .**214** C3
Wolstenholme HA7. . . . . .**25** B5
Wolstonbury N12. . . . .**29** C5
Wolvercote Rd SE2. . . . . .**124** D4
Wolverley St E2. . . . .**96** B4
Wolverton Ave SE17. . . . .**263** A2
Wolverton Ave KT2. . . . . .**176** C2
Wolverton Gdns
Brook Green W6. . . . .**112** D2
Ealing W5. . . . .**110** B6
Wolverton Mans W5. . . . .**110** B5
Wolverton Rd HA7. . . . . . .**25** B3
Wolverton Way N14. . . . . .**15** C6
Wolves La N22. . . . .**32** C4
Womersley Rd N4, N8. . . . .**50** B3
Wonford Cl KT2, KT3. . . .**177** C2
Wontner Cl **5** N1. . . . .**73** A1
Wontner Rd SW12, SW17. .**158** D2
Wooburn Cl UB8. . . . .**82** D3
Wooburn Ct N14. . . . .**15** D3
Woodall Cl
Chessington KT9. . . . . . .**213** D2
15 Poplar E14. . . . .**119** D6

Woodall Ho TW7. . . . .**130** D2
Woodall Rd EN3. . . . .**18** D5
Woodbank Rd BR1. . . . . .**164** D1
Woodbastwick Rd SE26. .**185** A5
Woodberry Ave
Edmonton N21. . . . .**16** D2
Harrow HA2. . . . .**42** A5
Woodberry Cl
Ashford TW16. . . . .**172** A4
Mill Hill NW7. . . . .**28** D3
Woodberry Cres N10. . . . .**49** B6
Woodberry Down N4. . . . .**51** A2
Woodberry Down Com Prim
Sch N4. . . . .**51** A2
Woodberry Gdns N12. . . . .**30** A4
Woodberry Gr
Finchley N12. . . . .**30** A4
Stoke Newington N4. . . . . .**51** A2
Woodberry View N6. . . . . .**49** A3
Woodberry Way
Chingford E4. . . . .**20** A4
Finchley N12. . . . .**30** A4
Woodbine Cl TW2. . . . . . .**152** B2
Woodbine Gr Enfield EN2. . .**5** B5
Penge SE20. . . . .**184** B3
Woodbine La KT4. . . . . . .**216** C5
Woodbine Pl E11. . . . .**55** A3
Woodbine Rd DA15. . . . . .**167** C3
Woodbines Ave KT1. . . . .**197** D6
Woodbine Terr E9. . . . . . .**74** C2
Woodborough Rd SW15. .**134** B1
Woodbourne Ave SW16. .**159** B1
Woodbourne Cl SW16. . . .**160** A1
Woodbourne Dr KT10. . . .**212** D2
Woodbourne Gdns SM6. .**219** B1
Woodbridge Cl
4 Dollis Hill NW2. . . . . . .**68** A5
10 Finsbury Pk N7. . . . . .**72** B6
Woodbridge Ct
Forest Gate E7. . . . .**77** D3
Stoke Newington N16. . . .**73** B5
Woodbridge High Sch
IG8. . . . .**37** B3
Woodbridge Ho E11. . . . . .**54** D1
Woodbridge Rd IG11. . . . .**79** D3
Woodbridge St
EC1. . . . . **94** D3 **241** C6
Woodbrook Rd SE2. . . . .**146** B2
Woodburn Cl NW4. . . . . . .**46** D4
Woodbury Cl
Croydon CR0. . . . .**221** D6
Wanstead E11. . . . .**55** B5
Woodbury Ct **1** W13. . . . .**87** B3
Woodbury Gdns
Bromley SE12. . . . .**187** B6
Eltham SE12. . . . .**165** B1
Woodbury Ho **4** SE26. . .**162** B1
Woodbury Park Rd W13. . .**87** B3
Woodbury Rd E17. . . . .**53** D5
Woodbury St SW17. . . . .**180** C5
Woodchester Sq W2. . . . . .**91** B2
Woodchurch Cl DA14. . . .**167** B1
Woodchurch Dr BR1. . . . .**187** D3
Woodchurch Ho **15**
SW9. . . . .**138** C4
Woodchurch Rd NW6. . . . .**69** D1
Wood Cl Bethnal Green E2. . .**96** A3
Harrow HA1. . . . .**42** B2
Kingsbury NW9. . . . .**45** B2
Woodclyffe Dr BR7. . . . . .**188** C1
Woodcock Ct HA3. . . . .**44** A2
Woodcock Dell Ave HA3. . .**43** D2
Woodcock Hill HA3. . . . . . .**43** C3
Woodcock Ho **4** E14. . . . .**97** C2
Woodcocks E16. . . . .**99** D2
Woodcombe Cres SE23. .**162** C3
Woodcote Ave
Mill Hill NW7. . . . .**28** C4
Thornton Heath CR7. . . .**204** D5
Wallington SM6. . . . .**219** B1
Woodcote Cl Enfield N9. . .**18** C5
Kingston u T KT2. . . . . . .**176** B5
Woodcote Ct **14** SM6. . .**219** B2
Woodcote Ho **4** SE8. . . .**141** B6
Woodcote Mews
Loughton IG10. . . . .**21** D4
Wallington SM6. . . . .**219** B2
Woodcote Pl **1** SE27. . . .**182** D5
Woodcote Rd
Wallington SM6. . . . .**219** C1
Wanstead E11. . . . .**55** A2
Woodcott Ho **1** SW15. . .**156** A4
Woodcroft SE9. . . . .**166** B1
South Croydon CR0. . . . .**221** C5
Southgate N21. . . . .**16** C3
17 Stanmore HA7. . . . . . .**25** C5
Wembley UB6. . . . .**65** A2
Woodcroft Ave
Edgware NW7. . . . .**27** C4
Stanmore HA7. . . . .**25** A2
Woodcroft Cres UB10. . . . .**82** D6
Woodcroft Mews SE8. . . .**119** A2
Woodcroft Prim Sch HA8. .**27** C3
Woodcroft Rd CR7. . . . . .**204** D3
Wood Dene **6** SE15. . . . .**140** B4
Wood Dr BR7. . . . .**188** A4
Woodedge Cl E4. . . . .**20** D3
Woodend
South Norwood SE19. . . .**183** A4

Woodend continued
Sutton SM1. . . . .**218** A6
Thames Ditton KT10. . . .**212** A6
WOOD END. **83** D1
Wood End UB3. . . . .**83** C1
Wood End Ave HA2. . . . . . .**64** A4
Wood End Cl UB5. . . . .**64** B3
Woodend Gdns EN2. . . . . . .**4** A1
Wood End Gdns UB5. . . . .**64** A3
WOOD END GREEN. **83** C2
Wood End Green Rd UB3. .**83** C1
Wood End Inf Sch UB5. . . .**64** B3
Wood End Jun Sch UB6. . .**64** B3
Wood End La UB5. . . . .**63** D3
Wood End Park Com Sch
UB3. . . . .**105** A6
Woodend Rd E17. . . . .**36** A1
Wood End Rd HA1, UB5. . .**64** B4
Wood End Way HA3. . . . . .**64** A3
Wooder Gdns E7. . . . .**77** A4
Wooderson Cl SE19. . . . .**205** C5
Wooderson Ct **9** BR3. . .**185** C2
Woodfall Ave EN5. . . . .**13** B6
Woodfall Rd N4. . . . .**72** C6
Woodfall St SW3. . . . . . .**257** C1
Woodfarrs SE5. . . . .**139** B1
Woodfield SW16. . . . .**182** B2
Wood Field NW3. . . . .**70** D3
Woodfield Ave
Colindale NW9. . . . .**45** C5
Ealing W5. . . . .**87** C3
Streatham SW16. . . . . . .**159** D1
Wallington SM5. . . . .**219** A1
Wembley HA0. . . . .**65** C5
Woodfield Cl
1 Enfield EN1. . . . .**5** C1
South Norwood SE19. . . .**183** A3
Woodfield Cres W5. . . . . . .**87** D3
Woodfield Cl SW16. . . . . .**159** D1
Woodfield Dr EN4. . . . .**15** A3
Woodfield Gdns KT3. . . . .**199** D4
Woodfield Gr SW16. . . . . .**159** D1
Woodfield Ho
11 Forest Hill SE23. . . .**162** D1
Hinchley Wood KT7. . . . .**212** D6
New Malden KT3. . . . . . .**199** D4
6 Upper Clapton E5. . . . .**74** B6
Wood Green N11. . . . .**31** D4
Woodfield La SW16. . . . . .**159** D1
Woodfield Pl W9. . . . .**91** B3
Woodfield Rd
Cranford TW4, TW5. . . . .**128** B3
Ealing W5. . . . .**87** C3
Hinchley Wood KT10, KT7. .**212** D6
Kensal Town W9. . . . .**91** B2
Woodfield Rise WD23. . . . .**8** B7
Woodfield Sch NW9. . . . . .**45** C1
Woodfields Ct SM1. . . . . .**218** A5
Woodfield Way N11. . . . . . .**31** D3
WOODFORD. **37** D5
Woodford Ave IG2, IG4, IG5,
IG8. . . . .**56** B5
Woodford Bridge Rd IG4. .**56** A5
Woodford Cres HA5. . . . . .**22** B1
Woodford Ct **12** W12. . . .**112** D4
Woodford Cty High Sch for
Girls IG8. . . . .**36** D4
Woodforde Ct UB3. . . . . .**105** B1
WOODFORD GREEN. **37** B3
Woodford Green Prep Sch
IG8. . . . .**37** A4
Woodford Green Sch
IG8. . . . .**36** D5
Woodford Ho **13** SE18. . .**144** D6
5 Wanstead E18. . . . . . .**55** A5
Woodford New Rd
Upper Walthamstow E17. . .**54** C6
Woodford E18. . . . .**36** D3
Woodford Pl HA9. . . . .**44** A1
Woodford Rd
Forest Gate E7. . . . .**77** B4
Wanstead E18. . . . .**55** A6
Woodford Sta IG8. . . . .**37** B4
Woodford Trad Est IG8. . . .**37** D1
WOODFORD WELLS. **21** B1
Woodgate Ave KT9. . . . . .**213** D3
Woodgate Cres HA6. . . . . .**22** A4
Woodgate Dr SW16. . . . .**181** D3
Woodgate Ho **12** KT6. . .**198** A3
Woodger Rd W12. . . . . . .**112** C4
Woodget Cl E6. . . . .**100** A1
Woodglen SM4. . . . .**202** C4
Woodgrange Ave
Ealing W5. . . . .**110** C5
Enfield EN1. . . . .**18** A5
Finchley N12. . . . .**30** B4
Harrow HA3. . . . .**43** D4
Woodgrange Cl HA3. . . . . .**43** D4
Woodgrange Ct **1** BR2. .**208** D1
Woodgrange Gdns EN1. . .**18** A5
Woodgrange Ho W5. . . . .**110** D5
Woodgrange Inf Sch E7. . .**77** B4
Woodgrange Mans HA3. . .**43** C4
Woodgrange Park Sta
E12. . . . .**77** D3
Woodgrange Rd E7. . . . . . .**77** A3
Woodgrange Terr EN1. . . .**18** A5
WOOD GREEN. **32** B2
Wood Green Sh City N22. .**32** C1
Wood Green Sta N22. . . . .**32** C1

Woodhall NW1. . . . .**232** A1
Woodhall Ave
Dulwich SE21. . . . .**161** C1
Pinner HA5. . . . .**23** A2
Woodhall Dr
Dulwich SE21. . . . .**161** D1
Pinner HA5. . . . .**23** A2
Woodhall Gate HA5. . . . . .**22** D3
Woodhall Ho SW18. . . . . .**158** B5
Woodhall La WD19. . . . . . .**23** A6
Woodhall Rd HA5. . . . .**22** D4
Woodhall Sch WD19. . . . . .**23** A6
Woodham Ct E11. . . . .**54** D5
Woodham Rd SE6. . . . . . .**164** A1
Woodhatch Cl **16** E6. . . .**100** A2
Woodhaven Gdns IG6. . . . .**57** A5
Woodhayes BR7. . . . .**188** D4
Woodhayes Rd SW19,
SW20. . . . .**178** C4
Woodhead Dr BR6. . . . . .**227** C6
Woodheyes Rd NW10. . . . .**67** C3
Woodhill SE7, SE18. . . . .**122** A4
Woodhill Cres HA3. . . . . . .**43** D3
Woodhill Prim Sch
SE18. . . . .**122** A2
Wood Ho
4 Clapham SW4. . . . . .**137** D3
6 Paddington NW6. . . . . .**91** B5
Woodhouse Ave UB6. . . . .**86** D5
Woodhouse Cl
Hayes UB3. . . . .**105** C3
Wembley UB6. . . . .**86** A5
Woodhouse Coll N12. . . . .**30** B4
Woodhouse Eaves HA6. . .**22** A5
Woodhouse Gr E12. . . . . . .**78** A2
Woodhouse Rd
Colney Hatch N12. . . . . . .**30** C4
Leyton E11. . . . .**76** D5
Woodhurst Ave BR5. . . . .**211** A3
Woodhurst Rd Acton W3. .**111** A6
SE2. . . . .**124** A2
Woodington Cl SE9. . . . . .**166** C5
Woodison St E3. . . . .**97** A3
Woodknoll Dr BR7. . . . . .**188** B2
Wood La Dagenham RM10. .**81** A5
Highgate N6. . . . .**49** B3
Hounslow TW7. . . . .**130** D5
Kingsbury NW9. . . . .**45** B2
Ruislip HA4. . . . .**61** C6
Shepherd's Bush W12. . .**112** C6
Stanmore HA7. . . . .**9** B2
Woodford IG8. . . . .**36** D5
Woodland App UB6. . . . . . .**65** A2
Woodland Cl
Kingsbury NW9. . . . .**45** A3
Uxbridge UB10. . . . .**60** D6
West Ewell KT19. . . . . . .**215** C2
West Norwood SE19. . . .**183** C4
Woodford IG8. . . . .**21** B1
Woodland Cres
18 Rotherhithe SE16. . .**118** D4
SE10. . . . .**142** C6
Woodland Ct
Cheam SM1. . . . .**217** C2
Temple Fortune NW4. . . .**47** A4
13 Wanstead E11. . . . . . .**55** A4
Woodland Gdns
Cranley Gdns N10. . . . . . .**49** B4
Isleworth TW7. . . . .**130** C2
Woodland Gr SE10. . . . . .**120** C1
Woodland Hill SE19. . . . .**183** C4
Woodland Hts SE3. . . . . .**142** C6
Woodland Rd
Chingford E4. . . . .**20** A3
Friern Barnet N11. . . . . . .**31** B5
Penge SE19. . . . .**183** C4
Thornton Heath CR7. . . .**204** C5
Woodland Rise
Cranley Gdns N10. . . . . . .**49** B5
Wembley UB6. . . . .**65** A4
WOODLANDS. **130** C2
Woodlands
Beckenham BR3. . . . . . .**185** B3
Bexley DA6. . . . .**169** D6
Clapham SW4. . . . .**137** B1
Finchley N12. . . . .**30** A4
Harrow HA2. . . . .**41** C5
Temple Fortune NW11. . . .**47** A4
Walthamstow E11. . . . . . .**54** B2
West Barnes SW20. . . . .**200** D5
Woodlands Ave
Acton W3. . . . .**110** D5
DA15. . . . .**167** C3
Dagenham RM6. . . . .**59** A2
Finchley N3. . . . .**30** A2
Kingston u T KT3. . . . . . .**177** B2
Ruislip HA4. . . . .**40** D2
Wanstead E11. . . . .**55** B1
Worcester Pk KT4. . . . . .**216** A6
Woodlands Cl BR1. . . . . .**188** B1
Claygate KT10. . . . .**212** D1
Temple Fortune NW11. . . .**47** A4
Woodlands Ct
9 Bromley BR1. . . . . . .**186** D2
Brondesbury Pk NW10. . . .**90** B4
Dulwich SE22. . . . .**162** B4
Southall UB1. . . . .**107** C6
Woodlands Dr
Harrow HA7. . . . .**24** D4

Woodlands Dr *continued*
Sunbury TW16 . . . . **172** C1
Woodlands Fst & Mid Sch
HA8 . . . . **26** B2
Woodlands Gdns E17 . . . . **54** C5
Woodlands Gr TW7 . . . . . . **130** C3
Woodlands Gt SW15 . . . . . **157** B6
Woodlands Jun & Inf Schs
IG1 . . . . **79** B3
Woodlands Par TW15 . . . . **171** A4
Woodlands Park Rd
SE10 . . . . **142** C6
Tottenham N15. . . . . **51** A4
Woodlands Rd
Barnes SW13 . . . . **133** D2
Bexleyheath DA7 . . . . **147** A2
Bickley BR1. . . . . **188** B1
Enfield EN2. . . . . **5** B4
Harrow HA1 . . . . **42** D4
Ilford IG1 . . . . **79** A5
Isleworth TW7 . . . . **130** C3
Lower Edmonton N9. . . . . **18** C3
Southall UB1. . . . . **106** D5
Surbiton KT6. . . . . **197** D2
Walthamstow E17 . . . . . . **54** A6
Woodlands St SE13 . . . . . **164** B4
Woodland St **2** E8. . . . . **73** D2
Woodlands The
East Barnet N14. . . . . **15** B3
Harrow HA1 . . . . **64** C6
Highbury N5 . . . . **73** A4
12 Hornsey N8 . . . . **50** A2
Isleworth TW7 . . . . **130** D3
Lewisham SE13 . . . . **164** B4
Mitcham CR4 . . . . **203** A6
South Norwood SE19 . . . **183** A3
Stanmore HA7 . . . . **25** B5
Thames Ditton KT10 . . . . **212** A6
Woodlands Way SW15 . . . **157** B6
Woodland Terr SE7. . . . . . **122** A2
Woodland Way
Abbey Wood SE2. . . . . . . **124** D2
Croydon CR0. . . . . **207** A1
Edgware NW7 . . . . **27** D4
Merton SM4 . . . . **201** B5
Mitcham CR4 . . . . **181** A3
Petts Wood BR5 . . . . **211** A4
Southgate N21 . . . . **16** C2
Tolworth KT5 . . . . **214** D6
West Wickham BR4 . . . . . **224** A5
Woodford IG8. . . . . **21** B1
Woodland Wlk
Chessington KT19 . . . . . . **214** C2
9 Greenwich SE10 . . . . **120** C1
Hampstead NW3 . . . . **70** C3
Wood Lane High Sch
W12 . . . . **90** B1
Wood Lane Sta W12 . . . . **112** C6
Wood La Sp Ctr RM8 . . . . **59** D1
Wood La Sta W12 . . . . . . **112** C6
Woodlawn CI SW15 . . . . . **157** B6
Woodlawn Cres TW2 . . . . **151** D2
Woodlawn Dr TW13 . . . . . **150** D2
Woodlawn Rd SW6 . . . . . **134** D4
Woodlea Dr BR2 . . . . **208** C4
Woodlea Lo EN1 . . . . **17** C5
Woodlea Rd N16. . . . . **73** C5
Woodleigh
1 Kingston u T KT5 . . . . **198** B4
3 Woodleigh E18 . . . . . . **37** A2
Woodleigh Ave N12. . . . . **30** C4
Woodleigh Ct N22 . . . . . . **32** B2
Woodleigh Gdns SW16 . . **160** A2
Woodley CI SW17 . . . . . . **180** D3
Woodley La SM1, SM5. . . **218** C5
Woodlodge **4** Gdns BR1. **188** A3
Wood Lodge La BR4. . . . . **224** A5
Woodman La E4 . . . . **20** C6
Woodman Mews W9 . . . . **132** D4
Woodman Par **4** E16 . . . . **122** C5
Woodmans Ct HA7. . . . . . **44** A6
Woodmans Gr NW10. . . . . **67** D3
Woodmans Mews W12. . . **90** B2
Woodman St E16 . . . . **122** C5
Woodmansterne Prim Sch
SW16 . . . . **181** D2
Woodmansterne Rd
Mitcham SW16 . . . . **181** D2
Sutton SM5. . . . . **218** C1
Wood Mead N17. . . . . **34** A4
Woodmere SE9 . . . . **166** B3
Woodmere Ave CR0. . . . . **206** D2
Woodmere CI
11 Clapham SW11 . . . . . **137** A4
Croydon CR0. . . . . **206** D2
Woodmere Ct N14. . . . . . . **15** B4
Woodmere Gdns CR0. . . . **206** D2
Woodmere Way BR3. . . . . **208** B4
Woodmill Rd E5 . . . . **74** C6
Woodnook Rd SW16 . . . . **181** B5
Woodpecker CI
Bushey WD23 . . . . **8** A3
Enfield N9. . . . . **18** B5
Harrow HA3 . . . . **24** D2
Woodpecker Ct TW2 . . . . **151** D4
Woodpecker Ho E17 . . . . **53** C6
Woodpecker Mews
SE13 . . . . **142** B1

Woodpecker Rd
6 SE14 . . . . **141** A6
Woolwich SE28. . . . . **124** C6
Wood Point **8** E16. . . . . **99** A2
Woodquest Ave SE24. . . . **161** A6
Wood Rd Littleton TW17 . . **192** C5
Willesden NW10. . . . . **67** A1
Wood Retreat SE18 . . . . . **145** B5
Wood Ride Barnet EN4 . . . **2** B4
Orpington BR5 . . . . **211** C5
Woodridge CI EN2 . . . . . . **4** C4
Woodridge Prim Sch
N12. . . . . **13** C1
Woodridings Ave HA5 . . . **23** B2
Woodridings CI HA5 . . . . . **23** B3
Woodridings Ct N22 . . . . **31** D2
Woodriffe Rd E11. . . . . . . **54** B2
Wood Rise HA5 . . . . **40** A4
Woodrow SE18 . . . . **122** B2
Woodrow Ave UB4 . . . . . . **83** D3
Woodrow CI UB6. . . . . **65** B1
Woodrow Ct **3** N17. . . . . **34** B3
Woodruff Ho E12 . . . . **160** C5
Woodrush CI **4** SE14 . . . **141** A5
Woodrush Way RM6 . . . . **58** D5
Woodseer St E1 . . . . **96** A2
Woodsford SE17 . . . . **262** C1
Woodsford Sq
W14. . . . . **113** A4 **244** B2
Woodshire Rd RM10 . . . . **81** D5
Woods Ho SW8 . . . . **269** A2
WOODSIDE **206** A4
Woodside
Buckhurst Hill IG9 . . . . . . **21** C2
Hampstead Garden Suburb
NW11. . . . . **47** C4
Muswell Hill N10. . . . . **49** A6
Walton-on-T KT12 . . . . . **194** A1
Wimbledon SW19. . . . . . . **179** B5
Woodside Ave
Chislehurst BR7 . . . . **189** A5
Croydon SE25. . . . . **206** B4
Fortis Green N6 . . . . **48** D5
North Finchley N12. . . . . . **30** A6
Thames Ditton KT10 . . . . **196** C2
Wembley HA0. . . . . **88** A6
Woodside CI Ruislip HA4 . . **39** A5
Stanmore HA7 . . . . **25** B5
Tolworth KT5 . . . . **199** A2
Wembley HA0. . . . . **88** A6
Woodside Court Rd CR0. . **206** A2
Woodside Cres DA15. . . . **167** C1
Woodside Ct Ealing W5 . . **110** A5
Enfield EN2. . . . . **4** D4
10 Finchley N12. . . . . . . **29** D6
Palmers Green N13 . . . . . **16** C1
Wanstead E12 . . . . **55** C1
Woodside End HA0 . . . . . **88** A6
Woodside Gdns
Chingford E4. . . . . **35** D4
Tottenham N17. . . . . **33** D1
Woodside Gn SE25. . . . . **206** A3
Woodside Gr N12 . . . . **14** A1
Woodside Grange Rd
N12. . . . . **29** D6
Woodside High Sch N22 . . **32** D3
Woodside Ho SW19 . . . . . **179** B4
Woodside Jun & Inf Sch
CR0. . . . . **206** A2
Woodside La DA5. . . . . . . **168** D5
Whetstone N12. . . . . **14** A1
WOODSIDE PARK **29** C6
Woodside Park Ave E17 . . **54** B5
Woodside Park Rd N12. . . **30** A6
Woodside Pk SE25. . . . . . **206** B3
Woodside Pk Sta N12 . . . **29** D6
Woodside PI HA0 . . . . **88** A6
Woodside Prim Sch E17. . **54** A6
Woodside Rd BR1. . . . . . . **210** A4
Coombe KT3 . . . . **177** C1
Croydon SE25. . . . . **206** B3
Kingston u T KT2. . . . . . . **176** A3
Newham E13 . . . . **99** C3
Northwood HA6 . . . . **22** A3
Sidcup DA15. . . . . **167** C1
Sutton SM1. . . . . **218** A5
Woodford IG8. . . . . **37** A6
Wood Green N22 . . . . **32** C3
Woodside Sch DA17 . . . . **125** D2
Woodside Sta SE25 . . . . . **206** B3
Woodside Way
Croydon CR0. . . . . **206** C3
Streatham CR4 . . . . **181** C2
Wood's Mews
W1. . . . . **115** A6 **248** A6
Woodsome Rd NW5. . . . . **71** B5
Wood's PI SE1. . . . . **263** B5
Woodspring Rd SW19. . . . **157** A2
Wood's Rd SE15 . . . . **140** B4
Wood St Barnet EN5 . . . . **1** A1
Carshalton CR4. . . . . **203** A2
Chiswick W4 . . . . **111** C1
City of London EC2 . . **95** A1 **242** B2
Custom Ho E16. . . . . **121** B4
Kingston u T KT1. . . . . . . **175** D1
Kingston u T KT2. . . . . . . **176** A2
Walthamstow E17 . . . . . . **54** B5
Woodstar Ho **3** SE15 . . . **140** A5
Woodstead Gr HA8. . . . . . **26** A4
Woods The Eastbury HA6 . . **22** A5

Woods The *continued*
Uxbridge UB10 . . . . **60** D4
Woodstock Ave
Brentford W13 . . . . **109** A3
Cheam SM3 . . . . **201** B2
Golders Green NW11. . . . **47** A2
Isleworth TW7 . . . . **153** A6
Southall UB1. . . . . **85** B4
Woodstock CI DA5. . . . . . **169** B3
Stanmore HA7 . . . . **26** A1
Woodstock Cres N9. . . . . **18** B5
Woodstock Ct
Kingston u T KT2. . . . . . . **176** D1
Lee SE12. . . . . **165** A5
Vauxhall SE11. . . . . **260** D2
Woodstock Dr UB10. . . . . **60** B4
Woodstock Gdns
Beckenham BR3. . . . . **185** D3
Hayes UB4 . . . . **83** D2
Ilford IG3 . . . . **80** A6
Woodstock Gr W12 . . . . . **112** D4
Woodstock Grange W5 . . **110** A5
Woodstock Ho Hayes UB3. . **83** B2
2 Highbury N5 . . . . **73** A4
Woodstock Lane N KT6. . . **213** C6
Woodstock Lane S KT6, KT9,
KT10. . . . . **213** C4
Woodstock Mews W1. . . . **238** B3
Woodstock Rd
Bedford Pk W4 . . . . **111** C3
Bushey WD23 . . . . **8** D4
Chingford E17. . . . . **36** B1
Finsbury Pk N4 . . . . **50** C1
Golders Green NW11. . . . **47** B1
South Croydon CR0. . . . . **221** B5
Upton E7. . . . . **77** C1
Wallington SM5, SM6. . . **219** A3
Wembley HA0. . . . . **66** B1
Woodstock Rise SM3. . . . **201** B2
Woodstock St W1. . . . . . . **238** C1
Woodstock Studios **17**
W12. . . . . **112** D4
Woodstock Terr E14. . . . . **119** D6
Woodstock The SM3 . . . . **201** B2
Woodstock Way CR4 . . . . **181** C1
Woodstone Ave KT17,
KT4 . . . . **216** A3
Wood Street Sta E17. . . . **54** B5
Woodsyre SE26 . . . . **183** D6
Woodthorpe Rd
Ashford TW15. . . . . **170** A6
Putney SW15 . . . . **134** B1
Woodtree CI NW4. . . . . . . **28** C1
Wood Vale
Cranley Gdns N10. . . . . . . **49** C4
Dulwich SE22 . . . . **162** B4
Woodvale Ave SE25 . . . . **183** D1
Woodvale Ct BR1. . . . . . . **187** B1
South Norwood SE25. . . . **205** D6
Woodvale Way NW11 . . . . **68** D5
Woodvale Wlk SE27. . . . . **183** A5
Woodview Ave E4. . . . . . . **36** A6
Woodview CI
Finsbury Pk N4 . . . . **50** D2
Kingston u T SW15 . . . . . **177** B6
Orpington BR6 . . . . **227** A6
Woodville CI SE12 . . . . . . **165** A6
Teddington TW11 . . . . **175** A6
Woodville Ct
3 Lewisham SE10 . . . . . **142** A4
Southgate N14 . . . . **15** C6
Woodville Gdns
Ealing W5 . . . . **88** A1
Hendon NW11 . . . . **46** D2
Ilford IG6 . . . . **56** D5
Ruislip HA4 . . . . **39** A2
Surbiton KT6. . . . . **197** D2
Woodville Gr **2** DA16 . . . **146** A2
Woodville Ho SE1. . . . . . . **263** C6
Sutton SM3. . . . . **217** D4
Woodville Rd Barnet EN5. . **1** D2
Ealing W5 . . . . **87** D1
Golders Green NW11. . . . **47** A2
Leytonstone E11. . . . . **54** D1
Morden SM4. . . . . **201** C5
Paddington NW6 . . . . **91** B5
Richmond TW10 . . . . **153** C1
South Norwood CR7. . . . . **205** B6
Stoke Newington N16. . . . **73** C3
Walthamstow E17 . . . . . . **53** B5
Woodford E18. . . . . **37** B1
Woodville St **18** SE18. . . . **122** A2
Woodville The W5 . . . . . . **87** D1
Woodward Ave NW4 . . . . **46** A4
Woodward CI KT10. . . . . . **212** D2
Woodwarde Rd SE22. . . . **161** C5
Woodward Gdns
Dagenham RM9 . . . . **80** C1
Harrow HA7 . . . . **24** D3
Woodward Rd RM9 . . . . . **80** C1
Wood Way BR6 . . . . **226** C6
Woodway Cres HA1. . . . . **43** A3
Woodwell St SW18. . . . . . **158** A6
Wood Wharf SE10. . . . . . **142** A6
Woodyard CI NW5. . . . . . **71** A3
Woodyard La SE21 . . . . . . **161** C4
Woodyates Rd SE12. . . . . **165** B6
Woolacombe Rd SE3. . . . **143** C3
Woolacombe Way UB3. . . **105** C2

Woolands Rd E11. . . . . . . **76** C6
Woolcombes Ct **4**
SE16 . . . . **118** D5
Woolden Ho **2** E4. . . . . . **20** C4
Wooler St SE17. . . . **117** B1 **262** D2
Woolf CI SE28 . . . . **124** B5
Woolf Ct **7** W3 . . . . **111** A3
Woolf Mews WC1. . . . . . . **240** A6
Woollaston Rd N4 . . . . . . **50** D3
Woolley Ho SW9 . . . . **138** D2
Woollon Ho **1** E1. . . . . . . **96** C1
Woolmead Ave NW9 . . . . **46** A2
Woolmer Gdns N18. . . . . . **34** A5
Woolmer Ho **2** E5. . . . . . **74** B6
Woolmer Rd N18 . . . . **34** A5
Woolmore Prim Sch **14**
E14. . . . . **120** A6
Woolmore St E14. . . . . . . **120** A6
Woolneigh St SW6. . . . . . **135** D3
Woolpack Ho **1** E9 . . . . . **74** C2
Wool Rd SW20. . . . . **178** B4
Woolridge CI TW14 . . . . . **149** A3
Woolridge Way E9 . . . . . . **74** C1
Woolstaplers Way SE16 . . **118** A2
Woolston CI E17. . . . . **34** D6
Woolstone Ho **7** E2. . . . . **96** A6
Woolstone Rd SE23 . . . . . **163** A2
Woolven Ho SE3 . . . . **142** D6
WOOLWICH **122** D3
Woolwich Arsenal Sta
SE18 . . . . **122** D2
Woolwich Church St SE7,
SE18 . . . . **122** A3
Woolwich Comm SE18 . . **144** C6
Woolwich Ct EN3 . . . . **7** C5
Woolwich Dockyard Ind Est
SE18 . . . . **122** A3
Woolwich Dockyard Sta
SE18 . . . . **122** B2
Woolwich High St SE18 . . **122** C3
Woolwich Manorway
E16 . . . . **122** D4
Woolwich Manor Way
Beckton E6 . . . . **100** C1
North Woolwich E16. . . . . **122** D5
Woolwich New Rd SE18 . . **122** D2
Woolwich Poly Sch
SE28. . . . . **124** A5
Woolwich Rd
Belvedere DA17 . . . . **125** C1
DA7. . . . . **147** C2
Erith SE2. . . . . **125** B1
Greenwich SE7, SE10. . . . **121** C2
Woolwich Tramshed The*
16 SE18 . . . . **122** D2
Wooster Gdns E14 . . . . . . **98** B1
Wooster Mews HA2. . . . . **42** A6
Wooster PI SE1 . . . . **262** D4
Wootton CI KT10 . . . . **212** A4
Wootton Gr N3 . . . . **29** C2
Wootton Ho SE9 . . . . **167** B5
Wootton St SE1. . . . . **116** C5 **251** B3
Worbeck Rd SE20. . . . . . . **184** C1
Worcester Ave N17. . . . . . **34** A3
Worcester CI
Croydon CR0. . . . . **223** C6
Dollis Hill NW2 . . . . **243** A5
Mitcham CR4 . . . . **181** A1
Worcester Cres
Edgware NW7 . . . . **11** C1
Woodford IG8. . . . . **37** C6
Worcester Ct
Ashford TW15. . . . . **170** D5
Ealing W7 . . . . **86** D1
Finchley N12. . . . . **29** D5
Harrow HA1 . . . . **42** C6
44 Paddington W2 . . . . . **91** C2
Walton-on-T KT12 . . . . . **194** C1
Worcester Park KT4. . . . . **215** C5
Worcester Dr
Ashford TW15. . . . . **170** D5
Bedford Pk W4 . . . . **111** C4
Worcester Gdns
Northolt UB6 . . . . **64** B2
Redbridge IG1 . . . . **56** A2
Wandsworth SW11 . . . . . **158** D6
Worcester Park KT4. . . . . **215** C5
Worcester Ho
Bayswater W2 . . . . **236** A1
3 Islington N1 . . . . **73** A1
Lambeth SE11. . . . . **261** A5
9 Putney SW15. . . . . . . **156** C4
Worcester Mews **2** NW6. . **69** D2
WORCESTER PARK **215** C4
Worcester Park Rd KT4. . . **215** B5
Worcester Park Sta KT4. . **200** A1
Worcester Rd
Belmont SM2 . . . . **217** D1
Higham Hill E17 . . . . **34** D1
Ilford E12 . . . . **78** B4
11 Wimbledon SW19 . . . **179** B5
Worcesters Ave EN1 . . . . . **6** A5
Worcesters Prim Sch EN1. . **5** D5
Wordsworth **50** C5
Wordsworth Ave
Greenford UB6. . . . . **86** B5
Plashet E12 . . . . **78** A1
Snaresbrook E18 . . . . **54** D6

Wordsworth Ct
Harrow HA1 . . . . **42** B2
New Barnet EN5. . . . . **14** A6
Wordsworth Dr KT4,
SM3 . . . . **216** C4
Wordsworth Gdns WD6 . . **10** C6
Wordsworth Ho
Maida Vale NW6 . . . . **91** C4
15 SE18 . . . . **144** C6
Wordsworth Par **1** N15. . **50** D5
Wordsworth PI **11** NW5. . **70** D3
Wordsworth Rd
Bermondsey SE1 . . . . **263** D3
Bexley DA16. . . . . **145** C4
Hampton TW12, TW13 . . . **173** B6
Penge SE20 . . . . **184** D3
Stoke Newington N16. . . . **73** C4
Wallington SM6 . . . . **219** D2
Wordsworth Way UB7. . . . **104** B2
Wordsworth Wlk NW11 . . **47** C5
Worfield St
SW11. . . . . **136** C5 **267** B3
Worgan St
Rotherhithe SE16 . . . . **118** D2
SE11. . . . . **116** B1 **260** C2
Working Men's Coll The
NW1. . . . . **93** C5 **232** B4
Worland Rd E15 . . . . **76** C1
World Bsns Ctr TW6. . . . . **127** A4
World Rugby Mus*
TW1 . . . . **152** C5
WORLD'S END **4** C1
Worlds End La EN4. . . . . . **227** D1
World's End La EN2 . . . . . **4** B1
World's End Pas SW10 . . **266** C4
World's End PI SW10. . . . **266** B4
World Trade Ctr London
E14. . . . . **119** D4
Worley Cl NW2 . . . . **68** D5
Worleys Dr BR6. . . . . **227** B4
Worlidge St W6. . . . . **112** C1
Worlingham Rd SE22. . . . **139** D1
Wormholt Park Prim Sch
W12 . . . . **112** A6
Wormholt Rd W12 . . . . . . **112** A5
Wormwood St EC2. . . . . . **243** A2
Wornington Rd W10 . . . . . **91** A2
Woronzow Rd
NW8. . . . . **92** C6 **230** A5
Worple Ave
Isleworth TW7 . . . . **153** A6
Wimbledon SW19. . . . . . . **178** D3
Worple CI HA2. . . . . **41** B1
Worple Ct SW19 . . . . **179** A4
Worple Prim Sch TW7 . . . **131** A1
Worple Rd
Isleworth TW7 . . . . **131** A1
Wimbledon SW19, SW20. . **178** D2
Worple Road Mews
SW19. . . . . **179** B4
Worple St SW14 . . . . **133** B2
Worple Way Harrow HA2. . . **41** B1
Richmond TW10 . . . . **132** A1
Worship St EC2. . . . . **95** C3 **243** A5
Worslade Rd SW17. . . . . . **180** B6
Worsley Bridge Jun Sch **25**
BR3. . . . . **185** C3
Worsley Bridge Rd BR3,
SE6 . . . . **185** C5
Worsley Ct N3 . . . . **29** D4
Worsley Gr E5 . . . . **74** A4
Worsley Grange BR7 . . . . **189** A4
Worsley Ho **9** SE23 . . . . **162** B2
Worsley Rd E11. . . . . **76** C4
Worsopp Dr SW4 . . . . **159** C6
Worth CI BR6. . . . . **227** C4
Worthfield CI KT19. . . . . . **215** B1
Worth Gr SE17. . . . . **262** C1
Worthing CI **3** E15. . . . . . **98** C6
Worthing Ho **1** Rd TW5. . **129** B6
Worthington CI CR4. . . . . **203** B6
Worthington Ho EC1. . . . . **234** B2
18 Streatham SW2. . . . . **160** C4
Worthington Rd KT6 . . . . . **198** B1
Wortley Rd Forest Gate E6. . **77** D1
Thornton Heath CR0. . . . . **204** C2
Worton Ct TW7 . . . . **130** C1
Worton Gdns TW7 . . . . . . **130** B3
Worton Hall Ind Est
TW7 . . . . **130** C1
Worton Rd TW7. . . . . **130** C2
Worton Way TW3, TW7. . . **130** B3
Wotton CI **14** E14 . . . . . . **120** A6
Wotton Rd
Cricklewood NW2. . . . . . . **68** C5
1 SE8 . . . . **141** B6
Wouldham Rd E16 . . . . . . **98** D1
Wragby Rd E11. . . . . **76** C5
Wrampling PI N9 . . . . **18** C4
Wrangthorne Wlk CR0 . . . **220** C4
Wray Ave IG5. . . . . **156** D3
Wrayburn Ho **28** SE16 . . . **118** A4
Wray Cres N4. . . . . **72** B6
Wray Ct N4. . . . . **72** B6
Wrayfield Rd SM3. . . . . . . **216** D5
Wray Ho **11** SW2 . . . . **160** A3
Wraysbury CI TW4 . . . . . . **151** B2

Wrays Way UB4............83 C3
Wrekin Rd SE18.........145 A5
Wren Acad N12...........30 B5
Wren Ave
  Cricklewood NW2.........68 C4
  Southall UB2...........107 B2
Wren Cl E16..............98 D1
  Lower Edmonton N9........18 D3
Wren Cres WD23...........8 A3
Wren Ct **1** Barnet EN4....14 D3
  Croydon CR0...........221 B4
Wren Gdns RM9...........80 D3
Wren Ho **29** Bow E3......97 A5
  4 Hampton TW12......173 D4
  SW1..................259 C1
Wren Landing E14........119 C5
Wrenn Ho SW13.........134 C6
Wren Path SE28.........123 B4
Wren Rd Camberwell SE5..139 B4
  Dagenham RM9...........80 D3
  Sidcup DA14...........168 C1
Wrens Ave TW15.........171 A6
Wren's Park Ho E5........74 B6
Wren St WC1.....94 B3 240 D6
Wrentham Ave NW10.......90 D5
Wrenthorpe Rd BR1.....186 C6
Wren View N6............49 C1
Wrenwood Way HA5........40 B5
Wrestlers Ct EC3.......243 A2
Wrexham Rd E3...........97 C5
Wricklemarsh Rd SE3....143 D4
Wrigglesworth St SE14..140 D5
Wright Cl SE13.........142 B1
Wright Gdns TW17.......192 C4
Wright Ho SW15.........156 B6
Wrighton Ct SM1........217 B2
Wright Rd TW5..........128 C5
Wrights Cl RM10.........81 D4
Wright's Gn SW4........137 D1
Wright's La W8...113 D3 255 C6
Wrights Pl NW10.........67 A2
Wrights Rd SE25........205 C6
Wright's Rd E3..........97 B5
Wright's Row SM5.......219 B4
Wrights Wlk SW14.......133 B2
Writtle Ho **36** NW9.....27 D1
Wrotham Ho
  Beckenham BR3........185 B3
  SE1..................262 D6
Wrotham Rd Barnet EN5...1 A3
  13 Camden Town NW1...71 C1
  DA16.................146 C4
  Ealing W13...........109 C5
Wrottesley Rd SE18.....145 A6
  Willesden Green NW10...90 A5
Wroughton Rd SW11......158 D5
Wroughton Terr NW4......46 B5
Wroxall Rd RM9..........80 C2
Wroxham Gdns N11........31 D3
Wroxham Rd SE28........124 D6
Wroxton Rd SE15........140 C3
Wrythe Gn **2** SM5......218 D5
Wrythe Green Rd SM5....218 D5
Wrythe La SM1, SM5,
  SM4.................218 C5
WRYTHE THE...........218 D6
Wulfstan St W12.........89 D1
Wyatt Cl Bushey WD23....8 C4
  Feltham TW13.........150 D3
  Hayes UB4.............84 A2
  Rotherhithe SE16.....119 B4
Wyatt Ct HA0............66 A1
Wyatt Dr SW13.........134 B5
Wyatt Ho
  Blackheath Vale SE3...142 D3
  NW8.................236 D5
Wyatt Park Mans **1**
  SW2.................160 A2
Wyatt Park Rd SW2......160 B2
Wyatt Rd Forest Gate E7..77 A2
  Highbury N5...........73 A5
Wyatt's La E17..........54 A6
Wybert St NW1..........239 A6
Wyborne Ho NW10........67 A1
Wyborne Prim Sch SE9...166 D3
Wyborne Way NW10.......67 A1
Wyburn Ave EN5..........1 B2
Wyche Gr CR2...........221 A1
Wycherley Cl SE3.......142 D5
Wycherley Cres EN5.....13 D5
Wychwood Ave
  Edgware HA8...........25 D4
  South Norwood CR7....205 A6
Wychwood Cl
  Ashford TW16.........172 A4
  Edgware HA8...........25 D4
Wychwood End N6.........49 C2
Wychwood Gdns IG5......56 C5
Wychwood Ho N4.........51 A2
Wychwood Way SE19.....183 B4
Wyclif Ct EC1..........234 C1
Wycliffe Cl DA16.......145 D4
Wycliffe Ho **13** N16....73 C4

Wycliffe Rd
  Battersea SW11.......137 A3
  Wimbledon SW19.......179 D4
Wyclif St EC1..........234 C1
Wycombe Ct SE3........143 A5
Wycombe Gdns NW11......69 C6
Wycombe Ho **1** NW8....237 A6
Wycombe Pl SW18.......158 A5
Wycombe Rd
  Redbridge IG2.........56 B4
  Tottenham N17.........34 A2
  Wembley HA0...........88 C6
Wycombe Sq W8.........245 A3
Wydehurst Rd CR0......206 B2
Wydell Cl SM4..........200 D3
Wydeville Manor Rd
  SE12................187 B6
Wye Cl Ashford TW15....170 D6
  BR6.................211 D2
  Ruislip HA4...........39 A3
Wye Ct W13.............87 B2
Wyemead Cres E4........20 C2
Wyersdale Ho N4........51 A2
Wye St SW11...........136 B3
Wyevale Cl HA5.........40 A6
Wyfold Ho **8** SE2....124 D4
Wyfold Rd SW6...135 A5 264 A3
Wyke Cl TW7...........130 D6
Wyke Gdns W7..........109 A3
Wykeham Ave RM9........80 C2
Wykeham Cl
  Chislehurst BR7......189 C4
  Hendon NW4............46 C4
Wykeham Gn RM9.........80 C2
Wykeham Hill HA9.......44 B1
Wykeham Ho SW19.......179 C2
Wykeham Prim Sch
  NW10.................67 C5
Wykeham Rd Harrow HA3..43 B5
  Hendon NW4............46 C4
Wykeham Rise N20.......13 A3
Wykehurst Rd SW11.....180 B5
Wyke Rd Hackney Wick E3..75 C1
  Merton SW20..........178 C1
Wylchin Cl HA5.........39 D6
Wyldes Cl NW11.........48 A1
Wyldfield Gdns N9......17 D2
Wyld Way HA9...........66 D2
Wyleu St SE23.........163 A4
Wylie Rd UB2..........107 C3
Wyllen Cl E1...........96 C3
Wylo Dr EN5............12 A5
Wymering **9** W9.......91 C4
Wymering Rd W9.........91 C4
Wymondham Ct NW8.....229 D6
Wymond St SW15.......134 C2
Wynan Rd E14..........119 D1
Wynash Gdns SM5.......218 C3
Wynaud Ct N22..........32 B4
Wynbourne Ct SE20.....184 B1
Wyncham Ave DA15......167 C3
Wynchgate Harrow HA3...24 C3
  Southgate N14.........16 A4
Wyncroft Cl BR1.......210 B6
Wyndale Ave NW9........44 C3
Wyndcliff Rd SE7......143 B6
Wyndcroft Cl EN2........4 D2
Wyndham Cl
  Belmont SM2..........217 C1
  Orpington BR6........211 A1
Wyndham Cres
  Camden Town N19.......71 C5
  Hounslow TW4........151 C5
Wyndham Ct
  Brentford W7.........109 A2
  1 Thornton Heath CR0..204 D3
Wyndham Deedes Ho 30
  E2...................96 A5
Wyndham Ho SW1........258 A3
Wyndham Lo TW7.......130 C4
Wyndham Mews W1......237 C3
Wyndham Pl W1........237 C3
Wyndham Rd Barnet EN4..14 D3
  Brentford W13........109 B3
  Forest Gate E6........77 D1
  Kingston u T KT2.....176 B3
  SE5.................139 A5
Wyndhams Ct **4** E8....73 D1
Wyndham St W1....92 D2 237 C4
Wyndham Yd W1.........237 C3
Wyndhurst Cl CR2......220 D1
Wyneham Rd SE24.......161 B6
Wynell Rd SE23........162 D1
Wynford Pl DA17.......147 C6
Wynford Rd N1....94 B5 233 D4
Wynford Way SE9.......166 B1
Wynlie Gdns HA5........22 B1
Wynndale Rd E18........37 B2
Wynne Ct **6** TW7.....131 A2
Wynne Ho SE14.........140 D4
Wynne Rd SW9..........138 C3
Wynn's Ave DA15.......168 A6
Wynnstay Gdns
  W8..............113 C3 255 B6
Wynter Ho **20** SW9....138 B3

Wynter St SW11........136 A1
Wynton Gdns SE25......205 D4
Wynton Pl W3...........88 D1
Wynyard Ho SE11.......260 D2
Wynyard Terr SE11.....260 D2
Wynyatt Ho EC1........234 C2
Wynyatt St EC1....94 D4 234 C2
Wyre Gr Edgware HA8....10 D1
  Hayes UB3...........106 A2
Wyresdale Cres UB6.....86 D4
Wyteleaf Cl HA4........39 A3
Wytham Ho NW8........236 D5
Wythburn Ct W1.......237 C2
Wythburn Pl W1.......237 C2
Wythenshawe Rd RM10....81 C5
Wythens Wlk SE9.......166 D5
Wythes Rd E16.........122 A5
Wythfield Rd SE9......166 B5
Wyvenhoe Rd HA2........64 A5
Wyvern Est The KT3....200 A5
Wyvil Prim Sch
  SW8...........138 A5 270 B4
Wyvil Rd SW8....138 A5 270 A4
Wyvis St E14...........97 D2

X

Xavier Ho E17..........35 B1

Y

Yabsley St E14........120 A5
Yaldam Ho SE1........263 A3
Yalding Ho **20** E5.....74 B3
Yalding Rd SE16.......118 A2
Yale Cl TW4...........151 B6
Yale Ct NW6............69 D3
Yarborough Rd **1**
  SW19.................180 B2
Yardley Cl E4..........19 D6
Yardley Ct SM3........216 D4
Yardley La E4..........19 D6
Yardley Prim Sch E4....20 A5
Yardley St WC1........234 A1
Yard The N1...........233 B3
Yarlington Ct N11......31 A5
Yarmouth Cres N17......52 B4
Yarmouth Pl W1........248 C3
Yarnfield Sq **15** SE15..140 A4
Yarnton Way DA17, DA18..125 B3
Yarrow Cres E6........100 A2
Yarrow Ho
  12 Cubitt Town E14...120 A3
  16 North Kensington W10..90 C2
Yateley St SE18.......121 D3
Yatesbury Ct E5........75 A3
Yates Ct NW2...........68 D2
Yates Ho **22** E2......96 A4
Yatton Ho **15** W10....90 C2
YEADING................84 D3
Yeading Ave HA2........41 A1
Yeading Ct UB4.........84 C3
Yeading Fork UB4.......84 C3
Yeading Gdns UB4.......84 B2
Yeading Ho UB4.........84 D2
Yeading Jun & Inf Schs
  UB4.................84 C2
Yeading La Hayes UB4...84 B2
  Northolt UB4, UB5.....84 C4
Yeadon Ho **14** W10....90 C2
Yeames Cl W13..........87 A1
Yearby Ho W10..........90 C3
Yeate St N1............73 B1
Yeatman Rd N6..........48 D3
Yeats Cl Ealing W7....108 D6
  London NW10...........67 C2
Yeend Cl KT8..........195 C5
Yeldham Ho W6.........112 D1
Yeldham Rd W6.........112 D1
Yellowhammer Ct NW9....27 C1
Yelverton Lo TW1......153 C4
Yelverton Rd SW11.....136 B3
Ye Market CR0.........221 B3
Yenston Cl SM4........201 C3
Yeoman Cl Newham E16..122 D6
  West Norwood SE27....160 D1
Yeoman Ct Heston TW5..129 B5
  8 Sutton SM1......218 B3
Yeoman Dr TW19........148 A3
Yeoman Rd UB5..........63 A1
Yeomans Acre HA4.......40 A3
Yeomans Mews TW7......152 B6
Yeoman's Row
  SW3..............114 C3 257 B5
Yeoman St SE8.........119 A2
Yeomans Way EN3........6 C3
Yeoman's Yd E1........253 D6
Yeo St E3..............97 D2
Yeovil Cl BR6.........227 C6
Yeovil Ho Finsbury Pk N7..72 B6
  North Kensington W10...90 C3
Yeovilton Pl KT2......175 C5
Yerbury Prim Sch N19...71 D5

Yerbury Rd N19.........71 D5
Yeshivo Horomo Talmudical
  Coll N16.............51 B1
Yesodey Hatorah Jun Sch for
  Girls **7** N16.......51 D2
Yesodey Hatorah Sec Sch for
  Girls **5** N16.......51 D2
Yester Dr BR7.........188 A3
Yester Pk BR7.........188 B4
Yester Rd BR7.........188 B3
Yet Lev Ct E5..........52 A1
Yew Ave UB7...........104 A6
Yew Cl IG9.............21 D2
Yewdale Cl BR1........186 C4
Yewfield Rd NW10.......67 D2
Yew Gr NW2.............68 D4
Yew Ho SE14...........141 B3
Yews The TW15.........170 D6
Yew Tree Ave N2........47 D6
Yewtree Cl Harrow HA2..41 D5
  Wood Green N22........31 C2
Yew Tree Cl DA16......146 A4
  3 Lewisham SE13....142 A2
  New Malden KT4.......199 C1
  Southgate N21.........16 C4
Yew Tree Cotts KT10...212 B6
Yew Tree Ct Elstree WD6..9 D5
  8 Stoke Newington N16..73 B6
  8 Sutton SM2......218 A1
  4 Temple Fortune NW11..47 B4
Yew Tree Gdns RM6......59 A4
Yew Tree Grange **2**
  W5.................109 C6
Yew Tree Ho
  New Malden KT4.......199 C1
  5 Surbiton KT6....198 A1
Yew Tree Lo **10** SW16..181 C6
Yewtree Rd BR3........207 B6
Yew Tree Rd
  East Acton W12......111 D6
  Hillingdon UB10.......82 B6
Yew Trees TW17........192 B5
Yew Tree Wlk TW4......151 B6
Yew Wlk HA1............42 C1
YIEWSLEY..............104 A6
Yiewsley Ct UB7.......104 A5
Yoakley Rd N16.........73 C6
Yoke Cl N7.............72 A2
Yolande Gdns SE9......166 A6
Yonge Pk N4, N7........72 C5
York Ave Ealing W7....108 C5
  Hayes UB3.............83 A1
  Mortlake SW14.......155 A6
  Sidcup DA15.........167 D2
  Stanmore HA7..........25 B1
  Walworth SE17.......262 B2
York Bldgs WC2...116 A6 250 B5
York Bridge NW1...93 A3 238 A6
York Cl
  17 Camberwell SE5...139 A3
  Ealing W7...........108 C5
  Morden SM4..........201 D5
  Newham E6...........100 B1
York Ct Beckenham BR3..186 B2
  Kingston u T KT2.....175 D4
  Palmers Green N13.....16 A1
  Wallington SM6.......219 C3
York Gate NW1.........238 B5
  Southgate N14.........16 A4
York Gr SE15..........140 C4
York Hall L Ctr E2.....96 C5
York Hill SE27, SW16..160 D1
York Ho Acton W3.....111 A6
  Chelsea SW3.........257 D2
  Chingford E4..........35 C6
  Edgware HA8...........26 B4
  Enfield EN2............5 B4
  Forest Hill SE26.....184 C5
  1 Hendon NW4......28 D1
  1 Ilford IG1......78 D6
  Islington N5..........72 C3
  Kensington W8........245 C2
  11 Kentish Town N7..71 D2
  Kew TW9.............132 C4
  4 Kingston u T KT2..176 B3
  Lambeth SE1.....116 B3 260 D5
  Marylebone W1........237 C4
  Pentonville N1.......233 C3
  Richmond TW10.......154 C6
  South Norwood SE25...205 C5
  10 West Acton W3...88 C1
York House Pl
  W8..............113 D4 245 C2
Yorkland Ave DA16.....145 D1
Yorkley Ho **3** W10....90 C3
York Mans
  Battersea SW11.......268 B2
  2 Hendon NW9......46 A3
  Marylebone W1........238 A4
  Walworth SE17.......262 B2
York Mews
  Camden Town NW5......71 B3
  Ilford IG1...........78 C5
York Par Brentford TW8..109 D1
  Hendon NW9...........46 A3
York Pl Battersea SW11..136 B2

York Pl continued
  Ilford IG1...........78 C6
  WC2.................250 B5
York Place Mans NW1...237 D6
York Rd
  Battersea SW11, SW18..136 B2
  Belmont SM1, SM2....217 C1
  Brentford TW8.......109 D1
  Chingford E4..........35 C5
  Dagenham W3...........89 B1
  Ealing W5...........109 C3
  Edmonton N18.........34 B5
  Forest Gate E7........77 A2
  Friern Barnet N11.....31 D4
  Hounslow TW3........129 D2
  Ilford IG1...........78 C6
  Kingston u T KT2.....176 B3
  Leyton E10............76 A5
  New Barnet EN5........14 B6
  Pinner HA6............22 A1
  4 Richmond TW10....154 B6
  SE1.............116 B4 250 D2
  Southgate N21.........17 B4
  Teddington TW11......174 C6
  Thornton Heath CR0...204 C2
  Walthamstow E17.......52 D4
  Wimbledon SW19.......180 A4
York Rise BR6.........227 C6
  Dartmouth Pk NW5.....71 B5
York Road Bsns Ctr
  SW11................136 B3
York St Chambers W1...237 C4
Yorkshire Cl N16.......73 C5
Yorkshire Gdns N18.....34 B5
Yorkshire Grey SE9...165 D6
Yorkshire Grey Pl **13**
  NW3.................70 A4
Yorkshire Grey Yd WC1..240 C3
Yorkshire Rd
  Limehouse E14.........97 A1
  Mitcham CR4.........204 A5
York Sq **12** E14......97 A1
York St Carshalton CR4..203 A2
  Paddington W1....92 D2 237 D4
  Twickenham TW1......153 A3
York Terr EN2...........5 A5
York Terr E NW1....93 A3 238 B5
York Terr W NW1....93 A3 238 A5
Yorkton St E2..........96 A5
York Way
  Barnsbury N1, N7, NW1..72 A1
  Chessington KT9......214 A1
  Friern Barnet N20.....14 D1
  N1..................233 B5
  Twickenham TW13......151 B1
York Way Ct Islington N1..233 C5
  Islington N1........233 B5
York Wr Gate* SW1.....250 B4
Youngmans Cl EN2........5 A4
Young Rd E16...........99 C1
Young's Bldgs EC1.....242 B6
Youngs Brewery Visitor Ctr*
  SW18................157 D6
Youngs Ct SW11........268 B1
Youngs Rd IG2..........57 B4
Young St W8......113 D4 245 C1
Yoxall Ho **2** W10.....90 C3
Yoxford Ct **6** RM6....58 B4
Yoxley App IG2.........57 A3
Yoxley Dr IG2..........57 A3
Yukon Rd SW12.........159 B4
Yunus Khan Cl E17......53 C4

Z

Zambezie Dr N9.........18 C1
Zampa Rd SE16........118 C1
Zander Ct E2...........96 A4
Zangwill Ho NW6........91 B5
Zangwill Rd SE18, SE3..143 D4
Zaskin Coll **13** HA1...42 D3
Zealand Ave UB7.......126 A5
Zealand Ho
  11 Camberwell SE5...139 A3
  4 Woolwich SE18....122 A4
Zealand Rd E3..........97 A5
Zenith Lo **7** N3......29 D3
Zennor Rd SW12........159 C3
Zenoria St SE22.......139 D1
Zermatt Rd CR7........205 A5
Zetland Ho W8.........255 C6
Zetland St E14.........98 A2
Zeus Ho N1............235 C1
Zion Ho **6** E1........96 C1
Zion Pl CR7...........205 B5
Zion Rd CR7...........205 B5
Zircon Ct N11..........31 D3
ZK Pk CR0.............220 B5
Zoar St SE1......117 A5 252 A4
Zodiac Ct CR0.........204 D1
Zodiac Ho **3** E3......97 C3
Zoffany St N19.........71 D4

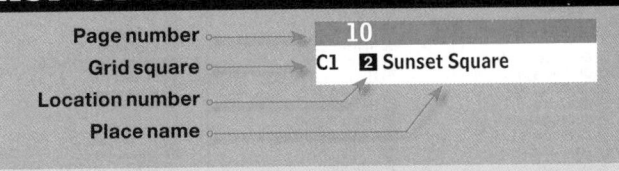

List of numbered locations

In some busy areas of the maps it is not always possible to show the name of every place.

Where not all names will fit, some smaller places are shown by a number. If you wish to find out the name associated with a number, use this listing.

The places in this list are also listed conventionally in the Index.

Page number → **10**
Grid square → **C1** **2** Sunset Square
Location number
Place name

1

A1 **1** Hertswood Ct
2 Abingdon Lo
3 Sunbury Ct
4 Meriden Ho
5 Norfolk Ct
6 Vanburgh Ct
7 Morrison Ct
8 Kingshill Ct
9 Baronsmere Ct
10 Chartwell Ct
11 St Martha's Convent Jun Sch
A2 **1** Richard Ct
2 Alston Ct
3 Ridgeleigh Ct
4 Bartletts Cotts
5 Leathersellers Cl
6 Holkham Ho
7 Leinster Mews
B1 **1** Olivia Ct
2 Tudor Ct
3 Gordon Mans
4 Montague Cl
B2 **1** Brake Shear Ho
2 Durham Ct
3 Huntingdon Ct
4 Cambridge Ct
5 Summit Ct
D1 **1** Cranleigh Ct
2 Valeside Ct
3 Sherwood
4 Bradbury Ct
5 Chester Ho
6 Graham Ho
7 Highfield Ct
8 Amberley Ho
9 Hadley View
10 Stratton Lo
11 Gainsborough Ct
12 Christopher Ct
13 Bowmar Lo

2

A1 **1** Hanover Ho
2 St Giles Ho
3 Henrietta Ho
4 Byron Ct
5 Preston Ct
6 Clivedon Ct
7 Battle House Mews
8 Phoenix Ct
9 Landsdown Cl
10 Comer Ho
11 Basil Ct
12 Russell Ct
13 Alice Cl
C1 **1** Braeburn Ct
2 Bramley Ct
3 Cox Ct
4 Golden Ct
5 Pippin Ct
6 Russet Ct
7 High Birch Ct
8 Joystone Ct
9 Mark Lo
10 Edgeworth Ct

4

D3 **1** Oakington Ct
2 Elderberry Ct
3 Blueberry Ct
4 Butterfield Ho

5

C1 **1** Woodfield Cl
2 Fielders Cl

7

A2 **1** Amethyest Ct
2 Bradmore Ct
3 Acer Ct
4 Cornell Ct
5 Durnsford Ct
6 Feldspar Ct
C6 **1** Whitworth Cres
2 Polsten Mews
3 Aldis Mews
4 Dundas Mews
5 Colt Mews
6 Warlow Cl
7 Barrass Ct
8 Rigby Pl
9 Gunner Dr
10 Colgate Pl
11 Baddeley Cl
12 Sten Cl
13 Pritchett Cl
14 Rubin Pl
15 Turpin Ct
16 Island Centre Way
17 Hispano Mews
18 Watkin Mews
19 Wallace Ct
20 Needham Ct
21 Dryer Ct
22 Webley Ct
23 Frosbery Ct
24 Jacob Ct
25 Peabody Ct
26 Greener Ct
27 Bren Ct

9

D5 **1** Watling Ct
2 Stuart Ct
3 Westview Ct

13

D6 **1** Rowan Wlk
2 Ford Ho
3 Glenwood Ho
4 Whitegates
5 Lisa Lo
6 South Lo
7 Hockington Ct
8 Lysander Ct
9 Ashwood Lo
10 Thornbridge Ct
11 Invergarry Cl
12 Eysham Ct
13 Warwick Ct
14 Chaucer Ct
15 Coleridge Ct
16 Springfields
17 Bure Ct
18 Florence Ct
19 Minetta Ct

14

A1 **1** Belmont Ct
2 Terrace Ho
3 Croft Mews
4 Bluebell Ct
5 North London Int Sch (Lower Sch)
A2 **1** Westview Ct
2 Oakleigh Mews
3 Mountview Ct
4 Mortimer Ct
5 Parklands
A6 **1** Chiltern Ct
2 Gills Ct
3 Beaufort Ct
4 St Augustines Ct
5 Somerset Lo
6 Carlyle Lo
7 Stirling Lo

8 St Mirren Ct
9 Wardrew Ct
10 Apex Lo
11 Westbury Ct
B2 **1** Davis Ct
2 Deerings Ct
3 Ashcroft Ct
B6 **1** Redrose Trad Ctr
2 Lancaster Road Ind Est
C2 **1** Mendip Ct
2 Purbeck Ct
3 Brendon Ct
4 Quantock Ct
5 Malvern Ct
6 Chiltern Ct
C5 **1** Feline Ct
2 Brookhill Ct
3 Littlegrove Ct
4 Desmond Ho
D1 **1** Springfield Ct
2 Victor Ho
3 Malborough Ho
4 Coopers Ct
5 Joiners Ct
D2 **1** Bantock Ct
2 Burgess Ct
3 Heaton Ct
4 Bordley Ct
5 Garside Ct
6 Cranston Ct
7 Gleave Ct
D3 **1** Wren Ct
2 Homerton Ct
3 Emmanuel Ct
4 Wolfson Ct
5 Robinson Ct
6 Gonville Ct
7 Magdalene Gdns
8 Fitzwilliam Cl

15

B4 **1** Salcombe Prep Sch (Junior Dept)
C6 **1** Tregenna Cl
2 Catherine Ct
3 Conisbee Ct
4 Ashmead
D3 **1** Dennis Par
2 Broadway The
3 Southgate Cir
4 Station Par
5 Bourneside
6 Bourneside Cres

17

C6 **1** Wade Ho
2 Newport Lo
3 Halcyon Ho
4 Lerwick Ct
5 Anchor Ct
6 Grassmere Ct
7 Datchworth Ct
8 Trentham Lo
9 Austin Ct
10 Cedar Grange
11 Brookview Ct
12 Chestbrook Ct
13 Paddock Lo
14 Hamlet Ct
15 Haven Lo

18

A1 **1** Plevna Ct
2 Lea Ho
3 Brook Ho
4 Valley Ho
5 Chiltern Ho
6 Blenheim Ho
7 Penn Ho
8 Romany Ho
9 Gilpin Ho

10 Anvil Ho
11 Well Ho
12 Passmore Ho
13 Durbin Ho
A2 **1** Market Par
2 Beechwood Mews
3 Keats Par
4 Cedars Rd
5 Cross Keys Cl
6 Dorman Pl
7 Concourse The
8 Hector Cl
B3 **1** St Edmund's RC Prim Sch
2 Phoenix Acad

20

A2 **1** Lea Ct
2 Park Ct
3 Conference Cl
4 Berrybank Cl
5 Russell Lo
6 Brunswick Lo
7 Kenilworth Ct
8 Trinity Ct
9 Kingsmead Lo
10 Fairlawns
A3 **1** Ridgeway The
2 Grant Ct
3 Pineview Ct
4 Ellen Ct
5 Leeview Ct
6 Chelsea Ct
7 Bramley Ct
8 Garenne Ct
9 Kendal Ct
10 Fairways
11 Avon Ct
B3 **1** Maddox Ct
2 Village Arc The
3 Cambridge Rd
4 Crown Bldgs
5 Pentney Rd
6 Scholars Ho
7 Cranworth Cres
8 St Mary's RC Prim Sch
9 Chingford CE Jun Sch
10 Chingford CE Inf Sch
C4 **1** Connaught Ct
2 Woolden Ho
3 Fairmead Ct
4 Lockhart Lo
5 Cavendish Ct
6 Oakwood Ct
7 Plains The
8 Hadleigh Ct
9 Forest Ho
10 Mathieson Ho

21

B2 **1** Stag Hts
2 Shore Point
3 Buckhurst Hill Ho
4 Beech Ave
5 High Road Buckhurst Hill
6 Highclears
C2 **1** Westbury Ct
2 Palmerston Ct
3 Ibrox Ct
4 Richard Burton Ct
5 Queens Mews
6 Gunnels Ct & Hastingwood Ct
7 Marlborough Ct
8 Avenue The
9 Tora Ct
10 Somerset Ct
11 Mirravale Ct
C3 **1** Rayburne Ct
2 Laurels The
3 Mablin Lo

4 Silvers
5 Makinen Ho
6 Roman Lo
D1 **1** Highview Ho
2 Hornbeam Ho
3 Highview Ho
4 Bourne Ho
D2 **1** Regency Lo
2 Kings Ct
3 Beech Ct
4 Sycamore Ho
5 Salisbury Gdns
6 Pegasus Ct
7 Buckhurst Ct
8 Mountbatten Ct
9 Atrium
D6 **1** Collins Ct
2 Lower Park Rd
3 Homecherry Ho

22

C1 **1** Daniel Ho
2 Hawthorn Ct
3 Northcote
4 Edwin Ware Ct
5 Chalfont Wlk
6 Maple Ct
7 Montesole Ct
8 Viewpoint Ct

23

B3 **1** Russettings
2 St Cuthberts Gdns
3 Cherry Croft Gdns
4 Claire Ct
5 Cornwall Ct
6 Falmouth Ho
7 Newlyn Ho
8 Chestnuts The
9 Dunford Ct
10 Stratton Ct
11 Hanover Ct
12 Tilbury Cl

25

C5 **1** Belgrave Gdns
2 Heywood Ct
3 Norfolk Ho
4 Garden Ct
5 Chatsworth Ct
6 Chartridge Ct
7 Hardwick Ct
8 Cheltenham Ct
9 Cargrey Ho
10 Holbein Ho
11 Goodwood Cl
12 Ascot Pl
13 Longchamp Ct
14 Halfacre
15 Burnham Ct
16 Dingle Ct
17 Woodcroft
18 Daneglen Ct
19 Buckingham Par
C6 **1** Bickley Ct
2 Elstree Ho
3 Brompton Ct
4 Kenmare Ct
5 Burlington Park Ho
6 Gressenham Ct
7 Amora

26

D5 **1** Penshurst Ct
2 Cranbourne Ct
3 Wilton Ct
4 Saxon Ct
5 Abbey Ct
6 Kenlor Ct

41

C2 **1** Buckingham College
Prep Sch

42

C2 **6** Harrovian Bsns Village
D3 **1** Nightingale Rd
2 St John's Ct
3 Gayton Ct
4 Wilton Pl
5 Murray Ct
6 Cymbeline Ct
7 Knowles Ct
8 Charville Ct
9 Lime Ct
10 Petherton Ct
11 Garth Ct
12 Chalfont Ct
13 Shepherds Ct
14 Zaskin Coll
D4 **1** Crystal Ctr The
2 Blue Point Ct
3 Ryan Ho
4 Rothwell Ct
5 Bruce Ho
6 Middlesex Ct
7 Ingram Ho
8 Arless Ho
9 Leaf Ho
10 Becket Fold
11 Brandan Ho
12 Robert Ho

46

A2 **1** Milton Rd
2 Stanley Rd
A3 **1** Mapesbury Mews
2 York Mans
3 Telford Rd
4 Beis Soroh Schneirer
(Sch)
A5 **1** Pilkington Ct
2 Cousins Ct
3 Seton Ct
4 Frensham Ct
5 Chatton Ct
6 Geraldine Ct
7 Swynford Gdns
8 Miller Ct
9 Roffey Ct
10 Peace Ct
11 Rambler Ct
12 Lion Ct
13 Wenlock Gdns
14 Dogrose Ct
15 Harry Ct
16 Tribune Ct
17 Bonville Gdns
18 Pearl Ct
B4 **1** Vivian Mans
2 Parade Mans
3 Georgian Ct
4 Florence Mans
5 Park Mans
6 Cheyne Cl
7 Queens Par
8 Central Mans
C5 **1** Courtney Ho
2 Golderton
3 Thornbury
4 Ferrydale Lo
5 Studio Mews
6 Brampton La
7 Short St
8 Belle Vue Rd
9 Longford Ct
10 Ashwood Ho
D4 **1** Hasmonean Prim Sch
2 Independant Jewish
Day Sch
D5 **1** Midford Ho
2 Rockfield Ho
3 Lisselton Ho
4 Acrefield Ho
5 London Sch of Jewish
Studies
6 Beth Jacob Gram Sch
7 Bell Lane Prim Sch
8 Nancy Reuben Prim
Sch

47

A2 **1** Talmud Torah Tiferes
Shlomo
B2 **1** Berkeley Ct
2 Exchange Mans
3 Beechcroft Ct
4 Nedahall Ct
B3 **1** Charlton Lo
2 Clifton Gdns
B4 **1** Hallswelle Par
2 Belmont Par
3 Temple Fortune Ho
4 Yew Tree Ct
5 Temple Fortune Par

6 Courtleigh
7 Arcade Ho
8 Queens Ct
9 Temple Fortune Ct
10 Crispin Mews
B5 **1** Monkville Par
2 Ashbourne Par

48

A6 **1** St Mary's Gn
2 Dunstan Cl
3 Paul Byrne Ho
4 Longfield Ct
5 Warwick Ct
6 Branksome Ct
7 Sherwood Hall

49

B6 **1** Dorchester Ct
2 Old Chapel Pl
3 Athenaeum Pl
4 Risborough Cl
5 Risborough Rd
C1 **1** Calvert Ct
2 Academy The
3 Whitehall Mans
4 Pauntley St
5 Archway Hts
6 Pauntley Ho
7 St Aloysius RC Coll
D1 **1** Louise White Ho
2 Levison Way
3 Sanders Way
4 Birbeck Ho
5 Scholars Ct
6 Mount Carmel RC Tech
Coll for Girls
D2 **1** Eleanor Rathbone Ho
2 Christopher Lo
3 Monkridge
4 Marbleford Ct
5 High London
6 Garton Ho
7 Hilltop Ho
8 Caroline Martyn Ho
9 Arthur Henderson Ho
10 Margaret Mcmillan Ho
11 Enid Stacy Ho
12 Mary McArthur Ho
13 Bruce Glasier Ho
14 John Wheatley Ho
15 Keir Hardie Ho
16 Monroe Ho
17 Iberia Ho
18 Lygoe Ho
19 Lambert Ho
20 Shelbourne Ho
21 Arkansas Ho
22 Lafitte Ho
23 Shreveport Ho
24 Packenham Ho
25 Orpheus Ho
26 Fayetville Ho
27 Bayon Ho
D4 **1** Kelland Cl
2 Truro Ct
3 Veryan Ct
4 Coulsdon Ct

50

A1 **1** Beeches The
2 Lambton Ct
3 Nugent Ct
4 Lambton Mews
5 Mews The
A2 **1** Marie Lloyd Gdns
2 Edith Cavell Cl
3 Marie Stopes Ct
4 Jessie Blythe La
5 Barbara Rudolph Ct
6 Hetty Rees Ct
7 Leyden Mans
8 Brambledown
9 Lochbie
10 Lyngham Ct
11 High Mount
12 Woodlands The
13 St Gildas' RC Jun Sch
A4 **1** Margaret Hill Ho
2 Manray Ct
3 Hermiston Ct
4 Carleton Ho
5 Rokesly Jun & Inf Schs
A5 **1** Mackenzie Ho
2 Stowell Ho
3 Campsbourne Ho
4 Palace Gate Mews
5 St Mary's CE Jun Sch
6 Greig City Acad
7 North London Rudolf
Steiner Sch
B1 **1** Lawson Ct
2 Wiltshire Ct
3 Fenstanton
4 Hutton Ct
5 Wisbech

6 Islington Arts & Media
Sch
B5 **3** St Mary's CE Inf Sch
D4 **1** South Harringay Jun &
Inf Schs
D5 **1** Wordsworth Par
2 Spanswick Lo
3 Barker Ho
4 St John Vianney RC
Prim Sch
D6 **1** Langham Cl
2 Sidi Ct
3 Ince Terr

51

A2 **1** Finmere Ho
2 Keynsham Ho
3 Kilpeck Ho
4 Knaresborough Ho
5 Leighfield Ho
6 Lonsdale Ho
7 Groveley Ho
8 Wensleydale Ho
9 Badminton Ct
B2 **1** Selwood Ho
2 Bnois Jerusalem Girls
Sch
3 Mendip Ho
4 Ennerdale Ho
5 Getters Talmud Torah
6 Delamere Ho
7 Westwood Ho
8 Bernwood Ho
9 Allerdale Ho
10 Farningham Ho
B5 **1** Wisdom Sch
C1 **1** Godstone Ct
2 Farnham Ct
3 Milford Ct
4 Cranleigh Ct
5 Haslemere Ct
6 Belmont Ct
7 Hockworth Ho
8 Garratt Ho
9 Fairburn Ho
10 Thorndale Ho
11 Oakdene Ho
12 Briardale Ho
C2 **1** Beis Rochel d'Satmar
Girls Sch
3 Our Lady's Convent RC
High Sch
C3 **1** Oatfield Ho
2 Perry Ct
3 Henrietta Ho
4 Bournes Ho
5 Chisley Rd
6 Twyford Ho
7 Langford Cl
8 Hatchfield Ho
D1 **1** Stamford Hill Mans
2 Montefiore Ct
3 Berwyn Ho
4 Clent Ho
5 Chiltern Ho
6 Laindon Ho
7 Pentland Ho
D2 **1** Regent Ct
2 Stamford Lo
3 Holmwood Ct
4 Bobov Foundation Sch
5 Yesodey Hatorah Sec
Sch for Girls
6 Lubavitch Boys Prim
Sch
7 Yesodey Hatorah Jun
Sch for Girls
8 Lubavitch Girls Prim
Sch
9 Lubavitch House Sch
(Jun Boys)
10 Skinners Company Sch
(Upper)
D3 **1** Sherboro Rd
2 Westcott Cl
3 Cadoxton Ave
D4 **1** Westerfield Rd
2 Suffield Rd
D5 **1** Laseron Ho
2 Greenway Cl
3 Earlsmead Prim Sch
4 Tottenham Gn E
5 Tottenham Gn E South
Side
6 Deaconess Ct
7 Elliot Ct
8 Bushmead Cl
9 Beaufort Ho
10 Tynemouth Terr
11 Green CE Sch Holy
Trinity (Inf Annexe)
The
D6 **1** Holcombe Rd
2 Rigby Ho
3 Chaplin Rd
4 Keswick Apartments
5 Ambleside Cl

6 Lauriston Apartments
7 Terrall Apartments
8 Old School Ct
9 Nicholson Ct
10 Reynardson's Ct
11 Protheroe Ho
13 North London Coll
14 Green CE Prim Sch The

52

A1 **1** Stamford Gr E
2 Stamford Mans
3 Grove Mans
4 Stamford Gr W
6 Talmud-Torah Yetev-
Lev
A6 **2** Welbourne Prim Sch
B1 **1** Hawkwood Mount
2 Holmbury View
3 High Hill Ferry
4 Leaside Ho
5 Courtlands
6 Tayyibah Girls Sch
7 Ivy Ho
7 Shelford Ct
8 Skinner's Company's
Lower Sch

53

A4 **1** Hammond Ct
2 St James Apartments
3 Grange The
A5 **1** Bristol Park Rd
2 Stoneydown Ho
3 Callonfield
4 Hardyng Ho
5 Stoneydown Park Sch
6 St Patrick's RC Prim
Sch
B5 **1** Palace Mews
2 Thomas Jacomb Pl
C1 **1** Wellington Mans
2 Clewer Ct
3 Cochrane Ct
C3 **1** Samira Ct
2 Walter Savill Twr
3 Boston Rd
C5 **1** Westbury Ho
2 Hatherley Ho
3 Vintry Mews
4 Tylers Ct
5 Merchants Lo
6 Gillards Mews
7 Blacksmiths Ho
8 Central Par
D1 **1** Fitzgerald Ct
2 Bechervaise Ct
3 Underwood Ct
D2 **1** Staton Ct
2 Howell Ct
3 Atkinson Ct
4 Russell Ct
5 St Catherines Twr
6 St Lukes Ct
7 St Matthews Ct
8 St Mark's Ct
9 St Elizabeth Ct
10 Emanuel Ct
11 St Thomas Ct
12 Beaumont Ho
13 Shelley Ct
14 St Paul's Twr
15 Flack Ct
16 King Ct
17 Osborne Ct
18 Muriel Ct
19 All Saints Twr
20 St Josephs Ct
D4 **1** Harriet Ho
2 Eastbank Cl
D5 **1** Nash Ho
2 St Columbas Ho
3 Attlee Terr
4 Astins Ho
5 Lindens The
6 Kevan Ct
7 Squire's Almshouses
8 Berry Field Cl
9 Connaught Ct
10 Holmcroft Ho
11 St Mary's Church Ho
D6 **1** Hallingbury Ct
2 Mace Ho
3 Gaitskell Ho
4 Hancocke Ho
5 Trinity Ho
6 Fanshaw Ho
7 Hilltop
8 Batten Ho
9 Bradwell Ho
10 Walton Ho
11 Temple Ho
12 Gower Ho
13 Maple Ho
14 Poplars Ho
15 Cedars Ho
16 Kimm Ho
17 O'Grady Ho

18 Latham Ho
19 Powell Ct
20 Crosbie Ho

54

A2 **1** Ayerst Ct
2 Dare Ct
3 St Edwards Ct
A4 **1** Collard's Almshouses
2 Ellen Miller Ho
3 Tom Smith Ho
A5 **1** Northwood Twr
2 Walnut Ct
3 Albert Whicher Ho
4 Pelly Ct
5 Ravenswood Ind Est
6 Holland Ct
7 Emberson Ho
8 St Mark's Ho
9 Alfred Villas
10 Leonard Ho
11 Old Station Yard The
A6 **1** St David's Ct
2 Golden Par
3 Chestnuts Ct
4 Matthew Ct
5 Gilbert Ho
6 Manning Ho
7 Southgate Ho
8 Boyden Ho
9 Prospect Ho
10 Newton Ho
C1 **2** Connaught Sch for
Girls
D2 **1** Buxton Ct
2 Hanbury Dr
3 Forest Lea
4 Watershipdown Ho

55

A3 **1** Aldham Hall
2 Parkside Ct
3 Mapperley Cl
4 Weavers Ho
5 Cyna Ct
6 Reed Mans
7 Thornton Ho
8 Hardwick Ct
9 St Joseph's Convent
Sch
A4 **1** Kingsley Grange
2 Station Par
3 Gwynne Ho
4 Staveley Cl
5 Thurlow Ct
6 Devon Ho
7 Wellington Pas
8 Wanstead Hts
9 Hollies The
10 Little Holt
11 Hunter Ct
12 Mountier Ct
13 Woodland Ct
14 Dudley Ct
15 Struan Ho
16 Westleigh Ct
A5 **1** Shernwood Ho
2 Orwell Lo
3 Hermitage Ct
4 Gowan Lea
5 Woodford Ho
6 Eagle Ct
7 Newbury Ct
8 Shelley Ct
9 Hardy Ct
10 Dickens Ct
11 Byron Ct
A6 **1** Millbrook
2 Half Acre
3 Elmbrook
4 Grange The
5 Glenavon Lo
6 Glenwood Ct
7 Ferndown
8 Embassy Ct
9 Orestes Ct
10 Walbrook
11 Helmsley
12 Snaresbrook Hall
B4 **1** Nightingale Ct
2 Chelston Ct
3 Grosvenor Ct
4 Louise Ct
5 St Davids Ct
6 Cedar Ct
7 Shrubbery The
8 Nightingale Mews
B5 **1** Great Hall The
2 Clock Ct
3 Langham Ho
B6 **1** Victoria Ct
2 Kenwood Gdns
3 Thaxted Lo
4 Albert Rd
5 Albert Ho

432 55 B6

6 Falcon Ct
7 Deborah Ct
8 Swift Ho
9 Pulteney Gdns
10 Spring Ct
11 Trinity Gdns
12 Foxdene Cl

56

B4 1 High View Par
2 Spurway Par
3 Florence Root Ho
4 Rohan Pl
5 Homeheather Ho
D4 1 St Augustine's RC Prim Sch

57

A3 1 Catherine Ct
2 Ivy Terr
3 Newbury Cotts

58

B1 1 Caledonian Cl
2 Talisman Cl
3 Norseman Cl
4 Frank Slater Ho
5 Brook's Mans
6 Brook's Par
B2 1 Mitre Ct
2 Coppins The
3 Stanetta Ct
4 Wilnett Ct
5 Wilnett Villas
B4 1 Sudbury Ct
2 Dunwich Ct
3 Cromer Terr
4 Norfolk Ct
5 Framlingham Ct
6 Yoxford Ct
C4 1 Swaffham Ct
2 Nacton Ct
3 Suffolk Ct
D2 1 Pavement Mews
2 Chadview Ct
3 Granary Ct
4 Bedwell Ct
5 Chapel La
6 Faulkner Cl
7 Maple Ct
8 Willow Ct
9 Cedar Terr

63

C2 1 Wimborne Ct
2 Haydock Green Flats
3 Brighton Dr
4 Blaydon Ct
5 Fakenham Cl
6 Rutland Ho
7 Windsor Ho

65

D3 1 Lowry Lo
2 Morritt Ho
3 Charles Goddard Ho
4 Snow Ct
5 Willow Tree Ct
6 Oak Lo

66

A2 1 Montrose Cres
2 Peggy Quirke Ct
3 Marylebone Ct
4 Waterloo Ct
5 Euston Ct
6 St Pancras Ct
7 Paddington Ct
8 Copland Mews
9 Coronet Par
10 Aylestone Ct
11 Charlotte Ct
A3 1 Wembley Mkt
2 Market Way
3 Lodge Ct
4 Central Sq
5 Manor Ct
6 Rupert Ave
7 Lily Ho
C4 1 Wembley Mkt

67

A5 1 Curie Ho
2 Darwin Ho
3 Priestley Ho
4 Rutherford Ho
5 Fleming Ho
6 Lister Ho
7 Edison Ho
B1 1 Biko Ho

2 Kingthorpe Terr
3 Scott Ho
4 Peary Ho
5 Shackleton Ho
6 Amundsen Ho
7 Brentfield Ho
8 Nansen Ho
9 Stonebridge Ct
10 Newcroft Ho
11 Magellan Ct
12 Leadbetter Ct
13 Jefferies Ho
14 Cowan Ct
15 Prothero Ho
16 Crawford St
17 Clark Ct
18 Diamond St
19 Mary Seacole Villas
C1 1 Beveridge Rd
2 Purcell Mews
3 George Lansbury Ho
4 Charles Hobson Ho
5 Reade Wlk
6 Westbury Ho
7 Bridge Ct
8 St Joseph's RC Prim Sch
9 Dixon Way
10 Armstrong Rd
11 Brittage Rd
C4 1 Grange Ct
2 Green Ct
C5 1 Hazelwood Ct
2 Winslow Cl

68

A2 1 Regency Mews
2 Tudor Mews
3 Utopia Ho
4 Bell Flats
5 Angel Ct
6 St Andrew & St Francis CE Prim Sch
A5 1 Bourne Ho
2 Carton Ho
3 Bidwell Ho
4 Woodbridge Cl
5 Mackenzie Ho
6 Banting Ho
B2 1 St Mary Magdelen's RC Jun Sch
2 Islamic Coll for Advanced Studies
C2 1 Rutland Park Gdns
2 Rutland Park Mans
3 Queens Par
4 Harcourt Ho
5 Solidarity Ho
6 Electra Ct
7 Cassandra Ct
8 Carlton Ct
9 Convent of Jesus & Mary RC Inf Sch
D4 1 Oaklands Mews
2 Acer Ct
3 Maple Ct
4 Argyle Mans

69

A1 1 Christ Church Ct
2 Paul Daisley Ct
3 Fountain Ho
4 Kingston Ho
5 Waverley Ct
6 Weston Ho
7 Mapes Ho
8 Athelstan Gdns
9 Leff Ho
10 Brondesbury Coll for Boys
B1 1 Alma Birk Ho
2 Brooklands Ct
3 Brooklands Court Apartments
4 Cleveland Mans
5 Buckley Ct
6 Webheath
B5 1 Mortimer Cl
2 Primrose Ct
3 Sunnyside Ho
4 Sunnyside
5 Prospect Pl
C1 1 Linstead St
2 Embassy Ho
3 Acol Ct
4 Kings Wood Ct
5 Douglas Ct
6 King's Gdns
7 Carlton Mans
8 Smyrna Mans
9 New Priory Ct
10 Queensgate Pl
11 Brondesbury Mews
12 St Eugene de Mazenod RC Prim Sch
C2 1 Dene Mans
2 Sandwell Cres
3 Sandwell Mans

4 Hampstead West
5 Redcroft
C3 1 Orestes Mews
2 Walter Northcott Ho
3 Polperro Mans
4 Lyncroft Mans
5 Marlborough Mans
6 Alexandra Mans
7 Cumberland Mans
8 Cavendish Mans
9 Ambassador Ct
10 Welbeck Mans
11 Inglewood Mans
12 Dennington Park Mansions
C4 1 Parsifal Coll
C5 1 Portman Hts
2 Hermitage Ct
3 Moreland Ct
4 Wendover Ct
D2 1 Beswick Mews
2 Worcester Mews
3 Minton Mews
4 Doulton Mews
5 Laurel Ho
6 Sandalwood Ho
7 Iroko Ho
8 Banyan Ho
9 Rosewood Ho
10 Ebony Ho
11 Rosemont Mans
12 Exeter Mews

70

A1 1 Harrold Ho
2 Glover Ho
3 Byron Ct
4 Nalton Ho
A2 1 Petros Gdns
2 Heath Ct
3 Imperial Twrs
4 Fairhurst
5 St John's Ct
6 New College Ct
7 Chalford
8 Rosslyn Mans
9 Sutherland Ho
10 Holy Trinity CE Prim Sch
11 Phoenix Sch The
12 North Bridge House Sch
13 Southbank International Sch
A3 1 Arkwright Mans
2 Hatstone Ct
3 Hampstead High Sch
A4 1 Windmill Hill
2 Highgrove Point
3 Gainsborough Ho
4 Holly Bush Hill
5 Heath Mans
6 Holly Bush Steps
7 Pavilion Ct
8 Holly Berry La
9 New Campden Ct
10 Holly Bush Vale
11 Benham's Pl
12 Prospect Pl
13 Yorkshire Grey Pl
14 Gardnor Mans
15 Ellerdale Cl
16 Monro Ho
17 Prince Arthur Mews
18 Prince Arthur Ct
19 Village Mount
20 Perrin's Ct
21 Wells Ct
22 Bakers Pas
23 Spencer Wlk
24 Bird In Hand Yd
25 Kings Well
26 New Ct
27 Streatley Pl
28 Mansfield Pl
29 Upper Hampstead Wlk
30 Hampstead Parochial CE Prim Sch
31 Univ Coll Jun Sch
32 Heathside Prep Sch
33 New End Prim Sch
34 Sisters of St Marcellina Sch
A5 1 Hampstead Sq
2 Stamford Cl
3 Mount Sq The
B1 1 New College Par
2 Northways Par
3 Noel Ho
4 Campden Ho
5 Centre Hts
6 Hickes Ho
7 Swiss Terr
8 Leitch Ho
9 Jevons Ho
10 Langhorne Ct
11 Park Lo
12 Avenue Lo
13 Frank Barnes Sch

14 Swiss Cottage Sch
B2 1 Belsize Park Mews
2 Baynes Mews
3 McCrone Mews
11 South Hampstead High Sch
B3 1 Belsize Court Garages
2 Roscommon Ho
3 Akenside
4 Fitzjohns Prim Sch
5 St Christopher's Sch
6 St Anthony's Sch
B4 1 White Bear Pl
2 Wells Ho The
3 Boades Mews
4 Flask Cotts
5 Coach House Yd
6 Pilgrim's Pl
7 Rosslyn Mews
8 Royal Sch Hampstead The
9 Academy Sch The
C2 1 Banff Ho
2 Glenloch Ct
3 Havercourt
4 Holmefield Ct
5 Gilling Ct
6 Howitt Cl
7 Manor Mans
8 Straffan Lo
9 Romney Ct
10 Lancaster Stables
11 Eton Garages
12 Hampstead Coll of Fine Arts & Humanities
C3 1 Hampstead Hill Sch
D1 1 Hancock Nunn Ho
2 Higginson Ho
3 Duncan Ho
4 Mary Wharrie Ho
5 Rockstraw Ho
6 Cleaver Ho
7 Chamberlain St
8 Sharples Hall St
9 Primrose Mews
10 Rothwell St
11 St Georges Mews
D2 1 Alder Ho
2 Hornbeam Ho
3 Whitebeam Ho
4 Aspen Ho
5 Rowan Ho
6 Beech Ho
7 Chestnut Ho
8 Oak Ho
9 Willow Ho
10 Sycamore Ho
11 Maple Ho
12 Hazel Ho
13 Elaine Ct
14 Faircourt
15 Walham Ct
16 Stanbury Ct
17 Priory Mans
18 Wellington Ho
19 Grange The
D3 1 Cayford Ho
2 Du Maurier Ho
3 Isokon Flats
4 Palgrave Ho
5 Garnett Ho
6 Stephenson Ho
7 Park Dwellings
8 Siddons Ho
9 Mall Studios
10 Park Hill Wlk
11 Wordsworth Pl
12 Fraser Regnart Ct
13 St Pancras Almshouses
14 St Dominic RC Prim Sch
15 Fleet Prim Sch

71

A1 1 Bridge Ho
2 Hardington
3 Mead Cl
4 Rugmere
5 Tottenhall
6 Beauvale
7 Broomfield
8 Camden Coll of English
A2 1 Silverbirch Wlk
2 Penshurst
3 Wingham
4 Westwell
5 Chislet
6 Burmarsh
7 Shipton Ho
8 Stonegate
9 Leysdown
10 Headcorn
11 Lenham
12 Halstow
13 Fordcombe
14 Cannington
15 Langridge
16 Athlone Ho
17 Pentland Ho

18 Beckington
19 Hawkridge
20 Edington
21 Rhyl Prim Sch
22 Haverstock Sch
B1 1 Ferdinand Ho
2 Harmood Ho
3 Hawley Rd
4 Hawley Mews
5 Leybourne St
6 Barling
7 Tiptree
8 Havering
9 Candida Ct
10 Lorraine Ct
11 Donnington Ct
12 Welford Ct
13 Torbay Ct
14 Bradfield Ct
15 Torbay St
16 Water La
17 Leybourne Rd
18 Haven St
19 Stucley Pl
20 Lawrence Ho
21 Chalcot Sch
22 Holy Trinity & Saint Silas CE Prim Sch
23 Hawley Inf Sch
B2 1 Ashington
2 Priestley Ho
3 Leonard Day Ho
4 Old Dairy Mews
5 Monmouth Ho
6 Alpha Ct
7 Una Ho
8 Widford
9 Heybridge
10 Roxwell
11 Hamstead Gates
12 Kingsway Coll
B4 1 Denyer Ho
2 Stephenson Ho
3 Trevithick Ho
4 Brunel Ho
5 Newcomen Ho
6 Faraday Ho
7 Winifrede Paul Ho
8 Wardlow
9 Fletcher Ct
10 Tideswell
11 Grangemill
12 Hambrook Ct
13 Calver
C1 1 Cherry Tree Ct
2 Chichester Ct
3 Durdans Ho
4 Philia Ho
5 Bernard Shaw Ct
6 Foster Ct
7 Bessemer Ct
8 Hogarth Ct
9 Rochester Ct
10 Soane Ct
11 Wallett Ct
12 Inwood Ct
13 Wrotham Rd
14 St Thomas Ct
15 Caulfield Ct
16 Bruges Pl
17 Reachview Cl
18 Lawfords Wharf
C3 1 Eleanor Ho
2 Falkland Pl
3 Kensington Ho
4 Willingham Cl
5 Kenbrook Ho
6 Aborfield
7 Great Field
8 Appleford
9 Forties The
10 Maud Wilkes Cl
11 Dunne Mews
12 Dowdeny Cl
13 Kentish Town CE Prim Sch
C4 1 Benson Ct
2 Tait Ho
3 Manorfield Cl
4 Greatfield Cl
5 Longley Ho
6 Lampson Ho
7 Davidson Ho
8 Palmer Ho
9 Lambourn Cl
10 Morris Ho
11 Owen Ho
12 Eleanor Palmer Prim Sch
C5 1 Hunter Ho
2 Fisher Ho
3 Lang Ho
4 Temple Ho
5 Palmer Ho
6 Carlisle Ho
7 Durham Ho
8 Suffolk Ho
9 Lincoln Ho
10 Llewellyn Ho
11 Fell Ho

12 Aveling Ho
13 Merryweather Ct
14 Brennands Ct
15 St Christophers Ct
16 Francis Terrace Mews
17 Tremlett Mews
C6 1 Flowers Mews
2 Archway Cl
3 Sandridge St
4 Bovingdon Cl
5 Cavell Ct
6 Torrence Ho
7 Rowan Wlk
8 Laurel Cl
9 Forest Way
10 Larch Cl
11 Pine Cl
12 Alder Mews
13 Aspen Cl
14 Hargrave Park Prim Sch
15 Middlesex Univ (Archway Campus)
D1 1 Hillier Ho
2 Gairloch Ho
3 Cobham Mews
4 Bergholt Mews
5 Blakeney Cl
6 Weavers Way
7 Allensbury Pl
D2 1 Rowstock
2 Peckwater Ho
3 Wolsey Ho
4 Pandian Way
5 Busby Mews
6 Caledonian Sq
7 Canal Bvd
8 Northpoint Sq
9 Lock Mews
10 Carters Cl
11 York Ho
12 Hungerford Rd
13 Cliff Road Studios
14 Cliff Ct
15 Camelot Ho
16 Church Studios
17 Camden Terr
18 Brecknock Prim Sch
19 Hungerford Prim Sch
D3 1 Blake Ho
2 Quelch Ho
3 Lee Ho
4 Willbury Ho
5 Howell Ho
6 Holmsbury Ho
7 Leith Ho
8 Betchworth Ho
9 Rushmore Ho
10 Dugdale Ho
11 Horsendon Ho
12 Colley Ho
13 Coombe Ho
14 Ivinghoe Ho
15 Buckhurst Ho
16 Saxonbury Ct
17 Charlton Ct
18 Apollo Studios
19 Barn Cl
20 Long Meadow
21 Landleys Field
22 Margaret Bondfield Ho
23 Haywood Lo
24 Torriano Jun & Inf Schs
D4 1 Fairlie Ct
2 Trecastle Way
3 Dalmeny Avenue Est
4 Hyndman Ho
5 Carpenter Ho
6 Graham Ho
7 Tufnell Mans
D5 1 Melchester Ho
2 Norcombe Ho
3 Weatherbury Ho
4 Wessex Ho
5 Archway Bsns Ctr
6 Harford Mews
7 Opera Ct
8 Rupert Ho
9 All Saints Church
D6 1 Bowerman Ct
2 Gresham Pl
3 Hargrave Mans
4 Church Garth
5 John King Ct
6 Ramsey Ct
7 St John's Upper Holloway CE Prim Sch
8 Byam Shaw Sch of Art

72
A2 1 Clock Tower Pl
2 Clock View Cres
3 Jim Veal Dr
4 Gower Sch The
A3 1 Kimble Ho
2 Saxonbury Ct
3 Poynder Ct
4 Pangbourne Ho
5 Moulsford Ho

A4 1 Arcade The
2 Macready Pl
3 Cardwell Rd
4 Mcmorran Ho
5 Crayford Ho
6 Whitby Ct
7 Prospect Pl
8 City & Islington Coll (Ctr for Bsns, Arts & Technology)
A5 1 Northview
2 Tufnell Park Mans
3 Fulford Mans
4 Tollington Ho
5 Grafton Prim Sch
A6 1 Bracey Mews
2 Christie Ct
3 Ringmer Gdns
4 Kingsdown Rd
5 Cottenham Ho
6 St Paul's Ct
7 Rickthorne Rd
8 Stanley Terr
9 Arundel Lo
10 Landseer Ct
11 St Mark's Prim Sch
B1 1 Kerwick Cl
2 Rydston Cl
3 Skegness Ho
4 Frederica St
5 Ponder St
6 Kings Ct
7 Freeling St
8 Coatbridge Ho
9 Tilloch St
B2 1 Burns Ho
2 Scott Ho
3 Wellington Mews
4 Roman Ct
5 Piccadilly Ct
6 Knowledge Point Sch
B3 1 Culverin Ct
2 Garand Ct
3 Mount Carmel
B4 1 Buckmaster Ho
2 Loreburn Ho
3 Cairns Ho
4 Halsbury Ho
5 Chelmsford Ho
6 Cranworth Ho
7 City & Islington Coll (Ctr for Health, Social & Child Care)
B5 1 Pakeman Prim Sch
2 London Meridian Coll
3 American Univ in London The
4 South Eastern Univ
5 Dean Coll of London
6 Montem Prim Sch
B6 1 Berkeley Wlk
2 Lazar Wlk
3 Thistlewood Cl
4 Tomlins Wlk
5 Andover Ho
6 Barmouth Ho
7 Chard Ho
8 Christ the King RC Prim Sch
9 Methley Ho
10 Rainford Ho
11 Woodbridge Cl
12 Allerton Wlk
13 Falconer Wlk
14 Sonderburg Rd
15 St Mark's Mans
16 Athol Ct
17 Pooles Park Prim Sch
C1 1 Mountfort Terr
2 Avon Ho
3 Buckland Ho
4 Dovey Lo
5 Carfree Cl
6 Mitchell Ho
7 New College Mews
8 Lofting Ho
9 Brooksby Ho
10 Cara Ho
11 Thornhill Prim Sch
12 North London Science Ctr
C2 1 London Metropolitian Univ (Spring Ho)
C3 1 Slaney Pl
2 Eastwood Cl
3 Milton Pl
4 Hartnoll Ho
5 St James School Flats
6 Widnes Ho
7 Tranmere Ho
8 Victoria Mans
9 Formby Ct
10 Mersey Ho
11 Birkenhead Ho
12 Drayton Park Mews
13 Drayton Park Prim Sch
C6 1 Brookfield
2 Churnfield
3 Cornwallis Sq
D1 1 Islington Park Mews

2 Evelyn Denington Ct
3 Bassingbourn Ho
4 Cadmore Ho
5 Adstock Ho
6 Garston Ho
7 Flitton Ho
8 Datchworth Ho
9 Battishill St
10 Almeida St
11 Edward's Cotts
12 Hyde's Pl
13 Tyndale Terr
14 Spriggs Ho
15 Barratt Ho
16 Spencer Pl
17 Chadston Ho
18 Whiston Ho
19 Wakelin Ho
20 Tressel Ho
21 Canonbury Ct
22 Halton Ho
23 Shillingford St
24 Highburty Mans
25 Premier Ho
26 Waterloo Gdns
27 William Tyndale Prim Sch
D2 1 Hampton Ct
2 Salisbury Ho
3 Canonbury Prim Sch
4 Laycock Prim Sch
D3 1 De Barowe Mews
2 Fieldview Ct
3 Viewpoint
4 Ashurst Lo
5 Highbury Fields Sch
6 London Metropolitan Univ (Ladbroke Ho)
7 Robinswood Mews
D4 1 Chestnuts The
2 Bowen Ct
3 Peckett Sq
4 De Barowe Mews
D5 1 Hurlock Ho
2 Blackstock Ho
3 Vivian Comma Cl
4 Monsell Ct
D6 1 Parkwood Prim Sch
2 Ambler Prim Sch
3 City & Islington Coll (Ctr for Lifelong Learning)

73
A1 1 Astey's Row
2 Lincoln Ho
3 Worcester Ho
4 Melville Pl
5 Wontner Ct
6 Hedingham Cl
7 Laundry La
8 Base Apartments
9 Walkinshaw Ct
10 New Bentham Ct
11 Bentham Ct
12 Haslam Ho
13 Horsfield Ho
14 Riverside Ho
15 Eric Fletcher Ct
16 Annette Cres
17 Ashby Ho
18 Lindsey Mews
19 Cardigan Wlk
20 Red House Sq
21 Orchard Cl
22 Queensbury St
23 Raynor Pl
A2 1 Crowline Wlk
2 Upper Handa Wlk
3 Handa Wlk
4 Lismore Wlk
5 Bardsey Wlk
6 Walney Wlk
7 Upper Bardsey Wlk
8 Upper Lismore Wlk
9 Sark Ho
10 Guernsey Ho
11 Guernsey Rd
12 Sybil Thorndike Ho
13 Clephane Rd
14 Florence Nightingale Ho
15 Jersey Ho
16 Jethou Ho
17 Islay Wlk
18 Upper Caldy Wlk
19 Caldy Wlk
20 Alderney Ho
21 Gulland Wlk
22 Nightingale Rd
23 Upper Gulland Wlk
24 Church Rd
25 Oransay Rd
26 Canonbury Yd E
A3 1 Pearfield Ho
2 Larchfield Ho
3 Beresford Terr
4 Pondfield Ho
5 Ashfield Ho

6 Elmfield Ho
7 Highbury Grove Sch
A4 1 Fountain Mews
2 Woodstock Ho
3 Henson Ct
4 Taverner Sq
B1 1 Downham Ct
2 Trafalgar Point
B2 1 John Kennedy Ho
2 John Kennedy Lo
3 Ball's Pond Pl
4 Haliday Wlk
5 Queen Elizabeth Ct
6 Canonbury Hts
7 Pinnacle The
8 Threadgold Ho
9 Wakeham St
10 Saffron Ct
11 Callaby Terr
12 Tilney Gdns
13 Westcliff Ho
14 Ilford Ho
15 Ongar Ho
16 Greenhills Terr
17 Romford Ho
18 Bute Wlk
19 Upper Ramsey Wlk
20 Rona Wlk
21 Thorndike Rd
22 St Pauls Steiner Sch
B3 1 Newington Green Prim Sch
B4 1 Ledo Ho
2 Salween Ho
3 Prome Ho
4 Arakan Ho
5 Rangoon Ho
6 Mandalay Ho
7 Karen Ho
8 Wingate Ho
9 Jubet Ho
10 Orde Ho
11 Chindit Ho
12 Mabel Thornton Ho
13 Crawshay Ho
14 Avon Ho
15 Connaught Mans
16 Jonson Ho
17 Herrick Ho
18 Donne Ho
19 Thirlmere Ho
20 Grasmere Ho
B5 1 Betty Layward Prim Sch
B6 1 Chestnut Cl
2 Sycamore Ho
3 Lordship Ho
4 Clissold Ho
5 Beech Ho
6 Laburnum Ho
7 Ormond Ho
8 Yew Tree Ct
9 Oak Ho
C1 1 Dorchester Ct
2 Wareham Ct
3 Dorset Ct
4 Stratton Ct
5 Swanage Ct
6 Blandford Ct
7 Portland Ct
8 Oscar Faber Pl
9 Metropolitan Bsns Ctr
10 Lancaster Cl
11 Palazzo Apartments
12 Watercress Pl
C2 1 Kingsland Gn
2 Kingsland Pas
3 Metropolitan Benefit Societies Almshouses
4 Nimrod Pas
5 De Beauvoir Ct
6 Warburton Ct
7 Buckingham Mews
8 Aztec Ct
9 Kerridge Ct
10 Isabella Mews
11 St Jude & St Paul's CE Prim Sch
12 De Beauvoir Prim Sch
13 Our Lady & St Joseph RC Prim Sch
14 Childrens House Upper Sch
C3 1 Hewling Ho
2 Matthias Ho
3 Port Royal Pl
4 Cressington Cl
5 King Henry's Yd
6 Bronte Ho
7 Sewell Ho
8 Lydgate Ho
9 Patmore Ho
10 Congreve Ho
11 Elton St
12 Conrad Ho
13 Southwell Ho
14 Neptune Ho
15 Campion Ho
16 Webster Ho
17 Meredith Ho

18 Beckford Ho
19 Ashley Ct
20 Hayling Cl
21 Millard Cl
22 Lydford Cl
23 Salcombe Rd
24 Truman's Rd
25 Templeton Cl
26 John Campbell Rd
27 Gillett Pl
28 Bradbury St
29 Thomas Crowell Ct
30 Shellgrove Rd
C4 1 Londesborough Ho
2 Knebworth Ho
3 Knebworth Rd
4 Bransby Ct
5 Imperial Ave
6 Leonard Pl
7 Shakspeare Mews
8 Binyon Ho
9 Shelley Ho
10 Browning Ho
11 Burns Ho
12 Andrew Marvell Ho
13 Wycliffe Ho
14 Blake Ho
15 Marlowe Ho
16 Fletcher Ho
17 Chaucer Ct
32 St Matthias's CE Prim Sch
C5 1 Gujarat Ho
2 Marton Rd
3 Painsthorpe Rd
4 Selkirk Ho
5 Defoe Ho
6 Edward Friend Ho
7 Sheridan Ho
8 Barrie Ho
9 Arnold Ho
10 Macaulay Ho
11 Stowe Ho
12 Carlyle Ho
13 Shaftesbury Ho
14 Lillian Cl
15 Swift Ho
16 Dryden Ho
17 Scott Ct
18 Kingsfield Ho
19 Uhura Sq
20 Hartopp Ct
C6 1 Denman Ho
2 St Mary's Stoke Newington CE Prim Sch
D1 1 Hilborough Rd
2 Shoreditch Ct
3 Evergreen Sq
4 Wyndhams Ct
5 Festival Ct
6 Fortune Ct
7 Rose Ct
8 Ability Plaza
9 Briar Ct
10 Lomas Dr
11 Queensbridge Inf Sch
D2 1 Prospect Ho
2 Woodland St
3 Crosby Wlk
4 Kirkland Wlk
5 Bowness Cl
6 Carlisle Wlk
7 Skelton Cl
8 Camerton Cl
9 Buttermere Wlk
10 Houghton Cl
11 Hayton Cl
12 Kingsland Sh Ctr
13 Springfield Ho
14 Parton Lo
15 Sanctuary Mews
16 Fenton Cl
D3 1 Miller's Terr
2 Chow Sq
3 Drysdale Flats
4 Gateway Mews
5 Birkbeck Mews
6 Winchester Pl
D4 1 Coronation Ave
2 Morris Blitz Ct
3 Shacklewell Ho
4 Alexandra Ct
5 Shacklewell Prim Sch
6 Princess May Prim Sch
D5 1 Lawrence Bldgs
2 Cottage Wlk
3 Batley Pl
D6 1 Graham St
2 Garnham St
3 Sanford La
4 Sanford Wlk
5 Abney Gdns
6 Fleet Wood
8 Simon Marks Jewish Prim Sch

9 William Patten Prim Sch

74

A1
1 Aldington Ct
2 Bayton Ct
3 Rochford Wlk
4 Windrush Cl
5 Gayhurst Prim Sch
A2 **3** Burdon Ct
4 Thomson Ct
5 Bruno Ct
6 Thackeray Mews
7 Madinah Rd
A3 **1** Kingsdown Ho
2 Glendown Ho
3 Moredown Ho
4 Blakeney Cl
5 Beeston Ct
6 Benabo Ct
7 David Devine Ho
8 Kreedman Wlk
9 Hermitage Row
10 Grafton Ct
11 Lushington Terr
12 Aspen Ct
13 Pykewell Lo
14 Albion Works Studios
A5 **1** Ravenscourt
2 Mellington Ct
3 Rendlesham Ho
4 Carroll Ct
6 St Scholastica's RC Prim Sch
A6 **1** Cazenove Mans
2 Chedworth Ho
3 Aldergrove Ho
4 Abbotstone Ho
5 Briggeford Cl
6 Inglethorpe Ho
7 Ashdown Ho
8 Epping Ho
9 Cypress Cl
B1 **1** Fortescue Ave
2 Pemberton Pl
3 Weston Wlk
4 Bayford St Ind Ctr
5 Bayford St
6 Sidworth St
7 Helmsley St
8 Cyntra Pl
9 Signal Ho
10 All Nations Ho
11 Vanguard Ho
12 Hacon Sq
B2 **1** Bohemia Pl
2 Graham Mans
3 Marvin St
4 Boscobel Ho
5 Royal Oak Rd
6 Colonnades The
7 Sylvester Ho
8 Sylvester Path
9 Doctor Spurstowe Almshouses
10 Great Eastern Bldgs
11 Sojourner-Truth Cl
B3 **1** Birchington Ho
2 Bicknor Ho
3 Boxley Ho
4 Adisham Ho
5 Cranbrook Ho
6 Marden Ho
7 Broome Ho
8 Crandale Ho
9 Cheriton Ho
10 Ditton Ho
11 Langley Ho
12 Dymchurch Ho
13 Elham Ho
14 Davina Ho
15 Pembury Pl
16 Downs Ct
17 Perrywood Ho
18 Staplehurst Ho
19 Pegwell Ho
20 Yalding Ho
21 Northbourne Ho
22 Monkton Ho
23 Milsted Ho
24 Athlone Cl
25 Clarence Pl
26 Gould Terr
27 Quested Ct
28 Brett Pas
29 Marcon Ct
30 Appleton Ct
31 Institute Pl
B4 **1** Ross Ct
2 Downs La
3 Gaviller Pl
4 Robert Owen Lo
5 Apprentice Way
6 Arrowe Ct
7 Gilwell Ct
8 Sutton Ct

9 St Andrews Mans
10 Kinnoull Mans
11 Rowhill Mans
12 Sladen Pl
13 Mothers Sq The
14 Richborough Ho
15 Sandgate Ho
16 Sheppey Ho
B5 **1** De Vere Ct
2 Redcliffe Ct
3 Greville Ct
4 Anthony Kendal Ho
5 Brook House Sixth Form Coll
6 Al Falah Sch
7 Baden Powell Sch
B6 **1** Wentwood Ho
2 Woolmer Ho
3 Warwick Ct
4 Winslade Ho
5 Morriss Ho
6 Woodfield Ho
7 Rossendale Ho
8 Ettrick Ho
9 Charnwood Ho
10 Boyne Ho
11 Whitwell Ho
12 Scardale Ho
13 Hendale Ho
14 Brampton Cl
15 Aveley Ct
16 Aldeburgh Cl
17 Dennington Cl
18 Chiltern Ct
C1 **1** Pitcairn Ho
2 Lyme Grove Ho
3 Shakespeare Ho
4 Upcott Ho
5 Loddiges Ho
6 Parkinson Ho
7 Sloane Ho
8 Vanbrugh Ho
9 Cambridge Pas
10 Lyttleton Ho
11 Victoria Park Ct
12 Tullis Ho
13 Fairchild Ho
14 Forsyth Ho
15 Tradescant Ho
16 Mason Ho
17 Capel Ho
18 Cordwainers Ct
19 Bridgeman Ho
20 St Thomas's Pl
21 Barclay Ho
22 Clayton Ho
23 Danby Ho
24 Sherard Ho
25 Catesby Ho
26 Petiver Ct
27 Leander Ct
28 Philip Turner Est
29 Grendon Ho
30 Shore Mews
31 Shore Bsns Ctr
32 Kendal Ho
33 Classic Mans
34 Tudor Ho
35 Park Ho
36 Enterprise Ho
37 Alpine Gr
38 Clarendon Cl
39 Rotheley Ho
40 Bernie Grant Ho
41 Orchard Prim Sch
42 St John of Jerusalem CE Prim Sch
C2 **1** Woolpack Ho
2 Elvin Ho
3 Thomas Ho
4 Hockley Ho
5 Retreat Ho
6 Butfield Ho
7 Brooksbank Ho
8 Cresset Ho
9 Brooksbank St
10 Lennox Ho
11 Milborne Ho
12 Collent Ho
13 Middlesex Pl
14 Elsdale Ho
15 Devonshire Hall
16 Brent Ho
17 Morningside Prim Sch
18 Hackney Free & Parochial CE Sec Sch
C3 **1** St John & St James CE Prim Sch
C6 **1** Haybridge Ho
2 Framlingham Ct
3 Halesworth Cl
4 Harleston Ct
5 Lowestoft Cl
6 Howard Ho
7 Templar Ho
D1 **1** Stuart Ho
2 Gascoyne Ho
3 Chelsfield Point
4 Sundridge Ho
5 Banbury Ho

6 Lauriston Ho
D2 **1** Musgrove Ho
2 Cheyney Ho
3 Haynes Ho
4 Warner Ho
5 Gilby Ho
6 Gadsden Ho
7 Risley Ho
8 Baycliffe Ho
9 Sheldon Ho
10 Offley Ho
11 Latimer Ho
12 Ribstone Ho
13 Salem Ho
14 Fieldwick Ho
15 Lever Ct
16 Matson Ho
17 Wilding Ho
18 Rennell Ho
19 Dycer Ho
20 Granard Ho
21 Whitelock Ho
22 Harrowgate Ho
23 Cass Ho
24 Lofts on the Park
25 Heathcote Point
26 Ravenscroft Point
27 Vanner Point
28 Hensley Point
29 San Ho
30 Berger Prim Sch
D4 **1** Cromford Path
2 Longford Ho
3 Overbury Ho
4 Heanor Ct
5 Wharfedale Ct
6 Ladybower Ho
7 Ilkeston Ct
8 Derby Ct
9 Rushmore Cres
10 Blackwell Cl
11 Belper Ct
12 Rushmore Prim Sch

75

A2 **1** Chigwell Ct
2 Wellday Ho
3 Selman Ho
4 Vaine Ho
5 Trower Ho
6 St Dominics RC Prim Sch
B2 **1** Mallard Cl
2 Merriam Ave
3 Gainsborough St
4 Palace Ct
5 St Anthony's Cl
6 Trowbridge Est
7 Wick Village
D6 **1** Hammond Ct
2 Sorensen Ct
3 Hinton Ct

76

A6 **1** Lantern of Knowledge Boys Sec Sch
B1 **1** Service Route No 2
2 Service Route No 3
7 Newham Sixth Form Coll (Stratford Ctr)
B4 **1** Mulberry Ct
2 Rosewood Ct
3 Gean Ct
4 Blackthorn Ct
5 Cypress Ct
C1 **1** Stratford Office Village The
2 Violet Ct
3 Mandrake Way
4 Brimstone Ho
5 Hibiscus Lo
6 Glasier Ct
C2 **1** Christ the Redeemer Bible Coll
C3 **1** Bordeaux Ho
2 Luxembourg Mews
3 Basle Ho
C5 **1** Acacia Bsns Ctr
2 Brook Ct
3 Gainsfield Ct
4 Artesian Wlk
5 Doreen Capstan Ho
6 Apollo Pl
7 Peppermint Pl
8 Denmark St
9 Mills Ct
10 Paramount Ho
11 Robinson Cl
C6 **1** Nansen Ct
2 Mallinson Ct
3 Barbara Ward Ct
4 Caradon Cl
5 Noel Baker Ct
6 Corigan Ct
7 Norman Ho
8 Willow Ct
9 Lime Ct
10 Owens Mews

11 Marnie Ct
12 Cotton Cl
13 Connaught Sch for Girls (Annexe)
14 East London Coll
D1 **1** Flint Cl
2 St Matthews Ct
3 Ammonite Ho
4 Stone Ct
D2 **1** Common The
2 Wolffe Gdns
3 College Pt
4 Onyx Mews
5 Candlelight Ct
6 Boltons The

77

A4 **1** Bronte Cl
2 Anna Neagle Cl
3 Brownlow Rd
4 Carrington Gdns
5 Vera Lynn Cl
C1 **1** Sarwan Ho
2 Bridgepoint Lofts
3 Vineyard Studios
C3 **1** Sandringham Prim Sch
2 Iman Zakaria Acad

78

A3 **1** Salisbury Prim Sch
C3 **1** Stewart Rainbird Ho
2 Abraham Fisher Ho
3 Redo Ho
4 George Comberton Wlk
C4 **1** Cardamom Ct
2 Annie Taylor Ho
3 Richard Fell Ho
4 Susan Lawrence Ho
5 Walter Hurford Par
6 John Cornwell VC Ho
7 Alfred Prior Ho
C5 **1** Charlbury Ho
2 Willis Ho
3 Arthur Walls Ho
4 Blakesley Ho
5 Twelve Acre Ho
6 Beech Ct
7 Golding Ct
D1 **1** Aveley Mans
2 Harlow Mans
3 Danbury Mans
4 Mayland Mans
5 Bowers Ho
6 Webber Ho
7 Paulson Ho
8 Collins Ho
9 Jack Cook Ho
D3 **1** St Luke's Path
2 Springfield Ct
D5 **1** Postway Mews
2 Oakfield Ho
3 Janice Mews
4 Kenneth More Rd
5 Clements Ct
6 Handforth Rd
7 Churchill Ct
8 Oakfield Lo
9 Langdale Ct
10 Ilford Chambers
D6 **1** York Ho
2 Opal Mews
3 Florentine Ho
4 Kingsley Mews
5 Hainault Bridge Par
7 Ilford Ursuline Prep Sch

79

A1 **1** Harvey Ho
2 Gower Ho
3 Apex Prim Sch
A6 **1** Spectrum Twr
2 Thames View
3 City View
4 Centreway
5 Axon Pl
D1 **1** Gibbards Cott
2 Upney Ct
3 Edgefield Ct
4 Manor Ct
5 Lambourne Gdns
6 Westone Mans
7 Loveland Mans
8 Edward Mans
9 Clarke Mans
10 Dawson Gdns
11 Sebastian Ct

80

A1 **1** Bristol Ho
2 Canterbury Ho
3 Durham Ho
4 Wells Ho
5 Winchester Ho
6 Rosalind Ct
7 Exeter Ho

8 Wheatley Mans
9 Greenwood Mans
10 Plymouth Ho
11 Graham Mans
12 Portia Ct

81

C5 **1** Markham Ct
2 Webb Ho
3 Preston Ho
4 Steadman Ho
5 Hyndman Ho
6 Clynes Ho
7 Henderson Ho
8 Blatchford Ho
9 Rogers Ho
10 Sylvia Pankhurst Ho
11 Mary Macarthur Ho
12 Ellen Wilkinson Ho
D2 **1** Picador Ho
2 Centurion Lodge
3 Louis Ct
4 Watsons Lo
5 Carpenters Ct
6 Bell Ho
7 Rounders Ct
8 Oldmead Ho
9 Jervis Ct
10 Bartletts Ct
11 Royal Par
12 Richardson Gdns
13 Forsyth Ct
14 Eldridge Ct
15 Madison Ct
16 Bowery Ct
17 Rivington Ct

82

D3 **1** Marlborough Par
2 Blenheim Par
3 Lea Ct
4 Westbourne Par
5 Whiteleys Par
6 Hillingdon Par
7 New Broadway

84

C4 **1** Dilston Cl
2 Wells Ct
3 Willett Cl
4 Merlin Ct
5 Glyndebourne Ct
6 Albury Ct
7 Osterley Ct
8 Hatfield Ct
9 Gayhurst Ct
D4 **1** Caravelle Gdns
2 Farman Gr
3 Viscount Gr
4 Tomahawk Gdns
5 Martlet Gr
6 Trident Gdns
7 Latham Ct
8 Jupiter Ct
9 Westland Ct
10 Seasprite Ct
11 Convair Wlk
12 Mayfly Gdns
13 Valiant Ct
14 Woburn Twr
15 Brett Cl
16 Friars Cl
D5 **1** Medlar Cl
2 Cranberry Cl
3 Lely Ho
4 Girtin Ho
5 Cotman Ho
6 Raeburn Ho
7 Gainsborough Twr
8 Stanfield Ho
9 Millais Ct
10 Hunt Ct
11 Poynter Ct
12 Hogarth Ho
13 Constable Ho
14 Bonnington Ct
15 Romney Ct
16 Landseer Ho

85

B1 **1** St Crispins Ct
B3 **1** Weaver Ho
2 Caldon Ho
3 Ashby Ho
4 Welford Ho
5 Hertford Ho
6 Wey Ho
7 Middlewich Ho
8 Stourbridge Ho
B4 **1** Netherton Ho
2 Keadby Ho
3 Tame Ho
4 Dorset Ct
D1 **1** Thurlestone Ct
2 Disley Ct
3 Burgess Ct

4 Bayliss Cl
5 Lytham Ct
6 Winford Par
7 Brunel Pl
8 Rutherford Twr
9 Rountree Ct

86
A1 1 Farnham Ct
2 Gleneagles Twr
3 Birkdale Ct
4 Verulam Ct
5 Hartsbourne Ct
6 Ferndown Ct
7 Deal Ct
8 St David's Ct
9 Portrush Ct
10 Alnmouth Ct
11 Panmure Ct
12 Peterhead Ct
13 Sunningdale Ct
D2 1 Denbigh Ct
2 Devon Ct
3 Dorset Ct
4 Glamorgan Ct
5 Gloucester Ct
6 Hereford Ct
7 Merioneth Ct
8 Oxford Ct
9 Monmouth Ct
10 Paddington Ct
11 Pembroke Ct
12 Chadwick Cl
13 Cotts Cl
D3 1 Berkshire Ct
2 Buckingham Ct
3 Cardigan Ct
4 Carmarthen Ct
5 Cornwall Ct
6 Merlin Ct
7 Osprey Ct
8 Pelham Pl
9 Puffin Ct
10 Fulmar Ct
11 Turnstone Terr
D5 1 Medway Par
2 Brabstone Ho
3 Cotswold Ct

87
B1 1 Ealing Coll
2 Avenue House Sch
B3 1 Woodbury Ct
2 Edward Ct
3 Park Lo
C1 1 Hurley Ct
2 Amherst Gdns
3 Tudor Ho
4 Hilton Ho
C2 1 Hutton Ct
2 Cain Ct
3 Langdale Ct
4 William Ct
5 Castlebar Ct
6 Warren Ct
7 White Lo
8 Queen's Ct
9 King's Ct
10 Cheriton Cl
11 Stanley Ct
12 Juniper Ho
13 Pendlewood Cl
15 St Benedict's Jun Sch
C3 1 Holtoake Ct
2 Pitshanger Ct
3 Holtoake Ho
D2 14 St Gregory's RC Prim Sch

88
A4 1 Nelson Ho
2 Gordon Ho
3 Frobisher Ho
4 Wellington Ho
5 Fairfax Ho
A5 1 Carlyon Mans
2 Ainslie Ct
3 Millers Ct
4 Priory Ct
5 Tylers Ct
6 Twyford Ct
7 Rose Ct
8 Laurel Ct
9 Sundew Ct
10 Campion Ct
11 Foxglove Ct
C1 1 Buckingham Ho
2 Chester Ct
3 Devon Ct
4 Essex Ho
5 Fife Ct
6 Gloucester Ct
7 Hereford Ho
8 Inverness Ct
9 Warwick Ho
10 York Ho
11 Suffolk Ho

12 Perth Ho
13 Norfolk Ho
14 Thanet Ct
15 Rutland Ct
16 Oxford Ct

89
A1 1 Avon Ct
2 Bromley Lo
3 Walter Ct
4 Lynton Terr
5 Acton Ho
6 Fells Haugh
7 Springfield Ct
8 Tamarind Ct
9 Lynton Ct
10 Aspen Ct
11 Pegasus Ct
12 Friary Park Ct
B1 1 Rosebank Gdns
2 Rosebank
3 Edinburgh Ho
4 Western Ct
5 Kilronan
B6 1 Carlyle Rd
2 Bernard Shaw Ho
3 Longlents Ho
4 Mordaunt Ho
5 Wilmers Ct
6 Stonebridge Ctr
7 Shakespeare Ave
8 Southcroft
9 Brent Adult Comm Education Service Coll
C5 1 Futters Ct
2 Barrett Ct
3 Elms The
4 Fairlight Ct
D5 1 New Crescent Yd
2 Harlesden Plaza
3 St Josephs Ct
4 Jubilee Cl
5 Ellery Cl

90
B1 1 Holborn Ho
2 Clement Danes Ho
3 Vellacott Ho
4 O'Driscoll Ho
5 King Ho
6 Daley Ho
7 Selma Ho
8 Garrett Ho
C1 1 Latimer Ind Est
2 Pankhurst Ho
3 Quadrangle The
4 Nightingale Ho
5 Gordon Ct
6 Ducane Cl
7 Browning Ho
8 Pavilion Terr
9 Ivebury Ct
10 Olympic Ho
C2 1 Galleywood Ho
2 Edgcote Ho
3 Cuffley Ho
4 Addlestone Ho
5 Hockliffe Ho
6 Sarratt Ho
7 Firle Ho
8 Sutton Est The
9 Terling Ho
10 Danes Ho
11 Udimore Ho
12 Vange Ho
13 Binbrook Ho
14 Yeadon Ho
15 Yatton Ho
16 Yarrow Ho
17 Clement Ho
18 Danebury
19 Coronation Ct
20 Calderon Pl
21 St Quintin Gdns
C3 1 Princess Alice Ho
2 Yoxall Ho
3 Yorkley Ho
4 Northaw Ho
5 Oakham Ho
6 Markyate Ho
7 Letchmore Ho
8 Pagham Ho
9 Quendon Ho
10 Redbourn Ho
11 Ketton Ho
12 Hillman Dr
D1 1 Kelfield Ct
2 Downing Ho
3 Crosfield Ct
4 Robinson Ho
5 Scampston Mews
6 Girton Villas
7 Ray Ho
8 Walmer Ho
9 Goodrich Ct
10 Arthur Ct
11 Whitstable Ho
12 Kingsnorth Ho

13 Bridge Cl
14 Prospect Ho
15 St Marks Rd
16 Whitchurch Ho
17 Blechynden Ho
18 Waynflete Sq
19 Bramley Ho
20 Dixon Ho
21 Oxford Gardens Prim Sch
22 Bassett House Sch
D2 1 Treverton Twr
2 Raymede Twr
3 Bruce Ho
4 Balfour Ho
5 Burleigh Ho
6 Sion-Manning RC Sch for Girls
7 St Charles RC Prim Sch
8 St Charles RC Sixth Form Coll
D4 1 Westfield Ct
2 Tropical Ct
3 Chamberlayne Mans
4 Quadrant The
5 Queens Park Ct
6 Warfield Yd
7 Regent St
8 Cherrytree Ho
9 Artisan Mews
10 Artisan Quarter

91
A1 1 Malton Mews
2 Lancaster Lo
3 Manning Ho
4 Galsworthy Ho
5 Hudson Ho
6 Cambourne Mews
7 Upper Talbot Wlk
8 Kingsdown Cl
9 Lower Clarendon Wlk
10 Talbot Grove Ho
11 Clarendon Wlk
12 Upper Clarendon Wlk
13 Camelford Wlk
14 Upper Camelford Wlk
15 Camelford Ct
16 Thomas Jones Prim Sch
17 Notting Hill Prep Sch
A2 1 Murchison Ho
2 Macaulay Ho
3 Chesterton Ho
4 Chiltern Ho
5 Lionel Ho
6 Watts Ho
7 Wheatstone Ho
8 Telford Ho
9 Golborne Mews
10 Millwood St
11 St Columb's Ho
12 Norfolk Mews
13 Lionel Mews
14 Kensington & Chelsea Coll
15 Bevington Prim Sch
16 Sion-Manning RC Sch for Girls
17 Lloyd Williamson Sch
A3 1 Sycamore Wlk
2 Westgate Bsns Ctr
3 Buspace Studios
4 Bosworth Ho
5 Golborne Gdns
6 Appleford Ho
7 Adair Twr
8 Gadsden Ho
9 Southam Ho
10 Norman Butler Ho
11 Thompson Ho
12 Wells Ho
13 Paul Ho
14 Olive Blythe Ho
15 Katherine Ho
16 Breakwell Ct
17 Pepler Ho
18 Edward Kennedy Ho
19 Winnington Ho
20 Queen's Park Prim Sch
21 Middle Row Prim Sch
22 St Mary RC Prim Sch
23 St Thomas' CE Prim Sch
A4 1 Selby Sq
2 Severn Ave
3 Stansbury Sq
4 Tolhurst Dr
5 John Fearon Wlk
6 Mundy Ho
7 Macfarren Ho
8 Bantock Ho
9 Banister Ho
10 Batten Ho
11 Croft Ho
12 Courtville Ho
13 Mounsey Ho
14 Bliss Mews
15 Symphony Mews

B1 1 Silvester Ho
2 Golden Cross Mews
3 Tavistock Mews
4 Clydesdale Ho
5 Colville Prim Sch
6 Melchester
7 Pinehurst Ct
8 Denbigh Ho
B2 1 Blagrove Rd
2 All Saints Ho
3 Tavistock Ho
4 Leamington Ho
B3 1 Octavia Mews
2 Russell's Wharf
3 Western Ho
4 Kelly Mews
5 Queen Elizabeth II Jubilee Sch
B4 1 Boyce Ho
2 Farnaby Ho
3 Danby Ho
4 Purday Ho
5 Naylor Ho
6 St Judes Ho
7 Leeve Ho
8 Longhurst Ho
9 Harrington Ct
10 Mulberry Ct
11 Kilburn Ho
12 Carlton Vale Inf Sch
B5 1 Claremont Ct
2 William Saville Ho
3 Western Ct
4 Bond Ho
5 Crone Ct
6 Wood Ho
7 Winterleys
8 Carlton Ho
9 Fiona Ct
10 Kilburn Park Sch
C1 1 Shottsford
2 Tolchurch
3 Casterbridge
4 Sandbourne
5 Anglebury
6 Weatherbury
7 Westbourne Gr Mews
8 Rosehart Mews
9 Viscount Ct
10 Hereford Mans
11 Hereford Mews
12 St Mary of the Angels RC Prim Sch
C2 1 Ascot Ho
2 Ashgrove Ct
3 Lockbridge Ct
4 Swallow Ct
5 Nightingale Lo
6 Hammond Lo
7 Penfield Lo
8 Harvey Lo
9 Hunter Lo
10 Barnard Lo
11 Falcon Lo
12 Johnson Lo
13 Livingstone Lo
14 Nuffield Lo
15 Finch Lo
16 Polesworth Ho
17 Oversley Ho
18 Derrycombe Ho
19 Buckshead Ho
20 Combe Ho
21 Culham Ho
22 Dainton Ho
23 Devonport Ho
24 Honwell Ho
25 Truro Ho
26 Sunderland Ho
27 Stonehouse Ho
28 Riverford Ho
29 Portishead Ho
30 Mickleton Ho
31 Keyham Ho
32 Moulsford Ho
33 Shrewsbury Mews
34 St Stephen's Mews
35 Westway Lo
36 Langley Ho
37 Brindley Ho
38 Radway Ho
39 Astley Ho
40 Willow Ct
41 Larch Ct
42 Elm Ct
43 Beech Ct
44 Worcester Ct
45 Union Ct
46 Leicester Ct
47 Kennet Ct
48 Oxford Ct
49 Fazerley Ct
C3 1 Westside Ct
2 Byron Mews
3 Sutherland Ct
4 Fleming Cl
5 Hermes Cl
6 St Peter's CE Prim Sch
7 Paddington Acad
C4 1 Pentland Rd

2 Nelson Cl
3 Pavilion Ct
4 Masefield Ho
5 Austen Ho
6 Fielding Ho
7 Argo Bsns Ctr
8 John Ratcliffe Ho
9 Wymering Mans
10 City of Westminster Coll, Queens Park Ctr
11 Essendine Prim Sch
C5 1 Wells Ct
2 Cambridge Ct
3 Ely Ct
4 Durham Ct
5 St Augustine's CE High Sch
6 Sch of the Islamic Republic of Iran The
C6 1 Ryde Ho
2 Glengall Pass
3 Leith Yd
4 Daynor Ho
5 Varley Ho
6 Sandby Ho
7 Colas Mews
8 Bishopsdale Ho
9 Lorton Ho
10 Marshwood Ho
11 Ribblesdale Ho
12 Holmesdale Ho
13 Kilburn Vale Est
14 Kilburn Bridge
15 Coll of NW London
16 St Mary's Kilburn CE Prim Sch
D1 1 Vera Ct
2 Alexander Mews
3 Gurney Ho
4 Burdett Mews
5 Greville Lo
6 Hatherley Ct
7 Bridge Field Ho
8 Ralph Ct
9 Peters Ct
10 Pickering Mews
11 Riven Ct
12 Inver Ct
13 Cervantes Ct
14 Bishops Ct
15 Newbury Ho
16 Marlow Ho
17 Lynton Ho
18 Pembroke Ho
19 Pickering Ho
20 College Park Sch
21 Hallfield Jun & Inf Schs
D2 1 Our Lady of Dolours RC Prim Sch
2 Edward Wilson Prim Sch
3 St Mary Magdalene CE Prim Sch
D3 1 Ellwood Ct
26 St Saviour's CE Prim Sch
D4 1 City of Westminster Coll, Maida Vale Ctr
D5 1 Tollgate Ho
2 Regents Plaza
3 Royal Langford Apartments
4 Naima Jewish Prep Sch
5 St Augustine's Prim Sch
D6 1 Sylvan Ct
2 Birchington Ct
3 Farndale Ho
4 Greville Mews
5 Goldsmith's Pl
6 Remsted Ho
7 Bradwell Ho
8 Cheshunt Ho
9 Haliwell Ho
10 Broadoak Ho
11 Philip Ho
12 Hillsborough Ct
13 Sandbourne
14 Wingreen
15 Toneborough
16 Silverthorn
17 Kington Ho
18 Marrick Ho
19 Rutland Mews

95
C4 1 Pimlico Wlk
2 Aske Ho
3 Hathaway Ho
4 Haberdasher Pl
5 Fairchild Ho
6 Burtt Ho
7 Enfield Cloisters
8 McGregor Ct
9 Royal Oak Ct

10 Hoxton Mkt
11 Bath Pl
12 Chapel Pl
13 Standard Pl
14 Cleeve Workshops
15 Cleeve Ho
16 Printing House Yd
17 Perseverance Works
18 Crooked Billet Yd
19 Drysdale Ho
20 Castlefrank Ho
21 School App
22 Basing House Yd
23 Mail Coach Yd
24 St Monica's RC Prim Sch
25 Symister Mews
33 Hackney Com Coll

C5 1 Bracer Ho
2 Scorton Ho
3 Fern Cl
4 Macbeth Ho
5 Oberon Ho
6 Buckland Ct
7 Crondall Ct
8 Osric Path
9 Caliban Twr
10 Celia Ho
11 Juliet Ho
12 Bacchus Wlk
13 Malcolm Ho
14 Homefield St
15 Crondall Pl
16 Blanca Ho
17 Miranda Ho
18 Falstaff Ho
19 Charmian Ho
20 Myrtle Wlk
21 Arden Ho
22 Sebastian Ho
23 Stanway Ct
24 Jerrold St
25 Rosalind Ho
26 Cordelia Ho
27 Monteagle Ct
28 John Parry Ct
29 James Anderson Ct
30 Ben Jonson Ct
31 Sara Lane Ct
32 Walbrook Ct
34 Burbage Sch

C6 1 Portelet Ct
2 Trinity Ct
3 Rozel Ct
4 St Helier Ct
5 Corbiere Ho
6 Kenning Ho
7 Higgins Ho
8 Cavell Ho
9 Girling Ho
10 Fulcher Ho
11 Francis Ho
12 Norris Ho
13 Kempton Ho
14 Nesham Ho
15 Crossbow Ho
16 Catherine Ho
17 Strale Ho
18 Horner Hos
19 Stringer Hos
20 Whitmore Ho
21 Nightingale Ho
22 Wilmer Gdns
23 Arrow Ho
24 Archer Ho
25 Meriden Ho
26 Rover Ho
27 Bowyer Ho
28 Tiller Ho
29 Canalside Studios
30 Kleine Wharf
31 Benyon Wharf
32 Quebec Wharf
33 Belvedere Ct
34 Portfleet Pl

D4 1 Gorsuch Pl
2 Strout's Pl
3 Vaughan Est
4 George Loveless Ho
5 Baroness Rd
6 James Brine Ho
7 Arthur Wade Ho
8 Robert Owen Ho
9 Sivill Ho
10 Georgina Gdns
11 Old Market Sq
12 Cuff Point
13 Bakers Rents
14 Leopold Bldgs
15 Dunmore Point
16 Wingfield Ho
17 Gascoigne Pl
18 Mandela Ho
19 Virginia Rd
20 Briggs Ho
21 Packenham Ho
22 Gowan Ho

23 Kirton Gdns
24 Chambord Ho
25 Ducal St
26 Strickland Ho
27 Alliston Ho
28 Gibraltar Wlk
29 Equity Sq
30 Shacklewell St
31 Rochelle St
32 Sonning Ho
33 Culham Ho
34 Hurley Ho
35 Palissy St
36 Taplow Ho
37 Chertsey Ho
38 Sunbury Ho
39 Sunbury Workshops
40 Datchett Ho
41 Hocker St
42 Coll Sharp Ct
43 Marlow Studio Workshops
44 Marlow Ho
45 Shiplake Ho
46 Wargrave Ho
47 Iffley Ho
48 Virginia Prim Sch
49 Bethnal Green Tech Coll
50 Columbia Prim Sch

D5 1 Queensbridge Ct
2 Godwin Ho
3 Kent Ct
4 Brunswick Ho
5 Weymouth Ct
6 Sovereign Mews
7 Dunloe Ct
8 Cremer Bsns Ctr
9 James Hammett Ho
10 Allgood St
11 Horatio St
12 Cadell Ho
13 Horatio Ho
14 Shipton Ho
15 Haggerston Sch
16 Randal Cremer JMI Sch

D6 1 Hilborough Ct
2 Scriven Ct
3 Livermere Ct
4 Angrave Ct
5 Angrave Pas
6 Benfleet Ct
7 Belford Ho
8 Orme Ho
9 Clemson Ho
10 Longman Ho
11 Lowther Ho
12 Lovelace Ho
13 Harlowe Ho
14 Pamela Ho
15 Samuel Ho
16 Acton Ho
17 Loanda Cl
18 Phoenix Cl
19 Richardson Cl
20 Thrasher Cl
21 Mary Secole Cl
22 Canal Path
23 Pear Tree Cl
24 Hebden Ct
25 Charlton Ct
26 Laburnum Ct
27 Mansfield Ct
28 Garden Pl
29 Amber Wharf
30 Haggerston Studios

96

A1 1 Whitechurch Pas
2 Manningtree St
3 Whitechurch La
4 Naylor Bldg W
5 Morrison Bldgs
6 Nayor Bldg E
7 Mulberry St
8 Albany Ct
9 Cornell Bldg
10 Dryden Bldg
11 Weyhill Rd
12 Colefax Bldg
13 Fordham St
14 Myrdle Ct
15 Buckle St
16 Plough St
17 Goodman's Stile
18 Ropewalk Gdns
19 Skyline Plaza Bldg
20 Minet Ho
21 Mitali Pas
22 Basil Ho
23 Bernhard Baron Ho
24 Hogarth Ct
25 Delafield Ho
26 Chandlery Ho
27 Berner Terr
28 Victoria Yd
29 Batson Ho
30 Harkness Ho
31 Drewett Ho

32 Dowler Ho
33 Everard Ho
34 Bicknell Ho
35 Danvers Ho
36 Philchurch Pl
37 Hadfield Ho
38 Kindersley Ho
39 Langmore Ho
40 Halliday Ho
41 Harry Gosling Prim Sch
42 London Metropolitan Univ (Commercial Rd)
43 Kobi Nazrul Prim Sch
44 London Metropolitan Univ (Central Ho)
45 European Coll

A2 1 Arthur Deakin Ho
2 Albert Cotts
3 Victoria Cotts
4 Boden Ho
5 Vollasky Ho
6 Daplyn St
7 Hobsons Pl
8 Hanbury Ho
9 Huguenot Ct
10 Links Yd
11 Casson Ho
12 Ramar Ho
13 Greatorex Ho
14 Chicksand Ho
15 Spelman Ho
16 Tailworth St
17 Monthope Rd
18 Evelyn Ho
19 Bloomfield Ho
20 Davenant Ho
21 Pauline Ho
22 Tannery Ho
23 Don Gratton Ho
24 Green Dragon Yd
25 Fieldgate Mans
26 Mosque Tower

A3 1 Bentworth Ct
2 Hawksmoor Pl
3 Kerbela St
4 Fuller Cl
5 Kinsham Ho
6 Menotti St
7 Barwell Ho
8 Grimsby St
9 Reflection Ho
10 Fleet Street Hill
11 Bratley St
12 Weaver Ho
13 Cornerstone Ct
14 Stuttle Ho
15 McGlashon Ho
16 John Pritchard Ho
17 Thomas Buxton Jun & Inf Sch
18 St Anne RC Prim Sch
19 William Davis Prim Sch

A4 1 Providence Yd
2 Lygon Ho
3 Brabner Ho
4 Delta St
5 Delta Point
6 Tillet Way
7 Mullet Gdns
8 Lampern Sq
9 Kite Pl
10 Elver Gdns
11 Cobden Ho
12 Eversley Ho
13 Lorden Wlk
14 Rapley Ho
15 Dence Ho
16 McKinnon Wood Ho
17 Satchwell Rd
18 Dickinson Ho
19 Hutton Ho
20 Simmons Ho
21 Swinton Ho
22 Yates Ho
23 Johnson Ho
24 Jeremy Bentham Ho
25 Waring Ho
26 St James Ct
27 Ebony Ho
28 Azure Ho
29 Westhope Ho
30 Hague St
31 Elizabeth Selby Inf Sch
32 Lawdale Jun Sch

A5 1 London Terr
2 Sturdee Ho
3 Maude Ho
4 Haig Ho
5 Jellicoe Ho
6 Ropley St
7 Guinness Trust Bldgs
8 Ion Ct
9 Columbia Rd
10 Moye Cl
11 Morrel Ct
12 Courtauld Ho
13 Drummond Ho
14 Gurney Ho
15 Atkinson Ho
16 Halley Ho

17 Goldsmith's Sq
18 Shahjalal Ho
19 Ken Wilson Ho
20 April Ct
21 Crofts Ho
22 Sebright Ho
23 Beechwood Ho
24 Gillman Ho
25 Cheverell Ho
26 Besford Ho
27 Dinmont Ho
28 Elizabeth Mews
29 Sebright Pas
30 Wyndham Deedes Ho
31 Sheppard Ho
32 Mary James Ho
33 Hadrian Est
34 Blythendale Ho
35 George Vale Ho
36 Lion Mills
37 St Peter's Ave
38 Pritchard Ho
39 Sebright Sch

A6 1 Broke Wlk
2 Rochemont Wlk
3 Marlborough Ave
4 Rivington Wlk
5 Magnin Cl
6 Gloucester Sq
7 Woolstone Ho
8 Marsworth Ho
9 Cheddington Ho
10 Linslade Ho
11 Cosgrove Ho
12 Blisworth Ho
13 Eleanor Ct
14 Wistow Ho
15 Muscott Ho
16 Boxmoor Ho
17 Linford Ho
18 Pendley Ho
19 Northchurch Ho
20 Debdale Ho
21 Broadway Market Mews
22 Welshpool Ho
23 Ada Ho
24 St Paul's with St Michael's Prim Sch

B1 1 Peter Best Ho
2 Mellish Ho
3 Porchester Ho
4 Dickson Ho
5 Joscoyne Ho
6 Silvester Ho
7 Wilton Ct
8 Sarah Ho
9 Bridgen Ho
10 Tylney Ho
11 Greenwich Ct
12 Damien Ct
13 Philson Mans
14 Siege Ho
15 Jacob Mans
16 Proud Ho
17 Sly St
18 Barnett St
19 Kinder St
20 Richard St
21 Hungerford St
22 Colstead Ho
23 Melwood Ho
24 Wicker St
25 Langdale St
26 Chapman Ho
27 Burwell Cl
28 Walford Ho
29 Welstead Ho
30 Norton Ho
31 Turnour Ho
32 Luke Ho
33 Dunch St
34 Sheridan St
35 Brinsley St
36 Spencer Way
37 Madani Girls Sch
38 East End Computing & Bsns Coll
39 Mayfair Sch for Girls
40 Jamiatul Ummah Sch
41 Bigland Green Prim Sch

B2 1 Wodeham Gdns
2 Castlemaine St
3 Court St
4 Ashfield St
5 London Hospital Dental Inst
6 Princess Alexandra School of Nursing The

B3 1 Rochester St
2 Weaver St
3 Greenheath Bsns Ctr
4 Glass St
5 Herald St
6 Northesk Ho
7 Codrington Ho
8 Heathpool Ct
9 Mocatta Ho
10 Harvey Ho

11 Blackwood Ho
12 Rutherford Ho
13 Bullen Ho
14 Fremantle Ho
15 Pellew Ho
16 Ashington Ho
17 Dinnington Ho
18 Bartholomew Sq
19 Steeple Ct
20 Orion Ho
21 Fellbrigg St
22 Hague Prim Sch
23 Eagle Ho
24 Sovereign Ho
25 Redmill Ho
26 Berry Ho
27 Grindall Ho
28 Collingwood Ho
29 Stewart Headlam Prim Sch

B4 1 Charles Dickens Ho
2 Adrian Bolt Ho
3 William Rathbone Ho
4 Southwood Smith Ho
5 Rushmead
6 William Channing Ho
7 John Cartwright Ho
8 Charles Darwin Ho
9 Thomas Burt Ho
10 John Fielden Ho
11 Gwilym Maries Ho
12 Joseph Priestley Ho
13 Wear Pl
14 John Nettleford Ho
15 Thornaby Ho
16 Stockton Ho
17 Barnard Ho
18 Gainford Ho
19 Stapleton Ho
20 James Middleton Ho
21 Kedleston Ho
22 Queen Margaret Flats
23 Hollybush Ho
24 Horwood Ho
25 Norden Ho
26 Newcourt Ho
27 Seabright St
28 Viaduct Pl
29 Sunlight Sq
30 Providence Row Cl
31 Oaklands Sec Sch
32 Raine's Foundation Lower Sch
33 Beatrice Tate Sch

B5 1 Dinmont St
2 Marian St
3 Claredale Ho
4 Keeling Ho
5 Maple St
6 Winkley St
7 Temple Dwellings
8 Argos Ho
9 Helen Ho
10 Lysander Ho
11 Antenor Ho
12 Paris Ho
13 Nestor Ho
14 Hector Ho
15 Ajax Ho
16 Achilles Ho
17 Priam Ho
18 Peabody Est
19 Felix St
20 Cambridge Cres
21 Peterley Bsns Ctr
22 Beckwith Ho
23 Brookfield Ho
24 Parminter Ind Est
25 Ted Roberts Ho
26 Cambridge Ct
27 Millennium Pl
28 William Caslon Ho
29 Hugh Platt Ho
30 West St
31 Mayfield Ho
32 Apollo Ho
33 Tanners Yd
34 Teesdale Yd

B6 1 Welshpool St
2 Broadway Ho
3 Regents Wharf
4 London Wharf
5 Warburton Ho
6 Warburton St
7 Triangle Rd
8 Warburton Ho
9 Williams Ho
10 Booth Cl
11 Albert Cl
12 King Edward Mans
13 Victoria Bldgs
14 Andrews Wharf
15 London Fields Prim Sch
16 Triangle The
17 Com Coll Hackney The

C1 1 Woollon Ho
2 Dundalk Ho
3 Anne Goodman Ho
4 Newbold Cotts
5 Kerry Ho

6 Zion Ho
7 Longford Ho
8 Bromehead St
9 Athlone Ho
10 Jubilee Mans
11 Harriott Ho
12 Brayford Sq
13 Clearbrook Way
14 Rochelle Ct
15 Winterton Ho
16 Swift Ho
17 Brinsley Ho
18 Dean Ho
19 Foley Ho
20 Robert Sutton Ho
21 Montpelier Pl
22 Glastonbury Pl
23 Steel's La
24 Masters Lo
25 Stylus Apartments
26 Arta Ho
27 St Mary & St Michael Prim Sch
28 Bishop Challoner Collegiate Sch
29 Morton Cl
30 James Voller Way
C2 1 Fulneck
2 Gracehill
3 Ockbrook
4 Fairfield
5 Dunstan Hos
6 Cressy Ct
7 Cressy Hos
8 Callahan Cotts
9 Lindley Ho
10 Mayo Ho
11 Wexford Ho
12 Sandhurst Ho
13 Addis Ho
14 Colverson Ho
15 Beckett Ho
16 Jarman Ho
17 Armsby Ho
18 Wingrad Ho
19 Miranda Cl
20 Drake Ho
21 Ashfield Yd
22 Magri Wlk
23 Jean Pardies Ho
24 St Vincent De Paul Ho
25 Sambrook Ho
26 Louise De Marillac Ho
27 Dagobert Ho
28 Le Moal Ho
29 Odette Duval Ho
30 Charles Auffray Ho
31 Boisseau Ho
32 Clichy Ho
33 Paymal Ho
34 Smithy Street Sch
35 Redlands Prim Sch
36 Cressy Ct
C3 1 William's Bldgs
2 Donegal Ho
3 Pelican Pas
4 Frederick Charrington Ho
5 Wickford Ho
6 Braintree Ho
7 Doveton Ho
8 Doveton St
9 Cephas Ho
10 Sceptre Ho
11 Bancroft Ho
12 Stothard St
13 Redclyf Ho
14 Winkworth Cotts
15 Amiel St
16 Hadleigh Ho
17 Hadleigh Cl
18 Ryder Ho
19 Mantus Cl
20 Kenton Ho
21 Colebert Ho
22 Ibbott St
23 Rickman Ho
24 Rickman St
25 Stothard Ho
26 Barbanel Ho
27 Stannard Cotts
28 St Peters Ct
29 Rennie Cotts
30 Pemell Cl
31 Pemell Ho
32 Leatherdale St
33 Gouldman Ho
34 Lamplighter Cl
35 Sherren Ho
36 Marlborough Lo
37 Hamilton Lo
38 Montgomery Lo
39 Cleveland Gr
40 Cromwell Lo
41 Bardsey Pl
42 Charrington Ho
43 Hayfield Yd
44 Allport Mews
45 Colin Winter Ho
46 John Scurr Prim Sch

C4 1 Mulberry Ho
2 Gretton Ho
3 Merceron Ho
4 Montfort Ho
5 Westbrook Ho
6 Sugar Loaf Wlk
7 Museum Ho
8 Burnham Est
9 Globe Terr
10 Moravian St
11 Shepton Hos
12 Mendip Hos
13 Academy Ct
14 Pepys Ho
15 Swinburne Ho
16 Moore Ho
17 Morris Ho
18 Burns Ho
19 Milton Ho
20 Whitman Ho
21 Shelley Ho
22 Keats Ho
23 Dawson Ho
24 Bradbeer Ho
25 Forber Ho
26 Hughes Ho
27 Silvester Ho
28 Rogers Est
29 Pavan Ct
30 Stafford Cripps Ho
31 Sidney Godley (VC) Ho
32 Butler Ho
33 Butler St
34 Thorne Ho
35 Bevin Ho
36 Tuscan Ho
37 Globe Prim Sch
38 Bangabandhu Prim Sch
39 Bonner Prim Sch
C5 1 Evesham Ho
2 James Campbell Ho
3 Thomas Hollywood Ho
4 James Docherty Ho
5 Ebenezer Mussel Ho
6 Jameson Ct
7 Edinburgh Cl
8 Roger Dowley Ct
9 Sherbrooke Ho
10 Calcraft Ho
11 Burrard Ho
12 Dundas Ho
13 Ponsonby Ho
14 Barnes Ho
15 Paget Ho
16 Maitland Ho
17 Chesil Ct
18 Reynolds Ho
19 Cleland Ho
20 Goodrich Ho
21 Rosebery Ho
22 Sankey Ho
23 Cyprus Pl
24 Royston St
25 Stainsbury St
26 Hunslett St
27 Baildon
28 Brockweir
29 Tytherton
30 Malmesbury
31 Kingswood
32 Colville Ho
33 St Elizabeth RC Prim Sch
34 Raine's Foundation Sch
35 St John's CE Prim Sch
36 Mowlem Prim Sch
C6 1 Halkett Ho
2 Christchurch Sq
3 Helena Pl
4 Swingfield Ho
5 Greenham Ho
6 Dinmore Ho
7 Anstey Ho
8 Weston Ho
9 Carbroke Ho
10 Bluebell Cl
11 Cherry Tree Cl
12 Georgian Ct
13 Park Cl
14 Regency Ct
15 Norris Ho
D1 1 Pattison Ho
2 St Thomas Ho
3 Arbour Ho
4 Bladen Ho
5 Antill Terr
6 Majorie Mews
7 Billing Ho
8 Dowson Ho
9 Lipton Rd
10 Chalkwell Ho
11 Corringham Ho
12 Ogilvie Ho
13 Edward Mann Cl
14 Reservoir Studios
15 Lighterman Mews
16 Tower Hamlets Coll
17 Marion Richardson Prim Sch
D2 1 Roland Mews

2 Beatrice Ho
3 Morecambe Cl
4 Stepney Green Ct
5 Milrood Ho
6 Panama Ho
7 Galway Ho
8 Jacqueline Ho
9 Crown Mews
10 Caspian Ho
11 Darien Ho
12 Riga Ho
13 Flores Ho
14 Taranto Ho
15 Aden Ho
16 Master's St
17 Rosary Ct
18 Stepney Green Maths & Computing Coll
19 Sir John Cass Foundation & Redcoat CE Sec Sch
D3 1 Raynham Ho
2 Pat Shaw Ho
3 Colmar Cl
4 Withy Ho
5 Stocks Ct
6 Downey Ho
7 Bay Ct
8 Sligo Ho
9 Pegasus Ho
10 Barents Ho
11 Biscay Ho
12 Solway Ho
13 Bantry Ho
14 Aral Ho
15 Pacific Ho
16 Magellan Ho
17 Levant Ho
18 Adriatic Ho
19 Genoa Ho
20 Hawke Ho
21 Palliser Ho
22 Ionian Ho
23 Weddell Ho
24 Carlyle Mews
25 Greencourt Ho
26 Sundra Wlk
D4 1 Stubbs Ho
2 Holman Ho
3 Clynes Ho
4 Windsor Ho
5 Gilbert Ho
6 Chater Ho
7 Ellen Wilkinson Ho
8 George Belt Ho
9 Ayrton Gould Ho
10 O'Brian Ho
11 Sulkin Ho
12 Jenkinson Ho
13 Bullards Pl
14 Sylvia Pankhurst Ho
15 Mary Macarthur Ho
16 Trevelyan Ho
17 Wedgwood Ho
18 Pemberton Ct
19 Leatherdale St
20 Walter Besant Ho
21 Barber Beaumont Ho
22 Brancaster Ho
23 Litcham Ho
24 Bradwell St
D5 1 Kemp Ho
2 Piggott Ho
3 Mark Ho
4 Sidney Ho
5 Pomeroy Ho
6 Puteaux Ho
7 Doric Ho
8 Modling Ho
9 Longman Ho
10 Ames Ho
11 Alzette Ho
12 Tate Ho
13 Norton Ho
14 St Gilles Ho
15 Harold Ho
16 Velletri Ho
17 Bridge Wharf
18 Gathorne St
19 Bow Brook The
20 Twig Folly Cl
21 Palmerston Ct
22 Lakeview
23 Peach Walk Mews
24 Caesar Ct
25 Gatehouse Sch
D6 1 Lauriston Prim Sch

97

A1 1 Hearnshaw St
2 Berry Cotts
3 Causton Cotts
4 Elizabeth Blount Ct
5 Carr St
6 Shaw Cres
7 Darnley Ho
8 Mercer's Cotts
9 Troon Ho

10 Ratcliffe Ho
11 Wakeling St
12 York Sq
13 Anglia Ho
14 Cambria Ho
15 Caledonia Ho
16 Ratcliffe La
17 Bekesbourne St
18 John Scurr Ho
19 Regents Canal Ho
20 Basin App
21 Powlesland Ct
22 Cayley Prim Sch
23 Stephen Hawking Sch
A2 1 Waley St
2 Edith Ramsay Ho
3 Andaman Ho
4 Atlantic Ho
5 Pevensey Ho
6 Solent Ho
7 Lorne Ho
8 Cromarty Ho
9 Dakin Pl
10 Greaves Cotts
11 Donaghue Cotts
12 Ames Cotts
13 Waterview Ho
14 Limehouse Fields Est
A3 1 Formosa Ho
2 Galveston Ho
3 Arabian Ho
4 Greenland Ho
5 Coral Ho
6 Anson Ho
7 Cambay Ho
8 Lindop Ho
9 Moray Ho
10 Azov Ho
11 Sandalwood Cl
12 Broadford Ho
A4 1 Imperial Ho
2 Newport Ho
3 Vassall Ho
4 Maurice Ct
5 Creed Ct
6 Christopher France Ho
7 Beaumont Ct
8 Pembroke Mews
9 Guardian Angels RC Prim Sch
10 Central Foundation Lower Girls Sch The
A5 1 Nightingale Mews
2 Bunsen Ho
3 Bunsen St
4 Beatrice Webb Ho
5 Margaret Bondfield Ho
6 Wilmer Ho
7 Sandall Ho
8 Butley Ct
9 Josseline Ct
10 Dalton Ho
11 Brine Ho
12 Ford Cl
13 Viking Cl
14 Stanfield Rd
15 Stoneleigh Mews
16 Ruth Ct
17 School Bell Cloisters
18 Schoolbell Mews
19 Medhurst Cl
20 Olga St
21 Conyer St
22 Diamond Ho
23 Daring Ho
24 Crane Ho
25 Exmoor Ho
26 Grenville Ho
27 Hyperion Ho
28 Sturdy Ho
29 Wren Ho
30 Ardent Ho
31 Senators Lo
32 Hooke Ho
33 Mohawk Ho
34 Ivanhoe Ho
35 Medway Mews
36 Chisenhale Prim Sch
37 Olga Prim Sch
B1 1 Dora Ho
2 Flansham Ho
3 Gatwick Ho
4 Ashpark Ho
5 Newdigate Ho
6 Midhurst Ho
7 Redbourne Ho
8 Southwater Cl
9 Andersens Wharf
10 Whatman Ho
11 Butler Ho
12 Fitzroy Ho
13 Salmon St
14 Mission The
15 Aithan Ho
16 Britley Ho
17 Cheadle Ho
18 Elland Ho
19 Wharf La
20 Docklands Ct
21 Park Heights Ct

22 Grosvenor Ct
23 Lime House Ct
24 Swallow Pl
25 St Anne's Trad Est
26 Stepney Greencoat CE Prim Sch The
27 Sir William Burrough Prim Sch
28 Our Lady RC Prim Sch
B2 1 Wearmouth Ho
2 Elmslie Point
3 Grindley Ho
4 Stileman Ho
5 Wilcox Ho
6 Huddart St
7 Robeson St
8 Couzens Ho
9 Perley Ho
10 Whytlaw Ho
11 Booker Cl
12 Tunley Gn
13 Callingham Cl
14 Bowry Ho
15 Perkins Ho
16 Printon Ho
17 Tasker Ho
18 St Paul with St Luke CE Prim Sch
B4 1 Trellis Sq
2 Sheffield Sq
3 Howcroft Ho
4 Astra Ho
5 Frye Ct
6 Byas Ho
7 George Lansbury Ho
8 Regal Pl
9 Coborn Mews
10 Tredegar Mews
11 Cavendish Terr
12 Lyn Mews
13 Buttermere Ho
14 Coniston Ho
15 Tracy Ho
16 Hanover Pl
17 St Clair Ho
18 Longthorne Ho
19 Vista Bldgs
20 Verity Ho
21 Icarus Ho
22 Whippingham Ho
23 Hamilton Ho
24 Winchester Ho
25 Malmesbury Prim Sch
26 Phoenix Sec & Prim Sch
27 Central Foundation Upper Girls Sch The
B5 1 Roman Road Mkt
2 John Bond Ho
3 McKenna Ho
4 Dennis Ho
5 McAusland Ho
6 McBride Ho
7 Libra Rd
8 Dave Adams Ho
9 Regency Ct
10 Tay Ho
11 Sleat Ho
12 Brodick Ho
13 Ewart Pl
14 Lunan Ho
15 Cruden Ho
16 Anglo Rd
17 Mull Ho
18 Sinclairs Ho
19 Driftway Ho
20 Clayhall Ct
21 Berebinder Ho
22 Partridge Ho
23 Barford Ho
24 Gullane Ho
25 Gosford Ho
26 Dornoch Ho
27 Dunnet Ho
28 Enard Ho
29 Fraserburgh Ho
30 Forth Ho
31 Stavers Ho
32 Rosegate Ho
33 Crowngate Ho
34 Queensgate Ho
35 Towergate Ho
36 Ordell Ct
37 William Pl
38 Old Ford Prim Sch
B6 1 Hampstead Wlk
2 Waverton Ho
3 Elton Ho
4 Locton Gn
5 Birtwhistle Ho
6 Clare Ho
7 Magpie Ho
8 Hornbeam Sq
9 Rowan Ho
10 Barge La
11 Walnut Ho
12 Birdsfield La

13 Atkins Ct
14 Willow Tree Cl
15 Jasmine Sq
16 Tait Ct
17 Ranwell Ho
18 Ranwell Cl
19 Tufnell Ct
20 Pulteney Cl
21 Vic Johnson Ho
22 Lea Sq
23 Iceni Ct
24 Tamar Cl
25 Roman Rd
26 Valentine Ho

C1 **1** Landin Ct
2 Thomas Road Ind Est
3 Vickery's Wharf
4 Abbotts Wharf
5 Limehouse Ct
6 Charlesworth Ho
7 Gurdon Ho
8 Trendell Ho
9 Menteath Ho
10 Minchin Ho
11 Donne Ho
12 Old School Sq
13 Anglesey Ho
14 Gough Wlk
15 Baring Ho
16 Gladstone Ho
17 Hopkins Ho
18 Granville Ho
19 Overstone Ho
20 Pusey Ho
21 Russell Ho
22 Stanley Ho

C2 **1** Bredel Ho
2 Linton Ho
3 Matthews Ho
4 Woodcock Ho
5 Limborough Ho
6 Maydwell Ho
7 Underhill Ho
8 Meyrick Ho
9 Ambrose Ho
10 Richardson Ho
11 Carpenter Ho
12 Robinson Ho
13 Bellmaker Ct
14 Lime Tree Ct
15 Bracken Ho
16 Bramble Ho
17 Berberis Ho
18 Bilberry Ho
19 Ladyfern Ho
20 Rosebay Ho
21 Invicta Cl
22 Phoenix Bsns Ctr
23 Metropolitan Cl
24 Busbridge Ho
25 St Paul's Way Com Sch
26 Stebon Prim Sch

C3 **1** Fairmont Ho
2 Healy Ho
3 Zodiac Ho
4 Buick Ho
5 Consul Ho
6 Bentley Ho
7 Cresta Ho
8 Daimler Ho
9 Riley Ho
10 Jensen Ho
11 Lagonda Ho
12 Ireton St
13 Navenby Wlk
14 Burwell Wlk
15 Leadenham Ct
16 Sleaford Ho
17 Bow Triangle Bsns Ctr
18 Clara Grant Prim Sch The

C4 **1** Bow Ho
2 Denmark Pl
3 Marsalis Ho
4 Lovette Ho
5 Drapers Almhouses
6 Mallard Point
7 Creswick Wlk
8 Bevin Ho
9 Huggins Ho
10 Williams Ho
11 Harris Ho
12 Marina Ct
13 Electric Ho
14 Matching Ct
15 Wellington Bldgs
16 Grafton Ho
17 Berkeley Ho
18 Columbia Ho
19 Bow Sec Sch
20 Wellington Prim Sch
21 Cherry Trees Sch The

C5 **1** Vincent Mews
2 Menai Pl
3 Heathfield Ct
4 Redwood Cl
5 Acorn Ct

6 Primrose Cl
7 Briar Ct
8 Springwood Cl
9 Lacey Mews
10 Matilda Gdns

C6 **1** Ironworks
2 Juno Ho
3 Chariot Cl
4 Saturn Ho
5 Hadrian Cl
6 Mercury Ho
7 Forum Cl
8 Venus Ho
9 Vesta Ho
10 Tiber Cl
11 Gemini Ho
12 Crown Close Bsns Ctr

D1 **1** Colebrook Ho
2 Essex Ho
3 Salisbury Ho
4 Maidstone Ho
5 Osterley Ho
6 Norwich Ho
7 Clarissa Ho
8 Elgin Ho
9 Shaftesbury Lo
10 Shepherd Ho
11 Jeremiah St
12 Elizabeth Cl
13 Chilcot Cl
14 Fitzgerald Ho
15 Vesey Path
16 Ennis Ho
17 Kilmore Ho
18 Cygnet House N
19 Cygnet House S
20 Lansbury Lawrence Prim Sch
21 Bygrove Prim Sch
22 Mayflower Prim Sch
23 Tower Hamlets Coll

D2 **1** Sumner Ho
2 David Hewitt Ho
3 St Gabriels Cl
4 Limehouse Cut
5 Colmans Wharf
6 Foundary Ho
7 Radford Ho
8 Manorfield Prim Sch
9 St Saviour's CE Prim Sch
10 Pioneer Cl

D3 **1** Broxbourne Ho
2 Roxford Ho
3 Biscott Ho
4 Stanborough Ho
5 Hillstone Ct
6 Marner Prim Sch

D4 **1** Bradley Ho
2 Prioress Ho
3 Alton Ho
4 Foxley Ho
5 Munden Ho
6 Canterbury Ho
7 Corbin Ho
8 Barton Ho
9 Jolles Ho
10 Rudstone Ho
11 Baxter Ho
12 Baker Ho
13 Insley Ho
14 Hardwicke Ho
15 St Agnes RC Prim Sch
16 Priory St
17 Sadler Ho
18 Ballinger Point
19 Henshall Point
20 Dorrington Point
21 Warren Ho
22 Fairlie Ct
23 Regent Sq
24 Hackworth Point
25 Priestman Point
26 Wingate Ho
27 Nethercott Ho
28 Thelbridge Ho
29 Bowden Ho
30 Kerscott Ho
31 Southcott Ho
32 Birchdown Ho
33 Upcott Ho
34 Langmead Ho
35 Limscott Ho
36 Moorey Cl
37 Huntshaw Ho
38 Chagford Ho
39 Ashcombe Ho
40 Shillingford Ho
41 Patrick Connolly Gdns
42 Lester Ct
43 Franklin St
44 Taft Way
45 Washington Cl
46 Veronica Ho
47 William Guy Gdns
48 Denbury Ho
49 Holsworthy Ho
50 Padstone Ho
51 Old Palace Prim Sch
52 Ian Mikardo Sch

E3 **21** London Metrocity Coll

98

A1 **1** Glenkerry Ho
2 Carradale Ho
3 Langdon Ho
4 Balfron Twr
5 St Frideswides Mews
6 Tabard Ct
7 Delta Bldg
8 Findhorn St
9 Kilbrennan Ho
10 Thistle Ho
11 Heather Ho
12 Tartan Ho
13 Sharman Ho
14 Trident Ho
15 Wharf View Ct
16 Culloden Prim Sch

A2 **1** Mills Gr
2 St Michaels Ct
3 Duncan Ct

B1 **1** Lansbury Gdns
2 Theseus Ho
3 Adams Ho
4 Jones Ho
5 Sam March Ho
6 Arapiles Ho
7 Athenia Ho
8 Julius Ho
9 Jervis Bay Ho
10 Helen Mackay Ho
11 Gaze Ho
12 Ritchie Ho
13 Blairgowrie Ct
14 Circle Ho
15 Dunkeld Ho
16 Rosemary Dr
17 Sorrel La
18 East India Dock Road Tunnel

B3 **1** Crescent Court Bsns Ctr
2 Ashmead Bsns Ctr
3 Forward Bsns Ctr The

B6 **1** Victoria Mills
2 Hallings Wharf Studios
3 Poland Ho
4 Peter Heathfield Ho
5 Burford Rd
6 John F Kennedy Specl Sch
7 Univ of East London (Duncan Ho)

C5 **1** Abbey Lane Commercial Est
2 Greenway Ct

C6 **1** Barnby Sq
2 Barnby St
3 Brassett Point
4 David Lee Point
5 Worthing Cl
6 Bexhill Wlk
7 Old Barrowfield
8 Elmgreen Cl
9 Stafford Morris Ho
10 Nina Mackay Cl
11 Lime Wlk

D1 **1** Newton Point
2 Sparke Terr
3 Montesquieu Terr
4 Crawford Point
5 Rathbone Ho
6 George St
7 Emily St
8 Fendt Cl
9 Sabbarton St
10 St Luke Prim CE Sch
11 Briary Ct
12 Shaftesbury Ho

D2 **1** Radley Terr
2 Bernard Cassidy St
3 Rathbone Mkt
4 Thomas North Terr
5 Mary St
6 Hughes Terr
7 Swanscombe Point
8 Rawlinson Point
9 Kennedy Cox Ho
10 Cooper St

D6 **1** Harris Cotts
2 Moorey Cl
3 Euro Bsns Ctr
4 Ladywell St
5 Caistor Ho
6 Redfern Ho
7 West Ham Church Prim Sch

99

A2 **1** Odeon Ct
2 Edward Ct
3 Newhaven La
4 Ravenscroft Cl
5 Douglas Rd
6 Ferrier Point
7 Harvey Point
8 Wood Point

9 Trinity St
10 Pattinson Point
11 Clinch Ct
12 Mint Bsns Pk
13 Keir Hardy Prim Sch

A3 **1** Webb Gdns
2 Eric Shipman Terr
3 Warmington St
4 Jellicoe Rd
5 Frank St
6 Seaton Cl
7 Tabernacle Ave
8 Upland Rd
9 Clove St
10 Edward St
11 Ravenscroft Prim Sch

A4 **1** Bob Anker Cl
2 Lea Ct
3 Third Ave
4 Suffolk Rd

A5 **1** Lettsom Wlk
2 Ashburton Terr
3 Grasmere Rd
4 Dimsdale Wlk
5 Rawstone Wlk
6 Scott Ho
7 Willett Ho
8 James Cl
9 Cordwainers Wlk
10 Victoria Point
11 Settle Point
12 Middle Rd
13 Steve Biko Lodge
14 Lady Helen Seymour Ho
15 Winifred Terr

A6 **1** Royston Ct
2 Chadd Gn
3 Tanner Point
4 Nicholls Point
5 Reindeer Cl
6 Selwyn Prim Sch
7 Portway Prim Sch

B4 **1** Barbers Alley
2 Grengate Lodge
3 Augurs La
4 Surrey St
5 Dongola Rd W
6 Bemersyde Point
7 Rowntree Clifford Cl

B5 **1** Lister Com Sch
2 Eleanor Smith Sch

C1 **1** St Joachim's RC Prim Sch

C2 **1** Alliance Rd
2 Salomons Rd
3 Barnes Ct
4 Triangle Ct
5 Moorings The

C5 **1** Wellby Ct
2 Northfield Ho
3 Bishop Wilfred Wood Ct
4 Castle Point
5 Moat Dr

C6 **1** Tolpuddle Ave
2 Crown Mews
3 Lilac Ct
4 Hamara Ghar
5 Greenleaf Rd
6 Massey Ct
7 Florence Rd
8 Sissulu Ct
9 Austin Ct
10 St Edwards RC Prim Sch

D2 **1** Partridge Cl
2 Vanburgh Cl
3 Meadowsweet Cl
4 St Michaels Cl
5 Long Mark Rd
6 Congreve Wlk

D5 **1** Foxcombe Cl
2 Rochford Cl
3 Kylemore Cl
4 Stondon Wlk
5 Imperial Mews
6 Dominica Cl
7 Central Park Prim Sch

D6 **1** Oldegate Ho
2 Gaitskell Ho
3 Cabot Way

100

A1 **1** Hadleigh Wlk
2 Hawksmoor Cl
3 Fraser Cl
4 Moncrieff Cl
5 Burlington Cl
6 Dundonald Cl
7 Oakley Cl
8 Ashwell Cl

A2 **1** Orchid Cl
2 Bellflower Cl
3 Partridge Sq
4 Larkspur Cl
5 Lobelia Cl
6 Stonechat Sq
7 Wintergreen Cl

8 Garnet Wlk
9 Mavis Wlk
10 Beacons Cl
11 Abbess Cl
12 Elmley Cl
13 Chetwood Wlk
14 Selby Cl
15 Denny Cl
16 Woodhatch Cl

A6 **1** Oakwood Cl
2 Harrow Rd
3 Ray Massey Way
4 Madge Gill Way
5 Pilgrims Way
6 St Bartholomews Ct
7 Hartley Prim Sch
8 Newham Acad of Music

B1 **1** Bowers Wlk
2 Barton Cl
3 Clayton Cl
4 Dixon Cl
5 Gautrey Sq
6 Wakerley Cl
7 Canterbury Cl
8 Goose Sq
9 Coventry Cl
10 Butterfield Sq
11 Winchester Cl

B2 **1** Fleetwood Ct
2 Lymington Cl
3 Holyhead Cl
4 Bondfield Rd
5 Tulip Cl
6 Ambrose Cl
7 Sage Cl
8 Lindwood Cl

B4 **1** Butterfly Cl
2 Cricket Ct
3 Sunningdale Cl
4 John Wesley Cl
5 Vicarage Prim Sch

B5 **1** Hastingwood Ct
2 Tippett Ct
3 Newham Coll of FE
4 St Michael's RC Prim Sch

D1 **1** Weymouth Cl
2 Founder Cl
3 Admirals Ct

101

A6 **1** St Ann's Rd
2 Cooke St
3 Gateway Ho
4 Ardleigh Ho
5 Skipper Ct
6 Hewetts Quay

B5 **1** Anderson Ho
2 Rookwood Ho
3 Tasker Ho
4 Crispe Ho
5 Oban Ho
6 Earlsdown Ho

B6 **1** Jarvis Cl
2 Mayflower Ct
3 Westbury Ct
4 Millicent Preston Ho
5 Louise Graham Ho
6 Grange Ho
7 Basing Ho
8 Barnes Ho
9 Lexham Ho
10 Ripple Ct
11 Waldegrave Ct
12 Howard Ct

104

A6 **1** Milburn Dr
2 Cousins Cl
3 Leacroft Cl

107

C4 **1** Decimal Ctr
2 Bridge Bsns Ctr The

108

C5 **1** Marlow Ct
2 Andrewes Ct
3 Vine Cotts
4 Benjamin Cl
5 Broadway Bldgs
6 Clocktower Mews
7 Amberley Ho
8 Diamond Ct
9 St Ann's Sch
10 St Josephs RC Prim Sch

D5 **1** Silverdale Cl
2 Burdett Cl
3 Hopefield
4 Maunder Rd
5 Clare Ho

109

A5 **1** Glastonbury Ct

2 Evesham Ct
3 Lacock Ct
4 Wigmore Ct
5 Melrose Ct
6 Brownlow Rd
7 Chignell Pl
8 Shirley Ct
9 Trojan Ct
10 Hatfield Rd
11 Pershore Ho
12 Hyde Ho
13 Hugh Clark Ho
14 Rosemoor Ho
15 Leeland Mans
16 Waterford Ct
17 O'Grady Ct
C1 1 Barrow Wlk
2 Mercury Rd
4 Our Lady & St John's RC Jun & Inf Sch
C3 1 Mt Carmel RC Prim Sch
2 Little Ealing Prim Sch
C6 1 Abbey Lo
2 Yew Tree Grange
3 Abinger Ct
D6 1 Sandringham Mews
3 St Savior's CE Inf Sch

110
A1 1 Burford Ho
2 Hope Cl
3 Centaur Ct
4 Phoenix Ct
A6 1 Watermans Mews
2 Hills Mews
3 Grosvenor Ct
4 Elton Lo
5 Hambledon Ct
6 Edwards Language Sch
C1 1 Surrey Cres
2 Forbes Ho
3 Haining Cl
4 Melville Ct
5 London Stile
6 Stile Hall Par
7 Priory Lo
8 Meadowcroft
9 St James Ct
10 Rivers Ho
C5 1 Grosvenor Par
2 Oakfield Ct
3 Hart Grove Ct
4 Grosvenor Ct
5 King Edwards Pl
D1 1 Churchdale Ct
2 Cromwell Cl
3 Cambridge Rd S
4 Oxbridge Ct
5 Tomlinson Cl
6 Gunnersbury Mews
7 Grange The
8 Gunnersbury Cl
9 Bellgrave Lo
D4 1 Cheltenham Pl
2 Beaumaris Twr
3 Arundel Ho
4 Pevensey Ct
5 Jerome Twr
6 Anstey Ct
7 Bennett Ct
8 Gunnersbury Ct
9 Barrington Ct
10 Hope Gdns
11 Park Road E
D5 1 Lantry Ct
2 Rosemount Ct
3 Moreton Ct
4 Acton Central Ind Est
5 Rufford Twr
6 Narrow St
7 Mount Pl
8 Sidney Miller Ct
9 Mill Hill Terr
10 Cheltenham Pl
11 Mill Hill Gr
12 Benjamin Ho
13 Arlington Ct
14 Lombard Ct
15 Steyne Ho
16 Acton & West London Coll

111
A1 1 Arlington Park Mans
2 Sandown Ho
3 Goodwood Ho
4 Windsor Ho
5 Lingfield Ho
6 Ascot Ho
7 Watchfield Ct
8 Belgrave Ct
9 Beverley Ct
10 Beaumont Ct
11 Harvard Rd
12 Troubridge Ct
13 Branden Lo
14 Fromow's Cnr
15 Heathfield House Sch

A2 1 Chiswick Green Studios
2 Bell Ind Est
3 Fairlawn Ct
4 Dukes Gate
5 Dewsbury Ct
6 Chiswick Terr
7 Mortlake Ho
A3 1 Blackmore Twr
2 Bollo Ct
3 Kipling Twr
4 Lawrence Ct
5 Maugham Ct
6 Reade Ct
7 Woolf Ct
8 Shaw Ct
9 Verne Ct
10 Wodehouse Ct
11 Greenock Rd
12 Garden Ct
13 Barons Gate
14 Cleveland Rd
15 Carver Cl
16 Chapter Cl
17 Beauchamp Cl
18 Holmes Ct
19 Copper Mews
A4 1 Belgrave Cl
2 Buckland Wlk
3 Frampton Ct
4 Telfer Cl
5 Harlech Twr
6 Corfe Twr
7 Barwick Ho
8 Charles Hocking Ho
9 Sunninghill Ct
10 Salisbury St
11 Jameson Pl
12 Castle Cl
A5 1 Rectory Rd
2 Derwentwater Mans
3 Market Pl
4 Hooper's Mews
5 Cromwell Pl
6 Locarno Rd
7 Edgecote Cl
8 Harleyford Manor
9 Coopers Ct
10 Avingdor Ct
11 Steyne Ho
B1 1 Chatsworth Lo
2 Prospect Pl
3 Townhall Ave
4 Devonhurst Pl
5 Heathfield Ct
6 Horticultural Pl
7 Merlin Ho
8 Garth Rd
9 Autumn Rise
B2 1 Disraeli Cl
2 Winston Wlk
3 Rusthall Mans
4 Bedford Park Mans
5 Essex Place Sq
6 Holly Rd
7 Homecross Ho
8 Swan Bsns Ctr
9 Jessop Ho
10 Belmont Prim Sch
C1 1 Glebe Ct
2 Devonshire Mews
3 Binns Terr
4 Ingress St
5 Swanscombe Rd
6 Brackley Terr
7 Stephen Fox Ho
8 Manor Gdns
9 Coram Ho
10 Flaxman Ho
11 Thorneycroft Ho
12 Thornhill Ho
13 Kent Ho
14 Oldfield Ho
15 William Hogarth Sch The
C2 1 Chestnut Ho
2 Bedford Ho
3 Bedford Cnr
4 Sydney Ho
5 Bedford Park Cnr
6 Priory Gdns
7 Windmill Alley
8 Castle Pl
9 Jonathan Ct
10 Windmill Pas
11 Chardin Rd
12 Gable Ho
13 Chiswick & Bedford Park Prep Sch
14 Arts Educational Sch The
15 Orchard House Sch
C3 1 Fleet Ct
2 Ember Ct
3 Emlyn Gdns
4 Clone Ct
5 Brent Ct
6 Abbey Ct
7 Ormsby Lo
8 St Catherine's Ct
9 Lodge The

C4 1 Longford Ct
2 Mole Ct
3 Lea Ct
4 Wandle Ct
5 Beverley Ct
6 Roding Ct
7 Crane Ct
D1 1 Miller's Ct
2 British Grove Pas
3 British Grove S
4 Berestede Rd
5 North Eyot Gdns
D2 1 Flanders Mans
2 Stamford Brook Mans
3 Linkenholt Mans
4 Prebend Mans
5 Middlesex Ct
D3 1 Stamford Brook Gdns
2 Hauteville Court Gdns
3 Ranelagh Gdns

112
A1 1 Chisholm Ct
2 North Verbena Gdns
3 Western Terr
4 Verbena Gdns
5 Montrose Villas
6 Hammersmith Terr
7 South Black Lion La
8 St Peter's Wharf
9 Eden High Sch
A2 1 Hamlet Ct
2 Derwent Ct
3 Westcroft Ct
4 Black Lion Mews
5 St Peter's Villas
6 Standish Ho
7 Chambon Pl
8 Court Mans
9 Longthorpe Ct
10 Charlotte Ct
11 Westside
12 Park Ct
13 London Ho
14 Latymer Upper Sch
15 St Peter's CE Prim Sch
16 Polish Univ Abroad
A3 1 Elizabeth Finn Ho
2 Ashchurch Ct
3 King's Par
4 Inver Ct
5 Ariel Ct
6 Pocklington Lo
7 Vitae Apartments
A4 1 Becklow Gdns
2 Victoria Ho
3 Lycett Pl
4 Kylemore Ct
5 Alexandra Ct
6 Lytten Ct
7 Becklow Mews
8 Northcroft Ct
9 Bailey Ct
10 Spring Cott
11 Landor Wlk
12 Laurence Mews
13 Hadyn Park Ct
14 Askew Mans
15 Malvern Ct
B1 1 Prince's Mews
2 Aspen Gdns
3 Hampshire Hog La
4 Blades Ct
B2 1 Albion Gdns
2 Flora Gdns
3 Lamington St
4 Felgate Mews
5 Galena Ho
6 Albion Mews
7 Albion Ct
8 King Street Cloisters
9 Dimes Pl
10 Clarence Ct
11 Hampshire Hog La
12 Marryat Ct
13 Ravenscourt Ho
14 Ravenscourt Theatre Sch
15 Cambridge Sch
16 Godolphin & Latymer Sch
17 Flora Gardens Prim Sch
B3 1 Ravenscourt Park Mans
2 Paddenswick Ct
3 Ashbridge Ct
4 Brackenbury Prim Sch
B4 1 Westbush Ct
2 Goldhawk Mews
3 Sycamore Ho
4 Shackleton Ct
5 Drake Ct
6 Scotts Ct
7 Raleigh Ct
8 Melville Court Flats
9 Southway Cl
B5 1 Arlington Ho
2 Lugard Ho
3 Shabana Ct

4 Sitarey Ct
5 Oaklands Ct
7 Davenport Mews
B6 1 Abercrombie Ho
2 Bathurst Ho
3 Brisbane Ho
4 Bentinck Ho
5 Ellenborough Ho
6 Lawrence Cl
7 Mackenzie Cl
8 Carteret Ho
9 Calvert Ho
10 Winthrop Ho
11 Auckland Ho
12 Blaxland Ho
13 Havelock Cl
14 Hargraves Ho
15 Hudson Cl
16 Phipps Ho
17 Lawson Ho
18 Hastings Ho
19 Wolfe Ho
20 Malabar Cl
21 Commonwealth Ave
22 Charnock Ho
23 Canning Ho
24 Cornwallis Ho
25 Commonwealth Ave
26 Champlain Ho
27 Grey Ho
28 Durban Ho
29 Baird Ho
30 Campbell Ho
31 Mitchell Ho
32 Denham Ho
33 Mackay Ho
34 Evans Ho
35 Davis Ho
36 Mandela Cl
C1 1 Bridge Avenue Mans
2 Bridgeview
3 College Ct
4 Beatrice Ho
5 Amelia Ho
6 Edith Ho
7 Joanna Ho
8 Mary Ho
9 Adela Ho
10 Sophia Ho
11 Henrietta Ho
12 Charlotte Ho
13 Alexandra Ho
14 Bath Pl
15 Elizabeth Ho
16 Margaret Ho
17 Peabody Est
18 Eleanor Ho
19 Isabella Ho
20 Caroline Ho
21 Chancellors Wharf
22 Sussex Pl
23 St Paul's CE Prim Sch
C2 1 Phoenix Lodge Mans
2 Samuel's Cl
3 Broadway Arc
4 Brook Ho
5 Hammersmith Broadway
6 Broadway Ctr The
7 Cambridge Ct
8 Ashcroft Sq
9 Sacred Heart High Sch
10 King Street Coll
C4 1 Verulam Ho
2 Grove Mans
3 Frobisher Ct
4 Library Mans
5 Pennard Mans
6 New Shepherd's Bush Mkt
7 Kerrington Ct
8 Granville Mans
9 Romney Ct
10 Rayner Ct
11 Sulgrave Gdns
12 Bamborough Gdns
13 Hillary Ct
14 Market Studios
15 Lanark Mans
16 Miles Coverdale Prim Sch
17 St Stephen's CE Prim Sch
18 London Coll of Fashion (Lime Grove)
C5 1 Linden Ct
2 Frithville Ct
3 Blomfield Mans
4 Poplar Mews
5 Hopgood St
6 Westwood Ho
7 Stanlake Mews
8 Stanlake Villas
9 Alexandra Mans
D2 1 St Paul's Girls' Sch
2 Bute House Prep Sch
3 Jacques Prevert Sch
4 Larmenier & Sacred Heart RC Prim Sch
D3 1 Grosvenor Residences

2 Blythe Mews
3 Burnand Ho
4 Bradford Ho
5 Springvale Terr
6 Ceylon Rd
7 Walpole Ct
8 Bronte Ct
9 Boswell Ct
10 Souldern Rd
11 Brook Green Flats
12 Haarlem Rd
13 Stafford Mans
14 Lionel Mans
15 Barradell Ho
D4 1 Vanderbilt Villas
2 Bodington Ct
3 Kingham Cl
4 Clearwater Terr
5 Lorne Gdns
6 Cameret Ct
7 Bush Ct
8 Shepherds Ct
9 Rockley Ct
10 Grampians The
11 Charcroft Ct
12 Addison Park Mans
13 Sinclair Mans
14 Fountain Ct
15 Woodford Ct
16 Roseford Ct
17 Woodstock Studios
D5 1 St Katherine's Wlk
2 Dorrit Ho
3 Pickwick Ho
4 Dombey Ho
5 Caranday Villas
6 Mortimer Ho
7 Nickleby Ho
8 Stebbing Ho
9 Boxmoor Ho
10 Poynter Ho
11 Swanscombe Ho
12 Darnley Terr
13 Norland Ho
14 Hume Ho
15 Boundary Ho
16 Norland Rd
17 Helix Ct
D6 1 Frinstead Ho
2 Hurstway Wlk
3 Testerton Wlk
4 Grenfell Wlk
5 Grenfell Twr
6 Barandon Wlk
7 Treadgold Ho
8 St Clements Ct
9 Willow Way
10 Florence Ho
11 Dora Ho
12 Carton Ho
13 Agnes Ho
14 Marley Ho
15 Estella Ho
16 Waynflete Sq
17 Pippin Ho
18 Baseline Business Studios
19 St Francis of Assisi Prim Sch
20 Nicholas Rd

118
A1 1 Hope Ct
2 West Point
3 Centre Point
4 East Point
5 Proctor Ho
6 Tovy Ho
7 Avondale Pavement
8 Brettingham
9 Colechurch Ho
10 Harman Cl
11 Avondale Ho
12 Lanark Ho
13 George Elliston Ho
14 Eric Wilkins Ho
15 Six Bridges Ind Est
16 St James Ind Mews
17 Winter Lo
18 Fern Wlk
19 Ivy Ct
20 Fallow Ct
21 Culloden Ct
22 Archers Lo
23 Eveline Lowe Prim Sch
A2 1 Cadbury Way
2 Robert Bell Ho
3 Robert Jones Ho
4 William Rushbrooke Ho
5 Helen Taylor Ho
6 Peter Hills Ho
7 Charles Mackenzie Ho
8 Drappers Way
9 Racs Flats
10 Abbey Gdns
11 Mayfair Ho

12 Windmill Cl
13 Maria Cl
14 Townsend Ho
15 Mason Ho
16 Kotree Way
17 Hannah Mary Way
18 Langdon Way
19 Whittaker Way
20 Cherry Garden Sch
21 Alma Prim Sch
A3 1 Rudge Ho
2 Spenlow Ho
3 Darnay Ho
4 Carton Ho
5 Giles Ho
6 Bowley Ho
7 Casby Ho
8 Sun Pas
9 Ness St
10 Voyager Bsns Est
11 Dockley Road Ind Est
12 Spa Ct
13 Discovery Bsns Pk
14 Priter Road Hostel
15 Salisbury Ct
16 William Ellis Way
17 John McKenna Wlk
18 Toussaint Wlk
19 Gillison Wlk
20 Bromfield Ct
21 Ben Smith Way
22 Major Rd
23 Old Jamaica Bsns Est
24 St James' CE Jun & Inf Sch
A4 1 Providence
2 Springalls Wharf
3 Flockton St
4 Meridian Ct
5 East La
6 Luna Ho
7 Axis Ct
8 Farthing Alley
9 Peter Butler Ho
10 Brownlow Ho
11 Tapley Ho
12 Copperfield Ho
13 Dombey Ho
14 Fleming Ho
15 Parkers Row
16 Wade Ho
17 Bardell Ho
18 Nickleby Ho
19 John Felton Rd
20 Flockton St
21 Pickwick Ho
22 Oliver Ho
23 Weller Ho
24 Haredale Ho
25 Havisham Ho
26 Tupman Ho
27 Micawber Ho
28 Wrayburn Ho
29 Dartle Ct
30 Waterside Cl
31 Burnaby Ct
32 Wickfield Ho
33 Fountain Ho
34 Fountain Green Sq
35 St Saviours Ho
36 Providence Sq
37 Riverside Prim Sch
38 St Michael's RC Sec Sch
39 St Joseph's RC Prim Sch
A5 1 Trade Winds Ct
2 Spice Ct
3 Leeward Ct
4 Bridgeport Pl
5 Tamarind Yd
6 Cape Yd
7 Nightingale Ho
8 St Anthony's Cl
9 Miah Terr
10 Seville Ho
11 Douthwaite Sq
12 Codling Cl
13 Hermitage Ct
14 Capital Wharf
15 Cinnabar Wharf East
16 Cinnabar Wharf Central
17 Cinnabar Wharf West
18 Bushell St
19 Hermitage Prim Sch
20 Waveney Cl
21 Welland Mews
A6 1 Conant Mews
2 Hanson Ho
3 Royal Tower Lo
4 Victoria Ct
5 Swan Pas
6 Royal Mint Pl
7 Peabody Est
8 Florin Ct
9 Flank St
10 Onedin Point

11 Liberty Ho
12 Ensign Ct
13 Sapphire Ct
14 Graces Alley
15 George Leybourne Ho
16 Fletcher St
17 Hatton Ho
18 Noble Ho
19 Shearsmith Ho
20 Wellclose St
21 Telford's Yd
22 Breezer's Ct
23 Pennington Ct
24 St Paul's CE Prim Sch
25 Shapla Prim Sch
B1 1 Hockney Ct
2 Toulouse Ct
3 Lowry Ct
4 Barry Ho
5 Lewis Ct
6 Gainsborough Ct
7 Renoir Ct
8 Blake Ct
9 Raphael Ct
10 Rembrandt Ct
11 Constable Ct
12 Da Vinci Ct
13 Gaugin Ct
14 Michelangelo Ct
15 Monet Ct
16 Weald Ct
17 Jasmin Lo
18 Birchmere Lo
19 Weybridge Ct
20 Florence Ho
21 Gleneagles Ct
22 Sunningdale Cl
23 Muirfield Cl
24 Turnberry Ct
25 St Andrews Cl
26 Kingsdown Cl
27 St Davids Cl
28 Galway Cl
29 Edenbridge Cl
30 Birkdale Cl
31 Tralee Ct
32 Woburn Ct
33 Belfry Cl
34 Troon Ct
35 Holywell Cl
B2 1 Market Pl
2 Trappes Ho
3 Thurland Ho
4 Ramsfort Ho
5 Hambley Ho
6 Holford Ho
7 Pope Ho
8 Southwell Ho
9 Mortain Ho
10 Radcliffe Ho
11 Southwark Park Est
12 Galleywall Road Trad Est
13 Trevithick Ho
14 Barlow Ho
15 Donkin Ho
16 Landmann Ho
17 Fitzmaurice Ho
18 Dodd Ho
19 Southwark Park Prim Sch
B3 1 Perryn Rd
2 Chalfont Ho
3 Prestwood Ho
4 Farmer Ho
5 Gataker Ho
6 Gataker St
7 Cornick Ho
8 Glebe Ho
9 Matson Ho
10 Hickling Ho
11 St Andrews Ho
12 Southwark Coll (Surrey Docks Ctr)
B4 1 Butterfield Cl
2 Janeway Pl
3 Trotwood Ho
4 Maylie Ho
5 Cranbourn Pas
6 Cranbourn Ho
7 Cherry Garden Ho
8 Burton Ho
9 Morriss Ho
10 Dixon's Alley
11 King Edward The Third Mews
12 Cathay St
13 Mission The
14 Millstream Ho
B5 1 China Ct
2 Wellington Terr
3 Stevedore St
4 Portland Sq
5 Reardon Ho
6 Lowder Ho
7 Meeting House Alley
8 Farthing Fields
9 Oswell Ho
10 Park Lo
11 Doughty Ct

12 Inglefield Sq
13 Chopin's Ct
14 Welsh Ho
15 Hilliard Ho
16 Clegg St
17 Tasman Ho
18 Ross Ho
19 Wapping Dock St
20 Bridewell Pl
21 New Tower Bldgs
22 Tower Bldgs
23 Chimney Ct
24 Jackman Ho
25 Fenner Ho
26 Franklin Ho
27 Frobisher Ho
28 Flinders Ho
29 Chancellor Ho
30 Beechey Ho
31 Reardon Path
32 Parry Ho
33 Vancover Ho
34 Willoughby Ho
35 Sanctuary The
36 Dundee Ct
37 Pierhead Wharf
38 Scandrett St
39 St Johns Ct
B6 1 Newton Ho
2 Richard Neale Ho
3 Maddocks Ho
4 Cornwall St
5 Brockmer Ho
6 Dellow Ho
7 Bewley Ho
8 Artichoke Hill
9 Queen Anne Terr
10 King Henry Terr
11 King Charles Terr
12 Queen Victoria Terr
13 Sovereign Ct
14 Princes Court Bsns Ctr
15 Kingsley Mews
16 Mulberry Sch for Girls
C1 16 Ilderton Prim Sch
C2 1 Damory Ho
2 Antony Ho
3 Roderick Ho
4 Pedworth Gdns
5 Banner Ct
6 Rotherhithe Bsns Est
7 Beamish Ho
8 Corbetts Pas
9 Gillam Ho
10 Richard Ho
11 George Walter Ho
12 Westlake
13 Adron Ho
14 Cavendish Sch
15 McIntosh Ho
C3 1 Blick Ho
2 Neptune Ho
3 Scotia Ct
4 Murdoch Ho
5 Edmonton Ct
6 Niagara Ct
7 Columbia Point
8 Ritchie Ho
9 Wells Ho
10 Helen Peele Cotts
11 Orchard Ho
12 Dock Offices
13 Landale Ho
14 Courthope Ho
15 Hithe Gr
16 China Hall Mews
C4 1 Mayflower St
2 St Mary's Est
3 Rupack St
4 Frank Whymark Ho
5 Adams Gardens Est
6 Hatteraick St
7 East India Ct
8 Bombay Ct
9 Stable Ho
10 Grannary The
11 Riverside
12 Cumberland Wharf
13 Seaford Ho
14 Hythe Ho
15 Sandwich Ho
16 Winchelsea Ho
17 Rye Ho
18 Kenning St
19 Western Pl
20 Ainsty St
21 Pine Ho
22 Beech Ho
23 Larch Ho
24 Turner Ct
25 Seth St
26 Risdon Ho
27 Risdon St
28 Aylton Est
29 Manitoba Ct
30 Calgary Ct
31 Irwell Est
32 St Olav's Sq
33 City Bsns Ctr
34 Albion Prim Sch

C5 1 John Rennie Wlk
2 Malay Ho
3 Wainwright Ho
4 Riverside Mans
5 Shackleton Ho
6 Whitehorn Ho
7 Wavel Ct
8 Prusom's Island
9 St Peter's CE Prim Sch
C6 1 Shadwell Pl
2 Gosling Ho
3 Vogler Ho
4 Donovan Ho
5 Knowlden Ho
6 Chamberlain Ho
7 Moore Ho
8 Thornewill Ho
9 Fisher Ho
10 All Saints Ct
11 Coburg Dwellings
12 Lowood Ho
13 Solander Gdns
14 Chancery Bldgs
15 Ring Ho
16 Juniper St
17 Gordon Ho
18 West Block
19 North Block
20 South Block
21 Ikon Ho
22 Blue Gate Fields Jun & Inf Schs
D2 1 John Kennedy Ho
2 Brydale Ho
3 Balman Ho
4 Tissington Ct
5 Harbord Ho
6 Westfield Ho
7 Albert Starr Ho
8 John Brent Ho
9 William Evans Ho
10 Raven Ho
11 Egret Ho
12 Fulmar Ho
13 Dunlin Ho
14 Siskin Ho
15 Sheldrake Ho
16 Buchanan Ct
17 Burrage Ct
18 Biddenham Ho
19 Ayston Ho
20 Empingham Ho
21 Deanshanger Ho
22 Codicote Ho
23 Buryfield Ct
24 Rotherhithe Prim Sch
D4 1 Schooner Cl
2 Dolphin Cl
3 Clipper Ct
4 Deauville Ct
5 Colette Ct
6 Coniston Ct
7 Virginia Ct
8 Derwent Ct
9 Grantham Ct
10 Serpentine Ct
11 Career Ct
12 Lacine Ct
13 Fairway Ct
14 Harold Ct
15 Spruce Ho
16 Cedar Ho
17 Sycamore Ho
18 Woodland Cres
19 Poplar Ho
20 Adelphi Ct
21 Basque Ct
22 Aberdale Ct
23 Quilting Ct
24 Chargrove Cl
25 Radley Ct
26 Greenacre Sq
27 Maple Leaf Sq
28 Stanhope Cl
29 Hawke Pl
30 Drake Cl
31 Brass Talley Alley
32 Monkton Ho
33 James Ho
34 Wolfe Cres
D5 1 Clarence Mews
2 Raleigh Ct
3 Katherine Cl
4 Woolcombes Ct
5 Tudor Ct
6 Quayside Ct
7 Princes Riverside Rd
8 Surrey Ho
9 Tideway Ct
10 Edinburgh Ct
11 Falkirk Ct
12 Byelands Cl
13 Gwent Ct
14 Lavender Ho
15 Abbotshade Rd
16 Bellamy's Ct
17 Blenheim Ct
18 Sandringham Ct
19 Hampton Ct
20 Windsor Ct

21 Balmoral Ct
22 Westminster Ct
23 Beatson Wlk
24 Peter Hills Sch
D6 1 Barnardo Gdns
2 Roslin Ho
3 Glamis Est
4 Peabody Est
5 East Block
6 Highway Trad Ctr The
7 Highway Bsns Pk The
8 Cranford Cotts
9 Ratcliffe Orch
10 Scotia Bldg
11 Mauretania Bldg
12 Compania Bldg
13 Sirius Bldg
14 Unicorn Bldg
15 Keepier Wharf

A1 1 Sir Francis Drake Prim Sch
2 Deptford Park Prim Sch
A2 1 Trafalgar Cl
2 Hornblower Cl
3 Cunard Wlk
4 Caronia Ct
5 Carinthia Ct
6 Freswick Ho
7 Graveley Ho
8 Husbourne Ho
9 Crofters Ct
10 Pomona Ho
11 Hazelwood Ho
12 Cannon Wharf Bsns Ctr
13 Bence Ho
14 Clement Ho
15 Pendennis Ho
16 Lighter Cl
17 Mast Ct
18 Rushcutters Ct
19 Boat Lifter Way
A5 1 Edward Sq
2 Prince Regent Ct
3 Codrington Ct
4 Pennington Ct
5 Cherry Ct
6 Ash Ct
7 Beech Ct
8 Hazel Ct
9 Laurel Ct
A6 1 St Georges Sq
2 Drake Ho
3 Osprey Ho
4 Fleet Ho
5 Gainsborough Ho
6 Victory Pl
7 Challenger Ho
8 Conrad Ho
9 Lock View Ct
10 Shoulder of Mutton Alley
11 Frederick Sq
12 Helena Sq
13 Elizabeth Sq
14 Sophia Sq
15 William Sq
16 Lamb Ct
17 Lockside
18 Adriatic Bldg
19 Ionian Bldg
20 Regents Gate Ho
B1 1 Gransden Ho
2 Daubeney Twr
3 North Ho
4 Rochfort Ho
5 Keppel Ho
6 Camden Ho
7 Sanderson Ho
8 Berkeley Ho
9 Strafford Ho
10 Richman Ho
11 Hurleston Ho
12 Grafton Ho
13 Fulcher Ho
14 Citrus Ho
B2 1 Windsock Cl
2 St George's Mews
3 Linberry Wlk
4 Lanyard Ho
5 Golden Hind Pl
6 James Lind Ho
7 Harmon Ho
8 Pelican Ho
9 Bembridge Ho
10 Terrace The
11 George Beard Rd
12 Colonnade The
13 Pepys Ent Ctr
B6 1 Hamilton Ho
2 Imperial Ho
3 Oriana Ho
4 Queens Ct
5 Brightlingsea Pl
6 Faraday Ho
7 Ropemaker's Fields
8 Oast Ct

9 Mitre The
10 Bate St
11 Joseph Irwin Ho
12 Padstow Ho
13 Bethlehem Ho
14 Saunders Cl
15 Roche Ho
16 Stocks Pl
17 Trinidad Ho
18 Grenada Ho
19 Kings Ho
20 Dunbar Wharf
21 Limekiln Wharf
22 Belgrave Ct
23 Eaton Ho
24 Cyril Jackson Prim Sch (North Bldg)
25 Cyril Jackson Prim Sch (South Bldg)
C1 1 Hudson Ct
2 Shackleton Ct
3 De Gama Pl
4 Mercator Pl
5 Maritime Quay
6 Perry Ct
7 Amundsen Ct
C2 1 Nova Bldg
2 Apollo Bldg
3 Gaverick Mews
4 Windmill Ho
5 Orion Point
6 Galaxy Bldg
7 Venus Ho
8 Olympian Ct
9 Poseidon Ct
10 Mercury Ct
11 Aphrodite Ct
12 Cyclops Mews
13 Neptune Ct
14 Artemis Ct
15 Hera Ct
16 Ares Ct
17 Ringwood Gdns
18 Dartmoor Wlk
19 Rothsay Wlk
20 Ashdown Wlk
21 Radnor Wlk
22 Ironmonger's Pl
23 Britannia Rd
24 Deptford Ferry Rd
25 Magellan Pl
26 Dockers Tanner Rd
C3 1 Bowsprit Point
2 St Hubert's Ho
3 John Tucker Ho
4 Broadway Wlk
5 Nash Ho
6 Fairlead Ho
7 Crosstrees Ho
8 Stanliff Ho
9 Keelson Ho
10 Clara Grant Ho
11 Gilbertson Ho
12 Scoulding Ho
13 Hibbert Ho
14 Cressall Ho
15 Alexander Ho
16 Kedge Ho
C4 1 Anchorage Point
2 Waterman Bldg
3 Jefferson Bldg
4 Pierpoint Bldg
5 Franklin Bldg
6 Vanguard Bldg
7 Edison Bldg
8 Seacon Twr
9 Naxos Bldg
10 Express Wharf
11 Hutching's Wharf
12 Tobago St
13 Bellamy Cl
14 Dowlen Ct
15 Cochrane Ho
16 Beatty Ho
17 Scott Ho
18 Laybourne Ho
19 Ensign Ho
20 Beaufort Ho
21 Spinnaker Ho
22 Bosun Cl
23 Topmast Point
24 Turner Ho
25 Constable Ho
26 Knighthead Point
27 Seven Mills Prim Sch
C6 1 West India Ho
2 Berber Pl
3 Birchfield Ho
4 Elderfield Ho
5 Thornfield Ho
6 Gorsefield Ho
7 Arborfield Ho
8 Colborne Ho
9 East India Bldgs
10 Compass Point
11 Salter St
12 Garland Ct
13 Bogart Ct
14 Fonda Ct
15 Welles Ct

16 Rogers Ct
17 Premier Pl
18 Kelly Ct
19 Flynn Ct
20 Mary Jones Ho
21 Cannon Dr
22 Horizon Bldg
23 Holy Family RC Prim Sch
D1 1 Slipway Ho
2 Taffrail Ho
3 Platehouse The
4 Wheelhouse The
5 Chart House The
6 Port House The
7 Beacon Ho
8 Blasker Wlk
9 Maconochies Rd
D2 1 Brassey Ho
2 Triton Ho
3 Warspite Ho
4 Rodney Ho
5 Conway Ho
6 Exmouth Ho
7 Akbar Ho
8 Arethusa Ho
9 Tasman Ct
10 Cutty Sark Ho
11 Harbinger Prim Sch
D3 1 Turnberry Quay
2 Balmoral Ho
3 Aegon Ho
4 Marina Point
D6 1 Westcott Ho
2 Corry Ho
3 Malam Gdns
4 Blomfield Ho
5 Devitt Ho
6 Leyland Ho
7 Wigram Ho
8 Willis Ho
9 Balsam Ho
10 Finch's Ct
11 Poplar Bath St
12 Lawless St
13 Storey Ho
14 Abbot Ho
15 Woodall Cl
16 Landon Wlk
17 Goodhope Ho
18 Goodfaith Ho
19 Winant Ho
20 Goodspeed Ho
21 Lubbock Ho
22 Goodwill Ho
23 Martindale Ho
24 Holmsdale Ho
25 Norwood Ho
26 Constant Ho
27 Tower Hamlets Coll

120

A2 1 St John's Ho
2 Betty May Gray Ho
3 Castleton Ho
4 Urmston Ho
5 Salford Ho
6 Capstan Ho
7 Frigate Ho
8 Galleon Ho
9 Barons Lo
A3 1 Cardale St
2 Hickin St
3 John McDonald Ho
4 Thorne Ho
5 Skeggs Ho
6 St Bernard Ho
7 Kimberley Ho
8 Kingdon Ho
9 Killoran Ho
10 Alastor Ho
11 Lingard Ho
12 Yarrow Ho
13 Sandpiper Ct
14 Nightingale Ct
15 Robin Ct
16 Heron Ct
17 Ferndown Lo
18 Crosby Ho
A4 1 Llandovery Ho
2 Rugless Ho
3 Ash Ho
4 Elm Ho
5 Cedar Ho
6 Castalia Sq
7 Aspect Ho
8 Normandy Ho
9 Valiant Ho
10 Tamar Ho
11 Watkins Ho
12 Alice Shepherd Ho
13 Oak Ho
14 Ballin Ct
15 Martin Ct
16 Grebe Ct
17 Kingfisher Ct
18 Walkers Lo
19 Antilles Bay
A5 1 Lumina Bldg

2 Nova Ct W
3 Nova Ct E
4 Aurora Bldg
5 Arran Ho
6 Kintyre Ho
7 Vantage Mews
8 Managers Ct
9 Horatio Pl
10 Concordia Wharf
A6 1 Discovery Ho
2 Mountague Pl
3 Virginia Ho
4 Collins Ho
5 Lawless Ho
6 Carmichael Ho
7 Commodore Ho
8 Mermaid Ho
9 Bullivant St
10 Anderson Ho
11 Mackrow Wlk
12 Robin Hood Gdns
13 Prestage Way
14 Woolmore Prim Sch
B2 1 Verwood Lo
2 Fawley Lo
3 Lyndhurst Lo
4 Blyth Cl
5 Farnworth Ho
6 Francis Cl
7 St Luke's CE Prim Sch
B6 1 Quixley St
2 Romney Ho
3 Pumping Ho
4 Switch Ho
5 Wingfield Ct
6 Explorers Ct
7 Sexton Ct
8 Keel Ct
9 Bridge Ct
10 Sail Ct
11 Settlers Ct
12 Pilgrims Mews
13 Studley Ct
14 Wotton Ct
15 Cape Henry Ct
16 Bartholomew Ct
17 Adventurers Ct
18 Susan Constant Ct
19 Atlantic Ct
C1 1 Bellot Gdns
2 Thornley Pl
3 King William La
4 Bolton Ho
5 Miles Ho
6 Mell St
7 Sam Manners Ho
8 Hatcliffe Almshouses
9 Woodland Wlk
10 Earlswood Cl
11 St Joseph's RC Prim Sch
D1 1 Baldrey Ho
2 Christie Ho
3 Dyson Ho
4 Cliffe Ho
5 Moore Ho
6 Collins Ho
7 Lockyer Ho
8 Halley Ho
9 Kepler Ho
10 Sailacre Ho
11 Union Pk
D3 1 Teal St
2 Maurer Ct
3 Mudlarks Blvd
4 Renaissance Wlk
5 Alamaro Lo

121

A1 1 Layfield Ho
2 Westerdale Rd
3 Mayston Mews
4 Station Mews Terr
5 Halstow Prim Sch
6 Holyrood Mews
A5 1 Capulet Mews
2 Pepys Cres
3 De Quincey Mews
4 Hardy Ave
5 Tom Jenkinson Rd
6 Kennacraig Cl
7 Charles Flemwell Mews
8 Gatcombe Rd
9 Badminton Mews
10 Holyrood Mews
11 Britannia Gate
12 Dalemain Mews
13 Bowes-Lyon Hall
14 Lancaster hall
15 Victoria Hall
A6 1 Clements Ave
2 Martindale Ave
3 Balearic Apts
4 Marmara Apts
5 Baltic Apts
6 Coral Apts
7 Aegean Apts
8 Capital East Apts
B1 1 Phipps Ho

2 Hartwell Ho
3 Nicholas Stacey Ho
4 Fossdene Prim Sch
5 Frank Burton Cl
B5 1 Beaulieu Ave
2 Charles Whincup Rd
3 Audley Dr
4 Julia Garfield Mews
5 Rayleigh Rd
6 Pirie St
7 Royal Victoria Pl
8 Pankhurst Ave
9 West Mersea Cl
10 Ramsgate Cl
11 Windsor Hall
12 Munning Ho
13 Drake Hall
14 Jane Austen Hall
15 Eastern Quay
16 Portsmouth Mews
17 Britannia Village Prim Sch
C1 1 Ransom Rd
2 Linton Cl
3 Cedar Pl
4 Gooding Ho
5 Valiant Ho
6 Chaffey Ho
7 Benn Ho
8 Wellesley Cl
9 Gollogly Terr

122

A2 1 Harden Ct
2 Albion Ct
3 Viking Ho
4 Zealand Ho
5 Glenalvon Way
6 Parish Wharf
7 Elsinore Ho
8 Lolland Ho
9 Denmark Ho
10 Jutland Ho
11 Tivoli Gdns
12 Rance Ho
13 Peel Yates Ho
14 Rosebank Wlk
15 Paradise Pl
16 Woodville St
B2 1 Bowling Green Row
2 Sarah Turnbull Ho
3 Brewhouse Rd
4 Red Barracks Rd
5 Marine Dr
6 Hastings Ho
7 Centurion Ct
8 Cambridge Ho
9 Churchill Ct
10 Elizabeth Ct
11 Cambridge Barracks Rd
12 Len Clifton Ho
13 Granby Ho
14 Harding Ho
15 Rutland Ho
16 Townshend Ho
17 Rendlebury Ho
18 Milne Ho
19 Mulgrave Ho
20 Murray Ho
21 Chatham Ho
22 Biddulph Ho
23 Carew Ho
24 Eleanor Wlk
25 Cardwell Prim Sch
C2 1 Preston Ho
2 Lindsay Ho
3 Fraser Ho
4 Pickering Ho
5 Watergate Ho
6 Grinling Ho
7 Glebe Ho
8 Elliston Ho
9 Sir Martin Bowes Ho
10 Jim Bradley Cl
11 Bathway
12 Limavady Ho
13 Slater Cl
14 Vista Bldg The
15 Greenwich London Coll
16 St Mary Magdalene CE Prim Sch
C5 1 Westland Ho
2 Queensland Ho
3 Pier Par
4 Woodman Par
5 Shaw Ho
6 Glen Ho
7 Brocklebank Ho
D1 1 Branham Ho
2 Ford Ho
3 Wilford Ho
4 Parker Ho
5 Stirling Ho
6 Twiss Ho
7 Hewett Ho
8 De Haviland Dr
9 Schoolhouse Yd
D2 1 Beresford Sq
2 Central Ct

3 Walpole Pl
4 Anglesea Ave
5 Troy Ct
6 Ormsby Point
7 Haven Lo
8 Green Lawns
9 Eardley Point
10 Sandham Point
11 Bingham Point
12 Anglesea Mews
13 Masons Hill
14 Maritime Ho
15 International Univ of America (London Campus)
16 Woolwich Tramshed The

123

A1 1 Glenmount Path
2 Claymill Ho
3 St James Hts
4 St Margaret's Path
5 George Akass Ho
A2 1 Abel Ho
2 Maynard Ho
3 Crown Ho
A3 1 Wayatt Point
2 Albert Ho
3 Building 50
4 Building 49
5 Building 48
6 Building 47
7 Building 36
8 Blenheim Ho
9 Wilson Ct
10 Romney Rd
B1 1 Bert Reilly Ho
2 Heavitree Rd
3 South Rise Prim Sch
B3 1 Apollo Way
2 Senator Wlk
3 Mallard Path
4 Fortune Wlk
C1 1 Fox Hollow Cl
2 Goldsmid St
C2 1 Gavin Ho
2 Richard Neve Ho
3 Bateson St
4 Lewin Ct
5 Conway Prim Sch

124

B5 1 Rowntree Path
2 Macaulay Way
3 Manning Ct
4 Chadwick Ct
5 Simon Ct
B6 1 Beveridge Ct
2 Hammond Way
3 Leonard Robbins Path
4 Lansbury Ct
5 Raymond Postgate Ct
6 Webb Ct
7 Curtis Way
8 Lytton Strachey Path
9 Keynes Ct
10 Marshall Path
11 Cross Ct
12 Octavia Way
13 Passfield Path
14 Mill Ct
15 Besant Ct
C3 1 Hermitage Cl
2 Chantry Cl
C4 1 Binsey Wlk
2 Tilehurst Point
3 Blewbury Ho
4 Coralline Wlk
5 Evenlode Ho
C5 1 Kingsley Ct
2 Wilberforce Ct
3 Shaftesbury Ct
4 Hazlitt Ct
5 Ricardo Path
6 Nassau Path
7 Malthus Path
8 Bright Ct
9 Cobden Ct
D4 1 Oakenholt Ho
2 Trewsbury Ho
3 Penton Ho
4 Osney Ho
5 St Helens Rd
6 Clewer Ho
7 Maplin Ho
8 Wyfold Ho
9 Hibernia Point
10 Duxford Ho
11 Radley Ho
12 Limestone Wlk
13 Masham Ho
14 Jacob Ho

125

A3 1 Harlequin Ho
2 Dexter Ho
3 Argali Ho
4 Mangold Way
5 Lucerne Ct
6 Holstein Way
7 Abbotswood Cl
8 Plympton Cl
9 Benedict Cl
B1 1 Shakespeare Ho
2 Tennyson Ho
3 Dickens Ho
4 Scott Ho
5 Lansbury Ho
6 Shaw Ho
7 Chestnuts The
C1 1 Stevanne Ct
2 Tolcairn Ct
3 Chalfont Ct
4 Alonso Ho
5 Ariel Ct
6 Miranda Ho
7 Prospero Ho
8 Laurels The
9 Camden Ct
10 Newnham Lo
11 Court Lo
12 Flaxman Ct
13 Hertford Wlk
14 Riverview Ct
15 Winchester Ct
C2 1 Brushwood Lo
2 Bletchington Ct
3 Upper Sheridan Rd
4 William Ct
5 Samson Ct
6 Cowper Rd
7 Venmead Ct
C3 1 Cressingham Ct
2 Telford Ho
3 Kelvin Ho
4 Faraday Ho
5 Jenner Ho
6 Keir Hardie Ho
7 Lennox Ho
8 Mary Macarthur Ho
9 Elizabeth Garrett
   Anderson Ho
10 William Smith Ho
11 Baden Powell Ho
12 Baird Ho
13 Boyle Ho

129

B2 1 St Michael & St Martin
   RC Prim Sch
D1 1 Bellview Ct
1 Heathwood Ct
2 Aldermead
3 Northumberland Ct
D2 1 Oak Hts Ind Sch

130

C4 1 Osterley Lo
2 St Andrew's Cl
3 Parkfield
4 Fairways
5 Granwood Ct
6 Grovewood Ct
D3 2 Beechen Cliff Way
3 Thurza Ct
4 Primrose Pl
5 Lanadron Cl
D4 1 Overton Cl

131

A2 1 Brewery Mews Bsns Ctr
2 Forge Lo
3 Pulteney Cl
4 Tolson Ho
5 Percy Gdns
6 Wynne Ct
7 Wisdom Ct
8 Swann Ct
9 Shrewsbury Wlk
10 King's Terr
11 Van Gogh Cl
12 Holme Ct
13 St Mary's RC Prim Sch
C5 1 Canute Ho
2 Spruce Ho
3 Moorings Ho
4 Jessops Wharf
5 Corsell Ho
6 Barnes Qtr
7 Dorey Ho
8 Tanyard Ho
9 Booth Ho
10 Oakbark Ho
11 Bordeston Ct
12 Shire Pl

D5 1 Galba Ct
2 Servius Ct
3 Maurice Ct
4 Leo Ct
5 Otho Ct
6 Nero Ct
7 Romulus Ct
8 Pump Alley
9 Caxton Mews
D6 1 Brockshot Cl
2 Westbury Pl
3 Brook La N
4 Braemar Ct
5 Brook Ct
6 Clifden Ho
7 Cedar Ct
8 Cranbrook Ct
9 Somerset Lo
10 Alexandra Rd
11 Berkeley Ho
12 Watermans Ct
13 Ferry Quays Ctyd
14 St Pauls CE Prim Sch

132

A1 1 St John's Gr
2 Michel's Row
3 Michelsdale Dr
4 Blue Anchor Alley
5 Clarence St
6 Sun Alley
7 Thames Link Ho
8 Benns Wlk
9 Waterloo Pl
10 Northumbria Ct
A6 1 Ferry Sq
2 Watermans Ct
3 Wilkes Rd
4 Albany Par
5 Charlton Ho
6 Albany Ho
7 Alma Ho
8 Griffin Ct
9 Cressage Ho
10 Tunstall Wlk
11 Trimmer Wlk
12 Running Horse Yd
13 Mission Sq
14 Distillery Wlk
B1 1 Towers The
2 Longs Ct
3 Sovereign Ct
4 Robinson Ct
5 Calvert Ct
6 Bedford Ct
7 Hickey's Almshouses
8 Church Estate
   Almshouses
9 Richmond International
   Bsns Ctr
10 Abercorn Mews
B4 1 Primrose Ho
2 Lawman Ct
3 Royston Ct
4 Garden Ct
5 Capel Lo
6 Devonshire Ct
7 Celia Ct
8 Rosslyn Ho
9 Branstone Ct
10 Lamerton Lo
11 Kew Lo
12 Dunraven Ho
13 Stoneleigh Lo
14 Tunstall Ct
15 Voltaire
C4 1 Clarendon Ct
2 Quintock Ho
3 Broome Ct
4 Lonsdale Mews
5 Elizabeth Cotts
6 Sandways
7 Victoria Cotts
8 North Ave
9 Grovewood
10 Hamilton Ho
11 Melvin Ct
12 Royal Par
13 Power Ho
14 Station Ave
15 Blake Mews
C6 5 Strand-on-the-Green
   Schs
D1 1 Hershell Ct
2 Deanhill Ct
3 Park Sheen
4 Furness Lo
5 Merricks Ct
D4 1 Terrano Ho
2 Oak Ho
3 Aura Ho
4 Maple Ho
5 Cedar Ho
6 Saffron Ho
7 Lime Ho
8 Lavender Ho
9 Juniper Ho
D6 1 Falcons Pre Prep
   school The

133

B2 1 Rann Ho
2 Craven Ho
3 John Dee Ho
4 Kindell Ho
5 Montgomery Ho
6 Avondale Ho
7 Addington Ct
8 Dovecote Gdns
9 Firmston Ho
10 Glendower Gdns
11 Chestnut Ave
12 Trehern Rd
13 Rock Ave
14 St Mary Magdalen's RC
   Prim Sch
D3 1 Melrose Rd
2 Seaforth Lo
3 St John's Gr
4 Sussex Ct
5 Carmichael Ct
6 Hampshire Ct
7 Thorne Pas
8 Brunel Ct
9 Beverley Path

134

D1 1 Olivette St
2 Mascotte Rd
3 Glegg Pl
4 Crown Ct
5 Charlwood Terr
6 Percy Laurie Ho
7 Our Lady of Victories
   RC Prim Sch
D2 1 Griffin Gate
2 Darfur St
3 John Keall Ho
4 Henry Jackson Ho
5 Felsham Ho
6 Ardshiel Cl
7 Ruvigny Mans
8 Star & Garter Mans
9 University Mans
10 Lockyer Ho
11 Phelps Ho
12 Princeton Ct
13 Kingsmere Cl
14 Felsham Mews
15 St Mary's CE Prim Sch
D6 1 Cobb's Hall
2 Dorset Mans
3 St Clements Mans
4 Bothwell St
5 Hawksmoor St
6 Melcombe Prim Sch

135

A3 1 Drive Mans
2 Romily Ct
3 Dwight Ct
4 Burlington Gdns
5 Fulham Prep Sch
6 Moat Sch The
7 All Saints CE Prim Sch
B3 1 Plato Pl
2 Mustow Pl
3 Laurel Bank Gdns
4 Ranelagh Mans
5 Churchfield Mans
6 Bear Croft Ho
7 Elysium Gate
8 Ethel Rankin Ct
9 Arthur Henderson Ho
10 William Banfield Ho
11 Melbray Mews
12 New King's Prim Sch
13 Eridge House Sch
D3 1 Brightwells
2 Broughton Road App
3 Bulow Ct
4 Langford Rd
5 Elizabeth Barnes Ct
6 Snowbury Rd

136

A2 1 Molasses Ho
2 Molasses Row
3 Cinnamon Row
4 Calico Ho
5 Calico Row
6 Port Ho
7 Square Rigger Row
8 Trade Twr
9 Ivory Ho
10 Spice Ho
11 Sherwood Ct
12 Mendip Ct
13 Chalmers Ho
14 Coral Row
15 Ivory Sq
16 Kingfisher Ho
B1 1 Burke Ho
1 High View Prim Sch
2 Centre Acad

2 Fox Ho
3 Buxton Ho
4 Pitt Ho
5 Ramsey Ho
6 Beverley Cl
7 Florence Ho
8 Linden Ct
9 Dorcas Ct
10 Johnson Ct
11 Agnes Ct
12 Hilltop Ct
13 Courtyard The
14 Old Laundry The
15 Oberstein Rd
16 Fineran Ct
17 Sangora Rd
18 Harvard Mans
19 Plough Mews
B2 1 Milner Ho
2 McManus Ho
3 Wilberforce Ho
4 Wheeler Ct
5 Sporle Ct
6 Holliday Sq
7 John Parker Sq
8 Carmichael Cl
9 Fenner Sq
10 Clark Lawrence Ct
11 Shaw Ct
12 Sendall Ct
13 Livingstone Rd
14 Farrant Ho
15 Jackson Ho
16 Darien Ho
17 Shepard Ho
18 Ganley Ct
19 Arthur Newton Ho
20 Chesterton Ho
21 John Kirk Ho
22 Mantua St
23 Heaver Rd
24 Candlemakers
25 Thames Christian Coll
26 Falconbrook Prim Sch
B3 1 Archer Ho
2 White Ho
3 Winfield Ho
4 Powrie Ho
5 Morgan Ct
6 Fairchild Cl
7 Musjid Rd
C2 1 Kiloh Ct
2 Lanner Ho
3 Griffon Ho
4 Kestrel Ho
5 Kite Ho
6 Peregrine Ho
7 Hawk Ho
8 Inkster Ho
9 Harrier Ho
10 Eagle Hts
11 Kingfisher Ho
12 Lavender Terr
13 Temple Ho
14 Ridley Ho
15 Eden Ho
16 Hertford Ct
17 Nepaul Rd
C3 1 Meecham Ct
2 McKiernan Ct
3 Banbury St
4 Colestown St
5 Crombie Mews
6 Frere St
D3 1 Stevenson Ho
2 Ambrose Mews
3 Harling Ct
4 Southside Quarter
5 Latchmere St
6 Dovedale Cotts
7 Roydon Cl
8 Castlemaine
9 Wittering Ho
10 Berry Ho
11 Weybridge Point

137

A2 1 Shaftesbury Park
   Chambers
2 Selborne
3 Rush Hill Mews
4 Marmion Mews
5 Crosland Pl
6 Craven Mews
7 Garfield Mews
8 Audley Ct
9 Basnett Rd
10 Tyneham Cl
11 Woodmere Cl
A3 1 Hopkinson Ho
2 Macdonald Ho
3 Rushlake Ho
4 Bishopstone Ho
5 Dresden Ho
6 Millgrove St
7 Farnhurst Ho
8 Walden Ho
9 Kennard St
10 Langhurst Ho

11 Atkinson Ho
12 Kennard Ho
13 Voltaire Ct
14 Barloch Ho
15 London Stone Bsns Est
16 Shaftesbury Park Prim
   Sch
17 John Burns Prim Sch
B2 1 Turnchapel Mews
2 Redwood Mews
3 Phil Brown Pl
4 Bev Callender Cl
5 Keith Connor Cl
6 Tessa Sanderson Pl
7 Daley Thompson Way
8 Rashleigh Ct
9 Abberley Mews
10 Willow Lodge
11 Beaufoy Rd
B3 1 St Philip Sq
2 Montefiore St
3 Gambetta St
4 Scott Ct
5 Radcliffe Path
6 Moresby Wlk
7 Victorian Hts
C1 1 Polygon The
2 Windsor Ct
3 Trinity Cl
4 Studios The
5 Bourne Ho
C2 1 Clapham Manor Ct
2 Clarke Ho
3 Gables The
4 Sycamore Mews
5 Maritime Ho
6 Rectory Gdns
7 Floris Pl
8 Clapham Manor Prim
   Sch
C3 1 Seymour Ho
2 Lucas Ho
3 Durrington Twr
4 Amesbury Twr
5 Fovant Ct
6 Allington Ct
7 Welford Ct
8 Ilsley Ct
9 Blake Ct
10 Brooklands Ct
11 Heathbrook Prim Sch
12 Michael Manley Ind Est
D1 1 Kendoa Rd
2 Felmersham Cl
3 Abbeville Mews
4 Saxon Ho
5 Gifford Ho
6 Teignmouth Cl
7 Holwood Pl
8 Oaklands Pl
9 Wilberforce Mews
10 William Bonney Est
11 London Coll of Bsns &
   Computer Studies
D2 1 Chelsham Ho
2 Lynde Ho
3 Greener Ho
4 Towns Ho
5 Hugh Morgan Ho
6 Roy Ridley Ho
7 Lendal Terr
8 Slievemore Cl
9 Cadmus Cl
10 Clapham North Bsns
   Ctr
D3 1 Haltone Ho
2 Surcot Ho
3 Kingsley Ho
4 Wood Ho
5 Dalemain Ho
6 Fallodon Ho
7 Dartington Ho
8 Esher Ho
9 Kneller Ho
10 Lostock Ho
11 Croxteth Ho
12 Donnington Ho
13 Farnley Ho
14 Hardwick Ho
15 Bradfield Ho
16 Brocket Ho
17 Colchester Ho
18 Clive Ho
19 Chessington Ho
20 Rushbrook Ho
21 Stanmore Ho
22 Newton Ho
23 Netherby Ho
24 Oakwell Ho
25 Rydal Ho
26 Rushton Ho
27 Harcourt Ho
28 Metcalfe Ho
29 Lydwell Ho
30 Raleigh Ho
31 Spencer Ho
32 Shipley Ho
33 Naylor Ho
34 Mordaunt Ho
35 Stanley Ho

36 Alderley Ho
37 Effingham Ho
38 Grant Ho
39 Wilson Ho
40 Fraser Ho

138

A1 1 Morris Ho
2 Gye Ho
3 Clowes Ho
4 Thomas Ho
5 Stuart Ho
6 Storace Ho
7 Bedford Ho
8 Ascot Ct
9 Ascot Par
10 Ashmere Ho
11 Ashmere Gr
12 Ventura Ho
13 Vickery Ho
14 Stafford Mans
15 Beresford Ho
A2 1 Callingham Ho
2 Russell Pickering Ho
3 Ormerod Ho
4 Lopez Ho
5 Coachmaker Mews
6 Brixton Day Coll
A3 1 Barling Ct
2 Jeffrey's Ct
3 Brooks Ct
4 Dalmeny Ct
5 Fender Ct
6 Fishlock Ct
7 Bedser Ct
8 Gover Ct
9 Clarence Wlk
10 Barton Ct
11 Allom Ct
12 Garden Ho
13 Otha Ho
14 Hayward Ct
15 Surridge Ct
16 Knox Ct
17 Jephson Ct
18 Holmes Ct
19 McIntyre Ct
20 Richardson Ct
21 Cassell Ho
22 Pakington Ho
23 Bain Ho
24 Enfield Ho
25 Fawcett Ho
26 Sidgwick Ho
27 Jowett Ho
28 Beckett Ho
29 Arden Ho
30 Pinter Ho
31 Barrington Ct
32 Union Mews
33 St Andrew's Prim Sch
B1 1 Freemens Hos
2 Roger's Almshouses
3 Gresham Almshouses
4 Exbury Ho
5 Glasbury Ho
6 Dalbury Ho
7 Fosbury Ho
8 Chalbury Ho
9 Neilson-Terry Ct
10 Pavilion Mans
11 Daisy Dormer Ct
12 George Lashwood Ct
13 Marie Lloyd Ct
14 Trinity Homes
15 Lethaby Ho
16 Edmundsbury Ct Est
17 Regis Pl
18 Marlborough Mews
19 Alpha Ho
20 Beta Pl
21 Cedars Ho
22 South Chelsea Coll
B2 1 Turberville Ho
2 Thrayle Ho
3 Percheron Ct
4 Draymans Ct
5 Lansdowne Ct
6 Stockwell Prim Sch
B3 1 Maurice Ho
2 Thring Ho
3 Paton Ho
4 Huxley Ho
5 Morell Ho
6 Mary Ho
7 Beale Ho
8 Rosa Parks Ho
9 Birrell Ho
10 Waltham Ho
11 Burford Ho
12 Thornicroft Ho
13 Addington Ho
14 Goffton Ho
15 Redmayne Ho
16 Norton Ho
17 Aytoun Ho
18 Colwall Ho
19 Burrow Ho
20 Wynter Ho

21 Crowhurst Ho
22 Lidcote Gdns
23 Cumnor Cl
24 Park View Mews
C1 1 Electric Mans
2 Electric La
3 Connaught Mans
4 Clifton Mans
5 Hereford Ho
6 Chaplin Ho
7 Brixton Oval
8 Lord David Pitt Ho
9 Marcus Garvey Way
10 Montego Cl
11 Bob Marley Way
12 Leeson Rd
C2 1 Buckmaster Cl
2 Albemarle Ho
3 Goodwood Mans
4 Angell Park Gdns
5 Fyfield Rd
6 Howard Ho
7 Harris Ho
8 Broadoak Ct
9 Burgate Ct
10 Witchwood Ho
11 Blacktree Mews
12 Chartham Ct
13 Chilham Ct
14 Northgate Ct
15 Westgate Ct
16 Dover Mans
17 St Helen's RC Sch
18 Dorrell Pl
C3 1 Norval Gn
2 Hilda Terr
3 Burton La
4 Church Gn
5 Lord Holland La
6 Sorrell Cl
7 Burton Rd
8 Holles Ho
9 Leys Ct
10 Warwick Ho
11 Fairfax Ho
12 Wayland Ho
13 Dudley Ho
14 Denchworth Ho
15 Fitzgerald Ho
16 Lambert Ho
17 Chute Ho
18 Bedwell Ho
19 Ferrey Mews
20 Serenaders Rd
21 Boatemah Wlk
22 Ireton Ho
23 Marston Ho
24 Morrison Rd
25 Fir Grove Rd
26 Shore Way
27 George Mews
28 St John's Angell Town CE Prim Sch
C4 1 Hector Ct
2 Jason Ct
3 Creon Ct
4 Hermes Ct
5 Argos Ct
6 Cadmus Ct
7 Appollo Ct
8 Mercury Ct
9 County Ho
10 Seasalter Ho
11 Downbarton Ho
12 Garlinge Ho
13 Moira Ho
14 Alvanley Ho
15 Woodchurch Ho
16 Durlock Ho
17 Hallam Ho
18 Whiteness Ho
19 Bromstone Ho
20 Penelope Ho
21 Melbourne Sq
22 Cloisters The
23 Cliffsend Ho
24 Sacketts Ho
25 Hanway Ho
26 Brickworth Ho
27 Redlynch Ho
28 Stodmarsh Ho
29 Kingsgate Ho
30 Chardin Ho
31 Annesley Ho
32 Knowlton Ho
33 Russell Gr
34 Eamann Casey Ho
35 Christ Church CE Prim Sch
C5 1 Swift Ho
2 Listowel Cl
3 Deal Wlk
4 Plover Ho
5 Aigburth Mans
6 Glencoe Mans
7 Glenshaw Mans
8 Cleveland Mans
9 Leda Ct
10 Jupiter Ct
11 Juno Ct

12 Healy Ho
13 Ashton Ho
14 Ramsey Ho
15 Annesley Ho
16 Cowley Rd
C6 1 Sherwin Ho
2 Pegasus Pl
3 Kilner Ho
4 Read Ho
5 Lohmann Ho
6 Hornby Ho
7 Abel Ho
8 Blythe Ho
9 Key Ho
10 Lockwood Ho
11 Alverstone Ho
12 Blades Ho
13 Rothesay Ct
15 Henry Fawcett Prim Sch
D1 1 Mahatma Gandhi Ind Est
2 Dylan Rd
3 Bessemer Park Ind Est
4 Pablo Neruda Cl
5 Langston Hughes Cl
6 Walt Whitman Cl
7 James Joyce Wlk
8 Alice Walker Cl
9 Louise Bennett Cl
10 Chadacre Ho
11 Burwood Ho
12 Pyrford Ho
13 Wangford Ho
14 Ashford Ho
15 Kenwood Ho
16 Moyne Ho
17 Elveden Ho
18 Carrara Cl
19 Broughton Dr
20 Angela Davis Ind Est
21 Tilia Wlk
22 County Ho
23 Hill Mead Prim Sch
D2 1 Mallams Mews
2 Amberley Ct
3 Harper Ho
4 Leicester Ho
5 Station Ave
6 Wellfit St
7 Loughborough Ct
8 Belinda Rd
9 Higgs Ind Est
10 Tham Cl
D3 1 Langport Ho
2 Iveagh Ho
3 Newark Ho
4 Edgehill Ho
5 Hopton Ho
6 Ashby Ho
7 Nevil Ho
D4 1 Fairbairn Gn
2 Hammelton Gn
3 Foxley Sq
4 Silverburn Ho
5 Butler Ho
6 Dalkeith Ho
7 Turner Cl
8 Bathgate Ho
9 Black Roof Ho
10 Charles Edward Brooke Sch (Dennen Site)
11 Charles Edward Brooke Sch
D6 1 Faunce Ho
2 Garbett Ho
3 Harvard Ho
4 Doddington Pl
5 Kean Ho
6 Jephson Ho
7 Cornish Ho
8 Bateman Ho
9 Molesworth Ho
10 Walters Ho
11 Cruden Ho
12 Brawne Ho
13 Prescott Ho
14 Chalmer's Wlk
15 Copley Cl
16 King Charles Ct

139

A3 1 Bergen Ho
2 Oslo Ho
3 Viking Ho
4 Jutland Ho
5 Norvic Ho
6 Odin Ho
7 Baltic Ho
8 Nobel Ho
9 Mercia Ho
10 Kenbury Gdns
11 Zealand Ho
12 Elsinore Ho
13 Norse Ho
14 Denmark Mans
15 Dane Ho
16 Canterbury Cl
17 York Cl

18 Kenbury Mans
19 Parade Mans
20 Winterslow Ho
21 Lilford Ho
22 Bartholomew Ho
23 Guildford Ho
24 Boston Ho
25 Hereford Ho
26 Weyhill Ho
27 Lichfield Ho
28 Lansdown Ho
29 Honiton Ho
30 Pinner Ho
31 Baldock Ho
32 Widecombe Ho
33 Nottingham Ho
34 Witham Ho
35 Barnet Ho
36 Empress Mews
A4 1 Bertha Neubergh Ho
2 Mornington Mews
3 Badsworth Rd
4 Pearson Cl
5 Elm Tree Ct
6 Samuel Lewis Trust Dwellings
7 Milkwell Yd
8 Keswick Ho
9 Mitcham Ho
10 Sacred Heart RC Sec Sch
A5 1 Boundary Ho
2 Day Ho
3 Burgess Ho
4 Carlyle Ho
5 Myers Ho
6 Thompson Ave
7 Palgrave Ho
8 Winnington Ho
9 Brantwood Ho
10 Lowell Ho
11 Jessie Duffett Ho
12 Otterburn Ho
13 Crossmount Ho
14 Venice Ct
15 Bowyer St
16 Livingstone Ho
17 Gothic Ct
18 Coniston Ho
19 Harlynwood
20 Carey Ct
21 Finley Ct
22 Grainger Ct
23 Hayes Ct
24 Moffat Ho
25 Marinel Ho
26 Hodister Cl
27 Arnot Ho
28 Lamb Ho
29 Kipling Ho
30 Keats Ho
31 Kenyon Ho
32 New Church Rd
33 Sir John Kirk Cl
34 Comber Grove Prim Sch
35 St Michael & All Angels CE Acad
36 St Joseph's RC Inf & Jun Schs
B1 1 Shaftesbury Ct
2 Mayhew Ct
3 Morris Ct
4 Swinburne Ct
5 Perth Ct
6 Tayside Ct
7 Matlock Ct
8 Hunter Ct
9 Turner Ct
B3 1 Selborne Rd
2 Hascombe Terr
B4 1 Joiners Arms Yd
2 Butterfly Wlk
3 Cuthill Wlk
4 Colonades The
5 Artichoke Mews
6 Peabody Bldgs
7 Brighton Ho
8 Park Ho
9 Peabody Ct
10 Lomond Ho
11 Lamb Ho
12 Kimpton Ct
13 Belham Wlk
14 Datchelor Pl
15 Harvey Rd
B5 1 Masterman Ho
2 Milton Ho
3 Pope Ho
4 Chester Ct
5 Marvel Ho
6 Flecker Ho
7 Landor Ho
8 Leslie Prince Ct
9 Evelina Mans
10 Langland Ho
11 Drinkwater Ho
12 Procter Ho
13 Shirley Ho
14 Drayton Ho

15 Bridges Ho
16 Cunningham Ho
17 Hood Ho
18 Herrick Ho
19 Dekker Ho
20 Houseman Way
21 Coleby Path
22 Brunswick Park Prim Sch
B6 1 Queens Ho
2 Arnside Ho
3 Horsley St
4 St Peter's Ho
5 St Johns Ho
6 St Marks Ho
7 St Stephens Ho
8 St Matthew's Ho
9 Red Lion Cl
10 Boyson Rd
11 Bradenham
C2 1 Harfield Gdns
2 Karen Ct
3 Seavington Ho
4 Appleshaw Ho
5 Birdsall Ho
6 Whitney Ho
7 Wheatland Ho
8 Wilton Ho
9 Walcot Ho
10 Whaddon Ho
11 Melbreak Ho
12 Ledbury Ho
13 Tidworth Ho
14 Riseholme Ho
15 Ringmer Ho
16 Petworth Ho
17 Stagshaw Ho
18 Ivybridge Ho
19 Inwood Ho
20 Gatcombe Ho
21 Felbridge Ho
22 Cowdray Ho
23 Dog Kennel Hill Sch
C3 1 Springfield Ho
2 Craston Ho
3 Walters Ho
4 Edgecombe Ho
5 Fowler Ho
6 Rignold Ho
7 Chatham Ho
C4 1 Barnwell Ho
2 Brunswick Villas
3 St Giles Twr
4 Bentley Ho
5 Dawson Ho
6 Dryden Ho
7 Mayward Ho
8 Longleigh Ho
9 Fairwall Ho
10 Bodeney Ho
11 Sandby Ho
12 Vestry Mews
13 Netley
14 Lakanal
15 Racine
16 Camberwell Coll of Arts
C5 1 Tower Mill Rd
2 Tilson Cl
3 Granville Sq
4 Edgar Wallace Cl
5 Potters Cl
6 Dorton Cl
7 Samuel Jones Ind Est
8 Dibden Ho
9 Marchwood Cl
10 Pilgrims Cloisters
11 Beacon Ho
12 Teather St
13 Stacy Path
14 Rumball Ho
15 Ballow Cl
16 Rill Ho
17 Southwark Coll (Camberwell Ctr)
18 St George's CE Prim Sch
C6 1 Downend Ct
2 Andoversford Ct
3 Pearse St
4 Watling St
5 Gandolfi St
6 Comfort St
7 Tower Mill Rd
D1 1 Dulwich Mews
1 New Hope Christian Sch
2 St James's Cloisters
D4 1 Colbert
2 Voltaire
3 Finch Mews
4 Charles Coveney Rd
5 Bamber Rd
6 Crane St
7 Curlew Ho
8 Mallard Ho
9 Tern Ho

10 Crane Ho
11 Falcon Ho
12 Bryanston Ho
13 Basing Ct
14 Marcus Ho
15 Sheffield Ho
16 Highshore Sch
17 St James The Great RC Prim Sch
18 Oliver Goldsmith Prim Sch

D5 1 Painswick Ct
2 Sharpness Ct
3 Mattingly Way
4 Hordle Prom N
5 Burcher Gale Gr
6 Calypso Cres
7 Hordle Prom S
8 Cinnamon Cl
9 Savannah Cl
10 Thames Ct
11 Shannon Ct
12 Amstel Ct
13 Danube Ct
14 Tilbury Cl
15 Hordle Prom E
16 Indus Ct
17 Oakcourt
18 Palm Ct
19 Rowan Ct
20 Blackthorn Ct
21 Pear Ct
22 Lidgate Rd
23 Whistler Mews
24 Boathouse Wlk
25 Camberwell Coll of Arts

D6 1 Willsbridge Ct
2 Cam Ct
3 Quedgeley Ct
4 Saul Ct
5 Quenington Ct
6 Westonbirt Ct
7 Wickway Ct

140

A2 4 St John's & St Clements CE Jun & Inf Sch
5 Bellenden Prim Sch

A3 1 William Margrie Cl
2 William Blake Ho
3 Quantock Mews
4 Choumert Sq
5 Parkstone Rd
6 Atwell Rd

A4 1 Canal Head Public Sq
2 Angelina Ho
3 Jarvis Ho
4 Richland Ho
5 Honeywood Ho
6 Wakefield Ho
7 Primrose Ho
8 Hardcastle Ho
9 Dunstall Ho
10 Springtide Cl
11 Purdon Ho
12 Flamborough Ho
13 Lambrook Ho
14 Witcombe Point
15 Yarnfield Sq
16 Winford Ct
17 Portbury Cl
18 Robert Keen Cl

A5 1 Thornbill Ho
2 Vervain Ho
3 Woodstar Ho
4 Tamarind Ho
5 Hereford Retreat
6 Haymerle Ho
7 Furley Ho
8 Thomas Milner Ho
9 Applegarth Ho
10 Freda Corbett Cl
11 Rudbeck Ho
12 Henslow Ho
13 Lindley Ho
14 Collinson Ho
15 Sister Mabel's Way
16 Timberland Cl
17 Hastings Cl
18 Sidmouth Ho
19 Budleigh Ho
20 Stanesgate Ho
21 Breamore Ho
22 Ely Ho
23 Gisburn Ho
24 Silkin Mews
25 Peckham Park Prim Sch
26 St Francis RC Prim Sch

A6 1 Bowles Rd
2 Western Wharf
3 Northfield Ho
4 Millbrook Ho
5 Denstone Ho

---

6 Deerhurst Ho
7 Caversham Ho
8 Battle Ho
9 Cardiff Ho
10 Bridgnorth Ho
11 Exeter Ho
12 Grantham Ho
13 Aylesbury Ho
14 Royston Ho
15 Haymerle Sch

B2 1 Tilling Ho
2 Goodwin Ho
3 Tyrells Ct
4 Citron Terr
5 Basswood Cl
6 Cheam St
7 Rye Oak Sch

B3 1 Walkynscroft
2 Ryegates
3 Hathorne Cl
4 Pilkington Rd
5 Russell Ct
6 Heaton Ho
7 Magdalene Cl
8 Iris Ct
10 St Mary Magdalene CE Prim Sch

B4 1 Willowdene
2 Pinedene
3 Oakdene
4 Beechdene
5 Hollydene
6 Wood Dene
7 Staveley Cl
8 Carnicot Ho
9 Martock Ct
10 Cherry Tree Ct
11 Kendrick Ct
12 John Donne Prim Sch

B5 1 Tortington Ho
2 Credenhill Ho
3 Bromyard Ho
4 Hoyland Ct
5 Willowdene
6 Ashdene
7 Acorn Par
8 Havelock Ct
9 Springall St
10 Harry Lambourn Ho
11 Grenier Apartments

C3 1 Honiton Gdns
2 Selden Ho
3 Hathway Ho
4 Hathway Ho
5 Station Ct
6 Symons Cl
7 Hollydale Prim Sch

C4 1 Trotman Ho
2 Boddington Ho
3 Heydon Ho
4 Boulter Ho
5 Astbury Bsns Pk

C5 1 Ambleside Point
2 Grasmere Point
3 Windermere Point
4 Roman Way
5 Laburnum Cl
6 Juniper Ho
7 Romney Cl
8 Hammersley Ho
9 Hutchinson Ho
10 Hammond Ho
11 Fir Tree Ho
12 Glastonbury Ct
13 Highbridge Ct
14 Filton Ct
15 Chiltern Ct
16 Cheviot Ct

C6 1 Penshurst Ho
2 Reculver Ho
3 Mereworth Ho
4 Camber Ho
5 Chiham Ho
6 Otford Ho
7 Olive Tree Ho
8 Aspen Ho
9 Lewis Silkin Ho
10 Richborough Ho
11 Dover Ho
12 Eynsford Ho
13 Horton Ho
14 Lamberhurst Ho
15 Canterbury Ind Pk
16 Upnall Ho
17 Sissinghurst Ho
18 Rochester Ho
19 Saltwood Ho
20 Leybourne Ho
21 Lullingstone Ho
22 Pilgrims Way Prim Sch

D1 1 Laxton Path
2 Barlings Ho
3 Bayfield Ho
4 Coston Wlk
5 Coverham Ho
6 Gateley Ho
7 Dereham Ho
8 Greenwood Ho
9 Hilton Ho
10 Goodall Ho

---

11 Horsley Ho
12 Jordan Ho

D5 1 Richard Anderson Ct
2 Palm Tree Ho
3 Edward Robinson Ho
4 Antony Ho
5 Gerrard Ho
6 Palmer Ho
7 Pankhurst Cl

D6 1 Harrisons Ct
2 Grantley Ho
3 Sunbury Ct
4 Tilbury Ho
5 Graham Ct
6 Connell Ct
7 St Clements Ct
8 Henderson Ct
9 Jemotts Ct
10 Verona Ct
11 Heywood Ho
12 Francis Ct
13 Hind Ho
14 Donne Ho
15 Carew Ct
16 Burbage Ho
17 Newland Ho
18 Dobson Ho
19 Dalton Ho
20 Greene Ct
21 Redrup Ho
22 Tarplett Ho
23 Stunell Ho
24 Gasson Ho
25 Bryce Ho
26 Barnes Ho
27 Barkwith Ho
28 Bannister Ho
29 Apollo Ind Bsns Ctr

141

A1 1 Turnham Prim Sch

A4 1 Archer Ho
2 Browning Ho
3 Hardcastle Ho
4 Brooke Ho
5 Wallis Ho

A5 1 Batavia Ho
2 Marlowe Bsns Ctr
3 Batavia Mews
4 Woodrush Cl
5 Alexandra St
6 Primrose Wlk
7 Vansittart St
8 Granville Ct
9 Cottesbrook St
10 Ewen Henderson Ct
11 Fordham Ho
12 Deptford Green Sch (Annex)

A6 1 Portland Ct
2 Phoenix Ct
3 Rainbow Ct
4 Hawke Twr
5 Chubworthy St
6 Woodpecker Rd
7 Hercules Ct

B5 1 Austin Ho
2 Exeter Way
3 Crossleigh Ct
4 Mornington Pl
5 Maple Ho

B6 1 Chester Ho
2 Lynch Wlk
3 Arlington Ho
4 Woodcote Ho
5 Cornbury Ho
6 Prospect Pl
7 Akintaro Ho
8 Mulberry Ho
9 Laurel Ho
10 Linden Ho
11 Ashford Ho
12 Wardalls Ho
13 Magnolia Ho
14 Howard Ho
15 Larch Cl
16 Ibis Ct
17 Merganser Ct
18 Wotton Rd
19 Kingfisher Sq
20 Sanderling Ct
21 Dolphin Twr
22 Mermaid Twr
23 Scoter Ct
24 Shearwater Ct
25 Brambling Ct
26 Kittiwake Ct
27 Diana Cl
28 Guillemot Ct
29 Marine Twr
30 Teal Ct
31 Lapwing Twr
32 Violet Cl
33 Skua Ct
34 Tristan Ct
35 Rosemary Ct
36 Cormorant Ct
37 Shelduck Ct
38 Eider Ct

---

39 Pintail Ct
40 Fulcher Ct
42 Grinling Gibbons Prim Sch

C3 1 Ashmead Mews
2 St Stephen's CE Prim Sch

C4 1 Admiralty Cl
2 Harton Lodge
3 Sylva Cotts
4 Pitman Ho
5 Heston Ho
6 Mereton Mans
7 Indiana Bldg
8 St John's Lodge
9 Dean's Gateway
10 Lucas Vale Prim Sch
11 Addey & Stanhope Sch
12 Lewisham Coll (Deptford Campus)

C5 1 Sandpiper Ct
2 Flamingo Ct
3 Titan Bsns Est
4 Rochdale Way
5 Speedwell St
6 Reginald Pl
7 Fletcher Path
8 Frankham Ho
9 Cremer Ho
10 Wilshaw Ho
11 Castell Ho
12 Holden Ho
13 Browne Ho
14 Resolution Way
15 Lady Florence Ctyd
16 Covell Ct
17 Albion Ho
18 Maritime Greenwich Coll
19 St Joseph's RC Prim Sch
20 Tidemill Prim Sch

C6 1 Dryfield Wlk
2 Blake Ho
3 Hawkins Ho
4 Grenville Ho
5 Langford Ho
6 Mandarin Ct
7 Bittern Ct
8 Lamerton St
9 Ravensbourne Mans
10 Armada St
11 Armada Ct
12 Benbow Ho
13 Oxenham Ho
14 Caravel Mews
15 Hughes Ho
16 Stretton Mans

D2 1 Pine Tree Way
2 Waterway Ave
3 Lewisham Bridge Prim Sch

D3 1 Morden Mount Prim Sch

D4 1 Washington Bldg
2 California Bldg
3 Utah Bldg
4 Montana Bldg
5 Oregon Bldg
6 Dakota bldg
7 Idaho Bldg
8 Atlanta Bldg
9 Colorado Bldg
10 Arizona Bldg
11 Nebraska Bldg
12 Alaska Bldg
13 Ohio Bldg
14 Charter Bldgs
15 Flamsteed Ct
16 Friendly Pl
17 Dover Ct
18 Robinscroft Mews
19 Doleman Ho
20 Plymouth Ho

D5 1 Finch Ho
2 Jubilee The
3 Maitland Cl
4 Ashburnham Retreat

142

A2 1 Bankside Ave
2 Elder Wlk
3 Yew Tree Cl
4 Mill Ho

A3 1 Ellison Ho
2 Pitmaston Ho
3 Aster Ho
4 Windmill Cl
5 Hertmitage The
6 Burnett Ho
7 Lacey Ho
8 Darwin Ho
9 Pearmain Ho

A4 1 Penn Almshouses
2 Jervis Ct
3 Woodville Ct
4 Darnall Ho
5 Renbold Ho
6 Lindsell St

---

7 Plumbridge St
8 Trinity Gr
9 Hollymount Cl
10 Cade Tyler Ho
11 Robertson Ho

A5 1 Temair Ho
2 Royal Hill Ct
3 Prince of Orange La
4 Lambard Ho
5 St Marks Cl
6 Ada Kennedy Ct
7 Arlington Pl
8 Topham Ho
9 Darnell Ho
10 Hawks Mews
11 Royal Pl
12 Swanne Ho
13 Maribor
14 Serica Ct
15 Queen Elizabeth's Coll
16 James Wolfe Prim Sch
17 Greenwich Coll

A6 1 Crescent Arc
2 Greenwich Mkt
3 Turnpin La
4 Durnford St
5 Sexton's Ho
6 Bardsley Ho
7 Wardell Ho
8 Clavell St
9 Stanton Ho
10 Macey Ho
11 Boreman Ho
12 Clipper Appts

B2 1 Our Lady of Lourdes RC Prim Sch

B6 1 Frobisher Ct
2 Hardy Cotts
3 Palliser Ho
4 Bernard Angell Ho
5 Corvette Sq
6 Travers Ho
7 Maze Hill Lodge
8 Park Place Ho
9 Meridian Prim Sch

D3 1 Heath House Prep Sch

D5 1 Westcombe Ct
2 Kleffens Ct
3 Ferndale Ct
4 Combe Mews
5 Mandeville Cl
7 Pinelands Cl

143

A5 1 Mary Lawrenson Pl
2 Bradbury Ct
3 Dunstable Ct
4 Wentworth Ho

A6 1 Nethercombe Ho
2 Holywell Cl

B6 1 Capella Ho
2 Collington Ho
3 Sherington Prim Sch
4 Our Lady of Grace RC Prim Sch

C6 1 Warren Wlk
2 Wilson Ho
3 Priory Ho
4 Mar Ho
5 Langhorne Ho
6 Games Ho
7 Erskine Ho
8 Ducie Ho
9 Downe Ho
10 Bayeux Ho
11 Elliscombe Mount
12 Harold Gibbons Ct
13 Mascalls Ct
14 Leila Parnell Pl
15 East Mascalls
16 Birch Tree Ho
17 Cherry Tree Ct
18 Elm Tree Ct
19 Cedar Ct

D5 1 Winchester Ho
2 Brentwood Ho
3 Shenfield Ho
4 Chesterford Ho

144

A4 1 Master Gunner's Pl
2 Ross Ho
3 Dickson Ho
4 Horne Ho
5 Pendlebury Ho
6 Roberts Ho
7 Maple Tree Pl
8 Berber Par
9 Centurian Sq

C6 1 Lawson Ho
2 Mabbett Ho
3 Petrie Ho
4 Memess Path
5 Ruegg Ho
6 Nile Path
7 Leslie Smith Sq
8 Spearman St
9 Siedle Ho

10 Watling Ho
11 O'Neill Path
12 Old Clem Sq
13 Jefferson Wlk
14 Milward Wlk
15 Wordsworth Ho
16 Fenwick Cl
D6 1 Acworth Ho
2 Griffiths Ho
3 Squires Ho
4 Cowen Ho
5 Turton Ho
6 Alford Ho
7 Boxshall Ho
8 Macallister Ho
9 Marvin Ho
10 Kelham Ho
11 Kimber Ho
12 Maxwell Ho
13 Woodford Ho
14 Penfold Ho
15 Butterfield Mews

146

A2 1 Wellingfield Ct
2 Woodville Gr
3 Midwinter Cl
4 St Leonards Cl

147

A1 1 Woburn Ct
2 Arundel Ct
3 Longleat Ct
4 Upton Villas
5 Whitehaven Ct
6 Shirley Hts
7 Louise Ct
8 Bethany Ct
B6 2 Bevercote Wlk
3 Lullingstone Rd
4 Benjamin Ct
5 Charton Cl
6 Terence Ct
8 Grove Rd
C1 1 Friswell Pl
2 Market Pl
3 Geddes Pl
4 Janet Ct
5 Broadway Sh Ctr
6 Mall The
7 Pincott Rd

148

A5 1 Stranraer Way
2 Deri Dene Cl
3 Lord Knyvetts Ct
4 Tudor Ct
5 Wessex Ct
6 Vanguard Ho
7 Shackleton Ct
8 Fleetwood Ct
9 Clifton Ct
10 Vickers Ct
11 Bristol Ct
12 Sunderland Ct

150

B3 1 Bergenia Ho
2 Azalea Ho
3 Hamlyn Ho
4 Highfield Rd
5 Cardinal Road Inf Sch

152

A4 1 Library Way
C2 1 Jack & Jill Sch
2 Archdeacon
Cambridge's CE Prim
Sch

153

A3 1 Katharine Rd
2 Sandringham Ct
3 Garfield Rd
4 Arragon Rd
5 Flood La
6 John Wesley Ct
7 King Street Par
8 Thames Eyot
A4 1 Perryn Ct
2 Ivybridge Cl
3 Heritage Ho
4 Brook Ho
5 Neville Ho
6 Latham Cl
7 March Rd
8 Berkley Ct
9 Cole Court Lo
10 Cheltenham Ave
11 Railway App
12 St Mary's CE Prim Sch
(Inf)
A5 1 Greenways The

2 Cole Park View
B4 1 Melton Ct
2 Amyand Park Gdns
3 Crown Ct
4 Burrell Ho
5 Owen Ho
6 Brentford Ho
7 Leeson Ho
8 Westbourne Ho
9 Orleans Ct
10 Lebanon Ct
B5 1 Grove The
2 Cumberland Cl
3 Westmorland Cl
4 Sussex Cl
5 Norfolk Cl
6 Nicol Cl
7 Old Lodge Pl
8 Kelvin Ct
9 St Margaret's Ct
10 Park Cotts
11 St Margarets Bsns Ctr
12 Amyand Cotts
C1 1 Benson Ho
2 Bowes Lyon Ho
3 Cavendish Ho
4 Bentinck Ho
5 Clarke Ho
6 Secrett Ho
7 Edwards Ho
8 Field Ho
9 Greig Ho
10 Hawkins Ho
11 Newman Ho
12 Leyland Ho
13 Hornby Ho
14 Hatch Ho
C5 1 Howmic Ct
2 Sefton Lo
3 Ravensbourne Ho
4 Arlington Ct
5 Georgina Ct
6 Trevelyan Ho
7 Caradon Ct
8 Green Hedges
9 Old House Gdns
10 Queens Keep
11 Beresford Ct
12 Langham Ct
13 Poplar Ct
D5 1 Richmond Bridge Mans
2 Heatherdene Mans
3 Kenton Ct
4 Lennox Ho
5 Leicester Ct
6 Turner Ho
7 Blanchard Ho
8 Arosa Rd
9 Ashe Ho
10 Bevan Ct
11 Lawley Ho
12 Darling Ho
13 Richmond Mans
14 Beaulieu Cl
15 Roseleigh Cl
16 Mallard Ct
D6 1 Garrick Cl
2 Old Palace Yd
3 Wardrobe The
4 Maids of Honour Row
5 Hunters Ct
6 Queensberry Ho
7 Green The
8 Old Palace Terr
9 Paved Ct
10 Golden Ct
11 Brewers La
12 Square The
13 Lower George St
14 St James's Cotts
15 Church Wlk
16 Church Ct
17 Victoria Pl
18 Castle Yd
19 Lewis Rd
20 Wakefield Rd
21 Church Terr
22 Warrington Rd
23 Ormond Ave
24 Glovers Lo
25 Holbrooke Pl
26 Northumberland Pl
27 Heron Sq
28 Whittaker Pl
29 Water Lane Ho
30 Riverside Ho
31 St Helena Terr

154

A5 1 Lancaster Cotts
2 Lancaster Mews
3 Bromwich Ho
4 Priors Lo
5 Richmond Hill Ct
6 Glenmore Ho
7 Hillbrow
8 Heathshott
9 Friars Stile Pl
10 Spire Ct

11 Ridgeway
12 Matthias Ct
13 Old Vicarage Sch
A6 1 Lichfield Terr
2 Union Ct
3 Carrington Lo
4 Wilton Ct
5 Egerton Ct
6 Beverley Lo
7 Bishop Duppa's
Almshouses
8 Regency Wlk
9 Clear Water Ho
10 Onslow Avenue Mans
11 Michels Almshouses
12 Albany Pas
13 Salcombe Villas
B5 1 Chester Cl
2 Evesham Ct
3 Queen's Ct
4 Russell Wlk
5 Charlotte Sq
6 Jones Wlk
7 Hilditch Ct
8 Isabella Ct
9 Damer Ho
10 Eliot Ho
11 Fitzherbert Ho
12 Reynolds Pl
13 Chisholm Rd
B6 1 Alberta Ct
2 Beatrice Rd
3 Lorne Rd
4 York Rd
5 Connaught Rd
6 Albany Terr
7 Kingswood Ct
8 Selwyn Ct
9 Broadhurst Cl

156

A3 1 Farnborough Ho
2 Rushmere Ho
3 Horndean Cl
4 Highcross Way
5 Timsbury Wlk
6 Foxcombe Rd
7 Ryefield Path
8 Greatham Wlk
9 Gosport Ho
10 Stoatley Ho
11 Milland Ho
12 Clanfield Ho
13 Fareham Ho
14 Grayswood Point
A4 1 Woodcott Ho
2 Lyndhurst Ho
3 Wheatley Ho
4 Allbrook Ho
5 Bordon Wlk
6 Chilcombe Ho
7 Vicarage Ct
8 Shawford Ct
9 Eastleigh Wlk
10 Kings Ct
11 Somborne Ho
A6 1 Theodore Ho
2 Nicholas Ho
3 Bonner Ho
4 Downing Ho
5 Jansen Ho
6 Fairfax Ho
7 Devereux Ho
8 David Ho
9 Leigh Ho
10 Clipstone Ho
11 Mallet Ho
12 Arton Wilson Ho
B3 1 Ramsdean Ho
2 Purbrook Ho
3 Portsea Ho
4 Blendworth Point
5 Eashing Point
6 Hindhead Point
7 Hilsea Point
8 Witley Point
9 Buriton Ho
10 Grateley Ho
11 Hascombe Ho
12 Dunhill Point
13 Westmark Point
14 Longmoor Point
15 Cadnam Point
C4 1 Cumberland Ho
2 Devonshire Ho
3 Cornwall Ho
4 Norfolk Ho
5 Leicester Ho
6 Warwick Ho
7 Sutherland Ho
8 Carmarthen Ho
9 Worcester Ho
10 Rutland Ho
11 Paddock Way
12 Putney Hill
C6 1 Inglis Ho
2 Ducie Ho
3 Wharncliffe Ho
4 Stanhope Ho

5 Waldegrave Ho
6 Mildmay Ho
7 Mullens Ho
D3 1 Sandringham Cl
2 Eastwick Ct
3 Oatlands Ct
4 Banning Ho
5 Grantley Ho
6 Caryl Ho
7 Duncombe Ho
8 Chilworth Ct
9 Kent Lo
10 Turner Lo
11 Marlborough
12 Parkland Gdns
13 Lewesdon Cl
14 Pines Ct
15 Ashtead Ct
16 Mynterne Ct
17 Arden
18 Stephen Ct
19 Marsham Ct
20 Doradus Ct
21 Acorns The
22 Heritage Ho
23 Conifer Ct
24 Spencer Ho
25 Chartwell
26 Blenheim
27 Chivelston
28 Greenfield Ho
29 Oakman Ho
30 Radley Lo
31 Simon Lo
32 Admirals Ct
33 Augustus Rd
D4 1 Brett Ho
2 Brett House Cl
3 Sylva Ct
4 Ross Ct
5 Potterne Cl
6 Stourhead Cl
7 Fleur Gates
8 Greenwood
9 John Paul II Sch
10 Our Lady Queen of
Heaven RC Prim Sch
11 Prospect House Sch
D5 1 Balmoral Ct
2 Glenalmond Ho
3 Selwyn Ho
4 Keble Ho
5 Bede Ho
6 Gonville Ho
7 Magdalene Ho
8 Armstrong Ho
9 Newnham Ho
10 Somerville Ho
11 Balliol Ho
12 Windermere
13 Little Combe Cl
14 Classinghall Ho
15 Chalford Ct
16 Garden Royal
17 South Ct
18 Anne Kerr Ct
19 Elmhurst
D6 1 Geneva Ct
2 Laurel Ct
3 Cambalt Ho
4 Langham Ct
5 Lower Pk
6 King's Keep
7 Whitnell Ct
8 Whitehead Ho
9 Halford Ho
10 Humphry Ho
11 Jellicoe Ho
12 South Thames Coll
(Putney Ctr)

157

A3 1 William Harvey Ho
2 Highview Ct
3 Cameron Ct
4 Galgate Ct
5 Green Ho The
6 King Charles Wlk
7 Florys Ct
8 Augustus Ct
9 Albert Ct
10 Hertford Lo
11 Mortimer Lo
12 Allenswood
13 Ambleside
14 Hansler Ct
15 Roosevelt Ct
16 Southmead Prim Sch
A4 1 Douglas Gracey Ho
2 Aman Dalvi Ho
3 Andrew Reed Ho
4 Stoford Ct
5 Ronald Ross Prim Sch
A6 1 Claremont
2 Downside
3 Cavendish Cl
4 Ashcombe Ct
5 Carltons The
6 Espirit Ho

159 B3 445

7 Millbrooke Ct
8 Coysh Ct
9 Keswick Hts
10 Avon Ct
11 Merlin Sch The
B6 1 Keswick Broadway
2 Burlington Mews
3 Cambria Lo
4 St Stephen's Gdns
5 Atlantic Ho
6 Burton Lo
7 Manfred Ct
8 Meadow Bank
9 Hooper Ho
10 Aspire Bld
C6 1 Pembridge Pl
2 Adelaide Rd
3 London Ct
4 Windsor Ct
5 Westminster Ct
6 Fullers Ho
7 Bridge Pk
8 Lambeth Ct
9 Milton Ct
10 Norfolk Mans
11 Francis Snary Lo
12 Bush Cotts
13 Downbury Mews
14 Newton's Yd
15 Roche Sch The
16 St Joseph's RC Prim
Sch
17 West Hill Prim Sch
18 St Michael Steiner Sch
The
D6 1 Fairfield Ct
2 Blackmore Ho
3 Lancaster Mews
4 Cricketers Mews
5 College Mews
6 Arndale Wlk
7 South Thames Coll
(Wandsworth Ctr)

158

A2 1 Bremans Row
2 St Andrew's Ct
3 Townsend Mews
4 Sheringham Mews
5 Rainbow Sch
6 Garratt Park Sec Specl
Sch
A6 1 St Faith's CE Prim Sch
C2 1 St Peters Cl
2 St Hildas Cl
3 St Edmunds Cl
4 St Hughes Cl
5 St Anthonys Cl
6 St Benets Cl
7 St Catherines Cl
8 Elsley Sch
D5 1 Staplehurst Ct
2 Teyham Ct
3 Honeywell Jun & Inf
Schs
D6 1 Clapham Computer &
Secretarial Coll

159

A2 1 Upper Tooting Park
Mans
2 Cecil Mans
3 Marius Mans
4 Boulevard The
5 Elmfield Mans
6 Holdernesse Rd
7 Lumiere Ct
A3 1 Heslop Ct
2 St James's Terr
3 Boundaries Mans
4 Station Par
5 Old Dairy Mews
6 Chestnut Grove Sch
7 Hornsby House Sch
8 Trinity St Mary's Prim
Sch
A4 1 Hollies Way
2 Endlesham Ct
3 Broomwood Hall Sch
(Upper Sch)
4 Holy Ghost RC Prim
Sch
A5 1 Rayne Ho
2 St Anthony's Ct
3 Earlsthorpe Mews
4 Nightingale Mans
5 Broomwood Hall
(Lower Sch)
B3 1 Holbeach Mews
2 Hildreth Street Mews
3 Coalbrook Mans
4 Hub Buildings The
5 Metropolis Apartments
6 Hildreth St

B4
1 Meyer Ho
2 Faraday Ho
3 Hales Ho
4 Frankland Ho
5 Graham Ho
6 Gibbs Ho
7 Dalton Ho
8 Ainslie Wlk
9 Rokeby Ho
10 Caistor Ho
11 Ivanhoe Ho
12 Catherine Baird Ct
13 Marmion Ho
14 Devonshire Ct
15 Blueprint Apartments
16 Royal Duchess Mews
17 Alderbrook Prim Sch
B5 1 Oliver House Prep Sch
C3 1 Henry Cavendish Prim Sch
3 Margaret Rutherford Pl
C4 1 Limerick Ct
2 Homewoods
3 Jewell Ho
4 Glanville Ho
5 Dan Bryant Ho
6 Olding Ho
7 Quennel Ho
8 Weir Ho
9 West Ho
10 Neville Ct
11 Friday Grove Mews
12 St Bernadette RC Jun Sch
C5 1 Joseph Powell Cl
2 Cavendish Mans
3 Westlands Terr
4 Cubitt Ho
5 Hawkesworth Ho
6 Normanton Ho
7 Eastman Ho
8 Couchman Ho
9 Poynders Ct
10 Selby Ho
11 Valentine Ho
12 Gorham Ho
13 Deauville Mans
14 Deauville Ct
C6 1 Timothy Cl
2 Shaftesbury Mews
3 Brook Ho
4 Grover Ho
5 Westbrook Ho
6 Hewer Ho
7 Batten Ho
8 Mandeville Ho
9 George Beare Lo
10 St Mary's RC Prim Sch
D3 1 Sinclair Ho
2 MacGregor Ho
3 Ingle Ho
4 St Andrews Mews
5 Telferscot Prim Sch
D4 1 Riley Ho
2 Bennett Ho
3 White Ho
4 Rodgers Ho
5 Dumphreys Ho
6 Homan Ho
7 Prendergast Ho
8 Hutchins Ho
9 Whiteley Ho
10 Tresidder Ho
11 Primrose Ct
12 Angus Ho
13 Currie Ho
D5 1 Parrington Ho
2 Savill Ho
3 Blackwell Ho
4 Bruce Ho
5 Victoria Ct
6 Victoria Ho
7 Belvedere Ct
8 Ingram Lo
9 Viney Ct
10 Bloomsbury Ho
11 Belgravia Ho
12 Barnsbury Ho

160
A1 1 De Montfort Ct
2 Leigham Hall Par
3 Leigham Hall
4 Endsleigh Mans
5 John Kirk Ho
6 Raeburn Ct
7 Wavel Ct
8 Homeleigh Ct
9 Howland Ho
10 Beauclerk Ho
11 Bertrand Ho
12 Drew Ho
13 Dowes Ho
14 Dunton Ho
15 Raynald Ho
16 Sackville Ho
17 Thurlow Ho
18 Astoria Mans
A2 1 Wyatt Park Mans
2 Broadlands Mans
3 Stonehill's Mans
4 Streatleigh Par
5 Dorchester Ct
6 Picture Ho
A3 1 Beaumont Ho
2 Christchurch Ho
3 Staplefield Cl
4 Chipstead Ho
5 Coulsdon Ho
6 Conway Ho
7 Telford Avenue Mans
8 Telford Parade Mans
9 Wavertree Ct
10 Hartswood Ho
11 Wray Ho
A4 1 Picton Ho
2 Rigg Ho
3 Watson Ho
4 MacArthur Ho
5 Sandon Ho
6 Thorold Ho
7 Pearce Ho
8 Mudie Ho
9 Miller Ho
10 Lycett Ho
11 Lafone Ho
12 Lucraft Ho
13 Freeman Ho
14 New Park Par
15 Argyll Ho
16 Dumbarton Ct
17 Kintyre Ct
18 Cotton Ho
19 Crossman Hos
20 Cameford Ct
21 Parsons Ho
22 Brindley Ho
23 Arkwright Ho
24 Perry Ho
25 Brunel Ho
26 New Park Ct
27 Tanhurst Ho
28 Hawkshaw Cl
29 Richard Atkins Prim Sch
A6 1 King's Mews
2 Clapham Court Terr
3 Clapham Ct
4 Clapham Park Terr
5 Pembroke Ho
6 Stevenson Ho
7 Queenswood Ct
8 Oak Tree Ct
9 Park Lofts
10 Ashby Mews
B1 1 Carisbrooke Ct
2 Pembroke Lo
3 Willow Ct
4 Poplar Ct
5 Leigham Cl
6 Mountview
7 Spa View
B3 1 Charlwood Ho
2 Earlswood Ho
3 Balcombe Ho
4 Claremont Cl
5 Holbrook Ho
6 Gwynne Ho
7 Kynaston Ho
8 Tillman Ho
9 Regents Lo
10 Hazelmere Ct
11 Dykes Ct
12 Hartwell Cl
13 Christ Church Streatham CE Prim Sch
14 Streatham Hill & Clapham High Sch
15 Orch Sch The
B4 1 Archbishop's Pl
2 Witley Ho
3 Outwood Ho
4 Dunsfold Ho
5 Deepdene Lo
6 Warnham Ho
7 Albury Lo
8 Tilford Ho
9 Elstead Ho
10 Thursley Ho
11 Brockham Ho
12 Capel Lo
13 Leith Ho
14 Fairview Ho
15 Weymouth Ct
16 Ascalon Ct
17 China Mews
18 Rush Common Mews
B6 1 Beatrice Ho
2 Florence Ho
3 Evelyn Ho
4 Diana Ho
5 Brixton Hill Ct
6 Austin Ho
7 Manor Ct
8 Camsey Ho
9 Romer Ho
10 Gale Ho
11 Byrne Ho
12 Farnfield Ho
13 Marchant Ho
14 Rainsford Ho
15 Springett Ho
16 Mannering Ho
17 Waldron Ho
18 Sudbourne Prim Sch
19 Corpus Christi RC Prim Sch
C3 1 Valens Ho
2 Loveday Ho
3 Strode Ho
4 Ethelworth Ho
5 Harbin Ho
6 Brooks Ho
7 Godolphin Ho
8 Sheppard Ho
9 McCormick Ho
10 Taylor Ho
11 Saunders Ho
12 Talcott Path
13 Derrick Ho
14 Williams Ho
15 Baldwin Ho
16 Churston Cl
17 Neil Wates Cres
18 Burnell Ho
19 Portland Ho
20 Fenstanton Prim Sch
21 St Martin-in-the-Fields High Sch
C4 1 Ellacombe Ho
2 Booth Ho
3 Hathersley Ho
4 Brereton Ho
5 Holdsworth Ho
6 Dearmer Ho
7 Cherry Cl
8 Greenleaf Cl
9 Longford Wlk
10 Scarlette Manor Wlk
11 Chandlers Way
12 Upgrove Manor Way
13 Ropers Wlk
14 Tebbs Ho
15 Bell Ho
16 Worthington Ho
17 Courier Ho
18 Mackie Ho
19 Hamers Ho
20 Kelway Ho
21 Harriet Tubman Cl
22 Estoria Cl
23 Leckhampton Pl
24 Scotia Rd
25 Charles Haller St
26 Sidmouth Ho
27 Hunter Ct
28 Onslow Lo
29 William Winter Ct
30 Langthorne Lo
C5 1 Eccleston Ho
2 Scarsbrook Ho
3 Purser Ho
4 Rudhall Ho
5 Heywood Ho
6 Hardham Ho
7 Haworth Ho
8 Birch Ho
9 Lansdell Ho
10 Lomley Ho
11 Laughton Ho
12 Woodruff Ho
13 Bascome St
14 Dudley Mews
15 Herbert Mews
16 Blades Lo
17 Dick Shepherd Ct
18 Charman Ho
19 Morden Ho
20 Bishop Ct
21 Blackburn Ct
22 Leigh Ct
23 John Conwey Ho
24 Bristowe Cl
C6 1 Crownstone Ct
2 Brockwell Ct
3 Nevena Ct
4 St George's Residences
5 Hanover Mans
6 Fleet Ho
7 Langbourne Ho
8 Turnmill Ho
9 Walker Mews
10 Cossar Mews
11 Carter Ho
12 Arungford Mews
D1 1 Thanet Ho
2 Chapman Ho
3 Beaufoy Ho
4 Easton Ho
5 Roberts Ho
6 Lloyd Ct
7 Kershaw Ho
8 Wakeling Ho
9 Edridge Ho
10 Jeston Ho
11 Lansdowne Wood Cl
12 Rotary Lo
D6 3 Poets Mews
4 St Jude's CE Prim Sch

161
B2 1 Welldon Ct
2 Coppedhall
3 Shackleton Ct
4 Bullfinch Ct
5 Gannet Ct
6 Fulmar Ct
7 Heron Ct
8 Petrel Ct
9 Falcon Ct
10 Eagle Ct
11 Dunnock Ct
12 Dunlin Ct
13 Cormorant Ct
14 Oak Lodge
15 Corfe Lodge
C6 1 Velde Way
2 Delft Way
3 Arnhem Way
4 Isel Way
5 Kempis Way
6 Terborch Way
7 Steen Way
8 Deventer Cres
9 Nimegen Way
10 Hilversum Cres
11 St Barnabas Cl
12 James Allen's Girls' Sch
13 James Allen's Prep Sch

162
A1 1 Tunbridge Ct
2 Harrogate Ct
3 Bath Ct
4 Leamington Ct
5 Porlock Ho
6 Cissbury Ho
7 Eddisbury Ho
8 Dundry Ho
9 Silbury Ho
10 Homildon Ho
11 Highgate Ho
12 Richmond Ho
13 Pendle Ho
14 Tynwald Ho
15 Wirrall Ho
16 Greyfriars
A6 1 Dorothy Charrington Ho
2 Keswick Ct
3 Kendall Ct
4 Halliwell Ct
B1 1 River Ho
2 Fordington Ho
3 Arbury Terr
4 Woodbury Ho
5 Gainsborough Mews
6 Forest Hill Ct
7 Kelvin Grove Prim Sch
B2 1 Bromleigh Ct
2 Parfew Ct
3 Thetford Ct
4 Attleborough Ct
5 Dunton Ct
6 Frobisher Ct
7 Julian Taylor Path
8 Grizedale Terr
9 Worsley Ho
C1 1 Forest Lo
2 Sydenham Park Mans
3 William Wood Ho
C2 1 Fitzwilliam Hts
2 Taymount Grange
3 McLeod Ho
4 Featherstone Ave
5 Kingswear Ho
6 Salcombe Ho
7 Glynwood Ct
8 Holy Trinity CE Prim Sch
C3 1 Harlech Ct
2 Angela Ct
3 Westwood Ct
4 New Belmont Ho
5 Pearcefield Ave
6 Waldram Pl
7 Horniman Grange
8 South View Ct
9 Heron Ct
10 Katherine Ct
D1 1 Standlake Point
2 Radcot Point
3 Newbridge Point
4 Northmoor
5 Kelmscott
6 Radnor Ct
7 Heathwood Point
8 Ashleigh Point
9 Deepdene Point
10 Rosemount Point
11 Woodfield Ho
12 Clairville Point
13 Trevenna Ho
14 Hyndewood
15 Brent Knoll Sch
16 Our Lady & St Philip Neri RC Infants Sch
D2 1 Pikethorne
2 Andrew Ct
3 Valentine Ct
4 Soper Cl
5 Perrymount Prim Sch
6 Christ Church CE Prim Sch

164
B5 3 Park Piazza
4 Birdwood Ave
C4 1 Beaumont Terr
2 Littlebourne
3 Verdant Ct
D2 1 Kinross Ct
2 Montrose Ct
3 Rattray Ct
4 Rothesay Ct
D3 1 Edinburgh Ct
2 McMillan Ct
3 Rowallan Ct
4 Meridian Ct
5 Braemar Ct
6 Barrow Ct
7 Blair Ct
8 Darlington Ct
9 Hamilton Ct
10 Inverness Ct
11 Oak Cottage Cl
12 Willow Ct
13 Keswick Ct

165
A4 1 Swallow Ct
2 Honeysuckle Ct
3 Venture Ct
4 Cheriton Ct
5 Askham Lo
6 Syon Lo

166
A2 1 Portland Cres
2 Bourdillon Ct
3 Hillary Ct
4 Tenzing Ct
5 John Hunt Ct
6 Everest Ct
7 Dorset Road Inf Sch
A6 1 Horsfield Gdns
2 Foxhole Rd
C5 1 Roper St
2 Arcade The
3 Elm Terr
4 Imber Ct
5 Ashcroft Ct
6 Fairlands Ct
7 Brecon Ct
8 Newlands Ct
9 Harvard Ct
10 Garden Ct
11 Chiltern Ct
12 Fairway Ct

167
A2 1 Mervyn Stockwood Ho
2 Michael Marshall Ho
3 Keith Sutton Ho

168
A1 1 Ham Shades Cl
2 Aspen Ho
3 Medlar Ho
4 Cornel Ho
5 Stanton Ct
6 Hornbeam Ho
7 Beech Ho
8 Spindle Ho
9 Hunters Lo
10 Edam Ct
11 Monica James Ho
12 Oak Ho
13 Crescent Ct
14 Benedict House Sch
B5 1 Rochester Cl
2 Cobham Cl
3 Shorne Cl
4 Warne Pl

169
C4 1 Close The
2 Parkhurst Gdns
3 Chichester Ct
4 Pound Green Ct

170
B6 1 Station Par
2 Queens La
3 Copthorne Chase
4 Canterbury Ct

11 Queenswood Ct
C4 **1** Northwood Way
2 High Limes
3 Valley Prospect
4 Plane Tree Wlk
5 City Prospect
6 Bankside Way
7 Ridge Way
8 Rochdale
9 Barrington Wlk
10 Gatestone Ct
11 Childs La
12 Carberry Rd
13 Norwood Heights Sh
Ctr
14 Paxton Prim Sch
C5 **1** Oakdene
2 Thorsden Way
3 Oakfield Gdns
4 Georgetown Cl
5 Bridgetown Cl
6 Mountbatten Cl
7 Brabourne Cl
8 Alexandra Wlk
9 Compton Ct
10 Battenburg Wlk
11 Burma Terr
12 Wiseman Ct
C6 **1** Linley Ct
2 Mellor Ho
3 Whitfield Ct
4 Michaelson Ho
5 Holberry Ho
6 Hovenden Ho
7 Huntley Ho
8 Telfer Ho
9 Markham Ho
10 Oldham Ho
11 Parnall Ho
12 Pierson Ho
13 Roper Ho
14 Roundell Ho
15 Sawyer Ho
16 Ransford Ho
17 Carmichael Ho
18 Bonne Marche Terr
Mews
D3 **1** Hetley Gdns
2 Claybourne Mews
3 Highland Lo
4 Mason Ct
5 Kendall Ct
6 High View
7 Stambourne Woodland
Wlk
D5 **1** Glenhurst Ct
2 Marlowe Ct
3 Grenville Ct
4 Raleigh Ct
5 Beechwoods Ct
6 Burntwood View

184

A3 **1** Hanover Ct
2 Brunswick Ct
3 New Church Ct
4 Regency Ct
7 Owen Wlk
8 Bargrove Cl
9 Beaver Ct
B2 **1** Dorset Ho
2 Collingwood Ct
3 Chartwell Way
4 Essex Twr
5 Appletree Cl
6 Ditton Pl
7 Kelvin Ct
8 Readman Ct
9 Glen Ct
10 Kingsbridge Ho
11 Carlton Ct
12 Benhurst Ct
13 Carole Ho
14 Dover Ho
15 Bettswood Ct
B3 **1** Avery Ct
2 Rossal Ct
3 Oakdene Lo
4 Ridgemount Cl
5 Blakewood Cl
6 Trenholme Cl
7 Oakleigh Ct
8 Upchurch Cl
9 Devon Ho
10 Westmoreland Terr
11 Oakfield Road Ind Est
B5 **1** Ragwort Ct
2 Firs The
3 Wingham Ho
4 Seath Ho
5 Ripley Ho
6 Lathwood Ho
7 Hurst Ho
8 George Ho
9 Browne Ho
10 Beacon Ho

11 Bailey Ho
12 Agate Ho
13 Sydenham High Sch
(Sec)
C2 **1** Challin St
2 Rutland Ho
3 Pine Cl
4 St Anthony's RC Prim
Sch
C3 **1** Watermen's Sq
2 St John's Cotts
3 Gladstone Mews
4 Middlesex Ho
5 Bethesda Ct
6 Ospringe Cl
7 Goudhurst Ho
8 Walmer Ho
9 Strood Ho
10 Greatstone Ho
11 John Baird Ho
12 St John's CE Prim Sch
C4 **1** Midhurst
2 Oliver Ct
3 Victoria Ct
4 Wakefield Ct
5 Fountain Ct
6 Newlands Ct
C6 **1** Homewalk Ho
2 Grace Path
3 Sycamore Ct
4 Sydenham Station App
5 Greenways
6 Faircroft
D3 **1** Groombridge Ho
2 Provincial Terr
3 Smithers Ho
4 West Ho
5 Swallows Ct
6 Hornbeam Ho
7 Blenheim Centre

185

A1 **1** Clock House Ct
2 Blandford Ave
3 Old School Cl
4 Lynsted Ct
5 Florence Rd
A6 **1** Paxton Ct
2 Kenton Ct
3 Grove Ct
4 Shirley Lo
5 St Michael's CE Prim
Sch
6 Our Lady & St Philip
Neri RC Prim Sch
B2 **1** Ashton Ct
2 Coombe Ct
3 Fontaine Ct
4 Richfield Ct
5 Sheridan Way
C1 **1** Christ Church Rd
2 Lea Rd
3 Stanmore Terr
C2 **1** Erindale Ct
2 Montgomerie Ct
3 Rebecca Ct
4 Sycamore Ct
5 Willow Ct
6 Marlborough Ct
7 Bearsted Terr
8 Berwick Ct
9 Wooderson Ct
10 Beck River Pk
11 Waterside
C3 **1** Gardenia Ct
2 Brackendale Ct
3 Daniel Ct
4 Moliner Ct
5 Chartwell Lo
6 Randmore Ct
7 Dover Ho
8 Lucerne Ct
9 Malling Ho
10 Westerham Lo
11 Brasted Lo
12 Milton Ho
13 Bradsole Ho
14 Sandgate Ho
15 Adelaide Ct
16 Nettlestead Cl
17 Warren Ct
18 Alton Ct
19 Rockingham Ct
20 Camellia Ct
21 Sinclair Ct
22 Regents Ct
23 Minshull Pl
24 South Park Ct
25 Worsley Bridge Jun
Sch
D1 **1** Parkside
2 Tudors The
3 Oakbrook
4 Tara Ct
5 Redlands The
6 Cambria
7 Hillworth
8 Kelsey Gate
9 Burrells

10 Lincoln Lo
11 Courtlands
12 Fairleas
13 Ashdown Cl
14 Barons
D2 **1** Clifton Ct
2 Mayfair Ct
3 Lait Ho
4 Fire Station Mews
5 Bromley Road Inf Sch
D4 **1** Warner Ho
2 Clifford Ho
3 Lloyd Ho
4 Thurston Ho
5 Byron Ho
6 Blake Ho
7 Keats Ho

186

A2 **1** White House Ct
2 Hunters The
3 Sandringham Ct
4 Glenhurst
5 Copperfields
6 Westgate Ct
A6 **1** Dedham Ho
2 Flatford Ho
3 Langthorne Ct
4 Radley Ct
5 Hoover Ho
6 Brunner Ho
7 Waterer Ho
8 Marriott Ho
9 Bourbon Ho
B5 **1** Longford Ho
2 Ingrebourne Ho
3 Brent Ho
4 Darent Ho
5 Beverley Ho
6 Wandle Ho
7 Rythe Ho
8 Ember Ho
9 Crane Ho
C1 **1** Warwick Ct
2 Maplehurst
3 Mount Arlington
4 Arundel Ct
D2 **1** Weston Gr
2 Gibbs Ho
3 Longfield
4 Hammelton Ct
5 Bracken Hill Cl
6 Townend
7 Treversh Ct
8 Cameron Ho
9 Woodlands Ct
10 Blythwood Pk
11 Bromley Pk
D3 **1** Homecoppice Ho
2 Linden Ct
3 Kimberley Gate
4 Inglewood Ct
5 Mavery Ct
6 Glen Ct
7 Marlborough Ct
8 Cawston Ct
9 Blendon Path

187

A1 **1** St James Ct
2 Court St
A2 **1** Mitchell Way
2 Harrington Ho
3 Newman Ct
4 Uno Apartments
5 Bromley Ho
B2 **1** Dainton Cl
2 Rothwell Ct
3 St Timothy's Mews
4 Andringham Lo
5 Kendall Lo
6 Summerfield
7 Winston Ct
8 Vogue Ct
9 Laurels The
C1 **1** Westland Lo
2 Eastland Ct
3 Dairsie Ct
4 Northlands
5 Beechfield Cotts
6 Oasis The
7 Cromarty Ct
8 Silverstone Ct

188

A6 **1** Beaconsfield Par
2 Cranley Par
3 Kimmeridge Gdns
4 King & Queen Cl
5 Ballantyne Cl
C2 **1** Ivybridge Ct
2 Greenbank Lo

190

A6 **2** Cyril Lo

3 Hazlemere
4 Milton Lo
5 Marlin Ct
6 Conroy Ct
7 Glenwood Ct
8 Culverton Ct
9 Holmbury Manor
B1 **1** Swanscombe Ho
2 Haverstock Ct
3 Arrandene Ho
4 Broomfield Ho
5 Headley Ho
6 Kenley Ho
7 Ladywell Ho
B6 **1** Chudleigh
2 Wimborne
3 St John's Par
4 Holly Ct
5 Rectory Bsns Ctr

193

D1 **1** Orchard Ct
2 Bridge Ct

197

A2 **1** Raleigh Ho
2 Leicester Ho
3 Gresham Ho
4 White Gates
D2 **1** Napier Ct
2 Darlington Ho
3 Charminster Ct
4 Mulberry Ct
5 Leander Ct
6 Clinton Ho
7 Hollingsworth Ct
8 Gloucester Ct
9 Palmerston Ct
10 Redwood Ct
11 Hursley Ct
12 Westmorland Ct
13 Lawson Ct
14 Alexander Ct
15 Winton Ct
16 Sydenham Ho
17 Caroline Ct
18 Ellswood Ct
19 Masefield Ct

198

A1 **1** Ash Tree Cl
2 Shrubbery The
3 Malvern Ct
4 Gate Ho
5 Yew Tree Ho
A3 **1** Station App
2 South Bank Lo
3 Bramshott Ct
4 Pandora Ct
5 Wellington Ct
6 Glenbuck Ct
7 Leighton Ho
8 Oakhill Ct
9 Downs View Lo
10 Osborne Ct
11 Surbiton Par
12 Woodgate Ho
13 Godwyn Ho
14 Ashby Ho
15 Newmans La
A4 **1** Effingham Lo
2 Maple Ho
3 Channon Ct
4 Falconhurst
5 Ferndown
6 Viceroy Lo
7 Frensham Ho
8 Kingsley Ho
9 Rannoch Ct
10 Stratton Ct
11 Moray Ho
12 Dulverton Ct
13 Westerham
14 Hill Ct
15 Assheton-Bennett Ho
16 Hatfield Ho
17 Oxford Ct
18 Pennington Lo
19 Austin Ho
20 Wentworth Ct
21 Priory The
22 Sheraton The
23 Christopher Ct
24 Hobart Ho
25 St Mark's Hts
26 Surbiton Boys Prep Sch
A5 **1** Marquis Ct
2 Garrick Ho
3 Surbiton High Sch Jun
Girls Sch
4 Surbiton High Senior
Sch
A6 **1** College Rdbt
2 Edinburgh Ct
3 Weston Ct
4 Grebe Terr
5 Heron Ct

6 Agar Ho
7 St James' Ct
8 Grove Ct
9 Springfield Ct
10 College Wlk
B3 **1** Percy Ct
2 Holmwood
3 Middle Green Cl
4 Herbert Ct
5 Alfriston Cl
B4 **1** Woodleigh
2 Highcroft
3 Caernarvon Ct
4 Regency Ct
D1 **1** Oakleigh Way
2 Chandler Ct

199

C2 **1** Goodland Ho
2 Furzeland Ho
3 Oakcroft Ho
4 Meadcroft Ho
5 Newhouse
C4 **1** Merryweather Ct
2 Roebuck Ct
3 Sable Ct
4 Holy Cross Sch The
C5 **1** Acacia Ho
2 Kingston Lo
3 Carrington Ct
4 Fairholme Ho
5 Marshall Ho
6 Norton Ho
7 Martin Ho

200

A1 **1** Brookside Cres
2 Beverley Gdns
3 Purdey Ct
4 Avenue The
5 Briarwood Ct
6 Station App

202

C6 **1** Cricket Green Specl
Sch
2 Melrose Specl Sch
D6 **1** Fair Green Ct
2 Regal Ct
3 Lewes Ct
4 Esher Mews
5 Sibford Ct
6 Deseret Ho
7 Standor Ho
8 Langdale Par
9 Newman Terr

204

A2 **1** Barcom Trad Est
2 Croydon Valley Trade
Pk
C3 **1** Rozelle Ct
2 Dunheved Ct
3 Truscott Ho
C4 **1** Brigstock Par
2 Terry Lodge
3 Justin Ct
D3 **1** Wyndham Ct
2 Byrne Cl
D5 **1** Nutfield Pl
2 Braidwood Ho
3 Elliott Ho

205

A6 **1** Beulah Jun Sch
2 Beulah Inf Sch
3 Maple House Ind
Montessori Sch
4 Vietory Day Sch
B1 **1** Tavistock Ct
2 Chartwell Cl
3 Speaker's Ct
4 Cumberland Ct
5 Viceroy Ct
6 Oriel Ct
7 Cherry Orchard Gdns
8 Sola Ct
9 Gamma Ct
10 Croydon Coll Annexe
11 Edwin Pl
B5 **1** Decimus Cl
2 Palace Ct
3 Reservoir Ct
4 Broxholme Cl
5 Whitehorse Manor Jun
Sch
6 Whitehorse Manor Inf
Sch
C1 **1** Windmill Bridge Ho
2 Squire Ct
3 Houston Ct
5 Warren Ct
6 Freemasons Pl
7 Al Khair Prim & Sec
Sch

8 Croydon Prim Independant Sch
D1 1 Hastings Pl
2 Grant Pl
3 Clive Ho
4 Havelock Ho
5 Bellmore Ct
6 Hereford Ct
7 Chequers Ct
8 Havelock Hall

206

A1 1 Farleycroft
2 Edgecumbe Ct
3 Wesson Ho
4 Sullivan Ct
5 Kenley Ho
6 Christopher Ct
7 Jayson Ct
8 Sundridge Pl
A3 4 St Thomas Becket RC Prim Sch
A5 3 St Mark's CE Prim Sch
A6 1 Leybourne Ct
2 Lestock Cl
3 Croftside The
D1 1 Cottongrass Cl
2 Oxlip Cl
3 Eyebright Cl

207

D1 1 North Rd
2 Sussex Rd
3 Riverside Wlk
4 Christie Ho
5 Windsor Ct
6 Sherwood Ct
7 Wheatsheaf Par
D6 1 Linden Ct
2 Park Ct
3 Chilchester Ct
4 Iveagh Ct

208

A6 1 Overbury
2 Wilton Pl
D1 1 Woodgrange Ct
2 Maycroft
3 Farnborough Cres
D4 1 Knowlton Gn
2 Speldhurst Cl
3 Bidborough Cl
4 Penshurst Wlk
D5 1 Wedgewood Ct
2 Birches The
3 Eccleshill
4 Tavistock Rd
5 Montpelier Ct
6 South Hill Rd

209

A5 1 Montague Terr
2 Chatsworth Ho
A6 1 Marina Cl
2 Cheveney Wlk
3 Bromley Manor Mans
4 Mall The
5 Westmoreland Pl
B5 1 Reflex Apartments
2 Wheeler Pl
3 Maxim Apartments
4 Exchange Apartments
5 Axiom Apartments
6 Weller Mews

211

B1 1 Gleneagles Gn
2 Tandridge Pl
3 Springfield Wlk
4 Pinehurst Wlk
5 Cromer Pl
6 Oakmont Pl

214

A6 1 St Bernards Ho

---

2 Wentworth Ct
3 Sunningdale Cl
4 Arklow Mews
5 Edward Pinner Ct

216

A6 1 Lansdowne Copse
2 Lansdowne Ct
D6 1 Edwards Cl
2 Pearing Cl
3 Churchlands Way
4 Langley Pl

217

A1 2 St Dunstan's CE Prim Sch
A2 1 Cheam Court Flats
2 Farnham Ct
3 Tabor Ct
5 Whyte Mews
6 Killick Mews
C1 1 Lancaster Ct
2 Redclyffe Terr
3 Kenilworth Terr
4 Lincoln Terr
5 Garden Ct
6 Ashwood Pk
7 Midsummer Apartments
8 Lyndhurst Ct
9 Lorraine Ct
10 Gloucester Ct
11 Banbury Ct
12 Camilla Ct
13 Lorac Ct
14 Kingswood Mans
15 Claremont Ho
16 Holly Ct
17 Castle Ho
18 Balmoral Ct
19 Davington Ct
20 Hereford Ct
C2 1 Norman Ho
2 Hawthorns The
3 Limes The
4 Alexa Ct
5 Kristina Ct
6 Beverley Ct
7 Chestnut Ct
D1 1 Holmeswood
2 Pebworth Lo
3 Addison Ct
4 Kingslee Ct
5 Raeburn Ho
6 Girtin Ho
7 Leith Towers
8 Courtlands
9 Thomas Ho
10 Grayshott Ct
11 Hadrian Ct
12 Sandown Ct
13 Magnolia Ct
14 Dunsfold Ct
15 Camberley Ct
16 Berrylands Ct
17 Brockham Ct
18 Alford Ct
19 Lansdowne Ho
20 Larchvale Ct
D2 1 Portland Ct
2 Durnston Ct
3 Barton Ct
4 Aplin Ct
5 Hannah Ct
6 Honeysuckle Ct
7 Rowans The
8 St Annes Ct
9 Bonnington Ho
10 Pamir Ct
11 Bradbourne Ct
12 Worcester Ct
D3 1 Marian Ct
2 Robin Hood Ct
3 Distin Ct
4 Queensmere
5 Grosvenor Ho
6 Cromer Mans
7 St Nicholas Ctr
8 Robin Hood Jun Sch

---

10 Sutton Coll of Learning for Adults
D5 1 Dorothy Pettingel Ho
2 Margaret Ho
3 All Saints' Benhilton CE Prim Sch

218

A1 1 Beaclere Ho
2 Melford Ct
3 Elmhurst Lo
4 Mansard Manor
5 Tranmere Ct
6 Beechcroft Lo
7 Savin Lo
8 Yew Tree Ct
9 Avondale Ct
10 Devonshire Ho
11 Hidcote Ho
12 Munstead Ct
13 Lodden Lo
14 Steetley Ct
15 Grampian Cl
16 Richard Sharples Ct
18 Devonshire Prim Sch
A2 1 Grosvenor Ct
2 Forest Dene Ct
3 Cedar Ct
4 Vanborough Ct
5 Shrub Ct
6 Evergreen Ct
7 Grasmere Ct
8 Heathfield Ct
9 Sherbourne Ct
10 Kinsale Grange
11 Linden Ct
12 Jubilee Ct
13 Langley Ct
14 Wilmot Ho
15 Farendon Ho
16 Alexander Ho
A3 1 Goossens Cl
2 Cliffe Wlk
3 Marlins Ct
4 Clowser Cl
5 Montana Gdns
6 Bournemouth Ct
7 Palmerston Ct
8 Manor Park Prim Sch
8 Sutton Gram Sch For Boys
A4 1 Lodge The
2 Hazelwood Ho
3 Chesterton Ho
4 Clevedon Ho
5 Staincliffe Ho
6 Denewood Ho
7 Newlyn Ho
8 Manor Ct
9 Glenrose Ho
10 Oak Lo
11 Briar The
12 Fernhead
13 Branch Ho
14 Thicket Ct
15 Adam Ct
16 Arndell Ho
17 Oakwood Ct
B3 1 Hogarth Ho
2 Gillray Ho
3 Cramhurst Ho
4 Ronald Ho
5 Blythewood
6 Hillsde
7 Weldon Ct
8 Yeoman Ct
D5 1 Kynersley Cl
2 Wrythe Gn
3 Bedford Villas
4 Chateau The
5 Nelson Ct
6 Errington Manor
7 Leeds Ct
8 Blair Ct

219

A4 1 Westcroft
2 Westcroft Ho
A5 1 Burnside Ct

---

2 Millpond Pl
3 Waterside Ct
4 Stable Ct
5 Manor Ct
6 Victor Seymour Inf Sch
B2 1 Runnymede Ct
2 Dolphin Ct
3 Kings Ct
4 Cheyne Ct
5 Hendfield Ct
6 Ellerslie Ct
7 Embassy Ct
8 Chandler Ct
9 Hambledon Ct
10 Wallington Ct
11 Jasmine Ct
12 Napier Ct
13 Rosswood Ho
14 Woodcote Ct
15 Surrey Ct
16 Stag Ct
17 Moorlands
18 Orchard Hill Coll
B3 1 Cornelion Cotts
2 Walpole Ct
3 Farmstead Ct
4 Derby Ho
5 Salisbury Ho
6 Chatham Ho
7 Collingwood Sch
B4 1 Loraine Ho
2 Harcourt Lo
3 Coniston Ct
4 Alcester Ct
5 Friars Ct
6 Campbell Ho
7 Brodie Ho
8 Lesley Ct
9 Birch Ct
10 Airborne Ho
C2 1 Rossendon Ct
2 Mulberry Mews
3 Nairn Ct
4 Wallington Sq
5 Rosemount Twrs
6 Connell Ho
7 Ashby Grange
8 Terry Ct
9 Leigham Ct
10 Clyde Works
11 Chandos Bsns Ctr
12 Beech Ho
13 Wendon Ct
C4 1 Holy Trinity CE Jun Sch
D3 1 Torquay Ho
2 Ashburton Ho
D5 1 Goodwood Lo
2 Haydock Lo
3 Kempton Lo

220

A1 1 Phoenix Ctr The
2 Ensign Way
3 Hunter Cl
4 Cirrus Cl
5 Mosquito Cl
D5 1 Latimer Rd
2 Cromwell Ho
3 Arundel Ct
4 Warrington Ct
5 Grace Ct
6 Stuart Ct
7 Bridge Par
8 Ridge's Yd
9 Parish Church CE Jun Sch
10 Parish Church CE Inf Sch
11 Old Palace of John Whitgift Sch (Seniors)

221

A3 1 Trent Ct
2 Sherwood Ct
3 Archers Ct
4 Keepers Ct
5 Lincoln Ct
6 Mount The
7 Fairhaven Ct

---

8 Brockham Ct
9 Chelwood Ct
10 Marey Ct
11 Landau Ct
A4 1 West Street Pl
2 Maple Ct
3 St Andrew's Rd
4 Albury Ct
5 Chestnut Ct
6 Elgin Ct
7 Beechfield Ct
8 Barham Ct
9 Whitstable Pl
10 Ledbury Pl
A5 1 Fellmongers Yd
2 Halstead Cl
3 Mann Cl
4 Waterworks Yd
5 Chanderia Ct
6 Katherine Ho
7 Smith's Yd
A6 1 Otterbourne Rd
2 Charrington Rd
3 Tamworth Pl
4 Priddy's Yd
5 Hospital of the Holy Trinity (Almshouses)
B6 1 Wellesley Court Rd
2 Norfolk Ho
3 Station App
4 Suffolk Ct
5 Cherry Orchard Gdns
6 Harrington Ct
D6 1 Cheyne Ct
2 Fourways
3 Princess Ct
4 Tierney Ct
5 Sinclair Ct
6 Guinness Ct
7 Mayfair Ct
8 Bishopscourt
9 Gloucester Lo
10 Beverley Hyrst
11 Melton Ct
12 Cecil Ct
13 Napier Ct

227

A3 1 Westfield
2 Farnborough Ct
3 Fern Hill Pl
4 Churchill Ct
5 Spencer Ct
6 Ladycroft Gdns
7 Crabbs Croft Cl
8 Clifton Ct
D2 1 Brittenden Cl
2 Wardens Field Cl
3 Winnipeg Dr
4 Superior Dr
5 Huron Ct
6 Manitoba Gdns
7 Lynne Cl
8 Flint Cl
9 Bakers Mews
D3 1 Osgood Gdns
2 Amberley Cl
3 Rawlings Cl
4 Beblets Cl
5 Fir Tree Cl
6 Raleigh Mews
7 King Henry Mews
D4 1 Healy Dr
2 Marsden Way
3 Taylor Cl
4 Strickland Way
5 Dryland Ave
6 Adcot Wlk
7 Lichlade Cl

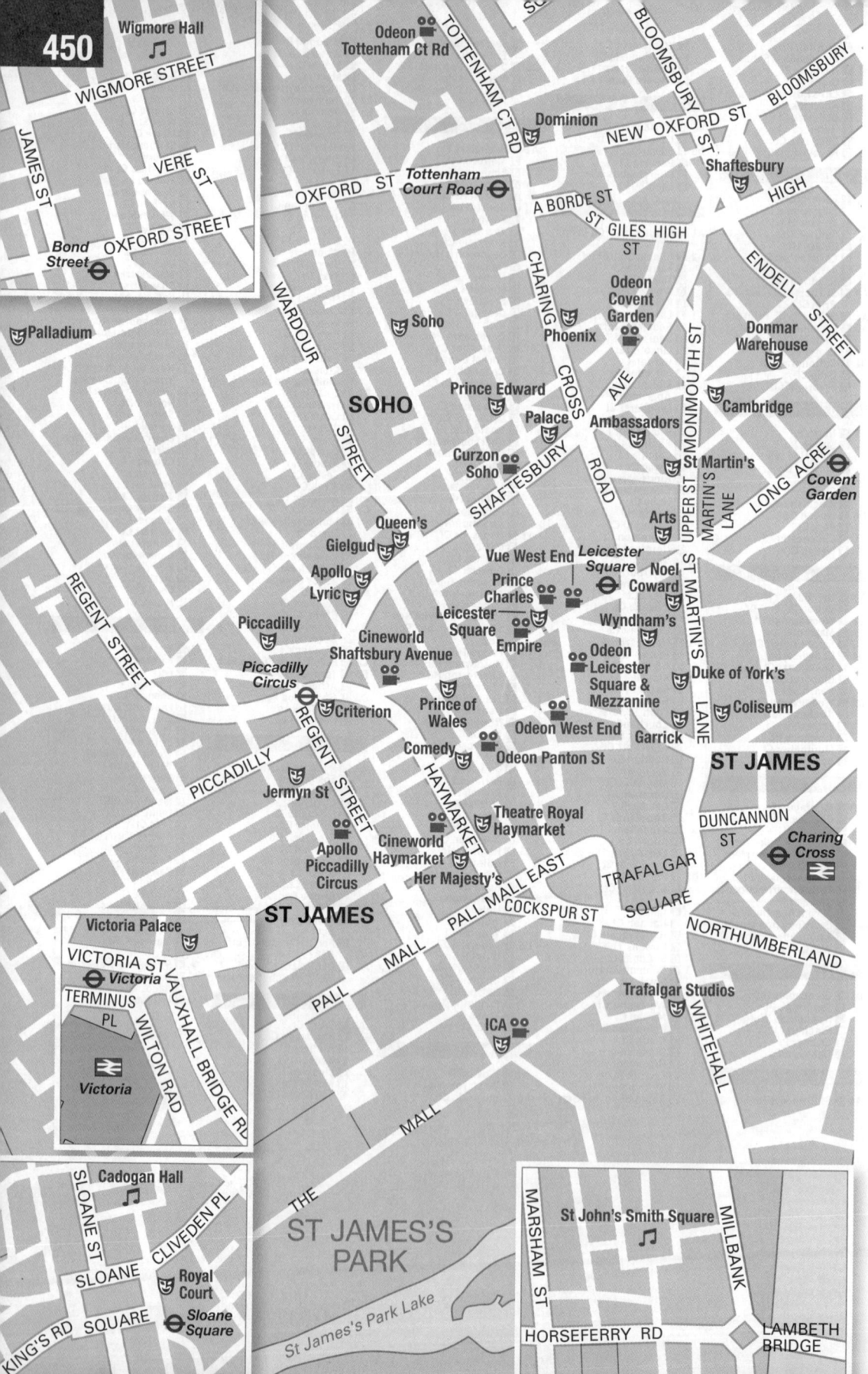

Wigmore Hall
WIGMORE STREET
VERE ST
JAMES ST
OXFORD STREET
Bond Street
OXFORD STREET
Palladium

Odeon Tottenham Ct Rd
TOTTENHAM CT RD
Dominion
NEW OXFORD ST
BLOOMSBURY
BLOOMSBURY
OXFORD ST
Tottenham Court Road
A BORDE ST
ST GILES HIGH ST
Shaftesbury
HIGH
ENDELL STREET

WARDOUR STREET
Soho
Phoenix
CHARING CROSS ROAD
Odeon Covent Garden
Donmar Warehouse
Cambridge
SOHO
Prince Edward
Palace
Ambassadors
St Martin's
UPPER ST MONMOUTH ST
LONG ACRE
Covent Garden
Curzon Soho
SHAFTESBURY
Arts
Queen's
Gielgud
Apollo
Lyric
Vue West End
Leicester Square
Noel Coward
Prince Charles
Wyndham's
Leicester Square
Empire
ST MARTIN'S LANE
Duke of York's
Piccadilly
REGENT STREET
Cineworld Shaftsbury Avenue
Odeon Leicester Square & Mezzanine
Garrick
Coliseum
Piccadilly Circus
Criterion
Prince of Wales
Odeon West End
Comedy
Odeon Panton St
ST JAMES
PICCADILLY
REGENT STREET
Jermyn St
HAYMARKET
Theatre Royal Haymarket
DUNCANNON ST
Charing Cross
Apollo Piccadilly Circus
Cineworld Haymarket
Her Majesty's
PALL MALL EAST
TRAFALGAR SQUARE
NORTHUMBERLAND
ST JAMES
COCKSPUR ST

Victoria Palace
VICTORIA ST
Victoria
TERMINUS PL
VAUXHALL BRIDGE RD
WILTON RD
Victoria
PALL MALL
Trafalgar Studios
WHITEHALL
ICA
THE MALL

Cadogan Hall
SLOANE ST
CLIVEDEN PL
SLOANE
Royal Court
Sloane Square
KING'S RD
SQUARE
ST JAMES'S PARK
St James's Park Lake
MARSHAM ST
St John's Smith Square
MILLBANK
HORSEFERRY RD
LAMBETH BRIDGE

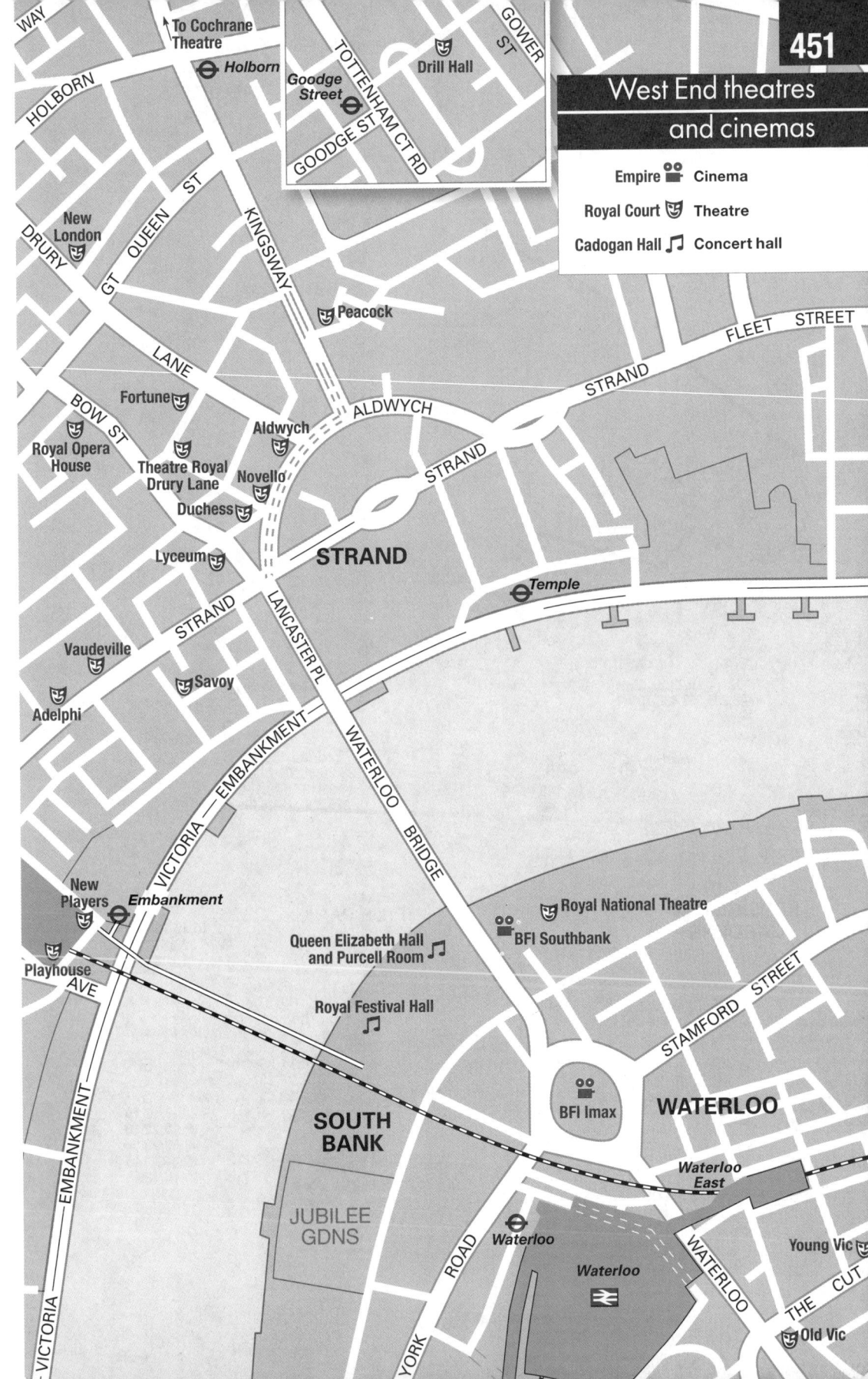

West End theatres and cinemas

Empire	🎥	Cinema
Royal Court	🎭	Theatre
Cadogan Hall	🎵	Concert hall

To Cochrane Theatre

⊖ Holborn

Goodge Street

Drill Hall

GOWER ST

TOTTENHAM CT RD

GOODGE ST

KINGSWAY

HOLBORN

WAY

New London

DRURY LANE

GT QUEEN ST

BOW ST

Royal Opera House

Fortune 🎭

Theatre Royal Drury Lane

Aldwych 🎭

Novello 🎭

Duchess 🎭

Lyceum 🎭

Peacock 🎭

ALDWYCH

STRAND

STRAND

FLEET STREET

STRAND

STRAND

⊖ Temple

STRAND

Vaudeville 🎭

Savoy 🎭

Adelphi 🎭

VICTORIA EMBANKMENT

LANCASTER PL

WATERLOO BRIDGE

New Players 🎭

Embankment ⊖

Playhouse 🎭

AVE

EMBANKMENT

VICTORIA

Queen Elizabeth Hall and Purcell Room 🎵

Royal Festival Hall 🎵

Royal National Theatre 🎭

BFI Southbank 🎥

SOUTH BANK

JUBILEE GDNS

BFI Imax 🎥

WATERLOO

STAMFORD STREET

Waterloo East

YORK ROAD

⊖ Waterloo

Waterloo 🚉

Young Vic 🎭

WATERLOO

THE CUT

Old Vic 🎭

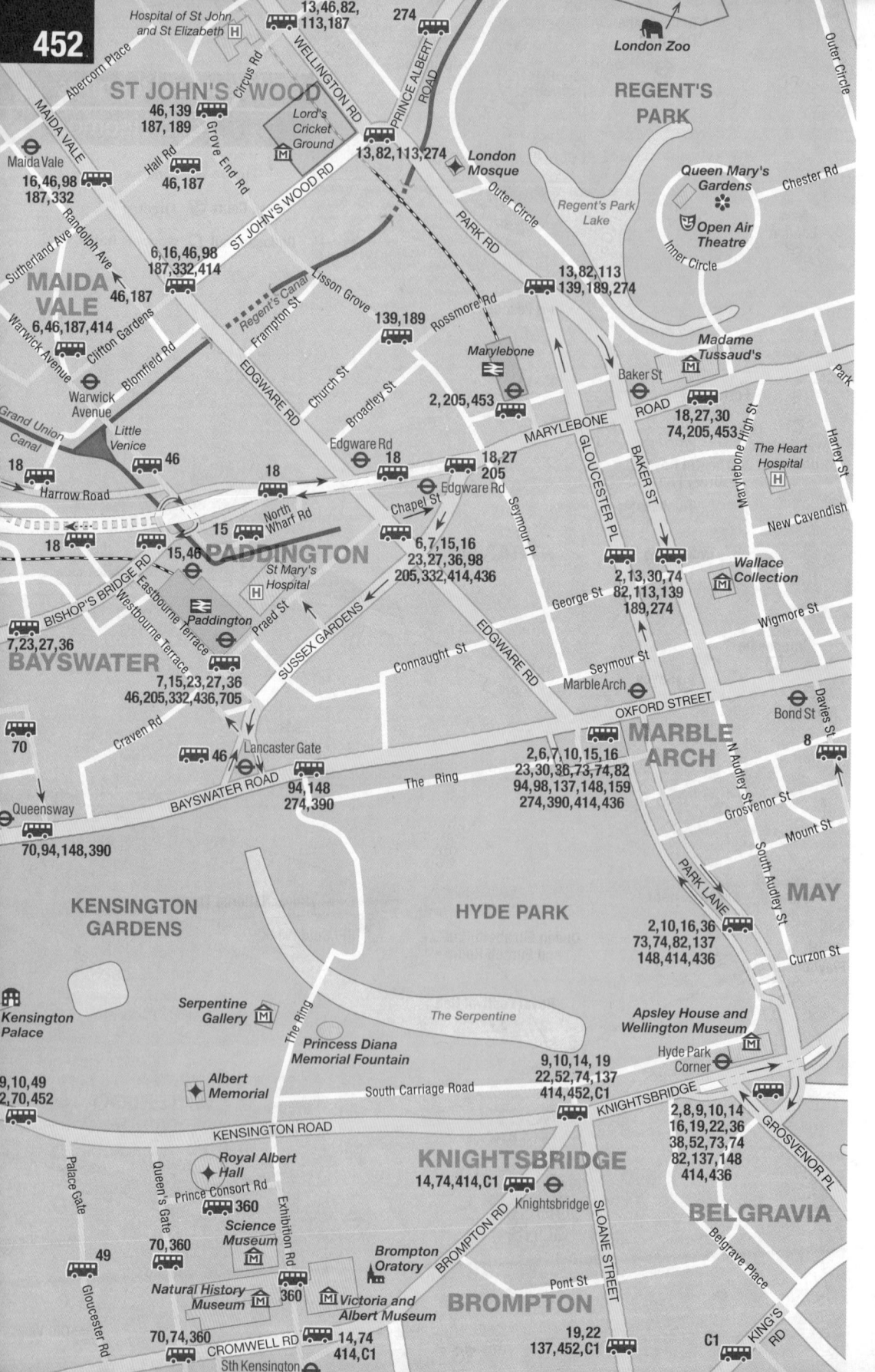

Hospital of St John
and St Elizabeth **H**

13,46,82,
113,187

274

London Zoo

ST JOHN'S WOOD

REGENT'S PARK

46,139
187,189

Lord's
Cricket
Ground

13,82,113,274

London
Mosque

Queen Mary's
Gardens

Chester Rd

Maida Vale

Grove End Rd

16,46,98
187,332

Hall Rd

46,187

ST JOHN'S WOOD RD

Outer Circle

Regent's Park
Lake

Open Air
Theatre

Inner Circle

MAIDA VALE

Randolph Ave

Sutherland Ave

6,16,46,98
187,332,414

Lisson Grove

Frampton St

PARK RD

13,82,113
139,189,274

Madame
Tussaud's

Park

Harley St

46,187

Regent's Canal

139,189

Rossmore Rd

Baker St

18,27,30
74,205,453

The Heart
Hospital **H**

6,46,187,414

Clifton Gardens

Blomfield Rd

Church St

Bradley St

Marylebone

Baker St
ROAD

New Cavendish

Warwick Avenue

EDGWARE RD

2,205,453

Warwick
Avenue

Little
Venice

Edgware Rd

18

18,27
205

GLOUCESTER PL

Wallace
Collection

Grand Union
Canal

18

46

18

Edgware Rd

Seymour Pl

2,13,30,74
82,113,139
189,274

Wigmore St

Harrow Road

15

North Wharf Rd

Chapel St

George St

18

15,46

PADDINGTON

St Mary's
Hospital **H**

6,7,15,16
23,27,36,98
205,332,414,436

Seymour St

Marble Arch

7,23,27,36

Westbourne Terrace
Eastbourne Terrace

Paddington

Praed St

SUSSEX GARDENS

EDGWARE RD

Connaught St

OXFORD STREET

Bond St

8

BAYSWATER

7,15,23,27,36
46,205,332,436,705

Craven Rd

Lancaster Gate

MARBLE ARCH

N Audley St

Davies St

70

46

BAYSWATER ROAD

The Ring

2,6,7,10,15,16
23,30,36,73,74,82
94,98,137,148,159
274,390,414,436

Grosvenor St

Mount St

Queensway

94,148
274,390

South Audley St

MAY

70,94,148,390

KENSINGTON GARDENS

HYDE PARK

PARK LANE

2,10,16,36
73,74,82,137
148,414,436

Curzon St

Kensington
Palace

Serpentine
Gallery

The Ring

The Serpentine

Apsley House and
Wellington Museum

9,10,49
2,70,452

Albert
Memorial

Princess Diana
Memorial Fountain

South Carriage Road

9,10,14,19
22,52,74,137
414,452,C1

Hyde Park
Corner

GROSVENOR PL

KENSINGTON ROAD

KNIGHTSBRIDGE

KNIGHTSBRIDGE

2,8,9,10,14
16,19,22,36
38,52,73,74
82,137,148
414,436

Palace Gate

Queen's Gate

Royal Albert
Hall

Prince Consort Rd

360

14,74,414,C1

Knightsbridge

SLOANE STREET

BELGRAVIA

Science
Museum

70,360

Exhibition Rd

BROMPTON RD

Brompton
Oratory

Pont St

Belgrave Place

49

Gloucester Rd

Natural History
Museum

360

Victoria and
Albert Museum

BROMPTON

KING'S RD

70,74,360

CROMWELL RD

14,74
414,C1

Sth Kensington

19,22
137,452,C1

C1

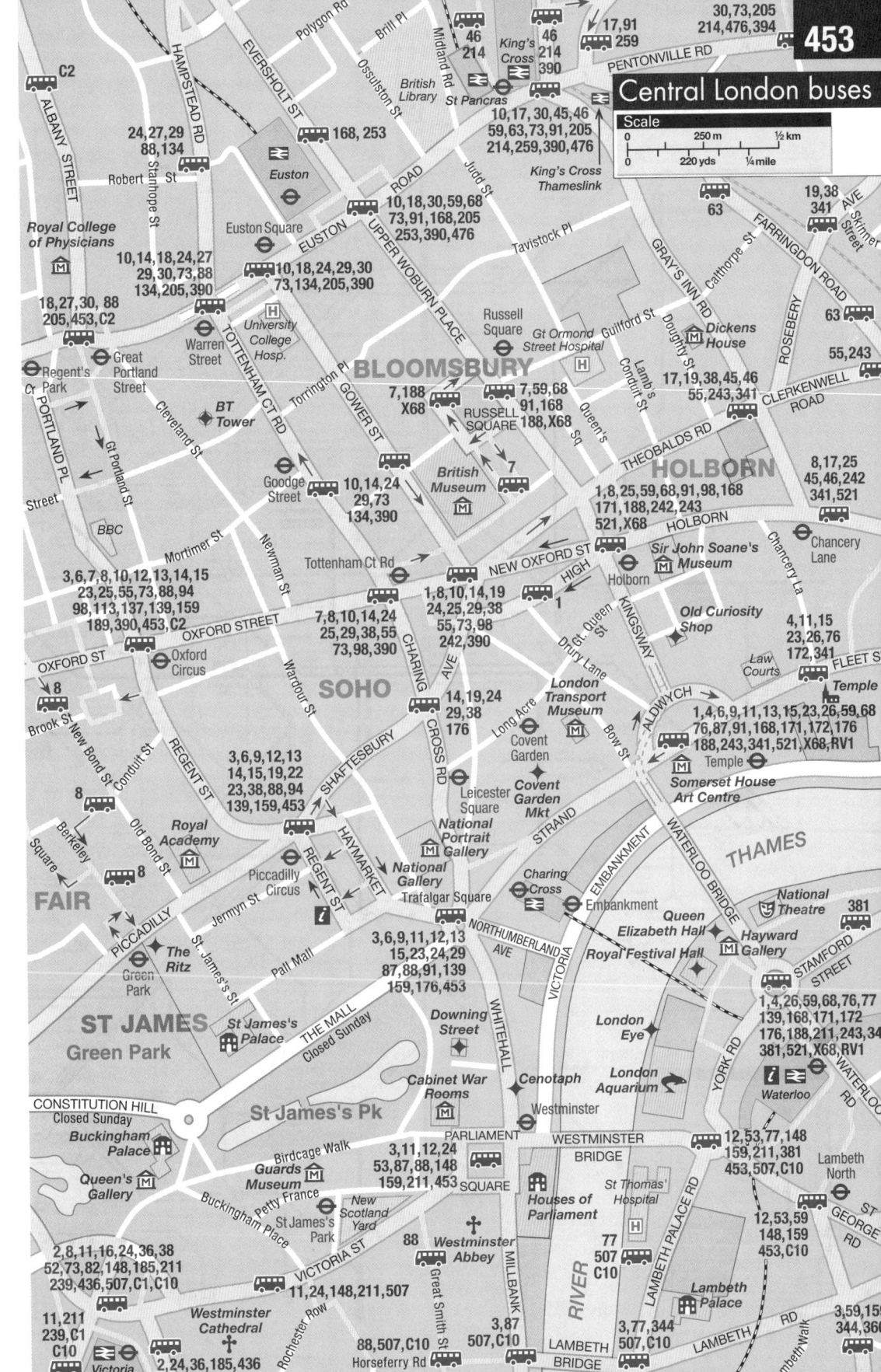

Central London buses

Scale

0 — 250 m — ½ km

0 — 220 yds — ¼ mile

C2

24, 27, 29
88, 134

Robert St

Royal College
of Physicians

10, 14, 18, 24, 27
29, 30, 73, 88
134, 205, 390

18, 27, 30, 88
205, 453, C2

Great
Portland
Street

Regent's
Ct Park

BT
Tower

BBC

3, 6, 7, 8, 10, 12, 13, 14, 15
23, 25, 55, 73, 88, 94
98, 113, 137, 139, 159
189, 390, 453, C2

OXFORD STREET

OXFORD ST

8

Oxford
Circus

Brook St

New Bond St

8

Berkeley
Square

8

FAIR

Royal
Academy

PICCADILLY

The Ritz

Green
Park

ST JAMES
Green Park

St James's
Palace

THE MALL
Closed Sunday

CONSTITUTION HILL
Closed Sunday

Buckingham
Palace

Queen's
Gallery

2, 8, 11, 16, 24, 36, 38
52, 73, 82, 148, 185, 211
239, 436, 507, C1, C10

11, 211
239, C1
C10

Victoria

Westminster
Cathedral

2, 24, 36, 185, 436

Polygon Rd

Brill Pl

46
214

46
214
390

17, 91
259

King's
Cross

30, 73, 205
214, 476, 394

PENTONVILLE RD

British
Library

St Pancras

168, 253

Euston

EUSTON

Euston Square

10, 18, 24, 29, 30
73, 134, 205, 390

University
College Hosp.

Warren
Street

Cleveland St

Gt Portland St

Goodge
Street

10, 14, 24
29, 73
134, 390

Tottenham Ct Rd

7, 8, 10, 14, 24
25, 29, 38, 55
73, 98, 390

SOHO

14, 19, 24
29, 38
176

3, 6, 9, 12, 13
14, 15, 19, 22
23, 38, 88, 94
139, 159, 453

Piccadilly
Circus

National
Gallery

Trafalgar Square

3, 6, 9, 11, 12, 13
15, 23, 24, 29
87, 88, 91, 139
159, 176, 453

Downing
Street

Cabinet War
Rooms

St James's Pk

Birdcage Walk

Guards
Museum

Buckingham Gate

St James's
Park

New
Scotland
Yard

Petty France

VICTORIA ST

11, 24, 148, 211, 507

Rochester Row

Horseferry Rd

10, 17, 30, 45, 46
59, 63, 73, 91, 205
214, 259, 390, 476

King's Cross
Thameslink

10, 18, 30, 59, 68
73, 91, 168, 205
253, 390, 476

Tavistock Pl

Russell
Square

Gt Ormond
Street Hospital

BLOOMSBURY

7, 188
X68

7, 59, 68
91, 168
188, X68

RUSSELL
SQUARE

7

British
Museum

Guilford St

Doughty St

Lamb's
Conduit St

Queen's

Queen's
Sq

Dickens
House

17, 19, 38, 45, 46
55, 243, 341

THEOBALDS RD

HOLBORN

1, 8, 25, 59, 68, 91, 98, 168
171, 188, 242, 243
521, X68

HOLBORN

NEW OXFORD ST

1, 8, 10, 14, 19
24, 25, 29, 38
55, 73, 98
242, 390

HIGH

1

Holborn

Sir John Soane's
Museum

Chancery
Lane

Chancery La

Old Curiosity
Shop

Law
Courts

FLEET ST

London
Transport
Museum

Long Acre

Covent
Garden

Covent
Garden
Mkt

Leicester
Square

National
Portrait
Gallery

Drury Lane

Gt Queen St

KINGSWAY

ALDWYCH

Temple

4, 11, 15
23, 26, 76
172, 341

Temple

1, 4, 6, 9, 11, 13, 15, 23, 26, 59, 68
76, 87, 91, 168, 171, 172, 176
188, 243, 341, 521, X68, RV1

Somerset House
Art Centre

THAMES

Charing
Cross

Embankment

EMBANKMENT

WATERLOO BRIDGE

Queen
Elizabeth Hall

Royal Festival Hall

National
Theatre

381

Hayward
Gallery

STAMFORD
STREET

1, 4, 26, 59, 68, 76, 77
139, 168, 171, 172
176, 188, 211, 243, 341
381, 521, X68, RV1

London
Eye

London
Aquarium

Cenotaph

Westminster

PARLIAMENT
SQUARE

WESTMINSTER
BRIDGE

VICTORIA

YORK RD

Waterloo

WATERLOO RD

3, 11, 12, 24
53, 87, 88, 148
159, 211, 453

Houses of
Parliament

St Thomas'
Hospital

88

Westminster
Abbey

Great Smith St

MILLBANK

77
507
C10

RIVER

3, 87

507, C10

88, 507, C10

LAMBETH
BRIDGE

12, 53, 77, 148
159, 211, 381
453, 507, C10

Lambeth
North

12, 53, 59
148, 159
453, C10

LAMBETH PALACE RD

Lambeth
Palace

LAMBETH RD

3, 59, 159
344, 360

3, 77, 344
507, C10

19, 38
341

Skinner St

AVE

FARRINGDON ROAD

63

63

ROSEBERY AV

CLERKENWELL
ROAD

55, 243

8, 17, 25
45, 46, 242
341, 521

GRAY'S INN RD

Catthorpe St

EVERSHOLT ST

HAMPSTEAD RD

ALBANY STREET

Stanhope St

PORTLAND PL

Gt Portland St

Newman St

Wardour St

REGENT ST

Old Bond St

Conduit St

HAYMARKET

REGENT ST

Jermyn St

St James's St

Pall Mall

WHITEHALL

NORTHUMBERLAND AVE

63

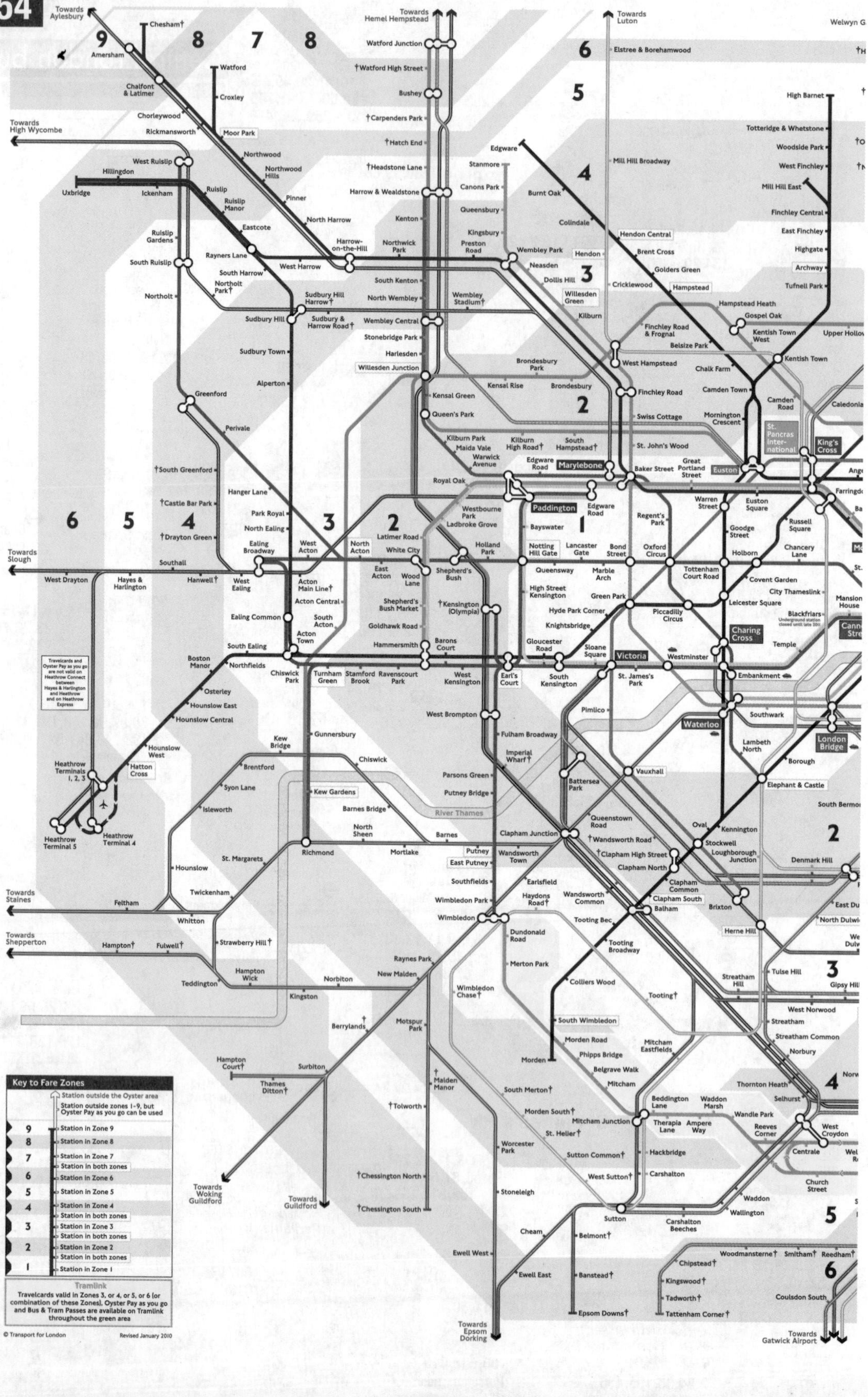

Towards Aylesbury
9
Chesham†
Amersham
Chalfont & Latimer
8
Watford
Croxley
7
8
Towards Hemel Hempstead
Watford Junction
†Watford High Street
Bushey
Towards Luton
6
Elstree & Borehamwood
Welwyn G
5
High Barnet
Totteridge & Whetstone
Woodside Park
West Finchley
Mill Hill East
Finchley Central
East Finchley
Highgate
Archway
Tufnell Park†

Towards High Wycombe
Chorleywood
Rickmansworth
Moor Park
Northwood
Northwood Hills
Pinner
†Carpenders Park
†Hatch End
†Headstone Lane
Harrow & Wealdstone
Edgware
Stanmore
Canons Park
Queensbury
Kingsbury
4
Mill Hill Broadway
Hendon Central
Brent Cross
Golders Green
Cricklewood
Hampstead
Hampstead Heath
Gospel Oak
Kentish Town West
Upper Hollow
Kentish Town

West Ruislip
Hillingdon
Uxbridge
Ickenham
Ruislip
Ruislip Manor
Eastcote
Rayners Lane
South Harrow
Northolt Park†
Ruislip Gardens
South Ruislip
Northolt
Harrow-on-the-Hill
North Harrow
West Harrow
Sudbury Hill Harrow†
Sudbury & Harrow Road†
Northwick Park
Preston Road
Kenton
South Kenton
North Wembley
Wembley Central
Stonebridge Park
Harlesden
Wembley Park
Neasden
Dollis Hill
3
Willesden Green
Kilburn
Finchley Road & Frognal
West Hampstead
Finchley Road
Belsize Park
Chalk Farm
Camden Town
Swiss Cottage
St. John's Wood
Mornington Crescent
Camden Road
St. Pancras International
King's Cross
Caledonia

Sudbury Hill
Sudbury Town
Alperton
Greenford
Perivale
†South Greenford
†Castle Bar Park
†Drayton Green
Hanger Lane
Park Royal
North Ealing
Ealing Broadway
West Acton
North Acton
2
Brondesbury Park
Kensal Rise
Brondesbury
Queen's Park
Kilburn Park
Maida Vale
Warwick Avenue
Royal Oak
West Hampstead
Kilburn High Road†
South Hampstead
Kensal Green
Edgware Road
Marylebone
Baker Street
Great Portland Street
Warren Street
Euston Square
Euston
Russell Square
Goodge Street
Farringdon
Ang

6
5
4
3
2
Towards Slough
West Drayton
Hayes & Harlington
Hanwell†
West Ealing
Ealing Common
South Ealing
Northfields
Boston Manor
Southall
Latimer Road
White City
East Acton
Wood Lane
Shepherd's Bush
Westbourne Park
Ladbroke Grove
Paddington
Edgware Road
Bayswater
Notting Hill Gate
Lancaster Gate
Queensway
Holland Park
Shepherd's Bush Market
Goldhawk Road
Acton Central
Shepherd's Bush
Kensington (Olympia)
High Street Kensington
Hyde Park Corner
Green Park
Marble Arch
Bond Street
Oxford Circus
Regent's Park
Tottenham Court Road
Holborn
Chancery Lane
Covent Garden
City Thameslink
Leicester Square
Me
Ba

Acton Main Line†
Ealing
Acton Town
South Acton
Chiswick Park
Turnham Green
Stamford Brook
Ravenscourt Park
Hammersmith
Barons Court
West Kensington
Earl's Court
Gloucester Road
South Kensington
Knightsbridge
Sloane Square
Victoria
Piccadilly Circus
Charing Cross
Temple
Mansion House
Blackfriars
Cann
Stre

Hounslow East
Hounslow Central
Osterley
Kew Bridge
Gunnersbury
Chiswick
West Brompton
Fulham Broadway
Imperial Wharf†
Pimlico
St. James's Park
Westminster
Embankment
Waterloo
Southwark

Heathrow Terminals 1, 2, 3
Hatton Cross
Brentford
Syon Lane
Isleworth
Kew Gardens
Barnes Bridge
North Sheen
Parsons Green
Putney Bridge
Battersea Park
Vauxhall
Lambeth North
Borough
London Bridge
Elephant & Castle
South Bermo

Heathrow Terminal 5
Heathrow Terminal 4
Hounslow
St. Margarets
Richmond
Mortlake
Barnes
Putney
East Putney
Queenstown Road
†Wandsworth Road
Clapham High Street
Clapham North
Oval
Kennington
Stockwell
Loughborough Junction
Denmark Hill
2
East Du

Towards Staines
Feltham
Twickenham
Whitton
Strawberry Hill†
Southfields
Wimbledon Park
Wandsworth Town
Earlsfield
Haydons Road†
Wimbledon
Clapham Junction
Wandsworth Common
Clapham Common
Balham
Clapham South
Brixton
North Dulwich

Towards Shepperton
Hampton†
Fulwell†
Teddington
Hampton Wick
Norbiton
New Malden
Raynes Park
Dundonald Road
Tooting Bec
Tooting Broadway
Herne Hill
Wes
Dulw

Towards Epsom Dorking
Worcester Park
Stoneleigh
Ewell West
Ewell East
Banstead†
Cheam
Belmont
Chessington North†
Chessington South†
Towards Guildford
Hampton Court†
Thames Ditton†
Surbiton
Berrylands
Motspur Park
Malden Manor
South Merton†
Morden South†
Merton Park
Colliers Wood
South Wimbledon
Morden Road
Phipps Bridge
Morden
Wimbledon Chase†
Mitcham
Mitcham Eastfields
Belgrave Walk
Mitcham Junction
St. Helier†
Sutton Common†
West Sutton†
Sutton
Carshalton Beeches
Beddington Lane
Waddon Marsh
Therapia Lane
Ampere Way
Wandle Park
Reeves Corner
West Croydon
Centrale
Church Street
Hackbridge
Carshalton
Waddon
Wallington
Tooting†
Streatham Hill
Tulse Hill
Gipsy Hill
West Norwood
Streatham
Streatham Common
Norbury
Thornton Heath
Selhurst
3
4
5
Epsom Downs
Tadworth†
Kingswood†
Chipstead†
Tattenham Corner†
Coulsdon South
Woodmansterne†
Smitham†
Reedham†
6
Towards Gatwick Airport

River Thames

Key to Fare Zones
Station outside the Oyster area
Station outside zones 1–9, but Oyster Pay as you go can be used
9 Station in Zone 9
8 Station in Zone 8
7 Station in Zone 7
   Station in both zones
6 Station in Zone 6
5 Station in Zone 5
   Station in both zones
4 Station in Zone 4
   Station in both zones
3 Station in Zone 3
   Station in both zones
2 Station in Zone 2
   Station in both zones
1 Station in Zone 1

Tramlink
Travelcards valid in Zones 3, or 4, or 5, or 6 (or combination of these Zones). Oyster Pay as you go and Bus & Tram Passes are available on Tramlink throughout the green area.

Travelcards and Oyster Pay as you go are not valid on Heathrow Connect between Hayes & Harlington and Heathrow and on Heathrow Express

© Transport for London   Revised January 2010

Oyster rail services in London

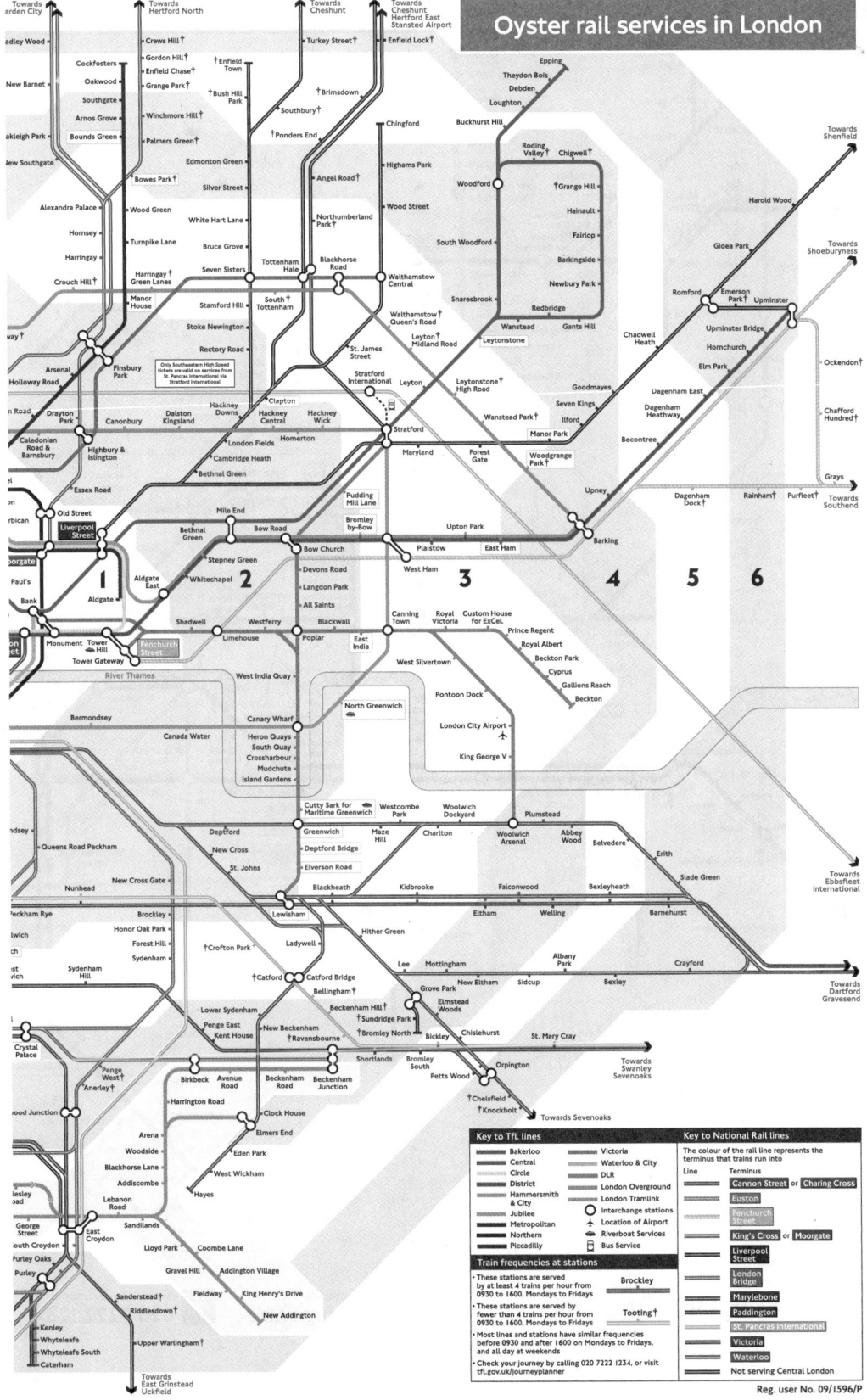

MAYOR OF LONDON

Website
tfl.gov.uk

24 hour travel information
020 7222 1234

© Transport for London   Reg. user No. 09/1596/P